HANDBOOK OF
PSYCHOPHYSIOLOGY

THE CONTRIBUTORS

A. A. ALEXANDER, Ph.D., Associate Professor of Psychiatry, University of Wisconsin Medical School

R. T. BLOCK, M.D., Fellow in Medicine, University of Oklahoma Medical Center

CLINTON C. BROWN, Ph.D., Director, Basic Science Research, Maryland Psychiatric Research Center; Associate Professor of Medical Psychology, Department of Psychiatry and Behavioral Science, Johns Hopkins University, School of Medicine

THOMAS D. CULLEN, Ph.D., Assistant Research Psychologist, Department of Psychology, University of California, Los Angeles

ELIZABETH DUFFY, Ph.D., Professor Emeritus of Psychology, University of North Carolina

ROBERT EDELBERG, Ph.D., Professor, Department of Psychiatry, Rutgers Medical School

BERNARD T. ENGEL, Ph.D., Chief, Laboratory of Behavioral Sciences, Gerontology Research Center, Baltimore City Hospitals

IRIS BALSHAN GOLDSTEIN, Ph.D., Lecturer, Loyola University, Los Angeles

DAVID T. GRAHAM, M.D., Professor of Medicine, University of Wisconsin Medical School

NORMAN S. GREENFIELD, Ph.D., Professor of Psychiatry, University of Wisconsin Medical School; Associate Director, Wisconsin Psychiatric Institute

C. G. GUNN, M.D., Professor of Medicine and Biological Psychology, University of Oklahoma Medical Center

ECKHARD H. HESS, Ph.D., Professor of Psychology, University of Chicago

LAVERNE C. JOHNSON, Ph.D., Head, Psychophysiology Division, Navy Medical Neuropsychiatric Research Unit, San Diego; Lecturer, Department of Psychology, San Diego State College; Adjunct Professor, Department of Psychiatry, University of California, San Diego

PETER J. LANG, Ph.D., Professor of Psychology, University of Wisconsin

ARDIE LUBIN, Ph.D., Research Psychologist, U.S. Navy Medical Neuropsychiatric Research Unit, San Diego, California

ROBERT B. MALMO, Ph.D., Professor, Departments of Psychiatry and Psychology, McGill University; Director, Neuropsychology Laboratory, Allan Memorial Institute, McGill University

JOHN W. MASON, M.D., Chief, Department of Neuroendocrinology, Division of Neuropsychiatry, Walter Reed Army Institute of Research, Walter Reed Army Medical Center

MARTIN T. ORNE, M.D., Ph.D., Director, Unit for Experimental Psychiatry, Institute of the Pennsylvania Hospital; Professor of Psychiatry, University of Pennsylvania

DAVID A. PASKEWITZ, Ph.D., Senior Psychophysiologist, Unit for Experimental Psychiatry, Institute of the Pennsylvania Hospital; Associate in Psychology in Psychiatry, University of Pennsylvania

R. J. PERSON, Ph.D., Research Fellow in Psychosomatic Medicine, University of Oklahoma Medical Center

DAVID G. RICE, Ph.D., Associate Professor of Psychiatry, University of Wisconsin Medical School

WILLIAM H. RICKLES, Jr., M.D., Assistant Research Psychiatrist, Neuropsychiatric Institute, UCLA Center for the Health Sciences

JIMMY SCOTT, Ph.D., Lecturer, Departments of Behavior Biology and Psychiatry, University of California Medical School, Davis

CHARLES SHAGASS, M.D., Professor of Psychiatry, Temple University Medical Center; Chief of Temple Clinical Service, Eastern Pennsylvania Psychiatric Institute

DONALD W. SHEARN, Ph.D., Professor, Department of Psychology, The Colorado College

FREDERICK SNYDER, M.D., Chief of Laboratory of Clinical Psychobiology, CBRD, National Institute of Mental Health, HSMHA

JOHN A. STERN, Ph.D., Professor of Psychology, Washington University, St. Louis, Missouri

RICHARD A. STERNBACH, Ph.D., Adjunct Associate Professor, Department of Psychiatry, School of Medicine, University of California, San Diego

CHARLES F. STROEBEL, Ph.D., Director, Gengras Laboratories of Experimental Psychophysiology, Institute of Living, Hartford, Connecticut

RICHARD I. THACKRAY, Ph.D., Chief, Stress Behavior Unit, Aviation Psychology Laboratory, Civil Aeromedical Institute, FAA, Oklahoma City

JACK D. WELSH, M.D., Chief, Gastroenterology Section; Professor, Department of Medicine, University of Oklahoma Medical Center

MARION A. WENGER, Ph.D., Professor of Psychology, University of California, Los Angeles

STEWART WOLF, M.D., Professor of Internal Medicine and Physiology, The University of Texas Medical Branch at Galveston; Director, The Marine Biomedical Institute, Galveston

MARVIN ZUCKERMAN, Ph.D., Professor of Psychology, University of Delaware

HANDBOOK OF PSYCHOPHYSIOLOGY

Editors

NORMAN S. GREENFIELD

University of Wisconsin

RICHARD A. STERNBACH

University of California, San Diego

HOLT, RINEHART AND WINSTON, INC.
New York • Chicago • San Francisco • Atlanta
Dallas • Montreal • Toronto • London • Sydney

Copyright © 1972 by Holt, Rinehart and Winston, Inc.
All rights reserved
Library of Congress Catalog Card Number: 72-158478
ISBN: 0-03-086656-1
Printed in the United States of America
2 3 4 5 6   071   9 8 7 6 5 4 3 2 1

PREFACE

Psychophysiology is an old idea but a new science. It is a likely assumption that ever since man began to experience himself as an object of his own awareness he has had some intuitive notion that bodily changes were, in some measure, related to his moods, his sentiments, his frustrations, his elations. How to relate these dual aspects of human functioning has been a concern of philosopher-scientists throughout the course of intellectual history.

The goal of translating tender-minded speculation and theorizing into tougher-minded models and methodologies was greatly spurred by the technological revolution which began in the late 1940s and has been burgeoning ever since. During this period crude instrumentations have given way to more sophisticated electronic techniques of data collection and the wonders of computer science have provided a means of dealing with the myriad problems of data reduction and analysis on which any science is dependent.

The first scientific periodical devoted exclusively to this field was the *Psychophysiology Newsletter* which was begun by Albert Ax in 1955 and subsequently became the journal *Psychophysiology*. The Society for Psychophysiological Research was founded in 1960 by a small but enthusiastic group of scientists of diverse disciplines who were dedicated to the belief that operational rapprochement between psychology and physiology

PREFACE

was necessary to any truly comprehensive study of man and his behavior.

The present volume was first conceived by the editors in 1965. Enthusiastic encouragement from John Lacey and Albert Ax gave us the courage to translate idea into action and the responses of potential contributors provided the critical reinforcement. The die was cast, the project launched.

The ensuing six years were beset by many trials and tribulations which we will spare the reader, since any detailed exposition would surely discourage publication of future handbooks for all time! Suffice to say we feel much like the Jewish Mother at her son's Bar Mitzvah: feelings of pride—today he is a man—but memories of the struggles and problems make it a somewhat bittersweet experience.

This *Handbook* was planned as a comprehensive though not encyclopedic view of the new science of psychophysiology. The field is too new, its knowledge too ephemeral and advances too rapid to attempt to present a definitive exegesis. And, despite the fact that chapters were revised during the past two years, we know that it is impossible to keep pace with progress. Thus we have endeavored to present foundations of physiological processes, empirical principles of psychophysiology, relationships between physiology and behavior, and applications to psychosomatic conditions and psychopathology which we hope will serve as a fundamental framework on which to build further knowledge. We address this book not only to those who wish to specialize and to work in the field but to those in related disciplines who wish to acquaint themselves with present knowledge, be they students of psychology or physiology, medical students or practitioners, or those who are seriously curious about new advances toward solutions of age-old problems.

We regret one notable omission: a chapter de-voted to Developmental Psychophysiology was originally planned and contracted but the author failed to meet his commitment at a time so late in the publication schedule that a replacement could not be arranged.

A book of this kind is dependent upon the help and cooperation of so many people that it is impossible to provide truly adequate acknowledgments or to express the depth of our gratitude. We chose the authors from among the leaders in the field as the quality of the chapters attests. Their cooperation, encouragement, and personal sacrifices during the painfully protracted period of deadlines, more deadlines, revisions, and then further deadlines have made them admired friends as well as respected colleagues.

We thank the many authors and publishers who have permitted reproduction of material throughout the text. Specific citations appear where appropriate.

Many of the early editorial chores were superbly handled by Helen Baldwin and the quality of this legacy was carried forward by Lyn Kimbrough.

Maureen Reimers, the project secretary, is the kind of person who combines pleasantness of personality, superior technical skills, and an uncanny ability to remember what's been done and where things are. Without her, confusion would have become chaos.

Brian Heald, Senior Project Editor of Holt, Rinehart and Winston, is a rare kind of man. Without his direction, his impressive grasp of material for which he had no formal training, his magnificent organizational talent, without these qualities all presented with candor, charm, and apparent imperturbability, we would have faltered many times.

Madison, Wisconsin NORMAN S. GREENFIELD
La Jolla, California RICHARD A. STERNBACH

vi

CONTENTS

PART 5 APPLICATIONS OF PSYCHOPHYSIOLOGICAL TECHNIQUES AND FINDINGS

PART
1 PHYSIOLOGICAL FOUNDATIONS

John W. Mason

ORGANIZATION OF PSYCHOENDOCRINE MECHANISMS*

A REVIEW AND RECONSIDERATION OF RESEARCH

1

THE SCOPE OF PSYCHOENDOCRINE RESEARCH

Psychoendocrine research has been limited so far largely to studies involving the adrenal and thyroid glands. As in other research concerned with endocrine regulation, there has also been a tendency to focus attention upon a *single* endocrine system at a time. During our early experience in this field, we became aware of some compelling reasons to believe that the conventional study of single endocrine systems in isolation may have some special limitations in psychoendocrine research. Several lines of evidence appeared to indicate that the study of endocrine regulation may uniquely require an approach which considers the *full scope* of activity in the many interdependent

*From the Department of Neuroendocrinology, Walter Reed Army Institute of Research, Walter Reed Army Medical Center, Washington, D.C.

All the authors associated with this Supplement are deeply indebted to David McKenzie Rioch for his encouragement and generous support of this project. Many helpful suggestions concerning the manuscripts and the analysis of data were made by Robert Rose, Edward Sachar, and Richard Poe. Mrs. Ruth Ernst helped in many valuable ways in the recording and statistical analysis of data and in the preparation of tables and graphs. We are also most grateful to Mrs. Barbara Weinberg and Mrs. Ernst for their careful preparation and proofreading of the manuscripts. Throughout all these experiments skillful and dependable technical assistance in the handling and care of the monkeys and in the processing of samples was given by Benjamin Jackson.

This chapter was adapted from a series of articles in Psychosomatic Medicine, Volume 30, Number 5, 1968, with the kind permission of Dr. Mason and the Hoeber Medical Division of Harper and Row, Publishers. The editors assume all responsibility for the accuracy of the reprinting and for the revisions of the original manuscript, which were made in order to conform to the style of this volume.

endocrine systems simultaneously. The experiments to be described are concerned with the *concurrent* measurement of levels of many different hormones in relation to a conditioned emotional disturbance in the monkey and represent an initial effort to test the usefulness of this conceptual approach. As this approach involves a departure in some respects from prevailing concepts and practices in the field of endocrine regulation, it may be appropriate in this introductory paper to review some of the events and theoretical considerations which led to the viewpoint underlying the present study.

Significance of New Biochemical Methods of Hormone Measurement

A historical development of utmost importance to psychoendocrine research has been the recent introduction of long-awaited, reliable, and specific biochemical methods of sufficient sensitivity to permit measurement of the minute amounts of many hormones in small samples of blood and urine. Over the past 50 years several major subdivisions have developed in the relatively young science of experimental endocrinology. A particularly active field has been that concerned with the study of the metabolic effects and actions of hormones. Progress in this area during the first quarter of the century was relatively slow, largely because only crude and impure glandular extracts were available for experimental work on the secretory products of most of the endocrine systems. Beginning about 1930, a series of brilliant biochemical advances resulted in the availability of many highly purified crystalline hormone preparations and opened the way for a period of extraordinary progress in the study of the effects of individual hormones on metabolic processes and body tissues.

Another area in experimental endocrinology is that concerned with the study of the regulation of hormone secretion. For many years, progress in this field was also slow and unsure, largely because the only available methods of evaluating rates of hormone secretion were indirect and lacked specificity. Just as the availability of highly purified hormone preparations was essential to major progress in the study of metabolic aspects of endocrinology, so the availability of highly sensitive, specific, and practicable methods of hormone measurement in body

fluids was a key prerequisite for major advances in the study of endocrine regulation. Such methods have become available, however, only during the past 15 years; thus in many instances there was a gap of 20 years or longer between the time that a crystalline hormone became available and the time that a reliable biochemical method for its measurement in body fluids became available. Research on endocrine regulation has consequently lagged considerably behind that in the field of metabolic endocrinology. It happens, then, that an unprecedented opportunity to participate in the early stages of development of a new era in research on endocrine regulation has fallen to the present generation of scientific workers as a result of very recent advances in hormone assay methodology.

Previous Emphasis on Pituitary-Adrenal Cortical System

At the time our own work on endocrine regulation began in 1953, attention in this field was concentrated heavily upon the pituitary-adrenal cortical system. This was largely a result of the influence of Selye's impressive presentation in 1950 of his earlier postulation that the response of this endocrine system has a unique, preeminent, and nonspecific character in relation to "stress." (Selye, 1950b). Approaching this field from a psychosomatic orientation, the issue of greatest immediate interest to us, raised almost as an incidental aspect of Selye's early work, was the possibility that emotional or psychological mechanisms may participate in the regulation of pituitary-adrenal cortical activity. (Selye, 1936a). This finding, if it were conclusively proved with relatively refined psychological and endocrinological methods, would represent the first extension of the scope of the psychoendocrine field beyond the sympathetic-adrenal medullary system, which up to that time—as a result of Cannon's systematic work many years earlier (Cannon, 1929; Cannon & de la Paz, 1911)—was the only endocrine system known to be responsive to psychological stimuli.

The decisive event which encouraged us to enter this field of research was the introduction in 1952 of the Nelson-Samuels' chromatographic method for measurement of plasma 17-hydroxycorticosteroid (17-OHCS) levels (Nelson & Samuels, 1952). This elegant but practicable method provided for the first time a direct and specific index of pituitary-adrenal cortical activity which could be used under natural conditions in the intact, living animal or human subject. Within a few years, research on this problem that was conducted in several different laboratories and is reviewed in detail later in this chapter, produced extensive evidence and virtually unanimous agreement that the pituitary-adrenal cortical system was indeed remarkably sensitive to psychological influences. Related neuroendocrine studies also demonstrated the existence of suprahypothalamic neural influences on plasma 17-OHCS levels (Mason, 1958, p. 645; 1959a; Mason, Nauta, Brady, Robinson, & Sachar, 1961), so that the basis for systematic psychoendocrine research involving the pituitary-adrenal cortical system was well established by 1960. We continued to devote a portion of our effort to exploring various applications of psychoendocrine approaches in psychiatric research, particularly to the study of emotions and related psychological processes, by using 17-OHCS levels as an index of the physiological reflection of affective distress or emotional arousal. These studies have been reviewed recently in some detail (Mason, 1964, p. 375; Mason & Brady, 1965).

Evidence for a Broader Scope of Psychoendocrine Relationships

Up to this last-mentioned point, then, our work followed the general tendency to concentrate almost exclusively on the pituitary-adrenal cortical system. As our experiments progressed, however, information converging from several directions seemed increasingly to indicate that this preoccupation with the adrenal gland, however fruitful, was serving to stifle further inquiries into the scope of the psychoendocrine field. It was troubling that the natural wave of interest in Selye's provocative concepts seemed to have the side effect of relegating Cannon's work on the adrenal medulla, along with a number of venerable clinical impressions suggesting psychological influences on still other endocrine systems, into the background. Thus, the situation tended, in a sense, to narrow vision in the psychoendocrine field. Also, recent advances in

several fields of experimental endocrinology were yielding information suggesting that endocrine regulation is very likely to be organized on a broad basis and that multiple endocrine systems, in addition to those involving the adrenal gland, may participate in psychoendocrine responses. Our research approach was accordingly reoriented in order that we might begin a survey of the extent to which the many other endocrine systems of the body may share with the adrenal systems a sensitivity to psychological influences. Some of the specific considerations which were most influential in our developing the view that the scope of psychoendocrine relationships may be relatively broad might be briefly summarized.

Neuroanatomical factors First, it appeared that the anatomical connections between various endocrine glands and the central nervous system might provide important clues to the scope of psychoendocrine relationships—assuming that a direct anatomical linkage, neural or neurohumoral, is a prerequisite for such relationships. Figure 1.1 presents a schematic diagram of known and suspected points of articulation between brain cells and the endocrine cells of many different glands.

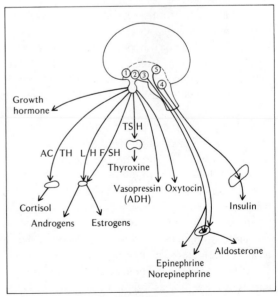

Figure 1.1 Points of anatomical contact between nervous and endocrine systems.

These contacts may be designated as localized in five general areas.

1. The hypothalamic-anterior pituitary neurohumoral linkage, through the portal-hypophyseal system. This linkage presumably could provide a pathway for neural or psychological influences on the anterior pituitary hormones, adrenocorticotropin, thyrotropin, the gonadotropins, growth hormone, and prolactin. While an anatomical connection cannot, of course, be assumed necessarily to have physiological significance, there is now considerable evidence of the functional importance of these linkages, particularly in the case of the tropic hormones, adrenocorticotropic hormone (Fortier, 1966, p. 195; Ganong, 1963, p. 92; Harris, 1955; Mangili, Motta, & Martini, 1966, p. 298; Mason, 1959c), thyrotropic hormone (D'Angelo, 1963, p. 158; Reichlin, 1966a, p. 445) and the gonadotropic hormones (Donovan, 1966, p. 49; Flerko, 1963, p. 211; Harris & Campbell, 1966, p. 99). There is also increasing physiological evidence of neural influences upon the secretion of prolactin (Everett, 1966, p. 166; Meites, Nicoll, & Talwalker, 1963, p. 238) and growth hormone (Pecile & Muller, 1966, p. 537; Reichlin, 1966b, p. 270).

2. The anterior hypothalamic-posterior pituitary neural linkage, involving neurosecretion of vasopressin (antidiuretic hormone) and oxytocin (Cross, 1966; Heller & Ginsburg, 1966, p. 330; Sawyer, 1963, p. 68; Sawyer & Mills, 1966, p. 187).

3. The posterior hypothalamic-sympathetic-adrenal medullary neural linkage, involving secretion of epinephrine and norepinephrine (Cannon, 1928; Euler, 1956; Folkow & Euler, 1954), shown in a highly schematic manner in Figure 1.1.

4. The possibility of a vagoinsulin or "vagoinsular" system has been considered since shortly after the discovery of insulin; the significance of such a possible linkage was of interest to Walter Cannon (1963). The early work on this problem, however, was inconclusive, principally because it was based upon the indirect estimate of insulin secretion as reflected in changes in blood sugar levels (Mason et al., 1968g). Since reliable radioimmunochemical assays have recently become available, the problem apparently has not as yet been systematically reevaluated. Subdiaphragmatic stimulation of the vagus presents some formidable experimental difficulties, particularly in dealing with certain compli-

cating variables, such as the blood glucose elevation secondary to surgical trauma in acute experiments. Evidence to be presented later in this series of papers indicates, however, that factors other than the blood glucose level are involved in the regulation of plasma insulin levels, so that the question of neural influences on insulin secretion still appears to be an open one, worthy of further study (Mason et al., 1968g).

5. The possibility of a posterior-diencephalic neurohumoral linkage, involving a hormone, "glomerulotropin," which can influence aldosterone secretion, in addition to the known renal and pituitary factors, has been suggested by the work of Farrell and his associates (Farrell, 1959; Taylor & Farrell, 1962). The existence or significance of such a neuroendocrine linkage has apparently not yet gained general acceptance and probably should be regarded as still awaiting definitive experimental evaluation (Mulrow, 1966, p. 408).

It is evident, then, that there are extensive anatomical linkages which provide points of contact for neural and presumably psychological influences upon a great many endocrine systems. In most instances the functional significance of these anatomical connections has already been demonstrated in neuroendocrine studies. From this viewpoint, then, there does not appear to be any justification for a selective or narrow focus on any single system, such as the pituitary-adrenal cortical system, in the study of brain-endocrine relationships. It appears, in fact, difficult at present to exclude on anatomical grounds any hormones from the neuroendocrine category, except possibly a few such as glucagon and parathyroid hormone. Even in these instances, however, neural or neurohumoral linkages have been discussed (Foa & Galansino, 1962; Morii, Fujita, Orimo, Okinaka, & Nakao, 1965) and may perhaps merit more study before they are conclusively ruled out. In any event, consideration of just the well-established neuroendocrine linkages alone seems to provide a strong argument for a broad, systematic survey of the extent to which the many endocrine systems are subjected to psychological influences.

Clinical impressions Another body of information which has suggested the influence of psychological factors on endocrine systems other than those involving the adrenal gland is provided by a number of long-standing clinical observations. These factors will be considered later in greater detail but a few examples may be briefly enumerated here. The recognition of a relationship between emotional states and menstrual and reproductive disorders has an ancient origin (Mason et al., 1968d). Such observations suggest the possibility that hormones such as the gonadotropins, estrogens, androgens, progesterone, and prolactin may be responsive to psychological factors. Parry's observation of the onset of hyperthyroidism following a severely frightening experience dates back to 1825. Clinical observations suggesting emotional influences on the secretion of still other hormones, including vasopressin and insulin, have also been reported (Mason et al., 1968a and 1968g). Clinical endocrinology, then, provides another set of impressions suggesting a relatively broad scope of psychoendocrine relationships.

Experimental findings In this enumeration of the factors underlying our present approach, it may be well to interject at this point two earlier experimental findings made in our own laboratory that were especially instrumental in promoting interest in the concurrent study of multiple endocrine systems. In our first effort in this direction, plasma epinephrine and norepinephrine measurements were added to our studies of plasma 17-OHCS responses to conditioned emotional stimuli in monkeys in order to study relationships between the pituitary-adrenal cortical and sympathetic-adrenal medullary systems. These experiments subsequently yielded evidence that these two major systems are under closely similar integrative control with regard to acute psychological stimuli. Some interesting evidence was also obtained, which suggested that two different patterns of hormonal response could be distinguished in a series of different stressful situations under study. In some situations only two hormones responded, while in other situations all three hormonal levels were elevated (Mason et al., 1961c; Mason, Brady, & Tolson, 1966, p. 227). It appeared, then, that information was obtained by the study of multiple, concurrent hormonal changes, providing a view of response "patterns" that could not have been obtained by studying a single hormone in isolation.

A second experimental finding which provided an important clue to the development of our present experimental approach occurred as a result of the measurement of changes in plasma and urinary pepsinogen levels in relation to sessions in which emotional disturbances were elicited in the monkey by using a conditioned "avoidance" procedure in which the monkey must, in the presence of a red light, press a hand lever in order to avoid an aversive stimulus. A striking and unexpected finding was the frequent occurrence of a marked and prolonged elevation in pepsinogen levels in the *aftermath* of these disturbing experimental sessions. Figure 1.2 shows that, while pepsinogen levels generally dropped during avoidance, a slow and prolonged elevation later ensued which often persisted for at least 5 days following a 3-day avoidance session (Mason et al., 1961a). While previous pattern studies had shown epinephrine, norepinephrine, and 17-OHCS levels to have generally similar dynamics in their response to acute emotional disturbances (in that the changes were in the same direction, although somewhat different in rate and duration), the dynamic features of the pepsinogen curves suggested a completely different class of regulatory phenomenon. While the corticosteroids

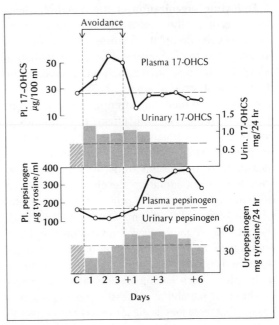

Figure 1.2 17-Hydroxycorticosteroid and pepsinogen responses to 72-hr avoidance sessions in the monkey.

and catecholamines predominate during the stressful period, the pepsinogen curves apparently indicate that significant regulatory changes also occur in a prolonged, second-phase recovery period. Although pepsinogen is, of course, not a hormone, its levels reflect neural and endocrine regulatory influences on the gastric function (Hirschowitz, 1957).

In searching for an explanation for a possible class of regulatory adjustments in the aftermath of a stressful period, the notion that reparative or restorative processes might logically follow the catabolic processes known to characterize the acute response period seemed worthy of consideration. The possibility, then, of a "catabolic-anabolic" sequence of regulatory events in relation to acute emotional disturbances became one of the specific working hypotheses underlying the present study. Whether this speculative extrapolation from pepsinogen changes to endocrine changes on a broad scale is justifiable or not, it was indeed this incident which most immediately brought the general concepts of the "organization" and "scope" of endocrine responses to the forefront of our thinking and provided a basis for visualizing a specific experimental approach to this problem.

Endocrine organization at the metabolic level
An account of the above experimental findings has also been interpolated in order to illustrate how we were led to still another body of information which has become increasingly influential in the development of our approach. The pepsinogen findings had turned our attention to the recent literature on the metabolic effects of hormones as we were seeking documentation for the selection of predominantly "anabolic" hormones to be measured in the present study. As our familiarity with this recent literature developed, it became evident that some general principles appear to be emerging from the field of metabolic endocrinology that almost certainly have implications of basic importance to the problem of endocrine organization. It is now known that most hormones are multipotent, each having a wide range of effects on different metabolic processes and tissues. It is known that most metabolic processes are subjected to the regulatory influence of many different hor-

mones. It is further known that these different hormones are closely interdependent, often bearing antagonistic, synergistic, additive, or permissive relationships to each other, which suggests that the activity of any given metabolic process at any given moment must be a resultant of the *over-all balance* between the cooperating and opposing hormonal influences which play upon it.

If endocrine function is organized in this manner at the *metabolic* level, it seems almost inescapable that the *regulation* of hormone secretion must be organized or coordinated on an over-all basis in general accordance with these close interdependencies of hormonal actions. The antagonistic nature of certain hormonal effects, such as that of epinephrine and insulin on carbohydrate metabolism, are reminiscent of the flexor-extensor relationships in the skeletal-muscular system or the sympathetic-parasympathetic relationships in the autonomic nervous system. The possibility suggests itself that the principle of reciprocal innervation as described by Sherrington for the skeletal-muscular nervous system and by Cannon (1929) for the autonomic nervous systems may also apply to the functional organization of the regulation of neuroendocrine systems. If there is coordination of neural control of flexor and extensor muscle action on bony levers or coordination of the dilator and constrictor innervation of the pupil, the gastrointestinal tract, etc., might there not be coordination of the secretory regulation of hormones with opposing actions in the body? In any event, it is clear that, in order to study such a postulated relationship or the more general question of *organized* changes in "over-all" hormonal balance experimentally, it will be necessary to make concurrent measurements of many different hormones in response to particular stimuli.

From the fields of neuroanatomy, clinical endocrinology, and metabolic endocrinology, then, one may derive support for suggesting a special necessity to explore the psychoendocrine field in terms of its full scope. As a first step in pursuing this goal, before the issue of endocrine organization may really be approached, it seems clear that a straight survey must be made of the number of endocrine responses that actually occur during emotional disturbances. If only a small percentage of hormones respond, then further interest in this approach would certainly be lessened. If, on the other hand, the scope of responses is broad, affecting many different hormones, then a basis for further study of the principles of endocrine organization would seem to be established.

The choice of hormone measurements for the study reported in 1968 (Mason, Brady, & Tolliver; Mason et al., 1968a–1968g, 1968i) was necessarily determined largely by the availability of suitable methods. Although the ideal goal of measuring levels of all the hormones, and hence of "over-all" hormonal balance, is not yet attainable, a survey of considerable scope is possible that involves just those hormones for which reliable methods of measurement are now available. In the first phase of this study we were able to measure plasma and urinary 17-hydroxycorticosteroids (17-OHCS), urinary epinephrine, norepinephrine, estrone, estradiol, estriol, androsterone, etiocholanolone, dehydroepiandrosterone, aldosterone, and plasma BEI (thyroxine) levels. Recently, largely because of our interest in comparing patterns of "anabolic" with "catabolic" hormones, we were able to add plasma insulin, plasma growth hormone, and urinary testosterone measurements to the battery.

The conditioned-avoidance procedure was chosen as a means of eliciting emotional disturbance in the monkey for several reasons. Considerable past experience with this procedure in our laboratory has substantiated its reliability and reproducibility. It elicits a disturbance which can be sustained over a long period of time—permitting the collection of urine in full 24-hr portions and allowing sufficient time for the more slow-moving endocrine systems to show appreciable responses. In addition, pilot studies had shown that the 17-OHCS elevations during 72-hr avoidance sessions were substantial and that lack of other hormonal responses in this situation would not likely be attributable to insufficient strength of the emotional stimulus.

The research papers appearing in 1968 and the present chapter deal primarily with the question, "How many endocrine systems are responsive to psychological factors?" Data on measurements of the hormones listed above in relation to 72-hr avoidance sessions appeared in 9 papers (Mason,

Brady, & Tolliver, 1968; Mason et al., 1968a–1968g, 1968i). The substantial body of published psychoendocrine data that deals with the corticosteroids, catecholamines, and thyroid hormones are reviewed in the next sections of this chapter. It is hoped that, while not exhaustive in its review of the literature, this chapter will not only give some idea of the impressive weight of the evidence supporting the sensitivity of the adrenal systems to psychological factors, but also will provide an indication of the highly selective focus that so far has been directed toward only a few endocrine systems. It may also become evident that the research models previously developed in psychoendocrine studies of the adrenal systems are ready and waiting to be applied to the many other endocrine systems.

While the following sections may be viewed mainly as an enumerative survey of the extent to which a number of different endocrine systems are subjected to psychological influences, it is hoped that, together with the data published in 1968, their relevance as the basis of a broad concept of endocrine organization will become evident. The theoretical discussion of our data appears in the last two sections of the chapter. Because the findings invite continued speculation and investigation along the lines which prompted the original work, and because such speculation appears to stimulate other new working hypotheses and experiments, it is hoped that its inclusion will seem justifiable.

THE PITUITARY-ADRENAL CORTICAL SYSTEM

Of all the endocrine systems, the pituitary-adrenal cortical system has been by far the most extensively studied from the standpoint of its subjection to the influence of psychological factors. The massive body of data which has accumulated on this system has led the way in establishing a solid foundation for a science of psychoendocrinology and has provided valuable methodological and conceptual models for future psychoendocrine research with many other endocrine systems.

Nearly all the experimental work in this field, furthermore, has been done in the past 20 years—with about 200 publications on the subject appearing during this period. This recent emphasis in psychoendocrine research on the pituitary-adrenal cortical system is perhaps particularly noteworthy when one considers the much longer history of folk, clinical, or experimental observations suggesting psychological influences on other endocrine glands, including the gonads (Mason et al., 1968d), the thyroid, and the adrenal medulla (Cannon & de la Paz, 1911). In contrast, observations suggesting psychological influences upon the pituitary-adrenal cortical system have a much shorter history.

An isolated report by Uno in 1922 described an increase in pituitary weight in rats following a 6-hr period of excitement. A speculative article by Hollingshead and Barton in 1931 suggested that the correlation between emotional instability and variability of blood nonprotein nitrogen levels in psychiatric patients, reported 10 years earlier by Hammett (1921a, 1921b), might indicate a relationship between the adrenal cortex and emotions (Hollingshead & Barton, 1931). No appreciable impetus was developed in this field, however, until 1936, when Selye reported morphological changes that included enlargement of the adrenal gland with loss of cortical lipoids in the rat after exposure to various experimental conditions, some of which were characterized as "merely causing nervous excitement." He also observed that the usual rapid involution of the thymus produced in rats when the legs are tied together for 48 hr does not occur following adrenalectomy or hypophysectomy. Similar findings were reported in rats subjected to fasting, various operative injuries, and drug administration (Selye, 1936a).

The implication of psychological stimuli in the regulation of the pituitary-adrenal cortical system by Selye appears to have intrigued many investigators, particularly those in psychiatric research, and to have provided the main initial stimulus for the recent heavy emphasis on adrenal cortical function in psychoendocrine research. In addition, the introduction about 15 years ago of excellent biochemical methods for measurement of the adrenal cortical hormones—among the first specific and practicable hormone assay methods to become available—was another major factor in the development of this trend.

Psychoendocrine research on the pituitary-adrenal cortical system might be viewed historically as being divided into two phases: the first including those early studies done prior to about 1955 with a great variety of indirect and nonspecific indices of adrenal cortical activity, and the second comprising those more recent studies that employ relatively specific and reliable, often chromatographic, methods for the biochemical measurement of the 17-hydroxycorticosteroids (17-OHCS) in blood or urine. In addition, perhaps three general approaches to the study of psychological disturbances may be identified: those that involve the study of experimental animals subjected to stressful conditions, the study of normal human subjects in stressful life and laboratory situations, and the study of patients in the course of psychiatric illnesses. While a number of reviews of this research have appeared in recent years, these have for the most part been selective in scope and do not individually really convey the full weight and extent of the data which have now accumulated in this field (Altschule, 1953; Bliss, Migeon, Branch, & Samuels, 1956; Bovard, 1959; Christian, 1961; Fox, 1960; Hamburg, 1962, p. 406; Hinde, 1959, p. 94; Hubble, 1963; Mason, 1959a, 1959c; Mason & Brady, 1964, p. 4; Mason, 1964, p. 375; Michael & Gibbons, 1963; Persky, 1962, p. 171; Rubin & Mandell, 1966; Sachar, 1967). Since a major objective of this chapter and our 1968 publications is to treat the issue of psychological influences on hormone secretion fully and critically, it may be appropriate to summarize the extensive data available from diverse sources, which now provide formidable support for the conclusion that psychological factors play a major role in pituitary-adrenal cortical regulation.

Studies with Experimental Animals

Stimulated by the work of Pavlov, Cannon, and others, Uno studied the effects of "general excitement" produced by fighting and electrical stimulation upon the weight and water content of the pituitary, adrenal, and thyroid glands in rats. In 1922 he reported that significant increases in pituitary weight occurred after "excitement" sessions of 6-hr duration, although adrenal and thyroid weights did not change during this period. Apparently no further experiments were done extending the duration of the sessions and this interesting lead was not followed up by others, although Rikimaru raised some questions about the significance of Uno's findings (Rikimaru, 1925).

Selye's initial experiments (reported in 1936), which showed an adrenal cortical response to psychological stimuli, were based upon immobilization of rats by tying the legs or wrapping them in a towel for 48 hr; the adrenal response was judged by morphological criteria, such as adrenal weight, as indirect indices of adrenal activity. Relatively few attempts to confirm or extend these observations on psychological stimuli in experimental animals were made for a number of years. Herrington and Nelbach (1942) reported an increase in adrenal weight of rats that were chronically disturbed by such stimuli as bell-ringing, air blasts, and cage vibration once each hour. Elmadjian and Pincus (1945) observed marked lymphopenia in mice immobilized by tying them to a wire grid. Long found a 40 percent drop in adrenal ascorbic acid levels in rats following brief painful stimulation of the sciatic or brachial nerves (1947).

In spite of these scattered early findings, several experiments reported around 1950, which demonstrated the release of ACTH from pituitary transplants in response to various agents, created some doubt as to the importance of the central nervous system in the regulation of the pituitary-adrenal cortical system (Fortier, 1951). In 1950, however, Colfer, de Groot, and Harris reported that marked lymphopenia is associated with the emotional stress of immobilization in the rabbit; it was further shown that this effect could be abolished by hypothalamic lesions (de Groot & Harris, 1950). Fortier reported some experiments in 1951 which appeared to provide a plausible basis for reconciliation of the differing viewpoints. He found that such "systemic" or humoral stimuli as adrenaline, cold, and histamine produced eosinopenia in normal rats and in rats with pituitary transplants in the anterior chamber of the eye, while "neurotropic" stimuli such as sound or immobilization induced a marked eosinopenia in the intact, but not in the grafted, animals. On the basis of these findings, he suggested that there is a dual control of adrenocorticotrophin release by both neural and humoral factors. Vogt (1951) also emphasized the effectiveness of emotional factors, such as those associated with the procedure of taking rectal temperature, in eliciting

ACTH release in the rat, as judged by a 60% drop in adrenal ascorbic acid levels. The association of lymphopenia with restraint was confirmed by Lavenda and co-workers in studies of both mice and rats (Lavenda, Bartlett, & Kennedy, 1956). Marsh and Rasmussen (1960) observed adrenal hypertrophy and drops in circulating leukocytes in mice exposed daily to emotionally disturbing shuttle box or confinement stress. Shapiro, Geller, and Eiduson (1962), in a study of neonatal rats, found that electric shock administration produced an adrenal cortical response, judged by adrenal corticosterone content, beginning at about 8 days of age.

It should also be pointed out that a series of neural studies of the effect of surgical ablation and electrical stimulation of the hypothalamus upon ACTH release, particularly those of Harris, helped to provide a foundation for psychoendocrine research in this field by establishing the functional significance of the portal-hypophysial capillary system and by beginning to elaborate the neurological pathways affecting anterior pituitary function (Harris, 1955; 1956, p. 31). The lack of secretomotor nerve supply to anterior pituitary cells had encouraged a concept of anterior pituitary functional autonomy, and the experimental demonstration of the significance of the unique neurohumoral, hypothalamic-hypophysial linkage was of special theoretical importance to the study of psychoendocrine relationships. The history of this field has recently been reviewed in some detail by Ganong (1963, p. 92) and the relevance of this approach to the psychoendocrine field has been emphasized (Mason et al., 1961d).

Beginning in about 1953 an interesting series of ecologically oriented studies developed some more support for the conclusion that psychological factors participate in pituitary adrenal-cortical regulation. In 1953 Clarke reported adrenal gland enlargement in fighting voles, in experiments suggested by a theoretical approach concerned with the dynamics of mammalian population cycles. In 1955 Christian found a direct relationship between population density and adrenal weight in mice, with adrenal cortical hypertrophy occurring in animals living under crowded conditions. The finding of evidence of increased adrenal activity with crowding or grouping of animals was subsequently confirmed in wild rats by Christian and Davis (1956) and by Barnett (1958); in mice by Thiessen, Zolman, and Rodgers (1962) and by Bronson and Eleftheriou (1963); in wild deer by Welch (1962); and in the monkey by Mason (1959). The phenomenon was thus demonstrated under both laboratory and field conditions. Barnett (1955) also commented upon the evidence of increased adrenal cortical activity in subordinate rats, as determined by the criterion of losing fights. This observation and Christian's finding of a significant correlation between adrenal weight and social rank (Davis & Christian, 1957) suggested that social and psychological factors might be involved in the mediation of population density effects upon the adrenal gland.

Southwick and Bland (1959) expressed a dissenting viewpoint; they failed to find a significant increase in mean adrenal weight in crowded animals and suggested that wounds resulting from fighting might be a principal factor in the adrenal enlargement of some animals. This possibility was also raised by the findings of Chitty and Leslie (1956). Christian (1959), however, found no correlation between injury from fighting and adrenal weight. Bronson and Eleftheriou reported that the adrenal cortical response to crowding may show strain differences in mice in relation to a genetic predisposition to aggressive or agonistic behavior. They showed, however, that mere exposure without physical contact of a subordinate mouse to fighters—particularly if the subject mouse has a previous history of defeat in combat—produces adrenal cortical responses as great as those observed in mice actually attacked and defeated (Bronson & Eleftheriou, 1964, 1965). Mason (1959b) also observed an adrenal cortical response in a small monkey who was merely a spectator to a fight between two large monkeys in an adjacent cage.

As most of the early studies of psychological influences on the pituitary-adrenal cortical system involved the use of nonspecific indices of ACTH activity and relatively crude methods of eliciting emotional distress, there was need for further evaluation of the findings of these studies with more specific and refined methods as the latter became available. In 1956 Mason and Brady employed operant conditioning techniques in order to elicit emotional distress relatively free of contaminating physical factors in the monkey; they used the

Nelson-Samuels method for the direct chromatographic measurement of plasma 17-OHCS levels as a relatively specific index of ACTH secretion. The resulting experimental findings showed that a conditioned emotional response, elicited simply by presentation of a mild clicking noise that had previously been paired with electric shock, was associated with marked plasma 17-OHCS elevations in the monkey. It was also found that this response was considerably reduced during the "tranquilizing" effect associated with administering reserpine to monkeys. Similar inhibition of the ACTH response to emotional stimuli in the rat following meprobramate administration was also reported by Makela, Naatanen, and Rinne (1959). Extension of studies in the monkey revealed that substantial changes in plasma or urinary 17-OHCS levels were associated also with conditioned avoidance, conditioned "punishment" extinction of food reward under special conditions, and with a variety of environmental disturbances—especially those involving novel or "first" experiences, including catching and handling, initial placement in a restraining chair, or transfer from one cage to another (Mason, 1959b, 1964; Mason, Brady, & Sidman, 1957; Mason, Harwood, & Rosenthal, 1957). Even subtle factors such as the day of the week, housing conditions, and the degree of surrounding environmental or social activity appeared to be sensitively reflected in plasma and urinary 17-OHCS changes, suggesting the concept of a tonicity exerted upon 17-OHCS levels by psychological factors (Mason, 1959b, 1964, p. 375; Mason & Brady, 1956, 1964, p. 4). Additional support for the specificity of the relationship between psychological factors and 17-OHCS changes was furnished by the demonstration of quantitative relations between certain parameters of avoidance behavior and 17-OHCS responses (Sidman, Mason, Brady, & Thach, 1962) and by the substantial decrease in the plasma 17-OHCS response to avoidance which accompanies the docility following amygdalectomy in the monkey (Mason et al., 1961d).

Biochemically measured plasma or urinary hormonal changes associated with environmental or psychological factors have also been observed in other species, although the use of chromatographic methods in psychoendocrine experiments with animals has been limited as yet. Holcombe reported in 1957 that marked and prolonged elevations of urinary "reducing corticoids" in cattle and sheep accompanied gross environmental changes such as those associated with introduction to a new environment or new experimental procedure. Using a fluorometric method, Fortier (1958; Fortier, de Groot, & Hartfield, 1959) observed marked plasma corticosteroid elevations in the rat in response to environmental transfer from one room to the next and in response to faradic stimulation. In the guinea pig, Burstein, Bhavanai, and Kimball (1964) reported two- to threefold increases in urinary corticosteroid excretion as a result of immobilization. Levine and Treiman (1964) demonstrated substantial plasma corticosterone elevations in mice as a result of the first immobilization experience and during repeated electric shock. Hill, Greer, and Felsenfeld (1967) observed plasma cortisol elevations in vervets subjected to irregular noise, light, and vertical movement. Ader, Friedman, and Grota (1967) have reported plasma corticosterone elevations in rats in response to an open field test and a reaction-to-handling test.

Comment It is clear, then, that experiments with direct biochemical measurement of plasma or urinary 17-OHCS elevations in response to a variety of psychological stimuli in many different animal species support fully the general conclusions of earlier work based upon less-refined methods of estimating ACTH release. There are some general features of this work with animals which may deserve comment.

First, many investigators have been impressed by the surprising sensitivity of the pituitary-adrenal cortical system to psychological stimuli, both in terms of the intensity of response to acute, dramatic stimuli, and the more subtle adjustments of basal 17-OHCS levels to everyday environmental factors.

While the system appears to respond to a wide variety of events and psychological stimuli, there do appear to be some conditions which tend to elicit responses of unusual intensity. The element of novelty, uncertainty, or unpredictability appears especially striking in this regard, as was demonstrated in the various "first experience" effects observed by many workers.

The study of conditioned emotional responses suggests that situations involving anticipation of,

or waiting for, something previously experienced as unpleasant, such as electric shock, are often associated with 17-OHCS responses larger than those associated with the unpleasant experience itself.

It also appears that the element of "involvement" or "trying" in situations in which the animal must master a difficult task in order to forestall aversive stimuli may have special relevance to the intensity of 17-OHCS response.

Finally, situations in which long-established rules are suddenly changed, and the behavior which previously was effective no longer accomplishes mastery of the task at hand, may lead to disorganized behavioral patterns which are likely to be associated with unusually intense 17-OHCS elevations.

Studies with Human Subjects

Because direct examination of the adrenal gland was precluded in human studies, the investigation of the effects of psychological stimuli on pituitary-adrenal cortical activity in humans was delayed considerably after Selye's early work with rats. Until about 1955 most of the studies attempted with human subjects involved the measurement of urinary 17-ketosteroid levels, blood eosinophil or lymphocyte levels, urinary electrolyte excretion, or the levels of a variety of urinary metabolites such as uric acid, creatinine, and phosphates. While these methods are lacking in specificity to a degree that their value as indices of pituitary-adrenal cortical activity is in serious question, the ingenuity of some of these early experiments and their influence on later work in the field may justify their inclusion in this survey. It should be particularly kept in mind, however, that the urinary 17-ketosteroid procedure involved in many of these studies is an ambiguous index, reflecting a variable mixture of adrenal cortical and gonadal secretory changes, and that the hematological and urinary metabolite measurements are also influenced by other hormones than those of the adrenal cortex (Bliss, Migeon, Branch, & Samuels, 1955; Sayers, 1950; Thorn, Jenkins, & Laidlaw, 1953). In terms of the approach to the study of psychological factors, these studies may be conveniently categorized according to whether normal human subjects or psychiatric patients were involved.

Normal subjects In a study of normal college students and aviators in 1943, Pincus and Hoagland demonstrated elevations in urinary 17-ketosteroid excretion during flight in test pilots and instructor pilots, as well as in normal subjects in the laboratory who were exposed to simulated flight situations involving performance with the serial coordination meter and pursuit meter. In a summary of this and related work in 1947, Pincus also describes an incident in which a nearly threefold increase in urinary 17-ketosteroid excretion was associated with a call to emergency hospital duty in a normal subject. Two similar examples of dramatic psychological disturbances associated with marked elevations in pituitary-adrenal cortical activity, as determined by a bioassay procedure, were mentioned by Browne in 1950.

In 1951 the admirable studies of Thorn and his associates, in which adrenal cortical activity was evaluated in Harvard oarsmen during the 2 weeks preceding the annual Harvard-Yale 4-mile race, were first reported. The demonstration of marked eosinopenia on the race day—not only in the crew members but also in the coach and coxswain as well—clearly implicated emotional factors in this physiological response (Renold, Quigley, Kennard, & Thorn, 1951). It was also reported by Frost, Dryer, and Kohlstaedt (1951) that marked eosinopenia and increased excretion of 17-ketosteroids occurred in auto race drivers participating in the 500-mile Indianapolis Speedway Race. Eosinopenia was also reported in association with such stressful experiences as performing mental calculations (Tatai, Mori, & Ito, 1951), parachute jumping (Basowitz, Persky, Korchin, & Grinker, 1955), and in taking final college examinations (Markkanen, Pekkarinen, Pulkkinen, & Simola, 1956). Recognizing the limitations of eosinophil count as an equivocal index of ACTH secretion, Thorn, Jenkins, Laidlaw, Goetz, and Reddy reported in 1953 that the eosinopenia in an oarsman and the coxswain were accompanied by substantial elevations in urinary 17-OHCS levels on the race day. A later summary of this work with urinary 17-OHCS measurements presents additional findings, such as corticosteroid elevations on time-trial days and correlations between psychological and hormonal observations, which convincingly implicate psychological factors in the determi-

nation of the observed changes in adrenal cortical activity (Hill et al., 1956).

A development of major importance was the application of chromatographic methods for plasma and urinary 17-OHCS measurement, with their relatively high degree of specificity, to the study of this problem, particularly in the studies made by Bliss and his co-workers in 1956. They surveyed 17-OHCS levels in a wide variety of stressful life situations, studying the relatives of emergency-room patients, medical students taking final examinations, day-to-day events in normal subjects, as well as through a number of contrived laboratory techniques of eliciting emotional disturbance. The general conclusion was drawn that the emotional disturbances associated with most of these situations caused modest but consistent increases in plasma and urinary 17-OHCS levels.

The pattern for future work in this field was thus established essentially along the lines traditionally employed in psychophysiological research with regard to the use of natural stressful life situations and laboratory attempts to elicit or isolate emotional disturbances in human subjects. These methodological categories, in fact, may serve as a convenient basis for summarizing the numerous psychoendocrine studies involving blood and urinary corticosteroid measurements in normal human subjects which have been reported in the past 10 years or so.

Stressful life situations The early studies of the effects of aircraft flight by Pincus and Hoagland (1943; Pincus, 1947) were followed by those of Murphy, Gofton, and Cleghorn (1954), who reported some inconclusive results from the measurement of corticoids in air crewmen by a phosphomolybdic acid reduction technique. Craven and Smith (1955) found an increase in the excretion level of phenolic steroids but not in formaldehydogenic steroids in airmen during flight periods. Substantial elevations in urinary 17-OHCS levels, as measured by the chromatographic method of Glenn and Nelson, were reported in long-range bomber crews by Marchbanks (1958, 1960) and Mason (1959b). Hale and co-workers also observed elevated plasma 17-OHCS levels in pilots and air crewmen after long flights (Hale, 1965, p. 527; Hale,

Duffy, Ellis, & Williams, 1964; Hale, Ellis, & Kratochvil, 1959; Hale, Kratochvil, Ellis, & Williams, 1958). Colehour and Graybiel (1963) reported that subjects with labyrinthine defects did not show the corticosteroid response observed in normal subjects during acrobatic flight. They suggested that the vestibular organs must be taken into account in evaluating flight effects on hormone excretion in instances such as acrobatic flight, in which "the gravitational inertial force environment is a variable." In a recent study, Hale et al. (1964) reported that urinary 17-OHCS levels were found to be higher in inexperienced pilots than in experienced pilots on training flights.

Preoperative period   The changes in 17-OHCS levels associated with mounting apprehension in surgical patients during the immediate preoperative period have been studied by several groups. In 1953 Moncrief, Weichselbaum, and Elman reported marked elevations in plasma corticosteroid levels in some patients during the 24-hr period before operation. Using the Nelson-Samuels chromatographic method, Fransson and Gemzell (1955) found preoperative increases in plasma 17-OHCS levels in 26 of 33 patients and suggested that this change was related to psychic tension. Significant 8:00 AM plasma 17-OHCS elevations the day before elective thoracic surgery were reported by Price, Thaler, and Mason (1957), who also found significant correlations between high 17-OHCS values and four Rorschach ratings which were interpreted as indicating a relatively undifferentiated state of "discomfort-involvement." Thomasson (1959) found elevated plasma 17-OHCS levels at 8:00 o'clock on the evening before operations, but not on the following morning. He also reviewed several other reports in which significant mean plasma 17-OHCS elevations were not observed in the preoperative period. It appears very likely, however, that in most instances such negative findings may be attributed to methodological factors, including failure to consider the diurnal rhythm of 17-OHCS levels, failure to consider the effect of preanesthetic medication, particularly the depressant effect on 17-OHCS levels of Nembutal or barbiturates given the night before operation, and the reliance upon the situational criterion of impending surgery rather than upon psychological evaluation of the marked

individual differences in the degree of preoperative disturbance experienced by different patients.

In a careful and well-controlled series of studies, Shannon and his associates have shown recently that significant preoperative plasma 17-OHCS elevations occur in dental patients routinely scheduled for simple extraction or oral surgery for impaction (Shannon, Isbell, & Hester, 1962; Shannon, Isbell, Prigmore, & Hester, 1962; Shannon, Prigmore, Hester, McCall, & Isbell, 1960, 1961; Shannon, Szmyd, & Prigmore, 1962). In addition, they found that such routinely scheduled patients ran 17-OHCS levels significantly higher than unscheduled patients who were brought to oral surgery without an appreciable anticipation period. In a study involving psychiatric and psychological evaluation of preoperative emotional state, Bursten and Russ (1965) found a significant positive correlation between 17-OHCS levels and degree of "discomfort-involvement," confirming the findings of Price, Thaler, and Mason (1957).

Final examinations of college students present another opportunity to study stressful situations. Schwartz and Shields (1954, 1956) reported a positive correlation between estimates of psychic tension and urinary formaldehydogenic steroid levels in medical students taking final examinations, but expressed some reservations about the interpretation of their data because of failure to observe similar correlations between the two measures under other conditions. Using the Nelson-Samuels method, Bliss et al. (1956) reported significant plasma 17-OHCS elevations in most medical students on the morning of an important final examination. The increase in adrenal cortical activity in association with final college examinations has also been reported by Venning, Dyrenfurth, and Beck (1957); by Melick (1960), who measured urinary 17-OHCS levels; by Connell, Cooper, and Redfearn (1958), who measured urinary 17-ketogenic steroids; by Hodges, Jones, and Stockham (1962), who measured plasma 17-OHCS and ACTH levels; and by Jensen and Ek (1962), who measured "TZR" reducing substances. Recent experience in our own laboratory with this approach has indicated the importance of continuous daily sample collection for at least 3 days prior to examinations, as well as during and after the time, as some subjects may show the greatest 17-OHCS response prior to examinations, some may do so during the examinations, and some only if examinations continue for several days. Marked individual differences in psychological reaction to examinations must also be evaluated (Mason et al., unpublished data).

A number of observations have been made in which unfamiliar or "first experience" situations have been associated with substantial 17-OHCS elevations, indicating that novelty is an especially potent stimulus to the pituitary-adrenal cortical system in man as well as animals. Elevated plasma 17-OHCS levels associated with the experience of hospital admission in elective surgery patients were reported in 1957 by Price, Thaler, and Mason. Also, Sabshin et al. (1957) observed plasma 17-OHCS levels in patients on the first day that they were brought to a laboratory for psychoendocrine experiments. Sloane, Saffran, and Cleghorn (1958) and Davis et al. (1962) also noted an elevation of corticosteroid levels in normal subjects who were brought into an unfamiliar laboratory for experimental study. An extensive study of urinary and plasma 17-OHCS levels in normal young adults revealed significant elevations in the majority of subjects on the first day of hospital admission to a normal control ward (Mason, Sachar, Fishman, Hamburg, & Handlon, 1965).

In these subjects correlations were also observed between several psychological and social factors and the adrenal cortical response (Fishman, Hamburg, Handlon, Mason, & Sachar, 1962). The hospital admission effect on 17-OHCS levels was also observed by Friedman, Mason, and Hamburg (1963) in another population of normal subjects. The studies of Wadeson, Mason, Hamburg, and Handlon (1963) further suggested that the impact, in terms of adrenal cortical response, of a novel situation may be lessened by reassurance and briefing aimed at reducing feelings of ambiguity and uncertainty. In a study of adolescent girls visiting Israel for 1 year, Shanan, Brzezinski, Sulman, and Sharon (1965) observed that subjects who subsequently became amenorrheic tended to have higher initial urinary 17-OHCS levels shortly after arrival from the United States.

Other situations The extensive, primarily psychological studies done on trainee paratroopers by Grinker and his associates included some obser-

vations of eosinopenia in relation to stressful training experiences (Basowitz, Persky, Korchin, & Grinker, 1955). Several studies of soldiers in combat in Korea made by Davis and Taylor (1954), Elmadjian (1955), and Howard et al. (1955) provided evidence of marked elevations in adrenal cortical activity in some men in response to acute battle danger. Following the studies on crew racing (Hill et al., 1956; Thorn, Jenkins, & Laidlaw, 1953; Thorn et al., 1953) and on auto racing (Frost, Dryer, & Kohlstaedt, 1951), there apparently have not been other reported studies of 17-OHCS responses related to athletic or sports competition. In 1955 Hetzel, Schottstaedt, Grace, and Wolff described a case in which the fearful anticipation of exposure to cold was associated with a greater urinary 17-OHCS response than the cold exposure itself. Mason (1959b) also observed substantial urinary 17-OHCS elevations in soldiers anticipating a 96-hr period of sleep deprivation.

A depression in adrenal cortical activity in human subjects on weekends, similar to that observed in the monkey, has been observed in human subjects by Mason and Brady (1964), who measured urinary 17-OHCS levels; and by Halberg, Engeli, and Hamburger (1965), who measured urinary 17-ketosteroid levels. These observations suggest the need to consider even subtle and routine aspects of the environment as having relevance to pituitary-adrenal cortical function. Observations by Shenkin (1964) on the effects of pain on plasma 17-OHCS levels, and by Arguelles, Ibeas, Ottone, and Chekherdemian (1962) on the effects of sounds of different frequencies on corticosteroid levels are also pertinent to the psychoendocrine field.

Chronic studies Most of the studies enumerated so far have been concerned primarily with the question of whether acute emotional responses are associated with concomitant pituitary-adrenal cortical responses. These studies on normal human subjects, however, particularly those conducted in a more chronic setting, inevitably led to the realization that psychological factors other than simply the current emotional state must be considered in psychoendocrine research. The repeated observations of a wide range of individual differences in hormonal levels of different persons exposed to the same situation led to a search for possible correlating psychological variables. The importance of the effectiveness of psychological defenses as a determinant of 17-OHCS response to situational factors was emphasized by Price, Thaler, and Mason (1957) in their study of preoperative 17-OHCS responses. Fox, Murawski, Bartholomay, and Gifford (1961) observed rather stable individual chronic mean urinary 17-OHCS levels in a large group of normal young men and found correlations between these individual differences in 17-OHCS levels and certain personality factors as determined by psychiatric interview and projective tests. A number of studies (Fiorica & Muehl, 1962; Sholiton, Wohl, & Werk, 1963; Tecce, Friedman, & Mason, 1965) have also been concerned with the possible correlation of relatively stable differences in 17-OHCS levels and psychological factors in individual subjects. The earlier study of Berkeley (1952), in which the extent of discrepancy between level of aspiration and achievement in test performance was related to 17-ketosteroid levels, also suggested involvement of personality characteristics in psychoendocrine response.

In long-term studies of the parents of leukemic children made during the course of their child's illness, a number of marked adrenal cortical elevations associated with emotional responses to life events were noted by Friedman, Mason, and Hamburg (1963) but the persistence of characteristic individual differences in chronic mean basal urinary 17-OHCS levels over periods of months or years was a more striking finding. Subsequently, a predictive psychiatric study by Wolff, Friedman, Hofer, and Mason (1964; also Wolff, Hofer, & Mason, 1964), concerned with an evaluation of the effectiveness of defenses in individual subjects, offered strong support for the hypothesis that defensive structure is an important determinant of chronic mean 17-OHCS level. In 1968 Rose, Poe, and Mason obtained quite similar results in a comparable study in which the urinary 17-OHCS levels of Army recruits were predicted on the basis of psychological factors; these workers also emphasized the importance of taking body weight into consideration in this type of study. One of the interesting findings in some of the chronic "low" 17-OHCS excretors has been a tendency to *suppress* 17-OHCS levels lower on stressful days than on uneventful days (Mason, 1964, p. 4). A striking example of this phenomenon was seen in a study of 17-OHCS levels in helicopter

medic and combat units in Vietnam (Bourne, Rose, & Mason, 1967). It is thus clear that future psychoendocrine studies must take into consideration not only emotional state, but also those psychological mechanisms which are concerned with counteracting or minimizing emotional arousal.

Experimentally induced stress The use of the operation of a pursuit meter as a stressful experience in the early studies by Pincus, Hoagland, and their collaborators, and Bliss's use of monotonous tasks, enforced self-analysis, stressful interviews, delayed speech feedback apparatus, and other contrived laboratory situations have already been mentioned (Bliss, Migeon, Branch, & Samuels, 1956; Hoagland, Bergen, Bloch, Elmadjian, & Gibree, 1955; Pincus & Hoagland, 1943; Pincus, 1947). The stressful interview technique has also been used by Hetzel et al. (1955) who observed substantial urinary 17-OHCS responses in some persons during interviews in which topics of special significance to the particular individual were discussed.

The use of motion pictures as a means of altering emotional state has been explored by a number of workers. In 1953 Thorn et al. observed variable degrees of eosinopenia in subjects observing movies of aboriginal ceremonial rites but they did not detect 17-OHCS elevations in short-term urine samples. Euler, Gemzell, Levi, and Strom (1959) failed to find significant increases in mean plasma 17-OHCS levels in subjects observing censored movies depicting violence, but they did observe mild elevations in urinary 17-ketosteroid levels. A study of plasma and urinary 17-OHCS levels in several small groups involved in a series of movie experiments showed mild but significant elevations in plasma 17-OHCS levels in response to a war movie in one group. A particularly interesting finding was the marked decrease in plasma 17-OHCS levels which consistently occurred during the viewing of Disney nature films. Because of the mild 17-OHCS changes usually observed in association with movie viewing, some crucial physiological aspects of experimental design appear to deserve special attention in future studies (Handlon et al., 1962; Wadeson et al., 1963).

The hypnotic induction of emotional distress has also been tried in psychoendocrine experiments. Persky, Grosz, Norton, and McMurtry (1959a) found that induction of the hypnotic trance significantly reduced plasma 17-OHCS levels in both sexes and that subsequent induction of anxiety raised the level in women by 75% but did not affect levels in men. Subsequently, Levitt and Persky (1960) also reported some indications that 17-OHCS responses in hypnotized subjects may be correlated with several factors scored on the Rorschach test. Grosz (1961) reported that plasma 17-OHCS levels rose significantly during a period of hypnotically induced anxiety in women but not in men. Sachar, Fishman, and Mason (1965) studied hypnotized subjects and confirmed that sharp decreases in plasma 17-OHCS levels are associated with the onset of the trance in some subjects. Attempts to predict, on the basis of several factors, which subjects were likely to show this trance effect suggested that the degree of the regressive relationship to the hypnotist may be a more useful criterion for prediction than estimates of suggestibility or susceptibility of trance induction (Sachar, Cobb, & Shor, 1966).

Another laboratory attempt to differentiate emotional responses by psychoendocrine methods was reported by Korchin and Herz (1960), who devised two experimental tasks in which "shame" and "disintegrative" threats might be perceived by normal college students. Subjects showed plasma 17-OHCS responses in both situations, with a greater response to the disintegrative threat, although this task was judged by the investigators to be associated with less affective change than the shame threat. Some recent studies by Frazier (1966b) provide encouragement that behavioral conditioning methods similar to those employed in studies with experimental animals may be profitably applied to the study of human subjects. Zuckerman, Persky, Hopkins, Murtaugh, Basu, and Schilling (1966) have also reported urinary 17-ketogenic steroid elevations in normal subjects exposed to 8-hr perceptual deprivation sessions.

While the finer degree of control and the experimental and practical advantages of the laboratory situation are well recognized, it is evident that relatively little effort has yet been devoted to this approach in comparison with the study of naturally occurring stressful life situations. In general, the results have confirmed the sensitivity of 17-OHCS levels to psychological factors—particularly that levels may be lowered as well as raised on a psychological basis. At the same time, the results have been somewhat disappointing in terms of the relatively small changes in 17-OHCS levels evoked and the substantial range of individual differences observed. It appears either that most subjects can maintain effective defenses against contrived stimuli presented in an artificial setting or that the stimuli presented so far have not been of sufficient intensity. It may be that future efforts in this direction should include consideration of small group social settings in an effort to overcome some of these problems (Mason & Brady, 1964, p. 4).

Disturbed patients   Except for the isolated report of Hollingshead and Barton (1931), in reference to work by Hammett (1921a, 1921b) and some scattered early hematological studies reviewed by Altschule (1953), apparently the investigation of adrenal cortical activity in psychiatric patients received little attention until about 1945. At this time, the extensive studies of Pincus, Hoagland, and their associates created a considerable interest in the study of schizophrenic patients that lasted for about a 10-year period. It is particularly relevant, in terms of the objectives of this review, to point out that these studies were not, however, primarily concerned with evaluating the sensitivity of the pituitary-adrenal cortical system to psychological influences but rather arose in a setting oriented in terms of the long-standing search for a biochemical abnormality which might distinguish schizophrenic patients from normal subjects (Hoskins, 1946). The principal focus was on the possibility of chronic abnormalities in adrenal cortical function in schizophrenic patients, rather than with the possibility of close relationships between changes in emotional or affective states and adrenal cortical hormone levels in schizophrenic patients. To this extent, some of the following studies involve a digression from the main issue under discussion, but it may be well to review them for the very purpose of emphasizing their delineation from other work in the psychoendocrine field.

The initial experiments reported (Elmadjian & Pincus, 1946; Freeman, Pincus, & Glover, 1944; Hoagland, Elmadjian, & Pincus, 1946; Pincus &

Elmadjian, 1946) were based upon comparisons between groups of normal and chronic schizophrenic subjects with regard to lymphocyte and urinary 17-ketosteroid levels under basal conditions and in response to such stressful experiences as exposure to cold, heat, anoxia, pursuit-meter operation, and psychological tests. The acute experiments were generally done in the morning and involved "prestress" and "stress" urine sample collection periods of relatively short, 2- or 3-hr duration. The findings in these studies led to the general conclusion that psychotic patients fail to show normal adrenal cortical responses to stress (Hoagland, 1947; Pincus, 1947). These studies were extended to include additional methods of attempting to elicit adrenal cortical activation, such as glucose ingestion, the targetball frustration test, and ACTH administration—as well as additional indirect indices of adrenal cortical activity, including urinary uric acid, potassium, sodium, inorganic phosphate, and neutral reducing lipid content (Pincus, 1949; Pincus & Hoagland, 1950; Pincus, Hoagland, Freeman, Elmadjian, & Romanoff, 1949a; Pincus, Schenker, Elmadjian, & Hoagland, 1949b). The resulting findings were interpreted as generally confirming earlier conclusions and as indicating a diminished adrenal cortical responsivity or a type of "hypoadrenalism" in the psychotic patient.

Attempts by other investigators to repeat or confirm these findings led to a period of considerable controversy and confusion. While some workers (Faurbye, Vestergaard, Kobbernagel, & Nielsen, 1951; Friedlander, Perrault, Turner, & Gottfried, 1950; Gottfried & Willner, 1949; Hemphill & Reiss, 1950) reported findings that appeared to provide at least partial support for the conclusions of Pincus, Hoagland, and their associates, a number of other investigators (Altschule, Promisel, Parkhurst, & Grunebaum, 1950; Bliss, Rubin, & Gilbert, 1951; Gildea, 1950, p. 565; Glaser & Hoch, 1951; Hiatt, Rothwell, & Horwitt, 1952; Parsons, Gildea, Ronzoni, & Hulbert, 1949; Stein, Ronzoni, & Gildea, 1951) did not find evidence of adrenal cortical abnormalities in their psychotic patients. In view of this controversy, attention was naturally turned to the many methodological details and experimental variables which might account for the conflicting findings and conclusions. The finer

study of nutritional factors (Pincus et al., 1949b) and of age (Freeman, Pincus, Elmadjian, & Romanoff, 1955; Hoagland et al., 1953; Mittleman, Romanoff, Pincus, & Hoagland, 1952) did not appreciably alter the position of Pincus, Hoagland, and associates regarding the existence of adrenal cortical abnormalities in schizophrenic patients.

The urgent need for more specific indices of adrenal cortical function at this point was increasingly recognized by most workers in the field. The report by Bliss and his co-workers in 1955, in which the newly introduced Nelson-Samuels chromatographic method for measuring plasma 17-OHCS levels was applied to the study of schizophrenic patients, was therefore an important milestone in the elucidation of this problem. Using this relatively direct and specific index of adrenal cortical activity, Bliss and his associates (1955) found no evidence of impairment of adrenal cortical function in chronic schizophrenic patients, as judged by the plasma 17-OHCS response to administration of ACTH, Piromen, or insulin. Similar studies of plasma 17-OHCS levels by Dohan, Winick, Purcell, Bennett, and Hecker (1955); by Tui, Riley, Columbus, and Orr (1956); and of urinary 17-OHCS levels by Sloane, Saffran, and Cleghorn (1958); and Eiduson, Brill, and Crumpton (1961) gave strong additional support for the conclusion that mean adrenal cortical responsivity in chronic schizophrenic patients was not significantly different from that of normal subjects.

Virtually all the psychoendocrine studies of schizophrenic patients reviewed up to this point utilized what has been called the *contrast* method of comparing mean values between groups of psychotic and normal subjects (Gornall, Eglitis, Miller, Stokes, & Dewan, 1953). Fortunately, the *longitudinal* method of studying individual patients throughout various phases of psychotic illnesses has also been applied more recently and has yielded valuable insight into some of the reasons for the confusion arising from the earlier "contrast" studies. The initial series of studies employing the longitudinal approach that were made by Reiss, Hemphill, Gordon, and Cook (1949), Gornall et al. (1953), Bryson and Martin (1954), and Rizzo, Fox, Laidlaw, and Thorn (1954) were concerned with patients with periodic catatonia or manic-depressive cycles and were largely limited by the use of crude biochemical methods for evaluating adrenal cortical activity. These studies did, however, indicate that hormone levels often changed in close relation to changing phases of clinical illness; they began to call attention to such important variables as the duration of psychotic illness, significant subgroup differences within the gross diagnostic categories of psychotic illness, the severity of illness, and, particularly, the importance of evaluating the degree of affective distress in patients in relation to endocrine measurements. It became increasingly evident that the study of heterogenous "chronic schizophrenic" groups was an unsound practice in psychoendocrine research unless careful estimates of emotional or psychological state in relation to hormone measurements were included in the experimental design.

The application of increasingly refined methods for plasma and urinary hormone measurements by Rizzo et al. (1954), Gunne and Gemzell (1956), Willcox (1959), Rey, Willcox, Gibbons, Tait, and Lewis (1961), and Suwa, Yamashita, Owada, Shinohara, and Nakazawa (1962) confirmed the consistent association of changes in the clinical phase of illness with changes in adrenal cortical hormone levels. In the studies of Rey et al. (1961), it was noted that urinary corticosteroid levels tended to be high in schizophrenic patients during periods of affective distress, subsiding during calm periods. In a study by Sachar, Mason, Kolmer, and Artiss (1963) of four patients seen over the several-month course of acute schizophrenic reactions, urinary 17-OHCS levels (measured by the Glenn-Nelson chromatographic method) were found to be high in "turmoil" and "depression" phases but lower in "psychotic equilibrium" and "recovery" phases, with striking consistency. It was found that 17-OHCS levels do not reflect the type or severity of the psychotic process per se, but rather the degree of emotional distress and the effectiveness of protective psychological defenses—whether the defenses be normal, neurotic, or psychotic. Thus, at the time the patient is the most severely psychotic and withdrawn, emotional distress is often minimal and adrenal cortical activity differs little, if any, from normal levels or from the patient's own level following eventual recovery. These observations suggest, therefore, the methodological corollary that

"contrast" studies of groups of normal subjects and psychotics in equilibrium would not be expected to show significant differences in 17-OHCS levels. Sachar, Harmatz, Bergen, and Cohler (1966), in a subsequent study, also found shifts in corticosteroid excretion in schizophrenic patients when defensive organization was disrupted during therapy, particularly when chronic psychotic defenses were challenged. The importance of taking into account the patient's relation with his milieu was also emphasized in this study. Recently, Matsumoto, Berlet, Bull, and Himwich (1966) have also reported shifting urinary 17-OHCS levels in relation to changes in symptoms in longitudinal studies of schizophrenic patients. Lovegrove, Melcalfe, Hobbs, and Stevenson (1965) have noted higher free corticosteroid excretion levels in acute than in chronic schizophrenic patients.

The early "contrast" studies, from which it was concluded that schizophrenic patients as a group show abnormally low adrenal cortical responsivity, appear, then, to have been misleading from a number of standpoints, as discussed above and earlier by Altschule (1953) and Bliss et al. (1955).

In summary, some of the principal limitations of these studies may be stated as follows: (a) the use of indirect or ambiguous methods, particularly the urinary 17-ketosteroid measurement, for estimating adrenal cortical function; (b) the fact that most subsequent studies with more specific 17-hydroxycorticosteroid measurements yielded nonconfirmatory findings; (c) the use of psychological tests as stressful stimuli in psychotic patients (of questionable validity; negative endocrine findings require evidence that the stimulus truly elicited emotional disturbance); (d) closely related to the previous point, the relatively indiscriminate use of patient groups of questionable homogeneity, particularly in the absence of clinical estimates of emotional state at the time of endocrine measurements; (e) the difficulty, in "contrast" studies of endocrine function in different groups, of evaluating or controlling such variables as body weight, nutritional status, age, seasonal factors, physical activity, drug administration, and other parameters as emphasized by Ingle (1951); and (f) the fact that the experimental design of acute psychoendocrine experiments from the standpoint of physiological dynamics is a more complex problem than is generally recognized. Such practices as the use of short-term, 2- or 3-hr urine collections, or of obtaining "prestress" urine samples during the morning (at a time when urinary 17-OHCS levels are apt to be high normally and often show marked diurnal variations between successive 1-hr periods), are particularly hazardous unless extensive control data are obtained (Romanoff, Rodriguez, Seelye, & Pincus, 1957; Sachar, Mason, Fishman, Hamburg, & Handlon, 1965; Wadeson et al., 1963).

Before dismissing this problem, however, it may be well to keep in mind that we do not yet have a complete understanding of the precise role that each of the above variables, or others, may have played in the conflicting results yielded by different individual studies. The possibility that the study of altered psychoendocrine responsivity in human subjects may yet prove to be a fruitful line of inquiry, particularly in longitudinal studies involving intensive psychiatric and psychological observations on individual subjects, should certainly remain open for future consideration.

The studies concerned with the quest for a constitutional abnormality or deficiency which might have pathogenetic significance in schizophrenia clearly must be regarded separately from the mainstream of psychoendocrine research concerned with emotional influences on the pituitary-adrenal cortical system, such as is represented by the extensive research with animals and normal human subjects reviewed earlier. It should be emphasized, however, that the studies of schizophrenic patients in whom emotional state was systematically evaluated in relation to endocrine measurements yielded generally consistent results, indicating close correlation between phases of psychological and hormonal change and thus providing another useful body of data that demonstrates the sensitivity of 17-OHCS levels to emotional factors.

Pincus reported some evidence in 1949 suggesting adrenal cortical hyperactivity in psychoneurotic subjects. Cleghorn and Graham (1950), also using indirect methods, reported that greater activation of the adrenal cortex was elicited by various tests, including controlled thermal pain and electroconvulsive therapy, in patients showing the greater degree of anxiety and tenseness. Shands and

Finesinger (1948) observed a mild lymphocytic response to a psychiatric "stress" interview in psychoneurotic patients. In 1956 Bliss et al. reported striking elevations in plasma 17-OHCS levels during a panic episode in a psychoneurotic patient.

Reports by Persky et al. (1956) and by Board, Persky, and Hamburg (1956) marked the first of a series of papers dealing with plasma 17-OHCS levels in acutely disturbed psychiatric patients. Morning plasma 17-OHCS levels were observed to be 60–70% higher in acutely anxious patients than in normal control subjects and elevated plasma and urine 17-OHCS levels were maintained in the anxious subjects over a 4-day period (Persky, 1957a). Psychiatric evaluation of the quality and intensity of emotional distress indicated that exceptionally high 17-OHCS levels were observed in those acutely disturbed patients with very intense distress and particularly with the development of extensive personality disintegration (Board, Persky, & Hamburg, 1956). Persky (1957a, 1957b) also reported that anxious patients show a considerably larger urinary 17-OHCS response to ACTH than normals in spite of the fact that they excrete a smaller proportion of a test load of hydrocortisone as dihydroxyacetone side-chain compounds, suggesting that the hydrocortisone secretion rate is much faster in anxious patients than in normal subjects. Persky's group, using two bioassay procedures, also obtained evidence that, in anxious patients, the mean ACTH level—judged by the concentration of the adrenal weight-maintenance factor—was more than twice as high as in normal subjects (Persky, Maroc, Conrad, & Den Breeijen, 1959c). In a study of the effects of stressful interviews upon anxious patients, they found that objective ratings of increase in anxiety, anger, depression, and combined affect were significantly and linearly related to the change in plasma hydrocortisone level associated with the interview, although diurnal changes in 17-OHCS levels complicate the interpretation of results somewhat (Persky et al., 1958). It was of particular interest that such relationships were observed even though the stimulus was generally of a mild or moderate intensity. The persistent elevation of plasma and urinary 17-OHCS levels in anxious patients was confirmed in another study in which the performance of two different psychological tasks failed to elicit much additional increase in levels on experimental days (Persky et al., 1959b).

The psychoendocrine study of depressed patients has been a particularly active field in recent years. As in the case of the studies of schizophrenic patients, some inconsistencies between the findings of different workers have been reported which seem very likely to be related to methodological problems and the lack of adequate control measures. In 1956, Board, Persky, and Hamburg reported that mean plasma 17-OHCS levels in depressed patients were elevated in comparison with normal subjects. It was also noted that higher 17-OHCS levels were found in the more intensely depressed and retarded group than in the less depressed group (Board, Wadeson, & Persky, 1957). This study was based upon 17-OHCS measurements in acutely depressed patients made shortly after hospital admission, in comparison both with similar measurements in the same patients made following clinical improvement and with levels in nonhospitalized normal subjects. Subsequently, a number of other workers confirmed the occurrence of high corticosteroid levels in depressed patients investigated under generally similar conditions (Bridges & Jones, 1966; Doig, Mummery, Wills, & Elkes, 1966; Ferguson et al., 1964; Gibbons, 1964; Gibbons & McHugh, 1962; Kurland, 1964a, 1964b; McClure, 1966a, 1966b; Pryce, 1964). In longitudinal studies which extended well beyond the hospital-admission period, other workers found, however, that positive correlations did not always obtain between 17-OHCS levels and the severity of depressive symptoms (Anderson & Dawson, 1965; Bunney, Mason, & Hamburg, 1965; Bunney, Mason, Roatch, & Hamburg, 1965c; Curtis, Cleghorn, & Sourkes, 1960; Gibbons, Gibson, Maxwell, & Willcox, 1960; Jakobson, Stenback, Strandstrom, & Rimon, 1966; Sachar, 1967; Sachar, Mackenzie, & Binstock, 1967; Sachar, Mackenzie, Binstock, & Mack, 1968; Stenback, Jakobson, & Rimon, 1966).

The study of Bunney, Mason, and Hamburg (1965b) identified two general subgroups of depressed patients in terms of 17-OHCS levels. One group, characterized by high and fluctuating 17-OHCS levels and high depression ratings, appeared to be more aware of, and involved in struggle with, their illness. The second group also showed high depression ratings but had relatively low and stable 17-OHCS levels. The latter group appeared to have differently organized psychological defenses, often employing extensive denial of their illness or related problems. In any event, this study made clear that the presence of severe depressive symptoms is not necessarily associated with elevated corticosteroid levels but that other psychological determinants were involved. In a related study of severe psychotic depressive crises, elevated 17-OHCS levels were found only in those periods in which there was associated awareness of illness and a breakdown of ego defenses (Bunney & Fawcett, 1965; Bunney et al., 1965c).

In a recent study by Sachar et al., intended to test the psychiatric hypothesis that certain depressive reactions serve a defensive function against the acknowledgment of painful disappointment, dynamic factors were carefully considered throughout the period of psychotherapy in six patients with reactive depression. Elevated 17-OHCS levels were generally not observed in these patients except during brief "confrontation" periods in psychotherapy, when the painful losses which precipitated their depressive reaction were considered. Otherwise, ratings of depressive symptoms which did not take into account dynamic factors did not correlate with 17-OHCS levels. Emphasis was placed on distinguishing the affects associated with loss and mourning from the organized syndrome of melancholia (Sachar, Mackenzie, & Binstock, 1967; Sachar et al., 1968).

Generally, similar findings were obtained in a larger study of 20 depressed patients before and after clinical recovery. In the report of this study, Sachar (1967) presents a penetrating critique of previous psychoendocrine research on depression which should clarify and guide future work in this field. The failure of many studies to consider important control issues, such as the psychoendocrine response to hospital admission or to the milieu throughout hospitalization, the interference of certain central-acting medications, and the choice of control data for comparison with illness data, is emphasized as a probable basis for many of the discrepancies in the findings of different research groups.

At present, it appears that the symptom of manifest depression alone is not, per se, necessarily associated with 17-OHCS elevations, but that other psychological factors such as the concomitant presence of anxiety or involvement and particularly the status of defensive ego functions from a dynamic standpoint must also be considered. The value of the longitudinal approach in a well-defined milieu in clinical psychoendocrine studies also now seems to be well established.

Psychoendocrine studies of several other categories of patients deserve mention. Longitudinal studies of manic-depressive patients by Rizzo et al. (1954), Bryson and Martin (1954), Fox, Murawski, Thorn, and Gray (1958), Bunney, Hartmann, and Mason (1965a), and Rubin, Young, and Clark (1968) have all indicated that the manic state is usually associated with low—often abnormally low—urinary corticosteroid levels in contrast to the higher levels during depressed phases. This was even true of a patient who showed a regular 48-hr manic-depressive cycle (Bunney, Hartmann, & Mason, 1965a). These findings have been interpreted as again indicating the need to consider defensive as well as emotional processes in psychoendocrine research and may, in this particular instance, provide some support for the clinical hypothesis that mania, with its elements of euphoria and denial, represents a counteracting, protective defense against the painful distress of depression.

The longitudinal study by Fox and his associates of a patient through a long period of psychoanalysis is also particularly worthy of mention (Fox, 1958; Fox et al., 1958). This study provided some of the earliest indications of the importance of considering ego functions in the interpretation of psychoendocrine data and stands as a model for the investigation of the complex qualitative aspects of emotional and related behavior which appears to be very much needed for the future systematic development of psychoendocrine research. The intensive longitudinal study of individual patients may well prove to be the single most fruitful source of clues to the many relevant and intimately interrelated variables—psychological, constitutional, and environmental—which must together be taken into account if we are eventually to understand the integration of psychoendocrine mechanisms.

Comment   In general, studies with human subjects have provided almost unanimous support for the conclusion that 17-OHCS levels sensitively reflect psychological influences. Pituitary-adrenal cortical activity is increased under conditions in which there appears to be a rather undifferentiated state of arousal, alerting, or involvement—perhaps in anticipation of activity or coping. The elimination of physical variables from the experimental conditions by many different approaches, along with the repeated demonstration of quantitative correlations between 17-OHCS changes and intensity of psychological disturbances, provide convincing evidence of the directness and specificity of relationships between psychological and endocrine factors. The precise nature of the psychological correlates of 17-OHCS response is in need of further study, however, with regard to such issues as, for example, the effect of experiences involving different types of pleasurable arousal, the effect of suppressed versus expressed anger, and the possible application of the concept of object relations (as developed by Engel, 1962) to the problem before general conclusions can be considered firmly established.

The evidence revealed in studies with human subjects for the particular effectiveness of novelty or unpredictability, of suspenseful anticipation, and of "involvement" or "trying" in the determination of adrenal cortical activity, together with the evidence of a "tonicity" exerted on this system by subtle, everyday influences, strongly reinforce the similar findings and conclusions from work with animals. The observations of unusually marked 17-OHCS responses in psychiatric patients in association with intense, disorganizing emotional reactions also concur with findings in animal experiments.

Some general guidelines appear to have been established concerning the absolute 17-OHCS levels or the magnitude of corticosteroid change associated with emotional disturbances in the human. Compared with an average 8:00 AM plasma 17-OHCS level of about 12 μg% under basal conditions, roughly twofold elevations to above 20 μg% have been repeatedly observed in normal human subjects in stressful situations, although levels of 30 μg% are rather rarely exceeded. In acutely and severely disturbed psychiatric patients, levels above

30 or even 40 μg% may be more frequently observed. In comparison with basal urinary 17-OHCS levels of about 5–8 mg/day, twofold elevations to between 10 and 15 mg/day are often observed in normal human subjects in stressful situations. While levels above 15 mg/day are rather uncommon in normal subjects, elevations above 20 mg/day are more frequently observed in psychiatric patients in states of severe, acute, disorganizing distress.

Perhaps some of the most valuable information emerging from the literature which has been reviewed concerns a number of methodological principles which should provide helpful guidelines for future psychoendocrine research, not only on the pituitary-adrenal system but on other endocrine systems as well. Many of these principles, however, have been slow to gain general recognition and it may be useful to review them briefly.

1. The importance of the selection of biochemical methods for the measurement of pituitary-adrenal cortical activity has often been underestimated. While many methods now available probably possess sufficient sensitivity and precision for psychoendocrine work, there is reason to question the specificity of many of these procedures. The total 17-ketosteroid method, which measures a variable, heterogeneous mixture of steroidal compounds from diverse sources, should be considered obsolete for psychoendocrine research. Currently used nonchromatographic urinary 17-OHCS methods, which do not exclude many nonsteroidal contaminants, are of questionable value. At present the methods of choice for psychoendocrine research appear to be the chromatographic procedures which are relatively specific for the 17-OHCS compounds as a class in blood and urine. In the future, however, the chromatographic measurement of the individual rather than the class of 17-OHCS compounds in both blood and urine and the increasing use of isotopic secretion rate methods remain desirable goals. The radioimmunochemical measurement of ACTH in body fluids would also represent a major future advance in methodology in this field.

2. The choice of blood and urine sample collection schedules, in a manner closely attuned with the dynamics of the endocrine response under study, is also a matter of special importance.

In acute psychoendocrine experiments, the collection of either blood or short-term urine samples is complicated greatly by the diurnal rhythm. The collection of "control" samples on the same schedule on a separate day does not necessarily counteract the problem. The diurnal pattern may well shift in its timing from one day to the next under "normal" conditions. Such measures as collecting several preexperimental or control samples on the same day immediately prior to the experiment and the use of the afternoon or early evening period when diurnal changes are less marked than in the morning have proved helpful in dealing with this problem. The reliability of 2–3-hr urine samples, in terms of completeness of voiding and variations in residual bladder urine, is also a very difficult problem to evaluate in short-term experiments—thus plasma determinations may be considered preferable for this reason.

In chronic experiments, particularly in those which involve characterization of individual subjects as having high, middle, or low 17-OHCS levels, the collection of full 24-hr samples appears to be highly advisable. Furthermore, a minimum of 6–10 daily samples, preferably spread out over a period of weeks or months, appears to be necessary for obtaining a reliable chronic mean basal individual value. Larger pools representing several days of urine output may add to the reliability of the mean value at the cost of relatively few biochemical analyses, but this procedure tends, of course, to obscure the range of daily variation in 17-OHCS levels in the event that there is interest in this parameter.

3. The diurnal variation is not only a variable to consider methodologically but it is also a biological parameter of probable importance in the psychoendocrine field. Collection of 24-hr urine samples in a sense presents a falsely simple picture of endocrine function because the diurnal variation is not delineated. Attempts to measure diurnal changes in either urine or blood, however, raise complicated practical problems. Diurnal 17-OHCS changes may be marked and rapid between about 3:00 and 11:00 AM; unless 17-OHCS levels are meas-

ured in about 2-hr segments during this period, misleading information may be obtained. It is particularly hazardous to work with urine samples of 6–12-hr duration and which divide the early morning period near its middle; a relatively slight shift in the 17-OHCS peak may be erroneously interpreted as involving a much greater physiological change than is actually the case.

4. It is now quite clear that situational criteria cannot be safely used as the sole basis for defining the psychological reaction in psychoendocrine experiments. It has been repeatedly shown with human subjects that there are wide individual differences in psychoendocrine response to the same situation or stimulus. No matter how seemingly threatening or drastic the life situation, it cannot be assumed that all, or even most, subjects will experience substantial emotional arousal or distress. The relevant question is "Do those individuals who become emotionally upset in this situation show significant hormonal response?" rather than "Do most people show hormonal responses in this situation?"

The fact that all or most individuals do not show the same emotional reaction to a given situation should not, of course, be confused or misinterpreted as indicating the failure of an endocrine system to be responsive to emotional stimuli. The lack of a significant mean hormonal elevation in a group of students taking scholastic examinations, for example, is not a sufficient basis alone to disprove the sensitivity of that hormone to psychological factors. Yet there is still a tendency for this approach to be used in psychoendocrine studies. The burden is on the investigator to establish by concurrent psychological measurements the quality and intensity of the emotional reaction in each subject so that hormonal changes may be related directly to psychological as well as to situational factors. This problem appears to apply primarily to research with human subjects, although it may sometimes complicate animal experiments as well.

5. Clinical ratings of the intensity of affective reactions, while valuable, do not represent a sufficient psychological evaluation in psychoendocrine studies. In addition, systematic assessment of the styles and effectiveness of psychological defenses and careful consideration of dynamic factors are essential in order to deal with the individual difference phenomenon. It is also important that all psychological measurements should be closely related in time to endocrine measurements.

6. In studies of psychiatric patients, attempts to relate hormonal levels to conventional diagnostic categories of illness by using mean group data have been unimpressive so far. In general, longitudinal studies of individual patients through various phases in the course of psychiatric illnesses, with close attention to current emotional state, defensive organization, and dynamic factors, have been more fruitful.

7. Novelty is an especially important variable to be taken into account in psychoendocrine experiments. In the study of hospitalized patients, at least 3 to 7 days should be allowed for adaptation to the new environment. The practice of bringing normal subjects into the hospital or laboratory for a single day or part of a day for "control" observations is hazardous, unless the "first-experience" effect is systematically evaluated.

8. Social factors deserve close attention as determinants of levels of endocrine activity, particularly in terms of the "milieu" of the hospital ward as it relates to the particular patient. There is also some indication that social factors are apt to be particularly important in studies dealing with acute psychoendocrine response in small, closely knit groups of human subjects.

9. Finally, nonpsychological determinants of 17-OHCS levels must be constantly considered. Body weight is one of the best established of these determinants and is of particular relevance in chronic studies in which high, middle, and low 17-OHCS level subgroups are compared. Sex and age may also be relevant variables. Drugs, particularly psychopharmaceutical compounds, may have marked and surprisingly prolonged effects on hormone levels, even after cessation of administration. If the drug factor cannot be eliminated from the study, then systematic control measures are required. Other factors such as environmental temperature, nutritional state, or muscular activity may also possibly be determinants of 17-OHCS levels, but conclusive data on these variables are not yet

available. With regard to "physical stress" factors, it may be well, in general, to bear in mind the increasing evidence that such elements may be less extensively involved in pituitary-adrenal cortical regulation than was previously thought. While it was generally assumed 15 years ago that adrenal cortical responses in any given stressful situation were caused by "physical" factors unless proved otherwise, it now appears increasingly important to take the position that concomitant emotional stimuli must be ruled out before it can be concluded that a "physical" stimulus is capable, by itself, of eliciting increased adrenal cortical activity. Selye's "stress" concepts, in fact, may well bear reevaluation in this light.

While the present review has dealt almost exclusively with the influence of psychological factors upon 17-OHCS levels, it should be borne in mind that interactions between the brain and the endocrine glands operate in both directions. It is known, of course, that many hormones exert significant influences upon the central nervous system, although our knowledge of such effects is still very limited owing largely to the considerable methodological difficulties in this field. Some of the earlier work to which the term *psychoendocrine* has been applied—particularly that of Reiss (1958) in England—was apparently conceived largely in terms of the possible clinical importance of the effects of abnormal hormone levels upon the brain in the pathogenesis of various psychiatric disorders. This approach has received relatively little attention in recent years with regard to the adrenal cortical hormones, but it is an aspect of psychoendocrinology which may deserve greater attention in the future, particularly as we can now consider broader patterns of hormonal change because of newer biochemical methods.

Summary

Massive evidence has now accumulated which indicates that the pituitary-adrenal cortical system responds sensitively to psychological influences. This evidence represents converging and reinforcing findings from diverse studies of many species, including man. It involved the use of many methods of eliciting, isolating, and evaluating emotional disturbances, relatively direct and specific biochemical measurements of endocrine activity, and control measures that permit exclusion of concomitant physical variables. It also appears that the principal experimental or methodological factors which were involved in the relatively few conflicting findings reported in this field have been largely identified, eliminated, or adequately taken into consideration.

There is no longer room for reasonable doubt as to the validity of the basic conclusion that psychological stimuli are capable of influencing the level of pituitary-adrenal cortical activity. It now appears to be time to consolidate our grasp of the knowledge that is firmly established in this field and to review the implications in order that we may logically decide the most likely directions for fruitful future work along these lines.

Some of the general biological conclusions emerging from the work covered in this review may be summarized as follows:

1. Psychological influences are among the most potent natural stimuli known to affect pituitary-adrenal cortical activity.

2. The remarkable sensitivity of 17-OHCS levels even to relatively subtle, everyday psychological influences suggests that the central nervous system exerts a constant "tonicity" upon this endocrine system, in much the same fashion as has been previously demonstrated for the autonomic and skeletal muscular effector systems.

3. Elevation of 17-OHCS levels is not related to a highly specific affective state, but rather appears to reflect a relatively undifferentiated state of emotional arousal or involvement, perhaps in anticipation of activity or coping.

4. The elements of novelty, uncertainty, or unpredictability are particularly potent influences in eliciting 17-OHCS elevations.

5. Intense, disorganizing emotional reactions with behavioral breakdown are associated with unusually marked 17-OHCS elevations.

6. Psychological factors may either raise or lower the level of pituitary-adrenal cortical activity. Some important variables to consider in relation to the direction of 17-OHCS response are the quality of the emotional reaction, the style and effectiveness of psychological defenses, and whether the threat is of an acute or chronic nature.

7. Marked individual differences in pituitary-adrenal cortical response to any given situation have been a striking and consistent feature of psychoendocrine studies. Definition of the multiple determinants, psychological and other, of these individual differences is a major goal in the future development of psychoendocrine research. The organization of psychological defenses has been shown to be an especially important factor to consider in the study of this problem.

8. The measurement of 17-OHCS levels provides the behavioral scientist with a sensitive, objective index of a physiological reflection of emotional state that represents a balance between forces promoting affective arousal or distress versus those of a protective or defensive nature which prevent, minimize, or counteract arousal or distress.

Experience in psychoendocrine research on the pituitary-adrenal cortical system has also yielded a number of important conclusions concerning methodological principles, which have been discussed at some length. These principles deserve wider recognition and should be useful in the future refinement of psychoendocrine research in general.

It is perhaps also important to realize that the recent burgeoning development of psychoendocrine research owes both its conception and support largely to psychiatry, and that the dissemination of psychoendocrine data has remained largely within the psychiatric literature—as clearly revealed by the inspection of the bibliography for this chapter. The many fruitful psychoendocrine approaches to a variety of basic issues in psychiatry that have now been delineated, as reviewed recently (Mason, 1964, p. 375), are gradually gaining recognition; thus it is likely that psychoendocrine approaches will be incorporated into psychiatric research programs to an even greater degree in the future as general awareness of their power and potential grows.

While the concept of psychological influences upon endocrine function has, in general, been readily accepted by behavioral scientists, it has, however, made very little headway as yet into other biological fields—particularly physiology and internal medicine. While psychoendocrine concepts may not yet provide the immediate promise of research tools and approaches for these fields as they do in the case of psychiatry, they have profound implications for the study and understanding of physiological integration and must, inescapably, be eventually incorporated into physiological thought. It may be true that the participation of psychological factors in endocrine regulation temporarily "muddies the waters" from the viewpoint of physiological theory, by complicating the servo-mechanism formulation of endocrine regulation, but this is not by any means the first instance in physiology in which a higher level regulatory mechanism has been found to be superimposed upon a lower level mechanism.

It should also be recognized that there are practical implications involved which the biological investigator concerned with measurement of metabolic or physiological functions in the conscious animal or human can no longer afford to ignore. There is clearly now a burden on such investigators to minimize extraneous environmental and psychological stimuli and to take necessary control measures to rule out the possibility that observed bodily responses are related to psychological or emotional reactions. What really appears to be needed, in fact, is a closer two-way relationship between psychoendocrinology and physiology. The endocrine glands are regulated in life by both physical and psychological stimuli, in varying combinations, and at present the psychoendocrinologist is perhaps as much in danger of ignoring physical or constitutional factors as the physiologist is of ignoring psychological factors in the experimental study and conceptualization of endocrine regulation.

A principal reason for including this review in the present series is to give an impression of the overwhelming weight of evidence for the superimposition of psychological mechanisms upon endocrine regulation. Definitive support for this conclusion in the case of the pituitary-adrenal cortical system should reasonably be expected to minimize contention over drawing similar conclusions for other endocrine systems if evidence along similar lines is obtained, even though it be on a smaller scale. It is also suggested that the evolution of psychoendocrine research on the pituitary-adrenal cortical system provides us with a valuable guide to the lines that similar research on other endocrine systems must very likely follow. Finally, a review of the extensive work on this system brings out the relative paucity of studies on most of the other endocrine systems.

THE SYMPATHETIC-ADRENAL MEDULLARY SYSTEM

The sympathetic-adrenal medullary system was the first endocrine system to be studied experimentally with regard to the possible participation of emotional factors in its regulation. The concept that the adrenal gland might be susceptible to emotional stimuli was developed by Walter Cannon with characteristic logic. He reasoned that (a) it was known that the adrenal medulla is linked to the sympathetic nervous system; (b) many physiological changes known to accompany emotional arousal such as dilation of the pupils, fast pulse, piloerection, and inhibition of gastrointestinal function, are all signs of increased sympathetic nervous system activity; and (c) therefore, as he put it, "Do not the adrenal glands share in this widespread subjugation of the viscera to sympathetic control?" (Cannon & de la Paz, 1911).

Cannon had been perhaps predisposed to think along these original lines as a result of the deep impression made upon him, in his early experience as an investigator, by noting the marked sensitivity of the stomach and intestines to psychological stimuli (1909). Together with de la Paz, he set about devising an experiment which would test the possibility that the adrenal medulla is activated by psychological stimuli of the type occurring in the natural course of events in an animal's life. In 1911 Cannon and de la Paz reported that when a cat, placed in a holder, was frightened by a barking dog, detectable amounts of "adrenalin"—measured by an intestinal strip bioassay—appeared in inferior venal caval blood obtained through an in-dwelling catheter, whereas none was detectable by this method under basal conditions. Cannon, Shohl, and Wright also reported in 1911 that normal cats, excited either by being bound in a holder for the first time or by being caged and barked at by a dog, showed glycosuria in about an hour, while adrenalectomized cats failed to show this response. Evi-

dence for "emotional glycosuria" in 4 of 9 medical students taking a difficult scholastic examination and in 12 of 25 members of the Harvard University football squad (including players on the bench) during the most exciting contest of the season also was reported from Cannon's laboratory (1914).

Elliott, who used a pharmacological approach, reported some evidence in 1912 suggesting that emotional stimuli influence the secretion of the adrenal medulla. Hitchings, Sloan, and Austin (1913), using cats frightened by dogs, confirmed the results of Cannon and de la Paz and found that the "adrenalin" response was abolished by section of the splanchnic nerves. These and other findings led Cannon in 1914 to propound the "emergency function" theory of adrenal-medulla function, based upon the view that the many physiological or metabolic consequences of "adrenalin" release are each "directly serviceable in making the organism more efficient in the struggle which fear or rage or pain may involve." This formulation of Cannon's and, in fact, his data, were shortly thereafter subjected to rather sharp criticism by Stewart and Rogoff (1917). Cannon responded to such criticism by repeating and confirming his basic findings on the stimulating effect of emotional excitement upon the adrenal medulla, using a new and more sensitive indicator of adrenal secretion, the denervated heart (1919). This ingenious study failed to forestall still further personal criticism from Stewart and Rogoff (1923), but the overall work of Cannon and others left very little doubt as to the validity of Cannon's conclusions concerning the sensitivity of the adrenal medulla to emotional stimuli (Cannon, 1953, p. 197; Cannon & Britton, 1927; Rikimaru, 1925).

Although research on the problem languished for many years after Cannon's contributions were made, the field was eventually reopened for study by some important biochemical discoveries. The demonstration of the natural occurrence of norepinephrine in the body by Euler (1946) and Holtz, Credner, and Kroneberg (1947), and the establishment shortly afterwards of its role as an adrenal-medullary hormone and chemical transmitter of adrenergic nerves, as reviewed by Euler and Floding (1955), made necessary the reassessment of adrenal-medullary function at this new level of insight.

The preparation of levoarterenol, an optically active form of norepinephrine, by Tainter, Tullar, and Luduena (1948) was also of considerable importance in establishing the physiological significance of norepinephrine, as only a physiologically inert racemic mixture of this compound had been available up to this point.

The knowledge that two separate hormones, epinephrine and norepinephrine, were involved in mediating the effects of the sympathetic-adrenal medullary system naturally raised the question of whether the two hormones are separately regulated or respond in a unitary fashion. Several different lines of early investigation appeared to lend support to the hypothesis that there may be differential secretion of epinephrine and norepinephrine. Histochemical evidence was reported by Hillarp and Hokfelt in 1953 and by Eranko in 1955, which indicated that separate types of cells in the adrenal medulla secrete predominantly epinephrine and norepinephrine, respectively. The selective release of epinephrine and norepinephrine upon stimulation of different hypothalamic areas in the cat was demonstrated by Redgate and Gellhorn in 1953, and by Folkow and Euler in 1954. The study of catecholamine content of the adrenal glands of various African mammals led Goodall to postulate in 1951 that aggressive animals have higher concentrations of noradrenaline in the adrenal than do typically nonaggressive animals. A large number of earlier studies in the psychosomatic field, reviewed by Cohen and Silverman (1959), had also generally suggested that anger, hostility, or aggressive impulses were associated with blood pressure elevation in stressful life or laboratory situations—which might be construed as indirectly suggesting the special association of norepinephrine release with those emotional factors.

In a series of experiments based upon blood pressure responses to injection of mecholyl or epinephrine, Funkenstein and his co-workers developed the concept that the response to psychological stress in persons who direct anger "inwardly" is characterized by predominantly epinephrine secretion, while the response associated with anger directed "outwardly" predominantly involves norepinephrine secretion (Funkenstein, 1955, 1956; Funkenstein, King, & Drolette, 1954, 1957). Using a variety of polygraphic measurements of autonomic functions, Ax (1953) reported different patterns of normal subjects' physiological response to laboratory situations designed to elicit fear versus those which elicit anger. These and other relatively early studies, done mostly prior to 1955, helped to establish a strong interest in the possibility that epinephrine and norepinephrine might be selectively related to different emotional states and served, particularly in the case of the concepts of Funkenstein and his associates, as a point of departure for many subsequent investigations.

As in the pituitary-adrenal cortical field, however, the early psychoendocrine studies of epinephrine and norepinephrine secretion were greatly limited by the lack of direct, specific, and reliable methods of hormonal measurement. The development, beginning in about 1950, of chromatographic-fluorimetric methods for measurement of epinephrine and norepinephrine in plasma by Lund (1949, 1950) and by Weil-Malherbe and Bone (1952, 1957) and in urine by Euler and his associates (Euler & Floding, 1955; Euler & Hellner, 1951; Euler & Lishajko, 1959, 1961) was therefore of particular importance in initiating the substantial advances of psychoendocrine research in this field during the past decade. Many other workers have also made important contributions in this especially difficult field of microanalytical chemistry and much of the history of this work, particularly the development of the relatively specific trihydroxyindole methods, has been reviewed by Euler (1959).

From the standpoint of psychological methodology, psychoendocrine experiments on catecholamine secretion have developed along lines similar to those just described for the pituitary-adrenal cortical field and may be considered according to the 3 categories: (a) studies of stressful life and laboratory situations in normal human subjects; (b) studies of psychiatric disorders in patients; and (c) studies of stressful situations in laboratory animals.

Studies of Normal Human Subjects

Urinary catecholamine studies The first systematic effort to study psychological influences on urinary epinephrine and norepinephrine levels was reported in 1954 by Euler and Lundberg, who used an aluminum hydroxide chromatographic technique coupled with a bioassay procedure. They found a selective increase in excretion of epinephrine—with little change in norepinephrine levels—in a group of military air transport passengers, while pilots showed an increase in excretion of both compounds during flight. These conclusions were based upon values in 4-hr urine samples collected usually between 7:00 and 11:00 AM, the period during which the actual 1- to 2-hr flight took place, and upon comparison between flight and nonflight days.

Elmadjian, Lamson, and Neri (1956), who also used a chromatographic-bioassay method, found urinary epinephrine and norepinephrine elevations in subjects performing on the pursuit meter, which simulates the tasks of aircraft flight. Klepping, Buisson, Guerrin, Escousse, and Didier (1963) attributed small increases in urinary epinephrine and norepinephrine levels in well-trained pilots to psychological rather than to physical factors. Colehour and Graybiel (1963) also found increased urinary epinephrine and norepinephrine excretion in normal men exposed to acrobatic flight. Such responses did not occur, however, in subjects with labyrinthine defects; the authors suggest that the vestibular organs may be involved in the catecholamine responses observed in normal subjects. Some instances of increased catecholamine excretion were reported by Ulvedal, Smith, and Welch (1963) in pilots during experiments in a space cabin simulator. Although systematic psychological observations were not available, it was noticed that increased excretion of epinephrine was related to a number of unscheduled, stressful incidents—including dysbarism, painful arterial punctures, and annoying malfunctions of equipment.

In an extensive series of studies by Elmadjian and his co-workers, based upon chromatographic-bioassay catecholamine measurements in short-term urine samples, it was found that urinary epinephrine and norepinephrine elevations often occurred in competing athletes in various sports, including professional hockey players, amateur boxers, and professional basketball players (Elmadjian, 1959; Elmadjian, Hope, & Lamson, 1957, 1958). Catecholamine elevations before as well as after competition indicated that psychological factors were major determinants of the endocrine

responses. Dissociation of epinephrine and norepinephrine levels were observed in some instances; high levels of one compound occurring either with or without concurrent elevation of the other compound. Marked differences in catecholamine responses between individual subjects were also noted in these studies. Psychological observations of these subjects yielded the impression, in keeping with Funkenstein's concepts, that active aggressive emotional states are related to increased excretion of norepinephrine, whereas tense, anxious, but passive emotional states are related to increased epinephrine excretion.

Gravitational stress situations   Cohen, Silverman, and their co-workers conducted a series of studies of catecholamine-excretion, blood pressure, and psychological responses in normal subjects in relation to experiences with the human centrifuge. On the basis of determinations in 1- to 3-hr urine samples with a bioassay method, along with focused interviews and projective tests for the psychiatric evaluation, it was generally concluded that the ratio between epinephrine and norepinephrine levels differs considerably between individual subjects exposed to the same situation and that the more aggressive subjects had higher norepinephrine and lower epinephrine urinary excretion levels than the more anxious subjects (Cohen & Silverman, 1959). Correlations between catecholamine excretion, psychological factors, and "g-tolerance" in the human centrifuge were also reported (Silverman & Cohen, 1960; Silverman, Cohen, Shmavonian, & Kirshner, 1961; Zuidema, Silverman, Cohen, & Goodall, 1957).

Goodall and Berman, (1960), using a bioassay method, studied the influence on catecholamine excretion of both psychological and physical factors associated with human centrifugation. They observed marked urinary epinephrine elevations in relation to the anticipation of centrifugation, i.e., in the waiting period just prior to actual or mock centrifugation and during mock rides. It was suggested that the physical effects of centrifugation play a relatively minor role in the release of epinephrine in comparison with emotional factors. On the other hand, it appeared that norepinephrine release was more closely related to the physical factors such as the hemodynamic changes associated with centrifugation. Conclusions were based upon short-term urine samples of 1-hr duration or less before and during the experience (the time of the day not being specified), and control urine samples were obtained 3 weeks following the experimental day. In a later paper, Goodall et al. also reported increased urinary epinephrine levels in normal subjects placed in a simulated weightless state by immersion in water; they suggested that this response may be related largely to emotional factors (Goodall, McCally, & Graveline, 1964). Frankenhaeuser, Sterky, and Jarpe (1962), in studies of habituation to gravitational stress, found that the level of urinary epinephrine excretion was almost directly proportional to the intensity of the subjective emotional reactions to the experimental situations and that both hormonal and emotional responses decreased with repetition of the experience.

In 1959, Euler et al., using a biochemical procedure, reported a pronounced increase in urinary epinephrine excretion and a slight increase in urinary norepinephrine excretion in normal subjects viewing censored cuttings from motion pictures depicting extreme forms of violence and cruelty. These experiments began at about 6:00 PM, thus minimizing the complicating factor of the diurnal rhythm, and conclusions were based upon comparison between control and experimental period urine samples of 2-hr duration each. More recently, Levi (1964b, 1965) observed urinary catecholamine responses in young women viewing four different types of motion pictures selected for "anxiety-provoking," "aggression-provoking," amusing, or bland qualities. He found significant increases in mean epinephrine excretion and similar epinephrine/norepinephrine ratios in response to both an "aggression-provoking" film and an amusing film, while the "anxiety-provoking" film was associated with both urinary epinephrine and norepinephrine elevations. The bland natural scenery films lowered urinary catecholamine levels significantly, an effect very similar to that previously reported by Wadeson et al. (1963) in relation to plasma 17-hydroxycorticosteroid levels. Levi (1966a) also reports that urinary catecholamine responses were observed in women viewing films with a predominantly erotic content.

The effect of psychological tasks, such as those included in conventional intelligence tests, upon catecholamine excretion was studied by Frankenhaeuser and Post (1962). Using a biochemical method, a 1-hr experimental urine sample, and a 2-hr control "inactivity" sample, they found significant elevations in urinary epinephrine—but not norepinephrine—excretion to be associated with the performance of these tasks (which included mental arithmetic). It is not clear whether the diurnal rhythm of catecholamine excretion was considered in these experiments. A similar study by Frankenhaeuser and Kareby (1962) does, however, employ three successive 40-min urine samples, a "before," "during," and "after" sample on the same day. In this study the intensity of the stressful experience was enhanced by rushing and unfairly criticizing the subjects during performance of their tasks. Both urinary epinephrine and norepinephrine elevations were observed not only during the experimental period but also in the anticipatory waiting period, as judged by comparison with "inactivity" samples taken on a different day. It was also found that the urinary catecholamine responses were diminished by the administration of meprobamate prior to the experiment. While, in general, epinephrine responses were more pronounced and consistent, the interesting observation was made in a subsequent study by Frankenhaeuser and Patkai (1964) that those subjects who showed the highest norepinephrine responses during mental work being performed under stressful conditions were also the subjects who showed the greatest improvement in performance during the stressful experience. The important problem of interindividual differences in catecholamine excretion during stressful situations has been also approached by Frankenhaeuser and Patkai (1965). In a study of 110 students, their results did not support the view that predominantly anxious versus aggressive individuals vary in their catecholamine response. Factor analysis, however, suggested that individuals with depressive tendencies had a relatively weaker epinephrine response on stressful occasions involving mental work.

Akabane (1962) has reported that two young men involved in the performance of a vigilance task for 4 hr a day excreted increased amounts of epinephrine and norepinephrine on a day of work as compared to an idle day, the change being most marked at the beginning of the work. Another group found increased urinary norepinephrine and VMA (3-methoxy-4 hydroxymandelic acid) excretion on workdays in a group of men exhibiting excessive competitive drive, aggressiveness, and an enhanced sense of time urgency—a behavioral pattern found to be often associated with coronary artery disease (Byers, Friedman, Rosenman, & Freed, 1962; Friedman, St. George, Byers, & Rosenman, 1960).

One of the most active workers in this field recently has been Levi, who has reported an extensive series of studies of urinary catecholamine excretion in relation to psychological factors. In 1961 he reported a study of urinary catecholamine excretion in normal subjects—divided into "low stress tolerance" and "high stress tolerance" groups on the basis of clinical evaluation—in relation to a 1-hr task of sorting 2000 steel balls of four different sizes, with an 0.8-mm difference between sizes, in the presence of harassment by noise, bright light, and criticism, as well as the pressure of time. Using a biochemical method and three successive 2-hr urine samples covering the periods before, during, and after the experimental task, he found an increase of epinephrine excretion in both groups during the stressful period. The "low-tolerance" group also showed a significant rise in norepinephrine excretion as well as generally higher mean epinephrine levels in all three samples.

Levi later repeated these experiments in another larger group, in which he used stressful motion pictures as well as the steel-ball-sorting tasks in an otherwise standardized situation. The elevations in mean epinephrine levels and the lesser change in norepinephrine levels associated with these situations were confirmed, but no significant difference was observed in catecholamine responses between the "low-tolerance" and "high-tolerance" groups. Some evidence was obtained of a relationship between the strain felt by an individual and his epinephrine excretion in the different situations. It is mentioned in this study that the control urine collection period started at 8:00 AM, which raises the question of the extent to which diurnal changes in catecholamine excretion may have complicated the interpretation of results (Levi, 1963).

In a subsequent study of young women who were performing their everyday work as invoicing clerks, Levi found that substantial increases in both urinary epinephrine and norepinephrine excretion (40 and 27%, respectively) occurred on days when the work was performed on a piecework rather than a salaried basis. Evidence of physical and mental discomfort also was associated with performance on a piecework basis (Levi, 1964a). In an hour-to-hour study of nine female telephone operators during 8 hr of work and rest periods, Levi concluded that the variations in work load correlated better with norepinephrine excretion than with epinephrine excretion. The raw data indicate, however, considerable individual variation in this study (Levi, 1967).

Scholastic examinations   Bogdonoff et al. studied the catecholamine responses to final college examinations, the experiment beginning at 11:00 AM and involving a 2-hr control urine sample and experimental and recovery urine samples of about 1-hr duration each. Increased epinephrine excretion was observed in all subjects during the examination period, but there was no consistent change in norepinephrine excretion as determined by a bioassay procedure. A positive correlation was found between the self-reported intensity of affective arousal and the change in epinephrine excretion during the examination (Bogdonoff, Estes, Harlan, Trout, & Kirshner, 1960; Bogdonoff, Harlan, Estes, & Kirshner, 1959). Substantial elevations in 24-hr urinary epinephrine and norepinephrine levels have also been observed by Mason et al. (unpublished data) in a small group of students taking final college examinations, although interindividual differences in response were considerable.

Other situations   In a study involving 24-hr urine collections and biochemical measurement of urinary catecholamine levels, Tolson et al. recently reported significant epinephrine and norepinephrine elevations on the first day of hospitalization in normal young adults, as compared with a later period following adaptation to the new environment (Tolson et al., 1965). As in the case of the pituitary-adrenal cortical system, it appears that the element of novelty is an especially important factor in relation to catecholamine regulation.

Mendelson et al. found elevation of both urinary epinephrine and norepinephrine levels in normal young men exposed to a laboratory situation in which some degree of sensory deprivation was produced by having the subject lie on his back in a respirator for a number of hours. Urine samples were collected in 12-hr portions and analyzed by a biochemical technique, but the results are expressed in such a way that it is not clear if the diurnal rhythm of catecholamine excretion was taken into account in the evaluation of results. It also appears difficult to separate possible effects of sensory deprivation per se from the psychoendocrine reaction of each subject to the situation as a whole, particularly with regard to the element of novelty. The investigators emphasize the limitations of mean group data and the importance of paying closer attention to the significance of individual differences in catecholamine response pattern—noting that a simple, two-valued system of "epinephrine responders" and "norepinephrine responders" is not adequate for the interpretation of the more complex response patterns they observed (Mendelson et al., 1960).

Metz, Schaff, and Grivel (1960) reported a marked increase in biochemically measured urinary epinephrine levels and a slight increase in norepinephrine excretion in normal subjects during a night of sleep deprivation. They also found that the urinary epinephrine and norepinephrine response to a workday on laboratory tasks was greatly exaggerated following a night of sleep loss, probably to a greater degree than can be accounted for by the effects of muscular work load and intense psychomotor activity.

In a study of paratroop trainees and officers in various stressful training situations, Bloom, Euler, and Frankenhaeuser (1963) found urinary epinephrine and norepinephrine levels to be generally increased in tower training and actual jump situations as compared with night-rest or ground-activity periods. No difference was found between officers and trainees and the data suggested that habituation does not occur very rapidly in these situations. Efforts to find correlations between catecholamine levels and personality traits, while promising in some respects, were inconclusive. In a preliminary report of a study of soldiers under conditions simulating combat, Levi (1966b) has observed marked rises in catecholamine excretion coinciding with periods of emotional turmoil in individual

subjects. Mason et al. (unpublished data) have also observed substantial urinary epinephrine and norepinephrine elevations in soldiers during stressful events associated with basic training in the army.

Changes in catecholamine excretion have been reported in relation to emotional reactions to dental treatment (Schmid, Suss, Zicha, Suss, & Weiss, 1964); to conditioned escape and avoidance procedures (Frazier, 1966a, 1966b; Graham, Cohen, Shmavonian, & Kirshner, 1963, 1967); in subjects anticipating laboratory tests involving repeated venipuncture (Elmadjian, Hope, & Lamson, 1957); in a psychiatrist during a series of psychotherapeutic sessions with a patient (Elmadjian, Hope, & Lamson, 1958); in physicians performing cardiac catheterizations (Ira, Whalen, & Bogdonoff, 1963); and in normal subjects receiving electric shock to the hand (Frankenhaeuser, Froberg, & Mellis, 1965–1966). The latter study demonstrated a quantitative relationship between epinephrine excretion, subjective reaction, and the intensity of the electric shock.

Incidental observations of urinary catecholamine responses in relation to emotional reactions during the course of studies primarily concerned with other aspects of catecholamine regulation have also been reported by Bischoff and Torres (1959) and by Feller and Hale (1964).

Plasma catecholamine studies A curious methodological feature of the psychoendocrine research on catecholamine responses in normal human subjects might be pointed out. Virtually all the studies reported so far have involved urinary measurement of epinephrine and norepinephrine levels, although methods have been available for measuring plasma catecholamine levels for more than 10 years and were applied successfully to human studies as early as 1956 by Renton and Weil-Malherbe, who reported that plasma epinephrine levels were higher during the waking state than during sleep. Several factors may account for this relative lack of studies of plasma catecholamine responses to psychological stimuli and this problem will be discussed in more detail later. An important factor in our own laboratory has been some early experimental observations on normal subjects in which two successive 25-ml blood samples were obtained in separate syringes through the same needle, each sample requiring about 2 min to be withdrawn. Analysis of these samples indicated that significant plasma norepinephrine responses just to the venipuncture procedure itself occurred in well over half the subjects (Mason, unpublished data). Coppen and Mezey (1960) also have found changes in metabolic rate and ventilatory equivalent in response to venipuncture in normal subjects, which they attributed to catecholamine release. It is very likely that this factor constitutes an important source of variance in studies of conscious subjects and that special methodological measures are required to minimize its interfering influence.

Studies of Psychiatric Patients

In connection with their other early work on blood pressure response to epinephrine and mecholyl, Funkenstein and his collaborators studied a large group of psychoneurotic and psychotic patients. There was indirect evidence of excessive secretion of "epinephrine-like" substances in many patients, particularly in those diagnosed as having manic-depressive or involutional psychoses, while most subjects in whom excessive norepinephrine secretion was suspected were diagnosed as schizophrenics and included those with paranoid tendencies. Some correlations between the suspected secretion pattern and response to electric shock therapy were also reported (Funkenstein, 1956; Funkenstein, Greenblatt, & Solomon, 1951–1952).

Urinary catecholamine studies   Using a bioassay procedure, Elmadjian, Hope, and Lamson (1958) found elevations in epinephrine excretion in a group of psychiatric patients during the period when they were presented at a staff conference. An increase in epinephrine excretion was also observed following LSD administration in patients with manic-depressive disorders or involutional depression but not in "chronic schizophrenic" patients. In an evaluation of 10 psychiatric patients with the Malamud-Sands rating scale tests, the same group (Elmadjian, Hope, & Lamson, 1957) derived some further support for the hypothesis that active, aggressive emotional displays are related to high norepinephrine excretion, while tense, anxious, but

passive, emotional displays are related to high epinephrine excretion. Some attempts have been made to determine experimentally whether the interpretation of Funkenstein's test as providing an index of epinephrine and norepinephrine levels was valid or not (Elmadjian & Hope, 1957; Elmadjian, Hope, & Freeman, 1956; Manger et al., 1957). However, Feinberg in 1958 concluded in a critical review of this field that the parameters of the Funkenstein test were still undefined and that the relevance of his findings to endocrine function was still undecided.

In one of the first longitudinal studies of urinary epinephrine and norepinephrine excretion in psychiatric patients, Strom-Olsen and Weil-Malherbe (1958) found that epinephrine excretion was significantly higher during the manic than the depressed phases in a series of manic-depressive patients. This finding was confirmed by Bergsman (1959), who also made extensive observations of other types of psychiatric patients. He found no differences in mean urinary output of catecholamines between chronic schizophrenic patients and normal subjects. When emotional outbursts occurred in schizophrenic patients, however, concomitant elevations in epinephrine excretion were observed. Patients with senile dementia had very low urinary epinephrine levels, but showed marked norepinephrine elevations when they were irritated or upset. Shinfuku, Omura, and Kayano (1961) reported a positive correlation between norepinephrine excretion and mania in a longitudinal study of a manic-depressive patient, but epinephrine excretion did not show similar correlations with mood. In studies of relationships between pyrocatecholamine excretion, measured fluorimetrically, and response to electroshock therapy in psychiatric patients, Sourkes, Sloane, and Drujan (1957, 1958) found that the majority of those patients who improve after therapy have lower catecholamine excretion in the morning than those who are not improved.

In 1960 Curtis, Cleghorn, and Sourkes measured daily urinary epinephrine, norepinephrine, and 17-OHCS excretion by biochemical methods in several different types of psychiatric patients classified principally according to the major affective content characterizing the illness. They found that norepinephrine is excreted preferentially in comparison with epinephrine and corticoids in depressed states, while epinephrine predominates in states of mixed affect—although they caution against generalizing too broadly from their findings. In summarizing a series of studies also focusing upon relationships between affective states and urinary catecholamine excretion in various types of psychiatric and medical patients, Silverman and Cohen and their associates (Cohen, Silverman, Waddell, & Zuidema, 1961; Silverman et al., 1961) reported a significant correlation between aggressiveness and norepinephrine and between anxiety and epinephrine excretion. The group also found some correlation between psychomotor activity and catecholamine excretion, and raised the question also whether increased muscular tension might be an important variable in evaluating catecholamine levels during emotional distress.

In a longitudinal study of patients made during acute schizophrenic reactions, Sachar et al. (1963) found that urinary epinephrine levels fluctuated during changing phases of psychotic illness, much in the same fashion as do the corticosteroids. During phases characterized by affective distress, such as "turmoil" or "depression" phases, epinephrine levels are high, while during calmer "psychotic equilibrium" or "recovery" phases, levels subside. No striking correlation between motor activity and catecholamine levels was noted in these patients. At times of extreme emotional upset, such as in turmoil phases, striking epinephrine elevations up to 40 μg per day, or about eight times the mean normal values, were observed. In an acutely disturbed patient with psychotic depression, Bunney and Mason (unpublished data) also observed urinary epinephrine levels up to 40 μg per day, and norepinephrine levels as high as 120 μg per day, or about four times the mean normal value.

Recently, the excretion of some of the major metabolites of epinephrine and norepinephrine have been studied in relation to psychological factors. In a group of psychiatric patients, Nelson, Masuda, and Holmes (1966) reported lower levels of metanephrine and normetanephrine during periods of calm, controlled behavior, whereas levels were elevated in association with agitated, unstable behavior. The findings of this study did not, inci-

dentally, support the Funkenstein concept. Some studies of the excretion of another less specific metabolite of epinephrine and norepinephrine, 3-methoxy-4 hydroxymandelic acid (VMA) have also been reported (McDonald & Weise, 1962; Schildkraut, Klerman, Hammond, & Friend, 1964), but another study in which lack of correlation between epinephrine, norepinephrine, and VMA excretion was found raises some question as to the interpretation of VMA changes (Pscheidt, Berlet, Bull, Spaide, & Himwich, 1964). In a longitudinal study of epinephrine, norepinephrine, and VMA excretion in nine schizophrenic patients seen over a period of several months, Pscheidt et al. found elevated epinephrine and norepinephrine excretion during periods of "worsened behavior" accompanied by anxiety and increased motor activity, confirming some earlier similar observations (Brune & Pscheidt, 1961). VMA excretion did not always parallel epinephrine and norepinephrine excretion, particularly in 24-hr urine samples.

Plasma catecholamine studies   As in the study of normal human subjects, there has been a notable lack of investigation of plasma catecholamine responses to emotional factors in psychiatric patients. In 1955 Weil-Malherbe studied mean plasma epinephrine and norepinephrine levels in various types of psychiatric patients and, on the basis of differences between the general classes of oligophrenic and nonoligophrenic patients, suggested a broad correlation between the plasma epinephrine level and "the level of consciousness or the extent of nervous activity." He postulated that the low plasma epinephrine level in oligophrenia is a reflection of the reduced mentation processes in these patients.

In 1958 Regan and Reilly reported an attempt to correlate plasma epinephrine and norepinephrine levels with changes in the emotional state of individual patients on two different occasions. They did not find differences in mean plasma catecholamine levels between different diagnostic categories of psychiatric illness. On the two different occasions changes in epinephrine and norepinephrine levels were in the same direction as the emotional rating in about two-thirds of the 60 subjects studied. Some descriptive and personality features, which appear to indicate the frequency with which this parallel relationship between catecholamine levels and emotional state will occur, were tentatively suggested. In a survey of various diagnostic categories of patients with psychiatric disorders, Manger et al. (1957) found no striking differences in mean catecholamine levels in comparison with those of normal subjects. Consideration of some other studies of the stability of catecholamines in plasma and of brain catecholamine metabolism in psychiatric disorders will be omitted as these studies do not bear directly upon the principal issue under discussion, the sensitivity of epinephrine and norepinephrine levels to psychological factors.

Studies of Experimental Animals

Although Cannon's pioneering work reported more than 50 years ago was based almost entirely upon the study of cats, it is curious that animals have been used relatively little in modern psychoendocrine research on the sympathetic-adrenal medullary system. Following the experience in our own laboratory of observing plasma catecholamine responses to venipuncture in human subjects, we turned to the chair-restrained rhesus monkey, which permitted the elimination of venipuncture by the use of a chronic cardiac catheterization technique. Behavioral conditioning procedures were used in an effort to elicit a variety of emotional responses relatively free of physical factors and under a considerable degree of control (Mason, Mangan, Brady, Conrad, & Rioch, 1961c).

In using this approach, we found that moderate plasma norepinephrine elevations occurred in a wide variety of acute, stressful conditioning procedures, but that comparable elevations in plasma epinephrine levels occurred considerably less frequently and apparently only under rather special conditions. While it was, of course, not possible to specify the type of affective reaction accompanying these different patterns of catecholamine response, several factors appeared to be related to the occurrence of marked epinephrine responses. The element of unpredictability or uncertainty appeared particularly relevant to epinephrine release, in combination with the threat of a noxious stimulus and with the element of "involvement" or "try-

ing" in the performance of a self-protective task. Procedures which were familiar to the animal and rather stereotyped, although presumably unpleasant, were usually associated with norepinephrine elevations but with relatively little change in plasma epinephrine levels. In those situations associated with substantial epinephrine elevations, both plasma norepinephrine and 17-OHCS responses were usually also of exceptional intensity, so that the question is raised as to whether one is concerned primarily with a qualitative or quantitative difference in psychoendocrine response. These findings in the monkey have recently been confirmed and extended to some degree but it is clear that the extent to which this problem can be pursued in the animal is limited (Mason, Brady, & Tolson, 1966, p. 227).

Comment

The many studies just reviewed are clearly in general agreement with the concept that the sympathetic-adrenal medullary system is highly sensitive to the influence of psychological factors. This conclusion rests not only upon observations of stimulus-response relationships, but also upon the roughly quantitative correlations between the magnitude of catecholamine response and the intensity of observed emotional response. The earlier conclusions of Walter Cannon concerning the subjection of this neuroendocrine system to psychological factors have therefore been amply borne out in studies employing modern biochemical and bioassay methods for catecholamine measurement in blood and urine. It is clear that elevations of both epinephrine and norepinephrine levels may occur in response to psychological stimuli, although in some instances selective responses of one hormone or the other may occur and the system is not unitary in this respect. Euler (1964) has recently emphasized the significance of the findings, showing graded catecholamine responses with increasing intensity of psychological stimulus. Levi (1967) has also concluded that a positive correlation exists between the intensity of emotional arousal (whether it be pleasant or unpleasant) and the urinary excretion of epinephrine, and possibly of norepinephrine. He has also emphasized that emotional stimuli of a considerably smaller intensity than those occurring in the everyday life of most people may be sensitively reflected in catecholamine levels.

While a number of studies, particularly those of Frankenhaeuser and Kareby (1962) and Levi (1966a, 1967) demonstrate convincingly the keen sensitivity of the sympathetic-adrenal medullary system to psychological influences, even in response to relatively subtle, everyday emotional reactions or mental activities, the question of the differential response of epinephrine and norepinephrine levels to emotional stimuli has not yet been fully clarified from a psychological standpoint. Perhaps the predominant urinary-response pattern observed in human subjects exposed to acute moderately stressful situations has been an elevation of epinephrine excretion, with smaller and more variable changes in norepinephrine excretion. Unfortunately, not many studies in which such acute catecholamine responses to stressful stimuli or situations have been observed have included systematic measurements of the quality and intensity of emotional reactions by multiple observer and self-rating procedures similar to those employed in comparable studies of corticosteroid responses.

In fact, most of the clinical data relating specific affective states to catecholamine excretion appear to be based largely upon general clinical impressions, supported in some instances by psychological test data, concerning rather stable personality differences in individual persons, such as being predominantly aggressive or passive, for example. The results of Elmadjian, Hope, and Lamson (1958), Silverman and Cohen (1960), and Silverman et al. (1961), who primarily used this approach, were in general agreement that individuals who tend to be active and aggressive and more apt to display hostility and anger tend to excrete more norepinephrine, while epinephrine excretion is more likely to predominate in individuals who characteristically react in a passive, anxious manner.

Most of the remaining psychoendocrine studies of urinary catecholamine responses in normal humans are based almost solely upon situational criteria: the occurrence of events or conditions which should presumably be stressful to most people; they lack attempts at objective assessment of emotional or other psychological factors in relation to the situation. Such studies, while useful in establishing in a general way the sensitivity of the system to environmental and psychological factors and in determining the degree of covariation between epinephrine and norepinephrine levels, have some substantial limitations. The resulting data are necessarily analyzed primarily in terms of group mean values, which tends to obscure the striking individual differences in response pattern that appear to provide some of the most promising clues at present to investigation of the differential relationships between psychological factors and epinephrine and norepinephrine responses. Studies of group mean values also invite the danger of misconstruing results as indicating a lack of catecholamine responsivity to emotional stimuli rather than as indicating that emotional reactions are not necessarily shown by all, or even most, persons in any particular stressful situation.

It appears very likely, then, that psychoendocrine research on the sympathetic-adrenal medullary system must in the future follow a course similar to that used for the pituitary-adrenal cortical system by gradually expanding the number of psychological parameters under observation—not only in the systematic, objective estimation of affective state but also in the direction of evaluating more fully some major differences in long-standing personality characteristics, particularly with regard to the type and effectiveness of psychological defenses and to dynamic factors. Mendelson et al. (1960) have called attention to the need for more detailed study of individual differences in this field and pointed out that their data suggested rather complicated patterns of individual response differences. While the few studies devoted to the question of the affective concomitants of epinephrine versus norepinephrine secretion have yielded encouraging results and have suggested some tentative general conclusions, it may be well to some extent to reserve judgment on this issue until further studies are available which relate catecholamine responses not only to specific affective states but also to specific aspects of ego structure, particularly the organization of psychological defenses and the use of tension-relieving mechanisms.

With regard to absolute urinary epinephrine and norepinephrine levels in response to stressful situations, some general guidelines appear to be emerging. Urinary epinephrine levels under basal conditions in normal adults average about 5 μg/day and twofold or threefold elevations are not uncommonly observed in relation to stressful life situations. Occasionally, more marked elevations up to 40 μg/day may be observed in association with intense emotional disturbances in psychiatric patients. Normally, urinary norepinephrine levels average about 30 μg/day under basal conditions and tend to show smaller percentage changes, with elevations seldom above 90 μg/day—except, again, in the case of severely disturbed patients in whom values up to 120 μg/day have been observed. Although it is difficult to generalize about absolute levels in the many studies involving short-term urine collections (because of differences in the manner of expressing the results and differences in the time of day experiments were performed), it does appear that twofold elevations in urinary epinephrine excretion rates have been rather frequently observed in stressful situations. Comparable elevations in norepinephrine excretion rate have perhaps been somewhat less commonly found.

Perhaps one of the principal obstacles to progress in this field is a basic methodological problem relating to the question of plasma versus urinary catecholamine measurements. As a general rule in studies of endocrine regulation, plasma hormone measurements, each representing a single point in time, have been regarded as more suitable for defining acute responses to stimuli in short-term experiments in terms of minutes or hours, while urinary measurements have been generally applied to experiments of longer duration, in terms of at least several hours, days, or even a longer period. Yet, psychoendocrine studies of catecholamine responses to acutely stressful situations have been limited so far almost exclusively to the measurement of urinary hormone levels in short-term urine samples, usually of 1- to 3-hr duration. Such a sampling design has substantial limitations—although, to be sure, its use has yielded much valuable information. Because of the variability in completeness of voluntary bladder-emptying, there is the trou-

blesome question of the reliability of any single urine sample collected without catheterization in a short period. Aside from that problem, the most serious limitation is the fact that even such short-term urine collections do not permit the point-to-point correlation between stimulus, psychological response, and hormone response which can be achieved by the measurement of plasma hormone levels. Urinary measurements cannot be expected to provide a fine analysis of the dynamics of response when one is dealing with a system in which enormous elevations or precipitous drops in levels can occur within a 5-min period.

Another important limitation of the short-term urine collection experiment, which apparently has not been taken into account with adequate control measures in some past studies, is the possible complication of results by the diurnal rhythm of catecholamine excretion. As most studies of the diurnal rhythm of catecholamine excretion have involved day–night comparisons of periods representing many hours of urine collection, it is apparently not generally recognized that diurnal changes in epinephrine and norepinephrine excretion may in some instances be extremely marked and abrupt in the morning hours as judged by the differences in levels between 2-hr samples. In the monkey we have observed epinephrine levels between 7:00 and 9:00 AM, for example, which show a twofold or greater difference in comparison with the levels between 9:00 AM and 3:00 PM under normal basal conditions. A number of studies on human subjects, however, have involved the use of early morning samples as "prestress" control samples for comparison with "stress" periods later in the morning or early afternoon. This is clearly a dangerous practice, unless additional control information is obtained, such as the collection of two successive "prestress" control samples to outline the direction and degree of diurnal change at the time the stimulus is presented, or at least a collection at exactly the same time period on a day when the subject is under basal conditions. The latter measure does not, however, take into account possible shifts in the position of the peak of the diurnal rhythm on different days that may occur in any particular subject. The problem can also be minimized, as in the movie study by Euler and Lishajko (1959), by sched-

uling the experiment in the afternoon or early evening well past the major, abrupt diurnal changes
in catecholamine excretion.

It seems likely that there are more profound
reasons for the almost exclusive reliance upon
urinary catecholamine measurements than the mere
following of precedent set by early psychoendocrine experiments in which this approach was necessarily used. Acute experiments with plasma epinephrine and norepinephrine measurements
present extraordinary and formidable technical
difficulties in at least two respects. First, biochemical methods sensitive enough to measure the extremely minute amounts of the catecholamines in
a reasonably small volume of blood are among the
most delicate and difficult of all hormone assay
procedures to set up and, especially, to maintain
in reliable operating condition week in and week
out. These methods require not just virtuoso performance of the biochemical technician in terms
of quantitative technique but also the most rigorous and meticulous attention to minute details in
such matters as the preparation of reagents and the
cleaning of glassware according to uniformly exacting standards, as well as the incorporation of
rather elaborate internal control measures which
assure a comprehensive check on the reliability of
each analytical run. It may take many months of
persistence and practice even for the initial setting
up and validation of a plasma catecholamine
method. Even after the method is thus established,
it may be expected that analytical losses and breakdowns will occur with annoying frequency and that,
while such problems may be detected with proper
routine internal controls, the precise source of error
may not always be tracked down so that recurrence
of similar trouble can be subsequently eliminated.
It would seem to be quite understandable, therefore, on just this basis alone, that so few psychoendocrine studies of plasma catecholamine levels
have appeared as yet. It should be pointed out,
however, that significant technical advances have
been made, that many methodological sources of
error have been discovered and eliminated in recent years, and that reliability is gradually improving
(Euler, 1959; Euler & Lishajko, 1961).

In addition, the technical problems faced from
the physiological standpoint are, unfortunately,
scarcely less difficult to cope with. The extreme
lability of the sympathetic-adrenal medullary system, which responds so rapidly that levels may
show more than a tenfold change in the human
or monkey in 2 min or may, on the other hand,
drop from a peak of 10 μg/L or more to less than
1 μg/L in a few minutes, places heavy technical
demands upon the physiological investigator
working with the conscious subject. It appears
almost obligatory, first of all, to use some type of
indwelling intravenous catheterization technique
to eliminate possible psychoendocrine responses to
repeated venipuncture. In addition, the use of
multiple prestimulus samples and recovery samples
and the rigorous control of extraneous environmental stimuli would appear to be essential.

This sobering appraisal of the difficulties attendant, in our own experience at least, to experiments
involving plasma catecholamine responses in conscious subjects is not meant to discourage others,
but rather to convey that the difficulties involved
are identifiable and surmountable and that the
importance and need for more work with this approach make it worthy of the special effort and
patience required. It is a curious fact, for example,
that well over 10 years after the provocative report
of Ax (1953), which described differential physiological responses to laboratory tests designed to
elicit fear and anger responses respectively, apparently there are no reported efforts to repeat his
experiments with the addition of direct measurement of plasma epinephrine and norepinephrine
levels. Other techniques of eliciting acute emotional reactions in the human such as the use of
hypnosis, motion pictures, psychological tests,
conditioning procedures, and small group interactions, in conjunction with intensive psychiatric
and psychological efforts to evaluate the actual
emotional reaction in each subject, may also well
deserve application to studies of plasma epinephrine and norepinephrine response patterns in the
human subject.

While the study of human subjects appears essential for the ultimate definition of possible relationships between catecholamine secretion and
specific emotional states, it seems likely that additional work with experimental animals may be useful. It would be of interest, for example, to know

if the finding of two general patterns of catecholamine response in the monkey (Mason et al., 1961b; Mason, Brady, & Tolson, 1966, p. 227) can be confirmed by other workers for this species and whether other species of animals may show these same two patterns or different patterns of plasma epinephrine or norepinephrine response to psychological stimuli. There is a need to obtain more data on catecholamine responses in animals to situations designed to elicit anger, preferably not with procedures involving the use of threat of painful stimuli but rather with one such as the sudden extinction of food reward to animals working on a difficult and exacting schedule like the "DRL" procedure (Mason, Brady, & Tolson, 1966, p. 227), for example. Most of the situations which we have studied in the monkey have involved negative reinforcement with foot shock and, although the conditions of shock administration varied considerably, it may be argued that the quality of the emotional response was similar as long as the threat remained similar, most likely in this instance representing a fearful or anxious type of response. At best, of course, we can only speculate regarding the subjective state of the animal, but it is possible that attempts to design experiments with these issues in mind may lead to further informative work in this field with experimental animals. It also appears that any attempts to evaluate the relative importance of the adrenal medulla and adrenergic nerve endings as possibly dissociable sources of catecholamine secretion in response to emotional stimuli may best be carried out in ablation experiments with laboratory animals. Little, if any, data bearing on this basic question are available as yet.

There are several physiological issues which deserve some mention for their relevance to future psychoendocrine research with the sympathetic-adrenal medullary system. It has often been pointed out that only a small percentage, roughly in the vicinity of 5%, of the epinephrine and norepinephrine secreted in the body appears as the unchanged parent compounds in the urine (Euler, 1956; Silverman et al., 1961). This raises the question, then, of the possibility that changes in urinary output of epinephrine and norepinephrine might under some conditions reflect changes in the metabolism or percentage of excretion rather than the rate of internal secretion of these compounds. Unfortunately, very little work has been done as yet to raise this issue from a theoretical to an experimental level. Presumably, most workers who have measured only the parent compounds in the urine have received reassurance from the general plausibility and reproducibility of the observed responses in relation to stimulus presentation and have felt little need from a practical standpoint to delve into this question. The major breakdown products of epinephrine and norepinephrine, however, are now known and measurable. It appears possible, then, to obtain data on this question by the concurrent measurement of urinary levels of epinephrine, norepinephrine, metanephrine, normetanephrine, and VMA under a variety of different conditions comparable to those employed in previous psychoendocrine studies. Until such data are obtained, the importance of this issue for psychoendocrine research will remain problematical, but it certainly cannot be fully dismissed at present.

The question of the importance of muscular activity as a variable in psychoendocrine studies of catecholamine responses is also in need of further clarification. Silverman et al. (1961) were impressed by the importance of this variable in some of their studies with normal human subjects. One of the obstacles in this field is the considerable difficulty in eliminating emotional or psychological reactions in experimental situations in which subjects are required to undergo muscular exertion. Recent work on corticosteroid regulation indicates that, when emotional reactions can be minimized, muscular activity per se may not elicit substantial changes in corticosteroid levels (Miller & Mason, 1964, p. 137).

We cannot assume the situation to be the same for catecholamines, of course, although most of the observations reported so far that relate catecholamine responses to muscular exertion involve situations in which the possibility of contaminating emotional reactions are not systematically considered. However, certain findings—such as the elevation of epinephrine levels in manic, hyperactive patients (Bergsman, 1959; Strom-Olsen & Weil-Malherbe, 1958), which contrasts with the low corticosteroid levels reported in similar patients, along with the results obtained by Silverman et al. (1961), suggest that this issue may deserve closer attention in future psychoendocrine studies. It is possible, of course, that if this dissociation between 17-OHCS and epinephrine levels can be confirmed in manic patients, it may also be explained on the basis of psychological factors—such as in relation to a distinction between distress and excitement for example.

Summary

There appears now to be no reasonable doubt that both epinephrine and norepinephrine belong to the category of hormones which are responsive to psychological influences.

Catecholamine levels, furthermore, appear sensitively to reflect relatively common, psychological reactions associated with everyday events, tasks, and activities. As in the case of the pituitary-adrenal cortical system, it appears that the central nervous system may exert an on-going "tonicity" on catecholamine levels which reflects environmental and psychological factors. The findings in this field have, in fact, suggested that systematic study of a wide variety of common tasks or activities and common methods of relaxation may reveal a surprisingly extensive range of diverse, on-going psychoendocrine adjustments in everyday life. The possibility that catecholamine responses to such events may further be correlated with performance effectiveness, as suggested by some studies, may be another fruitful area for future exploration. These approaches appear likely to have industrial and military, as well as physiological and medical, implications.

There is some evidence that psychological factors may lower as well as raise catecholamine excretion levels and that certain types of pleasant as well as unpleasant forms of emotional reaction may be associated with elevated catecholamine levels.

Dissociation between epinephrine and norepinephrine levels in relation to psychological influences has been demonstrated.

The precise psychological determinants of epinephrine versus norepinephrine release remain one of the most intriguing issues in the psychoendocrine field. While there are some indications, particularly in human studies, that aggressive versus anxious reactions are particularly relevant to the catecholamine excretion pattern, this problem is in need of further, more comprehensive study. Funkenstein's concept of the psychological basis of differential catecholamine secretion cannot yet be regarded as being definitively evaluated.

It appears that anticipation of experiences or situations involving a high degree of novelty or unpredictability may be associated with especially marked catecholamine responses.

Marked individual differences in catecholamine and psychological responses to a given situation have been found in many studies. The significance of mean group values based solely upon situational criteria is therefore rather limited. Increasing emphasis should be placed in the future on defining the psychological, constitutional, physical or other determinants of these differences in levels of response between individual subjects. From the psychological standpoint, this will require systematic assessment of multiple factors, including emotional state, the style and effectiveness of psychological defenses, dynamic factors in each individual's behavior, and cognizance of the social environment.

Many of the methodological principles which have emerged from psychoendocrine studies of the pituitary-adrenal cortical system also have been found to apply to the study of epinephrine and norepinephrine regulation. These principles pertain to such issues as the choice of reliable hormone assay methods, fitting the sample collection design to the dynamics of the response under study, taking the diurnal rhythm fully into account in acute experiments, the choice of control measures (e.g., eliminating novelty or "first experience" effects from clinical studies), the value of "longitudinal" versus "contrast" studies in patients, and the choice of methods for obtaining correlative psychological data.

Lack of systematic psychological measurements has been one of the principal deficiencies in psychoendocrine research on the sympathetic-adrenal medullary system.

There has been a strong emphasis in this field so far on the study of normal human subjects in stressful laboratory situations. In comparison with research on the pituitary-adrenal cortical system, catecholamine studies are not yet so well balanced in terms of studies of psychiatric disorders in patients, of normal human subjects in natural life situations, and of highly controlled stressful laboratory conditions with experimental animals.

There has also been a notable lack of studies of catecholamine levels in relation to chronic stressful situations that extend over periods of weeks, months, or years, similar to work concerned with 17-OHCS levels.

As in the case of the pituitary-adrenal cortical field, the findings reviewed here indicate an urgent need to incorporate the psychoendocrine aspect of sympathetic-adrenal medullary regulation more broadly into attitudes concerning physiology particularly from the practical viewpoint in work involving metabolic or endocrine measurements in conscious animal or human subjects. Much of our existing knowledge of the response of this system to physical stimuli, which has been gained by work in conscious subjects, may bear close reevaluation with regard to the possible role that psychological factors may have played in the determination of the observed catecholamine responses.

The findings in this field reinforce the conclusion that psychoendocrine research and concepts must not remain confined to the psychiatric and behavioral fields alone, but rather that they have important implications for future work in other biological fields as well.

THE PITUITARY-THYROID SYSTEM

The concept that psychological factors may influence the thyroid gland may be traced back at least to the publication in 1825 of Parry's classical clinical description of the onset of hyperthyroidism in a young woman following an unusual accident in which she was badly frightened but suffered little physical injury. In 1835 Graves also reported evidence of a relationship between emotional disturbance and the disease which now bears his name. Since these early reports, the frequent occurrence of severe emotional crises or disturbances just prior to the onset of thyrotoxicosis has been repeatedly and widely confirmed by many clinical investigators as reviewed by Ferguson-Rayport (1956), Lidz (1949), Gibson (1962), and others.

One of the most extensive series of patients studied was reported in 1927 by Bram, who found

"a clear history of psychic trauma as the exciting cause" in 85% of 3343 cases of exopthalmic goiters. Three categories of "exciting causes" were described by Bram. The first, observed in 13% of the cases, involved severe, life-threatening crises such as fires, earthquakes, shipwrecks, narrow escapes from accidents, or combat experiences. The second category, observed in 11% of the cases, involved reactions to the threat of impending surgery or parturition. The third and largest category by far, observed in 61% of the series, involved more sustained periods of emotional disturbance, such as worry, disappointment, or grief following sudden object loss. All of these categories appear to have in common, as pointed out by Ham, Alexander, and Carmichael (1951), a fear concerning biological survival.

In addition, a number of psychiatric and psychoanalytical studies, including those of Lewis (1923, 1925), Mittelmann (1933), Conrad (1934), Brown and Gildea (1937), Lidz (1949, 1955), Lidz and Whitehorn (1950), Mandelbrote and Wittkower (1955), Dongier, Wittkower, Stephens-Newsham, and Hoffman (1956), Ferguson-Rayport (1956), Alexander, Flagg, Foster, Clemens, and Blahd (1961), and Wallerstein, Holzman, Voth, and Uhr (1965), have indicated that particular personality or psychodynamic factors may be significant determinants of susceptibility to thyrotoxicosis. This work has been reviewed in some detail by Gibson and Willcox (1957). The relevance of certain psychological factors has been emphasized, based upon noting similarities from case to case in the lifelong patterns of psychological defense or modes of adaptation, in early developmental experiences, and in the types of situations which appear to precipitate the syndrome. Yet in spite of this massive clinical evidence, the precise psychoendocrine mechanisms involved in the etiology or pathogenesis of this disease remain to be defined conclusively.

As Lidz (1955) has put it, ". . . the accumulation of more and more case material cannot, in itself, prove whether emotional turmoil is an essential factor in the etiology of the disease or whether it plays a major or a subsidiary role among various other determinants."

The question of the effect of psychological stimuli upon the secretion of thyroid hormone, therefore, in addition to its general physiological interest and significance, presumably has special importance in relation to an eventual understanding of this long-standing clinical problem. Systematic experimental work in this field only became possible shortly after 1950, when reliable biochemical methods for the measurement of thyroid secretory activity were introduced. Since this time, however, relatively few experimental psychoendocrine studies on the pituitary-thyroid system have been reported, at least in comparison with the more extensive psychoendocrine research on the pituitary-adrenal medullary systems published during the same period. Furthermore, these experimental studies have yielded some curiously conflicting and, at times, apparently negative findings, so that considerable confusion now exists concerning the influence of psychological stimuli upon the secretion of thyroid hormone. Recent reviewers of this field, in fact, have been led not only to express doubt that significant thyroid responses to emotional stimuli occur in man but also to generalize that thyroid activity is principally *inhibited* by emotional stimuli in laboratory animals (Gibson, 1962; Hubble, 1963; Michael & Gibbons, 1963). In view of this unsettled state of affairs, it may be well in reviewing this experimental work to give special attention to methodological details or other practical or theoretical factors which may bear upon the present lack of general agreement and firm conclusions in this field.

As in the case of the adrenal systems, psychoendocrine research on the pituitary-thyroid system has involved several approaches: the study of stressful situations in normal human subjects and hyperthyroid patients, the study of psychiatric disorders in patients, and the study of laboratory animals exposed to stressful conditions. The experimental work also falls into two general phases: those recent studies which employed the relatively specific and reliable biochemical methods developed after about 1950, and those relatively few earlier studies in which indirect and less specific methods of evaluating thyroid activity were used.

Studies with Human Subjects

Normal and hyperthyroid subjects Early attempts at experimental evaluation of the influence of emotional stimuli on the thyroid gland in the normal human include the work of Ziegler and Levine, who reported in 1925 an increase in basal metabolic rate in ex-soldiers recalling unpleasant war experiences, and a study reported in 1932 by Wittkower, Sheringer, and Bay, who observed an increase in blood iodine level of more than 20% in 13 of 15 subjects in response to hypnotically induced emotional disturbances.

Using the relatively specific plasma protein-bound iodine (PBI) method for thyroid hormone measurement, Hetzel, de la Haba, and Hinkle reported (1952a, 1952b, p. 242) the case of a subject whose plasma PBI level fell from 8.4 to 6.1 μg% during an hour-long stressful interview in which the subject discussed his relationship to his father. The level then rose to 10 μg% 1 hr later and remained elevated for at least 3 hr. A similar pattern of PBI response, an initial brief fall followed by a prolonged rise, was reported in two other euthyroid subjects and in three hyperthyroid patients. A marked and sustained drop in PBI level from about 18 to 12 μg% was also observed 1 hr following a discussion in which a hyperthyroid subject freely ventilated feelings concerning his father. The authors found, then, surprisingly rapid and marked changes in plasma PBI levels in association with emotional reactions during stressful interviews, considering the long-standing impression that the thyroid is a rather "sluggish" organ. In 1956 Hetzel and colleagues (Hetzel, Grace, & Wolff, 1956; Hetzel, Schottstaedt, Grace, & Wolff, 1956) reported that mean plasma PBI levels, representing 14 "euthyroid" subjects, rose from 5.1 to 6.5 μg% during a 1-hr interview. There was a considerable range of individual difference in PBI response, with five subjects showing significant elevations and one subject a significant fall. Measurements of nitrogen and electrolyte metabolism and oxygen consumption were included in an effort to relate the observed changes in thyroid hormone levels to general body metabolism.

In 1958 Tingley, Morris, and Hill studied plasma PBI levels at 7:00 AM, 1:00 PM, and 5:00 PM in 11 medical students on a control day and on a day when medical oral examinations were given. A significant but slow elevation of PBI levels was observed on the examination day, evident only in the 5:00 PM sample.

Volpe, Vale, and Johnston (1960) studied serum

PBI levels in several groups of normal subjects in stressful life situations, including undergraduate and graduate students taking scholastic examinations, football players after games, surgical patients, and patients with myocardial infarction. The data were analyzed primarily in terms of group mean values and the significance of mean response was judged in terms of its relation to the "normal range" of fluctuation in PBI levels. Situational criteria of stress were employed and no attempt was made at psychological assessment of individual differences in emotional reactions in these situations. The authors report "no fluctuation beyond that observed in normal healthy persons in any of the groups studied, including the subjects undergoing major surgery." It is mentioned, however, that in 9 of the 11 undergraduate students, the PBI level reached its highest point during the examination period although the mean variation was not greater than 1 μg% over the whole period of study. In only 2 of the 11 graduate students were elevations observed. There were elements of both physical and psychological disturbances in the remaining groups studied. The authors concluded that their data provided no evidence that thyroid hormone secretion is readily affected by severe mental and physical stresses or strains.

Alexander et al. (1961) studied the plasma PBI and ^{131}PBI levels in normal subjects and hyperthyroid patients before and after viewing a stressful motion picture. Standard chemical PBI levels showed mean elevations of between 1 and 2 μg% immediately following the film in all three groups, with the largest rise occurring in the untreated hyperthyroid patient group. More marked and prolonged plasma ^{131}PBI responses occurred in the hyperthyroid patient group, with over 100% increases persisting for at least 2 hr following the film. In the control subjects, there appeared to be a transient drop in ^{131}PBI levels immediately after the film, followed by a moderate elevation. Neck-counting measurements taken during the showing of the films gave the impression that decrease in neck-counting rates, or loss of labeled thyroidal iodine into the circulation, coincided with melodramatic incidents in the film. There was generally a gradual fall in total counting rate during the film, followed by a recovery in counting-rate level after-

wards. Differences in the organization of psychological defenses between normal and hyperthyroid patient groups were also described. A subsequent study by this group confirmed the sensitivity of the plasma ^{131}PBI response in hyperthyroid patients to stressful movies (Flagg, Clemens, Michael, Alexander, & Wark, 1965).

In a group of five college students selected out of a larger group as showing the greatest urinary 17-hydroxycorticosteroid (17-OHCS) responses to final examinations, plasma BEI (butanol extractable iodine) elevations of between about 1 and 1.5 μg% were observed in all five subjects in relation to the examination period (Mason et al., unpublished data). The usefulness of concurrent 17-OHCS measurements as a means of assessing individual emotional reactions in a stressful situation is suggested by these observations. In a recent study, Zuckerman et al. (1966) have reported significant elevations of plasma thyrotropin (TSH) levels in a group of normal subjects in a laboratory perceptual isolation situation. Higher anxiety and depression levels, as determined by checklist scales and higher urinary corticosteroid levels were also observed in this group as compared with a control group.

Psychiatric patients For about a 10-year period beginning in 1922, there were a series of studies of basal metabolic rates in schizophrenic subjects by Bowman (1925, Bowman, Eidson, & Burladge, 1922; Bowman & Grabfield, 1923), Gibbs and Lemcke (1923), Farr (1924, 1931), Hoskins and Sleeper (1929), and Lingjaerde (1933) that were apparently inspired by Kraepelin's theory (1919) that endocrine disorders may play a role in the etiology of schizophrenia. As in the case of the later research on adrenal cortical function in schizophrenics, these studies were concerned primarily with the search for an etiological chronic endocrine abnormality rather than with the question of endocrine response to psychological stimuli. The finding in these studies of low mean basal metabolic rate in schizophrenic patients and the report by Gjessing in 1939 that thyroxine administration may have therapeutic value in periodic catatonia served further to maintain an interest in the study of thyroid function in schizophrenic subjects.

In 1942 Neustadt and Howard, using a crude

method which measured both inorganic and organic iodine in the blood, reported that manic patients have higher and depressed patients have lower blood iodine levels than do a group of normal controls. In individual manic-depressive subjects, they found a close correspondence between changes in mood and changes in blood iodine levels. Using a different method for measuring precipitable and total blood iodine levels, Man and Kahn (1945) found that levels were within the "normal range" of 3–8 μg% in 22 of 26 manic-depressive patients and all 17 depressed patients studied.

Following these isolated reports, the availability of radioiodine uptake techniques and the newly developed plasma PBI procedure led—beginning about in 1950—to another series of studies of thyroid activity in schizophrenic patients (Batt, Kay, Reiss, & Sands, 1957; Bowman et al., 1950a, 1950b; Brody & Man, 1950; Crammer & Pover, 1960; Cranswick, 1955; Faurbye, Munkvad, & Pind, 1958; Hare & Haigh, 1955; Kelsey, Gullock, & Kelsey, 1957; Lingjaerde, Skaug, & Lingjaerde, 1960; Reichlin, 1959; Reiss, 1954; Reiss et al., 1951; Simpson, Cranswick, & Blair, 1963, 1964; Stevens & Dunn, 1958; Stoll & Brack, 1957). Gibson (1962) and Michael and Gibbons (1963) have reviewed this work in some detail.

Certain general features of these studies may be briefly summarized.

1. The majority of the reports deal with *mean* thyroid activity levels in large, heterogeneous schizophrenic groups in comparison with *mean* normal group values.
2. Evaluation of emotional state at the time of the study of thyroid activity was seldom attempted.
3. Control of dietary factors, particularly iodine intake, was not consistent; the importance of this problem has been emphasized by Kelsey, Gullock, and Kelsey (1957).
4. The radioiodine techniques employed by different investigators varied considerably and the physiological significance of some of the isotopic measurements are open to question.

It is clear, then, that some of the same methodological problems are involved as those which appeared to confuse similar studies of adrenal-cortical function in schizophrenic patients reported in about the same period. In general, despite several

reports of increased mean iodine uptake in chronic schizophrenic patients (Bowman et al., 1950a; Cranswick, 1955; Lingjaerde, Skaug, & Lingjaerde, 1960), these findings have not been confirmed by others (Crammer & Pover, 1960; Kelsey, Gullock, & Kelsey, 1957; Reichlin, 1959; Stevens & Dunn, 1958), and no clear conclusions have emerged. Little, if any, differences in mean plasma PBI levels between groups of schizophrenics and normals were reported (Bowman et al., 1950a; Brody & Man, 1950; Kelsey, Gullock, & Kelsey, 1957; Reichlin, 1959; Starr et al., 1950).

Some limited attempts were made to differentiate between diagnostic subgroups of schizophrenics in a few studies. Bowman et al. (1950a) reported decreased ^{131}I uptake in manic patients and plasma PBI levels were low in manic and depressed patients, normal in catatonic patients, and high normal in paranoid patients. Reichlin (1959) noted increased iodine turnover in some paranoid patients and a tendency for higher plasma PBI levels than other patient subgroups.

As in the case of similar research on the pituitary-adrenal cortical system, it is important to recognize that these "contrast" studies, comparing groups of schizophrenics to normals, were addressed primarily to the question of chronic endocrine abnormalities as a causal factor in mental illness and, therefore, represent a digression from the question of psychological influences upon endocrine activity, which is the principal concern of the present review. It appears also, as is the case in the adrenal field, that the interpretability of clinical studies on this system is greatly enhanced when hormone levels are viewed in relation to concurrent, objectively estimated levels of emotional distress or when individual subjects are studied longitudinally through changing phases of clinical illness. Unfortunately, there are as yet only a few clinical studies of the pituitary-thyroid system which have employed these approaches and which do not rely largely on situational or static diagnostic criteria.

In 1949 Brody found that when he rated individuals in a heterogeneous patient population according to a clinical estimate of the degree of psychological tension, there were statistically significant, although small, mean differences in serum precipitable iodine levels between patients with higher and those with lower levels of tension, although all were within the "normal range." In a study of three patients with periodic catatonia, Gornall, Eglitis, Miller, Stokes, and Dewan (1953) observed changes in basal metabolic rate with changing phases of illness, but it is stated that no significant changes in serum PBI levels were found in one case, although no values or other details are given. Gunne and Gemzel (1956) also reported that the plasma PBI levels were "fairly constant and within normal limits" in two patients with periodic catatonia who were studied longitudinally, although the one patient on which the values are given appears to show a 2 μg% difference between about 6 μg% in the disturbed phase and 4 μg% in the following interval of improvement. A similar degree of change was reported by Gjessing (1964), who found PBI values of about 5 μg% during improved intervals and 7-8 μg% during the psychotic phases in three subjects with periodic catatonia. Libow and Durell (1965) also found a small but significant increase in PBI level from about 4-5 μg% during the mute and retarded phase in a patient studied through two cycles of a periodic psychosis. An increase in thyroid activity was also indicated by a doubling of thyroid 24-hr ^{131}I uptake on both occasions when the patient was studied in the mute and retarded phase.

In a study of depressed patients, Board, Persky, and Hamburg (1956) found significant PBI elevations in subjects immediately after hospital admission because of acute psychotic depression. In a related study, a mean PBI value of 6.7 μg% was observed in 9 patients rated as "most depressed" compared with a level of 5.7 μg% in all 33 depressed patients and a level of 4.9 μg% in 24 control subjects. On subsequent occasions of testing, the ratings of depression and the PBI levels both decreased as clinical recovery occurred (Board, Wadeson, & Persky, 1957). Gibbons et al. (1960) also noted a decline in PBI level in some depressed patients during clinical recovery but emphasized that the changes were generally small—seldom exceeding 1 μg%—and usually within the "accepted normal limits." In a longitudinal study of 6 psychiatric patients, including 3 with depression, Gibson and Willcox (1957) also reported phasic changes in

PBI level, with fluctuations of about 2 μg% in 3 subjects, 0.5 μg% in 1 subject, and 3-5 μg% in the other 2 subjects.

Apparently the only effort to study the thyroid response in psychiatric patients subjected to emotional stimuli in a laboratory setting was that of Dongier et al. in 1956. They found no significant change in plasma PBI levels at the end of 1-2 hr after 38 stressful interviews in a group of patients with anxiety. These experiments were based upon the expectation of very rapid PBI changes similar to those reported by Hetzel, de la Haba, and Hinkle (1952b) in normal subjects.

Studies with Laboratory Animals

Some of the early attempts to study relationships between emotional behavior and thyroid activity in animals yielded negative results. In 1914 Hatai reported no difference in thyroid weights between wild Norway rats and Wistar albino rats, a finding later confirmed by Donaldson and King (1929). In 1922 Uno found no increase in thyroid weight during a relatively brief 6-hr period of "excitement" in rats.

In 1932, however, Freudenberger found, as compared with Wistar rats, both heavier adrenals and thyroids in Long-Evans rats, which were regarded as a "nervous" strain. Anderson and Anderson (1938), using a similar approach, found no difference in thyroid weights between "emotional" and "nonemotional" subgroups selected from an apparently homogeneous colony of rats. Yeakel and Rhoades (1941), on the other hand, did find thyroid gland weights to be consistently heavier in "emotional" rats selected from a colony according to relatively systematic and objective criteria. These authors also mention that some preliminary experiments indicated a tendency toward thyroid enlargement in rats disturbed by repeated blasts of air. These few early studies based on thyroid gland weight, while somewhat suggestive of a relationship between thyroid enlargement and emotional behavior in rats, were certainly not conclusive.

The application of radioiodine techniques to studies of the effects of emotional stimuli on thyroid activity in the rabbit was reported by Brown-Grant, Harris, and Reichlin (1954). It was found that emotional disturbances produced by subcutaneous faradism, restraint, or abrupt changes in environmental lighting induced a prompt inhibition of 1–2 days' duration in thyroid activity, as judged by a decrease in the rate of release of ^{131}I from the thyroid gland. This response was not prevented by stellate ganglionectomy or by adrenalectomy. Brown-Grant later demonstrated (1957, p. 97) an abrupt decrease in the [131]PBI level, as well as the change in rate of ^{131}I release in response to restraint in the rabbit. Carriere and Isler (1959), working with mice, reported histological evidence of decreased thyroid activity in association with frequent housing changes. Badrick, Brimblecombe, Reiss, and Reiss (1954), measuring thyroid ^{131}I uptake, also found acute inhibition of thyroid activity under various conditions in rats, including electric shock to the ears. They question, however, the conclusions of Brown-Grant and his associates that this change represents decreased thyrotropic hormone secretion, as it is transitory and experiments with hypophysectomized rats indicate that it is independent of the anterior pituitary. They suggest, rather, that this acute, transitory inhibition of thyroid activity (also seen in some human subjects under severe mental tension) may be caused by increased release of vasoconstrictor substances. Furthermore, an increased uptake rate of ^{131}I by the thyroid was seen 24 hr after the acute stress, and these authors emphasize the importance of following the full time course of thyroid changes. This biphasic pattern of thyroid response, incidentally, fits with that described by Selye (1946) for various "stresses" in the rat, as judged largely by morphological criteria. Time relationships were also emphasized in a recent study by Ducommun, Vale, Sakiz, and Guillemin (1967), in which two plasma TSH response phases were observed over a 20-day period involving the repeated daily stressing of rats by location transfer, handling, sham injection, and brief ether anesthesia. During the first 10 days a drop in TSH levels was observed, while during the second 10 days TSH levels became elevated and acute stimuli superimposed upon this "chronic-stress" setting induced a further increase, rather than the usual decrease in levels.

Some other investigators working with animals have reported results which suggest increased thy-roid activity in response to psychological stimuli. Puntriano and Meites (1951) reported that continuous darkness for 4 weeks stimulated thyroid activity in the mouse. Kracht (1954) reported evidence of marked stimulation of thyroid activity in freshly captured wild rabbits, on the basis of both histological criteria and ^{131}I injection studies. Brown-Grant, Harris, and Reichlin (1954), incidentally, mention that they were unable to confirm these findings. Del Conte, Ravello, and Stux (1955) found an increase in blood thyrotrophin level, measured by bioassay, as well as histological evidence of thyroid activation in guinea pigs receiving electroshock; they also refer to work by others involving dogs and rabbits in which similar findings were reported. Amiragova (1957) observed that, while iodine storage by the thyroid was considerably delayed, iodine stored in the thyroid was released into the circulation in both dogs and cats during mutual confrontation.

In 1961, Mason et al. (1961b) reported preliminary experiments in which prolonged elevations in plasma BEI levels were associated with 72-hr conditioned avoidance sessions in the rhesus monkey. Recently, Harrison, Silver, and Zuidema (1966) have also found increased thyroid activity in monkeys subjected to chronic conditioned avoidance procedures, on the basis of elevated serum PBI and BEI levels and decrease in excretion of injected [131]I. Adrenal demedullectomy did not greatly influence this pattern of thyroid response. It was also recently reported by Falconer and Hetzel (1964), who used a rather elegant method of collecting venous blood from chronically exteriorized thyroid glands in undisturbed conscious sheep, that substantial elevations in thyroidal venous plasma PBI and [131]PBI levels occurred during emotional responses associated with exposure to exploding fireworks or a barking dog.

Comment

In contrast to the extensive research which has permitted virtually unanimous agreement concerning the sensitivity of the pituitary-adrenal cortical and sympathetic-adrenal medullary systems to psychological factors, psychoendocrine research on the pituitary-thyroid system is considerably less extensive and conclusive. In the human, the question at present appears to be whether the thyroid responds significantly to psychological stimuli or not. In laboratory animals, there is general agreement that a response occurs, but it is the direction of response that is in question. This unsettled state of affairs is rather surprising, if not disturbing, particularly in view of the venerable clinical association of emotional crises and onset of hyperthyroidism, and it seems advisable at present that we scrutinize various experimental and physiological parameters which may be relevant to this problem.

Considering the experiments with normal human subjects and hyperthyroid patients first, some general trends seem apparent. In the majority of these studies—those of Hetzel, de la Haba, and Hinkle (1952b); Tingley, Morris, and Hill (1958); Alexander et al. (1961); and Mason et al. (unpublished data)—thyroid hormone levels were found to be increased in response to emotional stimuli, although the increases were often small in terms of percentage change. The study of Volpe, Vale, and Johnston (1960), from which essentially negative conclusions were drawn, involved a rather conservative treatment of data in which changes in mean group values were primarily considered, although it was mentioned that 9 out of 11 undergraduate students in one of their groups showed their highest PBI level during the stressful period. The use of situational criteria and mean group values without evaluation of the actual emotional and defensive reactions of each individual has proved to be a hazardous practice in psychoendocrine research, as it cannot be assumed that all, or even most, individuals will be emotionally disturbed in a given "stressful" situation. The lack of a significant mean PBI rise in a group of students taking final examinations is an ambiguous finding without correlative data and might indicate either that the thyroid did not respond to emotional stimuli or that most individuals in the group did not manifest significant emotional reactions to the experience. It is of interest that, in our own small study of students taking final examinations, butanol extractable iodine (BEI) elevations were observed in all 5 subjects selected for study on the screening basis of concurrent 17-OHCS elevations that indicated that they each were substantially disturbed by the experience.

The findings in normal subjects, then, do not appear necessarily to be in serious conflict, and they generally support the conclusion that mild elevations in PBI levels are associated with acute emotional disturbances, possibly preceded by a brief, transitory decrease in levels, as suggested by the short-term experiments of Hetzel, de la Haba, and Hinkle (1952b) and Alexander et al. (1961). The dynamics of the response are particularly in need of further study in experiments in which a stimulus is maintained and levels of thyroid activity followed not just for the first 1 or 2 hr but for many hours or days.

The research on thyroid activity in schizophrenic patients can be largely dismissed from consideration here because, as discussed previously, this work was not appreciably concerned with thyroid responses to emotional stimuli. The longitudinal studies of psychiatric patients, however, do have considerable relevance and appear to permit some general remarks. It was rather consistently found in longitudinal studies of patients with periodic psychoses that PBI changes correlated with changing phases of illness, being higher during the disturbed phase than during the interval periods. The PBI changes, again, were relatively small, usually between 1 to 2 μg%. Most of the authors reported these findings as negative, however, because the changes usually fall in the "normal range."

As the criterion of the normal range has, curiously, been invoked in the interpretation of many psychoendocrine studies of thyroid activity in the human, it may be advisable to consider for a moment its validity in judging the significance of physiological changes. The normal range of PBI levels between 3–8 or 9 μg%, for example, was originally established largely on the basis of clinical and laboratory criteria with a view to setting lower and upper limits which would be useful in the diagnostic separation of individuals with pathological thyroid disorders, i.e., hypo- or hyperthyroidism. It is, however, not justifiable to assume that any fluctuations in levels occurring within this range have no physiological significance—which seems to have been the inference of some workers in this field. One of the most illuminating features of the extensive recent psychoendocrine research on the adrenal systems, for example, has been the recognition that relatively small differences between individuals or within normal individuals, all well within the "normal range," may have clear biological significance either in terms of correlation with stimuli, situational criteria, or with concurrent psychological measurements. It seems likely then that the failure of stimuli to raise PBI levels beyond the "normal range" into the hyperthyroid range is not a reasonable basis for judging the physiological significance of thyroid response to emotional or other stimuli.

This point might be considered in close conjunction with another general feature of thyroid physiology. Each endocrine system has its own peculiar dynamics and different hormones vary considerably with respect to the total range of fluctuation of their levels in blood or urine. Plasma epinephrine levels may vary in the monkey, for example, over a tremendous range—from less than 1 μg/liter to over 15 μg/liter with certain emotional stimuli, or over 100 μg/liter during hemorrhage. From a statistical standpoint, there is, of course, little problem in evaluating the significance of these changes which represent enormous percentage increases over basal levels. Thyroid hormone levels, however, represent a relatively "tightly regulated" system, very seldom exceeding a constricted range or seldom showing percentage increases greater than double the basal level. The possibility may deserve special consideration in the case of such a system that relatively small absolute or percentage changes in response to stimuli may have substantial physiological significance.

In connection with this point, it must be borne in mind that the precision of the biochemical method may become an important factor. For example, if a change of 0.3 μg% represents a reproducible, physiological response to a stimulus, and the biochemical method cannot distinguish in any single analysis a change of less than 0.6 μg%, then misleading conclusions may be drawn. Several measures may be taken in an effort to minimize such a problem. Duplicate or triplicate analyses will reduce the error in a single sample. The withdrawal of repeated blood samples during the stressful period, providing several points on the response curve, will strengthen the interpretation of small changes as significant. In a series of acute avoid-

ance experiments (Mason et al., 1968b), very small changes in BEI level, considerably less than 1 μg% in most instances, occurred at 2-, 6-, 12-, and 24-hr points during avoidance. These small changes, furthermore, were evident in 15 of 18 animals at the 24-hr point. The consistency of direction of change, together with the small magnitude of change, suggest that the use of nonparametric methods of data analysis may be particularly appropriate for evaluation of changes in PBI or BEI levels. Another approach to this problem which may deserve wider consideration in future studies is the use of the [131]PBI measurement, which has been found to show a substantially wider range of variation and to be a more sensitive index of thyroid activity than the standard PBI measurement.

Another matter which deserves emphasis in future psychoendocrine studies of thyroid activity in human subjects is the importance of concurrent psychological evaluation of emotional and defensive factors in the individual at the time of endocrine study. In studies such as those of Brody and Man (1950), Board, Wadeson, and Persky (1957), and Flagg et al. (1965), estimates of the degree of emotional distress or tension correlated well with the degree of hormonal elevation and served to minimize the misleading influence of the almost inevitable individual differences in response within any group defined by diagnostic category or by situational criteria.

If the above interpretative suggestions are accepted, particularly concerning the limitations of group mean values without correlative data and concerning the likelihood that relatively small changes in PBI levels well within the "normal range" may have significance, the findings in studies with human subjects really present a reasonably consistent picture of "small," 1–2 μg% elevations in association with emotional reactions in many individuals. The number of studies in normal human subjects is still exceedingly small and there is a pressing need for additional, well-controlled studies with several indices of thyroid activity and correlative 17-OHCS and psychological data.

In the case of the research with laboratory animals, the problem of interpreting the data appears to be more complicated. Some workers have reported in association with emotional stimuli unequivocal decreases, and others equally unequivo- cal increases in thyroid activity. Some general distinctions in methodological approach between these two groups of workers seem apparent. Exper- iments in which decreased thyroid activity was observed have involved small laboratory animals, mainly rodents, while those in which increased activity was found involved larger animals, includ- ing sheep and monkeys. Radioiodine uptake tech- niques were generally employed in the case of the small animals and plasma thyroid hormone meas- urement generally was the basis of experiments with the larger animals. Some very limited cross- checking with these two methods was done, how- ever, and it seems unlikely that this point alone could account for the differences in results— although some detailed studies in the future com- paring the various radioiodine indices with PBI or BEI measurements would be a valuable contribution to this field.

The suggestion made by Badrick et al. (1954) that the acute inhibition of thyroid activity observed in rabbits and rats subjected to emotional stimuli may represent the release of vasoconstrictor substances also appears worthy of consideration. Aside from the findings of Badrick and his co-workers that hypophysectomized rats continue to show this re- sponse, indicating that it is not a result of decreased TSH secretion, there is very little data bearing on this possibility and certainly not enough to refute it. The suggestion by Badrick et al. and by Ducom- mun et al. (1967) that a multiphasic response is involved and that much closer attention to time factors in experimental protocols may provide an alternative explanation for conflicting findings in animals also appears worthy of further experimental evaluation.

Perhaps one of the most appealing explanations for resolving the apparently discordant findings of various workers in this field is that of Gerwing (1958), Long (1957), and Gerwing, Long, and Pitt- Rivers (1958). They found that a single injection of endotoxin *depressed* the rate of release of ^{131}I from the thyroid gland of the rat, mouse, and rabbit but *increased* the release rate in the guinea pig and rhesus monkey. They suggest that there is an in- herent species difference affecting thyroid regula- tion which may also be somehow related to differ-

ences between these same species with regard to sensitivity to cortisone administration. While a species difference is usually invoked only as a last resort in explaining conflicting experimental find- ings, the demonstration in a single laboratory of a clear-cut species difference in thyroid response to injection of the same substance is not easily dismissed. The probability that coincidence might account for the same distribution of these species with regard to thyroid response to emotional stim- uli does not seem very high. Despite a dissenting report by Brown-Grant and Pethes (1960) against this formulation of Gerwing and her associates, it appears highly advisable that this question be kept in mind for future evaluation by other workers in the field.

Summary

At first glance, the present status of psycho- endocrine research on the pituitary-thyroid system may appear somewhat confusing. Yet if certain methodological issues are considered critically, the field may not be so unsettled as it first appears. It is perhaps particularly illuminating to view this work in the perspective of the more advanced but similar psychoendocrine research on the adrenal systems. If this is done, several conspicious defi- ciencies and limitations of the present data are evident, as are some special problems in thyroid physiology which appear to require special han- dling from an investigative standpoint.

One important deficiency in studies with normal human subjects has been the reliance upon situa- tional criteria of "stress" and upon mean group values, with a relative lack of systematic evaluation of the important and often marked individual differences between subjects in their emotional and defensive reactions to a given situation.

Likewise, studies with psychiatric patients have largely been based upon comparison or "contrast" between groups according to static diagnostic cri- teria and have often not included assessment of psychological state at the time hormone measure- ments were made.

In addition, some special problems complicate the experimental evaluation of thyroid activity that were not encountered in work with the adrenal systems and which require special measures in experimental design and data analysis. Perhaps a key issue is that relating to the relatively narrow range of fluctuation in absolute blood thyroid hormone levels. Different standards for judging the significance of changes in hormonal levels in this "tightly regulated" system are apparently indicated, in keeping with the difference in its dynamic characteristics as compared with other endocrine systems. The use of nonparametric methods of data analysis, for example, may be particularly suitable in dealing with this system. It also follows that the error of the biochemical method may assume greater importance here than in work with other endocrine systems. In view of this problem, it appears to be a highly questionable judgment to dismiss changes of 1–2 μg% in PBI or BEI levels as biologically unimportant.

The use of the "normal range" concept as a criterion for judging the biological significance of psychoendocrine responses of the pituitary-thyroid system is probably unsound and has been a misleading and confusing factor in this field. The extensive development of psychoendocrine relationships in the study of the adrenal systems has occurred largely within what might similarly be called the "normal range" of hormonal values.

Taking the above factors into consideration, the following conclusions are suggested.

1. The study of normal human subjects under stressful conditions indicates that "small" elevations in thyroid hormone levels, of the order of 1–2 μg%, possibly preceded by a transient decrease in some instances—are associated with acute emotional disturbances. The elevation in levels appears to be more marked in hyperthyroid patients.

2. Longitudinal studies of psychiatric patients suggest similar "small" PBI elevations in disturbed phases as compared with clinically less disturbed phases of illness.

3. There is general agreement that thyroid responses to emotional stimuli occur in laboratory animals, but the direction of such responses is in question. Generally, small animals such as rats, mice, and rabbits have shown decreases, while larger animals (including primates) have shown increases in thyroid activity in association with acute emotional disturbances. Some evidence has been presented suggesting that bona fide species

differences may be involved. Other evidence suggests that the reported discrepancies may be related to the lack of close attention to the time course of the thyroid response to emotional stimuli, and that a biphasic response may be involved. Further experiments will be needed to settle this question.

While the plasma PBI or BEI measurements are probably the most useful indices of thyroid hormone secretion available at present, methodological advances are needed in this field. The recent impressive progress in the radioimmunoassay of peptide and protein hormones offers hope that a reliable method for TSH measurement may soon be available. Meanwhile, it may be helpful if workers in this field include both blood hormone and radioiodine methods in the same study whenever possible. The concurrent measurement of plasma PBI or BEI, plasma [131]PBI, ^{131}I uptake, ^{131}I release rate, ^{131}I excretion, and inorganic iodine levels should help clarify the question of how closely these various indices correlate and also help to determine under what conditions they may become dissociated. [131]I turnover studies should be of interest. Assessment of the levels of thyroxine-binding protein and of "free" thyroxine may well also be included in this battery of measurements because of recent interest in the role of the protein as a determinant of plasma hormone levels.

Another need in this field is for more extensive investigation not only of acute disturbances and thyroid activity but also of possible relationships between chronic mean basal thyroid hormone levels and personality characteristics—particularly in relation to defensive organization in normal human subjects. Such studies have been among the most intriguing and provocative in recent psychoendocrine research on the pituitary-adrenal cortical system.

While consideration of the methodological and theoretical points discussed above may appear to have some explanatory value and to point to some general conclusions in the field, it is clear that further research is much needed before such conclusions can be regarded as firm. In any event, it certainly seems more defensible at present to regard the findings in this field as inconclusive rather than as negative or seriously conflicting. If the recent advances in psychiatric methodology from the adrenal psychoendocrine fields are used to proper advantage, and if energetic efforts are made to refine endocrine methodology to accommodate the special problems of thyroid physiology, particularly in relation to dynamics, it is likely that a more confident decision may soon be forthcoming concerning the placement of the pituitary-thyroid system in the psychoendocrine category.

ORGANIZATION OF THE MULTIPLE ENDOCRINE RESPONSES IN THE MONKEY

The question of *how many* endocrine systems are subjected to the influence of psychological factors has been considered in the preceding sections. It remains to summarize and evaluate this information and to consider its possible general implications with regard to the scope and the organization of psychoendocrine responses.

The Scope of Psychoendocrine Responses

The first step is perhaps simply to enumerate the endocrine systems which are responsive to psychological factors. Do psychological influences selectively affect only a few endocrine systems or is the scope of psychoendocrine relationships more extensive?

The evidence that the pituitary-adrenal cortical and sympathetic-adrenal medullary systems are both extremely sensitive to psychological influences is now overwhelming. The great bulk of previous psychoendocrine research, in fact, has been almost exclusively devoted to these two adrenal systems. The less extensive psychoendocrine research on the pituitary-thyroid system has been regarded as less conclusive so far. Close examination of the data in this field, however, also reveals that, while some differences in the direction of thyroid response in different species have been observed, there is rather general agreement that the secretion of thyroid hormone is responsive to psychological influences. It appears to be particularly important to take into account differences in dynamics when comparing the responsivity of the thyroid gland with that of other endocrine systems. Certainly our own data show with striking consistency a slow but prolonged pituitary-thyroid response in monkeys subjected to avoidance sessions (Mason et al., 1968c).

While very little experimental psychoendocrine research on other endocrine systems has been reported previously, our findings (Mason et al., 1968a–1968i) indicate that, in addition to the 17-hydroxycorticosteroids, epinephrine, norepinephrine, and thyroxine, a number of other hormones should probably be included in the psychoendocrine category. As shown in the overall summary of results in Figure 1.3, these include estrone, estradiol, estriol, testosterone, androsterone, etiocholanolone, dehydroepiandrosterone, aldoster-

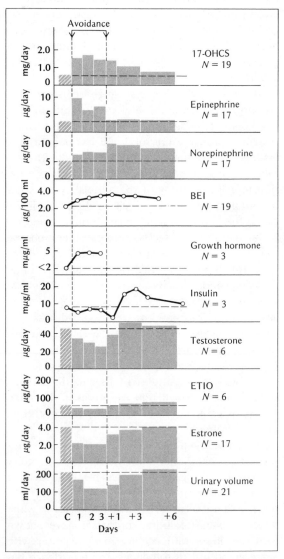

Figure 1.3 Pattern of multiple hormonal responses to 72-hr avoidance sessions in the monkey. Summary of data from Mason et al., 1968 a–h.

one, insulin, and growth hormone. It is evident, in fact, that substantial psychoendocrine responses occurred in the case of every hormone that our laboratory is able to measure at the present time. It remains for future studies to determine whether still additional hormones such as glucagon, prolactin, parathormone, progesterone, vasopressin, oxytocin, and others may also be included in the psychoendocrine category. In any event, our present data suggest that the scope of psychoendocrine relationships is considerably broader than has been generally recognized and support the conclusion that the responses of the adrenal systems, upon which so much attention has been lavished, are only integral parts of a larger, overall pattern of psychoendocrine adjustment.

Evidence for overall organization It is readily evident that the findings represented in Figure 1.3 raise questions which extend beyond that of the *scope* of psychoendocrine responses. The overall pattern is not that of a series of hormones responding in simple unison, as it were, with similar direction, duration, intensity, and configuration of response curves. There is, rather, evidence of a more complicated pattern of *organization,* with clusters of responses sharing common features in such a way as to suggest their possible functional alignment into subgroups.

Using direction of hormonal change as a criterion, it is evident that two general response subgroups may be distinguished. The levels of the 17-hydroxycorticosteroids, epinephrine, norepinephrine, thyroxine, and growth hormone all rise initially, while the levels of the estrogens, androgens, and insulin drop initially. With use of a temporal frame of reference, these same two hormonal response subgroups may also be generally distinguished. The hormones which rise initially tend to show a monophasic response curve while those hormones which drop initially tend to show a biphasic response curve. The former responses predominate in the avoidance period and the latter predominate in the recovery period. Within a particular subgroup there may also be a wide difference in duration of responses. Epinephrine responses sometimes were only 2 days in duration, for example, while thyroid responses lasted as long as 3 weeks following a single 72-hr session.

It seems reasonable to consider the possibility that these apparently orderly features of the hormonal response pattern may have a special physiological significance. Certainly many other types of possible response combinations and patterns can be conceived with a group of hormones this large. Does the particular type of patterning shown in Figure 1.3 indicate that these multiple hormonal responses are organized or coordinated in an overall manner towards a common functional end? The data appear to lead us, then, beyond the initial question of the scope of psychoendocrine responses into the very intriguing problem of their functional organization.

Interpretation An attempt to interpret the data in Figure 1.3 in terms of endocrine "organization" clearly involves a venture into territory in which there are few precedents to follow. In the past, interpretations of the significance of hormone responses have generally dealt with a single endocrine system at a time and not with complicated patterns of response. It seems reasonable, however, to begin with the same general premise which has been used in the analysis of single hormone responses—namely, that the adaptive significance of any hormonal response can be best understood in terms of the consequences of that response at the metabolic level.

It is customary, for example, to regard the insulin response to hyperglycemia as adaptively significant because it, in turn, acts to return the blood sugar level towards the normal range and thereby to maintain the homeostatic equilibrium. The adaptive value of many other hormonal responses, such as the aldosterone response to sodium deprivation, the catecholamine responses to hypotension, the parathormone response to hypocalcemia, or the vasopressin response to dehydration, can be reasonably formulated in the same way. This is not to say that every hormonal response necessarily has such clearly evident significance or adaptive value, but this approach probably provides the most useful and reasonable basis for interpreting such regulatory changes at the present time. The underlying principle might be stated in general terms as "change elicits hormonal response which counteracts change" or perhaps, more broadly, "need elicits hormonal response which satisfies need." A most intimate relationship is thus implied between the metabolic effects of a hormone and its regulation.

While this principle is easily adapted to the interpretation of many hormonal responses to various humoral or physiological stimuli, as indicated in the examples given above, its application to psychoendocrine responses is not quite so simple. We cannot specify with great certainty what the "change" or the "need" is that initiates psychoendocrine responses. The psychoendocrine response appears to differ in one fundamental respect from endocrine responses to other stimuli. Other stimuli to hormone secretion involve *actual* changes in chemical or physical composition of the blood or the peripheral activation of afferent neural pathways. These alterations are secondary either to activity of the organism itself or to changes or forces in the external environment which have direct physical impact upon the organism. In contrast, the most reasonable assumption in the case of the hormonal response to emotional stimuli appears to be that it is a response to *anticipated,* rather than actual change or need. Research with the adrenal systems has demonstrated, in fact, that the hormonal response to threat or to the anticipation of an unpleasant experience may often be more intense than the response to the actual experience itself.

If the assumption is accepted that the psychoendocrine response is basically anticipatory in character, the question remains as to what changes or needs are anticipated. For the most reasonable answer which has yet been given to this question we are indebted to Walter Cannon. In his studies of the sympathetic-adrenal medullary response to emotional stimuli, Cannon was struck by the fact that the metabolic effects of epinephrine, such as hyperglycemia, polycythemia, increased rate and amplitude of cardiac contraction, increased minute volume of respiration, and the like, seem all to have custom-made adaptive value as visceral preparations for muscular exertion. In animals exposed to emotionally arousing or pain-inducing situations, in turn, there is often strenuous muscular exertion associated with flight or struggle although this, of course, need not be an eventuality in every instance. The fact that flight or struggle do not always follow emotional stimuli, particularly in man and in laboratory animals, has sometimes been considered as militating against Cannon's formulation. This scarcely seems a valid basis, however, on which to argue against the adaptive significance or survival value of a bodily response. Certainly a great many common anticipatory or precautionary acts in human behavior can be cited which have unquestionable adaptive or survival value although the anticipated danger or event is rarely actually encountered.

Cannon (1953) further suggests a prominent metabolic need which concerns the organism in threatening situations: ". . . since the fear emotion and the anger emotion are, in wild life, likely to be followed by activities (running or fighting) which require contraction of great muscular masses in supreme and prolonged struggle, a mobilization of sugar in the blood might be of signal service to the laboring muscles." He thus singles out the need for mobilization of energy resources as a matter of special physiological importance to the animal in a threatening or "emergency" situation.

A Sequence of Coordinated Responses

Cannon's formulation provides us, then, with a specific working hypothesis which may be tested against the data in the present study. His concepts were, in fact, instrumental in the development of the notion of a possible "catabolic-anabolic" sequence of hormonal changes during the earlier stages of this study. If we use the criterion of the role of each hormone in energy metabolism, does Cannon's formulation provide a unifying explanation for the many hormonal responses comprising the overall pattern of response to avoidance?

As the multiple hormone responses summarized in Figure 1.3 are reviewed from this standpoint, it is indeed striking that the two general subgroups of hormone responses—previously differentiated on the basis of direction and temporal features of response—can also be generally separated on the basis of the relationships of each hormone to energy metabolism. Those hormones comprising the first response subgroup, which predominate during the avoidance period, including the corticosteroids, epinephrine, norepinephrine, growth hormone, and thyroxine, are all known to exert prominent "catabolic" effects on energy metabolism.

In addition to the hyperglycemia known to Cannon, epinephrine promotes the release of short-chain free fatty acids, which are now believed to have primary importance as fuel for increased energy metabolism (Ellis, 1956; Hagen & Hagen, 1964, p. 268). Although norepinephrine has little hyperglycemic effect, it has a strong free fatty acid releasing effect, perhaps even greater than that of epinephrine (Schotz & Page, 1959). The 17-hydroxycorticosteroids, particularly cortisol, promote hyperglycemia, probably because of increased gluconeogenesis in the liver (Renold & Ashmore, 1960, p. 194). Cortisol also increases free fatty acid release, apparently having both permissive and potentiating effects upon the free fatty acid release induced by epinephrine (Fajans, 1961). The importance of cortisol in supporting muscular work capacity has been well documented by Ingle (1950, p. 150). Some interesting recent evidence has also been presented by Grossfeld to indicate that high concentrations of cortisol increase the capacity of cells to produce energy anaerobically. The capacity for anaerobic energy metabolism is believed to be a critical factor in unusually strenuous muscular work (Grossfeld, 1959). Growth hormone accelerates triglyceride breakdown and induces fatty acid release (Knobil & Hotchkiss, 1964; Krahl, 1961; Randle, 1963). It appears, in fact, that there is a synergism between growth hormone and corticosteroids in fatty acid release.

Thyroxine also has some prominent effects which should be useful in providing increased amounts of utilizable energy, such as the increase of rates of oxidation and the potentiation of some of the major catabolic effects of epinephrine, including the release of free fatty acids (Hoch, 1962; Tepperman, 1962).

On the other hand, the hormones comprising the second response subgroup, which predominate during the recovery period and which include insulin, estrogens, testosterone, and the androgenic metabolites, are associated with predominantly "anabolic" effects with regard to energy metabolism. Insulin is particularly powerful in this respect, increasing the entry of glucose into the cell and promoting glycogenesis and lipogenesis. It also exerts a stimulating effect on protein synthesis which is apparently not linked to its effect on glucose transport (Krahl, 1961; Tepperman, 1962).

Metabolic research on the estrogens and androgens has been largely concerned with reproductive functions and relatively little is yet known of their possible roles in energy metabolism. It is, however, well established that testosterone and related androgens have potent anabolic properties, promoting protein synthesis in muscle and many other tissues (Dorfman & Shipley, 1956, p. 218; Kochakian, 1964). Beyond this, there is little either positive or negative information. There is some indication that both the estrogens (McKerns & Bell, 1960) and androgens (Talaat, Habib, & Habib, 1957) may potentiate some effects of insulin on carbohydrate metabolism. While the limited evidence available so far may suggest an anabolic role for the androgens and estrogens, whether these hormones play an appreciable role in general organic or energy metabolism largely remains to be clarified in future experimental work.

Thus in a very general way the unifying concept of a "catabolic-anabolic" sequence of coordinated hormonal adjustments in relation to avoidance appears to hold up. Levels not only of epinephrine but also of other hormones promoting glucose or free fatty acid mobilization rise acutely during the avoidance period. The level of insulin, the principal hormone known to oppose or antagonize the above changes and to promote synthesis and storage of carbohydrate, fat, and protein, drops during the avoidance period and then rises in the recovery period. All of these events appear to be oriented toward the common end of an efficient mobilization of energy resources during avoidance and replenishment of depleted stores afterwards.

While many of the hormonal changes associated with avoidance appear to be related primarily to energy metabolism, this should not be regarded as an exclusive explanation as it clearly does not encompass all the responses. Aldosterone and vasopressin, of course, are not believed to play an important or direct role in energy metabolism. It appears, rather, that the antidiuretic response (believed to be due largely to vasopressin release) and the aldosterone response are probably related primarily to water and electrolyte adjustments. Such adjustments, however, also may be viewed readily in terms of preparation for muscular exertion. Increased muscular activity is associated with increased heat production. The retention or conservation of water for dissipation of heat would thus seem clearly to have adaptive utility to the animal preparing for action. Water is also needed for the eventual excretion of waste by-products of increased muscular activity.

The findings of the present study should, then, not be misconstrued as indicating that mobilization of energy is the *sole* concern of endocrine responses to emotional stimuli. The likelihood that some hormonal responses, together with autonomic responses, contribute to still other adaptive adjustments to emotional stimuli should remain open to further consideration. The possibility has also been pointed out by Cannon that some of these adjustments, such as the increased rate of blood coagulation induced by epinephrine, may be better understood in terms of preparation for injury which may accompany struggle or flight (Cannon, 1953, p. 197).

Temporal Factors

The influence of some earlier observations on pepsinogen responses to avoidance in the conception of the present study was mentioned previously. The prolonged elevations of pepsinogen levels in the aftermath of avoidance first suggested to us the notion of two possible general classes of regulatory changes oriented in a "catabolic-anabolic" sequence (Mason et al., 1961a). Therefore, there was a predictive aspect to the present study which might be regarded as providing another form of support for the validity of the interpretation of results which has been suggested.

The pepsinogen findings also emphasized the need for directing greater attention to the full temporal course of events in relation to stressful experiences. There has been a tendency in the majority of endocrine studies of "stress" to focus primarily upon the initial, acute phases of response and to neglect later phases of endocrine adjustments, particularly during the recovery period. Many of the hormone response curves we have observed (Mason et al., 1968a–1968i), including those involving thyroxine, norepinephrine, insulin, testosterone, and the estrogens, certainly support the conclusion that the duration of endocrine responses may be remarkably prolonged following the termination of a stressful experience. The thyroid hormone response curve, in particular, indicated that the duration of endocrine changes may last in some in-

stances as much as seven times as long as the stressful period itself. Our findings suggest that phase duration may be, along with direction of response, a particularly important parameter in the organization of endocrine responses and can only be observed if all hormonal measurements extend through the full course of time until the levels again stabilize in the preexperimental baseline range.

Reciprocal Inhibition

The generally reciprocal character of the two hormone response subgroups in the present study seems to be an especially noteworthy finding that suggests the overall coordination of endocrine regulation on a broad scale. The drop in insulin level which is concomitant with corticosteroid and epinephrine elevations perhaps suggests a type of regulatory coordination of antagonistic elements similar to that which has been established for the skeletal-muscular and autonomic nervous systems.

Sherrington (1947, p. 84) described this principle of coordination in relation to simple muscle reflexes as follows:

> Reflex coordination makes separate muscles whose contractions act harmoniously, e.g., on a lever, contract together, although at separate places, so that they assist toward the same end. In other words, it excites synergic muscles. But in many cases it does more than that. Where two muscles would antagonize each other's action the reflex arc, instead of activating merely one of the two, when it activates the one causes depression of the activity . . . of the other. The latter is an inhibitory effect.

Cannon (1953, p. 197) also commented on this principle in relation to the coordination of autonomic nervous system function:

> *When the mid-part (sympathetic) meets either end-part (cranial or sacral) in any viscus their effects are characteristically antagonistic.* Thus the cranial supply to the eye contracts the pupil, the sympathetic dilates it; the cranial slows the heart, the sympathetic accelerates it.

Sherrington has demonstrated that the setting of skeletal muscles in opposed groups about a joint or system of joints, as in extensors and flexors, is associated with an internal organization of the central nervous system that provides for relaxation of one group of the opposed muscles, when the other group is made to contract. This "reciprocal innervation of antagonistic muscles," as Sherrington has called it, is thus a device for orderly action in the body. As the above description has shown, there are peripheral oppositions in the viscera, corresponding to the oppositions between flexor and extensor muscles. In all probability these opposed innervations of the viscera have counterparts in the organization of neurones in the central nervous system. Sherrington has noticed, and I can confirm the observation, that even though the sympathetic supply to the eye is severed and is therefore incapable of causing dilation of the pupil, nevertheless the pupil dilates in a paroxysm of anger, due, no doubt (because the response is too rapid to be mediated by the blood stream) to central inhibition of the cranial nerve supply to the constrictor muscle, i.e., an inhibition of the muscles which naturally oppose the dilator action of the sympathetic.

We now have evidence that psychoendocrine responses may be organized along precisely these same lines. The coelevation of the synergistic hormones, cortisol and epinephrine, concomitant with the "reciprocal inhibition" of their antagonist, insulin, appears to represent a striking parallel to the examples given by Sherrington and Cannon of the coordination of skeletal-muscular and autonomic responses. Whether this general principle that endocrine regulation is organized on the basis of a coordinated balance between opposing forces holds in other situations and with other combinations of hormones seems an important question for future research.

The Integrating Mechanism

A related question concerns the nature of the underlying integrating mechanism itself. Are all the hormonal responses initiated as a "package" by a common neural coordinating mechanism? Are some responses secondary to a smaller group of primary or preceding responses or the metabolic changes induced by the latter?

Perhaps the most relevant information now available is that concerned with the time relationships between the various hormonal changes. On this basis there appears to be little to suggest dependence of one hormonal change upon a prior hormonal change during the acute response period. The most rapid responses are apparently those involving insulin, growth hormone, and the catecholamines. The corticosteroid and thyroxine responses are slower to reach maximal development but probably also begin almost immediately after

presentation of the psychological stimulus. There is less information regarding the acute phases of the estrogen, androgen, and aldosterone response curves because only data on 24-hr urinary levels are available at present.

More detailed study of plasma levels of all these hormones (when possible) during the first avoidance day in monkeys with intravenous catheters should provide additional useful information on this question. It may also be of interest to determine if the second-phase elevations of insulin, testosterone, or other hormones during the recovery period are related to prior hormone responses during the avoidance period. Might the experimental infusion of exogenous cortisol or epinephrine, for example, produce a delayed but prolonged insulin or testosterone elevation similar to those seen in the avoidance pattern? Do the insulin and testosterone elevations in the recovery period following avoidance occur in adrenalectomized monkeys?

At present it appears to be reasonable to view the overall response pattern shown in Figure 1.3 as representing primarily a series of concomitant responses rather than a concatenation of changes following any single initial response such as that of the pituitary-adrenal cortical system, for example. Even if some of the observed hormonal responses eventually prove to be secondary in a temporal sense, it seems doubtful that such responses should be regarded as any the less "psychoendocrine" in nature if they invariably result from the presentation of a psychological stimulus.

Characteristics of the Response Pattern

Typicalness It has been implied in the preceding discussion that the hormone response pattern to avoidance may be generally characteristic of those seen in other situations involving acute emotional disturbances. It is certainly hazardous, however, to base such a broad generalization on the study of a single experimental procedure or set of conditions. What assurance do we have that the response pattern shown in Figure 1.3 is not peculiar to avoidance?

In an effort to obtain some information on this point, another series of experiments is currently underway in which the hormone response pattern in monkeys during adaptation to the restraining chair is being studied. Earlier work had indicated that the first transfer from the home cage to the restraining chair is usually an emotionally disturbing experience associated with substantial 17-hydroxycorticosteroid elevations, particularly in naïve monkeys without previous handling in the laboratory (Mason, Harwood, & Rosenthal, 1957). Preliminary results in current experiments indicate that the overall pattern of hormonal responses during chair adaptation is strikingly similar to that observed during avoidance. In these experiments monkeys are housed for several months in cages within a small, sound-resistant cubicle. When hormone levels have been found to be stable and basal for at least 2 months, the monkey is then transferred from the cage to a restraining chair-booth in the same cubicle. Figure 1.4 presents an experiment showing the multiple hormone responses during chair adaptation in comparison with the mean values for each hormone while the monkey was caged during the month immediately prior to placement in the chair. The similarity to the avoidance response pattern is evident. The 17-hydroxycorticosteroid, epinephrine, norepinephrine, and thyroxine levels rise initially, while the insulin, estrone, and testosterone levels fall initially (Mason et al., 1967). As this stress situation has temporal characteristics different from the avoidance session, which ceases abruptly after 72 hr, it is not possible to make further strict comparisons of the two situations with regard to the later phases of hormonal change. These data, however, do provide some support for the assumption that the avoidance hormonal response pattern may be more generally characteristic of acute emotional reactions in at least some other situations.

Modifying conditions While the pattern of hormonal response to avoidance was observed to be relatively stereotyped and consistent under the conditions of the present experiments, it should be emphasized that the pattern may be modified under certain conditions. The fact that a very similar response pattern was observed in monkeys adapting to the restraining chair, while suggesting that this pattern may be a common one, should certainly not be taken to indicate that this is the only acute

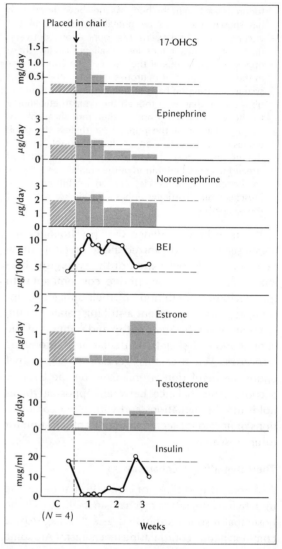

Figure 1.4 Pattern of multiple hormonal responses during restraining chair adaptation in Monkey M-005.

psychoendocrine response pattern observed in the monkey. Hopefully, other workers may attempt to repeat these experiments or to investigate other psychological stimuli in other species by using the general approach of this study. As we have already encountered some sources of variance in our own experiments, it may be well to review some of the known conditions under which the hormone response pattern shown in Figure 1.3 may be altered.

One of the critical conditions specified in the present study was the presence of "basal" hormone levels in the immediate preavoidance period. Thus all baseline urinary 17-OHCS values were below 1 mg/day and all baseline BEI values were below 4 μg%, for example. "Basal levels" have been established for each hormone on the basis of previous experience with normal, healthy male monkeys in the 10- to 15-lb weight range who have been kept for many weeks in a quiet, stable, and comfortable environment. It is likely that monkeys with baseline levels elevated markedly above these "basal" values may show an altered response to the avoidance stimulus. In the case of growth hormone, for example, when baseline values were above about 7 mμg/ml, the level dropped during avoidance while levels rose in the larger number of experiments in which baseline values were below 7 mμg/ml.

It is particularly important, therefore, to maintain animals in a quiet, comfortable, shielded environment during the baseline period as well as during the experimental manipulations in this type of study. In working with relatively labile systems such as those concerned with insulin or growth hormone secretion, it is also probably advisable to minimize confrontation and handling of the animal by using a chronic indwelling cardiac catheter instead of saphenous venipuncture. If the avoidance stimulus is superimposed in a period when hormonal responses to a preceding extraneous stimulus are still

in progress, replication of the pattern in Figure 1.3 cannot be expected.

We have also observed that a hormonal response to avoidance may be strikingly modified by experience. The monthly repetition of the 72-hr avoidance experience in the present study was associated with some moderate changes in the intensity and timing of the urinary 17-OHCS response, but the direction of response remained constant (Mason, Brady, & Tolliver, 1968). More recently, however, we have found that weekly repetition of 72-hr avoidance sessions may be associated with an actual reversal in the direction of the 17-OHCS response. Figure 1.5 shows the usual marked urinary 17-OHCS response in a monkey on the first 72-hr avoidance session. The responses to weekly repetition of the experience quickly diminish until, by the sixth session, the 17-OHCS levels do not rise but appear to decline slightly during avoidance. At Sessions 14 and 20 the same pattern persists with slightly lower levels during the 3-day avoidance period than during the 4-day rest period (Brady, 1964, p. 271). This observation is reminiscent of a similar phenomenon seen in some human subjects who tend to have low basal 17-OHCS levels during chronic, stressful life situations, and who often show a further drop in 17-OHCS levels during a superimposed, acutely stressful experience. The evidence in such subjects

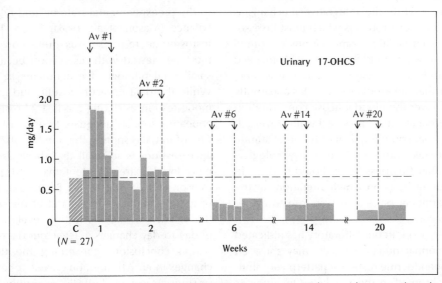

Figure 1.5 Modification of urinary 17-OHCS responses to 72-hr avoidance sessions in monkey with weekly repetition of sessions.

does not point to an endocrine "exhaustion" phenomenon but rather appears to indicate the operation of psychological suppressive mechanisms and to be related to individual differences in the organization of psychological defenses (Mason, 1964, p. 375).

It appears to be important, therefore, to give close attention to the temporal patterning of stressful experiences, particularly to their chronicity, in evaluating acute psychoendocrine response patterns. The timing of stimuli is, of course, considerably more difficult to specify and control in research with the human than in the experimental animal. While the question of individual differences in psychoendocrine responsiveness is less pronounced and less complicated in the monkey as compared with the human, it also appears to be advisable to consider the previous history of each animal as fully as possible in the design and interpretation of psychoendocrine experiments.

The endocrine systems are, of course, also subjected to the regulatory influence of factors other than psychological stimuli. The present study suggests that we need to determine whether these other stimuli also elicit multiple hormonal changes which appear to be organized on a relatively broad scale. In life there is probably very often a mixture of psychological and physical or humoral factors acting simultaneously in the regulation of endocrine secretion. How the integrative mechanisms handle the complex problems which must be associated with such variable combinations of stimuli is, in itself, a fascinating question much in need of further study. In the present study it was seen, for example, that the avoidance stimulus apparently took priority over the blood glucose concentration in the determination of plasma insulin levels. It seems likely that some physical or humoral stimuli may, in turn, take precedence over psychological factors and that this possibility should be kept in mind as another basis on which alterations in the observed hormonal pattern of response to avoidance may occur.

Preliminary work in our laboratory has indicated that some normal human subjects may show an acute psychoendocrine response pattern very similar to that observed in the monkey. Our findings also suggest, however, that considerably greater

variation in the response pattern may be found between human subjects than between individual monkeys. The definition of multiple determinants—psychological, metabolic, or other—that contribute to these individual variations is certainly one of the important future goals in psychoendocrine research. Our data suggest, however, that the response pattern observed in the present study is generally quite reproducible when working with naïve adult, male monkeys under highly standardized conditions. Accordingly, in the event that deviations from this pattern are observed, it seems advisable to suspect the presence of added experiential, metabolic, or environmental variables.

Limitations in the Research

The somewhat oversimplified interpretation of our data presented so far clearly needs to be tempered by the consideration of some limitations of both the experiments and their interpretation.

The question of the statistical significance of each hormonal response has been covered in the preceding individual papers. In general, most of the responses were extremely consistent from one experiment and one animal to the next. In the case of the estrogens, androgens, and aldosterone, some occasional variability of initial response direction was observed, but it appeared to be related systematically to urine volume changes and possibly to the preexperimental state of fluid or electrolyte balance (Mason et al., 1968a, 1968b, 1968d). The testosterone response was quite consistent, but must be viewed with reservation because of the small total number of experiments at this point. While the data on acute insulin and growth hormone responses during the first 2 hr of avoidance appear reasonably adequate to establish the direction of initial response, the number of 72-hr avoidance sessions is so small that these data must be considered extremely tentative and preliminary (Mason et al., 1968g, 1968i). Because of the lability of growth hormone levels and of the question of the validity of 9:00 AM fasting levels as an index of day-to-day changes in level, our data do not yet permit conclusions concerning the duration of changes in growth hormone levels following 72-hr sessions (Mason et al., 1968i). Accordingly, only the initial direction of growth hormone response has been indicated in Figure 1.1, enough to indicate its categorization with the other hormones which show elevated levels during the avoidance period.

For the most part, however, the reliability of the hormonal response pattern shown in Figure 1.3 appears to be reasonably well established. In recent experiments with partially amygdalectomized monkeys we have obtained still further data supporting the validity of the response pattern reported in the present study. While the partially amygdalectomized monkeys showed some moderate differences in quantitative and temporal features of response in comparison with normal monkeys, the overall pattern was identical to that shown in Figure 1.3 with regard to the direction of each hormonal response. It is, in fact, really rather remarkable that such a relatively complicated response pattern can be reproduced so consistently as a stereotyped whole—especially when one considers that the many hormones involved are also susceptible to the influence of a variety of other regulatory factors. This fact, in itself, perhaps suggests that psychological factors rank rather high in relative potency as compared with other factors capable of altering endocrine activity.

A crucial question in the present study concerns the extent to which measurements of plasma and urinary hormone levels may be regarded as valid indices of endocrine activity. These methods clearly represent dramatic and major biochemical improvements over the crude and indirect methods available prior to about 1950. The interpretation of plasma and urinary hormone levels as indices of hormone secretion rates, however, is certainly not without possible pitfalls from a physiological standpoint. The plasma level of a hormone is a resultant not only of the glandular secretion rate but also of other factors such as the physicochemical fate in the blood of the secreted hormone and the rate of removal of hormone from the plasma. The urinary levels of hormones reflect similar multiple determinants. In addition, the percentage of secreted hormone which appears unchanged in the urine as the parent compound may vary considerably from one hormone to the next; in the case of epinephrine, for example, this may be less than 5%. The question has been logically raised, therefore, whether small differences in metabolic or

renal handling of some hormones might conceivably result in large percentage differences in the quantity of hormone excreted in the face of a relatively constant secretion rate from the gland. So far this question has remained largely a theoretical one, and future systematic experimental work will be required to determine whether this is a matter of practical importance in the animal without renal or hepatic disease.

It seems advisable, therefore, not to regard our present measurements too complacently as definitive or even adequate indices of endocrine activity—in spite of their relative refinement from a biochemical standpoint. When possible, the concurrent measurement of both plasma and urinary levels of a given hormone should provide greater reliability in the estimation of glandular activity than either measurement alone. The increased use of isotopic techniques for hormone secretion rate or production rate measurements in conjunction with plasma and urinary hormone determinations is another measure which should be of great value in the future refinement of approaches in this field.

At the same time there is some good reason to believe that the plasma and urinary changes observed in the present study are probably not misleading. It is quite evident that, in the analysis of these data, the parameter of chief concern is the direction of change rather than the fine gradations of quantitative change in endocrine activity. Most of the reservations concerning plasma and urinary measurements as indices of hormone-secretion rate appear to involve primarily the question of quantitation and would seem less likely to result in a misleading indication of the direction of change in endocrine activity.

The response pattern defined in this study is based heavily upon 24-hr urinary excretion rates and 9:00 AM fasting blood levels of the various hormones. The corticosteroid data make it clear, however, that there may be considerable fluctuations in endocrine activity during each 24-hr period (Mason, Brady, & Tolliver, 1968). The 24-hr urinary excretion level presumably reflects the daily average of these diurnal fluctuations but, of course, does not delineate them otherwise. The 9:00 AM fasting levels presumably are less likely to reflect the average daily fluctuation, although in the case of the corticosteroids there was usually a very rough positive correlation between 9:00 AM plasma levels and 24-hr urinary levels. In the case of some of the more labile hormones, such as growth hormone and insulin, more data are needed with regard to what constitutes a daily sampling schedule that gives a reasonably valid picture of ongoing activity in these systems. Certainly our present sampling procedures convey an oversimplified picture of endocrine regulatory processes and future development of this work should include a closer look at the diurnal patterns of hormonal change in all phases of the experiment.

It is our assumption that the predominant independent variable in the present experiments is the psychological disturbance associated with the avoidance behavior required of the monkey. It is evident, however, that this experimental situation involves an admixture of several elements, including such factors as sleep deprivation, muscular activity, electric shock, and disturbances of food or water intake. As most of the available control information relevant to the evaluation of these factors has been obtained with 17-hydroxycorticosteroid measurements, the problem of these other variables has been discussed in some detail in connection with our corticosteroid data (Mason, Brady, & Tolliver, 1968). In general, on the basis of the corticosteroid data, alternative hypotheses that any of these factors played a prominent role in the study—particularly in the determination of the initial, acute response pattern—appear quite unlikely. It is also clear, however, that much more complete investigation of the possible effects of each of these individual variables on hormonal balance is needed in the future.

The "catabolic-anabolic" formulation outlined earlier was necessarily presented in an oversimplified manner. Certain metabolic effects of the various hormones were cited as the basis for their inclusion in either the "catabolic" or "anabolic" subgroups. These arbitrary selections may reasonably be questioned on several grounds. Some of these hormones have been reported, for example, to have both "catabolic" and "anabolic" effects in relation to organic metabolism. It is also true that some hormones selected as predominantly "catabolic" showed prolonged response curves extending

through both the avoidance and recovery periods. Is there any basis on which these facts can be reconciled with the suggested "catabolic-anabolic" sequence formulation?

It is clear that consideration of this problem requires that we delve much more deeply into the current state of knowledge in research on the metabolic actions and effects of hormones. Review of this complex field does suggest that some general principles of endocrine organization at the metabolic level are emerging which may have direct relevance not only to the present discussion but also to the study of endocrine regulation in general. Because of its scope, complexity, and importance, this issue is the subject of the final section of this chapter.

Future Directions for Research

As many of the concepts which have been suggested must certainly be regarded at present as hypothetical and tentative, it may be useful now to consider some ways in which these concepts can be subjected to further critical experimental tests.

One possible test of the validity of the "catabolic-anabolic" formulation may be in its power to predict the pattern of response to avoidance of additional hormones, as it becomes possible to measure them. Hormones such as glucagon, prolactin, and progesterone, for example, are known to have effects on general organic or energy metabolism and changes in all these hormones would therefore be predicted in relation to avoidance sessions. Because the most striking effect of glucagon is said to be a rise in blood glucose (Foa & Galansino, 1962), this hormone would be predicted, for example, to be aligned with the "catabolic" group. The validity of such "predictive" tests for this hypothesis would, of course, depend upon the validity of current conclusions concerning the metabolic effects of these less well-studied hormones.

One of the most direct approaches to the evaluation of the "catabolic-anabolic" formulation would appear to be through the addition of various metabolic measurements for comparison with the hormonal data. This should make it possible to determine if the metabolic changes postulated as likely consequences of the shifting phases in hormonal balance actually occur. Do elevations of glucose and free fatty acid levels indeed characterize the acute avoidance period or "catabolic" phase?

The fact that plasma glucose elevations usually occur during the avoidance session has already been discussed in connection with the plasma insulin data (Mason et al., 1968g). More recently we have also initiated some measurements of free fatty acid levels in 72-hr avoidance experiments. In all six experiments completed so far, free fatty acid levels have risen consistently during avoidance, the mean 9:00 AM value on all 3 avoidance days being roughly twice as high as the preavoidance baseline value of 0.34 mEq./liter. Additional determinations on partially amygdalectomized monkeys showed similarly consistent free fatty acid rises during 72-hr avoidance sessions.

While these findings confirm that some "catabolic" events promoting mobilization of energy resources do take place during the avoidance period, the question still remains as to whether the postulated "anabolic" changes can be demonstrated to occur during the recovery period. Little data are yet available on this point and we are presently involved in the problem of evaluating possible indices of "anabolic" activity with which we may pursue this question experimentally. It appears likely that more elaborate methods than the measurement of blood levels of substrates will be required for study of this question.

It seems likely that some of the more general concepts suggested by the present study may also apply to other aspects of research on endocrine regulation. For example, the concept that endocrine responses to stimuli are organized on a broad scale involving many endocrine systems concurrently and the concept that there must be intimate interrelationships between what a hormone does in the body and how it is regulated seem relevant not only to the study of psychoendocrine responses but also to the study of endocrine regulation in general. It appears, therefore, that the study of the possible application of these concepts to the regulation of endocrine secretion by humoral or physical stimuli may provide another basis for the future evaluation of the validity of these concepts. This question will be discussed in greater detail in the final section.

Summary

In the presentation of an interpretation of the findings in the present study a number of general issues have been discussed. The findings suggest that the scope of psychoendocrine responses is remarkably broad. The findings also suggest that the multiple hormonal responses to avoidance are organized on an overall basis. Some specific characteristics of this organization were suggested. The possibility that the multiple psychoendocrine responses were largely oriented to promote a "catabolic-anabolic" sequence of events in energy metabolism was suggested. The general importance of temporal factors in endocrine regulation was emphasized. Some basic similarities between the organization of endocrine, autonomic, and skeletal-muscular regulation were suggested—particularly with regard to the principle of a coordinated balance between opposing and cooperating forces. A number of limitations and critical questions concerning the present study were emphasized and some possible ways in which the concepts developed in this study might be further tested experimentally were discussed.

The one aspect of the present study that may deserve emphasis above all the others is simply the point that recent methodological developments have now made the concept of endocrine "organization" accessible to experimental study. Whether the more specific formulations suggested, such as those involving the "catabolic-anabolic" pattern or the principle of "reciprocal-inhibition" in endocrine regulation, should eventually prove valid is not the main issue at present. What is most important is that the concept of endocrine regulation as organized or coordinated on a broad "overall" basis—not only in relation to psychological stimuli but to other stimuli as well—is pursued in future experiments. The validity of this concept cannot be decided at present by argument, but only by new experiments carefully designed with this particular objective in mind.

Further experiments on isolated endocrine systems, with the conventional measurement of one hormone or one hormonal class at a time, cannot provide the needed insight into the question of endocrine organization as a whole. Achievement of this objective almost certainly requires a movement toward more studies of an increasingly broad range of *concurrent* hormone measurements so that patterns and interrelationships between the many endocrine systems can be defined. In the design and conception of such experiments, it seems likely that useful clues may be provided by current knowledge of the metabolic effects of hormones, on the basis that organization of endocrine function at the "metabolic" and "regulatory" levels must almost certainly be closely linked. Some recent experience in our laboratory has also suggested some other factors that may have practical implications for future work in this direction. The next section therefore, will be devoted to a review of some possible sources of useful guidelines for future attempts to extend the approach developed in the present study beyond the psychoendocrine field.

ENDOCRINE ORGANIZATION THROUGH OVERALL HORMONAL BALANCE

The question of how the many hormones in the body act together as a group to accomplish the homeostatic regulation of physiological processes is one of the major unsolved problems in endocrine physiology. It has been customary for most research on the effects of hormones and on the regulation of hormone secretion to be directed at the study of one endocrine system at a time. Our findings of multiple, concurrent hormonal responses in relation to avoidance sessions in the monkey suggest not only that a large number of endocrine systems respond in this situation but also that the response pattern may be organized on a broad overall basis, as discussed in the preceding section. It seems a logical next step to consider the possibility that this principle may also apply outside the psychoendocrine field in a more general way to the study of endocrine organization. Perhaps broad, coordinated patterns of hormonal responses are associated not only with psychological stimuli but with humoral or physical stimuli as well. Might the more general application of multiple, concurrent hormone measurements in studies of endocrine regulation provide a new level of insight into endocrine organization which has not been yielded by the

conventional study of a single endocrine system at a time?

Examination of this question, of course, can only be largely speculative at present. There are some reasons, however, why it may be useful at this stage to consider some of the more remote general implications of the present study. A principal reason is that this theoretical approach appears to provide a rich source of explicit working hypotheses and future experiments. While many of these suggested experiments lie outside the psychoendocrine field, they should provide direct testing of concepts upon which much of the interpretation of the present study is based. This approach also raises some practical questions about disciplinary boundaries which may have an important influence on future progress in this field. Finally, there is quite conceivably in this approach the potential for revolutionary changes of direction in physiological research more toward the study of coordinative or integrative processes and away from almost sole concern with isolated units of the organism.

The Intervolving of "Regulatory" and "Metabolic" Endocrinology

Our experience in the present study suggests that the interpretation of patterns of hormonal response to any stimulus must inevitably lead to consideration of the metabolic effects of the involved hormones. It is difficult to imagine any alternative basis for judging the significance of a hormone response other than by its consequences at the metabolic level. At the same time, it is difficult to imagine that the release of a hormone is unrelated to changes in the state of the metabolic processes which it regulates. As discussed earlier, this appears to be the principle with which we view many endocrine-metabolic relationships, e.g., the blood glucose-insulin relationship. Blood glucose elevation stimulates insulin release which, in turn, lowers blood glucose levels. The stimulus to hormone release is intrinsically related to the metabolic process upon which the hormone acts. While this principle seems implicit in the case of stimulus-response relationships involving many other hormones, it does not appear to have been carried to its logical conclusion in the field of endocrine regulation in general. This principle seems not to have been generally applied to the pituitary-adrenal cortical system, for example, although in 1959 Ingle remarked: "Twenty-one years ago, I suggested that the pituitary is sensitive to some physiological function regulated by the cortical hormones. I still think that a controlling center must be sensitive to the physiological consequences of cortical hormone action—how else can the body balance its supply of corticoids against its needs?"

The classical concept of humoral self-regulation of hormone secretion, as exemplified by the stimulation of ACTH secretion by low plasma 17-OHCS levels and the suppresion of ACTH secretion by high plasma 17-OHCS levels, is not a sufficient explanation for all the facts of endocrine regulation. There is no question but that this type of self-regulatory mechanism does exist, and it may well play a major governing role in the return of high or low levels of hormones towards the middle, "normal" range. This mechanism by itself, however, cannot account for the *initiation* of endocrine changes. It has been suggested that "utilization" of hormones during "stress" might be an initiating mechanism, but this concept has not been proved experimentally, despite a number of efforts and the availability of suitable methods to do so.

It is suggested, therefore, that we further explore the premise that the organization of endocrine function at the metabolic and regulatory levels must be intimately intervolved. If this is true, general principles emerging from the study of one of these aspects of endocrine physiology may very well have useful application to the other, i.e., *principles concerning how hormonal effects are organized at the metabolic level should apply to the study of endocrine regulation, and vice versa.* The present experiments have possibly provided some examples in support of this generalization, including the reciprocal regulation of hormones (such as epinephrine and insulin) that antagonize each other at the metabolic level. In any event, this approach suggests that the investigator of endocrine regulation has an investment in the current state of progress in research on the metabolic effects of hormones. Detailed knowledge of the effects of each hormone, knowledge of general principles of hormonal regulation of metabolism, and a critical appreciation of the limitations and technical diffi-

culties in this field are all matters which the present approach suggests are relevant to the study of endocrine regulation.

It does not take much exposure to be impressed by the almost overwhelming size and complexity of the field of "metabolic" endocrinology. It is a field which presents exceedingly difficult problems in regard to methods and the interpretation of data. Because of these problems it is much more difficult than one might think to establish with reasonable certainty the natural physiological effects of any particular hormone. It is beyond the scope of this paper and the competence of the author to attempt more than a brief summary of some of the major problems and limitations in this field and an outline of some general principles of hormone action which may have particular relevance to the present discussion.

Limitations in Research on Metabolic Effects on Hormones

Experimentally, the effects of a hormone may be studied either in vivo or in an in vitro system. If a hormone is administered in vivo, there is, for example, the problem of distinguishing between its direct, primary effects and those which are indirect or secondary. If a hormone is added to an in vitro system, the artificiality of the medium, variations in its composition, the need for attention to kinetics of reactions, and other problems complicate interpretation of data. In either type of approach, the dosage of hormone is a troublesome problem and the distinction between "physiological" versus "pharmacological" effects of hormones has constantly been a matter of serious concern to endocrinologists. In some instances a hormone may act in one direction at a low dosage and in the opposite direction in a larger dosage. It is understandable, therefore, that many authorities in this field have urged caution in making dogmatic generalizations about the effects of any particular hormone and have repeatedly emphasized these methodological problems (Astwood, 1957, p. 223; Bush, 1960, p. 92; Hoch, 1962; Munck, 1965; Thorn, 1960, p. 92).

Conclusions are arrived at slowly only after detailed and integrated study of a considerable amount of data from both in vitro studies and in vivo studies in animals and humans. While most of the hormonal effects on energy metabolism cited in connection with interpretation of the avoidance experiments are reasonably well established, it should be borne in mind that this is still a very active field of investigation and that varying levels of certainty are involved in the case of different hormonal effects.

Some General Principles of Hormonal Action on Metabolism

With the outlined limitations in mind, we may turn to the question of what is known at present with regard to the general principles underlying the functional organization of hormonal effects at the metabolic level. Curiously, in spite of all the data available, we do not have as yet a very clear picture of how the many hormones work together as a group to regulate the activity of so many processes and tissues. In the past there has been a tendency to "pigeonhole" many individual hormones in relation to a prominent specific effect. The association of growth hormone with growth, insulin with blood sugar, the "sex" steroids with reproduction, thyroxine with oxidation, norepinephrine with cardiovascular function, oxytocin with parturition, and so on, are cases in point. The general view of endocrine organization which seems implicit in this approach is that of a group of specialized agents which are called forth individually to meet individual needs of the organism, i.e., a special hormone for each special function. Several well-established facts of hormonal effects, however, now strongly militate against this simplistic view.

Multiplicity of effects of individual hormones
A massive amount of recent endocrinological data indicates that most hormones have a surprisingly broad range of effects on metabolic processes. The effects of cortisol, for example, include those on carbohydrate, lipid, protein, sodium, potassium, phosphate, chloride, calcium, magnesium, and water metabolism. It influences processes such as energy production, acid-base balance, growth, wound healing, lactation, and resistance to infection. It affects tissues and organs such as liver, muscle, adipose tissue, brain, kidney, gastrointestinal tract, bone, cartilage, connective tissue, blood cells, lymphoid tissue, skin, and the cardiovascular

system (Fajans, 1961; Noble, 1955). Other hormones, including thyroxine (Hoch, 1962), insulin (Krahl, 1961), growth hormone (Smith, Gaebler, & Long, 1954), and epinephrine (Ellis, 1956), similarly have a multiplicity of diverse effects. Thus the view that endocrine systems are generally organized as a group of specialized, largely independent agents, among which the responsibility for regulating different body processes is sharply divided, does not appear to be tenable at present.

We are faced, rather, with the question of how ·this widespread multipotence of hormones can be reconciled with the apparent economy, orderliness, and effectiveness of homeostatic regulation. Are the majority of these multiple effects observed with most hormones functionally significant? Are many of the lesser effects of various hormones merely "pharmacological side effects" related as artifacts to the research methods employed? If the majority of these reported effects are relevant to natural function, does it follow that the whole gamut of effects of a hormone necessarily ensues each time the level of that hormone in body fluids becomes elevated? Does inhibition of fibroblastic proliferation invariably accompany cortisol elevations? Does stimulation of the growth of articular cartilage always accompany the elevation of growth hormone levels? Does hypoglycemia invariably accompany insulin elevations? Does the principle of multipotence of hormones imply an indiscriminate, "shot-gun" character for hormonal regulatory responses or can it be reconciled with the concept that hormones make selective, economical metabolic adjustments appropriate to specific bodily changes or needs in a homeostatic sense? Certainly, answers to these questions are of great importance to the study of endocrine organization.

Staggered overlapping of hormonal effects
Hand-in-hand with the multipotence of hormones goes a considerable overlapping of hormonal effects. Lipid metabolism, for example, is subjected to the influence of many different hormones, including cortisol, epinephrine, norepinephrine, thyroxine, growth hormone, and insulin (Jeanrenaud, 1961; Winegrad, 1962). No metabolic process, in fact, appears to be regulated by only a single hormone. Does the general overlapping of hormonal

effects again suggest that endocrine systems are incapable of discriminating adjustments or is there evidence of an orderly organization of these overlapping effects between hormones? Clearly, interhormonal relationships thus emerge as an issue of central importance to an understanding of endocrine organization at both a metabolic and regulatory level.

Interhormonal relationships   In recent years, an increasing amount of attention in "metabolic" endocrinology has been devoted to the study of interrelationships between hormones. It is now clear that hormonal interactions are widespread and probably involve every hormone. At the metabolic level these interactions between hormones may be additive, synergistic, permissive, or antagonistic. Any two particular hormones are not necessarily involved in the same type of relationship across the board, i.e., they are not always antagonistic or synergistic in all areas of metabolism. Rather, there is considerable staggering in these relationships so that one hormone, for example, may be antagonistic to a second hormone in carbohydrate metabolism but synergistic with the same hormone in protein metabolism.

These staggered antagonistic and synergistic relationships seem to provide a means whereby different combinations of hormonal changes might selectively affect relatively narrow phases of metabolism. Let us take, for example, an instance in which an increase in the biosynthesis of protein is needed by the organism. Insulin has a potent stimulating effect on protein biosynthesis but it also has a strong effect on carbohydrate metabolism which would appear to be an undesirable or unnecessary "side-effect" in this instance. Growth hormone, on the other hand, while being synergistic with insulin in its effect on protein metabolism, antagonizes the effect of insulin on carbohydrate metabolism. Concurrent or coordinated elevations of both hormones might then logically be expected to exert a strong, selective effect on protein synthesis with minimal associated effects on carbohydrate metabolism. The adrenal corticosteroids are also known to counteract the effects of insulin on carbohydrate metabolism. In discussing this example, Korner (1960) adds a compelling

argument for the importance of these hormonal interactions from a metabolic standpoint: "This system of restraints on the hypoglycemic action of insulin enables insulin to stimulate protein synthesis without causing a dangerous hypoglycemia which would also be end-defeating in that the available amino acids would tend to be deaminated instead of being used as substrates for protein synthesis" [p. 38].

This particular formulation developed on the basis of metabolic considerations raises intriguing questions from the standpoint of endocrine regulation. While various experimental approaches may be required to evaluate its possible application to endocrine regulation, it is interesting that some data in the present study may bear upon this question. In the early recovery period of some of our recent 72-hr avoidance experiments, instances were indeed observed in which marked plasma insulin elevations were not associated with hypoglycemia at a time when growth hormone and corticosteroid levels were also elevated. Measurement of protein anabolism at this point would certainly be of interest in future experiments in order to determine the possible relevance of these observations to the present discussion.

Relevance of Hormonal Interactions to Study of Endocrine Regulation

If we proceed beyond such a single example of what hormonal interactions might achieve in a specific instance, it seems possible that the application of the underlying principle on a wider scale could provide an important strategic key to the understanding of endocrine regulation. Here is a remarkably efficient and versatile mechanism whereby a relative handful of hormones, by capitalizing upon their staggered interactions, might achieve a vast range of different, selective overall effects on metabolism. There are, moreover, apparently few other leads to follow at present which offer some hope of clarifying the inescapable problems raised by the multipotence and overlapping of the metabolic effects of the individual hormones. It is also likely, incidentally, that many important hormonal interactions remain to be discovered, particularly those that involve several hormones at the same time. Most attention up to now has been given to the study of interactions between just two hormones at a time. There is evidence, however, that there are more complicated interactions that involve several hormones simultaneously. A combination of four hormones, for example, has been found which exerts a marked synergistic effect on growth which greatly exceeds the effects of any other combinations of the same hormones (Bates, Miller, & Garrison, 1962).

The mechanism of interhormonal relationships might also, incidentally, provide an explanation for some of the troubling questions which can be raised concerning the "catabolic-anabolic" formulation in the present study. Some hormones placed in the "catabolic" group, for example, are reported also to have "anabolic" effects on organic metabolism. Some hormones in the "catabolic" group show responses which extend well into the recovery or "anabolic" phase of the experiment. Within the framework of the concept of hormonal interactions, however, a hormone having both "catabolic" and "anabolic" effects might well exert one effect or the other selectively depending upon the balance at a given time between various antagonistic or synergistic hormones with which it is interdependent. Long, Smith, and Fry (1960, p. 4) have pointed out, for example, that the "catabolic" gluconeogenetic effect and the "anabolic" deposition of liver glycogen effect of cortisol are not always or necessarily associated with each other. In the present experiments it is clear that because of the varying durations of different hormonal responses and because of the biphasic character of some responses, the balance between any single hormone and the others shifts markedly from one time to another. There is a period, for example, when epinephrine is high in relation to the corticosteroids and another period when it is low while corticosteroids remain elevated. There is a period when the corticosteroid level is high and one when it is low in relation to insulin, and so on. Shifting balances between any particular hormone and the other hormones over the full time course of the experiment appear, in fact, to be a prominent feature of the overall response pattern.

It seems reasonable, then, to consider the possibility that a single hormone may promote a "catabolic" effect at one point in time and an "anabolic"

effect at another time, depending upon shifts in the balance that involve the antagonists and synergists with which it is interdependent. It is interesting, incidentally, that some hormones which are reported to have both "catabolic" and "anabolic" effects, such as cortisol and thyroxine, show relatively prolonged elevations which extend through the avoidance period well into the recovery period. While this explanation involving interhormonal relationships in relation to the avoidance data certainly remains highly hypothetical at present, it does provide a plausible way of reconciling some puzzling facts with the suggested general interpretation which otherwise seems to fit the data rather well. Furthermore, some ways appear to exist by which this explanation can be tested critically in future experiments by the addition of appropriate metabolic measurements.

The Concept of "Overall" Hormonal Balance in Relation to Endocrine Regulation

There appear to be emerging from the study of hormonal effects on metabolism, then, some general principles underlying hormonal regulation of metabolism which may be profoundly relevant to the study of endocrine regulation. Most hormones have a broad spectrum or multiplicity of effects, have overlapping actions, and have multiple and staggered interdependencies. These characteristics taken together seem to suggest a unifying explanation of the modus operandi whereby the many endocrine systems could function as a coordinated unit. It appears to be a logical conclusion from consideration of these characteristics of hormones that *the state of any given metabolic activity at any given moment must be a function of the total combined hormonal influences acting upon it, i.e., a resultant of the varying balance between multiple cooperating and opposing hormonal influences.* The metabolic effects of hormones are dependent, then, not upon the absolute level of any single hormone but rather upon the *relative "overall" balance* between all participating hormones. This is not to say that every hormone plays a significant role in every metabolic change, of course, nor that all hormonal responses to a particular stimulus are equally important in a quantitative sense. It is implied, rather, that hormonal combinations of varying extent are involved in the determination of various specific metabolic changes. The number of hormones involved in the regulation of electrolyte balance or blood pressure, for example, may be considerably smaller than those involved in lipid or protein metabolism.

It is impressive that the findings of the present study fit so closely with the concept of the importance of the "overall" hormonal balance which can be independently derived from knowledge of endocrine organization at the metabolic level. Many examples in the present study, including that cited earlier concerning the reciprocal relationship of the acute insulin and adrenal hormone responses to avoidance, fit well with the concept that endocrine regulatory changes should be approached in terms of the "overall" hormonal balance. The fact that the concept of the "overall" hormonal balance as a key to endocrine organization may have implications which extend beyond the psychoendocrine field to the study of endocrine regulation in general also seems self-evident.

The concept of hormonal balance is, of course, by no means of recent origin. For example, basing his work upon observation of clinical endocrinopathies, Elliott wrote in 1913: "Increasing emphasis has been laid in the last few years on the need to look upon the ductless glands as parts of a connected whole. . . . The ductless glands do bear some functional relationship to one another; normal health and growth swing in the equal balance of their activities."

Houssay, whose pioneering work on experimental diabetes has been very much concerned with hormonal interactions for more than 20 years, has been one of the most forceful modern proponents of the strategic importance of the concept of hormonal balance. In a conference discussion published in 1957, Houssay expressed his viewpoint very clearly:

> Another question very important in physiology is that in the whole organism one hormone never works alone. In every case, the action of one hormone is related to the balance of hormones present. If we study any function we find that it does not depend on one hormone, but on a balance between hormones acting together or in a consecutive way. For instance, the mammary gland develops completely by action of estrogen, progesterone, prolactin and somatotrophin and not by one

of these hormones alone. The endometrial changes are due to the interplay of FSH, LH, estrogens, and progesterone.

> The carbohydrate metabolism is normally regulated by a balance of hormones of the pancreas, pituitary, adrenal, thyroid, and in some cases, gonadal hormones. The action of one hormone or gland is modified by the presence of another hormone or gland. Without the adrenal there is striking diminution of some actions of somatotrophin or thyroxin. In the organism we have always interaction between hormones, but never is one hormone action completely alone. This is an important concept to be kept in mind when working in endocrinology [p. 27].

Application of this viewpoint, however, has so far curiously been confined in a limited way to the study of clinical and metabolic aspects of endocrinology and it has had remarkably little impact on the study of endocrine regulation. In view of the almost inevitably close relationships between the organization of endocrine function at the metabolic and regulatory levels which have been discussed, however, it would seem that the time is overdue to carry the concept of hormonal balance to its logical conclusion in relation to endocrine regulation.

Application to physical and humoral stimuli. In a sense, it is a curious fact that a general theory concerning endocrine regulation should emerge from the study of hormonal responses to psychological stimuli. As discussed earlier, attempts to apply homeostatic concepts to psychoendocrine responses are somewhat awkward because it appears necessary to make the special assumption that the "need" which initiates these responses is *anticipation* of muscular effort. While this assumption may well be valid, it imposes an uncomfortable strategic disadvantage in the defense of the present chain of reasoning.

On the other hand, it is possible to specify with considerably greater certainty the "need" associated with most humoral or physical stimuli. The stimulus of glucose administration creates a "need" for the removal of glucose from the blood and for its conversion to other compounds for storage. The stimulus of cold creates a "need" for the increased production and conservation of body heat. Similar "needs" could be defined in regard to many other stimuli involving changes in the levels of such essential materials as oxygen, water, electrolytes, lipids, proteins, amino acids, and so on.

Being able to specify thus a "need" created by these stimuli in a homeostatic sense, one is in a reasonably sound position to test the hypothesis that each of these stimuli will elicit multiple hormonal responses organized generally in accordance with the effects of each hormone in relation to the principal "need" which has been created. In heat, for example, those hormones concerned with thermogenesis and heat conservation or dissipation should be prominently involved in an organized response pattern. This pattern should be quite different from that seen when the organism is exposed to a cold environment. In general, the "overall" response pattern should differ from one stimulus to the next depending on the physiological change or "need" which has been created.

In order to test the predictive power of this general hypothesis along these lines, we have recently initiated experiments with some humoral and physical stimuli. While these experiments are still in an exploratory stage, we have already encountered some methodological pitfalls which call for caution in future work in this area.

Admixture of elements in "physical stress" situations First of all, it has been difficult to interpret findings in certain classical, "physical stress" situations because they often involve a complex admixture of several different stimuli or "needs" in a homeostatic sense. In hemorrhage, for example, there is fluid loss, decreased oxygen-carrying capacity of the blood, protein loss, hypotension, etc. On what basis, then, can one decide which of these multiple metabolic problems may be principally related to any particular hormonal response to hemorrhage? Studies of surgical trauma may involve varying degrees of tissue damage, hemorrhage, pain, sleep loss, drug effects, and the like.

It seems advisable in the testing of this approach, therefore, to work initially with stimuli which are as simple or elemental as possible, in the sense that they elicit relatively selective, narrow, or specific metabolic disturbances. Once reproducible response patterns are identified for these simpler stimuli, it may be more feasible to attempt interpretation of patterns of response under more complex conditions in which there are various combi-

nations of metabolic disturbances. In approaching the problem of hemorrhage in such stepwise fashion, for example, it may first be helpful to study hypoxia without fluid loss and hypotension, or to study fluid loss with minimal disturbance of the oxygen-carrying capacity of the blood, or to study loss of red cells without fluid loss. In some situations it may, of course, be virtually impossible to separate certain elements even in the crude manner suggested above. Such situations would not seem well suited for the initial testing of this approach.

Frequent admixture of psychological and physical stimuli Perhaps the outstanding impression in our work so far with physical and humoral stimuli is the almost universal frequency with which psychological reactions may accompany the classical "physical stress" situations. As we began pilot experiments with the use of exercise, trauma, cold, heat, and fasting, we often encountered the same "psychoendocrine" response pattern reported in the present study. It then occurred to us that every one of these "physical stresses" to which conscious monkeys or humans were subjected was very probably associated with some degree of emotional disturbance, discomfort, or pain. We found, furthermore, that it is extraordinarily difficult to be certain that one is eliminating or minimizing such a factor, particularly in the laboratory animal. We have seen many instances of psychoendocrine responses occurring without overt signs of distress or disturbance in both monkeys and humans. It is perhaps particularly dangerous to make a clinical judgment as to which environmental stimuli "ought to" or "ought not to" elicit an emotional reaction in the laboratory animal. For this reason, we have attempted to reduce all extraneous environmental stimuli to the barest minimum by all possible measures.

Monkeys, for example, may show many obvious signs of displeasure and emotional reaction when they are forced to exercise on a treadmill or to lift heavy weights in order to get their daily food (Miller & Mason, 1964). Some of the largest adrenal cortical responses observed in such "exercise" experiments occurred on days when the monkey refused to do the hard labor, rather than on days when a substantial amount of muscular work was actually performed. Eventually, we found that monkeys appeared to be less upset by a climbing task—but even then it was difficult to determine whether there was still an unknown mixture of work and emotional reaction to the situation (Miller & Mason, 1964).

As another example, we recently obtained evidence that monkeys who are fasted but provided some bulk intake by substitution of a nonnutritive, heavily fruit-flavored pellet diet show a different hormonal response pattern than that in monkeys who are fasted by the conventional complete withdrawal of food that entails both lack of nutritive and bulk intake. This finding suggests the need for further work to determine if factors such as the discomfort of an empty stomach or the emotional reaction to the conventional fasting situation, in which the familiar animal caretaker repeatedly passes the hungry animal by without providing food, may be complicating variables in fasting experiments (Mason et al., 1968h).

Curiously, one of our major concerns 10 years ago was to isolate psychological influences on endocrine function as free as possible from contaminating physical stimuli. We now find ourselves in the diametrically opposite position and it begins to appear that it may be considerably more difficult in a practical way to eliminate psychological variables from experiments with physical stimuli than it was to do the converse.

Relevance to "stress" theory The problem discussed above raises a general doubt about the accuracy of much of our present knowledge concerning "physical" factors in endocrine regulation. It has apparently been assumed that most "physical stresses" were rather obviously more drastic or potent stimuli to endocrine activity than were psychological influences, and that the latter could be safely considered negligible under such conditions. Our recent experience, however, suggests that this may be a dangerous assumption because of the striking sensitivity of endocrine systems to psychological influences.

This problem also seems to bear very directly on some basic premises of "stress" theory as developed by Selye, such as the concept of the "General Adaptation Syndrome." On the basis of observations of morphological evidence of adrenal cortical responses to "diverse nocuous agents" including excessive muscular exercise, trauma, cold, fasting, spinal shock, acute infections, and intoxications with various drugs, Selye concluded that the pituitary-adrenal cortical system responds in a "nonspecific" manner *to many different stimuli or agents* as part of a General Adaptation Syndrome (Selye, 1936b, 1950). In the light of present knowledge of the keen sensitivity of the pituitary-adrenal cortical system to psychological influences, is it not disturbing to consider that most if not all of the situations described by Selye very likely involve some degree of *emotional reaction, discomfort, or pain as well as the designated "nocuous" stimuli?*

Does the widely occurring pituitary-adrenal cortical response, then, reflect a "general adaptive" or "nonspecific" endocrine response to many different "nocuous" stimuli or does it reflect a *specific* response to a *single* type of stimulus (psychological) that these various unpleasant situations share in common? Should the main conclusion drawn from Selye's observations have been simply that the pituitary-adrenal cortical system responds sensitively to the ubiquitous psychological influences in many "different" laboratory situations?

It may well be that the pituitary-adrenal cortical system responds to more than one stimulus at the hypothalamic or pituitary level, but it seems increasingly likely that the response is not so universal as concluded by Selye. One of the unfortunate consequences of the "stress" concept appears to be that it has served to allay critical thinking about the question of the actual *primary signals* capable of triggering ACTH release by exciting the final common pathway neurone or the pituitary cell. Somehow the categorical concept of "stressful" conditions seems to have circumvented work concerning systematic consideration of discrete stimuli, body receptors, and the underlying mediating mechanisms. Whatever the "stressful conditions," the environmental change, or the experimental manipulation may be, a *signal* must reach the hypothalamus or pituitary through neural or circulatory pathways in order for ACTH release to occur. What is the primary signal to the hypothalamic-pituitary-adrenal cortical axis in the case of a cold environment, for example? Is a different signal involved in the case of hemorrhage, and so on? Can the mediating pathway for one stimulus be interrupted without affecting the ACTH response to a different stimulus? How many different, discrete, primary stimuli or signals really are capable of initiating a response in the pituitary-adrenal cortical system?

It appears impossible to answer these questions conclusively at present, and only a thorough experimental reevaluation of the pituitary-adrenal cortical response to a variety of "physical" stimuli—with rigorous attempts to minimize attendant psychological reactions or other interfering factors—can clarify the problem. Experiments with human subjects may be particularly helpful, as evaluation of psychological factors is more feasible than in the laboratory animal. Bush (1962) has also emphasized the problem of psychological factors in "physical stress" situations and states that some work has already been done which indicates that ". . . severe exercise, cold, and fasting produce little or no effect on the secretion and metabolism of cortisol in man unless they are part of a situation that provokes emotion."

Certainly, this is a pivotal issue on which much of "stress" theory is founded, and its further experimental clarification would seem to rate a high order of priority.

The present study, in addition, raises the question of whether the pituitary-adrenal cortical system deserves a unique, preeminent status in our view of endocrine regulation according to Selye's formulation or whether it should more properly be regarded as an integral part of a larger, coordinated "overall" pattern of endocrine response in the various situations which have been studied in relation to "stress" concepts. Conclusive experimental confirmation or refutation of "stress" theory has long been impeded by the lack of highly refined methods for measuring hormone levels in the body. Such methods are now available and the time seems most opportune for a renewed evaluation of "stress" concepts in order to determine the extent to which they may need revision.

Need for a Field of Integrative Physiology

There appear to be some neglected implications of recent psychoendocrine research not only with regard to "stress" theory but also in a much more general way with regard to physiology itself. Psychoendocrine research has so far been nurtured by and almost exclusively confined to the behavioral sciences, principally psychiatry. Hormone measurements have been viewed by behavioral scientists as tools of potential importance in the experimental study of emotions and related psychological processes (Mason, 1964, p. 375; Mason et al., 1968h). On the other hand, appreciation of the important implications of psychoendocrine research for physiology has developed very slowly. Aside from theoretical considerations, the sensitivity of endocrine systems to psychological influences has a pervasive practical importance of concern to every investigator of metabolic or endocrine function, particularly for those who work with conscious laboratory-animal or human subjects. Yet many physiological investigators still fail to take into account such well-established critical variables as novelty, handling, or extraneous environmental stimuli in their experiments. Our disregard of psychoendocrine factors in the "physical stress" field certainly appears increasingly to have been a "bull in the china shop" affair. Psychological factors now merit a prominent place among the parameters of metabolic problems that have been so masterfully discussed by Ingle (1951, 1958).

The fact that endocrine regulation is determined in life by varying combinations or mixtures of physical, humoral, or psychological factors also suggests that the psychoendocrine investigator, in his preoccupation with behavioral processes, needs always to be conscious of the danger of overlooking important nonpsychological variables. The present situation, therefore, in which the investigation of psychological and physical factors in endocrine regulation is sharply fragmented between separate, traditional research fields, mainly psychiatry and endocrinology, has some unfortunate aspects. Cannon (1922–1923) commented many years ago that the study of physiological integrative processes lay in the "intermediate territory between sciences" and foresaw the formidable problems inherent in a field which embraces two or more normally distant scientific disciplines. This unfortunate fragmentation of research on integrative processes is still with us, and little progress appears to have been made in rectifying the situation since Cannon's time.

Modern physiology is still organized primarily in

terms of a regional view of the organism, with subdivisions according to the region, system, or other unit under study. While there has been some movement in the direction of more emphasis on regulatory mechanisms, the single-system model has usually been employed and there has been very little work on coordinative or integrative mechanisms on a broader scale within the organism. At the moment, perhaps we first need closer communication between the workers scattered throughout the fields of psychiatry, endocrinology, and physiology who are investigating various aspects of endocrine regulation. Ultimately, however, it is difficult to visualize any satisfactory long-term solution to the problem which does not include integration of research in this field so that the interrelations between physical, humoral, and psychological factors in endocrine regulation are systematically investigated in the same laboratory. One step beyond this would be the ideal of the concurrent study of autonomic and endocrine regulation as a coordinated effort. While these goals may seem distant at present, the development of such a unified science of "integrative physiology" seems an urgent need in the further development of biological research.

Endocrine Regulation and Biological Organization

It is interesting that the concept of a need for the study of integrative processes and biological organization enjoyed a great vogue during the first third of this century. It also seems rather ironic that these ideas were at a peak of popularity in a period before there were methods and approaches to permit the development of a viable experimental field of integrative physiology.

Since the establishment of a mechanistic view of biology during the past century, the direction of biological research has been inexorably toward a piece-by-piece analytical resolution of the complex living organism into its component parts and processes. The scientific method, so successful in the physical sciences, seems to apply most comfortably in biology when increasingly simpler units of the organism can be studied, preferably in isolation from the whole, so that greater control of experimental variables is possible. It has been an implicit premise of this approach that a full understanding of the living organism will ultimately be achieved when this dissection of unit processes is completed at a causal, physicochemical level. This front has advanced from the organ, tissue, cell, and cytoplasm levels to, in our own day, "molecular biology."

Around the turn of the century, some biologists began to question this assumption that the accumulation of a massive catalog of information about component functions alone was sufficient for biological science and to suggest that the paradigm borrowed from the classical physical sciences may have serious limitations in the study of living organisms. A renewed awareness of the profound and unexploited implications of Bernard's concept of the dependence of life upon the existence of precise regulatory mechanisms was an important factor in this movement. The foundation for any science of integrative physiology must certainly be the following section from Bernard's *Lessons on Reactions Common to Animals and Plants,* originally published in 1878 and quoted by A. Pi-Suner (1955) in *The Whole and Its Parts: Classics of Biology.*

> The stability of the internal medium is a primary condition for the freedom and independence of certain living bodies in relation to the environment surrounding them. Physiological mechanisms have to function therein assuring the maintenance of conditions necessary for the existence of the cell elements composing them. For we know that there exist neither liberty nor independence in the case of the simplest organisms in direct contact with immediate universal circumstances. The possibility of arranging their own internal medium is an exclusive faculty of organisms which have reached a higher stage of complexity and organic differentiation.
>
> Such stability in the internal medium implies an extremely perfect organism, able continuously to balance outside variations. The greater the freedom of the creature with regard to its external environment, the closer will be, on the other hand, the connection of its cells with such internal medium, which will necessarily have to maintain perfect regularity in its qualities, possible only if it has regulatory processes in operation as precise as the most sensitive chemical balances.
>
> The conditions necessary for existence which such internal medium must find will be, first of all, water, oxygen, warmth and food reserves. The same conditions are essential for the continued existence of even the simplest organism. In a polyplastid creature, maintenance of regularity in the qualities of the internal medium are achieved mainly by the intervention of the

nervous system, the agency of the functions producing harmony between the activities of the whole of the body. This is attained thanks to properly co-ordinated physiological mechanisms which consolidate the activities of even the most remote organs. To explain these remarkable facts, there is no need to resort to the agency of a vital principle opposed to the influence of physical conditions and possibly peculiar to and characteristic of living organisms. It can be shown that regulatory processes consist exclusively of interfunctional physiological mechanisms [p. 313].

Thus Bernard clearly foresaw and emphasized the need for study of interactions between bodily parts, i.e., the regulatory, coordinating processes which integrate the organism as a whole. At the same time, he was aware that the analytical and integrative approaches were complementary rather than antithetical and that the study of relationships between parts is obviously dependent upon prior study and characterization of individual parts.

During the period from about 1900–1935 there was a remarkable number of biologists concerned with the issue of physiological integration, including Haldane (1906, 1922), Driesch (1908), Sherrington (1947, p. 84), Pavlov (1955, p. 216), Pi-Suner (1955), Henderson (1917, 1928), Ritter (1919), White (1920), Cannon (1929), Barcroft (1934, p. 1), von Bertalanffy (1933), and others. Many of the early essays on the importance of biological organization are remarkable in their clarity, logical consistency, and strength of conviction. Von Bertalanffy has perhaps summarized most concisely the general position of this group of biological theoreticians (1933).

> Since the fundamental character of the living thing is its organization, the customary investigation of the single parts and processes, even the most thorough physicochemical analysis, cannot provide a complete explanation of the vital phenomena. This investigation gives us no information about the co-ordination of the parts and processes in the complicated system of the living whole which constitutes the essential "nature" of the organism, and by which the reactions in the organism are distinguished from those in the test-tube. But no reason has been brought forward for supposing that the organization of the parts and the mutual adjustments of the vital processes cannot be treated as scientific problems. Thus, the chief task of biology must be to discover the laws of biological systems to which the ingredient parts and processes are subordinate. *We regard this as the fundamental problem for modern biology.*

Von Bertalanffy (1952, 1959, p. 265) subsequently gave continuing attention to the establishment of the "organismic conception" in theoretical biology and developed a biological general-systems theory closely attuned to modern advances in physics and mathematics. Pi-Suner (1955, p. 300) and Adolph (1961) also have written recent reviews which pertain to this interest in biological organization that flourished about 50 years ago.

This movement, however, had more than a philosophical basis. Physiologists including Haldane, Sherrington, Henderson, and Cannon produced major experimental studies of regulatory or integrative processes during this period. In particular, one gains the impression in reading Cannon's later and lesser known essays, such as "New Evidence for Sympathetic Control of Some Internal Secretions" (1922–1923), "Some General Features of Endocrine Influence on Metabolism" (1926), "The Mechanism of Emotional Disturbance of Bodily Functions" (1928), "Organization for Physiological Homeostasis" (1929), and "Stresses and Strains of Homeostasis" (1935), that both substantial experimental and theoretical foundations for a field of integrative physiology were established more than 30 years ago. Yet it is difficult to find, during the past three decades, any clear historical continuity of interest in an experimental field of integrative physiology such as Cannon, or, for that matter, Bernard, conceived it.

An understanding of the reasons for the lack of interest in integrative physiology seems crucial to our future handling of this problem. Is it solely because the older theoretical approaches were not supported by sufficiently substantial experimental approaches that this field did not thrive? Does it in some measure reflect that there has been some overreaction against the use of scientific theory in the process of teaching the need for rigorous objectivity in the collection and analysis of data? Is it merely a question of the momentum of the analytical approach in biology? Whatever the reasons may be, the distinction between the analytical and integrative approaches seems clearly to be of such bedrock, fundamental importance that it is a matter of considerable urgency for at least the students representing the next generation of scientific workers to be made fully aware of this issue and of the historical forces which have determined the present direction of biological research.

Acquaintance with this older literature certainly raises the puzzling question of why a large and vigorous experimental field of integrative physiology did not evolve from such enthusiastic beginnings. It seems likely that, while several historical factors were probably involved, the timing of advances in endocrine research may have had a particularly crucial role. To pursue this point, it may be helpful to compare some general features of the endocrine system with the other effector systems involved in bodily integration.

It is generally accepted that the ultimate coordinating or integrating mechanisms probably reside principally in the central nervous system. The functions of such mechanisms can only be judged by the study of the effector systems through which coordinating effects are exerted at lower levels in the organism. Recent neuroendocrine research seems to leave little doubt but that the endocrine system should now be generally regarded as a third effector system of the brain, along with the skeletal-muscular, and autonomic systems.

Study of the integrative functions of the skeletal-muscular system has, of course, been concerned primarily with the behavioral interactions of the organism with the external environment and pertains to physiological homeostasis in a rather indirect and highly complicated manner.

Study of the autonomic system has been seriously hampered by methodological difficulties in concurrently making reliable assessments of activity in a number of different parts of the autonomic system in the intact, conscious organism. Also, autonomic activity has generally not been evaluated experimentally by measurement of the neural mediating influences themselves. This would presumably require the monitoring of activity directly in efferent autonomic nerve fibers in specific locations. Rather, autonomic regulation has generally been judged by measurement of activity in the tissues which have autonomic innervation, those with cardiac or smooth muscle or exocrine cells. Specificity is thereby lost to a considerable extent as activity in these tissues reflects the sum of multiple determinants, including sympathetic, parasympathetic, and humoral influences.

On the other hand, in the case of endocrine regulation, mediating changes in the effector system itself can be experimentally measured directly in the intact organism under relatively natural conditions. One is, in a sense, an important step closer to the central nervous system. Changes in hormone secretion rate are much more likely to be equivalent to changes in the final common pathway neurones in the brain itself than are changes in peripheral tissues regulated jointly by autonomic, endocrine, or humoral influences. Multiple, concurrent, hormone measurements can be made on single blood or urine samples and there is no need for surgical intervention in many regions of the organism in order to observe coordination of the various parts of the endocrine system. It appears, therefore, that the endocrine system provides unique, strategic advantages in the experimental study of physiological integration.

With this viewpoint, perhaps we may return now to the question of the failure of a major experimental field of integrative physiology to develop out of earlier theoretical interest in biological organization. At the time that this interest was most prevalent, between 1900 and 1935, knowledge of the significance of the endocrine systems was extremely limited and rudimentary. Availability of highly purified crystalline hormones was to come almost entirely after 1930—and it was this development perhaps more than any other which made possible the revolutionary advances in our understanding of endocrine physiology achieved in the past 30 years. The early physiologists were also missing other pieces of key information about the endocrine system, such as knowledge of the trophic hormones of the pituitary and the neuroendocrine linkage of the anterior pituitary, for example. From a practical standpoint, however, the most crucial limitation of all was certainly the lack of reliable biochemical methods for the measurement of the hormones in blood and urine. Cannon's success with the biological assay for adrenal medullary secretion was unfortunately an exceptional instance, and he later met great difficulties in attempting to study other endocrine systems. In 1922, he remarked rather wistfully, "Probably before many years have passed we shall have satisfactory tests for the internal secretion, and then shall know better the total expression of an emotional storm in our own bodies."

The importance of the new biochemical and immunochemical methods for hormone measurements which have become available within the past decade can scarcely be overemphasized. Experimental work on endocrine regulation could proceed only slowly and unsurely without them. Furthermore, they have been so long awaited that it appears historically that awareness has been gradually lost of their broader significance in relation to the issue of biological organization.

It would not be fair, however, to imply that failure to move more rapidly in the direction of studying the endocrine systems as an organized whole during the past 10 years has been solely related to a loss of contact with older concepts. In recent times Houssay (1957, p. 27), Hubble (1961), and others have again emphasized the need to view the endocrine systems as a whole. The fact is that, while revolutionary advances in hormone assay methods have been made recently, these methods are generally still unusually difficult and time-consuming microanalytical procedures. They require considerable laboratory space, superior technical skill, and scrupulous and consistently painstaking care week in and week out. Practical problems involving not only cost, space, and personnel but also quality control and supervisory management techniques multiply rapidly as establishment of a larger battery of hormone assay methods is attempted. Considerably higher space-investigator and technician-investigator ratios are required than conventionally prevail in most medical research centers at the present time.

Because of this situation it appears that the pace at which the study of hormonal balance and endocrine organization on a fuller scale can proceed may well be determined largely by the rate at which simpler, more rapid, more automated hormone assay methods can be developed without the sacrificing of specificity, precision, or sensitivity. The analytical principles of gas chromatography, isotopic procedures, protein-binding methods, and immunochemical techniques offer considerable promise of still more major advances and improvements in hormone assay methods in the near future.

Regardless of whether many of the more specific conclusions and concepts suggested in the present study stand up under future scrutiny, this study does demonstrate the feasibility of bringing broad patterns of hormonal responses—and, hence, the problem of endocrine organization—under experimental study at the present time. It does not seem too optimistic to hope that within the next decade or two it may be possible to determine whether this approach can provide the leverage it seems to promise at present for achieving a new level of insight into the organization of the mechanisms of physiological integration and for providing a firmer basic science foundation for the field of psychosomatic medicine.

REFERENCES

ADER, R., FRIEDMAN, S. B., & GROTA, L. J. "Emotionality" and adrenal cortical function: Effects of strain, test, and the 24-hour corticosterone rhythm. *Animal Behavior,* 1967, **15,** 37.

ADOLPH, E. F. Early concepts of physiological regulations. *Physiological Review,* 1961, **41,** 737.

AKABANE, K. Studies on the relation between mental and physical work load and urinary excretion of adrenaline and noradrenaline: 4. On the effect of mental load upon urinary excretion of Ad and NAd. *Rodo Kagaku,* 1962, **38,** 699.

ALEXANDER, F., FLAGG, G. W., FOSTER, S., CLEMENS, T., & BLAHD, W. Experimental studies of emotional stress: I. Hyperthyroidism. *Psychosomatic Medicine,* 1961, **23,** 104.

ALTSCHULE, M. D. *Bodily physiology in mental and emotional disorders.* New York: Grune & Stratton, 1953.

ALTSCHULE, M. D., PROMISEL, E., PARKHURST, B. H., & GRUNEBAUM, H. Effects of ACTH in patients with mental disease. *Archives of Neurology and Psychiatry,* 1950, **64,** 641.

ALTSCHULE, M. D., PROMISEL, E., PARKHURST, B. H., & GRUNEBAUM, H. Effects of intravenous injection of typhoid vaccine on blood leukocytes and adrenal cortex. *Archives of Internal Medicine,* 1950, **86,** 505.

AMIRAGOVA, M. G. Influence of so-called emotional excitement of the animal on the functional activity of the thyroid gland. *Fiziologicheskie Zhurnal SSSR Sechenov,* 1957, **43,** 65.

ANDERSON, E. E., & ANDERSON, S. F. The relation between the weight of the endocrine glands and measures of sexual, emotional and exploratory behavior in the male albino rat. *Journal of Comparative and Physiological Psychology,* 1938, **26,** 459.

ANDERSON, W. M., & DAWSON, J. The variability of plasma 17-hydroxycorticosteroid levels in affective illness and schizophrenia. *Journal of Psychosomatic Research,* 1965, **9,** 237.

ARGUELLES, A. E., IBEAS, D., OTTONE, J. P., & CHEKHERDEMIAN, M. Pituitary-adrenal stimulation by sound of different frequencies. *Journal of Clinical Endocrinology,* 1962, **22,** 846.

ASTWOOD, E. B. The adrenal cortex and energy metabolism. In L. W. KINSELL (Ed.), *Hormonal regulation of energy.* Springfield, Ill.: Charles C Thomas, 1957.

AX, A. The physiological differentiation between fear and anger in humans. *Psychosomatic Medicine,* 1953, **15,** 433.

BADRICK, F. E., BRIMBLECOMBE, R. W., REISS, J. M., & REISS, M. The influence of stress conditions on the uptake of ^{131}I by the rat thyroid. *Journal of Endocrinology,* 1954, **11,** 305.

BARCROFT, J. La fixité du milieu interieur est la condition de la vie libre (Claude Bernard). In *Features in the architecture of physiological function.* London: Cambridge University Press, 1934.

BARNETT, S. A. Competition among wild rats. *Nature,* 1955, **175,** 126.

BARNETT, S. A. Physiological effects of "social stress" in wild rats: I. The adrenal cortex. *Journal of Psychosomatic Research,* 1958, **3,** 1.

BASOWITZ, H., PERSKY, H., KORCHIN, S. J., & GRINKER, R. R. *Anxiety and stress.* New York: McGraw-Hill, 1955.

BATES, R. W., MILLER, R. A., & GARRISON, M. M. Evidence in the hypophysectomized pigeon of a synergism among prolactin, growth hormone, thyroxine and prednisone upon weight of the body, digestive tract, kidney and fat stores. *Endocrinology,* 1962, **71,** 345.

BATT, J. C., KAY, W. W., REISS, M., & SANDS, D. E. The endocrine concomitants of schizophrenia. *Journal of Mental Science,* 1957, **103,** 240.

BERGSMAN, A. The urinary excretion of adrenaline and noradrenaline in some mental diseases: A clinical and experimental study. *Acta Psychiatrica Scandinavica,* 1959, **34** (Suppl. 133).

BERKELEY, A. W. Level of aspiration in relation to adrenal cortical activity and the concept of stress. *Journal of Comparative and Physiological Psychology,* 1952, **45,** 443.

BERNARD, C. Quoted by A. PI-SUNER, in *The whole and its parts: Classics of biology.* New York: Philosophical Library, 1955.

BERTALANFFY, L. von *Modern theories of development.* Translated by J. H. WOODGER, London: Oxford University Press, 1933.

BERTALANFFY, L. von *Problems of life.* New York: Wiley, 1952.

BERTALANFFY, L. von Modern concepts on biological adaptation. In C. BROOKS & P. F. CRANEFIELD (Eds.), *The historical development of physiological thought.* New York: Hafner, 1959.

BISCHOFF, F., & TORRES, A. Fluorimetric determination of urinary adrenaline. *Journal of Applied Physiology,* 1959, **14,** 237.

BLISS, E. L., MIGEON, C. J., BRANCH, C. H., & SAMUELS, L. T. Adrenocortical function in schizophrenia. *American Journal of Psychiatry,* 1955, **112,** 358.

BLISS, E. L., MIGEON, C. J., BRANCH, C. H., & SAMUELS, L. T. Reaction of the adrenal cortex to emotional stress. *Psychosomatic Medicine,* 1956, **18,** 56.

BLISS, E. L., RUBIN, S., & GILBERT, T. The effect of adrenalin on adrenal cortical function. *Journal of Clinical Endocrinology,* 1951, **11,** 46.

BLOOM, G., EULER, U. S. von, & FRANKENHAEUSER, M. Catecholamine excretion and personality traits in paratroop trainees. *Acta Physiologica Scandinavica,* 1963, **58,** 77.

BOARD, F., PERSKY, H., & HAMBURG, D. A. Psychological stress and endocrine functions. *Psychosomatic Medicine,* 1956, **18,** 324.

BOARD, F., WADESON, R., & PERSKY, H. Depressive affect and endocrine functions. *Archives of Neurology and Psychiatry,* 1957, **78,** 612.

BOGDONOFF, M. D., ESTES, E. H., Jr., HARLAN, W. R., TROUT, D. L., & KIRSHNER, N. Metabolic and cardiovascular changes during a state of acute central nervous system arousal. *Journal of Clinical Endocrinology,* 1960, **20,** 1333.

BOGDONOFF, M. D., HARLAN, W. R., ESTES, E. H., Jr., & KIRSHNER, N. Changes in urinary catecholamine excretion accompanying carbohydrate and lipid responses to oral examination. *Circulation,* 1959, **20,** 674.

BOURNE, P. G., ROSE, R. M., & MASON, J. W. Urinary 17-OHCS levels: Data on seven helicopter ambulance medics in combat. *Archives of General Psychiatry,* 1967, **17,** 104.

BOVARD, E. W. The effects of social stimuli on the response to stress. *Psychological Review,* 1959, **66,** 267.

BOWMAN, K. M. Endocrine and biochemical studies in schizophrenia. *Proceedings of the Association for Research in Nervous and Mental Disease,* 1925, **5,** 262.

BOWMAN, K. M., EIDSON, J. P., & BURLADGE, S. P. Biochemical studies in ten cases of dementia praecox. *Boston Medical and Surgical Journal,* 1922, **187,** 358.

BOWMAN, K. M., & GRABFIELD, G. P. Basal metabolism in mental disease. *Archives of Neurology and Psychiatry,* 1923, **9,** 358.

BOWMAN, K. M., MILLER, E. R., DAILEY, M. E., SIMON, A., FRANKEL, B., & LOWE, G. W. Thyroid function in mental disease measured with radioactive iodine, I^{131}. *American Journal of Psychiatry,* 1950, **106,** 561. (a)

BOWMAN, K. M., MILLER, E. R., DAILEY, M. E., SIMON, A., & MAYER, B. F. Thyroid function in mental disease: A multiple test survey. *Journal of Nervous and Mental Disease,* 1950, **112,** 404. (b)

BRADY, J. V. Experimental studies of psychophysiological responses to stressful situations. In *Symposium on medical aspects of stress in the military climate.* Washington, D.C.: Walter Reed Army Institute of Research, 1964.

BRAM, I. Psychic trauma in pathogenesis of exophthalmic goiter. *Endocrinology,* 1927, **11,** 106.

BRIDGES, P. K., & JONES, M. T. The diurnal rhythm of plasma cortisol concentration in depression. *British Journal of Psychiatry,* 1966, **112,** 1257.

BRODY, E. B.   Psychologic tension and serum iodine levels in psychiatric patients without evidence of thyroid disease. *Psychosomatic Medicine,* 1949, **11,** 70.

BRODY, E. B., & MAN, E. B.   Thyroid function measured by serum precipitable iodine determinations in schizophrenic patients. *American Journal of Psychiatry,* 1950, **107,** 357.

BRONSON, F. H., & ELEFTHERIOU, B. E.   Adrenal responses to crowding in peromyscus and C57BL/10J mice. *Physiological Zoology,* 1963, **36,** 161.

BRONSON, F. H., & ELEFTHERIOU, B. E.   Chronic physiological effects of fighting in mice. *General and Comparative Endocrinology,* 1964, **4,** 9.

BRONSON, F. H., & ELEFTHERIOU, B. E.   Adrenal response to fighting in mice: Separation of physical and psychological causes. *Science,* 1965, **147,** 627.

BROWN, W. T., & GILDEA, E. F.   Hyperthyroidism and personality. *American Journal of Psychiatry,* 1937, **94,** 59.

BROWNE, J. S. L.   Discussion. In J. R. MOTE (Ed.), *Proceedings of the First Clinical ACTH Conference.* Philadelphia: Blakiston, 1950.

BROWN-GRANT, K.   The "feed-back" hypothesis of the control of thyroid function. In G. WOLSTENHOLME & E. MILLAR (Eds.), *Ciba Foundation colloquia on endocrinology, regulation and mode of action of thyroid hormones.* Vol. 10. Boston: Little, Brown, 1957.

BROWN-GRANT, K., HARRIS, G. W., & REICHLIN, S.   The effect of emotional and physical stress on thyroid activity in the rabbit. *Journal of Physiology,* 1954, **126,** 29.

BROWN-GRANT, K., & PETHES, G.   The response of the thyroid gland of the guinea pig to stress. *Journal of Physiology,* 1960, **151,** 40.

BRUNE, G. G., & PSCHEIDT, G. R.   Correlations between behavior and urinary excretion of indole amines and catecholamines in schizophrenic patients as affected by drugs. *Federation Proceedings,* 1961, **20,** 889.

BRYSON, R. W., & MARTIN, D. F.   17-ketosteroid excretion in a case of manic-depressive psychosis. *Lancet,* 1954, **2,** 365.

BUNNEY, W. E., Jr., & FAWCETT, J. A.   Possibility of a biochemical test for suicidal potential. *Archives of General Psychiatry,* 1965, **13,** 232.

BUNNEY, W. E., Jr., HARTMANN, E. L., & MASON, J. W.   Study of a patient with 48-hour manic-depressive cycles: II. Strong positive correlation between endocrine factors and manic defense patterns. *Archives of General Psychiatry,* 1965, **12,** 619. (a)

BUNNEY, W. E., Jr., MASON, J. W., & HAMBURG, D. A.   Correlations between behavioral variables and urinary 17-hydroxycorticosteroids in depressed patients. *Psychosomatic Medicine,* 1965, **27,** 299. (b)

BUNNEY, W. E., Jr., MASON, J. W., ROATCH, J. F., & HAMBURG, D. A.   A psychoendocrine study of severe psychotic depressive crises. *American Journal of Psychiatry,* 1965, **122,** 72. (c)

BURSTEIN, S., BHAVANAI, B. R., & KIMBALL, H. L.   Observations on urinary corticosteroid excretion patterns in individual guinea pigs. *Endocrinology,* 1964, **75,** 226.

BURSTEN, B., & RUSS, J. J.   Preoperative psychological state and corticosteroid levels of surgical patients. *Psychosomatic Medicine,* 1965, **27,** 309.

BUSH, I. E.   General discussion. In G. E. W. WOLSTENHOLME & C. M. O'CONNOR (Eds.), *Metabolic effects of adrenal hormones* (Ciba Foundation Study Group No. 6). Boston: Little, Brown, 1960.

BUSH, I. E.   Chemical and biological factors in the activity of adrenocortical steroids. *Pharmacological Review,* 1962, **14,** 317.

BYERS, S. O., FRIEDMAN, M., ROSENMAN, R. H., & FREED, S. C.   Excretion of 3-methoxy-4-hydroxymandelic acid in men with behavior pattern associated with high incidents of coronary artery disease. *Federation Proceedings,* 1962, **21,** 99.

CANNON, W. B.   The influence of emotional states on the functions of the alimentary canal. *American Journal of Medical Science,* 1909, **137,** 480.

CANNON, W. B.   The emergency function of the adrenal medulla in pain and the major emotions. *American Journal of Physiology,* 1914, **33,** 356.

CANNON, W. B.   Studies on the conditions of activity in endocrine glands: V. The isolated heart as an indicator of adrenal secretion induced by pain, asphyxia and excitement. *American Journal of Physiology,* 1919, **1,** 399.

CANNON, W. B.   New evidence for sympathetic control of some internal secretions. *American Journal of Psychiatry,* 1922–1923, **2,** 15.

CANNON, W. B.   Some general features of endocrine influence on metabolism. *American Journal of Medical Science,* 1926, **171,** 1.

CANNON, W. B.   The mechanism of emotional disturbance of bodily functions. *New England Journal of Medicine,* 1928, **198,** 877.

CANNON, W. B.   Organization for physiological homeostasis. *Physiological Review,* 1929, **9,** 399.

CANNON, W. B.   Stresses and strains of homeostasis. *American Journal of Medicine,* 1935, **189,** 1.

CANNON, W. B.   *Bodily changes in pain, hunger, fear and rage.* (2nd ed.). Boston: Charles T. Branford, 1953.

CANNON, W. B.   *The wisdom of the body.* New York: Norton, 1963.

CANNON, W. B., & BRITTON, S. W.   Studies on the conditions of activity in endocrine glands: Influence of motion and emotion on medulliadrenal secretion. *American Journal of Physiology,* 1927, **79,** 433.

CANNON, W. B., & de la PAZ, D.   Emotional stimulation of adrenal secretion. *American Journal of Physiology,* 1911, **27,** 64.

CANNON, W. B., SHOHL, A. T., & WRIGHT, W. S.   Emotional glycosuria. *American Journal of Physiology,* 1911, **29,** 280.

CARRIERE, R., & ISLER, H.   Effect of frequent housing changes and of muscular exercise on the thyroid gland of mice. *Endocrinology,* 1959, **64,** 414.

CHITTY, D., CHITTY, H., & LESLIE, P. H.   Changes in the relative size of the nucleus in the intervertebral discs of stressed Orkney voles (microtus orcadensis). *Journal of Pathology and Bacteriology,* 1956, **72,** 459.

CHRISTIAN, J. J.   Effect of population size on the adrenal

glands and reproductive organs of male mice in populations of fixed size. *American Journal of Physiology*, 1955, **182**, 292.

CHRISTIAN, J. J. Lack of correlation between adrenal weight and injury in grouped male albino mice. *Proceedings of the Society for Experimental Biology and Medicine*, 1959, **101**, 166.

CHRISTIAN, J. J. Phenomena associated with population density. *Proceedings of the National Academy of Sciences of the United States of America*, 1961, **47**, 428.

CHRISTIAN, J. J., & DAVIS, D. E. The relationship between adrenal weight and population status of urban Norway rats. *Journal of Mammals*, 1956, **37**, 475.

CLARKE, J. R. The effect of fighting on the adrenals, thymus and spleen of the vole (microtus agrestis). *Journal of Endocrinology*, 1953, **9**, 114.

CLEGHORN, R. A., & GRAHAM, B. F. Studies of adrenal cortical activity in psychoneurotic subjects. *American Journal of Psychiatry*, 1950, **106**, 668.

COHEN, S. I., & SILVERMAN, A. J. Psychophysiological investigations of vascular response variability. *Journal of Psychosomatic Research*, 1959, **3**, 185.

COHEN, S. I., SILVERMAN, A. J., WADDELL, W., & ZUIDEMA, G. D. Urinary catechol amine levels, gastric secretion and specific psychological factors in ulcer and non-ulcer patients. *Journal of Psychosomatic Research*, 1961, **5**, 90.

COLEHOUR, J. K., & GRAYBIEL, A. Excretion of 17-hydroxy-corticosteroids, catecholamines, and uropepsin in the urine of normal persons and deaf subjects with bilateral vestibular defects following acrobatic flight stress. *Joint Report, U.S. Naval School of Aviation Medicine*, May 10, 1963.

COLFER, H. F., de GROOT, J., & HARRIS, G. W. Pituitary gland and blood lymphocytes. *Journal of Physiology*, 1950, **111**, 328.

CONNELL, A. M., COOPER, J., & REDFEARN, J. W. The contrasting effects of emotional tensions and physical exercise on the excretion of 17-ketogenic steroids and 17-ketosteroids. *Acta Endocrinologica (Kobenhavn)*, 1958, **27**, 179.

CONRAD, A. The psychiatric study of hyperthyroid patients. *Journal of Nervous and Mental Disease*, 1934, **79**, 656.

COPPEN, A. J., & MEZEY, A. G. Metabolic effect of venipuncture in man. *Journal of Psychosomatic Research*, 1960, **5**, 56.

CRAMMER, J. L., & POVER, W. F. R. Iodine-132 uptakes by the thyroid in psychotics. *Journal of Mental Science*, 1960, **106**, 1371.

CRANSWICK, E. H. Tracer iodine studies on thyroid activity and thyroid responsiveness in schizophrenia. *American Journal of Psychiatry*, 1955, **112**, 170.

CRAVEN, C. W., & SMITH, C. S. Steroid excretion in airmen under stress. *Journal of Aviation Medicine*, 1955, **26**, 200.

CROSS, B. A. Neural control of oxytocin secretion. *Neuroendocrinology*, 1966, **1**, 217.

CURTIS, G. C., CLEGHORN, R. A., & SOURKES, T. L. The relationship between affect and the excretion of adren-aline, noradrenaline and 17-hydroxycorticosteroids. *Journal of Psychosomatic Research*, 1960, **4**, 176.

D'ANGELO, S. A. Central nervous regulation of the secretion and release of thyroid stimulating hormone. In A. V. NALBANDOV (Ed.), *Advances in neuroendocrinology*. Urbana: University of Illinois Press, 1963.

DAVIS, D. E., & CHRISTIAN, J. J. Relation of adrenal weight to social rank of mice. *Proceedings of the Society for Experimental Biology and Medicine*, 1957, **94**, 728.

DAVIS, J., MORRILL, R., FAWCETT, J., UPTON, V., BONDY, P. K., & SPIRO, H. M. Apprehension and elevated serum cortisol levels. *Journal of Psychosomatic Research*, 1962, **6**, 83.

DAVIS, S. W., & TAYLOR, J. G. Stress in infantry combat. *Technical Memorandum ORO-T-295*, 1954.

de GROOT, J., & HARRIS, G. W. Hypothalamic control of anterior pituitary gland and blood lymphocytes. *Journal of Physiology*, 1950, **111**, 335.

DEL CONTE, E., RAVELLO, J. J., & STUX, M. The increase of circulating thyrotrophin and the activation of the thyroid by means of electroshock in guinea pigs. *Acta Endocrinologica (Kobenhavn)*, 1955, **18**, 8.

DOHAN, F. C., WINICK, W., PURCELL, M., BENNETT, I. F., & HECKER, A. O. Response of blood eosinophiles and plasma 17-hydroxycorticoids to insulin shock therapy. *Archives of Neurology and Psychiatry*, 1955, **73**, 47.

DOIG, R. J., MUMMERY, R. V., WILLS, M. R., & ELKES, A. Plasma cortisol levels in depression. *British Journal of Psychiatry*, 1966, **112**, 1263.

DONALDSON, H. H., & KING, H. D. Life processes and size of the body and organs of the gray Norway rat during ten generations in captivity. *American Anatomical Memorandum, No. 14*, 1929.

DONGIER, M., WITTKOWER, E. D., STEPHENS-NEWSHAM, L., & HOFFMAN, M. M. Psychophysiological studies in thyroid function. *Psychosomatic Medicine*, 1956, **18**, 310.

DONOVAN, B. T. The regulation of the secretion of follicle-stimulating hormone. In G. W. HARRIS & B. T. DONOVAN (Eds.), *The pituitary gland*. Vol. 2. Berkeley and Los Angeles: University of California Press, 1966.

DORFMAN, R. I., & SHIPLEY, R. A. *Androgens*. New York: Wiley, 1956.

DRIESCH, H. *The science and philosophy of the organism*. Vol. 2. London: A & C Black, 1908.

DUCOMMUN, P., VALE, W., SAKIZ, E., & GUILLEMIN, R. Reversal of the inhibition of TSH secretion due to acute stress. *Endocrinology*, 1967, **80**, 953.

EIDUSON, S., BRILL, N. Q., & CRUMPTON, E. Adrenocortical activity in psychiatric disorders. *Archives of General Psychiatry*, 1961, **5**, 227.

ELLIOTT, T. R. The control of the suprarenal glands by the splanchnic nerves. *Journal of Physiology*, 1912, **44**, 374.

ELLIOTT, T. R. Ductless glands and the nervous system. *Brain*, 1913, **35**, 306.

ELLIS, S. The metabolic effects of epinephrine and related amines. *Pharmacological Review*, 1956, **8**, 485.

ELMADJIAN, F. Adrenocortical function of combat infantrymen in Korea. *Ciba Foundation Colloquia on Endocrinology,* 1955, **8,** 627.

ELMADJIAN, F. Excretion and metabolism of epinephrine. *Pharmacological Review,* 1959, **11,** 409.

ELMADJIAN, F., & HOPE, J. M. Methacholine test and epinephrine and arterenol excretion. *Archives of Neurology and Psychiatry,* 1957, **77,** 399.

ELMADJIAN, F., HOPE, J. M., & FREEMAN, H. The hemodynamics of the mecholyl test and its relation to the excretion of epinephrine and norepinephrine in normal and schizophrenic subjects. *Journal of Nervous and Mental Disease,* 1956, **123,** 408.

ELMADJIAN, F., HOPE, J. M., & LAMSON, E. T. Excretion of epinephrine and norepinephrine in various emotional states. *Journal of Clinical Endocrinology,* 1957, **17,** 608.

ELMADJIAN, F., HOPE, J. M., & LAMSON, E. T. Excretion of epinephrine and norepinephrine under stress. *Recent Progress in Hormone Research,* 1958, **14,** 513.

ELMADJIAN, F., LAMSON, E. T., & NERI, R. Excretion of adrenaline and noradrenaline in human subjects. *Journal of Clinical Endocrinology,* 1956, **16,** 222.

ELMADJIAN, F., & PINCUS, G. The adrenal cortex and the lymphocytopenia of stress. *Endocrinology,* 1945, **37,** 47.

ELMADJIAN, F., & PINCUS, G. A study of the diurnal variations in circulating lymphocytes in normal and psychotic subjects. *Journal of Clinical Endocrinology,* 1946, **6,** 287.

ENGEL, G. L. *Psychological development in health and disease.* Philadelphia: Saunders, 1962.

ERANKO, O. Distribution of adrenaline and noradrenaline in the adrenal medulla. *Nature,* 1955, **175,** 88.

EULER, U. S. von A specific sympathomimetic ergone in adrenergic nerve fibers (sympathin) and its relation to adrenaline and noradrenaline. *Acta Physiologica Scandinavica,* 1946, **12,** 73.

EULER, U. S. von *Noradrenaline: Chemistry, physiology, pharmacology and clinical aspects.* Springfield, Ill.: Charles C Thomas, 1956.

EULER, U. S. von The development and applications of the trihydroxyindole method for catecholamines. *Pharmacological Review,* 1959, **11,** 262.

EULER, U. S. von Quantitation of stress by catecholamine analysis. *Clinical Pharmacology and Therapy,* 1964, **5,** 398.

EULER, U. S. von, & FLODING, I. A fluorimetric micromethod for differential estimation of adrenaline and noradrenaline. *Acta Physiologica Scandinavica,* 1955, **33** (Suppl. 118), 45.

EULER, U. S. von, GEMZELL, C. A., LEVI, L., & STROM, G. Cortical and medullary adrenal activity in emotional stress. *Acta Endocrinologica (Kobenhavn),* 1959, **30,** 567.

EULER, U. S. von, & HELLNER, S. Excretion of noradrenaline, adrenaline, and hydroxytyramine in urine. *Acta Physiologica Scandinavica,* 1951, **22,** 161.

EULER, U. S. von, & LISHAJKO, F. The estimation of catecholamines in urine. *Acta Physiologica Scandinavica,* 1959, **45,** 122.

EULER, U. S. von, & LISHAJKO, F. Improved technique for the fluorimetric estimation of catecholamines. *Acta Physiologica Scandinavica,* 1961, **51,** 348.

EULER, U. S. von, & LUNDBERG, U. Effect of flying on the epinephrine excretion in air force personnel. *Journal of Applied Physiology,* 1954, **6,** 551.

EVERETT, J. W. The control of the secretion of prolactin. In G. W. HARRIS & B. T. DONOVAN (Eds.), *The pituitary gland.* Vol. 2. Berkeley: University of California Press, 1966.

FAJANS, S. S. Some metabolic actions of corticosteroids. *Metabolism,* 1961, **10,** 951.

FALCONER, I. R., & HETZEL, B. S. Effect of emotional stress and TSH on thyroid vein hormone level in sheep with exteriorized thyroids. *Endocrinology,* 1964, **75,** 42.

FARR, C. B. Results of basal metabolism tests in one hundred mental cases. *Archives of Neurology and Psychiatry,* 1924, **12,** 518.

FARR, C. B. Basal metabolism in the psychoses. *Proceedings of the Association for Research in Nervous and Mental Disease,* 1931, **11,** 221.

FARRELL, G. The physiological factors which influence the secretion of aldosterone. *Recent Progress in Hormone Research,* 1959, **15,** 275.

FAURBYE, A., MUNKVAD, I., & PIND, K. The thyroid function in chronic schizophrenia (hebephrenia). *Acta Endocrinologica (Kobenhavn),* 1958, **28,** 395.

FAURBYE, A., VESTERGAARD, P., KOBBERNAGEL, F., & NIELSEN, A. Adrenal cortical function in chronic schizophrenia (stress, adrenaline-test, ACTH-test). *Acta Endocrinologica (Kobenhavn),* 1951, **8,** 215.

FEINBERG, I. Current status of the Funkenstein test. *Archives of Neurology and Psychiatry,* 1958, **80,** 488.

FELLER, R. P., & HALE, H. B. Human urinary catecholamines in relation to climate. *Journal of Applied Physiology,* 1964, **19,** 37.

FERGUSON, H. C., BARTRAM, A. C. G., FOWLIE, H. C., CATHRO, D. M., BIRCHALL, K., & MITCHELL, F. L. A preliminary investigation of steroid excretion in depressed patients before and after electroconvulsive therapy. *Acta Endocrinologica (Kobenhavn),* 1964, **47,** 58.

FERGUSON-RAYPORT, S. M. The relation of emotional factors to recurrence of thyrotoxicosis. *Canadian Medical Association Journal,* 1956, **75,** 993.

FIORICA, V., & MUEHL, S. Relationship between plasma levels of 17-hydroxycorticosteroids (17-OH-CS) and a psychological measure of manifest anxiety. *Psychosomatic Medicine,* 1962, **24,** 596.

FISHMAN, J. R., HAMBURG, D. A., HANDLON, J. H., MASON, J. W., & SACHAR, E. J. Emotional and adrenal cortical responses to a new experience. *Archives of General Psychiatry,* 1962, **6,** 271.

FLAGG, G. W., CLEMENS, T. L., MICHAEL, E. A., ALEXANDER, F., & WARK, J. A psychophysiological investigation of hyperthyroidism. *Psychosomatic Medicine,* 1965, **27,** 497.

FLERKO, B. The central nervous system and the secretion and release of luteinizing hormone and follicle stimulating hormone. In A. V. NALBANDOV (Ed.), *Advances in neuroendocrinology*. Urbana: University of Illinois Press, 1963.

FOA, P. P., & GALANSINO, G. *Glucagon: Chemistry and function in health and disease*. Springfield, Ill.: Charles C Thomas, 1962.

FOLKOW, B., & EULER, U. S. von Selective activation of noradrenaline and adrenaline producing cells in the cat's adrenal gland by hypothalamic stimulation. *Circulation Research*, 1954, **2**, 191.

FORTIER, C. Dual control of adrenocorticotrophin release. *Endocrinology*, 1951, **49**, 782.

FORTIER, C. Sensitivity of the plasma free corticosteroid response to environmental change in the rat. *Archives of International Physiology*, 1958, **66**, 672.

FORTIER, C. Nervous control of ACTH secretion. In G. W. HARRIS & B. T. DONOVAN (Eds.), *The pituitary gland*. Vol. 2. Berkeley: University of California Press, 1966.

FORTIER, C., de GROOT, J., & HARTFIELD, J. E. Plasma free corticosteroid response to faradic stimulation in the rat. *Acta Endocrinologica (Kobenhavn)*, 1959, **30**, 219.

FOX, H. M. Effect of psychophysiological research on transference. *Journal of the American Psychoanalytic Association*, 1958, **6**, 413.

FOX, H. M. Some recent trends in psychophysiological research. *Medical Clinics of North America*, 1960, **44**, 1341.

FOX, H. M., MURAWSKI, B. J., BARTHOLOMAY, A. F., & GIFFORD, S. Adrenal steroid excretion patterns in eighteen healthy subjects. *Psychosomatic Medicine*, 1961, **23**, 33.

FOX, H. M. MURAWSKI, B. J., THORN, G. W., & GRAY, S. J. Urinary 17-hydroxycorticoid and uropepsin levels with psychological data: A three year study of one subject. *Archives of Internal Medicine*, 1958, **101**, 859.

FRANKENHAEUSER, M., FROBERG, J., & MELLIS, I. Subjective and physiological reactions induced by electrical shocks of varying intensity. *Neuroendocrinology*, 1965–1966, **1**, 105.

FRANKENHAEUSER, M., & KAREBY, S. Effect of meprobamate on catecholamine excretion during mental stress. *Perceptual and Motor Skills*, 1962, **15**, 571.

FRANKENHAEUSER, M., & PATKAI, P. Catecholamine excretion and performance during stress. *Perceptual and Motor Skills*, 1964, **19**, 13.

FRANKENHAEUSER, M., & PATKAI, P. Interindividual differences in catecholamine excretion during stress. *Scandinavian Journal of Psychology*, 1965, **6**, 117.

FRANKENHAEUSER, M., & POST, B. Catecholamine excretion during mental work as modified by centrally acting drugs. *Acta Physiologica Scandinavica*, 1962, **55**, 74.

FRANKENHAEUSER, M., STERKY, K., & JARPE, G. Psychophysiological relations in habituation to gravitational stress. *Perceptual and Motor Skills*, 1962, **15**, 63.

FRANSSON, C., & GEMZELL, C. A. Adrenocortical activity in the preoperative period. *Journal of Clinical Endocrinology (Kobenhavn)*, 1955, **15**, 1069.

FRAZIER, T. Effect of transitory behavior stress on urinary 17-hydroxycorticosteroid and catecholamine levels. *Proceedings of the 2nd Annual Biomedical Research Conference*, NASA, February 17–18, 1966. (a)

FRAZIER, T. W. Adrenal participation in conditioned arousal. Doctoral dissertation, Florida State University, 1966. (b)

FREEMAN, H., PINCUS, G., ELMADJIAN, F., & ROMANOFF, L. P. Adrenal responsivity in aged psychotic patients. *Geriatrics*, 1955, **10**, 72.

FREEMAN, W., PINCUS, G., & GLOVER, E. D. The excretion of neutral urinary steroids in stress. *Endocrinology*, 1944, **35**, 215. (Abstract)

FREUDENBERGER, C. B. A comparison of the Wistar albino and the Long-Evans hybrid strain of the Norway rat. *American Journal of Anatomy*, 1932, **50**, 293.

FRIEDLANDER, J. H., PERRAULT, R., TURNER, W. J., & GOTTFRIED, S. P. Adrenocortical response to physiologic stress in schizophrenia. *Psychosomatic Medicine*, 1950, **12**, 86.

FRIEDMAN, M., ST. GEORGE, S., BYERS, S. O., & ROSENMAN, R. H. Excretion of catecholamines, 17-ketosteroids, 17-hydroxycorticoids and 5-hydroxyindole in men exhibiting a particular behavior pattern (a) associated with high incidence of clinical coronary artery disease. *Journal of Clinical Investigation*, 1960, **39**, 758.

FRIEDMAN, S. B., MASON, J. W., & HAMBURG, D. A. Urinary 17-hydroxycorticosteroid levels in parents of children with neoplastic disease. *Psychosomatic Medicine*, 1963, **25**, 364.

FROST, J. W., DRYER, R. L., & KOHLSTAEDT, K. G. Stress studies on auto race drivers. *Journal of Laboratory and Clinical Medicine*, 1951, **38**, 523.

FUNKENSTEIN, D. H. The physiology of fear and anger. *Scientific American*, 1955, **192–193**, 74.

FUNKENSTEIN, D. H. Nor-epinephrine-like and epinephrine-like substances in relation to human behavior. *Journal of Nervous and Mental Disease*, 1956, **124**, 58.

FUNKENSTEIN, D. H., GREENBLATT, M., & SOLOMON, H. C. Nor-epinephrine-like and epinephrine-like substances in psychotic and psychoneurotic patients. *American Journal of Psychiatry*, 1951–1952, **108**, 652.

FUNKENSTEIN, D. H., KING, S. H., & DROLETTE, M. E. The direction of anger during a laboratory stress-inducing situation. *Psychosomatic Medicine*, 1954, **16**, 404.

FUNKENSTEIN, D. H., KING, S. H., & DROLETTE, M. E. *Mastery of stress*. Cambridge, Mass.: Harvard University Press, 1957.

GANONG, W. F. The central nervous system and the synthesis and release of adrenocorticotropic hormone. In A. V. NALBANDOV (Ed.), *Advances in neuroendocrinology*. Urbana: University of Illinois Press, 1963.

GERWING, J. The effect of continued toxic stress on the activity of the thyroid gland in the rat and the guinea-pig. *Journal of Physiology*, 1958, **144**, 243.

GERWING, J., LONG, D. A., & PITT-RIVERS, R. The influence of bacterial exotoxins on the activity of the thyroid gland in different species. *Journal of Physiology*, 1958, **144**, 229.

GIBBONS, J. L.   Cortisol secretion rate in depressive illness. *Archives of General Psychiatry*, 1964, **10,** 572.

GIBBONS, J. L., GIBSON, J. G., MAXWELL, A. E., & WILLCOX, D. R. C.   An endocrine study of depressive illness. *Journal of Psychosomatic Research*, 1960, **5,** 32.

GIBBONS, J. L., & MCHUGH, P. R.   Plasma cortisol in depressive illness. *Journal of Psychiatric Research,* 1962, **1,** 162.

GIBBS, C. E., & LEMCKE, D.   Study in basal metabolism in dementia praecox and manic-depressive psychoses. *Archives of Internal Medicine,* 1923, **31,** 102.

GIBSON, J. B., & WILLCOX, D. R. C.   Observations on thyroid adrenocortical relationships. *Journal of Psychosomatic Research,* 1957, **2,** 225.

GIBSON, J. G.   Emotions and the thyroid gland: A critical appraisal. *Journal of Psychosomatic Research,* 1962, **6,** 93.

GILDEA, E. F.   Discussion. In J. R. MOTE (Ed.), *Proceedings of the First Clinical ACTH Conference.* Philadelphia: Blakiston, 1950.

GJESSING, L. R.   Studies of periodic catatonia: I. Blood levels of protein-bound iodine and urinary excretion of vanillyl-mandelic acid in relation to clinical course. *Journal of Psychiatric Research,* 1964, **2,** 123.

GJESSING, R. Beitrage zur Kenntnis der pathophysiologic periodisch katatoner Zustande: Versuch einer Ausgleichung der Funktionsstorungen. *Achiv für Psychiatrie und Nervenkrankheiten,* 1939, **109,** 525.

GLASER, G. H., & HOCH, P. H.   Observations on effect of corticotrophin in schizophrenics: Preliminary report. *Archives of Neurology and Psychiatry,* 1951, **66,** 697.

GOODALL, McC.   Studies of adrenaline and noradrenaline in mammalian heart and suprarenals. *Acta Physiologica Scandinavica,* 1951, **24** (Suppl. 85).

GOODALL, McC., & BERMAN, M. L.   Urinary output of adrenaline, noradrenaline, and 3-methoxy-4-hydroxy-mandelic acid following centrifugation and anticipation of centrifugation. *Journal of Clinical Investigation,* 1960, **39,** 1533.

GOODALL, McC., McCALLY, M., & GRAVELINE, D. E.   Urinary adrenaline and noradrenaline response to simulated weightless state. *American Journal of Physiology,* 1964, **206,** 431.

GORNALL, A. G., EGLITIS, B., MILLER, A., STOKES, A. B., & DEWAN, J. G.   Long-term clinical and metabolic observations in periodic catatonia: An application of the kinetic method of research in three schizophrenic patients. *American Journal of Psychiatry,* 1953, **109,** 584.

GOTTFRIED, S. P., & WILLNER, H. H.   Blood chemistry of schizophrenic patients before, during and after insulin shock therapy: Preliminary studies. *Archives of Neurology and Psychiatry,* 1949, **62,** 809.

GRAHAM, L. A., COHEN, S. I., SHMAVONIAN, B., & KIRSHNER, N.   Sympathetico-adrenal correlates of avoidance and escape behavior in human conditioning studies. *Psychosomatic Medicine,* 1963, **25,** 488. (Abstract)

GRAHAM, L. A., COHEN, S. I., SHMAVONIAN, B. M., & KIRSHNER, N.   Urinary catecholamine excretion during instrumental conditioning. *Psychosomatic Medicine,* 1967, **29,** 134.

GRAVES, R. J.   Newly observed affection of the thyroid gland in females. *London Medical and Surgical Journal,* 1835, **7,** 516.

GROSSFELD, H.   Action of adrenalcortical steroids on cultured cells. *Endocrinology,* 1959, **65,** 777.

GROSZ, H. J.   The relation of serum ascorbic acid level to adrenocortical secretion during experimentally induced emotional stress in human subjects. *Journal of Psychosomatic Research,* 1961, **5,** 253.

GUNNE, L. M., and GEMZELL, C. A.   Adrenocortical and thyroid function in periodic catatonia. *Archives of Psychiatry and Neurology, Scandinavia,* 1956, **31,** 367.

HAGEN, J. H., & HAGEN, P. B.   Actions of adrenalin and noradrenalin on metabolic systems. In G. LITWACK & D. KRITCHEVSKY (Eds.), *Actions of hormones on molecular processes.* New York: Wiley, 1964.

HALBERG, F., ENGELI, M., & HAMBURGER, C.   The 17-ketosteroid excretion of a healthy man on weekdays and weekends. *Experimental Medicine and Surgery,* 1965, **23,** 61.

HALDANE, J. S.   Life and mechanism. *Guy's Hospital Gazette,* 1906, **20,** 212.

HALDANE, J. S.   *Respiration.* New Haven: Yale University Press, 1922.

HALE, H. B.   Plasma corticosteroid changes during space-equivalent decompression in partial-pressure suits and in supersonic flight. In *Hormonal steroids, biochemistry, pharmacology and therapeutics.* Vol. 2. New York: Academic, 1965.

HALE, H. B., DUFFY, J. C., ELLIS, J. P., Jr., & WILLIAMS, E. W.   Flying stress in relation to flying proficiency. *U.S. Air Force School of Aerospace Medicine,* 1964, 1–8.

HALE, H. B., ELLIS, J. P., Jr., & KRATOCHVIL, C. H.   Effects of piloting supersonic aircraft on plasma corticosteroids and bicarbonate. *Journal of Applied Physiology,* 1959, **14,** 629.

HALE, H. B., KRATOCHVIL, C. H., ELLIS, J. P., Jr., & WILLIAMS, E. W.   Plasma corticosteroid levels in aircrewmen after long flights. *Journal of Clinical Endocrinology,* 1958, **18,** 1440.

HAM, G. C., ALEXANDER, F., & CARMICHAEL, H. T.   A psychosomatic theory of thyrotoxicosis. *Psychosomatic Medicine,* 1951, **13,** 18.

HAMBURG, D. A.   Plasma and urinary corticosteroid levels in naturally occurring psychologic stresses. In *Ultrastructure and metabolism of the nervous system: Proceedings of the Association for Research in Nervous and Mental Disease.* Vol. 40. Baltimore: Williams & Wilkins, 1962.

HAMMETT, F. S.   Observations on the relation between emotional and metabolic stability. *American Journal of Physiology,* 1921, **53,** 307. (a)

HAMMETT, F. S.   Temperament and bodily constitution. *Journal of Comparative Psychology,* 1921, **1,** 489. (b)

HANDLON, J. H., WADESON, R. W., FISHMAN, J. R., SACHAR, E. J., HAMBURG, D. A., & MASON, J. W.   Psychological factors lowering plasma 17-hydroxycorticosteroid concentration. *Psychosomatic Medicine,* 1962, **24,** 535.

HARE, E. H., & HAIGH, C. P. Variations in the iodine avidity of the normal human thyroid as measured by the 24-hour ^{131}I uptake. *Clinical Science,* 1955, **14,** 441.

HARRIS, G. W. *Neural control of the pituitary gland.* London: Arnold, 1955.

HARRIS, G. W. Hypothalamic control of the anterior lobe of the hypophysis. In W. S. FIELDS, R. GUILLEMIN, & C. A. CARTON (Eds.), *Hypothalamic-hypophysial interrelationships.* Springfield, Ill.: Charles C Thomas, 1956.

HARRIS, G. W., & CAMPBELL, H. J. The regulation of the secretion of luteinizing hormone and ovulation. In G. W. HARRIS & B. T. DONOVAN (Eds.), *The pituitary gland.* Vol. 2. Berkeley: University of California Press, 1966.

HARRISON, T. S., SILVER, D. M., & ZUIDEMA, G. D. Thyroid and adrenal medullary function in chronic "executive" monkeys. *Endocrinology,* 1966, **78,** 685.

HATAI, S. On the weight of some of the ductless glands of the Norway and of the albino rat according to sex and variety. *Anatomical Record,* 1914, **8,** 511.

HELLER, H., and GINSBURG, M. Secretion, metabolism and fate of the posterior pituitary hormones. In G. W. HARRIS & B. T. DONOVAN (Eds.), *The pituitary gland.* Vol. 3. Berkeley: University of California Press, 1966.

HEMPHILL, R. E., & REISS, M. A.C.T.H. in psychiatry. *International Congress of Psychiatry,* 1950, **4,** 471.

HENDERSON, L. J. *The order of nature.* Cambridge: Harvard University Press, 1917.

HENDERSON, L. J. *Blood: A survey in general physiology.* New Haven: Yale University Press, 1928.

HERRINGTON, L. P., & NELBACH, J. H. Relation of gland weights to growth and aging processes in rats exposed to certain environmental conditions. *Endocrinology,* 1942, **30,** 375.

HETZEL, B. S., GRACE, W. J., & WOLFF, H. G. General metabolic changes during stressful life experiences in man. *Journal of Psychosomatic Research,* 1956, **1,** 186.

HETZEL, B. S., de la HABA, D. S., & HINKLE, L. E., Jr. Life stress and thyroid function in human subjects. *Journal of Clinical Endocrinology,* 1952, **12,** 941. (a) (Abstract)

HETZEL, B. S., de la HABA, D. S., & HINKLE, L. E., Jr. Rapid changes in plasma PBI in euthyroid and hyperthyroid subjects. In *Transactions of the American Goiter Association.* Springfield, Ill.: Charles C Thomas, 1952. (b)

HETZEL, B. S., SCHOTTSTAEDT, W. W., GRACE, W. J., & WOLFF, H. G. Changes in urinary 17-hydroxycorticosteroid excretion during stressful life experiences in man. *Journal of Clinical Endocrinology,* 1955, **15,** 1057.

HETZEL, B. S., SCHOTTSTAEDT, W. W., GRACE, W. J., & WOLFF, H. G. Changes in urinary nitrogen and electrolyte excretion during stressful life experiences, and their relation to thyroid function. *Journal of Psychosomatic Research,* 1956, **1,** 177.

HIATT, H. H., ROTHWELL, W. S., & HORWITT, M. K. Eosinopenia produced by ACTH in patients with schizophrenia. *Proceedings of the Society for Experimental Biology and Medicine,* 1952, **79,** 707.

HILL, C. W., GREER, W. E., & FELSENFELD, O. Psychological stress, early response to foreign protein, and blood cortisol in vervets. *Psychosomatic Medicine,* 1967, **29,** 279.

HILL, S. R., Jr., GOETZ, F. C., FOX, H. M., MURAWSKI, B. J., KRAKAUER, L. J., REIFENSTEIN, R. W., GRAY, S. J., REDDY, W. J., HEDBERG, S. E., ST. MARC, J. R., & THORN, G. W. Studies on adrenocortical and psychological response to stress in man. *Archives of Internal Medicine,* 1956, **97,** 269.

HILLARP, N. A., & HOKFELT, B. Evidence of adrenaline and noradrenaline in separate adrenal medullary cells. *Acta Physiologica Scandinavica,* 1953, **30,** 55.

HINDE, R. A. Some investigations on the responses of animals to stress in nature. In *The nature of stress disorders.* Springfield, Ill.: Charles C Thomas, 1959.

HIRSCHOWITZ, B. I. Pepsinogen: Its origins, secretion and excretion. *Physiological Review,* 1957, **37,** 475.

HITCHINGS, F. W., SLOAN, H. G., & AUSTIN, J. D. Laboratory studies of the activity of the brain and the adrenals in response to specific stimuli. *Cleveland Medical Journal,* 1913, **12,** 684.

HOAGLAND, H. The human adrenal cortex in relation to stressful activities. *Journal of Aviation Medicine,* 1947, **18,** 450.

HOAGLAND, H., BERGEN, J. R., BLOCH, E., ELMADJIAN, F., & GIBREE, N. R. Adrenal stress responses in normal men. *Journal of Applied Physiology,* 1955, **8,** 149.

HOAGLAND, H., ELMADJIAN, F., & PINCUS, G. Stressful psychomotor performance and adrenal cortical function as indicated by the lymphocyte response. *Journal of Clinical Endocrinology,* 1946, **6,** 301.

HOAGLAND, H., PINCUS, G., ELMADJIAN, F., ROMANOFF, L., FREEMAN, H., HOPE, J., BALLAN, J., BERKELEY, A., & CARLO, J. Study of adrenocortical physiology in normal and schizophrenic men. *Archives of Neurology and Psychiatry,* 1953, **69,** 470.

HOCH, F. L. Biochemical actions of thyroid hormones. *Physiological Review,* 1962, **42,** 605.

HODGES, J. R., JONES, M. T., & STOCKHAM, M. A. Effect of emotion on blood corticotrophin and cortisol concentrations in man. *Nature,* 1962, **193,** 1187.

HOLCOMBE, R. B. Investigations on the urinary excretion of "reducing corticoids" in cattle and sheep. *Acta Endocrinologica (Kobenhavn)* 1957, **26** (Suppl. 34).

HOLLINGSHEAD, L., & BARTON, J. W. The adrenal cortex and emotion. *Psychological Review,* 1931, **38,** 538.

HOLTZ, P., CREDNER, K., & KRONEBERG, G. Über das sympathicomimetische pressorische Prinzip des Harns ("Urosympathin"). *Archives of Experimental and Pathological Pharmacology,* 1947, **204,** 228.

HOSKINS, R. G. *The biology of schizophrenia.* New York: Norton, 1946.

HOSKINS, R. G., & SLEEPER, F. H. Basal metabolism in schizophrenia. *Archives of Neurology and Psychiatry,* 1929, **21,** 887.

HOUSSAY, B. C. Comments. In *Hormonal regulation of energy metabolism.* Springfield, Ill.: Charles C Thomas, 1957.

HOWARD, J. M., OLNEY, J. M., FRAWLEY, J. P., PETERSON, R. E.,

SMITH, L. H., DAVIS, J. H., GUERRA, S., & DIBRELL, W. H. Studies of adrenal function in combat and wounded soldiers. *Annals of Surgery,* 1955, **141,** 314.

HUBBLE, D. The endocrine orchestra. *British Medical Journal,* 1961, **1,** 523.

HUBBLE, D. The psyche and the endocrine system. *Lancet,* 1963, **2,** 209.

INGLE, D. J. Metabolic effects of adrenal steroids. In E. S. GORDON (Ed.), *A symposium on steroid hormones.* Madison: University of Wisconsin Press, 1950.

INGLE, D. J. Parameters of metabolic problems. *Recent Progress in Hormone Research,* 1951, **6,** 159.

INGLE, D. J. *Principles of research in biology and medicine.* Philadelphia: Lippincott, 1958.

INGLE, D. Current status of adrenocortical research. *American Scientist,* 1959, **47,** 413.

IRA, G. H., WHALEN, R. E., & BOGDONOFF, M. D. Heart rate changes in physicians during daily "stressful" tasks. *Journal of Psychosomatic Research,* 1963, **7,** 147.

JAKOBSON, T., STENBACK, A., STRANDSTROM, L., & RIMON, R. The excretion of urinary 11-deoxy- and 11-oxy-17-hydroxycorticosteroids in depressive patients during basal conditions and during the administration of methopyrapone. *Journal of Psychosomatic Research,* 1966, **9,** 363.

JEANRENAUD, B. Dynamic aspects of adipose tissue metabolism: A review. *Metabolism,* 1961, **10,** 535.

JENSEN, C. C., & EK, J. I. The excretion of certain adrenal steroids during mental stress in healthy persons. *Acta Psychiatrica Scandinavica,* 1962, **38,** 302.

KELSEY, F. O., GULLOCK, A. H., & KELSEY, F. E. Thyroid activity in hospitalized psychiatric patients: Relation of dietary iodine to I^{131} uptake. *Archives of Neurology and Psychiatry,* 1957, **77,** 543.

KLEPPING, J., BUISSON, O., GUERRIN, J., ESCOUSSE, A., & DIDIER, J. P. Urinary elimination of catecholamines in airplane pilots in action. *Comptes Rendus de la Société de Biologie (Paris),* 1963, **157,** 1727.

KNOBIL, E., & HOTCHKISS, J. Growth hormone. *Annual Review of Physiology,* 1964, **26,** 47.

KOCHAKIAN, C. D. Protein anabolic property of androgens. *Alabama Journal of Medical Science,* 1964, **1,** 24.

KORCHIN, S. J., & HERZ, M. Differential effects of "shame" and "disintegrative" threats on emotional and adrenocortical functioning. *Archives of General Psychiatry,* 1960, **2,** 640.

KORNER, A. The adrenal gland and *in vitro* protein synthesis. In G. E. W. WOLSTENHOLME & C. M. O'CONNOR (Eds.), *Metabolic effects of adrenal hormones* (Ciba Foundation Study Group No. 6). Boston: Little, Brown, 1960.

KRACHT, J. Fright-thyrotoxicosis in the wild rabbit: A model of thyrotrophic alarm-reaction. *Acta Endocrinologica (Kobenhavn),* 1954, **15,** 355.

KRAEPELIN, E. *Dementia praecox and paraphrenia.* Edinburgh: Livingston, 1919.

KRAHL, M. E. *The action of insulin on cells.* New York: Academic, 1961.

KURLAND, H. D. Steroid excretion in depressive disorders. *Archives of General Psychiatry,* 1964, **10,** 554. (a)

KURLAND, H. D. Urinary steroids in neurotic- and manic-depression. *Proceedings of the Society for Experimental Biology and Medicine,* 1964, **115,** 723. (b)

LAVENDA, N., BARTLETT, R. G., Jr., & KENNEDY, V. E. Leucocyte changes in rodents exposed to cold with and without restraint. *American Journal of Physiology,* 1956, **184,** 624.

LEVI, L. A new stress tolerance test with simultaneous study of physiological and psychological variables. *Acta Endocrinologica (Kobenhavn),* 1961, **37,** 38.

LEVI, L. The urinary output of adrenalin and noradrenalin during experimentally induced emotional stress in clinically different groups. *Acta Psychotherapica (Basel),* 1963, **11,** 218.

LEVI, L. The stress of everyday work as reflected in productiveness, subjective feelings, and urinary output of adrenaline and noradrenaline under salaried and piecework conditions. *Journal of Psychosomatic Research,* 1964, **8,** 199. (a)

LEVI, L. The urinary output of adrenaline and noradrenaline during different experimentally induced pleasant and unpleasant emotional states: A summary. *Journal of Psychosomatic Research,* 1964, **8,** 197. (b)

LEVI, L. The urinary output of adrenalin and noradrenalin during pleasant and unpleasant emotional states. *Psychosomatic Medicine,* 1965, **27,** 80.

LEVI, L. Life stress and urinary excretion of adrenaline and noradrenaline. In W. RAAB (Ed.), *Prevention of ischemic heart disease: Principles and practice.* Springfield, Ill.: Charles C Thomas, 1966. (a)

LEVI, L. Physical and mental stress reactions during experimental conditions simulating combat. *Forsvarsmedicin,* 1966, **2,** 3. (b)

LEVI, L. Sympatho-adrenomedullary responses to emotional stimuli: Methodologic, physiologic, and pathologic considerations. In E. BAJUSZ (Ed.), *An introduction to clinical neuroendocrinology.* White Plains, N.Y.: Karger (Phiebig), 1967.

LEVINE, S., & TREIMAN, D. M. Differential plasma corticosterone response to stress in four inbred strains of mice. *Endocrinology,* 1964, **75,** 142.

LEVITT, E. E., & PERSKY, H. Relation of Rorschach factors and plasma hydrocortisone level in hypnotically induced anxiety. *Psychosomatic Medicine,* 1960, **22,** 218.

LEWIS, N. D. C. A psychoanalytic study of hyperthyroidism. *Psychoanalytic Review,* 1923, **10,** 140.

LEWIS, N. D. C. Psychological factors in hyperthyroidism. *Medical Journal Record,* 1925, **122,** 121.

LIBOW, L. S., & DURELL, J. Clinical studies on the relationship between psychosis and the regulation of thyroid gland activity: I. Periodic psychosis with coupled change in thyroid function: Report of a case. *Psychosomatic Medicine,* 1965, **27,** 369.

LIDZ, T. Emotional factors in etiology of hyperthyroidism: The report of a preliminary survey. *Psychosomatic Medicine,* 1949, **11,** 2.

LIDZ, T. Emotional factors in the etiology of hyperthyroidism occurring in relation to pregnancy: Summary of eleven cases. *Psychosomatic Medicine,* 1955, **17,** 420.

LIDZ, T., & WHITEHORN, J. C. Life situations, emotions, and Graves' disease. *Psychosomatic Medicine,* 1950, **12,** 184.

LINGJAERDE, O. Investigations of basal metabolism in schizophrenics: Effects of thyroid treatment. *Acta Psychiatrica Neurologica,* 1933, **8,** 573.

LINGJAERDE, P., SKAUG, O. E., & LINGJAERDE, O. The determination of thyroid function with radioiodine (I-131) in mental patients. *Acta Psychiatrica Neurologica,* 1960, **35,** 498.

LONG, C. N. The relation of cholesterol and ascorbic acid to the secretion of the adrenal cortex. *Recent Progress in Hormone Research,* 1947, **1,** 99.

LONG, C. N. H., SMITH, O. K., & FRY, E. G. Actions of cortisol and related compounds on carbohydrate and protein metabolism. In G. E. W. WOLSTENHOLME & E. M. O'CONNOR (Eds.), *Metabolic effects of adrenal hormones* (Ciba Foundation Study Group No. 6). Boston: Little, Brown, 1960.

LONG, D. A. The influence of corticosteroids on immunological responses to bacterial infections. *International Archives of Allergy,* 1957, **10,** 5.

LOVEGROVE, T. D., MELCALFE, E. V., HOBBS, G. E., & STEVENSON, J. A. The urinary excretion of adrenaline, noradrenaline, and 17-hydroxycorticosteroids in mental illness. *Canadian Psychiatric Association Journal,* 1965, **10,** 170.

LUND, A. Fluorimetric determination of adrenaline in blood: III. A new sensitive and specific method. *Acta Pharmacologica (Kobenhavn),* 1949, **5,** 231.

LUND, A. Simultaneous fluorimetric determinations of adrenaline and noradrenaline in blood. *Acta Pharmacologica (Kobenhavn),* 1950, **6,** 137.

MAKELA, S., NAATANEN, E., & RINNE, U. K. The response of the adrenal cortex to psychic stress after meprobamate treatment. *Acta Endocrinologica (Kobenhavn),* 1959, **32,** 1.

MAN, E. B., & KAHN, E. Thyroid function of manic-depressive patients evaluated by determinations of the serum iodine. *Archives of Neurology and Psychiatry,* 1945, **54,** 51.

MANDELBROTE, B. M., & WITTKOWER, E. D. Emotional factors in Graves' disease. *Psychosomatic Medicine,* 1955, **17,** 109.

MANGER, W. M., SCHWARZ, B. E., BAARS, C. W., WAKIM, K. G., BOLLMAN, J. L., PETERSEN, M. C., & BERKSON, J. Epinephrine and arterenol (norepinephrine) in mental disease: Plasma and cerebrospinal fluid concentrations. *Archives of Neurology and Psychiatry,* 1957, **78,** 396.

MANGILI, G., MOTTA, M., & MARTINI, L. Control of adrenocorticotropic hormone secretion. In L. MARTINI & W. F. GANONG (Eds.), *Neuroendocrinology.* Vol. 1. New York: Academic, 1966.

MARCHBANKS, V. H., Jr. Effect of flying stress on urinary 17-hydroxycorticosteroid levels: Observations during a 22½ hour mission. *Journal of Aviation Medicine,* 1958, **29,** 676.

MARCHBANKS, V. H., Jr. Flying stress and urinary 17-hydroxycorticosteroid levels during twenty-hour missions. *Aerospace Medicine,* 1960, **31,** 639.

MARCHBANKS, V. H., Jr., HALE, H. B., & ELLIS, J. P. Stress responses of pilots flying 6-hour overwater missions in F-100 and F-104 aircraft. *Aerospace Medicine,* 1963, **34,** 15.

MARKKANEN, A., PEKKARINEN, A., PULKKINEN, K., & SIMOLA, P. E. On the emotional eosinopenic reaction caused by examination. *Acta Physiologica Scandinavica,* 1956, **35,** 225.

MARSH, J. T., & RASMUSSEN, A. F., Jr. Response of adrenals, thymus, spleen and leucocytes to shuttle box and confinement stress. *Proceedings of the Society for Experimental Biology and Medicine,* 1960, **104,** 180.

MASON, J. W. The central nervous system regulation of ACTH secretion. In H. JASPER et al. (Eds.), *International symposium on reticular formation of the brain.* Boston: Little, Brown, 1958.

MASON, J. W. Plasma 17-hydroxycorticosteroid levels during electrical stimulation of the amygdaloid complex in conscious monkeys. *American Journal of Physiology,* 1959, **196,** 44. (a)

MASON, J. W. Psychological influences on the pituitary-adrenal cortical system. *Recent Progress in Hormone Research,* 1959, **15,** 345. (b)

MASON, J. W. Visceral functions of the nervous system. *Annual Review of Physiology,* 1959, **21,** 353. (c)

MASON, J. W. Psychoendocrine approaches in stress research. In *Symposium on medical aspects of stress in the military climate.* Washington, D.C.: Walter Reed Army Institute of Research, 1964.

MASON, J. W., & BRADY, J. V. Plasma 17-hydroxycorticosteroid changes related to reserpine effects on emotional behavior. *Science,* 1956, **124,** 983.

MASON, J. W., & BRADY, J. V. The sensitivity of psychoendocrine systems to social and physical environment. In P. H. LEIDERMAN & D. SHAPIRO (Eds.), *Psychobiological approaches to social behavior.* Stanford, Calif.: Stanford University Press, 1964.

MASON, J. W., BRADY, J. V., POLISH, E., BAUER, J. A., ROBINSON, J. A., ROSE, R. M., & TAYLOR, E. D. Patterns of corticosteroid and pepsinogen change related to emotional stress in the monkey. *Science,* 1961, **133,** 1596. (a)

MASON, J. W., BRADY, J. V., & SIDMAN, M. Plasma 17-hydroxycorticosteroid levels and conditioned behavior in the rhesus monkey. *Endocrinology,* 1957, **60,** 741.

MASON, J. W., BRADY, J. V., & TOLLIVER, G. A. Plasma and urinary 17-hydroxycorticosteroid responses to 72-hr. avoidance in the monkey. *Psychosomatic Medicine,* 1968, **30,** 608.

MASON, J. W., BRADY, J. V., & TOLSON, W. W. Behavioral adaptations and endocrine activity. In R. LEVINE (Ed.),

Endocrines and the central nervous system. Baltimore: Williams & Wilkins, 1966.

MASON, J. W., BRADY, J. V., TOLSON, W. W., ROBINSON, J. A., TAYLOR, E. D., & MOUGEY, E. H. Patterns of thyroid, gonadal, and adrenal hormone secretion related to psychological stress in the monkey. *Psychosomatic Medicine,* 1961, **23,** 446. (b) (Abstract)

MASON, J. W., FISHMAN, J. R., MOUGEY, E. H., TAYLOR, E. D., ROBINSON, J. A., & HAMBURG, D. A. Hormonal response patterns associated with final college examinations. Unpublished data.

MASON, J. W., HARWOOD, C. T., & ROSENTHAL, N. R. Influence of some environmental factors on plasma and urinary 17-hydroxycorticosteroid levels in the rhesus monkey. *American Journal of Physiology,* 1957, **190,** 429.

MASON, J. W., JONES, J. A., RICKETTS, P. T., BRADY, J. V., & TOLLIVER, G. A. Urinary aldosterone and urine volume responses to 72-hr. avoidance sessions in the monkey. *Psychosomatic Medicine,* 1968, **30,** 733. (a)

MASON, J. W., KENION, C. C., COLLINS, D. R., MOUGEY, E. H., JONES, J. A., DRIVER, G. C., BRADY, J. V., & BEER, B. Urinary testosterone response to 72-hr. avoidance sessions in the monkey. *Psychosomatic Medicine,* 1968, **30,** 721. (b)

MASON, J. W., MANGAN, G. F., Jr., BRADY, J. V., CONRAD, D., & RIOCH, D. McK. Concurrent plasma epinephrine, norepinephrine and 17-hydroxycorticosteroid levels during conditioned emotional disturbances in monkeys. *Psychosomatic Medicine,* 1961, **23,** 344. (c)

MASON, J. W., MOUGEY, E. H., BRADY, J. V., & TOLLIVER, G. A. Thyroid (plasma butanol-extractable iodine) response to 72-hr. avoidance sessions in the monkey. *Psychosomatic Medicine,* 1968, **30,** 682. (d)

MASON, J. W., MOUGEY, E., WHERRY, F., COLLINS, D., TAYLOR, E., & WOOL, M. Organization of the multiple hormonal responses during restraining chair adaptation in the monkey. *Program of the Annual Meeting of the Endocrine Society, Bal Harbour, Fla.,* June 1967, 90. (Abstract)

MASON, J. W., NAUTA, W. J. H., BRADY, J. V., ROBINSON, J. A., & SACHAR, E. J. The role of limbic system structures in the regulation of ACTH secretion. *Acta Neurovegetativa (Wien)* 1961, **23,** 4. (e)

MASON, J. W., SACHAR, E. J., FISHMAN, J. R., HAMBURG, D. A., & HANDLON, J. H. Corticosteroid responses to hospital admission. *Archives of General Psychiatry,* 1965, **13,** 1.

MASON, J. W., TAYLOR, E. D., BRADY, J. V., & TOLLIVER, G. A. Urinary estrone, estradiol, and estriol responses to 72-hr. avoidance sessions in the monkey. *Psychosomatic Medicine,* 1968, **30,** 696. (f)

MASON, J. W., TOLSON, W. W., BRADY, J. V., TOLLIVER, G. A., & GILMORE, L. R. I. Urinary epinephrine and norepinephrine responses to 72-hr avoidance sessions in the monkey. *Psychosomatic Medicine,* 1968, **30,** 654. (g)

MASON, J. W., TOLSON, W. W., ROBINSON, J. A., BRADY, J. V., TOLLIVER, G. A., & JOHNSON, T. A. Urinary androsterone, etiocholanolone, and dehydroepiandrosterone responses to 72-hr avoidance sessions in the monkey.

Psychosomatic Research, 1968, **30,** 710. (h)

MASON, J. W., WHERRY, F. E., BRADY, J. V., BEER, B., PENNINGTON, L. L., & GOODMAN, A. C. Plasma insulin response to 72-hr avoidance sessions in the monkey. *Psychosomatic Medicine,* 1968, **30,** 746. (i)

MASON, J. W., WOOL, M. S., MOUGEY, E. H., WHERRY, F. E., COLLINS, D. R., & TAYLOR, E. D. Psychological versus nutritional factors in the effects of "fasting" on hormonal balance. *Program of the Annual Meeting of the American Psychosomatic Society,* Boston, March 1968. (j)

MASON, J. W., WOOL, M. S., WHERRY, F. E., PENNINGTON, L. L., BRADY, J. V., & BEER, B. Plasma growth hormone response to avoidance sessions in the monkey. *Psychosomatic Medicine,* 1968, **30,** 760. (k)

MATSUMOTO, K., BERLET, H. H., BULL, C., & HIMWICH, H. E. Excretion of 17-hydroxycorticosteroids and 17-ketosteroids in relation to schizophrenic symptoms. *Journal of Psychiatric Research,* 1966, **4,** 1.

McCLURE, D. J. The diurnal variation of plasma cortisol levels in depression. *Journal of Psychosomatic Research,* 1966, **10,** 189. (a)

McCLURE, D. J. The effects of antidepressant medication on the diurnal plasma cortisol levels in depressed patients. *Journal of Psychosomatic Research,* 1966, **10,** 197. (b)

McDONALD, R. K., & WEISE, V. K. The excretion of 3-methoxy-4-hydroxymandelic acid in normal and in chronic schizophrenic male subjects: Effect of reserpine and chlorpromazine. *Psychiatric Research,* 1962, **1,** 173.

McKERNS, K. W., & BELL, P. H. The mechanism of action of estrogenic hormones on metabolism. *Recent Progress in Hormone Research,* 1960, **16,** 97.

MEITES, J., NICOLL, C. S., & TALWALKER, P. K. The central nervous system and the secretion and release of prolactin. In A. V. NALBANDOV (Ed.), *Advances in neuroendocrinology.* Urbana: University of Illinois Press, 1963.

MELICK, R. Changes in urinary steroid excretion during examinations. *Australian Annals of Medicine,* 1960, **9,** 200.

MENDELSON, J., KUBZANSKY, P., LEIDERMAN, P. H., WEXLER, D., DUTOIT, C., & SOLOMON, P. Catecholamine excretion and behavior during sensory deprivation. *Archives of General Psychiatry,* 1960, **2,** 147.

METZ, B., SCHAFF, G., & GRIVEL, F. Psychophysiological effects of sleep loss. *16th International Congress of Psychology, Symposium on sleep loss,* Bonn, West Germany, 1960. (Abstract)

MICHAEL, R. P., & GIBBONS, J. L. Interrelationships between the endocrine system and neuropsychiatry. *International Review of Neurobiology,* 1963, **5,** 243.

MILLER, R. E., & MASON, J. W. Changes in 17-hydroxycorticosteroid excretion related to muscular work. In *Symposium on medical aspects of stress in the military climate.* Washington, D.C.: Walter Reed Army Institute of Research, 1964.

MITTLEMAN, A., ROMANOFF, L. P., PINCUS, G., & HOAGLAND, H. Neutral steroid excretion by normal and schizophrenic men. *Journal of Clinical Endocrinology,* 1952, **12,** 831.

MITTELMANN, B. Psychogenic factors and psychotherapy in hyperthyreosis and rapid heart imbalance. *Journal of Nervous and Mental Disease*, 1933, **77,** 465.

MONCRIEF, J. A., WEICHSELBAUM, T. E., & ELMAN, R. Changes in adrenocortical steroid concentration of peripheral plasma following surgery. *Surgical Forum*, 1953, **4,** 469.

MORII, H., FUJITA, T., ORIMO, H., OKINAKA, S., & NAKAO, K. Effect of sympathetic stimulation, epinephrine and phentolamine on recovery from induced hypocalcemia. *Endocrinology*, 1965, **76,** 58.

MULROW, P. J. Neural and other mechanisms regulating aldosterone secretion. In L. MARTINI & W. F. GANONG (Eds.), *Neuroendocrinology*, Vol. 1. New York: Academic, 1966.

MUNCK, A. Steroid concentration and tissue integrity as factors determining the physiological significance of effects of adrenal steroids *in vitro*. *Endocrinology*, 1965, **77,** 356.

MURPHY, C. W., GOFTON, J. P., & CLEGHORN, R. A. Effect of long-range flights on eosinophil level and corticosteroid excretion. *Journal of Aviation Medicine*, 1954, **25,** 242.

NELSON, D. H., & SAMUELS, L. T. A method for the determination of 17-hydroxycorticoids in blood: 17-hydroxycorticosterone in the peripheral circulation. *Journal of Clinical Endocrinology*, 1952, **12,** 519.

NELSON, G. N., MASUDA, M., & HOLMES, T. H. Correlation of behavior and catecholamine metabolite excretion. *Psychosomatic Medicine*, 1966, **28,** 216.

NEUSTADT, R., & HOWARD, L. G. Fluctuations in blood iodine in cyclic psychoses. *American Journal of Psychiatry*, 1942–1943, **99,** 130.

NOBLE, R. L. Physiology of the adrenal cortex. In G. PINCUS & K. V. THIMANN (Eds.), *The hormones*. Vol. 3. New York: Academic, 1955.

PARRY, C. H. (Ed.) *Collections from the unpublished writings of the late Caleb Hillier Parry*. Vol. 1. London: Underwoods, 1825.

PARSONS, E. H., GILDEA, E. F., RONZONI, E., & HULBERT, S. Z. Comparative lymphocytic and biochemical responses of patients with schizophrenia and affective disorders to electroshock, insulin shock and epinephrine. *American Journal of Psychiatry*, 1949, **105,** 573.

PAVLOV, I. P. *Natural science and the brain*, 1909. Translated in I. P. PAVLOV, *Selected works*. Moscow: Foreign Languages Publishing House, 1955.

PECILE, A., & MULLER, E. E. Control of growth hormone secretion. In L. MARTINI & W. F. GANONG (Eds.), *Neuroendocrinology*. Vol. 1. New York: Academic, 1966.

PERSKY, H. Adrenal cortical function in anxious human subjects: Effect of corticotropin (ACTH) on plasma hydrocortisone level and urinary hydroxycorticosteroid excretion. *Archives of Neurology and Psychiatry*, 1957, **78,** 95.

PERSKY, H. Adrenocortical function in anxious human subjects: The disappearance of hydrocortisone from plasma and its metabolic fate. *Journal of Clinical Endocrinology*, 1957, **17,** 760.

PERSKY, H. Adrenocortical function during anxiety. In R. ROESSLER & N. S. GREENFIELD (Eds.), *Physiological correlates of psychological disorders*. Madison: University of Wisconsin Press, 1962.

PERSKY, H., GRINKER, R. R., HAMBURG, D. A., SABSHIN, M. A., KORCHIN, S. J., BASOWITZ, H., & CHEVALIER, J. A. Adrenal cortical function in anxious human subjects: Plasma level and urinary excretion of hydrocortisone. *Archives of Neurology and Psychiatry*, 1956, **76,** 549.

PERSKY, H., GROSZ, H. J., NORTON, J. A., & MCMURTRY, M. Effect of hypnotically-induced anxiety on plasma hydrocortisone level of normal subjects. *Journal of Clinical Endocrinology*, 1959, **19,** 700. (a)

PERSKY, H., HAMBURG, D. A., BASOWITZ, H., GRINKER, R. R., SABSHIN, M., KORCHIN, S. J., HERZ, M., BOARD, F. A., & HEATH, H. A. Relation of emotional responses and changes in plasma hydrocortisone level after stressful interview. *Archives of Neurology and Psychiatry*, 1958, **79,** 434.

PERSKY, H., KORCHIN, S. J., BASOWITZ, H., BOARD, F. A., SABSHIN, M., HAMBURG, D. A., & GRINKER, R. R. Effect of two psychological stresses on adrenocortical function: Studies on anxious and normal subjects. *Archives of Neurology and Psychiatry*, 1959, **81,** 219. (b)

PERSKY, H., MAROC, J., CONRAD, E., & DEN BREEIJEN, A. Blood corticotropin and adrenal weight-maintenance factor levels of anxious patients and normal subjects. *Psychosomatic Medicine*, 1959, **21,** 379. (c)

PINCUS, G. Studies of the role of the adrenal cortex in the stress of human subjects. *Recent Progress in Hormone Research*, 1947, **1,** 123.

PINCUS, G. Adrenal cortex function in stress. *Annals of the New York Academy of Sciences*, 1949, **50,** 635.

PINCUS, G., & ELMADJIAN, F. The lymphocyte response to heat stress in normal and psychotic subjects. *Journal of Clinical Endocrinology*, 1946, **6,** 295.

PINCUS, G., & HOAGLAND, H. Steroid excretion and the stress of flying. *Journal of Aviation Medicine*, 1943, **14,** 173.

PINCUS, G., & HOAGLAND, H. Adrenal cortical responses to stress in normal men and in those with personality disorders: Part II. Analysis of the pituitary-adrenal mechanism in man. *American Journal of Psychiatry*, 1950, **106,** 651.

PINCUS, G., HOAGLAND, H., FREEMAN, H., ELMADJIAN, F., & ROMANOFF, L. P. A study of pituitary-adrenocortical function in normal and psychotic men. *Psychosomatic Medicine*, 1949, **11,** 74. (a)

PINCUS, G., SCHENKER, V., ELMADJIAN, F., & HOAGLAND, H. Responsivity of schizophrenic men to pituitary adrenocorticotrophin. *Psychosomatic Medicine*, 1949, **11,** 146. (b)

PI-SUNER, A. *The whole and its parts: Classics of biology*. New York: Philosophical Library, 1955.

PRICE, D. B., THALER, M., & MASON, J. W. Preoperative emotional states and adrenal cortical activity: Studies on cardiac and pulmonary surgery patients. *Archives of Neurology and Psychiatry,* 1957, **77,** 646.

PRYCE, I. G. The relationship between 17-hydroxycortico-steroid excretion and glucose utilization in depressions. *British Journal of Psychiatry,* 1964, **110,** 90.

PSCHEIDT, G. R., BERLET, H. H., BULL, C., SPAIDE, J., & HIMWICH, H. E. Excretion of catecholamines and exacerbation of symptoms in schizophrenic patients. *Journal of Psychiatric Research,* 1964, **2,** 163.

PUNTRIANO, G., & MEITES, J. The effects of continuous light or darkness on thyroid function in mice. *Endocrinology,* 1951, **48,** 217.

RANDLE, P. J. Endocrine control of metabolism. *Annual Review of Physiology,* 1963, **25,** 291.

REDGATE, E. S., & GELLHORN, E. Nature of sympathetico-adrenal discharge under conditions of excitation of central autonomic structures. *American Journal of Physiology,* 1953, **174,** 475.

REGAN, P. F., & REILLY, J. Circulating epinephrine and norepinephrine in changing emotional states. *Journal of Nervous and Mental Disease,* 1958, **127,** 12.

REICHLIN, S. Peripheral thyroxine metabolism in patients with psychiatric and neurological diseases. *Archives of General Psychiatry,* 1959, **1,** 434.

REICHLIN, S. Control of thyrotropic hormone secretion. In L. MARTINI & W. F. GANONG (Eds.), *Neuroendocrinology.* Vol. 1. New York: Academic, 1966. (a)

REICHLIN, S. Regulation of somatotrophic hormone secretion. In G. W. HARRIS & B. T. DONOVAN (Eds.), *The pituitary gland.* Vol. 2. Berkeley: University of California Press, 1966. (b)

REISS, M. Correlations between changes in mental states and thyroid activity after different forms of treatment. *Journal of Mental Science,* 1954, **100,** 687.

REISS, M. (Ed.) *Psychoendocrinology.* New York: Grune & Stratton, 1958.

REISS, M., HEMPHILL, R. E., GORDON, J. J., & COOK, E. R. Regulation of urinary steroid excretion: 2. Spontaneous changes in the pattern of daily excretion in mental patients. *Biochemical Journal,* 1949, **45,** 574.

REISS, M., HEMPHILL, R. E., MAGGS, R., SMITH, S., HAIGH, C. P., & REISS, J. M. Thyroid activity in mental patients: Evaluation by radioactive tracer methods. *British Medical Journal,* 1951, **1,** 1181.

RENOLD, A. E., & ASHMORE, J. Metabolic effects of adrenal corticosteroids. In R. H. WILLIAMS (Ed.), *Diabetes.* New York: Hoeber, 1960.

RENOLD, A. E., QUIGLEY, T. B., KENNARD, H. E., & THORN, G. W. Reaction of the adrenal cortex to physical and emotional stress in college oarsmen. *New England Journal of Medicine,* 1951, **244,** 754.

RENTON, G. H., & WEIL-MALHERBE, H. Adrenaline and noradrenaline in human plasma during natural sleep. *Journal of Physiology,* 1956, **131,** 170.

REY, J. H., WILLCOX, D. R., GIBBONS, J. L., TAIT, H., & LEWIS, D. J. Serial biochemical and endocrine investigations

in recurrent mental illness. *Journal of Psychosomatic Research,* 1961, **5,** 155.

RIKIMARU, J. Emotion and endocrine activities. *Psychological Bulletin,* 1925, **22,** 205.

RITTER, W. E. *The unity of the organism or the organismal conception of life.* Boston: Badger, 1919.

RIZZO, N. D., FOX, H. M., LAIDLAW, J. C., & THORN, G. W. Concurrent observations of behavior changes and of adrenocortical variations in a cyclothymic patient during a period of 12 months. *Annals of Internal Medicine,* 1954, **41,** 798.

ROMANOFF, L. P., RODRIGUEZ, R. M., SEELYE, J. M., & PINCUS, G. Determination of tetrahydrocortisol and tetrahydrocortisone in the urine of normal and schizophrenic men. *Journal of Clinical Endocrinology,* 1957, **17,** 777.

ROSE, R. M., POE, R. O., & MASON, J. W. Psychological state and body size as determinants of 17-OHCS excretion. *Archives of Internal Medicine,* 1968, **121,** 406.

RUBIN, R. T., & MANDELL, A. J. Adrenal cortical activity in pathological emotional states: A review. *American Journal of Psychiatry,* 1966, **123,** 387.

RUBIN, R. T., YOUNG, W. M., & CLARK, B. R. 17-hydroxycorticosteroid and vanillylmandelic acid excretion in a rapidly cycling manic-depressive. *Psychosomatic Medicine,* 1968, **30,** 162.

SABSHIN, M., HAMBURG, D. A., GRINKER, R. R., PERSKY, H., BASOWITZ, H., KORCHIN, S. J., & CHEVALIER, J. A. Significance of preexperimental studies in the psychosomatic laboratory. *Archives of Neurology and Psychiatry,* 1957, **78,** 207.

SACHAR, E. J. Corticosteroids in depressive illness: A reevaluation of control issues and the literature. *Archives of General Psychiatry,* 1967, **17,** 544.

SACHAR, E. J., COBB, J. C., & SHOR, R. E. Plasma cortisol changes during hypnotic trance. *Archives of General Psychiatry,* 1966, **14,** 482.

SACHAR, E. J., FISHMAN, J. R., & MASON, J. W. Influence of hypnotic trance on plasma 17-hydroxycorticosteroid concentration. *Psychosomatic Medicine,* 1965, **27,** 330.

SACHAR, E. J., HARMATZ, J., BERGEN, H., & COHLER, J. Corticosteroid responses to milieu therapy of chronic schizophrenics. *Archives of General Psychiatry,* 1966, **15,** 310.

SACHAR, E. J., MACKENZIE, J. M., & BINSTOCK, W. A. Corticosteroid responses to psychotherapy of depressions: I. Evaluations during confrontation of loss. *Archives of General Psychiatry,* 1967, **16,** 461.

SACHAR, E. J., MACKENZIE, J. M., BINSTOCK, W. A., & MACK, J. E. Corticosteroid responses to psychotherapy of depressions: II. Further clinical and physiological implications. *Psychosomatic Medicine,* 1968, **30,** 23.

SACHAR, E. J., MASON, J. W., FISHMAN, J. R., HAMBURG, D. A., & HANDLON, J. H. Corticosteroid excretion in normal young adults living under "basal" conditions. *Psychosomatic Medicine,* 1965, **27,** 435.

SACHAR, E. J., MASON, J. W., KOLMER, H. S., Jr., & ARTISS,

K. L. Psychoendocrine aspects of acute schizophrenic reactions. *Psychosomatic Medicine,* 1963, **25,** 510.

SAWYER, W. H. Neurohypophyseal secretions and their origin. In A. V. NALBANDOV (Ed.), *Advances in neuro-endocrinology.* Urbana: University of Illinois Press, 1963.

SAWYER, W. H., & MILLS, E. Control of vasopressin secretion. In L. MARTINI & W. F. GANONG (Eds.), *Neuroendocrinology.* Vol. 1. New York: Academic, 1968.

SAYERS, G. The adrenal cortex and homeostasis. *Psysiological Review,* 1950, **30,** 241.

SCHILDKRAUT, J. J., KLERMAN, G. L., HAMMOND, R., & FRIEND, D. G. Excretion of 3-methoxy-4-hydroxymandelic acid (VMA) in depressed patients treated with antidepressant drugs. *Journal of Psychiatric Research,* 1964, **2,** 257.

SCHMID, V. E., SUSS, G., ZICHA, L., SUSS, E., & WEISS, P. Influence of emotional stress connected with dental treatment on reactions of sympathoadrenergic system. *Arzneimittelforschung,* 1964, **14,** 852.

SCHOTZ, M. C., & PAGE, I. H. Effect of norepinephrine and epinephrine on nonesterified fatty acid concentration in plasma. *Proceedings of the Society for Experimental Biology and Medicine,* 1959, **101,** 624.

SCHWARTZ, T. B., & SHIELDS, D. R. Emotional tension and excretion of corticoids and creatinine. *American Journal of Medicine,* 1954, **16,** 608.

SCHWARTZ, T. B., & SHIELDS, D. R. Urinary excretion of formaldehydogenic steroids and creatinine: A reflection of emotional tension. *Psychosomatic Medicine,* 1956, **18,** 159.

SELYE, H. Thymus and adrenals in the response of the organism to injuries and intoxications. *British Journal of Experimental Pathology,* 1936, **17,** 234. (a)

SELYE, H. A syndrome produced by diverse nocuous agents. *Nature,* 1936, **138,** 32. (b)

SELYE, H. The general adaptation syndrome and the diseases of adaptation. *Journal of Clinical Endocrinology,* 1946, **6,** 117.

SELYE, H. *Stress.* Montreal: ACTA, 1950.

SHANAN, J., BRZEZINSKI, A., SULMAN, F., & SHARON, M. Active coping behavior, anxiety, and cortical steroid excretion in the prediction of transient amenorrhea. *Behavioral Science,* 1965, **10,** 461.

SHANDS, H. C., & FINESINGER, J. E. Lymphocytes in the psychoneuroses: Preliminary observations. *American Journal of Psychiatry,* 1948, **105,** 277.

SHANNON, I. L., ISBELL, G. M., & HESTER, W. R. Stress in dental patients: The effect of local anesthetic administration upon serum free 17-hydroxycorticosteroid patterns. *U.S. Air Force School of Aerospace Medicine,* 1962, **62-59.**

SHANNON, I. L., ISBELL, G. M., PRIGMORE, J. R., & HESTER, W. R. Stress in dental patients: The serum free 17-hydroxycorticosteroid response in routinely appointed patients undergoing simple exodontia. *U.S. Air Force School of Aerospace Medicine,* 1962, **62-27.**

SHANNON, I. L., PRIGMORE, J. R., HESTER, W. R., McCALL, C. M., & ISBELL, G. M. Stress patterns in dental patients: Local anesthesia and simple exodontia. *U.S. Air Force School of Aerospace Medicine,* 1960, **61-23.**

SHANNON, I. L., PRIGMORE, J. R., HESTER, W. R., McCALL, C. M., & ISBELL, G. M. Stress patterns in dental patients: I. Serum free 17-hydroxycorticosteroid, sodium and potassium in subjects undergoing local anesthesia and simple exodontic procedures. *Journal of Oral Surgery,* 1961, **19,** 486.

SHANNON, I. L., SZMYD, L., & PRIGMORE, J. R. Stress in dental patients: Serum and urine 17-hydroxycorticosteroid response in impaction patients. *U.S. Air Force School of Aerospace Medicine,* 1962, **62-59.**

SHAPIRO, S., GELLER, E., & EIDUSON, S. Neonatal adrenal cortical response to stress and vasopressin. *Proceedings of the Society for Experimental Biology and Medicine,* 1962, **109,** 937.

SHENKIN, H. A. The effect of pain on the diurnal pattern of plasma corticoid levels. *Neurology,* 1964, **14,** 1112.

SHERRINGTON, C. *The integrative action of the nervous system* (2nd ed.). New Haven: Yale University Press, 1947.

SHINFUKU, N., OMURA, M., & KAYANO, M. Catechol amine excretion in manic depressive psychosis. *Yonago Acta Medica,* 1961, **5,** 109.

SHOLITON, L. J., WOHL, T. H., & WERK, E. E., Jr. The correlation of 2 psychological variables, anxiety and hostility, with adrenocortical function in patients with lung cancer. *Cancer,* 1963, **16,** 223.

SIDMAN, M., MASON, J. W., BRADY, J. V., & THACH, J., Jr. Quantitative relations between avoidance behavior and pituitary-adrenal cortical activity. *Journal of Experimental Analysis of Behavior,* 1962, **5,** 353.

SILVERMAN, A. J., & COHEN, S. I. Affect and vascular correlates to catechol amines. *Psychiatric Research Reports of the American Psychiatric Association,* 1960, **12,** 16.

SILVERMAN, A. J., COHEN, S. I., SHMAVONIAN, B. M., & KIRSHNER, N. Catechol amines in psychophysiologic studies. *Recent Advances in Biology and Psychiatry,* 1961, **3,** 104.

SIMPSON, G. M., CRANSWICK, E. H., & BLAIR, J. H. Thyroid indices in chronic schizophrenia. *Journal of Nervous and Mental Disease,* 1963, **137,** 582.

SIMPSON, G. M., CRANSWICK, E. H., & BLAIR, J. H. Thyroid indices in chronic schizophrenia: II. *Journal of Nervous and Mental Disease,* 1964, **138,** 581.

SLOANE, R. B., SAFFRAN, M., & CLEGHORN, R. A. Autonomic and adrenal responsivity in psychiatric patients: Effect of methacholine and corticotropin. *Archives of Neurology and Psychiatry,* 1958, **79,** 549.

SMITH, R. W., GAEBLER, O. H., & LONG, C. N. H. (Eds.) *The hypophyseal growth hormone: Nature and actions.* New York: McGraw-Hill, 1954.

SOURKES, T. L., SLOANE, R. B., & DRUJAN, B. D. Pyrocatechol amine (catecholamine) metabolism and effects of electro-convulsive therapy. *Archives of Neurology and Psychiatry,* 1957, **78,** 204.

SOURKES, T. L., SLOANE, R. B., & DRUJAN, B. D. Relation between the rate of excretion of pyrocatecholamines in the urine and the outcome of electroshock therapy. *Confinia Neurologica,* 1958, **18,** 299.

SOUTHWICK, C. H., & BLAND, V. P. Effect of population density on adrenal glands and reproductive organs of CFW mice. *American Journal of Physiology,* 1959, **197,** 111.

STARR, P., PETIT, D. W., CHANEY, A. L., ROLLMAN, H., AIKEN, J. B., JAMIESON, B., & KLING, I. Clinical experience with the blood protein-bound iodine determination as a routine procedure. *Journal of Clinical Endocrinology,* 1950, **10,** 1237.

STEIN, M., RONZONI, E., & GILDEA, E. F. Physiological responses to heat stress and ACTH of normal and schizophrenic subjects. *American Journal of Psychiatry,* 1951, **108,** 450.

STENBACK, A., JAKOBSON, T., & RIMON, R. Depression and anxiety ratings in relation to the excretion of urinary total 17-OHCS in depressive subjects. *Journal of Psychosomatic Research,* 1966, **9,** 355.

STEVENS, J. D., & DUNN, A. L. Thyroid function in mental diseases. *Diseases of the Nervous System,* 1958, **19,** 338.

STEWART, G. N., & ROGOFF, J. M. The alleged relation of the epinephrin secretion of the adrenals to certain experimental hyperglycemias. *American Journal of Physiology,* 1917, **44,** 543.

STEWART, G. N., & ROGOFF, J. M. The average epinephrin output in cats and dogs. *American Journal of Physiology,* 1923, **66,** 235.

STOLL, W. A., & BRACK, K. E. Diagnostische und therapeutische Erfahrungen an schilddrusengestorten Anstaltspatienten. *Psychiatria Neurologia,* 1957, **133,** 167.

STROM-OLSEN, R., & WEIL-MALHERBE, H. Humoral changes in manic-depressive psychosis with particular reference to the excretion of catechol amines in urine. *Journal of Mental Science,* 1958, **104,** 696.

SUWA, N., YAMASHITA, I., OWADA, H., SHINOHARA, S., & NAKAZAWA, A. Psychic state and adrenocortical function: A psychophysiologic study of emotion. *Journal of Nervous and Mental Disease,* 1962, **134,** 268.

TAINTER, M. L., TULLAR, B. F., & LUDUENA, F. P. Levoarterenol. *Science,* 1948, **107,** 39.

TALAAT, M., HABIB, Y. A., & HABIB, M. The effect of testosterone on the carbohydrate metabolism in normal subjects. *Archives of International Pharmacodynamics,* 1957, **111,** 215.

TATAI, K., MORI, Y., & ITO, K. Response of the pituitary-adrenocortical system to mental strain in healthy women. *Japanese Journal of Physiology,* 1951, **1,** 316.

TAYLOR, A. N., & FARRELL, G. Effects of brain stem lesions on aldosterone and cortisol secretion. *Endocrinology,* 1962, **70,** 556.

TECCE, J. J., FRIEDMAN, S. B., & MASON, J. W. Anxiety, defensiveness and 17-hydroxycorticosteroid excretion. *Journal of Nervous and Mental Disease,* 1965, **141,** 549.

TEPPERMAN, J. *Metabolic and endocrine physiology.* Chicago: Yearbook Medical Publishers, 1962.

THIESSEN, D. D., ZOLMAN, J. F., & RODGERS, D. A. Relation between adrenal weight, brain cholinesterase activity, and hole-in-wall behavior of mice under different living conditions. *Journal of Comparative and Physiological Psychology,* 1962, **55,** 186.

THOMASSON, B. Studies of the content of 17-hydroxycorticosteroids and its diurnal rhythm in the plasma of surgical patients. *Scandinavian Journal of Clinical and Laboratory Investigation,* 1959, **11** (Suppl. 42).

THORN, G. W. General discussion. In G. E. W. WOLSTEN-HOLME & C. M. O'CONNOR (Eds.), *Metabolic effects of adrenal hormones* (Ciba Foundation Study Group No. 6). Boston: Little, Brown, 1960.

THORN, G. W., JENKINS, D., & LAIDLAW, J. C. The adrenal response to stress in man. *Recent Progress in Hormone Research,* 1953, **8,** 171.

THORN, G. W., JENKINS, D., LAIDLAW, J. C., GOETZ, F. C., & REDDY, W. Response of the adrenal cortex to stress in man. *Transactions of the Association of American Physicians,* 1953, **66,** 48.

TINGLEY, J. O., MORRIS, A. W., & HILL, S. R. Studies on the diurnal variation and response to emotional stress of the thyroid gland. *Clinical Research,* 1958, **6,** 134.

TOLSON, W. W., MASON, J. W., SACHAR, E. J., HAMBURG, D. A., HANDLON, J. H., & FISHMAN, J. R. Urinary catecholamine responses associated with hospital admission in normal human subjects. *Journal of Psychosomatic Research,* 1965, **8,** 365.

TUI, C., RILEY, E., COLUMBUS, P., & ORR, A. 17-hydroxycorticosteroid levels in the peripheral blood of schizophrenic patients. *Journal of Clinical and Experimental Psychopathology,* 1956, **17,** 276.

ULVEDAL, F., SMITH, W. R., & WELCH, B. E. Steroid and catecholamine studies on pilots during prolonged experiments in a space cabin simulation. *Journal of Applied Physiology,* 1963, **18,** 1257.

UNO, T. Effect of general excitement and of fighting on some ductless glands of male albino rats. *American Journal of Physiology,* 1922, **61,** 203.

VENNING, E. H., DYRENFURTH, I., & BECK, J. C. Effect of anxiety upon aldosterone excretion in man. *Journal of Clinical Endocrinology,* 1957, **17,** 1005.

VOGT, M. The effect of emotion and of β-tetrahydronaphthylamine on the adrenal cortex of the rat. *Journal of Physiology,* 1951, **114,** 465.

VOLPE, R., VALE, J., & JOHNSTON, M. W. The effects of certain physical and emotional tensions and strains on fluctuations in the level of serum protein-bound iodine. *Journal of Clinical Endocrinology,* 1960, **20,** 415.

WADESON, R. W., MASON, J. W., HAMBURG, D. A., & HANDLON, J. H. Plasma and urinary 17-OH-CS responses to motion pictures. *Archives of General Psychiatry,* 1963, **9,** 146.

WALLERSTEIN, R. S., HOLZMAN, P. S., VOTH, H. M., & UHR, N. Thyroid "hot spots": A psychophysiological study. *Psychosomatic Medicine,* 1965, **27,** 508.

WEIL-MALHERBE, H. The concentration of adrenaline in human plasma and its relation to mental activity. *Journal of Mental Science,* 1955, **101,** 733.

WEIL-MALHERBE, H., & BONE, A. D. The chemical estimation of adrenaline-like substances in blood. *Biochemical Journal,* 1952, **51,** 311.

WEIL-MALHERBE, H., & BONE, A. D. The fluorimetric estimation of adrenaline and noradrenaline in plasma. *Biochemical Journal,* 1957, **67,** 65.

WELCH, B. L. Adrenals of deer as indicators of population conditions for purposes of management. *Proceedings First National Deer Disease Symposium,* Athens, Ga., February 13–15, University of Georgia Center for Continuing Education Publication, 1962.

WHITE, W. A. The unity of the organism. *Psychoanalytical Review,* 1920, **7,** 71.

WILLCOX, D. R. The serial study of adrenal steroid excretion. *Journal of Psychosomatic Research,* 1959, **4,** 106.

WINEGRAD, A. I. Endocrine effects on adipose tissue metabolism. *Vitamins and Hormones* (New York), 1962, **20,** 142.

WITTKOWER, E. D., SHERINGER, W., & BAY, E. Über affektivsomatische Veranderungen: Zur affectiven Beeinflussbarkeit des Blutjodspiegels. *Klinische Wissenschraft,* 1932, **11,** 1186.

WOLFF, C. T., FRIEDMAN, S. B., HOFER, M. A., & MASON, J. W. Relationship between psychological defenses and mean urinary 17-OH-CS excretion rates: I. A predictive study of parents of fatally ill children. *Psychosomatic Medicine,* 1964, **26,** 576.

WOLFF, C. T., HOFER, M. A., & MASON, J. W. Relationship between psychological defenses and mean urinary 17-OH-CS excretion rates: II. Methodological and theoretical considerations. *Psychosomatic Medicine,* 1964, **26,** 592.

YEAKEL, E. H., & RHOADES, R. P. A comparison of the body and endocrine gland (adrenal, thyroid and pituitary) weights of emotional and nonemotional rats. *Endocrinology,* 1941, **28,** 337.

ZIEGLER, L. H., & LEVINE, B. S. The influence of emotional reactions on basal metabolism. *American Journal of Medical Science,* 1925, **169,** 68.

ZUCKERMAN, M., PERSKY, H., HOPKINS, T. R., MURTAUGH, T., BASU, G. K., & SCHILLING, M. Comparison of stress effects of perceptual and social isolation. *Archives of General Psychiatry,* 1966, **14,** 356.

ZUIDEMA, G. D., SILVERMAN, A. J., COHEN, S. I., & GOODALL, McC. Catechol amine and psychological correlates of vascular responses. *New England Journal of Medicine,* 1957, **256,** 976.

William H. Rickles, Jr.

CENTRAL NERVOUS SYSTEM SUBSTRATES OF SOME PSYCHOPHYSIOLOGICAL VARIABLES

2

Only a moment's reflection is required to realize that, during the past 200 years of the scientific study of physiology, the function of every system of the body has been found to be at least partially regulated and integrated with other systems by the brain. This control may be exerted directly via the peripheral nervous system or may have a more indirect pathway through the hypothalamus and/or medulla via the hormonal transmitters emanating from the pituitary. More recently, Sherrington has also conceptualized a primary function of the brain as "the mover of muscles," but even the ancients recognized the brain as being the organ of the mind. That these three principal functions of the brain, which we term *homeostasing, moving,* and *minding,* are interdependent and covarient is axiomatic; but how they are interrelated has been a classical puzzle for theologians, philosophers, and scientists. Neurophysiologists and neurologists have properly attacked the problems of homeostasing. Physiological psychologists aided by neurophysiologists and behaviorists have attempted to describe the natural laws governing moving functions. Phenomenologically oriented psychologists and philosophers have attempted to unravel the mysteries of the brain's minding behavior. To the psychophysiologist and the allied clinical field of psychosomatic medicine is left the Herculean feat of describing the interrelationships of these brain functions.

Many psychophysiologists come to their work well equipped

with the conceptual and factual tools provided by investigators of minding functions (i.e., phenomenologists) and moving functions (i.e., behaviorists); however, the latter use a "black box" conceptualization of the brain, even when homeostasing functions are described. It is my hope that this chapter will encourage the new group of psychophysiologists to take the lid off of the black box concepts of the brain and avail themselves of the "hows" of homeostasing and moving provided by neurophysiology to assist them in thinking about the "whats" of homeostasing, moving, and minding interactions.

Thus, in the extreme, all of neurophysiology is relevant to psychophysiology, but, at least during the present, some neurophysiological data are more relevant than others. Accordingly, we have chosen to concentrate on the central regulation of the autonomic nervous system (ANS) and the neurophysiological substrates of behavior. It became apparent that these topics were too ambitious when the MEDLARS[1] search of the literature from January 1964 through September 1967 for our subject retrieved almost 1500 citations. As a result of this considerable motivation, we decided to limit our task to describing two autonomic systems and to integrating neuroanatomical studies of behavior with these descriptions, as appropriate.

Central control of the cardiovascular system was chosen because of its primacy among homeostatic brain functions and the ease and frequency with which the psychophysiologists use the several available cardiovascular parameters. The electrodermal phenomenon (galvanic skin reflex, GSR) was chosen as a second ANS parameter because of the popularity it enjoys as a very reactive psychophysiological measure. We also wish to highlight the relative dearth of modern data concerning the central nervous control of phasically reactive electrodermal phenomena. The neurophysiology of behavior is such an enormous field that we have chosen to limit our discussion to studies directly referable to the physiological system under consideration. We concur with Lacey (1967, pp. 14–42), who writes of the need for new concepts and

[1]MEDLARS Search Nos. 093740 and 020608, *Neurophysiological Correlates of Psychophysiology*, National Library of Medicine, Washington, D.C.

theories in psychophysiology that are more congruent with modern neurophysiological knowledge and provide multidimensional concepts for organizing psychophysiological research theories. It is our hope that this chapter will provide further stimulus in this direction.

NEUROANATOMY

Although the autonomic nervous system (ANS) was first conceived as being separate and autonomous from the brain and spinal cord (Brazier, 1959, pp. 1–58), a prejudice that persists despite a long history of evidence to the contrary, now it is clear that the central nervous system (CNS) exerts a powerful influence on both homeostatic and reactive ANS behavior. The levels of central autonomic regulations, i.e., the spinal cord, brain stem, hypothalamus, and limbic systems, may be conceived in terms of the complexity of the regulation provided at each level. Thus the cord and brain stem subsume reflexive and homeostatic responses, respectively. The hypothalamus seems to integrate the various vegetative and somatic responses around gross, innate, emotional responses such as fear, anger, hunger, thirst, and sex; while the limbic system may be thought of as integrating emotional and vegetative responses with the learning process and with evoked, learned behavior. That the non-limbic cortex and basal ganglia can evoke autonomic activity is clear, but the functional significance of these responses is still obscure. Indeed, this outline of structure and function is simplistic in the extreme but it does provide some framework for thinking about these systems.

Two of these levels of integration, the hypothalamus and the limbic system, are comprised of several brain structures that have multiple and complex interconnections. Hence, a summary of the neuroanatomy of the hypothalamus and limbic systems is presented to provide a topographical orientation and reference for the chapter. Several reference works were used and may be consulted for greater detail (Adey, Dunlop, & Sunderland, 1958; Crosby, Humphrey, & Lauer, 1962, p. 392; Doty, 1967, pp. 125–143; Glasser, Perez-Reyes, & Tippet, 1964; Mitchell, 1953; Pribram, Lennox, & Dunsmore, 1950; Solinsky, 1964; and Wang, 1964).

The Limbic System

Limbic cortex The limbic cortex, which includes the temporal-insular, orbitofrontal, cingulate and retrosplenal cortex, has been divided by Doty (1967) into four systems on the basis of thalamic projection nuclei and the afferent connections of these nuclei:

1. The *hippocampal gyrus* (allocortex) receives no thalamic projections and serves as the primary afferent pathway to the hippocampus.
2. The *orbitofrontal cortex* receives fibers from the dorsomedial nucleus of the thalamus. This nucleus receives input from the piriform cortex, a major olfactory relay station; in primates, the dorsomedial nucleus receives afferents from the fornix system.
3. The *insular cortex* receives fibers from the ventral anterior nucleus, which in turn has input predominantly from the globus pallidus.
4. The *cingulate gyrus* receives afferents from the anterior thalamic nucleus, which receives heavy innervation from the medial mammillary nucleus by way of the mammillothalamic tract.

A large tract of fibers parallels the circle of limbic cortex and serves as its major output and associated pathway. Ventrally, this system is called the uncinate fasciculus, which forms a reciprocal pathway between orbitofrontal and insular temporal cortex. The main system, called the *cingulum,* runs an arching course within the white matter of the *cingulate gyrus.* This system arises in the prefrontal area (exclusive of the orbital cortex) and projects predominantly in an inferior caudal direction, although fibers run in both directions. Axons from cingulate cortex cells frequently branch when they enter the cingulum and send one collateral rostrally into the septal area or the striatum and the other caudally. A large number of cingulum fibers reach the entorhinal and subicular areas, which project to the hippocampus.

The cingulate cortices of the two hemispheres are connected via the *corpus callosum,* while the temporal cortices are joined by fibers passing through the *anterior commissure.* The temporal cortex also projects to the amygdala and by way of the *fornix,* to the lateral septal nucleus. The limbic cortex sends efferents to corresponding thalamic projection nuclei, as well as to the basal ganglia.

Hippocampal system The *cornu ammonia* is a curving strip of palisading neurons with apical dendrites projecting toward the center of the hippocampus. These precisely aligned cells are divided into four fields designated CA_1, CA_2, etc., because of morphological differences of the cells. The cells in CA_1 and CA_2 are the largest; they send other collaterals which end on the apical dendrites of CA_3 and CA_4 pyramidal cells. Three major efferent pathways from the hippocampus include: (a) a diffuse pathway to the adjacent neocortex, (b) the *hippocampal commissure* (*psalterium*) connecting the two hippocampi, and (c) the *fornix,* composed of hippocampal fibers passing by way of the *alveus* and *fimbria* to join fibers from the hippocampal gyrus descending into the septal area and hypothalamus. The septal projection of the fornix splits around the anterior commissure to form the *precommissural fornix* and passes into the septal and preoptic areas. The *postcommissural fornix* continues back through the hypothalamus into the *mammillary bodies,* and beyond into the central gray.

The alveus, fimbria, and fornix are all in direct contact with cerebral spinal fluid, since these structures form the ventromedial wall of the lateral ventricle. Not all fibers in the fornix are efferent. In man and other species, bundles of fibers from the area stria and the cingulate area pass through the corpus callosum to the dorsal fornix. The destination of these fibers is not precisely known but many pass to the septal area and hippocampus. The input pathways to the hippocampus are complex and not fully defined. In man, the *entorhinal cortex* provides the major source of afferent input. The entorhinal cortex (hippocampal gyrus) has connections with the parietal, occipital, and temporal lobes and thus receives general somatic visual, auditory, gustatory, and olfactory impulses.

The *mammillary bodies,* greatly enlarged in man, send fibers via the *mammillothalamic tract* to the anterior thalamic nucleus and thence to the cingulate cortex. The latter projects via the cingulate cortex to the hippocampal gyrus, and thus the Papez circuit is formed: hippocampus—fornix—mammillary body—anterior thalamic nucleus—cingulate cortex—cingulum—hippocampal gyrus—hippocampus. Doty (1967, pp. 125–143) warns that self-sustaining or reverberating activity in this circuit is unlikely, since the topographic projections of the pathways are too complex to permit simple avalanching activity.

The amygdala Within the *amygdala* exist over a dozen nuclei, which may be divided into two groups on the basis of embryological and comparative anatomical studies. The phylogenetically older of these groups, the *corticomedial* or *anteromedial group,* is comprised of the medial, cortical, and central nuclei. The *basolateral division,* comprised of the pars medialis parvocellularis, pars lateralis magnocellularis, and the lateral nuclei, first appears in reptiles and forms the major component in man. The projections of the *olfactory* tract onto the amygdala are confined to the anteromedial portion; it is primarily from this division that the fibers of the *stria terminalis* are drawn and project to the septal, preoptic, and hypothalamic areas. Nauta (1962) has described connections of the amygdala with the part of the dorsomedial thalamic nucleus that projects to the orbitofrontal cortex. The basolateral division contributes few fibers to the stria terminalis but does project widely by way of the connections with the hippocampal gyrus. Fibers from this division interconnect with the contralateral amygdala through the anterior commissure and may project directly to the preoptic and anterior hypothalamic areas by the *longitudinal association bundle.* In man, fibers from basolateral nuclei have been described passing to frontal and temporal cortex; Crosby, Humphrey, and Lauer (1962, p. 392) consider the connections of the basolateral group to resemble cortex more than the remainder of the amygdaloid complex. It is generally agreed, however, that the connections of the basolateral division are poorly known, and hence must be more complex and probably more related to contiguous structures such as other parts of the amygdala, hippocampus, hippocampal gyrus, and temporal cortex.

The habenula The *epithalamus* is formed by the *habenula, epiphysis* (pineal body), and the *posterior commissure.* The epithalamus resides in the posterior wall of the third ventricle above the level of the cerebral aqueduct. The habenula of the two sides contain two nuclei, the medial and lateral habenular nuclei, and the sides are connected by the short *habenula commissure* lying just rostral to the epiphysis. The afferent connections of the habenula arise chiefly from the limbic structures, i.e., the septal area, preoptic area, hippocampus, anterior thalamic nucleus, and basal ganglia; they arrive via the *stria medullaris thalami.* The efferent pathways are the *fasciculus retroflexus* and *habenal-peduncular tract.* The latter terminates in the *interpeduncular nucleus* located in interpeduncula fossa of the midbrain. The interpeduncular nucleus sends fibers to the tegmentum, particularly the central gray, and thus provides a pathway for limbic influence into the midbrain reticular formation. This area is relatively underdeveloped in man and has not been studied well in any species.

The rhinencephalon (basal forebrain) The *olfactory bulb, olfactory tract, olfactory trigone,* and *olfactory stria* are the only parts of the brain concerned exclusively with smell. In the past, the term "rhinencephalon" has been essentially synonymous with the limbic system; however, the realization that most limbic structures are equally well developed in anosmatic animals (cetaceans and birds), which lack olfactory input, has required a reconsideration of the role of the limbic system in olfaction. Phylogenetic observations leave no doubt that olfaction plays an important role in both feeding, fight-flight, and sexual behavior. Although in man the sense of smell no longer enjoys the primacy it holds in lower animals (insurance companies will not compensate for the loss of smell), the strong emotional associations elicitable by odors bear witness to the phylogenetic origins of the CNS areas concerned with emotional behavior.

The olfactory tract originates in the olfactory bulb and passes along the olfactory groove, separating the medial gyrus rectus from the lateral frontal gyrus of the orbital cortex. The olfactory tract enters the olfactory trigone and divides into medial and lateral stria. The lateral fibers spread diffusely into the *prepiriform* and *piriform cortex,* the corticomedial nucleus of the amygdala, and the *lateral anterior perforated substance.* The smaller, medial band of fibers cross in the anterior limb of the anterior commissure to the contralateral olfactory bulb and also to the *medial septal nucleus, nucleus of the diagonal band,* and *medial anterior perforated substance.*

The anterior perforated substance, also known as the *area olfactoria,* is "perforated" by a dense infiltration of small blood vessels and receives its major afferent supply from the septal area. Efferents from this area form a major component of the *median forebrain bundle,* and also project into the piriform and entorhinal cortex, medial septal nucleus, and olfactory bulb. From the posterior portion arises the *diagonal band of Broca,* which continues into the septal area and *subcallosal gyrus.*

The nuclei of the diagonal band are also continuous with the globus pallidus. The basal ganglia are further related to the limbic system in this region by the *nucleus accumbens septi,* which is a continuation of the caudate nucleus.

The septal area occupies the posterior portion of the medial surface of the frontal lobe. It is comprised of the *subcallosal gyrus* and *par-olfactory area.* The subcallosal gyrus is a narrow, short gyrus, closely applied to the inferior aspect of the rostrum by the corpus callosum. Inferiorly, the subcallosal sulcus separates it from the par-olfactory area. This area is prominent in lower animals but is rudimentary in man. The septal nuclei, nucleus of the diag-

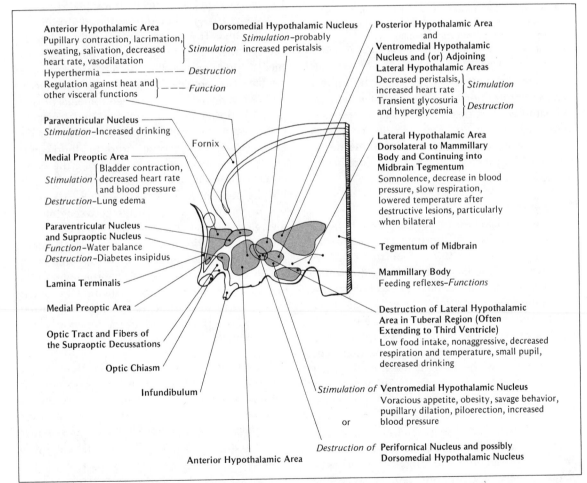

Figure 2.1 Diagram of hypothalamus and the functional areas obtained by stimulation and ablation studies. Redrawn from E. C. Crosby, J. Humphrey, and E. W. Lauer, *Correlative anatomy of the nervous system.* New York: Macmillan, 1962. Redrawn by permission of the Macmillan Company.

onal band, the anterior perforated substance, and *substantia imoninate* posteriorally shade over into the preoptic area, which in turn becomes the anterior hypothalamus. The major efferent pathway of the septal area is the medial forebrain bundle.

Doty (1967, pp. 125–143) summarizes these converging and transient systems as follows:

1. Olfactory input to piriform cortex.
2. Connections to and from the hippocampal system and the septal and preoptic areas.
3. Connections to and from the amygdala and the preoptic-septal regions.
4. Connections to and from the tegmentum and septal area.
5. Afferents to the habenular interpeduncular system.
6. Relations to the temporal lobes via the anterior commissure and the nucleus basalis.
7. Afferents from piriform cortex to the magnocellular component of n. medialis dorsalis and the projection of the latter upon orbitofrontal cortex.
8. Efferents into the hypothalamus via the median forebrain bundle.

Thus the basal forebrain can readily be appreciated as a vortex of emotional and behavioral relays and pathways. It is small wonder that simple concepts such as reverberating circuits or control centers are inadequate for describing the neurophysiological function of the substrate of the psychosomatic interface.

The Hypothalamus

The hypothalamus is a small collection of nuclei situated at the base of the brain, just above the pituitary and located near the geometric center of the head. It is bounded anteriorly by the *lamina terminalis* and *anterior commissure* and posteriorly by the *interpeduncular fossa.* Dorsally, the *hypothalamic sulcus* cleaves the boundary between the hypothalamus and the thalamus. The hypothalamus extends to the inferior surfaces of the brain and is represented by the floor of the third ventricle (just dorsal to the *optic chiasm*), the *tuber cinerium, infundibulum,* and *mammillary bodies.* This region is separated into two halves by the third ventricle. Laterally, it is bounded by several nuclear groups of the ventral thalamus and the optic tract. The *preoptic areas* anterior and superior to the optic chiasm provide a transition zone between the subcallosal septal area and the hypothalamus. The

remainder of the hypothalamus may conveniently be divided into supraoptic, tuberal, and mammillary regions.. For further reference, these areas, their nuclei and general function, are diagramed in Figure 2.1. The *supraoptic area* contains the *anterior hypothalamic nuclei* (well defined in some species but vague in humans) and the *supraoptic nucleus.* Two conspicuous groups of cells in this area, the *paraventricular nucleus* and *supraoptic nucleus,* are considered to be concerned with neurosecretion.

The *tuberal region* is separated into lateral and medial areas by the descending columns of the *fornix.* The lateral area contains many nerve fibers, collectively known as the *medial forebrain bundle.* These fibers have their origin not only in the hypothalamus but in the more anterior septal and olfactory areas as well; they run posteriorly to the tegmental area. The lateral nuclei of the tuber are found only in man and probably contribute to the medial forebrain bundle. The medial tuberal area contains two large nuclear groups, the *dorsomedial* and *ventromedial nuclei.* The ventromedial nucleus is quite conspicuous in carnivores and lower primates. Ventrally, the *arcuate nucleus* lies at the lateral edges of the ventral part of the third ventricle, near the *median eminence.* Along the dorsal aspect of the wall of the third ventricle in this area lies the *periventricular nuclear system.* The *posterior hypothalamic nucleus* lies between the two diverging mammillothalamic tracts and extends to the most posterior region of the hypothalamus.

The *mammillary area* contains the large *mammillary bodies* that are especially prominent in the human. The mammillary bodies themselves contain a complex of nuclei but they need not be listed, since so little is known about the function of this group of cells.

Input connections (afferent) The input/output anatomy of the hypothalamus has been studied in great detail, and the best interpretation of diverse data has not been resolved. The following, taken from Ingram (1960, pp. 951–978), is representative and reasonably accurate for the primate hypothalamus.

1. Medial forebrain bundle
   Origins: olfactory, parolfactory, septal, and striate

areas. The septal fibers probably relay impulses from frontal cortex and rhinencephalon.

2. Thalamohypothalamic fibers
Origin: medial and midline thalamic nuclei; periventricular system. This pathway is probably the major afferent pathway between the neocortex and hypothalamus. Direct connections from orbitofrontal cortex to ventromedial hypothalamic nucleus have been described, but not substantiated.

3. Fornix
Origin: hippocampus.
Terminus: thalamic areas.

4. Stria terminalis
Origin: amygdala.
Terminus: preoptic area, septal area, and diffusely elsewhere.

5. Pallidohypothalamic fibers
Origin: lentiform nuclei.
Terminus: ventromedial hypothalamic nucleus.

6. Subthalamohypothalamic connections

7. Mammillary peduncle
Origin: mesencephalon.
Terminus: lateral mammillary nucleus. Its existence in man is questionable.

8. Vagosupraoptic connection
Origin: demonstrated physiologically, presumably arises in tractus solitarius.

Output connections (efferent)

1. Mammillothalamic tract
Origin: mammillary nuclei.
Terminus: anterior thalamic nuclei with fibers projecting to the cingulate gyrus.

2. Mammillotegmental tract
Origin: mammillary nuclei.
Terminus: tegmental nuclei of lower brain stem.

3. Periventricular system and dorsal longitudinal fasciculus
Origin: throughout hypothalamus but especially posterior hypothalamic area.
Terminus: central gray, tegmentum, tectum, and reticular formation of medulla.

4. Diffuse descending connections
Origin: throughout hypothalamus.
Terminus: lower autonomic centers.

5. Hypothalamohypophesial connections
Origin: supraoptic nuclei, paraventricular nucleus, scattered cells in tuberal area.
Terminus: neurohypophysis, median eminence, and infundibular stem.

6. Diffuse cortical projection system
Origin: posterior hypothalamus, reticular formation of mesencephalon.
Terminus: diffuse neocortical areas, probably relayed through the thalamus.

NEUROPHYSIOLOGY OF THE CENTRAL AUTONOMIC NERVOUS SYSTEM

The experimental evidence that visceral and somatic functions are controlled and integrated by the CNS encompasses a voluminous literature that has developed over a period of about a hundred years. In their review of the cortical influence on cardiovascular function, Hoff, Kell, and Carroll (1963) discuss the early literature on this subject and emphasize the conceptual contributions of John Hulings Jackson based on the study of clinical material. In 1869, Jackson stated that "the highest nervous processes are potentially the whole organism [1958, p. 47]." He adds that support of this "extravagant statement" is based, not on reasoning from observations of bodily changes associated with emotions, but on observations "that gross disease, tumors for instance, of the 'organ of the mind' produce muscular, circulatory and visceral symptoms." Other authors, before and after Jackson, arrived at similar holistic views of the coordinating action of the central nervous system (CNS), but Jackson's contributions were particularly outstanding because of his wealth of clinical observations and extensive background of neurological insight. Similar ideas were developed by the Russian physiologist, Setchenow, who studied in the laboratories of Helmholtz, du Bois Raymond, and Ludwig. It is of particular historical interest that not only did Setchenow appreciate that involuntary functions may be coordinated at cortical levels but also his physiological concepts provided a basis upon which Pavlov began his work.

The Cardiovascular System

Cortex In 1960, Smith, Jabbur, Rushmer, and Lasher stated that the concept that the CNS participates in adaptive cardiovascular regulation is based on the facts that "(a) cardiovascular changes result from anticipation of exercise, eating, or emotional situations; (b) experimentally induced peripheral changes such as those following injection of epinephrine do not mimic cardiovascular changes typical of exercise; and (c) the latency of the cardiovascular responses to exercise is too short to result from peripherally initiated changes [p. 136]." Numerous studies have utilized methods of stimulation and ablation to determine further the influence of the cerebral cortex on autonomic function by direct laboratory experimentation, in addition to the above observational evidence. Bard (1960), Wall and Pribram (1950), and Baldwin (1963) have discussed the hazards of drawing conclusions from electrical stimulation of the cortex, as well as the artifacts induced by the use of anesthetics and paralyzing agents such as Flaxidyl and curare, but a large body of strong experimental evidence remains which indicates that the cerebral cortex is involved with the integrative function of the ANS.

1. Stimulation studies   Although many studies concerning the role of the cerebral cortex in the regulation of the ANS had been reported by the third decade of this century (see historical review by Hoff, Kell, and Carroll, 1963), Bard (1959) is considered to have expressed a widespread skepticism when he stated in 1929 that "many of the effects which were produced are to be accounted for on the basis of spread of strong stimulating currents to subcortical regions or to the production of cortical epilepsy in which a widespread and unphysiological discharge occurs." In 1936, Hoff and Green published the first modern work that began to dispel this view. They studied cats, monkeys, and a chimpanzee, utilizing controlled electrical stimulation and ether anesthesia, while recording blood pressure, heart rate, and respiration. They found both pressor and depressor points, but pressor results predominated. Stimulation in the motor region of the cortex regularly produced a rise in blood pressure of 10–80 mm Hg after latencies of about 10 sec. This effect was followed by a return to normal pressures after cessation of stimulus after a similar latency period. The pressor response reached a peak in 10–20 sec and then began to decline slowly. With this rise in pressure, there was often a cardioacceleration of 5–10%; sometimes a fall in heart rate of as much as 50% occurred during the poststimulatory decline in pressure.

Hoff and Green also reported that most stimulations did not produce a change in heart rate; however, in 3 out of 5 cats stimulated in the gyrus proreus, cardioacceleration with no change or only a slight fall in blood pressure was found. Motor responses frequently accompanied the stimulus in

this area but it was possible to find areas in which stimuli below motor response threshold gave only autonomic responses. In the cat, pressor responses occurred most frequently with the stimulation of posterior and anterior sigmoid gyri and adjacent gyrus proreus. Pressor points were also found on the anterior portions of the suprasylvian and ectosylvian gyri. Depressor responses were consistently obtained from gyrus lateralis medius, gyrus suprasylvius medius, gyrus ectosylvius medius, and gyrus sylvius. In the monkey, responses were most easily obtained in area 6 and parts of area 4. Rises in blood pressure were also obtained from the superior, inferior, and middle frontal gyri. Both pressor and depressor responses were obtained from stimulation of anterior cingulate gyrus. Results from the chimpanzee were similar to those obtained with monkeys. Exploration of the entire cortical convexity in both cats and monkeys revealed no other isocortical loci to produce vasomotor changes.

That the autonomic responses obtained by Hoff and Green were due to excitation of cortical elements was demonstrated by:

1. Obtaining pressor and depressor responses from discrete points located within 2–4 mm of each other.
2. Abolition of the response by applying a small cotton pledget soaked in local anesthetic to responsive cortical points.
3. Loss of the response by undercutting the cortex.
4. Finding that somatic and vasomotor components can be differentiated.

These results have been essentially confirmed by several similar studies (Bard, 1960; Delgado, 1960; Paine, 1965) in rabbits, cats, dogs, and monkeys. Stimulation of supplementary motor cortex in man by Penfield produced pupillary dilatation and occasionally cardioacceleration, in addition to motor and sensory effects (Penfield, 1950). Using chronically implanted electrodes, and thus freeing his results from contamination by anesthesia and restraint, Delgado (1960) found that there was cardiovascular representation in the hidden motor cortex of cats (sulci presylvius, coronalis, and cruciatus), but no systematic distribution of pressor and depressor areas could be discerned.

Most authors who have reviewed the subject of cortical influence of the cardiovascular system conclude that there is both pressor and depressor cardiovascular representation in the superficial cerebral cortex, discontinuously located in the motor and premotor area and loci of the frontal cortex. Wall and Pribram (1950) studied the blood pressure response in monkeys to cortical stimulation before and after trigeminal neurotomy. Before neurotomy they obtained maximal responses from stimulation around the cortical blood vessels and similar responses from the dura. In the intact animal, pressor and depressor points were widespread over the dorsal and lateral cortex; however, after trigeminal section, only depressor responses were evoked and were restricted to a region on both sides of the central sulcus and loci in the frontal lobe. One may conclude that participation of the superficial cortex in cardiovascular control has been demonstrated, but the nature of this control, whether pressor or depressor, is not clear and has probably been confounded by artifacts introduced by anesthesia, spread of current to dura and cortical vessels, paralyzing agents, and species differences between rabbit, cat, dog, monkey, and man.

In many of the studies concerning the cardiovascular representation of the cortex, electrocardiogram (EKG) alterations and heart rate changes were also reported. Recently, Baldwin (1963) has carried out a quantitative study of the cardiac response to cortical stimulation in the cat that confirms and extends the earlier studies. Using local anesthesia and d-tubocurarine, he found that maximal cardioacceleration and minimal latencies were evoked from a band of cortex formed by the anterior sigmoid gyrus and coronal gyrus. The coronal gyrus stimulation produced greater accelerations than anterior sigmoid ($p < .01$) with the largest heart rate change being 39 beats per min. The posterior sigmoid, posterior coronal, anterio-lateral, and anterior suprasylvian gyri, all gave significantly smaller and slower responses ($p < .01$) than both anterior sigmoid and coronal gyri. The shortest latencies were recorded during coronal gyri stimulation with a mean of 2.5 sec and a minimum of 0.5 sec. Stimulation of the superior gyrus proreus and anterior sigmoid gyrus sometimes gave a slight decrease in heart rate. He found cardioacceleration to occur with, and without, blood pressure changes; significant accelerations were recorded in spite of large blood pressure increases. Increasing stimulation intensity increased the magnitude of cardioaccelerations and decreased latency. Heart rate

responses were negatively correlated with initial heart rate and diastolic blood pressure in most of his preparations; 61% of the stimuli were associated with EKG alterations or pathological arrhythmias.

2. Ablation studies The stabilizing and modulating influence of the cerebral cortex on the sympathetic nervous system has been demonstrated by several studies of experimental lesions and clinical material. In 1955, Covian and Houssay (1955) found that 91% of hemidecorticate rats developed arterial hypertension in the course of a month following operation. The hypertension lasted about 2 months. Subsequently, Anand, Dua, and Chhina (1957; Anand & Dua, 1956a) reported that extensive lesions in the frontal cortex of monkeys and cats caused variability of blood pressure and heart rate, with a general depression of both. In 1961, Balitskii, Il'chevich, and Pridatko (1961) found that immediately following decortication in rabbits, cardiodeceleration ensued in some animals, but heart rate reverted to normal in about 1 week. Pituitrin injection produced a greater bradycardia with ectopic beats but less elevation of blood pressure in the operated animals than in controls. In 1945, Kennard reported that bilateral ablation of the frontal lobes in monkeys resulted in temporary cardiac, vasomotor, and pupillary changes. She also reported cardioacceleration associated with sham rage in decorticate cats (Kennard, 1945).

It is well known to physicians that cortical lesions are associated with an acute vasodilation of the affected extremity, which later subsides as the extremity becomes pale and cool and increased sweating occurs (Ingram, 1960, pp. 951–978). Patients with brain injuries frequently have multiple symptoms relating to vasomotor instability of the body as a whole, as well as circumscribed parts of the body. Permanent bradycardias and, more rarely, tachycardias, have been seen and often there is an abnormal orthostatic differential in heart rate (Hoff, Kell, & Carroll, 1963). In 1962, Ovcharova reported an interesting finding of the effects of frontal lobe lesions in man on the reflex responses to the oculocardiac reflex after giving atropine. He found that, in comparison to normal subjects, patients with frontal lesions had a sizable increase in cardioacceleration after atropine. The effects of frontal lesions on the orienting reflex will be discussed later (see section on neurophysiology of the GSR).

Brutkowski (1965) has recently reviewed the functions of prefrontal cortex in animals and advances the conclusion that, if motor and premotor areas are intact, there is little ANS projection to the prefrontal cortex. He supports this conclusion by the interpretation that most ablation studies of the prefrontal cortex in which ANS effects have been reported have sustained damage to motor or premotor areas.

3. Sympathetic muscular vasodilation Of particular interest to psychophysiologists are the properties of a sympathetic, cholinergic, vasodilator system that has the capability of inducing marked effects on the muscular blood flow (Uvnas, 1960, pp. 1131–1162). This system has representation in the motor cortex with relay stations in the hypothalamus and tectum. It bypasses medullary vasomotor centers and passes into the lateral fasciculus of the spinal cord. Vasoconstriction of the skin and intestine and liberation of adrenaline by the adrenals is associated with the activation of this system, and it has been shown to play no role in the tonic maintenance of vasomotor tone. The physiological significance of this system is by no means understood but it is considered to be concerned with the immediate adjustment of the muscular blood flow known to occur in anticipation to, or immediately with the onset of, exercise. The location of a relay station in the hypothalamus and the association of rage behavior concomitant with the stimulation of the hypothalamic representation of this system in chronically implanted cats further suggest that it participates in a physiologic preparation for fight or flight in stress situations. In support of this hypothesis are the reports by Blair, Glover, Greenfield, and Roddie (1959) and Kelly and Walter (1968), which indicate that vasodilator nerves to skeletal muscle are activated in humans who are emotionally stressed, and the report by Barcroft, Edholm, McMichael, and Sharpey-Schafer (1944) of muscular vasodilation in association with fainting. Of further interest, from a psychosomatic medical viewpoint, is the recent report that intense renal vasocardiovascular constriction is associated with activation of this system in the hypothalamus (Feigl, Johansson & Löfving, 1964).

4. Outflow pathways Although there are extensive connections between the hypothalamus and the cortex, the autonomic responses resulting from cortical stimulation are not mediated via the hypothalamus (Baldwin, 1963; Mitchell, 1953; Raisman, 1966). Landau (1953) demonstrated that autonomic responses evoked by medullary pyramid stimulation were abolished by section of the corticospinal tract in the medulla. Wall and Davis (1951) also found that arterial pressure changes evoked from the sensory motor cortex were abolished by section of the pyramid and that lesions of the hypothalamus did not alter these responses. Thus the corticofugal fibers passing chiefly from the motor strip to the reticular formation of the pons and medulla provide a nonhypothalamic route for cortical modulation of somatomotor and autonomic functions.

The limbic system In 1925 von Ecomomo and Koskinas noted the close relationship between smell and the ANS as the basis for their proposal that there exists an autonomic representation in the limbic region, as well as regulation of movements that might be either independent of, or associated with, olfaction. On the basis of neuroanatomical and clinical observation, in 1937 Papez put forth his now-famous hypothesis that the anatomical system composed of the hypothalamus, the anterior thalamic nucleus, the cingulate gyrus, the hippocampus, and their interconnections constituted a neurophysiological circuit underlying the functions of emotional expression. Two years later, in 1939, Kluver and Bucy reported their classic findings that extensive bilateral excision of the temporal lobes in the monkey is followed by dramatic changes of behavior and emotional responsiveness. These papers have stimulated extensive studies of this system in the past three decades, so that now the limbic system has been expanded to include the amygdala, orbitofrontal-basotemporal and insular cortex, and the septal area. Several recent reviews concerning the limbic system or parts of it are available (Douglas & Pribram, 1966; Gloor, 1960, pp. 1395–1420; Gloor & Feindel, 1963, pp. 685–715; Green, 1964; Ursin & Kaada, 1960).

1. Cortical areas within the limbic system Cardiovascular changes consisting of alterations in blood pressure, heart rate, and regional vasomotor changes have been demonstrated in chimpanzee, monkey, cat, dog, and rabbit by topical stimulation of the orbital cortex, insula, anterior cingulate gyrus, and basal temporal cortex (for reviews, see Delgado, 1960; Folkow, 1955; Hoff, Kell, & Carroll, 1963; Löfving, 1961). An extensive investigation of the somatomotor and autonomic effects of stimulation of the rhinencephalon in monkeys, cats, and dogs under various anesthetics was carried out by Kaada in 1951. In monkeys he found the greatest blood pressure responses from the anterior cingulate gyrus around the genu of the corpus callosum, posterior orbital gyrus, anterior insula, and olfactory tubercle. Marked responses were obtained from the anterior hippocampal gyrus and the ventricular medial part of the temporal pole. Less consistent changes, usually slow rises, were obtained from the lateral temporal pole, lower precentral region, posterior gyrus rectus, and posterior part of the anterior cingulate gyrus. In cats and dogs he found the greatest blood pressure responses from pre- and subgenual regions, the orbital and adjacent pyriform cortex, the depth of the lower end of the presylvian sulcus, the olfactory tubercle, and the frontal cortex covered by the olfactory tract. The most frequent blood pressure response was a 15–30 mm Hg fall, with a maximum fall of 60 mm Hg recorded. Less frequently, an increase in blood pressure was obtained and, occasionally, a reversal in response was observed when anesthesia was deepened or the preparation deteriorated. Maximal respiratory alterations, usually a result of inhibition, were found to coincide with the areas giving maximal blood pressure responses. Independence of respiration and blood pressure changes was demonstrated by the observation of rises and falls in blood pressure, with and without respiration alteration.

The cortical origin of the responses was demonstrated by the several maneuvers used by Hoff and Green (see section on the cortex) and the lack of effect of bilateral trigeminal section on the responses. Pressor points gave maximal response at stimulation frequencies of 4–80 Hz, while depressor points responded best to 15–40 Hz but were obtainable at all frequencies. The reversal of response to changes in frequency was only occasionally seen. Thus it appears that, at most of these loci, either pressor or depressor systems are solely or predominantly represented. Section of the vagus nerve abolished or greatly reduced depressor responses but did not influence the pressor response.

In the same year, Wall and Davis (1951) reported the results of cortical stimulation and ablation on blood pressure in a large number of monkeys and two chimpanzees. Their results were similar to those detailed above; however, they found that destruction of the hypothalamus abolished the blood pressure response from orbital stimulation but had no effect on the respiration response. In addition, they found that hypothalamic lesions had no effect on anterior temporal basal stimulation but that ablation of the ipsilateral temporal lobe would decrease the blood pressure response to anterior cingulate stimulation by 90%. On the basis of their results they postulated three independent cortical systems that influence the ANS via separate pathways: (a) the sensory-motor cortex, (b) the posterior orbital-insular system, and (c) the temporal-cingulate system.

Subsequently, a number of studies have been published reporting the effects of orbital stimulation in cats, monkeys, and chimpanzees on cardiovascular measures and respiration (Anand & Dua, 1956a, 1956b; Delgado, 1960). Apnea has been a consistent respiratory response, but the effects on blood pressure and heart rate, although consistently present, have varied in degree and direction. A recent series of studies by Newman and Wolstencroft (1960) has demonstrated a subtle but powerful innervation between the orbital cortex and the bulbar cardiovascular centers that does not involve a hypothalamic relay. In anesthetized cats, they found that the reflex fall in blood pressure which occurs in response to heating carotid blood could be totally inhibited by orbital stimulation with current strengths that are subliminal for autonomic effects. They have demonstrated a direct neurophysiological link between the orbital cortex and the temperature-sensitive cells in the medulla responsible for this reflex; they suggest that the orbital cortex must be considered as playing a role in the regulation of the circulation and body temperature.

Thus the influence of the limbic cortical areas on the ANS is well established; however, the function of these areas in integrating and influencing

ANS adjustment in the intact, conscious organism is a matter for future research. Kaada (1951) found inhibition and occasional facilitation of movement and reflexes with stimulation of the same areas outlined above. These effects were obtained at stimulation levels below those required for ANS effects. The inhibition of respiration could not be prolonged beyond 20–40 sec, but the inhibition of movement could be held by stimulation for several minutes. In addition, he found no constant relationship between the direction of blood pressure change and the facilitation or inhibition of movement.

The direction of blood pressure change is known to be a poor indicator of regional vasomotor changes, as first shown by Hoff and Green (1936), who found peripheral vasodilatation simultaneously with renal vasoconstriction in response to cortical stimulation. More recently, Löfving (1961) has carried out a detailed and extensive analysis of vasomotor changes resulting from stimulation of the anterior cingulate area in cats lightly anesthetized with chloralose. He found that the cingulate gyrus in the region of the genu of the corpus callosum gave vasodilation responses, and the subcallosal area responded with vasoconstriction. Although there was overlap of these responses, his studies showed a clear separation of the areas. Regional blood flow through the muscle, skin, foot pad, intestine, and kidney, as well as the heart rate and blood pressure, were monitored and were found to respond differentially when various areas of the vasoconstrictor region were stimulated. In contrast, the cingulate vasodepressor area consistently responded with a slowing of the heart rate, pronounced vasodilation within the skeletal muscles, moderate dilation of the intestinal vessels, a small response within the skin, and usually no response in the renal vessels. The sympatho-inhibitory fibers of the depressor area were found to pass through the hypothalamus, since small lesions of this structure selectively eliminated the cortically induced depressor effects. Pharmacologically, it was demonstrated that this system is not identical with sympatho-cholinergic muscular vasodilator pathways. The depressor effect was found to be mediated via the bulbar depressor area, but constrictor responses were unaffected by le-

sions in the bulbar vasodepressor reticular formation. Studies carried out in chronically implanted, conscious animals revealed the diffuse sympatho-inhibitory response to be associated with a generalized inhibition of spontaneous somatomotor activity, as well as a temporary respiratory inhibition. Löfving hypothesized that the vasoconstrictor component of this system is active in the alarm defense reaction, but that intense activation of the inhibitory cortical structures "may be responsible for phenomena like emotional fainting in man and the 'playing dead' reaction occurring in some species." Further, such a system as this may be well suited to play an important role in the differential rate of habituation of the various components of the orienting response.

2. Amygdala and septal area   Electrical stimulation experiments of the amygdaloid nuclear complex have demonstrated a large number of sexual, arousal, somatic, emotional, endocrine, and feeding responses (for reviews and sources see Gloor, 1954; Goddard, 1964). Thus, as might be expected, a number of studies have demonstrated autonomic responses to stimulation in this area in cat, monkey, and man. Independent changes in blood pressure and heart rate have been found, as well as alterations in respiratory activity (Gloor, 1960). Chapman et al. (1954) found increased blood pressure with stimulation of amygdala in man, but Anand and Dua (1956a) and others found a predominance of depressor responses in cat and monkey. They found no localization of the vasomotor changes, but others (Ursin & Kaada, 1960) found the basolateral division and periamygdaloid cortex to be optimal for pressor responses, while the most effective depressor points are located in the cortical and medial nuclei.

The detailed studies of the heart rate response to amygdaloid and periamygdaloid stimulation in the squirrel monkey recently reported by Reis and Oliphant (1964) are of particular interest because the animals were not anesthetized. They found that bradycardia was elicited primarily from points concentrated within the amygdaloid nucleus, particularly in the basolateral part. Tachycardia was more diffusely represented, being elicited most frequently from white matter, particularly the external and internal capsules and the depths of the temporal lobe. These heart rate responses are not considered to be reflexive in origin because they were found to occur independent of changes in blood pressure and respiration. The bradycardia, which was shown to be exclusively vagal in origin, usually appeared with a latency of 20–30 sec, would persist with stimulation for several minutes, and often was associated with cardiac arrhythmias, particularly ventricular extrasystoles. The tachycardia had opposite characteristics. Pressor responses were elicited from all subdivisions of the amygdala and adjacent cortex, and only once was a depressor response seen. Reis and Oliphant conclude that the heart rate as a single parameter of cardiovascular function is independently represented in the amygdaloid region of the monkey brain, and that the descending systems mediating the bradycardia and tachycardia induced from this area are organized differently. Also, they cite their finding that only 50% of the sites stimulated responded with heart changes as further support for the view that forebrain influences on autonomic regulation may be canceled by more compelling reflex adjustments arising from lower brain areas. Gloor (1960, pp. 1395–1420) reviewed much of the work on the amygdala up to that time and concluded that there was no topographical localization of autonomic and behavioral function of the amygdaloid complex.

In contradistinction to Gloor's position, Ursin and Kaada (1960) reported a group of stimulation experiments on unanesthetized cats and concluded that the desynchronization of the EEG and the "attention" response are localized in the basolateral group of nuclei and can be traced medially through the region of the central nucleus into the internal capsule. They also found fear and anger responses from two separate areas running approximately parallel within the attention zone and into the internal capsule and brain stem. They review a number of papers concerning autonomic and somatic responses elicited from the amygdala and conclude that none of them are mediated through the hippocampal-fornix system. Similarly, attention, fear, and anger seem to be unrelated to the stria terminalis.

In contrast to the profound behavioral changes found with amygdaloid lesions, the ANS mechanisms influenced by stimulation show minor deficits or none at all with bilateral destruction of the amygdala (Gloor, 1960, pp. 1395–1420). Thus, maintaining ANS tone and integration is not one of the functions of the amygdala, but integrating the appropriate phasic vegetative adjustments to emotional or behavioral states is an important aspect of amygdaloid nuclear activity.

Because of its close anatomical connections with the limbic structures, the septal area has come to be considered part of the limbic system. Using chloralose anesthesia, Covian, Antunes-Rodrigues, and O'Flaherty (1964) have recently reported the effects of septal stimulation on ANS variables in the cat. They found a long latency fall in blood pressure to be the most frequent response. A fall in heart rate of 4–36 beats per min was a frequent concomitant of the blood pressure change. Respiratory inhibitions with and without blood pressure changes were infrequently seen. The fact that the blood pressure fall reaches a maximum and persists for several minutes with the end of stimulation suggests that the response is chemically mediated. This conclusion is supported by the finding that vagotomy and cervical sympathectomy augments the bradycardia and vasodepressor response. It is virtually unaltered by atropine and abolished by infusion of norepinephrine. Thus the response is mediated by the inhibition of either vasoconstrictor fibers or catecholamine secretion. Further studies by this group have found this response maintainable with stimulation for periods up to 28 min (Covian & Timo-Iaria, 1966). Penile erections in the cat have been elicited by septal stimulation (MacLean, Ploog, & Robinson, 1960). This localized vasomotor change persisted for 3–5 min without continued stimulation, suggesting that the blood pressure and heart rate changes are not nonspecific changes but that part of the limbic system is concerned with expressive and feeling states that are conductive to the preliminaries of copulation and reproduction. They interpret these observations to indicate that this region is a CNS substratum for behaviors appropriate to preservation of the species, while the aggressive and feeding responses elicited from the amygdala suggest that the amygdaloid region is more concerned with self-preservational behavior. Further detailed characterization of the ANS responses to stimuli in the septal region would be of interest to psychophysiologists interested in positive feeling states, since Heath (1964) has demonstrated that septal stimuli in humans elicit states of pleasurable feeling, and sometimes sexual feelings, even to the point of orgasm. Heath's finding that psychosis and chronic schizophrenia (both highly dysphoric and unsociable states of being) are associated with evidence of malfunction in the septal area, if confirmed, would further highlight this region of the brain as extremely important for the psychophysiological adaptive functions of pleasure (Rickles, 1969).

   3. *Hippocampus, fornix, mammillary bodies, and anterior nucleus of thalamus*   Although Papez's theory of the limbic circuit concerning the neurophysiology of emotional behavior has stimulated considerable productive research, the hippocampus, fornix-mammillary-anterior nucleus part of the circuit has not been found to be directly concerned with mediation of motor or autonomic responses (Ursin & Kaada, 1960). In his review of hippocampus physiology, Green (1964) notes the lack of effect on emotions of the section of the fornix in humans. Others have reported a general absence of ANS responses to hippocampus and fornix stimuli. Kaada (1951) suggests that these essentially negative results of stimulation and ablation indicate that these structures are concerned with higher psychic activity. A broad base of diverse data suggests that these structures are concerned with memory functions (Green, 1964). Since the adequate recording of memory traces that include sensory-motor perceptions and the associated emotional reactions is strongly dependent upon appropriate emotional motivation, and its reduction by reinforcement, it is not surprising that the memory circuits are intimately interrelated with emotional circuits but are not directly efferent for the ANS. This concept finds some support in the recent reports that different types of evoked hippocampal electrical activity correlate with autonomic changes. Torii and Kawamura (1960) found that stimulation of the amygdala, septal region, and preoptic area generally cause a fall in blood pressure concomitant with the appearance of fast waves in the hippocampus, while posterior hypothalamic stimulation results in a rise in blood pressure concomitant with hippocampal slow waves. Yokota and

Fujimori (1964) extended these studies to include somatomotor and sudomotor reflexes, as well as vasomotor activity. They concluded that the slow wave components of hippocampal electrical activity bear a close relationship (facilitory) to somatomotor, sudomotor, and vasomotor activity. Desynchronization was usually associated with the inhibition of somatic and autonomic activity, but it was impossible to relate fast wave components of hippocampal electrical activity to either somatomotor and sudomotor or vasomotor functions. These findings correlate well with the report by Karmos, Grastyán, Losonczy, Vereczkey, and Grósz (1965) that hippocampal slow waves are associated with the orienting reaction, and Adey's (1963) report that ventral hippocampal slow waves are present during the decision period, while a discrimination task is being learned, but no longer appear after the task is mastered.

   In 1963 Gloor and Feindel reviewed the pathophysiology of the temporal lobe. They observe that in temporal-lobe epilepsy, a strong feeling of fear is a common symptom that is often associated with visceral sensations or activity. Ictal rage and depression have been described but are uncommon. Pleasurable emotions, sexual emotions, and feelings of hunger and thirst have also been described as ictal events in temporal-lobe epileptics but these ictal symptoms are extremely rare.

The hypothalamus   Beginning with the early studies done by Karplus and Kreidl (1927), a large body of literature has developed concerning the hypothalamic control of the vegetative nervous system. Workers such as Bard (1928), Ranson and Magoun (1939), Hess (see Gloor, 1954), and Gellhorn (1964) have contributed monumentally to the analysis of the hypothalamus in regulation of behavioral states such as sleep, fear and rage, as well as alimentary, sexual, and thermoregulatory responses. Recent reviews of these functions have been written by Bligh (1966), Cross (1964), Fitzsimons (1966), and Ingram (1960, pp. 951–958). The early workers produced marked elevation of blood pressure, hypernea, pupillary dilatation, and bladder constriction when they stimulated the walls of the third ventricle and the hypothalamus. Multiple discrete sites of the hypothalamus have been stereotaxically stimulated and a wide variety of vascular responses has been documented (Paine, 1965). Anterior hypothalamic excitation has produced hypertension, and ST-segment elevation and T wave inversion of the EKG. Stimulation of the lateral hypothalamic nucleus has caused, in addition to hypertension, atrioventricular dissociation and premature ventricular contractions. Postero-lateral stimulation has been followed by hypertension, A-V nodal rhythm, aberrant intraventricular conduction, and premature ventricular contractions. In the supraoptic area, stimulation has brought about 50–200% increase in the venous outflow of skeletal muscles without a change in arterial blood pressure, while other venous beds have shown a vasoconstriction. Many of these effects are found in quite discrete areas, while others can be elicited from many points of the hypothalamus. Obviously, other vegetative effects and behavioral effects are mingled with the same sites that will produce vascular responses.

Over a long series of experiments with cats, utilizing stimulation and ablation as well as local and systemic pharmacological tools, Gellhorn has contributed a large body of data concerning the hypothalamic regulation of the cardiovascular system (1964). As a result of his findings, he functionally divides the hypothalamus into a parasympathetic division located in the anterior hypothalamus, including nuclei preopticus, supraopticus, suprachiasmaticus, and hypothalamicus anterior; and a sympathetic division located in the posterior hypothalamus, including mammillaris, ventrolateralis, lateralis, and posterior nuclei. This division is based on alterations of heart rate and blood pressure induced by electrical or pharmacological stimulation or lesion. Parasympathetic responses are indicated by decreased heart rate and blood pressure and sympathetic responses by the reverse. He has developed the concept of autonomic "tuning" of the hypothalamus, which may be induced by hypothalamic lesions, stimulation, cortical impulses, or baroreceptor impulses resulting from peripheral cardiovascular adjustments. In "sympathetic tuning," most easily achieved by the injection of hypotensive drugs, the reactivity of the posterior hypothalamus to stimuli is increased. Injecting hypertensive drugs creates a state of

"parasympathetic tuning," in which the anterior hypothalamus has a lowered threshold to local, nervous, or peripheral stimuli. Of particular interest is his demonstration of the reciprocal relationship between these areas of the hypothalamus; i.e., parasympathetic tuning may be induced by diminishing anterior hypothalamic activity. His concepts and findings are congruent with Lacey's theory of fractional differentiation and also are relevant to the law of initial values.

Bard has criticized Gellhorn's division of the hypothalamus into parasympathetic (PNS) and sympathetic (SNS) parts on several counts. In 1960 he wrote.[2]

> Whatever the parasympathetic representation may be in the hypothalamus, it is surely something quite different from the sympathetic mechanisms located there, for the latter are capable of causing large fractions or even the whole of the thoracolumbar outflow to discharge. One of these mechanisms goes into action during the display of aggressive or defensive behavior, and the visceral alterations thus brought about are part of this patterned mode of response. Again, on exposure to cold, cutaneous vasoconstriction, piloerection and medulliadrenal secretion indicate a rather widespread, though by no means total, sympathetic discharge. There is no evidence that any comparable mechanism related to the parasympathetic system exists in this or any other part of the central nervous system. Such a mechanism could only produce visceral changes bearing no functional relation to one another; certainly constriction of the pupils, slowing of the heart, increased gastrointestinal activity, contraction of the urinary bladder and engorgement of erectile tissue are not changes that are bound by physiological ties of integration. As far as the circulatory system is concerned, the only established parasympathetic pathways of control are the vagal fibers to the heart, the sacral vasodilator outflow to the external genitalia and, in all probability, secretory fibers to salivary glands. In this connection, it is well to bear in mind that there is no valid experimental evidence that a reflex fall in arterial pressure can be due to any parasympathetic activity other than vagal cardiac inhibition. [p. 19]

Others have divided the hypothalamus into sagittal sections and described parasympathetic responses from lateral nuclei and sympathetic responses from the medial region (Ban, 1966), but blood pressure responses in both directions have been obtained both medially and laterally (Gloor, 1954; Ingram, 1960). Enoch and Kerr (1967) have recently traced vasomotor and vesicomotor pathways in the hypothalamus of the cat. They used both microelectrode stimuli and discrete electrolytic lesions to map the pathways of the different responses. They found pressor and depressor vasomotor responses evoked from all frontal planes from the optic chiasm to the rostral region of the mesencephalon. They conclude that vasomotor and vesicomotor pathways are intimately associated in the hypothalamus and do not support a division into SNS and PNS regions.

The hypothalamic control of cardiovascular responses to fear and rage reactions has been extensively studied and recently reviewed by Hilton (1965). These responses, also referred to as the defense reaction, are basic behavioral responses in all higher animals, and their details vary only a little from one species to another. The blood flow through most tissues and organs is controlled by the CNS solely through vasoconstrictor nerve fibers; but in the skeletal muscle of the cat and dog, there are, in addition, other nerve fibers of the sympathetic outflow that actively dilate the resistance vessels (cf. the section on cortical influence on cardiovascular system). These vasodilator fibers, which are cholinergic and therefore atropine-sensitive, are *not involved in any of the homeostatic circulatory reflexes*. They are, however, most readily activated by electrical stimulation of only a restricted area of the hypothalamus in the cat. Hilton localized this area as being as far anterior as the level of the optic chiasm and 1–2 mm lateral to the third ventricle and just dorsal to chiasm itself. At the level of the tuber, the vasodilator responses were larger and elicited from a region medial and ventral to the fornix and extended laterally as a narrow band toward the zona incerta. At the level of the mammillary bodies, responses were obtained from a strip dorsolateral to these structures. In addition to muscular vasodilatation, stimulation of acute preparations in these areas also produced vasoconstriction of the skin and intestines, tachycardia, pupillary dilatation, retraction of the nictitating membrane, widening of the palpebral fissure, piloerection, and tachypnea, i.e., autonomic features of the defense reaction. Stimulation of chronically implanted animals in the same regions using the same stimulus parameters produced defense reactions in conscious cats.

Using chronically implanted, blood-flow thermistors in the femoral vein of the cat, Hilton and coworkers demonstrated that at the threshold of hypothalamic stimulation for the early alerting stage of the defense reactions, atropine-sensitive vasodilatation is already well developed. This response has been shown to be a component of the orienting reflex, and it can be established as a very stable conditional response. Homeostatic mechanisms are inhibited under these conditions, since it has been shown that the reflex depressor effect of raising the pressure in a blind sac preparation of the carotid bifurcation is strongly inhibited and may be unobtainable during stimulation of the brain stem center for the defense reaction. Hilton points out that the vascular components of preparatory response in man seem similar to that described in the cat. It is of interest that muscular blood flow is significantly higher in hypertensives than in normal subjects. Apparently, the muscle vessels do not participate in the general increase in vascular tone in established hypertension.

The participation of the hypothalamus in cardiovascular adjustments to other behavior activities and states has been studied by Smith et al. (1960). After bilateral lesions of the paraventricular gray, changes in heart rate normally found in eating were not evidenced; changes in systolic pressure were actually reversed. In the same animal the heart rate response to exercise was not affected but the systolic blood pressure response was eliminated. In an animal with lesions bilaterally symmetrical and in the most medial portion of the field of Forel just dorsolateral to the mammillary bodies, the blood pressure and heart rate increases to exercise did not occur. Thus certain hypothalamic and subthalamic areas are essential for the emergence of normal cardiovascular adjustment patterns to eating and exercise.

Although most of the cardiovascular effects described here are neuronally mediated, it should be mentioned that not only can hypothalamic stimulation cause secretion of catecholamines by the adrenal medulla but Folkow and von Euler

(1954) have shown that the ratio of epinephrine to norepinephrine secreted can be changed and even reversed by stimulation in different hypothalamic sites.

Extensive studies by Hess (see Gloor, 1954) and others have made it clear that the cardiovascular alterations associated with behavioral responses are only a part of a total integration of autonomic, somatic, and arousal adjustments that are patterned in the hypothalamus to produce organized, adap-

tive behavior and the appropriate central and peripheral physiological support. More recent studies have shown that other brain areas participate with the hypothalamus to bring about this integration but their respective roles are only beginning to be understood.

Medulla and midbrain The reticular formation of the midbrain and medulla has received considerable attention in recent years as an important

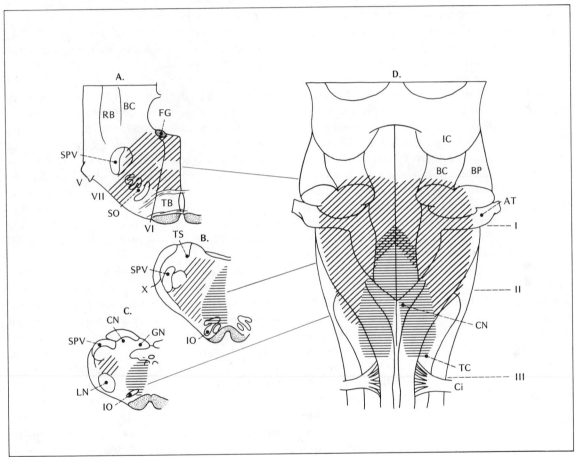

Figure 2.2 Localization of pressor and depressor centers in the brain stem of the cat. Pressor regions indicated by slanted lines; depressor regions by horizontal lines. A–C: cross sections through the medulla at levels indicated by guide lines to D; D: semidiagrammatic projection of pressor and depressor regions onto the dorsal surface of the brain stem viewed with the cerebella peduncles cut across and the cerebellum removed. AT = auditory tubercle; BC = brachium conjunctivum; BP = brachium ponti; C_1 = first cervical nerve; CN = cuneat nucleus; FG = facial genu; GN = gracile nucleus; IC = inferior colliculus; IO = inferior olivary nucleus; LN = lateral reticular nucleus; RB = rests-form body; SO = superior olivary nucleus; SPV = spinal trigeminal tract; TB = trapezoid body; TC = tuberculum cinereum; TS = tractus solitarius; V, VI, VII, X = corresponding cranial nerves; I, II, III = levels of transection discussed in text. Redrawn from R. S. Alexander, Toxic and reflex functions of medullary sympathetic cardiovascular centers. *Journal of Neurophysiology,* 1946, **9,** 205. By permission.

structure in regulating cortical arousal, somato-motor and autonomic tonus, reflexes, and sensory filtering. Reviews of these several functions are available (French, 1960, pp. 1281–1307; Moruzzi, 1964; Rossi & Zanchetti, 1957); they are interrelated with control of the cardiovascular system and should be considered jointly to appreciate the complex interplay of the arousal, the sensory-motor and the autonomic systems in the brain stem.

In his review of the cardiovascular centers of the brain stem, Oberholzer (1960) cites the early work of Flourens, Schiff, and Dittman spanning a period of 50 years during the nineteenth century. By the use of ablation techniques, they established the existence of centers for respiration and vasomotor control in the pontomedullary region. More recently, exploration of the bulbopontine region by electrical stimulation has led to the hypothesis that there are two half-centers dominating the spinal vasomotor outflow. Stimulation of the medial reticular formation between the inferior olive and hypoglossal nucleus produces inhibition of the peripheral sympathetic vasomotor tone and leads in general to a fall in blood pressure. The cells of this depressor area show little autonomous activity and seem dependent on input from the baroceptors for activation. Stimulating the lateral part of the medullary reticular formation results in blood pressure elevation. This pressor zone extends more cephalad than the depressor zone, reaching the pontine level. Utilizing stimulation and ablation techniques, Alexander prepared the diagram reproduced in Figure 2.2, which illustrates the demarcation of pressor and depressor centers in the cat medulla (Alexander, 1946). The three lines indicate the level of sections made from the cephalad to the caudad direction. The section at level I produced a slight fall in pressure, in II a marked fall in mean pressure, and in III a slight rise in pressure. These results indicate that the pressor region exerts significant tonic influence on spinal vasomotor neurons, whereas the slight rise after Section III suggests a slight tonic inhibition emanating from the depressor area. Oberholzer considers this schema to be representative of dogs, cats, and sheep. There is no sharp limit between medio-caudal depressor and laterocranial pressor areas; both overlap. Clinical data regarding medullary

cardiovascular control is sparse, but pathological study of poliomyelitis cases has shown that destruction of cells in the medial reticular formation correlates with the loss of vasomotor tone, and lesions in lateral reticular formation are associated with respiratory failure (Oberholzer, 1960). Using ischemic decerebration, Glasser (1960) demonstrated a blood pressure and heart rate depressor area in the anterior pons. Subsequent sections along the brain stem produced the same blood pressure pattern as already outlined, but some heart rate acceleration persisted after the fall of blood pressure to normal or below.

Inasmuch as the depressor area of the medullary reticular formation coincides with the respiratory apneustic center and the pressor area with the pneumotaxic center, it is not surprising to find that carotid, aortic, and other cardiovascular reflexes usually have a respiratory component. Respiration is not invariably linked with cardiovascular changes, however. Tan (1967), in his recent studies of stimulus-bound respiration in the cat, found areas of the medulla where periodic stimuli would capture respiration rhythms but had no effect on the blood pressure, heart rate, or motor responses. The phenomenon of stimulus-bound respiration could be elicited from the preoptic region to the caudal medulla.

Carotid sinus and sciatic nerve reflexes are not mediated solely by the medulla. Manning (1965) found that large lesions in the medullary vasomotor system did not significantly alter these reflexes but they were lost with decerebration. The maintenance of vasomotor tone in these preparations indicates that the hypothalamus participates independent of the medulla in supporting cardiovascular tone.

The interaction between the reticular formation mediated cardiovascular reflexes and the arousal/gating functions of the reticular formation is of major psychophysiological interest. The publication of Bonvallet, Dell, and Hiebel in 1954 was the first to demonstrate the activating influence of blood pressure elevation and adrenalin injection. They demonstrated that this effect is mediated by the mesencephalic reticular formation and is quite sensitive to small doses of anesthetic. They, as well as others, subsequently concluded that circulating adrenaline acted directly on the cells of the reticular formation to cause cortical activation. Several strong lines of evidence point away from this conclusion now (see Baust & Niemczyk, 1964; Baust, Niemczyk, & Vieth, 1963; Doty, Rutledge, & Larsen, 1956; Nakao, Ballin, & Gellhorn, 1956, for reviews of these topics). Recently, Baust, Niemczyk, and Vieth (1963) repeated much of this work in *encephale isolé* cats, and demonstrated that stabilization of the blood pressure during adrenalin injection greatly abbreviates and delays the cortical desynchronization. Further, they demonstrated that single units in the mesencephalic reticular formation and hypothalamus, which were influenced by mechanical changes in blood pressure, did not alter their firing rates when large amounts of adrenalin were injected during blood pressure stabilization (Baust & Niemczyk, 1963). The elevation of cerebral spinal fluid pressures does not influence these neurons; therefore, the effect is not mediated by pressoceptive neurons in the brain. They have shown that the increase or decrease of single-unit activity is not induced by other parts of the CNS, particularly not from the carotid baroceptors, but they are unable to elucidate how this phenomenon is mediated.

Parallel with the experiments concerning activation of the CNS by autonomic feedback, several investigations (Bonvallet, Dell, & Hiebel, 1954; Mazzella, Garcia-Austt, & Garcia-Mullin, 1956; Rothballer, 1959) have demonstrated that increased carotid sinus pressure causes cortical synchronization. In the firing of the medullary reticular formation, single units have been shown to be modulated by carotid and aortic baroceptors (Salmoiraghi, 1962). The importance of the baroceptors in regulation of CNS activity is further underlined by the report of Bartorelli, Bizzi, Libretti, and Zanchetti (1960) that the hypothalamic centers responsible for sham rage are under a tonic inhibitory influence from the carotic pressoceptors. They found that a transient interruption of baroceptor firing in decorticate cats was regularly followed by an outburst of sham rage and that, conversely, baroceptor stimulation could block or reduce the frequency and intensity of spontaneously occurring fits of sham rage. The relationship between this finding and a baroceptor modulation of emotional behavior in humans is problematical, but Passouant and Minvielle (1967) obtained cortical desynchronization sometimes associated with behavioral arousal by a pericarotid infiltration of Novocaine in human subjects. Reviewers have accepted this hypothesis reluctantly (Rossi & Zanchetti, 1957) and pointed out that it is the only known example of sensory influences exerting an inhibiting action in the ascending reticular formation and that unilateral sinusal distention produced a moderate slowing of the EEG that was exclusively or predominantly ipsilateral (Moruzzi, 1964). The latter finding suggests that the effect may be due to an interruption of the cerebral circulation, rather than via a neural mechanism. Still, the reticular activating system can act on the cortex in a unilateral fashion (Rothballer, 1959), and since single units within the medullary reticular formation are known to respond to baroceptor stimulation (Salmoiraghi, 1962), this effect may act through the inhibitory reticular system and be of real physiological significance.

Central nervous system activation by the reticular formation is not necessarily a nonspecific, generalized matter. Cortical activation, somatic or autonomic reflex modulation, or gating of sensory impulses may be differentially influenced by reticular stimulation (French, 1960, pp. 1281–1307; Moruzzi, 1964; Rossi & Zanchetti, 1957). Of particular psychophysiological interest is the recent report by Mészáros and Kukorelli (1965), who found that reticular stimulation in cats would progressively facilitate evoked potentials from sciatic stimulation, while first augmenting, then diminishing, evoked potentials from splenic stimulation. Thus, under some conditions, reticular activity may selectively facilitate reception from the external world, while inhibiting interoception.

Electrodermal System (GSR)

Cortex The influence of the sensory-motor cortex on GSR activity has been an area of neurophysiological interest since 1905, when Bechterew demonstrated that electrical stimulation of the cortex in the region of the sensory-motor projection area produces sweating in the footpad of the cat. These findings have been reproduced many times in the form of either phasic changes of skin potential (SP) or skin resistance (SR) (Darrow, 1937;

Langworthy & Richter, 1930; Wang, 1957, 1958; Wilcott, 1968). The majority of these studies indicate that the agranular premotor area 6 and posterolateral somatic area 2 are responsible for the footpad SP or SR responses to electrical stimulation of the cat cortex.

In a recent publication, Wilcott (1968) has challenged the concept that the excitation of cortical elements is responsible for the evoked GSR response when the cortex is stimulated electrically. He found evoked responses only when the stimulating electrode was near large blood vessels or within 5 mm of the dura. Trigeminal neurotomy abolished responses to cortical stimulation, but responses to peroneal nerve stimulation were also decreased. Earlier, Doty reported that GSRs were totally abolished after section of the 5th nerve but he found that complications of the surgery had damaged the brain stem, so no conclusion could be drawn regarding the neural mechanism of the diminished responses (Doty, Rutledge, & Larsen, 1956). Presumably, Wilcott's finding of a diminished response to peroneal stimulation was similarly mediated.

Although the participation of cortical neural elements in GSR responses to electrical stimulation of the premotor cortex is in question, ablation studies leave no doubt that this cortical area exerts a strong inhibiting effect on sweating and electrodermal phenomena. Wang (1957, 1958, 1964) found that area 6 stimulation in the cat reduced the amplitude of skin potential responses (SPRs) to peroneal nerve stimulation, and that decortication increased the amplitude of this response by 400%. Wilcott (1968) found SP levels and response amplitude well increased on the contralateral side after lesions in the sensory-motor area of the cat. Contralateral skin resistance levels and responses were *lower* in the same preparations. Schwartz (1937) found ipsilateral loss of the psychogalvanic reflex in cats whenever area 6 was included in cortical lesions, but these lesions had no effect on segmental reflexes. Stimulation and ablation studies of premotor cortex in monkeys and humans have demonstrated this area to be active in exerting considerable influence on the autonomic nervous system (Bucy, 1949; Darrow, 1937; Kennard, Viets, & Fulton, 1934; Terzuolo & Adey, 1960, pp. 797–835).

Lesions of area 6 in man and the monkey produce vasomotor changes of the extremities, profuse sweating over the contralateral side, and exaggerated grasping response to sensory stimulation of the palm.

The corticofugal pathway for GSR activity is fairly well established. In 1953, Landau found that stimulation of the pyramidal tracts produced sweating, pilo-erection, pupillary dilatation, alterations in blood pressure, heart rate changes, and gastrointestinal changes, and that section of the pyramids in the medulla abolished these responses. Earlier, in 1930, using a technique of coronal sections through the cat brain, Langworthy and Richter had found that only areas of the internal capsule and cerebral peduncles corresponding to the frontopontine and temporopontine tracts produced footpad SP responses to stimulation. No responses were found to stimulation of the red nucleus, but the rubrospinal tract below this area gave large responses. In the medulla they found the vestibular nuclei, nucleus gracilis and cuneatus, and cortical spinal tracts to produce SPRs. In the cervical cord stimulation of the posterior and lateral columns produced SPRs but none was obtained from the ventral column. It should be noted that they report biphasic SPRs from stimulation of the cortex, although only monophasic responses from stimulation of all other areas; but the significance of this interesting finding is difficult to understand. It might be considered further evidence for the reflexogenic origin of the evoked response from the cortex. Nevertheless, the findings by Langworthy and Richter require replication in chronically implanted preparations, since the mutilated nature of their preparation probably grossly distorted the normal physiology of the brain structures.

Although there are fugal connections between the frontal cortex and the hypothalamus, Wang (1957, 1958) has demonstrated that they play no part in cortical control of the footpad SP reflex in cats. Indirect evidence for the influence of these pathways on sweating in humans is the finding by Rickles and Day (1968), Wilcott (1967), and others that, under conditions of thermal or exertional sweating, evoked GSR responses can be elicited from areas of the body that are usually not active. These data suggest that hypothalamic centers responsible for nervous sweating receive impulses from the cortex but do not respond unless their threshold is lowered by thermal stimulation. An alternate hypothesis is that corticospinal pathways to nonpalmar spinal sudomotor neurons exist but are inadequate for the firing of these cells unless their threshold is lowered by tonic discharge emanating from hypothalamic-reticular formation circuits. In the cat, Wang (1957, 1958) and Wang and Brown (1956) have demonstrated that the cortical *inhibition* of the GSR is mediated through the reticular inhibitory system of the medulla. Although Wang adduced evidence that thalamic structures exert a facilitatory influence on the SP reflex, no studies have been found directly relating the unspecific activating system of the thalamus to GSR activity. Ojemann and Van Buren have recently reported that small GSR responses were found when they stimulated posterior inferior thalamus and parietal white matter in patients with movement disorder (Ojemann & Van Buren, 1967). They found GSR responses most frequently in association with induced sensations of various types and concluded that a direct effect on the GSR could not be assumed as long as there were associated sensory responses.

Ablation of the cerebellum does not alter GSR responses in the cat footpad to stimulation of peripheral nerves (Glasser, Perez-Reyes, & Tippet, 1964; Wang, 1964), but stimulation of the anterior lobe of the cerebellum does produce inhibition of the reflex response (Wang & Brown, 1956). Wang (1964) believes that the absence of a rebound effect (present in somatic reflexes), when both GSR and vasomotor reflexes are inhibited by cerebellar stimulation, indicates that the cerebellar output to the ANS is purely inhibitory. Stimulation of the caudate and hippocampus has been found to produce inhibition of the skin potential reflex to stimulation of peripheral nerve in the cat, but little else is known regarding the participation of these structures in GSR activity (Wang & Brown, 1956).

Limbic system Although over 30 years have passed since Papez (1937) published his historic paper describing this system and his speculations concerning its role in emotional behavior, surprisingly little work has been done relating structures of this system to GSR activity. In 1961 Isamat reported that stimulation of the anterior cingulate cortex produced GSR responses in the footpads of the cat. He found the subcallosal gyrus to be the most responsive area and found very few responses in the posterior two-thirds of the cingulate gyrus. Wilcott (1968) has challenged these findings, since he was not able to find any change in the SP or SR response to auditory or sensory stimulation after ablation of the anterior cingulate area in the cat. Lang, Tuovinen, and Valleala (1964) studied the relationship of amygdaloid after-discharges and GSR responses in the footpads of the cat. They found phasic GSR responses in the absence of after-discharges when the basolateral area of the amygdala was stimulated, but found a sustained GSR deflection in the presence of an after-discharge. This tonic GSR response was time-locked to the duration of the amygdala after-discharge to a much greater degree than other autonomic responses. They did not report on the effects of stimulation or ablation of fornix, mammillary bodies, anterior nucleus of the thalamus, and basal temporal cortex on GSR activity. Presumably, Langworthy and Richter, as well as Wang, stimulated the mammillary bodies without response. Stimulation of the baso-orbital cortex has been found to produce skin potential responses both in the cat and man (Langworthy & Richter, 1930; Sourek, 1965). Homskaya (1961, pp. 951–978) has studied several autonomic components of the orienting response in humans with cortical lesions in different areas of the brain. He found that, in lesions other than the frontal lobe, the ANS-orienting responses were diffuse, resistant to extinction, absent, or paradoxical (i.e., vasodilation instead of constriction). He found that giving the stimulus signal value would regularize these responses. Patients with frontal lobe lesions showed aberrations of the orienting response similar to those with nonfrontal lesions. However, giving signal value to the stimulus does not alter these aberrations in the frontal-lesioned patients. He found that with frontal lesions the GSR responses were usually absent or could be produced only by inspiration or strong auditory stimuli.

Recently, a series of papers from Pribram's laboratory has reported the effects of frontal lobe and limbic lesions in monkeys on the GSR and other components of the orienting reflex (Bagshaw & Benzies, 1968; Bagshaw, Kimble, & Pribram, 1965; Grueninger, Kimble, & Levine, 1965; Kimble, Bagshaw, & Pribram, 1965). These workers found that bilateral lesions of the amygdala and lateral frontal cortex greatly depress the GSR response to a tone stimulus. Dorsolateral, frontal lesions abolished the GSR response, but hippocampal, inferio-temporal cortex, and medial-frontal, anterior cingulate cortex lesions influenced neither the GSR response nor habituation of the response. None of these lesions affected the EEG activation associated with the orienting reflex. The authors observed that these results stand in opposition to what would be expected if the GSR component of the orienting reflex simply paralleled the behavioral alterations of hyperreactivity in frontal monkeys and resistance to habituation in amygdaloid-lesioned monkeys. They conclude that the GSR, and probably other autonomic components of the orienting response, represents a process of registering the stimulus, rather than focusing attention.

Hypothalamus Langworthy and Richter (1930), Wang (1957, 1958), and earlier authors reported that electrical stimulation of the tuber region of the hypothalamus produced SP responses in the footpads of the cat. More recently, Celesia and Wang (1964) have stimulated the hypothalamus of the intact cat with single stimuli and obtained high amplitude SPRs from the footpad. The reactive area was well circumscribed in the region of the tuber. Pairing these single pulses with subsequent cutaneous nerve stimulation, they found the hypothalamus stimulation to *facilitate* the reflexly evoked responses. Hypothalamic-evoked SPRs had a 50% *shorter* latency than those evoked by peripheral nerve stimulation, suggesting a direct hypothalamospinal pathway to spinal sudomotor neurons. Wang (1961) considers the anterior hypothalamus to be the most powerful GSR-facilitatory influence in the brain, inasmuch as this is the only area that will overcome inhibition of the GSR reflex resulting from ventromedial reticular formation stimulation. These findings are in keeping with the concept of Gellhorn and others that this area is an integrative center for the sympathetic nervous system. Presumably, GSR activity partici-

pated in the massive sympathetic discharge accompanying rage reaction resulting from medial hypothalamic stimulation.

Midbrain and medulla Several studies have clearly demonstrated that the mesencephalic reticular formation exerts a facilitatory influence, and the pontine and medullary reticular formation exerts an inhibitory influence on the skin potential reflex of the cat. Wang (1957, 1958) demonstrated that reflex SPRs of the footpad to stimulation of a peripheral nerve were augmented as much as 400% after decortication but that this augmentation was gradually diminished as the midbrain was serially sectioned and changed to inhibition after the midpontine region was reached. He elucidated the inhibitory nature of the medullary reticular formation on the skin potential reflex by demonstrating that injection of local anesthetic to the medullary reticular formation or cooling of the floor of the fourth ventricle near the obex results in increased GSR reflex amplitude.

In 1964, Glasser, Perez-Reyes, and Tippet further localized the extent of the brain stem influence on the footpad SP reflex. Using a preparation in which serial sections of the brain stem were made beginning at mesencephalic levels, they found a "powerful inhibitory system" for GSR activity in the medulla that extends upward into the midpontine region. They considered this system to be anatomically and physiologically distinct from the somatic inhibitory system described by Magoun (1950), because the latter system is largely restricted to the ventromedial reticular formation and, in contrast to the GSR system, it appears to lack an intrinsic activity but is dependent on excitatory influences from cerebral and cerebellar sources. Langworthy and Richter (1930) found SPRs when the region of the vestibular nucleus in the cat was stimulated. This finding is consonant with the common experience of profuse sweating and massive autonomic discharge (predominantly parasympathetic) associated with motion sickness. These authors also reported large SPRs to stimulation of nuclei cuneatus and gracilis, which must have been mediated through spinal and perhaps pontine reflexes, since the forebrain had been removed in their preparations.

Spinal cord In the spinal cat, Wang and Ladpli (1960; Ladpli, 1962) reported the presence of foot-pad responses elicited reflexly by stimulation of a peripheral nerve. High spinal transection (T-9) desynchronized the spontaneous SP waves in all four footpads. Spinal transection at the T-1 level desynchronized the SPs of the hindpaws but not the forepaws. SPRs to stimulation of the tail returned 3–38 days after spinal transections in contradistinction to the somatic areflexia which lasted only 1 day. Apparently, the dependence on higher centers and sensitivity to spinal shock is even greater in humans, as evidenced by the report of Sourek (1965), who found no return of reflex SP on the plantar surface of the foot after complete cord transection in humans.

SOME SPECULATIONS

In the introduction to this chapter, I stated that I hoped this review would stimulate some heuristically useful ideas for those concerned with psychophysiological problems. Several areas of speculation, drawn from the papers reviewed herein, follow to exemplify ways in which psychophysiological conceptualization may be modified to include neurophysiological data.

Lacey (1967, pp. 14–42) has suggested that psychophysiological conceptualizations are needed which are physiologically congruent with the way the brain *really* works. Expanding this concept, one may conceive of the nervous system as made up of modules of integrated organismic functions that include not only the somatic and autonomic sensory-motor functions but the feedback systems involved and the *minding capability* resulting from the operation of the module. According to this framework, Lacey's hypothesis that the CNS focuses perception either inwardly or outwardly via modulation of the heart rate is an example of such a *functional module*. The presence of neurophysiological patterns of response gives clues to the modules of behaving that the psychophysiologist must decode in terms of behavior and psychological conceptualization (minding). The preceding review is replete with examples of modular functioning in the CNS: (a) the studies by Smith et al. (1960), which demonstrate that blood pressure

and/or heart rate changes during eating or exercise could be selectively eliminated by, or even reversed by, various hypothalamic or subthalamic lesions; (b) by the separation of loci for bradycardia and tachycardia responses in the amygdala reported by Reis and Oliphant (1964); (c) the patterns of vasoconstriction and dilatation recorded when cingulate areas were stimulated by Löfving (1961); and, of course, (d) the complex patterns of fear, rage, sexual arousal, and feeding behavior that may be elicited by stimulating or destroying appropriate brain areas. The minding capabilities that arise as a result of these functional modules and their interaction remain a challenging problem.

The limitations or band width of applicability on the behavioral spectrum of a psychophysiological concept may be limited by mechanisms that alter an essential parameter of a psychophysiological response module. For example, Lacey's mechanism of autoregulation via the baroreceptor reflex is probably inactivated in extreme responses, since the baroreceptor reflex has been shown to be inhibited by hypothalamic stimulation in the area eliciting a defense reaction (Hilton, 1965).

Some systems might be used as special indicators, i.e., the highly specific sympathetic, cholinergic, muscle-vasodilator system has been shown to exhibit fractional differentiation (Kelly & Walter, 1968) and conceivably could be used to monitor the degree of defense preparation (? anxiety) contaminating experimental paradigms intended to stimulate other emotional responses. The implication of this system that (a) plays no part in homeostasis, (b) is conditionable, and (c) is well developed in very early mild defense reactions, seems to have been neglected thus far by psychophysiology. Also, the neuroanatomical and functional relationship between this system and another sympathetic, cholinergically innervated structure, the electrodermal system (GSR), would be of considerable interest.

In the various studies of autonomic responses to brain stimulation in the preceding sections, the consistent association of respiratory and somatomotor responses with autonomic reactions has become increasingly evident. One is thus struck with the implication that somatic movements, and respiratory excursions in particular, are intimately interrelated with autonomic systems in general and the cardiovascular system in particular, and that psychophysiological studies must be careful of contamination from these quarters. An example of this problem, the heart rate response, springs to mind immediately. Perhaps part of the difficulty in characterizing the cardiac component of the orienting response is due to the presence of respiratory "noise" in the heart rate. One cannot simply assume that, because no reflexic inspiration has occurred in association with a stimulus, there has been no cardiopulmonary contamination, for Clynes has shown that the heart rate transients to both inspiration and expiration have the same biphasic shape but different time constants (1961). Also, anticipation of movement (Baldwin, personal communication), even during sleep, is accompanied by changes in heart rate.

The unitary activation hypothesis equating autonomic and EEG arousal has been questioned recently (Lacey, 1967, pp. 14–42). Demonstration that autonomic responses may be greatly diminished without affecting the EEG activation response by bilateral amygdaloid lesion adds further evidence for a more sophisticated view. A limitation of these data arises from the fact that they are concerned with brief, presumably orienting responses, rather than tonic levels of activation. One assumes that the amygdala plays no part in tonic responses, since ablation studies have shown it to have little effect on baseline autonomic levels. It appears that there are both general and fractionated arousal systems. Stimulation in the appropriate areas of the reticular formation or hypothalamus may bring about tonic or phasic changes in behavioral, EEG, and autonomic arousal. The separation of these functions seems to occur, however, in the amygdala, the frontal cortex, and the hippocampus. The hippocampus seems to be uninvolved with autonomic arousal but is important in the modulation and habituation of EEG and behavioral components of the orienting response, while the amygdala and dorsolateral frontal cortex are required for elaboration of autonomic and, in the case of the amygdala, behavioral arousal, but are unconcerned with EEG arousal. It behooves the psychophysiologist to differentiate carefully the interpretation of experiments when comparisons among EEG, the behav-

ioral and autonomic responses, or baseline shifts are reported. These several dimensions of psychophysiological interest, though interrelated, are subserved by different neurophysiological systems and probably indicate important, different functional significance.

There are many other areas of central nervous system investigation that have only been mentioned in this chapter, among them, the unspecific thalamic activating system and the area of current active investigation concerning scalp EEG, alpha waves, theta waves, evoked responses, etc.; and the large literature on the anatomical substrates of conditioned behavior (both somatic and autonomic). Certain important brain areas such as the caudate and basal ganglia, which will produce autonomic and state of consciousness changes when stimulated (Divac, Rosvold, & Szwarcbart, 1967; Rubinstein & Delgado, 1963; Subberwal, Anand, & Singh, 1965) and the cerebellum, which can inhibit sham rage (Dow & Moruzzi, 1958) and has been recently implicated in aggressive behavior (Prescott & Essman, 1969), have received very little attention, as have the extensive studies of central autonomic control and representation of the gastrointestinal system (Boom, Chavez-Ibarra, Del Villar, & Hernandez-Peon, 1965; Fennegan & Puiggari, 1965) and temperature regulation (Andersson, Gale, Hokfelt, & Larsson, 1965; Bligh, 1966; Cooper, 1966). Also, we mention by citation only some papers on renal and bladder neurophysiology (Koikegami, Dodo, Mochida, & Takahashi, 1956; Lewin & Porter, 1965), CNS control of erythropoesis (Medado, Izak, & Feldman, 1967), and the CNS influence on experimental pancreatitis (Gilsdorf, Long, Moberg, & Leonard, 1965). The neuroendocrine is still another important system, and finally, the central control of respiration, which has been alluded to in different aspects of this review, has not been dealt with in proportion to its importance in the literature extant.

The theoretical importance of the neurophysiology described and noted here for the psychophysiologist is obvious, but how and if this diverse information obtained from multiple biological species can be practically applied to the tasks of psychophysiology remains for the scientist to decide.

REFERENCES

ADEY, W. R.   Computer analysis of hippocampal EEG activity and impedance in approach learning: Effects of psychotomimetic and hallucinogenic drugs. Proceedings 2nd International Pharmacological meeting, Prague, Czechoslovakia, August 1963.

ADEY, W. R., DUNLOP, C. W., & SUNDERLAND, S.   A survey of rhinencephalic interconnections with the brain stem. *Journal of Comparative Neurology*, 1958, **110**, 173-203.

ALEXANDER, R. S.   Tonic and reflex functions of medullary sympathetic cardiovascular centers. *Journal of Neurophysiology*, 1946, **9**, 205-218.

ANAND, B. K., & DUA, S.   Circulatory and respiratory changes induced by electrical stimulation of limbic system (visceral brain). *Journal of Neurophysiology*, 1956, **19**, 393-400. (a)

ANAND, B. K., & DUA, S.   Electric stimulation of the limbic system of brain (visceral brain) in the walking animals. *Indian Journal of Medical Research*, 1956, **44**, 117-119. (b)

ANAND, B. K., DUA, S., & CHHINA, G. S.   Changes in visceral and metabolic activities after frontal and temporal lobe lesions. *Indian Journal of Medical Research*, 1957, **45**, 345-352.

ANDERSSON, B., GALE, C. C., HOKFELT, B., & LARSSON, B.   Acute and chronic effects of preoptic lesions. *Acta Physiologica Scandinavica*, 1965, **65**, 45-60.

BAGSHAW, M. H., & BENZIES, S.   Multiple measures of the orienting reaction and their dissociation after amygdalectomy in monkeys. *Experimental Neurology*, 1968, **20**, 175-196.

BAGSHAW, M. H., KIMBLE, D. P., & PRIBRAM, K. H.   The GSR of monkeys during orienting and habituation and after ablation of the amygdala hippocampus and inferotemporal cortex. *Neuropsychologia*, 1965, **3**, 111-119.

BALDWIN, B. E.   Effects of stimulating the anterior-superior cerebral cortex of the cat on heart rate and the electrocardiogram. Unpublished doctoral dissertation, George Washington University, 1963.

BALITSKII, K. P., IL'CHEVICH, N. V., & PRIDATKO, O. E.   The changes in the activity of the cardiovascular system and respiration in decortication. *Bulletin of Experimental Biology and Medicine USSR*, 1961, **51**, 528-531. Cited in Baldwin, 1963.

BAN, T.   The septo-preoptico-hypothalamic system and its autonomic function. *Progress in Brain Research*, 1966, **21**(A), 1-43.

BARCROFT, H., EDHOLM, O. G., MCMICHAEL, J., & SHARPEY-SCHAFER, E. P.   Posthaemorrhagic fainting: Study by cardiac output and forearm flow. *Lancet*, 1944, **1**, 489-491.

BARD, P.   A diencephalic mechanism for the expression of rage with special reference to the sympathetic nervous system. *American Journal of Physiology*, 1928, **84**, 490-513.

BARD, P.   The central representation of the sympathetic system. *Archives of Neurology and Psychiatry*, 1959, **22**, 230-246.

BARD, P.   Anatomical organization of the central nervous system in relation to control of the heart and blood vessels. *Physiological Reviews*, 1960 (Suppl. 4), 3-26.

BARTORELLI, C., BIZZI, E., LIBRETTI, A., & ZANCHETTI, A.   Inhibitory control of sinocarotid pressoceptive afferents of hypothalamic autonomic activity and sham rage behavior. *Archives Italiennes de Biologie*, 1960, **98**, 308-326.

BAUST, W., & NIEMCZYK, H.   Studies on the adrenaline-sensitive component of the mesencephalic reticular formation. *Journal of Neurophysiology*, 1963, **26**, 692-704.

BAUST, W., & NIEMCZYK, H.   Further studies on the action of adrenergic drugs on cortical activity. *Electroencephalography and Clinical Neurophysiology*, 1964, **17**, 261-271.

BAUST, W., NIEMCZYK, H., & VIETH, J.   The action of blood pressure on the ascending reticular activating system with special reference to adrenaline-induced EEG arousal. *Electroencephalography and Clinical Neurophysiology*, 1963, **15**, 63-72.

BLAIR, D. A., GLOVER, W. E., GREENFIELD, A. D. M., & RODDIE, I. C.   Excitation of cholinergic vasodilator nerves to human skeletal muscles during emotional stress. *Journal of Physiology*, 1959, **148**, 633-647.

BLIGH, J.   The thermosensitivity of the hypothalamus and thermoregulation in mammals. *Biological Review*, 1966, **41**, 317-368.

BONVALLET, M., DELL, P., & HIEBEL, G.   Tonus sympathique et activité électrique corticale. *Electroencephalography and Clinical Neurophysiology*, 1954, **6**, 119-144.

BOOM, R., CHAVEZ-IBARRA, E., DEL VILLAR, J. J., & HERNANDEZ-PEON, R.   Changes of colonic motility induced by electrical and chemical stimulation of the forebrain and hypothalamus in cats. *British Journal of Neuropharmacology*, 1965, **4**, 169-175.

BRAZIER, M. A.   The historical development of neurophysiology. In J. FIELD, H. W. MAGOUN, & V. HALL (Eds.), *Handbook of physiology*, Section 1. Neurophysiology. Vol. 1. Washington, D.C.: American Physiological Society, 1959.

BRUTKOWSKI, S.   Functions of prefrontal cortex in animals. *Physiological Reviews*, 1965, **45**, 721-746.

BUCY, P. D. (Ed.)   *The precentral motor cortex*. Urbana: University of Illinois Press, 1949.

CELESIA, G. G., & WANG, G. H.   Sudomotor activity induced by single shock stimulation of the hypothalamus in anesthetized cats. *Archives Italiennes de Biologie*, 1964, **102**, 587-598.

CHAPMAN, W. P., SHROEDER, H. R., GEYER, G., BRAZIER, M. A. B., FAGER, C., POPPEN, J. L., SOLOMON, H. C., & YAKOVLEV, P. I.   Physiological evidence concerning importance of the amygdaloid nuclear region in the integration of circulatory function and emotion in man. *Science*, 1954, **120,** 949–950.

CHITANONDH, H. Stereotaxic amygdalotomy in the treatment of olfactory seizures and psychiatric disorders with olfactory hallucination. *Confinia Neurologica*, 1966, **27,** 181–196.

CLYNES, M. Respiratory sinus arrhythmia: Laws derived from computer simulation. *Journal of Applied Physiology*, 1961, **15,** 863–874.

COHEN, M. I., & HUGELIN, A. Suprapontine reticular control of intrinsic respiratory mechanisms. *Archives Italiennes de Biologie*, 1965, **103,** 317–334.

COOPER, K. E. Temperature regulation and the hypothalamus. *British Medical Bulletin*, 1966, **22,** 238–242.

COVIAN, M. R., ANTUNES-RODRIGUES, J., & O'FLAHERTY, J. J. Effects of stimulation of the septal area upon blood pressure and respiration in the cat. *Journal of Neurophysiology*, 1964, **27,** 394–407.

COVIAN, M. R., & HOUSSAY, H. E. J. Arterial hypertension in hemidecorticate rats. *Circulation Research*, 1955, **111,** 459–462.

COVIAN, M. R., & TIMO-IARIA, C. Decreased blood pressure due to brain septal stimulation: Parameters of stimulation, bradycardia, baroreceptor reflex. *Physiology and Behavior*, 1966, **1,** 37–43.

CROSBY, E. C., HUMPHREY, T., & LAUER, E. W. *Correlative anatomy of the nervous system.* New York: Macmillan, 1962.

CROSS, B. A. The hypothalamus in mammalian homeostasis. *Symposium of the Society for Experimental Biology*, 1964, **18,** 157–193.

DARROW, C. W. Neural mechanisms controlling the palmar galvanic skin reflex and palmar sweating. *Archives of Neurology and Psychiatry*, 1937, **37,** 641–663.

DELGADO, J. M. R. Circulatory effects of cortical stimulation. *Physiological Reviews*, 1960 (Suppl. 4), 146–178.

DIVAC, I., ROSVOLD, H. E., & SZWARCBART, M. K. Behavioral effects of selective ablation of the caudate nucleus. *Journal of Comparative and Physiological Psychology*, 1967, **63,** 184–190.

DOTY, R. W. The limbic system. In A. M. FREEDMAN & H. I. KAPLAN (Eds.), *Textbook of psychiatry.* Baltimore: Williams & Wilkins, 1967.

DOTY, R. W., RUTLEDGE, L. T., & LARSEN, R. M. Conditional reflexes established to electrical stimulation of cat cerebral cortex. *Journal of Neurophysiology*, 1956, **19,** 401–415.

DOUGLAS, R. J., & PRIBRAM, K. H. Learning and limbic lesions. *Neuropsychology*, 1966, **4,** 197–220.

DOW, R. S., & MORUZZI, G. *The physiology and pathology of the cerebellum.* Minneapolis: University of Minnesota Press, 1958.

ECONOMO, C. von, & KOSKINAS, G. N. *Die Cytoarchitektonic der Hirnrinde des Erwachsenen Menschen.* Wien: Springer, 1925. (Cited in Hoff, Kell, & Carroll, 1963.)

ENOCH, D. M., & KERR, W. L. Hypothalamic vasopressor and vesicopressor pathways: 1. Functional studies. *Archives of Neurology*, 1967, **16,** 290–320.

FEIGL, E., JOHANSSON, B., & LÖFVING, B. Renal vasoconstriction and the "defense reaction." *Acta Physiologica Scandinavica*, 1964, **62,** 429–435.

FENNEGAN, F. M., & PUIGGARI, M. J. Hypothalamic and amygdaloid influence on gastric motility in dogs. *Journal of Neurosurgery*, 1965, **24,** 497–504.

FITZSIMONS, J. T. The hypothalamus and drinking. *British Medical Bulletin*, 1966, **22,** 232–237.

FOLKOW, B. Nervous control of blood vessels. *Physiological Reviews*, 1955, **35,** 629–663.

FOLKOW, B., & EULER, U. S. von Selective activation of noradrenaline and adrenaline-producing cells in the cat's adrenal gland by hypothalamic stimulation. *Circulation Research*, 1954, **2,** 191–195.

FRENCH, J. D. The reticular formation. In J. FIELD, H. W. MAGOUN, & V. E. HALL (Eds.), *Handbook of physiology,* Section 1. *Neurophysiology.* Vol. 2. Washington, D.C.: American Physiological Society, 1960.

GELLHORN, E. The significance of the state of the central autonomic nervous system for quantitative and qualitative aspects of some cardiovascular reactions. *American Heart Journal*, 1964, **67,** 106–120.

GILSDORF, R. B., LONG, D., MOBERG, A., & LEONARD, A. S. Central nervous system influence on experimentally induced pancreatitis. *Journal of the American Medical Association*, 1965, **192,** 394–397.

GLASSER, R. L. Brain stem augmentation of cardiovascular activity. *American Journal of Physiology*, 1960, **198,** 421–423.

GLASSER, R. L., PEREZ-REYES, M., & TIPPET, J. W. Brain-stem inhibition of electrodermal (galvanic skin) activity. *American Journal of Physiology*, 1964, **207,** 1133–1138.

GLOOR, P. Autonomic functions of the diencephalon: A summary of the experimental work of Professor W. R. Hess. *Archives of Neurology and Psychiatry*, 1954, **71,** 773–790.

GLOOR, P. Amygdala. In J. FIELD, H. W. MAGOUN, & V. E. HALL (Eds.), *Handbook of physiology,* Section 1. *Neurophysiology.* Vol. 2. Washington, D.C.: American Physiological Society, 1960.

GLOOR, P., & FEINDEL, W. Psychische Funktionen und vegetativen Nervensystem. (b) Affective behavior and temporal lobe. In M. Monnier, *Physiologie und Pathophysiologie des vegetativen Nervensystem. II. Pathophysiologie.* Stuttgart, West Germany: Hippokrates-Verlag, 1963.

GODDARD, G. Functions of the amygdala. *Psychological Bulletin*, 1964, **62,** 89–109.

GREEN, J. P. The hippocampus. *Physiological Reviews*, 1964, **44,** 561–608.

GRUENINGER, W. E., KIMBLE, D. P., & LEVINE, S. GSR and corticosteroid response in monkeys with frontal ablations. *Neuropsychologia*, 1965, **3,** 205–216.

HEATH, R. G. Pleasure response of human subject to direct stimulation of the brain: Physiologic and psychodynamic considerations. In R. G. HEATH (Ed.), *The role of pleasure in behavior.* New York: Hoeber, 1964.

HILTON, S. Hypothalamic control of the cardiovascular responses in fear and rage. *Scientific Basis of Medicine: Annual Reviews,* 1965, 217–238.

HOFF, E. C., & GREEN, H. D. Cardiovascular reactions induced by electrical stimulation of the cerebral cortex. *American Journal of Physiology,* 1936, **117,** 411–422.

HOFF, E. C., KELL, J. R., Jr., & CARROLL, M. N., Jr. Effects of cortical stimulation and lesions on cardiovascular function. *Physiological Reviews,* 1963, **43,** 68–114.

HOMSKAYA, E. D. The effect of a verbal instruction on the autonomic components of the orienting reflex in brain lesions (Russian). Moscow: Doklady Akademiia Pedagogicheskikh Nauk RSFSR, 1961. (Cited in A. R. Luria, *Human brain and psychological processes.* New York: Harper & Row, 1966.)

INGRAM, W. R. Central autonomic mechanism. In J. FIELD, H. W. MAGOUN, & V. E. HALL (Eds.), *Handbook of physiology,* Section 1. *Neurophysiology.* Vol. 2. Washington D.C.: American Physiological Society, 1960.

ISAMAT, F. Galvanic skin responses from stimulation of limbic cortex. *Journal of Neurophysiology,* 1961, **24,** 176–181.

JACKSON, J. H. *Selected Writings of John Hulings Jackson.* Vol. 1. J. TARJAN (Ed.) New York: Basic Books, 1958.

JELASIC, F. Relation of the lateral part of the amgdala to pain. *Confinia Neurologica,* 1966, **27,** 53–55.

KAADA, B. R. Somato-motor, autonomic and electrocorticographic responses to electrical stimulation of "rhinencephalic" and other structures in primates, cat, and dog. *Acta Physiologica Scandinavica,* 1951, **24** (Suppl. 83), 1–285.

KARMOS, G., GRASTYÁN, E., LOSONCZY, H., VERECZKEY, L., & GRÓSZ, J. The possible role of the hippocampus in the organization of the orientation reaction. *Acta Physiologica Academiae Scientiarum Hungaricae,* 1965, **26,** 131–141.

KARPLUS, J. P., & KREIDL, A. Gehirn und Sympathicus. VII Mitteilung: Uber Beziehungen der Hypothalamus zentren zu Blutdruck und innerer Sekretion. *Pflugers Archiv für die gesamte Physiologie,* 1927, **215,** 667–670.

KELLY, D. H. W., & WALTER, C. J. S. The relationship between clinical diagnosis and anxiety, assessed by forearm blood flow and other measurements. *British Journal of Psychiatry,* 1968, **114,** 611–626.

KENNARD, M. A. Focal autonomic representation in the cortex and its relation to sham rage. *Journal of Neuropathology and Experimental Neurology,* 1945, **4,** 295–304.

KENNARD, M. A., VIETS, H. R., & FULTON, J. F. The syndrome of the premotor cortex in man: Impairment of skilled movements, forced grasping, spasticity, and vasomotor disturbance. *Brain,* 1934, **57,** 69–84.

KIMBLE, D. P., BAGSHAW, M. H., & PRIBRAM, K. H. The GSR of monkeys during orienting and habituation after selective partial ablations of the congulate and frontal cortex. *Neuropsychologia,* 1965, **3,** 121–128.

KLUVER, H., & BUCY, P. C. Preliminary analysis of functions of the temporal lobes in monkeys. *Archives of Neurology and Psychiatry,* 1939, **42,** 979–1000.

KOIKEGAMI, H., DODO, T., MOCHIDA, Y., & TAKAHASHI, H. Stimulation experiments on the amygdaloid nuclear complex and related structures: Effects on renal volume, urinary secretion, movements of the urinary bladder, blood pressure and respiratory movements. *Folia Psychiatrica et Neurologica Japonica,* 1957, **11,** 157–206.

LACEY, J. I. Somatic response patterning and stress: Some revisions of activation theory. In M. H. APPLEY & R. TRUMBULL (Eds.), *Psychological stress: Issues in research.* New York: Appleton-Century-Crofts, 1967.

LADPLI, R. Galvanic skin reactions of chronic spinal cats. *American Journal of Physical Medicine,* 1962, **41,** 15–22.

LANDAU, W. M. Autonomic responses mediated via the corticospinal tract. *Journal of Neurophysiology,* 1953, **16,** 299–311.

LANG, H., TUOVINEN, T., & VALLEALA, P. Amygdaloid after discharge and galvanic skin response. *Electroencephalography and Clinical Neurophysiology,* 1964, **16,** 366–374.

LANGWORTHY, O. R., RICHTER, C. P. The influence of efferent cerebral pathways upon the sympathetic nervous system. *Brain,* 1930, **53,** 178–193.

LEWIN, R. J., & PORTER, R. W. Inhibition of spontaneous bladder activity by stimulation of the globus pallidus. *Neurology,* 1965, **15,** 1049–1052.

LÖFVING, B. Cardiovascular adjustments induced from the rostral cingulate gyrus, with special reference to sympatho-inhibitory mechanisms. *Acta Physiologica Scandinavica,* 1961, **53** (Suppl. 184), 1–82.

MACLEAN, P. D., PLOOG, D. W., & ROBINSON, B. W. Circulatory effects of limbic stimulation with special reference to the male genital organs. *Physiological Reviews,* 1960, **40** (Suppl. 4), 105–112.

MAGOUN, H. W. Caudal and cephalic influences of the brain stem reticular formation. *Physiological Reviews,* 1950, **30,** 459–473.

MANNING, J. W. Cardiovascular reflexes following lesions in medullary reticular formation. *American Journal of Physiology,* 1965, **208,** 283–288.

MAZZELLA, E., GARCIA-AUSTT, E., & GARCIA-MULLIN, R. Carotid sinus and EEG. *Electroencephalography and Clinical Neurophysiology,* 1956, **8,** 155. (Abstract)

MEDADO, P., IZAK, G., & FELDMAN, S. The effect of electrical stimulation of the central nervous system on erythropoiesis in the rat: II. Localization of a specific brain structure capable of enhancing red cell production. *Journal of Laboratory and Clinical Medicine,* 1967, **69,** 776–786.

MÉSZÁROS, I., & KUKORELLI, T. Reticular control of

splanchnic afferentation. *Acta Physiologica Academiae Scientiarum Hungaricae,* 1965, **26,** 143–148.

MITCHELL, G. A. G. *Anatomy of the autonomic nervous system.* Edinburgh, Scotland: E. & S. Livingstone, 1953.

MORUZZI, G. Reticular influences on the EEG. *Electro-encephalography and Clinical Neurophysiology,* 1964, **16,** 2–17.

NAKAO, H., BALLIN, H. M., & GELLHORN, E. The role of the sino-aortic receptors in the action of adrenaline, noradrenaline, and acetylcholine on the cerebral cortex. *Electroencephalography and Clinical Neurophysiology,* 1956, **8,** 413–420.

NAUTA, W. J. H. Neural associations of the amygdaloid complex in the monkey. *Brain,* 1962, **85,** 505–520.

NEWMAN, P. P., & WOLSTENCROFT, J. H. Influence of orbital cortex on blood pressure responses in cat. *Journal of Neurophysiology,* 1960, **23,** 211–223.

OBERHOLZER, R. J. H. Circulatory centers in medulla and midbrain. *Physiological Reviews,* 1960, **40** (Suppl. 4), 179–197.

OBERHOLZER, R. J. G., & TOFANI, W. P. The neural control of respiration. In J. Field, H. W. MAGOUN, & V. E. HALL (Eds.), *Handbook of physiology,* Section 1. *Neurophysiology.* Vol 2. Washington, D.C.: American Physiological Society, 1960.

OJEMANN, G. A., & VAN BUREN, J. M. Respiratory, heart rate, and GSR responses from human diencephalon. *Archives of Neurology,* 1967, **16,** 74–88.

OVCHAROVA, P. Changes in some non-conditioned cardiovascular reflexes in lesions of the frontal lobes of the brain. *Zhurnal Neuropatologic i Psikhiatric,* 1962, **62,** 519–522. (Cited in Baldwin, 1963.)

PAINE, R. The nervous system and the heart: Part III. *Missouri Medicine,* 1965, **62,** 842–846.

PAPEZ, J. W. A proposed mechanism of emotion. *Archives of Neurology and Psychiatry,* 1937, **38,** 725–743.

PASSOUANT, P., & MINVIELLE, J. Étude de la réaction d'éveil provoqúee par l'infiltration pericarotidienne de Novocaine. *Revue de Neurologie,* 1954, **90,** 140–152. (Cited in Rossi & Zanchetti, 1957.)

PENFIELD, W. The supplementary motor area in the cerebral cortex of man. *Archiv für Psychiatrie und Nervenkrankheiten vereinigt mit Zeitschrift für die gesamte Neurologie und Psychiatrie, Berlin,* 1950, **185,** 670–674.

PRESCOTT, J. W., & ESSMAN, W. B. The psychobiology of maternal-social deprivation and the etiology of violent-aggressive behavior: A special case of sensory deprivation. Presented at the 2nd Annual Winter Conference, Brain Research, January 1969.

PRIBRAM, K. H., LENNOX, M. A., & DUNSMORE, R. H. Some connections of the orbito-fronto-temporal, limbic, and hippocampal areas of Macaca mulatta. *Journal of Neurophysiology,* 1950, **13,** 127–135.

RAISMAN, G. Neural connections of the hypothalamus. *British Medical Bulletin,* 1966, **22,** 197–201.

RANSON, S. W., & MAGOUN, H. W. The hypothalamus. *Ergebnisse der Physiologie,* 1939, **41,** 56–163.

REIS, D. J., & OLIPHANT, M. C. Bradycardia and tachycardia following electrical stimulation of the amygdaloid region in monkey. *Journal of Neurophysiology,* 1964, **27,** 893–912.

RICKLES, W. H., Jr. Depth implants in patients with chronic schizophrenia. *Annals of Internal Medicine,* 1969, **71**(3), 632–633.

RICKLES, W. H., Jr., & DAY, J. L. Electrodermal activity in non-palmar skin sites. *Psychophysiology,* 1968, **4,** 421–435.

ROSSI, G. F., & ZANCHETTI, A. The brain stem reticular formation: Anatomy and physiology. *Archives Italiennes de Biologie,* 1957, **95,** 199–435.

ROTHBALLER, A. B. Studies on the adrenaline-sensitive component of the reticular activating system. *Electro-encephalography and Clinical Neurophysiology,* 1956, **8,** 603–621.

ROTHBALLER, A. B. The effects of catecholamines on the central nervous system. *Pharmacological Review,* 1959, **11,** 494–547.

RUBINSTEIN, E. H., & DELGADO, J. M. R. Inhibition induced by forebrain stimulation in the monkey. *American Journal of Physiology,* 1963, **205,** 941–948.

SALMOIRAGHI, G. C. "Cardiovascular" neurones in brain stem of cat. *Journal of Neurophysiology,* 1962, **25,** 182–197.

SCHWARTZ, H. G. Effect of experimental lesions of the cortex on the "psychogalvanic reflex" in the cat. *Archives of Neurology and Psychiatry,* 1937, **38,** 308–320.

SMITH, O. A., JABBUR, S. J., RUSHMER, R. F., & LASHER, E. P. Role of hypothalamic structures in cardiac control. *Physiological Reviews,* 1960, **40** (Suppl. 4), 136–145.

SOLINSKY, O. The limbic system: Its relation to personality. *Georgetown Medical Bulletin,* 1964, **17,** 161–177.

SOUREK, K. *The nervous control of skin potential in man.* Translated by A. Hermann, Prague: Nakladatelstvi Ceskoslovenske Akademi Ved., 1965.

SUBBERWAL, U., ANAND, B. K., & SINGH, B. Effect of caudate stimulation on some vegetative functions. *Indian Journal of Medical Research,* 1965, **53** (11), 1034–1039.

TAN, E.-S. Brain-stem regions for stimulus-bound and stimulus-related respiration. *Experimental Neurology,* 1967, **17,** 517–528.

TERZUOLO, C. A., & ADEY, W. R. Sensorimotor cortical activities. In J. FIELD, H. W. MAGOUN, & V. E. HALL (Eds.), *Handbook of physiology,* Section 1. *Neurophysiology.* Vol. 2. Washington, D.C.: American Physiological Society, 1960.

TORII, S., & KAWAMURA, H. Effects of amygdaloid stimulation on blood pressure and electrical activity of hippocampus. *Japanese Journal of Physiology,* 1960, **10,** 374–384.

URSIN, H., & KAADA, B. R. Functional localization within the amygdaloid complex in the cat. *Electroencephalography and Clinical Neurophysiology,* 1960, **12,** 1–20.

UVNAS, B. Central cardiovascular control. In J. FIELD, H. W. MAGOUN, & V. E. HALL (Eds.), *Handbook of physiology,* Section 1. *Neurophysiology.* Vol. 2. Washington, D.C.: American Physiological Society, 1960.

WALL, P. D., & DAVIS, G. D. Three cerebral cortical systems affecting autonomic function. *Journal of Neurophysiology,* 1951, **14,** 507–517.

WALL, P. D., & PRIBRAM, K. H. Trigeminal neurotomy and blood pressure responses from stimulation of lateral cerebral cortex of Macaca mulatta. *Journal of Neurophysiology,* 1950, **13,** 409–412.

WANG, G. H. The galvanic skin reflex: A review of old and recent works from a physiologic point of view. Part 1. *American Journal of Physical Medicine,* 1957, **36,** 295–320.

WANG, G. H. The galvanic skin reflex: A review of old and recent works from a physiologic point of view. Part II. *American Journal of Physical Medicine,* 1958, **37,** 35–57.

WANG, G. H. *The neural control of sweating.* Madison: University of Wisconsin Press, 1964.

WANG, G. H., & BROWN, V. W. Suprasegmental inhibitions of an autonomic reflex. *Journal of Neurophysiology,* 1956, **19,** 564–572.

WANG, G. H., & LADPLI, R. Spontaneous variations of skin potentials in footpads of normal, striatal and spinal cats. *Journal of Neurophysiology,* 1960, **23,** 448–452.

WIDDICOMBE, J. G. Respiratory reflexes. In W. O. FINN & H. RAHN (Eds.), *Handbook of physiology,* Section 3. *Respiration.* Vol. 1. Washington D.C.: American Physiological Society, 1964.

WILCOTT, R. C. Arousal sweating and electrodermal phenomena. *Psychological Bulletin,* 1967, **67** 58–72.

WILCOTT, R. C. Cortical control of skin potential, skin resistance and sweating. *Psychophysiology,* 1968, **4,** 500. (Abstract)

YOKOTA, T., & FUJIMORI, B. Effects of brain-stem stimulation upon hippocampal electrical activity, somatomotor reflexes and autonomic functions. *Electroencephalography and Clinical Neurophysiology,* 1964, **16,** 375–382.

PART

2 EXPERIMENTAL DESIGN AND METHODS

Laverne C. Johnson and Ardie Lubin

ON PLANNING PSYCHOPHYSIOLOGICAL EXPERIMENTS

DESIGN, MEASUREMENT, AND ANALYSIS

3

The experimental design, the method of measurement, and the type of statistical analysis—all of these factors generally have a profound effect on the conclusions reached by the experimenter. For example, designs with two or more treatments on each subject may yield very different results from designs with a single treatment for each subject (Grice, 1966); counterbalancing the treatments will not eliminate the interaction bias caused by treatment carryover (Poulton & Freeman, 1966). Use of the heart period rather than its reciprocal, the heart rate, may change the correlation of the response level with the prestimulus level. Time series analyses such as the Fourier computation of spectral power, serial correlations, and interevent randomness tests of time intervals answer questions that cannot be posed within the usual analysis of variance model. The choice of experimental design, the measurement technique, and the method of statistical analysis tend to be restricted by the experimenter's limited knowledge about the alternatives open to him and about the differing results of each choice. Perhaps an even larger influence is exerted by the experimenter's conscious or unconscious acceptance of certain proposed principles of psychophysiology; e.g., homeostasis, the activation continuum, Wilder's law of initial value.

The purpose of this chapter is to present some theoretical and empirical considerations concerning the environmental and subject variables, choice of design, measurement method, and statistical analysis. All of these aspects of psychophysiological experimentation are intimately and intricately related; the choice of one has considerable effect upon the choice of others. We believe that the more the experimenter knows about the consequences of his choice, the better he will be able to select those procedures that will give unbiased answers to his questions.

EXPERIMENTAL VARIABLES

Based upon the results of his survey and his own research, Wenger (1962, pp. 97–114) concluded that five environmental variables have shown substantial relations to physiological results: time of testing, initial room temperature, external temperature at time of testing, lowest relative humidity, and highest barometric pressure in the 24 hr prior to testing. In addition, initial and partial correlations indicated that, for certain physiological variables, corrections for the maximal concentration of total oxidants on the day of testing must be considered.

INTERNAL VARIABLES

Variance within Subject

Set or attitude   The effect of environmental variables can usually be handled by experimental design, laboratory construction, or through statistical controls, but the variance introduced by the subject is difficult to identify and control. We are often unable to measure, or are unaware of, the subject's definition of the situation and how this influences his response by predisposing him to perceive or act in a certain way. Several studies have emphasized how the subject's set or cognitive appraisal mediates both physiological and behavioral response to stress or situations (Lazarus & Opton, 1966; Sternbach, 1966, pp. 111–138). Hodges and Spielberger (1966) showed the effects of the subject's cognitive appraisal of a stressor situation— in this case, the threat of shock. Subjects who had reported moderate to extreme fear of shock months prior to the experiment responded with greater heart rate acceleration than subjects who reported little or no fear. In addition to the subject's set, the experimenter's hopes and expectations may also influence the subject's response. Rosenthal (1964)

has discussed the role of experimenter outcome-orientation and the results of psychological experiments in general.

While the subject and the experimenter may be unaware of these unverbalized predisposing attitudes and expectations, the technique used by Hodges & Spielberger (1966), that of questioning their subjects on attitudes toward shock, a significant aspect of their study, is one way of possibly determining the effects of the subject's set. Another technique is that of controlling the attitude or set of the subject by deliberately structuring the situation to induce certain attitudes or emotional states. Ax (1953) deliberately induced a feeling of fear or of anger and reported differing physiological response patterns for these two emotional states. Hypnosis has been used to investigate the effects of varying attitudes on physiological response (Graham, Kabler, & Graham, 1962). Physiological responses of unhypnotized subjects to attitude suggestions have also been studied by Graham and Kunish (1965). They found that suggestions to the unhypnotized subjects could produce the same kind of differential physiological responses as do hypnotic suggestions but generally not to the same degree.

Level of activation   Another attribute of the subject that will affect physiological response is the level of arousal or activation, i.e., whether the subject is bored, alert, excited, drowsy, asleep, etc. The early conception of arousal as a unidimensional continuum ranging from coma to a highly disorganized state of behavior (Duffy, 1962; Lindsley, 1951; Malmo, 1959) has been challenged. This challenge has come primarily from the increasing body of evidence indicating that there is no consistent monotonic physiological change associated with the differing behavioral levels of arousal. In contrast to the earlier notions that the level of arousal would be reflected in all physiological variables, the data indicate that there is no single measure or combination of measures that can be consistently used as the best indicator of activation. Sternbach (1960) found no correlation between two indices of activation, Wenger's estimate of relative autonomic balance and percent time alpha. Drugs have been used to produce striking dissociation between the electroencephalogram (EEG) and motor behavior. Atropine produces a synchronized, slow wave EEG during alert and even excited waking activity (Wikler, 1952); whereas physostigmine produces the opposite effect: low voltage EEG activity in the presence of quiescence and, in some instances, during sleep (Bradley, 1958, pp. 123–149).

Nonspecific (spontaneous) autonomic responses (responses without known external stimuli) have been viewed as one of the best estimates of arousal; however, such responses as spontaneous heart rate, skin resistance, etc., have insignificant correlations with each other. Johnson (1963) found that the spontaneous activity of a specific variable, e.g., heart rate or skin resistance, predicted the level of response to stimuli for that variable, but it was not possible to predict the heart rate response (HRR) to external stimuli from the background spontaneous skin resistance responses (SRRs) or the evoked SRR from the background heart rate (HR) fluctuations. Since we cannot make inferences as to reactivity or basal level from one variable to another, such terms as general autonomic lability are of doubtful value.

Lacey (1967) has pressed for a revised activation theory, based on his belief that electrocortical, autonomic, skeletal muscle, and other behavioral systems are imperfectly coupled, interacting systems.

Despite disagreement over the physiological correlates of activation and the measures that should be used as criteria of activation, there is little disagreement over the need to control for changes in level of consciousness as measured by the EEG. We refer in particular to the transition from waking through the various stages of sleep. One can only guess at the number of studies that have been done using subjects who were supposed to be awake but actually dozed or even slept through the experiment. Until recently, few laboratories routinely monitored the EEG as part of their psychophysiological studies. The importance of monitoring the EEG as a measure of alertness was demonstrated by McDonald, Johnson, and Hord (1964). Cardiovascular behavior, the heart rate responses (HRRs), and finger pulse responses (FPRs) of the drowsy group showed little habituation, while the alert subjects showed the usual habituation curves. Further work (Johnson & Lubin, 1967) has confirmed the failure of the cardiovascular orienting

response (OR) to habituate and disappear when recorded from sleeping subjects. The autonomic OR habituated in the waking subject and returned with sleep onset but the degree to which it returned differed from variable to variable. While the cardiovascular OR during sleep often exceeded that when awake, the electrodermal OR during sleep was lower than during waking. Both ORs varied in the rate of occurrence over the various stages of sleep. In addition to differences in magnitude, the latency and shape of the response varied with the alertness of the subject.

Keefe, Johnson, and Hunter (1971), in a detailed study of the response hierarchy of EEG and autonomic variables to stimuli, found clear differences in the pattern of response for the awake and sleep states. In the awake state the response in all variables occurred as the auditory threshold was reached and a motor response to a tone was made. But during sleep there were clear responses to stimuli below the arousal threshold and the motor response, and further there was a definite ordering of the appearance of the various responses. EEG responses occurred to stimuli 30–25 dB below arousal threshold and preceded finger pulse and heart rate responses, which occurred 20–10 dB below arousal from sleep. Significant skin potential, skin resistance, and motor responses were seen only at arousal threshold, as indicated by EEG signs of awakening.

The importance of the level of consciousness for electrodermal responses has been noted also by Johnson and Davidoff (1964) and Ojemann and Van Buren (1967). Johnson and Davidoff found that during petit mal absence attacks the cardiovascular and respiratory changes were clearly present during the attack, but the electrodermal change (SRR) occurred only after the attack had ended and the subject was again aware and responsive.

Ojemann and Van Buren (1967), in a study of respiratory, heart rate, and electrodermal responses induced by electrical stimulation in the diencephalon, noted that while the respiratory and heart rate changes followed stimulation per se, electrodermal changes (SRR) were related to the presence of subjective sensations during stimulation.

Spontaneous activity further highlights the difference between waking and sleeping. During sleep the spontaneous activity for every autonomic variable thus far studied exceeds that seen during waking but the maximal rate for each variable does not occur during the same stage of sleep. Spontaneous electrodermal activity is maximum during slow wave sleep (Johnson & Lubin, 1966), while the cardiovascular variables and respiratory measures show maximal variability during *Stage* REM sleep (Johnson, 1966; Snyder, Hobson, Morrison, & Goldfrank, 1964).

In a review paper entitled "A Psychophysiology for All States," Johnson (1970) asked the question, "Can the same EEG and visceral changes occur in different states of consciousness [p. 501]?" A survey of EEG and autonomic activity led to the conclusion that the answer is "Yes," and the use of EEG and autonomic activity to define states of consciousness, especially when only one or two variables are used, was seriously questioned. "Instead of using our autonomic and EEG measures to define state, the reverse appears more appropriate. We must first determine the state before we can interpret our physiological measures [p. 515]."

Variance between subjects

Age The electrodermal systems of the newborn and the aged subject are relatively unresponsive (Cohen, Silverman, & Shmavonian, 1961; Richter, 1930; Surwillo & Quilter, 1965). For many years it was thought the SRR could not be obtained during the first few hours of life because of inactive eccrine sweat glands (Richter, 1930). Kaye's finding (1964) of a significant increase in skin conductance over the first 4 days of life supported Richter's conclusions; but Crowell, Davis, Chun, and Spellacy (1965) demonstrated an SRR to light, sound, and tactile stimuli in neonates. By the age of four (Jones, 1935), electrodermal activity appears to follow the adult pattern.

With aging, the spontaneous electrodermal responses decrease. Surwillo and Quilter (1965) and Cohen, Silverman, and Shmavonian (1961) found that the overall amplitude of the evoked SRR was lower in aged subjects. Elliott found more near zero correlations among physiological responses and lower habituation rates in kindergarten children than in young adults. Elliott raises the problems of maintaining a consistent "set" in young children. It is of interest that the dissociation and lack of

habituation in children is similar to that Johnson and Lubin (1967) found for the sleeping adult.

Brain activity as measured by the EEG is also influenced by age. The waking infant's EEG is characterized by dominant high amplitude delta (1–4 Hz) activity. As the child matures, the frequency increases and the amplitude decreases, until usually by the teens the waking alpha frequencies (8–12 Hz) dominate. As old age approaches, there is a general slowing, especially in the alpha range of the EEG (Obrist & Busse, 1965, pp. 185–205).

Several studies have conclusively demonstrated that the cardiac orienting response is influenced by age (Berg, Berg, & Graham, 1971; Clifton & Meyers, 1969; Graham et al., 1970; Gray & Crowell, 1968; Lipton, Steinschneider, & Richmond, 1961). During the first few months of life, the HR response to stimuli undergoes marked changes. In newborns, the response to stimuli is accelerative while in infants 2½–5 months old the response to the same stimuli is solely decelerative. For Graham and her colleagues (Graham & Clifton, 1966; Graham & Jackson, 1970, pp. 59–117), these changes support their view that deceleration is associated with an orienting system which facilitates stimulus intake and learning while acceleration can be interpreted as part of a protective-defensive system which mobilizes the organism but inhibits stimulus intake. An alternative explanation would be one involving neuronal maturation, and it is of interest that neonates' acceleratory response is similar to the HR OR during sleep (Johnson & Lubin, 1967).

These three areas alone, electrodermal activity, EEG, and HR, indicate the necessity of considering age in psychophysiological experiments. For a more extensive review of these variables, as well as respiration rate (RR) and muscle activity, the reader is referred to Elliott's monograph (1964).

Sex Studies comparing the electrodermal activity of men and women have consistently reported lower basal skin conductance values and less electrodermal responsivity to stimuli for women (Davis, 1932; Graham, Cohen, & Shmavonian, 1966; Kimmel & Hill, 1961; Kimmel & Kimmel, 1965; Plutchik, 1964; Shmavonian, Yarmat, & Cohen, 1965). McNair, Droppleman, and Pillard (1967) reported that, when age was controlled, women perspire less, as measured either by the sweat ring or the sweat weight techniques for the activity of eccrine sweat glands.

Shmavonian, Graham, and their colleagues have found that young men show a larger vasomotor response and that women have a higher HRR to stimuli. They conclude that it would be grossly erroneous to mix men and women in studies involving physiological measures.

Race and culture Electrodermal activity appears to be the only physiological variable that differs significantly among the races. Dark-skinned races appear to have lower basal skin conductance levels than do Caucasians, as reported from studies of Negroes (Johnson & Corah, 1963; Johnson & Landon, 1965) and Indians (Malmo, 1965). Wenger (personal communication) reported that the skin conductance level of Orientals fell between the levels of Caucasians and Negroes. Bernstein (1965) found higher basal skin level impedance in Negro subjects than in whites. Kugelmass and Lieblich (1966) have suggested that there may be lower electrodermal responsivity in dark-skinned races but these findings have not been supported (Bernstein, 1965; Johnson & Landon, 1965). Racial differences in responsivity found by Johnson & Landon were eliminated when differences in basal level conductance were controlled, suggesting that the difference in response reflected differing prestimulus levels.

The reasons for a racial difference in basal electrodermal values are still unknown. Malmo (1965) felt that this difference was in the sweat glands and reported lower finger sweat values for Negro, Indian, and Arab subjects than for Caucasians and Orientals. Johnson and Landon (1965) found a lower number of active eccrine sweat glands in Negroes than Caucasians but the difference between the races was not significant. Similar insignificant findings in the number and distribution of eccrine sweat glands for Africans and Europeans have been reported by Thomson (1954).

In studies of a related area, ethnic differences, Sternbach and Tursky (1965; Tursky & Sternbach, 1967) found that skin potential and other psychophysiological responses differ among Irish, Yankee (Protestants of British descent whose parents and grandparents were born in the United States), Jew-

ish, and Italian housewives, suggesting a possible need to control for ethnic, as well as racial, differences in psychophysiological studies. The need to control for cultural variables is indicated by the study of Japanese subjects, who, in contrast to Americans, showed the same high basal skin conductance during a benign film as during a stressful film. American subjects showed lower skin conductance during the showing of the benign film (Lazarus, Tomita, Kodama, & Opton, 1966).

Intelligence Higher basal conductance and decreased electrodermal responsiveness are the most consistent findings from psychophysiological studies on mentally retarded subjects (Ellis & Sloan, 1958; O'Connor & Venables, 1956). Berkson (1963, pp. 556–573) and Karrer (1966, pp. 57–83) have reviewed the psychophysiological studies in mental deficiency. Karrer and Clausen (1964) reported that mental defectives were less responsive to stimuli, especially in HR, with a greater prevalence of a deceleratory HRR than normal subjects. Karrer (1966) cites conflicting findings, however, and discusses the methodological problems in the study of intelligence as a correlate of psychophysiological variables.

Vogel and Broverman (1964) reviewed the literature on EEG and intelligence and concluded that the EEG indices distinguished among normal children, institutionalized geriatric patients, mental defectives, and brain-injured patients. The relation between EEG and intelligence was weakest for samples of normal adults, and in all cases the EEG indices were reported to be more strongly related to mental age than to IQ.

Ellingson (1966) disagreed with Vogel and Broverman's conclusions. He felt that the data on the relation between normal brain-wave phenomena and IQ in children and in the mentally retarded was contradictory and inconclusive, and that there was no relation between EEG and IQ in adults. A most important point made by Ellingson was that EEG abnormality and decreased intellectual capacity can both result from organic brain disorders and hence tend to be related to one another.

It is of interest that electrodermal activity, the psychophysiological variable which appears to be least relevant for survival and which is least subject to homeostatic control, is the variable most likely to be influenced by such factors as age, sex, race, intelligence, and sleep stage.

Interaction among Response Variables

While we are often sensitive to the influence of age, race, sex, etc., upon our response measure, we pay little heed to the influence of the various responses on each other. The internal environment is overlooked in our zeal to control external variables.

The psychophysiologist must be aware that excitatory processes coexist with inhibitory processes and that the response in one system influences the response of another. How this complex interaction among response systems will influence the crucial variables can best be determined by a multivariable approach.

The best-known example of this interaction is sinus arrhythmia, the increase in heart rate at the peak of inspiration and decrease toward the end of exhalation. Wescott and Huttenlocher (1961) controlled respiration experimentally and found that the HR increased with deep inspiration. With deep breathing at 6 cycles per min, an increase on the order of about 30 beats per min was recorded. They went on to demonstrate the importance of controlling respiration in conditioning studies. While the phenomenon of sinus arrhythmia is well known, it is often neglected in studies of cardiac conditioning, especially with regard to the shape of the cardiac response. Hord, Lubin, and Johnson (1966) found that, if an auditory stimulus occurred during inspiration or in the period just prior to inspiration, the heart rate response to a tone was facilitated. Simons (1964) also demonstrated the dependence of the heart rate reflex on respiration; Clynes (1966) has constructed an analog computer program to generate the heart rate pattern during a series of respiratory maneuvers and during normal respiration.

The importance of controlling for the influence of the cardiac and respiratory cycles, even when measuring responses in other systems, has been illustrated by Birren, Cardon, and Phillips (1963), as well as by Callaway and Buchsbaum (1965) for visual evoked responses recorded from scalp electrodes. Birren, Cardon, and Phillips found that the slowest

reaction time occurred to an auditory stimulus presented during the QRS component of the cardiac cycle. The fastest reaction time was to stimuli presented during the P wave. Callaway and Layne (1964) found that the reaction times to a visual stimulus were significantly faster in the latter half of the cardiac cycle. This was also found in patients whose heart rate was controlled by transistorized pacemakers and was thus not under the usual neuronal control. Callaway and Buchsbaum (1965) found that the cardiac and respiration cycles not only influence the magnitude of the response but also contribute to variability in the visual average evoked response. Pairs of averaged EEG responses, evoked by visual stimuli given at inspiration, correlated more highly than did pairs if one were evoked by stimulating at inspiration and the other by stimulating at expiration. Similarly, pairs of averaged EEG responses were most similar when evoked by stimulating at the same phase of the cardiac cycle.

The interaction and influence of one response system upon another does not end with the onset of sleep. An effect of respiration phase upon the response of heart rate to a tone stimulus was found during both waking and sleeping (Hord, Lubin, & Johnson, 1966). Hodes and Dement (1965) found that the H reflex was least likely during rapid eye movement (REM) bursts. Johnson and Lubin (1967) found that the evoked HRR and evoked finger pulse response (FPR) diminished during REM-bursts but that the electrodermal response was not affected. In contrast to the depressant effect of REM-bursts, the evoked EEG K-complex during Sleep Stage 2 was associated with an enhanced response in both the cardiovascular and electrodermal systems.

The examples in the preceding paragraph illustrate the point that psychophysiological response systems interact and influence each other. Whether this influence will facilitate or suppress depends upon the phase of the response cycle during which the stimuli are given. Interaction does not cease with the onset of sleep but the pattern of influence may differ. Lacey (1967) has speculated on the neurophysiology of the excitatory and inhibitory aspects of the cardiovascular system, and how its interaction with the central nervous system is reflected in psychophysiological variables. Sokolov (1963) has also speculated on the role of autonomic activity acting directly on receptors and indirectly by feedbacks to central mechanisms, altering the sensitivity of receptors and the response of the system they serve.

MEASUREMENT OF RESPONSES

We find it useful to think of psychophysiological responses to stimuli as being tonic or phasic. However, it is wise to modify these terms by specifying the psychophysiological variable involved. A multiphasic electrocortical response can be evoked by a variety of stimuli (auditory, visual, and tactile) and ordinarily returns to baseline in a second or less. If we saw a slow shift in cortical potential, triggered by an auditory stimulus, which took 30–60 sec to complete, then ordinarily we would talk about a tonic component of the evoked cortical response. But evoked cardiovascular responses and evoked respiratory responses often take 15–45 sec before they return to baseline, and yet we think of these as phasic responses. *Tonic* and *phasic* therefore are relative to the variable being studied. Nor are they mutually exclusive. If a subject is drowsy, an intense stimulus can awaken him, thus causing a tonic electrocortical response; at the same time it can cause a brief phasic electrocortical response lasting less than a second.

There is a very practical distinction when the parameters of the measuring apparatus are defined. The standard time constant for EEG amplifiers is 0.3 sec. If one wishes to measure a slow shift in potential that takes 15–30 sec to complete, then this time constant must be increased, perhaps to the equivalent of a direct current readout. Similarly, the apparatus that is best for the evoked SPR gives extremely poor measures of slow shifts, so poor that we use a different apparatus for measuring the basal skin potential. The same distinction arises when one wishes to measure finger pulse height as opposed to finger blood volume.

It must always be borne in mind that these evoked tonic and phasic responses are superimposed upon, and modulated by, the rhythmic physiological activity of the organism. Thus the evoked phasic electrocortical response may be a function of the EEG alpha cycle (about 0.1 sec), the heart beat cycle of about 1 sec, the breathing cycle of about 4–5 sec, the sleep-wake (circadian) cycle of about 24 hr, the menstrual cycle of about 28 days, the seasonal cycle of about 1 year, etc.

Such cycles can be considered a special case of tonic response to endogenous stimuli, since they can usually be maintained for days or weeks in constant environmental situations. However, it is perfectly possible for some environmental change to act as a stimulus, a *Zeitgeber,* which changes the phase of the cycle. For example, short periods of light during otherwise unbroken darkness will often entrain the circadian cycle. These cycles influence each other, as well as the tonic and phasic responses, and can cause confusion in the measurement of responses.

The circadian rhythm can easily be confounded with the tonic response to sleep loss or fatigue. One group of experimenters undertook to measure fatigue by testing subjects at 0800 hr before their workday started, and then at 1700 hr, at the end of the workday. They were startled to find that almost all of their physiological and performance measures showed improvement at 1700 compared with 0800. What they failed to consider was that most subjects show a strong metabolic cycle during the day. Body temperature and other metabolic indices are lowest in the early morning and highest in the late afternoon and evening. R. T. Wilkinson, an astute student of sleep loss, considers that almost all studies of sleep loss previous to 1956 or so were hopelessly vitiated by the neglect of such factors as circadian rhythm (1963).

Phasic Responses

There are two kinds of phasic responses, specific and nonspecific (spontaneous). The specific response is evoked by an external stimulus; the nonspecific phasic response occurs in the absence of a detectable external stimulus. If the external stimulus is under the control of the experimenter, then the measurement of the evoked response is relatively easy: the onset time of the stimulus is known and it is a matter of following the variable until the disturbance subsides and the level returns to the prestimulus baseline. In some instances, however, it is difficult to separate the spontaneous responses from specific responses to the stimuli, and knowledge of the stimulus onset time may not suffice. This problem becomes particularly acute when the spontaneous discharge rate is very high, as in states of high excitement or, paradoxically, during sleep. Figure 3.1 illustrates the problem of separating the specific electrodermal response to a tone from the background spontaneous activity for Sleep Stage 3. During REM sleep, the background spontaneous fluctuations in HR, RR, and finger pulse (FP) pose similar problems. Neither latency nor magnitude has been found sufficient to distinguish the spontaneous response from the evoked response.

We have utilized both a statistical method and a pseudostimulus method to control for the possibility that the change following the stimulus might be spontaneous. When the spontaneous rate is known, the statistical technique is feasible. Let us use electrodermal activity as an example. (This illustration would apply to either SPR or SRR.) First, we estimate the number of spontaneous electrodermal responses that would occur within 5 sec after stimulus onset if no stimulus were given during this period. (Generally, 5 sec is accepted as the maximal latency of electrodermal responses.)

Then we correct the observed rate of evoked responses for this spontaneous rate. The exact formula used is $R/N - C/t$, where R is the total number of observed responses within 5 sec after the stimulus onset, N the number of stimuli, C the number of spontaneous electrodermal responses per minute, and t is 60 sec divided by the maximum response latency in seconds (in this example, 5 sec).

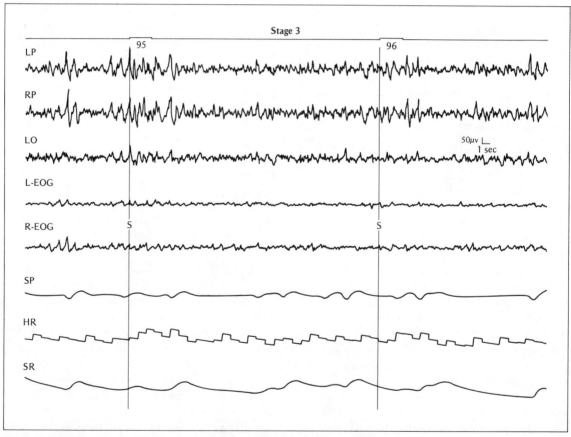

Figure 3.1 Illustration of difficulty in detecting specific SRRs and SPRs from nonspecific changes. The beat-to-beat variability in HR is also illustrated. Legend: S = tone stimulus, LP = left parietal (P3), RP = right parietal (P4), L-EOG = left oculogram, R-EOG = right oculogram, SP = skin potential, HR = heart rate, and SR = skin resistance. Redrawn from L. C. Johnson and A. Lubin, The orienting response during waking and sleeping, *Electroencephalography and Clinical Neurophysiology*, 1967, **22,** 11–21. By permission.

This formula gives the corrected proportion of responses.

The other control employs the pseudostimulus technique. Again, using electrodermal activity as an example, a pseudostimulus can be marked 5, 10, or 15 sec before the real stimulus. If HR, FP, or RR responses are scored, at least a 25-sec period is necessary to allow for the latency and duration of these responses. The criteria used for scoring a response to the real stimulus should be used for the pseudostimulus. To obtain the corrected evoked response to the real stimulus for each subject, his response to the pseudostimulus should be subtracted from that following the real stimulus. This use of the pseudostimulus control is illustrated in a study of the OR by Johnson and Lubin (1967). The statistical control method and the pseudostimulus control gave similar results. If the spontaneous rate is known, then the statistical control method simplifies the data analysis. Where the rate is not known, or varies, the pseudostimulus method is more precise, since it is time-locked to the real stimulus.

Shape of the phasic response Responses vary in latency, shape, and duration. According to Sokolov (1963a), responses fall into three classes: orientation (the what-is-it response), defense, and adaptation. These three classes of response differ not only in their physiological significance but also in their latency, shape, and response magnitude over repeated stimuli.

What aspects of the response should be measured? If we knew the mathematical form of the response, then we could calculate the best estimates of the parameters from the observed points. We would then have extracted all the relevant information. But this is exactly what we do not know: the necessary and sufficient parameters to describe a response.

Ordinarily, what we know of the response will consist of a set of deflections that varies in amplitude with the time after the stimulus onset. The amplitude may be measured in terms of millimeters, microvolts, ohms, beats, degrees per square centimeter, or some arbitrary scale. The abscissa may be clock time or it may be measured in terms of the number of heartbeats, breaths, etc., after the stimu-

lus onset. Whatever the units, ordinarily we shall end up with a tracing of amplitude against some sort of time scale.

For most variables the response will have a relatively fixed latency from stimulus onset and a consistent response form. For example, the SRR usually occurs 2–4 sec after the stimulus onset; its response is monophasic, a decrease in resistance. But the SPR may be monophasic, diphasic, or in some cases, triphasic; although its latency is relatively constant and similar to that of the SRR.

The finger pulse height OR also has a relatively fixed latency, and its response is usually monophasic vasoconstriction. Raskin, Kotses, and Bever (1969) have reported a forehead pulse response of vasoconstriction while Keefe and Johnson (1970) have reported vasoconstriction followed by vasodilation. Sokolov (1963a), however, reports that the pulse height OR recorded from the forehead is vasodilation. To complicate matters further, the defense response supposedly is vasoconstrictive in both the head and fingers.

The respiratory OR is generally monophasic, reflecting an increase or decrease in rate; but a recent study by Johnson and Lubin (1967) found that, during Sleep Stage 2 and Slow Wave Stages 3 and 4, the response was diphasic, a brief deceleration followed by acceleration.

Of all the autonomic responses, the cardiac response probably has the most complex shape. Techniques for measuring the HRR have differed considerably. Many investigators have used some form of poststimulus level minus prestimulus level for measuring the HR change. One such method takes the average of the 5th to the 15th poststimulus heartbeats minus the average of the 5th to the 15th prestimulus heartbeats. Some have taken the average of the three fastest beats for the 30-sec prestimulus period and subtracted this from the 3 fastest beats for the 30-sec poststimulus period.

A serious limitation of using average measures of HRR is that they do not take into account the fact that the HRR is usually not monophasic. If one averages over the 5th through the 15th beats in a fixed period before and following a stimulus, the diphasic response will be lost. If the response is diphasic, then the average of the highest and lowest HRs might be equal to the prestimulus level and the conclusion would be that no HRR occurred. The $Z - X$ technique first used by Lang and Hnatiow (1962) appears to be the most sensitive procedure for measuring the amplitude of diphasic HRRs. In this procedure the fastest HR (Z) in the first post-stimulus beats is determined. Then the slowest HR (X) following Z, in the first 20 beats after the stimulus, is found. The $Z - X$ difference is the HRR. This Lang-Hnatiow measure generally has a near-zero correlation with the prestimulus level, even when the post-minus-pre-measures of the HRR have a substantial correlation with the prestimulus level.

There is no general agreement on the shape of the HRR. Some investigators found that the HRR was diphasic (Davis, Buchwald, & Frankmann, 1955; Hord, Lubin, & Johnson, 1966; Lang & Hnatiow, 1962); some found only a decelerative component (Davis & Buchwald, 1957; Lewis & Spaulding, 1967; Zeaman, Deane, & Wenger, 1954); but Sokolov (1963a) reported it consists solely of an accelerative component. Lacey, Kagan, Lacey, and Moss (1963) have presented data to show that whether the HRR is accelerative or decelerative depends on the nature of the stimulus and the subject's set to respond. Berg and Graham (1971) have found that with mild stimuli the heart response is primarily decelerative, to moderate stimuli it is generally diphasic, and to intense stimuli it is solely accelerative.

Graham and Clifton (1966), in an extensive review, developed the thesis that the accelerative component of the diphasic HRR was a defensive response and that the early decelerative component was the OR. Solely accelerative responses are viewed as defensive responses and for Graham and Clifton only decelerative responses meet the criteria of an OR. Whether one supports the views of Sokolov, of Lacey, or the position of Graham and Clifton, clearly the shape of the HRR must be determined before the appropriate procedure for measuring change can be determined. This requirement holds not only for the HRR but for all psychophysiological responses.

The technique of averaging evoked responses has been extensively used by neurophysiologists to determine the shape of the evoked response from scalp, cortical, and subcortical electrode place-

ments. Averaging has also been used by a few psychophysiologists for autonomic responses (Lang & Hnatiow, 1962; Meyers, Valenstein, & Lacey, 1963; Newton & Perez-Cruet, 1967; Uno & Grings, 1965). One of the reasons why averaging has not been used extensively with autonomic variables is that in the waking subject the OR usually habituates quickly. To overcome this problem, the first response for a number of similar subjects can be averaged, or the responses can be averaged over each trial to determine how the shape of the response changes with the number of stimuli. During sleep, habituation is minimal or does not occur, so that the usual procedure of averaging over repeated stimuli can be used (Hord, Lubin, & Johnson, 1966).

There are at least two other difficulties with the averaging of evoked responses: (a) response latencies tend to vary, and (b) the average of the observed curves may not converge to the true function. Very often, individual electrocortical-evoked responses have amplitudes of 50–200 μV; yet the average response may only be 10 or 20 μV. When the time of occurrence of a crest and trough vary, amplitudes will be markedly reduced even if the response shape is preserved.

For certain nonlinear functions Sidman (1952) and Bakan (1954) have shown that the group average does not converge to the true curve. For example, when each subject has an exponential decay response, if the decay rate is not the same for all subjects, then the group average will tend to be a power curve, rather than an exponential.

In addition to the general question "What is the shape of the response?," the researcher should also determine whether the shape is constant for all subjects, whether it varies with the prestimulus level, and whether it depends on the intensity of the stimulus or varies with the interstimulus interval. How many parameters do we need to reproduce the response? Are these parameters differentially sensitive to stimulus intensity and to the state of the subject? The answers to most of these questions are unknown. Uno and Grings (1965) found that there was an increase in the number of diphasic SPRs with increase in stimulus intensity. A beat-by-beat analysis of the HRR indicated that the shape of the HR response also varied with stimulus intensity.

Tonic Responses

Monophasic tonic response   To measure a tonic response, the organism is generally exposed to a constant stimulus or constant multistimulus situation until the organism is judged to have adjusted to the new levels. The usual measure of tonic level is obtained from the level of one or more variables *averaged* over a given period of time and then compared to prestimulus averages over a comparable period of time. The difference is the tonic response. Another way is to compare the average level during stimulation with the asymptotic level after stimulation. This assumes that the tonic changes are reversible.

The problems of measuring tonic responses center around (a) response latency, (b) homogeneity of the tonic response, and (c) confusion with long-period cycles.

With the onset or offset of any prolonged stimulus, there will be momentary phasic responses (the phasic orienting reflex) throughout the CNS and the ANS. The experimenter must decide at what point after the stimulus onset the activity of the organism has become tonic. In other words, what is the *rise time* of the tonic response? At stimulus offset, there ordinarily will again be momentary phasic responses to this change in the environment. The phasic responses to the stimulus offset will usually coincide with the beginning of a slow drift in tonic level toward the prestimulus value. The interval between the stimulus offset and the return to baseline is called the *recovery time*.

Somewhere between the rise-time interval and the recovery-time interval, the tonic response will reach its maximum. Unless the rise time is known with some accuracy, tonic and phasic responses may be confused at the stimulus onset and stimulus offset.

When the tonic response rises smoothly to a maximum and remains at a plateau until the response offset, there is minimal difficulty in measurement. However, sometimes the tonic response consists of various states of the organism that occur at unpredictable times. For example, when a subject undergoes loss of sleep, there is no gradual increase in reaction time, errors of omission, errors of commission, etc. Instead, the subject alternates between alertness and drowsiness (see Williams, Goodnow, & Lubin, 1959).

How can the experimenter deal with heterogeneity of a tonic state? One way is to measure the heterogeneity directly by means of the standard deviation, the range, etc. These measures can be used to test whether the tonic state does differ from the previous prestimulus level. Thus, if a series of trials of reaction time is administered to a subject suffering from sleep loss, the standard deviation of the latencies will far exceed that of the subject before loss of sleep or after recovery sleep.

Another, rather similar idea is to use only extreme values. Suppose we make a distribution of the reaction times for the subject experiencing loss of sleep, and consider only the upper 10%, those trials with the longest reaction times. The average of such trials will be considerably greater for subjects undergoing sleep loss than for control subjects. On the other hand, if the shortest reaction times are considered, there will be little difference between the controls and subjects with moderate loss of sleep (Williams, Goodnow, & Lubin, 1959).

Occasionally, multivariate studies will reveal measures that can be used to discriminate among the various phases of a heterogeneous tonic state. For instance, Williams, Lubin, Granda, Jones, and Armington (1962) found that some of their sleep-loss subjects were alternating between an EEG with dominant alpha and an EEG with dominant theta rhythm. By correlating the reaction time and errors of omission with the EEG frequency (1 sec before the signal), they confirmed the supposition that the subjects were alternating between an alert and a drowsy state.

Circadian rhythms are present in many psychophysiological variables. If a tonic response takes an hour or more to develop, how can we distinguish it from the ordinary changes in heart rate, respiration, or EEG frequency that depend upon the time of day? Perhaps the simplest method is to design control periods without stimulation that occur at the same time of day as the stimulus periods. This is another use of the pseudostimulus method. In this way normal circadian variability can be measured and extracted from the tonic response.

Multiphasic tonic response As soon as there is more than one extreme value (e.g., two or more crests, two or more troughs), we face the same problem as for the phasic response—what is the shape? Since tonic states by definition have relatively long durations and change slowly, it is possible to use certain methods of time-series analysis to calculate those parametric estimates that are sufficient to describe the tonic response. In particular, the autoregressive linear model can be fitted to the data if we assume that we are dealing with a stationary time series (Kendall, 1946; Yule, 1921). Some of the characteristics of a stationary time series are that any segment of it has the same true mean, the same true variance, and the same true covariance with an external variable. The autoregressive model has rarely been used in psychophysiology, although learning theorists have made extensive use of the Markov process, the one-step autoregressive model. These models call for the calculation of serial correlations, the correlation of a set of observations with itself, displaced by one time unit (lag one), displaced by two time units (lag two), and so on.

The continuous spectral density model has been applied to characterize EEG tonic levels in terms of their spectral densities (see Walter, 1963). One basic difficulty with the spectral model is in the way it deals with transient nonrepeating responses. It transforms the phasic contributions of eye movements, K-complexes, and so on, to wave-forms that repeat themselves with constant amplitude and constant period throughout the time interval under analysis.

Another difficulty results from the stationarity assumption. If a certain EEG frequency, such as the alpha rhythm, is present in only part of the analyzed record, the spectral model does not distinguish it from the case in which a lower intensity of alpha is present during the entire record.

Measurement of Change

Even when the type and shape of the response have been determined, there are many ways to measure the parameters of the response. The choice among these many possible measures can be made by the experimenter in terms of his implicit or explicit acceptance of certain principles; principles of measurement such as the need for high validity and reliability, principles of physiology such as homeostasis and the activation continuum, and principles of faith in the desirability of normal distributions and homogeneous variances. Sometimes the principle of convenience of interpretation influences the choice of measurement units. All variables may be scored, so that a high score would conventionally be interpreted as high arousal. Thus respiration rate and heart rate are scored rather than period, and skin conductance rather than resistance.

Skin resistance response The wide variety in the number and kind of principles that can be used finds its natural consequence in the extremely large number of measures of change used for the same variable. Even though the SRR is probably the most commonly obtained measure in the psychophysiological laboratory, there is little agreement on how even this response should be measured.

C. W. Darrow (1934, 1964) justified the change from resistance to conductance on the grounds that the amount of perspiration of an area correlated better with conductance than resistance. He hypothesized a unifactor causal relation between sudomotor excitation and the SRR. This unifactor hypothesis has some difficulty in accounting for all the facts, and recently some experimenters have put forward a two-factor theory to account for the SRR (Edelberg, 1964).

E. A. Haggard (1949) was concerned about minimizing the correlation between the SRR and the prestimulus level. Log conductance change was one of the best measures from this point of view.

The nonnormality of resistance change as a measure has troubled some investigators. Lacey and Siegel (1949) found that log conductance change tended to be normally distributed, but Schlosberg and Stanley (1953) reported that the square root of the log conductance change was even better.

Let us list some commonly used measures of the SRR to see how different the definitions can be. Let R_x be the average skin resistance for some fixed time period before the stimulus. Let R_y be the lowest skin resistance within 5 sec after the stimulus. Then, in conductance units,

$$C_x = \frac{1}{R_x} \qquad \text{and} \qquad C_y = \frac{1}{R_y}$$

Some of the common transforms are: (a) resistance change, $R_x - R_y$; (b) conductance change, $C_y - C_x$; (c) log conductance change, $\log(C_y - C_x)$; (d) square root log conductance change, $\sqrt{\log(C_y - C_x)}$; (e) log resistance change, $\log(R_x - R_y)$; (f) percentage conductance change, (C_y/C_x); and (g) the autonomic lability score (ALS), $C_y - (a + bC_x)$ where a and b measure the linear regression of C_y on C_x.

Which of these measures is used generally makes a real difference. Any time a nonlinear transformation of a score is used (even if the transform is monotonic), validities, significance tests, and distribution shapes will change. The SRR to two drugs may differ significantly for one measure, and show little change for another measure.[1]

How is an experimenter to choose among the various scoring methods? Primarily, it must be in terms of the purpose of the experiment: the questions being asked. The originators of a scoring method will generally present logical and/or empirical criteria for concluding that their method is better than other scoring methods. By comparing the claims of each method with the goal of the experimenter, it is theoretically possible to make the best match. Actually, as we have noted in our introduction, the choice of the scoring method is inextricably bound up with the choice of experimental design, statistical analysis, variables to be measured, certain psychophysiological principles, etc. At this stage in our knowledge of psychophysiology, it is impossible to state rules that will always guide the experimenter to the best choice. Instead we shall study in detail one scoring method and some of the alternatives to demonstrate the complexity of criteria for choosing or rejecting a measure of change.

Autonomic lability score (ALS) In 1956, J. I. Lacey proposed a way of scoring autonomic responses to stimuli which he felt took into account certain physiological principles such as homeostasis and Wilder's (1950) law of initial value (LIV), as well as the statistical notion of equating treatment effects for pretreatment differences. The LIV states that the true response of a variable to a stimulus

decreases as the true prestimulus level increases; i.e., change has a negative correlation with initial level.[2] The general notion is that there is some optimal level for a variable. If the prestimulus level is above the optimal level, then stimulation tends to produce a negative response. Lacey argued that the reciprocal inhibition of the sympathetic and parasympathetic systems should lead directly to the LIV.

Let X be the observed prestimulus level and Y be the observed poststimulus level. Then $Y - X = D$ is the observed algebraic change. (The LIV states that the true algebraic change, G, has a negative correlation with T, the true value of X.) Lacey's ALS was devised to rid the change score of dependence upon the prestimulus level. Let $(a + bX)$ be the value of Y predicted from its linear regression on X. Then $Y - a - bX = Z$ is the residual gain score of Manning and DuBois (1962). When the residual gain score has been standardized to a mean of 50 and a standard deviation of 10, it becomes Lacey's ALS; Z and ALS have a correlation of unity.

Suppose we find the value of D predicted from its regression on X, and subtract the predicted D from the observed D. It is easy to prove that this deviation of the observed D from the predicted D equals Z. Earlier, it was noted that Z has a correlation of unity with ALS. The ALS is equivalent to the algebraic change, D, corrected for its regression on the prestimulus level X. It must have a zero correlation with X within the sample used to obtain the regression constants, a and b. Lacey's use of the regression model, therefore, has produced a score that is linearly independent of the prestimulus level in the analysis sample.

Are there other ways in which the ALS is better than conventional scores? Yes. Lacey claimed that, whenever the absolute and percent change scores showed a significant correlation with some criterion variable such as age, sex, intensity of shock, Rorschach responses, etc., the ALS always yielded clearer trends and greater interpretive clarity (1956,

---

[1] E. A. Haggard (1949) showed that for four different transformations of skin resistance measures, the F ratio varied from 1.71–118.11. Since the 0.05 significance level was 4.11, it made a real difference which transform was used.

[2] In his recent book, Wilder (1967) makes it clear that his definition of the change score excludes crests and troughs. For Wilder, change should always be measured as an integral of the poststimulus period. Therefore the reader should substitute "quasi-LIV" or some other term wherever we use "LIV." The term LIV is used throughout this chapter to mean that the true correlation, between the change score and the prechange level, is negative.

p. 143). Mathematically, it is difficult to work with absolute scores or percent change scores. This claim, therefore, has not been checked in toto, but Lubin, Hord, and Johnson (1964) proved that the ALS will always have higher validity than D, the algebraic difference, *if* the LIV holds. Furthermore, if X has a near-zero correlation with the criterion variable (i.e., is a suppressor variable), the ALS has a greater validity than any other linear combination of X and Y. How about the reliability of the ALS? Again *if* the LIV holds, then, in general, the retest reliability of the ALS will be greater than that of the difference score. However, Lubin, Hord, and Johnson (1964) had to impose side conditions equivalent to the usual psychometric assumption of parallel tests to obtain a rigorous proof that, when the LIV does not hold, then the ALS will have lower validity and reliability than a difference score.

So the ALS tends to be both valid and reliable if the LIV holds. The question now is, "Does the LIV hold?" Hord, Johnson, and Lubin (1964) investigated this for skin conductance (SC), HR, RR, and skin temperature (ST) and found that only HR and RR met the requirements for LIV. They stated that, if the results had been expressed in terms of skin resistance, rather than conductance, the LIV would have applied.

J. Wilder (1965) took a strong exception to this statement saying, "It is not logical . . . if one team concludes that the LIV is not valid for skin conductance but valid for skin resistance, since one is the reverse of the other. Therefore, if the correlation is positive for resistance, it must be *eo ipso* negative for conductance and vice versa." The simplest answer here is factual. For a sample of 29 naval aviators, Hord, Johnson, and Lubin (1964) found a correlation of 0.77 between the prestimulus *skin conductance* and change. This positive correlation implies that the LIV does not hold. The same correlation recalculated using *skin resistance* was −0.24. This negative correlation using skin resistance implies that the LIV may hold. Clearly, it does make a difference how change is measured.

It is extraordinarily difficult to say what will happen to a nonlinear transformation of X in terms of the changes in correlation, F ratios, etc. As we have seen, even a simple monotonic transform such as the reciprocal, $1/X$, can have unexpected conse-

quences. Hord, Johnson, and Lubin (1964) implied that the regression of reciprocals would equal the reciprocal of the original regression if the original regression went through the origin. Benjamin (1967) made a Monte Carlo study, which showed that taking the reciprocal did not necessarily cause a change in the sign of the correlation between the prestimulus level and the change score. In fact, for those cases with near-zero intercepts, only 19% showed a sign change. The most frequent (43%) sign changes occurred when the r_{xy} was greater than 0.50 and the variance of Y was greater than the variance of X. She found that Anova (analysis of variance) and Anacova (analysis of covariance) procedures were "robust" to the reciprocal transformation; i.e. the significance of the F ratios was changed by reciprocal transformation in only 2–11% of the cases.

Another objection to the 1964 article by Hord, Johnson, and Lubin was raised by Surwillo and Arenberg (1965). Hord, Johnson, and Lubin had assumed that r_{xd}, the correlation of the prestimulus level (X) with the change score, $(Y - X)$, was an adequate measure of the LIV. This meant that if r_{xd} was negative, then the LIV held. But Surwillo and Arenberg pointed out that r_{xd} has a negative bias due to the error of measurement in X: "As a consequence pairs of measurements with no stimulus would be classified as an instance of LIV using the Hord, Johnson and Lubin criterion." Since error of measurement is always present in the D score, this statement is certainly correct. Thorndike (1924) made essentially the same observation.

Surwillo and Arenberg (1965) suggested that a control group be added to whom no stimulus is presented (a pseudostimulus technique). The slope of Y on X for the experimental group is compared to the same slope in the control group, where there is no stimulus between the two measures. The LIV is accepted if the slope for the experimental group (with stimulus) is significantly less than the slope for the control group (without stimulus). This two-sample test has the virtue that there is no consistent bias for or against the LIV.

Lubin, Hord, and Johnson (1964) used this notion of comparing two slopes, one with and one without an intervening stimulus, to generate a one-sample test. As before, let Y be the poststimulus measure.

Let X_1 and X_2 be the prestimulus levels. Then r_{2d} is the correlation of X_2 with $D = Y - X_1$. The numerator of r_{2d} is proportionate to $b_{y2} - b_{12}$, the stimulus slope minus the control slope. If r_{2d} is significantly negative, the LIV is accepted.

So it is now possible to compare the LIV model with the data and use the t test to decide whether to accept or reject the LIV. Of course, the acceptance of the LIV implies the desirability of the ALS.

J. I. Lacey, in his 1956 article, did not stop with the ALS. The correlation of change with the initial level varies from group to group, and (when within-subject correlations can be calculated) from individual to individual. "Does this variation reflect individual differences in homeostatic efficiency, or is it mere sampling variation? [p. 149]" Hahn (1966), using the slope of Y on X, showed that asthmatic children had less homeostatic restraint on their heart rate orienting response than did the control subjects. Hord, Johnson, and Lubin (1964) reported a similar weakness of homeostatic restraint for adults with cardiovascular disease. The correlation of change with the prestimulus level is a crude but valuable approximation to the measurement of homeostatic strength within a system.

Ordinarily, we cannot use the correlation of change with prestimulus level to measure homeostatic strength within the subject, because the orienting response habituates so quickly. For neonates, however, Bridger and Reiser (1959) found that the heart rate OR showed little or no habituation. Therefore, they were able to calculate various parameters of the regression of Y (poststimulus level) on X (prestimulus level) within each subject. One interesting measure they developed was the crossover point, the prestimulus value below which change will tend to be positive, and above which change will tend to be negative. The crossover point is an estimate of the optimal level that the homeostatic mechanism is trying to maintain.

There are still other ways to measure homeostatic strength within the subject. One technique is to vary the characteristics of the stimulus (e.g., intensity, pitch, interstimulus interval) in such a way that habituation does not occur. Sokolov (1963a) Berlyne (1960), and others have suggested that the amplitude of the OR is some positive linear function of the information it contains for the subject.

If the information level of the stimulus can be held constant, then habituation would not take place.

Lubin, Hord, and Johnson (1964) suggested fitting an exponential equation to all the stimulus trials to estimate the homeostatic strength. As they point out, however, the solution will be extremely unstable, unless the responses decline very smoothly with the trial number.

If we adopt the notion that every set of consecutive measures on a subject constitutes an ordered series, then *time-series analysis* can be used to characterize the homeostatic process within each subject. Such an analysis can deal with measures that occur spontaneously, as well as measures that are evoked by stimuli. Suppose that we have a series of k measures: $X_1, X_2, \cdots X_j \cdots X_k$ with no stimulus intervening. Yule's (1921) autoregressive process assumes that each measure is generated by some finite set of preceding measures. The simplest case would be a linear, first-order autoregression, e.g., $X_j = a + bX_{j-1} + e_j$, where e_j is a random error term, with a Gaussian distribution. For a second-order autoregression, X_j would be a linear function of X_{j-1} and X_{j-2}.

For a linear autoregressive process of the kth order, the model would be completely determined, once the variance and the k serial correlations were known. The first order serial correlation is computed by pairing X_1 with X_2, X_2 with X_3, X_3 with X_4, and so on, to produce the correlation, r_1. By pairing X_1 with X_3, X_2 with X_4, X_3 with X_5, and so on, we can obtain the second order serial correlation, r_2. Proceeding in this way, one will generate r_1, r_2, r_3, r_4, etc., until all k serial correlations have been calculated (M. G. Kendall, 1946, paragraphs 30.12–30.53).

If the linear autoregressive model applies, then this set of serial correlations completely specifies the homeostatic strength of the subject in that time period. For example, we can correlate the change, $X_{j+1} - X_j$, with the initial level, X_{j-1}. The correlation of the initial level, X_{j-1}, with X_j is the first order serial correlation, r_1. The correlation of the initial level with X_{j+1} is the second order serial correlation, r_2. If we assume stationarity of the variance, the correlation of change with the prechange level will be $(r_2 - r_1) / \sqrt{2 - 2r_1}$, the serial correlation equivalent of r_{2d}. Therefore, $(r_1 - r_2) / \sqrt{2 - 2r_1}$ is a positive measure of homeostatic strength for the individual, just as $-r_{2d}$ is a positive measure of homeostatic strength for the group. However, the serial correlation function measures the nonspecific homeostatic strength, the amount of control over the spontaneous changes, rather than the control over responses to specific stimuli.

If it can be assumed that the series has what the statistician calls second order stationarity (e.g., r_1 will be the same no matter what subsequence of the series is used to calculate r_1; the same for r_2, r_3, r_4, etc.), then the set of serial correlations can be used to characterize the series in terms of the autoregressive linear model. In particular, a Fourier analysis can be done to find whether homeostasis is being maintained by means of rhythms and, if so, what rhythms dominate (Blackman & Tukey, 1958; Box & Jenkins, 1970; Goldberg, 1961).

There are many other aspects of the ALS and the LIV that merit study but space considerations limit us to a few: (a) If we have a series of measures in which the LIV holds, then a superdiagonal covariance matrix is generated. That is, the covariance of X_i and X_{i+1} will always be greater than the covariance of X_i and X_{i+2}. Since repeated measures almost always are observed to yield a superdiagonal matrix, the LIV will generally hold for repeated measures. (b) An amplitude measure of a multiphasic response will generally have a zero correlation with the prestimulus level. In particular, if the crest and trough components of the amplitude follow the LIV with the same degree of homeostatic strength, the correlation must be near zero. The Lang-Hnatiow (1962), zenith-minus-nadir $(Z - X)$ measure of HRR is a good example of such an amplitude score. (c) There are some misunderstandings about the relation of homeostatic strength to the value of r_{xy}, the correlation of the prestimulus level with the poststimulus level. A large positive correlation between the prestimulus level and poststimulus level does *not* imply homeostasis. Quite the contrary: as r_{xy} goes toward zero, homeostatic strength $(-r_{2d})$ is maximized. The limit of $-r_{2d}$ is generally r_{12}, the correlation between two successive measures when no stimulus intervenes. (d) If the LIV relation is reversed, i.e., if r_{2d} is positive, then an activation model with short-term positive feedback would give a better fit to the data than the LIV homeostatic model.

Recommendations This short survey of the facts and theories surrounding the ALS shows that the choice of the change score involves questions of experimental design, statistical analysis, and basic physiological postulates. Given these complex interactions between the components of an experiment, how should the experimenter proceed to select a measure of change?

We recommend that the experimenter adopt a pluralist point of view. For each question in his experiment there may be an optimal measure, but it does not follow that the measure which is best for answering one question is best for answering all questions.

How should we judge new scoring methods? Unless the advocate clearly states some logical and/or empirical criteria by means of which the new scoring method can be compared to standard methods, such new scores should not be considered. The number of scoring methods that can be generated by such ingenious minds as those of Block and Bridger (1962), Heath and Oken (1962), Benjamin (1963), Dykman, Ackerman, Galbrecht, and Reese (1963), and Lykken, Rose, Luther, and Maley (1966) is potentially infinite. We suggest that a variation of Ockham's razor be invoked: "Scoring methods should not be multiplied or complicated unnecessarily."

Generally, there are two criteria by which to judge new scoring systems: reliability and validity. Reliability is particularly important when the measurement of *traits* is involved. One can scarcely use a measure of schizophrenia, or honesty, or warmth, etc., without implying considerable stability over weeks, months, and perhaps even years. On the other hand, if the measurement of *state* is involved, e.g., if one wants a score that is especially sensitive to slight changes in anxiety, to sudden lapses of vigilance, etc., then probably this measure would show rather large changes within the subject from hour to hour, let alone day to day.

An excellent reliability study of 14 measures of the heart rate activity of the newborn human has been published by Clifton and Graham (1968). There were a number of important findings. The lowest heart rate of 15 samples had more day-to-day reliability than the average heart rate. Three measures of the prestimulus-poststimulus regression were studied; none gave significant day-to-day reliability. Simple difference measures of poststimulus activity were just as reliable as their ALS analogs.

To compare the validity of various SC and HR scores, R. D. Hare (1968) used autonomic measures to discriminate between psychopaths and non-psychopaths. The uncorrected difference scores for both HR and SC gave significant group differences. This was not generally true for the range-corrected, difference score of Lykken et al. (1966).

Such laborious studies (Clifton & Graham, 1968; Hare, 1968) will have to be done if logical, a priori criteria are lacking, but the findings from them should not be overgeneralized. Reliability is not validity and a measure of homeostatic strength that is unreliable for neonates may be perfectly fine for young adults.

For psychophysiologists, one constant quest is for scores that will be sensitive to stimuli, treatments, and experimenter-imposed changes in the environment. Generally, we design the experiment so that a difference between the pseudoresponse and the stimulus response can be calculated. If such a difference is calculated for each proposed kind of score, then a multivariate Anova can be used to see which measure, if any, is the most sensitive. Sometimes we find that a combination of the proposed scores is better than any single score.

We recommend that the psychophysiologist not only be pragmatic but that he be a pragmatic pluralist. For each purpose, the score which will best suit that purpose should be calculated. There is no one score that is best for all situations. If the investigator is doubtful about which of several scores to use, then probably all such scores should be tried out in an analysis sample. If there is any one score that is significantly better than the others, it can be used in subsequent samples. In any case, new scores can always be compared to the ALS and the difference score. If the LIV holds, the ALS can be used as a standard; if the LIV does not hold, the difference score can serve as a standard.

EXPERIMENTAL DESIGN AND ANALYSIS

In this section we shall examine some aspects of experimental design and analysis of data that are particularly relevant for psychophysiological research. Knowledge of statistical principles as ordinarily taught in a psychology department will be assumed, as well as access to the usual texts on statistical psychology.[3] Statistical assumptions will be studied from a pragmatic point of view. Which of them must be followed rigorously? Which can ordinarily be disregarded except under special circumstances? Experimental designs found frequently in psychophysiological research but rarely in statistical texts will be dealt with in detail; some more common designs will also be examined.

Roughly speaking, all experiments are univariate (i.e., one measure per subject) or multivariate (i.e., two or more measures per subject). For the moment we shall discuss only the univariate design. The necessary assumptions for statistical analysis can be stated simply: (a) random assignment of the subjects to each experimental condition, and (b) independence of the scores that result from each treatment. The random assignment of the subjects usually guarantees that the scores will be independent.

Why have we not mentioned any other assumptions? What about normality and homogeneity of variance? In large samples normality and variance homogeneity are not important. The independence of scores guarantees that the relevant statistics (means, regression coefficients, etc.) will be normally distributed as N increases indefinitely, even if the original distribution is very nonnormal. (This is a result of the Central Limit Theorem.) Variance heterogeneity implies a loss of degrees of freedom when the usual Anova tests are applied, but for large samples no difference in significance level will result (Box, 1954).

These facts are very reassuring for experimenters with large samples, but what about studies with small samples? Even for small samples with significant deviations from normality and homogeneity, the t and F tests may be "robust" to such violations, and the tabled values may be used for all practical purposes. How can we tell when and when not to use the normal-based statistics?

One solution is to calculate a rank-order analog for each of the classical statistics. The Spearman rank-order coefficient can be computed whenever

---

[3]When we refer to statistical inference in this chapter, we allude to the logical systems generally used by research workers today; i.e., the Fisher set of significance tests and the Neyman-Pearson approach. It is true that the posthumous work of Bayes is alive and doing well, but so far has had little effect on routine statistical analysis.

a Pearson product-moment correlation is obtained; the signed rank test can be used to check a zero-mu t ratio; the Kruskal-Wallis H test is a rank-order equivalent of the F ratio, and so on.

When the universe is bivariate normal (i.e., there is linearity, homoscedasticity, and marginal normality), and the product-moment correlation is zero, then the expected rank-order correlation is zero. If the universe product-moment correlation is nonzero, there will be a corresponding deviation for the expected rank-order correlation. As the rank-order coefficient has a larger sampling error, it will be less significant than the product-moment correlation. When the results for these two coefficients differ widely, the cause usually lies in the violation of one or more of the bivariate normal assumptions. A frequent cause for such a difference is a single observation that lies so far outside the range of the other observations that its removal may change the sign of the product-moment correlation. The rank-order correlation is insensitive to such bivariate skewness.

The t and F ratios are also sensitive to small-sample skewness, and wild observations usually decrease the significance level. Again, comparison with the analog rank-order test should warn the investigator when the deviation from the usual assumptions has reached the point where the robustness of the normal-based tests is threatened.

When both the rank-order and the normal-based tests give the same result, with slightly higher significance levels for the normal-based tests, then the classical statistics usually are the best summaries of the data. This is what we should expect to occur when the deviations from normality and homogeneous variance are not very great.

If the rank-order test gives a clearly significant result, and if the t or F ratio is clearly not significant, then the investigator must stop and consider both his data and his question very closely. It is very easy to construct cases in which the difference between two means is zero, so that the t ratio must be significant, but the medians are very different. This is done by introducing a skew into one of the distributions. In such a case, the investigator must decide which statistic he wishes to test: the mean or the median. But not all cases can be resolved that easily.

Generally, the rank-order statistics, such as Wilcoxon's $\mathcal{U}$, are complex functions of *all* the moments: the mean, the variance, the skew, the fourth moment, etc. Wetherill (1960) has shown that it is perfectly possible to have two distributions (one normal and the other nonnormal) with the same mean and median. Yet the Wilcoxon $\mathcal{U}$ would be very significant. This would result from differences in skew and fourth moment rather than in central tendency (as measured by the mean and median). So the investigator must be very careful to specify in such cases exactly what kind of differences he is looking for; otherwise he will be unable to decide which test to accept. The rank-order statistic and the normal-based statistic ordinarily do *not* answer the same question. ("How absolute the knave is! We must speak by the card, or equivocation will undo us." *Hamlet.*)

The remaining case is when the normal-based statistic is clearly significant and the rank-order statistic is clearly nonsignificant. Such results are rarely obtained. When the t ratio is at the 0.01 level or better, usually the rank-order statistic is close to, or exceeds, the 0.05 level. The one clear exception is when the sample sizes are very small. With a sample size of four or less, it is impossible to get a signed rank-order result that is significant at the 0.05 level. When dealing with sample sizes of two to five, we generally use the t and F ratios, since these are known to be robust (but we replicate before publishing).

Randomization and the Randomized Blocks Design

R. A. Fisher (1949) has emphasized that *randomization is necessary if one wishes to infer the effects of the treatments from the observed treatment averages.* He has also demonstrated that randomization suffices to justify an exact (if highly conditional) test of significance (1949, paragraph 21). The full hypothesis for Fisher's randomization (or permutation) test asserts that all samples are drawn from the same (possibly nonnormal) population. For independent scores, the Central Limit Theorem shows that Fisher's randomization test converges very rapidly to the usual Anova test as the number of subjects and number of blocks increase. The randomization test also forms the basis of all the rank-order tests with which we are familiar. Ordinarily, the randomization test is not applied to raw data because of the extreme laboriousness of computing all of the required combinations and permutations of the raw scores. However, the electronic computer may well make the randomization algorithm the test of choice.

What constitutes a random assignment of subjects to treatment? Ordinarily, we want an equal number of subjects for each treatment group. In such a case, random assignment is any method of allocation such that the probability of ending up in any treatment group is exactly equal to the probability of being placed in any other treatment group. Furthermore, knowledge of the subject's age, sex, pretreatment level, etc., does not change this probability; i.e., all conditional probabilities of assignment to a particular group are equal to the absolute probability of assignment. Occasionally, unequal frequencies for the various treatments are sought, which creates unequal assignment probabilities. Again the basic principle holds: all conditional probabilities of assignment to a particular treatment are equal to the absolute probability of assignment to that treatment. Randomization procedures must always include a physical act which guarantees that the assignment is dependent on purely chance phenomena: tossing a coin, rolling a die, using a table of random numbers, etc. An assignment is random if randomizing procedures have been used; it does not depend on the result of such procedures.

Indeed, one difficulty with these "completely randomized designs," as they are called, is that they must produce some extremely unbalanced results upon occasion. If 8 subjects are assigned with equal probability to one of two growth-producing drugs, then in 1 experiment out of every 14, the 4 tallest subjects will be assigned to 1 drug, the 4 shortest to the other. Thus unbiased results are guaranteed over all possible experiments at the cost of certain bias in a few experiments. We could require that all subjects be of the same height, but this would cut down the size of our experiment considerably and make it impossible to test for the existence of a height-by-drug interaction. R. A. Fisher (1949) speaks of the experimenter's dilemma: on the one hand, the utmost uniformity is desired to increase the sensitivity of each individual observation to the treatment effect; on the other hand, many observations are desired to test that the treatment effect is reliable and consistent.

One solution to this problem is to "block" the subjects into relatively homogeneous groups and then assign each block member at random to a treatment. In the example mentioned above, the subjects would be rank-ordered according to height and blocked into pairs. The toss of a coin would decide the treatment for the first subject of a pair; the other subject must then be assigned to the remaining treatment. The precision of the experiment will increase, the more the subjects within a pair resemble each other, but will not suffer if some pairs differ widely from other pairs. Clearly, the principle of the *randomized blocks design* may be applied to cases in which three or more treatments are being studied. If there are t treatments, then the subjects are divided into b blocks of t subjects each. Then each subject is assigned at random to one of the t treatments. When $t - 1$ treatments have been assigned to the $t - 1$ subjects in a block, the assignment of the tth treatment is completely determined. Such a randomized block design is sometimes called a *matched-group design* in the statistical psychology texts. Ordinarily at least two subjects from each block are assigned to the same treatment. This allows us to test for a block-by-treatment interaction.

Analysis of Correlated Means

A randomized block design can usually be analyzed by two-way Anova, as if it were a univariate design; even though the assumption of independent scores may not hold. The reason univariate Anova can be used is that, under the null hypothesis, the randomized block design generates t sets of treatment scores with equal variances and a constant correlation; therefore each pair of treatments has the same covariance. Randomized assignment to the t treatments within each block ensures that the expected correlation between any pair of treatment scores is due to the blocking and that the expected variances are equal.

A. Stuart (1958) proved that differences between the means of variates with equal covariances can be transformed into differences between the means of uncorrelated variates. The two-way, univariate Anova, blocks by treatments, essentially accomplishes this transformation.

When the null hypothesis is false, and the treatment effects do differ, Q. McNemar (personal communication) points out that the effects of nonadditive treatment may cause unequal variances and unequal correlations among the treatments. As soon as the equal covariance assumption fails, we must turn to multivariate Anova.

For a multivariate design, when the measures are unequally correlated, Hotelling's exact multivariate Anova is the best procedure, given that multivariate normality applies (Rao, 1952, pp. 239–244). However, there are some nonoptimal procedures that will often suffice without the labor involved in a complete multivariate Anova. In particular, Geisser and Greenhouse (1958) have shown that a conservative test can be applied to the usual univariate F-ratio. If the Geisser-Greenhouse result is significant, then it is not necessary to go any further, since it is a conservative test. If the univariate F-ratio is not significant under the usual univariate procedure, this also suffices, since *the univariate* F-*ratio is biased toward significance when the correlations are unequal.* If neither of these two criteria is met, Kendall's rank-order W coefficient of concordance can be computed. When the rank order of the treatment means can be specified, the rank-order correlation tests of Jonckheere (1954), Lubin (1961b), or Lyerly (1952) are very powerful.

The *repeated measures design* is used much more than the randomized blocks design. In the repeated measures design, each subject is usually tested t times, once for each treatment. Then a two-way Anova, subjects by treatments, is carried out to test for the differences between the treatment means (the symmetry test). This design is highly recommended by many statistical psychology texts as a way of eliminating between-subjects deviance from the comparison of treatment means. Actually, it results in introducing at least three major sources of error: (a) unequal correlations between treatments, (b) measurement carryover, and (c) treatment carryover.

Unequal correlations   Unequal correlations between treatments demand a multivariate Anova, rather than the usual univariate Anova, as pointed out previously. But would repeated measures on the same subjects lead to unequal correlations? Yes. Repeated measures have to be given in some fixed order and at some finite interval of time between trials. Trials close together in time generally have higher correlations than those with longer time intervals. The correlation between the first and the second trials is almost always greater than the correlation between the first and the last trials.

Lana and Lubin (1963) found that the repeated measures design dominated the papers appearing in three well-known journals studied over a period of three years: the *Journal of Experimental Psychology,* the *Journal of Comparative and Physiological Psychology,* and the *Journal of Abnormal and Social Psychology.* In one case only was an appropriate multivariate analysis used. In all other cases, the biased, two-way, subjects-by-trials, univariate Anova was applied.

Why is the univariate Anova incorrectly applied so universally? Because the commonly used statistical psychology texts recommend this incorrect procedure. At this time, we know of only one statistical psychology text (Winer, 1962, paragraph 4.4) that discusses the use of a multivariate Anova when correlated means are involved.

Multivariate procedures should be considered whenever each subject is tested three or more times. In particular, whenever the total univariate Anova degrees of freedom exceed $N - 1$ (N is the number of subjects) multivariate methods should be used. Multivariate analysis is unnecessary when each subject is tested twice, since degrees of freedom for the univariate Anova are exactly $N - 1$.

Measurement carryover   The effects of measurement carryover are familiar to psychophysiologists under such rubrics as habituation, learning, negative transfer, fatigue, warmup, and boredom. The effect of unequal correlation is to overestimate the significance of the univariate F ratio. The effect of measurement carryover is to bias the estimate of treatment effects, either by additive carryover or by interaction with the treatment. The additive bias in the treatment means may be positive (e.g., learning, warmup) or negative (e.g., habituation, negative transfer, fatigue).

Control groups (pseudotreatment groups) offer a straightforward way of assessing additive measurement carryover. No treatments should be administered to the control subject, but t measures should be obtained from each subject as if they had been treated; then a multivariate test for differences between the t correlated means (Rao, 1952) should be made. If the symmetry test is significant, there is additive measurement carryover.

This method, essentially the pseudostimulus method, suggests an experimental design and a statistical procedure for assessing the tonic effect of a continuous treatment free of additive measurement carryover. The subjects are paired on a blocking variable, and members of each pair are assigned at random to treatment and control groups. Then the treatments are administered, measuring both control and treated subjects at the same time intervals over t trials. The difference (treatment score minus control score) is then calculated for each pair, followed by a multivariate Anova to see if the t-correlated, average differences deviate significantly from zero (a zero-mu test). These average differences are free of additive measurement carryover; however, this design does not eliminate the interaction of measurement carryover with subsequent treatments.

Another device for eliminating measurement carryover is to measure each subject on repeated trials, until an asymptotic level has been reached, and then introduce the treatment. This works fairly well if the measurement carryover is due to such factors as learning or warmup. It does not work if habituation or sensory adaptation is involved. If the treatment introduces novel stimuli, this will generally dishabituate the subject and start the habituation process anew. Similarly, introduction of the treatment may involve stimuli that reduce fatigue and boredom and start these processes over again. Psychophysiologists, with their knowledge of the orienting reflex, should never underestimate the influence of novel stimuli or novel combinations of familar stimuli.

The most dangerous effect of measurement carryover is possible interaction with subsequent treatments. Solomon (1949) and Campbell and Stanley (1963) have discussed designs for assessing pretest-treatment interactions. Lana (1959, 1964) and Entwisle (1961) have used such designs in studies of training and attitude change.

Treatment carryover   Treatment carryover may occur whenever two or more treatments are given to the same subject; i.e., whenever a crossover design is used. Every time we cross over from Treatment A to Treatment B within the same subject, we risk two possible biases: (a) there may be an additive carryover effect of Treatment A; and (b) the carryover effect of Treatment A may interact with Treatment B. Many statistical texts mention the difficulties of the crossover design. For example, Kempthorne (1952) warns,

> The practical obstacle we encounter with this design is that there may be residual effects [treatment carryover] and the design we use is not a valid one in this case. It is essential to use every possible device to ensure that there are no residual effects, the simplest one being to allow an interval between each experimental period during which we hope that residual effects of the treatments will be used up. [p. 596]
>
> A basic assumption in the switchover design is that the effect of a treatment is the same in all the periods in which it may be applied. . . . The utility of the switchover design, or, in fact, of any design that involves different treatments on the same experimental unit, is limited because of the necessity of constant treatment effects and zero residual effects. [p. 607]

There is a widespread notion that counterbalancing the treatment order disposes of the treatment carryover problem. This is not so. Counterbalancing eliminates (a) additive order effects (learning, fatigue, etc.) that do not interact with the treatments, and (b) constant carryover effects that do not vary with the treatment. If the additive treatment carryover varies with treatment, or if the treatment carryover interacts with the subsequent treatments, counterbalancing fails.

Recently, some psychologists have been concerned enough about treatment carryover effects to run duplicate designs. They have studied single-treatment (between subjects) designs versus multiple-treatment (within subjects) designs. Many cases have been found in which multiple treatments have profoundly different results from the single-treatment-per-subject design. In experiments dealing with the relation of response strength to stimulus intensity, which used more than one intensity per subject, Grice (1966) found very different results for a within-subjects design and a between-subjects design. Poulton and Freeman (1966) have given many examples in which additive and interactive carryover effects have completely biased the experimental results.

As to procedures or experimental designs that will control or eliminate treatment carryover, the best established device was the one mentioned above by Kempthorne: a recovery interval between treatments that is long enough for the carryover effect to vanish. This leads to a multiphase treatment recovery design in which each treatment is preceded by a recovery (or washout) interval long enough for the subject to return to baseline.

In deciding what recovery interval is long enough, in drug studies, it is possible to determine the amount of the administered drug that is still present in the blood and urine. Consequently, the recovery interval used between drug treatments is usually set at the time necessary for the drug to reach some minimal blood-urine level. But it is well known that chemicals sometimes reach remote parts of the body such as the bone marrow and remain there, undetected, for long periods of time. There is also the peculiar effect known as "withdrawal," which occurs when certain drug treatments stop. Oswald and Priest (1965) administered sleeping pills to their subjects for about 2 weeks. When the drug was stopped, there were immediate changes in the sleep pattern (nightmares, excess of "dreaming" sleep, etc.)—these subjects took over 5 weeks to return to predrug sleep levels. During most of this 5-week interval, the blood and urine were free of the drug. Here is a case in which recovery occurred in terms of blood levels but the sleep behavior did not return to the baseline. The drug had caused some profound change in the sleep mechanisms; its withdrawal caused equally profound changes. If the organism manages to adjust its circadian rhythms to a treatment, we may expect significant responses to the offset of that treatment.

The multiphase treatment recovery design can be improved considerably by pretreatment testing to an asymptotic level, continuous testing of each subject on the physiological and behavioral criteria, and actively aiding the subject to return to pretreatment levels. The experimental design then involves: (a) a baseline period, when the subject is manipulated to yield a steady state baseline in which all the measured variables of interest reach

the asymptote, (b) a treatment period, (c) a recovery period in which the subject is manipulated to return to the pretreatment level (d) a treatment period, and (e) and so on. This design is commonly used by Skinnerians; they have developed great skill in using it (see Sidman, 1960).

This alternating treatment and recovery design is most appropriate and valid when the experimenter is interested in the effect of treatment on steady state (tonic) behavior, and if *the treatment effect is reversible*. If the effects of treatment carryover make it impossible to return to the pretreatment state, all subsequent treatments are affected. When treatment effects are irreversible, then recovery intervals are useless.

The assessment of reversibility can be difficult. The return of the measured behavior to the pretreatment *level* does not guarantee that the subject is in the pretreatment *state*. For example, extinction procedures can generally return a learned response to the prelearning level; but subsequent learning trials usually show significant savings, indicating that the subjects did not return to the naïve prelearning state.

If the effects of treatment carryover can neither be assessed nor eliminated, what are we to do with the multiple treatment (crossover, within-subjects, etc.) design? Our answer is simple—abandon it. If we are trying to assess the isolated effect of a particular treatment, why borrow trouble by deliberately inserting the possible carryover effect of other treatments? When we are trying to use the subject as his own control to eliminate the effects of age, sex, race, etc., there are two plausible alternatives: (a) if there are a small number of variables that might affect the treatment, then we use them as blocking variables in a randomized blocks design; and (b) if there are a large number of such blocking variables relative to a small number of possible subjects, then we use the *three-phase design,* discussed below.

Of course, if interactions due to treatment carryover or the cumulative effects of the measurement procedure are to be assessed, then a multiple-treatment, repeated-measures design is called for, but only as part of a larger experiment including sections in which measurement carryover and treatment carryover are vigorously excluded. These rotation designs or sequential treatment designs are routinely used in agricultural experiments.

Three-phase design If we abandon the multiple-treatment design in favor of only one treatment per subject, then the three-phase design is in many ways the most attractive single-treatment design. The three-phase design consists of (a) the baseline steady state, (b) the treatment, and (c) the recovery. Since only a single treatment is involved, we never need to worry about the carryover effect on subsequent treatments. When treatment effects are reversible, both pretreatment and recovery measures can be combined to decrease the between-subjects deviance in the assessment of treatment effects, but the primary use of these phases is to assure ourselves that the treatment effect is under experimental control. Multivariate Anova is the most appropriate statistical analysis, although special circumstances may make it possible to substitute an a priori linear function in a univariate Anova.

The logic of the three-phase design calls for the attainment of an asymptotic steady state during the baseline phase. Theoretically, it is possible to take account of a linear or monotonic nonlinear trend throughout the experiment; but we are on much safer ground, experimentally and statistically, if we can establish a constant pretreatment basal level. Although it is not necessary for the subject to return to baseline during recovery (i.e., the treatment effect can be irreversible), analysis is much easier if the asymptotic levels for the baseline and recovery periods are identical.

Skinnerians generally consider the establishment of an asymptotic baseline level as a necessary preliminary to the treatment phase. This is to demonstrate the experimenter's understanding and control of behavior, rather than to improve the statistical analysis. "The descriptive investigation of steady-state behavior must precede any manipulative study . . . in order to describe the changes (produced by treatments) we must be able to specify the baseline from which they occurred; otherwise we face insoluble problems of control, measurement, and generality (Sidman, 1960, p. 238)."

The investigator should remember that, even when an asymptotic baseline has been achieved, there is still the possibility of interaction between measurement carryover and the subsequent treatment. In this respect it is much like the "pretest-posttest control group design" of Campbell and Stanley (1963).

The three-phase design fails completely when the object is to study the parameters of growth, or learning, or habituation, or any other nonstationary state. Here the randomized block design (or stratified randomization, as it is sometimes called) becomes highly desirable, since there is no way of using the subject as his own control through baseline testing.

Intraindividual Statistics

One very hazy area is the question of experiments where $N = 1$. A common solution is to treat each measure as if it were an independent score. This leads to a t ratio or F ratio in which the number of measures plays the role of the number of subjects. As we have seen from our previous discussion of correlated means, this procedure is appropriate only when the correlations between the measures are equal. In the section on the autonomic lability score, we discussed the computation of serial correlations (autocorrelations) between consecutive measures on one subject. The use of the usual Anova procedure is equivalent to stating that all serial correlations are equal, a most unlikely phenomenon.

Box and Tiao (1965) have taken the special case in which there is a possible shift in the level of the measures caused by an imposed treatment; i.e., when the treatment adds a constant to the time series, making it a nonstationary process. First, they specify their model, an integrated, moving average process such that the first order differences have a positive first order serial correlation and all other serial correlations are zero. Once the serial correlations can be specified, a multivariate t ratio can be formed and tested for significance. Maguire and Glass (1967) have actually worked out a computer program for this procedure and applied it to an example. The chief problem comes in deciding whether the Box-Tiao model is appropriate. A periodic function or any monotonic asymptotic function such as an exponential, hyperbolic or power process would not fit the Box-Tiao model.

Theoretically, if one could describe the time

series as some finite autoregressive process, then the necessary set of serial correlations could be calculated and multivariate Anova applied. But even with our limited knowledge of possible time-series processes, there are too many to be able to test them all on the same set of data. Some a priori judgments must be made. Box and Jenkins (1970) have described an iterative approach to the selection of time-series models which leans heavily on the use of autocorrelation.

One psychophysiological variable, the EEG, has been treated intensively as a time series. As we mentioned in the section on the measurement of tonic states, the spectral model (a special case of the autoregressive process) has been applied very widely to time series within each subject. Even though the spectral model (by definition) fails to reproduce certain important phasic events, such as vertex-sharp waves and K complexes, it has given us significant quantitative differences between known states of consciousness (Hord, Johnson, Lubin, & Austin, 1965; Johnson, Lubin, Naitoh, Nute, & Austin, 1969). After all, a model does not have to be true to be useful. A partial truth is sufficient for many exploratory purposes.

It is customary to perform autospectral tests (e.g., Walter & Adey, 1963), which take account of correlations between adjacent spectral ordinates by comparing only those densities that are separated by several ordinates. Until we know more about the robustness of such tests under deviations from the spectral model, significance tests within a subject are *not* recommended. D. O. Walter (personal communication) has pointed out that the major criterion of physiological significance in spectral studies is repeatability (see also Hord et al., 1965).

What should be done about testing the significance of within-subject statistics? At the present time, there are few psychophysiologists who have the statistical skills or the computational time necessary for exact tests in a single subject. So, our first recommendation is to give up significance tests when $N = 1$. (We do *not* recommend giving up *experiments* in which the N is unity. As far as we know, there is not a single significance test in all the work of Ebbinghaus.)

Next, we recommend the strategy used by Rao (1952) in devising multivariate tests of significance.

Whenever possible, he reduces the problem to a univariate test by choosing an optimal linear function of the measures, and constructing a statistic suitable for the univariate case. In other words we could compute a statistic within each subject that is an appropriate test of the hypothesis, but the significance of this statistic would be determined by the usual between-subject methods. Each statistic is now a score. Under the usual null hypothesis, the expected average statistic over all subjects is zero. Perform the usual t test, or signed-rank test to see if the group average deviates significantly from zero. For example, one could calculate a t ratio within each subject, and then regard these ratios as scores to be subjected to the usual zero-mu t test. Similarly, a correlation could be computed within each subject, the z transformation applied to put the N correlations in quasinormal form and then the zero-mu test computed to see if the average z differs from zero. (See Spreng, Johnson, & Lubin, 1968, for a worked example of this.)

What difficulties arise from this suggestion? Of course, the primary problem is that now we can only make inferences about the group of subjects as a whole and cannot talk about the significance of any statistic for a single subject. Unless we are in a clinical situation, this should cause little discomfort. The between-subjects test is highly conditional, and much depends upon the variation found in the particular sample observed. But this is true of all Anova tests and of all statistical tests that rely upon estimating parameters from the sample values. Of course, any hope of testing for interaction between the subject and the treatment must be given up.

Double Sampling

Many statistical and experimental difficulties are eased considerably if the experimenter decides beforehand to do his study in two or more stages. The simplest, and possibly the most valuable, kind of double sampling is to run a pilot study on at least two subjects (in each treatment group). The results are used to correct procedural errors, change the apparatus, redesign the treatment, etc.; the pilot study is then thrown away and the full study is made. We routinely assume in our laboratory that the first two subjects in any new study will give results that have to be discarded because of procedural errors.

Even after the pilot study has been done (and discarded), there are many good arguments for using two samples rather than one. Experienced psychometricians always carry out multiple correlations or multivariate discriminating functions on an *analysis* sample and then apply the derived functions to a *cross-validation* sample. There are two reasons for this. At present, there is no published solution to the question of what correlation to expect when the derived multiple regression is applied to a universe of cross-validation samples. It is known that this expected cross-validity is considerably lower than the multiple correlation in the analysis sample and that it is somewhat lower than the true multiple correlation in the universe. Therefore, the cross-validation sample is used to fill in the gap in our statistical knowledge. The second difficulty is that we never know how closely our sample fits the multivariate normal assumptions of linearity and homogeneous error variance. Theoretically, it would be possible to analyze the deviations from multivariate normality and work out the effects on the expected cross-validity—in practice it is a lot easier to draw another sample and cross-validate. The cross-validation sample performs the same function for the multivariate discriminating function with the percent of agreement playing the same role as the cross-validity. About the only difference is that discriminating functions make even more assumptions than multiple regression models.

The notion of deriving parameter estimates in one sample, and then using these statistics to answer precise questions in a subsequent sample, has attracted some attention from statisticians but has not been used very much by experimenters. Walker and Lev (1953) give a clear, concise explanation of what might be called "precision sampling." Suppose that the null hypothesis is that a particular difference ($\bar{D}$) is equal to zero, on the average; i.e., a zero-mu test. The experimenter draws an analysis sample (we use two to five subjects), calculates $\bar{D}$ and s_d. Then $\bar{D}$ becomes the alternative to the null hypothesis. The experimenter must now fix his Type 1 error and decide on what power (1 − Type 2 error) he wants. This gives him the total number of obser-

vations he needs in the cross-validation sample. For example, suppose that he sets his Type 1 error at the 0.05 level and wants 50% certainty (power) of detecting a deviation from zero if the true mean equals $\bar{D}$. Then the number of cases needed for the cross-validation sample is $t^2 s_d^2 / \bar{D}^2$, where t is the t ratio at the 0.05 level for the needed N. If the needed value of N is small, then some iteration will be necessary before this function converges on fixed values of t and N. If greater than 50% power is wanted, then another t ratio must be added to the function (using the power table to obtain the t ratio) and the needed N is increased proportionately (Walker & Lev, 1953, pp. 165–166).

This is a very interesting procedure from the point of view of statistical inference. If one followed this precision-sampling method and were unable to detect a significant difference from zero, then one might say "I am 95% certain that the average difference from zero must be equal to or less than $\bar{D}$. My cross-validation sample size was such that, if the true mean were $\bar{D}$ and the true standard deviation s_d, then 95% of the time I should have obtained t ratios that were significant at the 5% level." Of course, the experimenter is not limited to the analysis sample estimate, $\bar{D}$. He can set up any deviation that he considers to be of practical significance and use s_d to derive the needed cross-validation N. Statisticians have worked out a number of variations on this theme, such as testing for the highest mean in a set of groups, testing for the order of the means, and combining both the analysis and the cross-validation samples so as to use all the data (e.g., Wormleighton, 1960).

There are many other uses of multistage sampling, such as sequential testing of treatments (Billewicz, 1958) and finding optimal combinations of treatments (Box & Wilson, 1951). We shall return to this topic when we consider the virtues of replication and the (Sherlock) Holmesian inference calculus used by epidemiologists.

COMMON PROCEDURAL AND INTERPRETATIONAL DIFFICULTIES

In this section we shall deal with some miscellaneous problems considered only briefly before. First, we shall ask what should be done with significant interactions. Our second emphasis will be on the problems that arise when the subjects have not been assigned randomly to the treatment groups.

Significant Interactions

Significant interactions are frequently found in psychological experiments. In these cases it is often recommended that the significant interaction be used as an error term for the main effects involved. There is a logical error here. If the interaction between treatments and blocks is significant, there is no need to ask if the treatment effect is significant—at least one pair of treatments must differ significantly within a block. If the interaction is not significant, then the residuals within each treatment-by-block cell form the appropriate error term.

The claim is often made that, if the block represents a random sample of the relevant population, and if the effectiveness of the treatments over the entire population is in question, then interaction is the only appropriate error term. But the answer to this question hinges on whether the significant interaction is *ordinal* (Lindquist, 1953) or *disordinal.* If the interaction is ordinal, then the treatment effects have the same rank order within each block and there will be a single most effective treatment regardless of block. If the interaction is disordinal, the rank order of the treatments varies from block to block, and there may not be a single, most effective treatment. In either case, the question cannot be answered by using the interaction as error. Instead, the interaction effects must be studied and, if possible, described mathematically. Detailed procedures for these analyses have been discussed by Lubin (1961a) and Cox (1958).

Disordinal interaction is very often viewed with dismay by the research worker. No monotonic function such as a square root or logarithmic transformation can rid the data of a significant disordinal interaction. However for most applied researchers, disordinal interaction (and the Anacova analog, slope heterogeneity) comes as a gift of Nature. Now instead of looking for *the* best drug, *the* best teaching method, he can apply the right drug to the right patient, assign the right student to the right teaching method. Disordinal interaction is a

magnificent answer to the question of individual differences in treatment effects. Research workers looking for such answers should note that when several correlated measures of treatment effect are used for each subject, by a slight variation of Hotelling's T^2 test, it is possible to find a linear combination of the criteria that will maximize the interaction effect.

Slope Heterogeneity

Although it is rarely thought of in this manner, inequality of slopes in an analysis of covariance is exactly equivalent to a significant treatment-by-block interaction. As long as the assumption of linearity is met, the covariate plays the part of a blocking variable. Significant inequality of slopes leads to exactly the same interpretation as significant treatment-by-block interaction. The treatment effects are certainly significant, and the question of rank-ordering the treatments depends on whether the slopes are ordinal (no crossovers within the observed range of the covariate) or disordinal.

Nonrandom Grouping

Very often, the psychologist matches the experimental groups in his design in such a way that ordinary statistical analysis is completely inappropriate. If a subject with low education is added to one group to decrease the average educational level, a subject of high education is added to another group to increase the average education level, and so on, then positive and negative dependencies are being created between successive subjects. When scores are correlated in such unpredictable ways, the Central Limit Theorem cannot be applied and most statistical procedures are invalid. Let us paraphrase Campbell and Stanley (1963) on this question: randomization may not be the perfect way of assigning subjects but it is the only way.

Quite apart from the statistical difficulties raised by the correlations between the scores, nonrandom allocation removes our logical basis for inductive inference. How can we be sure that the significant differences obtained are in fact due to the treatments? Why are they not attributable to chance differences between the groups on traits that we did not measure, that we did not control? Of course, we can never be sure in any particular situation that such irrelevant differences do not exist, but randomization guarantees us there can be no systematic effects of such irrelevant differences.

Ex post facto experiments The phrase "ex post facto experiment" was introduced by Chapin and Queen (1937) to designate the situation in which preformed groups such as men and women, paranoid and simple schizophrenics, good and poor sleepers, etc., are handed to the experimenter; his job is to test for differences in some criterion variable such as learning, lactate-pyruvic ratio, or alpha abundance. This kind of experiment has been discussed extensively by Greenwood (1945), Chapin (1955), and Campbell and Stanley (1963). From the standpoint of the logic of inductive inference, this is the most fascinating design of all. The subjects have not been randomly assigned to the groups, and the treatment is part of the definition of group membership, i.e., the treatment was not randomly assigned. By R. A. Fisher's criterion, these studies do not fall into the category of experiments at all, and there is no assurance whatsoever that any observed differences can be attributed to the ostensible criterion of group membership.

Yet, this is exactly the problem of most medical research, where the physician is confronted with the phenomena of lung cancer, cholera, diptheria, depression, etc., and is asked not only to come up with invariant correlates of these conditions but to find (and remedy) their causes. If the investigator can only perform experiments involving nonrandom allocation, then by most rules (and especially those of R. A. Fisher), this is a game he cannot win. It is also true that final acceptance or rejection of causal hypotheses for each disease usually involves a "true" experiment, in which lower animals are assigned randomly to various infective procedures, humans with the disease (or susceptible to it) are assigned at random to various treatment groups, etc. Yet there are cases in which the "crucial" experiments have never been done, as in the matter of lung cancer, but the scientific and government communities have decided to pick out a particular agent as being a cause, or proximate cause. (Fisher was faithful to his principles: to the

end he insisted that cigarette smoking could *not* be accepted as a cause of lung cancer, since all the evidence depended upon statistical studies, not experiments on humans.) How does it come about that a substantial number of scientists become convinced through a series of "mere" statistical studies?

The strategy used to play this game has been well worked out by epidemiologists. The steps are as follows: (a) form a control or comparison group; (b) find significant differences in variables X, Y, Z, etc., between the target group and the comparison group; (c) designate one of the variables, say Y, as a presumed "causal" variable; (d) reanalyze the study or redesign the study so as to test the average difference in Y, holding X constant.

At Step (d), there are a large number of possible variations in results. The one result that would probably stop the investigator is to find no difference in the Y averages for the target and comparison groups, holding X constant. If the average Y difference is significant, within the strata or blocks of X, then the experimenter must now repeat the analysis using Z, P, Q, · · ·, or whatever other variables have discriminated or are supposed to discriminate between the target group and the comparison group. From a logical point of view, this is a Sisyphean labor, a never-ending series of tests of alternative hypotheses. It is limited only by the ingenuity of those who oppose the causal variable favored by the experimenter. If the rules prohibit a direct test of the experimenter's hypothesis, then the only way he can increase the general confidence in his causal variable is to eliminate all plausible alternatives.

The crucial part of this iterative set of statistical studies is the formation of the comparison group. By definition, the experimenter cannot allocate subjects to the target group. But he can select subjects and allocate them to the comparison group. Criteria for such control groups have been stated by MacMahon, Pugh, and Ipsen (1960):

> A comparison group is a group of unaffected individuals believed to reflect the characteristics of the population from which the affected group was drawn. Ideally the comparison group should not differ from the affected group in any respect other than not being affected which might be likely to influence the frequency of

the variable or variables suspected of being causally connected. This means either that both the patient and comparison groups must be representative of the same population or that if selective factors enter into the choice of patterns, the same factors ought to enter into the selection of the comparison group [p. 235].[4]

Finding the appropriate comparison group is the main difficulty but it is not the only one. Another problem is the nature of the causal network. If all causal hypotheses are independent and mutually exclusive, testing each alternative is a relatively easy job. But if the disease is the sum of a set of effects, or contingencies and interactions among causal effects play a large role, then disentangling the causation web may involve intricate hypothesizing of a complexity level far above those dealt with by Sherlock Holmes and Hercules Poirot.

Nevertheless, the epidemiologist may reflect with some satisfaction that generally when a sequence of such studies has been carried out, meticulously selecting a different comparison group (or analyzing the data in a different way) for each alternative, there has been convergence on a very small set of postulated causes. It is doubtful that agreement about such causes has ever been unanimous, but a large enough degree of scientific consensus usually leads to governmental action to control or eliminate such potential health hazards. Doubt always remains and the epidemiologist can only be sure of one thing—there is no basis in statistical inference for his conclusions.

The Insignificance of the Significance Test

Most current statistical theories revolve about the power and sensitivity of the significance test; editors usually demand that significance test results be given; psychologists pride themselves on their copious use of such tests—what argument could possibly lead to the conclusion that formal significance tests are not necessary?

In determining what we want to find out from a significance test, Arthur W. Melton, editor of the *Journal of Experimental Psychology* for 12 years, has pointed out (1962) that the essential use of the significance test is to assess the chances that the

results of the experiment could be repeated. One way to find out is to repeat the experiment. If, in some five or six repetitions of the experiments, the results are essentially the same, then most critics would be confident that the results are indeed repeatable. No formal significance test would be necessary.

Within the set of appropriate significance tests, how necessary is it to choose the most efficient statistic? The selection of the most sensitive test of statistical significance is of great importance in some sciences such as astronomy or economics, in which observations can be made only with considerable expenditure of effort and sometimes cannot be repeated within the lifetime of the observer. But psychophysiology is an experimental science in which it generally costs relatively little to test another subject. We should take full advantage of nature's generosity in this respect. Any unbiased, appropriate significance test, no matter how insensitive, will tend toward the same result as the most sensitive test, as the number of subjects increases *if* (a) treatments are randomly assigned, and (b) scores are independent of one another.

How much novel information does a significance test give to the competent experimenter about the level of significance of his results? This question may confuse the student who has conducted few empirical studies; but every experienced investigator knows that, after he has computed and plotted the averages, slopes, correlations, percentages, etc., studied them, and compared them to his expectations and to previous results, there is very little the significance test can add in the way of surprises. Results that are consistent for most or all of the subjects will be very significant; results that are clearly inconsistent will be very insignificant. The results of borderline consistency will give borderline significance levels. (In fact one of the few ways we have found effective in checking computer, and computer programmer errors, is the systematic comparison of the significance level printout with our a priori expectations and our eyeball analysis of the results.)

When a significance test is in conflict with later attempts to confirm the results, scientists will almost always object to the conclusion suggested by the significance test. There are many good reasons

[4] B. McMahon, T. F. Pugh, and J. Ibsen, *Epidemiologic methods*. Boston: Little, Brown, 1960. Reprinted with permission.

for this. Among them is the argument that, if you adopt the X percent confidence level for your significance test, you are guaranteeing that, when the null hypothesis is true, you will reach the wrong conclusion X percent of the time.

But how can the significance test really be in conflict with the results from repeated experimentation? After all, R. A. Fisher (1949) states that the only way in which the error term (for the significance test) can be appropriately estimated is through replication. Of course, for the ordinary self-contained experiment, this is true. The difficulty arises from the fact that the significance level is a simple monotonic asymptotic function of the *number* of replications, whereas the level of confidence in the scientific community tends to be much more a function of the *kind* of replication.

Suppose that a study is challenged by critics and the experimenter answers by repeating the experiment in the same laboratory, using the same source of subjects, the same procedure, the same apparatus, etc. If this (literal) replication obtains the same results, generally critics will not shift much from their previous position. On the other hand, if the experiment is repeated in a different laboratory, where the criticized procedures are replaced by those considered more appropriate, a different source for subjects is used, and the same results are still obtained, then this will be regarded as conclusive by most of the scientific community. Current statistical methodology cannot distinguish between these two kinds of replication[5], the increase in the significance level would be exactly equal, whether the two studies were done in the same laboratory or in different laboratories.

The formal significance test is a relatively recent innovation dating back to Karl Pearson and the early twentieth century. There are large segments of biological research in which it is not customary to make formal significance tests. If we reject all results not bearing a certified confidence level, then we reject almost all of our heritage of biological research, including most of the work done by the winners of the Nobel Prize. Formal significance tests may be helpful, informative, and sufficient, but are they necessary?

[5] Lykken (1968) has designated these two procedures as "literal replication" and "constructive replication." The "alternative hypothesis" testing procedure of the epidemiologist does not fall in either of these two categories, but Sidman (1960) has used the phrase "systematic replication" to cover those situations in which the experimenter deliberately varies the supposedly irrelevant variables.

REFERENCES

AX, A. F.   The physiological differentiation between fear and anger in humans. *Psychosomatic Medicine*, 1953, **15,** 433–443.

BAKAN, D.   A generalization of Sidman's results on group and individual functions and a criterion. *Psychological Bulletin*, 1954, **51,** 63–64.

BENJAMIN, L. S.   Statistical treatment of the law of initial values (LIV) in autonomic research: A review and recommendation. *Psychosomatic Medicine*, 1963, **25,** 556–566.

BENJAMIN, L. S.   Facts and artifacts in using analysis of covariance to undo the law of initial values. *Psychophysiology*, 1967, **4,** 187–206.

BERG, W. K., & GRAHAM, F. K.   Reproducible effects of stimulus intensity on heart rate response waves. *Psychophysiology*, 1970, **6,** 653–654.

BERG, K. M., BERG, W. K., & GRAHAM, F. K.   Infant heart rate response as a function of stimulus and state. *Psychophysiology*, 1971, **8,** 30–44.

BERKSON, F.   Psychophysiological studies in mental deficiency. In N. R. ELLIS (Ed.), *Handbook of mental deficiency.* New York: McGraw-Hill, 1963.

BERLYNE, D. E.   *Conflict, arousal and curiosity.* New York: McGraw-Hill, 1960.

BERNSTEIN, A.   Race and examiner as significant influences on basal skin impedance. *Journal of Personality and Social Psychology*, 1965, **1,** 346–349.

BILLEWICZ, W. Z.   Some practical problems in sequential medical trials. *Bulletin of the International Statistical Institute*, 1958, **36,** 165–171.

BIRREN, J. E., CARDON, P. V., Jr., & PHILLIPS, S. L.   Reaction times as a function of the cardiac cycle in young adults. *Science*, 1963, **140,** 195.

BLACKMAN, R. B., & TUKEY, J. W.   *The measurement of power spectra.* New York: Dover, 1958.

BLOCK, J. D., & BRIDGER, W. H.   The law of initial value in psychophysiology: A reformulation in terms of experimental and theoretical considerations. *Annals of the New York Academy of Sciences*, 1962, **98,** 1229–1241.

Box, G. E. P. Effects of inequalities of variance and correlation between errors in the two-way classification. *Annals of Mathematical Statistics,* 1954, **25,** 484–498.

Box, G. E. P., & Jenkins, G. M. *Time series analysis forecasting and control.* San Francisco: Holden-Day, 1970.

Box, G. E. P., & Tiao, G. C. A change in level of a nonstationary time series. *Biometrika,* 1965, **52,** 181–192.

Box, G. E. P., & Wilson, K. B. On the experimental attainment of optimum conditions. *Journal of the Royal Statistical Society,* Series B, 1951, **13,** 31–66.

Bradley, P. B. The central action of certain drugs in relation to the reticular formation of the brain. In H. H. Jasper, L. D. Proctor, R. S. Knighton, W. G. Noshay, & R. T. Costello (Eds.), *Henry Ford Hospital symposium on reticular formation of the brain.* Boston: Little, Brown, 1958.

Brazier, M. A. B. Electrical activity recorded simultaneously from the scalp and deep structures of the human brain. *Journal of Nervous and Mental Disease,* 1968, **147,** 31–39.

Bridger, W. H., & Reiser, M. Psychophysiologic studies of the neonate: An approach toward the methodological and technical problems involved. *Psychosomatic Medicine,* 1959, **21,** 265–276.

Callaway, E., & Buchsbaum, M. Effects of cardiac and respiratory cycles on averaged visual evoked response. *Electroencephalography and Clinical Neurophysiology,* 1965, **19,** 476–480.

Callaway, E., & Layne, R. Interaction between the visual evoked response and two spontaneous biological rhythms. *Annals of the New York Academy of Sciences,* 1964, **112,** 411–431.

Campbell, D. T., & Stanley, J. S. Experimental and quasi-experimental designs for research on teaching. In N. L. Gage (Ed.), *Handbook of research on teaching.* Chicago: Rand McNally, 1963.

Chapin, F. S. *Experimental designs in sociological research.* (Rev. ed.) New York: Harper, 1955.

Chapin, F. S., & Queen, S. A. *Research memorandum on social work in the depression.* New York: Social Science Research Council, Bulletin 39, 1937.

Clifton, R. K., & Graham, F. K. Stability of individual differences in heart rate activity during the newborn period. *Psychophysiology,* 1968, **5,** 37–50.

Clifton, R. K., & Meyers, W. J. The heart-rate response of four-month old infants to auditory stimuli. *Journal of Experimental Child Psychology,* 1969, **7,** 122–135.

Clynes, M. Respiratory control of heart rate: Laws derived from analog computer simulation. *IRE Transactions on Medical Electronics,* 1960, **ME-7,** 2–14.

Cohen, S. L., Silverman, A. J., & Shmavonian, B. M. Influences on psychodynamic factors on central nervous system functioning in young and aged subjects. *Psychosomatic Medicine,* 1961, **22,** 123–127.

Corah, N. L., & Stern, J. A. Stability and adaptation of some measures of electrodermal activity in children. *Journal of Experimental Psychology,* 1963, **65,** 80–85.

Cox, D. R. *Planning of experiments.* New York: Wiley, 1958.

Crowell, D. H., Davis, C. M., Chun, B. J., & Spellacy, F. J. Galvanic skin reflex in newborn human. *Science,* 1965, **148,** 1108–1111.

Darrow, C. W. Quantitative records of cutaneous secretory reactions. *Journal of General Psychology,* 1934, **11,** 445–452.

Darrow, C. W. The rationale for treating the change in galvanic skin response as a change in conductance. *Psychophysiology,* 1964, **1,** 31–38.

Davis, R. C. Electrical skin resistance before and after a period of noise stimulation. *Journal of Experimental Psychology,* 1932, **15,** 108–117.

Davis, R. C. & Buchwald, A. M. An exploration of somatic response pattern: Stimulus and sex differences. *Journal of Comparative and Physiological Psychology,* 1957, **50,** 44–52.

Davis, R. C., Buchwald, A. M., & Frankmann, R. W. Autonomic and muscular responses and their relation to simple stimuli. *Psychological Monographs,* 1955, **69** (20, No. 405).

Duffy, E. *Activation and behavior.* New York: Wiley, 1962.

Dykman, R. A., Ackerman, P. T., Galbrecht, C. R., & Reese, W. G. Physiological reactivity to different stressors and methods of evaluation. *Psychosomatic Medicine,* 1963, **25,** 37–59.

Edelberg, R. Independence of galvanic skin response amplitude and sweat production. *Journal of Investigative Dermatology,* 1964, **42,** 443–448.

Ellingson, R. J. Relationships between EEG and test intelligence: A commentary. *Psychological Bulletin,* 1966, **65,** 91–98.

Elliott, R. Physiological activity and performance: A comparison of kindergarten children with young adults. *Psychological Monographs,* 1964, **78** (10, No. 587).

Ellis, N. R., & Sloan, W. The relationship between intelligence and skin conductance. *American Journal of Mental Deficiency,* 1958, **63,** 304–306.

Entwisle, D. R. Interactive effects of pretesting. *Educational and Psychological Measurement,* 1961, **21,** 607–620.

Fisher, R. A. *Design of experiments.* (5th ed.) Edinburgh, Scotland: Oliver and Boyd, 1949.

Geisser, S., & Greenhouse, S. W. An extension of Box's results on the use of the *F* distribution in multivariate analysis. *Annals of Mathematical Statistics,* 1958, **29,** 885–891.

Goldberg, S. *Introduction to difference equations.* New York: Wiley, 1961.

Graham, D. T., Kabler, J. D., & Graham, F. K. Physiological response to the suggestion of attitudes specific for hives and hypertension. *Psychosomatic Medicine,* 1962, **24,** 159–169.

Graham, F. K., Berg, K. M., Berg, W. K., Jackson, J. C.,

HATTON, H. M., & KANTOWITZ, S. R. Cardiac orienting response as a function of age. *Psychonomic Science,* 1970, **19,** 363–364.

GRAHAM, F. K., & CLIFTON, R. K. Heart rate changes as a component of the orienting response. *Psychological Bulletin,* 1966, **65,** 305–320.

GRAHAM, F. K., & JACKSON, J. C. Arousal systems and infant heart rate responses. In L. P. LIPSITT & H. W. REESE (Eds.), *Advances in child development and behavior.* Vol. V. New York: Academic, 1970.

GRAHAM, F. K., & KUNISH, N. O. Physiological responses of unhypnotized subjects to attitude suggestions. *Psychosomatic Medicine,* 1965, **27,** 317–329.

GRAHAM, L. A., COHEN, S. I., & SHMAVONIAN, B. M. Sex differences in autonomic responses during instrumental conditioning. *Psychosomatic Medicine,* 1966, **28,** 264–271.

GRAY, M. L., & CROWELL, D. D. Heart rate changes to sudden peripheral stimuli in the human during early infancy. *Journal of Pediatrics,* 1968, **72,** 807–814.

GREENWOOD, E. *Experimental sociology.* New York: King's Crown, 1945.

GRICE, G. R. Dependence of empirical laws upon the source of experimental variation. *Psychological Bulletin,* 1966, **66,** 488–498.

GULLIKSEN, H. *Theory of mental tests.* New York: Wiley, 1950.

HAGGARD, E. A. On the application of Anova to GSR data: I. The selection of an appropriate measure. *Journal of Experimental Psychology,* 1949, **39,** 378–392. (a)

HAGGARD, E. A. On the application of Anova to GSR data: II. Some effects of the use of inappropriate measures. *Journal of Experimental Psychology,* 1949, **39,** 861–867. (b)

HAHN, W. W. Autonomic responses of asthmatic children. *Psychosomatic Medicine,* 1966, **28,** 323–332.

HARE, R. D. Psychopathy, autonomic functioning, and the orienting response. *Journal of Abnormal Psychology,* 1968, **73** (Monograph Suppl. 3, Part 2).

HEATH, H. A., & OKEN, D. Change scores as related to initial and final levels. *Annals of the New York Academy of Sciences,* 1962, **98,** 1242–1256.

HODES, R. H., & DEMENT, W. C. Depression of electrically induced reflexes (*H*-reflexes) in man during low voltage EEG "sleep." *Electroencephalography and Clinical Neurophysiology,* 1964, **17,** 617–629.

HODGES, W. F., & SPIELBERGER, C. D. The effects of shock on heart rate for subjects who differ in manifest anxiety and fear of shock. *Psychophysiology,* 1966, **2,** 287–294.

HORD, D. J., JOHNSON, L. C., & LUBIN, A. Differential effect of the law of initial value (LIV) on autonomic variables. *Psychophysiology,* 1964, **1,** 79–87.

HORD, D. J., JOHNSON, L. C., LUBIN, A., & AUSTIN, M. T. Resolution and stability in the autospectra of the EEG. *Electroencephalography and Clinical Neurophysiology,* 1965, **18,** 305–308.

HORD, D. J., LUBIN, A., & JOHNSON, L. C. The evoked heart rate response during sleep. *Psychophysiology,* 1966, **3,** 46–54.

JOHNSON, L. C. Some attributes of spontaneous autonomic activity. *Journal of Comparative and Physiological Psychology,* 1963, **56,** 415–422.

JOHNSON, L. C. Spontaneous and orienting responses during sleep. *U.S. Navy Medical Neuropsychiatric Research Unit Report* No. 66-9, 1966.

JOHNSON, L. C. A psychophysiology for all states. *Psychophysiology,* 1970, **6,** 501–516.

JOHNSON, L. C., & CORAH, N. L. Racial differences in skin resistance. *Science,* 1963, **139,** 766–767.

JOHNSON, L. C., & DAVIDOFF, R. A. Autonomic changes during paroxysmal EEG activity. *Electroencephalography and Clinical Neurophysiology,* 1964, **17,** 25–35.

JOHNSON, L. C., & LANDON, M. M. Eccrine sweat gland activity and skin conductance. *Psychophysiology,* 1965, **1,** 322–329.

JOHNSON, L. C., & LUBIN, A. Spontaneous electrodermal activity during sleep. *Psychophysiology,* 1966, **3,** 8–17.

JOHNSON, L. C., & LUBIN, A. The orienting response during waking and sleeping. *Electroencephalography and Clinical Neurophysiology,* 1967, **22,** 11–21.

JOHNSON, L. C., LUBIN, A., NAITOH, P., NUTE, C., & AUSTIN, M. Spectral analysis of the EEG of dominant and nondominant alpha subjects during waking and sleeping. *Electroencephalography and Clinical Neurophysiology,* 1969, **26,** 361–370.

JONCKHEERE, A. R. A distribution-free k-sample test against ordered alternatives. *Biometrika,* 1954, **41,** 133–145.

JONES, H. E. The galvanic skin reflex as related to overt emotional expression. *American Journal of Psychology,* 1935, **47,** 241–251.

KARRER, R. Autonomic nervous system functions and behavior: A review of experimental studies with mental defectives. In N. R. ELLIS (Ed.), *International review of research in mental retardation.* Vol. 2. New York: Academic, 1966.

KARRER, R., & CLAUSEN, J. A comparison of mentally deficient and normal individuals upon four dimensions of autonomic activity. *Journal of Mental Deficiency Research,* 1964, **8,** 149–163.

KAYE, H. Skin conductance in the human neonate. *Child Development,* 1964, **35,** 1297–1305.

KEEFE, F. B., & JOHNSON, L. C. Cardiovascular responses to auditory stimuli. *Psychonomic Science,* 1970, **19,** 335–337.

KEEFE, F. B., JOHNSON, L. C., & HUNTER, E. J. EEG and autonomic response pattern during waking and sleep stages. *Psychophysiology,* 1971, **8,** 198–212.

KEMPTHORNE, O. *The design and analysis of experiments.* New York: Wiley, 1952.

KENDALL, M. G. *The advanced theory of statistics.* London: Griffin, 1946.

KIMMEL, H. D., & HILL, F. A. A comparison of two electrodermal measures of response to stress. *Journal of Comparative and Physiological Psychology,* 1961, **54,** 395–397.

KIMMEL, H. D., & KIMMEL, E. Sex differences in adaptation of the GSR under repeated application of a visual stimulus. *Journal of Experimental Psychology,* 1965, **70,** 536–537.

KUGELMASS, S., & LIEBLICH, I. Effects of realistic stress and procedural inference in experimental lie detection. *Journal of Applied Psychology,* 1966, **50,** 211–216.

LACEY, J. I. The evaluation of an autonomic response: Toward a general solution. *Annals of the New York Academy of Sciences,* 1956, **67,** 123–164.

LACEY, J. I. Somatic response patterning and stress: Some revisions of activation theory. In M. H. APPLEY & R. TRUMBULL (Eds.), *Psychological stress: Issues in research.* New York; Appleton-Century-Crofts, 1967.

LACEY, J. I., KAGAN, J., LACEY, B. C., & MOSS, H. A. The visceral level: Situational and behavioral correlates of autonomic response patterns. In P. H. KNAPP (Ed.), *Expressions of the emotions in man.* New York: International Universities, 1963.

LACEY, O. L., & SIEGEL, P. S. An analysis of the unit of measurement of the galvanic skin response. *Journal of Experimental Psychology,* 1949, **39,** 122–127.

LANA, R. E. Pretest-treatment interaction effects in attitudinal studies. *Psychological Bulletin,* 1959, **56,** 297–300.

LANA, R. E. The influence of the pretest on order effects in persuasive communications. *Journal of Abnormal and Social Psychology,* 1964, **69,** 337–341.

LANA, R. E., & LUBIN, A. The effect of correlation on the repeated-measurements design. *Educational and Psychological Measurement,* 1963, **23,** 729–739.

LANG, P. J., & HNATIOW, J. Stimulus repetition and the heart rate response. *Journal of Comparative and Physiological Psychology,* 1962, **55,** 781–785.

LAZARUS, R. S., & OPTON, E. M., Jr. The use of motion picture films in the study of psychological stress: A summary of theoretical formulations and experimental findings. In C. D. SPIELBERGER (Ed.), *Anxiety and behavior.* New York: Academic, 1966.

LAZARUS, R. S., TOMITA, M., KODAMA, M., & OPTON, E. M., Jr. A cross-cultural study of stress reaction patterns in Japan. *Journal of Personality and Social Psychology,* 1966, **4,** 622–633.

LEWIS, M., & SPAULDING, S. J. Differential cardiac response to visual and auditory stimulation in the young child. *Psychophysiology,* 1967, **3,** 229–237.

LINDQUIST, E. F. *Design and analysis of experiments.* Boston: Houghton Mifflin, 1953.

LINDSLEY, D. B. Emotion. In S. S. STEVENS (Ed.), *Handbook of experimental psychology.* New York: Wiley, 1951.

LIPTON, E. L., STEINSCHNEIDER, A., & RICHMOND, J. B. Autonomic function in the neonate: IV. Individual differences in cardiac reactivity. *Psychosomatic Medicine,* 1961, **23,** 472–484.

LUBIN, A. L'utilisation des correlations par rang pour eprouver une tendance dans un ensemble de moyennes. *Bulletin de Centre d'Étude pour Recherche Psychotechnique,* 1961, **10,** 433–444. (a)

LUBIN, A. The interpretation of significant interaction. *Educational and Psychological Measurement,* 1961, **21,** 807–817. (b)

LUBIN, A., HORD, D. J., & JOHNSON, L. C. On the validity

and reliability of the autonomic lability score. *U.S. Navy Medical Neuropsychiatric Research Unit Report No. 64-20,* 1964.

LYERLY, S. B. The average Spearman rank correlation coefficient. *Psychometrika,* 1952, **17,** 421–428.

LYKKEN, D. T. *Statistical significance in psychological research,* 1968, in press.

LYKKEN, D. T., ROSE, R., LUTHER, B., & MALEY, M. Correcting psychophysiological measures for individual differences in range. *Psychological Bulletin,* 1966, **66,** 481–484.

MACMAHON, B., PUGH, T. F., & IPSEN, J., Jr. *Epidemiologic methods.* Boston: Little, Brown, 1960.

MAGUIRE, T. O., & GLASS, G. V. A program for the analysis of certain time-series quasi-experiments. *Educational and Psychological Measurement,* 1967, **27,** 743–750.

MALMO, R. B. Activation: A neuropsychological dimension. *Psychological Review,* 1959, **66,** 367–386.

MALMO, R. B. Finger-sweat prints in the differentiation of low and high incentive. *Psychophysiology,* 1965, **1,** 231–240.

MANNING, W. H., & DUBOIS, P. H. Correlational methods in research on human learning. *Perceptual and Motor Skills,* 1962, **15,** 287–321.

MCDONALD, D. G., JOHNSON, L. C., & HORD, D. J. Habituation of the orienting response in alert and drowsy subjects. *Psychophysiology,* 1964, **1,** 163–173.

MCNAIR, D. M., DROPPLEMAN, L. F., & PILLARD, R. C. Differential sensitivity of two palmar sweat measures. *Psychophysiology,* 1967, **3,** 280–284.

MELTON, A. W. Editorial. *Journal of Experimental Psychology,* 1962, **64,** 553–557.

MEYERS, W. J., VALENSTEIN, E. S., & LACEY, J. I. Heart rate changes after reinforcing brain stimulation in rats. *Science,* 1963, **140,** 1233–1235.

NEWTON, J. E., & PEREZ-CRUET, J. Successive beat analysis of cardiovascular responses. *Conditional Reflex,* 1967, **2,** 37–55.

OBRIST, W. D., & BUSSE, E. W. The electroencephalograms in old age. In W. P. WILSON (Ed.), *Applications of electroencephalography in psychiatry.* Durham, N. C.: Duke University Press, 1965.

O'CONNOR, N., & VENABLES, P. H. A note on the basal level of skin conductance and Binet IQ. *British Journal of Psychology,* 1956, **47,** 148–149.

OJEMANN, G. A., & VAN BUREN, J. M. Respiratory, heart rate, and GSR responses from human diencephalon. *Archives of Neurology,* 1967, **16,** 74–88.

OSWALD, I., & PRIEST, R. G. Five weeks to escape the sleeping pill habit. *British Medical Journal,* 1965, **2,** 1093–1099.

PLUTCHIK, R. Effect of electrode placement on skin impedance related measures. *Psychological Record,* 1964, **14,** 145–151.

POULTON, E. C., & FREEMAN, P. R. Unwanted asymmetrical

transfer effects with balanced experimental designs. *Psychological Bulletin,* 1966, **66,** 1-8.

RAO, C. R. *Advanced statistical methods in biometric research.* New York: Wiley, 1952.

RASKIN, D. C., KOTSES, H., & BEVER, J. Cephalic vasomotor and heart rate measures of orienting and defensive reflexes. *Psychophysiology,* 1969, **6,** 149-159.

RICHTER, C. P. High electrical resistance of the skin of newborn infants and its significance. *American Journal of Diseases of Children,* 1930, **40,** 18-26.

ROSENTHAL, R. Experimenter-outcome-orientation and the results of the psychological experiment. *Psychological Bulletin,* 1964, **61,** 405-412.

SCHLOSBERG, H., & STANLEY, W. C. A simple test of the normality of twenty-four distributions of electrical skin conductance. *Science,* 1953, **117,** 35-37.

SHMAVONIAN, B. M., YARMAT, A. J., & COHEN, S. I. Relationship between the autonomic nervous system and central nervous system in age differences in behavior. In A. T. WELFORD & J. E. BIRREN (Eds.), *Behavior, aging and the nervous system.* Springfield, Ill.: Charles C Thomas, 1965.

SIDMAN, M. A note on functional relations obtained from group data. *Psychological Bulletin,* 1952, **49,** 263-269.

SIDMAN, M. *Tactics of scientific research.* New York: Basic Books, 1960.

SIMONS, D. G. Response patterns in biomedical monitoring. In *Medical education for national defense, Symposium on biomedical monitoring.* U.S. Air Force School of Aerospace Medicine, 1964.

SNYDER, F., HOBSON, J. A., MORRISON, D. F., & GOLDFRANK, F. Changes in respiration, heart rate, and systolic blood pressure in human sleep. *Journal of Applied Physiology,* 1964, **19,** 417-422.

SOKOLOV, E. N. Higher nervous functions: The orienting reflex. *Annual Review of Physiology,* 1963, **25,** 545-580. (a)

SOKOLOV, E. N. *Perception and the conditioned reflex.* New York: Macmillan, 1963. (b)

SOLOMON, R. L. An extension of control group design. *Psychological Bulletin,* 1949, **46,** 137-150.

SPRENG, L. F., JOHNSON, L. C., & LUBIN, A. Autonomic correlates to eye movement bursts during stage REM sleep. *Psychophysiology,* 1968, **4,** 311-323.

STERNBACH, R. A. Two independent indices of activation. *Electroencephalography and Clinical Neurophysiology,* 1960, **12,** 609-611.

STERNBACH, R. A. *Principles of psychophysiology.* New York: Academic, 1966.

STERNBACH, R. A., & TURSKY, B. Ethnic differences among housewives in psychophysiological and skin potential responses to electrical shock. *Psychophysiology,* 1965, **1,** 241-246.

STUART, A. Equally correlated variates and the multinomial integral. *Journal of the Royal Statistical Society,* Series B, 1958, **20,** 373-378.

SURWILLO, W. W., & ARENBERG, D. L. On the law of initial value and the measurement of change. *Psychophysiology,* 1965, **1,** 368-370.

SURWILLO, W. W., & QUILTER, R. E. The relation of frequency of spontaneous skin potential responses to vigilance and to age. *Psychophysiology,* 1965, **1,** 272-276.

THOMSON, M. L. A. A comparison between the number and distribution of functioning eccrine sweat glands in Europeans and Africans. *Journal of Physiology,* 1954, **123,** 225-233.

THORNDIKE, E. L. The influence of chance imperfections of measures upon the relation of initial score to gain or loss. *Journal of Experimental Psychology,* 1924, **7,** 225-232.

TURSKY, B., & STERNBACH, R. A. Further physiological correlates of ethnic differences in response to shock. *Psychophysiology,* 1967, **4,** 67-74.

UNO, T., & GRINGS, W. W. Autonomic components of orienting behavior. *Psychophysiology,* 1965, **1,** 311-321.

VOGEL, W., & BROVERMAN, D. M. Relationship between EEG and test intelligence: A critical review. *Psychological Bulletin,* 1964, **62,** 132-144.

VOGEL, W., & BROVERMAN, D. M. A reply to "Relationship between EEG and test intelligence": A commentary. *Psychological Bulletin,* 1966, **65,** 99-109.

WALKER, H. M., & LEV, J. *Statistical inference.* New York: Holt, Rinehart and Winston, 1953.

WALTER, D. O. Spectral analysis for electroencephalograms: Mathematical relationships from records of limited duration. *Experimental Neurology,* 1963, **8,** 155-181.

WALTER, D. O., & ADEY, W. R. Spectral analysis of EEGs recorded during learning in the cat, before and after subthalamic lesions. *Experimental Neurology,* 1963, **7,** 481-501.

WENGER, M. A. Some problems in psychophysiological research. In R. ROESSLER & N. S. GREENFIELD (Eds.), *Physiological disorder.* Madison: University of Wisconsin Press, 1962.

WESCOTT, M. R., & HUTTENLOCHER, J. Cardiac conditioning: The effects and implication of controlled and uncontrolled respiration. *Journal of Experimental Psychology,* 1961, **61,** 353-359.

WETHERILL, G. B. The Wilcoxon test and non-null hypotheses. *Journal of the Royal Statistical Society,* Series B, 1960, **22,** 402-418.

WIKLER, A. Pharmacologic dissociation of behavior and EEG "sleep patterns" in dogs: Morphine, n-allyl-normorphine and atropine. *Proceedings of the Society for Experimental Biology,* 1952, **79,** 261-265.

WILDER, J. The law of initial values. *Psychosomatic Medicine,* 1950, **12,** 392.

WILDER, J. Basimetric approach (law of initial value) to biological rhythms. *Annals of the New York Academy of Sciences,* **68,** 1211.

WILDER, J. Pitfalls in the methodology of the law of initial value. *American Journal of Psychotherapy,* 1965, **19,** 577–584.

WILDER, J. *Stimulus and response.* Bristol, England: John Wright, 1967.

WILKINSON, R. T. Aftereffect of sleep deprivation. *Journal of Experimental Psychology,* 1963, **66,** 439–442.

WILLIAMS, H. L., GOODNOW, J., & LUBIN, A. Impaired performance with acute sleep loss. *Psychological Monographs,* 1959, **73,** (14, No. 484).

WILLIAMS, H. L., LUBIN, A., GRANDA, A. M., JONES, R. C., & ARMINGTON, J. C. EEG frequency and finger pulse volume as predictors of reaction time during sleep loss. *Electroencephalography and Clinical Neurophysiology,* 1962, **14,** 64–70.

WINER, B. J. *Statistical principles in experimental design.* New York: McGraw-Hill, 1962.

WORMLEIGHTON, R. A useful generalization of the Stein two-sample procedure. *Annals of Mathematical Statistics,* 1960, **31,** 217–221.

YULE, G. U. On the time-correlation problem. *Journal of the Royal Statistical Society,* 1921, **84,** 497–508.

ZEAMAN, D., DEANE, G., & WENGER, N. Amplitude and latency characteristics of the conditioned heart response. *Journal of Psychology,* 1954, **38,** 235–250.

Clinton Brown

INSTRUMENTS
IN PSYCHOPHYSIOLOGY

4

While it is nearly impossible to conduct psychophysiological research without instrumentation, many researchers view their collections of expensive, complex, and fragile apparatus with mixed but nevertheless intense feelings. For some, instrumentation is a necessary evil like taxes. Breakdowns, inaccuracies, or the sheer obstinate behavior of the inanimate device are tribulations that must be suffered for the sake of an investigation. For others, the delightfully scientific appearance of flashing lights, clicking relays, and humming polygraphs is a gratification in itself; and the attendant research procedures are an accessory justification for the purchase, cultivation, and display of gadgetry. Most investigators admit, however, that nearly all research in psychophysiology requires instrumentation, that gadgets are a necessary means to the end of objectivity of observation, and that the instrument represents a type of sensory prosthesis enabling the investigator to observe, measure, and perceive the otherwise inaccessible phenomenon of biological behavior.

While electronics has achieved a phenomenal growth in the years since World War II through the impetus of space and military research, there has been an undue lag in the application of new devices and measuring principles to psychophysiology, and a limited number of means by which this information can be disseminated. Of the growing number of bioelectronic instrumentation texts and journals now being published, most presume a certain critical amount of background in electronics rarely found in the behavioral scientist.

Some means must be found for accelerating the use of new instrumentation in psychophysiology. Although it is presently impractical to require that the psychophysiologist learn the whole field of electronics engineering, it *is* feasible to provide him with a summary of instrument functions in which the details of circuit theory and operation are deleted. The latter are clearly the province of electronics, require special knowledge and skills for understanding, and are separate and distinct from the more important matters of *instrument function*. Such an approach delegates the problems of instrument design to the qualified electronics engineer and condenses the material that must be grasped by the psychophysiologist to an important minimum.

I have attempted such an approach in the preparation of this chapter. The primary emphasis has been placed on the description of instrumentation necessary for detecting, measuring, recording, or stimulating the types of biologic processes that are of present or future importance to the field. Chapter subheads will indicate the type of biologic process to be discussed, and the material presented will indicate appropriate instrumentation. The details of circuit analysis will be omitted, except where they are essential to the understanding of device capability.

BASIC DEFINITIONS AND CONCEPTS

Signals

A signal may be defined as coded intelligence. More specifically, in the following discussion "signal" will refer to the derived analog (frequently electrical) of the physiological phenomena. For example, the electrical potentials emitted by the active heart muscle are biophysical phenomena. The electrical energy resulting from this event and detected from electrodes attached to the chest wall is a signal. Such an electrical signal is inserted into the instrument system, passes from input to output, and may be identified at any point.

In a second sense, the term "signal" refers to electrical or physical energies generated within an instrument and applied either to other sections of the instrument for control purposes or directly to the subject for purposes of stimulation. In either sense, any signal may be defined with respect to the three dimensions of amplitude, frequency, and waveform.

Amplitude   This term denotes the magnitude of the signal and may be determined at any point in the instrument system. For example, the heart muscle may generate several millivolts (mV) potential during contraction. When this is detected on the chest, the maximum signal amplitude is I mV, a result of losses in the intervening tissues. This weak signal is amplified by an electrocardiograph (ECG) amplifier to develop sufficient power to drive a recording pen. The amplitude of the recorded wave form may be adjusted to any suitable value by the use of gain controls. Amplitude, therefore, may be expressed as the number of millimeters (mm) of pen excursion produced by any component of the ECG complex, the value in mV of potential at the pick-off electrodes or as the various values of voltage at any point in the instrument.

Amplitudes of various waveforms are shown in Figure 4.1. The *peak amplitude* is the amplitude measured from a zero potential reference point to the maximum attained in either the positive or the negative direction. The *peak-to-peak amplitude* is determined by adding together the values for succeeding positive and negative excursions of an alternating waveform. In Figure 4.1, the peak-to-peak value is that given by $A_1 + A_2$, etc. The *root mean square amplitude* (RMS) is derived by squaring the peak value of each wave, adding these values together, determining the mean, and extracting the square root.

Period and frequency   A single waveform is measured from any one point on the wave to a succeeding equivalent point. In Figure 4.1, a cycle begins at 1, where the potential is zero; is half completed at 2, where it has described a full negative inflection; is fully complete at 3, etc. The period of a waveform is defined as the *length of time* required for one complete cycle, e.g., 100 milliseconds. A 10-Hz waveform contains 10 complete

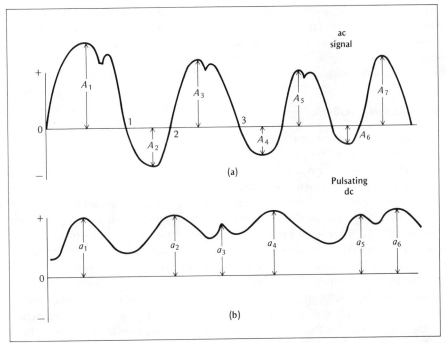

Figure 4.1 Idealized physiological waveform. (a): an ac-coupled phenomena that changes in both the positive and negative directions, passing through electrical zero; individual amplitudes are indicated. (b): a pulsating dc phenomenon that varies with respect to its positive potential.

is the number of waves per unit time, usually in seconds. A 10-H_3 waveform contains 10 complete cycles in 1 sec, and the average period of each wave is 0.100 sec or 100 msec.

Note that both the period and frequency of a wave are independent of the waveshape or of whether the fluctuations are about zero in alternating current (ac), or from zero to some positive or negative value in direct pulsating current (dc).

Waveform The remaining signal characteristic, waveform, is frequently the most difficult to determine, since it describes the generalized shape of a wave. While a variety of waveforms, e.g. sinusoidal, triangular, square, sawtooth, and spike, may be generated electronically, bioelectric signals are usually complex.

Absolute versus Relative Measures

It may be said with great generality that a bioelectric phenomenon may be measured in either absolute or relative terms. In the former, the derived values should be capable of definition in the same rigorous terms as any physical measurement, and there should be a zero referent. For example, blood pressure may be measured by cannulation; its instantaneous values may be expressed in terms of millimeters of mercury. By contrast, the finger pulse volume derived in optical plethysmography is a relative measure. While the output of the plethysmograph depicts a periodically varying waveform coincident with the heart cycle, the instantaneous values depicted are not referable to standard units of pressure, volume flow, etc. This does not diminish the utility of the relative measure, since it is possible to make: (a) *ratio* determinations such as the amount of change from pre-to-post stimulus; (*b*) derivation of a percent change score or; (c) determination of the amount of change from base level, representing the condition of no stimulation. The majority of the measures in psychophysiology are relative measurements.

The relativity of measures in no way reflects error, crudity, imperfection of the detection, or unwanted instrumental modification of signals. Rather it reflects the difficulty encountered in working with living systems, in which the process of measurement can intrude upon the nature or fidelity of the process being measured.

THE INSTRUMENTATION PROBLEM

The type and amount of equipment used in a research project is often determined by such factors as its immediate availability, cost, ease of operation, or even the esthetic appeal of the finished package when viewed in a manufacturer's display. Such considerations are frequently immaterial to more important requirements. Each research project requiring instrumentation should be considered as an instrumentation problem. The nature of the problem is not only that of determining how various variables may be detected, displayed, and measured, but the optimal amount and the types of instrument needed to accomplish this purpose. In fact, there are frequently a number of solutions to the instrumentation problem but only one or two of these represent optimum instrumentation. The selection of optimum instrumentation involves separate decisions concerning: (a) input sensitivity, (b) dynamic range of signal conditioning equipment, (c) complexity of operation, (d) degree of required resolution of the output, (e) amount of overall system accuracy, and (f) system reliability. Optimal instrumentation is not necessarily the most complex that can be devised or purchased. A series of examples will serve to illustrate these points.

A Hypothetical Problem and Possible Solutions

Assume that planned research requires a continuous measure of the beat-to-beat variation in the heart action of a group of subjects under experimental and control conditions. This information is needed to support hypothesized variations in heart rate (HR) produced by an external set of signals. The planning of optimal instrumentation requires that specific decisions be made about how the heart beat is to be detected, the means by which these signals are to be amplified, and finally, the manner in which the HR information is best displayed and the fineness of its resolution. A number

of alternate solutions will be presented, discussed, and evaluated; the order of presentation will be from the most simple to the most complex.

System 1. Direct observation The most simple and direct means for detecting the pulsations of the heart would be by the time-honored auscultatory means, by manual palpation of the pulse, especially that of the radial pulse, and subjective evaluation by the observer of changes in HR.

In this simplest case, the tactual senses of the observer are directly employed as a means for transducing the physical displacements of the partially occluded vessel into perceptible form and signal processing, i.e., the detection of the heartbeat itself and its variations in the rate of successive beats, is accomplished in the nervous system of the observer. The observer not only identifies each pulse by means of the recognition of the tactual pattern of the pulse (e.g., distinguished from the steady pressure required for palpation), but he must also perform the additional task of data reduction, analysis, and report by forming a mental image of the relative rate of pulse production and by defining an internal set of temporal standards for the detection of a change in rate (Figure 4.2).

In this simple case, all of the functions of detection, signal conditioning, and analysis have been made mentally by the observer. Instrumentation in terms of physical devices is absent. The entire attention of the observer-experimenter is spent in the task of observation; the crudity of the data restricts the fineness of resolution of the output, and the output is restricted to such verbal descriptions as "faster," "slower," or "about the same."

System 2. Simple, mechanical instrumentation The first refinement of System 1 would result from the use of two very simple instruments: a stethoscope as a transducer for the detection of the pulse beat and a stopwatch as an adjunct in signal processing and data reduction.

The stethoscope enables the observer to detect each heartbeat audibly and therefore permits him to note not only the occurrence of a beat but, with sufficient practice, to detect changes in the sound pattern of the beat, as evidenced by murmurs,

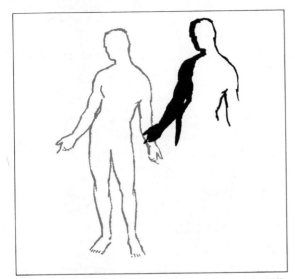

Figure 4.2 Instrument System 1. The observer manually palpates the radial pulse of the subject.

thumps, and other features that were not discernable by palpation. Signal processing is accomplished in the nervous system of the observer, but the addition of a stopwatch permits some quantification of the obtained data. Beats may now be counted over fixed periods of time and a simple calculation will yield the measure "beats per minute." The reverse technique may be used; a count may be made of a fixed number of beats and the time required for this may be measured and used to derive "average heart period." Finally, the experimenter may count the number of beats for fixed times during control, prestimulus, and poststimulus periods and use these numbers as data without converting into beats per minute. The minor increase in both cost and complexity of procedure from System 1 to System 2 has resulted in increased resolution, increased objectivity and variety of output data, increased sensitivity to multiple components of the phenomena being measured, and a decrease in the measurement error due to experimenter bias or other human fallibility.

System 3. Electrification and amplification This system is elaborated on the input side by the use of a microphone, piezoelectric detector, or other transducer that is sensitive either to the pulsatile

changes or directly to the sounds produced by the heart. Its output is an electrical analog of the pulse or sound. The output, of both low current and voltage, must be amplified electronically. The amplified signal is to be displayed on an oscilloscope screen as a series of vertical deflections of the beam as it is swept horizontally at a constant rate. A simultaneous auditory monitoring device may be used by feeding the amplified signal into a loudspeaker or headphones. See Figure 4.3.

These modifications represent changes in the system in its input, signal conditioning, and output sections. In System 1, each function was performed by the observer. If we consider him as an instrument system, his input transducer was the tactile sense of the fingertips; the signal conditioning section was his cortex and its functions; and the output, verbal statements, was mediated via the cortex and the functions of speech and language. Note that the human element has been almost entirely eliminated from System 3: pulse pickup, amplification, and visual and auditory display are accomplished automatically with minimal but constant error. Since the horizontal axis of the scope

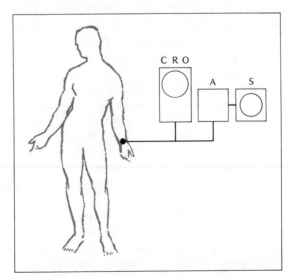

Figure 4.3 Instrument System 3. An input transducer has been substituted for the manual palpation and an oscilloscope (CRO) provides a visual monitor on the ECG potentials, which are simultaneously amplified by an amplifier (A) and displayed by a speaker (S).

may be calibrated in time units (e.g., mm per sec), the observer may directly read off the time per beat, beats per unit time (for a full sweep), and may observe the pictorial representation of the idiosyncrasies of each beat.

The output display is transient in nature, however. Although each successive sweep of the trace may be photographed, the process is costly and time consuming. The observer must therefore determine the change in the HR and its magnitude from the transient display and record it repetitively at frequent intervals. Aided by instruments, however, the observer can employ his perceptual skills and abstracting abilities in a highly accurate and reliable fashion. The integrating capacity of the trained observer in many respects exceeds that of the electronic computer. At present the expert diagnostician still employs his judgment and sensory acumen, based on past experience and multiple observations, to detect aberrant ECG and EEG patterns.

System 4. Addition of electronic counting Input and signal conditioning sections are retained from System 3, but a rapidly acting electronic counter is substituted as an output display device. The counter would be connected so that it advances by one count for each heartbeat and may be rapidly set to zero by an electrical control operated by the experimenter (Figure 4.4).

We have now relinquished for the first time the direct information contained in each heartbeat. The information available at the output is *only* a count of input pulses. Electrical noise, artifacts resulting from movement, etc., would be counted as a bonafide heartbeat. Precautions must now be taken to eliminate all possible sources of artifact from the input.

As an advantage, it is now possible to store an incremental count of HR beats over any epoch (defined as a predetermined period of time). Permanent storage of the data must be made manually by the observer, although he can do this rather conveniently before resetting the counter and during an epoch when a new count is being accumulated. Subsequently, the data may be converted into extrapolated HR, or the average time of each beat-to-beat interval by calculation.

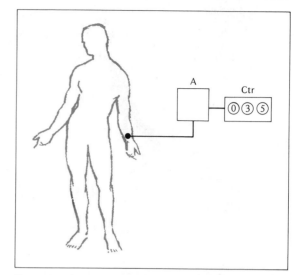

Figure 4.4 Instrument System 4. Transducer and amplifier have been retained, but a rapidly acting counter (Ctr) provides data storage.

System 5. Standard electrocardiograph This system will use the standard components of the ECG. Electrodes are attached to the body at various places to detect the small electrical signal at each heartbeat, a high gain, noise-free amplifier will amplify the power of each signal and the output will be graphically recorded by means of a moving pen on a continuous strip of paper transported beneath the pen at a fixed rate. The entirety of the ECG phenomenon is now permanently portrayed in the form of a Cartesian plot in which the ordinate is proportional to time (Figure 4.5).

The advantages of the system lie in its provisions for a graphic, permanent record of the whole physiological event. The fact that the complete electrical analog of the contraction of the heart is displayed is superfluous to the needs of the instrumentation as originally established. Any subsequent analysis of the beat-to-beat variability will ignore this redundant information. However, unlike System 4, the redundancy of information will enable the observer to eliminate noise signals or those from sources other than the heart. The decision of what differentiates a signal (heart contraction) from noise (any other signal source including extraneous artifact) is based upon the recognition of patterns characteristic of heart contraction and those of the artifact.

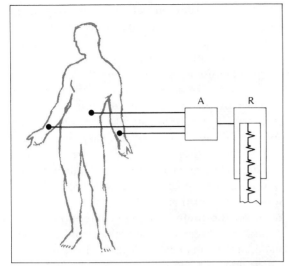

Figure 4.5 Instrument System 5 uses standard electro-cardiograph equipment, shown as an amplifier (A) and recorder (R). The consecutive heartbeats are displayed on continuous chart paper for either wave-form analysis or the computation of HR or *R–R* interval.

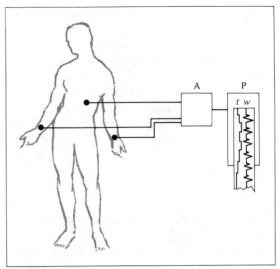

Figure 4.6 Instrument System 6 uses standard ECG components, an amplifier (A), and a polygraph recorder (P). Two channels are used on the recorder, one (*w*) displays the electrical analog of the heart contraction, while the other (*t*) provides tachometric information, i.e., the extrapolated beats per minute information for each *R–R* interval.

Since time is indicated along the length of the ECG recording, it is now possible to measure the beat-to-beat interval of the heart and collect the data in the form either of heart rate or of heart period (HP) during the experiment. Further, since the record is in permanent form, it can be reexamined at any time or used for other types of analysis.

System 6. Added measure of rate of change This system is modified from System 5 by the addition of a second channel of information on the recording chart, in the form of an integrated and continuous tracing of the *changes* in the beat-to-beat variation of the heart. This additional device, called variously a cardiotachometer or cardiotachograph, will indicate increases in HR as a positively inflected trace, decreases in the extrapolated HR as a negatively inflected trace, and a constant rate (no acceleration present) as a straight line at a position on the chart proportional to the value of the extrapolated HR (Figure 4.6).

This additional information is somewhat redundant, i.e., the values could be obtained by inspection of the beat-to-beat spacing of the ECG tracing, but it provides a visual record of the

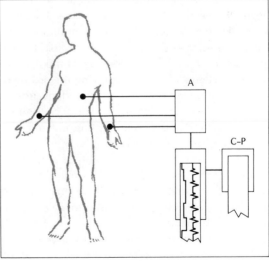

Figure 4.7 Instrument System 7 preserves both the waveform and rate information but adds a counter-printer unit (C–P) capable of presenting either heart rate or heart period information as a sequence of printed numbers on continuous paper tape.

changes in HR that may be grasped quickly by the untrained observer. Further, sampling the signal that the cardiotachometer produces will provide an auxiliary signal in which the voltage is proportional to the momentary heart rate. Such a signal may be used for online data reduction, to initiate signaling or stimulation at certain absolute values of HR, etc. Finally, the availability of both the ECG and cardiotachometer tracings enables the observer to examine suspected areas of the latter for the presence of the artifact, which the cardiotachometer cannot distinguish from a true signal.

System 7. Addition of a printed record This system is an elaboration of System 6 by adding to its output section a device known as a "counter-printer." The counter-printer (see Figure 4.7), by operations that will not be described at this point, produces one or the other of two types of output: (a) an exact measurement of the time lapse between two events (such as two heartbeats), or (b) an exact cumulative count of the number of events within an epoch. Both of these outputs are numerical, and either may be printed out on a continuous strip of paper in the form of numbers representing actual values.

The output from the system consists of: (a) a continuous tracing of the electrical activity of the heart muscle (ECG), (b) a continuous tracing of the integrated HR, (c) a continuous printout of the HP, heartbeats per epoch or, by derivation, the HR in numerical form. It therefore retains the features of the preceding one, i.e., preserving the analog of the original signal, providing its first derivation in graphic form and offering, in addition, a continuous succession of numbers representing either HP or number of beats per epoch.

If one accepts the numerical output as the final product of this system, it is in a form amenable to statistical computations, but this information must be manually extracted and subsequent calculations performed by hand.

The fidelity of the system is not improved over the former one but the resolution of the output, in terms of the fineness with which individual heart periods can be measured, is vastly increased. Resolutions of the HP in the range of 100 μsec to 1 msec are easily obtained.

System 8. Addition of a permanent tape record The final step in the evolution of an instrument designed to provide information on the beat-to-beat variation of the heart of subjects in a psychophysiological experiment is by no means the ultimate in complexity and elaboration. It does represent one means for measuring the phenomena of interest and of automatically deriving the data not only as raw scores but as final figures representing means within different conditions, variance, and statistical significance of the differences found.

This system employs the same configuration as System 7, except that an FM analog tape recorder has been substituted for the counter-printer unit (Figure 4.8). This means that the original ECG information is simultaneously registered on the ECG tracing and on magnetic tape, while the first derivative, acceleration, is recorded concurrently in graphic form. Neither the ECG nor the acceleration traces are final data sources; they are included to provide the experimenter with the means for maintaining a continuous visual check on the fidelity of the magnetic tape recording. The primary data on the magnetic tape recording must be passed through an analog-to-digital (A to D) converter

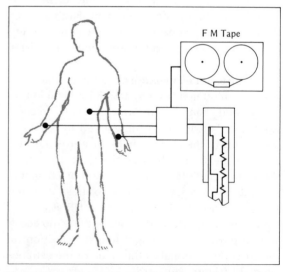

Figure 4.8 Instrument System 8 retains the features of the preceding system but adds an FM tape recorder to provide continuous storage of all of the features of the heartbeat. Tape storage permits unlimited analysis and reanalysis of the data after the termination of the experiment.

before computer analysis. The experimenter has not only the two graphic traces available for summary analysis but, in addition, the analog tape may be replayed into the appropriate recording equipment to produce a faithful copy of the original signal.

Analysis and Critique of a Theoretical System for Measuring Heart Rate

Each of the preceding eight instrument systems satisfied the instrumentation requirements of the research as originally postulated. Systems 1 through 5 provided increasing degrees of resolution in the output signal, but at the cost of increasing complexity of equipment and operating technique. The last three systems retained the input and signal conditioning sections of the former ones, but provided increasing facilities for the accurate, rapid automatic reduction of data. The introduction of the cardiotachometer tracing in System 6 provided the experimenter with a rapid, visual means for checking changes in heart rate *at the moment they were occurring.* The latter two systems reduced the involvement of the experimenter and technician in deriving numerical values representing the moment-to-moment status of the heart rate.

There is, however, almost an exponential progression of the costs of the instrumentation from Systems 1 through 8, a factor too seldom considered important in the design of instrument systems. If System 8 had been adopted, the increased costs could not have been justified if: (a) data analysis could have been performed at leisure, or (b) short time periods had been analyzed. On the other hand, it would have been the system of choice for recording the heart rate of astronauts engaged in a costly and unique experiment.

Some important conclusions can be drawn from the different solutions presented above for a single instrumentation problem. First, there is rarely a single, best solution to the problem of providing reliable, accurate information on psychophysiological processes. There are, instead, a number of solutions differing in complexity, cost, fineness of resolution, operator involvement, accessibility of data in a form suitable for statistical analysis, etc. The choice of an appropriate solution is contingent upon decisions by the experimenter at each of these points.

Second, it is evident that there are three logically distinct portions of an instrument. The first is the device that is attached to the subject and provides an input for the information derived from him to the second portion of the instrument. These devices are called *transducers;* literally, they "lead across" from the biological to the physical system. The second portion is the main body of the instrument in which such functions as amplification, timing, filtering, and the like, are performed. This is usually called the signal-conditioning or signal-processing section. It operates on the signal to sharpen, enlarge, restrict, or otherwise measure some of its aspects. It is usually entirely electrical in nature, requiring an electrical input and providing an electrical output. The direct nature of its operations and of its output are therefore imperceptible to the observer. The third and final section of the instrument, the output display, transforms these electrical signals into inked traces on paper, meter deflections, or printed numerical data that are accessible to human observation.

The three functions are sometimes termed "input," "throughput," and "output," for obvious reasons. Usually, it is the first and last functions that require the most ingenuity on the part of the systems designer; in a sense, they are the most important parts of the system. For example, the limitations on the fineness of resolution or the fidelity of reproduction of a system are initially determined by the characteristics of the input transducer. This element imposes a restraint upon the amount and kind of information that is subsequently processed and displayed. Deficiencies here cannot be adequately corrected in subsequent operations. If the input to the signal-conditioning section contains noise or distortion, little can be done to improve the signal quality, unless the sources of error are consistent and uniform. In a similar fashion, constraints are placed upon the amount and kind of emerging data by the output display. The characteristics of both input and output sections importantly restrict the amount of information in the data obtained, and particular care should be taken in their design or selection.

A third general conclusion can be deduced from this study: the most important consideration in selecting among the options of instrumentation is that of matching the complexity of the system to the *precision* (including the fineness of resolution, accuracy, and reliability) of the data required from the experiment. The relationship between the precision of an instrument and its cost or complexity is a near-geometric one. Unless justifiable on other grounds, one should not select an instrument that will provide an output in a more precise form than that required by the aims of the experiment. On the other hand, where high precision of output is actually needed, no amount of elaboration in signal processing or display instrumentation can compensate for imprecision or insensitivity of the input section. Appropriate instrumentation is neither more nor less complex than that required by the experiment. Neglect of this point may lead to the twin errors of over- and underinstrumentation.

Finally, the analysis of the instruments discussed above reveals that certain of them, because of their design, are inherently flexible, i.e., they may be adapted to a variety of purposes. The commercial polygraph is a good example. With suitable input transducers the function of this instrument may be changed to diverse recording purposes. By contrast, other instruments display a narrow range of sensitivities and functions. While they may be modified or supplemented, such alterations are usually impractical. For example, a hi-fi amplifier provides considerable amplification of recorded signals and is remarkably unprejudiced with respect to its reproduction of music and sound; however, it is poorly suited to the amplification of biological signals.

SOURCES OF BIOLOGICAL SIGNALS

The variety of measures used by psychophysiologists are usually classified in terms of the physiologic system that they monitor, e.g., the autonomic nervous system, the cardiovascular system, and the skeletal-muscular system. This is somewhat confusing from the instrumentation point of view, since it requires the reader to move unsystematically from one type of instrument or device to another, from direct-coupled amplifiers to integrators, etc. The following discussion will therefore be organized about the various *sources* of the input signals. In this classification, all physiologic sources may be included under three categories: (a) direct bioelectrical signals, (b) transduced bioelectric phenomena, and (c) physical biological phenomena. Information thus classified may be referred to more readily and may give the reader a better idea of the versatility of some of the techniques outlined.

For standards adopted by the Society for Psychophysiologic Research with respect to abbreviations of measures and measuring techniques, see the report of Brown (Brown, 1967, pp 260–264).

Direct Bioelectrical Signals

Direct bioelectrical signals are those originating in the tissues as the result of metabolic activity, which need only simple operations such as amplification before they can be observed and recorded. The category includes all of the direct biological sources of electrical energy. Measurements are usually made of potential differences between two points; the source of the energy is that of high metabolic activity, as is found in active muscle or nerve tissue. Since the phenomena are already electrical in form, the transducer in most cases will be a relatively simple electrode, i.e., a conductive pickup element fixed on or near the reacting tissue.

Electrode requirements The electrode is a deceptively simple device and merits considerable attention in the design of sensitive and accurate instrument systems. The main requirements for an electrode are that: (a) it must present a known and constant area of contact with the tissue; (b) it must not generate spurious signals, as from intermittent contact or from electrolytic sources arising in the electrode-tissue interface; (c) it must be quickly, securely, and comfortably attached; (d) its resistance, resulting in potential drops at the point of application, should be as low as possible and constant throughout the time of its use; (e) its adhesion must not be significantly affected by sweating, movement, or distension of the tissues; (f) its application should not disturb the preexisting physiological condition of the tissues under observation; and (g) it must be simple to construct, inexpensive, either reusable or disposable, and resistant to mechanical or chemical deterioriation. Since most existing electrodes fail to meet one or more of the above qualifications, there is the need for new and ingenious designs.

Electrode materials and configurations The most common electrode is a flat or curved disk or rectangle resembling the familiar ECG electrode. The area of the electrode is variable and is usually suited to its location. The EEG electrode, which must be placed between the parted hair on the scalp, is small; while the ECG electrode, placed on the arm or the wrist, is large in area. In general, the area of contact should be as large as possible in order to reduce contact resistance. Electrodes that are concave or flexible (such as wire mesh or metallized cloth) make more intimate contact than rigid, flat plates.

The newer materials for electrodes include metallized cloth, usually silvered nylon; extremely fine mesh materials of stainless steel, platinum, or tantalum; spray-on electrodes of silver powder in an adhesive vehicle similar to collodion; conductive vinyl plastic; disposable, adhesive-backed, silver-cloth electrodes; carbon disks; or a variety of liquid electrodes in which the metallic element is held above the skin and the intervening space filled with a liquid or gelled electrolyte. Each type of material and configuration is suited to a particular application.

The selection of electrode material for the measurement of direct bioelectric potentials is critical to the accuracy of measurement. Alloys of various types are completely unsuitable, for they generate large and variable potential differences. For this reason, solder connections to the electrode must be completely insulated, usually with a plastic coating. The precious metals are good with respect to resistance to chemical deteriorioration but they are expensive. Perhaps the best material is silver, preferably in the form of the 99.99% pure material sold as "fine" silver. These may either be chlorided before use or allowed to chloride in use.

Whatever materials or electrode shape is used, accurate recording of dc potentials requires that the electrodes be checked for bias potential before and after use. This is easily accomplished with either a high gain oscilloscope or the polygraph recorder set to its highest dc gain position with the electrodes connected to a differential input. A blob of saline paste, such as the Beckman or Grass electrode jelly, is placed on a clean glass surface and the electrode faces are brought into contact with the paste but are not allowed to touch each other.

The potential difference between the two should not exceed 10 μV. Noisy or high potential electrodes should be discarded or rechlorided. There are a number of good, commercially available, nonpolarizable electrodes. The ultimate test of the electrical quality of an electrode is that of low bias potential and electrical resistance not its construction or the materials used. Excessive chloriding or the presence of dried paste may produce low bias potentials but present such high resistance that the passage of the signal will be severely attenuated. Resistance between electrode pairs should *not* be checked with an ohmmeter, since the direct current applied will temporarily polarize them. Instead, an arrangement should be made whereby a low alternating current potential is applied to the pair and the drop in ac voltage calculated. The alternating current should be applied by slowly increasing and decreasing the source to prevent turn-off at either a positive or negative voltage value and consequent polarization. Geddes' discussion of electrodes (in Brown, 1967, pp. 411–433) remains the most comprehensive treatment in contemporary literature.

Transduced Bioelectric Phenomena

Transduced bioelectric phenomena are electrical properties of tissue that must be measured indirectly, frequently by comparison with known physical standards. They include six different measures of the variations of tissue resistance and impedance to applied currents: the familiar skin resistance phenomena (SR); the derived measure of skin conductance (SC); skin impedance (SZ), similar to SR but determined by means of applied alternating currents; the impedance plethysmogram and the rheoencephalogram, which are basically variations of the same technique for measuring the instantaneous value of blood in the tissue between two electrodes; and the impedance pneumogram, a complex continuous measure of the respiratory status of the subject.

Electrode requirements The electrode required for SR and SC measures must meet the same requirements as that used for skin potential (SP) measurement; i.e., it must not generate a bias potential and it must remain in intimate contact with the skin. In addition, all electrodes used for resistance or impedance measurements must present a known area of contact with the skin. The specification of basal resistance, impedance, or change in either is useless without indicating basal values or units of change in terms of ohms per unit area. The body is a volume conductor, and the impedance presented to the passage of an exogenous current is, among other factors, a function of the area of application. In the absence of standards for such measurements, the SR and SZ measures should be specified in ohms (or multiples) per square centimeter.

In SZ measures it is also necessary to specify the frequency of the applied alternating current in KHz, since this factor also determines in part the value of the measured impedance. The electrode materials for other impedance measures, plethysmography, pneumography, and rheoencephalography, are much less critical. Aluminum, stainless steel, plated rings, and adhesive-backed aluminum foil may be used as electrodes, since bias potential is not present as an artifact and polarization is prevented by the fact that the applied alternating current constantly reverses.

All of these electrodes must be constructed and attached so as to maintain a constant, low resistance contact with the skin. This is particularly important in the impedance measurements, where the maximum signal may be in the order of fractions of ohms and motion artifact may produce changes of several hundred ohms.

Physical Biological Phenomena

Physical biological phenomena are not necessarily unique to biological systems but represent physical phenomena such as pressure, acceleration, and color, which can be measured by methods of the physical sciences modified somewhat for biological purposes. These measures represent attempts to quantify and analyze various physical phenomena such as movement, pressure, velocity, temperature, etc. The transducers for these purposes are various and will be described in detail below. Many are commercially available or can be readily adapted from commercial devices.

INSTRUMENTAL DETECTION OF PSYCHOPHYSIOLOGICAL RESPONSES

Electrocardiogram (ECG or EKG)

The following discussion concerns the use of the ECG for *research,* not clinical or diagnostic purposes. This distinction is necessary, since recordings taken for clinical purposes must be made with standard electrode placements, amplifications, and amplifier time constants so that they can be interpreted for clinical significance. For research purposes, the main use for the ECG is as an index of heart action from which HR or HP may be derived. Electrode placement and amplifications are usually not standard.

Electrical impulses originating in the heart at each beat are the source of the ECG. When measured at standard locations on the body, the recorded signal exhibits a definite complex wave shape, shown in Figure 4.9. The tissues interposed between the heart and the surface recording electrodes are a volume conductor through which the impulses are transmitted. Modifications in the relative amplitude of the ECG constituents and of their temporal relationship are seen in each electrode location. In clinical electrocardiography, there are 12 standard locations: Lead 1, active electrodes located on the right and left arms of the subject;

TABLE 4.1   INSTRUMENTED SYSTEMS MEASURING DIRECT BIOELECTRIC SIGNALS

Instrumental system	Tissue origin of signal	Amplitude range	Frequency range
Electrocardiogram (ECG or EKG)	Heart muscle	10 μV–5 mV	1–100 Hz
Electroencephalogram (EEG)	Brain	1–100 μV	dc to 100 Hz
Electromyogram (EMG)	Skeletal muscle	10 μV–2 mV	10 Hz–2 KHz
Electrooculogram (EOG)	Dipole effect of eye	1–300 μV	dc to 5 Hz
Electrogastrogram (EGG)	Stomach and g.i. organs	150–500 μV	1 to 5 waves/minute
Skin potential (SP)	Skin	1.0–30 mV	dc to 5 Hz

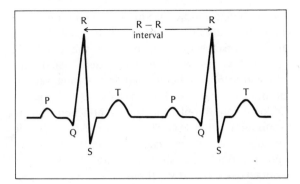

Figure 4.9 Somewhat idealized ECG waveforms.

Lead II, electrodes attached to the right arm and to the left leg; Lead III, electrodes attached to the left arm and the left leg. The amplifier is connected to these electrodes, so that when the latter limb of the pairs mentioned becomes positive, an upward deflection of the tracing will result. There are 9 additional pairs, V, through V_6, the precordial leads and the augmented leads AVR, AVL, and AVF.

Of the five components of the ECG, the P, Q, R, S, and T waves, the R wave is the most important for psychophysiological recordings (see Figure 4.9). The QRS complex represents the depolarization of the ventricular musculature and the R wave is the largest wave of this complex. Consequently, the R wave represents the most unambiguous signal that can be used for subsequent purposes of timing or counting.

While clinical electrocardiography is performed on a recumbent and cooperative patient, muscle and motion artifacts are a severe problem in seated, active human subjects or uncooperative animal subjects encountered in psychophysiological research. All standard leads include major muscle groups in the span between the two electrodes; the electrical output of these intervening muscles can obliterate the ECG recording. The use of a nonstandard location, chosen to exclude active muscle tissue so far as is possible, is recommended. Some experimentation will be necessary, but electrodes can be located on anterior and posterior locations on or near the midline of the body at about the level of the third to fifth intercostal space.

A variety of clinical-type electrodes are available for human work. These include solid steel or silver plates and disks held in place by punched rubber

strapping, suction-type electrodes which require little other support, or commercial, paste-on electrodes made from silvered-cloth patches backed with an adhesive plastic strip. The latter, although expensive, produce usable recordings during exercise. A slight variation in application technique permits the electrodes to be used underwater, with sweating subjects, etc. The cleaned skin is masked with a small patch of adhesive tape the size and shape of the conductive cloth of the commercial electrode, and the skin around the patch is lightly sprayed with a pressurized surgical adhesive material such as Vi-Drape. After drying for 60 sec, the mask is removed, the exposed area is lightly abraded with electrode paste, and the electrode is positioned carefully over the area. The resultant bond between the adhesive material of the electrode and that sprayed on the skin provides an excellent fixation. In all ECG applications, a conductive electrode paste or jelly, usually made from salt and thickeners, should be briskly rubbed into the skin site before applying the electrode.

The ECG may be measured from any amplifier-recorder capable of providing a pen deflection of 10–15 mm for each mV of signal and a frequency response from 0.1 to 125 Hz. Capacitor coupling is always used to eliminate the shifts in baseline caused by skin potentials, changes in electrode resistance, and other sources of artifact. Push-pull amplifiers with a high common mode rejection capability are used if electrical artifacts prove troublesome.

Some mention should be made of the derivation of continuous HR from ECG-type recordings. While the amplified R wave may be used to trigger subsequent counting or timing circuitry, a more foolproof technique is that of using the R wave of the ECG complex to activate a Schmitt trigger, which in turn operates a univibrator to provide a uniform pulse of 5–10 msec width. The pulse is a preferred signal input to subsequent integrators or cardiotachometers.

The data derived from the ECG recording may be manipulated in one of two ways to derive a measure related to the rate of the heart action. The first, HR, is computed on the basis of the number of beats per unit time, usually 1 min. Beats may be counted for any convenient period, i.e., 6 sec,

10 sec, etc.; but it should be kept in mind that this process imposes a severe amount of averaging on the HR response. In addition, if consecutive periods are counted, the assignment of fractions of inter-beat intervals to one or another period is a problem.

The HP, a more accurate and sensitive way of handling the same data, is determined by measuring the time lapse from one beat to another, usually from an *R* wave index point. This time, usually in seconds and milliseconds, is easily manipulated statistically and may be measured automatically by the use of an Event Per Unit Time (EPUT) meter. This commercially available device may be con-nected to a sequential printer to provide numeric printout of each heart period.

If a graphic record of the interbeat variability, which can be plotted on a polygraph record simul-taneously with other variables, is desired, there are several commercial cardiotachometers available that provide this information continuously, project-ing each heart period to a beat per minute basis. Beside the graphic record this provides, the voltage to the recording pen may be recorded on a mag-netic tape to provide a signal analog suitable for analog-to-digital conversion and computer analysis. (See Chapter 11 for a discussion of findings of electrocardiographic research.)

Electroencephalography (EEG)

Electroencephalography refers to the measure-ment of minute electrical potentials emitted from the brain and detected by means of electrodes attached to specific locations of the scalp. The electrical activity is amplified, sometimes filtered, and usually recorded graphically on strip chart paper for visual analysis and interpretation.

The primary information in the EEG is its fre-quency, which varies from 0.5 to 60 Hz. Attempts have been made to provide rough categories for the classification by frequency. The characteristic pattern in normal adults in the waking state is dominated by so-called alpha frequencies, roughly sinusoidal in shape and ranging from 8 to 12.5 Hz. Current usage, particularly in sleep research, iden-tifies 5 bands: *delta,* 0.5–4 Hz; *theta,* 4–8 Hz; *alpha,* 8–13 Hz; *beta 1,* 13–20 Hz; and *beta 2,* 20–40 Hz.

The maximum peak-to-peak amplitude in adults is approximately 100 μV. These are exceedingly small voltages and consequently require high am-plification, a voltage gain of 10^6. In general, there is an inverse relationship between the amplitude of the EEG and its frequency (Riehl, 1963); this characteristic has been used in devising various automatic means for EEG analysis.

Relatively simple electrodes attached to the scalp are used in EEG. Electrodes must be capable of attachment at any scalp location for periods of time up to 8 hr and should provide low resistance contact with the skin. There is a wide variety of electrode configuration available: flattened pellets of solder, metallic disks, precious metal cups of various shapes, and needles for subcutaneous in-sertion. To apply the cup, pellet, and disk elec-trodes, the hair must be parted or shaved at the electrode location, the scalp cleaned with acetone, the skin at the site abraded with a swab dipped in electrode paste, and the electrode attached and held in place by means of collodion alone or as a number of coats over a gauze patch helping to hold the electrode. Various modifications of this application procedure requiring special electrodes and glue (Skov & Simmons, 1965), are useful for long-term, high-reliability applications.

The placement of the EEG electrodes has been standardized for clinical usage and is accepted internationally (Jasper, 1958, pp 371–375). Irregular locations may be used for research purposes, par-ticularly when side-to-side differences in activity are not important.

Electroencephalograph recordings may be made on most modern, high-gain, polygraph recorders, and EEG input couplers that provide the means for switching between pairs are available. Push-pull (double-ended) amplifiers are nearly mandatory because they provide an inherently high, in-phase noise rejection. Electrical artifacts may be greatly reduced by electrical shielding of the recording room or, more inexpensively, by constructing a shielded enclosure to surround the subject only. Much electrical noise can be avoided by selecting a location for EEG recording not adjacent to motors, switches, solenoids, etc. and by *avoiding all fluo-rescent lighting.*

Electrode resistances between pairs should fall within the 5–30 KΩ range. The input impedance of the EEG amplifier should be as high as possible,

1–10 MΩ or better. The overall frequency response of the instrument is usually limited by that of the pen-writer, but it should provide a relatively flat response from dc to 70 Hz. If filtering controls are provided, the lower frequency response should be limited to 1–2 Hz.

When recordings are made from pairs of scalp electrodes, the electrical activity immediately beneath the electrode is most strongly represented, while the signal strength in the surrounding area declines as the square of its distance from the electrode because of the attenuation of the intervening tissues. Thus the activity seen in one location is due mostly to the potentials emanating from the cortex directly beneath it. A site on the ear lobe is relatively inactive because of its relative distance from cortical tissue. If a recording is made from one scalp site (active) to the ear lobe (inactive, reference), the mode of recording is said to be *monopolar*. Cortical activity is analogously viewed from a fixed and stable reference point. If two active electrodes are used, the recording is termed bipolar. The signal will reflect the algebraic sum and difference of the electrical activity beneath both sites at every instant.

Assume that a fairly large brain area is producing sinusoidal waveforms, and that a pair of electrodes is placed above it and a reference electrode on the ear lobe. A monopolar recording of either active electrode will reveal the sinusoidal activity, but a bipolar recording made from the two active electrodes will fail to show it. Only if either the phase or amplitude of the activity between two monopolar electrodes differs will the recording show this difference.

The use of monopolar or bipolar techniques depends upon the purposes of the study. Most clinical applications use bipolar arrangements because this provides the opportunity for detecting side-to-side differences or for localizing a *focus* of activity to a discrete area. An electroencephalographer should be consulted for recommended recording sites to suit the requirements of a particular research study.

The EEG, because of its low amplitude, is subject to numerous artifacts. The most common is that of 60 or 120 Hz electrical interference. This may be checked by replacing the subject with a "dummy," consisting of a 15-KΩ resistor and recording at a paper speed sufficiently fast to permit the frequency of the artifact to be counted. Unwanted signals from any other location in the body—EMG, ECG, SP, or SR—constitute artifacts when they appear in the EEG recording. The former two are easily recognized by their waveform, and the latter usually appears as a slow shift in baseline.

As noted above, visual analysis of the EEG is most commonly employed. Various average response computers have been used to reveal repetitive waveforms that were otherwise buried beneath noise. Phase relationships between anterior-posterior locations have provided some provocative data (E. H. Darrow, 1967, pp. 114–128). (See Chapter 7 for a discussion of the findings of EEG research.)

Skin Potential Measures (SP)

The measurement of the "endosomatic" skin phenomenon (also termed the "Tarchanoff effect"), or SP, has had as lengthy a history as that of skin resistance measurement. Various high and positive correlations have been reported between these two measures, and it was considered until relatively recently that SP and SR were manifestations of the same physiological phenomenon (Jeffress, 1928; Wilcott, 1958). The differentiation of these two phenomena and the occasions for their appropriate use are still under discussion (Forbes, 1964; Gaviria, Coyne & Thetford, 1969; Lykken, Miller, & Strahan, 1968; Venables & Martin, 1967; and Wilcott, 1969).

Both are essentially electrical phenomena that exhibit change when the subject is exposed to arousing or stressful stimuli. The major difference between the two measures is that the SP represents a small but measurable electrical *potential* difference between an active and a reference skin site. Consequently, in measures of SP, an external electrical potential is not impressed across the skin; the derived measure, usually expressed in mV, is independent of the area of tissue in contact with the electrode. Because of the very small amplitude of the signal in SP measurements, it is necessary to employ special electrodes, which are called nonpolarizable, i.e., they do not generate current in themselves. These electrodes are held in contact with the skin surface or immediately above it by plastic or rubber appliances. The intervening space is filled with a conductive paste or liquid, compounded from NaCl and thickening agents such as starch. This paste permits a low resistance contact to be made with the skin surface and practically eliminates artifact caused by intermittent contact between the electrode and the skin.

Dry metallic electrodes may not be used in SP measurement because the potentials generated in the interface between the electrode and the electrolyte would be greater than those constituting the SP. Instead, so-called nonpolarizable, silver-silver chloride electrodes (O'Connell & Tursky, 1960) are used. Care must be taken in handling such electrodes to ensure against accidental damage of the thin silver chloride coating, or against the artifact potential generated by the application of currents to the electrodes that would result in their polarization.

The magnitude of the potentials emitted from selected skin sites ranges from 1 or 2 to 40 or 50 mV. There is usually a fixed potential representing a basal level upon which are superimposed mono-, di-, or triphasic waves, which constitute the skin potential response (SPR). The location of both the active area (finger, palm, sole of foot) and the inactive area used as electrode sites should be specified. While the palm of the hand and the sole of the foot appear to be the most popular locations for the measurement of the SP, Edelberg (1967, pp. 1–53; Chapter 9 of this book) lists a number of other appropriate skin sites. The recording of the SP requires, in addition to nonpolarizable electrodes, a high gain, drift-free amplifier that is capable of registering very slow changes in potential, as well as the direct current level of the SP.

Various means have been devised to record the basal level of SP and the transient SPRs concurrently. This is difficult, because of the relatively high potential of the skin and the low levels of the responses superimposed upon it. Perhaps the simplest means is the use of two channels of polygraph recording, one at a relatively low gain level (e.g., 10 mV = 1 cm) for recording the basal level and a second at a higher gain (e.g., 1 mV = 1 cm) for detecting the SPR. If the first channel is adjusted to zero before attaching the electrodes, the absolute values of the SP may be read at any point in the experiment. Zero may be offset on the second channel, so that the basal level is located at the channel center and the trace may be recentered when required, since only the changes in SP are required. An alternate method is that of recording with a time constant in the order of 1–5 sec on a single channel. The disadvantages are that the basal SP is not recorded and the shape of the SPR waves may be somewhat distorted.

The question of the significance of positive and negative excursions of the SPR waveform is involved in scoring these responses. Recent evidence (Edelberg, 1966; Venables & Martin, 1967) suggests that there is a complex interaction between SC and SP, which accounts for the appearance of complex SPR waveforms. However, the amplitude of either positive or negative components of the SPR should be measured from the prestimulus baseline. They may then be collected individually or combined by addition, ignoring sign. (See Chapter 7 for a further discussion of electrical activity of the skin.)

Electromyography (EMG)

The EMG reflects the electrical activity of stimulated muscle fiber. This electrical activity consists of a wave of negativity resulting from a progressive change in polarization of the surface membrane of the muscle fiber that travels at approximately 4 m/sec from the neuromuscular junction to the distal ends of the fiber (Lambert, 1962, pp. 251–256). The electrical activity is not the result of the contraction of the muscle fiber proper.

Two contrasting approaches to electromyography are found. One uses surface electrodes similar to EEG electrodes located on the skin over the site of the muscle; the other uses monopolar needle electrodes inserted into the muscle mass to detect the action of one or a few fibers. The former technique will be discussed, since it seems most appropriate to psychophysiological measurement with human subjects.

The amplitude of the EMG recorded from surface electrodes is from 0.1 to 2.0 mV and the frequency range is from 2 Hz to 10,000 Hz. Waveforms are characteristically "spiky" and are usually found in trains. When recorded from surface electrodes, the average frequency is approximately 50–70 Hz because of the distortions imposed by the intervening tissue and the limitations of the pen-writer. The amplitude of the signal is roughly proportional to the tension produced by the muscle.

The EMG signals are frequently monitored by means of a parallel arrangement of a high speed recorder and an auditory monitor. The sounds of characteristic waveforms are frequently easier to identify than their graphically recorded pattern. A more accurate means for recording EMG data using typical ink-writing polygraphs, where the peak pen response is limited to 100–150 Hz, is that of integrating the waveforms and plotting this information. The resultant trace may be easily recorded on the average polygraph; it is in the form of an ascending ramp, indicating by its slope the summation of the EMG activity at each point in time. Some means must be provided for resetting the integrated trace, either at the point of maximum excursion of the pen or at fixed intervals in time. In the first case, a measure may be derived from the linear *distance* between resettings; in the latter, the *amplitude* of the pen displacement immediately before resetting is a summary of EMG activity in that epoch.

A high-gain oscilloscope may be used to display the envelope of EMG waveforms with full fidelity. However, the maximum dimensions of the envelope, not the waveforms, are the most significant aspect of EMG data for psychophysiological research. Permanent recording of this information can be made photographically.

Electromyography measures are particularly useful in estimating changes in tension levels of muscle groups, e.g., of the neck as an indication of the depth of sleep, of the forearm in motor reaction time studies, or in the assessment of the effect of CNS activating drugs on the startle response. An excellent although out-of-print reference is that of Davis (1952). (See Chapter 8 for the application of these techniques in psychophysiology.)

Electrogastrography (EGG)

Electrogastrography, along with salivary measures (Brown, 1970), are surprisingly unpopular in the United States but receive attention elsewhere. The EGG is a sensitive technique for recording intragastric motility which is quite acceptable to the subject. In essence, it consists of dc recording from electrodes located on the cleaned, lightly abraded surface of the abdomen, within any of the four quadrants, although most representative recordings are made from an active site 1 inch above and 2 inches to the left of the navel (Russell & Stern, 1967). The reference electrode is located on the lateral surface of the lower leg and provisions are made for the "bucking out" of high but constant dc potentials between the two sites.

The EGG thus recorded shows waves with a frequency of from 1 to 5 waves per minute (period of 12–60 seconds) at amplitudes between 150 and 500 volts. These have been classified into 3 types: Type I. simple, low-amplitude monophasic waves, 1 to 2 minutes in the fundus, presumably representing "mixing" type of motor activity; Type II. simple, monophasic waves of greater amplitude, from 2 to 5 waves per minute, presumably representing peristalsis; and Type III. more complex waves, consisting of a baseline shift of 1–5 minutes duration, upon which are superimposed waves of Types I and II (Hightower, 1959).

Alvarez, in 1922, first reported his attempt to monitor the electrical concomitants of gastric activity. Davis, Garafolo, and Gault (1957) and White (1964a, 1964b) explored the electrogastrographic (EGG) technique intensively. From their efforts we know that the electrical method is not only simpler than the older balloon techniques but also provides a potentially valuable gross summation of stomach and intestinal contractions. The technique consists of the measurement of potentials from nonpolarizable electrodes on the skin of the abdomen. The origin of these potentials is in doubt, although they seem to be characteristic of the bioelectricity found in sites of high metabolic activity such as secretory gland potentials and smooth muscle potentials of the stomach. The signals are quite large, 100–150 mV in amplitude, and consist of either slow dc drifts or periodic waves with a frequency range of 3–11 per min or greater.

Several ingenious attempts have been made to produce simultaneous electrical and mechanical recordings. Goodman, Ginsberg, and Robinson (1951) attached a nonpolarizable electrode to a stomach balloon and found a high degree of correspondence. Davis, Garafolo, and Gault (1957) measured the surface potentials and the signals produced by the movement of an ingested steel ball within the field of a magnetometer and found a similarity in the tracings.

It is not possible that the SP response from abdominal skin could account for the signals seen in electrogastrography, since the latter persist even when measured with subcutaneously implanted needle electrodes, and neither the frequency nor periodicity of the EGG is similar to the SP. While certain respiratory waves appear in the record, these are easily distinguished and probably arise from the motion imparted to the stomach and intestines by movement of the diaphragm. The ECG is always present as an artifact and may be removed or attenuated by the use of simple RC, low-pass filters.

Various electrode types and locations have been proposed. Davis used both plate and needle electrodes to measure either from two active locations on the abdomen, or from one active and one reference location on the dorsal surface of the forearm. While some investigators have noted large standing potentials that needed to be neutralized by equal and opposite externally applied potentials, it is probable that these arose from bias effects at the electrode and may be eliminated by the use of silver-silver chloride electrodes, similar to those used for the measurement of SP. The tendency in current work is to use a single active site on the abdomen and a reference site on the arm or leg, the latter prepared by skin drilling or puncture to reduce the contact resistance and eliminate SP from the recording. The active electrode has been successfully located "on the upper right quadrant of the abdomen on a line midway between the navel and the last rib" (White, 1964b). None of the active locations seems to have been centered over the stomach and consequently may reflect a major component of intestinal activity.

Electrooculography (EOG)

The technique of electrooculography is one of a number of means by which eye movement can be detected and to some extent, measured. In EOG, advantage is made of the fact that there is a potential difference of approximately 1 mV between the cornea and the retina of the eye. The cornea is positive with respect to the retina because of higher metabolic activity at the retina.

Brief mention should be made of other techniques that are generally more elaborate in instrumentation and result in greater disturbance to the subject. These include the older mechanical transducers that were attached directly to the corneal surface; various photographic methods that required a light focused in the eye and a tiny, bright spot of material adhering to the cornea; and various techniques of corneal reflection that take advantage of the bulging aspect of the cornea on the eyeball and its displacement during rotation. More recent techniques have used individually fabricated contact lenses for photographic or electrical registration. While each of these techniques is suited for a particular purpose, e.g., the study of nystagmus, of saccadic movements, and of sequences of eye fixation in a perceptual field, their complexity and the discomfort to the subject makes their use infrequent in psychophysiology.

If EEG-type electrodes are attached to the skin on the outer sides of each eye, and if the eyes are at rest in a forward fixation, no potential difference will be seen. If the eyes are moved horizontally, the dipoles represented by the eye will be aligned so that their potentials are summed. Movement of the eye to the left will bring the positive cornea into closer proximity to the left electrode and the negative retinal area of the right eye closer to the right electrode. This results in a positive deflection of the amplified output from a push-pull configuration. Eye movement to the right reverses the situation and produces an output of reversed polarity. In both cases, eye potential measures at the corners close to the nose (nasal aspects) are in series.

Very little of the vertical component of eye motion can be detected with this electrode placement, however, since there is little change in the relative positions of the corneal-retinal dipole in such movement. Equivalent electrodes mounted above and beneath the eyes are required for the detection of vertical movements. A compromise location may be made by attaching electrodes slightly outward from and above the outer canthi of both eyes with references to an electrode immediately above the bridge of the nose. Both horizontal and vertical components of eye motion can be recorded from this single location.

The advantages of the EOG technique are those of simplicity, greater comfort of the subject, and freedom from interference caused by head movements. It is difficult, however, to isolate the horizontal from the vertical components of eye motion. The relation between recorded potential and the extent of eye movement is generally linear only over a small extent of the total range ($\pm\frac{1}{2}°$ to $\pm 40°$); consequently, the EOG measure provides relative data only.

The recorded potentials are generally in the range of 50–200 μV (Young, 1963). Recording with direct coupling or a long time constant provides the clearest picture of the eye movement (Tursky & O'Connell, 1967). At the amplifications required, EEG activity is sometimes found superimposed upon the EOG record, as are the muscle action potentials (MAPs) from the face and the scalp. It is difficult to filter out this type of artifact, although relatively easy to restrict the higher frequency of the EMG artifacts. The galvanic skin phenomena are major sources of artifact in the EOG, according to Shackel (1960, pp. 323–335), who recommends skin drilling at the EOG sites to eliminate the major portion of this artifact.

The major present application of the EOG is that of detecting eye movements in sleep (Minard & Krausman, 1971) because of the simplicity and adequacy of EOG measures in detecting the relatively large eye movements in this state. There is a great need for standardization of this measure, particularly in the location and type of electrodes used in selecting an appropriate time constant of the amplifier. Precautions should be taken to eliminate the types of artifacts produced by skin resistance or potential changes at the site.

Skin Resistance (SR), Conductance (SC), and Impedance (SZ)

If a weak electric current is passed through a pair of electrodes contacting the skin surface at any two locations in the body, adequate instrumentation will reveal that the intervening tissues offer a resistance to the flow of this current. The major portion of this resistance can be localized to the skin layers and not in the subcutaneous tissue, body fluids, etc.

If the electrodes are placed on certain skin sites, such as the palm and the back of the hand, it will be seen that there are sharp and noticeable changes in resistance which accompany: (a) movement, (b) rapid changes in respiration or (c) emotion-producing stimuli. There are also identical

TABLE 4.2 PSYCHOPHYSIOLOGICAL MEASURES OF TRANSDUCED BIOELECTRIC SIGNALS

Instrumental system	Tissue origin of signal	Transducer type	Unit of measure
Skin resistance (SR)	Cutaneous tissue	Metal skin electrodes in Wheatstone bridge circuit	Kilohm (KΩ)
Skin conductance (SC)	Cutaneous tissue	Derived mathematically from SR	Micromho (μmho)
Skin impedance (SZ)	Cutaneous tissue	Metal electrodes, Kelvin double bridge	Ohms
Impedance plethysmogram	Tissue and blood	Metal skin electrodes, 15–25 kHz exciting current	Ohms
Impedance pneumograph	Tissue and blood	Metal skin electrodes, 15–25 kHz exciting current	Linear pen deflection
Rheoencephalogram (REG)	Cortical tissue and blood	Multiple scalp electrodes, continuous tracing, 15–75 kHz exciting current	Linear pen deflection

changes which occur spontaneously, i.e., in the absence of any apparent stimulus. The change in resistance in localized skin sites is the skin resistance response (SRR).

Because an external potential is applied to the skin to reveal these resistance changes, the SR is termed an *exosomatic response*. This is in contrast to the skin potential phenomenon (SP), in which an EMF is generated in the tissues; hence the term *endosomatic response*.

Resistance, in electrical terms, represents the relative amount of *hindrance* or opposition to current flow through a substance and is expressed in units of ohms. The term used to denote the opposite effect, that of the *ease* with which current flow is accomplished, is conductance. Conductance is the inverse or reciprocal of resistance ($C = 1/R$) and is usually derived mathematically and expressed in units of *mhos* (*ohms* spelled backward). Skin conductance (SC) is the reciprocal of SR. While care must be exercised in the transformation of one term to the other, the following discussion will deal with the more common term SR, although it will apply to either phenomena.

It is apparent from Ohm's law, $R = E/I$ (where R is resistance in ohms, E is the potential in volts, and I is the current in amperes), that the continuous measurement of resistance would require that either E or I should be held constant, while variations in the observed value of the other term would reflect changing resistance. This fact has led to the use of two contrasting types of instrument for SR measurement, the "constant voltage" and the "constant current" systems, which are shown schematically in Figure 4.10.

Each system requires that the unknown skin resistance, R_s, be placed in one arm of a Wheatstone bridge. In the constant voltage bridge, R_1 and R_s form a divider for the impressed potential, E. The division is proportional to the ratio, $R_s / (R_s + R_1)$. Since R_1 is fixed, the voltage at A is divided proportionally to changes in R_s, the resistance of the subject. This alone would be adequate for an output, except for the fact that the change in voltage at A produced by SR changes is only a tiny fraction of the much larger voltage at the same point, representing the basal skin resistance. The second half of the bridge, R_2 and R_k, is another potential divider, in which R_2 is fixed and equal to R_1. If R_k is adjusted to the same value as R_s, the potential *difference* between points A and B will be zero. The two advantages of a bridge circuit are now obvious: (a) it may be balanced by adjusting R_k, so that the basal value of SR may be read directly

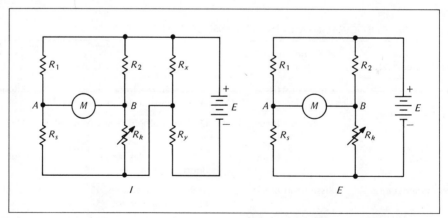

Figure 4.10 Two types of bridge circuit for measuring SR responses. The circuit at the left, marked *I*, is a constant current bridge; while the one on the right, marked *E*, is a constant voltage bridge. Note that the actual bridge arrangement is identical for both and that they differ most with respect to the arrangement for the potential to excite the bridge. Resistors R_1 and R_2 in either case are fixed in value; R_s, the resistance of the skin, is free to vary and is balanced by the adjustable resistance, R_k. Drawn as shown, the bridge arrangement is easily seen as a pair of voltage dividers with the sensing and display unit *M* arranged to read the *difference* between points A and B.

from this calibrated resistance; and (b) the initial balancing of the bridge cancels out the large residual signal and permits a high degree of amplification of the small variations in potential produced by SR activity.

Care must be taken to limit the maximum value of current allowed to flow through the skin segment because of the unusual electrical characteristics of the skin. In physical resistances the relationship between the change in applied current and the change in observed resistance is a linear one. In living tissue, including the skin, this linear relationship exists only for current densities below the value of $10 \mu A/cm^2$. Above this value, increasing the current through the skin produces a significant *fall* in the apparent basal skin resistance and diminishes the amplitude of the SR response. Note that the current has been specified in terms of its density, i.e., current applied to a given area. Spurious values of SR will be obtained if this limit is exceeded.

The nonlinear behavior of skin resistance follows from the fact that biological tissues present a complex type of resistance to applied electrical currents, a resistance that contains both resistive and capacitative components. The closest physical analogy to tissue resistance is that of a network of resistors and leaky capacitors. Electron flow through tissues is not simply resistive; the electrolytic contents of each cell in the current pathway polarize when current is passed through it. A finite time is required for this polarization to occur when the current is applied or removed. This polarization plays an important role in determining the unusual characteristics of the SR.

To return to the discussion of the relative merits of the constant current, constant voltage measurement of the SR, there are advantages and disadvantages in both approaches, which Edelberg (1967, pp. 1–53; also Chapter 9 of this book) discusses thoroughly. In either case, extreme care should be taken to ensure that the current density at the skin site does not exceed the above limits.

Sites for SR measurement Edelberg (1967, pp. 1–53) gives an extensive listing of skin sites for relative SR and SC activity. The most common locations are the palm and dorsal surfaces of the hand and the fingers. Other locations are not only feasible but may provide more sensitive measurement. Edelberg suggests the use of a site on the medial side of the foot directly beneath the ankle, which is not only a reactive site but allows the subject free use of the hands. Problems of attachment are relatively less in this location, and the amplitude of the SR response is equal to, or greater than, that derived from the palmar location.

Skin resistances are always measured from an active to an inactive site. Totally inactive sites are difficult to obtain, but relatively passive sites are found on the ear lobe and on the inner surface of the arm near the elbow. Activity may be greatly reduced in any site by procedures that break through the outer layer of skin and provide contact with subdermal layers. Such procedures involve abrasion of the skin with a gritty salt paste, multiple small punctures made with a fine gauge needle, or the technique of skin drilling (Shackel, 1959).

Electrodes for SR The electrodes used for SR measurement must meet very stringent requirements with respect to size, material, and the electrical factors of bias potential and polarization. Since SR must be expressed in ohms per unit area, the electrode area must be specified. Error frequently results from neglect of the fact that the actual electrode area includes the total area covered by the conductive paste. The simplest means to control the electrode area is to premask the skin site, apply rubber cement, adhesive rings or other insulating material to the peripheral areas, and apply the electrode to the masked area.

Various materials such as silver, zinc, stainless steel, and platinum have been used for SR electrodes. The best electrodes currently in use are made of chlorided silver, and silver/silver chloride electrodes are now available from several commercial sources.

Dry electrodes are useless for SR measurement, since eventual sweating beneath the electrode increases conductance. A thick conductive paste of common salt (NaCl) should form the interface between electrode and skin. This not only holds contact resistance fairly constant but also prevents intermittent contact caused by rocking the electrode. Electrocardiograph paste is commonly used but is probably too highly concentrated and will produce a progressive and spurious fall in both SR and response amplitude with time. Edelberg (1967) recommends a salt paste with a 0.5 molar concentration, approximately that of sweat.

Electrodes for long-term application are usually liquid electrodes, in which the metallic element is held in a cup-shaped depression a short distance above the skin with conductive paste filling the interface. Frequently, the edges of the cup are widely flanged and it is attached to the skin by means of double-faced adhesive O rings. Electrodes may be maintained for a week, although loosening will occur because of sweating or hair growth in the adhering area.

Bias potentials and polarization of the electrodes present serious problems in measuring SP. Bias potential is a small, sometimes variable, EMF resulting from a dissimilar half-cell potential generated at the interface between the electrode and the electrolyte. Polarization results from the passage of current through the electrodes and the generation of a counter EMF, somewhat similar to charging a battery. Both the bias potential and polarization introduce a random current that can, depending upon its polarity, add or subtract a varying amount from true readings. Polarization may be diminished by using relatively large area electrodes that reduce current density at any one point. Bias potential problems are avoided by the use of a nonpolarizable electrode such as chlorided silver.

Recording the skin resistance   The amplifier used for SR recording should have a high input impedance (SR levels are frequently 250 KΩ), a frequency response from 0–15 Hz, very low drift, and as high a gain as is consistent with the amount of electrical noise present in the recording situation. The choice of constant current or constant voltage systems will determine such instrumentation requirements as gain, single-ended or differential amplifiers, input impedance, etc. Edelberg (1967, pp. 1–53) has given an excellent discussion of these problems.

It is difficult to record both the slow shifts in "resting" resistance and the rapid transients that are the SRRs on a single channel. Frequently, two recording channels are used, one set to a relatively low gain to record basal resistance and its changes;

and the other, at higher level, coupled with a 3 sec time constant to record transient SRRs. The latter channel may be reset to zero at any time. Another solution is to make an initial determination of basal level from a calibrated variable resistor in the bridge circuit, and by subsequent resistance-capacitance (RC) coupling with a time constant of 6–12 sec to focus upon SR changes only. A third solution was devised by Simons and Perez (1965). This provides both types of information in one channel by an ingenious method of RC coupling. (See also Chapter 9.) A much more complex and sophisticated circuit with pulse coding of the basal skin resistance level is reported by McGraw (McGraw, Kleinman, Brown, & Korol, 1969).

Measurement of skin impedance (SZ)   The SZ measure is employed less frequently than the other electrical skin phenomena, partly because of its complex nature and its largely unknown relationship to SC and SR. The basis of the measure is in the polarizable elements contained in the cells of the skin. As noted in the discussion of the SR, this attribute of the skin requires that only limited amounts of current may be passed through it without disturbing the ionic status of the cells.

After a direct current has been passed through a skin segment for some time, the cell contents will have ionized to some degree, and the location of the ionized particles in each cell will be determined by the orientation of the positive and negative electrodes. If the current flow is now reversed, the charge carriers in the cell will rearrange in accordance with the new polarity. If an alternating current of low frequency is applied, there will be a periodic rearrangment of the charge carriers in accordance with the varying polarity of the applied current.

The process of polarization requires a fixed, minimum period of time, mainly due to the time required for the reorientation of charge carriers. If the frequency of alternation is increased, a point will be reached at which insufficient time is available for the reversals of ionization to occur. This occurs within the range of 5 kHz to 10 kHz; the residual hindrance presented by the tissues at this point is called the skin impedance.

The inner and outer layers of skin, as well as the tissues underlying them, are made up of cells whose interior is a reactance-free electrolyte of 300 ohm/cm² resistivity surrounded by a membrane that exhibits an average resistivity of 1000 ohms/cm² and a capacity value of 1–2 $\mu F/cm^2$ (Cole & Curtis, 1944, pp. 344–348).

Because of the capacitive property of the membrane, true resistivity of skin and tissue segments may be measured only at low values of direct current. When alternating currents are applied to the skin, the measured resistance (now properly termed "impedance") is lower than when the applied current is dc. The capacitive cell membrane effect is most pronounced when applied alternating currents are within the range of 20–20,000 Hz (Nyboer, 1950, pp. 736–743). Above 20 kHz, the capacitive membrane effect is negligible and the tissues present an impedance which is similar to that of a homogenous electrolytic solution. Advantage is taken of this fact in all the psychophysiological measurements of tissue impedance. At the lower frequencies the changes in the permeability of the cellular membranes that accompany electrodermal activity contribute significantly to the capacitive component of the skin impedance and permit the measurement of a response similar to that of the SR. These skin impedance measures can be made with alternating currents in the frequency range of 60–200 Hz.

One distinct advantage of the SZ measure is that it presents no problems of electrode polarization or bias potential, and a wide variety of electrode materials may be employed. Conductive pastes are necessary to reduce the contact resistance to a low and steady value.

The instrumentation required, in its simplest form, is an ac generator of the required frequency providing not more than 0.5V, the output of which is applied to a fixed resistor of 50–100 ohms in series with the subject's electrodes. An output is taken from across the fixed resistor, rectified, filtered, and recorded. This output will consist of a relatively high steady state voltage, representing the basal SZ upon which are imposed small fluctuations representing SZ responses. A variable "bucking" voltage may be inserted in series with the output to cancel out the basal SZ and permit higher amplification of the transient responses. Bagno and Liebman (1959) discuss a more complex bridge-type circuit

that provides a simultaneous measure of both the SZ and the phase angle. The SZ data should be expressed in ohms per square centimeter just as in SR. To carry the analogy with SC further, the reciprocal of impedance is admittance; conversions of the SZ measure could be made to this form. In general, the SZ technique remains largely unexplored and provides considerable promise for psychophysiology.

Impedance Plethysmography

Respiration, cutaneous skin impedance (SZ), and impedance plethysmography, are variations of the same basic measuring process made with essentially similar types of instruments and procedures. Each employs a high frequency oscillator to impose high frequency alternating currents across a skin or tissue site, in order to produce a continuous measure of impedance. Impedance is the equivalent measure to resistance, except that it is determined by the application of alternating, rather than direct, currents. The units of measurement in each is ohms per unit area, usually the square centimeter.

The measurement of impedance represents the opposition to the flow of electrical currents produced by resistive, capacitive, and inductive elements. When both the impedance and resistance of a *purely resistive* material are determined, their values are equal. If the material is other than purely resistive, impedance and resistance values differ. Living tissues, discussed in the section on SZ, contain capacitive as well as resistive components; thus the impedance of tissue is usually lower than its resistance. The value of the impedance depends in part upon the frequency of the alternating current applied.

The usual circuit for measuring impedance is that of a bridge arrangement fed from an ac source. The output of the bridge is demodulated and filtered to remove the carrier frequencies and is in the form of a steady or slowly changing value upon which transitory changes are superimposed. In impedance plethysmography, the basal values represent the sum of the impedance of the volume of both tissue and blood in the site. Since the volume of tissue is constant, slow changes in impedance are related to vasoconstriction and vasodilation in the tissue. The transitory changes reflect the sudden increases in blood in the tissue, coincident with the arrival of the blood volume pulse. A resultant tracing is shown in Figure 4.11.

Plethysmography is basically a volume measure, no matter what type of instrumentation is used. In older techniques the limb or digit under study was enclosed in a rigid chamber filled with either air or water. The enlargements of the limb produced by changes in the blood contained within it caused the fluid to be displaced from the chamber, and it was these displacements that provided an indirect measure of volume change.

Several objections can be made to this procedure. It has been demonstrated that changes in the blood volume in the skin and muscle are frequently in the opposite directions (Hertzman, 1950), but volume plethysmography summed these effects, obscuring the changes one wanted to observe. The identification of relative contributions from skin and muscle was nearly impossible. In addition, only protrusive parts of the body like arms, legs, and fingers could be measured. Finally, the technique was extremely subject to motion artifact, so that the subject had to hold the limb completely immobile.

Impedance plethysmography permits the measurement of essentially the same phenomena from any accessible skin site, is relatively insensitive to

motion artifact, requires much simpler instrumentation, and permits greater subject comfort. In contemporary impedance plethysmography, an ac current of 100–200 kHz is applied to a pair of electrodes located on the skin. Since polarization problems do not exist, the electrodes may be made from any appropriate metal such as copper, aluminum, or silver. The electrode configuration is usually that of an encircling ring for fingers, arms, etc., or plates of known area for other skin sites. Nyboer (1959) has used a Kelvin double-bridge arrangement, in which the exciting current is applied to one pair of electrodes bracketing an additional pair that is used to pick up the signal. This configuration effectively keeps the higher excitation voltages out of the detector circuit.

The detected signal is compared with the applied signal, amplified, demodulated to remove the carrier frequency, and recorded. Both impedance change and phase angle changes are available. The impedance tracing contains the typical blood volume pulse with its systolic peak, diastolic trough, and dicrotic notch on the descending limb of the waveform. If the recording has been made with direct coupled amplifiers, vasomotor changes are detected simultaneously as changes in the pulse amplitude and in absolute level. The values should be expressed in ohms per unit area; additional men-

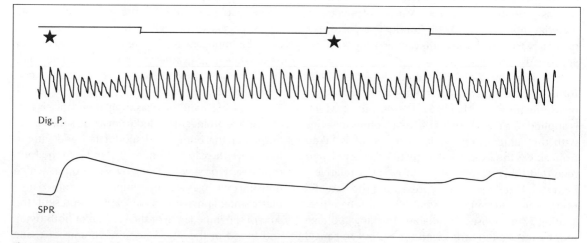

Figure 4.11 Sample of a record showing conditional plethysmographic reactions (Dig. P.) and skin potential responses (SPR). Stimuli are starred. The plethysmograph record is arranged so that filling of the tissue volume is upward, emptying downward. Systolic peaks are upward, diastolic troughs downward. Note that the latency of the two responses is somewhat different.

tion should be made of the frequency of the exciting current.

The volume of the interposed tissue segment may be calculated from the values for the specific resistivity of the blood, the measured impedance, and the distance between the electrodes (Brown, Giddon, & Dean, 1965). The contributions to the total impedance by blood and tissue are essentially those of resistances in parallel, of which only one, that contributed by the blood, is changing. The blood volume in the measured site at any moment is therefore available in the recorded output. While it is possible to derive absolute data from this measure, the usual practice in psychophysiological research is to compute a percentage or ratio measure of the response.

The advantages of impedance plethysmography are the ease and simplicity of the attachment of electrodes, contrasting with the bulky, cumbersome plethysmographic devices; the lack of restraint of the subject's movement; and the advantages of all-electrical instrumentation.

Impedance Pneumography

The measurement of respiration in man or animal is a deceptively simple problem that presents many difficult or insoluble problems in transducer instrumentation. Many simple devices have been employed and have proven unreliable, difficult to maintain, or inaccurate. One of the major difficulties lies in the fact that the ideal measure of respiration should time both the phases of inspiration and expiration and approximate the volume of air exchanged. This is a difficult problem in instrumentation, since the volumes and flow rates are small in magnitude, and many types of transducers obstruct the air flow enough to interfere seriously with the process being measured. Respiratory measures are therefore somewhat neglected in psychophysiological research and, when used, frequently provide information on rate only.

The usual approach to measuring respiration is to monitor changes in girth of the chest in either or both the costal and diaphragm areas, or to measure the velocity of air flow from the mouth or nasal passages. Girth measurements employ tubes filled with mercury, electrode paste, graphite, or some other electrolyte, and depend upon a change of resistance resulting from longitudinal stretching produced by the chest which they encircle. Velocity measurements are usually made with thermistors or thermocouples that are either mildly heated by current passage and cooled by the passage of respired air, or sense the temperature differential between inspired and warmer, exhaled air. Each system has its attendant difficulty, but the common defect in each is that they do not correlate well with the *volume* of air exchanged as measured by a spirometer. The relatively new technique of impedance pneumography holds great promise as a relatively simple technique that correlates exceedingly well with the standard spirogram.

While attempting to record impedance changes from chest to back and relate these to cardiac activity, Atzler (1935) noted respiratory artifacts. Not until 1959, with the report of Goldensohn and Zablow, were impedance devices used for measuring respiration. It is not entirely clear what causes the impedance change with respiration. The actual volume of tissues remains unchanged, despite the changes in air volume. The contributions of shifts in respiratory blood volume, tissue tension, or lymphatic volumes are not known (McCally, Barnard, Robins, & Marko, 1963).

The technique measures the variations in impedance of the tissues to the passage of a high frequency (20–60 kHz) carrier current applied to electrodes on opposite sides of the thorax. Both the low intensity (20 μA) and the high frequency of this current make it imperceptible and harmless to the subject. The mean impedance with adult human subjects varies from 100 to 750 ohms/cm^2. On this base is superimposed an impedance change of 1–2 ohms due to the respiratory cycle. The subject is usually placed in one arm of a bridge arrangement balanced for basal impedance. The subsequent imbalances are amplified and either demodulated and recorded or rectified, filtered, and recorded. Provision must be made for calibrating the trace by switching in precision resistors in the 100–700-ohm range. Silver or stainless steel electrodes may be used; or, for convenience with human subjects, commercial silver cloth or self-adhesive electrodes such as Telectrodes. McCalley et al. (1963) determined the relative output from locations varying from the fourth through the eighth intercostal space in the mid- or anterior axillary line bilaterally.

Artifacts of the system include a shifting baseline due to changes in electrode contact and variable resistance, and oscillatory movements superimposed upon the respiratory tracing due to motion. The advantages of the technique include a high correlation with both respiratory volume and rate, minimum encumbrance of the subject or his breathing, the possibility of using the same pair of electrodes for ECG recording, and the general simplicity of the technique.

Rheoencephalography (REG)

Rheoencephalography is a technique used to determine the instantaneous blood volume in the brain by means of continuous electrical impedance measurements. It was first developed as a research procedure, has been most extensively used, mainly for the localization of cerebrovascular anomalies in clinical work, and has now been perfected to the point at which it is again of considerable utility in research.

The technique is, in some respects, similar to that used for determining skin impedance (SZ) and in impedance plethysmography. In fact, the REG has been termed "cranial impedance plethysmography," indicating that it is a special application of the method. Whether the measure indicates cranial blood flow (as is indicated by the name *rheo-encephalography*) or only the changing volume of blood in the head (including scalp vessels) is a matter the experts debate. At the present time it seems best to assume that the REG is mainly a type of plethysmography, recognizing that the extent to which it reflects cerebral blood *flow* is not yet completely determined.

The technique was developed mainly by Jenkner (1962), who studied the pulse waves obtained from electrodes placed on the forehead and behind the ear on the mastoid process. A high frequency alternating current of low density was applied to the electrodes to determine basic impedance as well as transient variations produced by the pulse waves. In an extensive study of over 4000 clinical cases, he noted that no pulses were obtained from the hemispherectomized side of the head, and the effects of respiration and hyperventilation could be determined in the amplitude of the pulsatile re-

cordings. Hyperventilation produced decreased amplitude of the pulses, while the breathing of carbon dioxide increased the amplitude. Since this agrees with the known physiological bases for changes in the oxygen needs of the brain, it has been concluded that the REG reflects cerebral blood flow.

REG electrodes are applied to the surface of the scalp, an area that is richly supplied with blood. The relative amounts of the contributions of intra- and extracranial circulation to the REG may be questioned. While it is possible to restrict scalp circulation partially with a tightly fitting band about the head, this is quite uncomfortable for other than brief observations. Seipel (1967) has adopted a standard procedure in which individual and bilateral occlusions of the superficial temporal artery are routinely done, while the record is analyzed for alterations in the amplitude of the waveforms.

The frequencies of applied currents used by investigators have ranged from 10 to 100 kHz. The capacitative effect of the complex tissue impedance is minimized by the higher frequencies and those around 10 kHz produce a disagreeable sensation. The best of the available commercial instruments provide frequencies around 30 kHz at 10 mA. This rather high current level is used with electrodes of fairly large area (30 × 30 mm), which minimize the current density. Commercial rheoencephalographs incorporate ac bridge circuitry and provide controls for balancing the steady state resistive and capacitive components of the complex impedance. A low value, calibrating resistor, which can be switched into the circuit, is used to measure the height of the pulses seen in REG tracings.

Electrodes are applied with conductive paste and are held firmly on the scalp with rubber straps or mechanical holding devices. Two symmetrical areas about the midline are usually monitored simultaneously, together with a continuous pneumogram or other respiratory tracing, a single channel of ECG, and even markers. The respiratory tracing is necessary to evaluate the effects of hyperventilation or other respiratory effects, and the ECG provides an index point from which the propagation times of the observed pulses may be measured. Paper speeds from 10 to 30 or 40 mm/sec are used, the latter for the measurement of the pulse propagation time.

The amplifier and recorder for the REG need not

have a high frequency response or gains equivalent to that of the EEG machine. While the latter is commonly used in connection with a separate rheograph as an input, the relatively high levels of signal obtained from this instrument make it possible to use a regular clinical ECG recorder. The gain controls are usually set so that a 0.1-ohm change in the source produces a 10-mm pen deflection; calibration resistors of appropriate values are switched into the subject's circuit to obtain this deflection. While the impedance bridge and oscillator may be constructed, commercial equipment is more reliable and flexible.

Rheoencephalography, although little used by psychophysiologists, offers considérable promise in the study of cerebral vascular change during stress, in sleep, in the area of learning and conditioning, and particularly in studies of the orienting reflex.

Measurement of Temperature

The familiar, mercury-in-glass thermometers used clinically generally are unsuited for research applications because they unduly restrict the activity of the subject and do not provide a continuous, remotely recordable signal. All present temperature-sensing and recording devices for research use either thermistors or thermocouples as a sensing element.

Thermistors The thermistor is a type of semiconductor substance that changes resistance with changes in temperature. Widely used in industry, thermistors may be purchased in many sizes, configurations, and basic resistances from several manufacturers. Three shapes have been used with human subjects: (a) a flat disk sensitive on one of its faces, (b) spherical beads as small as several thousandths of an inch, and (c) elements sealed into the tip of a hypodermic needle for subcutaneous implantation. The bead and disk types may be either unclad, plastic-coated, or enclosed in a glass or metal waterproof housing. The disk type may be attached to the skin surface, in the notch of the fingers, the axillary area, etc. The probe or bead devices may be inserted into body cavities or implanted subcutaneously. At least one instrument company (Yellow Springs Instruments) provides a variety of complete units, including sensing probes, meter or graphic outputs and the option of sequentially sampling from a number of probes located in various sites.

A Wheatstone bridge circuit is usually used with the thermistor, which forms the unknown leg of the bridge and is balanced initially for a known temperature; the imbalances produced by thermally induced resistance change may be read out directly as temperature.

TABLE 4.3 PSYCHOPHYSIOLOGICAL MEASURES OF PHYSICAL BIOLOGICAL SIGNALS

Systematic measure	Tissue source of signal	Transducers
Temperature	Temperature of tissue, fluids	Thermocouple, thermistor, semiconductor gauge, electrical signal (either E or R).
Plethysmogram volume, girth	Whole body, limb, part	Girth measures with strain-sensitive gauge. Volume determined by displacement.
Motion, body or limb	Physical movement	Strain gauges, supersonic sonar systems, jiggle cages.
Gastric motility	Movements in bowel, stomach	Magnetometer detection of changes in location of ingested magnet.
Blood pressure (BP), indirect	Occlusion pressures	Sphygmomanometric measure of occluding pressure. Auditory, displacement, or pressure-pulse pickups.
Blood pressure (BP), direct	Intravascular pressure change	Strain-sensitive pressure transducer, cannulation.
Blood flow (BF)	Velocity of blood	Electromagnetic or supersonic (Doppler) transducers. Flow calculated from change in velocity in fixed bore.

The selection of a thermistor for a particular application must take into account not only the basal resistance value but a factor called the thermal time constant. This term refers to the relative rapidity with which the element can accurately detect a step change in temperature. There is a direct relationship between the thermal time constant and the element mass or bulk. Small elements have low thermal time constants. Coating the element with glass or other waterproofing increases this figure, as does mounting it in a housing or case. While the thermal time constant is relatively unimportant when the thermistor is used to detect slowly changing temperatures from the skin or body cavities, it frequently represents a limiting factor in applications for the measurement of respiration or fluid flow. If the rate of temperature change exceeds the thermal-time constant, the reproduction of temperature cycles will be distorted in the waveform or amplitude.

Thermocouples The thermocouple is a simple device formed by the junction of two wires made from dissimilar metals, usually copper and an alloy called constantan. When this junction is heated, a small potential is generated. While the thermocouple has been favored in the past for temperature detection because of its greater linearity of output versus temperature change, this has been largely overcome by the newer thermistor elements. The disadvantages of the thermocouple are its low output and consequent need for high amplification, and the necessity for using special alloys in the connecting cables to eliminate temperature artifacts.

The measurement of temperature is generally a simple problem in instrumentation, since inexpensive and high quality equipment is available commercially. Irregular uses of temperature-sensing devices have included the fabrication of fluid flow velocity probes with thermistor and heater elements in intimate contact and exposed to the cooling effect of the fluid, while the thermistor resistance is calibrated against flow velocity; the use of the thermistor as a negative resistance device in certain types of electronic instruments; and the indication of respiratory rate by detecting temperature differentials between inspired and expired air.

Plethysmography

Three plethysmography techniques, volume, impedance, and optical plethysmography, detect instantaneous blood volume changes but offer significant differences in the amount and type of tissue that they monitor. The volume and girth techniques summate the changes in the volume of blood for the same stimulus in both the skin and underlying muscle tissue, even though these may be in different directions, i.e., constriction and dilation. Electrical impedance methods permit positioning the electrodes so that changes in the skin and superficial tissues contribute a greater portion of the signal than the deeper tissues. The optical methods reveal changes in the cutaneous and superficial tissues almost exclusively.

Volume plethysmography, of the several means used to measure the variations in blood flow in a tissue segment, is the oldest technique (Sewall & Sanford, 1890), the simplest to instrument, and perhaps the most difficult to apply and interpret. In this technique a limb, usually the forearm, is inserted into a rigid fluid-filled container, closed at its lower end and cuffed at the upper, so as to entirely surround the arm or digit. An output tube is connected to devices that measure or record the displacements of the fluid resulting from changes in the limb volume. This technique has several shortcomings. (a) Motion artifact is very difficult to avoid unless the subject and device are rigidly constrained. This disturbs the naturalness of the situation and restricts the applications of the technique for psychophysiological experiments. (b) The volume changes seen in the limb are the algebraic sum of the contributions of both muscle tissue and skin. Since vasoconstriction may occur in the one, while vasodilation is taking place in the other in response to the same stimulus, the resulting measures are complex and difficult to interpret. (c) The pressure of the enclosing fluid and its temperature must be carefully considered, since it both modifies the rate of heat loss from the limb or, if it is perceptibly different from body temperature, may produce reflex vasomotor changes. However, much of the older literature on plethysmography represents volume measurement.

Venous Occlusion Plethysmography Venous occlusion plethysmography, devised by Brodie and Russell in 1905 (Greenfield, Whitney, & Mowbray, 1962), has continued to enjoy popularity as a research technique to the present day.

The basis of this technique is that of measuring, in absolute volume units, the *changes* in total volume of a limb produced by the brief and sudden arrest of the venous outflow while arterial inflow continues at a normal rate. The swelling in the volume of the limb is suitably transduced and recorded and describes a "ramp" the slope of which may be calibrated in terms of milliliters of blood per cubic centimeter of arm tissue per minute. (Kelly, Brown & Shaffer, 1970).

The venous occlusion is produced by the sudden inflation of a cuff, located immediately proximal to the volume plethysmograph, to a subdiastolic pressure, usually 60 mm Hg.

When this procedure is applied to the forearm, the tracing is predominantly reflective of the blood flow into the muscle due to the relatively low proportion of skin to muscle in the forearm.

The procedure has been used successfully to provide an index of stress-induced anxiety (Kelly, Brown, & Shaffer, 1969).

Rheoplethysmography The rheoplethysmograph, devised by Burch (1954), is a variation in the volume technique and is used to measure the rate of blood flow in a fingertip. A rigid, water-filled container encloses the finger tip and is connected by tubing to a manometric recording device. The proximal end of the container is fitted with a small inflatable cuff that encircles the finger. When this cuff is inflated to a pressure slightly above the venous occlusion pressure, blood outflow is halted while inflow is relatively unaffected. The tracing of increasing finger volume thus obtained is used by Burch to derive measures of the rate of blood inflow and outflow, and the differences between inflow and outflow.

Girth plethysmography In this procedure the transducer is a small elastic tube made of rubber or Silastic filled with a conductive fluid. Various filling materials have been used such as electrode paste, powdered carbon, copper sulfate solution,

or mercury. The ends are stoppered with metallic electrodes from which leads are brought to a Wheatstone bridge circuit. In use the device is wrapped lightly around a limb or a digit. Changes in the volume of the part produce changes in girth that in turn stretch the tube. This produces a change in the dimensions of the volume of electrolyte and a change in resistance. After initial balancing of the bridge, slight changes in girth produce changes in the bridge output.

The girth devices are extremely simple, inexpensive, and can reproduce changes from dc to 150 Hz without significant loss in amplitude. Despite the nonlinear nature of the stress-strain curves of the transducer, the output of these devices approaches linearity.

The shortcomings of this technique are those of its sensitivity to movement artifact, the fragile nature of the gauge and the restriction of its applications to portions of the body that may be encircled by the gauge. A critique of this technique may be found in Whitney (1954, pp. 45-52).

Optical plethysmography Photoplethysmography, while related to the older volume and impedance methods for studying the vasomotor status of a skin segment, represents such a radical departure in technique that comparisons with the former methods must be made cautiously. It has been suggested (Brown, 1967, pp. 54-74) that a new term, "peripheral vascular response" (PVR), should be applied to the data derived from its use. In the following discussion the more common term, photoplethysmogram, will be used to indicate that this is an optical method of measurement.

In this technique a constant-intensity light source is directed into or through the tissues. Changes in the amount of transmitted or backscattered light, due to variations in the interposed blood volume, are registered as changes in the resistance of a photoelectric cell used as a detector.

Tissue is relatively transparent to light in both the red and infrared areas of the spectrum (7000–9000 Å), while blood is relatively opaque to these wavelengths (Zijlstra, 1953, p. 24). Conveniently, incandescent light, which is maximal in the infrared, exhibits usable energies over this range. Photoresistive cells of cadmium sulfide and cadmium selenide are maximally sensitive in this region, small in size, and can respond rapidly to changes in illumination.

The receptor cell and the light source may be held in a number of ways, as shown in Figure 4.12. Transillumination of the tissue is possible only for protuberances such as the digits or ears, while the back-scattering technique can be used on any body location: forehead, chest, leg, etc. Transillumined light intensities must be adjusted to somewhat higher levels to compensate for greater opacity of bone or larger masses of tissue. Back-scattered light can be measured by small transducers attached lightly to the skin; transmitted and received light may be piped in by fiber-optic light guides that carry light to and from the site, permitting monitoring from otherwise inaccessible areas such as the dental gingiva (Brown, Giddon, & Dean, 1965).

Assuming that the relationship between the amount of light falling on the cell and its output in terms of the resistance change is a linear one, the absorption of light in the interposed tissues can be partitioned into two components: (a) an amount determined by the tissues alone, which is relatively constant for a particular area of application, and (b) a variable component contributed by changes in the quantity of blood in the light pathway. The latter variable component may be subdivided into two distinct phenomena: the blood volume (BV),

a relatively slow change reflecting the *mean* quantity of blood present; and the blood volume pulse (BVP), a series of minor pulsatile changes produced by the passage of the pulse wave through the monitored area. The tracing of the BVP resembles that of blood pressure waves obtained by cannulation and exhibits systolic and diastolic peaks, dicrotic notching, etc. It cannot be interpreted in the same way, however, since the data obtained by this technique is only relative. Figure 4.13 shows typical tracings.

Measurement from a site such as the finger tip of a resting subject will show that there are numerous small and large changes in the vasomotor status in the form of vasoconstrictions. Vasoconstriction produces both a lessening of the pulse amplitude and a reduction in mean blood volume, thereby permitting more light to be transmitted to the photocell. Emotional or thermal stimulation results in vasoconstrictions with approximately the same latency (1–1.5 sec), as is seen in SP and SR responses. The time for recovery from such stimulation is quite variable, although it is roughly proportional to the perceived intensity of the stimulation. While it is tempting to relate the digital plethysmographic response to the skin phenomena, Darrow (1929) has shown that there is no association with SR changes. There is however, some degree of relationship with the SP response (Wilcott, 1958; also see Figure 4.11).

Details of the construction of the back-scattered transducer may be found in Brown, Giddon, and Dean (1965). Most commercial transducers available are unsatisfactory because of their size and weight, and the excessive amounts of heat generated by the lamp. The optimum requirements for a transducer are:

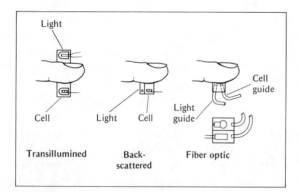

Figure 4.12 Three types of transducers for optical plethysmography. Transillumination is suitable for projecting body members only; back-scattered and fiber optic techniques are suited to any tissue surface. Redrawn from C. C. Brown, D. Giddon, and E. D. Dean, Techniques of plethysmography, *Psychophysiology*, 1965, **1**, 253–266. By permission.

1. It should be small and easily attached to any area.
2. The light intensity should be adjustable and of an appropriate color.
3. It should be firmly but lightly anchored to the skin to prevent motion artifact.
4. The photocell should display an appropriate spectral sensitivity and response time.
5. The light source and cell should be held in a fixed relation to each other.
6. The power to the light source must be constant, since variations in the level of illumination are indistinguishable from vasomotor changes.

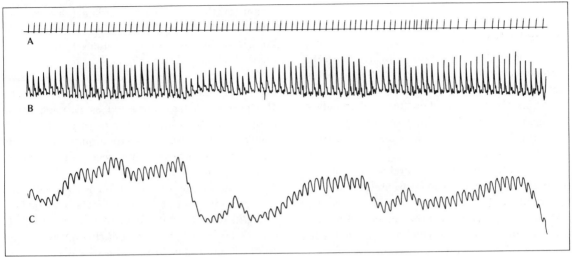

Figure 4.13 Tracing showing the digital plethysmogram recorded with ac coupling *B* and direct-coupled *C*; *A* is an event mark actuated by the *R* wave of the ECG. Vasoconstrictions are shown in both records as a diminution of pulse height, while the direct-coupled record also shows a downward movement as well. Note that the ac-signal waveform is sharper than that obtained by direct coupling. The latter is a more accurate rendition.

Nervous control of the plethysmographic response The type of nervous control of blood supply to the skin varies from location to location. In the hand and foot the contraction of cutaneous vessels is solely controlled by the sympathetic nervous system. However, in the skin of the forehead the vasoconstrictor response is weak or absent; on the trunk, face, arms, and legs, the dominant innervation appears to be vasodilative in action. This action is carried out mainly on the cutaneous veins (Hertzman, 1950).

Skin color is not normally dependent upon the most superficial vessels but upon the subpapillary venous plexi. These are parallel to the skin surface and therefore present a greater area than the capillary loops, which are right angles to the skin surface (Best & Taylor, 1961).

Studies of human hemidecorticates show that they possess equal vasomotor responsiveness on both sides, from which it may be concluded that the vasomotor response has no cortical station in man.

Factors affecting the plethysmographic response It is currently held that the digital vasoconstriction is evidence of an arousal or alerting reaction (Ackner, 1956). Sokolov (1963) and others state that the orienting response can be defined as a vasoconstriction in the finger and a simultaneous vasodilation in the forehead skin. Ackner (1956) has also related peripheral cutaneous vasoconstriction to the presence of anxiety. The extent and amount of change in BV, due to various physical and psychological stimuli, was correlated significantly with psychological test scores indicative of emotional stability and tension (Van der Merwe, 1948, 1950). The magnitude of spontaneous peripheral vasoconstrictions has been correlated with such personality traits as "phlegmatic" or "excitable" by Burch, Cohn, and Neumann (1942).

Perhaps the most interesting aspect of the PVR relates to its occurrence during sleep. Ackner and Pampiglione (1955) have shown both spontaneous changes and stimulus-induced responsiveness in sleeping individuals, while Johnson and Lubin (1966) found that spontaneous PVRs continue during the night and show little correlation with the depth of sleep. The latter finding concurs with our own unpublished work.

In summary, the PVR shows promise as another indicator of reactivity of the sympathetic nervous system in psychophysiological research. The techniques are in need of standardization, and new approaches need to be tried to provide absolute measures for the response.

Body or Limb Motion

The measurement of motion, in the sense that a numerical scale is provided for the extent of motion and its speed, is difficult to instrument. It is additionally difficult when the total activity of the subject cannot be restricted. The several approaches that follow represent only partial solutions to the problem.

Body sway, such as that produced in tests of hypnotic suggestibility, can be accurately measured with a kind of "proximity detector." This instrument takes advantage of the fact that an oscillator draws less current when it is oscillating. The circuit has been described in Brown and Whitman (1963) and consists of a one-tube oscillator operating at 100 kHz. The tank coil, which is commercially available, contains a tap that is brought out to a vertical sensor about 6 ft long and placed 1–2 ft behind the standing subject. The oscillator is tuned to the point at which it is about to go out of oscillation. The proximity of the body of the subject detunes the circuit and causes the tube to draw more plate current. The amount of detuning and increase in plate current is not linearly related to the extent of sway in degrees. The instrument is remarkably sensitive but must be retuned for each use.

Gross body movement of small animals may be detected and recorded by the use of a "jiggle cage." This is a round or square cage balanced on a pivot point above its center of gravity. The weight of the animal unbalances the cage by a small amount determined by constraint on the fulcrum. Microswitches are mounted at 90° stations beneath the cage, so that one is closed by the movement of the animal from one quadrant to another. Another variation uses small "reed switches" that are closed by the approach of a small permanent magnet mounted to the cage bottom. The advantage here is that moisture does not harm the totally enclosed switch element.

The motion of a free animal within an enclosure may be detected with an ultrasonic, Doppler effect device. Two elements, an ultrasonic transmitter and a detector, are mounted on the cage wall. Phase differences between the emitted and received signals provide a signal proportional to the speed and extent of the movement. Modifications of this device could be made to register motions of a human subject if they were limited to a single plane.

Various types of potentiometric devices have been used to record angular motion, as of a limb. The potentiometer, connected as two legs of a bridge, must be mounted at a pivot point so that angular motion results in its rotation. The resulting signal may be amplified and recorded (Brown & Thorne, 1963).

Various elaborations of these basic devices may be used as required, e.g., "switchmats" may be laid in a grid pattern on the floor of a room and each connected to a pen of a multichannel event recorder. There is a great need for new designs, perhaps using new devices, to record unrestricted motion.

Gastric Motility

Gastric motility has traditionally been measured by monitoring the pressure variations of a semi-inflated balloon swallowed by the subject and maintained within the stomach. While this is the most direct means for detecting the mechanical action of the stomach, there are numerous disadvantages. Among these are the discomfort felt by the subject, the possibility of interference with natural conditions, and the necessity for restrained activity. Consequently, the following discussion will emphasize more indirect electrical measures which, while they do not provide as good evidence of stomach activity, circumvent some of these problems, thereby offering considerable promise as psychophysiological measures.

An approach was developed by Wenger, Engel, and Clemens (1955). Subjects swallowed a small, plastic-coated, permanent magnet the size of a capsule that was then moved about by stomach contractions. A magnetometer, mounted in a fixed location above the abdomen, detected the changing field from the moving magnet and thus provided an output.

The endoradiosonde (MacKay & Jacobson, 1957) is an encapsulated, pressure-sensitive, radio transmitter that is swallowed by the subject and transmits pressure variations during its passage through the GI tract. The signal may be detected from a nearby receiver and the output recorded. Modifications of this device have been made in which the transmitter capsule was restricted to the stomach by means of a tether made of surgical thread tied to a tooth.

Whether or not these procedures reflect the stomach contractions alone as accurately as does the balloon method, they constitute a lesser disturbance to the subject and are recommended for much wider use in psychophysiological research. (See Chapter 10 for a discussion of the psychophysiology of the gastrointestinal tract.)

Blood Pressure Measurement (BP)

Indirect (auscultatory) technique This familiar technique employs an inflatable cuff wrapped firmly about the upper arm with a stethoscope or other device to detect the audible evidence of what are essentially occlusion pressures of the artery. A mercury or aneroid gauge connected into the cuff line provides an estimation of the pressures required to inhibit the pulsatile blood flow (the systolic peak), denoted by the disappearance of the pulse sound, and as the pressure is allowed to escape, the last moment of partial constriction of the artery accompanied by Korotkoff sounds (the diastolic pressure). A number of elaborations has been made on this simple technique by providing automatic increase and decrease of the cuff pressure, by the use of a microphone plus amplifier, or with displacement pulse detector to denote the systolic and diastolic pressure points, but none has overcome a number of basic shortcomings. These include the subjectivity of the operator's judgment of the proper sounds denoting the pressure points, the discomfort to the subject, and the difficulty in obtaining consecutive or continuous measures. The latter is probably the most serious shortcoming, since the blood pressure is a very labile phenomenon, as will be seen when appropriate direct pressure measurements are made. However, some variation of the intermittent occlusive technique is the only means at present for observing BP semicontinuously in the human subject. Successful automation of the occlusive technique was accomplished by Hinman, Engel, and Bickford (1962). (See Chapter 11 also.)

Direct blood pressure techniques While indirect methods provide a repeatable pressure reading with some degree of reliability, they reflect not only the external pressure required to overcome the bore pressure in the vessel but also that required to overcome the elasticity of the vessel wall and the surrounding tissues as well. By contrast, direct measures are made from within the bore of the vessel and consequently indicate the internal pressure with a high degree of accuracy. Furthermore, the indications are continuous and the tracing reveals the whole of the complex blood pressure curve. All contemporary direct techniques involve entry into the vessel through a puncture in the wall, involve discomfort and risk to the subject, and consequently are used rarely.

Three types of transducers are available: (a) the pressure transducer, basically a small, closed chamber with one elastic or distensible wall to which are attached strain gauge elements or the armature of a differential transformer. Movements of this distensible diaphragm are transmitted to the elements, and the consequent changes in stress produce an output proportional to pressure. (b) The strain gauge transducer, composed of four strain elements in a bridge configuration, arranged so that, while one pair is under compression, the other is elongated. The electrical output of the bridge is low and the elements are usually excited with an ac current. The output is a highly linear function of the monitored pressures. (c) The differential transformer type of transducer, in which the diaphragm is linked to the movable armature of a differential transformer. The differential transformer contains one primary winding and two secondaries. The latter are so wound and connected that their output is a function of the amount of magnetic coupling between the primary and secondary windings. The movements of the diaphragm and armature create variable coupling and changes in output voltage.

The strain gauge transducer (b) is used most often but is more susceptible to movement artifact than the differential transformer device. The latter, however, requires more complex and costly instrumentation to modulate and demodulate the signal. Both types are provided with Luer fittings from which the cannula is run to the subject. The bore of the cannula and its length determine the frequency response of the device and the fidelity of the recording.

Measurement of Blood Flow

Since all blood flow devices now known must be implanted surgically, the measurement is rarely made on normal human subjects. An extensive discussion of these devices has been given by Olmsted (1967, pp. 158–172).

All blood-flow transducers are essentially velocity detectors, sensitive to the velocity of blood flowing through them. Such transducers are perivascular, i.e., they surround the intact vessel; the bore of the blood vessel within the transducer is held constant, so that the flow rate can be derived directly with some accuracy. In the electromagnetic flowmeter, coils of fine wire, excited from an external source, generate magnetic lines of force perpendicular to the direction of blood flow. Immediately downstream is a pair of nonpolarizable electrodes held in intimate contact with the vessel wall. The blood is a conductor that, in its movement through the magnetic field, cuts its lines of force and generates a current proportional to the speed of flow. This signal is detected by the downstream electrodes and is led out to a recorder. The whole unit is encapsulated and is very small in size. Difficulties are sometimes encountered in establishing actual flow rate values, and the device has a tendency to cause erosion and damage to the enclosed vessel.

A second type of transducer, the ultrasonic, uses the Doppler effect to measure rates of blood flow. Again, the transducer is perivascular. It contains two tiny piezoelectric crystals, one upstream and the other downstream. The crystals are faced toward each other, so that their acoustic axes are common and at a slight angle to the axis of the enclosed blood vessel. A brief pulse applied to each crystal causes it to oscillate at a high natural frequency and to transmit supersonic energy at about 5 mHz. Each crystal alternately serves as a transmitter and a receiver at the rate of 400 Hz. The sound travels diagonally across the blood stream, first in one direction and then in the other. Associated electronic circuitry determines the *difference* between these two transit times and provides an output proportional to the difference. This is, in turn, proportional to the rate of blood flow. Ultrasonic transducers have recently been developed that can be applied to the unopened skin above a vessel, but these instruments are highly susceptible to movement artifact and provide relative measures only.

CONCLUSION

For various reasons, three years have elapsed between the first and final drafts of this chapter. The vista thus provided permits a critical evaluation of the procedures and instruments of psychophysiology and indirectly, of the directions which the field has taken in this time.

Some measures have declined in their popularity, e.g., blood pressure while all of the electrical skin phenomena have continued to preoccupy the field.

New techniques have emerged from elaborations of old: the "feedback" procedures for attaining autocontrol of covert bodily processes, the detection and isolation of the contingent negative variation (CNV) as an electrocortical phenomenon, on-line computer scoring of sleep stages to replace the trusty trained graduate student scorer—novel, yet in a sense familiar approaches.

It is questionable whether psychophysiology needs more new devices for detecting and transducing known bioelectric signals. It might be better if we searched instead for schemes and instruments for ordering known events into larger, more significant wholes—and for ways to observe and predict complex interrelationships between apparently discrete systems that would go beyond mere cross- and auto-correlations.

One might use, as an example, the present state of understanding with respect to the electrical activity of the brain manifested by the EEG. Outside of Darrow's attempts to plot the interarea phase relationships and their behavioral significance, beyond W. Grey Walter's observations of the CNV and a scattering of other techniques for spectral EEG analysis at various levels of consciousness, there is little in the way of attempts to relate all or part of the electrical activity of the brain to important cognative, conative, or affective processes in the behavior of the individual. In fact, it is quite possible that the important dynamic relationships between the EEG and various vascular, metabolic, bioelectric and environmental factors are of a complexity which might prevent their conceptualization by unassisted human mentality. Thus, new instrumentation should be that which permits the investigator to synthesize the already abundant discrete information at his disposal.

REFERENCES

ACKNER, B. Emotions and the peripheral vasomotor system. *Journal of Psychosomatic Research*, 1956, **1,** 3–20.

ACKNER, B. The relationship between anxiety and the level of peripheral vasomotor activity. *Journal of Psychosomatic Research*, 1956, **1,** 21–48.

ACKNER, B., & PAMPLIGLIONE, G. Combined EEG, plethysmographic, respiratory and skin resistance studies during sleep. *Electroencephalography and Clinical Neurophysiology*, 1955, **7,** 153.

ALVAREZ, E. C. New methods of studying gastric peristalsis: The electrogastrogram and what it shows. *Journal of the American Medical Association*, 1922, **78,** 1116–1119.

ATZLER, VON E. Dielektrographie. In URBAN & SCHWARZENBERG (Eds.), *Handbuch der Biologishen Arbeitsmethoden*, 1935, **5** (8), 1073. Cited in M. McCally, G. W. Barnard, K. E. Robins, & A. R. Marko (1963).

BAGNO, S., & LIEBMAN, F. M. Impedance measurements. *Electronics*, 1959, **32,** 62–63.

BEST, C. H., & TAYLOR, N. B. *The physiological basis of medical practice*. Baltimore: Williams & Wilkins, 1961.

BROWN, C. C. The techniques of plethysmography. In C. C. BROWN (Ed.), *Methods in psychophysiology*. Baltimore: Williams & Wilkins, 1967.

BROWN, C. C. A proposed standard nomenclature for physiologic measures: A committee report. *Psychophysiology*, 1967, **4,** 2, 260–264.

BROWN, C. C. The parotid puzzle: A review of the literature on human salivation and its applications to psychophysiology. *Psychophysiology*, 1970, **7,** 1, 66–85.

BROWN, C. C., GIDDON, D. B., & DEAN, E. D. Techniques of plethysmography. *Psychophysiology*, 1965, **1,** 253–266.

BROWN, C. C., & THORNE, P. The detection of vertical components of limb motion with a gravity sensing potentiometer. *Psychophysiology Newsletter*, 1963, **7,** 3–6.

BROWN, C. C., & WHITMAN, J. B. Apparatus for measuring restricted ranges of linear movement. *American Journal of Psychiatry*, 1963, **6,** 138–139.

BURCH, G. E. *Digital plethysmography*. New York: Grune and Stratton, 1954.

BURCH, G. E., COHN, A. E., & NEUMANN, C. Rheopneumoplethysmography, alpha and beta waves. *American Journal of Physiology*, 1942, **136,** 433–442.

COLE, K. S., & CURTIS, H. J. Electrical physiology: Electrical resistance and impedance of cells and tissues. In O. GLASSER (Ed.), *Medical physics*. Vol. 1. Chicago: Year Book Medical Publishers, 1944.

DARROW, C. W. The galvanic skin reflex and finer volume changes. *American Journal of Physiology*, 1929, **88,** 219–229.

DARROW, E. H. Interarea electroencephalographic phase relationships. In C. C. BROWN (Ed.), *Methods in psychophysiology*. Baltimore: Williams & Wilkins, 1967.

DAVIS, J. F., Manual of surface electromyography. Montreal, Canada: Laboratory for Psychological Studies, Allan Memorial Institute of Psychiatry, 1952.

DAVIS, R. C., GARAFOLO, L., & GAULT, F. I. An exploration of abdominal potentials. *Journal of Comparative and Physiological Psychology*, 1957, **50,** 519–523.

EDELBERG, R. Presidential address. Society for Psychophysiologic Research, Denver, 1966.

EDELBERG, R. Electrical properties of the skin. In C. C. BROWN (Ed.), *Methods of psychophysiology*. Baltimore: Williams & Wilkins, 1967.

FORBES, T. W. Problems in measurements of electrodermal phenomena: Choice of method and phenomena: Potential, impedance, resistance. *Psychophysiology*, 1964, **1,** 1, 26–30.

GAVIRIA, B., COYNE, L., & THETFORD, P. Correlation of skin potential and skin resistance measures. *Psychophysiology*, 1969, **5,** 5, 465–477.

GOLDENSOHN, S. S., & ZABLOW, L. An electrical impedance spirometer. *Journal of Applied Physiology*, 1959, **14,** 463.

GOODMAN, E. N., GINSBERG, I. A., & ROBINSON, M. A. An improved apparatus for measuring the electrogastrogram. *Science*, 1951, **113,** 682–683.

GREENFIELD, A. D. M., WHITNEY, R. J., & MOWBRAY, J. F. Methods for the investigation of peripheral blood flow. *British Medical Bulletin*, 1962, **19,** 2, 101–109.

HERTZMAN, A. B. Vasomotor regulation of cutaneous circulation. *Physiological Review*, 1950, **39,** 230–306.

HIGHTOWER, N. Motility of the alimentary canal of man. In J. A. RIDER & H. C. MOELLER (Eds.), *Disturbances of gastrointestinal motility*. Springfield, Ill.: Charles C Thomas, 1959.

HINMAN, A. T., ENGEL, B. T., & BICKFORD, A. F. Portable blood pressure recorder: Accuracy and preliminary use in evaluating daily variations in pressure. *American Heart Journal,* 1962, **63,** 663–668.

JASPER, H. H. (committee chairman) The ten twenty electrode system of the International Federation. *Electroencephalography and Clinical Neurophysiology,* 1958, **10,** 371–375.

JEFFRESS, L. A. Galvanic phenomena of the skin. *Journal of Experimental Psychology,* 1928, **11,** 130–144.

JENKNER, F. L. *Rheoencephalography.* Springfield, Ill.: Charles C Thomas, 1962.

JOHNSON, L. C., & LUBIN, A. The orienting response during waking and sleeping. Presented to the Pavlovian Society, November 11, 1966.

KELLY, B., BROWN, C. C., & SHAFFER, J. W. A controlled physiological, clinical and psychological evaluation of chlordiazepoxide. *British Journal of Psychiatry,* 1969, **115,** 529, 1387–1392.

KELLY, B., BROWN, C. C., & SHAFFER, J. W. A comparison of physiological and psychological measurements on anxious patients and normal controls. *Psychophysiology,* 1970, **6,** 4, 429–440.

LAMBERT, E. H. Electromyography. In O. GLASSER (Ed.), *Medical physics.* Vol. 3. Chicago: Year Book Medical Publishers, 1962.

LYKKEN, D. T., MILLER, R. D., & STRAHAN, R. F. Some properties of skin conductance and potential. *Psychophysiology,* 1968, **5,** 3, 253–268.

McCALLY, M., BARNARD, G. W., ROBINS, K. E., & MARKO, A. R. Observations with an electrical impedance respirometer. *American Journal of Medical Electronics,* 1963, **2,** 322–327.

McGRAW, E. R., KLEINMAN, K. M., BROWN, M. L., & KOROL, B. An accurate one-channel basal level/response signal separator for skin resistance, incorporating pulse coding of the basal level. *Psychophysiology,* 1969, **6,** 2, 209–213.

MACKAY, R. S., & JACOBSON, B. Endoradiosonde. *Nature,* 1957, **179,** 1239–1240.

MINARD, J. & KRAUSMAN, D. Rapid eye movement definition and count: An on-line detector. *Electroencephalography and Clinical Neurophysiology* 1971, **31,** 99–102.

NYBOER, J. Plethysmography: Impedance. In O. GLASSER (Ed.), *Medical physics.* Vol. 2. Chicago: Year Book Medical Publishers, 1950.

NYBOER, J. *Electrical impedance plethysmography.* Springfield, Ill.: Charles C Thomas, 1959.

O'CONNELL, D. N., & TURSKY, B. Silver-silver chloride sponge electrodes for skin potential recording. *American Journal of Psychology,* 1960, **73,** 302–304.

OLMSTED, F. Measurement of blood flow and blood pressure. In C. C. BROWN (Ed.), *Methods in psychophysiology.* Baltimore: Williams & Wilkins, 1967.

RICHTER, C. P. A study of the electric skin resistance and psychogalvanic reflex in a case of unilateral sweating. *Brain,* 1927, **50,** 216–235.

RIEHL, J. L. Analog analysis of EEG activity. *Electroencephalography and Clinical Neurophysiology,* 1963, **15,** 1039–1042.

RUSSELL, R. W., & STERN, R. M. Gastric motility: The electrogastrogram. In P. H. VENABLES & I. MARTIN (Eds.), *A manual of psychophysiological methods.* New York: Wiley, 1967.

SEIPEL, J. H. The biophysical basis and clinical applications of rheoencephalography. FAA, Office of Aviation Medicine, Georgetown Clinical Research Institute, Washington, D.C. 1967 (Report #AM 67-11).

SEWALL, H., & SANFORD, E. Plethysmographic studies of the human vasomotor mechanism when excited by electrical stimulation. *Journal of Physiology, London,* 1890, **11,** 179–207.

SHACKEL, B. Skin drilling: A method of diminishing galvanic skin potentials. *American Journal of Psychology,* 1959, **72,** 114–121.

SHACKEL, B. Electrooculography: The electrical recording of eye position. *Proceedings of the 3rd International Conference on Medical Electronics,* London, 1960.

SIMONS, D. G., & PEREZ, R. E. The B/GSR module: A combined recording to present base skin resistance and galvanic skin reflex activity patterns. *Psychophysiology,* 1965, **2,** 116–124.

SKOV, E. R., & SIMMONS, D. G. EEG electrodes for in-flight monitoring. *Psychophysiology,* 1965, **2,** 161–167.

SOKOLOV, E. N. *Perception and the conditioned reflex.* Translated by S. W. Waydenfield. New York: Pergamon, 1963.

TURSKY, B., & O'CONNELL, D. N. A comparison of ac and dc eye movement recording. *Psychophysiology,* 1967, **3,** 156–163.

VAN DER MERWE, A. B. Diagnostic value of peripheral vasomotor reactions in psychoneuroses. *Psychosomatic Medicine,* 1948, **10,** 347–354.

VAN DER MERWE, A. B. The value of the finger plethysmograph in diagnosing neurotic cases. *Proceedings of the South African Psychological Association,* 1950, **1,** 10–12.

VENABLES, P. H., & MARTIN, I. The relation of palmar sweat gland activity to level of skin potential and conductance. *Psychophysiology,* 1967, **3,** 302–311.

VIGOUROUX, R. Sur le rôle de la resistance électrique des tissus dans l'électrodiagnostique. *Comptes Rendus des Séances de la Société de Biologie,* 1879, **31,** 336–339.

WANG, G. H. The galvanic skin reflex: A review of old and recent works from a physiologic point of view. *American Journal of Physical Medicine,* 1957, **36,** 295–320.

WENGER, M. A., ENGEL, B. T., & CLEMENS, T. L. Initial results with the magnetometer method of recording stomach motility. *American Psychology,* 1955, **10,** 452.

WHITE, E. H. Additional notes on gastrointestinal activity during avoidance behavior. *Psychological Reports,* 1964, **14,** 343–347. (a)

WHITE, E. H. Surface recording of gastrointestinal motility. *Psychological Reports,* 1964, **14,** 321–322. (b)

WHITNEY, R. J. The electrical strain gauge method for measurement of peripheral circulation in man. In G. E. WOLSTENHOLME (Ed.), *Peripheral circulation in man.* Boston: Little, Brown, 1954.

WILCOTT, R. C. Correlation of skin resistance and potential. *Journal of Comparative and Physiological Psychology,* 1958, **51,** 691–696.

WILCOTT, R. C. Skin potential and skin resistance recording from the minimally restrained cat. *Psychophysiology,* 1969, **5,** 6, 727–729.

YOUNG, L. E. Measuring eye movements. *American Journal of Medical Electronics,* 1963, **2,** 300–307.

ZIJLSTRA, W. A. *Fundamentals and applications of clinical oximetry.* Ossen, Netherlands: Van Gorcum, 1953.

John A. Stern

PHYSIOLOGICAL RESPONSE MEASURES DURING CLASSICAL CONDITIONING

5

Interest in the area of classical conditioning of physiological response systems appears, at the present time, to be greater than it has been in the past 20 years. For example, in Prokasy's book, *Classical Conditioning: A Symposium,* we find 9 of the 19 chapters dealing specifically with such conditional responses. The eyeblink remains the most popular response, followed by heart rate and electrodermal conditioning. The reader is further referred to Dykman's chapter in *Progress in Experimental Personality Research* entitled "Toward a theory of classical conditioning: Cognitive, emotional, and motor components of the conditional reflex," and Razran's article, "The observable unconscious and the inferable conscious in current Soviet psychophysiology: Interoceptive conditioning, semantic conditioning, and the orienting reflex" (1961), for excellent reviews of various aspects of the classical conditioning problem.

PROCEDURES AND DEFINITIONS

Classical conditioning is here defined as that learning which takes place when two stimuli are presented in some temporal relationship in which a change in response to the first stimulus is contingent upon the presentation of the second stimulus. Whether the conditional response (CR), i.e., the response elicited by the first of the two stimuli, has to be identical or similar to the response produced by the unconditioned stimulus (UCS) or can be different from it, is a question that has not been satisfactorily resolved. For the purpose of the present exposition, any consistent change in response to the CS that can be attributed to the CS-UCS pairing and occurs with any regularity will be accepted as a conditional response (CR). Thus certain types of "sensitized" responses will be accepted as conditional responses. Before discussing the problem of conditioning, we shall review a few of the terms commonly used in the classical conditioning literature, as well as some of the conditioning paradigms in current vogue.

Since conditioning involves the presentation of stimuli over time, as well as responses to such stimuli, let us start by defining the stimuli that are under experimenter control. These are the *conditional* or *conditioned stimulus,* hereafter referred to as the CS; and the *unconditional* or *unconditioned stimulus,* hereafter referred to as the UCS. These stimuli produce responses appropriately labeled *conditional* or *conditioned responses* and *unconditional* or *unconditioned responses,* hereafter referred to as CR and UCR, respectively. My preference is for the *al* rather than the *ed* suffix, since it seems to describe more appropriately both the situation as well as the responses. However, let us remain flexible and accept and use these words interchangeably.

Since CS as well as UCS are presented over a period of time, we need recourse to two more notations, namely, ISI and ITI. The first of these is the *interstimulus interval,* the time elapsing between the onset of the two stimuli. Since in most conditioning experiments more than one conditioning trial is administered, we also need to define the *intertrial interval.* This is the time elapsing between the onset of a trial and the onset of the next trial.

Let us now briefly turn to a few of the conditioning paradigms in current use. *Forward conditioning* is defined as that conditioning in which the CS and the UCS occur either simultaneously or the UCS follows the CS by some definite time period. It is forward conditioning because the UCS follows the CS. *Backward conditioning* must then, of course, refer to the condition in which the UCS precedes the CS by some definite time period.

Returning now to forward conditioning, one can vary the temporal relation between the CS and the UCS in a number of ways. The most common procedures have involved *delayed conditioning;* in this procedure there is a delay between the onset of the CS and the UCS; the second procedure is *trace conditioning,* where a finite time period (trace) intervenes between termination of the CS and onset of the UCS. One further term will complete our basic conditioning vocabulary: *discriminant conditioning* is that type of conditioning in which one CS becomes the signal for a UCS (CS+), while another stimulus becomes the signal that no UCS will be presented (CS−). Discriminant conditioning can be further complicated by associating different CS with varying intensities of the UCS or even different UCS.

Let us also briefly discriminate between classical and instrumental conditioning, since the latter will be discussed in Chapter 6. In classical conditioning the pairing of the CS and UCS is completely under the experimenter's control, while in instrumental conditioning the organism's behavior is instrumental in determining whether he will or will not be presented with the UCS. In the latter situation both the CS and UCS can be thought of as under the organism's control, the experimenter's role here being the manipulation of the environment to increase the incidence of CRs.

In conditioning experiments I shall not talk of "the" CR but shall rather accept the possibility that a variety of conditional responses can be established when two stimuli are presented in a fixed order. This idea is more noted for its omission than for either tacit or explicit acceptance in the current American literature. The notion of the unitary nature of the conditioned response has its roots, in part, in the history of American learning theory with its strong emphasis on motor conditioning and in psychology's version of operationalism. That is, we define what we shall accept as evidence for the establishment of a conditional response, and any other behavior change that may be associated with and observed when one presents two stimuli in a specified order will be ignored. For example, in avoidance conditioning in which an animal has to cross from one side of the apparatus to the other side with the presentation of a CS in order to avoid shock, the only measure of conditioning commonly used is the number of avoidance responses. Animals that do not learn the desired (by the experimenter) response within a specified number of trials are categorized as nonlearners. That they are nonlearners only with respect to the avoidance response can be readily established if one measures their escape latency. Such animals often demonstrate typical learning curves with respect to escape from shock. They have learned to escape shock efficiently rather than learn the response upon which the experimenter is focusing his attention. They are not really nonlearners but simply are not learning the unique response the experimenter is willing to accept as evidence for the animal having learned anything. Thus, when the experimental subject outsmarts the experimenter, we are unwilling to dignify this behavior with the label "learning." Even though this type of behavior may, from a biological point of view, be more adaptive or homeostatic, we are unwilling to accept it as evidence for learning!

Let us dwell for a moment on this problem. If we train an animal in a shuttle box to go from one side of the box to the other whenever a tone is presented for a period of time followed by shock, two types of responses can develop: (a) animals can learn to avoid being shocked by going to the safe side during presentation of the CS and prior to the onset of shock stimulation, and (b) animals can also learn to escape shock more and more rapidly without ever learning to avoid shock. Is avoidance learning a higher order of learning than escape learning? The research literature would lead one to suspect that this is the case. However, if we turn to the extinction of the conditional response in this situation, we shall find that the speed of extinction is considerably more rapid in the animal that has learned to escape, rather than avoid, the shock. Although the avoidance of shock while it is potentially present is a bit of behavior to be lauded in lower animals as well as man, when such behavior persists in the absence of reinforcement, we should consider it to be an example of maladaptive or neurotic behavior. Thus, if our criterion of learning is the speed of extinction of a conditional response (or the learning of a new response to an old situation), we should all agree that escape training leads to a more rapid extinction than is true of avoidance

learning and is thus, in a sense, more adaptive.

I suggest that we behave less like narrowly programmed computers when studying the development of even relatively simple types of learned behavior such as conditional responses, and take a page out of the workbook of the ethologists, namely, to observe what is going on in the situation. My experience has convinced me that what is going on in the experimental situation defined as classical conditioning is considerably more complex (and interesting) than most textbooks and articles dealing with conditioning would lead us to believe. In a later section of this chapter I shall discuss the various types of conditioned responses possible in classical conditioning.

The focus of this chapter will thus not be on "the" classically conditioned response as measured in physiological response systems but will attempt to sketch a number of different responses that can and do become conditioned in any experiment utilizing the classical conditioning paradigm. The references will be restricted to the literature dealing with the conditioning of physiological measures in man, using the results of animal research only when no relevant examples in the human literature are available.

SOME PROBLEMS IN CLASSICAL CONDITIONING

Three further problems need to be resolved. The first deals with the question of what will be considered as appropriate content for a chapter dealing with conditioning of "physiological response systems." Obviously, all of man's activities have their basis in physiological activity. Thus, verbal conditioning, for example, might be considered within the rubric of physiological conditioning, since one is trying to get the subject to increase the emission of a particular array of sounds that obviously is mediated by physiological mechanisms. The recording of such sounds and their spectral analysis to determine whether the desired array of sounds is being produced with any greater degree of frequency after conditioning than prior to conditioning is one way, albeit a clumsy and expensive one, for assessing verbal conditioning. Whether it is more physiological than counting the number of times the desired word is emitted is also questionable.

The material in this chapter will concern measures that are recorded from the body by appropriately applied sensors recording physiological processes and will include only studies dealing with the recording of physiological measures during classical conditioning. In some studies such measures may be collected as ancillary information, with the principal emphasis perhaps on motor or verbal responses, or at the other extreme the dependent variable may be a specific physiological measure.

The physiological measures of concern here are those that can be objectively recorded by placing appropriate sensors (transducers) on, in, or at some distance from, the subject. Those measures that have been commonly obtained in such studies are the electroencephalogram; electrodermal activity (variously referred to as EDR, PGR, or GSR); vasomotor activity from various body sites; cardiovascular measures such as heart rate and blood pressure; responses associated with the eye such as pupillary diameter, eye movement, and eyelid responses; respiration; salivation; stomach contraction and intestinal motility; and electromyographic activity from diverse body sites and both internal, as well as external, body temperature.

A number of factors must be taken into consideration in experimenting with the conditioning of autonomic and interoceptive response systems, as compared to the classical conditioning of a motor response. The choice of the motor response to be conditioned is usually made on the basis of relative quiescence of the response to be conditioned. Thus, if one is interested in conditioning a gross motor response in the cat, one seldom, if ever, selects tail movement, since this appendage is seldom at rest; rather one selects a leg flexion response, a response relatively seldom emitted in the apparatus generally used for conditioning. Physiological response systems, unless the organism is dead, are seldom if ever quiescent, and the level of activity from which we are attempting to produce CRs may be a determiner of conditionability of the system. This problem is reviewed in other chapters of this handbook under such headings as the "law of initial values," "attention," and "activation," and thus need not concern us here.

The second problem is that physiological response systems in the absence of experimenter-controlled stimulation are not quiescent but variably active. This activity will be referred to as "spontaneous fluctuations" (SF). It is called spontaneous simply because we cannot specify (a priori) the factors that produce it. Some of the factors that produce such activity can be identified: thus extraneous stimuli in the environment, such as a person walking down the hall or apparatus noises, produce such responses; internally mediated material, such as erotic, frightening, pleasurable thoughts; hallucinatory or delusional material; daydreams; apprehension about the apparatus, the experiment, and the experimenter; the need to cough, sneeze, scratch an itch, etc.; can all be identified as cues that produce such responses. There are marked differences in the incidence of spontaneous fluctuations not only across the range of individuals but within individuals as well. Knowledge of a high level of SF in any one physiological response system tells you nothing about the level of SF in another response system. I shall return to SFs and their relationship to conditionability in a later section of this chapter.

The third problem in dealing with physiological measures of conditioning is the fact that all CS have unconditional responses associated with them, so that in many cases one cannot discriminate with respect to waveform between the unconditional response to the CS and possible conditional responses. These responses are referred to as orienting responses (OR) and will be discussed further in a section dealing with orienting responses.

Spontaneous Fluctuations

As I have said, one of the characteristics of living organisms is the cyclic activity of response systems. Circadian rhythms, menstrual cycles, seasonal cycles, etc., can be demonstrated in behavioral, as well as physiological, measures. In addition to such fluctuations one can identify other responses, especially in physiological response systems, that seem to bear no relationship to identifiable environmental events. These responses, which in waveform (spectral components) mirror responses evoked by specific stimuli (OR), can be observed in all physiological response systems. Thus alpha desynchronization occurs without known inputs into the organism, peripheral vasoconstriction and EDRs occur quite spontaneously, and all other response systems manifest such activity. If one records concurrently from a number of physiological response systems, one is struck by the fact that individuals differ markedly with respect to the physiological system in which they demonstrate such lability; and the fact that lability of one response system is of little or no predictive value with respect to such activity in other response systems, although theoretically they may both be mediated through the same branch of the autonomic nervous system. For example, although both peripheral vasoconstriction and electrodermal responses are believed to be principally mediated through the sympathetic branch of the autonomic nervous system, we find that a given subject may be extremely labile electrodermally and manifest a high degree of stability with respect to peripheral vascular activity. I suspect that the maintenance of lability in systems is under cortical control and that cortical centers associated with electrodermal activity may be quite distinct from those associated with vasomotor activity. No direct data bearing on this assumption are currently available. Indirect evidence is more readily found; e.g., if we conceive of sleep as being mediated through a decrease in cortical activity or cortical control of subcortical centers, we find that changes in such cortical activity have markedly different effects on electrodermal as compared to vasomotor SFs. Electrodermal SFs are markedly reduced or disappear during periods of medium or deep sleep, while vasomotor activity, as measured at the periphery, becomes more labile during sleep than during periods of wakefulness.

Johnson and Lubin (1966), as well as McDonald and Carpenter (1966), have reported on both electrodermal and plethysmographic activity during sleep. Johnson and Lubin suggest that electrodermal activity as measured by the skin potential method depicts some findings seldom seen in man, namely, a dissociation of SFs as measured bilaterally. Subjects during periods of deep sleep demonstrate differential SFs as measured from the left and right hand. Their results thus demonstrate that sleep may be a type of inhibition of higher nervous centers' control over lower (subcortical, spinal) brain

centers. As Wang (1964) has so ably demonstrated in studies of the cat, some SFs in the electrodermal system are organized at the spinal level, since animals with transected cords will still demonstrate SFs below the site of the transection. However, when recorded from bilaterally symmetrical sites (such as the pads of the two hind legs of the cat), these SFs are no longer time locked but occur quite independently of each other. Thus one can discriminate between CNS-controlled SFs and those mediated by more peripheral mechanisms by recording the response in question from a number of different body sites. If the responses are time locked, they are centrally mediated; if not time locked, they are under peripheral control.

What relationship does the incidence of SFs have to the subject matter of this chapter? Let us briefly review the literature with respect to the importance of SFs both to speed of habituation of ORs and to conditionability of specific response systems. Unfortunately, most of this literature is restricted to data obtained in the electrodermal response system. For example, in the typical studies conducted in our laboratories we evaluate SF during a period of rest prior to any type of stimulation, be it stimulation involving the habituation of ORs or that involved in conditioning experiments. We can thus evaluate SF during a period of rest. Intervals between trials of stimulation are also usually sufficiently long for us to assess SF between trials of stimulation, as well as between conditioning trials. As can be seen in the accompanying tables, the relationship between SF and OR as well as CRs are invariably positive, and generally statistically reliable.

Table 5.1 depicts the results of a study by Stern, Stewart, and Winokur (1961) that dealt with electrodermal conditioning. Subjects were presented with a series of trials of tone stimulation (CS only), a series of conditioning trials (CS plus UCS), followed by a series of extinction trials (CS only). In this study they also evaluated the incidence of SFs between trials of stimulation, and assessed the incidence of orienting responses (OR). Although ORs will be more fully described in the following section, let us simply state here that these are responses to the onset of a stimulus complex that decreases in amplitude as a function of successive

TABLE 5.1 CORRELATIONS (PRODUCT-MOMENT) BETWEEN SPONTANEOUS GSR RESPONSES AND OTHER GSR MEASURES

		Spontaneous fluctuations during		
		A	C	E
Spontaneous fluctuations during	A	X	0.18	0.05
	C		X	0.56*
	E			X
Response to tone during	A	0.68†	0.18	0.05
	C	0.50*	0.69†	0.44
	E	0.67*	0.67*	0.73†
Anticipatory response during conditioning	A	X	X	X
	C	0.55*	0.84†	0.77†
	E	0.20	0.89†	0.54

Note.—A = adaptation period; C = conditioning period; E = extinction period.
*p = .05.
†p = .01.

From J. A. Stern, M. A. Stewart, and G. Winokur, An investigation of some relationships between various measures of the galvanic skin response. *Journal of Psychosomatic Research*, 1961, **5**, 215–223. Reprinted by permission.

trials of stimulation. As is evident from Table 5.1, all the correlations are positive, indicating that associated with a high level of SF is the slow habituation of ORs. Also, the highest correlations are found between the incidence of SFs and the speed of habituation of ORs taken during comparable time periods. Thus, the correlation between SFs taken between trials of tone stimulation (SFt) and ORs to tone stimulation only (ORt) is the highest of all the correlations involving SFt. The same is true for SFc and SFe. As Martin points out (1963b), "It is worth emphasizing that such correlations have been found under a wide range of stimulus conditions, including shock (Stewart, Stern, & Fredman, 1961), tone UCS (Martin, 1960, 1963a) tone UCS plus RT reaction (Martin, 1963b) so that they are by no means findings specific to the present experimental conditions." According to Martin these results have to date been principally demonstrated in the electrodermal system. Similar comparisons involving spontaneous eyeblinks and conditional eyeblink responses were found by Martin (1963c) not to be statistically reliable.

The results from our laboratories, as well as those reported from other laboratories, indicate that the level of background activity in the electrodermal response system, as measured by SF, is a good predictor of the speed of habituation of ORs and is also a good predictor of the development of

various types of conditional responses in this response system. Gottschalk (1946) presents some data relating SFs in peripheral vasomotor activity to the speed of habituation of ORs; subjects with a high level of SF habituated more slowly. These results are thus consonant with those found in the electrodermal system.

To the best of my knowledge similar relationships have not as yet been demonstrated for other physiological response systems, although my conviction is that such relationship will be found. Whether the relationship between SF and OR is a causal relationship or only a co-relationship cannot be determined from the above type of study.

As indicated above, a high level of SF in one physiological response system is not predictive of the level of SF in other response systems. It is tempting to consider the incidence of SF as a measure of "arousal" or "alertness" of an organism; however, since the correlation of SF across physiological systems appears to be quite poor, we should at the present time only talk about alertness or arousal as measured in a given physiological response system. Any one individual probably manifests consistent patterns of lability across physiological response systems, so that we might, in the future, be able to talk of deviations from a basal level of SF in a number of response systems as measures of alertness or arousal; but unfortunately, at the present time, we can only speculate about this possibility, since no data are available either to confirm or refute this point of view.

The Orienting Response

The orienting or "what-is-it" response is defined by Sokolov (1963a) as the first response of the body to any type of stimulus, and according to Pavlov "tunes" sensory systems to ensure optimal conditions for the perception of stimuli with that sense modality. The orienting response to an auditory stimulus, for example, involves muscular activity resulting in such specific movements as orienting the head toward the stimulus, the pricking up of the ears, and the movement of the eyes in the direction of sound. It further involves secretory components such as salivation and sweating; autonomic components such as peripheral vascular constriction, pupillary dilation, electrodermal responses, and cardiac responses; and CNS components such as desynchronization of alpha activity, K complexes, and perhaps late components of the (averaged) evoked response. Under what conditions can these types of responses be identified as ORs? According to Sokolov three conditions have to be met in order for a response to be so characterized:

1. It must first of all be nonspecific with regard to the quality of the stimulus.
2. It must be nonspecific with regard to the intensity of the stimulus.
3. It must decrease in amplitude with repeated stimulus presentation.

The response can, however, be reinstated by any change in the stimulus. Thus, with an auditory stimulus, changing intensity, frequency, length, or the complexity of the stimulus all serve to reinstate a habituated OR.

I should like to add one further criterion for classifying a response as an OR, namely, that the response is time locked to the onset of a "stimulus." A stimulus is here defined as any change in stimulation. Thus the onset, as well as the termination, of a tone can be considered as a stimulus. Generally, however, we refer to the response to the onset of a stimulus, since the response to stimulus termination generally habituates quite rapidly. The

actual latency of the response to a given type of stimulus may vary considerably across individuals. However, in any one individual the response is quite tightly time locked to the onset of a stimulus. In the electrodermal system, for example, the latency of OR to tone stimulation varies between 1.5 and 4.0 sec across individuals. Within an individual, however, OR latency will not vary more than ±0.50 sec across blocks of 10 trials of stimulus presentation.

Orienting responses should be differentiated from adaptive (AR) or defensive (DR) responses. These discriminations cannot readily be made in all physiological response systems. For example, in the electrodermal system one cannot, on the basis of the type of response, discriminate any of these three responses from each other; the same is true of the EEG. Electrodermally, the response as measured with the induced current technique is one of a drop in skin resistance, regardless of the type of stimulus. Phasic increases in skin resistance simply do not occur. Similarly, in the EEG, the OR, AR, and DR is a desynchronization of alpha activity (in the moderately alert individual who demonstrates good alpha activity in his EEG). Hypersynchronization in response to such stimuli and under the condition stated simply does not occur. However, if we turn to the vasomotor system, or the cardiovascular system, such differentiations can be somewhat more readily made.

Two quite distinct techniques can be used to make this type of differentiation. The first of these is the one described by Sokolov (1963a), while the second technique is one currently being developed in our laboratory. According to Sokolov the vasomotor OR as measured at the periphery is one of vasoconstriction, while the OR as measured from the forehead is one of vasodilation. The response to a defensive stimulus, on the other hand, is one of vasoconstriction in both places. Thus one should be readily able to discriminate between defensive and ORs if one records plethysmographic activity from these two discrete body sites. It is apparent, however, from the published recordings emanating from Russian laboratories that the finger plethysmographic OR is readily discriminable from background fluctuations, while the response from the forehead is generally of much lower amplitude and, even in their published material, often difficult to define. I, as well as others, have attempted to record plethysmographic activity from both body sites and have been able to record the finger plethysmographic response but have had considerable difficulty in obtaining consistent examples of forehead vasodilation as measures of the vasomotor OR.

A second, but more restricted, technique is currently in use in our laboratory. The orienting response as measured in the peripheral vasomotor system (finger plethysmography) is vascular constriction and a decrease in pulse amplitude (pressure). In response to heat presented to a nonmuscular portion of the hand, we find that the vasomotor response as measured in a finger of the same hand is vasodilation, while generally the vasomotor response of the same finger on the nonstimulated hand will, after a few trials, be no response or an orienting response. The site of stimulation with heat appears to be critical here, since both Sokolov (1963b) and Zimny and Miller (1966) have demonstrated that warming of the forearm or back of the arm produces ORs for a relatively large number of trials (10–30) before the defensive response, vasodilation, becomes well elaborated. Warming of the back of the hand produces clear vasodilation responses after as few as 3–4 trials of heat stimulation. With this measure we then have two criteria that can be used to discriminate between an orienting and a particular adaptive or defensive response: (a) vasodilation rather than vasoconstriction in the stimulated hand, and (b) the fact that the response is localized, i.e., the fingers of both hands do not give the same response. The latter type of criterion can, of course, also be applied to the electrodermal response measure. In experiments performed in our laboratory we have, for example, demonstrated that in response to shock stimulation of the wrist many subjects will give a greater amplitude electrodermal response from the hand stimulated than from the contralateral limb. What we observe here is a summation of the orienting and adaptive or defensive response.

Sokolov, as well as Voronin et al. (1965), talk about the unitary nature of "the" OR and refer to the various physiological measures in which such responses can be elicited as "components of the OR." They need to do this because the habituation of ORs in the various systems does not proceed at the same pace. For example, in response to tone stimulation we shall find that the OR, as measured by desynchronization of alpha activity in the EEG, will habituate more rapidly than the electrodermal manifestations of the OR; while in response to photic stimulation the latter component of the OR will habituate more rapidly than electroencephalographic components. That Sokolov does not take the concept of "the" OR at face value is well exemplified by his need to introduce the concept of localized ORs. Localized ORs are orienting responses confined to the analyzer (response system) stimulated. Thus, in the above example of slow habituation of EEG signs of the OR to photic stimulation, the lack of such habituation in responses recorded from the occipital cortex (visual area) would be defined as the existence of a local OR. These responses apparently also habituate but at a much slower rate than is true of "the" OR. Since it does not meet the criterion of nonspecificity with regard to either quality or intensity of the stimulus, it should probably not be referred to as an OR at all.

It is my own preference not to attempt to discriminate between local ORs and the more generalized OR, but rather to refer to ORs in specific response systems. The fact that ORs habituate at different rates in different response systems and at different rates to different stimuli thus does not bother me as much as it should, and does, a doctrinaire Sokolovian or Pavlovian.

Another distinction made by Sokolov is between the "tonic" and "phasic" OR. Up to this point I have been talking principally about the phasic OR, i.e., the OR produced by the presentation of a specific stimulus. Tonic ORs are, in the American literature, generally referred to as measures of "arousal," "activation," etc. Tonic ORs are generally the responses that one can observe taking place over a relatively long period of time associated with a given experimental paradigm. For example, in experiments dealing with the habituation of electrodermal ORs to a series of tone stimulations, if one periodically monitors the resting level of skin resistance, one will find that it rises as a function of the passage of time in the experimental situation.

This increase in skin resistance would, by Sokolov, be taken as an example of the decrease of a tonic OR. To the extent that similar changes in skin resistance do not occur in a comparable group of subjects not so stimulated, but simply resting in the experimental situation, we should accept this definition of the tonic OR. We have convinced ourselves (Gross & Stern, 1966) that with respect to the above example Sokolov is correct. Subjects aperiodically stimulated with a tone of a constant frequency, intensity, and duration show a more rapid rise in the resting level of skin resistance than is manifested by a group of subjects who are simply resting in the experimental situation. Current experiments in my laboratory (on rabbits) suggest that the same is true with respect to electroencephalographic indices of "sleep," namely that the aperiodic presentation of 10-sec blocks of photic stimulation produces a higher incidence of EEG signs of sleep after a period of time than is true of subjects not so stimulated. Thus decreases in tonic ORs are associated with a lowering of arousal or attention.

The relationship between tonic and phasic ORs has not been clearly formulated. We do, however, know that marked differences in habituation of phasic ORs occur as a function of the tonic OR. Assuming, for the moment, that EEG stages characterizing the organism going from a state of extreme alertness to a state of deep sleep may be one continuum along which the tonic OR may be placed, we find different phasic ORs occurring at various points in this continuum. For example, during states of extreme vigilance the EEG is characterized by low voltage fast (LVF) activity, a period during which no EEG phasic ORs can be elaborated (since these involve desynchronization of alpha activity, there can be no such desynchronization when none of this activity is present). On the other hand, during stages of drowsiness, when EEG background activity is also desynchronized, but the pattern of desynchronization is different from that seen in the state of hypervigilance, we often find that an orienting stimulus produces an augmentation of alpha activity, rather than the desynchronization usually seen when an orienting stimulus is presented. In the electrodermal system things appear a bit more orderly (as the subject moves from a state of alertness to one of sleep, phasic ORs decrease in amplitude), while in the peripheral vasomotor system the relationship is again more complicated. A highly alert subject habituates more slowly than one less alert; but, interestingly, a sleeping subject also habituates more slowly than a less alert one, as measured by peripheral vascular activity (McDonald & Carpenter, 1966).

What role does the OR serve in conditioning? The Russian literature (Anokhin, 1965, pp. 3–16; Paramonova, 1965, pp. 114–121; Sokolov, 1963b; Vinogradova, 1965, pp. 45–53) is quite specific on this point. Vinogradova, for example, states, "A commonly accepted notion is that the existence of an OR to a stimulus that later on will become a CS is necessary for the establishment of a full-fledged conditioned connection [p. 65]." Sokolov points out that the habituation of ORs to a CS prior to conditioning interferes with the development of a CR. Although this appears to be a plausible position, and one with which we agree, we have not come across any specific data in either the Russian or American literature to verify this notion experimentally. According to Anokhin the principal role of the OR is in "linking the cortical representations of the analysers which partake in the series of stimulation between the CS and the terminal reinforcement [p. 15]." These connections (between cortical sites in which the CS and UCS are represented) are established early in conditioning and are maintained while the OR disappears.

Can habituation of ORs be considered as evidence of learning and conditioning? The answer to this question is "yes" with respect to learning, and "no" with respect to conditioning. What is learned when an organism demonstrates habituation to an OR? Within the Sokolovian model what is learned is a "cortical model" or representation of the stimulus. This model develops as a function of the number of trials of stimulation and can be considered to be completely developed when no ORs can further be elaborated to that stimulus. Development of the model is associated with the inhibition of subcortical mechanisms that mediate peripheral manifestations of the OR. That this model must be associated principally with short-term memory processes is attested to by the ease with which the model can be disturbed, or the adapted OR disinhibited, as well as by the fact that the length of the intertrial interval has profound effects on the speed of habituation of ORs. The longer the intertrial interval, the slower the habituation process. For example, after an OR to a specific stimulus has been habituated, the OR can readily, although temporarily, be returned by the presentation of a disinhibiting stimulus such as another tone. That it must, however, also be involved in longer-term storage of memory is attested to by the fact that the habituation of ORs to a specific stimulus proceeds more rapidly if the organism has had previous experiences, i.e., has previously been habituated to the same stimulus.

I believe that the habituation of ORs is a measure of some very rudimentary aspects of learning. The only reason we cannot consider them within the framework of classical conditioning, or conditioning in general, is the fact that we cannot identify what the UCS might be in such a situation.

A recent paper by Stein (1966) develops a model to account for the habituation of orienting responses based purely on a classical conditioning paradigm. Stein assumes that there are two antagonistic neural systems activated by the onset of a stimulus. The first of these is an excitatory system (*E*), which excites or facilitates the arousal reaction; the second is an inhibitory system (*I*), which inhibits the arousal reaction. It is the activity of the *I* system that is conditionable. According to Stein, although the *E* system does not habituate, the *I* system becomes conditioned to the onset of a stimulus. Since this system inhibits the arousal reaction, we see a diminution in the amplitude of the orienting response as a function of trials of stimulus presentation. He suggests some possible neurological and neurochemical mechanisms, through which these two different effects may be mediated, but no direct evidence of the presence of these two systems is given. Thus, although his explanation of the habituation phenomenon may be more parsimonious than that presented by Sokolov, the kinds of predictions that can currently be made within the framework of Sokolov's notions seem far more impressive than those made within Stein's framework. For further reviews dealing with the OR the reader is referred to Thompson and Spencer (1966) and Lynn (1966).

MEASURES OF CONDITIONING

It is my conviction that the notion of "the" conditioned response is as indefensible as the notion of "the" orienting response. Although writers like Smith (1954) convinced themselves and others that autonomic CRs are simply reflections of motor CRs and could not occur in the absence of motor responses, the current literature strongly challenges this hypothesis. It is, for example, demonstrable that the time history of development of a motor CR is quite different from the development of a cardiac CR (Dykman, 1965), and that cardiac conditional responses may bear no relationship to motor activity. The excellent series of studies by Notterman, Schoenfeld, and Bersh (1952a, b) are convincing evidence that cardiac decelerative responses can be conditioned in situations in which the UCS produces a marked motor response (as well as an increase in heart rate); exploratory research in my laboratory has convinced me that such cardiac deceleration cannot be interpreted as an artifact of changes in the respiratory pattern. Dykman (1965) reports, "In most dogs 'non-specific motor movements' to the positive CS (e.g., restlessness, looking down at shock electrodes or from side to side, eye opening, ear movements, posturing) appeared earlier in conditioning than the more 'specific' movements of the UCS leg and even before conditioned heart and respiratory changes [p. 265]."

Current interpretations of the relationship between the heart rate and water deprivation in the rat imply, and to a lesser extent demonstrate, that these changes are mediated through conditioning (Ducharme, 1966; Eisman, 1966; Goldstein, Stern, & Rothenberg, 1966). Again, the cardiac effects occur considerably later than the learned motor response. On the basis of the above evidence we are convinced that autonomic conditioning is not or is not necessarily an artifact of motor conditioning. That it is neither an artifact nor as simple a response as implied by some is well demonstrated in a recent series of experiments by Korol, Sletten, and Brown (1966) and Lang, Brown, Gershon, and Korol (1966). These authors demonstrated that a classically conditioned response to injection of an anticholinergic drug (atropine sulfate) occurs (mydriasis) in conjunction with a physiologically conditioned adaptive response (hypersalivation in anticipation of being injected with the drug). The UCR to atropine is mydriasis and the inhibition of salivary flow. Of the two conditioned responses observed by these authors, one was identical to the response produced by the UCS, while the other response was paradoxical, i.e., hypersalivation in response to the expectation of hypersalivation. How Smith (1954) might explain these results as artifacts of motor responses would make interesting reading.

CONDITIONING AND THE ORIENTING RESPONSE

As indicated earlier, one of the problems the experimenter has to face when attempting to condition physiological response systems is the fact that in most systems responses to novel stimuli occur. These responses have been identified as orienting responses (OR). One of the common procedures used in most conditioning studies is to "adapt-out" or habituate the response to the conditional stimulus prior to pairing it with the UCS. This is usually accomplished by presenting the CS for either a fixed number of trials or to a criterion of habituation—such as no OR for three consecutive CS presentations. Since the OR is a response to stimulus novelty, it should really surprise no one that, when the stimulus is changed, such as by pairing it with a UCS, the OR returns. Thus, if one considers the returned OR as a conditional response, it usually appears strongly by the second or third trial of conditioning. It is not apparent on the first trial, since the OR occurs to the onset of a stimulus complex and on the first trial the stimulus to which the subject responds has not as yet changed. However, since the OR demonstrates habituation, the CR wanes in amplitude as a function of the number of reinforced trials. Stewart, Stern, Winokur, and Fredman (1961) presented evidence that the return of this OR should not be considered as a conditional response in a simple classical conditioning paradigm, however, pointing out that there were other responses that could well be considered as CRs. Hilgard and Marquis (1940)

identify the augmentation of an original response to a CS through a conditioning procedure as "sensitization" or "pseudoconditioning." It was the contention of Stewart et al. (1961) that much of the research dealing with electrodermal conditioning described such sensitization phenomena, rather than conditional responses.

Knott and Henry (1941) demonstrated a similar phenomenon with respect to the conditioning of the EEG alpha desynchronization response, results that were apparently forgotten by many investigators studying the conditioning of physiological response systems. For example, Wells and Wolff (1960) conducted a study of conditioned alpha desynchronization of the EEG in which tone was paired with light. After habituating the unconditioned alpha desynchronization response to tone, they paired it with the UCS and described what they refer to as a conditioned alpha desynchronization response to the tone stimulus. Visser (1961, 1963) similarly describes a response labeled as "contingent alpha blocking," which appears to be a returned OR. Stern, Das, Anderson, Biddy, and Surphlis (1961) challenged the interpretation of Wells and Wolff and demonstrated that the conditioned response described by them was a returned OR, which was maximally present during the first five conditioning trials and decreased in incidence as a function of further CS-UCS presentation.

Zimny, Stern, and Fjeld (1966) presented data in a conditioning study involving four different groups of subjects. The conditioning procedure utilized the procedure claimed by many to produce optimal conditioning, namely a half-second ISI (Moeller, 1954; White & Schlosberg, 1952). The CS utilized was a tone, the UCS a shock. The four groups were constituted as follows: Group I, forward conditioning; Group II, backward conditioning; Group III, UCS alone; and Group IV, random presentation of the CS and UCS. Thus Groups I, II, and IV received equal numbers of CS and UCS presentations, while Group III received as many UCS presentations as were true of the other three groups. All groups received 42 acquisition trials with 8 test trials (CS only) interspersed between these conditioning trials. After the last conditioning trial, subjects were administered 4 extinction trials. The results of this study demonstrated that the first group to demonstrate any "conditioning" was the UCS only group. This group, when compared to the backward-conditioning group, demonstrated conditioning on the second test trial, which occurred after the second conditioning trial. The conditioned response was manifested by a greater amplitude response to the CS for the shock only as compared to any of the other groups.

This group, as well as the forward-conditioning group, demonstrates a conditioning effect during subsequent test trials, with the UCS-alone group demonstrating better differentiation from the other groups than was true of the forward-conditioning group. Thus, during conditioning, a group that gets only the CS on test trials demonstrates better "conditioning" than a group presented with CS-UCS pairing in a sequence leading to optimal conditioning. The reason why the UCS-alone group is superior in the demonstration of a CR during this phase of conditioning is probably that with this conditioning paradigm we are unable to discriminate between an OR and a conditional response. The UCS-only group, when presented with the CS on test trials, is giving an OR; while the group that is subjected to the forward-conditioning paradigm is giving conditional responses or a combination of ORs and CRs. One cannot, however, discriminate between these two responses. It is only under conditions of extinction trials (where the CS is presented by itself a number of times in succession) that one can demonstrate what appears to be a conditional effect, even though here the results are not as clear-cut as one would like. Figure 5.1 presents the results of this study. It is apparent that, during extinction trials, the forward-conditioning group demonstrates highest amplitude responses which can best be interpreted as evidence for retention of the CR in this group. This, however, could also be explained by invoking the notion that we are dealing with an OR, since nonpairing of CS with UCS constitutes a novel situation for this group. The same rationale should, however, also hold for the backward-conditioning group, yet we see that this group demonstrates significantly fewer responses than is true of the forward-conditioning group.

I thus cautiously interpret these results as evi-

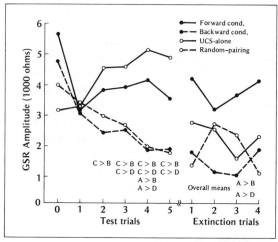

Figure 5.1 EDR amplitude on test and extinction trials for four conditions. Differences indicated are statistically significant: A, forward; B, backward; C, UCS alone; D, random. Redrawn from G. H. Zimny, J. A. Stern, and S. P. Fjeld, Effects of CS and UCS relationships on electrodermal response and heart rates, *Journal of Experimental Psychology*, 1966, **72,** 177–181. By permission.

dence for conditioning in the forward-conditioning group. However, alternate explanations for these results are equally feasible. For example, we could equally well hold that the discrimination observed between the forward- and backward-conditioning groups is due to the fact that the inhibition of the OR for the backward-conditioning group may be a conditional effect, while the greater amplitude responses of the forward-conditioning group can be accounted for by the return of the OR as a function of stimulus discrepancy between conditioning and extinction. As can be seen in Figure 5.1, backward conditioning leads to a relatively rapid suppression of the OR to tone on test trials. We have, in another study utilizing a backward-conditioning group in which the UCS-CS interval was considerably longer than in the present study, observed suppression of the OR to the CS. The interpretation given was that the CS was being presented during the refractory phase of the electrodermal response (Gale & Stern, 1967). If we can assume that in the study by Zimny, Stern, and Fjeld (1966) the CS in the backward-conditioning group was presented during a refractory period, then the suppression of the response to tone on extinction trials may well be a conditioned suppression response. Thus I suspect that one can, through conditioning procedures, suppress ORs, although the evidence for this conviction is far from unequivocal.

The analysis of EDR classical conditioning proposed by Stewart et al. (1961), has, of course, not gone unchallenged. Kimmel (1964), and Lockhart and Grings (1964), for example, have taken exception to some of the interpretations made in that paper. Their argument is not with respect to the return of the OR when a stimulus is changed, but rather concerns the definition of the conditional response. I shall return to these two papers in a subsequent portion of this chapter.

It is important to reiterate, in studies dealing with the classical conditioning of physiological response systems, that one must be careful not to confuse the return of an OR with a conditional response. This, of course, does not imply that the OR cannot be conditioned; however, under many experimental conditions one cannot discriminate between the return of an OR and a conditional response. What then are the types of responses that can be conditioned? Let us enumerate them here and then systematically explore the evidence for such responses: generalized conditional responses, conditional ORs, conditional anticipatory responses (CARs), and responses at the latency of the UCR when that stimulus is omitted on test or extinction trials (CR).

TYPES OF CONDITIONAL RESPONSE

Generalized Conditional Responses

The first response I am willing to accept as evidence for conditioning is a sensitized response to an experimental situation. These have elsewhere been referred to as generalized conditioned responses. These responses can be demonstrated in lower animals as well as man. One experiment involving cardiac conditioning in the rat will be used to describe this type of conditioning. Pavlov,

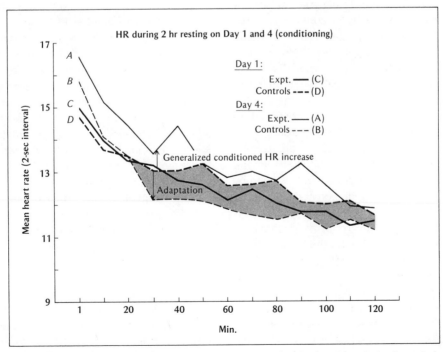

Figure 5.2 Mean HR adaptation (beats per 2-sec interval) as a function of 10-min periods during the 2-hr rest prior to conditioning, showing the development of a conditioned generalized HR increase over days. Redrawn from F. Fehr and J. A. Stern, Heart rate conditioning in the rat, *Journal of Psychosomatic Research*, 1965, **8**, 441–453. By permission.

of course, had described such sensitized responses in his work on experimental neurosis in the dog, and Liddell (1965, pp. 127–148) in sheep and goats. Anyone who has run rats in mazes with guillotine doors has observed such sensitized responses in animals whose tails were accidentally pinched by the guillotine door's descending behind them. Such animals demonstrate aversive behavior in the maze, and it takes a large number of trials to extinguish such aversive and generalized responses to the experimental situation.

These examples are all incidental observations occasioned by accidental or fortuitous conditioning or, in the case of experimental neuroses, the attempt at training animals to make discriminations apparently beyond their ability or by the application of "experimentally controlled stress" (Liddell, 1965, p. 131).

Let us briefly review an experiment in which a conditioned sensitized response could be clearly demonstrated (Fehr & Stern, 1965). These authors classically conditioned rats by pairing tone with unescapable shock, administering 50 trials per day for 5 days. Prior to each day of conditioning, the animals were placed into the conditioning apparatus 2 hr before the initiation of conditioning trials. The heart rate was periodically recorded during this 2-hr period. Two groups of animals were run in this situation, one group exposed only to the CS, the control group; and a second group exposed to tone-shock pairing, the conditioning group. Heart rate (HR) changes during the 2-hr preconditioning period, of course, did not discriminate between the two groups on Day 1 of conditioning. However, by Day 4 the control group demonstrated a more marked drop in HR during the 2-hr period than was true for the experimental group. As depicted in Figure 5.2, we see that the HR for the control group demonstrates a greater, as well as a more rapid, decrease over time on Day 4 as compared to Day 1, while the experimental group actually demonstrates an increase in HR when we compare Day 4 with Day 1. No sensitization group was run in this experiment (a group that received an equal number of non-temporally chained CS and UCS presentations). I believe that, as far as the generalized conditioned heart rate is concerned, such a group would have demonstrated as good conditioning on this measure as was true of our experimental group.

Korol, Sletten, and Brown (1966), in a recent series of studies in the dog, demonstrated a similar phenomenon with respect to salivary output. Dogs were placed into a Pavlovian conditioning camera and were daily injected with atropine, a drug that produces a marked inhibition of salivation. After a number of such experiences these dogs demonstrated a marked increase in salivary output when placed into the conditioning apparatus and prior to being injected with atropine; this response was restricted to the room in which injections were administered. Corson et al. (1962), again studying the dog, found that animals developed generalized conditional antidiuretic hormone secretory responses to being brought into the experimental room and being placed into the camera. That the response was localized to the experimental situation was tested by placing the animals into a similar apparatus in a room quite different from the room in which they were trained. In this situation they did not demonstrate the response.

Do such generalized conditional responses occur in man? At an anecdotal level we can find many examples of such responses, although experimentally they seem not to have been investigated as thoroughly, unless one casts the above results into a stimulus-generalization paradigm. The stimulus-generalization paradigm suggests that responses learned to a given stimulus will generalize to stimuli similar to the original stimulus, and in some situations to stimuli that are present when conditioning takes place. Thus, in the above examples the organism does not only become conditioned to the specific stimuli to which an experimenter is attempting to condition it, but also becomes conditioned to other stimuli present in the experimental situation.

M. C. Jones (1924), in a study quoted by most behavior therapists of the Wolpian school (Wolpe, 1958), demonstrated the generalization of a fear response from a toy rabbit both to other stimuli in the environment when the fear was established and to objects similar to the toy rabbit. What of course is most important to the behavior therapist is that these responses can be extinguished or replaced by more adequate responses. Thus today we see a resurgence and acceptance of classical conditioning techniques in psychotherapy. All of these techniques are based on the assumption that maladaptive or neurotic behavior was established through conditioning and that by utilizing such procedures we can get rid of undesirable behavior. Most work by behavior therapists is restricted to more narrowly conditioned responses than those being discussed here, which have been successfully extinguished or replaced by other responses. The generalized CR is, however, much more difficult for the behavior therapist to cope with, since the patient cannot identify the stimuli that bring on the CR. Thus pervasive anxieties and panic reactions are the most difficult to treat with behavior therapy (Lazarus, 1963), although Cautela (1966) reports success with a modified behavior therapy approach.

According to Wolpe (1958), the two conditions leading to the greatest degree of generalized fear responses are those in which a high level of anxiety is produced by a specific set of environmental stimuli; but, because of the intensity of anxiety, other stimuli in the environment acquire the property to elicit the anxiety response. A second condition suggested by him is that, at the time of establishment of the conditional response, environmental stimuli are poorly defined (i.e., only dimly visible), so that the CR through contiguity becomes associated with a wider array of stimuli than is true when the CS-UCS relationship can be well defined. Thus both parameters of the CS, as well as the UCS, appear to be important in determining whether generalized CRs will develop. Another parameter undoubtedly is the state of the organism, both genetic as well as situationally determined. Thus the conditioning of anxiety responses occurs much more poorly in relaxed than excited subjects, and this is one characteristic that behavior therapists capitalize on in the reduction of anxiety and other maladaptive responses in their therapeutic practice.

We find then that such generalized responses do occur in man and that, according to behavior therapists, such responses are the types of responses often associated with neurotic or maladaptive behavior. Factors that lead to their development in man inhere in the subject (genetic, motivation, arousal) in the intensity of the UCS, as well as the specificity of the CS (as identifiable by the subject being conditioned).

Edwards and Acker (1962) describe the long-term retention of a classically conditioned electrodermal response that would fit into the category of generalized CRs. Two groups of World War II veterans were selected, half of whom had seen service in the United States Navy and served aboard ship during combat conditions; the other half were Army veterans. Tests for retention of a CR developed during World War II consisted of the response to the GQ (general quarters) signal, as compared to other auditory stimuli. These tests were made 15–20 years after active service and discriminated between the two groups. This response can be considered as a generalized CR since it (a) generalized to situations markedly different from that in which the conditioning had occurred, and (b) was maintained over a long period of time.

The Conditional Orienting Response

This response can best be discriminated in a differential classical conditioning paradigm and will be illustrated from a study by Gale and Stern (1967). In a differential conditioning paradigm two CSs are used; one of these is reinforced with a UCS, while the second one is not so reinforced. These two CSs are referred to as the CS+ and CS−, respectively. In the Gale and Stern study, both of the CSs were tones; which of the two tones was reinforced was counterbalanced across subjects, so that half the subjects received Tone 1 in conjunction with the UCS, while the other half received Tone 2 in conjunction with the UCS. In order to discriminate between ORs and other possible responses in this type of conditioning, we utilized a long CS-UCS interval (7.8 sec). If the OR to the reinforced CS adapts at a slower rate, or actually increases in amplitude as a function of CS-UCS pairing as compared to the amplitude of the OR to the CS, one can talk about a conditional orienting response. For some authors a slower decrease in amplitude of the OR to the CS+ would not be acceptable as a CR and would be interpreted as a sensitized response. It is my conviction, which is shared by Dykman

(1965), that such *selectively* sensitized responses should be considered as conditional response. Prokasy and Ebel (1964) are apparently also willing to talk about CRs if response magnitude (OR) is maintained at a stable level, while that for a sensitization control group decreases. Although no control groups are really necessary to demonstrate the development of the conditional OR, since the subject essentially acts as his own control, the present study utilized a number of control groups, including a backward conditioning, as well as random CS-UCS presentation groups. The measure of conditioning utilized was the difference in amplitude of the OR to the CS+ and the CS−. It can be readily seen from Figure 5.3 (Gale & Stern, 1967) that the OR was conditioned in the forward-conditioning group; the difference in OR amplitude for the two control groups fluctuated around zero; while for the backward-conditioning group, the CS+ group demonstrated a significantly lower amplitude OR than was true of the two control groups.

According to Sokolov (1963a), such conditioning of the OR may explain the enhancement of the OR to verbal instructions. The reasonably well accepted finding that emotional stimuli produce larger electrodermal ORs (EDORs) than neutral stimuli may thus also be an example of conditioned ORs. For example, in a study by Gross and Stern (1966) involving the elaboration of EDORs to a word association task in patients hospitalized for alcoholism, it was found that the word "drink" (one that had been utilized as a neutral stimulus in studies with college students, as well as schizophrenic patients) produced markedly augmented ORs as compared to other neutral or emotion-arousing words in the list or as compared to the amplitude of ORs to the word "drink" in nonalcoholic subjects. Since I am unwilling to believe that these alcoholic subjects were born with a differential responsiveness to the word "drink" when compared to other words or the performance of nonalcoholic subjects, I assume that the response is a learned one. How such learn-

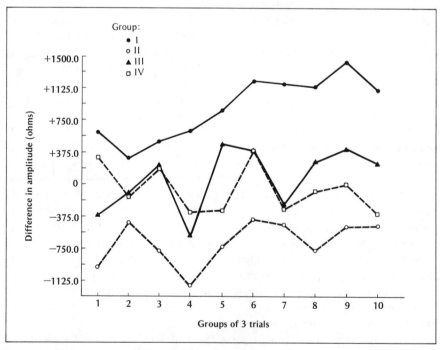

Figure 5.3 Difference in amplitude between reinforced and nonreinforced stimulus. Group I: forward conditioning; Group II: backward conditioning; Group III: sensitization control; and Group IV: sensitization control. Redrawn from E. Gale and J. A. Stern, Conditioning of the electrodermal orienting response, *Psychophysiology*, 1967, **3**, 291–301. By permission.

ing may occur is exemplified in the literature dealing with semantic conditioning.

Razran (1949) and Riess (1940, 1946) demonstrated the effectiveness of such semantic conditioning, and how conditioned responses generalize to words either similar in sound or meaning to the CS. Riess (1946) conditioned electrodermal responses to selected words in four groups of subjects ranging in age from 7 to 18 years. The UCS was a moderately loud buzzer that was sounded in conjunction with words to be reinforced, while nonreinforced words were presented alone. After conditioning, tests were run for transfer of the CR to synonyms, antonyms, and homonyms of the words previously conditioned. His results clearly indicate a conditioning effect, in that the reinforced word produced greater amplitude responses on nonreinforced trial than was true of the nonreinforced words. In addition, he found that young subjects gave greater amplitude responses to homonyms (words that sounded like the reinforced word), while older subjects gave greater amplitude responses to synonyms (words similar in meaning to the CS). Thus, in man, symbols cannot only become conditioned to unconditional stimuli but such conditioning generalizes in a predictable manner to other symbols. It is my contention that these studies deal with the conditioning of an OR to the stimulus word, since the latency of the electrodermal OR is tightly time locked to the onset of the stimulus word. It is not that the subject hears the stimulus word, "consciously" reflects on the similarity of the stimulus word and the word to which the conditional response has been elaborated, and then gives an electrodermal response, but that the association between the two stimuli is done so rapidly that the latency of the electrodermal response to the two stimulus words (CR and test for generalization word) cannot be differentiated.

Razran's work in this area deals principally with salivary conditioning and utilizes a technique of measuring salivary flow that is too crude to allow for the discrimination of ORs from other conditional responses. The technique utilizes the placement of dental rolls in the subject's mouth for specific periods of time and the measuring of salivary output by pre- and postweighing of the pledg-

ets. With this technique he was able to demonstrate that generalization in adults is greater to synonyms than homonyms and could be demonstrated for concepts as well as words. For example, generalization is good when the sentence to which salivation is conditioned is "poverty is degrading" and tested with the sentence "wealth is uplifting," and poor when the test sentence is the negative of the initial sentence, "poverty is not degrading." Razran (1961) reviews a large Russian literature dealing with semantic conditioning to which the reader interested in this problem is referred.

A study dealing with the extinction of a salivary conditioned response was conducted by Stern, Schwarz, and Gospodinoff (1966). With a group of alcoholic patients they used the Razran dental pledget technique to assess salivary output under conditions of rest, in response to instructions that they would be given a drink of lemon juice, and in actual response to lemon juice. This experiment was conducted daily for a 5-day period. In this group of patients salivary responses to instructions appear to have been generalized from past experience. On Day 1 of the study the patients gave a significantly larger salivary response to the instruction than to the rest condition. The response to instruction demonstrated a decrease over the 5-day period, while the response to both the rest and lemon juice condition remained stable over the period.

Sokolov (1963b) identifies another type of conditioned OR that is elaborated when two "nonsignal" stimuli are paired. The first stimulus is a tone of low intensity, followed after some seconds by a more intense tone stimulus. "It has been found that a weak stimulus reinforced by a strong one occasionally gives rise to a more persistent orienting reaction than the latter alone." Sokolov used a 1000-Hz tone presented at 70 and 90 dB above threshold. When the response to the weak sound had been extinguished, reinforcement with the louder sound produced an OR coupled with onset of the louder stimulus and disinhibition of the OR to the subsequently applied weak sound. With further pairing of the two stimuli, Sokolov observed a weakening of the OR to the intense sound (habituation of OR) and an intensification of the response to the weak sound (development of the conditioned OR). With further repetition of the stimulus complex, both of these ORs disappeared.

Thus this type of conditioned response demonstrates many of the attributes generally associated with conditioning. It differs from other classically conditioned responses in that the response builds up early in conditioning and then, as a function of further trials, disappears (Anokhin, 1965). Whether this disappearance of the response is a function of "conditioned inhibition" or whether it is truly extinguished cannot be answered at the present time.

That one must be extremely careful in defining what is and what is not a conditional response when one utilizes short ISI is well demonstrated in a study by Zimny and Miller (1966). Although their study does not deal with conditioning, but with habituation of ORs, it nicely demonstrates that a sensitization control group which only receives the CS on test trials produces more extreme vasoconstrictive ORs than is true of the response to two unconditional stimuli, hot and cold. Subjects were presented with 28 trials of either heat or cold stimulation of the forearm. The plethysmographic response was recorded from the middle finger of the right hand. Three test trials, consisting of tone stimulation, were interspersed between the 8–9th, 16–17th, and 24–25th trial of either heat or cold stimulation. The vasoconstrictive responses to the tone stimuli were consistently of greater amplitude than the responses to either heat or cold stimulation. If one compared the amplitude of the OR to the tone stimuli interspersed between heat or cold stimuli, to the amplitude of response to tone stimuli that had been paired with either heat or cold, and identified these responses as conditional responses, one would find that the response for the pseudo-conditioned or sensitization group would be greater than the response for the conditioned group.

Prokasy and Ebel (1964), studying electrodermal conditioning with a 0.5-sec ISI and 40 conditioning trials (75% reinforcement schedule), followed by 10 extinction trials, utilized a sensitization control group that received 40 trials of shock and 10 trials of CS presentation. These authors report that "with short ITIs (20 versus 40 sec), sensitization and conditioning performances were not distinct during early acquisition trials, but emerged as distinct mainly because response magnitude *decreased* across trials in the sensitization groups. There was, therefore, no evidence of the acquisition function (i.e., gradually increasing strength as a function of specific CS-UCS pairings) typically found with other classically conditioned response systems [p. 119]." Thus what appears to happen is that the difference between the conditioned and sensitized groups is a function more of habituation of the OR to the CS in the sensitized group than it is attributable to an increase in response amplitude of the conditioned group. Had these authors given fewer "test" trials, they might not have found any difference between the two groups. Prokasy, Fawcett, and Hall (1962) utilized a 0.5-sec ISI, with a 100% conditioning schedule; they found that, when 10 extinction trials were given, the conditioning group did not differ from a shock-only pseudoconditioning group. The authors conclude, "These results suggest that care must be exercised in the interpretation of GSR data, particularly with respect to inferences concerned with the specific pairing of CS and UCS [p. 106]."

In simple classical conditioning utilizing short ISIs, one must be extremely careful in designing one's experiment so that one can discriminate between ORs and conditional response. A paradigm utilizing a partial reinforcement schedule appears to be better than one utilizing a 100% schedule, since it allows for at least partial habituation of the OR in the sensitization group.

A paradigm utilizing a long ISI seems to be a promising way of identifying and discriminating between OR and other types of responses. The electrodermal system is a rather sluggish system with respect to the time interval between onset of a stimulus and the OR; latencies generally are greater than 1.5 sec, even with a relatively intense stimulus. An OR to tone in the audible and not unpleasant intensity range usually is accompanied by latencies of between 2 and 2.5 sec, with the latencies becoming somewhat longer as a function of habituation to the stimulus. Thus, when one utilizes a short ISI, it becomes impossible to discriminate between the OR to the CS and the OR or DR to the UCS. The most obvious solution to this problem is to use a longer CS-UCS interval.

Why has the half-second ISI been the interval most commonly employed in the conditioning of physiological measures? As Hilgard (1951) points out, "although for phasic responses, like finger withdrawal or eyelid reactions, the most favorable stimulus interval appears to be about half a second between conditioned and unconditioned stimulus . . . , it is quite possible that smooth muscle responses may call for longer intervals. The practice in conditioning salivation, galvanic skin responses, and pupillary reactions has been to use somewhat longer intervals, but the critical experiments on time intervals have not been done [p. 527]." Studies by Moeller (1954) and by White and Schlosberg (1952), indicated that the optimum interval between CS and UCS is at about 0.5 sec. However, more recent studies present evidence that conditioning with longer ISIs is not as impossible as the above authors had suggested. Thus Grings, Lockhart, and Dameron (1962), Kimmel (1963), Bridger and Lopez (1964), Fuhrer and Baer (1965), McDonald and Johnson (1965), Prescott (1965), are just a few of the authors who report conditioning of electrodermal and other physiological responses with ISIs longer than 0.5 sec. According to White and Schlosberg (1952), no conditioning is supposed to take place with ISIs greater than 2 sec, although Switzer (1934), as well as Rodnick (1937), demonstrated that electrodermal conditioning utilizing both delayed and trace conditioning procedures was possible with delay periods in excess of 20 sec. Of course, the Pavlovian literature dealing with the classical conditioning of salivary responses also suggests that conditioning can take place with longer than 0.5 sec ISIs.

I agree with Grings, Lockhart, and Dameron (1962), who suggest that the ready acceptance of the 0.5-sec ISI as the optimal interval for the conditioning of electrodermal responses occurred because these results fitted in well with the data of eyeblink conditioning, in addition to other motor responses. J. E. Jones (1962) reviews the literature on ISIs and comes to the conclusion that "actually there is less agreement in the literature on optimum intervals than the usual textbook statement implies." That the 0.5-sec ISI is not necessarily the optimal interval, even in eyeblink conditioning, is demonstrated in a study by Hartman and Grant (1962). Apparently, the 0.5-sec ISI may be optimal for simple classical conditioning but far from optimal when a differential conditioning paradigm is employed. Here is another example of the problems of overgeneralizing from restricted data, as well as the implicit assumption that there is such a thing as "the" conditioned response.

The Anticipatory Conditional Response (CAR)

If we allow longer ISIs between the onset of the CS and UCS, we find that a variety of responses can be observed between the onset of the CS and the UCS. Utilizing a 5-sec ISI, Grings, Lockhart, and Dameron (1962) could identify two basic types of responses and variations of these responses. If a response occurred during the 5-sec CS interval, it was identified as a Type A or "first interval response"; a response that started during the 5-sec period following CS termination was identified as a Type D or "second interval response." Variants of these two types of responses were identified as B and C. Both the B and the C response incorporate the A and D response; for the B response the first interval response is larger than the second, while for the C response the second interval response is larger than the first. A fifth type of response, Type E, was identified, which consisted of a trimodal response with a second response interpolated between the first and second interval response. Prokasy and Ebel (1965), using an 8-sec CS-UCS interval, identify three different responses, one early during the presentation of the CS, their "first response," one toward the latter portion of the CS presentation identified as the "second response," and a "third response" that occurs on nonreinforced trials after termination of the CS.

Stern, Stewart, and Winokur (1961) identified three different responses in their conditioning experiments utilizing a 7.5-sec ISI. They identified these responses as, first, the orienting response to the CS; the second response was identified as an "anticipatory response," and a third response on extinction trials as a "response to shock in the absence of shock." Lockhart (1966) labeled these responses as "multiple response phenomena" and they were identified by him with respect to where in the CS-UCS interval they occur. He feels that prejudging these various responses by labeling them as specifically as Stewart, Stern, and Fredman (1961) have done is rather premature. The first response identified by Lockhart is the "CS response," which occurs at the latency of the response to the CS prior to reinforcement. His second response is the "pre-US response," defined as any response(s) occurring in the interval 1.0–4.0 sec after the time of US onset on trials when the US is not presented. It is my belief, as well as Lockhart's, that the "first interval response," identified by Grings, Lockhart, and Dameron (1962), as well as by Prokasy and Ebel (1965), is identical to the OR to the CS identified by Stern, Stewart, and Winokur (1961). I also believe that the second interval response of Grings and his coworkers and Prokasy and Ebel's third interval response, are identical to the response I identify as the response to the UCS in the absence of that stimulus (UCS). Identifying responses as first interval, second interval, etc., responses will be quite confusing; e.g., there is no relationship between the second interval response of Grings et al. and Prokasy and Ebel's second interval response, since for the former the response follows termination of the CS, while for the latter it is the period immediately preceding termination of the CS. Although my labels (conditional orienting response, conditioned anticipatory response, and conditioned response at the latency of the UCS) may have excess meaning and not truly reflect the character of the response, I shall utilize them further in this chapter to describe some of the responses that can become conditional.

Stern, Stewart, and Winokur (1961), in a study dealing with the interrelationships between various measures of electrodermal responses, utilized a conditioning procedure to elaborate such responses. Their experiment consisted of the presentation of a series of tone trials (500 Hz, 65 dB), then a conditioning period during which the CS was presented for 6.5 sec, followed 1 sec after termination of the tone by the UCS (electric shock). The experiment was terminated with a series of extinction trials. The measures of conditioning utilized both in this and a later study (Stern, Winokur, Stewart, & Leonard, 1963), were: (a) response to tone on reinforced trials (OR); (b) anticipatory responses (CAR), defined as having to be of an amplitude greater than 500 ohms and having to occur

outside of the range of the OR to the tone and earlier than the UCR to shock; and (c) response to shock on nonreinforced trials, this response also having to be of an amplitude greater than 500 ohms and having to occur within the range of latencies of the UCR to shock (CRs).

The CAR in the first of these two studies developed during approximately the first 10 conditioning trials and then appeared to decay as a function of further reinforced trials. In the second study the CAR developed more precipitously, reaching peak of responsiveness after 6 trials, but decayed at a much slower rate than in the first study. In a study by McDonald and Johnson (1965), the CAR developed somewhat more slowly and persisted throughout the remainder of the conditioning trials. Lockhart and Grings (1964), questioned whether the CAR as defined and utilized by Stern et al. (1963) is really an anticipatory response or whether it might not be a sensitized response. If they include under the label of "sensitized" responses an increase in the incidence of SFs, I might well agree with them, since my anticipatory responses, unlike those reported by Kimmel, do not become localized in time to the period immediately preceding the onset of the UCS. Rather, my CARs occurred relatively randomly through the CS-UCS interval; thus I am willing to interpret these responses as an increase in SFs as a function of conditioning, rather than as truly anticipatory responses. In order for a response to be identified as truly anticipatory according to Pavlovian theory and the results of some other investigators (Kimmel, 1964; 1965), it should become time locked to the period immediately preceding the UCS. Thus we can identify two different anticipatory responses that can become conditioned in either a delay or trace conditioning procedure when relatively long ISIs are utilized. The first of these is a sensitized response, which we refer to as an increase in incidence of SFs during the ISI, and which occurs randomly during this interval. The second response is the CAR that becomes temporally localized to the period immediately preceding the UCS.

Kimmel (1964, 1965) presents data demonstrating that the CR latency increases as a function of the number of acquisition trials. One might question his conclusions and graphic presentations demonstrating a clear linear relationship between latency and acquisition trials (i.e., the response moves closer in time to the onset of the UCS as a function of reinforced trials) on the basis of his assigning maximum latency scores to trials on which subjects demonstrated no response. As a function of onset OR habituation one would expect that the early latency responses would drop out. Since they drop out at different rates across subjects and since he assigns an arbitrary value of 9 sec to nonresponse trials, the curve presented may well tell us more about habituation of onset ORs than it does about conditioned anticipatory responses. One cannot utilize this objection in discussing a second figure presented in the 1965 paper in which Kimmel omitted trials on which subjects did not respond. This curve demonstrates a relatively linear increase in latencies (although nowhere nearly as clear as in the earlier figure) as a function of trials, but unfortunately the final latency obtained (approximately 4.0 sec) is far removed from the onset of the UCS, which occurs 7.5 sec after CS onset. Kimmel concludes, "On the basis of the data shown in Figures 8.1 and 8.2 the conclusion appears justified that the latent period of the conditioned GSR [the latency as defined above] grows steadily throughout training of the sort involved in this experiment, in a way which supports the contention that inhibition of delay was operating. These data also strongly refute the assertion made recently by Stewart, Stern, and Fredman (1961) that the 'first' deflection following the CS is not a true CR but is a sensitized original response to the CS, an assertion based largely on the inability of those investigators to obtain changes in the latency of the "first" deflection in their sample of 19 Ss [p. 154]." Kimmel obviously adheres to the notion of the unitary nature of the CR and interprets his data accordingly.

In support of Kimmel's contention are the results of Switzer (1934) and Rodnick (1937), who, utilizing a trace conditioning procedure, demonstrated that the latency of the CR increased gradually with progressive trials. Kimmel (1963), however, also presents some data contrary to his later convictions. In an EDR conditioning study utilizing a 7.9-sec CS-UCS ISI, he finds, "GSR appears as a drop in skin resistance which lasts throughout the entire CS-UCS interval in the early training trials but in

the later conditioning trials, a tendency to recover from the drop is noticeable in the middle of the CS-UCS interval and another drop occurs near the end of the interval [p. 314]."

Those who are able to see multiple responses, rather than unitary responses that become localized in time in conditioning situations similar to those used by Kimmel (1963) and by Stewart, Stern, and Fredman (1961), appear to be increasing. Thus Grings, Lockhart, and Dameron (1962), Fromer (1963), Kimmel (1963), Martin (1963), Ellison (1964), Lockhart and Grings (1964), and Smith and Stebbins (1965) are but a few authors who are able to identify multiple responses in their conditioning records. Grings, Lockhart, and Dameron (1962), for example, point out, "It is probable that first and second interval responses are different kinds of CR's and will therefore be given separate consideration [in this paper] [p. 8]."

Not all of these authors are able to identify the development of conditioned responses in a delay or trace conditioning paradigm. Martin (1963a, 1963b), utilizing a 12-sec CS-UCS interval with a light CS and a loud tone UCS, demonstrated habituation of short latency EDRs (1.5–4 sec poststimulus onset), but no consistent pattern of change of later responses (those measured between 4–8 sec and 8–12.5 sec after CS onset). Martin, on the basis of these two studies, concludes, "The data provide little evidence for delayed conditioning, inasmuch as GSR's in the delayed CS-UCS interval show no increase in latency, and the increase in response frequency of long-latency GSR's over acquisition trials is slight [p. 366]." Whether Kimmel's interpretation or the multiple response interpretation of conditioning will persist can only be determined by further research, rather than by polemics.

I shall describe in some detail the study by Grings, Lockhart, and Dameron (1962), since it illustrates a number of points made earlier. These authors utilized a differential conditioning paradigm, in which the CS+ and CS− were tone or light. Two groups of subjects were conditioned (UCS shock): one utilizing a short (0.5 sec), the other a long (5 sec) ISI. Conditioning involved the presentation of the CS+ and CS− each for the 40 trials with 60% of the CS+ trials reinforced. All of their subjects were institutionalized for subnormal intelligence, and the groups were divided into a higher and lower IQ group.

With respect to the question of whether a 0.5-sec interval leads to better conditioning than a 5-sec interval, these authors conclude that, "The present study indicates that many past assertions concerning the efficacy of short versus long CS-UCS intervals may be based on the erroneous presupposition that a single CR definition is applicable at all points on the CS-UCS interval continuum. As demonstrated here, short interval conditioning leads to a definition of CR which is different from the definition demanded by long interval conditioning [p. 27]." The authors suggest that the differences in results between their study and those that have found no conditioning with ISIs longer than 2–3 sec may be a function of differences in conditioning procedures used. Other studies utilized group methods to control for sensitization and pseudoconditioning effects, while their study utilized a discrimination paradigm. They, as well as Lockhart (1966) and Prescott (1965), come to the conclusion that the discrimination conditioning paradigm is a more sensitive procedure for the elaboration of CRs than simple conditioning paradigms. I heartily concur in this opinion.

Let us now turn to the anticipatory CRs in their study. Although not so identified by them, we should classify their Type E or trimodal response as one including a CAR. Type E responses on nonreinforced CS+ trials were given by 7 of their 20 subjects. Six of these subjects also gave such responses to CS− trials. All of them, however, gave more such responses to the CS+ than to the CS− stimulus, suggesting that a discriminatory response probably did evolve as a function of successive conditioning trials. Another way of discriminating between ORs and CARs in this study is with respect to response latencies. First interval response latencies during conditioning tended to be somewhat longer than such responses in prior habituation trials and demonstrated an increase as a function of conditioning trials. Thus my interpretation of their results suggests that conditioned anticipatory responses are discriminable from conditioned orienting responses.

Whether this CAR evolves, as Kimmel (1965) suggests, through "inhibition of delay," i.e., the latency shifting in a relatively regular fashion from the short to the longer latency, or whether it is a function of the concurrent extinction of a conditioned OR to stimulus onset and the development of a CAR cannot, with assurance, be determined from their data. Grings, Lockhart, and Dameron, however, argue against such an interpretation, "First, there was no significant evidence of inhibition of delay in the present study. The first latency response continued to be elicited during the action of CS and showed little tendency to move closer in time to the UCS [p. 30]."

The Unconditioned Response in the Absence of Unconditioned Stimulus: A Conditional Response

Let us continue with the study by Grings, Lockhart, and Dameron, in which their Types B, C, D, and E response all include what we interpret as CRs. These are responses on nonreinforced trials that occur at the latency of the UCR.

In the studies reviewed in which such a response could be identified, a confounding factor emerges. As indicated before, whenever a stimulus complex is altered, one can observe the return of an OR. With a relatively long stimulus (5 sec or longer) one often observes ORs not only to the onset but to the termination of the stimulus as well. The OR at its most primitive level is a response to a change in stimulation. Termination of a stimulus is thus as much of a change as stimulus onset. However, the OR to stimulus termination generally habituates more rapidly than the OR to stimulus onset, indicating that the OR becomes a response to a stimulus complex, rather than a stimulus change (a somewhat more sophisticated response). One of the factors affecting the speed of habituation of the terminal OR is stimulus length, the longer the stimulus the slower the habituation of this response. Thus with a long CS-UCS interval, when test trials or extinction trials are presented, the response seen at the termination of the CS may either be a conditional response (CR) or the return of the terminal OR. A number of solutions to this problem are possible. The simplest one would be to utilize an even longer CS period (say 15 sec) and present the UCS after 8 sec of CS presentation for 0.5 sec. Under these conditions one can more readily discriminate between the CR and the OR to stimulus termination. A second procedure would use a trace conditioning paradigm in which the UCS is presented some time (say 5 sec) after termination of the CS. This, too, would allow for the discrimination of the CR and the OR to stimulus termination. A variant of the first procedure described above has been utilized by Lockhart and Grings (1964) and will be discussed later.

The response referred to by us as the CR is the second interval CR seen by Grings, Lockhart, and Dameron. That this interpretation is reasonable is attested to by comparing the latency of the UCR with the latency of the second interval response. The authors generally found that the latency of this CR is similar to the latency of the UCR and conclude, "These results point to the conclusion that, in general, no difference exists between CR and UCR latency in terms of second interval responding." That we are probably not dealing with an OR to stimulus termination but a conditional response is suggested by the finding that the latencies presented are generally shorter than those found for tone stimulation, either onset or termination. Their results indicate rather rapid conditioning of this response, in that it is observed in its full glory after 4 test trials (after 10 trials of each CS+ and CS− presentation) and is maintained throughout conditioning.

Lockhart and Grings (1964) essentially replicated the above study but used college students rather than mentally defective children as subjects. The only differences between the studies were (a) the inclusion of a third experimental group that received a 5-sec CS with a 0.5 sec shock occurring after 0.5 sec of CS presentation; (b) the fact that only 20 CS+ and 20 CS− conditioning trials were used in the study with college students; and (c) the fact that the college students were permitted to determine shock level to be used in the experiment (mentally defective subjects were unable to do this). The only difference in conditioning found between the two experiments was that the first interval CR increased as a function of the number of reinforcements in the defective group, while for the college students this response appeared early in conditioning and persisted throughout conditioning. With respect to the second interval response the two groups could not be discriminated, in that second interval response discrimination occurred at the same point in acquisition for both groups. The authors interpret their findings as suggesting (a) that second interval response discrimination represents a more basic process in classical conditioning, while (b) the first interval response may be modified by verbal perceptual factors. The authors hypothesize that, "While the GSR behavior of the mental defective represented a conditioned discrimination in the usual sense, GSR behavior of the college S's represented more nearly a response to an immediately developing perception of stimulus relations. More simply, the mental defectives attained 'perception through conditioning' (Razran, 1955), while the college S's showed conditioning-like behavior 'through perception' [p. 214]."

The conditioned discrimination (CR) referred to above is not, or need not be, a discrimination of which the subject is necessarily aware. Thus Bykov (1959) presents data dealing with interoceptive conditioning, the conditioning of internal organs that one would suspect more often than not occurs in the absence of the subject's perception of what is going on internally. In any case, there is a wealth of data suggesting that the subject's perception of his internal state may bear little relationship to internal events.

That perception can affect the CR is well demonstrated in a series of experiments by Bridger and Lopez (1964) and Bridger and Mandel (1964, 1965). These authors used a discrimination conditioning paradigm in which the CS was one of four different colored lights (Bridger & Mandel, 1964, 1965), or one of four different words (Bridger & Lopez, 1964), with a 4-sec CS-UCS interval in the latter and a 0.5 sec CS-UCS interval in the former studies. Upon termination of the conditioning series, subjects were either informed or not informed that they would receive no more shocks. In all studies extinction was more rapid in the informed than uninformed groups, suggesting that a perceptual component may well affect even this type of CR. Their data suggest that the perceptual component does not affect the speed of extinction per se, since the slope of the extinction curves for the informed and uninformed groups appear to parallel each other. Wishner

(1962) and Wishner, Peastrel, and Fishbein (1964) have demonstrated that instructions affect conditionability (of the EDR) and interact with motivational factors. Rate of conditioning is demonstrated by these authors to be a function of the interaction between motivational and task requirements. Berger (1962) also implicated the effect of instructions on electrodermal conditioning. Grings (1960) reviewed the literature dealing with preparatory set variables as they relate to classical conditioning of autonomic responses and discriminates between conditioning with perception and conditioning without perception.

These results are not unique to electrodermal conditioning but have been reported for cardiac conditioning (Notterman, Schoenfeld, & Bersh, 1952a), and more recently in studies involving eyelid conditioning as well (Spence & Spence, 1966). The study by Notterman, Schoenfeld, and Bersh is of interest in that extinction was carried out under three different instructions. The first group was not informed that no further shocks would be given; a second group was informed that they would receive no more shocks; and a third group was informed that, if they tapped a telegraph key to the onset of the CS, and tapped it "as soon as you hear the tone," they would not receive a shock. Conditioning was done under a partial reinforcement schedule, utilizing a trace conditioning paradigm. The response measured was the heart rate immediately preceding the UCS (last two sets of interbeat intervals). Whether the response we are dealing with here is a CAR or CR is debatable. If it is an anticipatory response, it is remarkably tightly time locked to the UCS, more closely time locked than we believe possible with the limited number of conditioning trials utilized. There is, however, also doubt about its being the CR, since the unconditioned response to shock is cardiac acceleration, while the CR reported by these authors was cardiac deceleration. In any case, extinction was affected not only by giving the subject a perceptual set (informing him that no more shocks would be given) but even more so by giving him a perceptual motor set, (informing him that whether he would not get shocked was under his control). Slowest extinction was under the no-information condition. The instructed versus noninstructed groups differed significantly from each

other after five extinction trials; the noninstructed versus instructed-avoidance group comparison resulted in significant differentiation between the two groups during the first five extinction trials, with similar results when the instructed group was compared to the instructed-avoidance group.

The studies involving eyelid conditioning have similarly reported effects of instruction, not only on the speed of extinction (Hartman & Grant, 1962; Spence, Honzie, & Rutledge, 1964; Spence & Spence, 1966), but on the speed of acquisition of CRs as well. All of these studies, however, deal with the conditioning of an anticipatory response. Grant (1939) demonstrated that an active, attentive attitude toward the CS produced more rapid conditioning than instructions that were passive in nature. McAllister and McAllister (1958) demonstrated that instructing subjects about the nature of classical eyelid conditioning affected the speed with which a CR developed, the effect being most noticeable in subjects who conditioned slowly.

Unfortunately, I find that eyelid conditioning studies do not discriminate between anticipatory responses and responses at the latency of the UCR when the UCS is not presented. The Hartman and Grant study, for example, although it used varying lengths of CS-UCS ISIs, only reported on the development of conditioned discrimination with a 100% reinforcement schedule to the CS+ and no extinction trials.

Spence, Honzie, and Rutledge (1964) presented data only on anticipatory responses. Whether CRs at the latency of the UCR do not occur in this situation, whether they are masked by the CAR in this response system, or whether investigators have not systematically looked for them, we do not know.

There is at least suggestive data in the literature indicating that different CRs may be differentially affected by such factors as instructions as measured during both conditioning and extinction.

OTHER FACTORS AFFECTING CONDITIONING

The Effect of Situation

The experimenter manipulation of instructions has marked effects on various conditional responses. Since man is a hypothesis-generating or self-instructing organism in the absence of instructions supplied by the experimenter, we should not be surprised to find that personality, as well as situation variables, markedly affect the conditioning process. As Spence and Spence (1966) have recently demonstrated, it is only under their "standard procedure" of eyelid conditioning that the Iowa group can demonstrate that highly anxious subjects condition more rapidly than subjects who score at the other extreme of the anxiety dimension of the Taylor Manifest Anxiety Scale. Their standard procedure involves a high level of situation-induced anxiety. The subject is naïve with respect to what is going to happen to him; he is given a minimum of information about the situation; he has various gadgets attached to him (for stimulation and eyeblink recording); he is seated in a dental chair and is isolated. Under these restrictive conditions the authors found that high anxiety subjects conditioned more rapidly than low anxiety subjects in 23 out of 27 studies, and that females conditioned better than males in 18 out of 19 studies. If the conditioning portion of the experiment is altered so that it is presented in the context of a masking probability learning task, the effect of anxiety and sex are completely eliminated. Although one can only make an inference from the Spence and Spence paper, it appears that if the conditioning task were spread out over more than one session, the effect similarly would not appear on the second session.

The fact that Franks (1956) and others (e.g., Gilberstadt & Davenport, 1960) have been unable to verify Spence's work relating eyeblink conditioning to manifest anxiety becomes, in view of the recent Spence and Spence paper, quite comprehensible. Their experimental conditions differed markedly from those used by the Iowa group. Subjects in the Franks study were (a) seated comfortably in an armchair as compared to being seated in a dental chair, and (b) were told that the test was a measure of how well they were able to relax under various conditions. The Iowa procedure involves maximizing situational anxiety, while Franks' procedure attempts to minimize such anxiety.

Personality attributes Franks was able to demonstrate, however, that under his experimental conditions subjects on the extraversion end of the extraversion-introversion continuum conditioned more poorly than introverted subjects. His measure of conditioning included both an electrodermal and eyelid-conditioned response. Franks, following Eysenck (1953), describes hysterics and psychopaths as falling on the extraversion end of the continuum; and anxiety neurotics, depressives, and obsessive compulsives on the introversion end of the continuum. Confirming evidence for poorer electrodermal conditioning in the psychopath has been presented by Lykken (1957), Welch and Hayes (1957), and Hare (1965), among others. In these studies psychopaths were compared to normal subjects. Nonconfirmatory evidence can be adduced from the study by Stewart et al. (1959), in which subjects hospitalized with the diagnosis of personality disorder demonstrated better conditioning of both an AR as well as CR than did subjects classified as manic-depressive and schizophrenic and conditioned at about the same rate as hospitalized anxiety neurotics.

The relationship between the introversion-extraversion dimension and conditionability is at least as controversial as the relationship between anxiety and conditioning (Becker & Matteson, 1961; Field & Brengelmann, 1961; Spence & Spence, 1964; Sweetbaum, 1963). To give but one example covering both the introversion and anxiety dimensions, I shall briefly review two studies by Davidson, Payne, and Sloane (1964, 1966). Utilizing an electrodermal and a finger withdrawal CR, these authors in their 1964 study of male and female college students were unable to obtain significant relationships between either of these CRs and measures of introversion, neuroticism, or manifest anxiety (MA). Their second study (1966) utilized a group of female hospitalized neurotic patients. All the correlations of "drive" measures (anxiety and neuroticism) with the measures of conditioning were positive; three of them statistically reliable, five more close to being reliable, with the best relationship found for the MA scale. Results for the introversion dimension were quite inconsistent.

A second and equally interesting finding emerged from the 1966 Davidson, Payne, and Sloane study, dealing with the generalizability of conditioning. In the study with hospitalized patients, there was a high correlation between the various conditioning measures used. In the normal college student population, no generality of conditioning was observable. They infer from their study that, "Extrapolating from our results it would seem that normal persons experiencing an unavoidable and unpleasant stimulus situation may develop *either* a conditioned withdrawal response or a conditioned autonomic response to that situation, whereas neurotics develop *both* a conditioned withdrawal response and a conditioned autonomic response [p. 313]."

Results from a study by Howe (1958) finds that patients hospitalized for anxiety reactions not only demonstrated better electrodermal conditioning but demonstrated more generalization to the CR. He also studied a group of schizophrenic subjects who demonstrated poorest conditioning as compared to both the anxiety reaction, as well as control, groups. He further reports an observation that this schizophrenic group could be divided into those who demonstrated habituation to shock and those who responded adequately to shock. Those who habituated had been hospitalized on the average of 7 years, longer than had those who responded adequately. Thus, in studies investigating the conditionability of schizophrenics, one must be sure that, when significantly poorer conditioning is reported for this group, it is a conditioning effect rather than nonresponding to the UCS. One would expect that, in the absence of a UCR, no conditioning would occur.

Current results would thus suggest that there are relationships between personality dimensions and various aspects of conditionability. Unfortunately, the results remain equivocal, in part because of the lack of specification of the type of conditional response being investigated, and in part because of the unreliability and unitary nature of the personality dimensions or dimensions of psychopathology to which we are attempting to relate the measures of conditioning.

Organic Brain Pathology

A number of studies have attempted to relate measures of brain damage with conditionability. Davidoff and McDonald (1964), utilizing populations of neurological patients and controls, found that with respect to habituation of EEG alpha desynchronization no differences between the groups emerged; while Wells and Wolff (1960) report a lower level of responsiveness, although again no differences in the slope of the habituation curve when comparing neurological patients with control subjects. Russian research, however, indicates that brain-damaged subjects should habituate more slowly than normal subjects. Davidoff and McDonald's conditioning situation utilized a 10-sec tone with 4 sec of light terminating concurrently with the end of tone as the UCS. Normal subjects demonstrated better conditioning of both an anticipatory response (alpha desynchronization in anticipation of light) as well as the CR; on non-reinforced trials, the control subjects gave more desynchronization responses at latency of response to light presentation. Interestingly, these differences could only be established with respect to EEG alpha desynchronization. Neither heart rate nor finger plethysmographic measures of conditioning differentiated the two groups, although in both of these measures habituation was more rapid in control subjects, thus offering limited support to the Russian literature in this area.

Elithorn (1955) studied a series of patients subjected to prefrontal leucotomy with respect to the development and maintenance of a conditioned anticipatory response in the electrodermal response system. He found that, following the operation, patients demonstrated poorer anticipatory CRs than was true prior to the operation. Goldstein, Ludwig, and Naunton (1954) divided a group of hard-of-hearing children into those who conditioned readily as compared to those who conditioned poorly. The response system used again was the electrodermal one. They found that "In a significant majority of the cases where conditioning was difficult, previous and independent diagnosis had suggested the presence of aphasia, and in a significant majority of the cases where conditioning was readily established no evidence of aphasia had been found [p. 75]."

Visser (1961) reported on contingent alpha blocking of the EEG as related to clinical diagnosis. Although we have some doubts as to whether he is dealing with a conditional response or habituation of an OR, he finds that patients diagnosed as having psychomotor epilepsy, organic psychosis, hysterical psychosis, symptomatic psychosis, or psychogenic depression all demonstrate poorer contingent alpha blocking than is true of either normal subjects or those diagnosed as manics. Thus conditionability or speed of habituation of ORs may cut across commonly accepted diagnostic categories and may not be diagnostic in the sense that it correlates highly with current psychiatric nosologies.

Intensity of CS and UCS

There has been little question about the importance of UCS intensity in conditioning (Spence, 1953; Spence, Haggard, & Ross, 1958; Taylor, 1956). That the relationship between UCS intensity and eyeblink conditioning, for example, is not a simple linear relationship is demonstrated in studies by Burstein (1965) and Spence and Platt (1966). Burstein presents evidence suggesting that the positive relationship between UCS intensity and conditionability is a statistical artifact. Rather than obtain better conditioning as a function of UCS intensity, Burstein believes that with a higher level of UCS intensity more *subjects* condition. Spence and Platt (1966) carefully analyzed Burstein's argument and demonstrated from data collected in the Iowa laboratories that their results are not an artifact attributable to the number of subjects who demonstrate CRs. In addition they reviewed a wealth of data, indicating that the relationship between UCS intensity and conditionability is a negatively accelerating function which approaches an asymptote within a relatively small range of UCS intensity.

Unconditioned stimulus intensity has similarly been found to be related to EDR conditioning. Doerfler and Kramer (1959), for example, found that with low shock intensity as the UCS, fewer subjects conditioned than did with a more intense UCS, and subjects getting the higher intensity UCS extinguished more slowly.

With respect to CS intensities the Russian literature again indicates that CS intensity is positively related to conditioning. The American literature is more equivocal. Beck (1963) and Grice and Hunter (1964), dealing with eyelid conditioning, conclude that the ability to demonstrate an effect of CS intensity is dependent on the experimental design used. When both intensities are used with the same subject with an irregular order of presentation of the two CSs, an intensity effect can be readily demonstrated. When different groups are used with different CS intensity levels, no effects, or minimal effects, attributable to CS intensity are obtained. Thus, in a discrimination conditioning paradigm, the effect of CS intensity can be demonstrated. As Grice and Hunter cogently point out, more than mere stimulus intensity is involved and some form of contrast effect is an important element in obtaining this effect.

CONCLUSION

In this review I have emphasized those aspects of classical conditioning of physiological responses that are currently being actively investigated. As is obvious, there are lacunas both in the coverage of this chapter as well as in the experimental literature. For example, no attempt was made to review systematically conditionability in various physiological response systems, nor to review the controversy dealing with respiratory factors in cardiac conditioning. An attempt to review conditionability in response systems would have demonstrated the paucity of studies in the American literature dealing with other than eyeblink, electrodermal, and heart rate conditioning. Thus, although Gottschalk demonstrated the feasibility of plethysmographic conditioning in 1946, few studies dealing with the conditioning of this response system have been reported in the American literature.

It is my distinct impression that studies dealing with the conditioning of physiological response systems in man are becoming more numerous in the American literature, and that more and more studies are not restricted to measurement in single response systems but include concurrent recording of conditioning in more than one system. Part of this broader coverage of response systems is attributable to the development of more adequate stimulus programming and recording techniques, and in part to advances in data reduction techniques. The latter range from semiautomatic data reduction equipment to the use of digital computers to reduce raw data. The use of digital computers in the latter role has, because of a host of technical problems, not progressed as rapidly as psychophysiologists had anticipated.

I believe that we are on the threshold of exciting days in the arena of classical conditioning of physiological systems. First, the relationship between spontaneous fluctuations in physiological systems, the habituation of orienting responses, and various conditional responses will elaborate reproducible factors across response systems. Second, factors affecting the conditioning of the various types of CRs elaborated in this chapter will be spelled out in greater detail, allowing for more reproducible results across laboratories and reducing fruitless polemics about the inability to reproduce results obtained in other laboratories. Third, the relationship of the conditionability of specific conditional responses in specific response systems will be more successfully related to personality and situationally determined factors than has been done in the past.

Parametric studies dealing with such factors as ISIs in simple and discriminant classical conditioning, the effect of varying ITIs, the effect of CS and UCS intensity, and the manipulation of motivational or drive variables are sorely needed.

REFERENCES

ANOKHIN, P. K. The role of the orienting-exploratory reaction in the formation of the CR. In L. G. VORONIN, A. N. LEONTIEV, A. R. LURIA, E. N. SOKOLOV, & O. S. VINOGRADOVA (Eds.), *Orienting reflex and exploratory behavior.* Washington, D.C.: American Institute of Biological Sciences, 1965.

BECK, S. B. Eyelid conditioning as a function of CS intensity, UCS intensity and manifest anxiety scale score. *Journal of Experimental Psychology,* 1963, **66,** 429-438.

BECKER, W. C., & MATTESON, H. H. GSR conditioning, anxiety and extraversion. *Journal of Abnormal and Social Psychology,* 1961, **62,** 427-430.

BERGER, S. Conditioning through vicarious instigation. *Psychological Review,* 1962, **69,** 450-466.

BRIDGER, W. H., & LOPEZ, T. Greater resistance to extinction after continuous reinforcement than after partial reinforcement. *Psychological Reports,* 1964, **15,** 563-569.

BRIDGER, W. H., & MANDEL, I. J. A comparison of GSR fear responses produced by threat and electric shock. *Journal of Psychiatric Research,* 1964, **2,** 31-40.

BRIDGER W. H., & MANDEL, I. J. Abolition of the PRE by instructions in GSR conditioning. *Journal of Experimental Psychology,* 1965, **69,** 476-482.

BURSTEIN, K. R. The influence of UCS upon the acquisition of the conditioned eyelid response. *Psychonomic Science,* 1965, **2,** 303-304.

BYKOV, K. *The cerebral cortex and the internal organs.* Moscow: Foreign Language Publishing House, 1959.

CAUTELA, J. R. A behavior therapy approach to pervasive anxiety. *Behaviour Research and Therapy,* 1966, **4,** 99-109.

CORSON, S. A., CORSON, E. O., DYKMAN, R. A., PETERS, J. E., REESE, W. G., & SEAGER, L. D. The nature of conditioned antidiuretic and electrolyte retention responses. *Activitas Nervoso* (Suppl.), 1962, **4,** 359-382.

DAVIDOFF, R. A., & McDONALD, D. G. Alpha blocking and autonomic responses in neurological patients. *Archives of Neurology,* 1964, **10,** 283-292.

DAVIDSON, P. O., PAYNE, R. W., & SLOANE, R. B. Introversion, neuroticism and conditioning. *Journal of Abnormal and Social Psychology,* 1964, **68,** 126-143.

DAVIDSON, P. O., PAYNE, R. W., & SLOANE, R. B. Cortical inhibition, drive level, and conditioning. *Journal of Abnormal and Social Psychology,* 1966, **71,** 310-314.

DOERFLER, L. G., & KRAMER, J. C. Unconditioned stimulus strength and the galvanic skin response. *Journal of Speech and Hearing Research,* 1959, **2,** 184-192.

DUCHARME, R. Effect of internal and external cues on the heart rate of the rat. *Canadian Journal of Psychology,* 1966, **20,** 97-104.

DYKMAN, R. A. Toward a theory of classical conditioning: Cognitive, emotional, and motor components of the conditional reflex. *Progress in Experimental Personality Research,* 1965, **2,** 229-317.

EDWARDS, A. E., & ACKER, L. E. A demonstration of the long-term retention of a conditioned GSR. *Psychosomatic Medicine,* 1962, **24,** 459-463.

EISMAN, E. Effects of deprivation and consummatory activity on heart rate. *Journal of Comparative and Physiological Psychology,* 1966, **62,** 71-75.

ELITHORN, A., PIERCY, M. F., & CROSSKEY, M. A. Prefrontal leucotomy and the anticipation of pain. *Journal of Neurology, Neurosurgery and Psychiatry,* 1955, **18,** 34.

ELLISON, G. D. Differential salivary conditioning to traces. *Journal of Comparative and Physiological Psychology,* 1964, **57,** 373-380.

EYSENCK, H. J. *The structure of human personality.* London: Methuen, 1953.

FEHR, F., & STERN, J. A. Heart rate conditioning in the rat. *Journal of Psychosomatic Research,* 1965, **8,** 441-453.

FIELD, J. G., & BRENGELMANN, J. C. Eyelid conditioning and three personality parameters. *Journal of Abnormal and Social Psychology*, 1961, **63**, 517-523.

FRANKS, C. M. Conditioning and personality: A study of normal and neurotic subjects. *Journal of Abnormal and Social Psychology*, 1956, **52**, 143-150.

FROMER, R. Conditioned vasomotor responses in the rabbit. *Journal of Comparative and Physiological Psychology*, 1963, **56**, 1050-1055.

FUHRER, M. J., & BAER, P. E. Differential classical conditioning: Verbalization of stimulus contingencies. *Science*, 1965, **150**, 1479-1481.

GALE, E., & STERN, J. A. Conditioning of the electrodermal orienting response. *Psychophysiology*, 1967, **3**, 291-301.

GILBERSTADT, H., & DAVENPORT, G. Some relationships between GSR conditioning and judgment of anxiety. *Journal of Abnormal and Social Psychology*, 1960, **60**, 441-443.

GOLDSTEIN, R., LUDWIG, H., & NAUNTON, R. F. Difficulty in conditioning galvanic skin responses: Its possible significance in clinical audiometry. *Acta Oto-Laryngologica*, 1954, **44**, 67-77.

GOLDSTEIN, R., STERN, J. A., & ROTHENBERG, S. J. Effect of water deprivation and cues associated with water on the heart rate of the rat. *Physiology and Behavior*, 1966, **1**, 199-204.

GOTTSCHALK, L. A. A study of conditioned vasomotor responses in ten human subjects. *Psychosomatic Medicine*, 1946, **8**, 16-27.

GRANT, D. A. The influence of attitude on the conditioned eyelid responses. *Journal of Experimental Psychology*, 1939, **25**, 393-402.

GRICE, G. R., & HUNTER, J. J. Stimulus intensity effects depend upon the type of experimental design. *Psychological Review*, 1964, **71**, 247-256.

GRINGS, W. W. Preparatory set variables related to classical conditioning of autonomic responses. *Psychological Review*, 1960, **67**, 243-252.

GRINGS, W. W., & LOCKHART, R. A. Effect of "anxiety-lessening" instructions and differential set development on the extinction of GSR. *Journal of Experimental Psychology*, 1963, **66**, 292-299.

GRINGS, W. W., LOCKHART, R. A., & DAMERON, L. E. Conditioning autonomic responses of mentally subnormal individuals. *Psychological Monograph*, 1962, **76**, 1-35.

GROSS, K., & STERN, J. A. Habituation of the OR as a function of "instructional set." *Conditional Reflex*, 1967, **2**, 23-36.

HARE, R. D. Temporal gradients of fear arousal in psychopaths. *Journal of Abnormal and Social Psychology*, 1965, **70**, 442-445.

HARE, R. D. Denial of threat and emotional response to impending painful stimulation. *Journal of Consulting Psychology*, 1966, **30**, 359-361.

HARTMAN, T. F., & GRANT, D. A. Differential eyelid conditioning as a function of the CS-UCS interval. *Journal of Experimental Psychology*, 1962, **64**, 131-136.

HILGARD, E. Methods and procedures in the study of learning. In S. S. STEVENS (Ed.), *Handbook of experimental psychology*. New York: Wiley, 1951.

HILGARD, E. R., & MARQUIS, D. G. *Conditioning and learning*. New York: Appleton-Century-Crofts, 1940.

HOWE, E. S. GSR conditioning in anxiety states, normals, and chronic functional schizophrenic subjects. *Journal of Abnormal and Social Psychology*, 1958, **2**, 183-189.

JOHNSON, L. C., & LUBIN, A. Spontaneous electrodermal activity. *Psychophysiology*, 1966, **3**, 8-17.

JONES, J. E. Contiguity and reinforcement in relation to CS-UCS intervals in classical conditioning. *Psychological Review*, 1962, **69**, 176-186.

JONES, M. C. A laboratory study of fear: The case of Peter. *Journal of Genetic Psychology*, 1924, **31**, 308-318.

KIMMEL, H. D. Management of conditioned fear. *Psychological Reports*, 1963, **12**, 313-314.

KIMMEL, H. D. Further analysis of GSR conditioning: A reply to Stewart, Stern, Winokur, and Fredman. *Psychological Review*, 1964, **71**, 160-166.

KIMMEL, H. D. Instrumental inhibitory factors in classical conditioning. In W. PROKASY (Ed.), *Classical conditioning*. New York: Appleton-Century-Crofts, 1965.

KNOTT, J. R., & HENRY, C. E. The conditioning of the blocking of the alpha rhythm of the human electroencephalogram. *Journal of Experimental Psychology*, 1941, **28**, 134-144.

KOROL, B., SLETTEN, I. W., & BROWN, M. L. Conditioned physiological adaptation to anticholinergic drugs. *American Journal of Physiology*, 1966, **211**, 911-914.

LANG, W. J., BROWN, M. L., GERSHON, S., & KOROL, B. Classical and physiologic adaptative conditioned responses to anticholinergic drugs in conscious dogs. *International Journal of Neuropharmacology*, 1966, **5**, 311-315.

LAZARUS, A. A. The results of behavior therapy in 126 cases of severe neurosis. *Behaviour Research and Therapy*, 1963, **1**, 69-80.

LIDDELL, H. S. The challenge of Pavlovian conditioning and experimental neuroses in animals. In J. WOLPE, A. SALTER, & L. J. REYNA (Eds.), *The conditioning therapies*. New York: Holt, Rinehart and Winston, 1965.

LOCKHART, R. A. Comments regarding multiple response phenomena in long interstimulus interval conditioning. *Psychophysiology*, 1966, **3**, 108-114.

LOCKHART, R. A., & GRINGS, W. W. Interstimulus interval effect in GSR discrimination conditioning. *Journal of Experimental Psychology*, 1964, **67**, 209-214.

LYKKEN, D. T. A study of anxiety in the sociopathic personality. *Journal of Abnormal and Social Psychology*, 1957, **55**, 6-10.

LYNN, R. *Attention, arousal and the orientation reaction.* New York: Pergamon, 1966.

MARTIN, I. Variations in skin resistance and their relationship to GSR conditioning. *Journal of Mental Science,* 1960, **106,** 281–287.

MARTIN, I. Delayed GSR conditioning and the effect of electrode placement on measurements of skin resistance. *Journal of Psychosomatic Research,* 1963, **7,** 15–22. (a)

MARTIN, I. A note on reflex sensitivity and the formation of conditioned responses. *Behaviour Research and Therapy,* 1963, **1,** 185–190. (b)

MARTIN, I. Eyelid conditioning and concomitant GSR activity. *Behaviour Research and Therapy,* 1963, **1,** 255–265. (c)

MARTIN, I. A further attempt at delayed GSR conditioning. *British Journal of Psychology,* 1963, **54,** 359–368. (d)

MCALLISTER, W. R., & MCALLISTER, D. E. Effect of knowledge of conditioning upon eyelid conditioning. *Journal of Experimental Psychology,* 1958, **55,** 579–583.

MCDONALD, D. G., & CARPENTER, A. F. Habituation of the OR in sleep. Paper presented at the annual meeting of the Society for Psychophysiological Research, 1966.

MCDONALD, D. G., & JOHNSON, L. C. A reanalysis of GSR conditioning. *Psychophysiology,* 1965, **1,** 291–295.

MOELLER, G. The CS-UCS interval in GSR conditioning. *Journal of Experimental Psychology,* 1954, **48,** 162–166.

NOTTERMAN, J. M., SCHOENFELD, W. N., & BERSH, P. J. A comparison of three extinction procedures following heart rate conditioning. *Journal of Abnormal and Social Psychology,* 1952, **47,** 674–677. (a)

NOTTERMAN, J. M., SCHOENFELD, W. N., & BERSH, P. J. Conditioned heart rate response in human beings during experimental anxiety. *Journal of Comparative and Physiological Psychology,* 1952, **48,** 1–8. (b)

PARAMONOVA, N. P. Influence of extinction and recovery of the OR on development of conditioned connections. In L. G. VORONIN, A. N. LEONTIEV, A. R. LURIA, E. N. SOKOLOV, & O. S. VINOGRADOVA (Eds.), *Orienting reflex and exploratory behavior.* Washington, D.C.: American Institute of Biological Sciences, 1965.

PRESCOTT, J. W. Neural timing mechanisms, conditioning and the CS-UCS interval. *Psychophysiology,* 1965, **2,** 125–131.

PROKASY, W. F. (Ed.) *Classical conditioning: A symposium.* New York: Appleton-Century-Crofts, 1965.

PROKASY, W. F., & EBEL, H. C. GSR conditioning and sensitization as a function of intertrial interval. *Journal of Experimental Psychology,* 1964, **67,** 113–119.

PROKASY, W. F., & EBEL, H. C. Three distinct components of the classically conditioned GRS in human subjects. *Journal of Experimental Psychology,* 1967, **73,** 247–256.

PROKASY, W. F., FAWCETT, J. T., & HALL, J. F. Recruitment, latency, magnitude, and amplitude of the GSR as a function of interstimulus interval. *Journal of Experimental Psychology,* 1962, **54,** 513–518.

PROKASY, W. F., HALL, J. F., & FAWCETT, J. T. Adaptation, sensitization, forward and backward conditioning, and pseudoconditioning of the GSR. *Psychological Reports,* 1962, **10,** 103–106.

RAZRAN, G. Semantic and phonetographic generalizations of salivary conditioning to verbal stimuli. *Journal of Experimental Psychology,* 1949, **39,** 642–652.

RAZRAN, G. Conditioning and perception. *Psychological Review,* 1955, **62,** 83–95.

RAZRAN, G. The observable unconscious and the inferable conscious in current Soviet psychophysiology: Interoceptive conditioning, semantic conditioning, and the orienting reflex. *Psychological Review,* 1961, **68,** 81–147.

RIESS, B. F. Semantic conditioning involving the galvanic skin reflex. *Journal of Experimental Psychology,* 1940, **26,** 238–240.

RIESS, B. F. Genetic changes in semantic conditioning. *Journal of Experimental Psychology,* 1946, **36,** 143–152.

RODNICK, E. H. Characteristics of delayed and trace conditioned responses. *Journal of Experimental Psychology,* 1937, **20,** 409–425.

SMITH, K. Conditioning as an artifact. *Psychological Review,* 1954, **61,** 217–225.

SMITH, O. A., & STEBBINS, W. C. Conditioned blood flow and heart rate in monkeys. *Journal of Comparative and Physiological Psychology,* 1965, **59,** 432–435.

SOKOLOV, E. N. Higher nervous function: The orienting reflex. *Annual Review of Physiology,* 1963, **25,** 545–580. (a)

SOKOLOV, E. N. *Perception and the conditioned reflex.* New York: Macmillan, 1963. (b)

SPENCE, K. W. Learning and performance in eyelid conditioning as a function of intensity of UCS. *Journal of Experimental Psychology,* 1953, **45,** 57–63.

SPENCE, K. W., HAGGARD, D. F., & ROSS, L. E. Intrasubject conditioning as a function of the intensity of the UCS. *Science,* 1958, **128,** 774–775.

SPENCE, K. W., HONZIE, M. J., & RUTLEDGE, E. F. Extinction of the human eyelid CR as a function of the discriminability of the change from acquisition to extinction. *Journal of Experimental Psychology,* 1964, **67,** 545–552.

SPENCE, K. W., & PLATT, J. R. UCS intensity and performance in eyelid conditioning. *Psychological Bulletin,* 1966, **65,** 1–10.

SPENCE, K. W., & SPENCE, J. T. Relation of eyelid conditioning to manifest anxiety, extraversion and rigidity. *Journal of Abnormal and Social Psychology,* 1964, **68,** 144–149.

SPENCE, K. W., & SPENCE, J. T. Sex and anxiety differences in eyelid conditioning. *Psychological Bulletin,* 1966, **65,** 137–142.

STEIN, L. Habituation and stimulus novelty: A model based on classical conditioning. *Psychological Review,* 1966, **73,** 352–356.

STERN, J. A., DAS, K. C., ANDERSON, J. M., BIDDY, R. L., & SURPHLIS, W. "Conditioned" alpha desynchronization. *Science*, 1961, **134**, 388–389.

STERN, J. A., SCHWARZ, L., & GOSPODINOFF, M. Salivary output of the alcoholic: Effect of treatment with amitriptyline. *Conditional Reflex*, 1968, **3**, 254–262.

STERN, J. A., STEWART, M. A., & WINOKUR, G. An investigation of some relationships between various measures of the galvanic skin response. *Journal of Psychosomatic Research*, 1961, **5**, 215–223.

STERN, J. A., WINOKUR, G., STEWART, M., & LEONARD, C. Electrodermal conditioning: Some further correlates. *Journal of Nervous and Mental Disease*, 1963, **137**, 479–486.

STEWART, M. A., STERN, J. A., WINOKUR, G., & FREDMAN, S. An analysis of GSR conditioning. *Psychological Review*, 1961, **68**, 60–67.

STEWART, M. A., WINOKUR, G., STERN, J. A., GUZE, S. B., PFEIFFER, E., & HORNUNG, F. Adaptation and conditioning of the GSR in psychiatric patients. *Journal of Mental Science*, 1959, **105**, 1102–1111.

SWEETBAUM, H. A. Comparison of the effects of introversion-extraversion and anxiety on conditioning. *Journal of Abnormal and Social Psychology*, 1963, **66**, 249–254.

SWITZER, C. A. St. Anticipatory and inhibitory characteristics of delayed conditioned reactions. *Journal of Experimental Psychology*, 1934, **17**, 603–620.

TAYLOR, J. Level of conditioning and intensity of the adaptation stimulus. *Journal of Experimental Psychology*, 1956, **51**, 127–130.

THOMPSON, R. F., & SPENCER, W. A. Habituation: A model phenomenon for the study of neuronal substrates of behavior. *Psychological Review*, 1966, **73**, 16–43.

VINOGRADOVA, O. S. On the dynamics of the OR in the course of closure of a conditioned connection. In L. G. VORONIN, A. N. LEONTIEV, A. R. LURIA, E. N. SOKOLOV, & O. S. VINOGRADOVA, (Eds.), *Orienting reflex and exploratory behavior*. Washington, D.C.: American Institute of Biological Sciences, 1965.

VISSER, S. L. Correlations between the contingent alpha blocking, EEG characteristics and clinical diagnosis. *Electroencephalography and Clinical Neurophysiology*, 1961, **13**, 438–448.

VISSER, S. L. Relationship between contingent alpha blocking and conditioned PGR. *Electroencephalography and Clinical Neurophysiology*, 1963, **15**, 768–774.

VORONIN, L. G., LEONTIEV, A. N., LURIA, A. R., SOKOLOV, E. N., & VINOGRADOVA, O. S. (Eds.), *Orienting reflex and exploratory behavior*. Washington, D.C.: American Institute of Biological Sciences, 1965.

WANG, G. H. *The neural control of sweating*. Madison: University of Wisconsin Press, 1964.

WELCH, L., & HAYES, R. F. Elements of conditioning in normal and pathological human behavior. *Journal of Genetic Psychology*, 1957, **91**, 263–293.

WELLS, C. E., & WOLFF, H. G. Formation of temporary cerebral connections in normal and brain damaged subjects. *Neurology, Minneapolis*, 1960, **10**, 335–340.

WHITE, C. T., & SCHLOSBERG, H. Degree of conditioning of the GSR as a function of the period of delay. *Journal of Experimental Psychology*, 1952, **43**, 357–362.

WISHNER, J. Studies in efficiency: GSR conditioning as a function of degree of task centering. *Journal of Abnormal and Social Psychology*, 1962, **65**, 170–177.

WISHNER, J., PEASTREL, A. L., & FISHBEIN, H. D. Studies in efficiency: MAP in reaction time as related to GSR conditioning. *Journal of Abnormal and Social Psychology*, 1964, **69**, 144–149.

WOLPE, J. *Psychotherapy by reciprocal inhibition*. Stanford, Calif.: Stanford University Press, 1958.

ZIMNY, G., & MILLER, F. L. Orienting and adaptive cardiovascular responses to heat and cold. *Psychophysiology*, 1966, **3**, 81–92.

ZIMNY, G. H., STERN, J. A., & FJELD, S. P. Effects of CS and UCS relationships on electrodermal response and heart rate. *Journal of Experimental Psychology*, 1966, **72**, 177–181.

Donald W. Shearn

OPERANT ANALYSIS
IN PSYCHOPHYSIOLOGY

6

An impressive range of phenomena is now in view as a result of operant analysis. Operant method has been put to work in such diverse regions as the control of single nerve cells (Fetz, 1969), psychophysics (Blough, 1966), verbal behavior (Greenspoon, 1962), the modification of abnormal behavior (Ullmann & Krasner, 1965), educational technology (Skinner, 1968), and social behavior (Azrin & Lindsley, 1956). It would be startling, therefore, if operant analysis had not touched psychophysiology.

This chapter takes up two issues that presently unite psychophysiology and operant analysis. The first of these concerns the psychophysiological by-products of traditional operant procedures, such as changes in steroid level during and after key pressing in a shock avoidance setting. The second bears upon more recent operant response contingencies that are directed at the psychophysiological responses themselves, in explicit attempts to strengthen or weaken such behaviors. The latter issue is sometimes known as the operant conditioning of autonomic responses. At some future time the division between these issues may seem to be unduly sharp but for now it provides a convenient organization.

In relating psychophysiology and operant conditioning it is difficult, if not impossible, to leave out a third area, classical conditioning. Chapter 5 should be consulted for further information on this topic.

A basic sketch of operant analysis is presented in this chapter before relevant psychophysiological matters are examined, but this sketch is not intended to provide the reader with the essential know-how of operant conditioning in its general form. There are several informative sources on the current principles, procedures, and terminology of operant analysis (Ferster & Perrott, 1968; Holland & Skinner, 1961; Honig, 1966; Reynolds, 1968; Sidman, 1960), its system and metasystem (Verplanck 1954), and its techniques (Dinsmoor, 1966; Sidman, 1962; Stebbins, 1966).

ELEMENTS OF OPERANT ANALYSIS

The Operant

Many responses are not elicited in the sense that orienting or conditional reflexes are elicited. Regarding such responses, Skinner said in 1938: "I do not believe that the 'stimulus' leading to the elaborate responses of singing a song or of painting a picture can be regarded as a mere substitute for a stimulus or a group of stimuli which originally elicited these responses or their component parts [p. 20]."

Operant behavior is emitted as spontaneous behavior, although the term "spontaneous" does not imply freedom. On the contrary, emitted response rates are noted for their orderliness and reproducibility, once controlling factors have been applied. Skinner has suggested that, in the face of such order and control, it may be unnecessary to search for causative agents in the environment (Skinner, 1938, p. 20). The operant, then, is an emitted response that can be controlled by contingencies of reinforcement, as discussed below.

The major dependent variable in operant analysis is the rate of responding, or its derivative, the interresponse time. Operant behavior is viewed typically as a single subject's response rate across time. These responses are graphed cumulatively, highlighting fluctuations in rate.

Response class The operant may be defined broadly (e.g., general body movement) or narrowly (e.g., between 25 and 30 μV EMG from the m. abductor pollicis brevis), depending on the aims of the investigator. Operants falling within limits of

a response class will be differentially affected by experimental procedures, since these procedures are intended to strengthen or weaken selected operants. Operant analysis is an aggressive method with respect to a designated dependent variable, in the sense that it aims for marked change; hence the specification of the response class is doubly important.

Autonomic operants Traditionally, only skeletal responses have been regarded as operants. If one considers visceral or glandular activities as operants, it would seem that he is at odds with traditional physiology, which prides itself on selecting and isolating antecedent events. Clearly, the evoking stimuli of many internal organ responses can be specified. Physiology has made this its business. On the other hand, a few seconds of observation of ongoing heart rate, sweat gland activity, or gastrointestinal movements is usually enough to make terms such as "spontaneous" or "emission" reasonably comfortable, at least for a considerable amount of internal organ behavior. How then can visceral and glandular responses be treated as operants? Using the same all-or-none logic for the occurrence of a response that one finds in operant pigeon laboratories, for example, where a disk must be pecked sufficiently hard to be counted as a response, it is a simple matter to count internal organ responses meeting amplitude criteria, and then to use the rate as the primary datum. The traditional arguments for excluding nonskeletal responses from operant conditioning have been more theoretical than empirical (e.g., Mowrer, 1947). For the empiricist there is no particular reason to exclude autonomic responses from operant analysis in the absence of laboratory data, and the operant researcher enjoys the reputation of empiricist rather than theorist (Skinner, 1950). The experimental evidence bearing on this point will be reviewed later in this chapter.

Contingencies of Reinforcement

The central principle of operant conditioning is that operants can be made to occur more or less frequently by certain events which follow them. Stimulation or its cessation, which occurs as a consequence of an operant, may strengthen or weaken that operant. This principle is essentially the same as that presented in the last moments of the nineteenth century by Thorndike (1898) as the Law of Effect. Reinforcement is the technical term for strengthening a response with consequent events.

Adventition The term "reinforcement" implies nothing about the purposive nature of a response in producing a reinforcer. Teleology is not involved (Skinner, 1966). It is unnecessary, of course, that these stimulus events be programmed knowingly, or even that there exists a cause and effect relation between the response and the consequent event. (Hence operants are not "instrumental.") A barely explored region of operant analysis is the adventitious contingency, in which an effective stimulus follows a response quite fortuitously (Herrnstein, 1966). As it turns out, the accidental contingency may be just as effective in strengthening the response as one that had been planned for weeks and delivered by a computer. Behaviors strengthened by such happenstance are called "superstitious." Clearly, many, if not most, response-contingent events in nature are not planned or caused; yet the antecedent behaviors are affected markedly. The extent to which "superstitious" behaviors are to be found within the domain of psychophysiology generally, and psychosomatic medicine especially, is purely a matter of guesswork at this time. Because psychophysiological responses are rarely monitored by other organisms (except in laboratories), we might expect that a considerable number of them would be reinforced accidentally.

Reinforcement is empirical The nature of reinforcement is operational and pragmatic. The list of effective reinforcers has been obtained through direct observation. No theory, as yet, predicts the reinforcing properties of particular stimulus events, whether they be 80 mg banana pellets, medial forebrain stimulation, or dim green numeral readouts. A stimulus event is called a positive reinforcer if its response-contingent presentation increases the response frequency. It is a negative reinforcer if its response-contingent presentation reduces the response frequency. Hence the concept of reinforcement suffers from the same sort of circularity as do such concepts as force and voltage. Some

proponents of operant analysis are interested in a theory of the nature of reinforcement, some less so. Many use reinforcement simply because "it works."

Response differentiation When one develops or shapes behavior by systematically shifting the limits of the reinforced response class, the extinction of undesirable behaviors is as important as the reinforcement of responses within the acceptable band. Responses that are not reinforced drop out, revealing the reinforced behavior more prominently. Hence the process of response differentiation requires both reinforcement and nonreinforcement.

Stimulus discrimination When reinforcement is presented or withheld systematically, depending upon the stimulus condition, discrimination develops. Behavior in the presence of the stimulus signaling reinforcement is strong, whereas behavior in the presence of the stimulus signaling extinction is weak. The absence of reinforcement (extinction), which is correlated with one stimulus condition, is as essential to the discrimination as is reinforcement, which is correlated with a different stimulus condition.

Schedules of reinforcement When only occasional responses are reinforced, without regard for the stimulus condition, intermittent reinforcement prevails. This situation is commonplace in nature. The programming rules by which occasional reinforcers are delivered according to the number of responses emitted and/or the elapse of time are called schedules of reinforcement. These schedules are important because they exert considerable control over the rate of responding and resistance to subsequent extinction (Ferster & Skinner, 1957).

Experimental Tactics

Operant research has made its headway by taking results from individual subjects, while eschewing statistical experimental designs and group data. In doing so, it has cut across the mainstream of psychophysiological and psychological research in the United States, while charting a course parallel to physiological research, which also concentrates on the individual subject. Without discussing the benefits of either mode, I suggest that it may be difficult to overestimate the effects of this choice of methodology upon the final character of a joint venture between psychophysiology and operant analysis. Any progress that operant analysis makes in psychophysiology ought to sharpen this issue considerably. For a discussion of this matter from the operant researcher's viewpoint, see Skinner (1938, p. 442) and Sidman (1960).

PSYCHOPHYSIOLOGICAL SIDE EFFECTS OF OPERANT PROCEDURES

Certainly, it would be unreasonable of us to assume that, when the experimenter is using contingent stimulation with a particular response class, a general bodily calm prevails elsewhere. So-called homeostatic mechanisms themselves imply adjustments to various disturbances, some of which are caused by reinforcers. These adjustments are so widespread in biological systems as to raise a question about the utility of homeostasis as a scientific concept (Davis, 1958).

Physiological Responses to Negative Reinforcers

Aversive conditioning procedures, including punishment, as a means to gain behavioral control, have been regarded as a possible source of deleterious side effects (Skinner, 1953, p. 187; Solomon, 1964).

Gastrointestinal effects The report that gastroduodenal ulcers were developed in primates as the by-product of a shock-avoidance situation (Brady, Porter, Conrad, & Mason, 1958) caused a considerable stir in both basic and applied psychosomatic research settings. One essential feature of this work indicated that the ulcers were produced by the avoidance contingency, in which pressing a key postponed a brief electric shock, and not simply by the delivery of electric shocks as such. Yoked-control animals without an avoidance opportunity received the same shocks as did their experimental partners but did not develop ulcers. In short, the lesion was not produced by "stress," but by a narrowly defined avoidance schedule. Subsequent investigations (Brady, 1963; Polish, Brady, Mason,

Thack, & Niemeck, 1962), in which fistulas were implanted in rhesus monkey subjects, showed that the buildup of stomach acid occurred, not in the course of the avoidance work-shift, but during a rest period following the avoidance behavior. A 6-hr rest period following avoidance appeared to be optimal for the buildup of stomach acid in monkeys, a result supported by rat data in a related study (H. K. Rice, 1963).

Puzzling information has emerged from human subjects working in a similar avoidance situation, if it is believed that increased stomach acidity and increased stomach activity go hand in hand. Davis (1959) observed that large increases in stomach activity were produced *during* an avoidance task in which key presses prevented intense noise. This finding was substantiated by another study in which controls sustained the same noxious events as experimental subjects without being able to avoid them (Davis & Berry, 1963). But a subsequent human study (White, 1964) showed less stomach activity during avoidance, a finding more in line with the data from Brady's monkeys than Davis's human subjects. The initial observations of Davis, however, were supported by Fedor and Russell (1965), in a detailed analysis, and by Stern (1966), who reviewed the evidence on both sides. When acid rather than activity was measured by means of a pH-telemetering device swallowed by human subjects (Norman, 1969), reliable differences in acid level between avoidance and control subjects were not produced, although both groups showed a higher rate of gastric acid secretion in the rest period after the shock period than during the shock period itself.

In comparing infrahuman and human experiments of this kind, an important detail in basic strategy ought to be emphasized. The monkeys in Brady's laboratory were run around the clock for many, many sessions, in order to achieve a steady state. The human subjects in the other studies, however, often were run for a single session only, with data analysis and conclusions depending heavily upon group averages during that session.

Endocrine changes The systematic elevation or depression of 17-hydroxycorticosteroids (17-OHCS), pepsinogen, norepinephrine, androsterone, estrone, and thyroid levels has been accomplished in a series of experiments employing noxious operant techniques (Mason & Brady, 1956; Mason, Brady, & Sidman, 1957; Mason et al., 1961a; Mason et al., 1961b; Mason, Brady, & Tolliver, 1968; Mason, Mangan, Brady, Conrad, & Rioch, 1961c; Mason, Nauta, Brady, Robinson, & Sachar, 1961d). Comparisons of procedures of positive reinforcement (fixed-ratio schedule) with those of aversive stimulation showed that only the latter were effective in increasing the adrenocortical response (Mason, Brady, & Sidman, 1957).

One aversive method that effected marked endocrinological changes was the conditioned emotional response (CER) procedure, in which a Pavlovian signal-shock sequence was superimposed upon a lever-pressing baseline maintained by occasional food reinforcers (Estes & Skinner, 1941). This paradigm has increased 17-OHCS and norepinephrine levels during the session (Mason et al., 1961b). A second aversive method, used more frequently in these researches, was the Sidman avoidance procedure, in which regularly occurring electric shocks could be delayed by lever presses. Sessions in which lever pressing rates are adequate enough to prevent virtually all shocks are commonplace with this method, even though the shocks could occur as often as every 20 sec in the absence of responses. This procedure elevated 17-OHCS in the absence of shocks; although shocks themselves, without the avoidance requirement, also increased this steroid (Sidman, Mason, Brady, & Thack, 1962). While 17-OHCS levels may be elevated during prolonged Sidman-avoidance sessions, pepsinogen levels dropped below control baseline levels (Mason et al., 1961a). Recovery of pepsinogen levels upon the removal of the Sidman schedule took the form of considerable overshooting beyond control levels. Similar elevations in norepinephrine, epinephrine, and thyroid levels, along with marked reductions in androsterone and estrone, have also been produced with the Sidman avoidance schedule (Mason et al., 1961b; see also Chapter 1).

In view of the effect of electric shock, as such, it is difficult to assign these endocrinological effects to any singular properties of aversive operant conditioning (Sidman et al., 1962). How much more or less could be accomplished with Pavlovian conditioning, or with other procedures not employing response-contingent events, is unclear at present.

General reactions An extensive analysis of human psychophysiology during aversive operant conditioning aligns rather well with the experiments involving nonhuman subjects discussed above (Frazier, Weil-Malherbe, & Lipscomb, 1969). In this investigation the subject's task was to detect changes in meter readings by repeatedly pressing an observing button that briefly illuminated a meter. When the meter pointer changed, a detection button was pressed. Deflections of the meter pointer were programmed by a variable interval schedule, and the subject's rates on the observing button were governed in accordance with this schedule, as found earlier by Holland (1958). Following one control detection session, punishing electric shocks were delivered to the subject if he failed to detect a meter change quickly, but only when a discriminative stimulus (light) was present. During the next session this discriminative stimulus, which had become a conditioned aversive stimulus, was used periodically, but the shock apparatus was turned off.

Reliable increases in button-pressing rates, the probability of meter change detection, heart rate, blood pressure, skin conductance, 17-OHCS, and norepinephrine and epinephrine levels were provoked by this discriminated avoidance procedure. These increases reflected differences between measures taken during avoidance periods, and those of the control session, nonavoidance periods (light-off), or other times during the day.

Again, how much of the operant procedure, as such, is necessary or sufficient to produce such marked physiological activities is a matter of guesswork at this time.

Blood flow and heart rate The conditioned emotional response procedure used successfully in the elevation of endocrine activity (e.g., Mason et al., 1961c) has proved to be a valuable technique in cardiovascular research (Stebbins & Smith, 1964). A distinct advantage of this procedure over others such as Sidman avoidance is that control baselines before and after each Pavlovian sequence of signal and shock are available many times during a given session for comparison. The alternating periods of control behavior, when the key-pressing rates maintained by reinforcement are robust, and of disrupted behavior, when the key pressing is dramatically suppressed by conditioned aversive stimuli, foster solid data analysis. Stebbins and Smith (1964) implanted flow transducers around the terminal aorta of monkeys and then examined the instantaneous blood flow and heart rate as the monkeys pressed keys in a conditioned emotional response setting. The expected suppression of response rates from the telegraph key was observed with the onset of a 1-min, conditioned aversive stimulus (light) followed by a brief shock. In addition, heart rate increases of 40 beats per min were not uncommon. Marked increases in blood flow were recorded.

These results were extended with a differentiation procedure, in which one stimulus was followed by shock (CS+), while another was not (CS−). Clear discrimination of the stimuli was marked by suppression of lever pressing, and increases in heart rate and terminal aorta blood flow, in the presence

of CS+ but not CS− (Nathan & Smith, 1968). Illustrative CS+ and CS− trials are shown in Figure 6.1. A similar procedure has been used by Toledo and Black (1966), but heart rate decelerations were obtained as the response to CS+ in their study. It is possible that the use of different subjects, hooded rats, accounts for the different heart rate response.

When a morphine substitute, nalorphine, was used instead of shock as the primary aversive event, the conditioned emotional paradigm brought on bradycardia, along with suppression of key pressing in rhesus monkeys (Goldberg & Schuster, 1967).

Additional cardiovascular measurement techniques for monkeys in aversive, free operant situations have been reported for heart rate (Perez-Cruet, Tolliver, Dunn, Marvin, & Brady, 1964) and blood pressure (Forsyth & Rosenblum, 1964). The analysis of blood pressure and key pressing using

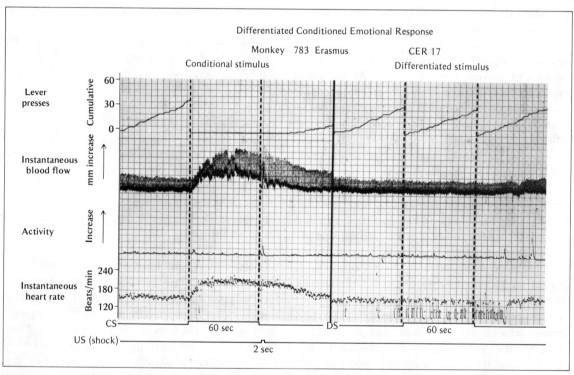

Figure 6.1 Cardiovascular and lever-pressing conditioned emotional responses (CERs) to a light (CS+) followed by shock (left) and to a different light (CS−) without shock (right). The major increases in blood flow and heart rate, and the suppression of lever pressing are brought on by the CS+ light, rather than by the shock itself. The CS− light is ineffectual after differentiation (discrimination) training. Some cardiotachometer artifacts are present. Adapted from M. A. Nathan & O. A. Smith, Differential conditional emotional and cardiovascular responses—a training technique for monkeys, *Journal of the Experimental Analysis of Behavior*, 1968, **11,** 77–82. By permission.

monkeys during Sidman avoidance suggests that the blood pressure wave may influence the time that avoidance key presses are made (Forsyth, 1965).

Psychophysiological responses may anticipate key pressing avoidance responses. In one study, only monkeys that first showed a discriminated heart rate response to shock learned a discriminated key-press avoidance response (Banks, Miller, & Ogawa, 1966). These data do not support those of an earlier human study which indicate that the discrimination of shock trials by heart rate did not occur until after the discriminated avoidance key press was learned (Graham, Cohen, & Shmavonian, 1964). The galvanic skin response, on the other hand, discriminated shock trials in anticipation of the discriminated avoidance key press. Species differences and procedural differences could easily account for the discrepancies between these two studies.

Blood pressure Blood pressure elevations brought about by the Sidman avoidance schedule (lever pressing) have been examined by Forsyth during short-term experiments of 15 days (1968) and during an investigation in which the schedule operated for over a year (1969). Blood pressures remained high during the days that the Sidman procedure was in effect but returned to control levels with its discontinuance after 15 days. In the long-term study, blood pressures at 7 months of avoidance behavior were increased over baseline values by 28 mm Hg, systolic, and 19 mm Hg, diastolic. Such changes were not seen in control subjects.

The potency of stimuli that have been allied with electric shock is underscored by an avoidance procedure, in which hypertensive blood pressure changes were produced (Herd, Morse, Kelleher, & Jones, 1969). In this study, lever pressing on a schedule of reinforcement turned off a warning light and the shock circuit. As the sessions continued, with many avoidance responses in the presence of the light, mean arterial blood pressure levels were elevated before, during, and after each session, even when few, if any, of the noxious stimuli were actually delivered. A long-term version of this approach has been taken by Findley and Brady (1969), in which the 24-hr-day environment

of baboons has been controlled, using escape-avoidance procedures. In this research the onset of the signal for the beginning of an escape avoidance period brought on 30–40 mm Hg increases in blood pressure and 60–80 beats per minute increases in heart rate.

Positive Reinforcement

In general, physiological reactions elicited by positive reinforcers are weaker than those brought on by negative reinforcers. A possible beginning in the analysis of the subtle responses evoked by positive reinforcers may be a look at electromyographic (EMG) responses in a manageable learning situation, using defined trials rather than free operant procedures. In one study human subjects guessed the onset of one of two lamps by pressing a corresponding key (Kent, 1958). When the response had been "correct," the responding arm showed a greater increase in muscle voltage than the other arm. When a response was "incorrect," the arms showed a nonsignificant difference in the opposite direction. In an investigation prompted by Kent's work (Shearn & Davis, 1961), subjects guessed the occurrence or nonoccurrence of a stimulus event by pressing or not pressing a single key. Reinforcement was the key-press response, followed by stimulus confirmation. Incidental stimuli appeared haphazardly during the session. Reinforcing stimuli caused slight increases in muscle tension, while incidental stimuli lessened the tension. The predominant heart rate response was a slowing for reinforcing stimuli, and an acceleration for the incidental.

Wenzel (1961) has observed that *discriminative* stimuli for food reinforcement of cats evoked cardiac acceleration, whereas conditioned aversive stimuli elicited bradycardia.

Several physiological responses of human subjects pressing buttons in a free operant situation have been recorded simultaneously (Doehring & Ferster, 1962). The reinforcing event was a counter tally, convertible to money. In both variable interval and fixed ratio schedules of reinforcement, galvanic skin responses elicited by reinforcement of button presses were larger than other kinds of responses (heart rate, volume pulse, and muscle potentials), perhaps because the high rate of presses and associated muscular activity tended to drown out any subtle electromyographic and cardiovascular responses (Doehring & Helmer, 1963a,b). When a pacing or time estimation procedure was tried, in which only responses following the preceding responses by 60 sec (plus or minus a few seconds) were reinforced, button-pressing rates dropped, allowing the evaluation of physiological responses evoked by the counter tallies. Reliable physiological responses evoked tended to vary with the subject: increased galvanic skin response, muscle potentials, heart rate, or volume pulse were noted.

There is, naturally, a question of what use these data might have for future researchers or theorists. In contrast to some of the marked psychophysiological and psychosomatic changes brought on by negative reinforcers, the mild responses produced by positive reinforcers appear to be little more than epiphenomena.

OPERANT REINFORCEMENT AND PUNISHMENT OF PHYSIOLOGICAL RESPONSES

Electromyographic Responses as Operants

Operant conditioning is best known for its control over the form and rate of striated muscle responses of animals. By means of response differentiation, using both reinforcement and extinction, skeletal behavior may be shaped to subtle and delicate topographies of varying amplitudes. In the traditional shaping of animal behavior, the limits imposed on the refinement of the behavior would seem to stem from the manual skill of the experimenter or trainer (Skinner, 1951) and the capacity of the species to make some designated response (Breland & Breland, 1961).

Hefferline's work With the improvement of high gain, low noise amplifiers for use in psychophysiology, and the development of switching logic instrumentation and technique in operant conditioning, the way was open for further testing of the limits of an operant response class. In the past, near maximal motor involvement had already been shaped routinely. The question now was just how small could an operant be? It was in this direction that the paramount investigations of Hefferline and his students were made (Hefferline & Keenan, 1961,

1963; Hefferline, Keenan, & Harford, 1959; Hefferline & Perera, 1963).

Hefferline proposed to use small EMG responses of human subjects as operants. In the first study (Hefferline, Keenan, & Harford, 1959), momentary EMG changes of 1–3 μV from the palmar base of the thumb were counted by the experimenters for a few minutes, in order to establish a baseline tally. The subject listened to music during this time. During the conditioning phase of the experiment, a noise was superimposed on the music; the same 1–3 μV EMG changes in this phase terminated the noise for 15 sec or postponed it for 15 sec, once it was off. Larger amplitude responses were ineffective in terminating or postponing the noise. Extinction periods, in which no responses were effective, followed conditioning. Cumulative records tallying emission rates of the small EMG responses of individual subjects showed that subjects who were given no instructions about the required response and the contingency increased the rates of these responses impressively during conditioning. Verbal reports after the session suggest that these subjects were ignorant of the response and the reinforcement contingency. Subjects who were instructed explicitly to make small thumb twitches to turn off the noise conditioned poorly, since they made few EMG responses that were small enough to meet the 1–3 μV requirement. Subjects who were given these instructions and were then allowed to watch a meter presenting their own EMG behavior ("augmented feedback") conditioned best of all.

Additional work has extended the control over tiny EMG operants from this escape-avoidance situation to settings employing positive reinforcers, money or points (Hefferline & Keenan, 1963; Hefferline & Perera, 1963). In one enlarged analysis, records of the reinforced, EMG-response class were supplemented with records of both smaller and larger amplitude-response classes, which were monitored but not reinforced. This study made it clear that differential reinforcement increases criterion EMG-response class, while decreasing larger EMG-amplitude rates. When reinforcement is withheld during extinction, the higher frequencies of large EMG amplitudes returned (Hefferline & Keenan, 1963). Figure 6.2 shows the cumulative records and frequency distributions from one subject in this study.

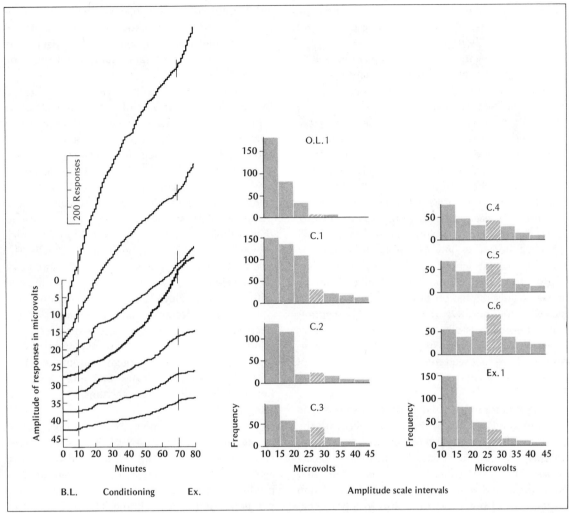

Figure 6.2 Amplitude induction of thumb EMG when the subject was reinforced for 25–30 μV responses. Cumulative records at the left show running totals of the reinforced response (dark record) and neighboring amplitudes (indicated by ordinate values). Frequency distributions on the right, taken during same sessions, again show effects of reinforcing 25–30 μV responses (barred) upon that response class and its neighbors (solid) during baseline, conditioning, and extinction. Adapted from R. F. Hefferline & B. Keenan, Amplitude-induction gradient of a small-scale (covert) operant, *Journal of the Experimental Analysis of Behavior*, 1963, **6,** 307–315. By permission.

In still another direction, discrimination procedures were tested, in which minute EMG responses themselves served successfully as discriminative stimuli for key-press responses of the other hand (Hefferline & Perera, 1963). The subject in this experiment was told to press a telegraph key with his right hand each time a tone sounded, in order to receive points that could be converted to money. Reinforcing key pressing in the presence of tone was a straightforward stimulus-discrimination procedure. The tone was presented, however, only

when the left thumb (m. abductor pollicis brevis) emitted an EMG response of less than 25 μV. As one might expect, there was a high incidence of left thumb, criterion EMG responses, immediately followed by right key presses, simply because of the role of the tone. In the next part of the experiment a fading procedure was used, in which the tone was gradually attenuated, leaving only trifling m. abductor pollicis brevis EMG as the discriminative stimulus for key pressing. Key presses following the minute proprioceptive cue (hits) were far more frequent than key presses occuring at other times (false alarms) or the key presses just after the EMG cue (misses).

These investigations of Hefferline could well be taken as an archetype of operant analysis in psychophysiology, whether the behavior in question be skeletal, neural, glandular, cardiovascular, or gastrointestinal. From a systematic point of view, the experiments were not quests for "indicants" of presumed entities, nor, for that matter, was there really any reductionistic intent at all (Hefferline, 1962, p. 107). The nature of the experiments obligated the experimenters to attain experimental control over each subject, rather than statistical control over a group of subjects. This control was demonstrated, not only by efforts to return the subject, via extinction, to the original baseline representing the original state of affairs, but by means of discrimination procedures as well. Both positive and negative reinforcement procedures were used successfully. Few subsequent attempts at operant conditioning of psychophysiological responses have followed these stringent examples of experimental analysis.

Single motor units Single motor units have been brought under control by human subjects with the aid of auditory or visual monitors of the behavior (Basmajian, 1963; Carlsöö & Edfeldt, 1963). Subjects learned not only to contract a particular fiber touching an indwelling electrode within 15–30 min of the start of the session but also to repress that unit and achieve control over another unit. In some instances subjects could contract particular units without the augmented feedback provided by the auditory or visual monitors.

Sutton and Kimm (1969) have trained subjects to emit a single motor unit spike in a reaction time experiment employing augmented feedback. Latency distributions of EMG versus the unit showed that the unit was slower than the gross measure.

Heart Rate

Human studies John Favill and Paul Dudley White examined subjects who reportedly could increase their heart rates and found that accelerations could be produced "one second after the word is given by the experimenter" (Favill & White,

1917). One of these subjects, apparently anticipating the practical psychosomatic implications of the procedure, had used it once during great fatigue in a hot operating room, and again when impending syncope was felt.

Some years later, Shearn (1960, 1962) conditioned increases in the heart rate of human subjects using a modified, Sidman avoidance schedule in which heart rate acceleration itself postponed an electric shock. Subjects watched the reset timer that programmed these shocks. Yoked-control subjects received the same pattern of shocks and shock postponements as did their experimental partners. The paradigm of these yoked subjects, in contrast to that of their operant partners, was Pavlovian, since they had no control over the timer and shocks. The operant subjects produced increasingly more heart rate accelerations over five sessions, as compared with the yoked controls. These accelerations were not enough to retard overall habituation of the heart rate. Respiratory responses, which were not controlled in this initial effort, were correlated with heart rate responses; although nothing could be said, of course, about cause and effect relations between these or skeletal reactions, and the heart rate.

Subsequent experiments bolstered these incipient findings (Brener, 1964, 1966; Brener & Hothersall, 1966; Engel & Chism, 1967a; Engel & Hansen, 1966). Either high or low heart rates were used to produce reinforcement in a Sidman avoidance experiment conducted by Brener (1966). Two out of three subjects reinforced by the delay of aversive noise for heart rates higher than resting baseline rates showed more high rate responses than their yoked-control subjects. All subjects reinforced for heart rates lower than resting baselines rates showed more low rate responses than their yoked-control subjects. A successive approximation of criterion rates to more difficult levels followed a period of successful avoidance behavior.

Engel and colleagues employed a feedback light and clock, which they told subjects to keep on as much as possible. In the first study (Engel & Hansen, 1966) the light and clock went on when the heart rate dropped below a criterion value established during an earlier baseline period. The final clock reading, indicating total time that the heart rate was below the criterion value, was converted to money reinforcement after the session. The clock measure is noteworthy, since the heart rate contingency does not distinguish rate changes beyond the cri-

terion value. Therefore, considerable conditioning may be evidenced by the clock reading, although heart rate changes are barely large enough to meet the criterion value. These investigators showed that

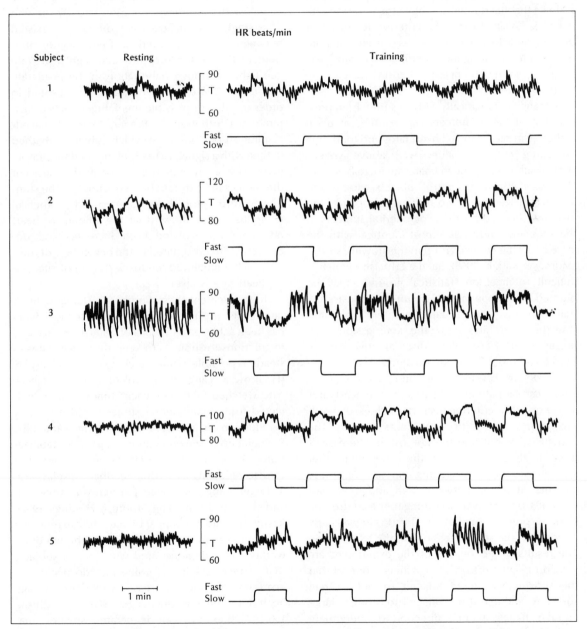

Figure 6.3 Differential operant conditioning of heart rate of human subjects, showing increases and decreases in rate when the discriminative stimuli signaled "up" or "down," respectively. The procedure illustrates the effects of using each subject as his own control, in that heart rate changes in both directions were produced. Adapted from H. I. Levene, B. T. Engel, & J. A. Pearson, Differential operant conditioning of heart rate, *Psychosomatic Medicine*, 1968, **30**, 837–845. By permission.

the heart rate could be slowed successfully by some subjects, apparently not by changes in breathing.

In another experiment subjects increased their heart rate by the same procedure, except that the positive reinforcers, light and clock, were presented at times that heart rate was above the criterion rate (Engel & Chism, 1967a). The criterion for onset of the light and clock reinforcers was shifted to a more stringent level during the experiment to shape performance. In the absence of criterion changes, the heart rate could change slightly while clock readings changed dramatically. Subjects for whom presentation of the reinforcers was contingent upon higher heart rates showed heart rates and total time exceeding criterion values well above yoked-control subjects, although heart rate increases were also observed among control subjects. Murray and Katkin criticized these two studies, noting that "the increase obtained for the experimental subjects in the speeding study was almost identical with the increase of the control group in the slowing study" (Murray & Katkin, 1968). Such a criticism, which is difficult to meet on statistical grounds, may be blunted with experimental results demonstrating that individual subjects can alternately speed and slow their heart rates during the same session upon presentation of controlling discriminative stimuli. Results of this kind were obtained in the same laboratory by Levene, Engel, and Pearson (1969) whose cardiac patient subjects kept their heart rates above or below criterion heart rate values, depending upon which of two cue lights was on. The patients were not told the purpose of the experiment. In the final stages of the experiment, after separate sessions on speeding and slowing, these patients alternated between high and low heart rates, at 1-min intervals according to the controlling stimulus present. The baseline heart rate was fairly steady over the several sessions of the experiment. The results of all subjects of the experiment are shown in Figure 6.3. The researchers reported that the slowing was more difficult to obtain than speeding, and that it was difficult to produce large enough changes in either direction to differentiate each clearly from a resting baseline.

The study by Levene, Engel, and Pearson (1969) was quite similar to one that had been run by Brener and Hothersall (1966), in which human sub-

jects increased or decreased their heart rates as one or the other cue lights came on during a single session. In the earlier study a cue light was on for 50 heart beats. Feedback, in the form of high or low tones, indicated that the heart rate was above or below the base level criterion rate. By the end of a single session, clear-cut differences existed between the cardiac interbeat frequency distributions in the presence of low and high heart rate cue lights, although habituation in the heart rate was clear. This experiment was then repeated in order to rule out possible mediating effects of respiration (Hothersall & Brener, 1969). A paced-respiration procedure, in which subjects breathed in time with a signal, virtually eliminated respiratory maneuvers as a mediating factor in the clear-cut differences in heart rate brought about by the stimulus control procedures. Brener and Hothersall (1967) have also shown that the amount of heart rate control, involving both increases and decreases, is directly related to the percentage of trials on which augmented feedback (tones) of successful heart rate is given.

To supplement these findings in changing heart rate levels, the reduction of heart rate *variability* has been achieved by means of visual feedback and instructions to subjects to keep their heart rates as steady as possible, while watching the visual display (Hnatiow & Lang, 1965). Yoked-control subjects, who watched fake "feedback" that had been collected from experimental subjects, did not show a reduction in cardiac interbeat time variability. Refinements in the procedures for learned stabilization of heart rate showed clear stimulus control of cardiac variability as a visual feedback display with a "target" range of 6 beats per min was turned on and off every 5 min (Lang, Sroufe, & Hastings, 1967). Respiration did not appear to play a role in reducing heart rate variability (Sroufe, 1969), although other workers have demonstrated with human subjects that, if increases in breathing rate do occur, the heart rate variance decreases while the average heart rate remains unchanged (Engel & Chism, 1967b). Other effects of deliberate respiratory maneuvers upon cardiovascular responses have been reported (Sharpey-Schafer, 1965; Stern & Anschel, 1968).

Substantial increases in the heart rate of human

subjects were produced during periods when a cue warned of shocks, unless avoidance responses were made (Frazier, 1966). The avoidance response was the heart rate above the previous period, when shocks and cue were omitted. In the absence of procedures employing heart rate decreases as well as increases, or yoked-control subjects, the shock cue may be interpreted easily as a Pavlovian conditional stimulus, instead of an operant discriminative stimulus, and hence the operant nature of the study is ambiguous.

Animal studies Aversive contingencies have been used with cardiac responses in rabbits such that heart rates that drifted either above or below criterion rates produced punishing shocks (Shearn & Clifford, 1964). Since the unconditioned response elicited by shock was acceleration, it was not surprising that the cardiac interbeat frequency distributions shifted initially to shorter intervals (higher rates) for punishment of either shorter or longer interbeat intervals when the shock period started. However, response-contingent shock following short interbeat intervals of other animals did, eventually, shift the interbeat distribution toward long values (lower rates) as compared with resting baselines, but only after many runaway sessions, when the shock elicited accelerations maintained a positive feedback loop of more shocks. The eventual success in punishing short interbeat intervals was confounded, however, by the possibility of habituation to shock, and tarnished by an unacceptable frequency of shock artifacts.

Miller and his associates (1969), using rat subjects, have substantially replicated the results of human operant cardiac conditioning reported earlier. To eliminate possible mediating effects of skeletal muscle activity, the replications employed curarization to interrupt the neuromuscular junction, an unwieldy technique for use with human subjects. In the first of these studies (Trowill, 1966, 1967), reinforcing stimulation was aimed via monopolar electrodes at the medial forebrain bundle of curarized rats. As in most of the human studies reported above, stimulation was contingent upon either high or low criterion heart rates, as determined from baseline rates, and yoked-control subjects were employed. Trowill obtained small but statistically

reliable differences between high and low rate contingency subjects and their yoked-control partners.

The essentials of Trowill's study were repeated (Miller & DiCara, 1967), but with shaping and discrimination procedures that had been used successfully with human subjects (Brener & Hothersall, 1966; Engel & Hansen, 1966). Differences in heart rates between high and low rate contingency animals were large and discrimination procedures were effective. The experiment was repeated again (Miller & Banuazizi, 1968), but now some rats were reinforced for either higher or lower intestinal contraction rates. Comparatively little interaction was observed between cardiac and intestinal behaviors during reinforcement of one system, although the rate of the reinforced response (either cardiac or intestinal) increased.

Operant conditioning of either increases or decreases in heart rate in curarized rats has been obtained by Hothersall and Brener (1969). Instead of the single conditioning session they ran four sessions, each with an adaptation, conditioning, and extinction phase. Stimulation directed at the medial forebrain bundle was again used.

To check against the possibility that stimulation aimed at the medial forebrain bundle of curarized rats was unique in reinforcing cardiac changes of rats, another reinforcement procedure, shock avoidance, was tried (DiCara & Miller, 1968c). Food reinforcement of rat cardiac rate changes had been attempted earlier in Harwood's laboratory (1962), but apparently the slow delivery time of food pellets, coupled with rapid changes in the rat heart rate, produced delays of reinforcement that counteracted the intended response contingency. DiCara and Miller (1968c) found that an avoidance procedure involving light followed by shock resulted in heart rate slowing or speeding, depending upon which behavior was programmed to avoid the shock. An attempt was made in this experiment to allay concerns about partial curarization. Black (1967b) had shown that EMG responses would occur under sizable doses of curare, and that these EMG responses were disturbingly correlated with changes in heart rate. Therefore, DiCara and Miller placed EMG electrodes on the lateral right gastrocnemius and were able to report an absence of

EMG activity during conditioning. Unfortunately, of course, monitoring EMG from a single location cannot rule out EMG activity elsewhere. Since it is reported that curare does not affect all muscle locations at the same rate (Goodman & Gilman, 1965, p. 603), this may not be a trivial point.

Blood Pressure

Animal studies Experiments using the avoidance of shock as negative reinforcement indicate that blood pressure can be changed either up or down by operant contingencies. In these studies a signal was followed some seconds later by an electric shock to the animal, unless it made the designated blood pressure response. DiCara and Miller (1968a) trained one group of rats to increase systolic blood pressure and another group to decrease it. Each avoidance rat was yoked to a control rat that received the same shocks delivered to his partner. Marked increases and decreases in pressure were produced by avoidance subjects but not their yoked controls, during the single experimental session. Heart rate responses were unrelated to the pressure changes.

Plumlee (1968) also conditioned increases in blood pressure with shock avoidance procedures, using a diastolic pressure response in rhesus monkey subjects. In his experiment an automatic adjusting schedule was employed over several sessions, so that increasingly greater changes in blood pressure were required to avoid shocks. A yoked-control subject did not show these increases in blood pressure. Attempts to decrease systolic blood pressure produced fluctuations, rather than reliable drops in pressure.

In the last of these animal studies using blood pressure avoidance responses, squirrel monkeys were first trained to press a lever during a signal to avoid shocks (Benson, Herd, Morse, & Kelleher, 1969). Once the lever-press response was established, a switch was made from lever pressing to blood pressure increases as the shock avoidance responses. Mean blood pressure rose to hypertensive levels during this phase. Finally, another switch in the response was made, so that drops in mean blood pressure avoided shocks. Blood pressure then decreased to control levels. Without controls for Pavlovian effects, especially habitua-

tion, it is not clear whether the results reflect operant or Pavlovian conditioning. The investigators, incidentally, did not frame the experiment in an operant conditioning context.

Human studies Human systolic blood pressure has been conditioned using positive reinforcement (D. Shapiro, Tursky, Gershon, & Stern, 1969). Either increases or decreases in pressure were reinforced with presentations of nude pictures. Substantial differences between the effects of increase and decrease contingency were produced across the session as overall blood pressure appeared to habituate. Analysis of heart rate and respiratory behavior made them unlikely mediators.

Vasomotor Conditioning

Human studies Successful vasodilatation conditioning, using termination of electric shock (escape) as the response-contingent event has been reported (Lisina, 1965). Lisina's human subjects were able to turn off electric shock via dilatation only when aided by a display of their own vasomotor behavior. The unconditioned response elicited by shock was vasoconstriction, opposite in direction to the selected operant.

Impressive operant conditioning of vasoconstriction of human subjects has been reported by Snyder and Noble (1965, 1966). These investigators excluded from their data analysis all criterion vasoconstriction responses that followed a light onset, used as a positive reinforcer, or any criterion response that followed a thoracic or abdominal respiration irregularity, or movement as detected by the EMG or plethysmograph polygraph channels. In doing so, their results depended upon vasomotor data collected in the absence of reinforcement-elicited constriction and detectable respiratory and skeletal mediation. As noted above, however, in connection with DiCara and Miller's recording (1968a) of EMG in curarized rats, a single EMG channel cannot refute even an ill-founded suspicion that skeletal activity is present somewhere on the body surface. The EMG channel of Snyder and Noble appeared to be many times more sensitive than that of DiCara and Miller (1968c) but, nevertheless, only one location was being monitored. Snyder and Noble's method produced a convincing divergence between vasoconstriction-contingent subjects and both yoked-control and unstimulated control subjects during conditioning, although the actual rate of vasoconstrictions of the experimental subjects did not go much above one response per minute.

Animal studies The differential vasomotor conditioning of rats using medial forebrain bundle stimulation as the positive reinforcer has been reported by DiCara and Miller (1968b). In this study vasodilatation-constriction differences between the two ears turned on the reinforcer during trials as defined by a tone. Substantial differences in vasomotor activity emerged during a single session.

Using medial forebrain stimulation as the positive reinforcer, Miller and DiCara (1968) reinforced curarized rats for increases or decreases in urine formation. As a function of these procedures, both the rate of urine formation and renal blood flow were increased or decreased according to the contingency, although no systematic changes were observed in additional cardiovascular measures or body temperature, which were not, of course, reinforced.

Galvanic Skin Response

Positive reinforcement Kimmel and his colleagues have done the most extensive work on operant conditioning of the galvanic skin response (GSR). The first effort to control this autonomic response made use of odor reinforcers given as a consequence of GSR amplitudes which exceeded values based upon shock-evoked GSRs obtained earlier (Kimmel & Hill, 1960). Despite the considerable delays of reinforcement that must have prevailed with odor delivery, and the necessary guesswork concerning a fertile response criterion, the results of this pioneering effort were encouraging enough to prompt a considerable number of increasingly refined experiments in Kimmel's and other laboratories. In later experiments any detectable GSR was reinforced with a light flash (Fowler & Kimmel, 1962; Kimmel & Kimmel, 1963) with the same general findings as before.

These experiments used control subjects who were presented with the same number of reinforcers as experimental subjects, but only when

they were *not* emitting criterion responses, a procedure known in operant circles as the differential reinforcement of other behavior (DRO). Greene (1966) employed the yoked-control procedure and obtained differences in criterion GSR rates between contingent and noncontingent treatments, but they were not so striking as those found when control subjects were reinforced for not giving GSRs (DRO). Kimmel has noted that the DRO procedure tends to reduce criterion GSR rates, as compared with the yoked-control procedure used by Greene, and therefore makes experimental–control differences even more impressive (Kimmel, 1967).

Operant conditioning of the GSR has come from another laboratory in which heart rate and respiratory movements (Shapiro, Crider, & Tursky, 1964) and slight body movements (Crider, Shapiro, & Tursky, 1966) were monitored during times of criterion GSRs. The analysis made these behaviors unlikely "causes" for the differences in GSR rates obtained between contingent and control groups. Had there been evidence that the other response measures *consistently* preceded criterion GSRs, an assertion that GSR was mediated by other response systems would still be questionable. Statistical correlation does not mean physiological cause and effect. The absence of correlation among response systems does, on the other hand, raise doubts about a mediation hypothesis in the particular experimental setting.

Additional studies demonstrate a lack of correspondence between other kinds of responses and the GSR. Gavalas (1967) detected no heart rate or finger blood volume changes associated with criterion GSRs. Van Twyver and Kimmel (1966) obtained GSR conditioning without increasing observable respiration or muscle action potential frequencies. As a double-check they replotted their conditioning curves after omitting all GSRs following EMG and respiratory responses. These conditioning curves still demonstrated convincing differences between contingent and noncontingent treatments.

In a heroic attempt to control for skeletal mediations, partial curarization was used by Birk, Crider, Shapiro, and Tursky (1966). Evidence for GSR conditioning was obtained from their subject, although overall GSR response rates were lower with curarization than without. Understandably, additional noncontingent control sessions under curare were omitted.

A particularly interesting and significant technique for unraveling physiological responses was used by D. G. Rice (1966). In one experimental condition he reinforced criterion GSRs only when they occurred in the absence of criterion EMG responses. That is, an EMG response precluded reinforcement for a GSR. The contingency operates as the logical arrangement, NAND, in which one input negates the output that is otherwise gated when a second input is applied. This contingency is a departure from already discussed techniques with the same goal, since it is part of the program in effect *during* the session, rather than a computational procedure employed afterward to rule out mediation effects.

When Rice used NAND in order to remove the effects of muscle responses upon GSR conditioning, ambiguous results were obtained. It is possible that a rather complex statistical design beclouded the question, but other difficulties were present. In examining only subjects who had showed a high baseline rate of GSRs before reinforcement started, conditioning under the NAND contingency was successful enough. For low GSR baseline subjects, however, no such conditioning was apparent; in fact, the noncontingent control treatment tended to show more "conditioning" than the contingent treatment. This part of the experiment was then rerun with longer sessions to boost the number of reinforcements. Again, conditioning was not demonstrated. A close examination of the results, however, suggests a likely reason for the absence of clear conditioning data. The average number of reinforcements delivered for the various treatment groups ranged from about 13 to 30. A skilled operant man would have difficulties with a NAND contingency in establishing even the most natural skeletal response with such niggardly quantities of reinforcement. (Imagine, e.g., attempting to shape a monkey during a single session to press a key only when he is holding his breath, using no more than 30 banana pellets.)

Negative attempts to condition the GSR as an operant have been reported from two laboratories. Stern and his associates were unable to replicate the sort of conditioning effects obtained by Kimmel (Stern, 1967; Stern, Boles, & Dionis, 1966). Mandler, Preven, and Kuhlman (1962) indicate that they did not obtain evidence for operant conditioning of GSRs. They posited "activation" brought on during the reinforcement part of the session as the cause of their GSRs, although an analysis of the records showed that reinforcers evoked GSRs only on one-third of the occasions. The control procedure in their study was a 10-min period of nonreinforcement just before reinforcement for 500-ohm GSRs was introduced, instead of a noncontingent treatment using the same or different subjects. Their results showed that both criterion GSR rates and conductance levels during the 10-min control period were lower than during the reinforcement period, despite the fact that the control period always preceded the experimental period. The opposite result would be expected in view of the greater toll of rate and conductance taken by habituation by the time the reinforcement period began. Just why activation was preferred over reinforcement as an explanation is not clear.

Noxious procedures Aversive control techniques have not been so effective in demonstrating operant control of the GSR as have positive reinforcement techniques. Kimmel and Baxter (1967) used a classical avoidance procedure in which GSRs during defined trials (tone followed 5.0 sec later by shock) would prevent shocks. Yoked controls received shocks whenever the avoidance subjects did but had no control over them. Slight but statistically significant GSR-rate differences between the treatments were found, but these could not be repeated in later attempts (Kimmel & Sternthal, 1967; Kimmel, Sternthal, & Strub, 1966). In another laboratory (Grings & Carlin, 1966), however, differences between avoidance and yoked-control GSR rates were obtained in the face of habituation of the response. The same study also showed, as expected, that the frequency of GSRs followed by shock punishment dropped below the frequency of GSRs emitted by yoked-control subjects. In another punishment study, Johnson and Schwartz (1967) obtained sizable differences between the GSR rates of contingent and noncontingent punishment groups. Electromyographic records tended to rule out skeletal mediation effects.

May and Johnson (1969), in a particularly convincing experiment, exposed subjects to both positive reinforcement and punishment during the same session. This procedure of using each subject as his own control is, of course, a mark of operant conditioning. A given subject would receive positive reinforcement (nude slide) following each criterion GSR for 16 min and then receive punishment (700 Hz at 99 dB SPL) following each criterion GSR by another 16 min. Other subjects received punishment first and then positive reinforcement. Extinction followed these treatments. As shown in Figure 6.4, the expected shifts in GSR rates as positive reinforcement and punishment conditions changed were substantial and impressive, although, once again, habituation was in evidence.

Salivation

Salivation in dogs has been increased and decreased by water reinforcement made contingent upon bursts of salivation or periods of quiescence, respectively (Miller & Carmona, 1967). Respiratory behavior, the heart rate, and general arousal tended

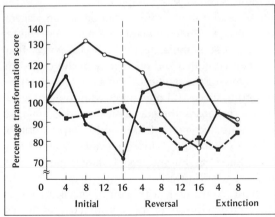

Figure 6.4 Operant conditioning of the GSR using positive reinforcement (nude slides) and punishment (loud noise) during the same session. Open-circle subjects were reinforced initially and then punished (reversal), following each criterion GSR. Other subjects (closed circles) were punished first and then reinforced. No response contingency was employed for control subjects (dotted lines). Conditioning, including the reversal of effect, was demonstrated in the presence of habituation. Redrawn from J. R. May & H. J. Johnson, Positive reinforcement and suppression of GSR activity, *Journal of Experimental Psychology*, 1969, **80,** 193–195. By permission.

to be correlated with these salivation responses. Brown and Katz (1967) used a similar procedure to condition high rates of salivation in humans using money reinforcers. An attempt to condition a low rate of salivation did not work so well as it had in the dog experiments.

Discrimination of increasing or decreasing salivation in human subjects has been achieved through an augmented feedback procedure in which a beep sounded with each drop of saliva (Delse & Feather, 1968). The subjects were told that a drop of saliva produced the beep and to increase saliva flow in the presence of one light and to decrease it in the presence of another. Three of ten subjects showed convincing discriminations, and the overall group differences were statistically significant. Conditioning was not obtained when the experiment was run without the auditory feedback.

The first operant analyses of salivation examined the operant discriminative functions of stimuli, rather than their reinforcing effects upon salivation (M. Shapiro, 1960; M. Shapiro & Miller, 1965). These systematic investigations, using dog subjects trained to press a lever, showed that a Pavlovian conditioned stimulus can act as an operant discriminative stimulus to control lever pressing. The strength of this operant role of the stimulus was a function of its potency to elicit conditioned salivation. Because discriminative stimuli not only guide behavior but serve as conditioned reinforcers for preceding behavior as well (Dinsmoor, 1950), the linkage among these stimulus functions is particularly noteworthy.

Neural Events

Stevens (1962) conditioned subjects to avoid shocks whenever their paroxysmal epileptiform activity was presented over a loudspeaker. One subject continued to discriminate his own paroxysmal pattern, even after the audio feedback was eliminated.

Using a meter that swung to the left with EEG desynchronization, and to the right with EEG alpha rhythm, Mulholland and Evans (1966) were able to train a subject to alternate rapidly between desynchronization and alpha by instructing him to try to keep the meter pointer centered. The subject then oscillated back and forth from alpha to no-alpha. Initially, the subject closed his eyes in order to produce alpha but this was unnecessary after training. This research followed a line of analysis in which EEG presentation was part of the subject's feedback loop (Mulholland & Runnals, 1962).

Kamiya and his associates have trained human subjects to produce high or low amplitude alpha rhythms using the conformation of correct behavior as a positive reinforcer (Kamiya, 1968). Auditory feedback, which was used at first, could be discarded once a subject was proficient. This technique was used later to evaluate the effects of light upon visual evoked responses in the presence of high or low alpha (Spilker, Kamiya, Callaway, & Yeager, 1969).

A related study made use of visual (oscilloscope) presentation of evoked potentials to human subjects. These subjects were able to learn small but reliable neural changes in the response produced by an evoking auditory pip, both with and without visual feedback (Rosenfeld, Rudell, & Fox, 1969). The results are similar to those obtained from animal subjects in the same laboratory (Fox & Rudell, 1969).

Increased depolarization rates of *single* nerve cells in the precentral cortex of awake monkeys have been conditioned by Fetz (1969), who used banana pellet reinforcers combined with neuronal activity presented visually or auditorily as augmented feedback. A similar procedure, in which bursts of spike potentials in rats were reinforced, had been used earlier by Olds and Olds (1961, p. 153). As control procedures, Fetz employed extinction and reconditioning, as well as noncontingent pellets delivered according to a yoked program taped from the same subject, during an earlier reinforcement phase.

CONTROVERSIAL ISSUES IN USING AUTONOMIC RESPONSES AS OPERANTS

In its briefest form the controversy about the operant conditioning of autonomic responses is whether or not so-called autonomic operants are really autonomic respondents—unconditioned, conditioned, orienting, or defensive reflexes— traveling in disguise. These respondents may be tripped by external stimulation, as well as internal stimulation provided by other body systems, particularly the somatic. No matter how psycho-physiologists elect to cross-list autonomic responses according to their experimental settings, it is rather obvious that these responses will always be furtive respondents. It is probable that detecting and severing respondent properties from ongoing visceral behavior will always be a difficult job.

Many of the issues arising from a consideration of visceral responses of operants were discussed by Skinner some years ago (1938, pp. 40, 61–66, 109–115, 258–282, 426–444). While he spelled out certain criteria to separate respondents and operants, Skinner did not at that time exclude the possibility that visceral responses might be treated as operants, and actually attempted, with Delabarre, to condition vasomotor responses with operant techniques (1938, p. 112). One of his central questions appears to have been whether particular responses— skeletal or visceral—were *conspicuous,* in the sense that they acted upon the environment noticeably (1938, p. 48). With the development, since 1938, of transducers, electronic instruments, and programming devices it would seem that many visceral responses can be made amply conspicuous. On the other hand, the environment upon which visceral responses act under operant contingencies is better represented by the gadgetry of the laboratory than the natural milieu and phylogeny of the organism.

Following the publication of a number of papers reporting successful operant conditioning of autonomic responses, three analytical reviews emerged that evaluated methodology and interpretation of those experiments (Crider, Schwartz, & Shnidman, 1969; Katkin & Murray, 1968; Kimmel, 1967). These important critiques are essential readings for the student concerned with controversial issues in operant conditioning of autonomic responses. Some of the points of these critiques are found below, supplemented with the additional ideas of this writer.

Reinforcer Mediation

A likely outcome of the presentation of a positive or negative reinforcer is the disturbance of the autonomic and related systems. When one is reinforcing some ongoing response such as lever pressing, the eddies and ripples in these other body systems may be viewed as secondary effects of the response contingency. Such events were discussed earlier in terms of the psychophysiological side effects of reinforcers. When one is reinforcing antecedent autonomic responses directly, however, any disturbances *evoked* by presentation of the reinforcer can only be confusing in the interpretation of the results. How many of the observed autonomic responses were due to the operant reinforcement contingency and how many were elicited by the reinforcer itself?

Yoked-control designs Although the separation of operant and respondent effects of a reinforcer may depend more upon substantial indirect evidence from various laboratories using diverse procedures than on a single coup de grâce from a given laboratory, one experimental design has been particularly helpful. This popular control procedure in operant autonomic conditioning is the yoked control, in which positive or negative reinforcers are delivered to a control subject whenever the experimental subject receives them. The reinforcers are therefore contingent upon, and are correlated with, some particular feature of the experimental subject's behavior, whereas they are uncorrelated with respect to that same behavior in the control subject. The yoked control is superior to the unstimulated control simply because the noncontingent presentation of reinforcers permits the evaluation of *evocative* effects of these reinforcers upon the response in question. Comparisons between unstimulated controls and yoked controls will allow us to make estimates of these evocative properties of the reinforcer. Comparison between response-contingent subjects and yoked-control subjects provides an evaluation of the additional contribution of *reinforcement* or *punishment*.

The yoked-control method has been roundly criticized by Church (1964), who argues that experimental subjects are favored with more opportunities to show *evoked* responses than control subjects in an experimental situation which is, in fact, respondent. Consider an experimental and yoked-control pair in which the experimental subject is more labile than his yoked-control partner with respect to the autonomic response in question. The yoked-control subject may fall behind the experi-

mental subject simply because the reinforcers delivered in equal numbers to both subjects fail to elicit as many respondents from him. The reverse situation, in which the yoked-control subject is more labile than the experimental subject, is also biased in favor of the experimental subject because the stabile experimental subject limits the number of reinforcers and, therefore, opportunities to which his labile yoked-control subject can respond.

While this logic seems to reduce the reliability of yoked-control designs in positive reinforcement settings, it may actually increase the trustworthiness of the design in aversive control settings (Black, 1967a). The stabile experimental subject, who does not make many escape or avoidance responses, allows many of the aversive stimuli to occur for himself, and for his more labile yoked-control partner, who will respond even more. When a stabile experimental subject is punished, his lower probability of responding will set a limit on the opportunities for yoked-control responses. Conversely, punishment of a labile experimental subject will evoke many more of the responses that are supposed to be suppressed by contingent punishment, while the sluggish yoked-control subject is less likely to respond anyway to the aversive stimuli (Crider, Schwartz, & Shnidman, 1969). Briefly then, any bias that may operate in yoked-control designs seems to work *against* the experimenter's attempts to demonstrate operant conditioning of autonomic responses if he is using aversive procedures.

Other experimental design procedures may assist the yoked-control method. For example, one may use the standard yoked-control subject procedure and then later systematically exclude from the data analysis all responses following reinforcers in the time span in which reinforcers might have elicited them. Possible mediating responses (respiratory and skeletal) may also be excluded at this time (e.g., Snyder & Noble, 1965, 1966). Or one may make the mediation of autonomic responses by reinforcers quite unlikely by using both positive and negative reinforcers in the same experiment and, possibly, as May and Johnson (1969) have done, using both with the same subject. When the alternating presentation of positive reinforcer and punishment first strengthens and then suppresses the autonomic response in question, an operant interpretation is not far fetched. Of course, using the same re-inforcer with differential cues to increase and de-crease the response in the same subject tends to remove reinforcer-elicited responses as a factor (Brener & Hothersall, 1966; Levene, Engel, & Pear-son, 1969).

Subjects may be matched as experimental and yoked-control partners on the basis of prior auto-nomic behavior (e.g., May & Johnson, 1969). Hope-fully, such matching handles varying habituation rates during the experiment proper. Almost perfect matching might be attained by employing each subject as his own yoked control, using a recorded program of reinforcers. These reinforcers would be uncorrelated with his behavior when played back at a later time (Fetz, 1969). The delayed yoked control amounts to a period of extinction following conditioning, in which reinforcers are delivered without respect to the ongoing behavior. One drawback in using this control is that the experi-menter may confront a considerable amount of hysteresis as he shifts from reinforcement to the yoked-control condition, and therefore may have limited chances for showing experimental and control differences. Such retardation of the "ex-tinction" process using noncontingent reinforcers has been reported by Herrnstein (1966, p. 36) in the context of skeletal operants.

Intracranial reinforcement   Because of the fre-quent use of intracranial stimulation (ICS) as re-inforcing stimulation in animal autonomic operant conditioning experiments (Miller & DiCara, 1969; Hothersall & Brener, 1969; Miller & Banuazizi, 1968; Trowill, 1967) a word of reservation about inter-pretation of these experiments may be in order. The target area of these investigations has been the medial forebrain bundle (although no data regard-ing histological confirmation have been presented). The numerous branches of this bundle project to myriad regions of the hypothalamus, brain stem, rhinencephalon, and limbic brain (Gurdjian, 1925; Krieg, 1932). Many of those structures associated with the medial forebrain bundle are known in a different context, that of central nervous system control of cardiovascular behavior. The hypothala-mus, for example, is a region of tremendous car-diovascular influence, as shown by stimulation and

lesion studies (Fuster & Weinberg, 1960; Smith, Jabbur, Rushmer, & Lasher, 1960).

Rat experiments, which bear directly upon the issue of brain stimulation reinforcers and the heart rate changes elicited by them, largely have been ignored, despite the caution signals that they have provided for workers in operant heart rate condi-tioning (Malmo, 1961, 1964; Meyers, Valenstein, & Lacey, 1964; Perez-Cruet, Black, & Brady, 1963). These studies, which have examined both septal and hypothalamus stimulation sites, have shown that the rate and intensity of stimulation at either site can affect overall heart rate, as well as the direction and form of heart rate change. For exam-ple, hypothalamic stimulation at low rates pro-duced a three-phase response of acceleration, de-celeration, then acceleration. Higher rates of stimulation produced only a shortened accelerative phase and reduced variability in the overall heart rate among subjects (Meyers, Valenstein, & Lacey, 1964). In operant autonomic conditioning studies, the absence of independent data that show cardio-vascular respondents evoked by stimulation at the intensities, *rates,* and brain loci actually used during conditioning will cause some uneasiness, whether or not subjects are assigned by random means to different treatment groups.

A curious interaction between brain stimulation reinforcers and the yoked-control design further impedes straightforward interpretation of experi-ments employing brain stimulation reinforcement (Steiner, Beer, & Shaffer, 1969). In this study rats first learned to press levers that delivered electrical stimulation to various hypothalamic sites. Later, the same pattern of electrical stimulation to the brain was played back to the animals by means of tape. The rats then showed strong escape behavior on a second lever, which briefly turned off the pattern that they had previously recorded, suggesting that a noncontingent or yoked pattern of such brain stimulation is actually aversive.

Habituation

To the investigator who has logged a few hours beside a polygraph machine, response habituation (adaptation) is not a mere verbal abstraction. This phenomenon, often taken for granted, is one of the most ubiquitous and powerful in all of psychophysiology. It would be surprising, therefore, if an investigator's plan to increase a response rate were enough, in itself, to erase this phenomenon. Many of the data of autonomic operant conditioning studies reflect the braking effects of habituation working against the effects of response-contingent events. One could not expect to see an increase in the rate of responding due to reinforcement, unless the motive effects of reinforcement were more powerful than the resistance afforded by habituation. To illustrate, if one gradually increased the force requirements of the levers of both a food-reinforced and a yoked rat, response rates of both animals could actually drop below the baseline rates obtained earlier. In the face of substantial differences between the rates of the two animals, however, no one would seriously question the effect of response-contingent food reinforcement upon lever-pressing behavior.

Data from operant autonomic conditioning can be brought to bear on this point. Results obtained by Schwartz and Johnson (1969) strongly suggest that, as more effective reinforcers are located, the resistive effects of habituation will be overcome. They reinforced 500-ohm GSRs with nude pictures.

For a discussion of this point and other related issues, the reader is again urged to read the arguments of Kimmel (1967), Katkin and Murray (1968), and Crider, Schwartz, and Shnidman (1969).

Somatic Mediation

Possible skeletal and respiratory mediation of operant autonomic conditioning of human subjects has been appraised by two methods. The first of these has entailed the scrutiny of data for correlations between the autonomic response, which has been reinforced, and respiratory or muscular responses (e.g., Crider, Shapiro, & Tursky, 1966; Hnatiow & Lang, 1965; Shearn, 1962). Respiratory responses may be paced by a signal to reduce further the chances of mediation due to respiratory maneuvers (Brener & Hothersall, 1966). Most of the published reports conclude that respiratory or muscular responses were not systematically related to the occurrence of the autonomic response that was reinforced. (Respiratory data of Shearn, 1962, were an exception.) An obvious concern, of course, is whether or not the location of transducers, the

gain of the amplifiers, and the techniques of analysis were up to the task of detecting such subtle correlations.

The second method is one of exclusion, in which portions of the polygraph record which show suspicious skeletal or respiratory activity are tossed out, so that the data analysis proceeds only with autonomic behavior which, presumably, is uncontaminated by such mediation (Snyder & Noble, 1965, 1966; Van Twyver & Kimmel, 1966). The rejection of data, nevertheless, must depend upon the insightful choice of transducer location, the accurate detection of skeletal or respiratory responses occurring at low levels, and a priori mediation criteria for exclusion.

The possibility of mediation still exists when a human subject is conditioned with operant stimulus control techniques first to increase and then to decrease (or vice versa) the rate of an autonomic response (e.g., Levene, Engel, & Pearson, 1968; May & Johnson, 1969). Conceivably, the mediator would work in one direction only, say, to increase the rate of the autonomic response. Relaxing or reducing the rate of the mediator, however, could still bring the autonomic rate below the baseline. Further, it is possible that a mediator such as respiration could both increase and decrease a response rate such as the heart rate (Stern & Anschel, 1968).

A convincing demonstration of operant autonomic conditioning that discredits skeletal or respiratory mediation might be one that shows autonomic conditioning across various kinds and levels of skeletal and respiratory activity. Unfortunately, it appears now that the only task more difficult than discounting skeletal or respiratory mediation in human operant autonomic conditioning is proving the null hypothesis.

A more reasonable approach might be to shift the burden of proof to those who espouse a somatic mediation interpretation of operant autonomic conditioning. Gavalas (1968) has provided solid experimental results on this point. Taking the mediation theorists at their word, he reinforced criterion GSRs only when they followed a particular respiratory maneuver, a twosome resembling cause and effect. The GSRs, rather than increasing in frequency via respiratory mediation, actually became uncoupled from respiration, decreasing in frequency. This experiment suggests many others in which the common aim would be to test the existence of mediation of autonomic responses within particular experimental settings.

Curare Many psychophysiologists and psychologists seem to be under the impression at present that curarization is a straightforward and decisive control procedure for ruling out somatic interaction with the autonomic system. It is not.

The investigator who intends to use curare in his autonomic conditioning research is urged to peruse the reports of Black (1967b) and colleagues (Black, Carlson, & Solomon, 1962) after reading his favorite pharmacological texts. First of all, the curarization procedure effects certain changes in the cardiovascular behavior that ought to be noted, although they would not necessarily operate systematically in favor of one treatment or another in a well-controlled experiment. These effects are an elevation in baseline heart rate, a reduction in heart rate variability, and a drop in blood pressure. Such changes are influenced by curare dosage, its rate of injection, and, of course, the rate and volume settings on the animal respirator. In addition to these cardiovascular effects, it is reported elsewhere that the time course of curarization of the skeletal musculature varies with the particular muscle group. Apparently, smaller, rapidly moving muscles are the first to be quieted during the administration of curare and the last to recover. Large muscles and respiratory control are affected last and recover first (Goodman & Gilman, 1965). Further, it has been demonstrated by Black (1967b) that operant heart rate conditioning under partial curarization can be influenced by muscular activity that shows up as low level EMG. In view of the large dosages Black used for partial curarization of the dog subjects (0.8 mg/kg/1.5 hr and 4.1 mg/kg/8 hr), a working definition of "partial" or "complete" curarization might be in order for future work.

There is a second concern that may be the pivotal issue in the future evaluation of somatic mediation. That issue is whether or not *skeletal* muscular mediation can be taken as the same thing as somatic mediation. In interrupting the neuromuscular junction, curare inhibits skeletal muscle activity and the proprioceptive afferent volleys that would

ensue otherwise. The effects of curare (*d*-turbocurarine) upon efferent volleys from the motor cortex, basal ganglia, or other parts of the somatic system seem, however, to be negligible or nonexistent. Miller and DiCara (1967), who have curarized rats in their studies of operant heart rate conditioning, have recognized this issue, noting that "It might be considered barely conceivable that *S*s learned to send out from the motor cortex central impulses for skeletal responses such as struggling, and that these impulses elicited innate or classically conditioned changes in heart rate [p. 17]." A similar stand has been taken by Katkin and Murray (1968) who indicate that, if motor cortex impulses were a factor, "the effect would have been general, influencing many autonomically innervated structures [p. 65]." Contrary to these ideas, however, direct and specific somatic mediation appears likely. Evidence in favor of selective, rather than general, somatic mediation of cardiovascular function, in the absence of skeletal mediation, has come from an investigation of primate motor cortex (Clarke, Smith, & Shearn, 1968). The skeletal activity of limbs to be tested was first eliminated by decamethonium bromide or surgical means. Stimulation of certain points of the somatic cortex (area 4) then produced increases in blood flow in the contralateral limb in the absence of *skeletal* activity. The control limb (ipsilateral) was relatively unaffected by stimulation. The selective responses elicited by such somatic stimulation rules out "indiscriminate . . . general arousal or by-products of the rate at which impulses to struggle are sent out from the motor cortex (Miller & Banuazizi, 1968)," and suggests that somatic control over cardiovascular, glandular, and gastrointestinal behavior could, to the contrary, be quite specific.

Additional evidence for somatic mediation comes from DiCara and Miller (1969), who used a procedure very much like one employed by Black (1967b) to analyze skeletal conditioning under curare. Black had found that the training of EMGs under curare influenced an overt skeletal response test after recovery. DiCara and Miller (1969) also tested conditioning under curare and after recovery, but their conditioning concerned the heart rate. They were interested in discounting "central commands" from the motor cortex from which "one would expect movements of the muscles to appear when Ss trained under curare are later tested and retrained without paralysis by curare." It appears that their data do, however, reflect such control during testing, immediately after recovery from curarization, although the investigators interpret their results differently (see Figure 6.5). The first tests after recovery from curarization show marked

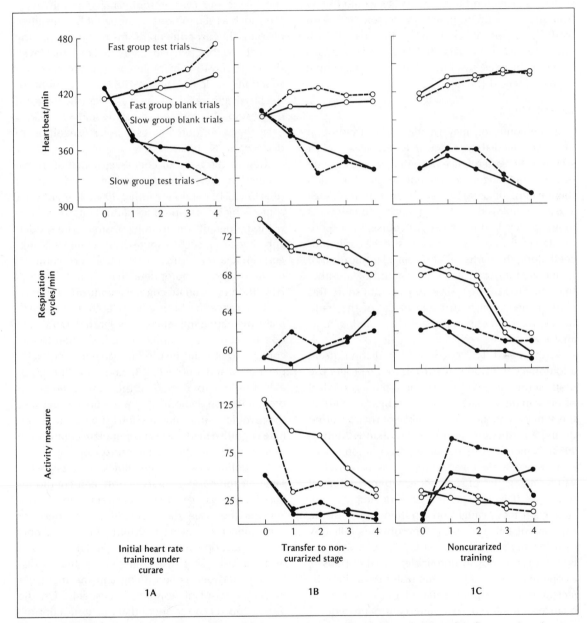

Figure 6.5 Transfer of conditioned heart rate from curarized to noncurarized stage. Note that first reactions in non-curarized stage (1B) show no effects of heart rate conditioning but marked effects of respiratory and activity conditioning. Redrawn from L. V. DiCara & N. E. Miller, Transfer of instrumentally learned heart rate changes from curarized to noncurarized state: Implications for a mediational hypothesis, *Journal of Comparative and Physiological Psychology*, 1969, **68,** 159–162. By permission.

differences in respiratory and activity measures, as one would expect if such "central commands" had been directed, in fact, to skeletal muscle during conditioning, albeit blocked at the last junction. On later post-curare tests, these marked differences in skeletal activity tend to disappear, as would follow from practice with an intact system complete with feedback loops. Black (1967b) anticipated such outcomes when he said that "curare only seems to block the overt response, and leaves the central state unaffected [p. 15]."

Central Mediation

Some confusion may emanate from the notion of central mediation, since it is not always clear whether the term refers to a central nervous system function or a cognitive concept. In this discussion the meaning of "central" will be held to the usage already employed regarding such structures as motor cortex. In this context, of course, the experimental analysis of mediation must necessarily proceed along the paths of laborious identification of neural anatomy and function (Smith, 1965), rather than the vista of the instructional set. In short, this kind of mediation is part and parcel of the traditional work of neurophysiologists and neuroanatomists.

With regard to "cognitive" mediation itself, additional confusion may exist as to the proper use of the term. Some writers appear to put a good deal of stock in the verbal behavior of subjects regarding the somatic and autonomic behavior that occurred during an experimental session (Katkin & Murray, 1968). A more or less standard procedure in evaluating these subject verbal reports is to correlate various categories of statements with physiological responses (Engel & Hansen, 1966) or simply to ask subjects if they "caught on" to the purpose of the experiment (Shearn, 1962). One obvious difficulty in using the subject's verbal behavior in this way is that it is notoriously unreliable; verbal responses, as operants, depend upon the histories of the subjects before the experimental session, as well as on nuances found in such stimulus control procedures as instructions. A review of the fortunes of procedures intended to enrich the understanding of conditioning experiments by means of analysis of post-experimental verbal behavior is well beyond

the objectives of this chapter. The reader is referred to other discussions of verbal behavior (Eriksen, 1962; Greenspoon, 1962; Holz & Azrin, 1966).

Quite aside from the methodological problems of correlating verbal reports and autonomic responses is the ever-present danger of reifying a term such as "cognition" as though it had meaning beyond the experimenter's instructions and the subject's verbal behavior. It is unlikely that even the most sensitive amplifiers will locate such abstractions. As R. C. Davis (1953) put it, "A hunt for the physical parallels of these entities (the 'physical dimensions of consciousness') would very likely have the same outcome as a polar expedition to discover St. Nicholas."

Tied to the issue of cognitive mediation is the distinction between conditioning and control (Black, 1967b; Katkin & Murray, 1968). It seems that some subjects can produce autonomic responses without operant conditioning sessions. The sudden appearance of such responses on command suggests that a term such as "control" or "conjure" might be more appropriate than "conditioning." How then to evaluate cognitive control? The prospect of canceling both cognitive control and somatic mediating influences in order to demonstrate operant autonomic conditioning is enough to discourage even stout-hearted researchers. For example, Katkin and Murray (1968) have said, "It is probably fruitless to pursue further any attempts at providing such demonstrations in humans, because they would require unconscious subjects to eliminate cognitive mediation and complete curarization to eliminate somatic mediation [p. 66]."

On definitional grounds, unless we assign the same meaning to voluntary control and conditioning, the terms necessarily refer to different events. Perhaps the issue then reduces to the need or convenience of having two terms instead of one. If we expect operant conditioning to take the form of a gradual S-shaped learning curve, then a distinction between conditioning and the more immediate control of response is desirable. On the other hand, it is no accident that the term "control" is part of a large operant literature known as "stimulus control" (Terrace, 1966). This literature shows that the gradual acquisition of a response is but a small and early part of the history of a selected behavior. More typically, responses are occasioned by particular discriminative stimuli, interoceptive, no doubt, as well as exteroceptive, and they often appear, fully blown, whenever the appropriate stimulus appears. Imagine a pigeon resting in an experimental chamber who suddenly begins furiously pecking a disk whenever a blue light goes on. An observer unfamiliar with the operant techniques of discrimination that brought about the phenomena might explain the bird's behavior with words such as "know," "want," and even "voluntarily." Similarly, as a child learns a language, including certain regional accents, the role of shaping by family, teachers, and culture in developing the repertoire is generally recognized. Once the behavior is well-established and discriminating, however, interpretations of it are likely to turn to internal conceptual entities rather than stimulus-control factors. The guileless tone of these interpretations hides, of course, centuries of mentalism in the usage of such explanatory concepts (Kantor, 1953). Perhaps it is not unreasonable to suppose that in the realm of "control" of an autonomic response we are, in fact, dealing with an individual's history of stimulus control.

SOME CONSIDERATIONS FOR FUTURE RESEARCH

Future investigators may well be puzzled by the present emphasis upon mediation in operant autonomic conditioning. On the one hand, such a concentration of effort on this problem will have meant a loss of experimental analysis elsewhere (Black, 1967b, p. 21). On the other hand, with mediation such a general property of bodily systems and psychophysiological settings anyway, the singling out of operant autonomic conditioning for this special scrutiny may seem curious. Most would agree that an organism without mediation of some sort is dead. Some would suggest that, when mediation begins to imply the primacy of one body system over another, the emphasis be shifted to integration. From the present vantage point it appears that the mediation issue in autonomic conditioning gradually may be forgotten rather than resolved, as small clusters of researchers drift off to other problems. Certainly one of these problem

areas is the practical one of psychosomatic medicine. Operant conditioning techniques are being employed with increasing effectiveness in the larger region of behavioral disorders under the label "behavior modification" (Ullmann & Krasner, 1965). Indications that a psychosomatic flank is developing in the behavioral modification phalanx are already present. Engel and Melmon (1967), for example, have reported success in modifying supraventricular atrial tachycardia with operant procedures. One rather expects now that a large number of diseases and malfunctions of various organ systems will be approached with response-contingent events.

A number of basic problems await solutions that could be assisted by operant procedures. Some of these pertain to the interaction of body systems, e.g., the effects of work upon cardiovascular function, the consequences of cardiovascular behavior upon somatic and sensory functions, and the reciprocity of body systems in providing interoceptive and proprioceptive cues for long and complex chains of responses. These are not new problems, of course (Forsyth, 1965; Lacey & Lacey, 1958; Peters & Gantt, 1953; Razran, 1961; Smith, King, Rushmer, & Ruch, 1962); but, as yet, the full use of operant methods has not been turned to them.

Analysis of autonomic and somatic afferent stimuli as *discriminative* stimuli in a detection setting has been slow in starting, despite considerable advances in animal psychophysics and operant applications of the theory of signal detectability (Blough, 1966, 1967; Green & Swets, 1966). The salivation of dogs has been viewed as an operant discriminative stimulus (M. Shapiro, 1960; M. Shapiro & Miller, 1965). Hefferline and Perera (1963) were successful in establishing exceedingly small muscle action potentials as S^Ds for overt key pressing by human subjects. Interoceptive stimulation provided by an implanted jejunum loop was used as an S^D in monkeys by Slucki, Adam, and Porter (1965). A noteworthy experiment by Mandler and Kahn (1960), in which heart rate discrimination by human subjects was unsuccessful, apparently has not generated much laboratory effort in this direction. Sensory detection experiments in vision and audition typically involve many, many sessions with a single object (Mandler and Kahn used but four sessions with changing experimental conditions); often little serious data collection begins until the subject reaches a reliable steady state. If sensory detection experiments using interoceptive stimuli are successful, it will be interesting to relate such detection to the control of autonomic behavior. The boosting of this weak, natural, proprioceptive and interoceptive feedback with various visual and auditory devices has already been noted in the earlier discussion of operant EMG and autonomic conditioning. One can easily see such augmented feedback techniques as part of cybernetics; but then, of course, the response contingencies of operant conditioning can also be viewed within this more general framework.

The reinforcement or feedback in operant conditioning of such skeletal responses as key pressing has been "all or none," rather than graded, with few exceptions (Notterman, 1965); i.e., a response is either followed by delivery of the full amount of the reinforcer or none at all. Some graded feedback has been used with psychophysiological responses (Hefferline, Keenan, & Harford, 1959; Hnatiow & Lang, 1965). The notion that graded responses such as GSR and heart rate might be reinforced with events that are proportional to response magnitude will, no doubt, provide some interesting experimental speculation in the future. Whether the current interest in meter panels, counters, jeweled lamps, and other feedback devices represents a fruitful trend, or one to be rele-

gated by time to the status of recorder-ink technology, remains to be seen.

There is also the problem of how skeletal and autonomic operants compare across the full range of criteria. To an experimenter who has applied operant techniques to both kinds of behavior, there is an obvious difference between a responsive skeletal operant and a sluggish autonomic response, particularly one that is wandering through a habituatory phase. Clearly, the time constants stand apart, and even with sharp response criteria in hand it somehow seems harder to ignore the magnitudes of autonomic responses. For the operant researcher who relishes a baseline or operant level frequency close to zero, as might be true of a lever-pressing experiment, the sudden flood of autonomic responses just as conditioning is about to start is more than disheartening: a soundproof room will probably be included in the next budget request. Additional comparisons between skeletal and autonomic conditioning will be suggested by the chapter headings of learning textbooks such as discrimination, schedules of reinforcement, and resistance to extinction, and experiments on these topics may be anticipated.

A final suggestion is offered. If the relationship between psychophysiology and operant conditioning is to flourish, any talk around the polygraph machine that operant analysis is "just a technique" had best be silenced. One man's technique is another man's science.

REFERENCES

Azrin, N. H., & Lindsley, O. R. The reinforcement of cooperation between children. *Journal of Abnormal and Social Psychology,* 1956, **52,** 100–102.

Banks, J. H., Miller, R. E., & Ogawa, N. The development of discriminated autonomic and instrumental responses during avoidance conditioning in the Rhesus monkey. *Journal of General Psychology,* 1966, **108,** 199–211.

Basmajian, J. V. Control and training of individual motor units. *Science,* 1963, **141,** 440–441.

Benson, H., Herd, J. A., Morse, W. H., & Kelleher, R. T. Behavioral induction of arterial hypertension and its reversal. *American Journal of Physiology,* 1969, **217,** 30–34.

Birk, L., Crider, A., Shapiro, D., & Tursky, B. Operant

electrodermal conditioning under partial curarization. *Journal of Comparative and Physiological Psychology,* 1966, **62,** 165–166.

Black, A. H. A comment on yoked-control designs. Technical Report No. 11, 1967, Department of Psychology, McMaster University. (a)

Black, A. H. Operant conditioning of heart rate under curare. Technical Report No. 12, 1967, Department of Psychology, McMaster University. (b)

Black, A. H., Carlson, J. J., & Solomon, R. L. Exploratory studies of the conditioning of autonomic responses in curarized dogs. *Psychological Monographs,* 1962, **76** (No. 548).

Blough, D. S. The study of animal sensory processes by

operant methods. In W. K. HONIG (Ed.), *Operant behavior: Areas of research and application.* New York: Appleton-Century-Crofts, 1966.

BLOUGH, D. S. Stimulus generalization as signal detection in pigeons. *Science,* 1967, **158,** 940–941.

BRADY, J. V. Further comments on the gastrointestinal system and avoidance behavior. *Psychological Reports,* 1963, **12,** 742.

BRADY, J. V., PORTER, R. W., CONRAD, D. G., & MASON, J. W. Avoidance behavior and the development of gastrointestinal ulcers. *Journal of the Experimental Analysis of Behavior,* 1958, **1,** 69–73.

BRELAND, K., & BRELAND, M. The misbehavior of organisms. *American Psychologist,* 1961, **16,** 681–684.

BRENER, J. M. The characteristics of heart rate during various conditioning procedures. Unpublished doctoral dissertation, London University, 1964.

BRENER, J. Heart rate as an avoidance response. *Psychological Record,* 1966, **16,** 329–336.

BRENER, J., & HOTHERSALL, D. Heart rate control under conditions of augmented sensory feedback. *Psychophysiology,* 1966, **3,** 23–28.

BRENER, J., & HOTHERSALL, D. Paced respiration and heart rate control. *Psychophysiology,* 1967, **4,** 1–6.

BRENER, J., KLEINMAN, R., & GOESLING, W. J. The effects of different exposures to augmented sensory feedback on the control of heart rate. *Psychophysiology,* 1969, **5,** 510–516.

BROWN, C. C., & KATZ, R. A. Operant salivary conditioning in man. *Psychophysiology,* 1967, **4,** 156–160.

CARLSÖÖ, S., & EDFELDT, A. W. Attempts at muscle control with visual and auditory impulses as auxiliary stimuli *Scandinavian Journal of Psychology,* 1963, **4,** 231–233.

CHURCH, R. M. Systematic effect of random error in the yoked control design. *Psychological Bulletin,* 1964, **62,** 122–131.

CLARKE, N. P., SMITH, O. A., & SHEARN, D. W. Topographical representation of vascular smooth muscle of limbs in primate motor cortex. *American Journal of Physiology,* 1968, **214,** 122–129.

CRIDER, A., SCHWARTZ, G. E., & SHNIDMAN, S. On the criteria for instrumental autonomic conditioning: A reply to Katkin and Murray. *Psychological Bulletin,* 1969, **71,** 455–461.

CRIDER, A., SHAPIRO, D., & TURSKY, B. Reinforcement of spontaneous electrodermal activity. *Journal of Comparative and Physiological Psychology,* 1966, **61,** 20–27.

DAVIS, R. C. Physical psychology. *Psychological Review,* 1953, **60,** 7–14.

DAVIS, R. C. The domain of homeostasis. *Psychological Review,* 1958, **65,** 8–13.

DAVIS, R. C. Environmental control of gastrointestinal activity. *Science,* 1959, **130,** 1414–1415.

DAVIS, R. C., & BERRY, F. Gastrointestinal reactions during

a noise avoidance task. *Psychological Reports,* 1963, **12,** 135–137.

DELSE, F. C., & FEATHER, B. W. The effect of augmented sensory feedback on the control of salivation. *Psychophysiology,* 1968, **5,** 15–21.

DICARA, L. V., & MILLER, N. E. Instrumental learning of systolic blood pressure responses by curarized rats: Dissociation of cardiac and vascular changes. *Psychosomatic Medicine,* 1968, **38,** 489–494. (a)

DICARA, L. V., & MILLER, N. E. Instrumental learning of vasomotor responses by rats: Learning to respond differentially in the two ears. *Science,* 1968, **159,** 1485–1486. (b)

DICARA, L. V., & MILLER, N. E. Changes in heart rate instrumentally learned by curarized rats as avoidance responses. *Journal of Comparative and Physiological Psychology,* 1968, **65,** 8–12. (c)

DICARA, L. V., & MILLER, N. E. Transfer of instrumentally learned heart-rate changes from curarized to noncurarized state: Implications for a mediational hypothesis. *Journal of Comparative and Physiological Psychology,* 1969, **68,** 159–162.

DINSMOOR, J. A. A quantitative comparison of the discriminative and reinforcing functions of a stimulus. *Journal of Experimental Psychology,* 1950, **40,** 458–472.

DINSMOOR, J. A. Operant conditioning. In J. B. SIDOWSKI (Ed.), *Experimental methods and instrumentation in psychology.* New York: McGraw-Hill, 1966.

DOEHRING, D. G., & FERSTER, C. B. Psychophysiological responses in a human operant situation. *Psychological Record,* 1962, **12,** 251–261.

DOEHRING, D. G., & HELMER, J. E. Psychophysiological response to variable interval reinforcement in a human situation. *Psychological Record,* 1963, **13,** 283–292. (a)

DOEHRING, D. G., & HELMER, J. E. Psychophysiological responses to fixed ratio reinforcement. *Psychological Record,* 1963, **13,** 389–397. (b)

ENGEL, B. T., & CHISM, R. A. Operant conditioning of heart rate speeding. *Psychophysiology,* 1967, **3,** 418–426. (a)

ENGEL, B. T., & CHISM, R. A. Effect of increases and decreases in breathing rate on heart rate and finger pulse volume. *Psychophysiology,* 1967, **4,** 83–89. (b)

ENGEL, B. T., & HANSEN, S. P. Operant conditioning of heart rate slowing. *Psychophysiology,* 1966, **3,** 176–187.

ENGEL, B. T., & MELMON, K. L. Modification of cardiac arrhythmias through voluntary control. Paper presented at the Pavlovian Society Meetings, 1967.

ERIKSEN, C. W. (Ed.) *Behavior and awareness.* Durham, N.C.: Duke University Press, 1962.

ESTES, W. K., & SKINNER, B. F. Some quantitative properties of anxiety. *Journal of Experimental Psychology,* 1941, **29,** 390–400.

FAVILL, J., & WHITE, P. D. Voluntary acceleration of the heart rate. *Heart,* 1917, **6,** 175–184.

FEDOR, J. H., & RUSSELL, R. W. Gastrointestinal reactions

to response-contingent stimulation. *Psychological Reports*, 1965, **16**, 93–113.

FERSTER, C. B., & PERROTT, M. C. *Behavior principles.* New York: Appleton-Century-Crofts, 1968.

FERSTER, C. B., & SKINNER, B. F. *Schedules of reinforcement.* New York: Appleton-Century-Crofts, 1957.

FETZ, E. E. Operant conditioning of cortical unit activity. *Science*, 1969, **163**, 955–958.

FINDLEY, J. D., & BRADY, J. V. Blood pressure and heart rate changes under a chronic stress-inducing escape-avoidance procedure. Paper presented at the American Psychological Association, 1969.

FORSYTH, R. P. Influence of blood pressure on patterns of voluntary behavior. *Psychophysiology*, 1965, **2**, 98–102.

FORSYTH, R. P. Blood pressure and avoidance conditioning. *Psychosomatic Medicine*, 1968, **30**, 125–135.

FORSYTH, R. P. Blood pressure responses to long-term avoidance schedules in the restrained Rhesus monkey. *Psychosomatic Medicine*, 1969, **31**, 300–309.

FORSYTH, R. P., & ROSENBLUM, M. A. A restraining device and procedure for continuous blood pressure recordings in monkeys. *Journal of the Experimental Analysis of Behavior*, 1964, **7**, 367–368.

FOWLER, R. L., & KIMMEL, H. D. Operant conditioning of the GSR. *Journal of Experimental Psychology*, 1962, **63**, 563–567.

FOX, S. S., & RUDELL, A. P. Operant controlled neural event: Formal and systematic approach to electrical coding of behavior in brain. *Science*, 1969, **162**, 1299–1302.

FRAZIER, T. W. Avoidance conditioning of heart rate in humans. *Psychophysiology*, 1966, **3**, 188–202.

FRAZIER, T. W., WEIL-MALHERBE, H., & LIPSCOMB, H. S. Psychophysiology of conditioned emotional disturbances in humans. *Psychophysiology*, 1969, **5**, 478–503.

FUSTER, J. M., & WEINBERG, S. J. Bioelectrical changes in the heart cycle induced by stimulation of diencephalic regions. *Experimental Neurology*, 1960, **2**, 26–39.

GAVALAS, R. J. Operant reinforcement of an autonomic response: Two studies. *Journal of the Experimental Analysis of Behavior*, 1967, **16**, 119–130.

GAVALAS, R. J. Operant reinforcement of a skeletally mediated autonomic response: Uncoupling of the two responses. *Psychonomic Science*, 1968, **11**, 195–196.

GOLDBERG, S. R., & SCHUSTER, C. R. Conditional suppression by a stimulus associated with nalorphine in morphine dependent monkeys. *Journal of the Experimental Analysis of Behavior*, 1967, **10**, 235–242.

GOODMAN, L. S., & GILMAN, A. *The pharmacological basis of therapeutics.* New York: Macmillan, 1965.

GRAHAM, C. A., COHEN, S. F., & SHMAVONIAN, B. M. Physiological discrimination and behavioral relationships in human instrumental conditioning. *Psychosomatic Medicine*, 1964, **26**, 321–355.

GREEN, D. M., & SWETS, J. A. *Signal detection theory and psychophysics.* New York: Wiley, 1966.

GREENE, W. A. Operant conditioning of the GSR using

partial reinforcement. *Psychological Reports*, 1966, **19**, 571–578.

GREENSPOON, J. Verbal conditioning and clinical psychology. In A. J. BACHRACH (Ed.), *Experimental foundations of clinical psychology.* New York: Basic Books, 1962.

GRINGS, W. W., & CARLIN, S. Instrumental modification of autonomic behavior. *Psychological Record*, 1966, **16**, 153–159.

GURDJIAN, E. S. Olfactory connections in the albino rat with special reference to the stria medullaris and the anterior commissure. *Journal of Comparative Neurology*, 1925, **38**, 127–163.

HARWOOD, C. W. Operant heart rate conditioning. *Psychological Record*, 1962, **12**, 279–284.

HEFFERLINE, R. F. Learning theory and clinical psychology—an eventual symbiosis? In A. BACHRACH (Ed.), *Experimental foundations of clinical psychology.* New York: Basic Books, 1962.

HEFFERLINE, R. F., & KEENAN, B. Amplitude-induction gradient of a small human operant in an escape-avoidance situation. *Journal of the Experimental Analysis of Behavior*, 1961, **4**, 41–43.

HEFFERLINE, R. F., & KEENAN, B. Amplitude-induction gradient of a small-scale (covert) operant. *Journal of the Experimental Analysis of Behavior*, 1963, **6**, 307–315.

HEFFERLINE, R. F., KEENAN, B., & HARFORD, A. Escape and avoidance in human subjects without their observation of the response. *Science*, 1959, **130**, 1338–1339.

HEFFERLINE, R. F., & PERERA, T. B. Proprioceptive discrimination of a covert operant without its observation by the subject. *Science*, 1963, **139**, 834–835.

HERD, J. A., MORSE, W. H., KELLEHER, R. T., & JONES, L. G. Arterial hypertension in the squirrel monkey during behavioral experiments. *American Journal of Physiology*, 1969, **217**, 24–29.

HERRNSTEIN, R. J. Superstition: A corollary of the principles of operant conditioning. In W. K. HONIG (Ed.), *Operant behavior: Areas of research and application.* New York: Appleton-Century-Crofts, 1966.

HNATIOW, M., & LANG, P. J. Learned stabilization of cardiac rate. *Psychophysiology*, 1965, **1**, 330–336.

HOLLAND, J. G. Human vigilance. *Science*, 1958, **128**, 61–67.

HOLLAND, J. G., & SKINNER, B. F. *The analysis of behavior.* New York: McGraw-Hill, 1961.

HOLZ, W. C., & AZRIN, N. H. Conditioning human verbal behavior. In W. K. HONIG (Ed.), *Operant behavior: Areas of research and application.* New York: Appleton-Century-Crofts, 1966.

HONIG, W. K. (Ed.) *Operant behavior: Areas of research and application.* New York: Appleton-Century-Crofts, 1966.

HOTHERSALL, D., & BRENER, J. Operant conditioning of changes in heart rate in curarized rats. *Journal of Comparative and Physiological Psychology*, 1969, **68**, 338–342.

JOHNSON, H. J., & SCHWARTZ, G. E. Suppression of GSR

activity through operant reinforcement. *Journal of Experimental Psychology,* 1967, **75,** 307–312.

KAMIYA, J. Conscious control of brain waves. *Psychology Today,* 1968, **1,** 57–60.

KANTOR, J. R. *The logic of modern science.* Bloomington, Ind.: Principia Press, 1953.

KATKIN, E. S., & MURRAY, E. N. Instrumental conditioning of autonomically mediated behavior: Theoretical and methodological issues. *Psychological Bulletin,* 1968, **70,** 52–68.

KENT, N. Muscle action potentials during verbal learning. Unpublished doctoral dissertation, Indiana University, 1958.

KIMMEL, E., & KIMMEL, H. D. A replication of operant conditioning of the GSR. *Journal of Experimental Psychology,* 1963, **65,** 212.

KIMMEL, H. D. Instrumental conditioning of autonomically mediated behavior. *Psychological Bulletin,* 1967, **67,** 337–345.

KIMMEL, H. D., & BAXTER, R. Avoidance conditioning of the GSR. *Journal of Experimental Psychology,* 1964, **68,** 482–485.

KIMMEL, H. D., & HILL, F. A. Operant conditioning of the GSR. *Psychological Reports,* 1960, **7,** 555–562.

KIMMEL, H. D., & STERNTHAL, H. S. Replication of GSR avoidance conditioning with concomitant EMG measurement and subjects matched in responsivity and conditionability. *Journal of Experimental Psychology,* 1967, **74,** 144–146.

KIMMEL, H. D., STERNTHAL, H. S., & STRUB, H. Two replications of avoidance conditioning of the GSR. *Journal of Experimental Psychology,* 1966, **72,** 151–152.

KRIEG, W. J. S. The hypothalamus of the albino rat. *Journal of Comparative Neurology,* 1932, **55,** 19–89.

LACEY, J. I., & LACEY, B. C. The relationship of resting autonomic activity to motor impulsivity. *Research Publications of the Association for Nervous and Mental Disease,* 1958, **36,** 144–209.

LANG, P. J., SROUFE, L. A., & HASTINGS, J. E. Effects of feedback and instructional set on the control of cardiac rate variability. *Journal of Experimental Psychology,* 1967, **75,** 425–431.

LEVENE, H. I., ENGEL, B. T., & PEARSON, J. A. Differential operant conditioning of heart rate. *Psychosomatic Medicine,* 1969, **30,** 837–845.

LISINA, M. I. The role of orientation in the transformation of involuntary reactions into voluntary ones. In L. G. VORONIN, A. N. LEONTIEV, A. R. LURIA, E. N. SOKOLOV, & O. S. VINOGRADOVA (Eds.), *Orienting reflex and exploratory behavior.* Washington, D.C.: American Institute of Biological Sciences, 1965.

MALMO, R. B. Slowing of heart rate after septal self-stimulation in rats. *Science,* 1961, **133,** 1129–1130.

MALMO, R. B. Heart rate reactions and locus of stimulation within the septal area of the rat. *Science,* 1964, **144,** 1029–1030.

MANDLER, G., & KAHN, M. Discrimination of changes in heart rate: Two unsuccessful attempts. *Journal of the Experimental Analysis of Behavior,* 1960, **3,** 21–25.

MANDLER, G., PREVEN, D. W., & KUHLMAN, C. K. Effects of operant reinforcement on the GSR. *Journal of the Experimental Analysis of Behavior,* 1962, **5,** 317–321.

MASON, J., & BRADY, J. V. Plasma 17-hydroxycorticosteroid changes related to reserpine effects on emotional behavior. *Science,* 1956, **124,** 983–984.

MASON, J., BRADY, J. V., POLISH, E., BAUER, J. A., ROBINSON, J. A., ROSE, R. M., & TAYLOR, E. D. Patterns of corticosteroid and pepsinogen change related to psychological stress in the monkey. *Science,* 1961, **133,** 1569–1598. (a)

MASON, J. W., BRADY, J. V., ROBINSON, J. A., TAYLOR, E. D., TOLSON, W. W., & MOUGEY, E. H. Patterns of thyroid, gonadal and adrenal hormone secretion related to psychological stress in the monkey. *Psychosomatic Medicine,* 1961, **23,** 446. (Abstract) (b)

MASON, J. W., BRADY, J. V., & SIDMAN, M. Plasma 17-hydroxycorticosteroid levels and conditioned behavior in the Rhesus monkey. *Endocrinology,* 1957, **60,** 741–752.

MASON, J. W., BRADY, J. V., & TOLLIVER, G. A. Plasma and urinary 17-hydoxycorticosteroid responses to 72-hr avoidance sessions in the monkey. *Psychosomatic Medicine,* 1968, **30,** 608–630.

MASON, J. W., MANGAN, G., BRADY, J. V., CONRAD, D., & RIOCH, D. McK. Concurrent plasma epinephrine, norepinephrine and 17-hydroxycorticosteroid levels during conditioned emotional disturbances in monkeys. *Psychosomatic Medicine,* 1961, **23,** 344–353. (c)

MASON, J. W., NAUTA, W. J. H., BRADY, J. V., ROBINSON, J. A., & SACHAR, E. J. The role of limbic system structures in regulation of ACTH secretion. *Acta Neurovegetativa,* 1961, **23,** 4–14. (d)

MAY, J. R., & JOHNSON, H. J. Positive reinforcement and suppression of spontaneous GSR activity. *Journal of Experimental Psychology,* 1969, **80,** 193–195.

MEYERS, W. J., VALENSTEIN, E. S., & LACEY, J. I. Heart rate changes after reinforcing brain stimulation in rats. *Science,* 1964, **144,** 1029–1030.

MILLER, N. E. Learning of visceral and glandular responses. *Science,* 1969, **163,** 434–445.

MILLER, N. E., & BANUAZIZI, A. Instrumental learning by curarized rats of a specific visceral response, intestinal or cardiac. *Journal of Comparative and Physiological Psychology,* 1968, **65,** 1–7.

MILLER, N. E., & CARMONA, A. Modification of a visceral response, salivation in thirsty dogs, by instrumental training with water reward. *Journal of Comparative and Physiological Psychology,* 1967, **63,** 1–6.

MILLER, N. E., & DiCARA, L. V. Instrumental learning of heart rate changes in curarized rats: Shaping, and specificity to discriminative stimulus. *Journal of Comparative and Physiological Psychology,* 1967, **63,** 12–19.

MILLER, N. E., & DiCARA, L. V. Instrumental learning of

urine formation by rats: Changes in renal blood flow. *American Journal of Physiology*, 1968, **215**, 677–683.

MOWRER, O. H. On the dual nature of learning—a reinterpretation of "conditioning" and "problem-solving." *Harvard Educational Review*, 1947, **17**, 102–148.

MULHOLLAND, T., & EVANS, C. R. Oculomotor function and the alpha-activation cycle. *Nature*, 1966, **211**, 1278–1279.

MULHOLLAND, T., & RUNNALS, S. Evaluation of attention and alertness with a stimulus brain feedback loop. *Electroencephalography and Clinical Neurophysiology*, 1962, **14**, 847–852.

MURRAY, E. N., & KATKIN, E. S. Comment on two reports of operant heart rate conditioning. *Psychophysiology*, 1968, **5**, 192–195.

NATHAN, M. A., & SMITH, O. A. Differential conditional emotional and cardiovascular responses—a training technique for monkeys. *Journal of the Experimental Analysis of Behavior*, 1968, **11**, 77–82.

NORMAN, A. Response contingency and human gastric acidity. *Psychophysiology*, 1969, **5**, 673–682.

NOTTERMAN, J. M., & MINTZ, D. E. *Dynamics of response*. New York: Wiley, 1965.

OLDS, J., & OLDS, M. F. In J. F. DELAFRESNAYE (Ed.), *Brain mechanisms and learning*. Oxford: Blackwell, 1961.

PEREZ-CRUET, J., BLACK, W. C., & BRADY, J. V. Heart rate: Differential effects of hypothalamic and septal self-stimulation. *Science*, 1963, **140**, 1235–1236.

PEREZ-CRUET, J., TOLLIVER, G., DUNN, G., MARVIN, S., & BRADY, J. V. Concurrent measurement of heart rate and instrumental avoidance behavior in the Rhesus monkey. *Journal of the Experimental Analysis of Behavior*, 1964, **6**, 61–64.

PETERS, J. E., & GANTT, W. H. Effect of graded degrees of muscular exertion on human heart rate and the role of muscular exertion in cardiac conditional reflexes. *Journal of General Psychology*, 1953, **49**, 31–43.

PLUMLEE, L. Operant conditioning of blood pressure increases and decreases in the monkey. *Psychophysiology*, 1968, **4**, 507–508.

POLISH, E., BRADY, J. V., MASON, J. W., THACK, J. S., & NIEMECK, W. Gastric contents and the occurrence of duodenal lesions in the Rhesus monkey during avoidance behavior. *Gastroenterology*, 1962, **43**, 193–201.

PORTER, R. W., BRADY, J. V., CONRAD, D., MASON, J. W., GALAMBOS, R., & RIOCH, D. McK. Some experimental observations on gastrointestinal lesions in behaviorally conditioned monkeys. *Psychosomatic Medicine*, 1958, **20**, 379–394.

RAZRAN, G. The observable unconscious and the inferable conscious in current Soviet psychophysiology: Interoceptive conditioning, semantic conditioning, and the orienting reflex. *Psychological Review*, 1961, **68**, 81–147.

REYNOLDS, G. S. *A primer of operant conditioning*. Glenview, Ill.: Scott, Foresman, 1968.

RICE, D. G. Operant conditioning and associated electromyogram responses. *Journal of Experimental Psychology*, 1966, **71**, 908–912.

RICE, H. K. The responding-rest ratio in the production of gastric ulcers in the rat. *Psychological Reports*, 1963, **13**, 11–14.

ROSENFELD, J. P., RUDELL, A. P., & FOX, S. S. Operant control of neural events in humans. *Science*, 1969, **165**, 821–822.

SCHWARTZ, G. E., & JOHNSON, H. J. Affective visual stimuli as operant reinforcement of the GSR. *Journal of Experimental Psychology*, 1969, **80**, 28–32.

SHAPIRO, D., CRIDER, A. B., & TURSKY, B. Differentiation of an autonomic response through operant reinforcement. *Psychonomic Science*, 1964, **1**, 147–148.

SHAPIRO, D., TURSKY, B., GERSHON, E., & STERN, M. Effects of feedback and reinforcement on the control of human systolic blood pressure. *Science*, 1969, **163**, 588–590.

SHAPIRO, M. M. Respondent salivary conditioning during operant lever pressing in dogs. *Science*, 1960, **132**, 619–620.

SHAPIRO, M. M., & MILLER, T. M. On the relationship between conditional and discriminative stimuli and between instrumental and consummatory responses. In W. F. PROKASY (Ed.), *Classical conditioning*. New York: Appleton-Century-Crofts, 1965.

SHARPEY-SCHAFER, E. P. Effect of respiratory acts on the circulation. In W. F. HAMILTON (Ed.), *Circulation. Handbook of physiology*. Vol. 3. Washington, D.C.: American Physiological Society, 1965.

SHEARN, D. W. Operant conditioning of the heart rate. Unpublished doctoral dissertation, Indiana University, 1960.

SHEARN, D. W. Operant conditioning of heart rate. *Science*, 1962, **137**, 530–531.

SHEARN, D. W., & CLIFFORD, G. Cardiac adaptation and contingent stimulation. *American Psychologist*, 1964, **19**, 491. (Abstract)

SHEARN, D. W., & DAVIS, R. C. Skeletal and cardiac reactions to reinforcing and incidental stimuli. Technical Report No. 4, Contract Nonr. 908–15, Indiana University, 1961.

SIDMAN, M. *Tactics of scientific research*. New York: Basic Books, 1960.

SIDMAN, M. Operant techniques. In A. BACHRACH (Ed.), *Experimental foundations of clinical psychology*. New York: Basic Books, 1962.

SIDMAN, M., MASON, J. W., BRADY, J. V., & THACK, J. Quantitative relations between avoidance behavior and pituitary-adrenal cortical activity. *Journal of the Experimental Analysis of Behavior*, 1962, **5**, 353–362.

SKINNER, B. F. *The behavior of organisms: An experimental analysis*. New York: Appleton-Century-Crofts, 1938.

SKINNER, B. F. Are theories of learning necessary? *Psychological Review*, 1950, **57**, 193–216.

SKINNER, B. F. How to teach animals. *Scientific American*, 1951, **185**, 26–29.

SKINNER, B. F. *Science and human behavior.* New York: Macmillan, 1953.

SKINNER, B. F. Operant behavior. In W. K. HONIG (Ed.), *Operant behavior: Areas of research and application.* New York: Appleton-Century-Crofts, 1966.

SKINNER, B. F. *The technology of teaching.* New York: Appleton-Century-Crofts, 1968.

SLUCKI, H., ADAM, G., & PORTER, R. W. Operant discrimination of an interoceptive stimulus in Rhesus monkeys. *Journal of the Experimental Analysis of Behavior,* 1965, **8,** 405–414.

SMITH, O. A., Anatomy of central neural pathways mediating cardiovascular functions. In W. C. RANDALL (Ed.), *Nervous control of the heart.* Baltimore: Williams & Wilkins, 1965.

SMITH, O. A., JABBUR, S. J., RUSHMER, R. F., & LASHER, E. P. Role of hypothalamic structures in cardiac control. *Physiological Review,* 1960, **40** (Suppl. No. 4, Part 2), 136–141.

SMITH, O. A., KING, R. L., RUSHMER, R. F., & RUCH, T. C. Techniques for determination of cardiovascular response to exercise in unanesthetized monkeys. *Journal of Applied Physiology,* 1962, **17,** 718–721.

SNYDER, C., & NOBLE, M. E. Operant conditioning of vasoconstriction. *Journal of Experimental Psychology,* 1968, **77,** 263–268.

SNYDER, C., & NOBLE, M. E. Operant conditioning of vasoconstriction. Paper presented at the meeting of the Psychonomic Society, St. Louis, Mo., October 1966.

SOLOMON, R. L. Punishment. *American Psychologist,* 1964, **19,** 239–253.

SPILKER, B., KAMIYA, J., CALLAWAY, E., & YEAGER, C. C. Visual evoked responses in subjects trained to control alpha rhythms. *Psychophysiology,* 1969, **5,** 683–695.

SROUFE, L. A. Learned stabilization of cardiac rate with respiration experimentally controlled. *Journal of Experimental Psychology,* 1969, **81,** 391–393.

STEBBINS, W. C. Behavioral technics. In R. F. RUSHMER (Ed.), *Methods in medical research,* Vol. 11. Chicago: Year Book Medical Publishers, 1966.

STEBBINS, W. C., & SMITH, O. A. Cardiovascular concomitants of the conditioned emotional response in the monkey. *Science,* 1964, **144,** 881–883.

STEINER, S. S., BEER, B., & SHAFFER, M. M. Escape from self-produced rates of brain stimulation. *Science,* 1969, **163,** 90–91.

STERN, R. M. A re-examination of the effects of response-contingent stimulation on gastrointestinal activity. *Psychophysiology,* 1966, **2,** 217–223.

STERN, R. M. Operant conditioning of spontaneous GSRs: Negative results. *Journal of Experimental Psychology,* 1967, **75,** 128–130.

STERN, R. M., & ANSCHEL, C. Deep inspirations as stimuli for responses of the autonomic nervous system. *Psychophysiology,* 1968, **5,** 132–141.

STERN, R. M., BOLES, J., & DIONIS, J. Operant conditioning of spontaneous GSRs: Two unsuccessful attempts. Technical Report No. 13, Contract Nonr. 908–15, Office of Naval Research, Indiana University, 1966.

STEVENS, J. R. Endogenous conditioning to abnormal cerebral electrical transients in man. *Science,* 1962, **137,** 974–976.

SUTTON, D., & KIMM, J. Reaction time of motor units in biceps and triceps. *Experimental Neurology,* 1969, **23,** 503–515.

TERRACE, H. S. Stimulus control. In W. K. HONIG (Ed.), *Operant behavior: Areas of research and application.* New York: Appleton-Century-Crofts, 1966.

THORNDIKE, E. L. Animal intelligence: An experimental study of the associative processes in animals. Unpublished doctoral dissertation, Columbia University, 1898.

TOLEDO, L. DE, & BLACK, A. H. Heart rate: Changes during conditional suppression in rats. *Science,* 1966, **152,** 1404–1406.

TROWILL, J. A. Instrumental conditioning of the heart rate. Unpublished doctoral dissertation, Yale University, 1966.

TROWILL, J. A. Instrumental conditioning of the heart rate in the curarized rat. *Journal of Comparative and Physiological Psychology,* 1967, **63,** 7–11.

ULLMANN, L. P., & KRASNER, L. *Case studies in behavior modification.* New York: Holt, Rinehart and Winston, 1965.

VAN TWYVER, H. B., & KIMMEL, H. D. Operant conditioning of the GSR with concomitant measurement of two somatic variables. *Journal of Experimental Psychology,* 1966, **72,** 841–846.

VERPLANCK, W. S. B. F. Skinner. In W. K. ESTES, S. KOCK, K. MacCORQUODAL, P. E. MEEHL, C. G. MUELLER, W. N. SCHOENFELD, & W. S. VERPLANCK (Eds.), *Modern learning theory.* New York: Appleton-Century-Crofts, 1954.

WENZEL, B. M. Changes in heart rate associated with responses based on positive and negative reinforcement. *Journal of Comparative and Physiological Psychology,* 1961, **54,** 638–644.

WHITE, E. H. Additional notes on gastrointestinal activity during avoidance behavior. *Psychological Reports,* 1964, **14,** 343–347.

PART

3 RESPONSE SYSTEMS

Charles Shagass

ELECTRICAL ACTIVITY
OF THE BRAIN*

7

HISTORICAL INTRODUCTION

Electrical brain activities may be placed into three general categories: (a) potential changes resulting from nerve impulses initiated by alterations in the internal or external environments; (b) the steady potential difference existing between the cortical surface and the white matter beneath it; (c) the oscillating potential of the brain, commonly called the electroencephalogram (EEG). All of these electrical events are interdependent (Brazier, 1958). The psychophysiologist can seldom study events in Category b, since they must be recorded directly from the brain. This chapter will deal with events in Categories a and c, which are accessible with electrodes placed on the scalp, although they may be much attenuated. Additional limitations arise from the fact that the recorded electrical events arise mainly in structures adjacent to the skull and scalp. In the case of the evoked potentials, falling into Category a, special recording techniques, which restrict the scope of observation, may be necessary.

Historically, human electrophysiology has followed discoveries of electrical phenomena in experimental animals, with a time lag dependent upon the invention of techniques for

*Research supported in part by the United States Public Health Service Grants MH02635 and MH12507. The advice and criticism of Donald A. Overton are also gratefully acknowledged.

similar observations in man. Brazier (1961) has provided an excellent account of the early history of electrophysiology, which begins with the experiments of Galvani with frogs and metals toward the end of the eighteenth century. Galvani concluded that nerves contain an intrinsic form of electricity. Volta believed that all the phenomena uncovered by Galvani were to be explained on the basis of bimetallic currents, whereas Galvani's view was that the electricity was derived in each case from the animal tissue. Both arguments were partly right and partly wrong, but the controversy led to two great achievements: the design of the electric battery from Volta and the science of electrophysiology from Galvani. A half century passed before DuBois-Reymond demonstrated that activity in a peripheral nerve was invariably accompanied by an electrical change, a "negative variation," in the standing potential found between the cut end of the nerve and its longitudinal surface. The demonstration that the passage of a nerve impulse involves a concomitant electrical signal gave electrophysiologists their most important tool for tracing the transmission of impulses through the nervous system, i.e., the action potential. This finding led directly to the discovery of the EEG, a discovery made independently, 15 years apart, in two separate countries.

The first to discover the EEG was Richard Caton (1875) at Liverpool University. He began his experiments to determine whether the negative variation that DuBois-Reymond had found in nerves could be demonstrated in the brain on the stimulation of sensory receptors. In other words, he was looking for an evoked potential in the brain. He not only found what he was seeking but he was also a sufficiently astute observer to note (and not discard, as the later workers did) an unexpected observation. When both electrodes were on uncut cortex, there were incessant fluctuations of potential, even when he eliminated all experimental stimulation of the animal. He named these the "electric currents of the brain" and reported them to the British Medical Association in 1875. Although his discovery appeared in journals of three countries, England, the United States, and Russia, it remained comparatively unnoticed. Fifteen years after Caton's discovery, Adolf Beck, a young instructor in physiology

at the University of Jagiellianski in Krakau, Poland, also set out to look for signs of action potentials in the brain, initiated by impulses in sense organs. He was as successful as Caton, though ignorant of his work.

Both Caton and Beck observed cerebral responses to photic stimuli, as did Fleischl von Marxow in Vienna, also working in ignorance of Caton's discovery. These early workers were dependent upon sensitive galvanometers for their recordings. With the invention of the vacuum tube and its use in electronic amplifiers, great magnification of fluctuating potentials of the brain "at rest" was possible, as observed by many workers.

The discovery that what was true for animals was also true for man was made by Hans Berger, a psychiatrist at Jena. He had made unpublished studies on the electrical activity of the brain in animals beginning in 1902; his studies in man started in 1924. Two types of rhythm, now known as alpha and beta, had been distinguished in the dog by Prawdicz-Neminski (1913); Berger found similar rhythms in man and gave them the same designations (1929). Berger was not only the first to demonstrate the EEG of man but he discovered that it is abnormal in epilepsy. He did not publish his findings until 1929. In that year and until 1938 a long series of his papers appeared.

Berger seems to have had a global concept of the electrical activity of the brain. In many of his experiments he used very large electrodes, one on the forehead and one on the occiput. His recordings were badly contaminated by muscle artifacts, and he did not realize the localizing potentialities of the EEG.

It took some time before there was general acceptance of the fact that the rhythms obtained by Berger really had their origin in the brain. A major event determining such acceptance took place in 1935 at a meeting of the Physiological Society in England. Adrian and Matthews attached leads from electrodes on Adrian's head to a Matthews amplifier and ink-writing oscillograph and proved that Berger had in fact discovered that the electrical rhythms of the human brain were accessible from the intact skull. They demonstrated that the larger rhythms, alpha, tended to stop when the subject opened his eyes or worked on a difficult problem. Adrian and Yamagiwa (1935) showed that the alpha rhythm in normal man originates in the occipital regions and not from the whole brain, a finding that Berger was unwilling to accept.

W. G. Walter (1936) demonstrated that slow potential swings, which he named delta waves, arose from the tissue surrounding brain tumors and that tumors could be localized by means of the EEG. This finding and the discovery by Gibbs, Davis, and Lennox (1935) of a 3/sec wave and spike discharge in petit mal epilepsy gave electroencephalography the status of a procedure relevant to clinical diagnosis.

Firm establishment that man's electrical brain activity could be recorded from the top of the scalp, the demonstration that such recordings could be of clinical value, and the rapid development of easily used recording instruments through advances in electronics combined to provide the basis for widespread adoption of electroencephalographic techniques. Well under way before the beginning of World War II, the development of electroencephalography was markedly accelerated after 1945. The appearance of the *EEG Journal* (*Electroencephalography and Clinical Neurophysiology*) in 1949 under the editorship of Herbert Jasper signaled its coming of age. There are now active EEG societies in many countries, all members of the International Federation of Societies for Electroencephalography and Clinical Neurophysiology.

The possibility of recording electrical signs of brain activity in intact, conscious, and reporting human beings generated much hope for new understanding of mind-brain relationships. Investigations of the EEG during various kinds of mental activity and attempts to correlate EEG characteristics with personal attributes on the behavioral level such as intelligence and personality were quickly undertaken. Although these were, for the most part, disappointing in their outcome, investigators have persisted. New concepts concerning "arousal" followed Moruzzi and Magoun's (1949) discovery that electrical stimulation of the mesencephalic reticular formation resulted in behavioral alerting and electrical changes like those following peripheral stimulation, and that these outlasted the stimulus. The central role of the EEG signs of arousal added strong impetus for the use of the EEG in psychophysiology.

The underlying physiology of the EEG became a major research interest of many investigators. As Brazier (1958) notes, the "all or nothing" law dominated neurophysiology during the first three decades of this century. However, attempts to explain the comparatively slow potential changes represented by the EEG in terms of action potentials of axons, which in the periphery have a duration of less than a millisecond, were not convincing. For example, it would require very many axon spikes slightly out of phase to give the envelope of one alpha wave. Electrophysiologists soon sought electrical events within the brain with a slower time course. Investigation of the possibility that dendritic potentials may give rise to the EEG was facilitated by development of techniques for recording from brain neurons with microelectrodes. Bishop and Clare (1953) demonstrated that normal activity of these dendrites appears to consist mainly of nonpropagated graded potentials spreading decrementally from the point at which the stimulus is received. These potentials are of long duration, and they reflect the strength of the stimulus, i.e., they are not all-or-nothing in character. They do not have a refractory period, so that they may sum with any consequent potentials that are set up before they die away. The discovery of graded responses in the central nervous system opened the way to flexible models of brain activity that were not possible with the all-or-nothing law. According to Brazier (1958), "The lack of a refractory period with the resultant effect that an incoming impulse could sum with the traces of a previous one gave a basis for the nonlinearity of response that is so typical of the biologic system [p. 314]."

The remarkable changes that take place in the EEG as the organism passes from the waking to the sleep state had been noted from the earliest days of electroencephalography (Loomis, Harvey, & Hobart, 1935), and had given rise to a number of studies and various classifications of the EEG stages of sleep. The discovery that rapid eye movements (REM) are associated with a particular stage of sleep and that the awakened sleeper will report dreaming with much higher frequency during this stage of sleep as compared with others (Aserinsky & Kleitman, 1955) was responsible for the remarkable proliferation of studies on sleep and dreams during the past decade. Chapter 17, which is devoted to the topic in this volume, is an indication of the great interest in the area.

Although the potentials evoked by sensory stimulation were the first electrical phenomena of the brain to be observed in animal studies, they are difficult to record from the scalp of man. This is because they are obscured by the oscillations of the "spontaneous" EEG and also because the conventional apparatus used in EEG recording will not reproduce the more rapid components of the evoked response. G. D. Dawson (1947) showed that responses evoked by stimulation of a peripheral nerve could be detected by application of the principle of averaging, using a cathode ray oscilloscope. He superimposed numerous traces following application of a sensory stimulus and showed that a time-locked waveform representing the evoked response could be detected against the background EEG activity, whose temporal distribution was random with respect to the stimulus. Over the following years, various instruments for automatic detection of evoked responses in the background EEG activity were devised (Barlow, 1957; Dawson, 1954; Kozhevnikov, 1958). The most sophisticated involved use of the general purpose digital computer. Specialized laboratory computers, which rendered averaging relatively simple, were introduced about 1960; this development was followed by widespread adoption of the method of recording sensory evoked responses.

The specialized application of the computer technology involved in instruments used for extracting averaged evoked responses is but one example of the rapidly expanding application of computer technology to the field of electrophysiology. The extremely large amount of information obtained in a relatively short multichannel recording of the EEG presents enormous problems of data reduction. The high speed computational capacity of digital computers, combined with the ability to bring EEG data to the computer by means of precision tape recorders, has made it possible for investigators to explore different models for summarizing a large amount of EEG information in compact quantitative form. Although still in relatively early stages of exploration, computer analysis of the EEG may offer the psychophysiologist his greatest hope of relating electrical brain activity to behavioral events.

TECHNIQUES

Instrumentation

General requirements for recording the EEG have been well stated by W. G. Walter and Parr (1963).

1. There must be at least 4 separate amplifying channels. Six are usually desirable and 8 are necessary for the best yield of information. As many as 30 have been used, and in specifying recording equipment it should be recalled that in many circumstances other variables besides the EEG have to be recorded, so that even if only 8 channels are envisaged for EEG apparatus, several more can easily be occupied by polygraphic recording.
2. The record should be immediately visible to the operator, and should not require extra processing to render it visible.
3. The record should be permanent and should not fade or smudge.
4. The material used for recording should be cheap and easily stored since records lasting for several minutes are usually required [p. 43].

Requirements 2 and 4 render the cathode ray oscilloscope unsuitable for use in electroencephalography, particularly since it requires photography of the trace.

The most commonly used recorders involve a moving coil with a movement similar to that of a conventional ammeter; with special design of the coils and magnetic assemblies, a frequency response up to 100 Hz can be achieved. The recording pen has to be of considerable length in order to avoid excessive arc distortion; its moment of inertia determines the upper frequency limit of the system. There must also be critical damping to avoid overswing when recording transients and exaggeration of the components at the natural frequency of the system.

The electrical signal picked up from the scalp must be amplified to an extent sufficient to move the recording pens. The amplitude range of activities in the normal EEG may be from 5 to over 100 μV; in the case of convulsive electrical discharges, amplitudes approaching 1 mV may be encountered. Hence voltage amplification between 1000 and 200,000 is required to achieve a nominal 1-V signal level. Although direct-coupled amplifiers are desirable on theoretical grounds, nearly all EEG record-ing is done with resistance-capacitance-coupled amplifiers to avoid base line drift and low frequency noise signals. To amplify the slow (1–2 Hz) changes in potential found in the EEG, particularly in sleep, without distortion, the time constant of the am-plifier should be of the order of 1 sec. With such a time constant, if a strong signal overloads the amplifier, it will remain blocked for several seconds, during which time it is unable to accept signals of normal value. Customarily, two amplifier units are used for each channel, the one to which the signal is brought being called the "preamplifier." The output of the preamplifier is led into a "power" or "driver" amplifier, the output of which goes to the recording oscillograph.

Conventional EEG apparatus generally includes the following controls to facilitate operation:

1. *Lead selectors.* These are switches by means of which any pair of leads may be connected to the input of a given channel; the switch markings correspond to those on a lead-input box, into which the subject's electrodes are plugged.
2. *Gain or amplitude controls.* These frequently involve a multiposition step switch for gross changes and a continuous potentiometer for fine adjustments.
3. *High frequency filter controls.* These allow the oper-ator to reduce fast activity that may be generated by muscle. Although useful in clinical work, they may introduce considerable distortion into the record. Special filters are also available to reduce mains hum.
4. *Low frequency cutoff setting.* This determines the lowest frequencies that will be amplified.

Special devices for switching entire sets of elec-trode montages are available in some instruments.

In general, the number of controls and adjust-ments provided in instruments used for clinical electroencephalography is less than those available on research polygraphs. These reflect the different requirements of the more specialized EEG record-ing, as opposed to the variety of applications to which a general purpose polygraph may be put. The psychophysiologist should consider this difference carefully when purchasing equipment, since the conventional EEG apparatus may be unduly restric-tive in its applicability. For example, amplifiers in some EEG instruments are less than optimal for evoked-response recording because of restricted frequency response. Another consideration influ-

encing the decision would be the ease with which the amplifier output may be led to magnetic tape for later computer processing; general polygraphs are more likely to be fitted with convenient jacks for this purpose.

The most commonly used medium for recording the EEG is inked paper. Other media, such as wax paper or heat-sensitive paper, offer certain advan-tages but these are generally outweighed by the combination of low cost, convenience in handling, and the ease of storage afforded by inked paper. The provision of recording paper in a folded packet facilitates location of any particular portion of the record.

The mechanism for moving the paper under the pens, i.e., the paper drive, should provide for different speeds of recording. For routine clinical recording the speeds most favored are 3.0 and 2.5 and 1.5 cm/sec, the last being in common use in Europe. For esthetic reasons the speed of recording will usually be adjusted to yield a ratio of 7:10 in the height of a given wave to its length (W. G. Walter & Parr, 1963, pp. 25–64). When additional variables that oscillate at a slow rate are recorded, the tendency will be to use slower recording speeds. On the other hand, for such problems as estimating time differences between signals from different regions of the brain, speeds up to 30 cm/sec may be desirable. The range of paper speeds offered on most clinical equipment is usually more restricted than that available on research poly-graphs. Whatever the speeds used, constancy is essential, and a time marker driven from a source independent of the paper drive mechanism is de-sirable.

Recording Procedure

Position of the subject Clinical recordings are usually made with the patient in the supine posi-tion, in order to maximize comfort and relaxation and to permit sleep if this is desired. On the other hand, in psychophysiological experiments the sub-ject is commonly required to engage in some form of activity. A comfortable chair, perhaps of the reclining variety, may be more suitable for this. To reduce extraneous stimuli, the subject is frequently placed in a room apart from the one in which the apparatus is located. Observation of the subject may be carried out through a viewing window, perhaps of the one-way variety. In order to alleviate anxiety when there are separate rooms, an inter-communication system, which has been demonstrated to the subject, is useful. If recording from the occipital area, the head should be elevated from either the bed or the chair by some form of comfortable neck support, so that the electrodes will not be subjected to pressure.

Electrodes Perhaps the most critical element in the recording system is the interface between the tissue and the electrodes. Although needles inserted under the skin of the scalp are used as electrodes in some laboratories, most workers depend upon leads applied at the surface. To be effective, the surface of the scalp must be cleaned, usually with alcohol, to remove the greasy film of sebum that interferes with electrical contact. Silver is the preferred metal for electrophysiological electrodes; the surface of the silver must be "chlorided" to make the junction nonpolarizable. A salt solution is placed between the electrode and the scalp, usually in the form of a gel to prevent rapid drying. One convenient arrangement is for the electrode to be a saucer-shaped disk with a hole in the center, through which a blunted hypodermic needle may be inserted; after the electrode is applied to the scalp, the salt gel is introduced from a syringe through the hole into the space between the electrode and the skin. This type of electrode is generally between 5 and 10 mm in diameter and is stuck to the scalp with a film of collodion or a gauze square saturated with collodion.

Another popular form of electrode is made by screwing a threaded silver tube into a triangular plastic base molded to fit the curvature of the head. Such an electrode is held in place on the head by a rubber band, and an array of electrodes may be held by a grid of rubber bands laced under the chin forming a *casque*. The rubber band attachment has the advantage of rapid application but is more subject to artifacts due to movement than are the collodion-applied leads. The rubber band type of attachment may also give rise to some discomfort during long recordings; some subjects are not able to relax with a pressure band on or under the chin. An adherant conducting paste (bentonite), into

which a small silver disk may be inserted and held, is widely used (Turner & Roberts, 1944). However, bentonite has the disadvantage of producing sensitivity reactions in a proportion of subjects; this may prove to be troublesome, particularly if recordings are to be made on several different days. Also, if the subject is likely to be moving, the probability of the lead's being lifted off the scalp is much greater than with the collodion attachment. The major complaint of subjects with collodion is the residue of collodion particles after removal of the electrode; a fine toothed comb will remove most of these. When electrodes of any type are properly applied, the resistance between any pair of scalp electrodes should not be more than 5000 ohms and preferably less than 3000.

Sources of Distortion

Defects in both amplifier and recorder may give rise to distortions of the record, many of which may be avoided by attention to the limitations of the equipment.

Amplitude distortion The most commonly encountered type of amplitude distortion is "clipping." An excessive input voltage may operate the tubes beyond the limits of the straight portion of their characteristic; in the recorder the same effect is produced when the pen reaches the limit of its movement. This often has the effect of making a sine wave square-topped. To avoid amplitude distortion, the amplification or gain controls must be adjusted to keep the signal within the linear range of all amplifier stages and of the recorder. When a very large signal is being handled, and the gain controls are at a minimum, amplitude distortion may be introduced in the early stages, even before the recorder has reached its limits. This should be remembered whenever the gain controls have to be set at a very low level.

Frequency distortion When the amplification at one frequency is different from that at another, frequency distortion is present. Distortion is bound to occur above the upper and below the lower frequency limits. The effects of changes in the time constant upon the recording of a square wave input pulse are shown in Figure 7.1(A), while Figure 7.1(B) illustrates the effects on a sine wave input. Figure 7.1(C) demonstrates the effect of varying the high frequency cutoff on amplification of square pulses, while the effect of the filter on a sine wave with a 40-Hz superimposed ripple is shown in Figure 7.1(D).

Phase distortion This refers to the alteration in phase or time relationship of different frequencies relative to one another as they are passed through the amplifier. Alteration in phase of the various components of a complex waveform is of considerable importance, as a false picture of the actual input may be rendered. In some respects phase distortion is a form of frequency distortion. Figure 7.1(B) gives an example of the effect; the amplitude of the slower component in Channel 3 is reduced and its phase is retarded.

Distortions arising in the recorder itself include malalignment of the pens, which can give an illu-

sion of phase shift that does not actually exist. Also, in most recorders the pen moves in the arc of a circle instead of a straight line, thus making the side of a wave appear curved.

Artifacts

Artifacts are of two main kinds, instrumental and physiological.

Instrumental Although various deflections may be produced by any of the several components in the equipment, some are more likely than others to do so. W. G. Walter and Parr (1963) list these in the following order of probability: batteries, switches, plugs, sockets and wiring, resistors, tubes, and capacitors. The probability of interference and artifacts from the input electrodes is proportional to the resistance between electrodes. The likelihood of high resistance is greater with bald sub-

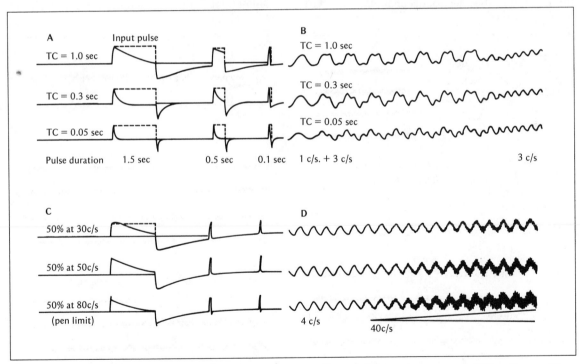

Figure 7.1 Distortions seen in electroencephalograms (EEGs). A: Effect of different time constants (TC) on the amplification of square input pulses; B: effect of time constants on sine wave input; C: effect of varying high frequency filter on amplification of square pulses; and D: effect of filter on sine wave with 40-Hz superimposed ripple. Adapted from W. G. Walter & G. Parr, Recording equipment and technique. In D. Hill & G. Parr (Eds.), *Electroencephalography*. New York: Macmillan, 1963. By permission.

jects, in whom sclerosis of the outer skin produces a horny layer, and with newborn babies.

Ripple or hum from the power mains is one of the most common problems encountered in the laboratory. It may be necessary to adjust the balance of the input stages and, particularly in evoked potential recording, the amplifiers in use should have balance controls that are checked daily. The so-called mains ripple (60 Hz in the United States) can be recognized by its extreme constancy of frequency and amplitude; physiological activity in the same frequency range will always fluctuate to some extent.

Movement artifacts may create much difficulty, although they usually are readily identified if the subject can be observed by the operator. They will be synchronous with breathing, scalp movement, etc.

Physiological artifacts Many bioelectric potentials recorded from the head originate outside of the brain, and the electroencephalographer must learn to recognize these and distinguish them from brain activity. Figure 7.2 gives examples of various types of biological artifacts.

Figure 7.2(A) shows slow swings due to the galvanic skin response (GSR) or psychogalvanic reflex (PGR). The changes are more likely to be seen on the forehead and are commoner on hot days with apprehensive subjects. This effect can be considerably reduced by using nonpolarizable electrodes. If very troublesome, it may be partially eliminated by using a time constant of 0.3 sec.

Figure 7.2(B) shows EEG tracings obscured by electromyographic (EMG) activity. The duration of muscle pulses is only about 10 msec, but they often merge into an apparent rhythmic pattern that can easily be mistaken for brain activity, particularly in the frontal areas. Although considerable muscle activity may be filtered out by using the high frequency cutoff, the best solution is to induce the subject to relax.

Figure 7.2(C) shows the changes produced by eyeblinks. These are generally attributed to the

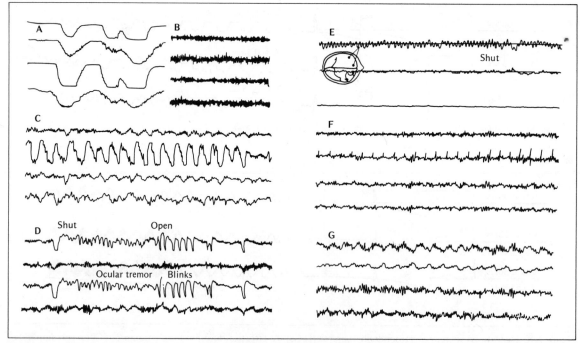

Figure 7.2 Artifacts in electroencephalograms (EEGs). The artifacts were produced by: A, psychogalvanic reflex; B, muscle potentials (EMG); C, eyeblinks; D, ocular tremors; E, nystagmus; F, EKG; G, movement of electrodes caused by pulse in scalp. Adapted from W. G. Walter & G. Parr, Recording equipment and technique. In D. Hill & G. Parr (Eds.), *Electroencephalography.* New York: Macmillan, 1963. By permission.

potential difference of about 100 mV between the cornea and the orbit, with the cornea positive. When the eyeball moves, the potential differences change, and a large deflection will be picked up by electrodes near the eye. In recent years such recordings have come to be called electrooculograms (EOG), and they are regularly made in studies of sleep. When the eye is shut, or the lids are blinked, the eyeball rotates upward, producing the deflections recorded particularly in the second line of Figure 7.2(C). When the eye is shut, the electrodes nearer to it become more positive to the posterior ones, and the reverse happens when it is open. Slow changes due to eyeblink are easy to recognize, but slight nystagmoid movement of the eyes may be associated with rhythmic voltage fluctuations that resemble brain rhythms. Examples are shown in Figures 7.2(D) and 7.2(E). This effect may be particularly confusing in conditions in which spasmodic eye movements commonly occur. One way of dealing with the problem is to place a pair of electrodes very close to the eyes, so that it picks up primarily the eye artifacts and can be used to identify deflections in other channels that may be attributable to them. The explanation of the eyeblink potential as arising from the retinal-corneal dipole has recently been challenged by the findings of Pasik, Pasik & Bender (1965), who showed that the EOG recovered after total ablation of the retina in monkeys. This suggests that much of the potential originates in the palpebral structures.

Figure 7.2(F) shows the presence of electrocardiographic activity in recordings from the scalp. This should not occur if the common mode rejection of the amplifier is adequate. Figure 7.2(G) shows the effects of movement of the electrodes caused by the pulse in the arteries in the scalp; the pattern is similar to that of the sphygmogram. This can be avoided by moving the electrode just off the artery.

Artifacts may sometimes be generated by unusual and unsuspected sources such as dental restorations (Milnarich, Tourney, & Beckett, 1957). Figure 7.3 shows an example of potentials originating from such restorations that were synchronous with discharges recorded from anterior temporal electrodes. Milnarich, Tourney, and Beckett have also demonstrated that slow oscillations of a regular nature may be recorded in the temporal electrodes as a consequence of tongue movements.

Electrode Linkages

There are three general methods of deriving potentials from electrodes on the scalp. These are designated as bipolar, unipolar, and average refer-

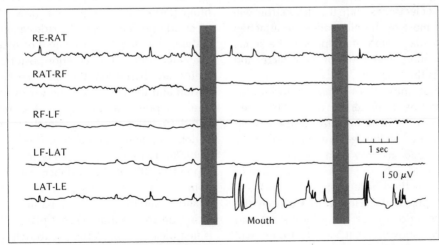

Figure 7.3 Synchronization of discharges from metal restorations in the mouth with discharges from anterior temporal electrodes. The last recording line was taken from electrodes placed on the subject's face over the area of the metals. Adapted from R. E. Milnarich, G. Tourney, & P. G. S. Beckett, Electroencephalographic artifact arising from dental restorations, *Electroencephalography and Clinical Neurophysiology*, 1957, **9,** 337–339. By permission.

ence methods. Bipolar recordings involve linkages between electrodes on the scalp and are so named because all electrodes are equally liable to be affected by potential differences on the surface of the head. Unipolar recordings involve a linkage between an electrode on the scalp and a common electrode, usually on the lobe of one ear or both ears connected together. The common electrode is sometimes called the "reference" or "indifferent" electrode, because it is assumed to be insensitive to potential changes within the head. The idea of the unipolar method is to simplify the record from each channel by indicating only those potential changes that occur under or near the electrode on the scalp. In the bipolar method the record contains components picked up by both electrodes. At any one point in time, the bipolar recording reflects the difference in potentials picked up by the two electrodes.

The average reference method was suggested by Offner (1950) and used first by Goldman (1950). A voltage equal to the average of the signals on all electrodes is produced by connecting every electrode to a common reference point through a high resistance (1 megohm). Each polygraph channel then records the difference between this average potential and the voltage on some specific electrode. The accuracy of this method increases with the number of electrodes, so that serious errors will occur only if most of the electrodes are attached to some particular region of scalp, or if the signal from one or more electrodes is very large and unduly affects the average.

The virtue of unipolar, as compared to bipolar, recording remains a matter of debate between some workers in the field. In many clinical laboratories both kinds of linkage are employed, the attitude being that each may yield significant information not provided by the other. The advantages of the bipolar method have been stated by W. G. Walter (1963, pp. 65–98). He points out that the reference electrode is never truly indifferent and gives examples showing that ear electrodes will pick up potential differences generated by the brain. He notes that, whenever a focus of activity is about midway between the ear and an exploring electrode, or about equally distant from them, little activity will be registered; although the exploring

electrode of the channel concerned may actually be nearer to the focus than any other electrode. Walter also indicates that the location of the source of electrical rhythm with unipolar leads can be accomplished only by observing the differences in amplitude of the rhythm in several channels, and that amplitude differences are trustworthy only as long as the interelectrode distances are approximately the same. With a bipolar linkage, in which one electrode is common to adjacent channels, a focus of activity under such a common lead will lead to reversals of phase in adjacent channels, thus facilitating localization. Walter favors the bipolar connection because it provides unequivocal information about potential differences between electrode pairs and is the method of choice for estimating potential gradient.

Osselton (1965) has recently pointed out that EEG data stored on tape for subsequent processing will yield the same information, whether recorded by bipolar, unipolar, or average reference methods. However, the bipolar method has some practical advantages over the others.

For clinical electroencephalography, some standardization of electrode placement was introduced by adoption of the 10–20 system proposed by the International Federation of Societies for Electroencephalography and Clinical Neurophysiology (Jasper, 1958). Figure 7.4 shows the standard electrode positions and their designations by this system, including the placement of special pharyngeal electrodes. The anterior-posterior measurements are based on the distance between the nasion and the inion over the vertex and the midline. Five points are marked on this line and designated frontal pole (Fp), frontal (F), central (C), parietal (P), and occipital (O). The Fp point is 10% of the nasion-inion distance above the nasion. The F point is 20% of this distance back from the Fp point. Similar 20% steps back are taken for the C, P, and O midline points. Lateral measurements are based on the central coronal plane. The distance is first measured from the left to right preauricular points (felt as depressions at the root of the zygoma just anterior to the tragus). The measuring tape should pass through the central point at the vertex; 10% of this distance is then taken for the temporal (T) point up from the preauricular point on either

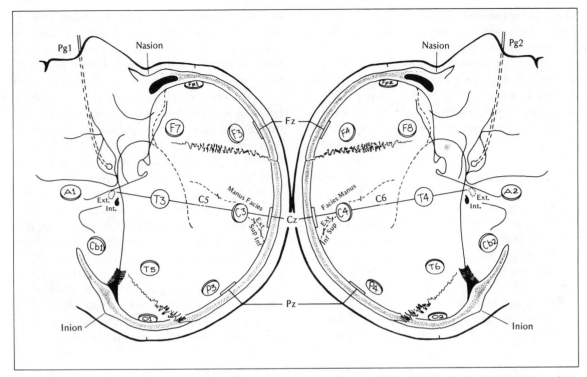

Figure 7.4 Standard electrode positions of the 10–20 system (lateral view of left and right hemispheres). Intermediate positions, such as C-5 and C-6, are omitted. The drawings were made from X-ray projections with true lateral views. The location of principal fissures was determined by silver clips placed at operation. Pg 1 and Pg 2 indicate pharyngeal electrodes. Adapted from H. H. Jasper, The ten-twenty electrode system of the International Federation, *Electro-encephalography and Clinical Neurophysiology,* 1958, **10,** 371–375. By permission.

side. The central points are marked 20% of the distance above the temporal points (C3, Figure 7.4).

The antero-posterior line of electrodes over the temporal lobe, frontal to occipital, is determined by measuring the distance between the *Fp* midline point through the *T* position of the central line and back to the mid-occipital point. The *Fp* electrode position is marked 10% of this distance from the midline in front, and the O position is 10% of the distance from the midline in back. The inferior frontal (F7) and posterior temporal (T5) positions fall 20% of the distance from the *Fp* and O electrodes, respectively. The remaining mid-frontal (*F3* and *F4*) and mid-parietal (*P3* and *P4*) electrodes are then placed along the frontal and parietal coronal lines, respectively, equally distant between the midline and the temporal line of electrodes on either side.

This system provides a total of 21 standard elec-

trode positions with approximately equal spacing between them. Figure 7.4 attempts to show the relation between the positions of the electrodes placed on the scalp and the underlying major fissures of the brain, as well as skull sutures. Rémond and Torres (1964) have proposed a more complicated electrode placement for use in topographical research.

Activation Methods

Most electroencephalographic recording in the clinical laboratory is done in a state of waking rest, generally with eyes closed; but increasing attention is being paid to the changes induced by various types of external stimulation, including responses to instructions and various chemical agents. Clinical EEG tests have usually included maneuvers to test alpha rhythm responsiveness to light (opening eyes) and sensitivity to CO_2 reduction (hyperventilation).

The latter maneuver generally produces increased slow activity and may elicit convulsive discharges in patients with epilepsy.

Intermittent photic stimulation, usually involving the presentation of trains of brief, but intense, flashes, is also routinely used in clinical work in an attempt to elicit convulsive activity. Such stimulation normally causes the brain rhythms to follow the frequency of the train of light flashes over a variable frequency range. Figure 7.5 illustrates this photic driving phenomenon. Since intermittent photic stimulation generally elicits a variety of subjective sensations, attempts have been made to relate these to the EEG changes (Mundy-Castle, 1953; V. J. Walter & W. G. Walter, 1949). Photic driving has also been studied in relation to emotional and personality variables (Shagass, 1955a, 1955b; Ulett, Gleser, Winokur, & Lawler, 1953). In addition to driving and true convulsive responses, intermittent photic stimulation may evoke electrical activity of an apparently convulsive character that does not,

however, represent activity of the brain. This involves myoclonic twitching, which may include only the periorbital structures, but may also extend to involve jerking of the entire body in rhythm with the light flashes. Bickford, Sem-Jacobson, White, and Daly (1952) have provided criteria for distinguishing between this photomyoclonic response and the true photic convulsive response. Driving effects somewhat similar to those obtained with intermittent photic stimulation have been obtained with intermittent auditory clicks (Neher, 1961).

The term "activation" has been applied in a somewhat paradoxical way to the deliberate induction of sleep during the EEG-recording session. This is because certain epileptiform discharges become more apparent during the early stages of sleep (E. L. Gibbs & F. A. Gibbs, 1946). The results appear to be similar, whether sleep is natural or induced by a hypnotic dose of a sedative such as secobarbital.

Many drugs have been employed in electroencephalography in an attempt to elicit seizure

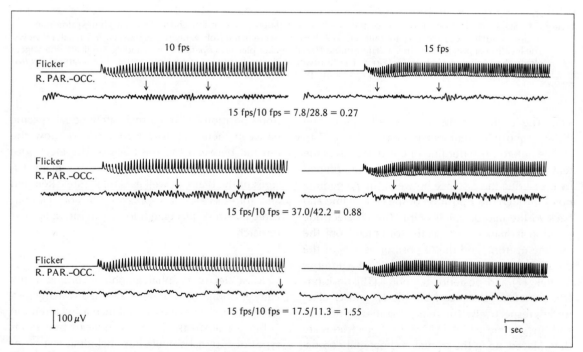

Figure 7.5 Photic driving to 10 and 15-Hz flashes in three subjects. Right parieto-occipital leads were used. Arrows designate samples of maximal driving response selected for measurement to give designated values. "Flicker" indicates signal from photoelectric cell. Adapted from C. Shagass, Differentiation between anxiety and depression by the photically activated electroencephalogram, *American Journal of Psychiatry*, 1955, **112**, 41–46. By permission.

discharges that were not otherwise apparent. Pentylenetetrazol (metrazol) is perhaps the best known of these.

In general the use of the EEG in psychophysiologic studies may be regarded as involving examination of the effects of activation procedures upon the brain rhythms. Changes induced by mental tasks of various sorts, exposure to emotionally charged statements, etc., may all be regarded as activation effects. These may then be related to changes in other physiological variables, such as heart rate and GSR; or an attempt may be made to relate the magnitude of such changes to individual differences in personality test scores, psychiatric diagnosis, etc. Liberson (1944) used the term "functional" electroencephalography to designate the range of activation procedures in general and suggested that the functional approach offered greater hope for psychologically relevant findings than one based on resting records.

ANALYSIS AND QUANTIFICATION OF THE EEG

For any given recording channel, the EEG represents a continuous time graph of the electrical potential difference between two locations in the head. The tremendous amount of information obtained in a relatively short time from one channel is more than arithmetically increased when multiple channels are taken simultaneously. There is an obvious need for extracting the most relevant data from the mass of available information. As high speed computation aids become available, issues of quantitative analysis center about the relevance of mathematical models upon which programs of analysis can be based. As long as one channel only is under consideration, these models involve temporal analysis of the EEG. With more than one channel, spatial-temporal analysis is required. Burch (1959) has reviewed and classified the systems for automatic EEG analysis.

Frequency Analysis

Fourier series Many complex wave shapes can be characterized as the sum of regular sine waves by use of the Fourier series, which accounts for

phase, amplitude, and frequency. This approach to analysis of the EEG was first attempted by Grass and F. A. Gibbs (1938). Data on Fourier transforms of the EEG during sleep were reported by Knott, Friedman, and Bardsley (1942), who described the EEG output in terms of the amount of energy at specific frequencies.

Tuned filters The Walter-type analyzer (Baldock & W. G. Walter, 1946) provides displays of electrical output for selected center frequencies, obtained by passing signals through a series of tuned filters. Since its introduction, this has continued to be a popular approach to the quantification of the EEG. A major problem with the Walter-type analyzer results from the difficulty of maintaining stable tuning of the filters. Various attempts to improve the filters have been made (Ulett & Loeffel, 1953). Knott (1953) has discussed some important problems inherent in automatic frequency analysis. These include the need to select arbitrarily a limited number of frequencies about which the filters are tuned, and the fact that, even with such restricted and arbitrary selection of frequencies, the amount of data generated by the analyzer is still too great for easy assimilation. Difficulties of data reduction caused most results of wave analyzer investigations to be treated subjectively, leading Knott (1953) to

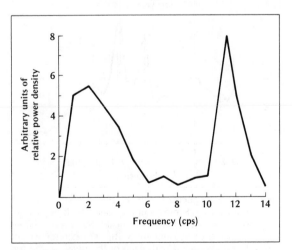

Figure 7.6   Representative power density spectrum showing two peaks of activity. Redrawn from D. J. Hord, Computers in brain research. *American Journal of EEG Technology*, 1964, **4,** 1–7. By permission.

state: "This is to be deplored, for an instrument designed to complement *visual* analysis should not lead just to further visual analysis [p. 19]."

Power Spectrum Analysis

Power spectrum analysis involves the square of the filter output of voltage integrated over time, which is called power density. The value of power density for a given frequency band will be high if components within that band have high amplitude within the analysis epoch. Figure 7.6 shows an example of a power density spectrum simplified for illustrative purposes (Hord, 1964). The spectrum indicates that a slow component exists at about 1 Hz and that the alpha component represented by the peak at 11 Hz contains more power. Figure

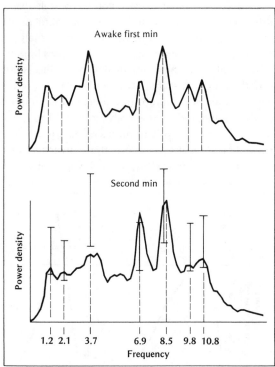

Figure 7.7 Autospectra obtained from the same subject during two 1-min sampling periods. Broken lines drawn to show stability of peaks. Solid vertical lines in bottom spectrum show the 90% confidence interval associated with each of the peaks in the top spectrum. Adapted from D. J. Hord, L. C. Johnson, A. Lubin, & M. T. Austin, Resolution and stability in the autospectra of EEG, *Electroencephalography and Clinical Neurophysiology,* 1965, **19,** 305–308. By permission.

7.7 shows two power density spectra obtained in an actual experiment (Hord, Johnson, Lubin, & Austin, 1965). Both of these spectra were obtained from the same person in one session; although not identical, the spectra are quite similar, indicating fair stability.

Period Analysis

The most easily delineated aspect of wave shape is the period, or duration, at certain amplitude points such as the baseline. Manual quantification of the EEG by measuring or counting wave periods has been the most commonly used and perhaps is the most generally accepted quantitative approach to the EEG. The alpha index, which is the percentage time occupied by waves of alpha frequency, also depends on measurement of the period.

Burch, Greiner, and Correll (1955) introduced an instrument for automatic period analysis of the EEG, analyzing the baseline cross to establish each half wave (major) period. The zero crosses of the second derivative yield the time position of inflection points in the EEG. The time between these points is displayed as the minor period and represents high frequency oscillations superimposed on the waves giving the major period. An interval histogram, representing the duration of major periods, may readily be obtained with some special purpose computers, used primarily for averaging to extract evoked responses. The EEG is passed through a zero-cross detector, and the averager will store the duration between successive zero-crosses and generate a histogram showing the number of periods of each duration.

Correlation Analysis

Cross-correlation and autocorrelation provide sensitive measures of frequency and phase. The autocorrelogram is obtained by determining the correlation between a given input and itself delayed by successive intervals. Figure 7.8 shows examples of autocorrelograms of 1-min EEG samples in a normal subject (Brazier & Barlow, 1956). The height of each pen deflection indicates the degree of correlation at that particular delay time. Delay times increase in length from left to right along the abscissa in steps of 5 msec from zero delay on the left to 925 msec on the right.

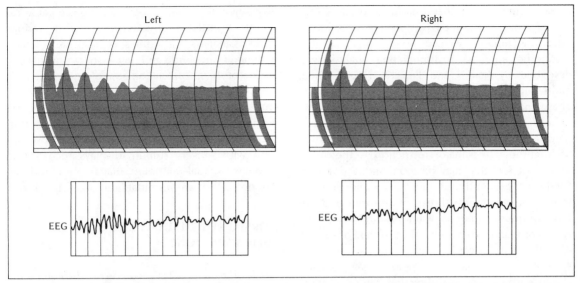

Figure 7.8 Autocorrelograms of 1-min samples of EEG from left and right parieto-occipital leads in a normal subject. The first and last three pen deflections in each correlogram represent the base line level when the correlator received no input. The height of each pen deflection indicates the degree of correlation at that particular delay time. Delay times increase in length from left to right in steps of 5 msec. A 3-sec sample of original EEG trace is below each correlogram. Vertical lines on the EEG are 200 msec apart. This figure represents a small fraction only of the total length of record analyzed. Adapted from M. A. B. Brazier & J. S. Barlow, Some applications of correlation analysis to clinical problems in electroencephalography, *Electroencephalography and Clinical Neurophysiology*, 1956, **8**, 325–331. By permission.

The cross-correlogram is obtained by applying the same procedure to two different inputs. The times of peaking of correlations may then provide information bearing on the delay between identical activities in two records from different sources; e.g., if a traveling wave takes 20 msec to move from point *A* to *B*, the cross-correlogram will show a peak at 20 msec. A relatively long EEG sample must be available for correlation analysis (Brazier & Casby, 1952; Burch, 1959).

Amplitude Analysis

One of the simplest approaches to automatic EEG quantification is provided by Drohocki's (1948) integrator, which summates electrical activity over wide frequency bands. Goldstein, Murphree, Sugarman, Pfeiffer, and Jenney (1963) have employed the variability in the Drohocki measure from one 20-sec interval to another to obtain an index of variation in EEG activity that appears to relate to psychiatric status.

Toposcopes

The Walter toposcope (W. G. Walter & Shipton, 1951) is a device that simultaneously displays the time of occurrence of voltage peaks from multiple recording sites. A faint radial line is synchronously rotated about the center point on each of several small oscilloscopes. When a peak amplitude point in the analyzed signal occurs, the radial line is intensified. If a peak point occurs once within the full cycle or sweep time of the synchronizing signal, one bright line will appear on the oscilloscope face. The radial displacement of the line from its starting position indicates the time position of the peak. Since the peak points of all analyzed signals are related to a single synchronizing signal, their phase or time relationship to one another is displayed. If one or more analyzed peak points occur within the sweep time, two or more bright lines will appear, indicating that harmonics or multiples of the sweep frequency are present in the analyzed signal. With 22 channels displayed, the problem of analysis is very formidable, so that it has been used by few investigators. A modified version has been introduced by Shipton (1963).

Another approach to topographic analysis was described by Marko and Petsche (1960). Their multivibrator toposcope allows visualization of phase shift across the head by recording simultaneously from several electrode positions and displaying the amplitude of the signals as a variation of brightness. The major restriction is the short sample of EEG that may be examined. Storm van Leeuwen (1964) utilized the Marko and Petsche toposcope, together with two other forms of analysis, continuous frequency analysis and auto- and cross-correlation, to examine the problem of spread of alpha waves over the scalp. His observations suggested that alpha waves appear to sweep, usually in a frontal-occipital direction. He concluded that, from a methodological viewpoint, the various methods of analysis are complementary to one another.

Another instrumental approach to the study of EEG phase relationships has been suggested by Darrow and Smith (1964). Their instrument provides continuous automatic scoring of phase relationships between areas. Darrow and his associates have used this method to relate EEG phase relationships to mental activity and other physiological events (Darrow & Hicks, 1965).

Computer Analysis Models

All forms of EEG analysis discussed above can be performed by means of a general purpose computer. For practical reasons it would be desirable to establish criteria for selecting one form of analysis over another and to determine the degree of redundancy of different analytic models in given situations. Fink, Shapiro, Hickman, and Itil (1966) have carried out a systematic comparison of EEG analysis methods, using an IBM 1710 computer system. Their test experiment, involving the induction of changes in the EEG by psychotropic drugs, compared four programs of analysis: period analysis, power spectrum density, amplitude analysis, and pattern identification using a random shapes model. The digital power spectral density was compared with results from an analogue electronic filter analyzer. Their results indicated that, for their

experimental problem, there was considerable redundancy in the information provided by various forms of analysis; e.g., quite similar information was obtained from period and power spectrum analysis.

The problem of relating suitably quantified activity in one brain area to that in another still presents great difficulties. These may be reduced somewhat by using a synchronizing point in time, as in the presentation of a sensory stimulus. However, even with sensory stimuli, displays such as the complex spatial-temporal maps presented by Rémond (1964) are formidable in their complexity.

NORMAL EEG RHYTHMS AND THEIR VARIATIONS

Classifications of EEG activity into the commonly used Greek letter categories refer mainly to frequency ranges. It should be recognized that any statement about normality must take into account many factors concerning the subject and the conditions of recording. The age of the subject and his state of alertness are particularly important.

Alpha

Alpha frequency varies between 8 and 13 Hz, with waves of 25 to 100 μV appearing mainly from parietal and occipital derivations. Alpha rhythm is reduced or desynchronized by sensory stimulation, especially light, and during attentive mental activity. A small number of people have little or no alpha activity; these were designated as the B type by P. Davis (1941). Another small proportion of normal individuals has persistent alpha activity, even during light stimulation (Walter's P type; Golla, Hutton, & W. G. Walter, 1943). Alpha variants are considered to be present when well-defined alpha rhythms within the 8–13 Hz range are associated with a fast or slow rhythm that is either a multiple or a submultiple of this frequency. These are the fast and slow alpha variants of Goodwin (1947). Fluctuations of alpha amplitude from moment to moment are usual. Although alpha rhythm sometimes appears sinusoidal, irregularities and dissimilarities from wave to wave are more commonly seen. These indicate the presence of harmonic or unrelated frequencies.

Alpha generators The location and number of alpha rhythm generators has engaged the attention of many investigators. Adrian and Yamagiwa (1935) noted that there were fluctuations of amplitude in the occipital region and that relative phase in adjacent channels altered. This suggested to them that the alpha focus was capable of movement over the cortex within a range of 5–6 cm laterally and 5 cm upward from the occipital region. Cohn (1948) advanced the view that there are actually two generators or sources in each hemisphere and that change of dominance of the activity of one to that of the other would give rise to apparent movement of a single focus. Walsh (1958) employed a special instrument to compare the polarity of signals from four channels of the EEG and paid special attention to the phase reversals demonstrable along a chain of electrodes running transversely through the parietal-occipital region. He found that there were usually two-phase reversals, although occasionally only one. The polarity of signals from either end of the chain was unrelated or in antiphase. He concluded that the two-phase reversals reflected the activity of autonomous generators. He also pointed out that the existence of more than two generators was not excluded by his findings.

The concept of several generators is compatible with the findings obtained by Cooper and Mundy-Castle (1960) in a toposcopic analysis of alpha rhythm. The results obtained by D. O. Walter, Rhodes, Brown, and Adey (1966), employing an elegant method of computer analysis of the EEG, also indicate that there are several generation processes for alpha, oscillating in similar frequency bands within the posterior part of the head. D. O. Walter et al. point out that this conclusion is compatible with the findings obtained from recordings taken from the depths of the human brain, which indicate that there are numerous, deep, bioelectric processes varying greatly in size, shape, strength, and orientation. They further suggest that recordings taken at the surface reflect only the average tendency of the deep generators.

It is commonly observed that, in the first second or so following the return of alpha rhythm on closing the eyes, its frequency may be about 1 Hz faster than at other times. Cobb (1963, pp. 232–249) points out that, although this appears to be an actual change in frequency of the dominant rhythm, it might be accounted for by a momentarily greater increase in amplitude of a faster component than of the slower. He takes this and a variety of other observations to support the concept of multiple alpha generators and suggests that we should speak of alpha *rhythms* rather than a single alpha rhythm.

Alpha amplitude and lateral dominance The mean alpha activity of the two hemispheres is different in perhaps 30% of normal adults, and markedly so in 5 or 10%; the difference is mainly in amplitude but sometimes only in forward spread (Cobb, 1963, p. 238). In most cases that show asymmetry, the greater amplitude is on the right side. This has been thought to reflect a smaller degree of activation or excitability on the nondominant than on the dominant side (Raney, 1939). However, in left-handed subjects the expected greater amplitude of left-sided alpha rhythm is not clearly seen (Cobb, 1963, p. 238). This may be due to recording during the resting state, since Wilson, Darrow, Vieth, and Maller (1959) found that, during writing movements with either the right or left hand, the percentage of alpha time was greater on the right in right-handed individuals. This tendency toward left lateralization of occipital blocking during writing suggests greater contribution of the dominant hemisphere in control of verbal-motor behavior.

Beta

Beta rhythm was so named by Berger. Next to alpha it is the most common component of the adult EEG. There is some disagreement about its frequency limits. Some workers designate all rhythms faster than alpha as beta, whereas others restrict its use to the range from 14 to 30 Hz.

It is usually frontal and central in distribution and varies greatly in amplitude, continuity, and wideness of distribution. In some individuals beta of fairly high amplitude is found posteriorly and may appear to block in response to stimuli. Amplitudes seldom exceed 20 μV.

In individuals who are nervous or tense, the alpha rhythm is often reduced, and the EEG is described as "low voltage fast"; beta activity then predominates. Although an increase of beta activity has been thought to occur in association with anxiety or tension, this observation may be due more to the suppression of alpha than to actual augmentation of beta. For example, comparison of frontal beta measurements prior to injection of amobarbital sodium for measurements of sedation thresholds in a group of healthy control subjects and a group of patients with pathological anxiety revealed a slightly greater amount of measurable beta in the control sample (Shagass, unpublished observations). It may be that the controls were responding with more anxiety to the anticipated injection than the patients, for whom this would be a more customary experience. In any event, the relationship between beta activity and anxiety is not definitely established.

Less Common Waveforms

Gamma This term has been used to cover the frequency range from 35 to 50 Hz; it is seldom encountered and the existence of gamma activity has never been generally accepted.

Delta W. G. Walter (1936) designated waves slower than alpha as delta, but delta activity is usually defined as less than 4 Hz. Delta waves are abnormal in the waking adult EEG.

Theta W. G. Walter and Dovey (1944) designated waves in the 4–7 Hz bands as theta rhythm. Theta rhythms are prominent, normal components of the EEG of children; they diminish in amplitude and amount throughout the second decade. They are usually detectable in the young adult but are few and small in the majority. They are usually symmetrical and mainly frontal-temporal in distribution if one excludes alpha variants, which are seen in the posterior areas. Their amplitude is usually less than 20 μV. In young children they are diffusely present; with increasing age they tend to be restricted to the parietal-temporal areas.

Mu This rhythm has been given various names: "comb," "wicket," *rythme en arceau*. It appears in the normal EEG of about 7% of subjects and is less frequent after the age of 30. H. Gastaut (1952) described it as being found in the Rolandic regions, sometimes near the vertex, and tending to occur in bursts, usually bilaterally asynchronous. The fre-

quency is 9–11 Hz; there is usually an associated beta rhythm at twice this frequency. The appearance is that of rounded negative aspects and sharp or pointed positive aspects, giving the pattern the appearance of a comb or a wicket fence. The mu rhythm is diminished by actual movement of, or intention of moving, the contralateral limbs, and is not affected by the usual stimuli that cause blocking of alpha rhythm.

Kappa Kennedy, Gottsdanker, Armington, and Gray (1948) described a rhythm at about 10 Hz, best seen in bipolar records of the temporal areas, which appears to be related to thinking; i.e., it is elicited by activity such as problem solving. It was found in about 30% of normal subjects. Harlan, White, and

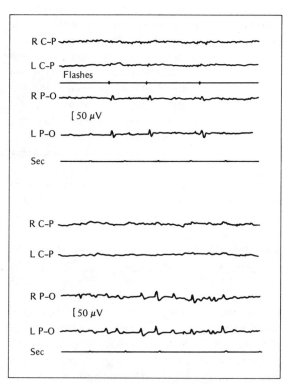

Figure 7.9 EEG of responses to single flashes in right and left parieto-occipital leads (upper tracing) and lambda waves (lower traces). Lower traces were taken from the same leads. The subject's eyes were open in a lighted room. From C. C. Evans, Spontaneous excitation of the visual cortex and association areas—lambda waves, *Electroencephalography and Clinical Neurophysiology*, 1953, **5,** 69–74. By permission.

Bickford (1958) have attributed it to eye movement, but Armington and Chapman (1959) have produced evidence to the contrary.

Lambda The term lambda has been used to designate single, sawtooth, random, surface-positive waves at the occiput, sometimes with a small negative afterswing. These are very prominent in the EEG of a few subjects and may be seen less clearly in many others. They were first described independently by Y. Gastaut (1951) and Evans (1952). They are not seen when the subject's eyes are closed or in the dark. They are blocked when the eyes are fixed on a point or if the field being viewed is uniform, and are best seen with a well-illuminated pattern. Their duration is about 250 msec. They are often correlated with marked photic responses, as demonstrated in Figure 7.9.

Vertex Waves

The vertex or *V* waves are electronegative waves of sharp appearance that can be seen in fully alert subjects, especially children, in the absence of overt stimulation (Y. Gastaut, 1953). The vertex waves

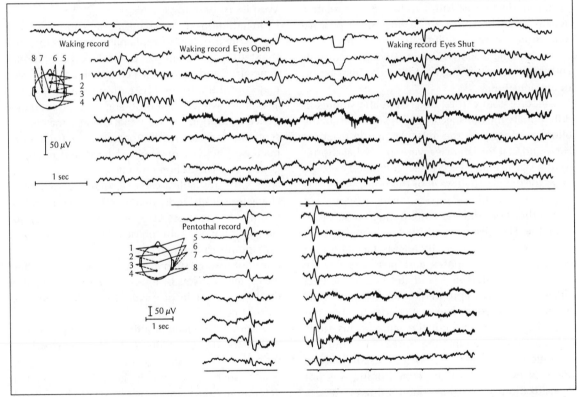

Figure 7.10 Vertex waves. The three upper responses were elicited during consciousness, the two lower ones under light barbiturate anesthesia. The first and third upper responses were recorded with the eyes shut, the middle one with the eyes open. No suppression of alpha follows the first response, while the third response is followed by brief suppression. The second response can be clearly differentiated in all areas owing to the absence of alpha rhythm. The blink artifact following the response is quite distinct in form from the frontal component of the vertex wave. No facial movements were observed to accompany any of the responses. The two lower responses are more complex and higher in voltage. Spindles are seen in the monopolar leads. Although the main deflection in the barbiturate responses shows negativity at the vertex in relation to the surrounding areas, there is a small deflection in an opposite sense preceding it, seen particularly clearly in the bipolar recordings. The stimulus is marked by an arrow on the time marker trace opposite the dot. Adapted from M. Roth, J. Shaw, & J. Green, The form, voltage distribution and physiological significance of the *K*-complex, *Electroencephalography and Clinical Neurophysiology*, 1956, **8**, 385–402. By permission.

have been related to the K complex by Roth, Shaw, and Green (1956). They may be distinguished from lambda by virtue of being maximum over the vertex, whereas the lambda waves are maximum over the occiput; the peak polarity also differs. Larsson (1956) has termed them the "nonspecific response" and has demonstrated that they may be aroused quite regularly by a variety of sudden stimuli. Roth, Shaw, and Green (1956) report detecting the response in 20% of normal subjects and in a similar proportion of psychiatric patients. They found that it infrequently exceeded a voltage of 25 μV and described it as a triphasic phenomenon, with the vertex initially becoming electropositive in relation to surrounding areas. This is followed by a relative negativity of the vertex and a final small positive deflection. Figure 7.10 illustrates the vertex phase reversal of the response under varying conditions and shows how it is augmented under light barbiturate anesthesia.

Larsson (1956) carried out systematic studies to differentiate the nonspecific EEG response from the blink component in the muscular startle reaction. He found that the latencies were somewhat shorter for the startle blink, 35–45 msec, compared to 50–90 msec for the negative wave of the nonspecific EEG response. The blink response had a somewhat higher threshold and was more frequency-sensitive than the EEG response. With two simultaneous stimuli of different type, there was facilitation or occlusion of the responses, and these effects were not similar for the blink and the EEG responses. Since the responses appeared to vary independently of one another under different conditions, he concluded that they were not the same. In his study Larsson also showed that the vertex wave could be conditioned by pairing it with various stimuli and adduced evidence that the conditioning was not "sensitization" or "pseudoconditioning."

PHYSIOLOGICAL BASIS OF THE EEG

A generally accepted physiological basis for the EEG is not yet available, although this problem has engaged many outstanding workers since the EEG was discovered. A systematic and detailed account of the information bearing on the problem would encompass much of neurophysiology and is beyond

the scope of this chapter. Whitteridge and Walsh (1963, pp. 99–146) present a comprehensive discussion. Among topics considered by them are electrical properties of peripheral nerve and single cells, propagation of spontaneous and induced activity, direct current fields, various specific cortical areas, fronto-parietal recruiting system, and the limbic system. The paper by Brazier (1958) also gives an indication of the range of neural mechanisms that may be involved in the genesis of the EEG. More general accounts of nervous system physiology that present the concepts required for considering the physiological basis of the EEG may be found in texts such as those of Ochs (1965) and Ruch, Patton, Woodbury, and Towe (1965).

In addition to mechanisms at various neural levels, the problem of explaining the EEG concerns the statistical operation of a population of neuronal generators and ways in which individual neurones may contribute to the EEG pattern. Adey (1966, pp. 1–43) has reviewed the problem. He presented evidence to support the view that the EEG may represent the normal distribution resulting from summation of activity of nonlinearly related neuronal generators. This scheme would predict, in accordance with available evidence, that the frequency characteristics of individual neurones would relate strongly to the gross EEG, but that the process of summation would blur phase relations. Adey, however, points to the many questions that the scheme does not resolve such as regional frequency differences, mechanisms of interneuronal coupling, and the locus of origin of waves within the individual cortical cell.

Although the lack of a firm physiological explanation for the EEG does not now seem to be a serious deterrent to psychophysiological EEG research, such basic knowledge will be crucial in determining the significance of EEG-behavior relationships uncovered by the psychophysiologist.

BIOCHEMICAL FACTORS INFLUENCING THE EEG

Brain function is highly dependent upon the cerebral blood supply and the mechanisms maintaining a stable chemical milieu. The effects of changes of blood supply or of alterations in the chemical milieu vary in different parts of the brain (Himwich, 1951). M. E. Dawson and Greville (1963, pp. 147–192) point out that interactions between chemical substances and electrical phenomena may be classified according to three general modes of action.

1. *Action elsewhere in the body* is exemplified by insulin. The central effects of insulin are secondary to the hypoglycemia caused by it. Another example is the action of thyroid hormone, in which EEG effects are probably secondary to changes in the body temperature brought about by this hormone.

2. *Substances that affect growth or maintenance of the brain* include water, inorganic salts, and vitamins. These are essential nutrients which, when lacking, alter the EEG. A deficiency of thiamine (vitamin B_1) changes the EEG at an early stage; the effects may be reversed if the vitamin is provided. Other substances in this category are toxic agents, including drugs.

3. *Substances acting on routes normally controlling the level of functional activity* include many synthetic drugs and some hormones. These substances initiate chemical processes that bring nerve cells into action. Examples are acetylcholine, noradrenaline, and serotonin, which appear to be involved in transmission of excitation at central synapses, and gamma-aminobutyric acid, which is involved in inhibition.

Oxygen

The maintenance of normal brain rhythms is dependent on an adequate supply of oxygen. When the available oxygen is reduced, as by breathing air at reduced pressure at high altitudes, there is a reduction of frequency and the appearance of slow activity (F. A. Gibbs, Williams, & E. L. Gibbs, 1940). High voltage slow rhythms in the EEG are also associated with arrest of the cerebral circulation. Rossen, Kabat, and Anderson (1943) used an inflatable cervical pressure cuff to stop cerebral circulation and showed that loss of consciousness occurred about 7 sec after arrest and coincided with the sudden appearance of delta waves. Similar effects may be observed in fainting from various causes. In these cases the loss of consciousness is almost invariably accompanied by high voltage,

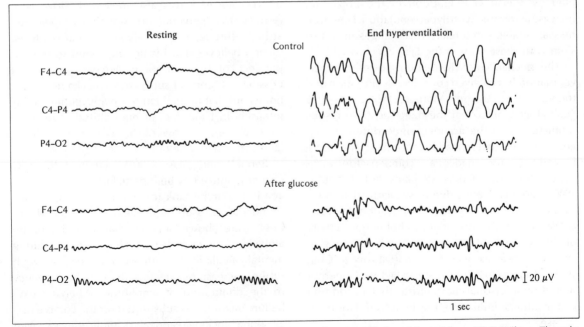

Figure 7.11   Effect of glucose in reducing slow wave response to hyperventilation. Adapted from W. P. Wilson, The role of potassium in the production of the slow wave response to hyperventilation in the electroencephalogram, *Electroencephalography and Clinical Neurophysiology*, 1958, **10**, 546–549. By permission.

slow EEG activity (Engel, 1945). A slight increase in frequency of cortical rhythms is caused by oxygen excess (Engel, Romano, Ferris, Webb, & Stevens, 1944).

Glucose and CO_2

Normal brain function requires an adequate supply of glucose. It is believed that the complete oxidation of glucose accounts for over 90% of the respiration of the brain. When blood sugar levels are low, slow rhythms appear in the EEG; the lower the blood sugar level, the slower the frequency. There is an important interaction between the effects of hyperventilation and the blood sugar level. Overbreathing may induce high voltage delta rhythms more readily in fasting subjects, in whom the blood sugar level is low. It is of diagnostic significance to relate the blood sugar level to the hyperventilation response. A delta response to hyperventilation at a blood sugar level above 130 mg per 100 cc is taken as abnormal (Brazier, Finesinger, & Schwab, 1944). Figure 7.11 illustrates the effects of glucose in reducing the slow wave response to hyperventilation. Wilson (1958) showed that the administration of glucose was accompanied by a marked diminution in the potassium increase associated with hyperventilation. However, he was unable to correlate the changes in potassium with those seen in the EEG.

The mechanism of the delta response to hyperventilation has received considerable attention and theoretical discussion (Morrice, 1956). There is general agreement that the delta response results ultimately from the acapnia. Three different suggestions have been made concerning the more immediate cause: inadequate compensatory vasoconstriction (F. A. Gibbs, Williams, & E. L. Gibbs, 1940), cerebral anemia due to vasoconstriction resulting in anoxia and glucose deprivation (H. Davis & Wallace, 1942), and reduced cholinergic activity of the cerebral vascular nerve supply resulting in excessive local vasoconstriction (Darrow & Graf, 1945). Morrice (1956) postulated a factor of inherent stability as a personal characteristic that, in addition to the others, influences the hyperventilation response.

High and Low Altitudes

Querol (1958, 1965) has made interesting observations on subjects accustomed to high and low altitudes in Peru. Sea level residents studied at 14,900 ft had lower voltage background activity than at sea level. Between the first and seventh day of their stay at high altitude, they showed an increase in mean frequency of background rhythms. Delta response to hyperventilation was not present at high altitude in subjects who had shown such a response at sea level. Theta waves also decreased in the course of adaptation to high altitude. Although glucose levels increased at high altitude, the reduced hyperventilation slow wave response could not be attributed to this factor. When the subjects returned to sea level in Lima, background rhythm frequency diminished and voltage increased. The slow wave response to hyperventilation also increased. In a second study, Querol (1965) examined subjects who were born and lived at high altitude and who descended to sea level. Recordings during rest at high altitude were within normal limits. On descent to Lima, the background activity was found to increase in voltage, and frequency decreased by 0.5 Hz. Slower waves also increased. Slow wave response to hyperventilation was almost never seen at high altitude, and was always seen at sea level. Querol believes that his findings point to the importance of the autonomic nervous system and possibly of cortical-subcortical mechanisms. He points out that his highlanders hyperventilated less intensely in Lima than at high altitude, and that, although they had lower levels of CO_2 in the highlands, they had a delta response at sea level.

Bennett and Glass (1961) examined the EEG changes induced by high partial pressures of nitrogen in a training tank for submarine escape. They found that pressure equivalent to a 200-ft depth of sea water showed an immediate abolition of the alpha blocking response, which was present during mental calculations at atmospheric pressure. With further increase of pressure, there was a tendency to the diminution of amplitude. When an oxyhelium mixture was substituted for the compressed air, alpha blocking reappeared, implicating nitrogen as the agent responsible. Bennett and Glass proposed that the effects they observed were due to the progressively increased saturation of the ascending reticular formation by nitrogen under pressure.

Ions

Many ions are undoubtedly important in maintaining normal electrical activity of the brain. From a theoretical standpoint, one would expect potassium to have a significant effect on the EEG, but this has not been found true in cases of hypopotassemia in man (Saunders, 1954). Roth and Nevsimal (1964) found that calcium deficiency in man associated with tetany was accompanied by EEG abnormalities: high voltage slow waves, frequently rhythmic. The injection of sodium chloride into animals apparently produces very little effect on the electrocorticogram. Conditions that give rise to a high ammonia concentration in the blood are associated with a peculiar triphasic wave if there also is a disturbance of consciousness (Poser, 1958).

Hormones

The importance of the endocrine balance in relation to maintaining normal electrical activity of the brain is indicated by a variety of disturbances in endocrine disorders. Thiebaut, Rohmer, and Wackenheim (1958) reviewed their clinical EEG findings in cases of endocrine disorder. They found slow rhythms in myxedema and rapid rhythms in hyperthyroidism. The changes in adrenal syndromes were variable. W. P. Wilson and Johnson (1964) found that hyperthyroid patients had a decreased duration of photically elicited, alpha-blocking responses and an increase in susceptibility to intermittent photic stimulation, which they often found unpleasant. W. P. Wilson, Johnson, and Fiest (1964) administered triiodothyronine to normal subjects and examined their EEG responses. They found no change in alpha frequencies, but the duration of the alpha-blocking response was shortened in all subjects. They thus reproduced experimentally some of the findings obtained in hyperthyroid patients. Hermann and Quarton (1964) studied hyper- and hypothyroid patients as their level of hormone changed. Alpha frequency correlated positively with protein-bound iodine and basal metabolic rate.

There were also high correlations of 0.83 and 0.85, respectively, between change in alpha and change in these two indices of thyroid activity.

Patients with inadequate adrenal-cortical function in Addison's disease tend to show slow rhythms (Engel & Margolin, 1942). The administration of cortisone corrects the EEG abnormality.

Although direct effects of sodium administration have been difficult to demonstrate, Margerison, Anderson, and J. Dawson (1964) showed relationships between plasma sodium and the EEG during the menstrual cycle of normal women. They found that the amount of activity from 7 to 9 Hz was less premenstrually than 12–14 days after the onset of bleeding. Plasma sodium was lower premenstrually. The changes in the amount of activity at 7 and 8 Hz were significantly associated with changes in plasma sodium; there was also a trend for such an association at 9 Hz. Other frequencies did not show such a correlation. These findings deserve particular interest in relation to the observation of Margerison, Anderson, J. Dawson, and Lettich (1962) in patients with depressive disorders. They found that urinary sodium-potassium ratios were correlated positively with amount of 7–10 Hz activity in the EEG. Reduced urinary sodium, associated with depression, would mean sodium retention and probably high intracellular sodium. The lower plasma sodium values during the premenstrual period may be explainable as due to a migration of sodium from the extra- to the intracellular compartments, perhaps leading to the common occurrence of premenstrual tension. This theory is compatible with EEG findings and with the probable sodium shifts. A point of methodological significance from this work is that, in using female subjects, consideration needs to be given to the variations in EEG amplitude which may be found in different phases of the menstrual cycle.

Temperature

A general metabolic factor of importance in relation to the EEG is the temperature of the brain. Hoagland (1936) investigated normal subjects, whose body temperature was lowered or was increased by diathermy, and found that the frequency of the alpha rhythm increased when body temperature rose. Changes associated with thyroid disturbance may be mediated by temperature effects.

It should be clear that EEG activity may be influenced by many chemical and environmental factors. Some of these may play a significant role in psychophysiological investigations and need to be controlled by the investigator or taken into account in experimental design. Examples are the phase of menstruation, temperature, blood sugar level (time since last meal), and hyperventilation during an experimental task.

AGE AND THE EEG

Investigations relating chronological age to characteristics of the EEG have concentrated on the early and late periods of life. Most have necessarily been cross-sectional or longitudinal over a relatively short time. The apparent stability of the EEG from early adulthood through middle age, suggested by cross-sectional studies, almost certainly indicates that whatever changes take place during this time are not dramatic. However, it would require longitudinal studies over many years to demonstrate subtle changes with age through adult life.

Fetal EEG

Several investigators have recorded electrical brain activity of fetuses of various ages removed at operation from the uterus. The results have been variable; some cases showing fast activity, and others, slow waves or convulsive activity. As Pond (1963, pp. 193–206) points out, it is difficult to be sure how much of the electrical activity recorded was actually cerebral in origin. This is because many of the fetuses had signs of cerebral hemorrhage a few hours after the tracings were obtained, and there was great variability in the amount of movement, the degree of cyanosis, and the presence of drugs.

Infancy and Childhood

The earliest records obtained from babies who later developed normally were taken about 24 weeks after conception, with body weight slightly more than 1000 grams. The main activity was at 5 Hz, and there were some slower waves. The activity appeared to be bilaterally synchronous and sym-

metrical. Within a few weeks there appeared to be some differentiation between one part of the hemisphere and another. The occipital region showed activity at about 1 Hz and some low voltage rhythms at 9–12 Hz. A regular rhythm appeared 26–32 weeks after conception. Full-term neonates tend to show uniform EEGs up to the age of 3 months; these are characterized by low voltage, irregular, arrhythmic activity, of somewhat larger amplitude and slower frequency in the posterior regions. At about 6 months, Lindsley (1936) found the frequency to be about 5 Hz and at about 1 year, 7 Hz. These findings were confirmed by Smith (1938), who also observed that frequencies of 6–8 and 12–16 Hz were found in the central regions at an age before the occipital rhythms became prominent. Smith observed activity in various frequency bands up to 14 Hz that increased in amplitude, persistence, and regularity up to the age of 4 to 6 years, after which the 3.5–6 Hz component decreased.

Lindsley (1939) followed 132 children through several years of development and showed that, in every case, the average frequency of the occipital rhythms increased steadily with age, following a roughly exponential curve. The average amplitude rose at first and then steadily declined. Henry (1944) also provided longitudinal data; one example is shown in Figure 7.12. His results are similar to those obtained by Lindsley. Henry found that alpha frequency in the majority of children stabilizes close to 8 years of age at about 9–11 Hz. The normal adult distribution of frequencies in the population was not reached until the age of 13 years.

Henry also measured the activity in the delta frequency range, which he defined as less than 7.5 Hz. He found that all 227 children studied between 6 and 19 years of age exhibited slow activity in their resting records, and that the amount of slow activity was greater in the central than in the occipital areas. With increasing chronological age, the percentage of delta time decreased, and delta frequency increased.

W. G. Walter (1950) surveyed 110 normal children using an automatic analyzer. In general, he confirmed the results of Lindsley, Smith, and Henry. He also demonstrated some interesting characteristics of theta rhythm: it was more prominent

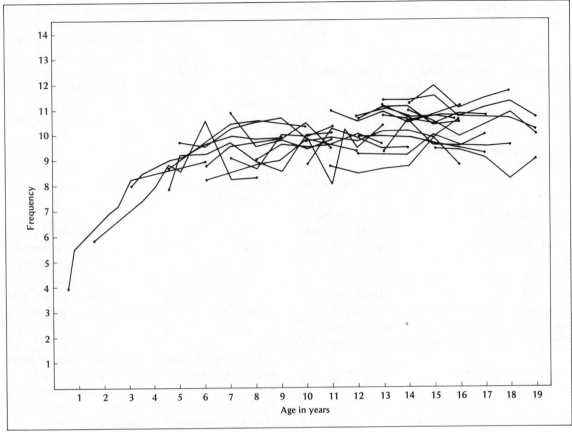

Figure 7.12   Longitudinal changes in occipital alpha frequency for 26 boys. The joined lines represent observations on
each individual. From C. E. Henry, Electroencephalograms of normal children. *Monograph of the Society for
Research in Child Development,* 1944, **9,** (Serial No. 39). By permission.

on the left side than on the right in all age groups;
in children up to the age of 2 to 3 years it was
usually augmented by closing the eyes and by such
emotions as laughing, crying, or hunger. Walter also
found that alpha rhythm is rarely responsive to
visual stimuli below 3 years of age but quite frequently so above that age. The *Atlas* of F. A. Gibbs
and E. L. Gibbs (1950) contains detailed, quantitative data concerning EEG characteristics at various
ages. Beta activity seems to be of low amplitude
in normal children and to change little in frequency
(Pond, 1963, p. 198).

In general, the EEG is much more sensitive to
overbreathing in children than in adults. Responses
to sensory stimuli may be seen in premature infants
32 weeks after conception. Ellingson (1958) confirmed earlier workers' descriptions of EEG patterns

during wakefulness and sleep in a large sample of
newborns. He also studied the effects of loud auditory stimuli and found two effects, flattening of the
tracings and a response resembling the adult *K*
complex. Single flashes of light to the eyes often
elicited evoked potentials in the occipital area.
These visual responses differed from those of
adults, in that they were more variable in waveform
and amplitude, showed greater "fatigueability," and
were of much longer latency (160–220 msec). Trains
of flashes of light at 2 per sec or faster elicited
responses at the beginning and end of stimulation;
driving effects were rarely observed. In a later report
on a larger series, Ellingson (1960) presented detailed observations on the development of the
flash-evoked response. He showed that there was
a high correlation between latency of this response

and body weight up to about 12 lb ($r = 0.80$). Curves relating response latency to age and body weight were found to be two-legged rather than monotonic, the breaks in the curves occurring at 4 weeks postterm and 9-lb body weight, respectively.

Old Age

The incidence of "abnormality" in the EEG tends to increase past the age of 60. Criteria for abnormality based on younger populations are probably not too relevant. Silverman, Busse, and Barnes (1955) found that, in 145 volunteers from the community without neurological disease, there was a high percentage of focal slow wave disturbance, which did not seem to be related to psychological impairment. There was also an interesting relation between high socioeconomic level and a low incidence of EEG abnormality. Obrist (1954) reported findings on 150 normal men from 65 to 94 years of age. Using the scheme devised by F. A. and E. L. Gibbs for classification of dominant frequency, he

found that elderly males had a much higher incidence of slightly slow (S1) EEGs than young adults. The occipital alpha frequency shifted toward the slow side, with an increase in the number of cases with 7-8 Hz activity. The percentage of time alpha was also reduced in old age. Beta waves were found in about half the subjects and were the dominant frequency in about 12%. The senile EEG appeared to be similar to that of middle age with respect to beta activity. Delta waves were somewhat increased in incidence, compared with a young group; there was relatively little response to hyperventilation, a finding similar to that in middle age.

Thus the major change characterizing the EEG of the aged adult without apparent illness appears to be a reduction of frequency. In addition, there is increased fast frequency or beta activity with its onset in middle age. Figure 7.13 shows the percentage distribution of alpha frequencies in different age groups.

Functional relations of EEG frequency changes with aging There is some indication that the slowing of the frequencies of brain waves with aging may be correlated with variations in mental functioning. This possibility comes from studies comparing psychiatric patients with brain syndromes to patients with functional disorders. Obrist and Henry (1958) found that patients with brain syndromes had more slow activity and significantly lower peak frequencies in the occipital and temporal areas than did functional cases. Individuals with brain syndromes are characterized by greater difficulties in memory, decreasing ability to pay attention, etc.

Surwillo has carried out an interesting series of studies relating EEG frequency to simple response time and age. His subjects were 100 males ranging in age from 28 to 99 years (mean, 55.3). Reaction times were measured using a 250 Hz tone to which a response key was pressed. In two of three stimulus sequences the duration of the signal was approximately 3 sec; whereas in the third, 10 signals of the standard 3-sec duration were followed by signals lasting only 0.3 sec. Between the second and third sessions the subject was informed that his level of vigilance had fluctuated during the course

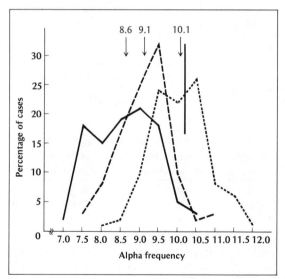

Figure 7.13 Distribution of occipital alpha frequency for three age groups. The arrows represent the means of the three samples. The vertical line indicates the mean of 10.2 Hz obtained for another sample of 75 young and middle-aged adults. . . . Age 13–19 ($N = 147$); --- age 65–79 ($N = 63$); —age 80–94 ($N = 62$). Adapted from W. D. Obrist, The electroencephalogram of normal aged adults, *Electroencephalography and Clinical Neurophysiology*, 1954, **6**, 235–244. By permission.

of the previous session. He was requested, therefore, to keep especially alert, and, as soon as the duration of the signals changed, to exert the greatest effort in pressing the response button as quickly as possible. This procedure resulted in a shorter reaction time in all but four subjects. The maneuver to obtain a high level of alertness was instituted in order to have data over the whole arousal continuum, from drowsiness to alertness.

Surwillo (1963a) found that the mean reaction time and the brain wave period were significantly correlated ($r = 0.72$), longer reaction time being associated with the greater duration of individual waves. The brain wave period was correlated with age to the extent of 0.57, but the partial correlation, in which the effect of age in relation to both the reaction time and the alpha period was statistically removed, gave a coefficient of 0.76. Surwillo also found that the correlations between the reaction time and the brain wave period for each subject individually were nearly all positive. He interpreted his findings to support the hypothesis that the brain wave cycle is the basic unit of time; any response is programmed by the central nervous system in terms of this unit of time.

Further analysis of his data permitted Surwillo (1963b) to show a significant positive correlation between the variability of reaction time and age, which appeared to be due to variations in the average brain wave period. Later he studied a more complex kind of reaction time, involving a decision, and compared disjunctive and simple reaction time relationships to the brain wave period (Surwillo, 1964). Subjects were required to press a response key only when the higher of two tones (1000 and 250 Hz) was presented. The correlations between the brain wave period and the simple and disjunctive reaction times were both 0.76. Figure 7.14 shows the scattergrams. The steeper slope of the time curve for the disjunctive reaction indicates that people with slow brain waves required more time to decide between two alternatives than people with fast brain waves. Decision time, measured as the difference between simple and disjunctive times, was also significantly correlated with the brain wave period ($r = 0.40$).

More recently, Surwillo (1966) demonstrated that the latent time for the blocking of alpha by flashes

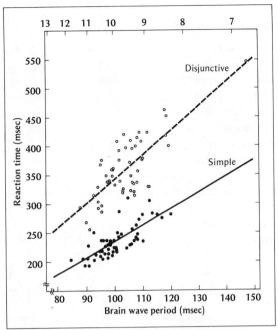

Figure 7.14 Scattergram of time required to make a discriminative response. Reaction time plotted against brain wave period for disjunctive responses (open circles, broken lines) and simple responses (solid circles, solid line). Each open circle represents the average disjunctive reaction time and the average brain wave period of a single subject and is derived from the mean of 11 observations. The solid circles are averages for simple reaction time and the EEG period from the same group, each point being derived from the mean of 16 observations. Numbers at the top of the graph refer to the corresponding EEG frequencies in Hz. Adapted from W. W. Surwillo, The relation of decision time to brain wave frequency and to age, *Electroencephalography and Clinical Neurophysiology*, 1964, **16**, 510–514. By permission.

of white light was significantly correlated with the EEG period. He also showed a decline of EEG reactivity with age.

If we accept Surwillo's view of the brain wave cycle as the basic unit of time underlying response programming by the brain, then the general slowing of frequencies with age would underlie the trend toward slower responsiveness in older persons. On the other hand, there appear to be great individual differences in the rate at which brain waves slow with aging, so that the reaction time-alpha frequency correlation is greater than the correlation of either variable alone with age.

SEX AND THE EEG

There has been surprisingly little study of sex differences in the EEG. Henry (1944) presented evidence showing that females tend to have faster alpha frequency than males and that the low voltage, fast type of record is more common in females. He found no consistent changes to accompany the presumed onset of puberty in 40 cases in which such a correlation was sought. The observations of Margerison, Anderson, and J. Dawson (1964), relating alpha abundance to the menstrual cycle, have been mentioned above; they suggest greater day-by-day variability in the female than male EEG. Studies of photic driving have revealed sex differences: over a broad frequency range, intermittent photic stimulation elicited higher amplitude driving responses in female than in male subjects (Shagass, 1955a).

THE EEG AND INDIVIDUAL DIFFERENCES

Stability of the EEG

Any attempt to relate individual differences in the EEG to individual differences on other physiological or behavioral dimensions assumes that the EEG of adults is stable over relatively long periods of time. Since it is clear that the characteristics of the EEG will change markedly under different conditions, conditions of recording must be specified in any statement of stability. Virtually all available data on stability appear to have been obtained under the usual, clinical resting conditions.

H. Davis and P. A. Davis (1939) found no change in the gross appearance of records obtained from subjects over a period of 4 years. Jasper and Andrews (1938a) made measurements on six normal individuals over a period of 6–18 months and reported only slight variations in these measurements from time to time. Rubin (1938) found a variation of less than 1 Hz in mean alpha frequency over periods up to 4 months. Engel, Romano, and Ferris (1947) studied three subjects over a 5-year period with 25–39 observations each. They found that the greatest range of variations in alpha frequency for any one subject was 0.8 Hz. They found no correlation between changes in alpha frequency and variations in blood sugar or rectal temperature.

One might expect the EEG to be particularly stable if its characteristics are heavily determined by genetic factors. Should this be so, there should be greater similarities between the EEGs of identical twins than between individuals with different genetic makeup. H. Davis and P. A. Davis (1936), Raney (1939), and Lennox, F. A. Gibbs, and E. L. Gibbs (1942) found this generally to be true. Raney's quantitative data did show variations from time to time, so that he found it necessary to point out that the similarity was greater only on a group basis. On the other hand, Lennox, F. A. Gibbs, and E. L. Gibbs found 87% concordance between the EEG and physical traits in 53 normal twins.

The twin studies support the concept that genetic factors underlie the relative stability of the individual EEG; however, notions about genetically determined differences in cortical organization and their contribution to stability of the EEG were cast into doubt by Henry's data (1941a, 1941b). In one study he recorded the all-night rhythms of 20 subjects. The population was selected for heterogeneity with respect to waking alpha index prior to sleep, but it proved to be homogeneous with respect to all-sleep rhythms. Even more striking was the discovery that the waking alpha index after sleep was quite similar among the subjects, so that the differentiation of subjects before sleeping into four alpha index groups was lost. In a study of the waking EEG, Henry (1941b) selected four subjects for extremes of alpha index in the resting record. The subjects were then engaged in activities such as reading and talking. He found that certain conditions of psychological activity, coupled with visual stimulation, reduced the differences between individuals to the point at which they did not significantly exceed fluctuations within the individuals' responses.

Johnson and Ulett (1959) carried out an extensive, quantitative study of the stability of the EEG activity over a 9-month period in 182 young men. They found that the shape of the EEG-activity profile, as determined by measuring 24 frequencies with their frequency analyzer, was highly stable over 9 months, but that the amount of activity was significantly lower in the initial record. Subjects with high alpha records showed the least change over time. Over 50% of the frequency-amplitude profiles were highly stable, but there were marked individual differences in stability.

The evidence, therefore, suggests that *under uniform conditions* there will be *relative* stability of various EEG characteristics. However, there may be great shifts in certain subjects, and individual differences may be virtually wiped out if records are taken shortly after sleep. This means that any attempt to correlate EEG characteristics with psychological characteristics of the individual must contend with considerable instability of the EEG measure.

Intelligence and the EEG

Kreezer (1939, 1940) reported a series of studies relating the EEG to intelligence in Mongolian-type mental deficients of adult age and nondifferentiated, familial-type mental deficients. He used adult subjects to limit the effect of chronological age. His results varied with the types of groups studied. For example, he found a significant correlation of 0.35 between mental age and alpha index in the Mongolians but no correlations between mental age and alpha frequency; whereas the reverse was true in familial-type mental deficients. Lindsley (1938) and Rahm and Williams (1938) failed to find correlations between EEG characteristics and intelligence. Knott, Friedman, and Bardsley (1942) studied 8- and 12-year-old children. Alpha frequency and intelligence level were significantly correlated ($r = 0.50$) in the 8-year-olds. They were unable to suggest a satisfactory explanation for the discrepant findings between the different age groups.

Shagass (1946) reported no correlation between alpha frequency and scores on a group intelligence test in 1100 adult subjects ranging in age from 18 to 33 years. H. Gastaut's group (1959; summarized in H. Gastaut, 1960) reported an absence of correlation between intelligence scores and EEG characteristics in a sample of 511 French recruits, aged 20.

Mundy-Castle (1958) attempted to test the hypothesis, based on various findings, that vocabulary performance and alpha frequency are related. The Wechsler-Bellevue Intelligence Test was administered to his sample of 34 adult subjects. Alpha frequency was found to be significantly correlated with the vocabulary score, verbal IQ, practical IQ, and general IQ. The correlation with general IQ was

highest ($r = 0.51$). Mundy-Castle did a factor analysis of the 11 Wechsler subtests, alpha frequency, alpha index, age and occupational level. He extracted five factors; of these, four were interpreted as (a) a visual-concrete aspect of intelligence, (b) a visual-abstract aspect of intelligence, (c) an age factor of intelligence, and (d) temperamental component of intelligence related to a central excitability factor. Mundy-Castle suggested that his data might be different from those of other workers because of the special properties of the Wechsler-Bellevue test. His factor analysis has been questioned (D. R. Saunders, 1960). Mundy-Castle and Nelson (1960) also reported a significant correlation of 0.34 between alpha frequency and Wechsler intelligence scores.

Ellingson, Wilcott, Sineps, and Dudek (1957) tested a hypothesis derived from W. G. Walter's (1953) observation that his more brilliant colleagues showed greater variation in their EEG-frequency spectrum than his duller patients. EEG measures obtained with a frequency analyzer were correlated with intelligence measures from a short form of the Wechsler-Bellevue scale. A single summary measure of frequency pattern variability was derived. No correlation between this measure and intelligence was found, so that the hypothesis was not confirmed. A somewhat different, but related, approach to the problem of the EEG and intelligence is found in the study of Wyspianski, Barry, and Dayhaw (1963), which correlated EEG amplitude with a classification of creative thinking based on five tests: word fluency, ideational fluency, associational fluency, expressional fluency, and alternate uses. Tests were derived from Guilford and Merrifield (1960). Wyspianski, Barry, and Dayhaw (1963) found that amplitude was significantly lower in the group with the highest creativity scores than it was in others. However, the group classified as having a middle creativity level actually had higher alpha amplitude than did the one classified as low creativity.

The issue of EEG correlates of intelligence does not yet appear to be resolved, although the bulk of the evidence suggests that relationships, if they exist, are slight. The positive findings that have appeared in the literature over the last 30 years have all involved relatively small samples, whereas studies using samples of several hundred subjects have failed to demonstrate significant relationships. Mundy-Castle's (1958) suggestion that the nature of the intelligence test may be a relevant factor is worthy of attention. It may be that some factor other than intelligence per se is tapped by both a given intelligence test and EEG activity. For example, on the basis of Surwillo's (1963a) findings, any test that emphasizes the speed of response could yield results correlated with alpha frequency.

EEG Correlates of Personality

Henry (1965, pp. 3–18) has reviewed the literature concerned with the relation of EEG to personality variables. In his review he adopted the reasonable course of avoiding attempts to obtain a unanimous definition of the word "personality," but interpreted it freely to include behavior tendencies, temperament, and attributes of the individual.

Psychodynamic correlates Henry drew attention to the fact that the earliest relationship reported between the EEG and personality is still the one most strongly supported by available evidence. In 1937 Saul, H. Davis, and P. A. Davis studied patients in psychoanalysis. The subjects were categorized according to their tendencies for activity versus passivity in habitual actions and in their attitudes toward other persons and toward food, work, sleep, and sex. Since trends of both activity and passivity could be found in the same individual, an assessment of relative strength was made. A high alpha index was found associated with a passive, dependent, receptive attitude toward other persons, provided this attitude was freely accepted and not thwarted or inhibited internally. Low alpha indices were usually found in association with a consistent, well-directed, freely indulged drive to activity, excluding, however, diffuse hypomanic activity, which is in the nature of a defense. In a later publication, (1949), the same group enlarged the number of cases studied to 136. The results still showed that very passive individuals had high alpha EEGs; there were three times as many men as women in this group. Women with strong masculine trends generally had low voltage fast or low alpha EEGs, and there were relatively few men with EEGs of this type. A third category was added, consisting largely

of frustrated, impatient, aggressive, demanding, and hostile women with mixed fast or mixed slow types of records. Only two men fell into the latter category. Despite the ongoing psychoanalysis, there was no pronounced shift from high to low alpha index in any case. The relative stability of the EEG over this period of time is a testimony to the standardized conditions of recording.

Palmer and Rock (1953) obtained findings that accord with those of Saul's group. They selected 25 men on the basis of high alpha activity in the EEG. Clinical studies showed that these men had very inadequate schizoid or immature personalities. In addition to being nonaggressive and conforming, they all had poor identification with fathers in early formative years. This lack of identification was interpreted as a deficiency of "crystallized experience," which could result in an "idling" brain that did not adequately deal with life's problems in a masculine fashion. A control group of 15 men with passive personalities but with adequate identification with their fathers at an early age did not have high alpha activity. Henry (1965, pp. 3–18) makes the point that Saul, H. Davis, and P. A. Davis did not claim to be able to predict personality from EEG but rather the converse, i.e., to predict EEG from personality.

Gottlober (1938) found a significant relationship between introversion-extraversion and alpha index. However, Henry and Knott (1941) reexamined Gottlober's data, added a larger group of subjects, used the same rating scale, and found only a chance distribution of alpha type versus personality type.

Test findings Although there have been many attempts to relate EEG characteristics to findings from complex personality tests such as the Minnesota Multiphasic Personality Inventory (MMPI) and the Rorschach Diagnostic Test, results on the whole have been either negative or inconsistent from one study to another. For example, Werre (1957) carried out an extensive study in which virtually all possible EEG variables were correlated with a number of psychological test procedures, including the Rorschach. He was forced to conclude: "There are no unique associations between any single electroencephalographic variable and any specific psychological parameter [p. 131]." The study of the relations between EEG variables and psychological findings in 511 French recruits corroborates the absence of relationships. Thus H. Gastaut (1960) concluded: "No relation exists between the EEG variables and those of the Rosenzweig test and the intelligence tests. Some rare relations, slight and poorly organized, sometimes absurd, exist between the EEG variables and those of the MMPI [p. 227]."

Photic driving   Ulett, Gleser, Winokur and Lawler (1953) measured the reaction to intermittent photic stimulation and found photic driving responses to be related to "anxiety proneness." They were able to discriminate a high proportion of anxiety-prone individuals by means of photic responses. However, they found their results difficult to replicate in later studies.

Shagass (1955a, 1955b) also studied the relationship between the photic driving response and affective state. Using flashes at rates of 15 and 10 Hz, he expressed relative driving to these two flash rates as a 15–10 ratio (Figure 7.5). A group of psychiatric patients classified as suffering from anxiety or depression were compared with a normal control group. Among female subjects the patients with anxiety showed significantly higher 15–10 driving ratios than the control subjects, who in turn had higher ratios than the depressed patients. Longitudinal studies on individual subjects showed that the driving response varied considerably from one session to another but that the variations appeared to be related to life experiences of an emotional nature. In subsequent work, however, the group results were difficult to replicate.

Sedation threshold   Data relating EEG responses to personality were obtained by Shagass with another experimental approach utilizing the intravenous injection of amobarbital sodium. While injecting the drug in a stepwise manner at the rate of 0.5 mg/kg every 40 sec, he recorded the EEG. The injection continued well beyond the time at which the subject responded to test words with an obvious slurring of speech. Measurement of the amplitude of frontal 15–30 Hz activity induced by the amobarbital yielded a curve roughly of S-shape, when the amplitude was plotted against the amount of drug given. The amount of amobarbital, in mg/kg, which had been administered at the time of maximal rise of the beta amplitude between two adjacent injections, was taken as the sedation threshold. This point corresponded roughly to the time of onset of slurred speech. Shagass (1954) found that the sedation threshold correlated well with clinical ratings of tension; the latter could be regarded as ratings of anxiety proneness, since they were based on factors in the patient's history, as well as his clinical status at the time of the test. Subsequent data indicated that the relationship between sedation threshold and anxiety proneness pertained only to nonpsychotic individuals. Entirely different relationships were found in psychoses (Shagass & Naiman, 1955).

Shagass and Naiman (1955, 1956) found that sedation thresholds were significantly higher in a group of psychoneurotic patients than in a group of volunteer controls. Within the control group the sedation threshold was related to symptoms of anxiety proneness elicited by clinical interview and by means of a standardized, self-administered questionnaire. Although the data relating the degree of anxiety to the sedation threshold in nonpsychotic subjects appeared reasonably clear, another interpretation appeared possible in the light of Eysenck's (1957) theory of anxiety and hysteria. One of Eysenck's dimensions of personality is that of extraversion-introversion. Hildebrand (1953) had independently showed that psychological measures of introversion-extraversion arranged the psychoneuroses in an order corresponding exactly to that obtained with the sedation threshold. Hysterics had low thresholds and high extraversion, whereas anxiety states had high thresholds and high introversion. The direction was also as predicted from Eysenck's theory. This suggested that the sedation threshold differences in psychoneuroses could just as readily be interpreted in terms of the introversion-extraversion dimension, or a related hysterical-obsessional continuum, as in terms of the level of anxiety.

Shagass and Kerenyi (1958) rated the case records of a large sample of psychoneurotic subjects on such a hysterical-obsessional continuum and confirmed the predicted relationship. They also applied the Guilford S and R scales, which contributed heavily to Hildebrand's introversion-extraversion battery, to a group of psychoneurotic patients who were tested for the sedation threshold. The results showed significant correlation between the sedation threshold and the degree of introversion: for a score combining the two scales, so that high introversion yielded a high value, r was $+0.60$. The findings relating sedation threshold to position on the hysterical-obsessional continuum have been confirmed by Claridge and Herrington (1963a; 1963b, pp. 131–168).

Mental Imagery and the EEG

The style of mental imagery, be it predominantly visual, verbal, kinesthetic, or whatever, may be considered a personality characteristic, although it may be less global in nature than such factors as extraversion-introversion. Possible relations between imagery style and the EEG merit special consideration, because of the obvious EEG changes usually associated with visual perception and attention to visual stimuli.

The fact that individuals differ in the amount of alpha and alpha blocking led Golla, Hutton, and W. G. Walter (1943) to classify alpha records into M, R, and P types. They found that subjects with M (minus, i.e., little alpha) records used mainly visual imagery in thinking; the P types (persistent alpha, even to light) chiefly used auditory or kinesthetic imagery; and either visual or nonvisual imagery was found in the R (responsive) type. Short (1953) showed that the alpha rhythms tended to block when the subject used visual imagery and to persist when he used verbal-motor imagery. Mundy-Castle (1958) also presented evidence supporting the presence of correlations between alpha characteristics and the mental imagery type. However, not all workers observed such relationships, so that Slatter (1960), in reviewing the literature, noted that about as many had failed to find it as had been able to demonstrate it.

Slatter's (1960) investigation of the EEG correlates of mental imagery in a group of 60 medical and dental students represented an attempt to explain the differences in results. In his study he paid particular attention to the relaxation and reassurance of the subjects, attempting to eliminate any apprehensions they might have about having their

EEG recorded. Furthermore, he selected his mental tasks with great care to avoid giving the anxiety-provoking impression that they were tests of intelligence. His inquiry into the visual imagery experiences of his subjects explicitly took into account their variable ideas of visualizing. With attention to these problems the EEG was recorded during a series of simple tasks involving arithmetic and various requests to imagine. An example of the latter was: "Think of an apple. Cut it in half; now cut it in halves again. How many sides of all the pieces will be white and how many will be colored?" Slatter found no subject with an extreme predominance of any one type of imagery, as described by Golla, Hutton, and W. G. Walter (1943). Instead he found a central group in which the individual's use of the various types of imagery was very evenly mixed, with gradations on either side in the direction of predominant visualization or verbalization. On this basis he classified his subjects into four groups: predominant visualizers, visualizers, verbalizers, and predominant verbalizers. He also assessed the quality of their imagery on a four-point scale.

Slatter's results showed clearly that visual imagery is associated with a reduction in the alpha rhythms, whereas verbal imagery is associated with their persistence. Of 264 instances involving visual imagery, about 94% involved an alpha response, compared to 16% of 148 instances involving verbal imagery. In tasks demanding purposive imagery, the visual task elicited an alpha response in 58 out of 60 instances; whereas the verbal imagery task elicited alpha response in only 7 of 60. Looking at a picture always elicited alpha blocking. Those subjects with higher amplitude rhythms showed the greatest percentage reduction in amplitude on actual visualization or visual recall; this may be due to operation of the law of initial value. However, Slatter found that the high amplitude records were especially associated with poor quality of visual appreciation, so that the actual degree of amplitude change bore no direct relation to the quality of the visual processes.

Slatter found a high degree of association between the classification of habitual imagery into visual or verbal and the average amplitude of the EEG. In 32 subjects classified as visual, amplitude was below average in 30; whereas it was above average in 21 of 28 classified as verbal. Another characteristic related to imagery style was the degree of intermittence of alpha. More than half of those with habitual verbal imagery had continuous or almost continuous alpha; whereas only 1 of 32 with habitual visual imagery showed the same characteristic. The degree of blocking, whether complete or incomplete, was also related to habitual imagery; the visual type showed predominantly complete blocking, whereas the opposite was true with the verbal type. The quality of visual imagery tended to be associated with amplitude; those with good and excellent quality tended to have lower amplitudes. Frequency analysis suggested a particular association between visual imagery and the frequency of 12 Hz. Of 12 students with a dominant frequency of 12 Hz, 11 were habitual visualizers; the average alpha amplitude was also below the median in all 12.

Slatter concluded that (a) active vision and visual recall are associated with blocking or attenuation of the alpha rhythm, with the former producing the greater change; (b) nonvisual imagery is associated with the persistence of alpha rhythms; and (c) alpha activity is blocked nonspecifically by anxiety. The fact that the EEG showed every grade of change between the M and P types suggested to him that these represent two extremes of a continuous gradation of changes. He expressed the view that individuals use different types of imagery with differing degrees of ease and preponderance, and that alpha rhythm properties in the record taken at rest correlate with the subject's ease and habitual use of visual imagery.

Slatter's study has been described in some detail because its extraordinarily clear results support a relationship between alpha characteristics and style of imagery, and because they seem to have been obtained by virtue of careful attention to many factors that can influence the EEG, which are often poorly controlled. Obviously, if apprehensiveness usually suppresses alpha, it is a factor that must be controlled when one wishes to relate alpha suppression to some other variable. Conversely, if the purpose of the experiment is to relate the level of anxiety to alpha, the experimental design must cope with the problems presented by the relationship between visual imagery and the suppression of alpha. Although controls for factors such as anxiety and visual imagery are difficult to institute, they are necessary for valid results.

Psychopathology

W. P. Wilson (1965) has edited a volume devoted to comprehensive reviews of the EEG in relation to various psychopathological states; no attempt will be made here to deal extensively with the topic. In general, evidence concerning EEG correlates of major "functional" psychiatric disorders, such as the schizophrenic and manic-depressive psychoses, is inconclusive, although there is a high incidence of EEG abnormalities in brain syndromes. The functional group which appears to be associated with EEG changes in a consistent way is that of psychopathic personality. The most commonly found deviation from normal consists of excessive theta activity. In recent years considerable attention has been given to the "14 and 6," positive-spike phenomenon, which is commonly found in young psychopaths. This is best seen in monopolar temporal derivations during light sleep; the spikes are relatively positive at the scalp lead. There is still incomplete consensus about the status of this EEG sign as an indicator of pathology, particularly in relation to aggressive behavior (Knott, 1965, pp. 19–29).

Although the results relating EEG findings to presence of psychopathologic states have been rather disappointing, this may be to some extent disappointment with the absence of clear relationships, as in epilepsy, rather than a true absence of differences. Kennard, in a number of studies, has found statistical differences between psychiatric patient populations and control groups (Kennard & Schwartzman, 1956, 1957; Levy & Kennard, 1953). Levy and Kennard (1953) reviewed more than 1000 EEG tracings from patients of four different institutions. They found that in childhood and adolescence more than 50% of the EEGs in both schizophrenics and patients with behavior disorders were abnormal. However, the incidence of abnormality in the behavior disorder group fell to 20–30% in the 20-year-olds and rose again after 55. In contrast, the incidence of abnormality in schizophrenia was high throughout all the age groups studied. Abnormal, fast, frontal activity was the most common finding in the schizophrenics; the possibility that this fast frontal activity could be myogenic cannot be fully discounted.

A quantitative study, using frequency analysis, by Kennard, Rabinovitch, and Fister (1955) displayed pattern differences among schizophrenics, normal subjects, and psychopaths. Longitudinal study of frequency analyzer patterns showed that the frequency pattern changed with clinical recovery such that a later record more clearly resembled normal than the first one. The most acutely disturbed individuals showed the most extreme disturbances of coordination among EEG frequency patterns on first examination, whereas the chronically ill had a steadier frequency pattern.

Most of the available data on the EEG in psychopathologic states rests upon visual inspection and limited measurements. It seems possible that computer methods, which have the potential of doing justice to the richness of the electrical information, may yield more positive outcomes. Among the few studies is that by Fink, Shapiro, Hickman, and Itil (1966). These workers applied a discriminant function analysis to the EEG frequency bands derived from frequency analysis. They found that schizophrenic subjects exhibited greater amounts of 3.0–4.5 Hz and less 22.5–33.0 Hz activity than did depressive subjects. Inadequate control of a number of important factors such as age, sex, and previous somatotherapy leave their specific results open to question. Nevertheless, it seems clear that analytic methods of at least the sophistication of those employed in their study must be tried before accepting the conclusion that the EEG is of little relevance to psychopathology.

EEG CORRELATES OF AWARENESS, MENTAL ACTIVITY, AND SENSORY-MOTOR RESPONSIVENESS

Awareness and Mental Activity

Probably the most striking behavioral correlates of the EEG are in relation to conditions of reduced awareness, notably sleep. The changes associated with sleep will be considered elsewhere in this volume. It may be noted here that slowing of the

background rhythms is characteristic not only of natural sleep but of conditions of impared awareness due to many causes. Examples are altered metabolism, as by insulin; depression of the central nervous system by drugs, as in barbiturate coma; and diseases of the central nervous system such as cerebral arteriosclerosis. Romano and Engel's (1944) classic studies of delirium, which is a state of impaired ability to integrate environmental cues, illustrate factors that may alter both the EEG and the level of awareness in a correlated manner.

Studies of sensory deprivation have also demonstrated that the maintenance of normal EEG characteristics is dependent upon normal sensory input. Thus Heron (1957) found that alpha frequency was slowed after 48 hr of isolation, slowed to a greater extent after 96 hr of isolation, and remained slow compared to control values in records taken 3 hr after the subject emerged from the isolation situation. These findings fit readily with the idea that the reticular formation influences alpha frequency and, in turn, is maintained at its usual level of functioning by constant sensory inputs.

The most commonly observed EEG correlate of heightened alertness consists of desynchronization of the alpha rhythm with the production of a "blocking" response or reduced amplitude. The alpha frequency also generally increases with mental work. Other EEG characteristics, such as lambda, mu, and kappa, appear to be elicited in only a certain proportion of subjects under special conditions of mental activity. The data of Tyler, Goodman, and Rothman (1947), showing a reduction of activity in the alpha band and some augmentation of fast frequency during the performance of mental arithmetic, are representative. These authors obtained their results in a study of experimental insomnia with a group of subjects kept awake for 100 hr. They found that the changes produced by prolonged wakefulness were in the same direction as those produced by the increased attention or alertness required for performance of the arithmetic problems. They interpreted the similarity of these effects as a paradox more apparent than real, since they believed that the subject was expending a great deal of effort or attention to remain awake. The same mental task after long wakefulness resulted in little further change in the EEG, suggesting that a fatigued brain has less capacity to further increase its rate of electrical activity in response to the stimulus of an additional problem. Tyler's results again underscore the fact that EEG responsiveness depends upon "initial value." A more dramatic EEG change with prolonged sleep deprivation was found by Ross (1965) in a 17-year-old boy who underwent a vigil lasting 264 hr. The subject showed marked reduction in alpha activity, which was evident when his eyes were closed as well as open, and an increase in both low voltage delta and theta activity. A record taken 10 days after the first recovery sleep showed normal alpha.

Adults, but not children, show the reduction in alpha rhythm associated with performance and mental activity (Elliott, 1964). Using a simple auditory reaction time task, Elliott found that the mean alpha amplitude actually increased in children compared with the expected decrease found in adults. Elliott attributed his findings to the difficulty of 6-year-olds in maintaining a prolonged set. Elliott found also that beta amplitude decreased in adults during attention. From this he reached a conclusion similar to the one stated earlier in this chapter: the apparent increase in beta during attention and anxiety may be due more to the blocking of alpha than to the actual increase in beta.

The functional significance of alpha blocking, particularly as a correlate of mental activity, has

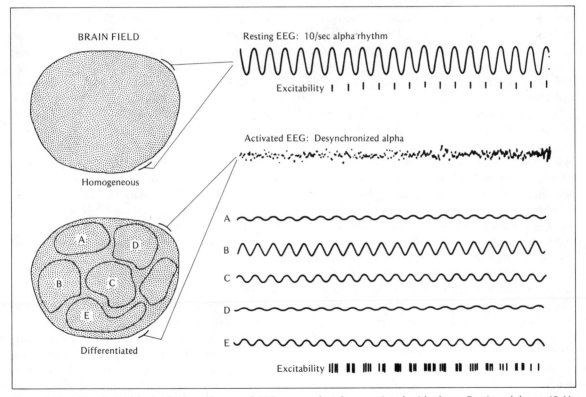

Figure 7.15 Hypothetical brain fields and type of EEG assumed to be associated with them. Resting alpha at 10 Hz characterizes the "homogeneous" or relaxed condition, while a desynchronized or activated EEG is associated with a "differentiative" state of brain function. The latter EEG is characteristic of attention and problem solving and, in general, more efficient perception and performance. According to the concept that an excitability cycle is associated with the waxing and waning phases of the waves, it is evident that there could be only 10/sec in the case of the resting EEG; whereas almost continuous points of excitability are represented in the case of the differentiated brain field and resulting EEG rhythms that are out of phase with one another. Adapted from D. B. Lindsley, Basic perceptual processes and the EEG, *American Psychiatric Association Psychiatric Research Reports,* 1956, **6,** 161–170. By permission.

received considerable theoretical attention. The speculations that have been put forth may also be applied to the related changes of reduced alpha amplitude and increased alpha frequency. One theory is that the alpha rhythm is a mechanism that continuously scans the visual projection areas in search of information (W. G. Walter, 1950). According to this theory, the alpha rhythm sweeps back and forth across the featureless projection areas when the eyes are shut, but when the eyes are opened it is broken up and desynchronized by the visual patterns; the extensive interruption of rhythms provides the basis for the temporal form of the spatial display. Although the scanning theory has had little direct experimental support, and some experiments carried out to test it have been negative (Mackay, 1953), it has generated many investigations attempting to relate alpha activity and visual perception. An example is the study of Mundy-Castle (1955a), who found that complex, nongeometric figures were more accurately perceived and subsequently recognized by subjects with high alpha frequencies.

A related theory is that of Lindsley (1952, 1956). Lindsley distinguished between alpha *rhythm* and alpha *activity*. He assumed that alpha activity is a basic cellular rhythm always present, whereas alpha rhythm is recorded only when the activity of large neuronal aggregates is synchronized. Lindsley's hypothesis is illustrated in Figure 7.15. He proposed that alpha activity represented an excitability cycle in particular aggregates of cells and suggested that the excitability cycle provides a means of pulsing and coding sensory impulses. Lindsley's hypothesis has also stimulated fruitful experimental work, e.g., Lansing's (1957) study, which will be described in the section on alpha phase and reaction time.

Autonomic Indicators of Arousal

The central role of the alpha-blocking response indicator in theories of activation or arousal suggests that it should be correlated with the peripheral indicators of arousal commonly employed in psychophysiologic studies. The evidence for this is not impressive. For example, Sternbach (1960) attempted to correlate Wenger's estimate of relative autonomic balance with percentage of time alpha in 42 male undergraduate subjects and found no

significant relationships. Wenger's measures include salivary output, sublingual temperature, palmar and volar forearm conductance, diastolic blood pressure, and heart rate. Sternbach concluded that "activation" as a concept in emotions cannot refer uniformly to central and autonomic nervous system activity. Stennett (1957) did find a relation of inverted-U form between levels of palmar conductance and alpha amplitude, but Sternbach found no evidence of systematic nonlinear relationships between his autonomic and EEG variables.

Mundy-Castle and McKiever (1953) also examined relationships between GSR responsiveness and EEG characteristics in 109 normal subjects but found no relationships between the alpha index and average resistance levels or between alpha frequencies and GSR records classified into stable and labile. Theta rhythm was also not related to GSR. A drawback of their study was that the GSR and EEG were recorded at different times. Elliott (1964) found that his EEG and somatic measures, recorded together during performance, were largely independent within age groups. The somatic measures, which included the heart rate, palmar conductance, respiratory rate, and EMG, were significantly interrelated, with the autonomic measures more highly correlated with one another than with the EMG. Davidoff and McDonald (1964) also failed to find clear-cut temporal relationships between EEG changes and a variety of autonomic measures during a study of conditional alpha blocking.

The absence of concomitant variation in measures of autonomic and central nervous system activity, all of which are interpreted as "activation," presents serious difficulties for any general activation theory. The available evidence suggests that different response systems, whether they be in the brain or in the peripheral structures, are set into action at different rates and levels in association with the behavioral changes taken to indicate activation. Since the activity of these systems must involve central controlling mechanisms, differential responsiveness of these central mechanisms must be inferred. It also follows that the EEG phenomena which have been studied are probably not intimately related to central mechanisms regulating peripheral responsiveness.

Critical Flicker Fusion

The concept that the timing of the EEG governs that of behavioral events naturally led to attempts to correlate critical flicker fusion (CFF) with EEG characteristics. Striking positive results were obtained by Chyatte (1954, 1958), who in two studies reported a correlation of 0.85 between the CFF and EEG percentage of time alpha. Reuning (1955) also reported a significant correlation. Unfortunately, these observations have not been confirmed by other investigators (Dondero, Hofstaetter, & O'Connor, 1956; Karp, Pollack, & Fink, 1962). Karp and his colleagues showed that the test-retest correlations for both CFF and EEG measures were high but they were unable to demonstrate intercorrelations between them. They suggested that a more fruitful approach to the relationship of EEG to behavior would be derived from direct measures of EEG reactivity to sensory and other stimuli.

The results of Claridge and Herrington (1963a) are of interest in relation to the suggestion of Karp, Pollack, and Fink (1962). They measured the alpha index and time required for alpha return after eye closure following fixation of a rotating spiral (Archimedes spiral). They found positive correlations between the subjectively reported duration of spiral aftereffect (contraction for an expanding spiral) and the extent to which the return of alpha was delayed by visual stimulation. They also obtained significant correlations between the duration of the spiral aftereffect and the alpha index. From this they concluded that subjects whose EEG records were more activated tended to report longer spiral aftereffects and to show greater delay in the return of alpha after visual stimulation. Claridge and Herrington also found differences related to personality, with obsessional subjects showing longer spiral aftereffects and more activated EEG records than psychopaths.

Motor Responsiveness

Jasper and Andrews (1938a) showed that spontaneous tremor movements corresponded to a significant extent with the alpha rhythm; they concluded that the normal control of spontaneous movement is probably caused by a delicate inte-

gration of cortical and subcortical areas, the extent of correspondence depending upon the degree to which cortical regions are dominant. Mundy-Castle (1955b) administered a series of motor tests designed to reflect aspects of a temperament factor designated as the primary-secondary function. He found significant positive correlations between the alpha frequency and the rate of tapping as fast as possible and at a self-preferred speed, these being of the order of 0.40. The speed of performing Thurstone's Repeated Letters Test was also positively correlated with the alpha frequency. Mundy-Castle suggested that the alpha frequency determined the speed of "unstructured motor activity." Herberg (1958) undertook an investigation to check this hypothesis by establishing whether the alpha frequency was significantly related to the speed of saccadic movements of the eyes, which he felt to be possibly the purest example of unstructured motor activity. He found that his mean fixation time and mean saccadic duration measures, derived from the eye movement tests, were significantly correlated with continuous arithmetic performance, and that mean fixation time was correlated with intelligence. However, he obtained no significant correlation between the eye movement scores and EEG alpha frequency, alpha index, or alpha amplitude. The relation between simple behavioral measures of motor tempo and EEG characteristics thus remains in some doubt.

The contrast between the clear results obtained by Surwillo (1963a), with the reaction time and alpha frequency measured during the performance, compared with the low or absent correlations obtained when the EEG and behavioral measures are recorded at different times, seems noteworthy. The greater productivity of the approach in which the EEG is measured at the same time as the performance is further supported by the studies on reaction time, to be described below.

Alpha Phase and Reaction Time

Lansing (1957) performed an experiment to test Lindsley's concept of an alpha excitability cycle. From a pool of 100 subjects he selected 8, in whom the alpha rhythm persisted while observing a dim red fixation light. The EEG from visual and motor areas and the tremor of the finger pressing the key in a reaction time situation were recorded. Figure 7.16 illustrates Lansing's oscillographic records. He found that the mean reaction times were related to the point of incidence of the stimulus on the occipital alpha cycle; significant differences between the reaction times associated with different phases of the cycle were apparent. The shortest and longest reaction times were found at points 50 msec apart, in opposite phases of the alpha cycle. The time of the finger response was also related to the phase of the motor alpha cycle. By correcting for the estimated conduction times the periods of enhanced response for the motor and occipital alpha cycle appeared to coincide. This suggested that the same phase of the alpha cycle in two different regions of the cortex represented an ex-

citable period. He also noted a low positive correlation between the alpha blocking time and the reaction time for individual responses and the occurrence of the motor response on the descending phase of the tremor cycle. The latter finding suggested the possibility of an excitability cycle in the spinal motor neuron pool.

Lansing's findings support the concept of excitability cycles at various levels of the central nervous system. However, they are open to the criticism that the subjects constituted a special group, selected for alpha rhythms resistant to blocking. This could possibly explain why Lansing obtained positive results in contrast to other workers such as Walsh (1952). From the standpoint of Lindsley's hypothesis, the objection is not crucial, since a recordable alpha *rhythm* would be expected in only a minority of subjects; but these subjects could be considered representative of the general population with respect to alpha *activity*. They can be regarded as selected only in the sense that their EEG provided an observable indicator permitting a test of the hypothesis.

Lansing's findings have been confirmed by Callaway (1961, 1962; Callaway & Yeager, 1960). He pointed out that the differences in reaction time from one alpha phase to another are small and that the alpha phase-reaction time relationships within a single subject vary to a considerable extent. On the other hand, he was able to demonstrate sufficient short-term consistency to permit pooling the data from several consecutive days on a single subject. Callaway also found it necessary to select subjects with relatively persistent alpha rhythm but found that he could use about one in three. He employed a technique that allowed the subject's own alpha to determine the stimulus presentation. Perhaps the most important conclusion emerging from Callaway's investigations is a negative one: "There is no clear-cut interindividual alpha phase-reaction time relationship consistency. In other words, given an unknown subject we still have no 'best guess' as to where on his alpha cycle stimuli should be given for fastest reaction times [Callaway, 1962, p. 680]." He also found that, although reaction times were speeded by increasing the intensity of the light stimulus, there was no corresponding shift in the alpha phase-reaction time

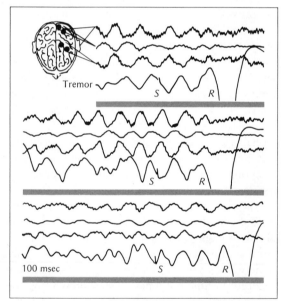

Figure 7.16   Brain and tremor rhythms recorded by a Westinghouse Oscillograph during response (*R*) to a visual stimulus (*S*). The top two lines are occipital EEGs from scalp to ear and scalp to scalp. Line 3 shows motor alpha rhythm. Line 4 shows the tremor rhythm and the response produced by depressing the finger. The interval between *S* and *R* is the reaction time. In the middle record, *S* falls in an excitable phase of the occipital alpha wave and results in a short reaction time, compared to the top and bottom records, when the stimulus falls in relatively inexcitable periods. Adapted from R. W. Lansing, Relation of brain and tremor rhythms to visual reaction time, *Electroencephalography and Clinical Neurophysiology*, 1957, **9**, 497–504. By permission.

relationship. This led him to suggest that the alpha phase may be indirectly related to cortical excitability or that the alpha phase may become related to the reaction time much earlier in the course of neural events than had been expected.

In further studies Callaway (1965, pp. 217–234) found that the judgment of brightness was also related to the alpha phase. In addition, he showed that alpha was time-locked to the cardiac cycle, the relationship holding for 200 msec or less after the Q wave of the electrocardiogram (EKG). Nevertheless, alpha-phase behavioral effects could be demonstrated when stimuli were restricted to portions of the cardiac cycle in which no alpha time-locking took place.

Callaway's subsequent experiments in this area were based on the idea that the autonomic cardiovascular cycle could account for alpha phase relationships without the necessity of postulating Lindsley's unrecordable alpha activity. The autonomic cardiovascular cycle theory is based on observations that, as blood pressure falls after mechanical systole, discharges from the carotid sinus and other pressure receptors diminish, and there tends to be a speeding of reaction time. This reaction time effect can also be found using subjects with artificial cardiac pacemakers, so that the possibility that some intrinsic central rhythm influences both the reaction time and the heartbeat is discounted. Electrocardiogram and alpha time-locking occurs during the 250-msec interval between the Q wave of the EKG and the carotid pulse, the same time during which relationships between the reaction time and the cardiac cycle are found. With the electrical systole, a series of inhibitory discharges starts bombarding the medulla; these reach a peak after the carotid pulse and fall to a minimum just before the next systole. These waves of inhibition are assumed to retard the discharge of motor reactions. Callaway's data on reaction time in relation to the cardiac cycle supported this formulation.

In Callaway's view, his experiments indicate that the autonomic cardiovascular cycle influences only the reaction time and is independent of stimulus modality. By contrast the alpha cycle influences responses only to visual stimuli, and this influence occurs early in the course of neural events, affecting reaction time and brightness judgment but with variable phase relationships. There may be some relationship between Surwillo's (1963a) findings on alpha frequency and reaction time and Lansing's and Callaway's results on reaction time and alpha cycle. Surwillo's correlations are based on the *mean* reaction time and the *mean* alpha frequency. With higher alpha frequency there would be a larger number of peak excitable phases and, other things being equal, more short reaction times.

Interarea Relationships

Findings such as those of Lansing and Callaway relate aspects of the alpha wave, which are precisely defined in time, to an equally well defined aspect of behavior, reaction time. There is a striking contrast between these studies and many discussed previously, such as those attempting to correlate alpha index and personality, with respect to knowledge of what is being studied at both physiological and behavioral levels. The work on EEG-phase relations to be considered here approaches the more complex problem of interarea relationships on a wave-to-wave basis with a precision resembling that of the reaction time investigations.

Darrow, J. P. Wilson, Vieth, and Maller (1960) employed an instrument that automatically compared active, negative or positive, ascents of waves in any two areas from zero or ground potential. This comparison permitted them to determine whether the activity in one electrode was leading the other. They examined a variety of behavioral conditions such as arousal from sleep, startling or ideational stimuli, and recovery following hyperventilation. Their results indicated that in stimulation or other conditions causing temporarily increased excitation or facilitation, the EEG waves from anterior or central brain areas tended to lead those from more occipital areas. In contrast, with the beginning of recovery from excitation, these time relations were reversed, and waves from the most posterior areas led those from the anterior for a time. They were also able to show that, during hyperventilation, there was a predominance of increased anterior leading during inspiration and occipital leading during expiration. The results with overbreathing were, therefore, in general agreement with the shifts in phase seen during psychologically defined situations. Figure 7.17 illustrates the data relating EEG phase to phase of respiration.

These findings seem related in some ways to those of Genkin (1966), who has studied the symmetry of EEG oscillations by measuring the durations of their ascending and descending phases. In normal subjects he found that the waves were usually symmetrical. Changes in symmetry appeared during mental activity such as arithmetic or imagining a picture. Under these conditions symmetry decreased in the frontal-central areas and increased in the parietal-occipital areas; changes could be demonstrated even when visual analysis did not show alterations in the EEG amplitude and frequency. Shifts in the pattern of symmetry also occurred between the right and left hemispheres. Genkin found that the symmetry usually returned to its initial value about 10–30 sec after the conclusion of activity. Studies of subjects with implanted electrodes revealed that the degree of symmetry differed considerably in different cortical layers, even though the EEGs had practically the same amplitude and frequency.

Perhaps the most complex interarea studies have been undertaken by Livanov, Gavrilova, and Aslanov (1966, pp. 31–38), who recorded from 50 electrodes simultaneously. With the aid of a computer they calculated correlation coefficients, reflecting the degree of coherent activity between recording sites, for the 1225 possible combinations of pairs; they employed a 1.5 sec analysis epoch. In normal subjects at rest, only a small number of points were synchronous with one another; these were generally in proximity. High correlations were more or less evenly distributed along the cortex. However, during mental activity, such as the multiplication of two- and three-digit numbers, they observed a marked increase in spatial synchronization. Under these conditions most of the points from which they recorded correlated with several

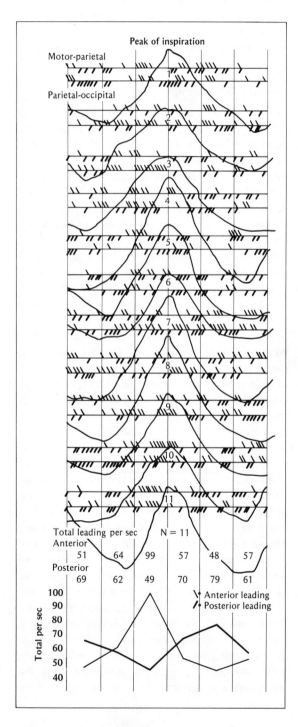

Figure 7.17 EEG phase relations during hyperventilation. Eleven successive respiratory cycles are aligned at the peak of inspiration and compared second by second by a summation technique for motor-parietal and parietal-occipital phase relations. Diagonal scoring for lead and lag is shown for each cycle. Second-by-second counts are totaled and graphed, and, relative to the mean, show a predominance of increased anterior leading during inspiration and occipital leading during expiration. Adapted from C. W. Darrow, J. P. Wilson, R. N. Vieth, & J. M. Maller, Acceleration and momentum in cerebral function reflected in EEG phase relations, *Recent Advances in Biological Psychology*, 1960, **2,** 51–59. By permission.

others. Furthermore, cortical points that were remote from each other, and often situated in different hemispheres, appeared to become connected. Different points became connected at different moments of the analysis, so that there was constant shift. Most of the high correlations involved the anterior frontal divisions of the brain. Livanov, Gavrilova, and Aslanov believe that their data demonstrate lawful relationships between the difficulty of solving problems and the increase of spatial synchronization, greater difficulty being associated with more increase. It is of some interest that these workers also found that patients in severe delusional states showed greater degree of synchronization while "at rest" than did normal subjects but that there was no frontal predominance in the synchronization. During the performance of a mental task, the delusional patients did not show as much synchronization as normal subjects.

CONDITIONING OF THE EEG

Observations suggesting that the alpha-blocking response in man could be conditioned were made in the early days of electroencephalography. Durup and Fessard (1935) used a camera to photograph the response of the alpha to a visual stimulus. Initially, the noise of opening the shutter had no effect on the EEG; however, this noise began to produce attenuation of the alpha activity after it had been succeeded a number of times by the visual stimulus. Loomis, Harvey, and Hobart (1936) made similar observations. More systematic studies were carried out by Travis and Egan (1938); they found that pairing a tone and light resulted in more frequent suppression of the alpha wave than presentation of the tone alone. Knott and Henry (1941) also studied alpha-block conditioning; they suggested that the absence of an acquisition curve indicated that the alpha blocking response was not true conditioning but rather a conditioned, anticipatory response based upon sensitization.

Jasper and Shagass (1941a) were able to demonstrate a variety of conditioned responses including cyclic conditioning, delayed conditioning, differential conditioning, trace conditioning, and backward conditioning. They considered sensitization to be ruled out by the demonstration of differential conditioning: i.e., the response was specific to frequency and was not elicited by just any stimulus of equal intensity. A feature of the procedure used by Jasper and Shagass, which may have an important bearing on their results, was that the subject was instructed to press a button each time that the visual stimulus appeared; there is evidence that cerebral desynchronization to the conditioned stimulus is easier to obtain and more consistent when the unconditioned stimulus represents a signal for a motor act (Anokhin, 1960).

Jasper and Shagass (1941b), Shagass (1942), and Shagass and Johnson (1943) also demonstrated conditioned alpha blocking to a voluntary stimulus. In the latter two studies the subject's EMG resulting from periodic fist clench was followed by light stimulation. Characteristic curves of acquisition and extinction were obtained.

Additional evidence supporting the existence of conditioned blocking of the alpha rhythm was provided by the studies of Motokawa and Huzimori (1949), Iwama (1950), and Morrell and Ross (1953). Morrell and Ross employed a tone stimulus followed after 1 or 2 sec by a light, their subjects having been instructed to press a key as soon as the light appeared. They were able to demonstrate conditioned alpha block and differential and delayed inhibition of the response.

A cooperative study of conditioned cerebral responses in man was undertaken by workers from several countries (H. Gastaut et al., 1957). The conditioned stimulus was a tone; the unconditioned stimulus was either light, light plus the active movement of the hand, or the passive movement of the wrist. After several presentations of the unconditioned stimuli, the diffuse desynchronization, which they caused initially, became restricted to a specific cortical region, the occipital region for visual stimulation. The pairing of conditioned and unconditioned stimuli resulted in a conditioned cerebral response, which involved desynchronization of the electrical activity only in the region in which the unconditioned stimulus would be expected to be recorded. For example, a sound combined with the passive movement of the wrist would block the contralateral Rolandic rhythm. If the paired stimuli were continued, the conditioned stimulus might come to be followed either by the increased amplitude of alpha or Rolandic activity, or even by slow waves, i.e., the enhancement of cerebral rhythms occupying the same region as that previously occupied by desynchronization. This was interpreted as "conditioned inhibition" in Pavlov's terminology. The investigators regarded desynchronization as a manifestation of central excitation, whereas the enhancement of rhythms or the appearance of slow rhythms was considered to be a manifestation of central inhibition.

Attempts to condition frequency-specific responses, like those of photic driving, have been relatively unsuccessful in man (A. Jus & C. Jus, 1959).

Since the proper exploration of central conditioning mechanisms requires depth electrodes, much investigation of electrographic conditioning has been carried out in animals. The excellent review of Wells (1963, pp. 60–108) summarizes the most relevant studies. According to Wells, EEG studies on conditioning "have been a disappointment in failing to provide a new concept of central neural function and in failing to provide either a firm scientific basis for the comprehension of behavior or a firm basis upon which a therapeutic approach to central nervous system dysfunction could be constructed [p. 94]." Some of the negative results are important, however. Conditioning studies have undermined notions that the "neural trace" of memory might be found within any one cerebral structure, and they have helped to reemphasize the position that brain function results from complex interrelationships between its various parts.

The fact that conditioned EEG responses may be established also has some bearing upon the issue of the genetic versus the acquired determination of EEG characteristics. It seems possible that conditioning mechanisms may play a significant role in determining such characteristics of the EEG as the alpha index.

SENSORY EVOKED RESPONSES

Recordings of human cerebral responses to sensory stimuli by the method of averaging have become a relatively commonplace laboratory procedure during the past decade. A symposium on the subject, held early in 1963, resulted in a large and informative volume (Katzman, 1964); the output of reports of research utilizing averaging methods has been increasing constantly since that time. The discussion to follow will attempt to summarize

some important methodological aspects of evoked response recording and to give some indication of problem areas to which the method has been applied.

Apparatus and Recording Procedures

Principle of averaging A desired signal is extracted from the biological noise of the spontaneous EEG by averaging or summing EEG samples

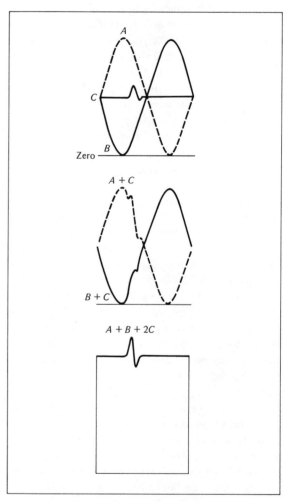

Figure 7.18 Illustration of the principle of summation to extract an evoked response. *A* and *B* are schematic alpha waves out of phase, and *C* represents a much smaller, evoked response. The middle drawing shows the appearance to be expected when *C* is superimposed on both *A* and *B*. The right-hand figure shows the result obtained by summing the activity represented in the middle figure. The out-of-phase alpha waves sum to a horizontal line and *C* is enhanced.

recorded for a specified period in relation to a fixed point in time, which is generally the onset of the stimulus. The signal-noise gain of an averaging system for a time-coherent signal is proportional to the square root of the number of observations. With a sufficient number of repetitions, the time-locked evoked response will consistently summate into a characteristic waveform, whereas the presumably random EEG oscillations will summate to an approximate horizontal line by addition of waves that are out of phase with one another. The principle is illustrated in Figure 7.18.

Some requirements The instruments most widely used for averaging carry out an analogue-to-digital conversion of the incoming electrical signals, storing the digital values in memory along a fixed number of data points. Successive incoming signals are digitized and stored. When the desired number of stimuli have been administered, the

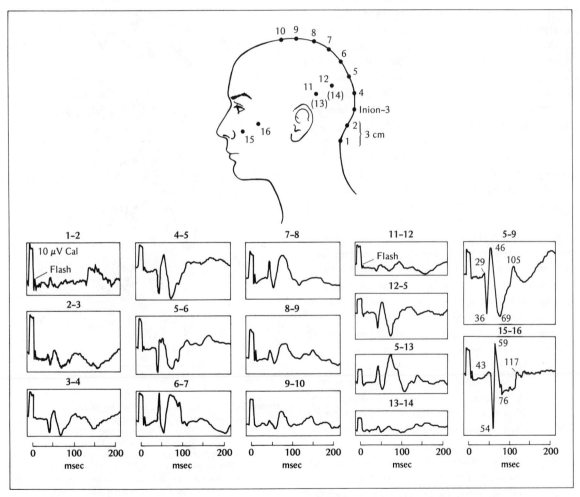

Figure 7.19 Localization by phase reversal of response evoked by flash in a patient with myoclonic twitches of face. Note that the entire early portion of the response reverses at Electrode 6. Center tracings show that reversal is in the midline (Electrodes 13 and 14 were located on *R* side in positions equivalent to 12 and 11, respectively). In addition to phase reversal of Lead 6 in the midline, amplitudes diminish anterior to Lead 8 and posterior to Lead 4. Tracings at the left compare midline head recordings with those from the face and illustrate latency differences (the numbers are peak latencies in msec) between cerebral and myogenic responses. Polarity: upward deflection indicates relative positivity of posterior or left-sided lead of pair. The initial square wave in all tracings in the 10 μV calibration signal.

digital average or sum is converted to analogue form and may be displayed on the face of a cathode ray oscilloscope or written out. The information may also be retrieved in digital form and either printed out or transferred to punched paper or digital magnetic tape.

The fixed total number of data points may be used for one, two, or four inputs, depending upon the type of instrument and the experimenter's needs. The period of signal analysis for a given number of data points should be determined by the degree of resolution required. Biological signals with rapid rise characteristics necessitate a short analysis time. For example, the earliest positive peak of the response to peripheral nerve stimulation may occur as little as 2 msec after the initial negative one. To obtain at least three data points for these 2 msec requires 200 data points for analysis time of 125 msec. Frequency response of amplifiers and tape recorders must at least match the degree of resolution required from the averager.

Amplitude calibration of averaged evoked responses is probably best performed by treating a standard calibration signal in the same way as the biological signal. The time-locked, low level calibrator developed by Emde (1964) permits a square wave of amplitude similar to the evoked response to be inserted in series with the recording leads and to be placed on each sweep entered into the computer memory. Gartside, Lippold, and Meldrum (1966) have used a photoelectric device that appears equally effective.

Simultaneous recording of multiple channels appears to be as necessary in evoked response work as it is for the EEG. The usually limited on-line capacity of laboratory computers may be supplemented by the use of instrumentation tape recorders. In addition, the recording of data on tape has the advantage of permitting several forms of subsequent analysis and the transportation of data to other computers. Multiple channel recordings allow the analysis of evoked response topography and have special value in helping to distinguish cerebral and extracerebral potentials that are so often intermingled. Figure 7.19 illustrates the localization by phase reversal of the response to a light flash in a patient who also reacted to each light flash with a myoclonic twitch of the facial muscles. The la-

tency differences between average cerebral and muscle responses in this case are demonstrated.

Statements made previously concerning the complexities of reducing EEG data apply as well to the information obtained with multiple channel, evoked-response recording. Automatic quantification by computer of average evoked-response information is obviously desirable. Rodin, Grisell, Gudobba, and Zachary (1965) and Shagass (1967) have made pilot efforts along these lines.

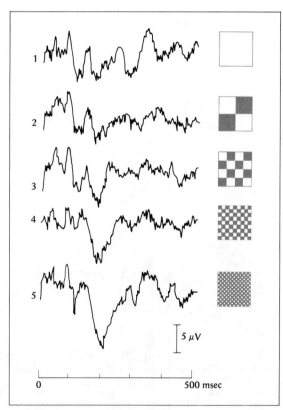

Figure 7.20 Responses to visual patterns of increasing contrast density in one subject. Each tracing is the average of 100 responses. The patterns used for Tracings 2–5 reflect the same amount of light, but the number of contrast borders on them increases in the relation of 1:2:16:32, as indicated by the sketches of the patterns on the right-hand side. Tracings were obtained in irregular sequence during the experiment. Note the increases in amplitude and latency to the peak of the surface-positive component at about 200 msec ("late wave"). Adapted from R. Spehlmann, The averaged electrical responses to diffuse and to patterned light in the human, *Electroencephalography and Clinical Neurophysiology*, 1965, **19**, 560–569. By permission.

Stimulus problems The need to average in relation to a fixed point in time necessitates sharply defining the onset of the stimulus. Furthermore, should the stimulus be effective over a lengthy period of time, additional responses may be generated before the first is completed. For this reason most investigators have employed rather brief stimuli, such as flashes of light, auditory clicks, or shocks to peripheral nerve. However, more complex stimuli, such as pictures presented by means of a slide projector, have been used with interesting results.

The standardization of stimuli, an obvious necessity, presents problems. For example, the most widely used electrical stimulators are neither constant current nor constant voltage at the intensity required for stimulation of the nerve through the skin. Schwartz, Emde, and Shagass (1964) found that both the constant current and the constant voltage stimulation yield about the same evoked-response results. However, one or the other must be pro-

vided to achieve a satisfactory degree of stimulus constancy.

The standardization of visual stimulation also involves a number of difficulties. One should maintain pupil size at a constant level, and the position of the eyes should be stabilized, usually with a fixation point when the eyes are open. Visual stimulation also introduces large bioelectric responses from extracranial structures, including the retina, those structures responsible for the potentials associated with eye movements, and the muscles about the eyes and neck. Auditory stimuli may vary unless presented in fixed relation to the ear; background noise in the room may present serious problems.

Auditory stimulation elicits myogenic potentials that R. C. Davis (1950) demonstrated may be picked up from the limbs. Bickford, Jacobson, and Cody (1964) have shown that averaged responses to loud auditory clicks from electrodes at the head contain a sequence of response peaks of myogenic origin;

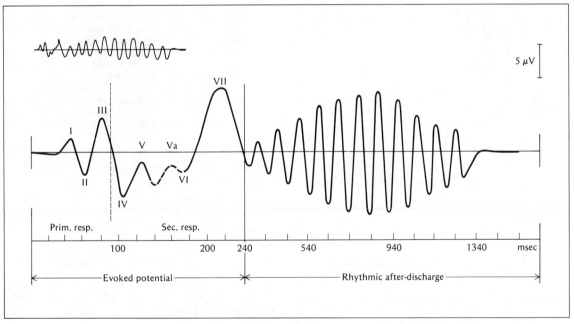

Figure 7.21 Scheme for the human EEG response to light flashes recorded with midline occipital-parietal electrodes. Negativity at electrode O_z results in an upward deflection of the graph. Because of the large disproportionality between the length of the normal evoked potential and the rhythmic after-discharge beginning from 240 msec after the stimulus, another scale is used. On the left at the top of the figure the scheme for the evoked potential with the real ratio of both constituents is reproduced. Adapted from L. Cigánek, The EEG response (evoked potential) to light stimulus in man, *Electroencephalography and Clinical Neurophysiology,* 1961, **13,** 165–172. By permission.

the earliest of these may occur within 6 msec of the stimulus. These myogenic responses are particularly prominent when sustained contraction is induced in the muscles over which the electrodes are placed. Their occurrence is not restricted to auditory stimuli, and they may be demonstrated with stimuli in other modalities. The possibility that averaged responses are contaminated by myogenic potentials must always be kept in mind, although it is somewhat reassuring that systematically averaged peaks of this type are seldom observed in subjects such as psychiatric patients, who cannot be made to relax. In such cases there is usually a great deal of "noise," and systematic average deflections of any kind are difficult to observe.

The need to repeat simple stimuli favors boredom and fluctuations in attention. Such variations in the level of alertness may have a profound influence upon evoked responses. Although the relation between evoked responses and attention is in itself

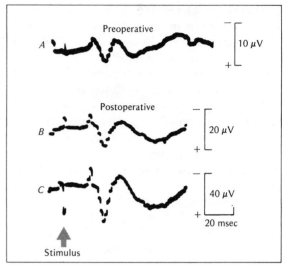

Figure 7.23 Comparison of evoked potentials recorded from the scalp and cortex in man. The stimulus was shock above the motor threshold, applied to the contralateral median nerve at the wrist. A: Record from electrodes on the scalp before operation; B: record from electrodes on scalp in same location after craniotomy; C: simultaneous record from electrode on the postcentral gyrus, 8 cm from the midline and directly beneath the recording electrode on the scalp; the same scalp electrode was used as reference. Records are from a patient without sensory loss and with apparently normal evoked potentials. The relative negativity in the active electrode gives an upward deflection. Adapted from D. R. Giblin, Somatosensory evoked potentials in healthy subjects and in patients with lesions of the nervous system, *Annals of the New York Academy of Sciences,* 1964, **112,** 93–142. By permission.

of investigative interest, such studies require independent criteria of attention. Evoked responses can change markedly with variation in the quality of the stimulus input. As shown in Figure 7.20, this can be dramatically illustrated by the different responses elicited by patterned and unpatterned visual stimuli of equal intensity (Spehlmann, 1965). Figure 7.20 also shows that the amplitude of the late wave introduced by patterned light stimuli is dependent upon the density of contrast borders between black and white lines of the stimulus pattern.

Description of Evoked Responses

The appearance of averaged evoked responses will vary, not only with characteristics of stimulus input such as intensity, duration, sensory modality,

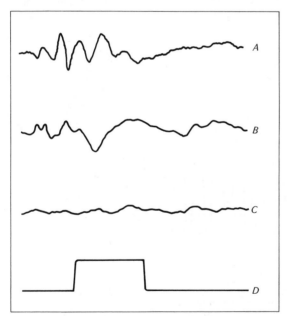

Figure 7.22 EEG differences between *on* and *off* responses to light. A: "On" response to onset of 800 msec flash (average of 1600); B: "Off" response to end of 800 msec flash; C: average of same number of traces not triggered by stimulus; D: calibration pulse 2 μV, 200 msec. Adapted from R. Efron, Artificial synthesis of evoked responses to light flash. In R. Katzman (Ed.), Sensory evoked response in man, *Annals of the New York Academy of Sciences,* 1964, **112,** 292–304. By permission.

and meaning, but with the location of the electrodes from which they are recorded. As with the EEG, there are adherents of the bipolar and unipolar points of view, and it seems equally probable that both types of linkage will give useful information for particular purposes. It may be noted, however, that reference electrodes placed on the ear or on the bridge of the nose are probably more likely to pick up extracerebral potentials.

Visual responses Cigánek (1961) and Kooi and Bagchi (1964) have presented normative data on flash-evoked responses. Figure 7.21 presents Cigánek's scheme for designating the various components of the visual response. It shows his division of the response into three major segments. He considers the first segment (components I to III) to be a primary response, and the second segment (components IV to VII) to have the character of a

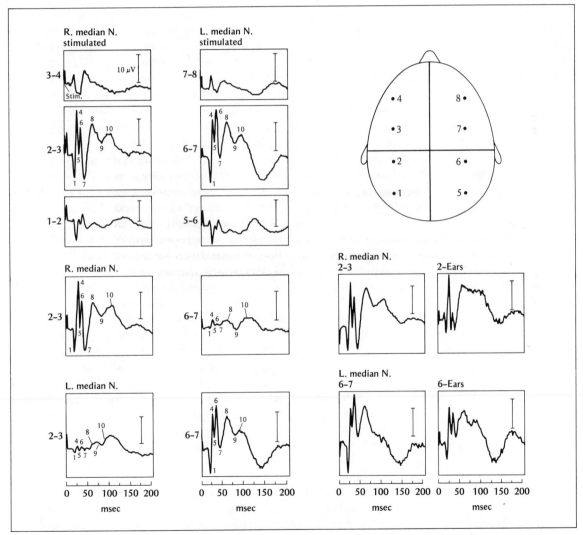

Figure 7.24 Averages of 100 responses to median nerve shocks at one or the other wrist. The relative positivity at the posterior electrode gives an upward deflection. The numbers in tracings indicate Shagass's designation of serial peaks in somatosensory response. Note also that Peaks 1 to 8 of the ipsilateral recordings are synchronous with the contralateral peaks and probably represent pickup at a distance of the contralateral response. The recordings at right, using the two ears tied together as a reference, differ in several respects from the scalp-to-scalp recordings.

response produced by nonspecific, perhaps diffuse, pathways. The third segment, designated by Cigánek "rhythmic after-discharge," has been called "ringing" by W. G. Walter (1962, pp. 222–257). The normal, visual-evoked potential is localized predominantly in the midline and in the occipital region.

Because of its duration, the repetition interval required to derive a full, averaged, visual response should exceed one second; much longer intervals would probably be desirable but would lengthen the duration of the averaging sequence and increase the probability of drowsiness. Cigánek (1961) demonstrated that a qualitatively new response originates when stimuli are given rapidly at the rate of 10–16 Hz. Studies of the visual recovery function using paired conditioning and test stimuli suggest that the response to the test stimulus is altered for a considerable period of time (Shagass & Schwartz, 1965b). Although the amplitude of the initial deflection to the test stimulus may approximate that of the conditioning stimulus at intervals as early as 30 msec, these deflections occur at a longer latency than the initial component of the conditioning response.

With visual stimuli of long duration it is possible to demonstrate both *on* and *off* responses (Efron, 1964). These have different characteristics, as illustrated in Figure 7.22.

Somatosensory responses Somatosensory responses have generally been elicited by applying brief pulses to the skin over the median or ulnar nerves at the wrist. The nerve response involves several modalities, although the greatest contribution appears to be made by fibers subserving joint position sense (Halliday & Wakefield, 1963). Tactile stimulation has also been employed; it tends to yield a simpler response (Debecker & Desmedt, 1964). The general similarity of scalp-recorded, averaged responses to those recorded epidurally or from the surface of the brain has been documented (Domino, Mödsuoka, Waltz, & Cooper, 1965; Giblin, 1964; Jasper, Lende, & Rasmussen, 1960).

Figure 7.23 illustrates comparative records from the scalp and the brain. Localization studies have been reasonably consistent, indicating that at least the initial components of the somatosensory

evoked response are recorded from the surface of the scalp overlying the post-Rolandic area in which the stimulated zone is represented; the largest deflections are seen on the side of the head contralateral to the stimulated area. Figure 7.24 illustrates the localization of responses to median nerve stimulation and also compares scalp-to-scalp with scalp-to-ear recordings. The numbering scheme is the one used by Shagass and Schwartz (1965a) to designate sequential peaks in the somatosensory response. Peaks 2 and 3 are not labeled because they were not visible in this instance. The records were from a 61-year-old subject; these peaks are rarely seen in subjects more than 30 years old.

Goff, Rosner, and Allison (1962) have attempted to relate the somatosensory response components to specific neurophysiological events. They have suggested that the initial component (composed mainly of Peak 1 in Figure 7.24) represents potentials in presynaptic thalamocortical fibers of the primary somatosensory projection pathway, and that the succeeding positive component (Peak 4, Figure 7.24) represents corresponding postsynaptic potentials. They suggested that the next positive component (probably Peaks 6 and 8 in Figure 7.24) might reflect extralemniscal activity, perhaps mediated by the reticular formation. Component 4 of Goff, Rosner, and Allison probably corresponds to Peaks 9 and 10 in Figure 7.24; their component 5 is visible as a deflection at the left of each tracing in Figure 7.24. Goff's group thought that the later electrical events might be representative of nonspecific mechanisms, since they do not appear to be modality-specific.

During surgery Domino et al. (1965) studied the effects of cryogenic lesions of certain thalamic nuclei on the somatosensory evoked response in over 100 patients undergoing cryothalamectomy. They found that lesions of the nucleus venteropostero-lateralis (VPL) of the thalamus produced the most dramatic changes in the evoked response, with reduction of all components occurring in the first 125 msec. Since all components were affected, they suggested that response events occurring within 125 msec following stimulation are primarily mediated through the nucleus VPL of the thalamus and questioned the contribution of the nonspecific pathways.

The strength of stimulus that is required to elicit the first evidence of a somatosensory response corresponds to the sensory threshold (Shagass & Schwartz, 1961). This relationship holds for responses recorded from both scalp and dura, but Libet, Alberts, Wright, and Feinstein (1967) have found responses to subthreshold stimulus intensities in recordings from electrodes placed on the cortex under the dura. As stimulus intensity is increased above the threshold, the amplitude of the response increases and there is some tendency for the shortening of latency. Maximal amplitude is generally achieved at an intensity about 5 mamp above the sensory threshold with a pulse of 0.1 msec duration (Schwartz, Emde, & Shagass, 1964); there is relatively little increase of response size with stimulus intensities well above this value.

In man, recovery functions determined with paired conditioning and test stimuli seem to differ from those measured with peripheral nerve stimuli in such animals as the cat. In the lower species the recovery curve tends to be monotonic, with the amplitude of the second response reaching that of the first at about 50 msec. In normal man an initial peak of amplitude recovery or facilitation usually takes place within the first 20 msec. As Figure 7.25 shows, this is followed by a period of amplitude suppression with interstimulus intervals from 25–50 msec or longer. The cortical response recovery functions are not correlated with those measured simultaneously at the peripheral nerve (Shagass & Schwartz, 1964), and latency recovery differs from amplitude recovery (Shagass & Schwartz, 1966).

Auditory responses These are most frequently recorded from the region of the vertex with the reference electrode at the ear or mastoid. Since the early portion of the response is difficult to distin-

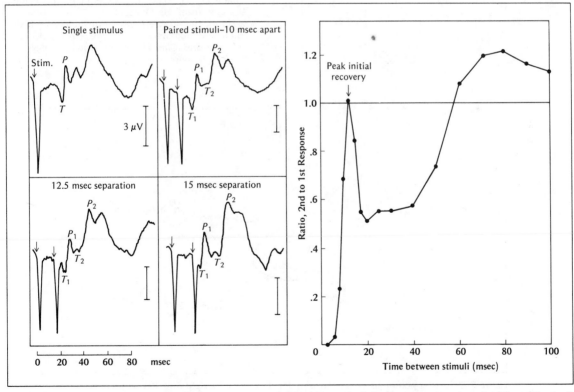

Figure 7.25 Recovery function of somatosensory response. Tracings at the left show responses to paired "conditioning" and "test" stimuli at varying intervals. Response amplitudes were measured from T_1 to P_1 and from T_2 and P_2 to yield the recovery curve on the right. Recovery is expressed as the ratio of amplitudes of the second to the first response; overlapping effects of the first response were corrected for.

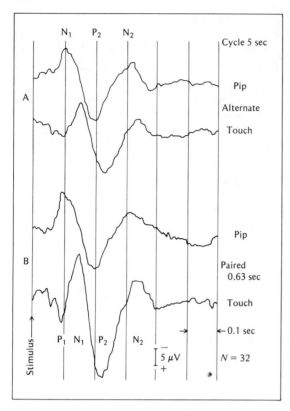

guish from the myogenic contaminants, workers such as H. Davis, Mast, Yoshie, and Zerlin (1966) have directed attention to the later components. Figure 7.26 compares the responses to tactile and auditory stimuli in one of their subjects. H. Davis and his colleagues describe a recovery function for auditory responses which suggests that the interval between stimuli should exceed 6 sec, and perhaps should be as long as 10 sec, to obtain the maximum amplitude of the averaged evoked response. The duration of suppression of auditory responses by a preceding stimulus thus appears to be longer than in the visual or somatosensory modalities.

Figure 7.26 Comparison of patterns of slow evoked responses to auditory and to tactile stimuli. For tactile stimuli, the latencies are longer and P_1 is very prominent. Electrodes were placed on the vertex-mastoid. In A the pip and touch are alternated at equal intervals of 2.5 sec; in B touch followed pip at 0.63 sec. The stimuli were nominally the same in A and B, but the tactile responses became systematically larger as the experiment proceeded. Adapted from H. Davis, T. Mast, N. Yoshie, & S. Zerlin, The slow response of the human cortex to auditory stimuli: Recovery process, *Electroencephalography and Clinical Neurophysiology*, 1966, **21,** 105–113. By permission.

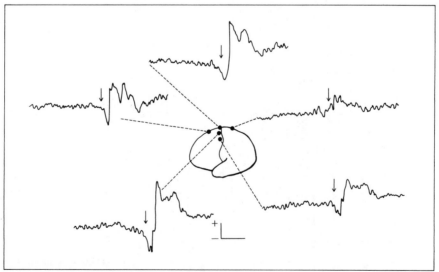

Figure 7.27 Motor potentials associated with dorsiflexion of the right foot. Records represent the sum of 400 contractions. Horizontal time line, 500 msec; vertical amplitude calibration, 2.5 μV. Adapted from H. G. Vaughan, Jr., I. D. Costa, & W. Ritter, Topography of the human motor potential, *Electroencephalography and Clinical Neurophysiology*, 1968, **25,** 1–10. By permission.

Potentials associated with voluntary movement
Averaging may also be employed to determine whether time-locked changes in the potential precede voluntary movement. One way of achieving this is to use the electromyogram (EMG) associated with movement to generate a trigger signal. The tape-recorded EEG may then be played backward, thereby reversing the temporal order of the EMG and EEG events. Gilden, Vaughan, and Costa (1966) utilized this method to demonstrate a "motor potential" in association with dorsiflexion of the foot and contraction of the fist. More recently, Vaughan, Costa, and Ritter (1968) have described the topography of the human motor potential. They indicate that there are four identifiable components: (a) a slow negative shift, normally between 5 and 25 μV maximum amplitude, which begins from 0.5 to 2 sec before onset of muscle contraction; (b) a small positive wave, seen inconstantly, which precedes the movement by an interval dependent on the muscle contracted; (c) a sharp negative wave, 10–15 μV amplitude, occurring 50–150 msec before the contraction; and (d) a complex positive wave that accompanies and follows the movement for a brief period. Figure 7.27 shows motor potentials recorded from various electrode locations in a single subject. Vaughan, Costa, and Ritter (1968) have demonstrated that the motor potential has a somatotopic distribution for contractions of various muscles which resembles that obtained by direct stimulation of the cortex.

Contingent negative variation (CNV) This response was originally described by W. G. Walter, Cooper, Aldridge, McCallum, and Winter (1964) as a slow potential shift occurring between the warning and response signals in a reaction time experiment. It is usually recorded between an active vertex electrode and a reference electrode on the mastoid. Because it is so slow, it must be recorded with either a direct-coupled amplifier or one with a time constant of several seconds. It appears as vertex negativity, which begins in the late phases of the response evoked by the first or warning stimulus, and persists until a response is made to the second stimulus. Figure 7.28 illustrates the response and shows that it depends upon significance being attributed to the forthcoming stimulus.

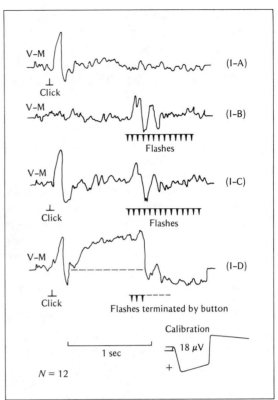

Figure 7.28 Contingent negative variation (CNV). Each tracing is the average of 12 trials. The responses were taken from the vertex-mastoid derivation. A: Clicks presented alone at random; B: series of 15-Hz flashes presented at random; C: flashes presented at interval of 1 sec after a click; D: flashes presented 1 sec after a click, but flashes are terminated by the subject pressing a button. CNV elicited. Vertex negative gives upward deflection. Adapted from J. Cohen & W. G. Walter, The interaction of responses in the brain to semantic stimuli, *Psychophysiology*, 1966, **2**, 187–196. By permission.

Walter has linked the response to the concept of expectancy; Irwin, Knott, McAdam, and Rebert (1966) have interpreted their data to indicate that it is associated with motivational variables. The same group has demonstrated that the CNV may be manipulated by experimenter-subjects at will (McAdam et al., 1966). Since the CNV appears to be an aspect of evoked-response activity that is extremely sensitive to psychological manipulation, it should find considerable popularity as a psychophysiological variable. Special measures must, however, be undertaken to distinguish it from eye-movement artifact.

The P300 Wave Sutton, Braren, and Zubin (1965) described an evoked potential event that seems to reflect psychological processes more than the physical characteristics of the stimulus. It consists of a positive wave, starting about 300 msec after the stimulus and lasting 300 or more msec. It is not ordinarily elicited when the subject knows the nature of the forthcoming stimulus, but rather when he is uncertain. For example, when loud and soft clicks are intermingled, and the subject is asked to guess which will come next, loud or soft, the P300 wave is elicited. Furthermore, its amplitude is a function of uncertainty, being greater when the probability of occurrence of a given stimulus is lower. The P300 wave may be elicited by the *absence* of expected stimulus (Sutton, Teuting, Zubin, & John, 1967). Figure 7.29 illustrates the nature of the positive response, its elicitation by an experimental condition producing uncertainty as to whether a stimulus would be delivered, and the effect of expected stimulus interval on its latency. All of the responses shown in Figure 7.29 were evoked by physically identical single clicks recorded between vertex and left ear lobe. In the first tracing (certain), the subject was informed in advance whether the click would be single or double. In the second tracing, the response also is to a single click, but the subject did not know whether the click would be single or if there would be a second click after 180 msec. In the third tracing, the alternative double click would have occurred with an interval of 580 msec after the first; the positive potential is seen to be shifted in latency. The fourth response shown in Figure 7.29 was obtained under conditions in which the stimuli could be either single click, a double click with a 180 msec interval, or a double click with a 580 msec interval. However, the subject was asked to guess only whether the forthcoming stimulus would be single or double. Since the absence of a click at 180 msec could still leave the possibility of a click at 580 msec, the positive process appears to be delayed until that time.

These results led Sutton, Braren, Zubin, and John to conclude that the large positive process was related to the resolution of uncertainty. This seems compatible with the views of Ritter, Vaughan, and Costa (1968) who demonstrated that long latency

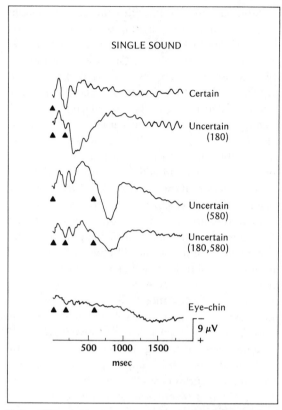

Figure 7.29 Average responses to single clicks obtained from one subject under several experimental conditions. First triangle indicates actual delivery of click. Subsequent triangles indicate points in time when a second click is anticipated at a later time. Adapted from S. Sutton, P. Tueting, J. Zubin, & E. R. John, Information delivery and the sensory evoked potential, *Science,* 1967, **155,** 1436–1439. Copyright 1967 by the American Association for the Advancement of Science. By permission.

positive responses occurred whenever the presentation of auditory stimuli was unpredictable. They concluded that the P300 component reflected the shift of attention associated with the orienting response.

Individual Differences

Stability of evoked responses There have been numerous demonstrations that evoked responses are highly subject to habituation or adaptation. With repeated presentation of stimuli, there may be considerable attenuation of the response during even a single averaging sequence. Responses may also be attenuated by distraction (Bogacz, Vanzulli,

& Garcia-Austt, 1962). However, even though intra-individual variability is great, it has been shown that there is a significant degree of long-term stability and that the interindividual variability exceeds the intraindividual (Dustman & Beck, 1963; Shagass & Schwartz, 1961).

It is probable that genetic factors play at least as much a role in evoked responses as in the EEG. Dustman and Beck (1965) compared the concordance between visually evoked responses of mono-zygotic and dizygotic twins and age-matched, un-related children. They found that the responses of identical twins were significantly more alike than those of subjects with differing genetic makeup.

Age Evoked responses are generally large during infancy and childhood and reach their lowest amplitude between 20 and 40 years, after which amplitude once again increases (Barnet & Goodwin, 1965; Dustman & Beck, 1966; Shagass & Schwartz,

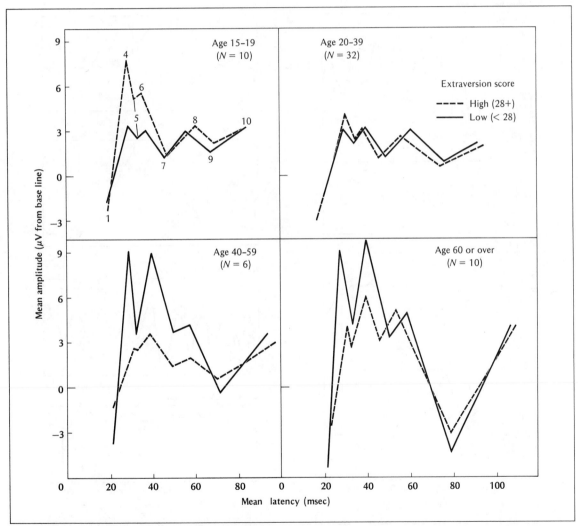

Figure 7.30 Mean somatosensory evoked responses for subjects of different age groups divided at the median on the extraversion (*E*) score of the Maudsley Personality Inventory. Note that mean responses are larger in high *E* subjects aged 15-19, whereas they are smaller in high *E* subjects over the age of 40 years. Adapted from C. Shagass & M. Schwartz, Age, personality, and somatosensory cerebral evoked responses, *Science,* 1965, **148,** 1359–1361. Copyright 1965 by the American Association for the Advancement of Science. By permission.

1965b; Straumanis, Shagass, & Schwartz, 1965). Latencies of evoked response peaks are prolonged early in life, decrease as maturation progresses, and finally tend to increase with advancing age in adults (Ellingson, 1960; Shagass & Schwartz, 1965a; Straumanis, Shagass, & Schwartz, 1965).

Sex   Females tend to have shorter latency responses in both visual and somatosensory modali-

ties, and there is some indication that their responses tend to be larger (Shagass & Schwartz, 1965a, 1965b; Straumanis, Shagass, & Schwartz, 1965).

Intelligence   Chalke and Ertl (1965) presented data suggesting that the latency of flash-evoked potentials may be correlated with psychometric intelligence; high IQ was associated with shorter

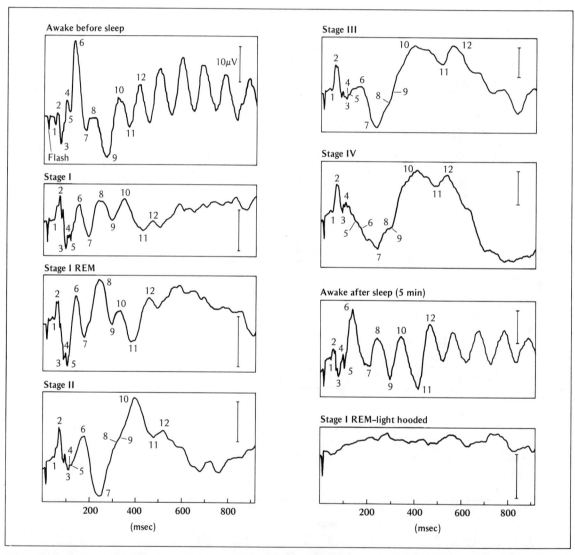

Figure 7.31   Flash-evoked responses of one subject in different stages of sleep as determined from the classification of concomitant EEG and EOG (electrooculogram). Leads are midline occipital-parietal with relative positivity in occipital lead giving upward deflection. Note the disappearance of "ringing" in Stage I, the progressive delay in occurrence of consecutive peaks with deepening sleep, and also the differences between the waking records taken after sleep and before sleep. Adapted from C. Shagass & D. Trusty, Somatosensory and visual cerebral evoked response changes during sleep, *Recent Advances in Biological Psychiatry*, 1966, **8,** 321–334. By permission.

latencies. They employed unusual lead placements, since they were recording responses to flash over the left motor area of each subject. Although their first averaging technique was somewhat unusual, Ertl's group has obtained confirmatory results with a more conventional averaging device (Ertl & Schafer, 1969). These findings are of great interest, but require additional confirmation. The present author has examined his own data from subjects for whom intelligence test scores were available

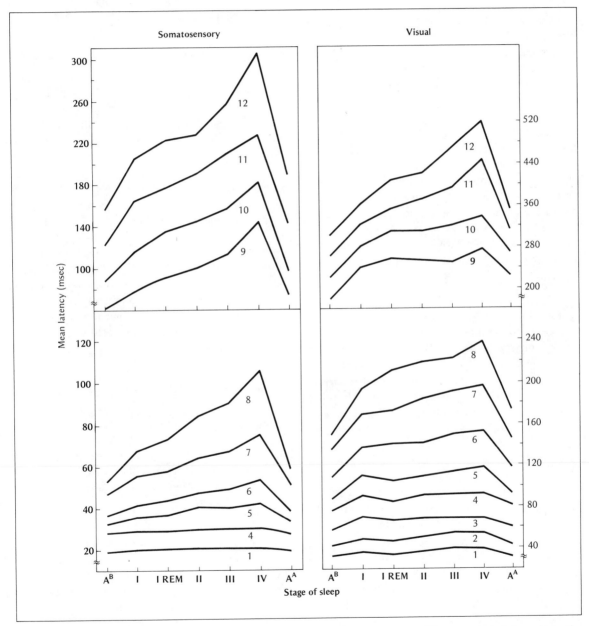

Figure 7.32 Mean latency measurements for somatosensory and visual responses at different stages of sleep. Note the progressive increase in latency of the various peaks for both responses with deepening sleep. Adapted from C. Shagass & D. Trusty, Somatosensory and visual cerebral evoked response changes during sleep, *Recent Advances in Biological Psychiatry,* 1966, **8,** 321–334. By permission.

and computed the correlations between IQ and latencies of visual and somatosensory peaks. The results were equivocal; Chalke and Ertl's findings were substantiated for some peaks, but significant correlations in the opposite direction were found for other peaks.

Personality Shagass and Schwartz (1965a) demonstrated a relationship in normal subjects between the amplitude of somatosensory responses and the extraversion measure (*E*) provided by the Maudsley Personality Inventory. This relationship was age dependent, so that the direction of differences was of opposite sign in a teen-aged group and in subjects over 40 years old. Figure 7.30 shows the results. Dividing the group at the median *E* score, amplitudes were about twice as great in the high *E* teenage subjects as in those with low *E*, whereas the converse was true for subjects over 40. Within a group of psychiatric patients, individuals with high field-dependence scores on the Witkin Rod-and-Frame test had larger evoked-potential amplitudes than subjects with lower scores (Shagass & Canter, 1966, pp. 47–52).

Psychopathology Shagass and Schwartz (1962, pp. 45–60) found that the recovery function of the somatosensory response was altered in certain kinds of psychiatric patients; the patients showed less recovery than control subjects, particularly in the first 20 msec of the recovery function. In other studies they showed that the amplitudes of somatosensory and visual responses were greater in psychiatric patients and that patients had less visual response "ringing" (Shagass & Schwartz, 1963, 1965a). More recent studies of the somatosensory response confirmed the previously found differences in recovery but suggested that the amplitude differences were caused by insufficient control for the factor of age (Shagass & Schwartz, 1966). Speck, Dim and Mercer (1966) have also found decreased visual response recovery in psychiatric patients.

Callaway and his group have used a different approach to study psychopathological correlates of evoked responses. Basing their method on the idea that schizophrenics will pay more attention to irrelevant stimuli than normal subjects, they recorded the responses evoked by auditory tones of 1000 and 600 Hz. In accordance with their hypothesis, schizophrenic subjects showed greater differences in their responses to the two tones than did normal subjects; their responses became more uniform when their clinical condition improved (Callaway, Jones, & Layne, 1965; Jones, Blacker, Callaway, & Layne, 1965).

Level of Awareness and Evoked Responses

Sleep Marked changes occur in the evoked responses of all modalities as the subject falls asleep. As Figure 7.31 demonstrates, there is an almost immediate loss of the late after-rhythm or ringing in the visual response. The latencies of all components tend to increase progressively with deepening sleep; the amplitude of initial components tends to increase (Shagass & Trusty, 1966). The systematic relationship between the latency of successive peaks and stages of sleep is illustrated in Figure 7.32 for visual and somatosensory responses. Similar findings have been obtained with auditory responses (Weitzman & Kremen, 1965). Recovery of presleep latencies of evoked response peaks may be delayed for 30 min after the subject has been wakened, even though the EEG appears to have regained its waking characteristics (Shagass & Trusty, 1966).

Delirium In conditions of impaired awareness that do not involve sleep, such as drug-induced delirium or disorientation occurring in chronic brain syndromes, there is also a relative absence of ringing and prolonged latency of the later evoked-response components (Brown, Shagass, & Schwartz, 1965; Straumanis, Shagass, & Schwartz, 1965).

Increased alertness One condition for the contingent negative variation must undoubtedly be heightened attentiveness, although a more specific psychological construct is needed to designate its correlates. The evoked-potential changes with stimulus uncertainty demonstrated by Sutton, Braren, and Zubin (1965) probably also involve attentive processes. Haider, Spong, and Lindsley

(1964) and Spong, Haider, and Lindsley (1965) have shown that the amplitude of the evoked potential increases when the subject is alert and attentive. Donchin and Lindsley (1966) also found that the amplitude of the averaged evoked potential was related to reaction time. Faster reactions were correlated with evoked potentials of larger amplitude. Furthermore, when subjects knew the results of their performance, reaction times were shortened and amplitudes were increased.

Hypnosis The ability to record sensory-evoked responses immediately suggests the possibility of testing whether hypnotic suggestion can selectively inhibit or enhance sensory transmission. There are some reports that this is so (Clynes, Kohn, & Lifshitz, 1964). However, systematic studies with groups of subjects have failed to reveal such changes (Beck, Dustman, & Beier, 1966; Halliday & Mason, 1964). Beck, Dustman, and Beier were unable to demonstrate significant changes from control values in 10 subjects, selected as adequately suggestible, who were given suggestions that flashes would either be brighter or dimmer.

Evoked responses and background EEG Since alterations in the state of awareness are generally correlated with EEG changes, fluctuations in the amplitude of evoked responses, which take place with changes in alertness, might be expected to be correlated with shifts in the background EEG pattern. That this may be so is suggested by the findings of Rodin et al. (1965), indicating a significant correlation between EEG and average evoked-response amplitudes. Levonian (1966) has shown that, even within the same stimulus sequence, amplitudes of visual-evoked responses differ in relation to subsequent alpha frequency (Figure 7.33). He interpreted this relationship to be based on the variation in attention from trial to trial.

CONCLUDING REMARKS

Although demonstrated relationships are far from perfect, electrical events recordable at the human scalp bear important relationships to many psychological variables of interest. These include consciousness, alertness, intelligence, personality, sensorimotor reactivity, and psychopathology. Most of the currently available data have been obtained by methods that are relatively primitive, compared to those now provided by advancing technology; hence the forthcoming decade will undoubtedly witness great progress in the definition of relationships between human brain function and behavior. At this moment the greatest foreseeable limitation of future research seems to lie in the uncertain ability of the psychophysiologist to use the tools made available to him. This limitation is probably less in knowing how to use the electrophysiological devices, than in knowing how to ask the appropriate behavioral questions. It will take much insight and wisdom to select the correct aspects of behavior to be related to electrical signs of brain activity. To paraphrase W. G. Walter's concluding remarks at the 1966 Symposium on Electrophysiological Correlates of Behavior at the International Congress of Psychology in Moscow: We now have the tools to answer almost any question; we need to ask the right questions.

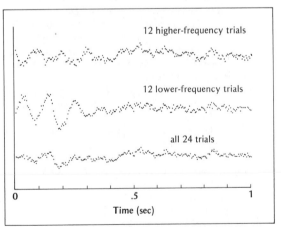

Figure 7.33 Averaged evoked potentials to a light flash associated with different subsequent alpha frequencies. The three curves are plotted to the same scale. The positive potential at the electrode near the inion is upward for each curve. Stimulus presented at onset of trace. Note the difference between the higher and lower alpha frequency trials and the canceling effect in the sum. Adapted from E. Levonian, Evoked potential in relation to subsequent alpha frequency, *Science*, 1966, **152,** 1280-1282. Copyright 1966 by the American Association for the Advancement of Science. By permission.

REFERENCES

ADEY, W. R. Neurophysiological correlates of information transaction and storage in brain tissue. In E. STELLAR & J. M. SPRAGUE (Eds.), *Progress in physiological psychology.* Vol. 1. New York: Academic, 1966.

ADRIAN, E. D., & YAMAGIWA, K. The origin of the Berger rhythm. *Brain,* 1935, **58,** 323–351.

ANOKHIN, P. On the specific action of the reticular formation on the cerebral cortex. *Electroencephalography and Clinical Neurophysiology,* 1960, **1,** (Suppl. 13), 257–270.

ARMINGTON, J. C., & CHAPMAN, R. M. Temporal potentials and eye movements. *Electroencephalography and Clinical Neurophysiology,* 1959, **11,** 346–348.

ASERINSKY, E., & KLEITMAN, N. Two types of ocular motility occurring in sleep. *Journal of Applied Physiology,* 1955, **8,** 1–10.

BALDOCK, G. R., & WALTER, W. G. A new electronic analyzer. *Electronic Engineering,* 1946, **18,** 339–344.

BARLOW, J. S. An electronic method for detecting evoked responses of the brain and for reproducing their average waveforms. *Electroencephalography and Clinical Neurophysiology,* 1957, **9,** 340–343.

BARNET, A. B., & GOODWIN, R. S. Averaged evoked electroencephalographic responses to clicks in the human newborn. *Electroencephalography and Clinical Neurophysiology,* 1965, **18,** 441–450.

BECK, E. C., DUSTMAN, R. E., & BEIER, E. G. Hypnotic suggestions and visually evoked potentials. *Electroencephalography and Clinical Neurophysiology,* 1966, **20,** 397–400.

BENNETT, P. B., & GLASS, A. Electroencephalographic and other changes induced by high partial pressures of nitrogen. *Electroencephalography and Clinical Neurophysiology,* 1961, **13,** 91–98.

BERGER, H. Über das Elektrenkephalogramm des Menschen. *Archiv für Psychiatrie und Nervenkrankheiten,* 1929, **87,** 527–570.

BICKFORD, R. G., JACOBSON, J. L., & CODY, D. T. R. Nature of average evoked potentials to sound and other stimuli in man. In R. KATZMAN (Ed.), *Sensory evoked response in man. Annals of the New York Academy of Sciences,* 1964, **112,** 204–223.

BICKFORD, R. G., SEM-JACOBSEN, C. W., WHITE, P. T., & DALY, D. Some observations on mechanism of photic and photo-metrazol activation. *Electroencephalography and Clinical Neurophysiology,* 1952, **4,** 275–282.

BISHOP, G. H., & CLARE, M. H. Responses of cortex to direct electrical stimuli applied at different depths. *Journal of Neurophysiology,* 1953, **16,** 1–19.

BOGACZ, J., VANZULLI, A., & GARCIA-AUSTT, E. Evoked responses in man: IV. Effects of habituation distraction and conditioning upon auditory evoked responses. *Acta Neurologica Latinoamericana,* 1962, **8,** 244–252.

BRAZIER, M. A. B. The development of concepts relating to the electrical activity of the brain. *Journal of Nervous and Mental Disease,* 1958, **126,** 303–321.

BRAZIER, M. A. B. *A history of the electrical activity of the brain.* New York: Macmillan, 1961.

BRAZIER, M. A. B., & BARLOW, J. S. Some applications of correlation analysis to clinical problems in electroencephalography. *Electroencephalography and Clinical Neurophysiology,* 1956, **8,** 325–331.

BRAZIER, M. A. B., & CASBY, J. U. Crosscorrelation and autocorrelation studies of electroencephalographic potentials. *Electroencephalography and Clinical Neurophysiology,* 1952, **4,** 201–211.

BRAZIER, M. A. B., FINESINGER, J., & SCHWAB, R. S. Characteristics of the normal electroencephalogram: The effects of varying blood sugar levels on the occipital cortical potentials in adults during hyperventilation. *Journal of Clinical Investigation,* 1944, **23,** 319–323.

BROWN, J. C. N., SHAGASS, C., & SCHWARTZ, M. Cerebral evoked potential changes associated with the ditran delirium and its reversal in man. *Recent Advances in Biological Psychiatry,* 1965, **7,** 223–234.

BURCH, N. R. Automatic analysis of the electroencephalogram: A review and classification of systems. *Electroencephalography and Clinical Neurophysiology,* 1959, **11,** 827–834.

BURCH, N. R., GREINER, T. H., & CORRELL, E. G. Automatic analysis of electroencephalogram as an index of minimal changes in human consciousness. *Federation Proceedings,* 1955, **14,** 23. (Abstract)

CALLAWAY, E. Day-to-day variability in relationship between electroencephalographic alpha phase and reaction time to visual stimuli. *Annals of the New York Academy of Sciences,* 1961, **92,** 1183–1186.

CALLAWAY, E. Factors influencing the relationship between alpha activity and visual reaction time. *Electroencephalography and Clinical Neurophysiology,* 1962, **14,** 674–682.

CALLAWAY, E. Response speed, the EEG alpha cycle, and the autonomic cardiovascular cycle. In A. T. WELFORD & J. E. BIRREN (Eds.), *Behavior, aging and the nervous system.* Springfield, Ill.: Charles C Thomas, 1965.

CALLAWAY, E., JONES, R. T., & LAYNE, R. S. Evoked responses and segmental set of schizophrenia. *Archives of General Psychiatry,* 1965, **12,** 83–89.

CALLAWAY, E., & YEAGER, C. L. Relationship between reaction time and electroencephalographic alpha phase. *Science,* 1960, **132,** 1765.

CATON, R. The electric currents of the brain. *British Medical Journal,* 1875, **2,** 278.

CHALKE, F. C. R., & ERTL, J. Evoked potentials and intelligence. *Life Sciences,* 1965, **4,** 1319–1322.

CHYATTE, C. The relation of cortical potentials to perceptual functions. *Genetic Psychology Monographs,* 1954, **50,** 189–226.

CHYATTE, C. A note on the relationship of alpha index to critical flicker frequency. *Electroencephalography and Clinical Neurophysiology,* 1958, **10,** 553–554.

CIGÁNEK, L. The EEG response (evoked potential) to light stimulus in man. *Electroencephalography and Clinical Neurophysiology*, 1961, **13**, 165-172.

CLARIDGE, G. S., & HERRINGTON, R. N. An EEG correlate of the Archimedes spiral after-effect and its relationship with personality. *Behaviour Research and Therapy*, 1963, **1**, 217-229. (a)

CLARIDGE, G. S., & HERRINGTON, R. N. Excitation-inhibition and the theory of neurosis: A study of the sedation threshold. In H. J. EYSENCK (Ed.), *Experiments with drugs.* Oxford: Pergamon, 1963. (b)

CLYNES, M., KOHN, M., & LIFSHITZ, K. Dynamics and spatial behavior of light-evoked potentials, their modification under hypnosis, and on-line correlation in relation to rhythmic components. *Annals of the New York Academy of Sciences*, 1964, **112**, 468-509.

COBB, W. A. The normal adult EEG. In D. HILL & G. PARR (Eds.), *Electroencephalography.* (Ch. 8.) New York: Macmillan, 1963.

COHEN, J. & WALTER, W. G. The interaction of responses in the brain to semantic stimuli. *Psychophysiology*, 1966, **2**, 187-196.

COHN, R. The occipital alpha rhythm: A study of phase variations. *Journal of Neurophysiology*, 1948, **11**, 31-37.

COOPER, R., & MUNDY-CASTLE, A. C. Spatial and temporal characteristics of the alpha rhythm: A toposcopic analysis. *Electroencephalography and Clinical Neurophysiology*, 1960, **12**, 153-165.

DARROW, C. W., & GRAF, C. G. Relation of EEG to photometrically observed vasomotor changes in the brain. *Journal of Neurophysiology*, 1945, **8**, 449-461.

DARROW, C. W., & HICKS, R. G. Interarea electroencephalographic phase relationships following sensory and ideational stimuli. *Psychophysiology*, 1965, **1**, 337-346.

DARROW, C. W., & SMITH, H. F. An instrument for automatic scoring of EEG phase relationships. *Electroencephalography and Clinical Neurophysiology*, 1964, **16**, 614-616.

DARROW, C. W., WILSON, J. P., VIETH, R. N., & MALLER, J. M. Acceleration and momentum in cerebral function reflected in EEG phase relations. *Recent Advances in Biological Psychology*, 1960, **2**, 51-59.

DAVIDOFF, R. A., & McDONALD, D. G. Alpha blocking and autonomic responses in neurological patients. *Archives of Neurology*, 1964, **10**, 283-292.

DAVIS, H., & DAVIS, P. A. Action potentials of brain in normal persons and in normal states of cerebral activity. *Archives of Neurology and Psychiatry*, 1936, **36**, 1214-1224.

DAVIS, H., & DAVIS, P. A. Electrical activity of the brain: Its relation to physiological states and to states of impaired consciousness. *Research Publications of the Association for Research in Nervous and Mental Disease*, 1939, **19**, 50-80.

DAVIS, H., MAST, T., YOSHIE, N., & ZERLIN, S. The slow response of the human cortex to auditory stimuli: Re-covery process. *Electroencephalography and Clinical Neurophysiology*, 1966, **21**, 105-113.

DAVIS, H., & WALLACE, W. Factors affecting changes produced in electroencephalogram by standardized hyperventilation. *Archives of Neurology and Psychiatry*, 1942, **47**, 606-625.

DAVIS, P. A. Technique and evaluation of the electroencephalogram. *Journal of Neurophysiology*, 1941, **4**, 92-114.

DAVIS, R. C. Motor responses to auditory stimuli above and below threshold. *Journal of Experimental Psychology*, 1950, **40**, 107-120.

DAWSON, G. D. Cerebral responses to electrical stimulation of peripheral nerve in man. *Journal of Neurology, Neurosurgery and Psychiatry*, 1947, **10**, 137-140.

DAWSON, G. D. A summation technique for the detection of small evoked potentials. *Electroencephalography and Clinical Neurophysiology*, 1954, **6**, 65-84.

DAWSON, M. E., & GREVILLE, G. D. Biochemistry. In D. HILL & G. PARR (Eds.), *Electroencephalography.* (Ch. 5.) New York: Macmillan, 1963.

DEBECKER, J., & DESMEDT, J. E. Les potentiels évoqués cérébraux et les potentiels de nerf sensible chez l'homme. *Acta Neurologica et Psychiatrica Belgica*, 1964, **64**, 1212-1248.

DOMINO, E. F., MATSUOKA, S. WALTZ, J., & COOPER, I. S. Effects of cryogenic thalamic lesions on the somesthetic evoked response in man. *Electroencephalography and Clinical Neurophysiology*, 1965, **19**, 127-138.

DONCHIN, E., & LINDSLEY, D. B. Averaged evoked potentials and reaction times to visual stimuli. *Electroencephalography and Clinical Neurophysiology*, 1966, **20**, 217-223.

DONDERO, A., HOFSTAETTER, P. R., & O'CONNOR, J. P. Critical flicker frequency and cortical alpha. *Electroencephalography and Clinical Neurophysiology*, 1956, **8**, 465-466.

DROHOCKI, Z. Lintegrateur de l'électroproduction cérébrale pour l'éléctroencéphalographie quantitative. *Revue Neurologique*, 1948, **80**, 619.

DURUP, G., & FESSARD, A. L'électroencéphalogramme de l'homme: Observations psycho-physiologique relatives à l'action des stimuli visuels et auditifs. *Année Psychologique, Paris*, 1935, **36**, 1-36.

DUSTMAN, R. E., & BECK, E. C. Long-term stability of visually evoked potentials in man. *Science*, 1963, **142**, 1480-1481.

DUSTMAN, R. E., & BECK, E. C. The visually evoked potential in twins. *Electroencephalography and Clinical Neurophysiology*, 1965, **19**, 570-575.

DUSTMAN, R. E., & BECK, E. C. Visually evoked potentials: Amplitude changes with age. *Science*, 1966, **151**, 1013-1015.

EFRON, R. Artificial synthesis of evoked responses to light flash. In R. KATZMAN (Ed.), *Sensory evoked response in man. Annals of the New York Academy of Sciences*, 1964, **112**, 292-304.

ELLINGSON, R. J. Electroencephalograms of normal, full-term newborns immediately after birth with observations on arousal and visual evoked responses. *Electroenceph-alography and Clinical Neurophysiology*, 1958, **10**, 31–50.

ELLINGSON, R. J. Cortical electrical responses to visual stimulation in the human infant. *Electroencephalography and Clinical Neurophysiology*, 1960, **12**, 663–677.

ELLINGSON, R. J., WILCOTT, R. C., SINEPS, J. G., & DUDEK, F. J. The EEG frequency-pattern variation and intelligence. *Electroencephalography and Clinical Neurophysiology*, 1957, **9**, 657–660.

ELLIOTT, R. Physiological activity and performance: A comparison of kindergarten children with young adults. *Psychological Monographs*, 1964, **78** (No. 10).

EMDE, J. A time locked low level calibrator. *Electro-encephalography and Clinical Neurophysiology*, 1964, **16**, 616–618.

ENGEL, G. L. Mechanisms of fainting. *Journal of the Mt. Sinai Hospital, New York*, 1945, **12**, 170–190.

ENGEL, G. L., & MARGOLIN, S. G. Neuropsychiatric disturbances in internal disease: Metabolic factors and electroencephalographic correlations. *Archives of Internal Medicine*, 1942, **70**, 236–259.

ENGEL, G. L., ROMANO, J. Delirium: II. Reversibility of the electroencephalogram with experimental procedures. *Archives of Neurology and Psychiatry*, 1944, **51**, 378–392.

ENGEL, G. L., ROMANO, J., & FERRIS, E. B. Variations in the normal electroencephalogram during a five-year period. *Science*, 1947, **105**, 600–601.

ENGEL, G. L., ROMANO, J., FERRIS, E. B., WEBB, J. P., & STEVENS, C. D. A simple method of determining frequency spectra in the electroencephalogram. *Archives of Neurology and Psychiatry*, 1944, **51**, 134–146.

ERTL, J., & SCHAFER, E. W. P. Brain response correlates of psychometric intelligence. *Nature*, 1969, **223**, 421–422.

EVANS, C. C. Comments on: "Occipital sharp waves responsive to visual stimuli." *Electroencephalography and Clinical Neurophysiology*, 1952, **4**, 111.

EVANS, C. C. Spontaneous excitation of the visual cortex and association areas—lambda waves. *Electroencepha-lography and Clinical Neurophysiology*, 1953, **5**, 69–74.

EYSENCK, H. J. *The dynamics of anxiety and hysteria*. London: Routledge, 1957.

FIELD, J. (Ed.) *Handbook of Physiology*. Vols. 1–3. Washington, D.C.: American Physiological Society, 1959.

FINK, M., ITIL, T., & CLYDE, D. The classification of psychoses by quantitative EEG measures. *Recent Advances in Biological Psychiatry*, 1966, **8**, 305–312.

FINK, M., SHAPIRO, D. M., HICKMAN, C., & ITIL, T. Quantitative analysis of the electroencephalogram by digital computer methods: III. Applications to psychopharmacology. St. Louis, 1966 (mimeo).

GARTSIDE, I. B., LIPPOLD, O. C. J., & MELDRUM, B. S. The evoked cortical somatosensory response in normal man and its modification by oral lithium carbonate. *Electro-encephalography and Clinical Neurophysiology*, 1966, **20**, 382–390.

GASTAUT, H. Étude électrocorticographique de la ré-activité des rythmes rolandiques. *Revue Neurologique*, 1952, **87**, 176–182.

GASTAUT, H. Correlations between the electroencephalographic and the psychometric variables (MMPI, Rosenzweig, intelligence tests). *Electroencephalography and Clinical Neurophysiology*, 1960, **12**, 226–227.

GASTAUT, H., BACHER, F., BERT, J., BLANC-GARIN, J., FESSARD, A., FRAISEE, P., LEE VAN GOETHEM, M., & ROGER, A. Relations entre les variables électroencéphalographiques et celles exprimant la personnalité et les fonctions sensorimotrices: Resultats d'une enquête effectuée sur une population homogène de jeunes adultes males age de 20 ans. *Revue Neurologique*, 1959, **101**, 320–390.

GASTAUT, H., JUS, A., JUS, C., MORRELL, F., STORM VAN LEEUWEN, W., DONGIER, S., NAQUET, R., REGIS, H., ROGER, A., BEKKERING, D., KAMP, A., & WERRE, J. Études topographiques des réactions d'électroencéphalographiques conditionées chez l'homme. *Electroencephalography and Clinical Neurophysiology*, 1957, **9**, 1–34.

GASTAUT, Y. Un signe électroencéphalographique peu connu: Les pointes occipitales survenant pendant l'ouverture des yeux. *Revue Neurologique*, 1951, **84**, 640–643.

GASTAUT, Y. Les pointes négatives evoquées sur le vertex: Leur signification psycho-physiologique et pathologique. *Revue Neurologique*, 1953, **89**, 382–399.

GENKIN, A. A. Statistical characteristics of phase durations of EEG oscillation and some mechanisms of human voluntary activity. *Proceedings of the 18th International Congress on Psychology*, 1966, Symposium No. 6, 86–90.

GIBBS, E. L., & GIBBS, F. A. Diagnostic and localizing value of electroencephalographic studies in sleep. *Proceedings of the Association for Research in Nervous and Mental Disease*, 1946, **26**, 366–376.

GIBBS, E. L., GIBBS, F. A., LENNOX, W. G., & NIMS, L. F. Regulation of cerebral carbon dioxide. *Archives of Neurology and Psychiatry*, 1942, **47**, 879–889.

GIBBS, F. A., DAVIS, H., & LENNOX, W. G. The electroencephalogram in epilepsy and in conditions of impaired consciousness. *Archives of Neurology and Psychiatry*, 1935, **3**, 1133–1148.

GIBBS, F. A., & GIBBS, E. L. *Atlas of electroencephalography*. Reading, Mass.: Addison-Wesley, 1950.

GIBBS, F. A., & GRASS, A. M. Frequency analysis of electroencephalograms. *Science*, 1947, **105**, 132–137.

GIBBS, F. A., WILLIAMS, D., & GIBBS, E. L. Modification of the cortical frequency spectrum by changes in CO_2, blood sugar and O_2. *Journal of Neurophysiology*, 1940, **3**, 49–58.

GIBLIN, D. R. Somatosensory evoked potentials in healthy subjects and in patients with lesions of the nervous system. *Annals of the New York Academy of Sciences*, 1964, **112**, 93–142.

GILDEN, L., VAUGHAN, H. G., Jr., & COSTA, L. D. Summated human EEG potentials with voluntary movement. *Electroencephalography and Clinical Neurophysiology*, 1966, **20**, 433–438.

GOFF, W. R., ROSNER, B. S., & ALLISON, T. Distribution of cerebral somatosensory evoked responses in normal man. *Electroencephalography and Clinical Neurophysiology*, 1962, **14,** 697–713.

GOLDMAN, D. The clinical use of the "average" reference electrode. *Electroencephalography and Clinical Neurophysiology*, 1950, **2,** 209–212.

GOLDSTEIN, L., MURPHREE, H. B., SUGARMAN, A. A., PFEIFFER, C. C., & JENNEY, E. H. Quantitative electroencephalographic analysis of naturally occurring (schizophrenic) and drug-inducted psychotic states in human males. *Clinical Pharmacology and Therapeutics*, 1963, **4,** 10–21.

GOLLA, F., HUTTON, E. L., & WALTER, W. G. Objective study of mental imagery; physiological concomitants: Appendix on new method of electroencephalographic analysis. *Journal of Mental Science*, 1943, **89,** 216–223.

GOODWIN, J. E. The significance of alpha variants in the EEG and their relationship to an epileptiform syndrome. *American Journal of Psychiatry*, 1947, **104,** 369–379.

GOTTLOBER, A. B. The relationship between brain potentials and personality. *Journal of Experimental Psychology*, 1938, **22,** 67–74.

GRASS, A. M., & GIBBS, F. A. Fourier transform of the electroencephalogram. *Journal of Neurophysiology*, 1938, **1,** 521–526.

GUILFORD, J. P., & MERRIFIELD, P. R. The structure of intellect model: Its uses and implications. *Report from the Psychological Laboratory*, University of Southern California, 1960, **24,** 1–27.

HAIDER, M., SPONG, P., & LINDSLEY, D. B. Attention, vigilance and cortical evoked-potentials in humans. *Science*, 1964, **145,** 180–182.

HALLIDAY, A. M., & MASON, A. A. The effect of hypnotic anesthesia on cortical responses. *Journal of Neurology, Neurosurgery and Psychiatry*, 1964, **27,** 300–312.

HALLIDAY, A. M., & WAKEFIELD, G. S. Cerebral evoked potentials in patients with dissociated sensory loss. *Journal of Neurology, Neurosurgery and Psychiatry*, 1963, **26,** 211–219.

HARLAN, W. L., WHITE, P. T., & BICKFORD, R. G. Electric activity produced by eye flutter simulating frontal electroencephalographic rhythms. *Electroencephalography and Clinical Neurophysiology*, 1958, **10,** 164–169.

HENRY, C. E. Electroencephalographic individual differences and their constancy: I. During sleep. *Journal of Experimental Psychology*, 1941, **29,** 117–132. (a)

HENRY, C. E. Electroencephalographic individual differences and their constancy: II. During waking. *Journal of Experimental Psychology*, 1941, **29,** 236–247. (b)

HENRY, C. E. Electroencephalograms of normal children. *Monograph of the Society for Research in Child Development*, 1944, **9** (Serial No. 39).

HENRY, C. E. Electroencephalographic correlates with personality. In W. P. WILSON (Ed.), *Applications of electroencephalography in psychiatry*. Durham, N.C.: Duke University Press, 1965.

HENRY, C. E., & KNOTT, J. R. A note on the relationship between 'personality' and the alpha rhythm of the electroencephalogram: I. *Journal of Experimental Psychology*, 1941, **28,** 362–366.

HERBERG, L. J. Eye-movements in relation to the EEG alpha rhythm, speed of work and intelligence score. *Journal of the National Institute for Personnel Research* (Johannesburg), 1958, **7,** 98–103.

HERMANN, H. T., & QUARTON, G. C. Changes in alpha frequency with change in thyroid hormone level. *Electroencephalography and Clinical Neurophysiology*, 1964, **16,** 515–518.

HERON, W. The pathology of boredom. *Scientific American*, 1957, **196,** 52–56.

HILDEBRAND, H. P. A factorial study of introversion-extraversion by means of objective tests. Unpublished doctoral dissertation, University of London, 1953.

HIMWICH, H. E. *Brain metabolism and cerebral disorders.* Baltimore: Williams & Wilkins, 1951.

HOAGLAND, H. Electrical brain waves and temperature. *Science*, 1936, **84,** 139–140.

HORD, D. J. Computers in brain research. *American Journal of EEG Technology*, 1964, **4,** 1–7.

HORD, D. J., JOHNSON, L. C., LUBIN, A., & AUSTIN, M. T. Resolution and stability in the autospectra of EEG. *Electroencephalography and Clinical Neurophysiology*, 1965, **19,** 305–308.

IRWIN, D. A., KNOTT, J. R., McADAM, D. W., & REBERT, C. S. Motivational determinants of the "contingent negative variation." *Electroencephalography and Clinical Neurophysiology*, 1966, **21,** 538–543.

IWAMA, K. Delayed conditioned reflex in man and brain waves. *Tohoku Journal of Experimental Medicine*, 1950, **52,** 53–62.

JASPER, H. H. The ten-twenty electrode system of the International Federation. *Electroencephalography and Clinical Neurophysiology*, 1958, **10,** 371–375.

JASPER, H. H., & ANDREWS, H. L. Brain potentials and voluntary muscle activity in man. *Journal of Neurophysiology*, 1938, **1,** 87–100. (a)

JASPER, H. H., & ANDREWS, H. L. Electroencephalography: III. Normal differentiation between occipital and precentral regions in man. *Archives of Neurology and Psychiatry*, 1938, **39,** 96–115. (b)

JASPER, H. H., LENDE, R., & RASMUSSEN, T. Evoked potentials from the exposed somatosensory cortex in man. *Journal of Nervous and Mental Disease*, 1960, **130,** 526–537.

JASPER, H. H., & SHAGASS, C. Conditioning the occipital alpha rhythm in man. *Journal of Experimental Psychology*, 1941, **28,** 373–388. (a)

JASPER, H. H., & SHAGASS, C. Conscious time judgments related to conditioned time intervals and voluntary control of the alpha rhythm. *Journal of Experimental Psychology*, 1941, **28,** 503–508. (b)

JOHNSON, L. C., & ULETT, G. A. Quantitative study of pattern and stability of resting electroencephalographic activity in a young adult group. *Electroencephalography and Clinical Neurophysiology*, 1959, **11**, 233-249.

JONES, R. T., BLACKER, K. H., CALLAWAY, E., & LAYNE, R. S. The auditory evoked response as a diagnostic and prognostic measure in schizophrenia. *American Journal of Psychiatry*, 1965, **122**, 33-41.

JUS, A., & JUS, C. Studies on photic driving conditioning in man. *Electroencephalography and Clinical Neurophysiology*, 1959, **11**, 178.

KARP, E., POLLACK, M., & FINK, M. Critical flicker frequency and EEG alpha: A reliability study. *Electroencephalography and Clinical Neurophysiology*, 1962, **14**, 60-63.

KATZMAN, R. (Ed.) Sensory evoked response in man. *Annals of the New York Academy of Sciences*, 1964, **112**.

KENNARD, M. A., RABINOVITCH, M. S., & FISTER, W. P. The use of frequency analysis in the interpretation of the EEGs of patients with psychological disorders. *Electroencephalography and Clinical Neurophysiology*, 1955, **7**, 29-38.

KENNARD, M. A., & SCHWARTZMAN, A. E. A longitudinal study of changes in EEG frequency pattern as related to psychological changes. *Journal of Nervous and Mental Disease*, 1956, **124**, 8-20.

KENNARD, M. A., & SCHWARTZMAN, A. E. A longitudinal study of electroencephalographic frequency patterns in mental hospital patients and normal controls. *Electroencephalography and Clinical Neurophysiology*, 1957, **9**, 262-274.

KENNEDY, J. L., GOTTSDANKER, R. M., ARMINGTON, J. C., & GRAY, F. E. A new electroencephalogram associated with thinking. *Science*, 1948, **108**, 527-529.

KNOTT, J. R. Automatic frequency analysis. *Electroencephalography and Clinical Neurophysiology* (Suppl. 4), 1953, 17-25.

KNOTT, J. R. Electroencephalograms in psychopathic personality and in murderers. In W. P. WILSON (Ed.), *Applications of electroencephalography in psychiatry*. Durham, N.C.: Duke University Press, 1965.

KNOTT, J. R., FRIEDMAN, H., & BARDSLEY, R. Some electroencephalographic correlates of intelligence in eight-year- and twelve-year-old children. *Journal of Experimental Psychology*, 1942, **30**, 380-391.

KNOTT, J. R., GIBBS, F. A., & HENRY, C. E. Fourier transforms of the electroencephalogram during sleep. *Journal of Experimental Psychology*, 1942, **31**, 465-477.

KNOTT, J. R., & HENRY, C. E. The conditioning of the blocking of the alpha rhythms of the human electroencephalogram. *Journal of Experimental Psychology*, 1941, **28**, 134-144.

KOOI, K. A., & BAGCHI, B. K. Observations on early components of the visual evoked response and occipital rhythms. *Electroencephalography and Clinical Neurophysiology*, 1964, **17**, 638-643.

KOZHEVNIKOV, V. A. Photo-electric method for the separation of weak electrical responses in the brain. *Sechenov Physiological Journal*, 1958, **44**, 765-773.

KREEZER, G. Intelligence level and occipital alpha rhythm in the mongolian type of mental deficiency. *American Journal of Psychology*, 1939, **52**, 503-532.

KREEZER, G. The relation of intelligence level and the electroencephalogram. *National Society for the Study of Education, Yearbook 39*, 1940 (Part I), 130-133.

LANSING, R. W. Relation of brain and tremor rhythms to visual reaction time. *Electroencephalography and Clinical Neurophysiology*, 1957, **9**, 497-504.

LARSSON, L. E. The relation between the startle reaction and the nonspecific EEG response to sudden stimuli with a discussion on the mechanism of arousal. *Electroencephalography and Clinical Neurophysiology*, 1956, **8**, 631-644.

LENNOX, W. G., GIBBS, F. A., & GIBBS, E. L. Twins, brain waves and epilepsy. *Archives of Neurology and Psychiatry*, 1942, **47**, 702-706.

LEVONIAN, E. Evoked potential in relation to subsequent alpha frequency. *Science*, 1966, **152**, 1280-1282.

LEVY, S., & KENNARD, M. A. The EEG pattern of patients with psychological disorders of various ages. *Journal of Nervous and Mental Disease*, 1953, **118**, 416-428.

LIBERSON, W. T. Functional electroencephalography in mental disorders. *Diseases of the Nervous System*, 1944, **5**, 357-364.

LIBET, B., ALBERTS, W. W., WRIGHT, E. W., Jr., & FEINSTEIN, B. Responses of human somatosensory cortex to stimuli for conscious sensation. *Science*, 1967, **158**, 1597-1600.

LINDSLEY, D. B. Brain potentials in children and adults. *Science*, 1936, **84**, 354.

LINDSLEY, D. B. Electrical potentials of the brain in children and adults. *Journal of Genetic Psychology*, 1938, **19**, 285-306.

LINDSLEY, D. B. A longitudinal study of the occipital alpha rhythm in normal children: Frequency and amplitude standards. *Journal of Genetic Psychology*, 1939, **55**, 197-213.

LINDSLEY, D. B. Psychological phenomena and the electroencephalogram. *Electroencephalography and Clinical Neurophysiology*, 1952, **4**, 443-456.

LINDSLEY, D. B. Basic perceptual processes and the EEG. *Psychiatric Research Reports*, 1956, **6**, 161-170.

LIVANOV, M. N., GAVRILOVA, N. A., & ASLANOV, A. S. Reflection of some mental states in the spatial distribution of human cerebral cortex biopotentials. *Proceedings of the 18th International Congress of Psychology*, 1966, Symposium No. 6.

LOOMIS, A. L., HARVEY, E. N., & HOBART, G. A. Potential rhythms of the cerebral cortex during sleep. *Science*, 1935, **81**, 597-598.

LOOMIS, A. L., HARVEY, E. N., & HOBART, G. Electrical potentials of the human brain. *Journal of Experimental Psychology*, 1936, **19**, 249-279.

MACKAY, D. M. Some experiments on the perception of patterns modulated at the alpha frequency. *Electro-*

encephalography and Clinical Neurophysiology, 1953, **5,** 559–562.

MAGOUN, H. W. Caudal and cephalic influences on the brain stem reticular formation. *Physiological Reviews,* 1950, **30,** 459–474.

MARGERISON, J. H., ANDERSON, W. McC., & DAWSON, J. Plasma sodium and the EEG during the menstrual cycle of normal human females. *Electroencephalography and Clinical Neurophysiology,* 1964, **17,** 540–544.

MARGERISON, J. H., ANDERSON, W. McC., DAWSON, J., & LETTICH, E. The relationship between sodium metabolism, verbal output and the EEG in 21 depressives. *Electroencephalography and Clinical Neurophysiology,* 1962, **14,** 853–857.

MARKO, A., & PETSCHE, H. The multivibrator toposcope: An electronic polygraph. *Electroencephalography and Clinical Neurophysiology,* 1960, **12,** 209–211.

MCADAM, D. W., IRWIN, D. A., REBERT, C. S., & KNOTT, J. R. Conative control of the contingent negative variation. *Electroencephalography and Clinical Neurophysiology,* 1966, **21,** 194–195.

MILNARICH, R. E., TOURNEY, G., & BECKETT, P. G. S. Electroencephalographic artifact arising from dental restorations. *Electroencephalography and Clinical Neurophysiology,* 1957, **9,** 337–339.

MORRELL, F., & ROSS, M. H. Central inhibition in cortical conditioned reflexes. *Archives of Neurology and Psychiatry,* 1953, **70,** 611–616.

MORRICE, J. K. W. Slow wave production in the EEG, with reference to hyperpnoea, carbon dioxide and autonomic balance. *Electroencephalography and Clinical Neurophysiology,* 1956, **8,** 49–72.

MORUZZI, G., & MAGOUN, H. W. Brain stem reticular formation and activation of the EEG. *Electroencephalography and Clinical Neurophysiology,* 1940, **1,** 455–473.

MOTOKAWA, K., & HUZIMORI, B. Electroencephalograms and conditioned reflexes. *Tohoku Journal of Experimental Medicine,* 1949, **50,** 215–223.

MUNDY-CASTLE, A. C. An analysis of central responses to photic stimulation in normal adults. *Electroencephalography and Clinical Neurophysiology,* 1953, **5,** 1–122.

MUNDY-CASTLE, A. C. The alpha rhythm and rate of visual perception. *Journal of the National Institute for Personnel Research (Johannesburg),* 1955, **6,** 38–43. (a)

MUNDY-CASTLE, A. C. The relationship between primary-secondary function and the alpha rhythm of the electroencephalogram. *Journal of the National Institute for Personnel Research* (Johannesburg), 1955, **6,** 95–102. (b)

MUNDY-CASTLE, A. C. Electrophysiological correlates of intelligence. *Journal of Personality,* 1958, **26,** 184–199.

MUNDY-CASTLE, A. C., & MCKIEVER, B. L. The psychophysiological significance of the galvanic skin response. *Journal of Experimental Psychology,* 1953, **46,** 15–24.

MUNDY-CASTLE, A. C., & NELSON, G. K. Intelligence, personality and brain rhythms in a socially isolated community. *Nature,* 1960, **185,** 484–485.

NEHER, A. Auditory driving observed with scalp electrodes in normal subjects. *Electroencephalography and Clinical Neurophysiology,* 1961, **13,** 449–451.

OBRIST, W. D. The electroencephalogram of normal aged adults. *Electroencephalography and Clinical Neurophysiology,* 1954, **6,** 235–244.

OBRIST, W. D., & HENRY, C. E. Electroencephalographic frequency analysis of aged psychiatric patients. *Electroencephalography and Clinical Neurophysiology,* 1958, **10,** 621–632.

OCHS, S. *Elements of neurophysiology.* New York: Wiley, 1965.

OFFNER, F. The EEG as potential mapping: The value of average monopolar references. *Electroencephalography and Clinical Neurophysiology,* 1950, **2,** 213–214.

OSSELTON, J. W. Acquisition of EEG data by bipolar, unipolar and average reference methods: A theoretical comparison. *Electroencephalography and Clinical Neurophysiology,* 1965, **19,** 527–528.

PALMER, D. M., & ROCK, H. A. Brain wave patterns and "crystallized experiences." *Ohio Medical Journal,* 1953, **49,** 804–806.

PASIK, P., PASIK, T., & BENDER, M. B. Recovery of the electrooculogram after total ablation of the retina in monkeys. *Electroencephalography and Clinical Neurophysiology,* 1965, **19,** 291–297.

POND, D. A. The development of normal rhythms. In D. HILL & G. PARR (Eds.), *Electroencephalography.* (Ch. 6.) New York: Macmillan, 1963.

POSER, C. M. Electroencephalographic changes and hyperammonemia. *Electroencephalography and Clinical Neurophysiology,* 1958, **10,** 51–62.

PRAWDICZ-NEMINSKI, W. W. Ein Versuch der Registrierung der elektrischen Gehirnerscheinungen. *Zentralblatt für Physiologie,* 1913, **27,** 951–960.

QUEROL, M. The electroencephalogram in a group of normal subjects at sea level and at 14,900 feet. *Electroencephalography and Clinical Neurophysiology,* 1958, **10,** 69–87.

QUEROL, M. The electroencephalogram in a group of native highlanders at 4540 meters altitude and at sea level. *Electroencephalography and Clinical Neurophysiology,* 1965, **18,** 401–408.

RAHM, W. E., & WILLIAMS, A. C. Aspects of electroencephalogram in epilepsy and feeblemindedness. *Psychiatric Quarterly,* 1938, **12,** 230–235.

RANEY, E. T. Brain potentials and lateral dominance in identical twins. *Journal of Experimental Psychology,* 1939, **24,** 21–39.

RÉMOND, A. Level of organization of evoked responses in man. *Annals of the New York Academy of Sciences,* 1964, **112,** 143–159.

X RÉMOND, A., & TORRES, F. A method of electrode placement with a view to topographical research: I. Basic concepts. *Electroencephalography and Clinical Neurophysiology*, 1964, **17**, 577-578.

REUNING, H. A new flicker apparatus for measuring individual differences. *Journal of the National Institute for Personnel Research (Johannesburg)*, 1955, **6**, 44-54.

RITTER, W., VAUGHAN, H. G., Jr., & COSTA, L. D. Orienting and habituation to auditory stimuli: A study of short term changes in average evoked responses. *Electroencephalography and Clinical Neurophysiology*, 1968, **25**, 550-556.

RODIN, E. A., GRISELL, J. L., GUDOBBA, R. D., & ZACHARY, G. Relationship of EEG background rhythms to photic evoked responses. *Electroencephalography and Clinical Neurophysiology*, 1965, **19**, 301-304.

ROMANO, J., & ENGEL, G. L. Delirium: Electroencephalographic data. *Archives of Neurology and Psychiatry*, 1944, **51**, 356-377.

ROSS, J. J. Neurological findings after prolonged sleep deprivation. *Archives of Neurology and Psychiatry*, 1965, **12**, 399-403.

ROSSEN, R., KABAT, H., & ANDERSON, J. P. Acute arrest of cerebral circulation in man. *Archives of Neurology and Psychiatry*, 1943, **50**, 510-528.

ROTH, B., & NEVSIMAL, O. EEG study of tetany and spasmophilia. *Electroencephalography and Clinical Neurophysiology*, 1964, **17**, 36-45.

X ROTH, M., SHAW, J., & GREEN, J. The form, voltage distribution and physiological significance of the K-complex. *Electroencephalography and Clinical Neurophysiology*, 1956, **8**, 385-402.

RUBIN, M. A. A variability study of the normal and schizophrenic occipital alpha rhythm. *Journal of Psychology*, 1938, **6**, 325-334.

RUCH, T. C., PATTON, H. D., WOODBURY, J. W., & TOWE, A. L. *Neurophysiology*. (2nd ed.) Philadelphia: Saunders, 1965.

SAUL, L. J., DAVIS, H., & DAVIS, P. A. Correlations between electroencephalograms and psychological organization of the individual. *Transactions of the American Neurological Association*, 1937, **63**, 167-169.

SAUL, L. J., DAVIS, H., & DAVIS, P. A. Psychologic correlations with the electroencephalogram. *Psychosomatic Medicine*, 1949, **11**, 361-376.

SAUNDERS, D. R. Further implications of Mundy-Castle's correlations between EEG and Wechsler-Bellevue variables. *Journal of the National Institute for Personnel Research (Johannesburg)*, 1960, **8**, 91-101.

SAUNDERS, M. C. Electroencephalograph findings in a case of familial periodic paralysis with hypopotassemia. *Electroencephalography and Clinical Neurophysiology*, 1954, **6**, 499-501.

SCHWARTZ, M., EMDE, J., & SHAGASS, C. Comparison of constant current and constant voltage stimulators for scalp-recorded somatosensory responses. *Electroencephalography and Clinical Neurophysiology*, 1964, **17**, 81-83.

SHAGASS, C. Conditioning the human occipital alpha rhythm to a voluntary stimulus: A quantitative study. *Journal of Experimental Psychology*, 1942, **31**, 367-379.

SHAGASS, C. An attempt to correlate the occipital alpha frequency of the electroencephalogram with performance on a mental ability test. *Journal of Experimental Psychology*, 1946, **36**, 88-92.

SHAGASS, C. The sedation threshold: A method for estimating tension in psychiatric patients. *Electroencephalography and Clinical Neurophysiology*, 1954, **6**, 221-233.

SHAGASS, C. Differentiation between anxiety and depression by the photically activated electroencephalogram. *American Journal of Psychiatry*, 1955, **112**, 41-46. (a)

SHAGASS, C. Anxiety, depression, and the photically driven electroencephalogram. *Archives of Neurology and Psychiatry*, 1955, **74**, 3-10. (b)

SHAGASS, C. Effects of LSD on somatosensory and visual evoked responses and on the EEG in man. *Recent Advances in Biological Psychology*, 1967, **9**, 209-227.

SHAGASS, C., & CANTER, A. Some personality correlates of cerebral evoked response characteristics. *Proceedings of the 18th International Congress of Psychology*, 1966, Symposium No. 6.

SHAGASS, C., & JOHNSON, E. P. The course of acquisition of a conditioned response of the occipital alpha rhythm. *Journal of Experimental Psychology* **33**, 201-209, 1943.

SHAGASS, C., & KERENYI, A. B. Neurophysiologic studies of personality. *Journal of Nervous and Mental Disease*, 1958, **126**, 141-147.

SHAGASS, C., & NAIMAN, J. The sedation threshold, manifest anxiety, and some aspects of ego function. *Archives of Neurology and Psychiatry*, 1955, **74**, 397-406.

SHAGASS, C., & NAIMAN, J. The sedation threshold as an objective index of manifest anxiety in psychoneurosis. *Journal of Psychosomatic Research*, 1956, **1**, 49-57.

SHAGASS, C., & SCHWARTZ, M. Evoked cortical potentials and sensation in man. *Journal of Neuropsychiatry*, 1961, **2**, 262-270.

SHAGASS, C., & SCHWARTZ, M. Excitability of the cerebral cortex in psychiatric disorders. In R. ROESSLER & N. S. GREENFIELD (Eds.), *Physiological correlates of psychological disorder*. Madison: University of Wisconsin Press, 1962.

SHAGASS, C., & SCHWARTZ, M. Psychiatric disorder and deviant cerebral responsiveness to sensory stimulation. *Recent Advances in Biological Psychiatry*, 1963, **5**, 321-330.

SHAGASS, C., & SCHWARTZ, M. Recovery functions of somatosensory peripheral nerve and cerebral evoked responses in man. *Electroencephalography and Clinical Neurophysiology*, 1964, **17**, 126-135.

SHAGASS, C., & SCHWARTZ, M. Age, personality, and somatosensory cerebral evoked responses. *Science*, 1965, **148**, 1359-1361. (a)

SHAGASS, C., & SCHWARTZ, M. Visual cerebral evoked response characteristics in a psychiatric population. *American Journal of Psychiatry*, 1965, **121**, 979-987. (b)

SHAGASS, C., & SCHWARTZ, M. Somatosensory cerebral

evoked responses in psychotic depression. *British Journal of Psychiatry*, 1966, **112**, 799–807.

SHAGASS, C., & TRUSTY, D. Somatosensory and visual cerebral evoked response changes during sleep. *Recent Advances in Biological Psychiatry*, 1966, **8**, 321–334.

SHIPTON, H. W. A new frequency-selective toposcope for electroencephalography. *Medical Electronics and Biological Engineering*, 1963, **1**, 483–495.

SHORT, P. L. The objective study of mental imagery. *British Journal of Psychology*, 1953, **44**, 38–51.

SILVERMAN, A. J., BUSSE, E. W., & BARNES, R. H. Studies in the processes of aging: Electroencephalographic findings in 400 elderly subjects. *Electroencephalography and Clinical Neurophysiology*, 1955, **7**, 67–74.

SLATTER, K. H. Alpha rhythms and mental imagery. *Electroencephalography and Clinical Neurophysiology*, 1960, **12**, 851–859.

SMITH, J. R. The electroencephalogram during normal infancy and childhood: I. Rhythmic activities present in the neonate and their subsequent development. *Journal of Genetic Psychology*, 1938, **53**, 431–453.

SPEHLMANN, R. The averaged electrical responses to diffuse and to patterned light in the human. *Electroencephalography and Clinical Neurophysiology*, 1965, **19**, 560–569.

SPECK, L. B., DIM, B., & MERCER, M. Visual evoked responses of psychiatric patients. *Archives of General Psychiatry*, 1966, **15**, 59–63.

SPONG, P., HAIDER, M., & LINDSLEY, D. B. Selective attentiveness and cortical evoked responses to visual and auditory stimuli. *Science*, 1965, **148**, 395–397.

STENNETT, R. G. The relationship of alpha amplitude to the level of palmar conductance. *Electroencephalography and Clinical Neurophysiology*, 1957, **9**, 131–138.

STERNBACH, R. A. Two independent indices of activation. *Electroencephalography and Clinical Neurophysiology*, 1960, **12**, 609–611.

STORM VAN LEEUWEN, W. Complementarity of different analysis methods. *Electroencephalography and Clinical Neurophysiology*, 1964, **16**, 136–139.

STRAUMANIS, J. J., SHAGASS, C., & SCHWARTZ, M. Visually evoked cerebral response changes associated with chronic brain syndromes and aging. *Journal of Gerontology*, 1965, **20**, 498–506.

SURWILLO, W. W. The relation of simple response time to brain-wave frequency and the effects of age. *Electroencephalography and Clinical Neurophysiology*, 1963, **15**, 105–114. (a).

SURWILLO, W. W. The relation of response-time variability to age and the influence of brain wave frequency. *Electroencephalography and Clinical Neurophysiology*, 1963, **15**, 1029–1032. (b)

SURWILLO, W. W. The relation of decision time to brain wave frequency and to age. *Electroencephalography and Clinical Neurophysiology*, 1964, **16**, 510–514.

SURWILLO, W. W. On the relation of latency of alpha attenuation to alpha rhythm frequency and the influence of age. *Electroencephalography and Clinical Neurophysiology*, 1966, **20**, 129–132.

SUTTON, S., BRAREN, M., & ZUBIN, J. Evoked-potential correlates of stimulus uncertainty. *Science*, 1965, **150**, 1187–1188.

SUTTON, S., TUETING, P., ZUBIN, J., & JOHN, E. R. Information delivery and the sensory evoked potential. *Science*, 1967, **155**, 1436–1439.

THIEBAUT, F., ROHMER, F., & WACKENHEIM, A. Contribution à l'étude électroencéphalographique des syndromes endocriniens. *Electroencephalography and Clinical Neurophysiology*, 1958, **10**, 1–30.

TRAVIS, L. E., & EGAN, J. P. Conditioning of the electrical response of the cortex. *Journal of Experimental Psychology*, 1938, **22**, 524–531.

TURNER, W. J., & ROBERTS, C. S. An adhesive nondrying electrode paste. *Journal of Laboratory and Clinical Medicine*, 1944, **29**, 81.

TYLER, D B., GOODMAN, J., & ROTHMAN, T. The effect of experimental insomnia on the rate of potential changes in the brain. *American Journal of Physiology*, 1947, **149**, 185–193.

ULETT, G. A., GLESER, G., WINOKUR, G., & LAWLER, A. The EEG and reaction to photic stimulation as an index of anxiety-proneness. *Electroencephalography and Clinical Neurophysiology*, 1953, **5**, 23–32.

ULETT, G. A., & LOEFFEL, R. G. A new resonator-integrator unit for the automatic brain wave analyser. *Electroencephalography and Clinical Neurophysiology*, 1953, **5**, 113–115.

VAUGHAN, H. G., Jr., COSTA, I.D., & RITTER, W. Topography of the human motor potential. *Electroencephalography and Clinical Neurophysiology*, 1968, **25**, 1–10.

WALSH, E. G. Visual reaction time and the alpha rhythm: Investigation of the scanning hypothesis. *Journal of Physiology*, 1952, **118**, 500–508.

WALSH, E. G. Autonomy of alpha rhythm generators studied by multiple channel cross-correlation. *Electroencephalography and Clinical Neurophysiology*, 1958, **10**, 121–130.

WALTER, D. O., RHODES, J. M., BROWN, D., & ADEY, W. R. Comprehensive spectral analysis of human EEG generators in posterior cerebral regions. *Electroencephalography and Clinical Neurophysiology*, 1966, **20**, 224–237.

WALTER, V. J., & WALTER, W. G. The central effects of rhythmic sensory stimulation. *Electroencephalography and Clinical Neurophysiology*, 1949, **1**, 57–86.

WALTER, W. G. The location of cerebral tumors by electroencephalography. *Lancet*, 1936, **2**, 305–308.

WALTER, W. G. Chapter 2. In D. HILL & G. PARR (Eds.), *Electroencephalography*. (1st ed.) London: Macdonald, 1950.

WALTER, W. G. *The living brain*. New York: Norton, 1953.

WALTER, W. G. Oscillatory activity in the nervous system: Spontaneous oscillatory systems and alterations in stability. In R. G. GRENELL (Ed.), *Neural physiopathology:*

Some relationships of normal to altered nervous system activity. New York: Harper & Row, 1962.

WALTER, W. G. Technique-interpretation. In D. HILL & G. PARR (Eds.), *Electroencephalography.* New York: Macmillan, 1963.

WALTER, W. G., COOPER, R., ALDRIDGE, V. J., McCALLUM, W. C., & WINTER, A. L. Contingent negative variation: An electric sign of sensorimotor association and expectancy in the human brain. *Nature,* 1964, **203,** 380–384.

WALTER, W. G., & DOVEY, V. J. Electro-encephalography in cases of subcortical tumour. *Journal of Neurology, Neurosurgery, and Psychiatry,* 1944, **7,** 57–65.

WALTER, W. G., & PARR, G. Recording equipment and technique. In D. HILL & G. PARR (Eds.), *Electroencephalography.* New York: Macmillan, 1963.

WALTER, W. G., & SHIPTON, H. W. A new toposcopic display system. *Electroencephalography and Clinical Neurophysiology,* 1951, **3,** 281–292.

WEITZMAN, E. D., & KREMEN, H. Auditory evoked responses during different stages of sleep in man. *Electroencephalography and Clinical Neurophysiology,* 1965, **18,** 65–70.

WELLS, C. E. Electroencephalographic correlates of conditioned responses. In G. H. GLASER (Ed.), *EEG and behavior.* New York: Basic Books, 1963.

WERRE, P. F. *The relationships between electroencephalographic and psychological data in normal adults.* The Hague: Nijhoff, 1957.

WHITTERIDGE, D., & WALSH, E. G. The physiological basis of the electroencephalogram. In D. HILL & G. PARR (Eds.), *Electroencephalography.* New York: Macmillan, 1963.

WILSON, J. P., DARROW, C. W., VIETH, R. N., & MALLER, J. M. Laterality of change in the EEG during right and left activity. *Electroencephalography and Clinical Neurophysiology,* 1959, **11,** 845–846.

WILSON, W. P. The role of potassium in the production of the slow wave response to hyperventilation in the electroencephalogram. *Electroencephalography and Clinical Neurophysiology,* 1958, **10,** 546–549.

WILSON, W. P. (Ed.) *Applications of electroencephalography in psychiatry.* Durham, N.C.: Duke University Press, 1965.

WILSON, W. P., & JOHNSON, J. E. Thyroid hormone and brain function: I. The EEG of hyperthyroidism with observations on the effect of age, sex, and reserpine in the production of abnormalities. *Electroencephalography and Clinical Neurophysiology,* 1964, **16,** 321–328.

WILSON, W. P., JOHNSON, J. E., & FIEST, F. W. Thyroid hormone and brain function: II. Changes in photically elicited EEG responses following the administration of triiodothyronine to normal subjects. *Electroencephalography and Clinical Neurophysiology,* 1964, **16,** 329–331.

WYSPIANSKI, J. O., BARRY, W. F., & DAYHAW, L. T. Brain wave amplitude and creative thinking. *Revue de l'Université d'Ottawa,* 1963, 269–276.

Iris Balshan Goldstein

ELECTROMYOGRAPHY

A MEASURE OF SKELETAL MUSCLE RESPONSE

8

The role of electromyography in psychology is somewhat different from its function in other fields. In psychological studies, interest centers on the tension of skeletal muscles; here the electromyogram (EMG) has provided a useful method of quantifying data. When used in this chapter, EMG will refer to the recording of electrical responses from muscles. While it is not the only means of recording muscle tension, it has definite advantages over other methods and is currently the most popular technique in muscle tension research.

Some clarification of the exact meaning of the term "muscle tension" is necessary. Jacobson's (1938) reference to it as a vaguely defined state of nervous hypertension or hyperexcitability has definite pathological connotations. While some writers identify tension with "tonus" others clearly distinguish between the two, confining tonus to sustained contraction caused by a continuous barrage of nerve impulses. Freeman (1948) finds the two words to be quite similar but reserves the usage of "tension" for certain events coming under cerebral control. Underlying the numerous definitions of "muscle tension" is the idea of muscular contraction. Because of this common concept, muscle tension will be used herein to refer to *the state of contraction of the muscles.* Where complete relaxation occurs, there is no muscular contraction, and, consequently, no tension (Broman, 1949). Stimulation of the muscle, on the other hand, leads to its contraction and to the simultaneous electrical, chemical, structural, and thermal changes that result in the muscle action potential (MAP). The record of the electrical events of the MAP or a series of MAPs makes up the EMG.

HISTORICAL BACKGROUND

When man first became aware of electric current, he began to search for a similar activating force in muscular movement. As a result, around the beginning of the nineteenth century, interest developed in the phenomena produced by the electrical stimulation of muscles. Soon "animal electricity" was proposed as a substitute for the earlier concept of "animal spirits." If we are to credit any single individual with giving impetus to this idea, it would probably be Luigi Galvani. His commentary, *Effects of Electricity on Muscular Motion* (Foley, 1954), revealed that (a) skeletal muscles contract in response to electricity, and (b) they produce detectable current when they do so.

Although many individuals contributed to the further development of the concept of muscle action potentials, it was Carlo Matteucci who laid the groundwork for muscle electrophysiology. In 1841 he demonstrated to the Académie des Sciences that a galvanometer connected from the surface of a muscle to a wound in the muscle indicated a flowing current. This idea, which may have seemed insignificant at the time, was the germ of the discovery of the action current. On the basis of this paper, du Bois-Reymond formulated a theory of the polarization of animal tissue and later confirmed Matteucci's demonstration that not only nervemuscle preparations but also the muscles themselves could produce electricity. In so doing, he claimed priority for naming this the muscular current. By means of liquid electrode jars, he also recorded the first human EMG, which was taken from the contracting arm of a man. (For further details on the history of both muscle and nerve action potentials, see Basmajian, 1967c; Boring, 1950; Brazier, 1959, pp. 1–58; Licht, 1961, p. 1–23; Norris, 1963; and Rasch & Burke, 1963.)

The use of liquid electrode jars, although quite primitive, was the beginning of the EMG. For the registration of smaller and more rapidly fluctuating MAPs, investigators had to await the development of more precise instrumentation. Among the first of such instruments was the capillary electrometer developed by Lippmann in 1872. Ten years later, d'Arsonval constructed the moving coil galvanometer by suspending a small coil of wire between opposed magnetic poles (Grings, 1954). Substituting a single straight fiber of silvered quartz for the loop or coil, Einthoven devised the string galvanometer in 1901. The quartz fiber was stretched tightly between the poles of a strong magnet in such a manner that a current from the muscles would be conducted along its surface, causing it to move in the magnetic field. Movements of the filament appeared as a magnified shadow on a screen, where they were recorded by moving photographic film (Galambos, 1962; Grings, 1954; E. Jacobson, 1938, 1941).

Increased sensitivity was provided in 1920 by Forbes and Thatcher, who electronically amplified the action potentials recorded with the string galvanometer. Although the combination of string galvanometer and electronic amplification produced excellent EMGs, a need for an inertialess system for recording physiological activity existed. This led to the adaptation of the cathode ray oscilloscope to biological research. The device was first employed for the EMG by Erlanger and Gasser. Unlike the electrometer and galvanometer, which required that a tiny biocurrent move a relatively large mass, the cathode ray tube uses a beam of electrons with negligible mass to write on a fluorescent screen (E. Jacobson, 1938; Licht, 1961, pp. 1–23; Norris, 1963).

MUSCLE ACTION POTENTIALS (MAPS) AND THEIR RELATIONSHIP TO MUSCLE TENSION

Electrochemistry of the MAP

The typical muscle is an elongated mass of tissue consisting of millions of separate muscle fibers bound together by a sheet of connective tissue. If two electrodes are on the skin or inserted into the muscle, and the muscle is stimulated, an electrical current flows, which is recorded as the EMG. The potential of the muscle fiber is actually responsible for most of the phenomena observed in the EMG. Each time an action potential passes along a muscle fiber, a small portion of electrical activity spreads from the muscle to the skin. If many muscle fibers contract simultaneously, the sum of the electrical potentials at the skin may be quite large and readily recorded.

During the resting state each fiber within the muscle maintains a negative intracellular potential of 50–100 mV. This negative potential underlies the electrical phenomenon of the MAP. While there are variations in thought concerning the origin of the MAP, the theory of muscle and nerve action based on the potassium-sodium pump has the widest general acceptance. Basic to the theory is a selectively permeable cell membrane and a system for active transport of the positive sodium and potassium ions. In the resting state, negative chloride and positive potassium ions move freely through the cell membrane in response to electrochemical gradients. Because of their greater hydration, sodium ions diffuse much less freely but they do enter the cell. In addition to this passive flux of ions, potassium is pumped into the cell and sodium out, in a 1:1 ratio, by an active transport system frequently called the sodium pump. By this means sodium ions, which have a low reentry rate, are concentrated outside the cell, and potassium ions inside. The latter diffuse out, building up a greater positive charge outside the cell, a corresponding negative intracellular charge, and causing polarization of the cell.[1]

The MAP is a brief reversal (depolarization) of the resting membrane potential. When the muscle cell becomes active, its permeability to sodium is increased and sodium pours into the cell (Figure 8.1). As the customary concentration gradient is destroyed and the resting potential abolished, the cell fails to hold its high ratio of potassium. This loss of potassium results in a momentarily larger concentration of sodium inside the cell, as compared to the outside.

The increased permeability to sodium during

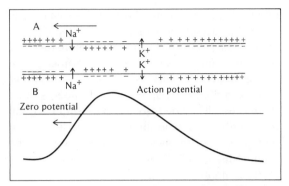

Figure 8.1 A: The postulated movement of sodium and potassium ions across the membrane during an impulse advancing in the direction of the arrow, the resulting alteration of charge on the membrane, and its recovery; B: potential distribution of the impulse along a nerve or muscle fiber. Redrawn from J. C. Eccles, Neuron physiology—introduction. In J. Field, H. W. Magoun, & V. E. Hall (Eds.), *Handbook of Physiology*, Section 1, Vol. 1. Washington, D.C.: American Physiological Society, 1959. By permission.

activity is transient and returns to resting values in a millisecond. In addition, when the membrane potential is near zero or becomes internally positive, permeability to potassium begins to increase. The combined increase in permeability to potassium and the decrease in permeability to sodium causes a rapid fall of the potential to the resting level.

Any sudden excitation not only causes a reversal of the membrane potential but also results in a traveling, self-propagated area of excitation on the cell membrane. This is accompanied by a wave of contraction that spreads over the fiber with constant velocity and undiminished amplitude. The contraction of the fibers exerts a force on the tendons. If the force is sufficient, shortening of the fibers occurs (Eccles, 1959; Galambos, 1962; Katz, 1966; Morgan, 1965; Richardson & Parry, 1957; Szumski, 1967; Woodbury, 1965, pp. 26–58; Woodbury, Gordon, & Conrad, 1965, pp. 113–152; Woolf, 1962).

Motor Unit

Basic to an understanding of the MAP is the concept of the motor unit, for muscle fibers in normal skeletal muscle do not contract individually but function as a group. Such a group of fibers is innervated by a single nerve fiber, the cell body

[1][Editors' footnote.] For a more complete explanation, the reader may wish to read Woodbury, J. W. The cell membrane: Ionic and potential gradients and active transport. In T. C. Ruch & H. D. Patton (Eds.), *Physiology and biophysics.* Philadelphia: Saunders, 1965, pp. 1–25.

of which is in the ventral horn of the spinal cord; or, in the case of the muscles of the head, in the motor nuclei of the brain stem. Just before reaching the muscle fibers, axons of the nerve fiber divide into a number of small branches, or axon fibrils. Each axon fibril ends upon a muscle fiber, so that there is usually a one-to-one relationship between muscle fiber and axon fibril. The complete motor unit consists of the nerve cell body, its axon, the axon fibrils, and all of the muscle fibers innervated by these fibrils.

While the ratio of muscle fibers to nerve axons (innervation ratio) may vary considerably, the actual size of the motor unit is related to the precision of movement of the particular muscles involved. The impulse in a nerve fiber with a high ratio will cause a large contraction, in contrast to an axon fiber with a small number of motor fibers. For example, the slowly acting postural muscles may have as many as 3000 muscle fibers in each motor unit. On the other hand, muscles that react rapidly and have more precise control, such as those of the eye, have a very low innervation ratio, perhaps 10:1 (Basmajian, 1967b, 1967c; Guyton, 1956; Lippold, 1967, pp. 244–297; Morgan, 1965).

Summation of Motor Units

By means of needle electrodes, single motor units have been recorded and their characteristic form described. Lindsley (1935a), for example, has indicated that a given motor unit at any specific intensity of contraction is characterized by a definite amplitude, waveform, and rhythm. Most EMG studies in psychology, however, are concerned with the activity of whole muscles, rather than discrete motor units. For this reason the psychologist uses surface electrodes that record the coarse pattern of rapidly occurring spikes over many units.

The magnitude of contraction, as measured by the surface EMG, varies as a function of the number of motor units participating, as well as with the frequency with which each fires. At low contraction there are only a few discrete motor units active at a low discharge rate. A slight increase in effort increases the contraction rate of these units up to about 40 discharges per sec. With greater tension, additional motor units are activated (Bigland &

Lippold, 1954; Gilson & Mills, 1941; Lindsley, 1935a; Norris & Gasteiger, 1955). According to Eason (1959), the gradual increase in the integrated surface EMG with time suggests that additional motor units are progressively recruited to compensate for the loss in contractility of fatigued units. In addition, the amplitude decrement of active units is more than offset by their summation with new units.

Muscle Tension Changes

A major assumption throughout this chapter is that the EMG varies with changes in muscle tension. It should be noted, however, that the EMG does not provide a direct measure of either muscle tension or muscular contraction. The electrical activity of the motor unit, which it does record, actually occurs prior to the contraction of the muscle, which is a mechanical event (Thompson, Lindsley, & Eason, 1966, pp. 117–182). In the recording of surface EMGs, a major variable of concern is the peak-to-peak amplitude of MAPs. There is sufficient evidence to indicate that, as muscle tension or muscular activity increases, peak amplitude changes proportionally. Basic to this occurrence is the requirement that the muscle being studied maintain constant length, while it gradually increases the force of its contraction (Inman, Ralston, Saunders, Feinstein, & Wright, 1952).

In studies relating variations in muscle tension to changes in EMG amplitude, the arm muscles frequently have been observed while the subject pressed a dynamometer. This relationship is demonstrated in Figure 8.2. Generally, the resulting correlations between the two variables have been somewhat linear and quite high. Wilcott and Beenken (1957), in fact, have reported correlations in the 0.80s and 0.90s. Electromyograms obtained from the calf muscles during 10 different strengths of contraction showed similar high correlations (Lippold, 1952). Nevertheless, there is some indication that the relationship between muscle tension (or muscle contraction) and EMG amplitude is linear only up to about 75–100 mV, or approximately 6 kg of pull. Malmo, Shagass, and J. F. Davis (1951) and Wilcott and Beenken (1957) note that this is well within the range of EMG recordings reported for most

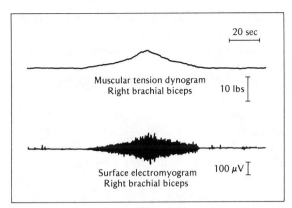

Figure 8.2 Parallel between pressure on a dynamometer and surface EMG of the right biceps. Adapted from J. E. Nidever, A factor analytic study of general muscular tension. Unpublished doctoral dissertation, University of California, Los Angeles, 1959. By permission.

behavioral studies and are satisfied that the EMG gives a fairly good indication of tension in skeletal muscles.

There is some evidence that the curves relating muscle tension to EMG changes differ between sexes. Although the differences are real, they are minimal and appear to be related to variations in strength. On the average, the same degree of muscular work is accompanied by more electrical activity in women (Malmo, Shagass, & J. F. Davis, 1951; Small & Gross, 1958; Wilcott & Beenken, 1957).

METHODS IN ELECTROMYOGRAPHIC RESEARCH

Apparatus

The recording of MAPs requires three components: (a) the electrodes, to transmit the electrical impulses from the muscles; (b) the amplifier, to provide enough sensitivity and power for recording; and (c) a mechanism to display the impulses from the amplifier (R. C. Davis, 1942; Schwartz, Heath, & Hudson, 1949).

Electrodes Although there are various types of electrodes, they generally fall into either of two broad categories: disks or plates (frequently metallic), which are anchored to the surface of the skin; and wire or needle electrodes, which penetrate the

skin. O'Connell and Gardner (1963) further divide the latter category, depending on the depth of penetration, into electrodes that extend into the muscle itself (intramuscular) and those that are inserted only through the skin (subcutaneous).

Intramuscular electrodes are important in clinical work or if one is primarily concerned with the activity of individual muscle units. Where interest centers on the combined spikes of muscle bundles or groups of muscles, either subcutaneous or surface electrodes may be utilized. As a consequence of their ability to respond to large groups of muscle fibers and their relative lack of stress to the subject, surface electrodes are ideal for most psychological studies. Surface electrodes normally consist of two active electrodes, but a ground or reference electrode may be used. Either use results in a potential difference that is amplified and recorded. Most surface electrodes are composed of metal but they can be made of almost any substance that will conduct electricity.

According to J. F. Davis (1959), a satisfactory lead for recording MAPs requires optimal choices of (a) the site for electrodes, (b) the type of electrode, (c) the means of attachment, and (d) the preparation of the skin. Since current flow through electrodes is generally negligible (with high impedance input), and since MAPs are momentary, R. C. Davis (1942) believes that the polarization of electrodes is of no importance. Further discussion of electrodes and their application can be found in several sources (Basmajian, 1967c; J. F. Davis, 1961; Inman et al., 1952; Lippold, 1967, pp. 244–297; O'Connell & Gardner, 1963; Rogoff & Reiner, 1961, pp. 24–65).

Amplification The major issue regarding amplification revolves about the question of what range of MAP frequencies are most important in muscle tension research. Buchthal, Pinelli, and Rosenfalck (1954) report that an upper limiting frequency of 10,000 Hz and a lower limiting frequency of 2 Hz allow undistorted recordings of MAPs. Rodriquez and Oester (1961) place the minimal frequency range from 40 to 5000 Hz. Other investigators admit that MAPs have a broad range but state further that the maximal activity occurs at the lower end of the spectrum. According to R. C. Davis (1942) the frequency response of the amplifier should be linear between 20 and 400 Hz; Hayes (1959) feels that the important range is between 30 and 100 Hz. A study by Friedmann (1951) indicates that the Type-D EEG (electroencephalograph) amplifiers impose certain frequency restrictions, causing some attenuation beyond 70 Hz. Although the frequencies of muscle units under surface electrodes may exceed this range, Friedmann states that the total spectrum for MAPs is adequately represented by frequencies between 10 and 70 Hz.

In addition, the equipment should be sensitive enough for the recording to appear on the scale used for measurement; it must have sufficiently low inherent noise level to permit distinguishing different signal levels from noise; and the scale of signal levels must be calibrated. The impedance of the recording system must be selected so that there is minimal loss of signal due to loading by the recording equipment.

A major difficulty is introduced by surrounding ac (alternating current) power lines, which may induce ac artifacts. In general, an amplifier with high, common-mode signal rejection, such as a differential amplifier, permits minute MAPs to be fairly accurately recorded. The overall problem of recording in the presence of 60-cycle and other interfering sources is somewhat complex and is discussed in Rogoff and Reiner (1961, pp. 24–65). Further evaluations of amplifiers for use in EMG work can be found in J. F. Davis (1959), R. C. Davis (1942), Schwartz, Heath, and Hudson (1949), and Whitfield (1953).

Recording systems   Where the experimenter has been particularly concerned about the accuracy of EMG recordings, the mirror-coil oscillographs or the galvanometers used in them (Grings, 1954) have proved to be useful. Low inertia, coupled with the ability to respond to fairly high frequencies, are to their advantage. Far superior to these instruments, however, is the cathode ray oscilloscope. Its lack of any appreciable inertia leads to an almost undistorted EMG, which makes it preferable to other recording systems for most contemporary physiological and clinical investigations. With regard to its use in psychology, the cathode ray oscilloscope is limited by the inability to record several channels

of EMG simultaneously. In addition, the necessity of obtaining permanent records photographically on paper makes the use of the cathode ray oscilloscope too costly for it to be considered practical in any lengthy experiments (J. F. Davis, 1959; R. C. Davis, 1942).

Frequently, when used in psychological studies, the cathode ray oscilloscope is accompanied by an inkwriting galvanometer. Despite its limited frequency response, the direct-writing oscillograph is the most widely used method of recording MAPs in psychological research. It provides an immediate record without the expense involved in photographic development. Furthermore, multiple channel recording is available, permitting EMGs to be taken simultaneously from several areas of the body. While almost all inkwriters will record some MAPs, according to J. F. Davis (1959), only a few will respond to high enough frequencies to record a really useful EMG. Galvanometers with noninkwriting styli have also been developed but they generally require specially prepared recording paper, which can become quite costly. More recently, data is being recorded on multichannel, frequency-modulated, tape recorders. This can be used to supplement other recording systems and permits quick analysis of data by means of computers (Thompson, Lindsley, & Eason, 1966, pp. 117–182).

Integration   Because the measurement of MAP amplitude from EMG recordings is quite time consuming, integrators have become an important part of any EMG equipment. Basically, they provide a measure of total electrical activity as some function of time. Their total output is proportional to the combined area under both positive and negative excursions of the waveform. The output of the amplifier is rectified, so that the positive and negative excursions appear in one direction. The signal is then fed into an accumulating device such as a long-period galvanometer, which maintains a deflection proportional to the sum of potentials in a short period of time. Other devices that have been commonly used operate over longer time intervals and consist of a circuit that employs a condenser to accumulate a charge and then operates to discharge the condenser after a fixed time. The accumulation at the time of discharge is then measured (R. C. Davis, 1942).

A newer device accumulates potential changes over a range of intervals of time. The closing of a relay, which sets the condensers back to their original charge, enables the experimenter to control the length of the cumulating interval. Once the potentials have accumulated across two condensers, they are passed to the deflection plates of a cathode ray oscilloscope and are then photographed as a series of notches. The total potential change in the interval is indicated by the height of each notch (Grings, 1954).

In spite of the convenience of an immediate numerical read-out, there are certain dangers inherent in the use of integrators. To begin with, since they fail to discriminate between artifacts and action potentials, artifacts are integrated along with muscle tension values. In this regard naked-eye examination of records is superior. Secondly, one cannot compare the integrated potentials from one channel with those from another (Basmajian, 1967c). Grossman and Weiner (1966) have insisted upon exercising care when using integrators with commercial polygraphs, since those polygraphs available are felt to be unsuitable in low input, high frequency ranges without modification. Other discussions of integrator units are found in J. F. Davis (1959), R. C. Davis (1948a), Eason and White (1959), Inman et al. (1952), Krusberg and Zimmer, 1966; Malmstadt, Enke, and Toren (1963), Rogoff and Reiner (1961, pp. 24–65), and Tursky (1964).

Experimental Difficulties

In EMG studies, as in any type of research, certain problems have a fairly high frequency of occurrence. For some, satisfactory solutions have been obtained; others still present major difficulties. Where solutions to problems have not been found, it is important that the investigator be aware of the problems and be able to minimize them whenever possible.

The concept of muscle tension   In a search of the literature it is possible to find numerous measures of muscle tension. They range from electrical recording devices to indirect means of assessment (R. C. Davis, 1942). Examples of some of the meas-

ures include the amount of resistance offered to the imposed flexion or extension of a limb (McKinley & Berkwitz, 1928), the magnitude of the knee jerk (Courts, 1939), eyeblink rate (D. R. Meyer, 1953), reaction time (R. C. Davis, 1940), tremor and motor irregularities (Travis & Hunter, 1931). Other indices of muscle tension rely on a more direct assessment of some property of a muscle or a limb, such as the posture of a limb, the amount of pressure on a lever or dynamometer, and the hardness of a muscle (Wendt, 1938).

If one were to search for a common element in all of these studies, it would probably have something to do with skeletal muscle activity. Beyond this, it is hard to see how all of the measures are related. Where MAPs have been correlated with other indices of muscle tension, i.e., muscle movements, grip pressure (Clites, 1936) and eyeblink rate (Malmo & Smith, 1955), the correlation coefficients have been insignificant. It seems possible that the various measures purporting to estimate muscle tension have assessed different aspects of muscular activity. Until more information has been gained about all of the reported measures of muscle tension, it seems reasonable to rely on the EMG, especially if one is restricted to a single index of muscle tension. This instrument offers a relatively sensitive direct method of measurement and provides quantification of tension. It has the added advantage of presenting little disturbance to the subject (R. C. Davis, 1935).

Selection of muscle groups and electrode sites   Because there are so many possible areas of the body from which MAPs could be recorded, a given investigator has almost unlimited choice in his selection of electrode placements. Obviously, he cannot record MAPs from every muscle, and sometimes he is limited by his equipment to one or two muscle groups. The question then arises as to which muscles, if any, would be predictive of the overall state of tension in the body.

Two investigators have studied this problem in some detail by searching for the possible existence of a general muscle tension factor. Nidever (1959), recording MAPs from 23 muscle groups in men, and Balshan (1961), examining MAP activity in women, revealed that such a factor did exist. During a resting state the factors for both men and women were highly similar, in that muscle tension was found to be centered about the limb musculature. Only the muscles of the head and neck were unrelated to either factor. With the introduction of a white-noise stimulus, Balshan found that tension in all parts of the body increased significantly, but the focus of tension remained the same. In other words, this factor was almost identical to the one obtained during the resting condition.

While the muscle factors during rest and in response to an auditory stimulus are quite similar, this does not mean that the pattern of tension will remain constant under all conditions. As a matter of fact, the muscle tension factor shifted from the limbs to the head and neck muscles, when Nidever's subjects engaged in serial learning. In contrast, Voas (1952) reported that the arm muscles were the best indicators of muscle tension during mental work. During stress and frustration, tension was found to be most prominent in the trapezius and masseter[2] muscles. The fact that there may not be just one muscle tension factor is further supported by R. C. Davis's (1956) statement that there are a great many different tension states in the body due to the many possible combinations of muscle contraction. Since there is no immediate answer to the problem of the selection of muscle groups, it probably would be best for the investigator to sample several muscles in different parts of the body. (see Figure 8.3).

Once the selection of muscle groups has been made, there should be some standard for the placement of electrodes. J. F. Davis (1959) feels that the electrode site may be quite crucial in recording MAPs from the desired area. In general, as the spacing between electrodes increases, so does the likelihood of getting higher MAPs and gaining more information from deeper layers. Unfortunately, the possibility of recording undesired signals from neighboring muscle groups increases as well.

Muscle depth The problem of muscle depth can be illustrated in the following manner. Suppose that we have two muscles lying at different depths under the skin that respond with the same MAP

[2]Muscles in the angle of the lower jaw.

amplitudes. We cannot say that these two muscles are responding equally because the conducting path to the electrode sites differs. J. F. Davis (1959) reports that the electrical activity at the surface of the skin is inversely related to the depth of the muscle, although the exact relationship is unknown. Depending upon the relationship of muscle to skin and other anatomical structures, the electrical field of muscle vectors will be squeezed and distorted.

Precisely what this means with regard to the interpretation of EMGs obtained by means of surface electrodes is not known at present. It certainly leads one to question the meaning of intermuscle comparisons. Furthermore, there is the problem of relating EMGs in people with varying body builds, where the same muscle in two individuals is not at comparable distances from the surface of the skin. Nidever (1959) and Balshan (1962) have accounted for this problem to some degree by entering an index of body build (weight over height cubed) into their determinations of general muscle tension factors. In both studies the index was found to have small negative loadings on the factors.

Controlling important physical variables Certain variables that are known to affect muscle tension cannot be eliminated completely but it is possible to control them by means of experimental design. The variable which has been investigated most fully is that of age. With advancing age there is a continuous increase in mean action potential duration during a slight voluntary effort. This results in almost a doubling of the duration of the individual spike potential in the period from 5 to 75 years (Buchthal, Guld, & Rosenfalck, 1954).

The increase in duration of MAPs with advanced age has been attributed to the fiber density in motor units caused by the decrease in the volume of muscle (Sacco, Buchthal, & Rosenfalck, 1962). Carlson, Alston, and Feldman (1964) have also found a considerable number of highly complex and long-duration motor potentials in a large number of elderly patients. Due to the greater synchrony of individual units during the larger time interval, one would expect to find a heightened amplitude of surface EMGs with increasing age. This is substantiated by investigations of MAPs in men

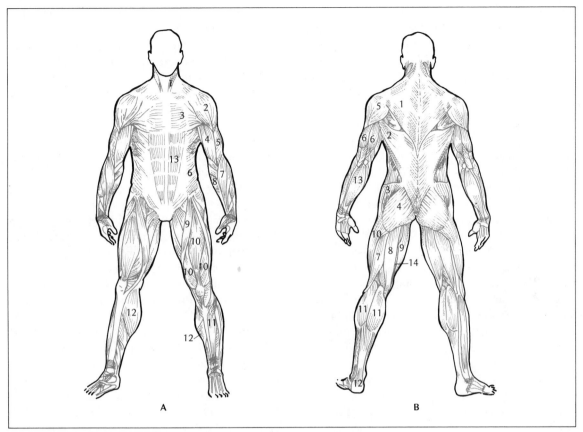

Figure 8.3 Major muscle groups of the human body. A: Front view—1, sternocleidomastoid; 2, deltoid; 3, pectoralis major; 4, biceps; 5, triceps; 6, external oblique; 7, brachioradialis; 8, flexor carpi ulnaris; 9, sartorius; 10, quadratus femoris; 11, anterior tibial; 12, gastrocnemius; 13, rectus abdominis. B: Back view—1, trapezius; 2, latissimus dorsi; 3, gluteus medius; 4, gluteus maximus; 5, deltoid; 6, triceps; 7, biceps femoris; 8, semitendinosus; 9, gracilis; 10, vastus lateralis; 11, gastrocnemius; 12, Achilles' tendon; 13, flexor carpi radialis; 14, semimembranosus. Adapted from Edith E. Sproul, *The science book of the human body* (illustrator, Kathleen Elgin). New York: F. Watts, 1955. By permission.

(Nidever, 1959) and in children (Missiuro, 1963). Other experimenters, attempting to relate age to MAP amplitude, have failed to find tension varying in any meaningful way with age (Bartoshuk, 1959; Martin, 1956). Although Malmo, Shagass, and J. F. Davis (1951) reported a significant relationship between forearm muscle tension and age, no other muscle groups that they sampled were affected in the same manner. The failure of some investigators to find age correlated with muscle tension may be due partially to the limited number of muscle groups selected, as well as the restricted age range of the subjects.

A consideration of temperature must also be involved in EMG research. With decreasing intra-muscular temperature, MAP amplitude decreases by as much as 2–5%/°C. At approximately 75° F (24° C) the contractile force of the muscle reaches a maximum (Buchthal, Guld, & Rosenfalck, 1954; Vargas, 1958). Apparently, muscular activity has similar effects in raising the intramuscular temperature of muscles. In addition, atmospheric temperature was found to be positively correlated with general muscle tension factors obtained during rest (Nidever, 1959; Balshan, 1962). By restricting the activity of subjects and maintaining a constant temperature level in the experimental room, it is possible to control for some of the effects of temperature on skeletal muscle.

The information available on sex, education, and

IQ indicates that they are unrelated to MAP changes (Bartoshuk, 1959; Martin, 1956). Where variations have been reported between the sexes, they appear to be caused by differences in strength (Buchthal, Guld, & Rosenfalck, 1954; Malmo, Shagass, & J. F. Davis, 1951; Malmo & Smith, 1955).

Artifacts Because of the relatively low level of MAPs, there is a likelihood of picking up electrical waveforms that do not originate in skeletal muscle. These artifacts can arise from numerous sources and sometimes create difficulties in the interpretation of records. Such artifacts are discussed by Cohen and Bramlik (1968), J. F. Davis (1959), O'Connell and Gardner (1963), Rodriquez and Oester (1961, pp. 286–341), and Schwartz, Heath, and Hudson (1949).

Depending upon the particular electrode site, the EMG record may show readings of other physiological signals in the area of the electrodes. The strongest and most easily recognized of these is the cardiac potential (EKG) but it is also possible to obtain recordings of brain activity, the movement of the eyelids, and skin resistance changes. Repositioning electrodes sometimes reduces or even eliminates these interfering signals. If not, they usually can be eliminated in the visual reading of the records.

Artifacts due to movement of leads, sliding electrodes, and open circuits can be detected quite easily and the appropriate correction made. The subjects' movements frequently create problems, however, which cannot be handled so effectively. Not only does vigorous movement make records difficult to read but it may lead to the breakage of pens and create a situation in which muscles slide over one another and skin slides over muscle. Such activity results in differing areas being recorded from the same electrodes from one moment to the next. Sometimes the problem is dealt with by creating a cutoff of electrical activity beyond a certain limit, but by such a technique important information may be lost. Probably the best way to deal with movement problems is to instruct the subject to remain as quiet as possible throughout the experiment; or when activity is an important variable, subcutaneous electrodes might be used (O'Connell & Gardner, 1963).

An extremely common artifact in EMG recordings is due to electrical power lines, which carry 115 V of 60-Hz line voltage. With amplifiers at maximum gain, 60-cycle artifact (which is in the middle of the frequency spectrum of MAPs) should generally be expected. Fortunately, it can be recognized easily by setting the recording chart at higher than normal speeds. This 60-cycle interference can be reduced by a firm ground connection and removal of nearby electrical connections. Grounding the subject and any large metal objects that might contact the subject will also help. Experimenters have sometimes found it necessary to shield the subject in a specially screened room. The power line and the EMG apparatus frequently require shielding, also. In some places an elaborate cage is needed, while in others no shielding at all has been necessary. The requirements are generally dependent upon the presence of electrical or electromagnetic interference in the vicinity of the test area. Some EMG-measuring instruments include filters that automatically reject 60-cycle current and reduce the effect of power line interference. While eliminating some artifacts, they also remove an important band of frequencies from the EMG and lead to some distortion of long-duration potentials (J. F. Davis, 1959; R. C. Davis, 1942; O'Connell & Gardner, 1963; Rodriquez & Oester, 1961, pp. 286–341; Rogoff & Reiner, 1961, pp. 24–65).

Another source of artifact originates within the amplifier itself and is termed "noise," since it can cover the complete spectrum of EMG responses. The selection of special amplifier components enables the experimenter to keep the noise levels low but it is not possible to eliminate noise completely (Rogoff & Reiner, 1961, pp. 24–65).

Many artifact problems can be minimized by reducing electrical skin resistance. Most of the high resistance is due to oil on the skin surface and the horny outer layer of the skin itself. By means of appropriate methods of electrode application (which are discussed in Basmajian, 1967c; J. F. Davis, 1959; Lippold, 1967, pp. 244–297; and O'Connell & Gardner, 1963), it is generally possible to reduce skin resistance to about 5000–10,000 ohms.

Obviously, the methods of recording EMGs are not perfect. In addition to the above-mentioned problems, individual spikes, particularly in the high frequency ranges, are distorted by attenuation effects. Furthermore, inkwriters are unable to follow these higher frequencies. Some investigators argue that this is not a significant problem, since there is ample evidence that the wave-peak amplitude of the EMG changes in proportion to the amount of muscular activity (J. F. Davis, 1959). Other writers urge caution in the use and interpretation of the EMG and are particularly concerned with the measurement of signals under 100 μV in the frequency range up to 100–200 Hz (Grossman & Weiner, 1966). Evidently more work must be done to answer all of these questions.

Reliability of Measurement

A final issue that must be considered before discussing the psychological meaning of the EMG is its reliability. Without some constancy from one experimental session to the next, any system of measurement becomes meaningless. Exploring this problem in some detail, Voas (1952) reported amazingly high test–retest reliabilities on MAPs over an average period of 9 days (see Table 8.1). Reliability coefficients ranged as high as .95 for the frontalis and the forearm extensors but were substantially lower for the leg muscles. In addition, the constancy of muscle tension levels is dependent upon the population of subjects and the stimulus conditions. Correlations between arm muscles were larger during active conditions (mental work and stress frustration) than during relaxation. For the masseter and the trapezius muscles, correlations were highest during mental work. Only the frontalis

maintained its high level of reliability throughout all conditions.

As a result of the high retest reliabilities for certain muscles (forearm flexors and frontalis), Voas believes that their usage is warranted for individual measurement. Further support comes from the work of Martin (1956, 1958a), who has found a fairly high consistency in the frontalis and forearm MAPs. Correlations between two separate rest periods were .81 for the frontalis and .52 for the forearm extensors.

Other muscle groups with lower reliabilities are felt to be sensitive enough for group prediction, particularly if the situations under which measurements are taken are carefully controlled (Voas, 1952). J. F. Davis (1959), realizing the variability in muscle measurement, stresses the importance of averaging EMG responses, so that reliable comparisons can be made from subject to subject or in a given subject on different occasions.

THE RELATIONSHIP BETWEEN THE ELECTROMYOGRAM AND PERFORMANCE

Most of the variables purporting to measure muscle tension have shown fairly consistent increases as the result of mental or muscular work (Courts, 1942). R. C. Davis (1939) reported an initial increase in forearm and calf MAPs at the onset of mental work, followed by a quick drop to a level somewhat above that of a resting condition, and then a more gradual rise in tension. Sidowski and Eason (1960) found that, while learning nonsense

TABLE 8.1 TEST-RETEST RELIABILITY COEFFICIENTS FOR VARIOUS EXPERIMENTAL CONDITIONS

	Relaxation	Mental work (addition)	Stress-frustration	Average for all conditions
Gastrocnemius	.306	.119[e]	.127[e]	.158[e]
Tibialis[a]	.231[e]	.414	.121[e]	.408[e]
Forearm flexors[b]	.460	.938	.798	.958
Forearm extensors[c]	.117[e]	.594	.699	.702
Trapezius	.300[e]	.690	.232[e]	.672
Masseter	.392	.873	.317[e]	.757
Frontalis[d]	.806	.905	.918	.954

Note.—From R. B. Voas, Generalization and consistency of muscle tension level. Unpublished doctoral dissertation, University of California, Los Angeles, 1952.
[a] Also referred to as tibial.
[b] Include flexor carpi radialis and flexor carpi ulnaris.
[c] Muscles of the back and lateral side of forearm.
[d] Muscles of the forehead.
[e] Not significantly different from zero.

syllables, the change in frontalis MAPs was related to the anxiety levels of the subjects. For the highly anxious subjects, MAPs decreased over trials; while the opposite occurred for subjects with little anxiety, showing the importance of taking the subject's motivational level into consideration.

While the subject was learning a stylus maze by means of kinesthetic cues, Daniel (1939) demonstrated a different course of muscle tension. Initially, there was a decrease in MAPs of the forearms and lower legs, followed by an increase up to cessation of practice. Here the drop in tension was associated with the elimination of errors and the development of a coordination pattern; rising tension seemed to accompany increased speed of performance and a more efficient use of coordination.

Although increases in tension are sometimes associated with more efficient performance, too much tension can diminish performance. Studies of induced tension are in general agreement that the relationship between tension and performance fits the inverted-U curve (either too much or too little tension may be detrimental to performance) (Courts, 1942; Malmo, 1957). Klein (1961), recording MAPs during induced tension, demonstrated the same sort of phenomenon. During an ergographic task, various levels of MAPs were induced in the forearm flexors. High MAP levels were associated with increased work output but decreased precision. Apparently, when tension became too great, the quality of work began to suffer. While a certain level of breakdown was characteristic of ergographic work, Klein believes that for other tasks there might exist optimal levels of tension above or below which performance is impaired.

Rather than record tension during a period of activity, Sharp (1941) has obtained EMG measures following 2 min of ergographic work. During this period action potentials in the resting but previously active arm followed a cyclical course, beginning with a sharp initial drop in tension. This was followed by a slow increase, which reached a peak at the end of 15 min and slowly fell to the prework level after 15 min more. Knowing that such a pattern existed, Sharp spaced a double work period so that it occurred at the peak of "recovery" tension, after 15 min. Working in this manner, individuals significantly increased their work output.

While tension generally increases during performance, not all studies indicate a continuing rise in MAPs. On the contrary, we have just seen that tension may follow a cyclical course. For this reason it is important to consider in some detail the factors that may affect changes in muscle tension during various tasks. The reader should bear in mind that only those studies directly involved in EMG recordings have been included in the discussion.

Degree of Effort Applied to a Task

Some experimenters have related changes in EMG to the amount of effort that a subject applies during some task. For example, MAPs in the biceps and the forearm flexors were found by Eason (1959) to vary with the subject's feelings of effort, rather than with the amount of physical force he applied during muscular contraction.

The attempt to attain high scores during rotary tracking resulted in increased MAPs in the back, trapezius, and biceps muscles. High scores were interpreted as reflecting the subject's degree of concentration or amount of effort. Increased effort also became apparent as the tracking became more difficult. When the subject was applying the greatest effort, MAPs were highest, particularly in the neck. Eason and White (1961) believe the neck muscles to be the best indicators of effort.

The EMG level may also be used to assess performance efficiency if one assumes that changes in amplitude of the MAP parallel changes in effort. With a performance index based on how well a task is performed relative to the amount of effort exerted, Eason (1963) has determined the effects of practice and variations in target size on the efficiency of a rotary tracking task. MAPs were recorded from the trapezius, the splenius,[3] the biceps, and the forearm flexors. For a given target, tension level (or amount of effort exerted) remained constant, in spite of the fact that performance in tracking improved. Eason felt that this might have been due to the subject's working within his own level of achievement, rather than for an imposed criterion. As the target became smaller, however, the exertion of more effort involved in making finer discriminations caused the MAPs to increase.

[3]Muscles at the back of the neck.

If a slight distraction is introduced while a subject is performing a task, he frequently counteracts the distraction by increased effort. This is reflected, in turn, in heightened muscle tension. Ryan, Cottrell, and Bitterman (1950) found such an occurrence when noise and glare distracted the performance of a visual task. Increments in MAPs were produced in all of the regions from which recordings were made (gastrocnemius, triceps, biceps, and the neck).

Eason, Beardshall, and Jaffee (1965) set up an easy discrimination task under semi-impoverished environmental conditions, thus inducing a progressive state of relaxation, as well as boredom. In addition, maintaining a constant posture for 1 hr was conducive to feelings of discomfort and muscular fatigue. Any of these factors could have led to an increase in neck MAPs as the subject attempted to exert more effort. In spite of the increased neck tension, performance level showed a decline. The authors felt, however, that the performance decrement would have been even more marked if there had been no increase in neck MAPs.

In combination, these studies present a convincing argument for a positive relationship between subjective effort and MAPs. Conditions that lead to increased effort have been found to bring about heightened MAPs, as well as improvements in performance. One could further predict some optimal level, above which additional effort would lead to a performance decrement, even though increases in MAPs would still be observed.

Muscle Tension As a Form of Set

Among the conditions under which muscle tension is generally high are those involving a state of anticipation. Accordingly, R. C. Davis (1940) observed that during the foreperiod in a reaction time experiment, the muscles that executed the hand movement (forearm extensors) showed a rise in tension. This rise began about 200–400 msec after the warning signal and increased up to the time of reaction. In general, it was found that the higher the MAP increase, the shorter the reaction time. Also, tension was higher and reaction time shorter with a regular foreperiod than with an irregular one. When the subject was given a warning signal, the foreperiod reactions in the forearms and upper arms

were much greater than to a tone for which he was unprepared (R. C. Davis, 1948c). Davis concluded that the tension increase during the foreperiod was actually a form of set. If such a set does exist in a reaction situation, Hathaway (1935) found no evidence for it. In trying to explain these results, Davis suggested that Hathaway may have been working at too low a sensitivity to record minute changes in tension.

Miller (1957) substantiated Davis's findings and cited evidence for a rise in MAPs in the right and left forearm extensors during the foreperiod in a two-choice reaction. Only the arm that made the overt behavioral response finally maintained the heightened activity. The other arm, which was not further involved in the response, exhibited a decrease in muscle tension. With EMGs recorded from the frontalis muscle, Kennedy and Travis (1947, 1948; Travis & Kennedy, 1949) studied the reaction time to aperiodic stimuli in a monotonous situation. With increased boredom, the reaction time became longer, and MAPs reduced correspondingly. Studying various reaction-time frequency distributions obtained under different stimulus conditions and in response to both auditory and visual stimuli, Harter and White (1968) found a modal period of approximately 25 msec. The same modal period was also present in EMGs of the forearm.

It has been hypothesized by Botwinick and Thompson (1966) that reaction time is composed of two components, one which is related and one which is unrelated to the preparatory interval. The first of these, premotor time, is the period from the presentation of the stimulus to the beginning of increased muscle firing. The time from the change in action potentials to the response of lifting a finger is called motor time. Premotor time was found to be highly correlated with reaction time and varied as a function of the preparatory interval. It was concluded that set is a premotor, rather than a motor, process.

Whether the muscle tension response in the foreperiod is a necessary condition for the successful performance of a choice response or not, Miller (1957) feels that it does improve performance. It appears to produce kinesthetic stimuli, adding to the number of possible factors that contribute to a successful performance. Furthermore, R. C. Davis

(1948c) is of the opinion that it operates in much the same manner as induced tension.

Whereas the muscles participating in the response are characterized by increased tension, muscles in other areas of the body sometimes exhibit a reduction in tension. During the initial response the subject not only presses a button but also contracts muscles in other parts of the body not immediately concerned in the reaction. With increased practice the responses of the other muscles gradually drop out, as has been demonstrated with the leg muscles (H. D. Meyer, 1949) and with the nonresponding arm (Henderson, 1952). Obrist, Webb, and Sutterer (1969) observed a decrease in MAPs of the muscles in and around the mouth during anticipation of an aversive stimulus and in a reaction time task. They felt that this represented the inhibition of irrelevant motor activity that might detract from more relevant motor acts (see Webb & Obrist, 1970).

Something similar to set has been observed in investigations of tracking, where the subject must attend closely to the stimulus in order to perform efficiently. In a rotary tracking task, Eason and Branks (1963) indicated that the EMG responses in the frontalis, trapezius, neck, and forearm flexors increased as the subject concentrated more intently. The addition of an irrelevant stimulus such as the lifting of a light weight increased the MAPs and led to a further increment in performance level. In effect, the additional stimulus had no distracting effects and actually aided performance efficiency. On the other hand, when the extraneous stimuli were intense enough to cause a further demand on the subject's attention, his performance suffered, despite an elevation in his muscle tension.

In a study of divided set subjects tracked manually but expected to shift from single (manual) to double (manual and foot pedal) tracking at a later time during a trial. As one might expect, subjects with divided set were poorer at tracking than subjects who expected to continue with manual tracking throughout the trial. In spite of this, there were no muscle tension differences between conditions of unified and divided set. In conclusion, Malmo (1966) stated that the performance decrement did not show any relationship to changes in physiological activation.

Whenever the subject gets drowsy or his alertness level drops, certain MAP amplitudes show a corresponding decrease. In a task simulating lookout performance (Travis & Kennedy, 1948), and during continuous tracking (Kennedy & Travis, 1948), the experimenters observed a gradually decreasing level of frontalis MAPs over a long period of time. When the muscle tension fell, there were many slow reactions, and even some failures to respond. It was hypothesized that the initial spurt of good performance and high muscle tension was followed by a period of disinterest as the task became boring. Accordingly, the experimenters devised a gadget to keep the subject informed regarding his state of alertness. As soon as the MAPs fell below a certain level, a warning red light flashed, indicating that his alertness and the consequent performance level were beginning to show changes.

If muscle tension is actually a form of set, as many studies show, investigators have a fairly accurate means of obtaining some indication of subsequent performance. To be sure, the results of investigations demonstrate that changes in MAP closely parallel variations in set. Furthermore, conditions known to contribute to the subject's set such as the regularity of the foreperiod and the use of a warning signal also act to increase MAPs. Boredom and drowsiness operate in an opposite manner. Probably the primary difficulty in using muscle tension as a form of set occurs when the experimenter has failed to consider other factors that may have brought about changes in muscular tension. While it may be accurate to state that rises in MAPs accompany heightened concentration and alertness, it does not necessarily follow that high muscle tension in a given person is the product of his set. In the pages to follow, the reader will see how many different conditions produce heightened muscle tension. Among these, the subject's level of motivation is extremely important.

Motivation

Lewin (1955) has postulated that, if a person undertakes a task with a definite goal and is not allowed to complete it, the muscle tension remains undischarged until the goal has somehow been reached. Using the EMG technique, Smith (1953) set up an experiment to learn something about the nature of this tension. Four drawings were presented to subjects as mirror-tracing tasks, while MAPs were obtained from the forehead, neck, chin, and the extensors of both forearms. Half of the tasks were interrupted; the others were completed. The decrease in MAPs tended to be greater after completion than after interruption. In addition, the subjects who showed the greatest rise in MAP while drawing were most likely to maintain this tension when interrupted.

Repeating Smith's procedure, Bartoshuk (1955a) obtained results that were in the same direction but were not significant. Bartoshuk felt that the difference in the two studies was due to the greater motivation of Smith's subjects. As a result they exhibited a greater tendency toward increased tension when interrupted. It is also conceivable that the tension that was so important to Lewin's hypothesis is not evident in the skeletal muscular system. Much of the usage of the term "tension" is rather vague and may or may not have reference to what is being discussed here as muscle tension.

The possibility that the high level of muscle tension occurring after interruption might be the somatic basis of the Zeigarnik effect was tested by Forrest (1959). As predicted by the Zeigarnik effect, task-oriented subjects remembered more of the interrupted mirror-drawing tasks; while the ego-oriented subjects showed a reversal, having a greater recall of the completed tasks. With both groups, however, higher MAP levels (active arm) occurred after interruption than after completion. Consequently, Forrest concluded that increased tension was not a necessary concomitant of enhanced recall, and that in his study, at least, increased MAPs were merely the result of the sudden restraint of a skeletal movement.

While the Zeigarnik effect has not been found related to muscle tension, Reuder (1956) has indicated that there are differences between the EMGs of task-oriented and ego-oriented subjects. The task-oriented subjects exhibited higher forearm MAPs on difficult problems than on easy ones. The reverse occurred with ego-oriented subjects, who responded to the easy problems with elevated MAPs. Explaining the results in terms of level of aspiration theory, Reuder stated that the task-oriented subjects worked as hard as the problem demanded, with minimal worry regarding the success or failure of their work. Ego-oriented subjects, on the other hand, being much more concerned with success, put their greatest effort into the easy problems in order to make certain they did not fail.

By manipulating aspiration levels in subjects, Leshner (1961) related them to MAPs in the biceps and the forearm. To begin with, MAPs increased when statements of aspiration were made. During the solution of mental problems those subjects who stated realistic aspirations and failed showed a greater rate of tension increase than those who failed but whose aspirations were unrealistic. This seemed to indicate that failure caused greater effort, while success resulted in less effort. For the subjects who succeeded, higher MAPs accompanied unrealistic as opposed to realistic aspirations. Here, the former subjects set a high goal level and may not have been prepared to meet it. The effects of failure and success upon MAPs are dependent upon whether or not an individual views his performance realistically.

Some investigators have noted a phenomenon called the EMG gradient—a progressive rise in muscle tension that starts with the initiation of a task and continues until the task is ended. Bartoshuk believes that the EMG gradient reflects an individual's level of motivation with regard to a given task. He has cited some evidence for the progressive increase in MAPs from some early studies of mental work, as well as from his own findings on the chin and active forearm during mirror tracing. Further confirmation has come from Malmo and Davis (1956). In addition, Bartoshuk (1955a) has shown that the slope of the EMG gradient recorded during mirror tracing bears a direct relationship to speed and accuracy of performance, two other indicators of motivation. Increasing the incentive was another factor that raised the EMG gradient. Pishkin and Wolfgang (1964) showed that monetary reward and mental activity during concept identification were related to EMG gradients in two inactive muscle groups (forearm flexors and extensors).

Bartoshuk (1956) reported that EMG gradients, obtained from the forehead of subjects listening to essays or stories, evinced their motivation. Such gradients were not observed in the EMGs from the forearm or the chin. Changes in the slope of the EMG gradients were hypothesized as being due either to the directional changes in the subject's motivation or to the intensity, or to a combination of the two. In another study EMG gradients were reported to vary with the subject's degree of interest while listening. So long as the subject was attending to the material, there was a continual rise of MAPs in the chin and the frontalis muscles. When he became bored or if the material were dull, MAPs began to fall (Smith, Malmo, & Shagass, 1954).

Although EMG gradients may be related to motivational level, Malmo (1965) has felt that they are part of a whole system of physiological activity necessary in maintaining an even level of attention for the entire duration of a task. While muscle tension shows progressive increases during a task, cortical activity is relatively constant. The assumption has been made that cortical neurons and circuits are more susceptible to adaptation or fatigue than the motor neurons. To keep activation level constant and to overcome the fatigue of cortical circuits, there must be increased activity in part of the arousal system. Consequently, rising gradients are produced in peripheral tonus. In a complex match-to-sample visual discrimination Vaughn and McDaniel (1969) noted a tonic neuromuscular adjustment of frontalis MAPs during performance, as Malmo would have predicted. At the same time, however, when an error was made, there were phasic shifts in activity that were similar to orienting reactions.

Bartoshuk, Alexander, and Kaswick (1966), in a further test of the meaning of EMG gradients, recorded tracings of the flexors and extensors of both forearms during pressure tracking with visual cues and while blindfolded. The results of their investigation were not in complete agreement with Malmo's arousal gradient hypothesis; for it was unclear to the experimenters how Malmo would have accounted for EMG gradients in the flexors but not in the extensors during visual tracking. Furthermore, it would be difficult for such a hypothesis to explain steeper gradients in the active than in the passive arm.

According to these investigations, carried out under different experimental conditions, the rela-tionship between muscle tension and motivation appears to be a significant one. In general, lack of motivation is associated with low muscle tension, while conditions that raise a subject's motivational level tend to bring about corresponding increases in muscle tension. As this relationship is studied more closely, similarities with previously discussed experiments become apparent; for attentiveness, increased effort, and a high motivational level all augment MAP activity. This is quite predictable, since the highly motivated subject seems to concentrate well and applies effort to the task at hand. In actuality, one cannot differentiate those effects on muscle tension that are due to motivation from the effects of effort and from set. Although somewhat artificial, such a division in this presentation was made for purposes of simplicity. For the most part, what one experimenter has discussed in terms of effort, another could have described as due to motivational level.

Success versus Failure

Directly related to studies on motivation are those concerned with success and failure. Clites (1936) found that, during successful work on a verbal problem from the Stanford-Binet, forearm MAPs were greater than during unsuccessful problem solving. Successful subjects showed a marked increase in MAPs as compared to a prior rest period; failing subjects, however, exhibited a constant low level of muscle tension. During the period following the mental work, the MAPs of failing subjects increased, while those of successful subjects subsided. Similarly, Eason and White (1961) showed that high scoring on a rotary tracking task was associated with increased EMG levels in the neck, trapezius, deltoid, and biceps muscles, as compared to low MAPs in subjects scoring poorly. Pishkin (1964) also found that MAPs in the forearm extensors were lower in the subjects who produced more errors while identifying concepts.

In a related study, Berry and R. C. Davis (1958) obtained MAPs from the masseter, frontalis, and forearm extensors, in three groups of subjects selected on the basis of their ability to learn nonsense syllables. The most successful performers exhibited high levels of MAPs in the head area during learning. As soon as subjects' responses were confirmed, tension dropped. When they were told that they had been wrong, their MAPs changed very little. Moderately successful learners were more like the failure group of Clites, displaying the lowest levels of muscular tension. When their responses were confirmed, they showed no change in MAPs; but once they had been corrected, there was a marked decrease in muscle tension. The greatest discrepancy between this investigation and the previous ones is found among the poor learners, who reacted like the successful group by showing a high EMG level during performance. Also, like the successful group, they responded to confirmation with a decrease in MAPs. When they were told they had made an error, however, there was a sizable increase in muscle tension. Because three groups of subjects were selected, rather than the two extremes of Clites' study, it is difficult to make direct comparisons of the two experiments.

Apparently, the subject's feelings regarding his performance are equally, if not more, important than the actual performance in determining subsequent EMG levels. Subjects who believed they had performed well on an ergographic task manifested a reduction in MAPs on later work, whereas those who failed showed elevated MAPs. Klein (1955) interpreted these results in terms of differences in effort that were applied to subsequent tasks. If, however, the subject was convinced that achieving success is hopeless, he might reduce his efforts, thereby producing smaller MAPs. Where there was less probability of success, the level of muscle tension (forearm flexors and biceps), as well as the rate of increase in muscle tension, was lower. Consequently, the expectation to succeed resulted in more muscle tension than the expectation to fail (Diggory, Klein, & Cohen, 1964).

Both task difficulty and the degree of success have been found to be important variables affecting MAP changes. For the most part high MAPs accompany success, while muscle tension remains low during failure. Furthermore, upon the successful completion of a task, MAPs drop rather than increase, as they do after failure. Perhaps even more crucial than actual success is the subject's feeling of having done well. Unfortunately, for experimental evaluation of these factors, one cannot really separate task difficulty from the frequency of success, as the latter is so dependent upon the former. R. C. Davis (1938) demonstrated this interdependence in his study of muscle tension while solving number-series problems. He reported that the important variable was the difficulty level, rather than actual failures or successes. However, the difficulty of a given problem was judged by the proportion of subjects who failed it. As the problems increased in difficulty, there was a corresponding rise in the MAPs in the forearm extensors and the sternocleidomastoid. Hadley (1941) found a similar relationship between forearm MAPs and difficulty of mathematical problems. In both studies, there must have been a concomitant increase in the incidence of failure. In a concept identification task Pishkin and Shurley (1968) indicated that the increase in frontalis muscle tension with increasing complexity was greater for a failure set than for the solvable conditions (see also Pishkin, Shurley, & Wolfgang, 1967). Shaw and Kline (1947) avoided some of the interdependence between task difficulty and failure by using an independent test of difficulty. When children tried to solve pregraded mental arithmetic problems, MAPs in the upper forearm rose as the problems became more difficult. Further, the more intelligent children exhibited the lowest EMG activity during performance and the subsequent rest. The investigators reasoned that the problems were probably less difficult for the brighter children.

In general, it has been found that subjects show higher MAPs while executing more difficult tasks. This is probably because the more difficult problems require greater effort and concentration. Eason and White (1961) related the increased tension found during a difficult tracking task to the amount of effort that the subjects were required to apply. Forrest (1958) associated difficulty with the length of the task and reported higher forearm MAPs with longer addition sums. Some of the subjects actually reported that a greater effort was made with the longer sums, except when they had been instructed to add at their own speed. The relationship is not a simple one, however, for not all subjects apply the same degree of effort to problems if the amount of ego involvement varies. (See the preceding section on motivation.)

The EMG Response As a Reflex

By demonstrating an involuntary increase in forearm MAPs less than 100 msec after the onset of an auditory stimulus, R. C. Davis (1935) showed that the EMG response displayed the characteristics of a reflex. Not only were instructions to inhibit the response ineffective but the subject's report regarding his intention to relax had almost no relationship to MAP activity, either before or after stimulation. While not subject to voluntary control, the response was definitely affected by previous conditions. Prior activity favored larger responses; previous inactivity produced smaller responses. In comparing the EMG reaction to a tendon reflex, Davis felt that the EMG response had a larger latency period and was more easily modified by stimulus repetition.

Later work on the EMG response revealed two components, which R. C. Davis (1948b) referred to as two discrete reactions. In response to a 500-Hz tone, there was a brief, sudden rise in forearm MAPs, followed by a more lasting reaction with lower amplitude. Only the initial reaction, Component a, was identified as a reflex and could be affected by such stimulus characteristics as intensity and repetition (see Davis, Buchwald, & Frankmann, 1955; Davis & Van Liere, 1949). In describing the EMG response as a reflex, certain likenesses to the startle pattern are brought to mind. In fact, Component a occurs at about the same time as the startle pattern reaches the arm. R. C. Davis, however, felt that the two were not identical, for they have different properties and Response a cannot be observed directly without the appropriate equipment.

The EMG response can be incurred by auditory stimuli, whether the subject has indicated that he heard anything or not. Recordings of MAPs from the forearm extensors, masseter, and the sternocleidomastoid revealed such a phenomenon, although the responses to unheard stimuli were generally smaller than those to more audible sounds. Other characteristics of the EMG response were unaltered by the low amplitude sounds (R. C. Davis, 1950).

More recently, Fjeld (1965) obtained MAPs from the forearm flexors in response to visual stimuli that subjects felt they could no longer perceive. The stimulus would appear either on the right or left and was presented at gradually changing levels of brightness. By pressing the appropriate key, the subject indicated the position of the stimulus. As the brightness level decreased, the proportion of correct MAP responses to correct overt responses increased. Apparently, when weakness of the stimulus made decisions difficult, muscle tension indicated the subject's accuracy better than his overt response.

Conditioning of Muscle Tension Responses

Because of its instantaneous, involuntary occurrence following a sudden stimulus, the EMG response has been compared to a reflex. Moreover, like a reflex, it can be affected by previous conditions and can occur without the subject's realizing that a stimulus has been introduced. One would further expect such a response to show the properties of conditioning. This is indeed the case, for sufficient evidence has been collected from many sources to warrant the conclusion that MAPs can be conditioned to a variety of stimuli. With light as the conditioned stimulus (CS) and shock as the unconditioned stimulus (UCS), Hilden (1937) conditioned an EMG response that had a latency approximately the same as an overt hand withdrawal but lasted much longer than the overtly measured conditioned response (CR). The progressive increase in the magnitude of the MAPs prior to the appearance of the overt response indicated the presence of conditioning, while the reverse was witnessed during the extinction process. R. C. Davis (1950) also suggested the involvement of a conditioning process. He observed that, after repeated trials, the MAP increments which normally precede and accompany an overt response tended to creep forward in time toward the initiation of the stimulus (warning signal) and the beginning of the overt response. He reasoned that this might have been a CR in an incomplete form.

To discover if an EMG response in the masseters and forearm extensors could be conditioned when no overt response was involved, Van Liere (1953) presented two different tones, one as the CS and one as the UCS, for 25 trials to an experimental group. The control group heard only the one tone, CS, for 25 trials. Although both groups initially responded with a rise in MAPs, on subsequent trials the experimental group showed a significantly greater amplitude of response to the CS than did the control group. In addition, there was evidence of a facilitative effect by the CS on the amplitude of the response to the UCS. Thus some kind of conditioning process was occurring in the skeletal muscles.

Paired auditory stimuli were also employed in an experiment modeled on the Pavlovian paradigm. The instructions were for the subject to give a key-pressing response with one hand if the tone were high pitched, and with the other if it were low pitched. While a warning sound preceded the high pitched tone, the subject did not expect this warning sound before the low pitched tone. Actually, the latter tone was preceded by a low level, white noise (CS). The CS did, in fact, elicit MAPs in the region of the forearm extensors (Fink, 1954).

In a somewhat different study of conditioning, Kimmel and Davidov (1967) gave their subjects either paired light and shock with a 5 sec interstimulus interval, or unpaired light and shock. Although there was evidence of galvanic skin response (GSR) conditioning, there was no difference in the frequency of EMG changes (forearm extensors) between the two groups. The failure to obtain evidence of EMG conditioning was felt to be due to the fact that the CS-UCS interval should have been closer to .5 sec. Furthermore, studies such as Fink's (1954), that have reported EMG conditioning, used an instructed voluntary response as the unconditioned response. This has led the investigators to question the effectiveness of electric shock in conditioning muscular responses. Obrist (1968), however, was able to demonstrate an increase in EMG activity from three different muscle groups (neck, chin, and forearm flexors) during classical aversive conditioning, when a 1 sec interstimulus interval was utilized. With a 7 sec interstimulus interval, bursts of EMG activity were attenuated.

Using an adaptation of Humphrey's guessing paradigm, Gelber (1957) brought out further evidence for the conditioning of MAPs. Accompanying the acquisition of an overt hand-pressing response, there was a general increase in MAPs of the forearm extensors, with a reduction in muscular activity during extinction. A similar trend was shown for the left gastrocnemius and the forehead muscles. Additional confirmation developed from recording MAPs from the sternocleidomastoid during eyelid conditioning. In this experiment Runquist and Spence (1959) showed a high positive correlation between the EMG response and performance during conditioning.

Fink and R. C. Davis (1951) demonstrated that EMG responses tend to accompany stimulus generalization gradients in the same manner as overt responses. As the duration of the stimulus sound varied from that of the practice tone, MAPs in the forearm extensors gradually decreased in amplitude.

These experiments and others seem to be sufficient evidence that MAP responses undergo classical conditioning. After repeated trials they occur in response to the CS with greater regularity and increased magnitude; moreover, they display a generalization gradient and extinction. No reports on the use of operant conditioning with MAPs have appeared so far. Some investigators, though, have been convinced that the operant conditioning of GSRs is actually brought about by muscle tension changes (see Edelman, 1970). Rice's (1966) findings have not supported this hypothesis, and he feels that a skeletal response, which frequently precedes alteration in skin conductance, is not required in operant GSR conditioning. This was shown by recording MAPs from the forearm during GSR conditioning, which was reinforced with a white light. Similar studies by Kimmel and his associates have provided further evidence that the GSR can be operantly conditioned in the absence of somatic mediation (Kimmel & Davidov, 1967; Kimmel & Sternthal, 1967; Van Twyer & Kimmel, 1966).

Time-Error Effects

In addition to studies of their likeness to reflexes, MAP responses have been studied in connection with the time-error effect. When two stimuli are presented successively in time and compared with one another, there is a tendency to over- or underestimate the second response in relation to the first (Underwood, 1949). It has been suggested that the error in judgment is caused by an occurrence in the time intervening between the two stimuli. The concept of a stimulus trace has been invoked to explain the phenomenon. R. C. Davis (1952) believed the trace to be a process aroused by the stimulus and lasting a few seconds after it. Moreover, he thought that it might be represented physiologically by the EMG response.

In a study of trace effects Payne and R. C. Davis (1940) used a fixed time interval between lifting each of a pair of weights and explored the relationship between the judgments expressed and the level of MAPs in the active arm. They observed an association between the ratio of MAPs recorded during pairs of lifts and the judgments that were made. When the muscular response was greater to the second weight than to the first, there was also a judgment that the second weight was "heavier." The muscular response to the second weight was less than the response to the first, in cases when the second weight was judged "lighter."

Freeman and Sharp (1941) claimed that judgments of comparison were not a function of both weights but were related to EMG changes occurring between the first and second weight lifting. After lifting the weight, MAPs in the active arm (biceps) decayed in a cyclical manner, corresponding to the general course of the time-error function. When the interval between the two lifts was as short as 4 sec, there was an increase in muscle tension and a preponderance of lighter judgments. As the interval increased in length from 8 to 30 sec, the MAPs decreased, with a tendency toward heavier judgments. Further lengthening up to 60 sec led to a gradual increase in MAPs toward the level observed before the first lifting. There was a concomitant diminution of the negative time-error (heavier judgments).

The time-error function has also been tested with auditory stimuli given in successive pairs. Under various conditions the subject was required to press a key with the right or left hand to indicate whether the second stimulus was stronger or weaker than the first. It was found that the percentage of judgments of strong or weak was related to the difference in the activity of the arms (forearm extensors) just before the second tone was delivered. The temporal course of excitation was similar to that usually attributed to the stimulus trace,

except that it was less bound to the stimulus. It tended to vary with the setting factors (i.e., simple versus choice reaction, regularity versus irregularity of the time interval between stimuli, and duration of the first stimulus) (R. C. Davis, 1952).

Thus some experimenters have attempted to explain the time-error function by demonstrating the existence of a muscular arousal mechanism that behaves very much like a stimulus trace. Evidence, which has come from comparative judgments of auditory stimuli and of weights, suggests that error in judgment may be due either to the ratio of MAPs following the two stimuli or to certain changes taking place between the occurrence of stimuli.

Imagination and Thought

Very early work on EMG activity indicated that MAPs occur during thought processes. According to the peripheral theory of thinking, all mental phenomena are related in some way to the activity of the skeletal musculature. Some adherants of this theory have insisted that thought processes are identified primarily with responses of the speech mechanisms. Accordingly, when someone is thinking, he is actually "talking to himself," and some activity is centered around the vocal organs. E. Jacobson (1931a) has obtained evidence that the speech musculature is involved in certain mental processes concerned with words; however, his view of the motor theory is much broader, suggesting that thinking is based upon implicit muscular contractions involving various muscle groups.

Max (1935) was concerned with the speech mechanisms involved in thinking and hypothesized that MAPs would be present not only during the solution of thought problems but during all of a person's conscious moments. By studying the hands of deaf mutes, Max hoped to take advantage of the fact that all of their speech originated in their fingers. He reasoned that MAPs from the hands would be present in their dreams. During the time that both normal and deaf subjects were falling asleep, MAPs from the arms decreased gradually. When MAPs reappeared in the arm and finger muscles, the subjects were wakened and reported that they had been dreaming. Dreaming was associated with hand MAPs in the deaf mutes but not in the normal subjects. Further evidence for a link between thinking in deaf mutes and motor activity of the hands came from investigations of the solution of abstract problems. During problem solving, MAPs in the arms occurred in 84% of the deaf mutes and in only 31% of the normal subjects (Max, 1937). Because of the difficulty that Max had in obtaining vocal organ records, the results of the study cannot be generalized to the thought processes of normal subjects. Using rapid eye movements, a more recent and reliable index of dreaming, Stoyva (1965) was able to demonstrate increased finger activity in deaf subjects during dreams. Contrary to Max's findings, however, there were no significant differences between deaf and hearing subjects.

In a further attempt to substantiate a motor theory of thinking, E. Jacobson (1932) tried to show that the processes of thought, reasoning, and ideation were not only dependent upon motor responses, but that without such motor responses none of these processes could occur. In a series of experiments, E. Jacobson (1930a, 1930b, 1930d) recorded MAPs during specific acts of imagination. For example, if a subject imagined that he was bending his right forearm, muscle tension increased in the right biceps but not in any other muscles. Similar results were obtained by Max (1937). During visual imagination, muscular activity shifted to the ocular muscles (E. Jacobson, 1930c). Imagination failed to occur when the subject was completely relaxed, a fact felt to be evidence that muscular excitation is essential for mental activity.

To determine the extent to which imagination depended upon muscular movement, E. Jacobson (1931b) recorded EMGs from subjects who had lost a body part by total amputation. Whereas the normal subject's imagination of limb movement involved the presence of MAPs in that area and no other, for the amputee there were "substitute contractions." This meant that imagining the movement of an amputated right arm could result in increased muscle tension in the left arm or in some other part of the body.

Using studies of imagined movement, Shaw (1938) provided support for a motor theory of thinking, but he did not find that EMG activity was confined to the specific muscles involved in an imagined act. Although the greatest increase in tension appeared over the active member, MAPs

occurred simultaneously in almost every area tested. This may be partially explained by the fact that Shaw's subjects had not been trained to relax as Jacobson's had.

Shaw (1940) also revealed a correspondence between the action potential in the forearm and the size of the imagined load. For both real and imagined weight lifting there was a linear increase in MAPs as the weights became heavier. Furthermore, higher MAP activity was associated with reports of more vivid images. Within the limits of the study, repetition had very little effect on muscular activity during imagination.

Considered as a whole, these studies indicate that MAPs do occur during thinking. They are not confined to the vocal mechanism, as some investigators have suggested, but can occur in almost any part of the body.

Sleep and Dreaming

Some experimenters tend to utilize changes in muscle tension as a signal that a dream is about to commence (Kales, Hoedemaker, Jacobson, & Lichtenstein, 1964). There is sufficient evidence that a decrease in tension characteristically occurs in some muscles just prior to, or concomitant with, the onset of a rapid eye movement (REM) phase, that phase of sleep most frequently associated with dreaming. Berger (1961) reported a rapid decrease in tension of the extrinsic laryngeal muscles just before subjects passed from non-rapid eye movement (N-REM) sleep to the REM phase. During REM sleep the diminished muscle tone was maintained. A. Jacobson, Kales, Lehmann, and Hoedemaker (1964) reaffirmed this pattern of muscle tension in most of the head and neck muscles, but the trunk and limbs of the body were found to react differently. Throughout the night the trunk and limb muscles exhibited a stable level of tonic activity, with no change associated with the REM phase.

In an attempt to gain an understanding of the pre-REM period of muscle relaxation in the head and neck region, Larson and Foulkes (1969) awakened their subjects during different phases of N-REM sleep. As a result, they discovered that pre-REM EMG suppression (under the chin) was accompanied by lower dream frequency and lower Dreamlike Fantasy Scale ratings than the preceding period of high EMG N-REM sleep. Furthermore, there seemed to be additional evidence of a deepening of sleep during EMG suppression; for it was more difficult to awaken the subject at such times. In order to explain this inhibition of muscle tone, the investigators have hypothesized that a momentary deepening of sleep may serve to protect individuals from wakefulness prior to the REM phase. A deep phase of sleep may thus allow one to experience intense mental and autonomic activity, which are otherwise incompatible with sleep.

The possibility that variations in sleeping EMG levels bear some relationship to differences in dream reports has been suggested by Aarons' (1968) investigation. On the basis of psychological test scores an A ("active") and a P ("passive") group of subjects were obtained. As compared with the P group, the A group exhibited greater verbal fluency, more idiosyncratic and perceptual types of responses in free word association, and a greater preference for positive evaluative responses in binary choice. With the exception of muscle tension under the chin, the A group exhibited more EMG activity (frontalis and one of the forearm extensor muscles) while awake than the P group. During sleep, however, there was a reversal; for then the P group exhibited greater activity. Differences between A and P groups lead one to suspect, as Aarons suggests, that the dream content would be quite different for the two groups. If this proves to be true, the implications of such a study are indeed far-reaching.

There is sufficient evidence of a definite pattern of muscle tension during sleep. Moreover, the onset of dreaming is marked by a clear reduction in tension in the head and neck area. As more information is gathered about the phenomenon of sleep, perhaps more will be learned about the relationship between skeletal muscle activity and the actual meaning and content of dreams.

ELECTROMYOGRAPHIC STUDIES RELATING TO PERSONALITY THEORY

Personality Characteristics

Since the early part of the twentieth century, various writers have suggested a relationship between muscle tension and certain aspects of personality. In general, the individual with low muscle tension has been found to approach situations in a very calm and deliberate manner. In contrast, the highly tense person is characterized by more hyperactive, excitable behavior (see Goldstein, 1964b). For the most part these results have come from observations of indirect and somewhat unreliable means of recording muscle tension. Using a factor estimate of general muscle tension obtained from MAPs of 16 different muscle groups, Balshan (1962) showed that tension during an auditory stimulus was negatively correlated with the Guilford-Zimmerman trait of restraint and positively correlated with general activity. This would seem to indicate that the person with heightened muscle tension is somewhat impulsive and happy-go-lucky, with a rather high energy level. There was no relationship with any of the other Guilford-Zimmerman temperaments.

On the basis of patterns of muscle tension (forearm flexors) during the solution of mental arithmetic problems, Harvey (1966) classified students into three groups. Group one displayed an initial increase in activity, which leveled off for the balance of the period, while the second group was characterized by bursts of activity interspersed with periods of reduced activity. A third group, which displayed a consistent increase in activity throughout measurement, was characterized as psychologically rigid on the Gough-Sanford Scale.

Using an index of general muscle tension based on the sum of standard scores for seven widely separated muscles (frontalis, trapezius, neck extensors[4], biceps, forearm flexors, quadriceps, and gastrocnemius), Shipman, Oken, Goldstein, Grinker, and Heath (1964) found an unexpected relationship between MAPs and personality. Those subjects whose EMGs during rest and stressful interviews were elevated tended to be emotionally stable and free from anxiety, with a clear sense of personal limits and good self-control. These results, which are contrary to most theoretical thinking and to earlier investigations, probably result from the selection of subjects, who were all from a psychiatric population in which intense depression and acute

---

[4]Muscles at the back of the neck, more specifically referred to as the splenius muscles.

illness were major factors. Among these highly depressed patients, the individuals who were in better control of their emotions were more tense than patients with low emotional stability. The authors suggested that the element of control was expressed through the skeletal muscles.

A further attempt to relate differences in muscle tension to personality traits was made by Martin (1958a, 1958b). She selected college students on the basis of extreme scores on a questionnaire that divided them into the following four groups: introverted neurotics, extraverted neurotics, introverted normal subjects, and extraverted normal subjects. None of these categories was significantly related to MAPs obtained from the frontalis and the forearm extensors. Possibly, the range in the college population was not extreme enough to show these differences.

There is some indication that a given individual has a characteristic pattern of muscle reaction and will respond to a variety of conditions with a maximal level of response in the same muscle (response specificity); he will also maintain a constant hierarchy of tension levels in different muscle groups (response stereotypy). Such an idiosyncratic pattern of response was maintained fairly well by seven different muscle groups during conditions of affect arousal, attempts at self-control, a nonstressful interview, and rest. In addition, when autonomic reactions of heart rate and systolic and diastolic blood pressure were analyzed, individuals were further categorized on the basis of a tendency to show a heightened response of either the autonomic nervous system or the skeletal muscular system (Goldstein, Grinker, Heath, Oken, & Shipman, 1964).

Consistent with these findings is Kempe's (1956) report of personality types differentiated on the basis of their primary response in one of these physiological systems. Recordings of the GSR, heart rate, respiration rate, and MAPs from the masseter, sternocleidomastoid, and forearm extensors, were taken during sensory stimulation and in response to pictures similar to those used in the Thematic Apperception Test. On the basis of intercorrelations obtained from 12 physiological measures and 26 personality test items, Kempe extracted clusters of significant intercorrelations. This led to a description of the skeletal muscular responder as one who remains aloof from others, denies emotion, and approaches life in an intellectual, unfeeling manner. In contrast, the autonomic responder is prone to worry a great deal, is more emotionally sensitive, and is highly concerned with his acceptance by others.

Experimental studies generally support the hypothesis that there are distinct differences in muscle tension among individuals, and that these differences tend to be maintained under varied conditions. Furthermore, although the results are not clear-cut, certain traits have been associated with high muscle tension. For the most part, excessive MAP activity has been found in the subject who is extremely responsive to a variety of stimuli. This individual is able to express his emotions freely and to act out his feelings.

Muscle Tension As Related to Psychopathology

Among psychologically maladjusted groups, frequent reports have been made of exaggerated skeletal muscular responses. Such individuals have stated that they feel "fidgety," "uncomfortable," and "tense." Reusch, Cobb, and Finesinger (1941) and Reusch and Finesinger (1943) observed that subjects with feelings of body tension had difficulty relaxing (as indicated by elevated MAPs of the forearm flexors and extensors) during the intervals between a simple hand exercise. These symptoms have been found by Lundervold (1952) to be more characteristic of women than of men. While some relaxation was possible, it could be accomplished only in a few positions. In addition, while typewriting, those subjects who had been judged as tense used more muscles to perform the activity and used them in a less efficient manner (Lundervold, 1951). Because EMG recordings were used originally to make judgments of the subjects' tension levels, there is some circularity to Lundervold's reasoning.

E. Jacobson (1934, 1938) believes that the inability to relax is responsible for the persistence of the mental state, and the excessive imagination and emotions of many neurotic and hypertense subjects. By constant practice in the contraction and relaxation of various muscle groups in response to a signal, Jacobson trained subjects to relax, thereby reducing MAPs and accompanying mental symptoms.

In addition to a difficulty in relaxation, many neurotics are characterized by persistent conflicts. Hoshiko and Grandstaff (1967) have provided evidence of some fairly definite trends in MAPs in conflict situations. Accompanying frequent conflicts is a tendency to respond to stress with extreme skeletal muscular reactions. The picture is further complicated by their tendency to perceive a number of situations as potentially stressful. For example, during a simple voluntary motor task in which a subject was required to push a button on the tenth beat of a metronome, MAPs in the inactive arm of the patients were higher than in normal control subjects. Also, MAP increases were greater during the anticipation of the pressing response, and then again after the response was made (Davidowitz, Brown-Meyers, Kohn, Welch, & Hayes, 1955).

Whether the stress is real or imagined, there is evidence that some of the physiological reactions are the same. Barber and Hahn (1964) found that increased frontalis muscle tension, resulting from a cold pressor stimulus, could be produced in a group instructed to imagine that they were receiving this pain-producing stimulus. Hypnosis had similar effects on muscle tension, in marked contrast to a group given an innocuous stimulus. Similarly, though the results were not significant, there was a consistent tendency for the imagination of fearful scenes to produce more muscle activity (frontalis) than neutral scenes (Grossberg & Wilson, 1968). Thus we perceive the neurotic, with his imagined fears and pains, as being in a constant state of heightened muscle tension.

From a series of investigations, Malmo, Shagass, Belanger, and Smith (1951) concluded that psychoneurotics can be characterized by some disturbance in motor function, perhaps as a result of a defect in the motor mechanism. They hypothesized that this defect would become apparent in almost any type of stress. Support for the hypothesis has come from situations involving mirror drawing, speeded size discrimination, and pain stimulation (Malmo, Shagass, & J. F. Davis, 1951). In response to all three stressors, psychotic and neurotic patients showed higher EMG reactions in the forearm flexors and

the neck than a comparable group of nonpatients. Evidence for an exaggerated muscle response was also found with other measures of motor activity (Malmo, Shagass, Belanger, & Smith, 1951). Malmo believes that the large amount of energy that the psychoneurotic expends via the musculature during stress may offer some explanation for the clinical complaints of fatigue and tension.

In an investigation by Martin (1956), MAP recordings of the frontalis and forearm extensors revealed no difference between neurotics and normal subjects at rest. It was found that dysthymics (anxious, depressed, or obsessional patients) were more tense than hysterics, while psychotics (schizophrenics in early stages of illness) showed higher EMG responses than normals. Among the various stress situations, only the requirement of responding to questions increased forearm MAPs of the neurotic group. The failure to obtain results more like those of Malmo may be partially due to sampling differences.

Anxiety   One frequently finds symptoms of anxiety accompanying excessive skeletal muscular responses. When a Hardy-Wolff pain stimulator was applied, patients with major complaints of anxiety exhibited greater physiological responses in the autonomic and skeletal muscular systems than normal control subjects or groups of patients in whom anxiety was either absent or was a minor symptom. Increased responsiveness was particularly evident among various measures of motor function, including MAPs from the neck area. As a result of this investigation and others, Malmo and Shagass (1949a) concluded that anxiety is to be associated with a "heightened state of expectation," reflected primarily in the skeletal muscular system. J. G. L. Williams and B. Williams (1967) provided evidence of this increased muscular activity when they compared the responses of anxious female psychiatric patients with those of normal female subjects. During delayed auditory feedback, EMGs of the forearm extensors were significantly higher among the patients.

It has been hypothesized by Brandt and Fenz (1969) that manifest anxiety is composed of a general factor of anxiety, as well as a specific factor involving muscle tension. By means of a modification of the Taylor Manifest Anxiety Scale, subjects were divided into two groups: one displaying symptoms of striated muscle activity and another characterized by autonomic arousal. Contrary to expectations, there were no significant differences with regard to EMG reactions to a noise stimulus or to the threat of shock. It should be noted, however, that recordings were taken only from the frontalis muscle.

Using a 1000-Hz tone lasting 3 sec, Malmo, Shagass, and J. F. Davis (1950) compared physiological responses in normal subjects and in severely anxious psychoneurotics. The initial startle reaction in the 0.2 sec following the sound was very similar for the forearm extensors in the two groups. The control subjects, however, quickly returned to their prior levels of tension, while the patients responded with a further increase in muscle tension, which lasted for the duration of the stimulus. Apparently, their peak response occurred at a later point in time than that of the control group.

Using a noise stimulus of 0.125-sec duration presented at 1-min intervals, J. F. Davis, Malmo, and Shagass (1954) again found the greatest amount of muscular activity among anxiety-state neurotics. Here it was possible to demonstrate larger initial responses to the stimulus, but the most significant differences occurred in the forearm extensors 0.4 sec after the stimulus, at a time when the responses of the control group had almost subsided. Muscle action potentials in the masseter and the sternocleidomastoid did not differentiate between groups. In conclusion, the authors stated that the after-response was a better discriminator between patients and control subjects than the immediate response. In a subsequent study Bartoshuk (1959) showed that the magnitude and habituation rate of EMG after-responses was significantly related to prior activation level (as inferred from the combined measures of EMG prelevels and EEG alpha amplitudes). When psychoneurotics were categorized on the basis of EEG-activation level, only those with low alpha amplitudes exhibited large EMG after-responses. During the experiment these psychoneurotics showed behavioral symptoms of fear and apprehensiveness.

In a study of normal women students, the present writer (Balshan, 1962) selected subjects on the basis of extreme scores on both the Freeman and Taylor Manifest Anxiety Scales. The two resulting groups of subjects were compared during a resting state and in response to 1 min of white noise. In none of the 16 muscle groups from which EMGs were taken was there a significant difference between subjects during the resting state. During the auditory stimulus, however, the more anxious group responded with significantly greater activity in 9 of the muscle groups. The autonomic measures that were used did not discriminate between the anxious and nonanxious subjects. By repeating the procedure with 7 EMG recordings on a group of normal women and chronically anxious women patients, most of the results of the earlier study were substantiated (Goldstein 1964a). This time, however, the autonomic measures revealed differences between the two groups of subjects, both at rest and during the white-noise stimulus. It was concluded that, as far as the skeletal muscular system is concerned, measurement during some form of stress discriminates better between anxious and nonanxious subjects than does measurement at rest.

Evidence of a somewhat contradictory nature was introduced by Sainsbury and Gibson (1954), who found elevated MAPs in the frontalis and forearm extensors of anxious patients during a resting state. On the basis of high muscle tension observed in these two widely separated areas, the investigators concluded that the muscle tension increase probably included all of the body musculature (a possible, but not necessary, conclusion). A serious difficulty arises from the fact that the patient group was selected originally on the basis of signs of tension, as well as symptoms of anxiety. In addition, adequate measures to eliminate anxiety from the experimental situation may not have been made. To ascertain that the subjects are responding at resting levels, it is necessary to see that the experimental situation is relatively free from stress. While this is not always possible, anxiety sometimes is alleviated by having the subject visit the laboratory prior to the actual experiment. Kelly, Brown, and Shaffer (1970) found no differences between anxious patients and normal subjects during either rest or experimental stress (mental arithmetic during harassment), but here again only one muscle group (forearm extensors) was measured.

In studies of anxiety, varying results have been obtained, often because of the difficulties involved in defining anxiety itself. Characteristically, experimenters have depended upon some psychological test of anxiety or the diagnoses of various experts (which are notoriously contradictory). In one investigation (Malmstrom, 1968) the Zuckerman Affect Adjective Check List (AACL) and the Nowlis Mood Adjective Check List (MCL) were utilized together. During a 12 min motion picture and during radio static noise, frontalis muscle tension was found to correlate positively with the AACL but negatively with the MCL. Apparently these two scales have tapped different aspects of the psychophysiological state of anxiety, as do numerous tests of anxiety.

Disorders associated with overt unresponsiveness The relationship between high muscle tension and hyperactive disorders such as anxiety has been discussed in the literature for some time (Goldstein, 1964b). It has been expected that the converse relationship also exists: more withdrawn individuals, showing little overt emotionality, would be physiologically unresponsive. To test this hypothesis, Goldstein (1965) recorded various physiological reactions (including EMGs from seven muscle groups) in different types of patients, all in acute stages of illness. During resting conditions and in response to a white noise, the psychiatric patients were at least as reactive as normal subjects in all areas from which MAPs were recorded, despite the apparent lack of behavioral response in some patients. In a comparison of psychotics, neurotics, character-disordered patients, and normal subjects, the psychotics (primarily schizophrenics) showed the highest levels of response, particularly with regard to the skeletal muscles (sternocleidomastoid, frontalis, biceps, and forearm extensors), during the auditory stimulus. The neurotic patients characteristically showed a slightly elevated EMG response to the noise, with levels somewhat higher than normal control subjects (although only frontalis MAPs were significantly different).

While many investigators have shown that the neurotic, rather than the psychotic, is the most physiologically reactive, this is generally due to the anxiety level of the neurotics. In this study (Goldstein, 1965) the anxiety of the two groups was quite similar, since they were matched in advance on the basis of anxiety test scores. It is particularly interesting that the individuals with character disorders responded at MAP levels that were equivalent to those of normal subjects. In contrast to the belief that schizophrenics are unreactive, Malmo and Shagass (1949a) demonstrated that these patients had exaggerated EMG neck reactions to pain. During rest Whatmore and Ellis (1958) found higher MAPs in the forehead, jaw, forearm, and leg muscles of schizophrenics than in a comparable group of normal subjects. The investigators hypothesized that disturbances in thinking and emotion, which are typical of the schizophrenic, might stem directly from a hyperactive motor system.

Because the degree of retardation is so extreme in the chronic schizophrenic, there was reason to believe that his physiological reactivity was correspondingly low. The research of Malmo, Shagass, and J. F. Davis (1951) and Malmo, Shagass, and Smith (1951) would seem to indicate that this is not true. In fact, the level of tension in the forearm flexors and in the neck of the schizophrenic during speeded size-discrimination and mirror drawing was at least as high as other psychiatric patients and higher than normal control subjects. When the necessary muscular response was a purposive act such as pressing a button in response to pain the schizophrenic found it difficult to react adequately. Presumably, while his emotional (physiological) responses were intact, voluntary reactions were subject to some loss.

In another study of chronic schizophrenics, 10 out of 13 showed some failure to suppress muscle tension during REM sleep, either in terms of very frequent bursts of EMG or sustained EMG activity during REM periods. This raised the question of some disturbance of the motor inhibitory component of REM sleep in schizophrenics (Gulevich, Dement, & Zarcone, 1967).

Rather than investigating schizophrenia as an entity, Fenz and Velner (1970) classified their patients either as acute or chronic on the basis of their premorbid level of development (Phillips Scale). In addition to other physiological measures, frontalis MAPs were recorded at rest and in response to intense audio and visual stimuli. In general, the two schizophrenic groups did not differ significantly among themselves with regard to muscle tension, but they did exhibit higher EMG responses than a normal control group. Furthermore, the patient groups showed greater muscle potential increases from rest to the stress situation.

Although hallucinatory behavior is common among schizophrenics, very little is known about the accompanying psychophysiological changes. Because of numerous difficulties involved in gathering data, McGuigan (1966) finally limited his sample to a single, cooperative psychotic patient. Although limited in their generality, his results at least give us some suggestions regarding the relationship between muscle tension and hallucinations. Immediately prior to the reported auditory hallucinations, there were significant increases in chin MAPs, with slight increases in tongue MAPs and sound production. At the same time, there were no EMG changes in the arm, indicating that the responses may be limited to the speech musculature. Whether or not covert oral behavior is related to hallucinations in a causal fashion remains to be seen.

Another maladjustive disorder, in which we generally see a decline in overt responsiveness, is depression. Although the group of depressed patients selected by Whatmore and Ellis (1959) was retarded to the point of being either mute or almost mute, their EMG responses (jaw, forehead, forearm, and leg) during relaxation were higher than in the control group. A second group of depressed patients with less visible signs of retardation was also characterized by exaggerated EMG activity, although MAPs were not so high as those in the first group. During psychiatric treatment with five of the retarded patients, muscular activity was found to drop. Some time after treatment, during a period of apparent excellent health, prior to relapse, significant increases in MAP levels occurred in the retarded patients, indicating that this is a general characteristic of the depressed person (Whatmore & Ellis, 1962).

Utilizing Beck's Depression Inventory (BDI) to measure degree of depression, Rimon, Stenback, and Hahmar (1966) recorded resting levels of muscle tension in the frontalis, masseter, forearm, and leg. Not only were there differences among the various muscles, but there were sex differences, as well. The slightly depressed women exhibited higher muscle tension levels than the more depressed women. Such an unexpected difference was felt by the investigators to have been due to the psychological tension produced in the women by a male physician. Among the males, greater EMG activity (frontalis and forearm) was more characteristic of deeply depressed patients. In contrast, the masseter muscle (associated by the authors with the wish to decide and concentrate) was more active among the slightly depressed patients of both sexes.

Because depression is so frequently accompanied by symptoms of anxiety, Goldstein (1965) compared depressed neurotic patients with a group of nondepressed neurotics of equivalent tested anxiety levels and a nonpatient sample. The depressed patients were differentiated by their autonomic responses and by their heightened MAPs (trapezius, frontalis, forearm extensors) in response to a white noise. The nondepressed neurotics and normals had similar physiological reactions and were less responsive than the depressed patients. It was concluded that the presence of a neurosis, by itself, or of some anxiety was not sufficient to account for the exaggerated physiological responses accompanying depression.

High muscle tension has been found to be prevalent among psychiatric patients, who not only react to stress with increased tension but perceive many situations as stressful. Among those patients for whom there is evidence of particularly extreme muscular activity are those with symptoms of anxiety. In addition, schizophrenics and depressives (groups once felt to be physiologically unresponsive) exhibit elevated MAPs. The fact that there is some lack of agreement about which psychiatric groups show the greatest amount of muscular disturbance is partially caused by the noncomparability of experimental conditions, the difficulty in pinning labels on patients, and the differences in chronicity of disorders.

Psychotherapy

The recording of skeletal muscular activity from various muscle groups during interview sessions enabled Malmo and his colleagues (F. H. Davis & Malmo, 1951; Shagass & Malmo, 1954) to study a patient intensively throughout the course of psychotherapy and to gain further knowledge about psychopathology in general. Typically, this method has involved multiple sessions in depth with a single patient. For example, one patient who was studied longitudinally displayed high EMG levels with a depressed mood, while low tension accompanied more cheerful mood ratings. Clinical improvement also was reflected in decreased MAPs.

Not only has this technique enabled the investigators to study the remarks of the patient objectively but it has provided information about the therapist as well. Malmo, Boag, and Smith (1957) discovered differential motor reactions to supportive versus threatening situations in both patients and in the examiner. MAPs in the speech muscles fell rapidly during a rest interval following praise, while they remained high after criticism. Neck muscle tension failed to discriminate between experimental conditions.

The reaction to verbal stimuli was tested in a somewhat different manner by Newman (1953). During the recording of MAPs from the temporal muscle[5], stimulating words were presented from Jung's list of "emotional" and neutral words. When a subject reacted to a word, a weak response elicited a few spikes, but a strong response resulted in the persistence of spike potentials for as long as the subject could concentrate or until another word was presented. This suggests that the emotional value of a word can be judged from the persistence of MAP spikes.

One of the more recent therapies which has been studied in relation to EMG work is that of systematic desensitization. A basic requirement of systematic desensitization is that the relaxation training, which is used, result in a reduction of physiological arousal. Three groups of subjects were studied on two separate occasions, one week apart.

[5]Muscle in the region of the temples of the head.

Each of the groups was given one of the following: (a) training in progressive relaxation; (b) hypnotic induction suggesting relaxation; (c) self-relaxation, which consisted of resting quietly. Both the hypnotic suggestion and the progressive relaxation resulted in decreased forearm muscle tension within one to two sessions, although the progressive relaxation was more effective in lowering tension (Paul, 1969). In another test of relaxation training, Mathews and Gelder (1969) found that frontalis muscle tension was significantly lower in response to instructions to relax, as compared with instructions to plan a new program at home.

In systematic desensitization a patient ranks a list of fear-evoking situations and is then trained to relax. During relaxation he is told to imagine first the mildest fear item on his list and so on up the hierarchy of more intense fears until there is no longer any subjective disturbance. Basic to this therapy is the assumption that the fearful scenes have produced more physiological arousal than neutral scenes. Grossberg and Wilson (1968) recorded frontalis muscle tension and other physiological variables during the imagining of a fearful and a neutral scene four times. While the fear scenes resulted in more muscle activity than the neutral scenes, these differences were not statistically significant. Apparently much can be learned about systematic desensitization, as well as various forms of therapy, by recording muscle tension during therapy sessions.

Symptom Specificity

While some maladjusted individuals react to stress by means of heightened muscle tension throughout the body, there are other persons who characteristically respond through a single muscle or group of muscles. The tendency for a given person to respond to a variety of stimuli, with the same maximal physiological response, has been referred to by Malmo, Shagass, and F. H. Davis (1950a, 1950b) as "symptom specificity." To cite an example, those patients with head, neck, or arm symptoms were found by Sainsbury and Gibson (1954) to have higher action potentials in the relevant muscle than subjects without such symptoms. In contrast, more generalized body symptoms, such as tremor or startle, were associated with significant increases of muscle activity in well-separated areas.

Wolff (1948) revealed sustained contractions of the skeletal muscles of the head and neck in certain individuals that bore a direct relationship to headaches and other head sensations. The pain nerve endings were stimulated by contractions that were identifiable by increased MAPs. Further pain was caused by reduction in the blood supply to the muscles. The headaches occurred most frequently during emotional tension, dissatisfaction, and anxiety, when the individual was poised for an action that did not take place. The subjective feeling was of stiffness and soreness radiating over the back of the head from the neck (Simons, Day, Goodell, & Wolff, 1943; Wolf & Wolff, 1953).

When subjected to a standard pain stimulus, psychiatric patients with head and neck complaints exhibited greater increases in MAPs recorded from those areas than did patients free of such complaints (Malmo & Shagass, 1949b; Malmo, Shagass, & F. H. Davis, 1950a). Similar MAP changes were observed during interview sessions when the examiner discussed critical material with headache-prone patients. There was a gradual increase in forehead tension, which was associated with the developing headache and was not necessarily accompanied by increased muscle tension in other areas. In fact, during the time headache symptoms were beginning, forearm tension actually declined (Malmo, Shagass, & F. H. Davis, 1950b). Periods of silence have also produced increases in muscle tension, while talking reduced the tension momentarily. Davis and Malmo (1951) observed that insulin therapy could be used to eliminate symptoms and reduce MAPs below the level associated with headaches.

Just as sustained contractions of the head muscles have been associated with headaches, so contractions of the trapezius, the lumbar sacro spinalis[6], and the hamstring muscles[7] play a role in the backache syndrome. Muscle action potential increases in these muscles have been shown by Holmes and Wolff (1950) to occur in situations of conflict, quiet, or during a threat to the individual's security.

[6]Longitudinal muscles running along the center of the back near the spine.

[7]Semitendinosus, biceps femoris, and semimembranosus.

Localized muscular contractions have also been observed in association with particular themes during interview sessions. When the discussion centered about hostility, increased forearm MAPs were noted. During a session concerned with sex, leg tension rose in two female patients. Shagass and Malmo (1954) believe these mechanisms to be unconscious because the impulses connected with the two themes have been repressed by conflict. In a sense, the increased muscle tension reflects a poor resolution of conflict within the individual (Malmo, Smith, & Kohlmeyer, 1956).

High EMG activity in symptomatic muscles has also been demonstrated among arthritics. Moos and Engel (1962) hypothesized that increased muscle tension in such individuals was related to the onset or to the course of their symptoms. Prior to an attack patients frequently reported pain and muscular rigidity. When compared with subjects characterized by essential hypertension, arthritics exhibited higher MAPs in their symptomatic muscles (the ones giving the greatest pain) during verbal learning but no increased responses in asymptomatic areas.

However, not all investigations have borne out these findings. In a comparison of individuals with rheumatoid arthritis and those with peptic ulcers, R. L. Williams and Krasnoff (1964) found very few differences in forearm EMG activity. They had hypothesized that individuals having such diverse attitudes toward their own bodies would show very different physiological patterns under stress. Following stress, muscle tension took longer to fall to resting levels in the rheumatoid arthritics than in the peptic ulcer subjects, giving limited support to their prediction. Following the administration of a word association test, Southworth (1958) demonstrated a longer persistance of trapezius MAPs in rheumatoid arthritics than in a group of peptic ulcer patients. No group differences were observed among frontalis MAPs, emphasizing the importance of selecting the appropriate muscle groups. Further results suggested that individuals who discharged emotional tension via the skeletal musculature were not so likely to express it by verbal means. Gottschalk, Serota, and Shapiro (1950) presented substantiating evidence that a decrease in muscle tension occurred when a patient's hostile impulses were expressed in a socially permissible manner. Conversely, the inhibition of aggression during the discussion of upsetting material led to increases in MAPs. Because no statistical evidence was presented, these results cannot be accepted unequivocally. As in the previous study, symptomatic muscle groups were not used. Instead, EMGs were recorded from the forearm flexors and extensors, the gastrocnemius, and the peroneal muscles.[8]

In one sense the development of various muscle symptoms can be viewed as an exaggeration of the idiosyncratic response pattern that frequently characterized a given individual. The previously discussed experiments have shown how a person can react to many different conditions with extremely high tension in one particular muscle. In addition, the greater the degree of stress, the greater the tension in the muscle. Extending the argument a step further, one can see how stress, continued over a long period of time, might lead to symptoms of pain in a given muscle.

MUSCLE CONTROL BY THE USE OF FEEDBACK MECHANISMS

Given impetus by the research of Basmajian and his associates, a relatively new role is developing for EMG. These researchers (Basmajian, 1963) have demonstrated fine conscious control of pathways to a single spinal neuron. Within 30 minutes most individuals in their sample were trained to fire single neurons, with active suppression of neighboring motor units. Since the twitch was triggered by one neuron, the motor unit response represented the minimal response possible in intact muscle. Once the skills were learned, however, they were retained after elimination of feedback. Furthermore, individuals could produce unique firing patterns, such as "gallop rhythms, drum-beat rhythms, doublets, and roll effects" (Basmajian, 1967a, 1967b, 1967c; Basmajian, Balza, & Fabrigar, 1965).

Apparently some form of proprioceptive memory, that is integrated at the spinal cord, accounts for the ability to gain such fine control over a single motor unit. In addition to some form of feedback,

Simard and Basmajian (1967) have concluded that it is necessary to have a calm atmosphere, skilled supervision, a step-by-step training schedule with short, clearly directed commands interspersed with specific tests and rest periods. As to personal characteristics that reveal reasons for quality of performance, none have been found. Attempts have been made to relate an individual's skill in motor unit control to special manual skills. Surprisingly enough, the manually skilled took longer to train single motor units than the less skilled. Scully and Basmajian (1969) felt that this may be due to a neuromuscular pathway acquiring a habit of responding in a certain way. Perhaps not until a habit is broken can a new skill be learned.

The possible applications of Basmajian's procedure of isolating individual motor units and gaining control of their firing are great indeed. E. E. Green, Walters, A. M. Green, and Murphy (1969) have described a feedback meter, which, by indicating to subjects their own tension level, has aided in the relaxation of skeletal muscle. Formerly, it had taken days or weeks before an individual could relax to a satisfactory degree. With a simple feedback mechanism, which showed each subject his own EMG tension level, zero firing for a single motor unit in the large forearm muscle bundles could be achieved in 20 min in 7 out of 21 subjects.

Not only can the feedback mechanism play a role in relaxation, but such a device has been utilized in work with reading problems. One of the major obstacles to being a fast reader is the problem of subvocalization, which includes a range of activities from inaudible articulation and vocalization to audible whispering while reading. In many instances activity is limited to the vocal musculature, and the individual may not even be aware that he is subvocalizing. Subvocalization is common in young children but has been found to persist in adults (McGuigan & Bailey, 1969). Hardyck, Petrinovich, and Ellsworth (1966; Hardyck & Petrinovich, 1969) have been able to determine the presence of subvocalization by means of electrodes applied over the thyroid cartilage. By channeling the output of an oscillograph amplifier to an audio amplifier, and then to earphones, the investigator can provide an individual with feedback on his own subvocalizations during reading. In a matter of one 30-min

---

[8]Muscles that occupy a lateral position on the lower leg.

session all 50 subjects showed complete cessation of subvocalization, whereas prior attempts to reduce speech muscle activity by instructions alone had been unsuccessful.

The basic assumption behind the use of the EMG in psychology is that it provides a measure of muscle tension. While such measurement is not exact, it is evident that MAP amplitudes recorded by the EMG show correlations with muscle tension which are linear and fairly high.

Among the difficulties in studying muscle tension is that the term itself has not been defined clearly. There are almost as many definitions of "muscle tension" as there are methods for recording it, and the latter are quite numerous. Even those using the EMG differ in their choice of the muscles to investigate and the placement of the electrodes. There are also problems due to artifacts; however, most of these can either be eliminated or recognized later in the visual reading of records. The evidence that is available indicates that the EMG is a reliable *instrument*. In fact, MAPs from certain muscles (i.e., the frontalis and the forearm flexors) are high enough to warrant their usage in measuring differences between individuals. Other muscle groups with lower reliabilities are probably sensitive enough for group prediction.

Where it has been used in psychology, the EMG has proved to be an important tool in providing information about behavior. Studies on performance have related changes in MAPs to the degree of effort that a subject applies to a task or how well he performs it, variations in set, level of motivation, and even the entire thought process. The EMG response has also been found to behave like a reflex and is capable of being conditioned. Moreover, because of its similarity to the stimulus trace, experimenters have used the EMG response to explain certain time-error effects.

The role of the EMG in the study of personality has been equally important. Many investigators have tried to relate MAP levels to a variety of personality traits. Distinct differences in muscle tension have been found between individuals. Extremely high levels of tension frequently have been associated with psychotic and neurotic symptoms. In schizophrenia and depression, which at one time were thought to be highly unresponsive disorders, experimenters have found exaggerated MAP activity throughout most of the body musculature. Unlike this generalized tension, studies on symptom specificity have indicated that some people respond to stress with high muscle tension in specific muscle groups.

REFERENCES

AARONS, L. Diurnal variations of muscle action potentials and word associations related to psychological orientation. *Psychophysiology*, 1968, **5,** 77–91.

BALSHAN, I. D. Muscle tension and personality in women. *Archives of General Psychiatry*, 1962, **7,** 436–448.

BARBER, T. X., & HAHN, K. W. Experimental studies in "hypnotic" behavior: Physiologic and subject effects of imagined pain. *Journal of Nervous and Mental Disease*, 1964, **139,** 416–425.

BARTOSHUK, A. K. Electromyographic gradients as indicants of motivation. *Canadian Journal of Psychology*, 1955, **9,** 215–230. (a)

BARTOSHUK, A. K. Electromyographic gradients in goal-directed activity. *Canadian Journal of Psychology*, 1955, **9,** 21–28. (b)

BARTOSHUK, A. K. EMG gradients and EEG amplitude during motivated listening. *Canadian Journal of Psychology*, 1956, **10,** 156–164.

BARTOSHUK, A. K. Electromyographic reactions to strong auditory stimulation as a function of alpha amplitude. *Journal of Comparative and Physiological Psychology*, 1959, **52,** 540–545.

BARTOSHUK, A. K., ALEXANDER, K., & KASWICK, J. A. Electromyographic gradients as a function of tracking cues. *Psychonomic Science*, 1966, **6,** 43–44.

BASMAJIAN, J. V. Control and training of individual motor units. *Science*, 1963, **141,** 440–441.

BASMAJIAN, J. V. Control of individual motor units. *American Journal of Physical Medicine*, 1967, **46,** 480–486. (a)

BASMAJIAN, J. V. Electromyography: Its structural and neural basis. *International Review of Cytology*, 1967, **21,** 129–140. (b)

BASMAJIAN, J. V. *Muscles alive: Their functions revealed by electromyography.* (2nd ed.) Baltimore: Williams & Wilkins, 1967. (c)

BASMAJIAN, J. V., BALZA, M., & FABRIGAR, C. Conscious control and training of individual spinal motor neurons in normal human subjects. *Journal of New Drugs,* 1965, **2,** 78-85.

BERGER, R. Tonus of extrinsic laryngeal muscles during sleep and dreaming. *Science,* 1961, **134,** 840.

BERRY, R. N., & DAVIS, R. C. Muscle responses and their relation to rote learning. *Journal of Experimental Psychology,* 1958, **55,** 188-194.

BIGLAND, B., & LIPPOLD, O. C. J. Motor unit activity in the voluntary contraction of human muscle. *Journal of Physiology, London,* 1954, **125,** 322-335.

BORING, E. G. *A history of experimental psychology.* New York: Appleton-Century-Crofts, 1950.

BOTWINICK, J., & THOMPSON, L. W. Premotor and motor components of reaction time. *Journal of Experimental Psychology,* 1966, **71,** 9-15.

BRANDT, K., & FENZ, W. D. Specificity in verbal and physiological indicants of anxiety. *Perceptual and Motor Skills,* 1969, **29,** 663-675.

BRAZIER, M. A. The historical development of neurophysiology. In J. FIELD, H. W. MAGOUN, & V. E. HALL (Eds.), *Handbook of physiology,* Section 1, Vol. 1. Washington, D.C.: American Physiological Society, 1959.

BROMAN, T. Electromyo-mechanographic registrations of passive movements in normal and pathological subjects. *Acta Psychiatrica Scandinavica,* 1949 (Suppl. No. 53).

BUCHTHAL, F., GULD, C., & ROSENFALCK, P. Action potential parameters in normal human muscle and their dependence on physical variables. *Acta Physiologica Scandinavica,* 1954, **32,** 200-218.

BUCHTHAL, F., PINELLI, P., & ROSENFALCK, P. Action potential parameters in normal human muscle and their physiological determinants. *Acta Physiologica Scandinavica,* 1954, **32,** 219-229.

CARLSON, K. E., ALSTON, W., & FELDMAN, D. J. Electromyographic study of aging in skeletal muscle. *American Journal of Physical Medicine,* 1964, **43,** 141-145.

CLITES, M. S. Certain somatic activities in relation to successful and unsuccessful problem solving: III. *Journal of Experimental Psychology,* 1936, **19,** 172-192.

COHEN, H. L., & BRUNLIK, J. *A manual of electromyography.* New York: Harper & Row, 1968.

COLE, K. S. *Membranes, ions, and impulses: A chapter of classical biophysics.* Berkeley: University of California Press, 1968.

COURTS, F. A. The knee-jerk as a measure of muscular tension. *Journal of Experimental Psychology,* 1939, **24,** 520-529.

COURTS, F. A. Relations between muscular tension and performance. *Psychological Bulletin,* 1942, **39,** 347-367.

DANIEL, R. S. The distribution of muscular action potentials during maze learning. *Journal of Experimental Psychology,* 1939, **24,** 621-629.

DAVIDOWITZ, J., BROWN-MEYERS, A. N., KOHN, R., WELCH, L. L., & HAYES, R. An electromyographic study of muscular tension. *Journal of Psychology,* 1955, **40,** 85-94.

DAVIS, F. H., & MALMO, R. B. Electromyographic recording during interview. *American Journal of Psychiatry,* 1951, **107,** 908-916.

DAVIS, J. F. *A manual of surface electromyography.* Allan Memorial Institute of Psychiatry, McGill University, 1959. (Republished at Wright-Patterson Air Force Base, Ohio, 1959, WADC Technical Rep. 59-184, USAF.)

DAVIS, J. F. Unipolar methods of electrophysiology. In *Instrumental requirements for psychophysiological research.* New York: Foundation for Instrumentation, Education, and Research, 1961.

DAVIS, J. F., MALMO, R. B., & SHAGASS, G. Electromyographic reaction to strong auditory stimulation in psychiatric patients. *Canadian Journal of Psychology,* 1954, **8,** 177-186.

DAVIS, R. C. The muscular tension reflex and two of its modifying conditions. *Indiana University Publications, Science Series,* 1935, No. 3.

DAVIS, R. C. The relation of muscle action potentials to difficulty and frustration. *Journal of Experimental Psychology,* 1938, **23,** 141-158.

DAVIS, R. C. Patterns of muscular activity during "mental work" and their constancy. *Journal of Experimental Psychology,* 1939, **24,** 451-465.

DAVIS, R. C. Set and muscular tension. *Indiana University Publications, Science Series,* 1940, No. 10.

DAVIS, R. C. Methods of measuring muscular tension. *Psychological Bulletin,* 1942, **39,** 329-346.

DAVIS, R. C. An integrator and accessory apparatus for recording action potential. *American Journal of Psychology,* 1948, **61,** 100-104. (a)

DAVIS, R. C. Motor effects of strong auditory stimuli. *Journal of Experimental Psychology,* 1948, **38,** 257-275. (b)

DAVIS, R. C. Responses to "meaningful" and "meaningless" sounds. *Journal of Psychology,* 1948, **38,** 744-756. (c)

DAVIS, R. C. Motor responses to auditory stimuli above and below threshold. *Journal of Experimental Psychology,* 1950, **40,** 107-120.

DAVIS, R. C. The stimulus trace in effectors and its relation to judgment responses. *Journal of Experimental Psychology,* 1952, **44,** 377-390.

DAVIS, R. C. Electromyographic factors in aircraft control: The relation of muscular tension to performance. U.S. Air Force School of Aviation Medicine 1956, Rep. No. 55-122.

DAVIS, R. C., BUCHWALD, A. M., & FRANKMANN, R. W. Autonomic and muscular responses and their relation to simple stimuli. *Psychological Monographs,* 1955, **69 :** No. 20 (No. 405).

DAVIS, R. C., & VAN LIERE, D. W. Adaptation of the muscular tension response to gunfire. *Journal of Experimental Psychology,* 1949, **39,** 114-117.

DIGGORY, J. C., KLEIN, S. J., & COHEN, M. Muscle-action potentials and estimated probability of success. *Journal of Experimental Psychology,* 1964, **68,** 449-455.

EASON, R. G. An electromyographic study of impairment and estimates of subjective effort associated with voluntary muscular contractions. U.S. Naval Electronics Laboratory 1959, Rep. No. 898.

EASON, R. G. Relation between effort, tension level, skill, and performance efficiency in a perceptual motor task. *Perceptual and Motor Skills,* 1963, **16,** 297–317.

EASON, R. G., BEARDSHALL, A., & JAFFEE, S. Performance and physiological indicants of activation in a vigilance situation. *Perceptual and Motor Skills,* 1965, **20,** 3–13.

EASON, R. G., & BRANKS, J. Effect of level of activation on the quality and efficiency of performance of verbal and motor tasks. *Perceptual and Motor Skills,* 1963, **16,** 525–543.

EASON, R. G., & WHITE, C. T. A photoelectric method for integrating muscle-action potentials. *American Journal of Psychology,* 1959, **72,** 125–126.

EASON, R. G., & WHITE, C. T. Muscular tension, effort, and tracking difficulty: Studies of parameters which affect tension level and performance efficiency. *Perceptual and Motor Skills,* 1961, **12,** 331–372.

ECCLES, J. C. Neuron physiology—introduction. In J. FIELD, H. W. MAGOUN, & V. E. HALL (Eds.), *Handbook of physiology,* Section 1, Vol. 1. Washington, D.C.: American Physiological Society, 1959.

EDELMAN, R. I. Effects of differential afferent feedback on instrumental GSR conditioning. *Journal of Psychology,* 1970, **74,** 3–14.

FENZ, W. D., & VELNER, J. Physiological concomitants of behavioral indexes in schizophrenia. *Journal of Abnormal Psychology,* 1970, **76,** 27–35.

FINK, J. B. Conditioning of muscle action potential increments accompanying instructed movement. *Journal of Experimental Psychology,* 1954, **47,** 61–68.

FINK, J. B., & DAVIS, R. C. Generalization of a muscle action potential response to tonal duration. *Journal of Experimental Psychology,* 1951, **42,** 403–408.

FJELD, S. P. Motor response and muscle action potential in the measurement of sensory threshold. *Psychophysiology,* 1965, **1,** 277–281.

FOLEY, M. G. (Translation). *Galvani: Effects of electricity on muscular motion.* Norwalk, Conn.: Bundy Library, 1954.

FORREST, D. W. Influence of length of task on rate of work and level of muscular tension. *Occupational Psychology,* 1958, **32,** 253–257.

FREEMAN, G. L. *Physiological psychology.* New York: Van Nostrand, 1948.

FREEMAN, G. L., & SHARP, L. H. Muscular action potentials and the time-error function in lifted weight judgments. *Journal of Experimental Psychology,* 1941, **29,** 23–26.

FRIEDMANN, N. E. Instrumentation requirements for continuous magnetic tape recording of muscle potentials. Unpublished doctoral dissertation, University of California, Los Angeles, 1951.

GALAMBOS, R. *Nerves and muscles.* Garden City, N.Y.: Doubleday, 1962.

GELBER, B. Electromyographic factors in aircraft control: Muscular tension in the learning and unlearning of a simple-choice response. U.S. Air Force School of Aviation Medicine, 1957, Rep. No. 55-134.

GILSON, A. S., & MILLS, W. B. Activities of single motor units in man during slight voluntary efforts. *American Journal of Physiology,* 1941, **133,** 658–669.

GOLDSTEIN, I. B. Physiological responses in anxious women patients. *Archives of General Psychiatry,* 1964, **10,** 382–388. (a)

GOLDSTEIN, I. B. Role of muscle tension in personality theory. *Psychological Bulletin,* 1964, **61,** 413–425. (b)

GOLDSTEIN, I. B. The relationship of muscle tension and autonomic activity to psychiatric disorders. *Psychosomatic Medicine,* 1965, **27,** 39–52.

GOLDSTEIN, I. B., GRINKER, R. R., HEATH, H. A., OKEN, D., & SHIPMAN, W. G. Study in psychophysiology of muscle tension: I. Response specificity. *Archives of General Psychiatry,* 1964, **11,** 322–330.

GOTTSCHALK, L. A., SEROTA, H. M., & SHAPIRO, L. B. Psychologic conflict and neuromuscular tension. *Psychosomatic Medicine,* 1950, **12,** 315–319.

GREEN, E. E., WALTERS, E. D., GREEN, A. M., & MURPHY, G. Feedback technique for deep relaxation. *Psychophysiology,* 1969, **6,** 371–377.

GRINGS, W. W. *Laboratory instrumentation in psychology.* Palo Alto, Calif.: National Press, 1954.

GROSSBERG, J., & WILSON, H. Physiological changes accompanying the visualization of fearful and neutral situations. *Journal of Personality and Social Psychology,* 1968, **10,** 124–133.

GROSSMAN, W. I., & WEINER, H. Some factors affecting the reliability of surface electromyography. *Psychosomatic Medicine,* 1966, **28,** 78–83.

GULEVICH, G. D., DEMENT, W. C., & ZARCONE, V. P. All-night sleep recordings of chronic schizophrenics in remission. *Comprehensive Psychiatry,* 1967, **8,** 141–149.

GUYTON, A. C. *Textbook of medical physiology.* Philadelphia: Saunders, 1956.

HADLEY, J. M. Some relationships between electrical signs of central and peripheral activity: II. During mental work. *Journal of Experimental Psychology,* 1941, **28,** 53–62.

HARDYCK, C. D., & PETRINOVICH, L. F. Treatment of subvocal speech during reading. *Journal of Reading,* 1969, **12,** 361–368, 419–422.

HARDYCK, C. D., PETRINOVICH, L. F., & ELLSWORTH, D. W. Feedback of speech muscle activity during silent reading: Rapid extinction. *Science,* 1966, **154,** 1467–1468.

HARTER, M. R., & WHITE, C. T. Periodicity within reaction time distributions and electromyograms. *Quarterly Journal of Experimental Psychology,* 1968, **20,** 157–166.

HARVEY, E. Psychological rigidity and muscle tension. *Psychophysiology,* 1966, **3,** 224–226.

HATHAWAY, S. R. An action potential study in neuromuscular relations. *Journal of Experimental Psychology,* 1935, **18,** 285–298.

HAYES, K. J. Wave analyses of tissue noise and muscle

action potentials. U.S. Naval Air Material Center, 1959, Rep. No. 404.

HENDERSON, R. L. Remote action potentials at the moment of response in a simple reaction-time situation. *Journal of Experimental Psychology*, 1952, **44**, 238–241.

HILDEN, A. H. An action current study of the conditioned hand withdrawal. *Psychological Monographs*, 1937, **49**: No. 1 (No. 217).

HOLMES, T. H., & WOLFF, H. G. Life situations, emotions, and backaches. *Research Publications of the Association for Nervous and Mental Disease*, 1950, **29**, 750–772.

HOSHIKO, M. S., & GRANDSTAFF, H. L. An electromyographic investigation of motor conflict. *Psychonomic Science*, 1967, **9**, 87–88.

INMAN, V. T., RALSTON, H. J., SAUNDERS, J. B., FEINSTEIN, B. F., & WRIGHT, E. W. Relation of human electromyogram to muscular tension. *Electroencephalography and Clinical Neurophysiology*, 1952, **4**, 187–194.

JACOBSON, A., KALES, A., LEHMANN, D., & HOEDEMAKER, F. S. Muscle tonus in human subjects during sleep and dreaming. *Experimental Neurology*, 1964, **10**, 418–424.

JACOBSON, E. Electrical measurements of neuromuscular states during mental activities: I. Imagination of movement involving skeletal muscle. *American Journal of Physiology*, 1930, **91**, 567–608. (a)

JACOBSON, E. Electrical measurements of neuromuscular states during mental activities: II. Imagination and recollection of various muscular acts. *American Journal of Physiology*, 1930, **94**, 23–34. (b)

JACOBSON, E. Electrical measurements of neuromuscular states during mental activities: III. Visual imagination and recollection. *American Journal of Physiology*, 1930, **95**, 604–702. (c)

JACOBSON, E. Electrical measurements of neuromuscular states during mental activities: IV. Evidence of contraction of specific muscles during imagination. *American Journal of Physiology*, 1930, **95**, 703–712. (d)

JACOBSON, E. Electrical measurements of neuromuscular states during mental activities: V. Variation of specific muscles contracting during imagination. *American Journal of Physiology*, 1931, **96**, 115–121. (a)

JACOBSON, E. Electrical measurements of neuromuscular states during mental activities: VI. Note on mental activities concerning an amputated limb. *American Journal of Physiology*, 1931, **96**, 122–125. (b)

JACOBSON, E. Electrical measurements of neuromuscular states during mental activities: VII. Imagination, recollection, and abstract thinking involving the speech musculature. *American Journal of Physiology*, 1931, **97**, 200–209. (c)

JACOBSON, E. Electrophysiology of mental activities. *American Journal of Psychology*, 1932, **44**, 677–694.

JACOBSON, E. Electrical measurements concerning muscular contraction (tonus) and the cultivation of relaxation in man: Studies on arm flexors. *American Journal of Physiology*, 1934, **107**, 230–248.

JACOBSON, E. *Progressive relaxation*. Chicago: University of Chicago Press, 1938.

JACOBSON, E. The neurovoltmeter. *American Journal of Psychology*, 1939, **52**, 620–624.

JACOBSON, E. Recording action potentials without photography. *American Journal of Psychology*, 1941, **54**, 266–269.

KALES, A., HOEDEMAKER, F. S., JACOBSON, A., & LICHTENSTEIN, E. L. Dream deprivation: An experimental appraisal. *Nature*, 1964, **204**, 1337–1338.

KATZ, B. *Nerve, muscle, and synapse*. New York: McGraw-Hill, 1966.

KELLY, D., BROWN, C. C., & SHAFFER, J. W. A comparison of physiological and psychological measurements on anxious patients and normal controls. *Psychophysiology*, 1970, **6**, 429–441.

KEMPE, J. E. An experimental investigation of the relationship between certain personality characteristics and physiological responses to stress in a normal population. Unpublished doctoral dissertation, Michigan State University, 1956.

KENNEDY, J. L., & TRAVIS, R. C. Prediction of speed of performance by muscle action potentials. *Science*, 1947, **105**, 410–411.

KENNEDY, J. L., & TRAVIS, R. C. Prediction and control of alertness: II. Continuous tracking. *Journal of Comparative and Physiological Psychology*, 1948, **41**, 203–210.

KIMMEL, H. D., & DAVIDOV, W. Classical GSR conditioning with concomitant EMG measurement. *Journal of Experimental Psychology*, 1967, **74**, 67–74.

KIMMEL, H. D., & STERNTHAL, H. S. Replication of GSR avoidance conditioning with concomitant EMG measurement and subjects matched in responsivity and conditionability. *Journal of Experimental Psychology*, 1967, **74**, 144–146.

KLEIN, S. J. The summation of muscle tensions due to stress. *American Psychologist*, 1955, **10**, 451–452.

KLEIN, S. J. Relation of muscle action potentials variously induced to breakdown of work in task-oriented subjects. *Perceptual and Motor Skills*, 1961, **12**, 131–141.

KRUSBERG, R. J., & ZIMMER, H. An integrator circuit for psychophysiological applications. *Psychophysiology*, 1966, **3**, 213–217.

LARSON, J. D., & FOULKES, D. Electromyogram suppression during sleep, dream recall, and orientation time. *Psychophysiology*, 1969, **5**, 548–555.

LESHNER, S. S. Effects of aspiration and achievement on muscular tensions. *Journal of Experimental Psychology*, 1961, **61**, 133–137.

LEWIN, K. *A dynamic theory of personality: Selected papers*. New York: McGraw-Hill, 1935.

LICHT, S. History of electrodiagnosis. In S. LICHT (Ed.), *Electrodiagnosis and electromyography*. Baltimore: Waverly Press, 1961.

LINDSLEY, D. B. Characteristics of single motor unit responses in human muscle during various degrees of contraction. *American Journal of Physiology,* 1935, **113,** 88–89. (a)

LINDSLEY, D. B. Electrical activity of muscle during contraction. *American Journal of Physiology,* 1935, **114,** 90–99. (b)

LIPPOLD, O. C. J. The relation between integrated action potentials in a human muscle and its isometric tension. *Journal of Physiology,* 1952, **117,** 492–499.

LIPPOLD, O. C. J. Electromyography. In P. H. VENABLES & I. MARTIN (Eds.), *Manual of psycho-physiological methods.* New York: Wiley, 1967.

LUNDERVOLD, A. Electromyographic investigations during sedentary work, especially typewriting. *British Journal of Physical Medicine,* 1951, **14,** 32–36.

LUNDERVOLD, A. An electromyographic investigation of tense and relaxed subjects. *Journal of Nervous and Mental Disease,* 1952, **115,** 512–525.

MALMO, R. B. Anxiety and behavioral arousal. *Psychological Review,* 1957, **64,** 276–287.

MALMO, R. B. Physiological gradients and behavior. *Psychological Bulletin,* 1965, **64,** 225–234.

MALMO, R. B. Cognitive factors in impairment: A neuropsychological study of divided set. *Journal of Experimental Psychology,* 1966, **71,** 184–189.

MALMO, R. B., BOAG, T. J., & SMITH, A. A. Physiological study of personal interaction. *Psychosomatic Medicine,* 1957, **19,** 105–119.

MALMO, R. B., & DAVIS, J. F. Physiological gradients as indicants of "arousal" in mirror tracing. *Canadian Journal of Physiology,* 1956, **10,** 231–238.

MALMO, R. B., & SHAGASS, C. Physiologic studies of reaction to stress in anxiety and early schizophrenia. *Psychosomatic Medicine,* 1949, **11,** 9–24. (a)

MALMO, R. B., & SHAGASS. C. Physiologic study of symptom mechanisms in psychiatric patients under stress. *Psychosomatic Medicine,* 1949, **11,** 25–29. (b)

MALMO, R. B., SHAGASS, C., BELANGER, D. J., & SMITH, A. A. Motor control in psychiatric patients under experimental stress. *Journal of Abnormal and Social Psychology,* 1951, **46,** 539–547.

MALMO, R. B., SHAGASS, C., & DAVIS, F. H. A physiological study of somatic symptom mechanisms in psychiatric patients. *Research Publications of the Association for Nervous and Mental Disease,* 1950, **29,** 23–261. (a)

MALMO, R. B., SHAGASS, C., & DAVIS, F. H. Symptom specificity and bodily reactions during psychiatric interview. *Psychosomatic Medicine,* 1950, **12,** 362–376. (b)

MALMO, R. B., SHAGASS, C., & DAVIS, J. F. A method for the investigation of somatic response mechanisms in psychoneurosis. *Science,* 1950, **112,** 325–328.

MALMO, R. B., SHAGASS, C., & DAVIS, J. F. Electromyographic studies of muscular tension in psychiatric patients under stress. *Journal of Clinical and Experimental Psychopathology,* 1951, **12,** 45–66.

MALMO, R. B., SHAGASS, C., & SMITH, A. A. Responsiveness in chronic schizophrenia. *Journal of Personality,* 1951, **19,** 359–375.

MALMO, R. B., & SMITH, A. A. Forehead tension and motor irregularities in psychoneurotic patients under stress. *Journal of Personality,* 1955, **23,** 391–406.

MALMO, R. B., SMITH, A. A., & KOHLMEYER, W. A. Motor manifestations of conflict in interview: A case study. *Journal of Abnormal and Social Psychology,* 1956, **52,** 268–271.

MALMSTADT, H. V., ENKE, C. G., & TOREN, E. C. *Electronics for scientists.* New York: W. A. Benjamin, 1963.

MALMSTROM, E. J. The effect of prestimulus variability upon physiological reactivity scores. *Psychophysiology,* 1968, **5,** 149–165.

MARTIN, I. Levels of muscle activity in psychiatric patients. *Acta Psychologica,* 1956, **12,** 326–341.

MARTIN, I. Blink rate and muscle tension. *Journal of Mental Science,* 1958, **104,** 123–132. (a)

MARTIN, I. Personality and muscle activity. *Canadian Journal of Psychology,* 1958, **12,** 23–30. (b)

MATHEWS, A. M., & GELDER, M. G. Psycho-physiological investigations of brief relaxation training. *Journal of Psychosomatic Research,* 1969, **13,** 1–12.

MAX, L. W. An experimental study of the motor theory of consciousness: III. Action-current responses in deafmutes during sleep, sensory stimulation and dreams. *Journal of Comparative Psychology,* 1935, **19,** 469–486.

MAX, L. W. An experimental study of the motor theory of consciousness: IV. Action-current responses in the deaf during awakening, kinesthetic imagery and abstract thinking. *Journal of Comparative Psychology,* 1937, **24,** 301–344.

McGUIGAN, F. J. Covert oral behavior and auditory hallucinations. *Psychophysiology,* 1966, **3,** 73–80.

McGUIGAN, F. J., & BAILEY, S. C. Longitudinal study of covert oral behavior during silent reading. *Perceptual and Motor Skills,* 1969, **28,** 170.

McKINELY, J. C., & BERKWITZ, N. J. Quantitative studies in human muscle tonus. *Archives of Neurology and Psychiatry,* 1928, **19,** 1036–1056.

MEYER, D. R. On the interaction of simultaneous responses. *Psychological Bulletin,* 1953, **50,** 204–220.

MEYER, H. D. Reaction time as related to tensions in muscles not essential in the reaction. *Journal of Experimental Psychology,* 1949, **39,** 96–113.

MILLER, J. D. Electromyographic factors in aircraft control: Differential muscle tension during a delayed response. U.S. Air Force School of Aviation Medicine, 1957, Rep. No. 55–129.

MISSIURO, W. Studies on developmental stages of children's reflex activity. *Child Development,* 1963, **34,** 33–41.

MOOS, R. H., & ENGEL, B. T. Psychophysiological reactions in hypertensive and arthritic patients. *Journal of Psychosomatic Research,* 1962, **6,** 227–241.

MORGAN, C. T. *Physiological psychology.* New York: McGraw-Hill, 1965.

NEWMAN, P. P. EMG studies of emotional states in normal subjects. *Journal of Neurology, Neurosurgery, and Psychiatry,* 1953, **16,** 200–208.

NIDEVER, J. E.   A factor analytic study of general muscular tension. Unpublished doctoral dissertation, University of California, Los Angeles, 1959.

NORRIS, F. H.   *The EMG.* New York: Grune & Stratton, 1963.

NORRIS, F. H., & GASTEIGER, E. L.   Action potentials of single motor units in normal muscle. *Electroencephalography and Clinical Neurophysiology,* 1955, **7,** 115-126.

OBRIST, P. A.   Heart rate and somatic-motor coupling during classical aversive conditioning in humans. *Journal of Experimental Psychology,* 1968, **77,** 180-193.

OBRIST, P. A., WEBB, R. A., & SUTTERER, J. R.   Heart rate and somatic changes during aversive conditioning and a simple reaction time task. *Psychophysiology,* 1969, **5,** 696-723.

O'CONNELL, A. L., & GARDNER, E. B.   The use of electromyography in kinesiological research. *Research Quarterly, American Association for Health, Physical Education and Recreation,* 1963, **34,** 166-184.

PAUL, G. L.   Physiological effects of relaxation training and hypnotic suggestion. *Journal of Abnormal Psychology,* 1969, **74,** 425-437.

PAYNE, B., & DAVIS, R. C.   The role of muscular tension in the comparison of lifted weights. *Journal of Experimental Psychology,* 1940, **27,** 227-242.

PISHKIN, V.   Electromyographic variation concomitant with concept identification parameters. *Perceptual and Motor Skills,* 1964, **18,** 649-652.

PISHKIN, V., & SHURLEY, J. T.   Electrodermal and electromyographic parameters in concept identification. *Psychophysiology,* 1968, **5,** 112-118.

PISHKIN, V., SHURLEY, J. T., & WOLFGANG, A.   Stress: Psychophysiological and cognitive indices in an acute double-blind study with hydroxyzine in psychiatric patients. *Archives of General Psychiatry,* 1967, **16,** 471-478.

PISHKIN, V., & WOLFGANG, A.   Electromyographic gradients in concept identification with numbers of irrelevant dimensions. *Journal of Clinical Psychology,* 1964, **20,** 61-67.

RASCH, P. J., & BURKE, R. K.   *Kinesiology and applied anatomy.* Philadelphia: Lea & Febiger, 1963.

REUDER, M. E.   The effect of ego orientation and problem difficulty on muscle action potentials. *Journal of Experimental Psychology,* 1956, **51,** 142-148.

REUSCH, J., COBB, S., & FINESINGER, J. E.   Studies on muscular tension in the neuroses. *Transactions of the American Neurological Association,* 1941, **67,** 186-189.

REUSCH, J., & FINESINGER, J. E.   The relation between electromyographic measurements and subjective reports of muscular relaxation. *Psychosomatic Medicine,* 1943, **5,** 132-138.

RICE, D. G.   Operant conditioning and associated electromyogram responses. *Journal of Experimental Psychology,* 1966, **71,** 908-912.

RICHARDSON, A. T., & WYNN PARRY, C. B.   The theory and practice of electrodiagnosis. *Annals of Physical Medicine,* 1957, **4,** 3-16, 41-58.

RIMON, R., STENBACK, A., & HAHMAR, E.   Electromyographic findings in depressive patients. *Journal of Psychosomatic Research,* 1966, **10,** 159-170.

RODRIQUEZ, A. A., & OESTER, Y. T.   Fundamentals of electromyography. In S. LICHT (Ed.), *Electrodiagnosis and electromyography.* Baltimore: Waverly Press, 1961.

ROGOFF, J. B., & REINER, S.   Electrodiagnostic apparatus in electrodiagnosis and EMG. In S. LICHT (Ed.), *Electrodiagnosis and electromyography.* Baltimore: Waverly Press, 1961.

RUNQUIST, W. N., & SPENCE, K. W.   Performance in eyelid conditioning related to changes in muscular tension and physiological measures of emotionality. *Journal of Experimental Psychology,* 1959, **58,** 417-422.

RYAN, T. A., COTTRELL, C. L., & BITTERMAN, M. E.   Muscular tension as an index of effort: The effect of glare and other disturbances on visual work. *American Journal of Psychology,* 1950, **63,** 317-341.

SACCO, G., BUCHTHAL, F., & ROSENFALCK, P.   Motor unit potentials at different ages. *Archives of Neurology,* 1962, **6,** 366-373.

SAINSBURY, P., & GIBSON, J. G.   Symptoms of anxiety and tension and the accompanying physiological changes in the muscular system. *Journal of Neurology, Neurosurgery, and Psychiatry,* 1954, **17,** 216-224.

SCHWARTZ, R. P., HEATH, A. L., & HUDSON, F. W.   Instrumentation in relation to electromyography. *Archives of Physical Medicine,* 1949, **30,** 383-400.

SCULLY, H. E., & BASMAJIAN, J. V.   Motor-unit training and influence of manual skill. *Psychophysiology,* 1969, **5,** 625-632.

SHAGASS, C., & MALMO, R. B.   Psychodynamic themes and localized tension during psychotherapy. *Psychosomatic Medicine,* 1954, **16,** 295-314.

SHARP, L. H.   Effects of residual tension output and energy expenditure in muscular work. *Journal of Experimental Psychology,* 1941, **29,** 1-22.

SHAW, W. A.   The distribution of muscular action potentials during imaging. *Psychological Record,* 1938, **2,** 195-216.

SHAW, W. A.   The relation of muscle action potentials to imaginal weight lifting. *Archives of Psychology, New York,* 1940, No. 247.

SHAW, W. A., & KLINE, L. H.   A study of muscle action potentials during attempted solution of problems of increasing difficulty. *Journal of Experimental Psychology,* 1947, **37,** 146-158.

SHIPMAN, W. G., OKEN, D., GOLDSTEIN, I. B., GRINKER, R. R., & HEATH, H. A.   Study in psychophysiology of muscle tension: II. Personality factors. *Archives of General Psychiatry,* 1964, **11,** 330-345.

SIDOWSKI, J. B., & EASON, R. G.   Drive, verbal performance, and muscle action potential. *Journal of Experimental Psychology,* 1960, **60,** 365-370.

SIMARD, T. G., & BASMAJIAN, J. V.   Methods in training the

conscious control of motor units. *Archives of Physical Medicine,* 1967, **48,** 12–19.

SIMONS, D. J., DAY, E., GOODELL, H., & WOLFF, H. G. Experimental studies on headache: Muscles of the scalp and neck as sources of pain. *Research Publications of the Association for Nervous and Mental Disease,* 1943, **23,** 228–244.

SMALL, A. M., & GROSS, N. B. Integrated muscle action potentials in a weight-lifting task as a function of weight and rate of lifting. *Journal of Comparative and Physiological Psychology,* 1958, **51,** 227–233.

SMITH, A. A. An electromyographic study of tension in interrupted and completed tasks. *Journal of Experimental Psychology,* 1953, **46,** 32–36.

SMITH, A. A., MALMO, R. B., & SHAGASS, C. An electromyographic study of listening and talking. *Canadian Journal of Psychology,* 1954, **8,** 219–227.

SOUTHWORTH, J. A. Muscular tension as a response to psychological stress in rheumatoid arthritis and peptic ulcer. *Genetic Psychology Monographs,* 1958, **57,** 337–392.

STOYVA, J. M. Finger electromyographic activity during sleep: Its relation to dreaming in deaf and normal subjects. *Journal of Abnormal Psychology,* 1965, **70,** 343–349.

SURWILLO, W. W. Psychological factors in muscle-action potentials: EMG gradients. *Journal of Experimental Psychology,* 1956, **52,** 263–272.

SZUMSKI, A. J. Mechanisms underlying normal motor behavior. *American Journal of Physical Medicine,* 1967, **46,** 52–68.

THOMPSON, R. F., LINDSLEY, D. B., & EASON, R. G. Physiological psychology. In J. B. SIDOWSKI (Ed.), *Experimental methods and instrumentation in psychology.* New York: McGraw-Hill, 1966.

TRAVIS, L. E., & HUNTER, T. A. Tremor frequencies. *Journal of General Psychology,* 1931, **5,** 255–260.

TRAVIS, L. E., & KENNEDY, J. L. Prediction and automatic control of alertness: II. Continuous tracking. *Journal of Comparative and Physiological Psychology,* 1948, **41,** 203–210.

TRAVIS, L. E., & KENNEDY, J. L. Prediction and automatic control of alertness: III. Calibration of the alertness indicator and further results. *Journal of Comparative and Physiological Psychology,* 1949, **42,** 45–57.

TURSKY, B. Integrators as measuring devices of bioelectric output. *Clinical Pharmacology and Therapeutics,* 1964, **5,** 887–892.

UNDERWOOD, B. J. *Experimental psychology.* New York: Appleton-Century-Crofts, 1949.

VAN LIERE, D. W. Characteristics of the muscle tension response to paired tones. *Journal of Experimental Psychology,* 1953, **46,** 319–324.

VAN TWYER, H. B., & KIMMEL, H. D. Operant conditioning of GSR with concomitant measurement of 2 somatic variables. *Journal of Experimental Psychology,* 1966, **72,** 841–846.

VARGAS, L. The contractile system in muscle. *McGill Medical Journal,* 1958, **27,** 67–73.

VAUGHN, A. O., & McDANIEL, J. W. Electromyographic gradients during complex visual discrimination learning. *Psychonomic Science,* 1969, **16,** 203–204.

VOAS, R. B. Generalization and consistency of muscle tension level. Unpublished doctoral dissertation, University of California, Los Angeles, 1952.

WALLERSTEIN, H. An electromyographic study of attentive listening. *Canadian Journal of Psychology,* 1954, **8,** 228–238.

WEBB, R. A., & OBRIST, P. A. The physiological concomitants of reaction time performance as a function of preparatory interval and preparatory interval series. *Psychophysiology,* 1970, **6,** 389–403.

WENDT, G. R. Methods of recording action. *Archives of Psychology,* New York, 1938, No. 228.

WHATMORE, G. B., & ELLIS, R. M. Some motor aspects of schizophrenia. *American Journal of Psychiatry,* 1958, **114,** 882–889.

WHATMORE, G. B., & ELLIS, R. M. Some neurophysiologic aspects of depressed states. *Archives of General Psychiatry,* 1959, **1,** 70–80.

WHATMORE, G. B., & ELLIS, R. M. Further neurophysiologic aspects of depressed states. *Archives of General Psychiatry,* 1962, **6,** 243–253.

WHITFIELD, I. C. *An introduction to electronics for physiological workers.* New York: Macmillan, 1953.

WILCOTT, R. C., & BEENKEN, H. G. Relation of integrated surface electromyography and muscle tension. *Perceptual and Motor Skills,* 1957, **7,** 295–298.

WILLIAMS, J. G. L., & WILLIAMS, B. The effect of meprobamate on the somatic responses of anxious patients and normal controls. *Psychophysiology,* 1967, **3,** 403–405.

WILLIAMS, R. L., & KRASNOFF, A. G. Body image and physiological patterns in patients with peptic ulcer and rheumatoid arthritis. *Psychosomatic Medicine,* 1964, **26,** 701–709.

WOLF, S., & WOLFF, H. G. *Headaches: Their nature and treatment.* Boston: Little, Brown, 1953.

WOLFF, H. G. *Headache and other head pain.* New York: Oxford University Press, 1948.

WOODBURY, J. W. Action potential: Properties of excitable membranes. In T. C. RUCH & H. D. PATTON (Eds.), *Physiology and biophysics.* Philadelphia: Saunders, 1965.

WOODBURY, J. W., GORDON, A. M., & CONRAD, J. T. Muscle. In T. C. RUCH & H. D. PATTON (Eds.), *Physiology and biophysics.* Philadelphia: Saunders, 1965.

WOOLF, A. L. The theoretical basis of clinical electromyography. *Annals of Physical Medicine,* 1962, **6,** 189–209, 241–260.

Robert Edelberg

ELECTRICAL ACTIVITY
OF THE SKIN

ITS MEASUREMENT AND USES
IN PSYCHOPHYSIOLOGY

9

BASES OF ELECTRODERMAL ACTIVITY

The cell membrane of an amoeba represents a well-defined boundary between that organism and its environment and serves as the primary screen controlling the interaction of the protoplasm and the external world. In the mammal the various functions of this membrane have been taken over by such specialized structures as the mouth, lungs, gastrointestinal tract, eyes, ears, nose, and the skin. This last organ still defines the external, physical limits of the body and, as such, has for its owner a special psychological significance. It also has the vital task of keeping bacteria, toxins, and other undesirable elements out, and the precious fluids in. Through its tactile and thermosensitive apparatus, it acts as a primary station for reception of information from the immediately adjacent outer world. If penetrated by foreign matter, the skin can become aware of the location of the penetration and sound the appropriate alarm. Finally, in response to signals from higher centers, and sometimes from local stations, it regulates the rate at which the heat generated within its bounds is lost to the outer world. Sometimes it must expedite this loss by a contribution of its own making, namely sweat.

Is it surprising, then, that an organ with such vital and dynamic functions should be constantly flooded with signals from an array of control centers? We would be well advised to monitor these signals if the proceedings in the control centers are of any interest to us. We can listen in on such signals by taking advantage of the fact that their arrival at the skin is heralded by measurable electrical changes that we call electrodermal activity. Since the electrical activity is, for the most part, an epiphenomenon of the physiological processes that ensue, it is perhaps more appropriate to term the collective action of the various skin effectors and their associated tracts and centers "neurodermal activity."

In discussing this topic, major emphasis has been placed on the examination of basic principles of interpretation. This reevaluation seems more necessary for the electrodermal field than for almost any other psychophysiological measure, in the light of the extensive and conflicting literature that has accumulated since Féré's description (1888) of the galvanic skin response to emotional stimuli. Controversy over the identification of the classes of adequate stimuli for this reflex has been especially acute. Early examples of this are seen in the papers of Peterson and Jung (1907), Wells and Forbes (1911), Pieron (1914), Waller (1918), Prideaux (1920), Wechsler (1925), Syz (1926), and Jones (1928).

Finally, a great deal of uncertainty over the nature of the peripheral processes involved in this response still exists. The controversy developed about 10 years after the discovery of the electrical variations of the skin by Vigouroux (1879). Tarchanoff's discovery (1890) of the skin *potential* response shed the first doubt on Féré's (1888) interpretation of the skin *resistance* response as a vasomotor phenomenon. The great debate continued during the next several decades, carried on by such notable participants as Sommer (1905) and Sidis and Nelson (1910), who defended a muscular basis; McDowall (1933), who defended a vascular basis; Veraguth (1909), Darrow (1927), and Jeffress (1928), who argued for the sweat gland; and Richter (1929) who supported a combined sweat gland and epidermal mechanism. The controversy, though past its climax, still continues. It is of more than academic interest, for, until the basic nature of the peripheral events in this reflex has been elucidated, the absence of a rational basis for appropriate quantitative treatment of electrodermal measures and for the behavioral interpretation of this form of biological adaptation will continue to be a barrier to progress.

Microstructure of the Skin

Any discussion of the biophysical, physiological, and even psychological aspects of neurodermal activity is best comprehended in the light of the overall histological organization of the skin (Figure 9.1). Four rather well-defined layers may be recognized. The innermost, the *corium* or dermis, is largely composed of connective tissue and also contains tactile elements, sebaceous glands, hair roots, the bodies of the sweat glands, most of their ducts, and the neural and vascular supply, including capillary loops that enter the little domes or dermal papillae forming the roof of this layer. This stratum, because of its generous intercellular spaces and network of blood vessels, has a high electrical conductivity. Above the corium is the *Malpighian* or *germinating* layer, which contains, in the deepest or basal layer, reproducing cells. The products of cell division metamorphose as they are displaced toward the surface and are destined to replace the keratinized cells of the horny layer or corneum lost through wear and tear. The cells of the germinating layer are separated by narrow spaces filled with a fluid in which free diffusion and perhaps circulation may take place (Nordquist, Olson, & Everett, 1966). Cell membranes usually constitute an effective

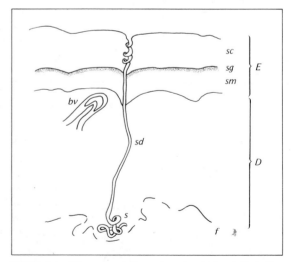

Figure 9.1 Diagram of the microstructure of the skin. *E*, epidermis; *D*, dermis or corium; *sc*, stratum corneum; *sg*, stratum granulosum; *sm*, stratum Malpighii; *bv*, blood vessel; *sd*, sweat duct; *s*, secretory portion of sweat gland; *f*, subcutaneous fat.

barrier against electric current, but it may be surmised that the conductivity of the layer is enhanced by the presence of this intercellular lacework of aqueous channels. Arthur and Shelley (1959) demonstrated that nerve fibers enter this layer; their concentration varies considerably over various parts of the body. The cells at the upper level of the Malpighian layer contain numerous deeply staining granules, from which is derived the name of the third or *granular* layer.

Above the granular layer lies the *corneum,* a compact stratum of flattened cell carcasses. In the skin of the palm and soles, where the corneum is unusually thick, 0.5–1.3 mm (Kuno, 1956), there is a thin glistening layer, the *stratum lucidum,* which separates the granular layer from the corneum proper. At the boundary between the granular layer and the corneum there lies a barrier to the passage of water and solutes (Blank & Gould, 1959).

Special attention should be given to the structure of the eccrine sweat gland, the type that produces a watery secretion. These are found on the palmar and plantar surfaces and over most of the body. This gland is a long tube with walls consisting of a double or triple cell layer. The deepest 2 mm of the tube is coiled up to form a compact body, the sweat gland proper, in which secretion actually takes place. The remainder is the duct. After a straight course through the corium and germinating layer, it spirals through the horny layer and opens to the surface as a small pore. Outside of the epithelial layers of the secretory region, but not of the duct, are longitudinal smooth muscle fibers, the myoepithelial cells. Also surrounding the secretory portion is a profuse, coiled, nerve supply. Montagna (1962, p. 354) states that, in man and most mammals, cholinesterase-containing nerves are not found on the straight portion of the duct, but Winkelmann (1960, p. 120) points out that it is technically extremely difficult to demonstrate neural elements along the sweat gland. Therefore, the statement that the long, straight duct leading from the secretory portion to the corneum is without innervation should be accepted with reservations.

In addition to the eccrine sweat gland, there is another type, the apocrine glands, located in the axilla, mammary areola, the labia majora, the mons pubis and in the circum-anal region. In these the secretion is formed by pinching off bits of the protoplasm of the secretory cells. Unlike eccrine glands, the expulsion of sweat from apocrine glands is achieved entirely by contraction of the myoepithelial fibers, which are under adrenergic control (Hurley & Shelley, 1954). According to Wang (1964, p. 7) the glands on the footpad of the cat are also apocrine, but this view is a controversial one.

Electrical Behavior of the Skin

Resistance or conductance If one places two electrodes on the skin surface and drives a small constant current through them, the skin behaves as a resistor. A voltage develops across these electrodes and by application of Ohm's law one can calculate the apparent resistance. A sudden noise, a sharp sniff by the subject, a question asked of him, or a statement made by him will, to varying degrees, be followed about 2 sec later by a rapid decrease in the measured voltage. The voltage drop indicates a fall in skin resistance. This transient response, commonly known as the galvanic skin reflex (GSR) or psychogalvanic reflex (PGR), has a characteristic waveform, taking about 0.5–5 sec to reach peak; 1–2 sec is typical (Figure 9.2). Recovery from peak to baseline is considerably slower and may have a variety of shapes, from a gently sloping plateau to an exponential-like descent that is almost as fast as the rising portion (Figure 9.2). The

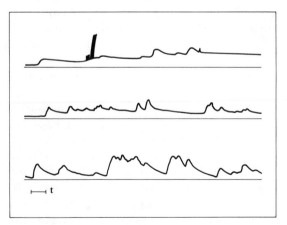

Figure 9.2 Various forms of skin conductance responses recorded from the volar surface of the finger. Note the increase of base conductance in the upper trace with few responses and the paradoxical absence of increase in the lower trace with many responses. Responses with rapid recovery are shown in the middle trace. Calibration: vertical, increase of 2 and 10 μmho; horizontal, 10 sec.

time required for the recovery limb to reach its point of 50% return to baseline varies greatly, from 1 to 30 sec. Response latency ranges from about 1.2–4 sec, depending on the temperature (Gilde-meister & Ellinghaus, 1923) and site of the body (Bloch, 1952). A typical latency for palmar responses at comfortable room temperature is about 1.8 sec.

Apparent resistance, which is commonly expressed in terms of its reciprocal, conductance, ranges between 10,000 and 500,000 ohm cm². Slow variations in resistance, sometimes of the order of 100–200%, may occur during changes of arousal in the waking state or upon falling asleep or awakening. Reflex changes may amount to as much as 50% of the base level, more commonly, up to 5%.

If the development of voltage across the skin during the passage of a current is measured on an oscilloscope, it is observed to rise exponentially, rather than instantaneously, when the current is turned on, indicating a capacitative component in the skin. Direct current continues to flow even after the skin capacitor is fully charged, indicating either that it is in parallel with an ohmic resistance or that it behaves as a leaky capacitor (Hozawa, 1928; Lykken, Miller, & Strahan, 1966).

Impedance   In a second type of measurement, a small alternating current is applied to a pair of electrodes on similar skin sites and the impedance measured. Such measurements furnish values that vary with frequency but possibly offer a means of avoiding the difficult problem of electrode polarization. Further evidence for a capacitative component is found in the progressive reduction of skin impedance with the increase in frequency of the applied current (Barnett, 1938; Plutchik & Hirsch, 1963). The unusual behavior of this reactive component as the frequency of the energizing circuit is increased indicates that the capacitance cannot be of the sort found in electronic circuits; i.e., it cannot be caused by the static capacitative properties of a fixed structure. A static capacitance in parallel with a fixed resistor would show a phase angle that increases with increasing frequency. In the case of the skin, however, the phase angle increases up to a value of about 72° at around 2000 Hz but remains essentially constant as the frequency continues to increase (Barnett, 1938). This situation can only

occur if the capacitative reactance remains constant with the frequency; i.e., if the capacity varies inversely with the frequency. According to Fricke (1932) such a condition occurs when the capacitative effect is produced by a polarization phenomenon such as occurs at the surface of a polarizing electrode. In the case of the skin it is due to membrane polarization resulting from the ion-selective permeability of one or more membranes within the skin. The behavior of the skin as an impedance network has been discussed elsewhere (Edelberg, 1967; Montagu, 1964).

Potential   There need be no external current source to observe these electrodermal changes. If one electrode is placed on the surface of the skin and a similar one inside the body, an electrical potential difference between the electrodes may be measured on a sensitive, high impedance voltmeter. This may vary from a few millivolts (mV) to as much as 50–60 mV, the surface being negative with respect to the interior. When stimuli are presented to the subject, the potential level changes, usually to a higher negativity, with time relations somewhat similar to those for the resistance response. Such potential responses may also be biphasic or even triphasic, with the amplitude of the negative and positive components varying greatly in relation to each other. The component waves may be as high as 25 mV.

It is, of course, inconvenient to place one of the pair of electrodes inside the body in human experiments, and in practice both are placed on the surface. Since only the *difference* in potential at the two sites can be measured, the potential difference between two areas, each having the same potential with respect to the interior, is zero. Similarly, if both electrode sites vary reflexly to the same degree, no response will be recorded because of cancellation. To observe activity, two sites of dissimilar activity are required. Unfortunately, if a positive wave is recorded from such a pair, one cannot determine whether it indicates a positive response in the first site or a negative one in the other. To circumvent this problem, the experimenter can use an inactive region such as the inner aspect of the ear lobe (Edelberg, 1967, pp. 1–53) for one of the electrodes or he can artificially "inactivate" one of the sites, as by perforation (Wilcott, 1959) or skin drilling (Shackel, 1959). These procedures reduce, but do not completely eliminate, activity (Takagi & Nakayama, 1959; Wilcott, 1959). If an inactive region is selected as a reference, base potential measurements will have an absolute error that depends on the potential from the reference to the inside of the body and a dynamic error due to the slow drift of the inactive potential.

The most commonly observed waveforms of the potential response are the uniphasic negative and the biphasic. The biphasic wave starts with a sharp negative wave, termed the a wave by Forbes (1936), followed by a sharp positive wave (Forbes's b wave), which has a slower recovery (Figure 9.3). Rise time ranges from 0.5 to 15 sec, and 50% recovery time from 1 sec to over 1 min. When a positive wave appears, the negative wave is invariably very rapid and frequently of low amplitude, despite its steep rate of rise (Figure 9.3). The recovery limb of the positive wave sometimes overshoots the baseline to produce a slow negative wave, sometimes of high amplitude, which may be termed the c or gamma wave. The c wave requires between 10 and 25 sec after onset of the response complex before it reaches its negative peak.

Internal circuit-currents There exists in the skin a situation causing distortion in measurements of potential made at the skin surface, namely, the opportunity for the flow of currents within the skin structure. A microelectrode survey of the skin surface reveals that the pores of the full sweat ducts

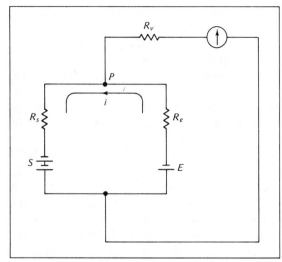

Figure 9.4 Schematic diagram of internal circuit currents in the skin. R_v, input resistance of voltmeter; R_s, internal resistance of sweat gland, including membrane and duct; R_e, internal resistance of epidermis, including membranes and horny layer; S, resting potential of sweat gland; E, resting potential of epidermis; P, potential at surface; i, internal current between the sweat gland and the epidermis. Redrawn from R. Edelberg, Biopotentials from the skin surface: The hydration effect. *Annals of the New York Academy of Sciences*, 1968, **148**, 252–262. Reproduced by permission.

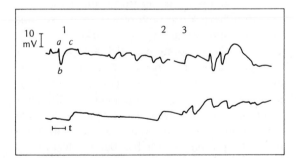

Figure 9.3 Various forms of skin potential responses recorded from the volar surface of the finger and referred to an inactive site. Upward deflections are negative. Response 1 is triphasic, Response 2 uniphasic positive, and Response 3 uniphasic negative. $t = 10$ sec.

are usually 5–20 mV more negative than the epidermal patches between sweat glands (Edelberg, 1968). Under these circumstances a current will flow, whether an electrode is present or not, between the sweat ducts and these less negative epidermal areas. When an electrode is placed on the skin surface, the observed potential is a composite of these two potentials, the value being determined by the relative resistances of the sweat duct and epidermal pathways.

The internal circuitry is represented in Figure 9.4. The resistance of the sweat gland path is made up of the resistance of the column of saline in the sweat duct and the resistance of the sweat gland membrane. The resistance of the epidermal path comprises that of the horny layer and of the living cellular layer. If, without changing either the sweat gland or the epidermal potential, we change the associated resistances, the potential recorded at the surface changes. This can occur wherever there are two spots with different potentials in parallel arrangement, as are the sweat gland and the epidermis. A somewhat similar situation is implied in a model presented by Darrow (1964). These considerations hold whether the epidermis is capable of active response or not. Their experimental justification and quantitative expression have been reported elsewhere (Edelberg, 1968) and some of the methodological implications have been pursued by Fowles and Venables (1970).

One can make certain predictions on the basis of this internal circuit-current model. First, the skin potential as commonly measured is a resultant not only of potentials present in the skin but of the fullness of the sweat ducts and the degree of hydration of the corneum. Secondly, the rise of sweat in the ducts should be associated with a negative shift in surface potential. This shift should last until the sweat level has receded. Finally, the overflow of sweat into the relatively dry corneum should produce a slow positive shift in potential that should slowly reverse as the horny layer dries out. These predictions were supported by the results of experiments on electronic and hydraulic models, as well as on the skin. A further prediction of this model is that an *external* shunt may under some circumstances significantly alter the form of the

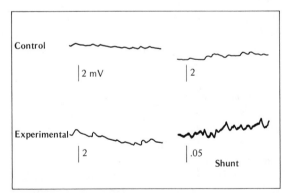

Figure 9.5 Change in polarity of SPR by addition of an external shunt. The left-hand traces are simultaneous conventional recordings from two palmar sites referred to inactive sites. In the lower right-hand trace, a shunt of one-tenth the skin resistance has been placed across that pair of sites. The upward deflections are negative. Redrawn from R. Edelberg, Biopotentials from the skin surface: The hydration effect. *Annals of the New York Academy of Sciences,* 1968, **148,** 252–262. Reproduced by permission.

surface reflection of events in the skin. A remarkable example of the transformation produced by this effect is shown in Figure 9.5. The upper and lower traces are from two nearby sites on human skin, each paired with an inactive one. In the right panel an external shunt, 10% of the skin resistance, has been placed across the lower pair. The previously negative responses have been converted to positive ones; the output reverts to normal when the shunt is removed. This phenomenon, it should be stressed, can only happen in the presence of different generators arranged in parallel.

Ebbecke waves   A little-known phenomenon discovered many years ago by Ebbecke (1921) is the transient, locally restricted change in skin resistance, which can be elicited from the forearm and other areas, but not from the palm, by a variety of local physical stimuli such as pressure, heat, or electricity. Ebbecke reported that these responses were independent of nerve activity and could be obtained from a cadaver for several hours after death and even a day later. They could be eliminated in the living subject by exposure of the skin to chloroform. He attributed them to the excitability of a nonglandular layer of epithelial cells in the epidermis. Rein (1929) subsequently obtained similar responses using the potential method. The responses were always in the positive direction and up to several mV in amplitude. The rise time of this response found by Rein was of the order of 5 sec and the duration about 12 sec. The slow rise time may have been a result of the low-frequency response of his galvanometer or prolonged stimulation; similar responses measured in this author's laboratory have a rise time of less than 1 sec and a total duration of about 4 sec. Shackel (1959) also reported short durations. Richter (1929), like Ebbecke, was unable to elicit local resistance responses from the palms but could obtain them easily from the dorsum of the hand. He therefore concluded that nonsweat gland areas do not play a significant role in controlling palmar skin resistance. The present author has been able to elicit not only local positive potential responses from the palms but could obtain local resistance responses as well (unpublished data).

It should be mentioned that Lewis and Zotterman (1926–1927) disclaimed Ebbecke's interpretation of the resistance drop, although they confirmed his observations, pointing out that all results, including those on cadaver skin, could be attributed to damage of the horny layer by the stimulus. This layer, they claimed, was the site of the skin's resistance. The work of these authors does not really appear to invalidate Ebbeck's interpretation. Their stimuli were primarily needle pricks, which could be calculated to cause damage. Further, they were unaware of the positive wave accompanying the response, and also, apparently, of the fact that a genuine local response is followed by quick recovery. These are not likely to be explained by the behavior of a layer of dead cells. Even their demonstration that the site of the skin's resistance resides in the epidermis is invalid, resting as it does on the erroneous assumption that the boundary of separation in blister formation is *above* the living cell layer. Actually, it is *within* the living epidermal layer or beneath it (Rothman, 1954, pp. 699–707).

Nomenclature

An unfortunately casual application of terms in the electrodermal literature has generated considerable confusion. While papers that fail to specify clearly whether the author is dealing with potential or resistance cause some anguish, these ambiguities can, in most cases, be resolved by close examination of the text. Much more serious is the common fault of discussing "GSR," "galvanic skin potential (GSP)," or "electrodermal activity" without specifying whether one is referring to the level or the response amplitude. One group of authors in a related field has, for example, published a series of at least five papers in which the term GSR was used throughout to signify base resistance, much to the confusion and ultimate dismay of the present author. Such inappropriate terminology has, in fact,

caused many misconceptions to arise with regard to the behavior of certain clinical groups. For instance, when one reports an observation that anxiety neurotics show "more GSR activity" than normal subjects, it is of great importance that the reader understand whether this refers to the base level, which may be indicative of diffuse, nondirected activation, or the response amplitude, which may perhaps be interpreted as effective responsivity (Burch & Greiner, 1960).

A related problem arises from the practice of calling each electrodermal wave a "response," the implication being that a stimulus, in the usual sense, has set it off. It is certainly possible that a given electrodermal excitatory center that is highly activated, perhaps pharmacologically, may discharge periodically if afferent bombardment, acting upon a spontaneously varying local excitatory state, causes the attainment of the discharge threshold at random points. If the nature of the discharge is a short burst, the cutaneous response will be a wave of a characteristic shape (Edelberg, 1967, p. 47; Fujimori, 1955). The organized appearance of such waves suggests to many that all responses are of a reflex origin, or at least represent responses to internal stimuli. In many cases, however, such as Stage 4 sleep, they may represent spontaneous discharge. Wang (1957, 1958) suggested that the electrodermal activity set off by excitation of a sensory organ or nerve should be called a galvanic skin "reflex," while that elicited by drugs or the stimulation of nonsensory pathways should be called a galvanic skin "response." The term "response" seems preferable to "reflex" for all electrodermal waves because of the unknown admixture of reflex and nonreflex activity. Consistent with this reasoning, it would seem desirable to refer to "spontaneous activity" rather than "nonspecific responses," which was used by Burch and Greiner (1958) and A. J. Silverman, Cohen, and Shmavonian

TABLE 9.1 ELECTRODERMAL TERMS AND ABBREVIATIONS

Level	Abbreviation	Response	Abbreviation
Skin resistance	SR	Skin resistance response	SRR
Skin conductance	SC	Skin conductance response	SCR
Skin potential	SP	Skin potential response	SPR
Skin impedance	SZ	Skin impedance response	SZR

(1959). Johnson and Lubin's (1966) general term, *electrodermal activity* (EDA) is very convenient and meaningful. To define further the sense in which electrodermal activity is used, it is useful to refer to activity in which the characteristic electrodermal wave form appears as "phasic EDA," and to baseline variations not clearly caused by phasic effects as "tonic EDA."

To reduce the confusion resulting from the endless variety of terms and abbreviations used for electrodermal measures, a committee of active workers in this field, working under the auspices of the Society for Psychophysiological Research, has suggested a group of terms and abbreviations that it felt worthy of standardization. These are shown in Table 9.1.

Venables and Martin (1967) suggest using SRL, SCL, etc., to indicate "level," a convention that appears to have considerable merit. In addition to those recommended, the generic term "electrodermal response" (EDR) is a very convenient one, which seems to deserve adoption. The generic terms "endosomatic" for describing measurements with no external current source, and "exosomatic" for all measurements using an external source, are distinctly advantageous. It appears that the terms GSR or PGR, despite a long tradition, may have to be sacrificed in the interest of standardization. One term that may be used in the future, if alternating current (ac) sources are adopted, is "admittance." This term used by Montagu (1964) in his analysis of ac effects is, for impedance measurements, the counterpart of conductance in resistance measurements, i.e., the reciprocal of Z. On the basis of the scheme presented above, the associated abbreviations would probably be SA and SAR.

Peripheral Variables

Temperature and humidity Of all the peripheral variables, temperature has probably contributed more to the variance of the measure than any other. Resistance increases with the decrease in temperature by about 3%/°C. Since skin cooling of several degrees may accompany vasoconstriction, this may introduce a substantial error into base-level measurements. The amplitude of the skin resistance response increases by about 5%/°C as the temperature drops, but this effect may be lost after a few

minutes (Maulsby & Edelberg, 1960). Lowering the skin temperature to 20°C for periods of 15 min or more depresses the resistance response, although this effect is characterized by great individual differences. The positive and negative components of the potential response were found to behave differently in response to temperature changes; the positive response was absent from the dorsum of the hand at 15°C and 20°C, appeared at 30°C, and increased in amplitude at 40°C. The negative response was most conspicuous at 20°C (Yokota, Takahashi, Kondo, & Fujimori, 1959). These results were obtained with changes in room temperature. Depression of the positive wave at lower temperature was also observed when skin temperature was changed locally, a finding also reported by Fujimori (1955). Wenger and Cullen (1962, pp. 106–112) reported positive correlations between forearm skin conductance and room temperature of .17, .22, and .12 for three large groups of subjects (total N above 900). Log conductance change showed a variable relation, and palmar skin conductance a negligible one. Venables (1955) also found an extremely variable relation between conductance response and temperature.

Latency of the electrodermal response is markedly increased by decreases in skin temperature. One wonders how well this parameter was controlled in experiments in which latency changes were measured as a function of central arousal. Latency can vary from 1.2 sec at a local temperature of 40°C to 4 sec at 10°C (Gildemeister & Ellinghaus, 1923). This implies that a significant portion of the total delay from stimulus to response is due to a peripheral delay, possibly to the diffusion of a chemical mediator, possibly to the time required to elaborate or express sweat, and possibly to the spread of an excitation wave through an epidermal cell layer. Since the skin temperature may easily change as a consequence of the vasoconstriction attending a state of central activation, the likelihood that latency measures are spurious seems high.

Humidity can be expected to exert an effect on skin conductance, insofar as it influences evaporative water loss, and consequently, the activity of the thermoregulatory system. One would expect higher humidity to reduce evaporation and, therefore, to cause a reflex increase in perspiration to promote heat loss. This would be accompanied by increased skin conductance. The negative correlation reported by Venables (1955) and by Wenger and Cullen (1962, pp. 106–112) between palmar skin conductance and relative humidity is therefore unexpected. It seems to indicate that the palms are not controlled by thermoregulatory requirements, a conclusion consistent with the insignificant correlation reported by these authors between palmar conductance and room temperature. It may indicate that palmar water output is in part regulated by the local requirements for maintaining hydration of the corneum.

Chemical environment The effector organ of the electrodermal response, whatever it may be, is sensitive to the composition of the solution at the electrode site and in this respect manifests the characteristics of a membrane. Certain salts such as Na_2SO_4, $CaCl_2$, and $AlCl_3$ may potentiate the resistance response significantly, e.g., by 240% in the case of 1M $CaCl_2$, and 600% for 1M $AlCl_3$. The degree of potentiation depends on the polarity of the current at the experimental site and is greatest when the larger ion of the electrolyte is tending to move into the skin (Edelberg, Greiner, & Burch, 1960). Thus, in the case of $AlCl_3$, the increase in response amplitude is twice as great at an anodal site as at a cathodal one. Conversely, the potentiation by Na_2SO_4 is greatest at the cathode. It should be stressed that, despite the potentiation of response, resistance is *decreased* by these compounds and is only slightly affected by polarity of the current (to a maximum of 15%). Other agents attenuated the response. For example, a cationic detergent mixture, Zephiran (Winthrop Laboratories), in total concentration of less than 0.005M, reduced the response amplitude to 45% of control, and a 1M KCl solution to 64%.

The specific effects of the various common electrolytes became weaker with decreasing concentration and were negligible at concentrations of the order of 0.1M. Acidity of the medium had a pronounced effect, with the greatest response amplitude occurring at pH 7 and falling off on either side. At pH 3 the amplitude was reduced to 30% of normal; at pH 11, to 60%.

The effect of the electrolyte medium upon the potential level can be predicted on the basis of the expected behavior of a surface membrane with a negatively charged, fixed structure. The negative charge is an electrostatic one and is caused by the ionization of the molecules that form part of the structure. In the case of the skin, the anionic portion remains fixed, while the cation is free to move. The net effect of this is a selective permeability of such structures to cations. For the skin this selectivity is evident but rather imperfect. When a concentrated solution of KCl is placed on the skin, potassium tends to diffuse through the membrane, while chloride tends to be excluded, the result being an increase in external negativity (Rothman, 1954, p. 12). A less concentrated solution produces a lesser increase. When one finger is dipped into 0.1M KCl and another into 0.01M KCl, the potential between these sites is of the order of 20 mV, as compared to a theoretical value of 58 mV if the membranes were perfectly selective (Edelberg, 1963b). In addition to the charge, the ionic size is also a determinant of the effect. Thus a site exposed to a molar solution of KCl is appreciably more negative (by 12 mV) than is one exposed to a molar solution of $AlCl_3$.

Despite this generally predictable behavior of skin exposed to such electrolytes, the effect on the transcutaneous potential is quite unpredictable in the individual case (Edelberg, 1963b). For example, the potential level is sometimes unchanged despite the variation of the external concentration from 0.005M–0.5M. In other instances the surface potential changes but remains highly negative, even when the external concentration of the electrolyte is reduced almost to zero. These variable results can best be explained if the site of the potential difference across the skin resides not in a single structure but in two separate structures having different properties and arranged in parallel. If one assumes that these are the sweat gland and the epidermis and, in agreement with Rothman (1954, p. 33), that the sweat gland membrane is not easily accessible to surface agents, one can explain such results by allowing for the fact that the sweat glands may be full or partially empty and may, therefore, contribute differently to the total surface potential.

The skin potential response is affected by surface

electrolytes in somewhat the same way as is the skin resistance response, but the quantitative relations have not been worked out. Recent experiments in the author's laboratory indicate that the effect on the positive and negative components of the potential response are different. For example, 1M AlCl₃, which had produced an average increase of 600% in the amplitude of the *resistance* response (Edelberg, Greiner, & Burch, 1960), produced, in a more recent study, an increase of 750% in the positive wave but no significant increase of the negative wave (Figure 9.6). A solution of 5M NaCl produced a dramatic potentiation of the c wave, even after 45 min of exposure. Figure 9.7 shows the effect after 15 min.

Various chemical agents other than inorganic electrolytes may affect the peripheral apparatus. For example, iontophoretically introduced formalin may block sweating for many days (Kuno, 1956, p. 356). A solution of 5% acriflavin may reduce base resistance to 11% of its control level; a 2% soap solution may reduce it to 40% (Edelberg, 1963a).

Pharmacologic effects   Although the literature on the local effects of atropine on EDA was controversial for a long period (Waller, 1919–1920; Leva, 1920; Aveling & McDowall, 1925; Richter, 1929; Perry, Mount, Hull, & Zeilenga, 1955), the introduction by Montagu (1958) of a reliable method for the local application of this agent by iontophoresis permitted consensual validation of the observation

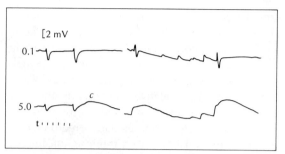

Figure 9.7   Potentiation of slow negative (c) waves after exposure to 5M NaCl. The upper traces show recordings of control site in 0.1M NaCl. Lower left trace is from a site which has been in 5M NaCl for 15 min. Lower right is same site 3 min later. Upward deflections are negative. The signals, t, are at 4 sec intervals.

that cholinergic blocking agents such as atropine (Lader & Montagu, 1962; Wilcott, 1964), hyoscyamine (Martin & Venables, 1964), and scopolamine (Edelberg, unpublished) all effectively block neurodermal activity in the human. Reports of the effects of the catecholamines on sweat secretion are conflicting. Darrow (1936) has reported a depression of EDA resulting from the systemic injection of adrenaline. Haimovici's pharmacological experiments (1950) on the human eccrine gland support the idea that the normally cholinergic sudomotor fibers manifest adrenergic activity. He was able to elicit prolonged sweating with the local introduction of adrenaline or noradrenaline and to inhibit spontaneous sweating with dibenamine, an adrenergic blocking agent. The sweat glands of the footpad of the cat, although possibly apocrine, are cholinergic (Dale & Feldberg, 1934), but surprisingly, systemic injection of norepinephrine (25 μg/kg), also consistently abolished the footpad response for periods up to 45 min (Gooch & Edelberg, unpublished), possibly because of spasm of the myoepithelial fibers. Pilocarpine acts directly on the end organ and causes profuse, continuing secretion of sweat and lowering of resistance (Aveling & McDowall, 1925). Richter (1927) demonstrated that pilocarpine eliminates spontaneous responses, but the response to intense startle stimuli is retained.

Centrally acting agents may produce an indirect effect on EDA via their action on neurodermal control and regulatory areas, but a direct effect on

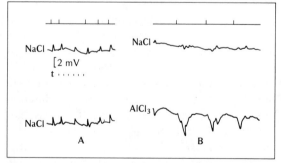

Figure 9.6   Potentiation of palmar positive SPR by 1M AlCl₃. In A, both experimental and control sites are in 0.1M NaCl. In B, the upper site has been transferred to fresh 0.1M NaCl, the lower to 1M AlCl₃. The upward deflections are negative. The top trace shows stimulus presentations. The time signals, t, are at 5-sec intervals.

the peripheral apparatus may also be involved, e.g., in the case of adrenaline and mecholyl (Haimovici, 1950). In interpreting such effects, one should consider the possible indirect effect on EDA resulting from alteration in the blood flow, since vasoconstriction per se may have a marked effect on the amplitude of the EDR (Edelberg, 1964a).

Current density and polarity The total current applied to a site is of no significance unless one knows how much of it passes through each unit area of skin, i.e., unless it is expressed in terms of current per unit area (current density). A linear relation between the voltage developed at a site and current density was reported by Fujimori (1955). Later, however, Edelberg, Greiner, and Burch (1960) pointed out that this apparently ideal behavior was determined over a range of current density considerably in excess of that commonly applied. At the lower levels of this curve, the apparent resistance and the amplitude of the response behaved linearly with the current up to a density of 8–12 $\mu A/cm^2$. Between this value and 40–50 $\mu A/cm^2$, occurred one, frequently two, deflections in the current resistance or current response curves. On this basis a maximum current density of 8 $\mu A/cm^2$ was adopted for use in the constant current system. Wilcott and Hammond (1965) subsequently demonstrated that at very high resistances the voltage developed across the skin can be considerable, even with fairly low current densities, and may cause a reduction in the apparent resistance of the skin. This may imply that we must monitor both current density and voltage. It may be demonstrated with the use of an X-Y plotter that for short-term application the extent of linear behavior of apparent resistance with increasing current density varies with base resistance. This range becomes greatly extended at very low resistances, to as high as 75 $\mu A/cm^2$ (Edelberg, 1965a, p. 38). Although this observation may seem to permit the establishment of a limited constant voltage level to prevent the reduction in resistance described by Wilcott and Hammond, it would possibly raise problems of electrode polarization at very low subject resistance.

The polarity of the current does not have an appreciable effect on either the base level or the response amplitude when the electrolyte medium is dilute NaCl in liquid or paste. With other electrolytes, there may be a pronounced polarity effect on response amplitude, although a minor one on base resistance. For example, in a solution of 1M $CaCl_2$, the response amplitude is 1.58 times as high at a positive site as at a negative site, but the corresponding resistance ratio is only 1.06:1. The corresponding ratios for 1M $AlCl_3$ are 2.04 and 1.15. With modern amplifiers employing common-mode rejection, it is desirable to use a pair of two similar sites, rather than a large arm reference; this will tend to reduce the polarity effect.

Anatomical differences The palmar and plantar surfaces are commonly the most active sites in exosomatic as well as endosomatic responses, although they are not the most conductive ones on the body. The forehead and scalp are substantially more so. The medial aspect of the foot over the hallucis abductor muscle is highly active. The relative activity of several other areas can be found in the same citation (Edelberg, 1967, pp. 14–17). Fisher (1960) has compared resistance levels on the hand with those on various points on the head and has related the gradients to the body image.

In comparing various parts of the body, one should bear in mind that the relative activity changes with the state of activity of the individual. For example, the lateral differences reported by Fisher (1958) may shift during sleep (Johnson & Lubin, 1966) or during hypnosis (Edelberg, unpublished data). The inactivity that generally characterizes skin potential and conductance in such regions as the chest or arm may give way to activity under temperature load or high emotional stress, (Rickles & Day, 1968; Wilcott, 1963). An interesting seasonal effect upon topographical differences in activity has been reported by Neumann (1968). It should be noted that the relation between endosomatic and exosomatic activity of an area varies considerably; some areas show little exosomatic response, despite the occurrence of potential responses of appreciable magnitude. The relative proportion of positive and negative components of the SPR from different areas also varies considerably (Edelberg, 1965a, p. 34). It is of interest that the plantar surface shows very little positive activity;

whereas the hypothenar and thenar eminences of the palm show the highest positive activity of the body, despite the fact that the negative activity of these areas is about equal.

Species differences Electrodermal activity has been allegedly observed in the skin of the frog, toad, and horse, and from the pads or paws of the rabbit, rat, cat, dog, and monkey (reviewed by Landis & DeWick, 1929). Not all of these citations are necessarily of genuine responses. For example, in the study on rabbits, Sidis and Nelson (1910) observed that no reflex was produced as long as the legs were held motionless; they interpreted this as evidence of the muscular basis of the response. This author was unable to elicit any response from the felt-covered pad of the rabbit, unless the preparation was such as to permit movement artifacts, a likely explanation for the earlier observations. Genuine responses are present in the rat, cat, and dog (at least in young dogs). The cat, which has been most studied, resembles man and monkey in its electrodermal behavior but rarely produces positive SPRs. Wilcott (1965) observed that the cat behaved differently from these primates in its response to small currents superimposed on the SPR (potential "driving").

EXPERIMENTAL METHODS AND FINDINGS

Specific Techniques

Numerous discussions of methodology, many of which are excellent, are already in the literature. General discussions include those of Wechsler (1925), Landis and DeWick (1929), Davis (1930), Thouless (1930), Landis (1932), Grings (1953), Edelberg and Burch (1962), Hume (1966), Montagu and Coles (1966), Venables and Martin (1967), and Edelberg (1967, pp. 1–53). Others deal with special topics such as endosomatic measurements (Venables & Sayer, 1963), skin electrodes (Lykken, 1959; O'Connell, Tursky, & Orne, 1960; Geddes, 1967, pp. 369–458), or instrumentation (Strohl, 1918; Strohl & Iodka, 1924; Davis, 1929; Darrow, 1932b; Hagfors, 1964; Simons & Perez, 1965). For the reader's convenience, however, it seems appropriate to describe briefly some recommended techniques. One par-

ticularly useful advance for the study of the EDR in conscious cats has been Wilcott's development of the carpal pad electrode (1969).

Electrodes and their application Nonpolarizable electrodes should be used for potential or conductance measurement, and even for low frequency impedance measurement. The two most popular types are the zinc/zinc sulphate (Darrow, 1929; Lacey, Bateman & Van Lehn, 1953; Lykken, 1959; Richter, 1929; Wenger, Engel & Clemens, 1957; Wilcott, 1962) and the silver/silver chloride (Ag/AgCl) (Edelberg, 1964b; Johnson & Lubin, 1966; Sternbach & Tursky, 1965; Venables & Sayer, 1963). The zinc sulphate is usually mixed with kaolin clay to provide a nonrunning electrode paste. The silver/silver chloride electrode is commonly made by anodizing a silver electrode in a chloride solution (Geddes, Baker & Moore, 1969; Janz & Taniguchi, 1953). The present author uses a standard method for their preparation that involves (a) cleaning the surface with an abrasive (scouring powder), (b) washing in hot water, (c) cathodizing at 1 mA/cm² for 1 min in 1M NaCl, and (d) anodizing at 1 mA/cm² for 5 min in the same bath.

Since the nature of electrolytes on the skin surface may have a marked effect on base levels and response amplitudes, one does well to use a paste whose electrolyte concentration resembles that of average sweat, i.e., 0.05M NaCl. One such paste can be made by suspending 6 grams of corn starch in 100 ml 0.05M NaCl and bringing the mixture to a gentle boil, while stirring. After boiling 30 sec, the mixture is removed from the heat, poured into containers, and capped.

Size, preparation, and location of site The size of the site does not influence potential measurements, but if too small, its resistance may become appreciable in comparison with the input resistance of the amplifier and attenuation of the signal results. A site of 1 cm² or more is recommended, unless amplifiers of exceptionally high input impedance are available. The area is very important in *exosomatic* measures, since SR and SRR decrease as area increases. SC and SCR increase with area. To circumscribe a specific area, one may use either a mask made of plastic, pressure-sensitive tape with a cutout, or a cup electrode fastened to the skin with adhesive or an elastic band (see Day & Lippitt, 1964). If the masking tape method is used, the skin is cleaned with acetone; the mask pressed into place; electrode paste applied; and a silver/silver chloride electrode somewhat larger than the cutout pressed gently over the site and held in place by pressure-sensitive tape with a layer of $\frac{1}{4}$-in. sponge rubber between it and the electrode. One should ensure that the application does not occlude circulation. It is desirable to wrap the prepared site in cloth or sponge rubber to insulate against temperature changes.

For exosomatic measures, a pair of sites on the volar surfaces of the middle segments of two fingers is a convenient arrangement. Alternatively, an active area on the foot is conveniently located just dorsal to the plantar surface, over the abductor hallucis muscle, midway between a point under the internal malleolus and the first phalange. Two electrodes may be located 2 cm apart in this region, since it is desirable when taking exosomatic measures to use similar skin for both sites to effect maximal cancellation of endosomatic effects. The abductor hallucis site is more active than the plantar area and is to be preferred if the subject will be walking at any time in the course of the experiment.

In endosomatic measures the same sites are recommended for the active electrode. There are three preferred "inactive" areas for the reference site: the inner aspect of the ear lobe; over the ulnar bone, one-fifth the distance from the elbow to the wrist; and over the tibial bone, one-fifth the distance from the ankle to the knee.

Current strength   If constant current is used, a current density of 8 μA/cm^2 is recommended. For a pair of sites the area used in calculation is that of one of the sites. With constant voltage a source of .75–1.0 V across two matched sites is recommended. Each of these values is optimum for general use but will have serious disadvantages under special conditions (Edelberg, 1967, pp. 22–27).

Associated circuitry   An array of circuits is presented in the papers on methodology cited in the introduction to this section. The following requirements should be kept in mind during selection of

a preferred circuit. First, if response amplitude or count is to be measured, one generally needs to cancel the large steady component of the signal, so that it is possible to use high amplification on the remainder for better observation of small fluctuations. Either a bridge circuit or a bucking circuit may be used for exosomatic purposes; but for endosomatic measures a bucking system is required, unless the amplifier has an unusual range of zero adjustment. Secondly, there are two major choices in the selection of an exosomatic circuit. If one uses a constant current circuit, deflections are proportional to resistance, and conversion of all data to conductance is usually required. Conductance and conductance changes can, however, be recorded directly if one uses a constant voltage system. While this has distinct disadvantages under some circumstances (Edelberg, 1967, pp. 26–27), its convenience in data reduction appears to outweigh its other problems.

Direct measurement of sweat   The measurement of sweat output is obtained by three principal methods. One of these includes a count of active (i.e., surface-wet) sweat glands; another measures total weight loss; and a third monitors the vapor output from a circumscribed area. The interested reader is referred for details of counting technique to papers by Minor (1928), Netsky (1948), Papa (1963), Randall (1946), J. J. Silverman and Powell (1945), Sutarman and Thomson (1952), and Wada and Takagaki (1948). For examples of the vapor method, refer to papers by Adams, Funkhouser, and Kendall (1963), Bullard (1962), Darrow (1927), Edelberg (1964b), and Wilcott (1962). An interesting application of the count method to a psychophysiological investigation is seen in a study by Malmo (1965). The weight-loss method has been used primarily by environmental physiologists, but an example of its application to psychophysiological research is that of Darrow and Freeman (1934).

Physiological Behavior of the Skin

Sweat secretion   Although sweat glands are found over most of the body, those on the palmar and plantar surface have been recognized as responding primarily to emotional or ideational stimuli, the remainder primarily to thermal stimuli. The secretion of apocrine glands has been associated with sexual behavior but appears to respond to a variety of emotional stimuli (Shelley & Hurley, 1953).

During the sweat response, the sweat rises rapidly and may commonly be seen on the volar surface of the finger, emerging as a small droplet at the sweat gland pore. Not all glands are active in any given EDR, nor are all EDRs necessarily accompanied by any visible sweat. The sweat glands are supplied with sympathetic nerve fibers that are paradoxically cholinergic. It is commonly believed that secretion is phasic, occurring at the time of the reflex. Kuno (1956, p. 296), however, argues that the secretion is continuous, the sweat being stored in the lumen of the gland or duct until it is forcibly expelled by the contraction of the myoepithelial cells, which are adrenergic. Since atropine blocks sweating, the production of sweat must be under neural control; but if Kuno is correct, this innervation must act as a tonic control that can change its level as the situation demands. Although apocrine glands appear to require myoepithelial contraction to force out the contents, it seems possible that secretory pressures in the eccrine gland may be adequate to force sweat up the narrow ducts. Myoepithelial contraction would, of course, be of substantial assistance, since it was found in the case of apocrine glands that an internal pressure of 225 mm Hg could be developed by this action (Shelley & Hurley, 1953). Evidence for the role of myoepithelial action in eccrine sweating is seen in unpublished results from my laboratory in which high systemic doses of norepinephrine, 25 μg/kg in anesthetized cats, caused prompt cessation of the electrodermal activity that normally occurred in response to electrical stimulation of the sympathetic supply to the footpad. Since arterial occlusion produced no such effect, vasoconstriction could not account for this result; it, therefore, was most likely caused by spasm of the myoepithelial cells.

Haimovici (1950) and others have demonstrated local stimulation of eccrine sweating by adrenergic agents and its inhibition by adrenergic blocking agents in humans. Although the evidence seems to implicate the myoepithelium as the mediator of these effects; as Kuno (1956, p. 289) pointed out,

the enhanced local sweating subsequent to a single injection of adrenaline may continue for 2 hr and cannot therefore be explained by the contraction of myoepithelial cells. He concludes that the secretory cells of the sweat gland respond to adrenaline, as well as acetylcholine. Kuno (1956, p. 294) and Rothman (1954, p. 157) cite the work of Takahara (1934), who cannulated single sweat glands on the human palm and recorded the behavior of the fluid level in a capillary tube. Spontaneous sweat discharge at rest occurred in waves that took about 15–20 sec to reach peak and slowly receded to the original level in a total time of 1 min. These occurred periodically in 2–3-min intervals. Kuno argues that the downward movement of the column after reaching peak is best explained by the relaxation of the myoepithelial fibers. He has calculated that the volume change in the capillary during each of these contractions is approximately equal to the volume of the lumen of the secretory portion of the sweat gland. Thus he regards the state of the gland at rest as characterized by a very low tonic secretion rate and a slow rhythmic contraction of the myoepithelium. During squeezing of a hand dynamometer, these waves increased in frequency to about 2/min. They had about the same rise time as in the rest condition. With relaxation of the myoepithelial cells, the height of the column no longer fell. This resulted in a staircase buildup of the height of the fluid level. Superimposed upon the slow waves were smaller perturbations that took about 5 sec to reach their peak effect. It seems likely that these may represent a phasic component in the activity of the cholinergic fibers controlling the rate of secretion. It is noteworthy that a similar pattern of slow and fast components can be observed in skin potential variation, with the potential becoming more negative in accordance with similar variations in vapor output (Figures 9.3 and 9.9).

Myoepithelial relaxation seems to me to be an improbable explanation for the retrograde movement of the fluid level in Takahara's experiment. Smooth muscle does not behave like a rubber syringe bulb. Relaxation would not cause suction at deeper levels but would simply permit refilling and distension of the lumen by secretory activity. Weiner and Hellmann (1960) have written an excellent review of the structure and function of the sweat gland and have pointed out the existence of other explanations than that proposed by Kuno to account for the backflow of sweat. Lobitz and Mason (1948), for example, have contended that water reabsorption in the duct may account for this effect, since the solutes in palmar sweat are found to be more concentrated when the secretion is slow. Contrary to Lobitz and Mason, Robinson and Robinson (1954) report that solute concentration is increased during copious sweating. Montagna (1962, pp. 358–359), in agreement with Lobitz and Mason, has taken the view that physiological and histochemical evidence appears to support the occurrence of duct reabsorption.

TABLE 9.2 SURVEY OF REPRESENTATIVE STUDIES SHOWING CORRELATION OF SWEAT MEASUREMENTS WITH ELECTRICAL MEASUREMENTS

Method	Sweat measure and site	Electrical measure	Individuals	Group	Source

Vapor:
  Resistance
  hygrometry
	Response
	amplitude
	(Palmar; Arm)
		Pos SPR
		SRR
		SCR
			.73
			.45
			—
				—
				.45
				.65
					Darrow
					(1927)

Sweat count:
  Colorimetric
    density scaling
    (Silverman & Powell)
	Level	SC	—	.31	Wenger &
					Gilchrist
					(1948)

Sweat count: Netsky prism	Count (Thermoregulatory sites)	SC	.44 to .96 (.91 median)		Thomas & Korr (1957)
Vapor: Coulometry	Level (Palmar)	SC SR SP	— — —	.26 −.22 .29	Wilcott (1962)
	Response amplitude (Palmar)	SRR Neg SPR Pos SPR	.82 to .95 (.87 median) .62 to .80 (.73 median) .81 to .95 (.86 median)	— .49 .45	

Vapor:
  Resistance
  hygrometry
	Response
	amplitude
	(Palmar)
		SCR
		
		SRR
			−.10 to +.62
			(.30 median)
			−.13 to +.64
			(.24 median)
				—	Edelberg
					(1964b)

Vapor: Thermal conductivity	Level (Palmar) Log level (Palmar) Response amplitude (Palmar)	SR Log SR SRR Log SRR	−.79 to −.92 (−.90 median) −.78 to −.96 (−.92 median) .92 to .95 (.94 median) .72 to .84 (.78 median)	— — — —	Adams & Vaughan (1965)
	Level	SP	.04	—	Martin & Venables (1966)
Sweat count	Level (Palmar)	SR	−.12 to −.96	−.74	Juniper, Blanton, & Dykman (1967)

Of special significance to the question of duct reabsorption is the occurrence of miliaria, a condition in which the ducts become plugged with keratin, either as a naturally occurring phenomenon or experimentally by the use of high electrical currents (Shelley, 1951). In this condition an engorgement of the duct occurs, eventually causing rupture and discharge of the contents into the surrounding tissue. When the plug occurs very close to the sweat pore, the expansion and rupture occur in the corneum (Miliaria crystallina). This perhaps implies that there is considerable resistance to lateral diffusion of water out of the coiled duct in the horny layer and that sweat normally issues from the pore and wets the corneum from the surface. However, it seems just as likely that rupture may result from the high intraductal pressure generated by myoepithelial contraction, in which the rate of buildup exceeds the capacity of the spiral portion to release water into the corneum, despite the fact that this rate of lateral diffusion is appreciable.

It is of interest that there is a passive, negative-feedback mechanism in the stratum corneum to restrict excessive sweating. The corneum is very hygroscopic and is capable of holding up to 70% of its own weight in water (Kligman, 1964, pp. 387–433). The swelling that results causes occlusion of the sweat ducts and reduction in sweating (Brebner & Kerslake, 1964). Sarkany, Shuster, and Stammers (1965) have shown that sweating does not occur in skin that has been soaking in water but does so when soaked in 15% saline. The effect was shown to be due to differential swelling of the horny layer.

There have been several studies that compared electrodermal activity either in terms of the level or the response amplitude with sweat gland activity, in some instances in terms of active sweat gland count, and others in terms of evaporative water loss. Correlations ranged from low to very high. Some results are tabulated for comparison in Table 9.2. It is clear that there is often a high enough correlation to suggest a causal relation between the two parameters. A considerable portion of the variance must be attributed either to the independence of these two measures or to factors of the sort that Adams discusses (1966; Adams & Vaughan, 1965). Although electrical measures may sometimes pre-sent a distorted picture of sweat gland activity, measurements of vapor output or count are also subject to serious distortion; the convenience and relative simplicity of electrical measures appear to make them the method of choice for psychophysiological studies.

Epidermal function The epidermis functions as a barrier against the movement of water and solutes across the skin, and in the human represents the area through which most heat exchange occurs. Kuno (1956, p. 18) estimated that a 94-cm^2 area of skin is occupied by sweat gland pores, plus the cavities in which they lie. Since the whole body surface is about 18,000 cm^2, it can be appreciated that under a heavy heat load the availability of the entire epidermal surface area for evaporative heat loss would be highly advantageous, perhaps imperative. The ease with which the corneum absorbs sweat secreted at the sweat pores can be readily observed under low power magnification; it is apparent that the evaporative surface area may considerably be extended by this process. The extent to which moisture is transpired directly from the corium through the Malpighian and horny layers is uncertain, but this surely represents one route, as demonstrated by the observation by Loewy and Wechselmann (1911) that individuals with the congenital absence of sweat glands behave like normal individuals in their rate of insensible perspiration (i.e., without a visible aqueous phase on the surface) and in the response of this perspiration to temperature changes. Pinson (1942) eliminated sweat gland activity by iontophoretic introduction of formaldehyde without altering the rate of insensible perspiration. According to Kuno (1956, p. 40), except for the palms and soles, the water loss from the epidermal layer is far greater than that from sweat gland activity.

Permeability to water and solutes Man as a land animal must maintain what Claude Bernard called his *milieu intérieur* in the face of a dessicating atmosphere. This requires an effective barrier against the outward movement of water. It is understandable, then, that the permeability of the skin to water is rather low. Under average conditions of temperature and humidity, the rate of loss of water to the outside is only of the order of 0.5–1 mg/cm^2/hr (Kligman, 1964, p. 423). At this rate it would take over 40 days to lose 1 gram of water through 1 cm^2 of skin. The barrier is not diffuse but seems to be concentrated in a very thin layer. If one strips off sequential layers of the corneum by applying cellophane tape and pulling (Szakall, 1958), the rate of water loss remains relatively constant until about the tenth strip, at which point the barrier is essentially removed (Blank, 1953). Buettner and Odland (1957) regard this as the level of the stratum corneum conjunctum, in the compact, deepest layers of the corneum. Kligman (1964) has argued that the barrier is diffusely distributed throughout the corneum. Several other workers, using radioactive tracers, have identified a second ion-barrier at the dermo–epidermal junction (e.g. Witten, Ross, Oshry, & Hyman, 1951).

As in the case of water, the permeability of the corneum to electrolytes is relatively high in the most superficial layers but becomes very low in the layer just above the granular layer. Blank and Gould (1959) demonstrated with the skin-stripping technique that this thin supergranular layer constitutes an effective chemical barrier. The layer of corneum above this barrier is rather freely permeable to many solutes. For example, this author has exposed skin to silver nitrate for a period of 30 min, exposed it to light, and reduced it with photographic developing solution (Edelberg, 1963a, pp. 9–17). Histological examination showed the entire corneum to be permeated by the heavy deposit of reduced silver. The lower boundary of this dark zone was just above the granular layer. Added evidence for the free permeability of this horny layer to solutes is seen in the work of Rein (1929), who demonstrated that neutral, acidic, or basic dyes penetrate the horny layer readily but come to a sudden halt at its lower boundary. These data appear to contradict the recent assertion that the corneum is permeable to water but not to salts (Rushmer, Buettner, Short, & Odland, 1966).

The question of whether the penetration of the skin by solutes occurs through the epidermis via the corneum and the Malpighian layer or via the sweat ducts is another matter and the subject of controversy. Rothman argues on the basis of his studies of percutaneous absorption that the route

of entry on hairy areas is primarily through the hair follicles and associated sebaceous glands. The epidermal route per se represents a rather restrictive one. Its permeability to solutes may, however, be increased by exposure to certain agents such as dimethyl sulfoxide (Sweeney, Downes, & Matoltsy, 1966) or by increasing the surface alkalinity to pH 10.5 (Blank & Gould, 1959). Rothman considered the sweat glands to be an improbable route of entry, a belief consistent with the poor absorptive capacity of palmar and plantar skin, the two areas of the body richest in sweat glands. Although Kuno defends the role of the sweat gland as an avenue of entry of solutes, pointing to the penetration of sweat ducts by methylene blue (Kuno, 1956, p. 311), his argument was seriously weakened by the demonstration by Flesch, Goldstone, and Urbach (1951) that this penetration was limited to the upper layers of the corneum, even when strong iontophoretic driving was used.

The resolution of this dilemma is of great importance to the clarification of the electrical properties of the skin discussed in this chapter. An experiment by Kuno (1956) strongly suggests that under some conditions the sweat duct represents an avenue of entrance to lower levels, even though perhaps not so far as the secretory portion. By using short pulses of high intensity current, he was able to drive methylene blue down the ducts and out into the upper regions of the corium, as indicated by histological examination. Suchi (1950) was able to obtain similar results with ferrous sulphate.

The absorption phenomenon   The bidirectional nature of the transepidermal movement of water was demonstrated by Buettner (1959). He placed, against the skin, containers that were partially filled with solutions having a range of vapor pressure. By measuring the change in weight he was able to demonstrate that water diffused from the skin into the air at relative humidity levels up to 86%. Above this level water moved into the skin. This simple behavior in the direction of a concentration gradient did not appear to be neurally controlled, but a subsequent finding raised the possibility that the permeability of the diffusion barrier perhaps showed reflex variations, as will be described below (Edelberg, 1966b; 1970).

When a device suitable for measuring changes in hydration of the skin is placed on its surface, a curious phenomenon may be observed. During the same time at which a conventional vapor detector (dry air flow) is indicating an increase in water output from the skin, the hydration detector frequently indicates a concomitant drying of the surface. This phenomenon is associated with the positive wave of the SPR. At first glance this observation appears to be an expected one; i.e., as evaporation occurs, the skin surface dries, while the air above it becomes moist. However, since the device used to measure hydration prevents evaporation, this simple explanation is untenable. The measurement of hydration is based on the relation of the current pathway to the lateral distance between two surface electrodes (Figure 9.8). Current between Wires A and B (seen in cross section) flows through the resistive network indicated. As these wires are brought closer together, resistances R_1 and R_3 decrease, while resistances R_2 and R_4 remain constant. As the distance between Wires A and B approaches zero, the resistance of this circuit becomes determined essentially by R_1, the lateral resistance across the surface of the corneum. Changes in this depend primarily on changes in its moisture content. In practice the two electrodes A

and B are fine wires pressed into a plastic plate and ground flush with its surface. The plate is fastened to the skin with the wires in contact with its surface.

Changes in the resistance (or preferably impedance at 1000 Hz) between the wires reflect both increases and decreases in moisture content of the corneum (Figure 9.9). Rapid, reflexly induced absorption of water was commonly observed, either by this method or by two others described in the same paper, one of which was a conventional vapor detector in which water-saturated air was used instead of dry air. Vapor increases were simultaneously indicated in the dry flow unit. These observations perhaps imply that the permeability of the skin to water frequently increases during the electrodermal response such that water will move in the direction of its concentration gradient. Difficulties are found in this interpretation when one attempts to reconcile it with the relative impermeability of the water-barrier layer. It would imply that the barrier may reside not only in the dead cells of the supergranular layer but also in the viable ones of the granular layer itself. An alternative possibility is that the absorption response reflects duct reabsorption with the consequent withdrawal of the droplets of sweat that accumulate at the sweat pore when evaporation is not permitted. Needless to say, there are many difficulties in such an explanation. An advantage would be served by this process in terms of the loss of heat without evaporation, since the sweat would be heated in the deeper regions and brought to the surface, where heat would be radiated. The cooled sweat would then be reabsorbed in the upper duct and a fresh portion of heated sweat brought to the surface.

Models of the Physiological Basis of Electrodermal Phenomena

Having reviewed the electrical and secretory behavior of the components of the skin, it should be possible to decide how the various changes in potential, resistance, impedance, and capacitance are related to physiological events. Several models have been proposed, and it seems appropriate to evaluate their consistency with experimental material.

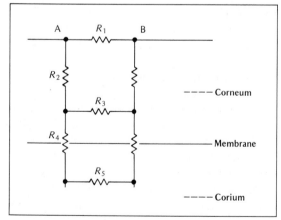

Figure 9.8 Schematic circuit of resistances in the skin as a basis for the measurement of surface hydration. Redrawn from R. Edelberg, Response of cutaneous water barrier to ideational stimulation: A GSR component. *Journal of Comparative and Physiological Psychology*, 1966, **61**, 28–33. Reproduced by permission.

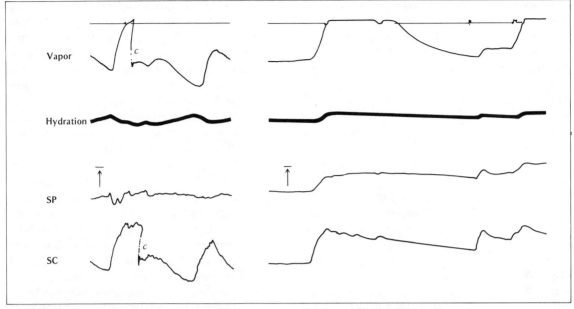

Figure 9.9 Changes in hydration of the surface of the skin accompanying electrodermal activity. On the left is a tracing from a subject showing positive SPRs and associated absorption responses (downward deflections in hydration tract). On the right, another subject with only negative SPR activity shows increased hydration at each response. The upper traces are vapor recordings from a nearby site using dry air flow. At c, manual baseline corrections have been made. The thickness of the hydration trace reflects unfiltered residue of the ac source. SP, skin potential; SC, skin conductance.

Other than the sweat gland hypothesis, the vascular hypothesis has received the most serious consideration; the muscular theory was discredited relatively early. A determined effort was made by Aveling and McDowall (1925), Densham and Wells (1927), and McDowall (1933), to demonstrate that the exosomatic electrodermal response depended upon a vasomotor reaction, but there is at present little doubt that such a mechanism falls far short of explaining the electrical behavior. A vital blow at this hypothesis was first struck by Darrow (1929), who showed electrodermal responses to be independent of plethysmographic changes. Some of my later studies (unpublished) have shown that engorgement of the blood vessels by a venous cuff produced no significant effect upon skin resistance, although the changes in blood volume were far greater than any encountered in normal vasomotor responses. In their examination of the vascular mechanism, Densham and Wells demonstrated that the SRR was not due to change in the rate of blood flow.

The experiments of Lader and Montagu (1962) have essentially laid the vascular theory to rest as far as its constituting a basis for resistance change is concerned. These authors introduced the cholinergic blocking agent, atropine, into the skin by iontophoresis and blocked the SRR, while leaving the vascular picture unaffected. They similarly introduced bretyllium tosylate, an adrenergic blocking agent, which produced a marked vascular paralysis in the dilated state but induced no electrodermal change. It should be noted that these authors measured only skin resistance; the relation of skin potential changes to vasomotor effects remains in doubt. Experiments by the present author suggest the possibility that vasomotor activity may be accompanied by potential changes measurable from the surface but these are not yet definitive. A most recent piece of evidence damaging to the vascular hypothesis was the demonstration by Prout, Coote, and Downman (1965) that the central controls for vasomotor and sudomotor responses in the footpad of the cat are independent.

Adams's hypothesis One old explanation for the EDR, readily adopted by many consumers of this new tool, but rarely considered seriously by investigators, was the simple effect of sweat on conductivity. Dry skin does not conduct well; moist skin does. Anyone who has touched a defective electric appliance with wet hands can testify to this. At first glance it seems that there are so many factors that are inconsistent with this model, such as the observation of EDRs from skin immersed in saline, the behavior of skin when a high frequency source is used, and the phenomenon of endosomatic responses, that we may immediately cast this explanation aside. Despite this, Adams, in an elegant series of experiments primarily on the cat, has made an excellent case for it (1966; Adams & Vaughan, 1965). He has stimulated the distal stump of the sectioned plantar nerve and recorded skin conductance and evaporative water loss from the footpad, using a newly developed instrument for precise measurement of water output (Adams, Funkhouser, & Kendall, 1963). His results, obtained under a large variety of initial states and stimulus schedules, are consistent in all respects with a model in which the conductance changes are a function of changes in hydration due to sweat production. He visualizes the corkscrew duct in the stratum corneum as rather freely permeable to water. Sweat may thus rise in the duct to an intermediate level and may hydrate the corneum. Due to the hydraulic capacitance of the corneum, little or no increase in moisture will be seen in the vapor tracing, but an increase in conductance will occur. As the sweat rises higher in the duct, the vapor given off becomes more highly correlated with resistance changes. Adams regards the horny layer as having a barrier that is located some distance out from its junction with the granular layer. Szakall (1958) has in fact claimed to have demonstrated such a barrier, using the skin-stripping technique. Thus there is an inner zone of the corneum that is isolated from surface solutions by a barrier layer and can be moistened by the lateral diffusion of sweat out of the duct. The drying of the inner zone is seen to take place by reabsorption through the underlying epidermis. This model does not seem capable of explaining potential responses, but even these may be explained if one considers the internal

circuit currents discussed earlier in this chapter.

To explain why changes in hydration that would produce essentially ohmic resistance changes should account for the reactive component evident in ac measurements, Adams points out (personal communication) that the dense keratinized horny layer may have intrinsic reactive properties. The experiments of Lawler, Davis, and Griffith (1960) on the effect of skin stripping on impedance support this. As successive layers of the corneum were removed, they found that capacitance increased. This still does not explain the constancy of the phase angle, unless possibly the behavior of the dielectric property of the horny layer is frequency dependent. There are, however, several objections to the Adams model that are more difficult to overcome. To explain the specific effect of the various ions on SRR amplitude, one must postulate, as has Adams (personal communication), that the horny layer has membranelike characteristics. It does in fact have a fixed negative charge (Edelberg, 1963b) and would to some extent exert a weak ion selectivity. Perhaps the barrier layer exerts even higher selectivity than the outer layer (stratum disjunctum). Some of the characteristics which Adams attributes to the corneum, though hypothetical, are not unreasonable; to the extent that this model explains many experimental data satisfactorily, at least for the cat, it should be seriously considered. Its application to the human is more questionable.

Darrow's model A model proposed by Darrow (1964; Darrow & Gullickson, 1970) views the sweat gland as the source of potential changes, both negative and positive, but implicates other structures as well. Leaning upon the observations of earlier workers on the parotid gland and pancreas, he assumes that the intraluminal potential of the sweat gland is positive, the exterior negative. He further assumes that neural impulses may cause increases in the permeability of the epidermis and corneum, as well as sweat gland activity. Either effect produces resistance changes. At high resistance and relatively empty ducts, the reflex change in extra–sweat gland resistance is seen as bringing the skin surface into better contact with the external negative surface of the sweat gland, thereby resulting in a negative potential wave. The eruption of sensible perspiration is seen as bringing the surface into better contact with the positive interior, thereby accounting for the positive wave. Darrow points to the relation between the steepness of the recovery limb of the response and the level of conductance to support this model.

Several difficulties appear in the way of reconciling Darrow's explanation with experimental data. For one thing, assuming that it applies to the cat as well as the human, it is difficult to understand why it is so rare to obtain a positive response from the cat footpad by electrical stimulation of the plantar nerve, even when the sweat ducts are relatively full (Richter, 1930; Wilcott, 1965). The positive responses reported by Shaver, Brusilow, and Cooke (1962) and by Lloyd (1961) are extremely slow (several minutes in rise time) and are not likely caused by the rise of sweat in the duct. A second difficulty is seen with regard to the cause of the increase in permeability of the corneum (unless this occurs as a result of the moisture entering the horny layer from the underlying granular layer).

A third difficulty is seen in data collected during the microelectrode survey of the potential of sweat pores and of areas between sweat pores (Edelberg, 1966a) in which the sweat pores were significantly more negative than the nonsweat gland areas. Darrow correctly argues (personal communication) that the higher degree of moisture in the vicinity of the sweat pore would allow for better contact with the external surface of the sweat gland in these areas, so that sweat pore measurements might actually be of external potentials. Furthermore, in all fairness to his model, it would not really be necessary that the intraductal potential be positive, only that it be less negative than the epidermis. In such a case the internal circuit-current model would predict a positive wave as the duct filled, followed by a slow negative wave as sweat overflowed into the corneum. Much more incompatible with Darrow's model is the report by Schulz and her co-workers (1965), who have shown by direct microelectrode measurement that the lumen of the sweat duct is highly negative with respect to the surrounding tissues.

Another weakness of this model is its inability to explain the action of aluminum chloride on the positive wave of the SPR. The average potentiation

of the positive wave in 7 subjects produced by 1M $AlCl_3$ was 750% (Edelberg, unpublished data). It did not significantly increase the negative wave. This effect cannot be due to concentration per se because 1M or even 5M NaCl does not potentiate the positive wave. It seems that a specific effect on a membrane is involved here and that the positive wave likely originates at a selective membrane.

Lastly, Darrow's model would predict that, in an area of many sweat glands, increased activity would be associated with decreasing negativity, as the intralumenal potentials are brought into better contact with the surface. In fact, the opposite is found (Leiderman & Shapiro, 1964).

Lloyd's hypothesis Still another model was postulated by Lloyd (1961). He attributed the negative potential response from the footpad of the cat to an action potential, essentially to what Darrow has termed the presecretory potential. With repeated stimulation a very slow positive wave of several minutes duration is generated. Lloyd terms this the secretory potential, and he further demonstrates that it is accompanied by a progressive fall in impedance, due to the filling of the ducts with sweat. The rise of sweat in the duct is seen as enabling better contact with the generator of the presecretory potentials and as causing an increase in the observed amplitude of these negative action potentials as repetitive stimulation continues. Lloyd used this model to explain the differences between recordings with ducts empty and ducts full. He notes that, when the sweat ducts have been filled by antecedent stimulation, the secretory potential reaches a steady level. A new stimulus then evokes a negative action potential but no secretory potential. His explanation for this is that, once the ducts are full, the secretory potential, which is a reflection of duct filling, reaches a ceiling.

Lloyd's observations may perhaps be stated more simply but just as accurately as follows:

As the footpad becomes wetter as a result of continued sweating, the base potential becomes more positive. When the pad has become thoroughly wet, further additions of moisture do not increase this positivity. If it is allowed to rest, that is, to dry, the positivity is reduced; subsequent stimulation will then increase its moisture and therefore its positivity.

These observations are exactly those that would be predicted by the circuit-current model, provided the interior of the sweat gland is more negative than the epidermis between sweat glands. As the corneum is progressively hydrated, its resistance is decreased and the epidermal potential makes a greater contribution to the surface potential. Added evidence for the validity of this explanation is seen in the appearance of the large negative wave that accompanied the first stimulation following a prolonged rest. This would be the effect predicted by the circuit-current model if the first stimuli fill the ducts but do not wet the corneum. As stimulation continues, the corneum becomes hydrated and the base potential becomes less negative. Since the impedance changes recorded by Lloyd closely follow the positive wave, rather than these negative action potentials, it would seem that the skin impedance of the cat footpad is determined not so much by the level of sweat in the ducts as by the hydration of the corneum, a conclusion consistent with the Adams model. Lloyd's interpretation of his data seems highly improbable, in view of the strong evidence that the interior of the sweat gland is highly negative rather than positive (Edelberg, 1968; Schulz et al., 1965).

Hypothesis of Martin and Venables   Various pieces of evidence have been examined by I. Martin and Venables (1966); and, largely on the basis of the high correlation frequently reported between sweat gland activity and conductance, and on the basis of the observation that cholinergic blocking agents abolish both the SRR and sweat production (Venables & Martin, 1967), they conclude that sweat gland activity is responsible for the SRR. They further point to the equal latencies of the negative SPR and the SRR, and to the fact that these are both abolished by hyoscyamine, as evidence that they have a common basis; both are viewed as reflecting a change in membrane permeability related to the presecretory activity described by Darrow (1927). In regard to the significance of the positive wave they remain more in doubt, suggesting in agreement with Darrow that it may represent a secondary aspect of sweat gland activity (it, too, is abolished by hyoscyamine), or that it may represent some aspect of epidermal activity. As they point out,

Wilcott's report of a high positive correlation between the positive wave amplitude and vapor production (1962) suggests that sweat gland activity is responsible for the positive wave. More recently, Fowles and Venables (1970) have suggested that reabsorption of sodium may account not only for the negative transductal potential but also for the positive SPR.

Martin and Venables have considered the overall picture carefully and have been fair in pointing out limitations to their hypothesis. There are, however, more ponderous obstacles to its acceptance than they have advanced. For one thing they must attribute the marked specific effects of various electrolytes and surface-active agents on the SRR to an effect on the sweat gland secretory membrane. This explanation is offered despite the evidence (Blank & Gould, 1959; Flesch, Goldstone, & Urbach, 1951; Malkinson & Rothman, 1963, p. 90; Rothman, 1954, pp. 33–34) that the sweat gland represents an unlikely route of entry of solutes, even under iontophoresis (possibly because an outward flow of sweat causes a retrograde movement that is more effective than the inward movement under diffusion and electrical forces). Furthermore, the contention by Martin and Venables (1966) that the specific ion effect on SPR amplitude can take place because these ions have been driven into the sweat gland during resistance measurements in the same experiments is easily challenged. The marked potentiation of the positive SPR wave by $AlCl_3$, described above, was accomplished without an external voltage source. One could also point to the observation that $AlCl_3$, which caused such a profound potentiation of both the SRR and the positive SPR, produced no significant effect on the negative SPR. If this negative "presecretory" wave is related to the membrane change responsible for the SRR, it is difficult to understand why it should be unaffected.

Another objection to this model is its inconsistency with the observations of Shaver, Brusilow, and Cooke (1965), who placed microelectrodes in the sweat duct of the cat and observed negative responses at epidermal level but no intraductal responses at all at the level of the upper corium. This seems to preclude presecretory potentials as the origin of the negative wave, at least in the cat. It may, of course, be invalid to extend these observations made on the glands of the cat footpad to the glands of the human palm, since those of the cat are supposedly apocrine (Wang, 1964, p. 7).

Wilcott's model By various correlative procedures involving resistance, potential, and sweat production, and by physiological and pharmacological manipulation of the electrodermal effector site, Wilcott (1958a, 1958b, 1959, 1962, 1963, 1964, 1965, 1966, 1967) has arrived at yet another model. He has developed a procedure called potential driving in which he imposes across two skin electrodes a small voltage that shifts the base potential somewhat. By this procedure he obtains predictable variations in the waveform of the SPR between these sites and concludes that the polarity of the SPR is determined by the SP level. An examination of his circuit arrangement, however, reveals that the imposed potential acts as an exosomatic current source. Therefore, when the resistance of the subject becomes appreciable with respect to that of the associated amplifier, variations in the subject resistance will be reflected as changes in potential across the amplifier. If adequate, these changes will alter the waveform of the associated skin potential response, as has been demonstrated elsewhere (Edelberg & Burch, 1962). Surwillo (1965) has analyzed Wilcott's circuit and arrived at a similar conclusion. The assertion by Wilcott that skin resistance is really a driving of the skin potential by the applied potential has a lot of merit but is essentially a restatement of the demonstrated fact that skin resistance is an apparent resistance, actually a polarization potential. Wilcott's experiments do not appear to demonstrate satisfactorily that SPR amplitude and polarity depend on the SP level.

In spite of some doubts as to the validity of these recent observations as a basis for a physiological model, Wilcott has drawn some telling deductions with regard to the origin of the skin potential and resistance change. Like Martin and Venables, he places the site of the SRR and some of the potential changes in the sweat gland but takes a firm stand in implicating epidermal depolarization as the origin of other potential responses. These, he believes, may be by-products of sympathetic impulses acting to modify tactile sensitivity. He points to the pain-sensitizing effects of local mecholyl injection and its associated effects on skin potential as evidence for this interpretation. This hypothesis, one also held by the present author (Edelberg, 1961b; Martin & Edelberg, 1963), seems to be in doubt. Subsequent unpublished observations on unilaterally sympathectomized individuals have shown that sensitivity is increased following an SRR almost as much on the operated side as on the intact one; hence most of this sensitizing effect must be central, although some peripheral effect does seem to be in evidence. Wilcott (1966) holds that the sympathetic supply to the epidermis, which presumably mediates the tactile function, produces increased polarization, a rise in negative SP, and an increase in negative SPR amplitude; sweating produces partial depolarization, the lowering of negative SP, and the positive wave.

As with the previous models, Wilcott's is tenable only if the marked effects of surface agents on SRR are due to action on the secretory portion of the sweat gland. With the evidence that this is a very unlikely effect, one is left on the horns of a dilemma. The dilemma can be resolved if one makes the assumption that the epidermis, or the epidermal portion of the sweat duct, participates not only in potential responses but in resistance responses as well. The following section will be devoted to consideration of a model that in most respects appears to be consistent with the large variety of experimental data already presented.

The sweat circuit model The sweat gland may be considered as a relatively steady source of sweat production, and its lumen as having a substantial negative potential with respect to the surrounding tissue. In response to external stimulation, this tonic level may increase somewhat or phasic neural discharges above the tonic level may occur. If the findings of Shaver, Brusilow, and Cooke (1965) are applicable to humans, these secretory events apparently are not accompanied by any potential change; for the purposes of this model they are also assumed to be unaccompanied by any resistance change and therefore not in evidence at the surface. When the glands are inactive, sweat is presumed normally to fill the ducts up to the level of the Malpighian layer, as observed by Shaver, Brusilow, and Cooke. When sudomotor activity commences, as a result either of increased secretion or of myo-epithelial contraction, the sweat rises up the coiled portion of the duct, reducing the resistance between the surface and the negative electrical generator. The result is an increase in conductance and, because of the less negative epidermal areas between sweat glands, and the internal circuit-current effect, a negative wave. Both the conductance and potential changes parallel the level of sweat in the duct. This is thought to be the origin of the first two waves seen in Figure 9.10. If secretion is halted, the sweat remains standing in the duct and the new levels of potential and conductance remain fairly stable. However, there will be a *slow* lateral diffusion of sweat into the horny layer, thereby gradually decreasing the sweat level, decreasing the negative potential, and decreasing the conductance level as seen in this record. So far, this model is almost identical to that of Adams.

Most SP and SR waves do not look like the first ones of Figure 9.10, but have a much more rapid recovery. How can the sweat-level effect account for this? The answer appears to be that most responses in the human are not produced by such a process alone. In an actively sweating subject, the ducts would be full most of the time and neither resistance nor conductance changes could be produced by this mechanism. Nevertheless, an actively sweating person does produce responses and if, as implied by Shaver's observations, these responses are not to be attributed to activity of the secretory membrane, they must be explained otherwise, ei-

ther *by epidermal activity or activity of the duct wall at the level of the Malpighian layer.*

The decision as to which of these is responsible cannot yet be made. The process is seen as a change in a selective membrane, initiated by intraepidermal fibers, by fibers innervating the dermoepidermal junction, or by stretching of the duct wall due to sweat pressure. Rothman, in the discussion section of a paper by Arthur and Shelley (1959), cites the work of J. Yamazaki, who with a silver technique demonstrated intraepidermal fibers only in the palms and soles. Apparently, these are different from the intraepidermal fibers which, in the study by Arthur and Shelley, took the methylene blue stain and were found everywhere *except* in the palms and soles. Microanatomical considerations suggest that an active *epidermal membrane* may be located in the granular layer, but the dermoepidermal junction is also a candidate for such a role. To the extent that the Ebbecke response also represents activity of this active membrane, the demonstration that it is still active in cadavers several hours after death implies that it does not depend on metabolism and therefore may well be located in the granular layer. In this position it would also be capable of controlling the passage of water. Moreover, it would be in the neighborhood in which the "barrier" layer has been identified. Unpublished experiments by this author show, in fact, that the Ebbecke response is, like the EDR, affected by surface electrolytes.

Several points argue in support of the hypothesis that the *upper duct wall* may be the responsible site for the membrane change. For one thing, Suchi (1950) demonstrated that the ferrous ion could be driven by electrophoresis down the sweat duct as far as the Malpighian layer, at which point it migrated across the duct wall, laterally through intercellular channels in this layer, and finally downward to the dermoepidermal junction. While the migration of surface electrolytes as far as the secretory portion of the sweat gland has been shown to be highly improbable, there is evidence that solutes may invade the upper region of the duct. In regard to the rapid passage of water and electrolytes through the skin, this route seems to be a more supportable one than that through the relatively impermeable epidermal barrier layer.

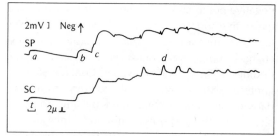

Figure 9.10 Example of transition from slowly recovering, pure negative (sweat) waves to rapidly recovering biphasic and uniphasic waves as membrane component becomes active. Upper record, skin potential; lower record, skin conductance; time line, *t*, represents 10 sec.

The membrane process, whether it takes place in the *dermoepidermal layer,* the *granular layer,* or the *wall of the upper sweat duct,* is viewed as functioning in the fine control of water movement, either to assist the sweat glands in thermoregulation or to regulate the moisture content of the horny layer by reabsorption of sweat. It is seen as a short-lived increase in the aqueous and ionic permeability of a cation-permeable membrane in response to a diffusing mediator, which, judging from the many reports that hyoscyamine and atropine block all electrodermal activity, is acetylcholine. The increase in permeability is reflected in a transient increase in conductance. Evidence that a membrane change does explain a large part of the phasic conductance response is indicated by the work of Lykken, Miller, and Strahan (1966). These authors applied square voltage pulses to the skin and by analysis of the transient changes attending the EDR showed that ohmic (i.e., nonmembrane) changes could account for only a small fraction of the total change in conductance. The reflex increase in permeability also reduces the potential of this normally surface-negative or, for the sweat duct, lumen-negative membrane, resulting in a positive-going wave.

Thus, according to this model, the normal bi- or triphasic SPR can be generated by a rapid uniphasic membrane wave, compounded with a uniphasic negative wave of slow recovery that originates in the rise of sweat in the sweat duct. Large negative waves of the sort seen in responses *a* and *b* of Figure 9.10 may result from the rise of sweat, perhaps due to myoepithelial contraction. Various combinations of these effects give the variations demonstrated so well in this figure and in Figure 9.3. The resistance response will also be some combination of these two effects, as seen in Figure 9.2 as well as Figure 9.10. A slow wave, produced by a change in sweat level, compounded with a fast wave from the upper membrane is illustrated in waves *c* and *d* of the sequence in Figure 9.10.

The model runs into difficulty in explaining the results of experiments involving arterial occlusion or exsanguination. Sweat may be almost completely interrupted by arterial occlusion with minimal effect on the SRR amplitude (Edelberg, 1964b). This finding is consistent with the model if sweat pro-

duction requires a greater supply of raw materials, and/or oxygen, than does the activity of the membrane, an assumption having a high physiological probability. The related observation by Wilcott (1958b) that the positive wave was abolished by exsanguination, while the negative wave was unaffected is, at face value, inconsistent with the model. In Wilcott's experiment, resistance response was greatly attenuated as well, as would be predicted if the membrane were the common site of resistance responses and positive potential responses. The absence of attenuation of the negative wave was unexpected and difficult to explain. A repeat of Wilcott's exsanguination experiment by this author has shown that, in fact, both negative and positive components are attenuated but the attenuation of the positive component eliminates part of the normal reversal effect on the negative wave. This results in an apparent maintenance of the negative amplitude during exsanguination. Evidence for this is seen in the dramatic potentiation of the negative wave immediately upon restoration of circulation.

Additional evidence of the capability of an epidermal structure to respond is afforded by the demonstration that potential responses can be recorded from the center of the nail bed, where no sweat glands occur (Edelberg, 1965b). Reflex resistance decreases were also apparently demonstrated from this area, although only under special conditions. Unfortunately, or perhaps fortunately, sweat glands have been discovered along the margin of the nail bed (Maricq, 1967). When the contribution of these marginal areas is eliminated by the use of small sites restricted to the center of the nail, potential responses are still clearly in evidence, but resistance responses disappear.

A major implication of this model is that base conductance level at an artificially hydrated site is determined primarily by the level of sweat in the ducts. There is good evidence that this depends upon a tonic control, since both unilateral sympathectomy and local administration of atropine cause an increase in resistance in the affected area. Responses that recover rapidly are judged to be of membrane origin and are seen as representing phasic activity only. Two pieces of evidence support this concept of different determinants of level and response. The first is the finding that intense vaso-constriction can markedly reduce response amplitude without affecting base level (Edelberg, 1964a). A second is the marked difference in the effects of polarity upon resistance level and response amplitude (Edelberg, Greiner, & Burch, 1960). For example, the ratio of anodal to cathodal response amplitude in the presence of 1M $AlCl_3$ was 2.04:1; the ratio for base levels, only 1.15:1. This observation is also consistent with the hypothesis that the base level is more ohmic in character, as expected for the behavior of sweat-filled tubes, while the response amplitude is characterized more by a membranelike behavior.

The function of nonpalmar, nonplantar, sweat gland secretory activity and of the superficial membrane activity of nonpalmar and nonplantar areas is, in agreement with Kuno (1956, p. 123), considered to be primarily thermoregulatory. Palmar and plantar sweat gland activity is thought to serve for emergency mechanical protection in addition to rendering the skin more pliable for optimal manipulative behavior, as proposed by Darrow and Freeman (1934). Palmar and plantar membrane activity is seen as primarily concerned with the reabsorption of sweat for control of the hydration of the corneum, again as an advantage in fine manipulative behavior.

Neurophysiological Processes and Behavior

Both the sympathetic and parasympathetic divisions of the autonomic system have been implicated as mediators of the skin reflex. Now, however, it is generally conceded that the control is, in fact, sympathetic, but with many parasympathetic characteristics, especially the involvement of acetylcholine as the mediator at the neuroeffector junction. The sympathetic nature of the reflex is deduced primarily from anatomical data, namely, that the reflex can be elicited by the stimulation of the sympathetic trunk, after the sectioning of the rami (Wang & Lu, 1930c), and further that a unilateral sympathectomy abolishes the reflex in the ipsilateral foot (Schwartz, 1934). The reflex can be elicited in the spinal animal by tactual stimulation (Richter, 1930).

Attempts have been made to implicate the parasympathetic system, e.g., by stimulation of the dorsal roots, which have been known to carry fibers of this division (Hara, 1929). Wang and Lu (1930b) effectively challenged these positive results as probably an effect on the blood vessels, perhaps by the influence of vasomotor changes on skin temperature and the rate of evaporation. As Darrow (1937a) pointed out, another reason for suspecting parasympathetic involvement is seen in the locus of central sites from which the EDR may be elicited. The stimulation of the premotor cortex activates not only the EDR but numerous other autonomic effects, most of which are clearly parasympathetic in nature. Moreover, the production of EDA by electrical stimulation of the hypothalamus is accomplished not by stimulating the posterior nuclei known to be associated with predominant sympathetic effects, but rather the anterior region (Langworthy & Richter, 1930; Wang & Richter, 1928). The stimulation of this area also provokes slowing of the heart, loss of blood pressure, enhanced gastrointestinal activity, and other parasympathetic influences. The control of the sweat activity thus has a paradoxical nature. Possibly, the reason for this lies in the dual function of sweating. Sweating for thermoregulatory purposes exerts a cooling effect that is trophotropic or vegetative in nature, having a routine homeostatic function. The posterior regions of the hypothalamus control sympathetic activity, commonly of an emergency nature. Heat production is one of the effects of such activation. If this heat production is simply a by-product of increased metabolism resulting primarily from intensified tonic activity in skeletal muscles, the concomitant mobilization of cooling effects would represent a synergistic activity. If, on the other hand, the heat production is in response to cold stress, the activation of the sudomotor units represents an undesirable antagonistic effect.

A second function of sweating is clearly to alter the physical characteristics of the skin surface (Darrow & Freeman, 1934). The pliability of the corneum is determined primarily by the water content of this region, which depends upon epidermal transpiration or sweat gland activity. Its importance in fine manipulative and tactile behavior is apparent. It is also important in an emergency, when flight, for example, requires the forceful contact of the extremities with abrasive objects. At such times it is a distinct advantage to activate a system for the emergency moisturizing of the horny layer, at least of the plantar and palmar surfaces.

Two somewhat independent systems participate in the initiation and control of the skin reflex. The premotor cortex, Area 6 of Brodmann, is the best recognized of the cortical areas capable of eliciting an EDR when stimulated (Schwartz, 1937; Wilcott, 1969). In addition, there is an area just posterolateral to the motor area that controls the contralateral foot (Langworthy & Richter, 1930), and, of special significance, another on the anterior limbic cortex (Isamat, 1961). The limbic area apparently constitutes a control center that is separate from the premotor area. The descending pathway from the premotor area courses through the pyramidal tract, bypassing the hypothalamus. Responses may be elicited by the stimulation of the pyramidal tract or the cerebral peduncles, and the section of one peduncle interrupts the responses elicited by stimulation of the ipsilateral Area 6 (Wall & Davis, 1951). On the other hand, ablation of the hypothalamus does not prevent the eliciting of EDRs by the stimulation of Area 6 (Wang & Lu, 1930a).

There is, in addition to this pyramidal route, a seemingly independent one in which the hypothalamus is involved. The stimulation of the tuber cinereum and of the lateral portions of the anterior hypothalamus elicits the electrodermal response (Hasama, 1929; Wang & Richter, 1928). The prechiasmic area is also an excitatory area that elicits an EDR when stimulated. Fibers from these areas impinge on the preganglionic spinal sympathetic neurones. The hypothalamic centers may be activated by direct warming (Hasama, 1929) and probably reflexly by temperature receptors in the skin (Kuno, 1956, p. 278). It therefore appears that this may be one of the primary means of thermoregulatory control of sudomotor activity. However, it seems likely that the hypothalamic centers also receive fibers from the limbic and infralimbic cortex, which have been shown to be facilitatory for the EDR (Isamat, 1961). Because of the involvement of limbic areas in emotional behavior (MacLean, 1955; Papez, 1937), this may represent a system for the initiation of electrodermal activity so commonly observed in response to emotional stimuli.

Other portions of the limbic system have also been implicated in the control of this reflex, perhaps more regulatory than primary. Lang, Tuovinen, and Valleala (1964) have shown that stimulation of the basolateral portions of the amygdala will evoke a single EDR with the typically observed wave shape. If, however, amygdaloid after-discharge occurs following this stimulation, the electrodermal response has a shape typical of many responses to emotional stimuli; i.e., a rapid rise of conductance which, instead of recovering, is maintained at peak level for a considerable time by a series of small flutterlike waves. Wang (1964, p. 105) has suggested that the hippocampus also plays a role in the control of the EDR by virtue of its connection via the fornix with the mammillary body of the posterior hypothalamus. There is evidence (Fujimori, 1961) that this is an inhibitory effect, as may be expected from the function of the posterior hypothalamus in heat conservation. However, Wang is uncertain whether this is the pathway mediating the inhibitory effect reported by Fujimori. An unexpected facilatory site has been identified by Wang (1964, p. 52) in the dorsal midline area of the thalamus.

The centers described above are subject to facilitation (Shimamura & Fujimori, 1961) or inhibition (Wang, Stein, & Brown, 1956) as a result of the activity of the reticular formation. For example, if the proximal stump of a sectioned cutaneous nerve of the cat is stimulated electrically, an EDR may be recorded from the footpad. If, however, a similar stimulus is imposed during stimulation of the ventromedial portions of the rhombencephalic (bulbar) reticular formation, a marked reduction in the amplitude of the response occurs, an indication of the inhibitory effect exerted by this area. If, instead, the lateral portion of the mesencephalic reticular formation or portions of the diencephalic reticular formation are stimulated, the responses to stimulation of the sensory nerve are potentiated. The stimulation of this area may, in fact, elicit an EDR per se. Bloch and Bonvallet (1961) have demonstrated that responses may be directly mediated by the mesencephalic reticular formation in response to activity in sensory collateral fibers. These same collaterals also activate the bulbar reticular formation to produce an inhibitory effect on the response that is normally masked by the predominating influence of the mesencephalic area. However, if the facilitatory area is depressed, e.g., by injection of novocaine, the inhibitory effects become manifest. It is interesting in this regard that emotionally depressed subjects will frequently be unresponsive to stimuli that normally evoke a marked orienting response in the electrodermal system.

The overall control systems mediating and moderating electrodermal activity have been comprehensively reviewed by Wang (1957, 1958, 1964) and by Bloch (1965). They involve, in addition to the premotor corticospinal system and the limbic-hypothalamic system, a control group involving the basal ganglia with a regulatory center in the pallidum. Only a few pathways in these systems have been anatomically identified, namely, those of the facilitatory fibers from the lateral mesencephalic reticular formation and from the sensorimotor areas to the spinal sympathetic neurones, and those of the inhibitory fibers from the bulbar ventromedial reticular formation to the spinal sympathetics. There are many interrelations with other centers, but the pathways remain to be identified. The inhibitory components include the frontal cortex, the caudate nucleus, the roof nuclei of the cerebellum, and possibly the hippocampus. The cerebellar nuclei have been shown to impinge directly on the bulbar ventromedial reticular formation. The behavioral significance of this connection was pointed out by Darrow (1937a) before the function of the reticular formation was recognized. He stressed the involvement of the cerebellum in orienting behavior and in preparing for manipulation, and pointed to the logical relation of these centers to sudomotor activity.

This last, when considered together with an experiment by Bieber and Fulton (1934), has special significance for the interpretation of the EDR. When a monkey with bilateral premotor lesions lies on its side, the forced grasping typically resulting from these lesions is inhibited on the downward side. Apparently, an inhibitory effect mediated by a postural control mechanism is able to substitute for the control formerly exerted by the premotor area. It seems directly relevant, as pointed out by Darrow (1937a), that the premotor lesion causes hyperactive sweating and that in the normal human, lying on one side depresses EDA on the downward side. Nakayama and Takagi (1958) have

shown that the positive wave of the SPR is selectively depressed on the under side when a subject lies on his side. The parallelism between fine motor control and control over sweating seems apparent.

The question arises, however, as to why extirpation of the premotor cortex, which is an excitatory area for sweating and EDA, should produce release from inhibition. The answer may be that this area, which functions in the control of fine coordination, has both facilitatory and inhibitory capabilities (Wilcott, 1969). An alternative explanation is that its action may, at a peripheral level, sometimes appear as a potentiating effect and sometimes as an inhibitory effect. If control of the sweat reabsorption mechanism resides in Area 6, damage to this region would permit the profuse wetting of the skin surface characteristic of the premotor syndrome. On the other hand, the stimulation of this area in the intact brain would, by activation of the epidermal reabsorption mechanism, cause a transient increase in electrical conductivity. The implication may be that hyperhydrosis can be caused as well by the failure of the reabsorption mechanism as by the hyperactivity of the secretory mechanism.

The appropriateness of the fine control exerted by the premotor area in the adaptation for manipulative activity may perhaps be manifested in the difference in plantar and palmar endosomatic activity in the human. While both are approximately equal in negative activity, the positive activity of the palm is about 20 times as great as that of the sole (Edelberg, 1965a, p. 34).

The multiplicity of control centers and their interconnections, and the evidence for independent corticospinal and hypothalamic-reticulo-spinal pathways, make it appear that the common utilization of EDA as a relatively monolithic arousal indicator is a gross and erroneous oversimplification.

Data Analysis

One consideration in the design of electrodermal experiments is the choice of measure. In most published studies, the selection appears to be based primarily on personal preference, but much of what has been discussed in this chapter implies that a rational choice may be made. Even on empirical grounds, however, the various electrodermal measures are not interchangeable and may show very low intercorrelations as well as high ones (Bonier & Hanley, 1965; Gaviria, Coyne, & Thetford, 1969).

The investigator faces several decisions when he considers how to treat electrodermal data. He must find answers to such questions as: Should levels and amplitudes be expressed in resistance or conductance units? Should a logarithmic transformation be used? How should one correct for the effect of the base level? How should one score the response amplitude when the response is a partially fused sequence of waves? How should one score the response amplitude when the baseline has a relatively steep drift rate? When one is counting the number of responses per epoch, should the criterion for minimum response be changed as a function of the base level and from person to person, or should it be an absolute standard? How should the negative and positive components of the potential response be scored?

The answers to these questions have, for the most part, been based on empirical findings or on personal bias; hence the variety of systems used is somewhat bewildering. While it does not yet seem possible to arrive at more definitive answers based on a rational approach, it is useful to discuss factors that are pertinent to choosing a method of evaluating electrodermal records. Most of the following discussion concerns exosomatic measurements, as these have been subjected to the greatest quantitative scrutiny.

Count of EDRs The frequency of phasic neurodermal discharges has been used as a measure of autonomic activity by several investigators (e.g., Burch & Greiner, 1958; McDonald, Johnson, & Hord, 1964; A. J. Silverman, Cohen, & Shmavonian, 1959). The count of spontaneous SRRs has been found to be unrelated to the base level during periods of relaxation, although it did vary with the base level over the arousal scale (Johnson, 1962). To the extent that the count of EDRs may be related to the variability of EDA, it is of interest that, in the resting state, variability was also found to be independent of the base level (Speisman, Osborn, & Lazarus, 1961).

The EDR count may have certain advantages over the analysis of complex conductance changes, despite the loss of amplitude data. There is, however, a continuous gradation of responses from clearly distinguishable ones down to almost imperceptible perturbations in the baseline, and an arbitrary threshold amplitude must be chosen. The selection of this threshold may alter results considerably, since a general reduction in the amplitude of all responses would cause a marked reduction in the count of large responses but possibly very little change in the count of the smaller ones. The threshold should not be a function of base level; the absolute criterion therefore should be modified as the conductance level changes (at least that part due to peripheral mechanisms). In practice it is convenient, when using a constant current system, to employ 0.1% of base resistance as a criterion. This is held as an absolute constant for all responses occurring within a base level range of 10% of the starting base level. When the base level exceeds this range, a new threshold amplitude is calculated. If a constant voltage source is used, deflections are directly proportional to the conductance change and a constant response criterion, e.g., 0.1 μmho, may be used throughout. These two approaches are used for practical reasons and are not equatable. Therefore, internal consistency requires that one or the other be used exclusively in a given study.

Measurement of response amplitude and base level Two general methods of determining the response amplitude are in common use. In one of these, the difference in conductance between the point of onset and the peak level of a single wave is measured. Some authors (e.g., Hagfors, 1964) suggest that a drifting prestimulus baseline be extrapolated along the curve it would have followed had the response not occurred, and the vertical distance between this line and peak amplitude then be measured. Data obtained from direct neural stimulation of the sympathetic nerve in the cat, however, indicate that this extrapolation is not necessary unless the response occurs within 2 sec after the peak of a preceding wave (Edelberg, 1967, pp. 46–47). The second approach is to determine the difference between two measures, one characterizing the prestimulus level, the other the poststimulus level. In some instances, especially when automatic A–D conversion is employed, a mean is used, but more commonly the average of the beginning, middle, and end base levels of a prescribed period (e.g., the last 15 sec prior to stimulus) is used. Many investigators take as the poststimulus level the highest conductance point reached within a fixed period following the stimulus. For base level measurement, most investigators sample at regular intervals and take an average of these samples. It should be appreciated that, if a conversion of resistance readings to conductance readings is to be made, the conversion must be made *prior* to averaging.

Normality of distribution   Statistical treatment of electrodermal data by parametric techniques demands a normal distribution, a requirement that is not often tested. O. L. Lacey (1947) found untransformed conductance to be most satisfactory in this regard. Schlosberg and Stanley (1953) examined conductance data from 20 women using various transformations, each examined for normality of distribution. He found that log conductance overcorrects for skewness. Half of his samples showed that conductance or the square root of conductance were equally good in regard to normality, while in the remaining 10 women, the square root of conductance was preferred. He concludes that, for most routine purposes, untransformed conductance constitutes an adequate measure. A similar conclusion was reached by O. L. Lacey and Siegel (1949).

Peripheral dependence of response amplitude on base level

1. Sudomotor activity   In terms of the all-or-none activity of individual sweat gland units, it is fortunate that conductances in parallel are directly additive and, as new units are brought into play, their contributions are equal, independent of the number already active. It should be stressed that this relation does *not* hold when resistances are used in the calculations. This constitutes a primary reason for selecting conductance as the preferred parameter in exosomatic measures.

From the experiments of Thomas and Korr (1957), which showed an excellent linear relation between sweat gland count and skin conductance, one would be inclined to view skin conductance as primarily a function of the number of units in play, i.e., as all-or-none behavior. This would imply a zero correlation of the response amplitude and base conductance at the peripheral level. However, there is reason to doubt this interpretation. In the measurements made by Thomas and Korr, an electrode was pressed *for 1–4 sec* to the paste-free, previously warmed, skin surface. Under these conditions, the surface of the corneum may be expected to be dry, and only those ducts filled to the brim, as it were, would make contact with the plate. It would therefore be surprising if the relation between the number of these parallel units making contact with the electrode and the sum of their conductances were anything *but* linear. Those units that are partially filled are excluded from the measurement, and the linearity is preserved. It seems clear that the behavior of the sweat glands must be dependent upon neural impulse frequency, as demonstrated by the experiments of Fujimori (1955) and Adams (1966). Even Wang, who demonstrated an apparent all-or-none behavior, argues for the likelihood of temporal summation. In Thomas and Korr's experiment, then, there must have been many, partly filled (less active) sweat duct units below the surface.

When an electrode paste is used, or when sweat is prevented from evaporating, the artificial hydration of the corneum puts the surface electrode in contact with these partially filled units. This process was studied by Blank and Finesinger (1946). Assuming that the individual sweat gland may in fact show graded responses to neural bursts of different frequencies, the prediction of the relation of the response amplitude to the conductance level becomes another matter. Here one is dealing with the summation of parallel conductances, whose individual values depend on the frequency of discharge. If the resistance of the sweat gland is determined primarily by the height of the column of sweat in the duct, additional increments of sweat cause a linear decrease in resistance, but a reciprocal increase in conductance. Thus, if each increment of sweat were to reduce the empty portion of the duct in equal decrements, the decrease in resistance at each increment of sweat would be the same. If each decrement of resistance were 100K, the corresponding change in conductance would be 0.5 μmho in going from 500 to 400K and 1.7 μmho in going from 300 to 200K. In this case the fall in resistance would be a much more linear measure than conductance and for the individual units would be independent of the base resistance. The conductance change would be positively correlated with the conductance level.

It appears that, for a system consisting of sweat gland activity only, in which all units operate, and each varies its resistance in equal increments for each neural impulse, skin *resistance* changes should be the linear measure of choice. The response amplitude would be independent of base *resistance*. If the situation is one in which individual units are being recruited in an all-or-none fashion, *conductance* values become a linear measure of activity. The response amplitude is then independent of the base *conductance* level. At times, one or the other of these conditions may prevail, but in practice both types of activation are probably involved. The opposing relations of these two types of increase in activity obviously make quantitative treatment difficult; from a peripheral standpoint one would be inclined not to make any baseline correction until more is known about the relative variation in active sweat units and neural impulse frequency.

2. Membrane activity   When a volley of nerve impulses arrives at the skin, acetylcholine, released at the nerve endings, is presumed to act on the cell membranes of the electrodermal effector to produce an increase in permeability. It can be appreciated that this change in permeability, as reflected in a transient change of conductance, might very well vary as a function of the state of the membrane when the parcel of acetylcholine arrives. The sieve model of the membrane structure leads one to expect that the change in permeability for a given ion per unit of acetylcholine would be greater when the permeability is low, rather than when a high degree of ionic admittance already exists. This fact can be appreciated by considering an outdoor enclosure with a normal distribution of holes of assorted sizes with all except a few of them slightly too small to admit the neighborhood cats. A slight increase in the size of each hole will convert many of them to cat-accessible holes. If, however, most of them have already been enlarged to cat proportions, an increase in the size of all the

holes has little effect on the rate at which cats can enter the enclosure. On the other hand, the increase in the rate at which dogs can enter by this last enlargement may be considerable. This is possibly the mechanism by which we can explain the observation that the degree of permeability increase as reflected in SCR amplitude is greater when larger ions are present (Edelberg, Greiner, & Burch, 1960). From these considerations one would predict a negative correlation between the conductance change and the conductance level.

3. Combined sweat gland and membrane activity   The two conductance effects, the filling of ducts and the change in membrane permeability, seem on a theoretical basis to be oppositely related to base level, when the individual sweat glands engage in graded activity (which they do). From this one can expect a variation in response-base level relations, depending on the relative activity of each type.

A further complicating factor is the degree of hydration of the corneum. If one repetitively stimulates the sympathetic supply to the cat foot-pad, conductance becomes very high, presumably as the thick horny layer is hydrated, thus increasing the area of contact with the coiled portion of the sweat duct. If stimulation is discontinued, conductance falls progressively over the period of 30–45 min, presumably because of the reabsorption of moisture. Small test stimuli at 30-sec intervals during this period cause progressively larger conductance changes as conductance level *decreases;* in fact, the relation determined empirically is that the conductance change varies inversely with the square of the conductance level (unpublished data).

This empirical finding is opposite to that predicted on the basis of a simple duct model. If one assumes that the slow recovery of the resistance of the cat foot-pad cannot be a membrane effect, the observation indicates that in the sweat effect one is not dealing with a change in series resistance, nor of units added in parallel, but rather of a more complex circuit effect. A possible one is the progressive hydration of the corneum, in which successive, additional parcels of sweat probably make a less significant contribution to the total conductivity as the moisture content of this layer approaches saturation. According to Adams (personal communication) this may even occur in a wet preparation.

The theoretical evaluation of peripheral base-level effects seems still to contain so many unknowns that an empirical approach is necessary. Nevertheless, Darrow (1964) has attempted to bring theory and empirical findings together to make a compelling case for the use of uncorrected change in conductance.

4. Relations of potential response amplitude to potential level   In view of the great complexity of the peripheral factors determining the potential response, it is not surprising that there has been little success in relating the amplitude of the SPR to the potential level (Wilcott, 1958a); although Trehub, Tucker, and Cazavelan (1962) have shown an increased occurrence of positive waves as the negativity of the base potential increased. More recently, Shapiro and Leiderman (1964) demonstrated a low correlation between the SPR and SP level. On empirical as well as on theoretical grounds, it does not appear reasonable to expect a satisfactory quantitative relation between SPR and SP to evolve.

Correction for base-line effects of central origin
Granted that the observation of electrodermal behavior affords the investigator a means of assessing the magnitude of sympathetic activity, one is inclined, on the basis of the discussion in the previous section, to consider conductance and the conductance change as measures of this effect without the base level correction. Thus, if one is using sympathetic activity as a measure of activation, there would be no reason to correct the data in making comparisons. However, let us suppose that one wishes to know whether anxious subjects are different from normal subjects in the degree of differentiation of their autonomic response to objects and persons. The anxious group may, like the one reported by Malmo and Shagass (1949), have a lower mean skin conductance than the normal. If the difference in the response amplitude to persons and objects were found to be less for the anxious than for the normal, the investigator would be left wondering whether this result reflected a difference in the discrimination of the two stimuli or whether it were simply an artifact of base-level

influence. Clearly, the solution demands an accounting of the base-level effect. This is ordinarily done empirically, in effect by determining for a large population the regression of response amplitude on the base level and, by a statistical maneuver, effectively bringing all subjects to the same base level (J. I. Lacey, 1956, pp. 160–208). The regression approach developed by Lacey was shown by Benjamin (1963) to be similar to treating the data by the analysis of covariance.

Although this approach seems rational and desirable, there is some reason to question its universal desirability. Let us suppose that the conductance change varies linearly with increasing intensity and frequency of peripheral neural activity, i.e., it is independent of the base level. Should one then correct for differences in the way the CNS responds? Consider the case in which we are comparing two groups for responsivity to a food stimulus. One group has been marching all day and is fatigued and has a low conductance. The other is rested and alert and has a high conductance. If the differences in the base level are related to differences in central arousal, it is to be expected that the response to *any* stimulus may be less for the group with lower conductance. Under these conditions it seems that, other than to satisfy a statistical appetite, it makes little sense to correct for base-level effects when the base level is related to the causal agent of the response difference. It is a bit like asking, "Do clerical workers read faster than third-grade students?" and correcting the data for age differences. Although there are many cases when a correction for the base-level effect is entirely in order, it should be appreciated that this is often a surefire method for elimination of any significant differences. In this regard the evaluation of treatment of various autonomic variables by Wenger, Clemens, Coleman, Cullen, and Engel (1961) is of interest. They concluded that uncorrected levels were as adequate a measure of response as were transformed or corrected ones, with the exception of electrodermal activity. For these they employed a change in log conductance.

J. I. Lacey (1956), in his treatment of autonomic responses, considered that the responses are base-level-dependent, because of the variation in homeostatic compensatory activity as a function of the prestimulus activity. His "autonomic lability score" has been used to great advantage for many measures, although its value has been questioned by Wenger et al. (1961) and by Lubin, Hord, and Johnson (1964). Its application to electrodermal measures in particular is subject to doubt, perhaps because of the complicated peripheral relations in this measure as compared with such others as heart rate, muscle action potential, skin temperature, and respiratory rate. In fact, Hord, Johnson, and Lubin (1964) point out that, for the SCR, the converse of the law of initial values seems to hold. Dykman, Reese, Galbrecht, and Thomasson (1959) have concluded that the Lacey approach *is* an effective one, even for electrodermal measures, but have modified it by using the prestimulus level as an independent variable in calculating the deviation of the subject's stimulus level from the predicted level. Part of the reason for the disagreement in this area may be explained by the work of Block and Bridger (1962). They concluded from observations of the regression of EDR amplitude on prestimulus level that the law of initial values operates independently for the individual and for the group.

There have been numerous attempts to provide empirical evidence for the most desirable transformations. For example, Hunt and Hunt (1935), after comparing five methods of scoring EDA, concluded that the use of absolute resistance change is as suitable as any measure. Bitterman, Krauskopf, and Holtzman (1954) found the square root of the percent resistance change to be a preferred measure, but their justification for it depended on a peripheral alteration of the base level by abrasion. Venables (1955) found the percent conductance change to be independent of the base level and normally distributed. It should be noted that the percent change in conductance is the same as the percent change in resistance for responses of about 5 percent or less. J. I. Lacey (1956) and Dykman, Reese, Galbrecht, and Thomasson (1959) have discussed many of these attempts, which include the consideration of resistance change, conductance change, percent resistance change, log of conductance change, log of resistance change, change in the log of resistance, and change in the log of conductance. Haggard (1949a, 1949b), who has been most active in this area, has concluded that the log

of the change in conductance is most suitable. At first glance this appears to be a means of compressing the range of response amplitudes without any correction for the base level. However, as has been shown elsewhere (Edelberg, 1967, p. 47), for a small response the change in conductance is equal to the change in resistance divided by the square of the resistance level. Thus, the use of conductance units automatically adjusts for the base *resistance* level whether the user intends to or not, and Haggard's transformation in this sense does contain a form of base level correction.

Darrow (1937b) argues that, for the application of conductance measures to psychological experiments, it is desirable to use the change in log conductance, a measure which has both statistical utility and a correction for base level. Moreover, as he has pointed out, the choice of conductance rather than resistance as a basis for measurement has intrinsic rationality, since the biological consequence of increased neurodermal activity is increased conductivity. Resistance then becomes a rather meaningless, reciprocal transformation of the manifest activity. Despite the advantages of this transformation, its incorporation of a powerful base-level effect should be well considered by the user. Whether its use is justified should appear to be a function of the particular focus of the problem under investigation.

Special approaches to treatment of electrodermal measures A few unorthodox methods have been proposed from time to time, some of which may have value for special purposes. One, the *Paintal index*, presents a means of reporting each response in terms of the proportion of the subject's total neurodermal capability which he has mobilized in that response (Paintal, 1951), and is apparently independent of base level. The subject is stimulated by a strong electrical shock. The response to this stimulus is considered to approximate the maximum amplitude characteristic of complete activation; subsequent responses in the course of the experiment are expressed in terms of their ratio to this amplitude. Elliott and Singer (1953) have examined the Paintal index as a measure and have confirmed its independence of base-level effects.

The SRR has been used by Freeman and Katzoff (1942) as a means of measuring the homeostatic capacity of an individual. The SRR is interpreted as indicating a neural disturbance in response to the stimulus, and the rate of recovery is considered to be a function of compensatory mechanisms that are brought into play to restore homeostasis. In practice those authors use the ratio of peak conductance change to the amount of recovery from peak in a prescribed time (recovery quotient or RQ). If recovery is in fact caused by a passive process such as the loss of water from the corneum one should not expect this measure to have much psychological significance. In many instances, however, recovery is retarded by a series of neurodermal "reverberations," which indicate that the neural disturbance is not being readily arrested. In such cases it seems apparent that the RQ approach could be useful, but results would be confounded by such responses as the first wave of Figure 9.10, which almost reaches a plateau, probably because sweat is not being reabsorbed.

The last comment introduces a *third special approach* to analysis, one proposed by this author (Edelberg, 1966b). If one examines the responses in Figure 9.10, a clearly apparent transition is observable in the skin potential response. At first, there are only single negative waves with very slow recovery periods, but by the third wave there is a disturbance on the ascending limb. With succeeding responses this disturbance evolves into a typical, fast, positive wave, superimposed on the slower negative waves. The positive component is sometimes strong enough to carry the potential below the base level, sometimes not. A gradual fading out of the slowly recovering component is observed as the record progresses.

The corresponding skin conductance responses on the lower trace show that the conductance level follows the slow component fairly faithfully, except for differences in the rate of recovery. In accordance with the sweat circuit model, the attainment and maintenance of a higher conductance level for an extended period after the response (see waves a and b) is in all likelihood an indication of an increase of sweat in the ducts that is not immediately reabsorbed. With the onset of the first positive-going component on the ascending limb of

wave c, the associated SCR develops a sharp peak, superimposed on the slower stepwise increment in conductance. Of special significance in the SCR is the flatter section of the recovery limb, which follows the steep section. It should be noted in waves c and d that this gently sloping portion is elevated above the level of the onset of the response.

As discussed earlier, the conductance response is seen as composed of two elements: One is a sharply peaked, rapid, fully recovering change in conductivity, associated primarily with the positive SPR and most likely with an epidermal or ductal membrane response. The other is a rounded prolonged shift in level, associated with the slow negative wave and probably with rise of sweat in the duct or hydrating of the corneum. Lasting changes in conductance then are considered to depend upon changes in the degree of filling of the ducts or hydration of the horny layer. The faster changes are looked upon as transient opening of a membrane without any enduring aftereffects (see p. 391). The fast, positive-going SPR component may be preceded by a brief sharp negative wave which probably represents the initial rise of sweat in the duct just *preceding* the membrane wave. The positive-going membrane wave may or may not overshoot the baseline.

The manner in which the components of the potential and conductance effects may interact is illustrated schematically in Figure 9.11. On the left the large, slow potential wave resulting from the rise of sweat in the duct combines with a fast, positive membrane wave to produce the triphasic wave at the bottom. As the sweat wave becomes relatively smaller, the third or c wave may not appear. Nakayama and Takagi (1958) have proposed a similar summation for the skin potential response, without suggesting a physical basis.

The corresponding conductance changes on the right show how the sharp increase in conductivity attending the membrane wave is superimposed on the sweat wave. By using the flat portion of the recovery limb, one may hope to get a measure of the sweat contribution by backward extrapolation, as shown in the lower right of Figure 9.11. It should then be possible to obtain a measure of the relative membrane effect by a subtraction process. From a quantitative standpoint this method has more value

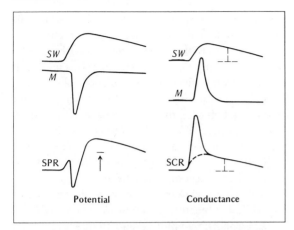

Figure 9.11 Schematic combination of potential components and corresponding conductance components when the filling of the sweat duct causes a slowly recovering wave (SW). The membrane potential response (M) is a uniphasic positive wave. Broken lines in the right-hand figures show elements of sweat duct resistance response reflected in the net SCR.

than the use of the potential difference, which is complicated by mutual cancellation and internal circuit-current effects. The use of conductance responses, however, is complicated by the fact that any absorption that occurs during the positive wave reduces the increment in the steady conductance level. This can be observed by comparing the prolonged increment in the conductance level with the amplitude of the negative potential wave both in the presence and in the absence of positive waves in Figure 9.10.

The preceding analysis has an important bearing on the measurement of skin potential responses. The magnitude of the positive response would appear to be most accurately measured as the difference between the peak of the first negative deflection and the peak of the positive deflection, without reference to the baseline and independent of whether the baseline is crossed. The absorption process cancels the negative sweat component to some extent, making it difficult to get a meaningful measure of the amplitude of the long lasting negative wave. An added complication is that the negative component is subject to electrical cancellation by any positive activity, even if no net positive deflections are observable (Holmquest & Edelberg, 1964). The best operational measure of the negative wave may be the sum of the initial negative deflec-

tion *plus* the second negative deflection, if the wave is triphasic.

This analysis of the contributions of the two components to the SCR explains why, under some circumstances, a continuous series of fast-recovering SCRs may be unaccompanied by any appreciable shift in base level, while at other times a few slowly recovering responses may result in a protracted increase in conductivity (Figure 9.2). It also introduces the notion that the initial rate of recovery of a given response is a function of the relative contributions of the membrane and duct-filling components. A study of the time course of the early portion of the recovery limb has in fact shown it to have excellent discriminating power for behavioral situations. It becomes more rapid in situations involving goal-directed behavior (Edelberg, 1970).

BEHAVIORAL CORRELATES AND APPLICATIONS

When an electrodermal measure is utilized either in an experiment or in a clinical evaluation, its use is almost entirely related to its characteristic as an indicator of autonomic (primarily sympathetic) nervous activity. Among dermatologists, however, it is more often used to evaluate the integrity of cutaneous structures, while its use by neurologists is commonly for the detection of nerve injury or degeneration (e.g., Herz, Glaser, & Moldover, 1946; Silver, Versaci, & Montagna, 1963).

While the most direct interpretation of the electrical behavior of the skin appears to be in its reflection of the sympathetic inflow to the cutaneous area under observation, it is clear that more often than not the investigator in a psychophysiological experiment conceptually bypasses this step and equates electrodermal activity either to the level of arousal or to emotional activity. It should be apparent that this is an abstraction based on an assumption that there is a direct relation between sympathetic activity and these behavioral correlates, an assumption which, in view of the neurophysiological substrate of the electrodermal reflex, may be unwarranted. For example, such conceptual leaps do not take into account the complex array of inhibitory centers, some of which represent limbic areas well known to be related to emotional behavior. Direct evidence for neurodermal inhibition is to be found in the anhydrotic response to stress, found in normals but absent in a schizophrenic population (MacKinnon, 1969).

The notion that arousal is a nonspecific dimension of human behavior also overlooks the fact that the autonomic correlates of the arousal associated with anger are not the same as those in the arousal associated with joyful anticipation. Ax (1953) and Schacter (1957) have clearly shown that they are not even the same in such closely related emotions as fear and anger (see Chapter 16).

The gross oversimplification of the significance of electrodermal activity, implicit in so many experimental designs, is probably in large part responsible for the astounding potpourri of assorted empirical findings in this area. The number of English language papers relating electrodermal activity to behavior is conservatively estimated at over 1500; the actual number may easily be twice this many. Needless to say, contradictions and blind alleys abound; nevertheless, it is possible to observe a pattern of consensual validation in certain areas. An attempt will be made to identify these emerging areas of agreement and to present a few representative studies in each case, but no effort will be made to review each area. Reviews have been made at intervals over the last 45 years. It is interesting that the most exhaustive ones were the earliest, despite the almost exponential growth in the number of studies incorporating this measure. The reader is referred to the reviews by Prideaux (1920), Wechsler (1925), Landis and De Wick (1929), Landis (1932), Darrow (1936), McCleary (1950), Woodworth and Schlosberg (1954, pp. 133–159), Rothman (1954, Ch. 2), Wang (1957, 1958), Bloch (1965) and Martin and Venables (1966).

Biological Significance of Electrodermal Behavior

Before proceeding to an overview of electrodermal measures in psychophysiological studies, it will be helpful to consider the biological significance of this type of activity. If a sensory nerve is stimulated, afferent collaterals to the facilitatory portions of the reticular formation may elicit a response either mediated directly by this area or

mediated at the spinal level but facilitated by this area. Such a neurophysiological observation has been used as a basis for equating EDA with reticular activation in an operational manner. This approach has in many instances been useful, possibly because reticular activation is frequently associated with modes of behavior that also are accompanied by EDA. The question boils down to one of the specificity of reticular facilitation of the skin reflex. Activation, evidenced in other autonomic channels, is not always accompanied by increased electrodermal activity. EDA may even be inhibited in cases of marked subjective irritation (R. Martin & Edelberg, 1963). The amplitude and frequency of EDA may for some subjects be considerably less during concentration on an absorbing task such as mirror drawing than during a relaxed rest period. Other types of tasks such as reading aloud may be accompanied by marked potentiation of such activity. If it is assumed that, in the performance of a task, one activates at least certain central neural functional systems, it must be concluded that not all of them necessarily invoke the electrodermal system as a concomitant. While one would generally view the sleeping individual as being in a very low state of arousal, it can be demonstrated that certain systems are hyperactivated and that in one type of sleep, Stage 4, there may be considerably more electrodermal activity than in the same subject when fully awake performing a task (Johnson & Lubin, 1966). Perhaps it is inappropriate to speak of arousal per se; rather, one might speak of cortical activation; or heightened amygdaloid, hippocampal, or pontine activity; or on a behavioral basis, of defensive arousal, cognitive activation, or alertness for information intake.

This qualification of the type of arousal implies that the autonomic concomitants represent part of an integrated adaptive complex. For the specific case of cutaneous activity, one might profitably consider the biological significance of the adaptation as an aid in qualitative interpretation. Given the overwhelming evidence that sweat gland activity plays a causal role in the production of an electrodermal response, certain inferences may be drawn with regard to its function. The moisturizing of the horny layer that results has been interpreted by Darrow (1936) as facilitating grasping and tactile manipulation. Katz (1925, pp. 176–178) had previously presented evidence of the greater sensitivity of moist, as opposed to dry, skin. The moisturizing process may also aid the organism by increasing the resistance of the corneum to tearing and abrasion. In microsurgical procedures designed to isolate a slab of epidermis (Edelberg, 1961a), it was found almost impossible to cut into the horny layer of a profusely sweating individual because of its rubbery, slippery texture. Drying the area with acetone immediately made cutting a simple matter. Wilcott (1966) pursued this observation further and demonstrated quantitatively that atropinized skin is more easily abraded than normal skin. This defensive adaptation perhaps explains why threatening situations are powerful stimuli for eliciting EDA. In one study (Wilson, 1967), perfect separation of a group of normals and a group of phobics was provided by comparing their relative responses to spiders and to landscapes.

While Darrow's view is clearly a valid one, it is also true that, if cutaneous moisture exceeds a certain limit, tactile exploration and manipulation is impeded. Adams and Hunter (1969) have in fact demonstrated that the frictional properties of skin reach a maximum at an intermediate level of surface moisture. This would imply that, under conditions in which the sweat glands are being activated as a tactile adaptation, one should be able to observe indications of a control mechanism to safeguard against excessive surface moisture. As discussed in an earlier section, the absorption reflex associated with the positive wave may mediate this type of control. Hence one would be inclined to interpret the positive skin potential response or reabsorption activity as an indication of the mobilization of task-oriented, finely coordinated motor activity. Added evidence for this may be seen in the demonstration that there is a regional association of SCR amplitude with specific muscular activity (Culp & Edelberg, 1966).

Still another interpretation of sudomotor activity may be made in relation to thermoregulation. Although Kuno (1956, p. 98) has claimed that the palmar and plantar surfaces from which most electrodermal activity is monitored are not involved in thermoregulatory activity, Wilcott (1963) has demonstrated thermoregulatory vapor production from

these areas. Furthermore, sweat glands on other areas of the skin, known to be activated by thermal control mechanisms, may also be activated by emotional or startle stimuli. A thermoregulatory adaptation of this type to a startle stimulus would suggest that an increased evaporative heat loss is of some advantage to the organism. It can be postulated that the individual is preparing a heat sink for an anticipated increase in metabolic activity. This would, in all likelihood, result from increased action or tonus of skeletal muscle, and would imply a real or displaced preparation for motor activity, i.e., active fight or flight. On the other hand, it should be noted that the startle reaction and responses to tension-arousing situations commonly produce cutaneous vasoconstriction that is largely arteriolar and, therefore, leads to reduced cutaneous blood flow (Graham, 1955). The adaptive value of this reflex is to raise the blood pressure for increased muscle perfusion and to reduce cutaneous bleeding in the event of surface injury. To prevent a rise of body temperature, this reduction in a primary route of heat loss must be compensated for; increased evaporative heat loss is one way of accomplishing this. Thus, in a sense, reflex thermoregulatory sweating may be nothing more than the servant of the cardiovascular system. A close relation between vasoconstriction and electrodermal activity has, in fact, been noted (Darrow, 1929), however, the control mechanisms for these have been demonstrated to be independent (Prout, Coote, & Downman, 1965).

Moisturizing the skin may not be the only means of increasing tactile acuity. Loewenstein (1956) demonstrated that the threshold of touch receptors in the frog may be reduced by the stimulation of efferent sympathetic fibers. The possibility that such a mechanism plays a role in the human was subsequently demonstrated (Edelberg, 1961b), by showing that tactile sensitivity was frequently enhanced following an electrodermal reflex. It was suggested that the electrical manifestations might in part be the by-product of the arrival of sympathetic impulses whose function was to sensitize the tactile receptors. Kaye and Lipsitt (1964) reported a positive correlation between the electrotactual threshold and the skin conductance. These relations are suggestive of the operation in the human of a mechanism like that demonstrated by Loewenstein. However, a recent unpublished study at this laboratory on unilaterally sympathectomized patients indicates that sensitization at central relays far surpasses any peripheral effect.

Another possible biological adaptation represented by psychogalvanic sweating is as a tracking aid. Far from being a simple salt solution, sweat contains a dilute but complex mixture of organic compounds (Rothman, 1954, Ch. 7). It is conceivable that such mixtures have a characteristic odor for a given species and can be used as an identifying tag for the tracks. Thus a stray offspring in search of its mother may leave an intensified tract of olfactory clues in addition to its vocalization. Needless to say, such tracks might also be of advantage to a predator, in much the same way that sweaty palms furnish useful information to a social antagonist. If there is any merit to this idea, emotional sweating would contain, in itself, some of the elements of a cry for help.

The skin reflex, then, may constitute a simple by-product of central processes or, much more likely, an adaptive response representing (a) thermoregulation to compensate for cutaneous vasoconstriction, (b) thermal preparation for a heat load of muscular origin, (c) the adjustment of physical properties to favor manipulative contact, (d) the adjustment of physical properties as a defense against abrasion, (e) the enhancement of tactual acuity either mechanically or neurochemically, or (f) the secretion of a characteristic odoriferous substance that facilitates tracking by other members of the species. The selection of the appropriate interpretation must await experiments designed to allow identification of the nature of the biological adaptation.

Electrodermal Activity As an Activation Index

Except for those focusing on response specificity, most behavioral studies that employ electrodermal measures utilize this response, rightly or wrongly, as a quantitative index of activation. There is no doubt that many of these studies have used the measure appropriately, since a relation between EDA and activation level has been demonstrated. Burch and Greiner (1960) have shown an S-shaped curve relating the increasing frequency of spontaneous activity to the increased level of arousal as manipulated pharmacologically. The amplitude of the response to a standard stimulus resembled an inverted U-shaped function with the maximal response at intermediate levels of arousal. The diminution in the response amplitude at higher levels of arousal was considered to reflect a breakdown in appropriate biological performance as a consequence of the loss of selective inhibition, but it should be pointed out that amplitude was measured as a resistance change without correction for base level. If base resistance fell at higher levels of activation, as is generally observed, the base-level correction might reduce or abolish the reduction in amplitude at this end of the curve.

Stennett (1957) has shown a direct relation of skin conductance to arousal as manipulated by tasks of graded difficulty. Electrodermal activity may, under some circumstances, serve as an arousal indicator; but it should be pointed out that McDonald, Johnson, and Hord (1964) found no differences in the amplitude of specific SRRs of alert and drowsy subjects, although SRR frequency was less in the drowsy group. Activation and vigilance are not synonymous, but the finding by Surwillo and Quilter (1965) that vigilance is positively related to the frequency of SPR in the interval just preceding the test stimulus appears to be consistent with that of McDonald, Johnson, and Hord (1964) on alert and drowsy subjects. It is of interest that efforts to correlate EDA with the anxiety level have been unsuccessful or contradictory. It is common to equate increasing anxiety with increased activation, but if so, one would have great difficulty in explaining the results of McDonnell and Carpenter (1960), who found that log skin conductance bore an inverted U-relation to anxiety, as measured with the Mandler-Sarason General Anxiety Scale. An example of the failure of electrodermal indices to correlate with anxiety indices is seen in the work of McReynolds, Acker, and Brackbill (1966) and Roessler, Burch, and Childers (1966).

The above discussion referred to three separate measures of EDA. When an investigator speaks of increased electrodermal activity, he may mean the skin conductance, the response frequency (i.e., the rate of occurrence), or the response amplitude. When he speaks of amplitude he may be referring to the amplitude of a single response to a specified stimulus, i.e., a specific response, to use the term proposed by Burch and Greiner (1958), or to the sum of the amplitudes of all responses occurring within a specified period. These various measures are not interchangeable, since they may have different relationships to a given variable. At higher levels of arousal, EDR spontaneous frequency remains relatively constant as the arousal increases, but the amplitude of specific responses falls off. The conductance varies in a parallel manner with EDR frequency as the activation level changes, but this relationship does not hold for relaxed subjects at rest (Johnson, 1962).

Many studies have correlated electrodermal activity with the *rate of learning,* either during the learning effort (Carrier & Orton, 1964; Obrist, 1962), or upon the attainment of criterion (Kintsch, 1965), with the hope of examining the relation between activation level and learning. Unfortunately, in most of these studies, there is no adequate basis for determining whether the activation reflects motivation or apprehension. Without such a qualitative label, one must expect a high degree of variance in such data.

Other examples of the implicit use of electrodermal measures as arousal indicators are those in which they serve as stress indicators (e.g., Learmonth, Ackerly, & Kaplan, 1959; Speisman, Lazarus, Mordkoff, & Davison, 1964), in lie detection (Gustafson & Orne, 1965), in measuring the tranquilizing or stimulating effects of pharmacologic agents (Schneider & Costiloe, 1957), or in assessing the state of autonomic balance (Wenger, 1957). Their use for these purposes has met with varying degrees of success, and again, the sources of contradictory findings are to be found primarily in the selection of different parameters for measuring the EDR or in failure to consider that qualitatively different types of arousal may be associated with different patterns of autonomic arousal (response specificity), as described by Davis (1957).

Relation of Electrodermal Activity to Emotional Experience

The plethora of experimental attempts to establish electrodermal activity as an emotion indicator has been curtailed in the past two decades as disillusionment and disrepute took over. As early as 1911, Wells and Forbes carefully examined the feasibility of its use as a criterion of emotional response to a word association test and concluded that its high variability renders the measure of limited value for application to the individual. McCurdy (1950) has discussed some of the limitations of these efforts but has also made a determined attempt to come to the rescue of this measure in such applications. J. I. Lacey (1959) has also presented cogent arguments, both for its limitations and its possibilities. One of the difficulties in much of the experimental work appears to have been in the failure to consider the specific meaning of a stimulus to a given individual when assigning it a value. It must also be realized that, even with highly reliable results, one cannot be certain that *emotion* is being indicated, as opposed to activation. Thus, in studies that show a difference in electrodermal activity during two different emotional states, for instance, anger versus fear (Ax, 1953), one is faced with the problem of deciding whether the differences are simply epiphenomena of the different levels of arousal associated with these emotions. Schlosberg (1954) has, in fact, suggested a model for classifying emotions in which one of the three dimensions is the activation level. If one accepts his theoretical framework, it would follow that the level of activation as reflected in EDA would be one of the coordinates which helps define the emotional state. Thus grief would be very low on the arousal scale, anger very high. To identify the emotion one would additionally require information regarding the coordinates on the other two orthogonal dimensions, namely acceptance-rejection and pleasantness-unpleasantness. This approach makes it all the more clear that, in many instances, efforts to distinguish emotional states by their autonomic concomitants are implicitly evaluating only the differences in the arousal level of these emotions.

One would expect, on a biological basis, that adaptive behavior plays a role in the determination of the autonomic profile associated with a given emotional state. For the case of the skin reflex, those emotions characterized by withdrawal from interaction with the external world would probably be characterized by diminished preparation for manipulative activity and, therefore, by the inhibition of those forms of electrodermal activity associated with such behavior (in particular, the positive SPR). On the other hand, emotions such as fear should appropriately be accompanied by the activation of any defensive elements represented in this skin reflex, such as sweating. Emotions (or affects) associated with exploratory behavior should be accompanied by activation of elements facilitating tactile and manipulative activity. This may be the significance of the enhanced EDA associated with perceptual novelty (Furedy, 1968) or perceptual conflict (Berlyne, 1966). The alternative to an adaptive interpretation of such behavior is that the attending EDA is merely part of a general outflow attending the reticular activation engendered by novel stimuli.

Personality Traits, Pathology, and Electrodermal Activity

Many studies have attempted to show a relation between personality traits and the intensity of electrodermal response to one type of stimulus or another. Wechsler (1925), Landis and DeWick (1929), Landis (1932), and J. I. Lacey (1959, pp. 160–208) have reviewed a number of these experiments. Electrodermal measures have been used in the study of psychoses (Bernstein, 1970; Lader & Wing, 1969; Venables & Wing, 1962) and in brain damage (Holloway & Parsons, 1969), in some cases to clarify the nature of the defect, in others to improve classification or diagnosis. Such studies commonly adopt an implicit arousal model in their interpretation.

Numerous attempts have been made to show significant differences in the EDA of groups selected on the basis of scores on psychological tests such as the Minnesota Multiphasic Personality Inventory (MMPI). While these are for the most part empirical, some genuine attempts have been made to interpret differences in terms of the significance of the type of behavior manifested in electrodermal activity. Lacey, for example, has viewed electrodermal activity as facilitating the transaction between an organism and its environment and has suggested that the pattern of response can be expected to vary in accordance with whether the individual is open to his environment or tends to reject it. Fisher (1958, 1960) has related the regional distribution of SRR to body image. Roessler, Alexander, and Greenfield (1963) have related physiological responsivity to ego strength on the basis of the adaptive function of autonomic responses.

It may be justifiable to expect that an individual with certain well-established behavioral patterns (personality traits) will deal with environmental demands in a characteristic manner. Such an assumption runs through a large portion of the literature on normal and especially pathological behavior. Thus, if an individual characteristically faces a threat by withdrawing from the situation, while another deals with the same threat by hostile action, we might expect the first to show a diminution in electrodermal activity and the second to show an increase. This comparison exemplifies an approach to the possible rational interpretation of response stereotypy and resembles that proposed by Wolff (1949) to explain the relations of psychosomatic symptoms to behavioral pattern. The particular application of this approach to the understanding of electrodermal responders and nonresponders appears to be a highly profitable one.

Stimulus-Response Specificity and Electrodermal Response

The phenomenon of stimulus response specificity, namely, a variation in response profile in accordance with the nature of the stimulus (Engel, 1960; J. I. Lacey, Bateman, & Van Lehn 1953; Wenger et al., 1961) may also operate. Early evidence presented by Darrow and Freeman (1934) demonstrated that muscular activity tended to elicit electrodermal responses primarily from the dorsal surface of the hand, while ideational stimuli elicited responses predominantly from the palms. This observation was followed up much later in comparisons of responses from the dorsal and volar surfaces of the finger, using simpler stimuli (Edelberg & Wright, 1964). The latter study demonstrated that differences in palmar and dorsal responses were a function of the nature of the stimulus and did not depend on muscular versus ideational activity. While regional response specificity of the EDR has since been demonstrated with localized motor activity (Culp & Edelberg, 1966), the earlier study afforded evidence that the observed effects did not depend upon this effect but rather on differences in the concentration of sweat glands in an area.

The volar response was selectively potentiated in accordance with relative sweat gland activity, and it was concluded that a second component was responsible for the disproportionate potentiation of the dorsal response to certain stimuli. These findings have since been in part confirmed by Katkin, Weintraub, and Yasser (1967) and have also been demonstrated with a different set of stimuli in a conditioning study (Mordkoff, Edelberg, & Ustick, 1965). The demonstration of a variation in the topographical pattern of a response in accordance with the nature of the stimulus is consistent with the notion that the response is an adaptive one, rather than a nonspecific reflection of central arousal.

The similar examination of the negative and positive components of the SPR suggests that these responses are stimulus-specific, but work by Forbes and Bolles (1936) indicates the differential factor is novelty rather than specificity. The differential behavior of these two components of the SPR has also been observed by Loveless and Thetford (1966) and by Shmavonian, Miller, and Cohen (1968) in conditioning studies. Paradoxically, although both papers demonstrate differences in the conditionability of the positive and negative components, they show opposite results. Unless this is due to the difference in UCS (light in the first study, shock in the second), it leads one to wonder whether one of these studies does not suffer from a polarity error. Raskin, Kotses, and Bever (1969) have also noted the differential behavior of the positive and negative SPR components in habituation series. They conclude, in agreement with Shmavonian, that the negative wave is associated with the orienting response. They further interpret the nonhabituating positive component at higher stimulus intensities as evidence of a defensive response. It should be noted that these conclusions run contrary to the implications of the functional model presented in a preceding section.

Electrodermal Activity in Conditioning Studies

It is not surprising, in view of the well-established demonstration of classical conditioning of autonomic activity, that the electrodermal response has been the focus of much study in this area (e.g., Ax, Beckett, Fretz, & Gottlieb, 1965;

Grings, Lockhart, & Dameron, 1962; I. Martin, 1962; Stern, Winokur, Stewart, & Leonard, 1963). Because of the well-defined form of the response, and the ease with which two separate responses in close sequence can be distinguished from a large single response, it has been particularly useful in examining the effect of the duration of the CS-UCS interval. Even at very short intervals, it is frequently possible to separate the conditioned response from the orienting response to the CS. For the same reason it has been particularly useful in distinguishing the anticipatory response from the unconditioned response. Instrumental conditioning of the GSR has also been reported (e.g., Fowler & Kimmel, 1962; Kimmel & Kimmel, 1963; and Rice, 1966). Although several investigators have apparently been able to discount mediation by motor activity, there is a high likelihood that operant EDR conditioning is mediated by cognitive events (Shean, 1970; Stern & Kaplan, 1967).

Electrodermal Activity in Sleep Studies

Until a few years ago, it had been relatively widely accepted that the EDR is essentially extinguished during sleep. Palmar and plantar resistances rise to very high levels (Johns, Cornell, & Masterson, 1968; Levy, Thaler, & Ruff, 1958), and the resistance of the skin of other areas tends to fall (Richter, 1926). With the relatively recent acceleration of the psychophysiological study of sleep, these views were revised. It was soon learned that, in Stage 4 sleep, palmar or plantar EDR phasic activity may be greater than in the walking state, becoming progressively less in other stages, with essentially none in Stage 1 REM (Johnson & Lubin, 1966). Lester, Burch, and Dossett (1967) showed that such activity depended upon the psychological climate of the preceding waking period, with anxiety-provoking situations tending to predispose toward more EDA during sleep.

Since the slow wave, EEG activity of Stage 4 suggests a decoupled cortex, the increased EDA of this stage has been interpreted as a release of subcortical facilitatory centers from cortical inhibitory control (Lester, Burch, & Dossett, 1967). This interpretation seems consistent with the neurophysiological state in this stage, but the simultaneous depression of other forms of autonomic activity throws some doubt on such an interpretation.

Johnson and Lubin (1966) have proposed a somewhat similar interpretation but have suggested that it is the rhombencephalic inhibitory center that is depressed during Stage 4 sleep. One also wonders why in most instances of REM sleep there is a virtual absence of electrodermal phasic activity at a time when other autonomic channels are displaying their most marked variation.

The relation of the skin potential to the stage of sleep does not appear to be consistent, although in general the palmar or plantar potential becomes less negative (Leiderman & Shapiro, 1964) during sleep and shows a rapid shift to a more negative level upon awakening. This probably indicates a shutting down of sweat gland activity in these areas during sleep, a process which would serve to conserve water during the long period without replenishment. The trend of potential shift on other portions of the body involved in thermoregulation has, to my knowledge, not yet been reported.

A significant phenomenon reported by Johnson and Lubin (1966) is the dissociation between potential responses and resistance responses in sleep. When a period of electrodermal activity starts, the skin potential responses are observable a few seconds to several minutes prior to the skin conductance responses. These potential responses, however, were recorded between the finger and the forearm, while the resistance responses were from a pair of fingers. Thus it is possible that the early responses originated in the forearm, a site that may be very active on occasion. The dissociation would then be a regional one, rather than one between the endosomatic and exosomatic responses. This interpretation is, in fact, consistent with the reversal of polarity relations that occurred in their sample record when SRR activity did appear.

Sex Differences

Rein (1926) demonstrated that female skin tends to depolarize faster than male skin in response to continuous high current and, further, that its polarization capacity is weaker. There is, however, no significant difference in the phase angles calculated for male and female skin (Barnett, 1938). Observations in my laboratory have demonstrated that males and females show opposite shifts in skin potential (recorded over the lower end of the tibial

bone), associated with changes in the level of arousal (Cook & Edelberg, unpublished observations).

The above comparisons may all reflect peripheral differences, but there are others which are probably of behavioral origin, such as that by Shmavonian, Miller, and Cohen (1968) in a conditioning study. It is almost certain that the menstrual cycle is responsible for some of the reported sex differences in EDA. Burr and Musselman (1936) found a marked increase in the potential between the right and left index fingers at mid-cycle. Barton (1940) found a periodic variation in skin potential related to this cycle that was not present in males or menopausal women. The periodic effects may be direct reflection of physiological effects, as occurs in the sleep cycle, but very likely some of the periodicity is a secondary effect of the psychological changes induced by endocrine variation (see Altmann, Knowles, & Bull, 1941). Evidence for the influence of endocrine hormone levels upon electrodermal activity has been presented by Fowles and Venables (1970).

Electrodermal Activity in Infants and Children

Literature concerning electrodermal activity in infants has been somewhat conflicting. For example, Richter (1930) found the skin resistance of infants to be considerably higher than that of adults, while Jones (1930) found it to be somewhat lower. Wenger and Irwin (1936), in a careful study on 15 neonates all under 10 days of age, found that their palmar and plantar resistance was slightly higher than that of adults. They also demonstrated rapid fluctuations in resistance that resembled the adult SRR. These were most evident when the infant apparently was going to sleep. Observations on infants are greatly influenced by their labile states of arousal; moreover, there is a changing pattern of EDA during the first few months (B. K. Lester, personal communication) that may also explain differences in observations. In this regard it should be noted that Jones's infant population was 3–11 months of age, while Richter's subjects were newborn. Infants were found to show characteristic resistance responses to pain, restraint, or loud noises, even at less than 6 months of age (Jones, 1928). More recently the SRR has been demonstrated in 1–3-day infants (Crowell, 1965) and the SPR in 2–6-day infants (Stechler, Bradford, & Levy, 1966). In the neonate chimpanzee, Berkson (1963) found no skin resistance response to light or sound stimuli but he did obtain a decrease with tickling. In a study on human neonates he found a progressive increase in skin conductance during the first 4 days after birth.

Jones (1950, pp. 161–168) has discussed the results of his earlier cross-sectional studies of young children and adolescents (1930, 1935) in an attempt to relate changes in the pattern of EDR to personality development. He found that, in general, maturation was associated with a tendency to show increasing EDA and less vocalization but that, even within the younger group, the more expressive children showed less EDA, and conversely. Other studies dealing with EDA in children have been reviewed by Landis (1932). One may also cite the studies by Grings, Lowell, and Rushford (1959) on conditioning of the EDR in children and by Corah and Stern (1963) on spontaneous activity in children.

CONCLUSIONS

The heavy emphasis placed here on theoretical considerations over 90 years after the first report of electrodermal activity, is perhaps symptomatic of a past overreliance on empiricism in its application to behavioral research. If nothing else, this chapter has underlined the great complexity of the neurodermal system, and the many unjustified assumptions adopted in the measurement of its activity. This discussion should not end on a note of pessimism, however, because implicit in the very reasons for the complexity of EDA are promises of potential sources of behavioral information that for the most part have not yet been tapped. In particular, the possibility of separating the neocortical and the limbic contributions to overall electrodermal activity is especially exciting, because of the qualitatively different modes of central processing reflected in these two areas. Another facet that appears most fruitful in the future development of this measure is the assessment and interpretation of the activity of its many inhibitory controls. On a more traditional note, it is hoped that the valuable application of neurodermal measures as activation indicators will grow in validity and reliability, as the many aspects of the neurodermal system are accounted for during measurement and interpretation. Very few answers, perhaps a few clues, have been given here. It appears that the conversion of this diffusely sensitive, highly qualitative tool to a specific, quantitative measure of central processes lies well in the future.

REFERENCES

ADAMS, T. Characteristics of eccrine sweat gland activity in the footpad of the cat. *Journal of Applied Physiology,* 1966, **21,** 1004–1012.

ADAMS, T., FUNKHOUSER, G. E., & KENDALL, W. W. Measurement of evaporative water loss by a thermal conductivity cell. *Journal of Applied Physiology,* 1963, **18,** 1291–1293.

ADAMS, T., & HUNTER, W. S. Modification of skin mechanical properties by eccrine sweat gland activity. *Journal of Applied Physiology,* 1969, **26,** 417–419.

ADAMS, T., & VAUGHAN, J. A. Human eccrine sweat gland activity and palmar electrical skin resistance. *Journal of Applied Physiology,* 1965, **20,** 980–983.

ALTMANN, M., KNOWLES, E., & BULL, H. D. A psychosomatic study of the sex cycle in women. *Psychosomatic Medicine,* 1941, **3,** 199–225.

ARTHUR, R. P., & SHELLEY, W. B. The innervation of human epidermis. *Journal of Investigative Dermatology,* 1959, **32,** 397–411.

AVELING, F., & McDOWALL, R. J. S. The effect of the circulation on the electrical resistance of the skin. *Journal of Physiology, London,* 1925, **60,** 316–321.

AX, A. F. The physiological differentiation between fear and anger in humans. *Psychosomatic Medicine,* 1953, **15,** 433–442.

AX, A. F., BECKETT, P. G. S., FRETZ, N. A., & GOTTLIEB, J. S. Development of a selection test for motivational aptitude. NASA Contractor Report NASA CR-156, Washington, D.C., January 1965.

BARNETT, A. The phase angle of normal human skin. *Journal of Physiology, London,* 1938, **93,** 349–366.

BARTON, D. S. Electric correlates of the menstrual cycle

in women. *Yale Journal of Biological Medicine,* 1940, **12,** 335–344.

BENJAMIN, L. S. Statistical treatment of the law of initial values (LIV) in autonomic research: A review and recommendation. *Psychosomatic Medicine,* 1963, **25,** 556–566.

BERKSON, G. Stimuli affecting vocalizations and basal skin resistance of neonate chimpanzees. *Perceptual Motor Skills,* 1963, **17,** 871–874.

BERLYNE, D. E. Curiosity and exploration. *Science,* 1966, **153,** 25–33.

BERNSTEIN, A. S. Phasic electrodermal orienting response in chronic schizophrenics: II. Response to auditory signals of varying intensity. *Journal of Abnormal Psychology,* 1970, **75,** 146–156.

BIEBER, I., & FULTON, J. F. A physiologic analysis of reflex grasping: I. The relation of forced grasping and the grasp reflex to the righting reflex. *Archives of Psychiatry and Neurology,* 1934, **32,** 433–434.

BITTERMAN, M. E., KRAUSKOPF, J., & HOLTZMAN, W. H. The galvanic skin response following artificial reduction of the basal resistance. *Journal of Comparative and Physiological Psychology,* 1954, **47,** 230–234.

BLANK, I. H. Further observations on factors which influence the water content of the stratum corneum. *Journal of Investigative Dermatology,* 1953, **21,** 259–271.

BLANK, I. H., & FINESINGER, J. E. Electrical resistance of the skin. *Archives of Neurology and Psychiatry,* 1946, **56,** 544–557.

BLANK, I. H., & GOULD, E. Penetration of anionic surfactants (surface active agents) into skin: I. Penetration of sodium laurate and sodium dodecyl sulfate into excised human skin. *Journal of Investigative Dermatology,* 1959, **33,** 327–336.

BLOCH, V. Nouveau aspects de la méthode psychogalvanique ou électrodermographique (EDG) comme critère des tensions affectives. *Année Psychologique, Paris,* 1952, **52,** 329–362.

BLOCH, V. Le contrôle central de l'activité électrodermale. *Journal de Physiologie,* 1965, **57,** Suppl. 13, 1–132.

BLOCH, V., & BONVALLET, M. Interactions des formations réticulaires méséncephalique et bulbaire. *Journal de Physiologie,* 1961, **53,** 280–281.

BLOCK, J. D., & BRIDGER, W. H. The law of initial value in psychophysiology: A reformulation in terms of experimental and theoretical considerations. *Annals of the New York Academy of Sciences,* 1962, **98,** 1229–1241.

BONIER, R. J., & HANLEY, C. Relationship among PGR indices. *Journal of Psychosomatic Research,* 1965, **9,** 285–289.

BREBNER, D. F., & KERSLAKE, D. McK. The time course of the decline in sweating produced by wetting the skin. *Journal of Physiology, London,* 1964, **175,** 295–302.

BUETTNER, K. J. K. Diffusion of water vapor through small areas of human skin in normal environment. *Journal of Applied Physiology,* 1959, **14,** 269–275.

BUETTNER, K. J. K., & ODLAND, G. F. Physical factors of the skin barrier layer and water diffusion into human skin. *Federation Proceedings,* 1957, **16,** 18. (Abstract)

BULLARD, R. W. The continuous recording of sweating rate by resistance hygrometry. *Journal of Applied Physiology,* 1962, **17,** 735–737.

BURCH, N. R., & GREINER, T. H. Drugs and human fatigue: GSR parameters. *Journal of Psychology,* 1958, **45,** 3–10.

BURCH, N. R., & GREINER, T. H. A bioelectric scale of human alertness: Concurrent recordings of the EEG and GSR. Psychiatric Research Report No. 12, American Psychiatric Association, 1960, 183–193.

BURR, H. S., & MUSSELMAN, L. K. Bioelectric phenomena associated with menstruation. *Yale Journal of Biological Medicine,* 1936, **9,** 155–158.

CARRIER, N. A., & ORTON, K. D. Skin conductance trends during learning by bright, normal and retarded children. *Journal of Comparative and Physiological Psychology,* 1964, **58,** 315–317.

CORAH, N. L., & STERN, J. A. Stability and adaptation of some measures of electrodermal activity in children. *Journal of Experimental Psychology,* 1963, **65,** 80–85.

CROWELL, D. H. Galvanic skin reflex in newborn humans. *Science,* 1965, **148,** 1108–1111.

CULP, W. C., & EDELBERG, R. Regional response specificity in the electrodermal reflex. *Perceptual and Motor Skills,* 1966, **23,** 623–627.

DALE, H. H., & FELDBERG, W. The chemical transmission of secretory impulses to the sweat gland of the cat. *Journal of Physiology, London,* 1934, **82,** 121–128.

DARROW, C. W. Sensory, secretory and electrical changes in the skin following bodily excitation. *Journal of Experimental Psychology,* 1927, **10,** 197–226.

DARROW, C. W. The galvanic skin-reflex and finger volume changes. *American Journal of Physiology,* 1929, **88,** 219–229.

DARROW, C. W. The relation of the galvanic skin reflex recovery curve to reactivity, resistance level, and perspiration. *Journal of General Psychology,* 1932, **7,** 261–271. (a)

DARROW, C. W. Uniform current for continuous standard unit resistance records. *Journal of General Psychology,* 1932, **6,** 471–473. (b)

DARROW, C. W. The galvanic skin reflex (sweating) and blood pressure as preparatory and facilitative functions. *Psychological Bulletin,* 1936, **33,** 73–94.

DARROW, C. W. Neural mechanisms controlling the palmar galvanic skin reflex and palmar sweating. *Archives of Neurology and Psychiatry,* 1937, **37,** 641–663. (a)

DARROW, C. W. The equation of the galvanic skin reflex curve: I. The dynamics of reaction in relation to excitation-background. *Journal of General Psychology,* 1937, **16,** 285–309. (b)

DARROW, C. W. The rationale for treating the change in galvanic skin response as a change in conductance. *Psychophysiology,* 1964, **1,** 31–38.

Darrow, C. W., & Freeman, G. L. Palmar skin-resistance changes contrasted with non-palmar changes, and rate of insensible weight loss. *Journal of Experimental Psychology,* 1934, **17,** 739–748.

Darrow, C. W., & Gullickson, G. R. The peripheral mechanism of the galvanic skin response. *Psychophysiology,* 1970, **6,** 597–600.

Davis, R. C. A vacuum tube for stabilizing the current during measurements of the galvanic reflex. *American Journal of Psychology,* 1929, **41,** 474–475.

Davis, R. C. Factors affecting the galvanic reflex. *Archives of Psychology, New York,* 1930, **18** (115), 1–64.

Davis, R. C. Response patterns. *Annals of the New York Academy of Sciences,* 1957, **19,** 731–739.

Day, J. L., & Lippitt, M. W., Jr. A long-term electrode system for electrocardiography and impedance pneumography. *Psychophysiology,* 1964, **1,** 174–182.

Densham, H. B., & Wells, H. M. The mechanism by which the electrical resistance of the skin is altered. *Quarterly Journal of Experimental Physiology,* 1927, **18,** 175–184.

Dykman, R. A., Reese, W. G., Galbrecht, C. R., & Thomasson, P. A. Psychophysiological reactions to novel stimuli: Measurement, adaptation and relationship of psychological and physiological variables in the normal human. *Annals of the New York Academy of Sciences,* 1959, **79,** 43–107.

Ebbecke, U. Die lokale galvanische Reaktion der Haut: Über die Beziehung zwischen lokaler Reizung und elektrischer Leitfähigkeit. *Pflügers Archiv für die gesamte Physiologie,* 1921, **190,** 230–269.

Edelberg, R. Microelectrode study of the galvanic skin response. *Federation Proceedings,* 1961, **20,** 326. (Abstract) (a)

Edelberg, R. The relationship between the galvanic skin response, vasoconstriction and tactile sensitivity. *Journal of Experimental Psychology,* 1961, **62,** 187–195. (b)

Edelberg, R. Development of an electrode for long term application in biological recording. NASA Manned Spacecraft Center, Contract Report NAS 9-445, September 1963. (a)

Edelberg, R. Electrophysiologic characteristics and interpretation of skin potentials. U.S. Air Force School of Aerospace Medicine, Tech. Doc. Rep. 63-95. 1963. (b)

Edelberg, R. Effect of vasoconstriction on galvanic skin response amplitude. *Journal of Applied Physiology,* 1964, **19,** 427–430. (a)

Edelberg, R. Independence of galvanic skin response amplitude and sweat production. *Journal of Investigative Dermatology,* 1964, **42,** 443–448. (b)

Edelberg, R. Development of methodology for bioelectric monitoring of human subjects. NASA Manned Spacecraft Center, Contract Rep. NAS 9-2839, September 1965. (a)

Edelberg, R. Electrodermal responses from the fingernail: An enigma. Paper presented at the 5th Annual Meeting of the Society for Psychophysiological Research, Houston, Tex., October 1965. (b)

Edelberg, R. Response of cutaneous water barrier to ideational stimulation: A GSR component. *Journal of Comparative and Physiological Psychology,* 1966, **61,** 28–33. (a)

Edelberg, R. Skin potential and skin conductance: An attempt at integration. Presidential address presented at the 6th Annual Meeting of the Society for Psychophysiological Research, Denver, Colo., October 1966. (b)

Edelberg, R. Electrical properties of the skin. In C. C. Brown (Ed.), *Methods in psychophysiology.* Baltimore: Williams & Wilkins, 1967.

Edelberg, R. Biopotentials from the skin surface: The hydration effect. *Annals of the New York Academy of Sciences,* 1968, **148,** 252–262.

Edelberg, R. The information content of the recovery limb of the electrodermal response. *Psychophysiology,* 1970, **6,** 527–539.

Edelberg, R., & Burch, N. R. Skin resistance and galvanic skin response: Influence of surface variables and methodological implications. *Archives of General Psychiatry,* 1962, **7,** 163–169.

Edelberg, R., Greiner, T., & Burch, N. R. Some membrane properties of the effector in the galvanic skin response. *Journal of Applied Physiology,* 1960, **15,** 691–696.

Edelberg, R., & Wright, D. J. Two GSR effector organs and their stimulus specificity. *Psychophysiology,* 1964, **1,** 39–47.

Elliott, D. N., & Singer, E. G. The Paintal index as an indicator of skin resistance change to emotional stimuli. *Journal of Experimental Psychology,* 1953, **45,** 429–430.

Engel, B. T. Stimulus-response and individual-response specificity. *Archives of General Psychiatry,* 1960, **2,** 305–313.

Féré, C. Note sur les modifications de la tension électrique dans le corps humain. *Comptes rendus des Séances de la Société de Biologie,* 1888, **5,** 28–33.

Fisher, S. Body image and asymmetry of body reactivity. *Journal of Abnormal and Social Psychology,* 1958, **57,** 292–298.

Fisher, S. Head-body differentiation in body image and resistance level. *Journal of Abnormal and Social Psychology,* 1960, **60,** 283–285.

Flesch, P., Goldstone, S. B., & Urbach, F. Palmar pore patterns: Their significance in the absorption of dyes. *Archiv für Dermatologie und Syphilis,* 1951, **63,** 228–231.

Forbes, T. W. Skin potential and impedance responses with recurring shock stimulation. *American Journal of Physiology,* 1936, **117,** 189–199.

Forbes, T. W., & Bolles, M. M. Correlation of the response potentials of the skin with "exciting" and "non-exciting" stimuli. *Journal of Psychology,* 1936, **2,** 273–285.

Fowler, R. L., & Kimmel, H. D. Operant conditioning of the GSR. *Journal of Experimental Psychology,* 1962, **63,** 563–657.

Fowles, D. C., & Venables, P. H. The effects of epidermal

hydration and sodium reabsorption on palmar skin potential. *Psychological Bulletin*, 1970, **73**, 363-378.

FREEMAN, G. L., & KATZOFF, E. T.   Methodological evaluation of the galvanic skin response, with special reference to the formula for R. Q. *Journal of Psychology*, 1942, **31**, 239-248.

FRICKE, H.   The theory of electrolytic polarization. *Philosophical Magazine*, 1932, **14**, 310-318.

FUJIMORI, B.   Studies on the galvanic skin response using the current and potential method. *Japanese Journal of Physiology*, 1955, **5**, 394-405.

FUJIMORI, B.,   1961. Cited by G. H. Wang, *The neural control of sweating*. Madison: University of Wisconsin Press, 1964. P. 105.

FUREDY, J. J.   Novelty and the measurement of the GSR. *Journal of Experimental Psychology*, 1968, **76**, 501-503.

GAVIRIA, B., COYNE, L., & THETFORD, P. E.   Correlation of skin potential and skin resistance measures. *Psychophysiology*, 1969, **5**, 465-477.

GEDDES, L. A.   Transducers and recorders. In C. C. BROWN (Ed.), *Methods in psychophysiology*. Baltimore: Williams & Wilkins, 1967.

GEDDES, L. A., BAKER, L. E., & MOORE, A. G.   Optimum electrolytic chloriding of silver electrodes. *Medical and Biological Engineering*, 1969, **7**, 49-56.

GILDEMEISTER, M., & ELLINGHAUS, J.   Zur Physiologie der menschlichen Haut: III. Über die Abhängigkeit des galvanischen Hautreflexes von der Temperatur der Haut. *Pflügers Archiv für die gesamte Physiologie*, 1923, **200**, 262-277.

GRAHAM, D. T.   Cutaneous vascular reactions in Raynaud's disease in states of hostility, anxiety, and depression. *Psychosomatic Medicine*, 1955, **17**, 200-207.

GRINGS, W. W.   Methodological considerations underlying electrodermal measurement. *Journal of Psychology*, 1953, **35**, 271-282.

GRINGS, W. W., LOCKHART, R. A., & DAMERON, L. E.   Conditioning autonomic responses of mentally subnormal individuals. *Psychological Monographs*, 1962, **76**, No. 39 (No. 558), 1-35.

GRINGS, W. W., LOWELL, E. L., & RUSHFORD, G. M.   Role of conditioning in GSR audiometry with children. *Journal of Speech and Hearing Disorders*, 1959, **24**, 380-390.

GUSTAFSON, L. A., & ORNE, M. T.   The effects of verbal responses on the laboratory detection of deception. *Psychophysiology*, 1965, **2**, 10-13.

HAGFORS, C.   Beiträge zur Messtheorie der Hautgalvanischen Reaktion. *Psychologische Beiträge*, 1964, **7**, 517-538.

HAGGARD, E. A.   On the application of analysis of variance to GSR data: I. The selection of an appropriate measure. *Journal of Experimental Psychology*, 1949, **39**, 378-392. (a)

HAGGARD, E. A.   On the application of analysis of variance to GSR data: II. Some effects of the use of inappropriate measures. *Journal of Experimental Psychology*, 1949, **39**, 861-867. (b)

HAIMOVICI, H.   Evidence for adrenergic sweating in man. *Journal of Applied Physiology*, 1950, **2**, 512-521.

HARA, K.   Über die Hemmung der Schweiss-secretion nach Reizung der hinteren Wurzel. *Pflügers Archiv für die gesamte Physiologie*, 1929, **221**, 692-694.

HASAMA, B.   Pharmakologische und physiologische Studien über die Schweisszentren: II. Über den Einfluss der direkten, mechanischen thermischen und elektrischen Reizung zuf die Schweiss-sowie Warmezentren. *Archiv für experimentelle Pathologie und Pharmakologie*, 1929, **146**, 129-161.

HERZ, E., GLASER, G. H., & MOLDOVER, J.   Electrical skin resistance test in evaluation of peripheral nerve injuries. *Archives of Neurology and Psychiatry*, 1946, **56**, 365-380.

HOLLOWAY, F. A., & PARSONS, O. A.   Unilateral brain damage and bilateral skin conductance level in humans. *Psychophysiology*, 1969, **6**, 138-148.

HOLMQUEST, D., & EDELBERG, R.   Problems in the analysis of the endosomatic galvanic skin response. *Psychophysiology*, 1964, **1**, 48-54.

HORD, D. J., JOHNSON, L. C., & LUBIN, A.   Differential effect of the law of initial value (LIV) on autonomic variables. *Psychophysiology*, 1964, **1**, 79-87.

HOZAWA, S.   Studien über die Polarisation der Haut: I. Die "Anfangszacke" des elektrischen Stromes durch den Menschenkorper, betrachtet als Ladungserscheining der Polarisationskapazität der Haut; II. Über oszillatorische Ladung der Polarisationskapazität der menschlichen Haut. *Pflügers Archiv für die gesamte Physiologie*, 1928, **219**, 111-158.

HUME, W. I.   Electrodermal measures in behavioral research. *Journal of Psychosomatic Research*, 1966, **9**, 383-391.

HUNT, W. A., & HUNT, E. G.   A comparison of five methods of scoring the galvanic skin response. *Journal of Experimental Psychology*, 1935, **18**, 383-387.

HURLEY, H. J., & SHELLEY, W. B.   The role of the myoepithelium of the human apocrine sweat gland. *Journal of Investigative Dermatology*, 1954, **22**, 143-155.

ISAMAT, F.   Galvanic skin responses from stimulation of limbic cortex. *Journal of Neurophysiology*, 1961, **24**, 176-181.

JANZ, G. J., & TANIGUCHI, H.   The silver-silver halide electrodes. *Chemical Reviews*, 1953, **53**, 397-437.

JEFFRESS, L. A.   Galvanic phenomena of the skin. *Journal of Experimental Psychology*, 1928, **11**, 130-144.

JOHNS, M. W., CORNELL, B. A., & MASTERTON, J. P.   Monitoring sleep of hospital patients by measurement of electrical resistance of skin. *Journal of Applied Physiology*, 1969, **27**, 898-901.

JOHNSON, L. C.   Stability and correlates of spontaneous autonomic activity. U.S. Navy Medical Neuropsychiatric Research Unit Rep. No. 62-6, 1962.

JOHNSON, L. C., & LUBIN, A.   Spontaneous electrodermal

activity during sleeping and waking. *Psychophysiology*, 1966, **3,** 8-17.

JONES, H. E. Conditioned psychogalvanic responses in infants. *Psychological Bulletin*, 1928, **25,** 183-184.

JONES, H. E. The galvanic skin reflex in infancy. *Child Development*, 1930, **1,** 106-110.

JONES, H. E. The galvanic skin reflex as related to overt emotional expression. *American Journal of Psychology*, 1935, **47,** 241-251.

JONES, H. E. The study of patterns of emotional expression. In M. L. REYMERT (Ed.), *Feelings and emotions.* New York: McGraw-Hill, 1950.

JUNIPER, K., Jr., BLANTON, D. E., & DYKMAN, R. A. Palmar skin resistance and sweat-gland counts in drug and non-drug states. *Psychophysiology*, 1967, **4,** 231-243.

KATKIN, E. S., WEINTRAUB, G. S., & YASSER, A. M. Stimulus specificity of epidermal and sweat gland contributions to GSR. *Journal of Comparative and Physiological Psychology*, 1967, **64,** 186-190.

KATZ, D. *Der Aufbau der Tastwelt.* Berlin: Barth, 1925. Cited by C. W. Darrow, The galvanic skin reflex (sweating) and blood pressure as preparatory and facilitative functions. *Psychological Bulletin*, 1936, **33,** 73-94.

KAYE, H. Skin conductance in the human neonate. *Child Development*, 1964, **35,** 1297-1305.

KAYE, H., & LIPSITT, L. P. Relation of electrotactual threshold to basal skin conductance. *Child Development*, 1964, **35,** 1307-1312.

KIMMEL, E., & KIMMEL, H. D. A replication of operant conditioning of the GSR. *Journal of Experimental Psychology*, 1963, **65,** 212-213.

KINTSCH, W. Habituation of the GSR component of the orienting reflex during paired-associate learning before and after learning has taken place. *Journal of Mathematical Psychology*, 1965, **2**(2), 330-341.

KLIGMAN, A. M. The biology of the stratum corneum. In W. MONTAGNA & W. C. LOBITZ (Eds.), *The epidermis.* New York: Academic, 1964.

KUNO, Y. *Human perspiration.* Springfield, Ill.: Charles C Thomas, 1956.

LACEY, J. I. The evaluation of autonomic responses: Toward a general solution. *Annals of the New York Academy of Sciences*, 1956, **67,** 123-164.

LACEY, J. I. Psychophysiological approaches to the evaluation of psychotherapeutic process and outcome. *Research in psychotherapy.* Vol. 1. Proceedings of the American Psychological Association Conference, 1958. Washington, D.C., 1959.

LACEY, J. I., BATEMAN, D. E., & VAN LEHN, R. Autonomic response specificity: An experimental study. *Psychosomatic Medicine*, 1953, **15,** 8-21.

LACEY, O. L. An analysis of the appropriate unit for use in the measurement of level of galvanic skin resistance. *Journal of Experimental Psychology*, 1947, **37,** 449-457.

LACEY, O. L., & SIEGEL, P. S. An analysis of the unit of measurement of the galvanic skin response. *Journal of Experimental Psychology*, 1949, **39,** 122-127.

LADER, M. H., & MONTAGU, J. D. The psycho-galvanic reflex: A pharmacological study of the peripheral mechanism. *Journal of Neurology, Neurosurgery, and Psychiatry*, 1962, **25,** 126-133.

LADER, M. H., & WING, W. Physiological measures in agitated and retarded depressed patients. *Journal of Psychiatric Research*, 1969, **7,** 89-100.

LANDIS, C. Electrical phenomena of the skin. *Psychological Bulletin*, 1932, **29,** 693-752.

LANDIS, C., & DeWICK, H. N. The electrical phenomena of the skin (psychogalvanic reflex). *Psychological Bulletin*, 1929, **26,** 64-119.

LANG, H., TUOVINEN, T., & VALLEALA, P. Amygdaloid afterdischarge and galvanic skin response. *Electroencephalography and Clinical Neurophysiology*, 1964, **16,** 366-374.

LANGWORTHY, O. R., & RICHTER, C. P. The influence of efferent cerebral pathways upon the sympathetic nervous system. *Brain*, 1930, **53,** 178-193.

LAWLER, J. C., DAVIS, M. J., & GRIFFITH, E. C. Electrical characteristics of the skin: The impedance of the surface sheath and deep tissues. *Journal of Investigative Dermatology*, 1960, **34,** 301-308.

LEARMONTH, G. J., ACKERLY, W., & KAPLAN, M. Relationship between palmar skin potential during stress and personality variables. *Psychosomatic Medicine*, 1959, **21,** 150-157.

LEIDERMAN, P. H., & SHAPIRO, D. Studies on the galvanic skin potential level: Some behavioral correlates. *Journal of Psychosomatic Research*, 1964, **7,** 277-281.

LESTER, B. K., BURCH, N. R., & DOSSETT, R. C. Nocturnal EEG-GSR profiles: The influence of presleep states. *Psychophysiology*, 1967, **3,** 238-248.

LEVA, J. Über einige Körperliche Begleiterscheinungen psychischer Vorgänge mit besonderer Berücksichtigung des psychogalvanischer Reflexphänomens. *Münchener Medizinische Wochenschrift*, 1913, Bd. XLIII, S. 2386. Cited by E. Prideaux, The psychogalvanic reflex: A review. *Brain*, 1920, **43,** 50.

LEVY, E. Z., THALER, V. H., & RUFF, G. E. New technique for recording skin resistance change. *Science*, 1958, **128,** 33-34.

LEWIS, T., & ZOTTERMAN, Y. Vascular reactions of the human skin to injury: VIII. The resistance of the human skin to constant currents, in relation to injury and vascular response. *Journal of Physiology, London*, 1926-1927, **62,** 280-288.

LLOYD, D. C. Action potential and secretory potential of sweat glands. *Proceedings of the National Academy of Sciences of the United States of America*, 1961, **47,** 351-358.

LOBITZ, W. C., & MASON, H. L. Chemistry of palmar sweat: VII. Discussion of studies on chloride, urea, glucose, uric acid, ammonia-nitrogen and creatinine. *Archiv für Dermatologie und Syphilis*, 1948, **57,** 907-915.

LOEWENSTEIN, W. R. Modulation of cutaneous receptors by

sympathetic stimulation. *Journal of Physiology, London,* 1956, **132,** 40–60.

LOEWY, A., & WECHSELMANN, W., 1911. Cited by Y. Kuno, *Human perspiration.* Springfield, Ill.: Charles C Thomas, 1956.

LOVELESS, E., & THETFORD, P. E. Interpretation and conditioning of the positive and negative components of the skin potential response. *Psychological Record,* 1966, **16,** 357–360.

LUBIN, A., HORD, D. J., & JOHNSON, L. C. On the validity and reliability of the autonomic lability score. U.S. Navy Medical Neuropsychiatric Research Unit. Rep. No. 64-20, 1964.

LYKKEN, D. T. Properties of electrodes used in electrodermal measurement. *Journal of Comparative and Physiological Psychology,* 1959, **52,** 629–634.

LYKKEN, D. T., MILLER, R. D., & STRAHAN, R. F. GSR and polarization capacity of the skin. *Psychonomic Science,* 1966, **4,** 355–356.

MACKINNON, P. C. B. The palmar anhydrotic response to stress in schizophrenic patients and control groups. *Journal of Psychiatric Research,* 1969, **7,** 1–8.

MacLEAN, P. D. Limbic system ("visceral brain") in relation to central gray and reticulum of brain stem: Evidence of interdependence in emotional process. *Psychosomatic Medicine,* 1955, **17,** 355–366.

MALKINSON, F. D., & ROTHMAN, S. Percutaneous absorption. In J. JADASSOHN (Ed.), *Handbuch der Haut- und Geschlechtskrankheiten,* Suppl. Vol. 3. Berlin: Springer, 1963.

MALMO, R. B. Finger-sweat prints in the differentiation of low and high incentive. *Psychophysiology,* 1965, **1,** 231–240.

MALMO, R. B., & SHAGASS, C. Physiologic studies of reaction to stress in anxiety and early schizophrenia. *Psychosomatic Medicine,* 1949, **11,** 9–24.

MARICQ, H. R. Observation and photography of sweat ducts of the finger in vivo. *Journal of Investigative Dermatology,* 1967, **48,** 399–401.

MARTIN, I. GSR conditioning and pseudoconditioning. *British Journal of Psychology,* 1962, **53,** 365–371.

MARTIN, I., & VENABLES, P. H. The contribution of sweat gland activity to measures of palmar skin conductance and potential. Paper presented at the 4th Annual Meeting of the Society for Psychophysiological Research, Washington, D.C., October 1964.

MARTIN, I., & VENABLES, P. H. Mechanisms of palmar skin resistance and skin potential. *Psychological Bulletin,* 1966, **65,** 347–357.

MARTIN, R. D., & EDELBERG, R. The relationship of skin resistance changes to receptivity. *Journal of Psychosomatic Research,* 1963, **7,** 173–179.

MAULSBY, R. L., & EDELBERG, R. The interrelationship between the galvanic skin response, basal resistance and temperature. *Journal of Comparative and Physiological Psychology,* 1960, **53,** 475–479.

McCLEARY, R. A. The nature of the galvanic skin response. *Psychological Bulletin,* 1950, **47,** 97–117.

McCURDY, H. G. Consciousness and the galvanometer. *Psychological Review,* 1950, **57,** 322–327.

McDONALD, D. G., JOHNSON, L. C., & HORD, D. J. Habituation of the orienting response in alert and drowsy subjects. *Psychophysiology,* 1964, **1,** 163–173.

McDONNELL, G. J., & CARPENTER, J. A. Manifest anxiety and prestimulus conductance levels. *Journal of Abnormal and Social Psychology,* 1960, **60,** 437–38.

McDOWALL, R. J. S. The physiology of the psychogalvanic reflex. *Quarterly Journal of Experimental Physiology,* 1933, **23,** 277–285.

McREYNOLDS, P., ACKER, M., & BRACKBILL, G. On the assessment of anxiety: IV. By measures of basal conductance and palmar sweat. *Psychological Reports,* 1966, **19,** 347–356.

MINOR, V. Ein neues Verfahren zu Klinschen Untersuchung der Schweissabsonderung. *Deutsche Zeitschrift für Nervenheilkunde,* 1928, **101,** 302–308. Cited by G. H. Wang, *Neural control of sweating.* Madison: University of Wisconsin Press, 1964.

MONTAGNA, W. *The structure and function of the skin.* (2nd ed.) New York: Academic, 1962.

MONTAGNA, W., & LOBITZ, W. C. *The epidermis.* New York: Academic, 1964.

MONTAGU, J. D. The psychogalvanic reflex: A comparison of ac skin resistance and skin potential changes. *Journal of Neurology, Neurosurgery, and Psychiatry,* 1958, **21,** 119–128.

MONTAGU, J. D. The psycho-galvanic reflex: A comparison of dc and ac methods of measurement. *Journal of Psychosomatic Research,* 1964, **8,** 49–65.

MONTAGU, J. D., & COLES, E. M. Mechanism and measurement of the galvanic skin response. *Psychological Bulletin,* 1966, **65,** 261–279.

MORDKOFF, A. M., EDELBERG, R., & USTICK, M. The differential conditionability of two components of the galvanic skin response. *Psychophysiology,* 1968, **4,** 40–47.

NAKAYAMA, T., & TAKAGI, K. Two components involved in galvanic skin response. *Japanese Journal of Physiology,* 1958, **8,** 21–30.

NETSKY, M. G. Studies on sweat secretion in man. *Archives of Neurology and Psychiatry,* 1948, **60,** 279–287.

NEUMANN, E. Thermal changes in palmar skin resistance patterns. *Psychophysiology,* 1968, **5,** 103–111.

NORDQUIST, R. E., OLSON, R. L., & EVERETT, M. A. The transport, uptake, and storage of ferritin in human epidermis. *Archives of Dermatology,* 1966, **94,** 482–490.

OBRIST, P. A. Some autonomic correlates of serial learning. *Journal of Verbal Learning and Verbal Behavior,* 1962, **1,** 100–104.

O'CONNELL, D. N., TURSKY, B., & ORNE, M. T. Electrodes for the recording of skin potential. *Archives of General Psychiatry,* 1960, **3,** 252–258.

PAINTAL, A. S. A comparison of the galvanic skin responses of normals and psychotics. *Journal of Experimental Psychology,* 1951, **41,** 425-428.

PAPA, C. M. A new technique to observe and record sweating. *Archives of Dermatology,* 1963, **88,** 732-733.

PAPEZ, J. W. A proposed mechanism of emotion. *Archives of Neurology and Psychiatry,* 1937, **38,** 725-743.

PERRY, D. J., MOUNT, G. E., HULL, C. D., & ZEILENGA, R. H. Effect of order of drug administration and repeat placebos on the galvanic skin resistance in human subjects. *Journal of Investigative Dermatology,* 1955, **25,** 179-185.

PETERSON, F., & JUNG, C. G. Psychophysical investigations with the galvanometer and plethysmograph in normal and insane individuals. *Brain,* 1907, **30,** 153-218.

PIERON, H. Sur les variations de la résistance du corps d'origine affective. *Comptes rendus des Séances de la Société de Biologie,* 1914, **77,** 332-334.

PINSON, E. A. Evaporation from human skin with sweat glands inactivated. *American Journal of Physiology,* 1942, **137,** 492-500.

PLUTCHIK, R., & HIRSCH, H. R. Skin impedance and phase angle as a function of frequency and current. *Science,* 1963, **141,** 927-928.

PRIDEAUX, E. The psychogalvanic reflex: A review. *Brain,* 1920, **43,** 50-71.

PROUT, B. J., COOTE, J. H., & DOWNMAN, C. B. B. Independence of central controls of vascular and sweat gland responses in the paw of the cat. *Journal of Neurology, Neurosurgery, and Psychiatry,* 1965, **28,** 223-227.

RANDALL, W. C. Quantitation and regional distribution of sweat glands in man. *Journal of Clinical Investigation,* 1946, **25,** 761-767.

RASKIN, D. C., KOTSES, H., & BEVER, J. Autonomic indicators of orienting and defensive reflexes. *Journal of Experimental Psychology,* 1969, **80,** 423-433.

REIN, H. Experimentelle Studien über Electroendosmose an überlebender menschlicher Haut. *Zeitschrift für Biologie,* 1924, **81,** 125-140.

REIN, H. Die Gleichstromleitereigenschaften und elektromotorischen Kräfte der menschlichen Haut und ihre Answertung zur Untersuchung von Funktionszuständen des Organes I-IV. *Zeitschrift für Biologie,* 1926, **85,** 195-247.

REIN, H. Die elektrophysiologie der Haut. In J. JADASSOHN (Ed.), *Handbuch der Haut und Geschlechtskrankheiten,* **1,** 43-91, Berlin: J. Springer, 1929. Cited by S. Rothman, *Physiology and biochemistry of the skin.* Chicago: University of Chicago Press, 1954.

RICE, D. G. Operant conditioning and associated electromyogram responses. *Journal of Experimental Psychology,* 1966, **71,** 908-912.

RICHTER, C. P. The significance of changes in the electrical resistance of the body during sleep. *Proceedings of the National Academy of Sciences of the United States of America,* 1926, **12,** 214-222.

RICHTER, C. P. A study of the electric skin resistance and psychogalvanic reflex in a case of unilateral sweating. *Brain,* 1927, **50,** 216-235.

RICHTER, C. P. Physiological factors involved in the electric resistance of the skin. *American Journal of Physiology,* 1929, **88,** 596-615.

RICHTER, C. P. Galvanic skin reflex from animals with complete transection of the spinal cord. *American Journal of Physiology,* 1930, **93,** 468-472.

RICHTER, C. P. High electrical resistance of the skin of new-born infants and its significance. *American Journal of Diseases of Children,* 1930, **40,** 18-26.

RICKLES, W. H., Jr., & DAY, J. L. Electrodermal activity in non-palmar skin sites. *Psychophysiology,* 1968, **4,** 421-435.

ROBINSON, S., & ROBINSON, A. H. Chemical composition of sweat. *Physiological Review,* 1954, **34,** 202-220.

ROESSLER, R., ALEXANDER, A. A., & GREENFIELD, N. S. Ego strength and physiological responsivity: I. The relationship of the barron ES scale to skin resistance, finger blood volume, heart rate and muscle potential responses to sound. *Archives of General Psychiatry,* 1963, **8,** 142-154.

ROESSLER, R., BURCH, N. R., & CHILDERS, H. E. Personality and arousal correlates of specific galvanic skin responses. *Psychophysiology,* 1966, **3,** 115-130.

ROTHMAN, S. (Ed.) *Physiology and biochemistry of the skin.* Chicago: University of Chicago Press, 1954.

RUSHMER, R. F., BUETTNER, K. J. K., SHORT, J. M., & ODLAND, G. F. The skin. *Science,* 1966, **154,** 343-348.

SARKANY, I., SHUSTER, S., & STAMMERS, M. C. Occlusion of the sweat pore by hydration. *British Journal of Dermatology,* 1965, **77,** 101-104.

SCHACHTER, J. Pain, fear and anger in hypertensives and normotensives. *Psychosomatic Medicine,* 1957, **19,** 17-29.

SCHLOSBERG, H. Three dimensions of emotion. *Psychological Review,* 1954, **61,** 81-88.

SCHLOSBERG, H., & STANLEY, W. C. A simple test of normality of 24 distributions of electrical skin conductance. *Science,* 1953, **117,** 35-37.

SCHNEIDER, R. A., & COSTILOE, J. P. Effect of centrally active drugs on conditioning in man: The inhibiting and facilitating effects of chlorpromazine and amobarbitol and methylphenidylactate on the conditioned GSR. *American Journal of Medical Science,* 1957, **233,** 418-423.

SCHULZ, I., ULLRICH, K. J., FRÖMTER, E., HOLZGREVE, H., FRICK, A., & HEGEL, U. Micropunction and measurements on electric potentials in human sweat glands. *Pflügers Archiv für die gesamte Physiologie,* 1965, **284,** 1, 360-372.

SCHWARTZ, H. G. Reflex activity within the sympathetic nervous system. *American Journal of Physiology,* 1934, **109,** 593-604.

SCHWARTZ, H. G. Effect of experimental lesions of the cortex on the "psychogalvanic reflex" in the cat. *Archives of Neurology and Psychiatry, Chicago,* 1937, **38,** 308-320.

SHACKEL, B. Skin-drilling: A method of diminishing galvanic skin potentials. *American Journal of Psychology,* 1959, **72,** 114-121.

SHAPIRO, D., & LEIDERMAN, P. H. Studies on the galvanic skin potential level: Some statistical properties. *Journal of Psychosomatic Research,* 1964, **7,** 269-275.

SHAVER, B. A., Jr., BRUSILOW, S. W., & COOKE, R. E. Origin of the galvanic skin response. *Proceedings of the Society for Experimental Biology and Medicine,* 1962, **110,** 559-564.

SHAVER, B. A., Jr., BRUSILOW, S. W., & COOKE, R. E. Electrophysiology of the sweat gland: Intraductal potential changes during secretion. *Bulletin of the Johns Hopkins Hospital,* 1965, **116,** 100-109.

SHEAN, G. D. Instrumental modification of the galvanic skin response: Conditioning or control. *Journal of Psychosomatic Research,* 1970, **14,** 155-160.

SHELLEY, W. B. Experimental miliaria in man: IV. Sweat retention vesicles following destruction of terminal sweat duct. *Journal of Investigative Dermatology,* 1951, **16,** 53-64.

SHELLEY, W. B., & HURLEY, H. J. The physiology of the human axillary apocrine sweat gland. *Journal of Investigative Dermatology,* 1953, **20,** 285-297.

SHIMAMURA, M., & FUJIMORI, B. Studies on effects of brain-stem stimulation upon motor and autonomic reflexes, with special reference to interrelationship between effects. *Japanese Journal of Physiology,* 1961, **11,** 238-251.

SHMAVONIAN, B. M., MILLER, L. H., & COHEN, S. I. Differences among age and sex groups in electro-dermal conditioning. *Psychophysiology,* 1968, **5,** 119-131.

SIDIS, B., & NELSON, L. The nature and causation of galvanic phenomena. *Psychological Review,* 1910, **17,** 98-146.

SILVER, A., VERSACI, A., & MONTAGNA, W. Studies of sweating and sensory function in cases of peripheral nerve injuries of the hand. *Journal of Investigative Dermatology,* 1963, **40,** 243-258.

SILVERMAN, A. J., COHEN, S. I., & SHMAVONIAN, B. M. Investigation of psychophysiologic relationships with skin resistance measures. *Journal of Psychosomatic Research,* 1959, **4,** 65-87.

SILVERMAN, J. J., & POWELL, V. E. A simple technic for outlining the sweat pattern. *War Medicine,* 1945, **7,** 178-180.

SIMONS, D. G., & PEREZ, R. E. The B/GSR module: A combined recording to present base skin resistance and galvanic skin reflex activity patterns. *Psychophysiology,* 1965, **2,** 116-124.

SOMMER, R. Elektromotorische Wirkungen der Finger. *Neurologisches Zentralblatt,* 1905, **24,** 290-295.

SPEISMAN, J. C., LAZARUS, R. S., MORDKOFF, A., & DAVISON, L. Experimental reduction of stress based on ego defense theory. *Journal of Abnormal and Social Psychology,* 1964, **68,** 367-380.

SPEISMAN, J. C., OSBORN, J., & LAZARUS, R. S. Cluster analysis of skin resistance and heart rate at rest and under stress. *Psychosomatic Medicine,* 1961, **23,** 323-343.

STECHLER, G., BRADFORD, S., & LEVY, H. Attention in the newborn: Effect on motility and skin potential. *Science,* 1966, **151,** 1246-1248.

STENNETT, R. G. The relationship of performance level to level of arousal. *Journal of Experimental Psychology,* 1957, **54,** 54-61.

STERN, J. A., WINOKUR, G., STEWART, M. A., & LEONARD, C. Electrodermal conditioning: Some further correlates. *Journal of Nervous and Mental Disease,* 1963, **137,** 479-486.

STERN, R. M., & KAPLAN, B. E. Galvanic skin response: Voluntary control and externalization. *Journal of Psychosomatic Research,* 1967, **10,** 349-353.

STERNBACH, R. A., & TURSKY, B. Ethnic differences among housewives in psychophysical and skin potential responses to electric shock. *Psychophysiology,* 1965, **1,** 241-246.

STROHL, A. La résistance électrique du corps humain et les nouvelles methodes d'électrodiagnostic. *Journal de radiologie et électrologie,* 1918, **3,** 207-213. Cited by C. Landis & H. N. DeWick, The electrical phenomena of the skin (psychogalvanic reflex). *Psychological Bulletin,* 1929, **26,** 64-119.

STROHL, A., & IODKA, H. Utilisation de la lampe à trois électrodes pour la mesure de la counterélectromotrice de polarization. *Comptes rendus des Séances de la Société de Biologie,* 1924, **91,** 183-184. Cited by C. Landis & H. N. DeWick, The electrical phenomena of the skin (psychogalvanic reflex). *Psychological Bulletin,* 1929, **26,** 64-119.

SUCHI, T., 1950. Cited by Y. Kuno, *Human perspiration.* Springfield, Ill.: Charles C Thomas, 1956.

SURWILLO, W. W. On the effects of artificial variation of the basal level of skin potential. *Psychophysiology,* 1965, **2,** 83-85.

SURWILLO, W. W., & QUILTER, R. E. The relation of frequency of spontaneous skin potential responses to vigilance and to age. *Psychophysiology,* 1965, **1,** 272-276.

SUTARMAN, & THOMSON, M. L. A new technique for enumerating active sweat glands in man. *Journal of Physiology, London,* 1952, **117,** 51P-52.

SWEENEY, T. M., DOWNES, A. M., & MATOLTSY, A. G. The effect of dimethylsulfoxide on the epidermal water barrier. *Journal of Investigative Dermatology,* 1966, **46,** 300-302.

SYZ, H. C. Observations on the unreliability of subjective reports of emotional reactions. *British Journal of Psychology,* 1926, **17,** 119-126.

SZAKALL, A. Experimentelle Daten zur Klärung der Funktion der Wasserbarriere in der Epidermis des lebenden Menschen. *Berufs-Dermatosen,* 1958, **6,** 171. Cited by A. M. Kligman, The stratum corneum. In W. MONTAGNA & W. C. LOBITZ (Eds.), *The epidermis.* New York: Academic, 1964.

TAKAGI, K., & NAKAYAMA, T. Peripheral effector mechanism of galvanic skin reflex. *Japanese Journal of Physiology,* 1959, **9,** 1-7.

TAKAHARA, K. Variation of the insensible perspiration due to cooling and warming of the skin. *Journal of Oriental Medicine,* 1934. Cited by Y. Kuno, *Human perspiration.* Springfield, Ill.: Charles C Thomas, 1956.

TARCHANOFF, J. Über die galvanischen Erscheinungen an der Haut des Menschen bei Reizung der Sinnesorgane und bei verschiedenen Formen der psychisohen Tatigkeit. *Pflügers Archiv für die gesamte Physiologie,* 1890, **46,** 46–55.

THOMAS, P. E., & KORR, I. M. Relationship between sweat gland activity and electrical resistance of the skin. *Journal of Applied Physiology,* 1957, **10,** 505–510.

THOULESS, R. H. The technique of experimentation on the psychogalvanic reflex phenomenon and the phenomenon of Tarchanoff. *British Journal of Psychology,* 1930, **20,** 219–240.

TREHUB, A., TUCKER, I., & CAZAVELAN, J. Epidermal b-waves and changes in basal potentials of the skin. *American Journal of Psychology,* 1962, **75,** 140–143.

VENABLES, P. H. The relationship between PGR scores and temperature and humidity. *Quarterly Journal of Experimental Psychology,* 1955, **7,** 12–18.

VENABLES, P. H., & MARTIN, I. Skin resistance and skin potential. In P. H. VENABLES & I. MARTIN (Eds.), *A manual of psychophysiological methods.* New York: Wiley, 1967.

VENABLES, P. H., & MARTIN, I. The relation of palmar sweat gland activity to level of skin potential and conductance. *Psychophysiology,* 1967, **3,** 302–11.

VENABLES, P. H., & SAYER, E. On the measurement of the level of skin potential. *British Journal of Psychology,* 1963, **54,** 251–260.

VENABLES, P. H., & WING, J. R. Level of arousal and the subclassification of schizophrenia. *Archives of General Psychiatry,* 1962, **7,** 116–119.

VERAGUTH, O. *Das psychogalvanische Reflex-phänomen.* Berlin: S. Karger, 1909.

VIGOUROUX, R. Sur le rôle de la resistance électrique des tissus dans l'électrodiagnostic. *Comptes rendus des Séances de la Société de Biologie,* 1879, **31,** 336–339.

WADA, M., & TAKAGAKI, T. New methods for detecting sweat secretion. *Tohuku Journal of Experimental Medicine,* 1948, **49,** 284. Cited by Y. Kuno, *Human perspiration.* Springfield, Ill.: Charles C Thomas, 1956.

WALL, P. D., & DAVIS, G. D. Three cerebral cortical systems affecting autonomic function. *Journal of Neurophysiology,* 1951, **14,** 507–517.

WALLER, A. D. The emotive response to ordinary stimulation, real and imaginary. *Lancet,* 1918, **96,** 380–381.

WALLER, A. D. Concerning emotive phenomena: III. The influence of drugs on the electrical conductivity of the palm of the hand. *Proceedings of the Royal Society of London,* Series B, 1919–1920, **91,** 32–40.

WANG, G. H. The galvanic skin reflex: A review of old and recent works from a physiologic point of view. *American Journal of Physical Medicine,* 1957, **36,** 295–320; 1958, **37,** 35–57.

WANG, G. H. *The neural control of sweating.* Madison: University of Wisconsin Press, 1964.

WANG, G. H., & LU, T. W. Galvanic skin reflex induced in the cat by stimulation of the motor area of the cerebral cortex. *Chinese Journal of Physiology,* 1930, **4,** 303–324. (a)

WANG, G. H., & LU, T. W. On "inhibition" of the secretion of sweat in the cat by stimulation of dorsal nerve-roots. *Chinese Journal of Physiology,* 1930, **4,** 175–182. (b)

WANG, G. H., & LU, T. W. On the intensity of the GSR induced by stimulation of postganglionic sympathetic nerve fibers with single induction shocks. *Chinese Journal of Physiology,* 1930, **4,** 393–400. (c)

WANG, G. H., & RICHTER, C. P. Action currents from the pad of the cat's foot produced by stimulation of the tuber cinerium. *Chinese Journal of Physiology,* 1928, **2,** 279–284.

WANG, G. H., STEIN, P., & BROWN, V. W. Brainstem reticular system and galvanic skin reflex in acute decerebrate cats. *Journal of Neurophysiology,* 1956, **19,** 350–355.

WECHSLER, D. The measurement of emotional reactions: Researches on the psychogalvanic reflexes. *Archives of Psychology, New York,* 1925, **12,** (76), 1–181.

WEINER, J. S., & HELLMANN, K. The sweat glands. *Biological Review,* 1960, **35,** 141–186.

WELLS, F. L., & FORBES, A. On certain electrical processes in the human body and their relation to emotional reactions. *Archives of Psychology, New York,* 1911, **2,** (16), 1–39.

WENGER, M. A. Pattern analyses of autonomic variables during rest. *Psychosomatic Medicine,* 1957, **19,** 240–244.

WENGER, M. A., CLEMENS, T. L., COLEMAN, D. R., CULLEN, T. D., & ENGEL, B. T. Autonomic response specificity. *Psychosomatic Medicine,* 1961, **23,** 185–193.

WENGER, M. A., & CULLEN, T. D. Some problems in psychophysiological research: III. The effects of uncontrolled variables. In R. ROESSLER & N. S. GREENFIELD (Eds.), *Psychophysiological correlates of psychological disorder.* Madison: University of Wisconsin Press, 1962.

WENGER, M. A., ENGEL, B. T., & CLEMENS, T. L. Studies of autonomic response patterns: Rationale and methods. *Behavioral Science,* 1957, **2,** 216–221.

WENGER, M. A., & GILCHRIST, J. C. A comparison of two indices of palmar sweating. *Journal of Experimental Psychology,* 1948, **38,** 757–761.

WENGER, M. A., & IRWIN, D. C. Fluctuations in skin resistance of infants and adults and their relation to muscular processes. *University of Iowa Studies in Child Welfare* 1936, **12,** 143–179.

WILCOTT, R. C. Correlation of skin resistance and potential. *Journal of Comparative and Physiological Psychology,* 1958, **51,** 691–696. (a)

WILCOTT, R. C. Effects of local blood removal on the skin resistance and potential. *Journal of Comparative and Physiological Psychology,* 1958, **51,** 295–300. (b)

WILCOTT, R. C. On the role of the epidermis in the production of skin resistance and potential. *Journal of
Comparative and Physiological Psychology,* 1959, **52,**
642–649.

WILCOTT, R. C. Palmar skin sweating vs. palmar skin resistance and skin potential. *Journal of Comparative and
Physiological Psychology,* 1962, **55,** 327–331.

WILCOTT, R. C. Effects of high environmental temperature
on sweating and skin resistance. *Journal of Comparative
and Physiological Psychology,* 1963, **56,** 778–782.

WILCOTT, R. C. The partial independence of skin potential
and skin resistance from sweating. *Psychophysiology,*
1964, **1,** 55–66.

WILCOTT, R. C. A comparative study of the skin potential,
skin resistance, and sweating of cat's foot pad. *Psychophysiology,* 1965, **2,** 62–71.

WILCOTT, R. C. Adaptive value of arousal sweating and the
epidermal mechanism related to skin potential and skin
resistance. *Psychophysiology,* 1966, **2,** 249–262.

WILCOTT, R. C. Arousal sweating and electrodermal phenomena. *Psychological Bulletin,* 1967, **67,** 58–72.

WILCOTT, R. C. Skin potential and skin resistance recording
from the minimally restrained cat. *Psychophysiology,*
1969, **5,** 727–729.

WILCOTT, R. C. Electrical stimulation of the anterior cortex

and skin-potential responses in the cat. *Journal of Comparative and Physiological Psychology,* 1969, **69,** 465–472.

WILCOTT, R. C., & HAMMOND, L. J. On the constant-current
error in skin resistance measurement. *Psychophysiology,*
1965, **2,** 39–41.

WILSON, G. D. GSR responses to fear-related stimuli.
Perceptual and Motor Skills, 1967, **24,** 401–402.

WINKLEMANN, R. K. *Nerve endings in normal and pathologic skin.* Springfield, Ill.: Charles C Thomas, 1960.

WITTEN, V. H., ROSS, M. S., OSHRY, E., & HYMAN, A. B.
Studies of thorium-X applied to human skin: I. Routes
and degree of penetration and sites of deposition of
thorium-X in selected vehicles. *Journal of Investigative
Dermatology,* 1951, **17,** 311–322.

WOLFF, H. G. Life stress and bodily disease: A formulation.
*Proceedings of the Association for Research in Nervous
and Mental Disease,* 1949, **29,** 1059–1094.

WOODWORTH, R. S., & SCHLOSBERG, H. Emotions: II. Energetics. In *Experimental psychology.* (2nd ed., Ch. 6). New
York: Holt, Rinehart and Winston, 1954.

YOKOTA, T., TAKAHASHI, T., KONDO, M., & FUJIMORI, B.
Studies on the diphasic wave form of the galvanic skin
reflex. *Electroencephalography and Clinical Neurophysiology,* 1959, **11,** 687–696.

Stewart Wolf and Jack D. Welsh

THE GASTROINTESTINAL TRACT AS A RESPONSIVE SYSTEM

10

The gastrointestinal tract has long been known to participate in man's behavioral response to meaningful events in his surroundings. Human cultures are replete with such evidence. Documentation of the mechanisms involved, however, has come along more slowly and is still partly presumptive.

To establish altogether satisfactory evidence would require data from the whole sequence of phenomena beginning with "input" in the form of an experience, the effect of which depends on its significance to the individual, continuing through the interpretive process in the brain, and ending with the "output" mechanism, whereby visceral effectors are either activated or inhibited. Present knowledge is spotty throughout, even with respect to the way in which the effector mechanisms act on individual gastrointestinal functions. A close coordination of effort is needed among those with special skills in behavioral science, neurophysiology, and clinical investigation. Relatively rarely are these areas of competence found in a single investigator; and too infrequently have experts in these fields worked closely together. Thus the information available at the present time is fragmentary and scattered, so that the student is faced with an almost impossible task to synthesize the available literature himself.

Nature of Stimuli

Because living forms are constantly responding to a variety of forces in the environment, one cannot study a set stimulus in pure culture. Indeed, just what a symbolic stimulus may elicit would be difficult to predict, since it may either reinforce or run counter to other forces acting on an end organ at the same time. Thus the effects of a stimulus on a living organism are not simply a function of the intensity of the stimulus. They depend also on the prevailing state of the affected organ and on the algebraic sum of other forces acting on it. Failure to recognize this principle has led to a good deal of confusion among medical scientists. Indeed, some have dismissed as impossible the study of psychophysiology. For example, Pasteur, on the occasion of his induction into the Académie Française, made the somewhat gratuitous remark that scientific method is not applicable to problems involving emotions (Pasteur, cited by Dubos, 1959).

Recognizing the difficulty of obtaining objective data in the psychosocial sphere, many investigators have made heroic efforts to provide a standard stimulus for their subjects. The difficulty, however, does not lie in accurately determining the amount of the stimulus. A harsh word can be measured in decibels or a sight in lamberts, lumens, or photons. It is the meaning of the sight or sound, the significance for a particular individual, and the ensuing reaction that elude measurement. It is possible to call an individual a coward, for instance, in a precisely modulated tone, so that the decibels can be accurately measured and hence the amount of energy transmitted through the ear drum and the middle ear to the organ of Corti can be as nicely determined as any stimulus in biological research. Such pains, however, would not reward the investigator with a uniformity of response from person to person or even from time to time in the same person. Energy fed via receptors into the nervous system actuates an integrative process that ultimately interprets the event in the light of individual proclivities and past experience as threatening, neutral, or pleasurable, and to what degree. It is by such integrative activity that the stimulus gains it force. The search for the standard stimulus is, therefore, a search for the will-o'-the-wisp (Wolf, 1954).

The Integrative Process

Since the quality and relevance of a stimulus situation are of more concern than its quantity, the most pertinent questions relate to the effects of the stimulus on the integrative processes of the brain. These are much more difficult to evaluate than the stimulus itself. A somewhat similar state of affairs is seen in the way microorganisms elicit to a greater or lesser degree a complex response in the body's immune apparatus. Their ultimate effect depends not so much on the quantity of the stimulus, i.e., on the actual number of organisms to which one is exposed, but on such other things as the nature of the organisms and the state of the host, including any past exposure. Thus, although quantity is a factor in the equation, it does not determine the presence or absence or even the severity of an infection. The quantity of stimulus, while important, is not therefore crucial. With either microorganic or symbolic stimuli, one need only establish their relevance to the particular effects observed, before undertaking the exploration of the processes involved.

The mechanisms that regulate the functions of the gastrointestinal tract appear to be distributed as a series of control circuits along most of the length of the central and peripheral nervous systems. At each level they are responsive reflexly to afferent impulses from below, as well as to information from higher centers. In the periphery, by virtue of specialized muscle and intrinsic nerve plexuses, there is considerable regulatory capability in the isolated tissues themselves. Thus digestive organs, separated from the nervous system, are capable to considerable extent of adaptive behavior with respect to secretion, motor activity, and membrane transport. In this situation the chemical composition of the perfusing fluid exerts a measure of control through the concentration of constituent ions, hormones, and biologically active polypeptides. In the intact organism, higher levels of control occur in the autonomic ganglia, the segmental areas of the cord, the brain stem, and finally in the cerebral hemispheres themselves. Presumably, at this level, there are circuits that make the visceral controls responsive to information of a symbolic nature. Evidence from stereotaxic studies on pathways and mechanisms in the hemispheres is sparse. By contrast, there is considerable published data derived from stimulation of various sites in the hypothalamus and medulla.

Much evaluative function occurs in the human brain without awareness, even during sleep. A mother may awaken to the faint cry of an infant but sleep through a much louder noise that lacks important meaning to her. Unconscious mental activity may, indeed, be much more precise than that undertaken during awareness. A fully alert man may miss by an hour or more in judging the time of day and yet discipline himself to awaken within a minute of a set time.

Important emotional conflicts are likely to be shunted out of awareness for the general comfort of the individual. The information remains in the brain, however, perfectly capable of being recruited on appropriate stimulation and of entering the complex process of behavior. Thus emotional responses may be aroused such as fear, anxiety, or resentment, with or without awareness of the original conflict. Responses may also be formulated with or without awareness of the stimulus and with or without an emotion or feeling state. These responses may be in terms of striving, creating, destroying, avoiding, and other patterns of behavior.

The frequent association of manifestations of physiological dysfunction with overt emotional disturbance has led to the widely accepted but confusing proposition that emotions are the cause of bodily reactions. The confusion is further compounded by the difficulty of defining *emotion*. Different writers use the term in different ways. Literally, the word implies movement of some sort. Thus an emotion is clearly a manifestation, not a cause. Many authors, however, equate the term with a feeling state. To them an emotion is a sort of sensation or at least an awareness, which may be pleasant or unpleasant; for example, joy, satisfaction, hope, and appetite fall into the category of emotions. But again emotion is part of the reaction to some circumstance that is pleasing, frightening, or frustrating, not the cause of the reaction.

Finally, some workers apply the term emotion to conscious or unconscious mental processes, whereby events are interpreted in view of personality and past experience. In this instance, as already discussed, neural connections are made because of the significance of the event but without the process necessarily being brought to awareness. An emotion viewed in this light would constitute an essential part of the neural integrative activity, and thus part of the mechanism of response, but it still would not be the cause. An emotion, therefore, may be looked upon variously as (a) a manifestation or part of the reaction pattern aroused as a consequence of the interpretation of a life experience, (b) a feeling state occurring because of the conscious or unconscious interpretation of a life experience, or (c) an often repressed but functioning aspect of the interpretation of a life experience. In any case, bodily changes appear to derive from the individual's evaluation of his experience, consciously or unconsciously, and with or without overt emotional expression.

Nature of Responses

Viscera have a limited number of ways in which they can react. Responses ordinarily concerned with alimentation or elimination may be evoked at each level of the gut by emotionally significant events that have no obvious relationship to the responses elicited. Nevertheless, the patterns of reaction observed appear to be at least quasipurposeful. Psychoanalysts contend that such changes are attributable to the resurgence of a regressive (infantile) pattern of psychosexual development. Whether or not this interpretation is correct, the functions have clearly taken on a figurative, verbal significance, as suggested by such emotionally expressive language as "I can't swallow that," "His attitude is nauseating," and "He gripes me."

The responses of digestive organs to meaningful situations result mainly from the patterned interplay of various elements of the autonomic nervous system. The manifestations observed are clearly not explained by the old simpler concept of alternative discharges, either parasympathetic or sympathetic. For example, during nausea there is gastric hypotonia and hyposecretion reflecting vagal inhibition, but at the same time hypersalivation occurs, showing increased parasympathetic activity.

METHODS OF INVESTIGATION

In contrast to the naturalist, who simply observes and records, the experimenter manipulates the circumstances surrounding the object he wishes to observe. He is thus limited by the fact that any contrived arrangement for experimental purposes, however simple, introduces artifacts and allows only an approximation of the natural responses of the subject under study (Hopkins & Edwards, 1964). Experience with human subjects has shown, however, that the use of uncomfortable apparatus that restricts movement and may inflict some degree of pain causes much less alteration in the bodily indicators than do subtler aspects of the experimental surroundings—the curt manner or inattentiveness of an assistant, the lack of poise and assurance on the part of the experimenter, maladroit questions, or awkward efforts at reassurance. By taking these factors into consideration, and assuming the skill and poise of the experimenters, it has been found generally preferable to use apparatus that requires relatively little attention, so that the experimenter can devote himself to the subject. Only thus can the nuances of the patient's responses be appreciated and utilized. It follows that the gathering of psychophysiological data requires far more than elegant and precise measuring devices.

The search for new knowledge demands an alertness and sensitivity to cues often subtle and sometimes occurring only once in many trials. Here the skill and intuition of the explorer is indispensable to the task of picking up and following leads. Fixity of purpose requires flexibility of method and often a readiness to abandon a question, a concept, or a direction for a more fruitful one. Creative imagination is perhaps the most valuable quality of the discoverer. It is important, too, that the tools of the investigator do not obscure a significant but subtle cue. Claude Bernard (1859) illustrated how, under some circumstances, statistical analysis can obliterate an important lead: in one animal he produced glycosuria by piqûre of the fourth ventricle; in the next nine trials he failed to do so.

The techniques applied to the study of the gas-trointestinal tract fall conveniently into the following categories: (a) the collection of secretions for chemical analysis, (b) absorption, (c) blood flow, (d) measurements of rate of travel through the intestinal tract, and (e) motor activity.

Collection of Secretions for Analysis

Saliva   The secretion of the parotid glands can be obtained in relatively pure form by catheterization of Stenson's duct, or more conveniently, by applying an especially designed suction cup over the papilla. Hormones, as well as inorganic substances, vasoactive peptides, and digestive enzymes, may be recovered from the saliva, and thus provide the possibility of relatively precise psychophysiological correlations.

Gastric juice, bile, pancreatic secretion   These substances can be obtained in a more or less contaminated state in intact humans by intubation. Gastric, biliary, or pancreatic fistulae in human subjects provide special opportunities to collect secretions in purer form.

Succus entericus and surface mucus   It has not been possible to make satisfactory collections of these materials in intact humans. The few observations that have been made have relied on the collection of material through tubes introduced into the intestine from portions of the intestinal tract that are outside the peritoneal cavity as a result of injury or surgical intervention.

Absorption

Most studies of absorption in the stomach have relied on the introduction of the material to be studied, together with a measured amount of a nonabsorbable marker. The amount of test substance withdrawn from the stomach after the period specified for absorption can then be corrected for loss through the pylorus on the basis of the amount of marker lost (Chapman, Lawrence, & Janowitz, 1967). Studies of absorption in the small intestine of intact humans require more elaborate methods, usually multichannel tubes equipped with a terminal balloon to reduce the loss of material beyond the level of the intestine being studied. The enzymes responsible for the absorption of various nutritive materials can be assayed on small bits of tissue obtained by peroral biopsy, utilizing a tube such as the Baker-Hughes multiple biopsy tube (Alvarez & Freedlander, 1924). The absorption of materials that are transported into the blood stream unchanged, such as glucose, can be determined by measuring blood glucose concentration before and after giving the test substance. The same principle can be applied to more complex substances that are broken down in the gut and absorbed as distinct components. These techniques have been used chiefly in the study of the absorption of disaccharides and iron-containing materials (Gray & Ingelfinger, 1966). The absorption of substances not destroyed in the gastrointestinal tract may be studied by measuring the residua in the stools, a classical method for the measurement of fat absorption (Van de Kamer, ten Bokkel Huinink, & Weyers, 1949). This method has also been applied to such substances as vitamin B_{12} (Heinle, Welch, Scharf, Meacham, & Prusoff, 1952). When the area of disposition of absorbed material in the body is known, one can feed radioactively labeled substances and count the quantity absorbed over the target organ. This technique has been used to determine the amount of absorbed vitamin B_{12} after it has been stored in the liver (Glass, Boyd, Gellin, & Stephenson, 1954).

Blood Flow

The problems of measuring the blood flow in the gastrointestinal tract have been completely reviewed recently (Jacobson, 1967). There are essentially no methods for studying the blood flow in the intact human. In animal preparations the major difficulty has been to distinguish the mucosal blood flow from the total blood flow through the organ. Efforts in this direction have been made in human subjects equipped with enteric fistulae of various sorts. Changes in color have perhaps been the most helpful indicators. Hyperemia may be of two types: a bright red color suggests increased mucosal blood flow; a deeper, more cyanotic red suggests stagnation and an increase in mucosal blood content. Although such changes cannot yet be satisfactorily measured quantitatively, carefully standardized color photography has been used to provide comparisons and permanent records; the

changes in brightness, as well as hue, have been shown to correlate with the surface flow as measured by a thermal gradient technique (Richards, Wolf, & Wolff, 1942).

Travel Along the Gut

The rate of passage (transit time) through the intestinal tract has been shown to be related to the type of food ingested; the amount of the residual; the dryness or wetness of the material; and a variety of environmental conditions, including the prevailing emotional state. There are wide intra- and interindividual differences and variations, depending on the methods used. All studies suggest that there is mixing of the intestinal content, so that each stool represents material eaten over a period of several days. Millet seeds first appeared in the stool from 15 to 39 hr after ingestion, while the final seeds appeared between 23 and 184 hr (Burnett, 1923). Studies with tiny colored glass beads given in gelatin capsules have demonstrated that about 80% of the residua from any one meal is passed by the end of the 4th day (Alvarez & Freedlander, 1924). Carmine ingested in a capsule first appeared after 65–98 hr (Mulinos, 1935). When barium was given with a meal, the majority of subjects eliminated all but a trace of the contrast material in 3 or 4 days, but one-third of the individuals took 5 days or more (Köhler, 1964).

Motor Activity

Direct observation The serosal or mucosal surface of the intestine has provided useful information on motor activity of the gut when it has been possible to observe it directly in human subjects with suitable fistulae.

Radiological methods Using a radiopaque contrast medium, such as barium sulfate or a water-soluble iodionated compound, makes it possible to visualize the gastrointestinal tract in relief radiologically. The use of an image intensifier requires a relatively small dose of radiation, and hence permits prolonged examinations with relative safety. When cineradiography is utilized, a permanent record is obtained that can be reviewed at leisure. The technique allows comparisons of intestinal activity from subject to subject or in the same subject under different experimental conditions.

Intraluminal pressure recordings Changes in the intraluminal pressures in the intestine have been recorded by at least four methods (Truelove, 1966). Differences in these methods make some more suitable for certain parts of the gut than others. Often it is helpful to use more than one method at a time.

1. Balloons, single or in tandem, and filled with water or gas, may be coupled to a system to register contractile activity of the intestine. This method has the advantage of simplicity; unfortunately, the ballon's presence itself may evoke motor activity and hence not accurately reflect spontaneous contractions. Furthermore, the accurate reflection of intraluminal pressure may not be possible because of the contribution of intraballoon (closed space) pressure related to variations in the size and shape of the segment of gut where the balloon is lodged.

2. Fluid-filled, open-end tubes may faithfully record the actual intraluminal pressure but will reflect only that activity which alters intraluminal pressure. Blockage of the tip by the contents of the intestinal tract or the mucosa itself may be minimized by having secondary holes or by "bleeding" out small amounts of fluid to maintain patency. Either a gas or liquid can be used. Liquid has the advantage of being incompressible within the range of physiological pressure changes occurring when the tube is coupled to a rigid manometer, so that the volume to pressure coefficient is high (Brody & Quigley, 1951, pp. 109–123).

3. Small electromagnetic transducers can be introduced into parts of the intestinal tract that cannot be plugged. As they come into actual contact with the mucosa, however, they may, like balloons, provide a stimulus for contraction (Gauer & Gienapp, 1950).

4. Radiotelemetering capsules, containing a small radio transmitter designed to emit signals that are modified by the pressure acting on a diaphragm, can be swallowed. A receiving set outside the body picks up the signals and converts them into electrical impulses. The results obtained from a telemetering capsule and an open-ended polythene tube located in the same segment of the pelvic

colon have been shown to be very similar. One of the disadvantages of this method is the problem of localization. The capsule provides only a single point recording and is free to move with the intestinal content from a high pressure zone to a low pressure zone (Connell & Rowlands, 1960).

5. Intraluminal pressure recording and cineradiography may be combined. Richie, Ardran, and Truelove (1962) have demonstrated that (a) balloons will register isotonic contractions of the bowel wall that are imperceptible on an open-ended tube tracing; (b) a differential unit (small balloon and open-ended tube coupled to the two sides of a differential manometer) provides an index of the movement of the bowel wall in the immediate vicinity of the balloon; and (c) a differential unit with an additional open-ended tube coupled to a second manometer to record the actual intraluminal pressures can distinguish a pressure rise due to contraction of the segment of the bowel from a rise of pressure due to the segment of the bowel's being distended by contents passing into it from the contraction of a neighboring segment.

The most direct studies of the psychophysiology of the gastrointestinal tract have been undertaken through fistulous openings, produced either accidentally or artificially. The first systematic study was that of William Beaumont (1833), followed by that of Charles Richet (1878), both in fistulous human beings. Pavlov (1910) worked extensively with dogs equipped with salivary and gastric fistulae. Most recently, subjects with gastric, duodenal, and colonic fistulae have been studied by Wolf and Wolff (1947; Grace, Wolf, & Wolff, 1951). In these investigations direct visualization of the mucous membrane was supplemented by measurements of secretion, of motor activity, and of blood flow using a thermal gradient technique. The measurement of secretory function has depended largely upon the recovery of secretion by intubation, the study of motor activity on balloons, open-tipped catheters, and other pressure-sensitive devices introduced into the lumen of the gut, and on X-ray techniques. These measures have yielded data on efferent neural activity. A variety of different stimuli have been used. These include naturally occurring events in the daily life of the individual, or contrived situations such as stress interviews covering areas of significant personal conflict, viewing of motion pictures, performing of difficult tasks, and undergoing harrassing or frightening experiences of various sorts. Hypnosis and Pavlovian conditioning procedures have also been used experimentally. It has been possible to standardize input and to measure output satisfactorily. However, the more difficult problem has been the study of the integrative process within the central nervous system. Evidence in this area is largely inferential, although some of the pathways have been mapped through the stereotaxic approach (McLean, 1955).

EFFECTS OF HUNGER AND SATIETY

Appetite is best understood as an emotional state characterized by the pleasurable anticipation of eating. The experience of appetite may be elicited by a variety of sights, sounds, and smells; may follow strenuous physical exertion; or may occur in the course of a thought process relating to food, especially if there has been a significant interval since the last meal. No somatic receptors have been identified as responsible for the sense of appetite. Appetite is, however, generally accompanied by increased secretory and motor activity in the stomach.

Hunger differs from appetite in that it has a peripheral sensory component, and also is not necessarily a pleasant experience. Indeed, hunger is perhaps more commonly unpleasant, even painful. Cannon and Washburn, in 1912, associated the pangs of hunger with contraction of the gastric antrum. Later, Patterson and Sandweiss (1942) showed that duodenal contractions could give rise to hunger sensations as well.

Hunger, as reflected in the drive to eat, appears to involve more than the production of sensation by contractions in the gut. The studies of Brobeck, Tepperman, and Long, in 1942, led to the recognition of collections of ganglion cells in the ventromedial and lateral hypothalamus that govern eating behavior. The lateral area is concerned with eating. Stimulation there leads to almost uninterrupted eating associated with increased gastric secretion and motor activity, while destruction of this area results in the refusal to eat and the absence of gastric acid secretion and motor activity (Anand,

1962, pp. 43–116; Smith & Brooks, 1967). The ventromedial area is ordinarily responsive to the concentration of blood glucose. Stimulation in this area inhibits feeding, while destruction of the area in animals leads to unrestrained eating. Neural activity in these areas of the hypothalamus is coordinated with that at higher levels. Stimulation in the amygdala can induce the same gastric changes as stimulation in the lateral hypothalamus. Also, in cats under urethane anesthesia, cortical activation present in an unfed animal can be blocked by feeding or by stimulation of the ventromedial area of the hypothalamus (Sudakov & Mnasin, 1965).

Regulatory processes that govern feeding are evident in animals along most of the phylogenetic scale. The removal of the brain in certain crustacea, for example, removes all restraints to eating (Waterman, 1960). The brainless animal will continue feeding, even when the stomach is completely filled; as a result it may eventually burst. The relative restraint that characterizes the intact animal implies the presence of a controlling mechanism of some sort in the brain.

SALIVARY GLANDS

Pavlov's studies of gastrointestinal function were focused first on salivary secretion (1910). He showed that auditory, visual, and tactile symbols associated with food could elicit copious secretion of the saliva. He also showed that other meaningful events could counteract this effect, and indeed inhibit salivary flow. He observed, e.g., that a dog which salivated reliably to conditional stimuli in the laboratory might fail altogether to respond with salivation during a demonstration before a large and imposing audience of students (Gantt, personal communication). On the occasion of such an inhibitory experience, Pavlov observed that the dog appeared somewhat frightened by the fixed attention of the group and stood immobile, secreting hardly a drop of saliva. When Pavlov rang his bell, the dog remained motionless, and his salivary glands failed to respond. Far from being discouraged by such experiences, Pavlov learned that meaningful experiences must compete in their effects on an end organ, and if in opposition, one or the other may predominate.

The structures of the mouth are involved in a great many interactions of a human being with his environment. It is not surprising, therefore, that they respond to circumstances of important symbolic significance. The suppression of saliva has long been associated with fear and guilt. In ancient times in China suspected criminals were forced to chew rice to reveal guilt.

Less obvious, but perhaps as frequent in emotionally charged situations, are increases in salivary secretion. M. D. Bogdonoff, M. M. Bogdonoff, and Wolf (1961) collected saliva directly from Stenson's duct before and during tooth drilling as their subjects sat in the dentist's chair. The individuals were independently evaluated with respect to their personality structure and way of life, and without knowledge of the salivary data, were classified as preponderantly assertive or passive. There was a highly significant correlation between these evaluations and the salivary data. The assertive group secreted increased amounts of saliva during the drilling procedure, while the salivary flow of the passive subjects decreased sharply and assumed a thick quality often associated with the sudden manifestation of halitosis (S. Wolf, unpublished observations). Such changes were brought on repeatedly in susceptible individuals during stress interviews.

ESOPHAGUS

The function of the esophagus is to expedite the passage of swallowed food into the stomach by nicely regulated peristaltic contractions and to prevent the regurgitation of acid material from the stomach by the action of the lower esophageal sphincter. The propulsive rhythm may be disturbed by obstruction and other circumstances, including emotionally troublesome situations (Schindler, 1926; Thieding, 1921; Weiss, 1946; Winkelstein, 1931). Sphincter mechanisms at both ends of the esophagus separate the positive intraluminal pressures of the pharynx and the stomach from the negative intraluminal pressure of the esophagus.

Anatomy

The esophagus is a downward continuation of the pharynx, starting at about the level of the sixth cervical vertebra and ending where it joins the cardia of the stomach at approximately the level of the tenth thoracic vertebra. An elastic membrane, the phreno-esophageal membrane, extends from the muscular wall of the esophagus a few centimeters above the diaphragm down to the rim at the diaphragmatic hiatus and tends to anchor the distal esophagus, thus preventing excessive shortening by the longitudinal muscles or esophageal displacement during increased intraabdominal pressure (Lerche, 1950).

The esophagus, like other parts of the alimentary canal, contains a mucosa, a submucosa, a muscularis, and an adventitia. The mucosa consists of epithelium, the lamina propria, and a muscularis mucosae. The surface lining is stratified squamous epithelium continued from the pharynx. The point of juncture between the stratified squamous epithelium of the esophagus and columnar epithelium of the stomach in adults is normally 20–25 cm from the incisor teeth (Barrett, 1958, pp. 147–162). The demarcation usually consists of a zigzag line formed by extensions of irregular tongues of stratified squamous epithelium. The secretory glands of the esophagus are of two types, the deep mucous glands and the superficial cardiac glands. The lamina propria consists of loose connective tissue, while the muscularis mucosae appears to be a muscular continuation downward from the pharyngeal aponeurosis. The submucosa is made up of dense elastic and collagen fibers. The musculature of the esophagus consists of an outer longitudinal layer, beginning as two distinct bundles that eventually fuse into a layer over the esophagus and an inner "circular" muscle layer. The inner muscular coat has a circular pattern in a 2-cm segment that is 7–8 cm below the cricopharyngeus; above and below this segment, the muscle fibers course elliptically (Lerche, 1950). In contrast to other parts of the gastrointestinal tract, the inner muscle layer is slightly thinner than the outer longitudinal coat. Although there is considerable variation, in general the upper one-fourth of the esophagus contains striated muscle; the second one-fourth has a mixture of a striated and smooth muscle; and the lower half is of smooth muscle only.

The main blood supply of the cervical portion of the esophagus is derived from the inferior thyroid artery. The thoracic segment is supplied by branches from the bronchial arteries, the aorta, and the right intercostals. The abdominal esophagus receives its blood supply through branches from the left gastric, from the short gastrics, and from the recurrent branch of the left inferior phrenic. Venous drainage is through tributaries that empty into various single veins and into the azygos and hemiazygos systems.

The esophagus is supplied by both sympathetic and parasympathetic divisions of the autonomic nervous system. The sympathetic fibers are derived from the superior and inferior cervical sympathetic ganglia, the fourth and fifth thoracic ganglia, and preganglionic fibers from the greater and lesser splanchnic nerves. The parasympathetic innervation is provided by the vagi. Although it is known that both sympathetic and parasympathetic stimulation cause contraction of the muscularis mucosae, the function of the muscularis mucosae remains unknown (Davenport, 1966). The upper esophageal sphincter appears to have a double innervation from cells in the nucleus ambiguous and the dorsal motor nucleus of the vagus in the medulla (Ingelfinger, 1958). The esophageal vestibule, located above the cardiac sphincter, is supplied by both the vagi and the sympathetic nerves. The intrinsic innervation of the esophagus consists mainly of the postganglionic parasympathetic neurons. The myenteric plexus of Auerbach, found between the longitudinal and circular muscle layers, has as many as 10 ganglion cells per section cut at 1-mm intervals (Netter, 1959). The ganglion cells of the submucosal plexus of Meissner are more sparsely scattered.

Function

Swallowing may be initiated voluntarily or it may be reflexly elicited by stimulation of the mouth and pharynx (Davenport, 1966). Afferent impulses traveling in the glossopharyngeal nerves and superior laryngeal branch of the vagus are integrated at the level of the medulla, and the complete act of swallowing is affected by discharge through six nuclei and motor neurons C-1 through C-3. Further integrative activity is responsible for the orderly manner in which the primary peristaltic wave moves down the esophagus.

Swallowing may be divided into three phases: oral, pharyngeal, and esophageal. The contact of material from the mouth with pharyngeal and peri-

pharyngeal structures initiates reflexes that complete the second and third stages of deglutition (Hightower, 1959, pp. 3–61). The oral phase is initiated by the voluntary movement of the tongue pushing the bolus backward. The jaw shuts; the forepart of the tongue is pressed against the roof of the mouth; and the anterior portion of the mouth is sealed off when the lips close. The soft palate and contracted palatopharyngeal muscle close the opening into the nasopharynx, and with posterior movement the tongue displaces the bolus into the oropharynx. Respiration is briefly inhibited. The larynx is brought upward and forward under the tongue, and the epiglottis is tilted downward, closing the larynx. A pressure of 4–10 mm Hg, produced by movement of the tongue, pushes the bolus over and around the epiglottis (Davenport, 1966). The anteroposterior diameter of the laryngopharynx is increased and the true and false vocal cords approximate. The contraction of the pharyngeal constrictors aids the movement of the bolus by a peristaltic wave, which moves downward over the cricopharyngeus and continues as the primary esophageal peristaltic contraction. The cricopharyngeus closes the esophagus above it, immediately after the bolus passes that level. Present evidence suggests that the cricopharyngeal muscle is supplied by a nerve from the pharyngeal branch of the vagus (Lund, 1965). The pharyngeal phase of swallowing occupies only 1 sec (Davenport, 1966). The larynx descends; the glottis is opened; the tongue moves forward; and respiration resumes when the bolus of food passes the level of the clavicle.

When a bolus of food is delivered into the pharynx by the tongue, air usually present in the pharynx is trapped. Most of the air passes into the trachea just before the glottis closes, and only occasionally is any air forced into the esophagus. If air is swallowed, it usually does not pass beyond the esophagus and is soon expelled by belching.

The events of the esophageal phase depend upon the nature of the swallowed material and the position of the individual. When an individual is in the upright position, liquids may travel through the esophagus faster than the primary peristaltic wave. Swallowed liquid usually is held up at the lower end of the esophagus until a peristaltic contraction allows it to enter the stomach. Transport by peristaltic action through the esophagus still occurs after swallowing when the subject is upside down. The primary peristaltic wave is the principal factor producing the gradient of pressure in the esophagus favoring proximal to distal transport; however, it is neither invariable nor all-or-none (Ingelfinger, 1958). Its presence is not consistently related to force, frequency, or the extent of propagation. When a rapid succession of swallows occurs, the primary peristaltic wave is inhibited until after the last swallow. The remaining contents are then emptied by a peristaltic wave. The main afferent limb for the reflex arc of the primary peristaltic contraction is the pharyngeal branch of the glossopharyngeal nerve, while the vagus provides the efferent limb. Local neural connections are also important in the propagation of the peristaltic wave. When the local muscular and neural elements are interrupted, the primary peristaltic wave ceases upon reaching the involved area, only to appear again below the lesion and to continue toward the stomach. The esophago-gastric junction has a zone of high basal pressure, and the entire vestibule segment performs as a sphincter. As the peristaltic wave approaches the vestibule, the latter relaxes to admit the bolus. Thereupon, slow contraction of the vestibule produces a higher pressure in its segment above the diaphragm than in its portion below the diaphragm, thus emptying the contents into the stomach.

If the character of the bolus is such that the primary peristaltic wave fails to move it alone, local distention produced by the bolus may initiate a secondary peristaltic contraction, or another primary wave may be initiated by deglutition. The only afferent nerve fibers that travel with the vagus are those concerned with secondary peristalsis. Secondary peristaltic contractions may appear spontaneously or in response to distention. They usually originate at the level of the arch of the aorta. The initiating distention may be localized or disseminated over a considerable portion of the esophagus, as occurs when liquids are swallowed. The contraction wave proceeds down the esophagus in a manner similar to the primary peristaltic wave. The rate of occurrence of secondary contractions produced by a small distended balloon is 6.5 and 8.1 waves/min in the upper, middle, and lower seg-

ments, respectively (Hightower, 1959, pp. 3–61). Recently, gastrin has been shown to play a part in the control of lower esophageal sphincter tone.

A third type of esophageal motor activity (tertiary waves) consists of a series of dysrhythmic contractions of the lower two-thirds, which may force the esophageal content in any direction but chiefly toward the mouth. Such irregular contractions, characteristic of achalasia, may be induced by the presence of obstruction, especially at the cardiac sphincter, and may occur in association with emotionally stressful situations in healthy subjects (Wolf & Almy, 1949). They are also seen commonly in elderly individuals (presbyesophagus).

Psychophysiological Data

In experiments with humans, Jacobson (1927) and Faulkner (1941) induced spastic contraction of the esophagus during emotional stress, followed by lessening contraction during recovery and reassurance. Wolf and Almy (1949) added further evidence of the participation of the esophagus in the adaptive behavior of man and of its control at the highest integrative levels of the central nervous system. Dysrhythmic motor activity and delay in esophageal emptying were displayed by several healthy subjects experiencing intense headaches caused by a steel headband, and also by students undergoing particularly difficult academic examinations. In patients with achalasia, delay in esophageal emptying was induced during stress interviews and dispelled by offering strong reassurance. The participation of the cardiac sphincter in this type of reaction is discussed in the next section.

STOMACH

Unlike the heart and lungs, the stomach is an intermittently active organ whose demands for nourishment vary greatly over the day. Like the heart and the lungs, however, its functions are fundamentally automatic. As the heart beats 70 times/min and the lungs breathe 16 times/min, the stomach, every few hours and for several minutes, undergoes a period of accelerated activity manifested by blood flow, the secretion of juices, and digestive movements. Also, like the heart and lungs, the automatic activities of the stomach are subject to major modifications in response to a variety of stimuli. Such stimuli, including events that have an emotional significance for the subject, may cause the heart or respiratory rate or the activities of the gastric glands and the musculature of the stomach to accelerate greatly or to decrease sharply.

The functions of the stomach are numerous and complex, being concerned not only with transporting but also with storing and processing of swallowed foods. Ingested material from the esophagus is modified in such a way as to present a fairly uniform product to the small intestine for further digestion and, finally, for absorption. The stomach must adjust the temperature, pH, osmolarity, and consistency of the ingesta, in addition to starting the process of protein digestion and providing an escort for certain molecular components, such as vitamin B_{12}, en route to their absorptive destination further down the gastrointestinal tract. If we consider the wide variety of foods and beverages eaten each day by human beings, and their temperature, texture, and corrosive and solvent properties, it seems incredible that one organ could perform the task of equalization and, in most instances at least, survive unscathed. To accomplish its functions, the stomach is equipped with the most flawlessly designed motor and secretory equipment, and is subject to an elaborate hierarchy of controls.

Anatomy

The wall of the stomach consists of three layers of smooth muscle, neatly coordinated so that the job of mixing and moving is largely carried out without the subject's awareness. There is an inner oblique, a middle circular, and an outer longitudinal layer. The inner oblique layer is continuous with the circular musculature of the esophagus and is most dense in the fundic region of the stomach, where it fans out to form a sort of suspensory. The outer longitudinal layer is continuous with that of the esophagus and forms primarily two bands of fibers extending along the lesser and greater curvatures of the stomach. They contribute a few fibers to the pyloric sphincter and continue on as the longitudinal muscle of the duodenum. The middle circular layer is the strongest and most continuous of the three. It becomes progressively heavier toward the antrum and is heaviest in the pyloric

region, where it functions as the pyloric sphincter. It is important to note that the circular musculature of the stomach is not continuous with that of the duodenum, but that the two are separated by a thin fibrous septum which allows each to engage in its independent motor function. The fundus and body provide a storage area for swallowed food, whereas the antrum is involved in triturating and kneading actions, and ultimately expels the chyme into the duodenum.

The cavity of the stomach is lined throughout by a single layer of columnar epithelial cells, which present an arrangement of alternating mounds and valleys in cross section. These cells produce the mucinous material that insulates them from the corrosive properties of the acid-proteolytic enzyme mixture of the gastric juice, and they may synthesize other substances as well. Scattered infrequently throughout the surface epithelium, and normally only at the antral end of the stomach, are mucus-secreting goblet cells, clear-staining with hematoxylin and eosin. However, there is disagreement as to whether or not the normal stomach may contain goblet cells. Goblet cells increase in number in atrophic gastritis and, in that condition, may appear in the fundus, as well as in the pyloric antrum.

Beneath the single layer of surface epithelial cells, the normal gastric mucosa of the fundus contains tubular glands closely packed together in linear fashion like a row of test tubes. The glands contain at least three cell types and produce HCl, as well as several protein and polysaccharide components. Among these are the proteolytic enzymes, pepsin and gastricsin, and Castle's intrinsic factor. The HCl is apparently secreted by parietal cells, which appear round and red-staining in the hematoxylin and eosin preparation. They were so named because originally they were thought not to communicate with the lumina of the glands but to be placed peripherally around the tubular glands. Their true relationship to adjacent cells was not recognized until the refined staining methods of Coles were introduced in the last decade of the last century (Conn, 1933). The zymogen, or chief cells, are smaller than the parietal cells and show paler-staining in the hematoxylin and eosin preparation. They are the source of pepsinogen and perhaps are responsible for providing other digestive enzymes of the gastric juice. Many of the cells near the surface of the tubular glands, the so-called mucous neck cells, stain even less than the chief cells. They are apparently progenitors of the surface epithelium and the parietal and chief cells of the gastric glands (Bertalanffy, 1962).

In the fundus and body of the stomach, the closely packed tubular glands are arranged in clusters with a thin strand of smooth muscle or connective tissue between each cluster and a slightly thicker septum separating groups of clusters. The antrum begins roughly two-thirds of the distance from cardia to pylorus. Here the parietal cells are much more scattered, and deep-lying clusters of mucous cells appear. Argentaffin-like cells are thought to secrete gastrin. Connective tissue is prominent and closely packed. The glands of the antrum are branched, so that the orderly, linear, test-tubelike arrangement no longer obtains. In the cardia near the entrance of the esophagus, the mucosa itself is relatively thin. Its appearance varies from place to place more than that of the antrum or fundus. In some portions of the cardia, parietal cells are relatively numerous, while a few millimeters away there may be a few parietal cells but more prominent connective tissue.

Beneath the tubular glands of the normal mucosa lies a thin sheet of smooth muscle, the muscularis mucosae, from which wisps of smooth muscle fibers extend upward to surround groups of two or three gastric glands. The muscularis mucosae is penetrated by blood vessels that send arches of smaller branches up to the surface, where the neck of each gland is ringed by a venous loop (Figure 10.1).

The lining membrane of the stomach, like that in the rest of the gastrointestinal tract, is frequently renewed. There is a circadian rhythm that governs mitosis, but over a 24-hr period in the fundus of the stomach approximately one-third of the surface epithelial cells are renewed by mitosis. The parietal and chief cells apparently last longer, but rarely, if ever, are found in mitosis; thus they must be replaced by differentiation of new mucous neck cells. In the pyloric area, cell replacement occurs somewhat more rapidly than in the fundus, so that approximately half of the pyloric epithelial and gland cells are renewed each day (Cantelli, 1962).

Function

With each beat the heart puts about 70 cc of blood into the aorta to supply the general circulation, and the same quantity into the vessels that lead to the lungs. Beating 70 times/min, the heart pumps roughly 5 liters of blood into the arterial channels each minute. The portion of the blood that is already oxygenated, having passed through the lungs, is taken up in widely differing amounts by the various organs. The brain, representing only 2% of the body weight, claims nearly 20% of the blood in any given minute. The kidneys, even smaller, claim in the neighborhood of 25%, and the less than 60% remaining is distributed among the liver, muscles, skin, and the intestinal tract. Here the volume of blood at any time is relatively great, but the speed of circulation is relatively slow. The stomach's share during its resting state is less than 0.5%, but the mucous membrane lining of the stomach varies enormously in its demand for blood. During digestive activity it increases greatly. The cycle of increased gastric function in the normal individual is marked not only by a stepping up of contractile activity and secretions but also by a great increase in blood flow. This is usually provided for by a temporary increase in the output of blood by the heart. At times of most intense activity, while producing secretions and during its kneading motions, the stomach rivals the brain and kidneys with respect to the rate at which it uses up oxygen and converts the nutrients in the blood to energy. Because these periods are brief, however, and because in the normal individual only 6 or 8 of them occur during the 24-hr period, the overall use of blood and oxygen by the stomach is relatively low.

Sensibility The sensory equipment of the stomach is responsible for supplying the afferent limb of numerous regulatory reflexes without any sensory experiences reaching consciousness. Those afferent stimuli which do reach consciousness provide the basis of symptoms. Periodically, since the pioneer studies of Richet in 1878 (see p. 437), in-

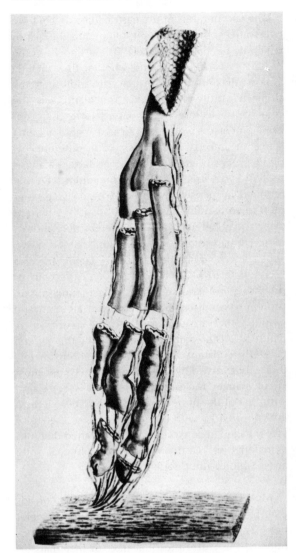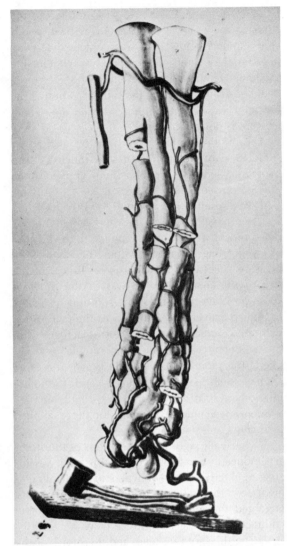

Figure 10.1 Wax reconstructions of gastric glands. Left: wisps of smooth muscle fibers extend upward from the muscularis mucosae. Right: the surrounding blood vessels. From J. Vial. Reproduced by permission.

vestigators have become interested in this problem, but only recently has an extensive, long-term study been reported. Tom, a fistulous subject with a uniquely accessible stomach, provided a suitable opportunity to explore the sensibility of the mucosa and deeper layers as well (Wolf & Wolff, 1947). Tom had undergone a surgical gastrostomy in 1895 at the age of nine because of an esophageal stricture that resulted from accidentally swallowing scalding hot clam chowder. From 1941 until his death in 1958

he was the subject of a series of experiments. Various sensory stimuli were applied to the wall within the cavity of Tom's stomach and to a redundant fold of mucosa protruding through the stoma. It was found that:

1. Touch sensation was absent in the gastric mucosa.

2. Pressure was sensed in the mucosa and roughly localized. Two pressure points could be distinguished at a distance of more than 9 cm.

3. A warm stimulus above 40°C applied to the stomach mucosa was appreciated as heat, and a cold stimulus below 18°C was perceived as cold. Between these limits no sensation was felt. Outside the limits, temperature differences of 3°C or more could be distinguished by the subject. Whether the sensation was felt in the mucosa or in the deeper layers was not established.

4. Painful sensations could not be elicited by stimulation of the normal gastric mucosa. With hyperemia and edema, minor stimuli applied to the mucosa caused pain.

5. Pain resulted from distention of the muscular and peritoneal coats of the stomach, either by pressure with a blunt object applied to the mucosa or by inflating a balloon within the viscus. The pressure necessary to elicit pain regardless of the size of the area stimulated was of the order of 100 g/cm². The strength of the stimulus necessary to induce pain and the intensity of the pain varied with the contractile state of the stomach and with the suddenness with which the stimulus was applied. The more contracted the organ, the more readily could pain be induced, and the more intensely was it felt. Moreover, stimuli applied suddenly were more painful than those applied gradually.

6. Unusually vigorous contractions of the stomach induced pain. Sensitivity to this pain was increased in the presence of hyperemia and engorgement of the mucous membrane. The more engorged the mucosa, the less forceful was the contraction necessary to induce pain.

7. The threshold for pain, and therefore for the occurrence of gastrointestinal symptoms, varied with the condition of the tissues. Vascular engorgement, inflammation, and edema lowered the pain threshold and were therefore often associated with abdominal complaints.

8. Nausea accompanied intense pain from whatever source and occurred most readily when the wall of the stomach was distended enough to put traction on the peritoneal coat.

Secretion Knowledge of the digestive process in the stomach has developed less rapidly than knowledge of other chemical processes in the body. Much remains unknown.

The components of the gastric juice derive from two sources, the lining epithelium and the glands which lie beneath. Relatively little is known of the products of the former and whether they include biologically important substances in addition to the stomach's protective mucus. The glands, via the chief cells, secrete pepsinogens, proteolytic enzyme precursors which in man are capable of being activated into two enzymes with different pH optima; pepsin and gastricsin. The latter catalyzes protein hydrolysis in a less acid medium than that required by pepsin, the proteolytic enzyme common to vertebrates. Lipase, and possibly other enzymes, may be elaborated by the gastric glands of men. Human infants secrete rennin. Blood group substances and Castle's intrinsic factor are also secreted into the stomach, although the cells of origin are not known. The stomach functions in protein catabolism, digesting serum albumin and globulin that are secreted into the gastric juice. Dilute HCl is presumably produced by the parietal cells in constant concentration, approximately 0.15N, but in widely varying amount. Under most circumstances the secretion of acid is correlated with that of the proteolytic enzymes. These in turn are coordinated with the movements of the stomach engaged in converting a widely varied diet into a material of reasonably uniform physical state acceptable to the duodenum.

Motor activity Smooth muscle may be considered phylogenetically more primitive than skeletal but it is peculiarly well adapted to serve the functions of the gastrointestinal tract of mammals. In insects and certain primitive fish, the stomach wall is composed of striated muscle, a design that may have been abandoned in the evolutionary branching that led to man. Smooth muscle lacks the capacity for elegant precision of skeletal muscle and cannot produce the modulated movements of a pianist's fingers. On the other hand, smooth muscle is far more versatile than skeletal muscle. A particularly impressive feature of smooth muscle is its capacity to contract effectively over a wide range of fiber length. The stomach of man maintains a degree of contraction at all times but will tolerate stretching and still exert orderly and forceful contractile activity on a contained volume as large as

1500 cc. Only when the stomach is greatly distended do the muscles lose their tone, so that the organ becomes lax and powerless. Of the stomach's many capabilities, one of the most intriguing is its ability to accommodate a very large ingested meal at one time, and at another to enclose and manipulate a small amount of swallowed material, exerting approximately the same force on the contents despite the difference in volume. This phenomenon, called receptive relaxation, was described in 1911 by Cannon and Lieb. As the stomach's contents increase in volume, the walls relax progressively, so that approximately the same intraluminal pressure (3–6 cm Hg) is maintained. The stomach's heavy muscular wall was found able to relax enough to accommodate about 6 qt of material. Usually, however, the muscular walls of the stomach were in a state of partial contraction, so that the organ appeared filled with only a pint of material ingested.

The Regulation and Control of Gastric Functions

In the exquisite adaptation of the human organism to its environment, the stomach plays a very significant and versatile role, one concerned not only with sustaining life and providing for growth but with protecting the individual against the ingestion of injurious agents.

The control of the digestive apparatus of man has reached a complexity which matches that governing his social behavior, his strivings, frustrations, and achievements. The motor, secretory, and vascular structures of the stomach display a wide range of functions from alerting the individual to the need for nourishment and processing what is ingested to resisting ingestion or actually rejecting the substance swallowed. This degree of discrimination is under intricate and sometimes contradictory mechanisms. The stomach is called upon to deal with an extraordinary variety of materials and textures that we call food. Some require a long treatment in the stomach; others can pass directly into the small intestine. The ability to control the period of gastric digestion and to provide the chemical environment most suitable rests in a complex hierarchy of regulatory mechanisms. At present these are only partly understood. The mechanisms range from processes that take place entirely at the molecular level to those that involve widespread neural and endocrine connections.

The control of rhythmic gastric motor activity is exercised at several levels of integrative function (Youmans, 1952) acting on a pacemaker mechanism in the upper third. At the tissue level, an isolated strip of smooth muscle from the stomach will contract rhythmically in vitro under appropriate circumstances, governed by much the same local biochemical factors that determine the behavior of other isolated strips of smooth muscle. At the organ level, periodic contractions also persist. Cannon (1907) divided the stomach of the cat, in vivo, from its extrinsic nerve supply. The stomach remained inactive for a period of days after operation, then recovered its capacity for a kind of periodic contractile activity but was less versatile in its reactions than the normal stomach. In the intact, healthy human subject, there is a basic pattern of motor

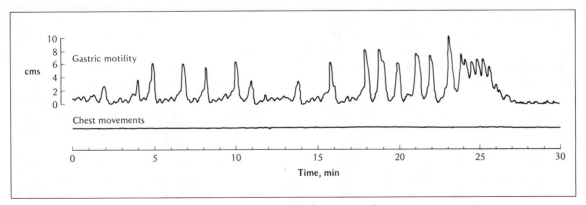

Figure 10.2 Motor activity in the gastric antrum showing the three types of waves.

activity characterized by 3/min rhythmic contractions of the stomach (Type I waves). These are interrupted every now and then by a period of vigorous contractile activity (Type II waves), lasting a matter of minutes, which generates the higher pressures that force the stomach's contents into the duodenum. Episodes of vigorous gastric contraction often terminate in a period of more or less sustained contraction or incomplete "gastric tetany" (Type III waves; Figure 10.2). One of the most frequent interruptions to the automatic activity of the stomach is provided by the eating of a meal. At the level of the medulla, motor fibers to the stomach derive from cells in the nucleus alae cinereae, the dorsal nucleus of the vagus. Semba, Noda, and Fuji's (1963) studies of dogs have shown that not only are fibers from this nucleus carried in the vagus nerves but some of them travel down the gray matter of the cord to the dorsal roots of the cervical and thoracic area, whence they are carried in sympathetic trunks to the stomach. Much of the complex skein of interconnected circuits that control and modulate gastric activity remains to be unraveled. Roughly speaking, the various stimulatory and inhibitory forces affect motor and secretory functions alike but not invariably so; there are also certain patterned responses in which differential effects are evident.

Many of the signals that govern gastric activity originate at other levels of the gut. The intercommunication among different levels and the versatile adaptive capacity of the gastrointestinal musculature are evident from the observation that contractions increase in force above a partial obstruction until a certain degree of pressure is reached. At that point contractions stop altogether. A stomach, passively distended because of an obstruction in the intestine below may hold several liters of material without a substantial increase in intragastric pressure.

The innervation of smooth muscle contains considerable numbers of inhibiting fibers. When inhibitory impulses from extrinsic nerves are acting, not only is the threshold for electrical stimuli elevated but conduction in the fiber is so impaired that the strength of contraction is reduced, so that finally the transmission of motor nerve impulses is blocked (Burnstock, personal communication).

The response of a smooth muscle structure to a stimulus depends in part on the previous state of the muscle. Page and McCubbin (1953) have shown that a contracted blood vessel may respond to serotonin or even epinephrine by relaxing, whereas these agents would bring about contraction in a relaxed vessel. Variability in response to stimuli may be observed in smooth muscle structures, however, when the circumstances seem identical. For example, a sudden distention of the gastric antrum in the fistulous subject, Tom, carried out in identical fashion 25 times during a phase of inactivity, elicited a contractile wave on 9 occasions but nothing on the other 16. Sudden distention of the stomach during a phase of already established contractile activity rarely altered the pattern at all (Wolf & Wolff, 1947).

One of the most reliable ways to inhibit gastrointestinal motor activity, including that of the stomach, is by intense noxious stimulation of any part of the body. The duration of impairment of gastric motor function that follows abdominal surgery correlates closely with the extent of manipulation of intraabdominal structures (Wells, Tinckler, & Rawlinson, 1964).

Cardia The act of swallowing, even if nothing is swallowed, induces relaxation of the esophagocardiac sphincter (Wolf, 1965). The presence of a bolus or liquid in the lower portion of the esophagus is equally effective. On the other hand, irritants in the esophagus cause the sphincter to constrict. Prolonged relaxation of the cardia may occur when a stomach tube is left in place, thus risking the hazard of esophagitis and possible stricture from the effects of regurgitated gastric juice, unless the constrictor action of the irritant predominates (Nagler & Spiro, 1963).

As already indicated, the cardiac sphincter is important in preventing reflux of gastric contents into the esophagus. When it fails to relax at the appropriate time, however, the contents of the esophagus are prevented from reaching the stomach. Wolf and Almy (1949) had shown that such constriction may be induced in healthy humans on swallowing extremely hot (63°C) or extremely cold (6.5°C) material, or an irritant substance such as Tabasco sauce. As long ago as 1883, Kronecker and

Meltzer and later von Mikulicz (1903) observed failure of the cardiac sphincter to relax in healthy subjects following noxious stimulation. Here, presumably, cardiospasm occurred as an adaptive reaction to protect the rest of the gastrointestinal tract from the effects of irritating materials. Other noxious stimuli not directed at the alimentary tract are similarly effective in inducing constriction of the cardiac sphincter in some individuals. Even symbolic stimuli, words or events that aroused emotional conflicts, were in some instances followed by tight closing of the cardiac sphincter.

The regulation of the cardiac sphincter and its coordination with the movements of the esophagus and with the act of swallowing itself is presumably accomplished through the post ganglionic autonomic fibers of the submucosal and myenteric plexuses of Meissner and Auerbach. This relationship is shown by the development of achalasia, when these structures are destroyed by such agents as diphtheria toxin or Chagas' disease. Such a denervated esophagus, in keeping with Cannon's law, may be unduly responsive to humoral agents that induce contraction. Kramer and Ingelfinger (1949) demonstrated such hypersensitivity by giving 10 mg acetyl-β-methylcholine to both healthy subjects and those with achalasia. The latter displayed unduly forceful and arrhythmic contractions under the influence of the parasympathomimetic agent. This violent response was not evident in healthy subjects or in those with esophageal obstruction secondary to diffuse systemic sclerosis. The data suggest that some degree of structural or functional denervation is a regular feature of cardiospasm.

Fundus The term "fundus" designates the portion of the stomach between cardia and pylorus, the part that some classify as body plus fundus. The functions of the fundus ventriculi consist mainly of secreting HCl and digestive enzymes, and the kneading and mixing of the gastric contents. The activation of the zymogen cells responsible for the digestive enzymes appears to be primarily under the control of the vagus nerves acting with the hormone gastrin. The regulation of the relative amounts of pepsin or gastricsin produced from their precursor zymogens may take place at the molecular level and depends on the pH and other characteristics of the activating medium.

The coordination of the behavior of the stomach with that of the rest of the intestinal tract is accomplished by a variety of local reflexes, mainly involving signals from the esophagus, the duodenum, and the stomach itself. The act of swallowing causes not only relaxation of the cardiac sphincter, but also momentary inhibition of gastric contractions. The stomach grasps or contracts around whatever has entered it, and at the same time adjusts to the new volume, so that a more or less uniform pressure is exerted by the gastric walls, irrespective of the volume of the contents. The mechanical effect always induces a certain amount of secretion of acid and pepsin; if the ingested material is beef broth or alcohol, the gastric glands are stimulated to an even greater degree of secretion.

Antrum Among the regulators of the secretion of HCl is the hormone gastrin, first identified by Edkins in 1906. Shortly thereafter, Popielski discovered that histamine, another substance occurring naturally in the human body, was a potent stimulator of gastric acid secretion. This finding forced the consideration of gastrin into the background, and for years many investigators believed gastrin to be histamine. The hormone's independent existence now is established beyond doubt. Gregory and Tracy (1964) have extracted two gastrins from hog antral mucosa, have identified them as polypeptides of about 2000 molecular weight, and have determined their amino acid sequences. Gastrin I does not contain sulfate, while Gastrin II has an ethereal sulfate on the phenolic hydroxyl radical of tyrosine.

No pure chemical substances from natural foods have been found to be reliable or effective stimulants for gastrin release. During the response to a meal, four recognized factors interact to control the rate of gastrin release: vagal stimulation from cephalic and gastric sources, local stimulation by distention, local stimulation by chemical agents, and inhibition of gastrin release by acidification of the antral contents (Grossman, 1966).

The biological effects of gastrin are not limited to the stomach, but include stimulation of esophageal and uterine musculature and inhibition of intestinal absorption (Bynum & Jacobson, 1971). Small doses of exogenous gastrin increase gastric acid and proteolytic enzyme secretion, stimulate pancreatic flow and bicarbonate secretion, stimulate pancreatic enzyme secretion, and stimulate hepatic biliary flow and bicarbonate secretion. Large amounts of gastrin administered intravenously in a single bolus in animals caused inhibition of gastric secretion of acid, marked stimulation of gastric proteolytic enzyme secretion, increased gastric motility, and initial stimulation followed by inhibition of small intestinal motility (Grossman, 1967, pp. 208–220).

Specialized receptors in the upper intestinal mucosa exert a constant restraint on the antrum. It is important to recognize that the pylorus itself functions as part of the gastric pump, relaxed at first and offering little resistance to the flow of chyme into the duodenum but closing tightly as the last of the bolus passes into the duodenal bulb, which in turn contracts with a force comparable to that in the antrum. The tightly closed pyloric sphincter thereby prevents regurgitation of chyme into the stomach.

The mucosa of the duodenum, and probably that of the jejunum as well, monitors the material that passes through. On the basis of its chemical and physical characteristics, the secretory and motor activities of the stomach are either stimulated or inhibited. Stimulation is accomplished by a reflex mechanism via afferents in the intestinal mucosa, efferents in the vagus, and by means of a gastrinlike hormone secreted in the wall of the intestine. Inhibition may also be effected through neural pathways, including the sympathetic nerves and probably certain fibers of the vagus, as well as by hormonal mechanisms including secretin and cholecystokinin.

In the small intestine the alkaline secretions of the pancreas and liver are added to the acid mixture from the stomach, effectively neutralizing it. As digestion proceeds in the small intestine, motor and secretory activities in the stomach gradually subside. By the time the last bit of the meal has been expelled from it, the stomach is limp and inactive, and remains that way until the next period of increased gastric function occurs.

The secretions of the pancreas also exert a modulating influence on gastric secretion, since the obstruction of the pancreatic ducts, atrophy of the pancreas, or diversion of the pancreatic secretion from the duodenum markedly accelerates the secretion of gastric acid (McIlrath, Kennedy, & Hallenbeck, 1963). On the other hand, certain islet cell tumors of the pancreas, which contain gastrin (Gregory & Tracy, 1961), cause the most pronounced hypersecretion that is encountered clinically. These tumors are associated, in most instances, with duodenal or jejunal ulcer (Zollinger & Ellison, 1955). The mechanism whereby disorders of the pancreas that impair its enzyme secretion also stimulate gastric secretion of HCl and proteolytic enzymes is particularly challenging. Impairment of liver function may be implicated in chronic cases but this is not the whole story. Stimulation of gastric secretion has been observed in the absence of liver damage and in pancreatic disease, even when pancreatic enzymes were present (Mason, Eigenbrodt, Oberhelman, & Nelsen, 1963). These findings suggest a regulatory process, perhaps triggered by undigested proteins, whereby gastric proteolytic activity may be enhanced in the presence of inadequate enzymatic activity in the pancreatic juice.

As already mentioned, obstruction in the duodenum or in the intestine below sets off a reflex that inhibits gastric functions. When obstruction persists, the consequent relaxation of the gastric walls may lead to great dilatation of the stomach. The intermediate steps involved in these processes are not understood, and there may be additional mechanisms that also govern gastric secretion. In any case, it is clear that much of the regulation of gastric secretory activity depends on signals from beyond the pylorus, acting to prepare the gastric contents optimally for the duodenum.

Central neural connections Electrical stimulation in selected areas of the hypothalamus may enhance gastric secretion and blood flow or reduce them, depending on whether vagal or sympathetic connections are activated. Puiggari (personal communication) has observed prolonged periods of gastric activity during stimulation of the amygdaloid complex. The results of stimulation or ablation of parts of the brain, as reported by various authors, are somewhat contradictory, perhaps because of species differences and subtle differences in the technical procedures (Anand & Dua, 1956; Davey, Kaada, & Fulton, 1950; Eliasson, 1960, pp. 1163–1171; Feldman & Birnbaum, 1965; Long, Leonard, Chou, & French, 1962; Long, Leonard, Story, & French, 1962; Maevskaya, 1964; Pearl, Ritchie, Gilsdorf, Delaney, & Leonard, 1966). The experimental work on hypothalamic control of gastric secretion in animals has been reviewed briefly (Smith & Brooks, 1967). Not only can stimulation or inhibition of various secretory functions be effected by manipulation in the central nervous system (Pearl et al., 1966) but chronic stimulation in the anterior hypothalamus even brought about an increase in the cell population in the glands of the cat's fundus with the ultimate development of ulceration.

Transsection of the vagus nerves interrupts afferent, as well as efferent, fibers. Following vagotomy in humans, periodic gastric activity continues, but in a modified form and with much less vigorous contractions, so that emptying of the stomach may not be accomplished at all effectively. The basic reflexes persist, including contraction in response to sudden stretching of a muscle and relaxation accompanying sudden distention or intense contraction of a more distal segment of gut. In fact contraction of the smooth muscle of the stomach in response to stretching occurs more predictably when control from higher neural centers is eliminated, presumably because the higher centers inhibit certain of the more primitive reflexes as they set their own pattern of contractile activity.

Inherent rhythms Underlying the elaborately coordinated responses that characterize human gastric function is a mechanism for biological periodicity that participates in the regulatory process. In the intact human the basic gastric rhythm of the biological clock is usually not clearly evident. Short periods of fasting enhance gastric contractions and thus produce hunger sensations. Presumably, through a reflex mediated at the level of the hypothalamus, the absence of adequate nourishment induces an increase in frequency and duration of vigorous waves of gastric contraction, gastric behavior characteristic of those suffering from peptic ulcer.

Endocrine glands Whether endocrine secretions are responsible for the periodicity in gastric functions is not known. Neither is it known whether the endocrine glands are implicated in moment-to-moment regulation and control of gastric functions during the course of a day. It has been established, however, that hormones of the pituitary, thyroid, and adrenal glands are required to maintain normal functioning and responsiveness of the glands of the gastric mucous membrane (Cannon, 1929).

Gastric Psychophysiology

Role of higher integrative levels Most important among forces that interfere with the basic periodic rhythm of gastric activity are impulses from the interpretive areas of the brain. Agreeable thoughts of food or situations that arouse aggressive attitudes are likely to set off a phase of increased gastric activity. Those that disgust, depress, or frighten, on the other hand, can halt the stomach's secretory and motor activities altogether.

Studies of fistulous subjects William Beaumont (1833), in his studies on the fistulous Alexis St. Martin, observed changes in the gastric mucosa associated with St. Martin's moods and irascible behavior. Small white flecks that were scattered about the mucous membrane were noted. Subsequent information suggests that these were probably fragments of rolled-up, precipitated mucus (Wolf & Wolff, 1947). Beaumont made no correlation with gastric secretory function, but the presence of precipitated mucus, if that is what it was, indicates that acid secretion was probably considerably accelerated.

Before Pavlov demonstrated "psychic" secretion of gastric juice in his dogs with the famous Pavlov pouches, Charles Richet (1878), a medical student in Paris, observed the phenomenon in a fistulous human being. The studies of this young boy, named Marcellin, provided Richet with his graduation thesis from the University of Paris. Richet focused his attention mainly on the sensibility of the stomach and on the character of the acid secretion. He observed in passing that the sight or thought of food was associated with an increased flow of gastric juice but failed to appreciate the significance of the observation, and reported it only many years later. Pavlov (1910), on the other hand, systematically explored the phenomenon and observed that psychic secretion could be inhibited for a relatively long time by terrifying events such as a flood that once occurred in his kennels.

Observations on motor and secretory activity in the stomach were undertaken by Walter Cannon (1929), who was among the first to exploit the potential of the marvelous Roentgen rays (X rays). He observed that digestive functions, as reflected by both motor activity and acid secretion in the stomach, were brought to a halt in animals, mainly cats, placed in threatening situations. From this he developed a unitary hypothesis concerning the effects of adverse emotions such as pain, hunger, fear, and rage on the digestive apparatus.

While William Beaumont (1833) had noticed changes in the appearance of the gastric mucosa associated with emotional turmoil in his famous fistulous subject, Alexis St. Martin, correlation with opposing types of emotional attitude was not made.

In 1940 Gordon and Chernya reported studies of three human subjects with gastric fistulae. One of them, who ordinarily displayed a low level of gastric acid secretion, became a hypersecretor when he was homesick, and resentful and impatient with the experimenter and with the experimental procedures. A year later the studies on the fistulous subject Tom appeared, which established clearly

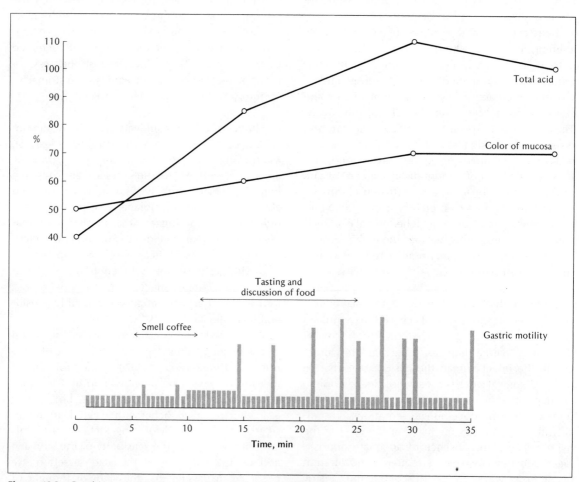

Figure 10.3 Graphic representation of increase of color, HCl secretion, and motor activity at the prospect of eating. In illustrations of experiments carried out prior to 1943, the old conventions of "free acid" and "total acid" are used instead of expressing acid in mEq per l. Color is matched to a standardized Tallqvist hemoglobin scale.

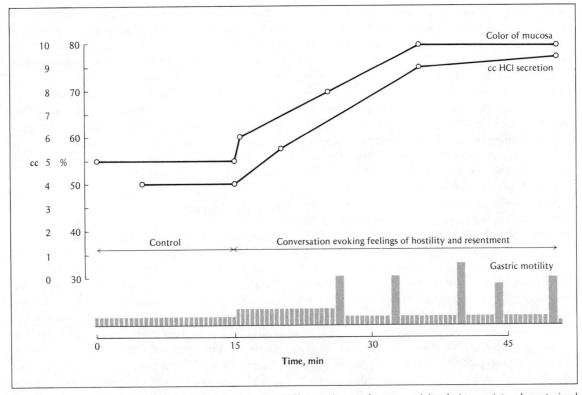

Figure 10.4 Graphic representation of increase in color, HCl secretion, and motor activity during anxiety, characterized by hostility and resentment.

that emotionally stressful situations might give rise to either hyper-or hypofunction of the stomach, depending on the nature of the circumstances and the subject's interpretation of the event. In Tom and in other fistulous subjects whom one of the present authors (Wolf, 1965) studied, fright, depression, and attitudes of being overwhelmed were associated with hypofunction of the stomach, as Cannon (1929) had shown some years before. Hyperfunction of the stomach accompanied more aggressive attitudes, including such feeling states as anger and resentment. These correlations were also observable when the subject was unaware of personal conflict or strong emotion, but when the examiner, through discussions of dreams, and from the stream of talk, associations, projections, and slips of the tongue was able to detect evidence of unconscious conflicts and emotions. Often there were associated alterations in general behavior: restlessness and quick movements accompanied gastric hyperfunction; listlessness and unresponsiveness were seen

with hypofunction. Cannon was so interested in this development that he came to New York to visit the laboratory and spent several days observing the experiments being conducted, often talking at length with Tom, while he watched the function of his stomach. Later Cannon wrote: "He had an emotional range and responsiveness that permitted nice discriminations which the authors have fully utilized. The interesting fact that frustration and repressed conflict were associated with hyperemia and with increase of motility and secretion will come as a surprise to many" (Foreword to Wolf & Wolff, 1947).

Ultimately, the observations on Tom were confirmed by Reichsman, Engle, and Segal (1955). Their study of a 6-year-old girl with a gastric fistula included documentation by motion pictures of aggressive or withdrawal behavior, associated with gastric hyper- or hypofunction, respectively. Further evidence of the contrasting patterns of gastric function under circumstances of emotional adjustment was presented by Farr and Lueders (1923), who found high levels of gastric acid secretion in hypomanic patients but low levels in those with mental depression.

It appeared to be significant that enhanced gastric activity during resentment, conscious or unconscious, corresponded to that induced by the prospect of eating. The opposite reaction, which might culminate in nausea and vomiting, was similar to the rejection reactions induced by the ingestion of toxic substances, answering a biological need to halt assimilation and reject the offending substance (Figures 10.3 and 10.4). From these data one may speculate that an individual's conscious or unconscious mental attitude or posture toward his world might habitually be more in one direction than the other and that such a sustained deviation from the normal might have pathogenic significance. This question still awaits settlement, but the available data continue to be in keeping with such a hypothesis.

Tom contributed several new items to our body of knowledge about the stomach. Perhaps the most significant concerned the relationship between emotions and visceral function. Of special interest also was the finding that sustained hyperemia and engorgement of the gastric mucosa were associated with a striking increase in fragility of the membrane, so that small erosions and bleeding points appeared spontaneously or in response to the most minor traumata. Mucosal hyperemia and engorgement were also found to be associated with a lowering of pain threshold. Pinching and pulling of the gastric mucous membrane in its average state did not induce pain. Neither did vigorous contractions of the muscular coats. Such stimuli applied when the mucosa was hyperemic or engorged, however, did induce pain. Moreover, the gastric juice contained in the stomach was found capable of digesting its mucous membrane. In fact, a peptic ulcer was induced in the mucosa of Tom by keeping a portion of the membrane with defective mucus production in contact with his own gastric juice for a 3-day period.

The study of Tom and his stomach also made possible identification of the afferent nerves that are stimulated when acid gastric juice is brought in contact with an eroded mucosal surface, thereby setting up a reflex hyperemia, engorgement, and hypersecretion. In this connection Zavodskaya (1960) has shown that mechanical trauma to the duodenum in rats activates a reflex mechanism that results in gastric erosions.

Finally, Tom provided the first quantitative evidence of the objective effects of placebos (Wolf, 1950). Measurable changes in Tom's gastric function occurred repeatedly following administration of placebos, changes as marked as those induced by potent pharmacodynamic agents.

SMALL INTESTINE

The small intestine engages in the process of nourishment by breaking down ingested foods and absorbing the metabolically useful constituents. The entire procedure takes place along the length of the duodenum, jejunum, and ileum. The important secretions of the liver and pancreas are added in the duodenum. Here and below, along the whole course of the small intestine, the mucosa itself engages in supplying a variety of digestive enzymes and in achieving absorption. The mechanisms that regulate these functions are but little understood, however, perhaps because of the small intestine's recondite situation in the body.

Anatomy

The duodenum is between 20 and 39 cm in length, with a diameter ranging from 3–5 cm. The average length of the remainder of the small intestine is 20 ft (range 16–30 ft) in the adult; the proximal two-fifths is the jejunum, and the remaining three-fifths, the ileum. Although there is no definite line of separation between these two portions, there are progressive structural differences between them. The thickness of the wall and the width of the lumen gradually decrease from the proximal to the distal intestine.

The mucosa has transverse folds of Kerckring (valvulae conniventes). In the duodenum and jejunum the folds are 0.8 cm in height, and are thick and numerous. The folds become progressively shorter toward the ileum, where they are fewer in number and do not encircle the lumen but extend only two-thirds of the way around its circumference. The mucosa has numerous villous projections, averaging 350 mμ in height (range 287–650 mμ) and 137 mμ in width (range 87–215 mμ), in the proximal jejunum (Roy-Choudhury, Cook, Tan, Banwell, & Smits, 1966). The connective tissue core of the villi (lamina propria) contains lacteals, capillaries, smooth muscle, nerve elements, and leucocytes. The latter may serve an important protective role. The villi are covered with columnar epithelial cells that merge with the crypts at their base. Absorptive and goblet cells cover the villi; undifferentiated, goblet, Paneth, and enterochromaffin cells line the crypts.

The structure of these specified epithelial cells has been clarified by electron-microscopic studies (Trier & Rubin, 1965), but their function remains obscure. The absorptive cells are columnar with microvilli on their apical end; the average length of the microvilli is 1 μ, and their width approximately 0.1 μ. It has been established that the microvilli increase the surface of the absorptive cells 14–39 fold (Brown, 1962; Zetterqvist, 1956). The cells covering the villous tip have the maximum absorptive capacity. The plasma membrane covering the microvilli is 95–115 Å wide and is a continuous triple-layered membrane. The cores of the microvilli are composed of fine filaments that extend into, and are continuous with, the underlying terminal web. It has been suggested that the terminal web stiffens and stabilizes the apical cell surface. The microvilli serve important digestive and absorptive functions and have been found in association with a variety of enzymes, including alkaline phosphatase, adenosine triphosphatase, disaccharidases, and leucine naphthylamidase (Eichholz & Crane, 1965; Overton, Eichholz, & Crane, 1965; Trier & Rubin, 1965). Applied to the plasma membrane of the microvilli are numerous fine filaments, perpendicular to the plane of the membrane, which are considered an integral part of the cells (Trier & Rubin, 1965). The lateral plasma membrane of the upper halves of the cells are closely apposed to each other, while there is a space between the basal portions of the cells. Typical goblet cells contain mucous granules, and the microvilli on their apical surface are few and irregular in shape and size.

Studies to date suggest that goblet cells secrete their mucus in a merocrine fashion (Trier, 1963, 1964). Undifferentiated cells are the most abundant type in the crypts; they proliferate and differentiate into absorptive cells to replace those lost at the villous tips. There is morphological evidence that the undifferentiated crypt cells engage in both merocrine and apocrine secretion (Trier, 1964). The Paneth cells have both apocrine and merocrine secretory capability but their function is unknown (Roy-Choudhury et al., 1966). The muscularis mucosae separates the mucosa from the submucosa. The submucosa consists of a dense connective tissue that supports the folds of Kerckring. As elsewhere in the gut, the autonomic nerve plexus of Meissner is located within the submucosa, and that of Auerbach between the muscle layers. The outer muscle coat, the thinnest, forms a loose longitudinal spiral; while the inner coat is a thicker, tight, almost circular spiral.

The jejunum and ileum are supplied by 12 or more branches of the superior mesenteric artery, which form loops (arcades) between the layers of the mesentery. The arcades are single and have straight large branches to most of the jejunum. In contrast, the arcuate pattern of the ileum becomes progressively more complex with 2, 3, or 4 arcades at the ileo-cecal junction. The straight arterial branches are therefore shorter.

The length of the small intestine is richly supplied by branches of the vagal and sympathetic outflows, as well as intercostal nerves that penetrate via mesenteric attachments. The vagus (parasympathetic) nerve synapses with postganglionic fibers in the myenteric plexus of the intestinal wall. The preganglionic sympathetic (splanchnic) nerves synapse with postganglionic fibers in the celiac and other preaortic ganglia.

Function

Many factors governing hydrolysis, absorption, and transport of dietary foodstuffs are still poorly understood. Extensive reviews of intraluminal digestion and absorption in animals and man have appeared (Saunders & Isselbacher, 1966; Wilson, 1962; Wiseman, 1964).

A physiologic gradient in the intestine is evident from the fact that the respiratory quotient, irritability, and frequency of segmental contractions decrease from the proximal to the distal end of the small intestine. Two types of electrical activity are observed: large spiking action potentials and slow waves of lower potential. The large spiking potential is associated with segmental contractions. The slow waves increase the excitability of the muscle and lower the threshold to other stimuli. Each smooth muscle fiber serves as a conducting fiber.

Farrar and Zfass have reviewed comprehensively the mechanisms that regulate small intestinal motility (1967); Kosterlitz and Lees (1964) have summarized the neuropharmacological phenomena involved. Food in the stomach stimulates gastric and ileal peristalsis, a reflex (gastro-ileal reflex) that persists after vagotomy. It appears to depend on connections among adjacent portions of the gut. Thus, in an isolated segment, the reflex is absent, despite intact blood and extrinsic nerve supplies. Distention of the jejunum inhibits gastric emptying (the jejuno-gastric inhibitory reflex). Impulses are initiated from pressure receptors in the jejunum, while the afferent and efferent fibers travel in the vagus. Marked distention of one segment of the intestine inhibits the tonus and motility of the adjacent segments (the intestino-intestinal inhibitory reflex). The center for this reflex is in the spinal cord, T-7 to L-6. It is mediated through the sympathetic pathway with efferent and afferent fibers passing along the thoraco-lumbar sympathetic pathways. A mild stretch stimulus of the anorectal region mediated through sympathetic fibers may inhibit gastric and intestinal motility (anorectal inhibitory reflex).

Psychophysiological Data

The relative inaccessibility of the small intestine has up to now precluded the collection of any significant amount of psychophysiological data. There have been radiographic demonstrations of typical "disordered motor function" patterns related to situations of emotional stress; Freedman (1954) has reported the typical radiographic appearance of a "malabsorption pattern" in healthy subjects under circumstances of emotional stress, a radiographic abnormality that disappeared after circumstances became more serene.

There is little evidence currently available on the control of intestinal secretion and absorption. Published data on the participation of the brain in regulating the functions of the small intestine relate almost exclusively to motor activity, and particularly to localized increases in the contractile state of the duodenum (Abbot, Mack, & Wolf, 1952), a phenomenon involved in the mechanism of nausea. Such duodenal spasms, occurring in the region of the ampulla vater, when sustained, may result in obstruction of biliary or pancreatic ducts, thus leading either to obstructive biliary colic or acute pancreatitis (Boba, Stein, Nakamura, & Powers, 1957), as the result of regurgitation of pancreatic enzymes into the parenchymatous tissue.

An unusual opportunity was afforded to study the human jejunal mucosa directly in a 45-year-old man, who had been discovered to have regional enteritis following a sudden bout of peritonitis at age 28. Following a series of operations extending over a period of several years, he developed a jejunal fistula that failed to close and ultimately led to a fourth operation with further intestinal resection. The fistula was successfully closed but he was left with a patch of jejunum unconnected to the remainder of the gut, the mucosa of which lay exposed on the abdominal wall. The isolated patch contained not only intact mucosa but muscular coats as well. It was observed that this patch of jejunal mucosa shared many of the characteristics of the gastric mucous membrane, but it was striking that it underwent a much narrower range of variation in color and turgidity. The resistance of the membrane to physical and chemical injury was tested in the same fashion as that of the stomach. First, it was noted that mechanical stimulation, with a forceps or blunt glass rod, did not elicit as much mucus secretion from the jejunal mucosa as is produced in the stomach. Nevertheless, the membrane withstood mechanical stimuli, including negative pressure, about as well as did the stomach without developing erosions that were detectable either grossly or with the dissecting microscope. On several occasions during the period of study the subject was frustrated and resentful because of problems with his wife's family. Each such occasion was associated with hyperemia and hypermotility of the exposed segment of intestine, indicating a similarity to findings in the case of Tom (Wolf, 1965). Also, as in the case of Tom, changes were induced by stress interview.

LIVER AND BILIARY PASSAGES

Only fragmentary data of a psychophysiological sort are available on the liver and biliary passages. The liver receives both sympathetic and parasympathetic innervation, but the details of nerve distribution and neural regulation of hepatic function remain obscure. The available information on hepatic circulation has been reviewed by Leevy (1965). In 1960 Calvert and Brody observed that the typical hepatic necrosis of chloroform poisoning failed to occur in animals when the sympathetic innervation had been interrupted. This observation has since been confirmed in monkeys with livers damaged by overwhelming malaria infection (B. K. Anand, personal communication).

Anatomy

The pear-shaped gallbladder rests on the inferior surface of the liver. The organ is from 7 to 10 cm long, and measures from 2.5 to 5 cm at its widest part. The gallbladder wall has four coats: the serosa, the perimuscularis, the muscularis, and the internal mucosa. The perimuscularis contains connective tissue, blood vessels, and lymphatics. The discontinuous smooth muscles of the muscularis are separated by connective tissue and pass longitudinally in the inner layer and in a spiral fashion in the outer layer. The muscularis invades the true mucosa and, with the deep layer of the mucosa, forms the fibromuscularis mucosa. The mucosa, which has mucous glands only in the neck of the gallbladder, is lined with tall, columnar, surface epithelial cells. Microvilli, convoluted lateral cell walls, terminal bars, and stratification of cytoplasmic organelles are identifiable by electron microscopy (Evett, Higgins, & Brown, 1964). Capillaries with fenestrated endothelium located beneath the basement membrane are thought to have an absorptive function. The cystic duct joins the common hepatic duct to form the common bile duct. The portion of the cystic duct connected to the gallbladder has mucosal duplications arranged in crescentric folds. This arrangement prevents the collapse or overdistention of the cystic duct and in addition allows the gallbladder to fill under low pressure but to empty under only high pressure. The gallbladder and bile ducts are innervated through the splanchnic group of nerve fibers and the right branch of the vagus. The splanchnic fibers (inhibitory and motor) arise from the sixth thoracic to the first lumbar segment of the spinal cord. The vagus supplies motor and some sensory fibers.

Function

Under fasting conditions bile is continuously secreted by the liver but is prevented from entering the duodenum because of contraction of the sphincter of Oddi. Bile accumulates in the common duct until a pressure of approximately 20 cm of water is reached; then it passes into the gallbladder. When food passes into the intestine, the sphincter of Oddi relaxes and the gallbladder contracts, thus allowing bile to enter the duodenum. As this occurs the pressure in the common bile duct decreases to about 10 cm of water or less. The gallbladder empties slowly, taking 15 min to several hours. Usually, the pace of evacuation is uneven, much of the contents of the gallbladder being squirted out in a sudden burst several minutes after the beginning of evacuation (Englert & Chiu, 1966). The coordinated dilatation of the sphincter of Oddi and contraction of the gallbladder are mediated by the hormone cholecystokinin released from the intestinal mucosa when fat, proteins, or saline cathartics enter the duodenum. Hormonal stimulation appears to be of more importance than nervous stimulation.

Bachrach (personal communication) demonstrated spasm of the common bile duct secondary to an anxiety-producing situation. Using a multichannel recording device, he demonstrated spasm in the common duct, sometimes accompanied by duodenal spasm, during a period of stress occasioned by the patient's fear of the procedure. Since then these studies have been repeated; it is now clear that biliary pain which arises from common duct spasm may be induced by the contemplation of troublesome life situations.

PANCREAS

The pancreas is an important biochemical factory that produces at least four hormones, a variety of digestive enzymes, and a carefully regulated mixture of inorganic ions. Its role in intermediary metabolism via the secretion of insulin and glucagon will not be dealt with here. Only the digestive intraluminal functions of the pancreas will be discussed.

Anatomy

The pancreas, 10–15 cm long, is situated in the retroperitoneal space at the level of the first and second lumbar vertebrae. The head of the pancreas fits in the duodenal loop, while the body and tail extend transversely behind the stomach to the spleen.

The pancreas has groups of acini divided into lobules. Intralobular ducts connect with the larger interlobular ducts. The main pancreatic duct of Wirsung starts in the tail of the gland by the confluence of several small ducts and extends into the head. Thereafter, it joins the common bile duct in the duodenum and terminates at the papilla, either entering the duodenum on the papilla of Vater through a separate orifice or with the bile duct through a common channel, the ampulla of Vater. The parenchyma of the pancreas is made up of closely packed acinae, each consisting of a line of columnar or pyramidal cells that encircle the lumen of the gland and open into a ductule. Small centroacinar cells also extend into the acinus. Flattened cells form the small intralobular ducts. They become cuboidal in the intermediate ducts and columnar in the large ducts. The acinar cells contain zymogen granules. Following stimulation of the gland, the cells become smaller and the number of granules is reduced. It is uncertain if the granules contain one or a mixture of enzymes. Islets of Langerhans lie adjacent to the acinar cells in the lobules.

The pancreas is supplied with blood from the hepatic, splenic, and superior mesenteric arteries along with the celiac trunk. All nerves to the pancreas, both afferent and efferent, pass through the celiac plexus. The sympathetic innervation originates from the fifth to the ninth (occasionally to the tenth or the eleventh) thoracic ganglia and reaches the pancreas through the greater and lesser splanchnic trunks (Netter, 1957). The preganglionic sympathetic fibers terminate in the celiac or superior mesenteric ganglia, the fibers passing from

these ganglia to the pancreas along the blood vessels. The vagi supply the parasympathetic fibers, and the preganglionic fibers terminate in intrinsic pancreatic ganglia. The smooth muscle of the duct is innervated by parasympathetic fibers. Afferent pain fibers follow the sympathetic and vagus pathways, as well as travel in neighboring somatic intercostal nerves. The nervous and hormonal regulation of the pancreas has been thoroughly reviewed by Grossman (1961). Like other parts of the digestive system, the pancreas, although under nervous control, is also capable of secreting in an appropriate way when nerve connections have been cut.

Function

As pancreatic juice passes into the duodenum, it consists of water, electrolytes, mucus, mucoproteins, and digestive enzymes. The hormone secretin stimulates bicarbonate and water secretion. The colorless fluid has a low viscosity and an alkaline pH (7.1–8.65) and includes the inorganic ions Na^+, K^+, HCO_3^-, Cl^-, Ca^{2+}, and Zn^{2+}; HPO_4^{2-} and SO_4^{2-} are present in lesser concentrations (Pearl, Ritchie, Gilsdorf, Delaney, & Leonard, 1966). The concentrations of Na^+ and K^+ are approximately equal to those in plasma and are independent of the rate of flow (Janowitz & Dreiling, 1961, pp. 115–133). The HCO_3^- concentration varies directly with the flow rate and inversely with Cl^- concentration; thus the sum of their concentrations remains constant (154 ± 10 mM/kg H_2O). The total volume of pancreatic secretion in man for 24 hr has been variously estimated from 1500 to 4000 cc. From 10 to 40 g of protein are secreted by the pancreas each day (Kukrol, Adams, & Preston, 1965). Secretions from the pancreas appear to be continuous in man, although this has not been completely verified. The pancreatic enzymes, secreted in response to the hormone cholecystokinin or to vagal stimulation, consist of an alphaamylase, lipase, lecithinase A, trypsin, chymotrypsin, carboxypeptidases, elastase, and possibly others not so well identified (Dreiling, Janowitz, & Perrier, 1964; Zieve, Vogel, & Kelly, 1963).

Psychophysiological Data

Edema of the pancreas was produced experimentally by thoracolumbar sympathetic stimulation by Mallet-Guy, Feroldi, and Reboul (1949). Others have also described pronounced edema sufficient to produce pancreatitis in response to neurovascular mechanisms (Helms & Meredith, 1961). For years clinicians have associated inflammatory reaction in the pancreas with stressful life situations with or without assistance from alcohol. There is, however, little concrete evidence as to the mechanisms involved. Sympathetic stimulation offers one possibility; the other, regurgitation of secretion secondary to duodenal spasm, was discussed in the section on the small intestine.

THE COLON

The colon, a versatile organ, is saddled with the ultimate disposition of much of man's generous, widely variegated, and often capricious diet. Moreover, the colon must adapt its behavior to the sometimes frantic timing problems of the complex society in which we live. The adaptation is accomplished by an elaborate hierarchy of controls that, in man, operate at every level from the peripheral tissue itself to the cerebral cortex.

The job of the colon, to harbor the waste products of digestion, to provide a medium for the proliferation of symbiotic microorganisms, to mix and dry the stool, and to deliver it to the rectum for evacuation, requires that it engage in a variety of differing but coordinated movements. Thus it is not surprising that the colon consists mainly of an arrangement of smooth muscles with a rich vascular network, but interestingly, a relatively small blood flow (Bynum & Jacobson, 1971; Horvath, Kelly, Folk, & Hutt, 1957).

Anatomy

The colon is a muscular tube that varies in length and width, depending on the work it is performing. Under resting conditions its length has been estimated to vary from 91 to 125 cm. The usual caliber of the colon diminishes from the cecum (about 8.5 cm) to the sigmoid segment (about 2.5 cm).

As the ileum enters the colon at the ileocecal junction, its lumen is directed horizontally or even slightly downward. The ileocecal valve consists of two protruding folds of tissue from the ileal side that form narrow transverse lips extending into the cecal lumen. Crescentic folds join them laterally, so that the valve itself encircles the stoma. The valve functions more like a flutter-type of mechanical valve than a true sphincter, with the lower fold assuming a more active role in the closure than the upper. The valve muscle is innervated by fibers from T-9 through L-2 (Palmer, 1963). Apparently, no resistance is presented to flow from the ileum to the cecum, but the mechanism resists the retrograde movement of the contents, since distention of the cecum closes the valve.

From the ileocecal junction the colon ascends a distance of about 20 cm to a level overlying the pole of the right kidney. At the undersurface of the right lobe of the liver the colon angulates acutely and passes medially and downward to form the hepatic flexure. The transverse portion is the longest (40–50 cm) and usually the most mobile segment of the colon. The colon is firmly attached high in the left hypochondrium at the junction (splenic flexure) between the transverse and descending segments. In its descent from the acute angle at the splenic flexure, the descending colon passes the lateral border of the left kidney and then turns somewhat medially, descending in the groove between the psoas and the quadratus lumborum muscles. The length of the descending colon is about 30 cm. The level of the adjacent pelvic brim is designated the dividing point between the descending colon and the sigmoid segment. From the pelvic brim to the beginning of the rectum at the peritoneal reflection, the colon often forms an S-shape or sigma from which it derives its name. The segment varies in length from 15 to 20 cm and usually has a mesentery permitting much mobility and variation in its course. The rectum, beginning where the pelvic mesocolon ends, curves down to the anus. The rectal lumen is fusiform, with its midportion forming the rectal ampulla. The course of the anal canal is short (3 cm) and extends to within 1 cm of the anal orifice. The external sphincter is attached posteriorly to the coccyx and anteriorly to the perineal body, and forms a collar around the anal canal with its fibers above mingling with the levator ani muscle. The internal and external sphincters are separated by the thin layer of elastic fibers and longitudinal muscle, which form an extension of the outer longitudinal muscle of the rectum. These fibers fan out below and penetrate the subcutaneous portion of the external anal sphincter and insert in the skin surrounding the anus.

The wall of the colon consists of four coats: the mucosa, submucosa, the muscular coat, and the serosa. The mucosa is covered by a single layer of tall, columnar, epithelial cells with numerous goblet cells. The surface of the mucosa is flat with closely packed epithelial crypts that form the glands of the Liberkuhn. The lamina propria, beneath the surface epithelium, contains connective tissue, blood and lymph vessels, unmyelineated nerve fibers, and round cells. Between the mucosa and submucosa is a thin muscularis mucosae. The inner circular muscle is well developed and forms a tight spiral. The outer longitudinal muscle is concentrated into thick bands (taenia coli), but a thin layer of longitudinal muscle persists in the intervening areas (Hamilton, 1946; Lineback, 1925). The muscle is divided into bundles; some of the muscle bundles

of the taenia penetrate to the circular muscle, so that the two muscles interdigitate. The longitudinal muscle becomes continuous over the rectum.

The colon derives its blood from two main sources: the superior mesenteric artery, which supplies the right side of the colon to approximately the middle of the transverse colon; and the inferior mesenteric artery, which supplies the rest of the colon to the rectum. The rectum and anal canal are supplied by branches from the internal iliac artery. In general the course of the veins parallels that of the arteries.

The main internal nerve plexuses of the colon are the myenteric (Auerbach's) plexus between the longitudinal and circular muscle coats and the submucous (Meissner's) plexus. The myenteric plexuses in man are relatively concentrated in the region of the taenia. Ganglion cells become more numerous from the proximal to the distal colon (Irwin, 1931), are densely distributed in the rectum, and extend to the internal sphincter ani. Present

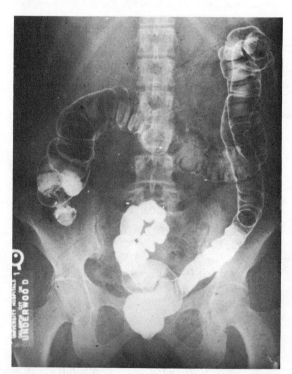

Figure 10.5 Normal colon showing segmental contractions extending throughout the sigmoid—drying activity.

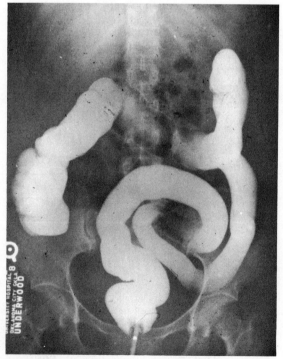

Figure 10.6 Normal colon of the same patient, showing smooth walls of sigmoid with temporary loss of haustral markings—transport activity.

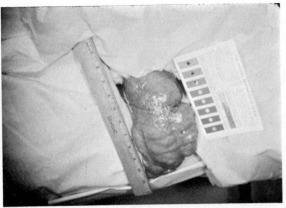 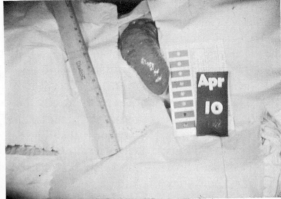

Figure 10.7 Sigmoid colon showing change from relaxed form (left) to the shortened, narrowed posture during fecal transport (right).

evidence suggests that the nerve fibers, ensheathed by Schwann cells, make contact with the surface of the smooth muscle cells to form neuromuscular junctions (Thaemert, 1963). The extrinsic nerves include sensory fibers for nice discriminations as well as both vagus and sympathetic fibers to the cecum, and to the ascending, and transverse portions of the colon. These nerves arise directly from the superior mesenteric plexus. The descending colon and proximal portion of the rectum are innervated by nerves arising from the inferior mesenteric plexus (Kuntz, 1953). The exact distribution of vagal efferent fibers in the human colon of man is uncertain but they apparently supply the ascending and transverse colon (Hollinshead, 1962). The parasympathetic innervation of the descending colon and rectum is through the sacral outflow (Kuntz, 1953). Preganglionic parasympathetic fibers traverse the visceral rami of either the second or the third and the fourth sacral nerves. The major parasympathetic innervation to the distal colon is derived from the pelvic nerves on either side, while the distal portion of the rectum receives postganglionic sympathetic fibers from the hypogastric plexus. The distal anal canal and the external sphincter are also supplied from the inferior hemorrhoidal branches of the pudendal nerve (third and fourth sacral).

Function

The colon, like the stomach, is an intermittently active organ in contrast to the continuously active heart. Associated with its periodic propulsive and eliminative activity, there occurs a transitory increase in blood flow with the engorgement of the mucosa and vigorous contractile activity of the muscular layers.

The heart, by virtue of communication among muscle fibers, is able to go on beating after its nerve connections have been cut. Organized contractile activity also persists in the colon after central nervous connections have been cut. The movements of the colon are, indeed, much more complex than those of the heart. In the first place, they are intermittent, not continuous. In the second place, more than one type of movement is required. In comparison contractions of the heart are relatively uniform. Contractions of the colon are propulsive or nonpropulsive, rhythmic or sustained. The right side is more frequently active than the left, and the motor patterns on the right side are clearly distinguishable from those on the left (Hertz & Newton, 1913).

Efforts to classify and describe movements of the colon on the basis of balloon or pressure tracings have yielded four types of contraction waves, distinguishable in terms of height, duration, and frequency (Code, Hightower, & Morlock, 1952). Such data, useful as they are, do not provide a full picture of the actual performance of the colon. X-ray studies with a barium filling from above or below afford other information but over only very short periods of time. They do, however, establish two very distinct patterns of motor activity. In one the left colon, like the right, engages in segmental non-propulsive contractions (Figure 10.5). The haustra that characterize this pattern indicate that segmental mixing contractions, like the kneading of bread, are taking place, drying the contents. Pressure in the segment closed off by the haustra is relatively high. Some textbooks say that such contractions do not occur on the left side of the colon. It is true that they are less frequent than on the right but they do occur. Exaggeration of the segmental, drying activity of the colon is associated with one form of constipation. The other form, found characteristically among depressed people, is accompanied by general hypomotility and redundancy of the colon (Kantor, 1924, 1925).

The second and distinctly different motor pat-tern of the colon is marked by shortening and narrowing on the left side without haustra or segmentation (Figures 10.6 and 10.7). This latter pattern subserves coordinated propulsive activity. During propulsion the smooth walls of the descending and sigmoid colon are contracted, but the lumen remains open, and pressure is low. Diarrhea is associated with exaggeration of this pattern.

Failure to understand the divergent motor patterns associated with the two contrasting functions of the colon, drying and propulsion, has led to confusion in the literature. Those who have focused on the interpretation of intraluminal pressure tracings have even considered the motility pattern associated with diarrhea and constipation as paradoxical (Connell, 1962). Since the pressure on the

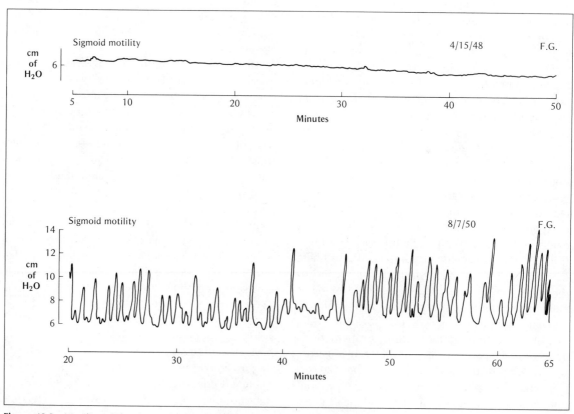

Figure 10.8 Motility of the sigmoid colon. The tracing at the top was made during a period of diarrhea. Two years later, the tracing below was obtained from the same patient when the ulcerative colitis was in remission without diarrhea. This tracing shows normal phasic activity. Redrawn from F. Kern, Jr., T. P. Almy, F. K. Abbot, and M. D. Bogdonoff, The motility of the distal colon in nonspecific ulcerative colitis. *Gastroenterology*, 1951, **19**, 492. Reproduced by permission.

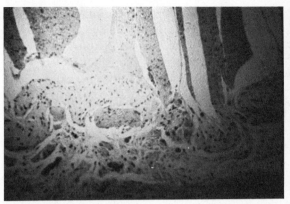
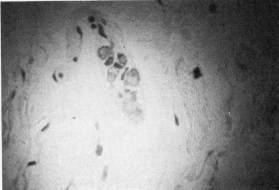

Figure 10.9 A: Auerbach's plexus between the circular and longitudinal muscle layers of the colon. B: Ganglion cells of Meissner's submucous plexus.

right is high during propulsion and is low on the left, one might conclude from pressure tracings that the narrowed, shortened left colon was not contracting.

Direct observations of the colon in unanesthetized man or animals afford further understanding of colonic movements. Four human subjects with different levels of the colon exposed and evaginated on the abdominal wall were carefully studied over periods of several weeks or months. In one who had undergone ileostomy for ulcerative colitis, the cecum and part of the ascending colon had prolapsed through an old cecostomy wound. A second patient with ulcerative colitis also had an exposed portion of cecum. The third subject's exposed segment was in the mid-transverse colon. His colostomy had been performed because of diverticulitis of the sigmoid. In the fourth subject a large segment of sigmoid had prolapsed through a left-sided colostomy. In the subject with ulcerative colitis, whose cecum and part of the ascending colon were exposed, transport consisted of coordinated movements of the circular and longitudinal muscles, which were clearly peristaltic. There were also occasional ringlike contractions of the circular muscles that simply traveled along the organ, as if stripping it. In this subject we rarely observed the nonpropulsive segmental contractions of the tinea and circular musculature that produce the haustral markings usually seen on radiographic examination. This observation corresponds well with the radi-

ologist's characteristic description of the colon involved in ulcerative colitis: "a loss of haustral markings." Segmental or haustral contractions were, however, identified in the descending and sigmoid colon of the subject, a 54-year-old man who 13 years before had undergone a sigmoid colostomy because of rectal stricture, due presumably to lymphopathia venereum. This case demonstrated clearly how differently the left colon and the right colon function in the gastrocolic reflex. During periods of fecal transport following meals, the entire distal colon shortened and narrowed and maintained this posture for a matter of 10 min or more. The wall of the colon was firm and tense, but the intraluminal pressure recorded from an inlying balloon was relatively low, and the tracing was perfectly flat, similar to that prevailing in the sigmoid during active ulcerative colitis with diarrhea (Figure 10.8). Almy, Kern, and Abbot (1950), among others, have studied healthy subjects, supplementing balloon tracings with direct observation through a sigmoidoscope. They emphasized that the characteristic posture of the left side of the colon during the gastrocolic reflex is distinctly different from that during the brief, rhythmic, high pressure, nonpropulsive, segmental contractions.

What governs the elaborately patterned activity of the colon is not really clear from the available evidence. It has been stated that the cells of the submucous (Meissner's) plexus and the myenteric (Auerbach's) plexus are mainly postganglionic, parasympathetic neurons. The former stimulate the secretion of mucus (Schoefield, 1960), while the latter are concerned with movements of the colon (Dupont & Sprinz, 1964) (Figure 10.9). Data in the literature concerning the regulation and control of the mammalian colon indicate that the muscles themselves are capable of a certain amount of coordinated movement independent of their nerve supply (Kosterlitz & Lees, 1964). An isolated strip of colon, deprived even of its intrinsic innervation, contracts rhythmically and will react to stimuli to some extent. If the plexuses of Meissner and Auerbach are left intact, however, the excised strip of colon is capable of a greater range of activity, including propulsive movements; as shown by Bayliss and Starling in 1899, it will respond to such stimuli as distention with a coordinated movement characterized by contraction above the stimulus and relaxation below.

The gastrocolic reflex has been said to occur in the totally extrinsically denervated colon (Alvarez, 1948). Whatever the limits of its versatility when entirely on its own, the colon, in order to effect coordinated purposeful movements, must possess an integrated system of afferent and efferent impulses in the plexuses of Auerbach and Meissner. There is very little in the literature, however, to suggest that sensory nerve cells may exist, or that effector postganglionic parasympathetic cells may be of different types, or that nerve cells capable of inducing inhibition are present in the myenteric plexus. Neither is there evidence that internuncial neurons are found in the plexuses. Richly ramifying connections between the ganglion cells of Meissner and Auerbach's plexuses have been demonstrated; but in view of the distance that messages must travel, it would be hard to conceive of a really effective operating system without internuncial neurons. In order to explain the coordinated activity of the isolated colon, several of the following alternative assumptions would have to be made:

1. a. Afferent fibers conduct antidromically.
   b. Sensory ganglion cells are present in myenteric plexuses.
2. a. Several types of parasympathetic cells are present in plexuses, including inhibitors.
   b. A group of chemical neuroeffectors are present.
   c. Postganglionic sympathetic cells occur in plexuses.

As one of these possibilities the afferent fibers, cut off from their cell bodies in the dorsal root ganglia, may nevertheless continue to conduct and are capable of antidromic conduction down a branch to activate a postganglionic parasympathetic cell. It is known that there are more afferent than efferent fibers connecting the central nervous system with the viscera. In fact, it appears that about 10% of all afferents that come into the cord are visceral afferents (Ruch, 1962, pp. 187–212).

The possibility of antidromic conduction gains support from the work of Toennies (1938), who demonstrated antidromic conduction in the saphenous nerve of the cat. Upon stimulating sensory fibers after their dorsal root had been cut, he was able to pick up action potentials in neighboring sensory and motor nerves. Lorente de No confirmed these findings, applying his stimulus to the trigeminal nerve whose root had been cut. In this connection, it may be significant that sensory and sympathetic neurons have their embryonic origin in the same anlage. It seems reasonable to suspect that sensory ganglion cells exist in the myenteric plexuses and, via internuncial neurons, are capable of relaying information to relatively distant levels. Encouragement for such speculations comes from two facts: (a) there are many more nerve cells in the plexuses than there are preganglionic parasympathetic fibers (Johansson & Langston, 1964); and (b) not all the cells in the plexuses contain cholinesterase (Menguy, 1964).

Interesting as it is to reflect on the capabilities of the extrinsically denervated colon, most of us still have our connections with the central nervous system. As a result, colonic behavior is all the more complicated. There is good evidence that adaptive colonic behavior in mammals is organized at several levels, segmental, brain stem, and supratentorial, each higher level taking precedence over the lower ones.

Babkin (1952) once observed that the proper way to understand the complicated functions of the mammalian autonomic nervous system is to follow its evolutionary development. If we go back to the amphioxus, the transitional form between invertebrate and vertebrate, we already find a double nerve plexus in the wall of the gut. Central connections of both sympathetic and parasympathetic types are evident in the cyclostomes (lamprey eels); but in these and other primitive vertebrates the two systems are more synergistic than opposed. A clear differentiation between the two systems appears first in the dogfish shark but there is no sacral parasympathetic outflow until we reach the amphibians. With respect to the dilemma concerning the composition of the cells in the myenteric plexus of man, it is interesting that Young (1936) has identified postganglionic sympathetic cells in the gut wall of teleost fishes. Perhaps the flexibility that they afford has been retained in man.

Psychophysiological Data

In the four fistulous subjects described above, in intact individuals with a variety of colonic disturbances, and in healthy subjects, it has been shown that the colon of man may participate in his reaction patterns to threatening events in his life situation, including those threats that arise out of problems of interpersonal adjustment. It further appears that changes involving colonic hyperfunction, at first altogether functional and transitory, may, when unduly sustained, result in structural damage and disease.

Thus it would appear from available data on the psychophysiology of the colon that at least three distinct patterns of behavior may be elicited under differing circumstances. These may be classified roughly as follows: (a) transport activity (the gastrocolic reflex) characterized by peristalsis on the right side and a sustained shortening and narrowing on the left; (b) desiccating activity (the haustral pattern) characterized by nonpropulsive segmental contractions; and (c) inactivity characterized by muscular relaxation, dilatation, and redundancy of the entire colon.

Typically, in association with sudden fright, or in susceptible individuals during emotional conflicts characterized by an attitude of petulant hostility, exaggerated transport activity becomes manifest. There is vigorous peristalsis on the right side and sustained contraction of longitudinal and circular muscles on the left, so that the lower portion of the colon assumes the posture of a stiff tube, shortened and narrowed. Such accentuated transport activity tends to preclude sufficient desiccating behavior, so that watery diarrhea results.

The colons of subjects with ulcerative colitis were found to be in the posture of the gastrocolic reflex continuously. Whether or not ulcerative colitis is the result of sustained maintenance of this posture has not been established. It has been shown, however, that the hyperfunctioning colon is hyperemic and the mucous membrane fragile, so that small bleeding points may appear in response to minor traumata. Enhanced transport activity is associated with relatively large concentrations of lysozyme in the colonic mucus.

The relationship of colonic hyperfunction to mucosal engorgement and fragility was explored in detail in 19 patients with ulcerative colitis and correlated with attitudes and reactions in response to day-to-day life situations. The subjects were found to be characteristically outwardly calm, superficially peaceful, and more than usually dependent. Beneath the calm exterior it became apparent that there was intense hostility, resentment, and guilt. Such feelings, when sustained and unrelieved, were associated with hyperfunction of the colon, with increased transport activity, increased vascularity, turgescence, and small hemorrhagic lesions, as well as with an increase in the concentration of lysozyme in the colonic mucus.

Exaggerated desiccating activity, on the other hand, characterized by persistent nonpropulsive segmental contractions, resulted in delayed transport and small, hard, dry stools and was usually accompanied by constipation. Such a reaction pattern has been encountered in association with mild depression and attitudes of grim persistence. A study of such individuals revealed that most of them were effectively engaged in work, or in assuming responsibility, showing no conspicuous outward evidence of strain. They often acknowledged, however, that their zest for the task, though effectively performed, had waned. They often actually complained of being depressed, of feeling discouraged and discontented, but were grimly determined to keep going. Often such individuals complained of feeling weary, all-in, tense, bored, blue, melancholy, down-in-the-dumps, or in need of a vacation. They commonly stated that they had "to drag themselves around," that they were short-tempered, irritable, or brusque. Complaints of headache, stiffness, and pain the back and neck were common; sexual interest and activity were reduced, concentration and attention span were short; and often memory was defective. In those who failed to complain or show overt evidence of fatigue or discouragement, it was usually possible, in skillfully conducted interviews, to elicit evidence of a basic attitude of sadness and pessimism. In the constipated subject there was usually an increase in contractile activity of skeletal muscles, as well as in the colon. This was true of the muscles in the neck, back, and extremities; and especially of the external rectal sphincter. Often there were tender hemorrhoids or fissure-in-ano, so that there was a fear of pain on defecation.

The third type of altered colonic function associated with emotional stress was manifested by hypotonia of the colon with reduction in all motor activity. Characteristic of megacolon and of post-operative ileus, this pattern of colonic behavior is also frequently seen among seriously depressed individuals, and usually is accompanied by obstinate constipation and striking psychomotor retardation.

The preceding discussion of the psychophysiology of the gastrointestinal tract has emphasized the importance of training in many fields for the reader and investigator of these complex phenomena. Knowledge of physiology, anatomy, neurosciences, behavioral sciences, and clinical biochemistry must combine to bring about an understanding of the interactions of this vital organic system. It is hoped that these challenges excite rather than discourage students to further study of the gastrointestinal system, one of the major crossroads of the human being.

REFERENCES

ABBOT, F. K., MACK, M., & WOLF, S. The relation of sustained contraction of the duodenum to nausea and vomiting. *Gastroenterology,* 1952, **20,** 238–248.

ALMY, T. P., KERN, F., & ABBOT, F. K. Constipation and diarrhea as reactions to life stress. *Proceedings of the Association for Research in Nervous and Mental Disease,* 1950, **29,** 724–731.

ALVAREZ, W. C., & FREEDLANDER, B. L. The rate of progress of food residues through the bowel. *Journal of the American Medical Association,* 1924, **83,** 576–580.

ANAND, B. K. Influence of the internal environment of the nervous regulation of alimentary behavior. In M. A. B. BRAZIER (Ed.), *Brain and behavior.* Vol. 2. *The internal environment and alimentary behavior.* Washington, D.C.: American Institute of Biological Sciences, 1962.

ANAND, B. K., & DUA, S. Effect of electrical stimulation of the limbic system ("visceral brain") on gastric secretion and motility. *Indian Journal of Medical Research,* 1956, **44,** 125–130.

BABKIN, B. P. Quoted by J. A. C. NICOL, Autonomic nervous systems in lower chordates. *Biological Review,* 1952, **27,** 1–49.

BARRETT, N. R. The lower esophagus lined by columnar epithelium. In F. A. JONES (Ed.), *Modern trends in gastroenterology* (2nd series). New York: Hoeber, 1958.

BAYLISS, W. M., & STARLING, E. H. The movements and innervation of the small intestine. *Journal of Physiology, London,* 1899, **24,** 99–143.

BEAUMONT, W. *Experiments and observations on the gastric juice and the physiology of digestion.* Plattsburg, N.Y.: F. P. Allen, 1833.

BERNARD, C. *Leçons sur les propriétés physiologiques et les altérations pathologiques des liquides de l'organisme.* Paris: Bailleurs, 1859.

BERTALANFFY, F. O. Cell renewal in the gastrointestinal tract of man. *Gastroenterology,* 1962, **43,** 472–475.

BOBA, A., STEIN, A. A., NAKAMURA, Y., & POWERS, S. R., Jr. A study of the relationships between alcoholic intoxication, vomiting, and acute hemorrhagic pancreatitis. *Surgical Forum,* 1957, **8,** 251–254.

BOGDONOFF, M. D., BOGDONOFF, M. M., & WOLF, S. Studies on salivary function in man: Variations in secretory rates as part of the adaptive pattern. *Journal of Psychosomatic Research,* 1961, **5,** 170–174.

BROBECK, J. R., TEPPERMAN, J., & LONG, C. N. H. Experimental hypothalamic hyperphagia in the albino rat. *Yale Journal of Biology and Medicine,* 1942, **15,** 831–853.

BRODY, D. A., & QUIGLEY, J. P. Registration of digestive tract intralumen pressure. In *Methods in medical research.* Vol. 4. Chicago: Year Book Medical Publishers, 1951.

BROWN, A. L., Jr. Microvilli of the human jejunal epithelial cell. *Journal of Cellular Biology,* 1962, **12,** 623–627.

BURNETT, F. L. The intestinal rate and the form of the feces. *American Journal of Roentgenology,* 1923, **10,** 599–604.

BYNUM, T. E., & JACOBSON, E. D. Blood flow and gastrointestinal function. *Gastroenterology,* 1971, **60,** 325–335.

CALVERT, D. N., & BRODY, T. M. Role of sympathetic nervous system in CCl_4 hepatotoxicity. *American Journal of Physiology,* 1960, **198,** 669–676.

CANNON, W. B. The motor activities of the stomach and small intestine after splanchnic and vagus section. *American Journal of Physiology,* 1907, **17,** 429–442.

CANNON, W. B. *Bodily changes in pain, hunger, fear and rage.* (2nd ed.) New York: Appleton-Century-Crofts, 1929.

CANNON, W. B., & LIEB, C. W.: The receptive relaxation of the stomach. *American Journal of Physiology,* 1911, **29,** 267–273.

CANNON, W. B., & WASHBURN, A. L. An explanation of hunger. *American Journal of Physiology,* 1912, **29,** 441–454.

CANTELLI, T. Cellular renewal of the epithelium of the esophageal mucosa in the mouse. *Gazzetta Internazionale di Medicina e Chirurgia, Roma,* 1962, **67,** 1678–1689.

CHAPMAN, M. L., LAWRENCE, W. J., & JANOWITZ, H. D. The reabsorption of acid in the human stomach: The effect of gastric corpus ulcers. Presented at the American Gastroenterology Association Meeting, 1967.

CODE, C. F., HIGHTOWER, N. C., Jr., & MORLOCK, C. G. Motility of the alimentary canal in man. *American Journal of Medicine,* 1952, **13,** 328–351.

CONN, H. J. *The history of staining.* Geneva, N.Y.: Biological Stain Commission, 1933.

CONNELL, A. M. The motility of the pelvic colon: II. Paradoxical motility in diarrhea and constipation. *Gut,* 1962, **3,** 342–348.

CONNELL, A. M., & ROWLANDS, E. N. Wireless telemetering from the digestive tract. *Gut,* 1960, **1,** 266–272.

DAVENPORT, H. W. *Physiology of the digestive tract.* (2nd ed.) Chicago: Year Book Medical Publishers, 1966.

DAVEY, L. M., KAADA, B. R., & FULTON, J. F. Effects on gastric secretion of frontal lobe stimulation. *Report of the Association for Research on Nervous and Mental Disease,* 1950, **29,** 617–627.

DREILING, D. A., JANOWITZ, H. D., & PERRIER, C. V. *Pancreatic inflammatory disease.* New York: Hoeber, 1964.

DUPONT, J., & SPRINZ, H. The neurovegetative periphery of the gut: A revaluation with conventional technics in the light of modern knowledge. *American Journal of Anatomy,* 1964, **114,** 393–402

EDKINS, J. S. The chemical mechanism of gastric secretion. *Journal of Physiology, London,* 1906, **34,** 133–144.

EDWARDS, D. A. W. (Ed.) Seventh Annual Conference of the Society for Psychosomatic Research. *Journal of Psychosomatic Research,* 1964, **8,** 167–352.

EICHHOLZ, A., & CRANE, R. K. Studies on the organization of the brush border in intestinal epithelial cells: I. Tris disruption of isolated hamster brush borders and density gradient separation of fractions. *Journal of Cell Biology,* 1965, **26,** 687–691.

ELIASSON, S. G. Central control of digestive function. In H. W. MAGOUN (Ed.), *Handbook of Physiology,* Section 1.

Neurophysiology. Vol. 2. Washington, D.C.: American Physiological Society, 1960.

ENGLERT, E., Jr., & CHIU, V. S. W. Quantitative analysis of human biliary evacuation with a radioisotopic technique. *Gastroenterology,* 1966, **50,** 506–518.

EVETT, R. D., HIGGINS, J. A., & BROWN, A. L., Jr. The fine structure of normal mucosa in human gall bladder. *Gastroenterology,* 1964, **47,** 49–60.

FARR, C. B., & LUEDERS, C. W. Gastric secretory functions in the psychoses. *Archives of Neurology and Psychiatry,* 1923, **10,** 548–561.

FARRAR, J. T., & ZFASS, A. M. Small intestinal motility. *Gastroenterology,* 1967, **52,** 1019–1037.

FAULKNER, W. B. Effect of emotions upon diaphragmatic functions: Observations in 5 patients. *Psychosomatic Medicine,* 1941, **3,** 187–189.

FELDMAN, S., & BIRNBAUM, D. The effect of brain stimulation on gastric secretion: An experimental study on unanesthetized dogs with permanently implanted electrodes. *Israel Journal of Medical Science,* 1965, **1,** 415–422.

FREEDMAN, J. Roentgen studies of the effects on the small intestine from emotional disturbances. *American Journal of Roentgenology,* 1954, **22,** 367–379.

FRENCH, J. D., LONGMIRE, R. L., PORTER, R. W., & MOVIUS, H. F. Extravagal influences on gastric hydrochloric acid secretion induced by stress stimuli. *Surgery, St. Louis,* 1953, **34,** 621–632.

GAUER, O. H., & GIENAPP, E. A. Miniature pressure-recording device. *Science,* 1950, **112,** 404–405.

GLASS, G. B. J., BOYD, L. J., GELLIN, G. A., & STEPHENSON, L. Uptake of radioactive vitamin B_{12} by the liver in humans: Test for measurement of intestinal absorption of vitamin B_{12} and intrinsic factor activity. *Archives of Biochemistry and Biophysics,* 1954, **51,** 251–257.

GORDON, O. L., & CHERNYA, Y. M. Physiology of the gastric secretion in man: Studies on patients with gastric fistula and artificial esophagus. *Klinicheskaya meditsina* (No. 12), 1940, **18,** 63–71.

GRACE, W. J., WOLF, S., & WOLFF, H. G. *The human colon: An experimental study based on direct observation of four fistulous subjects.* New York: Hoeber, 1951.

GRAY, G. M., & INGELFINGER, F. J. Intestinal absorption of sucrose in man: Interrelation of hydrolysis and monosaccharide product absorption. *Journal of Clinical Investigation,* 1966, **45,** 388–398.

GREGORY, R. A., & TRACY, H. J. The preparation and properties of gastrin. *Journal of Physiology,* 1961, **156,** 523–543.

GREGORY, R. A., & TRACY, H. J. Constitution and properties of two gastrins extracted from hog antral mucosa. *Gut,* 1964, **5,** 103–117.

GROSSMAN, M. I. Nervous and hormonal regulation of pancreatic secretion in the exocrine pancreas. In A. V. A. de REUCK & M. P. CAMERON (Eds.), *The exocrine pancreas: Ciba Foundation Symposium,* Boston: Little, Brown, 1961.

GROSSMAN, M. I. Gastrin: Reminiscence and speculation.

American Journal of Digestive Diseases, 1966, **11,** 90–95.

GROSSMAN, M. I. Some aspects of gastric secretion. *Gastroenterology,* 1967, **52,** 882–892.

HAMILTON, G. F. The longitudinal muscle coat of the human colon. *Journal of Anatomy,* 1946, **80,** 230 (abst.)

HEINLE, R. W., WELCH, A. D., SCHARF, V., MEACHAM, G. C., & PRUSOFF, W. H. Studies of excretion (and absorption) of Co⁶⁰-labeled vitamin B_{12} in pernicious anemia. *Transactions of the Association of American Physicians,* 1952, **65,** 214–222.

HELMS, C. H., & MEREDITH, J. H. Concerning neurovascular factors in pancreatitis. *American Surgeon,* 1961, **27,** 665–670.

HERTZ, A. F., & NEWTON, A. The normal movements of the colon in man. *Journal of Physiology,* 1913, **47,** 57–65.

HIGHTOWER, N. C., Jr. Motility of the alimentary canal of man. In J. A. RIDER & H. C. MOELLER (Eds.), *Disturbances in gastrointestinal motility.* Springfield, Ill.: Charles C Thomas, 1959.

HOLLINSHEAD, W. H. Embryology and surgical anatomy of the colon. *Diseases of the Colon and Rectum,* 1962, **5,** 23–27.

HOPKINS, P., & EDWARDS, D. A. W. (Eds.) Seventh Annual Conference of the Society for Psychosomatic Research. *Journal of Psychosomatic Research,* 1964, 8, 167–352.

HORVATH, S. M., KELLY, T., FOLK, G. E., Jr., & HUTT, B. K. Measurement of blood volumes in the splanchnic bed of the dog. *American Journal of Physiology,* 1957, **189,** 573–575.

INGELFINGER, R. J. Esophageal motility. *Physiological Reviews,* 1958, **38,** 533–584.

IRWIN, D. A. The anatomy of Auerbach's plexus. *American Journal of Anatomy,* 1931, **49,** 141–166.

JACOBSON, E. D. Spastic esophagus and mucous colitis: Etiology and treatment by progressive relaxation. *Archives of Internal Medicine,* 1927, **39,** 433–445.

JACOBSON, E. D. Recent advances in the gastrointestinal circulation and related areas: Comments on a symposium on gastrointestinal circulation. *Gastroenterology,* 1967, **52,** 332–337.

JANOWITZ, H. D., & DREILING, D. A. The pancreatic secretion of fluid and electrolytes. In A. V. S. de REUCK & M. P. CAMERON (Eds.), *The exocrine pancreas: Ciba Foundation Symposium.* Boston: Little, Brown, 1961.

JOHANSSON, B., & LANGSTON, J. B. Reflex influence of mesenteric afferents, on renal, intestinal and muscle blood flow and on intestinal motility. *Acta Physiologica Scandinavica,* 1964, **61,** 400–412.

KANTOR, J. L. A clinical study of some common anatomical abnormalities of the colon: I. Redundant colon. *American Journal of Roentgenology,* 1924, **12,** 414–430.

KANTOR, J. L. A clinical study of some common anatomical abnormalities of the colon: II. The low cecum. *American Journal of Roentgenology,* 1925, **14,** 207–215.

KERN, F., Jr., ALMY, T. P., ABBOT, F. K., & BOGDONOFF, M. D. The motility of the distal colon in nonspecific ulcerative colitis. *Gastroenterology,* 1951, **19,** 492.

KÖHLER, R. Evacuation of the normal large intestine. *Acta Radiologica,* 1964, **2,** 9–16.

KOSTERLITZ, H. W., & LEES, G. M. Pharmacological analysis of intrinsic intestinal reflexes. *Pharmacological Reviews,* 1964, **16,** 301–339.

KRAMER, P., & INGELFINGER, F. J. Motility of the human esophagus in control subjects and in patients with esophageal disorders: II. Cardiospasm, a generalized disorder of esophageal motility. *American Journal of Medicine,* 1949, **7,** 168–179.

KRONECKER, H., & NICOLAIDES, R. Ueber die Erregung der Gefassnervencentren durch Summation elektrischer Reize. *Archiv für Physiologie, Leipzig,* 1883, 27–42.

KUKROL, J. C., ADAMS, A. P., & PRESTON, F. W. Protein producing capacity of the human exocrine pancreas. *Annals of Surgery,* 1965, **162,** 63–73.

KUNTZ, A. *The autonomic nervous system.* (4th ed.) Philadelphia: Lea & Febiger, 1953.

LEEVY, C. M. Clinical aspects of the hepatic circulation. *Gastroenterology,* 1965, **48,** 790–804.

LERCHE, W. *The esophagus and pharynx in action.* Springfield, Ill.: Charles C Thomas, 1950.

LINEBACK, P. E. Studies on the musculature of the human colon, with special reference to the taeniae. *American Journal of Anatomy,* 1925, **36,** 357–383.

LONG, D. M., LEONARD, A. S., CHOU, S. N., & FRENCH, L. A. Hypothalamus and gastric ulceration: I. Gastric effects of hypothalamic lesions. *Archives of Neurology,* 1962, **7,** 167–175.

LONG, D. M., LEONARD, A. S., STORY, J., & FRENCH, L. A. Hypothalamus and gastric ulceration: II. Production of gastrointestinal ulceration by chronic hypothalamic stimulation. *Archives of Neurology,* 1962, **7,** 176–183.

LUND, W. S. A study of the cricopharyngeal sphincter in man and in the dog. *Annals of the Royal College of Surgeons of England,* 1965, **37,** 225–246.

MAEVSKAYA, N. C. Changes in the gastrointestinal secretion. (Russian.) *X S'ezd Vsesoyuznogo Fiziologiches-Kogo Obshchestva Imeni I. P. Pavlova,* 1964, **11,** 42.

MALLET-GUY, P., FEROLDI, J., & REBOUL, E. Recherches expérimentales sur la pathogénie des pancreatites aigues: Leur provocation par l'excitation du nerf splanchnique gauche. *Lyon Chirurgical,* 1949, **44,** 281–301.

MASON, G. R., EIGENBRODT, E. H., OBERHELMAN, H. A., Jr., & NELSEN, T. S. Gastric hypersecretion following pancreatitis. *Surgery, St. Louis,* 1963, **54,** 604–608.

MCILRATH, D. C., KENNEDY, J. A., & HALLENBECK, G. A. Relationship between atrophy of the pancreas and gastric secretion: An experimental study. *American Journal of Digestive Diseases,* 1963, **8,** 623–631.

MCLEAN, P. The limbic system ("visceral brain") in relation to central gray and reticulum of the brain stem. *Psychosomatic Medicine,* 1955, **17,** 355–366.

MELTZER, S.   Die Irradiationen des Schlickcentrums und ihre allgemeine Bedeutung. *Archiv für Physiologie, Leipzig.* 1883, 209-238.

MENGUY, R.   Motor function of the alimentary tract. *Annual Review of Physiology,* 1964, **26,** 227-248.

MIKULICZ, J. von   Beitrage zur Physiologie der Speiserohre und der Cardia. *Mitteilungen Grenzgebieten Medizin und Chirurgie,* 1903, **12,** 569-601.

MULINOS, M. G.   The value of selective drugs in the treatment of constipation. *Review of Gastroenterology,* 1935, **2,** 292-301.

NAGLER, R., & SPIRO, H. M.   Persistent gastroesophageal reflux induced during prolonged gastric intubation. *New England Journal of Medicine,* 1963, **269,** 495-500.

NETTER, F. H.   Digestive system: Part III. Liver, biliary tract and pancreas. *The Ciba collection of medical illustrations:* Vol. 3. Summit, N.J.: Ciba Pharmaceutical Co., 1957.

NETTER, F. H.   Digestive system: Part I. Upper digestive tract. *The Ciba collection of medical illustrations:* Vol. 3. Summit, N.J.: Ciba Pharmaceutical Co., 1959.

OVERTON, J., EICHHOLZ, A., & CRANE, R. K.   Studies on the organization of the brush border in intestinal epithelial cells: II. Fine structure of fractions of tris-disrupted hamster brush borders. *Journal of Cell Biology,* 1965, **26,** 693-706.

PAGE, I. H., & McCUBBIN, J. W.   The variable arterial pressure responses to serotonin in laboratory animals and man. *Circulation Research,* 1953, **1,** 354-362.

PALMER, E. D.   *Clinical gastroenterology.* (2nd ed.) New York: Hoeber, 1963.

PASTEUR, L.   Quoted by DUBOS, R. *Mirage of health.* New York: Harper & Row, 1959.

PATTERSON, T. L., & SANDWEISS, D. J.   Relationship between gastroduodenal motility phases and symptoms associated with duodenal ulcer in the human. *American Journal of Digestive Diseases,* 1942, **9,** 375-381.

PAVLOV, I.   *The work of the digestive glands.* Translated by W. H. Thompson. London: Griffin, 1910.

PEARL, J. W., RITCHIE, W. P., GILSDORF, R. B., DELANEY, S. P., & LEONARD, A. S.   Hypothalamus stimulation and feline gastric mucosal cellular populations: Factors in the etiology of the stress ulcer. *Journal of the American Medical Association,* 1966, **195,** 281-284.

REICHSMAN, F., ENGLE, G. L., & SEGAL, H. L.   Behavior and gastric secretion: The study of an infant with a gastric fistula. *Psychosomatic Medicine,* 1955, **17,** 481. (Abstract)

RICHARDS, C. H., WOLF, S., & WOLFF, H. G.   The measurement and recordings of gastroduodenal blood flow in man by means of a thermal gradientometer. *Journal of Clinical Investigation,* 1942, **21,** 551-558.

RICHET, C.   Des propriétés chimiques et physiologiques du suc gastrique chez l'homme et les animaux. Appendix A. *Journal d'Anatomie et Physiologie, Paris,* 1878, **14,** 170-333.

RICHIE, J. A., ARDRAN, G. M., & TRUELOVE, S. C.   Motor activity of the sigmoid colon in humans: A combined study by intraluminal pressure recording and cineradiography. *Gastroenterology,* 1962, **43,** 642-668.

ROY-CHOUDHURY, D., COOK, W. T., TAN, D. R., BANWELL, J. G., & SMITS, B. J.   Jejunal biopsy: Criteria and significance. *Scandinavian Journal of Gastroenterology,* 1966, **1,** 57-74.

RUCH, T. C.   Discussion of "the visceral afferents" by C. B. B. Dowman. In M. A. B. BRAZIER (Ed.), *Brain and behavior.* Vol. 2. *The internal environment and alimentary behavior.* Washington, D.C.: American Institute of Biological Sciences, 1962.

SAUNDERS, S. J., & ISSELBACHER, K. H.   Intestinal absorption of amino acids. *Gastroenterology,* 1966, **50,** 586-595.

SCHINDLER, R.   Mechanism and treatment of cardiospasm. *Münchener medizinische Wochenschrift,* 1926, **73,** 1612.

SCHOEFIELD, G. C.   Experimental studies on the innervation of the mucous membrane of the gut. *Brain,* 1960, **83,** 490-514.

SEMBA, T., NODA, H., & FUJI, K.   On splanchnic motor responses of stomach movements produced by stimulation of the medulla oblongata and spinal cord. *Japanese Journal of Physiology,* 1963, **13,** 466-478.

SMITH, G. P., & BROOKS, F. P.   Hypothalamic control of gastric secretion. *Gastroenterology,* 1967, **52,** 727-729. (Editorial.)

SUDAKOV, K. V., & MNASIN, L. S.   Characteristics of the mechanism of ascending activation of the cerebral cortex during mechanical irritation of the stomach. *Bulletin of Experimental Biology and Medicine, USSR,* 1965, **59,** 354-357.

THAEMERT, J. C.   The ultrastructure and disposition of vesiculated nerve processes in smooth muscle. *Journal of Cell Biology,* 1963, **16,** 361-377.

THIEDING, F.   Cardiospasm, atony and idiopathic dilatation of esophagus. *Bruns' Beiträge zur klinischen Chirurgie,* 1921, **121,** 237.

THOMAS, J. E.   *External secretion of the pancreas.* Springfield, Ill.: Charles C Thomas, 1950.

TOENNIES, J. G.   Reflex discharge from spinal cord over dorsal roots. *Journal of Neurophysiology,* 1938, **1,** 378-390.

TRIER, J. S.   Studies on small intestinal crypt epithelium: I. The fine structure of the crypt epithelium of the proximal small intestine of fasting humans. *Journal of Cell Biology,* 1963, **18,** 599-620.

TRIER, J. S.   Studies on small intestinal crypt epithelium: II. Evidence for mechanisms of secretory activity by undifferentiated crypt cells of the human small intestine. *Gastroenterology,* 1964, **47,** 480-495.

TRIER, J. S., & RUBIN, C. E.   Electromicroscopy of the small intestine: A review. *Gastroenterology,* 1965, **49,** 574-603.

TRUELOVE, S. C.   Movements of the large intestine. *Physiological Reviews,* 1966, **46,** 457-512.

VAN DE KAMER, J. H., TEN BOKKEL HUININK, D., & WEYERS, H. A. Rapid method for the determination of fat in feces. *Journal of Biological Chemistry,* 1949, **177,** 347–355.

VIAL, J. Personal communication.

WATERMAN, T. H. (Ed.) *The physiology of crustacea.* Vol. 2. *Sense organs, integration and behavior.* New York: Academic, 1960.

WEISS, E. J. Psychogenic peripheral basospasm: Case report. *Psychosomatic Medicine,* 1946, **8,** 274–278.

WELLS, C., TINCKLER, L., & RAWLINSON, K. Postoperative gastrointestinal motility. *Lancet,* 1964, **1,** 4–10.

WELSH, J. D., ROHRER, G. V., & PORTER, M. G. The Baker-Hughes gastrointestinal biopsy tube. *American Journal of Digestive Diseases,* 1966, **11,** 559–563.

WINKELSTEIN, A. Psychogenic factors in cardiospasm. *American Journal of Surgery,* 1931, **12,** 135–138.

WILSON, T. H. *Intestinal absorption.* Philadelphia: Saunders, 1962.

WISEMAN, G. *Absorption from the intestine.* New York: Academic, 1964.

WOLF, S. Effects of suggestion and conditioning on the action of chemical agents in human subjects: The pharmacology of placebos. *Journal of Clinical Investigation,* 1950, **29,** 100–109.

WOLF, S. A note on the cause of disease. *American Journal of Medicine,* 1954, **16,** 769. (Editorial.)

WOLF, S. *The stomach.* New York: Oxford University Press, 1965.

WOLF, S., & ALMY, T. P. Experimental observations on cardiospasm in man. *Gastroenterology,* 1949, **13,** 401–421.

WOLF, S., & WOLFF, H. G. *Human gastric function: An experimental study of a man and his stomach.* (2nd ed.) New York: Oxford University Press, 1947.

YOUMANS, W. B. Neural regulation of gastric and intestinal motility. *American Journal of Medicine,* 1952, **13,** 209–226.

YOUNG, C. M. Evolution and adaptation in the digestive system of the metazoa. *Biological Review,* 1936, **12,** 87–111.

ZAVODSKAYA, I. S. Action of central cholinolytics on the trophic processes in the gastric wall. *Medycyna,* 1960, **3,** 33–38.

ZETTERQVIST, H. *The ultrastructural organization of the columnar absorbing cells of the mouse jejunum.* (Monogr.) Stockholm, Sweden: Aktiebolaget Godvil, 1956.

ZIEVE, L., VOGEL, W. S., & KELLY, W. D. Species difference in pancreatic lipolytic and amylolytic enzymes. *Journal of Applied Physiology,* 1963, **18,** 77–81.

ZOLLINGER, R. M., & ELLISON, E. H. Primary peptic ulcerations of jejunum associated with islet cell tumors of the pancreas. *Annals of Surgery,* 1955, **142,** 709–728.

C. G. Gunn, Stewart Wolf, R. T. Block, and R. J. Person

PSYCHOPHYSIOLOGY OF THE CARDIOVASCULAR SYSTEM

11

For centuries man has perceived in himself, in his fellow man, and in animals, such physiological changes as pilo-erection, blushing, paresthesias, or altered respiration rate, heart rate, and pupil size. He has long associated these changes with emotionally significant experiences. Study of the relationship of these and other biological responses to meaningful events has been hampered by the reluctance or inability of investigators to acquire the necessary methodologic versatility to cross interdisciplinary lines. Recently, however, multidisciplinary teams have developed the interdisciplinary capabilities and aggressiveness necessary for such studies. This chapter will attempt to encourage the student, the investigator, and the clinician toward an interdisciplinary approach, so that they may consider the interrelationships of the nervous system to the cardiovascular system on several levels of description: the physical, chemical, anatomical, physiological, psychological (behavioral), and medical (pathological).

The reader is referred to such a multidisciplinary approach concerning cardio-somatic relationships pertinent to psychophysiology in a review by Obrist and his colleagues (1970).

The nervous system, by acting directly on the heart and blood vessels, produces rapid and powerful shifts in the circulation of the blood and causes major changes in regional nutrition (Folkow, 1960). Direct neural control of effector cells in the heart and blood vessels is faster, more potent, and more selective than that achieved indirectly through stimulation of glands and other tissues and the consequent elaboration of blood-borne chemical substances such as catechols, peptides, and prostaglandins. The central nervous system gains both versatility and selectivity from the availability of several effector systems with different latencies. The integrated response is influenced by sensory and chemical feedback, prior memory, and the evaluation of need. These integrative characteristics may be programmed in such a way that there is little or no representation on the conscious level. Patterned cardiovascular reactions involving the regulation of the heart beat and peripheral vasculature may be elicited in anticipation of running or playing, or among blood donors unaware of any fear or anxiety. A sharp rise in arterial pressure has been noted before the needle was inserted (Wolf et al., 1955). Thus the cardiovascular system of an individual may respond in a major way to life situations without the subject's awareness of any significant emotional relationships. One of the tasks of the psychophysiologist is to study the psychological and neurophysiological mechanisms of this autonomic life-style programming. The physician of the future will then be challenged to work with the psychophysiologist to alter those programs that lead to inappropriate psychophysiological responses or threaten an individual's well-being.

METHODOLOGY OF CARDIOVASCULAR PHYSIOLOGY

Heart Rate and Rhythm

The electrocardiogram (EKG) is a useful means of assessing the heart rate, rhythm, and the status of cardiac muscle (myocardium). Numerous textbooks (Dubin, 1970; Goldman, 1970; Lipman & Massie, 1965) cover the fundamentals of electrocardiography. We shall consider only its use in psychophysiology. Although the old problems of maintaining electrode skin contact, eliminating muscle artifacts, and occasional malfunctioning of either amplifier or tape recorder remain, it is now possible in psychophysiological studies either to escape the confines of the laboratory or to work

more conveniently within it. Miniature portable devices for continuous electrocardiographic recording have made it possible to record electrocardiograms outside the bounds of the laboratory as an individual goes about his daily activities. This independence has greatly enhanced its capabilities as an investigative tool in relating cardiac events to human behavior, especially when studying cardiac arrhythmias and events that possibly alter the blood flow to the heart muscle itself.

Even greater reduction of the amount of paraphernalia directly attached to the patient can be achieved by the use of wireless telemetry (Mackay, 1963 pp. 45–58). In this system the patient need not wear an actual recorder but only an FM or AM transmitter capable of sending signals to a recorder located at a distant site. Most portable recorders now commercially available weigh 2–5 lb, as opposed to telemetry transmitters, which weigh as little as 4 oz. The artifact introduced by the presence of gadgetry might be expected to be less with wireless telemetry than with recorders. When telemetry is used, however, the strength of the transmitter limits the operational area. The telemetry system is also susceptible to electrical interference of various sorts. The portable recorder is therefore useful if the area of operation exceeds the range of telemetry transmitters, or in areas of high interference to FM transmission. On the other hand, telemetry is more useful in studies performed in restricted geographical areas free of interference from radio signals because the patient is less burdened by equipment.

New and valuable techniques of data analysis have been developed to analyze the huge mass of data obtainable by means of the continuous EKG recording. Several reviews of data acquisition and analysis are available and should be consulted (Caceres, 1965; Slater, 1963; Zimmer, 1966). Some of the methods will be touched upon in this chapter.

The cardiotachometer provides a beat-to-beat measure of the heart rate, usually by recording the distance between R waves of the electrocardiogram. It is useful whenever a continuous rate measure is desired, as in operant conditioning of the heart rate. It enables one to correlate changes in rate with other variables. Rhythm patterns may also be studied with a cardiotachometer but it gives no direct information about arrhythmias, sites of the cardiac pacemaker, or morphological changes in the electrocardiogram.

Histograms of measured distances on electrocardiographic tracings, particularly the R–R interval, make it possible to scan for and measure arrhythmias rapidly (Simborg, Ross, Lewis, & Shepard, 1966). Present techniques using automatic data processing equipment allow 1 hr of recording to be processed in 2–4 min. The end product is a graph showing numbers of intervals on the ordinate and interval length on the abscissa. To date, the histogram has been used to study patterns of atrial fibrillation and sinus rhythm and to evaluate quantitatively the effect of drugs on cardiac rhythms (Horan & Kistler, 1961; Simborg et al., 1966). Histograms of R–R intervals are useful to study variability of the heart rate during different sleep stages in people with and without heart disease (personal observations).

Two rapid-display techniques offer the trained electrocardiographer ways to analyze quickly and quite accurately. One involves playing back taped electrocardiograms at rapid speeds, while the QRS complexes, displayed on an oscilloscope, are rapidly superimposed on one another. The rate is also continuously displayed during the playback. This technique is most useful in screening for changes in the morphology of QRS, ST segment, and T-waves, and also for ventricular arrhythmias. Other techniques involve the simultaneous display of entire electrocardiographic complexes by various means (Webb, 1963). By displaying as many as 60 complexes at one time, these methods permit quick analysis of large amounts of data concerning changes in rate, rhythm, and morphology, but they are probably not so rapid as the superimposition technique mentioned above.

Specific applications of the computer to psychophysiological data, including heart rate and blood pressure, are reviewed in a recent monograph (Zimmer, 1966). Certainly, computer programs for electrocardiogram analysis appear to hold great promise for the future (Sheffield, Holt, Lester, Conroy, & Reeves, 1969). Since computer programs can be patterned to various degrees of complexity and completeness, information about rate, rhythm, and electrocardiographic morphology may be obtained. Its broad versatility and capacity for huge amounts of data make its potential virtually unlimited in continuous recordings of psychophysiological experiments (Whiteman et al., 1967). However, such an operation requires computers and people trained in computer electrocardiogram applications, including both electrocardiographers and statisticians. This usually limits its usefulness to larger centers, unless data transmission to time-sharing computer centers is available to investigators.

Blood Flow and Pressure

The measurement of blood flow in the intact human continues to plague the researcher and the clinician. Although plethysmography and skin temperature techniques have been refined in recent years, they provide only approximate, although valuable, information on changes in flow. Recent electromagnetic techniques allow probes to be placed around arteries after surgical implantation, a technique not generally feasible in human psychophysiology. Newer ultrasonic flowmeters utilize the Doppler effect (Franklin et al., 1966) to reflect blood flow in superficial arteries. These noninvasive sensors can be applied without perforating the skin. Absolute quantification is not possible with such an external device, but changes in blood velocity and flow are nevertheless discernible without seriously restricting the patient's movements.

Cardiac output (Stead, Warren, Merrill, & Brannon, 1945) and cerebral blood flow (Kety, 1960, pp. 1751–1760) have been extensively studied by the Fick principle of analyzing arterial-venous differences of oxygen, injected dyes, carbon monoxide, nitrous oxide, and other substances not metabolized by the body. Because such elaborate techniques expose the subject to considerable discomfort and some hazard, they have a very limited application in general psychophysiological studies but have provided important information in carefully controlled situations.

Techniques involving external monitoring of injected radioisotopes are used to record cardiac output and blood flow in various organs, including the heart, brain, and kidneys (Sevelius, 1965). Changes in cardiac output and coronary flow in

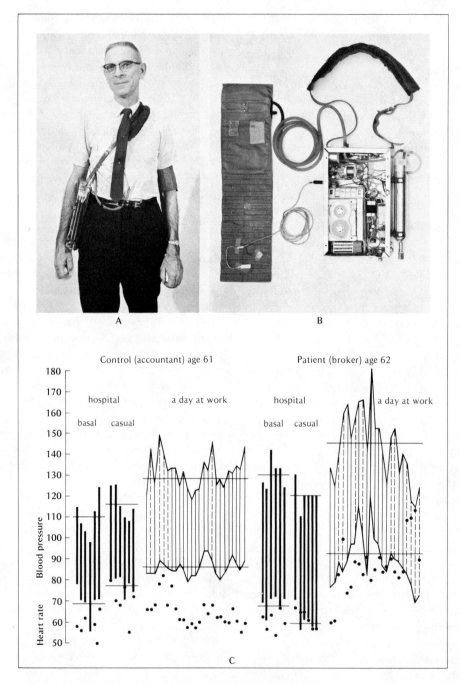

Figure 11.1 A. The fully automated portable blood pressure apparatus in operation, programmed to record every 15 min. B. The instrument itself, cover removed, showing tape recorder, timing circuits, and external nitrogen tank. C. Data obtained from ambulatory patient. Note the variability and event responsiveness. Redrawn from R. A. Schneider, A fully automatic portable blood pressure recorder. *Journal of Applied Physiology,* 1968, **24,** 115–118. Reproduced by permission.

situations of emotional stress have been observed by this method (Adsett, Schottstaedt, & Wolf, 1962). It is relatively innocuous, may be repeated several times in one session, and requires only an intravenous injection and regional monitoring with a radiodetector over the organ of interest. While the cardiac output and renal flow measurements by this method are generally accepted, there is some debate concerning the validity of coronary flow measurements with isotopes. Doubtless the problem will be resolved in the near future. This noninvasive technique and its refinements will undoubtedly offer much to the study of blood flow in human subjects when intermittent monitoring is sufficient.

Continuous blood flow data can be obtained from human subjects without restrictions using the ultrasonic Doppler technique with telemetry and surface or implanted probes (Franklin, Watson, Pierson, & Van Citters, 1966). Schneider (1968) has recently devised a portable, fully automatic, blood pressure measuring device that inflates a cuff on a programmed schedule and records the systolic and diastolic pressure and a calibrated signal on a miniature tape recorder. This instrument, the size of a woman's purse, will record for as long as 10 hr when attached to an ambulatory subject (Figure 11.1).

Measurement of Biochemical Factors

Catechols Catechols function as transaction mechanisms between local autonomic neurons or distant sympathetic neural elements and the smooth muscle in vascular beds and the myocardium. Thus their importance to cardiovascular function is very great. They also serve as intermediaries between neural mechanisms and biochemical systems of carbohydrate and lipid metabolism that play secondary roles in vascular integrity in health and disease. As such, the level of catecholamines in the urine or blood provides an indicator of sympathetic activity. Techniques are now available to measure epinephrine, norepinephrine, and their metabolic products, vanilmandelic acid, metanephrin, and noremetanephrin. At present fluorometric assays of urine collected during the experimental and control periods are most

often used, since analyses for plasma catechol are less reliable.

Various workers who have measured catechols during stressful life events have demonstrated differences in levels of either norepinephrine, epinephrine, or both related to the meaning of the events to the individual and the emotional responses felt and observed (Froberg et al., 1970). The consensus finds the increased excretion of norepinephrine in active aggressive emotional behavior and increased excretion of epinephrine in passive emotional responses of tenseness and anxiety (Elmadjian, Hope, & Lamson, 1957; Von Euler & Lundberg, 1954). Cohen and Silverman (1959) have verified the above concepts and extended the observations by studying the vascular variability under high gravitational forces. They found that the "anger out" responder excreted greater amounts of norepinephrine and was better able to resist the hypotension of increased gravity than those "anger in" subjects whose elevated urinary catechols were principally epinephrine.

Lipids and lipid metabolism Lipids and lipid metabolism have been adequately demonstrated to be responsive to central nervous system (CNS) stimulation (Gunn, Friedman, & Byers, 1960), peripheral nerve stimulation (Correll, 1963), psychological stresses in life situations (Cathey, Jones, Naughton, Hammarsten, & Wolf, 1962), and to conditions imposed during psychophysiological experiments (Bogdonoff et al., 1964). The relevance of lipid response to psychological reactions may have greater significance to the atherosclerotic involvement of various vascular beds in concert with neural and catechol effects (Gunn, Friedman, & Byers, 1960). The measurement of free fatty acids by Dole's technique (1956) offers another indicator of sympathetic activity, since the mobilization of free fatty acids from fatty tissue is very sensitive to epinephrine and norepinephrine (Havel, pp. 575–582). Although this mobilization probably occurs as a result of adrenergic innervation of adipose tissue, some denervation studies, so far unconfirmed, have suggested that the adrenergic lipid mobilization effect may, in fact, be secondary to blood-flow changes (Cantu & Goodman, 1967).

Polypeptides The peptides angiotensin (Page & Bumpus, 1961), bradykinin (Erdos, 1963; Erdos, Back, & Sicuteri, 1966), and Substance P (Lembeck & Zetler, 1962; Pernow, 1963) cause remarkable effects on the cardiovascular system. Angiotensin and Substance P act on the CNS as well. At present, difficulty in measuring and identifying these biological compounds hampers their study in psychophysiological experiments. In the future the interactions of neural mechanisms and the peptide system should be investigated together to understand better the variability and specificity of cardiovascular responses to internal and external environmental changes.

Renin is the enzyme that releases angiotensin from plasma proteins. This gives special interest to the indirect findings that neurogenic factors are important to renin release from the kidney in slow hemorrhage, which does not in itself produce a fall in blood pressure (Bunag, McCubbin, & Page, 1965). Angiotensin itself probably potentiates the sympathetic influence on vascular resistance in amounts that produce no direct vascular effect (McCubbin & Page, pp. 104–120, 1966). More recent work (Joy & Lowe, 1970) has shown that angiotensin in minute amounts activates medullary vasopressor mechanisms via area postrema chemoreceptor stimulation. Further evidence of the physiological alliance between angiotensin and the nervous system in vasoconstriction was adduced by the experiments of Zimmerman (1962). The stimulation of sympathetics to the hind limb of animals increased the response to angiotensin but decreased the response to norepinephrine. This suggests different mechanisms of vascular response for the two agents. Removing the sympathetics significantly reduced the vasoconstriction by angiotensin and had no influence on the response to norepinephrine. These mechanisms are complex in their biochemical interactions; especially so because angiotensin stimulates aldosterone secretion by the adrenals (Laragh, Angers, Kelly, & Lieberman, 1960). Aldosterone itself influences salt and water balance and secondarily promotes an increase in vascular tone in animals and man.

The kinins, including the potent vasodilatory substance, bradykinin, are known to be released directly at the site of local injury or indirectly by

an axon reflex (Chapman & Goodell, 1964). Kinins are potent stimulators of afferent pain fibers (Erdos, 1966) and as such may participate as an intermediary in painful vascular syndromes. Chapman, Goodell, & Wolff (1959) demonstrated that hypnotic suggestions of anesthesia reduced the vascular response to noxious stimulation of the skin and the degree of tissue damage. The suggestion of hyperalgesia increased them. This work provides strong evidence that the CNS and its autonomic integrative functions can modify the peripheral afferent axon reflex and release polypeptides such as bradykinin.

Substance P, another vasoactive peptide, was described by Gaddum and Von Euler in 1931. It is found in many tissues of man and animals and is capable of producing vasodilation, significant short-lived increases in blood flow in the skin and skeletal muscles, and constriction of the smooth muscle in the gastro-intestinal tract (Pernow, 1963). Its effects on the CNS have also been studied in pharmacological investigations (Lembeck & Zetler, 1962). It remains for the future to determine the role of Substance P in cardiovascular physiology.

Vasopressin is probably the most widely known of the biologically active peptides. It is a vasoactive and antidiuretic substance that is formed within the CNS in or near the supraoptic nucleus of the hypothalamus. It is released by the stimulation of "osmoreceptors" in the supraoptic nucleus by intravascular electrolyte concentrations, pain, various drugs, and emotional stress (O'Connor, 1946; Verney, 1947). It is thought to travel along the nerve fiber tracts to the posterior pituitary for storage or release. The cardiovascular effects of vasopressin include intense vasoconstriction of capillary beds, arterioles, and coronary arteries. Constriction of the latter vessels results in reduced cardiac output and peripheral blood flow. It does not seem to increase blood pressure in normal man when given in small pharmacological doses capable of altering diuresis. Vasopressin was one of the first peptides to be isolated and synthesized by du Vigneaud and his colleagues; it may well be the first to be measured by chemical tests. Bioassays are currently the only tests available for the other peptides.

While physiological functions of these peptides await further clarification, it is well to consider investigating them in future psychophysiological research when complex cardiovascular reactions with long latencies and prolonged effects are present.

Prostaglandins Comprehensive reviews of the prostaglandins are presented by Bergstrom, Carlson, and Weeks (1968) and Horton (1969).

These complex fatty acids exist in many tissues including brain, prostate, uterus, kidneys, adrenals and lungs. Some are vasodilators, others are vasoconstrictor agents. They have been found to be smooth muscle relaxants in bronchi, uterus, and placenta. Prostaglandins have potent CNS actions. Some of them have been considered to be actual neural transmitter substances in parasympathetic and sympathetic systems.

Prostaglandin E_1 is a potent inhibitor of lipolysis and gastric secretion. It dilates veins and arteries and lowers systemic vascular resistance and pressure. It also inhibits platelet aggregation and adhesiveness which in the presence of decreased blood flow and injury prevents the intravascular coagulation of blood. Many of these physiological interactions are thought to be mediated by inhibiting the adenyl cyclase activation of 3',5' cyclic AMP, the second messenger for catechols and other humoral agents. In this sense it may be an excellent local mediator of negative feedback in the peripheral cardiovascular system (Horton, 1969).

Prostaglandin F_2 has a vasoconstrictor and positive inotropic (increased strength of muscular contraction) and chronotropic (increased rate of contraction) influence on smooth and cardiac muscle. Certain of these compounds in minute amounts can potentiate many physiological responses in the CNS, cardiovascular, and reproductive systems (Bergstrom, Carlson, & Weeks, 1968). The prostaglandins certainly deserve a niche in the information system of present-day psychophysiologists. Probably in the research of tomorrow, psychophysiology laboratories will be measuring prostaglandins as important psychophysiological mediators of cardiovascular adaptation.

Cyclic AMP (cAMP) Adenosine 3',5'-monophosphate is now considered to be the intracellular mediator of many humoral and neurohumoral responses in both the central and the peripheral

nervous systems, and in the heart and blood vessels, as well as other organs. It can be measured in the body fluids of man (Sutherland, 1970) and has been found to elevate on the day of switching from depression to mania in patients with manic-depressive illness (Paul, Cramer, & Bunney, 1971).

The enzyme adenyl cyclase in different tissues responds to hormones or humoral agents such as the catechols, epinephrine, and norepinephrine to produce intracellular cyclic AMP, and it is broken down by phosphodiesterase, another enzyme widely present in the same tissues. In the heart and vascular system it activates energy phosphocylase systems, it produces a positive inotropic effect increasing the contractile force of the heart and blood vessels, and it mobilizes lipids (Greengard & Costa, 1970).

It mediates the ACTH and angiotensin stimulation of adrenal steriodogenesis. Many of the activities of cAMP, such as gastric secretion, blood platelet functions, lypolysis, and myocardial contraction, can be inhibited by prostaglandins and adrenergic blocking agents (Sutherland, Robinson, & Butcher, 1968).

In view of the close relationship of cAMP as a mediator system for the autonomic stimulation of cardiovascular responses and other adaptational efforts such as steroid activation, the cAMP system should be monitored in behavioral experiments correlating neural and emotional influences on the cardiovascular system.

Psychophysiological Techniques, Measurements, and Controls

Situational monitoring Attempts to classify people according to personality types correlated with cardiovascular physiological patterns or disease have been inconclusive. Attempts to make meaningful correlations at a single point in time encounter further difficulty caused by the variability in an individual's visceral reactivity and other behavior. On the other hand, correlations of behavior, attitudes, and reactions in the same individual over time offers considerable promise, especially if observations can be made as the subject goes about his day-to-day activities in his natural environment. Such studies enable one to observe an individual's psychophysiological responses to his own environment, both internal and external, but have not yet offered an opportunity for replication and comparison with the responses of different subjects, since the situational aspects can never be the same from person to person or from time to time. The subject may, however, serve as his own control, providing information as to how he reacts to his varying life situations.

Rapidly advancing technology has greatly increased the variety of data that can be continuously gathered at any one time by either telemetry or miniature recording devices. Persistent abnormal physiological changes have been documented as a response to troublesome life experiences. For example, using a portable EKG recorder, paroxysmal atrial tachycardia, an abnormally rapid heart beat, was recorded in 1965 when a hypertensive patient began a contract bridge tournament with his highly critical partner (his wife). It continued throughout the day until the tournament was over and a normal sinus rhythm returned. In 1971 he died suddenly in another stressful tournament. Using the same type of portable electrocardiographic recorder, abnormalities of both the cardiac rate and rhythm were seen in physicians and patients during the stress of driving an automobile (Burns, Baker, Simonson, & Keiper, 1966) or performing medical chores (Ira, Whalen, & Bogdonoff, 1963). Schneider's (1968) portable blood pressure device has shown dramatic blood pressure changes as patients go about their daily life impeded only by a cuff and a 6 lb holster containing a tape recorder (Figure 11.1C). Correlations in time are made with specific events noted by the patient in a diary. Daily measurements of urinary catechols (Levi, 1966, pp. 85–95), steroids (Bunney, Mason, & Hamburg, 1965), and other factors, have also been correlated with the general emotional states existing during the monitored periods.

Studies in the controlled environment of a research ward have afforded frequent daily observations of emotional content, individual behavior, group dynamics, and interpersonal reactions correlated with metabolic balance data, data on lipid metabolism (Cathey, Jones, Naughton, Hammarsten, & Wolf, 1962), and renal function (Barnes & Schottstaedt, 1960). Studies of the effects of naturally occurring conflict situations on different members of a more or less controlled group could be enhanced by using portable recorders and telemetry devices that provide continuous cardiovascular monitoring. Long-term as well as short-term changes, individual differences, and variability could be detected.

Although sensory isolation and other artificial environments have been available for psychophysiological studies for several years, new opportunities and new necessities are forced to our attention. Isolation in Antarctic stations, during prolonged underwater travel in atomic-powered submarines, in stationary sea laboratories, during space flights, and in manned orbiting space laboratories, place man in unusual physical, physiological, psychological, and social environments. These can produce marked physiological behavioral changes that merit study. Weightlessness, a new and unfamiliar dimension unique to space flight, may produce significant alterations in cardiovascular adaptation and psychomotor performance (DiGiovanni & Chambers, 1964). As indicated by short-term space flights, it is of vital importance to these missions that the relevant psychological, physiological, and behavioral factors in these exotic environments be determined and studied and that attempts be made to devise tests which have predictive value in the selection of personnel who might be most effective in such novel situations.

Short-term investigations involving the acute manipulation of the environment offer opportunities for the study of group dynamics and individual responses to artificial situations created by programmed devices. Behavioral changes, free fatty acids, and catechols have been monitored under such circumstances (Bogdonoff, Combs, Bryant, & Warren, 1959).

The psychodrama has been used to create emotionally significant situations during which to study blood pressure changes in normotensive young adults (Harris, Sokolow, Carpenter, Freedman, & Hunt, 1953). These investigators found that blood pressure elevations were significantly greater among subjects with hypertensive parents.

Motion picture films with emotional content of various sorts have been shown to individuals and groups during continuous monitoring of autonomic indicators (Lazarus, Speisman, & Mordkoff, 1963).

This method permits both inter- and intraindividual analysis, since the stimuli are the same, although the meaning may be different to each person.

The stress interview has been used by the Cornell and Oklahoma groups. Information with emotional significance from the patients' medical and social history is discussed in a guided interview, while the blood pressure, heart rate, electrocardiogram, blood flow, and other parameters are monitored (Adsett, Schottstaedt, & Wolf, 1962; Schneider & Zangari, 1951; Wolf, Cardon, Shepard, & Wolff, 1955). Cardiac arrhythmias have been precipitated by stress interviews (Meinhardt & Robinson, 1962; Wolf, 1958). A monitored grand mal convulsion has been precipitated by stress interviews in an individual without a prior history of seizures (Barker & Wolf, 1947). Unfortunately, the stimuli for these reactions cannot be measured or precisely duplicated. The patient's response is to a unique situation and depends on many variables, which include the skill of the interviewer in interpretating and manipulating the subject's reactions.

Hypnosis As a tool for psychophysiological investigations, hypnosis is considered elsewhere in this book (see Chapter 21). Its value lies in the ability to induce specific and differential autonomic reactions (D. T. Graham, Kabler, & F. K. Graham, 1962; F. K. Graham & Kunish, 1965; Stern, Winokur, D. T. Graham, & F. K. Graham, 1961), including regional differences in blood flow and vascularity, with some attitudinal specificity. As information increases about hypnosis and suggestibility, this form of experimental manipulation should become an even more useful technique. In this connection, the same heart rate responses have been observed during hypnotically induced emotional responses as in the simulated hypnotic state. This cautions against the use of autonomic monitors to assay the hypnotic state itself (Damaser, Shor, & Orne, 1963).

Conditioning techniques The usefulness of conditioning techniques in studying cardiovascular reactivity in rate and rhythm has been extensive in animals and more so in man in recent years (see Chapters 5 and 6). Even though it is felt that the galvanic skin resistance (GSR) can be conditioned without awareness of a contingent relationship between the conditional and unconditional stimulus, attempts to condition the heart rate seem to depend more on cognitive factors and awareness of the conditional stimulus-unconditional stimulus relationship (Chatterjee & Eriksen, 1962). The availability of additional sensory feedback, such as a visual or auditory signal that varies with the change in the beat-to-beat interval, increases the conditional learning of heart rate control (Brener & Hothersall, 1966).

Shearn (1962) and others have demonstrated that the heart rate could be operantly conditioned and showed that contingent punishment produced greater increases in heart rate than noncontingent punishment in controls, thus suggesting cognitive factors entering into autonomic control of the heart. The availability of new technology in the form of digital logic modules, computers, and other electronic programming devices has made operant conditioning available to the investigator interested in cardiovascular responses. Using these techniques, Engel and Hansen (1966) showed that man can learn to slow his heart rate by using a light reinforcement for slowing, even though the subjects were not aware of what they were learning. Respiration was shown to be not a relevant mechanism, although this may have an effect on changes in the rate and rhythm. Engel and Melmon (1967) have extended the operant techniques to patients with pathological rhythms. Previously, Hnatiow and Lang (1965) achieved operant stabilization of the heart rates in man by differential signals for slow and fast heart rate reinforcement.

To date cardiac deceleration has been achieved by conditioning less often than cardiac acceleration has been produced by avoidance conditioning. Frazier (1966) used an instrumental technique of shock delivered when the total number of beats per minute decreased from the previous minute's total during an instrument panel-monitoring task. With this method he was able to produce significant tachycardia in patients unaware of the biological avoidance contingency.

Following the leads of Gantt (1960), Pavlovian techniques have been readily applied to cardiovascular conditioning. They require less instrumentation than operant conditioning and are easier to apply to the human in a clinical setting to investigate the heart rate (Hein, Cohen, & Shmavonian, 1966) and rhythm (Perez-Cruet, 1962) and presumably vasomotor responses of vasoconstriction and vasodilation.

Experiments of nature Special populations provide unique opportunities for study. The ancient disciplines of yoga in controlling cardiovascular physiology have been studied by Anand, Chhina, and Singh (1961). During an 8 hr stay in an air-tight box of 2263 liters effective capacity, the yogi subject decreased his O_2 consumption and CO_2 production and heart rate with no change in respiratory rate. Simultaneous EEG recordings showed low voltage fast activity, characteristic of REM sleep or of arousal. These findings of lowered metabolic rate and heart slowing suggest a response similar to the oxygen-conserving "dive reflex" response. The yogi's voluntary ability to modulate his metabolic rate is indeed impressive and suggests a fruitful area for further research.

The Tarahumara Indians of Mexico, who have extraordinary capabilities as long distance runners, are currently being studied by psychiatrists, cardiologists, and psychologists in their habitat during their normal activities (Parades, West, & Snow, 1970).

Patients with various mental illnesses have been studied and offer rewarding opportunities to make serial observations at the various stages of recovery, exacerbation, and during significant psychological changes. The influence of psychotropic and autonomic compounds on these and control populations have been evaluated. The continual emergence of newer compounds that alter behavior constantly challenge the interested psychophysiologists, as well as others engaged in drug evaluation. Since most of these agents significantly alter autonomic and somatic functions, clinical pharmacological investigations of these agents are immeasurably improved by scientists interested in both psychological and physiological aspects of behavior.

Other patient groups, such as those with hypertension, orthostatic hypertension, fainting spells, hyperventilation syndrome, hyperthyroidism, hypothyroidism, adrenal disturbances, angina pectoris and myocardial infarction, Raynaud's phenomenon,

and anorexia nervosa, provide students of human biology with a wealth of material that can be contrasted with those assumed to be healthy and normal. For example, a psychophysiologic investigation correlated with the social, psychological, and medical histories of a population of healthy elderly patients, using those of the same age with chronic vascular disease as the control, should enlighten our concepts of aging and may even provide some clues as to how we all could age gracefully.

The epidemiological approach to cardiovascular studies has rarely included the evaluation of social and psychophysiological data. A few studies do include comparisons of various ethnic groups (Walker, Mortimer, Downing, & Dunn, 1960), and of the same ethnic groups in different environments (Gampel, Slome, Scotch, & Abramson, 1962; Scotch, 1960), with respect to differences in blood pressure and the prevalence of ischemic heart disease (Stout, Morrow, Brandt, & Wolf, 1964). Negroes are more prone to hypertension than whites, especially if urbanized (Gampel, Slome, Scotch, & Abramson, 1962), and American Indians on reservations appear to have little cardiovascular disease, specifically hypertension and coronary artery disease. These findings, if correct, would suggest that there may be significant differences in autonomic reactivity related to environment and social interactions in these peoples. Significantly, cardiovascular psychophysiology remains to be added to the broad field of epidemiology.

INNERVATION OF THE HEART AND VESSELS

Myocardium

The anatomical level of cardiovascular psychophysiology is reviewed in *Nervous Control of the Heart* (Randall, 1965). Other monographs provide details concerning the innervation of the heart (Khabarova, 1963; Mitchell, 1956), and the blood vessels (Grigor'eva, 1962).

The heart, in all vertebrates including man, has an intrinsic mechansim to maintain its beat. The pacemaker cells in the sino-atrial (SA) node undergo periodic excitation automatically and independent of any extrinsic connections. The action potentials are distributed from the SA node through the atrium to the atrioventricular (AV) node, then by conduction bundles into both the left and right ventricle exciting first the atrial and then the ventricular myocardium to contract. The propagation of the impulses generates the electrocardiogram as recorded from the body wall (Sher, 1962, pp. 287–322). The dominant pacemaker is normally the SA node which possesses the higher inherent rate. The second highest inherent rate is the AV node, which may become dominant and usurp the role of the pacemaker if the SA node is inhibited.

The denervated heart is capable of exciting itself to contract and during exercise conditions it can operate independent of extrinsic nervous control by increasing the stroke volume and, to some extent, the rate (Donald & Shepard, 1961). In the intact organism, however, it is continually influenced by extrinsic sympathetic and parasympathetic impulses that are distributed to the specialized tissues and alter the behavior of the heart from moment to moment in response to physiological and metabolic demand, with or without involvement at the psychological level.

The termination of the extrinsic nerves to and from the heart is a subject of much investigation. Present-day controversies exist because of difficulties inherent in the methods of histological identification of the sympathetic and parasympathetic components, as well as their afferent, efferent, preganglionic, or postganglionic character. Regardless of the problems involved, the nervous control of the heart cannot be properly understood, unless the terminal innervation is morphologically defined (Cooper, 1965).

The efferent vagus to the heart originates from either the dorsal motor nucleus or the area of the nucleus ambiguus, the latter being the primary source. There are bilateral communications in the medulla between each of these nuclei (Gunn, Sevelius, Puiggari, & Myers, 1968). Although few in number, the efferent vagal fibers that go to the heart produce very influential inhibitory effects on the SA and AV nodes. The left and right vagi produce an overlapping influence on the atria, the right predominantly to the SA node and the left predominantly to the AV node (Mitchell, 1956).

The preganglionic efferent sympathetics arise from the intermedio-lateral cell columns of the upper five thoracic levels. They make synaptic connections or pass through vertebral and cervical sympathetic ganglia to descend in the mediastinum to the cardiac plexus. Here they intermingle with vagal efferents and afferents carried in the vagus trunk before entering the heart, creating a difficult problem of identification (Mitchell, 1956). From physiological evidence the postganglionic fibers from the right sympathetic chain appear to innervate the SA node and the rest of the atria. The left-sided fibers are primarily distributed to both ventricles, since their stimulation produces mainly an inotropic augmenting effect on ventricular contraction with little or no influence on the heart rate (Randall & Rohse, 1956).

Vagal Innervation of the Ventricles

Still unsettled is the presence or absence of vagal terminals in the ventricles. There is excellent physiological evidence to suggest that vagal fibers directly inhibit myocardial contractile force, when the heart is paced externally (DeGeest, Levy, Zieske, & Lipman, 1965). These fibers appear capable of partially antagonizing the positive chronotropic effect (rate increase) of sympathetic stimulation (Levy, Ng, Martin, & Zieske, 1966). The experiments of Juhasz-Nagy and Szentivanyi (1961) suggest the presence of sympathetic cholinergic fibers in the ventricles. Cooper (1965) found axons of C fiber dimensions in the ventricle of the denervated heart. They were devoid of sympathetic membrane-limited granules and may be postganglionic parasympathetic fibers or sympathetic cholinergic fibers or even partially damaged sympathetic fibers. The last possibility seems the least likely. The ventricular myocardium also contains acetylcholine, the parasympathetic transmitter substance, but in lesser amounts than the atrial myocardium (Cooper, 1965). This further supports the concept that the vagus influences ventricular myocardium. The work of Cooper, Hirsch, Napolitano, and others, so well summarized in *Nervous Control of the Heart* (Randall, 1965), also emphasizes the wealth of nerve fibers in the ventricle. These are almost completely destroyed by removing the heart and reimplanting it, thus producing a complete denervation. This also destroys the plexiform neural investments that surround each myocardial fiber. This plexiform neuroeffector investment, described by Hillarp (1960, pp. 979–1006), permits either adrenergic or cholinergic transmitter substance to find intimate contact with every myocardial cell without penetrating the cell or using an end plate apparatus, as occurs in somatic neuromuscular units.

Coronary Innervation

The innervation of the coronary arteries is also incompletely understood. The fluorescence techniques of Hillarp, used by Dahlstrom, Fuxe, Mya-Tu, and Zetterstrom (1965), not only identify rich adrenergic plexi in the SA and AV nodes and atrial myocardium but also define rich plexiform arrangements around coronary arterioles and venules close to the outer muscle layers.

Although the physiological evidence is conflicting, it appears that both parasympathetic and sympathetic fibers innervate the coronaries. The most acceptable evidence at the present time is that the parasympathetic fibers dilate the coronary bed, independent of chronotropic and inotropic effects on the myocardium (Feigl, 1969), and the sympathetic fibers constrict them (Berne, DeGeest, & Levy, 1965). More recent evidence suggests that alpha adrenergic receptors constrict coronaries but the beta receptors probably dilate to support the beta inotropic facilitation (Brown, 1968; Feigl, 1967).

Afferent Nerves from the Heart

Afferent receptors in the heart and major arteries provide feedback information to the CNS, which in turn prompts reflex adjustments (modulation) as exemplified by either an increase in the heart rate from vena cava and right atrial distension (Bainbridge reflex) or a decrease in the rate from the carotid sinus and left ventricular distension. Opposite results or biphasic responses from the stimulation of these receptors suggest either that other types of receptors are also stimulated or that the CNS, operating with additional information, alters the response. The location and nature of many afferent receptors still await clarification. It appears likely, however, that a variety of receptors responding to changes in the chemical environment or to physical pressures are distributed widely throughout the heart and vessels. Although afferent endings have been studied for many years, decisive information has been slow in coming. Newer his-

tological techniques applied to the reflexogenous areas in the atria, aortic arch, carotid sinus, pulmonary artery, and the base of the renal artery, display complex unencapsulated endings that are regarded as stretch receptors; and encapsulated endings of the Vater-Pacinian type of pressure receptors are found in the walls of larger veins (M. R. Miller & Kasahara, 1964). The same techniques applied to the heart reveal afferent end nets and unencapsulated endings in the endocardium of the atria. The ventricular endocardium has only nerve nets derived from a rich plexus of myelinated nerves. The epicardium is more sparsely supplied with sensory endings. The myocardium probably contains afferents but assurance here is lacking.

The coronaries are well supplied with sensory fibers also, but the nature of the endings is not established (M. R. Miller & Kasahara, 1964). Woollard (1926), in fact, considered them to be more richly innervated than any other arteries but did not separate afferent from efferent fibers.

Not only are the atrioventricular valves innervated more than the pulmonary and aortic valves (M. R. Miller & Kasahara, 1964; Woollard, 1926), but recent workers have also assigned them afferent status while identifying a large myelinated nerve that comes through the mitral valves into cordae tendinae to the papillary muscles (Williams, 1964a, 1964b). This large fiber is capable of fast conduction, implying that it may be a proprioceptive and timing device. Evidence does not preclude its being a motor fiber to innervate the papillary muscle and open the valves. Williams also infers from their shape that the sensory nerve nets in the valves may sense the flow properties of the blood.

Alpha and Beta Adrenergic Cardiovascular Receptors

The concept of the alpha and beta adrenotropic receptor sites of the adrenergic effector cell (smooth muscle or gland) was a by-product of Ahlquist's (1948) search for a drug that would relax the nonpregnant uterus contracted by vasopressin. Instead of finding a cure for dysmenorrhea, he gave us a new pharmacological attitude toward the sympathetic nervous system. His general classification placed the adrenergic mechanisms producing arterial constriction as an alpha receptor function, and the arterial dilation and myocardial inotropic stimulation as a beta receptor. This schema took on new meaning recently after beta adrenergic blocking agents were synthesized. Epinephrine has both alpha and beta properties; both receptors are usually present in the tissue but have never been histologically verified per se. Norepinephrine is considered a potent alpha adrenergic compound with weak beta adrenergic properties, except on the heart.

This dual receptor hypothesis permits us to understand both stimulation and inhibition by catechol at a single effector cell. However, it is in danger of being complicated unduly if every new adrenergic blocking agent behaves differently from those before, suggesting to some investigators the need for more and different receptor sites. Ahlquist (1965, pp. 2457–2476) himself cautioned that indirect drug classification is but a preliminary to the exact knowledge of responsive mechanisms for adrenergic influences on the effector cell. Perhaps further caution is warranted, so that pharmacological information is not blindly accepted as physiological gospel.

The individuality of control of the vascular tone existing in the vascular beds of the various organs is seen in their different degrees of spontaneous myogenic tone, their capability for autoregulation, and in the different populations of adrenergic receptors shown by different responsivity to catechols. The smooth muscles from small coronaries

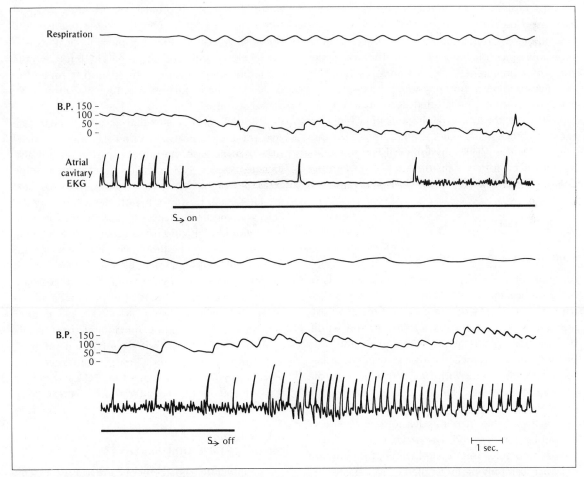

Figure 11.2 Stimulus-bound atrial fibrillation and tachypnea induced by stimulation of the nucleus ambiguous area in the medulla. S = Stimulus. Redrawn from C. G. Gunn, G. Sevelius, M. Puiggari, & F. K. Myers, Vagal cardiomotor mechanism in the hind brain of the dog and cat. *American Journal of Physiology,* 1968, **214,** 258–262. Reproduced by permission.

have little or no alpha receptor activity and predominant beta receptors (dilation), while the larger coronaries and the skeletal muscle arteries contain both alpha and beta receptors. The large coronaries contain more beta receptors than those of skeletal muscle. Therefore, in the in vitro system, epinephrine and norepinephrine produce dilation in coronaries and constriction in skeletal arteries (Bohr, 1967). We must not, however, lose sight of the likelihood that human coronaries may be markedly constricted by direct neural mechanisms and that myocardial infarcts do occur without coronary atherosclerosis.

There is a growing trend to consider various adrenergic blockers as selective agents that suppress the specific adrenergic functions in an all-or-none fashion. Data from blocking experiments have even been used to establish the identity of new adrenergic functions. Such inferences are not allowable since blocking occurs with varying degrees of completeness. Furthermore, as blockers are pharmacologic, not physiologic agents, they may give rise to unidentified secondary effects. Nevertheless, the use of alpha and beta blocking agents to block selectively specific adrenergic functions in clinical psychophysiological investigations may soon be a very valuable tool if interpreted pharmacologically rather than physiologically.

NEUROPHYSIOLOGY

Control of Rate and Rhythm

Regulation of the heart's rate and rhythm is of prime importance to the function and survival of man. A change in heart rate is one means of adjusting cardiac output and blood flow to the whole body. A change in rhythm varies in extent from being of no importance to causing a drop in cardiac output incompatible with life. Although the role of different areas of the nervous system will be discussed separately in cardiovascular control, the artificiality of the anatomic divisions or "centers" should be kept in mind. The nervous system operates as a complex interrelated whole, the function of which can only be incompletely appreciated by study of component parts. For greater detail than presented here, recent reviews should be consulted

(Eichna & McQuarrie, 1960; Korner, 1971; Randall, 1965).

The medullary sites of the vagal efferent outflow to the heart are sparsely found in the dorsal nucleus and are more importantly present in the area of the nucleus ambiguus (Gunn, Sevelius, Puiggari, & Myers, 1968). Stimulation of the above sites produces bradycardia. If the vagal suppression is severe, a stimulus-bound atrial fibrillation that is many times replicable in a susceptible animal may occur, when the medullary areas in or just lateral to the nucleus ambiguus area, or the peripheral vagus itself are stimulated (Gunn et al., 1968; see Figure 11.2).

The medullary cardioinhibitor vagus can be activated from subtectal areas in the mesencephalon, posterior lateral hypothalamus, orbital surfaces of forebrain, as well as in cingulate gyri areas and the insular cortex. In neurophysiological experiments bradycardia and abnormal rhythms are quite common when electrical stimulation is applied to cortex and diencephalon (Manning & Cotton, 1962; Parker, Gunn, & Lynn, 1962).

The CNS mechanisms that accelerate heart rate also produce a pressor response; however, many sites that increase the blood pressure do not also increase the rate. The sensorimotor cortex; some areas of the cingulate gyrus, septum, and amygdala; the lateral and posterior hypothalamus; the central gray and mesencephalic reticular formation; and the medullary reticulum are capable of producing rate increases when stimulated. Interesting alterations of the ST segments and the T wave, which suggest ischemic changes or infarction of the heart, occur and persist for hours after prolonged stimulation of the above sites; they also occur after neurosurgical procedures in man and are clinically confused with myocardial infarction (Porter, Kamikawa, & Greenhoot, 1962). Whichever the mechanism, it is obvious that the CNS can produce marked and prolonged alterations in the cardiac conduction system.

CNS Induction of Potentially Fatal Arrhythmias

The integrative character of cardiac arrest is seen in the work of Porter and French (1960). The excitability of the CNS is controlled by the reticular formation that also mediates many somatic and visceral, including cardiac, reflexes. Monitoring CNS excitability by observing reticular-formation–evoked potentials to sciatic stimulation, Porter and French found a diminution of the evoked potential in light anesthesia levels, a paradoxical increase in amplitude and latency of the response at moderate levels, and a disappearance at deep levels. When a short burst of stimulation to the afferent vagus was produced at each of these levels, only a slight decrease in cardiac rate was seen with light anesthesia. But when the sciatic-evoked potential marked a hyper-reflexive condition in the reticular formation at moderate levels, vagal stimulation produced cardiac arrest. This demonstrates how changing levels of

CNS excitability may amplify sensory input producing exaggerated ouput, a potential mechanism of sudden death.

The dive reflex as seen in animals (Scholander, 1962) and man (Wolf, Schneider, & Groover, 1956) is obviously a mixed system response with respiratory arrest, bradycardia, a rise in blood pressure, and oxygen conservation. Stimulation of the nucleus solitarius, an afferent way station for vagal, facial, and glossopharyngeal nerve input in the medulla, can produce at least the autonomic components of this reflex (Gunn et al., 1968; see Figure 11.3). Feigl and Folkow (1963) also produced the dive reflex by stimulating the more anterior mesencephalon of ducks, probably in the subtectal retic-

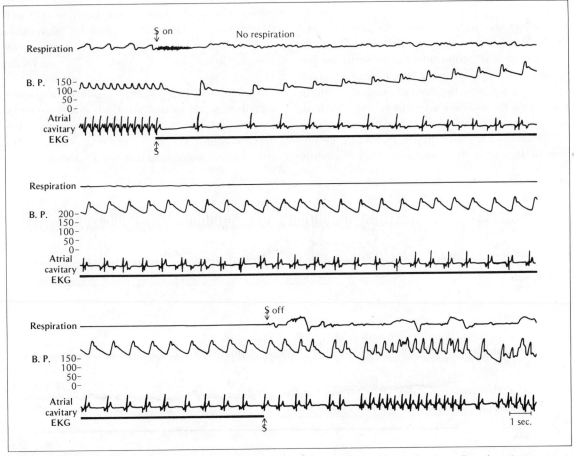

Figure 11.3 Stimulation of the multi-afferent nucleus of the tractus solitarius produces the dive reflex of respiratory arrest, a rise or no change in blood pressure, and bradycardia. S₋ = Stimulus. Redrawn from C. G. Gunn, G. Sevelius, M. Puiggari, & F. K. Myers, Vagal cardiomotor mechanism in the hind brain of the dog and cat. *American Journal of Physiology*, 1968, **214**, 258–262. Reproduced by permission.

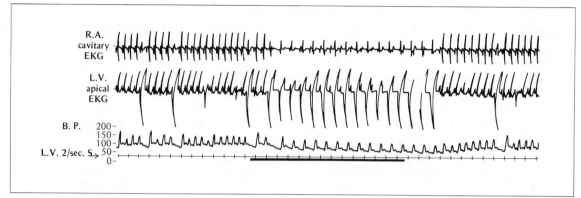

Figure 11.4 Continuous 2/sec electrical stimulation just below pacemaker threshold. Stimulation of the left vagus at 30. sec, suppressing normal conduction pathways, permits ectopic left ventricle focus to become the pacemaker. Redrawn from C. G. Gunn, P. Houk, & R. J. Person (to be published).

ulum that also contains supra nuclear vagal mechanisms.

Another way in which the CNS can influence the heart's rhythm is to inhibit the normal conduction system and permit an irritable focus already present (such as exists in the periphery of an infarct or in a heart muscle deprived of nutrients without infarction) to assume a pacemaker role. By simulating an ectopic focus with stimulating electrodes in the ventricular wall, currents that alone are unable to depolarize the entire ventricle and capture

the pacemaker function may become the pacemaker when the vagus to the heart is activated (Figure 11.4). At faster rates ventricular tachycardia and fibrillation are facilitated by the same vagal action (Gunn, Houk, & Person, 1971; see Figure 11.5).

Generalized hypoxia may produce ventricular arrhythmias and cardiac standstill in experimental animals if the heart is oxygenated by coronary bypass and pump procedures. The heart still develops arrhythmias, suggesting that the CNS may partici-

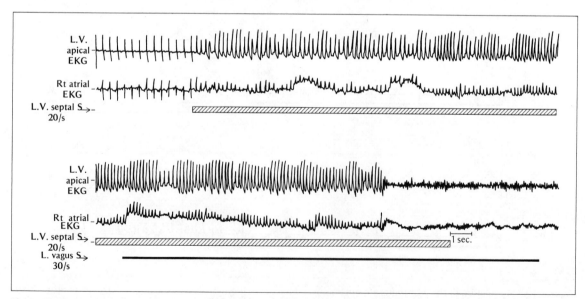

Figure 11.5 An ectopic septal focus is established by stimulating at 20/sec. Interaction of vagal stimulation to the heart facilitates ventricular rate until ventricular fibrillation supervenes. Redrawn from C. G. Gunn, P. C. Houk, & R. J. Person (to be published).

pate in their development. This can be proved by protecting the heart from these arrhythmias by cutting the vagi or giving large doses of atropine, a parasympathetic blocker (Austen, Ebert, & Greenfield, 1962). Even the severe and fatal ventricular arrhythmias following a myocardial infarction are markedly reduced or even prevented experimentally by freeing the heart from its extrinsic nerve supply (Ebert, Allgood, & Sabiston, 1967). It is clear that vagal mechanisms from cortex to the periphery can, if maximally activated, turn off the heart, producing cardiac standstill, or can participate in the production of ventricular autonomy and eventually fibrillation if irritable foci exist in the ventricles.

That the CNS possesses adequate mechanisms to modulate the rate and rhythm of the heart seems quite apparent. From the biological models of abnormal rhythms described above, it is also apparent that the CNS can indeed participate in their production, in either the presence or absence of organic heart disease. Thus we are looking at inappropriate neural mechanisms that may well be involved in causing death.

Cardiac Dynamics

The important functions of the heart include the ability to pump blood continually to the entire body and, by changing its rate and stroke volume, to alter its output to meet the changing demands of the body for continuous nutrition. Much physiology taught currently uses information derived from heart-lung and denervation experiments. These demonstrate that the heart does indeed have autoregulatory capability, but the fact remains that the nerves to the heart can and do modify the heart's function from moment to moment, as a response to the CNS integrative function to meet the demands of the body. One great advantage of CNS modulation is that cardiac output can be increased prior to exercise or during mental work, so that the sudden maximal demand for flow and nutrition can be met without cost to the tissues or the loss of rapid function.

Rushmer's (1962, pp. 533–550) summary of neurogenic influences on heart dynamics and the classic monograph by Heymans and Neil (1958) on cardiovascular reflexes should be consulted by all readers. Rushmer presents a cogent argument for extending our observations on cardiac dynamics beyond anesthetized animals, in which neural mechanisms are less important, to walking, moving, and mentating animals and man. This is now possible by virtue of technologic advances in telemetry and small portable recording systems.

Cardiac output, as determined by the venous return, the strength of cardiac contraction, and the cardiac rate, is influenced by afferent messages to the CNS, by central autonomic integration, and by the resultant efferent outflow to the heart and vasculature. Central cardiovascular integration occurs at all levels in the neuraxis from the spinal cord to the sensorimotor cortex, with important way stations in the medulla, mesencephalon, hypothalamus, and limbic system (Kaada, 1951; Randall, 1965; Rushmer, Smith, & Lasher, 1960). Perhaps the best example of this is shown by stimulating the lateral hypothalamus in the area of the H_2 field of Forel. This increases the cardiac output and mimics the cardiovascular pattern of exercise observed in the same conscious dog via previously implanted detectors (Rushmer, Smith, & Lasher, 1960). The patterns of cardiac activity with exercise, eating, the anticipation of exercise, and emotional situations can be markedly altered, and even abolished, by making bilateral periventricular lesions in the hypothalamus (Smith, Jabbur, Rushmer, & Lasher, 1960). These results indicate that the hypothalamus or pathways through it play an important integrative role in the heart's dynamic response to internal and external environmental demands.

Although the respiratory mechanisms were not investigated in the above work, others investigating autonomic mechanisms in the CNS have shown that stimulation of many areas, including the limbic system, produces stimulus-bound respiratory alterations accompanying vasomotor phenomena (Kaada, 1951). This implies that the integrative mechanisms involve not only cardiovascular but also pulmonary, somatomotor, and probably even biochemical systems that effect a compatible and efficient coordination of the total organism in its adaptation to changing needs. Stimulating the same lateral hypothalamic area in conscious dogs produces changes in blood-clotting factors (Gunn & Hampton, 1967) and also produces discrete differential norepinephrine and epinephrine responses, depending on the site being stimulated (Folkow & Von Euler, 1954).

The stroke volume is largely determined by the contractile force of the ventricular myocardium. The sympathetic innervation to the heart and the release of catecholamines to the myocardium increases its contractility. This positive inotropic (contractile) effect, as well as the positive chronotropic (rate) effect, increases the cardiac output as long as an adequate volume of blood is presented to the normal heart. These effects are well established, but variations in conduction, contraction, and synchrony of the various chambers of the heart do occur when cardiac nerves are stimulated. Such responses suggest another mechanism of variability due to the patterned innervation of the heart, which differs from the more universal response seen with norepinephrine infusions (Randall, 1965).

The influence of the vagus on the ventricular function is debated. Until recently, the presence of parasympathetic fibers in the ventricles was denied, and physiological workers considered the decreased cardiac output to be due entirely to either decreased heart rate or decreased atrial ejection into the ventricles. More recent and well-controlled work suggests that there is indeed a negative inotropic vagal effect on the ventricles, and their contractile force is decreased by vagal stimulation when the heart rate, aortic pressure, and cardiac input are controlled (Daggett, Nugent, Carr, Powers, & Harada, 1967; DeGeest et al., 1965). A CNS-provoked decrease in cardiac contractility and heart rate has been shown to occur from stimulation of the medial or lateral septal areas (limbic system) of the cat's brain. The effect apparently is not mediated by the vagus. Removing the stellate ganglia or using beta adrenergic blocking agents abolishes this response. This finding led Manning, Charbon, and Cotten (1963) to infer that the response was caused by inhibition of previously existing sympathetic tone. The function of such a central mechanism may also be involved in the integrated homeostatic mechanism involved in sleep, since slow stimulation of the same areas will produce sleep in a waking animal (Sterman & Clemente, 1962).

A clinical use for this physiological information has been found. Some patients who have angina have surgically implanted electrodes on the carotid sinus baroreceptor nerves and a radio frequency stimulator. When he or she has heart pain, stimulation delivered to these afferent nerves to the CNS in turn produces reflex vagal cardio-inhibition and a release of sympathetic tone that reduces the heart rate and decreases myocardial contractility. This relieves the myocardium of its work load and usually abolishes angina (Braunwald, Epstein, Glick, Wechsler, & Braunwald, 1967).

Although the experimental animal whose heart is completely deprived of extrinsic innervation has some ability to change his cardiac output in response to venous return during exercise, the importance of both the sympathetic and parasympathetic innervation to cardiac output has been demonstrated. The balance of the two systems, although partially competitive at the myocardium, also depends on central inhibitory mechanisms. For example, inhibition of vagal activity at central levels can increase the cardiac output by increasing the heart rate. Using a beta adrenergic blocking drug to block sympathetic inotropic effects helps to demonstrate this point nicely (Stone, Bishop, & Dong, 1967).

These findings point to a large integrative role of the CNS in regulating cardiac output by activating important central inhibitory or facilitatory mechanisms at multiple sites in the brain and spinal cord. These in turn inhibit or facilitate either the vagal inhibition or sympathetic facilitation, to change the blood flow to the body. Whether the change is appropriate to the situation or not depends upon the integrative character of the CNS to accept all the information input, both afferent and memory, concerning both the present situation and the estimated demands of the immediate future, and then to activate autonomic effectors according to the final appraisal of needs.

Integrative Regulation of Vascular Beds

Arterial tone   Blood flow to the body is pulsatile through distensible and contractile tubes. The physical characteristics of flow are quite complex and can be pursued in greater detail in various physiology texts, handbooks, and monographs. The neurogenic factors influencing cardiac output are coupled to those influencing peripheral vascular resistance, which in turn is primarily controlled by arteriolar and capillary constriction. Arterial pressure, therefore, results from the interplay of stroke volume and arteriolar constriction. Vasomotor tone of neurogenic origin is superimposed on the autoregulatory phenomena currently popular among physiologists who study isolated vascular beds principally in anesthetized animals (Johnson, 1964). Folkow (1964) has pointed out that the presence of adrenergic innervation of the outer muscle layers in arterioles probably modulates the autoregulatory myogenic tone of the inner layers of non-innervated smooth muscle when sympathetic discharge is increased. Others voice a similar opinion that neurogenic influences of vasodilation and vasoconstriction are superimposed upon the intrinsic autoregulatory processes in the muscle and skin (Jones & Berne, 1964) and in other vascular beds as well. There is some recent evidence that neurogenic control offers specificity of function in terms of increasing the blood flow to certain vascular beds, while decreasing flow to others which are less functional at that moment. Such an integrated action confers greater efficiency on the body and might easily be regarded as its wisdom, as Cannon (1939) long ago proposed. The CNS can be regarded as a console organ. With its many stops, pedals, and keys it produces at any single instant of play a pattern of vascular responses that gives differential flow through the brain, gut, and kidney (Pappenheimer, 1960) and through the skin and muscle (Hoff, Kell, & Carroll, 1963; Hoff, Kell, Hasings, Sholes, & Gray, 1951; Uvnas, 1960). It thus produces a complex and integrated functional tune of total behavior in animal or man, analogous to music rather than noise. The expressor mechanisms derive from sensorimotor cortex, amygdala, hypothalamus, or medulla and pass out through peripheral sympathetic constrictors or sympathetic cholinergic dilatory systems (Bard, 1960; Smith, 1965, pp. 34–53; Uvnas, 1960; Wall & Davis, 1951). As pointed out earlier, there are mechanisms within the CNS to facilitate or inhibit the outflow of each of these systems (Manning, Charbon, & Cotten, 1963). This persistent vascular tone, due to a constant adrenergic outflow to specific vascular beds, may be blocked by inhibition of that particular CNS-adrenergic mechanism within the CNS itself, or by isolated peripheral competition of dilator and constrictor influences.

A classical example of this functional autonomic specificity comes from the experiments of Hoff and his colleagues (1951 and 1963). In these experiments, stimulation of the sensorimotor cortex, which would move the leg, produced vasodilation of the muscle vascular bed, vasoconstriction of the skin of that leg, and decreased blood flow to the cortex of the kidney. Blood volume was preserved by decreasing the urinary output, while raising the blood pressure. Denervating the kidney reversed the renal cortical constriction, but curare, preventing leg movement, did not abolish the functional shunt in the leg. Further knowledge of functional specificity of vascular reactivity must come from neurocardiological laboratory investigations on waking animals and from psychophysiological experiments in man.

It seems no longer reasonable to speak of anatomically discrete CNS "centers" for vasomotor control. Recent evidence would argue that the autonomic functions are controlled by transactional and interactional mechanisms that involve several levels of the CNS. Their integrative behavior appears to fit the job to be executed, rather than reflect a regional autonomy. A similar view concerning respiratory regulation, heart rate modulation, and neuroendocrine function may be equally tenable.

Venous System

The venous system and its neural control have challenged few biological workers and thinkers in the past. But now, since we know that blood returns to the heart through capacitance channels that are directly innervated (Grigor'eva, 1962; Kuntz, 1953, pp. 135–151) and are more sensitive to locally released or circulating catechols than are the resistance arterioles (Folkow, 1960; Kelly & Visscher, 1956), this may change. Certainly, the neural regulation of the veins assumes greater importance to regulating blood flow and total circulation than the volume of research indicates.

The clinical importance of venomotor tone and venous return as contributory factors in congestive heart failure has been recognized in the studies of

Burch and Ray (1951). Maire and Patton (1956a, 1956b) later demonstrated that acute pulmonary edema was precipitated in exercising rats following hypothalamic lesions. This was a consequence of the sudden redistribution of the splanchnic blood pool into the venous return beyond the recirculation capabilities of the heart. Patterson and Langford (1955) observed the same acute left ventricular failure and pulmonary edema in dogs whose sensorimotor cortex was stimulated, producing transient rises in blood pressure, after experimental myocardial infarction. More recently, a positive relationship between the emotional response to life situations and an increase in both central venous pressure (Martin, Vernon, & White, 1958) and salt and water retention (Barnes & Schottstaedt, 1960) has been observed in patients in congestive failure. Since these psychophysiologic reactions increase the degree of congestive failure and the risk of death, the search for these and related factors assumes clinical importance.

In dogs' adaptation to exercise, the vena cava constricts and venous return increases before the heart rate and stroke volume increase, whereas a frightening situation produces demonstrable decreases in caval diameter with an initial decrease in flow, followed by an increase (Tafur & Guntheroth, 1966). One obvious extension of these findings would be to predict that situations that give rise to fear would delay the cardiovascular physical response in emergency situations, but after being cornered, the animal or man may fight well.

Veins are constricted by sympathetic innervation or adrenergic neurohumors (Burch & Murtadha, 1956; Page, Hickam, Sieker, McIntosh, & Pryor, 1955). Zimmerman's (1966) observations on the sympathetic influence on small vessels have demonstrated separate innervation for arteries and veins in the dog's limb. The fibers supplying veins are diffusely distributed from cutaneous areas, as well as from the nerves accompanying the arteries. This allows for some specificity of vascular response and resultant variability of the regional blood flow.

Burch, who measured segmental tone in the human isolated forearm vein, describes a decrease in venous pressure preceding syncope in patients experiencing fright and apprehension (Burch, 1960;

Burch & Murtadha, 1956). This was a fortunate observation of an important psychogenic phenomenon. Venous tone increases readily with body movement, anticipation of movement, change in attention, or reflexes from pain, liver compression, or bladder distension. The orienting reflex to sudden noises and changes in environment also produced increased venous tone. Simple conditioning of this venous constriction by meaningless words or other symbols, associated with an electric shock, can be produced (Burch, 1964).

Using a cuff technique, Duggan, Love, and Lyons (1953) and Cohen, Bondurant, and Silverman (1960) studied isolated forearm venomotor tone in young male subjects. They found that venous constriction began within 2–3 sec after presentation of stimulus words that were either "bland or charged," and increased to a maximum between 30 and 60 sec, returning slowly toward the prestimulus level. This pattern is similar to that produced by physical stimuli and reflects the use of similar mechanisms. The venopressor response to "charged" words was greater than to "bland" words. One patient, however, showed no increase in venous pressure to "charged" words, although the interview and concurrent GSR readings disclosed an acute anxiety reaction. The experimenters concluded that maximal venoconstriction was already present with his high level of physiological arousal and that further vasoconstriction was not possible. This supports the findings of Lacey, Bateman, and VanLehn (1953) that high autonomic excitement preceding stimulation limits further reactivity. Burch (1964) cautions that in the selection of patients for these and other autonomic experiments the experimenter should exclude those people who present obvious evidence of anxiety.

Shmavonian's vasomotor conditioning experiments on young and aged subjects, using digital plethysmography, points out the errors a researcher can fall into if he is not multidisciplined and observant. The younger subjects could be conditioned to vasoconstriction; the older ones could not. The possible age factor took on a new meaning when an increase in baseline values of the older subjects, which was initially felt to be caused by arteriolar vasodilation, was observed to follow a modified valsalva (breath holding and attempted exhalation) maneuver. A respiratory tracing then showed that the resultant increased venous pressure and peripheral venous distension was producing the increased finger blood volume (Shmavonian, 1959). This example demonstrates the psychophysiological researcher's needs for training, experience, and continuing curiosity in both psychology and physiology (Cohen, 1964).

PSYCHOPHYSIOLOGICAL MECHANISMS

Heart Rate

Significant work has been done by monitoring the heart rate of people in naturally occurring stress. For example, continuous EKG and psychological monitoring of experienced, carrier-based naval pilots showed that the take off and landing not only demanded more attention and produced more anxiety than bombing runs against small arms fire in the Viet Nam conflict but they also resulted in greater tachycardia than actual combat bombing (Roman, Older, & Jones, 1967). Similar results have been studied in the daily life of physicians during stressful periods that produce increase in catechols and prolonged tachycardia (Ira, Whalen, & Bogdonoff, 1963) and in ski jumpers (Imhog et al., 1969).

A part of the orienting response to any new stimulus may be an increase in the heart rate (Germana & Klein, 1968). This phenomenon is not necessarily related to anxiety (Tan, 1964) but is probably related to the arousal mechanisms so well documented by Magoun (1963) and others. If the arousal is inordinate and persistent, a psychological state of anxiety occurs, which activates inappropriate autonomic mechanisms. The mechanisms and degree of the rate reaction are related to the individual's conscious or unconscious evaluation of the situation, his prior experience, and his previously established reaction patterns. The degree and direction of the heart rate response are thus determined and allow for the individual differences seen (Hodges & Spielberger, 1966). A novel or rarely experienced stimulus or event frequently produces an increase in heart rate. When the event anticipated becomes known and routine, even though noxious, the heart rate may fall (Deane, 1966). Furthermore, man's heart rate response to his environment, although varying individually and temporally, seems to have some relation to his involvement. If he considers himself personally involved in survival or if he is excluding environmental stimuli while performing arithmetic or mental work, the heart rate may increase. The heart rate has been observed to decrease when attention is directed to the environment without a sense of involvement (Campos & Johnson, 1966; Obrist, 1963).

Either classical (Dykman & Gantt, 1956; Hein, Cohen, & Shmavonian, 1966) or instrumental techniques can slow or speed up the heart. These methods are always more effective if the autonomic feedback is augmented by giving the subject cues of his response, even though he has no knowledge of what he is to learn or what regulates the feedback cue (Brener, 1966; Brener & Hothersall, 1966; Engel & Chism, 1967; Engel & Hansen, 1966). By the use of a visual display of a simultaneous feedback of the heart rate, human subjects have learned to stablize their heart rate, reducing the variability that occurred during the experimental period. This did not involve any overall change in rate; neither was it related to respiratory changes (Hnatiow & Lang, 1965). These conditioning results suggest that man can, by physiological methods and physiological feedback, alter his heart rate.

In rats previously conditioned to bar press for a reward stimulation of the medial forebrain bundle (MFB), further instrumental learning to change the heart rate in either direction was obtained by delivering a rewarding MFB stimulation on reaching a criterion response of rate change. By progressively increasing the criteria, different groups achieved either 20% or more increases or decreases in the heart rate. Interestingly, the three rats that died in these experiments were all in the group learning to slow their hearts (N. E. Miller & Di Cara, 1967). They showed progressively greater declines in their heart rates than did those who survived (Miller, personal communication).

Further experiments from the same laboratory have shown that medial forebrain bundle stimulation reward can prompt instrumental learning and specificity for either visceral motility or cardiac rate depending upon which visceral activity is rewarded (N. E. Miller & Banuazizi, 1968). Additionally, cardiac rate changes, both speeding and slowing, can be operantly conditioned with negative, aversive, reinforcement (DiCara & Miller, 1968), and learning of these responses can be transferred from the curarized to the noncurarized state (DiCara & Miller, 1969).

Engel and Gottleib (1970) demonstrated differential heart rate conditioning in the monkey. Producing cardiac rate slowing or speeding on demand within the same animal, they found that cardiac rate and arterial blood pressure changes were positively correlated during slowing conditions but uncorrelated during speeding conditions. This suggests that different physiological mechanisms are responsible for the opposite changes.

Taken together these studies of instrumental conditioning or cardiac dynamics indicate the existence of mechanisms for strong central control over visceral function and provide insight into the mechanisms of cardiac derangement and sudden death with intense psychological experience; they also suggest means to correct psychosomatic cardiac disorders.

In human operant conditioning experiments where patients were instructed to increase or decrease their heart rate without externalized feedback, Bergman and Johnson (1971) found heart rate increases easier to condition. Those subjects with either high or low autonomic perception were less successful in heart rate conditioning than those with mid-range autonomic perception quotients without externalized feedback. This is a significant overture toward understanding the internal milieu of individual patients that contributes to individual differences in autonomic behavior.

The Rhythm of the Heart

The neurogenic factors involved in altering the cardiac rhythm and cardiac conduction (EKG morphology) were discussed earlier. The next level of description of CNS influence is the psychogenic, which in the human being has been shown to produce emotional changes in the ST and T segments of the electrocardiogram (Duncan, Stevenson, & Ripley, 1950; Sigler, 1961), blocks in the atrioventricular conduction (Benedict & Evans, 1952), atrial arrhythmias (Duncan, Stevenson, & Ripley, 1950), ventricular extrasystoles (Stevenson, Duncan, Wolf, Ripley, & Wolff, 1949), and atrial and ventricular tachycardias (Meinhardt & Robinson, 1962; Wolf, 1958). Most clinicians have seen these

psychogenic arrhythmias in patients with and without heart disease; frequently, they have difficulty determining the psychogenic relationships due to the lack of continuous monitoring equipment, sufficient time for a good psychological history, and psychophysiological screening techniques.

There have been successful attempts to modify the heart rhythm using classical conditioning techniques. Bykov (1957) and Perez-Cruet and Gantt (1964) have conditioned changes in the heart rhythm in experimental animals by using drugs as the unconditioned stimulus. Attempts to condition extrasystoles using direct myocardial stimulation as the unconditional stimulus were not successful, presumably because there was no CNS intermediary (Perez-Cruet, Jude, & Gantt, 1966). This information was applied to man: 105 people without a history of heart disease were tested for ventricular extrasystoles during respiratory maneuvers. Nineteen of them did develop extrasystoles, 6 with a high incidence. Using multiple light stimuli to signal inspiration and expiration as the conditioned stimuli and the respiratory maneuvers as the unconditional stimuli, Perez-Cruet (1962) was able to condition ventricular premature contractions in 3 persons. Engel and Melmon (1968) have demonstrated that instrumental conditioning technques can be applied to patients with pathological heart rhythms such as atrial fibrillation, tachycardia, and supraventricular tachycardia. These patients were conditioned to slow their hearts and in some instances reverted to a normal sinus rhythm. Weiss and Engel (1971) have recently reported stopping frequent ventricular premature contractions when the patient was taught to slow the heart using operant conditioning techniques. Another patient, when given feedback of his ventricular prematurities, was able to reduce them from 20 to 2 per min. These results definitely suggest that vagal mechanisms can be conditioned to inhibit ventricular irritable foci.

These efforts signal the growing importance of conditioning in cardiovascular psychophysiology. Even more important is its potential usefulness in clinical cardiology for the prophylaxis and therapy of patients with recurrent or continuous disturbances of heart rhythms, some of which may be life-threatening.

The monitoring of patients by continuous physiological recording, combined with nurses' observations, offers an opportunity to correlate behavior with physiological responses. During periods of emotional stress, which also included humor with a hostile flavor, patients recovering from myocardial infarctions displayed multifocal ventricular prematurities, short runs of ventricular tachycardia, and atrioventricular blocks. More sinus and ventricular arrhythmias were seen during the REM-sleep periods, demonstrating that sleep is not necessarily restful to the patient recovering from heart disease (Lester, Block, & Gunn, 1968).

Dynamics of Heart and Circulation

Psychological factors altering the work of the heart have received much less attention than have those concerned with changes in the heart rate. The use of the ballistocardiograph, although yielding only a very approximate estimate of cardiac output, has adequately shown that cardiac output increases during anxiety, both at rest and after exercise in people with or without heart disease. In some instances the anxiety-producing stimulations increased the cardiac output more than did exercise itself (Stevenson et al., 1949). This is similar in its effect to the anticipation of exercise and hypothalamic stimulation seen in experimental animals (Rushmer, Smith, & Lasher, 1960; Smith et al., 1960).

Anxiety accompanying cardiac catheterizations may produce marked alterations in cardiac output and increases in blood pressure (Stead et al., 1945). In some patients the anxiety brought circulatory collapse. Furthermore, in patients made anxious by direct intravenous and respiratory measurements, an increase in peripheral resistance and blood pressure was not always attended by an increase in cardiac output (Hickam, Cargill, & Golden, 1948).

Attempts have been made to delineate the influence of various affective states. Bogdonoff et al. (1959), using the dye dilution technique and role enactment to produce different affective states in healthy college subjects, found that the quantity of the emotion influenced the cardiac output more than the quality. Circumstances that induced marked anxiety were more effective than those that aroused only moderate anxiety. The stroke volume did not increase in all subjects; neither did the heart rate; although cardiac output did. The postexperimental interviews to determine the affect and

degree produced did not disclose the reasons for these variations. Hostility could not be distinguished from anxiety by the character of the cardiovascular responses. These results are similar to those in other experiments using role enactment for affect production, but where cardiac dynamics were measured by ballistocardiograph (Ax, 1953; Schachter, 1957).

Responses of anger, anxiety, and the combination of both were associated with statistically significant increases in cardiac output, as monitored by stress interviews and the radioisotope technique. Although depression decreased the cardiac output, the changes did not reach statistical significance in these experiments (Adsett, Schottstaedt, & Wolf, 1962). In another study utilizing serial determinations over a 5-year period, decreases in cardiac output and coronary flow were observed in patients with coronary artery disease and their matched controls at times when independent observers judged the patients to be depressed (Sevelius, 1967). The significance of these observations is apparent to observers of patients with compensated organic heart disease, whose acute heart failure was precipitated by emotional crises (Barnes & Schottstaedt, 1960) or by a sudden cerebrovascular thrombosis or hemorrhage, which also activates the neurophysiological autonomic outflow.

The sympathetic nervous system is a final common pathway to the heart and the vessels that secures rapid and sensitive changes in heart functions not only to increase the rate and venous return but also to increase the contractile capabilities of the myocardium by increasing both the velocity and strength of the contraction. It has been observed that patients with congestive failure have an increased excretion of norepinephrine at rest, possibly signaling an increased sympathetic activity. Measuring the myocardial stores of norepinephrine, however, shows that the formation of norepinephrine and the capacity of the tissues to bind norepinephrine decreased during heart failure. Whether these were causes or effects of the heart failure is not clear, but they do appear to reduce myocardial efficiency (Chidsey & Braunwald, 1966). Patients with angina and sedentary individuals excrete more norepinephrine during exercise than do trained and active people. Such responses suggest that maximal measures are being used to meet minimal physical demands in the poorly conditioned person. This is an extravagant price for the marginal heart to pay and one perhaps related to the development of congestive failure.

The arterial response to neurogenic, neurohumoral, and metabolic vasomotor effectors may all subserve psychogenic mechanisms that change vascular tone and may be radically different in different vascular beds, depending on the subject, the emotional stress, and its meaning to him at that moment. This may mean that the composite of cardiac output and resistances of the various vascular beds may raise or lower the blood pressure or even produce no change. Vasodilation in the muscles, simultaneous with vasoconstriction in the splanchnic beds, kidney, and skin, occurs in animals following cortical and hypothalamic stimulation (Hoff et al., 1951) and in man during anxiety, fear, strenuous exercise, and to a lesser extent in the orienting reflex (Brod, 1964). The hypertensive man displays greater blood pressure changes in response to emotionally stressful situations than does a normotensive individual (Schachter, 1957; Wolf & Wolff, 1951, pp. 228–330). Healthy subjects with hypertensive parents overreact to noxious stimuli by greater cardiac output and systolic pressure rises than those of control subjects (A. P. Shapiro, 1961). Such subjects later respond by developing a greater peripheral resistance, after they develop clinical hypertension (Widimsky, Fejfarova, & Fejfar, 1957).

College-age hypertensive subjects reacted to both the stress interview and psychodrama with greater pressor response and less social poise than control subjects, a pattern shared by those with established hypertension (Harris et al., 1953). In one study subjects were classified as anxious hyperreactors and nonanxious hyporeactors on the basis of blood pressure response to a psychiatric interview. Mecholyl tests then showed the hyperreactors to respond by a pressor and the hyporeactors by a depressor response. The control subjects fell in between these groups. This again shows that psychophysiological reactions can offer predictive information (Thurrel, Greenfield, & Roessler, 1961).

Using regressive hypnosis, A. P. Shapiro (1960) observed rises in blood pressure when discussing conflictual periods with unresolved resentment and hostility in hypertensive patients. This differs from the stress interview data only in the means used to present significant life stresses to the patient.

Variability of the vascular response to increased gravity in the human centrifuge, or to the Mecholyl test, was found to be related to the affective and behavioral response of the subjects. Anxious, nonaggressive responders possessed poorer compensatory blood pressure adjustments than those with less anxiety and more overt agression. Altering the affective response by instruction altered the vascular response, as well as the catechol excretion. The aggressors excreted relatively more norepinephrine and less epinephrine than the anxious subjects, thus accounting in part for physiological differences of vascular tone to physical stress from subject to subject and in the same subject from time to time. The differences appear to be related to specific affective states and behavioral responses (Cohen & Silverman, 1959).

Also pertinent are Obrist's (1963) studies of young college students, already cited. With only one exception, both noxious stimuli and conceptual tasks increased the heart rate and blood pressure, but decreased the peripheral blood flow (finger plethysmographic) and the GSR. Those stimuli that required attention to the environment and away from a self-decreased heart rate, had either no effect on, or decreased, the blood pressure and increased the peripheral blood flow. The specificity of the response was seen in the different pattern of responses to the cold pressor test and to white noise, considered noxious but unthreatening. These stimuli slowed the heart while raising the blood pressure levels. Patients with phobias, who were asked to imagine their situational fears, showed marked increases in forearm blood flow. In some people, forearm blood flow is an excellent measure of arousal (Gelder & Mathews, 1968).

Primates have been observed to gradually increase their blood pressures to hypertensive during chronic avoidance conditioning experiments in restraining chairs. These results suggest that operant conditioning schedules that continuously exert strong control over behavior of animal or man may induce markedly persistent elevations in the arterial pressure (Forsyth, 1969; Herd, Morse, Kelleher, & Jones, 1969).

Figure 11.1C shows in essence a natural conditioning situation in a stock broker who was hypertensive before his myocardial infarction, 8 yr. ago, but was never found to have elevated blood pressures in the doctor's office since. During very stressful economic conditions, the continuously recorded blood pressure notes the rise in blood pressure when the market opened, which persisted until the market closed (Schneider, 1968).

Since blood pressure can be conditioned to rise, it should be conditioned to persist at lower levels in those people with hypertension. Recent experiences using light and tone feedback and reward reinforcement demonstrate that man can learn to lower his blood pressure using operant techniques (D. Shapiro, Schwartz, & Tursky, 1970). This application of psychophysiology may soon find a role in hypertensive therapy.

Vascular Beds

As we have pointed out earlier, the regulation of coronary flow by neurohumors, neural input, autoregulatory or metabolic mechanisms still challenges the physiologist. Studies of intact animals with implanted flow probes on the coronaries have shown the possibility of establishing conditional changes in the coronary flow (Zakharzhevskii, 1965). Chronic stimulation of lateral hypothalamic areas resulted in more coronary atherosclerosis and less aortic involvement than the more medial stimulation areas in rabbits fed the same mildly atherogenic diet (Gunn, Friedman, & Byers, 1960). These findings, and other studies, suggest that the CNS has specific regulatory influences over the coronary tree in health and may produce responses which contribute to coronary artery disease.

Angina pectoris, first described by Heberden in 1772, was recognized to be related to psychic factors long before its relation to coronary artery insufficiency was recognized. Ostfeld, Lebovits, Shekelle, and Paul (1964) administered the MMPI test prospectively to healthy industrial employees. Those who later developed angina scored significantly higher on the hysteria and hypochondriasis scales than those who developed evidences of coronary artery disease without angina pectoris. This observation has since been confirmed by others. Significantly, more depression has also been re-

corded in the MMPI of patients with angina than is seen in normal populations (Cole, Griffith, & Kaye, 1965). An aura of hopeless depression frequently surrounds the chronic cardiac patient before his terminal event. Depression seems to be related to a decrease in coronary flow and cardiac output, as shown by serial radiocardiogram observations of patients who had previous myocardial infarctions. Adsett, Schottstaedt, and Wolf (1962) also reported that depression decreased or had no effect on coronary flow and cardiac output, whereas anger, anxiety, and their combination were associated with increases in both.

During coronary angiography on a young man with no cinearteriographic evidence of coronary atherosclerosis, Demany, Tambe, and Zimmerman (1968) observed that emotional stress was accompanied by temporary coronary spasm, followed by coronary insufficiency and cardiac standstill. This is a most interesting observation which further demonstrates that psychophysiological observations and experiments of great importance can be made in a clinical medical environment.

The renal vascular bed responds to neural, as well as autoregulatory, signals in the intact human and in the experimental animal. Renal function studies performed on people before, during, and after stress interviews disclosed significant decreases in renal blood flow and increases in the glomerular filtration fractions during the pressor response. The consequent rise in vascular resistance was found to be greater in hypertensive than in normotensive subjects. Following lumbodorsal and splanchnic sympathectomy, the interview still induced an elevation of blood pressure, but now it was associated with a fall in filtration fraction and a rise in renal plasma flow, indicating less vasoconstriction in the afferent glomerular arteriole (Pfeiffer & Wolff, 1950). These studies have been confirmed using a radioactive tracer technique. Acute anxiety or fear associated with the anticipation of pain was accompanied by a decrease in renal blood flow, more marked in the right kidney. This is potentially of pathological significance, since the right kidney is far more often involved in unilateral renal disease associated with hypertension (De Maria et al., 1963). If this difference is not an artifact, and there is no technical reason to believe that it is, then we must assume that the right kidney is predisposed to react to neurogenic stimuli more intensely than the left, and furthermore that the degree and frequency of the reaction may predispose it to renal infection, arteriosclerosis, and perhaps even sustained elevation of blood pressure.

An interesting series of observations on patients with the so-called autoerythrocyte sensitization syndrome was made by Agle, Ratnoff, and Wasman (1967). These patients experienced recurrent deep cutaneous bleeding episodes. They had no abnormalities in their coagulation system or any known evidence of trauma but they did show a sensitivity to fragments of their own erythrocytes. Psychiatric interviews and psychological testing demonstrated a predominance of hysterical and masochistic traits and a propensity to express psychological problems in physical form through conversion mechanisms and psychophysiological responses. Patient observations suggested a temporal relationship between life stress and the bleeding episodes. The investigators were able to induce typical inflammatory ecchymotic lesions in specific skin areas by hypnotic suggestion in four of these patients. In one patient who had had a right lumbar sympathectomy, they were unable to produce lesions on the right leg but were able to do so on the left leg, suggesting that the increased vascular permeability may in some way be related to the sympathetic system. These investigators also feel that the release of bradykinin may be involved in this vascular permeability syndrome, since Wolff, Tunis, and Goodell (1953) have already demonstrated its involvement in migraine headache and ecchymoses. The same group has shown release of bradykinin under hypnotic suggestion (Chapman, Goodell, & Wolff, 1959). Now, in addition to dilation, constriction, and blood flow, the dimension of vascular permeability comes within the sphere of psychophysiology, bringing with it the need for new investigative techniques.

The sexual response cycle in man is well described in the classical monograph by Masters and Johnson (1966) and involves far-reaching vascular responses to specific stimuli. The four phases of the complete cycle are the excitement phase, plateau phase, orgasm phase, and resolution phase, which occur in that sequence with some

variation in both male and female. Vascular reactions in genital and in extragenital organs are modulated by the nervous system and are important in every phase. During the excitement phase, congestion of the genital organs begins and persists to the end of the entire response cycle. This results in penile erection in the male and vascular engorgement of the clitoris and labia in the female. Penile erection is brought about by vascular engorgement by increased arterial flow, and, to a lesser extent, decreased venous outflow, of the special erectile tissue of the penis. This is composed of a system of sinuses separated by fibrous septi and endowed with a rich arteriolar blood supply and veins capable of marked venoconstriction and possibly possessed of valves.

Erection cycles, disregarding other components of the sexual response cycle, have been studied during normal sleep in college students (Karacan, Goodenough, Shapiro, & Starker, 1966); 80% of the erections occurred with REM sleep accompanied by reported dreams of low anxiety content. Studies of erection and ejaculation by stimulation of the nervous system have established that portions of the limbic system (MacLean, Ploog, & Robinson, 1960) are involved in this complex psychovisceral event. Extragenital sexual responses in both arterial and venous beds are parallel in male and female. During the excitement phase in the female, venous engorgement of the breasts begins and persists until late in the resolution phase. In both sexes blood pressure elevations and a cutaneous flush are characteristically seen in the late plateau and orgasm phases. Increases in arterial blood pressure of 20–40 mm Hg diastolic and 40–100 mm Hg systolic have been observed. Shifts in blood volume and blood flow in other organs undoubtedly occur but need documentation. (See also Chapter 18.)

Hyperventilation

The consensus holds that the arteries to the brain are innervated by cervical sympathetic constrictor and dilator fibers from the greater superficial petrosal nerves. These extrinsic vasomotor mechanisms can account for less than 20% of cerebral vascular resistance, the principal factor being the concentration of CO_2 in the blood. A high concentration of CO_2 produces the most potent cerebral vasodilation, while hyperventilation, which decreases the concentration of CO_2, is a powerful cerebral vasoconstrictor. In our society the hyperventilation syndrome occurs most commonly as a psychophysiological accompaniment of anxiety and depression, a response capable of producing intense cerebrovasoconstriction, dizziness, changes in the EKG, and even unconsciousness and seizures. Hyperventilation also decreases the blood flow through the heart and skeletal muscles. In most subjects hyperventilation produces no change or only a slight fall in blood pressure. In some, however, it may produce episodic rises in blood pressure and severe headaches, simulating the effects of the epinephrine-producing tumor, pheochromocytoma. Counseling and the explanation of symptoms due to overbreathing have been shown to reduce the incidence and intensity of symptoms, even though the blood gases and the monitored physiological state show no improvement (Saltzman, Heyman, & Sieker, 1963).

Hyperventilation is a worthwhile technique for cardiovascular and psychophysiological studies in patients who have histories of vasomotor instability, orthostatic hypotension, angina, and the hyperventilation syndrome itself.

CONCLUSION

This chapter attempts to summarize the major physiological, biochemical, and neurophysiological principles pertinent to cardiovascular functions and to discuss their relevance to cardiovascular psychophysiology.

We have attempted to describe those studies that relate the psychological and physiological dimensions of cardiovascular behavior in health, and especially disease. Where possible, we have stressed response specificity, variability, and individual differences.

We have attempted to encourage a multidisciplinary view toward the subject pointing out possible methodological errors, areas needing further work, and more importantly the relevancy of psychophysiology to clinical medicine.

REFERENCES

ADSETT, C. A., SCHOTTSTAEDT, W. W., & WOLF S. G. Changes in coronary blood flow and other hemodynamic indicators induced by stressful interviews. *Psychosomatic Medicine*, 1962, **24**, 331-336.

AGLE, D. P., RATNOFF, O. D., & WASMAN, M. Studies in autoerythrocyte sensitization: The induction of purpuric lesions by hypnotic suggestion. *Psychosomatic Medicine*, 1967, **29**, 491-503.

AHLQUIST, R. P. A study of the adrenotropic receptors. *American Journal of Physiology*, 1948, **153**, 586-599.

AHLQUIST, R. P. Effects of the autonomic drugs on the circulatory system. In W. F. HAMILTON & P. DOW (Eds), *Handbook of Physiology*, Section 2, *Circulation*, Vol. 3. Washington, D.C.: American Physiological Society, 1965.

ANAND, B. K., CHHINA, G. S., & SINGH, B. Studies on Shri Ramanand Yogi during his stay in an air-tight box. *Indian Journal of Medical Research*, 1961, **49**, 82-89.

ANDERSON, D. E., & BRADY, J. V. Preavoidance blood pressure elevations accompanied by heart rate decreases in the dog. *Science*, 1971, **172**, 595.

AUSTEN, W. G., EBERT, P. A., & GREENFIELD, L. J. Mechanisms of cardiac arrest in acute hypoxia. *Surgery*, 1962, **53**, 784-791.

AX, A. F. The physiological differentiation between fear and anger in humans. *Psychosomatic Medicine*, 1953, **15**, 433-442.

BARD, P. Anatomical organization of central nervous system in relation to control of the heart and blood vessels. *Physiological Reviews*, 1960, **40** (Suppl. 4), 3-26.

BARKER, S., & WOLF, S. G. Experimental induction of grand mal seizure during the hypnoidal state induced by sodium amytal. *American Journal of Medical Science*, 1947, **214**, 600-604.

BARNES, R., & SCHOTTSTAEDT, W. W. The relation of emotional state to renal excretion of water and electrolytes in patients with congestive heart failure. *American Journal of Medicine*, 1960, **29**, 217-227.

BENEDICT, R. B., & EVANS, J. M. Second degree heart block and Wenckebach phenomenon associated with anxiety. *American Heart Journal*, 1952, **43**, 623-633.

BERGMAN, J. S., & JOHNSON, H. J. The effects of instructional set and autonomic perception on cardiac control. *Psychophysiology*, 1971, **8**, 180.

BERGSTROM, S., CARLSON, L. A., & WEEKS, J. R. Prostaglandins: A family of biologically active lipids. *Pharmacological Reviews*, 1968, **20**, 1-48.

BERNE, R. M., DEGEEST, H., & LEVY, M. N. Influence of the

cardiac nerves on coronary resistance. *American Journal of Physiology*, 1965, **208**, 763–769.

BOGDONOFF, M. D., COMBS, J. J., BRYANT, G. D., & WARREN, J. V. Cardiovascular responses in experimentally induced alterations of affect. *Circulation*, 1959, **20**, 353–359.

BOGDONOFF, M. D., KLEIN, R. F., BACK, K. W., NICHOLS, C. R., TROYER, W. E., & HOOD, T. C. Effect of group relationship and of the role of leadership upon lipid mobilization. *Psychosomatic Medicine*, 1964, **26**, 710–719.

BOHR, D. F. Adrenergic receptors in coronary arteries. *Annals of the New York Academy of Sciences*, 1967, **139**, 799–807.

BRAUNWALD, E., EPSTEIN, S. E., GLICK, G., WECHSLER, A., & BRAUNWALD, N. S. Relief of angina pectoris by electrical stimulation of the carotid sinus. *New England Journal of Medicine*, 1967, **277**, 1278–1283.

BRENER, J. Heart rate as an avoidance response. *Physiological Record*, 1966, **16**, 329–336.

BRENER, J., & HOTHERSALL, D. Heart rate control under conditions of augmented sensory feedback. *Psychophysiology*, 1966, **3**, 23–28.

BROD, J. Circulation in muscle during acute pressor responses to emotional stress and during chronic sustained elevation of blood pressure. *American Heart Journal*, 1964, **68**, 424–426.

BROWN, A. M. Motor innervation of coronary arteries of the cat. *Journal of Physiology*, 1968, **198**, 311–328.

BUNAG, R. D., McCUBBIN, J. W., & PAGE, I. H. Neurogenic stimulation of renin release. *Pharmacologist*, 1965, **7**, 152.

BUNNEY, W. E., Jr., MASON, J. W., & HAMBURG, D. A. Correlations between behavioral variables and urinary 17-hydroxycorticosteroids in depressed patients. *Psychosomatic Medicine*, 1965, **27**, 299–308.

BURCH, G. E. Influence of central nervous system on veins of man. *Physiological Reviews*, 1960, **40** (Suppl. 4), 50–56.

BURCH, G. E. A critique of aspects of methodological approaches to the role of the central nervous system in cardiovascular disease. *Psychosomatic Medicine*, 1964, **26**, 432–453.

BURCH, G. E., & MURTADHA, M. A study of the venomotor tone in a short intact venous segment of the forearm of man. *American Heart Journal*, 1956, **51**, 807–828.

BURCH, G. E., & RAY, C. T. A consideration of the mechanism of congestive heart failure. *American Heart Journal*, 1951, **41**, 918–946.

BURNS, N. M., BAKER, C. A., SIMONSON, E., & KEIPER, C. EKG changes in prolonged automobile driving. *Perceptual and Motor Skills*, 1966, **23**, 210.

BYKOV, K. M. *The cerebral cortex and the internal organs.* Translated by W. Gantt, New York: Chemical Publishing, 1957.

CACERES, C. A. (Ed.) *Biomedical telemetry.* New York: Academic, 1965.

CAMPOS, J. J., & JOHNSON, H. J. The effects of verbalization instructions and visual attention on heart rate and skin conductance. *Psychophysiology*, 1966, **2**, 305–310.

CANNON, W. B. *The wisdom of the body.* (2nd ed.) New York: Norton, 1939.

CANTU, R. C., & GOODMAN, H. M. Effects of denervation and fasting on white adipose tissue. *American Journal of Physiology*, 1967, **212**, 207–212.

CATHEY, C., JONES, H. B., NAUGHTON, J., HAMMARSTEN, J. F., & WOLF, S. G. The relationship of life stress to concentration of serum lipids in patients with coronary artery disease. *American Journal of Medicine*, 1962, **244**, 421–441.

CHAPMAN, L. F., & GOODELL, H. The participation of the nervous system in the inflammatory reaction. *Annals of the New York Academy of Sciences*, 1964, **116**, 990–1017.

CHAPMAN, L. F., GOODELL, H., & WOLFF, H. G. Changes in tissue vulnerability induced during hypnotic suggestion. *Journal of Psychosomatic Research*, 1959, **4**, 99–105.

CHATTERJEE, B. B., & ERIKSEN, C. W. Cognitive factors in heart rate conditioning. *Journal of Experimental Psychology*, 1962, **64**, 272–279.

CHIDSEY, C. A., & BRAUNWALD, E. Sympathetic activity and neurotransmitter depletion in congestive heart failure. *Pharmacological Reviews*, 1966, **18**, 685–700.

COHEN, S. I. Comments, Timberline conference on psychophysiological aspects of cardiovascular disease. *Psychosomatic Medicine*, 1964, **26**, 437.

COHEN, S. I., BONDURANT, S., & SILVERMAN, A. J. Psychophysiological influences on peripheral venous tone. *Psychosomatic Medicine*, 1960, **22**, 106–117.

COHEN, S. I., & SILVERMAN, A. J. Psychophysiological investigations of vascular response variability. *Journal of Psychosomatic Research*, 1959, **3**, 185–210.

COLE, S. L., GRIFFITH, G. C., & KAYE, H. Anginal pain and depression: A preliminary investigation. *Diseases of the Chest*, 1965, **48**, 584–586.

COOPER, T. Terminal innervation of the heart. In W. RANDALL (Ed.), *Nervous control of the heart.* Baltimore: Williams & Wilkins, 1965.

CORRELL, J. W. Adipose tissue: Ability to respond to nerve stimulation in vitro. *Science*, 1963, **140**, 387–388.

DAGGETT, W. M., NUGENT, G. C., CARR, P. W., POWERS, P. C., & HARADA, Y. Influence of vagal stimulation on ventricular contractility, O_2 consumption and coronary flow. *American Journal of Physiology*, 1967, **212**, 8–18.

DAHLSTROM, A., FUXE, K., MYA-TU, M., & ZETTERSTROM, B. E. M. Observations on adrenergic innervation of dog heart. *American Journal of Physiology*, 1965, **209**, 689–692.

DAMASER, E. C., SHOR, R. R., & ORNE, M. T. Physiological effects during hypnotically requested emotions. *Psychosomatic Medicine*, 1963, **25**, 334–343.

DEANE, G. E. Human heart rate responses during experimentally induced anxiety: Effects of instruction on acquisition. *Journal of Experimental Psychology*, 1966, **71**, 772–773.

DeGEEST, H., LEVY, M. N., ZIESKE, H., & LIPMAN, R. I. Depression of ventricular contractility by stimulation of the vagus nerves. *Circulation Research*, 1965, **17,** 222–235.

DEMANY, M. A., TAMBE, A., & ZIMMERMAN, H. A. Coronary arterial spasm. *Diseases of the Chest*, 1968, **53,** 714–721.

DE MARIA, W. J., SHMAVONIAN, B. M., COHEN, S. I., KRUEGER, R. P., HAWKINS, D. M., BAYLIN, S. B., SANDERS, A. P., & BAYLIN, G. J. Renal conditioning. *Psychosomatic Medicine*, 1963, **25,** 538–542.

DICARA, L. V., & MILLER, N. E. Changes in heart rate instrumentally learned by curarized rats as avoidances responses. *Journal of Comparative and Physiological Psychology*, 1968, **65,** 8–12.

DICARA, L. V., & MILLER, N. E. Transfer of instrumentally learned heart rate changes from curarized to non-curarized state: Implications for a mediational hypothesis. *Journal of Comparative and Physiological Psychology*, 1969, **68,** 159–162.

DIGIOVANNI, C., & CHAMBERS, R. M. Physiological and psychologic aspects of the gravity spectrum. *New England Journal of Medicine*, 1964, **270,** 88–94, 134–139.

DOLE, V. P. A relation between non-esterified fatty acids in plasma and the metabolism of glucose. *Journal of Clinical Investigation*, 1956, **35,** 150–154.

DONALD, D. E., & SHEPARD, J. T. Heart rate and cardiac output in exercising dogs after partial and complete cardiac denervation. *Physiologist*, 1961, **4,** 29. (Abstract)

DUBIN, D. *Rapid interpretation of EKG's.* (12th ed.) Tampa, Fla.: Cover Publishing Company, 1970.

DUGGAN, J. L., LOVE, V. L., & LYONS, R. H. A study of reflex venomotor reactions in man. *Circulation*, 1953, **7,** 869–873.

DUNCAN, C. H., STEVENSON, I. P., & RIPLEY, H. S. Life situations, emotions, and paroxysmal auricular arrhythmias. *Psychosomatic Medicine*, 1950, **12,** 23–37.

DYKMAN, R. A., & GANTT, W. H. Relation of experimental tachycardia to amplitude of motor activity and intensity of motivating stimulus. *American Journal of Physiology*, 1956, **185,** 495–498.

EBERT, P. A., ALLGOOD, R. J., & SABISTON, P. C. Effect of cardiac denervation on arrhythmia following coronary artery occlusion. *Surgical Forum*, 1967, **18,** 114–115.

EICHNA, L. W., & MCQUARRIE, D. G. (Eds.) Symposium: Central nervous system control of circulation. *Physiological Reviews*, 1960, **40** (Suppl. 4).

ELMADJIAN, F., HOPE, J. M., & LAMSON, E. T. Excretion of epinephrine and norepinephrine in various emotional states. *Journal of Clinical Endocrinology*, 1957, **17,** 608–620.

ENGEL, B. T., & CHISM, R. A. Operant conditioning of heart rate speeding. *Psychophysiology*, 1967, **3,** 418–426.

ENGEL, B. T., & GOTTLEIB, S. H. Differential operant conditioning of heart rate in the restrained monkey. *Journal of Comparative and Physiological Psychology*, 1970, **73,** 217–225.

ENGEL, B. T., & HANSEN, S. P. Operant conditioning of heart rate slowing. *Psychophysiology* 1966, **3,** 176–187.

ENGEL, B. T., & MELMON, K. L. Operant conditioning of

heart rate in patients with cardiac arrhythmias. Presented at the Pavlovian Society Meeting, Princeton, N.J., November 1967.

ERDOS, E. G. (Ed.) Structure and function of biologically active peptides. *Annals of the New York Academy of Sciences*, 1963, **104,** 1–464.

ERDOS, E. G. Hypotensive peptides: Bradykinkin, kallidin, and eledoisin. *Advances in Pharmacology*, 1966, **4,** 1–90.

ERDOS, E. G., BACK, N., & SICUTERI, F. (Eds.) *Hypotensive peptides.* New York: Springer-Verlag, 1966.

FEIGL, E. O. Sympathetic control of coronary circulation. *Circulation Research*, 1967, **20,** 262–270.

FEIGL, E. O. Parasympathetic control of coronary bloodflow in dogs. *Circulation Research*, 1969, **25,** 509–519.

FEIGL, E. O., & FOLKOW, B. Cardiovascular responses in "diving" and during brain stimulation in ducks. *Acta Physiologica Scandinavica*, 1963, **57,** 99–110.

FOLKOW, B. Range of control of cardiovascular system by the central nervous system. *Physiological Reviews*, 1960, **40** (Suppl. 4), 93–99.

FOLKOW, B. Autoregulation in muscle and skin. *Circulation Research*, 1964, **15** (Suppl. 1), 19–24.

FOLKOW, B., & VON EULER, U. S. Selective activation of nor-adrenaline and adrenaline producing cells in the cat's adrenal gland by hypothalamic stimulation. *Circulation Research*, 1954, **2,** 191–195.

FORSYTH, R. P. Blood pressure responses to long-term avoidance schedules in the restrained rhesus monkey. *Psychosomatic Medicine*, 1969, **31,** 300–309.

FRANKLIN, D., WATSON, N. W., PIERSON, K. E., & VAN CITTERS, R. L. Technique for radiotelemetry of blood flow velocity from unrestrained animals. *American Journal of Medical Electronics*, 1966, **5,** 24–28.

FRAZIER, T. W. Avoidance conditioning of heart rate in humans. *Psychophysiology*, 1966, **3,** 188–202.

FROBERG, J., KARLSSON, C. G., LEVI, L., LIDBERG, L., & SEEMAN, K. Conditions of work: Psychological and endocrine stress reactions. *Archives of Environmental Health*, 1970, **21,** 789–797.

GAMPEL, B., SLOME, C., SCOTCH, N., & ABRAMSON, J. H. Urbanization and hypertension among Zulu adults. *Journal of Chronic Diseases*, 1962, **15,** 67–70.

GANTT, W. H. Cardiovascular component of the conditioned reflex to pain, food, and other stimuli. *Physiological Reviews*, 1960, **40** (Suppl. 4), 266–295.

GELDER, M. G., & MATHEWS, A. M. Forearm blood flow and phobic anxiety. *British Journal of Psychiatry*, 1968, **114,** 1371–1376.

GERMANA, J., & KLEIN, S. B. The cardiac component of the orienting response. *Psychophysiology*, 1968, **4,** 324.

GOLDMAN, M. J. *Principles of clinical electrocardiography.* Los Altos, Cal.: Lange Medical Publications, 1970.

GRAHAM, D. T., KABLER, J. D., & GRAHAM, F. K. Physiological response to the suggestion of attitudes specific for hives and hypertension. *Psychosomatic Medicine*, 1962, **24**, 159-169.

GRAHAM, F. K., & KUNISH, N. O. Physiological responses of unhypnotized subjects to attitude suggestions. *Psychosomatic Medicine*, 1965, **27**, 317-329.

GREENGARD, P., & COSTA, E. (Eds.) Role of cyclic AMP in cell function. *Advances in Biochemical Psychopharmacology*, 1970, **3**, 11-386.

GRIGOR'EVA, T. A. *Innervation of blood vessels*. Translated by C. Matthews & C. R. Pringle. New York: Pergamon, 1962.

GUNN, C. G., FRIEDMAN, M., & BYERS, S. O. Effect of chronic hypothalamic stimulation upon cholesterol-induced atherosclerosis in the rabbit. *Journal of Clinical Investigation*, 1960, **39**, 1963-1972.

GUNN, C. G., & HAMPTON, J. W. CNS influence on plasma levels of factor VIII activity. *American Journal of Physiology*, 1967, **212**, 124-130.

GUNN, C. G., HOUK, P. C., & PERSON, R. J. Vagal and sympathetic influence on a ventricular extopic focus. To be published, 1971.

GUNN, C. G., SEVELIUS, G., PUIGGARI, M., & MYERS, F. K. Vagal cardiomotor mechanisms in the hind brain of the dog and cat. *American Journal of Physiology*, 1968, **214**, 258-262.

HARRIS, R. E., SOKOLOW, M., CARPENTER, L. G., FREEDMAN, M., & HUNT, S. P. Response to psychologic stress in persons who are potentially hypertensive. *Circulation*, 1953, **7**, 874-879.

HAVEL, R. J. Autonomic nervous system and adipose tissue. In A. E. RENOLD & G. F. CAHILL, Jr. (Eds), *Handbook of physiology*, Section 5, *Adipose tissue*, Vol. 1. Washington, D.C.: American Physiological Society, 1965.

HEIN, P. L., COHEN, S. I., & SHMAVONIAN, B. M. Perceptual mode and cardiac conditioning. *Psychophysiology*, 1966, **3**, 101-107.

HERD, J. A., MORSE, W., KELLEHER, R. T., & JONES, L. R. Arterial hypertension in the squirrel monkey during behavioral experiments. *American Journal of Physiology*, 1969, **217**, 24-29.

HEYMANS, C., & NEIL, E. *Reflexogenic areas of the cardiovascular system*. Boston: Little, Brown, 1958.

HICKHAM, J. B., CARGILL, W. H., & GOLDEN, A. Cardiovascular reactions to emotional stimuli: Effect on the cardiac output, arteriovenous oxygen difference, arterial pressure, and peripheral resistance. *Journal of Clinical Investigation*, 1948, **27**, 290-298.

HILLARP, N. A. Peripheral autonomic mechanisms. In J. FIELD, H. W. MAGOUN, & V. E. HALL (Eds), *Handbook of physiology*, Section 1, *Neurophysiology*, Vol. 2. Washington, D.C.: American Physiological Society, 1960.

HNATIOW, M., & LANG, P. J. Learned stabilization of the cardiac rate. *Psychophysiology*, 1965, **1**, 330-336.

HODGES, W. F., & SPEILBERGER, C. D. Effect of threat of shock on heart rate for subjects who differ in manifest anxiety and fear of shock. *Psychophysiology*, 1966, **2**, 287-294.

HOFF, E. C., KELL, J. F., Jr., & CARROLL, M. N., Jr. Effects of cortical stimulation and lesions on cardiovascular function. *Physiological Reviews*, 1963, **43**, 68-114.

HOFF, E. C., KELL, J. F., Jr., HASTINGS, N., SHOLES, A. M., & GRAY, F. H. Vasomotor, cellular and functional changes produced in kidney by brain stimulation. *Journal of Neurophysiology*, 1951, **14**, 317-332.

HORAN, L. C., & KISTLER, I. C. Study of ventricular response in atrial fibrillation. *Circulation Research*, 1961, **9**, 305-311.

HORTON, E. W. Hypotheses on physiological roles of prostaglandins. *Physiological Reviews*. 1969, **49**, 122-161.

IMHOG, P. R. Beta-blockade and emotional tachycardia: Radiotelemetric investigations in ski jumpers. *Journal of Applied Physiology*, 1969, **27**, 366-369.

IRA, G. H., WHALEN, R. E., & BOGDONOFF, M. D. Heart rate changes in physicians during daily "stressful" tasks. *Journal of Psychosomatic, Research*, 1963, **7**, 147-150.

JOHNSON, P. C. Autoregulation of blood flow. *Circulation Research*, 1954, **15** (Suppl. 1), 2-9.

JONES, R. D., & BERNE, R. M. Local regulation of blood flow in skeletal muscle. *Circulation Research*, 1964, **15** (Suppl. 1), 30-38.

JOY, M. B., & LOWE, R. B. Evidence that the area postrema mediates the central cardiovascular response to angiotensin II. *Nature*, 1970, **228**, 1303-1304.

JUHASZ-NAGY, A., & SZENTIVANYI, M. Separation of cardioacceleration and coronary vasomotor fibers in the dog. *American Journal of Physiology*, 1961, **200**, 125-129.

KAADA, B. R. Somatomotor, autonomic and electrocorticographic responses to electrical stimulation of rinecephalic and other structures in primates, cat and dog. *Acta Physiologica Scandinavica*, 1951, **2** (Suppl. 83), 1-285.

KARACAN, I., GOODENOUGH, D. R., SHAPIRO, A., STARKER, S. Erection cycle in sleep in relation to dream anxiety. *Archives of General Psychiatry*, 1966, **15**, 183-189.

KELLEY, W. D., & VISSCHER, M. B. Effect of sympathetic nerve stimulation on cutaneous small vein and small artery pressures, blood flow and hindpaw volume in the dog. *American Journal of Physiology*, 1956, **185**, 453-464.

KETY, S. S. The cerebral circulation. In J. FIELD, H. W. MAGOUN, & V. E. HALL (Eds), *Handbook of physiology*, Section 1, *Neurophysiology*, Vol. 3. Washington, D.C.: American Physiological Society, 1960.

KHABAROVA, A. Y. *The afferent innervation of the heart*. Translated by B. Haigh. New York: Consultants Bureau, 1963.

KORNER, P. I. Integrative neural cardiovascular control. *Physiological Reviews*, 1971, **51**, 312-367.

KUNTZ, A. *The autonomic nervous system*. (4th ed.) Philadelphia: Lea & Febiger, 1953.

LACEY, J. I., BATEMAN, D. E., & VANLEHN, R. Autonomic response specificity: An experimental study. *Psychosomatic Medicine*, 1953, **15**, 8-21.

LARAGH, J. H., ANGERS, M., KELLY, W. G., & LIEBERMAN, S. Hypotensive agents and pressor substances: The effect of epinephrine, norepinephrine, angiotensin II, and others on secretory rate of aldosterone in man. *Journal of the American Medical Association*, 1960, **174,** 234–240.

LAZARUS, R. S., SPEISMAN, J. C., & MORDKOFF, A. M. The relationship between autonomic indicators of psychological stress: Heart rate and skin conductance. *Psychosomatic Medicine*, 1963, **25,** 19–30.

LEMBECK, F., & ZETLER, G. Substance P: A polypeptide of possible physiological significance especially within the nervous system. *International Review of Neurobiology*, 1962, **5,** 159–215.

LESTER, B. K., BLOCK, R., & GUNN, C. G. The relationship of cardiac arrhythmias to phases of sleep. *Clinical Research*, 1969, **17,** 456.

LEVI, L. Life stress and urinary excretion of adrenalin and nor adrenalin. In W. RAAB (Ed.), *Prevention of ischemic heart disease: Principles and practice.* Springfield, Ill.: Charles C Thomas, 1966.

LEVY, M. N., NG, M. L., MARTIN, P., & ZIESKE, H. Sympathetic and parasympathetic interactions on the left ventricle of the dog. *Circulation Research*, 1966, **19,** 5–10.

LIPMAN, B. S., & MASSIE, E. *Clinical scalar electrocardiography.* (5th ed.) Chicago: Year Book Medical Publishers, 1965.

MACKAY, R. S. The potential for telemetry in biological research in the physiology of animals and man. In L. E. SLATER (Ed.), *Biotelemetry.* New York: Pergamon, 1963, pp. 45–58.

MacLEAN, D., PLOOG, D. W., & ROBINSON, W. Circulatory effects of limbic stimulation, with special reference to the male genital organ. *Physiological Reviews*, 1960, **40** (Suppl. 4), 105–112.

MAGOUN, H. W. *The waking brain.* (2nd ed.) Springfield, Ill.: Charles C Thomas, 1963.

MAIRE, F. W., & PATTON, H. D. Neural structures involved in genesis of preoptic pulmonary edema, gastric erosions and behavioral changes. *American Journal of Physiology*, 1956, **184,** 345–350. (a)

MAIRE, F. W., & PATTON, H. D. Role of the spanchnic nerve and adrenal medulla in the genesis of preoptic pulmonary edema. *American Journal of Physiology*, 1956, **184,** 351–355. (b)

MANNING, J. W., CHARBON, G. A., & COTTEN, M. DE V. Central inhibition of tonic sympathetic activity on the heart. *American Journal of Physiology*, 1963, **205,** 1221–1226.

MANNING, J. W., & COTTEN, M. DE V. Mechanisms of cardiac arrhythmias induced by diencephalic stimulation. *American Journal of Physiology*, 1962, **203,** 1120–1124.

MARTIN, D. A., VERNON, C. R., & WHITE, K. L. Life situations and venous pressure in congestive heart failure. *North Carolina Medical Journal*, 1958, **19,** 513–523.

MASTERS, W. H., & JOHNSON, V. E. *Human sexual response.* Boston: Little, Brown, 1966.

McCUBBIN, J. W., & PAGE, I. H. A unifying view of renal hypertension. In W. M. MANAGER (Ed.), *Hormones and hypertension.* Springfield, Ill.: Charles C Thomas, 1966.

MEINHARDT, K., & ROBINSON, H. A. Stokes-Adams syndrome precipitated by emotional stress. *Psychosomatic Medicine*, 1962, **24,** 325–330.

MILLER, M. R., & KASAHARA, M. Studies of nerve endings in the heart. *American Journal of Anatomy*, 1964, **115,** 217–234.

MILLER, N. E., & BANUAZIZI, A. Instrumental learning by curarized rats of a specific visceral response, intestinal or cardiac. *Journal of Comparative and Physiological Psychology*, 1968, **65,** 1–7.

MILLER, N. E., & DiCARA, L. Instrumental learning of heart rate changes in curarized rats: Shaping and specificity to discriminative stimulus. *Journal of Comparative and Physiological Psychology*, 1967, **63,** 12–19.

MITCHELL, G. *Cardiovascular innervation.* Baltimore: Williams & Wilkins, 1956.

OBRIST, P. A. Cardiovascular differentiation of sensory stimuli. *Psychosomatic Medicine*, 1963, **25,** 450–459.

OBRIST, P. A., WEBB, R. A., SUTTERER, J. R. & HOWARD, J. C. The cardiac somatic relationship: Some reformulations. *Psychophysiology*, 1970, **6,** 569–587.

O'CONNOR, W. J. The effect of section of supraoptico-hypophyseal tracts on the inhibition of water diuresis by emotional stress. *Quarterly Journal of Experimental Physiology*, 1946, **33,** 149–161.

OSTFELD, A. M., LEBOVITS, B. Z., SHEKELLE, R. B., & PAUL, O. A prospective study of the relationship between personality and coronary heart disease. *Journal of Chronic Diseases*, 1964, **17,** 265–276.

PAGE, E. B., HICKAM, J. B., SIEKER, H. O., McINTOSH, H. D., & PRYOR, W. Reflex venomotor activity in normal persons and in patients with postural hypotension. *Circulation*, 1955, **11,** 262–270.

PAGE, I. H., & BUMPUS, F. M. Angiotensin. *Physiological Reviews*, 1961, **41,** 331–390.

PAPPENHEIMER, J. R. Central control of renal circulation, *Physiological Reviews*, 1960, **40** (Suppl. 4), 35–37.

PARADES, A., WEST, L. J., & SNOW, C. C. Biosocial adaptation and correlates of acculturation in the Tarahumara ecosystem. *International Journal of Social Psychiatry*, 1970, **16,** 163–174.

PARKER, I. T., GUNN, C. G., & LYNN, T. N. Experimental centrogenic arrhythmias. *Clinical Research*, 1962, **10,** 179.

PATTERSON, J. L., Jr., & LANGFORD, H. G. Dynamics of acute failure of the left ventricle during neurogenic hypertension. *Circulation*, 1955, **12,** 757. (Abstract)

PAUL, M. I., CRAMER, H., & BUNNEY, W. E. Urinary adenosine 3′,5′ monophosphate in the switch process from depression to mania. *Science*, 1971, **171,** 300–303.

PEREZ-CRUET, J. Conditioning of extrasystoles in humans with respiratory maneuvers as unconditional stimulus. *Science*, 1962, **137,** 160–161.

PEREZ-CRUET, J., & GANTT, W. H.   Conditional reflex electro-cardiographic changes to bulbocapnine. *American Heart Journal*, 1964, **67,** 61–72.

PEREZ-CRUET, J., JUDE, J. R., & GANTT, W. H.   An attempt to condition extrasystoles using direct myocardial electrical stimulation as an unconditional stimulus. *Conditional Reflex*, 1966, **1,** 104–116.

PERNOW, B.   Pharmacology of substance P. *Annals of the New York Academy of Sciences* 1963, **104,** 393–402.

PFEIFFER, J. B., Jr., & WOLFF, H. G.   Studies in renal circulation during periods of life stress and accompanying emotional reactions in subjects with and without essential hypertension: Observations on the role of neural activity in regulation of renal blood flow. *Proceedings of the Association for Research in Nervous and Mental Disease*, 1950, **29,** 929–953.

PITT, B., ELLIOT, E. C., & GREGG, D. E.   Adrenergic receptor activity in the coronary arteries of the unanesthetized dog. *Circulation Research*, 1967, **21,** 217–227.

PORTER, R. W., & FRENCH, J. D.   The physiologic basis of cardiac arrest during anesthesia. *American Journal of Surgery*, 1960, **100,** 354–357.

PORTER, R. W., KAMIKAWA, K., & GREENHOOT, J. H.   Persistent electrocardiographic abnormalities experimentally induced by stimulation of the brain. *American Heart Journal*, 1962, **64,** 815–819.

RANDALL, W. C. (Ed.)   *Nervous control of the heart*. Baltimore: Williams & Wilkins, 1965.

RANDALL, W. C., & ROHSE, W. G.   The augmentor action of the sympathetic cardiac nerves. *Circulation Research*, 1956, **4,** 470–475.

ROMAN, J., OLDER, H., & JONES, W., L.   Flight research program: VII. Medical monitoring of navy carrier pilots in combat. *Aerospace Medicine*, 1967, **38,** 133–139.

RUSHMER, R. F.   Effects of nerve stimulation and hormones on the heart: The role of the heart in general circulatory regulations. In W. F. HAMILTON & P. DOW (Eds.), *Handbook of Physiology*, Section 2, *Circulation*, Vol. 1. Washington, D.C.: American Physiological Society, 1962.

RUSHMER, R. F., SMITH, O. A., & LASHER, E. P.   Neural mechanisms of cardiac control during exertion. *Physiological Reviews*, 1960, **40** (Suppl. 4), 27–32.

SALTZMAN, H. A., HEYMAN, A., & SIEKER, H. O.   Correlation of clinical and physiologic manifestations of sustained hyperventilation. *New England Journal of Medicine*, 1963, **268,** 1431–1436.

SCHACHTER, J.   Pain, fear, and anger in hypertensives and normotensives: A psychophysiological study. *Journal of Psychosomatic Medicine*, 1957, **19,** 17–29.

SCHNEIDER, R. A.   A fully automatic portable blood pressure recorder. *Journal of Applied Physiology*, 1968, **24,** 115–118.

SCHNEIDER, R. S., & ZANGARI, V. M.   Variations in clotting time, relative vicosity and other physiochemical properties of blood accompanying physical and emotional

stress in normotensive and hypertensive subjects. *Psychosomatic Medicine* 1951, **13,** 289–303.

SCHOLANDER, P. F.   Physiological adaptation to diving in animals and man. *Harvey Lectures*, 1961–1962, Series 57, 93–111.

SCOTCH, N. A.   A preliminary report of the relation of socio-cultural factors to hypertension among the Zulu. *Annals of the New York Academy of Sciences*, 1960, **84,** 1000–1009.

SEVELIUS, G. (Ed.)   *Radioisotopes and circulation*. Boston: Little, Brown, 1965.

SEVELIUS, G.   The influence of affective tone on cardiac dynamic in patients who have had myocardial infarctions. Presented at S. G. Wolf Day, University of Oklahoma Medical Center, Oklahoma City, 1967.

SHAPIRO, A. P.   Psychophysiologic mechanisms in hypertensive vascular disease. *Annals of Internal Medicine*, 1960, **53,** 64–83.

SHAPIRO, A. P.   An experimental study of comparative responses of blood pressure to different noxious stimuli. *Journal of Chronic Diseases*, 1961, **13,** 293–311.

SHAPIRO, D., SCHWARTZ, G. E., & TURSKY, B.   Control of diastolic blood pressure in man by feedback and reinforcement. *Psychophysiology*, 1970, **8,** 262. (Abstract)

SHEARN, D. W.   Operant conditioning of the heart rate. *Science*, 1962, **137,** 530–531.

SHEFFIELD, L. T., HOLT, J. H., LESTER, F. M., CONROY, D. V., & REEVES, T. J.   On line analysis of the exercise electrocardiogram. *Circulation*, 1969, **40,** 935–944.

SHER, A. M.   Excitation of the heart. In W. F. HAMILTON & D. DOW (Eds.), *Handbook of physiology*, Section 2. *Circulation*, Vol. 1. Washington, D.C.: American Physiological Society, 1962.

SHMAVONIAN, B. M.   Methodological study of vasomotor conditioning in human subjects. *Journal of Comparative and Physiological Psychology*, 1959, **52,** 315–321.

SIGLER, L. H.   Abnormalities in the electrocardiogram induced by emotional strain. *American Journal of Cardiology*, 1961, **8,** 807–814.

SIMBORG, D. W., ROSS, R. S., LEWIS, K. B., & SHEPARD, R. H.   The R-R interval histogram. *Journal of the American Medical Association*, 1966, **197,** 145–148.

SLATER, L. E. (Ed.)   *Biotelemetry*. New York: Pergamon, 1963.

SMITH, O. A., Jr.   Anatomy of central neural pathways mediating cardiovascular functions. In W. C. RANDALL (Ed.), *Nervous control of the heart*. Baltimore: Williams & Wilkins, 1965.

SMITH, O. A., JABBUR, S. J., RUSHMER, R. F., & LASHER, E. P.   Role of hypothalamic structures in cardiac control. *Physiological Reviews*, 1960, **40** (Suppl. 4), 136–141.

STEAD, E. A., WARREN, J. V., MERRILL, A. J., & BRANNON, E. S.   Cardiac output in male subjects as measured by the technique of right atrial catheterization: Normal values with observations on the effect of anxiety and tilting. *Journal of Clinical Investigation*, 1945, **24,** 326–331.

STERMAN, M. B., & CLEMENTE, C. D.   Forebrain inhibitory mechanism: Sleep patterns induced by basal forebrain stimulation in the behaving cat. *Experimental Neurology,* 1962, **6,** 103–117.

STERN, J. A., WINOKUR, G., GRAHAM, D. T., & GRAHAM, F. K. Alterations in physiological measures during experimentally induced attitudes. *Journal of Psychosomatic Research,* 1961, **5,** 73–82.

STEVENSON, I. P., DUNCAN, C. H., WOLF, S., RIPLEY, H. S., & WOLFF, H. G. Life situations, emotions, and extrasystoles. *Psychosomatic Medicine,* 1949, **11,** 257–272.

STONE, H. L., BISHOP, V. S., & DONG, E. Ventricular function in cardiac denervated and cardiac sympathectomized dogs. *Circulation Research,* 1967, **20,** 587–593.

STOUT, C. MORROW, J., BRANDT, E., & WOLF, S. Unusually low death rate from myocardial infarction in an Italian-American community in Pennsylvania. *Journal of the American Medical Association,* 1964, **188,** 845–849.

SUTHERLAND, E. W. On the biological role of cyclic AMP. *Journal of the American Medical Association,* 1970, **214,** 1281–1288.

SUTHERLAND, E. W., ROBINSON, G. A., & BUTCHER, R. W. Some aspects of the biologic role of adenosine 3′,5′ monophosphate (cyclic AMP). *Circulation,* 1968, **37,** 279–306.

TAFUR, E., & GUNTHEROTH, W. G. Simultaneous pressure, flow and diameter of the vena cava with fright and exercise. *Circulation Research,* 1966, **19,** 42–50.

TAN, B. K. Physiological correlates of anxiety: A preliminary investigation of the orienting reflex. *Journal of the Canadian Psychiatric Association,* 1964, **9,** 64–71.

THURRELL, R. J., GREENFIELD, N. S., & ROESSLER, R. Prediction of physiological responsivity from psychological responsivity. *Journal of Psychosomatic Research,* 1961, **5,** 211–214.

UVNAS, B. Sympathetic vasodilator system and blood flow. *Physiological Reviews,* 1960, **40** (Suppl. 4), 69–76.

VERNEY, E. B. The antidiuretic hormone and the factors which determine its release. *Proceedings of the Royal Society of London,* Series B., 1947, **135,** 25–106.

VON EULER, U. S., & LUNDBERG, U. Effect of flying on the epinephrine excretion in air force personnel. *Journal of Applied Physiology,* 1954, **6,** 551–555.

WALKER, A. R. P., MORTIMER, K. L., DOWNING, J. W., & DUNN, J. A. Hypertension in African populations. *British Medical Journal,* 1960, **2,** 805.

WALL, P. D., & DAVIS, G. D. Three cerebral cortical systems affecting autonomic function. *Journal of Neurophysiology,* 1951, **14,** 507–517.

WEBB, G. N. The display of physiological data from extended periods of time. In L. E. SLATER (Ed.), *Biotelemetry.* New York: Pergamon, 1963.

WEISS, T., & ENGEL, B. T. Operant conditioning of heart rate in patients with premature ventricular contractions. *Psychophysiology,* 1971, **8,** 263. (Abstract)

WHITEMAN, J. R., GORMAN, P. A., CALATAYUD, J. B., ABRAHAM, S., WECHAER, A. L., & CACERES, C. A. Automation of ECG diagnostic criteria. *Journal of the American Medical Association,* 1967, **200,** 932–938.

WIDIMSKY, J., FEJFAROVA, M. H., & FEJFAR, Z. Changes of cardiac output in hypertensive disease. *Cardiologia,* 1957, **31,** 381–389.

WILLIAMS, T. H. Mitral and tricuspid valve innervation. *British Heart Journal,* 1964, **26,** 105–115. (a)

WILLIAMS, T. H. Fast conducting fibers in the mitral valve. *British Heart Journal,* 1964, **26,** 554–557. (b)

WOLF, S. G. Cardiovascular reactions to symbolic stimuli. *Circulation,* 1958, **18,** 287–292.

WOLF, S. G., CARDON, P. V., Jr., SHEPARD, E. M., & WOLFF, H. G. *Life stress and essential hypertension.* Baltimore: Williams & Wilkins, 1955.

WOLF, S. G., SCHNEIDER, R. A., & GROOVER, M. E. Further studies on the circulatory and metabolic alterations of the oxygen-conserving (diving) reflex in man. *Transactions of the Association of American Physicians,* 1965, **78,** 242–254.

WOLF, S. G., & WOLFF, H. G. A summary of experimental evidence relating life stress to the pathogenesis of essential hypertension in man. In E. T. BELL (Ed.), *Hypertension.* Minneapolis: University of Minnesota Press, 1951.

WOLFF, H. G., TUNIS, M. M., & GOODELL, H. Studies on headache: Evidence of tissue damage and changes in pain sensitivity in subjects with vascular headaches of the migraine type. *Transactions of the Association of American Physicians,* 1953, **66,** 332–341.

WOOLLARD, H. H. The innervation of the heart. *Journal of Anatomy,* 1926, **60,** 345–373.

ZAKHARZHEVSKII, V. B. Changes in coronary blood flow under action of alimentary conditional stimulus. (Russian) *Zhurnal vysshei nervoni Deiated Nostri I. P. Pavlova,* 1965, **15,** 453–457.

ZIMMER, H. *Computers in psychophysiology.* Springfield, Ill.: Charles C Thomas, 1966.

ZIMMERMAN, B. G. Effects of acute sympathectomy on responses to angiotensin and norepinephrine. *Circulation Research,* 1962, **11,** 780–787.

ZIMMERMAN, B. G. Separation of responses of arteries and veins to sympathetic stimulation. *Circulation Research,* 1966, **18,** 429–436.

Eckhard H. Hess

PUPILLOMETRICS

A METHOD OF STUDYING MENTAL, EMOTIONAL, AND SENSORY PROCESSES

12

"Pupillometrics" is a word that I invented in 1965 to describe a new research field which was started in 1960 (Hess & Polt, 1960). The subject matter of pupillometrics encompasses the effects of psychological influences, especially positive and negative affect states, perceptual processes, and mental activity, upon the size of the eye pupil. It ranges far beyond the classically and widely known effects of extreme fear or terror that produce a grossly dilated pupil as part of the fright reaction. Under these conditions the dilation persists even if intense light is shone into the eye, showing that such emotional processes abolish the constrictive light reflex of the pupil. This phenomenon has long been known; an early observation of it in the cat may be found in Fontana (1765). Similar observations upon humans were made by Gratiolet (1855) and by Schmidt-Rimpler (1899), both cited by Bumke (1911).

Pupillary behavior constitutes an objective physiological manifestation of psychological phenomena involved in sensory, emotional, and mental activity. Since it is a technique that can be used without recourse to verbal reports, research design becomes free from cultural biases and thus the pupil technique has considerable potential as a tool for the scientific study of the behavior of the human species. In recent years the results and possibilities of pupillometrics have generated tremendous enthusiasm in psychophysiological circles. In the succeeding years research findings in this area will greatly increase.

This chapter will deal in detail with some of the many psychological variables that can be reflected in pupil responses. The technology of pupillometrics is extremely important in permitting the conclusion that psychological activity, rather than brightness or other illumination factors such as contrast, is reflected in observed pupil size changes. Therefore, I shall attempt to be as detailed as possible in describing pupillometric technology. This information, which includes a review of the historical background and neuroanatomical bases of the psychopupil response, should serve as a convenient technical guide for those who wish to become "pupillometricians" themselves.

HISTORY OF RESEARCH ON THE PSYCHOPUPIL RESPONSE

For more than one hundred years the behavior of the pupil of the eye has been the subject of a tremendous quantity of scientific research, and several thousand research papers have been published. However, the psychopupil response has been discussed in only a relatively small portion of this literature.

Many decades ago Bumke (1911), summarizing the currently known observations of pupillary activity, emphasized that, for normal individuals, "in general every active intellectual process, every psychical effort, every exertion of attention, every active mental image, regardless of content, particularly every affect just as truly produces pupil enlargement as does every sensory stimulus [p. 60]." Bumke pointed out, e.g., that mentally counting the beats of a metronome will cause rhythmic pupillary dilations and contractions in time with the metronome beats, and that even a moderate handshake will elicit pupil enlargement. A. Westphal's student, Otto Lowenstein (1920), reaffirmed these facts as generally known and accepted, adding that even the very beginning of "volitional impulses" could be reflected in pupillary dilation. However well known they were in the German literature of that time, they were in obscurity in this country until a decade ago.

Furthermore, it appears that much of the underlying literature was observational, rather than quantitative or systematic. If the effect of intellectual processes such as mental arithmetic were being studied (Heinrich, 1896; Roubinovitch, 1900, 1901), we might find a report of the degree of dilation that occurred (Heinrich, 1896) but not the specific mathematical problems that were posed. Similarly, antecedent conditions of psychical pupil dilation might merely be described as "recalling a date," "suggestion of fear," and so on. This lack of adequate precision in experimental observations of pupillary responses to mental and mild affective processes may be still another reason that knowledge of these effects fell in relative obscurity for several decades; only the fact that *extreme* emotions dilate pupils and that abnormal bodily states such as narcosis will produce pupillary abnormalities appeared to remain generally known. Fortunately, recent research efforts have begun to produce more quantitative and systematic data upon these phenomena and to restore to general acceptance the credo that most, perhaps all, mental processes may be observed in pupillary activity.

The early observation of Fontana (1765), that eye pupils dilate upon awakening despite strong environmental illumination, certainly could be construed as showing that psychosensory stimulation at the moment of waking activates the observed dilation. Nevertheless, it was not until 1863, with C. Westphal's findings, that we see a systematic study of the effects of nonvisual sensory stimulation upon pupil behavior. He noted that, under the influence of chloroform, eye pupils become extremely constricted. Yet needle pricks could cause these pupils to widen tremendously, after which they returned to their former tiny size. Loud screams in the subject's ears elicited the same response. Under heavy chloroform narcosis, however, the phenomenon would not be manifested. C. Westphal also noted that the pupils dilated upon sudden awakening from the chloroform anesthesia.

The German physiologist Schiff (1874, 1875) regarded pupillary activity as an index of sensory stimulation, or as an esthesiometer, because the pupil could be seen to respond to even the lightest touch when experimental animals were curarized or chloroformed. Pupils dilated in response to sensory stimulation even if no pain were involved. Dilation was reported to be greater for stronger stimulation such as pressure than for the weaker stimulation of touch. Foa, who worked in Schiff's laboratory and gave a report and interpretation of his own experimental findings in Schiff's (1875) article, concluded "tels sont les résultats de ces recherches, ... afin de mieux établir les services que peut rendre la pupille comme *moyen esthési-omètre.*"[1]

At about the same time Charles Darwin (1872), in his book *The Expression of the Emotions in Man and Animals,* referred to the widening and narrowing of the eyes through the movements of the eyelids and eyebrows as indicators of human emotion. This is a phenomenon that I have also observed in pupillometric experiments. Later Mentz (1895, p. 568), a German physiologist, reported that multiplication problems (7 times 16 or 9 times 18) increased a subject's pupil diameter by 15%, and that just "thinking" could increase pupil diameter to the same degree, 14% in one subject and 15% in another.

Heinrich (1896), working in Exner's laboratories in Vienna, measured the pupil diameter of four male subjects (one with retinitis pigmentosa, the others apparently without ocular abnormalities) as they performed "difficult" mental multiplication and other calculations, while fixating centrally on a certain point 32.2 cm away. The consequent increases in pupil diameter that Heinrich reported varied both from individual to individual and from occasion to occasion. While Heinrich did not discuss these variations specifically, it may be that both the individual variability in mathematical ability and the differential difficulty of the problems were reflected in the differential degrees of dilation during mental calculation. With the retinitis patient, who had normal central acuity, mental calculation increased pupil diameter 7%; with the second subject, the pupil was found to dilate 40% in diameter. The third subject was tested on different occasions, with his pupil dilating 101% the first time a problem was presented and 49% upon repetition.

The pupil of the fourth subject changed 13% in diameter during the required calculation.

Ancillary research by Heinrich showed that fixation on an object in the peripheral portion of the visual field was accompanied by greater pupil size than was fixation on the same object in the central portion of the visual field. This finding he attributed to the greater attention required on the part of the subject to fixate in the periphery. Heinrich also confirmed that accommodation to far vision was accompanied by larger pupil size than was accommodation to near vision. One of the subjects mentioned above was also requested to fixate a point 384 cm away, more than ten times farther than before. Despite the 45% increase in pupil diameter caused by this shift in accommodation, there was an even further increase in pupil diameter, 23% greater than the size induced by the far accommodation itself, as the result of mental calculation (Heinrich, p. 372).

Similar and independent observations on mental activity and pupil size were reported by Roubinovitch (1900, 1901). Subjects of both sexes, mostly adults, were requested to maintain constant fixation on a small black ball that hung from the end of a rod attached to the subject's head. Accommodation to near vision was apparently used, approximately the same range as Heinrich's or closer, according to the diagram of the rod-and-ball holder published in Roubinovitch's 1901 article. While the subjects fixated upon the little black ball, they were asked to recall a date or a name, to solve a mathematical problem mentally, or to perform some other mental task. Roubinovitch reported that pupil dilation attended these mentally performed tasks and persisted as long as the question or arithmetical problem had not been answered. Upon solution, Roubinovitch found, the pupils of his subjects reverted to their previous size, and they gave the answer orally. In some of the cases, dilation became apparent even when the problem had not yet been completely posed to the subject. Furthermore, Roubinovitch stated that pupil dilation failed to occur only when the subjects considered the answer extremely easy, requiring no effort, or when the task was immediately judged as impossible. Also, in two neurasthenic subjects Roubinovitch observed that, at the moment the answer to the

---

[1] Freely translated into English, "this research clearly established the value of the pupil as an esthesiometer."

problem had been given, the pupils constricted to a smaller size. Roubinovitch concluded that both the extent and duration of pupil dilation serve to measure precisely the degree of intellectual effort exerted by a given subject.

Another pupillary phenomenon has been regularly observed in normal healthy subjects: dilation upon muscular exertion, as reported by Redlich (1892, 1897, 1908a, 1908b) and A. Westphal (1907, 1920; Lowenstein & Westphal, 1933), who found that muscular contractions and even the thought of performing them regularly evoked pupillary enlargement. Later observations on muscular exertion and pupillary dilation were made by Levine and Schilder (1942), May (1948), Parker and Mogyorosy (1967), and Nunnally, Knott, Duchnowski, and Parker (1967). Levine and Schilder (1942) emphasized that this phenomenon is present in all individuals who possess pupillary reactivity to light stimulation. As Redlich observed, muscular effort, like emotional or psychic stimulation, can supersede the light reflex to increased illumination.

At the turn of the century, there was a great deal of interest in pupillary abnormalities in mentally ill people (with or without organic symptomatology). Among the many researchers who published reports on pupillary phenomena in psychiatric patients were Redlich (1892, 1897, 1908a, 1908b), A. Westphal (1907, 1920; Lowenstein & Westphal, 1933), and Bumke (1911). Bumke's book was, in fact, a comprehensive and fascinating review of the work of a veritable multitude of researchers, including himself, who had reported upon pupillary disturbances in mental and nervous illnesses up to his time. These abnormalities not only included special forms of pupillary behavior among these patients but also the absence of pupillary phenomena that regularly appear in normal healthy persons. A rather wide range of organic and nonorganic conditions had been studied with respect to pupillary behavior even by Bumke's time: tabes dorsalis, paralytic dementia, imbecility, neurosyphilis, senile dementia, arteriosclerotic psychosis, idiocy, multiple sclerosis, tumors of the central nervous system (CNS), primary degeneration of motoric apparatus, encephalitis, polioencephalitis, myelitis, poliomyelitis, meningitis, alcoholism, drug addiction (opium, morphine, bromides), dementia praecox,

schizophrenia, epilepsy, hysteria, neurasthenia, migraine, chorea, functional psychosis. Many of these conditions have continued to be studied for pupillary abnormalities, particularly among Russian researchers (Voronin, Leontiev, Luria, Sokolov, & Vinogradova, 1965).

One of the best known of pupillary abnormalities was A. Westphal's (1907, 1920; Lowenstein & Westphal, 1933) "transitory catatonic pupillary abnormality" (also called "spasmus mobilis") found in catatonic schizophrenic patients. Such patients were observed by A. Westphal to have pupils fixedly dilated more than normal and often failing to respond to an increase in light to near and far accommodation changes. The reactivity to light was found to be rather variable from moment to moment or from day to day. Transient periods of high reactivity to light could also be observed in these patients. The mydriatic pupillary fixation phenomenon has been observed in other psychiatric classifications such as dementia praecox (Meyer, 1910; Reichmann, 1914), traumatic neurosis, epidemic encephalitis, syphilis, and alcoholism (Levine & Schilder, 1942). As Lowenstein's later studies indicated (1927; Lowenstein & Westphal, 1933), the catatonic pupil can be readily observed in schizophrenics upon the suggestion of fear or anxiety and is very exceptional in normal people. As Gang (1948) has noted, this fact was used as a "differential diagnostic aid, a bedside psychosomatic experiment to distinguish between a catatonic stupor and a depressive or other stupor." Lowenstein and Westphal (1933) suggested that the pupillary abnormalities found in schizophrenics were possibly caused by aberrant emotional expression involving both the loss of lability and spontaneity and the heightening of emotional suggestibility. This is in contrast to the normal condition in which pupillary dilation occurs in response to emotional processes but does not remain at the dilated level beyond removal of the instigating cause. Lowenstein (1927; Lowenstein & Westphal, 1933) also showed that manic depressive psychotics in the manic phase have exaggerated light reflexes.

Other pupillary abnormalities observed in the psychiatric population have included the diminution or abolition of the light reflex and gross inequality of pupil size. Characteristic pupillary behavior during specific phases of epileptic fits was observed and described by Klein and Early (1948). It was known earlier that the pupil becomes rather wide during epileptic fits (Bumke, 1911). He and several other writers have included the presence or absence of pupillary unrest movements as diagnostic signs. Lowenstein and Loewenfeld (1962), however, pointed out that pupillary unrest varies in normal subjects and that the conditions for the occurrence of pupillary unrest have not been generally understood, so that its usefulness as a positive or negative diagnostic sign was rather questionable.

May (1948) studied 343 schizophrenic males and 100 normal males for incidence of gross pupillary inequalities and for pupillary reactions to light, pain, and muscular effort. Gross pupillary inequalities were found to occur far more frequently in schizophrenics (19%) than in normal subjects (3%). Abnormalities in the light reflex, however, were found in 15% of the schizophrenics tested (i.e., those able to cooperate with the test procedure), as opposed to only 1% of the normal control subjects. Furthermore, fewer of the 211 schizophrenics tested showed the pupillary dilation response to pain: 66% in comparison with 83% of the control subjects. There was also an impairment of the pupil dilation response to muscular effort: 61% of the 212 schizophrenics tested showed no pupillary dilation upon mild muscular effort, with only 26% of the normal subjects in this category. With stronger but still moderate effort, 37% of the 220 schizophrenics tested failed to dilate their pupils and only 15% of the control subjects failed to dilate their pupils.

May (1948) also reported that the light reflex of mentally defective patients was impaired. May thought that constitutional or acquired somatic factors could have played some part in these pupillary abnormalities, but the severe emotional imbalance (i.e., hyporeactivity to external stimuli) of the schizophrenic patients might be significantly related to the higher incidence of pupillary anomalies. Furthermore, changes in muscular tension, a contributing factor toward pupillary dilation, are frequently a prominent feature of mental disorders. More recently, several researchers have been investigating pupillary phenomena in schizophrenics. Lidsky, Hakerem, and Sutton (1967) have shown that schizophrenics' pupil responses to single brief light pulses differ from those of normal people. Still other studies on schizophrenics have been conducted by Rynearson (1968), Sheflin (1970), and Rubin and Barry (1970).

Recently, Streltsova (1965) has reported that the pupillary dilation orienting reaction is considerably stronger in hysterical patients than in normal persons. This she attributed to subcortical excitation and weakening of cortical regulation. Streltsova also wrote that, in chronic alcoholics, schizophrenics, or epileptics (when not in fits), this reaction is weaker than normal or absent entirely. This latter phenomenon was thought to be linked with inhibition in the higher areas of the brain. It is also of interest that Streltsova found that some drugs such as strychnine or caffeine stimulate the pupillary dilation orienting reflex when given in small doses but inhibit it when given in larger doses; this led her to suggest that the pupillary orienting reflex could be used in determining individual medication and dosage.

Other recent investigations (Birren, Casperson, & Botwinick, 1950; Kumnick, 1954, 1956a, 1956b; Wikler, Rosenberg, Hawthorne, & Cassidy, 1965; Rubin, 1961, 1962) have brought out the fact that normal, healthy children have larger pupil sizes than do normal, healthy adults. Furthermore, children suffering from autistic disorders have smaller pupils than do their healthy peers, but still larger than those of normal adults (Rubin, 1961, 1962). However, Rubin, Barbero, Chernik, and Sibinga (1963) were unable to discern any effect of age upon pupil diameter when children were divided into the age groups of 6–8, 9–11, and 12–14 years. Differences in pupillary phenomena between children and adults have also been noted by Streltsova (1965). In research conducted in collaboration with Liberman, she found that the basic regularities of the pupillary orienting reflex are influenced by age factors. She also reported that Prikhod'ko has demonstrated a number of peculiarities in the pupillary orienting reflex of children.

Rubin (1965) has also studied adults and reported data indicating that the pupil size of adults suffering from psychoneurosis is smaller than that of normal, healthy adults. He found that the pupillary return to normal after the termination of a stress consisting of a 5° C hand bath was significantly slower in psychoneurotic and nonpsychotic patients than in normal control adults, even though the pupillary reactions during dark and light adaptation periods and in rest and stress states were identical for both groups (Rubin, 1964). The schizophrenic's deficient return to normal after stress is congruent with Westphal's mydriatic pupillary fixation phenomenon. Another study, by Rubin, Barbero, and Sibinga (1967), has suggested that, like the adult subjects above, children suffering from recurrent abdominal pain show aberrant recovery from the same type of stress in comparison with normal peers, as reflected in pupillary behavior.

The role of the lability of the autonomic nervous system in disposing toward greater pupil responsiveness in normal people who obtain high neuroticism scores on a personality assessment test has been indicated by Francis (1969).

In this brief review of pupillometric literature I have shown the wide range of psychological causes of pupil size changes. It is equally important to point out that changes in pupillary size are beyond *direct* voluntary control. Bumke (1911) noted that so-called voluntary pupil enlargement is done *indirectly,* i.e., through such means as changing accommodation from near to far vision; holding the breath for several seconds; performing appreciable muscular effort; or inflicting pain on oneself, as by biting the tongue. In other words other bodily functions which themselves can influence pupillary size may be utilized by persons attempting to give the impression that they can voluntarily control the size of their pupil. Another means of indirectly increasing pupil size, we may add, is by performing mental calculation.

Data obtained by Krueger (1967) and by Chapman, Chapman, and Brelje (1969) indicate that either explicit instructions not to dilate pupils to pictures or the presence of an experimenter whose manner appears to have the effect of inhibiting emotional responsiveness on the part of subjects can serve to reduce somewhat the extensiveness of pupil dilation to pictures. This reduction, however, is certainly not through direct control of pupil size. Clark and Johnson (1970) investigated the effects of actually instructing subjects (either correctly or erroneously) regarding the nature of pupillary dilations to be expected as the result of

mental effort. The pupil responses of both subjects given correct and incorrect information regarding pupillary phenomena were not significantly different from those of a control group that had not been given any instructional set. Hence this experiment did not demonstrate any material effect of prior instruction upon pupillary responses.

The research begun in 1960 by Hess and Polt was prompted by observing increases in pupil size despite strong illumination as a result of viewing interesting pictorial material. We were at that time well aware of the role of deep emotions in increasing pupil size. However, in our observed cases there did not seem to be any strong emotional involvement; the interest seemed intellectual, which did not seem to be a generally known cause of increases in pupil size. Our first published experiment (Hess & Polt, 1960), carried out before we had developed adequate techniques to control bright-

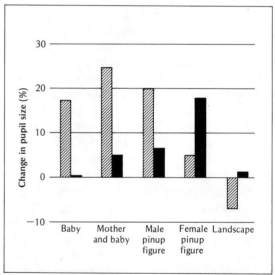

Figure 12.1 Changes in pupil size, in terms of percentage of decrease or increase in area, during the viewing of control patterns to various pictures. Different responses to the same picture by female subjects (solid bars) and male subjects (striped bars) established that the pupil response was independent of light intensity. The bars show changes in the average area of the pupils from the control period to the stimulus period. (From E. H. Hess & J. M. Polt, Pupil size as related to interest value of visual stimuli. *Science,* 1960, **132,** 349–350. Reproduced by permission of Scientific American, Inc. © 1965. All rights reserved.)

ness, tested four men and two women by showing each a series of five pictures while photographing their eyes. We reasoned that, if there were a significant difference in the pupil reactions of subjects of different sex to the same picture, then such a difference must be in response to something other than the intensity of illumination reaching the retina of the eye. Figure 12.1 shows the mean change in pupil area of male and female subjects from that during the previous control period upon presentation of one of the five photographs. The control presentation consisted of a plain slide with five numerals on it, of generally the same brightness as that of the stimulus slide (see Hess, 1965, p. 50). Both the control and stimulus presentation periods lasted for 10 sec, with a movie camera taking two photographs of the eye per second. We measured the pupil size by projecting a negative image of the film record on a screen and measuring the diameter of the pupil in each frame with a millimeter ruler.

The responses of the men and the women to the different pictures completely confirmed our expectation that factors other than light intensity can control the size of the pupil: the pupils of the four male subjects dilated considerably more at the sight of a female pinup than did the pupils of the two female subjects. Likewise, the women showed greater pupil dilation to the picture of the male pinup than the men did. They showed more dilation to a picture of a baby or a mother and baby than the men did. On the average the men's pupils showed practically no change in size when the baby was viewed.

Even though a very small number of subjects was used in this first study, the results have been more than reconfirmed by further unpublished studies of at least 45 subjects, which showed an extremely reliable result for the subjects retested after the interval of a day. Furthermore, among several hundred subjects, various pictorial stimuli of the same character as those used in this pilot study have always elicited pupillary responses of the same nature as did those in this initial study. In other words, pictures of babies, of mothers with young children, of "pinup" women or men characteristically elicit certain types of pupillary responses according to the sex of the viewer. An experiment

by Scott (1965) apparently confirms these findings. These responses, in fact, are so universal that they may readily be observed informally without using photographic recording techniques. Simply by showing a man a series of pictures, mostly landscapes and containing a female pinup, for example, one can, by watching the man's pupils, observe a distinctly noticeable pupil dilation when the pinup picture is seen.

Since these initial experiments, I have found that pupil size changes as a result of moderate emotional stimulation, i.e., positive and negative affect, are in two opposed directions (Hess, 1965). Positive affect will result in an enlargement of the pupils, while negative affect will cause constriction of the pupils. Not only do emotional states, but also various types of mental activity such as problem solving, and responses to stimulation in other sensory modalities such as taste appear to be accurately reflected in pupil size. Greater affect intensities, higher levels of mental activity, and stronger nonvisual sensory stimulation correlate with greater pupil size changes. Before discussing this research in detail, we shall consider the neuroanatomical bases of pupillary behavior.

NEUROANATOMICAL AND NEUROPHYSIOLOGICAL SUBSTRATES OF PUPILLARY ACTIVITY

The pupil of the eye is the aperture of the iris in front of the crystalline lens. The action of the muscles of the iris changes the size of this aperture. The iris contains two sets of muscles which together are responsible for the size of the pupil. These are the *sphincter pupillae* and the *dilator pupillae*. The sphincter pupillae consist of a ringed band of smooth muscle fibers that go completely around the pupil. The dilator pupillae are found in Bruch's membrane (which lines the entire posterior surface of the iris) and in the reinforcement bundles (which are radial fibers of smooth muscle tissue arranged like wheel spokes around the pupil).

The pupil of the eye constantly changes in size during the normal course of our waking hours. The pupil size is never stationary, except during sleep, when it is constricted. The pupil is highly sensitive

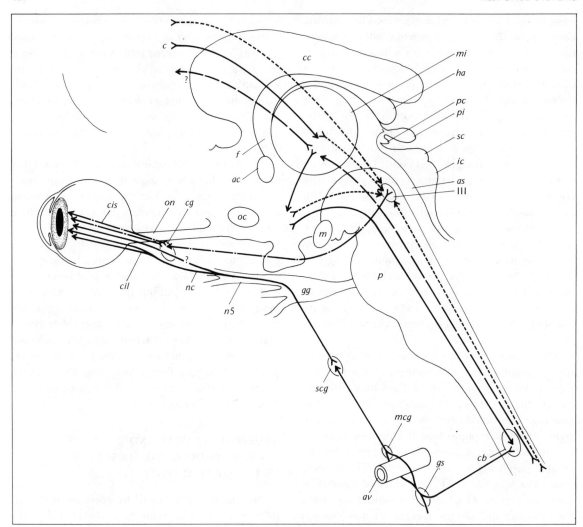

Figure 12.2   Schematic representation of mammalian brain, sagittal view. The solid lines represent the efferent sympathetic path from the cortex, thalamus, and hypothalamus via the cervical cord and peripheral sympathetic chain to the dilator pupillae. The broken lines represent the afferent sensory path to the thalamus and cortex. The dash-dot lines represent the efferent parasympathetic path from the oculomotor nucleus via the third nerve and ciliary ganglion to the iris sphincter. The short-dashed lines represent two inhibitory paths to the oculomotor nucleus, as follows: (a) direct afferent connections in the brain stem reticular formation and (b) descending connections from the cortex, thalamus and hypothalamus. Symbols: *ac,* anterior commissure; *as,* aqueduct of Sylvius; *av,* ansa of Vieussens; *c,* cortex; *cb,* cilio-spinal center of Budge (mostly T1 and T2); *cc,* corpus callosum; *cg,* ciliary ganglion; *cis,* short ciliary nerves; *cil,* long ciliary nerves; *f,* fornix; *gg,* Gasserian ganglion; *gs,* ganglion stellatum; *ha,* habenular nucleus; *ic,* inferior colliculus; *m,* mammillary body; *mcg,* middle cervical ganglion; *mi,* massa intermedia; *nc,* naso-ciliary branch of the opthalmic 5th nerve; *n5,* opthalmic division of the fifth nerve; *oc,* optic chiasm; *on,* optic nerve; *p,* pons; *pc,* posterior commissure; *pi,* pineal body; *sc,* superior colliculus; *scg,* superior cervical ganglion; *III,* oculomotor nucleus. (Redrawn from I. E. Loewenfeld, Mechanism of reflex dilatation of the pupil: Historical review and experimental analysis. *Documenta Opthalmologica,* 1958, **12,** 185–448. Reproduced by permission.)

and reactive to a number of influences, among which are the following (Lowenstein & Loewenfeld, 1962): (a) changes in environmental illumination that act upon the retinal cells; (b) closure of the eyelids; (c) accommodation to far and near vision; (d) general anesthesia, narcotic drugs, and other substances such as endogenous and exogenous compounds affecting the autonomic nervous system; (e) at least nine different specific types of neurological and brain damage; (f) spontaneous or reactive alterations in sympathetic and parasympathetic interaction, outside of those caused by changes in illumination or neurological insult, or by the administration of exogenous drugs.

Another very broad category, overlapping (f) to some extent, includes the factors that have been the focus of pupillometric research. The extremely wide implications of pupillometric research can be appreciated only by considering the fact that the iris muscles are innervated by both the sympathetic and parasympathetic divisions of the autonomic nervous system. In fact, the behavior of the pupil has already been used extensively for several decades as a tool for the study of autonomic neurophysiology, since the pupil is subject to the same influences as the autonomic nervous system. The sphincter muscles of the iris are controlled by parasympathetic nerve fibers from the ciliary ganglion, while the dilator muscles of the iris are controlled by the sympathetic nerves from the superior cervical ganglion. Thus the iris well represents the reciprocal innervation of the autonomic nervous system.

However, we must also remember that it has never been proved that the autonomic nervous system alone influences the constriction and dilation of the pupil. The anatomical bases of the total innervation of the pupil have not yet been delineated fully, so that we cannot categorically discount the possibility of extraautonomic neural influences in pupillary behavior. Figure 12.2, taken from Loewenfeld (1958), illustrates this point by depicting the complex interrelationships in the innervation of the iris and the possible existence of as yet unknown neural sources.

Within the brain, changes in hypothalamo-thalamo-cortical activity, which are themselves evoked by a large number of factors, affect pupil size. Sensory or emotional stimulation, either spontaneous or reactive (such as to electrical stimulation of that area), increases hypothalamo-thalamo-cortical activity. Under such conditions the pupil size increases, either through the sympathetic impulses that reach the dilator muscles of the iris via the cervical cord and the peripheral sympathetic chain, or through the inhibition of the activity of

the oculomotor nucleus, with consequent relaxation of the sphincter muscles of the iris. A decrease in hypothalamo-thalamo-cortical activity, and hence tendencies toward pupil enlargement, occur during fatigue. Such activity is at a minimal level during normal sleep or induced narcosis. In the sleep state, as has been known since Fontana (1765), eye pupils are contracted. Upon sudden awakening the pupils will dilate quite noticeably, even when environmental illumination is intense (Fontana, 1765; Raehlmann & Witkowski, 1878).

The importance of hypothalamic and thalamic functioning upon the pupil of the eye is indicated by Gellhorn's 1943 statement that "pupillary dilation is one of the most constant symptoms observed on [electrical] stimulation of the hypothalamus." Also, as Lowenstein and Loewenfeld (1962) have reported, destruction of the thalamus or hypothalamus results in the reduction of pupil dilation. The hypothalamus and thalamus, as is well known, are highly important anatomical substrates of emotional processes.

Sham rage or hyperemotionality in the cat is the result of certain brain operations such as the destruction of the ventro-medial hypothalamic nuclei, the removal of a rostral hemisphere, ablation of the bilateral cingulate, or cortical and forebrain removal. The literature on this phenomenon has noted that dilated pupils occur as a consequence of the operation or during the hyperemotional phases triggered off by mild handling or by encounters with other cats (e.g., Bard, 1928; Bard & Mountcastle, 1948; Fulton & Ingraham, 1929; Grinka & Serota, 1938; Kennard, 1945, 1955; Magoun & Ranson, 1938; Spiegel, Miller, & Oppenheimer, 1940). In other words, just as in man, events that set off "general visceral effects" in cats will also involve changes in pupillary behavior. Of course, as Bard and Mountcastle (1948) point out, pupillo-dilation is an important component of rage behavior in perfectly normal cats.

Several anatomical components of the brain have thus been found to be related to pupillary activity. For example, decorticated animals show maximal pupillary dilation because they are hypersensitive to autonomic and somatic functions (Lowenstein & Loewenfeld, 1962). Liberman (1965) has, on the other hand, interpreted the lively and inextinguishable pupil dilation orienting responses in decorticates to mean that this response has its executing mechanism in subcortical structures, with its regulation performed by the cortex. Liberman has, furthermore, suggested that the presence of the normal and easily extinguishable pupillary dilation reflex to stimulation should indicate that the cortex and subcortical structures are in a normal condition, that when this reflex is weakened and easily distinguishable both the cortex and subcortical structures have defects, and that a strengthened and inextinguishable reaction should indicate the disinhibition of cortical structures. Streltsova (1965, pp. 399–406) believes that the latter situation exists in hysterical patients, while the weakened reflex is characteristic of schizophrenics.

Russian researchers have found that activity in restricted brain areas is correlated with differential pupillary responses (Shaknovich, 1956). With an external light source serving to maintain a constant size of the pupil, the electrical stimulation of the occipital lobes caused constriction of the pupil; while the stimulation of the frontal and temporal areas produced dilation. Congruently, Smirnov (1952, reported in Sokolov, 1959) found differential constriction and dilation of the pupil in relation to brain damage. Damage to the occipital area, for example, resulted in pupil constriction, while damage in the temporal lobe caused dilation.

The intimate relation between the activities of the pupil and neurophysiological brain activities is further emphasized by the fact that the eye and the brain develop from the very same embryological neuroectodermal tissue. The pupil acts as a collateral tool of the brain in gathering and transmitting information. This transmission of information is a feature of pupillary behavior that generally operates at a nonverbal level and without conscious awareness. I shall discuss this phenomenon more fully in connection with interpersonal relationships. For the present it should be emphasized that the iris is constantly influenced by sympathetic, parasympathetic, and supranuclear cortical mechanisms. These are all simultaneously active to different degrees, and on this complex, various reflexes are superimposed.

The importance of psychological factors in pupillary behavior is underlined by Loewenfeld's finding (1958) of multiple humoral mechanisms that act to dilate the pupil of the eye. Classically, it has been known that extreme emotional stimulation causes adrenal epinephrine to be discharged into blood vessels and then reach the eye in about 8–15 sec, causing dilation. Under conditions of moderate emotional or physiological stimulation the eye may dilate in only 2 or 3 sec, and reach its maximum in less than 7 sec, before any adrenal epinephrine can possibly reach the eye through the blood vessels. Dilation in the pupillary orienting reflex studied by Liberman (1965) begins even more quickly, in 0.15–0.50 sec with maximum response reached in 0.5–1.0 sec. Our own data show a similarly fast response. Measurable dilation, when the subject views interesting visual material, can be observed to occur in less than 0.5 sec. According to Lowenstein and Loewenfeld, this faster acting response arises from the liberation of adrenergic substances upon the stimulation of sympathetic nerves to the heart and arteries.

Lowenstein and Loewenfeld (1962) have concluded that, since men and animals are subjected to moderate psychosensory stimulation during all their waking hours, and catastrophic emergency situations that bring the adrenal epinephrine mechanism into play occur relatively rarely, "the physiological role of the non-adrenal adrenergic humoral mechanism must be more important than is generally believed today." This implies that the normal range of psychosensory stimulation encountered in daily living greatly influences pupillary activity.

Psychological influences such as emotional excitement or psychosensory stimulation regularly appear to influence the pupil's reflex responses to light flashes (Lowenstein & Loewenfeld, 1961). Furthermore, hyperexcitable subjects characteristically manifest less extensive light reflexes than do calm subjects. In addition, hyperfatigable subjects show smaller pupils that respond more quickly to light than do those of less fatigable normal subjects. Lowenstein (1945) reported earlier that, when the pupillary constriction reflex response to light is fatigued, so that the pupil no longer shows a discernable response to increases in illumination, the administration of psychological stimulation will render the pupil again able to show the constriction effect clearly. This phenomenon, called the "psychical restitution effect," points again to the importance of psychological factors in the determination of pupillary behavior. According to Gang (1945), the restitution phenomenon itself can be exhausted, with the result that experimental animals fall asleep.

PUPILLOMETRIC RESEARCH METHODOLOGY

I shall describe the preparation of the stimuli for use in pupillometric experiments, the apparatus, the procedure for the experimentation, and lastly the measurement of the pupil responses on the film records.

Brightness and Contrast Influences

One of the most important factors in the methodology of pupillometric research is that contrast brightness and luminous flux factors must be strictly controlled. If a series of conditions is to be compared, contrast brightness and luminous flux must be kept at a rather constant level. Under these conditions, only reactive or spontaneous emotional states, i.e., the subject's psychological responses to the visual material being viewed or his endogenous affect processes, can be regarded as principally responsible for the observed pupil size changes.

While the importance of controlling the luminous flux or overall brightness is obvious, it is not so obvious why it is important to control the contrast brightness. My laboratory performed an unpublished study in which 16 different visual stimuli were projected in a series to the subjects. All consisted of a small square situated in the center of a uniformly colored background. The square was in one of four different achromatic intensities ranging from white to black, and the background was similarly one of these four achromatic shades. The pupil responses of the individual subjects to these stimuli were not correlated with the total amount of overall brightness of the stimuli. In fact, the responses of individual subjects to the same stimulus condition were very different. Apparently, both the foveal and peripheral retinal regions of the eye influence the pupillary response to changes in light intensity. The relative role played by each

region varies tremendously for different individuals, making it impossible to correct for differences in contrast brightness when analyzing responses to specific visual stimuli. It is, instead, necessary to minimize the contrast brightness down to a permissible level when stimuli are prepared.

Preparation of Stimulus Slides

In my laboratory all stimuli are prepared for photographing on 2 × 2 in. (35 mm) slides, the size used in the projector that is part of the perception apparatus for the actual experimentation. The overall brightness of all slides used in a single experiment is determined with an incident light meter (Gossen Lunasix) held at the aperture of the slide projector while the slides are projected. The readings obtained with the incident light meter for the entire series of stimulus and control slides must not fall outside the boundaries formed by two numerical values on the scale of this meter. The total range of Lunasix values used in our research lies between 14.8 and 20.6. No control slide has a Lunasix reading that deviates in value more than 0.25 from the corresponding stimulus slide.

Within the area of the pictorial stimulus, the difference between the darkest and lightest parts must not exceed one whole integer on the scale of a light meter that measures 3° of visual angle at a time (Honeywell Pentax spotmeter). This measurement is also taken with the completed slide projected on the screen of the perception apparatus and the light meter held at the viewing aperture of the perception apparatus.

The completed slides are tested for luminous flux and contrast brightness with the incident room illumination less than 5 ft-c, as determined by using a foot-candle light meter (Gossen Trilux).

To photograph the stimuli adequately, a single lens reflex camera with a 55 mm Micro-Nikkor lens should be used. I have found the Nikon F most satisfactory for this purpose. It is mounted on a standard animation or titling stand, after being loaded with professional Kodachrome Type 2 tungsten film. This film is used for all stimuli, whether composed of color or of black and white. The titling stand is illuminated by two 150-W reflectored bulbs placed obliquely 2 ft from the material to be photographed, so that no reflection from the stimulus material can enter the camera lens. This can be determined by looking through the viewfinder of the camera. After the bulbs have been on for 1 min, the voltage to them is increased by means of a Color-Tran converter. The voltage to the bulbs is stepped up until the color temperature on the scale of the converter reads 32A. According to the Norwood Director incident light meter, the use of this amount of illumination and the Kodachrome Type 2 tungsten film requires a lens speed of $\frac{1}{30}$ of a second and a lens aperture of f/5.6.

The next step in the preparation of stimuli is to measure the amount of contrast between the darkest and lighest part of the stimulus. The various parts of the stimulus are scanned with a meter like the Honeywell Pentax, which measures a 3° visual angle at a time. The small circle in the center of the ground glass in the Honeywell Pentax is positioned over the darkest area of the stimulus and the indicated reading on the Pentax scale noted. Then the circle is positioned in the same manner over the brightest area. If the difference between the readings for the darkest and the lightest sections does not exceed 1.0, the stimulus material is considered ready for photographing without further preparation.

Normally, however, this is not the case. To reduce the amount of contrast between the lightest and darkest areas of a stimulus, Bourges sheet overlays are used. These Bourges sheets, available from art supply stores, come in both black and white forms, covering 5, 10, or 20% of the total area. The white Bourges sheets serve to lighten the dark areas; the black Bourges sheets serve to darken the light areas. Bourges sheets are also used when the total brightness of the stimulus material falls outside the limits set for the stimulus series. If, for example, it is desired that all stimulus and control slides in a particular experiment have brightness values between 10 and 11, as measured by the Honeywell Pentax meter, and if a particular stimulus is brighter than this, going beyond the value of 11, then a Bourges black overlay is used over the entire material. The overlay is held in place with a nonreflecting, plate-glass platen that is part of the animation stand; this procedure prevents the blurring of images. In some instances Bourges overlays may reduce important detail such as the modeling and contours of a face. Whenever this occurs, the surface coating of the Bourges sheet in the face or other important detailed area must be removed by means of a stylus. This difficult procedure requires artistic skill and is needed for about one-third of the stimuli. Similarly, if a stimulus contains a rather large and uniform section of various dark shades, with a large patch of white inserted, it is necessary to use an adhesive black Bourges overlay that has been cut to fit the white area. Again, such a procedure requires artistic skill.

All control and stimulus slides should be in the same position with respect to the horizontal or vertical aspect of the $1\frac{1}{2} \times 1$ in. format of the slide. Mixing the positions of the slides of a specific series during the course of a single experiment renders the data difficult to analyze. If the stimulus happens to be of a size that will not adequately fill the $1\frac{1}{2} \times 1$ in. format, the stimulus must be mounted on a sheet of 50% gray cardboard or paper (Color-Aid or Tru-Tone). The use of 50% gray paper for borders prevents changes in brightness from one stimulus to the next.

For the control slides used in pupillometric research several different brightness intensities have been used, ranging from 14.8 to 20.6, according to the scale of the Gossen Lunasix. In most cases the Lunasix values of the control slides fall between 17.5 and 19.5. The background for control slides may be prepared from combinations of Bourges sheet overlays or from Color-Aid or Tru-Tone gray papers of various intensities. The numerals used in the control slides are either Prestype figures or high quality, typewritten numerals that are sharply cut, without blurred or ragged edges.

If actual living objects or other kinds of material are to be photographed for the stimulus slides, either the daylight or tungsten form of Kodachrome 2 film is used. From these slides 5×7 color prints are made, which are then treated as has just been described. However, under some conditions the original slides taken on Kodachrome 2 tungsten film may be used as they are, provided that they meet the criteria set up according to the test procedure.

This procedure tests and thus rechecks the slides that have been processed by Eastman Kodak. The 2×2 in. (35 mm) slides are placed into the individual holders supplied with the slide projector

(Bell and Howell Slide Master). With the incident room illumination at 5 ft-c or less, the slides are projected one at a time. The distance of the projector is such that the edges of the image being projected are 1–2 in. from the border of the screen. The Honeywell Pentax light meter is held at the viewing aperture of the apparatus, and then the readings on the scale of the meter for the lightest and darkest portions of the stimulus are taken. If these differ by no more than one whole unit, the slide is satisfactory. It is preferable, of course, that this difference be even less if possible.

When the perception apparatus is set up and the red light within the apparatus is on, the incidental illumination striking the screen should be such that the Pentax reading of the center of the screen is exactly 4. Thus no part of any slide projected will be less than 4.

After the contrast brightness has been checked, the total luminous flux of all control and stimulus slides is checked with the Lunasix light meter held at the viewing aperture of the projector. The Lunasix readings of all control and stimulus slides must fall between the same two whole number points. Furthermore, a control slide and the subsequent stimulus slide must not differ by more than ± 0.25.

This method of stimulus preparation and the measurements taken of the stimulus material are designed specifically for experimental conditions in which the incident illumination is not greater than 5 ft-c, particularly in the vicinity of the apparatus itself. It may at times be necessary to operate under conditions of greater illumination, e.g., it may be desired to test children in a schoolroom that cannot be sufficiently darkened. In such cases the slides may be prepared with greater contrast, which will be reduced by the incident room light. Testing can still be done under these conditions, using the Pentax spotmeter to determine whether or not the contrast within each stimulus falls within the prescribed limits. This is by no means a desirable method of experimentation, since it does not allow adequately for the manifestation of possible pupillary constriction effects. Precision can best be obtained by following the optimal conditions that were described previously.

In the experimental series of slides, two control slides appear first. The stimulus slides follow and are alternated with suitable control slides. One or two affectively neutral or irrelevant stimulus slides are added at the beginning of the stimulus series because the first pictorial stimulus shown to a subject always produces an unusually high pupil response. Thus the addition of an extra stimulus slide or two prevents contamination of the pupil response to the critical material through the novelty effect. This is not the same effect Shaknovich (1956, 1965) observed in response to certain novel visual stimuli (particularly in form or color). Shaknovich reported pupillary constriction as part of the adaptational orienting reflex to such stimuli. The orienting reflex proper, however, as described by Sokolov (1965), has pupillary dilation as a prominent component. Sokolov has noted that this orienting reflex is a characteristic response to a new stimulus. Data obtained by Kohn and Clynes (1969) suggest that opponent neural processes to color stimulation may be responsible for the initial pupillary contraction to color changes, a contraction which is subsequently followed by dilation in proportion to illumination level. Liberman (1965) has also emphasized the importance of novelty in maintaining the pupillary dilation orienting response; repeated presentation of the same homogenous stimulus within an experimental session will result in a diminution of the pupillary dilation orienting reflex. Woodmansee (1966) has also noted that adaptation causes a decrease in pupil size.

Another precaution observed in setting up the material to be used experimentally is that of not permitting the subject to become fatigued through the presentation of an excessive number of slides, since fatigue will cause the pupil to grow steadily smaller. The rate and duration of eye blinks also increase under such conditions, with consequent loss of data. For these reasons I never use more than 16 stimulus slides, with an equal number of control slides, and normally use fewer.

Perception Apparatus

There are many devices for measuring changes in size of the eye pupil (see Lowenstein & Loewenfeld, 1958). Mackworth (1968) has described a pupil apparatus which makes filmed pupil size records that also depict which area of a scene is being

Figure 12.3 Side view of the perception apparatus used for pupillometric research, with the slide projector shown in back of the apparatus.

fixated during each frame. Adaptations of pupillometric apparatus for use with human infants have been described by Fitzgerald (1968) and by Haith (1969). The equipment used in my laboratory was developed to record the pupil size during the viewing of specific pictorial material presented by means of a slide or movie projector.

Commercially manufactured pupil recording apparatus is available from the following companies: Smith-Kline Precision Company, 3400 Hillview Avenue, Palo Alto, California, 94306 (Electronic Pupillograph); Bausch & Lomb, Rochester, New York, 14602 (Pupillograph); Polymetric Company, 1415 Park Avenue, Hoboken, New Jersey, 07030 (Pupillometer System); Whittaker Corporation, Space Sciences Division, 301 Bear Hill Road, Waltham,

Massachusetts, 02154 (TV Pupillometer); Medidata Sciences, Inc., 140 Fourth Avenue, Waltham, Massachusetts, 02154 (MSI Oculo-Pupillometer); BioLogic Instruments, Inc., 1708 South Boulevard, Ann Arbor, Michigan, 48104 (BioLogic P-729 Pupillometer).

Figure 12.3 depicts the portable perception apparatus that my laboratory has devised for pupillometric research. The viewing aperture through which the subject looks may be seen at the left. It is cushioned with strips of foam rubber for comfort. To the right, in back of the apparatus, is the slide projector that rear-projects the images on the screen, so that the edges of the images are about 1–2 in. away from the edges of the projector screen. On the side is the mounted camera that photographs the subject's eye. The camera is bolted to the side of the apparatus in position to photograph the reflection of the subject's eye from a mirror inside the apparatus. The camera motor is plugged into an outlet on the far left of the control panel; to the right and below the camera are the control switches. The first switch on the control panel turns the red illumination for photographing the eye on and off. The second switch controls the timer; the third switch controls the camera motor; the fourth switch turns on and off the 40-W focusing light used to focus the lens of the camera; the fifth switch monitors the rear outlets to the slide projector. Next to the fifth switch are the apparatus indicator light and the fuse. The last switch, on the extreme right, is the main on-off switch for the entire apparatus, which also turns on the apparatus indicator light next to it. There is a carrying handle on the top of the apparatus, which is hinged to provide easy access to its interior. It is closed during the subject run, unless the room is extremely dark.

Figure 12.4 depicts the interior of the perception apparatus schematically. The apparatus itself is 68.6 cm long and has a 30.5 × 30.5 cm Transilwrap projection screen at its 38.1 × 40.5 cm rear wall. The hoodlike projection on the front of the apparatus contains the viewing aperture and is 38.1 × 30.5 cm. The eye is illuminated by a standard 25-W red bulb

(General Electric) in an aluminum reflector, 11 in. away. Since the red bulb must be on during the entire experimental session, we have found it wise to replace the bulb after 20–30 hr to prevent spoiling a film record if it were to burn out. This bulb provides illumination requiring a lens opening of f/4.0–f/5.6 when the rate of photographing is at 2 frames/sec.

The film used in the camera is 16-mm, Kodak High Speed, infrared film (ASA 500). Originally, I had used standard negative film (Eastman Royal Pan film, ASA 800) to record pupil behavior but found it difficult to measure subjects who had dark eyes, because of the lack of contrast between the pupil and the iris. The infrared film produces excellent pictures of any eye.

Only one eye need be photographed, since I have found from simultaneous photographs that the pupillary behavior of the two eyes usually follows each other perfectly. Other researchers have also observed this concordant behavior in normal subjects (Lowenstein & Loewenfeld, 1962).

The infrared movie film should be loaded into the camera in minimal light. I now use a 16-mm, Bolex II, movie camera, fitted with a 100-mm Macro-Yvar lens attached with 30 mm of extension tubes extending to 5.7 cm from the reflecting mir-

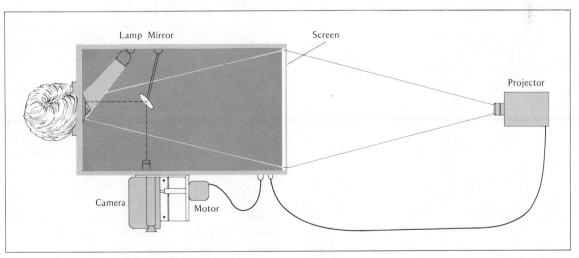

Figure 12.4 Diagram of the perception apparatus, showing essential interior components in relation to each other. A red lamp and infrared film are used. A timer advances the projector every 10 sec, flashing a control slide and a stimulus slide alternately. The mirror is below the eye level, so that view of the screen is clear. (Redrawn from E. H. Hess, Attitude and pupil size. *Scientific American*, 1965, **212,** No. 4, 46–54. Reproduced by permission of Scientific American, Inc. © 1965. All rights reserved.)

ror. The reflecting mirror, 5×7.5 cm in size, is placed directly in front of the subject's eye, just below the line of vision, 34.5 cm away. It can be adjusted slightly to suit the location of a subject's eyes. The Bolex camera is attached to a 15-rpm Bodine motor which drives the film at the rate of 2 frames/sec. A Veeder-Root counter records each frame of film as it is exposed.

Running of Subjects

The experimental slides are placed in the slide projector before the subject is brought to the apparatus. The master switch and the control switch for timing slide projection are turned on. One finger is kept on this switch until the slide changes; at the instant that the slide changes the switch is flicked off. This sets the timer, so that there will be a 10-sec interval between changing the second control slide, actually the first one that the subject sees, and projecting the first stimulus slide. After the timer has been set, the switch on the side of the projector is in the "on" position, the control slide is projected on the screen of the perception apparatus, and the red illuminating light is turned on. The loaded camera, if a new reel has just been placed in it, is allowed to run until the footage indicator is at 10 ft. Otherwise, the camera is allowed to run for a period of 20 sec to allow 1 ft of blank film between subjects and then is turned off again.

The subject is brought to the apparatus and given instructions as follows: "We would like to have you place your head so that you can comfortably see the numbers on this slide which we are showing. In a few moments we will show you a number of pictures. Each picture will be preceded by a control slide just like this one. Please look at each control slide when it appears by following the numbers 1, 2, 3, 4, and 5. The experimenter will pace you at first, and then you will follow the same procedure for each control slide. When the pictures come on, you of course look where you please. Do not look into the light or at the wall of the apparatus, etc. The entire run will take only a few minutes, so that even if you are not too comfortable after the session begins, please try to keep your head in the exact position into which the experimenter has helped you to place it."

After the subject places his head at the viewing aperture, with help from the experimenter if necessary, the focusing light switch is turned on and the subject is told to look steadily at the numeral 5 in the center of the screen. The reflecting mirror inside the apparatus is adjusted slightly if necessary. Looking through the viewfinder of the camera with its lens wide open at $f/3.3$, the experimenter focuses the lens on the iris of the eye. When the finer structure of the iris is clearly seen through the lens viewfinder, a $\frac{1}{4}$-in. clockwise turn of the focusing knob is made to compensate for the use of infrared film and red illumination, with longer average wavelengths than mixed white light. The pupil of the subject's eye appears in the center of the frame through the camera viewfinder as the subject views the numeral 5 on the control slide. Centering and focusing the subject's eye take approximately 10–15 sec. Then the focusing light is turned off, the lens of the camera narrowed down to $f/4.0$–$f/5.6$; after 5 or 10 sec, the actual running of the subject begins.

The timer and camera switch are flicked on simultaneously with one finger on each switch. This begins the timing. The control slide is on for 10 sec before the next, or first actual stimulus slide, is projected. The last holder in the run has no slide in it, so that the bright illumination and the resultant pupil constriction that appear on the film record signal the end of the actual run.

Most experiments use about 10 or 15 ft of film per subject. When the footage indicator shows that 90 ft of film have been used, no more subjects are run on that reel. The film is allowed to run in darkness until the footage indicator reads about 105 ft. If no further clicking is heard in the camera itself, the film has run through the camera. It is then carefully removed in minimal light, using a black cloth over the head of the experimenter in the way old-fashioned photographers viewed the image on their camera. The black cloth can also be used, if necessary, for loading the camera.

The film is then placed into its original film can, which is immediately closed and replaced in the yellow cardboard container in which it was purchased. The container is labeled with a serial number or the subjects' initials, a description of the experimental run, and the date.

I have developed a method of processing the

film in my own laboratory that obtains maximum and uniform contrast for this particular film and produces the best possible pictures under the conditions described. If commercial processing is necessary, the processor is instructed to treat the film as though Tri-X negative film were being developed.

Measurement of Pupil Size

The pupil diameter is measured and recorded for each single frame. Measurements from the 20 frames for the control slide determine the average size of the pupil for that slide, and then the average of the 20 frames for the stimulus slide following determines the size of the pupil for that stimulus slide. For any slide a few frames may not be measurable because of blinking or rapid eye movement. The sign and the absolute difference in the size from the control to the stimulus is converted to percentage of change to indicate the amount of positive or negative affect aroused by the stimulus slide. Since several steps have been taken to ensure that brightness or contrast factors are not appreciable influences in the observed pupillary changes, an indication of the essential affect value of the test stimulus is obtained.

The control slides, of course, also control for additional factors, such as accommodation, which can affect pupil size. Furthermore, the ten-second viewing intervals of both control and picture slides which have the same illumination level, permit the ever-present stochastic "pupil noise" (described by Stark, 1969) to be as small as possible a factor in pupil size when 20 frames are available for calculations. Finally, delays in dilation and contraction sequences, such as have been described by Hakerem and Lidsky (1969), do not materially affect the determination of pupillary reaction to picture slides since these delays are generally less than half a second in duration.

In the original report of Hess and Polt (1960) changes in pupil size were expressed in terms of *area;* percentage of changes in *diameter* is now used because changes in area are a function of the initial diameter. For example, a 1-mm *increase* in diameter produces a much larger change in area than does a 1-mm *decrease* in diameter if the original diameters are both the same. With percentage of diameter change, however, 1-mm changes in

diameter result in numerically smaller percentages when the original diameter is large than when the original diameter is small.

The frame-by-frame measurement of the pupil is carried out with a single frame animation projector[2] which will project 16-mm film one frame at a time without buckling it. The animation projector is placed on the floor, about 1 yd from a four-legged, desk-height table. On the white Formica surface of the table is a 9 × 12 in. plate glass inset, with a sheet of frosted plastic placed on it. A mirror on the floor beneath the table is inclined at a 45° angle, so that the image from the projector is directed up on the glass inset. Thus an accurate, enlarged representation of the pupil is transmitted, which can be measured with a transparent millimeter ruler. All measurements of pupil diameter are made to the nearest millimeter. The usual range is 30–80 mm, and the accuracy is ±1 mm, or from 96.7 to 98.8%. The pupil measurements can be made at a fairly rapid rate if one person measures and advances each frame of film with a remote control switch, while another person records the frame-by-frame data of the experiment.

An alternative method of measuring pupil size uses a photocell and records the changes in pupil area electronically. These readings are converted into pupil diameter mathematically.

It is also possible to analyze the movements of the eye on the film record to determine precisely what the subject is looking at during any given moment. The film negative is projected on a photograph of the stimulus. The beam that passes through the image of the pupil falls upon a particular spot on the stimulus, showing where the subject was looking during that particular frame. It is necessary, of course, to reproduce the original relationship between the subject's eye and the stimulus as projected on the screen of the perception apparatus. This can be done with precision by projecting the subject's sequential responses to the numerals on a control slide upon an image of the control slide and making the appropriate adjustments in height and distance.

The apparatus and technology in the University

---

[2] The PerceptoScope has been used for this purpose. It is no longer generally available.

508

of Chicago laboratories are versatile enough to permit use with nonvisual stimuli. For example, subjects have been asked to fixate upon an X or a 5 in the center of a control slide, while performing mental arithmetic or spelling, making anagrams, listening to music or other sounds, smelling various odors, taking puffs from various brands of cigarettes, or taking sips of flavored beverages. In these nonvisual experiments a control slide giving a Lunasix reading of 17.5 at the projector aperture is used. This level of illumination permits the pupil either to contract or to dilate as a consequence of stimulation. If complete darkness were used, the pupil would be at a maximal dilation state, so that little pupillary activity could occur.

Findings from these nonvisual situations have been extremely interesting and are highly suggestive of the tremendous potential of pupillometrics, particularly since the observed pupillary changes are obtained with absolutely no changes whatever in illumination. These findings, in addition to the ones obtained with visual material, startling as they are, indicate that the entire field of pupillometrics has scarcely been explored. It is as if we have so far taken only a tiny chip from a mammoth boulder.

RESEARCH FINDINGS BASED ON PUPILLOMETRICS

Affect and Classes of Pupil Response

One of the most intriguing results of the initial pupillometric research was the apparent constriction of the pupils of two women subjects when viewing a picture of a landscape (Hess & Polt, 1960). Negative pupil responses were subsequently observed in several other cases, when a subject was shown material that was for some reason distasteful to him. Distastefulness often appeared to depend on the individual, since what was distasteful to one person might not be so to other persons.

An example of both negative and positive pupillary responses can be seen in an experiment that attempted to eliminate the role of brightness. In this experiment no control slide at all was shown. Instead, there was a 10-sec blank interval between stimulus slides. Thus, whenever a stimulus slide was projected, every part of the screen was brighter than before, a factor that should act to decrease pupil size if brightness were the only factor con-

trolling the behavior of the pupil. This, however, was not the case. Positive responses for stimuli that had elicited a positive response in earlier experiments were observed. Negative responses were obtained for other stimuli, as may be seen in Figure 12.5. These negative responses were obtained only for stimuli that, for the person involved, might be expected to be distasteful or unappealing. As Figure 12.5 shows, male and female subjects had opposite responses, dilation and constriction, respectively, to the pictures of the sharks and of the female pinup. The relationship was reversed in the case of the male "pinup" picture. While this experiment does not, by itself, prove the existence of negative pupil responses, the negative reactions shown by most female subjects to the picture of the sharks and to the particular female pinup shown, and by some of the male subjects to the clothed male, have subsequently been shown not to be isolated phe-

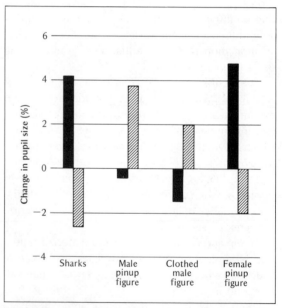

Figure 12.5 Changes in pupil diameter size in men and women in response to four different pictures. In this case the screen was unlighted before the presentation of the picture, a factor that, if operating alone, should have resulted in constriction. Yet, as may be seen, different pictures caused pupil dilation in the men (striped bars) and the women (solid bars). (Redrawn from E. H. Hess, Attitude and pupil size. *Scientific American*, 1965, **212**, No. 4, 46–54. Reproduced by permission of Scientific American, Inc. © 1965. All rights reserved.)

nomena. They are just as characteristic for these stimuli as the pupil dilation response is for certain other interesting or pleasant pictures, when the standard experimental procedure with appropriate control slides is used.

Pictures of a cross-eyed or a crippled child have almost universally produced negative responses in our subjects. Most of them report that they do not like to look at such pictures; one woman even closed her eyes when one of the pictures was projected on the screen of the perception apparatus. Negative responses have also been obtained regularly from abstract modern paintings, even if people who insisted that they liked modern art were used as subjects. Some of these people, in fact, showed strong negative responses to almost all of the examples of modern paintings that were shown to them. This finding accords with the observation of Shaknovich (1956, 1965) that the pupillary orienting (adaptational) reaction in the case of unfamiliar geometric patterns is one of constriction. Experiments by Bergum and Lehr (1966b) and by Barlow (1969, 1970) have confirmed that dilation and constriction responses can occur upon the presentation of pictorial stimuli with positive and negative affect, respectively.

However, not all persons respond with pupil constriction to pictures that have a certain degree of shock content. Examples of such pictures are those depicting dead soldiers on a battlefield, or the body of a murdered gangster. While such pictures produce extreme pupil constriction in many subjects, they also elicit a completely different pattern of pupil response in other subjects. In these subjects the pupil initially dilates considerably. However, with repeated exposure the pupil response declines, becoming negative after 3–5 exposures. The time interval between the successive exposures appears to make little difference in this pattern of change in the pupil response. These findings suggested that these essentially negative stimuli had an additional shock component that triggered off a strong emotional reaction. To check on this suggestion, electrodes were attached to the hands of some of the subject volunteers and their galvanic skin response (GSR), a measure of the electrical resistance of the skin that has been correlated with ongoing emotional level, recorded as

they were shown these pictures. The pictures with the high shock content did, indeed, produce a high GSR, as well as high pupil responses in these subjects. After repeated presentations of these pictures, however, both the GSR and the pupil response decreased, with the pupil response becoming negative.

The comparison of pupil response and GSR to "shock pictures" indicates that the pupil response is not merely a mirror of autonomic activity, even though the pupil is certainly influenced by autonomic activity. I have come to this conclusion because I have never been able to make pupil response data consistently equivalent to GSR data by altering the scales for units of measurement. While in any one case the scales of axes may be altered to make the graphed pupil response curve appear the same as the concurrent GSR curve, the same alteration of scales will not make the two curves superimposable for another set of stimuli exposed under the same conditions. Sometimes the pupil response curve is above the GSR curve; sometimes it is below. At other times, there may be no GSR changes in subjects that show good, differential pupil changes for various pictures.

Increased autonomic activity, as reflected in GSR changes, in itself appears to dilate the pupils. I have begun to suspect that this is the reason why the pupillary response to stimuli is so often positive. For example, with the shock pictures the pupil dilates strongly when GSR changes are high; but, as the GSR to these pictures drops, the dilation effect of autonomic activity diminishes, and the truly negative feature of the pupil response becomes evident. Thus, in many other cases, without the dilation effect of autonomic responses, pupillary behavior might very well be negative. It is as if the degree of dilation caused by autonomic activity might be subtracted from the total pupil size change to determine whether the pupil is actually reacting positively or negatively. For instance, both men and women may show high pupil responses to a specific picture of a nude female; however, the women may show high GSR, while the men do not. Since, as shown in Figure 12.5, women can show pupil constriction in response to pictures of their own sex, it may be that the seemingly positive pupil response of the women would turn out to be a negative one if the GSR were taken into account.

To test this hypothesis, we need to perform further research on the relationship between the GSR and pupil dilation. It should be determined empirically how much of a GSR response is correlated with how much pupil dilation. Such research, I am confident, will further indicate the bidirectional nature of the pupil response to affective processes. Ultimately, it appears that the maximal usefulness of the pupil response will be in conjunction with the simultaneous recording of other autonomic measures, as well as voluntary and verbal responses, even though Colman and Paivio (1969) have indicated that pupil responses are more sensitive measures of cognitive tasks than the GSR. Kahneman et al. (1969) have recorded pupillary responses, heart rate, and GSR simultaneously in a mental processing task. In my opinion, the simultaneous use of several different measures will certainly give us far more information than would any one of them alone. We cannot afford to be misled into thinking that any single dimension of measurement of behavioral response systems will provide complete information. Neither can we afford to be misled into discrediting any measurement simply because the results obtained with it do not fit our own theoretical preconceptions. For example, had we clung to the notion that men and women should show the *same* pattern of pupil responses to specific types of pictures, we would have concluded that the pupil response is not a measure of affect. Thus we must be ready to revise our notions regarding affective, attitudinal, or mental processes, rather than to summarily discard a specific measure for not producing results conforming to our viewpoint of a particular situation.

While most of my research has dealt with positively toned stimuli, I believe that the existence of negative pupil responses is an extremely important phenomenon. Such responses result, in effect, in the individual's perceptually avoiding such stimuli, much as a hand is withdrawn speedily from anything overly hot. The negative pupil response is not only an avoidance response but it is one that is accomplished involuntarily. Clearly, the existence of the negative pupil response independent of increases in visual illumination disproves any notion that the only normal physiological mechanism possible for the constriction of the pupil is through changes in the light level.

The reflection of positive and negative affect in dilation and constriction of the pupil has been still further demonstrated in an unpublished experiment conducted at the Pupil Research Center of the University of Michigan (personal communication, 1966). Subjects were first hypnotized and then told that they were going to be shown some slides. Actually, the slides projected in the perception apparatus were absolutely blank. The subjects were told that one of these slides was an extremely pleasant picture; its subject matter was unspecified. The pupils of the subject dilated, nevertheless. For another blank slide, the subjects were told that they were seeing unpleasant and distasteful pictures. Again, the actual subject matter was unspecified. This time pupil constriction resulted. When the blank slides were shown during the hypnotic state without instruction, the subjects' pupils showed no size changes.

Certainly, these results could not have been the product of changes in illumination or the patterning of visual stimulation. Congruent findings in nonhypnotized male subjects have been obtained by telling them, while they are looking in the perception apparatus, that they are going to be shown a "dirty" picture. Even though our subjects are never shown the suggested picture and continue looking at the control slide, their pupils can dilate even more than they usually do to pinup pictures.

The anticipation of other kinds of events has been shown to elicit pupillary dilation in normal subjects. Nunnally (1967) has observed pupillary responses in subjects anticipating visual displays varying in their emotion-provoking characteristics. Nunnally, Knott, Duchnowski, and Parker (1967) reported that the anticipation of a gunshot which did not occur produced strong pupil dilation, with a peak at the moment that it was expected.

In addition to positive and negative responses, a third category of responses was found—*indifference*—which occurs when subjects are shown uninteresting or boring stimuli. In such cases there are only slight, random variations in pupil diameter, which do not deviate more than 2% from the size produced by the previously presented control pattern. Thus there is a continuum of pupil responses to stimuli, ranging from extreme dilation for interesting or pleasing stimuli to extreme constriction for material that is unpleasant or distasteful to the viewer. To date, the greatest pupil dilation recorded in my experiments is 42% in diameter for a single subject and a single slide, and about 25% increase for a group of subjects. The greatest individual constriction of pupil diameter to a particular slide has been 19%. Individual and group responses to segments of animated material reach values twice as great as these.

Attitudes

One of the greatest values of pupillometric research is that it more reliably and easily measures a person's true attitudes toward some person, concept, or thing, than do other techniques when there is an involvement of cultural pressures, either to mask emotional responses or to profess only certain types of emotional feelings. The pupil response, one that is not under the direct voluntary control of the person being tested, may yield more accurate representations of a specific attitude than can be obtained even with a well-designed questionnaire or with an indirect projective technique in which a person's verbal or motor responses are recorded in an attempt to uncover his real feelings. That this is so has been rather strongly indicated by several studies.

For example, when 64 persons were shown 5 different pictures of food items that were essentially neutral insofar as social pressures are involved and were asked to rank the foods from favorite to least preferred, the verbal reports thus obtained correlated very highly with the pupil responses to the same 5 food items. Getting 61 positive correlations in 64 cases is a result that is highly significant statistically, on the .000001 level (Hess, 1965). Such good agreement between pupil and verbal responses was not obtained when women were shown pictures of seminude men. The verbal and pupil responses of men, as is well known, are both high to pinup pictures of seminude women. But according to the verbal rating obtained from the women tested, they did not think that the pictures of the seminude males were at all interesting. Nevertheless, they had large pupil responses to the seminude men. This disparity between the pupil response and the verbal response on the part of the women reflects the social values of our culture. While it is considered normal and healthy for a man to be interested in pictures of scantily clad women (indeed, it might arouse some speculation if he were not), it is not considered right for nice women to be interested in this type of picture of men. While it is well known that teen-aged girls collect pictures of actors and singers, it is noteworthy that these pictures are all of the face or fully clad.

Still another experiment demonstrates the effect of social pressures upon verbally expressed views. During the presidential election campaign of 1964 I showed photographs of President Johnson and Barry Goldwater to 34 University of Chicago students, faculty members, and employees (Hess, 1964, 1965). Everyone professed to be in favor of Johnson and against Goldwater. However, the pupil response test indicated that about a third of these people actually had a slightly more positive attitude toward Goldwater than toward Johnson. Since personal appearance may have influenced the pupil response, we cannot say that our data prove that the subjects with the more positive pupil response to Goldwater actually voted for him on election day. Nevertheless, the results raise the interesting possibility that at least some of them did, and that in the liberal atmosphere of the university these people found it difficult to utter any pro-Goldwater sentiment. Where there is no social climate of this sort, professed political sentiments do correspond with pupillary responses, as shown by Barlow (1969).

The greater effectiveness of pupillometric techniques over verbal self-reporting in eliciting actual attitudes has been found in marketing studies (Krugman, 1964). In one of these studies the pupil and verbal responses of women to silverware patterns were investigated. These women verbally indicated a preference for modern, simple designs. However, their pupil responses were more favorable toward the traditional patterns. Actual sales figures for the silverware patterns shown brought out the fact that the traditional designs outsold the newer, more avant-garde ones. The newer designs were eventually taken off the market. Congruent findings with a series of greeting cards were reported by Krugman. Results like these have led to a considerable development of pupillometrics in advertising and product studies. The method seems to make it possible to find what people truly like and to avoid the kind of fiascos suffered by the Henry J. Kaiser and Edsel autos, both of which had been researched and thought to have consumer appeal but which really did not. Examples of pupillometric application in advertising research are given in articles by Halpern (1967), Hess (1968), van Bortel (1968), and Coverdale and Leavitt (1968).

Psychosexual Response and Interpersonal Relationships

Another experiment further reveals the ability of pupillometric techniques to measure covert attitudes without the awareness of subjects (Hess, Seltzer, & Shlien, 1965). During the testing of a large number of subjects on pictures of babies, pinup females, pinup males, and other stimuli, it was found that a few subjects gave a larger pupil response to pictures of members of their own sex. It occurred to the experimenters that, if pupil dilation is really a measure of positive interest, these anomalous responses might be typical of homosexuals. A review of these incongruent cases further strengthened the plausibility of such a notion, which was then tested experimentally.

Ten young adult male subjects, between the ages of 24 and 34 years and of roughly the same educational level (all but one were graduate students), were shown a series of 15 picture slides all of which were representations of the human figure. Five of these subjects belonged to the heterosexual group and were students or workers in the laboratory. They were all known to the experimenters over a period of several years; their sexual outlet was judged to be exclusively heterosexual. The other 5 subjects were known to have overt homosexuality as their sole or primary sexual outlet as determined by one of us through observation, interview, and, in every case, by their own voluntary admission. None of the subjects was hospitalized or in therapy. They were all living in a normal environment, in school, at work, with friends. None of the homosexual subjects was informed of the purpose of the experiment nor of the nature of the stimuli to be shown before the experimental run.

Five of the 15 slides were classed as art slides; none of these was clearly male or clearly female. They ranged in style from a Michelangelo crucifixion to a Picasso. Three of them were abstracts and therefore sexually ambiguous; one showed both sexes; and the fifth was religious. Five other stimulus slides were classed as male pictures. They were considered to be the homosexual equivalent

TABLE 12.1 PUPIL SIZE INCREASE OR DECREASE WHEN COMPARING STIMULI TO CONTROLS EXPRESSED IN PERCENTAGE TOTALS[a]

Subject	Mean total response to male pictures	Mean total response to female pictures	Relative male-female response score
Heterosexuals			
A	−00.4	+05.9	+06.3
B	−54.5	−22.4	+32.1
C	+12.5	+19.2	+06.7
D	+06.3	+39.0	+32.7
E	−01.5	+23.1	+24.6
Homosexuals			
A	+18.8	+11.2	−07.6
B	−04.6	−38.0	−33.4
C	+18.9	+18.1	−00.8
D	+18.2	−05.6	−23.8
E	+15.8	+21.5	+05.7

[a]Responses to all five stimuli added together.

of pinups and were photographs culled from physique magazines. In general, they were artistically more crude than the pictures of females in the remaining 5 stimulus slides. Four of the 5 female slides were rather lush paintings of the female figure and the fifth, a nude female torso, was a photograph included as a partial compensation for the fact that all the male pinups were photographs or drawings.

Two of the art slides were presented first in the sequence of stimulus slides; two others were presented last in the series; the fifth was shown in the middle of the group. The art slides were included for several reasons. First, it was deemed desirable to place the sexual pictures in an artistic setting to reduce the threat to some subjects that might adhere in the obviously sexual material. Second, placing two art slides at the beginning of the series would protect the critical male and female pictures from the high response artifact to the first pictorial stimulus presented in a series. Third, it has often been thought that homosexuals have artistic interests.

Table 12.1 shows the total pupil response of individual subjects to the five male pictures, the five female pictures, and the difference between the total pupil response to the male and female pictures. The difference is expressed positively if the female pictures produced more positive response (dilation) than the male pictures, and negatively, if the male pictures caused more dilation than the female pictures. This last measure discriminates the most clearly between the two groups of subjects. Although one homosexual subject showed a slightly more positive attitude toward women than toward men, there is no overlap in the male-female difference scores of the heterosexual and homosexual subjects. Some of the female pictures drew a high and positive response from some of the homosexual subjects, and some of the male pictures drew a high and positive response from some of the heterosexual subjects. No single stimulus discriminated between the individual heterosexual and homosexual subjects; however, the average response of a homogenous group of subjects usually indicated whether a given picture had homosexual or heterosexual appeal. The total heterosexual response to three of the five female

pictures was positive; the total homosexual response to each of the five male pictures was positive.

Most of the homosexual subjects verbally expressed artistic inclinations. As a group the homosexuals showed a high response to the artistically good but sexually ambiguous art slides. They also showed a high response to the artistically crude male pictures. Furthermore, they showed a low response to the artistically good female pictures. It appears that pupillometrics may be of potential value in the study of esthetics.

This study lent even greater credibility to the notion that pupillometric techniques measure privately held attitudes directly, without depending on a verbal response that an individual may consciously or unconsciously falsify. The sexual preferences of the homosexual subjects were not obvious and were known only because one of the experimenters had gained their trust. These homosexuals were ordinarily most reluctant to talk about or reveal their sexual proclivities; yet their pupil responses, being both nonverbal and beyond ordinary voluntary control, differentiated them from the heterosexual subjects. It is of utmost importance to realize, of course, that I do not claim or suggest that the preferences shown by the pupil response are a predictive substitute for the behavior itself. I can only state that, in a very small sample in which both preference and behavior were homosexual, even though socially concealed, the pupil response has been shown to have discriminating power.

Our conclusions have been strengthened by the fact that Atwood and Howell (1971) obtained differential pupil responses from female-aggressing pedophiliacs who had been jailed for nonviolently molesting young girls. These pedophiliacs evidenced pupil dilation to pictures of young females but constricted slightly to pictures of adult females. In contrast, nonpedophiliac jail inmates dilated their pupils considerably to pictures of adult females and very little to pictures of young females, which is a normal heterosexual response pattern.

Another aspect of the pupil response as a measure of private attitudes and personality is the finding of more definite pupil responses in introverted subjects than in extraverted subjects. While I cannot state the basis of this apparent phenomenon, it seems possible that the extraverted personality has multiple modes of expressing responses to a situation, whereas the introverted personality channels the expression of responses more narrowly to the pupil response mechanism. Francis (1969) has indicated that there is a stronger relationship between normal neuroticism and tendency to have stronger pupil dilation responses than there is between introversion and pupil responsiveness. However, it is also true that Eysenck and Eysenck (1967a, 1967b, 1967c) have shown that introverts are indeed governed by greater autonomic lability, as shown by their "lemon juice" test for extensiveness of salivary responsiveness. The effect of personality variables upon pupil responses is further shown in research by Chapman, Chapman, and Brelje (1969) where the pupillary dilation responses of young men to pictures of females tended to be inhibited by an aloof and reserved experimenter and tended to be facilitated by an easy-going and friendly experimenter. Krueger (1967) has also shown that small inhibitory effects upon pupillary dilation of young men to female pictures can be obtained by certain experimental settings.

Results obtained with a pair of stimulus photographs also illustrate the relation between pupil behavior and personality (Hess, 1965). Two photographs of an attractive young woman were included in a series of pictures shown to a group of 20 men. The photographs were identical, except that one had been retouched to make the woman's pupils extra large and the other to make them very small. The average pupil response to the picture with the large pupils was more than twice as strong as the pupil response to the picture with the small pupils. Nevertheless, when the men were interviewed after the experimental session ended, we found that the majority of subjects thought the pictures were identical. Some subjects did say that one was "more feminine" or "prettier," or "softer." None remarked that one photograph had larger pupils than the other. In fact, this difference had to be pointed out to them.

As long ago as the Middle Ages women were known to take the drug belladonna (which means "beautiful woman" in Italian) to make their eyes more attractive. This drug dilates eye pupils. While it is evident from my experiments that large eye pupils are attractive to men, their response to large pupils is generally at a nonverbal level. It seems that large pupils in a woman imply to a man that she has an extraordinary and sexually toned interest in him. In effect, enlarged pupils act as a "signal" to another person. Several observations made by others have indicated that this can occur in the interpersonal relationship between a man and a woman, and without conscious awareness.

A subsequent study (Coss, 1965), based on the findings of Hess and Polt, attempted to evaluate pupillary responses to concentric circles that served as schematic eyes. Ten men and five women were used as homogeneously reacting subjects. The schematic eyespots were presented in sets of one, two, and three. The group of stimuli consisting of paired eyespots was found, on the average, to evoke greater pupil dilation than the groups consisting of single eyespots or tripled eyespots. The tripled eyespot group, in fact, produced the least pupil dilation, even though they provided a greater amount of dark area than the singleton or paired eyespots, a factor that should have served to increase the pupil size. Among the paired eyespots, the stimulus most resembling dilated pupils elicited considerably more pupil dilation than did the stimulus that most resembled constricted pupils. The differential in response to these two stimuli was greater in the women subjects than in the men subjects. These stimuli elicited pupil response scores of 1.900 and 1.550, respectively, from the women; whereas they elicited responses of 1.625 and I.550, respectively, from the men.

Stass and Willis (1967) have confirmed that pupil dilation in a person of the opposite sex has attractive value. Subjects were given a choice between two persons of the opposite sex for an experimental partner. One of these persons had pharmacologically dilated pupils and the other did not. Both male and female subjects were more likely to choose the person with the dilated pupils. Eye contact during the introduction of the subject to the prospective experimental partner was also a factor that influenced the selection of the partner, although the subjects did not necessarily report the use of the enlarged pupil or eye contact cues.

The findings of Hess (1965) on the effects of

perceiving enlarged and constricted pupils inspired a third study. Simms (1967) investigated the pupil response of men and women, all stably married and therefore presumably heterosexual, to four pictures, two each of a man or a woman with small or large pupils. As might be expected, the male subjects's pupils dilated the most to the picture of the woman with the large pupils. Similarly, the pupils of the female subjects dilated the most to the picture of the man with the large pupils. With both classes of subjects, dilation to the opposite-sex picture with the small pupils was markedly less than to the one with the large pupils. Even more interesting were the pupil responses of the subjects toward pictures of their own sex. The male subjects showed practically no increase in pupil size toward the pictures of the man, in comparison with their responses to the female pictures. The female subjects, on the other hand, responded to the same degree to the picture of the woman with small pupils as they had to the picture of the man with small pupils. There was an even smaller pupil response to the picture of the woman with large pupils. This latter fact is congruent with the recent finding of Hicks, Reaney, and Hill (1967) that women showed a verbal preference for a picture of a woman with a small pupil, rather than for a picture of the same woman with large pupils.

These interpretations have been supported by findings of Jones and Moyel (1971), who studied the effects of a male stimulus person's iris color and pupil size upon the affect expressed verbally by male subjects presented with photos of each condition. Not only did the subjects show less preference for pictures with the larger pupils but they also preferred pictures with light-colored irises in which the pupils could be more clearly seen and hence the nature of the communication signal more clearly apparent. Naturally, this last finding may hold more specifically only for photograph viewing conditions since in actual face-to-face interaction dark irises may not interfere with the adequate perception of the pupil size.

As suggested in the initial research of Hess (1965) these findings indicate rather strongly that dilated pupils in a person serves as an indicator of sexual interest. Furthermore, the perception of dilated pupils in a stimulus person, even though not at the

conscious level, will arouse a corresponding pupil dilation in an individual who finds the stimulus person's sex acceptable. The perception of the acceptable sexual object, with or without dilated pupils, produces greater pupil response than does the perception of an unacceptable sexual object. The responses of heterosexual men and women and of homosexual men to pictures of males and females as found in the studies of Hess, Seltzer, and Shlien and of Simms appear to bear out this conclusion.

Simms has done further research, as yet unpublished, which indicates that male homosexuals distinctly prefer a picture of a woman with constricted pupils to a picture of her with dilated pupils. This also supports our interpretation of the signal value of dilated pupils as an indicator of sexual interest. Interestingly, Simms has observed that men characterized as Don Juans show the same pattern of pupil response to women as homosexuals do. Simms has suggested that this indicates that both male homosexuals and Don Juans have an aversion to women whose pupils indicate sexual interest, even though their overt responses to women are very different.

Research by Sheflin (1969) has indicated that male schizophrenics display a heterosexual pupil response pattern. Hence their differential overt sexual patterns are not biologically evident in the pupil response pattern. Furthermore, paranoid schizophrenics were found to definitely have heterosexual pupil responses, a finding which casts considerable question on the validity of the long-held homosexual theory of paranoid schizophrenia.

Such research underscores the tremendous potential of pupillometrics as a tool for the study of all types of interpersonal relationships. The comparisons between homosexuals, Don Juans, schizophrenics and heterosexuals show that pupil response measurement can increase our understanding of personality dynamics in diagnostic categories. Not only is it possible to measure private attitudes toward other people but also to analyze the development of attitudes during interpersonal confrontations. The pupil response measure also is a valuable tool for longitudinal or cross-sectional studies of psychosexual development during the childhood years through adolescence.

A

B

Figure 12.6 Sequences of eye movements and pupil dilation in a female (A) and a male (B) subject when shown Leon Kroll's "Morning on the Cape" (Carnegie Institute, Pittsburgh). Black circles with white numbers indicate a pupil size about the same as that for a preceding control period; black circles with black numbers indicate a larger

An initial study in this direction, in fact, has been made in a doctoral dissertation by Bernick (1966) at the University of Chicago laboratories. Bernick investigated the pupil responses of boys and girls to pictures of babies, mothers with babies, mothers with a girl or a boy, fathers with babies, fathers with a girl or a boy, girls, boys, men, and women. He also obtained verbal preferences from them by asking them which pictures among those shown they liked the most and which they liked the least. All the children were school students, drawn from kindergarten and grades 1, 2, 4, 6, 8, 10, and 12, with approximately eight children of each sex in each grade.

The pupil responses elicited by the pictures in these boys and girls were very different from what has been long assumed to be the social-sexual preferences of young children and adolescents. The pictures of babies elicited high pupil responses from both sexes. Boys of all grades showed significantly greater pupil responsiveness to the babies than the girls did; in fact, the boys showed a stronger pupil response to pictures of babies than to any other class of stimuli. They showed more dilation to pictures of mothers than to pictures of fathers. The girls, on the other hand, showed more dilation to pictures of fathers than the boys did. Pictures of men and women elicited much less pupil dilation in boys and girls than did the pictures of babies, mothers, or fathers. Despite the smaller response to pictures of men and women, boys showed a stronger pupil dilation to the pictures of women than to the pictures of men, and the girls showed the converse. It appears that the pupil responses of boys and girls show the same type of opposite-sex interest as adults (Hess & Polt, 1960). This interest is relatively constant with respect to peers, adults, and parents from the age of 5 years to 18 years.

The verbally expressed preferences of the children and adolescents for these stimulus categories, however, were far more in conformity with the generally accepted beliefs regarding social preferences in children. The verbal data, in general, showed a preference for pictures of children of the same sex, contrary to the pupil data. While the verbal preferences of the boys and girls for pictures of babies was relatively high, the verbal preference of boys for pictures of mothers was extremely low. The verbal response data partially supported the notion of a latency period in the psychosexual development of the child, but the pupil response data did not at all. This discrepancy suggests that the so-called latency period may be no more than a reflection of socio-cultural pressures as expressed in some of the verbal responses. "One of the peculiar rules of our social value system is that while girls are relatively free to become tomboys or father's girls, boys who are sissies or mother's boys are usually condemned by their age-mates and adults as well (Kohlberg, 1965). The girls' responses to the father appear to be the only socially acceptable opposite-sex preference in the system," Bernick declared.

It is possible to study the development of interpersonal relationships in even younger children, as shown by Fitzgerald (1968). Fitzgerald showed that one- to four-month-old human infants had greater pupillary dilations to social stimuli than to nonsocial ones. In addition, four-month-old infants responded to their mother differently from the way they responded to a stranger.

Attitude Change

Attitude change has been studied in several experiments conducted at the University of Chicago laboratories. In one experiment the subjects were shown pictures of a popular movie actor. After obtaining their pupil responses in this fashion, half of the subjects were given some rather negatively toned material to read about him. The other subjects read an equal amount of neutral and unrelated material. All subjects were then retested on the pictures of the actor. Those subjects that had read the negative material showed a significantly lower pupil response on the retest than did the ones who had read the neutral material. This appeared to indicate that the negative material had changed the attitude of the subjects toward the actor. Similarly, some subjects were shown a picture of a man unknown to them. Then they were given reading material which indicated that this man was the former commandant of the concentration camp of Auschwitz. Again, the pupil response reflected a more negative attitude in the subjects as a result of the intervening reading.

During the 1964 election campaign, I showed 5 different photographs of President Johnson and 5 of Goldwater, along with a single photograph each of former presidents Kennedy and Eisenhower, to 3 groups of people (Hess, 1964, 1965). One group thereupon read anti-Johnson propaganda material, another read anti-Goldwater propaganda, and the third read some excerpts from a psychology journal that had no political content. Then each group was retested on the 12 photographs. The people who had read the anti-Johnson material had a slightly smaller response than they previously had to Johnson and a slightly larger response than they previously had to Goldwater. On the other hand, those who read the extremely bitter anti-Goldwater campaign propaganda (which had been made up for this experiment) were affected differently. This material caused the expected decrease in the response to Goldwater, but it also caused a large drop in the pupil response to Johnson, and even to Eisenhower. The only person unaffected was Kennedy. This result indicates that acrimonious campaign propaganda can lower a person's attitude toward politicians in general, Kennedy alone being spared, for obvious reasons.

The study of attitude changes through pupillometrics thus offers limitless possibilities. To pick a crude example, a patient seeking psychotherapy has a fear of people with beards. A pupillary measure of his initial attitude may be obtained by showing him photographs of bearded men, among others. The effectiveness of his treatment may be checked upon by repeating the test at appropriate intervals, since it will show whether there has been any diminution of the fear. The effect of any kind of experience, be it straightforward information, psychotherapy, conditioning, political propaganda, advertising, or any other means intended to influence or change attitudes can be measured quantitatively by recording changes in pupil size in a number of people at any desired interval. Pupillometrics can aid in developing more efficient diagnostic techniques in the mental health field, since

it bypasses handicaps that a patient may have in expressing the nature of his problems. It can also provide a valuable method of long-term followup and assessment after therapy is terminated.

The pupil response technique has been found to be even more valuable in conjunction with an eye motion analysis technique, earlier described, which plots the sequence of a subject's fixations upon stimulus material. One of the first findings produced by this technique was that the positive pupil response shown by men to a picture of a mother with her child in an earlier study (Hess & Polt, 1960) resulted primarily from the response to the mother and not to the child. Such directional analysis in terms of where the subject is looking during each frame of the film record and how large pupil diameter is in that frame confirms, extends, and elucidates the results obtained by the pupil response alone. Figure 12.6 shows an example of the responses of a female and a male subject to the same photograph. Although it is in its infancy, this combined technique promises to be vastly useful in increasingly sophisticated research involving personality, attitudes and attitude change, interpersonal relationships, and so on. It has already proven this in the study of the effectiveness of advertising material. It should have even more important applications in medical and psychological sciences.

Physiological States and Nonvisual Stimulation

Pupillary behavior can reflect changes in motivational states, not only the attitudinal ones earlier mentioned but also physiologically based ones. Hunger, for example, is very widely used as a standard variable in psychological research on motivation. To determine whether a person's physiological state might be a factor in the pupil response, I analyzed the results of a study in which several of the stimulus slides shown were attractive pictures of food. While the general response to the pictures of food was indeed positive, about half of the people tested had much stronger responses than the others. The logbook showed that 90% of the subjects who had evinced strong responses had been tested in the late morning or late afternoon; no doubt they were hungrier than the people tested soon after breakfast or lunch.

While not everyone is equally hungry a given

number of hours after eating, the pupil responses of two groups of people controlled for a length of time without food produced unequivocal results. The pupil responses of 10 subjects who had been without food for 4 or 5 hr were more than two and one-half times greater than those of 10 other subjects who had eaten a meal within a half hour before being tested. The mean pupil responses of the two groups were 11.3% and 4.4% of diameter, respectively.

Pupillary responses to pictures of food have also been tested through the hypnotic induction of hunger and satiation (Allan Seltzer, personal communication). Subjects were put into a hypnotic state and then shown pictures of food. The pupil response to the food objects was moderate. While remaining under hypnosis, the subjects were then made to feel hungry. They were again exposed to the food pictures in the perception apparatus. During this reexposure the pupil responses were much larger for the food pictures than for the other pictures. Then the subjects were led through a hypnotically suggested meal and told that they were now fully satiated. Then they were exposed to the food pictures for the third time. During this exposure the pupils constricted at the sight of the food pictures.

Not only are there pupillary responses to pictures of food but also to gustatory stimuli themselves. This is not surprising, since taste receptors are part of the nervous system of the organism. The perception apparatus was modified slightly, so that the subjects' mouths would be unobstructed as they held their heads at the viewing aperture and fixated on the screen. In this apparatus, the right eye was photographed instead of the left eye. Each subject was given a flexible straw to hold in the mouth, so that the experimenter could raise a cup of liquid to the straw as desired and the subject could sip the liquid as instructed. During the entire session the subjects trained their eyes on an **X** in the center of a control slide projected on the screen of the perception apparatus.

The first study involving gustatory stimuli utilized a variety of presumably pleasant-tasting liquids such as carbonated drinks, chocolate drinks, and milk, as well as some rather unpleasant-tasting ones such as concentrated lemon juice and a quinine solution. Surprisingly, both the pleasant and

unpleasant liquids, perhaps through increases in autonomic activity, elicited increases in pupil size as compared with the control of plain water. Subsequently, a series of similarly flavored beverages were tested, all presumably on the positive side of the "pleasant-unpleasant" continuum, to determine whether, as in the case of visual material, some of the stimuli elicited greater pupil responses than others (Hess & Polt, 1966). Five types of popular orange drinks were chosen as stimuli, since they were similar in flavor and yet each beverage differed somewhat from the others. The subjects were 4 female and 12 male graduate students from the University of Chicago. They ranged in age from 24 to 41 years. During the experiment the subjects held the straw constantly in their mouths. After the film record had run for 15 sec, a glass was raised into position so that the straw entered the liquid. Five seconds later the subject was told to "sip." After the subject had sipped and swallowed, the glass was removed. Sips of liquid were taken in this manner every 20 sec. The first and all remaining odd-numbered beverages were water. The remainder were all orange beverages. To take into account any possible effect of presentation order, the orange beverages were presented in a forward and reverse order, so that for half of the subjects the orange beverages were presented in the order of 1, 2, 3, 4, and 5, and for the other half in the order of 5, 4, 3, 2, 1. The measurement of the pupil diameter was done for the 5-sec period (10 frames) before a sip of liquid had been taken and the 5-sec period immediately after a sip had been taken by the subjects. These two periods provided the data on which the pupillary response to each sip of liquid was judged.

Table 12.2 shows the mean percent increase in

TABLE 12.2 MEAN INCREASES IN PUPIL DIAMETER SIZE IN RESPONSE TO FIVE PRESENTATIONS OF WATER AND TO FIVE DIFFERENT ORANGE-FLAVORED BEVERAGES

Water	Percent	Orange beverage	Percent
Water	8.1	Orange 1	5.4
Water	4.8	Orange 2	3.6
Water	3.7	Orange 3	10.6
Water	3.3	Orange 4	5.6
Water	4.5	Orange 5	3.7

pupil diameter to the five orange drinks. There was a definite difference in pupil response to the five orange drinks. Beverage 3 was associated with a marked increase in pupil size, even though it was not first in either of the two presentation orders. Beverages 1 and 4 elicited the second highest pupil responses, while 2 and 6 yielded the smallest percent increases in pupil diameter. With respect to the water stimuli, the 8.1% response to the first water presentation shows that the unusually large pupil response that normally occurs to the first presentation of pictorial stimulus material in an experimental run also happens when gustatory stimuli are used. The mean response to water stimuli was a 4.9% increase in the pupil diameter. The declining pupillary responses to water do not appear to indicate adaptation of the taste receptors, for Hahn, Kuckulies, and Taeger (1938) have demonstrated that almost complete recovery of the receptor can be expected in a 20-sec interval when stimuli of this type are used. The trend in our findings is completely congruent with Liberman's (1965) report that pupillary dilation orienting reactions to the same gustatory solution showed a tendency toward extinction with repeated 1.5-sec presentations of one solution at intervals of 15–20 sec.

Another method of analyzing the data is to take the 16 individual records and rank separately the responses to water and orange beverages with the highest obtaining a rank score of 1 and the lowest a rank score of 5. The average ranks obtained for the orange stimuli differentiated between the five stimuli at a .002 significance level, according to the Friedman two-way analysis of variance, while the average ranks obtained for the water stimuli fell well within the range of chance probability, at the .140 level. These data are all given in Table 12.3.

These findings offer strong evidence that pupillary activity, mediated by the sympathetic division of the autonomic nervous system, can be used as an indicator of taste sensitivity and perhaps taste preferences. The pupillary response to water, if the initial presentation were disregarded, proved to be relatively stable; while Beverage 3, which was not in the first position in either of the two orders, elicited the greatest response. The relative homogeneity of the stimuli used indicates considerable sensitivity of the pupillary response to taste stimuli,

TABLE 12.3 MEANS OF RANKED PUPIL RESPONSE FOR INDIVIDUAL SUBJECTS FOR FIVE PRESENTATIONS OF WATER AND FIVE DIFFERENT ORANGE-FLAVORED BEVERAGES

Stimulus number	Water	Orange
1	2.1	3.0
2	3.0	3.6
3	3.3	2.1
4	3.4	2.5
5	3.2	3.8
p differences between stimuli in series[a]	.140	.002

[a] Friedman two-way analysis of variance.

since one orange beverage was shown to be clearly superior to the others in eliciting a response. Obviously, there is still a great deal of work to be done on the taste modality, particularly with responses to unpleasant gustatory stimuli, but it already appears that the pupillary response can serve as a valuable tool in studies of food acceptance. Preliminary research with olfactory stimuli and pupillary behavior also indicates a relationship between neural activity, as initiated by olfactory stimulation, and pupillary responses.

Pupillary responses with respect to stimulation in still other sensory modalities have provided additional areas of profitable research. For example, we have had volunteers listen to taped excerpts of music while fixating on an **X** in the center of a control slide. During the procedure their eyes were monitored with the camera of the perception apparatus. Different compositions produced different responses. Apparently, individual preferences correlated with these differential responses. As was the case with taste stimuli, the response to music was always in a positive direction: the pupils of our subjects became larger no matter what kind of music was played. The control in this case was silence; in future studies the effect of the energy input from the music should be controlled by the use of "white noise." This might make it possible to find dilation and constriction effects in comparison with the white noise level. Other auditory stimuli such as taped speech and individual words also appear to elicit differential pupil responses, according to our preliminary research.

Nunnally, Knott, Duchnowski, and Parker (1967) presented a 2000 Hz tone at four different intensities in the order of 64.2 dB, 74.2 dB, 84.2 dB, 94.2 dB, 84.2 dB, 74.2 dB, and 64.2 dB, while subjects gazed at a homogeneous visual field. The highest pupil response was elicited by the 94.2 dB. presentation. In the descending part of the series there was a corresponding and regular decrease for each of the three decibel levels. A congruent rise was not elicited by the ascending portion of the series, probably because the first tone presented was subject to the dilating "first stimulus effect" so regularly observed.

Nunnally et al. (1967) and Parker and Mogyorosy (1967) also studied pupil dilation in response to muscular exertion. This phenomenon had also been observed by Westphal (1907), Redlich (1908a), Klein and Early (1948), and May (1948). May reported that greater muscular effort was more likely to produce pupil dilation in both schizophrenic and normal subjects, although schizophrenics frequently fail to give a pupil dilation response. However, he did not present quantitative data relating the degree of dilation to the degree of muscular effort. Nunnally et al. (1967) had 30 male subjects lift a series of 3 different iron weights to a height of 1 ft. Each subject lifted a given weight to this height for a period of 10 sec and then rested 10 sec before lifting another weight. The weights were lifted in the order of 10, 20, 30, 20, and 10 lb. In the ascending portion of the series the pupil size became greater as the weight increased. Furthermore, the resting pupil size increased but remained at a lower level than the dilation for the previously lifted weight. In the descending portion of the series the pupil size during the lifting periods decreased with weight, with resting pupil sizes following suit; in this case, however, the pupil sizes were slightly higher than the dilation for the succeeding weight lifting period, and markedly and consistently lower than for the preceding weight lifting period.

Parker and Mogyorosy (1967), enlarging on the above study, used 10 male subjects and 4 weights (10, 20, 30, and 40 lb). Each subject lifted the weights as in the first experiment, for 10-sec periods and to a height of 1 ft but in a *random* order on two separate occasions. The pupil dilation responses showed that the relationship between pupil size and weight lifted was statistically sig-

nificant: the heavier the weight, the larger the resultant pupil size. Isometric exercises such as fist clenching also elicited pupil dilation responses.

Mental Activity

Research in the various sensory modalities leads to the conclusion that pupillary behavior, outside of that instigated by changes in environmental illumination, reflects ongoing neurological activity in the brain. A study in which mental activity was investigated, exemplified by mental problem solving, further supports such notions (Hess & Polt, 1964). This excursion into the field of mental problem solving was prompted by reading in Bumke's (1911) book of the independent observations made more than half a century ago by two German psychologists, W. Heinrich (1896) and J. Roubinovitch (1900, 1901).[3] The phenomenon of pupil dilation during mental problem solving that they described can be readily observed on an informal basis, by simply gazing into a person's eyes and asking him to solve mentally a problem such as multiplying 8 by 13. This experiment can even be performed by oneself by looking into a mirror.

Four men and one woman served as subjects in an experiment at the University of Chicago laboratories. All subjects were presumed to be above average in intelligence; one held a PhD degree, two were at an advanced graduate level, one held a BA degree, and the fifth was an undergraduate research assistant. Two of these subjects seemed to be able to do mental arithmetic easily; the three others seemed to exert a great deal of effort to do even simple multiplication. Four problems, posed in the order of increasing difficulty, were mentally solved by the subjects as they sat in the perception apparatus and fixed their gaze on the numeral 5 in the center of the projection screen. While one experimenter operated the camera, a second gave the instructions and the problems. A third experimenter recorded the numbers of the frames at which each question was given and answered by observing the Veeder-Root frame counter attached to the camera motor. The film record was permitted to proceed for 30 sec before the first problem was given. After each answer, 5–10 sec were allowed to elapse be-

[3] Discussed on pages 492–494.

fore the next problem was given. Since the time taken for solving the problems varied from subject to subject, the questions were asked at different points during the filming with different subjects. The experiment was terminated 10 sec after the fourth problem had been solved. All subjects received the problems in the same order: (a) multiply 7 × 8; (b) multiply 8 × 13; (c) multiply 13 × 14; and (d) multiply 16 × 23. Since the stimuli were presented in a constant order with increasing difficulty, any adaptive effect in this particular situation would tend to minimize, rather than maximize, differences between the problems.

The film records of the pupillary behavior of the subjects during the mental problem-solving tasks confirmed the earlier findings of Roubinovitch (1900, 1901). Typically, the pupils of each subject gradually increased in diameter, reached a maximum dimension immediately before an answer was given, and then reverted to the previous control size. When the mean size of the pupil, as recorded in five frames immediately before a question was asked, is compared with the mean size of the pupil at the period of maximum dimension, as recorded on five frames immediately before the answer to that particular problem is given, the magnitude of the increase in pupil diameter among the four problems and the five subjects is found to range from 4.0% to 29.5%. Although there was not a perfect agreement between the amplitude of response and the apparent problem difficulty for individual subjects (Table 12.4), there is complete correlation between the difficulty and the mean response of the five subjects to the problems. In all cases of

nonagreement in the records of individual subjects, the reversals were between two problems adjacent to each other in difficulty.

The experimental situation was designed to eliminate any pressures, sense of competition, or anxiety insofar as the subject was concerned, so that extraneous factors would not enter as influences upon the pupillary behavior observed. It was felt that these factors were eliminated, since our preliminary research in this area led to the same type of response curve when subjects were instructed to pose and answer their own problems mentally without communication between the subject and the experimenter. Further unpublished research of Polt and Hess has demonstrated that emotional factors are minimally present in this problem-solving situation, since galvanic skin response recordings taken during mental problem-solving tasks failed to indicate any appreciable degree of autonomic response, even though the pupils of the subjects dilated considerably as before. This finding gives some support to the notion that there may be nonautonomic neural influences upon pupillary behavior (see p. 499).

In addition, subsequent research by Polt (1970) in which anxiety (threat of mild electric shock for incorrect answers) was deliberately introduced showed that its effect was principally in increasing the amount of effort performed in solving the problems and hence the pupil dilation during problem solving became even greater because of the additional mental effort. Pupil sizes between the problems themselves were not different.

In our original experiment, furthermore, the vis-

TABLE 12.4   PERCENTAGE OF INCREASE IN PUPIL DIAMETER AT POINT OF SOLUTION OF PROBLEM AS COMPARED WITH DIAMETER OF PUPIL BEFORE PROBLEM WAS POSED

| Subject | Problem | | | |
	7 × 8	8 × 13	13 × 14	16 × 23
A	15.2	15.8	20.2	22.9
B	9.8	14.1	24.9	21.9
C	10.0	8.9	13.5	23.1
D	4.0	8.8	7.8	11.6
E	16.2	9.1	25.1	29.5
Mean	10.8	11.3	18.3	21.6

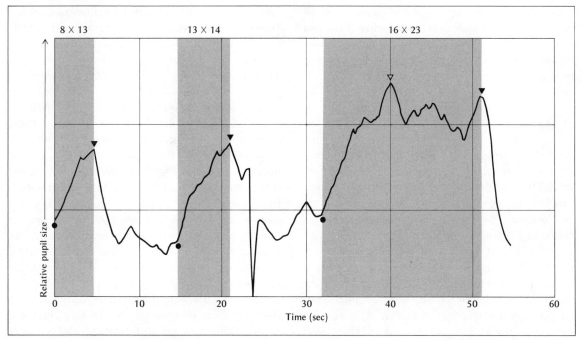

Figure 12.7 Changes in pupil diameter are traced in a subject during the solving of three mathematical problems. Beginning at the posing of the problem, as shown by the solid circles, the pupil dilated until the answer was given, as indicated by the solid triangles. In the case of the last mathematical problem, the subject appears to have arrived at an answer and then to have rechecked it before giving the solution. In every case the pupil size is seen to decrease after the giving of the solution to the mathematical problem. (Redrawn from E. H. Hess, Attitude and pupil size. *Scientific American*, 1965, **212,** No. 4, 46–54. Reproduced by permission of Scientific American, Inc. © 1965. All rights reserved.)

ual field was constant and the auditory stimulation consisted of the continuous sound of the camera motor and the voice of the experimenter giving the problems. It is evident from the subjects' records that they were not responding to the experimenter's voice, for had this been the case there would have been an immediate increase in pupil size when each problem was presented. In actual fact, the curve ascended rather slowly—and on occasion descended—from the point at which the question was asked and reached a peak immediately before the solution was given, anywhere from 3 to 30 sec later. Once the answer had been given orally, there was an immediate drop in pupil size, then a steady and slow decrease to a control level. These phenomena all agree with the ones reported by Roubinovitch (1900, 1901).

The observed peak in pupil diameter, together with variations in response latency, suggest that pupillary behavior may reflect "total mental activ-ity," as seen in a combination of both the amplitude and the latency of the response. I also observed, like Roubinovitch, that there is little or no pupil response if the problem posed is either extremely easy for the subject or if he judges it impossible to solve. Boersma et al. (1970) have made similar findings in a study comparing the pupil responses of normal and educable retarded children to three different difficulty levels of addition problems.

The pupil response records from this study (Hess, 1965) show individual differences in the course of problem solving. Most subjects show a marked drop in pupil size as soon as they give the answer. In some subjects, however, the pupil size has been observed to increase again, sometimes as high as the original peak, suggesting that the conscientious subject is working the problem over again to be sure of the solution's correctness. Other persons tend to recheck the answers before announcing them. This is illustrated by Figure 12.7, which depicts the changes in the pupil diameter of a subject as he was given the last three problems of the experiment. In the case of the final problem he appears to have reached a solution, as indicated by the open triangle, and then to have reconsidered, checking his answer before giving it.

Since electroencephalographs may be used for measuring activity in the brain, it would be expected that mental problem solving would also produce changes in electroencephalographic rhythms. Lorens and Darrow (1962) reported this to be true while their subjects mentally solved simple multiplication problems, as used in the study of Hess and Polt (1964). Their results indicated a significant decrease in occipital alpha activity during the period of problem solving, a decrease which correlated with increased activity in the association areas. There was more of an "on-off" effect in their results, which delineated the solution period regardless of the problem difficulty; while in the experiments of Polt and Hess the pupil responded differentially to problems of greater and lesser difficulty.

Research by Beatty and Kahneman (1966; Kahneman & Beatty, 1966, 1967b; Kahneman, Beatty, & Pollack, 1967) has provided additional facets of the relationship between pupillary response and mental activity. They found that the amount of pupil dilation during a digit-recall task was linearly related to the amount of material stored for immediate recall (Kahneman & Beatty, 1966). The pupils of the subjects enlarged while hearing a sequence of digits or words that they had been instructed to remember and report. Then the pupils progressively constricted as these items were reported by the subjects from short-term memory. The researchers considered the dilation and constriction to represent the mental "loading" and "unloading" of the subjects during the performance of the task. Since both the length of the material to be recalled and its difficulty were related to the total amount of dilation during the loading, the authors suggested that pupil dilation may measure the degree of the subject's load or mental activity.

In a second study Beatty and Kahneman (1966) gave five subjects two different types of memory tasks. One involved the recall of telephone numbers already well known to the subject, and the other the recall of unfamiliar telephone numbers. These were termed the "long-term" and "short-term" conditions, respectively. In both conditions there was an increase in pupil diameter and then a constriction to the base level. However, the peak pupillary diameter was much higher for the long-term condition than for the short-term condition. This does not necessarily mean, as the authors caution, that the recall of information from long-term memory will invariably produce a greater pupillary response than short-term memory tasks. It is rather that overlearning a task will diminish the associated pupil responses, as shown by a previous study (Kahneman & Beatty, 1966). We suspect that the personal associations involved with the familiar telephone numbers may have been responsible in large part for the observed enhancement of the pupil dilation response.

The mental activity involved in making a pitch discrimination was focused upon by Kahneman and Beatty (1967b). Male and female subjects were asked to report whether a tone was higher or lower than a standard tone. It was found that subjects had a substantial pupillary dilation immediately subsequent to the presentation of the comparison tone and that the degree of this dilation was rather closely related to the difficulty of the task. In fact, pupil size as a function of the frequency of the comparison tone was the highest when the comparison tone was the same frequency as the standard tone, with average pupil dilations for the comparison tone decreasing regularly as the distance between it and the standard increased, regardless of the direction of the difference. In addition, pupil responses to a redundant stimulus, a tone that served as a "ready" and "report" signal, decreased during the experimental session, which involved 55 trials (the tone was heard 110 times). The responses to the standard tone also decreased over the 55 trials.

As Kahneman and Beatty suggest (1967b), the pupil responses reflect the degree of mental activity required for the subject to perform the required task. "The magnitude of the responses that have been described here is clearly not determined by the arousing characteristics of any stimulus; rather it corresponds to what the organism does with the information conveyed by a particular stimulus."

While aroused by stimuli, an organism is placed under a "load" by its own responses to the stimuli, the authors contended. Emotionality or anxiety were not considered as underlying bases of the pupillary responses manifested in this study.

Kahneman and Peavler (1969) have shown that greater pupil dilation is evidenced by subjects when motivated by 5¢ rewards for correct responses in association learning tasks than when motivated by 1¢ rewards, because of the greater effort employed to solve problems in the 5¢ situation than in the 1¢ situation.

Several research papers have shown that extent of pupillary dilation and latency of pupillary dilation have a positive relationship to the degree of cognitive "load" in mental activity (e.g., Bradshaw, 1968; Colman & Paivio, 1970).

An interesting extension of the relation between mental activity and pupillary behavior has been provided in still another investigation by Kahneman, Beatty, and Pollack (1967). It is well known that a driver traveling alone may make no mistakes on a route he takes daily to and from work; however, if he has a companion riding with him and he is engrossed in conversation, he may fail to make the proper turns or even to observe a stop sign. The investigators, noting many similar observations, suggested that "intense involvement in thought may be detrimental to sensory and perceptual discriminations." To test this they set up two tasks for subjects to perform: a string of 4 digits auditorially presented were to be transformed by adding 1 to each digit of the string (e.g., 1345–2456), with the answer presented orally by the subjects in a paced fashion. Second, a display that flashed letters at the rate of 5 letters/sec was to be monitored with the goal of reporting whether or not the letter **K** had been presented in the series. All subjects performed under three conditions: both tasks simultaneously, transformation only, and monitoring concurrent with an extremely easy and repetitive transformation (e.g., 1111–2222).

Both the double task and the single transformation task produced the same sequence of pupillary behavior: pupil size increased slowly during the presentation of the digits, and then rose sharply to a higher level upon the giving of the transformed digits, where it remained until it began to diminish after the subjects' presentation of the second transformed digit, just as in the earlier study by Kahneman and Beatty (1966). Pupillary dilation during the "monitoring only" task, while generally rising during the 8-sec period, was much lower than when transformation was involved. While the interference between the monitoring and transformation tasks was mutual, the monitoring task suffered more from the interference. This may have been because of the relative reward value of the task, according to the authors. An analysis of the number of errors in failing to report the presentation of the **K** showed that many more were made during the double task situation than during monitoring alone. By far the largest number of errors were made from the time when subjects were just about to report the transformed digits until they had reported two of the four digits. Since errors did not decrease monotonically, the authors concluded that the interference was with the perception of the **K**, not with the memory of having seen the **K**. The widening of the pupils during the performance of the transformation task did not appear to be causally related to the increase in the number of monitoring errors, since the same pattern of errors was shown by the subjects who viewed the display through an artificial pupil 2.5 mm wide in diameter and by subjects who viewed it without such restriction.

Research by Paivio and Simpson (1966) at the University of Western Ontario and at Carleton University has further demonstrated the correlation between mental activity and pupillary behavior. In two experiments involving a total of 34 adult subjects, words were shown to the subjects in the same manner as in the University of Chicago laboratories. The selected words, all nouns, varied in two ways: concreteness versus abstractness and pleasantness versus unpleasantness. Subjects were requested to imagine an object or event related to each word as shown. It was found that subjects had greater pupil dilation to abstract words than to concrete words. Not only was pupil dilation consistently greater to abstract words, but it also took longer to return to control level than pupil dilation in response to the task of mental imagery to a concrete word. Paivio and Simpson consider these findings physiological evidence that it is more difficult to generate images to abstract than to concrete words. In another study (Simpson & Paivio, 1966), the differences between responses to abstract and concrete nouns were much less when there was no motor task involvement (key press response). Still, there was a difference. The greater difficulty of evoking images for abstract words than for concrete ones, as measured by the number of associations that may be elicited by each class, has been indicated by other research by Paivio (1966).

However, Paivio and Simpson (1966) did not find any differences in the pupillary behavior to pleasant versus unpleasant words. According to these investigations, the difference from the findings obtained in the University of Chicago laboratories with respect to pictorial stimuli may arise from the fact that different tasks were asked of the subjects and that the mental activity involved in the imagery task may have inhibited any constriction effects that might otherwise have occurred to unpleasant words. Stewart and Jensen (1966), Bergum and Lehr (1966b), Peavler and McLaughlin (1967), and Collins, Ellsworth, and Helmreich (1967) have also reported that responses to visually presented words differing in pleasantness were not the same as to the pictorial stimuli used in the University of Chicago laboratories. These findings indicate that the affect and mental processes evoked by visually presented words are not the same as those elicited by the presentation of pictorial stimuli.

For example, Guinan (1966) found that dilation to emotionally toned words is not significantly greater than that to neutral words until the 2.5–5.0 sec interval of the presentation period. In addition, our own work with visually presented words (Polt & Hess, 1968) has indicated that the pupil responses to these words is strongly idiosyncratic, making it difficult to differentiate pupil responses of groups of people when such stimuli are used. Research by Francis and Kelly (1969) has confirmed that there are strong individual differences in pupil responses to words. They were, however, able to obtain some degree of group differentiation in pupil responses. They suggested that neuroticism tendencies in normal subjects is related to their pupil response tendencies.

Koff (1966) has examined pupil responses of subjects while they chose one line out of three lines of different lengths to match to a standard. The pupil responses were measured before and after exposure to an Asch-type situation involving the same task. The Asch-type situation involves placing paid stooges in the same experimental situation with the subject. At some points the stooges unanimously give the wrong answer to the task. On the basis of this test, subjects were characterized as conformist or independent. The subjects characterized as independent showed more dilation to the stimuli involved in the task than they had before exposure to the Asch situation, while the subjects characterized as conformists showed less dilation to those stimuli after the Asch situation than they had before the Asch situation. Koff interpreted these results as showing that nonconformists have more interest in, and attention for, the task; and conformists have greater tension, lack of interest, and desire to avoid the task.

In the University of Chicago laboratories, informal experimentation has revealed that there are pupillary dilation responses to spelling tasks, with the degree of dilation correlated with the difficulty of the word. Such responses also appear when the subjects are asked to work an anagram. Other kinds of mental activity, such as decision making, certainly can, and should be, investigated with pupillometric techniques. The growing body of research results on mental activity and pupillary behavior suggests that pupillometric techniques will prove to be a valuable tool in the study of mental processes of all types, since they do not require the use of any introspective or other purely subjective responses on the part of the subject.

While I have described several ongoing research projects, both extensions of the ones described herein and completely new areas, there are still others that should be mentioned. These will illustrate still further the great possibilities of pupillometrics as a tool for the objective study of human behavior. In the University of Chicago laboratories and in other laboratories in the United States the pupil response has been used to analyze the nature of hypnotic induction and the hypnotic state itself (Seltzer, 1967); the effects of nonvisual stimulation such as sound (Beck, 1967); and the relationship between the pupil response and other psychophysiological measures such as the electroencephalogram, the galvanic skin response, the levels of adrenal steroids, and the heart rate. Other studies include the processes of sexual arousal, color perception (R. L. Miller, 1967), attitudes of equalitarian and racist white people toward Negroes (Woodmansee, 1967), tests of creativity, projective tests of personality (Oberlander, 1967), intelligence levels (M. B. Miller, 1967), verbal learning tasks (Kahneman & Beatty, 1967a), verbal problems, simple and complex problem solving, imagery (Simpson, 1967), and other cognitive processes. Pupillometric techniques are now being extensively applied to the evaluation of advertising material, both animated and still (van Bortel, 1968), and to product packaging.

During the eleven years since modern pupillometrics began, it has become increasingly apparent that pupillary activity reflects many different types of nervous system functioning. It now appears that pupillary behavior mirrors ongoing neurological activity in all parts of the brain. Pupillometric technology obviously provides inestimably valuable tools for studying and understanding man's behavior as a function of the total context in which it occurs. I feel certain that in the next few decades pupillometrics will become a firmly established means for unearthing much important information about the nature of man.

REFERENCES

ATWOOD, R. W., & HOWELL, R. J. Pupillometric and personality test score differences of female aggressing pedophiliacs and normals. *Psychonomic Science,* 1971, **22,** 115–116.

BARD, P. A diencephalic mechanism for the expression of rage with special reference to the sympathetic nervous system. *American Journal of Physiology,* 1928, **84,** 490–515.

BARD, P., & MOUNTCASTLE, V. B. Some forebrain mechanisms involved in the expression of rage with special reference to suppression of angry behavior. In ASSOCIATION FOR RESEARCH IN NERVOUS AND MENTAL DISEASE, *The Frontal Lobes.* Proceedings of the Association, December 1947. Research Publication of the Association for Nervous and Mental Disease No. 27. Baltimore: Williams & Wilkins, 1948.

BARLOW, J. D. Pupillary size as an index of preference in political candidates. *Perceptual and Motor Skills,* 1969, **28,** 587–590.

BEATTY, J., & KAHNEMAN, D. Pupillary changes in two memory tasks. *Psychonomic Science,* 1966, **5,** 371–372.

BECK, B. The effect of auditory stimulation on the photopupil reflex response. Unpublished doctoral dissertation, University of Chicago, 1967.

BERGUM, O., & LEHR, J. Prediction of stimulus approach: Core measures experiment I. Research Report R66-8. Rochester, N.Y.: Xerox Corp., 1966. (a)

BERGUM, O., & LEHR, J. Prediction of stimulus approach: Core measures experiment II. Research Report R66-36. Rochester, N.Y.: Xerox Corp., 1966. (b)

BERNICK, N. The development of children's preferences for social objects as evidenced by their pupil responses. Unpublished doctoral dissertation, University of Chicago, 1966.

BIRREN, J. E., CASPERSON, R. C., & BOTWINICK, J. Age changes in pupil size. *Journal of Gerontology,* 1950, **5,** 216–221.

BOERSMA, F., WILTON, K., BARHAM, R., & MUIR, W. Effects of arithmetic problem difficulty on pupillary dilation in normals and educable retardates. *Journal of Experimental Child Psychology,* 1970, **9,** 142–155.

BORTEL, F. J., VAN. Commercial applications of pupillometrics. In F. M. BASS, C. W. KING, & E. A. PESSEMIER (Eds.), *Applications of the sciences in marketing management.* New York: Wiley, 1968.

BRADSHAW, J. L. Load and pupillary changes in continuous processing tasks. *British Journal of Psychology,* 1968, **59,** 265–271.

BUMKE, O. *Die Pupillenstörungen, Bei Geistes—und Nervenkrankheiten.* (Physiologie und Pathologie der Irisbewegungen.) Jena: Fischer, 1911.

CHAPMAN, L. J., CHAPMAN, J. P., & BRELJE, T. Influence of the experimenter on pupillary dilation to sexually provocative pictures. *Journal of Abnormal Psychology,* 1969, **74,** 396–400.

CLARK, W. R., & JOHNSON, D. A. Effects of instructional set on pupillary responses during a short-term memory task. *Journal of Experimental Psychology,* 1970, **85,** 315–317.

COLLINS, B. E., ELLSWORTH, P. C., & HELMREICH, R. L. Correlations between pupil size and the semantic differential: An experimental paradigm and pilot study. *Psychonomic Science,* 1967, **9,** 627–628.

COLMAN, F. D., & PAIVIO, A. Pupillary response and galvanic skin response during an imagery task. *Psychonomic Science,* 1969, **16,** 296–297.

COLMAN, F. D., & PAIVIO, A. Pupillary dilation and mediation processes during paired-associate learning. *Canadian Journal of Psychology,* 1970, **24,** 261–270.

COSS, R. G. *Mood provoking visual stimuli: Their origins and applications.* Los Angeles. Industrial Design Graduate Program, University of California, 1965.

COVERDALE, H. L., & LEAVITT, C. Pupil size as a predictor of coupon return performance: A directional trend approach. *Proceedings, 76th Annual Convention, American Psychological Association,* 1968, 673–674.

DARWIN, C. *The expression of the emotions in man and animals.* London: Murray, 1872.

EYSENCK, H. J., & EYSENCK, S. B. G. On the unitary nature of extraversion. *Acta Psychologica,* 1967, **26,** 383–390. (a)
EYSENCK, S. B. G., & EYSENCK, H. J. Physiological reactivity to sensory stimulation as a measure of personality. *Psychological Reports,* 1967, **20,** 45–46. (b)
EYSENCK, S. B. G., & EYSENCK, H. J. Salivary response to lemon juice as a measure of introversion. *Perceptual and Motor Skills,* 1967, **24,** 1047–1053. (c)

FITZGERALD, H. E. Autonomic pupillary reflex activity during early infancy and its relation to social and nonsocial visual stimuli. *Journal of Experimental Child Psychology,* 1968, **6,** 470–482.
FOA, P., & SCHIFF, J. La pupilla come estesiometro. *Imparziale,* 1874, **14,** 617–626, 649–655, 691–702.
FONTANA, F. F. *Sui moti dell'iride.* Lucca: J. Giusti, 1765.
FRANCIS, R. D. Neuroticism and optical pupil changes in response to auditory stimuli. *British Journal of Social and Clinical Psychology,* 1969, **8,** 344–349.
FRANCIS, R. D., & KELLY, M. R. An investigation of the relationship between word stimuli and optical pupil size. *Australian Journal of Psychology,* 1969, **21,** 117–125.
FULTON, J. F., & INGRAHAM, F. D. Emotional disturbances following experimental lesions of the base of the brain (pre-chiasmal). *Journal of Physiology, London,* 1929, **67,** xxvii–xxviii. (Abstract: *American Journal of Physiology,* 1929, **90,** 353.)

GANG, K. Psychosomatic factors in the control of pupillary movement. *Journal of Clinical Psychopathology and Psychotherapy,* 1945, **6,** 461–472.
GELLHORN, E. *Autonomic regulations, their significance for physiology, psychology, and neuropsychiatry.* New York: Interscience, 1943.
GRATIOLET, L. P. *De la physiognomie et des mouvements d'expression suivi d'une notice sur sa vie et ses travaux et de la nomenclature de ses ouvrages.* Par Louis Gradeau. Paris: J. Hetzel, 1865.
GRINKA, R. R., & SEROTA, H. Studies on corticohypothalamic relations in the cat and man. *Journal of Neurophysiology,* 1938, **1,** 573–589.
GUINAN, J. F. An investigation on the relationship between pupil size and emotional words. Doctoral dissertation, Michigan State University, 1966. *Dissertation Abstracts International,* 1966, **27** (9-B), 3286–3287.

HAHN, H., KUCKULIES, G., & TAEGER, H. Eine systematische Untersuchung der Geschmacksschwellen. I. *Zeitschrift für Sinnesphysiologie,* 1938, **67,** 259–306.
HAITH, M. M. Infrared television recording and measurement of ocular behavior in the human infant. *American Psychologist,* 1969, **24,** 279–283.

HAKEREM, G., & LIDSKY, A. Pupillary reactions to sequences of light and variable dark impulses. *Annals of the New York Academy of Sciences,* 1969, **156,** 951–958.
HALPERN, R. Application of pupil response to before and after experiments. *Journal of Marketing Research,* 1967, **4,** 320–321.
HEINRICH, W. Die Aufmerksamkeit und die Funktion der Sinnesorgane. *Zeitschrift für Psychologie und Physiologie der Sinnesorgane,* 1896, **9,** 343–388.
HESS, E. H. Some relationships between pupillary activity and mental activity. Presented at the American Psychological Association Meeting, September, 1964.
HESS, E. H. Attitude and pupil size. *Scientific American,* 1965, **212,** No. 4, 46–54.
HESS, E. H. Pupillometrics. In: F. M. BASS, C. W. KING, & E. A. PESSEMEIER, (Eds.), *Application of the sciences in marketing management.* New York: Wiley, 1968.
HESS, E. H., & POLT, J. M. Pupil size as related to interest value of visual stimuli. *Science,* 1960, **132,** 349–350.
HESS, E. H., & POLT, J. M. Pupil size in relation to mental activity during simple problem-solving. *Science,* 1964, **143,** 1190–1192.
HESS, E. H., & POLT, J. M. Changes in pupil size as a measure of taste difference. *Perceptual and Motor Skills,* 1966, **23,** 451–455.
HESS, E. H., SELTZER, A. L., & SHLIEN, J. M. Pupil responses of hetero- and homosexual males to pictures of men and women: A pilot study. *Journal of Abnormal Psychology,* 1965, **70,** 165–168.
HICKS, R. A., REANEY, T., & HILL, L. Effects of pupil size and facial angle on preference for photographs of a young woman. *Peceptual and Motor Skills,* 1967, **24,** 388–390.

JONES, Q. R., & MOYEL, I. S. The influence of iris color and pupil size on expressed affect. *Psychonomic Science,* 1971, **22,** 126–127.

KAHNEMAN, D., & BEATTY, J. Pupil diameter and load on memory. *Science,* 1966, **154,** 1583–1585.
KAHNEMAN, D., & BEATTY, J. Pupillary changes in a paired-associate learning task. Presented at the Pupil Symposium, American Psychological Association Convention, Washington, D.C., 1967. (a)
KAHNEMAN, D., & BEATTY, J. Pupillary responses in a pitch discrimination task. *Perception and Psychophysics,* 1967, **2,** 101–105. (b)
KAHNEMAN, D., BEATTY, J., & POLLACK, I. Perceptual deficit during a mental task. *Science,* 1967, **157,** 218–219.
KAHNEMAN, D., & PEAVLER, W. S. Incentive effects and pupillary changes in association learning. *Journal of Experimental Psychology,* 1969, **79,** 312–318.
KAHNEMAN, D., TURSKY, B., SHAPIRO, D., & CRIDER, A. Pupillary, heart rate, and skin resistance changes during a mental task. *Journal of Experimental Psychology,* 1969, **79,** 164–167.
KENNARD, M. A. Effect of bilateral ablation of cingulate

area on behavior of cats. *Journal of Neurophysiology,* 1955, **18,** 159-169.

KLEIN, R., & EARLY, D. F.   Observations on the electrically produced epileptic convulsion: Part II. Pupillary phenomena in normal and pathological pupils. *Journal of Mental Science,* 1948, **94,** 805-808.

KOFF, R. H.   The relationship between two cognitive controls and selected voluntary and involuntary behavior. Unpublished doctoral dissertation, University of Chicago, 1966.

KOHLBERG, L.   A cognitive-developmental analysis of children's sex-role concepts and attitudes. In E. MACCOBY (Ed.), *The development of sex differences.* Stanford, Calif.: Stanford University Press, 1966.

KOHN, M., & CLYNES, M.   Color dynamics of the pupil. *Annals of the New York Academy of Sciences,* 1969, **156,** 931-950.

KRUEGER, L. M.   Voluntary control of pupillary responses to visual stimuli. *Dissertation Abstracts,* 1967, **28,** 6-B, 2644.

KRUGMAN, H. E.   Some applications of pupil measurement. *Journal of Marketing Research,* 1964 (November), **1,** 15-19.

KUMNICK, L. S.   Pupillary psychosensory restitution and aging. *Journal of the Optical Society of America,* 1954, **44,** 735-741.

KUMNICK, L. S.   Aging and pupillary response to light and sound stimuli. *Journal of Gerontology,* 1956, **11,** 38-45. (a)

KUMNICK, L. S.   Aging and the efficiency of the pupillary mechanism. *Journal of Gerontology,* 1956, **11,** 160-164. (b)

LEVINE, A., & SCHILDER, P.   The catatonic pupil. *Journal of Nervous and Mental Disease,* 1942, **96,** 1-12.

LIBERMAN, A. E.   Some new data on the pupillary component in man. In L. G. VORONIN, A. N. LEONTIEV, A. R. LURIA, E. N. SOKOLOV, & O. S. VINOGRADOVA (Eds.), *Orienting reflex and exploratory behavior.* Moscow: Academy of Pedagogical Sciences, RSFSR, 1958. Translated by V. SHMELEV & K. HANES. D. B. LINDSLEY (Ed.). Washington, D.C.: American Institute of Biological Sciences, 1965.

LIDSKY, A., HAKEREM, G., & SUTTON, S.   Psychopathological patterns of pupillary response to single light pulses. Paper presented at Fifth Colloquium on the Pupil, Philadelphia, 1967.

LOEWENFELD, I. E.   Mechanism of reflex dilatation of the pupil: Historical review and experimental analysis. *Documenta Opthalmologica,* 1958, **12,** 185-448.

LORENS, S., & DARROW, C.   Eye movements, EEG, GSR, and EKG during mental multiplication. *Electroencephalography and Clinical Neurophysiology,* 1962, **14,** 739-746.

LOWENSTEIN, O.   Experimentelle Beiträge zur Lehre von den katatonischen Pupillenveränderungen. *Monatsschrift für Psychiatrie und Neurologie,* 1920, **47,** 194-215.

LOWENSTEIN, O.   Über die Variationsbreite des Lichtreflexes und der Psychoreflexe der Pupille. *Archiv für Psychiatrie und Nervenkrankheiten,* 1927, **82,** 285-314.

LOWENSTEIN, O.   *Der psychische Restitutionseffekt: Das Princip der psychisch bedingten Wiederherstellung der ermüdeten, der erschöpften und der erkrankten Funktion.* Basel: Benno Schwabe, 1937.

LOWENSTEIN, O.   General principles of psychosomatic relations of the eye. *Journal of Clinical Psychopathology,* 1945, **6,** 433-436.

LOWENSTEIN, O. & LOEWENFELD, I. E.   Electronic pupillography: A new instrument and some clinical applications. *Archives of Opthalmology,* 1958, **59,** 352-363.

LOWENSTEIN, O., & LOEWENFELD, I. E.   Influence of retinal adaptation upon the pupillary reflex to light in normal man. *American Journal of Opthalmology,* 1961, **51,** 644-654.

LOWENSTEIN, O., & LOEWENFELD, I. E.   The pupil. In H. DAVSON (Ed.), *The eye.* Vol. 3. New York: Academic, 1962.

LOWENSTEIN, O., & WESTPHAL, A.   *Experimentelle und klinische Studien zur Physiologie der Pupillenbewegungen.* Berlin: Karger, 1933.

MACKWORTH, N. H.   The wide-angle reflection eye camera for visual choice and pupil size. *Perception and Psychophysics,* 1968, **3,** 32-34.

MAGOUN, H. W., & RANSON, S. W.   The behavior of cats following bilateral removal of the rostral portion of the cerebral hemispheres. *Journal of Neurophysiology,* 1938, **1,** 39-44.

MAY, P. R. A.   Pupillary abnormalities in schizophrenia and during muscular effort. *Journal of Mental Science,* 1948, **94,** 89-98.

MENTZ, P.   Die Wirkung akustischer Sinnesreize auf Puls und Athmung. *Philosophische Studien,* 1895, **11,** 61-124; 371-393; 562-602.

MEYER, E.   Pupillenstörungen bei Dementia praecox. *Berliner klinische Wochenschrift,* 1910, **47,** 1813-1815.

MILLER, M. B.   Pupil response variability as a function of stimulus meaningfulness in retarded and normal adolescents. Presented at the Pupil Symposium, American Psychological Association Convention, Washington, D.C., 1967.

MILLER, R. L.   The clinical validation of the pupillary response: The effect of chromatic and achromatic stimuli upon pupil responsivity. *Dissertation Abstracts,* 1967, **27,** 2515-B.

NUNNALLY, J. C.   Pupillary response in anticipation of emotion-provoking events. Presented at the Pupil Symposium, American Psychological Association Convention, Washington, D.C., 1967.

NUNNALLY, J. C., KNOTT, P. D., DUCHNOWSKI, A., & PARKER, R.   Pupillary response as a general measure of activation. *Perception and Psychophysics,* 1967, **2,** 149-155.

OBERLANDER, M. I.   Pupillary reaction correlates of adaptive regression. Unpublished doctoral dissertation, University of Chicago, 1967.

PAIVIO, A.   Latency of verbal association and imagery to noun stimuli as a function of abstractness and generality. *Canadian Journal of Psychology,* 1966, **20,** 378-387.

PAIVIO, A., & SIMPSON, H. M.   The effect of word abstractness and pleasantness on pupil size during an imagery task. *Psychonomic Science,* 1966, **5,** 55-57.

PARKER, R. K., & MOGYOROSY, R. S.   Pupillary response to induced muscular tension. Presented at the Pupil Symposium, American Psychological Association Convention, Washington, D.C., 1967.

PEAVLER, W. S., & MCLAUGHLIN, J. P.   The question of stimulus content and pupil size. *Psychonomic Science,* 1967, **8,** 505-506.

POLT, J. M.   Effect of threat of shock on pupillary response in a problem-solving situation. *Perceptual and Motor Skills,* 1970, **31,** 587-593.

POLT, J. M., & HESS, E. H.   Changes in pupil size to visually presented words. *Psychonomic Science,* 1968, **12,** 389-399.

RAEHLMANN, E., & WITKOWSI, L.   Über das Verhalten der Pupillen während des Schlafes nebst Bemerkungen zur Innervation der Iris. *Archiv für Anatomie und Physiologie (Physiologie),* Leipzig, 1878, 109-121.

REDLICH, E.   Zur Characteristik der reflectorischen Pupillenstarre bei der progressiven Paralyse. *Neurologisches Zentralblatt,* 1892, **11,** 307-312.

REDLICH, E.   *Die Pathologie der tabischen Hinterstrangerkrankung.* Jena: G. Fischer, 1897.

REDLICH, E.   Diskussion. *Zeitschrift für Augenheilkunde,* 1908, **19,** 171-172. (a)

REDLICH, E.   Ueber ein eigenartiges Pupillenphänomen; zugleich ein Beitrag zur Frage der hysterischen Pupillenstarre. *Deutsche medizinische Wochenschrift,* 1908, **34,** 313-315. (b)

REICHMANN, F.   Ueber Pupillenstörungen bei Dementia praecox. *Archiv für Psychiatrie und Nervenkrankheiten,* 1914, **53,** 302-321.

ROUBINOVITCH, J.   Du reflexe ideo-moteur de la pupille. *Revue neurologique,* 1900, **8:** 740-741.

ROUBINOVITCH, J.   Des variations du diamètre pupillaire en rapport avec l'effort intellectuel. In P. JANET (Ed.), *Quatrième Congrès Internationale de Psychologie* (1900). *Compte rendu des séances et textes des mèmoires, publiés par les soins du docteur Pierre Janet.* Paris: F. Alcan, 1901.

RUBIN, L. S.   Patterns of pupillary dilatation and constriction in psychotic adults and autistic children. *Journal of Nervous and Mental Disease,* 1961, **133,** 130-142.

RUBIN, L. S.   Autonomic dysfunction in psychoses: Adults and autistic children. *Archives of General Psychiatry,* 1962, **7,** 1-14.

RUBIN, L. S.   Autonomic dysfunction as a concomitant of neurotic behavior. *Journal of Nervous and Mental Disease,* 1964, **138,** 558-571.

RUBIN, L. S.   Autonomic dysfunction in neurotic behavior. *Archives of General Psychiatry,* 1965, **12,** 572-585.

RUBIN, L. S., BARBERO, G. J., CHERNIK, W. S., & SIBINGA, M. S.   Pupillary reactivity as a measure of autonomic balance in cystic fibrosis. *Journal of Pediatrics,* 1963, **63,** 1120-1129.

RUBIN, L. S., BARBERO, G. J., & SIBINGA, M. S.   Pupillary reactivity in children with recurrent abdominal pain. *Psychosomatic Medicine* 1967, **29,** 111-120.

RUBIN, L. S., & BARRY, T. J.   Dysautonomia in schizophrenic remission. *Psychosomatics,* 1970, **11,** 506-511.

RYNEARSON, R. C.   The pupillary reflex: An indication of autonomic dysfunction in process-reactive schizophrenia. Doctoral dissertation, Case Western Reserve University, 1968. *Dissertation Abstracts International,* 1970, **30,** (9-B), 3410-3411.

SCHIFF, J. M.   *La pupille considerée comme esthésiomètre.* Traduction de l'italien par Dr. R. G. de Choisity. Paris: Baillière, 1875.

SCHIFF, J. M. & FOA, P.   La pupille considerée comme esthésiomètre. Traduction de l'italien par Dr. R. G. de Choisity. *Marseille médicine* 1874, **2,** 736-741.

SCHMIDT-RIMPLER, H.   Die Erkrankung des -Auges im Zusammenhang mit anderen Krankheiten. In C. W. H. NOTHNAGEL (Ed.), *Handbuch der speciellen Pathologie und Therapie.* Vol. 21. Wien: Holder, 1898.

SCOTT, T. R.   Pupillary response: A fruitful research variable. *Newsletter for Research in Psychology,* 1965, **7,** (No. 2), 56.

SELTZER, A. L.   Pupil response in hypnosis. Presented at the Pupil Symposium, American Psychological Association Convention, Washington, D.C., 1967.

SHAKNOVICH, A. R.   Orienting, contracting reaction of the pupil to novelty in photic stimulation. *Fiziologicheskiĭ Zhurnal SSSR,* 1956, **42,** 632-638.

SHAKNOVICH, A. R.   On the pupillary component of the orienting reflex during action of stimuli specific for vision and nonspecific (extraneous) stimuli. In L. G. VORONIN, A. N. LEONTIEV, A. R. LURIA, E. N. SOKOLOV, & O. S. VINOGRADOVA (Eds.), *Orienting reflex and exploratory behavior.* Moscow: Academy of Pedagogical Sciences, RSFSR, 1958. Translated by V. SHMELEV & K. HANES. D. B. LINDSLEY (Ed.). Washington, D.C.: American Institute of Biological Sciences, 1965.

SHEFLIN, J. A.   An application of Hess' pupillometric procedure to a psychiatric population: An approach utilizing sexual stimuli. Doctoral dissertation, Purdue University, 1969. *Dissertation Abstracts, International,* 1969, **29,** 1907B.

SIMMS, T. M.   Pupillary response of male and female subjects to pupillary difference in male and female picture stimuli. *Perception and Psychophysics,* 1967, **2,** 553-555.

SIMPSON, H. M.   Pupillary activity during imagery tasks. Presented at the Pupil Symposium, American Psychological Association Convention, Washington, D.C., 1967.

SIMPSON, H. M., & PAIVIO, A.   Changes in pupil size during an imagery task without motor response involvement. *Psychonomic Science,* 1966, **5,** 405-406.

SIMPSON, H. M., & PAIVIO, A. Effects on pupil size of manual and verbal indicators of cognitive task fulfillment. *Perception and Psychophysics,* 1968, **3,** 185–190.

SOKOLOV, E. N. *Orientirovochniĭ reflex i. voprosy visshei nervnoi deiatelnosty.* Moscow: Academy of Pedagogical Sciences, RSFSR, 1959.

SOKOLOV, E. N. The orienting reflex, its structure and mechanisms. In L. G. VORONIN, A. N. LEONTIEV, A. R. LURIA, E. N. SOKOLOV, & O. S. VINOGRADOVA (Eds.), *Orienting reflex and exploratory behavior.* Moscow: Academy of Pedagogical Sciences, RSFSR, 1958. Translated by V. SHMELEV & K. HANES. D. B. LINDSLEY (Ed.). Washington, D.C.: American Institute of Biological Sciences, 1965.

SPIEGEL, E. A., MILLER, H. R., & OPPENHEIMER, M. J. Forebrain and rage reactions. *Journal of Neurophysiology,* 1940, **3,** 538–548.

STARK, L. Pupillary control system: Its nonlinear adaptive and stochastic engineering design characteristics. *Federation Proceedings,* 1969, **28,** 52–64.

STASS, W., & WILLIS, F. N., Jr. Eye contact, pupil dilation, and personal preference. *Psychonomic Science,* 1967, **7,** 375–376.

STEWART, R. W., & JENSEN, D. D. GSR, pupillary dilation, and response latency to words differing in entropy. Presented at the Midwest Psychological Association Meeting, Chicago, May 1966.

STRELTSOVA, N. I. The influence of some physiological and pharmacological factors on the pupillary orienting reflex. In L. G. VORONIN, A. N. LEONTIEV, A. R. LURIA, E. N. SOKOLOV, & O. S. VINOGRADOVA (Eds.), *Orienting reflex and exploratory behavior.* Moscow: Academy of Peda-

gogical Sciences, RSFSR, 1958. Translated by V. SHMELEV & K. HANES. D. B. LINDSLEY (Ed.). Washington, D.C.: American Institute of Biological Sciences, 1965.

VORONIN, L. G., LEONTIEV, A. N., LURIA, A. R., SOKOLOV, E. N., & VINOGRADOVA, O. S. (Eds.) *Orienting reflex and exploratory behavior.* Moscow: Academy of Pedagogical Sciences RSFSR, 1958. Translated by V. SHMELEV & K. HANES. D. B. LINDSLEY (Ed.). Washington, D.C.: American Institute of Biological Sciences, 1965.

WESTPHAL, A. Ueber ein im katatonischen Stupor beobachtetes Pupillenphänomen sowie Bemerkungen über die Pupillenstarre bei Hysterie. *Deutsche Medizinische Wochenschrift,* 1907, **33,** 1080–1084.

WESTPHAL, A. Über Pupillenphänomene bei Katatonie, Hysterie und myoklonischen Symptomenkomplexen. *Monatsschrift für Psychiatrie und Neurologie,* 1920, **47,** 187–193.

WESTPHAL, C. F. Ueber ein Pupillenphänomen in der Chloroformnarkose. *Virchows Archiv für Pathologische Anatomie und Physiologie,* 1863, **27,** 409–412.

WIKLER, A., ROSENBERG, D. E., HAWTHORNE, J. D., & CASSIDY, T. M. Age and effect of LSD-25 on pupil size and knee jerk threshold. *Psychopharmacologia,* 1965, **7,** 44–56.

WOODMANSEE, J. J. Methodological problems in pupillographic experiments. Presented at the American Psychological Association Convention, New York, 1966.

WOODMANSEE, J. J. Pupil reaction as an index of positive and negative affect. Presented at the Pupil Symposium, American Psychological Association Convention, Washington, D.C., 1967.

CONCEPTS OF HUMAN NATURE DEVELOPED THROUGH PSYCHOPHYSIOLOGY

Marion A. Wenger and Thomas D. Cullen

STUDIES OF AUTONOMIC BALANCE IN CHILDREN AND ADULTS

13

EARLY STUDIES OF CHILDREN AND ADULTS

Background for the Studies

The first author to postulate that dual control of involuntary muscle activity and glandular secretion is exerted through two antagonistic systems was Gaskell in 1885. He concluded that the viscera are innervated by two sets of nerve fibers, one set being anabolic and the other catabolic in function. This functional designation corresponded with the later anatomical division of the autonomic nervous system (ANS) by Langley (1905). Eppinger and Hess (1910) saw in the mutual antagonism of the two systems a principle that might account for many bodily disorders. If the normal functioning of the body were considered to be dependent upon a balance between sympathetic and parasympathetic (extended vagal system) activities, any shift in the balance to one side or the other might be expected to result in widespread disturbances.

Earlier suggestions of abnormal conditions or increased irritability of the vagus nerve as a cause of gastrointestinal disorders had been made by Rokitansky (1855) and by Von Noorden (1892), but it was Eppinger and Hess who formulated the idea of autonomic imbalance as a general concept. Their observations on the effects of certain drugs led them to conclude that individuals who react strongly to adrenalin are relatively insensitive to pilocarpine and atropine, and that individuals who react strongly to pilocarpine and atropine are relatively insensitive to adrenalin. They interpreted these differential drug reactions as indicating that in some individuals a condition of sympatheticotonia exists, characterized by hyperactivity or increased tonus of the sympathetic nervous system (SNS); in others a condition of vagotonia exists, characterized by hyperactivity or increased tonus of the extended vagal or parasympathetic nervous system (PNS). They also conceived of conditions of relative sympatheticotonia, characterized by parasympathetic hypoactivity without increased sympathetic activity, and of relative vagotonia, characterized by sympathetic hypoactivity without increased parasympathetic activity. Petren and Thorling (1911) pointed out that a condition in which both systems are hyperactive is also possible, since some individuals react strongly to both sympathomimetic and parasympathomimetic drugs.

Eppinger and Hess considered sympatheticotonia and vagotonia diseases of the ANS with symptoms similar to responses produced by stimulation of the SNS and PNS, respectively. Their methods of assessing the degree of autonomic imbalance included, in addition to testing the effects of drugs, the use of checklists of physiological symptoms and measurements of various reflexes such as the slowing of the pulse in response to pressure on the eyeball (Aschner's test) and in response to stooping (Erben's test). Some of the symptoms characteristic of the sympatheticotonic individual, according to Eppinger and Hess, are a rapid pulse, large pupils, and clammy hands and feet. Bradycardia, small pupils, and a dry skin, on the other hand, were held characteristic of the vagotonic individual. Behaviorally, the sympatheticotonic individual was described as lively and excitable, and the vagotonic individual as reserved and "cold-blooded."

The publication by Eppinger and Hess stimulated much research on individual differences in the functioning of the ANS. These studies have been well reviewed by Darrow (1943) and will not be cited here. Suffice it to say that none of them seemed to be conclusive and that the concepts of sympatheticotonia and vagotonia gradually fell into disuse, even disrepute. Not only was the concept

of tone in nerve fibers questioned but also the value of the concept of autonomic balance (Cannon, 1932). Nevertheless, when one of the present authors (Wenger) reached the conclusion in 1938 that the theory of Eppinger and Hess had never been adequately tested and proposed an attempt to do so by means of multiple tests and factorial analyses in supposedly normal children, he found Cannon to be most receptive to the idea. In fact, it was Cannon who urged that an attempt be made to include a measure of salivary output.

After this encouragement from Cannon, and after helpful discussions with Chester Darrow, Roland Davis, and many others, the Eppinger and Hess hypothesis was restated as follows (Wenger, 1941):

> The differential chemical reactivity and the physiological antagonism of the adrenergic and cholinergic branches of the autonomic nervous system permit of a situation in which the action of one branch may predominate over that of the other. This predominance, or autonomic imbalance, may be phasic or chronic, and may obtain for either the adrenergic or the cholinergic system. Autonomic imbalance, when measured in an unselected population, will be distributed continuously about a central tendency which shall be defined as autonomic balance. [p. 427]

The testing of this hypothesis was the beginning of the work described in this chapter. It will be seen that the formulation followed Dale (1934) in anticipating a general factor related to body chemistry, rather than to anatomy. The results reported in the next section, however, were more closely related to physiological differentiations based on anatomical divisions of the ANS and are regarded as supporting the original concept of Eppinger and Hess but making it applicable to health, as well as disease.

Initial Investigations

From 1939 through 1942, a series of physiological measurements were conducted during winter and summer months on the child subjects of the Fels Research Institute, Antioch College, Yellow Springs, Ohio. Several analyses of the data for children 6–13 years of age have been published (Wenger, 1941, 1942a, 1942b, 1943a, 1943b, 1943c; Wenger & Ellington, 1943). They described a factor composed of physiological responses that are mediated by the autonomic nervous system. It was shown that this "autonomic factor" could be estimated in terms of a battery of seven weighted tests, and that such derived estimates, termed scores of "autonomic balance" or $\overline{A}$, were more reliable than measurements of most single physiological variables. It was also shown that scores of autonomic balance varied considerably in a group of supposedly normal children but tended to remain constant for individuals over periods as long as 3 years. High scores of autonomic balance were regarded as representing a functional dominance of the parasympathetic branch of the autonomic nervous system, and low scores as representing a functional dominance of the sympathetic branch.

Effects of the season of measurement on these scores were studied (Wenger, 1943c). In general, individuals who had low $\overline{A}$ scores in winter had higher scores in summer; those with high scores in winter tended to demonstrate lower scores in summer; correlations between summer and winter measurements were low. In Ohio, as in most temperate latitudes, weather conditions that are known to affect the functions involved in such tests are more stable during the winter than during the summer months. For this reason, summer measurements were discontinued.

Evidence was beginning to accumulate concerning other factors that might affect the determination of autonomic balance. Excitement, apprehension, the onset of menstruation, fatigue, exercise just previous to examination, and extreme temperatures in the examining room, resulted in lowered $\overline{A}$ scores. More will be said about such factors later in this chapter.

Concerning some of the correlates of autonomic balance, an analysis of differences manifested by extreme deviates on the autonomic scale (Wenger, 1947) showed that children who had high scores, as compared with those who had low scores, tended to have lower basal metabolic rates, a more adequate diet, and a faster rate of physical development. Also, they were less emotional in terms of both frequency and intensity, showed a lower frequency of activity with less fatigue, and were more patient and neat, but were less friendly, less gregarious, and less distractible. Other data suggested that children manifesting difficulties in adjustment to their social environments appeared to have low, or occasionally extremely high, scores on this weighted battery of tests, while those who manifested adequate adjustment showed average or slightly higher than average scores. Moreover, when these children showed decreases or increases in $\overline{A}$ scores during the period of study, decreases appeared to be associated with deteriorating adjustment at home or in the school; increases appeared to be associated with improvement in overall adjustment.

Another unpublished study, conducted in the fall of 1941 (Neuropsychiatric Ward, Massachusetts General Hospital, Boston), reinforced the growing impression that scores of autonomic balance were related to psychological adjustment. At that time 24 adult patients of both sexes, all hospitalized with tentative diagnoses of psychoneurosis or prepsychosis, were tested. Anxiety was a prominent symptom in all. Although it was not known whether or not an autonomic factor could be measured in adults, nor what effect sex differences might have, the battery of tests that had been developed for children was given to these adult patients. The data were standardized against the norms for the oldest group of children from the Fels Research Institute and the regression equation for estimating $\overline{A}$ for children was applied.

The results were rather dramatic. For all but one of the patients an extremely low $\overline{A}$ score was obtained. The distribution curve was leptokurtic and had practically no overlap with the distribution curve for children. The exceptional patient had an extremely high score, almost 6 standard deviations above the mean. His tentative diagnosis was "prepsychotic." After further examination his diagnosis was changed to "hyperinsulinism," due to a tumor of the pancreas.

By this time it seemed clear that health and other environmental factors influenced the scores of autonomic balance. Nevertheless, the constancy of the scores for most of the Fels children from year to year was impressive. Further, an analysis by Jost and Sontag (1944) of the data concerning identical twins and siblings suggested that we were dealing with a physiological pattern that was in part genetically determined. Since the basic validity of the autonomic factor had been demonstrated by close

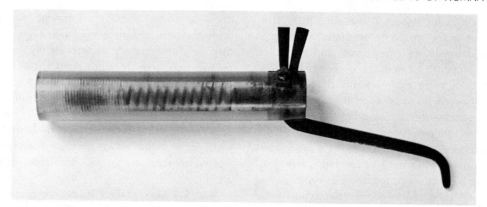

Figure 13.1 Dermographic stimulator. The end of the movable stylus is curved and rounded to a tip 2 mm in diameter, and the upright indicator is set at a right angle to the stylus arm. The plastic handle contains a fixed upright indicator and a spring whose tension against the stylus can be varied by a calibration screw. In use the movable indicator is brought parallel to the fixed indicator to deliver the required pressure.

correspondence between results from three separate analyses (Wenger, 1943a), and since a regression equation had been derived which so closely approximated any of the three original equations for weighting the tests that it could be recommended for general use with preadolescent children, Wenger and Ellington (1943) presented the normative data and described the methods of measurement in some detail. They are partly reproduced here.

Measurement procedures All measurements were made during the hours between 9 and 12 AM, at least an hour after breakfast, in a quiet room in which the temperature and humidity were controlled at 74–76°F and 40%, respectively. All were made during the winter months, and after the subject had been allowed to adjust to the room temperature for at least half an hour or, in severe weather, for 1 hr. Precautions were taken that the subject had not exercised just before the examination and was not excited or apprehensive. Measurement was undertaken only after excellent rapport had been gained, after the subject had seen the apparatus involved and had had it explained or demonstrated to him.

In the following description, the numbers appended to the tests are those used in previous reports and in the accompanying tables.

Persistence of red dermographia (*23*)   Red dermographia was elicited by applying two firm slow strokes over the biceps of the left arm with

the stimulator shown in Figure 13.1, calibrated to deliver approximately 250 grams pressure.

The rounded tip of the instrument was 2 mm

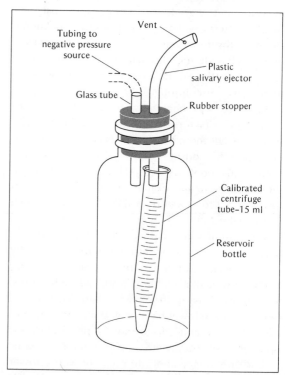

Figure 13.2 Apparatus for measurement of salivary output. Adapted from M. A. Wenger and M. Ellington, The measurement of autonomic balance in children: Method and normative data. *Psychosomatic Medicine*, 1943, **5**, 241–253. By permission of the publishers.

in diameter. The latency and persistence of the red response are more accurately observable if two strokes are made in the form of an **X**. Each stroke was about 3 in. in length and timed to require approximately 1 sec, the stop watch being started at the incidence of the first stroke. The latency was recorded in seconds as soon as the "crossing" was discernible; the persistence time was recorded to the nearest minute at which the location of the crossing was no longer a matter of certainty. The response was elicited as soon after reclining as the subject appeared to be at rest, since it persisted for 40 or more minutes in a few subjects. The more normal range was 3–30 min.

Salivary output (25)   Saliva was collected in a centrifuge tube using a water pump and apparatus similar to that shown in Figure 13.2. Wooden mouthpieces designed for use with a clinical spirometer were employed and were first moistened with water to prevent sticking to the subject's lips.

The subject, comfortably seated, was given the bottle to hold and the following instructions were presented orally: "We want to find out how much saliva (spit) you have. First swallow all that you have in your mouth now." (Pause until swallowing is observed.) "Now put the end of the glass tube just inside your lips and bring to the front of your mouth all the saliva you can. It will be sucked out of your mouth into the tube. Work hard and see how much you can get in the tube." When necessary, "Don't try to spit into the tube. Just get the saliva ready to spit and let the suction from the bottle draw it out of your mouth. . . . Work hard. The time is almost up." A warning was given as follows: "Only 1 minute yet. Work hard." For school-age children a time limit of 5 min was used. The stop watch was started at the first observed salivary flow. The score was the amount to the nearest 0.1 cc. If the sample could not be centrifuged, it was allowed to settle before recording the volume.

Heart period (28)   At least four samples of 1-min duration were taken over a 20-min period and were recorded electrocardiographically, with the subject reclining and in a resting state. Thirty beats were measured in seconds from peak QRS to QRS for each sample, and the mean of the 120 periods was recorded. If apparatus is not available for this form of recording, successive samples of

heart rate may be taken and the results converted to heart period.

Standing palmar skin conductance (37)   Darrow's (1932) constant 40-μamp current circuit was used and readings to the nearest KΩ were converted to μmho by means of a previously prepared table. The electrodes were attached to the center of the palms of the hands at least 10 min before the measurements were begun. Care was taken to rub the electrolyte into the skin only on the area to be covered by the electrode and not to abrade the skin. The mean of three measurements at 1-min intervals was regarded as the final measure. The subject was instructed to relax as much as possible, to stand erect and quietly, with his weight supported equally on both feet, and to let his hands and fingers relax. He faced a blank wall, and was instructed, "Try to think of nothing." Such standing measurements were more reliable than measurement while reclining or sitting because the influence of differing degrees of muscular tension is better controlled.

The electrode, a zinc disk 2 cm in diameter, was fastened inside a plastic cup with the same inside diameter and a depth of 0.5 cm. The unit could be attached with an adjustable rubber strap. As electrolytes, both kaolin and 1% zinc sulphate and finely powdered agar and 1% zinc sulphate have been used with similar results. The latter is cleaner and may be prepared in sufficient quantity to last for several months if stored in air-tight containers.[1]

Volar forearm skin conductance (39)   This measure was made in the same manner as that for palmar skin conductance, except that the electrodes were placed on the volar surfaces of the forearms, approximately 10 cm below the cubital fossa, before the subject reclined. The determination was made

---

[1]Electrodes and other apparatus used in this test battery now may be obtained from the Davis Instrument Co., North Hollywood, California. The agar jelly requires preparation—no commerical source has proved reliable. At first, Merck's reagent agar was used, and later their fine-powdered agar proved satisfactory. Recently, the best we have been able to procure is Pennick's. Since it seems to vary, no exact instructions can be given for its preparation. Use 356 cc distilled water, 4 grams ZnSO$_4$, and 40 grams fine-powdered agar. Thoroughly mix the above in a 600 ml open-mouth beaker at room temperature. Place 0.75 in. of water in a suitable receptacle and bring to boiling. Slowly place the beaker into the boiling water and stir the mixture continuously for 3–5 min; then transfer to a sealed container to cool. A consistency similar to a firm tooth paste is desired. Do not use a watery or an overly firm paste. Additional heating can correct the former; if the latter is the result, repeat with reduced heating time.

at the end of the experimental session before the subject arose. The mean of two readings at 1-min intervals, converted to μmho, was an adequate measure.

Respiration period (57)   Respiration was recorded pneumographically, and the respiration periods from inspiration peak to peak were measured for at least four samples of 1 min each over a 20-min period. The mean of all measures was utilized. Here, as in heart period, it was possible to substitute rate for period by conversion of the data. The data are recorded in seconds per mean respiration period.

Pulse pressure (80)   All readings were taken by remote auscultation, diastolic pressure being read at the fourth phase (first distinct muffling). The subject reclined in a resting state, with the cuff on the right upper arm. A stethephone diaphragm was strapped to the subject's arm over the brachial artery. For children 4–14 years old, a 9-cm cuff was employed. From a series of six or more readings taken over a 20-min period, the two lowest systolic measures that duplicated each other were employed as the minuend; the mean of their respective diastolic readings was employed as the subtrahend for the pulse-pressure determination. If the two diastolic readings were greatly disparate, the median of the three measures corresponding to the three lowest systolic readings was utilized.

Order of testing   Tests were given in the following order: salivary output, palmar skin conductance, red dermographia; then samples of heart period, respiration period, and pulse pressure at 3-min intervals, followed by volar forearm skin conductance.

Scores of autonomic balance   To obtain $\bar{A}$ scores the raw data for seven tests are converted into standard scores. To eliminate minus signs and decimal points, each score is multiplied by 10 and added to 50. Each distribution (T scores) then has a mean of 50 and a standard deviation of 10. The data then may be employed in the regression equation for the estimation of autonomic balance. The equation is:

$$\bar{A} = .1(T_{23}) + .2(T_{25}) + .4(T_{28}) + .3(T_{37^a})$$
$$+ .1(T_{39^b}) + .1(T_{57}) + .2(T_{80})$$

where $\bar{A}$ is the estimated score for the autonomic

factor and the T following each beta weight represents the standard score for the physiological test designated by the subscript. The superscript a following subscripts 37 and 39 indicates that these tests are reflected. A low raw score on these tests is represented by a proportionally high standard score.

If for each of these seven tests a T score of 50 is used in this equation, the mean score for autonomic balance is 70. Standard deviations for different samples have averaged about 6.7. Since our distributions have approached the normal curve, it may be said that approximately 68% of the children from such a sample may be expected to demonstrate an autonomic balance score of 70 ± 7. Of those individuals who have scores higher than 77, it may be said that they demonstrate an apparent functional dominance of the parasympathetic system. Likewise, those scores below 63 may be regarded as manifesting an apparent dominance of sympathetic function. It should be noted that such scores indicate nothing concerning the cause of deviations. A high score might result from weak sympathetic function, strong parasympathetic function, or both. A low score might indicate a hypoactive parasympathetic system, a hyperactive sympathetic system, or both. All that can be said from this test battery is that a high score is indicative of apparent dominance of parasympathetic function and a low score suggests apparent dominance of sympathetic function.

The normative data   We shall not present all of the data from Wenger and Ellington (1943) but only some of their tables. Table 13.1 shows the means and standard deviations for each variable of the seven-test battery, classified according to age and sex. It shows sex differences and critical ratios of the differences at each age. Only four age groups presented enough cases for this portion of that analysis. The data on systolic and diastolic blood pressure (variables 76 and 77) were included because of their general interest.

A critical ratio of 3.00 or more usually is regarded as statistically significant; however, such a criterion would seem unduly rigorous here. Rather, if each age group shows a sex difference in the same direction for a given variable, the possibility of a real

TABLE 13.1 MEANS, STANDARD DEVIATIONS, AND SEX DIFFERENCES FOR NINE PHYSIOLOGICAL MEASUREMENTS OF BOYS AND GIRLS, 7-10 YEARS OF AGE

Test variable	Age (yr)	7		8		9		10	
	N	19	23	19	16	19	23	15	21
	Sex	M	F	M	F	M	F	M	F
23 DP									
M		10.10	10.00	10.53	11.62	7.47	10.43	8.40	8.78
SD		10.77	9.54	10.50	9.97	6.73	8.77	10.67	11.01
Diff.		−.10		1.09		2.96		2.27	
CR		.03		.31		1.24		.69	
25 SO									
M		3.57	3.41	4.13	4.11	4.57	4.30	4.68	4.53
SD		1.19	1.16	1.82	2.12	1.81	1.72	1.41	2.30
Diff.		−.16		−.02		−.27		−.15	
CR		.44		.03		.49		.24	
28 HP									
M		.712	.676	.729	.708	.762	.723	.775	.746
SD		.093	.074	.092	.073	.075	.074	.079	.095
Diff.		−.036		−.021		−.039		−.03	
CR		1.37		.87		1.69		1.00	
39 VSC									
M		12.4	17.7	12.4	17.8	11.0	16.2	10.0	14.0
SD		5.34	9.05	4.30	6.39	4.07	8.9	2.73	4.27
Diff.		5.3		5.4		5.2		4.0	
CR		2.36		2.88		2.50		3.42	
57 RP									
M		3.05	3.31	2.97	3.33	3.35	3.31	4.13	3.46
SD		.57	.77	.48	.59	.63	.49	1.29	.59
Diff.		.26		.36		−.04		−.67	
CR		1.25		1.97		.02		1.87	
76 SBP									
M		98.6	96.4	98.0	97.0	99.8	98.1	101.1	101.4
SD		5.80	4.72	5.07	4.58	5.65	6.42	5.26	5.52
Diff.		−2.2		−1.0		−1.7		.3	
CR		1.34		.61		.91		.16	
77 DBP									
M		63.4	65.0	63.7	63.1	63.3	63.3	62.7	64.2
SD		6.96	6.14	8.08	5.76	9.99	8.14	8.46	7.61
Diff.		1.6		0.6		0.00		1.5	
CR		0.78		0.26		0.0		0.55	
80 PP									
M		35.2	30.5	34.4	33.9	36.5	34.4	38.4	36.2
SD		6.45	6.14	6.64	8.25	10.10	9.92	8.87	8.77
Diff.		−4.7		−0.5		−2.1		−2.2	
CR		2.92		.20		.68		.74	
	N	15	13	15	15	9	13	12	16
37 PSC[a]									
M		33.6	32.4	31.7	34.9	29.4	34.6	31.1	34.5
SD		13.2	8.7	13.0	12.2	13.0	7.9	12.9	10.1
Diff.		−1.22		3.20		5.18		3.42	
CR		.29		.70		1.07		.76	

[a]Subjects measured during 1942 were omitted from the treatment of this variable because of a slight change in the technique of measurement.

N, number in sample; M, mean; SD, standard deviation; diff., difference; CR, critical ratio.

23 DP = dermographia persistence; 25 SO = salivary output; 28 HP = heart period; 37 PSC = palmar skin conductance; 39 VSC = volar forearm skin conductance; 57 RP = respiration period; 76 SBP = systolic blood pressure; 77 DBP = diastolic blood pressure; 80 PP = pulse pressure.

Source: Adapted from M. A. Wenger and M. Ellington, The measurement of autonomic balance in children: Method and normative data. *Psychosomatic Medicine,* 1943, **5,** 241-253. By permission of the publishers.

TABLE 13.2 MEANS AND STANDARD DEVIATIONS FOR EIGHT PHYSIOLOGICAL MEASUREMENTS THAT SHOW NO SIGNIFICANT SEX DIFFERENCES FOR CHILDREN 6–12 YEARS OF AGE

Test variable	Age (yr)	6	7	8	9	10	11	12
	N	15	42	35	42	36	28	14
23 DP								
M		8.72	10.0	11.0	9.10	9.72	10.1	9.43
SD		8.94	10.10	10.30	8.05	10.20	9.92	9.13
25 SO								
M		3.13	3.49	4.12	4.43	4.54	4.64	4.85
SD		1.00	1.16	1.96	1.76	1.99	2.09	1.71
28 HP								
M		.67	.69	.72	.74	.76	.76	.80
SD		.07	.09	.08	.08	.09	.08	.07
57 RP								
M		3.16	3.19`	3.13	3.33	3.74	3.58	3.61
SD		.54	.70	.56	.56	1.01	.80	1.24
76 SBP								
M		96.3	97.4	97.6	98.8	101.3	103.8	109.1
SD		7.48	5.34	4.88	6.14	5.42	5.73	4.64
77 DBP								
M		60.8	64.3	63.4	63.3	63.6	67.9	71.1
SD		9.11	6.58	7.12	9.03	8.01	5.84	6.21
80 PP								
M		35.5	32.6	34.2	35.3	37.1	35.9	38.1
SD		10.80	6.69	7.42	10.00	8.88	6.76	5.56
	N	11	28	30	22	28	14	3
37 PSC[a]								
M		32.9	33.0	33.3	33.8	33.0	31.9	35.0
SD		7.8	11.4	12.7	10.1	11.5	9.4	6.7

[a] See note a, Table 13.1.

N, number in sample; M, mean; SD, standard deviation.

23 DP = dermographia persistence; *25* SO = salivary output; *28* HP = heart period; *57* RP = respiration period; *76* SBP = systolic blood pressure; *77* DBP = diastolic blood pressure; *80* PP = pulse pressure.

Source: Adapted from M. A. Wenger and M. Ellington, The measurement of autonomic balance in children: Method and normative data. *Psychosomatic Medicine,* 1943, **5,** 241–253. By permission of the publishers.

difference should be considered. This condition existed for tests of salivary output (*25*), heart period (*28*), volar skin conductance (*39*), and pulse pressure (*80*). In no instance does any critical ratio for the remaining variables approach 3.00. It may be concluded that persistence of dermographia, palmar conductance, respiration period, systolic blood pressure, and diastolic blood pressure manifested no consistent sex differences at these age levels.

The consistent differences for salivary output and pulse pressure (variables *25* and *80*) are seen to be slight and, although indicative of the existence of real differences, were disregarded for practical purposes.

TABLE 13.3 MEANS AND STANDARD DEVIATIONS OF THREE VARIABLES THAT REQUIRED NO CORRECTION FOR AGE OR SEX DIFFERENCES IN 87 CHILDREN OF AGE 6–12

Variable	M	SD
23 Dermographia persistence	10.17	9.85
37 Standing palmar skin conductance	33.08	11.04
80 Pulse pressure	34.60	9.72

Source: Adapted from M. A. Wenger and M. Ellington, The measurement of autonomic balance in children: Method and normative data. *Psychosomatic Medicine,* 1943, **5,** 241–253. By permission of the publishers.

The two remaining variables, heart period (28) and volar skin conductance (39), must be given more consideration. All critical ratios for the latter approached 3.00, and the differences in means were in some instances as large or larger than one standard deviation. It is clear that a significant sex difference obtains for this variable and this sample and must be taken into account in the derivation of standard scores. Judgment concerning the method of handling the data for heart period, however, cannot be so decisive. Here the greatest difference, at age 9, was .039 sec. The critical ratio at age 9 is seen to be 1.69, the highest for any age level for this variable. There can be no doubt that a true sex difference exists for this variable but it must be questioned whether or not it is sufficiently large to warrant the derivation of separate sets of standard scores. Since heart period is accorded the heaviest single weight in the normative regression equation, it is essential that its standard scores be as reliable as possible. For this reason it seemed advisable to use the entire group for the normative data for this variable, recognizing that slight sex

TABLE 13.5 CORRELATIONS FOR SCORES OF AUTONOMIC BALANCE (Ā) FROM SUCCESSIVE AND NONSUCCESSIVE YEARS

	N		
	60	56	68
Winter measures	1940	1940	1941
	1941	1942	1942
r for Ā from T scores by sample	.72	.67	.69
r for Ā from normative T scores	.70	.68	.69

Source: Adapted from M. A. Wenger and M. Ellington, The measurement of autonomic balance in children: Method and normative data. *Psychosomatic Medicine,* 1943, **5,** 241–253. By permission of the publishers.

differences, uncorrected here, may be apparent in the final scores of autonomic balance.

Next to be considered is the effect of chronological age on the data. Table 13.2 shows the means and sigmas for variables and age groups where *N* is greater than 12. It will be seen that all variables except dermographia persistence (23), palmar con-

TABLE 13.4 MEANS AND STANDARD DEVIATIONS OF FOUR VARIABLES CORRECTED FOR CHRONOLOGICAL AGE AND SEX DIFFERENCES IN CHILDREN

Variable	Age (yr)[a]						
	6	7	8	9	10	11	12
25 SO							
M	3.13	3.58	3.96	4.28	4.54	4.72	4.84
SD	1.32	1.47	1.63	1.78	1.94	2.09	2.25
28 HP							
M	.68	.70	.72	.74	.76	.78	.80
SD	.08 at each year						
57 RP							
M	3.11	3.19	3.28	3.36	3.43	3.52	3.60
SD	.55	.66	.78	.90	1.02	1.14	1.26
39 VSC							
Boys							
M	14.7	13.5	12.3	11.1	9.9	8.7	7.5
SD	6.2	5.4	4.5	3.7	2.8	2.8	2.8
Girls							
M	20.0	18.5	17.0	15.5	14.0	12.5	11.0
SD	9.2	8.4	7.5	6.7	5.8	5.0	4.1

[a]*N* at each age is the same as shown in Table 13.2, except for test *39*, where *N* is as shown in Table 13.1.
Source: Adapted from M. A. Wenger and M. Ellington, The measurement of autonomic balance in children: Method and normative data. *Psychosomatic Medicine,* 1943, **5,** 241–253. By permission of the publishers.

ductance (37), and pulse pressure (80) show a consistent change with increasing age. Since these three demonstrate no such age trend, standard scores may be derived for them from the mean and sigma of the entire group. Rather than weight the group means and sigmas unduly, an N of 87 was employed. The individual raw scores used involved the mean of one, two, or three measures, according to the amount of data available for a given subject. No subject appears more than once in the determinations. The means and standard deviations of these three variables are shown in Table 13.3. For complete conversion tables, see Wenger and Ellington (1943).

For each of the variables which demonstrated an age trend, an empirical method of correction was employed. Graphs were prepared of the means and standard deviations for all age levels and curves were fitted to the data. The corrected means and sigmas thus obtained are shown in Table 13.4. Wenger and Ellington (1943) show tables of T scores for all variables used in the $\bar{A}$ regression equation. These are not reproduced here but may be derived from the data presented in Tables 13.3 and 13.4.

Theoretically, estimates based upon standard scores derived from the combined data should be more reliable than those based upon standard scores derived from any one smaller sample, since more data are involved. Table 13.5, however, shows that the correlations between scores of autonomic balance obtained in successive years were not affected by the method of standardization. At least the use of the combined data did not lower the reliability of the measuring instrument. The coefficients in the first row are from a previous report (Wenger, 1943a) and involve data from three separate sets of standard scores.

It remained to determine whether the method of curve fitting that was employed for the normative data reduced the validity of the estimates. If it did not, we should expect to find very high correlations between estimates based on the normative standard scores and those based upon the standard scores for any one sample. Table 13.6 shows these correlation coefficients. Since all three coefficients approached unity, it was concluded that the normative standard scores may be used as validly as those for any one of our samples in the estimation of scores of autonomic balance.

TABLE 13.6 CORRELATION COEFFICIENTS BETWEEN SCORES FOR AUTONOMIC BALANCE BASED ON NORMATIVE STANDARD SCORES AND STANDARD SCORES BY SAMPLE

	N		
	62	74	81
Date of winter sample	1940	1941	1942
r	.98	.99	.98

Source: Adapted from M. A. Wenger and M. Ellington, The measurement of autonomic balance in children: Method and normative data. *Psychosomatic Medicine,* 1943, **5,** 241–253. By permission of the publishers.

Figure 13.3 shows a frequency distribution of the mean scores of autonomic balance for 87 children (the maximum N), as derived from the normative data and regression equation. It demonstrates that the distribution approaches the shape of the normal curve. When these data were correlated with chronological age, the resulting coefficient was .04. It was concluded that the relationship to age had been rendered negligible by the corrections. When the scores were analyzed for sex differences, the 49 girls showed a mean of 69.0 and a sigma of 5.8; while the 40 boys had a mean of 70.6 and a sigma

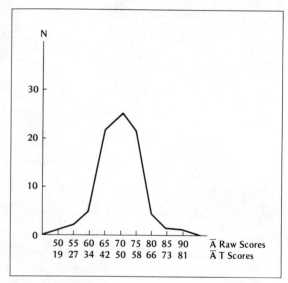

Figure 13.3 Frequency distribution of mean estimates of autonomic balance ($\bar{A}$) for 87 children 6–12 years of age. Adapted from M. A. Wenger and M. Ellington, The measurement of autonomic balance in children: Method and normative data. *Psychosomatic Medicine,* 1943, **5,** 241–253. By permission of the publishers.

of 7.0. This difference in means of 1.6 was found to have a critical ratio of 1.1. Apparently, the uncorrected, slight sex differences in heart period had only a slight effect upon the final scores. It is hoped, however, that any investigators who employ this test battery with children of different age and sex will consider and report on the adequacy of our so-called normative data. After all, the Ns for some of our subgroups were small.

The first study of young male adults

In 1944 it became possible to initiate an investigation of autonomic balance in young male adults at the Santa Ana Army Air Force (AAF) Base. J. P. Guilford was largely responsible for this program. He knew of the earlier work with children and of the belief that a factor of autonomic balance might prove of value in eliminating from those who aspired to aircrew positions some who would not prove efficient in such a stressful occupation. With his assistance and encouragement, a laboratory was quickly established and a crew of testers was trained in giving tests such as those described in the preceding pages of this chapter.

As a consequence of past experience, and with the advice of others associated with the testing of cadets and aviation students in the AAF program, other tests were added to the battery. Those that were not used in later work will not be described here. Instead, descriptions are given of the new tests that had further use, and of modifications of the tests previously described for children. The test numbers used in the following paragraphs are the numbers that appeared in the major publication of the Santa Ana work (Wenger, 1948).

Procedural modifications Changes in the tests detailed in the preceding pages are described first.

Salivary output (10) This test was reduced from 5 min to 3 min in duration because preliminary work showed that some of the adult subjects produced more than 10 cc of saliva in a 5-min period. Also, the longer test seemed to bore them. In some laboratory rooms running water was not available, so an electric vacuum pump or other means of producing negative pressure was employed instead of a water pump (see Figure 13.2). These forms of negative pressure made it necessary to incorporate an escape vent in the system, so that the pressure

did not attach the mouthpiece to the lips or tongues of the subjects. Moreover, since the wooden mouthpieces used for children were not available, various forms of sanitary glass or plastic mouthpieces were employed.

Dermographia latency (13) and persistence (14) The same method of stimulation was used except that the stimulator (see Figure 13.1) was calibrated to deliver 200 grams of pressure. This reduction in pressure was suggested by earlier unpublished work, in which a pressure of 250 grams had been found to abrade the skin of some adult subjects. The conditions of testing seldom permitted the observation of dermographia persistence for longer than 25 min; therefore, persisting results were recorded as 24+ min, 25+ min, etc.

Palmar skin conductance (15) The score was the mean of two measures at 1-min intervals. A Levine potentiometer was employed with a direct current of 40 μamps, impressed just long enough for the voltmeter to be read. The electromotive force required to impress the desired current through the subject was converted later to conductance units.

Volar forearm skin conductance (19) The Levine potentiometer was employed in the same way, but four measures were recorded at approximately 3-min intervals while the subject was reclining; only the lowest conductance obtained was used. This modification resulted from the fact that some adults proved to be reactive from the forearm skin area. In children, reactivity from this area had seldom been observed.

Systolic (21), diastolic (23), and pulse pressure (25) A standard, adult-size cuff was employed.

Heart period (28) In the absence of appropriate recording equipment, this measure was determined by auscultation immediately after the determination of the blood pressure. The operator inflated the blood pressure cuff to slightly over diastolic pressure and counted 11 consecutive pulse sounds, depressing a key that started an electric timer at the count of "one" and releasing the key at the count of "eleven." The time for 10 heart cycles thus was accumulated on the timer in milliminutes (mmin). At least four samples were recorded at intervals of approximately 3 min. The mean of all four was the recorded datum.

Respiration period (42) At the end of the

reclining period and before the subject had arisen, the various detector units were removed from the subject. Then a McKesson metabolator was wheeled into the room and attached to the subject by means of a standard mouthpiece with a nose clasp. (In a few instances it was necessary to employ a McKesson face mask.) The recording continued for 6 min. The respiration period was determined from the number of complete respiration cycles in the third and fourth minutes of the spirogram, and was expressed in seconds per cycle. Other measures also were determined from the spirogram but are not described here. In subsequent work with adults a metabolator has seldom been employed. Respiration has been recorded by more simple pneumographic equipment or by means of a pressure transducer attached to a flexible belt around the lower portion of the rib cage. Upon occasion, the respiration period has been determined by observing inspiratory movements and counting them for samples of 10 complete cycles, either with an electric timer or a stop watch started at the count of 1 and stopped at the count of 11.

Supplementary tests   The following tests had not been used consistently in work with children, but were used in this study and in later studies of adults.

Salivary pH (12)   The datum was determined by inserting a piece of Squibbs nitrazine paper in the saliva sample and comparing it with the color chart provided. The range of scores was 4.5–7.5 in 0.5 steps.

Change in log conductance (17)   This measure represents the difference in log units between the log of palmar skin conductance measured in a position of extreme muscular strain (described later) and the log of the lowest conductance obtained during a 12-min period of relaxation in a reclining position. The measure during strain was obtained immediately after the test of palmar skin conductance (*15*). The change in log conductance was included as an indicator of the ability to relax, but proved to be correlated with an autonomic factor and has been used consistently in later studies.

Sublingual temperature (30)   Body temperature was measured with an ordinary clinical thermometer, left in place under the tongue for at least

5 min, while the electrodes for skin conductance were being attached.

Finger temperature (32, first, and 34, second measures)   In the absence of more adequate apparatus for the determination of skin temperature, a laboratory thermometer (0–40°C) was used. The bulb was held by the subject between the thumb and distal phalanges of the first two fingers of the left hand. The first reading was taken while the seated subject was waiting in a reception room for the rest of the examination. The second was recorded at the end of the main testing period after the subject had been reclining for 12–15 min. The thermometer remained in position at least 5 min; the reading was made before the bulb was released.

Pupillary diameter (52)   The diameter of the pupil was measured by a relatively simple technique devised by Helmholtz. It required a black card 5 × 8 in. in size, on which a pair of converging lines were drawn, with the point of greatest divergence (approximately 20 mm) at the lower portion of the card. Along the converging lines, pairs of pinpoint holes were drilled at intervals, so that the center-to-center distance between any pair increased in 0.5-mm steps. The range of the test was 2.5–8.0 mm. The card was held by the subject in front of the preferred eye, the other eye being covered by the other hand. The subject was instructed to look at a distant object (30 ft or more away) and to move the card slowly up and down, until he found the pair of holes that were seen as just tangent the greater part of the time. He then held the card stationary, and the experimenter read the pupillary diameter from the distance between the holes marked on the opposite side of the card.

Testing procedures   Subjects in groups of four were scheduled at 30-min intervals for tests between 8:30 AM and 3:30 PM, with a slight break at noon. They were given prior instructions as follows: (a) Try to get a good night's sleep before you come for these psychophysiological tests. (b) Don't eat food or drink coffee, tea, or soft drinks for 1 hour prior to your testing time. (c) Don't engage in strenuous exercise for at least 1 hour prior to your tests. (d) Don't drink water or smoke for at least one-half hour prior to your tests.

Upon arrival the subjects were asked questions

about their health. If they were even slightly ill, they were not tested; an attempt was made to schedule them later. (Some who reported well-being but showed corrected sublingual temperatures of 99.7°F or above were tested, but their data were eliminated from the statistical analyses.)

The laboratory facilities for most of the AAF-testing program consisted of four small rooms in a comparatively quiet building. One was used as a reception room, where four subjects could be accommodated. They were seated at desks and requested to complete a questionnaire (Wenger, 1948). The general purpose of the tests was explained briefly, and assurance was given that the results of the tests would in no way effect their AAF classification for aircrew training and would cause no pain or discomfort. All were told that because of the unusual nature of these tests they might hear from us again.

Each subject was requested to remove his outer shirt and necktie. His sublingual temperature (30) and finger temperature (32, first recording) were determined, while electrodes were placed upon his palms and forearms. The pupillary diameter (52) and salivary output (10) and pH (12) were then measured. The subject was conducted to one of the three experimental rooms, each of which contained a hospital cot, a low wooden stool, and an apparatus desk and chair for the operator's use. Leads were connected to the electrodes previously attached to the subject's palms, and the palmar skin conductance (15) was measured. During this time the operator recorded the humidity and temperature of the room and the time of taking the measurements. The subject was next seated on the edge of a stool and was prepared for the measurement of palmar conductance during muscular strain (a portion of test 17) by the following oral instruction: "Extend your arms in front of you. Don't extend your fingers. Let your hands drop. Now raise your legs as high as you can. Keep them stiff at the knee. Don't lean back on the stool. Keep your head up. Get your legs up higher, higher! We want you straining in every muscle." The result is intense muscular strain. Immediately after this measurement, taken rapidly and at the lowest voltage achieved, the subject reclined on the cot, the dermographia stimulator was employed, and the latency (13) was recorded.

After putting on the blood pressure cuff and other attachments, and making certain that the subject was resting in a comfortable position, the operator instructed him to close his eyes and relax as much as possible for the next few minutes but not to go to sleep. Further reassurance of the benign nature of the tests was given at this point if the subject seemed apprehensive. In the following 12-min period, measurements of the blood pressure (21, 23, 25), heart period (28), palmar skin conductance (15), and volar forearm skin conductance (19) were made in that order, the operator watching between measurements for disappearance of the red dermographia and recording the total persistence time (14). The electrodes and blood pressure cuff were removed; the room temperature and humidity were recorded again; and the laboratory thermometer was placed for the second determination of finger temperature (34).

The experimenter then went to another room to work with another subject and was replaced by a second experimenter who brought a McKesson metabolator. After recording the finger temperature, the new operator prepared the subject for the metabolism test by a brief explanation. One 6-min spirogram was taken according to standard procedures; then the subject was returned to the reception room and was directed to another laboratory for blood tests, which are not described here.

This procedure was followed in three testing rooms, with subjects entering about 10 min apart. It thus was possible for two experimenters to be employed continuously in two rooms on the major group of measurements, while the metabolism operator was occupied in the third room. The program allowed a maximum of 20 min for the major measurements and 10 min for the metabolator measurements. With adequate assistance in the reception room and continuous attention by the experimenters, it was possible to test as many as 40 subjects daily. The number per day, however, rarely exceeded 25.

Subjects From March to May, 1944, a total of 632 aviation students and cadets were tested. They represented the lowest degree of selection that could be obtained under the conditions of the project. They had been accepted for general preflight training and already had passed a rigorous

TABLE 13.7 CORRECTIONS FOR VOLAR FOREARM SKIN CONDUCTANCE (in micromhos)

Room temperature scale[a]	Time[a]									
	0	1	2	3	4	5	6	7	8	9
0 (add)	2	2	2	2	2	2	1	1	1	1
1	2	2	2	2	2	1	1	1	1	1
2	2	2	2	2	1	1	1	1	1	1
3	2	2	2	2	1	1	1	1	1	1
4	2	2	2	1	1	1	1	1	1	1
5	2	2	1	1	1	1	1	1	1	0
6	2	1	1	1	1	1	1	1	0	0
7	1	1	1	1	1	1	1	0	0	0
8	1	1	1	1	1	1	0	0	0	0
9	1	1	1	1	1	1	0	0	0	0

Reduction scale	Mean room temperature in °C	Time of measurement	Reduction scale	Mean room temperature in °C	Time of measurement
9	30.0 or above	1530-1614	4	27.5-27.9	1130-1215
8	29.5-29.9	1445-1529	3	27.0-27.4	1045-1129
7	29.0-29.4	1400-1444	2	26.5-26.9	1000-1044
6	28.5-28.9	1315-1359	1	26.0-26.4	0915-0959
5	28.0-28.4	1230-1314	0	25.9 or below	0830-0914

[a] Reduction scale for room temperature and time

Source: Adapted from M. A. Wenger, Studies of autonomic balance in Army Air Forces personnel. *Comparative Psychology Monographs,* 1948, **19,** No. 4. By permission of the publishers.

TABLE 13.8 CORRECTIONS FOR FINGER AND SUBLINGUAL TEMPERATURES AND FOR SYSTOLIC BLOOD PRESSURE

Room temperature scale[a]	Time[a]									
	0	1	2	3	4	5	6	7	8	9
	Corrections for finger temperature in °C (2nd Test)									
0 (add)	2.4	2.2	2.0	1.9	1.8	1.7	1.7	1.7	1.7	1.7
1	2.1	1.9	1.7	1.6	1.5	1.4	1.4	1.4	1.4	1.4
2	1.8	1.6	1.4	1.3	1.2	1.1	1.1	1.1	1.1	1.1
3	1.5	1.3	1.1	1.0	0.9	0.8	0.8	0.8	0.8	0.8
4	1.3	1.1	0.9	0.8	0.7	0.6	0.6	0.6	0.6	0.6
5	1.1	0.9	0.7	0.6	0.5	0.4	0.4	0.4	0.4	0.4
6	0.9	0.7	0.5	0.4	0.3	0.2	0.2	0.2	0.2	0.2
7	0.7	0.5	0.3	0.2	0.1	0.0	0.0	0.0	0.0	0.0
8	0.7	0.5	0.3	0.2	0.1	0.0	0.0	0.0	0.0	0.0
9	0.7	0.5	0.3	0.2	0.1	0.0	0.0	0.0	0.0	0.0
	Corrections for sublingual temperature in °F									
(add)	0.5	0.4	0.4	0.3	0.3	0.2	0.2	0.1	0.1	0.0
	Corrections for systolic blood pressure in mm Hg									
(subtract)	0	0	0	0	0	−1	−2	−3	−4	−5

[a] Reduction scales for time and room temperature are shown at the bottom of Table 13.7.

Source: Adapted from M. A. Wenger, Studies of autonomic balance in Army Air Forces personnel. *Comparative Psychology Monographs,* 1948, **19,** No. 4. By permission of the publishers.

physical examination. None had been selected for specific aircrew training, and none had been eliminated from such training. It was from this group, therefore, that data for basic analyses were drawn.

Studies of uncontrolled variables   It seemed probable that the data collected with these tests under these conditions would show some effects of uncontrolled climatic conditions and possibly some diurnal effects. We had recorded only the room temperature and relative humidity, and the times of measurement. Other data were obtained from a nearby weather observation station.

When the first interruption occurred in testing, the available data were analyzed (at that time the maximum N was 180). The results convinced us that the data did exhibit uncontrolled effects and that we should explore these further. This was done at the time of the second interruption, after the completion of testing of the group of 632 students mentioned earlier. These laborious studies shall not be redescribed here (see Wenger, 1948); suffice it to say that it was decided to correct the data from only four test variables in terms of one, or in some cases two, uncontrolled variables. Differences in

room temperature and time of measurement influenced the data for volar skin conductance (19) and finger temperature (34, second test); time of measurement affected systolic blood pressure (21) and sublingual temperature (30). The derived corrections are shown in Tables 13.7 and 13.8.

Normative physiological data for young adult males   This sample is called normative only because it has been used as a comparison sample for many other studies. It does represent the largest sample of such measurements yet published for young adult males. The means and standard deviations for this sample, and reliability coefficients from two studies, are presented in Table 13.9. The age range for this sample of 632 healthy male adults was 17–34. Some were slightly ill or for other reasons were eliminated, so that the N for statistical analyses was reduced to 488.

The data for four test variables from this group of 488 adult males were corrected as described in Tables 13.7 and 13.8. All test data were then intercorrelated, and factorial analyses were conducted by the centroid method. No common factors were found by Thurstone's criteria. When certain modi-

TABLE 13.9   MEANS AND STANDARD DEVIATIONS OF NORMATIVE SAMPLE FOR ALL TEST VARIABLES AND TEST-RETEST RELIABILITY COEFFICIENTS FOR TWO SAMPLES

Test No.	Test variable	Mean ($N = 488$)	SD	$r34$[a]	$r39$[a]
10	Salivary output	4.2 cc	1.7	.88	.85
12	Salivary pH	7.2 pH	.4	.47	.62
13	Dermographia latency	13.3 sec	4.5	.35	.42
14	Dermographia persistence	16.8 min	9.2	.63	.19
15	Palmar conductance	16.8 μmho	7.1	.70*	.57
17	Log conductance change	30.1 log units	13.7	.65*	.70
19	Volar forearm conductance	7.3 μmho	2.2	.67	.27
21	Systolic blood pressure	111.1 mm Hg	9.0	.74*	.33
23	Diastolic blood pressure	70.0 mm Hg	7.4	.67	.33
25	Pulse pressure	41.1 mm Hg	10.0	.64	.44
28	Heart period	160.4 mmin/10 periods	23.5	.73*	.66
30	Sublingual temperature	99.0°F	.4	.11	.28
32	Finger temperature (1st)	34.9°C	1.9	.51	.73
34	Finger temperature (2d)	35.4°C	1.4	.55	.27
42	Respiration period	5.1 sec	1.4	.65	.68
52	Pupillary diameter	5.3 mm	.9	.71	.64

[a] During preliminary studies, tests were given on successive days to 37 subjects in an investigation of effects of the postabsorptive state. Coefficients marked with asterisks must be considered approximations, as these data were influenced by basal conditions. The last column involves 39 men of the normative sample, who were retested after 3–4 months.

Source: Adapted from M. A. Wenger, Studies of autonomic balance in Army Air Forces personnel. *Comparative Psychology Monographs,* 1948, **19,** No. 4. By permission of the publishers.

fications in procedure and criteria earlier suggested by Thurstone[2] were employed, a reasonable factor representing the autonomic nervous system was found (for details, see Wenger, 1948). The beta weights for the estimation of this factor are shown in Table 13.11 of the next section; data shown in Table 13.12 demonstrate that the autonomic factor for young adult males is similar to that previously described for children.

Summary Statement

The work reported here with children and adults led to several conclusions.

1. Individual differences in autonomic functioning during controlled conditions exist in both children and adults.
2. These differences, measured in terms of estimates of an autonomic factor, are continuously distributed and are presumed to be normally distributed in an unselected population. Vagotonia and sympatheticotonia, as described by Eppinger and Hess, are regarded as representing extremes in such a continuum.
3. Estimates of the autonomic factor for a given individual tend to remain constant from year to year but may be altered phasically or chronically by changes in external or internal stimulation.
4. Autonomic factor scores (estimates) are related to certain personality patterns and to certain diagnostic categories such as anxiety psychoneurosis and hyperinsulinism.

It was not possible in 1945 to compare the AAF data with either aircrew training performance or combat performance, but attempts continue in that direction (see pp. 556–558). Regardless, however, of the value of such tests for aircrew selection, the conclusions stated above served to stimulate many

---

[2]One of us (Wenger) was associated with Thurstone during 1935–1938 and had consulted with him about early factorial results from the Fels Research Institute. Thurstone's suggestions were, in essence:

1. Eliminate one of two, or two of three, tests that are highly related and tend to create a separate factor (e.g., use only one measure of blood pressure).
2. If you have reason to expect a common factor, do not strive for simple structure during rotation; strive for a common factor that is meaningful.
3. Perhaps you cannot achieve positive manifold with physiological tests; if not, forget about it.

The application of these suggestions made possible the description of the autonomic factor for children.

other investigations. Most of them are reported in the remainder of this chapter.

LATER STUDIES OF ADULT MALES[3]

Most of the investigations described here were conducted at the University of California in Los Angeles or at Veterans Administration Hospitals in or near Los Angeles. Frequent reference is also made to the Army Air Force data described in the preceding section and to other data collected at the Santa Ana Army Air Base during late 1944 and 1945 (Wenger, 1948).

One of the important findings in the AAF research was the discovery that individuals could show either mean or deviant $\overline{A}$ scores with clusters of functions deviating in nonpredicted directions. Functional patterns of relative sympathetic dominance, relative parasympathetic dominance, and autonomic balance (i.e., clusters about the group means) had been anticipated; but *mixed* patterns had not been expected, except through measurement error or other uncontrolled variance. Surprisingly, almost two-thirds of the many young males tested at the Santa Ana Army Air Base in 1944 showed such mixed patterns (Wenger, 1957). This finding gave one explanation for the low-order correlation coefficients that exist among many physiological variables, but it also suggested that the basis for the autonomic factor lay in about one-third of the sample.

Visual analysis of the test profiles defied assortment. Later, when modal patterns for separate abnormal groups were analyzed (Wenger, 1957), a mixed pattern termed "alpha" emerged. In time, a similar mixed pattern that was dominant for many groups of psychosomatic patients replaced alpha but, since it was a second, new pattern, it was called "beta." Later, Markwell (1963) and Tolmie (1958) discovered a different but consistent mixed pattern in tuberculous subjects, hospitalized or cured and tested as out-patients. It was called "Pattern TB."

This is the position today. We are able to speak

---

[3]This section is drawn largely from a previously published summary (Wenger, 1966). Many of the studies from 1954 on were supported in part by Research Grants M788 and M1281 from the Institute of Mental Health, National Institutes of Health, United States Public Health Service.

TABLE 13.10 PROFILE SHEET SHOWING BETA PATTERN

Name _____ Date _____ Group _____ No. _____ N488

	No.	Test	S	-3σ 20	-2σ 30	-1σ 40	M 50	1σ 60	2σ 70	3σ 80	P	M	Scores σ raw stand
CA	10	Salivary output	Low			X					High	4.2	1.7
C	14	Dermographia persistence	Short			X					Long	16.8	9.2
CA	15	Palmar conductance	High					X			Low	16.8	7.1
A	17	Log conductance change	Low								High	30.1	13.7
CA	19	Volar conductance	High								Low	7.3	2.2
	21	Systolic blood pressure	High			X					Low	111.1	9.0
A	23	Diastolic blood pressure	High								Low	70.0	7.4
C	25	Pulse pressure	Low								High	41.1	10.0
CA	28	Heart period	Short			X					Long	160.4	23.5
A	30	Sublingual temperature	High					X			Low	99.0	0.4
	32	Finger temperature (1st)	Low								High	34.9	1.9
	34	Finger temperature (2nd)	Low					X			High	35.4	1.4
C	42	Respiration period	Short								Long	5.1	1.4
	52	Pupillary diameter	Large								Small	5.3	0.9

80 70 60 50 40 30 20

Source: Adapted from M. A. Wenger, Pattern analyses of autonomic variables during rest. *Psychosomatic Medicine*, 1957, **19**, 240-244. By permission of the publisher.

TABLE 13.11 BETA WEIGHTS FOR ESTIMATING THE AUTONOMIC FACTOR ($\bar{A}$) IN THREE SAMPLES

Tests	$\bar{A}$ normal males	$\bar{A}$ operational fatigue	$\bar{A}$ children
Salivary output	0.14		0.23
Salivary pH		0.30	Not measured
Dermographia persistence[a]			−0.12
Palmar conductance[a]	0.09	0.27	0.29
Log palmar conductance change	0.17	0.07	Not measured
Forearm conductance[a]	0.09		0.14
Systolic blood pressure[a]		0.23	
Diastolic blood pressure[a]	0.18		
Pulse pressure			0.19
Heart period	0.41	0.17	0.45
Sublingual temperature[a]	0.30	0.21	Not measured
Respiration period			0.12
O_2 consumption[a]		0.07	

[a] Reflection of variable.

Source: Adapted from M. A. Wenger, Studies of autonomic balance in Army Air Forces personnel. *Comparative Psychology Monographs*, 1948, **19**, No. 4. By permission of the publishers.

of five known patterns of autonomic function in resting or standardized test conditions: relative sympathetic dominance (S), relative parasympathetic dominance (P), autonomic balance (or mean, M), the beta pattern (B), and the tuberculous pattern (TB). In addition, there are unclassified mixed patterns for most samples, but at least for the tuberculous samples (Markwell, 1963; Tolmie, 1958) these five patterns describe almost all the subjects.

Table 13.10 shows a profile sheet employed in pattern analyses on which selected individual test scores are entered in standard score form, based on the means and sigmas of the sample of aviation students previously mentioned. Some data are reflected, so that low scores indicate relative SNS dominance; Xs indicate the beta pattern. Also shown are the variables that are used to estimate the autonomic factor for children (C) and young male adults (A). The variables that appear in both equations are listed as CA.

The data for adult males reported in this summary have been corrected with the equations applied to those of the AAF normative sample, as shown in the first section of this chapter. It should be emphasized that the beta pattern is found with or without correction of the data. This also is true for the TB pattern, which differs from beta in four respects: fast respiration; *low* finger temperature; small pupillary diameter; and possibly, high sublingual temperature (Markwell, 1963; Tolmie, 1958).

As yet there is no physiological theory to account for these mixed patterns. It has been suggested that the beta pattern may represent merely the sedation of hospitalized patients, as compared to young, active males. However, at Santa Ana Army Air Base, young active males who had fainted on two occasions when taken to a simulated altitude

of 18,000 ft in a low compression chamber showed a higher frequency of beta pattern than any other (Wenger, 1957). Moreover, outpatients in other samples (Little, 1955; Markwell, 1963; Tolmie, 1958) showed this pattern as frequently as did hospitalized patients. In other words hospitalization or quiescence, per se, does not seem to provide the explanation. One related finding is of particular interest. Sherry (1959) showed that, under chlorpromazine, a sample of chronic catatonics shifted from 63% S pattern to 70% beta pattern. On the other hand, patients with psoriasis and urticaria showed the beta pattern not only as dominant but with a frequency of 62%, the highest yet reported in a drug-free patient group (Wenger, Clemens, & Cullen, 1962). It might be added that patterns beta, S, P, and M occur with approximately equal frequency in a subsample of the aviation students (15, 13, 14, and 11%, respectively) and that Pattern TB is rare (3%).

Before discussing patterns further, let us examine the results of a comparison of the autonomic factors found for three samples. The beta weights for the estimation of the factor in two of these samples have been published (Wenger, 1948; Wenger & Ellington, 1943). They are repeated in Table 13.11, with weights for an additional equation which were later derived for a factor from an analysis of data from 201 AAF personnel hospitalized in 1945 for "operational fatigue" (Wenger, 1948). Only one of any pair of highly correlated variables was employed in this centroid solution; and, unlike earlier practice, salivary pH (instead of output) and systolic (instead of diastolic) blood pressure were used. The obtained solution was different from that for normal males (Table 13.11) but still seems to represent the autonomic factor.

TABLE 13.12 INTERCORRELATIONS AMONG ESTIMATES OF THE AUTONOMIC FACTOR BY THREE EQUATIONS FOR THREE GROUPS

Group	N	$\bar{A}$-NM/$\bar{A}$-OF	$\bar{A}$-NM/$\bar{A}$-C	$\bar{A}$-OF/$\bar{A}$-C
			r	
NM	460	0.71	0.73	0.57
OF	225	0.76	0.76	0.63
PN	98	0.74	0.74	0.55

Source: Adapted from M. A. Wenger, Studies of autonomic balance: A summary. *Psychophysiology*, 1966, **2**, 173–186. By permission of the publishers.

Perhaps the best test of the belief that these three solutions describe the same factor is to apply all equations to the same data and to intercorrelate the obtained factor estimates. This has been done for three samples: 460 of the 488 cadets and aviation students (the normative male, group NM), the entire sample of 225 operational fatigue patients (group OF), and 98 AAF patients (cf. Wenger, 1948) with the diagnosis "psychoneurosis—anxiety state," or "psychoneurosis—mixed, with anxiety" (group PN). The comparison appears in Table 13.12. Since all the correlations are positive and statistically significant, it appears that the same factor has been described in the three solutions. It is obvious, however, that the three solutions are not equally valid. The factors for the Fels children and the operational fatigue patients appear to be most unlike, while that for the aviation students appears to be the most representative.

Next, something should be said about reliability and validity. Measurements of physiological functions are only relatively reliable. There is much variability. The consistently highest test-retest coefficient is for salivary output, which ranges from 0.88 to 0.79 over periods as long as 3 years. The reliability of $\overline{A}$ scores has not been that high, although coefficients of .66 have been reported over a 3-year period in children (Wenger, 1943a). For adults, and for shorter periods, test-retest coefficients have varied from a low of .28 to a coefficient of concordance of .83 for three sessions. The reliability of these factor estimates is quite adequate *if the tests are carefully administered*. The reliable testing of physiological functions requires extreme care and an appreciation of the psychological factors involved.

Early efforts to test the validity of the factor started with studies of the effects of drugs, initially with injections of epinephrine. Epinephrine lowered scores of autonomic balance and lowered reflected scores for all variables then tested, except skin resistance (unpublished results). A more recent study with intravenous infusion of epinephrine provided more accurate data for most of the measures (Wenger et al., 1960); an earlier study showed that amphetamine or atropine lowered $\overline{A}$ scores, while prostigmine increased them (Wenger, 1949).

Two investigations of paraplegics provided ad-

ditional validation evidence. Hohmann (1955) obtained a mean $\overline{A}$ score of 74.3 with an unselected group, significantly higher than the AAF mean. In the second, with subjects selected for clinically complete lesions at different levels of the spinal cord, McKelligott (1959) obtained the results shown in Table 13.13.

Still further validation evidence came from tests during phasic anxiety in graduate students on the day of an important oral examination (Smith & Wenger, 1965). Anxiety has been characterized as a generalized excessive reaction in the SNS (Wenger, F. N. Jones, & M. H. Jones, 1956). If this is correct, and if professors and students are correct in claiming, as they do, that students are in a state of anxiety before an oral examination, then low $\overline{A}$ measures should be found during this state. The results are clear: the mean $\overline{A}$ from tests just before the oral examination was 57.02. The comparison tests 1 month before or after the examination yielded a mean $\overline{A}$ of 69.36. All subjects showed lower $\overline{A}$ scores on the day of the examination than on the comparison test, and one very good student, who said his anxiety level was high, dropped from 78.3 to 51.5, a change of almost 4σ.

The investigations just cited have employed the data from the 488 AAF students and cadets described in the first section of this chapter as reference data. Since 1945 many studies of hospitalized patients have used this group for a normative reference group. The practice has been suspect, not only because patients are usually more sedentary but also because the aviation students were so carefully selected by physical examination. In 1958 an attempt was made to provide another reference group; data were collected from male students at the University of California—Los Angeles and from some university custodians (to increase the age

TABLE 13.13 AUTONOMIC BALANCE IN SUBJECTS WITH SPINAL CORD LESIONS

	N	Mean $\overline{A}$
Cervical lesions	8	76.2
Thoracic lesions	17	70.6
Lumbar lesions	10	67.6

Source: Adapted from M. A. Wenger, Studies of autonomic balance: A summary. *Psychophysiology*, 1966, **2**, 173–186. By permission of the publishers.

TABLE 13.14 AUTONOMIC BALANCE FOR THREE GROUPS OF ADULT MALES

Group	N	Mean	SD
AAF, 1944	460	69.89	7.36
UCLA students and custodians, 1958	81	71.55	7.45
UCLA students, 1962	44	71.79	5.88

Source: Adapted from M. A. Wenger, Studies of autonomic balance: A summary. *Psychophysiology,* 1966, **2,** 173–186. By permission of the publishers.

range to 45). In 1962 another smaller student sample was tested.

Table 13.14 shows the $\bar{A}$ means and standard deviations for the AAF and University of California groups. The only significant difference between the AAF data and the University of California data is at the .05 level and only with the small 1962 group. Although it may be attributable to the low variability and size of the group, it seems reasonable to suppose that there were enough "eager-beavers" in the Santa Ana AAF group to depress slightly the mean score. Although they were told that the tests would not influence placement in air crew positions, some surely did not believe this. Some, no doubt, were apprehensive—this state would tend to depress the mean $\bar{A}$ score. Therefore, for the remainder of this summary, data from patient groups are compared with both the AAF sample and the larger of the two University of California samples.

Table 13.15 compares a series of studies, showing $\bar{A}$ means, variabilities, and comparisons of means against two normative groups, for a number of patients hospitalized for psychoneuroses or psychoses. Probably, not all of those diagnosed as suffering operational fatigue in the Air Force terminology of 1944 were really sick persons. Some of them had no home, no goals. Some were malingerers. The results reflect this. Their mean score of autonomic balance is only slightly lower than the AAF sample mean. Not shown is the incidence of the beta pattern, which was higher in the operational fatigue group than in any other group represented in Table 13.15 (Wenger, 1957). The operational fatigue group of patients was tested because we had been told they were anxious. As a group they did not seem to be, nor did they show lower $\bar{A}$ scores. Two samples of psychoneurotics, both selected to include patients who manifested anxiety, did show predictably lower $\bar{A}$ scores.

The results with psychotic patients were surprising. Although Gunderson (1953) predicted the dominance of PNS activity for some groups of schizophrenic patients, he did not find this, nor did Sherry (1959). Most of the workers involved in these studies expected to find low $\bar{A}$ scores in some paranoid patients, and high $\bar{A}$ scores in at least some catatonics. Instead, both Gunderson and Sherry demonstrated that the physiological responses of most schizophrenic patients may be

TABLE 13.15 AUTONOMIC BALANCE IN PSYCHONEUROTIC AND PSYCHOTIC PATIENTS

Investigator	Patients	N	Mean	SD	CR_1[a]	CR_2[b]
Wenger (1948)	Psychoneurotics	98	64.95	7.5	5.95[c]	5.89[c]
Wenger (1948)	Operational fatigue	225	68.89	7.2	1.69	2.78[c]
Holt (1956)	Psychoneurotics	21	63.37	7.6	3.86[c]	4.42[c]
Gunderson (1953)	Young schizophrenics	81	67.17	7.2	3.13[c]	3.81[c]
Sherry (1959)	Chronic catatonics	72	61.93	8.0	6.13[c]	6.40[c]
Wenger, Clemens, &	Paranoid schizophrenics	44	54.06	10.5	9.79[c]	9.80[c]
Cullen (1965)	Catatonics	12	58.74	5.0	7.59[c]	7.76[c]
	Other schizophrenics	49	56.47	10.5	8.76[c]	8.83[c]

Note.—The studies cited in this table, except those by Wenger in 1948, were conducted in Veterans Administration Hospitals at Brentwood and Sepulveda.
[a] CR_1 = comparison with 1944 AAF sample.
[b] CR_2 = comparison with 1958 UCLA sample.
[c] Significant at .01 level of confidence.
Source: Adapted from M. A. Wenger, Studies of autonomic balance: A summary. *Psychophysiology,* 1966, **2,** 179. By permission of the publishers.

described as showing an apparent dominance of SNS activity. Moreover, Gunderson found no significant difference in $\overline{A}$ between patients with catatonic symptoms and those with paranoid symptoms. A later study (Wenger, Clemens, & Cullen, 1965) supported these earlier results but, under different laboratory conditions, found even lower $\overline{A}$ scores, especially for paranoid patients, than those reported by Gunderson and Sherry. According to these findings schizophrenic patients, in general, demonstrate relatively excessive SNS activity.

Table 13.16 shows a somewhat different picture. Psychosomatic disorders, whether of psychogenic origin or attitudinally influenced, produce less clear data. Because asthma is often treated with epinephrine, and peptic ulcer with a parasympatholytic drug, the prediction of high $\overline{A}$ scores for such patients seemed elementary. The results did not support the predictions. The first few asthma patients showed relative SNS dominance (Wenger, 1948). Further attempts to find suitable patients in a drug-free condition have been unsuccessful, so that the prediction for asthmatic patients has not yet been adequately tested.

Table 13.16 shows results for 3 groups of patients with peptic ulcer. The mean $\overline{A}$ scores, in 6 comparisons, show one significant difference from a normative group, and that opposite to the predicted direction; but Little's patients did demonstrate significantly higher $\overline{A}$ scores after vagotomy (1955). Little argued that these higher scores reflected the improved adjustment of the patients. When first tested, these patients were facing a major operation. Also, they were ill and in pain. The 40 who were retested on out-patient service, 6 months later, were free of pain and free of the apprehension associated with impending operation.

Little also tested a small control group, shown at the bottom of Table 13.16. It seems probable that neither hospitalization nor illness per se is necessarily responsible for lower scores on this scale. His control data are comparable to the normative data; this is true also for one patient group tested by Clemens (1954).

Clemens's study of patients with various types of carcinoma is of particular interest. Work by West (1954) and by Ellis and Blumberg (1954) had suggested that anxiety was a major factor in the progress of these diseases. This thesis led to Clemens's

TABLE 13.16 AUTONOMIC BALANCE IN PATIENTS WITH DISORDERS SOMETIMES CALLED PSYCHOSOMATIC

Investigator	Sample	N	Mean	SD	CR_1[a]	CR_2[b]
Wenger (1948)	Asthma	15	65.60	4.6	3.49[c]	4.13[c]
Wenger (1948)	Peptic ulcer	21	68.87	5.3	.85	1.89
Little (1955)	Peptic ulcer	51	69.40	7.68	.43	1.58
Wenger et al. (1962)	Peptic ulcer	30	66.99	8.2	1.89	2.67[c]
Little (1955)	Postvagotomy patients	40	75.88	8.72	4.22[c]	2.69[c]
Wenger et al. (1962)	Other GI patients	33	63.07	7.5	5.04[c]	5.47[c]
Wenger et al. (1962)	Neurodermatitis	17	66.18	11.2	1.36	1.89
Wenger et al. (1962)	Psoriasis and urticaria	15	66.26	6.9	2.01[d]	2.71[c]
Clemens (1954)	Cancer (fast growing)	23	64.99	6.9	3.33[c]	3.97[c]
Clemens (1954)	Cancer (slow growing)	24	68.66	7.6	.77	1.64
Markwell (1961)	Tuberculosis	105	61.30	7.2	11.00[c]	9.48[c]
Tolmie (1958)	Tuberculosis	67	64.50	6.9	5.92[c]	6.01[c]
Fink (1960)	Diabetics (White)	30	60.31	2.4	6.91[c]	6.99[c]
Fink (1960)	Diabetics (Black)	14	65.29	7.4	2.30[d]	2.53[c]
Little (1955)	Hernia and hemorrhoids (a hospitalized control group)	25	71.24	6.4	1.02	.20

Note.—The studies cited in this table, except those by Wenger in 1948, were conducted in Veterans Administration Hospitals at Birmingham, Long Beach, San Fernando, and Wadsworth
[a]CR_1 = comparison with 1944 AAF sample.
[b]CR_2 = comparison with 1958 University of California sample.
[c]Significant at .01 level of confidence.
[d]Significant at .05 level of confidence.
Source: Adapted from M. A. Wenger, Studies of autonomic balance: A summary. *Psychophysiology*, 1966, **2**, 173–186. By permission of the publishers.

investigation, and to a symposium on the psychological variables in human cancer (Gengerelli & Kirkner, 1954). Clemens sought to test the hypothesis that patients rated by physicians West and Ellis as having "fast growing" or "slow growing" cancers would demonstrate different $\overline{A}$ scores, with the fast growing group (those who were anxious) showing the lower scores. The results were in the predicted direction, but the small groups did not differ significantly, except by comparison with reference groups, as shown in Table 13.16.

Five years later Clemens made a follow-up study of his patients, not yet published. With continuing life or the time of death as the criteria, he has demonstrated significant $\overline{A}$ differences, even between small groups. Those with lower $\overline{A}$ scores died earlier; those who had high $\overline{A}$ scores were more likely to be still living. There is evidence that serenity helps to preclude death from cancer (Cutler, 1954). We have scattered evidence that serenity is associated with high $\overline{A}$ scores. Perhaps one goal for the future should be to test serene individuals instead of anxious patients.

Clemens's work stimulated Markwell in 1955 to conduct an investigation of autonomic balance with tuberculous patients. He found not only the lowest scores then obtained from any patient sample but described Pattern TB as mentioned previously (Markwell, 1961, 1963). Although he had excluded severely ill patients and had included out-patients in whom the disease was arrested, the latter sample was small. Tolmie (1958) questioned his results and repeated his study, but included more outpatients and even more carefully selected his inpatients. His results were not significantly different from Markwell's. Apparently, those who contract tuberculosis demonstrate relative SNS dominance to a significant degree and also show a particular mixed pattern of autonomic function.

These studies stimulated Fink (1960) to investigate autonomic balance in diabetics. Her main interest was in differences between so-called "brittle" and "stable" patients. Her results were unclear, possibly because of disproportionate numbers of black and white patients in her two groups. She did find, however, significant indications of autonomic imbalance and a predominance of Pattern beta.

This is the only study represented in this report in which black subjects have been used. Fink found this necessary in order to achieve a reasonable N, but the data led her to make separate analyses, as shown in Table 13.16. We have unpublished data on male black students that support her findings but have not directly investigated the question of racial differences in autonomic balance.

The patient groups shown in Tables 13.15 and 13.16 as reported by Wenger (1948) were tested in 1944 and 1945 at Santa Ana AAF Base in an attempt to obtain some indirect support for the hypothesis that led to the testing of aviation students. That hypothesis was that individuals with $\overline{A}$ scores from $-\frac{1}{2}\sigma$ to $+1\sigma$ about the mean would be best suited to withstand the stress of wartime aircrew positions (Wenger, 1948). Although 2112 students were tested in 1944, few of them were called to action during World War II, so that there was little opportunity for direct validation of the hypothesis.

Fortunately, all testees had been forewarned of a possible follow-up study. By 1960 several reasons indicated that a follow-up study should be undertaken. (a) Undoubtedly, some of the testees had seen service in Korea. (b) The accumulating data about autonomic balance added weight to the original hypothesis. (c) A new question had appeared: Were ANS patterns predictive of psychosomatic and other psychological disorders?

Locating the scattered subjects after the lapse of 15 years was not a small problem. The Air Force attempted to trace some of the records but had little success and did not encourage us. Later, with the help of Elston Hooper, then Chief of Research for Psychology in the Veterans Administration (VA), the VA claim files were located for 1861 of the 2112 subjects. While the largest concentration of files was in Los Angeles and San Francisco, the subjects were spread throughout the 50 states. Hooper also helped by appointing J. W. McKelligott to assist in the follow-up study.

After studying the claim files from Los Angeles and a number of other areas, McKelligott concluded that they would not provide sufficient information. He argued that only VA hospitalization was recorded, and that direct questionnaires were needed to test the value of $\overline{A}$ scores and pattern classification to predict psychosomatic and other

TABLE 13.17 INITIAL ANALYSIS OF AAF RESPONDENTS 1964: AUTONOMIC BALANCE FOR TOTAL GROUP AND PATTERN GROUPS

	N	Ā Mean	SD	Percent
Total group	534	68.35	7.89	100
Pattern S	59	59.44	5.32	11
Pattern P	73	76.43	5.93	14
Pattern B	83	67.83	5.98	16
Mean pattern	88	67.09	5.78	16
Other mixed patterns	231	68.75	7.67	43

Source: Adapted from M. A. Wenger, Studies of autonomic balance: A summary. *Psychophysiology*, 1966, **2,** 173–186. By permission of the publishers.

psychological disorders. Accordingly, questionnaires were sent in 1964 to 1032 men, for whom recent mailing addresses could be found. The response was excellent; 725 completed questionnaires were returned.

Tables 13.17 and 13.18 present some of the results from a preliminary analysis of the first 534 of the returned questionnaires. As may be seen in Table 13.17, the total group had a mean Ā score of 68.35 in 1944, not significantly different from the AAF normative mean. Also shown are mean Ā scores for each pattern classification and the pattern frequencies. Only one subject had developed tuberculosis, therefore Pattern TB was not included in this analysis.

Several of the results are of particular interest. First, the mean Ā score for respondents with Pattern S is lower than that obtained from any patient group, except the most recent samples of schizophrenics (Tables 13.15 and 13.16). Second, the mean Ā score for respondents with Pattern P is higher than that for any patient group. Third, except for the latter group, other scores are somewhat lower than the reference mean. Perhaps this reflects the temperament of those who respond to questionnaires; it was reported earlier that persons with higher scores of autonomic balance tend to be uncooperative (Wenger, 1947, 1948). Fourth, the percent frequencies of patterns among these 534 respondents are similar to those previously reported for a smaller sample (Wenger, 1957).

Table 13.18 briefly presents some of the reported disorders for which respondents had been treated, their mean Ā scores, and pattern distributions. Per-

TABLE 13.18 INITIAL ANALYSIS OF AAF RESPONDENTS 1964: AUTONOMIC BALANCE AND PERCENT OF FREQUENCIES OF PATTERNS FOR SPECIFIC DISORDERS

Disorder	N	Ā Mean	S	P	B	Mean	Mixed
High blood pressure	23	64.74	13	0	22	13	52
Persistent anxiety	33	66.47	24	0	15	21	39
Apprehension or fear	49	65.80	22	2	22	18	35
Excessive sweating	52	67.30	23	6	21	10	40
Heart trouble	21	67.66	24	10	19	14	33
Hay fever	52	68.27	15	12	10	12	52
Stomach pains	63	68.53	8	21	13	14	44
Allergies	78	68.55	12	9	19	15	45
Migraine headaches	15	68.99	13	27	27	7	27
Arthritis	28	69.74	0	18	29	29	25
Asthma	16	70.06	6	0	6	0	88
Peptic ulcer	40	70.38	0	15	23	25	38
Low blood pressure	12	73.54	0	33	0	17	50
No disorders reported	111	68.22	8	13	17	12	50

Source: Adapted from M. A. Wenger, Studies of autonomic balance: A summary. *Psychophysiology*, 1966, **2,** 173–186. By permission of the publishers.

cent frequencies for modal patterns other than mixed, are italicized.

Surprisingly, the beta pattern predominates for those who have suffered high blood pressure. More predictable was the modal S pattern and low $\bar{A}$ scores for those who had been treated for apprehension, anxiety, excessive sweating, and heart trouble. In partial support of the hypothesis that led to the measurements, the first three groups of Table 13.18 had, in 1944, mean $\bar{A}$ scores more than $\frac{1}{2}\sigma$ below the normative AAF mean. The high incidence of mixed patterns for some disorders (e.g., asthma, hay fever, high blood pressure) suggests that there may be specific mixed patterns that have not as yet been identified. Further studies of such patients are indicated.

It is not surprising that Pattern P predominates among those who reported stomach pains, headaches, and hypotension. On the other hand, it is of interest that some groups show a negligible incidence of Pattern P and others show little or no Pattern S. Possibly, the absence of Pattern S and the normal $\bar{A}$ in arthritics will provide new insight into the etiology of that disorder; hopefully, other meaningful relationships can also be detected.

These results have encouraged us to continue investigating the relationship between autonomic balance, autonomic patterns, and physical and psychological disorders. Additional results from another more extensive follow-up study will be reported in the near future.

RECENT INVESTIGATIONS

Our recent work has involved four areas: (a) a continuation of the follow-up study of 2112 males mentioned in the preceding section, (b) a search for better methods of ANS pattern description, (c) further analyses of the effects of uncontrolled variables on ANS measurements,[4] and (d) a study of autonomic balance in young adult females (Lucio and Wenger, 1961; Lucio, Wenger, & Cullen, 1967). Partial results from the last two areas of study are reported here.

[4]This work was supported in part by Research Grant HD 2933 from the National Institute of Child Health and Development, National Institutes of Health, United States Public Health Service.

Effects of Uncontrolled Variables on Measurements of Selected Physiological Functions

The existence of circadian, seasonal, and other cyclical variations in the physical and chemical properties of the internal environment presents a methodological problem of some importance for the measurement of physiological differences and of autonomic balance as an individual trait. The autonomic nervous system, as one of the chief agencies through which homeostasis is maintained, may be expected to show cyclical variations in its activities as the sympathetic and parasympathetic divisions are brought into play reciprocally to dampen the shorter and longer term oscillations in the controlled properties of the internal environment. Most biological rhythms are believed to involve entrainment by cyclical geophysical factors (Brown, 1960); but, as long as the identities of these factors remain uncertain, it is not possible to specify the times of measurement that are equivalent with respect to all the existing cycles. Consequently, the confounding of individual differences with the phases of these cycles cannot be avoided. Correlational studies, while pointing to the existence of cyclical influences, usually can provide little indication of which particular variables within a complex of interacting external conditions may be functionally related to biological phenomena and which may be only concomitants. Current theory in the field of bioclimatology (Tromp, 1962) tends to view electromagnetic radiation and field phenomena as the fundamental geophysical factors to which biological rhythms are linked, perhaps by way of direct effects on the rates of chemical processes that are involved in the maintenance of homeostasis at the cellular level (Piccardi, 1962). Mefferd (1966) has discussed in detail the problems of detecting and controlling the many kinds of cyclical and noncyclical extraneous factors that are either known or suspected to influence psychophysiological variables.

Apparently, there are interactions, not only between different cycles but also between cycles and individual differences. The seasonal trends in some physiological variables indicate a relatively increased level of SNS activity in winter, as compared to summer (Tromp, 1962); levels of epinephrine and norepinephrine secretion have been found to be higher in winter than in summer (Feller & Hale, 1963). Large individual differences exist in the amplitudes of seasonal and shorter term variations in many physiological variables (Schreider, 1966). Sargent and Weinman (1962) observed greater interindividual variability in the controlled properties of the internal environment in winter than in summer, while variability in the activities of the physiological controllers is greater in summer than in winter. Measurements of autonomic balance were less stable in summer than in winter, and seasonal trends interacted with individual differences in autonomic balance (Wenger, 1943c). In that study some individuals manifested relatively greater SNS activity in winter than in summer but others manifested relatively greater PNS activity in winter than in summer. It seems that, as Sargent and Weinman (1966) put it, problems of homeostasis do not have unique solutions, and a considerable range of quantitative variations exists in the compensatory responses of individuals to disturbances of the internal environment.

In the initial study of autonomic balance in adult males, an investigation was made of the effects of the time of day, temperature, humidity, and barometric pressure on physiological functions (Wenger, 1948). The only relations that appeared to be of importance were those of time of day with systolic blood pressure and sublingual temperature and those of time of day and room temperature with volar forearm skin conductance and finger temperature. Accordingly, corrections were applied only to these four physiological variables. The relation of age and weight to the physiological functions appeared inconsequential, possibly as a result of restricted ranges in the sample. Since then, Clemens (1954) found age to be a significant factor in measurements of autonomic balance for male subjects of about 50 years or more.

The corrections employed in 1944 at Santa Ana, California, were described in the first section of this chapter; later these were applied to the numerous smaller samples observed in Los Angeles and its environs as cited in the second section. After Clemens's study these observations were confined to an age range of 18–45 years; whenever female subjects were employed, an attempt was made to confine the measurements to a period of 7–14 days following the onset of menstruation, since Wieland, Cullen, and Wenger (1958) found that the phase of the menstrual cycle affected the measures of autonomic balance.

More extensive investigations of the effects of uncontrolled variables were made later for a group of 102 male college students and custodians, a group of 50 male college students who were tested on two occasions, and a group of 279 female college students (for the initial report of this work, see Wenger and Cullen, 1962). The environmental data[5] included measures of temperature, pressure, humidity, wind speed, inversion base height, solar radiation, geomagnetic activity, solar latitude and declination, and the concentrations of several atmospheric contaminants (oxidants, carbon monoxide, nitrogen monoxide and dioxide, ozone, sulfur dioxide and particulate matter), all of which follow both diurnal and seasonal cycles. Data for time of day, chronological age, height, and weight were also included.

Almost all of the physiological variables measured in these studies showed some degree of covariation with environmental conditions, but the correlations between physiological and environmental variables did not exhibit much consistency in magnitude and direction from one sample to another. This lack of consistency suggests that the environmental variables measured in these studies may be only concomitants of other variables, not yet identified, to which cyclical trends in the physiological variables are related. The correlations among the environmental variables varied considerably from one sample to another. Probably, their relations to the underlying variables whose influences are reflected in the observed covariations of physiological and environmental variables do not remain stable over any long periods of time. The "axioms for environmental research" listed by Platt and Griffiths (1964) strongly emphasize the limited degree to which effects observed at particular times

---

[5]The sources for environmental data were the U.S. Weather Bureau Local Climatological Reports, the U.S. Bureau of Standards Solar and Geophysical Data, the U.S. Ephemeris and Nautical Almanac, and the Los Angeles County Air Pollution Control District monthly reports.

and places may be generalized, and the results of the studies cited here point to the conclusion that any corrections applied to physiological measures should be based upon their observed regressions on environmental conditions at a specific locale and over a limited period of time.

The environmental variables that most often were significantly correlated with the physiological measures in these studies were time of day, experimental room temperature, external temperature, relative humidity, and barometric pressure. Further analyses with partial and multiple correlations indicated that the degree of covariation of the other environmental variables with these five variables was sufficient to account for all but a negligible proportion of their covariation with the physiological measures. It was concluded, therefore, that the five variables represented the observed apparent effects of environmental conditions and the

only other influences for which corrections might be necessary were chronological age and weight.

The physiological data for these three samples were corrected, therefore, for the effects of chronological age, weight, time of day, experimental room temperature, external temperature, relative humidity, and barometric pressure. The corrections were based upon the coefficients of the joint regressions of the physiological measures on the uncontrolled variables obtained in the specific sample. Those for the female sample are shown in the next section.

In view of these results, another analysis of the effects of uncontrolled variables was made for 1833 of the 2112 AAF students tested in 1944, to determine if these data ought to be corrected more extensively than the initial investigation involving a sample of 563 had indicated. The uncontrolled variables measured were chronological age, weight and height, experimental room temperature, exter-

TABLE 13.19 CORRELATIONS OF PHYSIOLOGICAL VARIABLES WITH TIME OF TESTING (TM), ROOM TEMPERATURE (RT), AND SOLAR LATITUDE (SL) FOR 1833 MALE AAF STUDENTS

	Correlations				Beta weights for corrections		
	TM	RT	SL	Mult. R	TM	RT	SL
SO	−01	02	−08	09	−03	03	−09
SP	−01	08	12	15	−02	08	12
DL	−05	−12	−33	35	−07	−08	−34
DP	05	04	−08	09	02	03	−08
PC	15	09	05	17	15	03	07
LC	−19	−09	12	21	−16	−04	10
VC	22	31	21	40	16	25	22
SB	19	05	07	21	21	−02	10
DB	−02	−03	15	15	01	−04	15
MB	12	02	13	19	15	−04	15
PP	19	07	−05	20	19	01	−03
HP	−23	−11	03	23	−22	−03	01
SA	03	05	−17	18	−01	06	−17
ST	−34	−16	28	42	−29	−07	24
OX	23	04	−15	26	23	−03	−11
PD	−05	−04	01	05	−04	−02	01
RR	06	00	01	07	07	−02	02
TM	09	03	−21	22	06	01	−20
TS	04	05	−05	07	02	04	−05
RL	−01	−01	07	07	01	−01	07
F1	−27	−23	−20	38	−26	−13	−23
F2	−25	−37	−14	42	−16	−31	−15

SO = Salivary output; SP = salivary pH; DL = dermographia latency; DP = dermographia persistence; PC = palmar conductance; LC = log conductance change; VC = volar forearm conductance; SB = systolic blood pressure; DB = diastolic blood pressure; MB = mean blood pressure; PP = pulse pressure; HP = heart period; SA = sinus arrythmia; ST = sublingual temperature; OX = oxygen consumption; PD = pupil diameter; RR = respiration rate; TM = tidal air mean; TS = tidal air sigma; RL = relaxation rating; F1 = first finger temperature; F2 = second finger temperature.

nal temperature, humidity, barometric pressure, solar radiation, and solar latitude and declination. Measures of atmospheric contaminants were not available for the period during which the physiological tests were made. As in the initial investigation (Wenger, 1948), no important effects of age, weight, height, humidity, or barometric pressure were detected. The only prominent covariations of the physiological measures were with time of day, room temperature, and time of year, as indicated by solar latitude. The correlations of the physiological variables with these three uncontrolled variables and the beta weights for the correction equations are shown in Table 13.19.

It should be noted that the use of such correction equations as a means of eliminating error variance attributable to the influences of uncontrolled variables may tend to decrease the covariances and reliabilities of some of the physiological measures. If there is a common factor underlying the degree of unity observable in autonomic functions, common tendencies in the trends followed by these functions in response to changes in environmental conditions may be expected. A portion of the variance eliminated by correcting for these trends, therefore, may represent common, rather

than specific, variance. Test-retest reliability coefficients of individual physiological variables similarly may be reduced if conditions are such that the correction of measures eliminates more common than specific error variance. The correction of a variable for correlations with age and weight, for instance, could be expected to reduce its reliability coefficient, since the corrections would reduce the interindividual variance while having little or no effect upon the intraindividual variance if the interval between measurements were not long.

Such considerations raise an interesting and perhaps important question. If one expects to discover a common factor among physiological variables, should the data be factor analyzed before or after correction for the extraneous influences not controllable experimentally? Or, to put the question in different form, if one expects to find a factor representing the autonomic nervous system, would such a factor be more clearly delineated if measurements were conducted during some form of general sympathicomimetic or parasympathicomimetic stimulation or inhibition?

At the moment such questions cannot be answered. Two relevant facts, however, may be mentioned. Among the factor analyses referred to in

TABLE 13.20 MEANS AND STANDARD DEVIATIONS OF CORRECTED PHYSIOLOGICAL MEASURES FOR 166 FEMALE STUDENTS

	Unit of measurement	Mean	SD
Salivary output	sq root cc	1.58	.49
Sublingual temperature	log (102.0 − °F)	.548	.055
Palmar conductance	log μmho	1.000	.256
Polar conductance	log μmho	.861	.156
Log conductance change	log μmho	.390	.246
Systolic blood pressure	mm Hg	101.7	8.0
Diastolic blood pressure	mm Hg	65.3	6.6
Pulse pressure	mm Hg	35.9	8.5
Heart period	μmin/10 cycles	144.6	18.8
Respiration period	log sec/cycle	.564	.074
Pupil diameter	mm	4.72	1.05
Dermographia persistence	log min	.414	.306
Dermographia latency	sec	16.2	5.0
Face temperature	log (39.0 − °C)	.764	.081
Auxillary temperature	log (40.0 − °C)	.593	.058
First finger temperature	log (39.0 − °C)	.940	.177
Second finger temperature	log (39.0 − °C)	.968	.161
Finger pulse volume	log (microliters × 100)	2.090	.205
Stomach period	sec/cycle	20.71	2.00

Source: Adapted from W. H. Lucio, M. A. Wenger, and T. D. Cullen, *Phychophysiological correlates of female teacher behavior and emotional stability: A seven-year longitudinal investigation.* CSE Rep. No. 44, University of California, Los Angeles, 1967.

TABLE 13.21 MEANS AND STANDARD DEVIATIONS OF SEVEN UNCONTROLLED VARIABLES, FOR WHICH CORRECTIONS WERE APPLIED TO PHYSIOLOGICAL MEASURES FOR FEMALE STUDENTS

Uncontrolled variables	Unit of measurement	Mean	SD	Correction baseline
Age (A)	log (years—18)	.598	.230	.600
Weight (W)	lb	122.4	13.9	120.0
Time of testing (Ti)	hr	12.2	2.7	12.0
Room temperature (RT)	°C	25.0	1.8	24.0
External temperature (T)	°F	64.2	7.3	65.0
Lowest relative humidity previous 24 hr (H)	percent	36.5	18.6	40.0
Highest pressure previous 24 hr (P)	barometric in.	30.10	.14	30.05

Source: Adapted from W. H. Lucio, M. A. Wenger, and T. D. Cullen, *Psychophysiological correlates of female teacher behavior and emotional stability: A seven-year longitudinal investigation.* CSE Rep. No. 44, University of California, Los Angeles, 1967.

the present chapter, that based on patients hospitalized with "operational fatigue" involved the highest intercorrelations yet reported for such physiological data and disclosed the greatest amount of common factor variance yet found. On the other hand, the study of females described below presents perhaps the least convincing autonomic factor yet reported; that analysis was based upon the most extensively corrected data so far employed.

Autonomic Balance in Young Adult Females

For the first extensive investigation of autonomic balance in adult females (Lucio, Wenger, & Cullen, 1967), the subjects were 279 young women, mean age 22.7 years, enrolled in the student teaching program at the University of California, Los Angeles. Testing was carried out by female operators, following the tests and procedures used in the study of AAF students (described in the first section of this

TABLE 13.22 BETA WEIGHTS IN THE EQUATIONS FOR CORRECTION OF PHYSIOLOGICAL MEASURES FOR FEMALE STUDENTS

Physiological measures	A	W	Ti	RT	T	H	P
Salivary output	−.08	.07	.08	−.15	.04	.06	.24
Sublingual temperature	.05	.03	−.28	.18	−.21	−.24	.02
Palmar conductance	−.16	−.05	.07	.10	.06	−.20	−.01
Volar conductance	.14	.08	−.01	.14	−.09	.01	.08
Log conductance change	−.08	.13	−.09	.18	−.02	−.17	−.04
Systolic blood pressure	−.05	.16	.03	−.13	.13	.11	.03
Diastolic blood pressure	−.01	.12	−.17	−.22	.05	.14	.30
Pulse pressure	−.01	.07	.15	.03	.05	−.04	−.20
Heart period	.01	.14	−.15	−.02	.04	.11	.04
Respiration period	−.04	.08	−.19	.04	.09	−.02	.22
Pupil diameter	−.05	−.03	−.03	−.20	−.04	−.07	.06
Dermographia persistence	−.22	−.01	−.19	−.02	−.05	−.12	.12
Dermographia latency	.13	.06	.18	−.18	.04	−.23	−.06
Face temperature	.01	−.01	−.18	−.38	.14	.03	−.12
Axillary temperature	−.20	.24	−.26	.03	.02	.18	.09
First finger temperature	.02	−.21	−.10	−.18	−.43	−.23	.12
Second finger temperature	.01	−.17	−.04	−.48	−.12	−.09	.07
Finger pulse volume	−.13	.19	−.06	.27	.32	.28	−.16
Stomach period	−.16	.11	−.14	.16	−.17	.20	.01

A = age; W = weight; Ti = time of testing; RT = initial room temperature; T = external temperature at time of testing; H = lowest relative humidity in previous 24 hr; P = highest barometric pressure in previous 24 hr.

Source: Adapted from W. H. Lucio, M. A. Wenger, and T. D. Cullen, *Psychophysiological correlates of female teacher behavior and emotional stability: A seven-year longitudinal investigation.* CSE Rep. No. 44, University of California, Los Angeles, 1967.

chapter). In addition, face and axillary temperatures, finger pulse volume, and stomach motility were measured using procedures described by Wenger, Engel, and Clemens (1957). The data recorded for these variables were the levels reached at the end of a 10-min period of rest with the subject reclining. Temperament (Guilford-Zimmerman Temperament Survey) and performance in supervised teaching were also assessed. Later follow-up studies provided data on in-service teaching performance and the incidence of psychosomatic and other disorders.

The first analyses of these data were based upon an N of 247, after exclusion of subjects who were unwell or under medication at the time of testing (Lucio & Wenger, 1961; Wenger & Cullen, 1962). To reduce the influences of race and phase of the menstrual cycle, the final sample, with an N of 166, was confined to subjects with Caucasian ancestry who had been tested within a period of 5–16 days following the cessation of menses. Table 13.20 shows the units of measurement, means, and standard deviations of the 19 physiological variables

measured. Normalizing transformations, as indicated in the table, were applied to several of the variables, and all were corrected for the effects of the seven uncontrolled variables, whose means and standard deviations are shown in Table 13.21. The equations for correction of the physiological variables were of the form:

$$Z_c = Z_x - B_1 Z_1 - B_2 Z_2 - \cdots - B_7 Z_7$$

where the values of Z_c and Z_x are the corrected and original standard scores for a physiological variable and the values of B_1 to B_7 are the beta weights from the multiple regression of the physiological variable on the seven uncontrolled variables, as given in Table 13.22. The standard scores for the uncontrolled variables (Z_1 to Z_7) were calculated as deviations from the correction baseline levels shown in Table 13.21, which were set at levels differing slightly from the mean levels for the sample.

The intercorrelations of the corrected physiological measures for the sample of 166 are shown in Table 13.23. The coefficients generally were low,

TABLE 13.23 INTERCORRELATIONS OF PHYSIOLOGICAL MEASURES FOR 166 FEMALE STUDENTS

	SO	ST[a]	PC[a]	VC[a]	LCC	SBP[a]	DBP[a]	PP	HP	RP	PD[a]	DP	DL[a]	FaT	AxT	FT$_1$	FT$_2$	FPV	SP
SO																			
ST[a]	10																		
PC[a]	−02	13																	
VC[a]	04	05	11																
LCC	01	02	−25	09															
SBP[a]	03	04	13	−01	−12														
DBP[a]	05	04	05	01	08	34													
PP	01	−01	−07	01	20	−68	44												
HP	−13	23	18	07	−09	27	12	−15											
RP	01	17	−02	−10	04	−09	−04	05	−01										
PD[a]	08	10	08	08	01	−03	05	09	16	−19									
DP	13	−07	11	02	00	00	12	10	−10	−04	02								
DL[a]	−06	07	01	−01	06	−01	−09	−04	−04	−01	−10	07							
FaT	−07	17	10	03	−10	16	−03	−18	23	−02	05	06	11						
AxT	−17	07	−02	−01	08	03	−13	−13	19	−05	19	01	01	16					
FT$_1$	11	15	12	06	−01	02	04	05	10	−07	09	12	15	22	00				
FT$_2$	04	03	09	−05	−05	09	05	−07	−03	00	04	−01	06	−10	10	35			
FPV	−07	03	01	20	06	00	04	06	02	−02	09	−03	07	00	−09	24	64		
SP	−17	12	−06	−18	−05	13	−02	−14	20	−15	01	−11	−10	20	18	02	−13	−07	

[a] Indicates reflection of variable.

SO = salivary output; ST = sublingual temperature; PC = palmar conductance; VC = volar forearm conductance; LCC = log conductance change; SBP = systolic blood pressure; DBP = diastolic blood pressure; PP = pulse pressure; HP = heart period; RP = respiration period; PD = pupil diameter; DP = dermographia persistence; DL = dermographia latency; FaT = face temperature; AxT = axillary temperature; FT$_1$ = first finger temperature; FT$_2$ = second finger temperature; FPV = finger pulse volume; SP = stomach period.

Source: Adapted from W. H. Lucio, M. A. Wenger, and T. D. Cullen, Psychophysiological correlates of female teacher behavior and emotional stability: A seven-year longitudinal investigation. CSE Rep. No. 44, University of California, Los Angeles, 1967.

TABLE 13.24 CENTROID SOLUTION OF FACTOR ANALYSIS OF PHYSIOLOGICAL MEASURES FOR 166 FEMALE STUDENTS

Variables	Factors						h^2
	I	II	III	IV	V	VI	
Salivary output	13	26	25	15	−19	19	24
Sublingual temperature[a]	27	−26	23	26	20	19	34
Palmar conductance[a]	41	−13	13	−17	05	−22	28
Volar conductance[a]	21	13	07	−11	20	04	12
Heart period	37	−35	−17	−10	28	20	42
Second finger temperature	08	−13	−07	13	−14	22	12
Respiration period	−19	−33	36	15	−02	04	30
Pupil diameter[a]	37	22	−16	25	24	−10	34
Dermographia persistence	11	21	18	−14	−17	−14	16
Systolic blood pressure[a]	36	−25	−19	−18	−30	21	39

[a] Indicates reflection of variable.

Source: Adapted from W. H. Lucio, M. A. Wenger, and T. D. Cullen, *Psychophysiological correlates of female teacher behavior and emotional stability: A seven-year longitudinal investigation.* CSE Rep. No. 44, University of California, Los Angeles, 1967.

but not so low as to be incompatible with the existence of a general autonomic factor. Some of the variables (e.g., finger temperature and finger pulse volume) represented different measures of the same underlying function; only one of each such pair was included in the matrix that was factor analyzed. The elimination of other variables, whose presence in the matrix was found to produce highly specific factors, finally reduced the number of variables to 10.

The centroid and varimax (Kaiser, 1959) rotated solutions for the final factor analysis are shown in Tables 13.24 and 13.25. The six factors obtained by the varimax method are not readily interpretable, and none seems to be very general. Additional rotations suggested by visual inspection, however, produced Factor IA (also shown in Table 13.25), which may be a general autonomic factor for adult females comparable to the one found by Wenger (1948) for adult males. The equation for the estimation of this factor is

$$\overline{A}_F = .25(T_{ST^a}) + .19(T_{PC^a}) + .10(T_{VC^a}) \\ + .37(T_{HP}) + .21(T_{SBP^a})$$

where $\overline{A}_F$ is the estimated factor score and the T following each beta weight represents the standard

TABLE 13.25 ROTATED SOLUTION OF FACTOR ANALYSIS OF PHYSIOLOGICAL MEASURES FOR 166 FEMALE STUDENTS

Variables	Factors						
	I	II	III	IV	V	VI	IA
Salivary output	06	47	07	05	04	04	02
Sublingual temperature[a]	14	01	52	14	15	−04	37
Palmar conductance[a]	07	−04	07	08	15	−49	33
Volar conductance[a]	−04	04	00	11	31	−10	16
Heart period	36	−34	20	13	32	−10	52
2nd Finger temperature	29	05	11	01	−06	12	05
Respiration period	−08	01	44	−27	−16	01	−01
Pupil diameter[a]	−02	02	01	56	13	−06	12
Dermographia persistence	−08	26	−15	−04	02	−23	03
Systolic blood pressure[a]	59	−03	−07	−05	03	−17	34

[a] Indicates reflection of variable.

Source: Adapted from W. H. Lucio, M. A. Wenger, and T. D. Cullen, *Psychophysiological correlates of female teacher behavior and emotional stability: A seven-year longitudinal investigation.* CSE Rep. No. 44, University of California, Los Angles, 1967.

TABLE 13.26 PATTERNS OF AUTONOMIC ACTIVITY FOR 166 FEMALE STUDENTS

	Pattern definitions					Percentage frequencies	
	Salivary output	Sublingual temperature	Palmar conductance	Heart period	Systolic blood pressure	Female students (N = 166)	Male AAF students (N = 100)
P	High(+)	Low(+)	Low(+)	Long(+)	Low(+)	10	14
PS1	Low(−)	Low(+)	Low(+)	Long(+)	Low(+)	6	—
Mean	Mean	Mean	Mean	Mean	Mean	25	11
S	Low(−)	High(−)	High(−)	Short(−)	High(−)	17	13
PS2	High(+)	High(−)	Low(+)	Short(−)	Low(+)	9	—
Beta	Low(−)	Low(+)	Low(+)	Short(−)	High(−)	3	15
Unclassified						30	47

+ Indicates a deviation from the normative mean of ½ σ or greater in a direction indicative of apparent dominance of parasympathetic nervous system activity (T score of 55.0 or greater).

− Indicates a deviation from the normative mean of ½ σ or greater in a direction indicative of apparent dominance of sympathetic nervous system activity (T score of 45.0 or less).

Source: Adapted from W. H. Lucio, M. A. Wenger, and T. D. Cullen, *Psychophysiological correlates of female teacher behavior and emotional stability: A seven-year longitudinal investigation.* CSE Rep. No. 44, University of California, Los Angeles, 1967.

score for the physiological variable designated by the subscript. The superscript *a* indicates reflection of a variable. While pupil diameter had a loading of 0.12 on the factor, its beta weight was only 0.02 and it therefore was omitted from the equation.

Individual patterns of autonomic activity in a set of five variables were analyzed according to the method developed by Wenger (1957). The criteria for classifying individual standard score profiles into patterns (cf. Table 13.10) when only five variables

are used were three consistent deviations with no inconsistent ones, or four consistent ones with one inconsistent deviation. The mean pattern was defined as fewer than three deviations of .5σ or more from the means for the female sample.

Table 13.26 shows the six patterns that appeared with the greatest frequencies in the female sample. The percentage frequencies of the sympathetic (S) and parasympathetic (P) patterns differed little from the corresponding frequencies observed in males,

TABLE 13.27 MEAN AUTONOMIC FACTOR SCORES AND FREQUENCIES OF AUTONOMIC PATTERNS WITHIN DISORDER CATEGORIES FOR 127 FEMALE STUDENTS

	ND	SK	GI	AX	HD	RP	MN
Mean factor score	53.4	48.1	47.3	46.5	49.9	47.9	50.8
P	7	0	2	0	2	0	3
PS1	4	1	1	0	2	1	1
M	10	3	7	1	2	10	7
S	5	5	9	5	6	4	7
PS2	0	2	0	4	2	8	3
B	1	2	2	1	1	0	1
Unclassified	12	4	8	3	4	5	8
P + PS1	11	1	3	0	4	1	4
S + PS2 + B	6	9	11	10	9	12	11
Chi-square		5.37[a]	5.81[a]	8.32[a]	3.39	7.78[a]	4.63[a]

Note.—Underlined mean factor scores differ significantly from the mean of group ND at the .05 level of confidence.

[a] Indicates that chi-square for the comparison of the pattern distribution with the distribution in group ND is significant at the .05 level of confidence.

ND = no disorders reported; SK = skin disorders (boils, eczema, shingles, skin rashes, excessive sweating); GI = gastrointestinal disorders (constipation, diarrhea, hemorrhoids, ulcers, etc.); AX = anxiety (anxiety, fear, depression, nervousness, nervous breakdown); HD = headaches (frequent headaches, migraine headaches); RP = respiratory disorders (hay fever, sinus trouble); MN = menstrual disorders (pain during menstruation, premenstrual tension).

Source: Adapted from W. H. Lucio, M. A. Wenger, and T. D. Cullen, *Psychophysiological correlates of female teacher behavior and emotional stability: A seven-year longitudinal investigation.* CSE Rep. No. 44, University of California, Los Angeles, 1967.

but the frequency of the beta pattern was much lower and was exceeded by the frequencies of two other mixed patterns (PS1 and PS2) which had not previously been identified in males. The reason for the low incidence of the beta pattern in this sample is not known. Further investigation will be required before concluding that the beta pattern is characteristic only of males. Additional studies are necessary also to confirm the existence of patterns PS1 and PS2. In particular, PS1 seems questionable. It may reflect Pattern P in individuals who experienced embarrassment during the determination of salivary output. Such a state inhibits salivation.

The major purpose of the study, in addition to establishing norms for adult females, was to investigate the value of measures of autonomic functioning for the prediction of teaching performance. The initial data gave little evidence that autonomic balance was related to performance in supervised teaching or in the first year of in-service teaching. While one of the physiological variables, finger temperature, was positively related to certain indices of performance, autonomic factor scores showed no significant relations with either performance or temperament.

At a later stage of the study, when data on professional status and on the incidence of psychosomatic and other disorders provided adequate criteria of performance, significant correlations were observed. Follow-up data were obtained from 127 of the subjects, surveyed by questionnaire 6 years after the initial physiological testing. Table 13.27 shows the mean autonomic factor scores (standardized with a total sample mean of 50 and a standard deviation of 10) and the distributions of autonomic patterns for certain categories of reported disorders. The relations of both factor scores and patterns to the occurrences of disorders indicated associations of relative SNS dominance with certain kinds of disorders and of relative PNS dominance with an absence of disorders. The mean factor scores for subjects with gastrointestinal disorders (GI), anxiety (AX), and respiratory disorders (RP) were below the normative mean and significantly lower than the mean score for subjects reporting no disorders (ND), which was above the normative mean. Also, the incidence of the S pattern was higher than that of the P pattern within

each disorder category but lower within the group having no disorders.

The chi-square tests in Table 13.27 show that among subjects within each disorder category, except headaches (HD), the ratio of the pure and predominantly parasympathetic patterns (P and PS1) to the sympathetic and mixed patterns (S, beta, and PS2) was significantly smaller than among subjects having no disorders.

The subjects in the anxiety category constituted the most deviant group. They had the lowest autonomic factor scores, the highest frequency of the S pattern, and zero frequencies of the P and PS1 patterns. These results, consistent with previous findings of low autonomic factor scores for males in anxiety states (Holt, 1956; Parker, 1955; Smith & Wenger, 1965; Wenger, 1948), provide further support for the belief that SNS activity is particularly prominent in anxiety and fear.

Although a relatively high frequency of the P pattern had been found in males with migraine headaches (Table 13.18), and some symptoms of hay fever and similar disorders suggest heightened PNS activity (Millonig et al., 1950), the autonomic factor scores and pattern distributions for the female subjects with headaches and respiratory disorders did not reveal relative PNS dominance for these disorders. While the percentage of subjects having the S pattern was low in the respiratory disorder group (14%), and about the same as the percentage in the group with no disorders, the percentage of subjects having the P pattern was not higher than in the other groups. The PS2 pattern, however, appeared to be rather strongly associated with respiratory disorders. Eight of the 12 subjects who showed this pattern of SNS dominance in some functions and PNS dominance in others reported having suffered from hay fever and/or sinus trouble. Moreover, 3 of the 4 subjects in the anxiety group, who showed this pattern, also had hay fever; while 3 of the 4 subjects in the group with respiratory disorders, who showed the S pattern, also had gastrointestinal disorders.

Differences between subjects who had or had not attained tenure in various school systems when surveyed later showed that ANS functioning bears some relation to success in the teaching profession. Table 13.28 compares mean autonomic factor scores

TABLE 13.28 MEAN AUTONOMIC FACTOR SCORES AND FREQUENCIES OF AUTONOMIC PATTERNS WITHIN TEACHING STATUS CATEGORIES FOR 127 FEMALE STUDENTS

	TT	NT	NR
Mean factor score	49.5	51.2	54.6
P	2	10	4
PS1	1	7	4
M	15	20	7
S	11	10	2
PS2	5	7	0
B	0	4	1
Unclassified	16	19	7
P + PS1	3	17	8
S + PS2 + B	16	21	3
Chi-square		4.79[a]	7.43[a]

Note.—The underlined mean factor score differs significantly from the mean of group TT at the .05 level of confidence.

[a]Indicates that chi-square for the comparison of the pattern distribution with the distribution in group TT is significant at the .05 level of confidence.

TT = tenured teachers; NT = nontenured teachers; NR = teachers who had left the profession and did not intend to return.

Source: Adapted from W. H. Lucio, M. A. Wenger, and T. D. Cullen, *Psychophysiological correlates of female teacher behavior and emotional stability: A seven-year longitudinal investigation.* CSE Rep. No. 44, University of California, Los Angeles, 1967.

and pattern distributions for tenured teachers (*TT*); nontenured teachers (*NT*); and a subgroup of the latter, who had left the profession and did not intend to return (*NR*). The results indicate that relative PNS dominance is associated with a lesser degree of success in teaching. The mean factor score of the group who had given up the profession (*NR*) was significantly higher than that of the group of tenured teachers (*TT*), which was close to the normative mean. Moreover, there were significant tendencies for the number of subjects with pure or predominantly parasympathetic patterns to be relatively greater, and the number with sympathetic and mixed patterns to be relatively smaller, in the *NT* and *NR* groups than in the *TT* group. Only 15% of the subjects who showed the P or PS1 patterns had obtained tenure at the time of the survey, and 40% had left the profession; whereas 43% of the subjects showing the S, PS2, or beta patterns had obtained tenure and only 8% had left the profession. These results emphasize the value of describing autonomic response patterns to supplement measures of autonomic balance. They also suggest the need to investigate possible relationships between autonomic patterns and measures of personality and temperament.

CONCLUDING STATEMENT

This chapter has attempted to collate our studies of autonomic balance in children and in adults and to describe the patterns of autonomic functions found for young adult males and females, making available in one reference studies that cover a span of 30 years. The chapter necessarily is incomplete, but the methods and most of the major results have been presented or cited. It is hoped that the chapter will stimulate others to replicate and test further some of the findings.

The studies described in the first section of this chapter and related factorial analyses have been summarized (cf. Cattell, 1966, pp. 666–683). This is not the place to criticize that summary but a few remarks may be appropriate. In the first place, we have never referred to the autonomic factor or factors described in this chapter as a *factor of autonomic balance.* Instead, autonomic balance was defined as the central tendency of the estimates of the autonomic factor. We have referred, perhaps somewhat loosely, to such estimates as "scores of autonomic balance," or imbalance.

Second, among the studies cited in Cattell, that by Darling (1940) seems to be most similar in approach to the work described in this chapter. Darling's reported discovery of both a sympathetic and a parasympathetic factor already has been criticized (Wenger, 1948). In essence, it is doubted that the commonly employed techniques of physiological measurement permit the discovery of separate ANS factors among autonomically controlled physiological functions. Such differentiation might prove possible if measurements were included of functions controlled solely by the PNS, but such functions are few in number, difficult to measure, and have not been included in factorial studies. Instead, the antagonistic control of most ANS functions by the two branches of the system automatically sets the stage for the appearance of a general factor of autonomic function.

Third, it remains to be determined whether or not the factor or factors described in this chapter are identical, or even similar, to others cited in

Cattell. Table 13.12 shows that three of the general autonomic factors obtained for three separate samples are similar. We doubt that other factors yet reported will prove to be that similar.

REFERENCES

BROWN, F. A., Jr.   Response to pervasive geophysical factors and the biological clock problem. *Cold Spring Harbor Symposia on Quantitative Biology,* 1960, **25,** 57-72.

CANNON, W. B.   *The wisdom of the body.* New York: Norton, 1932.

CATTELL, R. B.   (Ed.) *Handbook of multivariate experimental psychology.* Chicago: Rand McNally, 1966.

CLEMENS. T. L.   A preliminary report on autonomic functions in neoplastic diseases. In J. A. GENGERELLI & F. J. KIRKNER (Eds.), *The psychophysiological variables in human cancer.* Berkeley: University of California Press, 1954.

CUTLER, M.   The nature of the cancer process in relation to a possible psychosomatic influence. In J. A. GENGERELLI & F. J. KIRKNER (Eds.), *The psychophysiological variables in human cancer.* Berkeley: University of California Press, 1954.

DALE, H. H.   Chemical transmission of effects of nerve impulses. *British Medical Journal,* 1934, **1,** 835-841.

DARLING, R. P.   Autonomic action in relation to personality traits of children. *Journal of Abnormal and Social Psychology,* 1940, **35,** 246-260.

DARROW, C. W.   Physiological and clinical tests of autonomic function and autonomic balance. *Physiological Review,* 1943, **23,** 1-36.

ELLIS, F. W., & BLUMBERG, E. M.   Comparative case summaries with psychological profiles in representative rapidly and slowly progressive neoplastic diseases. In J. A. GENGERELLI & F. J. KIRKNER (Eds.), *The psychophysiological variables in human cancer.* Berkeley: University of California Press, 1954.

EPPINGER, H., & HESS, L.   *Die Vagotonie.* Berlin, 1910. (Translation) *Vagotonia.* New York: The Nervous and Mental Disease Publishing Company, 1917.

FELLER, R. P., & HALE, H. B.   Human sympathoadrenal responsiveness in autumn, winter and spring. U. S. Air Force School of Aerospace Medicine, Technical Documentary Rep. No. SAM-TDR-63-46, 1963.

FINK, J.   A psychophysiological comparison of brittle and stable diabetics. Unpublished doctoral dissertation, University of California, Los Angeles, 1960.

GASKELL, W. H.   On the structure, distribution and function of the nerves which innervate the visceral and vascular systems. *Journal of Physiology,* 1885, **7,** 1-80.

GENGERELLI, J. A., & KIRKNER, F. J. (Eds.)   *The psychophysiological variables in human cancer.* Berkeley: University of California Press, 1954.

GUNDERSON, E. K.   Autonomic balance in schizophrenia. Unpublished doctoral dissertation, University of California, Los Angeles, 1953.

HOHMANN, G. W.   Stress and spasticity in paraplegia. Unpublished doctoral dissertation, University of California, Los Angeles, 1955.

HOLT, J. M.   The treatment of chronic anxiety states by means of partial sympathetic blockade. Unpublished doctoral dissertation, University of California, Los Angeles, 1956.

JOST, H., & SONTAG, L. W.   The genetic factor in autonomic nervous system function. *Psychosomatic Medicine,* 1944, **6,** 308-310.

KAISER, H. F.   Computer program for varimax rotation in factor analysis. *Educational and Psychological Measurement,* 1959, **19,** 413-420.

LANGLEY, J. N.   Note on the trophic center of the afferent fibers accompanying the sympathetic nerves. *Journal of Physiology,* 1905, **33,** 27-28.

LEVINE, M.   Measurement of electrical skin resistance. *Archives of Neurology and Psychiatry,* 1933, **29,** 828-842.

LITTLE, K. B.   Effects of vagotomy on autonomic balance. *Psychosomatic Medicine,* 1955, **17,** 227-233.

LUCIO, W. H., & WENGER, M. A.   *Prediction of teacher performance and emotional stability: A psychophysiological pilot study of female student teachers.* Final report to U.S. Office of Education, Contract No. SAE 8311, September 30, 1961.

LUCIO, W. H., WENGER, M. A., & CULLEN, T. D.   *Psychophysiological correlates of female teacher behavior and emotional stability: A seven-year longitudinal investigation.* CSE Ref. No. 44, University of California, Los Angeles, 1967.

MARKWELL, E. D.   An investigation of autonomic balance in tuberculous patients. *Psychosomatic Medicine,* 1961, **23,** 392-399.

MARKWELL, E. D.   An investigation of resting patterns of autonomic function in the tuberculous. *Behavioral Science,* 1963, **8,** 28-33.

MCKELLIGOTT, J. W.   Autonomic functions and affective states in spinal cord injury. Unpublished doctoral dissertation, University of California, Los Angeles, 1959.

MEFFERD, R. B., Jr. Structuring physiological correlates of mental processes and states: The study of biological correlates of mental processes. In R. B. CATTELL (Ed.), *Handbook of multivariate experimental psychology.* Chicago: Rand McNally, 1966.

MILLONIG, A. F., HARRIS, H. E., & GARDNER, W. J. Effect of autonomic denervation on nasal mucosa. *Archives of Otolaryngology,* 1950, **52,** 359-368.

PARKER, A. G. Manifest anxiety and autonomic nervous system functions. Unpublished doctoral dissertation, University of California, Los Angeles, 1955.

PETREN, K., & THORLING, I. Untersuchengen über das Vorkommen von Vagotonus und Sympathikotonus. *Zeitschrift für klinische Medizin,* 1911, **73,** 27-46.

PICCARDI, G. *The chemical basis of medical climatology.* Springfield, Ill.: Charles C Thomas, 1962.

PLATT, R. B., & GRIFFITHS, J. F. *Environmental measurement and interpretation.* New York: Van Nostrand-Reinhold, 1964.

ROKITANSKY, C. *A manual of pathologic anatomy.* Philadelphia: Blanchard & Lea, 1855.

SARGENT, F., & WEINMAN, K. P. Variabilité physiologique chez l'homme jeune. *Biotypologie,* 1962, **23,** 137-171.

SARGENT, F., & WEINMAN, K. P. Physiological individuality. *Annals of the New York Academy of Sciences,* 1966, **134,** 696-720.

SCHREIDER, E. Typology and biometrics. *Annals of the New York Academy of Sciences,* 1966, **134,** 789-803.

SHERRY, L. U. Some effects of chlorpromazine on the physiological and psychological functioning of a group of chronic schizophrenics. Unpublished doctoral dissertation, University of California, Los Angeles, 1959.

SMITH, D. B. D., & WENGER, M. A. Changes in autonomic balance during phasic anxiety. *Psychophysiology,* 1965, **1,** 267-271.

TOLMIE, J. G. Patterns of autonomic function in tuberculous patients. Unpublished doctoral dissertation, University of California, Los Angeles, 1958.

TROMP, S. W. *Medical biometeorology.* New York: Elsevier, 1963.

VON NOORDEN, C. Beitrage zur Pathologie des Asthma Bronchiale. *Zeitschrift für klinische Medizin,* 1892, **20,** 98-106.

WENGER, M. A. The measurement of individual differences in autonomic balance. *Psychosomatic Medicine,* 1941, **3,** 427-434.

WENGER, M. A. A study of physiological factors: The autonomic nervous system and skeletal musculature. *Human Biology,* 1942, **14,** 69-84. (a)

WENGER, M. A. The stability of measurement of autonomic balance. *Psychosomatic Medicine,* 1942, **4,** 94-95. (b)

WENGER, M. A. A further note on the measurement of autonomic balance. *Psychosomatic Medicine,* 1943, **5,** 148-151. (a)

WENGER, M. A. An attempt to appraise individual differences in level of muscular tension. *Journal of Experimental Psychology,* 1943, **32,** 213-225. (b)

WENGER, M. A. Seasonal variations in some physiologic variables. *Journal of Laboratory and Clinical Medicine,* 1943, **28,** 1101-1108. (c)

WENGER, M. A. Preliminary study of the significance of measures of autonomic balance. *Psychosomatic Medicine,* 1947, **9,** 301-309.

WENGER, M. A. Studies of autonomic balance in Army Air Forces personnel. *Comparative Psychology Monographs,* 1948, **19,** No. 4.

WENGER, M. A. Autonomic balance under nine drugs. *American Psychologist,* 1949, **4,** 233.

WENGER, M. A. Recherches sur le système nerveux végétatif. *L'Encéphale,* 1952, No. 6, 493-504.

WENGER, M. A. Pattern analyses of autonomic variables during rest. *Psychosomatic Medicine,* 1957, **19,** 240-244.

WENGER, M. A. Studies of autonomic balance: A summary. *Psychophysiology,* 1966, **2,** 173-186.

WENGER, M. A., CLEMENS, T. L., & CULLEN, T. D. Autonomic functions in patients with gastrointestinal and dermatological disorders. *Psychosomatic Medicine,* 1962, **24,** 267-273.

WENGER, M. A., CLEMENS, T. L., & CULLEN, T. D. Patterns of autonomic response in schizophrenic patients. In preparation.

WENGER, M. A., CLEMENS, T. L., DARSIE, M. L., ENGEL, B. T., ESTESS, F. M., & SONNENSCHEIN, R. R. Autonomic response patterns during intravenous infusion of epinephrine and nor-epinephrine. *Psychosomatic Medicine,* 1960, **22,** 294-307.

WENGER, M. A., & CULLEN, T. D. Some problems in psychophysiological research: III. The effects of uncontrolled variables. In R. ROESSLER & N. S. GREENFIELD (Eds.), *Physiological correlates of psychological disorder.* Madison: University of Wisconsin Press, 1962.

WENGER, M. A., & ELLINGTON, M. The measurement of autonomic balance in children: Method and normative data. *Psychosomatic Medicine,* 1943, **5,** 241-253.

WENGER, M. A., ENGEL, B. T., & CLEMENS, T. L. Studies of autonomic response patterns: Rationale and methods. *Behavioral Science,* 1957, **2,** 216-221.

WENGER, M. A., JONES, F. N., & JONES, M. H. *Physiological psychology.* New York: Holt, Rinehart and Winston, 1956.

WEST, P. M. Origin and development of the psychological approach to the cancer problem. In J. A. GENGERELLI & F. J. KIRKNER (Eds.), *The psychophysiological variables in human cancer.* Berkeley: University of California Press, 1954.

WIELAND, B. A., CULLEN, T. D., & WENGER, M. A. The day-to-day stability of autonomic factor scores. Unpublished report, Western Psychological Association, 1958.

Bernard T. Engel

RESPONSE SPECIFICITY*

14

This chapter proposes to define the concepts of response specificity, to illustrate these definitions with examples from the psychophysiological literature, and to discuss some of the issues that need further clarification. It will not attempt to be exhaustive either in reviewing the literature or in identifying the issues.

The term "specificity" has existed in physiological psychology and its literature for more than a hundred years, in uses such as "the law of specific energies." Unfortunately, it has taken on a number of distinct and different meanings over this time. The use of the term in psychophysiology—the field of research defined by the contents of this handbook—is more recent (Lacey, Bateman, & Van Lehn, 1953), but even here it rests on historical precedents (e.g., Alexander, 1950). The multiple contexts in which specificity concepts have appeared and the various additional ways in which the term, response specificity, has been applied within psychophysiology (e.g., Ax, 1964; Engel, 1960) make it seem reasonable to conclude that one of its hallmarks is the confusion it has produced in the mind of the reader. It is hoped that this paper will help reduce some of this confusion by defining each of the concepts of psychophysiological specificity, and by showing how they interrelate.

*This chapter is an adaptation of an article by Engel and Moos (1967). We gratefully acknowledge our appreciation to the American Medical Association for the use of material from that paper.

DEFINITIONS

The most general division of the principle of response specificity is into two categories: stimulus (SR) specificity and individual (IR) specificity. *SR specificity* refers to the tendency that a stimulus or situation has to evoke characteristic responses from most subjects. *IR specificity* refers to the tendency that an individual has to emit characteristic responses to most stimuli. Stimulus and individual specificity are referred to as SR and IR specificity, respectively, rather than S and I specificity, to underscore the fact that specificity is always measured in terms of responses.

Stimulus Specificity

Stimulus uniqueness One characteristic of stimuli which gives them the property of specificity is that of uniqueness. Stimuli are either the same or different, depending on whether they do or do not evoke different effects from a group of subjects. Three necessary experimental conditions are therefore imposed by this concept: (a) a group of subjects, (b) more than one stimulus to which the group is exposed, and (c) a measurable response or set of responses (Table 14.1, A1). Specificity exists among a set of stimuli if each evokes different responses from the group.

This concept of SR specificity is an old and familiar one. When Ax (1953) showed that fear and anger evoked different autonomic responses from his subjects, he was showing that his two situations were unique. And when Lacey (1959) distinguished between the cardiac effects of outward-directed attention and inward-directed attention, he too was identifying some of the unique properties of stimuli. By the same token, Edelberg and Wright (1964)

showed that the galvanic skin response to an alerting stimulus was different, depending upon whether the altering stimulus was a prelude to an orienting response or to a reaction time response. This last study, incidentally, underscores the need for a careful definition of "the" stimulus. The role of instructional sets in psychophysiological research has been amply demonstrated (Sternbach, 1966). From a specificity point of view, explicit instructional sets must be part of the definition of the stimulus.

It should be clear that each of the three studies cited above has similar experimental designs. In each instance one group of subjects was exposed to two or more situations and the responses evoked by each of the stimuli were compared. This common link is not accidental, for each of the studies attempted to show that the stimulus had unique effects; the only way that can be done is by comparing the effects in the same subjects.

Stimulus consistency The other concept of stimulus specificity deals with the characteristics of a single stimulus. If a single stimulus evokes a consistent hierarchy of responses within a set of individuals, then it is said to have specificity. The necessary experimental conditions in this case are a single stimulus, a single group of subjects, and a set of response measures (Table 14.1, A2). There are several examples of stimulus consistency in the psychophysiological literature. Almost every response pattern that physiologists induce by external stimulation has the property of stimulus consistency. A few examples of these would be Valsalva's maneuver, hypercapnia, and hyperthermia. The reason a physiologist frequently studies consistent stimuli is simple: he is predominantly interested in studying the mechanisms that mediate peripheral

TABLE 14.1 NECESSARY CONDITIONS FOR DEMONSTRATING RESPONSE SPECIFICITIES

	A. Stimulus specificity				B. Individual specificity		
	Subjects	Stimuli	Responses		Subjects	Stimuli	Responses
1. Stimulus uniqueness	Single group	>1	$\geqq 1$	1. Individual uniqueness	>1 Group	1	$\geqq 1$
2. Stimulus consistency	Single group	1	>1	2. Individual consistency	1	>1	>1

physiological effects; to study such mechanisms, he must deal with reproducible (i.e., consistent) response patterns. Most theories of emotion are predicated on an assumption of stimulus consistency. Wenger, F. N. Jones, and M. H. Jones (1956, pp. 344ff.), for example, believe that there are a few discrete emotional states. In terms of an SR-specificity model, Wenger's theory means that there are a few unique classes of stimuli, and that within each class one can find a high degree of stimulus consistency.

A note of caution should be interpolated here. A measure of stimulus consistency can also be a measure of group similarity: i.e., to the extent that a stimulus evokes the same hierarchy of responses from one subject to the next, it is a consistent stimulus; to the extent that the hierarchy of responses is the same from one subject to the next, it is a homogeneous group. The application of this technique as an index of group homogeneity or of stimulus consistency will depend upon two factors: (a) the intent of the investigator—whether he is interested in measuring the specific properties of stimuli or whether he is more concerned with the characteristics of the group, and (b) how many stimuli and groups one uses to test his hypothesis—the only way to differentiate between a consistent stimulus and a homogeneous group is to test to see that either the group homogeneity is stable for many different kinds of stimuli or the stimulus consistency is stable for many different kinds of groups.

There is another concept of stimulus specificity closely related to the concept of similarity of total response patterns. It is often interesting to abstract one response from the total pattern because of its position in the hierarchy. In particular, it is useful to look at the response that is maximally evoked most frequently. An investigator would do this in a psychophysiological experiment if he were interested in selecting a stimulus (or situation) with a particular effect on heart rate, blood pressure, or some other response that was important in his experiment. The cardiac reflex occurring during diving (Elsner, Franklin, Van Citters, & Kenney, 1966) is one example of a maximal response that can be abstracted from the response hierarchy. The deceleration of heart rate that occurs consistently during

a reaction time foreperiod (Lacey, 1959, pp. 160–208) is probably part of a hierarchy of autonomic responses and probably has a stable position within that hierarchy.

Individual Specificity

The second broad class of specificities is that related to idiosyncratic responses. Whereas the essential characteristic of stimulus specificity is a group of subjects, the essential characteristic of individual specificity is a single subject.

Individual uniqueness   One concept of individual specificity (individual uniqueness) derives from the notion that it is feasible to collect a number of individuals into a group because they have similar characteristics, thereby creating a sort of super-individual. Often such a group is called an experimental group; the individual members of it are similar because they have all been subjected to the same experimental pretreatment. The concept of individual specificity arises because we think the subjects in our group will react differently from a control group to experimental treatment or a single stimulus. The experimental conditions necessary to demonstrate this form of individual specificity are three: two or more groups, each of which has certain, independently defined traits; a single stimulus; and a response or set of response measures (Table 14.1, B1).

There are at least two important differences between this concept of individual specificity and the concepts of stimulus specificity, which also deal with collections of individuals. First, if one is studying the properties of a *stimulus,* then one selects subjects who represent the general population; i.e., the subjects are assumed to be a random sample of the species. If, however, one is testing a hypothesis about certain kinds of *subjects,* then one chooses subjects for their similarities; i.e., the subjects are assumed to be a random sample of a specified subpopulation of the species. One difference between these concepts, then, is the difference in the way subjects are selected, which is based upon the intent of the investigator.

A second difference between the concepts of stimulus specificity and this concept of individual specificity lies in the experimental design: when the investigator tests for *stimulus uniqueness,* he uses one group of subjects and more than one stimulus. In the case of individual uniqueness the experimenter will use only one stimulus and more than one group of subjects. When an investigator tests for *stimulus consistency,* he uses one stimulus and one group of subjects. Thus, in the case of individual specificity, the crucial factors are that the investigator uses more than one group of subjects and it is his intent to differentiate among the groups.

This concept of individual specificity is a relatively common one, since it entails taking two or more groups of subjects, exposing them to the same stimulus, and then comparing their responses. The principle underlies medical diagnostic tests such as the "cold pressor" test, the "glucose tolerance" test, and the "Masters two-step" test. Moos and Engel (1962) revealed such individual uniqueness when they showed that patients with hypertension react more in blood pressure than patients with rheumatoid arthritis, whereas arthritic patients showed more reaction in the muscles spanning symptomatic joints than did hypertensive patients.

Individual consistency   The concept of stimulus specificity just cited, namely, that a single stimulus will evoke a consistent hierarchy of responses from a group of subjects, has a counterpart in individual specificity: a single individual will emit a consistent hierarchy of responses to a set of stimuli. The necessary experimental conditions to demonstrate this concept of specificity are therefore three: (a) a single individual, (b) a set of stimuli to which the individual is exposed, and (c) a set of responses (Table 14.1, B2).

The two concepts of stimulus and individual consistency may seem mutually contradictory but in fact they are independent. In the case of stimulus specificity, the experimental design requires a single stimulus, a group of subjects, and a set of response measures. Operationally, the demonstration of individual specificity requires a single subject, a set of stimuli, and a set of response measures. Therefore, both designs call for a set of response measures; in one case a single stimulus and a group of subjects are needed, while in the other a single subject and a group of stimuli are needed.

There is an important parallel between the concepts of individual and stimulus consistency. Earlier,

the distinction was made between consistency of the total response pattern and consistency in terms of the response that is maximally evoked. This distinction is especially important in the case of individual specificity because of its relationship to psychosomatic disease. When Lacey, Bateman, and Van Lehn (1953) first called attention to the concept of individual specificity, they distinguished between the similarity of total response patterns and the similarity in maximal response by referring to the former as "response stereotypy," and the latter as "response specificity." Malmo and Shagass (1949) used the term "symptom specificity" to refer to an individual's tendency to respond maximally in the same function, irrespective of the stimulus. Others have used the term "organ specificity" to refer to this phenomenon (Alexander, 1950, p. 69). The basic point all these investigators have attempted to make is that an individual tends to overreact in some physiological or psychological modality, irrespective of the situation. In the case of some individuals, this overreactivity is so consistent and marked that it is almost pathognomonic. For example, Malmo and Shagass (1949) have shown that the degree to which a psychiatric patient will react to a painful stimulus is related to the response measure that the investigator studies: the reaction is greatest in the modality about which the patient complains most. Engel and Bickford (1961) have shown that patients with essential hypertension react more in terms of systolic blood pressure (but not in other modalities such as heart rate, skin temperature, or galvanic skin response) to a series of stimuli than do normal subjects.

SOME INTERESTING PROBLEMS

In this section I shall consider two questions that are relevant to the response specificity principle: (a) the origins or bases of specific behavior, and (b) other kinds of psychophysiological responses to which the principles of response specificity might be applied.

The Origins of Specific Behavior

It should be clear from the outset that the definitions of specificity do not imply any etiology. Specific behavior could be innate or acquired or both. Although there is a tendency to consider stimulus-specific behavior as innate, and individual-specific behavior as acquired, neither of these relationships is necessary. An example of a stimulus-specific response that is acquired would be a conditioned response. In order to qualify as a specific stimulus, however, a conditional signal would have to have an equivalent significance for a large number of persons. Examples of such conditional signals would be traffic signals and fire alarms. Examples of individual-specific responses that are innate would be inborn errors such as familial dysautonomia, which affects responses mediated by the autonomic nervous system; and Huntington's chorea, which affects responses mediated by the somatic nervous system. An example of an acquired, individual-specific response would be a conditioned response. In contrast to a conditioned, stimulus-specific response, a conditioned, individual-specific response would be one with little generality (to other persons). Almost every laboratory-conditioned stimulus has this property.

Apart from specific responses that are known to be innate, very little is known about the origin of response specificities. A great deal has been written about the origins of IR specificity because of the relevance of IR specificity to psychosomatic disease; a great deal has been written about the origin of SR specificity because of the relevance of SR specificity to emotion. However, in neither case is much known. One major handicap to studies of etiology has been the fact that too much attention has been directed to human problems and not enough to animal research. It is very difficult to do longitudinal human studies, and even these may not answer the questions of origin unless siblings and parents, as well as propositi, are studied. This can be done in other animals. Ader (1963), for example, has done some fine work on the etiology of stress-induced gastric ulcers in the rat. Another area in which some potentially rewarding research could be done is in the role of imprinting on response specificity. What are the psychophysiological responses to an imprinted stimulus? Do different imprinted stimuli have similar effects?

Other Applications of the Specificity Principle

This chapter has dealt exclusively with the question of response specificity; however, it should be clear that the specificity principle could be generalized beyond responses. For example, Lacey, Bateman, and Van Lehn (1953) have referred to autonomic tension scores, by which they meant autonomic activity (in contrast to reactivity considered here). Another function that might have unique or consistent properties would be recovery from stimulation. Each of these functions—level, response, and recovery—present interesting problems for study. Conceptually, all are independent, although psychophysiologically they may be interrelated in important ways.

REFERENCES

ADER, R. Plasma pepsinogen level as a predictor of susceptibility to gastric erosions in the rat. *Psychosomatic Medicine,* 1963, **25,** 221–232.

ALEXANDER, F. *Psychosomatic medicine, its principles and applications.* New York: Norton, 1950.

AX, A. F. The physiological differentiation between fear and anger in humans. *Psychosomatic Medicine,* 1953, **15,** 433–442.

AX, A. F. Goals and methods of psychophysiology. *Psychophysiology,* 1964, **1,** 8–25.

EDELBERG, R., & WRIGHT, D. J. Two galvanic skin response effector organs and their stimulus specificity. *Psychophysiology,* 1964, **1,** 39–47.

ELSNER, R., FRANKLIN, D. L., VAN CITTERS, R. L., & KENNEY, D. W. Cardiovascular defense against asphyxia. *Science,* 1966, **153,** 941–949.

ENGEL, B. T. Stimulus-response and individual-response specificity. *Archives of General Psychiatry,* 1960, **2,** 305–313.

ENGEL, B. T., & BICKFORD, A. F. Response specificity: Stimulus-response and individual-response specificity in essential hypertensives. *Archives of General Psychiatry,* 1961, **5,** 478–489.

ENGEL, B. T., & MOOS, R. H. The generality of specificity. *Archives of General Psychiatry,* 1967, **16,** 574–581.

LACEY, J. I. Psychophysiological approaches to the evaluation of psychotherapeutic process and outcome. In E. A. RUBINSTEIN & M. B. PARLOFF (Eds.), *Research in psycho-*

therapy. Vol. 1. Washington, D.C.: National Publishing Co., 1959.

LACEY, J. I., BATEMAN, D. E., & VAN LEHN, R. Autonomic response specificity: An experimental study. *Psychosomatic Medicine,* 1953, **15,** 8–21.

MALMO, R. B., & SHAGASS, C. Physiologic study of symptom mechanisms in psychiatric patients under stress. *Psychosomatic Medicine,* 1949, **11,** 25–29.

MOOS, R. H., & ENGEL, B. T. Psychophysiological reactions in hypertensive and arthritic patients. *Journal of Psychosomatic Research,* 1962, **6,** 227–241.

STERNBACH, R. A. *Principles of psychophysiology.* New York: Academic, 1966.

WENGER, M. A., JONES, F. N., & JONES, M. H. *Physiological psychology.* New York: Holt, Rinehart and Winston, 1956.

Elizabeth Duffy*

ACTIVATION†

15

The description of behavior at a given moment requires the consideration of two basic aspects: (a) *direction,* approach or withdrawal with respect to persons, things, ideas, or any aspect of the environment; and (b) *activation, arousal,* or *intensity,* terms that are used as synonyms. As I have suggested (Duffy, 1934, 1941, 1949, 1951, 1957, 1962), especially in the 1941, 1949, and 1962 references, both the observation of behavior and the analysis of current psychological concepts suggest that these are the *only basic* ways in which behavior shows variation, although for a complete description of behavior, subheads of these cate-

*The editors, as do all of her colleagues, deeply regret the death of Dr. Duffy while this book was in production and before the final revision of this chapter. We wish to thank her co-worker, Dr. Robert Eason, for his advice and assistance.

†This project was supported by a grant from the research Council of the University of North Carolina at Greensboro, for which I should like to express appreciation.

A number of persons have assisted me in the work. Undergraduate students Sally Howard and Teresa Martin Leonhardt did much of the bibliographical work, and Donna Setzer assisted more recently. Graduate students Barbara Gold and John Reitzel helped in a very substantial way. I should like to thank Mr. Reitzel for assisting in the writing of a portion of the section on performance and Mrs. Gold for similar assistance on a portion of the discussion of individual differences, as well as for general supervision of the arrangement of the bibliography. My daughter, Elizabeth Bridgers, aided in the copying and revision of part of the manuscript. Mrs. Marjorie Ray and Miss Elizabeth Booker were most helpful and competent typists.

Dr. Robert Eason, of this department, was kind enough to read the manuscript for me.

gories are required. A few possible subheads have been mentioned, but no complete schema for behavioral description has as yet been worked out and published. Arguments have, however, been presented for the desirability of revising psychological concepts when they are employed for scientific purposes, as opposed to their use in general communication, which does not require the exactitude of scientific investigation.

The direction of behavior (goal direction) and the activation of behavior can be operationally defined: they apply to both overt and covert behavior; they interact with each other, yet can be measured separately; and they appear to constitute a good starting point for the terminology of a science of psychology. A complete psychology would specify both the antecedents and the consequents of the direction and the activation of the organism, as well as descriptive subheads under each of these basic categories. Many of our present concepts fit under these headings without change. Others are ambiguous or overlapping and should be abandoned in favor of more precise concepts. The references cited above discuss this topic.

The purpose of this chapter is to discuss the concept of activation, to counter some of the arguments that have been raised against it, and to cite some representative studies not included in my earlier publications. The concept that has been questioned appears to be that of an overall, undifferentiated activation of the sympathetic nervous system as described by Cannon (1915), which is scarcely related to the concept of activation as I presented it in 1962.

THE CONCEPT OF ACTIVATION

An individual, i.e., an organism as a whole, is sometimes excited, sometimes relaxed, and sometimes in one of a variety of intermediate conditions. Those obvious states suggested the concept of activation or arousal, which attempts to describe the physiology of these conditions and to consider their causes and effects.

Activation refers not to the overt activity of the organism but to the release of energy into various internal physiological systems, in preparation for overt activity. The overt activity need never occur; if it does, activation is its constant internal accompaniment and sustainer. Activation is not synonymous with "vitality," with the "ready availability of preparatory energy," or with "overt activity," although the first two are essential antecedents and the latter a usual outcome.

Activation is both general and specific (Duffy, 1962, Ch. 5). Changes constantly occur in the physiological functioning of the organism as it lives and meets, as best it can, the demands of the situations in which it finds itself. Since situations vary, the patterning of activation must necessarily vary to adjust to the particular conditions of the moment (Duffy, 1962, p. 83). A specific action requires a particular group of muscular movements, together with supporting internal conditions, including appropriate visceral and neural activities. Any change in the situation to which the organism is responding might be expected to cause, to some degree, a change in one or more of the systems of the organism. The same statement might be made in regard to any change in an attitude or a set for a particular kind of action. Dewey (1895), for example, has considered attitudes to be "reduced movements." The number of different patterns of physiological response employed by an organism must, then, be staggering in number.

A stimulus-response psychology that attempted to correlate physiological changes with every change in the stimulus situation (whether such a situation is described objectively or as presumed to be perceived by the organism) would be an endless, and therefore useless, list of particularities. Serving to multiply the infinite are the many factors of concomitant and of previous events that may alter the significance, or "cue-function," of the situation for the individual and the continual activity of the various systems of an organism. However, we would not deny that some grouping of situations may be useful in the study of physiological changes. For example, the patterning of physiological conditions in "approach" responses may be different from that in "withdrawal" responses. So-called "anger in," where the anger is not expressed, may differ in physiological patterning from "anger out," where expression is given to the individual's tendencies toward action. Both of these may be special cases of a broader principle: arousal accompanied by inhibition may show different patterning from arousal expressed overtly.

None of these facts or probabilities negates, however, the fact with which we are primarily concerned here, that whatever the patterning of the activation may be, the organism as a whole is more highly activated at some times than at others. Activation varies in *degree,* from a low point in deep sleep to a high point in extreme excitement. Intermediate degrees of activation represent intermediate effects of stimulus situations or conditions of the organism. There appears to be no point on the continuum of activation at which we can say, "Here sleep begins," or "Here emotion begins"; instead, continuous variation is the rule.

The changes that occur in the various physiological systems vary from time to time and from person to person. These changes will be discussed more fully later. It is equally certain that within an individual what is going on in one system is related to what is going on in another. The organism is, indeed, *integrated,* as Sherrington and other neurologists pointed out many years ago. Our problem, not yet near solution, is to discover to what extent and in what way the functioning of one system depends upon that of another, then to relate the integrated functioning of the organism to its stimulus antecedents and its response consequents. In this we may be sure that the functioning of the various systems is not basically dissociated under usual conditions. Such a situation, which would cause the organism to be highly aroused in one system and extremely relaxed in another, would probably only occur momentarily to maintain homeostasis.

So far we have here merely assertions, or logical argument. Evidence will follow. Unfortunately, the evidence is not always as clear-cut as one might wish. The field of investigation is relatively new and is beset with many problems. Only a few pioneers such as Darrow and Davis have worked in this area for a long time, consistently and carefully, although others are following now. What we do not know about basic problems is so great as almost to discourage the application of physiological measurements to areas in which they assuredly are of great practical importance. Yet the amazing fact is that, even with our very incomplete knowledge, practical application has usually proved rewarding.

Activation may be conceived of as a physiological intervening variable, produced by certain factors and resulting in certain effects upon various aspects of response. Activation is controlled by the neurohumoral system. (See Duffy, 1962, Ch. 3, for a detailed discussion.) Fortunately, knowledge of the functioning of the nervous system and the endocrine system is increasing daily, requiring us to amplify and modify our statements regarding neurohumoral control. In general, new information has emphasized, not denied, the closeness of the relationship between the functioning of the cortex and the subcortex, the somatic nervous system and the autonomic nervous system, and the endocrine system and the nervous system. Moreover, increased knowledge of the effects of drugs has further emphasized the importance of chemical factors in behavior. While some drugs appear to have predominantly stimulating (activating) effects upon behavior, and other drugs to have predominantly relaxing effects, the problem is far more complex than this statement suggests. Therefore, no attempt will be made to discuss the effect of drugs upon activation beyond stressing its great importance, particularly because of the successful use of drugs in the treatment of mental disorders. In fact, the study of drugs and of biochemical factors in general holds forth the hope of an ultimate understanding of behavior in chemical terms, even if the chemical condition may result from external environmental factors. (See Chapter 21.)

In the present chapter I shall discuss what the concept of activation now means. Although complete coverage of the literature was not possible, and even all of that covered could not be included, the studies cited are, I believe, reasonably representative of those that have been reported in English.

The concept of "activation" or "arousal" did not arise in the first instance from the work of electroencephalographers; they made the terms familiar by applying them to a certain pattern of the electroencephalogram (EEG) and made the concept plausible to many psychologists, who withheld acceptance of physiological and behavioral evidence until it was anchored in newly discovered aspects of the functioning of the nervous system. Prominent among the electroencephalographers who helped to advance the concept was Lindsley (1951, pp. 473–516; 1952) with his "activation theory of emotion" and detailed speculations about a continuum of psychological phenomena that might correspond to a similar continuum in the EEG. Both of these proposals had previously been made, using the term "energy mobilization" (Duffy, 1934, 1941a, 1941b, 1949, 1951).

Earlier, several investigators had been impressed with the organismic character of the excitation of the individual. Féré (1900) had been interested in what he called "dynamogenesis," or the energizing effect of increased muscular tension upon a wide variety of responses. Cannon (1915), in describing the physiological changes occurring during the excited "emotions," suggested a general increase in energy as one of the results. A discussion of the history of the concept may be found in Duffy (1966, pp. 278–281). A construct of this sort appears to account for the fact that an organism considered as a whole is sometimes excited, sometimes relaxed, and sometimes in one of a variety of intermediate conditions, even though the various systems of the organism may not be equally activated at a given moment. In fact, a thorough consideration of physiological functioning might indicate that no expectation of an equal degree of activation in different systems at a given moment would be reasonable, since different systems vary in the latency of their responses. Some systems operate in an antagonistic fashion to maintain homeostasis. Different situations, or interpretations of situations, may require maximal activity in different parts of the organism to secure an effective response.

It appears to the writer that the basic problems of activation at the present time rest in the area of methodology: (a) What should be measured and at what intervals (based on a physiological rationale)? (b) What techniques are adequate for such measurement? (c) How may measurements from different systems be combined to indicate overall activation, albeit not massive and undifferentiated? Despite the present imperfect measures and inadequate answers, almost staggering numbers of meaningful relationships have been reported between such measures as are now in use and an extremely wide variety of responses. Activation seems to be related to almost any response an organism gives. It apparently can be modified by almost anything done to the organism, such as observable stimulation (including drugs), or by the

organism, such as the symbolic activities of attending or thinking.

THE MEASUREMENT OF ACTIVATION

The most difficult and intricate of our problems is that of measurement. A wide variety of physiological measures has been employed, often obtained in different ways, and with results that have been conflicting. Nevertheless, on the whole, the concept of activation as a basic parameter of behavior seems to have survived very well.

Almost any physiological response might be considered an indicator (rough or refined) of the degree of activation. Among those that have been most frequently employed are measures of the brain potentials, muscle potentials, electrical conductivity of the skin, heart rate and blood pressure, temperature, and vasoconstriction and dilation of the extremities. More recently, there has been investigation of relationships with rapid eye movements (REM), the free fatty acid content of the blood, and other physiological conditions. Respiration has been used less frequently, no doubt because of the conflicting results of different investigators (Altschule, 1953). Techniques of measurement will not be discussed in detail here—they are covered in Chapter 3. Some discussion of measurement is necessary, however, for the concept of activation is an operational one.

Muscle action potentials continue to show a relation to situations that presumably involve a need for greater effort or activation. (For more details, see Chapter 8 and Duffy, 1962.) Muscle tension tends to be localized in that part of the body which will be most directly involved in making the response (Davis, 1939, 1952). Nevertheless, it spreads to other parts of the body. The squeezing of a hand dynamometer produced activity in the muscles of the arm, hand, and the leg on the opposite side of the body; in the foot on the same side of the body; and in the jaw, mouth, nose, ear, abdomen, chest, and neck (Shaw, 1938). Subjects instructed to relax the right arm during mental multiplication relaxed the muscles of other parts of the body as well (Davis, 1939). Apparently, more generalization of muscle tension occurs during stronger responses than during weaker ones

(Meyer, 1953), and during the early stages in the learning of a performance, which are probably in most cases accompanied by stronger responses (Daniel, 1939; Freeman, 1931). It seems probable, although not experimentally verified, that children show more diffuse tension than adults.

The search for "a most differentiating" muscle with respect to the general degree of muscular tension has led to various speculations. Duffy, at one time, following the suggestions of B. Johnson (1928), thought that the muscles involved in expression such as the hand muscles and perhaps those connected with speech might be most significant for sampling general muscle tension. Malmo, at one time, favored the frontalis muscle. More recently, Eason and Branks (1963) have reported that tension in the splenius and trapezius muscle of the back of the neck shows the same changes as the combination of the changes shown in the frontalis muscle, the trapezius muscle of the shoulder, and the forearm flexor of the right arm, at least during the task being performed in the investigation. Laville and Wisner (1965) found that, in all of 13 subjects working for 2 hr on a task involving precision and speed of movements, the general muscle tension (EMG) of the neck muscles increased progressively. The integrated EMG correlated with the subjective stress of the situation and was a more precise indicator of the situation than was posture or heart rate. Sheer and Kroeger (1961, pp. 116–144) stated, "The neck muscles appear to be key indicators of the general level of muscular tonus [p. 135]," although they also said that there was differential activity in muscle groups in various parts of the body.

The electrical resistance of the skin, or its reciprocal, conductance, which appears to be the better unit of measurement, has long been one of the most popular indicators of arousal. Most studies have used the Féré method, in which a minute electric current passes through the body; but recently, the Tarchanoff method, which employs no external current, has become increasingly popular. In both methods electrodes are placed upon the skin and differences in potential between two points are recorded. Wilcott (1958), like Jeffress (1928), found a high degree of correspondence between the skin resistance response (SRR, GSR)

and the skin potential response (SPR) but he was unable to find any relationship between the base levels of the two measures or between skin potential responses and the skin potential base level. While greater care is required in its measurement, the Tarchanoff method eliminates the problem of the polarization of the skin between the electrodes (Venables & Sayer, 1963). Sheer and Kroeger (1961, pp. 116–144) consider the Féré method, which is the more often used, to be more dependable. For further discussion of skin conductance, skin potentials, and sweating, see Wilcott (1959, 1962a, 1962b, 1965, 1966), Rachman (1960), Duffy (1962), Leiderman and Shapiro (1964), Broughton, Poire, and Tassinari (1965), Burnstein, Fenz, Bergeron, and Epstein (1965), Hume and Claridge (1965), Surwillo (1965), and Chapter 9 of this book.

The electroencephalogram, a measure of electrical potentials of the brain detected by electrodes placed on the scalp, has often been used as an indicator of activation. The frequency of the waves of the EEG is the measure most widely used, although amplitude, which usually varies with frequency, has also been studied. Darrow (1952) considered the relative strength or dominance of activity in various areas of the brain to be significant. He and Hicks reported that "EEG leading in anterior and central brain areas is found to characterize conditions of arousal (Darrow & Hicks, 1965)." Eason, Aiken, White, and Lichtenstein (1964) consider *evoked* potentials of the brain to be useful as a measure of activation.

Using electronic analysis of the data, Daniel (1966) has examined the many parameters of the EEG during relaxation, attention, arousal (hyperventilation), recovery, and relief (information that the session would be terminated). He reported that no single parameter matched his predicted model, a continuum correlated with the degrees of behavioral arousal incurred by the conditions described above. Statistically significant differences between conditions supported the hypothesis when he employed "correlograms of occipital recordings after interpretation by relative power ratios [p. 146]." Correlogram ratios analyze complex patterns of the EEG by measuring the total power, power at the dominant frequency, power at nondominant frequencies, synchronization, and rhythm. Thus the correlogram ratios represented multiparameter results and showed the value of going beyond single characteristics such as amplitude or frequency. Daniel suggested that "arousal as seen in the EEG is primarily a matter of the relative loss of power at the dominant frequency and a deterioration of its wave shape [p. 159]." His findings did not support the uniqueness of low voltage, fast activity to arousal. He pointed out that Elliott (1964) has shown that amplitudes of alpha and beta waves are positively, rather than negatively, correlated. If his findings are unchallenged, the interpretation of the relationship between characteristics of the EEG and activation must be somewhat revised. Duffy (1962) has discussed the earlier interpretations (see also Chapter 7 of this book).

Heart rate, blood pressure, vasoconstriction, and respiration have also been measured as indices of activation, as will be discussed later in the chapter.

Body temperature, which rises with increased activation, and skin temperature may indicate the degree of activation. The skin temperature usually falls in the hands and feet if the subject is immobile, but may rise in other parts of the body such as the face. These findings are reviewed in Duffy (1962). Teichner (1962), who has been particularly interested in the study of temperature, believes that the "thermal arousal index," a ratio of the difference between body and skin temperature to the difference between skin and air temperature, is an important index of activation. Values of the ratio that are greater than 1.00 are said to reflect most, if not all, other physiological changes that are indicators of arousal. This is because alterations in heat balance produce changes in the heart rate, the respiratory rate, and the thermal and electrical conductivity of the skin. Teichner suggested that consideration of any single one of the common arousal indices without relation to the total thermal regulatory process may have been responsible for the development of the concept of "autonomic response specificity" and for the failure of studies of metabolic rate to bear fruit. Teichner and Youngling (1962) reported that cold-acclimatized rats showed greater response strength and a higher metabolic rate than did rats acclimatized to optimal temperature conditions. They conclude, "This is consistent with a theoretical approach which ap-

peals to a concept of arousal level or generalized drive strength and suggests metabolic rate as an underlying factor. It is not consistent with an approach which makes no appeal to a generalized drive type of concept [p. 326]."

The free fatty acid (FFA) component of the blood plasma is said to be remarkably sensitive to the arousal of the individual (Eisdorfer, 1966). Powell, Eisdorfer, and Bogdonoff (1964) referred to studies indicating that lipid mobilization in man is strongly influenced by a number of neurohumoral factors. As a result of the activity of the autonomic nervous system and the adrenal medulla, adrenaline and noradrenaline release FFA into the blood stream. Their analysis of the FFA content of blood showed that the level of FFA of each of 48 subjects declined during control phases of an experiment and increased considerably after the beginning of a learning task. They concluded that "in the non-exercising nonobese, fasted individual, the higher the concentration of plasma FFA, the greater the degree of neurohumoral activation [p. 194]."

There are three significant, related aspects for most, if not all, measures employed: (a) the *level* of functioning, (b) changes or *fluctuations* in functioning, whether experimentally induced or called "spontaneous," and (c) the *recovery time* before the measure returns to its prestimulus level. Each of these has been shown in one or more studies to correlate with various aspects of behavior (discussed in Duffy, 1962).

In the measurement of changes in the level of functioning, the level from which the change takes place affects the extent of change. To take an example from the pioneer work of Dodge (1913), if we are to know the significance of a change in pulse rate when a man stands, we must know whether he was previously sitting or running. More recently, there has been a number of discussions involving the relation of a response to its base level, the problem Wilder (1957) called the law of initial value (LIV). Most investigators (e.g., Ellson, Davis, Saltzman, & Burke, 1952; Seward & Seward, 1935) have suggested that the relationship of a response to its base level, e.g., the GSR to the level of skin conductance from which it occurs, is linear, with less response at higher levels of conductance. Others have suggested that it may be curvilinear, with the greatest response occurring at intermediate levels of conductance (Duffy, 1962, interpreting the data of Staudt & Kubis, 1948), or may not apply to a given measure of change.

Surwillo and Arenberg (1965), measuring the heart rate, suggested that the regression effect must be taken into account when studying the LIV and that a control group is needed before applying the LIV model to any given data. When this was done, the law did not hold for their data. They suggested that this procedure also be applied to the results of Hord, L. C. Johnson, and Lubin (1964). In studies of the heart rate and respiration, these investigators observed that the usual finding, that stimuli increase the respiration and heart rate, held only to a point. Subjects who had prestimulus values above that point tended to show what Wilder (1957, p. 84) called "paradoxical" reactions—a decrease in the level of the measure rather than an increase when a stimulus is presented. Hord, L. C. Johnson, and Lubin referred to this as the crossover point, a term Bridger and Reiser (1959) had applied to the point "where the regression line crosses the line of equality." Hord, L. C. Johnson, and Lubin also found that skin temperature and skin conductance did not follow the LIV: the higher the prestimulus skin conductance, the greater was the GSR, while the skin temperature response was essentially unrelated to the prestimulus level.

PHYSIOLOGICAL SYSTEMS AS MEASURES OF ACTIVATION

The Interrelation of Measures of Activation

One of the more difficult questions for activation theorists is the degree to which various systems are integrated in their activation. One would not, of course, expect activation in all systems to be the same under all conditions. The current theory of dissociation of systems (J. I. Lacey, 1967, pp. 14–42), however, seems to be more untenable than the general activation theory that it questions. Determining the *degree* of generality and the *degree* of specificity of activation confronts us with problems of measurement, referred to earlier. These are seldom taken into account in the data available for drawing conclusions. For example, we know that the various responses with which we are concerned

vary in their latency, both for the beginning of the response and for the maximal response (Davis, Buchwald, & Frankmann, 1955; J. I. Lacey, 1956). Yet, experimentally, when they are compared and correlated with each other after simultaneous recording during continuous measurement, generally the correlations have been based on the value of each measure at a given instant in time, whether this finds one measure at its peak, another still on the rise, and a third perhaps beginning to decline, or even having returned to its level prior to stimulation. Taking measures during a resting or no-stimulation state does not solve the problem, for there is always stimulation, endogenous if not exogenous. It would appear more logical to use the peak response of each measure, taking into account the differences in the latencies of various systems and letting adequate time elapse after the presentation of a stimulus. Perhaps the degree of change that first appears after the stimulus, the recovery time, or some other indicator may be more reasonable.

We are all well aware of the significance of homeostatic mechanisms (Davis, Buchwald, & Frankmann, 1955), yet we seldom combine our measures to reflect this understanding. For example, heart rate and blood pressure may, at least at a certain point, react in a compensatory fashion to maintain homeostasis (Sheer & Kroeger, 1961, pp. 116–144), making it seem reasonable to combine these measures in some appropriate way, rather than consider them independently. Respiratory measures, which depend on many factors and apparently are notorious for yielding different results in different investigations, might be more dependable if the respiratory rate were combined with the amplitude, giving a measure of oxygen consumption. This has been done in some instances.

Integration of physiological systems is seen in Darrow and Graf's demonstration (1945) that cerebral vasodilation is associated with conditions which lead to increased potentials of fast waves in the EEG, while vasoconstriction is associated with conditions which lead to increased potentials of slow waves and decreased fast activity. They suggested that alpha rhythm depends on the maintenance of constrictor tone in the cerebral blood vessels and the resonant circuit between the cortical and subcortical centers; and on either increased sympathetic activity, coupled with the inhibition of parasympathetic activity, increased sympathetic activity alone, or the inhibition of parasympathetic activity alone. Bonvallet, Dell, and Hiebel (1954) confirmed their findings by showing parallel changes in the level of sympathetic tone and in the electrical activity of the cortex. Since the functioning of the central nervous system depends significantly on somato-visceral feedback influences, it is indeed difficult to conceive of the dissociation of these systems.

Evidence from many sources (see Duffy, 1962, Ch. 3) shows the close interrelation of functioning between the cortex and subcortex, and between these and peripheral responses, both those controlled most directly by the autonomic nervous system and those having more direct cortical control. Only a distorted picture of the functioning of the organism can be obtained by considering the functioning of the autonomic nervous system separately from the functioning of the cortex, or that of the cortex separately from that of the autonomic nervous system.

Since many studies have cited the influence of the autonomic nervous system (including endocrine secretions) upon the functioning of the cortex, it may be well to call attention to the fact that Gellhorn (1964) showed that *proprioceptive* discharges increase sympathetic discharges and, by way of collaterals from the specific afferent systems, reach the reticular formation and the hypothalamus, increasing the state of alertness (desynchronization of cortical potentials). The reduction or blocking of these proprioceptive impulses is said to reduce sympathetic discharge, increase parasympathetic discharge, and diminish cortical excitation.

The vast accumulation of evidence of interrelated functioning of the various parts of the organism makes it appear that, unless very limited, any concept of the "dissociation" of systems must be based upon inadequate measurement. Sequential action, for example, does not mean dissociation. The patterning of action, based upon the stimulus situation or the constitution of the individual, does not mean dissociation. It does mean that the individual does not respond as a massive undifferen-

tiated whole, but activation theory has never claimed that he does. Some of the pioneer work on the physiology of the excited "emotions" (Cannon, 1915) suggested massive, undifferentiated response of the sympathetic nervous system. Later theories, built upon this foundation, have taken account of the patterning of activation, including individual differences. The latter were studied most extensively by Lacey and his colleagues (J. I. Lacey, 1950; J. I. Lacey & B. C. Lacey, 1958b, 1962), who have reported that individuals show "idiosyncratic patterns of autonomic activity, in which the different physiological functions are differentially responsive [p. 72]," and that these individual patterns of response tend to be reproducible from one situation to another. Not all individuals maintain a given "hierarchy of response," or are consistently more activated in a particular system than another. However, one group of subjects was said to show a hierarchial ordering of the magnitude of response in systolic blood pressure, diastolic blood pressure, palmar conductance, heart rate, and variability of heart rate, which were reproduced with greater than chance expectancy over a four-year period (J. I. Lacey & B. C. Lacey, 1962). Only a single stress (cold pressor) was used. Individuals differed greatly in stereotypy of response, varying from almost rigid patterns to nearly random patterning of physiological reactions.

Dykman, Ackerman, Galbrecht, and Reese (1963) have reported consistency in individual responses, which they thought might be a function of innate differences in the lability of various systems in the same person. There was more evidence of specificity at initial or low levels of functioning than at high levels. The individuality in the degree of response of different systems tended to disappear and "conformity to the species pattern of mobilization" to appear when the stress was sufficiently great. Wenger, Clemens, Coleman, Cullen, and Engel (1961) also found support for "autonomic response specificity" and attributed it partly to the method of measurement and partly to significant individual differences in resting autonomic system functions. They cautioned against overgeneralizing "the significance and pervasiveness of autonomic response specificity and stereotypy [p. 192]."

At this point we should give further attention

to the question of the correlation of various physiological measures, both within the individual (intracorrelations) and between individuals (intercorrelations). It is obvious that determining the degree of correlation of measures, or at least observing their movement in a predicted direction following stimulation, is crucial for a general theory of activation. Errors in measurement, whether in what is measured or how the measures are treated, reduce the coefficients of correlation. Different investigators have varied greatly in the degree of correlation of measures reported, although almost all agree that a change in the stimulus conditions alters any given measure. We appear to have had little success in determining the best way to combine measures from different systems. In fact, Dykman et al. (1963, p. 54) found "single systems better in yielding consistent relations with psychological variables than combined results across systems." However, it would seem logical that a combination of measures would be preferable if only we knew the correct combination.

Early studies of the relationship of one measure to another used intercorrelations based on groups of subjects. Most of the coefficients of correlation were low, probably for the reasons cited earlier. A few were reported to be moderately high, and a few very high (see Duffy, 1962, Ch. 5). More recently, Venables (1963) has found significant linear correlations of $-.69$ for normal subjects, and $-.39$ for chronic schizophrenics between the skin potential and the electrocardiogram (EKG) amplitude. The reliability of both measures over a one-month period was fairly good, $+0.78$ and $+0.61$, respectively. Waller (1963) reported a high correlation between simultaneous recordings of GSR and thermal reactivity at the finger tips.

Davis, Lundervold, and Miller (1957, p. 57) thought it "legitimate to describe the general response pattern which [their] experimental conditions [tended] to produce, and the particular response patterns which [were] evoked by particular conditions." The general response pattern was described as consisting of "increased flexor and extensor activity [i.e., greater muscle tension], increased sweat gland activity, increased heart rate, peripheral vasoconstriction [finger], and increased respiration rate and amplitude." They commented that "except for the vasoconstriction, this complex is, on a small scale, the pattern which accompanies exercise," and similar to that supposed to be present in "emergency reaction."

Davis, Lundervold, and Miller (1957) had reported low, yet positive, correlations for their eight measures, except for the three that involved the volume pulse. Ford (1957), using the Davis group's data, found rather high correlations of each measure with the remaining seven. His procedure was to compute the rho value when the rank order of each physiological measure was correlated with the averages of the ranks of the remaining seven, re-ranked on the basis of the usual item validity measure of selection. He reported that the coefficient of correlation of each measure with the remaining seven was as follows: skin resistance, .801; EMG flexor, left hand, .71; EMG extensor, left hand, .43; pulse cycle time (time between beats), .50; volume pulse, .69; finger volume (capillary), .69; breathing amplitude, .60; and breathing cycle time, .69. In discussing his findings, he noted that the cardiac cycle is the reciprocal of the heart rate, and that a better measure of cardiac energy is the EKG, which is the product of both the frequency and the amplitude. The relatively low correlation of the electromyogram (EMG) extensor with the other measures may be accounted for by the fact that the extensor is an antagonist of the flexor. He also suggested that the demand for oxygen might better be measured by combining the breathing amplitude with the breathing cycle. When he correlated the product of the breathing amplitude and breathing cycle with the remaining six measures, he found a rho of .99. Ford's findings and his interpretations serve to emphasize the difficulty of determining precisely what should be measured and in what way the measurements should be combined.

Malmo (1959) has suggested that the *intra*individual correlations among physiological measures, rather than the *inter*individual correlations, provide the data crucial for a theory of activation. In other words, if, in a significantly large percentage of individuals, a number of physiological measures show a consistent increase or decrease under changes in stimulus conditions, we may conclude that these measures are indicative of the degree of activation of the individual, even though the *extent* of the change in one measure as compared with that of another is different in different individuals, thus reducing interindividual correlations. And, in fact, a somewhat closer correlation of measures has been found by the few investigators who have studied the intracorrelation of measures or the changes in various physiological responses within a given individual.

Schnore (1959) found that, during tasks of mental arithmetic and visual tracking, in one instance under "low arousal" conditions and in another instance under "high arousal," 56% of the 43 male subjects showed significant correlation among the following measures: EMG (right and left forearms and back of the neck), heart rate, systolic blood pressure, respiration, palmar conductance, skin temperature, and grip pressure. Dykman, Reese, Galbrecht, and Thomasson (1959) reported that individuals tended to maintain their group position in skin resistance, heart rate, and respiration from one stimulus to the next, although the individual's reaction in one autonomic system was not an adequate basis for predicting his reaction in another. Kuno, Golenhofen, and Lienert (1964) have reported that microvibration amplitude (MVA) discriminated intraindividual differences better than differences between subjects. The MVA measures were correlated with action potentials from the muscles and with pulse frequency.

Lazarus, Speisman, and Mordkoff (1963) also urged the use of intracorrelations of measures, rather than correlation across subjects (intercorrelations). Measuring skin conductance and heart rate during two motion picture films, one of which they designated as a "benign" and the other as a "stressor" film, and employing intraindividual correlations with 50 subjects, they found an average algebraic composite correlation across point means of +.545 and a curvilinear correlation (eta) of +.402 for the stressor film, with lower correlations for the control film. Interindividual correlations were lower. The correspondence between measures was sampled about every 10 sec. Again the thought occurs that closer relationships might have been found if a given instant in time had not been employed but, instead, latencies of responses had been taken into account and the peak response for each measure or some other indicator with a better physiological rationale had been employed.

Malmstrom, Opton, and Lazarus (1965) actually did find a closer relationship between the heart rate and skin conductance *within* individuals by employing a different measure of heart rate during the showing of the same films. With continuous recording of the two measures, the heart rate was measured by taking, not the first value in each 15-sec interval, but by taking the highest reading at the peak of each cyclic increase in the heart rate. The number of such peaks in a single 15-sec interval ranged from one to seven. The type of analysis was described as the *method of mean cyclic maxima.* "The group curve was smoothed by a method of moving averages of Order Three to reach a closer estimate of 'true' maximum heart-rate level at each point in time [p. 549]." Graphic analysis showed that the heart rate and skin conductance tended to rise and fall together over time, and that the responses were predictable both in direction and relative magnitude from the characteristics of the stimulus. A suitable method for expressing such relationships quantitatively has not been found, since the usual correlation coefficient requires independence between successive observations and chi-square is sensitive only to direction, not to magnitude. Two types of chi-square analysis were employed. In each, there was a strong tendency for the skin conductance and heart rate to decrease simultaneously. While this simultaneous decrease was strongest (higher value of chi-square), an increase of the heart rate with a concomitant decrease in the skin conductance was the next most frequent outcome, and it held for both the stressor film and the control film. It appears obvious that measurement is still the major problem for activation theory—not merely techniques, but *what* to measure and how to treat the data statistically.

Recent research appears to be concerned less with the coefficients of correlation between measures (a number of these are reported in Duffy, 1962, Ch. 5) and more with the concordance of measures, both among themselves and with the stimulus situation. For example, using 103 psychiatric patients as subjects, each tested on 2 consecutive days, Visser (1963) found a positive correlation between a contingent alpha block produced by combined acoustic and visual stimuli and a conditioned GSR produced by electric shock. For an individual, the intensity of the contingent alpha block was of the same order of magnitude as that of the conditioned GSR. He believed the facts supported the view that there is a characteristic individual degree of conditionability.

A number of negative findings has been reported with respect to the relationship of one physiological measure to another. Kreitman and Shaw (1965) obtained essentially negative results when alpha augmentation was related to arousal, which was defined as increased EMG responses from the forearm and an increase in the dominant alpha rhythm in the EEG. Apparently, there was only a chance association between the two measures selected as the criteria of arousal. Alpha frequency was also unrelated to alpha enhancement of blocking of the alpha rhythm. J. I. Lacey, Kazan, B. C. Lacey, and Moss (1963, pp. 161–196) found that the heart rate and the skin conductance measured as "spontaneous" bursts of activity behaved differently in the same stimulus condition.

In a study of a sleep-deprived subject, L. C. Johnson, Slye, and Dement (1965) concluded that there was a divergence of autonomic activity and central nervous system activity. Several autonomic measures indicated a high degree of arousal. While resting autonomic levels were high, the autonomic response to stimulation apparently was depressed, as was EEG responsiveness. It is of interest that the five autonomic measures employed seemed to move in the same direction with respect to responsiveness, although the degree of their responsiveness was different. From their work it seems likely that the EEG is the best indicator of sleep or near-sleep.

Eason, Harter, and Storm (1964) measured the skin conductance, heart rate, and neck and flexor forearm tension level, while the subjects memorized nonsense syllables under conditions of tension induced in different ways: lifting weights versus squeezing a hand dynamometer, with the amount of induced tension varying from 5 to 20 lb at 5-lb intervals. Correlations of the physiological variables were not significant within the subjects. All four measures showed orderly within-trial and between-trial changes, but the changes varied from decreasing to increasing functions, with individual difference scores unique for each subject. The authors conclude that differences in the level of activation between subjects are not adequately shown

by a single measure and that it is wise to use each individual as his own control in studies in which physiological measures are dependent variables. They also observe the regulating control of somatic and autonomic nervous systems upon each other. This interesting study might have yielded somewhat different results if the measures employed had been considered in relation to their various latency periods and not sampled simultaneously every 20 sec. The amount of induced tension did significantly affect the heart rate and the EMG from the neck and flexor muscles of the forearm. It is strange that no relationship was found with the skin conductance, since there is almost universal agreement that changes in the skin conductance show consistent variation with changes in muscle tension (Duffy, 1962, pp. 94–96). The conductance did show the usual decrease in the course of successive trials. There was also a linear increase in the heart rate, associated with progressive increases in induced muscle tension and a U-shaped change in the neck EMG level as a function of the amount of induced tension in the arm. In addition, the effect of the amount of induced muscle tension on verbal performance was said to resemble an inverted U-shaped curve. More clear-cut results might have been obtained if there had been fewer independent variables in the experiment, some of which have not been described here (even though a balanced Latin square was employed) and if the number of subjects had been greater than 16.

Sternbach (1960c) correlated the percent-time alpha in the records of 42 subjects with a score devised by Wenger for indicating relative autonomic balance through the use of seven measures of peripheral autonomic activity. The score, derived from a factor analytic study, is designed to indicate whether an individual has functional autonomic balance, relative sympathetic dominance, or relative parasympathetic dominance (see Chapter 13 for further discussion). Finding that some persons with apparent sympathetic dominance may show a high alpha index (presumably indicative of a high degree of cortical inactivity), and that some subjects with a relatively low alpha index may show apparent parasympathetic dominance, he remarks that the autonomic nervous system and the central nervous system "cannot be said to respond all of a piece, in the manner of a single effector [p. 611]." The product-moment coefficient of correlation for the two measures was −.179 and was not statistically significant. Nor could any curvilinear relationship be seen. I would certainly not support a theory of massive, undifferentiated activity within the organism, but, if the Wenger measure is indeed an adequate measure of the functioning of the autonomic nervous system, I should expect a somewhat closer relationship between the two measures than that reported. The Wenger factor, however, may not be a valid measure of autonomic functioning. An investigation by Wenger (1957) led him to conclude that it described somewhat less than one-third of each of several populations that he studied. By the criteria he employed for sympathetic and parasympathetic activity, most subjects showed mixed patterns of autonomic functions. In fact, Gellhorn reported evidence (1943) of simultaneous discharge over sympathetic and parasympathetic branches of the autonomic nervous system during excitement, with the sympathetic dominating and masking the effects of the parasympathetic.

When Sternbach (1960a) used 11 measures of autonomic response during various stimulus conditions (startle, cold pressor, exercise, infusion of epinephrine and infusions of norepinephrine) and compared the patterns of response, he found that all the patterns reflected some activation of the sympathetic system. Differences among them were sufficient to negate the concept of undifferentiated massive discharge of the sympathetic nervous system, which Cannon (1915) presented as a characteristic of emergency reactions, or at least to indicate that it is only a first approximation. The direction of startle responses was found to differ from those of cold pressor, exercise, and norepinephrine but was similar to that of epinephrine. The startle pattern was said to suggest "a somewhat general activation of the sympathetic nervous system, but with possible parasympatheticlike activity reflected by stomach contraction period [p. 210]." It seems likely to me that the intensity of response is a factor in determining the degree to which there is general sympathetic activation.

When various autonomic variables were recorded from sleeping subjects during stimulation above the auditory threshold, the responses of the cardiovascular system were not significantly corre-

lated with those of the electrodermal system, although the responses within each of the two systems were significantly correlated with each other (L. C. Johnson & Lubin, 1966). Apparently, sleep acted as a release for the heart rate response and a depressant for electrodermal activity. With the exception of the heart rate, most of the responses were minimal during the stage of 1-REM. Silverman, Cohen, and Shmavonian (1959), on the other hand, found that verbal chastisement had similar effects on GSR measures, blood pressure changes, venous tone, and increases of adrenalin and noradrenalin.

Sheer (1961, pp. 443–444) concludes, "It is clear that there is some relationship between an arousal pattern indicated by EEG and autonomic measures and somatic conditioning. . . . It is equally clear, however, that the relationship is a gross one. . . . Probably an important point to be made here, as Ricci et al. (1957) [pp. 401–415] have clearly demonstrated in a series of experiments, is that rigorous correlations between electrographic events and behavior depend upon a finer analysis of neural activity with microelectrode techniques as contrasted with the gross detection of electrical activity provided in surface records." Here again, the method of measurement appears to be a crucial factor.

Fluctuations in Measures of Activation

The discussion thus far has been concerned chiefly with the *level* of functioning of certain physiological measures and with the *change* in level produced by experimentally manipulated stimulation. Many investigators, including the writer (Duffy, 1932b), have long pointed out the significance of fluctuations in physiological measures. These are currently referred to by some as "spontaneous," because they do not result from stimulation by the experimenter. Such irregular and unpredicted changes may occur in almost any physiological measure, and they have been specifically demonstrated in a number of them, including muscle tension, skin conductance, and heart rate. Whether such fluctuations are merely another indicator of responsiveness, with no peculiar significance of their own, is a matter of some difference of opinion. J. I. Lacey and B. C. Lacey (1958a) reported "spontaneous" fluctuations of the heart rate and the skin resistance during rest as independent of the *level* of these measures, but as characterizing individuals and as correlated with impulsive responses in a discrimination task. I (1932c) found that irregularity (spontaneous changes) of the graphic record of muscle tension (grip pressure) during a discrimination task tended to accompany a high level of tension and to be characteristic of the individual, although the number of subjects was too small to offer dependable evidence. Impulsive responses during the task, or errors of commission rather than of omission, were reliably associated with such fluctuations. Malmo, Shagass, Belanger, and A. A. Smith (1951) found no relationship between the level of muscle tension and fluctuations in the measure. Later, however, Malmo and Smith (1955) reported that measures of motor irregularity, while correlating poorly with measures of muscular tension in the neck and forearm, showed a significant correlation with frontalis-muscle tension. Further discussion of studies of the problem prior to 1960 may be found in Duffy (1962, especially pp. 181–185, 255–266, 308–315).

Sternbach (1960b), measuring skin conductance, and referring to the study by J. I. Lacey and B. C. Lacey (1958b), reported that he could not agree that "tension, lability, balance, and spontaneous fluctuations are distinct dimensions of autonomic activity [p. 433]." He says, "It appears that they are not entirely independent of each other, although their covariation is generally modest [p. 433]." Autonomic balance (computed by the Wenger method described above), when measured during the resting state, was related to both the maximum response level (called lability) and to the prestimulus conductance level. The highest coefficient of correlation in his table was between the prestimulus level of conductance (called tension) and the maximum response level (called response lability)—an r of $+.788$. Subjects showing more spontaneous fluctuations of conductance had a more rapid reaction time (.05 level), but also those with higher prestimulus conductance levels showed faster reaction times at the same level of confidence, so that, for reaction time at least, it would seem to make little difference which measure is employed.

L. C. Johnson (1963) related measures of spontaneous changes in the heart rate and spontaneous GSR to each other and to certain other physiological measures during two different stimulating conditions: (a) the sounding of a tone, and (b) the presentation of a flickering light. A comparison of the types of stimulation revealed a significant relationship for both measures on both occasions, the flicker stimulation producing a rho of .57 for GSR and .72 for HR. Spontaneous GSR and diastolic blood pressure during stimulation by a tone showed a significant rho of .48; spontaneous heart rate during a tone and the same measure during flicker, a rho of .36. The relationship between spontaneous GSR and basal conductance during tone stimulation was represented by a rho of .37 ($p = .01$). Thus, although the agreement among measures was low (not a surprising fact, since neither the spontaneous GSR nor the spontaneous heart rate was very stable over a 48-hr period), some relationship of different physiological measures during the same type of stimulation was shown, a finding more in harmony with the concept of concordance of physiological activity than with that of complete dissociation of systems, although specificity as well as generality of response appeared. Although Johnson concluded that the spontaneous HR and the spontaneous GSR were independent of each other and showed no consistent relationship to the other measures, it is obvious from the data that a number of very interesting relationships did appear, so that one could emphasize at will either the relatedness or the unrelatedness of various measures. Both generality and specificity seem to have been indicated.

The study revealed individual differences, since the subjects could be divided into two groups with respect to spontaneous GSR and spontaneous HR, one group having a highly irregular, labile record and the other a smooth, stabile, regular record. The division held over time and during both stimulation and rest, with stimulation showing greater consistency in the records. This fact led Johnson to make the statement that "the relationships between physiological variables will depend in part upon the state of alertness or level of arousal of the S [p. 421]." Agreement with this conclusion comes easily, if for no other reason than the fact that higher values of the measures, as in greater arousal, provides more room for variability and hence for higher correlations. The writer found, for instance, that grip pressure scores from the used hand produced higher correlations with a number of factors than did scores from the unused hand, where the pressure was less (Duffy, 1932a).

Both Johnson (1963) and Mundy-Castle and McKiever (1953) reported that spontaneous GSR activity showed rapid adaptation (or decrease in the course of the experiment), the labiles showing less adaptation than the stabiles. More initial GSR activity was shown by the labiles, who would be considered by the writer (Duffy, 1962) to be more responsive. Although Johnson found a tendency for GSR labiles to show more reactivity in other autonomic systems also, he expressed the belief that it was unwarranted at this time to infer reactivity from one variable to another. With our present measurements, which appear to be inadequate on many grounds, this conclusion may well seem justified, though not beyond challenge. What to measure, how to measure it, how to test the relationships between measures, and how to treat the findings statistically—these are still our besetting problems. Errors of measurement must inevitably obscure relationships that may exist, rather than produce erroneous evidence of nonexistent relationships. To some extent we may obtain counterbalancing of errors when a large number of subjects is used, but many types of errors cannot be avoided in this way. Refinement of methodology seems essential if physiological measures (peripheral, autonomic, and central) are to fulfill their promise in the study of individuals, both normal and psychopathological. Nevertheless, I believe that even our present methods give more evidence of some degree of generality of response than of unrelated particularity of reaction by the various systems of the individual.

FACTORS AFFECTING ACTIVATION

Situational Influences

Situational influences on activation, referred to earlier, merit further discussion. Evidence of the effect of many different kinds of stimulus situations upon activation is so abundant that only a small portion of the available data and some of the more recent studies will be considered. A fairly extensive discussion of the topic may be found in Duffy (1962, Ch. 4).

Every response of the individual, internal as well as external, is a response to the particular demands of the stimulating situation; therefore, its patterning must vary from one situation to another. To quote from a statement made earlier (Duffy, 1962), "Nicety of adjustment is shown, however, not only in finely graded degrees of activation but also in the locus of activation. A goal-oriented organism, with a particular stimulus to be attended to, or a particular task to be performed in order to reach its goal, not only releases energy in appropriate degree (within the limits of its ability), but also in appropriate places within the organism. An organism set to carry on one type of activity requires a different pattern of activation from an organism set to carry on another type of activity. When, however, instructions to the subject are the same, but the stimulus varies in intensity, the locus of the covert response is likely to remain the same while the degree of activation varies [p. 83]." There follows a lengthy discussion of the patterning of activation and of the conditions under which a greater or a lesser degree of generalization versus localization of activation might be expected. Among the factors considered were the intensity of the response, the stage of learning, the age of the subject, and the relationship of one part or system of the body to another. Other factors emphasized were differences in the latencies of various responses, the role of homeostatic factors, and individual differences in the patterning of responses. Some group studies were also considered.

Measures of muscle tension Starting with activity of skeletal muscle, whose responses are closest to acting upon the external environment, we find an abundance of evidence for variation with the situation. Apparently, muscle tension ranges from a low point in deep sleep to a high point in situations that make heavy demands upon the organism, or may be interpreted to do so. Davis (1956) concluded that there seemed to be complete agreement that any sort of response implied some skeletal-muscle activity. He said, ". . . if we compare doing something with doing nothing (or as near as we can come to the latter) there is a positive relation between muscular activity and the occurrence of any of the activities tested."

A number of studies has shown that sensory stimuli of greater intensity produce more muscle tension than those of lesser intensity (Davis, 1948, 1950, 1953). Merely listening to material being read produced an increase in tension in certain muscles (Smith, Malmo, & Shagass, 1954; Wallerstein, 1954). Talking, as compared with listening, significantly increased tension not only in the chin muscles but also in those of the forehead, the neck, and both arms (Smith, Malmo, & Shagass, 1954).

An increase in the difficulty of number-series problems was accompanied by an increase in action potentials from the muscles of the arm and neck (Davis, 1938), and stepwise increases in the difficulty of mental arithmetic problems were accompanied by increased action potentials from the arm muscles of children for each of five categories of difficulty, except the final one (Shaw & Kline, 1947). Men undergoing flight training showed more grip pressure on the stick during the solo stage of the training and during the maneuvers of takeoff and landing (A. C. Williams, MacMillan, & Jenkins, 1947, p. 46). With habituation to a task, muscular tension decreases (Davis, 1937; Duffy, 1932c). The adaptation of muscle tension to tones is greatest for the most intense stimulus (Davis, Buchwald, & Frankmann, 1955). An opposite effect (i.e., an increase in tension with repetition) occurred when the subjects were listening to auditory stimuli near the threshold (Davis, 1950), perhaps because of increased alertness or an effort to hear sounds that were barely audible.

Further confirmation of the relation between muscle tension and the intensity of the stimulus situation is seen in a study by Eason and White (1961). Tension of the muscles was measured during a tracking task and showed in general that, when subjects attempted to attain a relatively high score, there was greater muscle tension in the neck and in several other muscle groups, including the biceps. The neck muscle showed the least variability from session to session, tended to show the most consistent changes when the level of aspiration was

varied, and therefore seemed to be the best single indicator of effort of those muscles studied. Tension in the neck muscles increased as the task was made more difficult. It decreased from trial to trial during each daily session of tracking (Eason, 1963). The neck muscle alone was found to be as good an indicator of the effort exerted as a combination of tension measures from the neck, shoulder, and arm. Variations in tension during the same task have been proposed as measures of alertness (Kennedy & Travis, 1948; Travis & Kennedy, 1947, 1949).

Depending on the requirements of the situation, muscle tension increases, decreases, or remains unchanged. For example, during the *learning* of a visuo-motor task, pressure on the keys was maintained at a constant level; but during *overlearning* there was a marked decrease in pressure (Ghiselli, 1936). Bills (1930, pp. 75–76), Stroud (1931), Duffy (1932b), and others have found that decreases in muscle tension accompanied the repetition of a performance. Also, as A. A. Smith (1953) reported, immediately after completed tasks, as compared with interrupted tasks, muscle tension showed a greater decrease.

Lundervold (1952) reported that his "labile" subjects showed a considerable increase in muscular activity (as recorded by needle electrodes) when they were angry or irritated, and a decrease when they became calmer. Malmo has pointed out similar effects. The therapeutic progress of patients during a series of psychiatric interviews was said to be associated with a decrease in muscle tension (Malmo, 1954, pp. 84–100). During a brief rest period following a thematic apperception test (TAT), speech-muscle tension was reported to drop rapidly in both the patient and the examiner after the examiner had praised the patient's story, but not after he had criticized it (Malmo, Boag, & A. A. Smith, 1957).

Fluctuations in muscle tension, reported as tremor or as irregular finger pressure, also vary with the stimulus situation. Finger tremor rose rapidly after a loud noise (French, 1944), and more irregular finger pressures accompanied work on more difficult arithmetic problems (Reymert & Speer, 1938–1939). Nervous movements also increase during stress (Olson, 1929; Sainsbury, 1955). The latter investigator made his recordings in the course of a psychiatric interview. In its most intense form, the startle response, there is a widespread and intense contraction of the musculature (Landis & Hunt, 1939).

Electrical conductance of the skin Turning to autonomic indicators of activation, we find evidence that the electrical conductance of the skin also reflects the demands, or the degree of significance, of the situation. During sleep, palmar skin conductance is very low. Changes occur in a continuum. There was found to be no particular moment at which it could be said that sleep had been reached, but, as the subject became more relaxed and drowsy, the skin conductance decreased. By watching changes in the electrical conductance alone, it was possible always to tell when drowsiness was coming over the individual (Kleitman, 1939). Low skin conductance did not occur at a particular moment when consciousness was lost; rather, it was characteristic of a general physiological condition that predisposed a person toward sleep (Darrow & Freeman, 1934). The degree of decrease in resistance was related to some extent to the depth and duration of sleep but appeared to be related to other factors also (Kleitman, 1939). It was reported that individual differences in the tendency to sleep soundly or to sleep lightly were related to the degree of change in this measure (Richter, 1926). Confirmation of these findings occurred in a study in which a graphic record of basal plantar conductance was made during drowsiness, alertness, fitful sleep, and periods of work (Levy, Thaler, & Ruff, 1958). Since the ability to respond to stimuli such as light flashes corresponded closely to the onset of sleep, the electronic monitoring of alertness seemed possible. There were, however, striking individual differences; the conductance of one person when he was asleep was higher than that of another when he was relaxed. It also appears that different stages of sleep show different patterns of autonomic activity (L. C. Johnson, 1965). Thus sleep is no more a uniform condition than the waking state.

Diurnal changes in skin conductance have been reported (Waller, 1919; Wechsler, 1925), as have changes accompanying sleep losses and fatigue from heavy muscular work (Ryan & Ranseen, 1944). However, in one study, the direction of change as a result of fatigue was not consistent for all individuals (Elbel & Ronkin, 1946). Perhaps some persons compensate or overcompensate for the fatigue.

Thermal stimulation, when reported as painful, produced a significant change in skin conductance; a greater incidence of central EEG blocking; a reduction in the amplitude of respiration, followed by an increase; a heart rate increase 40% of the time and a decrease 27% of the time (McKenna, as reported by Darrow, 1965). Blood pressure measures were not employed. The investigator emphasized *pain perception,* rather than the magnitude of the physical stimulus, concluding that the chief determinants of the physiological response to pain were central factors within the subject. In a conditioning experiment with human subjects (Wilson, 1964), basal skin conductance was increased by shock and by the threat of shock. The initially large GSR steadily diminished in the course of the experiment. In the case of rats, there was a significant increase in basal conductance level as a result of shock and a gradual decrease in level, both within a day and across days on 4 consecutive days (Kaplan, 1963).

It has long been known that the galvanic skin response is an excellent indicator of what has been called "emotion," though I think of it as an indicator of the high degree of activation likely to be found at such a time. Music judged to be exciting caused greater GSR responses than that presumed to be of a calming or neutral nature (Zimny & Weidenfeller, 1963). Heart rate measures showed no significant differences. W. Smith (1922) used the GSR as a measure of the emotion aroused by various words, and Bingham (1943) found reliably greater GSRs for words reported as very "meaningful, significant, and important," than for those reported as only slightly so. Murray (1938) and his co-workers made the interesting finding that GSRs accompanying expressions of agreement with the majority of the group in regard to provocative social questions were smaller than those accompanying disagreement; and that "no" responses, even in agreement with the group, elicited larger GSRs than "yes" responses in accord with group opinion.

Many different types of stressful situations have

been found to be related to skin conductance phenomena. Among these are a Ferris wheel ride (Laties, 1959), the telling of a lie (Ellson, Davis, Saltzman, & Burke, 1952), motion pictures showing scenes of danger (where the response of 1-year-olds was greater than that of 16-year-olds), and motion pictures of erotic scenes (where the 9-year-olds showed little response and the 16-year-olds had a strong reaction) (Dysinger & Ruckmick, 1933). A "stressor" film, as compared with a neutral film, produced large and significant increases in the skin conductance and heart rate in college students (Lazarus, Speisman, & Mordkoff, 1963). Skin conductance was the better indicator of changes in the content of various episodes of the film. Darrow (1936) has reviewed a number of studies showing extreme sweat gland activity during anxiety or stress.

Skin conductance changes occur, however, not only during sleep and emotion, but also during conditions that would be presumed to cause an intermediate degree of activation such as the performance of various tasks. Using subjects of wide variation in IQ level and tasks of differing degrees of difficulty, one study showed that all subjects tended to show increased skin conductance in the course of the series of tests (except for the rest period). However, the bright subjects showed the greatest increase in conductance during the most difficult tasks and the educable mentally handicapped showed the greatest increase during the least difficult task. The normal and the bright subjects appeared to be least affected by the task that was most arousing to the educable mentally handicapped (Carrier & Orton, 1964). Probably, the interest in, and the challenge of, the tasks—hence the degree of activation—depended upon the ability of the performer.

A conclusion of this sort is reinforced by a comparison of Navy enlisted men and college students, when biopotential responses were obtained during the learning of three lists of nonsense syllables of varying difficulty (Andreassi & Cavallari, 1965). The enlisted men, but not the college students, showed significant increases in heart rate and skin conductance with the easy lists, as compared with the moderately easy and the difficult lists, defined in terms of association value. Immediately

after making a response, the subject was told whether it was correct. It was believed that the Navy men were "more highly motivated" by success, since they were, on the average, 10 years older than the college students, were further removed from formal schooling, and showed a slower rate of learning. There were only 8 subjects and, in the case of the muscle action potentials, 2 of the subjects had to be omitted; hence it is not surprising that 2 of the measures (GSRs and muscle action potentials) showed nonsignificant changes.

A decline in skin conductance (adaptation) was found during successive presentations of a visual pattern and also during successive exposure of different patterns (Berlyne, Craw, Salapatek, & Lewis, 1963). This was interpreted by the investigators as a relationship between GSR incidence and novelty.

The requirements of the task affect the degree of activation, as shown by subjects learning nonsense syllables, then overlearning them, and finally being given further practice in a condition called "double overlearning," which produced corresponding changes in the three indicators of activation employed (Andreassi & Whalen, 1966). New learning produced an increase in the basal palmar conductance, GSR, and heart rate. All three measures decreased with overlearning, and decreased still further with "double overlearning." It was pointed out that these results were consistent with a study by L. W. Thompson and V. D. Thompson (1965) of EEG responses with overlearning; i.e., the EEG also indicated a decrease in physiological activity with overlearning.

Another study of the learning of nonsense syllables and of word lists (Schönpflug, 1965) led to the report that (a) subjects who *intended* to learn the material showed a rise in the GSR before learning had started; (b) subjects instructed to *learn* the lists, as compared with those instructed merely to *look* at the lists showed higher activation; and (c) subjects learning with distributed practice built up higher levels of GSR than those learning with massed practice.

The importance of task demands in determining the level of activation was also shown by Stern (1964), when a vigil group (reporting autokinetic "movements") was compared with a rest group with respect to skin conductance, heart rate, breathing, and muscle tension. The vigil group had a higher basal level of skin conductance and more spontaneous GSRs, a more rapid heart rate, and a breathing amplitude fluctuating around 100%, while that of the rest group fell. The breathing *rate* did not differentiate the groups. The EMG from the frontalis muscle of the forehead showed a significant decrease during the trials, although two other muscle groups (sternomastoid and forearm extensor) failed to do so. In another study competition increased both the level of palmar skin conductance and self-rated alertness (Church, 1962). When a subject learned the cue that allowed him to avoid an electric shock, there was, on subsequent trials, a significant decrease in the magnitude of the GSR (Grings & Lockhart, 1966), so that there was "anticipation of avoidance rather than anticipation of shock [p. 33]." Evidence could be multiplied that undertaking a task causes an increase in conductance and that difficult tasks cause a greater increase than easier ones (Davis, 1934; Kuno, 1930; White, 1930).

Adaptation of both the basal skin conductance level (decrease) (Conklin, 1951; Duffy & O. L. Lacey, 1946) and the GSR occurs with repetition of the stimulus situation (Blatz, 1925; Coombs, 1938; Darrow, 1936; Hovland & Riesen, 1940; H. D. Kimmel & E. Kimmel, 1965; Kubis, 1948; Montagu, 1963; Porter, 1938; Rasmus, 1936; J. P. Seward & G. H. Seward, 1935). This adaptation may be diminished or obliterated when successive sessions occur a week or more apart unless the stimulus is a strong one. In the case of a shock stimulus, there was an initial increase in the basal conductance level, followed by a plateau (Jones & Ayres, 1966).

Groups of measures A study of five repetitions of certain autonomic responses accompanying the "orienting response" to white noise of five different intensities led to the report that, in general, "response magnitudes and latencies were directly related to stimulus intensity and inversely related to number of repetitions" (Uno & Grings, 1965, p. 311). The measures employed were the GSR skin potential, heart rate, finger blood volume, and pulse volume. The greatest effect was usually obtained after the first exposure to each intensity; the lower

intensities (60 and 70 dB) seemed to be more susceptible to habituation. The effect of repetition on blood volume and pulse volume was not significant. Although this review does not permit the discussion of various interesting differences in the responses of the measures employed, it may be pointed out that correlations between the measures (Pearson *r*) were as follows: blood volume and skin potential (ac), .69; blood volume and pulse volume, .72; skin potential (ac) and pulse volume, .68; and GSR and skin potential (dc), .78. While the correlations were higher *within* response systems than *between* response systems, they were not significantly higher. Uno and Grings concluded that stimulus differences can be detected "by use of any one of the various response parameters of electrodermal or cardiovascular systems [p. 321]" but added that blood volume changes were related in more linear fashion to stimulus intensity and were more resistant to the effects of repetition.

L. C. Johnson and Lubin's findings (1966) of the events during sleep are rather different. The study of the orienting reflex during waking and sleeping, and the recording of electrodermal and cardiovascular responses revealed significant relationships between the measures within each system but not between the two systems. The interpretation of their findings is complicated by the fact that sleep appears to have different effects upon different autonomic variables and the scoring of responses to stimuli was complex, involving corrections of values that may or may not have been justified. It was concluded that sleep seemed to depress electrodermal activity, to have little influence on the finger plethysmograph response, and to serve as a release for the heart rate response. The investigators suggest that there is a reversal in responsiveness between sleeping and waking, with the direction of the change inconsistent from subject to subject. During sleep, no response habituation was found for any autonomic variable or for the K-complex. Least responsiveness for most measures, except the heart rate, was found during the period of 1-REM sleep.

When there were variations in task difficulty or in incentive level, there were concomitant changes in the skin conductance, the heart rate, and muscle tension (Eason, Harter, & Storm, 1964). However, there were unique changes within and between trials in each of the measures, showing that these measures reflected more than a general level of activation. In other words, there was specificity, as well as generality, of activation.

Measures of heart rate   The relationship of the heart rate to what I have called the "degree of significance of the situation" is shown by DuCharme (1966). Rats who had never been in a Skinner box showed no increase in heart rate with water deprivation, but those trained in the Skinner box showed an increase in heart rate with the degree of water deprivation when in the box and to a lesser degree while in their living cages 2 hr before being placed in the Skinner box. Presumably, we have here an anticipation response. Previous experience has given more significance to the cues in the situation. Incidentally, the number of instrumental responses in relation to the hours of water deprivation (24–72) follows an inverted U-curve, highly significant for the trend at the .01 level.

Heart rate deceleration on early trials, followed by acceleration on later trials, was reported to be the conditioned response to shock given by the rat (McDonald, Stern, & Hahn, 1963). In a rather different study of the conditioning of pulse rate to tones followed by shocks, the sustained pulse rate was depressed by the first few presentations in each series but gradually returned to the resting level (Wilson, 1964).

Controversy over whether the heart rate increases or decreases with stimulation continues. Graham and Clifton (1966) have given evidence that the rate increased with the orienting reflex, the function of which has been described as stimulus reception. However, a review of studies in which simple, "nonsignal" stimuli were used revealed deceleration to be the usual response.

While it may be hypothesized that deceleration makes the organism more receptive to new stimulation, and that an increase in the heart rate occurs only if the situation is found, after initial attention, to require an increase in energy release, all of the answers to the questions have not yet been received. J. I. Lacey (1967, pp. 14–42), for example, found that deceleration was sometimes only a prominent part of a polyphasic curve. A study by Campos and

H. J. Johnson (1966) suggested to them that verbalization versus nonverbalization by subjects might be the significant variable. Any requirement to verbalize, either at the time of presentation of the stimulus or afterwards, produced an increase in the heart rate and skin conductance. Conditions of no-verbalization produced a consistent but nonsignificant decrease in the heart rate. They interpreted their results as being opposed to the "intake-rejection hypothesis" such as has been proposed by J. I. Lacey (1967) to account for "directional fractionation of response and for heart rate decrements [p. 305]." They suggest instead that "the requirements to verbalize can produce important changes in degree and direction of autonomic activation [p. 305]," and suggest that "visual attention conditions not involving verbalization are simply not arousing [p. 310]." Mazes and landscapes were the scenes used. A later experiment by Campos and H. J. Johnson (1967) employed as stimuli a series of "Peanuts" cartoons and scenes from the motion picture, "Death on the Highways." It may be of some significance that all subjects were given instructions as to what they were to see 90 sec before each block of stimuli was presented. Hence, less close attention or less of the "What is it?" response might conceivably occur. In these experiments it was found that no-verbalization conditions were always accompanied by cardiac deceleration, without regard to the pleasantness or unpleasantness of the stimuli or the degree to which the stimuli were judged by a nonparticipator to be either pleasant or unpleasant. Later verbalization conditions produced cardiac acceleration, again without regard to pleasantness or unpleasantness. The investigators suggest that "cardiac activation depends more on the energy requirement of the task than on the kind of attention required [p. 288]." It has been my belief for some time that the energy requirement of the task was the determinant of the degree of activation.

Further support of this interpretation of changes in the heart rate was found by Diane (1964), who showed that acceleration of the heart rate occurred during a series of runs (1–8). On the tenth run deceleration occurred if the subject were told in advance to expect a shock on that run. Moreover, a comparison of subjects who were merely told to *expect* a shock with those who actually received the shock showed no difference between them in the amplitude of either the deceleration or the acceleration. A manipulation of an experimental situation in such a way as to produce frustration also produced an increase in the heart rate (Hokanson & Burgess, 1964).

Whatever the relationship between cardiac activity and skin conductance may be, it seems premature to conclude that the activation theory would be challenged, since this theory calls direct attention to *two* basic variables in response, activation and direction, which were said to interact with each other and to be specifically adjustable to particular situations, even though considerable communality in the activation of various systems is usually found (Duffy, 1962). Further investigation may reveal the specific details of a theory to which evidence now available gives only a very general form. However different specific responses prove to be, it is unlikely that the findings will support J. I. Lacey's theory (1967, pp. 14–42) that the physiological responses associated with attention to the external environment are to be *contrasted* in general with those associated with internalized problem solving.

Vascular and temperature responses   Vascular processes also indicate the degree of activation; changing, as the other measures do, with changes in the situation. In one study subjects with the hand immersed in cold water were given shocks of varying intensity and at varying periods on the second and third day of an experiment; they were told that there would be no shock on the fourth day (Teichner, 1965). Some subjects were placed in a strong shock group, some in a weak shock group, and some in a no-shock group. Vasodilation was assessed by a measure of finger temperature in a temperature-controlled chamber. The latency of vasodilation was increased by the threat of shock, and the degree to which the latency was affected depended on the intensity of the threat. Differences between individuals were found. The experimenter suggests that the extent of the ability to adapt to cold stress under conditions that permit a reflex vasodilation is related to high chronic arousal, characterized by a tendency to vasoconstrict under "emotion-producing" stress.

The cooling rate to vasodilation also showed differences. The same subjects were classified into 2 groups on the basis of cooling curves obtained after immersion of the hand in cold water. One group took more than 400 sec to reach the minimum temperature; the other group reached this point in 270–400 sec. These groups were placed in a situation in which they erroneously believed that they would receive a shock if they pressed the wrong one of a number of buttons. Continuous recordings were made of the index-finger temperature of the nonworking hand. By using latency to vasodilation as the criterion, the 41 subjects were classified into 3 groups. The greater than 400 sec group started with a higher finger temperature. With the initial shock, they dropped to, and remained at, a lower finger temperature than the 270–400 sec group, thus displaying a greater rate and degree of vasoconstriction. Progressively increasing vasoconstriction occurred in both groups, as the task progressed. Adaptation would not be expected, since the subjects continued to anticipate an electric shock. The experimenter suggested that the difference in finger temperature responses of the 2 groups may mean that individuals with delayed or no temperature-hunting reactions are highly or overly aroused in other characteristics. Apparently, they vasoconstrict more rapidly and to a greater degree following shock and when expecting shock. Their decision time (for pressing the button) was quite variable, while the other group showed a steadier decrease in reaction time.

Body temperature, as mentioned previously, is different from skin temperature. The body temperature of a group of boys and young men just before boxing was higher than that during training and higher than that of a matched sample in the audience (Renbourn, 1960). Mean pulse rates did not differ.

The electroencephalogram   Having examined skeletal-muscle changes and autonomic changes as they occur with changes in the situation, we may now turn to the more recently explored and less well understood changes in the EEG. In the intact organism, not stimulated electrically or pharmacologically, there appears to be considerable evidence of concordant changes in the EEG and in various aspects of behavior. The EEG is recorded from the scalp, not directly from responding neurons; hence it may not be sensitive enough to show relationships that may be revealed in the future. There is, nevertheless, an impressive body of evidence showing covariation in the EEG and in the situation, meaning the perceived situation and not merely the physical stimulus. For example, the alpha rhythm, which is blocked by opening the eyes and seeing something, is also blocked by the *expectation* of seeing something, even when the eyes are opened in a darkened room. If the individual does not expect to see anything, the rhythm continues as before (Loomis, Harvey, & Hobart, 1936). Only very meager evidence has been assembled to argue for dissociation between central and peripheral functions; the evidence to the contrary seems quite overwhelming, except where there is artificial intervention in the functioning of the organism.[1] Certainly, different systems *may* be dissociated if we employ the artificial means to bring this about, but, in general, the various systems of the organism cooperate to achieve its behavioral goals.

The EEG apparently varies in a continuum with respect to the frequency and amplitude of waves. For the most part, it appears to correspond with a continuum of behavioral arousal. Theta waves (4–7 to 15 Hz) seem to provide a puzzling exception, since they are often found under conditions in which waves of high frequency might be expected. They have, for example, frequently been found in anxiety-prone individuals and in behavioral problem children. Walter (1950, pp. 203–227) has ascribed them (if there is no organic brain disease) to neural immaturity, especially immaturity of the mechanisms linking the cortex with the thalamus and the hypothalamus.

Lying quietly for 2 hr or more has been said to reduce sharply the frequency of the alpha waves (Loomis, Harvey, & Hobart, 1936). Falling asleep causes the alpha rhythm (8–11 Hz) to drop out and slow waves of 4–5 Hz to appear (Lindsley, 1944, pp. 1033–1103). Varying depths of sleep, indicated by the duration or intensity of tones required to awaken the subject, are accompanied by changes

in the EEG (Simon & Emmons, 1956). Sounds or other disturbances during sleep cause the alpha rhythm to reappear, even when they do not awaken the subject (Loomis, Harvey, & Hobart, 1936; see also Chapter 17).

Viewing a stimulus and attempting to remain alert and attentive, as compared with simple viewing, generally produced shorter periods during which alpha waves occurred and longer periods without alpha waves (Mulholland & Runnals, 1962). In another experiment, alert subjects, instructed to respond regularly at 3-sec intervals, showed little variation in the time between successive responses (Anliker, 1963). However, as they became increasingly drowsy, the time between successive responses became longer and there was a decrease in the mean voltage of the peak alpha frequency. Judging from the amplitude of the alpha waves, it appears that here, too, we have evidence of a disappearing alpha as subjects become drowsy.

R. F. Thompson and Shaw (1965) showed that the amplitude of evoked responses from *cortical association areas* was inversely related to the degree of alertness or attention as indicated by behavioral orienting to a stimulus. Evoked potentials behaved in a fashion similar to the EEG frequency; i.e., they diminished with increased alerting. Their finding is not contrary to Anliker's report, since evidence mentioned elsewhere shows an *increase* in the amplitude of wave frequencies *below* the alpha in states of sleep.

Both the presentation of auditory stimuli and its removal caused sleeping cats to show behavioral arousal and electrocortical desynchronization (Weinberger & Lindsley, 1964). In other words, change in the environment alerts the organism. Longer-lasting desynchronization of alpha waves was produced by more complex or incongruous stimuli, in this instance with human subjects (Berlyne & McDonnell, 1965). The investigators state that the duration of desynchronization somehow measures the impact of a stimulus pattern upon the arousal system. Adaptation effects were found. High correlations were found between cortical activity, measured by the EEG, and perceptual condition in stabilized vision when the subjects were asked to report spontaneous fluctuations of a stabilized retinal image (Lehmann, Beeler, & Fender, 1965). At times, when the image was clearly

[1] Artificial dissociation of systems or parts of systems (by means of electrical stimulation or drugs) is very useful in showing the *mechanisms* by which certain results are produced but it does not necessarily show that these systems are dissociated in the intact animal responding to his environment.

visible, there was small-amplitude fast EEG activity.

More complex mental activities are also accompanied by changes in the EEG. The learning of nonsense syllables was accompanied by a decrease in alpha activity and an increase in beta and superimposed activity (Thompson & Obrist, 1964). The greatest changes occurred at the time when the nonsense syllables were first being anticipated correctly.

A further study of the learning and overlearning of nonsense syllables (Thompson & Thompson, 1965) showed that the EEG changed during learning, during overlearning, and during periods when errors were made after the syllables had been reasonably well learned. During learning (for each subject the quarter of the record when the syllable was first anticipated correctly on two successive trials) the percent alpha activity decreased and that of beta and superimposed activity increased as compared with the resting period. This finding is not only similar to that of other studies, but also to changes observed in animals when the reticular activation system is stimulated directly (Jasper, 1949; Moruzzi & Magoun, 1949). The EEG changed toward the pretraining level during adjusted overlearning. During the period when errors were made, alpha activity decreased, while beta and superimposed activity increased. All the error changes were statistically different from the EEG during overlearning and were comparable to, or greater than, the changes during the crucial stages of the learning process.

Habituation is rather generally found in the EEG. R. F. Thompson and Spencer (1966) reviewed studies that showed habituation of the "alpha blocking response" in human beings to tactile, visual, and auditory stimulation; and also showed habituation, spontaneous recovery, and dishabituation of cortical EEG arousal, when electrical stimulation of the mesencephalic reticular formation was employed. The reviewers concluded that, when other factors were equal, complex responses tended to habituate more rapidly than simpler responses.

During a paced auditory serial addition task and control trials that involved similar motor responses, EEG amplitude "usually tended to co-vary with other physiological functions in a manner expected from activation theory [MacNeilage, 1966, p. 344]." The other measures recorded were the heart rate, respiration, muscle tension, and palmar conductance. Physiological levels showed a sharp increase from the first rest period to the first experimental session, and a gradual decline (habituation) during succeeding sessions. Within trials, the various measures showed somewhat different gradients. This led the investigator to say that "such findings raise difficulties for the aspect of activation theory which requires concordance of the various physiological measures [p. 351]." This is a puzzling statement in view of statements on the same page to the effect that "the results show a considerable amount of concordance between alpha amplitude and other physiological indices of activation," and that "of all the measures, only muscle tension showed some departures from the over-all trends of the others." Moreover, it was said that, in spite of the different gradients within trials, "all tended to show lower physiological levels as the trial proceeded [p. 351]."

Activation theory does not demand that all measures march in step like an army but only that significant trends between most of the measures be concordant. There are many explanations for divergencies, and divergencies should, under various conditions, be expected. Again, however, it may be emphasized that the organism is not basically disintegrated or dissociated or "fractionated." It *does* show some patterning of activation, which is necessary for the adjustment of the organism to the situation (see Duffy, 1962, Ch. 5).

Investigators have traditionally used the amplitude of evoked potentials as an index of cortical excitability (Chang, 1959, pp. 299–313; Shagass & Schwartz, 1961). In a recent study, visually evoked cortical potentials varied systematically with variations in a task that was designed to change the degree of behavioral arousal (Eason, Harter, & Storm, 1964). The investigators suggest that this measure "may prove to be even more valuable than the conventional EEG in detecting changes in activation, since it appears to be highly sensitive to such changes [p. 894]." An increase in the amplitude of summated evoked potentials was produced by greater muscular activity such as exerting a sustained force on a dynamometer or by covert activity such as memorizing digits, adding by 13s, or silently saying the alphabet backward.

Thus it appears that the degree of activation of

the organism may be indicated by peripheral measures such as muscle tension; autonomic measures such as skin conductance and cardiovascular measures; and by central measures such as the EEG and evoked cortical potentials, which probably indicate the degree of cortical excitability.

Sensory Sensitivity and Activation

It has been argued that what occurs in one part of the organism affects, at least to some extent, what occurs in every other part of the organism. The functioning of the autonomic nervous system apparently affects the functioning of the cortex, other brain centers, and various other parts of the somatic nervous system, producing differences in the quality of responses and in the sensitivity of the organism to environmental influences. The functioning of the cerebral cortex impinges on the functioning of the autonomic nervous system. Thus the effect is circular.

Evidence from many sources suggests that, at least to some degree and up to a certain point, sensory sensitivity may be increased when the level of activation is higher. The neural basis for such an increase may be found in the diffuse, ascending projection system that sends collaterals to many parts of the brain.

Stimulation of one sense modality has been shown to alter the functioning of another. When recording electrical activity in the cat's brain, Gerard, Marshall, and Saul (1936) found an increased rate of electrical responses to sound as a result of visual stimulation. Also in cats, hypothalamic stimulation was shown to facilitate the response of the cortex to optic and acoustic stimuli (Gellhorn, Koella, & Ballin, 1955). With human subjects, Jacobson (1912) reported that his subjects experienced an odor to be more intense when it was accompanied by a sound; Cason (1936) found that a sound was judged to be more intense when it was accompanied by a light, and a light more intense when accompanied by a sound; and H. M. Johnson (1920) found tactual form discrimination, when the subject was wearing ground-glass lenses, to be reliably better (by 2%) in light than in darkness. Hartmann (1934) reported that tonal discrimination was about 3% finer under bright illumination than when it was dark or the light was dim. Kravkov (1930, 1933) presented evidence that si-

multaneous auditory stimulation affected visual discrimination. Many recent experiments in the Soviet Union have dealt with sensory interaction (London, 1954). The effect of a wide variety of sensory stimuli on visual sensitivity was examined by Symons (1963). A small but significant increase in sensitivity was produced by the following stimuli: olfactory, thermal, gustatory, "proprioceptive," and vestibular. Auditory stimulation and a control condition produced no significant change. Suggested interpretation is on the basis of a "priming" influence exerted on the cerebral cortex by means of the brain stem reticular formation.

It may be that too much, as well as too little, activation can interfere with the reception of sensory impulses. Bruner (1957) comments that psychophysical experiments on the whole show that "too alert an observer pays a price in a raising of sensory thresholds, and that a certain amount of relaxation in the observer yields the lowest thresholds." Experiments using direct stimulation of brain areas that produce electroencephalographic and behavioral arousal bear on this. Monkeys with electrodes implanted in their brains showed better tachistoscopic perception when the brain was stimulated at the level of the mesencephalon (Fuster, 1958). In comparison with control subjects they gave a higher percentage of correct responses and shorter reaction times. However, when the stimulation was of an intensity higher than the threshold for eliciting certain motor effects, sensory discrimination was adversely affected. The brain areas that, when they were mildly stimulated, improved discrimination were those shown by other investigators to produce electroencephalographic and behavioral arousal.

The effect of accessory stimulation upon tachistoscopic perception of geometric figures was studied by Andreassi (1965). Induced muscle tension, when it was one half of the maximum, was accompanied by significantly improved visual perception ($p = .01$). Using four levels of stimulation with white noise, Andreassi found that perception at the lowest level of difficulty was significantly improved ($p = .05$) at one-fourth of the maximum noise level. The investigator interpreted his findings "within the framework of the activation concept," commenting that "recent neurophysiological data point to the ascending reticular activating system as a possible mediator which could influence cortical and retinal areas in the facilitation of tasks such as tachistoscopic perception [p. 829]." A comparable relation is from Davis's report (1950) that an individual's auditory threshold depended in part on the logarithm of his prestimulus muscular tension in the arm and the jaws. The interaction is also shown by the converse situation; Edelberg (1961) found a reliable relationship between autonomic activity and cutaneous tactile sensory sensitivity. Increased GSR activity and finger pulse volume were associated with a decrease in the threshold for vibration, whether the autonomic changes were produced by specific stimulation or occurred spontaneously.

On the other hand, reduced sensitivity to stimulation as a concomitant of autonomic activity has also been reported (Clausen & Karrer, 1964). The visual threshold was studied in relation to blood pressure and the GSR. The same negative relationship between arousal and sensory sensitivity was suggested by the significantly lower resting finger volume in the high threshold group. The findings were contrary to the expectations of the investigators and led them to suggest that distracting effects of anxiety may be found in the high threshold group. I make no attempt to reconcile these conflicting reports, except to point out that they may be due to differences in methodology or to the effects one might presume to occur if there is an inverted U relationship between sensory sensitivity and arousal. However, there is no basis for concluding that the two studies were dealing with different levels of activation.

Some evidence for an inverted U relationship has already been mentioned. The following investigations are pertinent to this question. Corah (1962) divided his subjects on the basis of the skin conductance into a high, middle, and low group and tested for figure-reversal; he found that the middle-half group differed significantly from the combined outer-quarter groups. The two extreme conductance groups did not differ significantly from each other. The upper quarter differed from the middle half but the lower quarter did not. It was predicted (Corah, 1962) that subjects in the middle of the arousal continuum would give more figure reversals, larger kinesthetic figural aftereffects, and shorter reaction times than would subjects with either high or low arousal scores. These predictions were said by the investigator to be

generally confirmed when the palmar conductance measures associated with a given task were used in the analysis of that performance measure. The college students employed as subjects were considered to be within the normal limits of arousal. The relationships obtained were not particularly powerful and, understandably, there was some connection between the strength of the obtained relationship and the reliability estimates of the measures involved. To some extent, then, this study lends support to the hypothesis of an inverted-U relationship between arousal and sensory sensitivity. It also supports, with an eta of .52 ($p = .05$), a similar relationship between the arousal measure employed (skin conductance) and reaction time.

Conceivably interpretable in terms of the U curve is the finding (Anliker, 1966) that there is a systematic increase in the threshold for discrimination of two flashes of light as alpha voltage declines from the "normal alert level." Since a decline in alpha voltage may mean an increase in either lower or higher voltages such an interpretation is possible, though not certain. On the other hand, the estimation of visually presented point clusters was said to be monotonically related to GSR measures (Schönpflug, 1965, as reported in *Psychological Abstracts*).

It seems certain from these reports that there is some relationship, perhaps slight, between activation and sensory sensitivity, but the precise nature of the relationship—i.e., whether linear or curvilinear—remains in question.

ACTIVATION AND PERFORMANCE

Extensive investigation has shown that (a) the level of activation, as indicated by various physiological measures, is related to performance, and (b) activation is by no means the *only* factor affecting the quality of performance. Any statement made about the relationship between activation and performance must, therefore, assume that other factors are equal or that the relevant factors are adequately controlled in the investigation. A brief discussion of some of the pertinent factors will be presented here and, from the vast number of studies in this field, a few representative ones will be cited.

First, the nature of the task imposed is undoubtedly important, although we are not yet in a position to specify clearly the kinds of tasks that might be expected to profit from, and those which might be expected to suffer from, an increase in activation to one or another level. While almost any task might be expected to show improvement in performance as a subject changes from a very drowsy state to a state of alertness, changes in the level of activation beyond this point will no doubt have different effects upon performance, depending upon the nature of the task and the level of activation, among other things. The complexity of the task (meaning the number of cues to which the subject must respond) is presumably a factor of some importance in determining the outcome. Whether the task depends primarily upon muscular effort or upon muscular coordination may be another factor. The stage of learning of the task might be expected to be influential also, since performance requirements vary at different stages of learning, especially if the task is of even a moderate degree of complexity.

Set or attention, i.e., the directional aspect of behavior, interacts with the degree of activation in determining the outcome. A unitary direction, or set, might be expected to produce better results than a vacillating direction or changes in attention. Shifting the direction in response, or the distraction of attention, may be produced either by task instructions or by conflicts within the individual.

The degree of activation is probably of considerable importance in determining the quality of performance. Some investigators have reported an inverted **U**-shaped curve as representing this relationship, while others have found a linear relationship. It is often difficult to tell, when a linear relationship *is* found, if sufficiently high levels of activation were obtained in the laboratory. When the curvilinear relationship occurs, it is sometimes hard to tell whether it may not be due to factors other than activation such as distraction or conflict (changes in the direction of response). Whatever the findings, they are not crucial to activation theory, which does not demand the hypothesis of the **U**-shaped curve.

Individual differences and age differences might be expected to alter the relation between activation and performance, since the inhibitory abilities of different individuals and of different age groups are different. Performance of high quality demands the inhibition of tendencies to respond until all relevant cues can be taken into account and allowed

to influence the action. Hence a relative deficiency in inhibitory ability would lead to less adequate performance. The situation is further complicated by the fact that a high level of activation appears of itself to "press for action" or, in some instances, to produce compensatory inhibition that almost paralyzes action. The activation of response and the direction of response, although operationally different phenomena, are everywhere in close interaction.

The greatest hindrance to drawing conclusions about the relationship between activation and performance is, as with other aspects of the topic, the lack of satisfactory methodology, based upon a sound physiological and statistical rationale, by which to measure activation. Intriguing applications have been sought, before basic, and less glamorous, problems have been solved.

Those who have worked with autonomic variables, as opposed to central or peripheral variables, are particularly likely to doubt the relevance of activation, probably because autonomic variables are notably changeable and homeostatic in their functioning, and the means of measuring them and interpreting the findings has not progressed very rapidly. For example, there are at present differences of opinion in regard to the meaning of the heart rate and changes in the heart rate. The deceleration of the heart rate accompanied more rapid reaction times in a study by Coquery and Lacey (1966); however, we cannot interpret these findings yet. This is not an isolated case. Altschule (1953) became so discouraged about the variation in respiration studies that he suggested abandoning respiration as a measure of physiological response. Far from being surprised by the differences in results between some investigators, we may be surprised by the considerable extent of agreement found with physiological measures as yet imperfect and controls far from adequate. In the pages that follow, a few of the studies, using various types of performance and illustrating some of the problems mentioned above, will be described.

Reaction Time

Starting with one of the simpler types of performance, reaction time, we discover that findings even here are not uniform. Many factors, apparently, influence the results, according to Church (1962).

Using the palmar skin conductance as the measure, it was found that competition increased the skin conductance and lowered the reaction time, but, when self-rated alertness was partialed out, no relationship was found between the reaction time and the conductance. This scarcely seems surprising since, if activation *does* affect the reaction time, it would be presumed to do so through a general arousing or alerting of the individual, which would, of course, be experienced by him. Andreassi (1966) reported that the reaction time decreased as the GSR increased. In another study 18 subjects, selected with reference to their scores on an anxiety scale (6 from each extreme and 6 in the middle), had their reaction times measured while skin potential responses were recorded from the wrist and the palm of the passive hand (Nishisato, 1966). Discrimination reaction times were measured under two different conditions: (a) when the skin potential was steady (called nonarousal), or (b) when it showed a marked deflection (called arousal). Reaction time at the moment of arousal was found to be significantly longer than at the moment of non-arousal. Lansing, Schwartz, and Lindsley (1959) had reported the converse, that reaction time was shorter during arousal, as indicated by desynchronization of the EEG. Nishisato suggests that differences in the latencies of the two physiological measures may explain the discrepancy. The response latency of the EEG desynchronization is about 1 sec shorter than that of the skin potential response. Callaway and Yeager (1960) had found that a phase of the EEG cycle immediately preceding desynchronization was associated with a slow response. Nishisato suggested that differences in the phases of the two measures accounted for the differences in the results. (It should be pointed out, incidentally, that these differences in latencies support my contention that relatively low correlations between different physiological indices of arousal may well be due to differences in the latencies of the responses measured.) In the study under discussion, it was shown with statistical reliability that, under the nonarousal condition, the shortest reaction time was to be found in the intermediate anxiety group, while both of the other groups showed longer reaction times, the high anxiety group being slower than the low one. Under the arousal condition, there were no marked differ-

ences in the reaction time of the three anxiety groups. Apparently, momentary arousal contributes significantly to *intra*individual changes in reaction time, while the level of anxiety (general tendency toward high arousal?) contributes significantly to *inter*individual differences, the relationship being represented by the inverted **U** curve.

There are several recent studies of CNS measures and the reaction time. The amplitude of the average evoked cortical potentials from several different areas was reported to be greater when the reaction time was shorter (Haider, Spong, & Lindsley, 1964). Correlations ranged from −.44 to −.70. The EEG frequency has also been found to correlate with the reaction time (H. Williams, Grunda, Jones, Lubin, & Armington, 1962). In general, the correlation was higher after a longer period of sleep loss. In some subjects, the correlation after a sleep loss of 50 hr was −.70. Five subjects showed an average correlation of −.64 on the second day of sleep loss when peak measurements were the criterion. In this same study, finger vasodilation was significantly related to long reaction times but its predictive value for reaction time was small.

Reaction time appears to be directly influenced by the activity of the reticular activating system (RAS). Issac (1960) reported that stimulation of the RAS, either electrically or by increased sensory input, shortened reaction time. There is evidence that the reaction time follows diurnal cycles that parallel those of the pulse rate and respiration. Atkins (1964), measuring pulse and respiration rates and taking her measurements at 4:00 AM, 10:00 AM, 4:00 PM, and 10:00 PM, found both rates to reach a low point at 4:00 AM, to peak at 10:00 AM, and then to decline slowly. Similarly, the reaction time was longest at 4:00 AM, peaked at 10:00 AM, and then declined slowly.

Rotary Tracking

Although studies of the reaction time seem in most instances to show a positive linear relationship between activation and performance, such is not the case with the more complex task of rotary tracking. Subjects asked to perform a continuous tracking task before, during, and after experiencing the stress of the human centrifuge were found to perform best when the GSR suggested moderate activation (Silverman, Cohen, & Shmavonian, 1959).

Activation and performance appeared to be related in the form of an inverted U curve. Stennett (1957) had previously reported that tracking performance was optimal at moderate levels of the heart rate (changed by varying incentive conditions) and inferior at lower and higher levels, thus supporting the hypothesis of an inverted U curve.

Eason (1963), measuring the EMG from the trapezius, the deltoid, the biceps, and the neck muscles, found an inverted U-shaped relationship between the performance efficiency and the target size. The efficiency was defined in terms of the ratio of the degree of neuromuscular control, shown by the tracking, to the level of tension measured by the EMG. Neuromuscular control decreased in a linear fashion, and tension level exponentially, as the target size increased. The tension level was reported to be independent of the level of skill, i.e., subjects showed a similar tension level for a given target size over the several days of the experiment, despite the fact that, with practice, the subjects approached the imposed criterion of perfection. Eason's tentative explanation was that subjects set for themselves more realistic goals, increasing their goals in such a way as to keep their aspiration just above their current capabilities. Since the goal of perfection was not quite reached, a decrease in muscular tension, which might be expected to occur with overlearning, was not shown. Ghiselli (1936) had found overlearning to be associated with decreasing tension in a special multiple choice problem, involving constant choice time. In this task, three keys were paired with three lights, and the pressure with which the keys were depressed was the measure of neuromuscular tension.

Several investigators have concerned themselves with the relationship between induced muscle tension and performance. Unfortunately, methods of inducing tension seldom provide an increase in tension level that is uncomplicated by other factors which affect performance. More often than not, inducing tension provides an increase in activation and also a change in the directional aspect of behavior. This directional change was clearly seen in a study by Eason and White (1961), in which three methods of increasing muscle tension were employed: (a) raising the aspiration level of the subjects, (b) decreasing the target size, and (c) increasing the work load through a system of weights and pulleys on the active arm during a tracking task. The first two methods of raising muscle tension facilitated performance, while the latter disrupted performance, presumably by tying up certain muscle groups in a response incompatible with the tracking response. They reported that the attempt to attain a relatively high score in a tracking task was associated with a relatively high degree of muscle tension. Eason and Branks (1963) noted, however, that even though an increase in activation level was associated with improved performance, there was not a corresponding increase in efficiency.

Less obvious are the directional changes that may be introduced into learning tasks by other means of inducing tension. The two basic methods of inducing tension are to have the subject exert such a pull on a hand dynamometer as to keep the pointer in a certain position or to have the subject lift a weight of a certain magnitude. Clearly, the first method is distracting, since the subject must pay attention to the pointer in order to maintain the required pull. Eason, Harter, and Storm (1964) predicted and found that performance in the learning of nonsense syllables was poorer when tension was induced by squeezing a hand dynamometer than when lifting weights. Though not so obviously distracting, the weight-lifting method of inducing tension is certainly an additional task imposed upon the subject. Thus an inverted U relationship between tension and performance, when the tension is induced, is quite difficult to interpret. Eason et al. (1964), for instance, found the inverted U relationship between performance and induced tension in a nonsense-syllable learning situation but pointed out that that "a Duncan multiple range test revealed that the statistically significant effect of amount of induced tension on performance was due solely to the decrement in performance which occurred when Ss maintained a 20-lb. load." It is a matter of speculation whether this 20-lb decrement was due to the activation level or the distraction level, i.e., the interference with the directional aspect of performance.

Rote Learning

The evidence regarding the relationship between activation and performance in rote learning is quite contradictory. Furth and Terry (1961) found the pulse pressure to show a correlation of $-.92$ and the skin conductance level a correlation of $+.92$ with the learning of nonsense syllables by the anticipation method. No relation between learning and either diastolic or systolic blood pressure was reported. Berry and Davis (1960), however, found no relationship between the conductance level, frequency of GSRs, or heart rate in the learning of a series of digits by the anticipation method. They did find that subjects with less cutaneous vasoconstriction and smaller masseter muscle potentials were the better learners. In a partial replication of the Berry and Davis study, Thackray (1962) measured the heart rate, heart rate variability, skin resistance, pulse velocity, and frequency of GSRs under resting and learning conditions. He found no relationship between the mean T scores of any of these measures and the rate of learning.

Kleinsmith and Kaplan (1963, 1964) have demonstrated a differential effect of activation, as measured by the GSR, upon short-term versus long-term recall. Low activation was associated with high immediate recall, but poor long-term recall. High activation, on the other hand, was associated with poor immediate recall but good long-term recall. These effects were significant at the $<.001$ and $<.01$ levels, respectively, in the two studies. Using a recall interval of 1 week, they found a correlation coefficient of .54 between the skin conductance and recall. Unfortunately, their results do not clarify the discrepancy between those of Furth and Terry (1961) and Berry and Davis (1960). The two studies both used the anticipation method, although the interval between the stimulus presentations was 2 sec longer in the Berry and Davis study.

The findings are so contradictory that they neither support nor deny the hypothesis of an inverted U relationship between rote learning and activation within the range of the modest degree of activation investigated. Those studies which do suggest the inverted U relationship such as that of Hörmann and Todt (1960) and that of Eason et al. (1964) are not incompatible with an alternative explanation of directional change as the factor responsible for the results obtained. Eason and Branks (1963), using tracking and nonsense-syllable learning as tasks, offer convincing evidence that directional changes can quite strikingly affect performance, independently of the level of activation. This is not surprising, since it has never been suggested that activation alone determines performance but only that it can affect performance when other factors are constant.

Digit-Symbol Substitution and Other Tasks

The evidence for the inverted U relationship between activation and performance in the relatively complex motor task of digit-symbol substitution is more supportive. This task is similar to the Digit Symbol subtest of the Wechsler Adult Intelligence Scale (WAIS). Hokanson and Burgess (1964) investigated the relationship of the heart rate to performance using subjects at the high and at the low extremes of the heart rate and testing performance before and after a frustration manipulation that raised the heart rate about 20 beats/min. The results indicated that, prior to frustration, subjects with a high heart rate performed better than subjects with a low heart rate on tasks of relatively low complexity. Following frustration, with its accompanying increase in the heart rate, low heart rate subjects improved significantly more than subjects with a high heart rate, the latter group actually tending to decline in performance. Of further interest is the fact that, even though subjects with a high heart rate were significantly superior to subjects with a low heart rate on tasks of low complexity, the difference tended to disappear as task complexity was increased. It was predicted in this study that a low heart rate plus high frustration, a high heart rate plus low frustration, and a low heart rate plus physical exertion would show the greatest improvement in performance. Groups with a low heart rate plus low frustration, a high heart rate plus high frustration, and a high heart rate plus physical exertion would show the least improvement. The basis for the predictions for groups with a high heart rate plus high frustration and a high heart rate plus physical exertion was that subjects with high heart rates were already operating near the optimal activation level, so that further activation would perhaps place them on the decrement side of the inverted U. The predictions were almost completely upheld, with the exception of the group with high heart rate and physical exertion. Under this condition, improvement was much greater than with high heart rate plus high frustration and almost as great as low heart rate plus physical exertion. Hokanson and Burgess (1964) conclude, "In view of the general consistency of the data in this study it would be erroneous to assume that one discrepancy in the data would lead to a rejection of the inverted **U** function hypothesis altogether [p. 91]." Factors other than activation affect performance; these factors are sometimes difficult to identify, as they point out.

On a timed coding task following frustration or neutral instructions, subjects who had an initially low resting heart rate were said to show significant improvement in performance following frustration, while those with a high heart rate generally showed a decrement (Doerr & Hokanson, 1965). The investigators regarded the data as being generally consistent with the inverted **U** hypothesis. An entirely different measure, that of thermal regulation, as indicated by the time required for vasodilation in the hand under certain controlled conditions, has also been found to be related to paired associate learning. There was an "increase in performance with increasing time to vasodilation except for the > 400-sec group which exhibited a marked reversal [Teichner, 1962, p. 11]." The trend again was of the inverted **U**-shaped type. In this same study of vasodilation, Teichner reported that the hypothesis of poorer perception in the highly aroused group was also suggested. The perceptual measure was the discovery of hidden figures.

Forrest (1960), using arithmetic tasks and measuring EMG from the forearm and from above and below the point of the chin, found that tension, generated either by instructions to work at maximum rate or by pressing down on a spring balance, correlated with faster work when the measure analyzed was "the time taken over each addend of a sum and the tension accompanying it [p. 330]." Under certain conditions, however, increased tension was accompanied by slower response. This was especially noticeable when the subjects were told to work at a normal, easy rate. Considering the findings with individual subjects, Forrest reported that slow workers tended to have higher tension levels, which, as he says, has been reported by others working with anxiety neurotics, with nursery

school children, and with various other subjects. The investigator found it difficult to reconcile some of the various findings of his study.

Fiske and Maddi (1961, pp. 17–56), summarizing research in which the degree of arousal was related to the level of performance in various tasks, have reported general support for a curvilinear relationship between the two. Some studies failing to find such a relationship are open to methodological criticism. Sherwood (1965), who did not find the two factors related in the form of an inverted **U**-shaped curve, is aware of this fact. As a measure of arousal, he employed the rate of figure-reversals and, in a second experiment, the subjective report of feelings of arousal. Actually, he found a correlation of .87 (<.01) between the two presumed indicators of arousal. Nevertheless, in the absence of a physiological measure of what is a physiological construct, no conclusions can be drawn with respect to activation. Murphy (1966, pp. 1–2) also failed to find support for an inverted **U** relationship between auditory reaction time and activation, as defined by dynamometer-induced muscle tension. Again, the factor of direction (in this case, divided attention) must be considered.

Cue Utilization and Fluctuations in Activation

Not merely the general quality of performance but also specific characteristics of the response appear to be related to activation. Various hypotheses have been suggested in regard to "cue utilization" at high levels of activation and also with fluctuations in various indices of activation. It has been said that selectivity in the response to cues suffers under a high degree of activation, so that a relatively simple task such as a conditioned response might be facilitated, while a more complex task might be handicapped. When two groups of subjects, paired for total scores on a stylus maze test, and rated for anxiety (which was assumed to involve an increase in "drive strength"), were compared in their performance at easy choice points and more difficult choice points in the maze, it was found that the more anxious subjects performed better at the easier choice points and less well at the more difficult ones (Farber & Spence, 1953). It was hypothesized that dominant habit tendencies were facilitated at the expense of less dominant tendencies (Farber & Spence, 1953; Montague, 1953). This explanation was later challenged by Hill (1957).

Easterbrook (1959) suggested that the number of cues utilized in making a response becomes smaller during general covert excitement or increased activity in the brain stem reticular formation (Callaway & Dembo, 1958). Under such circumstances it was believed that the use of "central and immediately relevant cues" would be maintained, but the use of "peripheral (occasionally or partially relevant) cues" would be reduced. Some tasks would be improved by a reduction in the range of cue utilization, while, for other tasks, proficiency would require the use of a wide range of cues. Easterbrook was of the opinion that a mere increase in general excitement, in the absence of conflict, could disrupt complex action sequences. Task complexity was defined in terms of the number of cues that must be simultaneously utilized to achieve success in the performance. He referred to the reduced memory span for digits in anxiety (reported when anxiety was determined by questionnaire, induced by threat, or chronic as in neurosis), the reported shrinkage of the field of perception under stress, and the handicapping effect exerted by anxiety upon demanding serial operations such as tracing a complex maze, mirror drawing, and serial coding. He accounted for an inverted U-shaped curve representing the relationship between activation and performance by the fact that reduction in the range of cue use would first improve and then impair proficiency. Hence there would seem to be "an optimal range of cue utilization for each task."

Callaway and Stone (1960, pp. 393–398) showed that certain drugs which can produce electroencephalographic arousal make people less responsive to events occurring at the periphery of attention, while other drugs make them more responsive to peripheral stimulation. Thus the degree of arousal appears to be correlated with the extent of focus of attention.

There is some question as to whether such impairment in selectivity to cues as has been found during a high degree of activation is due to the activation per se or to the fluctuations in activation that frequently occur when the activation is high.

There is considerable evidence, reviewed elsewhere (Duffy, 1962), that these fluctuations are related to responsiveness. It has been suggested by me (1932c), and is implied in the work of Luria (1932), that the fluctuations may be due to a deficiency in inhibitory ability. Luria reported that children showed less inhibitory ability and more irregularity in the curve representing pressure on a key than did adults. He suggested that individuals who show irregular pressure responses have an "unconditioned sensibility of the nervous system" and "special defects in the cortical regulators of excitation, in consequence of which every arising excitation manifests the tendency to pass immediately to the motor sphere." Those showing irregular pressure were called "reactively labile," while those with smooth pressure curves were called "reactively stabile."

In a study (1932c) measuring grip pressure in nursery school children during a discrimination task, I found that the children who showed the greatest irregularity in their pressure curves, i.e., the most fluctuations, tended to commit more errors of "commission" than of "omission," while those with fewer fluctuations showed the opposite tendency, even though the number of correct responses might be the same for the two groups. A similar tendency had been noted in an earlier study (Duffy, 1930) with fewer subjects.

Since that time, differences in motor disorganization in different individuals have been noted by a number of psychologists, whose work will be mentioned later. The effect on performance was reported by James (1941, pp. 525–643) in a study of the conditioning of dogs, when the unconditional stimulus (UCS) was an electric shock. His "excitable" dogs responded to every signal presented, no matter how much it differed from the one used in the initial training, while his "lethargic" dogs did not react to all signals.

More recently, the relationship between performance and fluctuations in autonomic activity has been studied by J. I. Lacey and B. C. Lacey (1958). Continuous records of the heart rate and skin resistance showed bursts of activity, or more continuous aperiodic changes that were unconnected with the presentation of any stimulus. When the subjects were divided into those above and those below the median in number of half-minutes of activity in skin resistance during rest, it was found that those with more activity showed a statistically dependable difference from the others in the number of erroneous responses in their discrimination reactions. They made more responses to the lights to which no response was supposed to be made. The findings with respect to the cardiac measures were similar. Interpretation of the findings was that "autonomic labiles, driven by recurrent facilitatory volleys to the motor cortex and to brain stem formations, cannot voluntarily inhibit the speed of emission of an impulse along final motor pathways."

McNamara and Fisch (1964) tested the hypothesis that the number of cues utilized in a learning and performance task would be reduced under intense motivation, when these cues were relevant to completion of the task. Since there is much evidence that changes in "motivation" involve changes in activation, the study seems pertinent for present purposes, although there were no physiological measures of activation. The relevant motivation was receiving a monetary reward for a fast and accurate performance, while the "nonrelevant" motivation was the threat of electric shock. Both types of motivation adversely affected the receptor-effector span. A distinction was made between the span of attention and a scanning process described as the fixation and recall of specific cues relevant to the task. While the attention span was adversely affected by both highly relevant and highly nonrelevant motivation, the scanning efficiency was not severely disrupted by high nonrelevant motivation and was related to the intensity of the relevant motivational condition. It should be emphasized that activation in this situation must be inferred from manipulation of the stimulus, since it was not directly measured.

Age Differences

Eisdorfer (1966) has studied errors of "omission," as compared to errors of "commission," in older men and younger men. When the task was learning a list of eight words, an increase in the exposure time for the words caused a significant decrease in the omission errors of men between 60 and 80 years of age but not in a comparison group of younger men. Commission errors did not vary with exposure time. In a subsequent study, using the measurement of free fatty acid as an index of stress, it was shown that young subjects showed a more accelerated increase during the learning situation and a more rapid return to their resting level. Older persons (average age of 71.4 years) did not reach their peak elevation until 15 min after the learning terminated, and their free fatty acid levels remained high throughout the resting period. Eisdorfer concluded (1966), on the basis of this and other data not presented here, that the older person is made more anxious by having to learn and that "this anxiety and its physiologic correlates result in a tendency to withhold responses (even though learning has occurred), with an apparent decline in verbal learning." He comments, "It is almost as if the thermostat for stress in the elderly was impaired [p. 9]."

General Discussion

Although the inverted U relationship between activation and performance seems logically reasonable, not all attempts to demonstrate such a relationship have been convincing. Eason's (1963) finding of an inverted U relationship between activation and efficiency is of particular interest. Studies attempting to induce high degrees of tension have often shown an inverted U with regard to performance, but, as has been pointed out, it is often difficult to tell whether the performance inversion observed at the upper extremes of tension was due to induced activation or induced distraction. It seems that, if an inverted U relationship exists, the peak of the curve may not be reached in the rather narrow range of activation normally encountered in the laboratory.

With certain exceptions, it appears safe to say that increased activation facilitates performance within the range of activation generally encountered. Increased aspiration level seems associated with increased activation, as does increased task difficulty when the aspiration level is held constant. This latter statement would seem a parsimonious explanation for Forrest's finding that, within a given condition, the greatest tension was generated by an addend over which the subject took the longest time to react. In other words, when the problem becomes difficult, more effort is exerted. The consensus of findings would appear to be that greater effort results in greater activation and that greater activation results in better performance when the task difficulty is constant—at least within the limits of the performances studied.

While the relationship of activation to short-term retention may, at the moment, be ambiguous, Kleinsmith and his colleagues (1963) have documented the relationship of activation, as measured by GSR, to long-term retention in such a way as to leave little doubt that increased activation, within the range investigated, is facilitative with regard to this aspect of learning. The literature contains many other studies of the relationship between activation and performance that cannot be included here.

Only a few studies fail to find a relationship between these variables. Tentative conclusions have been presented throughout this discussion. Firm conclusions in regard to the U-shaped curve are difficult to draw. In at least some of the studies that have supported the hypothesis, other factors, such as the lack of control of the directional aspect of response (i.e., distraction) leave open the possibility that the changes in performance were due to factors other than changes in activation. In other instances, where no U-shaped curve was found, it is questionable whether the range of activation produced in the laboratory was sufficient to allow for the decrement in performance hypothesized for very high levels of activation. It is possible that the U curve holds for some types of performance and not for others. There are almost certainly individual and age differences in inhibitory ability, and hence in the degree of activation necessary to produce disruption, or disorganization, of the performance. It is an understatement to say that much remains to be learned.

INDIVIDUAL DIFFERENCES

A difference in responsiveness between individuals appears to be the basic behavioral correlate from which other correlates may be derived. The measures discussed in this chapter seem to be indicative of differences in the degree of excitability of the nervous system in both its higher and lower centers. While the measures may not be highly correlated with each other when taken over a brief interval of time, and especially when sampled simultaneously at a given moment, the general trend of the measures, continuously recorded, appears to give justification for the concept of a responsive or an unresponsive *individual,* and not merely responsive or unresponsive skin resistance, skeletal musculature, or cortical potentials. This relationship seems at times to have been obscured either by inadequate measurements or inadequate concepts. In some instances, for example, the directional aspect of behavior has not been distinguished from its arousal aspect. Research in this general area seems to be increasing, both in quantity and in quality.

Individuals apparently differ in their characteristic degree of activation, as well as in fluctuations in activation and in the length of time they require, after stimulation, to recover or return to the prestimulus level of activation. Different situations, of course, arouse different individuals to a different degree, but the variations in activation of one individual in different situations will, it seems, fluctuate around a different mean from those of another.

Problems in the measurement of the differences in activation *between* individuals are much greater than those of measuring differences *within* the individual. For example, levels in the skin conductance may be affected by differences in the thickness of the skin. To the extent that there is "response stereotypy" (J. I. Lacey & B. C. Lacey, 1958a), i.e., a consistent tendency on the part of one individual to respond to a stimulus with peak reactivity in one system and for another individual to respond with his maximum activation in another system, then sampling responses from many systems would be required before drawing conclusions in regard to individual differences in reactivity. Behavioral observations of men, dogs, rats, chimpanzees, and other species, as well as controlled studies of the various species, continue to support strongly the reality of such differences and their tendency to persist over time. A number of studies supporting these statements is described in Duffy, 1962 (Chs. 9, 10, 11).

Now, as earlier, there is support for the idea that differences in responsiveness between individuals of one sort are likely to be accompanied by differences in responsiveness of other sorts. For instance, as cited earlier, Kennard and Willner (1945) found specific differences in the EEGs between individuals whose deep reflexes were of high threshold and those with "easily elicited and active deep reflexes." Such differences, indicated by various measures, extend to more complex behavior such as the physical contacts of nursery school children on the playground (Duffy, 1932a), impulsiveness (defined as errors of "commission," as compared with those of "omission") (Duffy, 1932c; J. I. Lacey & B. C. Lacey, 1958a), irritability as a score on the Cason Common Annoyance Test (Freeman & Katzoff, 1932), and proneness to develop anxiety (Ulett, Gleser, Winokur, & Lawler, 1953.)

More recent studies continue to supply evidence for individual differences in responsiveness, measured in a number of ways, and for the maintenance of these differences over the time period of the studies. Some studies in which responsiveness was judged chiefly on the basis of overt behavior, rather than physiological measurements, provided evidence of differences between litters of dogs and of genetic influence upon these differences (Murphree & Dykman, 1965). The experimenters made behavioral studies of four litters of first generation dogs of the pointer breed and found that, although reared in the same laboratory under controlled conditions, the dogs showed within-litter similarities and between-litter differences: (a) in reactions to noise; (b) in the distance run during brief exploratory activity; (c) in reactions to persons assuming friendly, hostile, or neutral roles; and (d) in behavioral ratings by technicians working with the dogs. Stability of litter differences was also shown in spontaneous exploratory activity in an empty room over a period of 70 weeks. Physiological measures revealed differences in blood pressure levels and electrophoretic curves of blood serums. The original dogs had been selected "for the presence or absence of tendencies to retreat, cringe, tremble, and freeze when confronting an unfamiliar human [pp. 321–322]."

Second generation dogs, bred from A line (bold) dogs and E line (timid) dogs, showed that the A line, whether human or mother-reared, showed reliably more activity than E line dogs. They also differed reliably in approach reactions to a human being. In a conflict situation, the A litter had significantly higher systolic blood pressure scores than the D litter. Second generation litters were found to be much like their progenitors in reactions to sudden noises, reactions to human beings, and in activity levels.

Further work by Dykman, Murphree, and Ackerman (1966) on these litters of dogs revealed reliable differences between litters for various measures of conditioning. It was contended that the conditioned response is dependent upon "innate patterns of reactivity." Among the findings were the observation that A dogs (bold) were the most active and vigorous but were capable of inhibiting their activity in order to pay attention to relevant stimuli. C dogs, who were active and vigorous, lacked inhibitory constraints. E dogs (timid) were highly excitable and extremely active in the kennels but would inhibit reaction to almost any stimulus (people, other dogs, noises). Dykman suggests that "no explanation other than sensitization thresholds or some equivalent concept renders intelligible the idiosyncratic organization of the CR in different animals and the changes in form which occur with reinforcement and nonreinforcement [p. 430]." Could the required concept that is equivalent to sensitization thresholds be that of differences in responsiveness or activation?

Mason (1963), reporting on the social behavior of chimpanzees, states, "In the beginning, I had no special interest in the arousal concept but as the data accumulated, it became clear that some such construct was required . . . to explain the tendencies that emerged from the experimental work [p. 2]." He found that a given level of arousal predisposes an animal to engage in a characteristic pattern of social activity (i.e., grooming, clinging, play-fighting), and that social responses themselves influence the existing arousal level, either raising or lowering it [p. 3]. In general Mason's findings suggest that a "low or moderate level of arousal predisposes the young primate to engage in play; higher arousal produces the avoidance of physical activities and strengthens the tendency to cling. This is true whether the increase in arousal is brought about by social deprivation, the use of stimulant drugs, or by manipulation of situational novelty or noise level [pp. 7–8]." In the young chimpanzee play tends to increase arousal and clinging to decrease it. Thus the animal finds an important source of reinforcement in these activities, in that they assist him to maintain his level of arousal within an optimal range. We may conclude, so far as this evidence goes, that social behavior is influenced by the degree of arousal and that the latter is characteristic of the individual.

A longitudinal study of 130 children during the first years of life showed individual differences in a number of characteristics, including the activity level, intensity of reaction, threshold of responsiveness, approach or withdrawal, and distractibility (Thomas, Chess, Birch, Hertzig, & Karn, 1963). The characteristics (which were studied by general observation) were reported to remain relatively stable over the two-year period.

Experiments employing measures of physiological factors have augmented the observational studies of individuality of behavioral patterns from early infancy. Some time ago, Jost and Sontag (1944) reported a highly significant similarity in the GSRs of siblings, which they interpreted in terms of heredity, since half-siblings reared in the same home showed markedly less similarity.

Vandenberg, Clark, and Samuels (1965) compared the psychophysiological reaction of adolescent identical and fraternal twins in order to study the importance of heredity in the GSR, heartbeat, and breathing rate. They report a significant hereditary component in the heartbeat frequency and breathing rate in response to a startling event such as an unexpected flash of light or the sound of a hammer falling at a distance of several feet from the subject. In contrast, the reactions to the less startling stimulus of ringing a doorbell were smaller and slower, and, in general, showed little or no hereditary component. Although the study also revealed no hereditary component for the GSR, the authors point out that a particular experimental problem may have been responsible for the lack of significant findings.

There seems to be definite evidence for individual patterning in the maturation of autonomic functioning in the early months of life. Lipton, Steinschneider, and Richmond (1960) studied nine neonates, including three sets of identical twins,

during the second to fifth days of life. Using data from a cardiotachometer, they found that a response pattern of the cardiac rate could be defined by a series of parameters, including the peak response (maximum change in the rate after stimulation), the duration of the peak cycle, and the time required to return to the original level of the response. The nine infants differed in the parameters, with three statistically differentiated groups emerging. None of the twins was distinguishable on the basis of the data from his or her cotwin. Measures of respiratory responses indicated that infants who were very reactive in one autonomic system were relatively less so in another. Lipton says that this may represent early evidence of differential reactivity of end organs in the neonate.

The consistency over time of any physiological measure that has been used as an indicator of activation is obviously of interest. Skipping over evidence reported earlier (Duffy, 1962, Ch. 9), we should mention the study of spontaneous GSRs made by Docter and Friedman (1966). Measurements taken on 23 male university students on a *single occasion* failed to show a significant correlation with those taken 30 days later. However, the *average correlation* for successive days was .54, which was significant; when each subject's median for Week 1 was compared with his median for Week 2 (30 days later), a rho of .62 was found. Five separate measures had been taken during each week. This finding emphasizes the importance of making judgments of the differences between individuals on the basis of a number of repetitions of any measure.

Observing 48 women during rest periods between sessions of work on a pursuit-rotor, Kling and Schlosberg (1961) found considerable consistency in their individual conductance levels. The investigators suggest that the amplitude and latency of the rise in conductance are no more important than the subsequent recovery period in estimating the effect of various experimental situations. Other investigations have emphasized the importance of the recovery rate (Duffy, 1962, pp. 266–268).

A slower recovery rate from being startled was associated with greater autonomic responsiveness, as implied by indices computed from the systolic and diastolic blood pressures; finger, face, and axillary temperatures; palmar and volar skin resistances; heart and respiration rates; stomach motility; finger pulse volume; and frontal, temporal, parietal, and occipital brain potentials (Sternbach, 1960b). The indices were computed according to Wenger's mode of estimating autonomic balance, the percentage of time alpha, and the time required for the reappearance of the alpha rhythm. Thus it was shown that, according to these measures, more responsive individuals recovered more slowly from the effects of stimulation.

The level of the skin conductance, its degree of change, and its spontaneous fluctuations, may covary to only a modest degree; yet they do not seem to be entirely independent of each other (Sternbach, 1960b). He does not agree with the contention that these measures are separate and distinct dimensions of autonomic activity (J. I. Lacey & B. C. Lacey, 1958a), even though Sternbach found, as had J. I. Lacey and B. C. Lacey, that subjects with more "spontaneous" fluctuations in skin conductance had significantly more rapid reaction times. However, there was also a correlation (at the .01 level) between the reaction time and the change in conductance when a stimulus was presented, those with the slowest reaction time having the greatest difference between the log prestimulus conductance and the log response conductance. Therefore, Sternbach concluded that the subjects with the higher prestimulus conductance levels had the faster reaction times (at the .05 level). There were procedural differences between the studies, but a high prestimulus level of conductance has in other cases been found associated with less change in conductance upon the presentation of a stimulus, for possible reasons that have been discussed elsewhere (Duffy, 1962, pp. 31–32).

A previous study by Sternbach also indicated that slow responders showed greater differences between the prestimulus and the stimulus measures not only in skin conductance but also in the finger pulse volume, heart rate, pulse pressure, and systolic blood pressure. I tend to accept the speculation resisted by Sternbach: that more highly activated persons show more "spontaneous" fluctuations and higher prestimulus levels of conductance, as well as more rapid reaction times. The evidence offered against this conclusion is that

these individuals do not show the expected dominance of sympathetic activity (as measured by Wenger's formula for estimating autonomic balance), nor do they typically have an activated EEG pattern. It may be argued that Wenger's complex measure is not necessarily the best one to employ. The EEG pattern is more difficult to explain but there are some slight indications that the typical EEG pattern of the highly aroused person may contain either more fast activity or more slow activity than that of the less aroused person, who perhaps maintains a better balance in electrical activity of the brain, with more alpha waves present.

The foregoing section has pointed out that *both* the degree of activation and the responsiveness in a particular physiological system seem to be reliable and persistent characteristics of the individual.

Also characteristic of the individual are "spontaneous" fluctuations in physiological responses previously referred to, i.e., responses that occur without any observable stimuli. They seem to persist in the individual over a period of time and under various experimental conditions (Duffy, 1930, 1932c, 1962; J. I. Lacey & B. C. Lacey, 1958a). The question of whether these fluctuations are correlated with initial levels of physiological functioning is a difficult one. Experimental evidence on the point is contradictory. Mundy-Castle and McKiever (1953) reported a positive relationship between the two. J. I. Lacey & B. C. Lacey (1958a) found somewhat different results in two experimental groups but concluded that the measures are basically unrelated. Duffy (1946) found that the two measures appeared in different factors in a factor analysis. A lack of relationship between the two has been claimed by Malmo, Shagass, Belanger, and Smith (1951) and by Malmo and Smith (1955). In the latter study, however, while measures of muscle tension correlated poorly with the level of tension in the neck and forearm, they showed a significant correlation with frontalis-muscle tension.

Both the level of physiological functioning and fluctuations in functioning appear to be indicators of responsiveness. Procedural factors in the experiment are no doubt of importance in reaching a conclusion. In scoring motor irregularities, for example, a few large, long-lasting deviations from a baseline might have an entirely different significance from frequent, small deviations such as those observed in tremor; yet certain scoring systems have not taken this into account.

I suggest that the fluctuations indicate a lack of inhibitory ability or control. While not a necessary accompaniment of a high level of activation, they are frequently found in conjunction with it, depending upon the age and other characteristics of the subject. The behavioral significance of these irregularities in physiological measures has been discussed in part earlier in this chapter, where it was pointed out that all the available evidence tends to suggest that individuals showing such irregularities tend to be impulsive or to commit errors of "commission," rather than errors of "omission."

Studies of resting autonomic activity, EEG tracings, and motor impulsiveness have recently been made by Sternbach (1960b), Clements and Peters (1962), and Boyle, Dykman, and Ackerman (1965). In the last study 30 boys between the ages of 9 and 10 were tested on their ability to release a telegraph key when the correct one of a horizontal panel of 7 white lights came on. There was a green light directly above the central white light; only when the light under the green light came on was the key to be released. Since the subject could not anticipate which light would come on, he had to be on guard against releasing the key for one of the peripheral lights. Resting autonomic activity was recorded in a different room *after* the test. Measurement was made of the heart beat, skin resistance level and changes, respiration, muscle potentials, and EEG. There are complex problems involved in the scoring and comparison of variables, and only a reading of the original report will supply the information that is necessary. What is called "background activity" consists of "spontaneous" changes in these physiological responses, continuously recorded and scored, usually in terms of the number of fluctuations during 15-sec intervals. On this basis the subjects were divided into stabiles and labiles. The investigators concluded, "Overall there was a tendency for the labiles, regardless of how classified, to make more errors in responding to the peripheral lights than stabiles [p. 318]." This tendency was especially pronounced on the first

trial. In other words, it was reported that in all systems and all trials the labiles (subjects above the group median) made more false responses to peripheral lights than stabiles (subjects below the median). However, statistically significant results were found only for muscle potentials and "highest system dichotomies." It was suggested that the generalization of response in this experiment depended more upon the inhibitory than upon the discriminatory ability of the subjects.

The reaction times were also found to differ for stabiles and labiles. They were shorter for the labiles in all systems and at all foreperiods with the exception of one period for the respiratory cycle data. The investigators state that, although no one mean in any system differed reliably between the two groups, "there was no question about the reliability of the trend overall." A slower reaction time for stabiles appeared in 14 out of 15 pairs of means ($p < .01$ by binomial test). The subjects tended to hold their rank order position in the group across foreperiods. The coefficient of concordance was .86 ($p < .01$).

There are many other data in the study which are not recorded here. The investigators were acutely aware, as is the present writer, of the need of "some way of classifying subjects based on an appropriate weighting of BA [background, or "spontaneous" activity] in the different systems [p. 320]."

Other studies that have attempted to explore the relationship between activation and measures of behavior, especially anxiety, may be mentioned. I would define anxiety as a high degree of activation, with overt or symbolic responses directed *away* from something, whether it be an undesirable event or barriers to the occurrence of a desirable event.

Among those who have recently studied the relationship between anxiety and the amplitude of the GSR and have reported greater amplitude of response in anxious subjects are Beam (1955), Haywood and Spielberger (1966), Lader and Wing (1964), and Zahn (1964). Among those who have found less amplitude are Ax, Beckett, Fretz, and Gottlieb (1965), Goldstein (1964), and Weybrew (1963). Still other observers have not been able to find any clear-cut difference between subjects who were classified as high in anxiety and those classified as low in anxiety (Malmo & Shagass, 1949; D. B. D. Smith & Wenger, 1965). When this work is considered as a whole, little can be said with certainty about the relationship between the two variables. However, different indices of anxiety have been employed in these studies, and some of the studies have made use of both psychiatric and normal subjects. Who may be considered a "normal" subject, in the sense of being relatively free from anxiety, is in itself a difficult question, as was pointed out by Duffy (1962, p. 286). Merely using hospital personnel or other presumed normal groups is not necessarily a safe procedure.

Haywood and Spielberger (1966) employed college students as subjects and divided them into those with extremely high and those with extremely low scores on the Taylor Manifest Anxiety Scale. They measured arousal by means of the Palmar Sweating Index (PSI), which other studies have shown to correlate with, but not to be identical with, the GSR. The latter measure has been considered by most investigators to be better, although more difficult to obtain. The anxious, as compared with the nonanxious, subjects on the Taylor scale were selected in a nonanxiety-provoking experimental situation. Both groups were subjected to the same experimental procedure and given the same instructions. Palmar sweating was measured after a period of adaptation at the beginning of the verbal conditioning experiment and again later in the experiment. The data indicate that physiological arousal, as measured by the PSI, was significantly higher on both occasions for high anxiety subjects than for low anxiety subjects, and that the PSI declined proportionately for both groups as the experiments progressed. The authors concluded that the PSI is a sensitive measure of autonomic arousal and is significantly related to anxiety as measured by the Taylor Manifest Anxiety Scale.

Burnstein, Fenz, Bergeron, and Epstein (1965) compared gradients of the skin resistance and skin potential generated by different degrees of psychologically disturbing stimuli. The subjects were male and female undergraduate students. The stimuli were 42 tape-recorded words taken from clinical word association tests. Twelve words, 4 each of low, moderate, and strong emotional value, were randomly distributed among 30 neutral or buffer

words. The authors concluded that both the skin resistance and the skin potential were significantly related to the strength of stimulus-induced arousal. However, they noted considerable individual differences in correlations and somewhat lower intrasubject correlations than those reported in an earlier work of Wilcott (1958).

Roessler, Burch, and Childers (1966) reported on the personality correlates of galvanic skin responses. The basal skin resistance (BSR) and galvanic skin responses (GSR) to five stimulus intensities of light and sound were recorded under different experimental situations that were assumed to be analogous, respectively, to conditions of situational unfamiliarity, to basal conditions, and to real stress situations. Thirty-two male medical and dental students served as subjects. In general, the authors predicted that (a) the GSR amplitude would be greater under conditions of stress than under conditions relatively free from stress; (b) the greater the stimulus intensity, the greater the GSR amplitude; (c) the amplitude of the GSR to specified stimulation would be greater when the subjects were unfamiliar than when they were familiar with the experimental conditions; (d) that the GSR amplitude would decrease with time (habituation); and (e) alert subjects would show a greater GSR amplitude than drowsy subjects. By and large all but one of the specific predictions were supported. The authors failed to demonstrate any statistically significant difference between the stress and basal conditions. This failure was attributed to complications in the experimental sequence such as the anxiety aroused in the subjects by an impending comprehensive examination, rather than the actual absence of the predicted relationship.

Studies attempting to relate other physiological indices of arousal such as the cortical activity, heart rate, respiration rate, and level of muscle tension to personality variables have been reviewed in an earlier work (Duffy, 1962). A few of those concerned with anxiety in normal subjects will be discussed here. Maddi and Propst (1963) hypothesized that anxiety is an accompaniment of excessive activation, and boredom an accompaniment of insufficient activation. Individuals are assumed to differ in their characteristic activation and to engage in "impact-modifying behavior" when activation is very high or very low. This point of view is not unlike that of Leuba, who, in 1955, outlined a concept of optimal stimulation as a condition that he believed all organisms seek. L. C. Johnson and Ulett (1959) studied the resting EEG response over 24 frequencies (3–33 Hz) and the relationship of the EEG response to manifest anxiety. The subjects were 44 young adult males. Three recordings were taken over a 9-month period. The subjects with high manifest anxiety scores had significantly less EEG activity, especially in the 8–12 Hz band; however, there was no significant difference between high and low manifest anxiety groups in EEG responses on Records 2 and 3, although the general shape of the EEG profiles was the same as in Record 1. In their conclusions, the authors indicate the importance of the interaction of anxiety and the situation as the subject interprets it.

Recognizing the growing consensus that psychophysical response to stress is at least partly a function of how subjects in general view the situation (as I suggested in 1962), Hodges and Spielberger (1966) investigated differences within the individual subject's interpretation of a stressful situation. The subjects were 60 male undergraduates who were divided into high anxiety and low anxiety groups on the basis of scores on the Taylor Manifest Anxiety Scale. This test was given 20 months prior to the experiment to a large group of students, along with a test involving the fear of shock. Heart rate measures were taken for both groups as they were run in a verbal conditioning experiment under threat-of-shock or no-threat conditions. Immediately after the experiment the subjects were asked to fill out the Today form of the Zuckerman (1960) Affect Adjective Check List (AACL-Today). The data indicate that subjects in the threat-of-shock condition showed a marked increase in the heart rate, when compared to those in the no-threat condition. There was no difference in the magnitude of the increase in heart rate for low anxiety and high anxiety subjects. However, within each group those subjects who registered moderate to extreme fear of shock on the previous fear-of-shock test showed a significantly greater increase in heart rate in the threat condition than did those subjects who had reported little or no fear of shock. It would seem that, when anxiety as an individual characteristic is being investigated, care must be taken in assessing the amount of anxiety aroused in individual subjects by the experimental situation.

As pointed out earlier (Duffy, 1962), it is regrettable that little work has been done relating activation level (or responsivity) to other aspects of the normal personality. Personality still seems to be conceived of by many as comprised of the *directional* aspect of behavior only, with little attention given to differences in responsiveness and their probable correlates.

REFERENCES

ALTSCHULE, M. D. *Bodily physiology in mental and emotional disorders.* New York: Grune & Stratton, 1953.

ANDREASSI, J. L. Effect of induced muscle tension and auditory stimulation on tachistoscopic perception. *Perceptual and Motor Skills,* 1965, **20,** 829–841.

ANDREASSI, J. L. Skin conductance and reaction time in a continuous auditory monitoring task. *American Journal of Psychology,* 1966, **79,** 470–474.

ANDREASSI, J. L., & CAVALLARI, J. D. Biopotential signals as a function of learning task difficulty. Tech. Rep. IH-34, U.S. Naval Training Device Center, Port Washington, N.Y., 1965.

ANDREASSI, J. L., & WHALEN, P. M. Physiological correlates of learning and overlearning. Tech. Rep. IH-56, U.S. Naval Training Device Center, Port Washington, N.Y., 1966.

ANLIKER, J. Variations in alpha voltage of the EEG and time perception. *Science,* 1963, **140,** 1307–1309.

ANLIKER, J. Simultaneous changes in visual separation threshold and voltage of cortical alpha rhythm. *Science,* 1966, **153,** 316–318.

ATKINS, S. Performance, heart rate, respiration rate on the day-night continuum. *Perceptual and Motor Skills,* 1964, **18,** 409–412.

AX, A. F., BECKETT, P. G. S., FRETZ, N. A., & GOTTLIEB, J. S. Development of a selection test for motivational aptitude. NASA Contractor Rep. NASA CR-156, Washington, D.C., January 1965.

BEAM, J. C. Serial learning and conditioning under real-life stress. *Journal of Abnormal and Social Psychology,* 1955, **51,** 543–551.

BERLYNE, D. E., CRAW, M. A., SALAPATEK, P. H., & LEWIS, J. L. Novelty, complexity, incongruity, extrinsic motivation, and the GSR. *Journal of Experimental Psychology*, 1963, **66**, 560-567.

BERLYNE, D. E., & McDONNELL, P. Effects of stimulus complexity and incongruity on duration of EEG desynchronization. *Electroencephalography and Clinical Neurophysiology*, 1965, **18**, 156-161.

BERRY, R. N., & DAVIS, R. C. The somatic background of rote learning. *Journal of Experimental Psychology*, 1960, **59**, 27-34.

BILLS, A. G. Tensions in learning and association. In E. G. BARING (Ed.), *Proceedings of the 9th International Congress of Psychology*. Princeton, N.J.: Psychological Review, 1930.

BINGHAM, W. K., Jr. A study of the relations which the GSR and sensory reference bear to judgments of the meaningfulness, significance, and importance of 72 words. *Journal of Psychology*, 1943, **16**, 21-34.

BLATZ, W. E. The cardiac, respiratory, and electrical phenomena involved in the emotion of fear. *Journal of Experimental Psychology*, 1925, **8**, 109-132.

BONVALLET, M., DELL, P., & HEIBEL, G. Tonus sympathique et activité électrique corticale. *Electroencephalography and Clinical Neurophysiology*, 1954, **6**, 119-144.

BOYLE, R. H., DYKMAN, R. A., & ACKERMAN, P. T. Relationships of resting autonomic activity, motor impulsivity, and EEG tracings in children. *Archives of General Psychiatry*, 1965, **12**, 314-323.

BRIDGER, W. H., & REISER, M. F. Psychophysiologic studies of the neonate: An approach toward the methodological and theoretical problems involved. *Psychosomatic Medicine*, 1959, **21**, 265-276.

BROUGHTON, R., POIRE, R., & TASSINARI, C. A. Electrodermogram (Tarchanoff effect) during sleep. *Perceptual and Motor Skills*, 1965, **20**, 181-182.

BRUNER, J. S. Neural mechanisms in perception. *Psychological Review*, 1957, **64**, 340-358.

BURGESS, M., & HOKANSON, J. E. Effects of increased heart rate on intellectual performance. *Journal of Abnormal and Social Psychology*, 1964, **68**, 85-91.

BURNSTEIN, K. R., FENZ, W. D., BERGERON, J., & EPSTEIN, S. A comparison of skin potential and skin resistance responses as measures of emotional responsivity. *Psychophysiology*, 1965, **2**, 14-24.

CALLAWAY, E., III, & DEMBO, E. Narrowed attention: A psychological phenomenon that accompanies a certain physiological change. *Archives of Neurology and Psychiatry*, 1958, **79**, 74-90.

CALLAWAY, E., III, & STONE, G. Re-evaluating focus of attention. In L. UHR & J. G. MILLER (Eds.), *Drugs and behavior*. New York: Wiley, 1960.

CALLAWAY, E., III, & YEAGER, C. L. Relationship between reaction time and electroencephalographic alpha phase. *Science*, 1960, **132**, 1765-1766.

CAMPOS, J. J., & JOHNSON, H. J. The effects of verbalization in instructions and visual attention on heart rate and skin conductance. *Psychophysiology*, 1966, **2**, 305-310.

CAMPOS, J. J., & JOHNSON, H. J. Affect, verbalization, and directional fractionation of autonomic responses. *Psychophysiology*, 1967, **3**, 285-290.

CANNON, W. B. *Bodily changes in pain, hunger, fear, and rage*. New York: Appleton-Century-Crofts, 1915.

CARRIER, N. A., & ORTON, K. D. Skin conductance trends during learning by bright, normal, and retarded children. *Journal of Comparative Physiology and Psychology*, 1964, **58**, 315-317.

CASON, H. Sensory conditioning. *Journal of Experimental Psychology*, 1936, **19**, 572-591.

CHANG, H. T. The evoked potentials. In J. FIELD, H. W. MAGOUN, & V. E. HALL (Eds.), *Handbook of physiology*, Section 1, Vol. 1. *Neurophysiology*. Washington, D.C.: American Physiological Society, 1959.

CHURCH, R. M. The effects of competition on reaction time and palmar skin conductance. *Journal of Abnormal and Social Psychology*, 1962, **65**, 32-40.

CLAUSEN, J., & KARRER, P. Autonomic correlates of electrical excitability of the eye. *Perceptual and Motor Skills*, 1964, **19**, 753-754.

CLEMENTS, S. D., & PETERS, J. E. Minimal brain dysfunctions in school-age child. *Archives of General Psychiatry*, 1962, **6**, 185-197.

CONKLIN, J. E. Three factors affecting the general level of skin resistance. *American Journal of Psychology*, 1951, **64**, 78-86.

COOMBS, C. H. Adaptation of the galvanic response to auditory stimuli. *Journal of Experimental Psychology*, 1938, **22**, 244-268.

COQUERY, J. M., & LACEY, J. I. The effect of the foreperiod duration on the components of the cardiac response during the foreperiod of a reaction-time experiment. Presented at the Annual Meeting of the Society for Psychophysiological Research, October 15, 1966.

CORAH, N. L. Some perceptual correlates of individual differences in arousal. *Journal of Personality*, 1962, **30**, 471-484.

DANIEL, R. S. The distribution of muscle action potentials during maze learning. *Journal of Experimental Psychology*, 1939, **24**, 621-629.

DANIEL, R. S. Electroencephalographic pattern quantification and the arousal continuum. *Psychophysiology*, 1966, **2**, 146-160.

DARROW, C. W. The galvanic skin reflex (sweating) and blood pressure as preparatory and facilitative functions. *Psychological Bulletin*, 1936, **33**, 73-94.

DARROW, C. W. Psychological and psychophysiological significance of the electroencephalogram. *Psychological Review*, 1947, **54**, 137-168.

DARROW, C. W. A new frontier: Neurophysiological effects of emotion on the brain. In M. L. REYMERT (Ed.), *Feelings and emotions*. New York: McGraw-Hill, 1950.

DARROW, C. W. Cerebral concomitants of autonomic changes: Observations on anterior-posterior cerebral dominance. Paper presented at the American Psychological Association Meeting, Washington, D.C., September 1952.

DARROW, C. W. The psychophysiological reactions to pain. *Electroencephalography and Clinical Neurophysiology,* 1965, **19,** 201–202.

DARROW, C. W., & FREEMAN, G. L. Palmar skin resistance changes contrasted with non-palmar changes and rate of insensible weight loss. *Journal of Experimental Psychology,* 1934, **17,** 739–748.

DARROW, C. W., & GRAF, C. Relation of the electroencephalogram to photometrically observed vasomotor changes in the brain. *Journal of Neurophysiology,* 1945, **8,** 449–462.

DARROW, C. W., & HICKS, R. G. Interarea electroencephalographic phase relationships following sensory and ideational stimuli. *Psychophysiology,* 1965, **1,** 337–346.

DARROW, C. W., & PATHMAN, J. H. The relation of heart rate to slow waves in the electroencephalogram during hyperventilation. *American Journal of Physiology,* 1944, **140,** 583–588.

DARROW, C. W., PHILLIPS, M. L., & JOST, H. Simultaneous autonomic and electroencephalographic changes. *Psychological Bulletin,* 1941, **38,** 558–559.

DAVIS, R. C. Modification of the galvanic reflex by daily repetition of a stimulus. *Journal of Experimental Psychology,* 1934, **17,** 504–535.

DAVIS, R. C. The relation of certain muscle action potentials to "mental work." *Indiana University Publications, Science Series,* 1937, No. 5.

DAVIS, R. C. Relation of muscular action potentials to difficulty and frustration. *Journal of Experimental Psychology,* 1938, **23,** 141–158.

DAVIS, R. C. Patterns of muscular activity during "mental work" and their constancy. *Journal of Experimental Psychology,* 1939, **24,** 451–465.

DAVIS, R. C. Motor effects of strong auditory stimuli. *Journal of Experimental Psychology,* 1948, **38,** 257–275.

DAVIS, R. C. Motor responses to auditory stimuli above and below threshold. *Journal of Experimental Psychology,* 1950, **40,** 107–120.

DAVIS, R. C. The stimulus trace in effectors and its relation to judgment responses. *Journal of Experimental Psychology,* 1952, **44,** 377–390.

DAVIS, R. C. Response and adaptation to brief noises of high intensity. U.S. Air Force School of Aviation Medicine, Rep. No. 55–127, 1953.

DAVIS, R. C. Electromyographic factors in aircraft control: The relation of muscular tension to performance. U.S. Air Force School of Aviation Medicine, Rep. No. 55–122, 1956.

DAVIS, R. C., BUCHWALD, H. M., & FRANKMANN, R. W. Autonomic and muscular responses, and their relation to simple stimuli. *Psychological Monographs,* 1955, **69,** 20 (Whole No. 405).

DAVIS, R. C., LUNDERVOLD, A., & MILLER, J. D. The pattern of somatic response during a repetitive motor task and its modification by visual stimuli. *Journal of Comparative and Physiological Psychology,* 1957, **50,** 53–60.

DEWEY, J. The theory of emotion: II. *Psychological Review,* 1895, **2,** 13–32.

DIANE, G. E. Human heart rate response during experimentally induced anxiety: A follow up with controlled respiration. *Journal of Experimental Psychology,* 1964, **67,** 193–195.

DOCTER, R. F., & FRIEDMAN, L. F. Thirty-day stability of spontaneous galvanic skin responses in man. *Psychophysiology,* 1966, **2,** 311–315.

DODGE, R. Mental work: A study in psychodynamics. *Psychological Review,* 1913, **20,** 1–42.

DOERR, H. O., & HOKANSON, J. E. A relation between heart rate and performance in children. *Journal of Personality and Social Psychology,* 1965, **2,** 70–76.

DUCHARME, R. Effect of internal and external cues on the heart rate of the rat. *Canadian Journal of Psychology,* 1966, **20,** 97–104.

DUFFY, E. Tensions and emotional factors in reaction. *Genetic Psychology Monographs,* 1930, **7** (1), 1–79.

DUFFY, E. Muscular tension as related to physique and behavior. *Child Development,* 1932, **3,** 200–206. (a)

DUFFY, E. The measurement of muscular tension as a technique for the study of emotional tendencies. *American Journal of Psychology,* 1932, **44,** 146–162. (b)

DUFFY, E. The relationship between muscular tension and quality of performance. *American Journal of Psychology,* 1932, **44,** 535–546. (c)

DUFFY, E. Emotion: An example of the need for reorientation in psychology. *Psychological Review,* 1934, **41,** 184–198.

DUFFY, E. An explanation of "emotional" phenomena without the use of the concept "emotion." *Journal of General Psychology,* 1941, **25,** 283–293. (a)

DUFFY, E. The conceptual categories of psychology: A suggestion for revision. *Psychological Review,* 1941, **48,** 177–203. (b)

DUFFY, E. Level of muscular tension as an aspect of personality. *Journal of General Psychology,* 1946, **35,** 161–171.

DUFFY, E. A systematic framework for the description of personality. *Journal of Abnormal and Social Psychology,* 1949, **44,** 175–190.

DUFFY, E. The concept of energy mobilization. *Psychological Review,* 1951, **58,** 30–40.

DUFFY, E. The psychological significance of the concept of "arousal" or "activation." *Psychological Review,* 1957, **64,** 265–275.

DUFFY, E. *Activation and behavior.* New York: Wiley, 1962.

DUFFY, E. The nature and development of the concept of activation. In R. N. HABER (Ed.), *Current research in motivation.* New York: Holt, Rinehart and Winston, 1966.

DUFFY, E., & LACEY, O. L. Adaptation in energy mobilization: Changes in general level of palmar skin conductance. *Journal of Experimental Psychology,* 1946, **36,** 437–452.

DYKMAN, R. A., ACKERMAN, P. T., GALBRECHT, C. R., & REESE, W. G. Physiological reactivity to different stressors and methods of evaluation. *Psychosomatic Medicine,* 1963, **25,** 37–59.

DYKMAN, R. A., MURPHREE, O. D., & ACKERMAN, P. T. Litter patterns in the offspring of nervous and stable dogs: II.

Autonomic and motor conditioning. *Journal of Nervous and Mental Disease,* 1966, **141,** 419–431.

DYKMAN, R. A., REESE, W. G., GALBRECHT, C. R., & THOMASSON, P. J. Psychophysiological reaction to novel stimuli: Measurement, adaptation, and relationship of physiological and psychological variables in the normal human. *Annals of the New York Academy of Sciences,* 1959, **79,** 43–107.

DYSINGER, W. S., & RUCKMICK, C. A. *The emotional responses of children to the motion picture situation.* New York: Macmillan, 1933.

EASON, R. G. Relation between effort, tension level, skill, and performance efficiency in a perceptual-motor task. *Perceptual and Motor Skills,* 1963, **16,** 297–317.

EASON, R. G., AIKEN, L. R., Jr., WHITE, C. T., & LICHTENSTEIN, M. Activation and behavior: II. Visually evoked cortical potentials in man as indicants of activation level. *Perceptual and Motor Skills,* 1964, **19,** 875–895.

EASON, R. G., & BRANKS, J. Effect of level of activation on the quality and efficiency of performance of verbal and motor tasks. *Perceptual and Motor Skills,* 1963, **16,** 525–543.

EASON, R. G., HARTER, M. R., & STORM, W. F. Activation and behavior: I. Relationship between physiological "indicants" of activation and performance during memorization of nonsense syllables using differing induced tension conditions. *Perceptual and Motor Skills,* 1964, **19,** 95–110.

EASON, R. G., & WHITE, C. T. Muscular tension, effort, and tracking difficulty: Studies of parameters which affect tension level and performance efficiency. *Perceptual and Motor Skills,* 1961, **12,** 331–372.

EASTERBROOK, J. A. The effect of emotion on cue utilization and the organization of behavior. *Psychological Review,* 1959, **66,** 183–201.

EDELBERG, R. The relationship between the galvanic skin response, vasoconstriction, and tactile sensitivity. *Journal of Experimental Psychology,* 1961, **62,** 187–195.

EISDORFER, C. Psychophysiological aspects of learning in the aged: A tentative theory. Presented at the National Conference, Manpower Training and the Older Worker, Washington, D.C., January 17–19, 1966.

ELBEL, E. R., & RONKIN, R. R. Palmar skin resistance as a measure of physical fitness. *American Journal of Psychology,* 1946, **147,** 1–12.

ELLIOTT, R. Physiological activity and performance: A comparison of kindergarten children with young adults. *Psychological Monographs,* 1964, **78,** (10, No. 587).

ELLSON, D. G., DAVIS, R. C., SALTZMAN, I. J., & BURKE, C. J. Report of research on detection of deception. Contract No. NGONR-18011, Office of Naval Research, 1952.

FARBER, I. E., & SPENCE, K. W. Complex learning and conditioning as a function of anxiety. *Journal of Experimental Psychology,* 1953, **45,** 120–125.

FÉRÉ, C. *Sensation et mouvement: Études experimentales de psychomécanique.* (2nd ed., rev.) Paris: Ancienne Librarie German, Baillière et Cie, 1900.

FISKE, D. W., & MADDI, S. R. *Functions of varied experience.* Homewood, Ill.: Dorsey Press, 1961.

FORD, A. Foundations of bioelectronics for human engineering. U.S. Navy Electronics Laboratory Research Rep. No. 761, San Diego, Calif., 1957.

FORREST, D. W. Association between muscular tension and work output. *British Journal of Psychology,* 1960, **51,** 325–333.

FREEMAN, G. L. The spread of neuro-muscular activity during mental work. *Journal of General Psychology,* 1931, **5,** 479–494.

FREEMAN, G. L., & KATZOFF, E. G. Muscular tension and irritability. *American Journal of Psychology,* 1932, **44,** 789–792.

FRENCH, J. W. A comparison of finger tremor with the galvanic skin reflex and pulse. *Journal of Experimental Psychology,* 1944, **34,** 494–505.

FURTH, H. G., & TERRY, R. A. Autonomic responses and serial learning. *Journal of Comparative and Physiological Psychology,* 1961, **54,** 139–142.

FUSTER, J. M. Effects of stimulation of brain stem on tachistoscopic perception. *Science,* 1958, **127,** 150.

GELLHORN, E. *Autonomic regulations—Their significance for psychology and neuropsychiatry.* New York: Interscience, 1943.

GELLHORN, E. Motion and emotion: The role of proprioception in the physiology and pathology of the emotions. *Psychological Review,* 1964, **71,** 457–472.

GELLHORN, E., KOELLA, W. P., & BALLIN, H. M. The influence of hypothalamic stimulation on evoked cortical potentials. *Journal of Psychology,* 1955, **39,** 77–88.

GERARD, R. W., MARSHALL, W. H., & SAUL, L. J. Electrical activity of the cat's brain. *Archives of Neurology and Psychiatry,* 1936, **36,** 675–738.

GHISELLI, E. Changes in neuromuscular tension accompanying the performance of a learning problem involving constant choice time. *Journal of Experimental Psychology,* 1936, **19,** 91–98.

GOLDSTEIN, I. B. Physiological response in anxious women patients. *Archives of General Psychiatry,* 1964, **10,** 382–388.

GRAHAM, F. K., & CLIFTON, R. K. Heart-rate change as a component of the orienting response. *Psychological Bulletin* 1966, **65,** 305–320.

GRINGS, W. W., & LOCKHART, R. A. Galvanic skin response during avoidance learning. *Psychophysiology,* 1966, **3,** 29–34.

HAIDER, M., SPONG, P., & LINDSLEY, D. B. Attention, vigilance and cortical evoked-potentials in humans. *Science,* 1964, **145,** 180–182.

HARTMANN, G. W. The facilitation effect of strong general illumination upon the discrimination of pitch and intensity differences. *Journal of Experimental Psychology,* 1934, **17,** 813–822.

HAYWOOD, H. C., & SPIELBERGER, C. D. Palmar sweating as a function of individual differences in manifest anxiety. *Journal of Personality and Social Psychology,* 1966, **3,** 103–105.

HILL, W. F.   Comments on Taylor's "Drive theory and manifest anxiety." *Psychological Bulletin,* 1957, **54,** 490–493.

HODGES, W. F., & SPIELBERGER, C. D.   The effects of threat of shock on heart rate for subjects who differ in manifest anxiety and fear of shock. *Psychophysiology,* 1966, **2,** 287–294.

HOKANSON, J. E., & BURGESS, M.   Effects of physiological arousal level, frustration, and task complexity on performance. *Journal of Abnormal and Social Psychology,* 1964, **68,** 698–702.

HORD, D. J., JOHNSON, L. C., & LUBIN, A.   Differential effect of the law of initial value (LIV) on autonomic variables. *Psychophysiology,* 1964, **1,** 79–87.

HÖRMANN, H., & TODT, E.   Noise and learning. *Zeitschrift für experimentelle und angewandte Psychologie,* 1960, **1,** 422–426.

HOVLAND, C. I., & REISEN, A. H.   Magnitude of galvanic and vasomotor response as a function of stimulus intensity. *Journal of General Psychology,* 1940, **23,** 103–121.

HUME, W. I., & CLARIDGE, G. S.   A comparison of two measures of "arousal" in normal subjects. *Life Sciences,* 1965, **4,** 545–553.

ISSAC, W.   Arousal and reaction times in cats. *Journal of Comparative and Physiological Psychology,* 1960, **53,** 234–236.

JACOBSON, E.   Further experiments on the inhibition of sensations. *American Journal of Psychology,* 1912, **23,** 345–369.

JAMES, W. T.   Morphologic form and its relation to behavior. In C. R. STOCKARD (Ed.), *The genetic and endocrine basis for differences in form and behavior.* Philadelphia: Wistar Institute, 1941.

JASPER, H. H.   Diffuse projection system: The integrative action of the thalamic reticular system. *Electroencephalography and Clinical Neurophysiology,* 1949, **1,** 405–419.

JEFFRESS, L. H.   Galvanic phenomena of the skin. *Journal of Experimental Psychology,* 1928, **11,** 130–144.

JOHNSON, B.   Changes in muscular tension in coordinated hand movements. *Journal of Experimental Psychology,* 1928, **11,** 329–341.

JOHNSON, H. M.   The dynamogenic influence of light on tactile discrimination. *Psychobiology,* 1920, **2,** 351–374.

JOHNSON, L. C.   Some attributes of spontaneous autonomic activity. *Journal of Comparative and Physiological Psychology,* 1963, **56,** 415–422.

JOHNSON, L. C.   Spontaneous and orienting response during sleep. U.S. Navy Medical Neuropsychiatric Research Unit, Rep. 66-9, San Diego, Calif., 1965.

JOHNSON, L. C., & LUBIN, A.   The orienting reflex during waking and sleeping. Presented at the meeting of the Association for the Psychophysiological Study of Sleep, Gainsville, Fla., March 1966.

JOHNSON, L. C., SLYE, E. S., & DEMENT, W.   Electroencephalographic and autonomic activity during and after prolonged sleep deprivation. *Psychosomatic Medicine,* 1965, **27,** 415–423.

JOHNSON, L. C., & ULETT, G. A.   Stability of EEG activity and manifest anxiety. *Journal of Comparative and Physiological Psychology,* 1959, **52,** 284–288.

JONES, B. E., & AYRES, J. J.   Significance and reliability of shock-induced changes in basal skin conductance. *Psychophysiology,* 1966, **2,** 322–326.

JOST, H., & SONTAG, L.   The genetic factor in autonomic nervous system functions. *Psychosomatic Medicine* 1944, **6,** 308–310.

KAPLAN, R.   Rat basal resistance level under stress and nonstress conditions. *Journal of Comparative and Physiological Psychology,* 1963, **56,** 775–777.

KENNARD, M. A., & WILLNER, M. D.   Correlation between electroencephalograms and deep reflexes in normal adults. *Diseases of the Nervous System,* 1945, **6,** 337–342.

KENNEDY, J. L., & TRAVIS, R. C.   Prediction and control of alertness: II. Continuous tracking. *Journal of Comparative and Physiological Psychology,* 1948, **41,** 203–210.

KIMMEL, H. D., & KIMMEL, E.   Sex difference in adaptation of the GSR under repeated application of a visual stimulus. *Journal of Experimental Psychology,* 1965, **70,** 536–537.

KLEINSMITH, L. J., & KAPLAN, S.   Paired-associate learning as a function of arousal and interpolated interval. *Journal of Experimental Psychology,* 1963, **65,** 190–193.

KLEINSMITH, L. J., & KAPLAN, S.   Interaction of arousal and recall interval in nonsense syllable paired-associate learning. *Journal of Experimental Psychology,* 1964, **67,** 124–126.

KLEINSMITH, L. J., KAPLAN, S., & TARTE, R. D.   The relationship of arousal to short and long term verbal recall. *Canadian Journal of Psychology,* 1963, **17,** 393–397.

KLEITMAN, N.   *Sleep and wakefulness.* Chicago: University of Chicago Press, 1939.

KLING, J. W., & SCHLOSBERG, H.   The uniqueness of patterns of skin conductance. *American Journal of Psychology,* 1961, **74,** 74–79.

KRAVKOV, S. V.   Über die Abhängigkeit der Sehschärfe vom Schallreiz. *Albrecht v. Graefes Archiv für Ophthalmologie,* 1930, **124** (2), 334–339.

KRAVKOV, S. V.   Der Lichtirradiationseffert im Auge in seiner Abhängigkeit von den Gesichts-, Gehörs-, und Geruchsnebenreizen. *Albrecht v. Graefes Archiv für Ophthalmologie,* 1933, **129** (3), 440–451.

KREITMAN, N., & SHAW, J. C.   Experimental enhancement of alpha activity. *Electroencephalography and Clinical Neurophysiology,* 1965, **18,** 147–155.

KUBIS, J. F.   Adaptation of the psychogalvanic response (PGR) to a visual, auditory, and ideational stimulus. *American Psychologist,* 1948, **3,** 256. (Abstract)

KUNO, H., GOLENHOFEN, K., & LIENERT, G. A.   Reliability and validity of micro-vibration amplitude (MVA) measures as indicators of activation. *Zeitschrift für experimentelle und angewandte Psychologie,* 1964, **11** (B), 455-479.

KUNO, Y. The significance of sweating in man. *Lancet,* 1930, **218,** 912-915.

LACEY, J. I. Individual differences in somatic response patterns. *Journal of Comparative and Physiological Psychology,* 1950, **43,** 338-350.

LACEY, J. I. The evaluation of autonomic responses: Toward a general solution. *Annals of the New York Academy of Sciences,* 1956, **67,** 123-164.

LACEY, J. I. Somatic response patterning and stress: Some revisions of activation theory. In M. H. APPLEY & R. TRUMBULL (Eds.), *Psychological stress.* New York: Appleton-Century-Crofts, 1967.

LACEY, J. I., KAZAN, J., LACEY, B. C., & MOSS, H. A. The visceral level: Situational determinants and behavioral correlates of autonomic response patterns. In P. H. KRAPP (Ed.), *Expression of the emotions of man.* New York: International Universities Press, 1963.

LACEY, J. I., & LACEY, B. C. The relationship of resting autonomic activity to motor impulsivity. *Research Publications of the Association for Nervous and Mental Disease,* 1958, **36,** 144-209. (a)

LACEY, J. I., & LACEY, B. C. Verification and extension of the principle of autonomic response-stereotypy. *American Journal of Psychology,* 1958, **71,** 50-73. (b)

LACEY, J. I., & LACEY, B. C. The law of initial value in the longitudinal study of autonomic constitution: Reproducibility of autonomic responses and response patterns over a four-year interval. *Annals of the New York Academy of Sciences,* 1962, **98,** 1257-1290, 1322-1326.

LADER, M. H., & WING, L. Habituation of psycho-galvanic reflex in patients with anxiety states and normal subjects. *Journal of Neurology, Neurosurgery, and Psychiatry,* 1964, **27,** 210-218.

LANDIS, C., & HUNT, W. A. *The startle pattern.* New York: Holt, Rinehart and Winston, 1939.

LANSING, R. W., SCHWARTZ, E., & LINDSLEY, D. B. Reaction time and EEG activation under alerted and nonalerted conditions. *Journal of Experimental Psychology,* 1959, **58,** 1-7.

LATIES, V. G. Effects of meprobamate on fear and palmar sweating. *Journal of Abnormal and Social Psychology,* 1959, **59,** 156-161.

LAVILLE, A., & WISNER, A. An EMG study of the neck muscles during a precision task. *Journal of Physiology, Paris,* 1965, **57,** 260.

LAZARUS, R. S., SPEISMAN, J. C., & MORDKOFF, A. M. The relationship between autonomic indicators of psychological stress: Heart rate and skin conductance. *Psychosomatic Medicine,* 1963, **25,** 19-30.

LEHMANN, D., BEELER, G. W., Jr., & FENDER, D. H. Changes in patterns of the human electroencephalogram during fluctuations of perception of stabilized retinal images. *Electroencephalography and Clinical Neurophysiology,* 1965, **19,** 336-343.

LEIDERMAN, P. H., & SHAPIRO, D. Studies of the galvanic skin potential level: Some behavioral correlates. *Journal of Psychosomatic Research,* 1964, **7,** 277-281.

LEUBA, C. Toward some integration of learning theories: The concept of optimal stimulation. *Psychological Reports,* 1955, **1,** 27-33.

LEVY, E. Z., THALER, V. H., & RUFF, G. E. New technique for recording skin resistance changes. *Science,* 1958, **128,** 33-34.

LINDSLEY, D. B. Electroencephalography. In J. MCV. HUNT (Ed.), *Personality and the behavior disorders.* New York: Ronald, 1944.

LINDSLEY, D. B. Emotion. In S. S. STEVENS (Ed.), *Handbook of experimental psychology.* New York: Wiley, 1951.

LINDSLEY, D. B. Psychological phenomena and the electroencephalogram. *Electroencephalography and Clinical Neurophysiology,* 1952, **4,** 443-456.

LIPTON, E. L., STEINSCHNEIDER, A., & RICHMOND, J. B. Maturation of autonomic nervous system functions in the early months of life. *Psychosomatic Medicine,* 1960, **22,** 325-326. (Abstract)

LONDON, I. D. Research on sensory interaction in the Soviet Union. *Psychological Bulletin,* 1954, **51,** 531-568.

LOOMIS, A. L., HARVEY, E. N., & HOBART, G. Electrical potentials of the human brain. *Journal of Experimental Psychology,* 1936, **19,** 249-279.

LUNDERVOLD, A. An electromyographic investigation of tense and relaxed subjects. *Journal of Nervous and Mental Disease,* 1952, **115,** 512-525.

LURIA, A. R. *The nature of human conflicts: Or emotion, conflict, and will, an objective study of disorganization and control of human behavior.* Translated by W. H. GANTT (Ed.). New York: Liveright, 1932.

MACNEILAGE, P. F. Changes in electroencephalogram and other physiological measures during serial mental performance. *Psychophysiology,* 1966, **2,** 344-353.

MADDI, S. R. Activation and the need for variety. *Counseling Center Discussion Papers,* University of Chicago, 1963, **9** (No. 1).

MADDI, S. R., & PROPST, B. S. Activation and personality. Presented to the American Psychological Association Convention, Philadelphia, 1963.

MALMO, R. B. Research: Experimental and theoretical aspects. In E. D. WITTKOWER & R. A. CLEGHORN (Eds.), *Recent developments in psychosomatic medicine.* Philadelphia: Lippincott, 1954.

MALMO, R. B. Activation: A neurophysiological dimension. *Psychological Review,* 1959, **66,** 367-386.

MALMO, R. B., BOAG, T. J., & SMITH. A. A. Physiological study of personal interaction. *Psychosomatic Medicine,* 1957, **19,** 105-119.

MALMO, R. B., & SHAGASS, C. Physiological studies of reaction to stress in anxiety and early schizophrenia. *Psychosomatic Medicine,* 1949, **11,** 9-24.

MALMO, R. B., SHAGASS, C., BELANGER, D. J., & SMITH, A. A. Motor control in psychiatric patients under experimental stress. *Journal of Abnormal and Social Psychology,* 1951, **46,** 539–547.

MALMO, R. B., & SMITH, A. A. Forehead tension and motor irregularities in psychoneurotic patients under stress. *Journal of Personality,* 1955, **23,** 391–406.

MALMSTROM, E. J., OPTON, E., & LAZARUS, R. J. Heart rate measurement and the correlation of indices of arousal. *Psychosomatic Medicine,* 1965, **27,** 546–556.

MASON, W. A. The arousal concept and chimpanzee social behavior. Presented to the American Psychological Association Symposium, Some determinants and implications of activation level. September 4, 1963.

MCDONALD, D., STERN, J. A., & HAHN, W. H. Studies of classical heart rate conditioning in the rat. U.S. Navy Medical Neuropsychiatric Research Unit Rep., 1963, No. 63-3.

MCNAMARA, H. J., & FISCH, R. I. Effect of high and low motivation on two aspects of attention. *Perceptual and Motor Skills,* 1964, **19,** 571–578.

MEYER, D. R. On the interaction of simultaneous responses. *Psychological Bulletin,* 1953, **50,** 204–220.

MONTAGU, J. D. Habituation of the psycho-galvanic reflex during serial tests. *Journal of Psychosomatic Research,* 1963, **7,** 199–214.

MONTAGUE, E. K. The role of anxiety in serial rate learning. *Journal of Experimental Psychology,* 1953, **45,** 91–96.

MORUZZI, G., & MAGOUN, H. W. Brain stem reticular formation and activation of the EEG. *Electroencephalography and Clinical Neurophysiology,* 1949, **1,** 455–473.

MULHOLLAND, T., & RUNNALS, S. Evaluation of attention and alertness with a stimulus-brain feedback loop. *Electroencephalography and Clinical Neurophysiology,* 1962, **14,** 847–852.

MUNDY-CASTLE, A. C., & MCKIEVER, B. L. The psychophysiological significance of the galvanic skin response. *Journal of Experimental Psychology,* 1953, **46,** 15–24.

MURPHREE, O. D., & DYKMAN, R. A. Litter patterns in the offspring of nervous and stable dogs: I. Behavioral tests. *Journal of Nervous and Mental Disease,* 1965, **141,** 321–332.

MURPHY, L. E. Muscular effort, activation level, and reaction time. *Proceedings of the 74th annual convention of the American Psychological Association.* Washington, D.C.: American Psychological Association, 1966.

MURRAY, H. A. *Explorations in personality.* New York: Oxford, 1938.

NISHISATO, S. Reaction time as a function of arousal and anxiety. *Psychonomic Science,* 1966, **6,** 157–158.

OLSON, W. C. *The measurement of nervous habits in normal children.* Minneapolis: University of Minnesota Press, 1929.

PORTER, J. M., Jr. Adaptation of the galvanic skin response. *Journal of Experimental Psychology,* 1938, **23,** 553–557.

POWELL, A. H., Jr., EISDORFER, C., & BOGDONOFF, M. D.

Physiologic response patterns observed in a learning task. *Archives of General Psychiatry,* 1964, **10,** 192–195.

RACHMAN, S. Reliability of galvanic skin response measures. *Psychological Reports,* 1960, **6,** 326.

RASMUS, M. H. Degeneration of emotional response upon reshowing of motion picture situations. *Psychological Monographs,* 1936, **48,** 40–56.

RENBOURN, E. T. Body temperature and pulse rate in boys and young men prior to sporting contests: A study of emotional hyperthermia. *Journal of Psychosomatic Research,* 1960, **4,** 149–175.

REYMERT, M. L., & SPEER, G. S. Does the Luria technique measure emotion or merely bodily tension? *Character and Personality,* 1938–1939, **7,** 192–200.

RICCI, G., DOANE, B., & JASPER, H. H. Microelectrode studies of conditioning: Technique and preliminary results. *Proceedings of the 4th International Congress on Electroencephalography and Clinical Neurophysiology,* Brussels, 1957.

RICHTER, C. D. The significance of changes in the electrical resistance of the body during sleep. *Proceedings of the National Academy of Sciences, United States,* 1926, **12,** 214–222.

ROESSLER, R., BURCH, N. R., & CHILDERS, H. E. Personality and arousal correlates of specific galvanic skin responses. *Psychophysiology,* 1966, **3,** 115–130.

RYAN, A. H., & RANSEEN, E. L. Palmar skin resistance (PSR) during a standard period of controlled muscular activity as a measure of physical fitness and fatigue. *American Journal of Physiology,* 1944, **142,** 68–79.

SAINSBURY, A. Gestural movement during psychiatric interview. *Psychosomatic Medicine,* 1955, **17,** 458–469.

SCHNORE, M. M. Individual patterns of physiological activity as a function of task differences and degree of arousal. *Journal of Experimental Psychology,* 1959, **58,** 117–128.

SCHÖNPFLUG, W. Observations of the connection of activation and perception. *Zeitschrift für experimentelle und angewandte Psychologie,* 1965, **12** (2), 316–336. (As reported in *Psychological Abstracts,* 1966, **4,** No. 1191.)

SEWARD, J. P., & SEWARD, G. H. The relationship of galvanic skin reactions to preceding resistance. *Journal of Experimental Psychology,* 1935, **18,** 64–79.

SHAGASS, C., & SCHWARTZ, M. Reactivity cycle of somatosensory cortex in humans with and without psychiatric disorder. *Science,* 1961, **134,** 1757–1759.

SHAW, W. A. The distribution of muscle action potentials during imagining. *Psychological Record,* 1938, **2,** 195–216.

SHAW, W. A., & KLINE, L. H. A study of muscle action potentials during the attempted solution by children of problems of increasing difficulty. *Journal of Experimental Psychology,* 1947, **37,** 146–158.

SHEER, D. E. (Ed.) *Electrical stimulation of the brain.* Austin: University of Texas Press, 1961.

SHEER, D. E., & KROEGER, D. C. Recording autonomic responses as an index of stimulation effects. In D. E. SHEER (Ed.), *Electrical stimulation of the brain.* Austin: University of Texas Press, 1961.

SHERWOOD, J. J. A relation between arousal and performance. *American Journal of Psychology,* 1965, **78,** 461–465.

SICKEL, W. E. Human EEG's after prolonged mental activity. *Archiv für die gesamte Psychologie,* 1962, **114,** 1–54.

SILVERMAN, A. J., COHEN, S. I., & SHMAVONIAN, B. M. Investigations of psychophysiologic relationships with skin resistance measures. *Journal of Psychosomatic Research,* 1959, **4,** 65–87.

SIMON, C. W., & EMMONS, W. H. EEG, consciousness, and sleep. *Science,* 1956, **124,** 1066–1069.

SMITH, A. A. An electromyographic study of tension in interrupted and completed tasks. *Journal of Experimental Psychology,* 1953, **46,** 32–36.

SMITH, A. A., MALMO, R. B., & SHAGASS, C. An electromyographic study of listening and talking. *Canadian Journal of Psychology,* 1954, **8,** 219–227.

SMITH, D. B. D., & WENGER, M. A. Changes in autonomic balance during phasic anxiety. *Psychophysiology,* 1965, **1,** 267–271.

SMITH, W. *The measurement of emotion.* New York: Harcourt, 1922.

STAUDT, V. M., & KUBIS, J. F. The psychogalvanic response (PGR) and its relation to changes in tension and relaxation. *Journal of Psychology,* 1948, **25,** 443–453.

STENNETT, R. G. The relationship of performance level to level of arousal. *Journal of Experimental Psychology,* 1957, **54,** 54–61.

STERN, R. M. Electrophysiological effects of interaction between task demands and sensory input. *Canadian Journal of Psychology,* 1964, **18,** 311–320.

STERNBACH, R. A. A comparative analysis of autonomic responses in startle. *Psychosomatic Medicine,* 1960, **22,** 204–210. (a)

STERNBACH, R. A. Some relationships among various "dimensions" of autonomic activity. *Psychosomatic Medicine,* 1960, **22,** 430–434. (b)

STERNBACH, R. A. Two independent indices of activation. *Electroencephalography and Clinical Neurophysiology,* 1960, **12,** 609–611. (c)

STROUD, J. B. The role of muscular tensions in stylus maze learning. *Journal of Experimental Psychology,* 1931, **14,** 606–631.

SURWILLO, W. W. On the effects of artificial variation of the basal level of skin potential. *Psychophysiology,* 1965, **2,** 83–85.

SURWILLO, W. W., & ARENBERG, D. L. On the law of initial value and the measurement of change. *Psychophysiology,* 1965, **2,** 368–370.

SYMONS, J. R. The effect of various heteromodal stimuli on visual sensitivity. *Quarterly Journal of Experimental Psychology,* 1963, **15,** 243–251.

TEICHNER, W. H. The psychophysiology of thermal regu-

lation. Presented at the Psychonomic Society Meeting, August 1962.

TEICHNER, W. H. Delayed cold-induced vasodilatation and behavior. *Journal of Experimental Psychology,* 1965, **69,** 426–432.

TEICHNER, W. H., & YOUNGLING, E. Acclimatization, habituation, motivation, and cold exposure. *Journal of Comparative and Physiological Psychology,* 1962, **55,** 332–326.

THACKRAY, R. I. Rate of learning and autonomic divergence. *Psychophysiology Newsletter,* 1962, **8** (4), 21–28.

THOMAS, A., CHESS, S., BIRCH, H. G., HERTZIG, M. E., & KARN, S. *Behavioral individuality in early childhood.* New York: New York University Press, 1963.

THOMPSON, L. W., & OBRIST, W. D. EEG correlates of verbal learning and overlearning. *Electroencephalography and Clinical Neurophysiology,* 1964, **16,** 332–342.

THOMPSON, L. W., & THOMPSON, V. D. Comparison of EEG changes in learning and overlearning nonsense syllables. *Psychological Reports,* 1965, **16,** 339–344.

THOMPSON, R. F., & SHAW, J. A. Behavioral correlates of evoked activity recorded from association areas of the cerebral cortex. *Journal of Comparative and Physiological Psychology,* 1965, **60,** 329–339.

THOMPSON, R. F., & SPENCER, W. A. Habituation: A model phenomenon for the study of neuronal substrates of behavior. *Psychological Review,* 1966, **173** (1).

TRAVIS, R. C., & KENNEDY, J. L. Prediction and automatic control of alertness: I. Control of lookout alertness. *Journal of Comparative and Physiological Psychology,* 1947, **40,** 457–461.

TRAVIS, R. C., & KENNEDY, J. L. Prediction and control of alertness: III. Calibration of the alertness indicator and further results. *Journal of Comparative and Physiological Psychology,* 1949, **42,** 45–57.

ULETT, G. A., GLESER, G., WINOKUR, G., & LAWLER, A. The EEG and reaction to photic stimulation as an index of anxiety-proneness. *Electroencephalography and Clinical Neurophysiology,* 1953, **5,** 23–32.

UNO, T., & GRINGS, W. W. Autonomic components of orienting behavior. *Psychophysiology,* 1965, **1,** 311–321.

VALLER, V. Thermal microchanges as indicators of reactivity of organisms. *Psychological Studies,* 1963, **5,** 227–231.

VANDENBERG, S. G., CLARK, P. J., & SAMUELS, I. Psychophysiological reactions of twins: Hereditary factors in galvanic skin resistance, heartbeat, and breathing rates. *Eugenics Quarterly,* 1965, **12,** 7–10.

VENABLES, P. H. Amplitude of the electrocardiogram and level of skin potential. *Perceptual and Motor Skills,* 1963, **17,** 54.

VENABLES, P. H., & SAYER, E. On the measurement of the level of skin potential. *British Journal of Psychology,* 1963, **54,** 251–260.

VISSER, S. L. Relationship between contingent alpha blocking and conditioned psychogalvanic reflex. *Elec-*

troencephalography and Clinical Neurophysiology, 1963, 15, 768-774.

WALLER, A. D.   Concerning emotive phenomena: II. Periodic variations of conductance of the palm of the human hand. Proceedings of the Royal Society of London, Series B, 1919, 19, 17-32.

WALLERSTEIN, H.   An electromyographic study of attentive listening. Canadian Journal of Psychology, 1954, 8, 228-238.

WALTER, W. G.   Normal rhythms—their development, distribution and significance. In J. D. N. HILL & G. PARR (Eds.), Electroencephalography. London: Macdonald, 1950.

WECHSLER, D.   The measurement of emotional reaction. Archives of Psychology, New York, 1925, No. 76.

WEINBERGER, N. M., & LINDSLEY, D. B.   Behavioral and electroencephalographic arousal to contrasting novel stimulation. Science, 1964, 144, 1355-1357.

WENGER, M. A.   Pattern analysis of autonomic variables during rest. Psychosomatic Medicine, 1957, 14, 240-244.

WENGER, M. A., CLEMENS, T. L., COLEMAN, D. R., CULLEN, T. D., & ENGEL, B. T.   Autonomic response specificity. Psychosomatic Medicine, 1961, 23, 185-193.

WEYBREW, B. B.   Prediction of adjustment to prolonged submergence aboard a fleet ballistic missile submarine: IV. Psychophysiological indices. U.S. Naval Medical Research Laboratory, New London, Conn., 1963, 22, No. 18, Rep. No. 416.

WHITE, M. M.   The relation of bodily tension to electrical resistance. Journal of Experimental Psychology, 1930, 13, 267-277.

WILCOTT, R. C.   Correlation of skin resistance and potential. Journal of Comparative and Physiological Psychology, 1958, 51, 691-696.

WILCOTT, R. C.   Silverman-Powell index of sweating versus skin conductance and a humidity index of surface moisture. Journal of Comparative and Physiological Psychology, 1959, 52, 33-36.

WILCOTT, R. C.   Effects of exsanguination on sweating and skin potential responses. Journal of Comparative and Physiological Psychology, 1962, 55, 1136-1137. (a)

WILCOTT, R. C.   Palmar skin sweating vs. palmar skin resistance and skin potential. Journal of Comparative and Physiological Psychology, 1962, 55, 327-331. (b)

WILCOTT, R. C.   A comparative study of the skin potential, skin resistance, and sweating of the cat's foot pad. Psychophysiology, 1965, 2, 62-71.

WILCOTT, R. C.   A reply to Surwillo on artificial skin potential, basal level variation and skin potential response wave form. Psychophysiology, 1966, 2, 377-378.

WILDER, J.   The law of initial value in neurology and psychiatry: Facts and problems. Journal of Nervous and Mental Disease, 1957, 125, 73-86.

WILLIAMS, A. C., JR., MACMILLAN, J. W., & JENKINS, J. G.   Preliminary experimental investigations of "tension" as a determinant of performance in flight training. (CAA Division, Research Rep. No. 54, 1946; Publ. Bd. No. L50325.) Washington, D.C.: Department of Commerce, 1947.

WILLIAMS, H., GRUNDA, A. M., Jones, R. C., LUBIN, A., & ARMINGTON, J. C.   EEG frequency and finger pulse volume as predictors of reaction time during sleep loss. Electroencephalography and Clinical Neurophysiology, 1962, 14, 64-70.

WILSON, R. S.   Autonomic changes produced by noxious and innocuous stimulation. Journal of Comparative and Physiological Psychology, 1964, 58, 290-295.

ZAHN, T. P.   Autonomic reactivity and behavior in schizophrenia. Psychiatric Research Report 19, to the American Psychiatric Association Meeting, Washington, D.C., December 1964.

ZIMNY, G. H., & WEIDENFELLER, E. W.   Effects of music upon GSR and heart-rate. American Journal of Psychology, 1963, 76, 311-314.

ZUCKERMAN, M.   The development of an affect adjective check list for the measurement of anxiety. Journal of Consulting Psychology, 1960, 24, 457-462.

Peter J. Lang, David G. Rice, and Richard A. Sternbach

THE PSYCHOPHYSIOLOGY OF EMOTION*

16

While the term *emotion* has use and meaning for the layman, it is an unwieldly construct for the experimental psychophysiologist. The scientist's difficulty stems from the concept's origins in human subjectivity and the consequent difficulty in adapting it to the operational world of the laboratory. A long philosophic tradition holds that emotion or feeling is a primary function of the mind, along with willing, perceiving, and reasoning. All of these mind states are considered part of an individual's direct experience, and thus available to his own subjective analysis; however, they are unavailable to the laboratory investigator and are in fact outside the epistemological limits of natural science.

Nevertheless, man has long been sensitive to parallels between his subjective states or those inferred in others, and changes in organs innervated by the autonomic nervous system (ANS). This isomorphism is an impetus to the development of dualistic psychologies, in which the emotions are considered to be conjoint mental and physiological events. The two states have been held to interact, as Descartes suggested, when bodily events are occasionally touched by the soul; or as William James

*This work was supported in part by Research Career Grant 1-K3-MH-35,324 from the U.S. Public Health Service to P. J. Lang; and by U.S. Public Health Service Research Grant MH 12858-01 to D. G. Rice and R. A. Sternbach (A. A. Alexander, principal investigator; N. S. Greenfield, coinvestigator).

(1890) proposed, the mental event may be a perception of physiological responses. Theologians have tended to see them as two combatants, with man's animal nature (his physiology) contesting with his reasonable mind. It has often been noted that the passions differ from other subjective states, in that the individual does not feel himself to be in control but rather to be borne along by physical forces. The neuroanatomical partial independence of the ANS seems to offer a physical basis for this experience.

Psychoanalysis is a contemporary, dualistic theory that has stimulated considerable psychophysiological research. Analysts are concerned with the relationship between the patient's behavior and his subjective wishes, intentions, or desires. The fact that individuals are frequently unable to report what prompted specific acts is taken as evidence that some responses are motivated by unconscious purposes. The mental apparatus thus consists of two minds, one conscious and one unconscious. Desires that tend to be unconscious are identified with instinctual, physiological needs (primarily, sex or aggression). They tend to remain unconscious because they are unacceptable to civilized man's moral nature. However, the theory holds that, when an instinct is prompted to expression, it cannot be completely suppressed. Although unavailable to the patient's introspection, it may be betrayed in the covert, physiological responses of the organism. Thus, for many psychoanalysts, the study of autonomic events constitutes a royal road to the unconscious mind.

While the road has occasioned considerable traffic, nobody has yet located a terminus in human subjectivity. Experiments in the areas of "perceptual defense," "learning without awareness," and "unconscious anxiety" (Eriksen, 1958; Lacey & Smith, 1954; Lazarus & McCleary, 1951), have made extensive use of the physiological dependent variable. Reports demonstrating reliable discrepancies between these responses to emotional stimuli and overt behavior or verbal report have been frequent. However, as Eriksen (1958) pointed out, "When the nature of the stimulation is such as to give rise to weak or incomplete perceptual process . . . each of the response systems has a large margin of error, but as long as the different response systems are

partially independent of one another, these errors are not perfectly correlated. Thus we can expect, for example, that certain emotional responses may be appropriate to the stimulus in the absence of correct verbal responses and vice versa [p. 220]." The key concept here is the idea of *partial independence* of response systems. Such an interpretation of the data obviates the need for an unconscious receptacle to hold what is not apparent in verbal report. We do not need to assume that a "true" memory or the "complete" perception exists anywhere. In fact, a strict application of Ockham's razor encourages us not to make the assumption.

It is clear that constructs such as "consciousness" or "unconscious awareness" cannot be given scientific definition, without sacrificing their essence within a subjective or dualistic theory. This fact prompts researchers to leave aside the philosophies of experience and undertake the more austere, but potentially much more rewarding, task of developing a concept of emotion out of the measurable behavior observed in the clinic and laboratory. The contemporary psychophysiology of emotion is not a search for surface reflections of introspective life but an effort to find constructs that will integrate behavioral and physiological observations.[1]

In human subjects, emotional behavior includes responses in three expressive systems: verbal, gross motor, and physiological (autonomic, cortical, and neuromuscular). The responses of no single system seem to define or encompass an "emotion" completely. Verbal statements of hostility are obtained from subjects who show no tendency to overt attack. Individuals may report no fear of objects that they have systematically avoided for a lifetime. Subjects in a rage show elevated blood pressure, but the same reading can be caused by kidney failure or exercise. The clinical examples are legion, and the laboratory is yielding similar

[1]The principle applies broadly and must be considered when any experiment purports to seek objective indicants of subjective states. J. I. Lacey (1968) pointed out that a naïve application of this indicant or "lie detector" approach has flawed much of the psychophysiological study of psychotherapy over the previous two decades. Autonomic and neuromuscular responses are not most usefully considered as indicants of feeling but as a significant part of the emotional response under study. To put it another way, emotions are not entities independent of the responses held to assess them.

evidence of low correlation between systems, even when the subject population and the emotional stimuli are quite homogeneous (Lang, 1968, pp. 90–103). As Eriksen (1958) suggested, the different response systems are at least partially independent. Their independence is substantiated by accumulating evidence that they may be separately shaped by the environment and may change independently during the development of the organism. Recent experiments on both animals and human beings, demonstrating the operant control of autonomic activity, reveal this most dramatically (Lang, 1970; Miller, 1969).

Given these circumstances, and the necessity of abandoning subjectively based integrating concepts, we may ask what behavioral generalizations are present that can give meaning and value to the concept of an emotional response. Three such generalizations come to mind: (a) emotional behavior is intense behavior: the persistence and amplitude of responding are increased, as are the number of active response systems; (b) emotional behavior may be rigidly directional, as in intense fear or sexual responding; and (c) intense emotion is associated with behavioral disorganization, a breakdown in smooth functioning. A rough catalogue of stimuli or stimulus contexts that tend to prompt these response characteristics can be readily drawn up and would include physical danger, pain, sexual stimuli, conflict, attack, restraint, and interference with established patterns of responding.

The investigation of emotion has become a study of shifting patterns of responding to the classes of stimuli briefly listed above. "Patterns of responding" is a key concept. Emotional stimuli at their most intense are held to generate activity throughout the organism. An experiment that takes a simple stimulus-response (S-R) form is less clearly a study of emotional behavior than one which attempts to show not only a relationship of response to stimulus but also the coincident relationship between two or all three of the expressive systems referred to earlier. While our emphasis here will be on the measurement of physiological parameters, they must always be considered in context with the other behavioral output of the organism.

In the present chapter, we shall first consider theories of emotional stimuli and ways in which physiological data are being applied to their analysis; the succeeding section is devoted to theories of the emotional response and empirical problems in the analysis of relevant physiological data. Finally, we shall consider the instigation, alteration, and reduction of emotional states in the laboratory and clinic.

EMOTIONAL STIMULI

Theories that attempt to define emotional stimuli emphasize three different factors: intensity, novelty, and genetic prepotency. Theories based on the first two purport to show how the formal properties of certain stimuli or stimulus combinations can evoke emotion. Theories stressing the last factor are supported mainly by ethological research, which suggests that some stimuli may evoke emotion because of a genetically based, species-specific sensitivity in the observer.

Intensity Theories

The thesis that intense stimuli produce emotional responses is well documented. Loud auditory stimuli reliably initiate excited activity in normal infants (Jersild & Holmes, 1933), as the pain threshold is approached, this may be accompanied by whimpering and crying. Landis and Hunt (1939) found that the sound of a gunshot behind the adult subject's head reliably produced a startle response over repeated trials. Intense electric shocks (Solomon & Brush, 1956), heat (Malmo & Shagass, 1949a), cold (Malmo, Shagass, & Heslam, 1951), and high gravity stress (Silverman & Cohen, 1960), to name but a few, have been used to produce transient emotional behavior in experimental subjects. Schneirla (1959) argues that any intense stimulus will produce avoidance. He emphasizes the phylogenetic continuity of this behavior, pointing out that all primitive organisms avoid high intensity stimuli and approach low intensities of stimulation. Worms, ants, beetles, and the ontogenetically primitive human neonate avoid bright light, while responding positively to lower levels of illumination. Schneirla attempts to explain all emotional responding in terms of his intensity theory. Thus Tinbergen's (1951) finding that turkey chicks showed fear when a "hawk" model passed over them but not when a "goose" model was used (actually, the hawk reversed), is explained in terms of the rapid (and therefore intense) onset of the stimulus in the case of the hawk and, because the wings are to the rear, the relatively slower, less intense, approach of the goose. Schneirla (1959) has much greater difficulty applying a quantitative intensity theory to the complex stimuli that are often found to elicit emotional behavior in the adult human organism. Furthermore, once a scale of energy quanta is no longer appropriate, the definition of intensity becomes elusive. In dealing with specific fear situations, Schneirla argues that large stimuli are more intense than small; that a complex stimulus is more intense than a simple one; and that dark is more intense than light, or vice versa. So flexible a concept loses considerable explanatory power.

Novelty Theories

Theorists who view novelty as the central component of stimuli provoking emotional responses can cite a great variety of experiments supporting their thesis. Strange stimuli and strange environments reliably produce fear responses in rhesus monkeys more than 40 days old (Harlow, 1961). The 6-month-old human infant fears strangers (Bridges, 1932; Spitz, 1950). Unfamiliar stimuli may produce amusement, apprehension, or aggression in human adults, although not all unfamiliar stimuli produce emotional responses. Developmental age and past experience appear to be critical.

Hebb (1949) argues that emotion is elicited by the disruption of the response set. Emotional stimuli initiate a familiar response pattern, but the stimuli are distorted in ways that prevent the smooth completion of the response. The consequence is a behavioral disorganization that we call "emotion." Hebb argues that the basic effect of such stimuli is a disturbance of coordinated timing of neural activity in the brain. Hebb's concept is basically one of conflict, which attempts to explain the emotional responses produced both by frankly competing stimuli (e.g., the studies of approach-avoidance situations by Liddell, 1964; Masserman, 1943; Pavlov, 1927); and by stimuli that are simply novel or unfamiliar. Novelty theory is weakened by the fact that stimuli which elicit emotional re-

sponses often appear no more unusual than other, ignored stimuli. For example, Hebb (1949) found that a human skull and the cast of a snake produced avoidance in naïve rhesus monkeys, while a doll and a movable rubber tube did not. Similarly, Melzack (1952) found that puppies showed less apparent fear when confronted by a moving chair than when they were faced with an open umbrella. Thus, while the novelty theory explains elegantly the monkey's fear of an attendant who is wearing his colleague's lab coat (Hebb & Riesen, 1943), it strains credulity when enlisted to explain the different reactions obtained from what appear to be equally unusual events.

Theories of Genetic Prepotency

Ethologists developed the concept of releaser stimuli from experimental and naturalistic observation of animal behavior. Tinbergen's studies (1951) of the three-spined stickleback implicated specific releasers in the aggressive, avoidant, and sexual responses of this species. Lorenz (1952) showed how the potency of releaser stimuli may be determined by developmental periods and delineated the complex, sequential interaction between releaser and response in the courtship of birds. The hypothesis of intrinsically potent stimuli has less frequently been raised to explain emotional behavior in more complex animals. Nevertheless, data are accumulating which suggest that specific stimuli are innately activating for primates. Sackett (1966) found that "at least two kinds of socially meaningful visual stimuli, pictures of monkeys in threatening postures and pictures of infants, appear to have unlearned, prepotent, activating properties for socially naïve infant monkeys. From the second month of life these stimuli produced generally higher levels of all behaviors in all subjects. Furthermore, the visual stimulation involved in threat behavior appears to function as an 'innate releasing stimulus' for fearful behavior [p. 1473]." As in the studies of lower organisms by ethological investigators, stimulus potency interacts with maturation. Thus, pictures of monkeys in threatening postures released behavior in Sackett's rhesus monkeys 60–80 days after birth but failed to do so at a younger age.

Introductory textbooks in psychology pridefully assert man's independence from the biological restraints of instinct. Yet, if the hypothesis of phylo-genetic continuity is to be maintained, at least remnants of releaser mechanisms should be found in the emotional behavior of human beings. In fact, the stimuli of many of the gross fears of man are similar to those of other primates (snakes, being stared at, mutilated bodies, etc.). Human and non-human primates fear strangers at the same relative maturational age (Harlow, 1961).

Studies of reactions to a "visual cliff" by Gibson and Walk (1960) encourage the thesis that man shares with lower organisms an innate response to the visual perspectives evoked by high places. Their work reveals both species-specific responses and interaction between apparent biological pre-disposition and learning; in addition it suggests a phylogenetic ordering of species. In general, phylogenetically lower species show more stereo-typed and directly functional emotional responses with very high intraspecies reliability. Thus the response of nearly all chaffinch to the binocular stare of the owl is a ritualized "mobbing" behavior and a characteristic call. In phylogenetically higher species, more diverse behavior occurs. The response of some chimpanzees to being stared at is avoidant and fearful, while others become aggressive. Some human beings preen with pleasure when under an-other's gaze; others offer a hostile, "What are you looking at?" reaction. Our psychiatric clinics con-tain many whose greatest anxiety is stimulated by being watched. Studies of infants (Bridges, 1932; Kagan, 1970; Washburn, 1929) have confirmed that the human face is a potent stimulus, one that re-liably evokes smiling behavior in the neonate but produces fearful responses in many infants of 6 months. If binocularly set eyes have some innate releaser properties for a variety of animals including man, evidently the responses of higher organisms are basically much more varied or are more mal-leable under the press of experience. Despite di-versity in the observed responses, such stimuli ap-parently do instigate unusual nervous activity, perhaps in the diffuse projection system of the central nervous system and the autonomic nervous system, and furthermore, they seem to demand some adjustive response. These responses may be avoidant, aggressive, sexual: the specific charac-teristics are determined by context and learning.

Psychophysiological Studies of Emotional Stimuli

The psychophysiologist has potentially powerful tools available for analyzing the theoretical issues outlined above, and physiological dependent varia-bles figure prominently in recent thinking and re-search. An increasing number of experimenters are studying autonomic and cortical responding in neonates or young children (Graham, Clifton, & Hatton, 1968), in whom the initial development of emotional patterns might be observed. Thus, Campos, Langler, and Krowitz (1970) found signifi-cant differences in the heart rate response of crawling infants on the shallow and deep sides of the "visual cliff." Increasingly, studies of the effects of emotional stimuli on animals measure auto-nomic, as well as behavioral, responses (Toledo & Black, 1966). More and more, physiological meas-urement operationally defines "response" as it is used and understood in current theory.

Sokolov (1963) has developed a psychophysio-logical theory dealing with the relationship be-tween the intensity or novelty characteristics of stimuli and the responses of organisms. He suggests that, in addition to peripherally relevant adaptation of reflexes, stimuli prompt one of two primary response dispositions: orienting and defense. The orienting reflex is evoked by any change in the physical or signal characteristics of the environment and is associated with a set to attend or receive environmental input. The repetition of a stimulus leads to habituation of orienting, as the temporal and physical characteristics of the stimulus become less novel. In human subjects, orienting responses can be seen as changes in a variety of physiological systems (see Part 2 of this book, regarding alpha blocking in EEG, skin conductance, peripheral vasoconstriction, and cephalic vasodilation). The work of both Russian and Western investigators shows that increasing the intensity of a stimulus increases the amplitude and hastens the onset of the response. These effects can also be produced by increasing the novelty of the stimulus; i.e., within the range of nonaversive stimuli, larger re-sponses are associated with lower probability stim-uli (Berlyne, 1960; Sokolov, 1963). More recently, Kagan (1970) has suggested that as children develop intellectually, they generate representations (called schemas) of those temporal and spatial events that are more or less invariant in their environment. Stimuli which are moderately discrepant from such schema (different but not too different) occasion rapid orienting and greater attention, and presumably could lead to emotional responses. He notes that more deviant (less probable) stimuli often fail to prompt any reaction at all. This line of reasoning seems to take something both from orienting theory and from the speculations of Hebb (1949), to which we have previously referred.

The concept of the defensive reflex is of equal if not greater potential relevance to the psychology of emotion. According to Sokolov (1963), when very high intensity stimuli (particularly those exciting pain receptors) are presented, orienting is replaced by the defensive reflex. This response is associated with reduced sensitivity of the receptor and avoidance of the stimulus. The reflex is defined by yet higher amplitude sympathetic activity in a variety of systems, and specifically by cephalic vasoconstriction. The defensive reflex would presumably be an important part of what Western investigators consider to be fear behavior. It could also mediate inattention and breakdown in performance under stress, as this reflex is specifically associated with a reduction in the ability to discriminate and initially to process external input.

Despite these advantages, there are a number of difficulties in utilizing Sokolovian theory as a model for the analysis of emotional stimuli. Sokolov's neuronal model of the orienting and defensive reflexes is based on a conceptual nervous system, with few neurophysiological anchors in brain research. Furthermore, the theory does not handle selective attention or emotional specificity at all well. Finally, measuring the defensive reflex has proved to be a difficult task for psychophysiologists. Western investigators have only occasionally reported any consistent relationship between intensity of the stimulus and cephalic vascular changes (Royer, 1965). In an experiment from Graham's laboratory (Berg, 1968), diphasic and even triphasic patterns of constriction and dilation were noted in response to an auditory stimulus that Sokolov holds should evoke simple orienting (dilation) or defense (constriction).

Recently, Graham and Clifton (1966) suggested that orienting and defensive reflexes may also be represented by heartrate deceleration and acceleration, respectively. They further proposed an integration of Sokolov's concepts of orienting and defense with J. I. Lacey's speculations concerning the relationship between attention and cardiovascular activity. J. I. Lacey (1967, pp. 14–37) has noted a relationship between cardiovascular activity and the organism's "acceptance or rejection" of environmental input, which appears to be, at least in part, independent of the level of activity or arousal. Thus both painful, aversive stimuli and mental activity such as problem solving evoke cardiac acceleration and blood pressure increase, whereas stimuli that evoke attention and interest are associated with decreases in the cardiac rate and blood pressure. In some of the experiments reported, these findings were obtained when the stimuli used led to no differences in the amplitude of the skin conductance response. Basing his conclusions in part on the neurophysiological experiments of Bonvallet, Dell, and Hiebel (1954), J. I. Lacey (1967, pp. 14–37) has described a mechanism whereby increases in blood pressure, mediated by the baroreceptors of the aorta and the carotid sinus, alter the electrical activity in the brain stem and cortex, and hence the characteristics of the organism's overt motor behavior. Thus we are prompted to speculate that the organism's responses to emotional stimuli take place in many systems but they are not independently evoked by an external stimulus nor are they even independent consequences of central nervous system activity; rather, it would appear that feedback loops between the responding systems shape and modulate the behavior of the organism as it occurs. Such interaction complicates the analysis of emotional stimulus-response relationships enormously. It also encourages a research strategy which does not assume that autonomic activity is only a reflection of more central events, and further suggests that its understanding and control may have implications for techniques of changing emotional behavior.

It is to these other issues that we shall now proceed. The next section focuses on the physiological responses in emotion (autonomic and somatic) and on theories of their nature or function, and then outlines empirical problems in their measurement.

PHYSIOLOGICAL RESPONSE IN EMOTION

According to Wenger, emotion is the "activity and reactivity of the tissues and organs innervated by the autonomic nervous system. It may involve, but does not necessarily involve, skeletal muscular response or mental activity" (Wenger, F. N. Jones, & M. H. Jones, 1956, p. 343). Unlike earlier theories, Wenger's is concerned only with observable responses, not with the perception of them (as in James' theory), nor with perceptions of hypothalamic activity (as in Cannon's theory) (Wenger, 1950). Whether or not the response theory of Wenger is accepted *qua* theory, it directs the researcher to the measurement of autonomic behavior in various stimulus-situations. Hence it should be possible to demonstrate the existence of a unique pattern of autonomic responses for each emotion, where these are elicited by differing stimuli (emotional situations). A hypothesis of emotional specificity has not always met with acceptance, in part because of reluctance to accept an approach that does not encompass verbal report, and in part because of the assumption, based on earlier empirical evidence, that autonomic responses cannot be differentiated. Let us consider this concept.

Emotion As Activation

Since Cannon's (1936) early investigation of the sympathetic nervous system (SNS), we have been accustomed to think of it as serving emergency functions. The massive SNS discharges that occur in response to threatening stimulus situations facilitate fight-or-flight reactions. In less extreme conditions, the dual innervation of most viscera with SNS and parasympathetic (PNS) fibers, whose functions are typically antagonistic, maintains the homeostasis of the internal environment necessary for the organism's survival. Both the concept of emergency functions and that of homeostatic regulations place the operations of the autonomic nervous system (ANS) in a Darwinian (adaptational) framework which is easy to understand.

However, Cannon's early work, like that of Selye (1946) on biochemical responses to stressors, emphasized the unified and almost invarying pattern of responses to stimulation. Cannon described essentially the same physiological changes occurring in three states: fear, anger, and pain. More recently, Selye (1956) has described a single pattern of biochemical responses to prolonged stress: massive discharge of adrenal cortical steroids, destruction of the thymus, and bleeding gastric ulcers. This pattern would obtain whether the stressor were cold, exercise, fasting, injury, or any of several drugs. Such findings have led some writers such as Duffy (1962) and Malmo (1959) to develop a psychological construct of activation capable of explaining various emotional and motivational states. Neither Cannon nor Selye described any patterning of responses unique to the stimulus or to the individual organism, primarily because they were interested in the generality of their findings and in elucidating the mechanisms underlying the response patterns obtained. Other investigators, however, have demonstrated the existence of individual differences, of stimulus-response specificity, and of dissociation in activation patterns. We shall consider these in some detail, but first we must examine the nature of the changes that are generally referred to as "activation."

Let us consider the situation in which a sudden, intense, and unexpected stimulus produces a startle response. This is what happens: The heart beats faster. The amount of blood pumped out with each beat (cardiac stroke volume) is increased. The superficial blood vessels and those going to the gastrointestinal tract and to other viscera constrict, so that the blood pressure increases. The blood vessels serving the larger muscles dilate, increasing the blood supply to the muscles. The pupils of the eyes dilate, increasing the amount of light impinging on the retina, thus improving visual sensitivity. The adrenal medulla increases its secretion of epinephrine; beside reinforcing the other SNS effects as it circulates in the blood, epinephrine causes the liberation of bood sugar from the liver, making stored energy available for the muscles. Breathing becomes deeper and faster; the bronchioles of the lungs dilate; the secretion of mucus in the air passages decreases; and so more oxygen is available for the metabolism of the increased carbohydrates going to the large muscles (Sternbach, 1960a, 1960b, 1960c).

These are the immediate SNS effects in the brief startle response. If the stimulus is extended and responses prolonged, we might expect the subjects to report fear or anger and perhaps to show avoidance or attacking behavior: in most naturally occurring situations, this may well be the case. However, it is important to introduce here the first of several kinds of differential response patterns that make it difficult to retain the older concept of a unitary activation as the base for emotions. Massive SNS responses can be produced without accompanying reports of emotions or emotional behavior. It may be done artificially by the infusion of epinephrine, as reported by Wenger et al. (1960), or it may be done by simple physical exercises. Indeed, with effortful exercising, SNS responses may be greater than those occurring in the extreme emotions of terror and rage, and yet not necessarily be accompanied by any marked change in subjective feelings. The evident dissociation of physiological and verbal responses is a major difficulty for those who would equate the two or use the physiological changes to define the emotions.

Adaptation and Rebound

Another difficulty with a unitary concept of activation derives from the structure and function of the ANS. Most of the autonomically innervated organs receive dual innervation from the SNS and the PNS, two branches generally antagonistic. The SNS fibers cause pupillary dilatation, PNS fibers induce pupillary constriction; SNS fibers to the heart are cardiac accelerators, PNS fibers are cardiac decelerators; SNS fibers inhibit gastric activity, PNS fibers facilitate gastric activity; and so on.

Usually, the stimulus for increased activity in one branch is an increase in activity in the other. Thus an SNS increase in pupillary diameter is followed by a PNS constriction (assuming constant illumination). The constant oscillation about some ideal average diameter, observable in most normal subjects, is called "hippus," and is an example of homeostatic functioning. Homeostatic responses such as this make it difficult to specify the nature of the changes in a situation of prolonged stimulation. The changes occurring in startle, for example,

are intense but of brief duration. Even if the stimulus were extended over time, the physiological responses would not continue at their initial poststimulus levels. Several cardiovascular reflexes operate to return the blood pressure, pulse rate, and blood flow to normal levels.

It is not always correct to assume that the homeostatic reduction of responses to normal levels results from antagonistic PNS activity. Although many organs are dually innervated, not all of them are. The hair follicles, sweat glands, superficial blood vessels, and adrenal medulla receive only SNS innervation. In some instances, it is difficult to know whether the return of function to resting levels is due to the antagonistic action of the PNS, or to a decrease in SNS activity, especially since so many of the reflexes are functionally interrelated. The complexity of the control mechanisms prompted Darrow to observe that specifying the autonomic functions is like trying to "determine the weight on either side of a 'balance' when that on neither side is known" (Darrow, 1943).

The tendency of activation responses to return to prestimulus levels with continued or repeated stimulation is called *adaptation*. In the sense that activation is a set of responses to change or novelty, adaptation is the diminution of those responses in the face of constancy or familiarity. As the generalized activation pattern is one of mobilization of energy in response to changing stimuli (catabolism), adaptation refers to the conservation of energy in the presence of constant stimuli (anabolism). The adaptation of responses to continued or repetitive stimulation is not a smooth or steady decline in rate or magnitude. Occasionally, responses of initial magnitude will occur, or occasionally nonspecific responses will occur in the intervals between presentations of repetitive stimuli. In this the phenomenon of adaptation is rather analogous to the extinction of conditioned responses: the extinction curve is seldom smooth but contains bursts of occasional and apparently random responses, representing disinhibition or spontaneous recovery.

If the SNS responses to intense stimulation are great, the homeostatic reflexive responses are also likely to be quite large. Frequently, they return to and cross over the prestimulus baseline, so that the functioning is at slower or lower levels than preceded the onset of stimulation. Overshooting the prestimulus levels in a direction opposite to activation is called "rebound."

It is interesting that rebound most often occurs when the stimulation is stopped. Continued stimulation usually results in the adaptation of responses from maximal initial levels or slightly above prestimulus levels. Removing the stimulus often causes the rebound phenomenon to take place. It may be seen in both the dually innervated response variables (e.g., the heart rate) and the singly innervated ones (e.g., the skin conductance), so that rebound is not exclusively a result of antagonistic functioning.

These then are some of the complexities in activation. The activation responses diminish over time if the stimulus is prolonged or repeated (adaptation). They may "paradoxically" go the other way if the stimulus is abruptly terminated (rebound). The two variations are closely related to the nature of stimulation. Thus it is not possible to hold to a view that simply equates emotion with activation, without considering the fluctuating nature of activation per se. Let us now take a more detailed look at the extent to which activation responses are related to the stimuli that elicit them, in the sense of response patterning.

Specificity of Somatic Emotional Responses

Cannon had considered that essentially the same physiological responses occurred in pain, fear, hunger, and rage. For many years it was thought that only emergency and homeostatic functions were subserved by the ANS. Yet obvious and consistent differences in the verbal and motor responses in these states have prompted investigators to look for characteristic patterns of physiological responses to different emotion-producing stimuli. Our language has taught us that the vascular responses in our face are differentiable: the "pallor of fear," "purple with rage," and the "blush of shame" are a few examples. Similarly with gastric sensations: stage fright gives us "butterflies in the stomach"; the anxiety caused by looking down from great heights can "tie one's stomach in knots"; and the stench of decaying matter "turns one's stomach" in revulsion. On both subjective and clinical grounds, many investigators believed, as Alexander (1950) said, that "every emotional state has its own physiological syndrome." The difficulty lay in getting experimental data to support the hypothesis. It is difficult to induce authentic emotions in a standardized manner in the laboratory, while obtaining quantifiable physiological measures.

One of the first reports concerning differential physiological responses in emotions was by Wolf and Wolff (1947), who had the opportunity to make detailed observations of a patient's stomach through his chronic fistula. When the patient was anxious and wished to flee an emotionally charged situation, there was a decrease in his acid output, of his gastric blood flow, and of his gastric motility. When the patient was angry and resentful and wished to strike back, there was a marked increase in these gastric functions, to the point of engorgement and reddening of the mucosa, frequently seen in gastritis. Here was a clear differentiation of responses: an increase in gastric activity was associated with anger, and an inhibition of gastric functions was associated with fear. Both, clearly, occurred within the larger context of activation (see also Chapter 10).

Not all physiological variables are so easily accessible in a patient group, and more rigor is desired for an experimental study. Ax (1953) reported a controlled study with a normal population in which apparently authentic emotions of fear and anger were induced by staged situations. Ax found that the increases in diastolic blood pressure, decreases in the heart rate, increases in the muscle potentials and in the *number* of skin conductance responses were greater for anger than for fear. On the other hand, increases in the skin conductance levels, in respiration rate, and in the *number* of muscle action potentials, were greater for fear than for anger. Ax felt that the pattern in fear resembled that produced by injections of epinephrine, while that in anger was like the effect of combined epinephrine and norepinephrine (see Wenger et al., 1960).

Other investigators began reporting similar findings. For example, J. Schachter (1957) repeated Ax's study, adding hypertensive patients to the control subjects in his group, and adding pain from a cold pressor test to the fear and anger situations.

He found that fear produced a physiological pattern consistent with an epinephrine effect; cold pressor, a norepinephrine effect; and anger, a mixed effect.[2] Other investigators also reported differences in patterns of activation associated with different stimulus conditions. Davis, Buchwald, and Frankmann (1955) found differential response patterns to a variety of simple stimuli, as did Wenger and Cullen (1958). Engel (1959), taking advantage of recording and statistical techniques not available to Cannon, found clearly different patterns in hunger and pain. Sternbach (1960a) compared startle responses to those obtained during cold pressor, exercise, and epinephrine and norepinephrine infusions. The startle responses differed only in degree from epinephrine responses—confirming the observations of Ax and Schachter on the similarity between the patterns produced by fear and epinephrine. The patterns of responses to pain have been described in detail (Sternbach, 1968).

The attempts to differentiate some of the more subtle emotions have been less successful. The failure is a result, in part, of the difficulty (mentioned above) of inducing these emotions in controlled laboratory situations. Some investigators have used films for this purpose (Lazarus, Spiesman, Mordkoff, & Davison, 1962; Sternbach, 1962) but have encountered difficulties because of differences in the way the subjects were instructed or instructed themselves, and because the subjects must engage in perceptual tasks that tended to mask or override the response to the content of the film (J. I. Lacy, Kagan, B. C. Lacy, & Moss, 1963; Obrist, 1963).

On the other hand, D. T. Graham and his colleagues have reported encouraging results in inducing physiological response patterns specific to particular attitudes. Normal subjects, who were given hypnotic suggestions (D. T. Graham, Kabler, & F. K. Graham, 1962) or waking suggestions (F. K. Graham & Kunish, 1965) of attitudes verbalized by medical patients with particular psychosomatic disorders, responded with physiological changes underlying such disorders. For example, subjects given the suggestion of an attitude associated with hives responded with an elevation of skin temperature; when given the suggestion of an attitude associated with Raynaud's disease, the skin temperature decreased. An extension of D. T. Graham's method holds promise for the detailed analysis of the specificity of emotional responses (see also Chapter 21).

Let us summarize the preceding material. Given any resting subject, we find that virtually any change in stimulus conditions will result in "activation," i.e., a relative preponderance of responses in an SNS-direction. But, clearly, not all stimuli produce the same pattern of responses. This suggests that there must be at least several kinds of activation. They differ among themselves in the amount of change in the SNS direction; in some situations some variables change in the opposite, apparent PNS direction. Furthermore, considering the differences in responses to epinephrine and norepinephrine, it is no longer clear what is meant by an SNS pattern. Nevertheless, attempts have been made to find response patterns specific to emotional situations. Reliable configurations have been found for fear, anger, startle, hunger, pain, and a few specific interpersonal attitudes. It is now well demonstrated that patterning does occur within the nonspecific activation framework and that it takes the form of a specificity of response patterns, according to the demands of the stimulus-situation on the subject. It is unknown how far the S-R specificity extends across the range of response sets commonly labeled "emotion." Theorists favoring an extreme view of specificity (D. T. Graham, 1962) contend that every attitude (a verbal response) may be associated with a potentially definable pattern of physiological responses. They suggest that the difficulty in demonstrating such patterns is due to the artificiality of the experimental

---

[2] The chief difference in epinephrine and norepinephrine effects—both components of the secretion of the adrenal medulla—is their difference in impact on cardiovascular functioning. Epinephrine causes a marked increase in cardiac functioning, increasing the heart rate and stroke volume (amount of blood pumped out with each contraction of the cardiac muscles); it also produces a constriction in the superficial peripheral blood vessels. Norepinephrine, however, exerts its effect primarily on the large blood vessels supplying the muscles, causing a marked vasoconstriction there, and decreases the heart rate and stroke volume. The effect of both these hormones is to increase the systolic blood pressure but for different reasons: epinephrine chiefly because of the increased cardiac output, norepinephrine because of the increased peripheral vascular resistance. The latter effect of norepinephrine also results in a markedly increased diastolic blood pressure; while epinephrine has a negligible effect on diastolic blood pressure, since the increased cardiac output is accompanied by a dilatation of the large peripheral blood vessels, thus lessening the vascular resistance.

situation, and in part to the confounding effect of marked individual differences in the patterns suggested.

Individual Differences in the Physiological Response

Classifying people into emotional types is a favorite sport for many of us, and a serious pursuit for a few. The ancient Greeks had four types, based on the supposed dominance in one's system of certain body fluids: sanguinary (blood); phlegmatic (phlegm); choleric (yellow bile); and melancholic (black bile). Early in this century, Pavlov (1927) noted apparently constitutional differences in temperament in the dogs he worked with, by which he classified them as excitable or lethargic, a dimension supported by the work of W. T. James (1953), Scott and Charles (1954), and Fuller (1948). On the basis of factor analytic studies of psychological tests, Eysenck (1953) argues for a factor of neuroticism and another for introversion-extraversion, for which he finds corroborating evidence in physiological data. Sheldon (1944, pp. 526–549) used body builds as a predictor of temperament, with three ideal types: ectomorph (tall, thin, lonely, cerebral); endomorph (fat, jolly, visceral); and mesomorph (muscular, aggressive, dominant).

Some association with personality factors has been found for psychophysiological measures, too. Wenger (1947) reported that children with strong relative PNS dominance in the resting state showed more emotional inhibition, less emotional excitability, a lower frequency of activity with less fatigue, and more patience and neatness than those with strong apparent SNS dominance.

Individual differences have appeared also in studies of reactivity. Malmo and Shagass (1949a, 1949b) and Malmo, Shagass, and Davis (1950a, 1950b) compared the responses of psychiatric patients, with either a history of cardiovascular complaints or a history of head and neck pains, to painful stimuli. They found that the patients were most reactive to stressors of the system associated with their symptoms, even though the subjects were free of symptoms at the time of testing. These studies led Malmo and his colleagues to formulate a principle of symptom-specificity, which postulated that (for psychiatric patients with somatic symptoms) the physiological mechanism underlying the symptom is specifically responsive to activation by stressful stimuli.

J. I. Lacey and his co-workers extended these findings to normal subjects (adults and children, males and females) and used a variety of stimuli, including mental arithmetic, hyperventilation, word association, and cold pressor (J. I. Lacey, Bateman, & VanLehn, 1953; J. I. Lacey & B. C. Lacey, 1958a, pp. 144–209, 1958b). They found evidence for what they called autonomic response-stereotypy. Some individuals tended to respond in such a way that maximal activation occurred in the same physiological function, no matter what the stress. It further appeared that an individual's entire pattern of activation—the hierarchy of responses in standard score form—could be reproduced from one stimulus situation to another.

In addition to individual differences in the maximally reactive variable and in the rank order of the responses in activation, it also appears that there are individual differences in the degree of response-stereotypy. Some persons, whom we can call "rigid reactors," seem to respond to every stress with a highly consistent response hierarchy. Others, "random reactors," respond to different stimuli now with one pattern, now with another. These differences are intriguing, incidentally, for understanding the psychosomatic diseases (Sternbach, 1966). A prospective study should show whether the "rigid reactors," normal subjects who consistently show maximal activation in a single physiological variable (e.g., blood pressure) are those who later develop a related psychosomatic disorder (e.g., hypertension).

Engel (1960; Engel & Bickford, 1961) confirmed and extended the findings of J. I. Lacey et al. (1953, 1958a, 1958b) and showed how complicated the analysis of activation patterns can be. They were interested in the question of whether both a pattern of stimulus-response specificity and an individual, response-stereotypic pattern could occur simultaneously. The problem arises because, if responses in activation show one pattern for fear and another for anger, one would expect there to be little room for variation among individuals. On the other hand, if each person shows an activation pattern characteristic for him, then there can be no response patterns typical of fear and anger. Without going into detail (see Chapter 15), it is sufficient to say here that by employing an analysis-of-covariance design, it was possible to demonstrate the coexistence of response patterns specific both to the stimulus and to the individual.

A question has developed with respect to the stability of the phenomenon of individual response-stereotypy. Oken and his colleagues (1962) found that stereotypy, whether judged by the specific response showing maximal change, or by a hierarchy of responses, was not reproducible on another occasion of testing a week later. Johnson, Hord, and Lubin (1963) also found that half of their subjects, who showed stereotypy on one day, failed to show it when tested 48 hr later. While this is an embarrassment to specificity theorists, it is not a surprising result. Emotional responses may well be more stereotyped than other behavior; nevertheless, the relevant response systems (verbal, motor, and somatic) are all separately modifiable by learning and by genetically determined development. The latter facts suggest that high reliability of patterns may not be a reasonable expectation, except perhaps in psychosomatic disease.

We have come a long way from the idea of a single pattern of autonomic discharge in all emotions. No longer is it satisfactory to think of emotional activation as a generalized pattern of responses in an apparently sympathetic direction, since there are several SNS patterns known: those associated with epinephrine primarily, norepinephrine primarily, and with combined epinephrine and norepinephrine. Furthermore, while patterns of autonomic responses have been found that are typical of pain, fear, anger, and hunger, there also are patterns associated with unique individual differences. Both the response pattern associated with the emotion-producing stimulus situation and that associated with the individual's response hierarchy require involved statistical techniques to detect: they are not blatantly apparent to an observer. In fact, the somatic response that we have been discussing is defined operationally by the forms of data analyses used. Therefore, we can expect that the physiological patterns we find in emotion will be a complex set of responses deter-

mined in part by the unique properties of the stimulus situations, in part by the individual's unique response systems, and in part by the method of analysis. Furthermore, these patterns of response are not necessarily fixed but are subject to continuing modification with environmental change.

EMOTIONAL CHANGE AND CONTROL

In this chapter we have expressed the view that emotion is an operational construct, defined jointly by verbal, overt motor, and covert physiological responses. We have also suggested that these behavioral systems are partially independent; i.e., even in the context of emotional stimuli, correlations within and between subjects will tend to be low. Furthermore, in considering the characteristics of physiological responses in emotion, we outlined some of the special determinants of the system that have contributed to its independence.

Nevertheless, clinicians have traditionally operated on the basis of the dependence hypothesis. Their therapy is usually directed toward one response system, with the expectation that a change in this system will alter other relevant behavior. Thus it is expected that the administration of a muscle relaxant or sympathetic depressant drugs will produce more than a physiological change. Similarly, efforts to modify verbal or gross motor behavior through direct suggestion, conditioning, or interview psychotherapy are also expected to change the autonomic physiology of emotion. While the failures of the expectation are frequent, there are also dramatic individual successes, in which, for example, a new cognitive set may broadly modify the whole range of emotional responding.

Understanding the interrelation of response systems is fundamental to the psychology of emotion and to the development of effective treatment of emotional disorders. We need to know the conditions under which we can expect unit change, as well as the conditions that prompt disparate behavioral output. Therefore, in the final section we shall emphasize the research most relevant to this issue; particularly, experiments or clinical studies in which an attempt has been made to manipulate one system and to evaluate the effects of this intervention on the other emotional responses of the organism.

One subject of interest to investigators has been the modification of verbal or overt emotional responding as a correlate of spinal cord injury. McKelligott (1959) and Hohmann (1966) have interviewed patients with spinal lesions located at different cord levels. Few of McKelligott's subjects reported differences in emotional feelings after spinal cord injury. However, he noted that he had some difficulty in gaining rapport with his subjects, a finding that in itself suggests emotional alteration.

Hohmann (1966), who was able to overcome the difficulty of patient rapport, has given us a study worth considering in detail (see Table 16.1). We can summarize his findings in his own words: "[It] seems clear that spinal cord injury, at almost any level, may effect a reduction in feelings of sexual excitement, and a reduction in sexual drive.... Reports of experienced fear in this study followed a parallel course.... Only men with sacral lesions reported no decreased feelings of fear.... In regard to anger the experienced feelings also were markedly diminished.... The data presented here suggest that unless a person is neurologically intact at or above the sacral region, there will be a reduc-

tion in the experienced feelings, but not necessarily the acts, associated with the emotional behaviors called anger, fear, or sexual excitement. Experienced feelings of sentiment ... increased in all groups and no subject showed a decrease.... The other major area of emotional feeling investigated in this study, grief, showed no significant changes." Hohmann concluded that his data show "a direct relationship between decrease in general feelings and the degree of disruption of the autonomic nervous system [pp. 152–154]."

Hohmann contrasted his findings with clinical reports that patients with spinal cord lesions below the cervical region often show marked emotional, especially aggressive, behavior. He submits that the latter responses were learned prior to injury and are devoid of the appropriate emotional feeling. From the point of view of this chapter, his argument suggests that the gross motor responses in emotion are to some extent independent of reported feelings and less closely related to autonomic events than the verbal report of emotion. However, the data only permit speculation, without providing strong empirical support. It is regrettable that no investigator has examined the responses (verbal report, autonomic, and motor) of a popula-

TABLE 16.1 CHANGES IN EXPERIENCED EMOTIONS FOLLOWING SPINAL CORD INJURIES AT DIFFERENT LEVELS

	Sex			Fear			Anger			Sentiment			Grief			Σ		
	I[a]	N[b]	D[c]	I	N	D	I	N	D	I	N	D	I	N	D	I	N	D
Cervical N = 5	0	0	5	0	0	5	0	0	5	4	1	0	0	2	3	4	3	18
High thoracic N = 5	0	0	5	0	0	5	0	0	5	5	0	0	0	4	1	5	4	16
Low thoracic N = 5	0	0	5	0	1	4	0	1	4	5	0	0	0	4	1	5	6	14
Lumbar N = 5	0	0	5	0	1	4	1	1	3	5	0	0	2	3	0	8	5	12
Sacral N = 5	0	1	4	3	2	0	1	1	3	4	1	0	2	3	0	10	8	7
Σ	0	1	24	3	4	18	2	3	20	23	2	0	4	16	5	32	26	67

Note.—From G. W. Hohmann, Some effects of spinal cord lesions on experienced emotional feelings. *Psychophysiology*, 1966, **3**, 143–156. Reproduced by permission.
[a] I = increased.
[b] N = no change or unable to compare.
[c] D = decreased.

tion with spinal cord injuries in terms of responses to emotional stimuli presented in the laboratory setting. It would provide an ideal context in which to study the interdependence of responses and assess the significance of autonomic feedback in emotional learning.

Animal experiments have already demonstrated the importance of autonomic responses to the learning of overt emotional responses. Solomon and Wynne (1954) found that sympathectomized dogs learned to avoid shock, although the autonomic response in the conditioning was absent or minimal. Moreover, dogs who were deprived of autonomic response capability after avoidance conditioning were resistant to extinction of the conditioned response. Later experiments (Solomon & Turner, 1962) showed that curarization of the peripheral musculature was equally ineffective in disrupting avoidance learning. Thus the hypothesis of Mowrer (1947) that fear responses are exclusively autonomic, or Wenger's (1950) broader statement that autonomic events *are* emotion, or W. James's earlier speculations (1890) about the importance of posture to emotion are contradicted by the results of these careful experiments. Furthermore, they prompt us to reject, as Cannon did (1936), the concept of peripheral feedback modifying central states and could lead the student of emotion to devote himself exclusively to brain research.

On the other hand, in addition to the clinical studies cited earlier, a number of neurophysiological experiments suggest that changes in autonomic responses influence central states and motor responses. Bonvallet, Dell, and Hiebel (1954) found that, in chronically prepared dogs, increases in blood pressure or mechanical distention of the carotid artery at the carotid sinus reduced the frequency of EEG activity and also inhibited spinal reflexes. J. I. Lacey (1967, pp. 14–37) argues that variability in the blood pressure and heart rate influence cortical activity via such a pressor mechanism, and thus help determine the characteristics of individual temperament and also the responsiveness of the organism to various situations. The reaction time has been shown to depend on the heart rate during the foreperiod (Coquery & J. I. Lacey, 1966) and on the period in the cardiac cycle in which the stimuli are presented (Birren, Cardon,

& Phillips, 1963). From a more clinical perspective, Gellhorn (1964) has stressed the "modulating" role of autonomic and muscular events in emotion. He believes that proprioceptive stimulation of the posterior hypothalamus prompts the organism to be sympathetically balanced. Thus muscle tension may initiate or maintain emotional behavior at times when verbal or overt responses would not have occurred or continued.

The physiological responses of emotion may be manipulated through the administration of drugs. However, the effects are often both central and peripheral to an unknown degree, making the interpretation of these experiments difficult. Nevertheless, several investigators have administered epinephrine to human subjects and then monitored physiological responses and/or verbal report. In general, epinephrine increases the level of sympathetic activity throughout the system, a common response to emotional stimuli. On the other hand, there is less agreement about the effects of epinephrine on overt behavior or on verbal report in emotion. Hawkins, Monroe, Sandifer, and Vernon (1960) reported that the intravenous infusion of epinephrine produced physiological changes resembling those concomitant with an anxiety attack. Still, the verbal report of anxiety was relatively mild. The infusion of norepinephrine produced a physiological state they held to be similar to that of previously determined "anger directed outwardly." However, the change in verbal report of the experience was slight and nonspecific in direction. An important feature of the study by Hawkins et al. is that the two subjects were colleagues, who administered the drug to one another. Thus the experimental situation contained a variety of uncontrolled set and external social variables, in addition to the internal stimuli produced by the drug. The importance of these factors was subsequently shown by the work of S. Schachter and Singer (1962).[3]

After surveying the previous literature on physiological specificity in different emotional states (e.g., Ax, 1953; J. Schachter, 1957), S. Schachter and

[3]However, in the study by Wenger et al. (1960), subjects were unaware of the nature of the drugs being infused, and epinephrine and norepinephrine were alternated with saline infusions. These subjects also did not report subjective emotional changes.

Singer felt that the differences demonstrated were small and not causative. They theorized that cognitive factors (verbal sets) were more important in emotional differentiation. Specifically, they suggest that an individual ". . . labels, interprets, and identifies this stirred-up state in terms of the characteristics of the precipitating situation and one's apperceptive mass [p. 380]."

Marañon (1924) had reported that subjects injected with epinephrine reported arousal but not specific emotions, a finding similar to that of Hawkins et al. (1960). They had argued that the physiological state is nonspecific and an insufficient condition for emotion; cognitive factors are necessary to define direction and content. S. Schachter and Singer suggest that in Marañon's study the subjects knew they were getting a drug that would have physiological consequences; thus they had already a nonemotional label for whatever sensations were evoked. The experiment by Hawkins et al. and other studies failing to use a blind procedure may be similarly interpreted.

S. Schachter and Singer attempted to investigate systematically the role of response set in their own studies of drug effects. In a first experiment, subjects were told that they were participating in an experiment to see if a vitamin could improve eyesight. They were given subcutaneous injections of either epinephrine or a saline placebo. Subjects were further divided into three instruction subgroups, who were (a) told the actual side effects of the drug, (b) told nothing about what to expect in the way of side effects, and (c) misinformed as to the specific side effects.

Subjects were induced to behave emotionally during a 20-min waiting period, which was described as necessary for the injection to take effect. The emotional behavior was encouraged by a stooge in the waiting room (ostensibly a fellow subject), who behaved in one of two preplanned ways: (a) euphoria—the stooge "goofed off" and fooled around with play objects in the room; (b) anger—the stooge became increasingly irritated and "blew up" at a long questionnaire, finally tearing it up. At the end of the 20-min period, the subjects were asked to report their subjective feelings on various rating scales—happiness, tremor, etc.

In the euphoria condition, subjects given epinephrine and misinformed as to the drug's effect indicated the greatest self-report of euphoria; while those in the informed, epinephrine group reported the least euphoric arousal. Placebo subjects were roughly midway between these two groups on this dimension. In the anger condition, subjects seemed more reluctant to report feelings. However, the uninformed subjects who received epinephrine reported the greatest anger, the placebo subjects next; the subjects who knew that they received epinephrine reported the least anger.

In all groups, a higher pulse rate was associated with greater euphoria or with greater anger. S. Schachter and Singer concluded from the experiments that the presence of emotion is the product of two factors: (a) an undifferentiated state of physiological arousal, and (b) the availability of cognitive labels to arouse behavior along specifically emotional lines. These concepts would fit nicely with the two-component theories of activation (i.e., intensity and valence) such as that outlined by Duffy (1962). (See Chapter 15.)

While these data are consistent with a simple two-factor theory, they do not constitute strong evidence for it. Epinephrine may produce a state of undifferentiated autonomic arousal, onto which any emotional response may be grafted, but specific physiological states may be more likely to prompt one type of emotional behavior than another. Furthermore, there are many clinical instances in which changes in autonomic activity induce verbal or behavioral expressions of emotion, despite the subjects' awareness of their physiological origin and active efforts to suppress them (e.g., variations in temperament associated with the menstrual cycle, sexual arousal). In addition, other investigators may question whether evidence of psychophysiological specificity in emotion may be so lightly dismissed. As we have already pointed out, students of psychosomatic disorder have generated compelling evidence for specificity. Thus D. T. Graham, Stern, and Winokur (1958) found that the hypnotic induction of an emotional attitude held to be associated with hives (feeling unfairly treated and not knowing what to do) led to an increase in skin temperature, while suggesting to the *same* subjects the attitude for Raynaud's disease (feeling mistreated and actively hostile) led to a fall in the skin temperature. A further phase of the experiment indicated that systolic blood pressure might be similarly differentiated. Malmo and associates (Malmo & Shagass, 1949b; Malmo, Shagass, & Davis, 1950a) have reported differing distributions of muscle tension in different psychosomatic diseases and emotional states. The classic work of J. I. Lacey and B. C. Lacey (1958) and R. C. Davis (1957) on the relationship between patterns of physiological response and stimulus input also constitutes strong evidence for the physiological differentiation of emotions.

Like S. Schachter, Lazarus (1967, pp. 151–169) has emphasized the overriding importance of cognitive factors in emotion. He also studied the effects of a covertly administered instructional set on emotional responding but employed threatening external stimuli (filmed scenes of operation or injury), rather than drugs, to elicit an arousal response. When his subjects viewed a stress-inducing film with a sound track that encouraged "denial" of harmful consequences or "intellectualization" of the frightening events, both the level of autonomic activity and the level of verbal report of anxiety were attenuated. While not demonstrating the phenomenon conclusively, he also suggested that the effects of such "sets" interact with personality and temperament characteristics. Lazarus (1967, pp. 151–169) also found dramatic evidence of independence of verbal report and autonomic activity. When Japanese subjects were studied, only the data from their verbal reports followed the pattern of previous studies on American subjects; the skin conductance level did not clearly discriminate between the responses to control and stress films, as it had for American subjects. It is not clear whether the independence of responses is explicable on psychological or physiological grounds.

Lazarus and his colleagues (1962) have tended to treat autonomic activity as a unidimensional phenomenon (anxiety), which cognitive responses may increase or decrease. However, the evidence suggests that stress tolerance, cognitive set, and physiological response may interact in a more complex fashion. Silverman and Cohen (1960) explored the relationship between the functioning of subjects under high gravity (g) stress, their physiological responses, and observational evidence of emotion. They found that subjects who experienced high g without blackout tended to be more aggressive than subjects who showed lowered g tolerance. The latter were characterized by higher anxiety. Furthermore, bioassays of urine revealed that they had higher epinephrine levels, while the high g group had higher norepinephrine levels. When efforts to manipulate affect in a therapeutic interview were successful, the subjects showed the appropriate change in tolerance to gravity stress.

While the clinical studies of patients with spinal cord injury suggest that alteration of the physiological response will selectively alter other components of the emotional response, there is almost no supporting evidence from laboratory experimentation with human beings, with the possible exception of psychopharmacological studies of tranquilizing or energizing medications. As we suggested earlier, however, the neural consequences of drugs are often as much central as peripheral. Thus resulting changes in verbal or overt behavioral measures can hardly be considered specific to the associated changes in autonomic activity or tension in striated muscle.

Nevertheless, a number of theorists have suggested that efforts toward changing and controlling emotional behavior should center on the autonomic components of the emotional response. Wolpe (1958) urges that unwanted emotional responses may be eliminated by the substitution of competing or reciprocally inhibiting responses at the level of the autonomic nervous system. Jacobson (1938), Gellhorn (1964), and Schultz and Luthe (1959) have similarly argued the importance of peripheral muscular and autonomic control in the treatment of emotional disturbance. Traditionally, hypnotic suggestion, respiratory control, or training of muscle relaxation have been the main techniques applied. While anecdotal reports suggest that the hypnotic method can produce remarkably powerful and specific autonomic control (Bennett & Scott, 1949; Heyer, 1925, pp. 229–257; McDowell, 1959, pp. 101–115), the results of controlled experimentation have been less encouraging. Thus the suggestion of emotional attitudes may produce autonomic change (e.g., D. T. Graham, 1962), but direct suggestions to manipulate an autonomic system are not clearly any more effective during trance states than under more normal conditions of instruction (Barber, 1965). Jacobson (1938) has demonstrated that training in muscle relaxation has broad effects on the level of autonomic responding, but the result was a general lowering of sympathetic activity, rather than a precise instigation of a particular response or pattern.

Several investigators have demonstrated that control of specific autonomic systems may be acquired by operant conditioning methods (see Chapter 6). Lisina (1958), a Russian investigator, was one of the first to report this finding. He monitored the vascular activity of his subjects' arms with a plethysmograph. The subjects were given rather prolonged and moderately painful electric shock, which usually resulted in vasoconstriction. The experimenters set the apparatus so that any vasodilatation response (which occasionally occurred) would terminate the shock. Under these conditions, no subject showed evidence of learning the contingency, even after as many as 80 reinforcements. The experiment was then changed, so that the subjects could watch their plethysmographic records during the shock stimulation. Under these conditions, the subjects quickly learned the connection between vasodilation and the termination of shock. The response transformation from vasoconstriction to vasodilatation occurred in the course of several experimental sessions.

A somewhat more precise, avoidance-conditioning procedure was used by Shearn (1962) to demonstrate conditioned acceleration of the heart rate in human subjects. Other investigators have confirmed these results and shown operant control of cardiac deceleration and variability (Brener, 1966; Engel & Hanson, 1966; Frazier, 1966; Hnatiow & Lang, 1965). Lang, Sroufe, and Hastings (1967) and Sroufe (1969) found that such control could be obtained independent of respiratory change, and also that feedback of the heart rate had effects apparently independent of a specific instructional set. Hnatiow (1968) observed a lowering of blood pressure when feedback of this variable was provided to subjects. Similar control of skin conductance activity has been achieved by Rice (1966); Crider, Shapiro, and Tursky (1966); and Kimmel (1967).

Paralleling this work is the animal research of Miller and his colleagues (Miller, 1966, 1969; Miller & DiCara, 1967), who have demonstrated the operant conditioning of a broad spectrum of cardiovascular and other autonomically mediated responses, using brain stimulation as the reinforcer. The effects have been achieved in artificially respirated curarized animals, leaving little doubt that the method achieves autonomic conditioning without the direct mediation of the striated musculature (also see Chapter 6).

While the technique has been little explored in the context of emotional behavior, operant control of selected autonomic events should be a powerful tool for the investigation of relationships between the peripheral physiology and other systems of behavior. For example, will subjects who were trained to control autonomic responses be able to maintain such control when subjected to stress?

The method also has considerable potential as a treatment method. Engel, Melmon, and Hutchinson (1968) have applied operant techniques in the treatment of cardiac arrhythmias of organic origin. The operant conditioning of autonomic responses may also prove helpful in the treatment of those anxious or depressive states in which physiological responses are paramount in the symptom picture.

Given the present state of our knowledge, practical emotional control would seem to demand a treatment directed at multiple systems (Lang, 1968, 1970). Thus, if the individual subject's emotional response involves strong overt, behavioral components, such as phobic avoidance, an effort to shape these behaviors directly is prompted. Similarly, if verbal responses and feelings of anguish, depression, fear, and remorse dominate the symptom picture, then treatment should be concentrated on the cognitive responses or on modifying the verbal output of the patient. Strong, disruptive autonomic responses should also be dealt with directly, and the operant procedures described earlier may provide a vehicle of therapy.

Nevertheless, to be truly successful in treatment, we must know more about the way in which changing one system of responses affects other behavioral output of the organism. Some of the experiments reviewed suggest that feedback of gross change in autonomic levels modifies verbal report of emotion and observed behavior. However, other experiments suggest that the strong emotional behaviors such as avoidance can be learned and maintained in the absence of gross, peripheral physiological activity. Hohmann's (1966) study of spinal lesion cases argues that autonomic feedback from different points in the autonomic chain may differentially influence verbal report of emotion. In contrast, S. Schachter and Singer (1962) showed that the "meaning" of an emotional response can be determined exclusively by cognitive set. These apparent conflicts confirm the complexity of the phenomenon under study. Research already suggests that physiological responses are organized in

patterns unique both to stimuli and individuals. It is not unreasonable that the interaction between these responses and the verbal or overt behavior of the individual may be similarly complex.

Thus the response system of key importance will vary from subject to subject, and the best technique for its modification may prove to vary in a parallel fashion. If so, the task of the investigators of emotional behavior will be to explore the nature of these interactions and to develop diagnostic methods that will define the best program for positive emotional control.

REFERENCES

ALEXANDER, F. *Psychosomatic medicine: The principles and applications.* New York: Norton, 1950.

AX, A. F. The physiological differentiation between fear and anger in humans. *Psychosomatic Medicine*, 1953, **14**, 433–442.

BARBER, T. X. Experimental analysis of "hypnotic" behavior: A review of recent empirical findings. *Journal of Abnormal Psychology*, 1965, **70**, 132–154.

BENNETT, L. L., & SCOTT, N. E. The production of electrocardiographic abnormalities by suggestion under hypnosis: A case report. *American Practitioner*, 1949, **4**, 189–190.

BERG, W. K. Vasomotor and HR responses to nonsignal auditory stimuli. Unpublished master's thesis, University of Wisconsin, 1968.

BERLYNE, D. E. *Conflict, arousal, and curiosity.* New York: McGraw-Hill, 1960.

BIRREN, J. E., CARDON, P. V., Jr., & PHILLIPS, S. L. Reaction time as a function of the cardiac cycle in young adults. *Science*, 1963, **140**, 195–196.

BONVALLET, M., DELL, P., & HIEBEL, G. Tonus sympathique et activité électrique corticale. *Electroencephalography and Clinical Neurophysiology*, 1954, **6**, 119–144.

BRENER, J. Heart rate as an avoidance response. *Psychological Record*, 1966, **16**, 329–336.

BRIDGES, K. M. B. Emotional development in early infancy. *Child Development*, 1932, **3**, 324–354.

CAMPOS, J. J., LANGLER, A., & KROWITZ, A. Cardiac responses on the visual cliff in prelocomotor human infants. *Science*, 1970, **170**, 196–197.

CANNON, W. B. *Bodily changes in pain, hunger, fear and rage.* (2nd ed.) New York: Appleton-Century-Crofts, 1936.

COQUERY, J. M., & LACEY, J. I. The effect of foreperiod duration on the components of the cardiac response

during the foreperiod of a reaction-time experiment. Paper delivered at the annual Meeting of the Society for Psychophysiological Research, Denver, Colo., October 1966.

CRIDER. A., SHAPIRO, D., & TURSKY, B. Reinforcement of spontaneous electrodermal activity. *Journal of Comparative and Physiological Psychology*, 1966, **61**, 20–27.

DARROW, C. W. Physiological and clinical tests of autonomic function and autonomic balance. *Physiological Review*, 1943, **23**, 1–36.

DAVIS, R. C. Response patterns. *Transactions of the New York Academy of Sciences* (Series II). 1957, **19**, 731–739.

DAVIS, R. C., BUCHWALD, A. M., & FRANKMANN, R. W. Autonomic and muscular responses, and their relation to simple stimuli. *Psychological Monographs*, 1955, **69**, No. 20, 1–71 (Whole No. 405).

DUFFY, E. *Activation and behavior.* New York: Wiley, 1962.

ENGEL, B. T. Some physiological correlates of hunger and pain. *Journal of Experimental Psychology*, 1959, **57**, 389–396.

ENGEL, B. T. Stimulus-response and individual-response specificity. *Archives of General Psychiatry*, 1960, **2**, 305–313.

ENGEL, B. T., & BICKFORD, A. F. Response-specificity: Stimulus-response and individual-response specificity in essential hypertensives. *Archives of General Psychiatry*, 1961, **5**, 478–489.

ENGEL, B. T., & HANSON, S. P. Operant conditioning of heart rate slowing. *Psychophysiology*, 1966, **3**, 176–187.

ENGEL, B. T., MELMON, K. L., & HUTCHINSON, J. C. Learned slowing of heart rate in patients with atrial fibrillation. Prepublication manuscript, 1968.

ERIKSEN, C. W. Unconscious processes. In M. R. JONES

(Ed.), *Nebraska symposium on motivation*. Lincoln: University of Nebraska Press, 1958.

EYSENCK, H. J. *The structure of human personality*. New York: Wiley, 1953.

FRAZIER, T. W. Avoidance conditioning of heart rate in humans. *Psychophysiology*, 1966, **3**, 188–202.

FULLER, J. L. Individual differences in the reactivity of dogs. *Journal of Comparative and Physiological Psychology*, 1948, **41**, 339–347.

GELLHORN, E. Motion and emotion: The role of proprioception in the physiology and pathology of the emotions. *Psychological Review*, 1964, **71**, 457–472.

GIBSON, E. J., & WALK, R. D. The "visual cliff." *Scientific American*, 1960, **202**, 64–71.

GRAHAM, D. T. Some research on psychophysiologic specificity and its relation to psychosomatic disease. In R. ROESSLER & N. S. GREENFIELD (Eds.), *Physiological correlates of psychological disorder*. Madison: University of Wisconsin Press, 1962.

GRAHAM, D. T., KABLER, J. D., & GRAHAM, F. K. Physiological response to the suggestion of attitudes specific for hives and hypertension. *Psychosomatic Medicine*, 1962, **24**, 159–169.

GRAHAM, D. T., STERN, J. A., & WINOKUR, G. Experimental investigation of the specificity of attitude hypothesis in psychosomatic disease. *Psychosomatic Medicine*, 1958, **20**, 446–457.

GRAHAM, F. K., & CLIFTON, R. K. Heart rate change as a component of the orienting response. *Psychological Bulletin*, 1966, **65**, 305–320.

GRAHAM, F. K., CLIFTON, R. K., & HATTON, H. M. Habituation of heart rate response to repeated auditory stimulation during the first five days of life. *Child Development*, 1968, **39**, 35–51.

GRAHAM, F. K., & KUNISH, N. O. Physiological responses of unhypnotized subjects to attitude suggestions. *Psychosomatic Medicine*, 1965, **27**, 317–329.

HARLOW, H. F. The development of affectional patterns in infant monkeys. In B. FOSS (Ed.), *Determinants of infant behavior*. New York: Wiley, 1961.

HAWKINS, D. R., MONROE, J. T., SANDIFER, M. G., & VERNON, C. R. Psychological and physiological responses to continuous epinephrine infusion—An approach to the study of the affect, anxiety. In L. J. WEST & M. GREENBLATT (Eds.), *Explorations in the physiology of emotions*. Washington: American Psychological Association Psychiatric Research Rep. 12, January 1960.

HEBB, D. O. *Organization of behavior*. New York: Wiley, 1949.

HEBB, D. O., & RIESEN, A. H. The genesis of irrational fears. *Bulletin of the Canadian Psychological Association*, 1943, **3**, 49–50.

HEYER, G. R. Psychogene Functionsstörungen des Verdauungstraktes. In O. SCHWARZ (Ed.), *Psychogenese und Psychotherapie körperlicher Symptome*. Vienna: Springer, 1925.

HNATIOW, M. Learned control of heart rate and blood pressure. Unpublished doctoral dissertation, University of Pittsburgh, 1968.

HNATIOW, M., & LANG, P. J. Learned stabilization of cardiac rate. *Psychophysiology*, 1965, **1**, 330–336.

HOHMANN, G. W. Some effects of spinal cord lesions on experienced emotional feelings. *Psychophysiology*, 1966, **3**, 143–156.

JACOBSON, E. *Progressive relaxation*. Chicago: University of Chicago Press, 1938.

JAMES, W. *The principles of psychology*. New York: Holt, Rinehart and Winston, 1890.

JAMES, W. T. Morphological and constitutional factors in conditioning. *Annals of the New York Academy of Sciences*, 1953, **56**, 171–183.

JERSILD, A. T., & HOLMES, F. B. A study of children's fears. *Journal of Experimental Education*, 1933, **2**, 109–118.

JOHNSON, L. C., HORD, D. J., & LUBIN, A. Response specificity for difference scores and autonomic lability scores. U.S. Navy Medical Neuropsychiatric Research Unit, Rep. 63-12, August 1963.

KAGAN, J. Attention and psychological change in the young child. *Science*, 1970, **170**, 826–832.

KAGAN, J., & LEWIS, M. Studies of attention in the human infant. *Merrill-Palmer Quarterly*, 1965, **11**, 95–127.

KIMMEL, H. D. Instrumental conditioning of autonomically mediated behavior. *Psychological Bulletin*, 1967, **67**, 337–345.

LACEY, J. I. Psychophysiological approaches to the evaluation of psychotherapeutic process and outcome. In E. A. RUBINSTEIN & M. B. PARLOFF (Eds.), *Research in psychotherapy*. Washington, D.C.: American Psychological Association, 1959.

LACEY, J. I. Somatic response patterning and stress: Some revisions of activation theory. In M. H. APPLEY & R. TRUMBULL (Eds.), *Psychological stress: Issues in research*. New York: Appleton-Century-Crofts, 1967.

LACEY, J. I., BATEMAN, D. E., & VANLEHN, R. Autonomic response specificity: An experimental study. *Psychosomatic Medicine*, 1953, **15**, 8–21.

LACEY, J. I., KAGAN, J., LACEY, B. C., & MOSS, H. A. The visceral level: Situational determinants and behavioral correlates of autonomic response patterns. In P. H. KNAPP (Ed.), *Expression of the emotions in man*. New York: International Universities Press, 1963.

LACEY, J. I., & LACEY, B. C. The relationship of resting autonomic activity to motor impulsivity. In H. C. SOLOMON, S. COBB, & W. PENFIELD (Eds.), *The brain and human behavior*. Vol. 36. Baltimore: Williams & Wilkins, 1958. (a)

LACEY, J. I., & LACEY, B. C. Verification and extension of the principle of autonomic response-stereotypy. *American Journal of Psychology*, 1958, **71**, 50–73. (b)

LACEY, J. I., & SMITH, R. L.   Conditioning and generalization of unconscious anxiety. *Science,* 1954, **120,** 1045–1052.

LANDIS, C., & HUNT, W. A.   *The startle pattern.* New York: Holt, Rinehart and Winston, 1939.

LANG, P. J.   Fear reduction and fear behavior: Problems in treating a construct. In J. M. SHLIEN (Ed.), *Research in psychotherapy.* Vol. III. Washington D.C.: American Psychological Association, 1968.

LANG, P. J.   Autonomic control or learning to play the internal organs. *Psychology Today,* October 1970, 37–41.

LANG, P. J.   The application of psychophysiological methods to the study of psychotherapy and behavior change. In A. E. BERGIN & S. L. GARFIELD (Eds.), *Handbook of psychotherapy and behavior change: An empirical analysis.* New York: Wiley, 1971.

LANG, P. J., SROUFE, L. A., & HASTINGS, J. E.   Effects of feedback and instructional set on the control of cardiac-rate variability. *Journal of Experimental Psychology,* 1967, **75,** 425–431.

LAZARUS, R. S.   Cognitive and personality factors underlying threat and coping. In M. H. APPLEY & R. TRUMBULL (Eds.), *Psychological stress: Issues in research.* New York: Appleton-Century-Crofts, 1967.

LAZARUS, R. S., & MCCLEARY, R. A.   Autonomic discrimination without awareness: A study of subception. *Psychological Review,* 1951, **58,** 113–122.

LAZARUS, R. S., SPEISMAN, J. C., MORDKOFF, A. M., & DAVISON, L. A.   A laboratory study of psychological stress produced by a motion picture film. *Psychological Monographs,* 1962, **76** (Whole No. 553).

LIDELL, H. S.   The challenge of Pavlovian conditioning and experimental neuroses in animals. In J. WOLPE, A. SALTER, & L. J. REYNA (Eds.), *The conditioning therapies.* New York: Holt, Rinehart and Winston, 1964.

LISINA, M. I.   The role of orientation in the conversion of involuntary into voluntary reactions. In L. G. VORONIN A. N. LEONTIEV, A. R. LURIA, E. N. SOKOLOV, & O. S. VINOGRADOVA (Eds.), *The orienting reflex and exploratory behavior.* Moscow: Academy of Pedagogical Sciences, 1958.

LORENZ, K. Z.   *King Solomon's ring.* New York: Crowell, 1952.

MALMO, R. B.   Activation: A neuropsychological dimension. *Psychological Review,* 1959, **66,** 367–386.

MALMO, R. B., & SHAGASS, C.   Physiologic studies of reaction to stress in anxiety and early schizophrenia. *Psychosomatic Medicine,* 1949, **11,** 9–24. (a)

MALMO, R. B., & SHAGASS, C.   Physiologic study of symptom mechanisms in psychiatric patients under stress. *Psychosomatic Medicine,* 1949, **11,** 25–29. (b)

MALMO, R. B., SHAGASS, C., & DAVIS, F. H.   Symptom specificity and bodily reactions during psychiatric interview. *Psychosomatic Medicine,* 1950, **12,** 362–376. (a)

MALMO, R. B., SHAGASS, C., & DAVIS, F. H.   Specificity of bodily reactions under stress: A physiological study of somatic mechanisms in psychiatric patients. *Research*

Publications of the Association for Research in Nervous and Mental Disease, 1950, **29,** 231–261. (b)

MALMO, R. B., SHAGASS, C., & HESLAM, R. M.   Blood pressure response to repeated brief stress in psychoneurosis: A study of adaption. *Canadian Journal of Psychology,* 1951, **5,** 167–179.

MARAÑON, G.   Contribution à l'étude de l'action émotive de l'adrénaline. *Revue français d'Endocrinologie,* 1924, **2,** 301–325.

MASSERMAN, J. H.   *Behavior and neurosis.* Chicago: University of Chicago Press, 1943.

MCDOWELL, M.   Hypnosis in dermatology. In J. M. SCHNECK (Ed.), *Hypnosis in modern medicine.* (2nd ed.) Springfield, Ill.: Charles C Thomas, 1959.

MCKELLIGOTT, J. W.   Autonomic functions and affective states in spinal cord injury. Unpublished doctoral dissertation, University of California, 1959.

MELZACK, R.   Irrational fears in the dog. *Canadian Journal of Psychology,* 1952, **6,** 141–147.

MILLER, N. E.   Experiments relevant to learning theory and psychopathology. Paper presented at the meetings of the XVIII International Congress of Psychology, Moscow, 1966.

MILLER, N. E.   Learning of visceral and glandular responses. *Science,* 1969, **163,** 434–445.

MILLER, N. E., & DICARA, L.   Instrumental learning of heart rate changes in curarized rats: Shaping, and specificity to discriminative stimulus. *Journal of Comparative and Physiological Psychology,* 1967, **63,** 12–19.

MOWRER, O. H.   On the dual nature of learning—A reinterpretation of "conditioning" and "problem-solving." *Harvard Educational Review,* 1947, **17,** 102–148.

OBRIST, P. A.   Cardiovascular differentiation of sensory stimuli. *Psychosomatic Medicine,* 1963, **25,** 450–459.

OKEN, D., GRINKER, R. R., HEATH, H. A., HERTA, M., KORCHIN, S. J., SABSHIN, M., & SCHWARTZ, N. B.   Relation of physiological response to affect expression. *Archives of General Psychiatry,* 1962, **6,** 336–351.

PAVLOV, I. P.   *Conditioned reflexes: An investigation of the physiological activity of the cerebral cortex.* Translated by G. V. ANREP (Ed.). New York: Oxford, 1927.

RICE, D. G.   Operant conditioning and associated electromyogram responses. *Journal of Experimental Psychology,* 1966, **71,** 908–912.

ROYER, F. L.   Cutaneous vasomotor components of the orienting reflex. *Behavioral Research and Therapy,* 1965, **3,** 161–170.

SACKETT, G. P.   Monkeys reared in isolation with pictures as visual input: Evidence for an innate releasing mechanism. *Science,* 1966, **154,** 1468–1473.

SCHACHTER, J.   Pain, fear, and anger in hypertensives and normotensives. *Psychosomatic Medicine,* 1957, **19,** 17–29.

SCHACHTER, S., & SINGER, J. E.   Cognitive, social, and psychological determinants of emotional state. *Psychological Review*, 1962, **69**, 379-399.

SCHNEIRLA, T. C.   An evolutionary and developmental theory of biphasic processes underlying approach and withdrawal. In M. R. JONES (Ed.), *Nebraska symposium on motivation*. Lincoln: University of Nebraska Press, 1959.

SCHULTZ, J. H., & LUTHE, W.   *Autogenic training: A psychophysiological approach in psychotherapy*. New York: Grune & Stratton, 1959.

SCOTT, J. P., & CHARLES, M. S.   Genetic differences in the behavior of dogs: A case of magnification by thresholds and by habit formation. *Journal of Genetic Psychology*, 1954, **84**, 175-188.

SELYE, H.   The general adaptation syndrome and diseases of adaptation. *Journal of Clinical Endocrinology*, 1946, **6**, 217-230.

SELYE, H.   *The stress of life*. New York: McGraw-Hill, 1956.

SHEARN, D. W.   Operant conditioning of heart rate. *Science*, 1962, **137**, 530-531.

SHELDON, W. H.   Constitutional factors in personality. In J. McV. HUNT (Ed.), *Personality and the behavior disorders*. New York: Ronald, 1944.

SILVERMAN, A. J., & COHEN, S. L.   Affect and vascular correlates to catecholamines. In L. J. WEST & M. GREENBLAT (Eds.), *Explorations in the physiology of emotions*. Psychiatric Research Reports of the American Psychological Association, No. 12, January 1960.

SOKOLOV, Y. N.   *Perception and the conditioned reflex*. New York: Macmillan, 1963.

SOLOMON, R. L., & BRUSH, E. S.   Experimentally derived conceptions of anxiety and aversion. In M. R. JONES (Ed.), *Nebraska symposium on motivation*. Lincoln: University of Nebraska Press, 1956.

SOLOMON, R. L., & TURNER, L. H.   Discriminative classical conditioning in dogs paralyzed by curare can later control discriminative avoidance responses in the normal state. *Psychological Review*, 1962, **69**, 202-219.

SOLOMON, R. L., & WYNNE, L. C.   Traumatic avoidance learning: The principles of anxiety conservation and partial irreversibility. *Psychological Review*, 1954, **61**, 353-385.

SPITZ, R.   Anxiety in infancy: A study of its manifestations in the first year of life. *International Journal of Psycho-Analysis*, 1950, **31**, 138-143.

SROUFE, L. A.   Learned stabilization of cardiac rate under varied conditions of respiratory control. *Journal of Experimental Psychology*, 1969, **81**, 391-393.

STERNBACH, R. A.   A comparative analysis of autonomic responses in startle. *Psychosomatic Medicine*, 1960, **22**, 204-210. (a)

STERNBACH, R. A.   Correlates of differences in time to recover from startle. *Psychosomatic Medicine*, 1960, **22**, 143-148. (b)

STERNBACH, R. A.   Two independent indices of activation. *Electroencephalography and Clinical Neurophysiology*, 1960, **12**, 609-611. (c)

STERNBACH, R. A.   Assessing differential autonomic patterns in emotions. *Journal of Psychosomatic Research*, 1962, **6**, 87-91.

STERNBACH, R. A.   Psychophysiological bases of psychosomatic phenomena. *Psychosomatics*, 1966, **7**, 81-84.

STERNBACH, R. A.   *Pain: A psychophysiological analysis*. New York: Academic, 1968.

TINBERGEN, N.   *The study of instincts*. New York: Oxford, 1951.

TOLEDO, L. de, & BLACK, A. H.   Heart rate: Changes during conditioned suppression in rats. *Science*, 1966, **152**, 1404-1406.

WASHBURN, R. W.   A study of the smiling and laughing of infants in the first year of life. *Genetic Psychology Monographs*, 1929, **6**, 397-539.

WENGER, M. A.   Preliminary study of the significance of measures of autonomic balance. *Psychosomatic Medicine*, 1947, **9**, 301-309.

WENGER, M. A.   Emotion as visceral action: An extension of Lange's theory. In M. L. REYMERT (Ed.), *Feelings and emotions*. New York: McGraw-Hill, 1950.

WENGER, M. A., CLEMENS, T. L., DARSIE, M. L., ENGEL, B. T., ESTESS, F. M., & SONNENSCHEIN, R. R.   Autonomic response patterns during intravenous infusion of epinephrine and norepinephrine. *Psychosomatic Medicine*, 1960, **22**, 294-307.

WENGER, M. A., & CULLEN, T. D.   ANS response patterns to fourteen stimuli. *American Psychologist*, 1958, **13**, 423. (Abstract)

WENGER, M. A., JONES, F. N., & JONES, M. H.   *Physiological psychology*. New York: Holt, Rinehart and Winston, 1956.

WOLF, S., & WOLFF, H. G.   *Human gastric function*. (2nd ed.) New York: Oxford, 1947.

WOLPE, J.   *Psychotherapy by reciprocal inhibition*. Stanford, Calif.: Stanford University Press, 1958.

Frederick Snyder and Jimmy Scott

THE PSYCHOPHYSIOLOGY OF SLEEP

17

Where no part of the soul remained behind, concealed in the limbs, as fire remains concealed when buried under much ash, whence would sense be suddenly rekindled through the limbs, as flame can spring up from hidden fire?—Lucretius

Since the concept of sleep implies a relative absence of those complex mental functions and behaviors considered the proper subject matter of psychology, there is little wonder that in the past only death itself has been a less popular subject for psychological study. Nevertheless, sleep is not death (nor stupor nor coma) and two of its all-important distinctions constitute the bases for the psychophysiology of sleep. First, the absence of capacity for waking behaviors is only relative—as Lucretius expressed it, some part of the soul remains behind, ready to respond to appropriate external stimulation by awakening. The idea of depth of sleep, the degree to which mental capacities of waking persist during sleep, has been assessed behaviorly since the very beginning of experimental psychology. Second, sleep involves dreaming, that mode (or modes) of mental functioning intrinsic to sleep and more or less peculiar to it. The psychophysiology of sleep thus concerns the relationships between these two categories of concomitant mental and physiological events.

645

Sleep can only be defined by behavioral criteria, but, in the vast physiological literature concerning sleep, behavioral criteria were rarely measured or even stated. Consequently, despite heroic efforts and precise physiological measures, the results too often have little but historical importance. Most of the literature on dreams, equally great in volume and low in value, has been derived from anecdotal reports, remote from, and uncertainly relevant to, sleep itself. A physiology of sleep can be no better than the behavioral measures assessing sleep; a psychology of sleep must arise from the immediate context of that state, assessed in turn by objective (usually physiological) measures. Hence contemporary sleep research is inherently a psychophysiological enterprise, constituting a unique meeting ground for otherwise disparate disciplines, ranging from psychoanalysis to electrical engineering, and not excluding para-psychology.

Much of what is relevant to the topic is less than 15 years old and stems from E. Aserinsky and N. Kleitman's demonstration (1953, 1955b) of associations between certain physiological characteristics of sleep and the recall of dreaming. Their discovery was the effective beginning of a psychophysiology of dreaming, and its catalytic influence upon scientific interest in sleep cannot be overestimated. Nevertheless, the possible scope of the subject extends beyond the focal issues of its brief history to other problems deriving from its much older heritage. Viewed in that larger context, the psychophysiology of dreaming, which is the central theme of most of the recent work, must follow a discussion of the depth of sleep and its general psychophysiology, even though the complex interrelations among these aspects of sleep must eventually transcend these arbitrary divisions.

We have limited this chapter to descriptive evidence of the psychophysiological relationships actually found during sleep, so (except in passing) it will not encompass those developments concerning the physiological mechanisms of sleep, the content and psychological significance of dreams, or even the new knowledge of sleep psychology obtained by psychophysiological methods. Nevertheless, to interpret some of the relationships described, they must be placed finally in the context of comparative and neural physiology.

THE NATURE AND DEPTH OF SLEEP

Ordinary experience has always insisted that sleep has a dimension of intensity or depth, reflected primarily by the degree of difficulty in awakening the sleeper. The physiologist Burdach (1830) made a number of astute naturalistic observations about depth of sleep. "The sleep itself is in its beginning deepest, in its continuation smooth and quiet, toward its end slightest"; "Children sleep very soundly, old people have light sleep; men sleep more soundly than women, and after great fatigue the sleep becomes sounder." Burdach also recognized that awakening is a function of the meaning of the disturbing stimulus, as well as its strength, anticipating recent studies of perception during sleep, which will be discussed in a later section. We shall find that all of these commonplace impressions have some experimental support, although the scientific effort of a century has not developed a completely satisfactory means of assessing depth of sleep.

The first systematic approach to measuring the depth of sleep, the stimulus-response or arousal threshold method, was described by Fechner in *Elemente der Psychophysik* (1860), but it was credited to his student Kohlschütter, the founder of the experimental psychology of sleep, who reported on its first application 2 years later (Kohlschütter, 1862). He reasoned that depth of sleep should be proportional to the intensity of sound necessary to produce awakening, measuring the sound by the arc of a pendulum set to strike against a slate block. The "classical" curve of sleep depth over the course of the night obtained by Kohlschütter (Figure 17.1A) was distinguished by a very striking increase in the threshold until the end of the first hour, followed by a rapid and then gradually slower decline. The early peak of this first graph of the course of nightly sleep confirmed Burdach's impression that sleep "is in its beginning deepest," and has been confirmed both by subsequent stimulus-response studies and by more recent psychophysiological evidence. However, subsequent studies of the arousal threshold have progressively altered the remainder of Kohlschütter's curve (Czerny, 1891; De Sanctis & Neyroz, 1902; Endres & von Frey, 1930; Hass, 1923;

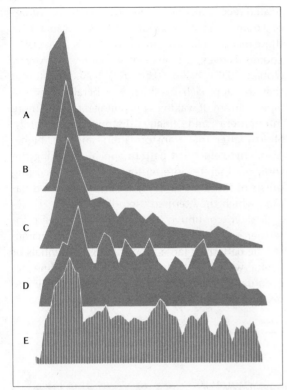

Figure 17.1 Evolution of sleep depth curves. This illustrates representative curves of sleep depth and their transformation over the past century. A is the "classic" curve of Kohlschütter (1862) and B is the curve of Monninghoff and Piesbergen (1883), both based upon averaged data from multiple nights. By contrast, C (Michelson, 1891) and D (De Sanctis & Neyroz, 1902) are examples of individual subject nights, and resemble contemporary estimates of the course of sleep based upon EEG criteria, such as E (adapted from Lester, 1958).

Lambranzi, 1900; Michelson, 1891; Monninghoff & Piesbergen, 1883; Mullin, N. Kleitman, & Cooperman, 1937: see also reviews by H. M. Johnson & Swan, 1930; N. Kleitman, 1963; Woehlisch, 1954). In general, after the first few hours, arousal thresholds have been higher, on the average, and much less regular than in Kohlschütter's curve.[1] Curves

[1]The earlier curves based upon composite data from multiple nights and multiple subjects could not have reflected the irregular fluctuations in threshold found on individual nights, but there were other methodological pitfalls. H. M. Johnson and Swan (1930) pointed out that Kohlschütter awakened his subjects as often as 17 times a night, probably explaining why sleep was so light after the first few hours. They also stated that he fulfilled Fechner's preconception about the smooth progression of the curve by disregarding almost half of his determinations.

based upon individual subject nights, such as those appearing at the turn of the century (Figure 17.1D) look entirely similar to present day estimates based upon electroencephalographic (EEG) criteria (Figure 17.1E). Today's accumulated psychophysiological evidence fully supports N. Kleitman's conclusion (1963) that the older depth of sleep curves may be a statistical expression of the incidence of deeper versus lighter sleep; but any actual night of sleep can best be characterized by a wavelike succession of curves, gradually but irregularly decreasing in amplitude and length.

Although measuring the arousal threshold to determine depth of sleep has yielded reasonably consistent estimates of the usual course of sleep, the method has several obvious limitations. Aside from being inordinately arduous, the procedures inevitably disturb the phenomenon they attempt to assess. Thus the natural course of sleep might not bear any close resemblance to that estimated by multiple experimental awakenings. Yet without multiple awakenings such approaches have little usefulness for comparisons among individuals or in the same persons under differing conditions. As an alternative to the stimulus-response methods, investigators have long sought an objective measure that does not disturb the natural course of sleep. One or another bodily index, applied in the parallel history of strictly physiological studies, has been suggested as such a measure. Unfortunately, in most instances the relevance of these measures to sleep depth was assumed, without comparison with any systematic behavioral testing, making the claims arbitrary and the results conflicting. Scientific interest in the concept of sleep depth suffered accordingly.

If sleep depth, or as we prefer to think of it, "general arousal level within sleep,"[2] is a meaningful or important dimension, it would seem that its ultimate definition necessarily rests upon behavioral assessment, and that physiological indices could be substituted only after they had been carefully correlated with such measures. The extent to

[2]Authors who conceptualize a continuum of arousal or activation in waking life are content to treat sleep simply as the lowest point on such continua (Duffy, 1962; Malmo, 1959). To our minds it must be considered a broad zone, and we emphasize the variations in the levels of general arousal within the range behaviorally characterized as "sleep."

which this has now been achieved rests upon studies employing the EEG. The importance of the EEG to the investigation of sleep goes beyond the issue of sleep depth to the more basic problem of determining whether or not sleep occurs. Therefore, we shall deal first with what has been learned about the relationship of the EEG to the behavioral condition of sleep and then go on to discuss other physiological functions in the light of their relationships to EEG findings.

The Electroencephalogram of Sleep

Observations of sleep were included in some of the very earliest studies of human EEG activity (Adrian & Yamagiwa, 1935; H. Berger, 1930), but characterization of the EEG waveforms of sleep as we now know them, and as they are illustrated in Figures 17.2 and 17.3, had to await more sophis-

ticated recording equipment. The extensive studies of Loomis and his co-workers took advantage of these technical improvements (H. Davis, P. A. Davis, Loomis, Harvey, & Hobart, 1938; Loomis, Harvey, & Hobart, 1935a, 1935b, 1936, 1937, 1938). They found that the approach of sleep was heralded by the alpha pattern of waking's becoming more and more intermittent and finally disappearing entirely. Shortly after that transformation, another, highly distinctive, electrical pattern appeared, taking the form of discrete, intermittent, regularly recurring bursts of fast activity, 13–15 Hz and 0.5–1 sec duration, which they termed "spindles."

If sleep continued, the spindles soon were interspersed with an equally striking and characteristic pattern of large, slow, random potentials or "delta waves." As these waxed in prominence, eventually dominating the entire record (like the heaving of a restless sea), the spindles waned and,

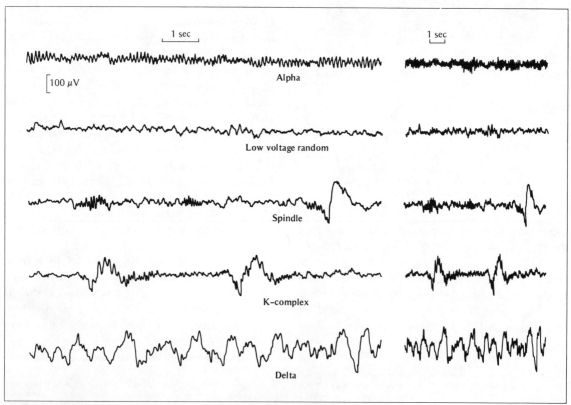

Figure 17.2 EEG waveforms distinguishing sleep from waking. The same patterns are shown at two recording speeds, on the left a conventional rate of 25 mm/sec, and on the right a rate of 10 mm/sec, widely used in sleep research.

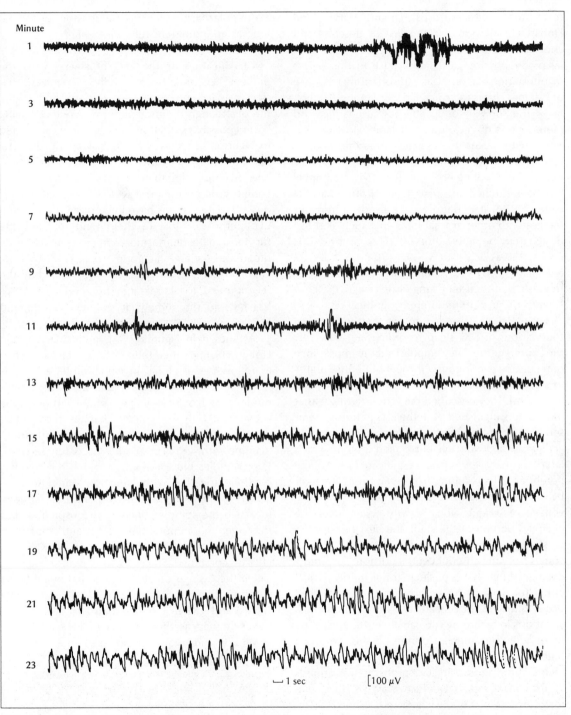

Figure 17.3 EEG progression at the beginning of sleep. Here the progressive transformation of EEG patterns is exemplified from full waking to "deep" sleep, in terms of samples taken every other minute at the very beginning of the night. In the Loomis, Harvey, and Hobart (1936) classification, Stage A would be represented by Minute 5, Stage B by Minutes 7 and 9, Stage C by 11 and 13, Stage D by 15, 17 and 19, and Stage E by 21 and 23.

for a time, were almost lost. Loomis, Harvey, and Hobart (1938) were also the first to describe still another waveform during sleep, which has particular psychophysiological significance in that it is a manifestation of arousal, like the orienting response of waking. This is the so-called "*K* complex," which takes the form of brief, abruptly appearing, and more or less discrete trains of large, slow oscillations with faster frequencies superimposed. It recurs intermittently and apparently spontaneously during the spindling phase of sleep. The *K* complex has been studied in great detail (Roth, Shaw, & Green, 1956); it is not always a fixed pattern but merges with other arousal transients such as those designated "bi-parietal humps" (F. A. Gibbs & E. L. Gibbs, 1950a) or vertex *V* waves (Bancaud, Bloch, & Paillard, 1953) and is sometimes difficult to distinguish from transient runs of delta activity, considered to have quite different significance.

Little has been added to the methodological foundations of EEG sleep recording laid down by the Loomis group. They emphasized the importance of recording continuously throughout entire nights of sleep (accomplished then on a slowly revolving 8-ft drum). They described the various artifacts that must be distinguished from the EEG patterns themselves such as those due to movement, muscle activity, swallowing, eye blinks, and the one which later assumed very special significance, the large potential shifts resulting from rotation of the eyeballs. They recognized that, while the maximal voltage of waking alpha activity occurs over the occipital portion of the skull, the best registration of sleep spindles, *K* complexes, or delta activity comes from the anterior central portion. For simply distinguishing phases of sleep, this is hardly critical either for delta waves or *K* complexes, since they occur diffusely; but small, and often individual, variations in recording site can affect the recording of spindles very much. Contrary to the prevailing tendency to use more and more electrode placements for diagnostic EEG purposes, the Loomis group considered that only two active sites were really necessary for the characterization of sleep EEG patterns, the occiput for maximal registration of alpha activity, and the vertex or midline central area for the best recording of slow waves and spindles—provided that the recording was done in

a "unipolar fashion," using the mastoid or the ear lobe as an indifferent reference area.[3]

Classification of the EEG of sleep Thus the pioneer EEG investigators fully recognized that sleep was accompanied by a continuously changing flux of strikingly different patterns. While observing "every possible gradation" among them (illustrated in Figure 17.3), they classified sleep by discrete, discontinuous categories of EEG states or stages. The fivefold alphabetical classification of the Loomis group is the most widely used, but numerous alternate systems have been offered for particular purposes. Most of them tend to subdivide further and to define more precisely their rather broad and general categories (E. L. Gibbs & F. A. Gibbs, 1950b; Simon & Emmons, 1956), but the recent need to score large numbers of records has favored the somewhat simpler Dement and N. Kleitman (1957a) classification.

As shown in Figure 17.3, Loomis, Harvey, and Hobart (1936) defined their states or stages of sleep as follows: A or alpha, in which alpha activity is no longer continuous but appears in trains of various lengths; B or low voltage, a phase without alpha activity and only low voltage changes in potential; C or spindle stage, characterized by a slightly irregular line with 12–14 Hz spindles every few seconds; D or spindles plus random, in which the spindles continue together with large random potentials, 0.5–3/sec and as high as 300 μV; and E or random, in which the spindles become inconspicuous but the large random potentials persist and come from all parts of the cortex. Dement and N. Kleitman (1957a) combined Stages A and B into Stage 1; called the C stage, Stage 2; and added quantitative criteria to define Stage 3 from D (10–50% delta waves) and 4 from E (more than 50% delta), delta being defined as those waves of at least 100 μV amplitude and frequency slower than 2 Hz.[4]

[3]Other particularly challenging technical aspects of EEG sleep recording are outside the scope of this discussion but have been assayed elsewhere (A. Jacobson, A. Kales, J. R. Zweizig, & J. Kales, 1965b).

[4]Recently, the Association for the Psychophysiological Study of Sleep (APSS) has formulated explicit standards for EEG sleep recording and scoring that should do much to allay the present confusion. These are available from the U.S. Government Printing Office, "A Manual of Standardized Terminology, Techniques and Scoring System for Sleep Stages of Human Subjects." U.S. Public Health Service Publication No. 204.

The standardization of scoring criteria among various studies is clearly desirable, yet it cannot be assumed that any existing classification distinguishes the most important functional differences within the sleep EEG, and clearly none of them adequately captures the myriad subtleties of individual variation. Hope for future refinement lies in much more sophisticated and continuous quantification of EEG parameters, such as would be feasible only by electronic assessment. Efforts to achieve automated analysis of sleep EEG patterns have been reported by a number of authors (Agnew, Parker, Webb, & Williams, 1967; Hord, L. C. Johnson, Lubin, & Austin, 1965; Koga, 1965; D. Lester, 1958; Walter, Rhodes, & Adey, 1967). Many others are underway.

Correlation between the EEG patterns and behavioral sleep Little of the huge literature of the physiology of sleep (N. Kleitman, 1963; Pieron, 1913, p. 520) is based upon any exacting behavioral criteria of the state. For most older studies it sufficed that subjects looked asleep or reported having slept; for many it was enough to assume that sleep occurred if persons were left recumbent in a dark room. Moreover, since any sleep was usually equated with all sleep, many of the most widely accepted generalizations are based upon whatever fleeting respite subjects obtained, despite the torture chamber atmosphere of the typical physiology laboratory. To the extent that precise temporal correlations have been sought recently between sleep and bodily measures, EEG criteria of sleep usually have been substituted for behavioral measures; hence the question of correlation between EEG and behavioral criteria is basic to the physiology of sleep in general and deserves rather detailed examination.

The relationship of EEG to behavior after sleep is well established and is really inseparable from the problem of depth of sleep; therefore it will be considered in that context. Here we shall consider studies of the temporal correlation between EEG and behavioral measures at the time of sleep onset. Basing their conclusions on tests of responsiveness to periodic auditory and visual stimuli, Loomis, Harvey, and Hobart (1937) stated that sleep begins somewhere in the latter part of the A state. However, they commented that subjects frequently

began to respond again after the signal was stopped. H. Davis et al. (1938) asked their subjects to signal whenever they felt that the state of consciousness had "floated" or "drifted." They obtained a "surprising" degree of correlation between such signals and interruptions in the continuity of the alpha rhythm during Stage A, the response usually occurring immediately after alpha returned, although occasionally just before it returned. Blake, Gerard, and N. Kleitman (1939) approached this question by noting the point at which subjects dropped a wooden spool held between their fingers; they concluded that muscle tone diminished almost immediately after the alpha rhythm disappeared, yet awareness of having dropped the spool might continue up to 25 sec longer.

More recent extensive studies by Simon and Emmons (1956), testing responsiveness to auditory stimuli and later recall, led to a comparable conclusion: both indications of awareness dropped progressively in parallel with the decline in the percentage of alpha, and no evidence of consciousness persisted after the appearance of the flat pattern of Stage B. Kamiya (1961, pp. 145–174), employing an operant technique (thumb pressing on a hand switch to avoid an unpleasant auditory stimulus), observed that the rate of pressing generally declined to zero, concomitant with the dropping out of alpha activity. W. T. Liberson and C. W. Liberson (1966) reported a linear increase for the latency of key pressing to auditory stimuli during the first 30 sec after the blocking of alpha activity but did not specify their criteria of alpha blocking. In general, the available evidence is quite consistent; at the onset of sleep, full waking consciousness correlates closely with the presence of EEG alpha activity. Unfortunately, this is not a useful criterion in subjects who do not exhibit strong waking alpha patterns, although many such subjects may reveal alpha activity when sufficiently relaxed prior to sleep (Knott, Henry, & Hadley, 1939).[5]

The transition to behavioral sleep is not really

[5]While the beginning of Stage B or 1 might thus be the most precise indicator of behavioral sleep onset, because of the ambiguity resulting from subjects deficient in waking alpha activity, the onset of "spindling" sleep (Stage C or 2) is more commonly taken as the point of sleep onset in quantitative studies. In most instances there is no more than a few minutes difference, and the spindle is a more dependable criterion.

so abrupt as these studies imply. Loomis, Harvey, and Hobart pointed out (1937) that designating the exact moment of sleep is necessarily arbitrary, depending upon the criterion of response, the nature and significance of the stimulus, and perhaps the sensory modality involved. With regard to the last possibility, Burdach (1830) suggested that the senses are differentially obtunded in sleep, e.g., vision fails earlier than audition. Recently, Rechtschaffen and Foulkes (1965) found that recall of visual imagery from stimuli held before taped-open eyes ceased before alpha activity did. While many aspects of these relationships would justify more careful study, existing evidence indicates clearly that the correlation between disappearance of alpha activity at sleep onset and marked diminution in the critical responsiveness of waking is as reliable and precise as any psychophysiological relationship. That it is influenced by a variety of factors of the psychological order of complexity merely suggests that the mind is not simply turned off during the transition from waking to sleep—a conclusion we shall return to on many occasions.

Over the past few years there has been increasing emphasis upon special conditions under which the correlation between EEG and behavioral criteria of sleep and wakefulness no longer hold, e.g., the sleeplike EEG patterns of atropinized but behaviorally awake animals, first described by Wikler (1952), and the persistence of some degree of motor performance in the presence of EEG sleep rhythms.[6] Although we would agree with N. Kleitman (1963) that the ultimate criteria of sleep are behavioral, yet under any natural circumstances the EEG is a precise and objective indicator of that state, and no contemporary studies of sleep are complete without it.

Nightly progression of the EEG of sleep For several good reasons Loomis and his collaborators inferred that their five stages represented successively deeper levels of sleep. One was the regular progression from A through E at sleep onset (as illustrated in Figure 17.3), together with the fact that the disturbance of sleep usually produced a reversion to a previous stage. In addition they noted that the ease of changing stages by external stimulation decreased as the sleeper approached the E level, although they reported no systematic exploration of that point. They were also impressed that "the content of the sound is important" in determining the results of stimulation and that the lack of a stimulus to which the sleeper is accustomed may itself act as a disturbance of sleep.[7]

With respect to the temporal sequence of EEG patterns of sleep over the course of the night, Loomis, Harvey, and Hobart emphasized only the frequency of shifts from one state to another, noting that downward progressions (toward deeper sleep) were usually gradual, although reverse changes were often abrupt and were usually associated with gross body movements. The all-night curves or "hypnograms" that they published displayed a succession of large peaks and troughs, resembling those in the stimulus-response curves of Michelson (1891) or De Sanctis and Neyroz (1902). Blake and Gerard (1937) emphasized the similarity to the older depth-of-sleep curves. They observed the same large oscillations of EEG patterns across the night but specifically noted that the first few hours of sleep generally appeared very deep, with an irregularly progressive lightening trend thereafter.

Nothing fundamental was added to the description of the sleep EEG progression until Aserinsky and N. Kleitman discovered the REM phase of sleep (1953), and Dement and N. Kleitman (1957a) demonstrated that it was implicated in regularly evolving cycles of EEG change during the night. Developments emerging from those observations will occupy much of the remainder of this chapter.

---

[6]Davis et al. (1939) describe a 14-year-old subject who continued to squeeze a rubber bulb in response to a tone without interruption of well-developed sleep potentials. Derbyshire and McDermott (1958) reported motor responses proportional to the intensity of stimulation in all stages of sleep, while Granda and Hammack (1961) found that sleep-deprived subjects occasionally performed rather complex response sequences in all EEG stages. Further studies from the Walter Reed laboratory (H. L. Williams et al., 1964, 1966) have shown that such behavioral responses are complex functions of the stimulus intensity, EEG stage, amount of elapsed sleep, prior sleep loss, and subject motivation.

[7]Burdach (1830) designated the latter phenomenon "miller's sleep," the idea being that the miller awakened if his mill wheel stopped turning for any reason.

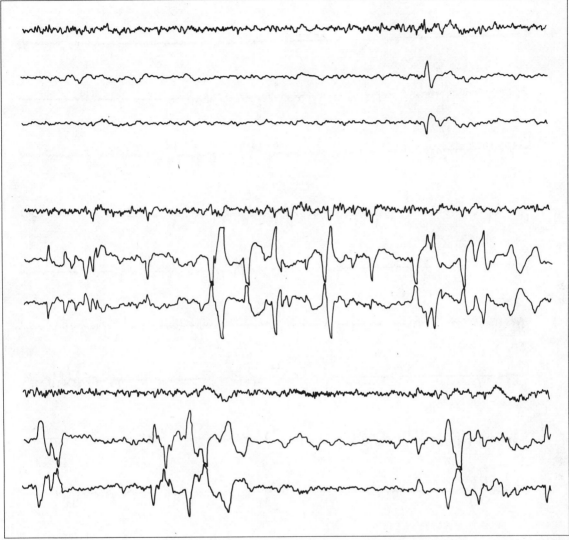

Figure 17.4 Electrooculographic patterns of REM. Three 15-sec samples of eye movement activity and accompanying EEG patterns during REM periods. The first trace in each group of three is the parietal EEG; the second and third reflect lateral movement of the right and left eyes, respectively. With appropriate electrode placements, vertical eye movement can be registered as well but for the most purposes the lateral component alone is a sufficient indicator of the occurrence of REM periods. The fact that these lateral displacements are conjugate is shown by the mirror image form of the patterns; it is therefore highly useful for distinguishing isolated REM from other random oscillations which they sometimes resemble. Note the great variation both in quantity and form of REM traces from one interval to the next.

The discovery of REM sleep While observing eye motility in sleeping infants at the physiology laboratories of the University of Chicago in 1952, Aserinsky and N. Kleitman noted that bodily repose and ocular quiescence alternated with periods of sporadic, twitching movements of all parts of the body, which were particularly prominent in the active motion of the closed eyes (Aserinsky & N. Kleitman, 1955a). The alternation occurred with great regularity for roughly equal intervals within

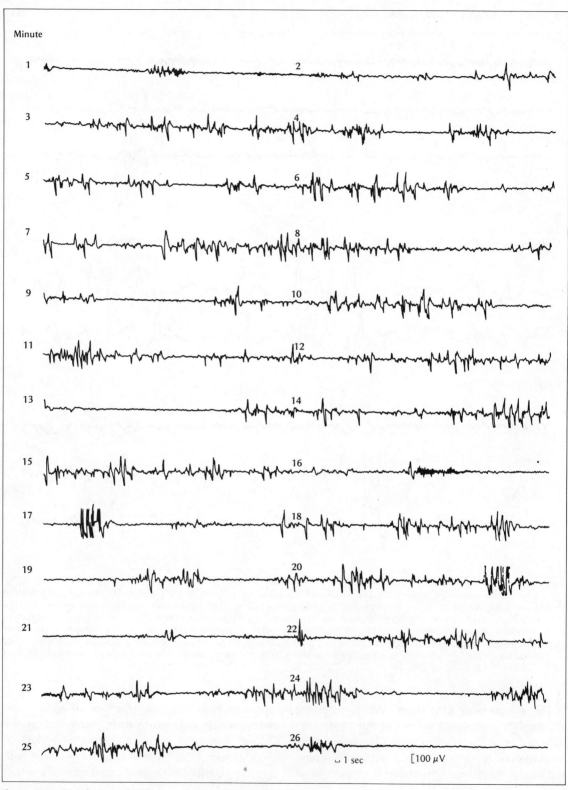

Figure 17.5 Distribution of REM throughout an REM period. One channel of eye movement is shown over 26 consecutive minutes of a single REM period. Note the artifacts caused by small body movement at the beginning and end of the period, as well as another in Minute 16, which divides the REM period into two parts.

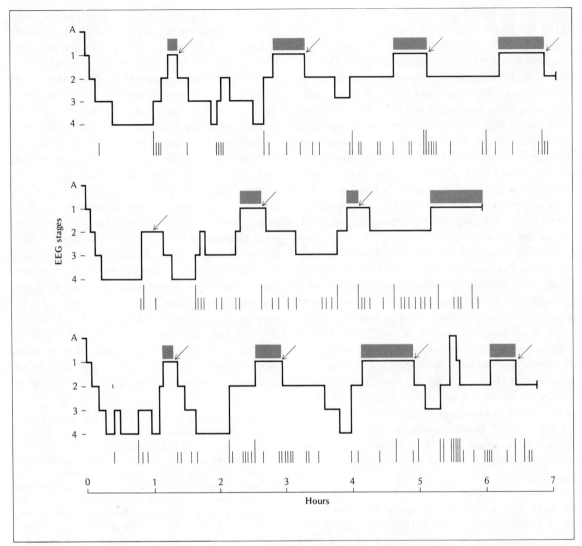

Figure 17.6   Cyclic variations in the EEG of sleep in relation to REM periods. Plottings from three representative nights to indicate variations in EEG stages (as indicated by the numerical categories on the left), in relation to REM periods (shown by the heavy bars above each graph). The arrows indicate demarcation of cycles, as they are designated from the end of one REM period to the end of the next. The vertical strokes indicate occurrence and intensity of body movements. Redrawn from W. Dement & N. Kleitman, Cyclic variations in EEG during sleep and their relation to eye movements, body motility, and dreaming. *Electroencephalography and Clinical Neurophysiology,* 1957a, **9,** 673–690, Fig. 3. Reproduced with permission.

each hour. While this observation had been almost completely anticipated by two Russian scientists several decades earlier,[8] the importance of Aser-

[8]In translated summary the report of Denisova and Figurin (1928) was as follows: "Thus it was determined that the breathing of infants during sleep is alternately accelerated and retarded with regular periodicity. Simultaneously with the acceleration, there

begins also a deeper breathing. The periods of acceleration and retardation may alternate in perfect rhythm, the average duration of a cycle being about 50 minutes, but they vary with the individual and with age. Moreover, the period of accelerated breathing is accompanied by motor phenomena as follows: Movements of the eyelids and pupils under the lids begin invariably at this time. In the same period there occur often, but not always, general movements of the head and hands and turning of the body. Expressive movements and smiling (common in children during sleep) are also observed in the period of accelerated breathing. [pp. 117–118]" insky and Kleitman's rediscovery was that they went on to search for comparable manifestations in the sleep of adults and, in doing so, supplemented behavioral observation with psychophysiological methods. To document the movement of the eyes during sleep, they employed the method of electrooculography, which is based upon the existence of a potential difference between the cornea and fundus of the eye, and the consequent changes in the electrical fields of fixed periorbital electrodes as the globes shift positions in the surrounding volume conductor of the head. Kris (1960, pp. 692–700) and Shackel (1960, pp. 323–335) discussed the method in detail, and Dement (1964b) commented on its use in sleep research.

As early as 1877, Raehlmann and Witkowski had described eye movements during sleep but these were slow, drifting, often disconjugate oscillations starting just before the onset of sleep and most prominent at its very beginning or after any transient disturbance of sleep (De Toni, 1933; Miles, 1929, pp. 308–309; Pietrusky, 1922). Aserinsky and N. Kleitman observed these random, roving eye movements lasting 3–4 sec but they also found a distinctly different kind of ocular movement that had not been noted previously.[9] These were rapid (1 sec or less), always conjugate, and of variable direction or amplitude, like the jerky fixational shifts of waking. Rapid eye movements (REM) occurred in sporadic bursts during discrete periods of sleep lasting from a few minutes to a half-hour or more, and not at all during the rest (Aserinsky & N. Kleitman, 1953, 1955b). Figure 17.4 illustrates the ever-changing form of the records of REM during sleep, while Figure 17.5 exemplifies their temporal distribution throughout a typical REM period.

In the brief paper in *Science* that first described the REM periods of sleep, Aserinsky and N. Kleitman also reported that subjects who were awakened during such periods had detailed and vivid memories of dreams in 74% of the instances, whereas only 7% of the awakenings from the rest

of sleep yielded such reports. Their finding effectively initiated the psychophysiology of dreaming and gave rise to many of the developments to be discussed in the remainder of this chapter. Before proceeding to these, however, there is considerably more to be said about depth of sleep and about the psychophysiology of sleep in general.

In their initial reports Aserinsky and N. Kleitman (1953, 1955b) recognized that periods of REM activity were accompanied by slight elevations in heart and respiratory rates, and by low voltage EEG patterns, although they were uncertain whether the EEG patterns were entirely characteristic. Much more extensive observations of Dement and Kleitman established that REM periods were indeed distinguished by a type of EEG pattern unlike any previously described during sleep, except at its very onset, the Stage B, (or Stage 1) pattern of low voltage, irregular activity, entirely devoid of spindles or *K* complexes (Dement & N. Kleitman, 1957a).[10] The further importance of their report lay in its clear exposition of the regular cyclic progression of sleep EEG patterns across the night. These were first illustrated as in Figure 17.6 and described as follows:

> The usual sequence was that after the onset of sleep, the EEG progressed fairly rapidly to stage 4, which persisted for varying amounts of time, generally about 30 minutes, and then a lightening took place. While the progression from wakefulness to stage 4 at the beginning of the cycle was almost invariably through a continuum of change, the lightening was usually abrupt and coincident with a body movement or series of body movements. After the termination of stage 4, there was generally a short period of stage 2 or 3 which gave way to stage 1 and rapid eye movements. When the first eye movement period ended, the EEG again progressed through a continuum of change to stage 3 or 4 which persisted for a time and then lightened, often abruptly with body movement, to stage 2 which again gave way to stage 1 and the second rapid eye movement period.

Dement and N. Kleitman (1957a) found that this cyclical variation of EEG patterns occurred repeat-

---

[9]The apparent discontinuity between slow and rapid eye movement is probably a function of our usual methods of recording (Tursky & O'Connell, 1966). With electrodes and recording equipment capable of detecting both components, Kamiya (1961) found that slower eye movements often built up in magnitude and speed over a 5–10 min interval into the REM periods, and that slow components are present throughout them.

[10]Blake, Gerard, and Kleitman (1939) had introduced the term "null" phase to describe a low voltage pattern that they found predominant during the third quarter of the night, after delta had become infrequent but before the return of waking alpha. From their characterization of null phase it is not clear whether this was identical with the later described Stage 1 pattern, or also included the long stretches of flat but spindling sleep (Stage 2), which are also present at that time.

edly throughout the night with intervals of 90–100 min from the end of one eye movement period to the end of the next. Usually, the "deepest" sleep patterns were observed only in the first and second cycles, although transient periods of Stages 3 or 4 sometimes appeared later in the nights. The outstanding aspect of these findings was that the same predictable progression of events, including the quite regularly recurring REM periods, were found every night in all subjects, as they have been found in innumerable studies since then.

EEG Stages and the Capacity to Respond

Blake and Gerard's (1937) attempt to relate EEG patterns of sleep to a behavioral measure was the first, and for 20 years the only, study of EEG-behavior correlates. Using a 1000-Hz tone of constant intensity as a stimulus to awaken, they determined the time necessary for subjects to answer "Yes" to the question "Are you awake?" They concluded that the EEG potential patterns of sleep reflected changes in depth in proportion to the extent of high voltage, slow activity. The authors presented only a small sample of data and did not specify how consistently the relationship obtained. They found marked individual differences in both behavioral and electrical measurements. In the light of subsequent developments their passing mention of occasional instances when the test sound was entirely ineffective in the presence of "feeble, irregular potentials" is especially interesting. On the basis of that single, rather impressionistic, report the validity of EEG sleep patterns as indicators of depth of sleep became generally accepted, and no more rigorous evaluation of that correlation appeared for the next 20 years.

Variability of the response capacity The study of the relationship between EEG stages and variation in the capacity to respond has been reopened during the past decade, mainly as a result of interest in the depth of REM sleep. The early assumption that the periodic REM phenomenon simply represented cyclically recurrent periods of light sleep was soon challenged. Shortly after Dement's (1958) recognition of REM sleep in the cat, numerous reports appeared that arousal thresholds were much higher during the REM-equivalent condition than

during the rest of sleep (Benoit & Block, 1960; Hara, Favale, Rossi, & Sacco, 1960; M. Jouvet, Michel, & Courjon, 1959). (Hence the REM phenomenon is frequently referred to as "deep" sleep in neurophysiological studies.)[11] Recent efforts have demonstrated the complexity of the problem, not only with regard to the REM and non-REM distinction but also in relation to EEG patterns of sleep.

The most obvious procedural approach is the old one of determining thresholds to stimuli of random intensity. In practice, this involves either an excruciatingly protracted procedure or so many tests that sleep is unduly disturbed (cf. Kohlschütter). One alternative is to present stimuli of gradually increasing intensities, until the response occurs (the method of limits). In general the results obtained in either fashion have been highly variable. Dement and N. Kleitman (1957a) found in humans that arousal thresholds to sound stimuli were at least two or three times higher during REM periods than they were during Stage 1 at sleep onset but they did not try to examine the remainder of sleep in the same manner. In a study employing the method of limits, thresholds for Stage 3 or 4 awakenings tended to be higher than those for Stage 2 or REM, but differences between the latter two stages were very slight and variable in direction (Snyder, 1960). The unpredictability of thresholds, either among subjects or in the same subject from night to night, independent of any apparent difference in EEG stage, was most striking. Some Stage 4 thresholds were much lower than other REM or Stage 2 thresholds. After a pilot study, Rechtschaffen, Hauri, and Zeitlin (1966) reached similar conclusions and abandoned the method of limits. Goodenough, Lewis, Shapiro, and Sleser (1965) did find generally lower average thresholds during REM trials than from non-REM awakenings, although the difference was not statistically significant. On the other hand, Pisano, Rosadini, Rossi, and Zattoni (1966), using electrical pain stimuli of progressively increasing intensity, reported a general tendency

[11]Dement (1965) has questioned this interpretation of the feline studies on the grounds that most are based upon direct electrical stimulation of the reticular formation, which is obviously not a physiological stimulus. In his own initial study of REM in the cat (1958), Dement found auditory thresholds varying over a tenfold range in both REM and non-REM sleep, although averaging slightly less in REM.

for higher mean thresholds from REM periods. Still, there were no statistically significant differences among any of the EEG categories, except for an increase in threshold between Stage 1 (sleep onset) and Stage 2.

The interpretation of the marked variability and unpredictability of arousal thresholds during sleep points up a basic conceptual distinction between old and new approaches to the psychophysiology of sleep. In the framework of *Psychophysik* from which the early studies arose, it was natural to seek a dimension of sleep depth measurable as a straightforward function of the strength of stimulus necessary to produce arousal, the assumption being that sleep merely involved a progressive loss of the capacity to awaken. The limitation of *Psychophysik* soon proved to be that only the most elementary sensory or reflex components of animal nervous activity actually conform to such simple physical principles. All others are continuously complicated by intrinsic nervous processes determined by a myriad of past influences. Similarly, there is nothing surprising about the variability of arousal thresholds during sleep if sleep has its own intrinsic mental life, and if the readiness of response to external stimuli is a complex function of the manner in which these two interact. With regard to the REM condition, H. L. Williams, Hammack, Daly, Dement, and Lubin (1964) suggested that absorption in the dream experience might serve to distract the dreamer from external disturbance, so tending to heighten arousal thresholds at such times. It also appears likely that the method of gradually increasing stimuli would be particularly prone to the incorporation of the stimulus into the ongoing dream experience, although both factors would obviously depend upon the highly variable nature of dream content.[12]

Assessing the frequency of response to strong stimuli of fixed intensity in relation to EEG stage may be less affected by the distracting or buffering effects of intrinsic mental activity during sleep.

Without considering the REM condition as a separate entity, Fischgold and Schwartz (1961, pp. 209–231) found that responses dropped from a level of 85–100% during Stage 1 (presumably, Stage 1 at sleep onset) to 27% during Stage 2, and 0% during Stage 3. Similarly, Zung and Wilson (1961; Wilson & Zung, 1966) found progressively decreasing rates of response in reaction to complex sound stimuli, in accordance with increasing EEG "depth." More recently, H. L. Williams et al. (1964) confirmed these observations in a study that required their subjects to close a microswitch whenever they heard a tone stimulus that was repeated periodically or aperiodically during the night. Rechtschaffen et al. (1966) also found that responses to an auditory stimulus of fixed intensity (empirically selected for each subject because of marked intersubject variability) were much less frequent from delta sleep (Stages 3 and 4) than from spindling sleep (Stage 2).

The depth of REM sleep continued to prove elusive: H. L. Williams et al. (1964) found that lever-pressing responses to tone stimuli were least frequent during REM periods. Wilson and Zung (1966) obtained a slightly lower rate of response during REM periods than during Stage 2. Rechtschaffen, Hauri, and Zeitlin (1966) found no statistically significant difference between REM and Stage 2 in the frequency of awakenings.

Reaction time in relation to sleep EEG stages
Another closely allied approach employs various tests of reaction time to stimuli of fixed intensity. The first such study comparing the reaction time to an integrated measure of EEG amplitude (Coleman, Gray, & Watanabe, 1959) disclosed a positive, but very low, relationship between the two ($r = .32$). The integrated measures of waking alpha activity were higher than were some measures of integrated sleep patterns, which may partly explain the surprisingly low correlation. The study is helpful, as it emphasizes the lack of predictability in the reaction time method by pointing out instances when responses were difficult to evoke in the presence of an EEG pattern characteristic of light sleep. The REM pattern was not specifically identified but it has been the subject of special interest in several subsequent studies. Goodenough et al. (1965a) reported significantly shorter reaction times from

[12]One of our REM awakenings following a very high arousal threshold yielded the account of a dream in which the subject was riding a horse across a stream, when a fly began to buzz around the horse's head intermittently, like our intermittent arousal stimulus. The buzzing became louder and louder and the horse more and more annoyed, until finally the dreamer was thrown off—and abruptly awakened (Snyder, 1960).

REM awakenings than from non-REM trials, although inspecting their data shows that REM versus Stage 2 differences were slight. Their study involved the rather complex response of picking up a telephone. Employing a simpler response to determine reaction time, Okuma, Majamura, Hayashi, and Fujimori (1966) obtained quite comparable results: reaction times increased progressively through sleep onset, spindling sleep, and delta sleep; standard deviations increased in parallel. Standard deviations of reaction times during REM periods were among the highest obtained. The means of the reaction times in REM trials were significantly less than those of delta sleep trials but they did not differ significantly from those of spindling sleep (Stage 2) or sleep onset, again confirming the study of Goodenough et al. (1965a). We have recently compared reaction times and EEG sleep stages in an extensive study, with results that were quite similar to those just described (Scott & Snyder, 1967).[13]

Thus, accumulating evidence confirms the existence of a relationship between EEG patterns and variable response capacity during sleep but fails to explain the striking degree of individual and intra-individual differences in such behavioral measures. In the next section we shall discuss progress in identifying other relevant variables.

Factors affecting response capacity within EEG stages It is part of the common-sense concept that sleep depth is enhanced after sleep deprivation. Despite experimental study of the effects of loss of sleep on the overall EEG patterning of sleep, there has been little attention to its influence upon differing capacities to respond within the several EEG stages. H. L. Williams et al. (1964) found that 64 hr without sleep almost eliminated behavioral response to a tone stimulus, regardless of its intensity or the attendant EEG stage, though the highest rate of response (4%) was still found in Stage 2.

Under circumstances of extreme deprivation, sleep does, indeed, resemble coma. In our studies of reaction time, a significant increase was found in all stages if subjects were limited to 4 hr of sleep on the previous night. Perhaps related to the accumulated need for sleep, but confounded by adaptational effects, were the conflicting reports of differences in response capacity at varying times of night but falling within a single stage. One group of experimenters remarked on a dramatic decline in response rates in Stage 2 sleep from the first to the fourth hour (H. L. Williams et al., 1964), while another found significantly higher response rates from Stage 2 during the second half of the night than in the first (Rechtschaffen, Hauri, & Zeitlin, 1966).

In keeping with Burdach's impression that women's sleep is lighter than men's, Wilson and Zung (1966) observed that female subjects responded much more rapidly to complex sound stimuli during all stages except REM. Our own data of reaction times completely confirmed this interesting sex difference (Scott & Snyder, 1967). Domestic experience suggests that subjects of varying ages would show even greater differences in response capacity during sleep, regardless of EEG pattern. Young children are notoriously difficult to awaken; older people seem to sleep very lightly. No systematic investigation of age and behavioral sleep depth has been published, although Gastaut and Broughton (1965) noted that the extreme confusion of abruptly awakened children is not seen after REM awakenings.

In all instances of great variation in response capacity in the presence of the same EEG pattern, the EEG pattern may only appear to be the same in our crude categories. There may be subtle, but critical, differences not yet distinguished that would provide much more precise psychophysiological relationships. While an important reservation, it would not explain the evidence of dependency between response and the meaningfulness of the stimulus to the subject, a phenomenon which argues that perception and discrimination persist to some extent throughout sleep.

The effect of significance of stimuli Anecdotal observations of the pioneer electroencepha-

[13]Our studies distinguished between the interval before the first movement in response to an awakening stimulus, and the longer interval required to signal a response by pressing a switch. The former increased very little with the increasing depth of sleep, while the latter increased markedly. This suggests to us that the initial reflex component of the response sequence is little affected by sleep EEG stage but that the orienting and coordinating aspects are affected much more.

lographers confirmed the early belief that arousal from sleep depends not only upon the strength of stimulus but also on its significance to the sleeper. Experimental analyses are recent, dating back hardly more than a decade to initial studies of cats. In their investigations of habituation of the arousal reaction, Sharpless and Jasper (1956) found that animals which no longer responded at all during sleep to repeated tone stimuli could be aroused immediately if presented with a slightly different tone. Rowland (1957) and Christake (1957) found that differential arousal to a stimulus previously paired with shock occurred in both cats and rats. A number of studies have demonstrated that the cessation of sound stimuli can be as arousing as their novelty (Rowland, 1957; Sommer-Smith, Galeano, Pineyrua, Roig, & Segundo, 1962; Weinberger & Lindsley, 1964). Buendia, Gooden, Sierra, and Segundo (1963) have suggested that pitch discrimination in sleeping cats is actually better than in awake ones.

Soon after the beginning of these studies of arousal, Toman, Bush, and Chackes (1958) briefly described the discrimination of "loaded" words during human sleep, an observation that Oswald, Taylor, and Treisman (1960) carefully documented. The Oswald group found that the subject's name, played on a tape recorder while he slept, was much more likely to evoke EEG and behavioral responses than other names or the same stimulus played backward. Several investigations added evidence of the importance of motivational variables to perception and response during sleep. Zung and Wilson (1961) observed that, although the familiarity or unfamiliarity of sounds seemed to make little difference in terms of arousal during sleep, motivation by monetary incentives enhanced the responsiveness to any sounds, and in all EEG stages. H. L. Williams, H. C. Morlock, and J. V. Morlock (1966) obtained similar results by punishing the failure to respond (sounding a fire alarm next to the subjects' heads). Beh and Barratt (1965) paired tones to painful stimuli, while the subjects were awake. These tones elicited K complex responses during sleep, demonstrating a discriminative capacity in the human subjects. The same investigators also confirmed the special significance of the subjects' own names in producing these physiological responses. Discrimination during sleep is highly relevant to

learning during sleep, a question that we can only mention here.[14] A more basic issue is the capacity for differential discrimination in relation to the EEG stage of sleep and to the REM condition.

In their earlier work Zung and Wilson (1961) found that, in the "motivated condition," subjects invariably awakened out of Stages D and E (delta sleep) but with less discrimination of motivated and neutral stimuli than they did in Stages B or C. That study did not specifically identify the REM condition.

As already cited, H. L. Williams et al. (1964) originally reported that, during REM periods, subjects responded less often to tone stimuli than during any other EEG sleep stage other than Stage 4. A later report from the same laboratory (H. L. Williams et al., 1966), however, indicated that, if the stimulus were a warning of impending punishment, responsiveness during REM was as good or better than during any other stage of sleep. Their finding is somewhat at variance with a report of Wilson and Zung (1966), who found that motivating subjects to produce an EEG arousal to particular auditory stimuli had the least effect during REM. Since the amount of the monetary incentive was not specified, we are left with the possibility that, in comparison to the subjects' dreams, it weighed less than did the threat of Williams's fire alarm. Yet several feline studies support the inference that conditioned responses are diminished during REM (Buendia, Gooden, Sierra, & Segundo, 1963; Siegel & Langley, 1965).

[14]The question of learning during sleep, while not necessarily a psychophysiological matter, is an excellent example of the necessity for psychophysiological methods in any research problem relating to sleep. Commercial exploitation of this idea is not without encouragement from the scientific literature, but, as the review by Simon and Emmons revealed (1955), none of the older studies in which learning was claimed actually demonstrated that the learning took place during sleep. In their own experimental approach employing very precise EEG control, they found no evidence of learning complex verbal material, as long as the EEG pattern was truly that of sleep (Simon & Emmons, 1956). No subsequent study has contradicted that conclusion, although there are now several studies demonstrating the acquisition of simple responses during sleep. Beh and Barratt (1965) claimed that K complexes during spindling sleep, induced by chloral hydrate, could be conditioned to tone stimuli paired with shock, while the continuity of sleep monitored by EEG remained unbroken. Moreover, when tested after the subjects were awake, the conditioned tone produced significantly greater alpha blocking than did a neutral tone. Similarly, Weinberg (1966) has reported success in training subjects during EEG-monitored sleep to discriminate among, and differentially respond to, tone stimuli.

A recent report points the inquiry in a new direction. Subjects were instructed to press a button during sleep in response to a series of photic flashes; they were awakened and questioned about their experience if they failed to comply (Okuma et al., 1966). The stimulus was rarely perceived and almost never responded to in delta sleep but was frequently perceived and responded to in REM. The most interesting aspect, however, was that, in terms of correct responses, the differences between trials in REM and Stage 2 were not significant, but the instances of correct perception without motor responses were significantly higher during REM than in any other stage of sleep. The authors interpreted the dissociation in terms of the distracting and incorporating capacities of dreaming consciousness. This indication of enhanced perception during REM corroborates the preliminary finding of M. P. Mandell, A. J. Mandell, and A. Jacobson (1965). They reported that numbers spoken 5 sec before awakening seemed to be heard and remembered during the REM condition but not during the rest of sleep. Both studies are compatible with others that imply the existence of unique response capacities in the REM state. One by Antrobus, Antrobus, and Fisher (1965) disclosed that, when subjects were instructed to signal whether they were dreaming or not dreaming, most of the signaling occurred with Stage 1 EEG patterns present. Another by Cobb et al. (1965) showed that highly hypnotizable subjects will respond behaviorally to verbal suggestions only during emergent Stage 1. Arkin, Hastey, and Reiser (1966) found that sleep talking can be produced during Stage 1 periods as the result of posthypnotic suggestion.[15]

While renewing experimental interest in variation of the capacity for response during sleep, the REM phenomenon has also highlighted the difficulty of finding any satisfactory operational approach to that issue. Findings still to be reviewed suggest that not only the REM condition but all of sleep is psychologically active; i.e., the sleeper is more or less occupied with inner mental events. If this is so, and if his response to external events

depends upon the degree to which they are not only perceived but also judged significant by comparison with inner events, then the very unpredictable relationships between strength of stimulus and likelihood of response during sleep are understandable. In these terms the complex interaction of "general arousal level" and "selective attention" during sleep is simply an extension of the same interaction present in waking, which J. A. Deutsch and D. Deutsch (1963) discussed. The extreme variability in readiness to respond to external stimulation during sleep, either among individuals or in the same persons at different times, correlates little with present categories of EEG patterns during sleep. Much more probably, it reflects a comparable variation in preoccupation with the mental life of sleep. Consideration of "sleep depth" (both in the sense of ordinary experience and in the framework of older experimental work) necessarily requires some means of isolating measures of "general arousal level" from the play of psychological processes for which it provides the stage. It has been assumed, but the assumption scarcely justified, that the EEG measures general arousal level during sleep. Perhaps no physiological measure does, but that cannot be concluded before considering the many other physical indices available.

Other Physiological Correlates of Sleep

Differences between sleep and waking have been described in terms of almost every physiological function, and at one time or another virtually all have been put forward as measures of sleep depth or intensity (N. Kleitman, 1963). In general, changes characteristic of sleep have been the diminution of the particular parameter. The degree of diminution has been assumed to vary with depth or intensity of sleep, an assumption obviating comparison with behavioral measures. While this premise had the virtue of simplicity, the time of appearance of the maxima and minima of various bodily measures did not always coincide during the typical night of sleep. From this came a legacy of confusion and discouragement concerning the entire issue of sleep depth (H. M. Johnson & Swan, 1930; N. Kleitman, 1963; H. L. Williams, 1967).

Whether there are distinctive changes in any measure associated with behavioral sleep could

---

[15]Like all the rest of sleep, and perhaps even more frequently, REM periods are punctuated by transient awakenings, so it is possible that the performance described in these reports has more to do with these brief arousals than with REM itself.

hardly be resolved without an objective indication of when sleep occurred. Now that EEG patterns can provide such an indication, these possible indices of sleep can be reexamined. There has been little effort to assess somatic functions in relation to arousal capacity, and comparatively little concern about how they correlate with EEG estimates of sleep depth. These are simply neglected issues in present-day sleep research. In the light of available information, however, it appears to us that one group of physiological measures is most unlikely to have any simple relationship to general arousal level and another group of functions deserves further examination. The former category includes those that reflect primarily the overall level of metabolic activity, e.g., body temperature, baseline changes in pulse or respiratory rates, and basal skin resistance.

Metabolic measures The much-studied circadian rhythm of body temperature generally reaches its nadir during the customary period of sleep, but the decline begins long before sleep, and some investigators report that the slope of the downward curve is actually less steep during the sleeping period than during the night as a whole (Mellete, Hutt, Askovitz, & Horvath, 1951). The 24-hr periodicity of body temperature depends upon abiding patterns of rest and activity, and is generally independent of immediate conditions of sleep and waking, at least over intervals of several days or longer.[16] One factor determining body temperature is metabolic rate, usually measured by oxygen consumption (rate of heat loss is the other). Recent studies during sleep (Brebbia & Altshuler, 1965; Kreider, Buskirk, & Bass, 1958), have confirmed earlier reports of a gradual decline of oxygen consumption during sleep. The assertion of Grollman (1930), that samples taken immediately after awakenings across the night also show nocturnal decline, has not been tested. See Figure 17.7.

The daily cycle of pulse rate is partly dependent upon the actual alternation of rest and activity (N. Kleitman & H. Kleitman, 1953), but under usual

circumstances it parallels the daily temperature curve very closely (N. Kleitman & Ramsaroop, 1948). The circadian decline in pulse rate begins long before sleep and is affected by the attendant conditions of bodily rest and relaxation. Whether sleep itself contributes to the extent or rate of the decline is an old and controversial question that has not been clarified by any new experimental evidence.

Daily periodicity in respiratory rate has not been studied, but it is apparent that the onset of sleep ordinarily occurs at a time of gradually slowing respiration. The older data of Reed and N. Kleitman (1926) and the only published examination of respiratory rates at sleep onset monitored by EEG (Birchfield, Sieker, & Hayman, 1959) revealed no consistent change. Indeed, in the latter study, rates generally increased rather than decreased. However, in subjects deprived of sleep, slowing and flattening of respiratory patterns has been noted as a more constant correlate of transient lapses of alertness than EEG changes (Mirsky & Cardon, 1962). Other, more consistent, changes in respiration at sleep onset have been described and will be considered later.

Regardless of whether there are changes specific to sleep, recent EEG studies confirm the observations of Aristotle and Galen that respiration and heart rates do undergo a gradually progressive decline throughout most, if not all, of the sleeping period (Batini, Fressy, & Coquery, 1965; Rohmer, Schaff, Collard, & Kurtz, 1965; Shapiro, Goodenough, Biederman, & Sleser, 1964; Snyder, Hobson, & Goldfrank, 1963). Figure 17.7 shows the similarity of the average baseline curves of body temperature, and direct measures of oxygen consumption, respiration, and heat rates (Brebbia & Altshuler, 1965; Kreider, Buskirk, & Bass, 1958). The tendency of these metabolic functions to level off or even ascend toward the end of sleep has been described and merits further explanation; nevertheless, the general downward trend probably reflects either immediate or more enduring adaptations to the sustained period of bodily rest that is ordinarily accompanied by sleep. It appears quite unrelated to depth of sleep, either as it was estimated earlier in stimulus-response studies or currently by EEG. Schaff, Marbach, and Vogt (1962) reached the same conclusion from finding that sleep deprivation,

---

[16]Despite its potential importance to psychophysiology, the vast subject of circadian rhythms is beyond the scope of this chapter. An review of the extensive and rapidly growing literature on that topic is provided by Mills (1966).

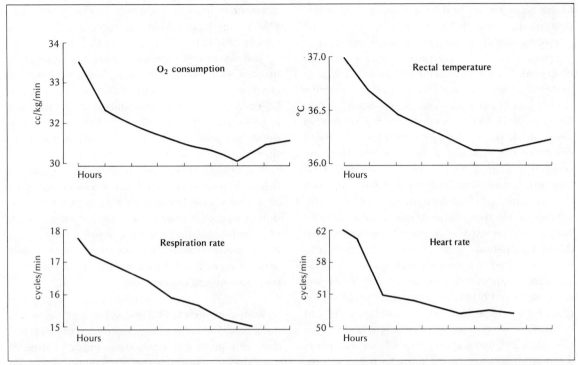

Figure 17.7 Typical curves of "metabolic" measures during sleep. Oxygen consumption and rectal temperature curves are adapted from Kreider, Buskirk, and Bass (1958), while respiration and heart rate curves are from the report of Schaff, Marbach, and Vogt (1962). Note the general similarity of the nightly trends. The apparent tendency for an upward inflection to occur in such measures toward the end of the night is difficult to evaluate in the absence of EEG control, since some individual subjects contributing to such grouped data may not have slept as long or as continuously as others.

which might be expected to increase the depth of sleep, did not significantly alter the all-night curves of pulse and respiratory frequency.

A number of authors have noted the striking fluctuations of pulse and respiration rates during sleep and have suggested that, if separated somehow from the long-term baseline trends, these alterations might relate to general arousal level (Batini, Fressy, & Coquery, 1965; C. McC. Brooks et al., 1956). To us it seems that these measures are usually quite stable during periods of spindling or slow wave sleep marked by stable EEG patterns; their often abrupt oscillations almost invariably accompany sharp transitions in EEG, body movements, or brief arousals, all of which regularly punctuate the entire course of sleep. The recurrent REM phase of sleep abides by different rules, as we shall mention shortly, but within the remainder of sleep we have been unable to demonstrate any

significant differences related to the EEG stages, even in the regularity of these vegetative measures (Snyder, Hobson, Morrison, & Goldfrank, 1964).

Basal skin resistance Our reason for considering the slow component of electrodermal resistance in sleep with the previously mentioned "metabolic measures" is based entirely upon the apparent similarity of their nightly sleep curves. There has never been a complete consensus about the course of basal skin resistance during sleep; most of the recent studies (Batini, Fressy, & Coquery, 1965; Hawkins, Puryear, Wallace, Deal, & Thomas, 1962; Kamiya, 1961, pp. 145–174) report curves similar to that first described by Farmer and Chambers (1925) showing a progressive trend toward higher resistance (diminished conductivity) throughout the night. Others (Regelsberger, 1942; Richter, 1926; Titelbaum, 1941) found a point of inflection late in the night, similar to the point of upward inflection usually found in temperature curves.

Noting that skin resistance mounts gradually as subjects become drowsy prior to sleep and may drop gradually after awakening, Darrow (1936) suggested that high palmar resistance is not specific for the loss of consciousness but relates to certain physiological conditions which predispose toward sleep. Similarly, Regelsberger (1942) found a rise in resistance that typically occurred before sleep and sometimes many hours before; while Levy, G. E. Johnson, Serrano, Thaler, and Ruff (1961) observed that the point of sleep onset could not be distinguished on the rising curve of resistance associated with relaxation. Levy et al. found similar patterns during long periods of concentration in which subjects "insulated" themselves from external stimuli. The same authors cited occasions when sleepers were awakened briefly to perform some automatic task and the expected drop in resistance did not occur. We have also seen individuals awaken spontaneously and make appropriate verbal comments without any change taking place in their high resistance levels. Immediately after they were spoken to, the resistance plummeted.

Whether basal skin resistance reflects anything at all about sleep itself, the measure certainly is influenced by many methodological factors. Landis (1927) insisted that, under the conditions of sleep studies, the increased levels found were entirely attributable to polarization and the drying of electrodes. This would not explain the drops in resistance generally observed at times of awakening, and most of the studies cited here have used electrodes (zinc electrodes, with zinc sulphate paste) relatively free of polarization (Lykken, 1959). Wenger (1962) reported that a number of differing curves could be obtained during sleep, depending upon the current strength, or whether the current were continuously or intermittently applied. An intermittent $40\text{-}\mu\text{A}$ current caused a continuous rise throughout the night, while a continuous current of the same strength yielded a smaller initial rise during the first few hours, followed by a gradual fall across the rest of the night. The latter course suggests a parallel with the typical EEG progression across the night, but such a relation is unlikely. Using the same recording conditions when investigating individual differences in skin resistance during sleep, Tart (1967) found both kinds of curves, as well as a variety of others.

The psychophysiological significance of changes in basal skin resistance during sleep will not be clarified until critical methodological variables can be controlled. In the meantime, most of the data appears unrelated to other indicators of sleep depth, yet parallel to the course of metabolic functions during the night.

It is unfortunate that body temperature, rates of respiration, pulse, or basal skin resistance offer so little promise for estimating general arousal level during sleep, for they are among the most readily obtained of all physiological indices. One other, more easily obtained and therefore more widely used, is really a behavioral measure: the extent of body movement during sleep.

Body movement Obviously, body movement is not a good indicator of the occurrence of sleep and does not provide a continuous index of arousal level during sleep. On the other hand, it can be easily recorded by a variety of means with little or no encumbrance to the sleeper (Coleman, Gray, & Watanabe, 1959; Cox & Marley, 1959; N. Kleitman, Cooperman, & Mullin, 1933), and for that reason has been examined in relation to a number of other criteria. Systematic observations of the motility of sleeping adults were pioneered by Szymanski (1922), as an extension of the method he had applied earlier to the activity cycles of animals and infants. As N. Kleitman pointed out (1963), we may assume that Szymanski's recording device was less than perfect, since he found one class of subjects whose rest was "absolute" throughout the night. Some degree of intermittent, postural readjustment always occurs during normal sleep. Although the total duration of gross motility during sleep is no more than 3–5 min, it may include from 20–60 discrete movements (N. Kleitman, Cooperman, & Mullin, 1933). We have already noted that movement is generally, though not invariably, associated with abrupt lightening of the EEG. Brazier and Beecher (1952) described an anticipatory cardiac acceleration beginning 6 min before body movements.

Mullin, N. Kleitman, and Cooperman (1937), in

the only systematic investigations relating the behavioral measure of response capacity to sleep motility, established several important generalizations. Based on 325 tests on 6 subjects, there was a regular curve of variation in the auditory threshold during the intervals between body movements; thresholds were lowest immediately after a movement, ascended to a peak often more than twice as high between 16 and 20 min later, and then tended to decrease before the next expected movement. The longer the interval of quiescence between pairs of successive movements, the higher the auditory threshold rises, so that deeper sleep might be expected to correlate with less frequent movements. See Figure 17.8.

Undoubtedly, the typical course of arousal threshold variations closely parallels the progression of EEG patterns and the average frequency of

body movements, for, as shown in Figure 17.8, the intervals between movements have a tendency to diminish the longer sleep continues (Batini, Fressy, & Coquery, 1965; C. McC. Brooks et al., 1956; Cathala & Guillard, 1961; Coleman, Gray, & Watanabe, 1959; N. Kleitman, Cooperman, & Mullin, 1933; Schaff & Marbach, 1960). Two groups of investigators have directly correlated body motility with EEG stages (Cathala & Guillard, 1961; Rohmer, Schaff, Collard, & Kurtz, 1965). Both found that frequency of movement diminishes progressively with "deeper" EEG stages; Rohmer et al. also emphasized important intra- and interindividual variations. The likelihood that motility reflects sleep depth, at least to some degree, was strengthened by the finding of Schaff and Marbach (1960), who found that one night of sleep deprivation significantly affected a number of indices of movement,

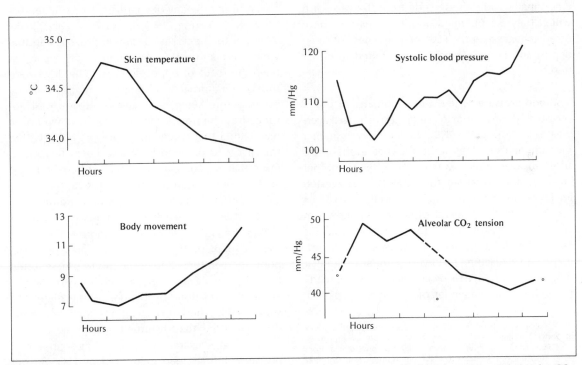

Figure 17.8 Typical curves of skin temperature, body movement frequency, systolic blood pressure and alveolar CO_2 tension during sleep. The skin temperature curve is adapted from the mean weighted skin temperature data of Kreider, Buskirk, and Bass (1958); the CO_2 curve is adapted from an example reported by Robin et al. (1958); while the graphs of systolic blood pressure and frequency of body movement are based on the means of determinations at 30-min intervals of 12 subjects studied with EEG control in our laboratory. The points to be noted are the direct parallelism of blood pressure or body movement curves on the one hand, and skin temperature or CO_2 tension on the other. The latter pair of measures would also correspond to EEG measures of sleep "depth," while the former would be inversely related.

particularly that based upon the duration of intervals of immobility.

Motility measures are especially appropriate for intraindividual studies and have been utilized to distinguish the effects of many experimental variables (see the extensive literature cited by N. Kleitman, 1963). Yet almost all investigators have emphasized the wide range of individual variation in nocturnal motility patterns, apparently unrelated to any other measures. Mullin, N. Kleitman, and Cooperman (1937) found that their most quiet sleeper was also the most easily aroused; C. McC. Brooks et al. (1956) found little correlation between EEG estimates of sleep depth and motility on any given night; Cox and Marley (1959) found no significant correlation between patients' estimates of soundness of sleep and motility scores; Lienert and Othmer (1965) report that emotionally labile subjects have less body movement during sleep than emotionally stable ones. Aside from the ease with which they are obtained, motility measures have no advantages over the EEG for assessment of sleep depth, and provide much more limited information.[17]

Blood pressure The earliest estimates of blood pressure during human sleep (Brush & Fayerweather, 1901; Hill, 1898), like the even earlier measurements in dogs, indicated that arterial pressure subsided to its lowest levels in sleep. Another classical study at about the same time suggested an explanation for that fact (Howell, 1897).[18] As illustrated in the smoked drum record shown in Figure 17.9, Howell found that the volume of his hand dilated during sleep. The descending kymograph curve, reaching its lowest point after the first hour or two and then rising gradually and irregularly throughout the remainder of the sleeping period,

traced the changes in peripheral vascular resistance. The curves of blood pressure that Brush and Fayerweather (1901) made 4 years later took the same form. The relation between the two is apparent, since blood pressure would be expected to vary with changes in peripheral vascular resistance. Howell also noted "periodic waves" superimposed on the general course of the plethysmograph curve at approximately hourly intervals, thus being the first to call attention to that intriguing rhythm in the physiological progression of sleep that was to become of such great interest to researchers more than half a century later.

While many have studied blood pressure during sleep (N. Kleitman, 1963), the results are most inconclusive, probably reflecting the difficulties of estimating blood pressure without disturbing sleep. It has been agreed that arterial tension falls steeply, concomitant with sleep, and tends to rise progressively during the day (Richardson, Honour, Fenton, Stott, & Pickering, 1964; Weysee & Lutz, 1915). Whether the nocturnal decline is greater than that which rest and relaxation alone might cause has been the focus of opposing views. The downward turn of the diurnal curve begins as much as several hours before sleep does and is already well advanced by the time sleep ensues. Those who have maintained that it reaches its lowest point within the first 2 hr of sleep have also been inclined to insist that no comparable drop resulted from rest alone (Brooks & Carroll, 1912; Brush & Fayerweather, 1901). Others, claiming that the descending curve of blood pressure reached a minimum a few hours before the end of sleep (Blankenhorn & Campbell, 1925; Grollman, 1930), as do measures of pulse, body temperature, and respiration, also reported that the same levels could be obtained after awakening at corresponding periods of the night. We suggest that these investigations included many determinations that disturbed sleep.

The first reexamination of changes in blood pressure during sleep monitored by EEG (Snyder et al., 1964) supported the very early observations. Blood pressure fell roughly 20%, to a minimum, 1.5-2.5 hr after the beginning of sleep, and then rose gradually and irregularly over the remainder of the night. Direct measures of arterial blood pressure have substantiated these curves (Khatri &

---

[17]Typical artifacts on the EEG record are a very sensitive index of body movement, and probably as satisfactory as any other.

[18]The account by Howell, the distinguished physiologist from Johns Hopkins, of his efforts to make plethysmographic observations in relation to sleep is a delightful human document, as well as an excellent scientific report. In order to examine the previous claim by Mosso that the volume of the extremities increased during sleep, Howell devised a water plethysmograph in which his hand and forearm were enclosed, and suspended from an over-head sling while he slept. In order to sleep at all under these conditions, he had to make himself unusually tired, and of 20 attempts only 4 or 5 were considered satisfactory, thus typifying the often heroic efforts required in the study of sleep.

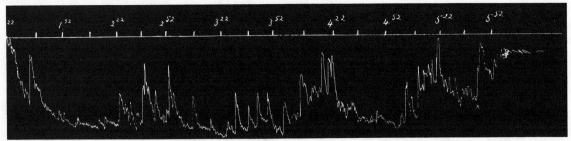

Figure 17.9 Plethysmography record of the hand and lower forearm. This is one of the original records from Howell's heroic plethysmograph studies, in which he was the first to note periodic waves (in this case intervals of varying vasoconstriction) at roughly hourly intervals during the night of sleep. From W. H. Howell, A contribution to the physiology of sleep, based upon plethysmographic experiments. *Journal of Experimental Medicine,* 1897, **2,** 313–345.

Freis, 1967; Nowlin, personal communication). Curves from any individual night, based on determinations taken once per minute, are much more irregular, but the form of a composite curve of mean levels across the night, as shown in Figure 17.8, is remarkably similar to those Brush and Fayerweather made more than 60 years ago, using a very different method. Our studies were not specifically concerned with changes in blood pressure at the onset of sleep, but the records show a gradual and irregular decline from the time when subjects first go to bed and recording begins. We find no consistent change over the few minutes when the EEG patterns of sleep first appear. Like the curves published in 1901, our average curve rises well above the level at sleep onset, while sleep continues to the end of the night.

Taken together, the studies supply good evidence of a rough correspondence between the typical progression of EEG depth across the night of sleep and the typical course of systolic blood pressure. We must, however, maintain some reservations: the frequency of body movements conforms to the same pattern, so that the lowering of blood pressure may simply reflect the degree of immobility. The explanation put forward by Howell cannot be entirely discounted either, for there is new, as well as old, evidence that the extent of peripheral vasodilatation (in the extremities at least) is the inverse of the sleep curves of blood pressure.

Peripheral vasomotor tone The changes in peripherovascular tone of the extremities brought out by Howell's classic study have been confirmed by plethysmography (L. C. Johnson & Lubin, 1967; Khatri & Freis, 1967; Magnussen, 1939; Mirsky & Cardon, 1962; Uhlenbruck, 1924) and by measures of skin temperature (N. Kleitman, Ramsaroop, & Engelmann, 1948; Kreider, Buskirk, & Bass, 1958; Magnussen, 1939; Snyder, 1967, pp. 469–487). All agree that sleep is associated with vascular dilatation of the hands and feet. Kleitman's group stressed that this does not imply generalized relaxation of sympathetic tonus, but the curve published by the Kreider group showed an average increase of the mean weighted skin temperature (taken from 10 skin points) over the first few hours of the night, followed by a more steep drop than appeared in the overnight trend of rectal temperature (Figure 17.8). Magnussen (1939) emphasized that vascular dilatation preceded sleep, sometimes by as much as 2 hr, thus constituting part of what he described as "vegetative preparedness" for sleep. We cannot attest to that point, but 6 EEG-controlled observations on as many subjects did show that sleep onset occurred at a time of rapidly rising finger temperature. The finger temperature reached a level 0.8–2.2°C higher than the presleep level within the first hour, then declined irregularly over the remainder of the night in a manner described further in the section on REM concomitants. By contrast, forehead temperature tended to fall slightly at sleep onset and otherwise behaved in an inverse fashion to finger temperature, aside from a gradually declining trend over the night. Although local skin temperature obviously depends upon many factors difficult to control under the conditions of natural sleep,[19] nevertheless, there is enough evidence that it bears some relationship to the course of EEG stages and blood pressure levels through the night to warrant further examination of its relation to the intensity of sleep.

Respiratory depression and sleep Despite the inconsistent changes in the rate of respiration at sleep onset, there is agreement that sleep is associated with decreased ventilation of the lungs and increased levels of carbon dioxide (CO_2) in expired air (N. Kleitman, 1963).[20] This results from the diminished responsiveness of the respiratory center, and thus might be considered a natural prototype of the stimulus-response method of assessing sleep depth—to whatever degree that part of central nervous system functioning is obtunded, higher levels of CO_2 are tolerated and less oxygen is required to maintain them. There remains the question of how well changes in that vegetative aspect of nervous functioning might correlate with changes in nervous functioning underlying "general arousal level." Some data have been obtained under EEG control (Birchfield, Sieker, & Heyman, 1959; Bülow, 1963), settling past doubt that elevated alveolar CO_2 tensions are specifically related to sleep (Mangold et al., 1955; Mills, 1953), and incidentally illustrating the virtual necessity for EEG monitoring in the study of sleep physiology. Bülow (1963) documented an extremely precise correlation between decreased ventilation and EEG signs of sleep for even transient changes in wakefulness of no more than a few seconds. The same investigator cites some evidence of a relationship between the amount of respiratory depression and EEG stages of sleep, supporting earlier reports that maximal

elevation in CO_2 tensions typically occurs during the first few hours of sleep (Bass & Herr, 1922; Robin et al., 1958). This is also exemplified in Figure 17.8.

Clearly, some correspondence exists between the degree of respiratory depression and EEG developments across the night. It remains to be determined whether measures of alveolar CO_2 tension or pulmonary ventilation might be in any way superior to the EEG as correlates of variable arousal capacity. Undoubtedly, such an assessment has been prevented until now by the very cumbersome methods required for estimation of these respiratory parameters.[21]

Thus far we have pointed out repeatedly the lack of distinctive changes in the various bodily measures that might distinguish sleep from wakefulness as precisely as they are distinguished by the EEG. One possible exception involves the *form* of respiration. Without EEG control and using a valve that increased the resistance to expiration, Magnussen (1944) found that a relative prolongation of the expiratory phase of the breathing cycle accompanied even transient intervals of apparent sleep. Other investigators, employing simultaneous EEG monitoring (Bülow, 1963; Mirsky & Cardon, 1962; Oswald, 1959) have described a close correspondence between periods of sleep and a particular form of respiration marked by sharper transitions between inspiration and expiration, increased rapidity of expiration, and longer pauses after expiration. Bülow observed that this characteristic form of respiration was often more conspicuous at the onset of sleep than later, and that it did not occur in all individuals. Many authors in the past have emphasized the instability of respiration at sleep onset. Bülow found that these variations coincided with comparable fluctuations in the EEG patterns between waking and sleep, which may be more prominent under laboratory conditions than in the usual process of falling asleep.

---

[19]If ambient temperature is high, arterioles of the skin tend to be constantly dilated, so that demonstrations of changes associated with sleep require room temperatures lower than about 20°C (Magnussen, 1939). The position of the extremity and the microclimate determined by the bed covering are equally important.

[20]The agreement concerning the increase in CO_2 tension contrasts with reports about the extent of diminished blood oxygen (O_2) saturations during sleep. On the basis of oximetric measures, Doust and Schneider (1952) claimed drops in arterial oxygen saturation with deepening sleep amounting to 6% or more. Due to the shape of the oxygen-hemoglobin dissociation curve, very marked decreases in alveolar O_2 tension would be required to produce that much desaturation in normal persons; in fact, subsequent studies employing direct blood sampling revealed much smaller and inconstant levels of desaturation during sleep (Birchfield, Sieker, & Heyman, 1959; Robin, Whaley, Crump, & Travis, 1958).

[21]One answer to this problem may be the replacement of uncomfortable face masks and mouthpiece arrangements by catheter sampling of expired air from the naso-pharynx and continuous infrared CO_2 analysis (Collier, Affeldt, & Farr, 1955). Still another may be forthcoming from estimates of pulmonary ventilation, based upon changes in the electrical resistance of mercury capillary length gauges about the chest and abdomen (Shapiro & Cohen, 1965).

This brief review should suffice to indicate that many aspects of the descriptive physiology of sleep have been insufficiently studied by modern methods, particularly the correlations of various measures with EEG changes. In the meantime, however, a new dimension has been added to sleep physiology by recognition of the unique bodily concomitants of the REM state.

Rapid Eye Movement Sleep

Since Aserinsky and N. Kleitman first described human REM periods, the physiological definition of the state has gradually extended. As mentioned earlier, Dement and N. Kleitman (1957a) established that the distinctive EEG pattern is generally continuous from the beginning of such a period to the end; hence it has become conventional to include the entire interval distinguished by this EEG pattern, when referring to REM periods. Aside from satisfying the criteria of being of low voltage and without *K* complexes or sleep spindles (though isolated spindles may be interspersed, especially in the first minutes), different individuals exhibit a considerable range of EEG rhythms during these periods, often including a conspicuous, intermittent, alpha-like component (Goodenough, Shapiro, Holden, & Steinschriber, 1959) and occasionally very fast activity 18–25 Hz, usually most prominent in the frontal regions. Lester and Edwards (1966) believe the latter to be more common in the REM patterns of schizophrenics than of normals. Although not well defined in all subjects, the most distinctive EEG characteristic consists of bursts of 2–3 saw-tooth–shaped waves per second, best seen in the anterior central regions, and usually preceding or overlapping clusters of REMs (M. Jouvet, Michel, & Mounier, 1960). It appears to be entirely confined to REM periods and may be comparable to the discrete pattern found in the visual cortex of cats during REM in association with unique spiking activity from the pontine reticular formation (D. C. Brooks & Bizzi, 1963) or to occipital lambda waves in humans, generally interpreted as evoked cortical responses.

In their original observations of infants, Aserinsky and N. Kleitman were as much impressed by the motor activity as by the eye movements of REM periods, but whether gross motor activity in adult humans is increased or decreased probably depends upon how the question is posed. Dement and N. Kleitman (1957a) reported a rise in the frequency of gross bodily motility just before the REM period, an abrupt drop once REM began, and an increased level immediately after each REM period. In the most detailed analysis of that point, Kamiya (1962) found that REM periods were quiescent relative only to the high levels of motility found a few minutes immediately preceding or following but tended to involve more movement than any other periods of sleep.

There is no doubt that REM periods are accompanied by a great deal of abrupt and diffuse twitchlike movement, especially evident about the face and hands (Baldridge, Whitman, & Kramer, 1965; Dement & N. Kleitman, 1957a; Stoyva, 1965b; Wolpert, 1960). Nothing comparable is found in other phases of sleep. While Max (1935) had concluded that muscle activity of the hands of deaf subjects signaled dreaming, Stoyva (1965b) now finds no difference between deaf and normal subjects in that respect. Phasic twitching is much more prominent during the REM condition in human infants and in adults of other mammals. Frequently, it is accompanied by motor components resembling coordinated but abortive behavioral manifestations. As Lucretius noted, this sometimes takes the form of walking or running movements of the extremities, or may involve licking and chewing. In newborn human infants there is almost continual evidence of athetoid stretching, smiling, frowning, brief vocalizations, and sucking (Delange, Castan, Cadilhac, & Passouant, 1962; Roffwarg, Dement, & Fisher, 1964, pp. 60–72).

Among the most unusual characteristics of the REM state is another motor phenomenon, first observed in the cat. When recording muscle activity from the back of the cat's neck, M. Jouvet, Michel, and Courjon (1959) noted that some degree of tonic muscle activity persisted throughout non-REM sleep; at the onset of REM periods it completely disappeared, only to return again afterward. It is very obvious in the sleeping cat, which abruptly drops the head into a posture of utter limpness, signaling the onset of a REM period. The presence or absence of this sign in other species appears to depend upon their customary sleeping position.

Sleep in man is ordinarily associated with complete disappearance of tonic muscle activity in the dorsal neck muscles, and there is no further change during REM; but a comparable phenomenon occurs in other muscle groups. In the course of an unsuccessful attempt to detect "subvocal speech" during dreaming, Berger (1961) found that a certain amount of tonic muscle activity could be recorded from beneath the chin throughout non-REM sleep but that it disappeared during REM periods. A. Jacobson, A. Kales, Lehmann, and Hoedemaker (1964) found varying degrees of this characteristic change in muscle tonus in many of the head and neck muscles of humans but not the trunk or limb muscles, which are persistently flaccid during sleep. We have also found a change in tonic muscle activity in the anterior neck muscles during REM in many subjects. Typically, we observe minimal muscle tone during REM periods, but in some subjects comparable low levels often long precede or outlast the REM state, or may occur during other noncontiguous periods of sleep. Despite its variability the low level of muscle tonus found during REM is of particular theoretical interest, since it is one manifestation that is not compatible with a concept of REM as a period of light sleep or one of physiological arousal secondary to the psychic state of dreaming. The finding that certain spinal reflexes are dramatically reduced during REM periods in humans and cats, apparently due to an active inhibitory process in the brain stem (Giaquinto, Pompeiano, & Somogyi, 1964; Hodes & Dement, 1964) seems to have the same significance.

In their first report, Aserinsky and N. Kleitman noted that pulse and respiratory rates were somewhat elevated during REM periods, as compared with the preceding periods of sleep. Their observation has been widely confirmed. A much more distinctive change is the marked variability of these measures during REM sleep (Batini, Fressy, & Coquery, 1965; L. C. Johnson & Lubin, 1967; M. Jouvet, Michel, & Mounier, 1960; Kamiya, 1962; Rohmer et al., 1964; Shapiro et al., 1964; Snyder, 1960; Snyder et al., 1964). With the onset of REM periods, and often slightly before, respiration and pulse rates become extremely irregular; the same is true of systolic blood pressure (Khatri & Freis, 1967; Nowlin, personal communication; Richardson et al., 1964; Snyder, Hobson, & Goldfrank, 1963). The na-

ture of these vegetative changes during REM periods is illustrated in Figure 17.10.

When pulse, respiration, or blood pressure are recorded over any long interval of sleep, the curves present a rather jagged appearance overall. Inspecting intervals of unchanging or gradually deepening EEG patterns reveals only minor oscillations around a quite stable baseline; the major irregularities almost always coincide with body movements or abrupt upward shifts in EEG patterns. We found no significant differences in these measures (based upon change with 5-min periods) among the non-REM phases of sleep. During REM the variability of all three functions increased by an average of 50%—even neglecting the overall variance from baseline that had been apparent throughout the entire REM period. Variability of heart rate and blood pressure tended to increase over the successive REM periods of the night, but the extent of such changes in variability differed considerably among REM periods, and they were not always discernible (Snyder et al., 1964).

The vegetative characteristics of REM are essentially similar in various species, yet certain differences summarized by Snyder (1967, pp. 469–487) have been noted. The variability of respiratory and heart rates, as well as of blood pressure, is heightened in all of the species in which this has been studied, but average levels of these functions in relation to non-REM sleep appear to vary. A drop in blood pressure during REM periods in the cat is particularly striking (Candia, Favale, Giussani, & Rossi, 1962), although not entirely consistent (Kanzow, Krause, & Kuhnel, 1962); and there have been contradictory reports on that point in humans. Systolic blood pressure is usually elevated during human REM periods, a finding originally based upon indirect measures taken once each minute throughout sleep from a large artery of the foot (Snyder, Hobson, & Goldfrank, 1963), and now confirmed by other indirect measures (Richardson et al., 1964) and by direct methods employing arterial catheterization (Khatri & Freis, 1967; Nowlin, personal communication).

The relationships among the various "phasic" components are of great interest but need further clarification. After a long respite from sleep studies, Aserinsky has returned to them, examining in detail the vegetative changes during REM periods. He has

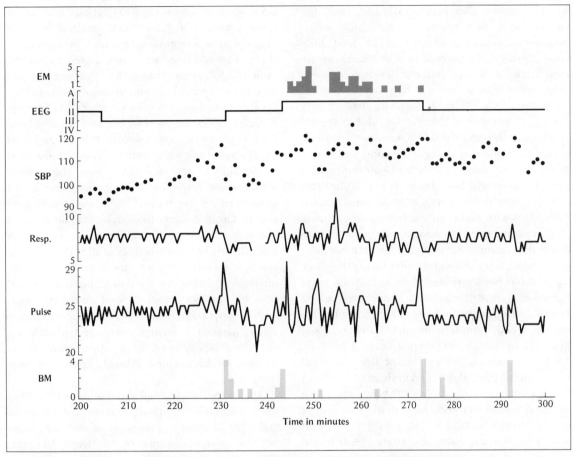

Figure 17.10 Characteristic irregularity of autonomic indices during REMS. Systolic blood pressure, respiration, pulse rate changes, and body movements over a 100-min sample of uninterrupted sleep are shown; the REM period consists of the interval between Minutes 242 and 273. Redrawn from F. Snyder, et al., Changes in respiration, heart rate, and systolic blood pressure in human sleep. *Journal of Applied Physiology*, 1964, **19,** 417–422, Fig. 2. Reproduced with permission.

described (1965) a very constant relationship between bursts of eye movements and irregularities of respiration. As discussed elsewhere (Snyder, 1967, pp. 469–487), they are frequently, but not always, associated.

Relaxation of vasomotor tone during sleep, evidenced by increased amplitude of plethysmograph pulse and elevation of skin temperature, has been mentioned earlier. Studies in our laboratory (Snyder, 1967, pp. 469–487) and elsewhere (L. C. Johnson, 1966; Khatri & Freis, 1967) have revealed a marked waxing and waning of pulse amplitude in the fingers during REMs, periods of constriction often accompanying particularly active bursts of eye movements and blood pressure elevations. Our

studies show a simultaneous lowering of finger skin temperature with an increased level of minute-to-minute fluctuations (Snyder, 1967, pp. 469–487).

In view of the many characteristics of REM periods suggesting a highly activated state, it might be expected that basal skin resistance would be lowered and galvanic skin responses much more prominent than during the remainder of sleep. In fact, more in keeping with the loss of tonic muscle activity, neither occurs. Several laboratories have reported elevations in basal skin resistance associated with REM periods (Batini, Fressy, & Coquery, 1965; Hawkins, Puryear, Wallace, Deal, & Thomas, 1962) and more have found no consistent change (L. C. Johnson & Lubin, 1967; Kamiya, 1961, pp.

145–174; Snyder, 1965, pp. 275–315; Tart, 1967), but clearly basal skin resistance does not reflect heightened arousal at those times. Indeed, brief spontaneous deflections of skin resistance or potential are much less frequent during REM sleep than during slow wave sleep in humans (Asahina, 1962; Broughton, Poire, & Tassinari, 1965; Burch, 1965; L. C. Johnson & Lubin, 1967), and in the cat (Tokizane, 1965, pp. 151–185). Consistently, spontaneous electrodermal changes are most prominent during Stages 3 and 4 of sleep and least during REM periods, although Broughton, Poire, & Tassinari (1965) found some during REM periods, usually coincident with particularly active eye movement.

Comparatively little is known with regard to REM about that classical autonomic index, the behavior of the pupil. Since the eighteenth century (Fontana, 1765), it has been repeatedly noted that the pupil is markedly constricted during sleep. Some recent observations have been made either by gently lifting the eyelids from time to time (Roffwarg, 1965) or by taping them open (Rechtschaffen & Foulkes, 1965), both approaches confirming that the pupil is constricted throughout human sleep but without any apparent changes during REM periods. More intensive studies in the cat have yielded somewhat contradictory results. Both M. Jouvet (1962) and Berlucchi, Moruzzi, Salvi, and Strata (1964) found maximal pupillary constriction during REM periods, although Berlucci et al. observed abrupt pupillary dilations synchronous with bursts of REM. Hodes (1964) also observed these fluctuations associated with eye movements but stated that there was actually a small increase in pupillary diameter and retraction of the nictitating membrane during REM periods, arguing that it is a state of greater sympathetic activity than the rest of sleep.

One other peripherally observable concomitant of REM in humans is the associated occurrence of penile erection.[22] Oswald (1962) noted that erec-

[22]The regular appearance of REM periods during the course of mammalian sleep and the marked bodily changes accompanying them are such striking phenomena that it is strange that they have not been studied much earlier. Beginning with the observations of Howell (1897) on the periodic variation in the plethysmograph curve of the arm, a number of very comparable periodicities were described for other modalities. For example, the periodic occurrence of penile erection during adult human sleep (appearing at 85-min intervals with an average duration of 25 min) was reported by Ohlmeyer, Brilmayer, and Huellstrung (1944).

tions accompanied some REM periods, and subsequent investigators have found measurable penile engorgement accompanying a high percentage of them. Fisher, Gross, and Zuch (1965) found the same results in more than 95% of REM periods, and erection was entirely absent during non-REM sleep, except immediately before or after REM periods. Karacan, Goodenough, Shapiro, and Starker (1966) have made similar observations but claimed only an 80% association and noted occasional instances of erection during non-REM sleep. The present evidence indicates that this phenomenon is not influenced by the recency of sexual gratification (Fisher, Gross, & Zuch, 1965) or by bladder pressure (Karacan et al., 1966), but rather it appears to be an intrinsic part of the physiology of REM sleep. Penile erection during sleep has not been studied adequately in other species, although limited observations of monkeys suggest at least some correlation with REM periods (Gross, Weitzman, Fisher, & Byrne, 1966a; Karacan & Snyder, 1966), and in still unpublished observations of a single infant chimpanzee, we have found a highly consistent relationship.

The further physiological definition of the REM state seems to be limited only by the technical feasibility of obtaining appropriate measures without the undue disturbance of sleep. All-night, EEG-controlled metabolic studies (Brebbia & Altschuler, 1965) indicate that REM periods are generally marked by a slight increase in both oxygen consumption and CO_2 production and that the same is true of the variability of these measures. The ventilation rate and alveolar CO_2 tension of REM periods were most similar to those in the stage of drowsiness prior to spindling sleep (Bülow, 1963), although the observations were very limited. Biochemical correlations with the EEG phases of human sleep are being sought by a variety of means. Assessment of urinary constituents obtained from catheterized patients has suggested that the kidneys produce less volume of more concentrated urine during REM periods (Mandell et al., 1966). Excretion of 17-hydroxycorticosteroids and catecholamine increased sharply (Mandell & Mandell, 1965). Corticosteroid levels in blood plasma followed a similar pattern of jagged peaks (Weitzman, Schaumburg, & Fishbein, 1966), although the temporal relationship to REM periods was not entirely clear. Similar EEG-controlled studies of plasma fatty acid levels during sleep have been made but did not reveal any consistent change, coincident with REM periods (Scott, 1966).

Arousal Reactions During Sleep

The stimulus-response studies of sleep described earlier did not always depend upon behavioral measures, but some included an EEG indicator of partial arousal, either the appearance of K complex,

or "lightening" of a stage (Oswald, Taylor, & Treisman, 1960; Zung & Wilson, 1961). Whether such EEG signs of transient arousal are evoked by experimental stimuli or are "spontaneous" (perhaps evoked by incidental or internal stimuli), they are frequently followed in a few seconds by a generalized vegetative reaction entirely similar to that of the "orienting reaction" of waking. The association of these autonomic changes to EEG events is not constant, nor are the various components always evident to the same degree, but they include a

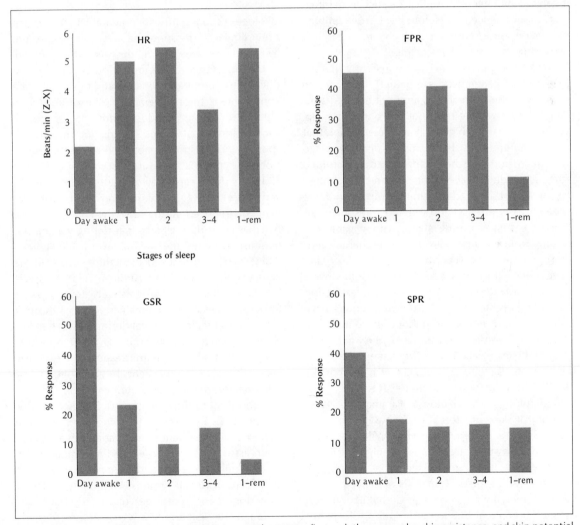

Figure 17.11 Autonomic responses to tones. Average heart rate, finger plethysmographs, skin resistance, and skin potential changes in response to tone stimuli are shown here in relation to the EEG stages of sleep. Redrawn from L. C. Johnson & A. Lubin, The orienting reflex during waking and sleeping. *Electroencephalography and Clinical Neurophysiology*, 1967, **22**, 11–21, Fig. 4. Reproduced with permission.

vasoconstriction response (VCR) of the fingers recorded with a plethysmograph, a galvanic skin resistance (GSR) or skin potential change (SPR), as well as transient acceleration of heart rate (HRR) and slowing of the respiration rate (RR.) Since, as already discussed, spontaneous changes in these modalities vary in degree among the EEG sleep stages (and particularly so between REM and the remainder of sleep), the systematic comparison of evoked reactions in relation to EEG stage is a natural development. As in the parallel study of such responses in the waking condition, the study in sleep involves a number of complexities such as habituation, the influence of baseline level on magnitude of the response, and the difficulty of separating evoked from spontaneous changes.

Jung (1954, pp. 310–344) was apparently the first to note that generalized sympathetic reactions to repetitive stimuli which had already become habituated during waking return at the onset of sleep. While there has been general agreement upon that point, opinion has been much divided as to whether habituation then reappears after continued stimulation during sleep. Pampiglione and Ackner (1958) emphasized the seemingly unaccountable variability of both EEG and vegetative responses to repetitive stimuli during sleep, with waxing and waning from one minute to the next. There is general agreement that such measures as VCR or GSR dishabituate at the onset of sleep, but some investigators have described their eventual extinction (Sokolov & Paramonova, 1961), while others have found them to persist throughout entire nights of sleep (L. C. Johnson & Lubin, 1967; Oswald, 1962; H. L. Williams et al., 1964). The same controversy involves the K complex itself, claims being equally divided that it does habituate (Oswald, 1962; Pampiglione, 1952; Sokolov & Paramanova, 1961) and that it does not (L. C. Johnson & Lubin, 1967; Roth, Shaw, & Green, 1956; H. L. Williams et al., 1964). If we assume the value of all-night coverage of the gamut of changes in sleep EEG patterns and of the careful statistical analysis employed in the latest studies, it would now appear that habituation is not a prominent phenomenon during sleep, but results may be highly dependent upon the precise nature of the stimulus and its manner of presentation, as well as the motivational set of the subjects.

If it is granted that habituation can be disregarded during sleep, then the relations between EEG stages and variations in response to repetitive stimuli are amenable to study. Unfortunately, reports in that respect are also somewhat contradictory. Ackner and Pampiglione (1957) found that the VCR was no longer present in deeper sleep, whereas H. L. Williams et al. (1964) found it present and of constant duration throughout all stages. Although Oswald (1962) described GSR to stimulation only after sleep had reached deeper stages, L. C. Johnson and Lubin (1967) observed them in all stages.

Since responses to experimental stimuli are entirely similar to the spontaneous responses present to varying degrees throughout sleep, the problem of distinguishing one from the other poses major difficulties. In one of the latest and most elaborate approaches to this problem, L. C. Johnson and Lubin (1967) utilized a "pseudostimulus" 15 sec before each of the actual stimuli, subtracting the rates of spontaneous response obtained at these points from the rates scored after stimulation (Figure 17.11). By this means they found that VCR changed very little between waking and sleep but was markedly reduced during REM; the HRR was about twice as great during Stage 2 as during waking but diminished below the waking level in delta sleep (Stages 3–4) and reached its highest levels during REM. In contrast with both cardiovascular measures, the GSR diminished progressively from waking through Stages 1 and 2, remained low in 3 through 4, and was at its lowest level during REM. The SPRs were unchanged throughout REM and non-REM sleep. Still different was the respiratory response, taking the form of a transient slowing, followed by a gradual return to baseline during waking and REM conditions, but during Stages 2 or 3–4 by an acceleration. L. C. Johnson and Lubin noted that the response of every autonomic variable was higher when associated with an evoked K complex, and, if the stimulus were presented during an actual REM burst, cardiovascular responses tended to be lower than during the remainder of the REM periods, although the GSR and SPR were not affected.

These striking differences among response modalities in relation to the EEG stages of sleep raise several additional issues. The first is whether the law of initial value (Wilder, 1958) applies during sleep, i.e., whether the extent, or rate, of a criterion response might be negatively correlated with the baseline level of the variable. McDonald, L. C. Johnson, and Hord (1963) have considered and rejected that possibility as an explanation for the apparent lack of HRR habituation in drowsy subjects but they did not specifically consider it with regard to the stage differences described above. The second problem is that the use of a pseudostimulus does not entirely obviate the difficulty of distinguishing "signal" (evoked response) from "noise" (spontaneous changes) if the amount of noise varies systematically among the EEG stages. With high levels of spontaneous fluctuation, as in the case of the VCR during REM, the likelihood of evoked responses might also be high, even though any given response would be undistinguishable. In that regard the same group has made another promising contribution (Hord, Lubin & L. C. Johnson, 1966), using the method of averaging large numbers of evoked HRR during sleep. In that procedure, all values not time locked to the stimulus average to zero, leaving for consideration only that part of the response consistently related to the stimulus.[23] By this means a diphasic response was demonstrated with an accelerating peak on the fourth poststimulus beat and a decelerating trough on the tenth beat; this technique also demonstrated a larger HRR during REM than in any other stage of sleep. Physiological responsiveness during sleep appears to be different from that of waking but certainly no less complex.

Factors Affecting the EEG Patterning of Sleep

The notion of sleep as a simple or unitary physiological entity was first challenged by revelations of the highly variegated EEG patterning of sleep states and has been made still more obsolete by recognition of the REM state, yet the significance and interrelationships of these disparate electrical forms need much further clarification. Although not psychophysiological in the strict sense, this distinctly new field of functional analysis promises to

be of basic importance for future psychophysiological understanding of sleep. Even though the temporal unfolding of nightly EEG sleep patterns is remarkably consistent in broad outline, there is also a noteworthy degree of variation among individuals or in the same person on different nights. Attempts to identify some of the factors affecting this dynamic progression will be the concern of the next sections.

Individual differences in sleep patterns Recent systematic and quantitative evaluation of the all-night EEG progression of sleep has been directed primarily to the relative proportions of the several stages (particularly, REM and Stage 4), and to a lesser extent to their temporal sequence. Broad ranges of variation are found in the percentage of total sleep spent in a given sleep stage, yet several reports indicate that the proportion of REM tends to be individually characteristic from night to night (Antrobus, 1962; Rechtschaffen & Verdone, 1964). Another study (R. L. Williams et al., 1964) extends the same generalization to all stages. Individual differences in the distribution of EEG frequencies and waveforms *within* stage criteria are readily apparent but have not been examined systematically. From either standpoint the exploration of differences in sleep patterns in relation to other stable individual differences, or even to genetic or ethnic influences, is a beckoning frontier.

In a first application of the traditional genetic approach, Zung and Wilson (1967) were unable to distinguish between monozygotic and dizygotic twin pairs by the proportions of time spent in various EEG sleep stages but felt that they could do so by the temporal concordance of stages across the night. Attempts to relate variations in sleep patterns to dimensions of psychological assessment have also been few. Antrobus, Dement, and Fisher (1964) found that individuals who habitually did not recall dreams tended to have low levels of REM time during undisturbed sleep. Other evidence has indicated that those who did not remember dreams were particularly repressive and less liable to manifest anxiety (Lachmann, Lapkin, & Handelman, 1962; Schonbar, 1959; Tart, 1962). Rechtschaffen and Verdone (1964), however, could not demonstrate significant correlations between time in REM sleep and Minnesota Multiphasic Personality Inventory

---

[23]The same approach has been widely applied to evoked scalp potentials, and in a number of studies such averaged evoked potentials have been compared among the EEG stages of human sleep (Davis & Yoshie, 1963; Weitzman & Kremen, 1965; Williams, Tepas, & Morlock, 1962). (See also Chapters 3 and 7 in this book.)

(MMPI) scores, except for an isolated correlation of .50 with the anxiety scale, which may have been a result of chance and could not be replicated later in the same laboratory (Monroe, 1967). Rechtschaffen and Verdone (1964) had remarked that those MMPI scores associated with extraversion showed small but negative correlations with time in REM sleep, while those associated with introversion were positively correlated at low levels. In Monroe's comparison of the sleep of "good" and "poor" sleepers, the latter spent markedly less time in REM sleep and had generally pathological scores on the MMPI, as well as on the Cornell Medical Index. Cartwright, Monroe, and Palmer (1967) reported that the proportion of REM sleep to total sleep correlated with a factor comprised of a number of psychological measures, including ratings of imaginativeness of dream reports and scores on Remote Association, Draw-A-Person, and Visual Imagery Flexibility Tests, but not including scores on the Cattell Anxiety Scale, the Wechsler Adult Intelligence Scale, or the Thematic Apperception Test (TAT). Individual correlations of these measures with percentages of REM sleep were not published, but the authors made them available to us. They are uniformly modest, except for a rank-order correlation of .53 with the Draw-A-Person Test.

Obviously, much further examination is needed to decide whether a propensity to the REM state during sleep is importantly related to any psychological dimension of waking, but the same is true in relation to even the broadest categories of biological variables. Thus far only age and sex have been appraised at all in that context. The systematic comparison of males and females with regard to EEG sleep patterns has been reported from just one laboratory and one age group, that of young adults (R. L. Williams et al., 1964, 1966), but there is general agreement that there are no striking or significant quantitative differences between the sexes among EEG categories of sleep, despite other evidence of differing response capacities during sleep.

Age comparisons   Age affects both the waveforms and their relative predominance in the sleep EEG. Considering the former first, recent studies of premature infants confirm older observations that the earlier the developmental age, the simpler and

less differentiated is EEG activity generally; therefore, the less distinctive are the patterns accompanying apparently different behavioral states (Dreyfus-Brisac, Samson, Blanc, & Monod, 1958; Parmelee, Wenner, Akiyama, Stern & Flescher, 1967b, pp. 459–476; Parmalee, Wenner, Akiyama, Schultz, & Stern, 1967a). Nevertheless, two distinct patterns within sleep become evident as soon as the distinctive pattern of wakefulness does. In full-term newborn infants, quiet behavioral sleep is more or less distinguished from waking by clusters of high voltage, slow waves separated by inactive intervals, although slow waves do not become continuous or associated with typical spindles or *K* complexes until 3 months of age. On the other hand, a low voltage, irregular rhythm, very similar to that of wakefulness, clearly distinguishes REM intervals at term. During the last few months of gestation this newer pattern emerges from the undifferentiated EEGs of earlier periods. The characteristics of the EEG patterns of sleep that are most tardy in their development, spindles and slow waves, also suffer the greatest attrition with old age (E. L. Gibbs & F. A. Gibbs, 1950b; Lairy, Cor-Mordret, Faure, & Ridjanovic, 1962).

At present, almost all normative data concerning the proportionate distribution and temporal patterning of sleep stages across the night have come from young adults, the age group most readily available for laboratory study of sleep. There is significant variation among laboratories in the conditions and procedures of study and in the scoring criteria for the quantitative estimation of EEG stages; nevertheless, the average percentages of time that young adults spent in REM sleep in several representative studies were consistent to within about 2%, ranging from 22 to 24% (Table 17.1). Similarly, there is close agreement among the average percentages of Stage 4 sleep, which ranges from 11 to 16%. When Stages 3 and 4 are combined to provide an estimate of average delta sleep for young adults, the totals amount to 21, 22, 23, and 24% in four of the studies tabulated. It is worth noting that the range of these average percentages is almost precisely the same as that for the REM state in the same group of studies, yet there is approximately a twofold range among individual subjects for either measure.

TABLE 17.1 PROPORTION OF TIME SPENT IN REM AND STAGE 4 SLEEP BY YOUNG ADULT SUBJECTS

REM % Time			Stage 4 % Time			
Male	Female	Male and Female	Male	Female	Male and Female	Source
22.5						Berger & Oswald, 1962a
21.7			14.5			H. L. Williams et al., 1964
24.1	21.9		13.2	16.2		R. L. Williams, Agnew, & Webb, 1964, 1966
	23.7					Antrobus, Dement, & Fisher, 1964
		24			11.2	A. Kales, Jacobson, J. D. Kales, Jun, & Weissbuch, 1967b
		22				Roffwarg, Muzio, & Dement, 1966

The first and still most encompassing comparison of age differences in REM manifestations is that of Roffwarg and his colleagues (Roffwarg, Dement, & Fisher, 1964; Roffwarg, Muzio, & Dement, 1966), which will serve as the basis for the present discussion. As shown in Figure 17.12, the most striking change in the proportion of REM sleep to total sleep occurs in the first year of life. The average of 46% that they found in neonates is fully supported by all comparable estimates (Delange et al.,

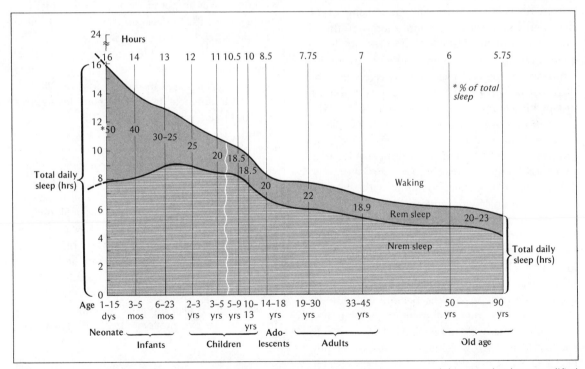

Figure 17.12 REM sleep/NREM relationship throughout human life. The old age portion of this curve has been modified by Roffwarg on the basis of subsequent data. From H. P. Roffwarg et al., Ontogenetic development of the human sleep-dream cycle. *Science,* 1966, **152,** 604–619, Fig. 1. Copyright 1966 by the American Association for the Advancement of Science.

1962; Parmelee et al., 1967a; Weitzman, Fishbein, & Graziana, 1965). Studies of premature infants reveal still higher percentages of REM sleep, although scoring criteria become increasingly ambiguous with diminishing gestational age (Parmelee et al., 1967a). Other characteristic features of the sleep cycle in neonates are the relatively short cycle lengths (about 50 min) and the tendency of infants to go immediately from waking to REM, without any intervening period of slow wave sleep.

As total sleep diminishes over the first 3 years of life, there is a progressive fall in the percentage of time in REM sleep to approximately adult levels, accompanied by a corresponding lengthening of sleep cycles and an increasing latency of the first REM period after sleep onset. In the 3- to 5-year-old age range, the further reduction in total sleep associated with the elimination of naps is accompanied by a marked prolongation of first REM latency (120–180 min after sleep onset); in effect, the first period of REM sleep is omitted. From infancy to adolescence, this interval is a rather distinctive feature of sleep patterns, although many of its characteristics tend to linger until young adulthood (the missing of the first REM period is not infrequent even in the late teens and early twenties). Although the percentages of REM sleep may be slightly lower in children than in adults, the more striking difference is the predominance of delta patterns; one recent study (A. Kales et al., 1967d) reported finding 30% Stage 4 and 29% Stage 3, as compared with 11% and 10%, respectively, in a young adult group studied in the same laboratory.

Changes in EEG sleep patterns with aging in adults are now receiving much more attention. Lairy et al. (1962) found an average of only 14% REM sleep in nine 66- to 81-year-old women, but mean levels above 20% have been obtained in other recent studies (Feinberg, Koresko, & Heller, 1967; Kahn & Fisher, 1966). The most striking change is progressive loss of the delta patterns, beginning in adolescents and continuing to the point of complete loss of Stage 4 in many elderly persons (Agnew, Webb, & R. L. Williams, 1967b; Feinberg, Koresko, & Heller, 1967; J. D. Kales, A. Kales, A. Jacobson, Po, & Green, 1967c). If it is granted that the delta component is an expression of sleep depth, then Burdach's statement that children sleep very soundly and old people have light sleep is certainly confirmed.

Whether this is a function of diminished need or diminished capacity cannot be settled at present, although the next section on the experimental alteration of EEG sleep patterns also bears upon that question.

Deprivation of REM sleep The experimental alteration of EEG sleep patterns had a late and singular beginning. For a long time after the discovery of REM it was generally assumed that this peculiar physiological pattern simply represented "light" sleep, a kind of transitional state between sleep and waking. Other reasons for rejecting that assumption will be discussed, but among the most cogent were the effects of an extraordinary experimental intervention first termed "dream deprivation" (Dement, 1960). Out of his interest in the function of dreaming, Dement set out to determine the effects of preventing its occurrence by awakening subjects at the very onset of each REM period over a series of consecutive nights. To his surprise he found that a progressively increasing number of awakenings was required to accomplish this; i.e., if there were 7 REM onsets on the first night, there might be 30 by the fifth night. Secondly, when the subjects were once again left to sleep undisturbed at the conclusion of these awakening nights, there were marked increases in the amount of REMs as compared to subjects' normal baseline levels. This amounted to an overall average of 50% in the original study, though it was as high as 80% in some cases. Neither effect appeared when comparable awakenings were made during any other EEG phase of sleep. Still another effect of REM deprivation that was not so apparent initially is a shortening of latency between sleep onset and the beginning of the first REM period (Rechtschaffen & Maron, 1964; Sampson, 1965). Increased intensity of phasic REM components such as eye movements and muscle twitches has been demonstrated in animals after REM deprivation (Dement, Henry, Cohen, & Ferguson, 1967) and is also reported in humans, at least with regard to eye movements (Pivik & Foulkes, 1966).[24]

[24]In both respects it is of interest that many severely depressed patients, who might be assumed to be suffering from chronic REM deprivation, show both extremely short REM latencies and extraordinarily intense REM activity (Snyder, 1968, pp. 272–301); "REM storms" are also described in the sleep of patients with delirium tremens (Gross et al., 1966b), as well as in chronic schizophrenics in remissions (Gulevich, Dement, & Zarcone, 1967).

Although these very striking and tangible effects of REM deprivation have been quite consistently confirmed (Agnew, Webb, & R. L. Williams, 1966; Cartwright, Monroe, & Palmer, 1967; A. Kales, Hoedemaker, A. Jacobson, & Lichtenstein, 1964; Sampson, 1965; Snyder, 1963) their interpretation has been much discussed ever since. Emphasis upon the dream deprivation aspect gave way to a purely physiological interpretation, after the very same results had been demonstrated in lower animals (Dement, 1964a, pp. 129–162; D. Jouvet, Vimont, Delorme, & M. Jouvet, 1964; Khazan & Sawyer, 1963; Siegel & Gordon, 1965). The one construction that could not be applied was that the experimental interruption of "light" sleep would specifically increase the propensity for "light" sleep to occur, rather than result in "deeper" sleep. The inappropriateness of such an explanation was even more apparent when the same recovery increases in REMs were demonstrated after total sleep deprivation (Berger & Oswald, 1962a; H. L. Williams et al., 1964), partial deprivation of total sleep (Sampson, 1965), or suppression of REM by pharmacological means (Rechtschaffen & Maron, 1964). Thus far, the most coherent explanation of these findings rests upon the assumption that the normal occurrence of REM periods depends upon the periodic accumulation and expenditure of some neurohumoral substance (M. Jouvet, 1961, pp. 188–208). When this is prevented, there is a progressively increasing tendency for REMs to occur (Dement, 1965, pp. 634–638; Snyder, 1963). New evidence that is particularly relevant indicates that compensatory increases in REM need not follow the deprivation procedure immediately but can be delayed deliberately for at least 5 nights by holding REM to baseline levels (Dement, Greenberg, & Klein, 1966).

With just one possible exception (Wood, 1962), no other experimental approaches have substantially increased the ratio of REM time to sleep time, nor, with few exceptions, has any reduced it very strikingly. By contrast, other aspects of the EEG during sleep are decidedly responsive to a variety of influences. Much attention is now focused upon Stage 4, but this could as well include Stage 3, or the delta component of sleep in general.[25] Of the

factors affecting both REM and delta sleep, total sleep deprivation has been the one most extensively studied. Berger and Oswald (1962a) reported that 4 nights of total sleep loss increased Stage 4 from 6 to 26% on the first recovery night (with a comparable increase in Stage 3), while reducing REM from 22 to 7%. After 2 nights of sleep loss, H. L. Williams et al. (1964) also found a substantial increase in Stage 4, from 15 to 25%, and a smaller decrease in REM (22 to 19%). This might suggest that enhancement of delta sleep and diminution of REM in recovery sleep are proportional to the duration of sleep deprivation. Although that issue has not been examined directly, evidence from a single subject totally deprived of sleep for a record length of time, 11 nights, confounds it in both respects (Gulevich, Dement, & L. Johnson, 1966). The young man showed almost a sixfold elevation of Stage 4 during his first 6 hr of recovery sleep, not vastly greater than the increase found by Berger and Oswald after just 4 nights without sleep. While a comparable figure for REM cannot be derived from the published data, the percentage of the entire first night of recovery (almost 15 hr) was strikingly *higher* than that of control nights (27% versus an average of 17%).

After such experimental deprivations, compensatory elevations of delta sleep continue at diminishing levels over at least several additional recovery nights. Usually, on the second night of recovery the REM level is most elevated above baseline measures. The accepted interpretation is that after the total deprivation of sleep, the need for Stage 4 is prepotent and initially tends to depress REM, but when that need is partially satisfied the accumulated need for REM sleep asserts itself (H. L. Williams et al., 1964). Although this may be true for relatively short periods of sleep loss, the findings of the 11-day study suggest that the need for REM sleep becomes increasingly peremptory the longer the deprivation.

A number of recent studies have been concerned with the effect of what is probably the more important naturally occurring condition, partial sleep deprivation. Sampson (1965) found that, when sleep was limited to 2.5 hr over 3 consecutive nights, substantial elevations of REM occurred during recovery nights in four of six subjects, even beginning on the first recovery night for three of them. Rush,

[25]One of the most dramatic of recent findings in human subjects is the observed association between Stages 3 and 4 sleep and peaks of plasma growth hormone (Sassin et al., 1969).

Muzio, and Roffwarg (1966) also reported increases in the percentage of REM after 7 days of sleep limited to 4 hr and again after 7 days limited to 6 hr. On the other hand, after 8 days of sleep restricted to 3 hr, Webb and Agnew (1965) did not observe any average increase in REM on the first recovery night and apparently did not assess it on subsequent nights. None of these studies revealed any general tendency for larger proportions of REM to be compressed into the abbreviated periods of sleep, as occurs in cats on restricted sleep regimes (Ferguson & Dement, 1967), although it did occur in individual subjects (Rush, Muzio, & Roffwarg, 1966; Webb & Agnew, 1965). Perhaps it might occur more consistently if partial sleep deprivation were continued over longer intervals.

There is general agreement that the proportion of Stage 4 is markedly increased under conditions of partial sleep deprivation, even though no actual deprivation of Stage 4 has occurred (Dement & Greenberg, 1966; Rush, Muzio, & Roffwarg, 1966; Webb & Agnew, 1965). By partially arousing subjects repeatedly over a series of nights before Stage 3 patterns could develop to Stage 4, Agnew, Webb, and R. L. Williams (1964) demonstrated that the resulting deprivation of Stage 4 was followed by compensatory increases in that stage on subsequent nights. However, the widely accepted comparison of that finding to the effects of REM deprivation is misleading, since it would not be surprising that deprivation of any period of sleep should bring about a greater tendency for "deep" sleep. The evidence that curtailment of total sleep without interference with Stage 4 has the same effects clearly supports that interpretation. We shall soon take up other reasons for assuming that Stage 4 represents an extreme of the EEG continuum of sleep depth. In that context all of the foregoing merely confirms Burdach's statement, "After great fatigue the sleep becomes sounder."

Other influences   Possible effects of physical exercise upon EEG sleep are of obvious relevance but the data are meager and equivocal. Hauri (1966) was unable to alter the EEG evolution of the first 3.5 hr of sleep either by 6 hr of strenuous exercise immediately before or by the same interval of concentrated study, although the prior study slightly delayed sleep onset. On the other hand, when Baekeland and Lasky (1966) compared the sleep of college athletes on nights after their customary daytime workouts with that after days of rest they found a significant increase in the percentage of delta sleep (40 versus 32%). Evening exercise of the same subjects, as in Hauri's study, was followed by an intermediate level of delta (35%) but significantly increased the number of brief periods of wakefulness, suggesting that sleep was more disturbed.

The effects of abiding levels of "stress" or "anxiety" on the sleep profiles are particularly interesting to psychophysiologists; unfortunately, they are especially difficult to study in the laboratory, and the effects of stress cannot be considered settled at present. The most extensive data relate to predictable changes in the sleep patterns accompanying adaptation to sleeping in the laboratory setting (Agnew, Webb, & R. L. Williams, 1966; Dement, Greenberg, & Klein, 1966; A. Kales et al., 1967b; Rechtschaffen & Verdone, 1964). The consistently lower proportion of REM found on the first night of laboratory sleep probably is attributable to increased tension or apprehension arising out of the newness of the experience, especially since other indications of disturbed sleep (increased amounts of spontaneous awakening during sleep and diminished percentages of delta patterns) support the same interpretation. However, the fragmentation of sleep by awakening and the curtailment of REM is seen much more strikingly in initial sleep records of experimental animals (Faure, Vincent, LeNouene, & Geissmann, 1963; Snyder, 1966) and may be prolonged over many weeks. The term "first night effect" should not encourage the optimistic assumption that 1 or 2 nights will be sufficient laboratory adaptation for all subjects. Some individuals may require 3 or more nights for adaptation and others none at all (Dement, Greenberg, & Klein, 1966).

Further support for the assumption that heightened states of arousal are associated with the reduced occurrence of REM is the evidence that poor sleepers spend less of their sleep in the REM state than good sleepers (Monroe, 1967), as well as the experimental effects of immobilization induced stress, injections of ACTH, or exposure to continuous white noise on the proportion of REM in animal sleep (Kawakami, Negoro, & Terasawa, 1965; Khazan & Sawyer, 1963). Yet the few investigations specifically directed at the analysis of such relationships in humans do not encourage that assumption. Baekeland, Koulack, and Lasky (1967) found that viewing a stressful moving picture had no significant effect on any of the parameters of sleep studied: the minor changes were that time in the REM state was slightly reduced; the density of eye movements within REM periods was heightened; and the number of spontaneous awakenings in the midst of, or terminating, REM periods was significantly increased. Longitudinal studies of the sleep patterns of normal subjects at the time of experimental and natural life stress (such as medical school examinations), revealed no significant relation between apparent stress and REM percentages, although the percentage of Stage 4 sleep was significantly lowered on stress nights (Lester, Burch, & Dossett, 1967). Similarly, a longitudinal study of psychiatric patients in our laboratory has disclosed no predictable relation between the extent of REM occurrence and the transient episodes of particular turmoil (Hartmann, Verdone, & Snyder, 1966).

Other kinds of psychological influences may also affect the occurrence of REM. Wood (1962) noted that social isolation appeared to increase the proportion of REM; Stoyva (1965b) reported that subjects who dreamed in accordance with topics suggested during presleep hypnosis had reduced levels of REM during the first half of the night; Rechtschaffen and Verdone (1964) claimed that the percentage of REM could be slightly influenced by offering subjects monetary incentives to dream more or less. It is impossible to guess how direct or remote such effects may actually be, so that little is now known about the factors responsible for the wide range of normal variability in the occurrence of REM.

Sufficiently complex at this time is the matter of changes in EEG sleep patterns within a single night, particularly as reflected in the unequal and complementary distributions of delta sleep and REM sleep. Since experimental deprivation of sleep immediately enhances delta sleep at the expense of REM, the normal progression of nightly patterns may simply result from the sleep deficit that must first be repaid. There is no such regular develop-

ment in the *ad lib* sleep of other species, and the long initial interval of delta sleep first appears in human sleep patterns at the time when napping ceases (Roffwarg, Muzio, & Dement, 1966). In adults taking morning naps after a full night of sleep, slow wave patterns are almost absent, percentage REM is high (38% in habituated subjects), and REM periods tend to begin very soon (Webb, Agnew, & Sternthal, 1966).

The same kind of explanation fits the data of Maron, Rechtschaffen, and Wolpert (1964), which showed that sleep patterns during early evening naps closely approximate the beginning of nocturnal sleep, while patterns during early afternoon naps are intermediate between the evening and the above described morning patterns. Nevertheless, such variations do raise the possibility that sleep patterns may be influenced to some extent by more stable circadian rhythms of bodily functioning such as those reflected by curves of adrenal steroid excretion or body temperature, a possibility enhanced by a number of still unpublished studies. When J. Davis (1965) induced a subject to divide his sleep into two 4-hr periods over a series of days, one at night and one in the afternoon, she found that night sleep continued to resemble the first part of typical nocturnal sleep, whereas afternoon sleep resembled the second half of the full night's sleep; this contrast persisted even when particular afternoon or night sleep periods were omitted. Similarly, Weitzman et al. (1967) found that REM time increased and the latency of the first REM period diminished during the early hours of daytime sleep, when sleep waking periods are acutely reversed, even though the extent of prior sleep deprivation was as great as, or initially greater than, that preceding nocturnal sleep. In a similar vein, Scherrer, Lille, and Gabersek (1968) have documented what sleep researchers have long suspected, that the daytime sleep of night workers tends to be foreshortened, disturbed, and deficient in the full quota of REM.

Pharmacological and hormonal influences
Whatever naturally occurring factors shape the variability of EEG sleep patterns, it is clear that they can be modified profoundly by many commonly used drugs. The rapidly growing, but still very con-

fusing, literature related to this topic has been reviewed by Kramer, Whitman, Baldridge, and Ornstein (1966, pp. 102–116) and by Hartmann (1967). Detailed consideration of it would carry us far afield from psychophysiology, but at least a few generalizations are in order. Almost all of the drugs assessed in this respect so far (largely those within the psychiatric pharmacopoeia) reduce the proportion of REM within sleep.[26] However, the degree of this effect varies widely among the drugs and undoubtedly involves a variety of mechanisms: for any given drug, the effects depend very much upon the dosage and upon the acuteness or chronicity of administration. In addition, the results of REM deprivation are such that the sleep cycle may reflect the intake of drugs long after their actual pharmacological action has ceased.

Possible hormonal influences upon the sleep patterns deserve special consideration, since they are important naturally changing variables that might require consideration in any studies, particularly those employing female subjects. Unfortunately, information relevant to that point is still minimal, being limited to a single report that the length of REM time changes throughout the menstrual cycle, reaching peak levels just before menstruation, and falling abruptly thereafter (Hartmann, 1966a) and to a finding of no significant deviations in the sleep patterns of hypothyroid patients before or after thyroid treatment (Heuser et al., 1966).

Animal studies in this area were earlier stimulated by observations in female rabbits that sleep and REM appeared to follow with unusual promptness after copulation, and that spontaneous REM appeared to be increased after injection of pituitary and placental gonadotrophins (Faure, 1965, pp. 241–282; Khazan & Sawyer, 1964). Somewhat at variance with these findings in rabbits and the unconfirmed relationship to the human menstrual cycle are new reports of minimal REM occurrence during estrogen-induced behavioral estrus in ovariectomized rats (Yokoyama, Ramirez, & Sawyer, 1966) or guinea pigs (Malven & Sawyer, 1966). The authors of the last two studies make the important point

that any such effects might be secondary to such others as changes in general activity level.

In the past, the nature of sleep as a general biological phenomenon has been a much neglected subject of empirical study. The works reviewed in this section are but the beginning of the extensive attention this problem undoubtedly will elicit in the future.

THE PSYCHOPHYSIOLOGY OF DREAMING

Der Blick unseres Auges dient ja auch nicht bloss der Wahrnehmung der äussern Welt—The glance of our eyes does not merely serve observation of the external world.—Griesinger, 1868

While the once more popular issue of sleep depth still has not received adequate psychophysiological study, that is more than compensated at present by the degree of attention to a topic formerly much neglected, that of physiological correlations with mental experience intrinsic to sleep. As indicated at the outset of this chapter, that aspect of psychophysiology arises almost entirely from the discovery of Aserinsky and N. Kleitman in 1953, although there had been a few isolated historical precursors.[27]

Plato located that part of the soul concerned with dreaming in the liver; other very early psychophysiological reports, although conflicting in many regards, agreed that dreaming was related in some way to motility of the stomach. Luckhardt (1915) found that gastric hunger contractions stopped when sleeping dogs moved in ways suggestive of dreaming. Wada (1922), however, claimed that dreaming in humans occurred only at times of gastric motility, a view McGlade (1942) supported on the basis of rather dubious evidence. Scantlebury, Frick, and Patterson (1942) reported that dreaming did not occur in the absence of hunger contractions, even though its immediate effect was to inhibit them. A recent telemetric study supports Wada's position, since REM periods were associated with increased peristalsis during sleep, almost as great as that of waking (Baust & Rohrwasser, 1969).

---

[26]Reserpine (Hartmann, 1966b; Tissot, 1965) and LSD (Muzio, Roffwarg, & Kaufman, 1966) are possible exceptions, tending to enhance REM occurrence.

[27]The scant scientific interest in dreaming before 1953 was emphasized by Ramsey in a review of empirical studies appearing in that year.

Incidental observations purportedly concerned with dreaming are common throughout the older literature of sleep physiology. For example, Farmer and Chambers (1925) reported that a subject who later recalled dreaming had a low and variable skin resistance. Max (1935) described characteristic patterns of muscle action currents in the fingers and forearms of deaf subjects prior to their spontaneous recall of dreams, a point to which Stoyva (1965a) has brought new evidence (see p. 669). Quite exceptional in its thoroughness and insight was the detailed and purposeful study of MacWilliam (1923), a professor of physiology at Aberdeen University, who carried out extensive measures of pulse, respiration, and blood pressure in sleeping subjects. MacWilliam concluded that there were two distinct conditions of sleep: "(1) Undisturbed sleep attended by lowering of blood pressure, heart and respiratory rates, etc. and (2) disturbed sleep, modified by reflex excitations, dreams, nightmares, etc., sometimes accompanied by extensive rises in blood pressure, increased heart action, changes in respiration and various reflex effects." MacWilliam did not note the regular alternations of these two kinds of sleep during the night, and his measurements of blood pressure made after awakening the sleeper were of uncertain relevance; yet, his report was remarkably prophetic of findings during the past few years.

A few casual observations concerned with dreaming appeared during the period when the various EEG patterns of sleep were first intensively studied. Loomis, Harvey, and Hobart (1937) cited two instances of awakenings from the B stage (1) of sleep that were associated with reports of dreams, which might be considered anticipatory of the Aserinsky and N. Kleitman discovery, but the same laboratory soon reported similar associations with C stage (or 2) also (Davis et al., 1938). Blake, Gerard, and N. Kleitman (1939) were the first to test such relationships experimentally by awakening a subject. They concluded that dreaming was minimal during the delta phase but otherwise present most of the night. Henry (1941) noted eight occasions of spontaneous dream recall from six subjects following EEG patterns ranging from the low voltage (B or 1) to spindle plus random (D or 3) categories. He also observed that bursts of alpha activity were constantly present and surmised that dreams might be related to transient upward shifts in the level of sleep. A decade before the Aserinsky and Kleitman report, and in the same laboratory, Teplitz (1943) approached this question in the most systematic of the early investigations. She obtained dream reports from all stages of sleep, but with a frequency diminishing from 100% in Stage B to 70% in Stage C and 50% in the small number of Stage D or E awakenings.

Thus there did not appear to be any specific EEG correlates of dreaming; available evidence suggested that it occurred throughout sleep, perhaps somewhat less commonly during the delta or deep sleep phases. Yet the association of eye movements with dreaming was conjectured not once but repeatedly. The earliest of these surmises appears in the introspective discussion of the distinguished psychiatrist, Griesinger (1868), quoted in part at the beginning of this section. He also included the flat statement, "One cannot observe on oneself how the globes move with the pictures and fantasies of our dreams. I believe, however, that with vivid dreaming movements of the eyes occur." The same association between eye movements and dreaming was suggested by Ladd (1892), Max (1935), and E. Jacobson (1938).

The Relationship of the REM State to Dreaming

There would be little occasion for this chapter if the association between REM periods and dreaming had never been claimed. Its value as a catalyst to the emergence of a psychophysiology of sleep is unquestionable. In addition, it is the outstanding psychophysiological relationship during sleep thus far posited and therefore requires much closer examination. As Malcolm (1959) points out, no evidence can really prove that a mental experience such as we call "dreaming" takes place during REM periods or any other condition of sleep. What we mean by "dreams" are always "dream reports," products of waking minds, and a corresponding psychic process during prior sleep can be only inferred. Even assuming the existence of a psychic life of dreaming, there could be no certainty that dreaming occurs only at those times when it appears to be remembered, for some conditions of sleep or awakening might simply be more favorable for its translation into waking memory, while some might preclude it. Since these uncertainties cannot be settled on any conceivable empirical basis, we must be content to ignore them in favor of issues appearing more amenable to experimental test, in this case the problems of whether REM periods are *invariably* or *uniquely* associated with dream reports. Nevertheless, as we review the considerable body of evidence directed toward these questions, we might anticipate that its ultimate inconclusiveness is inherent in the limitation just mentioned; i.e., the data from which all inference derives are the products of a wrenching transition between disparate states of consciousness.

Since the 1953 report of Aserinsky and Kleitman, the recall of dreaming after REM and non-REM awakenings has been reexamined in at least 15 studies, most of them considerably more elaborate than the original one. As summarized in Figure 17.13, the incidence of "dream" reports from REM awakenings varies between 60 and 89%, the 74% first reported being a "happy median." Although the range is considerable, the wide differences in subjects, procedures, and criteria employed in the various studies readily account for it. Dreams are not always recalled from REM awakenings, but most investigators would be willing to concede the margin of failure to the fallibility of memory, especially dream memory, or the perversity of subjects, especially under the circumstances of these studies.

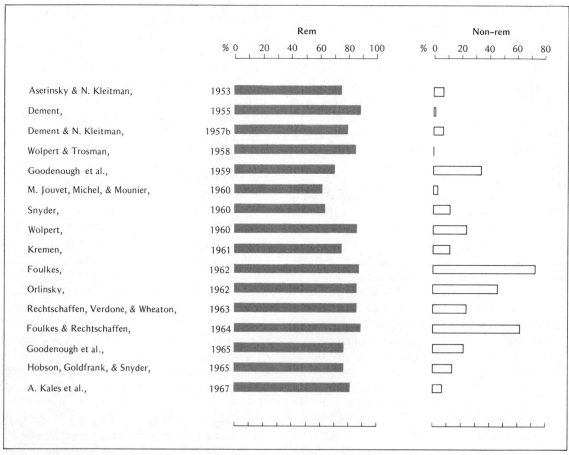

Figure 17.13 Systematic studies of percentage dream recall after REM and Non-REM awakenings. We have attempted to extract comparable figures from each of the studies listed here, although the form in which results were reported sometimes required our own interpretation of what the comparable categories might be.

Clearly, the laboratory study of dreaming involves complex and often subtle interpersonal interaction between subjects and experimenters, which may sometimes prevent dream recall, but more often could tend to exaggerate it. Subjects have been noted to withhold "too personal" dreams from the experimenter (Whitman, Kramer, & Baldridge, 1963) and the importance of "transference" in these studies has been pointed out (Keith, 1962). The lengths to which subjects will go in trying to comply with any experimenter's expectations have been emphasized (Orne, 1959) and might well be relevant to dream studies. Since subjects are generally volunteers, usually motivated by monetary incentives, and since it obviously is expected that they produce dreams, it is hardly surprising that they usually do so (Orne, 1962). This variable might have an overall inflationary effect upon estimates of dream recall, but it could not explain the differential results from REM and non-REM awakenings. Many reports are such highly detailed and complex narratives that it seems most unlikely that they could have been wholly the product of the very brief interval of waking imagination at the time of testing; many others are brief and vague, thus carrying correspondingly little conviction as descriptions of dreams.

As we shall elaborate later, the intensity of dreaming may vary with the intensity of the REM process, but it is equally likely that dream recall is strongly influenced by a variety of factors, possibly including the depth of sleep from which it emerges. When subjects appear unusually tired or are exceptionally sound sleepers, the waking process is difficult and dream recall is usually minimal (Snyder, 1960). This common laboratory observation is substantiated by the available data relating arousal thresholds to the incidence of dream reports (Goodenough et al., 1965a), as well as to the finding that abrupt awakening enhances recall (Goodenough et al., 1965b).

After REM awakenings, some subjects rarely report anything resembling dreams and others almost unfailingly report elaborate sagas. Except for the few studies that have deliberately included non-dreamers (Goodenough et al., 1959), probably most have included a disproportionate number of "good" subjects. Those who have volunteered for dream studies are usually well-educated, articulate, psychologically minded young adults who are likely to be interested in dreams. When the studies are extended to populations lacking those characteristics, the incidence of dream recall in the laboratory will probably suffer accordingly.[28] In view of such considerations, evidence is never likely to be conclusive regarding the invariability of association between REM and dreaming. The convincing importance of the relation between REM and dreaming thus rests largely on the differential results of REM and non-REM awakenings, which unfortunately are far from consistent (see Figure 17.13). The findings from some would suggest that mental activity is diffusely present during sleep, tending to minimize the importance of REM in relation to dreaming. At the same time they imply that cognitive functioning may be continuous throughout sleep (and more important, that a method is available for studying this). Since these are crucial issues in the recent psychophysiology of sleep, they must be dealt with at some length.

With very few exceptions, all studies, even the earliest, obtained a modicum of apparent dream recall from non-REM awakenings. The number was relatively small, so that it could be regarded as falling within the assumed limits of error of the procedure, the "noise level" of the system, as it were. Subjects are almost always more or less bewildered momentarily after awakenings in the laboratory, and are more or less assured and articulate about what they claim to remember from prior sleep. Whether or not the ensuing report should be considered an instance of dream recall often seems quite clear but sometimes requires a judgment on the part of the experimenter. Most investigators have attempted to base such judgments upon explicit, albeit rather vague, criteria: in the earlier studies the reports had to be "detailed dream descriptions" (Aserinsky & N. Kleitman 1953), "coherent, fairly detailed descriptions of dream content" (Dement & N. Kleitman 1957b), or "detailed recall of complete dramas" (Wolpert & Trosman, 1958). About half of the subsequent tests

---

[28]There have been two recent studies of laboratory dreams in children, one finding a rate of recall similar to that in young adults (Foulkes, Pivik, Steadman, Spear, & Symonds, 1967), but the other reporting considerably less (A. Kales et al., 1967b).

yielded very similar results (Hobson, Goldfrank, & Snyder, 1965; A. Kales et al., 1967a; Kremen, 1961; M. Jouvet, Michel, & Mounier, 1960; Snyder, 1960), on the basis of roughly similar criteria. However, using an equally vague but not too dissimilar sounding criterion, "a dream recalled in some detail," Goodenough et al. (1959) reported an overall rate of 34% dream recall from non-REM awakenings (including an incidence of 53% from their subgroup of subjects who ordinarily recalled dreams almost every night).

The next group of studies, all from the University of Chicago psychology laboratories, further highlighted the prevalence of reports from non-REM awakenings, but their criteria of dreaming were explicitly different, and in the most exceptional instances the reporting procedure was also. In general, what was judged in these studies was the presence or absence of "specific content" in the reports, although within that framework other distinctions were usually made which emphasized the problem of defining "dreaming." It seems that the longer, the more detailed, and the more coherent the account provided by the subject immediately after experimental awakenings, the more justified is the presumption that a subjective experience has been remembered from prior sleep (rather than an artifact or confabulation from the process of awakening). But the more stringent the minimal criteria imposed, the lower would be the incidence of qualifying REM reports, as was most clearly illustrated in the study involving the largest number of subjects (25), subject nights (204), and awakenings (908) (Kamiya, 1961, pp. 145–174; Orlinsky, 1962). Orlinsky rated the verbal reports obtained from over 400 non-REM awakenings with the following results:

(1) in 43% subjects could not remember dreaming at all; (2) in 11% they thought they had been dreaming, but could not remember any specific content; (3) in 14% they remembered a specific topic but in isolation, for example fragmentary actions, scenes, objects, words or ideas unrelated to anything else; (4) in 5% they remembered several such disconnected thoughts, scenes or actions; (5) in 14% they reported a short but coherent dream, the parts of which seemed related to one another; (6) in 5% they recalled a dream sequence, in which something happened, followed by some consequence (7) and in 7% they described a long detailed

dream sequence involving three or more discernible stages of development.[29]

Orlinsky's categories (6) and (7) (totaling 13% of non-REM reports) would have been considered "dreaming" by anyone's criteria, while Categories (4), (3), (2), and (1) (73%) probably would have been excluded by a definition such as "coherent fairly detailed descriptions of dream content" (Dement & N. Kleitman, 1957b). Thus the debatable margin would consist of the 14% in Category (5) that were judged, in this evaluation, to be "short but coherent dreams," and the range of the reported results of non-REM awakenings is of just this magnitude among the majority of studies.

There are only two papers in which a considerably higher range of non-REM dream reports were described (Foulkes, 1962; Foulkes & Rechtschaffen, 1964) but these are of particular interest because discussion concerning cognitive activity throughout sleep has been so largely based upon them. The first study fround specific content in 74% of non-REM awakenings, and the latter, 62%, although only that portion (54%) involving the "altered sensory imagery or altered identity of physical setting" was considered dreaming. These studies imply, therefore, that more often than not, some mental content can be elicited, regardless of the time when subjects are awakened. A number of investigations of mental experience during sleep have been based upon that conclusion (Foulkes & Rechtschaffen, 1964; Foulkes & Vogel, 1965).

In evaluating Foulke's (1962) results, consideration of the procedure employed is of paramount importance. He has described his approach to eliciting reports as follows: "To ensure that subjects, faced with the somewhat unpleasant experience of successive awakenings in the middle of the night, would not attempt to return to sleep immediately by grunting out a few drowsy, one-syllable replies, a continued arousal technique was used. Subjects faced a reporting session of several minutes length, even if initially upon awakening they definitely felt that nothing has been going through their mind prior to the awakening bell" [p. 16]. Other investi-

[29]Unfortunately, for our purposes, Orlinsky apparently did not subject his 500 REM reports to the same analysis, although we know that his figure of 86% for REM dream-recall included all reports with any "specific content."

gators have not found such a procedure necessary, but perhaps it might be to elicit subtle fragments of thought from the context of sleep, if such were present. However, what assurance can there be that these thoughts existed prior to awakening, rather than arising from the harassed imagination of the subjects during those several minutes of interrogation?

Other possible explanations of recall of non-REM dreams have received some measure of systematic testing. If non-REM recall depended upon the memory of earlier REM dreams, it would be expected to decline as a function of time since the last REM period. The available data (Dement & N. Kleitman, 1957b; Goodenough et al., 1965a; Kamiya, 1962; Wolpert & Trosman, 1958) quite consistently establishes that dream recall is much more frequent within the 5–10-min interval immediately after REM periods than later in non-REM sleep. While the data suggests that some non-REM dream recall may represent enduring memory of earlier REM dreams, there is other evidence that this is an insufficient explanation for all non-REM reports. In the extensive data of Kamiya (1962), the lowest incidence occurred from 10 to 19 min after undisturbed REM periods. In the succeeding intervals before the next expected REM period, the percentages of dream reports actually tended to rise. Foulkes (1962) reported that the proportion of non-REM recall was almost the same whether or not there had been an intervening REM period since the last awakening.

Similarly, if non-REM recall depended upon the memory of hypnagogic experience at the time of sleep onset, it would decline as a function of time elapsed. Kamiya's data (1962), however, indicated that the incidence of dreaming recall was higher 20–80 min later than it was in the first 4 min after sleep onset. Goodenough and co-workers (1965b) reasoned, following the "delayed remembering" hypothesis, that non-REM reports after intervals of waking should be more "thoughtlike"; while those following undisturbed REM periods should be more "dreamlike." Their expectations were not confirmed by the results.

If non-REM reports represent artifacts of awakening (hypnopompic experience), they would occur more frequently when awakening was difficult and

prolonged, an assumption that has received some measure of support. Foulkes (1962) mentioned that recall was rarely obtained from those awakenings with the longest arousal time, but in a series of studies in which the abruptness of awakening was experimentally varied (Shapiro, Goodenough, & Gryler, 1963; Shapiro, Goodenough, Lewis, & Sleser, 1965; Goodenough et al., 1965b), when the level of sound stimulus was gradually increased to awaken subjects, "thinking" type reports occurred more commonly in both REM and non-REM intervals. If arousal resulted from an abrupt and loud sound stimulus, "thinking" reports from REM periods were largely replaced by a higher rate of dream reports; those from non-REM periods were significantly diminished in favor of "no-content" responses. This alone does not account for the considerable incidence of dream reports from non-REM awakenings, since they occurred as often with abrupt as with gradual arousals, and most studies use abrupt awakening techniques.

The Definition of Dreaming

We have already seen that the weight of evidence for an exclusive relationship between the recurring REM periods of sleep and dreaming depends greatly upon the investigator's definition of dreaming, since that in turn determines what is accepted as evidence of dreaming. If dreaming is "any mental activity during sleep," then available knowledge regarding specific physiological associations is nebulous; but if the term is limited to a qualitatively distinctive kind of subjective experience, a much clearer psychophysiological relationship emerges. The concept of dreaming is so imbedded in the matrix of common experience that few authors have ever troubled to define it. Aristotle wrote, "Nor should the true thoughts, as distinct from the mere presentations, which occur in sleep [be called dreams]. The dream proper is a presentation based upon the movement of sense impressions, when such presentation occurs during sleep, taking sleep in the strict sense of the term [p. 706]." Thus he pointed to the perceptual, rather than the cognitive, quality of dreaming as its experiential essence. The same emphasis upon dreaming as a hallucinatory process was accepted by Freud (1953) as the consensus of most earlier authors. Naturally, we would ignore these authorities if we did not agree with them, but we also assume that when people say, "I had a dream last night," they mean to convey memories of a complex, perceptual, usually visual, experience which they believe occurred in the midst of sleep. Moreover, they almost always imply that this was not an amorphous fragment of imagery, but a more or less coherently organized facsimile of reality, and that it was not a mere tableau, but a progressively unfolding narrative. Perhaps this definition is as arbitrary as any other, but it happens to conform to a high percentage of the descriptions obtained from REM and to a very low percentage arising out of non-REM awakenings.

Three general approaches have been taken to distinguishing differences between REM and non-REM reports. As already mentioned, in the first a definition of dreaming reasonably similar to the one just presented was at least implicit, and vague or fragmentary impressions were rejected (Aserinsky & N. Kleitman, 1953; Dement, 1955; Dement & N. Kleitman, 1957b; M. Jouvet, Michel, & Mounier, 1960; A. Kales et al., 1967a; Snyder, 1960; Wolpert & Trosman, 1958).

In the second approach, the much more liberal criterion of "any content" was used, accompanied by further subdivision and qualitative assessment of the reports. In their first study the Brooklyn investigators (Goodenough et al., 1959) noted occasions when subjects were unsure whether they had been asleep and dreaming or awake and thinking. In that first analysis, all such reports were considered "mislabeling," not formally distinguished from the rest, and therefore contributed to the high incidence of non-REM dreams. Subsequent studies from the same laboratory (Shapiro, Goodenough, & Gryler, 1963; Goodenough et al., 1965b) separated reports of being awake and thinking from occasions of recalling specific dream content. Since the report of thinking accounted for approximately half of the non-REM content responses, the later results appear much like earlier studies elsewhere.[30] Foulkes

---

[30]One of these studies (Goodenough et al., 1965b) provides a particularly revealing indication of the extent of subject confusion. After 19% of abrupt awakenings coincident with clear EEG evidence of non-REM sleep, the subjective experience was that of having been awake.

(1962) classified his reports as "thoughts" if they did not contain perceptual imagery or if there were no evidence that the subject assumed another identity or felt he was thinking in a setting other than the laboratory. His category of "thought" contributed 20% of the incidence of specific content from non-REM awakenings versus 5% of the REM incidence. Rechtschaffen, Verdone, and Wheaton (1963) reported a much lower rate of specific content from non-REM awakenings (23%), and almost one-third of them could be separated as "thought" responses, a proportion almost five times greater than that found among REM content reports. Therefore, it is not disputed that, when mental content is reported from non-REM awakenings, a very considerable share of it is, by any criteria, *thoughtlike* rather than *dreamlike*.

The same investigators have attempted a number of formal analyses of content (Foulkes, 1962; Goodenough et al., 1965b; Rechtschaffen, Verdone, & Wheaton, 1963). To the extent that the results can be compared, agreement is general that content from non-REM reports differs characteristically from REM content: it is more poorly remembered; it tends to be much less vivid, visual, and emotional; and is more plausible and concerned with contemporary events. As Rechtschaffen, Verdone, and Wheaton (1963a) described it, "NREM mentation resembles that large portion of our waking thoughts which wander in seemingly disorganized, drifting, undirected fashion whenever we are not attending to external stimuli or actively working out a problem or daydream."

The third approach to distinguishing on qualitative grounds between REM and non-REM experience most closely approximates "real life" decisions about the occurrence of dreaming, since it involves simply a global judgment. These judgments are made without knowledge of the corresponding physiological patterns and thus are the least liable to experimenter bias. Two such investigations included the subject's own judgment as to whether he had been dreaming, independent of content recall. Their results were somewhat conflicting: in the first (Kremen, 1961) dreaming was reported in 75% of the REM awakenings and 12% of the non-REM tests, a result highly comparable to the Aserinsky and N. Kleitman percentages; in the second (Rechtschaffen, Verdone, & Wheaton, 1963) dreaming was claimed in 87% of REM awakenings, and in 41% of the non-REM awakenings. In the former study, Kremen was especially concerned about minimizing the subject's assumptions regarding his expectations and reasoned that this was best accomplished by requiring him to state only whether or not he had been dreaming prior to awakening, without any demand for the description of content. This was a comparatively small scale study but may suggest the degree to which the usual requests for descriptions of content influence the subjects to strive to produce "dreams" whenever awakened.

In still another group of studies, the investigators made global judgments on a "blind" basis from transcripts of the awakening reports. Unfortunately, these are also subject to varying preconceptions as to what constitutes a dream. In the first application of this approach (Goodenough et al., 1959) 34% of non-REM transcripts were considered to contain dream recall, but in the second comparison by the same workers (Goodenough et al., 1965b), that incidence fell to 21%, reflecting the subtraction of a category deemed "thought" (and perhaps differences in the subjects as well). A comparable study from our laboratory (Hobson, Goldfrank, & Snyder, 1965) employed an explicit model of dreaming, that of "a complex, visually experienced situation which had undergone some progression or unfolding." The REM period transcripts were blindly identified as dreaming in 76% of the instances, while non-REM reports were similarly designated in 14%.

Although not lending itself to inclusion in Figure 17.13, the most recent evidence that the REM state is associated with qualitatively distinctive recall also involved the ability of investigators to guess whether the reports had come from REM or non-REM awakenings. The decisions were based entirely on the transcripts but this time under a number of prescribed conditions (Monroe, Rechtschaffen, Foulkes, & Jensen, 1965).

In the first phase 227 mixed REM and non-REM reports were assessed by two judges; 73% correct discrimination was obtained from one of them previously unacquainted with such reports, and 87% success by the second, an experienced sleep researcher. The accuracy of the "naïve" judge was matched by a "mechanical" discrimination analysis based entirely on the presence or absence of content and the perceptual versus conceptual nature of the reports. It was assumed that inter- and intra-individual differences in reports (the latter among nights, or at different times of the night) might affect such judgments; in the second phase of analysis the judges were presented with 77 pairs of reports, each pair from the same subject, the same night, and roughly the same time of night. In that comparison the average success of the two judges in making correct discriminations was 89%. Next they were given 46 pairs of reports matched as in the previous phase, but limited to the "specific content" category; this (presumably more difficult) discrimination was achieved in 92% of instances. Finally, the last discriminations, otherwise similar to the preceding two, included only those reports which the subjects themselves had labeled as "dreams"; yet between them the judges correctly identified the corresponding physiological condition in 94%, and the experienced judge did so in 100%. The authors of that report conclude, "These results seem to complete a full circle started with the work of Aserinsky, Kleitman and Dement. It appears that REM periods are, after all, highly diagnostic of a kind of sleep mentation which has all of the characteristics associated with the term dreaming, of the kind of vivid, distorted, elaborated, visual-hallucinatory mentation which has been the major interest of the clinician."

The association between dream reports and the REM periods of sleep would seem to have been examined as thoroughly as any psychophysiological correlation. Although still imperfect, the relation appears as clear as we might hope for, considering the difficulty of the question. Detailed descriptions of complex, hallucinatory dramas emerge convincingly from REM awakenings in a high percentage of instances, although they are lacking from the remainder. From non-REM awakenings, an equally high percentage either produce no content at all, or very vague, thoughtlike, fragmentary reports, quite lacking in conviction as dreams. Nevertheless, in any large study, there have been occasional non-REM responses that sounded quite indistinguishable from typical REM reports, and the ultimate psychophysiological uniqueness of the REM state remains as uncertain as our experimental approach is fallible.

Carryover Effects from Sleep and Critical Reactivity

To whatever extent the evidence reviewed suggests specific relationships between mental experience reported after awakening and prior physiological patterns of sleep, the basic uncertainties remain. Perhaps dreaming is random or continuous during sleep and the REM condition is somehow more conducive to the persistence of its memory into waking; or perhaps there is no psychic life during sleep, but effects of the REM state are somehow carried over into waking to enhance the immediate capacity for confabulation. Before discussing arguments against those alternatives, we shall digress briefly to consider some new reasons for taking them seriously.

That confusion follows abrupt awakening from sleep is a commonplace observation and was the subject of experimentation before the beginning of this century (de Manaceine, 1897, pp. 229–335), as it has been recently (Webb & Agnew, 1964). Current research has begun to correlate such confusion directly with physiological events and to indicate that it may vary systematically according to the prior conditions of sleep. Gastaut and Broughton (1965) remarked that the confusion typically seen in children after abrupt awakenings from sleep is never present after REM awakenings, although it should be noted that their comparison has not included spindling (Stage 2) sleep. Similarly Fiss, Klein, and Bokert (1966) reported that the thought content was markedly impoverished, blocked, and perseverative after non-REM awakenings, as contrasted with REM awakenings. Since they parallel increasing knowledge of the contrasting physiological patterns of sleep and REM, such indications suggest the importance of continuing to evaluate performance capacity after abrupt awakenings from various conditions of sleep. There has been just one published finding in this area, that muscular strength is diminished after REM awakenings (Tebbs & Foulkes, 1966). Results from studies in progress in our own laboratory (Scott & Snyder, 1967) indicate that performance after REM awakenings is more like waking performance than

after any non-REM sleep awakening. The differences are quite marked in relation to delta sleep but they now appear rather minimal and inconstant when compared to spindling sleep.[31]

There are also indications of enhanced memory registration during REMs as compared with the remainder of sleep, although differences in perception cannot be excluded (M. P. Mandell, A. J. Mandell, & A. Jacobson, 1965; Okuma et al., 1966). In addition, the finding of Fiss, Klein, and Bokert (1966) suggests that there may be a greater capacity for confabulation after REM awakenings. Subjects who were asked to create TAT stories immediately after awakenings from interrupted REM periods told stories with qualities more like dream reports; i.e., the imagery was more vivid, there was greater emphasis on the visual modality, and there were more intense affects, more perceptual distortion, and more bizarre, intrusive thoughts. Such factors may well affect the nature of reports elicited after awakenings from the several conditions of sleep, but there are reasons for thinking that they do not suffice to explain them all. Another sort of evidence, that correlating specific physiological events before waking with the psychological events reported afterward, bears upon the same issue.

More Specific Psychophysiological Relationships

One of the first claims to a more specific correlation between the bodily characteristic of REM periods and subsequent dream reports had to do with variations in the extent of REM intervals and judgments of dream duration (Dement & N. Kleitman, 1957b); when subjects were awakened either 5 or 15 min after the onset of REM and asked to decide which had been the duration of their dreams, they guessed correctly in 92 out of 111 instances. By contrast, little or no relationship between the duration of REM periods and the length of dream reports or of subjects' estimates of dream length was found in a recent study, and the estimates of dream duration were markedly lower than the duration of the corresponding REM periods

---

[31]So far, these generalizations apply to certain perceptual measures (two-flash discrimination and flicker fusion thresholds), a cognitive test (solution of simple arithmetic problems), and a motor performance index (rapidity in turning off the arousal bell).

(Hall et al., 1966). Perhaps the earlier procedure of systematically varying REM durations between two extremes and requiring only a dichotomous judgment was a more reasonable expectation, although this kind of correlation probably involves additional complexities. The REM periods are sporadically interrupted by gross body movements; Dement and Wolpert (1958b) observed instances in which quite short reports of dreams sometimes followed soon after such a juncture. Data from a systematic examination of that point suggested that the absence or occurrence of such body movements correlated with the continuous or fragmented nature of the ensuing dream reports.[32] No replications of this relatively simple but important comparison have been published.

The first attempts to correlate the nature of reported dream content with the amount or nature of observed rapid eye movement also came early in the REM era. Dement and Wolpert (1958b) confirmed the less systematic earlier impressions (Dement & N. Kleitman, 1957b) that eye movement correlated with judgments concerning some gross aspect of the dream reports, and that the direction and timing of particular eye movements or eye movement clusters can be compared with much more specific elements of dream narrative. The first relationship has been widely confirmed, even though the dream dimension selected has varied from physical activity (Berger & Oswald, 1962b; Dement & Wolpert, 1958b; Goodenough et al., 1965a; Hobson, Goldfrank, & Snyder, 1965; Verdone, 1965) through emotionality (Hobson, Goldfrank, & Snyder, 1965; Karacan et al., 1966; Verdone, 1965) or bizarreness (Goodenough et al., 1965a; Verdone, 1965) to vividness (Dement & Wolpert, 1958b; Hobson, Goldfrank & Snyder, 1965; Verdone, 1965). Any of these studies which considered multiple dimensions together shows that they covary. Thus there is an overall dimension of dream intensity to which each such aspect contributes, and there is little basis at present for assuming that the intensity of eye movement relates more closely to one than to the other, or to "dream intensity" as a global measure. Although not reexamined in these terms, the

same interpretation might well apply to Wolpert's observation (1960) of a correlation between the amount of motor activity in the reported dream content and the amount of isolated muscle activity from the wrist prior to awakening in some subjects, or equally well to observations that the amount of respiratory irregularity is predictive of the vividness of subsequent dream recall (Shapiro et al., 1964; Snyder, 1960).

To some degree both intensity of physiological measures and dream content appear to vary systematically in the course of the normal night of sleep, and probably as the result of certain prior conditions as well. From the first it was noted that the initial REM period of the night is generally the shortest, the least active in eye movement, and the least likely to yield elaborate or vivid dream reports (Dement & N. Kleitman, 1957b). Evidence is now accumulating of a progressive, increasing trend as the night continues, both in physical measures such as the intensity of REMs (Antrobus, 1962; Goodenough et al., 1965a; Verdone, 1965), the incidence of penile erection (Karacan, 1965), or the variability of the pulse rate or blood pressure level (Snyder et al., 1964), and also in the intensity of reported dream content (Verdone, 1965). Such a nightly change is possibly confounded, however, by another factor apparently affecting both REM intensity and dream intensity, the effect of REM deprivation. There is evidence from animal studies that selective REM deprivation results not only in qualitative increases in the amount of REM time but also in much more intense or active REM periods (Dement, Henry, Cohen, & Ferguson, 1967). In at least one recent study with human subjects the same has been found in terms of rapid eye movements, as well as intensity of dream content (Pivik & Foulkes, 1966).

A dimension of intensity of REM functioning merits examination in relation to a variety of experimental manipulations. From still unpublished studies, Bokert (1965) reported that deprivation of water was followed by heightened density of rapid eye movements within REM periods, while Baekeland, Koulack, and Lasky (1967) have now found the same effect when subjects viewed a stressful motion picture just before sleeping. On the other hand, although Foulkes and Recht-

---

[32]In these terms, a "dream" as a more or less coherent story would not usually be the experience of an entire REM period but rather of one fragment of such a period.

schaffen (1964) reported clearer, more emotional, and more imaginative dreams after exposure to a violent film, they did not find significant differences in the rate of eye movements as a function of the experimental variable.

The intensity relationships described could be interpreted simply as an extension of the general relationship between the REM condition and the recall of dreaming, perhaps indicating merely that cerebral cortical functioning is being activated by the same mechanism and to a comparable degree as are many other parts of the brain. In contrast to these quite general parallels is the possibility of much more specific relationships between the details of dream experience and changes in particular physiological indices. Variations in the several phasic components of REM periods tend to occur together, but not constantly so, and their permutations and combinations present continuously changing patterns. It has been tempting to think of these varying patterns as a physiological code from which inferences might be made about the dream experience as it occurs, but thus far the evidence encouraging such a view has been largely confined to a single relationship, that between the nature of the dream recalled and the direction and timing of eye movements just before awakening. Dement and Wolpert (1958b) were able to predict the direction of the last eye movement from the subject's description of his last dream action in 17 of 23 instances. The same type of comparison was pursued by Roffwarg et al. (1962), who claimed success in their predictions in 75–80% of instances, as long as dream recall was vivid. Figure 17.14 gives some examples of varying movement patterns and the dream activities corresponding to them from this study. The only attempt on the part of different investigators to replicate that finding was reported recently as a failure (Moskowitz & Berger, 1969).

Whether any aspect of dream experience might correlate with the striking vegetative variations during REM is a question of particular psychophysiological interest. Unfortunately, it is fraught with at least as many difficulties as are comparable questions with regard to waking psychophysiology. If such changes reflected affects, their nature would be hard to predict from the present knowledge of waking psychophysiology. The matter is complicated even more by the fact that strong affects are comparatively rare in the dream reports obtained in the laboratory (Snyder, Karakan, Tharp, & Scott, 1967), and because they may reflect such dimensions as physical activity portrayed in the dream experience or simply its overall intensity. With respect to the last possibility, relationships between the vividness of dream recall and the variability of respiration during REM periods have already been cited (Shapiro et al., 1964; Snyder, 1960). A more recent study from our own laboratory (Hobson, Goldfrank, & Snyder, 1965) tested the possibility of correspondence between very brief and striking changes in respiratory patterns and the last events in subjective recall after immediate awakening. Positive relationships were found between rate and, to a lesser extent, variability of immediately previous respiration and the degree to which corresponding mental content was judged to be vivid and emotional and to involve imagery of physical activity. Such relationships were highly apparent in the data of certain subjects but they were minimal in others. The only aspect of that study at all comparable to the specific relationships described in eye movement studies was a correspondence found between episodes of apnea and reports of "respiratory content," by which we meant physical activities particularly involving the respiratory system (e.g., speech, laughter, choking); such reports followed apneic respiratory patterns twice as often as any other respiratory category. Studies of circulatory variations in relation to dream content have not been extensively pursued but neither have they been encouraged by the results of studies in our own laboratory and elsewhere (Kamiya, 1962; Verdone, 1965). One of us has reported a single anecdotal observation of an instance of marked and sustained acceleration of pulse and respiration during a REM period, followed by a report of an overtly erotic dream ending in ejaculation (Snyder, 1965).[33] Only one very recent study has examined physiological correlates of nightmares, either the rare *pavor nocturnus,* arising out of Stage 4 sleep, or the more common anxiety dreams colloquially called nightmares, arising out of REM periods (Fisher, Byrne, Edwards, & Kahn, 1970). That study found a remarkable absence of autonomic activa-

[33]Two other instances of nocturnal emission recorded in sleep laboratories were not related to overtly sexual dream content (Fisher, Gross, & Zuch, 1965; Karacan, 1965).

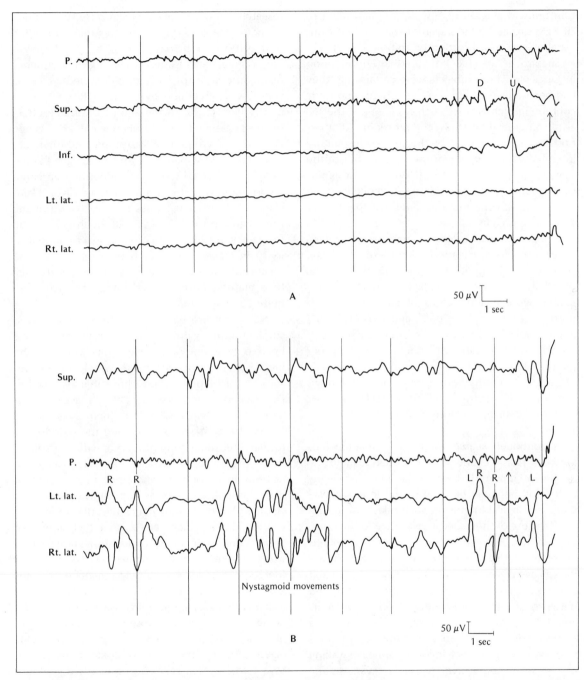

Figure 17.14 REM correlations with dream imagery. These are two examples of ac electrooculographic patterns correlated with details of dream imagery. A: the long period of REM quiescence preceding the brief burst of vertical deflections just prior to the awakening (indicated by the arrow) corresponded to the dream report of the subject's watching a violin recital on a stage, the deflections occurring at the point when the subject watched someone sit down just in front of her. B: the to-and-fro horizontal movements correlated with a report of looking back and forth along the opposite spectator stands at a football game. *E*, parietal EEG; *Sup.*, superior eye movement deviations; *Inf.*, inferior eye movement deviations; *Lt. lat.* and *Rt. lat.*, left and right lateral eye movement deviations. Redrawn from H. P. Roffwarg et al., Dream imagery: Relationship to rapid eye movements of sleep. *Archives of General Psychiatry*, 1962, **7**, 235–258, Figs. 4 and 7. Reproduced with permission.

tion prior to Stage 4 nightmares, while only 8 of 20 REM anxiety dreams were associated with unusual elevation of heart and respiration rates.

Shapiro et al. (1964) focused attention upon instances in which subjects were certain that they had been dreaming but were unable to report any content; in each of three such cases among the 160 awakenings in their study, the preceding REM periods were accompanied by the greatest respiratory irregularity found in any of the REM periods of the same subjects. Karacan et al. (1966) found a significant negative relationship between penile erection during the REM period and ratings of the anxiety content of dreams.

Gottschalk, Stone, Gleser, and Iacono (1966) have presented biochemical evidence of adrenergic stimulation during REM periods. In their study, blood levels of free fatty acids were positively correlated with anxiety scores of subsequently reported dreams. Lester, Burch, and Dossett (1967) implied relationships of a different order, when they found that rates of spontaneous GSR per minute were highest on nights following naturally occurring stress situations. It must be noted, however, that this was true of all sleep stages, and that no specific relation to dream content can be assumed.

A continued search for discrete relationships between phasic elements of REM periods and the details of reported dream experience is clearly called for, not only because of the inherent psychophysiological interest of such relationships but also because of their special relevance to the question of whether the reported mental activity is generated during sleep at the time of these physiological events. At present the assumption that it does rests heavily upon the relationships found between direction and timing of eye movements and subsequent dream reports. In addition, the correspondence between apneic episodes and reports of dream incidence involving apnea in waking life is clearly supportive. Equally relevant to the same issue is another category of studies involving the presentation of stimuli while sleep continues and the identification of the effects of that stimulation in the subsequent dream narratives, thus introducing "time markers" into the dreaming experience. This is a venerable approach in dream research, although the effectiveness of such stimuli in modifying dream content is as much disputed now as it was in the past. Prior to the psychophysiological era, conclusions concerning the frequency of incorporation of such stimuli varied from the very low levels found by Calkins (1893) or Weed and Hallam (1896) to the almost invariable effectiveness claimed by Cubberley (1923). When Dement and Wolpert (1958b) stimulated their subjects during REM periods with tones, light flashes, or sprays of cold water, they identified apparent incorporations of the water spray in 14 of 33 instances, of the light flashes in 7 of 30, and of the tone signal in only 3 of 35. Although the overall frequency of stimulus incorporation was quite low, in 10 instances, when such time markers in the dream narratives could be compared with the actual time elapsed prior to awakening, the two were quite commensurate.

No recent use has been made of incorporated stimuli for timing dream experience, and there have been only a few additional applications of the incorporation procedure, with widely varying results. After taping open the subjects' eyelids, Rechtschaffen and Foulkes (1965) placed illuminated stimulus cards before their eyes during different EEG stages of sleep and then attempted to match ensuing content reports with the stimuli presented. Since there was not a single instance of obvious incorporation, and since they could not match stimuli and reports with much better than chance frequency, they concluded that retinal excitation did not have any clear effect upon the dream content. In an analogous study, however, in which spoken personal names were the stimuli (Berger, 1963), subjects correctly matched dreams and stimulus names in 32 of 78 instances, while independent judges did almost as well, the majority being linked by certain words in the dream narratives having similar sounds to those of the stimulus name. Although the extent of dream modification by external stimuli seems to be highly dependent upon the sensory modality involved and upon the total experimental procedure, it is quite clear that stimuli presented during the course of REM do sometimes modify the dream narratives obtained after awakening.

On such a basis the conviction appears justified

that dreaming actually does unfold during the course of the REM periods. The same conviction is more difficult to achieve with regard to non-REM sleep mentation both because the reports themselves are much less detailed or elaborate and because there are less distinctive and discrete physiological changes involved. Nevertheless, similar relationships between non-REM periods and mental activity might be demonstrated throughout sleep if looked for, and some have already been described. Rechtschaffen, Vogel, and Shaikun (1963) reported instances in which tone stimuli repeated at varying intervals before non-REM awakenings were woven into remembered mental activity in correct temporal sequence. The relation between the vividness of the mental content that was remembered and the degree of respiratory acceleration during sleep immediately before experimental awakenings was even clearer in non-REM awakenings than in REM (Hobson, Goldfrank, & Snyder, 1965; Kamiya & Fong, 1962). Obviously, the second kind of evidence is less crucial than the first, since the variations in respiration just before awakening might be a nonspecific indication of the tendency toward arousal at that particular point of sleep.

Perhaps the most compelling evidence for the reality of intrinsic mentation during any sleep is that provided by the phenomenon of sleep talking, not generally occurring during REM periods, but rather during any other stage of sleep (Arkin, Hastey, & Reiser, 1966; Gastaut & Broughton, 1965; Kamiya, 1961, pp. 145–174; Rechtschaffen, Goodenough, & Shapiro, 1962). While these spontaneous utterances are taking place, the EEG is that of a transient state of waking, yet it is usually immediately preceded by unmistakable sleep patterns. It would be difficult to fathom how these often complex verbalizations could arise without some mental context, but the time relationships are such that this context must originate during prior sleep. In the same vein it has now been reported that sleep walking and nocturnal anxiety attacks do not arise out of REM periods, but rather out of the remainder of sleep (Gastaut & Broughton, 1965; A. Jacobson et al., 1965a).

Thus there are excellent reasons for inferring the existence of intrinsic mental events throughout sleep, but deciding whether such mental activity is intermittent or could be continuous is beyond our present abilities. At least equally well grounded is the working assumption that REM manifestations are distinctive physiological concomitants of a particular mode of mental event in the midst of sleep, that complex hallucinatory experience long known as dreaming. Indeed, if the timing and direction of REMs can be accurately predicted from dream reports, then it is as striking a psychophysiological correlation as has been found in any state of consciousness and strongly argues that the eye movements themselves precisely follow hallucinatory imagery. Somehow, this purely psychophysiological conclusion must be reconciled with equally good evidence that indistinguishable eye movements occur during REM periods under a variety of conditions, in which reports of complex hallucinatory experience can neither be reported nor even imagined: (a) in the congenitally blind (Amadeo & Gomez, 1966; Gross, Byrne, & Fisher, 1965); (b) in newborn animals prior to the opening of the eyelids (D. Jouvet, Valatx, & M. Jouvet, 1961); (c) in anencephalic infants (Pierce, Mathia, & Jabbour, 1965); or (d) in decorticate adults (D. Jouvet, Valatx, & M. Jouvet, 1961). This paradox is the reason why we cannot conclude this discussion, primarily concerned with the description of psychophysiological relationships during sleep, without at least brief consideration of certain questions about their nature. Do the peripheral physiological events of REM periods result from the psychological (cerebral cortical) events of dreaming, or is the converse possible, or could both be the manifestations of some underlying bodily processes quite outside the defined limits of psychophysiology?

REM Sleep as a Biological State

When the regularity, predictability, and universality of REM periods came to be recognized in human sleep, it began to appear highly unlikely that such physiological manifestations simply followed from the mental experience of dreaming (Snyder, 1960, 1963). The characteristics of the REM state all suggest an elemental biological mechanism, rather than an unpredictable psychic process, particularly one as capricious as dreaming has generally been thought to be. As described in other reviews (Roffwarg, Muzio, & Dement, 1966; Snyder, 1966) subsequent demonstration that the phenomenon is common to all mammals has greatly strengthened that impression. Most conclusive of all, over the same period it has been confirmed by remarkable neurophysiological developments.

It would carry us far from psychophysiology to consider the burgeoning neurophysiological literature on this subject; therefore it is fortunate that it has been reviewed authoritatively by M. Jouvet (1967). We believe, however, that the main points relevant to psychophysiology can be summarized as follows:

1. Both the peripheral and the central physiological correlates and mechanisms of REM sleep appear to be as different from those of the remainder of sleep as sleep is from waking; hence we construe the REM state as a "third basic organismic state." (Snyder, 1963; 1965, pp. 275–315; 1966).

2. REM sleep seems to reflect a relatively primitive condition of nervous function, as indicated not only by the crucial involvement of structures in the pontine brain stem but also by the patterning of neuronal activity similar to that found even during waking in the immature cerebral cortex (Huttenlocher, 1967).

3. REM sleep apparently accompanies a general heightening of brain excitability, together with extraordinary intensification of many aspects of spontaneous neuronal activity and marked inhibition of others. More and more it begins to look like the most remarkable phenomenon yet encountered in the normal functioning of the central nervous system.

Patently, dreaming is not the cause of this biological process, nor is there a basis in present evidence for assuming that it is invariably their accompaniment. On the other hand, emphasis upon the biological primacy of REM sleep does not preclude the possibility that something fundamental to dreaming may occur whenever REM sleep occurs (Snyder, 1966). Nor does there need to be any inherent incompatibility between this concept of a primordial biological process and the "higher nervous activities" (such as those involved in complex perception, thought, or memory) obviously operating in human dreaming. We have only to assume that these have been integrated during the evolutionary elaboration of the nervous system,

although the functional details of such integration are beyond any present knowledge.[34]

Challenging as it is that the brain mirrors reality for the waking mind, it is all the more mysterious that it creates its own reality in dreaming. Surely, this has always been and will long remain one of the supreme enigmas of nature, but, while its abiding difficulty should temper present enthusiasm (Snyder, 1967), we cannot but be inspired and encouraged by a quest so well begun.

The Application of Psychophysiological Methods to the Study of Dreaming

Regardless of its ultimate validity, the premise that REM periods of sleep are objective correlates of dreaming is of indisputable heuristic value in stimulating the experimental study of dreaming. If that private aspect of experience is at all worthy of serious consideration, there is everything to be gained by examining it systematically and immediately after the fact, and this is precisely what the REM discovery has brought about. Although adequate discussion of the application of psychophysiological methods in the study of dreaming would too much extend this already lengthy chapter, this subject has been treated somewhat more fully elsewhere (Foulkes, 1966; Witkin & Lewis, 1967). Just a few of the topics thus far approached in this manner have included changes in dream content over the course of the night (Verdone, 1965); the interrelatedness of dream reports on the same night or across nights (Dement & Wolpert, 1958a; Kramer, Whitman, Baldridge, & Lansky, 1964; Offenkrantz & Rechtschaffen, 1963; Rechtschaffen, Vogel, & Shaikun, 1963; Trosman, Rechtschaffen, Offenkrantz, & Wolpert, 1960); differences in dream content among clinical diagnostic groups (Dement, 1955; Kramer, Whitman, Baldridge, & Lansky, 1965); effects of drugs upon the dream content (Whitman,

[34] Recent observations do begin to suggest interactions between higher and lower nervous mechanisms in determining peripheral REMS characteristics. Although the cerebral cortex is not necessary for the occurrence of REM, it is reported that frontal lobe decortication in cats results in increased REM bursts and occipital decortication has the opposite effect (Jeannerod, Mouret, & Jouvet, 1965), or similarly that human patients with bilateral parietal and anterior occipital lesions show an almost complete absence of eye movements during REM periods (Greenberg, 1966). These are very gross effects but they point the way for future study of much more subtle interactions involving the entire brain, and perhaps the entire organism.

1

Kramer, & Baldridge, 1963), hypnotic suggestion (Stoyva, 1965b) or presleep stimulation (Foulkes & Rechtschaffen, 1964; Witkin & Lewis, 1965); and differences between home and laboratory dream reports (Domhoff & Kamiya, 1964; Hall et al., 1966).

Thus far, comparatively little use has been made of the psychophysiological approach as a tool in obtaining dream content for clinical uses (Offenkrantz & Rechtschaffen, 1963; Whitman, Kramer, & Baldridge, 1963), nor has full advantage been taken of it simply for further defining the phenomenology of dreaming consciousness. One aspect of the latter that has been examined is the incidence of color in dream reports (Berger, 1963; Kahn, Dement, & Fisher, 1962; Snyder, 1970, pp. 124–151). From a recent assessment of more than 600 REM dream reports collected in our laboratory, we found reason to conclude that dreaming may be richer than ordinarily imagined as a mode of experience, involving a great deal of verbal and auditory, as well as elaborate visual imagery, together with a more or less continuous background accompaniment of attitudes and reflections related to the hallucinatory imagery (Snyder, 1970, pp. 124–151). This conclusion agrees entirely with the reports of nineteenth-century introspective studies (Calkins, 1893;

Weed & Hallam, 1896), but we also agree with their conclusions concerning the very prosaic and ordinary nature of the majority of dreams. Typical examples of dream reports collected in the laboratory are not very "dreamlike," and naturally this raises the question of whether they are representative of dream experience or whether they might be highly distorted by effects of the experimental situation itself. Since there is no comparable access to dreams outside of an experimental situation, this question is probably unresolvable. Nevertheless, if we do assume that each nocturnal REM period represents at least one dream episode, and probably several, it is apparent that no one spontaneously remembers more than a minute fraction of this total dream life. It would seem to be least a strong possibility that factors determining the recall of this fraction may be highly selective.

Until now the subject of dreaming has remained one of the lost sanctuaries of poetic fancy, almost untouched by the rude hand of Science. Whatever may be gained by the further progress of psychophysiological research on sleep, much is bound to be lost from the realms of cherished illusion, romance, and mystery dreaming has so long imparted to our daily round.

REFERENCES

ACKNER, B., & PAMPIGLIONE, G. Some relationships between peripheral vasomotor and EEG changes. *Journal of Neurology, Neurosurgery, and Psychiatry*, 1957, **20**, 58–64.

ADRIAN, E. D., & YAMAGIWA, K. The origin of the Berger rhythm. *Brain*, 1935, **58**, 323–351.

AGNEW, H. W., Jr., PARKER, J. C., WEBB, W. B., & WILLIAMS, R. L. Amplitude measurement of the sleep electroencephalogram. *Electroencephalography and Clinical Neurophysiology*, 1967, **22**, 84–86.

AGNEW, H. W., Jr., WEBB, W. B., & WILLIAMS, R. L. The effects of stage four sleep deprivation. *Electroencephalography and Clinical Neurophysiology*, 1964, **17**, 68–70.

AGNEW, H. W., Jr., WEBB, W. B., & WILLIAMS, R. L. The first night effect: An EEG study of sleep. *Psychophysiology*, 1966, **2**, 263–266.

AGNEW, H. W., Jr., WEBB, W. B., & WILLIAMS, R. L. Comparison of stage four and 1-REM sleep deprivation. *Perceptual and Motor Skills*, 1967, **24**, 851–858. (a)

AGNEW, H. W. Jr., WEBB, W. B., & WILLIAMS, R. L. Sleep patterns in late middle age males: An EEG study. *Elec-

troencephalography and Clinical Neurophysiology*, 1967, **23**, 168–171. (b)

AMADEO, M., & GOMEZ, E. Eye movements, attention and dreaming in subjects with lifelong blindness. *Canadian Psychiatric Association Journal*, 1966, **11**, 500–507.

ANTROBUS, J. S. Patterns of dreaming and dream recall. Unpublished doctoral dissertation, Columbia University, 1962.

ANTROBUS, J. S., ANTROBUS, J. S., & FISHER, C. Discrimination of dreaming and nondreaming sleep. *Archives of General Psychiatry*, 1965, **12**, 395–401.

ANTROBUS, J. S., DEMENT, W., & FISHER, C. Patterns of dreaming and dream recall: An EEG study. *Journal of Abnormal and Social Psychology*, 1964, **69**, 341–344.

ARISTOTLE. On dreams. In R. M. HUTCHINS (Ed.), *Great books of the western world*. Vol. 8. Chicago: Encyclopaedia Britannica, 1952.

ARKIN, A. M., HASTEY, J. M., & REISER, M. F. Post-hypnotically stimulated sleep-talking. *Journal of Nervous and Mental Disease*, 1966, **142**, 293–309.

ASAHINA, K. Studies on sleep: I. Paradoxical phase and

reverse paradoxical phase in human subjects. *Journal of Physiological Society of Japan*, 1962, **24**, 443–450.

ASERINSKY, E. Periodic respiratory pattern occurring in conjunction with eye movements during sleep. *Science*, 1965, **150**, 763–766.

ASERINSKY, E., & KLEITMAN, N. Regularly occurring periods of eye motility, and concomitant phenomena, during sleep. *Science*, 1953, **118**, 273–274.

ASERINSKY, E., & KLEITMAN, N. A motility cycle in sleeping infants as manifested by ocular and gross bodily activity. *Journal of Applied Physiology*, 1955, **8**, 11–18. (a)

ASERINSKY, E., & KLEITMAN, N. Two types of ocular motility occurring in sleep. *Journal of Applied Physiology*, 1955, **8**, 1–10. (b)

BAEKELAND, F., KOULACK, D., & LASKY, R. Effects of a stressful presleep experience on electroencephalograph-recorded sleep. Paper presented at the meeting of the Association for the Psychophysiological Study of Sleep, Santa Monica, Calif., April 1967.

BAEKELAND, F., & LASKY, R. Exercise and sleep patterns in college athletes. *Perceptual and Motor Skills*, 1966, **23**, 1203–1207.

BALDRIDGE, B. J., WHITMAN, R. M., & KRAMER, M. The concurrence of fine muscle activity and rapid eye movements during sleep. *Psychosomatic Medicine*, 1965, **27**, 19–26.

BANCAUD, J., BLOCH, V., & PAILLARD, J. Contribution E. E. G. à l'étude des potentiels evoqués chez l'homme au niveau du vertex. *Revue Neurologique*, 1953, **89**, 399–418.

BASS, E., & HERR, K. Untersuchungen über die Erregbarkeit des Atemzuntrums im Schlaf-gemessen an der Alveolarspannung der Kohlensaeure. *Zeitschrift für Biologie*, 1922, **75**, 279–288.

BATINI, C., FRESSY, J., & COQUERY, J. M. Critères polygraphiques du sommeil lent et du sommeil rapide: Le sommeil de nuit normal et pathologique. *Études Électrocencéphalographiques: Électroencéphalographie et Neurophysiologie Clinique*, 1965, **2**, 156–183.

BAUST, W., & ROHRWASSER, W. Das Verhalten von pH und Motilität des Magens im natürlichen Schlaf des Menschen. *Pfluegers Archiv; European Journal of Physiology* (Berlin), 1969, **305**, 229–240.

BEH, J. C., & BARRATT, P. E. H. Discrimination and conditioning during sleep as indicated by the electroencephalogram. *Science*, 1965, **147**, 1470–1471.

BENOIT, O., & BLOCH, V. Seuil d'excitabilité retriculaire et sommeil profond chez le chat. *Journal de Physiologie*, Paris, 1960, **52**, 17–18.

BERGER, H. Über das Elektroenkephalogramm des Menschen. *Journal für Psychologie und Neurologie*, Leipzig, 1930, **40**, 160–179.

BERGER, R. J. Tonus of extrinsic laryngeal muscles during sleep and dreaming. *Science*, 1961, **134**, 840.

BERGER, R. J. Experimental modification of dream content by meaningful verbal stimuli. *British Journal of Psychiatry*, 1963, **109**, 722–740.

BERGER, R. J., & OSWALD, I. Effects of sleep deprivation on

behaviour, subsequent sleep, and dreaming. *Journal of Mental Science*, 1962, **108**, 457–465. (a)

BERGER, R. J., & OSWALD, I. Eye movements during active and passive dreams. *Science*, 1962, **137**, 601. (b)

BERLUCCHI, G., MORUZZI, G., SALVI, G., & STRATA, P. Pupil behavior and ocular movements during synchronized and desynchronized sleep. *Archives Italiennes de Biologie* (Pisa), 1964, **102**, 230–244.

BIRCHFIELD, R. I., SIEKER, H. O., & HEYMAN, A. Alterations in respiratory function during natural sleep. *Journal of Laboratory and Clinical Medicine*, 1959, **54**, 216–222.

BLAKE, H., & GERARD, R. W. Brain potentials during sleep. *American Journal of Physiology*, 1937, **119**, 692–703.

BLAKE, H., GERARD, R. W., & KLEITMAN, N. Factors influencing brain potentials during sleep. *Journal of Neurophysiology*, 1939, **2**, 48–60.

BLANKENHORN, M. A. & CAMPBELL, H. E. The effect of sleep on blood pressure. *American Journal of Physiology*, 1925, **74**, 115–120.

BOKERT, E. The effects of thirst and a related auditory stimulus on dream reports. Paper presented at the meeting of the Association for the Psychophysiological Study of Sleep, Washington D.C., March 1965.

BRAZIER, M. A. B., & BEECHER, H. K. Alpha content of the electroencephalogram in relation to movements made in sleep, and effect of a sedative on this type of motility. *Journal of Applied Physiology*, 1952, **4**, 819–825.

BREBBIA, D. R., & ALTSHULER, K. Z. Oxygen consumption rate and electroencephalographic stage of sleep. *Science*, 1965, **150**, 1621–1623.

BROOKS, C. McC., HOFFMAN, B. F., SUCKING, E. E., KLEYNTJENS, F., KOENIG, E. H., COLEMAN, K. S., & TREUMANN, H. J. Sleep and variations in certain functional activities accompanying cyclic change in depth of sleep. *Journal of Applied Physiology*, 1956, **9**, 97–104.

BROOKS, D. C., & BIZZI, E. Brain stem electrical activity during deep sleep. *Archives Italiennes de Biologie* (Pisa), 1963, **101**, 648–665.

BROOKS, H., & CARROLL, J. H. A clinical study of the effects of sleep and rest on blood-pressure. *Archives of Internal Medicine*, 1912, **10**, 97–102.

BROUGHTON, R. J., POIRE, R., & TASSINARI, C. A. The electrodermogram (Tarchanoff effect) during sleep. *Electroencephalography and Clinical Neurophysiology*, 1965, **18**, 691–708.

BRUSH, C. E., Jr., & FAYERWEATHER, R. Observations on the changes in blood-pressure during normal sleep. *American Journal of Physiology*, 1901, **5**, 199–210.

BUENDIA, N., GOODEN, M., SIERRA, G., & SEGUNDO, J. P. Responsiveness and discrimination during sleep. *Experientia*, 1963, **29**, 208–209.

BÜLOW, K. Respiration and wakefulness in man. *Acta Physiologica Scandinavica*, 1963, **59**, 1–110 (Suppl. 209).

BURCH, N. R. Data processing of psychophysiological recordings. In L. D. PROCTOR & W. R. ADEY (Eds.), *Symposium on the analysis of central nervous system and cardiovascular data using computer methods*. Washington, D.C.: NASA, 1965.

BURDACH, K. F.   *Die Physiologie als Erfahryngswissenschaft.* Vol. 3. Leipzig: bei Leopold Bob, 1830.

CALKINS, M. W.   Statistics of dreams. *American Journal of Psychology,* 1893, **5,** 311-343.

CANDIA, O., FAVALE, E., GIUSSANI, A., & ROSSI, G. F.   Blood pressure during natural sleep and during sleep induced by electrical stimulation of the brain stem reticular formation. *Archives Italiennes de Biologie (Pisa),* 1962, **100,** 216-233.

CARTWRIGHT, R. D.   Dream and drug-induced fantasy behavior. *Archives of General Psychiatry,* 1966, **15,** 7-15.

CARTWRIGHT, R. D., MONROE, L. J., & PALMER, C.   Individual differences in response to REM deprivation. *Archives of General Psychiatry,* 1967, **16,** 297-303.

CATHALA, H. P., & GUILLARD, A.   La réactivité au cours du sommeil physiologique de l'homme. *Pathologie et Biologie, Paris,* 1961, **9,** 1357-1375.

CHRISTAKE, A.   Conditioned emotional stimuli and arousal from sleep. *American Psychologist,* 1957, **12,** 405. (Abstract)

COBB, J. C., EVANS, F. J., GUSTAFSON, L. A., O'CONNELL, D. N., ORNE, M. T., & SHOR, R. E.   Specific motor response during sleep to sleep-administered meaningful suggestion: An exploratory investigation. *Perceptual and Motor Skills,* 1965, **20,** 629-636.

COLEMAN, P. D., GRAY, F. E., & WATANABE, K.   EEG amplitude and reaction time during sleep. *Journal of Applied Physiology,* 1959, **14,** 397-400.

COLLIER, C. R., AFFELDT, J. E., & FARR, A. F.   Continuous rapid infrared CO_2 analysis. *Journal of Laboratory and Clinical Medicine,* 1955, **45,** 526-539.

COX, G. H., & MARLEY, E.   The estimation of motility during rest or sleep. *Journal of Neurology, Neurosurgery, and Psychiatry,* 1959, **22,** 57-60.

CUBBERLEY, A. J.   The effects of tensions of the body surface upon the normal dream. *British Journal of Psychology,* 1923, **13,** 243-265.

CZERNY, A.   Physiologische Untersuchungen ueber den Schlaf. *Jahrbuch für Kinderheilkunde und physische Erziehung. Neue Folge.,* 1891, **33,** 1-29.

DARROW, C. W.   The galvanic skin reflex (sweating) and blood pressure as preparatory and facilitative functions. *Psychological Bulletin,* 1936, **33,** 73-94.

DAVIS, H., DAVIS, P. A., LOOMIS, A. L., HARVEY, E. N., & HOBART, G.   Human brain potentials during the onset of sleep. *Journal of Neurophysiology,* 1938, **1,** 24-38.

DAVIS, H., & YOSHIE, N.   Human evoked cortical responses to auditory stimuli. *Physiologist, Washington,* 1963, **6,** 164. (Abstract)

DAVIS, J.   Effects of alteration of the sleep-waking cycle on the EEG sleep pattern. Paper presented at the meeting of the Association for the Psychophysiological Study of Sleep, Washington D.C., March 1965.

DELANGE, M., CASTAN, P., CADILHAC, J., & PASSOUANT, P.   Les divers stades du sommeil chez le nouveau-né et le nourrisson. *Revue Neurologique,* 1962, **107,** 271-276.

DE MANACEINE, M.   *Sleep: Its physiology, pathology, hygiene and psychology.* London: Walter Scott, 1897.

DEMENT, W. C.   Dream recall and eye movements during sleep in schizophrenics and normals. *Journal of Nervous and Mental Disease,* 1955, **122,** 263-269.

DEMENT, W. C.   The occurrence of low voltage, fast electroencephalogram patterns during behavioral sleep in the cat. *Electroencephalography and Clinical Neurophysiology,* 1958, **10,** 291-295.

DEMENT, W. C.   The effect of dream deprivation. *Science,* 1960, **131,** 1705-1707.

DEMENT, W. C.   Experimental dream studies. In J. MASSERMAN (Ed.), *Science and psychoanalysis.* Vol. 7. *Development and research.* New York: Grune & Stratton, 1964. (a)

DEMENT, W. C.   Eye movements during sleep. In M. B. BENDER (Ed.), *The oculomotor system.* New York: Hoeber, 1964. (b)

DEMENT, W. C.   Discussion generale. In M. JOUVET (Ed.), *Aspects anatomo-fonctionnels de la physiologie du sommeil.* Paris: Centre National des Recherches de Science, 1965.

DEMENT, W. C., & GREENBERG, S.   Changes in total amount of stage four sleep as a function of partial sleep deprivation. *Electroencephalography and Clinical Neurophysiology,* 1966, **20,** 523-526.

DEMENT, W. C., GREENBERG, S., & KLEIN, R.   The effect of partial REM sleep deprivation and delayed recovery. *Journal of Psychiatric Research,* 1966, **4,** 141-152.

DEMENT, W. C., HENRY, P., COHEN, H., & FERGUSON, J.   Studies on the effect of REM deprivation in humans and in animals. *Research Publications of the Association for Research in Nervous and Mental Disease,* 1967, **45,** 456-468.

DEMENT, W. C., & KLEITMAN, N.   Cyclic variations in EEG during sleep and their relation to eye movements, body motility, and dreaming. *Electroencephalography and Clinical Neurophysiology,* 1957, **9,** 673-690. (a)

DEMENT, W. C., & KLEITMAN, N.   The relation of eye movements during sleep to dream activity: An objective method for the study of dreaming. *Journal of Experimental Psychology,* 1957, **53,** 339-346. (b)

DEMENT, W. C., & WOLPERT, E. A.   Relationships in the manifest content of dreams occurring on the same night. *Journal of Nervous and Mental Disease,* 1958, **126,** 568-577. (a)

DEMENT, W. C., & WOLPERT, E. A.   The relation of eye movements, body motility and external stimuli to dream content. *Journal of Experimental Psychology,* 1958, **55,** 543-553. (b)

DENISOVA, M. P., & FIGURIN, N. L.   Periodic phenomena in the sleep of children. (Russian.) *Psychiatric Abstracts,* 1928, **2,** 117-118.

DERBYSHIRE, A. J., & McDERMOTT, M.   Further contributions to the EEG method of evaluating auditory function. *Laryngoscope (St. Louis),* 1958, **68,** 558-570.

DE SANCTIS, D., & NEYROZ, U.   Experimental investigations concerning the depth of sleep. *Psychological Review,* 1902, **9,** 254-282.

DE TONI, G. I movimenti pendolari dei bulbi oculari dei bambini, durante il sonno fisiologico, ed in alcuni stati marbosi. *Pediatria (Napoli)*, 1933, **41,** 489–498.

DEUTSCH, J. A., & DEUTSCH, D. Attention: Some theoretical considerations. *Psychological Review*, 1963, **70,** 80–90.

DOMHOFF, B., & KAMIYA, J. Problems in dream content study with objective indicators: I. A comparison of home and laboratory dream reports. *Archives of General Psychiatry*, 1964, **11,** 519–524.

DOUST, J. W. L., & SCHNEIDER, R. A. Studies on the physiology of awareness: Anoxia and the levels of sleep. *British Medical Journal*, 1952, **1,** 449–455.

DREYFUS-BRISAC, C., SAMSON, D., BLANC, C., & MONOD, N. L'électroencéphalogramme de l'enfant normal de moins de 3 ans: Aspect fonctionel bioélectrique de la maturation nerveuse. *Études Néo-Natales*, 1958, **7,** 143–175.

DUFFY, E. *Activation and behavior.* New York: Wiley, 1962.

ENDRES, G., & VON FREY, W. Über Schlaftiefe und Schlafmenge. *Zeitschrift für Biologie*, 1930, **90,** 70–80.

FARMER, E., & CHAMBERS, E. G. Concerning the use of the psychogalvanic reflex in psychological experiments. *British Journal of Psychology*, 1925, **15,** 237–254.

FAURE, J. Le sommeil "paradoxal" du lapin dans ses aspects anatomo-functionnels et hormonaux. In M. JOUVET (Ed.), *Aspects anatomo-fonctionnels de la physiologie du sommeil.* Paris: Centre National des Recherches de Science, 1965.

FAURE, J., VINCENT, D., LE NOUENE, J., & GEISSMANN, P. Sommeil lent et stade paradoxal chez le lapin des deux sexes: Rôle du milieu. *Comptes Rendus des Séances de la Société de Biologie*, 1963, **157:** 799–807.

FECHNER, G. T. *Elemente der Psychophysik: 1. Dritte umveranderte Alflage.* Vol. 2. Leipzig: Breithopf und Hortel, 1860.

FEINBERG, I., KORESKO, R., & HELLER, N. EEG sleep patterns as a function of normal and pathological aging in man. *Journal of Psychiatric Research*, 1967, **5,** 107–144.

FERGUSON, J., & DEMENT, W. C. The effect of variations in total sleep time on the occurrence of rapid eye movement sleep in cats. *Electroencephalography and Clinical Neurophysiology*, 1967, **22,** 2–10.

FISCHGOLD, H., & SCHWARTZ, B. A. A clinical electroencephalographic and polygraphic study of sleep in the human adult. In G. E. W. WOLSTENHOLM & M. O'CONNOR (Eds.), *Ciba Foundation symposium on the nature of sleep.* Boston: Little, Brown, 1961.

FISHER, C., BYRNE, J., EDWARDS, A., & KAHN, E. A psychophysiological study of nightmares. *Journal of the American Psychoanalytic Association*, 1970, **18:** 747–782.

FISHER, C., GROSS, J., & ZUCH, J. A cycle of penile erection synchronous with dreaming (REM) sleep. *Archives of General Psychiatry*, 1965, **12,** 29–45.

FISS, H., KLEIN, G. S., & BOKERT, E. Waking fantasies following interruptions of two types of sleep. *Archives of General Psychiatry*, 1966, **14,** 543–551.

FONTANA, F. *Dei moti dell' iride.* Lucca, Italy: Stamperia Jacopo Giusti, 1765.

FOULKES, D. Dream reports from different states of sleep. *Journal of Abnormal and Social Psychology*, 1962, **65,** 14–25.

FOULKES, D. *The psychology of sleep.* New York: Scribner, 1966.

FOULKES, D., PIVIK, T., STEADMAN, H. S., SPEAR, P. S., & SYMONDS, J. D. Dreams of the male child: An EEG study. *Journal of Abnormal Psychology*, 1967, **72,** 457–467.

FOULKES, D., & RECHTSCHAFFEN, A. Presleep determinants of dream content: The effect of two films. *Perceptual and Motor Skills*, 1964, **19,** 983–1005.

FOULKES, D., & VOGEL, G. Mental activity at sleep onset. *Journal of Abnormal Psychology*, 1965, **70,** 231–243.

FREUD, S. The interpretation of dreams. Translated by J. Strachey. *Standard edition of complete psychological works of Sigmund Freud.* Vol. 4. London: Hogarth, 1953.

GASTAUT, H., & BROUGHTON, R. A clinical and polygraphic study of episodic phenomena during sleep. *Recent Advances in Biological Psychiatry*, 1965, **7,** 197–221.

GIAQUINTO, S., POMPEIANO, O., & SOMOGYI, I. Descending inhibitory influences on spinal reflexes during natural sleep. *Archives Italiennes de Biologie (Pisa)*, 1964, **102,** 282–307.

GIBBS, F. A., & GIBBS, E. L. *Atlas of electroencephalography.* (2nd ed.) Reading, Mass.: Addison-Wesley, 1950. (a)

GIBBS, E. L., & GIBBS, F. A. Electroencephalographic changes with age during sleep. *Electroencephalography and Clinical Neurophysiology*, 1950, **2,** 355. (Abstract) (b)

GOODENOUGH, D. R., LEWIS, H. B., SHAPIRO, A., & SLESER, I. Some correlates of dream reporting following laboratory awakenings. *Journal of Nervous and Mental Disease*, 1965, **140,** 365–373. (a)

GOODENOUGH, D. R., LEWIS, H. B., SHAPIRO, A., JARET, L., & SLESER, I. Dream reporting following abrupt and gradual awakenings from different types of sleep. *Journal of Personality and Social Psychology*, 1965, **2,** 170–179. (b)

GOODENOUGH, D. R., SHAPIRO, A., HOLDEN, M., & STEINSCHRIBER, L. A comparison of "dreamers" and "nondreamers": Eye movements, electroencephalograms and the recall of dreams. *Journal of Abnormal and Social Psychology*, 1959, **62,** 295–302.

GOTTSCHALK, L. A., STONE, W. N., GLESER, G. C., & IACONO, J. M. Anxiety levels in dreams: Relation to changes in plasma free fatty acids. *Science*, 1966, **153,** 654–657.

GRANDA, A. M., & HAMMACK, J. T. Operant behavior during sleep. *Science*, 1961, **133,** 1485–1486.

GREENBERG, R. Cerebral cortex lesions: The dream process and sleep spindles. *Cortex*, 1966, **2,** 357–366.

GRIESINGER, X. X. Physio-psychologische Selbstbeobachtugen. *Archiv für Psychiatrie und Nervenkrankheiten*, 1868, **1,** 200–204.

GROLLMAN, A. Physiological variations in the cardiac output of man. *American Journal of Physiology*, 1930, **95,** 274–284.

GROSS, J., BYRNE, J., & FISHER, C.   Eye movements during emergent stage I EEG in subjects with lifelong blindness. *Journal of Nervous and Mental Disease,* 1965, **141,** 365-370.

GROSS, J., WEITZMAN, E. D., FISHER, C., & BYRNE, J.   Penile erection in the monkey during REM sleep periods. Presented at the meeting of the Association for the Psychophysiological Study of Sleep, Gainesville, Fla., March 1966. (a)

GROSS, M., GOODENOUGH, D., TOBIN, M., HALPERT, E., LEPORE, D., PERLSTEIN, A., SIROTA, M., DIBIANCO, J., FULLER, R., & KRISHMER, I.   Sleep disturbances and hallucination in the acute alcoholic psychoses. *Journal of Nervous and Mental Disease,* 1966, **142,** 493-514. (b)

GULEVITCH, G., DEMENT, W. C., & JOHNSON, L.   Psychiatric and EEG observations on a case of prolonged (264 hours) wakefulness. *Archives of General Psychiatry,* 1966, **15,** 29-35.

GULEVITCH, G., DEMENT, W. C., & ZARCONE, V.   All-night sleep recording of chronic schizophrenics in remission. *Comprehensive Psychiatry,* 1962, **8,** 141-149.

HALL, C. S., VAN DE CASTLE, R. L., HESS, R., DERTKE, M., DAVERSO, G., DUPONT, G., Jr., NORDBY, V. J., & SCOTT, J.   Studies of dreams reported in the laboratory and at home. *Institute for Dream Research Monograph Series,* 1966, No. 1.

HARA, T., FAVALE, E., ROSSI, G. F., & SACCO, G.   Ricerche sull' attivita elettrica cerebrale durante il sonno nel gatto. *Rivista di Neurologia* (*Napoli*) 1960, **30,** 448-460.

HARTMANN, E.   Dreaming sleep (the D-state) and the menstrual cycle. *Journal of Nervous and Mental Disease,* 1966, **143,** 406-416. (a)

HARTMANN, E.   Reserpine: Its effect on the sleep-dream cycle in man. *Psychopharmacologia,* 1966, **9,** 242-247. (b)

HARTMANN, E.   *The biology of dreaming.* Springfield, Ill.: Charles C Thomas, 1967.

HARTMANN, E., VERDONE, P., & SNYDER, F.   Longitudinal studies of sleep and dreaming patterns in psychiatric patients. *Journal of Nervous and Mental Disease,* 1966, **142,** 117-126.

HASS., A.   Über Schlaftiefenmessungen. *Psychologische Arbeiten,* 1923, **8,** 228-264.

HAURI, P.   Effects of evening activities on subsequent sleep and dreams. Unpublished doctoral dissertation, University of Chicago, 1966.

HAWKINS, D., PURYEAR, H., WALLACE, C., DEAL, W., & THOMAS, E.   Basal skin resistance during sleep and dreaming. *Science,* 1962, **136,** 321-322.

HENRY, C. E.   Electroencephalographic individual differences and their constancy: I. During sleep. *Journal of Experimental Psychology,* 1941, **29,** 117-132.

HEUSER, G., KALES, A., JACOBSON, A., PAULSON. M. J., ZWEIZIG, J. R., WALTER, R. D., & KALES, J. D.   Sleep patterns in hypothyroid patients. *Physiologist* (*Washington*), 1966, **9,** 203. (Abstract)

HILL, L.   Arterial pressure in man while sleeping, resting, waking, bathing. *Journal of Physiology* (*London*), 1898, **22,** 26-29.

HOBSON, J. A., GOLDFRANK, F., & SNYDER, F.   Respiration and mental activity in sleep. *Journal of Psychiatric Research,* 1965, **3,** 79-90.

HODES, R.   Ocular phenomenon in the two stages of sleep in the cat. *Experimental Neurology,* 1964, **9,** 36-42.

HODES, R., & DEMENT, W. C.   Depression of electrically induced reflexes ("H-reflexes") in man during low voltage EEG "sleep." *Electroencephalography and Clinical Neurophysiology,* 1964, **17,** 617-629.

HORD, D. J., JOHNSON, L. C., LUBIN, A., & AUSTIN, M. T.   Resolution and stability in the autospectra of EEG. *Electroencephalography and Clinical Neurophysiology,* 1965, **19,** 305-308.

HORD, D. J., LUBIN, A. & JOHNSON, L. C.   The evoked heart rate response during sleep. *Psychophysiology,* 1966, **3,** 36-54.

HOWELL, W. H.   A contribution to the physiology of sleep, based upon plethysmographic experiments. *Journal of Experimental Medicine,* 1897, **2,** 313-345.

HUTTENLOCHER, P. R.   Development of cortical neuronal activity in the neonatal cat. *Experimental Neurology,* 1967, **17,** 247-262.

JACKSON, M. M.   Anticipatory cardiac acceleration during sleep. *Science,* 1942, **96,** 564-565.

JACOBSON, A. KALES, A., LEHMANN, D., & HOEDEMAKER, F. S.   Muscle tonus in human subjects during sleep and dreaming. *Experimental Neurology,* 1964, **10,** 418-424.

JACOBSON, A., KALES, A., LEHMANN, D., & ZWEIZIG, J. R.   Somnambulism: All-night electroencephalographic studies. *Science,* 1965, **148,** 975-977. (a)

JACOBSON, A., KALES, A., ZWEIZIG, J. R., & KALES, J.   Special EEG and EMG techniques for sleep research. *American Journal of EEG Technology,* 1965, **5,** 5-10. (b)

JACOBSON, E.   *You can sleep well: The ABC's of restful sleep for the average person.* New York: Whittlesey, 1938.

JEANNEROD, M., MOURET, J., & JOUVET, M.   Étude de la motricité oculaire au cours de la phase paradoxale du sommeil chez le chat. *Electroencephalography and Clinical Neurophysiology,* 1965, **18,** 554-566.

JOHNSON, H. M. & SWAN, T. H.   Sleep. *Psychological Bulletin,* 1930, **27,** 1-39.

JOHNSON, L. C.   Spontaneous and orienting responses during sleep. *U.S. Navy Medical Neuropsychiatric Research Unit,* Rep. No. 66-9, 1966.

JOHNSON, L. C., & LUBIN, A.   The orienting reflex during waking and sleeping. *Electroencephalography and Clinical Neurophysiology,* 1967, **22,** 11-21.

JOUVET, D., VALATX, J. L., & JOUVET, M.   Etude polygraphique du sommeil du chaton. *Comptes Rendus des Séances de la Société de Biologie,* 1961, **155,** 1660-1664.

JOUVET, D., VIMONT, P., DELORME, F., & JOUVET, M.   Étude de la privation selective de la phase paradoxale de sommeil chez le chat. *Comptes Rendus des Séances de la Société de Biologie,* 1964, **158,** 756-759.

JOUVET, M.   Telencephalic and rhombencephalic sleep in the cat. In G. E. W. WOLSTENHOLME & M. O'CONNOR (Eds.), *Ciba Foundation symposium on the nature of sleep.* Boston: Little, Brown, 1961.

JOUVET, M.   Recherches sur les structures nerveuses et les mechanismes responsables des differentes phases du sommeil physiologique. *Archives Italiennes de Biologie (Pisa)*, 1962, **100,** 125-206.

JOUVET, M.   Neurophysiology of the states of sleep. *Physiological Review*, 1967, **47,** 117-177.

JOUVET, M., & JOUVET, D.   A study of the neurophysiological mechanisms of dreaming. *Electroencephalography and Clinical Neurophysiology* (Suppl.), 1963, **24,** 133-157.

JOUVET, M., MICHEL, F., & COURJON, J.   Sur un stade d'activité électrique cérébrale rapide au cours du sommeil physiologique. *Comptes Rendus des Séances de la Société de Biologie*, 1959, **153,** 1024-1028.

JOUVET, M., MICHEL, F., & MOUNIER, D.   Analyse électro-encéphalographique comparée du sommeil physiologique chez le chat et chez l'homme. *Revue Neurologique (Paris)*, 1960, **103,** 189-204.

JUNG, R.   Correlation of bioelectrical and autonomic phenomena with alterations of consciousness and arousal in man. In *Brain mechanisms and consciousness: A symposium.* Oxford: Blackwell, 1954.

KAHN, E., DEMENT, W. C., & FISHER, C.   Incidence of color in immediately recalled dreams. *Science*, 1962, **137,** 1054-1055.

KAHN, E., & FISHER, C.   Sleep characteristics and REM period erections of healthy elderly male subjects. Presented at the meeting of the Association for the Psychophysiological Study of Sleep, Gainesville, Fla., March 1966.

KALES, A., HOEDEMAKER, F. S., JACOBSON, A., & LICHTENSTEIN, E. L.   Dream deprivation: An experimental reappraisal. *Nature*, 1964, **204,** 1337-1338.

KALES, A., HOEDEMAKER, F. S., JACOBSON, A., KALES, J. D., PAULSON, M. J., & WILSON, T. E.   Mentation during sleep: REM and NREM recall reports. *Perceptual and Motor Skills*, 1967, **24,** 555-560. (a)

KALES, A., JACOBSON, A., KALES, J. D., JUN, T., & WEISSBUCH, R.   All-night EEG sleep measurements in young adults. *Psychonomic Science*, 1967, **7,** 67-68. (b)

KALES, J. D., KALES, A., JACOBSON, A., PO, J., & GREEN, J.   Baseline sleep and recall studies in children. Presented at the meeting of the Association for the Psychophysiological Study of Sleep, Palo Alto, Calif., April 1967. (c)

KALES, A., WILSON, T., KALES, J. D., JACOBSON, A., PAULSON, M. J., KOLLAR, E., & WALTER, R. D.   Measurements of all-night sleep in normal elderly persons: Effects of aging. *Journal of the American Geriatric Society*, 1967, **15,** 405-414. (d)

KAMIYA, J.   Behavioral, subjective and physiological aspects of sleep and drowsiness. In D. W. FISKE & S. R. MADDI (Eds.), *Functions of varied experience.* Homewood, Ill.: Dorsey, 1961.

KAMIYA, J.   Behavioral and physiological concomitants of dreaming. Unpublished progress report, February, 1962.

KAMIYA, J., & FONG, S.   Dream reporting from non-REM sleep as related to respiration rate. Paper presented at the meeting of the Association for the Psychophysiological Study of Sleep, Chicago, March 1962.

KANZOW, E., KRAUSE, D., & KUHNEL, H.   Die Vasomotorik der Hirnrinde in den Phasen desynchronisierter EEG-Aktivitat im naturlichen Schlaf der Katze. *Pflüegers Archiv für die gesamte Physiologie des Menschen und der Tiere (Berlin)*, 1962, **274,** 593-607.

KARACAN, I.   The effect of exciting pre-sleep events on dream reporting and penile erections during sleep. Unpublished doctoral dissertation, Downstate Medical Center, State University of New York, 1965.

KARACAN, I., GOODENOUGH, D. R., SHAPIRO, A., & STARKER, S.   Erection cycle during sleep in relation to dream anxiety. *Archives of General Psychiatry*, 1966, **15,** 183-189.

KARACAN, I., & SNYDER, F.   Erection cycle during sleep in *Macaca mulatta*. Preliminary report presented at the meeting of the Association for the Psychophysiological Study of Sleep, Gainesville, Fla., March 1966.

KAWAKAMI, M., NEGORO, H., & TERASAWA, E.   Influence of immobilization stress upon the paradoxical sleep (EEG afterreaction) in the rabbit. *Japanese Journal of Physiology*, 1965, **15,** 1-16.

KEITH, C. R.   Some aspects of transference in dream research. *Bulletin of the Menninger Clinic*, 1962, **26,** 248-257.

KHATRI, I. M., & FREIS, E. D.   Hemodynamic changes during sleep. *Journal of Applied Physiology*, 1967, **2,** 867-873.

KHAZAN, N., & SAWYER, C. H.   "Rebound" recovery from deprivation of paradoxical sleep in the rabbit. *Proceedings of the Society for Experimental Biology and Medicine*, 1963, **144,** 536-539.

KHAZAN, N., & SAWYER, C. H.   Mechanisms of paradoxical sleep as revealed by neurophysiologic and pharmacologic approaches in the rabbit. *Psychopharmacologia*, 1964, **5,** 457-466.

KLEITMAN, N.   *Sleep and wakefulness.* (Rev. ed.) Chicago: University of Chicago Press, 1963.

KLEITMAN, N., COOPERMAN, N. R., & MULLIN, F. J.   Studies on the physiology of sleep: IX. Motility and body temperature during sleep. *American Journal of Physiology*, 1933, **105,** 574-584.

KLEITMAN, N., & KLEITMAN, H.   The sleep-wakefulness pattern in the Arctic. *Scientific Monthly*, 1953, **76,** 349-356.

KLEITMAN, N., & RAMSAROOP, A.   Periodicity in body temperature and heart rate. *Endocrinology*, 1948, **43,** 1-20.

KLEITMAN, N., RAMSAROOP, A., & ENGELMANN, T.   Variations in skin temperature of the feet and hands on the onset of sleep. *Federation Proceedings*, 1948, **7,** 66. (Abstract)

KNOTT, J. R., HENRY, C. E., & HADLEY, J. M.   Brain potentials during sleep: A comparative study of the dominant and nondominant alpha groups. *Journal of Experimental Psychology*, 1939, **24,** 157-168.

KOGA, E. A new method of EEG analysis and its application to the study of sleep. *Folia Psychiatrica et Neurologica Japonica,* 1965, **19,** 269–278.

KOHLSCHÜTTER, E. Messungen der Festigkeit des Schlafes. *Zeitschrift für rationelle Medizin,* 1862, **17,** 209–253.

KRAMER, M., WHITMAN, R. M., BALDRIDGE, B., & LANSKY, L. M. Patterns of dreaming: The interrelationship of the dreams of a night. *Journal of Nervous and Mental Disease,* 1964, **139,** 426–439.

KRAMER, M., WHITMAN, R. M., BALDRIDGE, B., & LANSKY, L. M. Depression: Dreams and defences. *American Journal of Psychiatry,* 1965, **122,** 411–419.

KRAMER, M., WHITMAN, R. M., BALDRIDGE, B. J., & ORNSTEIN, P. H. The pharmacology of dreaming. In G. J. MARTIN & B. KISCH (Eds.), *Enzymes in mental health.* Philadelphia: Lippincott, 1966.

KREIDER, M. B., BUSKIRK, E. R., & BASS, D. E. Oxygen consumption and body temperatures during the night. *Journal of Applied Physiology,* 1958, **12,** 361–366.

KREMEN, I. Dream reports and rapid eye movements. Unpublished doctoral dissertation, Harvard University, 1961.

KRIS, C. Vision: Electro-oculography. In O. GLASSER (Ed.), *Medical physics.* Vol. 3. Chicago: Year Book Medical Publishers, 1960.

LACHMANN, F. M., LAPKIN, B., & HANDELMAN, N. S. The recall of dreams: Its relation to repression and cognitive control. *Journal of Abnormal and Social Psychology,* 1962, **64,** 160–162.

LADD, G. T. Contribution to the psychology of visual dreams. *Mind,* 1892, **1,** 299–304.

LAIRY, G. C., COR-MORDRET, M., FAURE, R., & RIDJANOVIC, S. Étude EEG du sommeil du vieillard normal et pathologique. *Revue Neurologique* (Paris), 1962, **107,** 188–202.

LAMBRANZI, R. Sulla profondita del sonno. *Rivista sperimentale di Freniatria e di Medicina legale in Relazinoe con l'Antropologia e le Scienze Giuridiche e Sociali,* 1900, **26,** 828–830.

LANDIS, C. Electrical phenomena of the body during sleep. *American Journal of Physiology,* 1927, **81,** 6–19.

LEIDERMAN, P. H., & SHAPIRO, D. Studies on the galvanic skin potential level: Some behavioral correlates. *Journal of Psychosomatic Research,* 1964, **7,** 277–281.

LESTER, B. K., BURCH, N. R., & DOSSETT, R. C. Nocturnal EEG-GSR profiles: The influence of presleep states. *Psychophysiology,* 1967, **3,** 238–248.

LESTER, B. K., & EDWARDS, R. J. EEG fast activity in schizophrenic and control subjects. *International Journal of Neuropsychiatry,* 1966, **2,** 143–156.

LESTER, D. Continuous measurement of the depth of sleep. *Science,* 1958, **127,** 1340–1341.

LEVY, E. Z., JOHNSON, G. E., SERRANO, J., Jr., THALER, V. H., & RUFF, G. E. The use of skin resistance to monitor states of consciousness. *Aerospace Medicine,* 1961, **32,** 60–66.

LIBERSON, W. T., & LIBERSON, C. W. EEG records, reaction times, eye movements, respiration, and mental content during drowsiness. *Proceedings of the Society for Biological Psychiatry,* 19, **8,** 295–302.

LIENERT, G. A., & OTHMER, E. Objective correlates of the refreshing effects of sleep. *Progress in Brain Research,* 1965, **18,** 170–177.

LOOMIS, A. L., HARVEY, E. N., & HOBART, G. Further observations on the potential rhythms of the cerebral cortex during sleep. *Science,* 1935, **82,** 198–200. (a)

LOOMIS, A. L., HARVEY, E. N., & HOBART, G. Potential rhythms of the cerebral cortex during sleep. *Science,* 1935, **81,** 597–598. (b)

LOOMIS, A. L., HARVEY, E. N., & HOBART, G. Electrical potentials of the human brain. *Journal of Experimental Psychology,* 1936, **19,** 249–279.

LOOMIS, A. L., HARVEY, E. N., & HOBART, G. Cerebral states during sleep as studied by human brain potentials. *Journal of Experimental Psychology,* 1937, **21,** 127–144.

LOOMIS, A. L., HARVEY, E. N., & HOBART, G. Distribution of disturbance patterns in the human electroencephalogram, with special reference to sleep. *Journal of Neurophysiology,* 1938, **1,** 413–430.

LUCKHARDT, A. B. Contributions to the physiology of the empty stomach: XXXII. The effect of dreaming on the gastric hunger contractions. *American Journal of Physiology,* 1915, **39,** 330–333.

LYKKEN, D. R. Properties of electrodes used in electrodermal measurement. *Journal of Comparative and Physiological Psychology,* 1959, **52,** 629–634.

MACWILLIAM, J. A. Blood pressure and heart action in sleep and dreams. *British Medical Journal,* 1923, **2,** 1196–1200.

MAGNUSSEN, G. Vasomotorische Veränderungen in den Extremitäten im Verhältnis zu Schlaf und Schlafbereitschaft. *Acta Psychiatrica et Neurologica,* 1939, **14,** 39–54.

MAGNUSSEN, G. *Studies of the respiration during sleep.* London: Lewis, 1944.

MALCOLM, N. *Dreaming.* London: Routledge, 1959.

MALMO, R. B. Activation: A neuropsychological dimension. *Psychological Research,* 1959, **66,** 367–386.

MALVEN, P. V., & SAWYER, C. H. Sleeping patterns in female guinea pigs: Effects of sex hormones. *Experimental Neurology,* 1966, **15,** 229–239.

MANDELL, A. J., CHAFFEY, B., BRILL, P., MANDELL, M. P., RODNICK, J., RUBIN, R. T., & SHEFF, R. Dreaming sleep in man: Changes in urine volume and osmolality. *Science,* 1966, **151,** 1538–1560.

MANDELL, A. J., & MANDELL, M. P. Biochemical aspects of rapid eye movement of sleep. *American Journal of Psychiatry,* 1965, **122,** 391–401.

MANDELL, M. P., MANDELL, A. J., & JACOBSON, A. Biochemical and neurophysiological studies of paradoxical sleep. *Recent Advances in Biological Psychiatry,* 1965, **7,** 115–122.

MANGOLD, R., SOKOLOFF, L., CONNER, E., KLEINERMAN, J., THERMAN, P. G., & KETY, S. S. The effects of sleep on the cerebral circulation and metabolism of normal young men. *Journal of Clinical Investigation,* 1955, **34,** 1092–1100.

MARON, L., RECHTSCHAFFEN, A., & WOLPERT, E. A. Sleep cycle during napping. *Archives of General Psychiatry,* 1964, **11,** 503–508.

MAX, L. W. An experimental study of the motor theory of consciousness: III. Action current responses in deaf-mutes during sleep, sensory stimulation and dreams. *Journal of Comparative Psychology,* 1935, **19,** 469–486.

McDONALD, E. G., JOHNSON, L. C., & HORD, D. J. Habituation of the orienting response in alert and drowsy subjects. *Psychophysiology,* 1963, **1,** 163–173.

McGLADE, H. E. The relationship between gastric motility, muscular twitching during sleep and dreaming. *American Journal of Digestive Diseases,* 1942, **9,** 137–140.

MELLETTE, H. C., HUTT, B. K., ASKOVITZ, S. U., & HORVATH, S. M. Diurnal variation in body temperatures. *Journal of Applied Physiology,* 1951, **3,** 665–675.

MICHELSON, F. Untersuchungen ueber die Tiefe des Schlafes, Darpat. *Schnakenburg's Buchdruckevei,* 1891. (Dissertation.)

MILES, W. R. Eye movements during profound sleepiness. *Proceedings of the 9th International Congress on Psychology,* Princeton: Psychological Review Company, 1929.

MILLS, J. N. Changes in alveolar carbon dioxide tension by night and during sleep. *Journal of Physiology (London),* 1953, **122,** 66–80.

MILLS, J. N. Human circadian rhythms. *Physiological Review,* 1966, **46,** 128–171.

MIRSKY, A. F., & CARDON, P. V., Jr. A comparison of the behavioral and physiological changes accompanying sleep deprivation and chlorpromazine administration in man. *Electroencephalography and Clinical Neurophysiology,* 1962, **14,** 1–10.

MONNINGHOFF, O., & PIESBERGEN, F. Mussungen über die Tiefe des Schlafes. *Zeitschrift für Biologie,* 1883, **19,** 114–128.

MONROE, L. J. Psychological and physiological differences between good and poor sleepers. *Journal of Abnormal Psychology,* 1967, **72,** 255–264.

MONROE, L. J., RECHTSCHAFFEN, A., FOULKES, D., & JENSEN, J. Discriminability of REM and NREM reports. *Journal of Personality and Social Psychology,* 1965, **2,** 246–460.

MOSKOWITZ, E., & BERGER, R. J. Rapid eye movements and dream imagery: Are they related? *Nature,* 1969, **224,** 613–614.

MULLIN, F. J., KLEITMAN, N., & COOPERMAN, N. R. Changes in irritability to auditory stimuli during sleep. *Journal of Experimental Psychology,* 1937, **21,** 88–98.

MUZIO, J. N., ROFFWARG, H. P., & KAUFMAN, E. Alterations in the nocturnal sleep cycle resulting from LSD. *Electroencephalography and Clinical Neurophysiology,* 1966, **21,** 313–324.

OFFENKRANTZ, W., & RECHTSCHAFFEN, A. Clinical studies of sequential dreams: I. A patient in psychotherapy. *Archives of General Psychiatry,* 1963, **8,** 497–508.

OHLMEYER, P., BRILMAYER, H., & HUELLSTRUNG, H. Periodische Vorgaenge im Schlaf. *Pflügers Archiv für die gesamte Physiologie,* 1944, **248,** 559–560.

OKUMA, T., MAJAMURA, K., HAYASHI, A., & FUJIMORI, M. Psychophysiological study on the depth of sleep in normal human subjects. *Electroencephalography and Clinical Neurophysiology,* 1966, **21,** 140–147.

ORLINSKY, D. E. Psychodynamic and cognitive correlates of dream recall. Unpublished doctoral dissertation, University of Chicago, 1962.

ORNE, M. T. The nature of hypnosis: Artifact and essence. *Journal of Abnormal and Social Psychology,* 1959, **58,** 277–299.

ORNE, M. T. On the social psychology of the psychological experiment: With particular reference to demand characteristics and their implications. *American Psychologist,* 1962, **17,** 776–783.

OSWALD, I. Experimental studies of rhythm, anxiety and cerebral vigilance. *Journal of Mental Science,* 1959, **105,** 269–294.

OSWALD, I. *Sleeping and waking: Physiology and psychology.* Amsterdam: Elsevier, 1962.

OSWALD, I., TAYLOR, A. M., & TREISMAN, M. Discriminative responses to stimulation during human sleep. *Brain,* 1960, **83,** 440–453.

PAMPIGLIONE, C. The phenomenon of adaptation in human EEG (a study of K-complexes). *Revue de neurologie,* 1952, **87,** 197–198.

PAMPIGLIONE, G., & ACKNER, B. The effects of repeated stimuli upon EEG and vaso-motor activity during sleep in man. *Brain,* 1958, **81,** 64–74.

PARMELEE, A. H., Jr., WENNER, W. H., AKIYAMA, Y., SCHULTZ, M., & STERN, E. Sleep states in premature infants. *Developmental Medicine and Child Neurology,* 1967, **9,** 70–77. (a)

PARMELEE, A. H., Jr., WENNER, W. H., AKIYAMA, Y., STERN, E., & FLESCHER, J. Electroencephalography and brain maturation. In *Regional development of the brain in early life: A symposium.* Oxford: Blackwell, 1967. (b)

PIERCE, C. M., MATHIA, J. L., & JABBOUR, J. T. Dream patterns in narcoleptic and hydranencephalic patients. *American Journal of Psychiatry,* 1965, **122,** 402–404.

PIERON, H. *Le probleme physiologique du sommeil.* Paris: Masson et Cie, 1913.

PIETRUSKY, F. Das Verhalten der Augen im Schlafe. *Klinische Monatsblatter für Augenheilkunde,* 1922, **68,** 355–360.

PISANO, M., ROSSADINI, G., ROSSI, G. F., & ZATTONI, J. Relations between threshold of arousal and electroencephalographic patterns during sleep in man. *Physiology and Behavior,* 1966, **1,** 55–58.

PIVIK, T., & FOULKES, D. "Dream deprivation": Effects on dream content. *Science,* 1966, **153,** 1282–1284.

RAEHLMANN, E., & WITKOWSKI, L. Über atypische

Augenbewegungen. *Archiv für Physiologie,* 1877. Pp. 454-471.

RAMSEY, G. V. Studies of dreaming. *Psychological Bulletin,* 1953, **50,** 432-455.

RECHTSCHAFFEN, A., & FOULKES, D. Effect of visual stimuli on dream content. *Perceptual and Motor Skills,* 1965, **20,** 1149-1160.

RECHTSCHAFFEN, A., GOODENOUGH, D. R., & SHAPIRO, A. Patterns of sleep talking. *Archives of General Psychiatry,* 1962, **7,** 418-426.

RECHTSCHAFFEN, A., HAURI, P., & ZEITLIN, M. Auditory awakening thresholds in REM and NREM sleep stages. *Perceptual and Motor Skills.,* 1966, **22,** 927-942.

RECHTSCHAFFEN, A., & MARON, L. Effect of amphetamine on sleep cycle. *Electroencephalography and Clinical Neurophysiology,* 1964, **16,** 438-445.

RECHTSCHAFFEN, A., & VERDONE, P. Amount of dreaming: Effect of incentive, adaptation to laboratory, and individual differences. *Perceptual and Motor Skills,* 1964, **19,** 947-958.

RECHTSCHAFFEN, A., VERDONE, P., & WHEATON, J. Reports of mental activity during sleep. *Canadian Psychiatric Association Journal,* 1963, **8,** 409-414.

RECHTSCHAFFEN, A., VOGEL, G., & SHAIKUN, G. Interrelatedness of mental activity during sleep. *Archives of General Psychiatry,* 1963, **9,** 536-547.

REED, C. I., & KLEITMAN, N. Studies on the physiology of sleep: IV. The effect of sleep on respiration. *American Journal of Physiology,* 1926, **75,** 600-608.

REGELSBERGER, H. Die Veraenderungen des elektrischen Gleischstromwiderstandes im Schlaf: Ein Beitrag zur Innervationsfrage der Perspirato insensibilis. *Zeitschrift für die gesamte Neurologie und Psychiatrie,* 1942, **174,** 66-79.

RICHARDSON, D. W., HONOUR, A. J., FENTON, G. S., STOTT, F. H., & PICKERING, G. W. Variation in arterial pressure throughout the day and night. *Clinical Science,* 1964, **26,** 445-460.

RICHTER, C. P. The significance of changes in the electrical resistance of the body during sleep. *Proceedings of the National Academy of Sciences, United States of America,* 1926, **12,** 214-222.

ROBIN, E. D., WHALEY, R. D., CRUMP, C. H., & TRAVIS, D. M. Alveolar gas tensions, pulmonary ventilation and blood pH during physiologic sleep in normal subjects. *Journal of Clinical Investigation,* 1958, **37,** 981-989.

ROFFWARG, H. P. Pupillary behavior during sleep and dreaming. Paper presented at the meeting of the Association for the Psychophysiological Study of Sleep, Washington, D.C., March 1965.

ROFFWARG, H. P., DEMENT, W. C., & FISHER, C. Preliminary observations of the sleep-dream pattern in neonates, infants, children and adults. In E. HARMS(Ed.), *Problems of sleep and dream in children: International series of monographs on child psychiatry.* Vol. 2. New York: Macmillan, 1964.

ROFFWARG, H. P., DEMENT, W. C., MUZIO, J. N., & FISHER, C. Dream imagery: Relationship to rapid eye movements of sleep. *Archives of General Psychiatry,* 1962, **7,** 235-258.

ROFFWARG, H. P., MUZIO, J. N., & DEMENT, W. C. Ontogenetic development of the human sleep-dream cycle. *Science,* 1966, **152,** 604-619.

ROHMER, F., SCHAFF, G., COLLARD, M., & KURTZ, D. La motilité spontaneé, la fréquence cardiaque et la fréquence respiratoire au cours du sommeil chez l'homme normal: Le sommeil de nuit normal et pathologique. *Études électroencéphalographiques. Électroencéphalographie et Neurophysiologie Clinique,* 1965, **2,** 156-183.

ROTH, M., SHAW, J., & GREEN, J. The form, voltage distribution and physiological significance of the K-complex. *Electroencephalography and Clinical Neurophysiology,* 1956, **8,** 385-402.

ROWLAND, V. Differential electroencephalographic response to conditioned auditory stimuli in arousal from sleep. *Electroencephalography and Clinical Neurophysiology,* 1957, **9,** 585-594.

RUSH, J., MUZIO, J. N., & ROFFWARG, H. P. The sleep pattern under the influence of controlled sleep limitation. Presented at the meeting of the Association for the Psychophysiological Study of Sleep, Gainesville, Fla., March 1966.

SAMPSON, H. Deprivation of dreaming sleep by two methods: I. Compensatory REM time. *Archives of General Psychiatry,* 1965, **13,** 79-86.

SASSIN, J. R., PARKER, D. C., MACE, J. W., GOTLIN, R. W., JOHNSON, L. C., & ROSSMAN, L. G. Human growth hormone release: Relation to slow-wave sleep and sleep-waking cycles. *Science,* 1969, 165: 513-515.

SCANTLEBURY, R. E., FRICK, H. L., & PATTERSON, T. L. The effect of normal and hypnotically induced dreams on the gastric hunger movements of man. *Journal of Applied Physiology,* 1942, **26,** 682-691.

SCHAFF, G., & MARBACH, G. Recherche d'une methode d'évaluation de la quantité de sommeil: I. Influence de la privation de sommeil sur differentes expressions quantitatives de la motilité spontanée du dormeur. *Comptes Rendus des Séances de la Société de Biologie,* 1960, **154,** 202-206.

SCHAFF, G., MARBACH, G., & VOGT, J. J. Variations concomitantes de la motilité spontanée, de la fréquence cardiaque et de la fréquence respiratoire au cours du sommeil sous l'influence de divers états de fatigue. *Comptes Rendus des Séances de la Société de Biologie,* 1962, **156,** 1517-1522.

SCHERRER, J., LILLE, F., & GABERSEK, V. Étude électrophysiologique du sommeil de jour. In P. WERTHEIMER, (Ed.), *Rêve et conscience.* Paris: Presses Universitaires de France, 1968.

SCHONBAR, R. A. Some manifest characteristics of recallers and nonrecallers of dreams. *Journal of Consulting Psychology,* 1959, **23,** 414-418.

Scott, J. Blood plasma free fatty acids and sleep. Unpublished doctoral dissertation, University of North Carolina, 1966.

Scott, J., & Snyder, F. Critical reactivity after abrupt awakenings in relation to EEG stages of sleep. Presented at the meeting of the Association for the Psychophysiological Study of Sleep, Santa Monica, Calif., April 1967.

Shackel, B. Electro-oculography: The electrical recording of eye position. *Proceedings of the 3rd International Conference on Medical Electronics.* London: Iliffe; Springfield, Ill.: Charles C Thomas, 1960.

Shapiro, A., & Cohen, H. D. The use of mercury capillary length gauges for the measurement of the volume of thoracic and diaphragmatic components of human respiration: A theoretical analysis and a practical method. *Transactions of the New York Academy of Sciences,* Series 2, 1965, **27,** 634–649.

Shapiro, A., Goodenough, D. R., Biederman, I., & Sleser, I. Dream recall and the physiology of sleep. *Journal of Applied Physiology,* 1964, **19,** 778–783.

Shapiro, A., Goodenough, D. R., & Gryler, R. B. Dream recall as a function of method awakening. *Psychosomatic Medicine,* 1963, **25,** 174–180.

Shapiro, A., Goodenough, D. R., Lewis, H. B., & Sleser, I. Gradual arousal from sleep: A determinant of thinking reports. *Psychosomatic Medicine,* 1965, **27,** 342–349.

Sharpless, S., & Jasper, H. H. Habituation of the arousal reaction. *Brain,* 1956, **79,** 655–680.

Siegel, J., & Gordon, T. P. Paradoxical sleep: Deprivation in the cat. *Science,* 1965, **148,** 978–980.

Siegel, J., & Langley, T. D. Arousal threshold in the cat as a function of sleep phase and stimulus significance. *Experientia,* 1965, **21,** 1–5.

Simon, C. W., & Emmons, W. H. Learning during sleep. *Psychological Bulletin,* 1955, **52,** 328–342.

Simon, C. W., & Emmons, W. H. Responses to material presented during various levels of sleep. *Journal of Experimental Psychology,* 1956, **51,** 89–97.

Snyder, F. Dream recall, respiratory variability, and depth of sleep. Paper presented at the Round Table on Dream Research, Annual Meeting of the American Psychiatric Association, Atlantic City, N. J., May 1960.

Snyder, F. The new biology of dreaming. *Archives of General Psychiatry,* 1963, **8,** 381–391.

Snyder, F. The organismic state associated with dreaming. In N. S. Greenfield & W. C. Lewis (Eds.), *Psychoanalysis and current biological thought.* Madison: University of Wisconsin Press, 1965.

Snyder, F. Toward an evolutionary theory of dreaming. *American Journal of Psychiatry,* 1966, **2,** 121–136.

Snyder, F. Autonomic nervous system manifestations during sleep and dreaming. In S. S. Kety, E. V. Evarts, & H. L. Williams (Eds.), *Sleep and altered states of consciousness.* Association for Research in Nervous and Mental Disease. Vol. 45. Baltimore: Williams & Wilkins, 1967.

Snyder, F. Electrographic studies of sleep in depression. In E. S. Kline & R. Lasky (Eds.), *Computers and other electronic devices in psychiatry.* New York: Grune & Stratton, 1968.

Snyder, F. The phenomenology of dreaming. In L. Madow & L. H. Snow (Eds.), *The psychodynamic implications of the physiological studies on dreams.* Springfield, Ill.: Charles C Thomas, 1970.

Snyder, F., Hobson, J. A., & Goldfrank, F. Blood pressure changes during human sleep. *Science,* 1963, **142,** 1313–1314.

Snyder, F., Hobson, J. A., Morrison, D. F., & Goldfrank, F. Changes in respiration, heart rate, and systolic blood pressure in human sleep. *Journal of Applied Physiology,* 1964, **19,** 417–422.

Sokolov, E. N., & Paramonova, N. P. Dynamics of the orienting reflex in man during the development of sleep inhibition. *Zhurnal Vysshei Nervnoi Deiatel 'Nosti imeni L. P. Pavolova (Moskva),* 1961, **11,** 206–215.

Sommer-Smith, J. A., Galeano, C., Pineyrua, M., Roig, J. A., & Segundo, J. P. Tone cessation as conditioned signal. *Electroencephalography and Clinical Neurophysiology,* 1962, **14,** 869–877.

Stoyva, J. M. Finger electromyographic activity during sleep: Its relation to dreaming in deaf and normal subjects. *Journal of Abnormal Psychology,* 1965, **70,** 343–349. (a)

Stoyva, J. M. Posthypnotically suggested dreams and the sleep cycle. *Archives of General Psychiatry,* 1965, **12,** 287–294. (b)

Szymanski, J. S. Aktivität und Ruhe bei den Menschen. *Zeitschrift für angewandte Psychologie und psychologische Sammelforschung.,* 1922, **20,** 192–222.

Tart, C. T. Frequence of dream recall and some personality measures. *Journal of Consulting Psychology,* 1962, **26,** 467–470.

Tart, C. T. Patterns of basal skin resistance during sleep. *Psychophysiology,* 1967, **4,** 35–39.

Tebbs, R. B., & Foulkes, D. Strength of grip following different stages of sleep. *Perceptual and Motor Skills,* 1966, **23,** 827–834.

Teplitz, Z. An electroencephalographic study of dreams and sleep. Unpublished master's thesis. University of Illinois, 1943.

Tissot, R. The effects of certain drugs on the sleep cycle in man. *Progress in Brain Research,* 1965, **18,** 175–177.

Titelbaum, S. The electrical skin resistance during sleep. Unpublished doctoral dissertation, University of Chicago, 1941.

Tokizane, T. Sleep mechanism: Hypothalamic control of cortical activity. In M. Jouvet (Ed.), *Aspects anatomo-fonctionnels de la physiologie du sommeil.* Paris: Centre National des Recherches de Science, 1965.

Toman, J. E. P., Bush, I. M., & Chackes, J. T. Conditional features of sound-evoked EEG responses during sleep. *Federation Proceedings,* 1958, **17,** 163. (Abstract)

TROSMAN, H., RECHTSCHAFFEN, A., OFFENKRANTZ, W., & WOLPERT, E. Studies in psychophysiology of dreams: IV. Relations among dreams in sequence. *Archives of General Psychiatry*, 1960, **3**, 602-607.

TURSKY, B, & O'CONNELL, D. N. A comparison of ac and dc eye movement recording. *Psychophysiology*, 1966, **3**, 157-163.

UHLENBRUCK, P. Plethysmographische Untersuchung am Menschen: I. Ueber die Wirkung der Sinnesnerven der Haut auf den Tonus der Gefaesse. *Zeitschrift für Biologie*, 1924, **80**, 35-70.

VAUGHAN, C. J. Behavioral evidence for dreaming in rhesus monkeys. *Physiologist (Washington)*, 1964, **7**, 275. (Abstract)

VERDONE, P. Temporal reference of manifest dream content. *Perceptual and Motor Skills*, 1965, **20**, 1253-1268.

WADA, T. Experimental study of hunger in its relation to activity. *Archives of Psychology (New York)*, 1922, **8**, 1-65.

WALTER, D. O., RHODES, J. M., & ADEY, W. R. Discriminating among stages of consciousness by EEG measurements: A study of four subjects. *Electroencephalography and Clinical Neurophysiology*, 1967, **22**, 22-29.

WEBB, W. B., & AGNEW, H. W., Jr. Reaction time and serial response efficiency on arousal from sleep. *Perceptual and Motor Skills*, 1964, **18**, 783-784.

WEBB, W. B., & AGNEW, H. W., Jr. Sleep: Effects of a restricted regime. *Science*, 1965, **150**, 1745-1747.

WEBB, W. B., AGNEW, H. W., Jr., & STERNTHAL, H. Sleep during the early morning. *Psychonomic Science*, 1966, **6**, 277-278.

WEED, S. C., & HALLAM, F. M., III. A study of the dream-consciousness. *American Journal of Psychology*, 1896, **7**, 405-411.

WEINBERG, H. Evidence suggesting the acquisition of a simple discrimination during sleep. *Canadian Journal of Psychology*, 1966, **20**, 1-11.

WEINBERGER, N. M., & LINDSLEY, D. B. Behavioral and electroencephalographic arousal to contrasting novel stimulation. *Science*, 1964, **144**, 1355-1357.

WEITZMAN, E. D., FISHBEIN, W., & GRAZIANI, L. Auditory evoked responses obtained from the scalp electroencephalogram of the full-term human neonate during sleep. *Pediatrics*, 1965, **35**, 458-462.

WEITZMAN, E. D., GOLDMAKER, D., KRIPKE, D., MacGREGOR, J., KREAM, J., & HELLMAN, L. Reversal of sleep-waking cycle: Effect on sleep stage pattern and certain neuroendocrine rhythms. Paper presented at the meeting of the Association for the Psychophysiological Study of Sleep, Santa Monica, Calif., April 1967.

WEITZMAN, E. D., & KREMEN, H. Auditory evoked responses during different stages of sleep in man. *Electroencephalography and Clinical Neurophysiology*, 1965, **18**, 65-70.

WEITZMAN, E. D., SCHAUMBURG, H., & FISHBEIN, W. Plasma 17-OHCS levels during sleep in man. *Journal of Clinical Endocrinology and Metabolism*, 1966, **26**, 121-127.

WENGER, M. A. Some problems in psychophysiological research. In R. ROESSLER & N. S. GREENFIELD (Eds.), *Physiological correlates of psychological disorders*. Madison: University of Wisconsin Press, 1962.

WEYSEE, A. W., & LUTZ, B. Diurnal variations in arterial blood pressure. *American Journal of Physiology*, 1915, **37**, 330-347.

WHITMAN, R. M., KRAMER, M., & BALDRIDGE, B. Which dream does the patient tell? *Archives of General Psychiatry*, 1963, **8**, 277-282.

WIKLER, A. Pharmacologic dissociation of behavior and EEG "sleep patterns" in dogs: Morphine, N-allylnormorphine, and atropine. *Proceedings of the Society for Experimental Biology and Medicine*, 1952, **79**, 261-265.

WILDER, J. Modern psychophysiology and the law of initial value. *American Journal of Psychotherapy*, 1958, **12**, 199-221.

WILLIAMS, H. L. The problem of defining depth of sleep. *Proceedings of the Association for Research in Nervous and Mental Disease*, 1967, **45**, 277-287.

WILLIAMS, H. L., HAMMACK, J. T., DALY, R. L., DEMENT, W. C., & LUBIN, A. Responses to auditory stimulation, sleep loss and the EEG stages of sleep. *Electroencephalography and Clinical Neurophysiology*, 1964, **16**, 269-279.

WILLIAMS, H. L., MORLOCK, H. C., Jr., & MORLOCK, J. V. Instrumental behavior during sleep. *Psychophysiology*, 1966, **2**, 208-216.

WILLIAMS, H. L., TEPAS, D. I., & MORLOCK, H. C., Jr. Evoked responses to clicks and electroencephalographic stages of sleep in man. *Science*, 1962, **138**, 685-686.

WILLIAMS, R. L., AGNEW, H. W., Jr., & WEBB, W. B. Sleep patterns in young adults: An EEG study. *Electroencephalography and Clinical Neurophysiology*, 1964, **17**, 376-381.

WILLIAMS, R. L., AGNEW, H. W., Jr., & WEBB, W. B. Sleep patterns in the young adult female: An EEG study. *Electroencephalography and Clinical Neurophysiology*, 1966, **20**, 264-266.

WILSON, W. P., & ZUNG, W. W. K. Attention discrimination and arousal during sleep. *Archives of General Psychiatry*, 1966, **15**, 523-528.

WITKIN, H. A., & LEWIS, H. B. The relation of experimentally induced presleep experiences to dreams. *Journal of the American Psychoanalytic Association*, 1965, **13**, 819-849.

WITKIN, H. A., & LEWIS, H. B. *Experimental studies of dreaming*. New York: Random House, 1967.

WOHLISCH, E. Die Schlaftiefenzahl: Theorie und Anwendung. *Zeitschrift für Biologie*, 1954, **106**, 330-376.

WOLPERT, E. A. Studies in psychophysiology of dreams: II. An electromyographic study of dreaming. *Archives of General Psychiatry*, 1960, **2**, 231-241.

WOLPERT, E. A., & TROSMAN, H. Studies in psychophysiology of dreams: I. Experimental evocation of sequential dream episodes. *Archives of Neurology and Psychiatry,* 1958, **79,** 603–606.

WOOD, P. B. Dreaming and social isolation. Unpublished doctoral dissertation, University of North Carolina, 1962.

YOKOYAMA, A., RAMIREZ, V. D., & SAWYER, C. H. Sleep and wakefulness in female rats under various hormonal and physiological conditions. *General and Comparative Endocrinology,* 1966, **7,** 10–17.

ZUNG, W. W. K., & WILSON, W. P. Response to auditory stimulation during sleep. *Archives of General Psychiatry,* 1961, **4,** 548–552.

ZUNG, W. W. K., & WILSON, W. P. Sleep and dream patterns in twins: Markov analysis of a genetic trait. *Recent Advances in Biological Psychiatry,* 1967, **9,** 119–130.

Marvin Zuckerman

PHYSIOLOGICAL MEASURES
OF SEXUAL AROUSAL
IN THE HUMAN*

18

In an article about sex research appearing in the *New York Times*, Gebhard is quoted as saying to Masters, during an automobile trip, "Watch where you're going, Bill. If you get us all killed, there goes sex research in the United States [Buckley, 1969, p. 106]." Although Gebhard's statement is somewhat exaggerated, it is true that the Kinsey Institute and the Reproductive Biology Research Foundation represent the major sources of scientific information about human sexual patterns. However, many investigators are now becoming active in this field, and it may be helpful to survey some of the physiological methods currently in use. A later review will deal with psychological methods. This article deals with quantifiable physiological methods of measuring sexual arousal in the human. Many of the methods are still in developmental stages, and details about them were provided by generous investigators. It is hoped that by facilitating scientific communication, more research will be stimulated in this vital area.

Many important questions seem to be awaiting the development of appropriate methodology. One example which involves

* This review was supported by the Commission on Obscenity and Pornography. A summary of the review was read at the Ninth Annual Meeting of the Society for Psychophysiological Research, Monterey, California, October 1969.

Reprinted by permission of the author and the American Psychological Association from the *Psychological Bulletin*, 1971, **75,** 297-329. Copyright © 1971 by the American Psychological Association.

an area of public debate is the question of pornography. Every investigation of this problem from a legal or social standpoint has concluded with the statement that not enough scientific information is available. It is obvious that scientists cannot answer questions, such as how arousing pornography is, or who is most aroused by pornography, until they can decide on reliable methods for measuring sexual arousal. Theoretical issues must also await the development of suitable methodology.

Whalen (1966) has made a useful distinction between sexual arousal, the momentary or current level of sexual excitement, and sexual arousability, or "an individual's characteristic rate of approach to orgasm as a result of sexual stimulation [p. 152]." The distinction is similar to that made between state and trait by other investigators concerning other emotions (Cattell & Scheier, 1961; Spielberger, 1966; Zuckerman, Persky, & Link, 1967). Zuckerman et al. (1967) have suggested that a trait may be measurable as the average and variation in a series of state measures. Applying this to sexual arousability it would be possible to define arousability by a series of measures of sexual arousal to standard stimulation. Beach (1956) has reported high reliabilities for various behavioral indexes of sexual arousal in rats. Comparable data on humans are not available.

Sexual arousability can be measured by behavioral and verbal report measures. Latency to orgasm, frequency of orgasm, subjective estimate of arousal are some alternatives to physiological recording. However, physiological measures offer some obvious advantages in their objectivity, continuous sampling, and the fact that they can be used to measure arousal without the necessity of inducing orgasm. Although some mechanical devices have been developed for inducing orgasm in a somewhat standard fashion (Masters & Johnson, 1966; Sobrero, Stearns, & Blair, 1965), most measurements which rely on orgasm introduce many uncontrolled variables, the least of which is movement. The social nature of conventional sexual stimulation and the influence of the setting in which orgasm is induced, as well as the volunteer selection problem, are problems in this kind of experiment. Psychological, or visual and auditory stimuli are more easily

standardized and offer the possibility of sampling a wider variety of subjects. Furthermore, it is questionable that arousal can be measured by orgastic ejaculation since the two may depend on different neural mechanisms. This problem is discussed later in this review.

It should be pointed out that the tremendous fund of data collected by Kinsey and his co-workers (Kinsey, Pomeroy, & Martin, 1948, 1953) was based on retrospective reports. The data presented by Masters and Johnson (1966) are physiological and anatomical, but not very quantitative. In describing the course of physiological reactions during the various stages of arousal, Masters and Johnson reported modal and ranges of reactions with little indication of normal variation. Some of the changes described may be intrinsically difficult to measure, but most, such as blood volume changes, temperature changes, muscle tension, hyperventilation, tachycardia, and sweating are accessible to measurement by standard psychophysiological techniques. Special applications of these techniques of measuring sexual arousal are described in this paper. The description of modal patterns is useful, but more quantitative specificity is necessary in studying relationships between variables and comparing individuals or groups of individuals.

CENTRAL NERVOUS SYSTEM

Sexual arousal is undoubtedly mediated through the central and autonomic nervous systems and may also involve the pituitary gonadotropic and gonadal system.[1] Money (1961) has summarized:

> among the coordinates of sexual function there are three: local genital surfaces, the brain, the hormones, any of which can fail in its contributions without total destruction of sexual function . . . Nonetheless, it is evident that loss of any one of the three constituents is an immense handicap to effective sexual functioning [p. 1396].

Beach (1958) has noted that there are species and sex differences in the dependence of sexual arousal on the neocortex and hormones. The evolutionary

---

[1] Although the gonadotropic and gonadal hormones have been shown to play an essential role in the anatomical development of the sexual systems, their role in sexual arousal in man is less clearly understood.

trend is toward more stress on the former and less on the latter.

MacLean (1965) has discussed the psychosexual functions of the brain. Visual and olfactory senses are important in the initial stimulation of sexual arousal. MacLean suggested that the visual sense has become more important in the course of evolution. However, the importance of visual and auditory stimulation in the displays and calls of mating birds would suggest that the crucial roles of these senses are not confined to higher species of mammals. More specific sexual arousal centers have been found in the limbic system of the squirrel monkey, using the method of intracranial stimulation. Penile erections were elicited by stimulation of hippocampal projections to parts of the septum, anterior thalamus, and hypothalamus; parts of the Papez circuit (mammillary bodies, mammillo-thalamic tract, anterior thalamic nuclei, and anterior cingulate gyrus); and parts of the medial orbital gyrus, medial dorsal nucleus of the thalamus, and regions of their connections. The medial part of the medial dorsal nucleus and medial septopreoptic region are said to be modal points for erection. Stimulation in the septum and rostral diencephalon which result in erection is also noted to be associated with afterdischarges in the hippocampus during which time erections become throbbing in character and reach maximum size. Following these hippocampal afterdischarges, the monkeys appear to be calm and placid for some time. There is a strong suggestion that the hippocampal discharges are linked to the phenomenon of orgasm and post-orgastic decline of arousability in the male. However, ejaculation is not associated with the hippocampal afterdischarges. Stimulation in the thalamus or other points within and bordering on the caudal intralaminar region and along the course of the spinothalamic pathway elicit seminal discharge with motile sperm and quasipruritic scratching of the genitalia. The seminal discharge could occur without the appearance of throbbing penile erection. Beach (1956) suggested a distinction between a sexual arousal mechanism (SAM) and intromissive and ejaculatory mechanism (IEM) in the male[2] and MacLean's evidence shows the

[2]In the later articles Beach referred to these as the arousal mechanism (AM) and consummatory mechanism (CM).

neural separation of these mechanisms. Sobrero et al. (1965) used a vibrating cup applied with gentle pressure to the glans penis to obtain semen samples from schizophrenic males and males with infertility problems. Although ejaculation was eventually induced in all 40 infertile males "no full erection was ever observed, although in some instances a partial, very soft erection was observed at the time of ejaculation [p. 767]." Similar results were obtained with five normal subjects. Only 5 of these 45 subjects reported erotic fantasies or orgasmic feelings. In Hohmann's (1966) study of the effects of spinal cord lesions on emotional feelings, 15 of the 25 subjects were still able to have erections, but only 3 reported ejaculation, and 4 reported the experience of orgasm. These data provide behavioral evidence for the separation of SAM and IEM. Other findings relevant to the independence of ejaculation and orgasm are discussed by Beach, Westbrook, and Clemens (1966). The implication of the independent functioning of these systems is that latency of ejaculation cannot be equated with penile erection as alternate indexes of sexual arousal. The IEM seems to be more dependent on autonomic and sensory feedback than the SAM.

AUTONOMIC NERVOUS SYSTEM

The limbic structures which are involved in sexual arousal have connections with the hypothalamus which in turn may involve the autonomic and pituitary-gonadotropic systems. Gellhorn and Loofbourrow (1963) stated that appropriate hypothalamic lesions may abolish sexual behavior; but if the hypothalamus is intact, destruction of large parts of the cerebral cortex has little effect (in rats and rabbits). Sex hormones may sensitize the hypothalamic centers involved in the sex drive. These authors maintain that the sex act is accompanied by simultaneous parasympathetic and sympathetic discharges. Wenger, Jones, and Jones (1956) have suggested that the sacral portion of the parasympathetic nervous system dominates in the initial phases of sexual arousal, but that the sympathetic system becomes more prominent as orgasm approaches. After orgasm there is an overcompensatory phase of parasympathetic dominance.

Kinsey et al. (1953) reviewed the literature (what

there was of it) on autonomic components of sexual arousal. What is interesting in this review is the contrast of the autonomic patterns in sexual arousal with those in anger, fear, epilepsy, and pain. The problem of emotional specificity is an important one to consider in measuring responses to sexual stimuli since these stimuli might also elicit secondary reactions whose affects might be mistaken for those of sexual arousal. Both anger and sexual arousal may elicit increases in pulse rate, blood pressure, hyperventilation, adrenaline secretion, muscle tension, and inhibition of gastro-intestinal activity. However, sexual arousal is distinct in the "invariable increase" in surface temperatures, color, tumescence, genital secretions, rhythmic muscular movements, and orgasm. Fear may also increase pulse, blood pressure, breathing rate, adrenaline secretion, and muscle tension; but the increase in peripheral circulation of blood, vasodilation, genital secretions, salivary secretions, and rhythmic muscle movements are more characteristic of sexual arousal. The muscular tensions and rigidities of epileptic seizure are common to both epileptic fits and sexual responses as orgasm is approached. In some cases, orgasm may actually occur during epileptic seizures. In general, only tumescence, vasodilation, genital secretions, and rhythmic muscular movements are characteristic of sexual arousal alone. The rhythmic muscular movements are a spinal neural mechanism and generally are limited to the postintromission phase of sexual arousal just prior to and during orgasm.

Masters and Johnson (1966) have summarized their findings for the four phases of sexual arousal: excitement, plateau, orgasmic, and resolution. In the excitement phase, penile erection, thickening, flattening, and elevation of the scrotal integument, and moderate testicular elevation and size increase are the only typical reactions in the male. Nipple erection, vaginal lubrication, thickening of vaginal walls, flattening and elevation of major labia, and expansion of the vaginal barrel are found in women. Only penile erection and vaginal lubrication are found in the immediate response (3 to 15 seconds) to sexual stimulation. Sympathetic system responses such as hyperventilation, tachycardia, and muscle tension are not characteristic until the plateau phase of arousal (approaching orgasm). Cowper's gland emissions in the male and Bartholin's gland

emissions in the female are also found in this phase. Sympathetic reactions reach peak during the brief orgasmic phase when involuntary muscle contractions appear. Various contractions in genital and accessory organs and in the external rectal sphincter are seen during orgasm. Sympathetic reactions and vasocongestion diminish gradually during the resolution phase. A sweating reaction is seen in 30% to 40% of subjects. According to these authors, the only specific indexes of sexual arousal which could be used early in the excitement phase of sexual arousal would be penile erection in the male and vaginal lubrication and possibly nipple erection in the female. A "sex tension flush" is seen in a minority of females (25%) during the excitement phase, but only comes into prominence in a majority (75%) of females in the plateau phase. Masters and Johnson's description of the stages of arousal seems to support Wenger et al.'s (1956) theory of the predominance of parasympathetic phenomena during the early stages of arousal and the appearance of sympathetic phenomena during the later preorgasmic phases of arousal.

Perhaps Wenger's theory may be applied to the two mechanisms postulated by Beach: parasympathetic activity stimulating SAM and sympathetic activity associated with IEM. Some interesting and relevant data are available on the sexual effects of tranquilizing and antidepressant drugs. Blair and Simpson (1966) reported that tranquilizing drugs (Perphenazine, Trifluoperazine, Butaperazine, and Reserpine), which act as central sympathetic nervous system depressants, interfere with emission and ejaculation, often resulting in interference with ejaculation. The authors[3] have also reported that only 6 of 60 chronic patients on the drug Thioridazine (also a central autonomic depressant) could experience ejaculation; and 10 normals on Tofranil all had some degree of retarded ejaculation. Many other investigators have reported inhibitions of ejaculation produced by Thioridazine (Cohen, 1964). Money and Yankowitz (1967) found that the sympathetic inhibiting drug Ismelin produces ejaculation problems.

On the other hand, Simpson, Blair, and Amuso (1965) found that antidepressant MAO-inhibitors,

[3]G. M. Simpson and J. Blair, personal communication, August 1, 1969.

which have indirect sympathetic stimulation effects, and antiparasympathetic effects, can interfere with erection and cause impotence. When the drugs are discontinued, potency usually returns.

The possibility that sympathetic dominance may inhibit arousal and facilitate ejaculation may explain why sexual anxiety may be expressed in an inability to attain or maintain an erection, or premature ejaculation. Assuming that anxiety creates a state of heightened autonomic arousal these effects would follow.

HORMONES

Although a large amount of data has been collected on the role of hormones in sexual behavior in lower species (Beach, 1948, 1958, 1965) their role in human sexual arousal is not well defined. One of the reasons for the state of affairs is that extirpation experiments can be done freely with animals, but human data must be obtained from clinical case studies. Another reason is that sex hormone determinations have only recently been improved so that their total production rate can be measured. Formerly, investigators had to rely on unstable plasma measures or the metabolic end products of the hormones.

Money (1961) has reviewed the evidence from clinical studies including his own extensive series of cases. Sex hormones play a crucial role in the growth of the genital structures in man, as in lower species. However, anatomy is not necessarily destiny, Freud to the contrary. The gender role and erotic orientation of hermaphrodites, for instance, is determined by the social role assigned to them after birth. While hormones do not seem to play an important role in determining the direction of sexual interests, they may have crucial consequences for the strength of the sex drive or sexual arousability. Androgen stimulates growth and dilation of the vasculature of the penis and clitoris. The maintenance of erection by engorgement of the penis with blood is facilitated by androgen. "Tumescence of the penis can occur in the absence of androgen, but the erection is generally not complete and long lasting [p. 1387]." "Erotic drive" in hypogonadal males is generally heightened by androgen administration. Withdrawal of androgen, or substitution of placebo, generally results in a loss

of arousability. In one group of hypogonadal cases where androgen administration was stopped, the ejaculate diminished in volume until no fluid was emitted, and the men reported that they had fewer erections and less urge to masturbate or initiate heterosexual activity. Even reports of erotic imagery and daydreams were reduced.

The ovaries in women do not seem to be crucial for sexual arousability. Estrogen in women facilitates vaginal lubrication, but lack of lubrication is not an insurmountable problem in sexual intercourse. Money (1961) marshalls considerable clinical evidence to support the hypothesis that androgen is the hormone which is related to sexual arousability in women as well as in men. Androgens in women probably originate in the adrenals. Many women who receive androgen therapy report increased sexual desire. Androgen sensitizes the clitoris and, if prolonged, may result in hypertrophy of the clitoris. Hyperadrenal pseudohermaphroditic females produce high levels of androgen, but the effects on erotic behavior are variable.

Most cases of impotence in males and frigidity in women are not expressions of hormonal insufficiencies and do not respond to treatment with additional exogenous hormone. Sex hormones probably operate to lower thresholds for sexual arousal, but beyond a certain level additional hormone supplies may not make much difference.

Despite the importance of sex hormones (and probably the gonadotropic hormones) in sexual arousability, this writer has been unable to locate a single published study of the effects of sexual arousal on sex hormone levels in the human. Masters reported that such studies are going on in his laboratory, but it will be several years before these data will be made available.

Because of the important role of the autonomic nervous system in sexual arousability the adrenal medullary hormones may play a role in general arousal. Several studies on the effect of sexual arousal on these hormones are discussed later in this review.

ELECTRODERMAL MEASURES

It is of some historical interest to note that Wilhelm Reich (1937) experimented with skin potential measurement in an attempt to provide empirical evidence for a theory of the electrical nature of sexual excitement. He applied electrodes to various body parts including the penis, vaginal mucosa, tongue, lips, anal mucosa, nipple, palm of the hand, earlobe, and forehead. He claimed that erogenous zones (all of the aforementioned were considered erogenous) have a much higher potential than nonerogenous zones of the body and that sensations of pleasure are associated with rises in potential while sensations of displeasure are associated with falls in potential. His crude apparatus and unusual experimental techniques, such as using the electrode itself to stimulate the site, make his data questionable. Little need be said about the somewhat grandiose theory extrapolated from the data.

Davis and Buchwald (1957) used electrodermal and other autonomic measures of response to see if different types of pictures produce different kinds of somatic response. Twelve pictures were projected on lantern slides. There were two pictures for each of six categories: cartoons, landscapes, female nudes, horror, (e.g., photograph of a starving man), fear, (e.g., photograph of alligator head), and geometrical abstractions. Each picture was presented for 1 minute followed by a 1-minute rest period. Three electrodermal measurements were made from palmar electrodes: (a) maximum skin resistance decrease in the first 10 seconds of picture presentation expressed in percentage of base level; (b) skin resistance change from the beginning to the end of each stimulus presentation expressed as percentage change; (c) number of galvanic skin responses (GSRs) during the stimulus. The 12 stimuli were ranked in order of the mean magnitudes of response for each of the 11 physiological measures used including the 3 electrodermal measures. The ranks of the mean responses to the 12 stimuli for each measure were correlated with sums of the ranks on all measures to provide a measure of response generality. The ranks of pairs of stimuli ($N = 6$) were also correlated to see if the responses to classes of stimuli differ in a reliable fashion. For the males there was significant concordance among response variables, for females there was not. Similarly, for males, there was significant group reliability of combined responses to the pairs of pictures, for females there was not. For both sexes the two pictures of nudes elicited greater combined response than the other pictures. For males this was

also true for the initial galvanic skin response, and the net skin resistance change where Ranks 1 and 2 were assigned to the nudes. Both of these measures also correlated highly and significantly with the combined ranks and yielded significant correlations between pairs of pictures. The number of GSRs did not yield significant correlations with variables or across pairs of pictures. While the method of data analysis in this paper leaves something to be desired (individual data, even rankings, were not examined), it does tend to show that differential autonomic responses do occur to categories of pictures, that female nudes have a highly stimulating value, and that GSR and skin resistance seem to offer a reliable way of measuring arousal in response to pictures. However, these conclusions apply only to males. There is some evidence that males are more responsive on electrodermal measures than females, even to meaningless stimuli (Kimmel, 1965). This lower electrodermal responsiveness of females was found in the Davis and Buchwald experiment as well.

Loisselle and Mollenauer (1965) used male and female pictures as stimuli. Within each set there were three clothed, three seminude, and three nude figures. The subjects were 20 female seniors. These women showed significantly greater GSRs to nude than to clothed figures, and greater GSRs to nude male figures than to nude female figures. The authors were careful to say that the GSR may be measuring negative reactions as well as sexual arousal. It would be of great value in this type of experiment to obtain self-ratings of sexual arousal and other feelings in order to see the relations between physiological response and subjective reactions. An interesting sidenote to this study is that women scoring as more masculine on the MMPI scale gave stronger GSRs than more feminine subjects to both clothed and nude figures. This result parallels the sex difference in GSR responsivity noted above.

Although women in the aforementioned study showed greater GSRs to opposite-sexed nudes than to same-sexed ones, males in an experiment by Hain and Linton[4] failed to show a difference be-

[4] Hain, J. D., & Linton, P. H. Physiological response to visual sexual stimuli. Paper presented at the National Association for Mental Health Scientific Conference, New Orleans, November 1966.

tween response to male and female nudes. This failure of GSR discrimination is even more significant in view of the fact that there were large differences in Semantic Differential ratings of the two types of stimuli by another group of males.

Martin (1964) added another dimension to the standard experiment comparing reactions to nudes and landscapes. In half of his subjects the presentation of pictures was preceded by a permissive set, and in the other subjects by an inhibitory set. The measure of response was the change in skin conductance from the beginning to the end of an entire series of pictures. One group was shown six pictures of Playboy-type nudes interspersed with six pictures of landscapes. Another group was shown 12 pictures of landscapes.

In the first experiment, both picture type and the interaction between set and picture type were significant. There was less drop in skin conductance when nudes were being shown, and this difference between stimuli was more marked after an inhibitory set. In the second experiment, only the set variable was significant. This experiment underlines the importance of the social setting in which an experiment is performed.

Autonomic variables are not immune from this type of effect. For instance, Zuckerman, Persky, and Link (1969) showed that breathing and electrodermal responses to sensory deprivation may depend on the set given to subjects in the instructions and by the total experimental setting.

Speisman, Lazarus, Davison, and Mordkoff (1964) attempted to separate the effects of male nudity from those of mutilation in the film depicting Australoid Aborigine circumcision rites. The film was analyzed by dividing it into three sections: neutral, nudity, and mutilation. The subjects were 12 male and 12 female undergraduates. All subjects viewed all three sections of the film in a counterbalanced order. Skin conductance and heart rate were sampled at 10-second intervals during the film periods and for 2.5 minute base-line periods. Analysis of covariance was used to eliminate the influence of base-line levels. Mutilation scenes elicited greater skin conductance and heart rate increases than neutral scenes; nude scenes did not elicit responses different from those to neutral scenes on either measure. The predominant mood, elicited by both mutilation and nudity sections of film relative

to the neutral section, was tension. The fact that nude Australoid Aborigines elicit little sexual arousal in young female or male undergraduates is not surprising.

Koegler and Kline (1965) used the aborigine circumcision rite film along with two sexual films and three neutral films to compare the responses of 20 male medical students, 10 male undergraduates, and 20 female undergraduates. The film intended to induce heterosexual arousal in males showed nude and seminude women in striptease sequences. Another film showed two seminude males in wrestling and massage sequences and was aimed at homosexual arousal. They used measures of palmar skin resistance, GSR lability (number of fluctuations), heart rate, finger pulse volume, and respiration. Unfortunately their data were not presented in a form that would make comparison on the separate autonomic measures between films and subject groups easy to evaluate. The following discussion of their results is merely taken from the text of the article. The subincision film resulted in significant changes in GSR level and lability and heart rate, particularly in the male and female college students. Little effect was seen on blood volume and respiration measures. The medical students showed less subjective and autonomic reaction to this film, viewing it more intellectually and less empathically. However, all males enjoyed the heterosexual movie and found it exciting. They showed autonomic reactions of a magnitude comparable to those of the girls to the subincision movie. The authors felt that arousal in positive and negative affective states is not distinguishable: "Thus it seems that the direction of autonomic change is independent of the nature of the psychologic stress [p. 274]." However they noted that the males showed more autonomic reaction to the heterosexual than to the homosexual movie, and they found the latter unpleasant. Three homosexuals showed a stronger reaction to the homosexual movie than to the heterosexual movie. The results suggest that intensity of nonspecific autonomic reactions might be used to differentiate sexual arousal to preferred and nonpreferred sexual objects, but cannot be used to distinguish between positive and negative affective arousal. However, the stimuli and the affective reactions are confounded. Homosexual and heterosexual movies are likely to stimulate both positive and negative arousal, depending on the type of subject and the style of the movie itself.

Romano (1969) compared the electrodermal responses of 39 married male subjects to (a) control stimuli consisting of neutral slides, (b) an erotic motion picture depicting a couple engaged in coitus, (c) a film showing scenes from World War II Nazi concentration camps (gas chambers, corpses). The sexual and atrocity films were presented in a counterbalanced order with half of the subjects watching one film first, while the others viewed the other film first. Both of the films resulted in significant increases in spontaneous GSR activity relative to the control stimuli. Although the change was greater to the sexual film, the difference in responses to the two films was not significant even though the two films were rated differently on an affect checklist. Neither film produced significant changes in basal skin resistance. The results indicate a lack of affect response specificity. Although the subjects reported that the concentration camp film aroused unpleasant affect, and the sexual film aroused pleasant affect, the spontaneous GSR activity did not differentiate these affective reactions.

Roessler[5] examined the responses of male subjects to a sexual movie and a control movie (a piano recital). His subjects showed greater skin conductance increase in response to the erotic film than to the piano recital although the difference only approached significance. Data from an affect checklist test indicated that the erotic film also elicited more anxiety than the control film.

Fisher and Osofsky (1968) recorded skin resistance and spontaneous GSRs in 42 married women during three sessions: a control session while they were fully clothed and lying quietly; a second session during which a male gynecologist examined electrodes placed on the breast and labia and made "touch threshold" determinations; and a third session in which a standard gynecological examination was made. It is possible, but not probable judging from most womens' reports, that the gynecological

examinations produced sexual arousal. At any rate, no self-ratings were made by the subjects on their state of arousal during the examinations. Whatever the cause, anxiety or sexual arousal, the examinations produced greater GSR frequency and amplitudes, and lower palmar and leg skin resistance than the control session. The authors also measured skin resistance of the labia and breast in Sessions 2 and 3. While there was no base line to assess these comparisons against, it is interesting that skin resistance on the labia was lower than on the palm, while skin resistance on the breast was higher. These authors were the first since Reich to make electrical recordings in these erogenous areas of skin.

Another method of stimulating sexual arousal is to visually present erotic passages in printed form. This method demands more imagination from the subject. However, in view of the fact that women report less arousal than men in response to pictures and movies, but report comparable arousal in response to erotic passages in literature (Kinsey et al., 1953), this method of presentation may be useful in making comparisons of the sexes. Jordan and Butler (1967) used four passages from fiction presented on cards: two descriptions of sexual seduction and two neutral scenes. The subjects were 32 females: 16 high on the hysteria scale of the MMPI and 16 low. The experimenter was female. Sex and neutral themes were alternately presented with a 45-second pause between them. Significant differences in skin resistance change were found for diagnoses (high versus low hysteria scores), passages (sex versus neutral), and the interaction. Sexual material elicited more response in skin resistance than neutral material. High hysteria scorers showed more response than low scorers to the sexual passages, but these groups did not differ in response to the neutral passages.

Wenger, Averill, and Smith (1968) studied the reactions of 16 male subjects while reading erotic and innocuous passages presented on slides. Palmar skin conductance was 1 of 10 autonomic functions measured; it proved to be the most sensitive one, yielding highly significant differences between the erotic and control passages. Number of GSRs during presentation of the passages was also tabulated, but no results on this variable were reported.

---

[5] Roessler, R., and Collins, F. Physiological responses to sexually arousing motion pictures. Paper delivered at Ninth Annual meeting of the Society for Psychophysiological Research, Monterey, California, October 1969.

Physiological indexes have been increasingly employed in the study and treatment of sexual deviants. Solyom and Beck (1967) used three fetishists and one homosexual as subjects in a study of electrodermal reactions to pictures of the fetish objects (a seminude male in the case of the homosexual patient). Neutral geometrical designs and seminude female figures were also used as stimuli. Each picture was presented on a slide for a period of 1 minute. The electrodermal indexes of reaction included fall in skin resistance during the first GSR (percentage of prestimulus level), latency of first GSR, latency of maximum fall in skin resistance, recovery time to regain prestimulus level, change in skin resistance of 1-minute intervals (expressed as percentage of base line), and number of GSRs over each of the 1-minute intervals. Of the six electrodermal measures used, only amplitude of first GSR, recovery time, and change in basal skin resistance showed much variation from picture to picture. Analysis of variance was used to compare the effects of stimuli and trials (each type of stimulus was presented four times). Significant differences were obtained between stimuli: the fetish (seminude male in the case of the homosexual) object and the seminude female elicited a greater GSR amplitude than the neutral object, but did not differ significantly from each other. A somewhat weaker trials effect was also found, with habituation from the first to the fourth trial.

Steffy[6] has been attempting to develop a Sexual Attractiveness Scale (SAS), which measures physiological (GSR) arousal and verbal report of preference to a range of visual sexual stimuli. The stimuli consist of pictures in 18 categories representing the combinations of the following 3 major categories: sex (male, female), age (child, pubescent, adult), and state of dress (dressed, partially dressed and nude). Five pictures represent each of the categories and 10 geometrical forms are added as neutral items. The subjects observe each picture for 10 seconds, at which time GSR is recorded from finger electrodes. At the end of each 10-second period, the subject rates the attractiveness of the picture on a 10-point scale. Mean conductance-change data

[6]Steffy, R. A. Progress report on the treatment of the pedophile sex offender. Paper delivered at Fourth Annual Conference on Addictions and Sexual Deviation, Mimico, Ontario, April 1967.

are presented on some male subjects. The normal control group showed a major interest in adult female pictures in all stages of dress as reflected in both ratings and conductance change. There was only a slight indication of a gradient going from dressed to partly dressed to undressed. Heterosexual prisoners showed a pattern of response similar to normal males. The homosexual prisoners showed somewhat more response to nude adult and pubescent males than the heterosexual prisoners, but their greatest response was still to nude adult females. Heterosexual pedophiles rated all females higher than all males, and their GSRs showed greater response to females than to males; however, only the GSR to the nude and dressed female children was significantly different from the response to male figures. Homosexual pedophiles expressed greater interest in both pubescent males and adult females than in other categories, and the GSR reflected this interest. Both homosexual groups in the experiment expressed interest in both males and females, but the authors cautioned that the GSR may be measuring negative, as well as positive affective responses. The psychophysiological technique developed by the author is a promising one; but the sampling of stimuli is not balanced by a sampling of autonomic responses. Better discrimination of sexual types has been achieved using penile erection measurements; these techniques are discussed in a later section.

Barlow, Leitenberg, and Agras (1969) have used an electrodermal method to measure changes in response to imagined scenes during the course of behavioral therapy. They reported on two subjects—a male pedophiliac and a male homosexual. The therapy consisted of an association of the fantasy arousal stimuli with a covert noxious stimulus (imagining nausea and vomiting). Electrodermal arousal was measured as change in log conductance over each of the four experimental periods: base line, acquisition, extinction, and reacquisition. During acquisition, fantasied sexual stimuli were associated with fantasied nausea and vomiting. In the pedophiliac, there was a dramatic drop in conductance during acquisition, a rise during extinction, and a drop during reacquisition. In the homosexual, conductance declined during acquisition, but did not recover during extinction even though reports of subjective homosexual arousal increased during that period.

Galvanic skin reactions to pictures of nude females are quite pronounced in most studies, exceeding responses to clothed figures and neutral forms. Similarly, electrodermal reactions seem to be sensitive measures of response to the reading of erotic material, fantasying of erotic scenes, and the viewing of movies. Attempts to show differential GSRs to male and female sexual stimuli have not generally been successful. Female nudes seem to have a great arousal effect for heterosexual, homosexual, and fetishist males. Several authors have cautioned against interpreting electrodermal responses as specific measures of sexual arousal since they are known to be equally responsive in negative affective reactions. This caution is well taken. It is conceivable that a group of males might show equal electrodermal responsivity to male and female nudes because the former might elicit anxiety or surprise while the latter might elicit sexual arousal. From the electrodermal responses alone, there might be no way to differentiate these reactions.

CARDIOVASCULAR CHANGES

Cardiovascular responses during sexual arousal may be divided into two kinds: local vasocongestion in the primary and secondary erogenous zones and more general reactions, such as increased heart rate and blood pressure. The vasocongestion is the cause of tumescence of the penis, and the clitoral glans, increase in diameter of the clitoral shaft, increase in breast size, and other changes occurring in the labia, vagina, and uterus (Masters & Johnson, 1966). The initial sexual excitement is expressed in a dilation of blood vessels carrying blood to the primary erogenous zones of the body, and probably in a vasoconstriction of vessels leading away from these zones. Pronounced tachycardia and elevations in blood pressure are said to be more characteristic of the plateau phase of arousal, reaching a peak in the orgasmic phase of arousal. Masters and Johnson (1966) reported recorded heart rates in males and females averaging from 100 to 175 beats per minute (bpm) during the plateau phase and 110 to 180+ bpm during orgasm. Systolic blood pressure elevations of 20–60 millimeters in the orgasmic phase are reported in the female; and 20–80 millimeters in the plateau phase, and 40–100 millimeters in the orgasmic phase are reported for the male. Masters and Johnson claimed that heart rate and blood pressure elevations in the excitement phase increase "in direct parallel to rising tension," but it is not clear if these reactions would be useful in measuring responses to visual stimuli. Presumably, the authors are referring to increases occurring with genital manipulation.

Masters and Johnson (1966) presented sample electrocardiogram recordings of one male and one female during manipulation, orgasm, and postorgasm resolution. It is apparent that marked increase in heart rate occurs within about half a minute after the start of manipulation and reaches a peak during orgasm. Clearer recordings of rate are presented by Bartlett (1956). This author recorded heart and breathing response in three couples during foreplay, coitus, and orgasm. Each subject signaled intromission, orgasm, and withdrawal by pressing a button. Marked heart rate fluctuation is seen in both sexes during foreplay prior to intromission, but the constant acceleration to orgasm is not apparent until after intromission. Marked hyperventilation also occurs after intromission. Heart rates approaching 170 bpm were recorded during orgasm. A marked parallelism of heart rates of the sexual partners was seen after intromission although orgasms were not simultaneous. A sharp decrease in rates occurred following orgasm. Both the movement and the hyperventilation may account for some of the heart rate increase during coitus. However, Masters and Johnson reported comparable increases following manipulation, which involves much less muscular activity.

Davis and Buchwald (1957) measured volume pulse amplitude from the finger, pulse cycle time, pressure pulse amplitude, bone cardiogram amplitude, finger volume, and chin volume in their study of responses to pictures (described in the previous section on electrodermal measures). Volume pulse, pressure pulse, and pulse time showed reliability for responses to pairs of pictures of similar content. Only volume pulse and pulse time showed a correlation with combined ranks for all pictures (a measure of generality of arousal). Only pressure pulse showed the high arousal to both sexual stimuli found in the GSR variables.

Wenger et al. (1968) used systolic and diastolic blood pressure, heart rate, and finger pulse volume in their study of reactions of visually presented erotic prose (described in prior section). Only systolic and diastolic blood pressure significantly differentiated responses to erotic and control slides. Maximal mean rises of about 4 millimeters of mercury were found for systolic blood pressure, and about 5 millimeters of mercury for diastolic blood pressure. Mean heart rate showed no change in response to erotic or control slides. Finger pulse volume showed a slight biphasic response, first decreasing then increasing; however, the change was not significant. While the mean changes in blood pressure were significant, they were minimal compared to the changes reported by Masters and Johnson during manipulation.

Heart rate changes to visual or auditory input may be biphasic (Lacey, Kagan, Lacey, & Moss, 1963) first showing deceleration, then acceleration in the return to base line. Procedures which use average heart rate may average out significant responses if the biphasic nature of the heart rate is not considered.

Wood and Obrist (1968) used *Playboy* nude pictures as unconditioned stimuli in a conditioning task. A red light was used as a conditioned stimulus which preceded the nudes by 7 seconds. Heart rate was recorded for each second subsequent to the conditioned stimulus and following the unconditioned stimulus, which was presented for 8 seconds. Our main interest is in reinforced trials where the nudes were actually presented. In the first experiment with the nude unconditioned stimuli, no significant trends were found on reinforced trials. In postexperimental reports some subjects reported the nudes to be monotonous or tedious (Hugh Hefner take note!). A second experiment was designed to increase the subjects' motivation to look more carefully at the nudes by offering money as a reward for answering a postexperimental questionnaire regarding pictures. Using this procedure, a significant effect was found on reinforced trials. A deceleration was found in the second prior to the stimulus presentation and during the first second of the unconditioned stimulus presentation.

In the next 3 seconds, an acceleration was seen, followed by another deceleration in the last 3 seconds. The data of these authors suggest that (a) *Playboy* nudes are not very arousing stimuli for North Carolina undergraduate males; (b) even when subjects were motivated to attend to the nudes, the heart rate response is a very brief biphasic one; (c) if one wishes to use heart rate as a measure of sexual response to pictures, heart rate must be recorded beat by beat using a cardiotachometer.

Bernick, Kling, and Borowitz (1971) measured heart rate in nine male subjects during presentation of neutral slides, a heterosexual "stag" film, a homosexual "stag" film, and an Alfred Hitchcock suspense film. Mean heart rates were calculated for the 4-minute slide periods and the 16 minutes of each film. Using the heart rate during the slides as a base line, the mean changes were +7 bpm during the heterosexual film, +6 bpm during the homosexual film, and +4 bpm during the suspense film. The increases were significant for the heterosexual and suspense films but not significant for the homosexual film; none of the differences between films was significant. Subjects reported the percentage of viewing times that they had an erection. Seven of the eight subjects reported more erection during the heterosexual than the homosexual movie. While such self-reports may be of dubious reliability, it is interesting that there was no significant relationship between reports of erection and increases in heart rate, and the correlation was actually negative in the heterosexual film session.

Corman (1968) examined the effect of slides of *Playboy* nudes and an erotic motion picture on eight autonomic variables including heart rate. The subjects were 10 young married men. Reactions were measured in response to a sound stimulus, 50 control slides (Expo '67), 15 *Playboy* nude slides, and an erotic motion picture. The materials were presented in the sequence listed. The motion picture was made for the experiment and portrayed two people making love in bed, without explicit views of genitalia. Soft music was played with the movie. These details of the movie presentation are interesting in view of the positive results obtained. Apparently "hard-core" pornography is not necessary to elicit arousal. The physiological data were examined for the sound stimulus response and at standard points in the slide presentations and during crucial scenes in the motion picture. Heart rate did not increase significantly going from the control slides to the *Playboy* slides. However, the erotic movie significantly increased heart rate by an average of 5 bpm during the most arousing scene. Heart rate was significantly higher during the movie scenes than during the control slides, the nude slides, and the noise stimulus. Both systolic and diastolic blood pressures showed significant increases of about 5 millimeters going from control slides to slides of nudes, and further significant increases of 11 millimeters (systolic) and 6 millimeters (diastolic) going from the nudes to the peak scenes of the movie. The response to the movie was significantly greater than the response to the slides of nudes and the noise stimulus.

Romano (1969) used the same erotic motion picture used by Corman, but Romano's subjects also viewed a concentration camp movie which aroused negative affect. The details of this experiment were described in the prior section on electrodermal measures. As in Corman's experiment, the erotic movie resulted in significant increases in both systolic and diastolic blood pressure. The negative-affect arousing film also resulted in significant increases in blood pressure, and the differences between the films in the blood pressure effects were not significant. The changes in heart rate and heart rate variability produced by either film were not significant, disconfirming the heart rate effects of the erotic movie found by Corman.

Roessler (see Footnote 6) found significantly greater increases in pulse amplitude and heart rate in response to an erotic film than to a control film.

Fisher and Osofsky (1968) in their experiment comparing reactions in a control session and after gynecological exams, found that the latter produced significant heart rate increases. As was mentioned in the GSR section, it is not clear whether this autonomic arousal was produced by anxiety, sexual arousal, or both.

The research using heart rate as a measure of sexual arousal indicates that this measure is not very sensitive to sexual arousal prior to intromission or genital manipulation. Erotic motion pictures may stimulate a small increase in heart rate, but even

these effects are not consistent across experiments. Part of the problem may lie in the biphasic nature of the heart rate response to exteroceptive stimuli, but in the one study where rates were taken every second the amount of acceleration was small and briefly sustained. Even with the highly erotic stimulus of a stag movie, heart rate changes were minimal in most subjects and, where pronounced, were not associated with a more direct measure of arousal, penile erection. Furthermore, heart rate increases were not different in response to sexual and suspense movies.

Of the other cardiovascular variables examined in these experiments, only blood pressure showed any significant response to erotic stimuli. The response to pictures of female nudes or printed erotic passages was not pronounced, amounting to significant changes of a few millimeters of pressure, but larger systolic blood-pressure changes were produced by an erotic motion picture. Blood pressure seems to be one of the few variables that shows a graded reaction, with some response to still pictures of nudes, greater response to erotic motion pictures, and even greater response during coitus and orgasm.

RESPIRATORY CHANGES

Masters and Johnson (1966) stated that hyperventilation is a late plateau phase reaction for both sexes with peaks as high as 40 per minute for both sexes.

Bartlett (1956) measured respiratory rate, minute volume, and tidal volume in couples during coitus. "A simple mouthpiece was valved so that atmospheric air was inhaled, and the expired air was passed through a dry-gas test meter. Respiratory volumes were obtained by reading the volume of expired air at $\frac{1}{2}$-minute intervals. Respiratory rate was recorded on a smoked drum by a tambour which was attached to the exhalation side of the mouth piece to record pressure changes. From a knowledge of the minute volume and rate, the tidal volumes were calculated. The nose was lightly clamped to prevent an error in the measurement of the expired air [p. 469]." One must admire the heroic performance of Bartlett's subjects under these conditions of recording. The results on the three respiratory measures were similar to those for heart rate: (a) fluctuations before intromission but no accelerating trend until after intromission, (b) marked peaks at orgasm with rates of 20 to 70 reached during orgasm, (c) a parallelism of male and female rates. The authors speculated that this extreme hyperventilation at orgasm could account for the partial lapse of consciousness in some persons at this time.

Returning to the more gentle arousal induced by visual stimuli, we find breathing measures considerably less responsive. Davis and Buchwald (1957) measured breathing cycle time (duration of first breathing cycle in the stimulus interval) and maximum breathing amplitude of inspiration or expiration during the stimulus interval. Breathing cycle amplitude was reliable across pairs of pictures of similar content; breathing cycle time was not reliable. One of the sexual stimuli elicited a strong response on both measures, the other did not.

Wenger et al. (1968) found no differences between respiration rates recorded while reading erotic and control passages. Hain and Linton (see Footnote 5) measured depth of respiration and the inhalation rates (time taken for largest depth of respiration divided by the time taken from the complete inhalation–exhalation cycle) in response to pictures of male and female nudes. Neither measure yielded a difference between male and female nudes. The *I*-fraction showed no habituation, but the depth of respiration measure diminished with repeated stimulus presentations. Koegler and Kline (1965) reported that respiration changes were rarely seen in response to erotic or stressful movies. Corman (1968) whose experiment was described in the preceding section, found no significant changes in respiratory rate or variability produced by slides of nudes or an erotic movie. When base-line respiratory measures were compared to the scene designated by each subject as the most subjectively arousing, significant *decreases* in rate and increases in respiratory variance were found. Romano (1969) also found no effects of his erotic film on respiration rate or variability. The only positive result reported for respiration rate was in the study by Roessler (see Footnote 6) who found a greater increase in response to his erotic film than

to his control film. Apparently respiratory measures will not be useful in assessing sexual arousal to visual stimuli.

PENILE ERECTION MEASURES

Masters and Johnson (1966) have summarized what is known about the anatomy and physiology of the penis. Running through the body of the penis are three cylindrical bodies of erectile tissue. Two of these cylinders, the corpora cavernosa, lie parallel to each other, and a third, the corpus spongiosem, runs along the ventral portion of the penis and contains the urethra. Stimulation of the splanchnic nerves dilates the penile arteries, blood flows into arterioles in the corpora cavernosa and fills the sinuses. A center for reflex erection is said to exist in the sacral section of the spinal cord. (In Hohmann's study of the effects of spinal cord lesions, four of five cases with damage in this area were incapable of reflexive erections.) Of course, stimulation of erection may also be directed from higher cortical centers. "Erection is lost when the sympathetic nerve supply causes constriction of the penile arteries [p. 179]." Active constriction of the arterioles allows the trapped blood to escape from the cavernous sinuses through the penile veins. Thus, penile erection is a function of a localized vasodilation stimulated from spinal or higher neural centers. Sympathetic innervation results in a vasoconstriction which may inhibit erection or cause detumescence following erection. This description fits Wenger's theory of the predominance of parasympathetic activity in the initial phase of sexual arousal. However, the apparent sympathetic dominance during the plateau and orgasmic phases leading to ejaculation does not seem to interfere with erection. The relative roles of sympathetic and parasympathetic systems is obviously complex and some local autonomy of autonomic response is apparent. Sensory distractions, such as loud sudden noises, stimulating the central nervous system, may also impair penile erection.

Masters and Johnson have pointed out that penile erection may occur in states other than sexual excitement. One of these states, the rapid eye movement (REM) arousal stage of sleep, is discussed later in this section. However, in the presence of sexual stimulation, penile erection would seem to have some "face validity" as a specific measure of sexual arousal in the male. (It is conceivable that a male may be psychically aroused, but penile erection may be inhibited by anxiety-related sympathetic system reaction. This is one reason why the term "arousal" must be qualified by operational definition.) Several investigators have developed devices for measuring penile erection, and these are discussed in the following paragraphs.

Freund, Sedlacek, and Knob (1965) have described a transducer for mechanical plethysmography of the male genital. The penis is inserted through a flat, soft sponge-rubber ring and an elastic rubber tube, made from a condom, into a glass cylinder. The cylinder tapers down at the end to a narrow funnel which connects by tube with the volumetric instrument. The sponge-rubber ring which acts as a pad for the cylinder is fitted on the penis. The glass cylinder is attached to the body of the subject with straps. The elastic cuff is inflated with air to fill up the broad end of the cylinder to make its base airtight. The supply of air to the cuff is shut off, and the funnel of the cylinder is connected by tube to the volumetric device. Freund et al.'s study provides a diagram of the device and instructions for its construction.

Freund has applied his device to the diagnosis of various sexual deviancies including homosexuality and pedophilia. The technique consists of exposing subjects to pictures of nude males and females in five age categories ranging from children to adults.

Penile volume recordings are made to measure reactions to pictures in each of the categories. In the first study (Freund, 1963) the method was applied using 58 homosexuals and 65 heterosexuals. These groups were further subdivided into those who preferred adults, adolescents, or children as sex objects. Each picture was exposed for 13 seconds with an interval of 19 seconds between pictures. If the tracing of penile volume was still falling or rising, or if it was still some distance from its original level, the presentation of the next stimulus was postponed. Summed reactions in each category of pictures correctly diagnosed 48 of the 58 homosexuals and all 65 of the heterosexuals. Of the 10

misdiagnoses of homosexuals 6 occurred in records where responses to the stimuli were flat, or almost flat. There was also significant agreement among the age preferences in sexual objects and reactions to adult and child figures of the appropriate sexes; that is, subjects who preferred adolescents or children showed greater penile volume responses to younger age figures than to older age figures. A retest of 86 cases showed high consistency of the size of volume changes. A second experiment used a modification of the presentation method by using a paired-picture technique with a short interval between exposures of the two pictures in each pair. This method correctly diagnosed all 31 heterosexual neurotics and all 39 homosexuals. A final experiment was performed to test the effects of simulation. Heterosexuals were asked to simulate homosexuality, and homosexuals were asked to simulate heterosexuality. Of the 42 heterosexuals 5 were able to simulate homosexual responses on two diagnostic criteria, and another 5 simulated response on one of the criteria or showed obvious simulation efforts. Of 24 homosexuals 6 were able to simulate, and 5 others were partially successful.

Freund (1965) applied a new form of his test to the diagnosis of heterosexual pedophilia using 20 heterosexual pedophiliacs and 20 heterosexual controls who were alcoholics. Alcoholics are not a good control group for studies of sexual arousal. The cirrhosis in chronic alcoholics may cause difficulties in the metabolism of estrogen, resulting in high plasma levels and testicular atrophy (Korenman, Perrin, & McCallum).[7] In the new modification of the techniques, 20 male and 30 female pictures are used and divided into three age groupings. Each picture is exposed for 7 seconds, and measurement of volume is taken at the beginning and end of the exposure, and at a third time 7 seconds after the slide is turned off. New slides are not presented until reaction has subsided. Diagnosis is made using proportions of 10 slides of highest response which are either male or female or which fall into the adult or child groups. In all 40 subjects in this experiment, the proportion of female to male pic-

[7]Korenman, S. G., Perrin, L. E., and McCallum, T. Estradiol in human plasma: demonstration of elevated levels in gynemastia and in cirrhosis. Paper presented at the 61st annual meeting of the American Society for Clinical Investigation, Atlantic City, May 1969.

tures stimulating high reaction exceeded 2 to 1. None of 35 homosexual males reached this proportion. When the two groups of this study, pedophiliacs and normal heterosexuals, were compared for age of high-reaction pictures there was little overlap or misdiagnosis. Freund (1965, 1967) has extended his studies to more groups of pedophiliacs and homosexuals with results showing good differentiation of age and sex preferences in sexual objects.

The successful simulation of some of Freund's subjects raises the question of whether penile erection or inhibition of erection can be voluntarily controlled. Laws and Rubin (1969) tested the ability of normal subjects to inhibit erection while watching an erotic film and to produce erection without an external stimulus. Four subjects who developed full penile erections when watching erotic films were able to inhibit erection when instructed to do so. Subjects differed in their ability to inhibit erection, but when erection occurred during "inhibit" instructions it was always of less magnitude and longer latency to peak than in the "no inhibit" conditions. All subjects reported that they inhibited their erections by concentrating on irrelevant, nonsexual mental tasks, for instance, doing multiplication tables. Instructions to produce erections in the absence of stimulation resulted in weak erections of short duration. No subject was able to maintain any level of partial erection for more than a few minutes. Subjects induced erections by concentrating on sexual thoughts. The results of these experiments show that penile erection is under some voluntary control which subjects exert indirectly through their mental activity rather than directly through muscle control. While distraction is very successful in inhibiting erection, fantasy in some subjects does not seem to produce the magnitude of erection in any subject comparable to that produced by visual erotic stimuli. It would be interesting to see how much inhibition or facilitation of erection could be accomplished by feedback of erection information combined with operant reinforcement. The results of such studies might be useful in the treatment of sexual deviates. The efforts in this area have so far used classical conditioning methods.

McConaghy (1967) has also described a simple penile plethysmograph device. The end of a finger stall was cut off, and the cut end was stretched over the open end of a cylindrical tin. A nipple was soldered into the closed end and connected by a plastic tube to a Grass pressure transducer. The penis was inserted through the open end of the finger stall which maintains an airtight connection. The author used movies of singly appearing nudes, 10 males and 10 females, engaged in nonsexual activity. These stimuli were shown at 1-minute intervals and incorporated into a travelogue-type of movie. The subjects consisted of 22 male homosexuals referred for aversion-type behavioral therapy and 11 heterosexual medical students. Of 19 homosexuals 14 showed a greater response to male nudes than to female nudes, and 10 of 11 heterosexuals showed a greater response to female nudes.

Bancroft, Jones, and Pullan (1966) described a simple transducer for measuring penile erection. The device consisted of a strain gauge made of 18 centimeters of silicone rubber tubing filled with mercury and fitted with platinum electrodes. Two transistors were mounted in a brass block. The circuit was powered by two 1.5-volt batteries which were kept outside of the box. (A circuit diagram was provided in the article.) The strain gauge was fitted around the penis and changes in circumference of the penis were registered on a 50 microammeter as changes in current. The initial tension could be standardized by tightening the gauge and setting the reading to zero. The strain gauge could easily be put into position by the subject and worn under normal clothes. The authors reported that movement artifact was not a problem with the subjects comfortably seated. With the gain setting used, a change of 2 microamperes is equivalent to an alteration of .63 millimeters in circumference of the penis. The authors reported an average increase of about 25 millimeters in full erection. A case was described where the device was used to measure changes in arousal during aversive conditioning in behavioral therapy of a pedophiliac. The use of the device in the electric aversion treatment of sexual deviants was described in two articles (Bancroft & Marks, 1968; Marks & Gelder, 1967).

Barlow[8] and his colleagues described a strain

---

[8] D. H. Barlow, personal communication, July 17, 1969.

gauge for measuring penile volume changes. They claimed their device was less cumbersome and restrictive than Freund's. The authors stated that in Bancroft's device the mercury tended to separate at the upper range of volume displacement. They also claimed Bancroft's device was temperature sensitive and somewhat difficult to build and seal. Their own device consisted of a simple rugged strain gauge encompassed in a ring of plastic material. The ring surrounded the penis, but they claimed it did not constrict and caused no discomfort. Changes in the diameter of the ring were recorded on a Grass preamplifier. Recordings from the ring were said to be linear with volume changes within a range of 25–40 millimeters.

The authors reported using the device to measure changes in response to colored slides of nudes. They noted that volume displacement may take as long as 5 minutes to return to base line after stimulation, and it may not return to the previous base line, but may level off at a greater displacement, necessitating a resetting of the base line. Measurements on seven subjects over a period of 18 months yielded stable and reliable individual reactions. Reliable increases of about 1 millimeter may be recorded even though the subject is unaware of the change.

Abel, Levis, and Clancy[9] used a modification of the penile transducer developed by Bancroft et al. (1966) in a preliminary study of the effects of aversive therapy on sexual deviants. Voyeurs, exhibitionists, and transvestites were used as subjects. Subjects made tapes which recorded incidents of their deviant sexual behavior. Shock was used as an unconditioned stimulus to parts of the deviant tapes. Before treatment strong sexual arousal to deviant and nondeviant tapes was measured with the penile transducer. Stronger response was associated with deviant than with nondeviant tapes. One week after the conditioning treatment the responses to the shock-conditioned deviant tape and nonconditioned parts of the deviant tapes were minimal, while the response to the nondeviant tape remained strong. Eight weeks after treatment the

[9] Abel, G. C., Levis, D. J., and Clancy, J. Effects of aversive therapy on sexual deviants. Paper presented at meeting of American Psychiatric Association, May 1969.

responses to the deviant tapes were still minimal while the responses to nondeviant tapes were even stronger.

Other methods of measuring penile erection have been devised by sleep researchers interested in the association between penile erections during sleep and the REM stage of sleep. Fisher, Gross, and Zuch (1965) have experimented with a number of methods of recording penile erection during sleep. Their first attempt consisted of a polyvinyl tube about the size and shape of a doughnut. The tube was filled with water and fitted around the base of the penis. During erection the pressure on the tube resulted in a rise in the water level of a smaller tube attached to it. Apparently the size and bulk of the tube caused stimulation of the penis. Their second attempt involved the use of a small thermistor attached to the penis which recorded the changes in temperature produced by the increased blood flow during erection. This device proved to be too difficult to keep attached to the penis, and valid recordings were obtained in only 2 of 17 cases. The most successful device proved to be a mercury strain gauge developed by Shapiro and Cohen at the Downstate Medical Center. This device consisted of an elastic silicon plastic tube 1 millimeter in diameter which was filled with mercury and sealed at both ends with platinum electrodes to form a loop. The gauge formed one leg on a Wheatstone bridge circuit, and minute variations in resistance were measured as the tube was stretched during erection. The resistance changes were monitored on an Offner Type T electroencephalogram through a dc amplifier. The strain gauge may be calibrated by measuring the amount of deflection on the graphic tracing per unit change and circumference of the gauge as it is moved down on a tapering cone-shaped device graduated in centimeters. The authors stated that the rise in tracing was roughly linear to increase in circumference. Degree of erection for each subject was estimated by having the subject take measurements of the flaccid and erect penis. Using the more sensitive gain, minute increases of fractions of a millimeter were measurable. Using all devices, full or partial erection was found to be associated with 95% of the 86 REM periods studied. A close temporal relationship between REM periods and erections was noted. Increases in circumference of 2 centimeters or more were found to represent full or nearly full erection in most subjects. Partial erections ranged from 2 millimeters to 2 centimeters.

Shapiro and Cohen's strain-gauge device was used in a study of the relation between the erection cycle during sleep and dream anxiety (Karacan, Goodenough, Shapiro, & Starker, 1966). Most, but not all of the REM periods were accompanied by erection, but of these periods which were accompanied by erection, 95% yielded dream reports as opposed to 85% of nonerection REM periods. REM awakening reports with a high anxiety content were less likely to be accompanied by erection.

The techniques of pneumatic plethysmography were discussed by Lader (1967). Until recently these methods have been primarily used with a digit, usually a finger. The application of this method to the penis, as in the methods of Freund and McConaghy, may create certain kinds of problems. Since the penis is quite sensitive to stimulation, the stimulation from the device itself could result in an initial arousal reaction. Asking subjects to insert their penises in such devices might cause some anxiety in subjects. Shapiro and Cohen's and Bancroft's strain-gauge devices would seem to be preferable since they are simpler to apply and do not stimulate as large an area of the penis. Furthermore, calibration is simpler with a near linear relationship between circumference and change in current. Freund and McConaghy seem to rely on relative measures of penile volume rather than measures on a known scale. Freund has indicated some problem with movement artifacts which he says are detectable as rapid oscillations. The strain-gauge method is probably less vulnerable to such movement artifact which makes it the device of choice in sleep studies where the subject would be turning considerably during the night. However, despite the drawbacks of the pneumatic plethysmographic devices, they have proven to be highly reliable and discriminating in studies of sexual arousal, more so than any other physiological method discussed in prior sections. Measures of penile erection will probably be the methods of choice in future studies of sexual arousal in the male. Is there a similar specific measure of arousal available for the female? Here is an area where the methodology is currently evolving and mostly unpublished. The work on this area is described in a later section.

SCROTUM AND TESTES

Masters and Johnson (1966) have noted changes in the scrotum and testes during sexual arousal. During the excitement phase there is a tensing and thickening of scrotal integument, an effect of localized vasocongestion, and contraction of the smooth-muscle fibres of the dartos layer. There is an elevation of both testes toward the perineum, accomplished by shortening of the spermatic cords. The constricted scrotal sac provides secondary support to the reaction of testicular elevation. The testicular elevation progresses during the plateau phase until preejaculatory positioning where the testes are in apposition with the male perineum. Masters and Johnson stated that this elevation of the testes is essential to ejaculation.

> If the testes do not undergo at least partial elevation the human male will not experience a full ejaculatory sequence . . . When the testes do rise to a position of close apposition to the male perineum, an orgasmic phase is certain to follow if effective sexual stimulation is maintained. Full testicular elevation is pathognomic of impending ejaculation [p. 208].

Another arousal phenomenon is an increase of testicular size (about 50%) also attributed to the vasocongestive reaction.

Bell and Stroebel[10] have attempted to record the scrotal and testicular reactions. In addition to the penile strain-gauge developed by Shapiro and Cohen (see prior section) they have used a scrotal strain-gauge placed around the neck of the scrotum. Muscle activity was measured in the cremaster and dartos muscles using Beckman electrodes placed slightly below the lower inguinal ring and right and left about two-thirds of the way toward the bottom of the sac. Palmar GSR and cardiac rate were recorded along with the scrotal reactions. The authors have studied responses to emotionally

---

[10] A. I. Bell and C. F. Stroebel, personal communication, May 20, 1969.

charged interviews. They have theorized that the testicular elevation may occur in states of stress, as well as in sexual arousal. If this is true, then testicular elevation would not be useful as a specific indicator of sexual arousal. The authors are still in the data-collection phase, but they have reported the following in a personal communication:

> So far, some scrotal retraction highly correlated with GSR has been observed. Analysis of the data is still incomplete. There is a suggestion of localized dartos activity preceding retraction and GSR. There is a suggestion of dartos rhythm between one and three seconds of each cycle. It tended to be pronounced at the beginning of recording sessions; however it gradually disappeared. We are not sure yet whether it is an artifact or real activity. We have seen it in two-thirds of the subjects. We find one to three seconds per fluctuation; amplitude decreases as session proceeds [see Footnote 10].

Further results on this new psychophysiological method should be of great interest to investigators interested in sexual arousal. The fact that the authors found responses during emotionally charged interviews suggests that this measure may be a generalized stress indicator rather than a specific measure of sexual arousal.

VAGINAL BLOOD FLOW

Masters and Johnson (1966) have found that the first physiological evidence of the human female's response to any form of sexual stimulation is the production of vaginal lubrication. They suggested that this "sweating" phenomenon is not glandular but is the result of marked dilation of the venous plexus which encircles the entire vaginal barrel. "Apparently the transudation-like material which lubricates the vagina develops from the activation of a massive localized vasocongestive reaction [p. 70]." It is notable that the transudate appears even in artificial vaginas, which are sections of bowel transplanted with blood vessels intact to the vagina site. These vaginas have no connection with the cervix.

As sexual excitement progresses there is a lengthening and distention of the inner two-thirds of the vaginal barrel and an alteration of the color of the vaginal wall from a normal purplish-blue to the darker purplish hue of vasocongestion. The

labia majora and labia minora also show color and size signs of vasocongestion and a separation as if in involuntary preparation for penetration. The initial reaction of the clitoris during arousal is tumescence, with a vasocongestive increase in the diameter of the clitoral shaft and an increase in diameter and length of the shaft. During the plateau phase there is a withdrawal of the clitoral body and a retraction against the anterior body of the symphysis.

Shapiro, Cohen, DiBianco, and Rosen (1968) have asked whether the association between penile erection and REM periods in the male might have a parallel in the female vaginal responses. They first attempted to measure secretions from the vaginal wall. They used a platinum electrode held in a tampon saturated with hypotonic saline. A reference electrode was located on the pubic symphysis. An attempt was made to measure production of lactic acid in the vagina by measuring pH. Intravaginal temperature was also measured. These procedures have not produced reliable data because of movement and position artifact, and because the measurable responses were not large enough to be differentiated from the basal levels involved. For some subjects the process of attaching or inserting electrodes proved to be erotically stimulating so that arousal was present before measurement was started.

In order to induce arousal the authors selected female subjects who could sexually arouse themselves through fantasy. The subjects indicated when they were "turned on" or "turned off" by pressing a button which marked the record. At times the reading of erotic materials was used as a stimulant.

The last, and to date, most successful of the methods was a thermal flowmeter designed to measure changes of blood flow in the vaginal wall. A vaginal diaphragm with the center cut out was used to hold the measuring instrument in place. Subjects were fitted with the proper size diaphragm and inserted the diaphragm themselves. This ingenious method solved the problem of holding a sensor in place and reduced the problems of stimulation and movement artifact. Two thermistors mounted in a plastic holder about 1 centimeter apart were attached to the outside of the ring and held against the vaginal mucosa by the diaphragm. The matched thermistors were operated in a low current dc bridge in such a way that ambient temperature changes did not affect the bridge output. One of the thermistors was heated a few degrees above body temperature by square wave pulses to a heating element inbedded in its glass envelope. After initially establishing a heating level and rebalancing the bridge to zero output, an electronic negative feedback loop was closed which then varied the external heating to the thermistor, maintaining the null output condition. Since changes in blood flow alter the thermal conductivity of the tissue in contact with the heated thermistor, monitoring the power (heating) supplied to this thermistor yielded an indication of relative blood flow changes in the underlying tissue system.

The results obtained from a small number of subjects seem to indicate that the vaginal blood flow technique is sensitive to reported changes in sexual arousal. At present it is not certain how generalizable these results are, and work is going on at the Downstate Medical Center to perfect the technique. The use of the diaphragm ring to hold electrodes has led to a reexamination of the other techniques, vaginal pH and conductance measurements, which were given up in part because of the problems of holding electrodes in place.

Tart[11] has invented a device to measure blood flow in the clitoris: a "clitoroplethysmograph." The device was attached to a vaginal stabilizing rod which fits into the vagina. The device was mounted surrounding the clitoral tissue mass. A photocell recorded blood volume changes in the clitoris. Provision was also made for a photocell in the stabilizing rod, to measure vaginal blood flow, and silver cloth electrodes for impedance plethysmography voltage or resistance measurement.

A modification of Tart's device using only the photoelectric cell for the vagina has been developed by Fisher and Davis[12] at Mount Sinai Hospital. A photocell was used to record fluctuations in light transmission through tissue. The light reflected back to the photocell from the vaginal capillary bed was measured. A solid state light source was used instead of incandescent bulbs which generate heat.

[11] C. T. Tart, personal communication, April 29, 1969.
[12] D. M. Davis, personal communication, June 30, 1969.

The light source emitted light in the red spectrum without heat. The complete device also included a thermistor to measure temperature changes and a strain gauge to indicate intravaginal movements. Silicone rubber was used as a platform for the plethysmograph components in order to make the device comfortable for the subject and sterilizable. Fisher and Davis investigated changes in vaginal blood flow during sleep. The investigators expected to find a progressive increase in pulse volume during REM periods on the assumption that the vasocongestion seen in sexual arousal would characterize REM periods in females. They found marked fluctuations in REM periods rather than progressive changes, but these fluctuations were also found in a peripheral site, the toe. The implication is that the fluctuations in pulse volume were expressions of the general cardiovascular changes seen during REM periods.

UTERINE CONTRACTIONS

Masters and Johnson (1966) stated that as excitement-phase levels of sexual tension progress toward the plateau, the entire uterus is elevated from its position in contact with the posterior vaginal floor to a posterior and superior plane in the false pelvis. Full elevation is not achieved until the plateau phase. Corpus irritability increases from early in excitement and resolves into an identifiable contraction pattern that has specific orgasmic-phase orientation.

A study by Bardwick and Behrman (1967) suggests that uterine contractions might have some significance for sexual arousal early in the excitement phase. They used 10 paid volunteers as subjects. On the basis of psychological tests the subjects were divided into one group of subjects who were sexually anxious, passive, and neurotic, and another group who were not high on these traits. The subjects were studied at various points in their menstrual cycles. Sexual stimuli used included erotic passages from books, double entendre words, and cartoons from *Playboy*. The device used to measure uterine contractions consisted of a thick-walled polyethylene tube connected to the tip of a rubber balloon which was inserted through the cervix into the uterus and filled with water. The pressure on the water was standardized to atmospheric pressure through a transducer and led into a Sanborn Type R recorder. A half hour was allowed for stabilization before stimuli were presented. Measures included amplitude, tonus (tonus as defined appears to be interchangeable with amplitude) contraction duration, and number of contractions. Menstrual cycle phase seemed to affect the duration of the contractions more than the amplitude or tonus. Psychological stimulation seemed to affect the amplitude and tonus, but not the duration of contractions. The authors stated:

> The present data indicate that the uterus, *at any cycle phase* will respond to anxiety and sexual stimulation with an increased mean amplitude and amplitude variance . . . When the *S* [subject] data were pooled, there were no consistent differences in uterine motility between sessions in which the psychological stimuli had sexual content and those in which the content was neutral. When the *S*s were divided into those who were highly sexually anxious, we found that the sexually anxious *S*s reacted more strongly to the sexually relevant stimuli [p. 476].

Highly anxious women tended to extrude the intrauterine balloon while low-anxious subjects merely had uterine spasms without balloon extrusion. Balloon extrusion in high-anxious subjects occurred particularly when sexual material was being presented.

The data from the experiment suggest that uterine contractions are a joint function of sexual arousal and anxiety. From the Bardwick and Behrman article it is not clear if sexual arousal and anxiety reaction could be distinguished using this technique. Insertion of a balloon in the cervix is quite painful for many women which would limit the usefulness of this technique.

TEMPERATURE

Masters and Johnson (1966) have noted the "sex flush" that develops in response to sexual stimulation. In the female the flush appears late in the excitement phase, first over the epigastrium, then spreading rapidly over the breasts. In the plateau phase the flush is said to have a widespread distribution. Males show no evidence of the flush in the excitement phase, but in some it appears over the

epigastrium in the plateau phase and spreads to the anterior wall, near neck, face, and forehead. The sex flush is not universal, appearing in 75% of females and only 25% of males. However the phenomenon suggests that skin temperature measurements might have some usefulness as measures of sexual arousal. Masters stated that skin temperature changes are unreliable as measures of arousal, not being constant within subjects on different occasions.[13]

Wenger, Averill, and Smith (1968) measured face and finger temperatures in their study of autonomic responses to erotic literary passages. Finger temperature showed a significant decrease during the reading of erotic materials; face temperature did not yield significant differences between erotic and control materials.

Corman (1968) found similar results on temperature measures. Face temperature was not significantly affected by either slides of nudes or the erotic motion picture. Finger temperature showed a significant decrease in response to the motion picture, but no significant change in response to the *Playboy* nudes. Romano (1969) did not find significant effects of the same erotic movie on finger, face, or chest temperatures.

Fisher et al. (1965) attempted to measure penis and groin temperature during REM phases of sleep. There was considerable difficulty in keeping thermistors attached to the penis. An interesting finding of an inverse relationship between penis and groin temperatures (groin temperatures tend to fall when penile temperatures rise and vice versa) suggests that blood is withdrawn from adjacent areas to fill the penis during erections.

Shapiro et al. (1968) have used a thermal flowmeter as an index of vaginal blood flow. Their technique was described in a prior section.

Fisher and Osofsky (1968) measured head and leg temperatures of females during control sessions and after gynecological examinations. Rectal and vaginal temperatures were measured only after the genital stimulation of the examinations. As was mentioned previously, there is no reason to believe that the gynecological examinations were sexually arousing, although they did affect GSR, skin resist-

---

[13]W. Masters, personal communication, May 1969.

ance, and heart rate. No changes were found in head and leg temperatures. Rectal and vaginal temperatures after the examination were almost identical. Vaginal temperature correlated significantly with GSR frequency, heart rate, and rectal temperature.

Although not enough data are available on skin temperature as a measure of sexual arousal in the excitement phase, it would appear that such measurement would be valuable only on or in the genitals. The vasocongestive response during erection appears to involve some diversions of blood from surrounding tissues and a drop in skin temperature might be recorded from these tissues or even in more peripheral areas such as the finger. Care must be taken during temperature measurement to keep the ambient room temperature and humidity constant since skin temperature changes are liable to be small.

PUPILLARY RESPONSE

Studies by Hess and Polt (1960) and Hess, Seltzer, and Shlien (1965) have stimulated research in the use of pupillography as a method of measuring sexual arousal or interest. Hess (1968) has reviewed some of this work. The anatomy and physiology of the pupil are described in a chapter by Lowenstein and Loewenfeld (1962). The main function of the iris is to regulate the amount of light entering the eye, to increase depth of focus of the eye, and to reduce chromatic and spherical aberrations especially in bright light. The size of the pupil is controlled by sphincter pupillae and the dilator pupillae. The pupillary sphincter is an annular band of smooth muscle which encircles the pupil. It is activated by parasympathetic fibres and can constrict from 8 millimeters (dark) to 2 millimeters (light) in seconds. The dilator pupillae are radial strands of smooth muscle which converge upon the pupil "similar to wheel spokes." These muscles are controlled by sympathetic fibres. The size of the pupil is a function of spontaneous or reactive shifts of the dynamic equilibrium of sympathetic and parasympathetic innervation. Specific reflexes are imposed on this equilibrium. Increase of light, and convergence of the eyes and accommodation of the lens when viewing a near object, cause contraction

of the pupil. Decrease in illumination and sensory or emotional stimuli result in dilation. Dilation is the result of two neural effects: (a) sympathetic discharges which reach the dilator pupillae and cause it to contract and (b) inhibitory impulses which cause the sphincter pupillae to relax.

The reciprocal innervations of the iris by the sympathetic and parasympathetic systems make it an organ of some interest to psychophysiologists. However, the great sensitivity of the organ to changes in illumination has resulted in methodological problems which have not always been sufficiently recognized. This is particularly true when complex visual stimuli are used to stimulate emotional changes. Woodmansee (1966) has pointed out the methodological problems in the use of pupillography to measure psychophysiological reactions. He noted that controlling the overall illuminance of visual displays is not sufficient because the pupil may contract 1% to 5% in size when the gaze shifts from a relatively dark to a relatively brighter area of a test stimulus. Since the reactions to emotionally arousing stimuli rarely exceed 5%, they might easily be accounted for by a subject's shift of fixation. Pupillary responses are similar to GSR in the marked "arousal decrement effect" or habituation. In experiments where several control and test stimuli are presented, the major responses are to the first stimuli, and the differences between test and control stimuli may become smaller as the subject becomes less interested in the experiment. The near vision reflex can also account for shifts in pupillary size. If the subject focuses on test stimuli but allows his vision to blur on control stimuli, by fixating behind the plane of projection, constriction may occur on the control stimuli and dilation when he fixates the test stimuli. Finally, the author stated that the high variability of spontaneous pupillary activity (1% to 20%) can produce considerable "noise" in an experiment. The test-retest reliability of pupil size is said to be only about .30. However, the reliability of response to a constant stimulus may be greater. Bender (1933) found marked consistency of individual reactions in a day-to-day response to a standard light stimulus. Woodmansee has suggested various ways of reducing these extra-experimental influences, and these are discussed later after examination of the experiments which have used pupillography to measure responses to sexual stimuli.

Hess and Polt (1960) presented "pilot" data on two females and four males. Parenthetically, it is amazing how the labeling of an experiment as "pilot" has so little effect in inhibiting the tendency to play up the results. Generalizations about pupillographic sex differences based on these two females and four males have been widely promulgated despite the fact that the author has not yet published an extended study based on an adequate number of subjects.[14] The stimuli in this experiment were pictures of a baby, a mother and baby, a nude male, a nude female, and a landscape. The female subjects showed more dilation than males to the baby, mother and baby, and nude male pictures; the males dilated more in response to the nude female. The authors concluded "men are more interested in partially nude women, women are more interested in partially nude men [p. 132]." While there might be some truth in this conclusion, the data presented are hardly sufficient to make such a sweeping generalization.

Another "pilot study" by Hess and his co-workers (Hess et al., 1965) compared the responses of five known homosexual and five heterosexual males to 15 slides including 5 nude males, 5 nude females, and 5 art slides. The authors made an index of the relative responses to male and female stimuli. All five heterosexuals had a positive index, showing relatively greater pupil dilation to females than to males; four of the five homosexuals had a negative index, indicating greater dilation to nude males. The author's theory claims that dilation is an expression of positive arousal, and contraction is an indication of negative arousal. It is interesting, in view of this theory, that two of the five heterosexuals actually dilated to male stimuli, and only four of the five heterosexuals actually dilated to female stimuli. Also, while four of the five homosexuals dilated to male stimuli, three of the five also dilated to female stimuli.

The assumption that contraction indicates negative arousal is questionable. There is little indication

that anything but light or other visual reflexes can cause constriction. Bender (1933) studied the effect of loud noise (gunshot), pin-pricks, electric shocks, and the negative stimulus of a white rat presented just preceding or simultaneous with the exposure to light. All of the emotional stimuli resulted in inhibition of the normal contraction to light, with longer latencies, more extensive responses, and a longer time for the pupil to reach maximum contraction. While painful stimuli cause some oscillation of response, the dominant response in most subjects to most stimuli was a "dilatory" contraction. In no case did a stimulus do more than slightly delay the powerful contraction response to light. This maximal response is reached rather quickly without other stimulation: 3.5 seconds in four subjects and 3.0 seconds in two subjects. Emotional stimuli merely extend the duration of response a few seconds. It is easy to see how differences in illumination of stimuli presented could mislead investigators to assume they are measuring differences in emotional reactions. Hess claimed that illumination differences would affect all subjects similarly, but, as Woodmansee (1966) pointed out, shifts in fixation within each stimulus might vary from subject to subject.

Hess (1968) has gone so far as to suggest that "pupil response can serve as a more accurate representation of an attitude than can responses to well-drawn questionnaires or to projective techniques . . . [p. 580]." The following studies suggest that this claim may be premature. Seven experiments have been published which provide data relevant to Hess's hypotheses: three of these used male subjects only, while four of them compared responses of males and females.

Sims (1967) investigated the responses of 12 pairs of married subjects to clothed pictures of men and women. There were two pictures of each sex: one in which the pupils of the picture subject were retouched to appear dilated, and the other in which the pupils appeared constricted. The pupils of the subjects dilated significantly more in response to opposite-sex pictures than to same-sex pictures. Furthermore, the subjects showed greater response to pictures of the opposite sex with dilated pupils than to pictures of persons with constricted pupils. The opposite was true for same-sex pictures. While

---

[14] In a personal communication (July 17, 1969) Hess stated that the Hess and Polt (1960) study has been "consistently replicated" "with a few thousand subjects." In a second communication (August 5, 1969) Hess said that he has "personally run several hundred subjects" and found similar results.

the author did not use nude pictures, the results tend to substantiate the Hess hypothesis of greater pupil dilation to pictures of the opposite sex. The results due to the portrayal of the pupils in the pictures tended to indicate that the dilated pupil in the opposite sex is an arousal stimulus. A paper by Hicks, Reaney, and Hill (1967) tends to support the latter finding although preferences were expressed verbally, and pupil measurements were not made in this study.

Scott, Wells, Wood, and Morgan (1967) used four pictures in each of four categories: clothed males, clothed females, female nudes (from *Playboy*), and seminude males (from *Muscleboy*). Gray rectangles were used as control stimuli; these were trimmed so they reflected the same amount of light as the pictures. The pupillary responses of 10 male and 10 female undergraduates were compared. No significant effects were found attributable to sex of subject, sex of pictures, nudity of pictures, or any of the interactions of these variables. Four of 10 males dilated more to male seminude pictures than to female seminudes; 3 of 10 females dilated more to the female than to the male pictures. These data clearly provide no support for Hess's hypothesis of male–female differences. The second experiment tested the responses of five homosexual and five heterosexual males to these stimuli. Two of the five subjects in each group dilated more in response to male pictures than to female pictures. The difference between groups was not significant. A third experiment examined the responses of independent groups of 10 males and 10 females to (a) a pistol shot, (b) seminude male pictures, (c) seminude female pictures. Again, no significant sex differences in response to the different stimuli were found. Males actually showed more dilation in response to male pictures than to female pictures.

Peavler and McLaughlin (1967) examined the responses of four male and four female college students to various stimuli, one of which was a female nude "pin-up." Control stimuli were blank slides made darker than the darkest points on the test stimuli. The mean response to the nude was 2.2% dilation while all other stimuli produced constriction, as would be expected from the brightness differences between the test and control stimuli. No mention was made of sex differences. In the

second experiment, words rated on a "good–bad" continuum were presented as visual stimuli. No relationship was found between pupil diameter and rated evaluations of the words, casting some doubt in Hess's hypothesis of direction of arousal and dilation-contraction of the pupil.

Lawless[15] used 14 airmen and 7 female nurses as subjects. The stimuli were photographs and paintings and included male and female nudes and clothed figures. There were no significant differences in the relative male–female response (Hess's index) of male and female subjects to male and female stimuli. Male subjects actually showed significantly more dilation to male pictures than to female pictures, and reacted faster with a shorter latency to male pictures. Both groups reacted faster to nude figures than to clothed figures.

Nunnally, Knott, Duchnowski, and Parker (1967) examined the responses of 30 male students to a series of four slides showing a girl getting undressed. In the first picture the girl was clothed, and in the last three pictures she was in various stages of undress. Control slides were numbers on a gray background and were constructed darker than the test slides, setting a bias against finding greater dilation to the test stimuli. A significant increase of 7% dilation change was found going from the clothed-girl slide to the first stage of undress. Further progressions in the strip-tease produced no increase in dilation. All test slides taken together produced significantly more dilation than control slides. Another experiment showed that dilation was produced by novel as opposed to nonnovel stimuli, particularly on the first presentation of a novel stimulus. Positive affect pictures (faces of pretty girls) produced more dilation than neutral or negative affect pictures (faces with cancerous growths), but negative affect did not produce constriction as postulated by Hess. Dilation was also produced by muscle strain, auditory stimuli, and expectancy of gunshot. The results show that pupillary dilation may be produced by many kinds of arousal, one of which is the pleasant reactions of males to semiclothed or pretty girls.

Bernick et al. (1971) measured pupil re-

---

[15]Lawless, J. C. Sex differences in pupillary response to visual stimuli. Paper presented at the meeting of Society for Psychophysiological Research, Washington, D.C., October 1968.

sponses of nine male medical students to slides of clothed males and females and to three movies: a heterosexual stag movie, a homosexual stag movie, and a suspense movie. Brightness and contrast variations within each subject were said to be effectively eliminated by the illumination of the rear projection screen to a constant minimum brightness level. The brightest and darkest area were limited to a range of 24–26 footcandles. There were no significant differences in pupillary response to male and female slides. All of the movies produced more pupillary dilation than the slides. Significant differences were found between movies, with less dilation to the suspense movie than to the sexual films. Significant correlations were found between self-reported erection durations to sexual films and pupillary dilation. It should be noted that the design of the experiment confounded novelty (the heterosexual film was presented on the first occasion for all subjects) and the stimuli. The lack of differences on male and female slides, and between heterosexual and homosexual films does not support Hess's hypothesis (assuming that the subjects were not bisexual).

The final study by Chapman, Chapman, and Brelje (1969) points up a variable that is too often ignored in these experiments: examiner influence. The subjects were 51 male undergraduates. The stimuli were slides of nude, seminude, and clothed men and women, plus control slides of numbers and landscapes. Two experimenters were used: one a serious-looking older graduate student who dressed and behaved in a formal manner; the other a younger undergraduate who dressed informally and conducted the experiment in a "breezy" manner. The formal experimenter elicited greater dilation to female than to male slides in 14 out of 22 subjects; the informal examiner elicited greater pupillary dilation in 20 out of 25 subjects. The difference between stimuli was significant in the case of the informal examiner and was not significant for the subjects of the formal examiner. However, for both examiners the primary direction of response to the male stimuli, as well as to the female stimuli, was dilation, with 44 of 47 male subjects showing dilation to male pictures. The authors pointed out that if the examiners had been working in different laboratories one would have

reported positive results and the other negative results, concerning the differential response of males to female stimuli. The question raised by this experiment (assuming that the experimenter difference was real and generalizable) is, How does a subject voluntarily inhibit pupillary response? The pupillary response is considered to be involuntary. Perhaps the lack of response to pinups with a formal experimenter is due to a general inhibition of sympathetic activity through inhibition of fantasy response to the stimuli. The study bears replication with additional data on subjective responses to the stimuli.

Simpson[16] and his co-workers examined the pupillary constriction response and the delay of ejaculation time in response to antidepressive drugs. They found some suggestion of negative correlation between these variables: as the ability of the pupil to constrict lessens, the ejaculation time tends to increase.

In the experiments most relevant to Hess's hypotheses, those using male and female subjects, or heterosexual and homosexual subjects, only the study by Sims (1967) confirmed Hess's findings. From all of these studies, it would seem that pupillographic measures like other peripheral autonomic measures, such as GSR, are sensitive to the arousal produced by pictures of nudes or movies of sexual activity, but do not reflect the differential interest patterns of males and females in male and female figures. Furthermore, there is no support of Hess's hypothesis that dilation reflects positive interest and contraction negative interest. Rather, the magnitude of dilation seems to reflect sympathetic arousal value of novel, intense, or interesting stimuli. However, Hess (1968) has stated that "all of our subsequent research, involving a large number of subjects has more than confirmed these initial findings [p. 575]." Hess should collate and publish these findings to resolve the doubts raised by the published research of others. The results of the third study of Scott et al. (1967) suggest that GSR may be more sensitive to stimulus differences than pupil response. If this is true, one should consider the relative expense and methodological problems

---

[16] Unpublished study by G. M. Simpson, P. Harper, & E. Beckles entitled "The Effects of Three Antidepressant Drugs on Pupil Response to Light and Ejaculation Time," 1969.

in the two methods. Neither seems to yield responses which discriminate between different types of stimuli, and both show response to novelty and rapid habituation. However, GSR is cheaper and there are fewer methodological problems in the use of visual stimuli. Hess (1968) suggested that GSR might profitably be used to supplement pupillographic measurement. It should be pointed out that some of the problems with pupillography could be surmounted if auditory stimuli were used instead of complex visual stimuli, if lengthy trials were avoided, if the response were corrected for basal changes during the series, and if the reliability of responses to specific categories of stimuli were checked. The one hopeful note in the possibility of pupillographic response as a measure of sexual arousal is in the high correlations with reported erection in the Bernick et al. (1971) experiment. But these correlations were based on a sample of nine cases, and erections were not actually measured or observed. These correlations certainly need replication with an adequate number of cases, and one of the objective penile erection measures mentioned in the previous section on this method.

EVOKED CORTICAL RESPONSE

Lifshitz (1966) has studied the effect of various kinds of pictorial stimuli on the average evoked cortical response. Among other stimuli he used bland, scenic photographs, a "negative affective" series of photographs of ulcerated legs, and a "positive affective" series of "art studies" of nude females. The subjects were 10 young males. Slides were projected in focused or defocused presentations. It was possible to distinguish the focused or defocused presentations from the form of the average evoked cortical response, but the author could not tell which set of slides was being viewed from the average evoked cortical response.

> However in any particular individual the form differences between the AERs [average evoked cortical responses] for the different subject slide groups tended to be consistent and in the four individuals who were subjected to repeated runs of the different slide groups it was possible, once their "code" was known, to tell from the AER which slide group they were looking at [p. 61].

This is an interesting example of individual response specificity within a recording technique. However, the technique would not be useful in studying sexual arousal unless responses to other kinds of stimuli were studied within each individual subject.

BIOCHEMICAL DETERMINATIONS

As was mentioned in the introductory section on hormones, the author has failed to find any studies of the effects of sexual arousal on sex hormones in the human. In fact only two studies have been found on the effects of sexual arousal on any hormone. This is a neglected area of research. It is possible that the sex hormones influence arousability but are unaffected by arousal or sexual activity. But it would seem biologically feasible that sexual arousal would stimulate the production of luteinizing hormone from the pituitary which in turn might stimulate the release of testosterone from the gonads in the male. Seventeen ketosteroids, a metabolite of testosterone in women, could also be an indicator of sexual arousal.

Levi (1967) has studied the catecholamine excretion of subjects in response to many different kinds of stress or positive arousal. One of these studies concerns reactions to visual sexual stimulation (Levi, 1967, 1969). An experiment examined the effect of high quality "love films" which depicted sensual love scenes without showing human sexual organs. These scenes were shown to 15 female office clerks. Urinary adrenaline and noradrenaline were measured after a control period prior to watching the films, after the film period, and after a second control period following the film. The self-reported reactions were moderate and pleasant; the adrenaline and noradrenaline reactions were minimal or absent.

Levi then examined the effects of a more blatantly erotic movie, confiscated by the Swedish legal authorities and presented to the author for research purposes. The movie was shown to 53 females and 50 males, physiotherapy and medical students. Urine samples were collected for three 90-minute periods: one prior to the film, one during the film, and one 90 minutes after the film. The first and third samples were used to provide a base line for measurement of cathecholamine reactions to the film. Both males and females showed a significant increase in adrenaline, but the increase in the male was significantly greater than that in the female. Both sexes also demonstrated a significant increase in noradrenaline, but the difference in the magnitude of increase was not significant. Both sexes also had a significant increase in urine volume and a decrease in specific gravity of urine during the film. There were no significant changes in creatinine.

Subjects also rated their subjective reactions. Both sexes reported an increase in sexual arousal during the film, but the increase was significantly greater in males as were reports of pleasurable sensations. Both groups also reported increases in unpleasant sensations and general emotional arousal, but whereas in the males unpleasant sensations were minor compared to pleasurable sensations, in females the two kinds of sensations were about equal in intensity. Anxiety reactions and emotional upset showed small increases in both sexes. In the female group, low but significant correlations were found between self-ratings of sexual arousal and adrenaline and noradrenaline increases. Correlations with other affects were not reported. In males these correlations were minimal and nonsignificant. There were no significant differences between sexually experienced and nonexperienced females in adrenaline increase.

The authors interpret the adrenaline and sexual arousal self-rating data as supporting Kinsey's (1953) hypothesis that men are more responsive to visual sexual stimulation than are females. It should be noted that significant increases in cathecholamines were also found in response to movies portraying violence, sadism, cruelty, and even comedy. The cathecholamine response to sexual stimulation is no more specific to sex than is sympathetic system arousal.

Bernick et al. (1971) measured plasma 17-hydroxycorticoids (17 OHCS) in eight male subjects who watched a heterosexual stag movie, a homosexual stag movie, and a suspense movie on three different occasions. Blood samples were drawn before the movies, 10 minutes after the movies, and 1 hour after the movies. The changes in 17-OHCS

levels from the first to the second sample were small and insignificant, and there were no significant differences between reactions to the three movies. The lack of adrenocortical reaction to the erotic movies in this experiment is interesting in view of the marked adrenomedullary response in the Levi experiment. However Levi used urine samples from the entire period of stimulation to measure cathecholamines whereas Bernick et al. (1971) drew their second blood sample after a 10-minute postmovie interview. Plasma levels of hydrocortisone can change rapidly and the postmovie level may just as well have reflected responses to the interviews as well as responses to the movie.

Clark and Treichler (1950) first suggested that urinary acid phosphatase (AP) may be an indication of sexual arousal in males; and Gustafson, Winokur, and Reichlin (1963) assessed AP and plasma nonesterified fatty acids (NEFA) as possible indicators of sexual arousal in men and women. AP in men may come from prostatic secretions and therefore might be influenced by sexual arousal. Stimulation of the prostate gland causes AP to be secreted into the urethera. The subjects consisted of 17 men and 7 women. Three homosexual men were also tested. The stimulus was an 11-minute film portraying heterosexual relations. AP was determined from urine, and NEFA from blood samples taken before and after the film. Following the film there was a significant mean increase in urinary AP in men of 72% and a nonsignificant mean increase in women of 11%. Three of the five men who did not show the increase had higher initial levels than the other men, which may have limited their change (Law of Initial Values). Only one of the three homosexuals showed an increase in AP. Serum NEFA was tested in eight of the men, and only five of the eight had increased levels after the film. All subjects reported being sexually aroused. Eleven more male subjects were exposed to the film with concomitant electric shocks. Only 29% of this group had an increase in AP as opposed to 72% in the other heterosexual male group. The authors speculated that an emotionally induced cholinergic discharge over the nervi erigens stimulates secretion of epithelial cells of the prostatic acini and that the AP found in urine came from the prostatic secretion.

The sex differences and differences between heterosexuals and homosexuals in this experiment are interesting, but like so many other experiments in this field the generality of findings is limited by the low sample number, inadequate matching of samples, and lack of comparisons with other types of stimulation.

Barclay has used the AP measure in three studies attempting to validate various forms of projective techniques. In the first study, (Barclay, 1969) an attempt was made to arouse anger in college students in order to demonstrate a connection between aggression and sexual arousal.[17] The subjects were fraternity men and sorority women, and anger was induced by an experimenter insulting the quality of students in these organizations. Urine samples were collected before the anger arousal and after TAT stories were written following the anger arousal. Males subjected to the anger arousal procedure showed more aggression in questionnaires and TAT stories than control males. Aroused males also had more sexual content on appropriate pictures and secreted more AP in urine than nonaroused males.

In Barclay's second study (1970) an attempt was made to test the response of urinary AP to more direct sexual stimulation. Fifty-five male subjects were assigned to one of three conditions: arousal with information, arousal with false information, and control. Subjects in the arousal conditions were shown pictures of nude females taken from nudist magazines; control subjects were shown pictures of buildings. The arousal with information group was told the purpose of the sexual stimulation, while the other arousal group was given false information in which the sexual arousal procedure was construed as irrelevant to the urine collection. The author hypothesized that subjects who know their physiological sexuality is being assessed may become defensive and this may actually reduce their AP measured arousal. The differences between the three groups on AP was not significant. However, subjects differed in their reported arousal by the pictures. Subjects who rated the pictures as more sexually arousing showed significantly more increase on AP than controls, while subjects who found few of the pictures arousing did not differ from controls. Unlike Gustafson et al. (1963) who found no relation between self-reported arousal and AP, Barclay found that the self-rated arousal was crucial. Perhaps this is because the nude photographs used by Barclay were not as uniformly arousing as the sexual movie used by Gustafson.

Barclay's third study[18] did use an erotic movie to test the hypothesis of AP as a measure of sexual arousal and the influence of information or set on physiological sexual arousal. This study also examined the effect of the subjects' sexual experience on AP response. Nonexperienced subjects showed little or no AP response, regardless of whether they were stimulated or not, or what information was provided beforehand. Among the sexually experienced males the aroused, noninformed group showed a significant AP response, and the aroused informed and the control noninformed groups did not, as predicted by the authors. However a "paradoxical" finding emerged in the control-informed group, which knew that other subjects were watching erotic movies: these subjects showed an increase in AP following a noneerotic boring film. The author speculated that the information alone may have stimulated erotic fantasies in this group. High "sexual drive level" subjects (drive measured by number of reported orgasms per month) secreted significantly more AP overall than low-drive subjects. This last intriguing finding suggests that AP secretion may be related to sexual arousability as well as to sexual arousal.

Barclay[19] reported a fourth study underway to test the specificity of AP secretion as a measure of sexual arousal. The effects of sexual-, aggressive-, anxiety-, and euphoria-arousing conditions on AP are being compared.

The findings from the series of studies by Barclay are complicated, implicating arousal conditions, information or set, subjects' sexual experience and drive levels as influences on AP secretion. However

---

[17] A recent finding by H. Persky of a substantial positive correlation between testosterone production rate and a questionnaire aggression scale in young males tends to support this hypothesized connection.

[18] Unpublished study by A. M. Barclay entitled "Information as a Defensive Control of Sexual Arousal," 1969.

[19] A. M. Barclay, personal communication, August 20, 1969.

there are presently strong indications that urinary AP secretion may be a useful measure of sexual arousal. The results of Barclay's study in progress will be crucial in determining the affect-response specificity of AP secretion.

CRITIQUE AND CONCLUSIONS

An examination of the publication dates of the references shows that the study of the physiology of the human sexual response is new. Kinsey and Masters and Johnson deserve much of the credit for the breakthrough in this taboo area. However, as with most new areas, much of the research is exploratory rather than hypothesis testing. Inadequate numbers of subjects are too often used to make generalizations of any import. How can one generalize about "sex differences" based on sample sizes of a few subjects of each sex? Techniques are still being evolved, particularly in the measurement of female sexual arousal. Much of the research is poor in quality, lacking adequate controls, methodology, or matching of comparison groups. But this author has not bothered to address many specific criticisms to the individual studies reviewed. One reason is that such criticism would make the review rather monotonous and carping. The other reason is charity. In a new area every little bit of information is helpful, and if these researchers have the courage to breach the wall of taboo they may be permitted the indulgence of some "lets look and see" data collecting. Hopefully, as more investigators enter the field, the competition for journal space will result in a "natural selection" of better designed and conceived research.

The research review has attempted to answer some simple questions concerning sexual arousal. Do psychological sexual stimuli elicit physiological responses of greater magnitude than stimuli with nonsexual content? Do physiological responses distinguish the subjects favored sexual objects, that is, males for female subjects, females for heterosexual male subjects, males for homosexual male subjects, children for pedophiles, fetish objects for fetishists, etc.? What is the effect of the experimental set or atmosphere on physiological responses to sexual stimuli?

Some other important questions have rarely been asked. What is the relation between quantity and variety of experience and sexual arousal? What is the effect of relative deprivation (time since last orgasm) on sexual arousal? What are the ingredients of a sexual stimulus which make it relatively more or less arousing?

In many studies the authors seem to assume that the stimuli they are using are sexually arousing. *Playboy* nudes are a favorite type of stimulus. But in this era of public nudity such stimuli may become quite humdrum. The study of Corman (1968) showed considerably more arousal to erotic movies than to *Playboy* nudes. If discrete slides are used, why not use pictures of actual coitus? In a study by Brady and Levitt (1965) pictures of "ventral-ventral" coitus were rated by males as more arousing than nudes or portrayals of other forms of sexual contact. Movies of sexual activities are probably more arousing than static pictures, but there are problems in measuring physiological reactions during such complex visual presentations. Lazarus (1966) and his group in California have evolved a psychophysiological methodology for measuring reactions to movies which should be studied by persons using such stimuli. The typical low-grade "stag" movie may elicit hilarity or disgust along with sexual arousal. The type of erotic movie used by Corman (1968) and Romano (1969) may be preferable to "stag" movies. Some attention should be given to the stimulus dimension of sexual arousal studies. The scaling of sexual stimuli such as that done by Brady and Levitt (1965) is an example of what needs to be done. Other modes of presenting stimuli have not been explored, that is, auditory presentation, or combined visual and auditory. While measurements of arousal during actual coitus pose many problems for physiological measurement, autoerotic manipulation or the use of mechanical masturbatory devices might yield valuable data.

This review has not dealt extensively with psychological methods used to measure subjective arousal. Many authors have even neglected to obtain such self-reports. Without this kind of data it is impossible to assess whether the stimuli used were actually sexually arousing, and if physiological reactions were more related to subjective sexual arousal or to some other types of affective reaction.

Experimenters attempting to use psychophysiological methods to measure sexual arousal face some old problems familiar to those who have attempted to use psychophysiological methods to study other emotions. Most measures from different peripheral autonomic systems are minimally or inconsistently correlated across subjects. One reason for the state of affairs is individual specificity of response. Most subjects seem to have a most likely, or most powerful, channel of response. One subject may be an electrodermal responder, another subject a heart responder, and so on. When one compares all GSR responses with all heart rate responses the relationship will be attenuated by the individual differences in lability of each system. For this reason it is unlikely that the same peripheral autonomic indicator will be sensitive to sexual arousal in all persons. Evidence for individual specificity of autonomic response during sexual arousal may be found in a study by Hain and Linton.[20] These investigators found interindividual differences in physiological measures correlating with self-rated reactions to sexual stimuli. Individuals tended to be consistent within themselves in their physiological patterns of response.

Another problem is that of habituation. When the same type of stimulus is presented repeatedly over a lengthy series of trials, physiological responses are typically large to the first presentation and thereafter diminish in intensity. The reaction of the first trial may be as much a function of novelty or surprise as the nature of the stimulus itself.

Shifting base lines of response are a problem. The magnitude of response in many systems is inversely related to the base line from which the response began. Results may be radically different depending on what kind of response or change measure is used. Covariance techniques and Lacey's Autonomic Lability Score (1956) can be used to remove the influence of the base-line measure from the response measure.

Stimulus–response specificity can only be assessed by comparing the responses to more than one type of stimulus. This involves more than comparing sexual stimuli to blank slides or neutral stimuli. The question posed by Kinsey et al. (1953) in their review of autonomic findings is, Are there any autonomic reactions that can distinguish sexual arousal from other states of arousal such as fear and anger? Stimuli calculated to arouse emotional states other than sexual should be included in studies of this problem. Most of the studies using negative stimuli in addition to sexual stimuli have not found differences in response magnitude (Bernick & Kling, 1967; Koegler & Kline, 1965; Levi, 1967; Lifshitz, 1966; Peavler & McLaughlin, 1967; Romano, 1969). Even if only sexual stimuli were used it would be helpful to have verbal reports on other possible reactions to such stimuli.

The effects of the general experimental situations on the subjects have not been considered in most experiments. The experiments that considered these set factors (Barclay, 1970; Chapman et al., 1969; Martin, 1964) have found that even physiological responses, GSR, pupil size, and urinary acid phosphatase secretion, may be influenced by set induced by instructions, or the characteristics and behavior of the experimenter. Until recent times sexual response has been considered a semi-private matter beyond the realm of scientific study. Confronted with prying experimenters attaching electrodes, penile plethysmographs, vaginal devices, and showing pornographic stimuli, many subjects might be inclined to inhibit voluntary response. Such inhibition can also have consequences for physiological responses. A *Playboy* cartoon shows a naked man and woman all wired up and under the eye of the researchers' television camera. The man plaintively says: "I just don't feel like it." Failure to consider the human qualities of subjects can often lead to erroneous conclusions in psychological experiments.

Certainly, GSR has been the most favored psychophysiological toy of psychologists. In most of the experiments, the nude adult female figure has proven to be a powerful stimulus for GSR. But the amplitude of GSRs did not reflect the favored sexual object in several studies. Since sweaty palms are not specifically involved in the adaptive sexual reaction it is clear that the GSR may reflect the novelty of nude stimuli, or even negative reactions, as much as sexual arousal. This may be particularly

---

[20]Unpublished paper by J. D. Hain and P. H. Linton entitled "Physiological correlates and predictors of cognitive emotional response."

true of the reaction of women to male nudes, since Kinsey (1953) reported that most women say they are not aroused by the mere sight of the nude male body.

Although heart and breathing rates are remarkably accelerated during actual coitus, they do not seem to be very sensitive to the milder arousal produced by psychological stimuli; erotic movies affect some increase. Blood pressure was the only cardiovascular measure which showed a graded responsiveness to erotic stimuli.

Hess's studies generated a flurry of interest in pupil size as an index of positive arousal in general, and sexual arousal in particular. However, the research has failed to support his hypotheses about the stimulus specificity of the responses of males and females, and heterosexuals and homosexuals. As with GSR, the nude figure does elicit larger responses than clothed figures, but the sex of the nude figure is not very relevant. In fact, there is a tendency in several studies for the male subjects to show more dilation in response to male nudes than to female nudes. Rather than doubting the sexual orientation of the subjects, one might consider the novelty quality of the stimuli. Pictures of totally nude males are less common than the sight of nude females. The "wide eyed" response of males to male nudes may reflect more surprise than interest or sexual arousal. Like the GSR the pupil is a labile system, but unlike the GSR it poses many methodological problems when visual stimuli are used. Probably the only satisfactory way of controlling luminance is to keep the general illumination constant and present stimuli in auditory form.

Penile erection measures have proven to be the most sensitive indexes of arousal in the male, and these measures are quite sensitive to differential arousal to favored and nonfavored sexual objects. The extensive series of studies by Freund has shown good discrimination of homosexuals, heterosexuals, and pedophiliacs. Comparable devices for measuring female sexual arousal are still in developmental stages. The development of the vaginal blood flow measure mounted on a diaphragm ring (Shapiro & Cohen, 1968) and the Fisher and Davis modification of Tart's device seem to be promising methods.

In the biochemical area there has been a sad neglect of the sex hormones as possible indicators of sexual arousal. Levi has shown that adrenaline and noradrenaline show responses to erotic films, but they are elevated by other types of films as well. A suggestive finding by Gustafson et al. (1963) using urinary acid phosphatase has been followed up in a series of studies by Barclay. This measure of prostatic secretion might offer a more specific biochemical index of arousal in males.

The potential applications of some of the methods being developed are already apparent in the diagnosis and treatment of sexual deviants. Many theoretical questions concerning human sexual behavior await the development of objective and quantitative methodology. This methodology is evolving and if research continues to grow in this field, one day Gebhard and Masters may be able to take auto trips together in the security of knowing that what they pioneered will go on without them.

REFERENCES

Bancroft, J. H., Jones, H. G., & Pullan, B. P. A simple transducer for measuring penile erection with comments on its use in the treatment of sexual disorders. *Behavior Research and Therapy*, 1966, **4**, 239–241.

Bancroft, J. H., & Marks, I. Electrical aversion therapy of sexual deviations. *Proceedings of the Royal Society of Medicine*, 1968, **61**, 796–799.

Barclay, A. M. The effect of hostility on physiological and fantasy responses. *Journal of Personality*, 1969, **37**, 651–667.

Barclay, A. M. Urinary acid phosphatase secretion in

sexually aroused males. *Journal of Experimental Research in Personality*, 1970, **4**, 233–238.

Bardwick, J. M., & Behrman, S. J. Investigation into the effects of anxiety, sexual arousal, and menstrual cycle phase on uterine contractions. *Psychosomatic Medicine*, 1967, **29**, 468–482.

Barlow, D. H., Leitenberg, H., & Agras, S. The experimental control of sexual deviation through manipulation of the noxious scene in covert sensitization. *Journal of Abnormal Psychology*, 1969, **74**, 596–601.

BARTLETT, R. G., Jr.   Physiologic responses during coitus. *Journal of Applied Physiology,* 1956, **9,** 469-472.

BEACH, F. A.   *Hormones and behavior.* New York: Hoeber Inc., 1948.

BEACH, F. A.   Characteristics of masculine sex drive. *Nebraska Symposium on Motivation,* 1956, **4,** 1-32.

BEACH, F. A.   Neural and chemical regulation of behavior. In H. F. HARLOW & C. N. WOOLSEY (Eds.), *Biological and biochemical bases of behavior.* Madison: University of Wisconsin Press, 1958.

BEACH, F. A.   *Sex and behavior.* New York: Wiley, 1965.

BEACH, F. A., WESTBROOK, W. H., & CLEMENS, L. G.   Comparisons of the ejaculatory response in men and animals. *Psychosomatic Medicine,* 1966, **28,** 749-763.

BENDER, W. R. G.   The effect of pain and emotional stimuli and alcohol upon pupillary reflex activity. *Psychological Monographs,* 1933, **44**(2, Whole No. 198), 1-32.

BERNICK, N., KLING, A., & BOROWITZ, G.   Physiologic differentiation of sexual arousal and anxiety. *Psychosomatic Medicine,* 1971, **32,** 341-351.

BLAIR, J. H., & SIMPSON, G. M.   Effects of anti-psychotic drugs on reproductive functions. *Diseases of the Nervous System,* 1966, **27,** 645-647.

BRADY, J. P., & LEVITT, E. E.   The scalability of sexual experiences. *Psychological Record,* 1965, **15,** 275-279.

BUCKLEY, T.   All they talk about is sex, sex, sex. *New York Times Magazine Section,* April 20, 1969, 28, 106.

CATTELL, R. B., & SCHEIER, I. H.   *The meaning and measurement of neuroticism and anxiety.* New York: Ronald Press, 1961.

CHAPMAN, L. J., CHAPMAN, J. P., & BRELJE, T.   Influence of the experimenter on pupillary dilation to sexually provocative pictures. *Journal of Abnormal Psychology,* 1969, **74,** 396-400.

CLARK, L. C., & TREICHLER, P.   Psychic stimulation of prostatic secretion. *Psychosomatic Medicine,* 1950, **12,** 261-263.

COHEN, S.   Thioridazine (Mellaril): A review. *Mind,* 1964, **2,** 134-145.

CORMAN, C.   Physiological response to a sexual stimulus. Unpublished bachelor's thesis, University of Manitoba, Canada, 1968.

DAVIS, R. C., & BUCHWALD, A. M.   An exploration of somatic response patterns: Stimulus and sex differences. *Journal of Comparative Psychology,* 1957, **50,** 44-52.

FISHER, C., GROSS, J., & ZUCH, J.   Cycle of penile erection synchronous with dreaming (REM) sleep. *Archives of General Psychiatry,* 1965, **12,** 29-45.

FISHER, S., & OSOFSKY, H.   Sexual responsiveness in women, physiological correlates. *Psychological Reports,* 1968, **22,** 215-226.

FREUND, K.   A laboratory method for diagnosing predominance of homo- and hetero- erotic interest in the male. *Behavior Research and Therapy,* 1963, **1,** 85-93.

FREUND, K.   Diagnosing heterosexual pedophilia by means of a test for sexual interest. *Behavior Research and Therapy,* 1965, **3,** 229-234.

FREUND, K.   Diagnosing homo- and heterosexuality and erotic age preference by means of a psychophysiological test. *Behavior Research and Therapy,* 1967, **5,** 209-228.

FREUND, K., SEDLACEK, F., & KNOB, K.   A simple transducer for mechanical plethysmography of the male genital. *Journal of the Experimental Analysis of Behavior,* 1965, **8,** 169-170.

GELLHORN, E., & LOOFBOURROW, G. N.   *Emotions and emotional disorders.* New York: Harper & Row, 1963.

GUSTAFSON, J. E., WINOKUR, G., & REICHLIN, S.   The effect of psychic and sexual stimulation on urinary and serum acid phosphatase and plasma non-esterified fatty acids. *Psychosomatic Medicine,* 1963, **25,** 101-105.

HESS, E. H.   Pupillometric assessment. *Research in Psychotherapy,* 1968, **3,** 573-583.

HESS, E. H., & POLT, J. M.   Pupil size as related to interest value of visual stimuli. *Science,* 1960, **132,** 349-350.

HESS, E. H., SELTZER, A. L., & SHLIEN, J. M.   Pupil response of hetero- and homosexual males to pictures of men and women: A pilot study. *Journal of Abnormal Psychology,* 1965, **70,** 165-168.

HICKS, R. A., REANEY, T., & HILL, L.   Effects of pupil size and facial angle on preference for photographs of a young woman. *Perceptual & Motor Skills,* 1967, **24,** 388-390.

HOHMANN, G. W.   Some effects of spinal cord lesions on experienced emotional feelings. *Psychophysiology,* 1966, **3,** 143-156.

JORDAN, B. T., & BUTLER, J. R.   GSR as a measure of the sexual component in hysteria. *Journal of Psychology,* 1967, **67,** 211-219.

KARACAN, I., GOODENOUGH, D. R., SHAPIRO, A., & STARKER, S.   Erection cycle during sleep in relation to dream anxiety. *Archives of General Psychiatry,* 1966, **15,** 183-189.

KIMMEL, H. D.   Sex differences in adaptation of GSR under repeated applications of a visual stimulus. *Journal of Experimental Psychology,* 1965, **70,** 536-537.

KINSEY, A., POMEROY, W., & MARTIN, C.   *Sexual behavior in the human male.* Philadelphia: W. B. Saunders Co., 1948.

KINSEY, A., POMEROY, W., MARTIN, C., & GEBHARD, P.   *Sexual behavior in the human female.* Philadelphia: W. B. Saunders Co., 1953.

KOEGLER, R. R., & KLINE, L. Y.   Psychotherapy research: An approach utilizing autonomic response measurement. *American Journal of Psychotherapy,* 1965, **19,** 268-279.

LACEY, J. I.   The evaluation of autonomic responses: Toward a general solution. *Annals of the New York Academy of Sciences,* 1956, **67,** 123-164.

LACEY, J. I., KAGAN, J., LACEY, B., & MOSS, H. A.   Situational determinants and behavioral correlates of autonomic response patterns. In P. J. KNAPP (Ed.), *Expression of the emotions in man.* New York: International Universities Press, 1963.

LADER, M. H. Pneumatic plethysmography. In P. H. VENABLES & I. MARTIN (Eds.), *A manual of psychophysiological methods.* Amsterdam: North Holland Publishing Co., 1967.

LAWS, D. R., & RUBIN, H. B. Instructional control of an autonomic sexual response. *Journal of Applied Behavior Analysis,* 1969, **2,** 93–99.

LAZARUS, R. S. *Psychological stress and the coping process.* New York: McGraw-Hill, 1966.

LEVI, L. Sympatho-adrenomedullary responses to emotional stimuli: methodologic, physiologic and pathologic consideration. In E. BAJUSZ (Ed.), *An introduction to clinical neuroendocrinology.* Basel, N.Y.: S. Karger, 1967.

LEVI, L. Sympatho-adrenomedullary activity, diuresis and emotional reactions during visual sexual stimulation in human females and males. *Psychosomatic Medicine,* 1969, **31,** 251–268.

LIFSHITZ, K. The averaged evoked cortical response to complex visual stimuli. *Psychophysiology,* 1966, **3,** 55–68.

LOISSELLE, R. H., & MOLLENAUER, S. Galvanic skin responses to sexual stimuli in a female population. *Journal of Genetic Psychology,* 1965, **73,** 273–278.

LOWENSTEIN, O., & LOWENFELD, I. E. The pupil. In H. DAVISON (Ed.), *The eye.* New York: Academic Press, 1962.

MACLEAN, P. D. New findings relevant to the evolution of psychosexual functions of the brain. In J. MONEY (Ed.), *Sex research: New developments.* New York: Holt, Rinehart and Winston, 1965.

MARKS, I. M., & GELDER, M. G. Transvestism and fetishism: clinical and psychological changes during faradic aversion. *British Journal of Psychiatry,* 1967, **113,** 711–729.

MARTIN, B. Expression and inhibition of sex motive arousal in college males. *Journal of Abnormal and Social Psychology,* 1964, **68,** 307–312.

MASTERS, W., & JOHNSON, V. *Human sexual response.* Boston: Little, Brown & Co., 1966.

MCCONAGHY, N. Penile volume change to moving pictures of male and female nudes in heterosexual and homosexual males. *Behavior Research and Therapy,* 1967, **5,** 43–48.

MONEY, J. Sex hormones and other variables in human eroticism. In W. C. YOUNG (Ed.), *Sex and internal secretions:* VIII. Baltimore: Williams & Wilkins, 1961.

MONEY, J., & YANKOWITZ, R. The sympathic-inhibiting effects of the drug Ismelin on human male eroticism with a note on Mellaril. *Journal of Sex Research,* 1967, **3,** 69–82.

NUNNALLY, J. C., KNOTT, P. D., DUCHNOWSKI, A., & PARKER, R. Pupillary response as a general measure of activation. *Perception and Psychophysics,* 1967, **2,** 149–155.

PEAVLER, W. S., & MCLAUGHLIN, J. P. The question of stimulus content and pupil size. *Psychonomic Science,* 1967, **8,** 505–506.

REICH, W. Experimentelle Ergebnisse über die elektrische Funktion von Sexualitat und Angst. Institut für sexualokonomische forschung klinishe und experimentelle Berichte. No. 4, 1937. (Translated in *Journal of Orgonomy,* 1969, **3,** 4–29.)

ROMANO, K. Psychophysiological responses to a sexual and an unpleasant motion picture. Unpublished bachelor's thesis, University of Manitoba, Canada, 1969.

SCOTT, T. R., WELLS, W. H., WOOD, D. Z., & MORGAN, D. I. Pupillary response and sexual interest reexamined. *Journal of Clinical Psychology,* 1967, **23,** 433–438.

SHAPIRO, A., COHEN, H. D., DIBIANCO, P., & ROSEN, G. Vaginal blood flow changes during sleep and sexual arousal. *Psychophysiology,* 1968, **4,** 394. (Abstract)

SIMPSON, G. M., BLAIR, J. H., & AMUSO, D. A. Effects of antidepressants on genito-urinary function. *Diseases of the Nervous System,* 1965, **26,** 787–789.

SIMS, T. M. Pupillary response of male and female subjects to pupillary difference in male and female picture stimuli. *Perception and Psychophysics,* 1967, **2,** 553–555.

SOBRERO, A. J., STEARNS, H. E., & BLAIR, J. H. Technic for the induction of ejaculation in humans. *Fertility and Sterility,* 1965, **16,** 765–767.

SOLYOM, L., & BECK, P. R. GSR assessment of aberrant sexual behavior. *International Journal of Neuropsychiatry,* 1967, **3,** 52–59.

SPEISMAN, J. C., LAZARUS, R. S., DAVISON, L., & MORDKOFF, A. M. Experimental analysis of a film used as a threatening stimulus. *Journal of Consulting Psychology,* 1964, **28,** 23–33.

SPIELBERGER, C. D. Theory and research on anxiety. In C. D. SPIELBERGER (Ed.), *Anxiety and behavior.* New York: Academic Press, 1966.

WENGER, M. A., AVERILL, J. R., & SMITH, D. D. B. Autonomic activity during sexual arousal. *Psychophysiology,* 1968, **4,** 468–478.

WENGER, M. A., JONES, F. N., & JONES, M. H. *Physiological psychology.* New York: Holt, Rinehart and Winston, 1956.

WHALEN, R. E. Sexual motivation. *Psychological Review,* 1966, **73,** 151–163.

WOOD, D. M., & OBRIST, P. A. Minimal and maximal sensory intake and exercise as unconditioned stimuli in human heart-rate conditioning. *Journal of Experimental Psychology,* 1968, **76,** 254–262.

WOODMANSEE, J. J. Methodological problems in pupillographic experiments. *Proceedings of 74th Annual Convention of the American Psychological Association,* 1966, **1,** 133–134.

ZUCKERMAN, M., PERSKY, H., & LINK, D. Relation of mood and hypnotizability: An illustration of the importance of the state vs. trait distinction. *Journal of Consulting Psychology,* 1967, **31,** 464–470.

ZUCKERMAN, M., PERSKY, H., & LINK, K. E. The influence of set and diurnal factors on autonomic responses to sensory deprivation. *Psychophysiology,* 1969, **5,** 612–624.

PART

5 APPLICATIONS OF PSYCHOPHYSIOLOGICAL TECHNIQUES AND FINDINGS

Martin T. Orne, Richard I. Thackray, and David A. Paskewitz

ON THE DETECTION
OF DECEPTION*

A MODEL FOR THE STUDY OF PHYSIOLOGICAL
EFFECTS OF PSYCHOLOGICAL STIMULI

19

It is widely believed that lying is accompanied by specific perceptible physiological or behavioral alterations. Thus a mother tells her child, "Look at me," in order to assure his telling the truth, because she believes that lying is associated with averting the gaze. Other idiosyncratic behavioral manifestations may be recognized by those close to an individual when he purposefully decides to lie. These may include signs of tension, agitation, respiratory changes, a catch in one's voice, blanching, blushing, etc. In addition to physiological changes readily visible to an observer, more subtle ways of determining physiological responsivity may be used. In ancient China an individual was required to speak with his mouth full of rice in order to test the truth of his statement (Boring, 1942). This rather primitive "lie detector" might have worked, in some instances at least,

*The preparation of this review, as well as the substantive research conducted at the Unit for Experimental Psychiatry, was carried out at the Institute of the Pennsylvania Hospital, University of Pennsylvania, and was supported in part by the United States Army Research and Development Command, Contract No. DA-49-193-MD-2647 and Contract No. DA-49-193-MD-2480, and by the Institute for Experimental Psychiatry. The authors also wish to express their appreciation to Robert A. Brisentine, Jr., Frederick J. Evans, Kenneth R. Graham, Charles H. Holland, Frank Horvath, Fred E. Inbau, Aaron Katcher, Joseph F. Kubis, Sol Kugelmass, Edgar P. Nace, Duane R. Nedrud, Donald N. O'Connell, Jesse Orlansky, Emily Carota Orne, Campbell W. Perry, John E. Reid, and Mae C. Weglarski for their helpful comments during the preparation of the manuscript.

because emotion could interfere with salivation, thus differentially increasing the liar's difficulty in enunciating under those circumstances. (See Larson, 1932, for an excellent review of the history of the detection of deception.)

Shortly after the turn of the century, modifications of Galton's (1879) word association technique were used to detect lying by investigating associations and differential reaction times to stimuli associated with material about which an individual hopes to deceive (Jung, 1906; Wertheimer & Klein, 1904). Somewhat later, Luria (1932) showed that psychomotor coordination can be impaired while lying, using a technique which required subjects to hold one hand steady while depressing a plunger with the other. These techniques, while of theoretical interest, have had very limited practical application. It remained for Keeler (1930) to develop and combine the work of several previous workers in a simple polygraph to measure physiological responsivity as a technique for the detection of deception. His device measured respiration, "relative blood pressure," and the galvanic skin response (GSR).

PRINCIPLES UNDERLYING THE DETECTION OF DECEPTION

Despite the widespread use of the polygraph technique by police, governmental agencies, and industry to detect deception, considerable misunderstanding persists about its mode of operation. Contrary to popular superstition, no specific physiological response has ever been identified that is unique to lying. On the contrary, the kinds of behavioral and physiological responses associated with deception are also characteristic of arousal, anxiety, stress, etc. The detection of deception depends upon a comparison of the subject's responses to two or more stimuli matched in their presumed ability to arouse the subject. Some of these stimuli are known not to be associated with deception, whereas one or more of the others may be associated with deception. If the individual's responses to these basically similar stimuli are considerably different in the case of those stimuli about which deception is suspected, a diagnosis of lying is made. The parameter on which this comparison

is made can range from reaction time (as in Jung's experiments); to psychomotor coordination (as in Luria's); and to physiological parameters, as in a more typical "lie detection" procedure. Regardless of the parameter being measured, the model remains a comparison of matched stimuli, one set of which may involve deception. The procedure rests on a number of assumptions, which include an adequate matching of stimuli, as well as differential responsivity on one or more of the parameters being measured.

The Usefulness of the Paradigm

It is striking that a phenomenon such as the detection of deception has received so little systematic investigation. Perhaps this is partly explained by the psychologist's irritation with laymen who characteristically refer to all polygraphs as "lie detectors." Yet the phenomenon is probably a fundamental paradigm for psychophysiology. Consider the card test, a demonstration used both in certain field applications and in laboratory studies. A subject is asked to select and remember one of six cards. As the experimenter names each of the cards, he is required to answer "No" each time, thereby "lying" about the card he actually did select. The physiological response (typically GSR) to each of the stimuli is compared with the other responses and, under appropriate conditions, the greatest GSR will have been evoked by the card selected. Such a simple procedure remains one of the best illustrations of psychosomatic relationships. One assumes that prior to the selection of any one card, each of them would have evoked an essentially similar response, whereas afterward a greater physiological response is elicited by the card that has been selected. The process of selecting the card, then, differentially alters the individual's physiological responsivity to it. This procedure presents a rather simple way of studying the differential effect of past experience on the physiological responsivity of the individual. It should be emphasized that this simple procedure will not automatically guarantee that the greatest physiological response is associated with a selected card. On the contrary, as will be discussed later, situations varying the consequences of deception, the kind of response required of the subject, his antecedent experience, the kind of parameters being tested, etc., will dramatically affect the incidence with which a selected card will evoke a differentially greater physiological response.

It is possible, therefore, to view the apparently simple detection of deception situation as a meaningful way of investigating the contingencies under which an apparently matched stimulus can, by specifiable previous experience, become capable of arousing differential physiological responsivity. Whereas in most psychophysiological research one attempts to infer the fact that a stimulus has been meaningful from the physiological response of the individual, this paradigm allows an investigator to specify the meaningful stimulus (i.e., the selected card) and determine the particular kind of psychological situation under which it will lead to a differentially augmented physiological response. As will be shown later, psychological rather than physiological factors tend to determine the presence of differentially greater responsivity. This paradigm then becomes a technique for systematically investigating the contingencies under which previously neutral stimuli become capable of eliciting alterations in physiological responses.

Sources of Information Concerning the Detection of Deception

There are essentially two bodies of literature dealing with the detection of deception: a small number of studies by psychologists published in professional journals and a relatively large number of manuals, journals, and reports written by "professional lie detection experts." The concerns of these two groups have, as a rule, been dissimilar. The practitioner involved in "lie detection" tries to structure a situation in which he can successfully make a diagnosis of deception. His concern typically centers about reducing the number of cases in which he cannot make a clear-cut decision in his own mind on whether an individual is guilty or innocent. Because of a variety of reasons, not the least of which is the technical difficulty of establishing "truth" in an absolute sense, few reports deal with attempts at validating findings. No attempts are made to vary procedures in a systematic fashion, in order to establish the relative contribution of different aspects of the procedures to

the diagnosis of deception. The diagnosis of guilt or innocence is not typically made on the basis of a single measure or test, but represents a global decision, including all of the information known about the case.

In direct contrast to reports from the field are laboratory studies that are characteristically concerned with varying procedures and studying the effect on detection, using explicitly defined criteria as dependent variables. Not only are the motivations of subjects and the context in which these studies are carried out different, but neither the procedures nor the dependent variables are readily comparable. The problems raised by using, in one context, the data derived from another will become more evident in later sections. It seems most appropriate to discuss the field situation separately, since it is more closely akin to a clinical art developed by practitioners who are faced with the task of making the diagnosis of deception. In order to evaluate the field situation, it is necessary to appreciate the context in which the detection of deception is carried out, the procedures that are utilized, and the kinds of criteria that are employed.

LIE DETECTION IN THE FIELD

Typically, "lie detection" procedures are carried out by individuals who are trained interrogators but who may have only limited formal training in psychology, psychophysiology, and related fields. The technology has developed empirically, largely through the influence of Keeler (1930), his associates and successors, Inbau and Reid (1953), and Backster (1963). A body of knowledge, phrased in interrogation terminology, has been developed to explain and teach the rationale and the application of this technique. Usually, the interrogators have taken one or more courses from individuals who have had considerable experience with the technique. Currently, various attempts are being made to specify standards of training for interrogators who are to use this procedure.

Polygraphic interrogation techniques have been used in three major contexts: (a) the interrogation of suspects during criminal investigation procedures; (b) the screening of individuals for security purposes in the government; and (c) the screening of individuals who are or may be placed in positions to convert goods or defraud their employers on a more or less routine basis, in order to identify individuals guilty of crimes, who might not otherwise be detected.

Interrogation Procedure

For a detailed discussion of various procedures the reader is referred to Reid and Inbau (1966). It seems useful, however, to summarize certain aspects of the procedure. We shall describe the situation characteristic of lie detection in the context of criminal investigation. Typically, the polygraph operator sees the suspect in a relatively quiet, plainly furnished, comfortable office. He is acquainted with the suspect's dossier and has obtained as much factual information as he can. He is introduced to the suspect and is usually alone in the room with him, although the interview may be recorded and observed through a one-way screen.

The pretest interview Once the interrogator meets the suspect, he explains that he will shortly conduct a polygraph examination and that the "lie detector" is a scientific instrument which will record his physiological reactions and indicate when he is lying. He tends to state flatly that this can be done with certainty, implying that deception is pointless because the record will reveal this deception. A concerted effort is made to structure the interview as an opportunity for the suspect to prove himself innocent by telling his side of the story. The machine is usually visible in the background but is not directly mentioned at this point. The whole tone of the initial conversation is designed to maximize the suspect's belief in the infallibility of the "lie detector," a belief that, to some extent at least, tends to be shared by the interrogator. In the context of the impending polygraph examination, the interrogator goes over the material in the suspect's history. Since he is trained in his task, he will typically sympathize with the suspect, provide face-saving rationalizations for any crimes that might have been committed, and indicate subtly that he can understand how someone might murder but that lying is the lowest form

of degeneracy. Such a procedure may sound farfetched, yet in the hands of an expert it is remarkably convincing. Against the background of the forthcoming examination, he goes over all of the crucial points and at various stages casually indicates that the suspect might as well tell the truth now, since it will certainly come out later, and that by confessing he will earn the interrogator's respect.

Unlike other interrogation procedures, inconsistencies in the suspect's answers and possibly deceptive replies are not challenged by the interrogator during the pretest interview, except perhaps subtly during the course of formulating questions. It is important that the suspect not feel that the interrogator is trying to obtain admission of guilt, but merely eliciting information essential for the conduct of an adequate examination. This behavior is quite different from the usual behavior of an interrogator, where inconsistencies are used as leverage to force the suspect to reveal the truth. Since interrogators are trained to bear down when they suspect deception, and the pretest interview specifically prohibits such behavior, many polygraph practitioners are genuinely convinced that interrogation is not the real purpose of this interview. The examiner's belief that this is the case helps maximize the effectiveness of the interview, which often, in fact, elicits unexpected admissions of guilt prior to the actual test. It is, of course, a matter of semantics whether one wishes to consider these cases as examples of successful lie detection. While the polygraph record does not lead to the detection of deception in these instances, the existence of the polygraph creates a context without which a confession might not have been obtained.

The interrogator will then carefully discuss with the suspect the questions he will ask. There are, of course, different procedures used by different individuals in this regard, but the most widely used procedures, "peak of tension," "zone of comparison," and their various adaptations, all employ a similar pretest strategy. Approximately 12 questions are usually formulated, including a number of known, neutral control items such as: "Is your name John Doe?" "Are you now in the United States?" "Is today _____?" Also included will be certain questions designed to elicit a nonspecific emotional response, questions such as: "Have you ever stolen anything?" Finally, two or three crucial questions relating to the specific purpose of the interrogation will be included.

The interrogator will go over these questions in detail with the suspect, defining for him exactly what each aspect of the question should mean, to be certain that it will not be necessary for him to lie unless he is guilty. The pretest interview and the discussion of the questions to be asked during the test provide an unusual opportunity to elicit information. The interrogator usually approaches the suspect in a very calm, matter-of-fact fashion. The questions he asks in the process of clarifying the subsequent "lie detection" test are for the ostensible purpose of protecting the individual from giving a false guilty response.

The formulation of questions The formulation of appropriate questions is considered to be a crucial part of the procedure. It is in the formulation of questions that an attempt is made to take into account the individual's overall state of tension. An innocent individual may have cause to be highly aroused and very frightened in the test situation. The interrogator will attempt to include several emotion-arousing questions, not related to the specific crime, in order to have an estimate of the individual's responsivity to embarrassing questions. In an examination concerning a particular murder, for example, he might ask the individual about some other murder. This second murder might well be a fiction made up by the interrogator but to the innocent suspect it will be as real as is the first murder. Asking about a fictitious murder permits the interrogator to compare the responses to the two questions about the murders, one in which the suspect is known to be innocent and the other in which his involvement is questioned. It is, of course, essential that the interrogator ask questions in a manner which convinces the person that he is really suspected of each crime.

In an ideal case, some crucial questions may be asked about material that is known only to the guilty person and the interrogator. If, for example, the murdered person has been stabbed with a letter opener, and this fact has not been released to the public, questions may be formulated asking whether the victim was shot, strangled, or stabbed. The innocent individual's responses should be similar for all these questions, whereas the guilty individual can be expected to respond differently to the relevant item.

It is difficult to provide a real picture of the pretest interview that is such a crucial part of "lie detection." This interview carried out prior to the test, with the machine discreetly in the background and yet very much present as the ultimate scientific arbiter of truth, is useful not only to elicit information but also allows a quasi-alliance to be formed between the interrogator and the suspect vis-à-vis the machine. The very process of formulating questions and clarifying them with the suspect is immensely effective in maximizing the conviction that the machine will, in fact, detect lying unless both the interrogator and the suspect make absolutely certain that no lie is involved. In this context, a lie is carefully defined. As an example, an individual might be accused of stealing several hundred dollars from his employer. During the pretest interview, the interrogator asks him about a previous job in a supermarket. While formulating the questions, the interrogator asks, "Did you ever steal from the market?" If the suspect says, "No," the interrogator asks, "Did you ever, for example, run out of cigarettes and take a pack off the shelf?" If the suspect admits, after a few minutes, that he probably has, although he cannot remember specific instances, the interrogator then asks whether perhaps he might have helped himself to some cookies from a broken package. Again the suspect might admit that this could have happened. The interrogator then explains that this is not what was meant by stealing, but that stealing meant only the actual taking of money or merchandise of significant value, say in excess of $5, for his own use or to sell. He would not, then, mean an occasional cookie, cigarette, or piece of chewing gum. Thus he says, "When I ask you, 'Did you ever steal from the market?', you now know that I will be referring to taking merchandise valued in excess of $5 or to taking a similar or greater amount of money." Note that the interrogator apparently takes great care to prevent the suspect from giving responses not elicited by the issue in question. In so doing he implies that it is vital that there be no confusion about the meaning of the questions, lest the polygraph pick up lying, and, incidentally, that he, himself, has some understanding of trivial transgressions. He provides ample opportunity for the suspect to mention that he might have stolen, just so that there will be no confusion, since this stealing was quite irrelevant to the crime under investigation. The situation is so designed that a truthful interchange seems obviously essential for the suspect's own good.

Only after the questions that are to be asked have been carefully worked out does the actual examination begin. The pretest discussion may take an hour or more. It is emphasized that the suspect should be put at ease as much as possible prior to the examination; he should be properly rested and not medicated. The pretest interview is intended to reassure the suspect about the infallibility of the polygraph, in the hope that this will reduce the anxiety of the innocent and maximize the responsivity of the guilty.

The test procedure The typical commercial polygraph measures respiration using a pneumograph, a form of occlusion plethysmography of the arm often erroneously called "relative blood pressure" because it uses a pneumatic system with a blood pressure cuff,[1] inflated to a point midway between systolic and diastolic pressure, and GSR with simple, stainless steel electrodes without paste. Because the inflated blood pressure cuff soon becomes uncomfortable, the actual test is limited to about 10 or 12 questions taking only about 2 or 3 minutes.

After the polygraph has been attached, the interrogator may demonstrate its use by asking the suspect to select one of a number of cards and requesting that he answer "No" to all questions about these cards, forcing him to lie. He will then run through a number of questions concerning which card the suspect selected. At the conclusion of this demonstration, he will invariably be able to tell the suspect which card he selected. Certainty is possible in this instance because the interrogator ascertains the card in advance, the purpose of this procedure being to underline the infallibility of the

polygraph. While a card test helps in these measures, it is far less important—or effective—than the pretest interview. If it is felt that the suspect already has the right attitude, the card test may be omitted.[2]

During the actual test the suspect is seated so that he cannot see the record on the machine or the interrogator. Each of the questions the suspect is to answer has been discussed in detail in advance and is formulated to require a simple "Yes" or "No" answer. The interrogator waits long enough between each question to allow the three measures to return to a fairly stable baseline. After the interrogator has gone through the 12 questions once, the blood pressure cuff is deflated, and the suspect is given a rest period which, however, may be used as an integral part of the procedure. If, for example, a response to some item suggests guilt, the interrogator may well ask the suspect about it, in an attempt to account for this physiological response. Here again the interrogator takes the role of trying to help the suspect vis-à-vis the machine. In the case discussed earlier, for example, the suspect might have shown a reaction to the question, "Did you ever steal from the supermarket?" The interrogator might say, "Look, what really happened? You didn't tell me. You have a response there." The suspect may then recall that on one particular day he did, in fact, take $10 because he was short of money. He might say that he had always meant to return the money and hadn't thought of it as theft but he didn't get around to it. The interrogator might then say, "Fine, now let's be clear that the next time I ask you about this we will not think of stealing as meaning this $10 which you borrowed and intended to return." The test is then repeated, after clarifying what is meant by stealing, and the physiological response previously associated with the question may now no longer be elicited. Any apparent unexplained responses in the test are utilized in this manner to elicit more information. Such, of course, is also the case for the material concerning the crime. In most cases, the suspect is tested at least twice on the questions. Between the first and second tests, however, the interrogator may attempt to have the suspect reconcile and

---

[1] See p. 764 for a further discussion of this point.

[2] This test may instead be given following an initial examination on the relevant material.

explain the reason for any undue physiological response that might indicate knowledge of the crime.

Scoring The scoring of the physiological parameters is not specified in quantitative terms. Although examples of various types of deceptive responses are given in sources such as Reid and Inbau (1966), it is difficult to say that they indicate much more than an undue response. A change in respiration, blood pressure, or GSR beyond what would seem normal is considered important, but no specific physiological change is uniquely associated with lying. Instead, deception is diagnosed by comparing the subject's response on relevant items with his response on items that should be equally arousing or anxiety-provoking to an individual who is not lying.

If some particular item of information is available that would be known to the suspect but not to an innocent individual, the "peak of tension" technique may be used. In this procedure, a series of questions is asked in an order previously established with the suspect; the crucial item is typically placed third or fourth. The operator looks for a gradual increase in the amount of tension elicited by each item as the crucial one is approached and a sudden relaxation once it is passed. Items of information that involve numbers are particularly suited to this procedure. If, for example, $212 were taken in a theft and this amount is not generally known, the suspect might be asked, "Was the amount taken $56, $102, $160, $212, $418?" The suspect who knows the correct amount should not only show his maximal response to $212 but also demonstrate a gradual increase in tension that peaks at $212, with a sudden relaxation as the crucial item is passed.

Screening procedures When the polygraph is used in screening employees or prospective personnel, the procedures are much the same as in criminal investigations but there are certain differences. The problem facing the interrogator in a criminal case is to develop appropriate control questions to enable him to interpret the responses to questions concerning the crime. In screening, the interrogator does not have a set of ready-made questions about a specific event. The interview for pre-employment (or "routine" screening) is designed to discover whether or not the particular person being tested is guilty of certain transgressions, involvements, or tendencies that would render him unsuitable for the position. The polygraph, then, not only serves as a powerful lever in the pretest situation but serves as an "independent" measure of the veridicality of statements concerning the questions asked. The kinds of issues that are explored in the screening procedure tend to include material of a private, personal, and confidential nature, which under most circumstances would not legitimately be viewed as relevant to an individual's normal employment. The use of the polygraph in screening has been subject to considerable criticism (House of Representatives, 1964). The issues, however, relate less to its utility in such a context than to the kinds of questions explored. It should be realized that the questions asked, rather than the attempted validation of the answers, are objectionable to individuals. The issue of what aspects of an individual's life may be searched, and under what conditions, either by an employer or by the government, is an ethical and moral problem, separate from the problem of the effectiveness of the instrument and, therefore, beyond the scope of this presentation.

Evaluation of the Technique

When one considers the use of the polygraph in a real life situation, it becomes clear why it is difficult to evaluate. The interrogation procedure is an art rather than a science—much depends upon the manner in which the individual interrogator formulates his questions, the tone of his voice, and the subtle cues he may provide in the interrogation, etc. The experienced interrogator must intuitively deal with problems inherent in such issues as individual differences in reactivity, response specificity, and the overall state of the person being questioned. Interrogators who have worked with "lie detection" will readily admit that the psychological edge the machine provides during the pretest interview is, from their point of view, of major importance. Some go on to say that, even if the machine were out of order, it would still be a major asset. Scientific evaluation of the validity of the "lie detection" procedure is very difficult, since the test itself is only a small part of the total procedure, and much of the interrogator's attachment to the polygraph undoubtedly is related to the psychological effect it will have on the suspect.

In the past, the literature on "lie detection" written by the professional expert has tended to emphasize the scientific aspect of this technique. The polygraph is presented to the suspect as a scientific way of recording his physiological responses, which indeed it is. It is also implied—and at times even stated—that the polygraph is a scientific way to record lying. No adequate evaluation of the validity of the polygraph in this regard is yet available (Orlansky, 1962). Perhaps there has been an unfortunate disinclination toward evaluation by practitioners in this area, yet it must also be acknowledged that to do so is extremely difficult. How does one appropriately determine percentages of correct detection? Assume that one individual admitted a theft and polygraph examinations were carried out among 100 suspects, with all individuals apparently innocent; does this justify the claim of 99% accuracy that has been made in one instance? If, indeed, the interrogator considered the contingencies in each instance to be 50-50 instead of 100 to 1, such a claim might not be quite as absurd as it seems.

In evaluating "lie detection," it would perhaps be most appropriate to ask not how well the procedure works under ideal circumstances but rather to consider the whole technique as a unit—the interrogator, the test, and his interpretation of the test—and ask how effective this combination is in determining the truth. In the absence of any satisfactory way of establishing what truth really is, such an evaluation cannot be carried out. To validate against a jury's decision of guilt is a dubious procedure at best since criminal trials are adversary proceedings carried out in a highly formalized manner. The courts are, of necessity, more concerned about making certain that only legally obtained evidence is used according to correct procedure than in the guilt or innocence of any one particular individual. The purpose of a jury is to provide a socially useful criterion of fact in the absence of more reliable ways of determining truth. A panel of experts evaluating all of the facts in a case, including those

inadmissible in court, might be more accurate. A criterion measure of this sort was employed by Bersh (1969), who found better than 90% agreement between polygraph examiners' judgments of deception, based on both examinations and knowledge of details of the case, and unanimous judgments of guilt made by a panel of four Judge Advocate General attorneys. This panel independently reviewed case files from which all polygraph material was deleted. Bersh felt that such a panel provided the best practical criterion against which to compare examiner judgments. Although an excellent study, errors of classification are possible, even with such a panel. Other ways have been proposed to validate the procedure. These include subsequent confessions, the uncovering of evidence that would prove innocence after the test, and uncovering circumstantial proof of crimes by such a procedure. Each of these presents serious problems. In real life, polygraph examinations given during a period when some doubt as to guilt exists are seldom those in which such doubt is subsequently resolved.

An evaluation of the total procedure in such a retrospective fashion is greatly complicated by the fact that the procedure has an effect on the disposition of the case; thus in some instances the fact that a suspect appears to be telling the truth during a polygraph test is the basis upon which further investigation is deemed unnecessary. Obviously, a high correlation between apparent innocence on a polygraph examination and innocence in real life is virtually guaranteed. The same problem exists in the determination of guilt or lying. As has been pointed out, the interrogator has available to him as much information as possible and this information will include the investigative findings and convictions of his colleagues about the guilt of a suspect (Orlansky, 1962). These beliefs and convictions could certainly bias the interpretation of the records.

If the bias affected only the interpretation of the polygraph record, it would be possible to circumvent this bias by blind analysis of the records or a reevaluation by judges after the fact. The problem is far more complex. The procedure is by no means standardized, and the importance of the pretest interrogation in making the test itself work is uni-

versally acknowledged. The importance of formulating proper questions is also stressed in all of the
literature written by "lie detection" experts. Since
the technique depends upon the comparison of
physiological responses to critical questions with
those to control questions, the choice of control
questions is of crucial importance. The manner in
which questions are asked can certainly influence the physiological response. The interrogator
wishing to obtain a record with physiological evidence of deception is likely to be able to do so.
In view of the work by Rosenthal (1966) on experimenter bias, it seems extremely likely that the interrogator could unwittingly communicate some
aspects of his conviction to the subject. In fact,
suspects whom the interrogator believes to be
innocent might well be taking quite a different test
from that taken by those about whom the interrogator has strong convictions regarding their guilt.
If there were some way of knowing absolute truth
and if one could evaluate a large series of decisions
for their accuracy, this issue would be less serious.
In any retrospective attempt at evaluation, however,
where one is using primarily the polygraph record
itself, it cannot be ignored. The extent to which
experimenter bias enters into a decision can be
investigated. It is possible to ask polygraph operators to administer examinations to individuals who
are definitely innocent, and by providing accurate,
but slanted, investigative material convince the
interrogator that the individual is probably guilty.
A group of individuals tested in this fashion would
yield evidence about the extent to which the polygraph examiner might unwittingly bias the test in
actual practice. It would not be possible to obtain
evidence about the effect of the interrogator's
conviction of innocence on the guilty subject's
record, but this is perhaps of less concern than
false-positive tests.

Experimenter bias is not the only factor that may
cause innocent individuals to be classified as guilty.
An excellent example of the problem is cited by
Dearman and Smith (1963), in which an individual
felt guilty about legitimate financial dealings and
was, as a result, suspected of stealing from his
employer. Research directed at the problem of
false-positive classifications seems of great importance.

The reliability of the procedure may also be
evaluated. The record of physiological responses
that is obtained can be examined by different individuals and judged as to whether deception is or
is not present. Such studies, although not presently
available, would seem feasible. A high degree of
concordance in judgments, however, would in no
way deal with the problems of validity outlined.
It seems likely that different practitioners develop
different feelings of what might be indicative of
deception, partially based on an awareness of the
kind of interrogation they carried out. The importance of interrogator reliability about the purely
physiological evidence of lying could thus be overestimated.

No fully satisfactory way is available at this time
for evaluating the overall effectiveness of the technique, and it is probable that no such answer will
be forthcoming in the near future from real life
situations. Perhaps most sensibly, one must compare the total technique with alternative ways of
ascertaining whether an individual is telling the
truth. One could, for instance, compare the effectiveness of clinical interviews with that of polygraph interviews, although no comparative data are
yet available. In the clinical setting, the professional
makes certain that there is little if any advantage
to the patient in lying. The interrogator questioning
a suspect, however, tends to feel that the polygraph
yields a considerable increment to his effectiveness.
Just what proportion of this increment is based on
the physiological record, and what proportion on
the psychological leverage provided by the technique itself, remains an open question.

Ethical issues, as well as practical ones, are raised
by the use of polygraphs in a real life situation
(Sternbach, Gustafson, & Colier, 1962). Whether
such a technique ought to be used is beyond the
scope of a scientific discussion. The matter of
whether or not the technique works is, however,
subject to scientific inquiry. If, as the preponderance of evidence seems to indicate, the technique
is effective—at least more effective than alternative
methods of ascertaining truth—it still remains to
be determined how accurately and under what
conditions. It should be noted, however, that were
further research to establish a technique which is
100% effective in determining the truthfulness of

a statement, the ethical difficulties would not be diminished. Thus wire-tapping, when it yields incriminating evidence, is 100% effective, but by no means does this accuracy resolve the ethical issues raised by its use.

LABORATORY RESEARCH

The mechanisms involved in the detection of deception are subject to laboratory research, although major differences exist between laboratory situations and those in the field, and inferences from one to the other will need to be drawn cautiously (Orne, 1969). Yet, to the extent that we are investigating mechanisms, they may be meaningfully explored under controlled conditions. When the polygraph is used for criminal interrogation, security screening, or in pre-employment interviews, the consequences of the test are significant and real. These consequences are in sharp contrast to those in most laboratory research, where the consequences of detection tend to be minimal. Even if they are maximized by experimental manipulations, they tend to be from a universe of discourse different from that of the field situation. These differences in consequence are by no means the only differences, however. Researchers have rarely used situations that are comparable in any way to those found in the field. The tendency has been to use the kind of situation characterized by the card test described earlier. The subjects are asked to select one of several cards and then requested to lie about the identity of the one selected. The GSR to the selected card is typically compared with that evoked by cards not selected. Occasionally, investigators such as Lykken (1959), Kubis (1962), and Davidson (1968) have used a pseudocrime which is enacted by the subject, or in which he might participate. Here, again, a fixed number of stimuli are given to the subject, stimuli that include some highly relevant to the crime he observed and others less relevant to it. In the laboratory experiment, therefore, the formulation of questions characteristic of the field situation and a discussion of the reasons for a suspect's undue response are replaced by the use of closely matched stimuli. The psychological leverage characteristic of the field situation is typically not exploited in the laboratory.

With some exceptions (Ben Shakhar, Lieblich, & Kugelmass, 1970; Kugelmass & Lieblich, 1966), the subjects tend to be college students, a group that differs markedly from the clients of the "lie detection" experts. Finally, the relationship between the experimenter and the subject is radically different from that of the interrogator and the suspect.

The Effect of Motivation

In a field situation the suspect's concern about the test and its consequences for him may be taken for granted. The consequences of being detected have been emphasized repeatedly as significant determinants of detection (Burtt, 1921; Chappell, 1929; Marston, 1917). Because this view is widely held, a number of investigators have offered rewards to subjects who could successfully deceive during a polygraph examination (Davidson, 1968; Kubis, 1962; Lykken, 1960), or have administered electric shock during the experiment, presumably to increase the affective response to the relevant question (Lykken, 1959). The effectiveness of such manipulations is not known, however, since these investigators have not compared the detection rates obtained under these circumstances to those which have been obtained without such motivating techniques.

In a study designed to explore the role of motivation as a determinant of detection, Gustafson and Orne (1963) compared two groups of normal, paid college volunteers in a card experiment, using GSR as the response variable. Both groups were asked to select one card and were then played a tape recording that included a reference to the critical card, as well as to control cards. Before selecting the card, one of the two groups listened to a tape that contained the following information: (a) the experiment was designed to see how well the subject could keep information from the experimenter; (b) that this was extremely difficult and only persons with superior intelligence and great emotional control could succeed; (c) they were to try as hard as they could to beat the experimenter and the equipment; and (d) if they were successful, they would be paid an extra dollar. The experiment was carried out in a very impersonal fashion. Detection rates were found to be no greater than chance in the control group but significantly greater than chance in the motivated group. It would appear, then, that detection is in large part a function of the subject's *attempt to deceive* and that incentives to do so result in an increased ease of detection.

On the basis of these findings it could be hypothesized that motivated subjects who are told they had not been successful in their attempt to deceive, and who are thereby even more highly motivated to escape detection, are more easy to detect. This logic would seem to be the implicit assumption underlying the use of the card test in a field situation, where the interrogator goes to considerable pains to convince the subject of the virtual infallibility of the polygraph in the hope of maximizing the differential responsivity.

The wide use of the card test in field situations makes the results obtained by Ellson, Davis, Saltzman, and Burke (1952) puzzling. In a study on the consequences of previous detection, they report that subjects detected on an earlier trial and informed of this fact are more difficult to detect on a subsequent trial. Gustafson and Orne (1965a) attempted to resolve this apparent paradox. They observed that there is a widely held conviction among college students that lie detection techniques are effective with all normal subjects, and that only habitual liars or psychopaths fail to be detected. In a laboratory situation, therefore, subjects might be motivated to be detected. Once they

had obtained proof that detection was possible, their level of motivation would decrease, and they would then become more difficult to detect. If they were given proof that they were not detected, however, their concern about possibly having psychopathic tendencies would heighten the level of motivation and facilitate detection. In a real life context, any such problem would be overshadowed by concern for the consequences of detection, so that the results might be reversed.

To test these concepts, Gustafson and Orne (1965a) designed a study using GSR as an indicator of deception. Two groups of subjects were treated identically, except for different pre-experimental instructions designed to create two different mental sets toward the experiment. One group was told: "This is a study of lie detection. As you know, a lie detector is a scientific instrument. However, psychopaths and habitual liars are very difficult to detect. In the study we are assessing the adequacy of the technique. We want you to try to fool the lie detector. It is your job to fool the machine. Good luck!" The other group was presented a tape with motivating instructions similar to those employed in the earlier study, omitting only the monetary reward. The tape said: "This is a study in lie detection. Only very stable and emotionally mature individuals are able to fool the lie detector. We want you to try your best to fool the machine.

TABLE 19.1 SUCCESSFUL AND UNSUCCESSFUL DETECTION ON THE FIRST TRIAL OF SUBGROUPS TRYING TO BE DETECTED OR TO DECEIVE[a,b]

| Motivation | Feedback | | χ^2 between feedback groups |
	Told detected subsequently	Told not detected subsequently	
"Need to be detected"			
Detected	9	13	1.31
Not detected	7	3	n.s.
"Need to deceive"			
Detected	13	11	0.17
Not detected	3	5	n.s.
χ^2 between motivation groups	1.31 n.s.	0.17 n.s.	

[a] The subjects were informed about the success of detection only *after* the trial yielding these data.
[b] A multiple square contingency analysis (Sutcliffe, 1957) was used to determine the departures from expected frequencies in the entire table. Neither the chi-square components for each variable alone, nor the interaction between variables, was significant.

Note.—Reprinted after an article by Lawrence A. Gustafson and Martin T. Orne published in the December 1965 *Journal of Applied Psychology*. Copyrighted by the American Psychological Association, Inc., 1965.

Good luck!" All subjects were shown cards with numbers and were asked to select one, apparently without the experimenter's knowledge. A tape recording was then played on which all the possible numbers were repeated in the form of questions. The subject was instructed to reply "No" to each number, so that one of his responses would necessarily be a lie. Table 19.1 illustrates that on this first trial the two groups were not significantly different.

After the first trial, regardless of the subject's actual physiological responses, the experimenter entered the room and told half the subjects what their card had been—thus indicating that they had been detected. To the other half, the experimenter named the wrong card, so that they believed they had gone undetected. A second trial was then given to each subject in order to determine the effect of feedback on subsequent detection. Table 19.2 summarizes the findings.

The two groups showed exactly opposite reactions to the same information. For those subjects who had been striving to be detected because "psychopaths are difficult to detect," the information that they had been detected eliminated the differential responsivity the next time that they were required to lie. The identical information given to those subjects who hoped to go undetected because "only mature and stable individuals are able to fool the lie detector," however, greatly

augmented the response the next time that they were required to lie, making their detection much easier. Exactly the opposite result occurred when the experimenter purposely picked an incorrect card, communicating to the subject that he had effectively deceived the machine.

It should be emphasized that the physiological criterion for detection was the GSR, objectively scored, and that the experimental treatment was identical for both groups once the pre-experimental instructions had been given.

These findings illustrate the problems of inferring from laboratory findings to the field situation. Clearly, the identical experimental treatment and stimulus conditions can yield exactly opposite results depending upon the subject's attitude and set as he enters the experiment (Orne, 1962). In the above study, the subject's set was manipulated, but in many studies it is not investigated and can be inferred only with difficulty. In the field situation the individual's beliefs, attitudes, and sets are of great importance, but the suspect's motivations tend to be to prove himself innocent. A similar motivation must be assumed for laboratory studies from which we expect to draw inferences to a real life context. Recent work by Thackray and Orne (1967) underscores the need for care in generalizing about motivation. In the context of one of several studies altering the consequences of detection, the

TABLE 19.2 SUCCESSFUL AND UNSUCCESSFUL DETECTION ON THE SECOND TRIAL OF SUBGROUPS TRYING TO BE DETECTED OR TO DECEIVE[a]

Motivation	Feedback		χ^2 between feedback groups
	Told detected	Told not detected	
"Need to be detected"			
Detected	4	14	10.28
Not detected	12	2	$p < .005$
"Need to deceive"			
Detected	15	3	15.36
Not detected	1	13	$p < .001$
χ^2 between motivation groups	12.96 $p < .001$	12.55 $p < .001$	

[a] A multiple chi-square contingency analysis here shows that neither feedback nor motivation have significant effects by themselves. The relevant chi-square values, calculated from partitioned subtables, are .25 ($p > .95$) and .00, respectively ($df = 1$). However, successful detection does depend significantly on the *interaction* between feedback and motivation ($\chi^2 = 30.94$; $p < .001$; $df = 1$).

Note.—Reprinted after an article by Lawrence A. Gustafson and Martin T. Orne published in the December 1965 *Journal of Applied Psychology.* Copyrighted by the American Psychological Association, Inc., 1965.

subjects were administered "need to deceive" instructions and then were divided into several subgroups receiving differential feedback of information regarding the polygraph's effectiveness. The subjects receiving information that they were detectable were easier to detect in a subsequent interrogation than those subjects who believed that they were not detected. This difference was true, however, only for the later part of the interrogation. These studies used a situation in which an attempt was made to create a high degree of subject involvement. It is possible that, when a high level of arousal exists, the effect of differential feedback of information may be masked, becoming evident only after the subjects habituate sufficiently to the interrogation procedure. In summary, it appears that not only degree of subject motivation but the object of the motivation as well are important determinants of deception. The task that the subject perceives to be his in an experiment and the subject's perception of the total situation can exercise a profound influence on the outcome of an experimental treatment.

The Experimental Paradigm in the Detection of Deception

As has been indicated earlier, no specific physiological responses are pathognomic of lying. If one asked a suspect, "Did you murder Mr. X?" and observed a physiological response to the question, one could not infer deception, since any suspect could be expected to respond to such a question. The problem is to find additional questions which, when asked of innocent persons, would lead to responses equivalent to those obtained from questions related to the crime under investigation. The development of questions that will have a differential impact only on the individual possessing what Lykken (1959) calls "guilty knowledge" constitutes the major effort on the part of the interrogator employing this technique. His task is made considerably more difficult, as Lee (1953) points out, by the fact that the suspect has usually been questioned extensively prior to the test regarding the details of the crime and, further, that relevant details are often known to both innocent and guilty alike through news media. The situation in the laboratory, however, is more easily controlled. If a

subject is asked to choose a card, the alternative choices that he did not make provide ready-made questions. It is easy to lose sight of the major differences between such a laboratory paradigm and the field situation.

When the subjects are asked to take a card, and the names of these cards are then presented to the individual, all the subjects are known to be guilty and the experimenter wishes to know the specific nature of the information about which they are guilty. This situation has been termed the "guilty information paradigm" (Gustafson & Orne, 1964). On the other hand, the usual field situation is most typically one in which the examiner and the suspect know the nature of the critical questions and the intent of the procedure is to determine whether or not the individual is lying about these questions. This situation has been called the "guilty person paradigm" (Gustafson & Orne, 1964); the task of the experimenter is to differentiate the guilty person(s) from those who are innocent. An analogous distinction is made by Ben Shakhar, Lieblich, and Kugelmass (1970) in a discussion of the altered criteria of detection necessary in applying a signal detection model to the detection of deception situation.

The task that a subject in the laboratory faces is very different for one paradigm as opposed to the other. In one instance he sees his task as concealing specific information that he is known to have; in the other instance he sees his task as one of convincing the interrogator that he does not have any special information at all. The paradigm employed will determine to a large extent the kind of strategy subjects use to avoid detection. In a study of possible countermeasures to avoid detection, Kubis (1962) indicates that it is easier for subjects to produce willfully augmented autonomic responses to irrelevant questions than to suppress their responses to the critical questions. The typical laboratory study using the guilty information paradigm invites the use of this countermeasure. Under the guilty person paradigm, however, such attempts would lead an operator to suspect deception. Moreover, when a polygraph examination is carried out by an interrogator in a real life situation, the effectiveness of this strategy is even more severely limited because the suspect is asked about the reason for any undue physiological response and the situation constrains him to explain such a response. Having done so, the question may be rephrased in such a manner as to reduce the possibility of responses occurring for such a reason. It would appear that in the hands of a good interrogator a suspect's attempt purposively to augment his responses to neutral stimuli has distinct limitations as a countermeasure.

It is not necessary for the subject and the experimenter to view the experiment as following the same paradigm. In the laboratory one may create a situation that, when seen from the subject's point of view, has many of the elements of the guilty person paradigm, while retaining the structure of the guilty information paradigm in the manner of stimulus presentation and selection of control questions. Such a mixed paradigm is applicable to both of the commonly used laboratory tasks, the card or number test and the mock crime. In the usual card or number test situation (Alpert, Kurtzberg, & Friedhoff, 1963; Block, 1957; Block et al., 1952; Burtt, 1921; Geldreich, 1941; Kubis, 1962; Kugelmass, 1967; Landis & Wiley, 1926; Langfeld, 1921; Obermann, 1939; Van Buskirk & Marcuse, 1954; Violante & Ross, 1964), all possible cards (including the one that the subject has selected) are presented as stimuli, a procedure which automatically requires that the subject lie concerning the card he actually selected. This situation is clearly one in which the subject and the experimenter both know that the subject has some special knowledge and that the experimenter is attempting to identify the nature of that knowledge. Under these circumstances, if the subject voluntarily produces an augmented physiological response, he successfully interferes with detection. The identical experimental procedure may be transformed into the guilty person paradigm, from the subject's point of view, by explaining that there are blank cards as well as numbered cards in the deck from which he is to draw a card. His task will be to convince the interrogator that he has selected a blank card. If he shows an undue response to any of the cards, regardless of whether he selected it or not, he will convince the interrogator of his guilt. This is much the same situation as is met in real life, where the suspect's task is to convince the interrogator that

he is innocent of any crime, rather than that he has committed another crime from that of which he is accused. The subject is thus constrained from responding to neutral stimuli as a countermeasure, in that he sees the task of the experimenter not as that of determining which card was chosen but rather whether or not the card chosen contained any significant information.

Gustafson and Orne (1964) carried out a study comparing the successful detection of information under two conditions, one in which the subject saw the experiment as attempting to detect guilty information and the other in which he saw the experiment as attempting to detect whether he had information or not. Subjects operating under the guilty person paradigm were significantly easier to detect, overall, than were subjects operating under the guilty information paradigm. In addition, the way in which the subject perceived his task interacted with the manner in which the stimuli (cards) were presented in the interrogation. Clearly, it is important to consider the subject's perception of his task as it relates to the type of information which he believes the experimenter seeks to uncover.

Next to the rather simple card selection procedure, the most frequently used experimental model is one in which the subject observes or participates in a mock crime and is subsequently interrogated concerning this crime (Baesen, Chung, & Yang, 1949; Berrien, 1942; Berrien & Huntington, 1943; Burtt, 1936; Chappell, 1929; Davidson, 1968; Kubis, 1962; Landis & Wiley, 1926; Lykken, 1959; Marston, 1917; Obermann, 1939; Runkel, 1936). This experimental procedure can also be presented to the subject as two different paradigms. In the guilty information paradigm the subject can be told that several crimes are possible and that the interrogator will try to find out which crime he committed. In the guilty person paradigm, the subject can be told that the interrogator will try to discover whether or not he has committed the crime. Most of the mock crime situations involve the use of the guilty person paradigm. Some, however (Baesen, Chung, & Yang, 1949; Burtt, 1936; Davidson, 1968; Kubis, 1962; Lykken, 1959), provide situations where several crimes or several roles in a crime are involved. In such situations it is possible for the subject to see his task as either to appear innocent or to avoid revealing his role in the crime. In the Baesen, Chung, and Yang (1949) study, pairs of subjects committed the mock crime; one of the subjects actually carried it out and the other observed. The subjects were told that the purpose of the experiment was to find out which of them had carried out the crime and which had observed. No subject was innocent of the crime. In contrast, Lykken (1959) had some of his subjects commit two crimes, some only one, and some committed no crime. The subjects were told that they were to be questioned about the two crimes, but no report was given concerning their perceived task in the situation. Burtt (1936) required his subjects to look into one of two boxes containing several miscellaneous articles. The investigators then attempted to identify the box into which the subject had looked, clearly a guilty information paradigm. Davidson (1968) ran four groups of subjects, one actually committing a crime, one attempting the crime but failing, one planning the crime but not attempting it, and one group of naïve subjects. The subjects were told that they could keep the proceeds of the crime if they could successfully avoid detection. Kubis (1962) created three roles: thief, lookout, and innocent suspect. The subjects who were assigned to the thief and lookout roles were told to appear completely innocent when questioned.

Apart from the obvious necessity of being aware of the paradigm under which these studies were run, it is also important to examine the degree of stimulus control present in each situation. As Lykken (1959) indicates, the subject in a mock crime situation cannot always be relied upon to notice all of the details about which he is questioned. Furthermore, certain aspects of the crime may have a greater impact on the subject than others. Orne and Thackray (1967) have developed an experimental situation that allows for a high degree of stimulus control and yet is flexible in terms of the paradigm. The subjects are asked to play the role of a courier with secret information in the form of code words. The words are thoroughly learned by the subjects and may be assigned without the knowledge of the interrogator. Furthermore, the code words may be words with little meaning to the subject outside of the experimental context.

The subjects can be told either to appear innocent of being a courier or to avoid revealing the code words. Orne and Thackray (1967) found that such a model led to high subject motivation and involvement and felt that a realistic interrogation resulted when the subjects played the courier role. The results of experiments using this procedure may be easily considered either in terms of identifying the guilty person or the guilty information.

The lack of uniformity between the various investigations in regard to the paradigm used has made cross comparisons of the results difficult. It is important to consider the paradigm under which the research is conducted, in light of the demonstrated effects of subject motivation and expectancies on detection. It would seem that to render the laboratory situation more like that encountered in the field, the subject should view his task as following the guilty person paradigm. For purposes of statistical treatment of results, however, one can seek to identify both information and guilty subjects.

The Nature of the Stimulus Material

Since the detection of deception depends upon the comparison of significant stimuli with neutral control stimuli, the nature of the critical stimuli used will affect the probability of a physiological response. On one end of a continuum is the selection of a card or number about which the individual is expected to lie. The stimulus has only the affective value given it by the experimental situation. On the other end of the continuum, the individual's actual name or similar pertinent facts about him, his family, or other aspects of his identity possess considerable affective value apart from the laboratory. Using personal material (mother's name, father's name, name of high school) Lykken (1960) was able to obtain 100% accuracy in matching subjects to arrays of stimuli. This high degree of success was probably a function not only of the nature of the stimuli but also the level of motivation and the limited number of subjects with whom the subject was compared.

Mock crimes have been used to provide stimuli that have affective value because of their association with the totality of an involving context. Baesen, Chung, and Yang (1949), Berrien and Huntington (1943), Davidson (1968), Ellson et al. (1952), Kubis (1962), Lykken (1959), and Marston (1921) reported rates of detection in studies employing mock crimes ranging from 94% (Lykken, 1959; Marston, 1921) to 50% (Landis & Wiley, 1926). The median rate of detection from these studies is 80%. If we compare this rate with the rates in most studies that have used neutral stimuli such as numbers, letters, or geometric designs (Alpert, Kurtzberg, & Friedhoff, 1963; Block, 1957; Block et al., 1952; Burtt, 1921; Geldreich, 1941; Landis & Wiley, 1926; MacNitt, 1942; Ruckmick, 1938; Van Buskirk & Marcuse, 1954), detection rates range from 40% (Landis & Wiley, 1926) to 83% (Ruckmick, 1938) with a median rate of 73%. While this might appear to be slightly lower, comparisons of this kind have little meaning. In a mock crime situation the subject may be told that a $26 sum was stolen, thereby causing the number 26 to become a meaningful stimulus because of its association with the context. This manipulation is not much different from having a subject select a card, thereby making the stimulus meaningful. Furthermore, as has already been pointed out, differences between studies in experimental paradigms, methods of presentation, physiological response used, etc., make valid comparisons impossible.

A systematic attempt to compare contextual and personal stimuli in the same situation, matching for involvement, was carried out by Thackray and Orne (1968b) using the courier situation. The subjects were told that they would play the role of couriers and would overlearn three critical code words. Having done so, they were told that they would be interrogated by someone who, because of a leak in the courier system, had the first names, last names, and dates of birth of six agents and their respective code words. The interrogator, however, would not know the subject's actual identity nor would he know whether the subject was one of the couriers or one of the subjects whose names he did not have and who were not familiar with any code words. They were told that their task would be to appear innocent; i.e., to appear not to be one of the individuals about whom they would be interrogated, nor were they to recognize any of the code words. Each subject was introduced to the interrogator as subject Number 26. Further,

the interrogator was in fact blind as to the identity of the subjects. Using this situation it was possible to compare the rate of detection to first name, last name, and date of birth with the rate to three random words that the subject had overlearned. The mean detection rank for the personal material (1.44) was significantly better ($p < .025$) than for the code words (1.62).

Lieblich (1966, 1969) systematically varied the relevance and frequency of usage of stimuli in an information detection situation. He found striking and consistently ordered differences in detection between conditions using the subject's own name and conditions using either an irrelevant name or one that is rare. Detection was greatest when the subject's own name was compared to alternative names known not to be related to the subject. Lower rates of detection were found when the subject's name was compared with names from within his family circle, and still lower rates when an irrelevant or rare name given to the subject was compared with names from within his family circle.

These findings support the common-sense assumption that subjects should be more responsive to personally relevant stimuli reinforced by the context than to previously neutral stimuli made relevant only within the experimental context. Even before any experimental manipulation, the subject's own name or date of birth should evoke a physiological response. This component is probably additive to that component engendered by the experimental situation.

In the field setting, one deals with stimuli that tend to be of great concern to the individual, and which have usually been associated in the individual's mind with their involving context many times. Such stimuli are not briefly associated with the context, as in an experiment, nor are they typically as enduring a part of an individual as is his own name. There are no systematic studies relating the ease with which differential physiological responses may be elicited under varying degrees of association between a stimulus and the context within which it became meaningful. It would be of great interest to know the effects of time on such an association and the effects of repeated interrogation. Probably some of the increase in detection rate with the courier situation used by Thackray and

Orne (1967), when compared to the usual card selection situations (84% versus 73%) results from the procedure of requiring the subjects to overlearn the stimulus words. Even the spontaneous rehearsal of such connections may ease the task of detection. Such rehearsal may form the basis for the suggestion made by Reid and Inbau (1966) that, after each question session, the examiner leave the room for a few minutes to allow "a lying subject . . . [to] . . . develop greater concern with respect to whatever lies he may be contemplating . . . [p. 28]." In the laboratory context the results of such incubation are probably much more closely approximated by the subject's own name or personal material than by a card, number, or other similar stimuli.

For the most part, laboratory studies have not begun to concern themselves with the nature of the stimuli used in the detection of deception and their effect on the rates of detection. Several studies (Jones & Wechsler, 1928; Smith, 1922; Syz, 1926) have explored differential responsivity in other contexts, but laboratory studies within the detection of deception framework are rare. It would seem that, in light of the central role played by the stimulus material in detection, such studies are in order.

Methods of Stimulus Presentation

Most laboratory research has utilized what has been called the "relevant-irrelevant" method of stimulus presentation (Inbau & Reid, 1953; Lee, 1953), where critical and neutral stimuli are presented to the subject either in a completely random order or in some other sequence unknown to the subject. Such a procedure has many obvious design advantages, including the facilitation of counterbalancing and the equating of stimuli.

In field situations, on the other hand, the tendency has been to use questions that the suspect knows in advance; both the nature of the questions and the order in which they are presented are familiar to him. Such techniques arise from the use of the pretest interview and are partly the consequence of having to develop appropriate control questions. They also permit the interrogator to discuss the meaning of the questions in such a manner as to minimize misunderstandings.

Each of the procedures has certain advantages.

In the case of the relevant-irrelevant method, it is difficult for the individual to prepare himself in advance, since he does not know what question to expect. The element of surprise plays a role in all of his answers. On the other hand, the overall level of responsivity remains very high, since the subject does not know exactly what to expect next. In a situation of high motivation and concern, the response to the relevant question may be augmented, but even the irrelevant questions will, because of the manner in which they are presented, evoke considerable physiological response.

A procedure in which a suspect knows what to expect, especially when the questions are discussed in great detail, has the advantage that little or no response should be evoked by the neutral control questions. Any undue response, even to neutral questions, can therefore become a meaningful indication of possible deception. The overall level of responsivity can be greatly reduced and, while this would also affect the responsivity to the critical items, the remaining response to these items would tend to be far more conspicuous in relation to the control questions once the surprise element is eliminated. Such a procedure, on the other hand, permits the suspect to prepare himself for the critical items and, to the extent that he is able to suppress a response, might make detection more difficult. In the most characteristic form of interrogation of this kind, the peak-of-tension technique, the interrogator not only compares the relative response to the critical item but takes advantage of the suspect's tendency to relax once it has passed, looking for (as the name implies) a peaking of tension at the time of the critical item.

Marcuse and Bitterman (1946), discussing the peak-of-tension technique, feel that experimenter biases (voice inflections, subtle mannerisms, etc.) may unduly influence the course of an examination. The same sources of error are, however, inherent in the relevant-irrelevant method as well. In the laboratory these can be controlled by making certain that the person conducting the examination is unaware of the identity of the critical items; in the field no such ready solution is available.

Any comparison between stimulus methods of presentation must be carried out under comparable conditions. Gustafson and Orne (1964) compared the two procedures by asking subjects to select a numbered card. Numbers were then presented either in a random fashion, following the relevant-irrelevant procedure, or in ascending and descending order, following the peak-of-tension procedure. Each of these methods of stimulus presentation was studied under both the guilty person and the guilty information paradigms. When the guilty information paradigm was used, the relevant-irrelevant method was significantly more effective than the peak-of-tension technique; when the guilty person paradigm was employed, however, both techniques became more effective and any advantage of the relevant-irrelevant method was obviated. The peak-of-tension method appeared particularly vulnerable to the creation of false-positive responses in the laboratory context. Such responses, however, would not be a very effective stratagem in the real life situation and, when the laboratory design restrains subjects from their use, the findings appear more in line with the reported experience of professional interrogators that the two techniques are similar (Reid & Inbau, 1966).

The Effect of Habituation

As will be discussed later, the probability of detection is raised by increasing the number of trials available comparing different significant stimuli to neutral controls. One simple way in which such an increase may be augmented is to repeat the same stimuli. To the extent that one is dealing with random responses, a repetition will tend to clarify which stimuli evoke a differentially greater response. Habituation, however, may diminish the differential responsivity. The crucial question, then, concerns the relative rates of habituation between significant and control stimuli. If the critical stimuli habituate more rapidly than do control stimuli, little will be gained by extensive repetition of the same stimuli.

A study reported by Ellson et al. (1952) compared 10 subjects who were administered two series of five trials, each consisting of the names of six months, one of which the subject had previously selected. The average number of successful detections was 80% for the first series and 70% for the second series. Although somewhat inconclusive due to the small N, this finding suggests greater

habituation to the critical stimuli and is similar to a finding of Gustafson and Orne who, in an unpublished study, repeated a simple card test five times, motivating the subjects as described earlier. It was observed that combining the first and second repetition yielded a somewhat increased accuracy of detection over the first alone but that adding the third repetition did not augment detection. The addition, in turn, of the fourth and fifth repetitions actually decreased accuracy, indicating that in that situation at least, detection was not facilitated by habituation.

The relationship of habituation to detection, however, is by no means simple. As mentioned earlier, Thackray and Orne (1967) observed that a differential treatment effect became clear only at the end of a long series of stimuli. This study was characterized by a great deal of responsivity to neutral stimuli, which seemed to attenuate more rapidly under those circumstances than the responsivity to the significant stimuli. The effect of habituation on differential responsivity may be a function of the involvement of the individual. Peterson and Jung (1907) report the results of three successive trials on a word association test, during which the skin potential response (SPR) was monitored. During the first trial a number of stimuli elicited responses, one of which was to a stimulus with which the subject was emotionally involved. On the second trial the response to this stimulus was the largest and only a few other stimuli evoked significant responses. On the third trial, the same stimulus led to an only slightly attenuated response, while the other stimuli now produced very little response. Jones and Wechsler (1928), again using the word association technique, found differential habituation even within one trial. When a list of mixed emotional and neutral words was given, the responses to the neutral words became less for words at the end of the list when compared to the same words when placed at the front of the list, while emotion-provoking words showed no such position effect. These results, different from those of the Ellson et al. (1952) and the unpublished Gustafson and Orne studies, both obtained with card selection tests, raise the possibility that successive trials may serve to accentuate the signal-to-noise ratio when more involving stimuli are utilized.

If it is possible to habituate a subject to the neutral stimuli while minimizing or preventing habituation to the critical stimulus, then detection should be dramatically improved. Geldreich (1941) demonstrated this process. The subjects in one group were asked to choose a card from a set of five and then were administered a single series of questions concerning which card they had drawn. Using the GSR, he correctly identified the chosen card for 74% of the subjects. The other group was also required to select a card, following which they were administered from 20 to 50 cards, none of which were in the original set of five, until virtually no GSR was elicited. Then the original set of five cards was presented. Under these conditions, the subjects differentially habituated to the noncritical stimuli and essentially failed to habituate to the critical stimulus. As one would predict, the GSRs to the noncritical stimuli in the final set were substantially less than GSRs to comparable noncritical stimuli in the group without habituation. The average response to the critical stimulus, however, was essentially the same in both groups. As a result, the correct card was identified for 100% of the subjects in the second group.

The studies mentioned so far in this section have used the GSR as a measure of responsivity. The detection of deception in the field, however, typically employs the heart rate, "relative blood pressure," and respiration changes in addition to, or in place of, the GSR. Differential habituation is likely to vary with the parameter being examined. In an unpublished study, Solomon et al. (1958), focusing on the conditioning of the heart rate in humans to highly dramatic stimuli, observed that the heart rate and respiratory changes were difficult to condition and extinguished very rapidly, whereas differential GSRs persisted over a long period of time. J. P. Seward and G. H. Seward (1934) supported these observations in a study tracing the course of habituation to shock stimuli. They found that, within the same session, body movement and respiration responses to the shock diminished more quickly than did the GSR.

It seems likely that differential responsivity on parameters such as the heart rate or blood pressure would demand a very high level of arousal in the subject, perhaps sufficiently great to interfere with the easy recognition of a differential GSR responsivity. A lower level of arousal, on the other hand, might facilitate the recognition of differential GSR responsivity, while even lower levels of arousal again reduce differential responsivity. Darrow (1936) felt that adrenin (natural secretion of which adrenalin is an analog) inhibited the GSR and that blood pressure might therefore be a better measure at high levels of activation. Systematic work on the differential responsivity of measures with differing levels of activation is lacking.

The Role of Verbal Response

Although a few studies have not required a verbal response (Gustafson & Orne, 1963; Lieblich, 1966; Lykken, 1959), most studies require subjects to respond "Yes" or "No" to the questions. The procedure is usually arranged such that the subject will be forced to lie concerning the critical item. The extent to which verbal lying influences detection rates has been investigated in several studies (Ellson et al., 1952; Gustafson & Orne, 1965b; Kugelmass, Lieblich, & Bergman, 1967; Lieblich, 1966), all employing the GSR as the physiological measure. The conclusions to be reached from examining these studies are, at best, equivocal. Part of the confusion arises out of the diversity of procedures among the studies. Some studies have compared saying "Yes" to each question with saying "No" to each question (Ellson et al., 1952; Kugelmass et al., 1967). Others have compared saying "No" to remaining mute (Gustafson & Orne, 1965b; Lieblich, 1966). Gustafson and Orne (1965b) have also compared these two latter conditions with a condition in which subjects were required to respond with the first word that came to mind in a free association procedure.

The results are as varied as the procedures. Ellson et al. (1952) found in their pilot study that four of their eight subjects were detected when required to say "No" to each question, while only two of the eight (chance) were detected when replying in the affirmative. No assessment of significance was possible because of the small N and the use of the subjects as their own controls. Kugelmass, Lieblich, and Bergman (1967) replicated these conditions and compared trials in which individuals were required to say "No" to all questions with trials in which they were required to say "Yes" to all questions, counterbalancing for order. Under both conditions, the subjects were detected at a level well above chance, and no significant difference was found between conditions.

Gustafson and Orne (1965b), in a study comparing three groups of separate individuals, in which all subjects were motivated to deceive the experimenter, found that both those subjects who responded with "No" and those remaining silent were detected at a level significantly above chance, with the "No" group exhibiting the higher detection rate. The subjects in the free association group, however, were not detected better than chance. Lieblich (1966) ran two conditions out of six, in which his subjects were requested to remain mute. Although the material used in these two conditions was rather neutral, detection in the mute conditions was reduced from that in similar conditions in which the subjects were required to lie.

Clearly, the differentially augmented physiological response that forms the basis for the detection of deception is not contingent upon the subject's actual lying. It can occur in the absence of any verbal response and may also occur when subjects tell the truth to critical stimuli and lie to irrelevant ones (Kugelmass et al., 1967; Reid & Inbau, 1966). It is tempting to explain these discrepancies by indicating that it is the deceptive intent, rather than an overt lie, that is responsible for the increased physiological response. There appear, however, to be at least two other components in the detection of deception situation that are often confounded with the effect of lying or deception. The first of these components is that the subject is sensitized to an essentially neutral stimulus by the mere fact of drawing attention to it as the selected stimulus. This effect is in contrast to that seen when a stimulus has inherent arousal value, which has been discussed earlier. The sensitization effect is a situation-specific arousal inherent in the process of selecting any given stimulus as critical in the set of stimuli. The selected material becomes the figure in a figure-ground relationship among stimuli, with the remaining stimuli constituting the ground.

Only when the stimuli are all intrinsically neutral, and both lying and deceptive intent are eliminated, does the effect of sensitization become self-evident. If a subject is asked to select a numbered card from among several, to place it in full view of the experimenter, and then to respond honestly when asked by a tape recording about several numbers, the mere selection of a particular number will result in some increase in the GSR to the chosen number. In such an experiment, the subject responds "No" to each number except the one he had selected, and it could be argued that the augmented physiological response is a function of the different verbal response rather than of the sensitization to a particular number. Similar findings are obtained, however, if the same experimental procedure is followed, the chosen number exposed in full view, and the subject then asked to say "No" to each number in a context where his "lie" could not conceivably have deceptive intent. This type of sensitization to a selected number is present in all card test situations, and is generally confounded with the consequences of attempting to deceive. It is an effect which becomes obvious only in the kind of situation described above, where the stimuli are truly neutral and matched, the situation simple, and the time interval between card selection and the presentation of the stimuli is kept very brief to prevent the effect from being swamped by other factors.

The same kind of an experimental procedure can be easily altered to demonstrate the effect of trying to deceive. Merely instructing the subject not to show the card to the experimenter and to try his best to conceal its identity in his physiological responses—adding perhaps that this is difficult but some intelligent subjects are able to do so—leads to a significantly greater physiological response to the selected card. The sensitization effects, the effects of the intrinsic arousal value of the stimuli, and the motivation to deceive, as well as the consequences of detection, all appear to be independent and additive in the degree they augment the differential physiological response.

The second component is the amount of attention the subject pays to the entire set of stimuli. While this effect is partly determined by the motivational factors discussed earlier, instructing the subject to respond "No" (or "Yes") identically to each stimulus allows a strategy of ignoring the saliency of the selected stimulus. (This is why in a field context questions are phrased to require both yes and no answers in order to assert innocence.)

The effect of whether or not the subjects pay attention to the stimuli was noted in the Gustafson and Orne study (1965b). Postexperimental inquiries with subjects revealed that, when the individual had the task of providing free associations, it was possible for the subject to decide in advance on a number of associates which he then used as responses in a mechanical fashion; this strategy actually helped the subjects to ignore the content of the stimuli. Subjects reported that they found it easier to ignore the stimuli when carrying out this task than when they were required either to say "No" to every stimulus or to attend without giving any verbal response.

It may also be possible, however, for subjects who are required to say "No" to each stimulus to do so in a completely mechanical fashion, responding with "No" to the sound rather than to the actual word. Instances have been observed, for example, where subjects answered "No" when instructed that the test was completed, or when they heard some extraneous noise. No such response is observed with subjects who are differentially verbalizing, since it is essential for these subjects to listen to the stimuli as they are presented in order to respond correctly.

The additional factors that seem to play a major role in laboratory situations appear less relevant in the field situation because of the profound consequences of the interrogation. Furthermore, questions in the field situation are frequently arranged so that both "Yes" and "No" answers may be required, depending on the way in which the question is asked. Such a procedure forces attention to the questions asked, so as not to answer incorrectly. Even during procedures in which all answers may be the same, the suspect is so deeply involved in the situation that he is likely to attend to every cue and stimulus present in order to avoid making a mistake. In the laboratory the role of lying and the response required of the subject is, as yet, an unsettled question. Studies must separate the factors of involvement and attention from those concerning the response. It appears that, in the labora-

tory, either a "Yes" or a "No" response facilitates detection over an unrelated response or no response. Detection is possible, however, at a level significantly better than chance without any verbal response, provided that the subject is motivated to deceive and the stimuli have sufficient impact. The clarification of the specific effect of the verbal response on the likelihood of detection remains a task for future research.

Response Variables

To evaluate the state of the subject with respect to the stimuli presented him, one must have some measure of his emotional response. By far the most frequently used measures are those several correlates of autonomic nervous system activity which are subject to rapid change and a rapid return to baseline. Some investigators have used motor activity of the hand, eye movements, or verbal responses, measures usually considered to be more nearly under voluntary control. Such experiments rely on the psychological effect of the stimuli to produce abnormalities in these more usual modes of response. In view of the reliance placed on autonomic measures in the field, these will be discussed first.

Measures of autonomic activity While studies have demonstrated differences between individual patterns of autonomic activity (Lacey & Lacey, 1958; Schnore, 1959; Wenger, Clemens, Coleman, Cullen, & Engel, 1961) and differences between various emotional states and the patterns produced (Ax, 1953; Sternbach, 1960), there is no evidence at the present time that the autonomic changes which accompany deception differ qualitatively from those produced in other emotional states involving sympathetic nervous system activation. In general investigators feel that deception responses most closely resemble those characteristic of emotional excitement (Chappell, 1929) or fear (Marston, 1917), although even simple, auditory stimuli have been shown to produce autonomic patterns which are essentially the same as those occurring during deception (Davis, Buchwald, & Frankmann, 1955). A great deal of the research that has been done on the psychophysiological correlates of emotion is relevant to the detection of deception problem, but a discussion of most of this work is beyond the scope of this section. (See Arnold, 1960; Woodworth & Schlosberg, 1954.)

Most studies in the detection of deception use the detection rate as the validating criterion for judging the usefulness of the measures employed. As the preceding sections of this chapter tried to make clear, however, both subject and task variables are significant determinants of detection rates. Since few studies have concerned themselves exclusively with response variables per se, the effectiveness of any given physiological or behavioral measure of deception is generally confounded with these other experimental manipulations. Only when several response variables are included in a single study is it possible to draw meaningful conclusions concerning their relative effectiveness. To the extent possible, emphasis will be given to those studies which provide a comparison of more than one response variable within a single design.[3]

Cardiovascular measures Commercial "lie detectors" have used a measure often referred to as "relative blood pressure," obtained by inflating an arm or wrist cuff to a point approximately halfway between systolic and diastolic pressure. Davis (1961) has pointed out that this technique can be both painful and dangerous, unless frequently interrupted, and is not a true measure of either systolic or diastolic pressure. Perhaps for this reason, attempts are currently underway among field experts to change from the term "relative-blood-pressure" tracing to the term "cardio" tracing. This change reflects the growing awareness that this tracing does not really reflect changes in blood pressure but volumetric changes in the arm and heart rate. It is important that cardio measures and true measures of systolic pressure not be confused, since the two are quite different. Most laboratory studies and several early field studies have used systolic blood pressure rather than the cardio tracings, taking measurements intermittently during the course of questioning (Chappell, 1929; Landis & Gullette, 1925; Landis & Wiley, 1926; Langfeld, 1921; Marston, 1917). A frequent response is a rise in

---

[3]Even when a hierarchy has been established within a single study, however, there is no assurance that the relationships will remain invariant with other levels of activation.

pressure that is greater during deception than when the subjects are telling the truth. As expected, because of individual differences in reactivity and differences in procedure, the magnitude of the mean difference varies across the studies. Using systolic blood pressure alone, Chappell (1929) obtained 87% correct discrimination between subjects telling the truth or lying concerning details of a mock crime. Marston (1921), also using a mock crime, obtained 94% accuracy in differentiating between liars and those choosing to tell the truth. Recent investigators have not reported results as outstanding as these. Ellson et al. (1952) found systolic blood pressure measures about equal to respiration measures, and far inferior to the GSR. Thackray and Orne (1968a) found no evidence of discrimination with a measure of systolic blood pressure.

A reason for the differences may stem from the temporal relationships between the stimuli and measures of systolic blood pressure. The time necessary for a maximal rise in systolic pressure following a stimulus has not been well established, although Rushmer (1961) notes that rises in blood pressure are rapidly modulated through the baroreceptor reflex. The ability of a procedure, such as systolic pressure monitoring, to detect deception may well depend largely upon the time at which the pressure is measured. Both Ellson et al. (1952) and Thackray and Orne (1967) used devices to measure systolic pressure automatically at relatively fixed intervals. When the lack of success with the measure in these two studies is contrasted with the success reported by Chappell (1929) and Marston (1917), it seems possible that the manual determination of blood pressure is effective because it time-locks the measure in a fixed relationship to the stimuli, whereas an automatic system introduces a variable time interval between the stimulus and the point of measurement.

In the past few years a number of measures have been investigated for the purpose of augmenting or replacing blood pressure as a measure of cardiovascular changes during deception. Perhaps the most common technique is digital plethysmography. Brown (1967) has covered this measure in detail and states that "the plethysmogram is an extremely sensitive measure of internally and externally induced changes, surpassing even the electrical skin phenomena in this respect [p. 55]." The experience of investigators in the area of the laboratory detection of deception does not, however, show the measure to be as useful as GSR.

Although the heart rate is easily derived from either the electrocardiogram (EKG) or from records of finger or pulse volume and is a commonly used measure in psychophysiology, it has received little attention in laboratory studies of deception. Changes in the heart rate are difficult to see unless special circuitry is employed to convert the inter-pulse time into a measure of rate.

None of these cardiovascular measures appears to discriminate well between guilty and innocent individuals in the laboratory setting, as indicated in the few studies comparing these measures with others, notably with the GSR. Kubis (1962) reported pulse volume to be slightly superior to respiration in supplying cues to examiners attempting to differentiate guilt from innocence. Violante and Ross (1964), on the other hand, found respiration to be superior to pulse volume and found little or no discrimination with finger volume. In a study comparing several measures of autonomic activity during deception, Thackray and Orne (1968a) observed that finger volume discriminated between innocent and guilty subjects at a better than chance level, while pulse volume did not. In all of these studies the GSR was the best discriminator. While Kugelmass and Lieblich (1966) and Kugelmass, Lieblich, Ben-Ishai, Opatowski, and Kaplan (1968) found the heart rate to discriminate no better than chance, Ellson et al. (1952) indicated that heart rate was slightly superior to pulse volume but inferior to the GSR and systolic pressure. Even pulse volume was found to discriminate at a level better than chance. They indicated that the heart rate response consisted of an initial acceleration, followed by deceleration, with the magnitude of the deceleration becoming greater during lying than during truth. Maximum discrimination with the plethysmographic technique occurred when they measured the rate at which subjects recovered from increased peripheral resistance during the 12–22 sec post-stimulus period, with non-lie responses recovering more rapidly than lie responses. This measure was employed after discovering that equal vasocon-

striction responses were evident to both critical and noncritical stimuli. They suggested that a maximal response may have occurred in both cases. In the light of these data, Brown's (1967) statement that the plethysmogram is highly sensitive to change may indicate that the measure is too sensitive to yield a differential response in the detection of deception. The lack of agreement across studies concerning the usefulness of these measures suggests that greater effort should be directed toward an understanding of cardiovascular changes during deception.

Psychological changes in the subject are reflected both in changes in the cardiac output and in the amount of peripheral resistance. Blood pressure itself is the end product of the complex interplay of heart rate, stroke volume, and vasomotor influences. An increase in the heart rate alone, unaccompanied by other circulatory changes, affects diastolic blood pressure but has relatively little effect on systolic pressure. On the other hand, an increase in the volume of blood pumped per beat will affect primarily the systolic blood pressure, consequently increasing pulse pressure. An increase in peripheral resistance results in an increase in the mean blood pressure, but the more intense effect is on diastolic pressure, due to the longer period of the diastole relative to the systole (Best & Taylor, 1950). The primary cause of increased cardiac output may be an increase in stroke volume, rather than in the heart rate (Rushmer, 1961). The "cardio" measure, used with success in the field situation, is largely a plethysmographic measure. The record reflects complex interactions between the blood pressure and volumetric changes in the arm (Woodworth & Schlosberg, 1954). Reid and Inbau (1966) indicate that the usual criterion for deception consists of a rise in the baseline of the tracing; a decrease in pulse amplitude may or may not be present. Changes in the baseline level of the tracing are likely to reflect an increase in blood flow, which in turn may be accompanied by various different kinds of blood pressure changes. During emotionally mediated activation of the sympathetic nervous system, vasoconstriction takes place in the skin and in the splanchnic viscera, while vasodilation occurs in the skeletal muscles (Brod, 1964). At least part of the increase in cuff pressure observed during deception in the field situation is probably a result of the increase in volume produced by the increased blood flow to the muscles that make up the bulk of the upper arm tissue and greatly outweigh any reduction in blood flow to the skin of the upper arm (Brod, Hejl, & Ulrych, 1963). Ansley (1959) gave some support to this contention. He compared records taken with the standard arm cuff to those taken with a wrist cuff; in most cases the wrist cuff records showed markedly reduced responses, although the majority of records could be readily scored for deception. Placing the cuff over the musculature of the upper arm rather than the forearm may increase responsivity, since about 85% of the tissue in this area is skeletal muscle (Barron & Ruch, 1960). If some measure of the relative concentrations of blood in the viscera and skeletal musculature were available, it might serve as a sensitive measure of deception. The measurement of visceral vasoconstriction, however, would seem difficult at best.

A few other measures of cardiovascular activity have been suggested for use in the detection of deception, among which are pulse velocity (Dana & Barnett, 1957; Ellson et al., 1952; J. G. L. Williams & B. Williams, 1965) and blood flow. Reid and Inbau (1966) suggest the use of blood flow on the basis of preliminary investigations using an infrared sensor placed on the neck over the carotid artery. Their evidence indicates that the measure is differentially sensitive to stimuli during a card test and suggests that a Doppler shift measurement of blood flow in the arm might prove useful as well.

Respiratory measures   Measures of respiration were among the first to be used in the detection of deception (Trovillo, 1939). With the exception of the early work of Benussi (1914), virtually no studies of deception have used respiration measures as a sole physiological index, perhaps because of the difficulty involved in an attempt to quantify the respiratory pattern. Although the practice among field examiners is to regard any marked change in respiratory patterns following critical questions as indicative of deception (Joseph, 1957; Reid & Inbau, 1966; Trovillo, 1942), laboratory studies have usually employed either Benussi's inspiration-expiration (*I/E*) ratio (Burtt, 1921; Landis & Gullette, 1925; Landis & Wiley, 1926) or more

simple measures of average respiration amplitude and breathing cycle time (Ellson et al., 1952). There seems to be an increase in the ratio of the time of inspiration to the time of expiration (*I/E* ratio) following deception. This increase is closely related to the increase in breathing cycle time found by Ellson et al. following deception. These latter investigators also found breathing amplitude to be reduced during deception, when compared to nondeception responses. Some of the difficulties in quantifying respiration may be the result of difficulties in obtaining the *I/E* ratio. Ellson et al. (1952) reported that they attempted to determine the ratio from several records and found that no clear delineation existed between periods of inspiration, expiration, and rest. The lack of a distinctive point of change, they feel, can easily lead to large random variations in the ratio.

Apart from the measurement of respiratory parameters by means of a sensor stretched around the thoracic or abdominal region, very little work has been done on monitoring respiration within the area of deception detection. Reid and Inbau (1966) report the use of Doppler techniques to obtain the usual respiration tracing without sensor contact. Ellson et al. (1952) employed a thermocouple placed so as to measure the temperature of the subject's breath as he inhaled and exhaled. They found that baseline changes in breath temperature occurred but they were not significantly related to the stimuli. Measures of tidal volume or gaseous saturations in the breath, which require the subject to breathe through a mouthpiece, would seem to be impractical in the detection of deception situation. Impedance pneumography, however, may have potential as an alternative technique (Stein & Luparello, 1967).

Galvanic skin response   The galvanic skin response has long been recognized to be one of the most sensitive indicators of autonomic activity.[4] (See Edelberg, 1967, and Chapter 9 of this book for techniques and theory.) Its use in the detection of deception has had an interesting and controversial history. Many persons with field experience claim

[4]Because the results with other measures of the electrodermal response, such as the SPR, have thus far closely paralleled those obtained with the GSR in detection of deception situations (Thackray & Orne, 1968a), only the GSR will be discussed.

the GSR to be useful in the laboratory but of much less value than respiration and blood pressure in criminal investigations (Larson, 1932; Lee, 1953; Marston, 1938; Reid & Inbau, 1966). They appear to reflect the belief that the GSR is too responsive to any stimulus, making unequivocal decisions difficult in real life situations. Others, however, have supported the use of the GSR in the field. Kugelmass et al. (1968) found both relative blood pressure and the GSR about equal in detecting card choices with criminal suspects. Summers (1939) strongly supported the use of the GSR in both laboratory and field applications, and reported detection rates of over 98% with this measure alone. Likewise, MacNitt (1942) also supported the GSR and reported detection rates of equal magnitudes in both laboratory and field situations.

Interestingly enough, most of the laboratory studies that have compared GSR with one or more additional variables agree that the GSR is superior to other variables in the detection of deception. Ellson et al. (1952), for example, found it far superior to all of the other variables they investigated, as did Thackray and Orne (1968a). Likewise, Kubis (1962) reported GSR to be considerably better than either pulse volume or respiration, while Violante and Ross (1964), using measures similar to those of Kubis, also found GSR to discriminate better than other measures. Kugelmass and Lieblich (1966) obtained significant discrimination with GSR but not with pulse rate.

All of these studies tried to create highly motivating or involving situations for the subjects, in an attempt to approximate the real life situation. Ellson et al. (1952) and Kubis (1962) employed mock crimes, while Violante and Ross (1964) used aversive stimuli (noise) in a conditioning paradigm. Kugelmass and Lieblich (1966) specifically tried to create a highly stressful situation by employing policemen as subjects and informing them, as one of the experimental conditions, that their future occupational advancement might depend upon their success in controlling emotions in the polygraph test. Despite the variety of conditions and stresses, all found the GSR to be highly effective.

It is, of course, possible that the highly emotional circumstances of actual examining conditions in a criminal case were not even approached in

these studies, and thus they offer no real argument against the contentions of field authorities. The problems of simulating real life situations are too well known to require elaboration. A lack of involvement on the part of the subjects in all of the studies, however, particularly the Kugelmass and Lieblich (1966) study, is difficult to believe.

It has been argued that the equipment employed for measuring GSR in the field is inadequate, accounting for the lack of success with this measure (Ellson et al., 1952; Higley, 1958). In an unpublished study conducted by Gustafson, GSR detection rates based upon measures obtained from a Stoelting Deceptograph (an instrument typical of those used in the field) were compared to those obtained using a Beckman Dynograph with a constant current bridge and zinc-zinc sulphate electrodes. No difference in detection rates was found. While the equipment employed by field examiners to measure GSR may leave much to be desired in terms of current psychophysiological practice, it is doubtful that its inadequacies are the sole explanation for the convictions held by field personnel regarding the effectiveness of the GSR in guilt detection.

The relative effectiveness of GSR in both laboratory and field situations remains to be evaluated. No simple explanation such as equipment insufficiencies or level of arousal can fully account for the discrepancies. It is clear, however, that in laboratory settings, particularly with low subject involvement, GSR has been the most effective discriminator. It is also true that GSR is difficult to interpret with extremely anxious subjects; and under these circumstances respiration and the cardio tracings remain easily interpreted by inspection. The tendency to discount the GSR in the field situation is probably also related to the fact that some individuals are very unresponsive on this variable. Whether this lack of GSR responsivity is situational or a matter of autonomic specificity has not been investigated in this context. Despite all this, some individuals with extensive field experience are convinced that GSR is the most useful index of deception. In the absence of definitive data, the possibility that reports concerning the effectiveness of the GSR as a discriminator in field situations are related in large part to operator preference and response specificity cannot be excluded.

Oxygen saturation   A measure of the oxygen saturation in the blood can easily be obtained by means of a photoelectric sensor attached to the pinna of the ear or placed on the neck (Dana, 1958; Dana & Barnett, 1957). This measure has been shown to reflect emotional changes (Lovett Doust & Schneider, 1955), although changes in oxygen saturation take place at a rate somewhat slower than the rate for other measures (Dana & Barnett, 1957). Thackray and Orne (1968a) compared discrimination with the oxygen saturation measure to discrimination with several other measures; they found the discrimination significantly better than chance for experimental material (code words) but not for personally relevant material. The relatively slow rate of change in this measure, however, probably precludes its use in field situations.

Pupillary response   The response of the pupil to changes in autonomic activity in emotional states has been known for some time (Bender, 1933; Löwenstein & Friedman, 1942) and has more recently become the object of considerable research (Hess, 1965; Hess, Seltzer, & Shlien, 1965; Woodmansee, 1966). Berrien and Huntington (1943) compared pupillary responses to a measure of relative blood pressure in a deception situation involving a mock crime. The most typical response consisted of a slow, negatively accelerated dilation, lasting 1–5 sec, followed by a rapid constriction. Although this response also occurred spontaneously following control questions, it was most frequent when deception was involved. A second pupillary indicator of deception consisted of an increase in pupillary fluctuation in guilty subjects when the critical questions were introduced. When scored independently, both pupillary response and blood pressure yielded correct discrimination in over 70% of the cases and, since misidentifications of subjects on one measure were not necessarily the same as those on the other measure, the authors note that the two measures serve to complement each other, in combination yielding about 80% detection. Simultaneous significant changes to critical stimuli in both measures occurred in only 48% of the responses.

The most severe drawback in the use of the pupillary response is the problem of measurement. Photographic recording of the response has long been common (Bender, 1933), sometimes employing infrared lighting and film to avoid illumination differences (Lindsley, 1951); recently, devices have been developed using photocells to scan the eye (Löwenstein, 1956). Such techniques, in addition to the possible use of closed circuit television, should facilitate further research with this interesting and potentially significant measure.

Electroencephalogram   A number of investigators have reported a blocking or reduction in the alpha activity of the electroencephalogram (EEG) with stimulation of an emotion-producing sort (Lindsley, 1951; Thiesen, 1943; Williams, 1939). The only known study employing the EEG in the detection of deception was conducted by Obermann (1939), with two separate experiments reported, one involving neutral stimuli (numbered cards) and the other involving knowledge of the details of a fictitious crime. Monopolar recordings from a left occipital placement were obtained with the eyes closed, and judges were asked to rank the records on the basis of their likelihood of being indicative of deception, using as a criterion any disturbance in the record. Although the statistical treatment of the data makes them difficult to interpret in terms of the discrimination achieved, the detection of deception with EEG criteria seems possible. Interestingly enough, more objective measures of amplitude or percentage of alpha activity did not prove as efficient as did the subjective judgment.

Miscellaneous autonomic measures   The use of several other measures of autonomic nervous system activity has been suggested, among them salivary secretion, pilomotor response, and gastrointestinal motility. No evidence is available, however, concerning the use of these measures in the detection of deception. It would seem that the understanding and refinement of some of the more usual measures would be of greater value than would the proliferation of a number of esoteric measures, unless a significant improvement in detection can be demonstrated (Orlansky, 1962).

Behavioral measures of deception   Although the emphasis in current interrogation seems to focus on physiological measurements that are recorded during the examination period, field operators have long recognized the important information to be gained from observations of a suspect's actions, manner, and vocal responses (Reid & Arther, 1953; Reid & Inbau, 1966). While aspects of the subject's behavior no doubt add to the interrogator's ability to classify him correctly (Kubis, 1950), a number of studies have specifically investigated overt behavioral measures in the detection of deception situation. A clear separation does not exist between these measures and those covered previously. Respiration, for instance, is under voluntary control, as well as subject to autonomic influences, and several of the measures in the present section are probably influenced, in part, by autonomic activity. Nevertheless, the following behavioral measures have been employed to detect the presence of deceptive responses.

Reaction time   The use of associative reaction time to indicate deception was one of the earliest methods employed (Jung, 1907; Jung, 1910; Wertheimer, 1905; Wertheimer & Klein, 1904; Yerkes & Berry, 1909). A review of this early literature has been compiled by Crosland (1929). If a subject is asked to associate freely to a list of words, some critical to a crime and others neutral, it is expected that he will either give himself away through revealing or bizarre responses or, in suppressing such reponses, will give long reaction times and signs of emotion. As Woodworth and Schlosberg (1954) point out, however, it is vital that normative data from known innocent subjects be available, since critical words are typically less common than are the neutral words and will result in long reaction times, due to a lack of associations.

Marston (1920) studied reaction time in a laboratory situation, in which the subjects were instructed to either obey or disobey requests concerning arithmetic operations to be performed on sets of numbers. The time required to answer each item was measured, and it was predicted that response times would be longer when the subject disobeyed the experimenter and tried to deceive him. He found three groups of subjects: those whose responses were longer as predicted, those whose reaction times were inconsistent, and those who gave consistently shorter reaction times. He felt that both those subjects with shorter reaction times and those with longer response times were displaying a typical deception response. Goldstein

(1923), however, felt that those subjects with shorter reaction times were simply not involved in the task of deceiving the experimenter. The whole argument raised considerable controversy (English, 1926; Goldstein, 1923; Marston, 1925; Rich, 1926) but, as a general conclusion, whenever considerable affect is generated with deception, reaction times will probably increase.

The use of associative reaction time as an indicator of deception has been both supported and questioned by investigators. In a statistical combination with other indicators, Crosland (1929) found reaction time to be useful in determining the guilt of a person in an actual dormitory theft. Winter (1936) likewise found increased reaction times to critical words in a person guilty of an actual dormitory theft, although several innocent suspects also exhibited increases. Respiratory and blood pressure measures were also used in this instance; blood pressure was found to be the most useful, while respiration records were the least useful. In a study comparing deception responses to a mock crime, Runkel (1936) measured both the reaction time and motor response disturbances and found that for every subject the mean reaction time was greater to critical stimuli than it was to noncritical stimuli. Larson (1922) feels that the reaction time measure is not as satisfactory as is a respiration tracing and gives evidence that reactions occur in the tracings which are not reflected in longer reaction times.

In addition to measuring the reaction time to a word association task, the reaction time in answering questions has been measured. Ellson et al. (1952) instructed subjects to remove a sum of money from a box and then questioned them concerning the amount taken. The subjects responded by pressing a lever to the right for an affirmative answer and to the left for a negative answer. In addition to measuring reaction times, muscle potentials were obtained from the right forearm, since the authors felt that deception would result in motor conflict which would be reflected both in the reaction time and in the electromyogram (EMG). Measures of the reaction time significantly differentiated between truthful and deceptive responses. A measure of EMG amplitude, weighted and combined across five time periods during the stimulus presentation and the response, enabled the investigators to discriminate deceptive affirmative responses 90–95% of the time and deceptive negative responses 65–70% of the time.

Interference with voluntary motor behavior Considerable interest was generated in the early 1920s concerning the use of semivoluntary muscular indicators of deception. This interest was primarily engendered by the considerable success in criminal interrogation reported by the Russian psychologist Luria (1932) in recording the voluntary and involuntary movements of both hands in response to word associations. The rationale underlying this technique is that during heightened emotion there is a breakdown in motor control. When, as in Luria's case, the subject is required to press on a rubber bulb with his right hand as he responds verbally and to keep his left hand on another bulb, variations in response patterns and tremors or disturbances of the left hand may be recorded pneumatically. Significant responses usually consisted of tremors in both the right and left hands and rough or partial responses on the part of the right hand. Often a motor response would begin with the termination of the stimulus and fail to be completed, being followed later by a complete motor response and a verbal response. Luria felt that these premature responses indicated that certain words were being suppressed on the part of the subjects. Luria's techniques stimulated considerable research, most of which has been concerned with the nature of disturbance in abnormal subjects. Yates (1961) has summarized much of this literature, coming to the conclusion that increasing degrees of mental disorder are related to increasing levels of both left- and right-hand motor disturbance.

Few studies have specifically applied the technique to the detection of deception. Burtt (1936) found the most diagnostic measure of deception to be the extent to which the motor response in the right hand preceded the verbal response and was able to discriminate correctly in 69% of the cases. The nature of the responses, if any, elicited by the other hand was not reported. Runkel (1936) also found responses in the left hand of little discriminative value, being infrequent. He attributes this lack of distinctive left-hand responses to the relatively weak emotion generated by the experi-

mental procedure. He found distinctive right-hand motor responses to occur to critical stimuli an average of 50% of the time across subjects, the responses consisting of a wavelike tremor preceding the motor response. As Morgan and Ojemann (1942) point out, the determination of significant responses depends to a large extent upon the skill of the investigator.

Voice quality Quite a number of studies have explored the relationship between aspects of vocal expression and the emotional state of the person speaking (Kramer, 1963). Only two known studies have explored the use of vocal measures of deception, one employing subjective judgments of deception, the other an objective amplitude analysis. Using the subjective judgments of persons hearing other persons lie or tell the truth over a public address system, Fay and Middleton (1941) found that the two types of statements could be differentiated correctly about 55% of the time (chance was 50%). Alpert, Kurtzberg, and Friedhoff (1963) employed a deception situation with neutral stimuli and measured the amplitude of the subject's verbal responses with a voltmeter. Both a full frequency band (100–6000 Hz) and a filtered low frequency band (100–250 Hz) were measured. No differences were found in the full frequency band during deception, but amplitude increases in the low frequency band to the critical stimuli were significantly different from those to noncritical stimuli. Such an easily obtained and potentially useful measure should not be ignored.

Eye movements Eye movements and eye blinks have been noted as possible indicators of emotion (Lindsley, 1951; Orlansky, 1962). While no evidence exists on the use of eye blinks in the detection of deception, recordings of eye movements have been made and found useful in the differentiation of guilty and innocent subjects. Eye movements may be recorded by placing appropriate electrodes near the eye and amplifying the resulting signals, or by shining a light onto the cornea and projecting the reflected light through lenses onto photographic film. Using this corneal reflection method, Berrien (1942) explored eye movement variations in response to questions concerning a mock crime situation, but found no differences between the amount of eye movement present during critical questions and during neutral questions. During the prequestion period, however, guilty subjects seemed to decrease in ocular tremor, while innocent subjects did not. When judges were asked to classify as guilty those subjects whose records showed this decrease and as innocent those subjects who exhibited no change or an increase, the judges were, on the average, about 70% correct in discriminating guilty from innocent subjects. Differences in steadiness during the question period did not separate the subjects as well as did this criterion. Furthermore, the criterion successfully discriminated between guilty and innocent subjects when both groups were told the details of the mock crime before the crime was carried out, and between two subjects who were not tested until the day after performance of the mock crime.

Ellson et al. (1952) report a somewhat different approach to the determination of guilty responses. The subjects were instructed to remove a coin located in one quadrant of a box, and their eye movements were recorded during questioning, again using the corneal reflection method. Some subjects were instructed to tell the truth during questioning, while others were told to lie concerning the quadrant from which they had taken the coin. Eye movements to the guilty quadrant were greater in number than to the other quadrants for all subjects. The difference, however, was greater for lying subjects than for truthful subjects. Critical questions caused more eye movements and eye movements of greater magnitude toward the guilty quadrant for subjects who were told that they could keep the coin if successful in deceiving the experimenter than for subjects not told this. During neutral questions the subjects who had taken the coin made fewer movements toward the guilty quadrant than did a group of subjects who were not presented a coin in the box. It may be that in cases in which guilty subjects know details of crime not known to innocent subjects, an analysis of eye movements in response to the simultaneous presentation of several similar stimuli, one of which is critical, might provide evidence of guilty knowledge.

Muscular tension   Reid and Inbau (1966) report that the measurement of the pressure with which the suspect bears down on the arms of the chair can often serve as an indicator of deception. These authors have developed pneumatic and Doppler sensors for detecting these movements, as well as movements of the thighs. They report that suspects will, at times, tense their muscles in an attempt to raise blood pressure and thereby confuse the polygraph operator. They consider such deliberate actions indicative of guilt. As noted earlier, Ellson et al. (1952) were able to derive a measure of muscular activity from EMG recordings that allowed some discrimination between truthful and deceptive responses.

Nonverbal behavior   Based on data derived from observations of psychiatric patients, Ekman and Friesen (1969) have studied those aspects of a subject's behavior that communicate deception to the observer. In studying strictly nonverbal behavior, they find that persons who observed the hands and feet were more likely to detect what they refer to as deception cues and leakage of genuine underlying affect than those persons who observe the face alone. Furthermore, they reported that facial expression, when studied in slow motion, reveals another kind of deception clue. Observed at normal speed, the face will reveal one affect, while the very rapid "micro" expressions that become clearly visible only in slow motion may show the very opposite expression.

It would seem that these studies address themselves to the kinds of cues which allow an observer to become suspicious about the presence of deception. Certainly, this approach is of great interest, but as yet little is known about the power of these techniques. Further, such an approach must still be compared with other techniques that have been used to study the presence of deception.

Quantitative Evaluation of Responses

The current practice of field examiners is to rely on subjective impressions of whether or not deception has occurred. The examiner studies the record and notes any significant changes or differences in the patterns of responses between the critical and control stimuli. The tendency to consider as potentially significant almost any change in the response pattern (Joseph, 1957) leads to problems in interpretation. To the experienced examiner working on-line, small changes may have greater significance than do larger, more observable changes. Such may not be the case for the inexperienced examiner or someone examining the record post facto. In addition, examiners differ in the emphasis they place on the various measures, some relying primarily on respiration, some on "cardio," and some on the GSR (see Hathaway & Hanscom, 1958).

Laboratory studies, on the other hand, have tended to rely heavily on objective and quantifiable information such as the magnitude of the GSR (Block et al., 1952; Geldreich, 1941), GSR ranks (Lykken, 1959, 1960; Thackray & Orne, 1967), the I/E ratio (Burtt, 1921; Landis & Wiley, 1926), and systolic blood pressure (Chappell, 1929; Marston, 1917). Kugelmass et al. (1968) have attempted to score the "cardio" channel by connecting the "notches" of the tracings and measuring deflections from the baseline. Subjective impressions of several judges have even been quantified (Kubis, 1962). In order to quantify the responses, however, experimenters are forced to choose those measures that are obvious and amenable to quantification. With respiration, for example, laboratory studies generally rely on relatively crude measures of amplitude, frequency, or time relationships. Many possibly significant changes such as suppression, blockage, irregularities, or other subtle pattern changes are lost because they seem to defy ready quantification. Furthermore, invariant criteria are often applied to the responses of all subjects. In discarding much of the information available to the field examiner, however, a gain in reliability may be offset by the possible loss in validity. Kubis (1950) reports higher detection rates for independent experts who analyzed records resulting from an experimental situation than for persons using purely objective criteria, and the highest detection rates of all for operators interpreting the records on-line. Studies are needed exploring the possibility of quantifying the less regular aspects of changes in physiological records. While it is possible that a computer analysis might reveal measures contained in the variables, the computer must be programmed to derive these measures. The human investigator, therefore, is responsible for initially specifying the relationships and can rely on the computer only for information

as to their usefulness in the differentiation between guilty and innocent subjects.

Another use of the computer is as an aid in discovering combinations of measures that will allow increased differentiation. Kugelmass and Lieblich (1968) applied a discriminant function analysis to data derived from the three channels of a field polygraph but found poorer detection with this combination than with a simpler sum of ranks. They felt that the low intercorrelations they obtained between channels in many subjects was a contributing factor in this poorer detection. Kubis (1962) applied individual discriminant analyses to examiner's ratings of the significance of GSR, respiration, and pulse volume responses. For the individual subjects, higher rates of detection were achieved with these discriminants. Because of the subjective criteria employed in the ratings, however, there was little equivalence in the discriminant weights among those who rated the same records. Kubis (1962) concludes, "In view of the fundamental problems which are yet to be solved in the objective measurement of the physiological patterns . . . the concern for obtaining optimal discriminant functions is a small matter indeed [p. 60]."

Definition of the Detection Rate

As mentioned earlier, the analysis of data gathered in a detection of deception experiment depends upon the paradigm under which the study has been conducted. The definition of the detection rate differs for the two paradigms. When all of the subjects in a study are known to possess guilty information (the guilty information paradigm), it is the *information* rather than the *individuals* that the investigator seeks to detect. Studies of this sort usually compare the relative rates of detection resulting from experimental treatments such as different levels of motivation, the subject's perception of his task, or orders of presentation. In such cases, it is quite satisfactory and appropriate to define the detection rate as the percentage of times the significant stimulus evokes the greatest response when compared to otherwise matched control stimuli.[5] The fact that by chance alone this percentage could be, for instance, 20% does not diminish the importance of findings in which the experimental manipulation significantly affects detection. When all of the subjects are known to have guilty information, a greater response to a noncritical stimulus is a failure to detect the information sought and should affect the detection rate. Large responses to critical items result in the detection of the information and are thus successes.

An entirely different state of affairs exists when innocent subjects are introduced into an experiment. Such an experiment, following the guilty person paradigm, seeks to detect both guilty and innocent subjects, i.e., to discriminate between the two groups. To define the detection rate in such an experiment in the same way as for an experiment involving only guilty subjects, or even to redefine it as the percentage of individuals who exhibit their greatest response to the critical stimulus, is to ignore the chance factors operating in the case of the innocent subjects. Given a situation employing five stimuli, one of which is critical, and where some subjects may be innocent, all of the guilty subjects could exhibit their largest response to the critical stimulus. Detection of the guilty group, therefore, would be 100%. By chance alone, however, 20% of the innocent subjects would also show their largest response to the critical stimulus and would be misclassified as guilty. Such a situation results from overlapping response patterns in the two groups. In selecting the response pattern that allows maximal detection of the guilty subjects, in this case the greatest response to the critical stimulus, innocent subjects are unavoidably misclassified.

The Use of Multiple Indices of Guilt

There are a variety of strategies applicable in the laboratory situation to maximize the discrimination

[5] In this discussion we are dealing with ranked data, rather than with ratio scores or other procedures that take into account the magnitude of differences. Under most conditions in our own research we have found, somewhat to our surprise, that ranked scores are as effective as more complex scoring systems which take the magnitude of a response into account. Ratio scores may be appropriate under some conditions, but in the absence of data indicating this to be the case this discussion is limited to a consideration of scoring by ranks. Furthermore, the methods of stimulus presentation and record analysis discussed in this section are in no way comparable to those in the field situation.

between guilty and innocent subjects. Each of these strategies involves changing the situation from the simple example just presented. Each also demands an understanding of the parameters that enter into making the decision of guilt or innocence. Perhaps the simplest way to increase discrimination is to increase the number of neutral stimuli (Lieblich, Kugelmass, & Ben Shakhar, 1970). With the same 100% detection of the guilty subjects, if the number of stimuli is increased to 10, one of which is critical, the percentage of innocent subjects misclassified will drop to 10%. It is just as possible to increase the number of critical stimuli, but, in such a case, the detection of guilt would require either a greater response to all critical stimuli when compared with responses to the neutral stimuli, or at least some proportion of the responses must be greater. The probability of classifying an innocent subject as guilty would depend upon the criterion used for determining guilt; chance factors would involve joint probabilities of occurrence (assuming that each stimulus is independent). Suppose that 8 neutral and 2 critical stimuli were presented and that those subjects who responded with GSRs greater to the 2 critical stimuli than to the others were classified as guilty. Then by chance, 10% of the innocent subjects would respond most to 1 of the 2 critical stimuli and 10% of 10%, or 1%, of the innocent subjects would respond more to both critical stimuli than to the neutral stimuli and would be misclassified as guilty. As the number of critical stimuli is increased, the likelihood of an innocent subject's reacting significantly to all of the stimuli would decrease rapidly. In reality, however, it would be unlikely for all of the guilty subjects to show their greatest responses to all of the critical stimuli. To maximize discrimination, therefore, it is often desirable to widen somewhat the definition of a guilty subject to include response patterns in which only a specified number of stimuli yield greater responses. In this way the number of false-negative subjects (guilty subjects classified as innocent) is reduced, while the number of false-positive subjects (innocent subjects classified as guilty) is increased. Similar arguments could be advanced for the case of additional trials. If several trials are given, each with the same stimuli, continued high responses to critical stimuli would be unlikely to occur by chance, assuming minimal adaptation to the stimuli.

Separate distributions of guilty and innocent subjects can be established in the laboratory situation and each response pattern can be expressed in terms of the probabilities of falling into the guilty and innocent distributions. Each subject, then, could be classified as falling into that group for which the probability was highest (Hathaway & Hanscom, 1958). It is also possible to take into account factors such as the relative importance of avoiding false-positives and false-negatives. The elimination of false-positives would be more important in criminal investigations than in screening for a sensitive security position (Ben Shakhar et al., 1970). Much of the difference between the two situations arises from the fact that in criminal investigations only a few individuals, often only one, properly belong in the guilty group, whereas in screening, a large number of individuals may be in this category. The mechanism at work here is analogous to the concept of the selection ratio found in personnel selection (Cronbach & Gleser, 1965). Little work has been done in the laboratory with regard to the selection ratio problem. One would expect that, if the laboratory interrogator knew that only one subject in a group could be correctly classified as guilty, his approach would differ from his approach in the usual situation in which a number of subjects may be assigned to this category.

The process of combining probabilities to increase discrimination may be used not only across stimuli within one individual but also across individuals presented the same stimulus, provided that a response is available which can be readily averaged. The idea is analogous to that used in studying evoked cortical potentials with intact human subjects except that instead of time-locking multiple stimuli within the same individual, one observes simultaneously the response of multiple individuals to the same stimulus. If these individuals share the same guilty information, the averaged response to the critical stimuli should be maximized. Responses to the control stimuli, which may have idiosyncratic meaning to one subject or another, will tend to be minimized by averaging the responses. As a result, the signal-to-noise ratio will be markedly augmented.

A study by Orne and Thackray (1967) illustrates the use of this procedure. In this experiment the subjects were interrogated in groups of six subjects each, some groups being innocent and some guilty. Both individual and group GSRs, averaged across the individuals, were taken. The separation between the guilty and innocent subjects was shown to be very significantly improved through averaging. One would expect that with larger groups discrimination would improve still more, provided that all subjects are known to be either guilty or innocent. When the groups may contain both guilty and innocent subjects, one should be able to discriminate those groups containing guilty subjects, i.e., subjects with shared information, even if only a small proportion of the group consists of these individuals. The innocent subjects would merely add to the overall level of noise. While individual responsivity is difficult to predict, the responsivity of groups might well approach a mathematical function.

The Effect of Awareness

All of the research discussed so far is based on the assumption that the subject knows that someone is measuring physiological parameters to detect whether or not he is telling the truth. We have indicated, moreover, that motivation to deceive appears to be a major factor in making detection possible. One may legitimately wonder, therefore, how effectively we could detect deception if we had access to the physiological responses of an individual without his awareness that he was being recorded. This question, in view of present-day technology, cannot be considered totally unrealistic. It would be possible to sense at a distance parameters such as facial temperature, respiratory rate, and pupillary size. Appropriate concealed sensors could also measure the degree of fidgeting, some form of the cardioballistogram, and heart rate. Reid and Inbau (1966) report the results of research into techniques for recording respiration and body movements without the use of attached sensors. They report that results with the Doppler technique, whereby sound energy reflected from the subject may be analyzed to reveal relative movement, corresponded closely to respiration tracings obtained in the usual manner, and that movements of the limbs could be accurately recorded. These measurements can be obtained without the knowledge of the subject if the sensors are concealed. Even ignoring the ethical considerations, one might wonder how helpful such equipment would be in the detection of deception. Some preliminary indication concerning this problem was yielded in the course of a study by Thackray and Orne (1967). Prior to a peak-of-tension series in a group experiment, the stimuli were presented to the subjects, ostensibly so that they would know the stimulus order in the subsequent test. During this presentation the subjects were led to believe that the equipment, located in an adjacent room, was turned off. Immediately after the presentation, the subjects were interrogated about these same words; i.e., they were requested to answer "No" to each item. The difference in detection rates between the preinterrogation presentation and the actual interrogation, while in favor of the actual interrogation situation, only approached significance ($p < .10$). Any interpretation of this finding must be tempered by the realization that the procedure confounded a number of variables and no systematic effort was made to establish whether or not the subjects believed the experimenter when they were told that they were not being recorded.

In the context of another study an attempt was made to get at the latter issue more directly. Thackray and Orne (1968b) arranged the courier situation so that as the subject was entering the interrogation room a technician was turning off the polygraph. A number of electrodes were then attached to the subject, and it was explained to him that it would be necessary for some of the sensors, particularly the oximeter, to stabilize over a period of time before the test could take place. Prior to turning on the polygraph and actually taking the test, the subject and the interrogator discussed the questions in a way similar to that of a real life detection situation, ostensibly in order to avoid confusion and surprise. During this time the subject's GSR responses were telemetered to another polygraph four rooms away. Once the discussion was completed, the actual examination took place. A subsequent attempt was made to determine

whether the subjects believed that a recording was made during the pretrial test period. Only one subject reported such a belief. Nevertheless, it was not possible to demonstrate a significant difference between detection rates under these two conditions. Novelty and habituation worked against the hypothesis, there being no easy way to make plausible a reversal in the order of presentation. Furthermore, in talking with the subjects it became clear that, while they tended to believe that they were not being recorded during the initial presentation, they were very uncomfortable and felt strange with all of the sensors attached. It is difficult, therefore, on the basis of these studies, to answer the question of how subjects would behave if they were not in a polygraph situation. The findings do suggest that not merely the conscious belief that one is being monitored but the situation in its totality may be sufficient to evoke differential responsivity.

Studies are needed that allow monitoring of physiological responses, particularly the GSR, without the subject's feeling that he is being monitored, preferably with little or no electrode attachment. We know remarkably little about the effect of being monitored. One suspects that the extensive habituation characteristic of physiological recording is partly a result of habituation of the subjects to the psychological situation of being recorded (Woodworth & Schlosberg, 1954). This response is usually confounded with the experimental treatment itself. With the development of small, portable, and easily carried telemetering equipment, it should be possible to minimize the effects of being monitored and approximate the recording of physiological responses in an unaware individual. There has been some recording of physiological parameters over many sessions during the course of psychotherapy (Coleman, Greenblatt, & Solomon, 1956; Malmo, Boag, & Smith, 1957). Watson and Kanter (1956) report an experiment in which both the patient and the therapist were monitored throughout the treatment. While the therapist reported the monitoring as having a considerable effect on him, at least initially, the patient was able to make therapeutic progress despite this situation. The importance of the material to him was probably such that it made less salient any concern he might have had about the physiological monitoring. His major concern with the experimental situation centered around the presence of human observers, not the physiological measures. Again the heart rate, respiration, and EEG of astronauts have been monitored routinely throughout their flights, and without their reporting concern about the attached electrodes (Adey, Kado, & Walter, 1967; NASA Manned Spacecraft Center, 1962).

The issue of monitoring without awareness, however, is of importance in order to clarify some of the mechanisms involved in the detection of deception. The field situation is designed to take advantage of any psychological effects on the physiological response resulting from the suspect's awareness of being recorded on a machine. Many of the laboratory data mentioned here support the view that detection is possible only because of the individual's attempt to prevent detection. It is not clear whether this effort on the part of the subject is directed toward preventing detection through the physiological measures, or if he attempts to escape detection in the more general sense of controlling his tone of voice, manner, and overall behavior. Differences in physiological responsivity to highly affect-laden stimuli might emerge even more clearly if the individual were not aware that he was being monitored. In a like manner, conditioned GSR responses or anticipatory GSRs associated with the threat of shock should occur regardless of the subject's awareness of being monitored. On the other hand, there is no clear reason why a selected card or number should evoke a differential physiological response simply because an individual is required to "lie" and deny its selection.

The effectiveness of the lie detection procedure probably depends both on the subject's response to the content about which he is lying, as well as his awareness that his physiological responses are actually being recorded. Furthermore, there may be an interaction between the response to the arousal quality of the stimulus and the awareness of trying to deceive. The field interrogation takes place under conditions in which the stimuli have high intensive meaning, and the subject is made maximally aware of his attempt to deceive and the consequences of being detected, probably the situation that most favors detection. Studies by Gustafson and Orne (1963) and Thackray and Orne (1967, 1968b) have compared this situation with others in which involvement or awareness was manipulated, but no studies have specifically investigated the situation in which the subject is not concerned with the evasion of detection and is unaware of being monitored. Such a study could clarify the relative importance of both variables in the detection of deception.

Means of Minimizing Detection

The problem of minimizing detection is the obverse of procedures whereby detection is made more likely. Implicit in considering factors of subjects and situations that enhance detection is a consideration of factors that may also serve to minimize detection. These factors have often been grouped together under the heading of "countermeasures." Inasmuch as successful detection involves responses to relevant stimuli that differ in some way from responses to nonrelevant stimuli, countermeasure techniques attempt to reduce this difference. There are two principal means to reduce the difference in responses, increasing the level of response to irrelevant items or reducing the level of response to the critical items. Either method would bring about a reduction in the signal-to-noise ratio. The first method implies either an increase in the overall activation level, until additional responsiveness to critical items is small, or the production of false-positive responses to irrelevant items. The second method implies a reduction in responsivity on either a general or a specific level, brought about by voluntary suppression or by techniques involving drugs, hypnosis, or conditioning.

The voluntary production of false-positive responses The experimental literature on countermeasures has focused on the production of false-positive responses to neutral stimuli (Kubis, 1962; Lykken, 1960). Kubis (1962) trained subjects in three types of countermeasures, two of which involved the production of false-positive responses. The subjects were told either to generate exciting mental imagery to the neutral stimuli or to clench their toe muscles in response to the same stimuli. Using

GSR, respiration, and pulse volume as response measures, both imagery and muscle tension resulted in a significant reduction in detection rates. Kubis (1962) concluded that "the most important result underlying the successful use of countermeasures is the inability of a lie detection operator to distinguish the physiological reactions in deception from those in simulated deception. In other words, the tensing of the muscles and the bringing to mind of exciting thoughts produce a physiological pattern that cannot be distinguished readily from that found in lying [p. 104]." More (1966), however, claims to have replicated the Kubis (1962) study and reported that the same countermeasures led to a much smaller reduction in the detection rate than found by Kubis. More argues that his results "indicate that a carefully trained examiner can interpret a polygram even though countermeasures are being taken by the subject [p. 75]."

Block et al. (1952) used a conditioning paradigm to produce false-positive GSR responses to neutral stimuli. During a card test the subjects were shocked for "No" responses to cards other than the one they had chosen, presumably on the assumption that shocking subjects for telling the truth would lead to heightened autonomic activity when telling the truth in subsequent trials without shock. Responses to neutral stimuli did not increase relative to critical stimuli, as was expected, but there were fewer measurable responses to all stimuli and an increase in the magnitude of the GSR during deception.

A primary disadvantage in using false-positive responses as a countermeasure stems from the nature of the field examination. As Reid and Inbau (1966) point out, unusual responses, particularly those to irrelevant stimuli, should be discussed with the suspect in an attempt to uncover plausible explanations for these responses. Unexplainable responses, movement, or a lack of attention to the interrogator may be considered prima facie evidence of guilt. These authors endorse the use of arm and thigh movement detectors to uncover evidence of muscle tension (Reid, 1945) and caution operators to be constantly aware of the possibility of conscious acts by the suspect to distort the record. An individual with a good knowledge of the examination procedure may produce responses

at appropriate times and thus deceive the operator. Such an effort would require a knowledge of the order of the questions presented, as pointed out by Gustafson and Orne (1964). These investigators also note that detecting guilty information, such as the card choice in the Kubis (1962) study, allows the subject to mislead the experimenter by producing false responses, but the detection of a guilty person does not lend itself to such a strategy. The least suspicious pattern of false responding would seem to be the production of responses to all stimuli, relevant and irrelevant alike.

Experimental work dealing with increased general activation as a countermeasure has not been reported, although it is known that highly anxious subjects are often difficult to detect (Reid & Inbau, 1966). It would seem that increasing the activation of a subject should lead to a lessened difference between critical and noncritical responses because the subject is already at a level where further stimulation would have little effect. Obviously, however, a person would have to be capable of sustaining a high level of activation throughout an entire examination period. Reid and Inbau (1966) suggest that highly anxious or overly reactive suspects should be questioned about a fictitious crime, as well as about the crime in question. A lack of reactivity to questions concerning the fictitious crime would indicate deception concerning the actual crime.

The suppression of autonomic responses The entire basis for the detection of deception rests on the premise that the autonomic nervous system responds in an involuntary fashion; i.e., the conscious control of this system is difficult. There is, however, an increasing body of literature concerning the control of autonomic activity, by means of drugs, hypnosis, and particularly conditioning techniques. (See, for instance, Razran, 1961, for a review of Russian literature on conditioning.) Little research, however, has been directly concerned with response suppression in detection of deception situations.

The voluntary suppression of responses Kubis (1962) has published the only study directly involved with the voluntary suppression of responses during the detection of deception. As part of the previously mentioned study on countermeasures, his subjects attempted to assume a detached, "yoga" sort of attitude. He found these subjects no more difficult to detect under this condition than when given the usual instructions. Numerous authors have speculated on the inability of subjects to suppress affect at will (see Gustafson & Orne, 1964; Lykken, 1959).

The most important factor in this seeming inability to control autonomic responses is probably that the subject receives no feedback from the response he gives (Brener & Hothersall, 1966). Several studies indicate that providing feedback to subjects of heart rate information allows them to reduce heart rate variability (Hnatiow & Lang, 1965) and to increase or decrease the heart rate (Brener & Hothersall, 1966). Such feedback may take place naturally with the GSR (Reiser & Block, 1965). Kamiya (1969) has demonstrated that alpha activity in the EEG may be controlled by subjects who are informed of its appearance. The process by which subjects may learn to control autonomic activity is dependent upon providing appropriate feedback to the individual about changes and/or their direction in the parameter under investigation. Much of this work has been conceptualized as instrumental conditioning since in human studies the presentation of the appropriate feedback stimulus can serve as a reinforcer, and little effort has been made to separate reinforcement from informational aspects of the feedback stimulus. Again, partial reinforcement schedules are difficult to distinguish from intermittent feedback. It remains to be established, however, whether changes in the amount of feedback parallel those observed with varying the ratio of reinforcement contingencies. Nonetheless, it seems likely that learning to control autonomic functions in man is best understood as the consequence of feedback in individuals motivated to achieve such control rather than being due to the effects of discrete simple reinforcers.

The conditioned suppression of responses   A great deal of research has been done concerning the conditioning of autonomic responses, primarily the GSR (Crider, Shapiro, & Tursky, 1966; Grings & Carlin, 1966; Kimmel & Hill, 1960; Stewart, Stern, Winokur, & Fredman, 1961) and heart rate (Brener, 1966; Notterman, Schoenfeld, & Bersh, 1952), al-

though work has been done with other responses as well (Razran, 1961). These efforts have involved both classical and instrumental paradigms. The majority of these investigators have sought to establish responses to previously neutral stimuli, rather than extinguish responses already present. No one appears to have used the classical paradigm to suppress an autonomic response.

Several operant conditioning studies have examined the suppression of a response, particularly the GSR. Shapiro and Crider (1966) report that they were able to demonstrate increases in GSR activity with reinforcement (money) contingent upon the production of GSRs and also decreases in GSR activity with the reinforcement contingent upon inhibition of GSRs. An inspection of their data, however, shows the increase in activity to be much more striking than the decrease in activity. When reinforcement was contingent upon a lack of response, activity decreased greatly from the level during reinforcement for responding. The level during reinforcement for lack of responding was not, however, much less than it was during periods of nonreinforcement. Senter and Hummel (1965) performed an experiment in which one group of subjects received an electric shock each time a spontaneous GSR occurred. A control group received similar shocks at times when their experimental partners had received them. During the subsequent test period the experimental subjects showed a significant reduction in the number of spontaneous GSRs emitted, when compared to the number emitted by their yoked control subjects, whose number of GSRs actually increased. They also found that abrupt changes in the GSR consistently occurred between the spontaneous GSR and the shock in the experimental subjects and conclude that the spontaneous emission of a GSR "bears a sensory correlate which can act as a stimulus element in operant conditioning [p. 4]." Using the heart rate as a response, Engel and Hansen (1966) demonstrated that some subjects, particularly those who were not aware of the contingency between the feedback and their heart rate, were able to lower their rate significantly below that of their yoked control subjects.

The ability of operant conditioning techniques to suppress a response pattern to critical emotional stimuli has not been demonstrated. Even if a person is conditioned to suppress responses to GSR, heart rate, respiration, and other variables separately, he could experience difficulty in the simultaneous control of all of these measures while maintaining normal external appearance to the interrogator (Orlansky, 1962). It may be possible to condition a lack of concern for the critical issues of the examination. There is some evidence that a lack of concern leads to low rates of detection, both in laboratory settings (Gustafson & Orne, 1963) and in field settings involving abnormal personalities (Floch, 1950; Kubis, 1957). Outside of the one laboratory study just mentioned, though, little research has been directed toward this topic. Studies of subjects who are difficult to detect or who show low reactivity to critical stimuli indicate them to be less theoretical and abstract in their thinking than sensitive subjects (Iwahara, Miseki, Shiokawa, & Yoshida, 1960). They are also characterized as cool, independent, opportunistic, practical, and realistic by their responses to the Gough adjective checklist (Block, 1957). Ethnic background also seems to be a determiner of differential reactivity (Kugelmass, 1967; Kugelmass & Lieblich, 1966).

The use of drugs The use of drugs as aids to interrogation has been adequately reviewed elsewhere (Gottschalk, 1961) and will not be considered. This literature has dealt with the use of sedatives, stimulants, tranquilizers, or hallucinogenic drugs as possible aids in maximizing the effects of interrogation. The use of drugs to minimize detection, on the other hand, especially when the polygraph is employed, has not received much attention in print. Davis (1961) considers alcohol, barbiturates, and perhaps tranquilizers to be of possible use in minimizing detection, but the lack of empirical investigation renders this view speculative. On the basis of known evidence relating the effects of various depressants and tranquilizers to autonomic and central nervous system activity and behavior (Trouton & Eysenck, 1961), it could be predicted that the use of such drugs would impair detection. One of the more troublesome aspects of the use of drugs as countermeasures, however, is the possibility that the interrogator will discover that drugs have been taken. Unless a plausible reason can be found for the taking of a drug, this act may be considered prima facie evidence of the intent to deceive. Reid and Inbau (1966) state that doses of tranquilizers sufficient to depress responsivity usually produce obvious behavior abnormalities and suggest that the examination be postponed until the interrogator can be sure that no drugs have been taken which would alter the effectiveness of the test.

The use of hypnosis Hypnosis has been considered as a technique for either maximizing or minimizing detection (Orlansky, 1962), although evidence suggests that the use of posthypnotic amnesia to suppress autonomic responses is generally ineffective. Germann (1961), for example, induced posthypnotic amnesia in five subjects, screened for deep trance capability. Clinical evaluation of the GSR, blood pressure, and respiration responses to the critical stimuli showed that amnesia did not prevent an increased autonomic response to these items. Bitterman and Marcuse (1945), in a series of hypnotic inductions with one subject, were likewise unable to demonstrate any reduction in autonomic response resulting from posthypnotic amnesia. However, no data are available about other possible uses of the hypnotic phenomenon to prevent detection. Hypnosis might, for example, be used as a means of decreasing an individual's anxiety, either by direct suggestion or along the lines of systematic desensitization, making the subject more sensitive about a pseudocrime that was never committed by the use of appropriate suggestions. Alternatively, it could be used to induce a state of high anxiety that would make differential responsivity difficult to recognize, or to vary the effect of the meaning of the stimulus, rather than its recognition. Studies of this kind, carried out with appropriate waking controls, might help clarify the nature of hypnosis, as well as help to shed light on some of the mechanisms involved in causing the differential responsivity upon which the detection of deception is based.

CONCLUSIONS

In this review independent variables have been categorized for the purpose of organization. It must be recognized, however, that such categorization distorts some of the more complex effects these variables may have. For example, there is almost no increase in responsivity when subjects are asked to lie about a card they have selected, unless they are motivated to deceive; yet in another study in which the stimulus material has great intrinsic meaning, differential responsivity occurs even when the subject is telling the truth. Such findings are not contradictory, although one might well be tempted to draw such a conclusion; rather, they indicate that several factors play a role in the detection of deception. Either the attempt to deceive or the intrinsic significance of the stimulus may be responsible for the physiological response, and an experimental study may emphasize one or the other factor by the nature of its design.

Most studies to date have only begun to examine the effect of independent variables singly, and certainly such research is essential. Yet a full understanding of the phenomena involved in the detection of deception will need to take into account some of the significant interactions between these variables. Many of the apparent inconsistencies found between studies may ultimately be resolved when the effects of these interactions are clarified. We have tried to discuss the factors that seemed likely to play a role in this process, but it has become clear that even the apparently simple laboratory situation is highly complex and many aspects of the field situation remain to be subjected to meaningful analysis.

The detection of deception has not, however, been an area of much systematic research. Perhaps because of its applied implications, the field has been avoided by psychologists and physiologists alike. Psychophysiologists, in the search for professional identity, have seemed least interested in the phenomenon that the public most closely identifies with the polygraph. As a result of the increased status of psychophysiology, the intrinsic interest of the problem may receive the attention it deserves. There is little doubt that both psychological and physiological variables play large roles in determining the ability of a person using polygraphic techniques to judge whether or not another individual is guilty of deception. The conditions prevailing in the detection of deception situation seem to provide an almost unparalleled opportunity for psychologists to study those contingencies under which a psychological stimulus will or will not evoke an augmented physiological response. Clarification of these problems may be of interest to individuals professionally engaged in "lie detection." This in no way, however, diminishes the scientific importance of the phenomenon. It provides a paradigm for studying the effect of cognitive, motivational, attentional, and learning factors upon the physiological responsivity to verbal stimuli. It would seem appropriate that, instead of viewing the practical application as a detriment, we recognize its potential advantage in providing a means of testing the ecological validity of our findings outside the laboratory context. Because the detection of deception model allows systematic quantitative analysis, it provides a meaningful way of learning about the variables involved and the interactions, at least as they relate to one set of psychophysiological contingencies. An understanding of these relationships is likely to facilitate the use of physiological techniques to clarify other, and perhaps ultimately more important, aspects of psychological functioning.

REFERENCES

ADEY, W. R., KADO, R. T., & WALTER, D. O. Computer analysis of EEG data from Gemini flight GT-7. *Aerospace Medicine*, 1967, **38**, 345–359.

ALPERT, M., KURTZBERG, R. L., & FRIEDHOFF, A. J. Transient voice changes associated with emotional stimuli. *Archives of General Psychiatry*, 1963, **8**, 362–365.

ANSLEY, N. A comparison of arm-cuff and wrist-cuff blood pressure patterns in polygraph charts. *Journal of Criminal Law, Criminology, and Police Science*, 1959, **50**, 192–194.

ARNOLD, M. B. *Emotion and personality.* New York: Columbia University Press, 1960.

AX, A. F. The physiological differentiation between fear and anger in humans. *Psychosomatic Medicine*, 1953, **15**, 433–442.

BACKSTER, C. Polygraph professionalization through technique standardization. *Law & Order*, 1963, **11**(4), 63–64.

BAESEN, H. V., CHUNG, C. M., & YANG, C. Y. A lie-detector

experiment. *Journal of Criminal Law and Criminology,* 1949, **39,** 532–537.

BARRON, D. H., & RUCH, T. C. Circulation through special regions. In T. C. RUCH & J. F. FULTON (Eds.), *Medical physiology and biophysics.* (18th ed.) (Ch. 33.) Philadelphia: Saunders, 1960.

BENDER, W. R. G. The effect of pain and emotional stimuli and alcohol upon pupillary reflex activity. *Psychological Monographs,* 1933, **44,** No. 2(No. 198).

BEN SHAKHAR, G., LIEBLICH, I., & KUGELMASS, S. Guilty knowledge technique: Application of signal detection measures. *Journal of Applied Psychology,* 1970, **54,** 409–413.

BENUSSI, V. Die Atmungssymptome der Lüge. *Archiv für die gesamte Psychologie,* 1914, **31,** 244–273.

BERRIEN, F. K. Ocular stability in deception. *Journal of Applied Psychology,* 1942, **26,** 55–63.

BERRIEN, F. K., & HUNTINGTON, G. H. An exploratory study of pupillary responses during deception. *Journal of Experimental Psychology,* 1943, **32,** 443–449.

BERSH, P. J. A validation of polygraph examiner judgments. *Journal of Applied Psychology,* 1969, **53,** 399–403.

BEST, C. H., & TAYLOR, N. B. *The physiological basis of medical practice.* (5th ed.) Baltimore: Williams & Wilkins, 1950.

BITTERMAN, M. E., & MARCUSE, F. L. Autonomic response in posthypnotic amnesia. *Journal of Experimental Psychology,* 1945, **35,** 248–252.

BLOCK, J. D. A study of affective responsiveness in a lie-detection situation. *Journal of Abnormal and Social Psychology,* 1957, **55,** 11–15.

BLOCK, J. D., ROUKE, F. L., SALPETER, M. M., TOBACH, E., KUBIS, J. F., & WELCH, L. An attempt at reversal of the truth-lie relationship as measured by the psychogalvanic response. *Journal of Psychology,* 1952, **34,** 55–66.

BORING, E. G. *Sensation and perception in the history of experimental psychology.* New York: Appleton-Century-Crofts, 1942.

BRENER, J. Heart rate as an avoidance response. *Psychological Record,* 1966, **16,** 329–336.

BRENER, J., & HOTHERSALL, D. Heart rate control under conditions of augmented sensory feedback. *Psychophysiology,* 1966, **3,** 23–28.

BROD, J. Circulation in muscle during acute pressor responses to emotional stress and during chronic sustained elevation of blood pressure. *American Heart Journal,* 1964, **68,** 424–426.

BROD, J., HEJL, Z., & ULRYCH, M. Metabolic changes in the forearm muscle and skin during emotional muscular vasodilation. *Clinical Science,* 1963, **25,** 1–10.

BROWN, C. C. The techniques of plethysmography. In C. C. BROWN (Ed.), *Methods in psychophysiology.* (Ch. 2.) Baltimore: Williams & Wilkins, 1967.

BURTT, H. E. The inspiration-expiration ratio during truth and falsehood. *Journal of Experimental Psychology,* 1921, **4,** 1–23.

BURTT, H. E. Motor concomitants of the association reaction. *Journal of Experimental Psychology,* 1936, **19,** 51–63.

CHAPPELL, M. N. Blood pressure changes in deception. *Archives of Psychology, New York,* 1929, **17,** 1–39.

COLEMAN, R., GREENBLATT, M., & SOLOMON, H. C. Physiological evidence of rapport during psychotherapeutic interviews. *Diseases of the Nervous System,* 1956, **17,** 71–77.

CRIDER, A., SHAPIRO, D., & TURSKY, B. Reinforcement of spontaneous electrodermal activity. *Journal of Comparative and Physiological Psychology,* 1966, **61,** 20–27.

CRONBACH, L. J., & GLESER, G. C. *Psychological tests and personnel decisions.* (2nd ed.) Urbana: University of Illinois Press, 1965.

CROSLAND, H. R. The psychological methods of word-association and reaction-time as tests of deception. *Oregon University Publications, Psychology Series,* 1929, **1**(No. 1).

DANA, H. J. It is time to improve the polygraph: A progress report on polygraph research and development. In V. A. LEONARD (Ed.), *Academy lectures on lie detection.* Vol. 2. (Ch. 8.) Springfield, Ill.: Charles C Thomas, 1958.

DANA, H. J., & BARNETT, C. C. The emotional stress meter. In V. A. LEONARD (Ed.), *Academy lectures on lie detection.* (Ch. 7.) Springfield, Ill.: Charles C Thomas, 1957.

DARROW, C. W. The galvanic skin reflex (sweating) and blood-pressure as preparatory and facilitative functions. *Psychological Bulletin,* 1936, **33,** 73–94.

DAVIDSON, P. O. Validity of the guilty-knowledge technique: The effects of motivation. *Journal of Applied Psychology,* 1968, **52,** 62–65.

DAVIS, R. C. Physiological responses as a means of evaluating information. In A. D. BIDERMAN & H. ZIMMER (Eds.), *The manipulation of human behavior.* (Ch. 4.) New York: Wiley, 1961.

DAVIS, R. C., BUCHWALD, A. M., & FRANKMANN, R. W. Autonomic and muscular responses, and their relation to simple stimuli. *Psychological Monographs,* 1955, **69,** No. 20 (No. 405).

DEARMAN, H. B., & SMITH, B. M. Unconscious motivation and the polygraph test. *American Journal of Psychiatry,* 1963, **119,** 1017–1020.

EDELBERG, R. Electrical properties of the skin. In C. C. BROWN (Ed.), *Methods in psychophysiology.* (Ch. 1.) Baltimore: Williams & Wilkins, 1967.

EKMAN, P., & FRIESEN, W. V. Nonverbal leakage and clues to deception. *Psychiatry,* 1969, **63,** 88–106.

ELLSON, D. G., DAVIS, R. C., SALTZMAN, I. J., & BURKE, C. J. A report of research on detection of deception. Tech. Rep. prepared for Office of Naval Research, Contract N6onr-18011, Indiana University, 1952.

ENGEL, B. T., & HANSEN, S. P. Operant conditioning of heart rate slowing. *Psychophysiology,* 1966, **3,** 176–187.

ENGLISH, H. B. Reaction-time symptoms of deception. *American Journal of Psychology,* 1926, **37,** 428–429.

FAY, P. J., & MIDDLETON, W. C. The ability to judge truth-telling, or lying, from the voice as transmitted over a public address system. *Journal of General Psychology*, 1941, **24**, 211–215.

FLOCH, M. Limitations of the lie detector. *Journal of Criminal Law and Criminology*, 1950, **40**, 651–653.

GALTON, F. Psychometric experiments. *Brain*, 1879, **2**, 149–162.

GELDREICH, E. W. Studies of the galvanic skin response as a deception indicator. *Transactions of the Kansas Academy of Science*, 1941, **44**, 346–351.

GERMANN, A. C. Hypnosis as related to the scientific detection of deception by polygraph examination: A pilot study. *International Journal of Clinical and Experimental Hypnosis*, 1961, **9**, 309–311.

GOLDSTEIN, E. R. Reaction times and the consciousness of deception. *American Journal of Psychology*, 1923, **34**, 562–581.

GOTTSCHALK, L. A. The use of drugs in interrogation. In A. D. BIDERMAN & H. ZIMMER (Eds.), *The manipulation of human behavior*. (Ch. 3.) New York: Wiley, 1961.

GRINGS, W. W., & CARLIN, S. Instrumental modification of autonomic activity. *Psychological Record*, 1966, **16**, 153–159.

GUSTAFSON, L. A., & ORNE, M. T. Effects of heightened motivation on the detection of deception. *Journal of Applied Psychology*, 1963, **47**, 408–411.

GUSTAFSON, L. A., & ORNE, M. T. The effects of task and method of stimulus presentation on the detection of deception. *Journal of Applied Psychology*, 1964, **48**, 383–387.

GUSTAFSON, L. A., & ORNE, M. T. Effects of perceived role and role success on the detection of deception. *Journal of Applied Psychology*, 1965, **49**, 412–417. (a)

GUSTAFSON, L. A., & ORNE, M. T. The effects of verbal responses on the laboratory detection of deception. *Psychophysiology*, 1965, **2**, 10–13. (b)

HATHAWAY, S. R., & HANSCOM, C. B. The statistical evaluation of polygraph records. In V. A. LEONARD (Ed.), *Academy lectures on lie detection*. Vol. 2. (Ch. 11.) Springfield, Ill.: Charles C Thomas, 1958.

HESS, E. H. Attitude and pupil size. *Scientific American*, 1965, **212**(4), 46–54.

HESS, E. H., SELTZER, A. L., & SHLIEN, J. M. Pupil response of hetero- and homosexual males to pictures of men and women: A pilot study. *Journal of Abnormal Psychology*, 1965, **70**, 165–168.

HIGLEY, B. R. Interrogation with instrumentation. In V. A. LEONARD (Ed.), *Academy lectures on lie detection*. Vol. 2. (Ch. 10.) Springfield, Ill.: Charles C Thomas, 1958.

HNATIOW, M., & LANG, P. J. Learned stabilization of cardiac rate. *Psychophysiology*, 1965, **1**, 330–336.

HOUSE OF REPRESENTATIVES, EIGHTY-EIGHTH CONGRESS, Subcommittee of the Committee on Government Operations. *Use of polygraphs as "lie detectors" by the federal government*. Washington, D.C.: U.S. Government Printing Office, 1964.

INBAU, F. E., & REID, J. E. *Lie detection and criminal interrogation*. (3rd ed.) Baltimore: Williams & Wilkins, 1953.

IWAHARA, S., MISEKI, H., SHIOKAWA, N., & YOSHIDA, R. GSR to forced lying and personality traits. *Psychological Abstracts*, 1960, **6**, 269. (Abstract)

JONES, H. E., & WECHSLER, D. Galvanometric technique in studies of association. *American Journal of Psychology*, 1928, **40**, 607–612.

JOSEPH, C. N. Analysis of compensatory responses and irregularities in polygraph chart interpretation. In V. A. LEONARD (Ed.), *Academy lectures on lie detection*. (Ch. 9.) Springfield, Ill.: Charles C Thomas, 1957.

JUNG, C. G. Die psychologische Diagnose des Tatbestandes. *Juristisch-psychiatrische Grenzfragen*, 1906, **4**(2), 1–61.

JUNG, C. G. On psychophysical relations of the associative experiment. *Journal of Abnormal Psychology*, 1907, **1**, 247–255.

JUNG, C. G. The association method. *American Journal of Psychology*, 1910, **21**, 219–269.

KAMIYA, J. Operant control of the EEG alpha rhythm and some of its reported effects on consciousness. In C. TART (Ed.), *Altered states of consciousness: A book of readings*. (Ch. 35.) New York: Wiley, 1969.

KEELER, L. A method for detecting deception. *American Journal of Police Science*, 1930, **1**, 38–51.

KIMMEL, H., & HILL, F. Operant conditioning of the GSR. *Psychological Reports*, 1960, **7**, 555–562.

KRAMER, E. Judgment of personal characteristics and emotions from nonverbal properties of speech. *Psychological Bulletin*, 1963, **60**, 408–420.

KUBIS, J. F. Experimental and statistical factors in the diagnosis of consciously suppressed affective experience. *Journal of Clinical Psychology*, 1950, **6**, 12–16.

KUBIS, J. F. Instrumental, chemical, and psychological aids in the interrogation of witnesses. *Journal of Social Issues*, 1957, **13**(2), 40–49.

KUBIS, J. F. Studies in lie detection: Computer feasibility considerations. Tech. Rep. 62–205, prepared for Air Force Systems Command, Contract No. AF 30 (602)-2270, Project No. 5534, Fordham University, 1962.

KUGELMASS, S. Reactions to stress. Air Force Office of Scientific Research Rep. 67-0530, filed with Defense Documentation Center AD-647467, January 1967.

KUGELMASS, S., & LIEBLICH, I. Effects of realistic stress and procedural interference in experimental lie detection. *Journal of Applied Psychology*, 1966, **50**, 211–216.

KUGELMASS, S., & LIEBLICH, I. An analysis of mechanisms underlying psychophysiological detection. Paper presented at the 16th International Congress of Applied Psychology, Amsterdam, The Netherlands, August 18–22, 1968.

KUGELMASS, S., LIEBLICH, I., BEN-ISHAI, A., OPATOWSKI, A., & KAPLAN, M. Experimental evaluation of galvanic skin response and blood pressure change indices during criminal investigation. *Journal of Criminal Law, Criminology and Police Science,* 1968, **59,** 632–635.

KUGELMASS, S., LIEBLICH, I., & BERGMAN, Z. The role of "lying" in psychophysiological detection. *Psychophysiology,* 1967, **3,** 312–315.

LACEY, J. I., & LACEY, B. C. Verification and extension of the principle of autonomic response-stereotypy. *American Journal of Psychology,* 1958, **71,** 50–73.

LANDIS, C., & GULLETTE, R. Studies of emotional reactions: III. Systolic blood pressure and inspiration-expiration ratios. *Journal of Comparative Psychology,* 1925, **5,** 221–253.

LANDIS, C., & WILEY, L. E. Changes of blood pressure and respiration during deception. *Journal of Comparative Psychology,* 1926, **6,** 1–19.

LANGFELD, H. S. Psychophysical symptoms of deception. *Journal of Abnormal Psychology,* 1921, **15,** 319–328.

LARSON, J. A. The cardio-pneumo-psychogram and its use in the study of the emotions, with practical application. *Journal of Experimental Psychology,* 1922, **5,** 323–328.

LARSON, J. A. *Lying and its detection: A study of deception and deception tests.* Chicago: University of Chicago Press, 1932.

LEE, C. D. *The instrumental detection of deception.* Springfield, Ill.: Charles C Thomas, 1953.

LIEBLICH, I. Identification of variables related to the efficiency of the detection of information within the organism, using a physiological index. Unpublished doctoral dissertation, Hebrew University of Jerusalem, 1966.

LIEBLICH, I. Manipulation of contrast between differential GSR responses through the use of ordered tasks of information detection. *Psychophysiology,* 1969, **6,** 70–77.

LIEBLICH, I., KUGELMASS, S., & BEN SHAKHAR, G. Efficiency of GSR detection of information as a function of stimulus set size. *Psychophysiology,* 1970, **6,** 601–608.

LINDSLEY, D. B. Emotion. In S. S. STEVENS (Ed.), *Handbook of experimental psychology.* (Ch. 14.) New York: Wiley, 1951.

LOVETT DOUST, J. W., & SCHNEIDER, R. A. Studies on the physiology of awareness: An oximetrically monitored controlled stress test. *Canadian Journal of Psychology,* 1955, **9,** 67–78.

LÖWENSTEIN, O. Pupillography: Methods and diagnostic system. *Archives of Ophthalmology,* 1956, **55,** 565–571.

LÖWENSTEIN, O., & FRIEDMAN, E. D. Pupillographic studies: I. Present state of pupillography; its method and diagnostic significance. *Archives of Ophthalmology,* 1942, **27,** 969–993.

LURIA, A. R. *The nature of human conflicts: Or emotion, conflict and will.* Translated by W. H. Gantt. New York: Liveright, 1932.

LYKKEN, D. T. The GSR in the detection of guilt. *Journal of Applied Psychology,* 1959, **43,** 385–388.

LYKKEN, D. T. The validity of the guilty knowledge technique: The effects of faking. *Journal of Applied Psychology,* 1960, **44,** 258–262.

MACNITT, R. D. In defense of the electrodermal response and cardiac amplitude as measures of deception. *Journal of Criminal Law and Criminology,* 1942, **33,** 266–275.

MALMO, R. B., BOAG, T. J., & SMITH, A. A. Physiological study of personal interaction. *Psychosomatic Medicine,* 1957, **19,** 105–119.

MARCUSE, F. L., & BITTERMAN, M. E. Minimal cues in the peak of tension procedure of determining guilt. *American Journal of Psychology,* 1946, **59,** 144–146.

MARSTON, W. M. Systolic blood pressure symptoms of deception. *Journal of Experimental Psychology,* 1917, **2,** 117–163.

MARSTON, W. M. Reaction-time symptoms of deception. *Journal of Experimental Psychology,* 1920, **3,** 72–87.

MARSTON, W. M. Psychological possibilities in the deception tests. *Journal of Criminal Law and Criminology,* 1921, **11,** 551–570.

MARSTON, W. M. Negative type reaction-time symptoms of deception. *Psychological Review,* 1925, **32,** 241–247.

MARSTON, W. M. *The lie detector test.* New York: R. K. Smith, 1938.

MORE, H. W. Polygraph research and the university. *Law & Order,* 1966, **14**(3), 73–78.

MORGAN, M. I., & OJEMANN, R. H. A study of the Luria method. *Journal of Applied Psychology,* 1942, **26,** 168–179.

NASA MANNED SPACECRAFT CENTER. *Results of the first U.S. orbital space flight, February 20, 1962.* Washington, D.C.: U.S. Government Printing Office, 1962.

NOTTERMAN, J. M., SCHOENFELD, W. N., & BERSH, P. J. Conditioned heart rate response in human beings during experimental anxiety. *Journal of Comparative and Physiological Psychology,* 1952, **45,** 1–8.

OBERMANN, C. E. The effect on the Berger rhythm of mild affective states. *Journal of Abnormal and Social Psychology,* 1939, **34,** 84–95.

ORLANSKY, J. An assessment of lie detection capabilities. Tech. Rep. 62-16, prepared for Institute for Defense Analysis, Research and Engineering Support Division, AD 603860. Springfield, Va.: Clearing House of Scientific and Technical Information, 1962.

ORNE, M. T. On the social psychology of the psychological experiment: With particular reference to demand characteristics and their implications. *American Psychologist,* 1962, **17,** 776–783.

ORNE, M. T. Demand characteristics and the concept of design controls. In R. ROSENTHAL & R. ROSNOW (Eds.), *Artifact in behavioral research.* (Ch. 5.) New York: Academic, 1969.

ORNE, M. T., & THACKRAY, R. I. Group GSR technique in the detection of deception. *Perceptual and Motor Skills,* 1967, **25,** 809–816.

PETERSON, F., & JUNG, C. G. Psycho-physical investigations with the galvanometer and pneumograph in normal and insane individuals. *Brain,* 1907, **30,** 153–218.

RAZRAN, G. The observable unconscious and the inferable conscious in current Soviet psychophysiology: Interoceptive conditioning, semantic conditioning, and the orienting reflex. *Psychological Review*, 1961, **68**, 81–147.

REID, J. E. Simulated blood pressure responses in lie-detector tests and a method for their detection. *Journal of Criminal Law and Criminology*, 1945, **36**, 201–214.

REID, J. E., & ARTHER, R. O. Behavior symptoms of lie-detector subjects. *Journal of Criminal Law and Criminology*, 1953, **44**, 104–108.

REID, J. E., & INBAU, F. E. *Truth and deception: The polygraph ("lie detector") technique.* Baltimore: Williams & Wilkins, 1966.

REISER, M. F., & BLOCK, J. D. Discrimination and recognition of weak stimuli: III. Further experiments on interaction of cognitive and autonomic-feedback mechanisms. *Psychosomatic Medicine*, 1965, **27**, 274–285.

RICH, G. J. Dr. Marston on deception types. *American Journal of Psychology*, 1926, **37**, 307–309.

ROSENTHAL, R. *Experimenter effects in behavioral research.* New York: Appleton-Century-Crofts, 1966.

RUCKMICK, C. A. The truth about the lie detector. *Journal of Applied Psychology*, 1938, **22**, 50–58.

RUNKEL, J. E. Luria's motor method and word association in the study of deception. *Journal of General Psychology*, 1936, **15**, 23–37.

RUSHMER, R. F. *Cardiovascular dynamics.* Philadelphia: Saunders, 1961.

SCHNORE, M. M. Individual patterns of physiological activity as a function of task differences and degree of arousal. *Journal of Experimental Psychology*, 1959, **58**, 117–128.

SENTER, R. J., & HUMMEL, W. F. Suppression of an autonomic response through operant conditioning. *Psychological Record*, 1965, **15**, 1–5.

SEWARD, J. P., & SEWARD, G. H. The effect of repetition on reaction to electric shock: With special reference to the menstrual cycle. *Archives of Psychology, New York*, 1934, **25** (No. 168).

SHAPIRO, D., & CRIDER, A. Operant electrodermal conditioning: Some effects of multiple schedules of reinforcement. Tech. Rep. 14, prepared for Office of Naval Research, Group Psychology Branch, AD 641699. Springfield, Va.: Clearing House of Scientific and Technical Information, 1966.

SMITH, W. *The measurement of emotion.* London: Paul, 1922.

SOLOMON, R. L., BLACK, A. H., WATSON, P. D., HUTTENLOCHER, J., TURNER, L., & WESTCOTT, M. R. Some autonomic correlates of human traumatic avoidance learning. U.S. Public Health Service Progress Rep. USPHS M-1246, February 1958.

STEIN, M., & LUPARELLO, T. J. The measurement of respiration. In C. C. BROWN (Ed.), *Methods in psychophysiology.* (Ch. 3.) Baltimore: Williams & Wilkins, 1967.

STERNBACH, R. A. A comparative analysis of autonomic responses in startle. *Psychosomatic Medicine*, 1960, **22**, 204–210.

STERNBACH, R. A., GUSTAFSON, L. A., & COLIER, R. L. Don't trust the lie detector. *Harvard Business Review*, 1962, **40**, 127–134.

STEWART, M. A., STERN, J. A., WINOKUR, G., & FREDMAN, S. An analysis of GSR conditioning. *Psychological Review*, 1961, **68**, 60–67.

SUMMERS, W. G. Science can get the confession. *Fordham Law Revue*, 1939, **8**, 334–354.

SUTCLIFFE, J. P. A general method of analysis of frequency data for multiple classification designs. *Psychological Bulletin*, 1957, **54**, 134–137.

SYZ, H. C. Observations on the unreliability of subjective reports of emotional reactions. *British Journal of Psychology*, 1926, **17**, 119–126.

THACKRAY, R. I., & ORNE, M. T. Methodological studies in detection of deception. U.S. Army Medical Research and Development Command Research Rep., filed with the Defense Documentation Center, AD-645102, January 1967.

THACKRAY, R. I., & ORNE, M. T. A comparison of physiological indices in detection of deception. *Psychophysiology*, 1968, **4**, 329–339. (a)

THACKRAY, R. I., & ORNE, M. T. Effects of the type of stimulus employed and the level of subject awareness on the detection of deception. *Journal of Applied Psychology*, 1968, **52**, 234–239. (b)

THIESEN, J. W. Effects of certain forms of emotion on the normal electroencephalogram. *Archives of Psychology, New York*, 1943, **40** (No. 285).

TROUTON, D., & EYSENCK, H. J. The effects of drugs on behaviour. In H. J. EYSENCK (Ed.), *Handbook of abnormal psychology: An experimental approach.* (Ch. 17.) New York: Basic Books, 1961.

TROVILLO, P. V. A history of lie detection. *Journal of Criminal Law and Criminology*, 1939, **29**, 848–881.

TROVILLO, P. V. Deception test criteria: How can one determine truth and falsehood from polygraph records. *Journal of Criminal Law and Criminology*, 1942, **33**, 338–358.

VAN BUSKIRK, D., & MARCUSE, F. L. The nature of errors in experimental lie detection. *Journal of Experimental Psychology*, 1954, **47**, 187–190.

VIOLANTE, R., & ROSS, S. A. Research in interrogation procedures. Office of Naval Research, Rep. No. 707-65, filed with Defense Documentation Center, AD-467624, October 1964.

WATSON, P. D., & KANTER, S. S. Some influences of an experimental situation on the psychotherapeutic process: A report, based on 44 treatment interviews, of the reactions of a patient and therapist to observation, recording, and physiological measurement. *Psychosomatic Medicine*, 1956, **18**, 457–470.

WENGER, M. A., CLEMENS, T. L., COLEMAN, M. A., CULLEN, T. D., & ENGEL, B. T. Autonomic response specificity. *Psychosomatic Medicine,* 1961, **23,** 185–193.

WERTHEIMER, M. Experimentelle Untersuchungen zur Tatbestandsdiagnostik. *Archiv für die gesamte Psychologie,* 1905, **6,** 59–131.

WERTHEIMER, M., & KLEIN, J. Psychologische Tatbestandsdiagnostik. *Archiv für Kriminalanthropologie und Kriminalistik,* 1904, **15,** 72–113.

WILLIAMS, A., Jr. Some psychological correlates of the electroencephalogram. *Archives of Psychology, New York,* 1939, **34**(No. 240).

WILLIAMS, J. G. L., & WILLIAMS, B. Arterial pulse wave velocity as a psychophysiological measure. *Psychosomatic Medicine,* 1965, **27,** 408–414.

WINTER, J. E. A comparison of the cardio-pneumo-psychograph and association methods in the detection of lying in cases of theft among college students. *Journal of Applied Psychology,* 1936, **20,** 243–248.

WOODMANSEE, J. J. Methodological problems in pupillographic experiments. *Proceedings of the 74th Annual Convention of the American Psychological Association,* 1966, 133–134.

WOODWORTH, R. S., & SCHLOSBERG, H. *Experimental psychology.* (Rev. ed.) New York: Holt, Rinehart and Winston, 1954.

YATES, A. Abnormalities of psychomotor functions. In H. J. EYSENCK (Ed.), *Handbook of abnormal psychology: An experimental approach.* (Ch. 2.) New York: Basic Books, 1961.

YERKES, R. M., & BERRY, C. S. The association reaction method of mental diagnosis (*Tatbestandsdiagnostik*). *American Journal of Psychology,* 1909, **20,** 22–37.

Charles F. Stroebel

PSYCHOPHYSIOLOGICAL PHARMACOLOGY*

20

I often say that when you can measure what you are speaking about, and express it in numbers, you know something about it; but when you cannot measure it, when you cannot express it in numbers, your knowledge is of a meagre and unsatisfactory kind; it may be the beginning of knowledge, but you have scarcely, in your thoughts, advanced to the stage of Science whatever the matter may be.
—Lord Kelvin

The study of drugs that affect behavior is more complicated than the study of drugs that do not. This is because the vast majority of complex behavior consists of functional relationships among stimuli and responses that have been acquired through learning, or at least modified by the learning process. In other words, a subject's behavior and past history must be taken into consideration as complex variables that may alter the outcome of drug administration. From the viewpoint of a psychophysiologist who is interested in the translation functions between physiological

*The author is deeply indebted to Miss Dorthie McIntyre, Mrs. Deborah Prior, and Mrs. Dorothy Reiss for their devoted efforts in assembling the manuscript, bibliography, and illustrations. In addition, the following individuals are thanked for their ideas and advice: B. C. Glueck, Jr., G. T. Heistad, F. Halberg, P. E. Meehl, J. Donnelly, F. J. Braceland, William Zeller, Dean Clyde, A. Shapiro, D. F. Klein, M. Fink, Gay Luce, and E. Johnson. This research was supported by NIMH grant MH-08552 and by the Gengras Foundation.

and behavioral processes, a simple paradigm serves to make the point clear, as shown in Figure 20.1.

Interindividual or surface (phenotypic) behavior may be divided into components assignable to heredity (*H*), environment (*E*), and their interaction (*I*) (Hirsch, 1962, pp. 3–23; Stroebel, 1967b, pp. 453–458). It is clear that, in analyzing the effects of a drug on an individual's behavior (*P*), the effect of the last term, (*I*), is crucial in interpreting the other two. For, when the interaction is zero, the environmental and genetic components are related to phenotypic variance in a simple additive fashion; but, when nonzero, vastly more complicated multiplicative relationships must be considered as well.

To take advantage of the simplicity of the additive relationship, neurophysiologists classically study the effects of drugs on nervous system functioning with immobilized (curarized or anesthetized) animal preparations with the environment held constant; this familiar black environment experiment holds interactive effects relatively constant. Similarly, pharmacologists study the effect of drugs on some aspect of physiological functioning in situations in which the environment is clearly limited such as with isolated gut or isolated nerve preparations. Using comparable logic but a different strategy, experimental psychologists have studied the effects of drugs on the behavior of inbred animals with similar genetic constitutions, where

H equals a constant; this is the familiar black box experiment. In either the black box or the black environment experiments, the complexities of interpreting the multiplicative effects (exponential, logarithmic, rank reversal, or other) ascribable to interaction variance are minimized. Psychophysiologists, on the other hand, favor more realistic designs approximating real life in which both behavioral and physiological factors may vary; this situation is more like that faced by the clinician, who is confronted with a sick patient who needs help *now*, despite the presence of many complicating nonadditive factors.

In choosing an "ultimate" research strategy that denies him the efficacy of the black box or black environment approaches, the psychophysiologist has adopted a multivariate strategy in studying drug effects (Ax, 1962, pp. 29–44; Lader & Wing, 1966; Schnore, 1959; Stroebel, 1967a, pp. 215–241; Wenger, 1957). The pharmacologist-psychophysiologist is not interested in how drugs affect a laboratory artifact that he has arranged for convenience of study, but in how they change the interfunctioning of behavioral and biological mechanisms. His concern is a multidisciplinary one, ranging from the study of basic biochemical integration; the interrelationship of ascending reticular, midline thalamic, and limbic system influences; cerebellar modification; direct and indirect measures of autonomic and central arousal; sleep and wakefulness; and other more complex factors introduced by the circulatory and hormonal systems—all as physiological processes underlying sensation, perception, thinking, and emotion, and viewed against the past history of the organism. The suggestion has been made that longitudinal studies will be required to resolve interaction effects in the more complicated psychophysiological situations (Stroebel & Glueck, 1965, pp. 451–459).

It is apparent that the multidisciplinary approach and philosophy of psychophysiologists are ambitious. As the authors of other chapters of this handbook clearly indicate, psychophysiologists have only recently acquired workable tools with which to make their experiments congruent with their visions of experimental reality. A good case of such a tool is the digital computer, used as an interactive component in our experiments. Once

$$\underbrace{\sigma_P^2}_{\substack{\text{Interindividual} \\ \text{variance}}} = \underbrace{\sigma_H^2}_{\substack{\text{Heredity} \\ \text{variance}}} + \underbrace{\sigma_E^2}_{\substack{\text{Environmental} \\ \text{variance}}} + \underbrace{[\sigma_H \times \sigma_E]}_{\substack{\text{Interaction} \\ \text{variance}}}$$

Black environment model

$$\sigma_P^2 = \sigma_H^2 + K^2 + \sigma_H K$$

Black box model

$$\sigma_P^2 = K^2 + \sigma_E^2 + K\sigma_E$$

Figure 20.1 Schematic paradigm showing hereditary, environmental, and interaction components of interindividual variance. In the black environment model, environmental variance is held constant; in the black box model, genetic variance is held constant.

programmed, the computer can sample, calculate, store, and combine many variables, even presenting new behavioral stimuli, on the basis of "real"-time data calculations (Stroebel, 1970, pp. 79–81). Previously, such data often required weeks or months for scoring and analysis, making it unavailable in usable form for real-time experimental use.

A review of the vast literature on drug effects reveals few studies that fulfill even partially the design philosophy for psychophysiological experiments. This may partly reflect the undeveloped nature of our knowledge of basic psychophysiological relationships *without* drugs and also the controversies about psychophysiological techniques and methodology that still preoccupy many of our colleagues. If a scientist's basic recording techniques, e.g., the galvanic skin response (GSR), suffer from problems of reliability and validity within or between laboratories, would it be wise to complicate experiments further by adding drug conditions?

Recognizing that the psychophysiological approach is philosophically realistic but relatively untested, I have written this chapter with an optimistic view toward the future contributions of psychophysiologists to the study of drug effects. An attempt has been made to provide a compact summary of the relevant basic models, problems, drug effect information, methodology, and design considerations.

DEFINITION OF A DRUG

A drug may be defined as any externally supplied, solid, liquid, or gaseous substance that is eaten, injected into, inhaled, or absorbed by a living organism. Such substances may be biologically viable (bacteria, viruses) and may or may not result in any noticeable change in behavioral or physiological functioning. Drug effects may be direct or indirect (primary or secondary), depending on whether a response change is specifically attributable to the substance itself or whether the presence of the substance alters the role of other agents in exerting their usual effects. Thus, in addition to the agents usually defined as drugs, such as aspirin, adrenalin, or digitalis, we must include the usual respiratory gases and any contaminants they con-

tain, foods, beverages, and even inert substances such as carbon granules, which may or may not be radioactive.

Clearly, so broad a definition of a drug makes every psychophysiological experiment a study of drug effects, unless many variables are carefully controlled. Hence, to control diet; the hours since the last meal; smoking, caffeine, and alcohol habits; and present and past medication history, most psychophysiologists use advance instructions and questionnaires to screen subjects before testing them. A subject's deliberate suppression of past experience with LSD, marijuana, and other taboo drugs may pose problems in the future. Considerable debate exists as to the length of time subjects must be off various medication to be regarded as drug free; for example, data from the NIMH collaborative drug studies (Goldberg, Cole, & Klerman, 1966, pp. 69–84) demonstrate residual phenothiazine effects many weeks after the cessation of drug administration.

Precautions are usually taken by experimenters to provide fresh air adjusted for a comfortable temperature and humidity in the testing area. Tobacco as a drug-contaminant sometimes poses a difficult problem, since denying an inveterate smoker his cigarettes during an experimental session may lead to nervousness and activation that alters experimental results. Some investigators regularly record barometric pressure (reflecting by weight the amount of respiratory gases present in a unit volume) as a part of their data and cancel experiments when pressure is unusually low or high (Wenger, 1962, pp. 97–114); others have even suggested controlling the negative ion content of the air in testing areas (Duffee & Koontz, 1965).

Even when the independent variable in a study is a "real" drug agent (sometimes called a behaviorally active drug), ordinary food substances may significantly interact with a drug in a way that seriously alters the results. Kety (1959, 1965) reviews biochemical studies of schizophrenic patients in which the differences between the patients and the control subjects were attributed to a lack of vitamin C in the diet of patients in one study, and to unusually high coffee consumption in another. Hedberg, Gordon, and Glueck (1966) observed a hypertensive crisis in six psychiatric patients under treatment with tranylcypromine (Parnate) after they had eaten chicken livers containing tyramine, an amine also found in cheddar cheese, Chianti wine, and beer, and frequently associated with hypertensive reactions in combination with monoamine oxidase (MAO) inhibitors (Asatoor, Levi, & Milne, 1963). They also found that patients simultaneously receiving larger doses of various phenothiazines were apparently "protected" from the hypertensive crisis resulting from tyramine. In summary, meaningful research must take this broad definition of drugs into consideration, regardless of whether the effects of a behaviorally active drug are being tested or not.

THE PLACEBO EFFECT: DRUG EFFECTS WITHOUT DRUGS

Placebo procedures permit the psychophysiologist to resolve those effects of treatment which are primary, i.e., produced by the active drug principle, from effects which may result from implicit or explicit response predispositions on the part of the subject (Sternbach, 1966) and/or the experimenter (Rosenthal, 1965). Such resolution bears not only upon the study of drugs but also on many related issues such as hypnosis, suggestion, the patient-physician mystique, and psychosomatic illness. The consideration of the placebo effect must be two-sided, since it involves not only "drug" effects when no active drug, in fact, is given but also the failure to achieve a drug effect when an active drug *is* given in sufficient doses.

A brief review of psychophysiology methods and goals will clarify this point. Psychophysiological studies may be broadly classified into two types: (a) basal nonreactive steady state studies in which the subject behaves as normally as possible, usually while lying quiescently on a bed (e.g., EEG studies of the sequence and duration of different stages of sleep in normal control subjects); and (b) non-steady state, reactive experiments in which the subject is presented with a stimulus situation designed to alter his physiological and behavioral responses (e. g., he is given a drug or a learning task or is presented with a stimulus situation that leads to fear, anger, sorrow, guilt, etc.). Depending

on time limitations, a baseline of nonreactive recording is often collected as a control before introducing the independent variable.

Subjects come to either situation with implicit sets or expectations as to what will happen. The duality aspect of the placebo phenomena becomes apparent when we recognize that naïve subjects may be tense and fearful, making even a basal study a reactive one; on the other hand, experienced subjects often become bored, habituated, or blasé, making reactive studies more typically basal. These dual effects can often be isolated in psychophysiological experiments by repeating the measurements on the subjects over a series of occasions.

When additional factors such as drug conditions are added to psychophysiology designs, it is not unexpected that the placebo effect would become very complicated. This expectation is borne out by the results of Beecher's studies (1965, pp. 111–128) on quantification of the subjective experience of pain. These studies are particularly provocative because of the greater subjective intensity of the pain stimuli as compared to milder experimental manipulations (Sternbach, 1968). Beecher finds that the average effectiveness of placebos when dealing with pathological pain (tissue pathology) is 35%, while the effectiveness of placebos with experimentally contrived pain (such as tourniquet, heat) is only 3.2%. Hence the placebo is 10 times more effective in relieving pain of pathological, as opposed to experimentally contrived, origin. A presumed explanation is that when anxiety and stress are severe, placebos are more effective than when stress is of a smaller degree or absent. Beecher suggests a new principle of drug action: "Some drugs (morphine) are effective only in the presence of an appropriate mental state." He concludes that pain depends on two factors: (a) the actual stimulation of pain receptors, and (b) the *meaning* of the sensations to the individual, the latter being a secondary or reactive component to pain. Beecher's work represents a contribution to our understanding of the role of *implicit* sets on the part of the patient in the placebo effect, since every subject, whether receiving the placebo for pathologic or contrived pain, was under the impression that an active analgesic agent would be given. In other words, the observed differences in effectiveness must be attributed to the individual's own response predispositions.

Placebo effects resulting from *explicit* response sets have been examined by Sternbach (1964). He gave three sets of instructions in a "drug" experiment, stating that one kind of pill would relax the stomach, that a second was a placebo pill having no effect (in order to get a baseline recording of stomach activity), and that the third pill was a stimulant to the stomach. In actuality, all three pills were plastic-coated magnets used to monitor gastrointestinal activity. Sternbach's results are shown in Figure 20.2, indicating that four out of six subjects (1, 2, 5, and 6) showed significant differences in the rate of contractions in the directions predicted on the basis of the explicit instructions presented. Although the sample size is small, it is interesting that in the situations displaying the explicit response set, two-thirds of the subjects demonstrated a placebo effect, a figure about double the ratio of those reported as placebo reactors to pathological pain, and 20 times that to experimental pain with Beecher's implicit set condition.

In summary, psychophysiological drug studies should be carefully controlled or so designed that effects attributable to implicit or explicit response

sets may be analyzed. Perspicacious investigators may rightly insist that subjects for drug studies be pretested to determine their predispositions to implicit and explicit responses prior to the introduction of a drug condition (Lasagna, Mosteller, von Felsinger, & Beecher, 1954; Liberman, 1967, pp. 557–566; Wolf, Doering, Clark, & Hagans, 1957). Covariance analyses based on such reactivity indices could add considerable precision to the study of drug effects (Ax, 1962, pp. 29–44; Clyde, 1967).

THE STIMULUS ROLE OF DRUGS

While drug effects are usually attributed to complex alterations and interactions involving biochemical and physiological mediators of behavior, such effects may also be viewed at a more distinctly behavioral level, namely, as producing novel psychophysiological states that may serve as stimulus events. As stimuli, drugs can gain control of behavior through association with reinforcing environmental events; in other words, the drug state itself may acquire habit loadings or associative connections to responses. Any change in the drug condition would then alter the stimulus complex associated with learning or extinction; these changes,

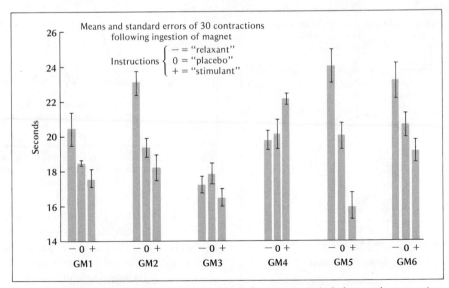

Figure 20.2 Effect of explicit sets (instructions) on the average period of stomach contractions (in seconds) for six subjects under three instruction conditions. Redrawn from R. A. Sternbach, The effects of instructional sets on autonomic responsivity. *Psychophysiology, 1964, **1**, 67–72.* Reproduced by permission.

when measured behaviorally, could be interpreted as a drug effect without specific biochemical mediation.

The stimulus role of drugs in a psychophysiological sense has only recently been recognized experimentally. Heistad (1957) has proposed a Pavlovian model in which the gradient of stimulus generalization for emotional behavior lies along an implied continuum of activity of the autonomic nervous system with relative sympathetic and parasympathetic dominance representing the tails, and autonomic balance the middle, as shown in Figure 20.3. The inverted U-shaped curve may be considered as a performance versus activation function or as a typical gradient of stimulus generalization in a Pavlovian experiment, in which the balance state would represent the stimulus complex present during the original learning. For example, a specific tone (previously neutral) might be temporally associated with a salivation response induced by placing food or acid on a subject's tongue. After a number of trials, the tone alone elicits salivation without the acid or food. However, maximum salivation requires the exact reproduction of the stimulus conditions that prevailed during learning, a situation which would be represented by the "balanced" state in Figure 20.3. A change in frequency or intensity of the tone, a change in the background noise level, the presence of addi-

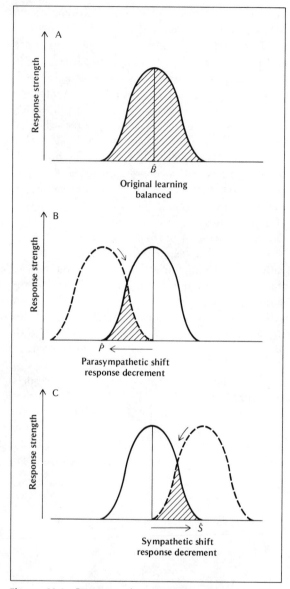

Figure 20.4 Response decrements occur when either parasympathetic or sympathetic agents alter the stimulus complex present during learning.

tional or different experimenters, moving to a different laboratory, or more specifically (referring to Figure 20.3), a change in autonomic nervous system balance toward relative parasympathetic or sympathetic dominance—all would interfere to some extent with the performance of the conditioned response. In each of these instances, we see a change in the stimulus conditions, so that the stimuli presented during test trials will be more or

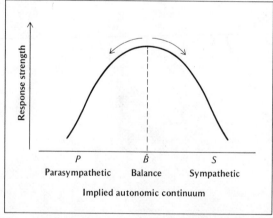

Figure 20.3 Gradient of stimulus generalization along an implied autonomic continuum, where any shift in balance produces a reduction in the response strength of learning that took place under the balanced condition.

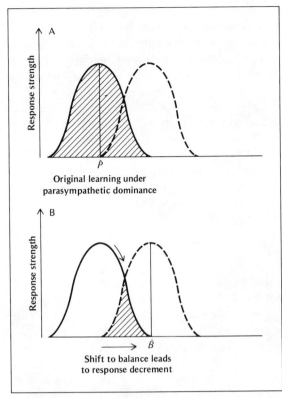

Figure 20.5 When original learning takes place under an unbalanced state, the mere return to balance produces a response strength decrement.

less similar to the original stimulus but not identical with the entire stimulus complex. Such changes in the original stimulus condition that prevailed during learning yield an attenuation of the response proportional to the degree of change along the arrows in Figure 20.3.

Heistad's model suggests that somatic alterations such as electroconvulsive shock, psychoactive drugs, coronary occlusions, pregnancy, surgical trauma, hot baths, or *any manipulation* that changes internal stimulus conditions so that they are different from those associated with emotional responses during learning, will reduce the strength of that emotional response along a gradient of stimulus generalization. Further, a learned emotional response that appears weakened by stimulus changes will recover in strength if the stimulus conditions during the learning process are reinstated.

Figure 20.6 New learning or insight gained through psychotherapy under a drug condition may be lost when the drug is suddenly withdrawn.

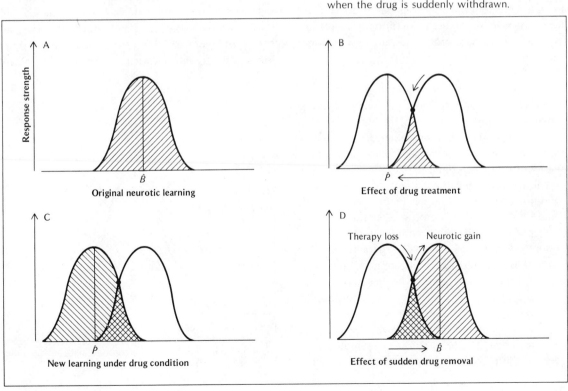

A number of interesting predictions, which have been partially confirmed in animal experiments by Heistad (1957), Grossman and Miller (1961), and Otis (1964), can be derived from this model. The first prediction is that an emotional response acquired under a balanced state will be attenuated if a drug or other treatment is used to alter the original stimulus complex. Figure 20.4 illustrates this situation, where Panel A represents the gradient of stimulus generalization associated with learning under the balanced condition; Panel B shows a decrement in strength of the original response along the original gradient of stimulus generalization after the subject is treated with a parasympathetic agent; and Panel C illustrates a comparable attenuation had the treatment been with a predominantly sympathetic agent such as electroconvulsive shock. Except for the nonspecific variety of treatments expected to produce a decrement in response strength, this finding is not unexpected.

The second prediction suggests that, when a response is acquired under an unbalanced state (shown as parasympathetic dominance in Figure 20.5), the return of the subject to a balanced condition will reduce the original response strength along the gradient of stimulus generalization. Thus, when rats were trained to a conditioned emotional response under chlorpromazine and tested under saline, they showed a *reduced* response (Heistad, 1957).

Further predictions may be applied to the combined treatment of psychiatric patients with drugs and psychotherapy. If we accept the hypothesis that mental illness involves a biochemical abnormality and/or an abnormal social and personal learning history, the model predicts that gains made from psychotherapy while the patient is under a drug condition may become largely ineffective or be lost when he stops taking the drug, or if some natural event presents him with a counterdrug stress. For example, Figure 20.6, Panel A, characterizes the gradient of stimulus generalization of a patient *without* a biological defect who has acquired an emotional behavior under a *balanced* condition. His disturbed behavior is attenuated along a gradient of stimulus generalization as shown in Panel B by a psychoactive drug (e.g., chlorpromazine); subsequently, the psychiatrist encourages new learning

of more acceptable behavior under the drug condition as shown by the shaded area in Panel C. If the patient is subsequently discharged as being well and terminates his medication, he then will return to the balanced state, experiencing a loss of the new behavior and a relapse to the old as shown in Panel D. By the gradual withdrawal or reduction of the drug while behavior therapy or psychotherapy is continued, the danger of such a relapse would be minimized, since the new learning would gradually replace the old, becoming attached to the balanced stimulus complex. This mechanism can also be used as a rationale for a problem that has recently been reported (Glueck, 1967) as follows: Although the release of "back-ward patients" from state hospitals has been widely ascribed to the use of psychoactive drugs, a new group of "chronic" psychotic patients, who have repeatedly been readmitted after stopping medication, apparently is growing. Many of these individuals no longer respond to the usual psychoactive agents, posing the danger of a new drug-insensitive, chronic population in state hospital systems. The stimulus-generalization model would suggest that, as a result of repeated drug-nondrug transitions, the abnormal behavior of these individuals has become conditioned to both the drug and nondrug states, as shown in Figure 20.7; hence the usual drugs are no longer effective in producing novel stimulus complexes.

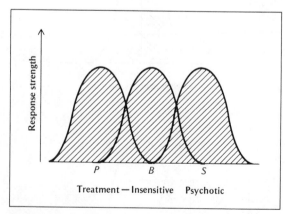

Figure 20.7 Stimulus generalization explanation of the treatment-insensitive psychotic, whose abnormal behavior has become associated with all possible internal stimulus complex states.

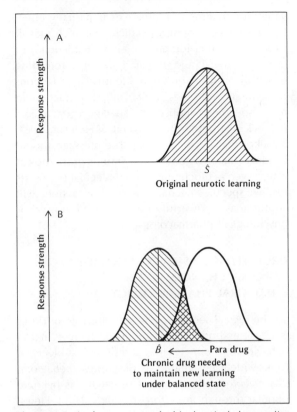

Figure 20.8 In the presence of a biochemical abnormality in mental illness (shown here as producing sympathetic activation), chronic administration of an antagonist drug agent is needed to maintain balance.

In the two-factor situation in which a biochemical (genetic?) defect and abnormal learning are both important aspects of the mental disease process, the model can be applied to make differential predictions, depending on whether abnormal learning occurred under a balanced or an unbalanced condition. Under the *unbalanced* learning condition shown in Figure 20.8, Panel A, chronic, lifelong administration of an effective drug will be required to compensate for the metabolic defect (cf. insulin for juvenile-onset diabetes), while also retaining the patient in the balanced state, where the new learning has taken place (Panel B).

The *balanced* learning condition has been advanced by Stroebel (1967b, pp. 453–458) to establish a rationale for the increasingly widespread but poorly understood practice of combining antago-

nistic drug treatments. (Examples of such combinations are chlorpromazine and electroconvulsive shock, Parnate and Stelazine, Melaril and imipramine, Elavil and Trilifon, imipramine and reserpine; these combinations apparently permit smaller doses of each drug than if given alone and also tend to reduce side effects.) He suggests that one of the drugs may serve as an active antipsychotic agent with the biochemical effect of correcting a brain malfunction or deficit, while the second, "antagonistic" drug merely serves to maintain relative balance in physiological functioning. Figure 20.9 illustrates this case, in which the parasympathetic drug might be the active antipsychotic agent, suitably balanced in dosage by a sympathetic drug or energizer to maintain a balanced stimulus complex condition. Experimental support for this hypothesis can be drawn from a report by Hedberg, Gordon, and Glueck (1966), in which Stelazine (a neuroleptic

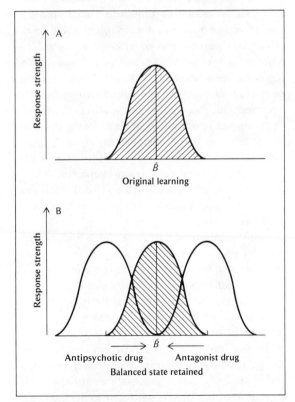

Figure 20.9 Application of the stimulus generalization model as a basis for the effectiveness of combined drug treatments in psychiatry.

drug) protected patients who were also receiving tranylcypromine (an energizer drug) from a tyramine challenge; and from Heistad (1957), who trained rats to criterion on a conditioned emotional response under saline, then eliminated the response with a series of electroconvulsive shock treatments (sympathetic dominance), and subsequently partially restored the response by merely administering chlorpromazine, which apparently served as an antagonistic "balancing" agent to reinstate the original learning conditions.

While the foregoing discussion suggests a stimulus role for drugs in a classical conditioning sense, similar if more distinct stimulus properties have also been demonstrated in instrumental learning situations with animals. Stewart (1962) found that cats could use a drug condition as a discriminative stimulus in a two-choice compartment situation. In separate experiments, he found that cats could discriminate chlorpromazine versus saline and imipramine versus saline. Cook, Davidson, Davis, and Kelleher (1960) used the infusion of epinephrine or acetylcholine as a warning stimulus to establish avoidance behavior in dogs. Polygraph recordings of respiration, electrocardiogram, and jejunal activity showed "that the [drug-induced] physiological changes consistently preceded the occurrence of the avoidance response." Caution in these studies is warranted in considering the finding of Schuster and Brady (1964) that, while using the intravenous infusion of epinephrine as a discriminative stimulus for lever pressing for food in monkeys, the subjects could also use the infusion of saline during control trials as a discriminative stimulus.

The stimulus model of drug effects is especially relevant for psychophysiology because of its general potential for integrating the somatic treatment and psychotherapeutic approaches of modern psychiatry. It presents a conceptual basis for the unusual range of treatments, including drugs with different pharmacological characteristics, which are seemingly effective in combination with psychotherapeutic intervention in ameliorating psychotic symptoms. Alternative explanations for these observations of nonspecificity clearly exist; the mediational variables of psychotic behavior may be so generalized and variable in nature that each of a

variety of treatment alternatives is partially effective. Impressions of nonspecificity might also result from the imprecision and objective inadequacy of present clinical and research designs, reflecting especially our inability to identify homogenous behavioral syndromes, which might, in fact, yield more specific responses to specific drug agents (Glueck & Stroebel, 1969; Overall & Hollister, 1964; Stroebel, 1967b, pp. 453–458). The message should be clear that analyses of the stimulus properties of drugs, even as biochemists and molecular biologists resolve specific mechanisms of drug action, will continue as a powerful integrative tool in psychophysiological pharmacology.

DRUG EFFECTS AS OVERT BEHAVIORAL RESPONSE CHANGES: BEHAVIORAL PHARMACOLOGY

The logical sequel to the stimulus role of drugs is consideration of drug-induced changes in the behavioral *responses* in conditioned subjects, a topic widely designated as descriptive *behavioral pharmacology*. This field of research has become popular through the efforts of Brady, Hunt, Dews, Sidman, and their colleagues (see Brady, 1956) in response to the practical need for infrahuman testing of behaviorally active drugs intended for clinical use. (See Kelleher and Morse, 1968, pp. 1–56 for an excellent recent review.) Behavioral pharmacologists depend heavily upon the techniques of operant conditioning originally developed by B. F. Skinner; these powerful procedures are both operational and pragmatic. By regulating the reinforcement contingencies of both animal and human subjects in controlled environments, a wide variety of behavioral responses may be produced in a highly consistent, reliable, and quantitative form. Because of the consistency of such behavior, subtle variations in responding attributable to drug effects should be clearly identifiable. While experiments in this field tend toward the purely behavioral, black box type (i.e., concomitant physiologic responses are seldom measured), behavioral pharmacologists perspicaciously use knowledge of pharmacological effects to formulate experiments, select drugs for comparison, and interpret results.

Despite the simplicity and elegance of this approach, several problems arise: first, apparently no general agreement has been reached among investigators as to which of the wide variety of possible responses should be brought under reinforcement control to resolve most sensitively the different drug effects and dosages (Weissman, 1966, pp. 617–641). Brady (1956) suggested that this problem might be solved by studying single and combined drugs with a battery of such responses, producing a drug profile or a drug interaction profile. While the profile approach is an ingenious one, objective procedures for comparing and classifying individual profiles are still relatively complicated and require large initial samples and further validation (Glueck & Stroebel, 1969). Second, despite the quantitative nature of data from response-change experiments, very few investigators manipulate or display their data in an easily generalizable form. In those instances in which the experimenter has serendipitously extended his conclusions beyond the raw

cumulative record (either statistically or graphically), the meaningfulness of the data is more apparent (Kornetsky, 1967, pp. 948–954; Rushton & Steinberg, 1967, pp. 464–470; Weiss, 1967). A third difficulty is that a majority of investigators using the response-change technique have studied the acute component of drug-induced response changes, even when studying drugs such as phenothiazines, which apparently exert their most unique clinical effect after a period of chronic administration (Stroebel, 1967b, pp. 453–458). A final problem, usually cited by clinicians, is that few of the clinical applications of psychoactive drugs were predicted initially on the basis of pharmacological actions in animals; also, that animal behavior models for evaluating recognized antipsychotic and antidepressant actions of drugs are relatively inadequate (Hollister, 1968; Klerman, 1966, pp. 183–200; May, 1966, pp. 147–155).

Behavioral pharmacologists are frequently criti-

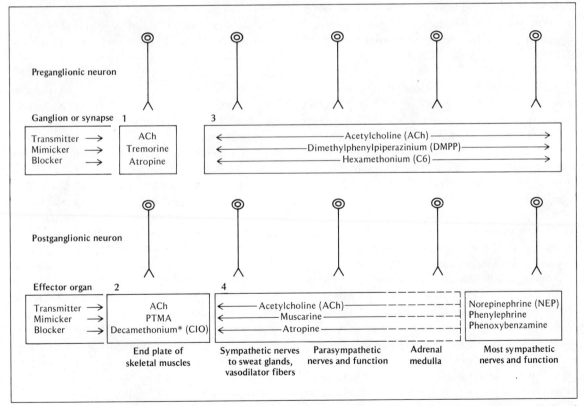

Figure 20.10   Five basic types of synaptic configurations categorized on the basis of the neurotransmitter involved and agents that specifically mimic or block it. Additional types, as well as combinations of the five shown, may exist.

cal of psychophysiological pharmacology because it attempts "to undertake too much, to be too encompassing, to be a jack-of-all-trades and master-of-none." Psychophysiologists, on the other hand, have specifically chosen a multilevel approach precisely *because* of their concern about complexities inherent in the whole functioning organism, rejecting more superficial and potentially more elegant approaches. The psychophysiologist is experimentally cognizant of the reality that many clinically important drug effects do not produce purely overt behavioral response changes; multiple measurement procedures sensitive to both overt *and* covert functioning are needed.

NEUROCHEMICAL MECHANISMS

Many psychophysiological drug studies assume a normal control condition characterized by the relative balance of the adrenergic and cholinergic mechanisms in the body. It is our expectation that imbalances produced by drugs, disease, trauma, or emotions should be detectable with psychophysiological methods. The ability to predict the effect of Drug X, or to understand Disease Y, strongly depends upon knowledge of those neuromechanisms that are most significantly affected by drugs or by a drug-sensitive disease process. It is logical that synapses, as gaps in the neural net especially subject to chemical mediation (if not largely chemically mediated), should receive primary attention. The major focus of this section on neuromechanisms of drugs will be devoted to drugs affecting acetylcholine at cholinergic synapses and norepinephrine at adrenergic synapses. What follows is an attempt to present an overview and consensus of a vast and rapidly changing literature made complicated by numerous conflicting reports.

From a pharmacological point of view, drugs mimicking or blocking cholinergic or adrenergic synapses may be used to distinguish five basic types of synaptic configurations in the nervous system, as shown in Figure 20.10. As presently understood, acetylcholine (ACh) is the neurotransmitter at most preganglionic and ganglionic synapses, in postganglionic nerves at the effector end plate of skeletal muscles, at parasympathetic effector organs, and at certain postganglionic sympathetic effector organs (e.g., sweat glands). Norepinephrine

is a primary neurotransmitter at postganglionic sympathetic effector organs; recent drug studies relating norepinephrine excess or deficiency to manic-depressive syndromes have also implicated it in processes of the central sympathetic nervous system (Bunney & Davis, 1965). Many other substances secreted by neural tissues (epinephrine, dopamine, serotonin, histamine) may act as neurotransmitters under localized conditions (e.g., in specific brain nuclei or organs), but are poorly understood because of the difficulties of studying these minute processes directly (only 10^{-18} moles of acetylcholine are required to produce a spike potential at the neuromuscular junction in many vertebrates, Ackerman, 1962).

Synaptic Transmission

The following sequence of events may be visualized in the ongoing function of a synapse: (a) the neurotransmitter substance is synthesized in the axonal terminal and stored there within synaptic vesicles or granules, either in highly concentrated ionic form (acetylcholine) or as readily dissociable salts (norepinephrine). (b) During the resting state, there is a continual slow release of packets of the transmitter into the synaptic cleft, normally insufficient to cause propagation of a nerve action potential at the postsynaptic site. (c) The nerve action potential (NAP) releases a larger number of packets of the transmitter substance into the synaptic cleft through a mechanism that is as yet unclear but is probably contingent both on depolarization of the presynaptic axonal membrane and the mobilization of calcium ions. (d) The transmitter substance diffuses across the synaptic cleft, a distance of about 100–1000 Å, and combines with receptor sites on the postsynaptic membrane, producing a localized increase in ionic permeability. Two types of permeability change apparently occur: either a generalized increase in permeability to all sizes of ions, resulting in a localized depolarization of the membrane or an excitatory postsynaptic potential (EPSP); or a selective increase in permeability to only the smaller ions such as potassium (K^+) or chloride (Cl^-) resulting in stabilization or actual hyperpolarization in the membrane, constituting an inhibitory postsynaptic potential (IPSP). (In cardiac muscle, acetylcholine, released by the inhibitory vagus nerve, increases the permeability to potassium (K+) and larger cations but does not alter the sodium (Na+) or lithium (Li+) permeability; as a result, a greater summation of local responses is necessary to initiate an action potential.) (e) Alternatively, the transmitter substance may be catalytically degraded in the synaptic cleft or be recaptured via an active transport process back into the presynaptic terminal. If an EPSP exceeds the membrane threshold, it will initiate a propagated action potential in a nerve or a muscle action potential (MAP) in most skeletal and cardiac muscles. In those tonic skeletal muscles and in smooth muscles in which propagated impulses do not occur, the EPSP initiates a localized contractile response; in gland cells, it initiates secretion.

Acetylcholine as a neurotransmitter As illustrated in Figure 20.10, acetylcholine has been implicated as a neurotransmitter substance at the motor end plate of the skeletal muscle, at the presynaptic terminal of autonomic nervous system ganglia, at the postsynaptic effector terminals of parasympathetic neurons, and very likely at many sites in the central nervous system. The primary action of acetylcholine at each of these sites is probably the depolarization of the postsynaptic cell membrane.

Although a wide variety of drugs can be used to influence differentially the physiology of each step of the neurohumoral transmission process, the general behavioral effect of two different drugs can

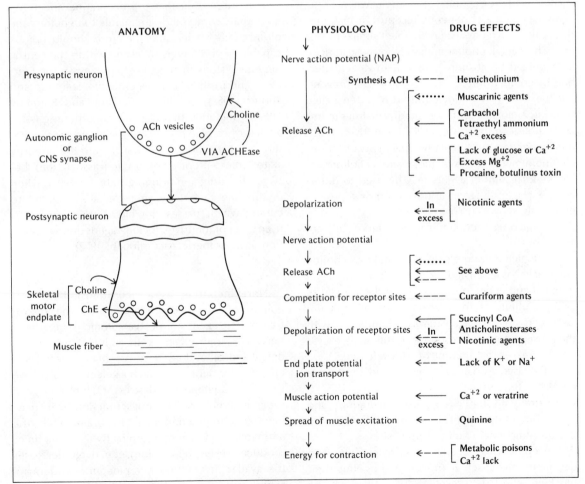

Figure 20.11 Schematic summary of anatomy, physiology, and drug effects at cholinergic synapses. Key: ◄••••, mimic; ◄——, enhance; ◄– –, block. After Holmstedt, cited by Koelle, in L. S. Goodman & A. Gilman (Eds.), *The pharmacological basis of therapeutics.* (3rd ed.) New York: Crowell-Collier-Macmillan, 1965. Reproduced by permission.

APPLICATIONS OF TECHNIQUES AND FINDINGS

often be similar (e.g., cause arousal). Figure 20.11 schematically presents the anatomy of typical cholinergic synapses, with the physiology of various drugs in mimicking, enhancing, or blocking neurotransmitter functioning. The figure is largely self-explanatory, except in providing a rationale for drug effects on the postjunctional receptor sites. Because acetylcholine is secreted as an effective neurotransmitter substance by the presynaptic terminal in each of the synapse configurations previously indicated (Figure 20.10), it could be expected that the postjunctional membrane of each would share certain common features. In addition, each of the synaptic types has distinctive special features, apparently based on specific chemical groupings or steric factors in the membrane that account for specificity of drug action. For example, when a drug combines with a cholinergic receptor, it may produce one of two effects: (a) an effect similar to that of ACh (called cholinomimetic or muscarinic if antagonized by atropine); or (b) no direct effect but, by competition for the receptor site, preventing the action of endogenous ACh (often called nicotinic agents; nicotine or curariform drugs mimic acetycholine in low doses and competitively block it in higher doses). The relative specificity of various cholinomimetic (muscarinic) and cholinergic-blocking (nicotinic) agents may be used to differentiate classically the various receptor types, as previously shown in Figure 20.10.

Specific drug effects indicated in Figure 20.11 are as follows:

1. Hemicholinium blocks the uptake of choline (10^5 weaker as a transmitter than ACh) by the nerve terminal and hence prevents the synthesis of ACh.

2. Botulinus toxin, procaine, lack of calcium Ca^{+2}, and excess magnesium Mg^{+2} interfere with the release of ACh in response to the MAP; excess Ca^{+2} increases the amount of ACh released.

3. Released ACh may be converted to choline by ACh-esterase (ChE).

4. Curare alkaloids (e.g., d-tubocurarine) and other competitive agents block by combining with the postjunctional cholinoceptive sites.

5. Depolarizing agents, succinylcholine and decamethonium, act at the same sites, but their blocking effect is preceded by activation; the antiChE agents, neostigmine and difluorophenyl-

alanine (DFP), produce the same effects through the accumulation of endogenous ACh; in the case of neostigmine, by its direct action as well.

6. K^+, like Ca^{+2} and veratrine, can act both at the postjunctional membrane and at distant parts of the muscle membrane to initiate the MAP. A lack of K^+ and Na^+ reduces the flow of current associated with the end-plate potential (EPP), so that it becomes insufficient to initiate the MAP.

7. Quinine blocks conduction of the MAP; it may also exert a curariform action at the muscle end plate.

8. Metabolic poisons (e.g., iodoacetate, fluoroacetate) interfere with the production of available energy for contraction; Ca^{+2} is essential for the immediate contractile process.

It is interesting that d-tubocurarine and other quaternary compounds are unable to penetrate the blood-brain barrier, and therefore should not be capable of cholinergic blockade within the central nervous system. In an extensive review of the literature and in their own experiments, Solomon and Turner (1962) and Black, Carlson, and Solomon (1962) concluded that classical conditioning (such as that of cardiac responses to electric shock stimuli) under d-tubocurarine transfers to the nondrug state. Transfer *does not occur* (dissociation) between the drug and nondrug state, however, when erythrydine (a tertiary amine alkaloid related to curare, which passes the blood-brain barrier) is used as a competitive blocking agent during conditioning (Gardner & McCollough, 1962).

Norepinephrine as a neurotransmitter Norepinephrine has been identified as the neurotransmitter agent in postganglionic sympathetic nervous system effectors. In addition, recent evidence indicates that those psychiatric treatments effective for depression such as electric convulsive therapy, monoamine oxidase (MAO) inhibitors, and the imipramine class of drugs, function by increasing free norepinephrine in the brain; while the antihypertensive agent reserpine (which sometimes produces severe depression) effectively decreases the availability of free norepinephrine (Klerman, Schildkraut, Hasenbush, Greenblatt, & Friend, 1963; Pare & Sandler, 1959; Rosenblatt, Chanley, Sobotka,

& Kaufman, 1960; Schildkraut, 1964). Biochemical and histochemical studies have demonstrated heavy concentrations of norepinephrine, dopamine, and serotonin in specific structures throughout the brain (Bunney & Davis, 1965).

Our present hypotheses about norepinephrine as a neurotransmitter possess both similarities and dissimilarities with the acetylcholine model. The various steps of the adrenergic transmission process, along with drug mechanisms mimicking, de-

pleting, enhancing, blocking, or displacing this process are shown in Figure 20.12.

1. Norepinephrine is synthesized from the amino acid tyrosine with dihydroxyphenylalanine (DOPA) and dihydroxyphenylethylamine (DOPA-mine) as intermediate steps. The synthesis of norepinephrine may be blocked by inhibitors of dopa-decarboxylase or dopamine beta-hydroxylase, e.g., alpha-methylmetatyrosine.

2. It is thought that norepinephrine is continu-

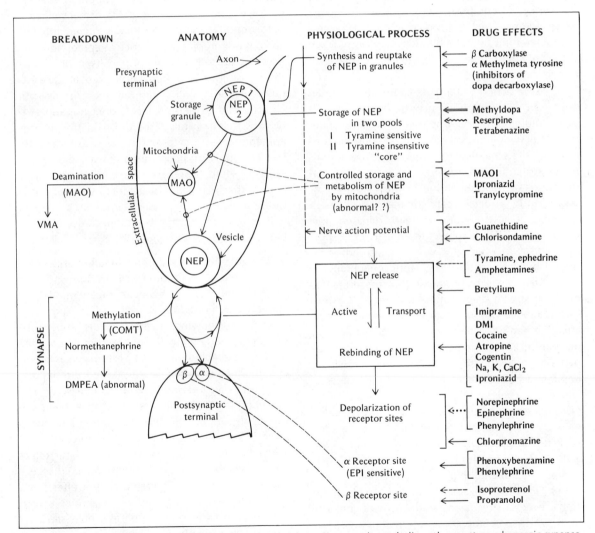

Figure 20.12 Schematic summary of anatomy, physiology, drug effects, and metabolic pathways at an adrenergic synapse. Key: ◄——, blockade; ◄----, enhance; ◄•••• mimic; ◄∿∿∿, deplete; ◄===, displace. Schematically redrawn with additions, from W. E. Bunney & J. M. Davis, Norepinephrine in depressive reactions. *Archives of General Psychiatry*, 1965, **13**, 483–494.

ously being synthesized and stored as an active process at the nerve terminal. Storage associated with the nerve membrane seems to be in two pools, organized somewhat like concentric rings of an onion. The outer pool appears to be tyramine sensitive, while the core is tyramine insensitive. Reserpine, an antihypertensive agent that frequently produces a depressive reaction, and tetrabenazine both operate by depleting the storage of norepinephrine in granules. The norepinephrine thus released is deaminated via MAO (monoamine oxidase) in mitochondria, thus producing a relative deficiency of norepinephrine in the adrenergic nerve endings. Metabolic deamination of excess norepinephrine by mitochondria may be blocked with MAO inhibitors (MAOI) such as iproniazid or tranylcypromine.

3. Nerve action potentials leading to eventual release of norepinephrine may be enhanced with guanethidine or blocked by the drug chlorisondamine. A nerve action potential releases norepinephrine into the synaptic cleft, where the free norepinephrine may follow a number of pathways. Normal quantities of norepinephrine in the cleft are not destroyed by a specific catalytic mechanism, as in the case of acetylcholine. Instead, released norepinephrine (NEP) is subject to an active transport mechanism, in which it may be recaptured or rebound by sites on the presynaptic membrane; if norepinephrine is in considerable excess, it may be methylated via catecholamine transferase to form the metabolic product normethanephrine. Drugs affecting various aspects of this active transport mechanism are amphetamine, which apparently enhances norepinephrine release, and bretylium, imipramine, dimethylimpramine and cocaine, which block release.

4. Norepinephrine reaching the postsynaptic membrane produces depolarization and a graded EPSP. It is suspected that phenylephrine mimics the action of norepinephrine in depolarizing the postsynaptic membrane, thus serving as a "false transmitter." Phenoxybenzamine is thought to block the alpha receptor sites (associated with vasoconstriction), which are epinephrine sensitive on the postsynaptic membrane. Pletscher and Da Prada (1967, pp. 304–311) have suggested that chlorpromazine may generally block the depolarization of the postsynaptic membrane. Beta receptor sites on the postsynaptic membrane (associated with vasodilation), which are isoproterenol sensitive, can be blocked with the drug propranolol. (See Ahlquist, 1968, for a recent review of beta-receptor pharmacology.)

5. Because epinephrine and other catecholamines may, in fact, be more effective than norepinephrine in stimulating the receptor sites on the postsynaptic membrane, there is reason to suspect that a considerable amount of the mechanism involved in adrenergic nerve transmission is dedicated to maintaining a "pure" norepinephrine system; e.g., the monoamine oxidase mechanism in mitochondria is maximally effective in metabolizing analogs of norepinephrine such as epinephrine and may operate on norepinephrine itself only when the transmitter is being synthesized in excessive quantities. In a similar fashion, the enzyme catecholamine transferase (COMT) does not appear to be an efficient catalyst for the oxidation of norepinephrine; it may primarily serve to reduce the concentration of norepinephrine analogs in the synaptic cleft (Kopin, 1968). For example, it is known that pyrogallol, a competitive inhibitor of COMT, enhances the physiologic effects of injected epinephrine and delays its disappearance from the blood (Axelrod & LaRoche, 1959).

The role of acetylcholine in adrenergic neurons A new concept introduced by Burn and Rand in 1962 complicates the neat, binary models of cholinergic and adrenergic synapses. They suggested the following chain of events when postganglionic adrenergic fibers are stimulated: NAP releases acetylcholine, which in turn releases norepinephrine. In other words, acetylcholine may function as an *intermediary* in the release of norepinephrine. The following data have been advanced to support this proposal: when atropine is given in sufficient doses to block a direct effect of acetylcholine as a transmitter on autonomic effector cells via the autonomic ganglia, injected acetylcholine still produces sympathomimetic effects. But when animals are pretreated with reserpine, which depletes available norepinephrine, no sympathomimetic effect is observed.

Summary A summary of pharmacologic agents depressing and stimulating cholinergic and adrenergic synapses is presented in Table 20.1. While

TABLE 20.1 SUMMARY OF DRUGS EXERTING STIMULANT AND DEPRESSANT ACTIONS ON VARIOUS AUTONOMIC NERVOUS SYSTEMS SITES*

Site of action	Depressant (inhibitory)	Stimulant (excitatory)
At parasympathetic effectors	Natural belladonna alkaloids Atropine sulfate Belladonna (tincture and extract) Scopolamine hbr. (hyoscine) d-hyoscyamine Synthetic allied related drugs Homatropine hbr., oral Homatropine mbr. (Mesopin[a], Novatrin[a]), subcut. Amprotropine phosphate (Syntropan[a]) Eucatropine hcl. (Euphthalmine[a]) Adiphenine hcl. (Trasentine[a]) Pavatrine[a]	Choline esters Acetylcholine Methacholine br. or cl. (Mecholyl[a]) Carbachol (Doryl[a]) Bethanechol cl. (Urecholine[a]) Furtrethonium iodide (Furmethide[a]) Cholinesterase inhibitors Physostigmine salicylate (eserine) Neostigmine br. (Prostigmin[a]), oral Neostigmine methylsulfate (Prostigmin[a]), subcut. Isoflurophate (DFP, Floropryl[a]) Octamethylpyrophosphoramide (OMPA)
	Dibutoline sulfate (Dibuline[a]) Methantheline br. (Banthine[a]) Oxyphenonium br. (Antrenyl[a]) Diphemanil methylsulfate (Prantal[a])	Other parasympathetic stimulants Pilocarpine nitrate Muscarine Arecoline
At ganglia (parasympathetic-sympathetic)	Nicotine (large doses) Quaternary ammonium compounds Hexamethonium cl. (Methium[a]) Hexamethonium br. (Bistrium[a]) Chlorisondamine cl. (Ecolid[a]) Mecamylamine hcl. (Inversine[a]) Pentolinium (Ansolysen[a])	Nicotine (small doses-transient effect)
	Curare (large doses)	
At sympathetic effectors	Central and peripheral depressants Ergotamine tartrate (Gynergen[a]) Ergonovine maleate (Ergotrate[a]) Ergotoxine Dihydroergotamine (DHE 45) Dihydroergocornine (DHO 180) Sympatholytic agents Dibenamine[a] Yohimbine Tolazoline hcl. (Priscoline[a]) Phentolamine hcl. (Regitine[a]) Piperoxan hcl. (Benodaine[a])	Epinephrine hcl. (adrenalin) Levarterenol (norepinephrine) Isoproterenol sulfate (Isuprel,[a] Aludrine,[a] Norisodrine[a]) Ephedrine sulfate Synthetic ephedrine-like amines Phenylephrine hcl. (Neo-Synephrine[a]) Phenylpropanolamine hcl. (Propadrine[a]) Pseudoephedrine
	Hydralazine hcl. (Apresoline[a])	Amphetamines Amphetamine sulfate (Benzedrine[a]) Dextro amphetamine sulfate (Dexedrine[a]) Methamphetamine hcl. (Desoxyn[a]) Hydroxyamphetamine hbr. (Paredrine[a])

Note.—From M. J. Chatton, S. Margen, & H. Brainerd, *Handbook of medical treatment.* (7th ed.) Los Altos, Calif.: Lange Medical Publishers, 1960. Reprinted by permission.
*Based upon pharmacological and not necessarily clinical relationships.
[a] Denotes trade names.

the drug effects presented in this section may be viewed as primary, this does not preclude the possibility of direct effects at sites other than those indicated, especially since many of the "primary" effects were identified in isolated preparations, in which the possibility of secondary or side effects was minimized. Recommended references presenting more detailed information can be found in chapters by Koelle (1965, pp. 399–440), Innes and Nickerson (1965, pp. 477–545), Wurtman (1966), Eccles (1964), in review articles appearing regularly in the *Annual Review of Pharmacology,* and in articles appearing in the current psychiatric and neurochemical literature.

NEUROTRANSMITTERS, DRUGS, AND BIOCHEMICAL THEORIES OF MENTAL ILLNESS

Our knowledge of cholinergic synaptic mechanisms stems largely from basic neurophysiological investigations of the neuromuscular junction and autonomic ganglia, relationships that have been presented in various stages of development to students of physiological psychology for several decades. Concepts about adrenergic mechanisms have evolved more recently from studies by neurochemists interested in a possible biochemical etiology for mental illness. A major impetus for the latter was the introduction of psychoactive drugs in the middle 1950s, emphasizing the involvement of a drug-sensitive biological substrate in mental disease processes.

Neurotransmission is probably much more complex than the neurophysiologists or neurochemists usually imply in their models. Usually, they investigate isolated "pure" preparations uncontaminated by the many variables that have created an obvious need for the multiple approaches of psychophysiology (Ax, 1962, pp. 29–44). Drug effects are very likely to serve as the vital bridge between the basic neurochemical mechanisms and the complexities of clinical treatment, thereby providing access to the psychophysiological etiology of mental illness. The "bridge" is not yet secure—it might be envisioned as a pontoon type that is not quite attached to either bank.

In contrast to the apparent elegance of bio-chemical models, clinical theories range from one extreme, in which a disease such as schizophrenia is attributed entirely to physiological or chemical malfunctioning (constitutional basis), to another that claims mental illness to be primarily an environmental or behavioral aberration (psychodynamic basis). Although a theory capable of securely unifying these approaches has not been presented, a majority of psychophysiologists assumes that constitutional and environmental factors interact (Meehl, 1962; Sternbach, Alexander, & Greenfield, 1968).

Regardless of one's position on this issue, we do know that drugs can modify behavior. Additionally, all behavior, whether normal or abnormal, has a biochemical basis, since all neurological processes are dependent upon neurochemical functioning. Ultimately, therefore, abnormal brain functioning in various mental diseases is mediated in some manner by changes in local biochemical events, events which themselves may be influenced by behavior. To clarify this apparently circular logic, an attempt will be made here to show how the various biochemical theories of mental illness might be integrated within a psychophysiological schema.

Some biological theories of mental illness reflect a *qualitative* alteration in brain chemistry, e.g., the various proposals of abnormal psychotogenic proteins such as taraxein (Heath & Krupp, 1968; Heath, Martens, Leach, Cohen, & Angel, 1957), alpha globulin (Frohman, Latham, Beckett, & Gottlieb, 1960), ceruloplasm (Akerfeldt, 1957) or proposals of a "neurotoxin" such as Friedhoff and Van Winkle's (1962) abnormal amine metabolite (namely, 3,4-dimethoxythemethylamine [DMPEA]), or of psychotomimetic substances such as bufotenine or dimethyltryptamine. Other biochemical changes might only be *quantitative*, reflecting an abnormal rate at which a neurotransmitter is released or metabolized (Bunney & Davis, 1965). Examples of *quantitative* mechanisms were presented in an earlier discussion of drug effects at the adrenergic synapse. Extensive, critical reviews of biochemical theories of schizophrenia have been published by Kety (1959, 1965) and Eiduson, Geller, Yuwiler, & Eiduson (1964).

The theories proposing a qualitatively abnormal protein are sufficiently elusive so as to contribute

TABLE 20.2 USUAL RESPONSES OF AUTONOMIC EFFECTOR SYSTEMS TO ADRENERGIC AND CHOLINERGIC NERVE STIMULATION

Effector organ	Receptor type	Adrenergic impulses	Cholinergic impulses
Eye			
Iris	α	Mydriasis	Miosis (contraction)
Ciliary muscle	β	Slight relaxation for far vision	Accommodates for near vision
Heart			
Rate	β	Accelerates	Decreases; vagal arrest
Output	β	Increases	Decreases
Rhythmicity	β	Tachychardia Fibrillation	A-V block; vagal arrest
Blood vessels			
Coronary		Dilation (passive)	? (dilation)
Skin and mucosa	α	Constriction	? (dilation)
Skeletal muscles	α, β	Constriction	Dilation
Cerebral	α	Slight constriction	? (dilation)
Pulmonary	α	Constriction	? (dilation)
Abdominal muscles	α, β	Constriction	? (dilation)
Salivary glands	α	Constriction	Dilation
Lungs			
Bronchial muscles	β	Relaxation	Contraction
Bronchial glands		? (inhibition)	Stimulation
Stomach			
Mobility and tone	β	Decreases	Increases
Sphincters	α	Usually contraction	Usually relaxation
Secretion		? (inhibition)	Increases
Intestine			
Mobility and tone	α, β	Decreases	Increases
Sphincters	α	Usually contraction	Usually relaxation
Secretion		? (inhibition)	Stimulation
Ureter			
Tone and mobility		Usually increases	?
Sex organs		Ejaculation	Erection
Skin			
Pilomotor muscles	α	Contraction	
Sweat glands	α	Slight localized secretion	Generalized secretion
Adrenal medulla			Secretion of epinephrine and norepinephrine
Liver		Glycogenolysis	
Salivary glands	α	Thick viscous secretion	Profuse watery secretion
Lacrimal glands			Secretion
Nasopharyngeal glands			Secretion
Autonomic ganglion cells			Stimulation
Gallbladder		Relaxation	Contraction
Urinary bladder			
Detrusor	β	Usually relaxation	Contraction
Trigone and sphincter	α	Contraction	Relaxation

Note.—From G. B. Koelle, Neurohumoral transmission and the autonomic nervous system. In L. Goodman & A. Gilman (Eds.), *The pharmacological basis of therapeutics.* (3rd ed.) New York: Crowell-Collier-Macmillan, 1965, pp. 399–440. Reprinted by permission.

little to our understanding of drug mechanisms; whereas the models suggesting quantitive neurochemical change provide a useful basis for hypotheses, especially in suggesting treatment modalities for mania and depression. This observation should not be taken as evidence for disqualifying the qualitative data, since tentative information linking both approaches is now visible. For example, autoimmune processes have been implicated in several of the theories of abnormal protein. Heath and Krupp (1968) have presented electroencephalographic and immunological evidence suggesting that serum fractions (such as taraxein) isolated from the blood of acute schizophrenics may operate as antigens against specific brain structures. Exemplifying a conceivably similar mechanism, Watson, Quigley, and Bolt (1966) have identified a lymphocyte extract from children with ulcerative colitis that is specifically cytotoxic for the epithelial cells of the colon. Further, the appearance of lesions in patients with autoerythrocyte sensitization, a chronic purpuric state of adult and adolescent females, may be exacerbated with hypnotic suggestion (polypeptide *vasodilator* has been implicated as a possible intermediary between psychological factors and the production of lesions). See Agle, Ratnoff, and Wasman (1967). Although the similarity has not been established, immunosympathectomy, an experimental procedure in animals, can be achieved by administering an antigen to a nerve growth factor (an antinerve growth factor) to newborn rats or mice, producing a 30% reduction in the adult compliment of sympathetic nerve endings (Wurtman, 1966). This defect produces a decline in the usual norepinephrine content of various organs with a predictable hypersensitivity to catecholamines; organ specificity depends on *when the antigen was administered during the developmental process,* in other words, an immunologically produced sympathectomy. The implication is clear that a *qualitative,* abnormal protein factor could influence the developmental process with great specificity, to produce organ- or receptor-specific *quantitative* abnormalities in catecholamine metabolism that would be sensitive to specific drugs. Space limitations restrict further speculation on these possibilities, except to note that immunosympathetic organ or receptor sensitization should be both easily and elegantly detectable in psychophysiological studies of response specificity and stereotypy in which sensitized effector organs are involved. Although no evidence has as yet been advanced to link immunosympathectomy with a naturally occurring disease, it does provide a possible pathway for integrating the qualitative and quantitative quests for a biochemical basis for mental illness.

DRUGS AND AUTONOMIC RESPONSE PATTERNS

While depending heavily upon neurochemical evidence derived from in vivo and in vitro animal experiments, the psychophysiologist's own research emphasis is on the study of drugs in wholly intact functioning subjects. Unfortunately, this more realistic situation introduces many additional sources of variation that complicate the interpretation of results. Examples of extra sources of variation might be implicit and explicit response sets, patterns of response specificity, levels of arousal, previous learning, etc.

An immediate problem is deciding which of the many possible physiological response variables will, in fact, be measured. Some of the possibilities are shown systematically in Table 20.2, indicating the usual responses of autonomic effector organs to adrenergic and cholinergic nerve stimulation. These "usual" patterns of response are complicated by significant interindividual variations in response specificity (i.e., in a given situation, individuals vary in the specific autonomic effector organs that are maximally activated). Synergistic innervation can also lead to difficulties; for example, can one definitely attribute pupillary dilation to an increase in sympathetic activity, or alternatively, to a decrease in parasympathetic activity? Psychophysiologists have partially solved some of these problems by measuring a number of autonomic effector responses, using the over-all pattern of response as an indicator (Schnore, 1959; Wenger, 1957). The necessity for this multiple-variable technique was anticipated by Darrow (1943), who was one of the first modern psychophysiologists to record electroencephalographic and autonomic nervous system variables simultaneously:

To attain significance a test of autonomic functions must circumvent the mutually antagonistic action of the two branches of the autonomic nervous system so that it may be clear whether an observed peripheral event is due to increase of activity in one branch of the autonomic system or to decrease of activity in the other. There must be no question for example whether an observed pupillary dilation is due to sympathetic excitation or to inhibition of the parasympathetically determined irido-constrictor tone. The problem is literally to determine the weight on either side of a "balance" when neither side is known. The mere knowledge that the balance has been upset by a given condition as afforded by many so-called tests of autonomic function, may be physiologically or clinically of little value except as indication that something has been disturbed. It does not necessarily define the foregoing events in the neural and neurohumoral systems, and in consequence may even be misleading in determining proper corrective procedures. Furthermore, peripheral autonomic events which now may bear one relation and now another to initiating processes in the nervous system need have no consistent relation to those manifestations of nervous system function known as "behavior." This may explain the sterility which, with few exceptions, has beset attempts to correlate measurements of peripheral autonomic changes with human "behavior" [p. 1].

Implicit in many studies of autonomic responses is a simplifying assumption of autonomic balance between the parasympathetic and sympathetic branches in normal individuals. As early as 1915, Eppinger and Hess introduced the concepts of sympathicotonia and vagotonia to describe conditions of unbalance. An individual exhibiting sympathicotonia (an exaggerated tonus of the sympathetic nervous system) would be expected to show strong sympathetic nervous system responses to sympathomimetic agents such as epinephrine and sympatholytic drugs such as ergotamine. Similarly, weaker responses to parasympathomimetic drugs such as pilocarpine and parasympatholytic drugs such as atropine would be expected. The reverse would be true of vagotonic individuals. Unfortunately, the simple dichotomy of the sympathicotonic-vagotonic concept is often difficult to apply in conditions in which both branches of the autonomic system are hypo- or hyperexcitable (e.g., in some autonomic disease states such as Raynaud's disease, characterized by sympathetic dominance; or in bronchial asthma, characterized by parasympathetic dominance; in both instances,

the opposite autonomic branch is also found to be hyperexcitable; similarly, some "normal" individuals show exaggerated responses to both parasympathetic and sympathetic drug agents). Additionally, specific responses of parasympathetic or sympathetic effector organs are not of an either/or type; for example, the sweat glands, a sympathetic effector organ, show greatest sensitivity to parasympathomimetic drugs such as atropine and pilocarpine, since the neurotransmitter mechanism involves acetylcholine.

Wenger (1941) proposed that the concept of adrenergic-cholinergic balance be used to replace the sympathicotonic-vagotonic dichotomy, a convention that has become widely accepted. The adrenergic-cholinergic concept is a heuristic one in providing a common basis for both biochemical and psychophysiological drug studies; in recognizing that imbalance could be of a continuous (chronic) or of a reactive (to some stress) phasic nature; and in clarifying that an adrenergic-cholinergic measure of a population of individuals would be continuously distributed about a measure of central tendency, where individuals at the extremes of the distribution could be designated as "vagotonic" or "sympathicotonic" in a statistical sense. The adrenergic-cholinergic model is also useful in integrating data from peripheral effector responses as collected in most human studies with evidence for the central control of autonomic functioning collected in acute animal experiments. (The hypothalamus, which has chemoreceptors sensitive to epinephrine, acid-base balance, and many other blood constituents, has been implicated as the central control unit regulating autonomic balance [Gellhorn & Loofbourrow, 1963].)

Psychophysiological drug studies of autonomic response patterns may be classified into two types:

1. *Type A:* Investigations that use the drug as an independent variable to produce a reactive change in the autonomic response pattern. Variations in drug response patterns are then used to categorize subjects into treatment or diagnostic groups.
2. *Type B:* Investigations that do not directly use drugs as an independent variable; instead, response patterns are measured under basal (tonic) and/or reactive (phasic, e.g., cold stress) conditions to classify a subject's autonomic reactivity into one of several

categories of balance and unbalance. The nature of the unbalance is then used to predict a drug or drug combination that could be used to restore balance.

A classical example of Type A is the mecholyl test, as developed by Funkenstein and his colleagues (Funkenstein, Greenblatt, & Solomon, 1948, 1952). Altman, Pratt, and Cohen (1943) had noted that the fall in blood pressure after an injection of mecholyl could be correlated with certain psychiatric states. Funkenstein refined this technique, classifying individuals into six groups based on the shape of the blood pressure curve after the combined injection of mecholyl and epinephrine. Prolonged hypotension after the injection correlated with a favorable prognosis for electroconvulsive shock treatment in chronic schizophrenics.

Gellhorn (1953) clarified a possible mechanism with animal experiments showing that levels of central sympathetic tonus were correlated with the response of systolic blood pressure (called "mecholyl area") to a standard injection of mecholyl. Hypertensive responses (designated as "norepinephrine-like") elevated sympathetic tonus; while prolonged hypotensive responses (designated "epinephrine-like") suggested depressed sympathetic tonus. Subsequently, many investigators omitted the epinephrine stress from the test.

Investigations by Funkenstein, Greenblatt, and Solomon, (1952), Gellhorn (1953), Ax (1953), Schachter (1957), Hoagland (1961, pp. 40–64), and L. Berger (1964) extended the concept of the mecholyl test to differentiate two general behavioral states; the hypertensive, norepinephrine-like, arousal state, associated with urinary excretion of metabolites of norepinephrine, has been correlated with aggressive, hostile, outward-directed behavior, designated also as "anger-out," the use of aggression and projection as preferred ego defenses, with infantile and paranoid personality tendencies. The hypotensive, epinephrine-like, arousal state, correlated with urinary metabolic products of epinephrine, has been associated with fear, timidity, depression, guilt, designated also as "anger-in," with irritation and annoyance toward oneself; with reaction formation as a major ego defense; and with a strong attachment to the mother. Cohen and Silverman (1959) have reported that, when the test is made on the same individual under different emotional states, the vascular effects of mecholyl varied with the emotion in question (anxiety versus aggression).

Ostensibly, these studies suggest a relationship between the ways an individual responds physically to a chemical stress and the way his underlying personality structure responds to psychological stress. Despite the attractiveness of this apparently simple model, a large number of conflicting reports have been published about the mecholyl test and experimental, sampling, and measurement difficulties (see Blumberg, 1960; Blumberg & Klein, 1965). For example, when the blood pressure response to mecholyl was studied in 338 psychiatric patients, the mecholyl area was found to be significantly correlated with age, diagnosis, and blood pressure (Blumberg & Klein, 1966). However, age was more effective in discriminating among diagnoses than was the basal blood pressure, which was in turn more effective than the mecholyl area. Although evidence relating the mecholyl response and age in normal subjects is not as yet available, the point is clear that the use of a single autonomic response variable such as the blood pressure alone does not permit the resolution of the many possible sources of variation, as noted earlier. Regrettably, only a few psychophysiological drug studies of Type A have been published in which age, sex, and other demographic variables have been analyzed, along with the simultaneous measures of several peripheral autonomic responses. Both the EEG and the GSR have been used with injected sodium pentothal to measure sedation thresholds in psychiatric classification procedures similar in design to the mecholyl area test (Perez-Reyes, Shands, & Johnson, 1962; Shagass, 1967, pp. 921–925).

Noteworthy among Type A studies is that by Wenger et al. (1960). In this carefully designed experiment, Wenger et al. studied the autonomic response patterns of 9 variables (systolic and diastolic blood pressure; heart rate; respiration rate; palmar skin conduction; finger pulse volume; finger, face and axillary temperatures; ballistocardiograph; stomach motility; and salivary output) simultaneously while intravenously infusing various doses of saline, epinephrine, and norepinephrine. The mere fact that drugs in the study were infused via a catheter and not abruptly injected (with confounding reactions to the needle) is noteworthy. Neither age nor sex were confounding variables, since the study was made on young, healthy adult males who were viewed as "emotionally stable." Statistically significant differences between the maximum responses to epinephrine and norepinephrine were identified in the diastolic blood pressure, heart rate, finger pulse volume, finger temperature, face temperature, and heart-stroke volume. Epinephrine produced a marked increase in both the heart rate and stroke volume; norepinephrine decreased both. The vasoconstrictor action of norepinephrine was apparently greater in blood vessels supplying the skeletal musculature, but less than that of epinephrine upon the blood vessels of the skin. In other words, 6 of the 12 autonomic nervous system variables that were investigated showed statistically significant differences between the maximal responses to epinephrine and norepinephrine. While the heart rate response to norepinephrine has been described in the literature (von Euler, 1956) as showing no change or only a slight decrease, all subjects in the Wenger study showed a decrease comparable in magnitude with the increase in response to epinephrine. The anxiety hypothesis of "anger-out" and "anger-in," advanced by Funkenstein et al. (1952), Ax (1953), and Schachter (1957), suggests that anger results from a combined epinephrine-norepinephrine response, and fear from an epinephrine-like response. In contrast, none of the subjects in the Wenger study reported any emotional experience with either drug.

One of the problems as seen in the Wenger study with multiple response patterns is the difficulty of conveniently summarizing the many individual responses to present a *gestalt* of experimental outcome. From studies of the infusion of epinephrine and norepinephrine (Gellhorn, 1957; Wenger et al., 1960) and from his own studies of the physiological patterns of fear and anger, Ax (1953) suggested a physiologic pattern index that would simulate the epinephrine–norepinephrine ratio. He proposed that the numerator or epinephrine part of the index would be composed of the sum in standard scores of increments of the heart rate, systolic blood pressure, ballistocardiogram, and respiration rate. The denominator or the norepinephrine term would

consist of increments of the diastolic blood pressure, muscle tension, number of GSRs and decrements of heart rate (Ax, 1962). Because the eight measures were expressed in standard score units, they could be combined into a single algebraic sum, so that a positive score would represent an epinephrine-like response, and a negative score, a norepinephrine response.

Ax's physiological pattern index is appealing in that (a) it has significant construct validity based upon the presumed mechanisms underlying adrenergic-cholinergic effector responses; (b) it is self-standardizing (experimental standard deviations are used to calculate standard scores); (c) covariants such as age can be used to adjust individual response measures; and (d) it produces a single number analogous to the syndrome concept that is easy to understand, at least superficially, a significant advantage when relating such results to nonpsychophysiologists. On the other hand, a problem with a priori composite indices is the preconceived nature of their construction, which may not be valid except with subjects whose autonomic responses are in the "classical" direction.

Alternate procedures for creating composite psychophysiological pattern scores are frequently achieved by combining empirical data with multivariate statistical procedures (multiple regression, factor analysis, discriminant function, etc.). An example in a study evaluating psychoactive drugs is the use of a discriminant function composite (consisting of total PGR conductance, rate of PGR habituation, and spontaneous skin conductance fluctuations at the end of the experimental trial) to assess the effect of two sedative drugs (amobarbital sodium and chlordiazepoxide) on overt anxiety in patients and control groups (Lader & Wing, 1966). In this study, the discriminant function composite correlated +.93 with behavioral ratings of anxiety and was moderately stable over time with a test-retest reliability over a period of three weeks of +.76. The Lader and Wing study is an exemplary one in so many regards that it should be consulted as a model for psychophysiologists undertaking or planning to undertake drug studies. For example, uncertainty exists in the vast majority of human drug studies as to the comparability of drug doses when two or more drugs are being compared. Even in single drug studies, investigators rarely take the opportunity of expressing dosages according to both absolute (total mg) and relative (mg/kg) bases. The ensuing confusion that this creates in attempting to reconcile conflicting reports is a matter of concern. One of the outstanding features of the Lader and Wing study is their incorporation of a psychophysiological bioassay into the research design, based on the fact that sedative drugs accelerate the rate of habituation to auditory clicks in anxious subjects. As a result of this bioassay, some assurance is gained that the two drugs are being compared with equivalent doses. For example, Lader and Wing found no significant difference between amobarbital sodium and chlordiazepoxide in the degree to which they altered the physiological composite score or relieved overt anxiety, when equivalent doses of 9 mg of chlordiazepoxide and 65 mg of amobarbital sodium were compared. On a cost basis, however, a significant difference does exist; an equivalent dose of chlordiazepoxide is about five times more expensive than amobarbital sodium.

Type B designs use nondrug-induced psychophysiological response patterns to evaluate or suggest the choice of a drug or treatment strategy, usually for psychiatric patients. Because the Type B design does not use drugs as independent variables, it is especially valuable in evaluating the course of pharmacological treatment of patients already receiving medications (i.e., the test drug used in Type A designs would only serve to confound the medication condition). The basis for Type B strategy has been derived from the hope that, in addition to overt behavioral deviations, covert physiological deviations might be found in patients with various kinds of mental disorder which would be of assistance in classifying, understanding, and treating an illness. In keeping with this possibility, the hypothesis has often been advanced that an imbalance of the autonomic nervous system exists in schizophrenics that might produce abnormal sensitivity to life stresses, perhaps hypersensitivity to punishment and criticism, and hyposensitivity to reward and praise (Ax, 1962). It has been suspected that measurements of sympathetic and parasympathetic balance might confirm or deny portions of this hypothesis.

Of the many attempts that have been made to discover such a physiological index (whether derived from single or multiple autonomic measures), few have emerged from replication testing as likely candidates. The equivocal nature of single variable indices (Darrow, 1943), along with insights gained from response specificity studies, suggest that autonomic balance indices to predict drug choice ideally should be derived from multiple response pattern data. Because multiparameter physiological recording and analysis has not yet been reliably and validly automated for the routine clinical screening of patient populations, an example of a single variable, Type B design must suffice.

The pupillary mechanism of the eye is antagonistically innervated by adrenergic (dilation) and cholinergic (constriction) influences. Separate rates of pupillary reaction to light and dark may be conveniently measured without attaching instrumentation to subjects to provide separate estimates of cholinergic and adrenergic reactivity. Rubin (1962) developed a Type B rationale, using pupillary reactivity as an index of autonomic balance. He defined "balance" as the 96% confidence intervals calculated for adrenergic and cholinergic reactivities of normal, control subjects, as shown by the center cell in Figure 20.13. Individuals at the ex-

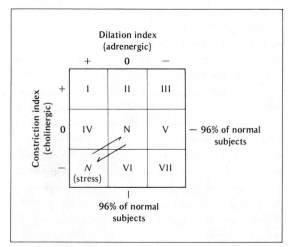

Figure 20.13 Paradigm used to classify psychiatric patients based upon measures of pupillary dilation and constriction. Redrawn from A. McCawley, C. F. Stroebel, & B. C. Glueck, Jr., Pupillary reactivity, psychologic disorder and age. *Archives of General Psychiatry,* 1966, **14,** 415–418. Reproduced by permission.

treme ends of one or both of the adrenergic and cholinergic indices would fall into one of the eight outlying cells. Normal subjects subjected to a cold pressor test predictably reacted by moving from Cell N to Cell N (stress) with adrenergic excitation and cholinergic depression.

The basis for the choice of drug therapies is suggested by Figure 20.13. For example, individuals in Cell I (+, +) should receive sympatholytic and parasympatholytic medication to restore normal balance; individuals falling in Cell III (−, +) should receive sympathomimetic and parasympatholytic medication, etc. Rubin (1962) found that all 47 psychotic patients tested fell into one of the abnormal outlying cells; although tests of drugs to restore normal balance were not performed, the procedure is an efficacious one in that it could easily be used at weekly intervals to evaluate the physiological effect and course of pharmacological treatment in mental patients.

When they attempted to replicate Rubin's work, McCawley, Stroebel, and Glueck (1966) found approximately twice as much variability in their normal control subjects over a similar distribution of age as Rubin had found. The additional age-dependent variability reduced the precision of the pupillary measure in discriminating among normal and abnormal individuals to the extent that only 20% of their patient sample could be classified as abnormal. Unfortunately, the two studies are not fully comparable, since Rubin's technique apparently involved considerably more experimental stress over a longer measuring session. It is possible that Rubin's results represented a differential response of psychiatric patients to a situation more stressful for them than for control subjects.

Noteworthy is the fact that age emerged as a significant variable for both Type A (Blumberg & Klein, 1966) and Type B (McCawley, Stroebel, & Glueck, 1966) procedures. This should not be sur-

TABLE 20.3 CLASSIFICATION SCHEME AND PROTOTYPE EXAMPLES FOR CLASSES OF DRUGS COMMONLY ENCOUNTERED IN PSYCHOPHYSIOLOGICAL LITERATURE

Drug classification	Prototype drugs
Hypnotics and sedatives	Barbiturates
Aliphatic alcohols	Ethyl alcohol
Narcotic analgesics	Morphine, codeine
Sympathomimetic agents	Epinephrine, amphetamine
Sympatholytic agents	Phenoxybenzamine, isoproterenol, reserpine
Parasympathomimetic agents	Muscarine, pilocarpine
Parasympatholytic agents	Atropine
Neuromuscular blocking agents	Curare, succinylcholine
Ganglionic stimulants and blockers	Nicotine, hexamethonium
Anticholinesterase drugs	Physostigmine
Common drugs	Caffeine, salicylates, nicotine, antihistamines
Psychiatric drugs	
Hypnotics and sedatives	Barbiturates
Tranquilizers	Meprobamate
Neuroleptics	Chlorpromazine
Antidepressants	MAOI, imipramine
Antimania agents	Lithium carbonate
Psychotomimetic drugs	LSD-25
Drugs that enhance learning	Strychnine
Drugs that block memory	Puromycin

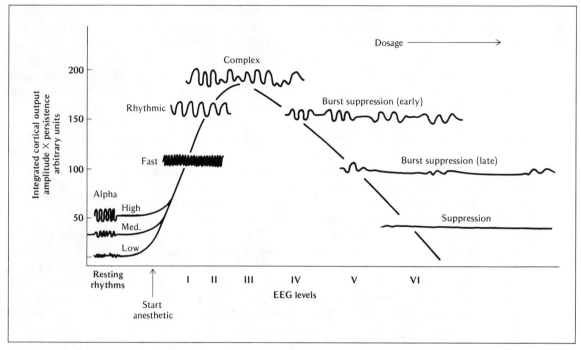

Figure 20.14 Typical changes in EEG pattern associated with increasing barbiturate dosage or anesthesia depth. The ordinate is an index of energy. Courtesy R. Dripps. From L. S. Goodman & A. Gilman (Eds.), *The pharmacological basis of therapeutics.* (3rd ed.) New York: Crowell-Collier-Macmillan, 1965. Reproduced by permission.

prising in view of the age correlations of many of the psychiatric illnesses and the very nature of the aging process itself. The monotonic relation between age and pupillary variability from ages 20 to 45 in the McCawley, Stroebel, and Glueck (1966) study suggests that age to the nearest semidecade should be matched between control and experimental groups in both Types A and B studies. In fact, insistent consideration of this simple, easily recorded covariable should be a requirement for all psychophysiological research studies.

GUIDE TO CLASSES OF DRUGS AND DRUG EFFECTS

This guide to classes of drugs and drug effects presents a systematic overview of the various drug types likely to be encountered by psychophysiologists. Because of space limitations, the material presented is not encyclopedic in detail. However, familiarity with nuances underlying the basic classification scheme and prototype drug examples

shown in Table 20.3 represents a minimal background knowledge of drugs that should be expected of psychophysiologists at the doctoral level. The classification scheme is neither infallible nor absolute but is a convenient starting point for simplifying and categorizing the incredibly large number of pharmaceutical agents with which we must deal.

Hypnotics and Sedatives

Hypnotics and sedatives operate by depressing general physiological activity nonspecifically in proportion to dosage. Widely used to reduce tension and promote sleep, minimal (sedation) doses characteristically lower sensory irritability; medium (hypnotic) doses further lower irritability with drowsiness and reduced motor activity; high doses may produce anesthesia or death. Usually classified by duration of action, common examples are chloral hydrate, paraldehyde, and derivatives of barbituric acid, e.g., phenobarbital (longest acting), amo- and pentobarbital (intermediate), secobarbital (short) and hexobarbital (ultrashort). Effects on the electro-encephalogram (EEG) are similar to those for anesthetics, as shown schematically in Figure 20.14.

In lower doses, idiosyncratic effects (excitement and activation, rather than depression) are not uncommon in emotionally disturbed patients. Chloral hydrate often produces irritation of the skin and mucous membranes.

Aliphatic Alcohols

Ethyl alcohol primarily affects the CNS by depressing the inhibitory control mechanisms used in fine discrimination and self-restraint. Responses are related to dosage with analgesic and hypnotic effects at medium doses, and anesthesia and death at higher doses. Characteristic EEG slowing is dosage related but is followed during withdrawal by a period of hyperexcitability. Moderate doses of alcohol interact synergistically with psychoactive medications to impair judgment dangerously

(Forney, Hughes, & Halpien, 1963). Increased sweating is associated with an attendant fall of body temperature if the ambient temperature is low. During early stages of intoxication alcohol may reduce the catecholamine content of the nervous system, producing transient hyperglycemia, pupillary dilation, and a slight increase in blood pressure (Kalant, 1962). Aliphatic alcohols other than ethyl are distinctly poisonous.

Narcotic Analgesics

Narcotic analgesics including morphine, codeine, papaverine, heroin, and their synthetic variants (methadone) all possess narcotic (producing sleep and analgesia) and addicting (psychological and physiological dependency) properties. The biphasic physiological mechanism (first stimulation and nausea, then depression) on CNS and bowel (peristalsis is blocked) is not well understood; behavioral effects are analgesia, drowsiness, mood

TABLE 20.4 DIFFERENTIAL EFFECTS OF INFUSED EPINEPHRINE AND NOREPINEPHRINE IN MAN

Function	Epinephrine	Norepinephrine
Cardiac		
Heart rate	+	−
Stroke volume	+ +	+ +
Cardiac output	+ + +	o, −
Arrhythmias	+ + + +	+ + + + +
Coronary blood flow	+ +	+ + +
Blood pressure		
Systolic	+ + +	+ + +
Diastolic	+, o, −	+ +
Mean	+	+ +
Peripheral circulation		
Peripheral resistance	−	+ +
Cerebral flow	+	o, −
Muscular flow	+ +	o, −
Cutaneous flow	− −	+, o, −
Metabolic effects		
Oxygen consumption	+ +	o, +
Blood sugar	+ + +	o, +
Central nervous system		
Respiration	+	+
Subjective sensations	+	o, +

Note.—After M. Goldenberg et al., Pheochromocytoma and essential hypertensive vascular disease. *Archives of Internal Medicine*, 1950, **86**, 823–836. Reprinted by permission.
+ = increase; o = no change; − = decrease.

changes (euphoria-dysphoria), and mental clouding. Therapeutic doses produce pupillary miosis (counteracted by atropine), EEG slowing, skin vasodilation, sweating, and respiratory depression. Although codeine possesses only one-fifth the analgesic potency of morphine, it is widely used clinically because of its lower addiction liability and efficacy in reducing the cough reflex. Beecher, in his classical studies of the placebo effect (1965, pp. 111–128), has demonstrated that the analgesic properties of morphine depend upon both physiological and behavioral mechanisms.

Sympathomimetic Agents

Sympathomimetic drugs mimic the effect of adrenergic nerve stimulation to produce a wide variety of autonomic nervous system effects, including skeletal muscle vasodilation, cutaneous vasoconstriction, pupillary dilation, cardiac acceleration, glycogenolysis, pilomotor contraction, and intestinal relaxation. The pharmacological prototypes for the catecholamines are epinephrine and its precursor, norepinephrine (levarterenol). The complex combinations of effects that can be achieved using these drugs or their blockers singly and/or in combination, suggest at least two kinds of adrenergic receptor mechanisms (Ahlquist, 1968): (a) the largely excitatory alpha receptors are from 2 to 11 times more sensitive to epinephrine than norepinephrine; and (b) the beta receptors respond to isoproterenol (specifically blocked by propranolol) to yield vasodilation and smooth muscle relaxation effects (except for the heart). Table 20.4 compares the differential effects of infused epinephrine and norepinephrine on a variety of effector mechanisms (Goldenberg, Aranow, Smith, & Faber, 1950). Effects of epinephrine on the EEG are sometimes idiosyncratic but most commonly yield acceleration and desynchronization with a facilitation of mono- and polysynaptic transmission pathways. Intradermal, but not systemic, injection of dilute epinephrine solutions induces sweating, which can be blocked with alpha-blocking agents (phenylephrine).

Important noncatecholamines that act by enhancing the release of stored adrenergic transmitters are the amphetamines, which can exist in two steric forms or as a mixture: d-amphetamine (Dexedrine) is twice as potent as the racemic mixture (amphetamine) which is in turn more potent than l-amphetamine (Benzedrine). The ability of the amphetamines to resist gastric destruction permits their administration orally, while the usual routes for epinephrine are intramuscular (IM) or subcutaneous (SC) (resulting vasoconstriction can impede uptake); norepinephrine is usually given intravenously (IV).

Sympatholytic Agents

Sympatholytic agents may be classified into: (a) those drugs blocking the effect of sympathomimetic drugs at alpha and beta effector receptor sites, and (b) antiadrenergic agents that inhibit the release of catecholamines from nerve terminals and chromaffin tissues. Phenoxybenzamine and dibenamine are prototype alpha blockers, producing stimulation of the CNS (nausea, motor excitement, hyperventilation), while reducing basal sweating in the hands and feet (re adrenergic component in the control of sweating; Haimovici, 1950). Certain ergot alkaloids (ergotamine) also produce competitive alpha blockade but directly stimulate smooth muscle as well. Propranolol is a prototype beta blocker, producing persistent blockage of vasodepressor responses to isoproterenol (Ahlquist, 1968). Prototype antiadrenergic agents and their suspected modes of action are bretylium and guanethidine, which at first enhance and then block the release of norepinephrine from storage pools, and the Rauwolfia alkaloids (reserpine), which operate by depleting norepinephrine from storage pools. Reserpine is an antihypertensive agent, simultaneously inducing psychic depression and increased gastric motility. Its popularity as one of the earliest of the "tranquilizers" (calming or sedative agents) has been displaced by the phenothiazine drugs, except in patients who cannot tolerate the latter.

Parasympathomimetic Agents

Parasympathomimetic agents such as acetylcholine and its derivatives and the cholinomimetic alkaloids, muscarine and pilocarpine, produce direct depolarization of cholinergic receptor sites, differentiating them from agents producing similar effects through other mechanisms (anticholinesterases or ganglionic stimulants). The relative specificity of the action of muscarine in mimicking acetylcholine at autonomic effector cells has been used to designate these sites as muscarinic (blocked by atropine). Acetylcholine itself is ineffective as a therapeutic drug because of the widespread distribution of acetylcholinesterase in the body; methacholine is less susceptible to esterase metabolism. The injection of pilocarpine produces activation of all parasympathetically innervated glands, inducing profuse sweating and salivation, cutaneous vasodilation, and pupillary constriction.

Parasympatholytic Agents

Parasympatholytic agents (antimuscarinic or atropinic) competitively combine (reversibly) with muscarinic receptors to block the action of acetylcholine, thus depressing the salivary, bronchial, and sweat gland secretions; at higher doses, atropine or scopalamine may also block transmission at autonomic ganglia and at skeletal neuromuscular junctions, producing pupillary dilation, blockade of vagal inhibition of the heart (eventually resulting in an increased heart rate) and depressed gastric secretion. Atropine is a racemic mixture of *d*- and *l*-hyoscyamine; the *d*-isomer reportedly has no effect on sweat gland activity, while similar doses of the *l*-isomer eliminate sweating entirely (Venables & Martin, 1967). Lader and Montagu (1962) and Wilcott (1964) have shown that skin conductance and skin potential responses are eliminated with atropine. The article by Venables and Martin (1967) is recommended for further consideration of the complexities involved in studying the effects of cholinergic drugs on skin conductance and skin potential. Progressive atropine blockade of the postganglionic cholinergic nerves often produces sympathetic overreactivity or rebound. Drowsiness, amnesia, euphoria, and dreamless sleep are associated with scopolamine in therapeutic doses. Both atropine and scopolamine depress spontaneous EEG activity, EEG arousal to photic stimulation (Ostfeld & Arguete, 1962), and cause the skin to feel hot and dry by inhibiting the activity of sweat glands. The nonspecific blockage of muscarinic receptors by the belladonna alkaloids has encouraged the development of a moderately large number of synthetic compounds designed for greater therapeutic selectivity for which fewer side effects are claimed.

Neuromuscular Blocking Agents

Neuromuscular blocking agents interfering with the action of acetylcholine at the motor end plate of skeletal muscles are differentiated on the basis of mechanism into drugs such as curare and/or *d*-tubocurarine, which compete for cholinoceptive receptor sites, as contrasted to agents such as decamethonium (C10) or succinylcholine, which depolarize the muscle membrane, rendering it insensitive to the effects of acetylcholine. Curariform drugs produce a rapid fall of blood pressure, tachycardia, loss of skeletal-muscle control at low doses, and skeletal and respiratory paralysis in higher doses. The inability of quaternary curariform drugs (above) to penetrate the blood-brain barrier was substantiated by Smith, Brown, Toman, and Goodman (1947), who could find no central depressant, stimulatory, or analgesic effects with high doses of *d*-tubocurarine in man. Tertiary curare-like drugs (erythrydine), which can penetrate the blood-brain barrier, act as central depressants.

Ganglionic Stimulators and Blockers

Agents serving to stimulate or block the autonomic *ganglia* are classified as *nicotinic*—first stimulating, then blocking by depolarization or hyperpolarization the postsynaptic membrane (e.g., nicotine); or *competitive*—competing with acetylcholine for receptor sites (e.g., hexamethonium or tetraethyl ammonium (TEA)). Multiple cholinoceptive sites of different types have been suggested to explain some of the interactive drug effects of stimulant-antagonist drugs at sympathetic ganglia (Eccles & Libet, 1961). Intradermal injection of dilute nicotine produces piloerection, sweating, and vasoconstriction, effects that may be blocked by atropine or TEA. Nicotine (frequently as tobacco smoke) causes peripheral vasoconstriction, increase in the heart rate and blood pressure, and parasympathomimetic gastrointestinal effects.

Antiacetylcholinesterase Agents

Drugs inactivating or inhibiting the metabolic breakdown of acetylcholine by acetylcholinesterase (called *anticholinesterase* drugs) exert both muscarinic and nicotinic types of cholinomimetic influence. The short-acting "reversible" agents, physostigmine (eserine) and neostigmine, have been used in the treatment of glaucoma and myasthenia gravis, while longer-acting "irreversible" organophosphates have been developed as insecticides (parathion or malathion) and as chemical warfare agents. The pervasive systemic action of these drugs is apparent from the widespread distribution of acetylcholine mechanisms in the body (see Figure 20.10 and Table 20.2).

Common Drugs

Coffee, tea, cola drinks, aspirin, tobacco, and "cold pills" are nonprescription drugs so widely consumed by the public as to be of interest by themselves, and as confounding variables. The actions of nicotine in tobacco as a ganglionic blocker have already been discussed. The active drug in coffee and cola drinks is caffeine, which like theobromine and theophylline is a member of the *xanthine* class. Caffeine acts as a CNS stimulant with effects on the cerebral cortex and the respiratory, vasomotor, and vagal centers in the medulla. Excessive consumption of caffeine beverages may produce tremors, nausea, tachycardia, motor overactivity, and restlessness.

Aspirin and its variants, phenacetin and antipyrine, are widely consumed for a variety of reasons. This *salicylate* class of drugs possesses useful analgesic, antipyretic, and antiinflammatory properties at therapeutic dosages. The depression of body temperature occurs only under febrile conditions and is usually accompanied by sweating. Salicylate toxity produces CNS depression and hyperventilation, followed by respiratory acidosis and seizures. Compared to other kinds of analgesics, salicylates have little if any effect on the sensorium, and chronic use does not lead to tolerance or addiction. Aspirin is frequently combined with antihistaminic agents, which reduce allergic and anaphylactic reactions, as a medication for the common cold.

Psychiatric Drugs

Prior to 1952, psychiatrists used sedative-hypnotic drugs to reduce anxiety and tension in their patients, despite the undesirable tendency of these agents to induce drowsiness, ataxia, dysarthia, mental clouding, and sleep. The report by Delay and Deniker (1952, pp. 22–26) that chlorpromazine produced a "chemical lobotomy" without hypnotic-sedative side effects in psychotic patients initiated a major revolution in pharmacological approaches to mental illness. Pharmaceutical research efforts since then have produced an extensive array of psychoactive drugs and an incredibly vast experimental literature describing their chemistry and behavioral effects. (See Gordon, 1964, 1967.)

Because of the variety of agents, mechanisms, and effects produced by psychiatric drugs now available, the earlier practice of labeling all of these agents "tranquilizers" has now been refined. The most satisfactory scheme for classification clusters those drugs with similar chemical structures (implying a common mode of action) according to their most important psychiatric application, as shown in Table 20.5, which lists the trade name, generic name, and manufacturer of the drugs in widespread use. Neuroleptic agents (sometimes called major tranquilizers) ameliorate psychotic symptoms but also elicit extrapyramidal side effects and autonomic reactions, and lower the convulsive threshold. Minor tranquilizers produce few of the side effects of neuroleptics, while *raising* the convulsive threshold, and find major application in relieving neurotic anxiety and tension.

The distinction between minor tranquilizers and sedative-hypnotics (discussed earlier) is less clear, since both kinds of agents induce muscle relaxation, relieve anxiety, and cause drowsiness and sleep at higher doses (Lader & Wing, 1966). In general, the margin of safety at very high doses is much greater for the minor tranquilizers—an important consideration in suicide-prone patients. Even toxic doses of the minor tranquilizers, of which meprobamate is a prototype, do not slow the EEG to frequencies below 6 Hz as do the barbiturates (Berger, 1963). Lehmann (1967, pp. 131–137) suggests that the biphasic disinhibition-inhibition action of sedatives might be used to differentiate tranquilizers and sedatives. (Many sedatives cause a disinhibited state of behavioral excitement and pseudofacilitation prior to general behavioral in-

TABLE 20.5 TRADE NAME, GENERIC NAME, AND MANUFACTURER OF COMMONLY USED PSYCHIATRIC DRUGS

Trade name	Generic name	Manufacturer	Use[a]
	A. Neuroleptics		
	Phenothiazine Derivatives		
Dimethylamines			
Thorazine	chlorpromazine	SK & F	PN
Sparine	promazine	Wyeth	PN
Vesprin	triflupromazine	Squibb	PN
Mellaril	thioridazine	Sandoz	PN
Piperazines			
Tindal	acetophenazine	Schering	PN
Proketazine	carphenazine	Wyeth	PN
Permitil	fluphenazine	White	PN
Prolixin	fluphenazine	Squibb	PN
Trilafon	perphenazine	Schering	PN
Compazine	prochlorperazine	SK & F	PN
Dartal	thiopropazate	Searle	PN
Stelazine	trifluoperazine	SK & F	PN
Quide	piperacetazine	Dow	PN
Thioxanthenes			
Taractan	chlorprothixene	Roche	PND
Navane	thiothixene	Roerig	PN
Butyrophenones			
Haldol	haloperidol	McNeil	PN
	Rauwolfia Alkaloids		
Rauwiloid	alseroxylon	Riker	PN
Harmonyl	deserpidine	Abbott	PN
Moderil	rescinnamine	Pfizer	PN
(many)	reserpine	(many)	PN
	B. Minor Tranquilizers		
	Substituted Diol Carbamates		
Listica	hydroxyphenamate	Armour	N
Equanil	meprobamate	Wyeth	N
Miltown	meprobamate	Wallace	N
Ultran	phenagylcodol	Lilly	N
Solacen	tybamate	Wallace	N
	Diphenylmethanes		
Suavitil	genactyzine	Merck	N
Atarax	hydroxyzine	Roerig	N
Vistaril	hydroxyzine	Pfizer	N
	Miscellaneous		
Frenquel	azacyclonol	Merrell	P
Softran	buclizine	Stuart	N
Suvren	captodiamine	Ayerst	N
Librium	chlordiazepoxide	Roche	NPD
Trancopal	chlormezanone	Winthrop	N
Valium	diazepam	Roche	ND
Levanil	ectylurea	Upjohn	N

TABLE 20.5 (Continued)

Trade name	Generic name	Manufacturer	Use[a]
Placidyl	ethchlorvynol	Abbott	N
Trepidone	mephenoxalone	Lederle	N
Lenetran	mephenoxalone	Lakeside	N
Quiactin	oxanamide	Merrell	N
Serax	oxazepam	Wyeth	N
Dalmane	flurazepam	Roche	N

C. ANTIDEPRESSANTS

MAO Inhibitors

Marplan	isocarboxazid	Roche	DPN
Niamid	nialamide	Pfizer	D
Nardil	phenelzine	Warner-Chilcott	D
Parnate	tranylcypromine	SK & F	D

Amphetamines

Benzedrine	amphetamine	SK & F	D
Dexedrine	d-amphetamine	SK & F	D
(many)	methamphetamine	(many)	D

Iminodibenzyl Derivatives

Elavil	amitriptyline	Merck	D
Norpramin	desipramine	Lakeside	D
Pertofrane	desipramine	Geigy	D
Tofranil	imipramine	Geigy	D
Sinequan	doxepin	Pfizer	D
Vivactil	protriptyline	Merck	D
Aventyl	nortriptyline	Lilly	D

Miscellaneous Antidepressants

Deaner	deanol	Riker	D
Ritalin	methylphenidate	Ciba	D

Combinations

Deprol	benactyzine and meprobamate	Wallace	D
Triavil	perphenazine and amitriptyline	Merck	PDN

[a]The final column indicates primary use in order of importance. P = psychotic; N = neurotic; D = depressed.

hibition.) Table 20.6 summarizes a number of characteristics that differentiate sedatives, tranquilizers, and neuroleptics.

Chlorpromazine is an appropriate prototype neuroleptic. Phenothiazine analogs of chlorpromazine were used as early as 1935 with livestock for their antihelmintic, urinary antiseptic, and insecticide actions. The antipsychotic and barbiturate-potentiating effects of the phenothiazines were not discovered until the 1950s. The acute sedative action of chlorpromazine when patients first start tak-

ing the drug becomes unnoticeable with prolonged administration. The antipsychotic effect (slowing of responses to external stimuli and the lessening of initiative, motor activity, and anxiety without impairing basic arousal, intellectual, or sensory functioning) may not become apparent for several weeks (Kornetsky, Vates, & Kessler, 1959) and may persist for months after the medication is stopped. Although the CNS mechanism of chlorpromazine is not clear, it has been suggested that it interferes with norepinephrine and/or dopamine re-uptake and transport, at both pre- and postsynaptic receptor sites (Pletscher & Da Prada, 1967, pp. 304–311). Autonomic reactions suggest strong alpha adrenergic and weaker peripheral cholinergic blocking activity. The body temperature is depressed or fluctuates more freely with changes in ambient temperature. Many of the phenothiazines possess weak antihistaminic and potent antiemetic activity. The extrapyramidal side effects common at the high dosages used to treat psychotic patients were once thought necessary for therapeutic effectiveness, a theory that has not been substantiated (Cole & Clyde, 1961).

Antidepressive drugs act by stimulating the nervous system directly (amphetamines), indirectly (MAO inhibitors and imipramine), or by combined bimodal action (nonhydrazine, MAO inhibitors such as tranylcypromine). The agents most widely used in the treatment of psychiatric depression operate indirectly; like the neuroleptics, they may require several weeks of administration to exert their antidepressive effects. Direct-acting drugs such as amphetamines and methylphenidate were discussed under the heading of sympathomimetic agents. Examples of indirect, prototype, antidepressive drugs are the MAO inhibitors and imipramine.

Monamine oxidase inhibitors elevate the mood of depressed patients by blocking the mitochondrial enzyme that metabolizes excess norepinephrine in adrenergic nerves; this blockade elevates brain levels of DOPAmine, norepinephrine, and serotonin. In general, the action of sympathomimetic amines, especially the noncatecholamines such as amphetamines or tyramine, is greatly potentiated by MAO inhibitors. While the mood-

TABLE 20.6 CHARACTERISTICS DIFFERENTIATING HYPNOTIC-SEDATIVES, TRANQUILIZERS, AND NEUROLEPTICS

Differentiating characteristics	Hypnotics	Tranquilizers	Neuroleptics
Sleep induction	Common	Common	Sometimes
Disinhibition in small doses	Usually	Sometimes	None at any dose
Increased hostility	No change	Sometimes	No change
Ataxia or dysarthria	At higher doses	At higher doses	None
Extrapyramidal side effects	None	None	Frequent
Convulsive threshold	Raised	Raised	Lowered
Autonomic reactions	Seldom	Seldom	Frequent
Habit forming	Frequent dependence	Frequent dependence	None
Cross tolerance to alcohol, barbiturates	Yes	Yes	No
Effect on neurotic anxiety	Effective	Effective	Inconsistent
Effect on psychotic anxiety	Inconsistent	Inconsistent	Effective
Ego defense mechanisms mobilized by drug	Denial, regression, projection	Denial, regression, projection	Rationalization, isolation, paranoia reaction formation, sublimation
Suppression of avoidance behavior	Suppresses passive	Suppresses passive	Suppresses active
Depression of motor activity	Enhanced at low doses	Enhanced at low doses	Depressed
Withdrawal symptoms	Yes	Yes	Occasionally
Afferent reactivity	Lowered	Lowered	Lowered
Body temperature	No change	No change	Lowered
Muscle tension	Decreased	Decreased	No change
Antihistaminic activity	No	No	Yes
Blood pressure	No change	No change	Lowered
Suicidal danger	Raised	No change	Lowered

Note.—After H. E. Lehmann, Differences in behavioral effects in humans. In H. Brill (Ed.), *Neuro-psycho-pharmacology.* Proceedings of the Fifth International Congress, Neuro-Psycho-Pharmacologium. New York: Excerpta Medica, 1967, pp. 131–137. Reprinted by permission.

elevating effects of MAO inhibitors may require several weeks to become manifest, toxic effects are frequently acute, including tremors, insomnia, excessive perspiration, orthostatic hypotension, and hypertensive crises associated with the ingestion of foods (cheese) containing the pressor amine, tyramine. Dibenzazepine compounds (imipramine) are also effective in the treatment of depression but involve a mechanism different from the MAO inhibitors. Imipramine apparently increases levels of brain norepinephrine by blocking the reuptake of norepinephrine released at the synapse. The pronounced cholinergic blocking action of imipramine produces side effects (dry mouth, blurred vision, constipation, urinary retention) similar to atropine. Schelkunov (1967, pp. 910–911) has suggested that the neuroleptic and antidepressant properties of drugs like imipramine can be evaluated by calculating a trophotropic index (antiadrenergic actions divided by anticholinergic actions) based upon relatively simple measurements. Even though none of the neuroleptic, MAO inhibitor, or dibenzazepine agents produces psychological or physiological dependence, withdrawal effects after a long period of administration are not uncommon.

In contrast to the more complex compounds now used to treat depressive illnesses, a simple salt, lithium carbonate ($LiCO_3$) is being scrutinized for its ability rapidly to reverse and prophylactically prevent manic states. It has been suggested that the drug decreases the exchange of sodium across the cell membrane, increases serum magnesium, and decreases the levels of free norepinephrine at synapses (Bunney, Goodwin, Davis, & Fawcett, 1968).

Psychotomimetic Drugs

Psychotomimetic drugs producing sensory distortions (hallucinations) include compounds such as mescaline, lysergic acid diethylamide (LSD-25), bufotenine, cannabinols (marijuana), yohimbine, harmine, peyote, psilocybin, and toxins such as lead and the organophosphates. The name "psychotomimetic" is not entirely appropriate, since it incorrectly implies that these agents produce effects mimicking the symptoms of natural psychoses. For example, schizophrenic hallucinations tend to be auditory, while those produced by LSD-25 are predominantly visual. Hence little credence is now given to the hypothesis that psychotomimetics are "model" psychosis simulators. The drug LSD-25 has sympathomimetic properties, producing hyperthermia, pupillary dilation, hyperglycemia, piloerection, and tachycardia. The tolerance to LSD develops rapidly in as few as three daily administrations. Also, LSD effects are counteracted by chlorpromazine and facilitated by reserpine. The drug is a potent antagonist of the peripheral actions of serotonin. Many of the religious, consciousness-expanding, and other so-called "desirable" effects of psychotomimetic agents apparently depend upon suggestion and require a sympathetic social environment for expression. The widespread adolescent proclivity for surreptitious, illegal, and medically unsupervised experimentation with these agents can only be viewed with alarm.

Drugs That Enhance Learning

A number of agents have been studied because of their apparent ability to facilitate the learning process. Four classes of drugs and their apparent mechanisms can be identified:

1. Low doses of strychnine and amphetamine may change the threshold for a behavioral response by facilitating synaptic transmission. Strychnine causes widespread CNS excitation by selectively blocking inhibitory synaptic influences. Strychnine does not excite nervous tissues such as the autonomic ganglia, which lack specific inhibitory fibers (Purpura & Grundfest, 1957). Low doses of amphetamine increase CNS arousal and may lower the threshold for reinforcement-motivational mechanisms (Stein, 1964, pp. 91–118). Amphetamines most distinctly improve performance in tasks involving fatigue and boredom (Laties & Weiss, 1967, pp. 800–808).

2. Electrolytes such as K^+, which are involved in many aspects of nerve transmission, have been manipulated to facilitate avoidance learning in rats (Sachs, 1962).

3. Exogenous ribonucleic acid (RNA) and promoters of endogenous RNA synthesis-tricyanoaminopropene (TRIAP) and magnesium pemoline (CYLERT) reportedly facilitate learning, ostensibly by enhancing the macromolecular protein or nucleotide mechanism of memory formation (Quarton, 1967).

4. Jenkins and Dallenbach (1924) showed that

recall was promoted when subjects slept immediately after learning, to minimize competing stimuli or interfering tasks. Nitrous oxide administered to human subjects after a learning task also improves retention apparently in an analogous fashion (Summerfield & Steinberg, 1957). Scopalamine exerts an antimuscarinic effect at cholinergic synapses to produce memory loss; however, it apparently enhances memory in situations in which learning trials are massed.

The uncertainty of present information about the chemical facilitation of learning is not surprising in view of the complexity of the learning process itself. The importance of dosage, route of administration, and interspecies variations all serve to make this an especially difficult research area.

Drugs That Block Memory

The CNS neuron is exceptional in that (a) it does not replicate itself, and (b) its production of ribonucleic acid (RNA) is proportionately much greater than for somatic cells (Hydén, 1967, pp. 765–771). Ribonucleic acid itself or RNA-specified proteins have been implicated as the molecular basis of memory. To test this hypothesis, a wide variety of microbial antimetabolites has been used to block RNA and/or protein synthesis to resolve the time constants and stages of the memory mechanism (Agranoff, 1967, pp. 756–764). Rats, mice, worms, and goldfish (whose optic tracts are completely crossed, making the animal a natural visual "split-brain" preparation) are widely used as experimental subjects. Representative drugs used in these studies are 8-azaguanine, acetoxycycloheximide (AXM), and the antibiotics, puromycin, chloramphenicol, and actinomycin-d. Memory-blockage experiments are complicated because of the apparent importance of neuroanatomical locus in short and long-term memory mechanisms, requiring direct cerebral injection of the blocking agent to achieve specific, nonsystemic effects.

THE ELECTROENCEPHALOGRAM, DRUGS, AND SLEEP

The scalp-recorded EEG is relatively easy to measure and rapidly reflects changes in attention, vigilance, and levels of sleep. While the clinical EEG is moderately sensitive to noxious agents and changing conditions, this sensitivity tends to be relatively nonspecific, dose related, and difficult to evaluate quantitatively. Recent advances in computer approaches to EEG quantification (Fink, 1969; Fink, Itil, & Shapiro, 1967) and increasing awareness of the importance of the background reactivity of the subject in making normative comparisions (Brazier, Killam, & Hance, 1961, pp. 699–716) will greatly increase the usefulness of the EEG as a psychophysiological tool for studying drug effects.

The earlier, electronic analog approaches to

TABLE 20.7 EFFECTS OF SIX PSYCHOACTIVE AGENTS ON EEG SPECTRUM AS DETERMINED WITH COMPUTERIZED PERIOD ANALYSIS

Drug	EEG spectrum					
	Delta	Theta	Alpha	Spindles	Beta	Gamma
	0	5	10	15	20	25 / 50
Amobarbital	←————————— With higher dosage ———				+	
Chlordiazepoxide		←——— With higher dosage ———			+	+
Imipramine (6 wk)			−		+	
Chlorpromazine (6 wk)	+	+		−	−	−
Ditran-atropine (anticholinesterases)	+		−		+	
LSD-25			⟶+		+	+

Note.—Data from M. Fink, T. Itil, & D. Shapiro, Digital computer analysis of the human EEG in psychiatric research. *Comprehensive Psychiatry*, 1967, **8**, 521–538. + = enhanced; − = decreased.

quantitative EEG analysis (frequency band analysis, amplitude integration, and baseline-cross analysis) tended to be technically limited, inflexible, and unstable. More recent, digital computer techniques for signal averaging, autocorrelation, and analysis of power-spectrum, pattern, amplitude, and period have been compared and reviewed by Fink (1969). He suggested that measuring only the amplitude does not provide adequate information and that power spectral analysis (including the fast Fourier transform) requires sufficiently large amounts of on-line computer time to reduce seriously the frequency of sampling. (Too few samples would vitiate the recent progress in scoring stages of alertness comparable to stages of sleep.) On the other hand, period analysis (Burch, Nettleton, Sweeny, & Edwards, 1964) appears to be a happy medium in providing enough information for differential classification, while allowing many samples to be collected so that the stage of alertness can be used as a covariable. Table 20.7 summarizes the effects of six pharmacological agents on the EEG spectrum as evaluated by period analysis (Fink, Itil, & Shapiro, 1967).

The precise quantification of the EEG may significantly change our understanding of the *pharmacological dissociation* between the EEG and behavioral arousal observed in animals (Bradley & Elkes,

1953). Such dissociation occurs with peripheral injections of low doses of atropine, which do not impair overt behavioral responsiveness to the environment but are accompanied by high voltage, slow wave, EEG activity characteristic of slow-wave sleep. Other examples of dissociation can be seen with reserpine, which induces drowsiness and reduces responsiveness in the waking subject without changing the EEG, and with physostigmine, an atropine antagonist, which produces EEG changes similar to "paradoxical sleep." Atropine elevates the threshold for EEG alerting, without altering the threshold for behavioral arousal; physostigmine has opposite effects. The interpretation of dissociation has become a contested issue; for example, Fink and Itil (1967) have applied computer analysis to their data to conclude "that the problem of dissociation is largely one of quantification of the EEG and definition of the significant aspects of behavior, suggesting that the usual definitions of behavior by motor functions alone are too restrictive, and that tests of learning, consciousness, and alertness (as applied to studies in man) are more directly related to EEG changes associated with anticholinergic drugs."

The role of cortical and brain-stem influences in producing pharmacological dissociation has been studied in *encéphale isolé* and *cerveau isolé* cats

TABLE 20.8 EFFECT OF VARIOUS DRUGS ON THE ANATOMICAL LOCUS OF PHARMACOLOGIC DISSOCIATION OF EEG AND BEHAVIOR

| Drug | Conscious animal | | Encéphale isolé | Cerveau isolé |
	Behavior	Electrical activity	Electrical activity	Electrical activity
Physostigmine	Normal	Fast, low amplitude activity	Fast, low amplitude activity	Fast, low amplitude
Atropine	Normal or excited	High amplitude slow waves and spindles	High amplitude slow waves and spindles	High amplitude slow waves and spindles
Amphetamine	Excited	Fast, low amplitude activity	Fast, low amplitude activity	No effect
LSD-25	Excited	Fast, low amplitude activity	No effect	No effect
Chlorpromazine	Drowsy and indifferent	Slow and 5–8 Hz activity	Increased slow activity and spindles	No effect

Note.—From P. B. Bradley, Central action of certain drugs in relation to the reticular formation of the brain. In H. H. Jasper (Ed.), *The reticular formation of the brain.* Boston: Little, Brown, 1958. Reprinted by permission.

TABLE 20.9 SPECULATIVE PATTERNS OF EEG SLEEP-STAGE ALTERATION BY VARIOUS PHARMACOLOGICAL AND BEHAVIORAL STATES

Pattern	Drug-behavior pattern	% REM sleep	% Slow sleep	Possible mechanism	Interpretation
F	Fatigue from exercise	n.c.	↑	Serotonin related	Catecholamine metabolism? hypnotoxin?
S	Sedative-hypnotic minor tranquilizers	↓	↓		By increasing total and transitional sleep time
D	Reserpine-depression	↑	↓	Depleted NEP	REM pressure
M	Antidepressants-mania	↓	n.c.	Excess NEP	Depressed REM pressure

by Bradley (1958, pp. 123–149). The results are summarized in Table 20.8.

Drug effects have already begun to play an important role in the comparatively recent but widespread interest by psychophysiologists in relationships among autonomic response patterns, EEG states, dreaming, and sleep (see Chapter 17). Most commonly, drugs are used as an independent variable in sleep studies to alter the onset, sequence, or percentages of time a subject spends in the various EEG-defined sleep stages. Even cautious generalization of the drug results now available is difficult because of the varieties of species, controls, methodologies, and the methods of EEG scoring and analysis used by different investigators. Based upon summaries of recent research (Association for the Psychophysiological Study of Sleep, Abstracts, 1967, 1968), four speculative patterns of sleep EEG response to drugs or behavioral states can be suggested, as shown in Table 20.9. The table is probably oversimplified in suggesting a biphasic drug-sleep interaction (i.e., percent REM versus percent slow sleep, with other stages regarded as transitional), but the methodological problems noted above make more detailed speculation unwise. Recent efforts to standardize the methodology, scoring, analysis, and reporting of EEG sleep data should greatly accelerate our understanding of drug effects in this interesting area of research (Rechtschaffen & Kales, 1968).

Oswald (1969, pp. 308–316) has recently summarized data showing that drugs which tend to produce dependency (e.g., barbiturates, morphine, glutethimide, amphetamines, alcohol) suppress the percentage of REM sleep during administration and induce REM rebound during withdrawal. Drugs which do not lead to dependency (e.g., amitryptyline, diphenylhydantoin, chlorpromazine) may produce REM suppression, but are not followed by REM rebound.

DESIGN OF DRUG EXPERIMENTS

Psychophysiological drug experiments may be classified into one of three broad design categories as follows:

Type I. These experiments investigate the drug itself, its physiological mechanisms, and its behavioral effects as the primary object of study. Two or more drugs are often compared with an active or passive placebo in a single study.

Type II. These experiments use the drug as an independent variable to manipulate, block, or isolate a psychophysiological response pattern (anxiety) or process (short-term memory, GSR). The drug condition may be only one of several independent variables used.

Type III. These experiments are investigations into the basic nature of a psychophysiological response pattern or process, in which drugs are confounding (and frequently undesirable) variables. This situation is common with subjects on any kind of medication, especially psychiatric patients. Because of the pervasive psychological and somatic effects of progestational and estrogenic hormones (Jackson & Schneider, 1968), the widespread use of oral contraceptives will place many "nondrug" studies of females in the Type III class.

Although Type I experiments usually precede Type II, it is frequently possible to combine them through perspicacious planning. One of the great virtues of the multivariate strategy used by psychophysiologists is that, with good design, many alternative hypotheses may be tested in the same experiment without greatly increased expense. Hence drug experiments need not be "one-shot" affairs from which a unitary hypothesis is either confirmed or rejected; regardless of the direction of results or outcome, information sensitive to a number of contingencies can be collected to provide evidence for an alternate rationale, model, or new hypothesis. (Perceptive awareness of errors stemming from multiple inference and a posteriori analyses is assumed.) The study by Lader and Wing (1966) comparing the effects of two drugs, amobarbital sodium and chlordiazepoxide, on habituation of psychophysiological measures in anxious subjects may be cited as a prototype Type I design. An example of a prototype Type II design is that by Venables and Martin (1967), in which the steric forms of atropine (d-and l-hyoscyamine) and neostigmine were used to elucidate the complex relationships among sweat gland activity, skin potential, and skin conductance.

The importance of careful planning and good design cannot be overemphasized; as Clyde (1967) noted, "A good experimental design will yield clear answers to an important problem at a reasonable cost. It is surprising how many published psychiatric [drug] studies do not fulfill any of these requirements." Important considerations for good experimental design in psychophysiological drug studies follow.

Subjects The specific type of drug research undertaken by a psychophysiologist is frequently influenced by the kinds of subjects available. Type I studies with major psychoactive agents are practicable in psychiatric settings in which such drugs are being evaluated with psychiatric patients and the psychophysiologist is an influential member of the research team. If he is not, Type III confounding becomes a serious issue because of the polypharmacy widely practiced by modern psychiatrists (Hollister, 1968). Both Type I and Type II studies using reversible, short-acting drugs are feasible with normal subjects; Type III confounding may be controlled by preexperimental screening instructions and/or covariance analysis. For any of the design types, however, anything but the random preclassification of subjects into groups is a difficult and critical problem because of the uncertainties

of somatic and behavioral nosology. Glueck, in Stroebel and Glueck (1965, pp. 437–459), has described the typology problem as a crucial issue in interdisciplinary psychiatric research:

> On the one hand, the chemists have developed relatively exact techniques for extracting minute quantities of various substances, but for the most part have been perfectly willing to accept the clinical material from which they obtain their samples in a most uncritical fashion, accepting a sample of 10, or 20, or 50 "schizophrenics" as really representing a single diagnostic entity, and as being reasonably similar individuals with similar disease processes. The clinicians, on the other hand, have been equally naive in turning to the biochemist or psychophysiologist and saying, "Okay, find us a sample of 10, 20, or 50 people who have the same metabolic substances in their urine, or the same physiological responses to test X, Y, or Z, and we will then appraise their clinical state assuming we have a homogeneous sample that will give us a clear-cut diagnostic entity." The result has been confusion piled upon confusion, and, I am afraid, repeated instances of the blind leading the blind [p. 457].

While the expediency of objective behavioral rating scales or lists of target symptoms is often used as a basis for preexperimental grouping, the diversity and noncomparability of techniques available, as well as the geographic and egocentric provincialism of the developers of scales, frequently provide a basis for criticism of experimental results even before the experiment is begun. An appropriate metaphor from Jaynes (1966) may be cited in this regard: "Physics may be likened to mountain climbing. The direction (through blizzard, mist, or searing sun) is always upward. Each new generation gets equipment, ropes up and follows the leader. By contrast, psychology is like a huge entangled forest. The multitudes pass through, each one equipped with ear-plugs and blinders, certain that he alone has found the way, and calls on others to follow."

Even if the rating instrument used for classification possesses clear construct validity, the critical issue of objective grouping of similar profiles is still uncertain and under extensive development (Glueck & Stroebel, 1969). To obviate these problems some investigators administer a rating instrument (e.g., the Taylor Manifest Anxiety Scale) to a large pool of subjects, selecting polar subsamples (e.g., top 10% and bottom 10%) to form experimental groups. A danger here is the inevitable but also unpredictable regression toward the mean that will occur on the occasion of a second testing, treatment or no.

Choice of drug and dosage Previous sections devoted to biochemical mechanisms and specific drug effects should provide guidelines as to drug options for investigators seeking to manipulate or isolate a psychophysiological process or mechanism through primary drug actions (Type II design). Once a general decision has been made as to an appropriate drug choice, immediate consideration should be given to the sorts of possible conclusions anticipated at the end of the study. Knowledge of the assumptions underlying the traditional statistics of bioassay, (e.g., the parallel line or slope ratio) will significantly assist in this process (Finney, 1952; Laska & Simpson, 1967, pp. 79–84). Briefly, the assumptions are that:

1. The drugs under comparison are qualitatively similar, differing only by an inert dilution factor that is expressed as relative potency.
2. The relationship of dose to response is a logarithmic, linear, or other known scale amenable to transformation. This implies that the dose-response curves for the drugs under study are parallel.
3. Errors of estimation are independent, possess homogenous variance, and are distributed normally (the last is required if fiducial limits are to be estimated). See Cornfield (1964) for distribution-free techniques.

Considerations of these assumptions will add considerable rigor to an investigator's decisions about the exact drug choice(s), dosage, importance of a pilot experiment to provide systematic dose-response estimates of relative potency, interactions between primary and side effects of the drugs, statistical analysis techniques, and expectations of outcome. Three examples of such considerations may clarify these points:

I. If Drug A has a logarithmic dose relationship with physiological response X, can we assume it will have a comparable relation with responses Y and Z? Intraindividual and interindividual response specificity data (Schnore, 1959; Sternbach, 1966) would suggest the contrary. In other words, which response variable with which subject would one use to establish an effective dose level? One potential solution is to create a multiple response score composite that is predictably related to dose

(for a discriminant function procedure, see Lader & Wing, 1966).

2. Can one assume that different psychoactive agents tested in a typical Type I study are qualitatively similar, or that they possess any kind of monotonic dose-response relationship to the psychotic response state? Does the usual "ceiling basis" for phenothiazine drug administration (the highest dose tolerable with a minimum of side effects and a maximum of altered, more socially acceptable behavior) provide a satisfactory kind of titration end point for evaluating comparable dosage levels of different drugs? Which responses are used to judge the end point objectively? Are the same responses appropriate for each drug or for each subject?

3. What design strategy would be used when several behavioral and physiological mechanisms are nonadditively involved in producing a global drug response? An illustrative instance of the effects of such interaction can be extrapolated from a paper by Kornetsky (1967, pp.948–954). He postulates that chronic schizophrenics are in a state of continual arousal, placing their basal level on the descending limb of the usual **U**-shaped activation or performance curve shown in Figure 20.15. The

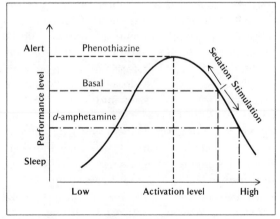

Figure 20.15 Paradoxical effects of phenothiazine and d-amphetamine on the performance level of chronic schizophrenics in a hyperactivated basal state. Schematically redrawn from C. Kornetsky, Attention dysfunction and drugs in schizophrenia. In H. Brill (Ed.), *Neuro-psycho-pharmacology.* Proceedings of the Fifth International Congress, Neuro-Psycho-Pharmacologium. New York: Excerpta Medica, 1967, pp. 948–954. Reproduced by permission.

figure demonstrates the paradoxical finding that administration of a stimulant, *d*-amphetamine, produced more sleep in three of the nine schizophrenics tested. On the other hand, phenothiazines, drugs thought to decrease the arousal or activation level, paradoxically improved the level of performance.

The fact that few of the restrictions of the traditional bioassay model can completely be met in a typical psychophysiology drug experiment should not serve as a deterrent. Hopefully, it will stimulate eventual generalization of these models to a multivariate form really appropriate for psychobioassay. In the interim, prior awareness by the investigator of why the assumptions cannot be met in a specific experimental procedure will almost inevitably yield more precise and rigorous designs with more meaningful results.

Practical considerations relating to drug potency Many drugs are available in a variety of dosage forms that are designed for various routes of administration and duration of action, factors affecting their applicability in psychophysiological experiments (see Goodman & Gilman, 1965). The dosage form of a drug is the physical state in which the drug is administered, usually in combination with a vehicle. Examples are (*a*) solid—the drug plus starch compounded as a tablet or capsule; (*b*) liquid—oil, syrup, aqueous, alcoholic, or saline solutions of the drug; (*c*) liquid suspensions—drugs insoluble in water; (*d*) aerosols—a liquid solution of the drug dispersed in a gas; and (*e*) gaseous— usually anesthetics. The dosage form frequently determines the route of administration. Common pathways are oral (PO for peroral), intravenous (IV), intramuscular (IM), subcutaneous (SC), intraperitoneal (IP). Parenteral pathways (through the skin) require a sterile technique; are usually more rapid (direct) than oral routes; and are also more certain, since the drug may not be surreptitiously stashed, vomited, or variably destroyed by strong gastric juices.

Broad generalizations about the effect of the route of administration on absorption rates and the duration of drug action are shown in Figure 20.16. The rank order for the rate of absorption is IV, IM, SC, and PO; for the duration of effect, SC, PO, IM,

and IV. Distribution in the body and the ultimate fate of the active drug are complex issues that should be investigated for each substance. For example, thiobarbiturates are rapidly distributed in adipose tissue because of their solubility in fat; chronic administration of chlorpromazine yields high levels of the drug in organs containing the pigment melanin, the lens and cornea of the eye, the skin (the Purple People Syndrome), and also the viscera (Greiner & Nicolson, 1964); of the two curariform drugs, *d*-tubocurarine and erythrydine, only the latter passes the blood-brain barrier (Gardner & McCollough, 1962).

Many drugs of interest to psychophysiologists are available in relatively limited dosage forms for various reasons such as lability, toxicity, acidity or alkalinity, insolubility, or the quantity of the drug needed for therapeutic effect. When drug experiments are repeated in studies on single subjects, in which a short-acting drug requires repeated or continuous (IV) administration to maintain a constant level during a recording session, drug adaptation or *tolerance* should be considered; i.e., higher doses may be needed to achieve the same effect on successive administrations. Drug tolerance may easily be misinterpreted as the adaptation of psychophysiological responses themselves. When prior doses of the drug are stored in inactive body tis-

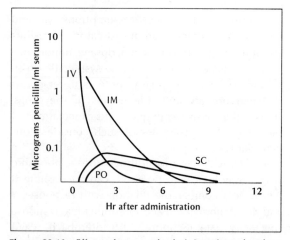

Figure 20.16 Effect of route of administration of a drug on the rate of absorption and duration of action for penicillin. Redrawn from D. F. Marsh, *Outline of fundamental pharmacology*. Springfield, Ill.: Charles C Thomas, 1951, p. 85. Reproduced by permission.

sues, or are incompletely detoxified and excreted, *cumulation* effects may occur, requiring a longer time for buildup of the drug and/or apparently enhanced potency with each new administration. Examples of cumulation are commonly observed with thiobarbiturates and most phenothiazines. In Type III situations in which a confounding drug is present, or when combinations of drugs are being tested, consideration should be given to effects attributable to *summation* (simple addition of effects), *synergism* (effect is greater than either drug alone but not equal to their summated effect), *potentiation* (the joint effect is greater than the summated effect), or *antagonism* (the joint effect is less than either drug alone).

Common omissions in drug experiment designs and reports The doubtful comparability, meaningfulness, and generalizability of a distressingly high percentage of drug research reports reviewed for this chapter may be attributed to several common oversights or omissions in experimental designs.

1. Failure to consider drug-behavioral interactions resulting from the physical act of drug administration is common. Such interaction effects may be created by past associations with medication (illness, pain, dependency), interindividual variations in reacting to the mystique of the experimenter-doctor who administers the drug, hypodermic needle stress and injection pain, distrust of the unknown, and physical discomfort (psychiatric patients under heavy medication may be forced to swallow as many as 32 capsules daily). Failure to consider the needle effect is especially prevalent in animal studies in which the arousal level induced by the injection process hardly produces a predictable or basal state in either placebo or experimental subjects (observe the wide varieties of behavior used by rats or monkeys to escape or "brace against" an injection). In those instances in which a short-acting drug is being studied, activation from injection stress may totally obscure the response under study. Comparable questions can be raised at the human level, in view of interindividual variations in response specificity (Schnore, 1959).

2. Failure to report dosage, form, vehicle, route, frequency, occasions, and the amount of the drug administered on a drug weight per unit of body weight and total body weight basis is also common. This error is especially frequent in Type I clinical psychopharmacology studies in which drugs are compared at ceiling dosages. Without even minimal dose/weight information, judgments and generalizations of relative potency and specific qualitative differences are questionable.

3. A third problem is failure to consider the assumptions underlying the independent random sampling in choosing control subjects or defining control groups (see Pollin, 1962, pp. 143–155, for an excellent review). For drug experiments, many errors of this type can be avoided by relying upon the encompassing definition of a "drug" presented earlier to assess the degree of Type III confounding in an experimental design. For example, differences in diet, vitamin intake, and exercise may clearly be expected to differentiate institutionalized and normal volunteer controls (Kety, 1959).

4. Failure to consider the interaction of the drug state with varying levels of homeostatic reactivity in subjects is especially widespread. The most obvious omission is failing to report or hold constant the time when the drug is administered and/or when measurements are made. Several reasons may be advanced to account for this common design defect. First, the diverse range of adaptive behavior exhibited by higher organisms has encouraged a natural and widespread interest in the more reactive mechanisms of central and autonomic nervous system control (e.g., EEG or GSR correlates of behavior). This interest, along with an attempt to simplify experimental designs, leads many investigators to assume a background of relative constancy in the less reactive mechanisms that apparently control the ongoing metabolic functioning of the body, i.e., biological rhythms. Thus if a psychophysiologist is aware of the possible relevance of biological rhythms, he attempts to hold their role invariant by selecting subjects who follow a regular social regimen, and by presenting drugs and experimental trials at the same clock hour each day. Awareness of this control is apparently rare, since it is reported in fewer than 5% of the reports in the experimental psychology, neuropsychology, and neurophysiology literature between 1960 and 1964 by actual tabulation (Stroebel, 1967a, pp. 158–172). A

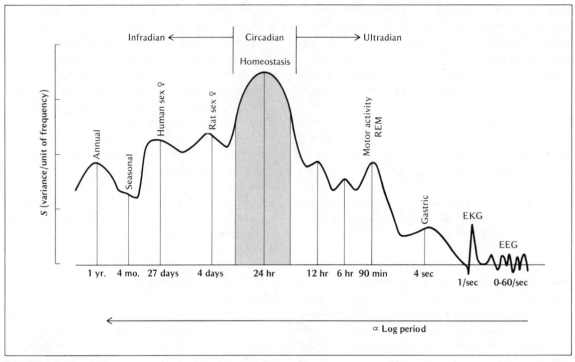

Figure 20.17   Schematic spectrum of biological periodicities. Biological rhythms with periods longer than 24 hr are labeled infradian; those with periods shorter than 24 hr are labeled ultradian. Redrawn from C. F. Stroebel, Behavioral aspects of circadian periodicity. In J. Zubin & H. Hunt (Eds.), *Comparative psychopathology.* New York: Grune & Stratton, 1967a, pp. 158–172. Reproduced by permission.

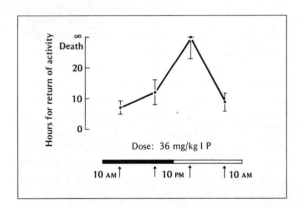

Figure 20.18   Circadian susceptibility rhythm observed when identical doses of a phenothiazine (TPS-23) are injected into independent groups of rats at the points specified by arrows. The experiment was conducted under constant light conditions. The light-dark cycle shown was preexperimental. Redrawn from C. F. Stroebel, Behavioral aspects of circadian periodicity. In J. Zubin & H. Hunt (Eds.), *Comparative psychopathology,* New York: Grune & Stratton, 1967a, pp. 158–172. Reproduced by permission.

second reason for neglect stems from a confusion of the distinction between circadian (*circa,* about; *dies,* day) and diurnal rhythms. Diurnal rhythms may be viewed as "autonomous systems whose oscillations decay if the inevitable losses of energy are not restored periodically from outside the system" (Aschoff, 1963). Circadian rhythms, then, are "autonomous systems capable of auto-oscillation" (self-sustained oscillations that persist even in a constant environment). Under normal environmental conditions, the correlation among an adaptive organism's circadian rhythms and light, dark, eating, drinking, sleeping, and reproductive cycles is very high; the circadian versus diurnal confusion frequently occurs via application of stimulus-response logic, wherein these correlations are (erroneously) assumed to be causal.

Virtually every physiological variable that has been sampled longitudinally has demonstrated a 24-hr periodicity; if no periodicity is found, the measurement technique is (a) not sufficiently sensitive or (b) "noisy" (Stroebel, 1969, pp. 91–105). The orderly sequence of crest and trough of the component rhythms (not all in phase) creates a unique succession of internal physiological states that is repeated once every 24 hr. This orderly sequence—a kind of internal temporal coordination or interlocking of metabolic functioning—can be viewed as the body's own timing mechanism or biological clock. As can be seen in Figure 20.17, many physiological and behavioral functions fluctuate with regular periods.

Halberg and his colleagues (Halberg, 1960; Reinberg, 1967; Savage, Rao, & Halberg, 1962; Stroebel, 1967c) have demonstrated startling variations in drug effects depending on the time of administration (circadian phase) during a 24-hr period. Figure 20.18 illustrates the results of a drug susceptibility study for an identical dose of a phenothiazine drug, administered IP to four independent groups of rats at the times indicated by arrows in the figure. The response variable was hours for return of normal activity. Whereas this dose was

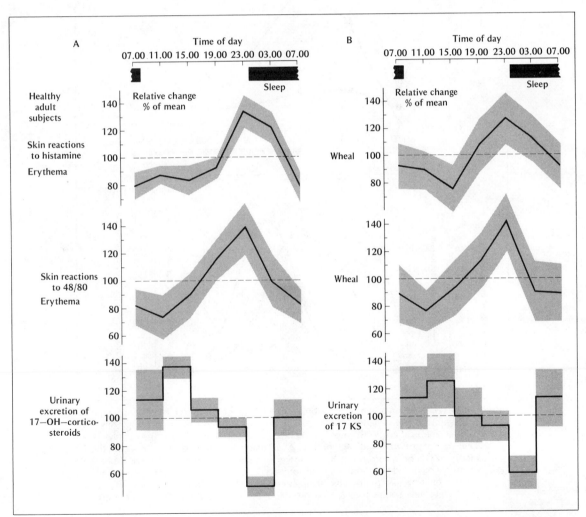

Figure 20.19 Circadian rhythms of skin reactions to intradermal injections of histamine (upper) and 48/80 (middle) as correlated with urinary excretion of 17-OH-corticosteroids (lower). The values shown are the means ±SEM for six subjects. Redrawn from A. Reinberg, The hours of changing responsiveness or susceptibility. *Perspectives in Biology and Medicine*, 1967, **10**, 111–128. Reproduced by permission.

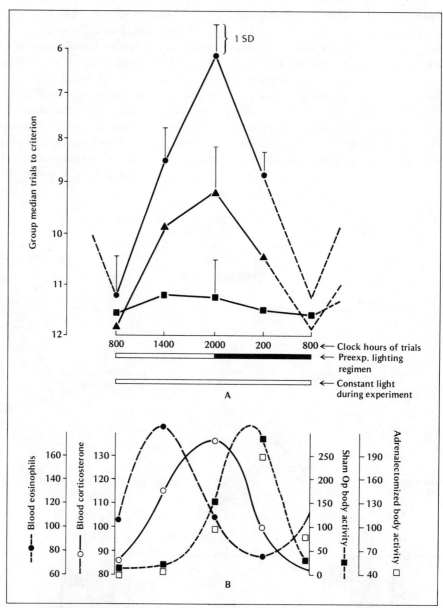

Figure 20.20 A. The circadian susceptibility rhythm to conditioned emotional response acquisition in rats is partially abolished by adrenalectomy, and more completely with pretrial medication with methopyrapone (a drug that blocks the synthesis of 11-β-corticosteroids). Key: ● control; ▲ adrenalectomized; ■ 100 mg/kg methopyrapone IP 1½ hr before trials. B. The lower panel shows other physiological behavior measures recorded from independent subjects. Redrawn from C. F. Stroebel, Behavioral aspects of circadian periodicity. In J. Zubin & H. Hunt (Eds.), *Comparative psychopathology.* New York: Grune & Stratton, 1967a, pp. 158–172. Reproduced by permission.

lethal for 75% of the animals receiving it at a time corresponding to the onset of the light cycle, it was totally nonlethal for the three groups injected at other times. Another example of interest to psychophysiologists is shown in Figure 20.19, demonstrating the circadian reactivity of human skin to intradermal injections of histamine and 48/80 (a histamine liberator) (Reinberg, 1967). The steroid data, also shown, suggests that corticosteroid levels in the blood are on the average lowest when the cutaneous response to histamine is the highest (the curve for urinary excretion lags behind the plasma curve by several hours).

The importance of controls for biological rhythm effects can be visualized in the instance in which two investigators in different laboratories are testing the effect of histamine on skin wheal in synchronized subjects, the first at 1200 hr and the second at 2400 hr; they could obtain results in exactly opposite directions. For synchronized subjects, such effects could at the least be held constant in minimal designs by administering drugs and tests at the same clock hour each day. Studies on desynchronized psychiatric patients will require frequent longitudinal sampling to identify the clock process, its amplitude, and correlates (Stroebel, 1967c). Such longitudinal designs tend to be very costly and tedious.

The role of biological rhythms in good experimental design is further complicated by reports that the rate of learning for behaviors involving peripheral autonomic arousal is highly dependent on the circadian phase, as shown in Figure 20.20 (Stroebel, 1967a). Longitudinal studies are now under way to resolve the drug-by-clock-by-behavior interactions stemming from simultaneous drug-clock and behavior-clock variance. Such designs and experiments may be essential for a full understanding of variations in psychophysiological functioning among normal and behaviorally disturbed individuals.

Response measures and data analysis Multiple response measures providing several criterion indices of the effect of a treatment are a characteristic feature of psychophysiological drug studies. The application of univariate statistical techniques (in which each variable is considered by itself) to such data can lead to several problems:

1. Multiple inference errors may occur when a number of univariate significance tests are computed using the same data. By chance, meaning is attached to differences that are really not significant (Spitzer & Cohen, 1968).
2. The single variables taken one at a time may not be significant, while a combination or pattern of them is (an analogy would be a disease *syndrome* that is more meaningful than each symptom by itself). For example, Clyde, Cramer, and Sherrin (1965, pp. 11–12), used five psychiatric history variables to predict drug response. None of the individual variables was significantly related to drug response but the combination was significant at the .01 level.

Multivariate statistics provide an optimal means for analyzing multiple variable data (Hall, 1966). In fact, many psychophysiological pharmacology experiments are sufficiently complicated to be pointless if multivariate analysis is not contemplated. Table 20.10 shows several common multivariate procedures with their univariate analogs.

The discriminant function is used to evaluate the differences between two independent random groups based upon multiple measures; the multiple discriminant function is used for three or more groups. MANOVA (actually a combination of discriminant function, analysis of variance, and canonical correlation) is used to test group differences in the presence of confounding or other overlying factors such as sex, age, or diagnosis. Each

TABLE 20.10 SOME MULTIVARIATE PROCEDURES AND THEIR UNIVARIATE ANALOGS

Univariate	*Multivariate*
Product-moment correlation	Canonical correlation
Students' *t* test	Discriminant function
Analysis of variance	MANOVA (multivariate analysis of variance)
Analysis of covariance	Multivariate analysis of covariance

of the multivariate procedures might be applied to a battery of response measures to form a weighted composite-response–subset to maximize predictive variance and minimize error variance. Pilot experiments to derive response composites in multiple response designs will frequently permit a reduction in the number of variables measured in the experiment proper. The rationale for this strategy stems from the awareness that highly predictive response measures may be obscured by useless ones, yielding an erroneous conclusion of nonsignificance; i.e., inadvertently including useless variables for the sake of "completeness" often reduces the power of multivariate tests. One especially helpful technique, stepwise multiple discriminant function, may be used to rank variables in order of their importance, so that useless measures can be eliminated from the experiment proper. A detailed description of the development of a discriminant function response composite is presented by Lader and Wing (1966) in a monograph describing an exemplary psychophysiological drug study.

Highly vocal criticism of multivariate statistics is usually misdirected; while it is true that misapplications are not uncommon, most of the difficulties stem from over- or misinterpretations of computed results by investigators. For example, the orthogonal (varimax) solution in factor analysis is both unique and objective, while the meaning or interpretation *attached* to each factor is a subjective task for the investigator that not infrequently requires a sense of imagination.

A widespread problem stems from the intrinsic complexity of psychophysiological experiments; i.e., the temptation is great to accept hypotheses derived *after* analyzing the results as proven (a posteriori analysis), rather than validating them with a new independent random sample in an expensive replication experiment. Shrewd use of mechanism-oriented pilot studies as a replication strategy (the measurement-prediction-measurement process) is especially appropriate in complicated multiple criteria experiments in which the influence of biasing or confounding variables cannot be precisely controlled or anticipated. The studies by J. I. Lacey (1967) may be viewed as classical in this regard.

A distinctive feature of psychophysiology research is an awareness of the role of individual differences in determining experimental outcome. Individual differences (of interest themselves) are frequently "corrected for" by making measurements on a subject before and after a treatment is applied; this obvious correction is most frequently accomplished by calculating a difference score—a procedure that seems to vitiate a large number of published drug studies. For example, in studying the effect of diet pills on the mechanism of weight loss, it should be intuitively obvious that a 75-lb loss by a 300-lb man should not automatically be grouped with the same loss by a 150-lb man. The complexities and applicability of difference scores and their more sophisticated variants, the law of initial values (LIV) (Wilder, 1950) and autonomic lability scores (ALS) (J. I. Lacey, 1956, pp. 47–64) are beyond the scope of this discussion (Harris, 1963; Hord, Johnson, & Lubin, 1964; Surwillo & Arenberg, 1956; Wilder, 1965). We can recommend that, prior to initiating a drug experiment, the investigator attempt to anticipate the range of shapes, magnitudes, and directions of possible individual responses that will lead to alternative conclusions, testing these mentally in a "Gedanken experiment" to visualize how various individual differences and scoring procedures may bias the outcome.

Experimental plans A number of excellent sources give detailed advice on overall plans (crossover, latin squares, incomplete blocking, etc.) relevant for drug studies (Beyer, 1966; Lasagna & Meier, 1959, pp. 37–60; Winer, 1962). The choice of a plan will frequently be dictated by the availability of a tested computer program to be used for eventual data analysis (Cramer & Bock, 1966). In general, the complexity of data collection inherent in multiple criteria studies strongly argues for the simpler experimental plans to minimize complexities at other levels (a common problem in complex drug study plans is incomplete or missing data from subjects who do not finish the entire planned sequence).

One plan, the crossover design, which is widely used in drug research, should usually be avoided, unless it is explicitly obvious that the *treatment effect is reversible.* In this design, a given subject receives several treatments in sequence, sometimes separated by recovery intervals ("drying-out periods") to determine which treatment is best for him. Investigators using this plan rely upon proven statistical procedures for detecting the carryover of effect from one treatment to the next. While it is of interest to know that a carryover has occurred, the resultant confounding of effects is not only difficult to unravel but also of questionable validity because of the need for extensive a posteriori analysis. Only the data from the first treatment period

are clearly uncontaminated. Unless clear evidence is available that the treatment effect is completely reversible, so that subjects return to both their pretreatment level and state (physiologically and behaviorally), crossover designs should be avoided.

While we can conclude that crossover drug designs are seldom appropriate with mental patients, we note that many of these individuals now arrive at the hospital or laboratory so replete with crossover and carryover effects from varied and extensive treatment histories as to present not only a rationale but a challenge for the future application of audacious psychophysiological methodology.

REFERENCES

ACKERMAN, E. *Biophysical science.* Englewood Cliffs, N.J.: Prentice-Hall, 1962

AGLE, D. P., RATNOFF, O. D., & WASMAN, M. Studies in autoerythrocyte sensitization. *Psychosomatic Medicine,* 1967, **29,** 491–543.

AGRANOFF, B. W. Agents that block memory. In G. QUARTON, T. MELNECHUK, & F. O. SCHMITT (Eds.), *Neurosciences.* New York: Rockefeller University Press, 1967.

AHLQUIST, R. P. Agents which block adrenergic β-receptors. *Annual Review of Pharmacology,* 1968, **8,** 259–272.

AKERFELDT, S. Oxidation of *N,N*-dimethyl-*p*-phenylenediamine by serum from patients with mental disease. *Science,* 1957, **125,** 117–118.

ALTMAN, L. L., PRATT, D., & COHEN, J. M. Cardiovascular responses to acetyl-β-mecholyl choline in mental disorders. *Journal of Nervous and Mental Disease,* 1943, **97,** 296–309.

ASATOOR, A. M., LEVI, A. J., & MILNE, M. D. Tranylcypromine and cheese. *Lancet,* 1963, **2,** 733–734.

ASCHOFF, J. Comparative physiology: Diurnal rhythms. *Annual Review of Physiology,* 1963, **25,** 581–600.

ASSOCIATION FOR THE PSYCHOPHYSIOLOGICAL STUDY OF SLEEP. Abstracts of 1967 Meeting. *Psychophysiology,* 1967, **4,** 361–398.

ASSOCIATION FOR THE PSYCHOPHYSIOLOGICAL STUDY OF SLEEP. Abstracts of 1968 Meeting. *Psychophysiology,* 1968, **5,** 198–245.

AX, A. F. The physiological differentiation between fear and anger in humans. *Psychosomatic Medicine,* 1953, **15,** 433–442.

AX, A. F. Psychophysiological methodology for the study of schizophrenia. In R. ROESSLER & N. S. GREENFIELD (Eds.), *Physiological correlates of psychological disorders.* Madison: University of Wisconsin Press, 1962.

AXELROD, J., & LAROCHE, M. J. Inhibitors of *o*-methylation of epinephrine and norepinephrine in vitro and in vivo. *Science,* 1959, **130,** 800.

BEECHER, H. K. Quantification of the subjective pain experience. In P. HOCH & J. ZUBIN (Eds.), *Psychopathology of perception.* New York: Grune & Stratton, 1965.

BERGER, L. Interrelationship between blood pressure responses to mecholyl and personality variables. *Psychophysiology,* 1964, **1,** 115–118.

BERGER, M. Similarities and differences between meprobamate and sedatives. *Clinical Pharmacology and Therapeutics,* 1963, **4,** 209–231.

BEYER, W. H. (Ed.) *Handbook of tables for probability and statistics.* Cleveland, Ohio: Chemical Rubber Co., 1967.

BLACK, A. H., CARLSON, M. J., & SOLOMON, R. L. *Physiological Monographs,* 1962, **76,** 1–31.

BLUMBERG, A. G. Reproducibility of the mecholyl test. *Psychosomatic Medicine,* 1960, **22,** 32–41.

BLUMBERG, A. G., & KLEIN, D. F. Methoxy-catecholamine excretion and the mecholyl test. *Journal of Psychiatric Research,* 1965, **3,** 239–254.

BLUMBERG, A. G., & KLEIN, D. F. Age, base blood pressure, diagnosis, and mecholyl test response. *Psychosomatic Medicine,* 1966, **28,** 789–794.

BRADLEY, P. B. Central action of certain drugs in relation to the reticular formation of the brain. In H. H. JASPER (Ed.), *The reticular formation of the brain.* Boston: Little, Brown, 1958.

BRADLEY, P. B., & ELKES, J. Effect of atropine, hyoscyamine, physostigmine, and neostigmine on the electrical activity of the brain of the conscious cat. *Journal of Physiology, London,* 1953, **120,** 14P–15P. (Abstract)

BRADY, J. V. A comparative approach to the evaluation of

drug effects upon affective behavior. *Annals of the New York Academy of Sciences,* 1956, **64,** 632–643.

BRAZIER, M., KILLAM, K., & HANCE, J. Reactivity of the nervous system in the light of the past history of the organism. In W. ROSENBLITH (Ed.), *Sensory communication.* New York: MIT Press and Wiley, 1961.

BUNNEY, W. E., Jr., & DAVIS, J. M. Norepinephrine in depressive reactions. *Archives of General Psychiatry,* 1965, **13,** 483–494.

BUNNEY, W. E., Jr., GOODWIN, F., DAVIS, J. M., & FAWCETT, J. A behavioral biochemical study of lithium treatment. *American Journal of Psychiatry,* 1968, **125,** 91–104.

BURCH, N., NETTLETON, W., SWEENY, J., & EDWARDS, R. Period analysis of the electroencephalogram on a general purpose digital computer. *Annals of the New York Academy of Sciences,* 1964, **115,** 827–843.

BURN, J. H., & RAND, M. J. A new interpretation of the adrenergic nerve fiber. *Advances in Pharmacology,* 1962, **1,** 1–30.

CHATTON, M. J., MARGEN, S., & BRAINERD, H. *Handbook of medical treatment.* (7th ed.) Los Altos, Calif.: Lange Medical Publishers, 1960.

CLYDE, D. J. Experimental design and statistics. *Comprehensive Psychiatry,* 1967, **8,** 539–543.

CLYDE, D. J., CRAMER, E., & SHERRIN, R. *Multivariate statistical programs.* Coral Gables, Florida: University of Miami Press, 1966.

COHEN, S. I., & SILVERMAN, H. J. Psychophysiological investigation of vascular-response variability. *Journal of Psychosomatic Research,* 1959, **3,** 185–210.

COLE, J. O., & CLYDE, D. J. Extrapyramidal side effects and clinical response to phenothiazines. *Review of Canadian Biology,* 1961, **20,** 565–574.

COOK, L., DAVIDSON, A., DAVIS, D., & KELLEHER, R. Epinephrine, norepinephrine, and acetylcholine as conditioned stimuli for avoidance behavior. *Science,* 1960, **131,** 990–991.

CORNFIELD, J. Comparative bioassays and the role of parallelism. *Journal of Pharmacology and Experimental Therapeutics,* 1964, **144,** 143–149.

CRAMER, E. M., & BOCK, R. D. Multivariate analysis. *Educational Research,* 1966, **36,** 604–617.

DARROW, C. W. Physiological and clinical tests of autonomic functioning and autonomic balance. *Physiological Review,* 1943, **23,** 1–36.

DELAY, J., & DENIKER, P. Trente-huit cas de psychoses traitées par la cure prolongée et continue de 4560 R. P. Luxembourg: *Comptes Rendus du Congrès médical des Alienistes et Neurologistes,* 1952.

DRIPPS, R. Signs and stages of anesthesia. In L. S. GOODMAN & A. GILMAN (Eds.), *The pharmacological basis of therapeutics.* (3rd ed.) New York: Crowell-Collier-Macmillan, 1965.

DUFFEE, R. A., & KOONTZ, R. H. Behavioral effects of ionized air on rats. *Psychophysiology,* 1965, **1,** 347–359.

ECCLES, J. C. *The physiology of synapses.* New York: Academic, 1964.

ECCLES, J. C., & LIBET, B. Origin and blockade of the synaptic responses of curarized sympathetic ganglia. *Journal of Physiology, London,* 1961, **157,** 484–503.

EIDUSON, S., GELLER, E., YUWILER, A., & EIDUSON, B. T. *Biochemistry and behavior.* New York: Van Nostrand Reinhold, 1964.

EPPINGER, H., & HESS, L. *Vagotonia. Nervous and Mental Disease Monograph.* New York: Nervous and Mental Disease Publication, 1915.

EULER, U. S., VON. *Noradrenaline: Chemistry, physiology, pharmacology, and clinical aspects.* Springfield, Ill.: Charles C Thomas, 1956.

FINK, M. EEG and human psychopharmacology. *Annual Review of Pharmacology,* 1969, **9,** 241–258.

FINK, M., & ITIL, T. Anticholinergic hallucinogens and their interaction with centrally active drugs. In H. BRILL (Ed.), *Neuro-psycho-pharmacology.* Proceedings of the International Congress, Neuro-Psycho-Pharmacologium. New York: Excerpta Medica, 1967. (Abstract)

FINK, M., ITIL, T., & SHAPIRO, D. Digital computer analysis of the human EEG in psychiatric research. *Comprehensive Psychiatry,* 1967, **8,** 521–538.

FINNEY, D. J. *Statistical method in biological assay.* New York: Hafner, 1952.

FORNEY, R. B., HUGHES, F., & HALPIEN, H. Potentiation of ethanol-induced depression in dogs by representative ataractic and analgesic agents. *Quarterly Journal of Studies on Alcohol,* 1963, **24,** 1–8.

FRIEDHOFF, A. J., & VAN WINKLE, E. Isolation and characterization of a compound from the urine of schizophrenics. *Nature,* 1962, **194,** 897–898.

FROHMAN, C. E., LATHAM, L. K., BECKETT, P. G., & GOTTLIEB, J. S. Evidence of a plasma factor in schizophrenia. *Archives of General Psychiatry,* 1960, **2,** 255–262.

FUNKENSTEIN, D. H., GREENBLATT, M., & SOLOMON, H. C. Autonomic nervous system changes following electric shock treatment. *Journal of Nervous and Mental Disease,* 1948, **108,** 409–422.

FUNKENSTEIN, D. H., GREENBLATT, M., & SOLOMON, H. C. Nor-epinephrine-like and epinephrine-like substances in psychotic and psychoneurotic patients. *American Journal of Psychiatry,* 1952, **108,** 652–661.

FURNESS, F. N., & DEWS, P. B. (Eds.) Conference on techniques for the study of behavioral effects of drugs. *Annals of the New York Academy of Sciences,* 1956, **65,** 247–356.

GARDNER, L., & McCOLLOUGH, C. A reinvestigation of the dissociative effect of curariform drugs. *American Journal of Psychology,* 1962, **17,** 398–406.

GELLHORN, E. Hypothalamic-cortical system in barbiturate anesthesia. *Archives of Internal Pharamacodynamics,* 1953, **93,** 434–442.

GELLHORN, E. *Autonomic imbalance and the hypothalamus.* Minneapolis: University of Minnesota Press, 1957.

GELLHORN, E., & LOOFBOURROW, G. *Emotions and emotional disorders.* New York: Hoeber, 1963.

GLUECK, B. C., Jr. Personal communication, 1967.

GLUECK, B. C., Jr., & STROEBEL, C. F. The computer and the clinical decision process: II. *American Journal of Psychiatry*, 1969, **126,** 2–7.

GOLDBERG, S. C., COLE, J. O., & KLERMAN, G. L. Differential prediction of improvement under three phenothiazines. In J. R. WITTENBORN & P. R. A. MAY (Eds.), *Prediction of response to pharmacotherapy.* Springfield, Ill.: Charles C Thomas, 1966.

GOLDENBERG, M., ARANOW, H., SMITH, A. A., & FABER, M. Pheochromocytoma and essential hypertensive vascular disease. *Archives of Internal Medicine*, 1950, **86,** 823–836.

GOODMAN, L. S., & GILMAN, A. (Eds.) *The pharmacological basis of therapeutics.* (3rd ed.) New York: Crowell-Collier-Macmillan, 1965.

GORDON, M. (Ed.) *Psychopharmacological agents.* Vol. 1. New York: Academic, 1964.

GORDON, M. (Ed.) *Psychopharmacological agents.* Vol. 2. New York: Academic, 1967.

GREINER, A. C., & NICHOLSON, G. A. Pigment deposition in viscera associated with prolonging chlorpromazine reaction. *Canadian Medical Association Journal*, 1964, **81,** 627–635.

GROSSMAN, S. P., & MILLER, N. E. Control for stimulus-change in the evaluation of alcohol and chlorpromazine as fear-reducing drugs. *Psychopharmacologia*, 1961, **2,** 342–351.

HAIMOVICI, H. Evidence for adrenergic sweating in man. *Journal of Applied Physiology*, 1950, **2,** 512–521.

HALBERG, F. Temporal coordination of physiologic function. *Cold Spring Harbor Symposia on Quantitative Biology*, 1960, **25,** 289–310.

HALL, C. E. A technique for predicting effect of treatment. *Psychophysiology*, 1966, **2,** 316–321.

HARRIS, C. W. (Ed.) *Problems in measuring change.* Madison: University of Wisconsin Press, 1963.

HEATH, R. G., & KRUPP, I. M. Schizophrenia as a specific biologic disease. *American Journal of Psychiatry*, 1968, **124,** 1019–1027.

HEATH, R. G., MARTENS, S., LEACH, B. E., COHEN, M., & ANGEL, C. Effect on behavior in humans with the administration of taraxien. *American Journal of Psychiatry*, 1957, **114,** 14–24.

HEDBERG, D. L., GORDON, M. W., & GLUECK, B. C., Jr. Six cases of hypertensive crisis in patients on tranylcypromine after eating chicken livers. *American Journal of Psychiatry*, 1966, **122,** 933–937.

HEISTAD, G. T. A bio-psychological approach to somatic treatments in psychiatry. *American Journal of Psychiatry*, 1957, **114,** 540–545.

HIRSCH, J. Individual differences in behavior and their genetic basis. In E. L. BLISS (Ed.), *Roots of behavior.* New York: Harper & Row, 1962.

HOAGLAND, H. Some endocrine stress responses in man. In E. SIMON, C. C. HERBERT, & C. H. KEENE (Eds.), *The physiology of emotions.* Springfield, Ill.: Charles C Thomas, 1961.

HOLLISTER, L. Human pharmacology of antipsychotic and antidepressant drugs. *Annual Review of Pharmacology*, 1968, **8,** 491–516.

HORD, D. J., JOHNSON, L. C., & LUBIN, A. Differential effects of the law of initial value (LIV) on autonomic variables. *Psychophysiology*, 1964, **1,** 79–87.

HYDEN, H. Biochemical changes accompanying learning. In G. C. QUARTON, T. MELNECHUK, & F. O. SCHMITT (Eds.), *The neurosciences.* New York: Rockefeller University Press, 1967.

INNES, I. R., & NICKERSON, M. Drugs acting on postganglionic adrenergic nerve endings and structures innervated by them (sympathomimetic drugs). In L. S. GOODMAN & A. GILMAN (Eds.), *The pharmacological basis of therapeutics.* (3rd ed.) New York: Crowell-Collier-Macmillan, 1965.

JACKSON, H., & SCHNEIDER, H. Pharmacology of reproduction and fertility. *Annual Review of Pharmacology*, 1968, **8,** 467–490.

JAYNES, J. The routes of science. *American Scientist*, 1966, **54,** 94–102.

JENKINS, J., & DALLENBACH, K. Ogliviscence during sleep and waking. *American Journal of Psychology*, 1924, **35,** 605–612.

KALANT, H. Some recent physiological and biochemical investigations on alcohol. *Quarterly Journal of Studies on Alcohol*, 1962, **23,** 52–93.

KELLEHER, R. T., & MORSE, W. H. Determinants of the specificity of behavioral effects of drugs. *Reviews of Physiology, Biochemistry, and Experimental Pharmacology*, 1968, **60,** 1–56.

KETY, S. S. Biochemical theories of schizophrenia. *Science*, 1959, **129,** 1528–1532.

KETY, S. S. Biochemical theories of schizophrenia. *International Journal of Psychiatry*, 1965, **1,** 409–430.

KLERMAN, G. L. Relationship between clinical practice and laboratory sciences. In J. R. WITTENBORN & P. R. A. MAY (Eds.), *Prediction of response to pharmacotherapy.* Springfield, Ill.: Charles C Thomas, 1966.

KLERMAN, G. L., SCHILDKRAUT, J., HASENBUSH, L., GREENBLATT, M., & FRIEND, D. Clinical experience with dihydroxyphenylalanine (DOPA) in depression. *Journal of Psychiatric Research*, 1963, **1,** 289–297.

KOELLE, G. B. Neurohumoral transmission and the autonomic nervous system. In L. GOODMAN & A. GILMAN (Eds.), *The pharmacological basis of therapeutics.* (3rd ed.) New York: Crowell-Collier-Macmillan, 1965.

KOPIN, I. J. Relationship of psychotropic drug action to

the metabolism and transport of catecholamines. In H. BRILL (Ed.), *Neuro-psycho-pharmacology*. Proceedings of the Fifth International Congress, Neuro-Psycho-Pharmacologium. New York: Excerpta Medica, 1967.

KOPIN, I. J. False adrenergic transmitters. *Annual Review of Pharmacology*, 1968, **8**, 377–394.

KORNETSKY, C. Attention dysfunction and drugs in schizophrenia. In H. BRILL (Ed.), *Neuro-psycho-pharmacology*. Proceedings of the Fifth International Congress, Neuro-Psycho-Pharmacologium. New York: Excerpta Medica, 1967.

KORNETSKY, C., VATES, T. S., & KESSLER, E. K. A comparison of hypnotic and residual psychological effects of single doses of chlorpromazine and secobarbital in man. *Journal of Pharmacology and Experimental Therapeutics*, 1959, **127**, 51–54.

LACEY, J. I. The evaluation of autonomic responses: Toward a general solution. *Annals of the New York Academy of Science*, 1956, **67**, 125–163.

LACEY, J. I. Somatic response patterning and stress: Some revisions of activation theory. In M. H. APPLEY & R. TRUMBULL (Eds.), *Psychological stress: Issues in research*. New York: Appleton-Century-Crofts, 1967.

LADER, M. H., & MONTAGU, J. D. The psycho-galvanic reflex: A pharmacologic study of the peripheral mechanism. *Journal of Neurochemical and Neurosurgical Psychiatry*, 1962, **25**, 126–133.

LADER, M. H., & WING, L. *Physiological measures, sedative drugs, and morbid anxiety*. New York: Oxford University Press, 1966.

LASAGNA, L., & MEIER, P. Experimental design and statistical problems. In S. O. WAIFE & A. P. SHAPIRO (Eds.), *The clinical evaluation of new drugs*. New York: Hoeber, 1959.

LASAGNA, L., MOSTELLER, F., von FELSINGER, J., & BEECHER, H. K. A study of the placebo response. *American Journal of Medicine*, 1954, **16**, 770–779.

LASKA, E., & SIMPSON, G. M. Dose response and bioassay for evaluation of psychopharmaceuticals. In H. BRILL (Ed.), *Neuro-psycho-pharmacology*. Proceedings of the Fifth International Congress, Neuro-Psycho-Pharmacologium. New York: Excerpta Medica, 1967.

LATIES, V. G., & WEISS, B. Performance enhancement by amphetamines: A new appraisal. In H. BRILL (Ed.), *Neuro-psycho-pharmacology*. Proceedings of the Fifth International Congress, Neuro-Psycho-Pharmacologium. New York: Excerpta Medica, 1967.

LEHMANN, H. E. Differences in behavioral effects in humans. In H. BRILL (Ed.), *Neuro-psycho-pharmacology*. Proceedings of the Fifth International Congress, Neuro-Psycho-Pharmacologium. New York: Excerpta Medica, 1967.

LIBERMAN, R. The elusive placebo reactor. In H. BRILL (Ed.), *Neuro-psycho-pharmacology*. Proceedings of the Fifth International Congress, Neuro-Psycho-Pharmacologium. New York: Excerpta Medica, 1967.

MARSH, D. F. *Outline of fundamental pharmacology*. Springfield, Ill.: Charles C Thomas, 1951.

MAY, PHILIP. Prediction of psychiatric outcome: Animal subjects and individual differences in response—a clinician's view. In J. R. WITTENBORN & P. R. A. MAY (Eds.), *Prediction of response to pharmacotherapy*. Springfield, Ill.: Charles C Thomas, 1966.

MCCAWLEY, A., STROEBEL, C. F., & GLUECK, B. C., Jr. Pupillary reactivity, psychologic disorder and age. *Archives of General Psychiatry*, 1966, **14**, 415–418.

MEEHL, P. E. Schizotaxia, schizotypy, schizophrenia. *American Psychologist*, 1962, **17**, 827–838.

OSTFELD, A. M., & ARGUETE, A. Central nervous system effects of hyoscine in man. *Journal of Pharmacology and Experimental Therapeutics*, 1962, **137**, 133–139.

OTIS, L. S. Dissociation and recovery of a response learned under the influence of chlorpromazine or saline. *Science*, 1964, **143**, 2347–2348.

OSWALD, I. Sleep and dependence on amphetamine and other drugs. In A. KALES (Ed.), *Sleep: Physiology and pathology*. Philadelphia: Lippincott, 1969.

OVERALL, J. E., & HOLLISTER, L. E. Computer procedures for psychiatric classification. *Journal of the American Medical Association*, 1964, **187**, 583–588

PARE, C., & SANDLER, M. A clinical and biochemical study of a trial of iproniazid in the treatment of depression. *Journal of Neurological and Neurosurgical Psychiatry*, 1959, **22**, 247–251.

PEREZ-REYES, M., SHANDS, H. C., & JOHNSON, G. Galvanic skin reflex inhibition threshold: A new psychophysiologic technique. *Psychosomatic Medicine*, 1962, **24**, 274–277.

PLETSCHER, A., & DA PRADA, M. Mechanism of action of neuroleptics. In H. BRILL (Ed.), *Neuro-psycho-pharmacology*. Proceedings of the Fifth International Congress, Neuro-Psycho-Pharmacologium. New York: Excerpta Medica, 1967.

POLLIN, W. Control and artifact in psychophysiological research. In R. ROESSLER & N. S. GREENFIELD (Eds.), *Physiological correlates of psychological disorder*. Madison: University of Wisconsin Press, 1962.

PURPURA, D. P., & GRUNDFEST, H. Physiological and pharmacological consequences of different synaptic organizations on cerebral and cerebellar cortex of cat. *Journal of Neurophysiology*, 1957, **20**, 494–522.

QUARTON, G. C. The enhancement of learning by drugs and the transfer of learning by macromolecules. In G. QUARTON, T. MELNECHUK, & F. SCHMITT (Eds.), *The neurosciences*. New York: Rockefeller University Press, 1967.

RECHTSCHAFFEN, A., & KALES, A. (Eds.). *A manual of standardized terminology, techniques, and scoring system for sleep stages of human subjects*. Washington, D.C.: Public Health Service, United States Government Printing Office, 1968.

REINBERG, A. The hours of changing responsiveness or susceptibility. *Perspectives in Biology and Medicine*, 1967, **10,** 111–128.

ROSENBLATT, S., CHANLEY, J., SOBOTKA, H., & KAUFMAN, M. Interrelationships between electroshock, the blood-brain barrier, and catecholamines. *Journal of Neurochemistry*, 1960, **5,** 172–176.

ROSENTHAL, R. Experimenter outcome-orientation and the results of the psychological experiment. *Psychological Bulletin*, 1965, **61,** 405–412.

RUBIN, L. S. Autonomic disfunction in psychosis. *Archives of General Psychiatry*, 1962, **7,** 1–14.

RUSHTON, R., & STEINBERG, H. Drug combinations and their analysis by means of exploratory activity in rats. In H. BRILL (Ed.), *Neuro-psycho-pharmacology*. Proceedings of the Fifth International Congress, Neuro-Psycho-Pharmacologium. New York: Excerpta Medica, 1967.

SACHS, E. *The role of brain electrolytes in learning and retention.* Doctoral dissertation, University of Rochester, 1962.

SAVAGE, I. R., RAO, M., & HALBERG, F. Test of peak values in a physiopathic time series. *Experimental Medicine and Surgery*, 1962, **20,** 309–324.

SCHACHTER, J. Pain, fear, and anger in hypertensives and normotensives. *Psychosomatic Medicine*, 1957, **19,** 17–29.

SCHELKUNOV, E. Integrated effect of psychotropic drugs in the balance of cholin-, adren-, and serotoninergic synapses as a basis of their gross behavioral and therapeutic actions. In H. BRILL (Ed.), *Neuro-psycho-pharmacology*. Proceedings of the Fifth International Congress, Neuro-Psycho-Pharmacologium. New York: Excerpta Medica, 1967.

SCHILDKRAUT, J. J. Excretion of 3-methoxy-4-hydroxy-mandelic acid (VMA) in depressed patients treated with antidepressant drugs. *Journal of Psychiatric Research*, 1964, **2,** 257–266.

SCHNORE, M. M. Individual patterns of physiological activity as a function of past differences and degree of arousal. *Journal of Experimental Psychology*, 1959, **2,** 117–128.

SCHUSTER, C. R., Jr., & BRADY, J. V. Pavlov J. A. *Higher Nervous Activity* (Russian), 1964, **4,** 448–458.

SHAGASS, C. Sedation threshold: Technique and concept. In H. BRILL (Ed.), *Neuro-psycho-pharmacology*. Proceedings of the Fifth International Congress, Neuro-Psycho-Pharmacologium. New York: Excerpta Medica, 1967.

SMITH, S., BROWN, H., TOMAN, J., & GOODMAN, L. The lack of cerebral effects of *d*-tubocurarine. *Anesthesiology*, 1947, **8,** 1–14.

SOLOMON, R. L., & TURNER, L. H. Discriminative classical conditioning in dogs paralyzed by curare can later control discriminative avoidance responses in the normal state. *Psychological Review*, 1962, **69,** 202–219.

SPITZER, R., & COHEN, J. Common errors in quantitative psychiatric research. *International Journal of Psychiatry*, 1968, **6,** 109–117.

STEIN, L. Amphetamine and neural reward mechanisms. In H. STEINBERG, A. V. S. DE REUCK, & J. KNIGHT (Eds.), *Animal behavior and drug action*, Ciba Foundation Symposium. Boston: Little, Brown, 1964.

STERNBACH, R. A. The effects of instructional sets on autonomic responsitivity. *Psychophysiology*, 1964, **1,** 67–72.

STERNBACH, R. A. *Principals of psychophysiology.* New York: Academic, 1966.

STERNBACH, R. A. *Pain: A psychophysiological analysis.* New York: Academic, 1968.

STERNBACH, A. A., ALEXANDER, A. A., & GREENFIELD, N. S. Autonomic and somatic reactivity in relation to psychopathology. In J. ZUBIN & C. SHAGASS (Eds.), *Neurobiological aspects of psychopathology*. New York: Grune & Stratton, 1969.

STEWART, J. Differential responses based on the physiological consequences of pharmacological agents. *Psychopharmacologia*, 1962, **3,** 132–138.

STROEBEL, C. F. Behavioral aspects of circadian periodicity. In J. ZUBIN & H. HUNT (Eds.), *Comparative psychopathology*. New York: Grune & Stratton, 1967. (a)

STROEBEL, C. F. Biochemical, behavioral, and clinical models of drug interactions. In H. BRILL (Ed.), *Neuro-psycho-pharmacology*. Proceedings of the Fifth International Congress, Neuro-Psycho-Pharmacologium. New York: Excerpta Medica, 1967. (b)

STROEBEL, C. F. Biologic rhythm approach to psychiatric treatment. In R. STEINBECK (Ed.), *Proceedings of the Seventh IBM Medical Symposium*. Yorktown Heights, N.Y.: IBM Corp., 1967. (c)

STROEBEL, C. F. Biologic rhythm correlates of disturbed behavior in the rhesus monkey. In F. H. ROHLES (Ed.), *Circadian rhythms in nonhuman primates*. New York: S. Karger, 1969.

STROEBEL, C. F. Computer techniques for studying biologic rhythms: Quantitative chronobiology. *Behavioral Research Methods and Instrumentation*, 1970, **2,** 79–81.

STROEBEL, C. F., & GLUECK, B. C., Jr. Measurement and prediction in interdisciplinary psychiatric research. In R. TAYLOR (Ed.), *Proceedings of the Fifth IBM Medical Symposium*. Yorktown Heights, N.Y.: IBM Corp., 1965.

SUMMERFIELD, A., & STEINBERG, H. Reducing interference in forgetting. *Quarterly Journal of Experimental Psychology*, 1957, **9,** 146–154.

SURWILLO, W. W., & ARENBERG, D. L. On the law of initial value and the measurement of change. *Psychophysiology*, 1965, **1,** 368–370.

VENABLES, P. H., & MARTIN, I. The relation of palmar sweat gland activity to level of skin potential and conductance. *Psychophysiology*, 1967, **3,** 302–311.

WATSON, D. W., QUIGLEY, A., & BOLT, R. J. Effect of lymphocytes from patients with ulcerative colitis on human adult colon epithelial cells. *Gastroenterology*, 1966, **51,** 985–993.

WENGER, M. A. The measurement of individual differences

in autonomic balance. *Psychosomatic Medicine*, 1941, **3,** 427–434.

WENGER, M. A.   Pattern analysis of autonomic variables during rest. *Psychosomatic Medicine*, 1957, **14,** 240–242.

WENGER, M. A.   Some problems in psychophysiological research. In R. ROESSLER & N. S. GREENFIELD (Eds.), *Physiologic correlates of psychological disorders.* Madison: University of Wisconsin Press, 1962.

WENGER, M. A., CLEMENS, T. L., DARSIE, M. L., ENGEL, B. T., ESTESS, F. M., & SONNENSCHEIN, R. R.   Autonomic response patterns during intravenous infusion of epinephrine and norepinephrine. *Psychosomatic Medicine*, 1960, **22,** 294–307.

WEISS, B.   Digital computers in the behavior laboratory. *Decus Biomedical Symposium.* Maynard, Mass.: Digital Equipment Co., 1967, p. 31.

WEISSMAN, A.   Behavioral pharmacology. In M. RINKEL (Ed.),

Biological treatment of mental illness. Boston: L. C. Page, 1966.

WILCOTT, R. C.   The partial independence of skin potential and skin resistance from sweating. *Psychophysiology,* 1964, **1,** 55–66.

WILDER, J.   The law of initial values. *Psychosomatic Medicine,* 1950, **12,** 392. (Abstract)

WILDER, J.   Pitfalls in the methodology of the law of initial value. *American Journal of Psychotherapy,* 1965, **19,** 577–584.

WINER, B. J.   *Statistical principles in experimental design.* New York: McGraw-Hill, 1962.

WOLF, S., DOERING, C. R., CLARK, M. L., & HAGANS, J. A.   Chance distribution and the placebo "reactor." *Journal of Laboratory and Clinical Medicine,* 1957, **49,** 837–841.

WURTMAN, R. J.   *Catecholamines.* Boston: Little, Brown, 1966.

David T. Graham

PSYCHOSOMATIC MEDICINE

21

THE PSYCHOSOMATIC PROBLEM DEFINED

What is now called "psychosomatic medicine" arose from the discovery that psychological considerations apply to traditionally "medical" diseases. The present chapter will therefore concentrate on those states of the organism that are called "diseases" and the processes that culminate in those states. Other states and processes are dealt with elsewhere in this volume. This is, of course, a distinction that is arbitrary in the extreme and is often only quantitative. Psychosomatic medicine is psychophysiology in a clinical context, and it is hoped that what follows may serve to bring to the attention of psychophysiologists some of the psychosomatic research that is apparently not well-known to them.

In writing for a *Handbook of Psychophysiology*, the emphases will be somewhat different from those appropriate to a discussion of psychosomatic medicine for other purposes. This chapter will consider only those physiological questions most immediately related to the peripheral processes responsible for the disease in question, without discussing details of mechanism, or more central processes, notably those in the central nervous system (CNS), that may be involved. Work with animals other than man will not be considered. We shall try to remain fairly close to reported data, avoiding many theoretical problems. The reason for this omission is not that these problems are without interest or importance, but rather that a serious discussion requires so much preliminary work in the definition of terms, in order to understand what assertions are being made, that including them would put the chapter out of balance.

We shall not consider all illnesses about which something "psychosomatic" has been said, but rather, because the present book is addressed primarily to psychophysiologists, shall limit discussion to those for which reasonably systematic biochemical or physiological measurements correlated with data of psychological interest have been made. This criterion excludes, for instance, psychosomatic work on cancer, but it is difficult to apply it rigorously. Rheumatoid arthritis is included, despite a paucity of physiological data, because psychophysiologists have been interested in it. Further, diseases outside of my area of competence such as those of the eye or the female reproductive system are not included, even when there are some psychophysiological data available. Finally, such diseases as anorexia nervosa, obesity, and coronary artery disease with myocardial infarction are also excluded because current knowledge about them is too confused to permit reasonably clear and brief expositions. One hopes that the current active investigation of the processes involved will lead to enough clarity to make useful summaries possible in the near future.

There are two useful general sources of information about research in psychosomatic medicine before 1955. The first is the 1950 Proceedings of the Association of Research in Nervous and Mental Disease (Wolff, Wolf, & Hare, 1950) which contains many papers by different authors and gives a good picture of the status of the field at that time. The second is Hamilton's analytic review (1955) of most of the relevant literature. The present chapter will not deal in detail with material covered by Hamilton, except where individual contributions may have special importance. Two other well-known authors who have produced rather comprehensive discussions of psychosomatic medicine are Dunbar (1947a, 1947b), who reviewed an enormous quantity of literature in a pioneering book and also presented formulations of her own; and Alexander,

who in 1950 published a summary of his psychoanalytic approach to the subject.

In order to present a sensible picture of the present state of the field, it is necessary to attempt logical clarification of two important issues. These are the mind-body problem and the problem of etiology.

Mind-Body Problem

Confusion about the mind-body problem is a serious obstacle to understanding psychosomatic medicine and has interfered with its growth. Although a discussion of the problem may seem an unnecessary philosophical digression, it is necessary to be clear about the meanings of words like "mental" and "physical" in order to avoid many useless debates. In particular, preoccupation with trying to show that "psychological factors" cause "physical disease" has led to much difficulty because of failure to examine what such an assertion means. The treatment of the problem to be followed has been given in detail elsewhere, under the name "linguistic parallelism" (D. T. Graham, 1967), and only the essentials will be repeated here.

Anyone, physician or psychologist, who makes statements about another person must be doing so on the basis of some sorts of observations he has made, directly or indirectly, concerning that person. There is no conceivable observation that could not be described in ways that we would call "physical." A patient's statement of his symptoms, for instance, must be produced by his organs of speech, which are certainly well-recognized anatomic structures, and transmitted through the air by sound waves to the listener's ear. We must therefore ask ourselves what it means to say that an illness is "all psychological," or that disease processes, or observed changes in blood pressure or in electrical skin resistance, have "emotional" or "psychological" causes.

It is suggested that a satisfactory approach to these kinds of problems requires the recognition that "psychological" and "physical" are the names of different *languages,* like Latin and Sanskrit, that are applied to observations of persons. This chapter will hereafter emphasize this point of view by following ordinary English usage for names of languages, which means capitalizing "Psychological," "Physical," and some other similar words, when they are used in that way. Psychological and Physical are both in *principle* applicable to exactly the same phenomena, although in *practice* Psychological tends to be used for the limited class of observations made on patients' or subjects' speech. Physical tends to be used for the outputs of other organs of the body, although it may be perfectly well used also for the organs of speech, as when laryngeal movements or speech energy levels are analyzed. It is this difference in practice that presumably has led to the implicit idea that there are *physical events* and *psychological events*, a point of view that will not withstand careful examination. Further, there are many events in persons for which no Psychological description at present exists.

A "psychological reaction" or "psychological illness" is, then, a state or process that we choose, for the moment, to describe in Psychological language. If we say, for example, that a man is "angry," we are summarizing a number of observations of his speech, of the movements of his arms, of his answers on psychological tests, etc., by using a word from the Psychological language. We could, however, if we wished, describe the same events in Physical language, by referring to the energies of the various frequencies making up his speech pattern, the various muscle contractions required for the movements we observe, etc. It is therefore impossible that there be a "nonphysical" state of an organism.

There is nothing intrinsically more "scientific" about one language than the other, and both may be used for directly expressing the results of observations, and for conceptualizing and theorizing at various levels. Convenience, convention, or other reasons dictate the choice between them.

Both languages have subdivisions. Biochemical, Physiological, or Anatomic statements, for instance, make up languages within the Physical group. Various sets of Psychoanalytic concepts are examples of languages within the Psychological group. One other language in common use in psychosomatic discussions is Sociological. "The patient is a middle class Lutheran" is an example of a statement in that language.

An "emotion" is a state of the organism. It is usually given a name from the Psychological language. Why some states are called "emotions," and others not, is not always clear. One criterion, however, appears to be that a psychological stimulus (see below) has evoked the state.

Etiology and Causation

The concept of "psychogenesis," contained in statements about "psychological causes" of "physical diseases," is so central to discussions of psychosomatic medicine that it needs to be carefully examined. The basic issues in Psycho-Physiological discussions are identical.

The first point to emphasize is that there are two common general meanings of statements about the causation of any disease. The first of these refers to the response of an organism to an external (environmental) stimulus. An example is, "Pneumonia is caused by the pneumococcus." The second refers to the production of one state of the organism (the disease) by another state. An example is, "Hypoglycemia causes convulsions." It would, of course, be possible to consider these states as, respectively, stimulus and response, but to do so is likely to invite confusion with the first meaning.

We wish, then, to investigate the cause of a disease (or other state or process). For present purposes, let us assume that this disease is described in the Physical language, e.g., as a duodenal ulcer or essential hypertension. (The argument is essentially the same, however, if the disease is described in Psychological language, e.g., depression.) The major trouble with the frequent assertion, or its denial, that a given disease is "psychogenic," is that it is not clear which of the two general meanings of statements about causation is intended.

If it is the first, the assertion is that the disease is a response to what we shall call a *psychological stimulus*. It should be noted, to begin with, that the latter must certainly be describable in Physical terms as light rays, sound waves, etc. Its special features, leading to the application of the word "psychogenic" to the responses it elicits, appear to be (D. T. Graham, 1954b, 1967) that it has a description in Psychological language, derived from a

Psychological description of the response (e.g., "a green tree," "a frightening cat"), and also that its effect is mediated through peripheral sense organs. These two conditions are highly correlated; it would probably serve well for all practical purposes to say that a "psychological stimulus" is an external sensory stimulus. It must be emphasized that we are not searching for a correct definition of the term "psychological stimulus" but are instead trying to answer an empirical question about linguistic usage.

The second possible meaning of "psychogenic" is that a state of the organism, described Psychologically, is responsible for another state, in this case a disease described Physically. This meaning occurs in such a sentence as, "His anger is causing his ulcer." The evidence for the existence of the causative state "anger" necessarily consists of signals emitted by the patient's body. The observer has chosen to lump together a large set of data, which could also be described in Physical terms under a single name, "anger." Probably, he also wants to imply that the essential feature of the state, with respect to its ability to cause an ulcer, is a particular pattern of activity in the CNS. At least theoretically, he could have described this pattern in Physical terms, too. Used in this way "psychogenic" says nothing about the presence of external stimuli; in other instances these are implied, as in the statement, "His wife's shouting made him angry, and that caused his ulcer."

In summary, statements about "psychological causes of physical diseases" frequently confuse two distinct meanings. The commonest consequence is that an investigator may find that some state described in Psychological terms such as "neurosis" or "anxiety" is not present in a group of patients, asthmatics, for instance, and therefore concludes that the disease asthma is not "psychogenic." He thereby obscures the possibility that it may nevertheless be a response to psychological stimuli. If he had looked for some *other state*, a specific emotion, for instance, he might have found it present. Even if this were the case, however, it would *not* tell us whether or not psychological stimuli were responsible for either the Psychological state or the disease.

In fact, the question of stimulus is generally more important and more productive. Its significance has been emphasized by several authors (e.g., D. T. Graham, 1954a; Guze, Matarazzo, & Saslow, 1953; Wolff, 1950, pp. 1059–1094), and its understanding is the primary issue of psychophysiological research today. Probably, psychosomatic medicine would profit from more concern with the stimulus question, and less preoccupation with the question of state; i.e., does a Psychologically described state cause a Physically described one?

In the psychosomatic context and with our present investigative resources the "state" question is almost impossible to answer. It is difficult to deal with in any context. Sometimes it is proposed that a prospective study will resolve it and avoid the supposed defects of a retrospective study. This proposition needs examining.

The aim of the usual prospective study in psychosomatic medicine is to discover whether a Psychologically described state, often called the "personality," is the cause or the effect of a Physically described state, the disease. Both states are ordinarily observed in the patient at the same time. For instance, patients with ulcerative colitis are said to be dependent. Critics often assume that this is intended to be a claim for the etiologic role of "dependency," and they point out that perhaps the colitis has produced the dependency. In rebuttal, attempts are made to show that the personality long antedated the disease. This is thought at least to make it impossible that the disease is the cause of the personality trait, even though it may not establish that the personality trait is the cause of the disease. The reason for the interest in prospective investigations is that they investigate the personalities of groups of persons before any disease is known to be present. If, thereafter, individuals with particular personality characteristics do develop particular diseases, one is thought to know more certainly which came first than he does if he must rely only on the recollections of patients who already have the disease when they are first investigated.

There is a serious flaw in that argument, however: it is impossible to know when the disease begins. It may have been present, though concealed, from birth. The problem, therefore, hinges on deciding exactly what phenomena comprise the disease. Sometimes a particular event can be located fairly precisely in time, e.g., the perforation of a duodenal ulcer or the onset of diabetic coma. If one wishes to call this event "the disease," then the time of occurrence of the disease can be specified. But such an episode is ordinarily thought of as only a single event in a long disease process. Suppose that a disease is genetically determined, even though it may not become clinically manifest until many years after birth, as may be the case with diabetes. Certainly then, there must be *something* present in the person all his life that might perfectly well be called "the disease."

It is often forgotten that it is equally impossible to know when the "personality" began. Consider a trait like "irritability," for instance. Suppose it was first noted in a man after he had had a myocardial infarction. We might then say that the infarction was the cause of the irritability. But suppose that the event irritability was but the manifestation of something latent; just as the myocardial infarction itself was but the manifestation of an arteriosclerotic process, long latent and finally manifest in this sudden form. Which underlying process started first and so could be considered the cause of the other? It is impossible to know by any technique now available.

It is true that an experimental approach is at least theoretically possible. That is, if one could isolate with sufficient precision the events that one has in mind as defining a disease or process, one could then experimentally manipulate exactly those events and see what happened to another process of interest. One could, for instance, experimentally shut off a coronary artery, thus producing a myocardial infarction, and, provided one were certain that the direct effect was on the heart, and not on that part of the body that makes up the state "irritability," produce evidence to suggest that the infarction was or was not the cause of the irritability. Similarly, one might directly alter those parts of the body, presumably of the brain, immediately responsible for the production of the behavioral phenomena called "irritability," and see whether myocardial infarction resulted. Some of the arguments, derived from the treatment of disease, which are often cited to show that "the body influences the mind, instead of the other way around," depend

for their force, such as it is, on the resemblance of the therapeutic procedure to such an experiment. In short, if surgical removal of a diseased colon in ulcerative colitis is followed by a disappearance of dependency, this is regarded as evidence that the colitis caused the dependency, because it is thought that the surgical manipulation must clearly have had its effect first on the colon and only indirectly on the personality.

This reasoning may, in fact, be sound, although it must also be pointed out that almost any therapeutic procedure is sufficiently complicated to make it hard to know which aspects of it were responsible for which effects. In other words, the surgery may have directly affected the "dependency" part of the person, so to speak. On the other hand, if someone wishes to show that by psychotherapy he has cured dependency and that the colon was restored to health *as a result of* the relief of dependency, his position is essentially hopeless. There is no way to know that his procedure did not *first* affect the colon, which in turn affected the dependency.

There is an additional complication. It may well be that there is an exchange of effects between the parts of the body involved in the two states under discussion; i.e., there may be feedback. In that case, nothing short of an experiment, and certainly no crude effort at deciding by observation which process came first, could ever provide the answer sought. Each process is the cause of the other, and the very first step might occur in either.

It is a mistake to think that the essence of psychosomatic medicine is to show that Psychologically described states cause Physically described states. It is often not realized that this whole question is simply a revival of the dispute over the James-Lange theory of emotion. Scientific interest in the physiology of emotions does not require that it be shown that the "emotion" (in this context, the word usually means a central state described Psychologically) causes the peripheral changes, rather than the reverse. This is a question of interest, but it is not critical to the continued existence of psychology.

The *etiologic question* of most interest and importance is the *stimulus* question: which responses of the organism, and especially which medical diseases, are responses to psychological stimuli? Similarly, if one's interest is in therapy, and particularly in so-called psychotherapy, why should he get involved in a controversy over whether the colon affected the dependency, or the dependency the colon? His major interest is certainly the effect of his *procedure* on the patient, and specifically, in knowing whether he is able to improve all the states he is trying to treat, without worrying about which improvement comes first.

We need to consider briefly the very common use of the word "stress" in etiologic discussions (Wolff, 1950). It usually refers, especially in the expression "life stress," to what we have called psychological stimuli. The situation is complicated, however, by the popular use of Selye's concept of stress (Selye, 1959). The value of Selye's usage depends on the similarity of response to different kinds of stimulus situations, a similarity apparently resulting from the common action of these on the pituitary-adrenal system. It has no intrinsic relation to the concept of psychological stimulus, but the unwary sometimes suppose that, if a psychological stimulus evokes a response described Physically, especially a disease, the stimulus is a "stress" in Selye's sense and must therefore activate that endocrine apparatus. In fact, however, there is no reason to think that all, or even most, of the psychogenic diseases have any special dependence on the pituitary and adrenal mechanisms that Selye investigated.

Table 21.1 outlines the position I have been developing in this chapter with illustrative examples in each column. Column 1 contains examples of stimuli. Some of these are psychological and some are not. Columns 2–4 contain, respectively, examples of long-term Psychological (e.g., personality), Physical, and Sociological statements about the person. Columns 5 and 6 contain examples of Psychological and Physical statements about the response (disease). It is not implied that the particular items on any row in this diagram have any connection with each other. Efforts to establish such connections will be discussed throughout the remainder of the chapter. The diagram is intended to facilitate thinking, and to help clarify the kinds of questions and statements encountered in discussions of psychosomatic medicine.

The fundamental scheme is of stimuli, acting on an organism, to elicit responses. We can describe in any language we choose the characteristics of the organism that lead to those responses, rather than others, and we can also describe, in any language we choose, the responses.

Role of Psychological Stimuli

The kinds of evidence that diseases are responses to psychological stimuli may, for convenience, be divided into five classes (D. T. Graham & Stevenson, 1963, pp. 115–136).

1. Life histories obtained from individual persons or groups of persons, indicating temporal correlations

TABLE 21.1 RELATIONS BETWEEN STIMULI, PERSONS, AND RESPONSES, DESCRIBED IN DIFFERENT LANGUAGES

Stimuli	Persons			Responses	
	Psychological language	Physical language	Sociological language	Psychological language	Physical language
Streptococcus	Passive-dependent	Obese	Lutheran	Anger	Asthma
X-radiation	Unresolved Oedipus complex	XYY chromosome pattern	Middle class	Activation of oral conflict	Tachycardia
Digitalis			Married		Rise in blood pressure
Wife leaves	Paranoid personality	Labile blood pressure	Uneducated	Attitude	
Pay decreased				Schizophrenic episode	Tuberculosis
Husband shouts	Careless	Inborn metabolic error			
	Response set				

Note.—Under each heading are given examples of appropriate items. It is not implied that items on the same horizontal line have any relation to each other.

between exposure to what are usually called "stress-ful life situations" and the onset or exacerbation of disease, or between such life situations and changes in physiological variables relevant to disease. "Stressful life situations" here refers to psychological stimuli, with the implication that the latter evoke some response, such as "feeling upset," in addition to the illness in question.

2. Experiments in which physiological observations are made while the patient is reacting to psychological stimuli presented as words or pictures. The experimental interview is a special case of this technique; usually, the stimuli used are symbols of other psychological stimuli, namely, the events presumed to have produced the patient's illness.

3. Observations of subjects during or after exposure to disturbing stimuli of a real life sort. These stimuli may be either experimentally manipulated or naturally occurring.

4. Correlations between major social variables and differences in the incidence of various diseases. This is essentially an epidemiologic approach, in which large groups are studied. Usually, it is very difficult to know whether the etiologically relevant features of the social situations are psychological stimuli.

5. Predictive studies of the outcome of illness according to the occurrence of disturbing psychological stimuli known to be present in the patients' lives.

1. The life history approach This common clinical procedure is the method reported most frequently in psychosomatic literature. It takes various forms; most often the patient simply recounts the events in his life, his conscious reactions to them, and the time relations of these to episodes of his illness. There are more sophisticated versions. One of these is the careful diary, in which a record is kept of particular kinds of life events (Metcalfe, 1956).

It is interesting that some of the most striking examples of temporal correlations between psychological stimuli and illness come from studies of diseases that are not conventionally thought of as psychosomatic. Meyer and Haggerty (1962) reported that acquisition of Beta-hemolytic streptococci, illness due to such streptococci, and nonstreptococcal respiratory infections, were all about four times as likely to be preceded as to be followed by acute stress. These stresses were various forms of crisis in the family such as deaths, illnesses in family members, loss of job, etc. Eylon (1967) reported significantly greater numbers of what he

called "birth events" (i.e., births of babies or pregnancies involving the patient's family, or weddings in the family at which the patient was present) in the lives of patients undergoing appendectomy for a confirmed appendicitis than in the lives of those having other surgical procedures.

Mutter and Schleifer (1966), comparing recent life experiences of 42 ill children and 45 well children, found that the ill children had been exposed to significantly more changes in the "psychosocial setting" than were the well children. It is particularly interesting that, apparently because of the intentional selection of cases, only three of the children were ultimately given diagnoses usually considered to be "psychosomatic" (peptic ulcer, bronchial asthma, and rheumatoid arthritis once each). The other illnesses, many of them infectious, were divided among 28 diagnostic categories. Holmes (1956) and Kissen (1958) have reported a significant occurrence of social stresses immediately preceding the development of pulmonary tuberculosis. In each case there was a suitable control group, in which comparable stresses were not found immediately preceding the onset of illness. Hinkle and his associates (Hinkle et al., 1958; Hinkle & Wolff, 1957, 1958) studied various groups of persons and found that illness of all kinds was more likely to occur when a person was exposed to psychological stimuli to which he had difficulty in adapting than when he was not so exposed.

This way of doing things has not gone unchallenged. For instance, it has been reported that women hospitalized for normal deliveries give a history of a large number of "potentially stressful" experiences in the preceding year (Murphy, Kuhn, Christensen, & Robins, 1962) and that patients with diseases not thought to be related to "stressful events" have as many such events in their lives as do patients with diseases that are usually thought to be so related (Papper & Handy, 1956). The implied assumption here that pregnancies and "nonstress-induced" illnesses are not responses to psychological stimuli is questionable. The phenomenon of temporal clustering of stresses just prior to the onset of illnesses and the addition of the concept of difficulty in adapting to the stresses provide other arguments in rebuttal of this criticism. Additional responses are given later.

In a refinement of the life history approach, Schmale (1958; 1964, pp. 433–443) concluded from patients' reports or investigators' interpretations that 151 of 190 patients with a large variety of "medical" (i.e., Physically defined) diseases had experienced an event which was an actual, threatened, or symbolic "object loss" within months prior to disease onset. For 31 patients in one group of 42 (Schmale, 1958), the intervening period was a week or less. He reported (1964) that all 151 had reacted to their losses with feelings of "giving up." A study of separation experiences of 455 "ostensibly normal" subjects (Imboden, Canter, & Cluff, 1963), however, found them in 25% of the group, as compared to the 33% of Schmale's patient population with actual or threatened rather than symbolic losses. These authors correctly point out that such control studies are necessary if simple percentages of positive findings in a patient population are to be used as evidence for etiology. They also discuss the possibility that illness may affect the *reporting* of disturbing events, a difficult problem to deal with. In rebuttal, however, Schmale could point to his finding (1964, pp. 433–443) that 21 of 59 "healthy individuals" had developed feelings of "giving up" in the year prior to interview, and that 16 of these reported illnesses, though not serious ones, at those times. This obviously shows the care required in the selection of control groups.

Holmes and his associates (Rahe, Meyer, Smith, Kjaer, & T. H. Holmes, 1964) have developed a very promising improvement on the usual life history approach. Two advantages over less formal methods are that the data are obtained from a self-administered form, as opposed to an interview, thus eliminating most of the effects of the doctor-investigator on the results, and that the events asked about are fairly clear-cut. That is, recollections of a marriage, a bankruptcy, or a jail sentence are, one supposes, less liable to distortion than those of less discrete events such as a gradually developing coolness between spouses.

Developments so far reported include construction of a Social Readjustment Rating Scale, based on values assigned by groups of judges to 43 kinds of events in life histories. The judges were asked to weight these in terms of the intensity and length of time necessary to accommodate to them,

and were given an anchor point of "marriage" with which to compare the others. The resulting estimates are called Life Change Units (T. H. Holmes & Rahe, 1967; Masuda & T. H. Holmes, 1967). The lives of patients or research subjects can then be scored for total Life Change Units by adding the weights of all the events reported.

Many of the correlations of Life Change Unit scores with subsequent Physically described illnesses have not yet been published, but those now available are of the greatest importance in adding to the evidence that psychological stimuli produce disease.

Rahe, McKean, and Arthur (1967) studied the health records in military service of 50 Navy and Marine Corps personnel who had been discharged from the service because of psychiatric illness. The records included all kinds of illness, not only psychiatric, and also permitted estimation of number of Life Change Units in the subjects' lives. There were more Life Change Units in the 1-yr periods prior to major health changes than in the 1-yr periods prior to minor health changes, and more in the latter periods than the mean number for all years in the group. The differences were statistically significant. Another retrospective investigation (Rahe & Arthur, 1968), studying virtually the entire crews of three naval vessels, and relying on the men's memories of both health changes and life changes, found clustering of life changes both immediately before and immediately after periods of illness of all kinds. The authors' conclusion was that life changes caused illness, and also that illness produced life changes.

Such studies are more convincing if at least the illness records do not depend on the subjects' recollections. Rahe, McKean, and Arthur (1970) met this condition by collecting health data on what seem to have been essentially the same naval personnel (2684 men) from the official records of medical attention given them during cruises 6–8 months in duration. These data were then compared with the life events the men had reported before the cruise started, for the preceding 2-yr period. Only the 6-month period immediately before the cruise showed a significant positive correlation between Life Change Units and number of illnesses of all kinds during the cruise. The men were divided into decile subgroups according to their Life Change Units during that 6-month period; a positive linear relationship was then found between these decile groupings and the illness rates during the cruise. In short, the men with the highest life change scores before the cruise had the most illnesses during the cruise. T. S. Holmes and T. H. Holmes (1970) studied the relation between daily events and the minor illnesses and symptoms of everyday life that do not ordinarily lead to seeking medical attention. Their 80 subjects were students, laboratory technicians, and secretaries, not selected because they were patients, who kept records of their life events and symptoms over periods of 2 to 9 weeks. It was found that symptoms and minor illnesses were much more likely to occur on days of high than of low life change; supporting the finding of Rahe and Arthur (1968), high life change scores were also found on the day before and the day after a symptomatic day. There were significant positive correlations between the subjects' Life Change Unit scores and the frequency with which they had symptoms.

It should be clear, of course, that life change does not necessarily operate through psychological stimuli. There may be changes in diet, in exposure to pathogenic microorganisms, etc. The involvement of these mechanisms does not make the outcome less significant or less interesting; it simply eliminates the responses from those we are considering here. In any case, it is likely that the life changes themselves were the results of responses by the persons concerned to various psychological stimuli.

The Holmes technique helps to dispose of the criticism already mentioned, based on the occurrence of stresses in the lives of persons who do not manifest any of the diseases usually thought to be psychosomatic. If early results are confirmed, this objection can be simply refuted on empirical grounds. Another answer to it, based on Psycho-Physical specificity, will be discussed below. Finally, it may be pointed out that, no matter how many stressful events other persons have in their lives, such events may be etiologic in the illness of a particular patient under study, a possibility that can be tested experimentally (see the discussion below of the experimental interview technique).

One advantage of obtaining careful life histories of this sort is that they may be used for prospective purposes; i.e., the occurrence of stressful events may be ascertained before the population studied has shown any sign of illness. Prior knowledge prevents retrospective distortion resulting from what we call the illness (the particular manifestations that lead us to say that the person is ill) but it does *not* get away from the problems raised earlier about what is to be considered the first step in the illness. In other words, it is always possible that the illness caused the life change. Our willingness to believe that it did not will depend on considerations other than simple time relationships. For instance, the loss of a job because of frequent absences resulting from abdominal pain is one thing; on the other hand, the loss of a job because the company closed its factory would be interpreted as quite another, even though in the second case also the patient might have been having abdominal pain at the time. An increase in the severity of an illness—such as perforation of a peptic ulcer—would be more likely to be considered a *consequence* of the loss of the job in the second case than in the first. In the first, one might always say that the stomach process was simply following a course uninfluenced by the life change, even though in its entirety it might very well be a response to some other psychological stimulus or another event. The value of the experimental methods of investigation, discussed below, is that they provide much less equivocal evidence about causation.

It is well to mention here the warning by Mechanic and Volkart (1961), that the sick persons who consult physicians, i.e., become patients, may not be a random sample of all sick persons. They emphasize the importance of the "tendency to adopt the sick rôle" in determining who will be available for the usual clinical research, and therefore in biasing the research results.

This is a suitable place to introduce a preliminary consideration of specificity in psychosomatic medicine, although it will be discussed more thoroughly later. The establishment of one kind of specificity relation is strong evidence for the importance of psychological stimuli in the etiology of disease. The kind of specificity relation important here is between the Psychological and Physical descriptions of, respectively, two parts of a response. For the sake of clarity, it is well to point out that the precise parts of the response described Physically will not, in this instance, be those described Psychologically.

We need to consider first what evidence we require in order to say that an event of any kind is etiologic in an illness. The principles are the same, whether the event is exposure to a psychological stimulus, to a microorganism, or to a drug. *One* logical requirement is that there be at least some circumstances under which the occurrence of the event makes the probability of the occurrence of the disease greater than it is when the event does not occur. In the present context we want to be able to say this about exposure to psychological stimuli. It is not necessary to say it of *all* psychological stimuli but only of some subgroups of such stimuli. In other words, in order to assert that a disease occurs in response to psychological stimuli, we do not have to say that *all* of these stimuli have the same effect.

Other considerations will certainly be invoked before a conclusion about etiology is reached. As is repeatedly and tiresomely pointed out, an association between events does not of itself suffice to establish causation. However, the objection to the belief in the etiologic role of psychological stimuli with which we are now dealing is directed only to this "association" question.

The reasoning is quite parallel to that employed in connection with infectious disease. To say that a disease is caused by a virus does not imply that *all* viruses produce it. It does not even imply that all viruses indistinguishable to us as observers produce it, since there may be undiscovered differences among virus particles that appear identical to us. It also does not imply that exposure to the truly pathogenic virus will necessarily lead to disease in all persons at all times. Immunity may vary; there may be other concurrent exposures—to low or high temperatures, for instance; and, in general, an infinity of other variables may influence a person's response to the virus. What we do want to say is that, at least under some conditions, exposure to a virus increases the probability that the disease we are interested in will develop.

At this point, we are considering only nonexperi-

mental approaches to this question and, in particular, history-taking, i.e., obtaining retrospective data by talking with the patient or with persons who know him. The parallel in infectious disease is recovery of a suspected organism from the patient with the disease. A difference, not important for the present purpose, is that obtaining a history of an event directly from the person concerned tells us not only that there was exposure to it but also that there was some response to the event, that is to say, it was at least remembered. The recovery of a microorganism, on the other hand, does not necessarily mean that the person reacted to it at all; it may simply have been present and even multiplying, without influencing the patient's physiological processes in any way, in which case it was not a stimulus.

The relevance of establishing one kind of Psycho-Physical specificity is that it permits the following conclusion: Given the occurrence of a psychological stimulus that evokes a certain kind of Psychological response, the probability of a certain kind of Physical response is increased. The kind of specificity relation necessary is between a Physical disease and something Psychological that is clearly a response to a psychological stimulus. If there is an association between the Psychological response and a Physical disease, *and* if the Psychological response is to a psychological stimulus, then the natural conclusion is that the disease is likewise a response to a psychological stimulus.

The specificity-of-attitude proposal of Grace and Graham (1952), discussed in more detail in the next section, and to some extent the nuclear conflict theory of French and Alexander (Alexander, 1950), are assertions of specific Psycho-Physical relations in response to a psychological stimulus. *They are therefore also assertions that the diseases they deal with are responses to psychological stimuli.* Suppose that all persons with Disease A express some feeling, X, toward the respective events that occurred shortly before the onsets or exacerbations of the disease. Suppose also that persons with Disease B all express Feeling Y toward the respective events that occurred shortly before the onset or exacerbation of B. Feelings X and Y are clearly responses to psychological stimuli. The associations between A and X and B and Y therefore make A and B also responses to psychological stimuli. Note that if there were no specific connection between particular diseases, on the one hand, and particular Psychological responses to psychological stimuli, on the other, then the fact that the Psychological responses were to psychological stimuli would not provide any evidence that the diseases were responses to psychological stimuli. That is, if A and B were each equally associated with X and Y, then there would be no link between a psychological stimulus and either disease. It is also true that Psycho-Physical specificity tells us nothing about the role of psychological stimuli in Physical disease, unless the Psychological statement about the patient implies a reaction to such stimuli.

The argument can be summarized and put somewhat more formally as follows. To support the assertion that a psychological stimulus is etiologic to a disease, one wants evidence that there are circumstances in which, given a psychological stimulus of a specified kind, the probability of the occurrence of the disease is increased. The appropriate kind of Psycho-Physical specificity relation says that, given a particular illness, the probability that a particular Psychological statement about the person is true is greater than when some other illness is given. It is therefore also necessarily true in the patient sample studied that, given this kind of Psychological statement, the probability of a particular illness is greater than when some other Psychological statement is given. For example, given the "ulcer" attitude, the probability of ulcer is greater than if the "asthma" attitude is given. The kind of Psychological statement involved here describes the patient's response to a psychological stimulus. Therefore, given exposure to a psychological stimulus that elicits a particular Psychological response (attitude), the probability of occurrence of the associated disease is increased.

Strictly analogous reasoning is used for infectious disease, although it has become so familiar that its structure is not often explained. Suppose a patient has pharyngitis, and streptococci have been recovered from his throat. Many persons have been exposed to streptococci, and many even have them in the throat, without acquiring pharyngitis. How, therefore, does one know that the exposure to streptococci was responsible for this patient's disease? Very commonly, the investigator looks for antibodies to streptococci in the patient's serum. In this analogy antibodies correspond to the Psychological statement. They show that the patient responded to streptococci, which increases one's confidence that the pharyngitis was likewise a response to streptococci. One may therefore say that an exposure to streptococci *that leads to antibody production* increases the probability that pharyngitis will occur. Of course, no amount of reasoning based on the historical method of data-gathering can eliminate the intrinsic weaknesses of any nonexperimental investigation of causation. One could, for instance, suppose that the disease occurred quite independently of psychological stimuli, and that it so affected the patient that he produced a false account of a psychological stimulus and of a specific Psychological response to that stimulus. The only real answer to this problem is an experimental approach.

We have so far considered only the situation within the patient samples studied. It is possible to draw certain inferences about the whole population, even without assurance that the patients represent a random sample of all persons ill with the disease studied, and without knowing anything about patients with other diseases or about well persons. If the specificity relation is established in the patient sample for a variety of illnesses, it would require a sampling bias almost impossible to conceive, for the conclusion about the etiologic role of psychological stimuli to be overthrown by a study of the complete population. For this to occur, it would be necessary that the relation between attitude and disease in the population be such that it exactly undid the relation in the sample. A merely random assortment of diseases and attitudes in the unstudied population would still leave a slight preponderance of specific associations for the total population, which includes the sample. A specific relation between disease and psychological response, even though different from that of the sample, would still support the belief in the role of psychological stimuli.

2. Use of experimentally controlled stimuli The second chief class of evidence comes from experiments in which Physiological observations are made while the subject is reacting to psychological stimuli. In its simplest form the experiment produces the desired effect if a relevant reaction occurs. More often, the point is to show that *particular* psychological stimuli are responsible for the Physiological changes seen in the experiment, and hence, by inference, for the disease of which these Physiological changes are a part. This is done through the well-known and important technique of the *experimental interview,* which has been extensively used in the many investigations carried out by H. G. Wolff and S. Wolf and their group at Cornell University. The investigator chooses topics of conversation in accordance with his impressions, gained from prior knowledge of the patient's history, of the psychological stimuli that precipitated the attacks of whatever illness he is dealing with. He wishes to contrast the response to the presentation of these stimuli in symbolic form, i.e., the words of the interviewer, with the response to discussions of other events, not thought to be related to the illness. A large number of experiments of this kind are summarized in *Life Stress and Bodily Disease* (Wolff, 1950, pp. 1059–1094). Physiological variables that have been measured include gastric acidity, heart rate and rhythm, blood pressure, changes in the mucous membrane and the motility of the colon, changes in the nasal mucous membrane, concentration of glucose and ketone bodies in the blood, behavior of blood vessels in the skin, sebum secretion, etc.

The technique has sometimes been criticized on the grounds that the same Physiological variables are not measured in the "normal" person, an observation that the critics believe to be necessary as a "control." This is a misunderstanding. The purpose of the experiment is to show that, in *this* patient, the circumstances being discussed had something to do with bringing on an attack of his illness. In other words, the patient is his own control; the investigator compares the state of the stomach, for instance, when he is not discussing disturbing events, with the state when he is. For this purpose, there is no need to compare the patient with anybody else.

Another kind of psychological stimulus experiment is the exposure of all of a number of patients to the *same* stimulus. An example is the work of

Alexander and his associates (Alexander, Flagg, Foster, Clemens, & Blahd, 1961) in which a disturbing motion picture was shown to patients with hyperthyroidism. If one wishes to show, as these investigators did, that patients with one disease differ in their responses from those with another, or from healthy persons, it is of course necessary to have a control group. The results of their study are presented in detail later in this chapter.

Other experiments illustrate a different technique in which the same stimulus is applied to all members of a group of subjects (D. T. Graham, Kabler, & F. K. Graham, 1962; D. T. Graham, Stern, & Winokur, 1958; Stern, Winokur, D. T. Graham, & F. K. Graham, 1961). The stimuli were hypnotic suggestions of specific attitudes that the subjects were to adopt toward aspects of the experimental situation. Predicted Physiological responses were obtained when attitudes previously found to be associated with Raynaud's disease, with hives, or with essential hypertension were suggested. The reasoning involved, with respect to our present interest in showing that psychological stimuli can elicit disease, is that the experimenter's words produce "miniature attacks" of the disease. These experiments are discussed more fully later in this chapter.

3. Real-life stimuli   A third major line of investigation is the study of subjects exposed to "real-life" situations, rather than to verbal or visual symbols of them. The experimental interview itself can be used as a "real-life" stress if the interviewer behaves in a way that is intended to disturb the patient, perhaps by indicating doubt about his truthfulness.

The famous study by S. Wolf and H. G. Wolff (1947) of Tom, a man with a gastric fistula, discussed later in this chapter, is of this type. So is the work of G. L. Engel, Reichsman, and Segal (1956), showing the changes in the behavior of an infant girl's stomach in response to changes in the person interacting with her or to changes in the behavior of that person. Both of these studies also contained elements of what have been called "experiments of nature"; i.e., some of the observed reactions occurred in response to events that had not been deliberately planned by the observers. In such circumstances, however, it is hard to be sure that the reported stimulus really was the significant element in evoking the observed bodily changes. Ax (1953) and Schachter (1957) carried out more precisely designed experiments, in which the subjects were exposed to situations in the laboratory arranged to appear accidental. They are discussed later.

It is also possible to follow changes in Physiological variables in groups of persons as they meet naturally occurring stimuli (not arranged for purposes of the investigation). One example is the report by Wertlake, Wilcox, Haley, and Peterson (1958) that serum cholesterol in medical students was higher on examination days than on control days. Another is the finding of elevated blood pressures in soldiers after combat (J. D. P. Graham, 1945), and in persons exposed to the Texas City explosion (Ruskin, Beard, & Schaffer, 1948).

4. Epidemiologic evidence The next class of evidence is the association between such events as wars or economic depressions and differences in disease incidence. It is an extension of "real-life" evidence, but knowledge of the circumstances is less precise, with consequently greater doubt about what stimuli were really responsible for any observed differences. Also, the measurement of changes in the population is much more difficult, especially with respect to "before" as opposed to "after" measurements. Halliday (1948) gives examples of the method. One variation of it is the comparison of the prevalence of illness in various social groups, exemplified in the study of duodenal versus gastric ulcer in different social classes (Doll & Jones, 1951), or of the frequency of myocardial infarction among doctors with practices differing in degree of stress (Russek, 1960).

5. Prediction of the course of illness The last kind of evidence for the etiologic relevance of psychological stimuli is the successful prediction of the course and outcome of illness by considering the patient's life situation and his success in adapting to it (e.g., Querido, 1959). This approach is of relatively little interest to psychophysiologists, and therefore will not be further considered here.

THE SPECIFICITY PROBLEM AND OTHER ISSUES

Almost all questions that have been asked in psychosomatic research up to this time fall under one of two chief headings. The first, which has just been discussed in detail, is the effort to show that external sensory stimuli (psychological stimuli) are significant in evoking responses that are called "diseases"; the second is the specificity problem, which can be subdivided in various ways. The etiologic question had to be dealt with first because it is central, even to the definition of psychosomatic medicine. The specificity question will be considered in the present section, together with other issues and problems that have received more than passing attention in the psychosomatic literature. While there are others that are logically entitled to places here, the research and intellectual effort devoted to them has been too small to justify including them.

The specificity problem may be thought of, in its broadest sense, as an inquiry into possible predictable relationships between "medical diseases" on the one hand, and variables thought of as "psychological" on the other. There is said to be "specificity" when the variables within classes are not considered to have any particular ordering; if they were ordered, we would have numerical relations.

Specificity statements in psychophysiology and psychosomatic medicine have been concerned with five classes of variables. In most psychophysiological discussions of specificity problems, these are reduced to three; namely, stimuli, persons (individuals), and responses. Two more are used for clinical statements, made by subdividing "persons" and "responses" into Psychological variables and Physical variables. By these we mean variables that are described by statements in Psychological or Physical terms. In a clinical context, the responses usually are "diseases." This subdivision, which gives us the total of five variables, helps to clarify the problem of specificity and also the more general problem of the logical relations among nonpsychiatric medical fields, psychiatry, and psychosomatic medicine.

Theoretically, one could look for predictable

relations among any of these sets of variables. In psychosomatic discussions, however, one typically starts with some member or members of the *disease* category and then attempts to predict members of other sets. In short, the question usually is: "Given that this person has Disease X, what will I find out about the stimulus that activated it, or about his personality (i.e., the Psychological description of the person), or other things?" In strictly psychophysiological settings the question is the same, except that one starts with a response, described Physically, such as an increase in the heart rate.

The two kinds of specificity relationships that have been discussed in Psycho-Physiological writing are stimulus-response (S-R) specificity and individual-response (I-R) specificity, also called stereotypy (B. T. Engel, 1960; J. I. Lacey & B. C. Lacey, 1958). The first of these is a statement that one can find the same predictable relationships in different persons between *stimuli* and Physiologically described responses. In clinical terms, there is stimulus specificity to the extent that the same stimuli elicit the same diseases in different persons. Individual-response specificity, or stereotypy, is a statement that a given individual tends to respond similarly to a variety of stimuli. As Sternbach (1966) has pointed out, this can be regarded as a manifestation of a "set" to respond in a certain way. Clinically, this is saying that a person gets the same disease no matter what different things happen to him. Put in this way, the statement makes no distinction between Psychological and Physical descriptions of the person.

Despite what is sometimes thought, S-R and I-R specificity statements are not the only kinds possible. Many specificity statements in psychosomatic medicine have nothing to do with either of them. One productive approach is to search for specific relations between Psychological and Physical statements about the person's responses. These relations could be present or absent, quite independent of the presence of S-R specificity, I-R specificity, or both.

S-R specificity is seldom seriously considered in psychosomatic medicine, although it is a theoretical possibility: it certainly exists in infectious diseases and in responses to drugs. It appears at present that knowledge only of psychological stimulus situations, without information about previous response history, is of almost no help in predicting what illnesses a person will develop; nor can one, knowing what disease is present, guess what stimulus evoked it. While not usually clinically important, S-R specificity was shown in experimental settings that were suggested by clinical observations (D. T. Graham, 1962).

Individual-response specificity is quite commonly proposed in clinical contexts. One simple form is the "organ-weakness" theory, the idea that a person has a weak or otherwise predisposed part of the body in which illness develops, no matter what the stressful situation may be. No special characteristic of the reacting person is named. Other forms of I-R specificity theories may associate some attribute of the person with his tendency to react in a stereotyped way. Attempts to find "personality types" typical of persons with specified diseases also exemplify I-R specificity theory. The early efforts of Dunbar (1947b) and Gildea (1949) in this direction should be mentioned. Although such formulations have not fared especially well, there is nevertheless a good deal of evidence in at least partial support of this kind of relation; much of the evidence is discussed under the separate disease headings. Another kind of I-R specificity is that between body types (i.e., Physical descriptions of persons) and diseases. This relationship has never aroused enough intensive investigative effort to establish it securely on any broad basis. On the other hand, if we look with a lens of higher resolving power, there seem to be many kinds of Physically described characteristics that have more or less specific relations with the other Physically described characteristics that define the disease. For instance, persons with high levels of plasma pepsinogen are more likely to have peptic ulcers than those with lower levels; there are chemical tests for a prediabetic state; and lability of blood pressure is said to predict the later occurrence of essential hypertension.

A third kind of specificity is Psychological-Physical specificity applied to an organism at the time it is responding. This is a search for predictable relations between Physical statements to make about the response and Psychological statements to make about it. Identical events need not be included in each description: Psychological may be used for describing what a person says, and Physical for changes in his viscera. This kind of specificity is implied in statements about specific Physiological changes in each emotion (Grace & D. T. Graham, 1952; D. T. Graham, Stern, & Winokur, 1960; Wenger, F. N. Jones, & M. H. Jones, 1956), or about activation of a particular nuclear conflict (Alexander, 1950) in association with the onset or exacerbation of an illness, or about a specific attitude associated with exacerbation of a disease (Grace & D. T. Graham, 1952; D. T. Graham et al., 1962).

Unlike these examples, a statement that each patient with a given disease has a particular nuclear conflict, without a necessary association between the activation of the conflict and the disease, belongs under the heading of I-R specificity.

There are still other assertions of specificity possible. We could suppose that predictable relations could be found between stimuli and Psychological descriptions of the response, or between Psychological or Physical descriptions of the person and Psychological descriptions of the response. Such possibilities are not of major concern in a chapter about psychosomatic medicine. More to our present purpose, we could look for evidence that a given person showed stimulus specificity, thus giving predictability for any single individual, but that different persons each had their own different characteristic stimulus-response relations. In other words, we should then know what each person would do in response to a given stimulus but we could not predict from this knowledge how other persons would react. This state of affairs could be called individual S-R specificity. We might predict, for instance, what illness a man would develop when he lost a job if we knew how he had reacted when he lost previous jobs. It is also conceivable that there exists individual Psychological-Physical specificity in the response. This would be the case if, for any single individual, there were predictable relations between appropriate Psychological and Physical statements about the response, but these relations differed from person to person.

It is also possible, and some work of this sort has been done, to describe persons in another language, the Sociological. Specific relations may then be sought between diseases and Sociological variables such as social class. This approach has been used as evidence that psychological stimuli are etiologic to disease, and will be discussed in that section.

There is some evidence supporting several of the possible kinds of specificity. Much of it is mentioned in the discussion of the various illnesses. It is also desirable to look at some of the overall formulations of specificity that have been offered. The "symptom specificity" of Malmo et al. (Malmo & Shagass, 1949; Malmo, Shagass, & Davis, 1950) is *in part* a statement of I-R specificity, although they also included in the term a very different idea, referring to psychophysical specificity in the response. As they used it, the term includes not only the tendency for one person to react always with the same organ (muscle rather than heart, or one muscle group instead of another) but also the specific association of symptoms with particular physiologic mechanisms. An example is a patient's report of "tightness" in the head when the muscles of the head showed increased electrical potential. The nuclear conflict theory of French and Alexander (Alexander, 1950) and the "body-image" views of Fisher and Cleveland (1958) are other examples of I-R specificity. A further refinement of I-R specificity is the position of Weiner, Thaler, Reiser, and Mirsky (1957), in connection with peptic ulcer. They associated ulcer with the Psychological characteristic, "oral conflicts," and the Physical characteristic, "high plasma pepsinogen." In short, they reported a specific association among three variables, two of which are attributes of a person. Wenger's (1966) work also illustrates a kind of I-R specificity. He used a number of autonomic variables to establish in human subjects "scores of autonomic balance," intended to reflect varying degrees of sympathetic or parasympathetic dominance. Later, he found that various mixed patterns occurred, which were not described well by the single autonomic score. The five patterns now recognized are relative sympathetic dominance, relative parasympathetic dominance, autonomic balance, a so-called beta pattern, and a pattern characteristic of patients with tuberculosis. There is some tendency to specific association between these patterns and various psychosomatic diseases, either present at the time of testing or developing later. Patients with peptic ulcer, for instance, showed most frequently the beta pattern, while patients with neurodermatitis (included under "eczema" in the present chapter) showed most frequently the sympathetic pattern. A large number of subjects in all disease categories had, however, unclassified mixed patterns (Wenger, Clemens, & Cullen, 1962). As Wenger points out, the connection between these patterns and their associated illnesses is obscure.

A study by Ring (1957), which has not received the attention that would have been expected, provides strong support for I-R specificity in psychosomatic disease. He interviewed a total of 134 patients who were in one of 15 possible categories (rheumatoid arthritis, peptic ulcer, diabetes, hypertension, hyperthyroidism, coronary occlusion, ulcerative colitis, migraine, asthma, neurodermatitis, dysmenorrhea, degenerative arthritis, glaucoma, backache, or some other disease). After an interview of 15–25 min, the examiner decided in which of the 15 categories a patient belonged. There were varying numbers of patients in each category. Each patient "had his entire body and extremities covered" to prevent the examiner's receiving visual diagnostic clues, and patients were instructed not to mention symptoms, treatment, etc. If a patient made such a statement and it helped the examiner, the case was removed from the study.

Patients were divided into four personality categories, apparently established by the author's previous observations of other patients. The categories and the illnesses believed to be associated with them were: (a) excessive reactors (coronary occlusion, peptic ulcer, degenerative arthritis); (b) deficient reactors (rheumatoid arthritis, ulcerative colitis, neurodermatitis; (c) restrained reactors (hypertension, hyperthyroidism, migraine, asthma, diabetes; and (d) unknown (dysmenorrhea, glaucoma, backache). The decision about placement of a patient in one of these four groups was based on the answers to the five following questions.

1. If you were sitting on a park bench on a nice warm spring day, very well relaxed and enjoying the sunshine, watching the birds flit around on the grass in front of you, and someone just your size, age, and sex, whom you have never seen, walked up, said nothing, and kicked you in the shins, what would you do?

2. If you were given your choice of a great deal of any one of these four things, and very little of the others, which would you want a lot of: (a) religion, (b) education, (c) money, or (d) opportunity to help other people? Why?
3. If suddenly you were awarded (a large sum of money), what would you do with it?
4. What is your greatest ambition? Greatest fear? Greatest anger? Greatest enjoyment?
5. What kind of people do you like most? Dislike most?

How individual illnesses within the groups were distinguished from each other is not reported.

The author's success rate of 66% (88 patients) in making the correct diagnosis as his first choice is most impressive. Further, most (27) of those incorrect on the first choice, were correct on the second choice, and seven were correct on the third. Statistical significance is not given and would be a little complex to calculate, since it depends on the distribution of diseases and on the distribution of diagnostic choices, but the outcome is obviously well outside the range of chance expectation. One may wonder whether the examiner could unconsciously have received some clues from unintended sources; nevertheless, it is a noteworthy study and it is surprising that it has apparently not stimulated further work.

The final specificity position, Psycho-Physical specificity in the response, refers to an association between Physical and Psychological descriptions of the response, i.e., the disease. To avoid confusion, it should be emphasized that we are not talking about descriptions of identical events but of two different sets of events, each of which is a part of the total response. One set, usually but not always the verbal output of the patient, is described Psychologically; the other, described Physically, is the group of findings that define the disease. This kind of relation is completely independent of either I-R or S-R specificity.

In general, any formulation that associates a specific emotion with a particular disease is an example of this sort of specificity position. For instance, if it is said that "repressed anger" is associated with essential hypertension, the presence of "repressed anger" is inferred from the patient's words, perhaps from certain facial expressions, etc.; the hypertension is discovered by sphygmomanometer. There seem to have been no systematic efforts to produce a general specificity theory correlating names of emotions with disease, although individual exceptions are mentioned in the subsequent discussions of individual diseases. However, an evaluation of such formulations depends heavily on the definition of "emotion," so that the views about to be considered are essentially examples of this approach.

The position of Schmale is the simplest possible example under this heading, since in effect it divides the entire population into only two groups, sick and well. In his original paper he reported on 42 almost consecutive hospital admissions of "medical" patients (1958); later (1964) he reported on 190 (apparently not including the original 42). They, of course, had many kinds of illnesses, though these are not specified. Of them, 151 reported, and/or the investigators interpreted interview data to mean, that they had "experienced a stress to which they had reacted with feelings of 'giving up'." "Giving up" could be either "helplessness" or "hopelessness." Of 59 healthy subjects who were studied, only 29 reported feelings of "giving up" in the year prior to interview. The difference between the two groups by the chi-square test is highly significant.

French and Alexander's nuclear conflict theory has already been mentioned under I-R specificity. It can also be thought of as a theory of Psycho-Physical specificity in the response, if emphasis is placed on activation of the specific conflict at the time of exacerbation of the illness. The conflicts proposed by the theory to be associated with various illnesses are discussed in detail in the sections on individual diseases. For ease of reference, they are given here, sometimes in abbreviated form (Alexander, 1950). They are based in varying degrees on the studies of Alexander and his associates.

1. Nervous vomiting. Intense feelings of guilt motivated by aggressive, grabbing, incorporating tendencies. The nervous vomiting is the expression of guilt feelings aroused by these wishes.
2. Duodenal ulcer. Frustration of oral receptive longings leading to oral aggressive response, followed by overcompensation by successful accomplishment in responsible activities, leading to increased unconscious oral-dependent cravings as reactions to excessive effort and concentration; or, prolonged frustration of oral receptive longings, with repression of these wishes.
3. Ulcerative colitis. Frustrated tendency to carry out an obligation, and frustrated ambition to accomplish something which requires a concentrated expenditure of energy. Alexander appears not to distinguish between ulcerative colitis and other forms of diarrhea. The specific dynamic pattern listed for diarrhea in general is: frustration of oral dependent longings, leading to oral aggressive responses, with overcompensation by the urge to give (restitution) and to accomplish, followed by inhibition and failure of the effort to give and accomplish.
4. Constipation. "I cannot expect anything from anybody, therefore I do not need to give anything. I must hold on to what I have."
5. Asthma. Excessive unresolved dependence upon the mother, a dependence that is a wish to be encompassed or protected. Asthma occurs when there is a threat of separation of the patient from the protective mother. It represents a suppressed cry for the mother.
6. Essential hypertension. Hostile competitive tendencies leading to intimidation, due to fear of retaliation, and failure, with consequent increase of dependent longings, leading to inferiority feelings, leading to reactivation of hostile competitiveness, leading to anxiety and resultant inhibition of aggressive hostile impulses.
7. Migraine. Repressed hostile impulses, perhaps when the repression or inhibition occurs during the planning and preparation for a hostile attack.
8. Urticaria. Inhibited dependent longing for a parental object, with suppression of weeping.
9. Eczema. (In part) Showing the body in order to obtain attention, love, and favor (i.e., exhibitionism) used as a weapon in competition, leading to arousal of guilt feelings, leading to punishment inflicted on the skin.
10. Hyperthyroidism. Frustration of dependent longings and threat to security, leading to unsuccessful premature attempts to identify with the object of dependent cravings, leading to an effort toward premature self-sufficiency and an effort to help others, followed by failure of these strivings.
11. Rheumatoid arthritis. Restrictive parental influence leading to rebellion against restrictions, with repression of rebellious tendencies followed by expression of rebellion in sports and outdoor activities, followed by expression of hostility while both serving and controlling the environment in later life, together with rejection of the feminine role in women. Arthritis occurs when the successful pattern of serving and dominating the environment is interrupted.

These ideas have been very influential in the development of psychosomatic medicine, but they have resisted testing and verification by experimental or other methods of the kind usually thought of as "objective." Experimental approaches seem to have been limited to work on hyperthyroidism, and are discussed below under that heading. It has also been possible to use formal psychological tests in attempts to evaluate the hypothesis, with reasonable success in at least the case of duodenal ulcer (Weiner, Thaler, Reiser, & Mirsky, 1962). One difficulty that always arises is the decision about the extent to which results of such procedures as Rorschach testing are equivalent to the concepts derived from psychoanalytic interviewing. The base of evidence for these ideas is still largely interpretations by psychoanalysts of the utterances of patients. Of course, some of the latter have been reported literally in various publications, but such evidence is necessarily difficult to give in sufficient detail to permit a reader to be sure that he is seeing all the relevant facts. Complete transcriptions of analytic sessions are too long to reproduce; without them, there is always the danger of unintentionally biased selection by the author. Even if this problem is solved, there remains the possibility that the analyst has unwittingly influenced the patient to produce data in support of the analyst's hypothesis.

A systematic attempt to solve the problem of selection of evidence, by obtaining agreement among judges rating entire interviews, was carried out for many years at the Chicago Institute for Psychoanalysis, where the specificity formulations just given originated. The results were not published until 1968 (Alexander, French, & Pollock, 1968). All of the interviewers knew the diagnoses for the patients they interviewed, and also knew the hypotheses under investigation. Unintentional illegitimate influence on the patient was therefore not excluded. In addition, a new difficulty was introduced, the possible transmission of cues from the interviewer to the judges by the kinds of questions he asked. An elaborate retrospective study produced reasonably good evidence that such cues did not account for most of the judges' decisions. A significant omission was study of the effect on the patient of the interviewer's knowledge. Perhaps the only satisfactory way to deal with that problem is to employ, as D. T. Graham et al. (1962) did, an interviewer who is unaware of the specificity formulations being tested.

The Chicago study included interviews with 83 patients, each with one of the following illnesses: bronchial asthma, neurodermatitis, rheumatoid arthritis, essential hypertension, ulcerative colitis, duodenal ulcer, or hyperthyroidism. Each disease was represented by at least 5 patients of each sex. The psychological formulations tested, as they are given in the report of the study, sometimes differ slightly from those listed above. Two of the differences are that, for ulcerative colitis, the hopelessness of a struggle for achievement is emphasized, and for hyperthyroidism, there is a shift of emphasis to make fear of death the central theme.

Interviews were recorded, edited to remove references identifying diseases, and submitted to from 5 to 9 judges, all of them psychoanalysts, who knew the hypotheses under investigation. Each judge listed the most likely diagnosis for each patient: 41% of these diagnoses were correct. Further, diagnoses were correct to a statistically significant degree in 13 of the 14 categories created by dividing all the cases according to disease, and then considering separately male and female patients with each disease. Female patients with ulcer were the only exceptional group. Seventy of the interviews were judged also by a panel of nonpsychiatric physicians (internists), selected "partly on the basis of lack of familiarity with the 'specificity' formulations," who attempted to make diagnoses from any standard medical clues remaining in the edited interview transcripts. Their success rate was only 22%. The study therefore supports the specificity hypotheses that inspired it.

Another specificity view was proposed by Grace and D. T. Graham (1952) and subsequently tested experimentally and clinically. The original empirical finding was that each different psychogenic (in the sense of being a response to psychological stimuli) illness or symptom was associated with a *specific attitude* expressed by the patient toward the stimulus situation that evoked the illness. The hypothesis derived from these observations was that the same specific associations occur in all other patients. A more sweeping hypothesis, not in fact formally proposed, would be that similar specific associations occur in patients with all psychogenic diseases. It is important to distinguish between a set of alleged facts and the various theories related to these facts, but in what follows we shall use the term "specificity-of-attitude hypothesis" a little loosely to refer to any of the ideas associated with this approach.

An *attitude* was defined as a statement containing two parts: (a) what the person feels is happening to him, and (b) what he wishes to do about it. The attitudes reported for the various illnesses, together with some added later, have been summarized (D. T. Graham et al., 1962) as follows:

1. Urticaria (hives): felt he was taking a beating and was helpless to do anything about it.
2. Ulcerative colitis: felt he was being injured and degraded and wished he could get rid of the responsible agent.
3. Eczema: felt he was being frustrated and could do nothing about it except take it out on himself.
4. Acne: felt he was being picked on or at and wanted to be let alone.
5. Psoriasis: felt there was a constant gnawing at him and that he had to put up with it.
6. Asthma and rhinitis: felt left out in the cold and wanted to shut the person or situation out.
7. Hyperthyroidism: felt he might lose somebody or something he loved and took care of, and wanted to prevent loss of the loved person or object.
8. Vomiting: felt something wrong had happened, usually something for which he felt responsible, and wished it hadn't happened, and wanted to undo it.
9. Duodenal ulcer: felt deprived of what was due him and wanted to get even.
10. Constipation: felt in a situation from which nothing good could come but kept on with it grimly.
11. Essential hypertension: felt threatened with harm and had to be ready for anything.
12. Migraine: felt something had to be achieved and then relaxed after the effort.
13. Multiple sclersosis: felt he was forced to undertake some kind of activity, especially hard work, and wanted not to, but to have help and support.
14. Metabolic edema (idiopathic edema of females): felt she was carrying a heavy load and wanted somebody else to carry all or part of it.
15. Rheumatoid arthritis: felt tied down and wanted to get free.
16. Raynaud's disease: wanted to take hostile gross motor action.
17. Regional enteritis: felt he had received something harmful and wanted to get rid of it.
18. Low backache: wanted to run away.

The nature of the evidence supporting the individual statements varies from disease to disease. The original formulations were based on statements made by patients in clinical interviews, chiefly conducted for therapeutic purposes. In the original report, 128 patients were included, with varying numbers in 10 diagnostic categories. Acne, psoriasis, hyperthyroidism, multiple sclerosis, metabolic edema, rheumatoid arthritis, and regional enteritis were added later, without enumerating instances. In any case the conviction carried by this form of reporting is low, for the reasons given in connection with Alexander's work (1950) on nuclear conflicts. It is therefore desirable to proceed to other kinds of evidence. The first to consider is carefully and systematically collected clinical data, at which the study of the Chicago Institute group was also aimed. D. T. Graham et al. (1962) conducted two interview studies with hospitalized patients. In the first there were 16 patients with 8 diseases: essential hypertension, bronchial asthma, duodenal ulcer, eczema, hyperthyroidism, multiple sclerosis, rheumatoid arthritis, and ulcerative colitis. In the second study there were 20 patients with 10 diseases, the 8 just listed plus migraine and metabolic edema. Half of the patients were interviewed by a psychologist unfamiliar with the specific predictions of the hypothesis (blind interviews). The other half, matched for disease, were interviewed by one of the authors of the hypothesis, who of course knew what he was looking for (nonblind interviews). The interviews were tape-recorded and the transcripts edited to remove references identifying diseases. The edited transcripts were then submitted to two physician and two nonphysician judges. The judges selected from the above list of 18 attitudes the 3 most like that expressed in each interview. They also ranked all 18 attitudes in the order of their applicability to the patient.

The percentage of predicted choices was significantly greater than the chance expectation in both studies and in both blind and nonblind interviews. The predicted attitude was judged to be among the three most prominent in an interview in 28% of the blind interviews in the first study, and in 48.5% of the blind interviews in the second; corresponding figures for nonblind interviews were, as might be expected, higher: 38% and 62% for the two studies separately. Three judges listed among their top three choices the predicted attitudes significantly often from the blind interviews, and all four judges did so from the nonblind. Judges showed significant agreement with one another.

In the companion procedure of ranking the entire 18 attitudes, the judges ranked a particular attitude lower (i.e., rated it more applicable) when the patient had the associated disease than when he did not. The ranks for attitudes predicted by the hypothesis were significantly lower in the blind interviews of the second study (4.75 versus 9.0) and in the nonblind interviews of both studies (5.0 versus 9.25, 2.0 versus 10.0). A physician who did not know the attitude hypothesis was able to make correct diagnoses as often as the judges selected the predicted attitudes but his correct interviews were *not,* in general, the same as those of the judges.

It was therefore concluded that different psychosomatic diseases are associated with different attitudes. It is, of course, obvious that the fit between the predicted and found attitudes was far short of perfect, although statistically satisfactory levels of significance were reached. It is also true that, although one may say that the hypothesis as a whole was supported, it is not possible to say just which of the attitude-disease associations have been corroborated, since the individual pairs were not evaluated statistically.

Since there were 10 diseases in the study, there were 10 attitudes that the hypothesis predicted would be present. For what it is worth, each of these 10 attitudes was chosen more often by the judges for interviews in which the hypothesis called for its presence than for other interviews. Similarly, each of the 10 was given a lower rank (i.e., in the predicted direction) for interviews in which the hypothesis called for it than for other interviews. These differences in choices and in ranks were sometimes small, however.

The hypothesis has also been tested by the experimental approach. In a series of three experiments (D. T. Graham et al., 1962; D. T. Graham, Stern, & Winokur, 1958; Stern, Winokur, D. T. Graham, & F. K. Graham, 1961), three of the attitudes were suggested to hypnotized subjects, while appropriate physiological measurements were made. In other words, the measurements were of variables relevant to the diseases thought to be associated with the attitudes. The attitudes used were those for Raynaud's disease, urticaria, and

essential hypertension; the physiological measurements were skin temperature and arterial blood pressure. In Raynaud's disease the skin temperature is low; in urticaria it is high. In essential hypertension, the blood pressure is high. In the experiments, then, the expectation was that suggesting Raynaud's attitude would evoke a reduction in skin temperature; that suggesting the urticaria attitude would evoke an increase in skin temperature; and that suggesting the hypertension attitude would evoke an increase in blood pressure, especially the diastolic pressure.

In the first series of experiments, it was found that suggesting the Raynaud's attitude produced a steady decline in the skin temperature of the back of the hand, while suggesting the hives attitude produced, after an initial drop, a steady rise in skin temperature. Statistical analysis showed that the differences between temperatures during the control periods prior to the attitude suggestion were not significant but that the differences between the curves during the 10-min period of attitude suggestions were significant after the third minute (D. T. Graham, Stern, & Winokur, 1958).

The second series of experiments included suggestions of the attitude associated with hypertension, as well as the attitudes associated with hives and Raynaud's disease. Problems in interpretation arose because the behavior of skin temperature during the control periods preceding the various attitude suggestions varied. Statistically significant differences in the direction predicted by the hypothesis were found in three of five possible physiological comparisons; the other two comparisons were in the predicted direction. Of 10 comparisons for which no predictions were made, 1 could not be tested because of technical difficulties in recording respiratory data; only 1 showed a significant difference between periods of attitude suggestion and this with only 1 of 2 measures of change; the remaining 8 showed no statistical difference (Stern, Winokur, D. T. Graham, & F. K. Graham, 1961).

In the third series of experiments, the experimental design consisted of a double, 2 × 2, Latin square. This permitted analysis of variance for effects of attitude suggestion, of experimental day (first or second), order of presentation of attitude, intersubject differences, and differences between 2 experimenters. The 2 attitudes used in the study were those associated with hives and essential hypertension. The 5 Physiological measures used were the skin temperature, diastolic and systolic blood pressures, heart rate, and respiratory rate. The specificity-of-attitude hypothesis predicted that there would be a rise in the skin temperature in response to the hives attitude suggestion greater than the rise, if any, which occurred in response to the hypertension attitude suggestion; similarly it predicted that, in response to the hypertension attitude suggestion, there would be a rise in the diastolic blood pressure greater than the rise, if any, which occurred in response to the hives attitude suggestion. The subjects were 20 male volunteer university students. Measures of change during the attitude suggestion period were the mean absolute change, maximal rise, and rate of change per minute. Statistically significant differences in predicted directions were found for the two variables, diastolic blood pressure and skin temperature, for which predictions were made, in all three of the methods of measuring such differences. No differences were found for the variables for which there was no prediction of differential effect. Further, there were no significant differences in any of the variables in the control periods preceding the attitude suggestions.

It must be emphasized that these experiments all tested the effect on Physiological variables of *suggesting* the attitudes, that is, of administering particular *stimuli*. They did not test the effect of such suggestions on the adoption of attitudes, and they have no bearing on the question whether attitudes cause Physiological changes, or the reverse is true.

In addition to supporting the specificity-of-attitude theory, these data show that there is *stimulus specificity*. Since each subject received both attitude suggestions in counterbalanced order, differences in Physiological response must have been the consequence of stimulus differences (D. T. Graham et al., 1962).

Hives and hypertension attitude suggestion were given to unhypnotized subjects in two experiments carried out by F. K. Graham and Kunish (1965). In the first, the design and procedure of the hypnotic

experiment just discussed was employed with 20 subjects, and differential responses in skin temperature and blood pressure were not obtained. In the second, in which 40 subjects took part, the procedure was modified to elicit greater involvement of the subjects, and differential responses in the directions predicted by the hypothesis were found. These were statistically significant for maximal change in skin temperature, but not for change in blood pressure. Semantic differential ratings by subjects of the degree to which they succeeded in feeling the suggested attitudes did not correlate with Physiological changes.

There has been some additional support of the specificity-of-attitude hypothesis in connection with the development of inguinal hernia (Rahe & Holmes, 1965) and with skin temperature (Gottlieb, Gleser, & Gottschalk, 1967; Tjossem, Leider, Deisher, Holmes, & Ripley, 1959). An experimental study in which the Raynaud's and hives attitudes were suggested to hypnotized subjects was conducted by Gottlieb, Gleser, and Gottschalk (1967). They found differences in the predicted direction in the responses to these suggestions. The interpretation is a little more difficult because, during their control period before the suggestions were made, the skin temperature was rising. The investigators concluded that suggesting the hives attitude evoked a rise in the skin temperature and suggestion of the Raynaud's attitude caused no consistent change. In fact the results could be interpreted equally well as showing no change with the hives suggestion but a fall (i.e., a sharply decreased rate of rise) with the Raynaud's suggestion.

Kogan, Dorpat, and Holmes (1965) have discussed methodological problems in ascertaining whether, and to what degree, an attitude is present. In attempting to construct rating scales for nine of the attitudes, they found that, when medical students assigned various statements to one or another attitude, there was very substantial overlapping, so that most items were assigned to more than one attitude. A cluster analysis showed that the attitudes appeared to belong to three groups; the authors suggest that the cluster composed of the attitudes for backache, asthma and rhinitis, diarrhea, and vomiting corresponds to Rosenzweig's class of ego-defensive responses to frustration. The cluster composed of the attitudes for urticaria, eczema, and duodenal ulcer appears to belong to the class of obstacle-dominated responses, and the cluster composed of the attitudes for constipation and for headache to the class of need-persistive responses. (They attribute the classification of responses to Rosenzweig, 1938. It seems not to be included in the reference they cite.)

Emotion

Because it is so common to hear that psychosomatic medicine is the study of diseases with emotional causes, it will be worthwhile to comment on the concept "emotion," without analyzing it exhaustively. An emotion is simply a state of the organism, given a name in the Psychological language. Why some states are considered emotions, and others not, is not always clear. One criterion appears to be that emotions are responses to psychological stimuli. The question of whether a disease is caused by an emotion is nothing but a special form of the general "state" problem of etiology treated earlier.

We are free to refer to "emotional causation," either when we know that a psychological stimulus is etiologically important or when we believe that a Psychological state is important in the development of the illness, depending on the meaning we choose to assign to "emotional causation." However, there are very grave difficulties in deciding that one state is the cause of another state; furthermore, it is not obvious that this is a vital question.

It is, however, important to recognize that the question of specificity in psychosomatic disease is essentially the same as the question of whether different emotions have different Physiological concomitants. To approach this question, it is necessary first to define "emotion" precisely enough to permit a test. It has been pointed out (Grace & D. T. Graham, 1952; D. T. Graham, Stern, & Winokur, 1960) that suitably defining "emotion" leads to the hypothesis that each emotion has its own specific set of Physiological processes, and also that each psychosomatic illness may be regarded as part of a specific emotion, different for each illness. Both of these assertions are consequences of the specificity-of-attitude hypothesis in psychosomatic disease.

The exact form of the statement chosen will depend on whether one thinks of the peripheral Physiological changes being measured as part of the same state, indicated usually by verbal behavior, that is called the "emotion," or whether one thinks of them as making up a separate state. If they are thought of as a separate state, one is considering their association with the central "emotional" state. In the first case, one will say that there are specific peripheral Physiological changes *in* each emotion; in the second, that there are specific Physiological changes *associated with* each emotion. Either way, the specificity-of-attitude hypothesis asserts that there is Psycho-Physiological specificity in emotion, that each emotion has its own unique set of bodily changes.

The attitudes just discussed can all be looked on as refinements of the names of usually recognized emotions, permitting finer subdivisions. For instance, "anger" can be examined more closely to see what the person is angry at, and what action he wishes to take. One then finds, to the extent that the specificity-of-attitude hypothesis is substantiated, that one can say either that each emotion has its own specific Physiological concomitants or that there are different specific Physiological changes *in* each emotion. One obstacle to recognizing the relation between this approach to disease, and the question of specificity of Physiological changes in emotions seems to be the failure to recognize that diseases do not suddenly appear full blown, or get into the body like implanted foreign objects, but are either consequences of Physiological processes or names for those processes themselves. This conclusion about the specificity of Physiological changes in different emotions is strengthened by the number of emotional states recognized by the attitude theory, which provides some advantages over the same conclusion reached by Ax (1953), working with two emotional states, fear and anger.

Homeostasis and Adaptation

The concept of homeostasis has been frequently invoked in connection with health and disease, and particularly with psychosomatic disease, but it is not always clearly defined. That is, it implies that something about the organism is to be kept constant but is often stated as though the organism were trying to keep *everything* constant. Maintaining constancy in one respect, however, may require variation in others. For instance, if the plasma pH is to be kept fairly constant despite variations in the amount of carbon dioxide entering the plasma, the concentration of bicarbonate must change. In short, if homeostasis is to be a meaningful concept, one must specify what is being maintained.

The body temperature is often thought of as being kept within a narrow range but it certainly rises in many conditions. Even if we leave out of consideration those states usually called illnesses, we can consider exercise, in which it increases significantly. One must be cautious in regarding any departure from "normal" as "failure of homeostasis." It is especially common to think of diseases in this way. We then might believe that the fever of infection or of exercise is a failure of homeostasis, not realizing that the high temperature is in fact desirable for the organism, and that the regulatory mechanisms are reset so that the temperature is held to a higher level. Similarly, many of the manifestations of disease may not represent a failure to maintain constancy in some parameter but rather a change in the desired value of that parameter. It is, of course, true that, if the disease progresses to the point of tissue destruction, as in duodenal ulcer, it is probably satisfactory to look on this as a failure to maintain the mucous membrane intact. It may, however, be the unfortunate price of an effort to keep some other variable, e.g., gastric secretory activity, at a high level. We shall not understand the illness as a reaction to life events if we do not recognize this relation among the various bodily processes.

The idea of homeostasis leads naturally into the important, interesting, and difficult question of the relation of illness to *adaptation* to the environment. A full discussion of it would take us rather far afield from the central direction of the present chapter but it should be noted that there are two somewhat different principal lines of thought about it. One is that an illness is the consequence of a failure of adaptive effort. The patient has been trying to get along in his environment, eventually becomes unable to do so, and falls ill. The second is not a denial of the first but is rather a significant variation

of it. It considers the illness as an extreme form of the adaptive effort itself. That is, the patient has been trying to get along in his environment by means that include a particular Physiological response (e.g., nasal hyperfunction); if more prolonged and intense adaptive efforts are called forth, the components of the Physiological response become sufficiently intense to be symptoms (e.g., nasal obstruction and discharge). This point of view should be credited especially to H. G. Wolff (1950, pp. 1059–1094). He also emphasized that, even though the illness is in a sense a consequence of, or a *part of,* an adaptive effort, nevertheless the particular kind of effort chosen by the patient is likely to be inappropriate to his actual situation. In short, he is using defensive, protective, or other adaptive mechanisms that would be helpful in certain circumstances but not in those which are, in fact, threatening him.

Conditioning and Learning

Although there has been occasional discussion of learning in general, and conditioning in particular (almost always of the classical sort), in connection with psychosomatic diseases; there has been very little concrete outcome of this speculation. Guze, Matarazzo, and Saslow (1953) give a particularly careful theoretical treatment of the role of learning in illness. Apparently, asthma is the only psychosomatic disease that has undergone serious investigation in terms of a conditioning model. The results are equivocal, so it is not clear whether such a model has helped to understand any of the diseases with which this chapter is concerned.

By extension, this question leads into the general problem of whether psychosomatic diseases can be regarded as learned responses. If they are, is the learning best conceptualized in terms of conditioning? In a general way it is self-evident that they must be learned, in the sense that the particular stimulus leading to the exacerbation of the disease would not have done so if the patient had had different life experiences. A girl who responds by an attack of asthma to a letter from her fiancé saying that he wishes to break their engagement, clearly would not react in this way if she had never had an opportunity to learn to read.

At present, it seems safe to say that we know

so little about the role of learning in psychosomatic disease that it is fruitless to discuss what sort of learning model is most applicable.

Discharge and Symptom Substitution

Another important question, as yet hardly approached systematically, is the extent to which one state of the organism can substitute for another. If both states in question are thought of as illnesses or symptoms, then "symptom substitution" is usually spoken of; if the second state is thought of as not an illness, then reference is usually made to the discharge of emotion or of tension. The issue is difficult to conceptualize clearly and often becomes involved with psychodynamic concepts such as "conversion," about which there is not very good agreement. Seitz (1951), in an experimental attack on this problem, was able hypnotically to substitute itching and scratching with excoriation for choreiform movements; suggestions that the patient was sad, unable to weep, and would develop hives, were followed instead by the appearance of coryza and eczematous dermatitis, both of which disappeared after the suggestions were withdrawn.

SPECIFIC DISEASES

This section will deal with individual diseases that are traditionally defined in Physical language. This is an arbitrary limitation, followed because of tradition and to keep the discussion within reasonable bounds. From the standpoint of logic, schizophrenia might just as well be included; although it is defined Psychologically, there are Physical things to say about it, just as there are about peptic ulcer. Anxiety, strictly defined, will not be considered either, even though its physiology has been investigated extensively, it is an illness often described Physically, and is managed by physicians without regard to Psychological considerations. It is, however, defined Psychologically.

The illnesses included will be chiefly those for which Psychological statements are based on what seems to me to be reasonably good evidence. The evaluation of evidence is clearly subject to much difference of opinion. Many persons object to statements made purely on the basis of clinical observations (which, in this context, usually means

the results of psychoanalytic interviews); others appear to put a good deal of reliance on them. In general the principle followed will be to report such observations if there is meaningful agreement among several authors, even though desirable control groups, quantitation of data, etc., are lacking. Observations not subsequently confirmed or tested by others will be excluded unless the reporting author seems to have been unusually careful in his study or there is some other reason to consider his findings intrinsically plausible.

There will be no consideration of CNS processes involved in the illnesses or of the Physiological steps in the development of the illness, except insofar as this is necessary to clarify points. The discussion of each illness will be divided into three major parts:

1. The role of psychological stimuli in producing the disease.
2. The long-term characteristics of the person who has the disease, especially with respect to the Psychological description called "personality." (Here will be included studies of responses to psychological stimuli, even when these do not appear to be integral parts of the process leading to what is ordinarily called the disease itself.)
3. Psychological descriptions of the person at, or close to, a time at which he has attacks of his illness.

Before proceeding, we should mention with respect to (3) that Schmale (1964) found feelings of "giving up" present at the time of onset of a very large number of illnesses.

Rheumatoid Arthritis

A recent review by Moos (1964) covers most of the publications relevant to the present section, so that earlier work will be separately discussed only if it is of special interest. In general, it can be said that the experimental investigation of the role of psychological stimuli in rheumatoid arthritis has been almost impossible because of the lack of any relevant Physiological variable that can be monitored while such stimuli are applied. This is in contrast to, for example, peptic ulcer, essential hypertension, or many skin diseases.

Role of psychological stimuli   As is the case with other illnesses, many authors who speak of "psychological factors" are not very explicit in distinguishing between external psychological stimuli and long-term Psychological statements about patients (i.e., personality descriptions) or short-term emotional changes. However, a large number of investigators (Moos, 1964) have reported on the basis of histories, usually from patients themselves, that psychological stimuli were important in producing the onset or exacerbation of the disease.

As is not true of most illnesses, one large scale control study of the significance of disturbing life events (i.e., psychological stimuli) has been carried out for rheumatoid arthritis (Empire Rheumatism Council, 1950). This study is worth looking at carefully because it illustrates some of the problems involved in evaluating the importance of psychological stimuli. The study included 584 persons; half were patients with rheumatoid arthritis and half were control subjects, who were healthy or "suffering from a disease or condition not relating to rheumatoid arthritis (fracture, injury, hernia)." There was careful matching of the groups with respect to age, sex, and socioeconomic status. The control subject was asked about possible disturbing events at a time prior to the date of the interview equal to that at which the matched patient had developed disease. There were no significant differences between groups in the frequency of occurrence of various life events such as death in the family or financial difficulty. This is certainly evidence against the idea that psychological stimuli are etiologic to rheumatoid arthritis but it is questionable that it is very strong evidence.

For one thing, the skill of the interviewer probably influenced to a substantial extent the willingness of the patient to tell of disturbing events. This is perhaps of relatively little consequence when one is asking about well-defined major changes such as deaths in the family or changes of residence, but it is obvious from clinical experience that the most important events may be more subtle or occur as parts of a long series of disturbances. Examples are changes in the behavior of spouses or children or a shift in the persons with whom one associates at work. Events of this sort may not be revealed at all by a simple question-and-answer technique, in part because the patient himself is not fully aware of their importance. Indeed, about 90% of both patient and control groups denied the pres-

ence of any of the events asked about in the 3 months preceding onset, and about 60% in the 2 years preceding onset. It is almost impossible for anyone to live 3 months without encountering some disturbing situations; we may therefore conclude either that the interviewing technique was unsatisfactory or that the kinds of events asked about were too gross. On the other hand, there is now evidence that a similar technique is of value in predicting all kinds of illness (Rahe, McKean, & Arthur, 1967; Rahe, Meyer, Smith, Kjaer, & Holmes, 1964). Although rheumatoid arthritis did not occur in the population studied in Rahe's work, one might expect at least some increased reporting of disturbing events in the arthritis patients as opposed to the controls if psychological stimuli were indeed important.

Further, as King (1955) remarks, an equal incidence of "disturbing" events in patients and control subjects does not imply that the events that *did* occur in the patients were not stimuli to their disease. What is essential in this connection is to study individual patients to see whether, in *each* patient, exacerbations appear to be precipitated by disturbing events. This is the technique of using the "patient as his own control."

Two studies (Gottschalk, Serota, & Shapiro, 1950; Moos & B. T. Engel, 1962) investigating the response of skeletal muscle to psychological stimuli need mention here because of the possibility that increased muscle tension is part of the process that leads to rheumatoid arthritis. If it is, and if one sees it increase in response to psychological stimuli, then confidence that such stimuli are important in evoking arthritis is strengthened.

Gottschalk, Serota, and Shapiro (1950) found no differences between rheumatoid muscle potentials in arthritics and hypertensives during voluntary movements and imagination of movements (the stimuli here are to be understood as the experimenter's instructions). However, arthritics in analytic therapy showed more muscle tension than a control group of psychiatric residents also in analytic therapy. The same patients showed sharp muscle tension increases when hearing a story of emotional significance read aloud and on overhearing a feigned disagreement in the laboratory. Since comparisons were not made between the patients and others with respect to these stimuli, or with respect to different stimuli, one cannot say that arthritics differ from other persons. One may feel that the findings provide some evidence that stimuli of this sort play some part in inducing rheumatoid arthritis if muscle tension is involved in its pathogenesis.

Moos and B. T. Engel (1962) measured muscle potentials in two different groups of muscles in arthritic and hypertensive patients. In each arthritic a muscle group was chosen from an area that had recently been painful, as well as a muscle group from an asymptomatic area; in each hypertensive, a group that was symptomatic in a corresponding arthritic and a group corresponding to the asymptomatic one in the arthritic (forearm flexors in all cases). The latter muscles were active in all patients in the button pressing that was part of the procedure. The arthritics showed a consistently higher potential in the symptomatic muscle than did the hypertensive; there were no differences in the asymptomatic muscles. The arthritics showed no adaptation (i.e., decrease) in muscle potential over the course of the experiment, although the hypertensives did. The results were reversed for blood pressure, in which the arthritics adapted, and the hypertensives did not. The stimuli used were phrases selected to be especially meaningful for arthritics or hypertensives, or to have no special meaning for either group. It was hoped that conditioning of the muscle potential response would occur but it did not. No data were given about the relative sensitivity of the patients to hypertensive versus arthritic phrases.

What conclusions can be drawn from these findings? They suggest, first, that arthritics show greater response in some muscles to some stimuli than do hypertensives. Unlike the usual experimental interview, however, this kind of experiment does not investigate the hypothesis that particular psychological stimuli were of etiologic significance in the illness. Its results may be taken as showing that at least some psychological stimuli produce responses that may be part of the pathogenesis of the illness in question.

If the muscle tension phenomena were not regarded as an essential part of the process leading to rheumatoid arthritis, we could discuss this sort of finding under the heading of long-duration characteristics of the person. Then we could say: "Rheumatoid arthritics are persons who have a tendency to respond to many stimuli by increases in muscle tension." Since response specificity is discussed elsewhere in this book, this aspect of the study will not be further elaborated on here.

Long-term characteristics Moos (1964) reports that at least two investigators appear to agree on each of the following conclusions: (a) rheumatoid arthritics are righteous, rigid, moral, conforming, and conscientious; (b) they have been hyperactive and are interested in athletics; (c) they commonly describe their parents as domineering, demanding, rigid, and strict. King and Cobb (1958) interviewed 1323 persons, using as an "index" of rheumatoid arthritis a list of symptoms found to correlate well with the actual presence of the disease in a smaller sample examined medically. They found that women who scored high had low education, four or more children, no spare time in the third decade of life, and said that they worried more than other people. High scoring men were characterized by low income, low education, and termination of marriage. There were especially high scores for those with disparity in either direction between education and income, suggesting that this may be a particularly difficult social position to endure.

Johnson, Shapiro, and Alexander (1947), on the basis of psychoanalytic or other interviews, reported that women with rheumatoid arthritis had masochistic needs, often manifested by a need to serve others, and that they showed "masculine protest," i.e., rejected the feminine role and competed with men. While their finding is open to the usual criticisms of this method of data gathering it should be pointed out that the real objection is not to the absence of a control group. The same technique has been applied to the study of persons with other diseases, resulting in findings different from those in rheumatoid arthritics, so that the existence of a control group may at least be inferred. The real problem is in evaluating the investigative procedure employed, especially in knowing whether it was applied in exactly the same way to patients with all the diseases studied. For example, did they all have the same opportunity to reveal "masculine protest"? At least partial reassurance is provided by the inclusion of rheumatoid arthritics in the Chicago interview study reported above. The results supported the psychoanalytic conclusions about personality.

A quite different approach by Fisher and Cleveland (1958), employed Rorschach test results for the determination of the way in which the patients perceived their body-boundaries, as one significant dimension of the total "body-image." Various kinds of Rorschach responses were used to make up a "barrier" score and a "penetration of boundary" score. The former was thought to reflect the patient's view of the body-boundary as a barrier against penetration from outside; the latter his view that the body-boundary was fragile and easily penetrated. The results were that rheumatoid arthritics had higher barrier scores and lower penetration scores than patients with "stomach disturbance" (mostly stomach ulcers), and higher barrier (but not lower penetration) scores than patients with ulcerative colitis. The differences in the distribution of scores were statistically significant by chi-square analysis.

Moos and Solomon (1964) found that female rheumatoid arthritics scored higher than their female relatives on Minnesota Multiphasic Personality Inventory (MMPI) scales reflecting physical symptoms; depression, apathy, and lack of motivation; general "neurotic" symptoms; psychological rigidity; and similarity to patients with ulcer and hypertension. Because of the problems involved in assessing significance levels when a total of 125 scale score comparisons were made, they determined how many significant differences would be expected to turn up by chance and found that their results showed a much larger percentage. In a study only of asymptomatic *relatives* of patients with rheumatoid arthritis, Solomon and Moos (1965) also found that those with the rheumatoid factor in their blood serum had higher scores than relatives without rheumatoid factor on scales reflecting impulse control, concern about social desirability of their responses, concern about socioeconomic status, and ego strength. Those without rheumatoid factor scored higher on scales reflecting somatic complaints, admission of psychiatric symptoms, social and self-alienation, lack of self-acceptance,

anxiety, and rigidity. The authors suggest that the findings could be explained if one supposed that the presence of the rheumatoid factor indicated a potentiality for developing the disease, but that the disease only appeared in the presence of "emotional conflict and psychologic distress." Asymptomatic persons with rheumatoid factor would then necessarily have "well-functioning psychological defenses"; those with the rheumatoid factor and collapsed defenses would be found in the group with overt disease.

The same authors (Moos & Solomon, 1965a, 1965b) compared 16 rheumatoid arthritic women with their nonarthritic sisters, some of whom, however, had a few findings suggestive of rheumatoid arthritis. The group of sisters was not subdivided according to the presence or absence of the rheumatoid factor. The personality trait dimensions were measured by various MMPI scales, by ratings of interviews, and by especially constructed personality tests. The patients showed greater compliance and subservience, nervousness and restlessness, depression, and sensitivity to anger. A content analysis of the interviews was also carried out. The following conclusions were based on actual word counts, but the method of deriving them from the counts is not given. The "typical" arthritic patient was "depressed, moody, nervous, worried and tense; masochistic, self-sacrificing, inhibited in her expression of anger, and oversensitive to manifestations of anger in others; reserved and introverted, compliant and subservient, compulsive and perfectionistic; oriented to work, duty, conscientiousness and productivity." She did not manifest overtly dependent behavior. She had not, as a child, manifested "a different amount of physical activity than her siblings." The authors also conducted a short psychodrama, in which the patients also showed masochism, self-sacrifice, and denial of hostility. The sisters were quite different, in general, from the patients, although there was no difference in the degree of manifest dependency. It should be remarked that the self-descriptions of both the sisters and the patients tended to agree with the descriptions of them given by their siblings. The patients were bothered more by the rejection they perceived from their mothers and the strictness they perceived from their fathers, although they did not consistently differ from their sisters in their actual descriptions of the parents' behavior.

The comparison group used in this study raises an important general question. When one says that patients with arthritis, or with any other disease, have such and such characteristics, there is necessarily implied a comparison with some other group, from which the patients in question differ. The statements about the patients would be of little interest if all the characteristics existed to the same extent in all other persons. It is therefore important to be clear about what the comparison group is. In many such studies, unfortunately, it is not explicitly described, and one supposes that it is "all other people" that are being compared with the patient group, although it may be "all other patients."

Psychological statements at the time of disease One of the points in which Moos (1964) finds agreement among investigators is that rheumatoid arthritics "tend to over-somaticize, i.e., they tend to complain more than necessary about their somatic problems." Since this sort of thing is often said, not only about arthritics, but also about other patients, it is worthwhile to examine the statement. The principal problem is to decide how much complaining is excessive. The assumption often appears to be that an arthritic says he has more pain or discomfort than he really has, but such an assertion is impossible to defend logically. How can anyone know how much pain someone else really has? In the particular case in question, what is apparently implied is a comparison of rheumatoid arthritics with some other group of people, patients or nonpatients. It is then possible to decide whether the arthritics complain more or less than the other group. One cannot, however, sensibly ask whether they complain more or less than another group with the same amount of discomfort, since there is no way to answer such a question. It is perhaps possible to find out whether they complain more than persons with "the same amount" of joint disease of some other sort, such as osteoarthritis, but since this is, by definition, not exactly the same *kind* of joint disease, it would be perfectly possible

to maintain that it was of an intrinsically less painful sort.

Of more interest is discovering what psychological statements of psychodynamic interest can be made at the time of exacerbation of the disease. Alexander (1950) suggests that a frustration of the need to serve is the most relevant Psychological variable. D. T. Graham et al. (1962) reported that the attitude of "being tied down and struggling to get free" was specifically associated with flareups of the arthritis. This association, to a certain extent, was confirmed as part of the general confirmation of the attitude hypothesis in this study. It has some intuitive attractiveness, in that it seems plausible that some sort of muscle and joint disturbance would be associated with such an attitude, but, in fact, information about the pathogenesis of rheumatoid arthritis is so scanty that it is not clear that alterations of muscle function around the joint are involved. Such involvement has, however, been proposed (Glick, 1967).

It should be mentioned also that rheumatoid arthritis has been regarded as a symbolic expression of Psychological problems (Alexander, 1950; King, 1955), a view which introduces the unsatisfactory concept of conversion reaction. One could, of course, view the arthritic changes as preventing some form of feared or forbidden activity, but the criteria for making such judgments, and hence for naming something "conversion," are, as stated previously, not at all well defined.

Summary In summary, personality descriptions in connection with rheumatoid arthritis are clearer and better studied than those applied to most of the diseases mentioned in this chapter, to a large extent because of the careful work of Moos. On the other hand, the evidence that psychological stimuli are important is based almost exclusively on histories from individual patients. This is in large part true because no one has been able to apply a technique like the experimental interview to evoke processes that are clearly related to the disease, chiefly because of the general lack of knowledge of what such processes are. There is no satisfactory agreement on psychological statements to be made about the patient at the time of exacerbations of the illness.

Essential Hypertension

Essential hypertension is not altogether easy to define. In practice, the name is applied whenever arterial blood pressure is found to be sufficiently far above whatever is considered normal, *and* when there is no evidence of one of the disease processes thought of as preceding and leading to high blood pressure. In other words, high blood pressure occurs in many patients; in some of these, there are identifiable processes called "diseases" that are thought of as causes of the hypertension. When one of these processes is not present, the hypertension is called "essential." Obviously, this terminology is largely the result of historical accident; in due course, when more is understood about pathophysiology, probably all instances of hypertension will be named according to the underlying processes.

Particularly with hypertension, the question of the relation between mild and transitory bodily changes and sustained deviations from normal has been raised with particular force. It is not clear whether or not brief elevations of blood pressure, induced by psychological stimuli, reflect fundamentally the same processes as those responsible for the sustained elevation of pressure and its complications such as kidney disease and cerebral hemorrhage that make up the disease "essential hypertension." There is a still further problem in deciding whether the so-called "accelerated" or "malignant" phase of essential hypertension is a response to the same sorts of things that produce the preceding "benign" phase.

There are reviews of Psychological discussions of essential hypertension by Shapiro (1960) and McGinn, Harburg, Julius, and McLeod (1964), and also in the books cited at the beginning of this chapter.

Life events There are many reports of persons in whom the onset of essential hypertension was preceded by disturbing life events. The problem in deciding whether these events are stimuli that evoke the disease is the same as that for all the other illnesses in which this sort of temporal correlation is relied on. Reiser, Brust, and Ferris (1951) reported that, in 41 of 80 patients for whom the time of onset of the disease was known, significant psychological stimuli preceded the onset of hypertension. They included in this decision the criterion that the "dynamic factors in the personality structure of the patient's reaction pattern to related experiences are such that the life events would have special emotional meaning to the patient." This is an overall rate, and the investigators add that "the more sustained the relationship with a patient, the more frequently was a significant preceding situation discovered." It needs to be emphasized that changes in blood pressure may occur without the patient's awareness, so that there is a particular difficulty in using the life history method for deciding about the role of psychological stimuli in this illness. The situation is, obviously, different with respect to *symptoms*. Reiser, Brust, and Ferris (1951) found correlations between events and symptoms in 119 of 182 patients.

The improvement in the percentage of patients reporting a significant preceding life event as a result of the experimenter's increased knowledge of the patient suggests that, in many investigations of various diseases, actual figures given may be minimal estimates that would have been higher had the investigator known the patients better. Reiser, Rosenbaum, and Ferris (1951) found that essentially similar events preceded the onset of the malignant phase of the disease, which of course suggests that it is no less psychogenic than the benign. The unusual feature of Reiser's work is that the actual percentages of positive findings are given. Many other reports (Alexander, 1950; Binger, 1951; Hambling, 1951; Wolf, Cardon, Shepard, & Wolff, 1955) report similar findings but without specifying the success rate.

Hypertension is one of the few illnesses for which there is some reasonable evidence about psychological stimuli derived from a study of the whole population exposed to a disturbing event. Levels of diastolic blood pressure above 95 mm Hg sustained for 1–2 weeks have been reported in 56% of persons exposed to the Texas City explosion of 1947 (Ruskin, Beard, & Schaffer, 1948). Similarly, it was found that 27% of soldiers who had seen protracted combat in the African desert in World War II showed diastolic pressures greater than 100 mm Hg for several months thereafter (J. D. P. Graham, 1945). In discussion of findings such as these, one sometimes sees questions raised about whether the effects are "purely physical" or "psychological." As the earlier discussion of the mind-body problem should show, such a question is confused. Presumably, the question is whether the effects of the entire stimulus situation were mediated by sense organs or not, and, if they were, whether this mediation required the production of a state in the organism that we might call Psychologically an "emotion." As has been pointed out earlier, it is hopeless to try to answer the second question on the basis of present-day knowledge. The answer to the first question is quite speculative, but probably such things as the direct impact of blast waves on the kidney, for instance, were not solely responsible for the elevated blood pressure, and some effects mediated through sense organs participated.

Scotch's (1963) survey of blood pressure in Zulu populations is a good illustration of a sociologic approach to illness. Such characteristics as church attendance, family type, length of urban residence, and marital status were related to the prevalence of hypertension.

There is a great deal of experimental evidence bearing on the role of psychological stimuli in evoking hypertension. One must bear in mind, however, that it is not certain that acute and brief rises in blood pressure are closely related to the disease essential hypertension; and also that there are two important mechanisms by which blood pressure is raised. One of these is increase in cardiac output, and the other, increase in peripheral resistance. The latter is probably more important in the actual disease.

Many authors have reported that rises in blood pressure, including diastolic, occur in hypertensives in response to psychological stimuli experimentally manipulated in interviews. The stimulus usually was the introduction by the experimenter of a topic thought to be "disturbing" to the subject, especially if there was reason to think that it was related to previous life events believed from the subject's history to have been of etiologic significance in the illness (Hambling, 1952; Moses, Daniels, & Nickerson, 1956; Shapiro, 1961; Van der Valk, 1957; Wolf, Cardon, Shepard, & Wolff, 1955).

Many studies included Physiological measurements, permitting analysis of the mechanism by which the blood pressure was elevated, and showed that such interviews may increase the peripheral resistance as well as the cardiac output.

Of particular interest is the study by Pfeiffer and Wolff (1950), which shows that during their experimental interviews the kidney function changed in directions to be expected on the assumption that the interview was producing a temporary increase in the disease process. That is, renal processes characteristic of hypertension became more pronounced in the 23 hypertensive subjects in whom they were already present and appeared in 13 subjects with normal blood pressures. The renal changes found were a fall in effective renal blood flow and a rise in filtration fraction, indicating an increase in the resistance offered by the renal glomerular arterioles, probably both afferent and efferent.

This sort of finding raises a problem when it is compared with studies of other kinds of Physiological processes in which persons with an illness are compared with control groups without the illness. A not uncommon report is that the normal subjects show the same kinds of changes as persons with the illness but to a lesser degree. Unless there was some very special selection of stimuli, which seems most unlikely, it is hard to understand how normal subjects could respond in every organ with changes like the disease process of special interest in the respective experiments. In view of the fact that many organs are capable of response in at least two directions, one would expect normal subjects to have a somewhat random distribution of responses within a single organ system.

Long-term characteristics Much has been written about the personality of patients with essential hypertension. As is almost inevitable, the statements that provide the most pleasing overall synthesis are those which are least satisfactorily documented. On the other hand, studies conducted more rigorously deal with rather narrow personality characteristics, and their findings are not integrated into an overall dynamic hypothesis.

The difficulty that hypertensives have with the expression of hostility has always been emphasized but it is not clear that this is any more true of hypertensives than of persons with any other diseases. Investigations of most persons whose illnesses are thought to be "psychogenic" usually indicate that problems of aggression or hostility are important.

The well-known formulation of Alexander (1950), based on psychoanalytic investigation, states that hostile competitive feelings lead to anxiety and inhibition of aggressive hostile impulses, and that in this setting hypertension develops. The competitive feelings and efforts are thought to be overcompensation for unsatisfied dependent wishes. As is true of most psychoanalytic hypotheses, this one has proved very hard to test because of the difficulty of specifying relationships between raw data and concepts. Hypertensives were, however, included in the Chicago interview study and the results supported Alexander's hypothesis.

A well-known, careful study of Saslow, Gressel, Shobe, DuBois, and Schroeder (1950) compared hypertensives with a group of normotensive, "psychiatrically ill," but not psychotic patients who had none of the "commonly accepted psychosomatic disorders," and with a group of normotensive patients with chronic diseases in which "psychological factors were thought to have low etiologic relevance." There was careful matching for age, sex, race, and sociological variables. On the basis of interviews, all subjects were rated on the following characteristics: impulsiveness, subnormal assertiveness, obsessive-compulsive behavior, depressive behavior, anxiety, and hysteria.

The ratings of obsessive-compulsive behavior and of subnormal assertiveness significantly differentiated the hypertensives from the psychiatrically ill group, and all the ratings except impulsiveness differentiated them from the "chronic medical and surgical" group. It is interesting, however, in view of other studies to be cited below, that anxiety differentiated the hypertensives from the second control group slightly better than did obsessive-compulsive behavior. Of particular interest is the finding that there were no significant differences between the patients thought to have "neurogenic" (roughly equivalent to "essential") hypertension and those with other types, such as "endocrine" and "renal."

Matarazzo (1954) wished to test the hypothesis that hypertensives show less aggression under stress than do normotensives. To do this, he gave 40 normotensive and 40 hypertensive patients a selection of cards from the Thematic Apperception Test (TAT), while harshly criticizing the responses. He made no measurements of blood pressure during the experiments, so it is solely a personality study, rather than a search for psychological correlates of changes in blood pressure. The two groups of subjects were roughly equivalent in age and in various socioeconomic respects. He defined *hostility* as "a motivational state of the organism which may or may not lead to aggression." *Aggression* was defined as "observable, quantifiable behavior which is directed toward harming another person, object or thing, or directed to protecting one's self against threat or injury." This distinction is potentially important and might lead to some clarification of the literature on hypertension, and on psychosomatic disease in general. One wonders, however, whether behavior "directed toward protecting one's self" should be put in the same class as an overt attack on someone.

On the Allport Ascendance-Submission Scale and the Rosenzweig Picture-Frustration Test, administered before the experimental criticism, the groups showed no significant differences. In other words, hypertensives did not appear on these tests to be less aggressive than other patients. The groups did not differ significantly in the number of aggressive words used in giving TAT responses, either before or after the criticism. In fact, contrary to expectation, both groups used *fewer* after the criticism than before. There was significant difference in one item of behavior: only one hypertensive, but 12 normotensives, refused to continue with the task. Their refusal may be interpreted as one form of aggression. If this finding were confirmed, it would be of considerable interest, especially since measures of gross behavior have been so rarely employed in psychosomatic investigations, despite their obvious relevance to real life situations. One possible objection to the study is that the criticizing experimenter knew which of the patients were hypertensive. This knowledge might have influenced his behavior, leading to differences in the subjects' behavior.

R. E. Harris, Sokolow, Carpenter, Freeman, and Hunt (1953) studied young women who were "potentially hypertensive," i.e., those whose blood pressures were higher than normal for their ages, and yet not high enough to be conventionally classified as having essential hypertension. Since there is evidence that such persons have a high probability of developing the kind of fixed high blood pressure that definitely qualifies them for the "disease" label later in life, it is probably legitimate to consider this investigation as having to do with personality characteristics of persons with the disease. In other words, they were showing the first stages of the disease.

In the first part of the study, the "prehypertensives" and a group of normotensives were interviewed by a psychiatrist, who had previously arrived at hypotheses about Psychological features in persons with fixed hypertension. These hypotheses are not precisely described but they had to do with "his evaluations of the dynamics and economics of conscious and unconscious hostility." Without knowing blood pressures, he was able to distinguish the two groups at a significantly better than chance level. This result is interesting because there are few reports of similar efforts.

The most unusual part of this work was the conduct of two-person psychodramas, in which one of two roles was assigned to a subject in the research and the other to a staff member. The behavior of the subject was judged by staff members, who checked as many adjectives as they thought applicable from a list of 389. There were statistically significant differences (the method of statistical analysis is not given) between the adjectives checked for the prehypertensives and for the normal subjects. Since 85 of them appear in the final list, it is not easy to state the results briefly and clearly. The authors' summary is that the prehypertensives brought more anxiety to the situations, became more emotionally involved, were less effective in achieving their ends, and created an undesirable social impression. Both groups of subjects were asked to check the adjectives that described themselves in general. Their self-ratings do not lend themselves to ready comparison with the observers' ratings: many of the adjectives are the same, but many are different, and it is not clear what the criteria of significant correspondence should be. One interesting item is that the prehypertensives saw themselves as submissive, al-

though observers did not so rate them during the psychodramas.

Kalis, Harris, Sokolow, and Carpenter (1957) extended this work, using slightly different psychodramas in studying 14 women who qualified for the diagnosis "essential hypertension." The 14 patients differed from the 22 control subjects, who were not being treated for any illness, in ratings of their behavior by observers and in ratings of typescripts made from sound recordings of the psychodramas. It is not explicitly reported whether the observers and the professional actors knew which of the subjects were patients. Observers rated the normotensives as more effective, and as showing more organization and control, in both psychodramas used. In particular, when the solution to the problem in the psychodrama called for self-assertion, the hypertensives were "appeasing, denying guilt, uncertain and confused, submissive, repetitive and perseverative." When the problem called for tact and conciliation, the hypertensives were "hostile and attacking." From the typescripts also the hypertensives were rated more hostile, more assertive, and more tense than the control subjects. The authors gave a list of adjectives that discriminated the prehypertensives, as well as the hypertensive patients, from their appropriate control groups. There is no estimate of the number of such agreements that should occur by chance.

Confining their attention to systolic blood pressure, Harburg, Julius, McGinn, McLeod, and Hoobler (1964) classified subjects according to a scheme rather too complex to summarize here. In general, their group is roughly equivalent to prehypertensives, as was Harris's group. On the whole, those with higher systolic readings rated themselves as "submissive" and "sensitive," on Cattell's 16 PF questionnaire. There was also some correlation of systolic pressure with neuroticism, introversion, anxiety, and being "warm-hearted and sociable." This combination is interpreted by the authors as indicating motivation to "obtain social contacts but in a 'sensitive' and 'anxious' manner."

The most interesting part of this work was an experimental, contrived argument. Subjects with high systolic pressures yielded in the argument more often than those with low, and furthermore afterwards privately changed their opinions more often also. This agrees nicely with their view of themselves as submissive, and with the self-ratings of Harris's prehypertensives.

Saul and Sheppard (1956) reported that the dreams of hypertensives showed more hostility than those of normotensives, according to their Dream Hostility Count Scoring System. Kaplan, Gottschalk, Magliocco, Rohovit, and Ross (1961) applied this system, and also a second devised by Gottschalk, to verbal samples produced by 10 hypertensives and 10 normotensive subjects who were told to speak uninterruptedly for 5 min about any dramatic or personal experience. According to both systems, there was significantly greater hostility in the speech of the hypertensives. The particular contribution of this study is the use of Gottschalk's scoring system for verbal samples , which represents a substantial advance over gross intuitive ratings.

An older piece of work, which seemed to be extremely promising but has apparently not been followed up, was carried out by M. L. Miller (1939). Miller was able to *predict* successfully the blood pressures of depressed and of paranoid psychiatric patients from the hypothesis of a positive correlation between pressure and hostility. Roughly speaking, and as predicted, the most depressed and the most paranoid patients had the highest pressures. Predictions were more successful, however, with respect to systolic than to diastolic pressure.

Summarizing, we can say that there is agreement that hypertensives have hostile impulses that they do not act on, that anxiety is frequently observed in them, and that they do not assert themselves effectively. Perhaps the last is because self-assertion implies hostility and may elicit hostile retaliation. This formulation agrees roughly with those of Wolf et al. (1955), Binger (1951), Dunbar (1947b), and others summarized by Hamilton (1955). Two epitomizing statements are worth quoting. Hambling (1951) concludes that hypertensives "behaved as though the environment were dangerous. They constantly sought to secure attachment to a stronger person who dominated the environment." Ackerman (1950) says that hypertensives "exhibit a pervasive sense of trapped, helpless exposure to the danger of aggressive injury, usually in a context in which the threat seems to derive from the very person on whom the patient depends for security.

They are ever alert to such danger, and their psychic energies are continuously absorbed with the effort to counteract it."

In a study very different from most of those cited, in that there was no assessment of conventional "personality" variables, B. T. Engel and Bickford (1961) found that hypertensives showed more individual-response specificity (stereotypy) than normotensives. This seems to lend support to the clinically derived descriptions of "rigidity" and "obsessive-compulsiveness."

Psychological statements at the time of disease Essential hypertension, unlike illnesses involving inaccessible viscera, provides an opportunity to make Psychological statements about the organism at the time of acute changes in the Physiological variable, provided one has appropriate measuring devices attached to the subject. On the other hand, reports by patients of changes in their own state are less useful than in most other illnesses, because the patients are typically not aware of increases in blood pressure.

The kind of Psychological statement made has usually been the name of an "emotion"; the discussion that follows shows how often investigators put the question in this way. To make this section more meaningful, findings in connection with blood pressure rises in normotensive persons will be included. The relevance of these to the disease "essential hypertension" depends on the assumption, discussed above, that the disease is closely related to the transient elevations of blood pressure seen in normal persons.

The paper of Kaplan et al. (1961), previously cited, reports that there was a rise in systolic pressure (mean 6.7 mm Hg) and in diastolic (mean 2.1 mm Hg) in the hypertensive subjects when they were asked to talk for 5 min. The systolic rise was statistically significant; the diastolic was not. There were significant differences between hypertensives and normotensives in both pressures, because the normotensives had a mean fall in diastolic. Since the rises occurred while the patients were speaking in a way judged to be hostile, one may tentatively conclude that hostility was a correlate of the rise in blood pressure. Additionally, one hypertensive patient who was intensively studied provided a total of 13 verbal samples. In his record there was significant association between diastolic, as well as systolic, pressures and the Dream Hostility Count. Another hypertensive patient produced 25 dreams under hypnosis, without suggestion of dream content. Again, there was significant association between the Dream Hostility Count and diastolic pressure, although the association with systolic pressure was not quite significant at the usually accepted levels.

Clinically, it is often reported that elevations in blood pressure occur in association with unexpressed or suppressed anger or hostility (e.g., Hambling, 1952; Wolf et al., 1955). The evidence is that the patient describes his feelings in some such terms during periods of elevated pressure, either induced experimentally or occurring without the investigator's intervention. Also, there is a striking case report, essentially an anecdote with documentation, that one patient's blood pressure fell from 165/100 to 125/85 after he had beaten up his brother-in-law. This might suggest that the expression of hostility reduces blood pressure (Wolf, Pfeiffer, Ripley, Winter, & Wolff, 1948). Hokanson, Burgess, and Cohen (1963) have produced experimental evidence tending to support such a conclusion, although they measured only systolic blood pressures. College-age subjects who were counting backward by twos were harassed and interrupted by an experimenter. They showed a significantly greater increase in systolic blood pressure than did control subjects who were not frustrated (15.6 mm Hg versus 4.4). It was furthermore found that when some of the frustrated subjects were later permitted to administer electric shocks to the experimenter or other persons as part of a "guessing game," the pressure dropped most (to a level representing an increase over the baseline of 7.3 mm Hg) in those who shocked the experimenter himself, least (to a level representing an increase over the baseline of 12.5 mm Hg) in those given no opportunity to shock anyone, and to intermediate degrees in those who shocked persons other than the experimenter.

In another experiment, Hokanson (1961) interfered with the backward counting his subjects had been instructed to do and threatened them with electric shock if they did not do their best, thereby inducing frustration and anxiety about retaliation by the experimenter. Subjects later administered shocks to the experimenter. During the period when they could shock the experimenter, the pressure they exerted on the plunger causing shocks correlated .39 ($p < .05$) with changes in systolic pressure. There was a $-.42$ ($p < .05$) correlation between pressure per shock and elevation of the systolic blood pressure at the final rest period. While the results would have been more informative if the diastolic blood pressure had also been reported, it is interesting that the vigor of expression of aggression was positively correlated with the systolic blood pressure while that expression was occurring, but negatively correlated with blood pressure measured after it occurred.

We shall now take up work indicating that there are different Psychological correlates of acute elevations in blood pressure, depending on the underlying Physiological mechanism. It will be recalled that there are two major processes by which blood pressure is elevated: increased cardiac output, which is ordinarily seen in exercise; and increased peripheral resistance, which is the major mechanism acting in essential hypertension. Hickam, Cargill, and Golden (1948) were apparently the first to call attention in a psychophysiological context to the difference between these processes. They did not mention any associated psychological difference, but simply reported that both processes occurred in "anxiety."

Moses, Daniels and Nickerson, (1956), using a ballistocardiograph for their hemodynamic investigations, concluded that large elevations (160–200/100–130 mm Hg) of blood pressure are associated with rage and resentment and are mediated by increased peripheral resistance with normal stroke volume and heart rate; that the minor elevations of blood pressure (140–160/90–100 mm Hg) associated with "anxiety with minimal overt expression" are mediated by increased peripheral resistance; and that the minor blood pressure elevations found in association with overtly expressed anxiety are mediated by increased stroke volume and heart rate (i.e., increased cardiac output) without change in peripheral resistance. They had only 10 subjects in their entire study, the number of instances of the various patterns is not given, and it is not clear that the persons judging the emotion were unaware of the hemodynamic findings. However, Wolf et al. (1955) came to essentially the same conclusions with respect to overtness of expression of emotion, although they did not differentiate anger from fear.

Further support comes from an extensive series of studies by Funkenstein, King, and Drolette (1957). They employed two experimental situations: (a) criticism by the experimenter as the subject attempted to solve problems, and (b) exposure of the subject to delayed auditory feedback while he was telling a story. During the latter he was given painless electric shocks if he stopped speaking or spoke very slowly. The authors' formulation is that each of these situations "principally used frustration." The blood pressures were measured, and the ballistocardiograph was used to provide evidence for hemodynamic mechanisms. In view of the serious doubt about the correct interpretation of ballistocardiographic tracings, the authors were cautious about making interpretations in terms of cardiac output and peripheral resistance.

The interviewer assessed the subjects' emotional states immediately after the experiment. The interviewer was the experimenter and, so far as one can tell, was aware of the physiological data obtained. The recording of the interview was subsequently judged by him and by another person. The latter had not been present during the experiment or interview; it is not explicitly stated that he was unaware of the Physiological data. Some of these are reported in terms of percentage change from basal levels; others are in terms of standard scores but without specification of the distribution from which those scores were obtained. The desirability of adjusting final scores by regression on the initial level (Benjamin, 1963) was apparently not considered.

The general pattern of the results was that with "anger-out"—anger directed outward—diastolic blood pressure, as well as systolic, rose; with "anxiety," there was a rise in systolic pressure but much less rise or even a fall in diastolic pressure. Hemodynamically, the anger-out state seemed to involve increased peripheral resistance and the anxiety state was marked by increased cardiac output, to which both increased stroke volume and increased heart rate contributed. These findings differ from those mentioned previously in that overtness of expression of emotion is not considered, so it is not clear whether or not the correlation of "anxiety" with increased cardiac output runs counter to the conclusions of the workers previously cited. There was also a category that we shall not consider, anger directed inward, "anger-in," hemodynamically intermediate to the other two.

The Psychological correlates of changes in blood pressure were also investigated by Ax (1953) and by Schachter (1957) in two similar studies. A situation designed to arouse *fear* consisted of an elaborate hoax in which the persons performing the experiment pretended that, because of a mishap with the equipment, the subject might receive a dangerous electric shock. He was then given small shocks, which he was allowed to interpret as signs of malfunction of the apparatus. In order to arouse *anger*, the subject was exposed to insulting criticism by the experimenter and his staff. Schachter added a *pain* stimulus, the "cold pressor test," in which one of the subject's hands was inserted in a bucket of ice water for 1 min. In both studies a variety of physiological measurements were made but we are concerned here only with blood pressure. Ax analyzed his data in a way that makes it a little difficult to get a clear picture of the outcomes. He reports only those instances in which pressures rose and gives means of those rises, without reporting occurrences of drop in pressure. Further he discusses only the maximal rises during the experimental periods. His data show that maximal rises in diastolic pressure were, on the average, greater in response to the "anger" than to the "fear" stimulus, and that maximal rises in systolic pressure were, on the average, greater to the "fear" than to the "anger" stimulus. He does not mention any systematic Psychological assessment of the subjects' reactions. Naming their states "anger" and "fear" appeared to be inferences from the stimuli employed. On the basis of general human experience, this seems a reasonable assumption, although an unwise one to make experimentally.

Schachter used some of the same subjects in a total group of 48. Of these, 18 were hypertensive and 15 "potentially hypertensive," i.e., they had transient elevations of blood pressure that returned to normal on rest. His method of analysis makes his data easier to interpret than those of Ax, although again only the maximal change from control to stimulus period is reported. There were substantial rises in both the systolic and diastolic pressures in all three stimulus conditions. "Pain" had the smallest effect, while "fear" and "anger" were about equal. The direction of the average changes differed according to the processes underlying the pressure changes. In pain the peripheral resistance increased and the cardiac output fell slightly; in fear the peripheral resistance decreased and the cardiac output rose; and in anger the peripheral resistance remained almost unchanged, while the cardiac output rose. It should be noted that peripheral resistance and cardiac output assessment depended on ballistocardiographic tracings, which, as we have noted, do not lead to clear-cut Physiological interpretations.

In contrast to Ax, Schachter made systematic Psychological evaluations of the subjects during the stimulus situation. Three judges, of whom one had no knowledge of the design or hypotheses of the experiment, and one had no knowledge of the blood pressure classifications, rated the degree of verbal and nonverbal emotional reaction exhibited during the exposure to the stimulus; the degree of response stated by the subject during an interview after the experiment; and the degree of response inferred by the judge from a combination of behavior during the experiment and the results of the interview. (Speech during the experiments was tape recorded. It is not stated whether the records of other behavior were made by someone who knew the aims of the experiment and the blood pressure classifications of the subjects, or whether the interview after the experiment was conducted with such knowledge.) Schachter's results give direct information about the Psychological correlates of pressure change, although one must bear in mind that Psychological statements about persons made in experimental situations may not be directly related to those about persons in nonexperimental situations. Since only the *intensity* of the response was evaluated, it is not known how the data were handled if a subject showed "fear" in the "anger" situation, for instance. Perhaps such inappropriate responses did not occur.

The hypertensives showed greater rises in pressure than normotensives in all three experimental conditions; but, of the six possible rises (systolic and diastolic in each condition), only three were significant. The hypertensives also received higher ratings in all three measures of emotional intensity. This, of course, runs counter to the usual belief that hypertensives do not express anger. There are, no doubt, many possible explanations of this discrepancy. Schachter suggests that it may, in part, be the result of sampling bias, in that hypertensives who come to psychoanalysis or other forms of psychotherapy, from whom some of the ideas about personality structure were first derived, are a selected group.

The differences between hypertensives and normotensives in the amount of blood pressure rise were apparently not a reflection of consistent differences in the underlying Physiological mechanisms, since increases in peripheral resistance and increases in cardiac output appeared to be responsible for the rise to approximately the same extent in the two groups.

From this study one might conclude that increases in both systolic and diastolic pressure are correlated with either fear or anger, but that the underlying mechanisms may be different, with an increase in cardiac output playing a greater role in fear. Since it is peripheral resistance that is typically elevated in the disease "essential hypertension," it is not necessarily true that the fear shown by these subjects is relevant to the psychological state of patients with the disease.

For the sake of clarity, it should be pointed out that the last three studies mentioned report slightly different kinds of correlations: Funkenstein reports a correlation between Psychological and Physiological statements about his subjects; Ax reports one between stimuli and Physiological statements; Schachter reports a three-way relation among stimuli, Psychological statements, and Physiological statements. In general the patterns of results obtained by all three workers seem to agree, especially if we identify Funkenstein's "anger-out" with the "anger" of the other two authors. With anger, there was elevation of diastolic blood pressure as well as systolic; with "anxiety," there was a rise in systolic pressure but much less rise or even a fall in diastolic. Hemodynamically—and remembering the doubts about the ballistocardiograph—the anger state involves increased peripheral resistance, while the anxiety state is chiefly a matter of increased cardiac output, to which both increased stroke volume and increased heart rate contribute. Therefore, although there may be procedural flaws in these and in other individual studies, they are consistent with the idea that anger is a significant Psychological correlate of increased blood pressure in the hypertensive. This does not necessarily mean that anger is the *most* significant correlate. Further research might well show that something else correlated even better. For instance, it might prove possible to subdivide anger into various kinds and show that one of these is more closely related than others to blood pressure rises. Also, it may be that anger, although common, is not the essential kernel of the Psychological state. Hambling (1952) and Binger (1951), particularly, mention the relation between hostility and anxiety in hypertensives. It is, of course, a familiar psychoanalytic idea that hostile feelings lead to anxiety (fear) about retaliation.

There is one report, available only as an abstract, which appears to contradict the conclusion that there are cardiovascular differences between fear and anger (Harris, Schoenfeld, Gwynne, Weissler, & Warren, 1964). In 20 experiments with 9 hypnotized subjects, similar cardiovascular responses to suggestions of fear and suggestions of anger were found. The work is important because cardiac catheterization, which made possible the direct assessment of relevant behavior of heart and blood vessels was used. This is a significant advance over techniques used in most psychophysiological work. These results, if confirmed, do not invalidate the actual *findings* of the earlier investigators, but different physiological *interpretations* might be required.

The studies to be discussed next provide some evidence that anxiety may be important in the blood pressure changes of essential hypertension. Blood donors about to have venipuncture performed, and especially those who later faint, show such changes, as do persons who develop the common emotional vasovagal faint in other situations (D. T. Graham, Kabler, & Lunsford, 1961). This is a

stimulus-response correlation, not a Psycho-Physiological one, and its force as evidence in this connection depends on the belief that anxiety rather than anger is the state likely to develop in one who is about to undergo venipuncture. Donors who said they were "nervous" were more likely to faint than those who did not (D. T. Graham, 1961), and if one interprets "nervous" as essentially equivalent to "anxious," this may be some evidence that "anxiety" is the appropriate name for the state of the donors whose blood pressure rises. In any case, the stimulus is one that seems at face value to be a threat of bodily harm.

Grace and D. T. Graham (1952) gave as the characteristic, specific attitude of hypertensive patients "an awareness of threat of bodily harm, without any possibility of running away or fighting back." This seems to be a statement of one kind of anxiety, namely, the kind associated with the possibility of bodily harm, the "castration anxiety" of psychoanalysis. This attitude was one of the group tested in the study of interviews (D. T. Graham et al., 1962) with patients with many diseases, which supported the general specificity-of-attitude formulation.

In two different experimental studies, blood pressures of hypnotized normal subjects rose in response to suggestion of the hypertension attitude. The first of these (Stern et al., 1961) compared responses to suggestions of the hypertension attitude with responses to suggestions of those for urticaria and for Raynaud's disease. The second (D. T. Graham, Kabler, & F. K. Graham, 1962) more carefully designed, compared responses to suggestions of the hypertension attitude with the suggestion of the urticaria attitude. The subjects were 20 male volunteer university students without hypertension or urticaria; the design consisted of a double, 2 × 2, Latin square, permitting analysis of variance for effect of attitude suggestion, experimental day (first or second), order of presentation of attitude, intersubject differences, and differences between two experimenters. Both the urticaria attitude (being mistreated and helpless to do anything about it) and the Raynaud's attitude (wanting to take hostile physical action) might be considered anger, although the latter is probably closer to the usual meaning. In the first of these studies, the diastolic pressure rose more in response to the hypertension suggestion than to the Raynaud's attitude but not to a statistically significant degree, and, in any case, methodological problems make interpretation difficult. In the second study, where more equivalent control periods were obtained before each attitude suggestion, diastolic pressure in response to the hypertension attitude rose more than in the response to the urticaria attitude, and to a statistically significant degree. The absolute values were small; the average change during the hypertension suggestion was 2.98 mm Hg as compared to .65 in the urticaria. The maximal change and rate of change were also significantly greater during the hypertension than the urticaria period. The changes in skin temperature were also in predicted directions, with a greater rise during the urticaria suggestion than during the hypertension (see the section on urticaria). It is difficult, though perhaps not impossible, to fit the findings into a framework based on the concept of general arousal, to the effect that the hypertension attitude suggestion was simply more arousing than the urticaria or the Raynaud's.

Strictly speaking, these experiments do not belong in a discussion of the Psychological correlates of blood pressure changes because they are concerned only with Physiological responses to a stimulus. However, the stimulus was chosen *because of* the observed Psychological correlate (i.e., the attitude statement made by patients) of the disease essential hypertension, and the work is therefore relevant to the question of Psychological correlates.

These results may be considered as evidence that some form of anxiety, rather than hostility, is central in the Psychological state of persons with hypertension at times of elevated pressures. On the other hand, it must be conceded that the anxiety that presumably developed in response to the fear situations of Ax (1953) and Schachter (1957), although it should have been of the same body-harm kind, was not accompanied by significant evidence of diastolic pressure increases.

It is pleasing to find, in association with attacks of a disease (in this case, rises in blood pressure), intensifications of the same Psychological characteristics that are typical of persons with the disease and still more pleasing to find these present at the

time of attacks in persons who do not ordinarily have the disease at all. That is, we hope to find the same "emotions" in normotensive subjects when their blood pressures rise as are chronically present in hypertensive patients. It would be attractive to regard what are ordinarily called "personality traits" as chronic emotions.

How near to this goal are we in essential hypertension? The descriptions of hypertensives as having difficulty with self-assertion, hostility, and anxiety, seem to fit with the association of acute rises with anger and anxiety. The relation between anxiety and anger, however, remains cloudy. Further, as in many other illnesses, one has to be sure that the personality descriptions are precise enough to be really meaningful, in the sense that they would not apply to everyone.

In one careful and rather elaborate study (Innes, Millar, & Valentine, 1959), increases of blood pressure observed during experimental interviews with a group of adult women in various clinical categories, including hypertension of pregnancy and hypertension without pregnancy, could not be correlated with the emotions of rage, anger, or fear. Neither could they be correlated with "emotional strength" and "degree of repression." There were significantly more self-references by the subject during periods of blood pressure peaks than during periods of troughs. All subjects showed increases in both systolic and diastolic pressures at the start of the interview; in the control group, these tended to fall again. The hypertensive and "neurotic" groups showed sustained rises of pressure. Perhaps the most important lesson from this study is hardly a new one: methods of making Psychological assessments need to be worked out and specified much more carefully, so that one investigator can replicate another's work. It should be mentioned, for instance, that Innes, Millar, and Valentine did not specify the method by which they judged the presence or strength of an emotion. The conceptual units of Psychological assessment probably need to be made smaller, and the use of global names of emotions avoided, since these in practice always present difficulty. One advantage of a formulation like the specificity-of-attitude hypothesis is that the attitudes are defined more precisely and are smaller segments of the Psychological conceptual scheme than are the names of emotions or other variables often used.

Hypertensive patients, as compared to those with duodenal ulcer and to normal subjects, responded less in heart rate, blood pressure, and maximum cardiac force to the presentation of TAT cards, with instructions to tell stories about them. This unresponsiveness was related by the investigators (Weiner, Singer, & Reiser, 1962) to the hypertensives' remaining "distant, uninvolved, and 'insulated.'" Since there is no analysis of the relation of the response to the initial level, one is not certain of the true extent of the "unresponsiveness."

Summary There is much clinical historical evidence that the sustained elevations of blood pressure that make up the disease "essential hypertension" are responses to life situational stimuli. There is very good evidence obtained under controlled conditions that Psychological stimuli elicit increases in both systolic and diastolic pressures, by increases in cardiac output and/or peripheral resistance, and there is one study showing that within the kidney itself changes are elicited that are like those found in the hypertensive kidney (Pfeiffer & Wolff, 1950).

Psychologically, there is agreement that hypertensives have difficulty asserting themselves, and that conflicts about the expression of hostility, which are associated with anxiety, are important. Several authors stress the hypertensives' sense of living in danger from the environment. Some believe that the hostility is generated by the loss of a dependent relationship. The Psychological correlate of acute rise in blood pressure is frequently reported as "anger," but there is reason to think that "anxiety" is also important, and may be crucial.

Vasovagal Fainting

Many faints have long been known to be "emotional," and the commonest of these is certainly the vasovagal, also called vasodepressor, faint. Its cardinal manifestations are a fall in blood pressure and a slowing of the heart rate. Fainting in general, including vasovagal fainting, is discussed in a monograph by G. L. Engel (1962). The actual faint has

been said to be the second half of a diphasic response (D. T. Graham, Kabler, & Lunsford, 1961); the first half consists of a rise in blood pressure and acceleration of the heart rate.

Role of psychological stimuli The occurrence of fainting in response to psychological stimuli is so well known that there do not seem to be any studies particularly aimed at establishing this event as a fact, probably because it has seemed to be laboring the obvious.

It is particularly crucial to be clear about the definition of "psychological stimuli" in considering their relationship to fainting. Most of the examples of vasovagal fainting given in physiological reports (G. L. Engel, 1962, and references cited therein; D. T. Graham, Kabler, & Lunsford, 1961), have occurred in response to manipulations of the subject's body in such maneuvers as venipuncture (although there is ample anecdotal evidence that simply the sight of blood may precipitate a faint). It might be suggested that such fainting is not truly "psychogenic," but is rather a response to the stimulation of pain endings by a needle. The reply to this is that such a state of affairs is included in our definition of "psychogenic," provided that we describe an essential part of the total response to the stimulus in psychological language, by such words as "pain" or "fear." One would presumably not call the fainting "psychogenic" if he knew it was mediated entirely through a reflex arc from the skin to the spinal cord and back to the heart and blood vessels, although there is nothing in logic to forbid doing so. If, however, we say that someone faints because "he is afraid of pain," or because "he is afraid of needles," we are essentially saying that the state "fainting" is a consequence of another state, "fear." The fear is in turn a response to the external sensory stimuli provided by the needle, the doctor, the room in which the venipuncture is occurring, etc.

Long-term characteristics There are very few data about the personality of fainters but it has been reported (Ruetz, Johnson, Callahan, Meade, & Smith, 1967) that blood donors who faint score higher on the Hypochondriasis and Depressive Scales of the MMPI than donors who do not faint.

It has been estimated (G. L. Engel, 1962) that 15 to 25% of young men have had at least one episode of vasovagal fainting since early adolescence. Whatever the relevant underlying personality characteristics, they are clearly not very unusual.

Psychological statements at the time of disease One of the states called "fear" or "anxiety" is obviously closely related to vasovagal fainting. The exact relation needs clarification. One obvious difficulty with a simple correlation of anxiety and fainting is that ordinarily tachycardia and elevated blood pressure are thought to be associated with anxiety. The diphasic character of the total fainting response may resolve this difficulty, if anxiety is associated with the first phase, and another Psychological description such as "relief from anxiety," with the second (D. T. Graham, Kabler, & Lunsford, 1961). Certainly, the blood pressure changes of the first phase are like those of essential hypertension, which suggests that the "hypertensive attitude" (see the section on hypertension) may apply and blood donors who say they are "nervous" before the procedure begins are more likely to faint than those who deny it (D. T. Graham, 1961). Urinary excretion of epinephrine and norepinephrine is higher in donors who later faint than in those who do not (Chosy & D. T. Graham, 1965). While the relations between these catecholamines and such emotions as fear and anger are by no means clear, this result at least suggests that anxiety before fainting is important.

The proper interpretation of the second phase, the faint proper, is an unsettled question. Engel's early position (G. L. Engel, 1947) stressed the importance of a combination of anxiety and inhibition of action in bringing about the cardiovascular changes in the faint. His most recent statement (G. L. Engel, 1962) conforms with D. T. Graham et al., in including the view that the correct Psychological statement about the patient at the time the fainting starts is not anxiety. He suggests that "helplessness" and "giving up" are appropriate descriptions.

Migraine

The classical migraine headache is but one form of a wider class of vascular headaches, in which the mechanism of pain production involves dilatation and distention of the arteries of the head.

Authors have not always been careful in describing the headaches about which they were writing but it is probable that small differences in the manifestations of *vascular* headache from person to person make no essential difference for the purposes of the present chapter. The possible exception is the so-called histamine or cluster headache, which may perhaps represent a slightly, though significantly, different Psycho-Physiological response. Migraine is one of the illnesses that occur, at least in many instances, as the second phase of a diphasic response. Others may be vasovagal fainting, asthma, and acne vulgaris. It should be mentioned that the two phases referred to in connection with migraine probably do not correspond to the successive periods of vasoconstriction and vasodilatation that physiologically underlie an acute attack.

Role of psychological stimuli Histories from patients are, again, the primary source of information about the role of psychological stimuli in this illness. There is an opportunity for confusion, since one must consider the patient's circumstances at the proper time. There is reason to think that an episode of migraine occurs at the end of a period of striving, as the subject begins to relax or "let down" (Grace & D. T. Graham, 1952; Wolff, 1963). The critical stimulus to the actual development of an attack is the signal to end the effort, and this signal may not be properly identified in taking a clinical history. The unwary may therefore conclude that psychological stimuli are unimportant because nothing "disturbing" happened to precipitate the headache.

Although there are occasional reports of the experimental induction of migraine by the use of psychological stimuli (e.g., Wolff, 1963), experimental methods have not been much employed in Psycho-Physiological investigations of this illness. The technique of inducing minor changes in the relevant organ by experimental interviews, of so much value in connection with other illnesses, has not been significantly exploited. This may be in part because of the difficulties involved in observation of the state of the temporal arteries. Pulse wave tracings from these vessels can be obtained, however; Wolff (1963) found that there was increased pulsation during headache, and even between attacks there was irregularity and a generally high amplitude of pulsation in headache-prone persons. A more important reason for the lack of data is probably the diphasic nature of the response, requiring that the experimenter bring the subject through both the striving and the "let-down" phases, an obviously difficult task.

Long-term characteristics There is so much agreement among investigators about the salient personality traits in migrainous persons that the relative lack of carefully controlled studies need not result in skepticism concerning the findings. With migraine, the precise words used by different authors may differ but they are obviously quite close in meaning. The description by Wolff (1963) is as satisfactory as any. He lists ambition, striving, perfectionism, efficiency, orderliness, a tendency to repetitions of behavior and doubts, inflexibility, and caution. Others might make some changes in this list but it is clear that something close to the "compulsive personality" of standard psychiatric diagnostic terminology is being described. Migraine provides perhaps the best example of a generally accepted specific relation between a collection of traits sufficiently comprehensive to be called a "personality," and one of the illnesses usually called "psychosomatic." There is less agreement on the psychodynamic foundations of these traits, although they have been discussed at some length. The pursuit of this topic would be somewhat far afield from the purposes of the present chapter.

Psychological statements at the time of disease There has not been much discussion of relevant Psychological statements to make at the precise onset of the migraine headache. The available evidence suggests that the headache begins when the subject is "letting down," i.e., ceasing to strive, after a period of intense effort. Wolff (1963) commented on this attitude, which has been described by Grace and D. T. Graham (1952) as a feeling that it was necessary to strive to accomplish something, followed by a feeling that relaxation was in order, whether the effort had been a failure or a success. Again, we are not dealing with a deeper meaning of the effort to accomplish, or of the signal that efforts should cease. Apparent disagreements with the formulation just given often reflect a difference in the psychological level of the author's discussion, so that no real contradiction is involved.

Peptic Ulcer

Peptic ulcer has perhaps received more attention as a psychosomatic disorder than any other illness. Indeed, the psychophysiological investigation of the stomach by S. Wolf and H. G. Wolff, reported in *Human Gastric Function* (1947), was a major impetus to subsequent work in psychosomatic medicine and clinical psychophysiology, and much of the reason for their investigations was interest in the etiology and pathogenesis of the ulcer.

However, especially in earlier writing, it is not always clear whether the ulcer referred to is of the stomach or the duodenum. About seven times as many chronic peptic ulcers are in the duodenum as are in the stomach, so one might ordinarily suppose that, of a random sample of ulcer cases, most will be duodenal. The distinction is important because there are many respects in which the two illnesses differ. For our purposes, let us note that the stomachs of persons with duodenal ulcer usually secrete more hydrochloric acid than normal, while those of persons with gastric ulcers secrete a normal or less than normal amount. Therefore, comments about the role of hypersecretion of acid and pepsin in ulcer formation apply only to duodenal, and not to gastric ulcers. There is also evidence that the social background of persons with gastric ulcer differs from that of persons with duodenal ulcer (Doll & Jones, 1951). Further, the kind of ulcer that was common in the early part of this century, and found more often in women than men, was in the stomach. Its relation, therefore, to the kind of ulcer seen today is not clear, and statements about the sex shift in ulcer prevalence must be read with this in mind.

The pathogenesis of ulceration is still very unsatisfactorily understood but at least it seems clear that the secretion of acid and pepsin by the stomach is extremely important, and that this secretion is the result of vagal activity.

Role of psychological stimuli As usual, much of the evidence is what is derogatorily called "clinical anecdote." Despite this fact, most observers agree that psychological stimuli are important in producing the onset or exacerbation of ulcer.

The study of ulcer has the very distinct advantage that at least some of the relevant Physiological variables are known. One can, therefore, increase one's confidence in the historical material by observing changes in these variables in response to manipulations of stimuli of interest. The experimental interview is the major technique used for this purpose. Variables susceptible of measurement include gastric acid secretion, gastric pepsin secretion, engorgement of the gastric mucous membrane, and gastric motility. Although it is not known precisely how these are related to ulcer formation, it is, nevertheless, fairly clear that they have substantial relevance to it.

Gastrointestinal psychophysiology is discussed elsewhere in this volume, so we shall mention only those research results that have the most immediate bearing on clinical problems. One of these issues is the extent to which there is parallelism among the various gastric Physiological variables. Wolf and Wolff (1947) proposed that acid, pepsin, and increased blood content of the mucosa tended to rise and fall together. Margolin (1951), however, reported that these varied independently in his study of a young woman with a gastrostomy.

There are many reports of increases in gastric activity of the sort presumably involved in the pathogenesis of ulcer, in response to psychological stimuli. Most of these come from experimental interviews (Mittelmann & Wolff, 1942), some with patients with ulcer or other gastrointestinal disease, and some with healthy subjects. Subjects like Tom of the Wolf and Wolff study, who were under continuing observation provided an opportunity to study the effects of planned and unplanned external events. The activity in Tom's stomach often changed dramatically in response to such stimuli, some of which were laboratory occurrences and others conversations about disturbing events. G. L. Engel and his coworkers (1956) carried out an extensive investigation of a baby girl with a gastrostomy. They measured changes in gastric acidity associated with various states described Psychologically such as "depression," or occurring in response to such environmental changes as the arrival or departure of the experimenter. The departure of the experimenter with whom she was familiar evoked a decline in gastric acidity; his arrival induced the opposite changes.

Long-term characteristics Despite the enormous number of Psychological statements about ulcer in the literature, there are very few careful studies of concomitant personality characteristics. A problem of "too many adjectives" seems to be especially prominent in writings about this disease, so that it seems hardly worthwhile to list all the things that have been said about ulcer patients, nor is it clear to what extent different authors agree or disagree with each other, or to what extent their personality descriptions differ from those that might be given for patients with any other disease. This confusion can be partially reduced by noting that problems about *dependency* are evident in many cases (see Hamilton, 1955). This dependency is associated with varying outward personality manifestations, depending on the extent to which the patient tends to deny it, acting in an exaggeratedly independent way; or, conversely, is openly dependent. It should be stressed that this overall statement is an effort to make sense out of a rather confused area and cannot be supported at this time by data rigorously obtained. It is, nevertheless, consonant with the more specific psychodynamic formulations about *oral* dependency discussed earlier. These formulations are supported by the results of the Chicago Interview study already discussed.

Among the more carefully controlled studies is one by Cleveland and Fisher (1969). They compared 33 male veterans with duodenal ulcer with 26 male veterans with rheumatoid arthritis, using the Holtzman Ink Blot Test, rather than the Rorschach, and also conducted an interview focused on areas of behavior they had previously found characteristic of rheumatoid arthritics. Since the interviewer presumably knew what disease the patient had, and also expected certain answers, the possibility of bias from these sources is not excluded. The results for the arthritics were similar to those the authors had reported earlier. The patients with ulcer, on the other hand, had much lower barrier scores and higher penetration scores than the arthritics. The authors' conclusion is that the person with ulcer perceives his body as not having a firm boundary, and as therefore being easily penetrated. They also, because of interest in the importance of oral deprivation in ulcer patients, noted references to food, eating, and parts of the mouth and upper gastrointestinal tract. Ulcer patients tended to have more of these than arthritics, at a borderline level of statistical significance.

Williams and Krasnoff (1964) confirmed these body-image findings. In addition they found that, in general, ulcer patients had higher heart rates than arthritics; contrary to expectation, they did not have lower galvanic skin response (GSR) or electromyographic activity. When the *diagnostic* categories were disregarded, and comparisons were made directly between patients with low barrier and those with high barrier scores, it was found that those with high barrier scores had higher muscle activity under stressful stimulation than those with low barrier scores, while the low barrier group had higher heart rates. This comparison is different from the diagnostic one because the correlation between barrier score and diagnostic category was by no means perfect.

Fisher and Cleveland (1960) had similarly reported that ulcer patients tended to have higher heart rates and lower GSR activity than arthritics. Their method of data handling is, however, not clear. Their general hypothesis was that persons with high barrier scores (i.e., those who perceived their bodies as having a firm boundary) would have greater reactivity in the body exterior, and less in the interior, than persons with low barrier scores. On the other hand, Weiner, Singer, and Reiser (1962) found that ulcer patients were less reactive in terms of heart rate and blood pressure than healthy subjects. It seems unlikely that the healthy subjects would have shown, if the test had been made, body images with weaker boundaries than the ulcer patients.

Approaching the study of overt behavior, Hecht (1952) tested the level of aspiration of 30 patients with peptic ulcer (location not stated) and 30 with ulcerative colitis. The ulcer patients more often (at the usually accepted statistical significance levels) than the colitis patients believed they would improve their scores on the pegboard test used. He further reported that spontaneous verbalizations during the test were usually rated "aggressive" for ulcer patients and "passive" for colitis patients.

Weiner, Thaler, Reiser, and Mirsky (1957), in a well-known paper, reported their investigation of 2073 Army inductees. Because of prior evidence that persons with duodenal ulcer have higher levels of pepsinogen[1] in their blood than do those without ulcer, they selected for special study 120 men with especially high or low concentrations of blood pepsinogen. To this group they administered various psychological tests (Cornell Medical Index, Saslow Screening Inventory, an especially devised sociological rating scale, Rorschach, Blacky pictures, and Draw-A-Person). A psychiatrist and a social worker interviewed each man briefly. Each man had a gastrointestinal X-ray examination for duodenal ulcer, at the time of induction and again between the eighth and the sixteenth week of basic training. Four men had evidence of healed or active ulcer at the time of the initial examination; five others had X-ray evidence of ulcer at the second examination. The major findings were: (a) All of the men with ulcer were in the upper 15% of the blood pepsinogen distribution; 8 of them were in the top 5%, thus supporting the relevance of the pepsinogen level to ulcer formation. (b) The Psychological material, evaluated without knowledge of the pepsinogen levels or of the presence or absence of ulcer, could be used to predict pepsinogen levels. By using a cluster of 20 criteria derived from the psychological tests, it was possible to assign correctly 102 of the 120 men to the class "hypersecretor" or the class "hyposecretor." It must be emphasized that this assignment was worked out *with* knowledge of the subject's pepsinogen levels; therefore, the accuracy of prediction would almost certainly show significant attenuation upon replication. Using less well defined, impressionistic criteria, without knowledge of the pepsinogen levels, three evaluators were able to classify correctly only 73 (61%) of the subjects. (c) Ten men of the 120 were selected as those most likely to have or develop an ulcer "because their test material not only suggested that they belong to the group of hypersecretors but also showed evidences of intense needs to maintain relationships with others." Seven of these did have or develop an ulcer, which appears to be a high rate of successful prediction, inasmuch as there were only nine men with ulcers in the entire group of 120. The Psychological bases

---

[1] Pepsinogen is secreted by the stomach and converted by acid to pepsin, an enzyme assisting in the digestion of protein. How it gets into the blood is controversial and need not concern us here.

used for this prediction were the impressionistic ones, and not the cluster of 20 criteria.

The authors' summary of the Psychological characteristics of the persons who had high pepsinogen levels is that they showed "intense needs that are principally 'oral' in nature." When attempts to satisfy these needs fail, "the resultant frustration arouses anger that cannot be expressed lest there ensue a loss of supply for their needs." It is not quite clear from the discussion whether or not those who actually develop ulcer have some *additional* characteristic reflecting a "need to maintain relationships with others."

Because this study is so well known and so widely quoted, it is worthwhile to consider the final point in the authors' summary: "neither a high rate of gastric secretion nor a specific psychodynamic constellation is independently responsible for development of peptic ulcer. Together, however, these two parameters constitute the essential determinants in the precipitation of peptic ulcer on exposure to social situations noxious to the individual." We may note, first, that the study is really not concerned with the question of whether social situations are involved in precipitating the ulcer, and contains no evidence for or against that belief. Second, one is not altogether sure what is meant by "independently responsible" and "together these two parameters . . . etc." The passage might be interpreted to mean that the two parameters *vary* somewhat independently of each other and that the development of ulcer was some function of both of them. It is more reasonable to view the data as showing that the two parameters, psychodynamic constellation and high rate of gastric secretion, are so highly correlated that they both reflect the presence of the same "essential determinant." In short, one must guard against thinking, contrary to the actual data, that there are separate and independent "psychological" and "physiological" factors that must combine in some way to produce ulcer.

Psychological statements at the time of disease The best-known formulation concerning Psychological correlates of ulcer is that by Alexander (1950). In essence, Alexander states that the frustration of oral-receptive longings is associated with gastric hyperfunction which, if sufficiently intense and prolonged, leads to peptic ulceration. The frustration may be simply because the world refuses to supply what the patient wants, or because the patient denies and represses his longings, and by so doing increases them. Alexander suggests that oral-aggressive response to oral-receptive longings, leading to guilt and anxiety, is one of the reasons for overcompensation for the receptive wishes, and hence for their failure to be satisfied. As in many of the formulations of this school, it is not altogether clear whether the emphasis is on the description of a long-term personality characteristic or on an assertion that the activation of a specific unconscious conflict accompanies exacerbations of the disease. The latter seems to be implied in this case, explaining its inclusion here.

Grace and D. T. Graham (1952) described the ulcer attitude to be the feeling that "one has been deprived of what he is due and wants revenge," which agrees very well with Alexander's view. This attitude was included in the later confirmatory interview study (D. T. Graham et al., 1962). Since actually getting even for deprivation would require taking something forcibly, it may not be farfetched to think of biting and eating as unconscious referents that amount to the "oral-aggressive" part of Alexander's statement. The attitude statement, of course, refers to the patient's feelings (i.e., the Psychological description of part of his total state) at the time of exacerbation of the ulcer disease.

Perforation of ulcer may be regarded as an especially severe exacerbation of the illness (although caution requires the warning that perforation may reflect a slightly different process). Castelnuovo-Tedesco (1962) reported, on the basis of interviews with 20 patients, that perforation occurred when the patient was faced with situations "which . . . he felt to be grossly damaging to his self-esteem, and to which he reacted, predominantly, with impotent rage." The author also refers to "bitter, vengeful anguish." While the theme of frustrated oral-dependency is not obviously present here, the second part of the attitude statement, the desire for revenge, is.

If we look at Psycho-Physiological studies in which gastric activity was correlated with such Psychological statements about the patients or experimental subjects as the names of emotions, the picture is not at all clear. In general, it is a reasonable working hypothesis that increased acid and pepsin are relevant to increased activity in ulcer disease. It is then of interest to see what emotions are present at times of increases or decreases in these functions. This could be rephrased by saying that it is of interest to see what Psychological statements apply at such times.

Wolf and Wolff (1947) reported that their fistulous subject, Tom, showed increases in gastric acid secretion, motility, and vascularity in association with "pleasurable thoughts of eating," and "reactions and emotions involving conflict, hostility, resentment and anxiety. . . . Fear, sadness, and other feelings involving desire for withdrawal were associated with decrease in these functions." The authors suggested that the pattern of increased gastric activity could be understood as associated with an "unfulfilled desire for aggression and fighting back," whereas decreased activity was associated with flight or withdrawal.

In working with an infant girl with a gastric fistula, G. L. Engel, Reichsman, and Segal (1956), found that secretion of gastric acid was higher in rage then in any other of the affect states they observed (contentment, joy, irritation, depression, and depression-unpleasure). It was lowest in depression. When "interest in things or persons in the environment" (object-relations) was scaled, it was found that the highest secretory rates occurred with the greatest degree of interest.

Mahl (1950) proposed that *chronic anxiety* is the appropriate psychological name for the state associated with gastric hypersecretion of acid. Support for his view came from his finding more free hydrochloric acid in the stomachs of 6 college students who were anxious about an examination scheduled for later in the day than in 2 students who were not anxious about the examination, or in the same students on a control day when no examination was scheduled. Mahl believed that *acute* anxiety was associated with decreased gastric activity. The decision about anxiety was based on an interview. Kehoe and Ironside (1963) conducted 78 hypnotic experiments with 7 healthy subjects, during which the secretory rate of total gastric acid was measured. In the main part of the experiment

the subjects were instructed to feel "depression," but they did not always do so. Since there were also other parts of the experiment, it was possible to compare various affects, rated by judges who did not know the results of the gastric juice measurements, in terms of total gastric acid. "Anger" was associated with the highest rate, followed in order by "anxiety," "contentment," "depression," and "helplessness-hopelessness." Anger was, at p values of .07 or less, significantly different from all the other states. These results fit with many of the Psychological statements made about persons with ulcer.

Margolin (1951) studied psychoanalytically a woman with a gastrostomy. Physiological observations were made but *not* simultaneously with the psychological ones. He concluded that, when a repressed instinctual need was about to become conscious, the stomach showed high activity in all measured dimensions (acid secretion, pepsin secretion, volume of secretion, motility, and redness); that when reaction-formation was the dominant defense, there were low values in all of these variables; and that when defense mechanisms had established psychic equilibrium, there was no correlation among the changes in the several variables, i.e., there was dissociation. He states, unfortunately without providing the supporting evidence, that from the Psychological data he could predict correctly the state of gastric function "in each instance." If this last statement were substantiated, it would be of the highest importance. Further, the concept of dissociation of function in the presence of "psychic equilibrium" is of great interest and deserves further study.

Summary The clinical observations of persons with ulcer give a more coherent picture than the reports involving only changes in gastric secretory activity. The following cautious statement seems justified: Most investigators who have carefully examined persons with ulcer, and with an eye to saying something in Psychological terms more meaningful than the simple application of names of emotions, agree that something in the nature of unsatisfied oral-dependent wishes is prominent, and probably crucial. Further, some state that may be considered as a form of anger seems to be involved as a reaction to the frustration of dependent wishes. Studies of changes in gastric secretory activity have failed to fit any single hypothesis very well, perhaps for several reasons. One possibility is that actual ulcer production requires additional Physiological steps besides excessive and sustained gastric hypersecretion, so that many Psycho-Physiological studies may have been missing the point to some extent. Another is that applying emotional names is too crude a classification method, especially when the defining criteria for the names are not sharp, so that more refined subdivisions are necessary.

It would, therefore, be helpful to try to correlate changes in gastric secretion with the presence or absence of frustrated oral-dependent wishes and consequent anger, in short, with a state described Psychologically by the "ulcer attitude." Particularly difficult to understand from present data is the relation between "anxiety" and gastric function. This difficulty is possibly the consequence of gross uncertainties in the definition of "anxiety," especially with relation to "fear." One could, perhaps, summarize the Psycho-Physiological (as opposed to Psycho-Disease) correlations by saying that an increase in gastric secretory activity is associated with Psychological states described by G. L. Engel et al. (1956) as "outgoing," whereas states of "depression-withdrawal" are associated with low gastric activity.

Ulcerative Colitis

The obscurity of the steps in the pathogenesis of ulcerative colitis has made the relevance of psychophysiological investigation of persons with this illness a little uncertain. The disease ulcerative colitis includes disturbances of intestinal motility and of the vascularity of the intestinal mucous membrane. Both of these phenomena have been studied in psychophysiological experiments but it is not clear how they combine to produce the ulceration of the mucous membrane that is the defining characteristic of the illness. As with many other clinical conditions, there is increasing interest in subdividing what was ordinarily thought of as a single "entity." In particular, ulcerative proctitis is now frequently considered a special category. Further, it is becoming apparent that many cases

formerly called "ulcerative colitis" probably should be thought of as examples of a quite different process. These display the kind of granulomatous change originally described in the small intestine as part of the disease now usually called "regional enteritis." In the sections that follow, one should recall that some discrepancies may have arisen as a result of placing two rather distinct illnesses under the same name.

Psychosomatic discussions of ulcerative colitis have, as G. L. Engel (1954) pointed out, suffered from too much preoccupation with diarrhea, whereas, in fact, bleeding is a more common presenting symptom and constipation is frequently present at the onset. Some implications of these facts for understanding the illness follow.

Role of psychological stimuli   There are many clinical reports of onset or exacerbation of ulcerative colitis following disturbing life situations (cf. G. L. Engel, 1955; Fullerton, Kollar, & Caldwell, 1962; Hamilton, 1955; Lindemann, 1950). Fullerton, Kollar, and Caldwell (1962) give the clearest actual count. Their study included 47 patients; precipitating psychological stimuli were found for 52 episodes in 40 patients. The total number of episodes studied is not given, so that one cannot arrive at the percentage of the total for which such stimuli were found. G. L. Engel (1955) had 30 patients in whom the time of onset was precisely established. Sixteen of these had an acute onset immediately preceded by a well-defined event. In 10 others, the onset was "insidious," preceded not by a clear-cut precipitating event but by "a period during which mounting pressures threatened previous psychologic compensation." It is clear from the context that these pressures were from external events.

There are a few studies in which psychological stimuli were applied experimentally, while various aspects of colonic function were monitored. The work that is most directly relevant to ulcerative colitis is that of Grace, Wolf, and Wolff, 1951. Four patients with colostomies, permitting direct observations of change in the colonic mucous membrane and its motility, were studied. Two of them had ulcerative colitis; the two others had had colostomies for other reasons. The findings in the two subjects without colitis were essentially the same as in the two who had the disease, but the latter had more frequent and more sustained hyperfunction of the colon than the former.

Observations were made of color, contractile state, motor activity, and secretion of lysozyme in the portions of the colon accessible to observation. At the time these studies were made, the enzyme lysozyme was thought to be important in the pathogenesis of ulcerative colitis; later evidence suggests that it is not, although its presence reflects inflammation in the colon. The distinction between contractile state and motor activity is the difference between what we may think of as "baseline" tension and superimposed additional contractions of various kinds. The contractile state was estimated from the area of the colon exposed; motor activity, by inspection of the exposed area and also from pneumographic records of pressures on a balloon inserted into the colon. Observations were made after the subject had been exposed to disturbing stimuli occurring naturally outside the laboratory and also disturbing topics deliberately introduced in experimental interviews. After such exposure, hyperfunction of the colon was sometimes observed, "manifested by increased rhythmic contractile activity, and ultimately by intense and frequent waves in the cecum and ascending colon and replacement of rhythmic activity on the left side by sustained contraction of longitudinal muscles with shortening and narrowing of the colonic lumen, hypermotility and hypersecretion of lysozyme." In two subjects sustained hyperfunction was associated with the appearance of petechial lesions and in three with an increase in the fragility of the mucous membrane. In one subject mucosal erosions and ulceration occurred during a period of sustained conflict. It is not stated whether the experimental discussions of events thought from their time relations to have been important in attacks of the disease were more powerful in producing colonic changes than were other topics.

Since the steps in the development of ulcerative colitis are not known, one cannot be sure just which of these findings are directly relevant to the question of the role of psychological stimuli in the etiology of the disease. Nevertheless the illness is certainly characterized by disturbances of motility and by increased fragility of the mucous membrane.

Wener and Polonsky (1950) made similar observations of the effect of psychological stimuli on the colon of a patient with ulcerative colitis and a colostomy. They also believed that the responses they saw might well have been steps in the development of the disease.

Other investigations showing the effects of verbal stimuli on the motility of the colon are by Almy and his associates (Almy, Abbot, & Hinkle, 1950; Almy, Hinkle, Berle, & Kern, 1949; Almy, Kern, & Tulin, 1949; Almy & Tulin, 1947), but these do not have an immediately obvious relevance to ulcerative colitis.

A recent paper by Feldman, Cantor, Soll, and Bachrach (1967), although it deals chiefly with the question of personality descriptions of patients with ulcerative colitis, appears to cast some doubt on the importance of psychological stimuli in the etiology of the disease. The authors report that in only 4 of 34 cases studied was a "significant precipitating factor thought to have occurred close in time to the first attack of ulcerative colitis. In three cases there was a possible substantial emotional conflict. In 15 cases a moderately eventful emotional factor was present within 6 months of a *relapse* of the disease but not before its first occurrence." One problem here is the common confusion between external stimuli and internal states. Another, of course, is that one needs to know what sort of "precipitating factor" was considered significant. In any case, and with respect to either the state of the organism or an external stimulus it is hard to believe that something close in time to the first attack of ulcerative colitis, something that was at least potentially a source of illness, occurred in only 4 out of 34 cases. The usual criticism of assertions of the etiologic role of external stimuli is based on exactly the reverse and more correct belief, namely, that everyone is encountering significant situations, and having emotional conflicts, all the time, so that the problem is to decide how one knows that any of them is really responsible for an illness.

Long-term characteristics G. L. Engel (1955) has thoroughly reviewed the literature on the subject of Psychological descriptions of persons who have ulcerative colitis, and much of what follows is a summary of his paper. He includes observations that he had made on 39 patients of his own. One finds, of course, the usual difficulty in deciding just what adjectival phrases used by various authors are essentially synonymous, and also in assessing the methods by which these labels are applied. Further, it is hard to know whether the same labels could or could not be applied to persons with other diseases.

Obsessive-compulsive character traits, so-called anal characteristics, are commonly mentioned. Well-directed, aggressive action and clear-cut expressions of anger are uncommon. Patients are also said to be very sensitive to hostile or rejecting attitudes in other persons, with consequent efforts to ward off or avoid rebuffs. "Immaturity" is very frequently commented on, referring to dependent attitudes, low frustration tolerance, low capacity to assume responsibility, lack of adult sexuality, and restricted character of relationships with people. These relationships are said to be characterized essentially by intense and ambivalent dependence (Sperling, 1946) on one person, most commonly a parent. The mother is usually mentioned much more prominently than the father, who is often inconspicuous in the patients' accounts, although male patients may describe him as brutal and punitive. (A few experiences of the present author suggest that harsh behavior by the father may be more important in producing ulcerative colitis in some patients than the usual statements in the literature indicate.) G. L. Engel appropriately warns that parents are almost always known only from patients' descriptions, so that caution is necessary in concluding that they would be described in the same way by other observers.

The paper by Feldman et al. (1967), cited previously, is principally directed to the question of personality structure in persons with ulcerative colitis. The investigative method was interviewing 34 patients with ulcerative colitis, unselected except for the presence of the illness, by at least three physician members of a team. A psychiatrist, who was also a psychoanalyst, always took part in at least some of the interviewing, which averaged 10–12 hr for each patient.

For each patient, 65 variables, not detailed in the paper, were scored. Ultimately, each patient was designated normal or abnormal by methods "too compendious to describe" in the paper. The authors concluded that 29 of the patients were essentially normal and 5 abnormal. There are obscurities in the description of this study and of the way in which conclusions were reached, but it is most important to notice the low utility of such a concept as "normal" in this context. What one is really interested in is whether there are things that can be said about the personalities of patients with ulcerative colitis that distinguish them from those of persons with other illnesses, or with no illness. "Normality" is not nearly precise enough for this purpose. One could easily find 65 biochemical variables that did not distinguish patients with gout from those without gout, and one might then say that patients with gout were biochemically "normal." If there were no measurement of uric acid, a highly important difference in the two groups would remain unknown. "Normality" is too loosely defined to be of much assistance in dealing with the important questions in psychosomatic medicine.

As mentioned in the section on peptic ulcer, Hecht (1952) found patients with ulcerative colitis less likely than patients with peptic ulcer to believe that their performance on the pegboard test would improve and reported that their spontaneous verbalizations were likely to be rated "passive." Psychoanalytic views already mentioned of the personality of patients with ulcerative colitis, were supported by the outcome of the Chicago interview study.

Psychological statements at the time of disease A major problem in connection with Psychological descriptions of the patient at the time of an attack of ulcerative colitis is the concentration on the presence of diarrhea, although bleeding is in fact the characteristic feature of the disease (G. L. Engel, 1954). Thus psychological formulations based on diarrhea are somewhat off the mark in connection with ulcerative colitis. Engel suggests that the process in the bowel appears to be a response to injury and that motility disturbances, whether constipation or diarrhea (and both may occur in ulcerative colitis), are secondary, We might expect Psychological statements about persons with ulcerative colitis at the times they are having constipation or diarrhea, when the latter are part of the colitic process, to be different from similar statements about persons with constipation or diarrhea that is not part of ulcerative colitis.

G. L. Engel summarizes his own work and that of others by saying that the "major psychologic phenomena which have been found to be associated with this transition to the tissue change which marks the onset of ulcerative colitis are (1) some disturbance in a key relationship, real, threatened or phantasied, and (2) an affective state characterized by such terms as helplessness or despair." The helplessness he regards as "evidence of a traumatic separation process." The tissue correlates of such a process would permit the "initiation of a variety of pathological processes in tissues, including those characteristic of ulcerative colitis."

There are some possible objections to the two Psychological correlates he mentions, however. In the first place, it would probably be possible to find that the events precipitating many psychogenic illnesses are to some extent disturbances in a key relationship; in the second, it is not clear from the statements of all authors that "helplessness" or "despair" is really always an appropriate name for the state of persons developing ulcerative colitis or that it is significantly more common in connection with that illness than with others. Feldman et al. (1967) reported that helplessness in their patients was "considered to be present only secondary to the illness itself," and often found none even in seriously ill patients. We have commented previously on the problem of trying to decide whether one state is the cause or effect of another, the two states being in this case "helplessness" and "ulcerative colitis."

It would be desirable to find some Psychological statement to make at the time of the exacerbation that would be more specific to ulcerative colitis. One can agree with G. L. Engel's conclusions that it should bear some relation to processes related to injury of the mucous membrane of the colon, and that explanations in terms only of diarrhea and constipation are not enough.

It is interesting that one of the most specific statements is that by Groen (1947), who said that the onset of ulcerative colitis occurred at times of "acute love loss and painful humiliation." The specific attitude reported by Grace and D. T. Graham (1952), and included in the later interview study (D. T. Graham et al., 1962), was that the patient "felt he was being injured and degraded, and wished he could get rid of the responsible agent." The agreement here is obvious, although the second part of this attitude statement essentially has to do with diarrhea, and, in view of G. L. Engel's comments, is probably not an integral part of the attitude. If it is not, it is not clear what the second part should be. Further, such a Psychological description of the patient is obviously highly compatible with Engel's emphasis that the bowel process is to be regarded as a reaction to injury. It is true that he concluded that the bowel behaved as though it were responding to "a noxious agent of microscopic and molecular size," but this appears unnecessarily restrictive and seems from the context to be in part intended to contrast with the expulsive response to a bolus-sized agent.

Other formulations that have attained some prominence are the conclusions of Lindemann (1950) that the loss of a key person and consequent morbid grief are important; the view of Sperling (1946) that essentially makes ulcerative colitis a pregenital conversion reaction representing "expressions of and defenses against aggressive incorporation of the frustrating object," and the emphasis of Grace, Wolf, and Wolff (1951) on the ejection-riddance pattern in the bowel in ulcerative colitis. The incompleteness, at least, of the last view has been discussed above. The experimental evidence of Grace and his associates is relevant here, in that they report that there is an association between hypermotility (which is presumably related to diarrhea) and increased blood content of the mucous membrane, with increased fragility. The fragility is probably more closely related to the essential process in ulcerative colitis. Whether the motor and vascular changes necessarily always occur in the same direction is an interesting question that has not apparently been answered to date.

This question leads to another set of problems, concerned with the nature of the colonic processes associated with various Psychologically described states, such as anger or fear, and the possible relevance of these to the disease ulcerative colitis. Unfortunately, it is not as easy as with some other organs to find evidence concerning the correct emotional name to apply in association with various changes in the colon, in part because many of the studies were carried out at a time when less attention was paid to careful techniques in the specification of emotional states than is now the case. Grace, Wolf, and Wolff report (1951) that "abject fear and dejection" were associated with hypofunction of the colon, whereas "conflict with feelings of anger, resentment and hostility, or of anxiety and apprehension" were associated with hyperfunction of the colon, i.e., with those colonic changes thought to be characteristic of ulcerative colitis. As G. L. Engel points out (1954), that is at variance with his conclusion that states of "helplessness" and "despair" are associated with the onset or exacerbation of ulcerative colitis. He suggests, however, that Grace's Psychological statements may be mistaken and that the data given are not adequate to support them. (There are, however, more data than he mentions in his review.) Wener and Polonsky (1950) studied a patient with a transverse colostomy and concluded that "pain, fear and anxiety" were associated with pallor and reduced motility of the colon; while anger, resentment and hostility were associated with hyperemia and engorgement of the colon. Depression was associated with pronounced hypermia and engorgement. There are important disagreements here with the conclusions of Grace but they may result mostly from the small number of available names of emotions.

Almy and his colleagues (Almy, Abbot, & Hinkle, 1950; Almy et al., 1949; Almy, Kern, & Tulin, 1949; Almy & Tulin, 1947) observed the colons of healthy subjects and of persons with the "irritable colon" and "spastic constipation" (ill-defined conditions, incidentally) through a proctoscope, and also measured motility and pressure in the colon by the use of inflated balloons. Although they obtained rather clear evidence that psychological stimuli, i.e., discussions of emotionally disturbing events, produce changes in colonic motility and in the blood content of the mucous membrane and in mucus secretion, it is difficult to apply most of their findings to the particular question that concerns us here. Almy, Abbot, and Hinkle (1950) report a sudden reduction in tone and wavelike motility in association with a change of mood "to one of personal inadequacy, self-reproach and hopelessness," which seems to conform to the results of Grace. It is, however, by no means necessarily true that these motility changes correspond to Grace's "hypofunction."

Summary By and large, recent years have not seen much psychophysiological investigation of ulcerative colitis. There are, however, suggestions that the central Psychological statement to make about the person in an attack of ulcerative colitis is that he feels injured in a way that makes the colon the natural site of illness. G. L. Engel points to the resemblance of the colonic process in the disease to a reaction to injury but does not indicate that he believes that there is a Psychological statement to be made about patients, based on their own words, suggesting that they feel injured.

Asthma

Excellent reviews of the psychosomatic literature concerned with asthma have been presented recently by Freeman, Feingold, Schlesinger, and Gorman (1964), Feingold, Singer, Freeman, and Deskins (1966), and Lipton, Steinschneider, and Richmond (1966). The last especially emphasizes children but discusses many findings obtained from studies of adults. Hamilton's book (1955) reviews much of the slightly older material. The present section, therefore, will concern itself primarily with recent work, mentioning only those earlier papers that seem to have been the most interesting, or the most important, or to report the most carefully conducted research.

The special question in connection with asthma is the extent to which the underlying process is really the same in all patients called "asthmatic." This problem of subdivision is, of course, theoretically important in any disease; it is especially important in asthma because of the existence of two etiologic hypotheses, the psychological and the allergic, which appear to be at least to some extent in competition.

Although much has been written about asthma as a psychosomatic disease, there exist very few Physiological data pertinent to the questions with which this chapter deals. This is apparently because there is no Physiological variable that can easily be measured at frequent intervals and is known to be relevant to the disease. The reason, of course, is the inaccessibility of the bronchioles to observations that do not grossly disturb the subject. Sophisticated modern methods of measuring respiratory function reveal a good deal about the state of the bronchioles, but they can only be carried out rather infrequently and require the full cooperation of the subject. It is therefore not possible to observe minute by minute changes in response to psychological stimuli, and the methods of making even those measurements that are possible require the subject's full attention, so that he is likely to be distracted from the experimental stimuli of interest. Investigators have therefore usually relied on patients' statements about their symptoms, frequently combined with occasional opportunities to hear wheezing breath sounds. The hazards in so doing are that the patient may not be able to distinguish between asthmatic dyspnea and that resulting from some other process such as the "hyperventilation syndrome," and that an increase even in wheezing may not necessarily reflect the kind of decrease in bronchiolar diameter that is the essence of asthma. For instance, forcing air more rapidly through bronchioles that have not changed in caliber will increase wheezing. Further, hyperventilation may even produce some bronchiolar constriction, even though this is presumably not the same sort as that which defines the disease asthma.

Role of psychological stimuli   As is true of many psychosomatic diseases, the evidence that psychological stimuli are important in asthma is largely historical; i.e., it is derived from what patients with asthma say. Many older reports provide more or less systematic accounts of this kind. Indeed, the centuries-old recognition of the importance of disturbing life events as stimuli to attacks of disease was probably responsible for the opinion that asthma was a "respiratory neurosis."

Rees (1956a) attempted to estimate the importance of various etiologic factors—psychological, infective, and allergic—in 441 asthmatics of both sexes and various ages. He found that "psychological factors" were dominant in 37%, subsidiary in 33%, and unimportant in 30%. He also reported that the

"emotional precipitation of attacks of asthma" was definite in from 20–57%, depending on the age group. In a random sample of 50 patients aged 60 or more, he found "psychological factors" dominant in 44%, subsidiary in 34%, and unimportant in 22% (Rees, 1956b). In 388 children, he found "psychological factors" dominant in 42%, subsidiary in 30%, and unimportant in 28% (Rees, 1964). These are pioneering efforts to deal with an important problem, but, as is often true of such efforts, some important points are left obscure. The definition of "psychological factors" is not clear, partly because of the common failure, mentioned previously, to distinguish states of the organism, i.e., emotions, from external psychological stimuli. Apparently, both the extent to which patients were "neurotic," and the finding of "emotional precipitants" were taken into account in the final judgments. Further, exactly how either of these was assessed is not explained, although presumably some attention was paid to external stimuli.

There have been some improvements in technique over simple anecdotal assertions about life histories. Knapp and Nemetz (1960) found what we are calling psychological stimuli antecedent to 94% of 406 attacks of asthma in 9 patients who were studied in intensive psychotherapy. Metcalfe (1956) asked a young woman patient with asthma to keep a diary. This record revealed that attacks of asthma occurred on 9 of the 23 occasions when she had been with her mother within the preceding 24 hr; asthma occurred only on 6 of 62 days when she had not been with her mother. The difference is statistically significant, but there is a real possibility of distortion in the patient's recording.

There are scattered observations of the occurrence of asthma in response to psychological stimuli not clearly of the sort usually thought to have "emotional significance." Thus Dekker and Groen (1956) reported "frank asthmatic attacks" in two patients when they were shown a goldfish in a bowl, and in a third when she looked at a picture of a horse. The attacks apparently consisted of dyspnea and clearly audible wheezing; during them the vital capacity was significantly decreased. It therefore seems likely that they represented true asthma, and not some other respiratory disturbance. It is not implied that the goldfish and the horse, respectively, had no meaning to the patient but they were not in themselves important indicators of change in interpersonal relationships such as would be, for instance, a wife's behavior. Subsequently, Dekker, Pelser, and Groen (1957) were able to produce in two asthmatic patients repeated attacks of asthma (dyspnea, wheezing, and decrease in vital capacity) merely by attaching to them the same kind of apparatus through which they had *previously* received the allergen to which they were sensitive. Various control procedures appear to have completely eliminated the possibility that trace contaminants of allergens were responsible. The authors remark that other patients developed no such "conditioned response" to the apparatus.

Experimental interviews with 17 asthmatic patients produced development of increased wheezing in 7 (Masuda, Notske, & Holmes, 1966). Although an increase in wheezing does not *necessarily* reflect an increase in the actual asthmatic process, there seems no special reason to doubt that it did in these cases. (Though it is peripheral to our chief point here, it is of interest that those patients who reacted "asthmatically" in the interview had lower excretions of metabolic products of epinephrine than the others, suggesting a less responsive adrenal medulla.)

Rees (1963) compared 330 asthmatic children with a control group of 160 children who had been involved in accidents, with matching for sex, age, and, as far as possible, socioeconomic status. Although he reports that "psychological and psychiatric aspects," including parental attitudes, were assessed without knowing the results of the "physical investigations," it appears that he must have, on at least some occasions, known that the children he was studying were asthmatic, since the disease is obvious to an observer. He used Kanner's (1957) criteria for classifying parental attitudes and found satisfactory attitudes in the parents of 44% of the asthmatic and 82% of the accident children. The unsatisfactory attitudes he divided into "overprotection," "perfectionism," and "overt rejection." The difference in the two groups may be regarded as evidence for the importance of psychological stimuli, to the extent that one feels that the parental attitudes and behavior evoked asthma in the children. Rees presents historical evidence that over-

protective attitudes antedated the onset of asthma in about three-quarters of the 44% of mothers who had such attitudes. Perfectionism was found in only 7% of mothers, and rejection in only 5%. In more than half of the last two categories, the attitudes antedated the onset of asthma. These findings are, however, not an answer to the possible objection that mothers who, for genetic reasons, have asthmatic children also develop overprotective attitudes but without the latter's having any influence on the child's respiratory system.

Subgroupings   Because of its relevance to the question of the etiologic role of psychological stimuli, it is necessary to pause here to consider ways in which the whole group of asthmatics has been subdivided by various workers.

Purcell, Bernstein, and Bukantz (1961) reported a subdivision of the group of asthmatic children, which Purcell and his colleagues have subsequently used in various ways. It is based on the response of such children to coming to live in a special residential institution designed for their care. Those who recover rapidly, without much need for medication, are called "rapidly remitting" (RR) and those who need steroid medication to remain symptom free, "steroid dependent" (SD). This division, then, is based on the response to treatment. We shall not deal with a third, intermediate group.

Block, Jennings, Harvey, and Simpson (1964) divided their 62 asthmatic children on the basis of scores on what they called the Allergic Potential Scale (APS). This was designed to be an "index of the individual's somatic or constitutional predisposition to asthma." Conceptually, this statement is perhaps not completely clear. A "predisposition" is a state of the organism, and, as such, *is* neither psychic nor somatic. Also, the meaning of "constitutional" is a little obscure, although it may be intended to imply something hereditary. The items on the scale included the family history of allergy, blood eosinophile percentage, skin test reactivity, total number of allergic symptoms in the patient, and ease of recognition that specific allergens (such as a particular pollen or house dust) were responsible for symptoms. The authors do not state how the skin test allergens were chosen for any individual patient, although perhaps the patient's clinical history was the guide. (Since the cornerstone of allergic theory is that patients have specific reactivities, it should follow that a patient might have high reactivity to one skin test substance and low to another, so exactly how the "skin test reactivity" criterion was used needs a little clarification.) In summary, this division is based on the degree to which the patient fits into the traditional clinical concept of "allergy."

The third system of classification of asthmatic children was used by Pinkerton (1967). He measured lung function and used the measurements to rate the children according to the severity of their disease. Although there seems to be no necessary reason for so doing, he divided the total group into three subgroups. It appears that it would have been almost as satisfactory simply to leave them scattered along a single scale. He measured the forced expiratory volume (FEV), which reflects the degree of obstruction of airways due to broncho-constriction, and also the change in the FEV in response to constricting and dilating influences. This is a physiological division, without regard to allergic concepts.

In evaluating the findings of studies employing any of these various groupings, one should remember that the relationships among the methods of grouping are by no means clear. It is not, for example, safe to conclude that the "physiologically" mildly affected child in Pinkerton's scheme would be a rapidly remitting one in the classification of Purcell. With this warning, we can resume examination of the evidence that psychological stimuli are of etiologic consequence. Differences in home situations and parental attitudes and behavior will be considered in this section of our discussion because they are stimuli acting on the children. Purcell and Metz (1962) found that, for RR children only, a relatively late age of onset was associated with autocratic and restrictive attitudes of mothers. Further, mothers of RR children scored significantly higher on "breaking the will" and "excluding outside influence" scales than mothers of SD children, and fathers of RR children scored higher on a "harsh punishment" scale than fathers of SD children. The authors suggest, but do not conclude, that these data support the view that asthma in RR children is functioning as a learned, adaptive response to

"psychologically defined" stimulation. It should be pointed out that, even if it were established that maternal attitudes caused asthma in RR children, it would not necessarily follow that the asthma had an adaptive function. Whether or not it would be regarded as "learned" would depend on an examination of the exact meaning of "learning" in this context. The authors conducted their study to investigate the hypothesis that asthma in RR children is a response to psychological stimuli, but in SD children to infectious or allergic stimuli.

Block et al. (1964), working without knowledge of the childrens' APS scores, compared mothers of a group of low and a group of high (i.e., more allergic) children. The two groups did not differ in the severity of their illness. The data are difficult to summarize; but, on the whole, mothers of low APS children seemed to have more undesirable characteristics such as anxiety, insecurity, and discomfort in relation to other people. Observations on the mother-child interactions indicate that mothers of the low APS group generally intruded into their children's lives, and that both they and their children were frustrated by their interactions. They were disappointed if the children failed to live up to their expectations, which confirms a finding of Little and Cohen (1951). In interactions between husband and wife, judged both by the interview and direct observation, parents of the low APS group showed more "friction, conflict, deprecation, ambivalence, and dissatisfaction," than those of the high group. These findings are of great interest, although the problem of deciding how many would be significant by chance is not considered.

Pinkerton, like Rees, found three kinds of unsatisfactory parental attitudes in the parents of his asthmatic children. He refers to these under the heading of "parental psychodynamic investment." In his group of 25 children, 8% had parents with satisfactory investment; 44% of the group had parents with an overprotective investment; 28%, parents with an ambivalent investment; and 20%, parents with a rejective investment. To what extent his three categories of unsatisfactory investment correspond to the three categories of Rees is not clear but at least two of them seem to be similar if not identical. He states that the child and his family were psychodynamically evaluated "independently" of Physiological information, although he does not say that the Physiological findings were unknown to the psychodynamic evaluators. He then compared these evaluations of parents with his Physiological data. The latter are arranged according to the forced expiratory volume at rest, or the maximum forced expiratory volume (FEV), plotted against what he called the Lability Factor (LF), a measure of the amount of change in FEV the child showed. He then used a combination of the LF and the FEV to arrange the cases. There is, however, a very marked positive correlation between resting (and maximum) FEV and LF, so that it is not clear that using both in any way improves the correlations he obtained. He found a remarkably consistent relationship, such that all the 13 Physiologically mildest cases (those with high FEV) had parents with an overprotective investment; all 6 Physiologically intermediate cases had parents with an ambivalent investment; and 5 of the 6 Physiologically most severe cases had parents with a rejective investment. One of the severe cases had ambivalent parents. He would have had the same results if he had considered only the FEV at rest and had ignored the LF. His statistical analysis does not quite do justice to this remarkable finding because of arbitrary division points used in his chi-square tables.

One hopes that these important results, which surely are among the most clear-cut ever obtained in psychosomatic medicine, will be confirmed by others.

It may not at first glance be obvious how the findings of these studies involving subgroups support the position that asthma is a response to psychological stimuli. Although the point is not explicitly made by any of the authors cited, the reasoning is that, if differences are found in the psychological stimuli to which two subgroups of asthmatics are exposed, then it is sensible to think that these stimuli are etiologic in at least one of the subgroups. The subgroups are now analogous to two groups of patients with diseases totally different from each other, such as cirrhosis of the liver and cancer of the kidney. If it is found that exposure to alcohol is greater in patients with cirrhosis, it is sensible to think either that alcohol is etiologic in cirrhosis, or that the lack of such expo-

sure is etiologic in kidney cancer. Additional information, of course, leads to the former conclusion. With respect to asthma we do not have the analogous additional information that would permit us to know in which subgroup psychological stimuli play a part, if they do so in only one, or whether they do so in both.

For example, the conclusion of Block et al. (1964) that "psychopathological factors [were] . . . observed significantly more often in the children identified by the low APS scores," needs to be examined carefully, if "factor" is interpreted to mean "cause." It is true that more items that everyone would probably consider "pathological" were found for the low APS children, but it is *not* true that there is any evidence that the asthma is more "psychogenic" in either possible sense of the word, in the low than in the high APS group. In other words, for all one now knows, the behavior of the high APS mothers may have been just as much a stimulus to their children's asthma as was the different behavior of the low APS mothers to *their* children's asthma. This point is emphasized because it also applies to investigations of other psychosomatic diseases. It may be objected that it is more probable that a "pathological" mother is the "cause of" (i.e., stimulus to) asthma, than is a "healthy" mother. Reflection will show, however, that we have no grounds for such an assertion. Evidence to support it would have to come from observing the relative frequencies with which pathological mothers and healthy mothers have asthmatic children, and we have no such evidence at present. One must therefore beware of concluding that the low APS group has psychogenic asthma, and the high APS group does not. Light could be thrown on these questions if one knew the exact circumstances in which the attacks of asthma occurred because one could then look for either relevant psychological or relevant allergic stimuli, but such data are not reported in this paper. Further, it is certainly theoretically possible that one individual was susceptible to both kinds of stimuli; therefore, even if one took the position that the presence of high APS scores clearly indicated that the asthma *did* occur in response to allergic stimuli, this would in no sense exclude the participation of psychological ones.

One negative result with respect to external psychological stimuli should be mentioned. Dubo et al. (1961) reported that family adjustment was not related to the age of onset or severity of asthma in children. While this finding might be considered evidence that psychological stimuli were not etiologically relevant, it is quite possible that a more refined analysis would reveal some specific aspect of family adjustment that *was* related to the onset or severity of the disease.

Long-term characteristics Knapp and Nemetz (1957) found a correlation of .81 between independent ratings of severity of pulmonary disability and severity of personality disturbance in 40 patients. In general, even for individual subjects studied across time, the relation between Psychological disturbance and severity of asthma was positive, although there is no formal calculation of this relationship. On the other hand, Dubo et al. (1961) had found that the behavioral adjustment of asthmatic children was not correlated with severity of asthma.

French and Alexander (Alexander, 1950) suggest that the constant feature of the personalities of asthmatics is "conflict centering in an excessive, unresolved dependence upon the mother"; this dependence is a wish to be protected, or "encompassed," rather than, for instance, to be fed. They state that a "history of maternal rejection in the lives of asthma patients is found as a recurrent motif." J. Miller and Baruch (1948) had reached similar conclusions. They were supported by the outcome of the Chicago interview study. In this connection one should mention a series of papers by Knapp and his colleagues (Knapp, 1960; Knapp, Carr, Mushatt, & Nemetz, 1966; Knapp, Mushatt, & Nemetz, 1966; Knapp & Nemetz, 1960) reporting their careful, intensive, psychoanalytic study of asthmatic patients, together with Physiological and Biochemical measurements. This research is cited again in the discussion of the asthmatic episode.

Reasoning that, if the above formulation were true, patients with allergic rhinitis or asthma should have a greater need for recognition than other persons, Greenfield (1958) found that in fact they did, as judged by recall of pictures representing that need.

Perhaps it is worthwhile to mention the obvious

point that, in personality or similar studies of a group of persons of whom all have the same disease, it is implicit that the patients are being compared with some sort of indefinite group of persons who do not have the illness in question; for if what were said of asthmatics, for instance, were also true of every person, it would be of no interest in the present context.

Purcell, Turnbull, and Bernstein (1962) studied 84 asthmatic children, divided into RR, intermediate, and SD subgoups according to the scheme mentioned above. A variety of psychological tests and behavior-rating data showed no significant differences among the subgroups. In connection with these findings, the authors make a comment that has a much broader application, and is relevant particularly to the formerly common technique of applying tests of "neuroticism" to groups of persons with various Physically defined illnesses. The comment is "that the creation of specialized research instruments for the testing of specific relationships between Psychologically defined variables and asthma might represent an advance over the research use of the usual diagnostic psychological test." The importance of this point is that "normal" results in a particular psychological test are often taken to mean that there are *no* differences that can be described Psychologically. The fallacy here can be made clear by analogy: consider a conclusion that there are *no* biochemical abnormalities in a patient, made on the basis of five biochemical laboratory procedures. Baraff and Cunningham (1965) later found, using Osgood's semantic differential technique for rating the concepts "me," "mother," "father," and "asthma" (or "illness" for healthy subjects), that RR children differed more from normal children than SD children did.

The subgrouping used by Block, Jennings, Harvey, and Simpson (1964), based on the APS, was used for correlation with scores on a Children's Apperception Test, with scores in a doll-play situation, and with descriptions of the children by their parents. These were independent of any knowledge by the investigators of the children's APS scores. It is not easy to summarize the differences found between the high and low APS groups, but it can in general be said that the low APS children had more of what one might consider undesirable characteristics, subsumed by the authors under the heading "psychopathology." Included were such traits as pessimism, anger in response to frustration, conforming, and preoccupation with themes of orality and aggression. Their parents described the children as rebellious, clinging, intelligent, jealous, nervous, and whining. There is no statistical treatment of data obtained from this part of the study. Pinkerton (1967), who developed the Physiological scheme of subdivision of asthmatics mentioned above, did not correlate it with characteristics of the patients themselves.

We may include here the study by Owen (1963) of the respiratory response of asthmatic children to hearing tape recordings of the voices of their mothers and of unfamiliar persons. If the changes in respiration are important parts of the actual pathogenesis of the asthmatic attack, then perhaps the work could be included in the "psychological stimuli" section. Each of 40 children, 20 of them asthmatic, heard a "threatening" story and a neutral one. Distribution of the kind of voice versus the kind of story was appropriately arranged in the experimental design, although the unfamiliar voice always came first. The respiratory rate, amplitude, and variability of amplitude were measured by pneumography. It was found, to a statistically significant degree, that asthmatic children showed more variability of amplitude on hearing their mothers' voices than did control subjects on hearing theirs. Further, asthmatic children showed more abnormal patterns of respiration as a result of hearing their mothers' voices than did control subjects. These patterns had to be rated by judges, instead of being derived from simple measurements of the respiratory tracings. The first finding was true for both threatening and nonthreatening material. It is interesting that responses to threatening material were not significantly different from those to nonthreatening. Therefore, one can say that the asthmatic children differentiated more between mothers' and unfamiliar voices than did control subjects.

Stevenson and Ripley (1952) also conducted a pneumographic study, using 22 patients, 15 of whom had asthma and 7 had anxiety states. The stimuli used were requests by the experimenters to think of disturbing topics, although it is not clearly said how these topics were chosen. Some were selected because they were known by the interviewer, on the basis of the patient's history, to be related to the development of symptoms. The way the results were reported makes it uncertain whether the findings should be considered under "rôle of psychological stimuli" or in the present section, or even in connection with Psychological statements about acute episodes. In any case, the authors found that a prolongation of expiration as compared with inspiration during periods of emotional disturbance occurred in 10 of the 11 asthmatic patients whose records permitted this comparison to be made, and in only 3 of 7 patients with anxiety. (Difficulty in expiration is particularly characteristic of asthma.) In three asthmatic patients this change was associated with wheezing and dyspnea, and in one with dyspnea alone.

Psychological statements at the time of disease French and Alexander (Alexander, 1950) concluded that a "repressed desire for the mother" produced spasm of the bronchioles. A case is cited, from which the conclusion is drawn that "activation of the longing to run back to mother," plus defense against this longing, precipitated attacks. They introduce the additional hypothesis, following an earlier suggestion by E. Weiss, that the attack "represents a suppressed cry for the mother." These ideas have had a good deal of influence on later writers, although they have never been put to anything that could reasonably be called a rigorous test. Nevertheless, it seems to me that the question of dependence and defense against it is indeed central to the explanation of attacks of psychogenic (in either sense) asthma.

The papers by Knapp, cited above, represent an effort to work out the psychodynamics of the asthma attack itself in more detail. Of particular interest is his view that there is an initial phase of drive arousal and excitement, followed by a later phase of drive restraint and inhibition. The asthma itself occurs in association with the second phase, when the earlier strong drives and emotions have been "altered into sadness and longing." This is therefore a proposal that understanding the disease requires looking at a diphasic sequence of events, a suggestion that is also appropriate in connection with migraine and with vasovagal fainting. He suggests that the asthma attack is a partial discharge of the originally aroused drives.

The attitude reported for asthma by Grace and D. T. Graham (1952), and included in the confirmatory review study of attitudes (D. T. Graham et al., 1962), is "felt left out in the cold and wanted to shut the person or situation out." This can clearly be read as a statement that the mother had separated herself from the child, and that the patient was defending himself against his most basic feelings in response to the separation, (i.e., among other feelings, against his wish to run back to her) by excluding the mother from himself.

Purcell (1963) found by interviewing that 15 of 20 RR children described emotional arousal with negative affect as a triggering event for asthmatic attacks, while 6 of 18 SD children did so. One must be careful to recognize that this is not, as it stands, a statement that there were emotionally significant external precipitating events (i.e., psychological stimuli). He does not state, in other words, that the "emotional arousal" occurred in response to psychological stimuli, although he mentions some such instances, without dealing with the question systematically. This is important because one can assert the theoretical possibility, as indeed it has been asserted (Hebb, 1949), that the emotion is a response to some allergen such as ragweed.

Summary For technical reasons, true psychophysiological experimentation has been rather limited in asthma; yet there seems to be substantial evidence that psychological stimuli evoke the chain of processes that terminates in the clinically recognized disease. This etiologic view does not exclude the participation of such other stimuli as allergens. There is very good agreement concerning one important Psychological common denominator: a "nuclear theme in most [conceptualizations] has been the conflict in the child over dealing with independence from the maternal figure" (Lipton, Steinschneider, & Richmond, 1964). Still more basically, one could perhaps say that the problem has to do with separation from the maternal figure. There is beginning to be confirmatory evidence that asthmatics have parents whose behavior is, in fact, of a kind one might expect to give rise to this sort

of problem. Finally, the subdivision of asthmatics into various groups seems already to have proved fruitful, and the same technique might well be applied to other illnesses.

Rhinitis

We shall use the term "rhinitis" to cover processes in the nasal mucous membrane characterized by dilatation of blood vessels, leading to swelling, and increases in secretion, and will avoid so far as possible the question of whether, and to what extent, these changes are "allergic." They may, by obstruction or other means, facilitate the development of infection. We are concerned with evidence that, whether or not allergens or microorganisms are also involved, psychological stimuli play a significant part, and with possible Psychological statements to make about the person whose nose is reacting. There is clearly a close connection between rhinitis and asthma, since both frequently occur in the same person and the Physiological changes are similar in both. Therefore much of what was said in the section on asthma may also apply here.

Role of psychological stimuli By far the most extensive investigations under this heading have been conducted by Holmes and his colleagues (Holmes, Goodell, Wolf, & Wolff, 1950). Their techniques for studying nasal reactions consisted of grading swelling and secretion of the nasal mucous membrane on five point scales, and comparing mucosal color changes, which reflected changes in blood flow, with a standard color scale. None of these methods is very precise, of course, but there is no reason to think that their unreliability grossly distorts the findings. They are more careful than the observations ordinarily made by physicians in clinical work, which presumably have some value. T. H. Holmes et al. studied 136 persons, of whom 129 were patients. The other 7 were "trained investigators," but it is not clear whether they ever had significant nasal symptoms. (With respect to an organ so frequently the site of symptoms as the nose, searching for "normals" who never have symptoms may be almost hopeless.) Although the numbers of experimental attempts are not given, there were many striking examples of increases in swelling, secretion, and redness of the nasal mucosa when the experimenter introduced discussions of disturbing life situations, especially when the latter were thought from the patients' histories to be relevant to their nasal difficulties (T. H. Holmes, Treuting, & Wolff, 1951). The redness diminished if the total reaction was intense and long lasting, because the blood vessels were obscured by secretion and by swelling of the mucosa. By manipulating both the topics discussed in the interview and the concentration of ragweed pollen in the air, it was found that the two kinds of stimuli had additive effects. There is also at least one example of an experimental interview (without pollen) that elicited increases in eosinophilic cells in the nasal secretion and in the blood, a response which would ordinarily be thought to suggest an allergic reaction. In some experiments there was an increase in neutrophilic cells in the secretion, which is the cellular reaction typical of inflammation.

Holmes et al. (1950) also stated that, in a group of 100 patients with nasal disease, "a close temporal correlation between symptoms and life situations was observed."

Long-term characteristics Except insofar as statements about asthmatics apply also to persons with rhinitis, little can be gleaned from the literature under this heading. Holmes et al. (1950) described their patients as "defensive, insecure, sensitive and dependent."

Psychological statements at the time of disease Holmes arrived at no special psychological statement to be correlated with exacerbations of the disease beyond saying that the pathogenic stimuli induce interpersonal conflict with "resultant anxiety, resentment, anger, guilt, humiliation, and feelings of frustration," in various patients at various times. He also noted that the physiological changes of "rhinitis" were often seen in association with weeping. He characterized the nasal response as a "shutting out–shutting in" pattern, which one might also consider to apply to asthma. The attitude statement listed by Grace and D. T. Graham (1952) for rhinitis is the same as that for asthma, namely, "felt left out in the cold and wanted to shut out the person or situation." Rhinitis was not, however, included in the systematic interview study.

Holmes reports that the opposite nasal changes, vasoconstriction and shrinking of the mucous membrane, were found in association with "feelings of being overwhelmed, of fear, sadness and other emotions which, however strong, involve minimal conflict."

Eczema

The skin disease most discussed in psychosomatic writing is certainly eczema. Differences among authorities, however, pose serious difficulties in defining the word. Their differences may evaporate when the investigators are concerned with concrete instances because the conflicts often reflect different ideas about etiology, rather than differences about the nature of the skin lesions. The word in this section will be used to mean chronic skin lesions characterized by redness, thickening, itching, sometimes by weeping, and sometimes by the appearance called "lichenification." This definition avoids etiologic implications. An extensive review of the psychosomatic literature on skin disease up to the early 1950s is provided by Obermayer (1955), with many references to the condition, or group of conditions, we are calling "eczema."

The role of itching in this illness has led to a good deal of discussion, and also probably of confusion, because of an easy transition to the idea that itching can occur "nonphysiologically," or "purely psychically." Debate also has developed over whether itching or scratching comes first, and over whether the visible lesions in persons with psychogenic itching are the consequence of scratching. The classification of skin diseases may be based on the classifier's view on this question, but it is my opinion that such questions have not always been properly put. It may well be that a vascular change in the skin is associated with attacks of itching, and that this same vascular change intensifies the response of the skin to scratching or other mechanical trauma, in such a way that lesions develop (D. T. Graham, Goodell, & Wolff, 1957; D. T. Graham, & Wolf, 1953). I shall attempt to avoid this entire controversy, and also remind the reader that, when considering any disease in which allergy may be involved, a discussion of the role of psychological stimuli does not imply in any way that allergic stimuli are not also important.

Role of psychological stimuli   There are a number of papers reporting rather large numbers of patients in whom psychological stimuli appear to be etiologically important in producing either the onset or exacerbation of the eczema. Wittkower and Edgell (1951), for instance, found a correlation between "emotional disturbances" (it seems to be implied that these are responses to psychological stimuli) and eczematous manifestations in 77 out of 90 patients. There was a subgroup of 50 in whom there was "a clear association between significant emotional stimuli and onset or relapses. . ." They report a total of 174 episodes of which this was true. D. T. Graham and Wolf (1953) found an association between psychological stimuli and attacks of eczema in 26 of 31 patients. Many authors refer to or imply such relationships, without providing numerical data. They often concentrate instead on emotional disturbances, without clearly stating whether or not these are responses to psychological stimuli, and emphasize the kinds of personality variables taken up in the next part of this section.

Experimental investigations of the role of psychological stimuli have been concerned with cutaneous vascular responses (D. T. Graham & Wolf, 1953; Kalz, Wittkower, Vavruska, Telner, & Ferguson, 1957), and exudation into the skin of fluid from blood vessels (Kepecs, Rabin, & Robin, 1951). D. T. Graham and Wolf (1953) measured the skin temperature, which is an index of the amount of blood flowing in the skin, and the reactive hyperemia threshold, which is an index of the tonus (resistance to dilatation) of the capillaries and venules of the skin. These small vessels are chiefly responsible for the intensity of skin color. Since the lesions of eczema are both warm and red, it is obvious that dilatation of both the arterioles and the minute vessels must be occurring. Therefore, an increase in skin temperature and reduction in minute vessel tone, i.e., lowered reactive hyperemia threshold, are Physiological changes relevant to eczema, in the same way that an increase in gastric acidity is relevant to peptic ulcer.

Nineteen experimental interviews were carried out with 16 of the eczema subjects. In 15 of these experiments there was an increase in skin temperature on the discussion of life events known to have been associated with exacerbations of the eczema. In 8 of these 15, and in one additional experiment,

it was technically possible to measure the reactive hyperemia threshold and show decreased minute vessel tone. All measurements were made on the volar surface of the forearm, whether or not lesions were clearly present on it. If they were too pronounced, the reactive hyperemia threshold could not be measured. When the changes were "marked, the subjects complained of itching and often scratched," but a count of such instances is not given. Although skin temperature measurements are quite reliable, the reactive hyperemia threshold is much less so and can only be estimated sufficiently well to detect changes of the magnitude reported in the paper. In brief, the experimental interviews could be thought of as evidence that psychological stimuli can produce miniature attacks of the disease.

Reasoning that fluid production in blisters may be a process similar to that occurring in eczema, Kepecs, Robin, and Brunner (1951) applied cantharides to the skin to produce a blister. The top was then cut off, leaving a surface from which blister fluid, not blood, oozed. The quantity of fluid accumulated in known time periods was estimated by weighing filter paper that had absorbed it. The relevance of this to the present discussion is that there is increased fluid in the skin in eczema. While fluid production in an artificial blister may not reflect the same process as that which occurs in eczema, it is not necessarily completely unrelated.

Kepecs, Robin, and Brunner conducted 24 experiments, with 12 subjects, of whom 5 had conditions that fitted into the general class "eczema," one had urticaria, and 6 had no skin disease. The subjects were hypnotized and then asked to talk about emotionally charged topics. In this series of experiments, there were 38 episodes of weeping associated with an increase in the exudation rate from the blister and 9 episodes without such association. There was no evidence that the association was stronger in patients with skin diseases than in those without. Relaxing suggestions or conversation were associated with a drop in the exudation rate in 40 of 42 instances (apparently counting all those occasions "when the subject was tense and the fluid level . . . high"). After abreaction, weeping was no longer associated with significant rises in the exudation rate.

It is pertinent to the present discussion that the

exudation of fluid, a process presumably included in the pathogenesis of eczema, can be induced by psychological stimuli. On the other hand, since no special attention was paid to discussions of events thought to have precipitated attacks of the illness, the results do not confirm belief in the importance of those particular events.

Kalz et al. (1957) observed that 6 patients with eczema who had previously shown normal cutaneous flare (reddening surrounding a site of trauma) following intradermal injection of histamine, did not have a flare after "upsetting incidents." This absence of flare is common in eczema, evidently therefore reflecting some part of the pathogenic process, and was found in 15 of the 32 patients in the study. These 15, who were at least partially "restricted in emotional expression," all developed flares when retested after an interview "directed to relieve and discharge previously inhibited aggression." This is perhaps not direct evidence that psychological stimuli evoke processes involved in eczema, since the opposite effect, improvement, was produced. In addition, interpretation is complicated by the findings in patients who showed normal flares to begin with, and who were classified as "free in emotional expression." Interviews designed to be stressful, not tension relieving, with these patients increased the size of the flare, but subsequent tension-relieving interviews then decreased flaring in some patients, and increased it in others, depending on their freedom of emotional expression, and the degree of the flaring before the interview. It may be possible to consider all these results as showing the ability of a tension-relieving interview to "normalize" the reaction to histamine. Similar increases in the size of the flare in three of four patients with eczema was found by West, Kierland, and Litin (1961) following hypnosis with suggestions of comfort and relaxation. The patients were told what the expected normal results were. Testing again in waking states showed the original abnormal response.

Long-term characteristics There are in the literature a very large number of statements about personality variables in eczema; many of these are summarized by Obermayer (1955). Most authors give formulations with illustrations but without actual counts or measurements. There are a few studies with quantification of varying degrees. On the whole, there is some consensus, although it is not so striking as in some of the other illnesses discussed.

Allerhand, Gough, and Grais (1950) found 26 questionnaire items (of 108 tested) that differentiated 30 eczema patients from 30 patients with other skin diseases (" of presumed nonpsychogenic origin"), and from 30 general medical patients without skin disease. The authors summarize these as indicating restlessness, impatience with others and irritability over minor frustrations, moderate dominance and brusqueness, emphasis on inner strength and resourcefulness, and declared confidence in own health and vitality. The study deserves special mention because of its care and objective character. On the other hand, the traits listed are not obviously similar to those characteristics brought out by others who used less objective methods such as interview findings.

Seitz, Gosman, and Craton (1953) tested two psychodynamic hypotheses in a way that is both interesting and unusually careful. The hypotheses were that patients who excoriate the skin excessively tend to have strict, punitive superegos, and that they are masochistic, tending to turn hostile-aggressive feelings and impulses back against themselves. There were 35 patients with eczema (in this study, circumscribed neurodermatitis), and a control group of 29 patients with a variety of "presumably nonpsychogenic" itching skin disorders. Both groups were given the Rosenzweig Picture-Frustration Test to determine the degree of punitiveness of the superego and the degree of masochistic expression of aggressiveness. The eczema group showed significantly ($p < .01$) higher "intropunitive superego" scores, but slightly and insignificantly lower "extrapunitive superego" scores. Tests were scored without knowledge of dermatologic diagnosis. When *all* responses pertaining to the direction of aggression were considered, not just the superego responses, there were no significant differences between the two groups. The results therefore support the first hypothesis, and to a lesser extent the second, since at least the superego aggressiveness was masochistic.

McLaughlin, Shoemaker, and Guy (1953) studied

30 patients, though without careful quantitative methods, and concluded that the "general pattern of personality defects seen in these patients is . . . excessive passivity and clinging dependency coupled with a crippling inhibition of aggressive and erotic drives." The authors remark that this pattern is seen in "a variety of psychosomatic disorders," a statement very reminiscent of the common belief that the same things are said of persons with all psychosomatic diseases. As a matter of fact, however, as a review of the other illnesses discussed in this chapter will show, such a description is *not* given for all of them. The authors also comment on the masochistic element in scratching, and its relation to the psychodynamics of depression. Wittkower and Edgell (1951, cited in Wittkower and Russell, 1953) say that the "basic character" of their 90 patients was that of the "insecure clinging child, always in need of reassurance and affection." Musaph (1964) also refers to dependence and masochism, and Mohr, Tausend, Selesnick, and Augenbraun (1963), to the "passivity, submissiveness and extreme dependency" of three children with eczema they studied.

Kepecs, Robin, and Brunner (1951) found that their 20 patients with eczema fell into two different groups, one emotionally labile and "hysterical," the other rigid and compulsive. D. T. Graham and Wolf (1953) thought that such terms might apply to their patients, though without a sharp line of demarcation between groups. The significance of these and similar distinctions may turn out to lie in correlations with location (Heseltine, 1963) or other characteristics of the skin and skin lesions.

Kalz et al. (1957) divided their patients into those who were "free" and those who were "restrained" in emotional expression, a division which they suggested corresponded to that made by Kepecs, Robin, and Brunner (1951). They predicted correctly in 9 of 12 cases that the free group would show a flare on histamine injection, and in 6 of 7 restrained patients that flare would be absent. No prediction was made for a partially restrained group.

Using the technique of evaluation of body image (described in the section on rheumatoid arthritis), Fisher and Cleveland (1958) investigated a group of 25 men with skin disease they considered to be "neurodermatoses." Twenty-one of them appar-

ently had lesions that we are including under the heading "eczema." Since the statistical summaries include all 25, it is possible that the outcomes might be different if only the eczema cases were included. The skin patients had significantly higher barrier scores than those with either "stomach disturbance" (18 of whom had stomach ulcers) or with ulcerative colitis. They had significantly lower penetration-of-boundary scores than the stomach patients but not than the colitis patients. Another report concerning what is apparently the same group of skin patients (Cleveland & Fisher, 1956), compares their Rorschach responses with those of patients with industrial skin lesions, and their TAT themes with those of rheumatoid arthritics and of patients with low back pain. The authors consider the results, together with interview impressions (not quantified) and figure drawings (not quantified), to justify six conclusions about the group with "neurodermatoses." The following headings refer to various psychodynamic hypotheses about persons with "dermatitis," which can be read here as equivalent to eczema.

1. Masochism: they had a depreciatory self-concept and showed themes of masochistic pleas to those in authority.
2. Exhibitionism: they did not show evidence of especially strong fantasies involving bodily exhibition, although they did score high on fantasies involving *defense* against exhibitionism.
3. Repressed hostility: their Rorschach responses contained little reference to hostile symbols or feelings, but TAT stories were "filled with negative feelings for both parental figures." The hostile expression tended to be "masochistically directed toward figures who represent the self."
4. "Armorplate" defense: like rheumatoid arthritics, they unconsciously think of their bodies as surrounded by an impermeable barrier.
5. Authoritarian father: a powerful, successful, and distant father was found in both their conscious descriptions and their TAT stories.
6. Rejecting mother: they felt resentment toward their mothers because the mothers never gave adequate love and attention.

All of these conclusions are supported by statistically significant differences from at least one of the control groups.

Many authors discuss the special importance of feelings toward the mother, although the father (contrary to a statement made in the paper just cited) has not received much attention. Kepecs et al. (1951) write of the "strongly hostile-dependent relation to the mother," which is a good summary statement of a theme referred to in many other discussions. Without a careful assessment of statements made about persons with other diseases, or, still better, control studies focused on this question, one cannot, of course, be certain that it is distinctive of the eczema patient, although one gains the impression that it is. It is probably not necessary, however, that the mother rather than the father be involved.

Condensing again the reports of many authors, there is a clear consensus that hostility in eczema patients is a consequence of their unsatisfied dependency needs. In particular, the idea that the unsatisfied wish is specifically for skin contact has long been entertained. Rosenthal (1952) therefore interviewed mothers of 25 infants with eczema and of 18 with illnesses not involving the skin. Although he knew at the time of interview to what group the infant belonged, it is nevertheless impressive that the mothers of infants with eczema reported much less often than the control mothers that they picked up the baby when it cried (24% versus 61%). There are striking similarities between this finding and a report of Spitz (1951) that the mothers of 22 infants with eczema, among 222 infants studied, revealed unconscious hostility toward their children, had overt anxiety about them, and therefore "were afraid to touch their children or refused to touch them." Unfortunately, the available reference does not include the quantitative evidence in support of these conclusions.

It should be noted that a conclusion, such as Obermayer's (1955), that patients show no consistent Psychological structure, and that persons without cutaneous disease show the same personality qualities as the patients, needs to be carefully examined. It applies, of course, only with respect to the methods used for testing. Furthermore, this statement is essentially a reference to only the very global categories of obsessive-compulsive and hysterical personalities. This becomes clear, when Obermayer reports that in fact there were certain characteristics "in common" in the patients. These included masochism, dependency, marked sexual

conflicts, and preoccupation with skin as "the safeguarding wall between their inner insecurity and the threatening outside world." The last supports the body-image studies of Fisher and Cleveland (1958). Exhibitionism is mentioned by some authors (e.g., Obermayer, 1955) as a prominent characteristic of patients with eczema, and as not so by others (D. T. Graham & Wolf, 1953; Kepecs, Robin, & Brunner, 1951). The discrepancy may result from different definitions of the term or from differences in the patient populations sampled. Alexander's (1950) formulation, emphasizing exhibitionism, masochism, and the need for love, was supported by the Chicago interview study.

Psychological statements at the time of disease
The consideration of attacks of eczema is complicated by the problems arising from the need to consider relations among the three variables, itching, scratching, and skin lesions, relations that have been much debated, and often not in a very lucid way. In other words, it is quite possible (and, in the opinion of D. T. Graham & Wolf, 1953, fairly likely) that these three aspects of the process "eczema" vary somewhat independently. It might well follow that the Psychological correlates of one of them were not exactly the same as those of another. We shall try to avoid too much involvement with these issues. It is at least a tenable hypothesis that the typical attack of eczema begins with vasodilatation, that this is associated with itching, that scratching follows, and that the scratching is largely responsible for the visible skin lesions (D. T. Graham & Wolf, 1953). Sometimes scratching may precede itching and act as a stimulus perhaps to both vasodilatation and itching. Because of the uncertainty of the relationship among these factors, "attacks" of any of the components of the illness will be included in the following discussion.

D. T. Graham and Wolf (1953) reported that exacerbations occurred when the patient felt that he "was prevented from doing as he wished, and was unable even to think of a way to deal with the frustrating circumstances." There is no statement of the fraction of all attacks in which this attitude was observed. In at least a great many of the instances cited, the "frustration" involved was of the effort to win love, approval, or attention. This obviously fits well with the statements quoted earlier about the place of this frustration in the general personality picture of the person with eczema. It also conforms to the summary statement of Brown (1967), that "there is one consistent theme in the literature, that of inhibition or suppression of aggressive impulses, particularly those springing from frustrated dependency needs, and often leading to exacerbations of the eczema." Eczema was included in the diseases studied in the attitude interview study previously cited (D. T. Graham et al., 1962), and the positive results of that study may therefore be considered as supportive of the "frustration" formulation.

Kepecs, Robin, and Brunner (1951) state that attacks in their "hysterical" group occurred when heterosexual strivings were frustrated. They mention that in their "rigid" group, conflicts about work situations were associated with exacerbations, without going further into Psychological statements to be made about the patients at that time. If we consider increased exudation into a blister site as the sign of an exacerbation of eczema, then their finding that exudation occurs with weeping suggests that exacerbations occur in association with those emotional states that accompany weeping. They also reported that the inhibition of weeping, as the result either of the experimenter's suggestion or of the subject's own reluctance to weep, was "in several instances" associated with a pattern consisting of a fall in exudation rate, followed by a rise. Kalz et al. (1957) reported differences in the size of flare response to histamine in association with differences in emotional state but without specifying the states other than to imply that flare response increased (in general, this would appear to be in the direction of an improvement in the skin) with free emotional expression.

D. T. Graham and Wolf (1953) did not deal explicitly with the question of what emotional state was present when their patients showed the cutaneous vasodilatation pattern during interviews dealing with life events etiologic for their illness. The assumption is, however, that it was the frustration reported as associated with the acute attacks of disease. In a later paper (D. T. Graham, 1955), it was reported that the cutaneous vascular changes in hostility, anxiety, and depression were different

from the pattern seen in eczema, and that psoriasis, which was associated with its own specific attitude (i.e., emotion) had a still different pattern. It therefore seems safe to conclude that not every emotional state, whether or not freely expressed, will be found associated with attacks of eczema. A more general conclusion is reached by McLaughlin, Shoemaker, and Guy (1953), who report that the common factor, Psychologically speaking, in response to events that provoke eczema is that they represent "an actual or threatened disruption of the emotional ties between the patient and the object of his excessive dependency." This is in no sense in opposition to the opinions of the other authors cited. Neither is it very different from what has been said about some other illnesses. McLaughlin, Shoemaker, and Guy also suggest that an attack of eczema is psychodynamically similar to a depression.

If we focus more closely on itching and scratching, additional, but not opposing, interpretations may be offered. If it is accepted that neural pain mechanisms for itching are closely related to those for pain, then there is experimental evidence linking vasodilatation with itching, since vasodilatation lowers the pain (and presumably thereby also the itch) threshold (D. T. Graham, Goodell, & Wolff, 1957). Itching is likely to occur at times of vasodilatation, and it was reported by patients during experimental interviews (D. T. Graham & Wolf, 1953) when vasodilatation developed. It may well be, of course, that itching is at least partially independent of the vascular changes, so that we are justified in looking for partially independent Psychological correlates.

Kepecs and Robin (1955) proposed that itching was a mixture of pleasure and pain, reflecting a state of the skin suitable for giving masochistic satisfaction when scratched. The combination of self-destructive impulses (i.e., hostility directed against the self) and pleasure in various degrees is mentioned by almost all authors who have discussed eczema Psychologically.

The act of scratching, then, may be considered as somewhat independent of the degree of itching, to judge by patients' reports. It appears to have several Psychologically stated correlates at different times and for different persons: acting out of self-destructive impulses; the relief of itching, giving pleasure which may have a masochistic quality; induction of further pleasure from increased itching and further scratching; attention-getting; and the discharge of tension, as in such other acts as table tapping. Scratching is unquestionably important in producing skin lesions and also, sometimes, further itching. Finally, several authors (D. T. Graham & Wolf, 1953; Wittkower & Russell, 1953) suggest that the location of lesions may be related to the precise emotional problem concerned: e.g., on the genitalia when there is sexual difficulty, on the ring finger at a time of marital infidelity, on the face when the patient's position in the eyes of others is the important issue, etc. The interpretation of such phenomena is complicated by the role of contact and mechanical trauma (as in the case of the ring), and by efforts to apply the unsatisfactorily defined concept "conversion."

Summary   There is abundant historical evidence that eczema is a response to psychological stimuli, and there is a measure of experimental confirmation of this conclusion. There seems to be a consensus that common to patients with the disease are strong, but ambivalent, dependency wishes and self-directed hostility. There is reason to think that attacks of the disease may occur in association with a state that can be described Psychologically as frustration of dependency and an increase in self-directed aggression. The evidence that deficient or faulty skin contact in infancy may be etiologically important is so interesting and promising that it is surprising that this lead has not been systematically followed.

Urticaria

Urticaria or hives has received less systematic attention in the psychosomatic literature than has eczema. It is physiologically distinct from eczema; it is also closely related to it (D. T. Graham & Wolf, 1953); and there appear to be patients with skin disorders transitional between the two. As in eczema, an important part of the pathophysiological process is dilatation of arterioles, capillaries, and venules ("minute vessels") of the skin. In pure urticaria there are no chronic skin lesions.

It has been said that patients with what was

called "psychogenic urticaria" might really have had only "dermographism," a condition in which the lesions appear only after mechanical trauma of the skin and do not itch. One reason for raising the question is the belief on the part of some that only one unusual kind of urticaria, characterized by a particular form and distribution of lesions, is psychogenic. This was called "cholinergic," because it was thought, probably correctly, to be due to release of acetylcholine at nerve endings on the blood vessels. Since most of the patients discussed in the psychosomatic literature did not have lesions of this form and distribution, the contention is that their urticaria was not cholinergic, and was therefore not psychogenic. There is, however, no reason to assume that only urticarial lesions of this form are cholinergic, nor is there any reason to assume that only cholinergic urticaria is psychogenic. Aside from the improbability that patients whose lesions looked and acted like urticaria, and who were *not* selected because of known emotional disturbances or for any reason other than the presence of the lesions, had "dermographism" instead, it is not even altogether clear exactly what the criticism is. It appears to arise from difficulty in believing that lesions can be produced by what are called "purely psychic mechanisms," which means in this case, without rubbing or scratching. It is immediately apparent that it is impossible to know about any patient that there was *no* mechanical stimulation of the skin. Further, it is admitted by all that persons with urticaria tend to develop more lesions at sites of minor trauma. Therefore, the rational approach is to look into the evidence that the illness in any patient or group of patients is psychogenic, and arguments about whether rubbing is or is not a necessary step in the pathogenesis of the lesions are, as Obermayer (1955) points out, of no decisive importance with respect to this question.

Role of psychological stimuli   There seem to be only a few reports in the past 20 years of clinical investigation of the role of psychological stimuli in any significant number of patients with urticaria. D. T. Graham (1950) reported that in 29 of 30 patients, selected insofar as possible only because they had chronic urticaria, and not because emotional factors were thought to be important, traumatic life situations precipitated attacks of hives. There is no statement concerning the total number of attacks of which this was true. Wittkower and Russell (1953) studied 35 patients but seem to have inquired into significant psychological stimuli in only 25. In 19 of these, "disturbing events" preceded the onset of the illness but very little is said about subsequent attacks. Kraft and Blumenthal (1959), reporting a study of 22 patients, say that psychological stimuli provoked attacks of urticaria, although they do not give actual counts. D. A. Miller, Freeman, and Akers (1968) report that "emotional factors" were significant in 23 of 50 consecutive cases of chronic urticaria but the criteria for their decision are not stated.

There is also experimental evidence that psychological stimuli are important. Experimental interviews (D. T. Graham, 1950) with 20 patients showed reduction of the reactive hyperemia threshold[2] in all cases and an increase in the skin temperature in 11 of the 13 instances in which it was measured while significant life events were discussed. Both of these changes are steps in the pathogenesis of urticaria, and the reasoning is analogous to that employed when small increases in blood pressure or gastric acidity are found in experimental interviews with patients with essential hypertension and peptic ulcer, respectively. The two "failures" occurred when the patients developed an emotion other than that present when their urticaria had appeared. During the interviews 5 patients developed urticarial lesions. Sensitivity to pilocarpine and histamine applied to the skin increased during the stressful portion of the interview with one subject, returning to the original level when bland topics were discussed, and there were similar changes in the response to stroking the skin of 3 subjects. The study would have been improved by quantitative summary of the amount of change in the measured variables and by stating the criteria for scoring the changes.

Additional evidence comes from three experiments in which the "urticaria attitude" ("being mistreated and helpless to do anything about it") was suggested to hypnotized subjects without skin disease. The aim of these studies was to produce

[2]See section on eczema, p. 897.

Physiological changes relevant to urticaria through the use of psychological stimuli having a reasonable connection with the disease. In the first experiment (D. T. Graham, Stern, & Winokur, 1958), in which 8 subjects were used, the urticaria attitude was suggested on a total of 23 occasions, and the Raynaud's disease attitude ("wish to take hostile physical action") on 18 occasions. As far as skin temperature goes, Raynaud's disease is the direct antithesis of urticaria, in that the skin temperature falls. The averaging of all the responses to the urticaria suggestions produced a curve that showed a preliminary fall, followed by a steady and statistically significant rise in temperature, whereas the response to the Raynaud's attitude suggestions was a steady and significant fall. This strengthens the belief that the warming of the skin when the urticaria attitude was suggested is a true response to that stimulus and not merely a consequence of sitting in the laboratory for a period of time.

In a second experiment (Stern et al., 1961) the urticaria attitude was suggested 11 times but only when the skin temperature in the control period was falling, in an effort to show that the suggestion could reverse that trend. This is a tactic of doubtful merit; in fact, the temperatures during the suggestion period were lower than during the control period, although the *slope* of the change was reversed. Conversely, a rising slope in the control period was reversed by suggesting the Raynaud's attitude, so that, if differences in control slopes are taken into account, the results confirm those of the first study.

Improvements in experimental design were incorporated into a third study (D. T. Graham et al., 1962) which is also described in the hypertension section of this chapter. Twenty subjects were given urticaria and hypertension attitude suggestions on each of two days, with the order of presentation reversed on the second day. Suggestion of the urticaria attitude evoked a significant rise in skin temperature, which was significantly different from the slight fall in skin temperature during suggestion of the hypertension attitude. Even though the absolute increases were small, the differences between responses to the two attitude suggestions were statistically significant for all three measures of change: maximal change, average change, and rate of change. The maximal change averaged over all 40 trials was 0.199° C. Suggestions of the same attitudes to subjects who were not hypnotized (F. K. Graham & Kunish, 1965) produced changes in the same directions but not quite at statistically significant levels. Gottlieb, Gleser, and Gottschalk have published a very similar study (1967) of hypnotized 16- and 17-year-old males, in which the skin temperatures rose in the control periods. During the suggestion of the urticaria attitude, this rise continued with very little change in slope; during suggestion of the Raynaud's attitude, especially when this was to be toward the experimental assistant, rather than toward the hypnotist, the slope abruptly leveled off, although the temperature did not actually fall. The difference in the effects of the two suggestions was statistically significant when the attitudes were to be toward the hypnotist but not when they were to be toward the assistant. The authors considered that the urticaria attitude produced a rise in temperature and that the Raynaud's attitude produced no change. It seems preferable, however, in view of the previous experiments discussed, to consider the sharp change in slope on suggesting the Raynaud's attitude to be equivalent to a fall in temperature. The results with the hives attitude appear to be uninterpretable because of the already rising temperature. D. T. Graham et al. (1962) had reported difficulty in producing an increase in slope if the control slope were already positive—i.e., if the temperatures in the control period were already rising.

Long-term characteristics There is little published material to discuss under this heading; most of it has been mentioned by Hamilton (1955). Although he states that there is wide disagreement among various authors, closer examination suggests that this is not really the case. At least some of the apparent differences result from describing different aspects of the total personality, rather than true discordance with respect to the things that are said. The paucity of literature, as well as some lack of precision in what is written, makes it difficult to determine whether there is any real consensus comparable to that which can be found for eczema or for hyperthyroidism.

Part of the difficulty is in a blending of statements in the literature about the personality in general with those about Psychological statements to be made at the time of the attack of the disease. That is, what is being described may be a state prevailing during the periods of urticaria but not necessarily characteristic of the patient at other times in his life. At the risk of distorting by abstracting and oversimplifying, it is possible to find some consistencies in published descriptions. The patients are passive and submissive with respect to some persons or situations, although not necessarily in all aspects of their lives; they feel resentment (i.e., a sense that something unjust is happening to them) but usually not overt hostility. Their tendencies to get into situations in which they are mistreated, and to fail to take effective action to end the mistreatment, may be regarded as a form of masochism (D. T. Graham, 1950; Hamilton, 1955; Musaph, 1964; Wittkower & Russell, 1953).

Psychological statements at the time of disease According to D. T. Graham (1950), the attitudes of patients with hives toward the situations responsible for their attacks was that they were unfairly treated and were helpless to do anything about it, or even to think of anything to do about it. Although Musaph (1964), for instance, remarks that no confirmation of this has ever been reported by others, it does not seem that real attempts to do so have been made. Most authors do not report carefully just what events precipitated attacks; therefore they cannot report the attitudes of patients toward those events.

Some support for the attitude formulation given here comes from a study by Tjossem, Leider, Deisher, Holmes, and Ripley (1959) of children's skin temperature responses to experimental situations. It was reported, though apparently without systematic data analysis, that increased skin temperature was observed "in response to threats productive of resentment for which adaptive actions were not taken." Decreased skin temperature was associated with "anxiety, fear and anger." All three of these words as used by the investigators imply either preparation for action or actual overt action. (See section below on Raynaud's disease.)

L. J. Saul and Bernstein (1941) suggest that urticaria is an equivalent of weeping. This explanation has been proposed for such other conditions as eczema (Kepecs, Robin, & Brunner, 1951) and asthma (Alexander, 1950). The question arises, what does "equivalent" mean? In effect, the statement amounts to saying that the pathogenic situation was one that might well have provoked weeping in some other person, or in the patient at some other time, and that, if weeping had occurred, urticaria would not have. Probably, a different Psychological statement could have been made if weeping had in fact taken place. In short, if a different emotion had developed, weeping would have replaced urticaria. It remains to be shown that this is any more true of urticaria, asthma, or eczema than of many other illnesses.

Raynaud's Disease

Raynaud's disease, much commoner in women than in men, is characterized by attacks of coldness and pallor of the extremities, especially the hands. These changes necessarily reflect constriction of both minute vessels (capillaries and venules) and arterioles. Exposure to cold is effective in producing attacks but it has long been known that psychological stimuli are also effective. If the same changes occur as part of a larger disease process, they are called "Raynaud's phenomenon," a usage that restricts the name "Raynaud's disease" to cases in which a generalized disease is not present. It is not clear whether this distinction is fundamental in our present context, because it is not known whether or not the same Psychological discussion applies to the changes in both instances. The relation of Raynaud's disease to the disease, or diseases, to which the name "scleroderma" is applied, is of particular interest. Mufson (1953) regards scleroderma as both Psychologically and Physiologically only an especially severe form of Raynaud's disease.

Role of psychological stimuli   There are numerous anecdotes and case reports in the medical literature giving examples of precipitating psychological stimuli. The comparative rarity of the disease is the probable reason for the scarcity of systematic studies. It seems likely that it is fairly common in mild forms that do not lead to medical consultations or to formal diagnosis.

Mittelmann and Wolff (1939) report the occurrence of Raynaud's disease in apparent response to disturbing life situations, Mufson (1944) gives six

such case reports, and D. T. Graham (1955) four. The Mittelmann and Wolff paper is especially interesting because it also reports one of the first uses of the experimental interview to support a belief that psychological stimuli are etiologically important in illnesses described Anatomically and Physiologically. Disturbing interviews in five patients with Raynaud's disease led to profound decreases in the temperature of the skin of the hands, although illustrative data from only one case are presented. D. T. Graham reported (1955), on the basis of eight interviews with three patients with Raynaud's disease, that a pattern of increased tone of minute vessels (capillaries and venules) and constriction of arterioles (shown by a fall in skin temperature) developed in the skin of the forearm when disturbing life events, thought from the patient's history to be of etiologic consequence, were discussed. The difference in interpretation of the two studies is that a drop in temperature occurring in response to an interview is a response to psychological stimuli, and therefore is evidence that such stimuli may be responsible for the disease. On the other hand, if the drop in temperature occurs in response to a discussion of some events only, then that is evidence that those events are etiologically important.

The same pattern occurs in persons without Raynaud's disease (perhaps one should say "without sufficient Raynaud's disease to lead to a clinical diagnosis"), since the occurrence during the interview of constriction of both sets of vessels could itself be considered to be a miniature attack of the disease in experimental interviews (D. T. Graham, 1955; Mittelmann & Wolff, 1943).

Long-term characteristics   Mufson (1944, 1953) says that "the basic personality" of patients with Raynaud's disease is "one of commensalism." He means by this that they are "susceptible to threats of death, indigence, or loss of a significant protective love object upon whom they [are] emotionally over-dependent." They are therefore chronically anxious. No other author seems to have discussed the personalities of these patients.

Psychological statements at the time of disease   Although Mufson (1944) says that, when the patient's commensalistic existence is destroyed, "the dread fear" initiates the illness, it must be remarked that his case reports do not always seem to support this statement.

Mittelmann and Wolff (1943) reported a great variety of emotional states in association with decreases in skin temperatures during their experimental interviews. D. T. Graham (1955), however, concluded on the basis of interviews with 19 patients, including 4 with Raynaud's disease, that a fall in skin temperature (due to arteriolar constriction) and an increase in the tone of minute vessels was associated with either *hostility* (a wish to take directly aggressive action) or *anxiety*. He also reported that actual major attacks of Raynaud's disease always occurred when hostility was present. This is not necessarily incompatible with Mufson's conclusion, since it is certainly common to have movement from fear to hostility, or the reverse, or to have what appear to be mixtures of the two states. The common denominator in "vasoconstrictive" emotions may be *action,* either overt or prepared for (see reference to Tjossem et al., 1959, in the section on urticaria).

Additional supporting evidence for the "hostility" formulation comes from the studies of the effects of suggesting attitudes to hypnotized subjects discussed above (Gottlieb, Gleser, & Gottschalk, 1967; D. T. Graham, Stern, & Winokur, 1958; Stern et al., 1961), in which suggesting hostility lowered the skin temperature. These findings obviously say nothing about whether or not anxiety is also important.

Psoriasis

Psoriasis is a very common skin disorder, characterized by scaling lesions, most commonly occurring on extensor surfaces. Itching is variable. Despite many references to some sort of connection with "emotional disturbances," there has been very little systematic psychosomatic investigation.

Role of psychological stimuli   D. T. Graham (1954b) reported that attacks of psoriasis seem to be responses to "stressful life situations" (i.e., psychological stimuli) in 9 of 10 patients studied. In Wittkower and Russell's discussion (1953) of etiology in 86 patients, the distinction between psychological stimuli and states of the organism described Psychologically is not always made.

Wittkower and Russell seem to have concluded that such stimuli were probably etiologically important in the onset in 29 patients and were possibly so in 20 others. There is no discussion of the etiology of subsequent exacerbations.

There is some experimental support of these clinical conclusions (D. T. Graham, 1954b). Interviews concerning events, thought from the history to be of etiologic significance, evoked a pattern of change in cutaneous blood vessels different from that seen in association with urticaria, eczema, Raynaud's disease, or depressive states. It consisted of dilatation of arterioles, together with *increased* tone of minute vessels (capillaries and venules). Since it is not immediately clear that this pattern is necessarily related to the production of psoriatic lesions, one must ask how it supports the contention that such lesions are responses to psychological stimuli. The reasoning is that the tone of minute vessels has been found consistently elevated in patients with psoriasis (Milberg, 1947), and that this pattern of vascular change is apparently unique to psoriasis. This, of course, suggests that it is an important part of the pathogenesis.

Long-term characteristics   Wittkower and Russell (1953) found five personality types among their patients. There seems to be very little careful discussion of personality dimensions by other authors, and hence no consensus.

Psychological statements at the time of disease   D. T. Graham (1954) said that the nine of his patients whose psoriasis was a response to psychological stimuli all had the same attitude toward the pathogenic events: they felt that they were exposed to constant "gnawing" or irritation, which they had to try to tolerate or "put up with." Other authors have hardly dealt with this question.

Acne Vulgaris

There are sporadic references, without much systematic investigation, to the importance of emotional states or of disturbing life circumstances in acne. It is included here because there are some experimental psychophysiologic data. Although its pathogenesis is not agreed on, it is certainly a disease of the sebaceous glands and therefore is presumably related in some way to changes in sebum secretion.

Role of psychological stimuli Lorenz, D. T. Graham, and Wolf (1953) reported correlations between disturbing events and exacerbations of acne in 30 patients, who were not selected because of any known emotional problem. The method used was the correlation of events listed in a diary kept by the patient with the number of pustules on the face. The death of the senior author prevented publication of the detailed results, so that the only findings available from this part of the study are illustrative examples of two patients followed over 6-week periods (Lorenz, D. T. Graham, & Wolf, 1953; Wolff, Lorenz, & D. T. Graham, 1951). Each patient, however, went through several outbreaks during the period of study.

The same authors report experimental interviews in which discussions of disturbing topics evoked changes in the amount of facial sebum, as well as similar interviews in which such topics were deliberately avoided. Each interview, whether "stress" or "nonstress," began with a control period, in which only neutral topics were discussed. Differences between "control" and "stress" interviews were, in short, confined to the second half of the experimental period. Stress interviews were likewise conducted with 10 patients who did not have acne. Topics chosen with these patients were those known to be important to them and to refer to situations that had produced symptoms of their respective illnesses in the past. Further, they were observed to react in various ways such as by headache or respiratory disturbance during the experiments.

These interviews, occurring rather late in the development of this technique, show a desirable improvement in design, since the decision about the kind of interview was made before the experiment was actually conducted, thus minimizing the possibility of biased reporting of outcomes to make them conform to the experimenters' expectations. One difficulty remains: the interviews with the acne patients are divided according to whether "anger" or "remorse" was mobilized in the patient, a judgment that was apparently not made in ignorance of the outcome of the physiological measures. Fur-

ther, criteria for designating the emotional states are not given.

The physiological measure during the experiments was the estimation of the amount of sebum produced on the face. The sebum was transferred to the end of a glass rod, and thence to a monomolecular layer of oil on water, thus permitting measurement of the area of the fatty sebum, which spread out within the oil as a readily visible film (Lorenz, D. T. Graham, & Wolff, 1952). It is probably not possible to use this technique to give any very good estimate of the absolute amount of sebum produced during a known period of time but very marked differences were apparent, from subject to subject, and between experimental conditions in single subjects.

The experimental manipulations were very successful in producing changes in sebum secretion, which one may take as an indication that psychological stimuli do influence the activity of sebaceous glands and may therefore play a part in the development of acne. Further, in those 12 interviews in which a period of reassurance was added to the control and stress periods, there was uniformly a substantial return of sebum values toward those prevailing in the control period, which is additional evidence that the mere passage of time was not the reason for the change.

During the 38 "nonstress" interviews with acne patients and the 10 stress interviews with patients without acne there were only slight changes in the amount of sebum obtained from the face. During the 29 interviews with acne patients in which "anger" was mobilized, however, there were very substantial increases in sebum obtained, and during 5 experiments in which "remorse" was mobilized, there were very substantial decreases. Statistical analysis is not presented because, as the authors point out, the differences between the stress experiments with the acne patients and the other two kinds of experiments are so great as to make such analysis superfluous. There was, in fact, no overlap in percentage change between the acne stress experiments, and the other two kinds. In other words, during anger, every acne patient showed more increase in sebum secretion than did any acne patient in a nonstress interview, or any nonacne patient; similarly, every acne patient during a remorse pe-

908

APPLICATIONS OF TECHNIQUES AND FINDINGS

riod showed a greater decrease than any acne patient in a nonstress period, or any nonacne patient.

Robin and Kepecs (1953) likewise studied sebum secretion, although by a quite different method, involving the application of osmic acid to the skin. With this technique, black dots appear when sebum is present. None of their subjects had acne. Their experimental manipulation was discussion with the patients of disturbing topics, although how these were chosen is not stated. They succeeded in obtaining emotional disturbance in 14 interviews, in 12 of which there were parallel increases in the rate of production of sebum. The emotional states were said to be "fear" and "weeping." This is in some contrast with the report just mentioned of the lack of changes in sebum secretion in experimental interviews in nonacne patients but it may be that the states of the nonacne patients of Lorenz et al. were neither "fear" nor "weeping." In fact, several of Robin and Kepec's patients appeared to be reacting to the experimental procedure as a threat, a situation that may not have prevailed in the patients of Lorenz et al. Of 9 experiments in which no emotional fluctuations occurred, sebum secretion remained essentially constant in 7.

Long-term characteristics There is little to report under this heading. Wittkower and Russell (1953) studied 64 patients, aged 18 or older, and found that 55 of them could be classified in one of the four categories rigid persons, rebels and dreamers, overgrown children, or persons showing gross psychological disorders. Nine patients could not be classified. The feature that they found "common to a majority" of their patients was an "inhibition of their sexuality." They did not, however, attempt to correlate any events leading to the activation of sexual conflict, or intrapsychic changes in the sexual conflict, with changes in the state of the acne. If the conclusion about sexuality in these patients could be confirmed and shown to distinguish them from patients with other illnesses, it would be of considerable interest. Lucas and Ojha (1963) used the Maudsley Personality Inventory in pursuing an earlier investigation (Lucas, 1961). Patients with acne showed no significant differences from English norms of neuroticism or extraversion. However, the 14 patients who *reported* exacerba-

tion of the disease with "strain and fatigue" had significantly higher neuroticism scores than the 29 who did not. How to interpret this result is not clear. We do not know, for instance, that no such association existed in those who failed to report it. Further, as this chapter has emphasized, such an association is not the same as a statement that exacerbations were responses to psychological stimuli.

Psychological statements at the time of disease Lorenz, D. T. Graham and Wolf (1953) say that the prevailing attitude of acne patients at the time of attack was that they felt they were being "picked on or at, and wanted to be let alone." They go on to distinguish between "anger" and "remorse" and suggest that the actual attack of acne did not occur until the patient had gone through alternations between anger and remorse. It must be said, however, that it would have been desirable to express the states "anger" and "remorse" more precisely in terms of attitudes if that had been possible. It may be that the attitude statement given really applies only to the anger stage. It will be recalled that the experimental interviews suggested that anger was associated with hypersecretion of sebum, and remorse with hyposecretion.

It has been objected that this technique might reflect, not changes in sebum produced, but changes in sweat on the face or changes in the properties of existing sebum when facial temperatures increased as vasodilatation occurred. However, Lorenz, D. T. Graham, and Wolff (1952) concluded after various control studies that neither of these could account for the increase in sebum estimated by this method.

Diabetes Mellitus

Psychosomatic investigation of diabetes appears to have waned in recent years. A chronic problem is the distraction of attention from the central focus on the diabetic metabolic state itself to such subsidiary issues as the failure of patients to take insulin or to follow a prescribed diet, or their reactions to the discovery that they have diabetes. These matters are certainly important in the treatment of a person with diabetes but it is not clear that they shed much light on the more basic question. The study is also complicated by the existence of at least two major kinds of diabetes mellitus, "maturity onset" and "juvenile," which may have different metabolic mechanisms. To what extent, if any, there are associated Psychological differences is unknown. Treuting (1962) has reviewed much of the relevant psychological literature about the disease.

Role of psychological stimuli There are a number of reports of the onset or exacerbation of diabetes occurring soon after some significant event, i.e., after what is often called "a significant life stress" (Hinkle, Evans, & Wolf, 1951a, 1951b; Slawson, Flynn, & Kollar, 1963; Treuting, 1962). These are of much the same character as other reports based on clinical histories, although the work of Hinkle, Evans, and Wolf increases the strength of the evidence by attention to the relation between psychological stimuli and remission or exacerbations of the disease in individual persons followed over a period of time.

Almost all of the significant experimental work has been carried out by Hinkle and his colleagues, and is summarized by Hinkle and Wolf (1952). There have been other reports of changes in blood sugar in association with various emotional states or in response to psychological stimuli, but there is little reason to think that such changes are necessarily closely related to the metabolic events making up the essence of diabetes. Hinkle also measured the level of ketones in the blood, a variable that probably comes substantially closer than blood sugar to the heart of the diabetic process.

He found in nine tests with five nondiabetic subjects, that neither blood ketones nor blood sugar changed significantly over a 3-hr period when there was no effort to apply stressful stimuli; and that in seven tests with seven nondiabetic subjects (some of whom were also in the previous group) "under stress" there were higher initial levels of, and also definite rises in, blood ketones (Hinkle, Conger, & Wolf, 1950). In two of these cases, the stress was an event not manipulated or observed by the experimenter but in the other five it was an interview deliberately initiated by him. The logic of these two situations is quite different, since only the latter is a true experiment.

The diabetic subjects showed essentially the same changes. Those whose levels of blood ketones were approximately normal to begin with had stress levels approximately the same as those of nondiabetic subjects; those who had high levels developed much more striking increases. There was a total of 21 stress interview experiments with 20 subjects, to be compared with 12 nonstressful interviews with 10 subjects. Though it is not explicitly stated, it is probable that the decision about the stressfulness of the interview was made *before* it was conducted, an important point in evaluating the results.

It is of particular interest that changes in blood sugar were not consistent, and in particular often dropped while the ketones rose. It is also of interest that, in the hour after the stressful interview, the ketones returned to approximately their initial values. Although the data are not analyzed statistically, inspection of the tables and graphs leaves little doubt that differences between stress and initial levels, and between stress and control interviews, are statistically significant for both diabetic and nondiabetic subjects.

Since these were acute experiments, conducted on diabetic subjects who had omitted their morning breakfast and insulin dosage, the changes induced clearly cannot be the result of those often-invoked mechanisms, failure to take insulin or to follow a diet. In short, these experiments provide excellent evidence that metabolic changes making up the diabetic state can occur in response to psychological stimuli.

Long-term characteristics There is substantial agreement (Alexander, 1950; Dunbar, 1947b; Hinkle, Evans, & Wolf, 1951a, 1951b; as well as earlier authors) that diabetics have special concerns about food, even before what is clinically recognized as the disease, with the consequent emphasis on diet, develops. This is presumably a reflection of one kind of dependency conflict. Obesity is common in life histories of diabetics, and overeating was found to be a characteristic response to stress of the six diabetics studied longitudinally by Hinkle, Evans, and Wolf (1951a, 1951b).

Slawson, Flynn, and Kollar (1963) found that their diabetics scored high on the *D* scale (depression scale) of the MMPI but point out that this may not distinguish this group from any other hospitalized patients, or, one may add, perhaps not from nonhospitalized patients.

Psychological statements at the time of disease Slawson, Flynn, and Kollar (1963) found that 14 of their 25 patients gave a history of a definite object loss, and 6 additional patients told of an experience that could reasonably be inferred to be an object loss, prior to onset of their diabetes. It is probably not possible to go from these findings to a generally applicable Psychological statement about diabetes, since only 10 of the patients were considered to show unresolved grief. The whole group tended to show depression in MMPI testing, but, as the authors point out, this may be true of other diseases also. Loss has been said to be important for many illnesses (Schmale, 1958).

Hinkle, Evans, and Wolf (1951a, 1951b) elaborate on this interpretation in connection with diabetes. They suggest that their patients reacted "to significant stresses as if they were deprivations," and had an "unconscious or conditioned identification of 'food' with 'love and security.'" Their evidence, however, is not so definite as that which has led to analogous conclusions in more recent work concerned with other illnesses, as the necessity of the validation of Psychological statements has become more apparent. Their point of view is associated with an "adaptational" interpretation offered by Hinkle, Evans, and Wolf, which is interesting enough to be mentioned, although we have avoided such discussions in connection with most illnesses. They pointed to the many similarities between the diabetic state and the metabolism of the nondiabetic starving person, and suggested (1951a) that "persons showing this disorder react to various life stresses with a physiologic response which is appropriate to starvation, but inappropriate to the deprivations which they have suffered."

Hyperthyroidism

Hyperthyroidism, which occurs much more often in women than in men, has been recognized from the time of its earliest descriptions as, in some instances at least, a response to psychological stimuli. Subsequent discussions of the disease have not, in general, distinguished between the hyperthyroidism associated with diffuse toxic goiter and that associated with toxic nodular goiter. In the former, there are typically certain characteristic changes in the eyes, in which case the name "Graves' disease" is often applied; in the latter these are absent. It is not at present clear whether or not this distinction is important with respect to the role of psychological stimuli and of particular personality descriptions. It may be important because the nodules of toxic nodular goiter are thought to be independent of control by any other organ, although the diffusely toxic gland of Graves' disease is probably under the control of the pituitary or the hypothalamus. It should be remembered, in reading the remainder of this section, that there is evidence that the mechanism by which the thyroid is "driven" in hyperthyroid patients is different from that in euthyroid persons.

Mandelbrote and Wittkower (1955) provide a brief summary of the psychosomatic literature on hyperthyroidism through 1953.

Role of psychological stimuli Despite the fairly large number of psychological discussions of hyperthyroidism, most of the reports focus on descriptions of the personalities of the patients, rather than on the role of external psychological stimuli (e.g., Ham, Alexander, & Carmichael, 1951; Mandelbrote & Wittkower, 1955). The latter are mentioned in passing, so to speak, in connection with some of the cases reported, and it seems to be implied that they were usually found to be present. The importance of this point has been discussed elsewhere in this chapter but it may be justifiable to consider it again here. Alexander's (1950) formulation is to the effect that the disease occurs with the failure of adaptive efforts made by the patient to defend against the "frustration of dependent longings and persistent threats to security." Such a statement could be true, and yet it would not follow that this failure was a response to a psychological stimulus—it might occur because the defense mechanisms had simply "worn out" after many years of overuse, irrespective of any particular changes in the total stimulus situation. Of course, if psychological stimuli early in life were thought to be responsible for the use of these mechanisms in the first place, one could view the disease, even under these cirumstances, as simply a response with a very long latency.

The experimental approach to hyperthyroidism is represented by only a small number of reports, probably because of technical problems in estimating the small changes in thyroid function that an experimenter can reasonably hope to induce within practical time limits. Wittkower, Scheringer, and Bay (1932) found in a pioneering study that an emotional stress resulted in an increase in the blood iodine in 13 of 15 subjects without thyroid disease. The total blood iodine is, however, so imperfectly related to thyroid function that the interpretation of results such as these is difficult. Dongier, Wittkower, Stephens-Newsham, and Hoffman (1956) used variations in the amount of circulating, radioactive, protein-bound iodine as an index of short-term changes in thyroid function during experimental interviews. Radioactive iodine, which can be traced in the body, had previously been administered to the subjects, and had been taken up by their thyroid glands and incorporated into thyroid hormone. Changes in thyroid function are reflected in changes in the release of thyroid hormone into the blood. The level of circulating hormone can be estimated by determining the quantity of iodine bound to protein, an estimation easier to carry out by measuring radioactivity than by other methods.

Dongier et al. conducted 36 stress interviews with 27 psychiatric patients with anxiety, none of whom was diagnosed as hyperthyroid at the time of the study. The interviews were designed "to break down psychological defenses, previously evaluated, in order to induce overt anxiety." They were then rated in terms of the degree of stressfulness, judged by the patients' verbal responses. Blood radioactive protein-bound iodine was measured before and after each interview; differences were essentially the same for the 10 most stressful as for the 10 least stressful interviews. This study, therefore, contrary to the conclusion of the earlier one, certainly provides no evidence that psychological stimuli can influence thyroid function, and by extension, induce hyperthyroidism. On the other hand, even if hyperthyroidism is a response to psychological stimuli, there is no special reason to think that stimuli that induce "anxiety," not further classified, are those that will induce changes in thyroid function. Put another way, to say that hyperthyroidism is psychogenic is not the same as to say that there is a special connection between it and the kind of anxiety seen in most psychiatric patients.

The most elaborate investigations of the effects of psychological stimuli on thyroid function (Alexander, Flagg, Foster, Clemens, & Blahd, 1961; Flagg, Clemens, Michael, Alexander, & Wark, 1965) employed motion pictures as stimuli. One was a commercial film chosen because its theme was struggle against the fear of death, thought to be of special significance to hyperthyroid persons; the others were bland travelogues.

In the first study, seven persons with hyperthyroidism, seven who had been treated for it but had normal thyroid function at the time of the experiment, and five controls, not known ever to have had thyroid disease, were studied. The indications of increased thyroid function were a rise in blood levels of radioactive protein-bound iodine (PBI) and decreases in radioactivity over the thyroid gland (neck-counts). The ill hyperthyroid patients showed substantially more blood radioactive PBI after the films than before; the treated hyperthyroid patients showed smaller increases; the control subjects showed a decrease. The raw data are not given, nor is there statistical evaluation, so that the significance of the findings cannot be estimated. There is no formal report of the neck-count results.

In the second study, in which various procedural modifications were introduced, 43 patients with hyperthyroidism, 7 with treated hyperthyroidism, and 31 without past or present evidence of hyperthyroidism were studied. Statistical analysis of the data is given. The hyperthyroid patients had significantly more decreases in neck-counts and increases in radioactive blood PBI during and after viewing the stressor film than during and after the bland film. Unfortunately, the criteria for judging "increases" and "decreases" are not spelled out but apparently the authors thought it more meaningful to consider that abrupt changes reflected increased thyroid function than to rely on differences between the beginning and end of the experiment. They state, without giving the data, that none of the first 11 control subjects responded to the films with evidence of increased thyroid activity, so that thyroid tests were not done on the remaining 20. On the basis of data from psychological tests, behavioral observations, and psychiatric interviews, variously obtained before, during, or after the films, the hyperthyroid subjects were classified according to the degree of "disturbance." The 18 "more disturbed" patients showed significantly greater decrease in neck-counts than the 19 "less disturbed" patients, and a significantly greater increase in blood radioactive protein-bound iodine during the films (for this analysis, results from watching the stressor and the bland films were combined). Both of these findings presumably reflect the increased release of hormone from the thyroid gland.

Let us now ask what bearing these findings have on the significance of psychological stimuli in hyperthyroidism. One film consistently produced greater changes than the others; the changes were therefore not entirely the result of passage of time. They indicate that psychological stimuli do influence thyroid activity in persons who are already hyperthyroid and thus certainly lend some weight to the belief that they could have been important in producing the disease in the first place. The difference between more and less disturbed patients, however, has no bearing on this point.

Long-term characteristics   There is reasonable agreement about the important personality characteristics of persons with hyperthyroidism, although the formulations are often based entirely on interview material, rather than on results from more manageable but probably less relevant "objective" tests. More important, the characteristics mentioned are sufficiently distinctive to separate them from those that are allegedly found in persons with other diseases. Statements differ somewhat from author to author (Dongier et al., 1956; Ham, Alexander, & Carmichael, 1951; Lidz, 1949; Mandelbrote & Wittkower, 1955), and it would be tedious to quote them all extensively. The more recent reports are generally quite compatible with earlier ones. We shall mention only those features that have not also been generally reported in connection with other illnesses and are cited by more than one author. Lidz (1949), for example, on the basis

of study of 15 patients, discusses the need for affection derived from some early experience of rejection, and ultimately satisfied by taking on the "over-solicitous characteristics (as the mother) in exaggerated and obsessive form." He continues, *"Without evidence of their own importance to others they feel hopeless and helpless.* The childrens' attention replaces the needed affection of the parents." Ham, Alexander, and Carmichael (1951) found, on interviewing 24 patients, that the latter showed a "premature need for self-sufficiency and maturity, in taking care of self, siblings and parents" as a result of losses of affection or frustrated dependence as children; a struggle against fear, most characteristically by counterphobic attitudes; and a significantly greater urge to bear children than in the average population. It is interesting that the last statement in the list is supported by an average number of 3.5 pregnancies per married woman in the patient group, as opposed to census figures for Chicago, where the study was carried out, of an average number of 1.7 pregnancies per woman. The paper also says, however, that this figure of 1.7 is for "living children" per woman, so there is some confusion. Further, the comparison of "married women" with "women" may obscure the picture.

It is also interesting that 50% of the patients were the oldest among their siblings, which was very significantly greater than the chance expectation. This was confirmed, although only for hyperthyroid patients who had relatives with the disorder, by Pilot and Kormos (1964), who point out that such a nonrandom distribution of disease in sibships suggest that "other than purely genetic determinants" are involved. In a series of 25 cases, Mandelbrote and Wittkower (1955), however, found neither a significantly large number of oldest children nor of only children among their patients. There is no obvious reason for this discrepancy, and as is true of many other research findings not confirmed by subsequent workers, one is simply left puzzled.

With respect to the basic question of the personalities of hyperthyroid patients, Mandelbrote and Wittkower (1955) confirmed by somewhat more precise methods many of the findings of Lidz (1949) and of Ham, Alexander, and Carmichael (1951).

Their patients were more anxious on the Saslow Rating Scale than the control group of patients with other diseases. They also showed more of each of the following: "inordinate need for children, with frustration of desires," feelings of rejection, feelings of insecurity, hostile-dependent relationships with mothers, need to remain with mothers to win their approval, and inability to accept dependency as a solution for insecurity. Differences between hyperthyroid patients and control subjects in premature striving for self-sufficiency did not quite reach conventional levels of statistical significance. Exactly how the ratings on which these statistical findings were based were made is not made clear. Both the interviews with patients and psychological tests (including projective tests) are mentioned as methods used; presumably, some combination of these was employed to make the final ratings.

Because of its relation to the discussion below of the Psychological correlates of the disease itself, the following passage from Mandelbrote and Wittkower (1955) deserves quotation (the discussion is of the patients' feelings toward children): "Reaction formations against the revived hostile feelings lead to anxious over-concern lest harm befall the needed love object. The theme of warding off the loss of a person they need, lest they be isolated, runs through their lives."

The psychoanalytic description article by Alexander (1950), summarized earlier in this chapter, is highly congruent with this statement. The hypothesis that was apparently tested in the Chicago interview study, however, together with the other psychoanalytic hypotheses, already mentioned, is shifted significantly toward making the patient's fear of death the central issue.

Dongier et al. (1956), on the basis of various published studies, listed the following characteristics of hyperthyroid patients: premature striving for independence; denial of hostility; undoing of hostile impulses by overconcern regarding the needed and ambivalently regarded objects; gaining affection by doing for others; desire and need for children (conflicting with fears of pregnancy and childbearing); feminine identification in male patients; and feebleness of defenses, leading to anxiety-proneness. They interviewed 44 patients with anxiety and predicted that those who, "on the basis of intuitive assessment," satisfied these criteria would have a shorter half-life of radioactivity in the thyroid gland (i.e., evidence of greater thyroid function) than those who did not. Using an arbitrary dividing line of a half-life of 45 days, 9 of 12 patients judged to have personality configurations like those of hyperthyroid patients did in fact have short half-lives, while only 7 of 32 judged to be not like hyperthyroid patients had short half-lives. The success rate was very significant statistically ($.001 < p < .01$). It is implied, though not made perfectly explicit, that the iodine data were not known to the 2 (occasionally, 3) judges who made the personality assessments. The authors' statement is, "After a decision had been made and duly recorded, the psychopathological findings were correlated with the experimental findings."

This study is unique in its successful correlation of an entire "personality" with a *predicted* Physiological finding. Perhaps one note of caution is necessary. There may be some danger that the arbitrary division at 45 days happens to capitalize on chance variations in the particular sample, so that the separation of the two groups may seem firmer than it really is. On the other hand, a preliminary series of 27 patients studied in the same way, but without a *prediction* of thyroid function, also showed what seems to be a significant separation at the 45-day point.

A correlation of personality variables with a measure of thyroid function that *may* be related to hyperthyroidism was reported by Wallerstein, Holzman, Voth, and Uhr (1965). They found a personality pattern that they called "inhibited martyrdom" in persons who, although without clinical evidence of thyroid disease, had areas ("hot spots") in the thyroid that put out greater than normal amounts of radioactivity after radioactive iodine had been administered. The 25 characteristics making up this personality pattern do not seem strikingly like the features listed by previous authors as typical of hyperthyroid persons. The list does not contain items referring specifically to attitudes toward children; but it is not stated whether these were simply absent from the 74 original items containing the 25 that were later found to be "salient" or whether they were present but not found salient.

The judges were successful at statistically significant levels in "blind" predictions of the presence or absence of hot spots on the basis of the personality picture. They also report that 8 of 9 subjects with hyperthyroidism "unmistakably showed the personality qualities that characterized the 15 pilot patients with 'hot spots.'" This is an important finding that should certainly be tested in further work. As the authors point out, this is desirable especially because the hyperthyroid patients were known to be such when the personality judgments were made.

In searching for a common denominator in the studies discussed, and in earlier reports, one finds a significant agreement that the central theme in the personality of the hyperthyroid person has to do with the fear of loss of a dependent relationship. This is a rather broad statement, however, applicable to too many persons to be very distinctive of hyperthyroidism. However, a closer examination of the literature suggests that there is an additional, distinctive feature of the dependency problem in the case of hyperthyroidism, a special concern about children. Not all authors make this the major focus of their presentations but it can be found in almost all, and, in my opinion, may well be the most important characteristic of the personality in hyperthyroidism. In other words, a person who is destined to become hyperthyroid seems to have reacted to an early personal loss by trying to achieve closeness with his children or with other persons who stand to him in somewhat the same relation as children.

Psychological statements at the time of disease   There is no consensus about appropriate Psychological statements to make about persons at the times of pathological increases in thyroid function. The experiments of Flagg, Clemens, Michael, Alexander, and Wark (1965) were inspired by the emphasis in the report of Ham, Alexander, and Carmichael (1951) on the fear of death as critically important in hyperthyroid patients. The finding of increased thyroid activity in such patients, in response to the motion pictures selected specifically to provoke such fear, shows that, to some extent, the Psychological correlate of acute increases in thyroid function, and, by extension, of exacerba-

tions of the disease hyperthyroidism, is in fact the fear of death. Of course, one does not know that other stimuli might not have been still more effective. Perhaps a stimulus designed to provoke a more precisely limited fear, connected with the loss of a close relationship, particularly to children, would have produced more striking changes. It is interesting that the investigators (Ham, Alexander, & Carmichael, 1951) themselves say, "In [hyperthyroid] women the struggle against anxiety caused by frustrated dependent needs manifests itself primarily in the wish to take care of and give birth to children." The actual disease syndrome develops when the defense against frustrated dependence breaks down. Lidz (1949) found "events that terminated or threatened to terminate an essential relationship" to have occurred immediately prior to the onset of hyperthyroidism in 14 of his 15 cases. In 4 of these cases it is obvious that the essential relationship was with a child. Mandelbrote and Wittkower (1955) say that hyperthyroidism is "apt to ensue" when efforts to obtain love fail "by actual loss of the mother or mother-substitute or through irrevocable rejection or desertion." They make it clear earlier in their paper that children may be "mother-substitutes."

The attitude listed by D. T. Graham et al. (1962) for hyperthyroidism is that the patient feels he might lose something or somebody he loves and takes care of, and tries to prevent the loss. This is based on the clinical observation of an unstated number of patients, and was the least successfully recognized attitude in the interview study. Although it is obviously similar to the views already mentioned, it differs in emphasizing the threat of loss rather than actual loss. In this respect it recalls the previously cited statement by Mandelbrote and Wittkower (1955) about "warding off" loss. It is still my opinion that this emphasis is sound, and that when deaths or similar "irrevocable" losses occur, a closer examination of the patient's response reveals increased anxiety about whoever is left to him (or her).

There is little experimental work to assist in psychosomatic formulations about hyperthyroidism. The evidence for the role of psychological stimuli is chiefly based on clinical histories; apparently there is no dissent from the belief that they are important. There is a satisfying agreement that the fundamental issue in life for the hyperthyroid person is to protect herself (or himself) from separation anxiety by loving and taking care of children or child substitutes.

SUMMARY

We have considered some of the major issues involved in psychosomatic medicine, as well as what appears to be the present state of knowledge and opinion in a number of those illnesses which may be called "psychosomatic," according to the possible sensible definitions of that word. Many illnesses have been omitted, for a variety of reasons, including the lack of psychophysiological data or imprecise definition. Since this chapter is concerned with *clinical* matters, it has seemed wise to confine specific discussions of illnesses to those that are reasonably well defined and also are not dealt with at length elsewhere in this volume. Therefore, the very large number of muscle tension states, for instance, are not included. The requirement of sharp clinical definition boils down, in most but not all cases, to the presence of a criterion in histopathology, and in the remainder to a Physiological disturbance that can be clearly stated (vasovagal fainting, hypertension) or a clear symptomatic picture (migraine).

What can be said about the present status of psychosomatic medicine as an area of investigation? Much of psychosomatic research has been concerned with the three problems that are emphasized in the individual disease sections of this chapter: to produce evidence that psychological stimuli are important, to find long-term psychological statements (e.g., about "personality") to make about persons with various illnesses, and to find Psychological statements applicable at the times of attacks of illness.

The evidence supporting the etiologic importance of psychological stimuli is actually firmer than many persons realize. While it needs to be improved and one may concede that it contains weaknesses, it is easy to exaggerate its defects. With respect to life histories, for instance, it should be pointed out that these are widely regarded as sources of useful information in most of clinical

medicine and there is no reason to assume that they are totally valueless when they are of the form, "when such and such happened, I got sick." It is, of course, highly desirable to try to corroborate such information by experimental approaches. Even without such corroboration, however, there are substantial improvements possible in their use; the work of Holmes, Rahe, and their associates (Holmes & Rahe, 1967; Rahe et al., 1964; Rahe, McKean, & Arthur, 1967) is likely to prove a very important step in this direction.

The use of the experimental interview is of immense importance, exactly comparable in principle to the experimental injection of microorganisms to produce disease. Indeed, in some ways it is better than that, since the experiment is being conducted directly on a human being and not on a guinea pig or mouse, as has usually been the case when testing microorganisms. On the other hand, much of the evidence obtained by the experimental method, and especially by the experimental interview technique, is open to the criticism that the research design was not rigorous.

The weakness is not in the lack of control periods within the interviews, because these are present. The trouble is that there is usually no count of the occasions on which the investigator introduced disturbing topics and found the expected Physiological changes, as opposed to the occasions on which he introduced nondisturbing topics. Many of the studies are now rather old; they stand in need of repetition with appropriate design and improved data handling; presumably, those who did them in the first place have little inclination for what would be for them a rather tedious task, and other workers have not, in general, chosen to take it up.

It must be remembered that the experimental interview may have any or all of three purposes: (a) to show that there are at least *some* psychological stimuli that evoke Physiological changes; (b) to show that *particular* psychological stimuli do so, usually discussions of life events that are thought to be stimuli to the illness of the patient under study; and (c) to reveal an association between Psychological and Physiological statements about the patient. The last occurs if the patient becomes, let us say, "angry," and concomitant changes occur in, for instance, his blood pressure. We then correlate the Psychological and Physiological statements. If there is reason to think that these responses develop because of the stimuli of the experimental interview, then, of course, the results are evidence that both the response we call "Psychological" and that which we call "Physiological" are responses to psychological stimuli, but that is a separate question. We may also believe that the particular event which the patient is discussing was etiologic to his illness, even though we may not wish to assume that the discussion of it was necessarily a response to the stimulus-complex of the interview.

With respect to the second of the two questions to which most of psychosomatic research has been directed, it seems fair to say that the situation is not as confused as many seem to believe. A review of the literature does not indicate that all conceivable personality statements are made about patients with all diseases, but rather shows that distinctions are drawn among diseases. Likewise, there is some consensus that *different* Psychological statements are applicable to patients at the times of attacks of different illnesses. A major problem continues to be that the most reliable and easiest psychological testing procedures are not well adapted to answering the questions of most concern in this context. One therefore finds, on one hand, quite objective and reproducible results which suggest that there are no specific Psychological statements to be made about the persons who have various diseases. On the other hand, there are results of interest obtained by procedures that, even if they are shown to be reliable (as in the case of interrater agreement, for instance), are cumbersome.

In summary, there is substantial evidence supporting specificity in psychosomatic medicine. The same evidence likewise supports Psycho-Physiological specificity in emotion. This positive evidence, combined with evident gaps and weakness, should encourage more investigation of these problems. With respect to the role of psychological stimuli, the repetition of some of the older work, with better criteria for a positive history and with more careful experimental interview techniques, is highly desirable. As an earlier section points out,

establishment of the right sort of specificity relationship is additional evidence supporting the importance of psychological stimuli. Techniques for making Psychological statements need to be examined and improved. The multiplication of psychological testing instruments has not so far solved the problem of translating among the results of these instruments and of finding bridges between them and the real-life behavior that is often of greatest interest. It is important, however, not to ask for too much here because there must always be some sacrifice of the "richness" of real life in order to obtain precision. More could probably be done with gross behavioral observations, i.e., the correlation of nonlanguage behavior with disease. It would also be highly desirable to do the kind of work on psychoanalytic interview material that would permit the production of confirmable statements, those that could be tested by others. The problem is to state the rules by which a particular set of utterances by a given patient can be translated into a more compact concept such as "repressed oral-dependent drives."

Are there still other directions in which psychosomatic investigations could move? Some of the concepts of psychophysiology, not ordinarily associated with diseases, could certainly be transferred to clinical investigation. The notion of "arousal," for instance, might well be investigated for its applicability to clinical problems, beyond those that are initially thought of as Psychological, such as schizophrenia. There is also room for much more investigation of Sociological variables, such as the relation of social class to such illnesses as coronary artery disease or peptic ulcer.

There are some conceptual questions that badly need clarification and investigation. Prominent among these is the complex of related problems referred to by such terms as "homeostasis," "psychological defense," "equilibrium," "coping mechanism," and "adaptation."

There has been a substantial shift in research emphasis in the past 15 years. In 1951, of 29 papers published in *Psychosomatic Medicine,* about 23 were studies of persons selected because they had something called an illness—in other words, the state of the person (usually defined Physically) was the independent variable and this state was a "disease entity." In 1967, only 21 of 50 papers published were of that sort. (There is some uncertainty in these figures, of course, since it is not always easy to classify individual papers.) The difference between the two years reflects the recognition that, for many purposes, progress will have to come through looking at smaller segments of the human being, both Physically and Psychologically, than a "disease." For instance, personality descriptions may need to be resolved into their component parts

(e.g., traits, motives, attitudes, defense mechanisms), and Physically-defined processes (illnesses) into theirs (e.g., hypersecretion, hypermotility), in order to find consistent relationships among the several variables of interest. It is likely that much future research will concern itself with looking for subdivisions of what have been considered unitary wholes, and therefore with smaller and more manageable pieces of the field of study than those with which investigators have struggled in the past.

REFERENCES

ACKERMAN, N. W. Character structure in hypertensive persons. *Proceedings of the Association for Research in Nervous and Mental Disease*, 1950, **29,** 900–928.

ALEXANDER, F. *Psychosomatic medicine: Its principles and applications.* New York: Norton, 1950.

ALEXANDER, F., FLAGG, G. W., FOSTER, S., CLEMENS, T., & BLAHD, W. Experimental studies of emotional stress: I. Hyperthyroidism. *Psychosomatic Medicine*, 1961, **23,** 104–114.

ALEXANDER, F., FRENCH, T. M., & POLLACK, G. H. (Eds.) *Psychosomatic specificity.* Vol. 1. Chicago: University of Chicago Press, 1968.

ALLERHAND, M. E., GOUGH, H. G., & GRAIS, M. L. Personality factors in neurodermatitis: A preliminary study. *Psychosomatic Medicine*, 1950, **12,** 386–390.

ALMY, T. P., ABOTT, F. K., & HINKLE, L. E., Jr. Alterations in colonic function in man under stress: IV. Hypomotility of the sigmoid colon, and its relationship to the mechanism of functional diarrhea. *Gastroenterology*, 1950, **15,** 95–103.

ALMY, T. P., HINKLE, L. E., Jr., BERLE, B., & KERN, F., Jr. Alterations in colonic function in man under stress: III. Experimental production of sigmoid spasm in patients with spastic constipation. *Gastroenterology*, 1949, **12,** 437–449.

ALMY, T. P., KERN, F., & TULIN, M. Alterations in colonic function in man under stress: II. Experimental production of sigmoid spasm in healthy persons. *Gastroenterology*, 1949, **12,** 425–436.

ALMY, T. P., & TULIN, M. Alterations in colonic function in man under stress: Experimental production of changes simulating the "irritable colon." *Gastroenterology*, 1947, **8,** 616–626.

AX, A. F. The physiological differentiation between fear and anger in humans. *Psychosomatic Medicine*, 1953, **15,** 433–442.

BARAFF, A. S., & CUNNINGHAM, A. P. Asthmatic and normal children. *Journal of the American Medical Association*, 1965, **192,** 99–101.

BENJAMIN, L. S. Statistical treatment of the law of initial values (LIV) in autonomic research: A review and recommendation. *Psychosomatic Medicine*, 1963, **25,** 556–566.

BINGER, C. On so-called psychogenic influences in essential hypertension. *Psychosomatic Medicine*, 1951, **13,** 273–276.

BLOCK, J., JENNINGS, P. H., HARVEY, E., & SIMPSON, E. Interaction between allergic potential and psychopathology in childhood asthma. *Psychosomatic Medicine*, 1964, **26,** 307–320.

BROWN, D. G. Emotional disturbances in eczema: A study of symptom-reporting behavior. *Journal of Psychosomatic Research*, 1967, **11,** 27–40.

CASTELNUOVO-TEDESCO, P. Emotional antecedents of perforation of ulcers of the stomach and duodenum. *Psychosomatic Medicine*, 1962, **24,** 398–416.

CHOSY, J. J., & GRAHAM, D. T. Catecholamines in vasovagal fainting. *Journal of Psychosomatic Research*, 1965, **9,** 189–194.

CLEVELAND, S. E., & FISHER, S. Psychological factors in the neurodermatoses. *Psychosomatic Medicine*, 1956, **18,** 209–220.

CLEVELAND, S. E., & FISHER, S. A comparison of psychological characteristics and physiological reactivity in ulcer and rheumatoid arthritis groups: I. Psychological measures. *Psychosomatic Medicine*, 1960, **22,** 283–289.

DEKKER, E., & GROEN, J. Reproducible psychogenic attacks of asthma. *Journal of Psychosomatic Research*, 1956, **1,** 58–67.

DEKKER, E., PELSER, H. E., & GROEN, J. Conditioning as a cause of asthmatic attacks: A laboratory study. *Journal of Psychosomatic Research*, 1957, **2,** 97–108.

DOLL, R., & JONES, F. A. Occupational factors in the aetiology of gastric and duodenal ulcers with an estimate of their incidence in the general population. Medical

Research Council Special Report Series No. 276, London: His Majesty's Stationery Office, 1951.

DONGIER, M., WITTKOWER, E. D., STEPHENS-NEWSHAM, L., & HOFFMAN, M. M. Psychophysiological studies in thyroid function. *Psychosomatic Medicine,* 1956, **18,** 310–324.

DUBO, S., MCLEAN, J. A., CHING, A. Y. T., WRIGHT, H. L., KAUFFMAN, P. E., & SHELDON, J. M. A study of relationships between family situation, bronchial asthma, and personal adjustment in children. *Journal of Pediatrics,* 1961, **59,** 402–414.

DUNBAR, F. *Emotions and bodily changes: A survey of literature on psychosomatic interrelationships 1910–1945.* (3rd ed.) New York: Columbia University Press, 1947. (a)

DUNBAR, F. *Psychosomatic diagnosis.* New York: Hoeber, 1947. (b)

EMPIRE RHEUMATISM COUNCIL. A controlled investigation into the aetiology and clinical features of rheumatoid arthritis. *British Medical Journal,* 1950, **1,** 799–805.

ENGEL, B. T. Stimulus-response and individual-response specificity. *Archives of General Psychiatry,* 1960, **2,** 305–313.

ENGEL, B. T., & BICKFORD, A. F. Response specificity: Stimulus-response and individual-response specificity in essential hypertensives. *Archives of General Psychiatry,* 1961, **5,** 478–489.

ENGEL, G. L. Studies of syncope: IV. Biologic interpretation of vasodepressor syncope. *Psychosomatic Medicine,* 1947, **9,** 288–294.

ENGEL, G. L. Studies of ulcerative colitis: II. The nature of the somatic processes and the adequacy of psychosomatic hypotheses. *American Journal of Medicine,* 1954, **16,** 416–433.

ENGEL, G. L. Studies of ulcerative colitis: III. The nature of the psychologic process. *American Journal of Medicine,* 1955, **19,** 231–256.

ENGEL, G. L. *Fainting: Physiological and psychological considerations.* Springfield, Ill.: Charles C Thomas, 1962.

ENGEL, G. L., REICHSMAN, F., & SEGAL, M. L. A study of an infant with a gastric fistula: I. Behavior and the rate of total hydrochloric acid secretion. *Psychosomatic Medicine,* 1956, **18,** 374–398.

EYLON, Y. Birth events, appendicitis and appendectomy. *British Journal of Medical Psychology,* 1967, **40,** 317–332.

FEINGOLD, B. F., SINGER, M. T., FREEMAN, E. H., & DESKINS, A. Psychological variables in allergic disease: A critical appraisal of methodology. *Journal of Allergy,* 1966, **38,** 143–155.

FELDMAN, F., CANTOR, D., SOLL, S., & BACHRACH, W. Psychiatric study of a consecutive series of 34 patients with ulcerative colitis. *British Medical Journal,* 1967, **3,** 14–17.

FISHER, S., & CLEVELAND, S. E. *Body image and personality.* New York: Van Nostrand Reinhold, 1958.

FISHER, S., & CLEVELAND, S. E. A comparison of psychological characteristics and physiological reactivity in ulcer and rheumatoid arthritis groups: II. Differences in psychological reactivity. *Psychosomatic Medicine,* 1960, **22,** 290–293.

FLAGG, G. W., CLEMENS, T. L., MICHAEL, E. A., ALEXANDER, F., & WARK, J. A psychophysiological investigation of hyperthyroidism. *Psychosomatic Medicine,* 1965, **27,** 497–507.

FREEMAN, E. H., FEINGOLD, B. F., SCHLESINGER, K., & GORMAN, F. J. Psychological variables in allergic disorders: A review. *Psychosomatic Medicine,* 1964, **26,** 543–575.

FULLERTON, D. T., KOLLAR, E. J., & CALDWELL, A. B. A clinical study of ulcerative colitis. *Journal of the American Medical Association,* 1962, **181,** 463–471.

FUNKENSTEIN, D. H., KING, S. H., & DROLETTE, M. E. *Mastery of stress.* Cambridge, Mass.: Harvard University Press, 1957.

GILDEA, E. F. Special features of personality which are common to certain psychosomatic disorders. *Psychosomatic Medicine,* 1949, **11,** 273–281.

GLICK, E. N. Asymmetrical rheumatoid arthritis after poliomyelitis. *British Medical Journal,* 1967, **3,** 26–28.

GOTTLIEB, A. A., GLESER, G. C., & GOTTSCHALK, L. A. Verbal and physiological responses to hypnotic suggestion of attitudes. *Psychosomatic Medicine,* 1967, **29,** 172–183.

GOTTSCHALK, L. A., SEROTA, H. M., & SHAPIRO, L. B. Psychologic conflict and neuromuscular tension: I. Preliminary report on a method, as applied to rheumatoid arthritis. *Psychosomatic Medicine,* 1950, **12,** 315–319.

GRACE, W. J., & GRAHAM, D. T. Relationship of specific attitudes and emotions to certain bodily diseases. *Psychosomatic Medicine,* 1952, **14,** 243–251.

GRACE, W. J., WOLF, S., & WOLFF, H. G. *The human colon: An experimental study based on direct observation of four fistulous subjects.* New York: Hoeber, 1951.

GRAHAM, D. T. The pathogenesis of hives: Experimental study of life situations, emotions and cutaneous vascular reactions. *Proceedings of the Association for Research in Nervous and Mental Disease,* 1950, **29,** 987–1009.

GRAHAM, D. T. Psychosomatic medicine—What are we talking about? (Editorial.) *American Journal of Medicine,* 1954, **16,** 163–167. (a)

GRAHAM, D. T. The relation of psoriasis to attitude and to vascular reactions of the human skin. *Journal of Investigative Dermatology,* 1954, **22,** 379–388. (b)

GRAHAM, D. T. Cutaneous vascular reactions in Raynaud's disease and its states of hostility, anxiety and depression. *Psychosomatic Medicine,* 1955, **17,** 200–207.

GRAHAM, D. T. Prediction of fainting in blood donors. *Circulation,* 1961, **23,** 901–1906.

GRAHAM, D. T. Some research on psychophysiologic specificity and its relation to psychosomatic disease. In R. ROESSLER & N. S. GREENFIELD (Eds.), *Physiological correlates of psychological disorders.* Madison: University of Wisconsin Press, 1962.

GRAHAM, D. T. Health, disease, and the mind-body problem: Linguistic parallelism. *Psychosomatic Medicine,* 1967, **29,** 52–71.

GRAHAM, D. T., GOODELL, H., & WOLFF, H. G. Studies of pain: The relation between cutaneous vasodilatation, pain threshold, and spontaneous itching and pain. *American Journal of the Medical Sciences,* 1957, **234,** 420–430.

GRAHAM, D. T., KABLER, J D, & GRAHAM, F. K. Physiological response to the suggestion of attitudes specific for hives and hypertension. *Psychosomatic Medicine,* 1962, **24,** 159–169.

GRAHAM, D. T., KABLER, J D, & LUNSFORD, L., Jr. Vasovagal fainting: A diphasic response. *Psychosomatic Medicine,* 1961, **23,** 493–507.

GRAHAM, D. T., LUNDY, R. M., BENJAMIN, L. S., KABLER, J D, LEWIS, W. C., KUNISH, N. O., & GRAHAM, F. K. Specific attitudes in initial interviews with patients having different "psychosomatic diseases." *Psychosomatic Medicine,* 1962, **24,** 257–266.

GRAHAM, D. T., STERN, J. A., & WINOKUR, G. Experimental investigation of the specificity of attitude hypothesis in psychosomatic disease. *Psychosomatic Medicine,* 1958, **20,** 446–457.

GRAHAM, D. T., STERN, J. A., & WINOKUR, G. The concept of a different specific set of physiological changes in each emotion. *Psychiatric Research Reports,* 1960, **12,** 8–15.

GRAHAM, D. T., & STEVENSON, I. Disease as response to life stress: (a) The nature of the evidence. In H. I. LIEF, V. F. LIEF, & N. R. LIEF (Eds.), *The psychological basis of medical practice.* New York: Harper & Row, 1963.

GRAHAM, D. T., & WOLF, S. The relation of eczema to attitude and to vascular reactions of the human skin. *Journal of Laboratory and Clinical Medicine,* 1953, **42,** 238–254.

GRAHAM, F. K., & KUNISH, N. O. Physiological responses of unhypnotized subjects to attitude suggestions. *Psychosomatic Medicine,* 1965, **27,** 317–329.

GRAHAM, J. D. P. High blood-pressure after battle. *Lancet,* 1945, **1,** 239–242.

GREENFIELD, N. S. Allergy and the need for recognition. *Journal of Consulting Psychology,* 1958, **22,** 230–232.

GROEN, J. Psychogenesis and psychotherapy of ulcerative colitis. *Psychosomatic Medicine,* 1947, **9,** 151–174.

GUZE, S. B., MATARAZZO, J. D., & SASLOW, G. A formulation of principles of comprehensive medicine. *Journal of Clinical Psychiatry,* 1953, **9,** 127–136.

HALLIDAY, J. L. *Psychosocial medicine.* New York: Norton, 1948.

HAM, G. G., ALEXANDER, F., & CARMICHAEL, H. T. A psychosomatic theory of thyrotoxicosis. *Psychosomatic Medicine,* 1951, **13,** 18–35.

HAMBLING, J. Emotions and symptoms in essential hypertension. *British Journal of Medical Psychology,* 1951, **24,** 242–253.

HAMBLING, J. Psychosomatic aspects of arterial hypertension. *British Journal of Medical Psychology,* 1952, **25,** 39–47.

HAMILTON, M. *Psychosomatics.* New York: Wiley, 1955.

HARBURG, E., JULIUS, S., MCGINN, N. F., MCLEOD, J., & HOOBLER, S. W. Personality traits and behavioral patterns associated with systolic blood pressure levels in college males. *Journal of Chronic Diseases,* 1964, **17,** 405–414.

HARRIS, R. E., SOKOLOW, M., CARPENTER, L. G., Jr., FREEMAN, M., & HUNT, S. P. Response to psychologic stress in persons who are potentially hypertensive. *Circulation,* 1953, **7,** 874–879.

HARRIS, W. S., SCHOENFELD, C. D., GWYNNE, P. H., WEISSLER, A. M., & WARREN, J. V. Circulatory and humoral responses to fear and anger. *Journal of Laboratory and Clinical Medicine,* 1964, **64,** 867. (Abstract)

HEBB, D. O. *Organization of behavior: A neuropsychological theory.* New York: Wiley, 1949.

HECHT, I. The difference in goal-striving behavior between peptic ulcer and ulcerative colitis patients as evaluated by psychological techniques. *Journal of Clinical Psychology,* 1952, **8,** 262–265.

HESELTINE, G. F. The site of onset of eczema and personality trait differences: An exploratory study. *Journal of Psychosomatic Research,* 1963, **7,** 241–246.

HICKAM, J. B., CARGILL, W. H., & GOLDEN, A. Cardiovascular reaction to emotional stimuli: Effect on the cardiac output, arteriovenous oxygen, arterial pressure, and peripheral resistance. *Journal of Clinical Investigation,* 1948, **27,** 290–298.

HINKLE, L. E., Jr., CHRISTENSON, W. N., KANE, F. D., OSTFELD, A., THETFORD, W. N., & WOLFF, H. G. An investigation of the relation between life experience, personality characteristics and general susceptibility to illness. *Psychosomatic Medicine,* 1958, **20,** 278–295.

HINKLE, L. E., Jr., CONGER, G. B., & WOLF, S. Studies on diabetes mellitus: The relation of stressful life situations to the concentration of ketone bodies in the blood of diabetic and non-diabetic humans. *Journal of Clinical Investigation,* 1950, **29,** 754–769.

HINKLE, L. E., Jr., EVANS, F. M., & WOLF, S. Studies in diabetes mellitus: III. Life history of three persons with labile diabetes, and relation of significant experiences in their lives to the onset and course of the disease. *Psychosomatic Medicine,* 1951, **13,** 160–183. (a)

HINKLE, L. E., Jr., EVANS, F. M., & WOLF, S. Studies in diabetes mellitus: IV. Life history of three persons with relatively mild, stable diabetes, and relation of significant experiences in their lives to the onset and course of the disease. *Psychosomatic Medicine,* 1951, **13,** 184–202. (b)

HINKLE, L. E., Jr., & WOLF, S. The effects of stressful life situations on the concentration of blood glucose in diabetic and non-diabetic humans. *Diabetes,* 1952, **1,** 383–392.

HINKLE, L. E., Jr., & WOLFF, H. G. The nature of man's adaptation to his total environment and the relation of this to illness. *Archives of Internal Medicine,* 1957, **99,** 442–460.

HINKLE, L. E., Jr., & WOLFF, H. G. Ecological investigations of the relationship between illness, life experiences and the social environment. *Annals of Internal Medicine,* 1958, **49,** 1373-1388.

HOKANSON, J. E.   The effects of frustration and anxiety on overt aggression. *Journal of Abnormal and Social Psychology,* 1961, **62,** 346-351.

HOKANSON, J. E., BURGESS, M., & COHEN, M. F.   Effects of displaced aggression on systolic blood pressure. *Journal of Abnormal and Social Psychology,* 1963, **67,** 214-218.

HOLMES, T. H.   Multidiscipline studies of tuberculosis. In P. J. SPARER (Ed.), *Personality, stress and tuberculosis.* New York: International Universities, 1956.

HOLMES, T. H.   Short-term intrusions into the life-style routine. *Journal of Psychosomatic Research,* 1970, **14,** 121-132.

HOLMES, T. H., GOODELL, H., WOLF, S., & WOLFF, H. G.   *The nose. An experimental study of reactions within the nose in human subjects during varying life experiences.* Springfield, Ill.: Charles C Thomas, 1950.

HOLMES, T. H., & RAHE, R. H.   The social readjustment rating scale. *Journal of Psychosomatic Research,* 1967, **11,** 213-218.

HOLMES, T. H., TREUTING, T., & WOLFF, H. G.   Life situations, emotions, and nasal disease. *Psychosomatic Medicine,* 1951, **13,** 71-82.

IMBODEN, J. B., CANTER, A., & CLUFF, L.   Separation experiences and health records in a group of normal adults. *Psychosomatic Medicine,* 1963, **25,** 433-440.

INNES, G., MILLAR, W. M., & VALENTINE, M.   Emotion and blood-pressure. *Journal of Mental Science,* 1959, **105,** 840-851.

JOHNSON, A. M., SHAPIRO, L. B., & ALEXANDER, F.   Preliminary report on a psychosomatic study of rheumatoid arthritis. *Psychosomatic Medicine,* 1947, **9,** 295-300.

KALIS, B. L., HARRIS, R. E., SOKOLOW, M., & CARPENTER, L. G.   Response to psychological stress in patients with essential hypertension. *American Heart Journal,* 1957, **53,** 572-578.

KALZ, F., WITTKOWER, E. D., VAVRUSKA, G. W., TELNER, P., & FERGUSON, S.   Studies on vascular skin responses in atopic dermatitis: The influence of psychological factors. *Journal of Investigative Dermatology,* 1957, **29,** 67-78.

KAPLAN, S. M., GOTTSCHALK, L. A., MAGLIOCCO, E. B., ROHOVIT, D. D., & ROSS, W. D.   Hostility in verbal productions and hypnotic dreams of hypertensive patients. *Psychosomatic Medicine,* 1961, **23,** 311-322.

KANNER, L. *Child psychiatry.* Springfield, Ill.: Charles C Thomas, 1957.

KEHOE, M., & IRONSIDE, W.   Studies on the experimental evocation of depressive responses using hypnosis: II. The influence of depressive responses upon the secretion of gastric acid. *Psychosomatic Medicine,* 1963, **15,** 403-419.

KEPECS, J. G., RABIN, A., & ROBIN, M.   Atopic dermatitis. *Psychosomatic Medicine,* 1951, **13,** 1-9.

KEPECS, J. G., & ROBIN, M.   Studies on itching: I. Contri-

butions toward an understanding of the physiology of masochism. *Psychosomatic Medicine,* 1955, **17,** 87-95.

KEPECS, J. G., ROBIN, M., & BRUNNER, M. J.   Relationship between certain emotional states and exudation into the skin. *Psychosomatic Medicine,* 1951, **13,** 10-17.

KING, S. H.   Psycho-social factors associated with rheumatoid arthritis: An evaluation of the literature. *Journal of Chronic Diseases,* 1955, **2,** 287-302.

KING, S. H., & COBB, S.   Psychosocial factors in the epidemiology of rheumatoid arthritis. *Journal of Chronic Diseases,* 1958, **7,** 466-475.

KISSEN, D. M.   *Emotional factors in pulmonary tuberculosis.* London: Tavistock, 1958.

KNAPP, P. H.   Acute bronchial asthma: II. Psychoanalytic observations of fantasy, emotional arousal and partial discharge. *Psychosomatic Medicine,* 1960, **22,** 88-105.

KNAPP, P. H., CARR, H. E., MUSHATT, C., & NEMETZ, S. J.   Asthma, melancholia, and death: II. Psychosomatic considerations. *Psychosomatic Medicine,* 1966, **28,** 134-153.

KNAPP, P. H., MUSHATT, C., & NEMETZ, S. J.   Asthma, melancholia, and death: I. Psychoanalytic considerations. *Psychosomatic Medicine,* 1966, **28,** 114-133.

KNAPP, P. H., & NEMETZ, S. J.   Personality variations in bronchial asthma. *Psychosomatic Medicine,* 1957, **19,** 443-465.

KNAPP, P. H., & NEMETZ, S. J.   Acute bronchial asthma: I. Concomitant depression and excitement, and varied antecedent patterns in 406 attacks. *Psychosomatic Medicine,* 1960, **22,** 42-56.

KOGAN, W. S., DORPAT, T. L., & HOLMES, T. H.   Semantic problems in evaluating a specificity hypothesis in psychophysiologic relations. *Psychosomatic Medicine,* 1965, **27,** 1-8.

KRAFT, B., & BLUMENTHAL, D.   Psychological components in chronic urticaria. *Acta Allergologica,* 1959, **13,** 469-475.

LACEY, J. I., & LACEY, B. C.   Varification and extension of the principle of autonomic response-stereotypy. *American Journal of Psychology,* 1958, **7,** 50-73.

LIDZ, T.   Emotional factors in the etiology of hyperthyroidism. *Psychosomatic Medicine,* 1949, **11,** 2-8.

LINDEMANN, E.   Modifications in the course of ulcerative colitis in relationship to changes in life situations and reaction patterns. *Proceedings of the Association for Research in Nervous and Mental Disease,* 1950, **29,** 706-723.

LIPTON, E. L., STEINSCHNEIDER, A., & RICHMOND, J. B.   Psychophysiological disorders in children. In L. W. HOFFMAN & M. L. HOFFMAN (Eds.), *Review of child development research.* Vol. 2. New York: Russell Sage Foundation, 1966.

LITTLE, S. W., & COHEN, L. D.   Goal-setting behavior of asthmatic children and of their mothers for them. *Journal of Personality,* 1951, **19,** 377-389.

LORENZ, T. H., GRAHAM, D. T., & WOLF, S.   The relation of life stress and emotions to human sebum secretion and to the mechanism of acne vulgaris. *Journal of Laboratory and Clinical Medicine,* 1953, **41,** 11-28.

LORENZ, T. H., GRAHAM, D. T., & WOLFF, H. G. A method for the collection and quantitative determination of sebum: Its application to an investigation of human sebum secretion. *Journal of Laboratory and Clinical Medicine,* 1952, **39,** 91-104.

LUCAS, C. J. Personality of students with acne vulgaris. *British Medical Journal,* 1961, **2,** 354-356.

LUCAS, C. J., & OJHA, A. B. Personality and acne. *Journal of Psychosomatic Research,* 1963, **7,** 41-43.

MAHL, G. F. Anxiety, HCl secretion, and peptic ulcer etiology. *Psychosomatic Medicine,* 1950, **12,** 158-169.

MALMO, R. B., & SHAGASS, C. Physiologic study of symptom mechanisms in psychiatric patients under stress. *Psychosomatic Medicine,* 1949, **11,** 25-29.

MALMO, R. B., SHAGASS, C., & DAVIS, F. H. Sympton specificity and bodily reactions during psychiatric interview. *Psychosomatic Medicine,* 1950, **12,** 362-376.

MANDELBROTE, B. M., & WITTKOWER, E. D. Emotional factors in Graves' disease. *Psychosomatic Medicine,* 1955, **17,** 109-123.

MARGOLIN, S. G. The behavior of the stomach during psychoanalysis: A contribution to a method of verifying psychoanalytic data. *Psychoanalytic Quarterly,* 1951, **20,** 349-373.

MASUDA, M., & HOLMES, T. H. Magnitude estimations of social readjustments. *Journal of Psychosomatic Research,* 1967, **11,** 219-226.

MASUDA, M., NOTSKE, R. N., & HOLMES, T. H. Catecholamine excretion and asthmatic behavior. *Journal of Psychosomatic Research,* 1966, **10,** 255-262.

MATARAZZO, J. D. An experimental study of aggression in the hypertensive patient. *Journal of Personality,* 1954, **22,** 423-447.

McGINN, N. F., HARBURG, E., JULIUS, S., & McLEOD, J. M. Psychological correlates of blood pressure. *Psychological Bulletin,* 1964, **61,** 209-219.

McLAUGHLIN, J. T., SHOEMAKER, R. J., & GUY, W. B. Personality factors in adult atopic eczema. *Archives of Dermatology and Syphilology,* 1953, **68,** 506-516.

MECHANIC, D., & VOLKART, E. H. Stress, illness behavior, and the sick role. *American Sociological Review,* 1961, **26,** 51-58.

METCALFE, M. Demonstration of a psychosomatic relationship. *British Journal of Medical Psychology,* 1956, **29,** 63-66.

MEYER, R. J., & HAGGERTY, R. J. Streptococcal infections in families. *Pediatrics, Springfield,* 1962, **29,** 539-549.

MILBERG, I. L. The reactive hyperemia response of the uninvolved skin of patients with psoriasis. *Journal of Investigative Dermatology,* 1947, **9,** 31-39.

MILLER, D. A., FREEMAN, G. L., & AKERS, W. A. Chronic urticaria. A clinical study of fifty patients. *American Journal of Medicine,* 1968, **44,** 68-86.

MILLER, J., & BARUCH, D. W. Psychosomatic studies of children with allergic manifestations: I. Maternal rejection. *Psychosomatic Medicine,* 1948, **10,** 275-278.

MILLER, M. L. Blood pressure findings in relation to inhibited aggression in psychotics. *Psychosomatic Medicine,* 1939, **1,** 162-172.

MITTELMANN, B., & WOLFF, H. G. Affective states and skin temperature: Experimental study of subjects with "cold hands" and Raynaud's syndrome. *Psychosomatic Medicine,* 1939, **1,** 271-292.

MITTELMANN, B., & WOLFF, H. G. Emotions and gastroduodenal function: Experimental studies on patients with gastritis, duodenitis, and peptic ulcer. *Psychosomatic Medicine,* 1942, **4,** 5-61.

MITTELMANN, B., & WOLFF, H. G. Emotions and skin temperature: Observations on patients during psychotherapeutic (psychoanalytic) interviews. *Psychosomatic Medicine,* 1943, **5,** 221-231.

MOHR, G. J., TAUSEND, H., SELESNICK, S., & AUGENBRAUN, B. Studies of eczema and asthma in the preschool child. *Journal of the American Academy of Child Psychiatry,* 1963, **2,** 271-291.

MOOS, R. H. Personality factors associated with rheumatoid arthritis: A review. *Journal of Chronic Diseases,* 1964, **17,** 41-55.

MOOS, R. H., & ENGEL, B. T. Psychophysiological reactions in hypertensive and arthritic patients. *Journal of Psychosomatic Research,* 1962, **6,** 227-241.

MOOS, R. H., & SOLOMON, G. F. Minnesota Multiphasic Personality Inventory response patterns in patients with rheumatoid arthritis. *Journal of Psychosomatic Research,* 1964, **8,** 17-28.

MOOS, R. H., & SOLOMON, G. F. Psychologic comparisons between women with rheumatoid arthritis and their nonarthritic sisters: I. Personality test and interview rating data. *Psychosomatic Medicine,* 1965, **27,** 135-149. (a)

MOOS, R. H., & SOLOMON, G. F. Psychologic comparisons between women with rheumatoid arthritis and their nonarthritic sisters. *Psychosomatic Medicine,* 1965, **27,** 150-164. (b)

MOSES, L., DANIELS, G. E., & NICKERSON, J. L. Psychogenic factors in essential hypertension: Methodology and preliminary report. *Psychosomatic Medicine,* 1956, **18,** 471-485.

MUFSON, I. The mechanism and treatment of Raynaud's disease: A psychosomatic disturbance. *Annals of Internal Medicine,* 1944, **20,** 228-238.

MUFSON, I. An etiology of scleroderma. *Annals of Internal Medicine,* 1953, **39,** 1219-1227.

MURPHY, G. E., KUHN, N. O., CHRISTENSEN, R. F., & ROBINS, E. "Life stress" in a normal population: A study of 101 women hospitalized for normal delivery. *Journal of Nervous and Mental Disease,* 1962, **134,** 150-161.

MUSAPH, H. *Itching and scratching: Psychodynamics in dermatology.* Philadelphia: Davis, 1964.

MUTTER, A. Z., & SCHLEIFER, M. J. The role of psychological and social factors in the onset of somatic illness in children. *Psychosomatic Medicine,* 1966, **28,** 333-343.

OBERMAYER, M. E.   *Psychocutaneous medicine.* Springfield, Ill.: Charles C Thomas, 1955.

OWEN, F. W.   Patterns of respiratory disturbance in asthmatic children evoked by the stimulus of the mother's voice. *Acta Psychotherapeutica,* 1963, **2,** 228-241.

PAPPER, S., & HANDY, J.   Observations in a "control" group of patients in psychosomatic investigation. *New England Journal of Medicine,* 1956, **255,** 1067-1071.

PFEIFFER, J. B., Jr., & WOLFF, H. G.   Studies in renal circulation during periods of life stress and accompanying emotional reactions in subjects with and without essential hypertension: Observations on the role of neural activity in regulation of renal blood flow. *Proceedings of the Association for Research in Nervous and Mental Disease,* 1950, **29,** 929-953.

PILOT, M. L., & KORMOS, H. R.   Ordinal position in asthma and hyperthyroidism. *Archives of General Psychiatry,* 1964, **11,** 181-184.

PINKERTON, P.   Correlating physiologic with psychodynamic data in the study and management of childhood asthma. *Journal of Psychosomatic Research,* 1967, **11,** 11-25.

PURCELL, K.   Distinctions between subgroups of asthmatic children: Children's perceptions of events associated with asthma. *Pediatrics, Springfield,* 1963, **31,** 486-494.

PURCELL, K., BERNSTEIN, L., & BUKANTZ, S. C.   A preliminary comparison of rapidly remitting and persistently "steroid-dependent" asthmatic children. *Psychosomatic Medicine,* 1961, **23,** 306-310.

PURCELL, K., & METZ, J. R.   Distinctions between subgroups of asthmatic children: Some parent attitude variables related to age of onset of asthma. *Journal of Psychosomatic Research,* 1962, **6,** 251-258.

PURCELL, K., TURNBULL, J. W., & BERNSTEIN, L.   Distinctions between subgroups of asthmatic children: Psychological test and behavior rating comparisons. *Journal of Psychosomatic Research,* 1962, **6,** 283-291.

QUERIDO, A.   Forecast and follow-up: An investigation into the clinical, social and mental factors determining the results of hospital treatment. *British Journal of Preventive and Social Medicine,* 1959, **13,** 33-49.

RAHE, H., & ARTHUR, R. J.   Life-change patterns surrounding illness experience. *Journal of Psychosomatic Research,* 1968, **11,** 341-347.

RAHE, R. H., & HOLMES, T. H.   Social psychologic and psychophysiologic aspects of inguinal hernia. *Journal of Psychosomatic Research,* 1965, **8,** 487-492.

RAHE, R. H., MAHAN, J. L., & ARTHUR, R. J.   Prediction of near-future health change from subjects' preceding life changes. *Journal of Psychosomatic Research,* 1970, **14,** 401-406.

RAHE, R. H., McKEAN, J. D., Jr., & ARTHUR, R. J.   A longitudinal study of life-change and illness patterns. *Journal of Psychosomatic Research,* 1967, **10,** 355-366.

RAHE, R. H., MEYER, M., SMITH, M., KJAER, G., & HOLMES, T. H.   Social stress and illness onset. *Journal of Psychosomatic Research,* 1964, **8,** 35-44.

REES, L.   Physical and emotional factors in bronchial asthma. *Journal of Psychosomatic Research,* 1956, **1,** 98-114. (a)

REES, L.   Psychosomatic aspects of asthma in elderly patients. *Journal of Psychosomatic Research,* 1956, **1,** 212-218. (b)

REES, L.   The significance of parental attitudes in childhood asthma. *Journal of Psychosomatic Research,* 1963, **7,** 181-190.

REES, L.   The importance of psychological, allergic, and infective factors in childhood asthma. *Journal of Research,* 1964, **7,** 253-262.

REISER, M. F., BRUST, A. A., & FERRIS, E. B.   Life situations, emotions, and the course of patients with arterial hypertension. *Psychosomatic Medicine,* 1951, **13,** 133-139.

REISER, M. D., ROSENBAUM, M., & FERRIS, E. B.   Psychological mechanisms in malignant hypertension. *Psychosomatic Medicine,* 1951, **13,** 147-159.

RING, F. O.   Testing the validity of personality profiles in psychosomatic illnesses. *American Journal of Psychiatry,* 1957, **113,** 1075-1080.

ROBIN, M., & KEPECS, J. G.   The relationship between certain emotional states and the rate of secretion of sebum. *Journal of Investigative Dermatology,* 1953, **20,** 373-380.

ROSENTHAL, M. J.   Psychosomatic study of infantile eczema: I. Mother-child relationship. *Pediatrics, Springfield,* 1952, **10,** 581-592.

ROSENZWEIG, S.   A general outline of frustration. *Journal of Personality,* 1938, **7,** 151-160.

RUETZ, P. P., JOHNSON, S. A., CALLAHAN, R., MEADE, R. C., & SMITH, J. J.   Fainting: A review of its mechanisms and a study in blood donors. *Medicine,* 1967, **46,** 363-384.

RUSKIN, A., BEARD, O. W., & SCHAFFER, R. L.   Blast hypertension: Elevated arterial pressures in the victims of the Texas City disaster. *American Journal of Medicine,* 1948, **4,** 228-230.

RUSSEK, H. I.   Emotional stress and coronary heart disease in American physicians. *American Journal of the Medical Sciences,* 1960, **240,** 711-721.

SASLOW, G., GRESSEL, G. C., SHOBE, F. O., DuBOIS, P. H., & SCHROEDER, H. A.   The possible etiological relevance of personality factors in arterial hypertension. *Proceedings of the Association for Research in Nervous and Mental Disease,* 1950, **29,** 881-899.

SAUL, L. J., & BERNSTEIN, C., Jr.   The emotional setting of some attacks of urticaria. *Psychosomatic Medicine,* 1941, **3,** 349-369.

SAUL, S., & SHEPPARD, E.   An attempt to quantify emotional forces using manifest dreams: A preliminary study. *Journal of the American Psychoanalytic Association,* 1956, **4,** 486-502.

SCHACHTER, J.   Pain, fear and anger in hypertensives and

normotensives: A psychophysiological study. *Psychosomatic Medicine,* 1957, **19,** 17-29.

SCHMALE, A. H., Jr. Relationship of separation and depression to disease: I. A report on a hospitalized medical population. *Psychosomatic Medicine,* 1958, **20,** 259-277.

SCHMALE, A. H., Jr. Object loss, "giving up" and disease onset: An overview of research in progress. In *Medical aspects of stress in the military climate.* Washington, D.C.: U.S. Government Printing Office, 1964.

SCOTCH, N. A. Sociocultural factors in the epidemiology of Zulu hypertension. *American Journal of Public Health,* 1963, **53,** 1205-1213.

SEITZ, P. F. D. Symbolism and organ choice in conversion reactions: An experimental approach. *Psychosomatic Medicine,* 1951, **8,** 254-259.

SEITZ, P. F. D., GOSMAN, J. S., & CRATON, J. Super-ego and aggression in circumscribed neurodermatitis. *Journal of Investigative Dermatology,* 1953, **20,** 263-269.

SELYE, H. The physiopathology of stress. *Postgraduate Medicine,* 1959, **25,** 660-667.

SHAPIRO, A. P. Psychophysiologic mechanisms in hypertensive vascular disease. *Annals of Internal Medicine,* 1960, **53,** 64-83.

SHAPIRO, A. P. An experimental study of comparative responses of blood pressure to different noxious stimuli. *Journal of Chronic Diseases,* 1961, **13,** 293-311.

SLAWSON, P. F., FLYNN, W. R., & KOLLAR, E. J. Psychological factors associated with the onset of diabetes mellitus. *Journal of the American Medical Association,* 1963, **185,** 166-170.

SOLOMON, G. F., & MOOS, R. H. The relationship of personality to the presence of rheumatoid factors in asymptomatic relatives of patients with rheumatoid arthritis. *Psychosomatic Medicine,* 1965, **27,** 350-360.

SPERLING, M. Psychoanalytic study of ulcerative colitis in children. *Psychoanalytic Quarterly,* 1946, **15,** 302-329.

SPITZ, R. A. The psychogenic diseases in infancy: An attempt at their etiologic classification. *Psychoanalytic Study of the Child,* 1951, **6,** 255-275.

STERN, J. A., WINOKUR, G., GRAHAM, D. T., & GRAHAM, F. K. Alterations in physiological measures during experimentally induced attitudes. *Journal of Psychosomatic Research,* 1961, **5,** 73-82.

STERNBACH, R. A. *Principles of psychophysiology.* New York: Academic, 1966.

STEVENSON, I., & RIPLEY, H. S. Variations in respiration and in respiratory systems during changes in emotion. *Psychosomatic Medicine,* 1952, **14,** 476-490.

TJOSSEM, T. D., LEIDER, A. R., DEISHER, R. W., HOLMES, T. H., & RIPLEY, H. S. Emotional reactions and skin temperature responses in children aged two to four years. *Journal of Psychosomatic Research,* 1959, **4,** 32-43.

TREUTING, T. F. The role of emotional factors in the etiology and course of diabetes mellitus: A review of the recent literature. *American Journal of Medical Science,* 1962, **244,** 93-109.

VAN DER VALK, J. M. Blood pressure changes under emotional influences in patients with essential hypertension and control subjects. *Journal of Psychosomatic Research,* 1957, **2,** 134-146.

WALLERSTEIN, R. S., HOLZMAN, P. S., VOTH, H. M., & UHR, N. Thyroid "hot spots": A psychophysiological study. *Psychosomatic Medicine,* 1965, **27,** 508-523.

WEINER, H., SINGER, M. T., & REISER, M. F. Cardiovascular responses and their psychological correlates: I. A study in healthy young adults and patients with peptic ulcer and hypertension. *Psychosomatic Medicine,* 1962, **24,** 477-498.

WEINER, H., THALER, M., REISER, M. F., & MIRSKY, I. A. Etiology of duodenal ulcer: I. Relation of specific psychological characteristics to rate of gastric secretion (serum pepsinogen). *Psychosomatic Medicine,* 1957, **19,** 1-10.

WENER, J., & POLONSKY, A. The reaction of the human colon to naturally occurring and experimentally induced emotional states: Observations through a transverse colostomy on a patient with ulcerative colitis. *Gastroenterology,* 1950, **15,** 84-94.

WENGER, M. A. Studies of autonomic balance: A summary. *Psychophysiology,* 1966, **2,** 173-186.

WENGER, M. A., CLEMENS, T. L., & CULLEN, T. D. Autonomic functions in patients with gastrointestinal and dermatologic disorders. *Psychosomatic Medicine,* 1962, **24,** 267-273.

WENGER, M. A., JONES, F. N., & JONES, M. H. *Physiological psychology.* New York: Holt, Rinehart and Winston, 1956.

WERTLAKE, P. T., WILCOX, A. A., HALEY, M. I., & PETERSON, J. E. Relationship of mental and emotional stress to serum cholesterol levels. *Proceedings of the Society for Experimental Biology and Medicine,* 1958, **97,** 163-165.

WEST, J. R., KIERLAND, R. R., & LITIN, E. M. Atopic dermatitis and hypnosis. *Archives of Dermatology,* 1961, **84,** 579-588.

WILLIAMS, R. L., & KRASNOFF, A. G. Body image and physiological patterns in patients with peptic ulcer and rheumatoid arthritis. *Psychosomatic Medicine,* 1964, **26,** 701-709.

WITTKOWER, E., & EDGELL, P. G. Eczema: A psychosomatic study. *Archives of Dermatology and Syphilology,* 1951, **63,** 207-219.

WITTKOWER, E., & RUSSELL, B. *Emotional factors in skin disease.* New York: Hoeber, 1953.

WITTKOWER, E. D., SCHERINGER, W., & BAY, E. Über affektivsomatische Veranderungen zur affektiven Beeinflussbarkeit des Blutjodspiegel. *Klinische Wochenschrift,* 1932, **11,** 1186-1187.

WOLF, S., CARDON, P. V., Jr., SHEPARD, E. M., & WOLFF, H. G. *Life stress and essential hypertension.* Baltimore: Williams & Wilkins, 1955.

WOLF, S., PFEIFFER, J. B., RIPLEY H. S., WINTER, O. S., & WOLFF, H. G. Hypertension as a reaction pattern to stress: Summary of experimental data on variations in blood pressure and renal blood flow. *Annals of Internal Medicine,* 1948, **29,** 1056–1076.

WOLF, S., & WOLFF, H. G. *Human gastric function.* (2nd ed.) New York: Oxford University Press, 1947.

WOLFF, H. G. Life stress and bodily disease—a formulation. *Proceedings of the Association for Research in Nervous and Mental Disease,* 1950, **29,** 1059–1094.

WOLFF, H. G. *Headache and other head pain.* (2nd ed.) New York: Oxford University Press, 1963.

WOLFF, H. G., LORENZ, T. H., & GRAHAM, D. T. Stress, emotions and human sebum: Their relevance to acne vulgaris. *Transactions of the Association of American Physicians,* 1951, **64,** 435–444.

WOLFF, H. G., WOLF, S. G., Jr., & HARE, C. C. (Eds.) Life stress and bodily disease. *Proceedings of the Association for Research in Nervous and Mental Disease,* 1950, **29.**

A. A. Alexander

PSYCHOPHYSIOLOGICAL CONCEPTS OF PSYCHOPATHOLOGY

22

I would like to have titled this chapter "Psychophysiological *theories* of psychopathology." It would have spoken of a maturity of the endeavor to relate physiological function to psychological disorder; it would have been considerably shorter, more easily organized, less redundant of other reviews in the general area, and ultimately more palpable to the reader. But while the attempt to relate bodily processes to psychological states has a long history, we have been left with little in the way of a heritage. No theoretical formulation put forth has as yet been broad enough to account more than selectively for a rather extensive literature, or precise enough to claim validly that the evidence in support of it is of such a critical nature that it takes precedence over contradictory findings or opposed notions. Nor has it been possible to survey the literature in hopes that a theory will present itself from the reported results. If one does not enter the literature with a particular conceptual bias from which to select some findings and ignore others, he is soon frustrated by the many inconsistencies and ambiguities to be found therein. This is so, I believe, not only because both domains, psychopathology and psychophysiology, are notorious for their complexity—difficulties in measurement, lack of reliability in certain parameters, reliance on subjective judgment or technological advances, and shifting nosologies—but because too few research studies have themselves been products of a systematic theoretical formulation on the part of the experimenter. It is because of the abundance of concept-free research which has been published that this chapter has been written.

What will be attempted here is not a catalogue of the vast number of findings in a broad literature but a delineation of certain concepts which emerge, take shape, submerge, recur, appear in disguise, obstruct the development of other conceptual paradigms, and sometimes lead to solid gains in scientific knowledge. The emphasis and structure of this chapter will be on recurrent concepts and formulations that may not have the elegance of true scientific theory or carry its credentials in the form of logical precision, ultimate testability, and explicit assumptions, but nevertheless are capable of generating hypotheses, answering some questions, and raising others. Psychophysiology is itself very much a discipline in process—young, at times immature, often premature or presumptive in its explanations, and in regard to psychopathology nascent in its potential. Yet there seem to me to be psychophysiological contributions to our understanding of abnormal psychology which are persistent enough and intriguing enough to warrant citing them here with their relevant literature. The reader may thereby compare their relevance, validity, consistency, and most important, testability. By bringing together in one source the many points of view put forth separately in other publications, my hope is that the highlighting of conceptual trends operating at the moment will facilitate their development into theories of the future.

The chapter is organized along the following lines. After considering the "mind-body" problem from a historical and methodological point of view, the few relatively well established psychophysiological findings on psychopathological groups will be reviewed. These can be taken, in a sense, as atheoretical; or as data any theoretical formulation should encompass. Subsequent sections will then deal with various physiological concepts that have been employed to understand psychopathology. The grouping of studies within categories of concepts will often reflect my understanding of them, or bias, as well as the original authors' intentions. When formulations are discussed which are attributed to specific individuals,

the particular evidence cited in their support will for the most part reflect that individual's biases. Investigations of various psychophysiological phenomena (such as stimulus-response specificity and habituation) will be covered only when they have been studied in relation to psychopathology. Other physiological findings in regard to psychoactive drugs, psychotherapy, changes in psychiatric states of patients, etc., will be reported when relevant, and represent data to be incorporated by the truly ambitious theoretician or to be appreciably extended by the aspiring experimentalist. For the most part, however, the studies reviewed are those which have dealt with clinically disordered human subjects or with explicit hypotheses dealing with psychopathology. The areas of "emotion," "stress," "conflict," "defense" and like processes or dynamics, which may be assumed to be related to disabling psychological disorder, are better charted elsewhere in this handbook and other publications (e.g., Martin, 1961, pp. 417–456). The heterogeneity inherent in psychiatric diagnosis itself does not allow the luxury of trying to deal with that introduced by inferences to psychopathology, or by including studies of subjects of dubious pathology. Due to the many sources of uncontrolled variation in any given psychophysiological experimental procedure, this review is also generally limited to those investigations that employed "normal" control groups in assessing the physiological function of psychiatric patient samples. Considerations of length dictated excluding the literature that did not relate directly to those physiological parameters traditionally investigated within psychophysiology: autonomic and somatic nervous system variables. The reader who wishes to explore the many pathways to the central nervous system (CNS) from the primarily autonomic nervous system (ANS) studies included here, will often find appropriate references in the studies cited. And finally, there were the many studies passed over because of glaring methodological failures, redundancy, or lack of repeatability, and most often, because they did not appear to fit within any conceptual framework obvious to me. The psychophysiological body of knowledge of psychopathology is too frequently buried in random results that seem to have been generated free of forethought and barren of possibilities. In those cases in which my perspective has been too limited to comprehend the theoretical relevance of a study, I apologize for its exclusion. No doubt significant results have been overlooked—it is sometimes difficult to see over the clutter. The attempt to group works on the basis of the concepts that underlie them, rather than by the physiological measure employed or the psychiatric phenomenon studied, will perhaps make it easier for others to see the support, difficulties, and insights inherent to each, as well as the promise of the endeavor to discern the physiological concomitants of psychopathology.

The foregoing may not seem overly restrictive when one considers the difficulties inherent in physiological approaches to psychopathology. First, and too often foremost, is the problem of reliable psychiatric diagnosis. Psychiatric taxonomies are not noted for their consistency; freedom from fads; exclusiveness of categories; basis in objective measurement; or reliability over time, across schools, beyond geographic areas, betwixt hospitals, and between diagnosticians. (It would be more accurate perhaps to say that "human behavior" is not noted for most of the above characteristics.) Furthermore, even if a psychiatric label such as "schizophrenic" is attached to the experimental subject population with some confidence, it is incumbent upon the investigator to further distinguish his patient group along dimensions such as acute-chronic and mild-severe. Sometimes even sex differences are ignored in reporting the composition of patient groups, as if to become psychiatrically ill is to lose one's sexual identity as far as the experimenter is concerned. More frequently, diagnostic subclassifications have been disregarded by investigators altogether. And even a breakdown of the experimental group into diagnostic subcategories may not be sufficient, since a number of authors have suggested that paranoid schizophrenia, for example, may be characterized differentially on a physiological level at different stages of the paranoid process (Glaser, 1952; Syz, 1926; Syz & Kinder, 1928; Venables & Wing, 1962). Psychodynamically, of course, diagnostic subcategories have been devised on the basis of assumed differences in perceptual and reactive processes. While

the clinician may at times make too much of these differences, the experimentalist most often makes too little of them in the composition of his patient samples.

The use of physiological measures to assess psychopathology also involves the problems relevant to any area of psychophysiology. J. I. Lacey has perhaps been our most consistent conscience in reminding contemporary investigators of the need to evaluate autonomic activity not only as to its tension level but also relative to physiological lability and initial values, nonspecific activity, the generally low intercorrelation among autonomic measures, the complete absence of response in any one variable shown by some subjects, and the various stereotypic patterns of response possible ("intrastressor, interstressor, and situational") (J. I. Lacey, 1956, 1962, pp. 160–208; J. I. Lacey & B. C. Lacey, 1958). As well as seriously questioning the use of a single physiological variable for the study of individuals, or the use of only one parameter of that variable (such as peak response) to measure responsivity, arousal, habituation, and the like, account must be taken of the greater physiological variability often shown by schizophrenic compared to normal experimental subjects (cf. reviews by Duffy, 1962; Martin, 1961, pp. 417–456). General methodological considerations such as these may be accentuated when schizophrenics are used as experimental subjects; single measures of physiological function may be even more misleading in patients than in normal subjects. Further variance is undoubtedly contributed through widespread use of psychotropic drugs in patient groups. The variance that is due to drugs is not eliminated with simple discontinuation, since drug effects are often long term. To add an even further experimental complication, significant interactions between tranquilized and nontranquilized process and reactive schizophrenics have been reported (Reynolds, 1963). Lang and Buss (1968, pp. 400–452), among others, also point out the increased possibility that the psychiatric patient may be differentially affected by the laboratory situation, the demand characteristics of the experiment, and interpersonal relations with the experimenter. One must keep in mind that the experimental session itself may be such a unique experience for institutionalized schizophrenic patients that the experimental results may not be at all indicative of day-to-day physiological function for these patients. This would be especially so in the case of the most chronic schizophrenic, since many of the studies reviewed here were conducted before the advent of tranquilizing medications, milieu therapy, and a heightened interest in general in the treatment and involvement of patients in more usual day-to-day activities. Differences due to hospitalization may exist not only between the patient and the normal control but also within or between experimental sessions for the same patient. The psychophysiologist, like the biochemist in search of a chemical basis of schizophrenia, must not forget to control for the effects of institutionalization. He must consider not only issues such as diet and relative sensory deprivation but the effect of hospitalization on psychological parameters such as motivation, set, anxiety, and dependency.

Some aspects of the problems facing the psychophysiological experimenters dealing with psychiatric patient groups may be summarized as follows: If the subjects in his experimental group are out of the hospital, they are likely to be on drugs; if they are hospitalized, experimental results should be compared with other hospitalized control subjects; and if only recent admissions are recruited, there is likely to be a confounding based on acute-chronic differences. An adequate sample size, with proper attention paid to diagnostic subcategories, and the adequate representation of physiological parameters is essential, ideally accompanied by tests of inter- and intrasession variability. Since few investigators have the money, resources, or time available to accomplish all of the above before they begin to study the particular hypotheses they may be interested in, it is especially important that they report precisely what they did do and be aware of what was not done when they interpret their own results.

To compound matters further, there are problems involved in the selection of normal control subjects in the study of psychopathology, beside the usual ones of proper matching for age, sex, and socioeconomic status. Pollin (1962, pp. 143–156), for example, maintains that it is unwarranted optimism to assume that differences are randomly distributed between experimental and control groups on variables other than the specific ones under study. He suggests that an objective assessment of personality characteristics and extent of pathology be undertaken for the control group as much as for the experimental group. The use of brief interviews and short questionnaires subsequent to the experimental procedures is recommended. By letting his subjects tell him, the investigator can quickly and sometimes painfully realize what he has overlooked.

Since diagnostic precision can rarely be obtained in the selection of the experimental population, it is critically important that the uncontrolled physiological variation due to environmental and procedural factors be held to an absolute minimum. Literally, volumes have been written cataloguing the care that should be taken in psychophysiological research procedures to minimize artifact and heterogeneity of measurement (e.g., Brown, 1967; Venables & Martin, 1967). Instrumentation; the control of environmental factors ranging from temperature to smog; electrode selection and placement; diurnal and seasonal variations in physiological levels and function; the effects of diet, menstruation, or smoking; the relevance of the physiological variables selected for study; units and means of measurement; and scoring and analysis procedures are only some of the considerations that must be kept in mind by the careful investigator.

There are also a number of logical difficulties awaiting investigators in this area. Foremost among them is a form of "dualism," by which one aspect of the individual or his function is attributed to another aspect of that same individual or function. Classically, this argument is of the form: "Hysteria is caused by a floating uterus." No doubt, many studies have been launched on the wish to discover the underlying physiological "cause" of various psychological disorders. To date no such wish has been fulfilled. Stern and McDonald (1965) can summarize more than 2000 years of trying by saying, "To the best of our knowledge no physiological bases for any of the major mental diseases can be found." They go on to state that they will "lower their sights" and consider research dealing with physiological *correlates* of psychiatric disturbance. It is my contention here that such an approach is not so much less noble as it is more in accord with reality. For there is no logical reason to believe that attempts to relate physiological functions to psychological ones represent anything more than a search for equivalent languages to describe one and the same organismic process. Psychiatric formulations themselves often contain relatively arbitrary "causes" or "effects" within the strictly psychological realm (e.g., paranoia as the result of latent homosexuality) and yet psychophysiologists for the most part still hope to explain away all behavioral and emotional symptomatology on the basis of physiological disease states. Implicit in much of the research is the James-Lange notion that bodily states can produce or cause emotions or psychological states (cf. Stern and Fehr, 1970, for the most recent treatment of this premise); or its opposite, that emotions can cause bodily states. The most parsimonious explanation of why this has never been demonstrated seems to me to be simply that they are not separate events. D. T. Graham (1967) has put forth the most complete and compelling analysis of the futility of trying to relate, rather than translate, one way of talking about the individual's function to what is merely another language for dealing with the same phenomena. His article is highly recommended, as is his chapter in this Handbook.

Other explanations have been given for the lack of success in finding a particular physiological disturbance in any mental disease (Ax, 1962, pp. 29–44). One possibility is that any psychiatric syndrome such as schizophrenia is not a single disease but several different disorders, each with its own physiological cause. Another possibility is that, if there is a single cause, it may produce a variety of clinical pictures. Finally, one might consider that two or more primary causes must be operative simultaneously for the symptomatology to be manifested. Ax goes on to discuss how each of these possibilities might be approached methodologically but no one has yet systematically done so.

Some of the logical aspects of physiological research into psychopathology have been briefly mentioned here in the hope that future research reports will more clearly state their intentions and assumptions; and in the hope of avoiding past mistakes such as performing colectomies on psy-chiatric patients because it was noticed around the turn of this century that colonic stasis occurred in depression and schizophrenia (Altschule, 1953).

It is almost as difficult to categorize the ideas that are embedded in the reported research as it sometimes is to categorize the results themselves. Most often, reviews of the literature have been organized around the physiological parameter investigated, the type of stimulus employed, or the category of experimental subjects used. While such an approach is undoubtedly useful, it seems that enough progress has been made in psychophysiology, and enough research has been conducted, to warrant an accounting, and perhaps sharpening, of underlying themes. The major difficulty in that particular endeavor is in separating ideas that logically and historically may be very much intertwined. Since it is the intellectual matter of the psychophysiology of psychopathology that I propose to dissect, it is obvious that it cannot be done cleanly or exhaustively: concepts are not exclusive of other, even opposing, concepts; the ideational overlap in a burgeoning discipline is considerable; and theoretical perspectives are more often complementary than they are distinct. What follows, therefore, must be understood to be only one particular organization of the conceptual currents in this area of interest—there are many others that hopefully will occur to the reader.

While headings may appear boldfaced in the text, conceptual distinctions cannot be made as boldly when going from, for example, considerations of the general reactivity or responsivity of psychiatric patients to notions of activation or arousal in their various guises. (Indeed, it is interesting to follow the work of the better investigators from one conceptual framework to another.) If questions are asked as to whether the psychologically disturbed are hyper- or hypoaroused, are we so far from those considered originally by Cannon as issues of energy mobilization and homeostasis? Implicitly and explicitly, a search for defective physiological regulation has generated an enormous amount of research, although there are some who argue that defects lie more in the realm of perceptual processes and only use ANS variables as a means of monitoring "openness" or "input dysfunction." To talk of dysfunction in any sphere, however, has cued many an investigator to emphasize brain structures and organic conditions as the underlying "cause" of disordered psychic or physiological function. But it has been difficult to confine such speculation to the CNS alone, and one finds the basic "source" spreading throughout the entire body, usually via hormonal mechanisms. Not even the psychophysiological research that has learning theory as its foundation stands distinct from other enabling formulations, since much of that work has been Pavlovian in nature and hardly free of neurologizing. Taken together, the ways we have of thinking about the disturbed individual, or the normal one for that matter, reflect perfectly the way he functions—as a whole, of a piece, complexly, and interdependently. No summary given here of a way to view that individual is to be taken as exclusive of any other.

Nor should the categories of concepts discussed in this chapter suggest that considered as a whole they would constitute a complete theoretical formulation of the individual. There are many other possibilities. J. I. Lacey, for example, concluded in 1963 that since it was clear that traditional and traditionally derived concepts such as sympathetic versus parasympathetic dominance failed to encompass much data, emphasis should be given to new concepts that do not merely utilize the ANS for its indicant function. In his typically independent fashion he first disclaimed the possible validity of any unidimensional approach and has since set out to unravel the "differential" significance of ANS function (J. I. Lacey, Kagan, B. C. Lacey, & Moss, 1963, pp. 161–196). This work will be discussed in its turn but mention is made of it as an illustration that the level of complexity of the concepts covered here can always be escalated.

RESPONSIVITY-REACTIVITY CONCEPTS

Perhaps the most frequent organizing concept that psychophysiologists have employed in considering psychopathology is whether psychiatric patients evidence different levels of physiological response than do normal control subjects. One form of the argument has been that, since schizophrenics are often withdrawn and blunted from the

clinical point of view, a physiological hyporeactivity may underlie the syndrome (e.g., Angyal, H. Freeman, & Hoskins, 1940). A causal relationship has most often been implied in even this most simple view, in that an unresponsive nervous system is assumed to prohibit the appearance of appropriate emotion or behavior. This is not a logically necessary aspect of such formulations, and some of the reported results on responsivity are better understood if causality is not assumed.

Rather than begin with the earliest research on general autonomic response in patients, let us start with some of the best. Malmo and Shagass and their coinvestigators have extensively studied the physiological reactions of chronic and acute schizophrenic, nonschizophrenic, psychotic, neurotic, anxiety-state, and control subjects to a variety of stimuli. One of their first reported findings (Malmo & Shagass, 1949) on this question was that "early" schizophrenics generally responded in much the same way as anxious neurotic patients in heart rate, galvanic skin response (GSR), neck muscle potentials (EMG), and respiratory rate to heat-induced forehead pain stimuli. This was taken as an indication of a high level of anxiety for both groups. Malmo, Shagass, and Davis (1951) went on to report a lower responsivity for chronic than for acute schizophrenic patients to pain stimuli of relatively low intensity, whereas the reactivity of chronic schizophrenics at high pain intensities was equal to that of the acute patients. Compared to normal subjects, they also found that psychoneurotic and psychotic patients responded to stress with a greater degree of muscle tension. In 1952 Malmo and Shagass reported their investigations of blood pressure responses to both physiological (pain) and psychological (rapid discrimination and mirror-drawing tasks) stress. The rise in systolic blood pressure was greater for psychoneurotic subjects than for either chronic schizophrenic patients or normal control subjects—the latter groups were similar. They conclude from these and other studies that schizophrenic patients are not abnormally sluggish under stress. (These studies will not be reported in greater detail here in the hope that the reader who is not already familiar with them will go to the original sources. In all the literature they are among the most worthy of study for their interest, methodological sensitivity, and overall thoughtfulness.)

From an historical point of view, data relative to the James-Lange theory, wherein emotions are conceived of as the perceptions of bodily changes, have been available for quite awhile. Early work which tested the hypothesis that schizophrenics should exhibit reduced visceral reactions to various sensory stimuli include that of Pollock and Dollear in 1916 (1944, pp. 971–1032) and Bender and Schilder (1930), who found changes in respiration in patients about equal to those of normal subjects; DeBruyn (1909) and Gordon (1930), who discerned no differences in blood pressure responses; and Coriat (1910) and Cohen and Patterson (1937), who measured changes in pulse rate as great or greater in patients than that in normal subjects following painful stimulation. Landis in 1932 reviewed studies of GSR response to stimuli such as noise and electrical shock and felt there were no consistencies. Freeman pointed out in 1933 the subsequently consistent finding of greater intraindividual variability for patients than for controls. Perhaps the most straightforward test of whether schizophrenics are apathetic, behaviorally and somatically, were Strauss's observations in 1929 of the startle response (1944, p. 1001) utilizing speed photography, in which he reported an intensified startle pattern in schizophrenic patients, especially a subgroup of catatonics.

While much of this early work did not offer James and Lange much support, there are data that indicate a diminished ANS response in hospitalized schizophrenics. These have been well summarized by Lang and Buss (1968, pp. 400–452). The following is a representative list of stressors to which patients have been found to be hyporeactive: the inhalation of heated air (H. Freeman & Rodnick, 1940), cold baths (Buck, Carscallen, & Hobbs, 1950), reduced rotational and ocular nystagmus (Angyal & Blackman, 1940, 1941; Angyal & Sherman, 1942; Colbert, Koegler, & Markham, 1959; Leach, 1960), pupillary hypofunction in response to pain, light, or exercise (May, 1948), inadequate vascular responses to cold (Astrup, 1962), the threat of pain (Paintal, 1951), and higher thresholds to thermal pain (Hall & Stride, 1954). Stengel, Oldham, and Ehrenberg (1955), however, also studied reactions to pain in a large group of patients and did not find differences in reactivity in various diagnostic subgroups that included schizophrenia. Although there is a wide variability in results with the cold pressor test as a stimulus, most likely due to the test itself, a diminished blood pressure response with schizophrenics is the more usual finding (e.g., A. Earle & B. V. Earle, 1955; Ingersheimer, 1953). Glaser (1952) found diminished pressor responses to be more characteristic of hebephrenic than paranoid patients. (A somewhat consistent exception to results on schizophrenics seems to be those for paranoid patients, at least lucid ones, who more often resemble normal subjects physiologically.) The Funkenstein test (blood pressure responses to injected mecholyl) has also passed from the scene after a spate of studies. Relative to responsivity of psychopathological groups, psychotic depressives tended to show a hypotensive reaction (prolonged fall in blood pressure) (cf. Funkenstein, Greenblatt, & Solomon, 1948, 1949; C. H. Jones, 1956). Gellhorn and Loofbourrow (1963) summarized their own investigations with mecholyl by stating that both hypo- and hyperreactors can more frequently be found in patient groups than in control groups.

Many of the seemingly contradictory findings cited above might well have been resolved had proper experimental attention been paid to initial levels preceding the measured responses, had more than one variable been employed to assess "responsivity," and had the experimental subjects been better defined on an acute-chronic dimension. The effect of the last factor is one for which we have experimental data other than that provided by Malmo and his co-workers. An early investigation of the general problem was conducted by Pfister (1938), who noted cardiovascular responsivity diminished from the early stages of schizophrenia to the chronic. In the current terminology of "process" versus "reactive" schizophrenia, employing usual laboratory stimuli, DeVault (1957) recorded positive increases in heart rate, similar to control subjects, for reactive schizophrenics as opposed to negative heart rate changes with process schizophrenics. King (1958) also demonstrated physiological differences between process and reactive schizophrenic subjects. His finding was that the maximum fall in systolic blood pressure in response to mecholyl injected intramuscularly was significantly different for reactive schizophrenics as compared with normal subjects, and significantly greater than for process patients. Zuckerman and Grosz (1959), however, found the opposite results: process schizophrenics showed a significantly greater fall in blood pressure following mecholyl injection than did reactive schizophrenics. A comparison of chronic schizophrenics selected on the basis of "adequate" and "inadequate" overt verbal behavior showed no differences in the level of autonomic reactivity to "threat-pain" thresholds (Ray, 1963).

A few investigators have reported studies of reactivity in psychopathological groups relative to the properties of the stimulus. Venables (1960) has been the most systematic. Schizophrenic and normal subjects were presented with visual and auditory stimuli, alone or in combination, of high and low intensities. Patients categorized as "active" had more GSRs in the low illumination and quiet condition than in the high illumination and noisy condition. "Withdrawn" schizophrenics, however, had the same number of GSRs in both stimulus conditions, although latencies were shorter in the bright-noisy situation. Venables suggests that active schizophrenics function at an optimal level with moderate stimulation and show diminished responsiveness with increased stimulus intensity. For withdrawn schizophrenics moderate stimuli are less effective, but responsiveness is improved with an increase in stimulus intensity. Data from a study by Roessler, A. A. Alexander, and Greenfield (1963) indicate that acutely hospitalized psychiatric patients respond somatically as do control subjects at the threshold and high intensity ends of a range of auditory stimuli but differ through a middle decibel range. Confirmation of decreased physiological deficit in schizophrenia with increased intensity of the stimulus is also provided in a study by Leach (1960) of ocular nystagmus with accelerated rotation.

Russian investigators have been actively involved in research on autonomic correlates of schizophrenia. Titaeva (1962) found catatonic schizophrenic patients falling into one of two groups, the first group having a reduced electroencephalogram (EEG) desynchronization response to repeated presentations of stimuli and increased polyphasic skin potential responses. A second group showed larger EEG responses but tended not to have skin potential responses. The diagnoses of these patients generally put those acutely disturbed into the first group, whereas the more chronic patients fell into the second group. In an investigation of autonomic responsivity of paranoid schizophrenic patients (Tirkeltaub, 1962), those patients who were acutely disturbed tended to show a variable vasomotor response, unstable arterial pressure, and irregular pulse and sinus arrhythmia. Greater cardiovascular irregularity was noted by Arutynov (1962), followed by more stable pulse and blood pressures, with clinical improvement following insulin coma therapy (ICT.) Morozov (1961) noticed a greater variability with catatonic patients, paralleling that found with paranoids. To move to other variables, Savitskii (1963) reports greater EMG activity at rest for catatonic patients and greater increases in skin temperature following movements. Rokhlin (1962) maintains that a thorough study of a patient's vascular system "permits a useful analysis of the illness of schizophrenia."

Emphasizing the notion that autonomic responsivity may be as important as the tonic level in differentiating psychopathic and nonpsychopathic individuals, Tong (1959) found that he was able to divide psychopathic subjects into those who were hyporeactive and those who were hyperreactive. With the use of the threat of electric shock as a stimulus, psychopaths have also been found to be relatively unresponsive in electrodermal activity (Hare, 1965a, 1965c; Lippert & Senter, 1966; Lykken, 1957). Hare (1965b) suggests that cues implying impending pain may be less capable of generating sufficient conditioned fear in the psychopath. This is consistent with the formulation of other investigators in its assumption that the psychopath has a hypoactive ANS, with the result that he is deficient in those autonomic correlates of anxiety necessary for the development and maintenance of certain patterns of behavior (Eysenck, 1964; Lykken, 1957; Tong & Murphy, 1960). Studies of resting levels in psychopathic subjects have been inconclusive or inconsistent (Lippert & Senter, 1966; Ruilmann & Gulo, 1950). Fewer spontaneous or nonspecific GSRs for a psychopathic group have been reported, however (Fox & Lippert, 1963). Stern and McDonald (1965) point out that perhaps the critical dimension in research with psychopaths is one of whether they demonstrate symptoms of anxiety or not.

A summary of the studies cited here and of the vast literature on the autonomic responsivity of psychopathological groups that they represent need not be long. The chronic schizophrenic patient seems to be slower or deficient in his response to stimuli to which normal subjects respond. At higher levels of stimulus intensity or stress the schizophrenic may mobilize autonomically to the same degree as control individuals. The psychiatric patient is not necessarily physiologically sluggish or apathetic, and there is no compelling evidence of a diminished capacity of physiological reactivity. Reactivity is often less in chronic than in acute schizophrenia, or lower in process than reactive patients. Early or acute schizophrenics may be hyperreactive in comparison to control subjects to a degree that resembles the hyperresponsivity of anxiety states.

Furthermore, it is clear from the literature that, in assessing responsivity, account must be taken of the initial level of the physiological variate, the lack of reliability of single measures of responsivity, the differential effects due to stimulus quality and intensity, the composition of the experimental groups as to diagnostic category and chronicity, and the nature and definition of terms such as "withdrawal." The definitive study of responsivity has yet to be done. But the one concept that has added the greatest bulk to the literature perhaps holds the least potential today for our understanding of psychopathology. This is not only because studies of responsivity probably encompass the most methodologically unsound research, but because they are too simplistic in their premises and in their view of the behavioral and physiological function of the human organism. The greatest contribution of studies which attempt to relate responsivity, per se, to psychopathology may be that they have forced us to accept a more complex view.

Basal Levels

Issues of physiological reactivity cannot be separated from consideration of the basal level from which these responses start. J. I. Lacey made this most forcefully clear in 1956, drawing on the original formulation by Wilder (1950) of the law of initial values. The principle involved is that the magnitude of change in a physiological variate may be expected to diminish as the initial, or basal, level increases. Homeostatic function implies that responses are reduced, or absent, or even paradoxical in direction when stimulation is added to an already high resting, or prestimulus, level in comparison to stimulation which occurs when initial levels are low. Lacey emphasized, and demonstrated statistically, that a 5 beat/min increase in heart rate, occurring on a high initial level of say 100 beats/min may have the same "responsivity" equivalence as a 20 beat/min increase occurring on a basal level of 60. While Lacey has made his point very clearly, too few experimenters have attended to it, and very few of the early studies of responsivity even report the prestimulus levels of their patient groups. Since the hyporeactivity often reported for chronic schizophrenics may be a function of higher basal levels, a brief summary of findings relative to resting levels in psychopathological groups is in order.

The earliest hypothesis as to basal activity in schizophrenia was similar to that for responsivity: flat behavior should be reflected in attenuated resting autonomic activity levels. A review 25 years ago of studies of resting level autonomic activity in schizophrenic and normal subjects reported no consistent differences (G. L. Freeman & Pathman, 1943; Hunt & Cofer, 1944, pp. 971–1032). A contemporary review by Lang and Buss (1968, pp. 400–452) concludes that studies of basal skin resistance (SR) in schizophrenics indicates relatively higher, the same, or lower resistance levels for these patients, as compared to normal control subjects. Representative studies of higher levels are those of Hoch, Kubis, and Rouke (1944), Jurko, Jost, and Hill (1952), and Howe (1958). Some studies that have reported no differences are those of Malmo and Shagass (1949), DeVault (1957), Ray (1963), and Pishkin and Hershiser (1963). Two studies have found lower basal SR in schizophrenics than in normal subjects (Williams, 1953; Zahn, Rosenthal, & Lawlor, 1963). Studies of heart rate, on the other hand, are relatively consistent in reporting resting rates generally elevated for schizophrenics as compared to normal subjects. Typical results are those of Jurko, Jost, and

Hill (1952) and Williams, 1953. Higher resting tonus of skin vessels is also generally reported in studies of vasoconstriction in schizophrenia (cf. the review by Altschule, 1953; also Henschel, Brožek, & Keys, 1951). Respiratory rates have also been found to be higher in schizophrenic patients than in normal subjects (Gunderson, 1953; Jurko, Jost, & Hill, 1952; Williams, 1953). Measures of muscle activity are also generally found to be in the direction of higher levels in patient groups. The series of studies by Malmo (1950, pp. 169–180; Malmo & Shagass, 1949; Malmo, Shagass, & Smith, 1951) all indicated a high resting EMG in schizophrenics, with the highest levels found in the chronic patients. This finding has been supported by others (Jurko, Jost, & Hill, 1952; Petursson, 1962; Reynolds, 1963; Whatmore & Ellis, 1958).

Taken as a group and across physiological systems, the studies reported above seem to indicate that generally higher basal levels are to be found in schizophrenic subjects than in control subjects. The hypothesis that the flattened affect or blunted behavior seen in schizophrenia has a physiological parallel in basal levels is not supported—at least by studies in which comparisons are made on single variables within one testing session. Many of the reports of no significant differences may reflect methodological shortcomings of the type discussed for studies of responsivity, rather than confirmation of a null hypothesis.

A few experiments have paid attention to diagnostic subgroups and found differences between them. Among the earliest were Syz (1926) and Syz and Kinder (1928), who reported higher basal SR for catatonic than for paranoid schizophrenics. On the reactive-process dimension of schizophrenia, DeVault (1957) reports a higher heart rate than normal subjects in long-term reactive patients, but not in process schizophrenics. Reynolds (1963) found both process and reactive patients to have higher pulse rates than control subjects but with the process group showing more acceleration than reactive schizophrenics. Differences associated with chronicity have already been mentioned for EMG studies conducted by Malmo, who also reports higher resting diastolic blood pressure levels in chronic schizophrenia (Malmo & Shagass, 1952).

A variable that has received particular attention recently, especially in affective disorder, is that of salivary output. A number of studies seem to agree that psychotic depression is associated with a significant decrease in salivary output, both while the subject is at rest or responding to stimulation (Busfield & Wechsler, 1961; Davies & Gurland, 1961; Gottlieb & Paulson, 1961; Peck, 1959). Stern and McDonald in their 1965 review of physiological correlates of mental illness point out, however, that this finding is not diagnostic of depression, since a similar decrease is found in schizo-affective disturbances (Busfield, Wechsler, & Barnum, 1961; Giddon & Lisanti, 1962). Stern and McDonald are also intrigued by a notion that hyperponesis makes a person more prone to develop depression. This suggestion was made by Whatmore and Ellis (1959, 1962) after finding that patients with a functional depression had significantly more activity in four muscle groups than was the case for a control group, whereas patients with a psychotic depression demonstrated no relationship between the clinical state and EMG.

Altschule has provided the most comprehensive survey of research up to 1953 that covers resting activity in various psychiatric patient groups. It is of primarily historical, rather than scientific, interest, however, since it is characterized by a quaint sense of the archaic in style, material covered, and logical perspective. Much of the research reviewed is organized around the concept of "neurocirculatory asthenia," a diagnosis that reached some prominence in the 1950s, especially in England (cf. Cohen & White, 1951; Miles & Cobb, 1951). The most valid conclusions to be abstracted from Altschule are as follows: Groups of (unspecified) neurotic subjects evidenced normal or accelerated cardiac rates, normal or slightly elevated venous blood pressure, and excessive vasoconstrictor activity. Normal or increased pulse rate and occasionally elevated arterial pressure is found in manic depressive patients, often elevated arterial pressures in psychotic depressions, hypertension as a rule in involutional psychosis, and normal or below normal blood pressure for schizophrenic patients.

A few investigators have reported changes in basal levels accompanying changes in psychopathology. Funkenstein, Greenblatt, and Solomon (1951) found that, as schizophrenic processes ameliorate, there is an associated reduction in basal systolic blood pressure, a finding supported by

Gellhorn (1953) and Gunderson (1953). Polygraphic profiles of schizophrenic subjects on tranquilizing medication are more like those of normal subjects than those of patients off medication (Reynolds, 1963). Studies of changes in habitual level, however, have been done in a vacuum of knowledge as to the reliability of this function over time in psychiatric groups. A few attempts have been made, with inconsistent results (Acker, 1964; Carrigan, 1963).

Spontaneous Activity

Polygraphers who have attempted investigations of basal levels have had to contend with spontaneous, or nonspecific, activity as well. Some have incorporated measures of these spontaneous fluctuations into their research into psychopathology. The greatest experimental emphasis has been on muscle activity, and Duffy as early as 1930 suggested that while the degree of muscle tension may indicate the degree of excitation of the subject, the irregularity of motor responses may reflect deficient inhibition. She cites evidence for a factor that determines irregularity of level independently of that which determines the general level (Duffy, 1946), a conclusion generally supported by Malmo and his colleagues (Malmo, Shagass, Belanger, & Smith, 1951; Malmo, Shagass, & Davis, 1951; Malmo & Smith, 1955). Jost, in 1941, also reported significantly less hand tension in 20 "well-adjusted" children before and after stimulation than in 18 children with "adjustment problems." Sainsbury (1955) speculates recklessly that the tremors seen in anxiety patients suggests "disorganization of central motor coordinating mechanisms," while Edwards and Harris (1953) report that finger tremor decreased significantly in schizophrenic subjects who showed improvement over 33 months, while those patients who did not improve had significantly more tremor. Objective measures of anxiety were not included in this study.

Research utilizing measures of spontaneous activity in other physiological variates with patient groups has been methodologically spotty. While Whitehorn and Richter (1937) concluded that psychotics have the most stable heart rates, and neurotics have the least stable, Altschule (1953) comments that it is well-known that the cardiac rate shows marked variability in psychotic patients without regard to the type of psychosis. It is the latter view that has the most subsequent support, a situation which also obtains with measures of regularity of respiration (Finesinger, 1944; Jurko, Jost, & Hill, 1952; Williams, 1953). Malmo and Shagass (1949) report that the greatest respiratory irregularity is found in anxiety patients and early schizophrenics, as compared to control and mixed patient groups. Chronic schizophrenics were less irregular in respiration immediately after pain stimulation than control subjects (Malmo, Shagass, & Smith, 1951). Studies of nonspecific fluctuations in the electrical resistance of the skin with patient groups began more than 40 years ago with a report of "spontaneous galvanic waves" in 78% of paranoid schizophrenics, 38% of catatonics, 32% of depressives, and only a small percentage of normal subjects (Syz, 1926); and more SR fluctuations in a group of "psychopathic" individuals than in normal subjects (Ödegaard, 1932). Studies on this specific issue have been few and far between since then and are as yet not conclusive. The experimenter interested in this area would do well to begin with some few investigations on normal subjects (Burch, Cohn, & Neuman, 1942; S. I. Cohen, Silverman, & Burch, 1956; J. I. Lacey & B. C. Lacey, 1958a).

Periodicity

One other facet of spontaneous autonomic activity has received intermittent experimental attention: the relationship of the rhythmic components of such nonspecific activity to psychopathology. Spontaneous ANS activity has been shown to sometimes include a component that is repetitive, or periodic, in nature (A. A. Alexander, Roessler, & Greenfield, 1963b). Levels of physiological variables which fluctuate regularly over 24-hr or longer cycles have long been documented (e.g., diurnal heart rate changes, hormonal cycles, and body temperature oscillations). But little is known of second-to-second or minute-to-minute rhythms and their possible meaning to psychological function. Doust (1962, pp. 61–96) reports that work from his laboratory demonstrates that spontaneous, nonspecific biological oscillating systems exist within the ANS, as well as within the CNS, and both are seemingly dependent upon the basal reticular formation for their pacemaking and feedback functions. Literature reviews for this concept have been provided by Doust (1959, pp. 45–60; 1960) and

J. I. Lacey and B. C. Lacey (1958a). The work from the Fels Institute is in terms of SR and heart rate spontaneous rhythmic activity; Doust's work in Toronto has been with spontaneous rhythms seen in skin temperature, capillary blood pressure, capillary blood-oxygen saturation, capillary blood flow, alveolar pCO_2, and intercapillary "ground substance" changes of the tissue cells of the skin. The rhythms analyzed in both of these laboratories were measured in minutes and are therefore markedly different from the microseconds involved in EEG monitoring of basal reticular formation activity or from the current investigations of circadian rhythms (e.g., Chovnick, 1961; Sollberger, 1965). The Fels experiments were with healthy subjects; that of Doust involved 182 psychiatric patients falling into six diagnostic categories. These diagnostic categories were shown to be the significantly differentiating factor between the group mean physiological frequencies. The longest resting sine waves were found in patients with schizophrenia, and the shortest in patients with epilepsy; mental health and other types of mental ill health fell between these extremes. Doust contends that longer periodicities imply an increased time spent at the trough of a continuously repetitive sine wave cycle. Since each of the measures employed is an index of relative capillary anoxemia, it is postulated that the schizophrenic will spend more of his life in an anoxemic state than any of the other five psychiatric conditions, and is consequently less susceptible to environmental stimulation (Doust, 1963). Laboratory work from the University of Wisconsin, on the other hand, has found that, for even shorter period intervals, measured in seconds, mixed psychiatric inpatient groups are characterized by the presence of high frequency oscillations in one or more physiological systems, when compared to normal control subjects (A. A. Alexander, Roessler, & Greenfield, 1963a).

CONCEPTS OF ACTIVATION/AROUSAL

Duffy began earnestly developing the concept of activation in the 1950s and was its leading proponent up to the time of her recent death. (See Chapter 15 for the latest statement from this thoughtful and very energetic woman.) As she pointed out in her book, *Activation and Behavior* (1962), the construct has been previously referred to as "energy mobilization," "excitation," and "arousal," all of which she considered to be identical. The activation construct "derives from and emphasizes the fact that a living organism is characteristically an energy system . . . The level of activation of the organism may be defined, then, as the extent of release of potential energy, stored in the tissues of the organism, as this is shown in activity or response [p. 17]." Duffy went on to point out that the degree of activation of the organism is not synonymous with the degree of overt activity, although the two phenomena bear a necessary relationship to each other; "rather, [activation is] the extent of release of the stored energy of the organism through metabolic activity in the tissues. The variations which are observed in the degree of activation appear to occur in a continuum, one end of which is found in the condition of deep sleep or of coma, and the other end of which is found during the performance of tasks requiring extreme effort or during states of great excitement [p. 18]."

Duffy discussed in detail associated issues such as the measurement of the level of activation, the measurement of changes in activation, neuro-humoral bases of activation, variations in activation with variations in the situation, the patterning of activation, the effects of variations in activation, and individual differences in activation. For Duffy the relevant dimensions of behavior were direction and intensity. Activation is a form of energy mobilization determined by the significance of stimuli, and the meaning of those stimuli to the individual. While she felt that intensity is the determining factor in patterns of physiological response, she allowed for the possibility that patterns may be different for the same individual, dependent on whether he is approaching or avoiding the situation.

Malmo (1959) held much the same view as Duffy; the primary difference between them was that activation was defined by him in terms of excitation of the ascending reticular activating system. Such an assumption was consistent with Hebb's (1955) formulation which relates Q-function, or performance, to arousal. In this sense Malmo saw activation as a general drive without directional aspects. For Malmo, like Duffy, the activation level is determined by the nature of the stimulus and the conditions that surround it, such as fatigue or hunger.

In discussing a divided set experiment, Malmo later pointed out that there have been other experiments in which performance (and learning) were significantly affected by conditions that were unaccompanied by any observable shift in physiological indicants (Malmo, 1963). Such findings would clearly limit generalizations concerning the relationship between physiological activation and performance, and Malmo's own divided set experiments provide a clear example of dissociation between these factors. Malmo suggests that this dissociative phenomenon in normal subjects seems related to a dissociation found early in schizophrenics. As far as neural mediation of these behavioral phenomena is concerned, the physiological evidence seems mainly to suggest cortical mechanisms, whose facilitation of autonomic effectors is probably much less strong than that of "the arousal system." However, he states, it is undoubtedly an oversimplification to assign all activation or arousal phenomena to the reticular system, since it has been shown that the posterior hypothalamus is at least as important in the mediation of these phenomena (e.g., Feldman & Waller, 1962).

The relationship of activation to the functional disorders will be of primary interest here, since Duffy's position, relative to psychopathology, is that neuroses and psychoses often differ from "normal" in the degree of arousal, as reflected by differences in levels, fluctuations, and patterning of physiological variables. Characteristic individual differences in activation, or responsiveness, are suggested as the basis from which certain other differences in behavior may be derived. Extreme differences in the degree of activation, the variability of activation, or the speed of return of activity to a lower level are suggested as characteristic of the functional disorders.

Over- and Underarousal

Schizophrenics have been held to be both underaroused and overaroused. While the hypothesis that schizophrenics suffer from an underactive arousal mechanism seems to receive support from studies demonstrating psychomotor and physiological hyporeactivity in chronic patients, Malmo in 1958 argued that activation is measured more directly in terms of basal physiological level than in research on responsivity. Thus studies showing high resting somatic activity in schizophrenia would indicate that schizophrenics are generally hyperaroused, rather than the opposite. Malmo (1958, pp. 44–105), J. I. Lacey (1956), and Wilder (1950) have all presented evidence that responsivity progressively decreases when plotted on an abscissa of increasing activation, as defined by the basal activity level. The underarousal theory of schizophrenia, in terms of diminished activity in nonspecific projection systems, is largely contradicted by most of the psychophysiological research reviewed by Lang and Buss (1968, pp. 400–452), and they conclude that it may be considered incorrect.

Venables (1964, pp. 1–47) summarizes a review by also saying that many false conclusions have been drawn because of the failure to distinguish the level of ongoing activity from reactivity to stimuli. Attempts to define the precise relationship of one to the other tend to be inconclusive, however. Whereas Wilder (1957) argues for an inverse linear relationship between the size of response and the level from which it starts, others (e.g., Silverman, S. I. Cohen, & Shmavonian, 1959) have argued for a curvilinear relationship between level and responses. It is by invoking the law of initial value, or the initial part of a curvilinear relationship between level and response, that what first appears to be a discrepancy between reports in clinical literature and the concept of a physiologically aroused state of the patient may be reconciled. Thus it is held that acute schizophrenic patients show large emotional reactions, while the affect of the chronic patient tends to be "flat." It is against the proposed low level activity of the acute schizophrenic that a large emotional response may be seen, while because of a high existing level of activity of the chronic patient, only a small response may be induced.

An experimental study of this notion is that of Fulcher, Gallagher, and Pfeiffer (1957), who assumed that, if chronic patients are in a high state of arousal, one would expect that the use of depressant drugs would lead to an improvement in their behavior, as well as a more appropriate response level of physiological variables. Their data indicate a greater effect in the behavioral realm than in the physiological one, however, since the findings were primarily that lucid periods became more frequent with the administration of depressant drugs. Stevens and Derbyshire (1958) obtained remission of catatonic stupor with amobarbital and found that there was a corresponding reduction in the levels of arousal as measured by EEG and polygraphic recordings. Shagass (1954), utilizing sedation-threshold techniques to measure resting levels of arousal, provides support for some of these notions in his findings that there are predictably higher thresholds for chronic schizophrenics than for simple schizophrenics or for normal subjects, whereas acute schizophrenic patients had lower sedation thresholds than any other group. Shagass (1954) defined the sedation threshold as that point at which the inflection occurs in the amplitude curve of barbiturate-induced fast frontal activity in the EEG. This inflection point is said to coincide with the onset of slurred speech, a behavioral sign of anesthesia. One of the original claims for the sedation threshold technique was that it could be used as a diagnostic tool to differentiate neurotic and psychotic depression. There is some agreement that an increased bartiturate sensitivity occurs in psychotic depression (Boudreau, 1958; Nymgaard, 1959; Perris & Brattemo, 1963; Seager, 1960), although equivocal findings have been reported by Ackner and Pampiglione (1959) and Martin and Davies (1962). Relative to schizophrenia, sedation thresholds are reported to be low in acute psychiatric states and high in patients who might be characterized as in a high arousal condition, as inferred through measures of tensions or manifest anxiety (Krishnamoorti & Shagass, 1964; Shagass, 1957). It should be noted here that the sedation-threshold technique itself has been called into question by some investigators, e.g., Bradley and Jeavons (1957).

Malmo (1957) has drawn a distinction between pathological and transient anxiety, and restricts the term to the chronic pathological condition. His studies indicate that standard stimulation, or stress, accentuated the differences in arousal between anxiety patients and control subjects. Under resting conditions such differences may be insignificant.

He suggests that anxiety may be produced in an individual by a high level of arousal over a long period of time. He also hypothesizes that some central inhibitory mechanism may be weakened in pathological anxiety.

General Literature

It is difficult to categorize precisely research relating to concepts of arousal because of the overlap and confounding with data dealing with other concepts such as sympathetic nervous system imbalance, responsivity, and neurophysiological function. Duffy made the attempt in 1962, and the following is a recapitulation of the conclusions she considered relevant. In addition to considering a number of physiological variables such as SR, muscle tension, and cardiovascular functions as indicants of arousal or activation level, she also addressed herself to findings of differences in the functional disorders in fluctuations in activation, patterns of measures, and recovery from the effects of stimulation.

Duffy concluded that consistent generalized levels of muscle tension are shown by individuals across situations. She also held that low but statistically reliable correlations of degree of muscle tension occur across different sites such as frontalis, forearm extensors, and posterior cervical muscles. Her own research and that of others led her to believe that individuals can be characterized by the degree of generalized muscle tension, whereby consistently higher degrees of skeletal tension are found in neurotics and psychotics than in normal subjects (e.g., Duffy, 1946; Lundervold, 1952; Malmo, Shagass, & Davis, 1951; Ruesch & Finesinger, 1943; Wishner, 1953). She also acknowledged that the differences appear primarily during response to stimulation and that some investigators question the use of generalized muscle tension measures that are largely independent of the situation and activity of the subject (Davis, Malmo, & Shagass, 1954; Malmo & Smith, 1955; Shagass & Malmo, 1954; Smith, Malmo, & Shagass, 1954). Some qualifications which must be pointed out in discussing measures of muscle tension are that chronic schizophrenics are more like normal subjects in response to pain stimuli than they are in response to tasks requiring active interaction with the environment; the lower the pain intensity, the greater the differences between normal subjects and patients; "preparation for activity" also discriminated between neurotic and normal subjects, as well as the activity itself; and forearm tension differentiated between normal and abnormal groups better than neck muscle potentials. Most of these details have been provided through the work of Malmo and his colleagues.

In reviewing the literature on SR measures of activation, Duffy noted that the contradictory findings in both normal and abnormal experimental populations may reflect differences in techniques of measurement and differences in the rigor of classification of subjects. She stated that it is probable that some abnormal states are characterized by unusually high degrees of activation (as in anxiety) and others by an unusually low degrees of activation (as in depression). Equal mixtures of such groups in the same experimental sample would result in no significant differences when compared to normal subjects, whereas high or low proportions of a particular diagnostic category would give positive or negative findings. Her ultimate argument was that classification on the basis of the degree of activation may be as meaningful as any other means of defining the experimental population.

Other than those studies of SR already cited in the previous section, the following may be of interest as they relate to the activation concept. Richter in 1928 found low SR in paranoids, higher SR in normals, and highest SR in catatonic and depressed patients. The Syz and Kinder (1928) study previously cited was consistent with Richter's findings, with the added comparison that catatonic and depressed patients evidenced fewer galvanic skin responses (GSRs), whereas normal subjects gave frequent GSRs to stimuli even though they had the same level of SR as schizophrenics. Ödegaard (1932) added the information that patients with well-formed psychoses were less reactive than neurotics, whereas organic and schizophrenic patients were the least active. Both Ödegaard (1932) and Westburgh (1929) reported decreased GSRs to stimulation in catatonic and depressive conditions. Darrow and Solomon (1940) confirmed aspects of this early work in their findings of low SR levels in paranoid and depressed subjects.

Interest in skin resistance as a measure was revived toward the close of World War II. In examin-

ing 1160 Army Hospital patients who were being discharged with psychoneurotic diagnoses, Silverman and Powell (1944) discerned strong or intense palmar sweat responses in 83% of their patients. Hoch, Kubis, and Rouke also reported in 1944 that, based on a study of their own and a survey of research on neurotic populations, greater GSR reactivity was evident in neurosis. Wenger, who is noted for his careful and refined research technique, however, reported in 1948 that no significant differences between neurotics and normal subjects on SR could be found. Altschule, in his review of the literature (1953), concluded that overt palmar sweating is generally higher for neurotics but SR measures are less consistent. For psychotic patient samples he concluded that SR is generally described as normal or high, with the greatest variance in manic depressive groups. Some of the most significant differences reported in the literature are those of Howe (1958), who found basal SR consistently lowest for chronically anxious subjects, highest for chronically schizophrenic subjects, and intermediate in control experimental populations. Perhaps the most obvious conclusion from all the skin resistance studies reported in this chapter is that this seems to be the variable most subject to artifact, improper instrumentation, motivations and expectations of the subject, and perhaps even biases of the experimenter.

The picture is somewhat clearer in studies of blood pressure as an index of activation. This is perhaps because Malmo's group has done much of the work relative to neuroses. In general one might say that the blood pressure level is not generally found to be elevated in psychoneurosis, although responses under stress are excessively elevated and more prolonged (Malmo & Shagass, 1952). In studying blood pressure responses to a series of psychomotor tests, Malmo, Shagass, and Heslam (1951) report that almost all individuals show a blood pressure elevation to the tests; diastolic changes parallel systolic changes; normal subjects show greater adaptation of systolic blood pressure over the series of tests than do neurotic subjects; and mean systolic pressure was higher for patients than control subjects for all of the tests. For a rapid discrimination task Malmo, Shagass, Belanger, and Smith (1951) noted higher systolic levels in both neurotic and chronic schizophrenic than in normal subjects. With a mirror-drawing test, Malmo, Shagass, and Davis (1951) found that, during instruction for mirror drawing, both patients and control subjects show an increase in blood pressure, from which they conclude that the autonomic preparatory responses are equal in both groups. Finally, Malmo, Shagass, and Smith (1951) found that systolic blood pressures of chronic schizophrenic subjects were not sluggish in response to stress, and that diastolic responses to pain were higher for chronic schizophrenic patients than normal subjects. There is general agreement that neurotic subjects show less adaptation in blood pressure responses or slower recovery from stimulation than normal subjects, in most but not all experiments. Neurotics show a greater blood pressure response to stimulation. Examples are Wenger's 1948 study, in which both systolic and diastolic pressures are significantly higher for operational fatigue and neurotic patients than for aviation students; and Hirschstein's 1955 study, in which significant negative correlations were found between poor behavioral adjustment, as measured by the Gardner Behavioral Scale, and increases in blood pressure to mecholyl injection, and significant positive correlations between good adjustment and decreases in blood pressure to mecholyl injection.

In considering heart rate responses, a general statement may be made that neurotics sometimes show higher heart rate and greater changes than control subjects, while certain psychotic subjects resemble neurotic subjects in their response but with much more variability. Some representative studies are those of Wenger (1948), in which significantly faster heart rate was found in his mixed neurotic group, with less arrhythmia than aviation students; Malmo, Shagass, and Smith (1951) who found a small selected group of chronic schizophrenic patients had a reliably higher mean heart rate during pain stress than control subjects; and Jurko, Jost, and Hill (1952), who found significantly higher heart rates in early paranoid schizophrenic subjects' responses to the Rosenzweig Picture-Frustration Test, generally higher heart rate in neurotic groups than for control subjects, and a smaller percentage change in heart rate from initial levels to the test period for the schizophrenic than for either the neurotic or control

group. Altschule (1953) also concluded in his review that heart rate is normal or accelerated in patients with neurosis or neurocirculatory asthenia, with marked rises under stress. Manic depressive subgroups evidenced normal or increased heart rates, whereas schizophrenic patients were normal, high, or low compared to control subjects.

Some findings relative to fluctuations in individual ANS variables are as follows. Luria (1932) reports that 61% of subjects with "neuropathic symptoms" were "reactively labile," as compared to 13% of normal subjects. He hypothesized that neurotics had greater "mobilization of excitation" and decreased (inhibitory) "activity of the higher regulative mechanisms." Duffy's own work was along this same line (1930, 1932), in which she speculated that the degree of muscle tension may indicate the degree of excitation, whereas irregularity of motor responses reflects deficient inhibition. In 1946 Duffy also concluded that there is a different factor which determines the regularity of response than that affecting the general level, a conclusion concurred in by Malmo and his coinvestigators (Malmo, Shagass, Belanger, & Smith, 1951; Malmo, Shagass & Davis, 1951; Malmo & Smith, 1955). Some other conclusions from these latter studies were that there was no correlation between irregularity of finger movement and total forearm tension; that psychiatric patients showed more irregularity of finger movement and total forearm tension; that psychiatric patients showed more irregularity than control subjects; and that control subjects showed less irregularity than neurotics, acute psychotics, or chronic schizophrenics. While psychiatric patients can be differentiated from control subjects by both the irregularity of motor response and the degree of muscle tension, Malmo suggests that measures of irregularity are more discriminative. Duffy also concurred that spontaneous changes in level and general irregularity in response and variability in physiological function not only have been found more frequently in neurotic and psychotic conditions but may also be more important in pathology than differences in the intensity of response.

When one considers groups of response measures, the conclusion is much the same. Jost (1941) found that poorly adjusted children were physiologically unstable in response to frustration and during a control period, using a criterion of one-half of the physiological variables falling more than one standard deviation outside of the mean of the control group. Sherman and Jost (1945), in examining EEG, SR, heart rate, and respiration variables, found neurotics to be physiologically unstable, in that they scored above the fiftieth percentile of a control group on all measures except heart rate. When Malmo and Shagass (1949) examined the entire group of variables in their study (muscle potentials, EEG, heart rate, respiration, SR, and finger movement), they found early schizophrenics more like markedly anxious neurotics than either the control or mixed patient experimental groups. A small and selected group of chronic schizophrenic subjects were as responsive as a control group, except in respiratory irregularity (Malmo, Shagass & Smith, 1951). They concluded that "background physiological responsiveness was not low, but purposive acts were less frequent and less well executed."

The general conclusion as to recovery from stimulation as an index of arousal is that maladjusted individuals ordinarily require a longer period of time to recover than do control subjects. They differ not only in the extent of response but in the persistence of disturbed physiological conditons. Equilibrium is restored less quickly, and the longer recovery time is not attributable merely to the extent of the response. Freeman has made use of a recovery quotient to assess the extent of recovery in a given time; he finds that significant correlations exist between the recovery quotient and clinical ratings of emotional stability (Freeman & Katzoff, 1942); and suggests that neuroticism may be related to "unreleased and self-perpetuating internal nervous excitement."

In general a number of physiological functions have been found to show slower recovery to stimulation in groups of psychiatric patients. The group of Malmo studies indicates that psychoneurotics had a greater "after response" with startle reflexes to strong auditory stimuli; whereas control subjects were recovering by 0.3 sec, and a sample of neurotics were still responding or showing a secondary increase in physiological levels (Davis, Malmo, & Shagass, 1954; Malmo, Shagass, & Davis, 1950). Similarly, chin muscle tension was maintained in neurotic patients at a time when it was dropping, i.e.,

recovering, in normal subjects following questions related to their feelings (Smith, Malmo, & Shagass, 1954). Psychoneurotic subjects also showed a longer continuation of blood pressure responses to stress (Malmo & Shagass, 1952); systolic blood pressure in control subjects showed better recovery to "nonspecific stress" than it did with psychoneurotics, both during performance and postperformance (Malmo, Shagass, & Heslam, 1951).

Personality and Arousal

Claridge published in 1967 an attempt to integrate general arousal theory and Eysenck's analysis of personality (1964). Claridge takes "corticoexcitation" as synonymous with "arousal," and argues further that the counterpart to arousal is Eysenck's dimension of neuroticism. Consistent with this view is Eysenck's statement (1955) that neuroticism is associated with instability of the ANS. Claridge's research objectives were an elucidation of some of the psychophysiological processes underlying dysthymic hysteria, following Eysenck's notion that the introvert and dysthymic neurotic have naturally low levels of cortical inhibition. Claridge hypothesized that dysthymic subjects should therefore resist the effect of depressant drugs more than extrovert and hysterical neurotics, whose natural levels of cortical inhibition are already said to be high. Utilizing Shagass's sedation-threshold technique, with some modifications, he found that dysthymics had significantly greater resistance to barbiturate anesthesia than did hysterical psychopaths (Claridge, 1967; Claridge & Herrington, 1966). Significant relationships with sedation thresholds were confined to measures of reactivity or stress arousal level, rather than with basal scores. The ultimate result of Claridge's review of the research from an Eysenckian point of view is a model of psychiatric disorder that proposes the existence of two functionally related arousal mechanisms. The first, identified as a *tonic* arousal system, is considered responsible for maintaining the individual's gross level of arousal. The second, termed by him the "arousal modulating system," (a) controls directly through suppressor influences the level of activity in the tonic arousal system, and (b) integrates the stimulus input into both systems by appropriate facilitation and suppression of incoming information. It is postulated that, in psychosis, the two systems become functionally dissociated (Claridge, 1967).

DEFECTIVE PHYSIOLOGICAL REGULATION

The hypothesis that psychiatric patients may suffer from a defect of some regulatory mechanism has appeared in many forms. All the studies of responsivity of patient groups can be considered, explicitly or implicitly, a test of some such premise. Malmo's series of research reports, for example, specifically asks the question of whether there is disordered physiological regulation in responses to stress. Support for the basic regulatory deficiency concept is claimed with various diagnostic groups, using measures of muscle tension, heart rate, and blood pressure (Malmo & Shagass, 1949, 1952; Malmo, Shagass, & Heslam, 1951). Defective regulation is thought by them to be present in acute schizophrenia and psychoneurotics in two primary forms: an increased magnitude of response and a low degree of adaptation to repeated stresses. (As far as I know no one has investigated directly the question of why an individual may be deficient in the regulation of responses in one organ system and not in another. The notion of a *differential* deficiency is embedded in the individual-response stereotypy phenomenon, for instance, yet how such differentials may come into existence is completely unresearched.)

Clinical and experimental observations of excessive peripheral vasoconstriction (cold or blue extremities) in schizophrenic patients (Ackner, 1956; Shattock, 1950) have led to speculation that impairment of the mechanism of vascular control implicates the hypothalamus (e.g., Gellhorn, 1953; Richter, 1957). Henschel, Brožek, and Keys (1951) have also studied peripheral circulation in schizophrenic patients by means of skin temperature and finger plethysmographic measures; they conclude that there was no fundamental abnormality of either circulation or of peripheral vessels.

Temperature regulation in schizophrenia has also received considerable attention. An illustrative finding is that of Buck, Carscallen, and Hobbs (1950), who noted significantly lower rectal temperature for a large group of schizophrenic patients, compared to a small group of normal control subjects. The mean daily range of temperatures was significantly less for the patients, as was their day-night differential. In 1951 these same authors report that temperature patterns revert to a more normal, less rigid, type after lobotomy. Since this was especially the case with patients categorized as acute rather than chronic, "chronicity" is equated, by these investigators, to a loss of influence of the frontal lobes on autonomic centers. Findings of excessive drops in skin temperature in schizophrenic subjects, as a result of external cooling (Finkelman & Stephens, 1936; G. L. Freeman, 1939), have contributed to the view that temperature-regulatory centers may be less responsive in schizophrenic than in normal subjects. Wenger's finding (1948) that skin temperature was one of the two best measures which reflected improvement in operational fatigue patients is consistent with this view, as is the data that finger temperature measures could be used to discriminate between mixed anxiety and neurotic patients and a normal control group.

Shattock (1950) concludes from his studies of the somatic manifestations of schizophrenia that the vascular disturbance depends on compensatory vasoconstrictor reactions. Body temperature is sufficiently maintained to assure survival, although peripheral structures may be injured by excessive reduction of their blood supply. When external temperature is lowered, the surface temperature of schizophrenic subjects falls to lower levels than that of other psychotics. Schizophrenics fail to respond to increased demands of the environment. As the average blood pressure of refractory (mainly catatonic) schizophrenic subjects was found to be lower than that of paranoid and socialized patients, and as improvement in systemic circulation coincided with onset of the remission, it is possible that abnormalities of behavior in refractory patients may be related to relatively inadequate cerebral circulation. Shattock also found evidence of minor and reversible endocrine disturbance in many of the schizophrenics examined. Cutaneous changes (as seen in thyroid deficiency) or the occurrence of asthenic states suggested a pituitary or adrenocortical dysfunction. Changes in appearance of vaginal mucosa and prolonged periods of amenorrhea give evidence of diminished ovarian function. Disturbance of cortical function is thought to be indicated by changes of mental awareness such as stupor, altered reactions to painful stimuli, and dissociation of conjugate eye movements in catatonic patients.

An interesting approach to questions of regulation is that put forth by Ax (1962, pp. 29–44). While noting that neither heart rate nor respiration rate is by itself significantly correlated with any clinical variable in schizophrenia, he maintains that if the functional relationship between the two, sinus-arrhythmia, is now treated as a single variable it may be involved in schizophrenia in the following way. Since respiration can influence heart rate by means of proprioceptive signals from the chest, diaphragm, and lungs, it is possible that the utilization of such proprioceptive information is impaired in some schizophrenic patients. Ax holds that the impairment reported by Angyal and Blackman (1940) and Leach (1960) of the vestibular response in schizophrenic patients is indicative of a lack of utilization of proprioceptive information. The importance of sensory input to reality testing is also highlighted by sensory deprivation studies. Ax seems to be extrapolating to psychopathological states abnormalities in the pathways between respiratory and cardiac centers which have been traced by J. I. Lacey (1967, pp. 14–36) in normal individuals. Unlike many other investigators who speculate about neurophysiological mechanisms, Ax suggests ways of testing hypotheses having to do with disordered empathy and interpersonal processes.

Interference Interpretations

Lang and Buss (1968, pp. 400–452) have concluded from their review of the psychophysiological literature that there is "remarkably consistent" support for the existence of physiological deficit in schizophrenia. Since many of the studies they have considered have also been reported here, the reader is left to judge for himself the degree of consistency of such support. The relevant data for these two authors are findings of reduced latency and/or amplitude of vestibular, cardiovascular, and sweat gland responses; intraindividual variability of response; and high somatic tension in the schizophrenic compared to normal subjects. Lang and

Buss also feel that the positive relationship between reduced responsivity and increased activation to the degree of withdrawal and exacerbation of the illness has been established. They note that these physiological deficits are more marked for chronic than for acute patients.

In choosing between activation and interference interpretations of the somatic deficits they seem to see so clearly, theories of underarousal are rejected, since research has shown that even chronic patients who appear withdrawn and passive may be physiologically hyperaroused. In the context of a paper championing interference formulations relative to schizophrenic deficit in attention, set, mental associations, and drive, they also choose interference as the explanatory construct for somatic aspects of schizophrenic deficit. They point out that competing stimuli such as those which might be due to excessive feedback of ANS activity would be disruptive of organized behavior. In this sense they seem to be embracing a concept of overarousal in schizophrenia as the source of internally competing and interfering stimuli.

Input Dysfunction

Schizophrenic deficit has also been attributed to diminished or excessive input or feedback from peripheral sensory or afferent systems. The clinical picture described is of an acute stage of psychosis with an excess of sensory input and behavioral responsiveness, and a chronic state with diminished awareness of external stimuli and behavioral and psychological withdrawal. Venables (1964, pp. 1–47) has pointed out that the transition from the one stage to the other has been explained by somewhat contradictory underlying mechanisms such as parasympathetic overactivity in the acute period, followed by sympathetically and cortically activated conditions in the chronic state; or excessive reticular activity while the patient is acute, which subsides as he becomes chronic. (Very few theorists seem to consider the patients who do not pass invariably from one stage to another.) The size constancy experiments cited previously (Callaway & Thompson, 1953; Weckowicz & Hall, 1958) were positive though indirect findings of high levels of sympathetic tonus related to a narrowing of the span of attention in schizophrenic subjects. E. Callaway has recently broadened his concept of physiological aspects of schizophrenia to include hypersensitivity, effects of defective short term memory, and "system noise" (Callaway, 1970, pp. 11–15). It has also been argued that stimulus modality may play a part in the degree of input dysfunction (Venables, 1964, pp. 1–47), and that the nature and frequency of microcirculation, as measured by the cutaneous blood flow, may relate to differing individual states of consciousness (Doust, 1962, pp. 61–96).

Emergency Reactions

Cannon's (1920) classical work with cats has generated a class of psychophysiological concepts about, most broadly, "emotion," and more specifically, about psychopathology. His thalamic theory stressed the activation of the sympathetic nervous system via downward discharge, the upward discharge from thalamus to cortex, and the usefulness of bodily changes as emergency functions. He believed diffuse sympathetic nervous system activity was characteristic of states of fear and anger, and that well-defined and localized sensations signaled conditions such as thirst and hunger. In making the distinction between the appetitive and emergency functions of the ANS, Cannon provided a way of viewing disordered personality.

The early studies in the series by Malmo previously cited were prompted by the hypothesis that psychiatric patients reacted to ordinary life situations as though they were emergencies. The premise was first tested utilizing muscle tension measures in various diagnostic groups (Malmo & Shagass, 1949) and then in response to stress (Malmo, Shagass, & Davis, 1951). General conclusions were that greater muscle tension in response to stress was found in psychoneurotic and psychotic patient groups as compared to control groups; that there was considerable individual consistency in muscle tension levels from one stress situation to another; and that frontalis muscle tension measures were more discriminative between patient and control groups than were neck and forearm muscle potentials (Malmo & Smith, 1955).

Measures of vasoconstriction have also been utilized in research based on "emergency response" concepts. Employing subjects with symptoms of anxiety, hysteria, and neuroasthenia, Van der Merwe

(1948) claimed that greater vasoconstriction was to be found in anxious patients than in hysterics, relative to control subjects. Ackner (1956), assuming that neurotic subjects would be less emotional and mobilized while asleep than they were awake, demonstrated significant differences in pulse volume between groups under Seconal-produced sleep, while awake measurements were not significantly different. Differential responsiveness to the drug itself is not taken into account in his statement that vasoconstriction is a "bodily alerting reaction to stress . . . diverting blood to areas which are becoming mobilized for offensive or defensive action." Martin (1961, pp. 417–456) summarizes peripheral blood flow findings in psychiatric disorders by stating that the many observations that schizophrenics are characterized by excessive peripheral vasoconstriction is most likely a consequence of normal physiological preservation of body heat, and that there is evidence of greater vasoconstriction in anxious patients.

PHYSIOLOGICAL IMBALANCE

Sympathetic-Parasympathetic Nervous System Dominance

Several research studies have been generated from the hypotheses that the functional psychoses will indicate a malfunctioning of either the sympathetic or parasympathetic nervous system, or both. While Cannon's legacy included the knowledge that emotional disturbance may be accompanied by excitation of the parasympathetic system as well as sympathico-adrenal discharge, the major experimental emphasis has been on the latter. Examples of investigators who have taken parasympathetic innervation into account directly, rather than merely as a reciprocal of sympathetic phenomena, are Gellhorn, Cortell, and Feldman (1941), who document that parasympathetic discharge may occur even in mild states of emotional excitement; and Rubin (1960, 1962), who suggests that patients with impaired parasympathetic nervous system responsiveness be treated with parasympathomimetic drugs. Many of the studies cited in this chapter's section on responsivity are based, of course, on the premise of a disordered sympathetic discharge; only a few additional ones will be considered here.

One of the most casual attempts to empirically relate sympathetic activity to mental disorder was documentation of the clinical observation that patients often had cold, moist, cyanotic hands. Altschule (1953) reviewed some of the studies related to this phenomenon and concluded that it was due to sympathetic activity which stimulates the sweat glands while simultaneously lowering cutaneous temperature by inducing vasoconstriction. Sympathetic nervous system response, as reflected in pupillary mechanisms, was investigated by May (1948) in a large sample of male schizophrenic patients and control subjects. He described a deficiency of sympathetic response at rest, in the light reflex, and in response to muscular effort, in his patient group. In an attempt to broaden the independent variables, Bockhoven, Greenblatt, and Solomon (1953) concluded that parasympathetic dominance could be seen in schizophrenic patients who engaged in constructive social activity, whereas relative dominance of the sympathetic division of the nervous system accompanied an impairment of organized activity. Only somewhat less broad strokes are taken by those who suggest that acute stages of schizophrenia evidence a parasympathetic overactivity, which is followed by a sympathetically aroused and cortically activated picture in chronic patients (e.g., Hoffer & Osmond, 1959; Weckowicz & Hall, 1958). Callaway and Thompson (1953) slightly narrow the field by considering the relationship of sympathetic nervous system activity and attention as one in which a perception of threat to the individual induces sympathetic discharge, which brings about a rise in input system threshold, which reduces the perception of threat, which in turn then reduces sympathetic discharge. This somewhat psychic "initial values" effect has been tested in perceptual experiments in which induced sympathetic activation results in reduced size constancy and size judgment (Callaway, 1959; Callaway & Dembo, 1958).

Changes in sympathetic reactivity have also been noted with ICT. Following ICT there have been reports of improved reactivity of the sympathetic nervous system (Gellhorn, 1938; Gold, 1943), the sympathetico-adrenal (Cameron, 1941), and the ANS as a whole (Fortuyn, 1941; Parker, 1940). The Cameron study was of blood pressure and pulse at rest; Gold measured blood pressure responses to mecholyl injections before and after ICT; and Parker found that patients categorized as predominantly sympathetically or parasympathetically aroused improved their autonomic balance after ICT. Scheflen, Reiner, and Cowitz (1953), in a later and methodologically more sound study, report, however, that they found no reliable differences in vital signs between patients who improved or failed to change with ICT. This held for measurements of level, change, pattern of response, and variance of their physiological measures.

Autonomic Balance

Perhaps the earliest study of the concept that individuals would differ in the degree in which sympathetic or parasympathetic function would be dominant was that by Eppinger and Hess (1910). But the most thorough and extensive work is that of Wenger (e.g., 1941, 1948, 1957) who has published a 25-year retrospective review of his own work (1966). (See also Chapter 13.) His contributions have been not only to theory but to the discipline itself, in the number of other investigators he has stimulated and trained, and as a model of experimental exactitude and control to be emulated.

The largest scale studies of autonomic balance were carried out during World War II, utilizing air crews and military hospital patients. The study reported in 1948 was of sympathetic imbalance in operational fatigue and in psychoneurotic patients. Ten of 20 physiological measures differed significantly between the 2 groups. Some of the findings were that the neurotic subjects had a lower and more acid salivary output, faster and shallower respiration, faster heart rate with little sinus arrhythmia, lower finger and sublingual temperature at pretest, and higher systolic and diastolic blood pressure. (No evidence was found for parasympathetic dominance in asthmatic and peptic ulcer patients.) A number of factor analyses has been conducted on the battery of physiological measures employed, and an "autonomic" and a "muscular tension" factor emerged which have not, however, related consistently to various personality scales. The many studies of autonomic balance in the literature have in common the goal and the problem of attempting to pierce the complex interaction of the various branches and factors within the ANS by means of only selected measures. J. I. Lacey's findings (J. I. Lacey, Bateman & Van Lehn, 1953; J. I. Lacey & Van Lehn, 1952) as to individual differences in the preferred response system and differing individual patterns of response possible with stimulation, the problems with the physiological criteria employed in autonomic balance studies pointed out by Darrow (1943), and the many studies previously cited which indicate the absence of a "mass action" of the sympathetic nervous system, have all lessened the impact of the autonomic balance formulation on contemporary thinking. Similarly, Lang and Buss (1968, pp. 400–452) point out that the inconsistency of findings with SR and schizophrenia have not supported Wenger's formulation (Wenger, 1959; Wenger, N. F. Jones, & M. H. Jones, 1956) that the autonomic activity of schizophrenics is dominated by the sympathetic nervous system. Rather, the emphasis currently is on the functional rather than the morphological classification of physiological responses.

Adrenergic-Cholinergic Formulations

A specific hypothesis relating schizophrenia to hormonal functions has evolved from Funkenstein's mecholyl test (Funkenstein, Greenblatt, & Solomon, 1951). Gellhorn (1957), Ax (1953; Ax et al., 1962), and Schachter (1957), among others, have held that schizophrenic patients, especially those who may be thought to be chronic, are considered to be in a norepinephrine-like arousal state. Collectively, they have demonstrated a relationship between the norepinephrine-like state and aggressive, hostile, and outwardly directed activity. In contrast, epinephrine-like states are associated with fear, passivity, and depression. Ax et al. (1962), for example, devised a physiological pattern index which simulates the epinephrine-norepinephrine ratio. The majority of a schizophrenic patient group had negative or norepinephrine-like indices, whereas almost all his nonschizophrenic subjects had positive indices, indicating an epinephrine-like response to the stress of pain apprehension.

Interest in epinephrine balances by psychiatrists was in part generated by psychotic patients with asthma: it was noticed that, when psychosis devel-

oped in patients with asthma, the asthma disappeared, only to return when the psychosis remitted; and that the asthmatic syndrome in some psychiatric patients is markedly influenced by emotions. What seems to Altschule (1953) the most likely explanation is that the adrenocortical hyperactivity that occurs commonly in manic depressive, schizophrenic, and involutional psychoses has the same effect on asthma as the administration of cortisone or adrenocorticotropic hormone. He claims that strong rage or fear may abort an asthmatic attack, apparently through the liberation of epinephrine during the emotional reaction, or more commonly, that asthmatic attacks are precipitated by emotional upsets.

Indirect data implicating epinephrine and psychopathology has been gathered with the use of electroconvulsive therapy. For example, L. Alexander (1953) describes successful ECT as a strong cholinergic stimulus which lowers sympathetic activity if that sympathetic activity was induced by epinephrine. At the same time successful treatment reduces the pressor response to mecholyl and enhances the response to epinephrine. Other investigations (Funkenstein, Greenblatt, & Solomon, 1952; Funkenstein & Mead, 1954) of the mecholyl reaction in psychotic patients and normal control subjects with elevated blood pressure showed the reactions falling into two groups: those in whom the blood pressure remained below the preinjection level throughout a 25-min observation period, who were interpreted as having excessive secretion of an ephinephrine-like substance and who had a good outcome with ECT; and a second group considered to have an excessive secretion of a norepinephrine-like substance and who did not improve with ECT. The first group consisted of patients diagnosed as manic depressive or involutional, whereas the second group consisted primarily of schizophrenic patients. Successful ECT has been said to decrease resting blood pressure, increase the pressor response to epinephrine, and decrease the depressor response to mecholyl (Funkenstein, Greenblatt, & Solomon, 1948, 1949, 1950). The concordance of psychological and physiological changes is also said to obtain when the patient recovers spontaneously, or with psychotherapy, or after insulin treatment (Funkenstein,

Greenblatt, & Solomon, 1951). It goes without saying that the estimation of autonomic balances by drug reactions is problematical because of the many factors involved.

Funkenstein and his associates at the Boston Psychopathic Hospital have also devised pharmacological prognostic tests (Funkenstein, Greenblatt, & Solomon, 1953; Meadow & Funkenstein, 1952, pp. 131–149; Meadow, Greenblatt, Funkenstein, & Solomon, 1953), using the systolic blood pressure response to injections of epinephrine chloride and mecholyl to divide psychiatric patients into seven categories. They claim a reciprocal relationship between the immediate response to the adrenergic and cholinergic stimulation, finding that schizophrenic patients most commonly show striking pressor reactions to epinephrine and mild depressor reactions to mecholyl. Catatonic cases tend to fall into a group which has a mild reaction to epinephrine and a marked reaction to mecholyl, with normal control subjects usually showing marked reactions to adrenalin and mild to moderate reactions to mecholyl (Funkenstein, Greenblatt, & Solomon, 1948, 1949, 1950; Funkenstein, Greenblatt, Root, & Solomon, 1949). Control subjects were said to show a moderate response to the drugs with a tendency to reestablish homeostasis quickly, whereas most of the neuropsychiatric cases had either exaggerated or weak responses and an often deficient capacity to reestablish homeostasis. The finding of most prognostic value was that those patients whose reaction was striking in response to both drugs, or for whom anxiety or a chill was precipitated by mecholyl, responded well to ECT. L. Alexander (1955) has provided supporting evidence for the breakdowns given above, although this group of studies taken as a whole is not without a number of internal inconsistencies.

One study has been done that attempted to measure plasma epinephrine levels directly, immediately after ECT seizure (Weil-Malherbe, 1955). The fluorometric measuring techniques indicated a 75% increase in plasma epinephrine for a period of 10 min after seizure, and a lower level increase in plasma norepinephrine which declined more slowly. When levels were measured with peripheral seizure eliminated, the same general rise in epinephrine levels was found, but the norepinephrine

elevations were eliminated. Weil-Malherbe therefore concluded that the epinephrine rise was primarily due to stimulation of brain autonomic centers, rather than as a secondary concomitant to the motor, cardiovascular, or anoxic aspects of the unmodified seizure.

HOMEOSTATIC CONCEPTS

From Cannon's work it was evident that the secretion of adrenalin was a powerful mechanism of sympathetic discharge. The question was then raised of whether central regulatory mechanisms are called into action that tend to terminate the sympathetic-adrenal discharge. Gellhorn (1953) concluded from a variety of primarily animal experiments that although the secretion of adrenalin acts at first as a powerful synergist for sympathetic excitation, it may, through its depressor action on sympathetic ganglia, including the adrenal medulla, reduce discharges over the sympathetic system and thereby contribute to homeostasis. This mechanism would have a tendency to restore hypothalamic reactivity to normal levels and to reduce the responsiveness of the hypothalamic-hypophysial system. The role of the hypothalamus in homeostasis will be considered specifically in a later section, but it should be stated here that Cannon's demonstration of the overall contribution of the ANS in homeostasis was again the impetus for a search for defective regulation as a concomitant to mental disorder. An example is the work of Funkenstein and his colleagues, previously mentioned, which demonstrated a failure or deficiency of homeostatic capacity in the responses of neuropsychiatric subjects to mecholyl and adrenalin, whereas control subjects were capable of reestablishing homeostasis more quickly even though their response to the drug may have been greater (cf. Funkenstein, Greenblatt, & Solomon, 1948, 1949, 1950).

When one considers homeostatic functions, issues of physiological rhythms are not far behind. Sollberger (1965) has given a great deal of thought to what he terms "chronopathology," the rhythms found in disease. Although much of his thinking is based on the normal individual, he states that there is a general tendency toward instability in the sick organism, either from overload of the regulating system or from exhaustion. He sees instability tending to create or enhance oscillations. If neural and endocrine stress mechanisms are overburdened, either transient or sustained oscillations may be expected. He feels that oscillatory diseases are especially common in the neurological realm, since most regulatory mechanisms in the living organism are themselves neural. Central nervous system rhythms which are pathological are thought to be roughly subdivided into hypothalamic and cortical disturbances. Psychic diseases are associated with cortico-malfunction which may invoke endocrine and autonomic nervous apparatus; whereas rhythmic malfunction in the hypothalamic region may not involve the psychic apparatus, according to Sollberger (1965). Menninger-Lerchenthal (1960) and Richter (1960) have pointed out that disordered endocrine and vegetative functions may alternate with psychotic symptomatology. There is said to be no real borderline between hypothalamic and psychic rhythmic disturbances, and Sollberger claims that periodic psychotic symptoms are followed by signs of hypothalamic disturbance, whether rhythmic or not. He points out as well that periodic changes in psychosis may appear at periods of life when the regulatory mechanisms are already out of balance, as in puberty or the climacterium.

Energetics of Human Behavior

G. L. Freeman (1948) has held a thesis that those persons regarded as emotionally unstable have low physiological recovery, high physiological variability, and a discrepancy in the ratio of arousal and discharge factors in neuromuscular homeostasis. In comparing small groups of neurotics, manic patients, and schizoidal subjects with control subjects, the neurotic group showed by far the greatest individual variability in neuromuscular homeostasis and the slowest physiological recovery from experimental displacements as measured by palmar skin conductance and general restless movement. It appeared to Freeman that the anxiety neurotics showed the greatest discrepancy between energy mobilization and its discharge, when compared to the fixated psychotic or the more flexible normal subject. Freeman also felt that the longer a psychotic had been confined in a hospital, the less

energy he was capable of mobilizing. Some of the implications of his work, which views behavior disorder and therapy from a homeostatic point of view, are that the nervously unstable personality is one that does not adequately discharge aroused excitation in a fashion to give lasting relief and equilibration. Freeman believes that while the neurotic has great discrepancies in the ratio of bodily energies mobilized and the degree of equilibrium obtained, his behavior toward many situations is still adaptive compared to the psychotic, who may achieve complete physiological equilibrium by bizarre, nondiscriminatory reactions at the expense of response flexibility and social reality.

G. L. Freeman (1948) has carried Cannon's original conceptions the furthest along as applied to the dimension of psychiatric illness. He argues that all behavior is an attempt to preserve organismic integrity by maintaining homeostasis. Any displacement from an equilibrium (rest) will be followed by mobilization, or arousal of internal bodily energies; discharge, or expression of these energies by overt response; and recovery, or the return to prestimulus condition. The individual was therefore said to have some of the attributes of an electronic capacitor. Contemporary thought places him physiologically at least at the level of a servomechanism.

Adaptive Deficiency

Hoskins (1946) has also emphasized an adaptive deficiency found in schizophrenia. He has reviewed his own and others' research on temperature regulation, circulatory functions, and measures of equilibrium reflexes for their bearing on the problem of homeostasis. He points out that one of the most important adaptive characteristics of man is an ability to maintain a steady state despite the stresses that constantly impinge upon him from the internal and external environment, and that the existence of such a steady state is the more remarkable in that the organism is made up of "materials that are notable for their instability." Homeostasis is said to have two important aspects as regards schizophrenia. First are the systematic differences between schizophrenics and normal persons in regard to the levels at which different functions are "set." Second is the extent to which the "steady state" is actually steady. A correlated problem is of how promptly an imposed distortion is corrected, since adaptation would be handicapped if ultimate restoration to normality were very slow. Adaptation also is not served best by an invariable pattern, since the adaptive value of some functions depends upon their ability to meet new needs very suddenly. Relative to the first issue of functional level, Hoskins's own research has indicated that patients and control subjects give essentially identical values in the aforementioned variables. The few measures in which differences were found were in oxygen consumption rate and rate of blood flow (Hoskins, 1946). Hoskins considers the evidence striking, however, that the schizophrenic patient is less than normally competent in holding to the steady state under ordinary conditions of existence. Extensive studies of variability in schizophrenics, which he conducted at Worcester State Hospital, indicate a reduced ability of patients to "maintain metabolic steadiness under conditions in which such steadiness would be regarded as a mark of psychosomatic stability." He points out, too, that others in his research group have reported a similar variability in psychological functions (Shakow & Huston, 1936; Shakow, Rodnick, & Lebeaux, 1945). Hoskins also reports two instances in which the ability to maintain differential levels is thought to be defective as compared to normal subjects. One of these was the oral-rectal temperature differential, which normal subjects maintained at about twice the efficiency as schizophrenics; the other was a systolic-diastolic blood pressure correlation, which was higher for the patients than for normal controls.

The view that Hoskins represents may be summarized as follows. Schizophrenic psychosis is marked by numerous defects of adaptive efficiency, which result in inadequate responses to changing stimuli. The "physiological clumsiness" may serve as a "decompensation factor," in that the prodigious effort required in organic adaptation may leave the patient with inadequate energy for social adaptation. An example of a more contemporary investigator in the same camp is Wishner (1955; 1962, pp. 161-187), who maintains that a positive correlation can be found between psychopathology and increases and decreases in efficiency. Efficiency is defined as the ratio of focused to diffuse activity.

CENTRAL NERVOUS SYSTEM STRUCTURE

Theoretical postulates, such as those under discussion in this chapter, have often been attributed to an assumed functional deficiency of some central regulatory mechanism such as the hypothalamus, the cortex, or the ascending reticular activating system. No direct relationship of any central mechanism to psychopathological states has ever been uncovered. A discussion of experimental and morphological relationships between central mechanisms and emotion, and the cortex and autonomic functions, has been covered by others (for example, Martin, 1961, pp. 417-456); this section will be limited to speculations about CNS involvement which are not covered elsewhere in the chapter.

Hypothalamic Involvement

The hypothalamus periodically is mentioned as a structural source of disordered autonomic function (e.g., Gellhorn, 1957). Indications of hypothalamic-hypophysial dysfunction that have been noted are the disturbances in the sexual sphere and in food intake which occur in schizophrenia and other functional psychoses; the lack of decisive hyperglycemia in the face of very dramatic emotional display; and the phasic and periodic aspects of some of the psychoses (Brožek, 1964; Gildea, Mailhouse, & Morris, 1935; Whitehorn, 1934). Gellhorn concluded that schizophrenia is characterized physiologically by a deficient reaction of the sympathetic nervous system, as indicated by decreased blood pressure and a lessened circulatory adjustment reaction. This led him to advocate treatment procedures which would increase and maintain hypothalamic reactivity for an extended period of time so that hypothalamic-cortico relations approach normality. While he acknowledges that the failure of the hypothalamus to adequately regulate hypophysial secretions leads to endocrine disturbances, he rejects as logically and physiologically simplistic the notion that the secretion of adrenalin is the sole important effect. For this reason he maintains that efforts to supplement deficient "downward discharge" by the injection of adrenalin or various hormones are bound to fail. (That conclusion, at least, has been supported by data; Cameron, 1941; Himwich & Fazekas, 1942.) Gellhorn believes that electroconvulsive and insulin shock treatments, however, satisfy the requirements of providing compensatory action on hypothalamic imbalance. The imbalance which must be corrected with psychosis is that of the relative predominance of the vago-insulin system over the sympathetico-adrenalin system. Other treatments which Gellhorn maintains induce a sympathetico-adrenalin discharge are electronarcosis, anoxia, induced fever therapy, and shock precipitated by an insulin-histamine combination (Bowman & Simon, 1948; Gellhorn, 1943; Gellhorn & Kessler, 1942; Hill, 1940; Rees, 1949; Sargant & Slater, 1948). Disinhibition of cortical control of the hypothalamus is thought to be a primary or secondary effect in all these treatment procedures. One might expect, then, that similar disinhibition and consequent hypothalamic excitation is the result of frontal lobotomy.

While there is agreement that both ECT and ICT have an effect on diencephalic centers, particularly hypothalamic regulative nuclei, there is a wide range of opinion as to the type of effect and the therapeutic mechanism that may be involved (Ashby, 1953; Kalinowsky & Hoch, 1952; Roth, 1952). Differences are in part due to the absence of a consistent correlation between any effects of ECT on autonomic centers and clinical improvement (Brill et al., 1957). A summary 20 years ago of the literature implicating the hypothalamus and ECT (Roth, 1952) points out the frequent association of recovery with improvement of menstrual function in female patients and the reestablishment of sleep rhythms, body weight, water retention, and appetite; the similarity of post-ECT and postconcussion amnesic syndromes; the occasional occurrence of Korsakoff syndromes following ECT and diencephalic lesions; and pentothal-EEG data. The probability that the convulsant current passes principally through basal brain structures, and evidence that direct central action is responsible for the blood pressure rise, hyperglycemia, and elevation of plasma epinephrine and 17-hydroxycorticosteroid (17-OHCS) seen with ECT further implicates the hypothalamus (Hoch & Pennes, 1958, pp. 423–455).

Gellhorn added a unique notion in 1964 when he pointed out that, since anterior portions of the hypothalamus influence parasympathetic activity and posterior hypothalamic function is largely involved in sympathetic nervous system activity, and since the hypothalamus discharges both "up" and "down," the balance of all of these hypothalamic functions in a large measure will contribute to underlying emotions. He goes on to state that since proprioceptive stimuli (tension or relaxation of striated muscle) tie in with the hypothalamus, they help set its balance. Facial contraction patterns would therefore lead to efferent discharges via hypothalamic-cortical systems and contribute to the physiological processes underlying emotions. As clinical evidence he points out that paranoids show a rigidity of facial expression and muscle tone and that treatment with phenothiozines consists largely of stimulation of extrapyramidal diencephalic (i.e., muscle) centers, rather than direct enhancement of autonomic effects, which are small.

Although, in general, it is assumed that the anterior and posterior hypothalamus operate in reciprocal fashion, in that activity in the posterior portion which mediates sympathetic function will tend to inhibit anterior innervation of parasympathetic functions, it is not always the case that both these branches of the ANS may not be operative with acute emotional disturbance. As central sympathetic nervous system mechanisms are innervated, cortical arousal is also produced. Drugs such as tranquilizers which may shift the balance between the anterior and posterior hypothalamus, would therefore also decrease the intensity of discharges from the hypothalamus and reticular formation to the cortex and lower the arousal level of the cortex. Some direct evidence for this formulation was reported by Stevens and Derbyshire (1958), in which remission of catatonic stupor under amobarbital was accompanied by decreased levels of cortical and autonomic activity, as measured by EEG and EKG recordings. Hyperarousal is therefore postulated for chronic or catatonic patients, since the action of a depressant drug is to improve the patient's condition.

Neuropsychological Bases of Schizophrenia

In a 1969 review article, Mirsky puts forth the concept of an inverted **U** function relating arousal or activation level and performance. His expectation is that maximum performance is to be found with intermediate activation levels, whereas performance should deteriorate at both high and low activation levels. He also presumes the basal activation level to be higher in schizophrenics. Therefore, chlorpromazine, which is said to reduce activation the same amount in schizophrenic and normal subjects, should result in less performance deficit in schizophrenics. Conversely, increasing the arousal level should result in a greater deficit for schizophrenics. Using Rosvold's Behavioral Test, Kornetsky and Mirsky (1966) found schizophrenics to be less affected by chlorpromazine. Mirsky's attempt to integrate the variability found in physiological measures of schizophrenics, issues of brain damage, and hyperarousal concepts leans somewhat on Russian diagnostic schemata. He contends that there is a "nuclear" schizophrenia, characterized by early onset, poor prognosis, and a profound degree of withdrawal (similar to "process" schizophrenia in this country), and a "periodic" schizophrenia, which has a later onset, is episodic, florid, assaultive, depersonalized, and delusional (comparable to the "reactive" or acute schizophrenic). He also theorizes that there are two types of brain pathology involved. For nuclear schizophrenia he posits long-standing, diffuse frontal lobe and associated subcortical structure damage—what he calls the "badly made" brain. The brain damage thought to be associated with periodic schizophrenia is in the septal, hippocampal, and temporal lobe areas, and may be undetectable with EEGs. He goes on to claim that hyperarousal is characteristic of all schizophrenias and that all schizophrenia begins with a basic fault of an obscure nature in the ascending reticular activating system (ARAS). The functional outcome of such a fault depends on the mechanisms remaining to cope with the overintense barrage of stimuli from the ARAS. If the cortical mantle is damaged as well, especially the frontal and temporal systems, the individual will be unable to adapt; the resulting syndrome is that of the chronic schizophrenic. For the more acute schizophrenic group, overexcitation of the ARAS may be less, cortical damage may be less, or both. Onset may be delayed until the individual is stressed in adolescence, or with head trauma, which may damage cortical inhibition. He also assumes that for para-

noid schizophrenics, about which the least is known, there is no cortical damage except that in the ARAS, and that the hyperaroused state is kept rigidly in check.

S. A. Mednick has lately been postulating hippocampal damage, and a resulting inadequacy to inhibit ACTH secretion, to explain his data on GSR responsivity in a group of mentally ill children (1970). He found that a great majority of what he termed his sick group differed from a well group in that their GSRs did not habituate to repeated stimuli; they were highly resistant to extinction of a conditioned GSR; and the mentally ill children demonstrated remarkably fast recovery of GSR responses. Moreover, 70% of the subjects with abnormal GSRs were those whose mothers had suffered pregnancy or birth complications. He relies heavily on animal ablation studies to make the link to disordered hippocampal function.

Freud's Model

Karl Pribram has been advocating that Freud's 1895 Project, which dealt with neurological aspects of the psychoanalytic model, should be taken seriously. He maintains that, although Freud himself abandoned this aspect of the model and neurophysiologists have failed to study it, the neurophysiological hypotheses derived from the model are now testable (Pribram, 1963). He believes that current neurophysiological, neurobehavioral, and experimental behavioral techniques will allow tests of constructs such as "cathexis" on neuropsychological grounds. While the research he cites in support of his position does not deal specifically with psychopathology, the task he is proposing is a provocative one and the reader is referred to the following sources for a fuller explication: Freud, 1954; Pribram, 1962, pp. 442–468; 1963, pp. 209–229; 1965, pp. 81–92.

APPROACH AND AVOIDANCE HYPOTHESES

Activity-Withdrawal

Several studies have related ANS function to the "active-withdrawn" dimension of schizophrenia. Paramount among these are those of Venables (1960) and Venables and Wing (1962). In response to stimulation, "withdrawn" schizophrenic patients were found to be less responsive in palmar skin potential than "active" schizophrenic patients or control subjects. Resting levels did not differ between any of the groups. Differences in responsiveness were also observed when background stimulation (dim and quiet or bright and noisy) was varied—the active schizophrenic subjects demonstrated more responsiveness in the low level background condition. The conclusions from these results were that the active schizophrenic patients were basically at an already high level of arousal, which is reduced in the quiet-dim condition, so that they respond more efficiently. Conversely, the withdrawn schizophrenic is thought to be at a low arousal level, which is increased and optimized by the bright-noisy background. Basal level measures do not support these assumed differences in arousal level, however. The study conducted in collaboration with Wing is interpreted by Venables in a review (1964, pp. 1–47) as indicating higher arousal levels to be associated positively with the degree of social withdrawal. Arousal was measured in terms of a two-flash threshold determination or decreased skin potential response to stimulation. Paranoid patients who were coherent were exceptions to the general finding, and indeed showed the opposite relationship. While inconsistencies between these two studies remain unresolved by the investigators, they have suggested that schizophrenic withdrawal is a form of conditioned avoidance.

Shattock (1950) also has argued that schizophrenic reactions may assume one of two forms: paranoid projection or gross catatonic withdrawal. The withdrawal is said to have a somatic, as well as a mental, aspect which facilitates or initiates schizophrenic nonparticipation. A lowering of metabolic level; vascular deficiency; the reduction of endocrine function; and local, instead of general, responses are examples of this somatic detachment. Paranoid reactions are more circumscribed and more limited to a mental level, but also demonstrate the "isolation of physical functions necessary to cognitive appraisal."

Orienting Responses

J. I. Lacey was one of the first to consider seriously the concept of psychophysiological states of "openness to the environment" and "rejection of the environment" (J. I. Lacey, 1969; J. I. Lacey, Kagan, B. C. Lacey, & Moss, 1963, pp. 161–196) in a study of "directional fractionation," wherein stimuli were employed that could be expected to call for selective acceptance or rejection of those stimuli by the subject. In the careful way so typical of him, J. I. Lacey found evidence that increases in heart rate or blood pressure responses accompanied "mental concentration," while attention to the environment was accompanied by cardiac deceleration. Skin conductance increases tended to be associated in their effect opposite to those for heart rate increases. The cardiac acceleration concomitant with rejection of painful incoming stimuli, along with elevated blood pressure, may lead to decreased sensory sensitivity by means of an "inhibitory effect of increased pressure within the carotid sinus on cortical and sensory-motor functions" (J. I. Lacey et al., 1963, p. 173). Pribram (1963, pp. 209–229) has also developed a neuropsychological model of the normal orienting response and habituation process.

J. I. Lacey's formulations always generate studies by other investigators and generally receive support (e.g., Obrist, 1963; Stewart & Dean, 1965). Unfortunately, a battery of studies dealing specifically with psychopathological states has not yet emerged, although Stern, Surphlis, and Koff (1965) have found that hospitalized psychiatric patients who habituated most rapidly in electrodermal orienting responses (immediate decreases in SR of at least 100 Ω within 0.5 sec of tone or word stimulus presentations) had the better prognosis, and that patients who were most responsive demonstrated the least pathology. Bernstein's results (1964, 1965) are consistent with the above, in that regressed schizophrenic subjects had markedly reduced frequencies and amplitudes of GSR orienting responses to light flashes, compared to both control subjects and remitted schizophrenics; but inconsistent with the study of Stern, Surphlis, and Koff, in that habituation was faster in the pathological group than in the normal subjects.

Russian research on the orienting response also indicates attenuated responses in schizophrenia, compared to normal control subjects. If the speed of habituation of the orienting response is taken as a measure of level of arousal, the general Russian finding with depressive patients is of higher arousal levels than in control subjects (Stern & McDonald, 1965).

Protective Inhibitions

Investigations of autonomic functions in schizophrenia conducted in the Soviet Union are almost always interpreted in Pavlovian terms. The concepts most relied upon are those of "protective inhibition" and "internal inhibition," the dulling of responsiveness with use and the extinction of response when it is not reinforced. These hypothesized phenomena are, in turn, used to support the contention that the schizophrenic state is one of excessive or failed inhibition of cortical and midbrain structures. The autonomic orienting response (OR) employed to test the presence or degree of either protective inhibition or internal inhibition in schizophrenic subjects sometimes bears a great deal of similarity to measures used to define activation in this country. (The majority of Russian studies cited here are from secondary sources, especially Lynn, 1963.) Traugott, Balonov, Kaufman, and Luchko (1963) report finding poor ORs in chronic schizophrenics, variable ORs in hallucinating paranoids, and overactive ORs with the institution of insulin treatment. Gamburg (1963) found that with simple schizophrenic subjects no ORs were elicited, whereas paranoid schizophrenics were characterized by defensive reactions.

Russian work also indicates that there is a depression of the sympathetic nervous system function, both in level and reactivity, in schizophrenia. Ekolovia-Bagalei (1963) reports a lowering of sympathetic tone; Vertogradova (1963) finds lower sympathetic responsiveness to hot and cold stimuli; and Streltsova (1963) finds less pupillary reaction to various stimuli. "Protective inhibition" is invoked as the explanatory concept, whereby it is held that reactions may be extinguished as a result of an excessive buildup of protective inhibition, that caffeine administration increases ORs by dissipating protective inhibition, and that reactivity differs from early to late in the day because of the accumulation of protective inhibition. Stanishevskaya (1963) theorizes that the increased spontaneous activity he found in simple schizophrenic and anxious "paranoiac" subjects was due to deficient cortical inhibitory control of high levels of activation. He maintains that catatonic schizophrenics and non-anxious paranoiacs show little or no spontaneous activity. As to reactivity, the finding is that catatonic subjects show none whatsoever, whereas hallucinated paranoids are equivalent to normal subjects. Schizophrenics show a generalized vascular reaction but not local ones.

There are some claims that autonomic conditioning is poor or unattainable in schizophrenia as a function of an excessive inhibitory process in the cortex (Trekina, 1963; Vertogradova, 1963). Lynn (1963) concludes from Russian work that there are two types of schizophrenia: (a) the majority characterized by low sympathetic tone and reactivity, consisting primarily of catatonic and simple schizophrenic individuals; and (b) the minority group in which sympathetic tone and reactivity are unusually high, consisting of acute and agitated patients, especially "paranoiacs." These classifications are seen as similar to Gellhorn's high and low sympathetic reactivity breakdown (1957), Venables' high and low arousal states (1960), and Mednick's high and low anxiety formulations (1958). The Russian work with stimulants such as caffeine, which demonstrates that small quantities improve performance in schizophrenia and large quantities corrupt it, is consistent with Venables' arousal formulations in which schizophrenics are seen as operating within a narrower range of arousal than do normal subjects.

Defense

Oken (1962, pp. 193–210) has discussed the role of defense in psychological stress, as illustrated by an earlier study (Oken, Grinker, Heath, Sabshin, & Schwartz, 1960). Chronically ill patient subjects chosen for their remarkable resistance to change by the use of denial and avoidance of the environment, were prevented from using these defensive styles in the experimental situation. Physiological and psychological responses thereby evoked were characteristic of a stress response, although somewhat more limited. Oken concludes that psychological avoidance mechanisms can effectively limit physiological responses to what is assumed to be the patient's desired minimum of disruption.

Oversensitivity–Undersensitivity

In an attempt to reconcile the seemingly contra-dictory hypotheses that schizophrenics are chroni-cally anxious because of an excessively sensitive ANS, or that they are essentially unmotivated be-cause of low, insensitive, levels of ANS function, Ax (1962, pp. 29–44) suggests that a differential sensitivity may be operative. The distinction would be in an overresponsiveness to punishment and criticism and an underresponsiveness to reward and praise. The hypothesis developed is that there may be an early oversensitive stage of schizophrenia, and a later phase characterized by defensive with-drawal or exhaustion, resulting in lower sensitivity. The notion approaches that of "protective inhibi-tion," of which Russian investigators are so fond, but Ax himself relates the idea to the aggressive norepinephrine-like and passive epinephrine-like states discussed elsewhere in this chapter (Ax, 1953; Funkenstein, Greenblatt, & Solomon, 1951; Schachter, 1957).

PSYCHOANALYTIC FORMULATIONS

Surprisingly little psychophysiological research has been conducted as a direct outgrowth of psy-choanalytic theories of psychopathology. While psychoanalytic formulations have undoubtedly en-tered into the clinical thinking of many investi-gators, they seem for the most part to have been left outside the laboratory. One wonders, for in-stance, why there have not been studies of physio-logical levels or responses of patients who are fixated at extremely "oral" levels of development, or what physiological functions may accompany a "tyrannical superego." Psychoanalytic concepts have not yet lost their currency in the clinical sphere, and it seems that concepts of use in a hospital may well be of some value in a laboratory. Most of the studies that have been based on Freud-ian models have dealt with dimensions of person-ality function such as "defensiveness," and "con-flict," rather than with severe psychological disorder. The best single source of contemporary thought and research along these psychoanalytic lines is the volume edited by Greenfield and Lewis

(1965), which covers topics such as the autonomic monitoring of ego defenses, biological assumptions and analytic theory, and the mind-body problem.

Ego Differentiation

On the basis of experimental results, which in-dicate that relatively high frequency spontaneous autonomic nervous system activity is characteristic of psychiatric inpatient groups when compared to normal populations (A. A. Alexander, 1962), Green-field and A. A. Alexander (1965, pp. 201–214) have hypothesized that such periodicities may be a physiological concomitant to ego development. The premise rests on a form of an energy model derived from Freudian theory in which ego binding of instinctual energies facilitates the creation of structure which is essential for secondary process function. They point out that the reverse sequence occurs in the pathological process of regression in which structure dissolves, controls and defenses weaken, free energy is liberated, and primary proc-ess maladaptive behavior assumes ascendency with a resultant disturbance of homeostasis. The hy-pothesis states that low ego-strength subjects should demonstrate physiological periodicities paralleling primary process activity, i. e., less or-dered, less controlled, more mobile, and opera-tionally defined as higher in frequency. The posited relationship between lowered ego strength and physiological periodicity has been found in a variety of patient groups (A. A. Alexander, Greenfield, & Roessler, in press; A. A. Alexander, Roessler, & Greenfield, 1963a, 1963b) and studies of the predic-tive power of periodicity, as well as its genetic loading, are now underway.

BEHAVIORAL CORRELATES OF AUTONOMIC RESPONSE PATTERNS

J. I. Lacey (1967, pp. 160–208), like many others who are dissatisfied with the traditional view link-ing autonomic response primarily to such concepts as stress, emotion, and homeostasis, is the leading investigator in attempts to establish *differential* significance for different physiological functions. He begins his search on the basis of the frequently low correlation coefficients found among auto-nomic responses, and the finding of reliable individual differences in patterns of autonomic response to a given stressor and to different stressors (J. I. Lacey, 1956; J. I. Lacey & B. C. Lacey, 1958; Dykman, Reese, Galbrecht, & Thomasson, 1959; Engel, 1960; Schnore, 1959; Wenger, Clemens, Coleman, Cullen, & Engel, 1961). By attempting to establish principles to explain situational determination of response patterns (a form of stimulus stereotypy) J. I. Lacey hopes to provide a more specific understanding of the behavioral significance of autonomic activity than is provided by the traditional concept of "arousal." By emphasizing "directional fractionation," i.e., changes in patterns of response to stimulus changes that are not mere quantitative modifications, he is taking a position contrary also to the view based in Cannon's formulation of overall sympathetic activation by "stress." It is in discussing somatic responses during psychotherapy that he is most eloquent (J. I. Lacey, 1962, pp. 160–208).

Research studies that deal with physiological changes during psychotherapy are beyond the intentions of this chapter and have been very adequately summarized elsewhere by J. I. Lacey (1962, pp. 160–208), but the work of Mowrer and his colleagues should be mentioned as the earliest truly scientific investigation in this area (Mowrer, Light, Luria, & Seleny, 1953, pp. 546–640). One of his findings was that palmar sweating measures differentiated between a group of patients who "stayed" in psychotherapy and patients who left prematurely; another was a demonstration of congruence between palmar sweating and ratings of tension of the patients. J. I. Lacey's 1962 review should be consulted by the reader interested in this area because of its discussion of the problems of interpreting data in the psychotherapeutic context. He does not have the simple faith that autonomic and skeletal-motor responses have clear, uncomplicated meaning such as that a decrease in "physiological tension" is indicative of a decrease in "psychological tension." His position is rather that the somatic response may be related at one time to subtle motivations underlying the patient's behavior to the therapist, but at another time this relation may be overshadowed by the relation of the somatic response to the importance of the material being explored by the patient. His emphasis is on interpreting the autonomic responses in terms of the *total* behavior of the organism, something very rarely done in the reported literature. He has summed up his position by saying that while he is pessimistic about a substitutive use of somatic response as an index of change, he is not as pessimistic about "the utilization of somatic responses in the study of the *process* of psychotherapy."

CONCLUSION

To fashion a theory from the mass of data available in this one area of psychophysiology having to do with psychopathology has challenged some of the best minds in the field. None has yet succeeded in devising one that carries within it the means by which it could be disproved—the critical experiment by which it could be confirmed or denied. Anyone who submerges himself in the psychophysiological literature quickly notices that the same, relatively few, studies are cited by theorists of many different persuasions. While this may be a tribute to the soundness of these particular investigations, it does not speak well of the exclusiveness of the theoretical formulations. Before there can be critical experiments, there must be more precise formulations.

Lest it sound as though those who have attempted theories are being unduly taken to task, let me hasten to say that the difficulty seems to me to lie with the experimenter in this area, as much as with the inherent difficulties of trying to conceptually mate two enormously complicated disciplines. (Perhaps computer dating holds the greatest promise at this stage.) For while the thinking in regard to psychopathology has not been noted for its crispness, and although our accumulated knowledge of psychophysiological function is primarily that it is more complex than we had feared, the difficulty in attempting to relate them has not been helped by research which is either concept-free or utterly simplistic. One might expect such approaches early in the history of an idea, but the mind-body notion has been with us for centuries. The literature, with a few notable exceptions, is studded with groundless hypotheses or random hunches. Too many experienced clinicians have naïvely turned to physiological indices to demonstrate what they feel they know, learned nothing, and then published anyway. Too many physiological researchers have set forth on crusades into psychiatric domains, retreated to the safety of their laboratories, and then published anyway. This

chapter was written in the hope that the clinician or the psychophysiologist might find in it a formulation that suits him and that he can extend; or that he will find none satisfactory and develop one of his own.

REFERENCES

ACKER, C. W. An investigation of the variability in repeated psychophysiological measurements in tranquilized mental patients. *Psychophysiology,* 1964, **1,** (2), 119.

ACKNER, B. Emotions and the peripheral vasomotor system: A review of previous work. *Journal of Psychosomatic Research,* 1956, **1,** 3-20.

ACKNER, B., & PAMPIGLIONE, G. An evaluation of the sedation threshold test. *Journal of Psychosomatic Research,* 1959, **3,** 271-280.

ALEXANDER, A. A. Physiological periodicity: Analyses, psychological and psychopathological correlates. *Dissertation Abstracts,* 1962, **23,** (6), 2213.

ALEXANDER, A. A., GREENFIELD, N. S., & ROESSLER, R. Psychopathological correlates of physiological periodicity. *Psychophysiology* in press.

ALEXANDER, A. A., ROESSLER, R., & GREENFIELD, N. S. Ego strength and physiological responsivity: III. The relationship of the Barron Es scale to spontaneous periodic activity in skin resistance, finger blood volume, heart rate and muscle potential. *Archives of General Psychiatry,* 1963, **9,** 142-145. (a)

ALEXANDER, A. A., ROESSLER, R., & GREENFIELD, N. S. Periodic nature of spontaneous nervous system activity. *Nature,* 1963, **197,** 1168-1170. (b)

ALEXANDER, L. *Treatment of mental disorder.* Philadelphia: Saunders, 1953.

ALEXANDER, L. Epinephrine-mecholyl test (Funkenstein test). *Archives of Neurology and Psychiatry,* 1955, **73,** 496-514.

ALTSCHULE, M. D. *Bodily physiology in mental and emotional disorders.* New York: Grune & Stratton, 1953.

ANGYAL, A., & BLACKMAN, N. Vestibular reactivity in schizophrenia. *Archives of Neurology and Psychiatry,* 1940, **44,** 611-620.

ANGYAL, A., & BLACKMAN, N. Paradoxical vestibular reactions in schizophrenia under the influence of alcohol, of hyperpnea and CO_2 inhalation. *American Journal of Psychiatry,* 1941, **97,** 894-903.

ANGYAL, A., FREEMAN, H., & HOSKINS, R. G. Physiologic aspects of schizophrenic withdrawal. *Archives of Neurology and Psychiatry,* 1940, **44,** 621-626.

ANGYAL, A., & SHERMAN, M. A. Postural reactions to vestibular stimulation in schizophrenic and normal subjects. *American Journal of Psychiatry,* 1942, **98,** 857-862.

ARUTYNOV, Y. S. Change in autonomic functions and certain aspects of higher nervous system activity in patients with schizophrenia during active therapy. In I. F. SLUCHERSKU (Ed.), *Problems of psychiatry and neurology.* New York: Pergamon, 1962, **3,** 277-293.

ASHBY, W. R. The mode of action of electroconvulsive therapy. *Journal of Mental Science,* 1953, **99,** 202-215.

ASTRUP, C. *Schizophrenia: Conditioned reflex studies.* Springfield, Ill.: Charles C Thomas, 1962.

AX, A. F. The physiological differentiation between fear and anger in humans. *Psychosomatic Medicine,* 1953, **15,** 433-442.

AX, A. F. Psychophysiological methodology for the study of schizophrenia. In R. ROESSLER & N. S. GREENFIELD (Eds.), *Physiological correlates of psychological disorder.* Madison: University of Wisconsin Press, 1962.

AX, A. F., BECKETT, P. G. S., COHEN, B. D., FROHMAN, C. E., TOURNEY, G., & GOTTLIEB, J. S. Psychophysiological patterns in chronic schizophrenia. *Recent Advances in Biological Psychiatry,* 1962, **4,** 218-233.

BENDER, L., & SCHILDER, P. Unconditioned and conditioned reactions to pain in schizophrenia. *American Journal of Psychiatry,* 1930, **10,** 365-384.

BERNSTEIN, A. S. The galvanic skin response orienting reflex among chronic schizophrenics. *Psychonomic Science,* 1964, **1,** 391-392.

BERNSTEIN, A. S. The reliability of electrodermal arousal measures over extended periods in normals, and as a function of tranquilizing drugs and regression in chronic schizophrenia. *Journal of Nervous and Mental Disease,* 1965, **140,** 189-195.

BOCKHOVEN, J. S., GREENBLATT, M., & SOLOMON, H. C. Social behavior and autonomic physiology in long-standing mental illness. *Journal of Nervous and Mental Disease,* 1953, **117,** 55-58.

BOUDREAU, D. Evaluation of the sedation threshold test. *Archives of Neurology and Psychiatry,* 1958, **80,** 771-775.

BOWMAN, K. M., & SIMON, A. Studies in electronarcosis therapy. *American Journal of Psychiatry,* 1948, **105,** 15-27.

BRADLEY, P. B., & JEAVONS, P. M. The effect of chlorpromazine and reserpine on sedation and convulsive thresholds in schizophrenic patients. *Electroencephalography and Clinical Neurophysiology,* 1957, **9,** 661-672.

BRILL, N. Q., CRUMPTON, E., EIDUSON, S., GRAYSON, H. M.,

HELLMAN, L. I., RICHARDS, R. A., STRASSMAN, H. D., & UNGER, A. A. Investigation of the therapeutic components and various factors associated with improvement with electroconvulsive treatment: A preliminary report. *American Journal of Psychiatry*, 1957, **113**, 997–1008.

BROWN, C. C. *Methods in psychophysiology.* Baltimore: Williams & Wilkins, 1967.

BROŽEK, J. Psychorhythmics: A special review. *Psychophysiology*, 1964, **1**, 127–141.

BUCK, C. W., CARSCALLEN, H. B., & HOBBS, G. E. Temperature regulation in schizophrenia: I. Comparison of schizophrenic and normal subjects. II. Analysis by duration of psychosis. *Archives of Neurology and Psychiatry*, 1950, **64**, 828–842.

BUCK, C. W., CARSCALLEN, H. B., & HOBBS, G. E. Effect of prefrontal lobotomy on temperature regulation in schizophrenic patients. *Archives of Neurology and Psychiatry*, 1951, **65**, 197–205.

BURCH, G. E., COHN, A. E., & NEUMAN, C. A. Study by quantitative methods of spontaneous variations in volume of the finger-tip, toe-tip, and postero-superior portion of the pinna of resting normal white adults. *American Journal of Physiology*, 1942, **136**, 433–447.

BUSFIELD, B. L., & WECHSLER, H. Studies of salivation in depression: A comparison of salivation rates in depressed, schizoaffective depressed, nondepressed hospitalized patients, and in normal controls. *Archives of General Psychiatry*, 1961, **4**, 10–15.

BUSFIELD, B. L., WECHSLER, H., & BARNUM, W. J. Studies of salivation in depression: II. Physiological differentiation of reactive and endogenous depression. *Archives of General Psychiatry*, 1961, **5**, 472–477.

CALLAWAY, E. The influence of amobarbital (amylobarbitone) and methamphetamine on the focus of attention. *Journal of Mental Science*, 1959, **105**, 382–392.

CALLAWAY, E. Arousal and schizophrenia. *Transactions*, 1970, **2**, 11–15.

CALLAWAY, E., & DEMBO, D. Narrowed attention: A psychological phenomenon that accompanies a certain physiological change. *Archives of Neurology and Psychiatry*, 1958, **79**, 74–90.

CALLAWAY, E., & THOMPSON, S. V. Sympathetic activity and perception. *Psychosomatic Medicine*, 1953, **15**, 443–455.

CAMERON, D. E. *Objective and experimental psychiatry.* (2nd ed.) New York: Macmillan, 1941.

CANNON, W. B. *Bodily changes in pain, hunger, fear and rage.* New York: Appleton-Century-Crofts, 1920

CARRIGAN, P. M. Selective variability in schizophrenia. *American Psychologist*, 1963, **18**, 427. (abst.)

CHOVNICK, A. (Ed.) Biological clocks. *Cold Spring Harbor Symposia on Quantitative Biology*, 1961, **25.**

CLARIDGE, G. S. *Personality and arousal.* Oxford: Pergamon, 1967.

CLARIDGE, G. S., & HERRINGTON, R. N. Excitation-inhibition and the theory of neurosis: A study of the sedation threshold. In H. J. EYSENCK (Ed.), *Experiments with drugs.* Oxford: Pergamon, 1963.

COHEN, L. H., & PATTERSON, M. Effect of pain on the heart rate of normal and schizophrenic individuals. *Journal of General Psychology*, 1937, **17**, 273–289.

COHEN, M. E., & WHITE, P. D. Life situations, emotions, and neurocirculatory asthenia (anxiety, neurosis, neurasthenia, effort syndrome). *Psychosomatic Medicine*, 1951, **13**, 335–357.

COHEN, S. I., SILVERMAN, A. J., & BURCH, N. R. A. A technique for the assessment of affect change. *Journal of Nervous and Mental Disease*, 1956, **124**, 352–360.

COLBERT, E. G., KOEGLER, R. R., & MARKHAM, C. H. Vestibular dysfunction in childhood schizophrenia. *Archives of General Psychiatry*, 1959, **1**, 600–617.

CORIAT, I. H. Certain pulse reactions as a measure of emotions. *Journal of Abnormal Psychology*, 1910, **4**, 261–279.

DARROW, C. W. Physiological and clinical tests of autonomic function and autonomic balance. *Physiological Reviews*, 1943, **23**, 1–36.

DARROW, C. W., & SOLOMON, A. P. Mutism and resistance behavior in psychotic patients: A physiologic study. *American Journal of Psychiatry*, 1940, **96**, 1441–1454.

DAVIES, B. M., & GURLAND, J. B. Salivary secretion in depressive illness. *Journal of Psychosomatic Research*, 1961, **5**, 269–271.

DAVIS, J. F., MALMO, R. B., & SHAGASS, C. Electromyographic reaction to strong auditory stimulation in psychiatric patients. *Canadian Journal of Psychology*, 1954, **8**, 177–186.

DEBRUYN, J. W. A study of emotional expression in dementia praecox. *Journal of Abnormal Psychology*, 1909, **3**, 378–385.

DEVAULT, S. Physiological responsiveness in reactive and process schizophrenia. *Dissertation Abstracts*, 1957, **17**, 1387.

DOUST, J. W. L. Recent investigations in selected aspects of the physiological dimensions, and the implications for psychiatry. In R. J. OJEMANN (Ed.), *Recent contributions of biological and psychosocial investigations to preventive psychiatry.* Iowa City: State University of Iowa Press, 1959.

DOUST, J. W. L. Spontaneous endogenous oscillating systems in autonomic and metabolic effectors: Their relation to mental illness. *Journal of Nervous and Mental Disease*, 1960, **131**, 335–347.

DOUST, J. W. L. Consciousness in schizophrenia as a function of the peripheral microcirculation. In R. ROESSLER & N. S. GREENFIELD (Eds.), *Physiological correlates of psychological disorder.* Madison: University of Wisconsin Press, 1962.

DOUST, J. W. L. Aspects of development and the changing settings of a biological clock: Psychiatric implications. *Recent Advances in Biological Psychiatry*, 1963, **5**, 103–113.

DUFFY, E. Tensions and emotional factors in reaction. *Genetic Psychology Monographs,* 1930, **7,** 1–79.

DUFFY, E. The measurement of muscular tension as a technique for the study of emotional tendencies. *American Journal of Psychology,* 1932, **44,** 146–162.

DUFFY, E. Level of muscular tension as an aspect of personality. *Journal of General Psychology,* 1946, **35,** 161–171.

DUFFY, E. *Activation and behavior.* New York: Wiley, 1962.

DYKMAN, A., REESE, W. G., GALBRECHT, C. R., & THOMASSON, P. A. Psychophysiological reactions to novel stimuli: Measurement, adaptation, and relationship of psychological and physiological variables in the normal human. *Annals of the New York Academy of Sciences,* 1959, **79,** 43–107.

EARLE, A., & EARLE, B. V. The blood pressure response to pain and emotion in schizophrenia. *Journal of Nervous and Mental Disease,* 1955, **121,** 132–139.

EDWARDS, A. S., & HARRIS, A. C. Laboratory measurements of deterioration and improvement among schizophrenics. *Journal of General Psychology,* 1953, **49,** 153–156.

EKOLOVIA-BAGALEI, E. M. The effect of cocaine on catatonics, 1954. Cited by R. LYNN, Russian theory and research on schizophrenia. *Psychological Bulletin,* 1963, **60,** 486–498.

ENGEL, B. T. Stimulus-response and individual-response specificity. *Archives of General Psychiatry,* 1960, **2,** 305.

EPPINGER, H., & HESS, L. *Die Vagotonie.* Berlin: 1910.

EYSENCK, H. J. A dynamic theory of anxiety and hysteria. *Journal of Mental Science,* 1955, **101,** 28–51.

EYSENCK, H. J. *Crime and personality.* London: Routledge, 1964.

FELDMAN, S. M., & WALLER, H. J. Dissociation of electrocortical activation and behavioral arousal. *Nature,* 1962, **196,** 1320–1322.

FINESINGER, J. E. The effect of pleasant and unpleasant ideas on the respiratory pattern (spirogram) in psychoneurotic patients. *American Journal of Psychiatry,* 1944, **100,** 659–667.

FINKELMAN, I., & STEPHENS, W. M. Heat regulation in dementia praecox: Reactions of patients with dementia praecox to cold. *Journal of Neurological Psychopathology,* 1936, **16,** 321–340.

FORTUYN, J. Hypoglycemia and the autonomic nervous system. *Journal of Nervous and Mental Disease,* 1941, **93,** 1–15.

FOX, R., & LIPPERT, W. Spontaneous GSR and anxiety level in sociopathic delinquents. *Journal of Consulting Psychology,* 1963, **27,** 368.

FREEMAN, G. L. Towards a psychiatric Plimsoll mark: Physiological recovery quotients in experimentally induced frustration. *Journal of Psychology,* 1939, **8,** 247–252.

FREEMAN, G. L. *The energetics of human behavior.* Ithaca, N.Y.: Cornell University Press, 1948.

FREEMAN, G. L., & KATZOFF, E. T. Individual differences in physiological reactions to emotional stimulation and their relation to other measures of emotionality. *Journal of Experimental Psychology,* 1942, **31,** 527–537.

FREEMAN, G. L., & PATHMAN, J. H. Physiological reactions of psychotics to experimentally induced displacement. *American Journal of Psychiatry,* 1943, **100,** 406–412.

FREEMAN, H. The effect of "habituation" on blood pressure in schizophrenia. *Archives of Neurology and Psychiatry,* 1933, **29,** 139–147.

FREEMAN, H., & RODNICK, E. H. Autonomic and respiratory response of schizophrenic and normal subjects to changes of intra-pulmonary atmosphere. *Psychosomatic Medicine,* 1940, **2,** 101–109.

FREEMAN, H., & RODNICK, E. H. Effects of rotation on postural steadiness in normal and schizophrenic subjects. *Archives of Neurology and Psychiatry,* 1942, **48,** 47–53.

FREUD, S. Project for a scientific psychology. In M. BONAPARTE, A. FREUD, & E. KRIS (Eds.), *The origins of pscyhoanalysis: Letters to Wilhelm Fliess, drafts and notes, 1887–1902.* New York: Basic Books, 1954.

FULCHER, J. H., GALLAGHER, W. J., & PFEIFFER, C. C. Comparative lucid intervals after amobarbitol, CO_2, and arecoline in chronic schizophrenics. *Archives of Neurology and Psychiatry,* 1957, **78,** 392–395.

FUNKENSTEIN, D. H., GREENBLATT, M., ROOT, S., & SOLOMON, H. C. Psychophysiological study of mentally ill patients: II. Changes in reaction to epinephrine and mecholyl after electric shock treatment. *American Journal of Psychiatry,* 1949, **106,** 116–121.

FUNKENSTEIN, D. H., GREENBLATT, M., & SOLOMON, H. C. Autonomic nervous system changes following electric shock treatment. *Journal of Nervous and Mental Disease,* 1948, **108,** 409–422.

FUNKENSTEIN, D. H., GREENBLATT, M., & SOLOMON, H. C. Psychophysiological study of mentally ill patients: I. The states of the peripheral autonomic nervous system as determined by the reaction to epinephrine and mecholyl. *American Journal of Psychiatry,* 1949, **106,** 16–28.

FUNKENSTEIN, D. H., GREENBLATT, M., & SOLOMON, H. C. Test which predicts clinical effects of electric shock treatment in schizophrenia patients. *American Journal of Psychiatry,* 1950, **106,** 889–901.

FUNKENSTEIN, D. H., GREENBLATT, M., & SOLOMON, H. C. Autonomic changes paralleling psychological changes in mentally ill patients. *Journal of Nervous and Mental Disease,* 1951, **114,** 1–18.

FUNKENSTEIN, D. H., GREENBLATT, M., & SOLOMON, H. C. Non-epinephrine-like and epinephrine-like substances in psychotic and psychoneurotic patients. *American Journal of Psychiatry,* 1952, **108,** 652–662.

FUNKENSTEIN, D. H., GREENBLATT, M., & SOLOMON, H. C. Prognostic tests indicating the effectiveness of treatment. *Proceedings of the Association for Research in Nervous and Mental Disease,* 1953, **31,** 245–266.

FUNKENSTEIN, D. H., & MEAD, L. W. Nor-epinephrine-like

and epinephrine-like substances and elevation of blood pressure during acute stress. *Journal of Nervous and Mental Disease,* 1954, **119,** 380–397.

GAMBURG, A. L. The orientating and defensive reaction in simple and paranoid schizophrenia, 1958. Cited by R. LYNN, Russian theory and research on schizophrenia. *Psychological Bulletin,* 1963, **60,** 486–498.

GELLHORN, E. The action of hypoglycemia on the central nervous system and the problem of schizophrenia from the physiologic point of view. *Journal of the American Medical Association,* 1938, **110,** 1433–1434.

GELLHORN, E. *Autonomic regulations—their significance for psychology and neuropsychiatry.* New York: Interscience, 1943.

GELLHORN, E. *Physiological foundations of neurology and psychiatry.* Minneapolis: University of Minnesota Press, 1953.

GELLHORN, E. *Autonomic imbalance and the hypothalamus.* Minneapolis: University of Minnesota Press, 1957.

GELLHORN, E. Motion and emotion: The role of proprioception in the physiology and pathology of emotions. *Psychological Review,* 1964, **71,** 457–471.

GELLHORN, E., CORTELL, L., & FELDMAN, J. The effect of emotion, sham rage, and hypothalamic stimulation on the vago-insulin system. *American Journal of Physiology,* 1941, **133,** 532–541.

GELLHORN, E., & KESSLER, M. The effect of hypoglycemia on the electroencephalogram at varying degrees of oxygenation of the blood. *American Journal of Physiology,* 1942, **136,** 1–6.

GELLHORN, E., & LOOFBOURROW, G. N. *Emotions and emotional disorder.* New York: Hoeber, 1963.

GIDDON, D. B., & LISANTI, V. F. Cholinesterase-like substance in the parotid saliva of normal and psychiatric patients. *Lancet,* 1962, **1,** 725–726.

GILDEA, E. F., MAILHOUSE, V. L., & MORRIS, D. P. The relationship between various emotional disturbances and the sugar content of the blood. *American Journal of Psychiatry,* 1935, **92,** 115–130.

GLASER, G. H. The effects of frontal topectomy on autonomic nervous system stability in schizophrenia. *Journal of Nervous and Mental Disease,* 1952, **115,** 189–202.

GOLD, L. Autonomic balance in patients treated with insulin shock as measured by mecholyl chloride. *Archives of Neurology and Psychiatry,* 1943, **50,** 311–317.

GORDON, A. Mental and emotional phenomena of some psychoses in their relation to blood pressure: Diagnostic and prognostic significance of latter. *Journal of Nervous and Mental Disease,* 1930, **72,** 396–404.

GOTTLIEB, G., & PAULSON, G. Salivation in depressed patients. *Archives of General Psychiatry,* 1961, **5,** 468–471.

GRAHAM, D. T. Health, disease, and the mind-body problem: Linguistic parallelism. *Psychosomatic Medicine,* 1967, **29,** 52–71.

GREENFIELD, N. S., & ALEXANDER, A. A. The ego and bodily responses. In N. S. GREENFIELD & W. C. LEWIS (Eds.), *Psy-choanalysis and current biological thought.* Madison: University of Wisconsin Press, 1965.

GREENFIELD, N. S., & LEWIS, W. C. (Eds.) *Psychoanalysis and current biological thought.* Madison: University of Wisconsin Press, 1965.

GUNDERSON, E. Autonomic balance in schizophrenia. Unpublished doctoral dissertation, University of California, 1953.

HALL, K., & STRIDE, E. The varying responses to pain in psychiatric disorders: A study in abnormal psychology. *British Journal of Medical Psychology,* 1954, **27,** 48–60.

HARE, R. D. A content and learning theory analysis of psychopathic behavior. *Journal of Research in Crime and Delinquency,* 1965, **2,** 12–19. (a)

HARE, R. D. Acquisition and generalization of a conditioned fear response in psychopathic and non-psychopathic criminals. *Journal of Psychology,* 1965, **59,** 367–370. (b)

HARE, R. D. Temporal gradient of fear arousal in psychopaths. *Journal of Abnormal Psychology,* 1965, **70,** 442–445. (c)

HEBB, D. O. Drives and C.N.S. (conceptual nervous system). *Psychological Review,* 1955, **62,** 243–254.

HENSCHEL, A., BROŽEK, J., & KEYS, A. Indirect vasodilation in normal man and in schizophrenic patients. *Journal of Applied Physiology,* 1951, **4,** 340–344.

HILL, H. *The histamine and insulin treatment of schizophrenia.* London: Baillière, 1940.

HIMWICH, H. E., & FAZEKAS, J. F. Factor of hypoxia in the shock therapies of schizophrenia. *Archives of Neurology and Psychiatry,* 1942, **47,** 800–807.

HIRSCHSTEIN, R. The significance of characteristic autonomic nervous system responses in the adjustment, change and outcome of schizophrenia. *Journal of Nervous and Mental Disease,* 1955, **122,** 254–262.

HOCH, P. H., KUBIS, J. F., & ROUKE, F. L. Psychogalvanometric investigations in psychosis and other abnormal states. *Psychosomatic Medicine,* 1944, **6,** 237–243.

HOCH, P. H., & PENNES, H. H. Electroconvulsive treatment and its modifications. In L. BELLACK (Ed.), *Schizophrenia: A review of the syndrome.* New York: Logos Press, 1958.

HOFFER, A., & OSMOND, H. R. Schizophrenia—an autonomic disease. *Journal of Nervous and Mental Disease,* 1955, **122,** 448–452.

HOSKINS, R. G. *The biology of schizophrenia.* New York: Norton, 1946.

HOWE, E. S. GSR conditioning in anxiety states, normals, and chronic functional schizophrenic subjects. *Journal of Abnormal and Social Psychology,* 1958, **56,** 183–189.

HUNT, J. MC.V. & COFER, C. Psychological deficit in schizophrenia. In J. MC.V. HUNT (Ed.), *Personality and the behavior disorders.* New York: Ronald, 1944.

INGERSHEIMER, W. W. Cold pressor test in functional psychiatric syndromes. *Archives of Neurology and Psychiatry,* 1953, **70,** 794–810.

JONES, C. H.   The Funkenstein test in selecting methods of psychiatric treatment. *Diseases of the Nervous System,* 1956, **17,** 37–43.

JOST, H.   Some physiological changes during frustration. *Child Development,* 1941, **12,** 9–15.

JURKO, M., JOST, H., & HILL, T. S.   Pathology of the energy system: An experimental clinical study of physiological adaptiveness capacities in a nonpatient, a psychoneurotic, and an early paranoid schizophrenic group. *Journal of Psychology,* 1952, **33,** 183–189.

KALINOWSKY, L. B., & HOCH, P. H.   *Shock treatments, psychosurgery, and other somatic treatments in psychiatry.* (2nd ed.) New York: Grune & Stratton, 1952.

KING, G. F.   Differential autonomic responsiveness in the process-reactive classification of schizophrenia. *Journal of Abnormal and Social Psychology,* 1958, **56,** 160–164.

KORNETSKY, C., & MIRSKY, A. F.   On certain psychopharmacological and physiological differences between schizophrenic and normal persons. *Psychopharmacologia,* 1966, **8,** 309–318.

KRISHNAMOORTI, S. R., & SHAGASS, C.   Some psychological test correlates of sedation threshold. *Recent Advances in Biological Psychiatry,* 1964, **6,** 256–266.

LACEY, J. I.   The evaluation of autonomic responses: Toward a general solution. *Annals of the New York Academy of Sciences,* 1956, **67,** 123–164.

LACEY, J. I.   Psychophysiological approaches to the evaluation of psychotherapeutic process and outcome. In E. A. RUBINSTEIN & M. B. PARLOFF (Eds.), *Research in psychotherapy.* Washington, D.C.: American Psychological Association, 1962.

LACEY, J. I.   Somatic response patterning and stress: Some revisions of activation theory. In M. H. APPLEY & R. TRUMBULL (Eds.), *Psychological stress.* New York: Appleton-Century-Crofts, 1967.

LACEY, J. I., BATEMAN, D. E., & VANLEHN, R.   Autonomic response specificity: An experimental study. *Psychosomatic Medicine,* 1953, **15,** 8–21.

LACEY, J. I., KAGAN, J., LACEY, B. C., & MOSS, H.   The visceral level: Situational determinants and behavioral correlates of autonomic response patterns. In P. H. KNAPP (Ed.), *Expressions of the emotions in man.* New York: International Universities, 1963.

LACEY, J. I., & LACEY, B. C.   The relationship of resting autonomic activity to motor impulsivity. *Research Publications of the Association for Nervous and Mental Disease,* 1958, **36,** 144–209. (a)

LACEY, J. I., & LACEY, B. C.   Verification and extension of the principle of autonomic response stereotypy. *American Journal of Psychology,* 1958, **71,** 50–73. (b)

LACEY, J. I., & VANLEHN, R.   Differential emphasis in somatic response to stress: An experimental study. *Psychosomatic Medicine,* 1952, **14,** 71–81.

LANDIS, C.   Electrical phenomena of the skin. *Psychological Bulletin,* 1932, **29,** 693–752.

LANG, P. J., & BUSS, A. H.   Psychological deficit in schizophrenia: II. Interference and activation. In D. S. HOLMES (Ed.), *Reviews of research in behavior pathology.* New York: Wiley, 1968.

LEACH, W. W.   Nystagmus: An integrative neural deficit in schizophrenia. *Journal of Abnormal and Social Psychology,* 1960, **60,** 225–233.

LIPPERT, W. W., & SENTER, R. J.   Electrodermal responses in the sociopath. *Psychonomic Science,* 1966, **4,** 25–26.

LUNDERVOLD, A.   An electromyographic investigation of tense and relaxed subjects. *Journal of Nervous and Mental Disease,* 1952, **115,** 512–525.

LURIA, A. R.   *The nature of human conflicts; or emotion, conflict and will, an objective study of disorganization and control of human behavior.* (Translated from Russian by W. H. Gantt.) New York: Liveright, 1932.

LYKKEN, D. T.   A study of anxiety in the sociopathic personality. *Journal of Abnormal and Social Psychology,* 1957, **55,** 6–10.

LYNN, R.   Russian theory and research on schizophrenia. *Psychological Bulletin,* 1963, **60,** 486–498.

MALMO, R. B.   Experimental studies of mental patients under stress. In M. L. REYMERT (Ed.), *Feelings and emotions.* New York: McGraw-Hill, 1950.

MALMO, R. B.   Anxiety and behavioral arousal. *Psychological Review,* 1957, **64,** 276–287.

MALMO, R. B.   Measurement of drive: An unsolved problem in psychology. In M. R. JONES (Ed.), *Nebraska symposium on motivation.* Lincoln: University of Nebraska Press, 1958.

MALMO, R. B.   Activation: A neurophysiological dimension. *Psychological Review,* 1959, **66,** 367–386.

MALMO, R. B.   On central and autonomic nervous system mechanisms in conditioning, learning, and performance. *Canadian Journal of Psychology,* 1963, **17,** 1–36.

MALMO, R. B. & SHAGASS, C.   Physiological studies of reaction to stress in anxiety states and early schizophrenia. *Psychosomatic Medicine,* 1949, **11,** 9–24.

MALMO, R. B. & SHAGASS, C.   Studies of blood pressure in psychiatric patients under stress. *Psychosomatic Medicine,* 1952, **14,** 82–93.

MALMO, R. B., SHAGASS, C., BELANGER, D. J., & SMITH, A. A.   Motor control in psychiatric patients under experimental stress. *Journal of Abnormal and Social Psychology,* 1951, **46,** 539–547.

MALMO, R. B., SHAGASS, C., & DAVIS, J. F.   A method for the investigation of somatic response mechanisms in psychoneurosis. *Science,* 1950, **112,** 325–328.

MALMO, R. B., SHAGASS, C., & DAVIS, J. F.   Electromyographic studies of muscular tension in psychiatric patients under stress. *Journal of Clinical and Experimental Psychopathology,* 1951, **12,** 45–66.

MALMO, R. B., SHAGASS, C., & HESLAM, R. M.   Blood pressure response to repeated brief stress in psychoneurosis: A study of adaptation. *Canadian Journal of Psychology,* 1951, **5,** 167–179.

MALMO, R. B., SHAGASS, C., & SMITH, A. A. Responsiveness in chronic schizophrenia. *Journal of Personality*, 1951, **19**, 359–375.

MALMO, R. B., & SMITH, A. A. Forehead tension and motor irregularities in psychoneurotic patients under stress. *Journal of Personality*, 1955, **23**, 391–406.

MARTIN, I. Somatic reactivity. In H. J. EYSENCK (Ed.), *Handbook of abnormal psychology*. New York: Basic Books, 1961.

MARTIN, I., & DAVIES, B. M. Sleep thresholds in depression. *Journal of Mental Science*, 1962, **108**, 466–473.

MAY, P. R. Pupillary abnormalities in schizophrenia and during muscular effort. *Journal of Mental Science*, 1948, **94**, 89–98.

MEADOW, A., & FUNKENSTEIN, D. H. The relationship of abstract thinking to the autonomic nervous system in schizophrenia. In P. H. HOCK & J. ZUBIN (Eds.), *Relation of psychological tests to psychiatry*. New York: Grune & Stratton, 1952.

MEADOW, A., GREENBLATT, M., FUNKENSTEIN, D. H., & SOLOMON, H. C. Relationship between capacity for abstraction in schizophrenia and physiological response to autonomic drugs. *Journal of Nervous and Mental Disease*, 1953, **118**, 332–338.

MEDNICK, S. A learning theory approach to research in schizophrenia. *Psychological Bulletin*, 1958, **55**, 316–327.

MEDNICK, S. A breakdown in individuals at high risk for schizophrenia: Possible predispositional perinatal factors. *Mental Hygiene*, 1970, **54**, 50–63.

MENNINGER-LERCHENTHAL, E. *Periodizitat in der Psychopathology*. Vienna: Maudrich, 1960.

MILES, H. H. W., & COBB, S. Neurocirculatory asthenia, anxiety and neurosis. *New England Journal of Medicine*, 1951, **245**, 711.

MIRSKY, A. F. Neuropsychological bases of schizophrenia. *Annual Review of Psychology*, 1969, **20**, 321–348.

MOROZOV, G. V. The pathogenesis of catatonic stupor, 1961. Cited by J. STERN & D. McDONALD, Physiological correlates of mental disease. *Annual Review of Psychology*, 1965, **16**, 238.

MOWRER, O. H., LIGHT, D. H., LURIA, Z., & SELENY, M. P. Tension changes during psychotherapy. In O. H. MOWRER (Ed.), *Psychotherapy: Theory and research*. New York: Ronald, 1953.

NYMGAARD, K. Studies on the sedation threshold: A. Reproducibility and effect of drugs. B. Sedation threshold in neurotic and psychotic depression. *Archives of General Psychiatry*, 1959, **1**, 530–536.

OBRIST, D. A. Cardiovascular differentiation of sensory stimuli. *Psychosomatic Medicine*, 1963, **25**, 450–459.

ÖDEGAARD, O. The psychogalvanic reactivity in affective disorders. *British Journal of Medical Psychology*, 1932, **12**, 132–150.

OKEN, D. The role of defense in psychological stress. In R. ROESSLER & N. S. GREENFIELD (Eds.), *Physiological correlates of psychological disorder*. Madison: University of Wisconsin Press, 1962.

OKEN, D., GRINKER, R. R., HEATH, H. A., SABSHIN, M., & SCHWARTZ, N. Stress response in a group of chronic psychiatric patients. *Archives of General Psychiatry*, 1960, **3**, 451.

PAINTAL, A. S. A comparison of the galvanic skin responses of normals and psychotics. *Journal of Experimental Psychology*, 1951, **41**, 425–438.

PARKER, C. S. Observations on autonomic functionings during hypoglycemic treatment of schizophrenics. *Journal of Mental Science*, 1940, **86**, 645–659.

PECK, R. E. The S.H.P. test: An aid in the detection and measurement of depression. *Archives of General Psychiatry*, 1959, **1**, 35–40.

PERRIS, C., & BRATTEMO, C. The sedation threshold as a method of evaluating anti-depressive treatments. *Acta Physiologica Scandinavica*, (Suppl. 169), 1963, **39**, 111–119.

PETURSSON, E. Electromyographic studies of muscular tension in psychiatric patients. *Comprehensive Psychiatry*, 1962, **3**, 29–36.

PFISTER, H. O. Disturbances of autonomic function in schizophrenia and their relations to insulin, cardiazol and sleep treatments. *American Journal of Psychiatry*, 1938, **94**, 109–118.

PISHKIN, V., & HERSHISER, D. Respiration and GSR as functions of white sound in schizophrenia. *Journal of Consulting Psychology*, 1963, **27**, 330–337.

POLLIN, W. M. Control and artifact in psychophysiological research. In R. ROESSLER & N. S. GREENFIELD (Eds.), *Physiological correlates of psychological disorder*. Madison: University of Wisconsin Press, 1962.

POLLOCK, L. J., & DOLLEAR, A. H. Pneumographic studies of emotional reactions in dementia praecox. *Inst. Quarterly, Springfield, Pa.*, 1916, **7**, 73–78. Reported by J. M. HUNT & C. N. COFER, Psychological deficit. In J. M. HUNT (Ed.), *Personality and the behavior disorders. Vol. 2.* New York: Ronald, 1944.

PRIBRAM, K. H. The neuropsychology of Sigmund Freud. In A. J. BACHRACH (Ed.), *Experimental foundations of clinical psychology*. New York: Basic Books, 1962.

PRIBRAM, K. H. A neuropsychological model: Some observations on the structure of psychological processes. In P. H. KNAPP (Ed.), *Expression of the emotions in man*. New York: International Universities, 1963.

PRIBRAM, K. H. Freud's project: An open, biologically based model for psychoanalysis. In N. S. GREENFIELD & W. C. LEWIS (Eds.), *Psychoanalysis and current biological thought*. Madison: University of Wisconsin Press, 1965.

RAY, T. S. Electrodermal indications of levels of psychological disturbance in chronic schizophrenia. *American Psychologist*, 1963, 18, 393. (Abstract)

REES, L. Physiological concomitants of electronarcosis. *Journal of Mental Science*, 1949, **95**, 162–170.

REYNOLDS, D. J. An investigation of the somatic response

system in chronic schizophrenia. *Dissertation Abstracts,* 1963, **23,** 4746.

RICHTER, C. P.   The electrical skin resistance: Diurnal and daily variations in psychopathic and normal persons. *Archives of Neurology and Psychiatry,* 1928, **19,** 488-508.

RICHTER, C. P.   Biological clocks in medicine and psychiatry: Shock-phase hypothesis. *Proceedings of the National Academy of Sciences, United States,* 1960, **46,** 1506.

RICHTER, D.   Biochemical aspects of schizophrenia. In D. RICHTER (Ed.), *Schizophrenia: Somatic aspects.* London: Pergamon, 1957.

ROESSLER, R., ALEXANDER, A. A., & GREENFIELD, N. S.   Ego strength and physiological responsivity: I. The relationship of the Barron Es scale to skin resistance, finger blood volume, heart rate, and muscle potential responses to sound. *Archives of General Psychiatry,* 1963, **8,** (2), 142-154.

ROKHLIN, L. L.   Investigations of the vascular changes in schizophrenic patients, 1962, Cited by J. STERN & D. MCDONALD. *Annual Review of Psychology,* 1965, **16,** 238.

ROTH, M. R. A.   A theory of ECT action and its bearing on the biological significance of epilepsy. *Journal of Mental Science,* 1952, **98,** 44-59.

RUBIN, L. S.   Pupillary reactivity as a measure of adrenergic-cholinergic mechanisms in the study of psychotic behavior. *Journal of Nervous and Mental Disease,* 1960, **130,** 386-400.

RUBIN, L. S.   Autonomic dysfunction in psychoses: Adults and autistic children. *Archives of General Psychiatry,* 1962, **7,** 1-14.

RUESCH, J., & FINESINGER, J. E.   Muscular tension in psychiatric patients. *Archives of Neurology and Psychiatry,* 1943, **50,** 439-449.

RUILMANN, C. J., & GULO, M. J.   Investigations of autonomic responses in psychopathic personalities. *Southern Medical Journal,* 1950, **43,** 953-956.

SAINSBURY, P.   Gestural movement during psychiatric interview. *Psychosomatic Medicine,* 1955, **17,** 458-469.

SARGANT, W. W., & SLATER, E. T. O.   *Introduction to physical methods of treatment in psychiatry.* (2nd ed.) Baltimore: Williams & Wilkins, 1948.

SAVITSKI, V. V.   The bioelectrical activity of muscles and body temperature in psychiatric conditions with a catatonic syndrome, 1962. Cited by J. STERN & D. MCDONALD, Physiological correlates of mental disease. *Annual Review of Psychology,* 1965, **16,** 238.

SCHACTER, J.   Pain, fear and anger in hypertensives and normotensives. *Psychosomatic Medicine,* 1957, **19,** 17-29.

SCHEFLEN, A. E., REINER, E. R., & COWITZ, B.   Therapeutic response in insulin coma therapy: A study of vital signs and sensitivity. *Journal of Clinical and Experimental Psychopathology,* 1953, **14,** 57-67.

SCHNORE, M. M.   Individual patterns of physiological activity as a function of the task differences and degree of arousal. *Journal of Experimental Psychology,* 1959, **58,** 117-128.

SEAGER, C. P.   Problems of technique concerning the sedation threshold. *Electroencephalography and Clinical Neurophysiology,* 1960, **12,** 910-913.

SHAGASS, C.   The sedation threshold: A method for estimating tension in psychiatric patients. *Electroencephalography and Clinical Neurophysiology,* 1954, **6,** 221-233.

SHAGASS, C.   A neurophysiological study of schizophrenia. *Congress Report of the Second International Congress for Psychiatry,* 1957, **2,** 248-254.

SHAGASS, C., & MALMO, R. B.   Psychodynamic themes and localized muscular tension during psychotherapy. *Psychosomatic Medicine,* 1954, **16,** 295-313.

SHAKOW, D., & HUSTON, P. E.   Studies of motor function in schizophrenia. *Journal of General Psychology,* 1936, **15,** 63.

SHAKOW, D., RODNICK, E. H., & LEBEAUX, T.   A psychological study of a schizophrenic: Exemplification of a method. *Journal of Abnormal and Social Psychology,* 1945, **40,** 154.

SHATTOCK, F. M.   The somatic manifestations of schizophrenia: A clinical study of their significance. *Journal of Mental Science,* 1950, **96,** 32-142.

SHERMAN, M., & JOST, H.   Quantification of psychophysiological measures. *Psychosomatic Medicine,* 1945, **7,** 215-219.

SILVERMAN, A. J., COHEN, S. I., & SHMAVONIAN, B. M.   Investigations of psychophysiologic relationship with skin resistance measures. *Journal of Psychosomatic Research,* 1959, **4,** 65-87.

SILVERMAN, J. J., & POWELL, V. E.   Studies of palmar sweating: III. Palmar sweating in an Army general hospital. *Psychosomatic Medicine,* 1944, **6,** 243-249.

SMITH, A. A., MALMO, R. B., & SHAGASS, C.   An electromyographic study of listening and talking. *Canadian Journal of Psychology,* 1954, **8,** 219-227.

SOLLBERGER, A.   *Biological rhythm research.* Amsterdam: Elsevier, 1965.

STANISHEVSKAYA, N. N.   A plethysmographic investigation of catatonic schizophrenics. 1955. Cited by R. LYNN, Russian theory and research on schizophrenia. *Psychological Bulletin,* 1963, **60,** 486-498.

STENGEL, E., OLDHAM, A. J., & EHRENBERG, A. S. C.   Reactions to pain in various abnormal mental states. *Journal of Mental Science,* 1955, **101,** 52-69.

STERN, J. A., & FEHR, F. S.   Peripheral physiological variables and emotion: The James-Lange theory revisited. *Psychological Bulletin,* 1970, **74,** 411-424.

STERN, J. A., & MCDONALD, D. G.   Physiological correlates of mental disease. *Annual Review of Psychology,* 1965, **16,** 225-264.

STERN, J. A., SURPHLIS, W., & KOFF, E.   Electrodermal responsiveness as related to psychiatric diagnosis and prognosis. *Psychophysiology,* 1965, **2,** 51-61.

STEVENS, J. M., & DERBYSHIRE, A. J.   Shifts along the alert response continuum during remission of catatonic stupor with amobarbitol. *Psychosomatic Medicine,* 1958, **20,** 99-107.

STEWART, K. D., & DEAN, W. H.   Perceptual-cognitive behavior and autonomic nervous system patterns. *Archives of General Psychiatry,* 1965, **12,** 329–335.

STRAUSS, H. Das Zusammenschrecken. *Journal of Psychology and Neurology,* 1929, **39,** 111–231. Reported by J. M. HUNT & C. N. COFER, in J. M. HUNT (Ed.), *Personality and the behavior disorders.* Vol. II. New York: Ronald, 1944.

STRELTSOVA, N. L. The characteristics of some unconditioned reflexes in schizophrenics, 1955. Cited by R. LYNN, Russian theory and research on shizophrenia. *Psychological Bulletin,* 1963, **60,** 486–498.

SYZ, H. C. Psychogalvanic studies in schizophrenia. *Archives of Neurology and Psychiatry,* 1926, **16,** 747–760.

SYZ, H. C., & KINDER, E. F. Electrical skin resistance in normal and in psychotic subjects. *Archives of Neurology and Psychiatry,* 1928, **19,** 1026–1035.

TIRKELTAUB, Y. A. Data on the investigations of the higher nervous activity, the cardio-vascular system and its re-activity in the acute stage of paranoid schizophrenia, 1962. Cited by J. STERN & D. MCDONALD, Physiological correlates of mental disease. *Annual Review of Psychology,* 1965, **16,** 238.

TITAEVA, M. A. EEG investigations of the reactivity of the central nervous system in patients with a catatonic form of schizophrenia, 1962. Cited by J. STERN & D. MCDONALD, Physiological correlates of mental disease. *Annual Review of Psychology,* 1965, **16,** 237.

TONG, J. E. Stress reactivity in relation to delinquent and psychopathic behavior. *Journal of Mental Science,* 1959, **105,** 935–956.

TONG, J. E., & MURPHY, I. C. A review of stress reactivity research in relation to psychopathology and psychopathic behavior disorders. *Journal of Mental Science,* 1960, **106,** 1273–1295.

TRAUGOTT, N. N., BALONOV, L. Y., KAUFMAN, D. A., & LUCHKO, A. E. O. On the dynamics of the destruction of orienting reflexes in certain psychotic syndromes, 1958. Cited by R. LYNN, Russian theory and research on schizophrenia. *Psychological Bulletin,* 1963, **60,** 486–498.

TREKINA, T. A. The clinical manifestations and course of schizophrenia with the maniacal syndrome, 1955. Cited by R. LYNN, Russian theory and research on schizophrenia. *Psychological Bulletin,* 1963, **60,** 486–498.

VAN der MERWE, A. B. The diagnostic value of peripheral vasomotor reaction in the psychoneuroses. *Psychosomatic Medicine,* 1948, **10,** 347–354.

VENABLES, P. H. The effect of auditory and visual stimulation on the skin potential response of schizophrenics. *Brain,* 1960, **83,** 77–92.

VENABLES, P. H. Input dysfunction in schizophrenia. In B. A. MAHER (Ed.), *Progress in experimental personality research.* New York: Academic, 1964.

VENABLES, P. H., & MARTIN, I. (Eds.) *Manual of psychophysiological methods.* New York: Wiley, 1967.

VENABLES, P. H., & WING, J. K. Level of arousal and the subclassification of schizophrenia. *Archives of General Psychiatry,* 1962, **7,** 114–119.

VERTOGRADOVA, O. D. Conditioned and unconditioned vaso-reflexes in schizophrenia, 1955. Cited by R. LYNN, Russian theory and research on schizophrenia. *Psychological Bulletin,* 1963, **60,** 486–498.

WECKOWICZ, T. E., & HALL, R. Skin histamine reaction in schizophrenic and non-schizophrenic mental patients. *Journal of Nervous and Mental Disease,* 1958, **126,** 415–420.

WEIL-MALHERBE, H. The concentration of adrenaline in human plasma and its relation to mental activity. *Journal of Mental Science,* 1955, **101,** 733–755.

WENGER, M. A. The measurement of individual differences in autonomic balance. *Psychosomatic Medicine,* 1941, **3,** 427–434.

WENGER, M. A. Studies of autonomic balance in Army Air Forces personnel, *Comparative Psychology Monographs,* 1948, **19,** No. 4.

WENGER, M. A. Pattern analysis of autonomic variables during rest. *Psychosomatic Medicine,* 1957, **19,** 240–244.

WENGER, M. A. *Evaluation of project 6, summary of proceedings: Second co-operative psychological research conference.* Veterans Administration Hospital, Cincinnati, Ohio, 1959.

WENGER, M. A. Studies of autonomic balance: A summary. *Psychophysiology,* 1966, **2,** 173–186.

WENGER, M. A., CLEMENS, T. L., COLEMAN, D. R., CULLEN, T. D., & ENGEL, B. T. Autonomic response specificity. *Psychosomatic Medicine,* 1961, **23,** 185–193.

WENGER, M. A., JONES, N. F., & JONES, M. H. *Physiological psychology.* New York: Holt, Rinehart and Winston, 1956.

WESTBURGH, E. M. Psychogalvanic studies on affective variations in the mentally diseased. *Archives of Neurology and Psychiatry,* 1929, **22,** 719–736.

WHATMORE, G. B., & ELLIS, R. M. Some motor aspects of schizophrenia: An EMG study. *American Journal of Psychiatry,* 1958, **114,** 882–889.

WHATMORE, G. B., & ELLIS, R. M. Some neurophysiological aspects of depressed states: An electromyographic study. *Archives of General Psychiatry,* 1959, **1,** 70–80.

WHATMORE, G. B., & ELLIS, R. M. Further neurophysiologic aspects of depressed states: An electromyographic study. *Archives of General Psychiatry,* 1962, **6,** 243–253.

WHITEHORN, J. C. The blood sugar in relation to emotional reactions. *American Journal of Psychiatry,* 1934, **13,** 987–1005.

WHITEHORN, J. C., & RICHTER, H. Unsteadiness of the heart rate in psychotic and neurotic states. *Archives of Neurology and Psychiatry, Chicago,* 1937, **38,** 62–70.

WILDER, J. The law of initial values. *Psychosomatic Medicine,* 1950, **12,** 392–401.

WILDER, J. The law of initial value in neurology and psychiatry. *Journal of Nervous and Mental Disease,* 1957, **125,** 73–86.

WILLIAMS, M.   Psychophysiological responsiveness to psychological stress in early chronic schizophrenic reactions. *Psychosomatic Medicine,* 1953, **15,** 456–462.

WISHNER, J.   Neurosis and tension: An exploratory study of the relationship of physiological and Rorschach measures. *Journal of Abnormal and Social Psychology,* 1953, **48,** 253–260.

WISHNER, J.   The concept of efficiency in psychological health and in psychopathology. *Psychology Review,* 1955, **62,** 69–80.

WISHNER, J.   Efficiency: Concept and measurement. In *Proceedings of the Fourteenth International Congress of* *Applied Psychology. Vol. 2. Personality research.* Copenhagen: Munksgaard, 1962.

ZAHN, T. P., ROSENTHAL, D., & LAWLOR, W. G.   GSR orienting reactions to visual and auditory stimuli in chronic schizophrenia and normal subjects. *Psychophysiology Newsletter,* 1963, **9,** 43–50.

ZUCKERMAN, M., & GROSZ, H. J.   Contradictory results using the mecholyl test to differentiate process and reactive schizophrenia. *Journal of Abnormal and Social Psychology,* 1959, **59,** 145–146.

PART

6 OVERVIEW AND INDEXES

Robert B. Malmo

OVERVIEW

Psychophysiology is a relatively recent arrival among the life sciences. The Society for Psychophysiological Research is only ten years old; the Society's Journal, *Psychophysiology,* and the first textbook in the field, Sternbach's *Principles of Psychophysiology,* are half as old. Publication of the first *Handbook of Psychophysiology* now is timely and significant.

EMOTIONS AND BODILY CHANGES

The title of Flanders Dunbar's classic book (1954) denotes a major area in psychophysiology, besides being its likely point of origin historically. As the chapter by Lang, Rice, and Sternbach shows, clinical problems of emotions and related physiological reactions provide challenging and exciting work for the psychophysiologist.

"Emotion" merely denotes an area of behavioral observation, of course. It is essential, therefore, to state precisely what the variables are for each investigation within this area. One may describe a change in skeletal-muscle tension as measured electromyographically, for instance. Now, it is well established that the EMG reaction to a loud sound is abnormally prolonged in psychiatric patients suffering from chronic anxiety. It may seem tempting to consider this prolonged EMG reaction as a clinical sign of "anxiety." Since the EMG reaction can be quantified, it may also be tempting to go one step further, and speak of a measure of "anxiety." But as the authors of this book repeatedly show, to yield to a temptation of this kind is to oversimplify a problem like that of anxiety.

The problem of pathological anxiety will be discussed later. It is introduced at the outset in order to point out one of the serious obstacles to sound progress in psychophysiology. Oversimplification of problems was a prevalent liability in the early days of this discipline; and unfortunately, it still persists to some extent today, for instance in relation to the concept of "stress."

STRESS

Writers frequently object to the concept of "stress" (see, e.g., Wenzel, 1970) but they rarely say exactly what is wrong with it. Mason's discussion clearly points to the trouble: overdependence on the concept of "stress" makes one neglect the "stimulus side" of the problem.

Mason criticizes endocrinological research on "stress" for failing to deal adequately with the following kind of question: What exactly are the stimulus conditions that cause the anterior pituitary gland to secrete the adrenocorticotrophic hormone (ACTH), which in turn stimulates the adrenal cortex to produce corticoids? Mason continues, "Whatever the 'stressful conditions,' the environmental change, or the experimental manipulation may be, a *signal* must reach the hypothalamus or pituitary through neural or circulatory pathways in order for ACTH release to occur [p. 71]."

It will be easier to understand Mason's criticism of research involving the *anterior* pituitary if we look at research on the *posterior* pituitary. Sensory aspects of posterior pituitary function are under active investigation. This contrasts sharply with the lack of attention paid to sensory aspects of *anterior* pituitary function, prior to Mason's work.

One main function served by the posterior pituitary is conservation of water in the body, under conditions of dehydration. In dehydration, sodium concentration in the fluids surrounding the cells is increased. The resulting increased osmotic pressure causes water to be drawn from the cells into the extracellular fluids. There are receptor cells

(*osmoreceptors*) in the supraoptic and paraventricular nuclei of the anterior hypothalamus that are specialized to signal (by firing at a faster rate) when they are losing water. In other words, they are "dehydration receptors."

Osmoreceptor neurons in the hypothalamus discharge into the posterior pituitary, causing this gland to release antidiuretic hormone. When the antidiuretic hormone reaches the kidneys, it promotes reabsorption of water by the kidney tubules, thus conserving water for the body.

Considered in the context of this chain of events involving the *posterior* pituitary, the perspicacity of Mason's criticism of research on *anterior* pituitary functions is obvious. Research on afferent neural mechanisms involving the anterior pituitary is clearly needed. In Mason's words: "One of the unfortunate consequences of the 'stress' concept appears to be that it has served to allay critical thinking about the question of the actual *primary signals* capable of triggering ACTH release by exciting the final common pathway neurone or the pituitary cell. Somehow the categorical concept of 'stressful' conditions seems to have circumvented work concerning systematic consideration of discrete stimuli, body receptors, and the underlying mediating mechanisms [p. 71]."

Endocrine and autonomic nervous system functions in avoidance behavior (including considerably more than hypothalamic-pituitary mechanisms) are, of course, far more extensive than those mediating the antidiuretic reflex. Furthermore, the relevant environmental stimuli are more numerous and more complex in behavioral situations than in reflexes. This means, as Mason insists, that precise control of environmental stimulation is crucial for valid and reliable psychoendocrine research.

A recent experiment by Frankenhaeuser, Fröberg, Hagdahl, Rissler, Björkvall, and Wolff (1967) exemplifies this precision of control, in human research on adrenal medullary secretion. (See Euler's Nobel Prize lecture [1971] for relations between this research and his own.)

On the response side, the thorough way Mason deals with multiple psychoendocrine responses could well serve as a model for psychophysiological research, where there are dangers inherent in too limited a coverage of physiological responses. Psychophysiology should avoid proliferation of studies employing only one physiological measure in a limited way. Paul Weiss (1970), in likening the development of a new life science to a growing organism, pointed out that a danger sign common to both is mass increase of a limited area to tumorous dimensions.

By following Mason's example we can work toward a comprehensive and integrated psychophysiology. It is important to note here Mason's acknowledgement of Cannon's contribution to integrative physiology, and of the present-day usefulness of Cannon's classic concepts. Mason found, during the avoidance period, a predominance of hormones that exert strong catabolic effects on energy metabolism. On the other hand, during the recovery period, he found mainly hormones associated with anabolic effects. Patterning of hormonal responses was very much as would have been expected on the basis of Cannon's classical physiology of preparation for muscular exertion: orientation toward efficient mobilization of energy resources during avoidance, and replenishment of depleted stores afterwards.

It seems appropriate here to stress tributes in this handbook to Cannon's great contributions to psychophysiology, especially in order to bring to light some aspects of his writings that are rarely referred to in secondary sources. Mason, whose own working hypotheses were derived from Cannon's formulations, calls attention to Cannon's lesser known essays that established substantial experimental and theoretical foundations for a field of integrative physiology more than 30 years ago. Furthermore, in the chapter by Wolf and Welsh on the gastrointestinal tract, there is frequent reference to Cannon, in some cases to research areas in which his work still stands as the most complete work to cite.

A major thrust of Mason's advance beyond Cannon's pioneering work lies in the area of perception. In the course of his investigations, Mason observed that various situations were perceived by monkeys in such a way that physiological mechanisms preparing them for muscular exertion were activated. In some situations, well-organized muscular exertion followed, but in other situations, the physiological activation was followed by displays

of emotion and by disorganized behavior. Related observations in children were the basis of Duffy's early writings on energy mobilization and behavior.

ELIZABETH DUFFY (1904-1970)

Duffy's important contributions to psychophysiology extend over a period of 40 years. Her early theoretical writings were influenced by Cannon's physiology. In applying this physiology to psychological problems in the areas of emotion and motivation, Duffy predicted the growing usefulness of recording techniques in psychology, stressing the advantages of knowing the degree to which a particular individual was aroused physiologically in a given situation. She was one of the first to study relations between physiological arousal and behavior in children.

Those early observations impressed on her the fact of relative continuity of energy mobilization in emotional and motivational aspects of behavior. That is, Cannon's physiological mechanisms were often just as much activated during work under high motivation as they were in an emotional situation. When there was a difference, it was one of degree. With reliable physiological recording, it should be possible, Duffy reasoned, to gauge degree of physiological activation, and to treat this measure as an independently defined variable. The problem was to find physiological methods that could be applied to a human subject in order to determine the extent to which perception of a given situation activated Cannon's energy mobilization system in that particular individual. She was a keen observer of individual differences in her own psychophysiological research, and an erudite student of this important aspect of behavioral science.

Duffy's writings have had considerable influence. This is evident in textbooks (see, for example, Woodworth & Schlosberg, 1954, p. 111), and in the many studies that she reviewed in her book (Duffy, 1962), and in her chapter in this handbook. One example of her influence is the current research on physiological arousability in schizophrenia. Shagass (1969, pp. 172-204) lists hyperarousal first in "a relatively small number of dominant interpretive ideas" concerning schizophrenic disorders. Other recent writers stressing the potential importance of hyperarousal in schizophrenia are King (1969); Kornetsky and Eliasson (1969); and Sternbach, Alexander, and Greenfield (1969, pp. 78–95).

ON LEVELS OF FUNCTION IN THE AUTONOMIC NERVOUS SYSTEM

In her handbook chapter, Duffy discusses J. I. Lacey's criticisms of her writings. Since the issue is a current one in psychophysiology, it should be useful to examine it again here, in the light of recent developments, in order to work toward a resolution.

Recall that Duffy's original focus was on physiological mechanisms that support skeletal-muscle activity. In concrete terms, this focus involves the following chain of events: In a situation calling for strong muscular exertion, cortical-hypothalamic-midbrain mechanisms initiate a sequence of physiological reactions including dilation of blood vessels in the muscles, constriction of vessels in the skin, increasing blood flow through the muscles, and (to the same end of providing metabolic support for the muscles) increased cardiac output.

It is essential to keep this focus in mind as we proceed. Also to be kept in mind is the fact that these circulatory changes generally commence in preparation for exertion; i.e., they usually anticipate muscular action. In his handbook chapter, Rickles stresses the importance of anticipation of exertion in relation to cardiovascular changes.

Now when an individual is placed in a situation calling for increased muscular exertion, heart rate generally increases, of course. For this reason and because it is easy to record, heart rate is frequently used as a physiological monitoring device. There are obvious dangers in recording heart rate alone, since it is cardiac output (Heart Rate $\times$ Stroke Volume) that is critical for metabolism. Still, in an individual who is preparing for muscular action, if there is a heart-rate change, we expect mainly an increase (although beat-by-beat curves for heart rate may show a compensatory heart-rate decrease following an initial sharp rise). It was somewhat surprising, therefore, when the Laceys and their collaborators first reported phasic heart-rate

changes in the opposite direction (i.e., slowing) during brief periods of heightened attention.

The writings of the Laceys (J. I. Lacey, 1967, pp. 14–42; J. I. Lacey & B. C. Lacey, 1970, pp. 205–227), have left some psychophysiologists with the impression that heart-rate deceleration has a direct facilitating effect on the brain and behavior. It is possible to see how a reader might gain the impression that the Laceys believe heart-rate slowing actually initiates, or is directly involved in, a facilitatory central process; because they repeatedly refer to the influence of the carotid sinus mechanism (and the possible influence of other autonomic mechanisms) on the state of the central nervous system. However, on careful reading, one finds that they regard the heart-rate slowing merely as a sign that the inhibitory mechanism of the carotid sinus reflex (and associated central inhibition) is inoperative at that particular time.

The carotid sinus reflex is part of a mechanism that normally prevents blood pressure from remaining at high levels over long periods of time. The main receptors for this reflex are in the carotid sinus (an enlarged section of the carotid artery, going to the head). These receptors (called pressoreceptors or baroreceptors) are, as their names indicate, pressure-sensitive. They change their rate of firing with changes in the arterial blood pressure: the higher the pressure, the greater the rate of firing. The pressoreceptors discharge their impulses into the carotid sinus nerve, joining the glossopharyngeal nerve, which enters the brain stem and goes to cardiovascular centers in the medulla oblongata. From the medulla, impulses go via the vagus nerve to the heart, causing it to slow down. Lowered heart rate and decreased peripheral resistance (also produced by the reflex) act to reduce blood pressure level.

The Laceys may be correct in suggesting that the phasic heart-rate decelerations during foreperiods in reaction-time, and related experiments, are produced by the carotid sinus mechanism. If so, phasic heart-rate deceleration, preceded as it is by stimulation of the pressoreceptors, should sometimes be part of a polyphasic beat-by-beat heart-rate curve. In other words, since heart-rate acceleration is often involved in pressoreceptor activation, one should look for phasic heart-rate acceleration preceding deceleration. Increased arterial blood pressure is, of course, more critical for pressoreceptor stimulation than heart-rate increase, but the two often go together.

A recent report by Hord and Barber (1971) described a polyphasic heart-rate curve with foreperiod heart-rate decrease regularly following a heart-rate increase. They state, "This result is generally not consistent with that of Coquery and Lacey, who found that, for experimenter-controlled warning signals, an acceleratory limb followed the signal, but tended to disappear with decreasing foreperiod durations [p. 15]." The lead provided by the Hord and Barber experiment obviously should be followed up.

On dominance of a "higher" functional system The carotid sinus reflex, which normally serves a protective function (guarding against excessively high blood pressure), is frequently overridden by cortical-hypothalamic and midbrain mechanisms, for instance when the individual is working on a task under high motivation, or is engaged in muscular exertion. For a wide range of behaviors, these brain mechanisms appear to be more important than those depending principally on the carotid sinus reflex. Obrist, Webb, Sutterer, and Howard (1970) appear to recognize this in their discussion of the experiments by Abrahams, Hilton, and Zbrozyna (1960), on those brain mechanisms in hypothalamus and midbrain that are concerned with integrated behavioral reactions. Uvnäs (1960, pp. 1131–1162) has provided a comprehensive review of these brain mechanisms.

In short, these cortical-hypothalamic and midbrain mechanisms appear to be more relevant for our particular focus than the carotid sinus reflex mechanism and associated physiological changes, on which the Laceys focus.

Generally, one can predict that any reflex-centered psychological formulation will be severely limited. As Miller, Galanter, and Pribram (1960, p. 30) point out, John Dewey's classic article on the reflex arc concept in psychology made this very point in 1896! Present-day behavior theorists all seem agreed that stimuli and responses should be seen as inextricably tied together: two continuously interacting factors in a continuous process. EMGs are extremely useful in following this continuity on the response side.

EMG MONITORING OF BEHAVIOR

Skeletal-muscle activity is a *sine qua non* of behavior. There is good evidence that it is even essential for thinking (Humphrey, 1951). Goldstein, in her handbook chapter, provides further documentation for association between thinking and muscle tension.

An experiment by Pinneo (1961) demonstrated surprisingly generalized effects from squeezing on a hand dynamometer. Significant effects were noted not only in remote muscles, heart rate, respiration, and palmar conductance, but even in quantified EEG.

Sperry (1952) has stated that the entire output of our thinking machine goes into the motor system, which controls the skeletal muscles. Speaking from the standpoint of a neuropsychologist, he says it is readily apparent that the sole product of brain function is muscular coordination. For those who remember the old outmoded peripheral theories of mental activity, it should be clearly stated that our conception of the role of skeletal muscles is in the context of central neural activity and the brain. But the swing away from theories that were overdependent on peripheral muscle reactions may have gone too far in the direction of central nervous system autonomy.

Considering the key significance of the skeletal muscles, the advantage of recording EMG along with cardiovascular measures such as heart rate is obvious. The discussion in the previous section referred to relations between heart rate and muscular exertion. However, these relations are also often observed in situations where the exertion is mild. In a tracking task, for example, heart rate correlated nearly as highly with EMG measures as the EMG measures correlated with each other (Malmo, 1965b). This tracking task requires only slight muscular effort.

EMG gradients Goldstein discusses EMG gradients in her handbook chapter. On the basis of further research since my review (Malmo, 1965c) to which she refers, I have revised my views about EMG gradients.

For illustration, it will be useful to refer to our tracking task. In tracking, the person turns a knob while listening to tones that inform him moment-to-moment how to proceed. The tracker has an expectation of about how long he must work at the task before rest (i.e., how long the tracking trial will be). This sets a goal, and the tracking trial may be regarded as a continuous progression toward the goal. This kind of continuous sequence is typical of tasks that produce EMG gradients (i.e., progressive rises in muscle tension from beginning to end of the task, usually with pronounced fall in tension at the goal-end).

In my experiment (Malmo, 1965c) I found gradients in heart rate and respiration, along with EMG gradients, during tracking trials. I now consider that gradients in heart rate and respiration reflect the usual support of skeletal-muscle activity by autonomic nervous system mechanisms. That is, they provide favorable conditions for progressively increasing muscle contractions (i.e., for the EMG gradients).

Now, EEGs do not show gradients, and quality of performance stays about the same throughout the trial. These are well-documented findings. Looking at all the evidence, it appears possible that the muscles participate in a positively accelerating activity that keeps certain brain functions on level course.

EMG gradients are apparently reflecting the operation of a positive-feedback mechanism (typically one whose output is fed back into a neural system of loops that increases the input more and more, causing progressive rise in neural activation over time). There are structures within the muscles, which, in combination with those in the motor (and related) parts of the nervous system, could participate in a positive-feedback system by sending impulses into the nervous system during muscular activity. These are the receptors in the muscles and the tendons.

Electromyographic and behavioral evidence supports the conclusion that feedback into the brain from tensed muscles is essential for staying alert. This conclusion is supported also by neurophysiological evidence. Hodes (1962) found that when he injected Flaxedil into the veins of cats they became sleepy and their EEGs changed from a desynchronized to a synchronized type of record.

Hodes proved that Flaxedil was in fact producing its effect through blocking muscle activity. When he injected the drug into the brain directly through the carotid artery, which is the direct supply route for blood to the brain, the effect was not produced. Hodes believes that the feedback system originating in the muscle receptors involves circuitous paths in the cerebellum with inputs to the cerebral cortex. It is known that impulses from muscle and tendon receptors are carried in the spinal column directly to the cerebellum.

Part of the total voltage recorded from the muscle (i.e., part of the amplitude of the EMG) is produced by intrafusal muscle fibers, which do not contract. (Their motoneurons are often referred to as "gamma" motoneurons.) When the intrafusal motor system is fired, it causes stretching and firing of receptors inside the muscle spindle, and the sensory impulses so generated are carried into the dorsal (sensory) roots of the spinal cord. The intrafusal motor system is thus part of a feedback system. Its amount of input back into the central nervous system reflects the degree of muscle tension.

There appear to be excellent opportunities for devising neurophysiological experiments that could bear critically on the specific neural mechanisms responsible for EMG gradients. Ingenious recording techniques developed by Evarts (1966, 1968) should be exceedingly valuable in such experiments. Evarts combines unit recording, from pyramidal tract neurons, with electromyography.

EMGs and phasic heart-rate deceleration It is possible that the phasic cardiac decelerations in foreperiods of reaction-time experiments (and in related situations) may be meaningfully related to skeletal-muscle activity in a way that can be convincingly demonstrated with electromyography, as suggested by Obrist et al. (1970). But it seems that a convincing demonstration would be difficult. In the first place, heart-rate changes and EMG reactions will probably be out of phase with one another. In the next place the adequate sampling of muscles over the body would pose a problem.

Finally, it should be pointed out that the Obrist group employs EMGs in order to investigate metabolically significant relations between cardiovascular activity and skeletal-muscle contractions. For investigating these relations it is clearly important to have a measure of cardiac output.

Dissociations between heart-rate changes and bodily movements Lest we oversimplify the problem, we should note some exceptions to close coupling of heart rate and bodily movements. As Obrist, Webb, and Sutterer (1969) recognize, rats show heart-rate changes that appear to be uninfluenced by ongoing somatic activity. Moreover, in all species, heart-rate rise is frequently observed in anticipation of movement or exertion (and when movements are inhibited, the heart-rate increase alone may be observed). A third instance of dissociation is seen in elicitation of phasic heart-rate change by electrical brain stimulation (see Malmo, 1964; 1965a).

MOTIVATION AND PHYSIOLOGICAL MEASURES

The muscular exertion required for low-incentive tracking is exactly the same as for high-incentive tracking. Why then should heart and breathing rate, muscle tension, and hand sweating be greater for high- than for low-incentive tracking (Malmo, 1965b)? One possible answer is that somehow the person's autonomic nervous system mechanisms react to the high-incentive situation *as though* greater muscular exertion is going to be required. EMG gradients, too, though clearly distinguishable from rapid rises in EMG level, possibly obey a related principle, in rising more steeply when motivation is high than when it is low. (See Goldstein's references to Bartoshuk's writings; and see also Bélanger, 1957.)

In other words, the person's perception of the high-incentive situation somehow activates neurophysiological mechanisms that prepare him for greater *muscular* exertion than is actually required (e.g., to turn the knob in tracking). This is purely descriptive, of course, but it is easy to see that these preparatory mechanisms, if overactivated, could conceivably impair efficiency. Further documenta-

tion for this point is included in Duffy's handbook chapter.

Boredom: Falling physiological levels and declining performance An example of waning motivation and its effects is drawn from our work on tracking (Malmo, 1966a). Comparing performance scores and physiological measures from early in the session with those from later in the same session, we found that performance declined late in the session and so did the physiological levels. Heart rate and breathing rate were lower, and palmar sweating was less. In addition, EMG level, recorded from the left leg, was significantly lower later in the session than earlier. Davies and Krkovic (1965) have reported similar findings in a study of vigilance. References to other related studies are included in Duffy's handbook chapter.

This kind of efficiency loss is opposite to the kind where overly strong demands of the situation are observed to impair performance. As Duffy's handbook chapter makes clear, it is apparent that our motivational mechanisms function poorly at the two opposite extremes of high and low effective situational facilitation. If we are to reach a deep understanding of why this is so, we must learn more about the relevant neurophysiological mechanisms.

Earlier, references were made to cortical-hypothalamic-midbrain mechanisms that are involved in motivated behavior. It is now well established that the reticular system is an important part of these mechanisms. An experiment by Goodman (1968) provides positive evidence and encourages further research in this area.

Goodman trained monkeys to perform in a visual reaction-time task while recording from multiple units in the reticular system. He found that there was a level of reticular-neuron activity that was optimal for performance. Above and below this optimal level, performance was relatively poor. Steady firing at a moderate level, just prior to stimulation, was a necessary condition for a short reaction time.

It is important to note that the aspect of background neural activity critical for efficient performance was presence of a plateau or level of reticular activity and not some kind of abrupt facilitatory change in reticular activity. Actually, Goodman found that a sudden burst of multiple-unit activity was unfavorable, even when this burst brought the averaged activity within the restricted (moderate) range. In short, it appeared to be the *level* of reticular activity that was critical for performance. Fast reaction times were never observed when this level departed from the optimal range.

Goodman's findings, it will be noted, are in accord with Hebb's (1955) classic paper on arousal, and with my suggestion in 1959 that in this research area, direct recording from the reticular system would have distinct advantages over other measures.

My views have, of course, changed since 1959. It will be clear from the previous discussion that I now place greater stress on dominance of the skeletal-motor system than formerly. But it is a dominance that somehow seems unnecessarily strong in some human psychophysiological functions. For instance, why should normal reclining persons listening to an entertaining detective story show EMG gradients (Bartoshuk, 1956; Wallerstein, 1954)? Nevertheless, the skeletal muscles apparently are more involved in psychological functions than I recognized in 1959, although our laboratory used EMGs extensively. Therefore, it seems that theory construction in psychophysiology now should strive toward an understanding of the human nervous system (central and autonomic), focusing on the key role of the skeletal-motor system.

In relation to the pivotal role of facilitation on the motor system, which I have been stressing, it is interesting to note that the points in the midbrain that Goodman chose for recording were ones where association with the motor system was clear. Electrodes were left only at sites in the midbrain reticular formation where multiple-unit activity increased as the animal moved spontaneously or showed withdrawal movements to pinch.

In short, the Goodman experiment, in addition to its importance in showing the relation between reticular activity and performance, is valuable in pointing the way toward a more integrated approach to the problem. We are also encouraged to use more precise language. Instead of referring to "level of reticular-neuron activation" we refer to quantity of multiple-unit activity recorded from midbrain sites that were selected because of their demonstrated connections with the skeletal-motor system.

The term "activation" may be retained to denote an area of investigation. This would place it in the same denotative class as the term "emotion." In agreement with Obrist et al. (1970, p. 575) and with Vanderwolf (1971, p. 106), I believe that heart rate should be used as a clue to what is going on in the nervous system (especially in the skeletal-motor system), rather than as an index of a "state."

This shift of emphasis has its parallel in current movement of theory away from "drive state" to theories based on detailed study of separate content areas such as thirst, hunger, and sex (Campbell & Misanin, 1969; Finger & Mook, 1971). Investigations of hypothalamic osmoreceptor discharge in dehydration, for instance, are beginning to replace the earlier quest for indirect measures of "thirst drive." The reader will note the similarity between the weakness of this categorical "drive" concept, and that of "stress," previously discussed.

With the new terms of reference proposed, it is meaningless to conclude that psychophysiological data do or do not support "activation theory." From our discussion, it is obvious that this would be like saying that certain data supported "emotion theory" or "motivation theory." Again, terms like emotion, motivation, and activation (or arousal) seem useful chiefly in referring to areas of research.

Lindsley, who was the first to call psychologists' attention to the importance of the nonspecific reticulo-thalamo-cortical systems, has recently reviewed the history and recent progress in this neuropsychological area (Lindsley, 1970, pp. 147–188). His references to theory, according to my understanding of them, are chiefly concerned with suggestions about how these brain systems may be involved in behavior. His suggestions have a strong empirical basis.

ON PHYSIOLOGICAL MONITORING IN THE AREA OF ACTIVATION

Podvoll and Goodman (1967) reported good agreement between observations of behavioral alertness in cats and accompanying degree of multiple-unit activity recorded from midbrain-reticular formation and other brain areas. Furthermore, they found that multiple-unit activity levels were closely correlated with the animal's observed behavior even under conditions when the electroencephalogram appeared dissociated from behavior. For work with animals, multiple-unit recording is obviously superior to EEG.

Direct methods of recording from subcortical structures in the brain can be used only rarely, of course, with human subjects; and consequently it is necessary to fall back on measures like the EEG. Mirsky and Pragay (1967, pp. 514–534) have reviewed human EEG-behavior dissociations. In their chapter Johnson and Lubin stress the point that, imperfect as the EEG is in its correlations with behavior, it is needed as a monitor in psychophysiological studies. However, it seems desirable to record additional physiological measures.

The contingent negative variation (CNV) has been used as a monitor in psychophysiological experiments (see Chapter 7). Most investigators of the CNV have recognized the problem of control of eye movement contamination. A recent article by Wasman, Morehead, Lee, and Rowland (1970) stresses the importance of this control. These authors have made an important contribution, which will undoubtedly strengthen methodology in this area of research. They urge that, in addition to controlling for EOG contamination, research workers pay particular attention to individual differences and to trial-to-trial reliability.

A recent experiment by Eason and Dudley (1970) clearly demonstrates the advantages gained by recording EMGs and autonomic measures along with recordings from the brain (evoked cortical potentials in their experiment). As handbook references indicate, the work of Eason and his collaborators in the activation area has been outstanding.

Schubert (1969) found that simple psychomotor-task rate was an increasing function of body temperature. This study is of particular interest in relation to the handbook chapter by Wenger and Cullen.

SLEEP AND AROUSAL

Snyder and Scott, in their excellent chapter on sleep, object strongly (and correctly, of course) to the idea of sleep as a single point on the "arousal continuum." In general, Snyder and Scott consider sleep a broad zone, and they "emphasize the variations in levels of general arousal within the range behaviorally characterized as 'sleep.'" They present

curves of some physiological measures, showing downward trends throughout sleep. Confirmatory data from at least one other laboratory have been published: Movement-monitored all-night measures of heart rate, respiration, palmar conductance, and quantified EEG declined progressively over hours during sleep (Malmo, 1959). Incidentally, these data, and my related discussion of sleep, contradict the statement by Snyder and Scott, in their chapter, that I regard sleep as a point on a continuum.

Snyder and Scott point out, furthermore, that "the peripheral and the central physiological correlates and mechanisms of REM sleep appear to be as different from those of the remainder of sleep as sleep is from waking; hence we construe the REM state as a 'third basic organismic state' [p. 696]."

A collection of papers on sleep and altered states of consciousness (Kety, Evarts, & Williams, 1967) is an important supplementary source.

ANXIETY

The term "anxiety" must be clearly defined in order to avoid confusion (see Alexander's handbook chapter). While normal emotions in threatening situations are frequently referred to as "anxiety," the prolonged exposure to threatening or extremely demanding situations can produce a state of "pathological anxiety." In order to avoid confusion, I use the term in the restricted sense of "pathological anxiety."

Recently, attention has again been focused on the cumulative effects of battle conditions. Reports indicated that during the Tet offensive, people in Saigon began showing the deleterious effects of prolonged exposure to these conditions. With the onset of indiscriminate bombing, burning, and rocketing, symptoms that were commonplace in World War II (combat fatigue, flying fatigue, war weariness) apparently became widespread. In World War II it was found that, if at the first symptoms of stress reaction—lack of appetite, insomnia, high heart rate, increasing irritability—the soldiers were withdrawn from active combat and rested for a period of time, many could go back and fight again. However, when the symptoms were not heeded and the soldiers were subjected to continuous tension and danger, eventually they would reach the breaking point and rest treatment would not bring relief. Instead, a chronic anxiety condition would develop.

The same kind of condition is found in civilian populations far removed from anything resembling battle conditions. Severe and conflicting demands in civilian life, when they are prolonged, appear to produce similar effects, although the precise etiological conditions are sometimes hard to identify. One distinguishing feature of pathological anxiety is that the person afflicted with it reacts to ordinary life situations as though they were emergencies.

Psychophysiology has produced convincing evidence of significant objective deviations in psychiatric patients with "anxiety." Goldstein's chapter summarizes evidence from electromyographic research, and Lader's review (1969, pp. 53–61) covers the general topic of psychophysiological research with anxiety-patients. Lader exposes the fallacy of assuming that it is possible to devise a "measure of anxiety" (as we define it). In his excellent chapter, Edelberg makes essentially the same point. The point is that "anxiety" and "arousal" have been used indiscriminately. Both writers agree on the utility of physiological arousal as an *operational* construct in psychophysiological research on anxiety. Other authors (e.g., Claridge, 1967; Eysenck, 1967) have expressed similar views.

Although we still do not know what "anxiety" is, psychophysiology has furnished important clues. There is evidence suggesting that anxiety involves an impaired regulatory mechanism in the brain (Malmo, 1966b, pp. 157–177).

PSYCHOPHYSIOLOGICAL INVESTIGATION OF BODILY SYMPTOMS

The observations made on patients with anxiety, as I have just noted, suggest that long-continued exposure to stressful situations may impair central regulatory mechanisms. The problem is always to identify the precise nature of the stress, and to try to understand the physiological changes produced.

D. T. Graham's discussion of Raynaud's disease may be taken as an objective point of reference. Raynaud's disease sufferers have painfully cold extremities, a condition which is produced by excessive peripheral vasoconstriction, especially in the hands.

As D. T. Graham explains in his handbook chapter, it is a common clinical assumption among physicians that Raynaud-disease patients often show their symptoms during emotion. D. T. Graham and co-workers have made a careful study of the kinds of emotional situations that produce Raynaud-type symptoms. They concluded that the most effective situations were those that made the person want to take action (often hostile action) against another person who was behaving in an unacceptable way.

There is little doubt that this kind of emotional reaction would activate the cortical-hypothalamic-midbrain mechanisms referred to earlier, and described by Uvnäs (1960, pp. 1131–1162). Constriction of the blood vessels in the skin is an integral part of the overall physiological mechanism that is designed for action. It is also, of course, part of the physiological reaction to cold.

In one of Mittelmann and Wolff's (1939) patients there was an interesting interaction between environmental cooling and emotional reaction. When room temperature was lowered to 41° Fahrenheit, temperature alone produced pain. At a moderately cool environmental temperature (around 68° Fahrenheit), although temperature alone did not precipitate a painful attack, it was much easier for an emotional reaction to do so there, than in a warmer room. Because of poverty, this patient was forced to live in a poorly heated apartment. This cold place and frequent emotional upsets combined to produce her symptoms.

It is understandable how being constantly exposed to life situations that engender an attitude of hostility in an individual could make that individual prone to Raynaud's disease. Of course, structural idiosyncrasies and other factors enter into the development of any specific symptom, whether it be cold hands, tension headaches, or whatever. Engel's handbook chapter, read in conjunction with D. T. Graham's chapter, fully documents these points.

It is important to realize that symptom specificity is a multifactor problem. How much weight we attach to each factor depends on how we interpret the many relevant research findings from investigations of a wide variety of symptoms. Buss (1966), who has provided a comprehensive summary of these findings, stresses the importance of laboratory research and physiological recordings. The laboratory research of D. T. Graham and his co-workers on relations between attitudes and psychophysiology of diseases represents one important contribution to this area.

There is now substantial objective proof that patients' subjective bodily complaints frequently have a real basis in specific physiological manifestations: that is, evidence that a patient with a specific bodily symptom shows a clear physiological overreaction which is also specific, and is appropriate to the particular symptom. Shearn's chapter is important for the application of many of these psychophysiological findings to the developing area of feedback training.

Both Shearn and Engel stress the importance of coordinated animal research. Engel's plea for more animal research (especially longitudinal studies) focused on problems of clinical relevance, should certainly be heeded.

BRAIN STIMULATION AND EMOTIONAL BEHAVIOR

Most brain research on emotion must, of course, be done with animals; and the results of this animal research can be cautiously applied to the problems of brain functions underlying human emotions. But it is fortunate that clinical investigators are taking advantage of opportunities (when in the patient's interest) to observe emotional reactions produced by direct stimulation of subcortical loci in the brain of waking patients (Ervin, Mark, & Stevens, 1969, pp. 54–65; Hassler, Ore, Dieckmann, Bricolo, & Dolce, 1969, pp. 306–310; Nashold, Wilson, & Slaughter, 1969). As Ervin, Mark, and Stevens (1969) point out, there are difficulties with the technique of brain stimulation that force caution in interpretation. But there is general agreement that brain stimulation in various areas can reliably produce striking emotional reactions such as strong fear and expressions of aversion, including pain. Rage reactions associated with brain stimulation have also been observed (Ervin, Mark, & Stevens, 1969).

Among the brain areas stimulated in clinical studies of centrally produced emotion are the following: intralaminar nuclei of the thalamus, anterior thalamus, medial forebrain bundle, anterior hypothalamus, hippocampus, amygdala, and areas in the dorsolateral midbrain, especially in the central gray region. Control stimulations in primary relay nuclei of the somatosensory system have produced well-localized sensations clearly referred to the body surface (e.g., certain fingers of one hand), without emotional concomitants.

There is thus a specificity about the brain areas that are associated with emotional reactions upon stimulation. Even in the midbrain of a rat, a distance as small as a half millimeter between stimulation sites has been found to make a significant difference in the speed of escape following stimulation (Gardner & Malmo, 1969). These midbrain areas are heterogeneous structurally and functionally, and their connections with other parts of the brain are intricate and extensive. The midbrain "reticular activating" system is itself exceedingly complex. Therefore it clearly is an oversimplification to refer to the reticular system as though it were relatively homogeneous.

To recognize such pitfalls is in keeping with Alexander's caution in discussing the CNS structures related to emotion. My chapter echoes that caution, but at the same time, I believe that we should recognize some notable advances in brain research that are relevant for psychophysiology. For example, Hunsperger (1969) has provided a flawless integration of behavioral, autonomic, and neurophysiological observations in the study of "rage" reactions following hypothalamic stimulation in the cat. These observations extend the pioneering work of Hess, Ranson, and others in the 1930s. The experiment by Abrahams et al., (1960) was noted earlier.

Closely related research is being carried out in other laboratories by Flynn and co-workers (Flynn, 1969; Wasman & Flynn, 1962) and by Glusman and co-workers (Glusman & Roizin, 1960, pp. 177–181; Stokman & Glusman, 1970). Delgado (1964) has reviewed neuropsychological studies of attack behavior in animals, beginning with the pioneering work of Hess in 1928. This aggressive behavior is regularly produced by stimulation of certain hypothalamic sites, although stimulation in other regions of the brain (e.g., thalamus and midbrain) may evoke similar behavior. In short, there is a substantial basis for proceeding with research on brain-behavior correlations, related to the area of emotion.

FURTHER COMPLEXITIES IN THE RESEARCH AREA OF EMOTION

The old question of whether there is an invariant pattern of physiological reactions associated with laboratory-produced emotions such as fear and anger is examined by Lang, Rice, and Sternbach. Their discussion draws on the major psychophysiological findings in this area, dealing constructively with a number of important problems. From the experiments by S. Schachter and Singer and those by Lazarus and co-workers, the authors stress the importance of interactions. Certainly, it is naive to approach these problems in any other way.

Schlosberg's model (1954) for classifying emotions took these complex interactions into account; and Edelberg points this out when he criticizes Ax (1953) for neglecting the variable of intensity. This criticism is clearly supported by Levi's (1965) experiment. Schnore's article (1959) is also relevant to the intensity question.

The importance of stimulus-response interactions for psychophysiology in relation to clinical psychology has been emphasized recently by Stern and Plapp (1969, pp. 197–254).

APOLOGIA AND LOOKING AHEAD

In writing an overview chapter, the selection of topics for discussion is bound to be somewhat arbitrary, although I deeply appreciate the importance of all topics covered in the handbook. Of course, much of the volume requires no discussion, being valuable compilations of foundation literature, methodologies, and of other such materials, which one expects to find in a handbook.

However, there are a few omissions in the handbook itself. For instance, the field of developmental psychophysiology is not represented by a chapter devoted to the topic, although several chapters refer to work with children.* For a recent review of psychophysiological research with infants, the reader is directed to F. K. Graham and Jackson (1970, pp. 59–117). Brackbill's ingenious new approach represents another important contribution to this field (Brackbill, 1971).

Longitudinal studies, commencing with children at a very early age, are obviously important for developmental psychophysiology (see Elliott, 1966).

Clearly, a supplement to the handbook some time in the future, adding topics omitted from this one, would be valuable.

---

*EDITORS' NOTE: Such a chapter was planned, but the author failed to honor his commitment at a time so late in the publication schedule that a replacement could not be arranged.

REFERENCES

ABRAHAMS, V. C., HILTON, S. M., & ZBROZYNA, A. Active muscle vasodilation produced by stimulation of the brain stem: Its significance in the defence reaction. *Journal of Physiology,* 1960, **154,** 491–513.

AX, A. F. The physiological differentiation between fear and anger in humans. *Psychosomatic Medicine,* 1953, **15,** 433–442.

BARTOSHUK, A. K. Electromyographic gradients and EEG amplitude during motivated listening. *Canadian Journal of Psychology,* 1956, **10,** 156–164.

BÉLANGER, D. "Gradients" musculaires et processus mentaux supérieurs. *Canadian Journal of Psychology,* 1957, **11,** 113–122.

BRACKBILL, Y. Cumulative effects of continuous stimulation on arousal level in infants. *Child Development,* 1971, **42,** 17–26.

BUSS, A. H. *Psychopathology.* New York: Wiley, 1966.

CAMPBELL, B. A., & MISANIN, J. R. Basic drives. *Annual Review of Psychology,* 1969, **20,** 57–84.

CLARIDGE, G. S. *Personality and arousal.* London: Pergamon, 1967.

DAVIES, D. R., & KRKOVIC, A. Skin-conductance, alpha-activity, and vigilance. *American Journal of Psychology,* 1965, **78,** 304–306.

DELGADO, J. M. R. Free behavior and brain stimulation. *International Review of Neurobiology,* 1964, **6,** 349–448.

DUFFY, E. *Activation and behavior.* New York: Wiley, 1962.

DUNBAR, F. *Emotions and bodily changes.* New York: Columbia University Press, 1954.

EASON, R. G., & DUDLEY, L. M. Physiological and behavioral indicants of activation. *Psychophysiology,* 1970, **7,** 223–232.

ELLIOTT, R. Physiological activity and performance in children and adults: A two-year follow-up. *Journal of Experimental Child Psychology,* 1966, **4,** 58–80.

ERVIN, F. R., MARK, V. H., & STEVENS, J. Behavioral and affective responses to brain stimulation in man. In J. ZUBIN & C. SHAGASS (Eds.), *Neurobiological aspects of psychopathology.* New York: Grune & Stratton, 1969.

EULER, U. S. V. Adrenergic neurotransmitter functions. *Science,* 1971, **173,** 202–206.

EVARTS, E. V. Pyramidal tract activity associated with a conditioned hand movement in the monkey. *Journal of Neurophysiology,* 1966, **29,** 1011–1027.

EVARTS, E. V. Relation of pyramidal tract activity to force exerted during voluntary movement. *Journal of Neurophysiology,* 1968, **31,** 14–27.

EYSENCK, H. J. *The biological basis of personality.* Springfield, Ill.: Charles C Thomas, 1967.

FINGER, F. W., & MOOK, D. G. Basic drives. *Annual Review of Psychology,* 1971, **22,** 1–38.

FLYNN, J. P. Neural aspects of attack behavior in cats. *Annals of the New York Academy of Sciences,* 1969, **159,** 1008–1012.

FRANKENHAEUSER, M., FRÖBERG, J., HAGDAHL, R., RISSLER, A., BJÖRKVALL, C., & WOLFF, B. Physiological, behavioral, and subjective indices of habituation to psychological stress. *Physiology and Behavior,* 1967, **2,** 229–237.

GARDNER, L., & MALMO, R. B. Effects of low-level septal stimulation on escape: Significance for limbic-midbrain interactions in pain. *Journal of Comparative and Physiological Psychology,* 1969, **68,** 65–73.

GLUSMAN, M., & ROIZIN, L. Role of the hypothalamus in the organization of agonistic behavior in the cat. *Transactions of the American Neurological Association,* 1960.

GOODMAN, S. J. Visuo-motor reaction times and brain stem multiple-unit activity. *Experimental Neurology,* 1968, **22,** 367–378.

GRAHAM, F. K., & JACKSON, J. C. Arousal systems and infant heart rate responses. In H. W. REESE & L. P. LIPSITT (Eds.), *Advances in child development and behavior.* Vol. V, New York: Academic, 1970.

HASSLER, R., ORE, D. G., DIECKMANN, G., BRICOLO, A., & DOLCE, G. Behavioural and EEG arousal induced by stimulation of unspecific projection systems in a patient with post-traumatic apallic syndrome. *Electroencephalography and Clinical Neurophysiology,* 1969, **27,** 306–310.

HEBB, D. O. Drives and the C.N.S. (conceptual nervous system). *Psychological Review,* 1955, **62,** 243–254.

HODES, R. Electrocortical synchronization resulting from reduced proprioceptive drive caused by neuromuscular blocking agents. *Electroencephalography and Clinical Neurophysiology,* 1962, **14,** 220–232.

HORD, D., & BARBER, J. Heart rate *pre-action:* Anticipatory change associated with self-pacing. Report Number 71-13, Navy Medical Neuropsychiatric Research Unit, San Diego, California, 1971, 1–18.

HUMPHREY, G. *Thinking: An introduction to its experimental psychology.* New York: Wiley, 1951.

HUNSPERGER, R. W. Postural tonus and cardiac activity during centrally elicited affective reactions in the cat. *Annals of the New York Academy of Sciences,* 1969, **159,** 1013–1024.

KETY, S. S., EVARTS, E. V., & WILLIAMS, H. L. (Eds.) *Sleep and altered states of consciousness.* Baltimore: Williams & Wilkins, 1967.

KING, H. E. Psychomotility: A dimension of behavior disorder. In J. ZUBIN & C. SHAGASS (Eds.), *Neurobiological aspects of psychopathology.* New York: Grune & Stratton, 1969.

KORNETSKY, C., & ELIASSON, M. Reticular stimulation and chlorpromazine: An animal model for schizophrenic overarousal. *Science,* 1969, **165,** 1273–1274.

LACEY, J. I. Somatic response patterning and stress: Some revisions of activation theory. In M. H. APPLEY & R. TRUMBULL (Eds.), *Psychological stress.* New York: Appleton-Century-Crofts, 1967.

LACEY, J. I., & LACEY, B. C. Some autonomic-central nervous system interrelationships. In P. BLACK (Ed.), *Physiological correlates of emotion.* New York: Academic, 1970.

LADER, M. H. Psychophysiological aspects of anxiety. In M. H. LADER (Ed.), *Studies of anxiety.* Ashford, Kent: Headley Brothers, 1969. (*British Journal of Psychiatry, Special Publication No. 3*)

LEVI, L. The urinary output of adrenalin and noradrenalin during pleasant and unpleasant emotional stress. *Psychosomatic Medicine,* 1965, **27,** 80–85.

LINDSLEY, D. B. The role of nonspecific reticulo-thalmocortical systems in emotion. In P. BLACK (Ed.), *Physiological correlates of emotion.* New York: Academic, 1970.

MALMO, R. B. Activation: A neuropsychological dimension. *Psychological Review,* 1959, **66,** 367–386.

MALMO, R. B. Heart rate reactions and locus of stimulation within the septal area of the rat. *Science,* 1964, **144,** 1029–1030.

MALMO, R. B. Comment on the exchange of theoretical notes between Smith, and Black and Lang. *Psychological Review,* 1965, **72,** 240–241. (a)

MALMO, R. B. Finger-sweat prints in the differentiation of low and high incentive. *Psychophysiology,* 1965, **1,** 231–240. (b)

MALMO, R. B. Physiological gradients and behavior. *Psychological Bulletin,* 1965, **64,** 225–234. (c)

MALMO, R. B. Cognitive factors in impairment: A neuropsychological study of divided set. *Journal of Experimental Psychology*, 1966, **71**, 184–189. (a)

MALMO, R. B.   Studies of anxiety: Some clinical origins of the activation concept. In C. D. SPIELBERGER (Ed.), *Anxiety and behavior.* New York: Academic, 1966. (b)

MILLER, G. A., GALANTER, E., & PRIBRAM, K. H.   *Plans and the structure of behavior.* New York: Holt, Rinehart and Winston, 1960.

MIRSKY, A. F., & PRAGAY, E. B.   The relation of EEG and performance in altered states of consciousness. In S. S. KETY, E. V. EVARTS, & H. L. WILLIAMS (Eds.), *Sleep and altered states of consciousness.* Baltimore: Williams & Wilkins, 1967.

MITTELMANN, B., & WOLFF, H. G.   Affective states and skin temperature: Experimental study of subjects with "cold hands" and Raynaud's syndrome. *Psychosomatic Medicine*, 1939, **1**, 271–292.

NASHOLD, B. S., Jr., WILSON, W. P., & SLAUGHTER, D. G.   Sensations evoked by stimulation in the midbrain of man. *Journal of Neurosurgery*, 1969, **30**, 14–24.

OBRIST, P. A., WEBB, R. A., & SUTTERER, J. R.   Heart rate and somatic changes during aversive conditioning and a simple reaction time task. *Psychophysiology*, 1969, **5**, 696–723.

OBRIST, P. A., WEBB, R. A., SUTTERER, J. R., & HOWARD, J. L.   The cardiac-somatic relationship: Some reformulations. *Psychophysiology*, 1970, **6**, 569–587.

PINNEO, L. R.   The effects of induced muscle tension during tracking on level of activation and on performance. *Journal of Experimental Psychology*, 1961, **62**, 523–531.

PODVOLL, E. M., & GOODMAN, S. J.   Averaged neural electrical activity and arousal. *Science*, 1967, **155**, 223–225.

SCHLOSBERG, H.   Three dimensions of emotion. *Psychological Review*, 1954, **61**, 81–88.

SCHNORE, M. M.   Individual patterns of physiological activity as a function of task differences and degree of arousal. *Journal of Experimental Psychology*, 1959, **58**, 117–128.

SCHUBERT, D. S. P.   Simple task rate as a direct function of diurnal sympathetic nervous system predominance: A law of performance. *Journal of Comparative and Physiological Psychology*, 1969, **68**, 434–436.

SHAGASS, C.   Neurophysiological studies. In L. BELLAK & L. LOEB (Eds.), *The schizophrenic syndrome.* New York: Grune & Stratton, 1969.

SPERRY, R. W.   Neurology and the mind-brain problem. *American Scientist*, 1952, **40**, 291–312.

STERN, J. A., & PLAPP, J. M.   Psychophysiology and clinical psychology. In C. B. SPIELBERGER (Ed.), *Current topics in clinical and community psychology.* Vol. 1. New York: Academic, 1969.

STERNBACH, R. A.   *Principles of psychophysiology.* New York: Academic, 1966.

STERNBACH, R. A. ALEXANDER, A. A., & GREENFIELD, N. S.   Autonomic and somatic reactivity in relation to psychopathology. In J. ZUBIN & C. SHAGASS (Eds.), *Neurobiological aspects of psychopathology.* New York: Grune & Stratton, 1969.

STOKMAN, C. L. J., & GLUSMAN, M.   Amygdaloid modulation of hypothalamic flight in cats. *Journal of Comparative and Physiological Psychology*, 1970, **71**, 365–375.

UVNÄS, B.   Central cardiovascular control. In J. FIELD, H. W. MAGOUN, & V. E. HALL (Eds.), *Handbook of physiology. Neurophysiology.* Vol. II. Washington: American Physiological Society, 1960.

VANDERWOLF, C. H.   Limbic-diencephalic mechanisms of voluntary movement. *Psychological Review*, 1971, **78**, 83–113.

WALLERSTEIN, H.   An electromyographic study of attentive listening: *Canadian Journal of Psychology*, 1954, **8**, 228–238.

WASMAN, M., & FLYNN, J. P.   Directed attack elicited from hypothalamus. *Archives of Neurology*, 1962, **6**, 220–227.

WASMAN, M., MOREHEAD, S. D., LEE, H.-Y., & ROWLAND, V.   Interaction of electro-ocular potentials with the contingent negative variation. *Psychophysiology*, 1970, **7**, 103–111.

WEISS, P. A.   Whither life science? *American Scientist*, 1970, **58**, 156–163.

WENZEL, B. M.   A word in search of a meaning. Review of M. H. APPLEY & R. T. TRUMBULL (Eds.), *Psychological stress: Issues in research. Contemporary Psychology*, 1970, **15**, 38–39.

WOODWORTH, R. S., & SCHLOSBERG, H.   *Experimental psychology.* (Rev. ed.) New York: Holt, Rinehart and Winston, 1954.

NAME
INDEX

SUBJECT
INDEX

*An asterisk is a suggestion to "See" or "See
also." Italic page numbers indicate illustrations. A
page number followed by a t is a table; followed
by an n is a footnote.